P9-DLZ-499

Algebra 2

Edward B. Burger
David J. Chard
Paul A. Kennedy
Steven J. Leinwand
Freddie L. Renfro
Tom W. Roby
Bert K. Waits

HOLT McDOUGAL

HOUGHTON MIFFLIN HARCOURT

Printed in the U.S.A.

ISBN 978-0-547-64707-4

8 9 10 0868 20 19 18 17 16 15 14

4500501896 D E F G

Cover photo: © Art by Vladimir Bulatov/Bulatov Abstract Creations/ Photo by Victoria Smith/HMH

Authors

Edward B. Burger, Ph.D., is Professor of Mathematics at Williams College and is the author of numerous articles, books, and videos. He has won several of the most prestigious writing and teaching awards offered by the Mathematical Association of America. Dr. Burger has made numerous television and radio appearances and has given countless mathematical presentations around the world.

David J. Chard, Ph.D., is the Leon Simmons Dean of the School of Education and Human Development at Southern Methodist University. He is a past president of the Divison of Research at the Council for Exceptional Children, a member of the International Academy for Research on Learning Disabilities, and has been the Principal Investigator on numerous research projects for the U.S. Department of Education.

Paul A. Kennedy, Ph.D., is a professor and Distinguished University Teaching Scholar in the Department of Mathematics at Colorado State University. Dr. Kennedy is a leader in mathematics education. His research focuses on developing algebraic thinking by using multiple representations and technology. He is the author of numerous publications.

Steven J. Leinwand is a Principal Research Analyst at the American Institutes for Research in Washington, D.C. He was previously, for 22 years, the Mathematics Supervisor with the Connecticut Department of Education.

Freddie L. Renfro, MA, has 35 years of experience in Texas education as a classroom teacher and director/coordinator of Mathematics PreK-12 for school districts in the Houston area. She has served as a reviewer and TXTEAM trainer for Texas Math Institutes and has presented at numerous math workshops.

Tom W. Roby, Ph.D., is Associate Professor of Mathematics and Director of the Quantitative Learning Center at the University of Connecticut. He founded and directed the Bay Area-based ACCLAIM professional development program. He also chaired the advisory board of the California Mathematics Project and reviewed content for the California Standards Tests.

Bert K. Waits, Ph.D., is a Professor Emeritus of Mathematics at The Ohio State University and cofounder of T^3 (Teachers Teaching with Technology), a national professional development program. Dr. Waits is also a former board member of the NCTM and an author of the original NCTM Standards.

CONTRIBUTING AUTHORS

Linda Antinone
Fort Worth, TX
Ms. Antinone teaches mathematics at R. L. Paschal High School in Fort Worth, Texas. She has received the Presidential Award for Excellence in Teaching Mathematics and the National Radio Shack Teacher award. She has coauthored several books for Texas Instruments on the use of technology in mathematics.

Carmen Whitman
Pflugerville, TX
Ms. Whitman travels nationally helping districts improve mathematics education. She has been a program coordinator on the mathematics team at the Charles A. Dana Center, and has served as a secondary math specialist for the Austin Independent School District.

REVIEWERS

Mary Anderson
Mathematics Department Chair
Community High School District 99 South
Downers Grove, IL

Dave Barker
Mathematics Department Chair
Los Alamitos High School
Los Alamitos, CA

MaryLane Blomquist
Mathematics Department Chair
Kewaskum High School
Kewaskum, WI

William L. Bonney
Mathematics Department Chair
Ballard High School
Seattle, WA

Suzanne Castren
Mathematics Teacher
Williamsville South High School
Williamsville, NY

Lala Geraldine Chambers, NBCT
Mathematics Department Chair
Forest Hill High School
Jackson, MS

Joan Chrismer-McNatt
Mathematics Teacher
Clear Creek High School
League City, TX

Roy L. Conwell, Jr.
Mathematics Department Chair
Sam Houston High School
Houston, TX

Patricia Daley
Mathematics Teacher, retired
Fairfield High School
Fairfield, CT

Mohamad Elkhatib
Mathematics Department Chair
Jones High School
Houston Community College Instructor
Houston, TX

Marti Freihofer
Mathematics Department Chair
Scott High School
Taylor Mill, KY

Mary Gesino
Mathematics Department Co-Chair
R. L. Turner High School
Carrollton, TX

Marilyn Gutman
Mathematics Department Chair
Mayfield High School
Las Cruces, NM

Jim Harrington
Supervisor of Mathematics
Omaha Public Schools
Omaha, NE

Marieta W. Harris
Mathematics Specialist
Memphis, TN

Jere Hassberger, PhD
Mathematics Department Chair
Saline High School
Saline, MI

Reviewers

James Patrick Herrington
Mathematics Department Chair
O'Fallon Township High School
O'Fallon, IL

Margie Hill
District Coordinating Teacher for Mathematics, K-12
Blue Valley USD 229
Overland Park, KS

Dr. Douglas Lohnas
Director of Mathematics
Niskayuna Central School District
Niskayuna, NY

Brenda Lynch
Mathematics Department Chair
Montgomery High School
Montgomery, TX

Dr. Charlotte May
Mathematics Teacher
Austin ISD
Austin, TX

Ruth Harbin Miles
K-12 Coordinator of Mathematics
Olathe USD 233
Olathe, TX

Saundra Paschal
Mathematics Department Chair
Lake View High School
San Angelo, TX

Carolyn Randolph
Mathematics Department Chair
Academic Director
Kendrick High School
Columbus, GA

Sarah Ritch
Mathematics Department Chair
Hebron High School
Carrollton, TX

Paul Schwiegerling
Gifted Mathematics Program
SUNY at Buffalo
Buffalo, NY

Katie Smith
Mathematics Department Chair
Berea High School
Greenville, SC

Stephanie Turner
Former Mathematics Teacher
Colleyville Heritage High School
Colleyville, TX

Field Test Participants

Gerri Chambers-McGee
Forest Hill High School
Jackson, MS

Stephanie Cundiff
Mesa Ridge High School
Colorado Springs, CO

Eddie Hancock
Navasota High School
Navasota, TX

Brenda Lynch
Montgomery High School
Montgomery, TX

Lisa Pope
Jacobs High School
Cincinnati, OH

Niki Robinson
Navasota High School
Navasota, TX

Piper Singleton
Pershing High School
Detroit, MI

Dierdre M. Watkins
Dunwoody High School
Dunwoody, GA

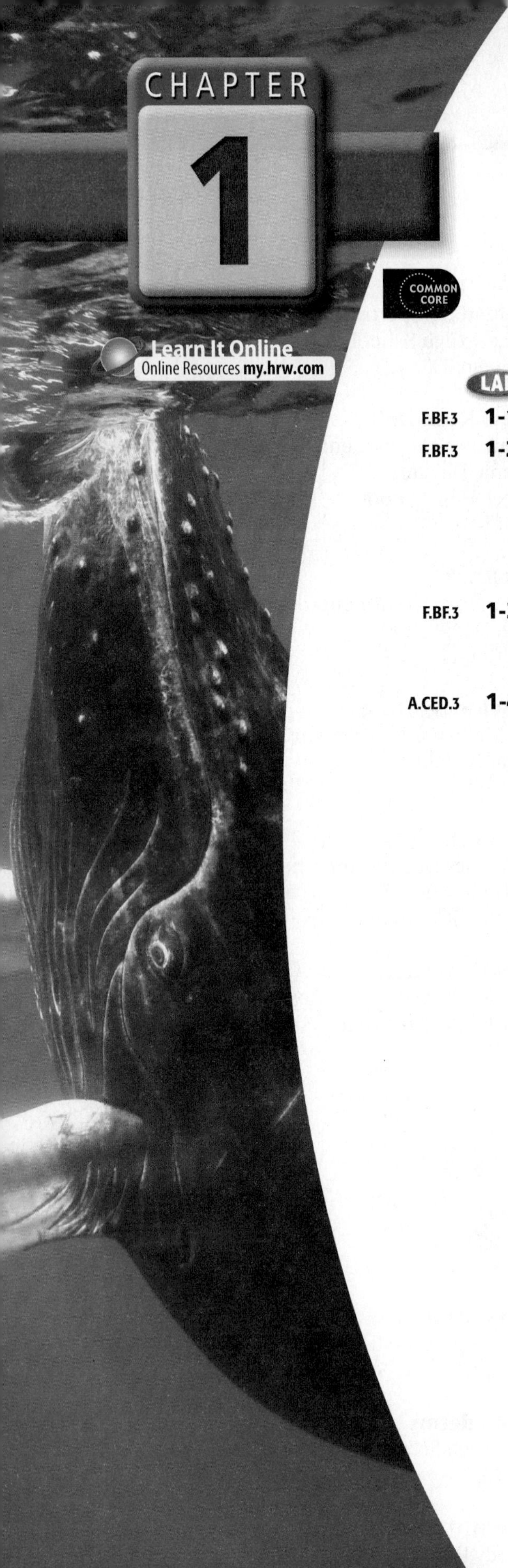

Foundations for Functions

WaterFrame/Alamy

Quadratic Functions

CHAPTER 2

COMMON CORE

Learn It Online
Online Resources my.hrw.com

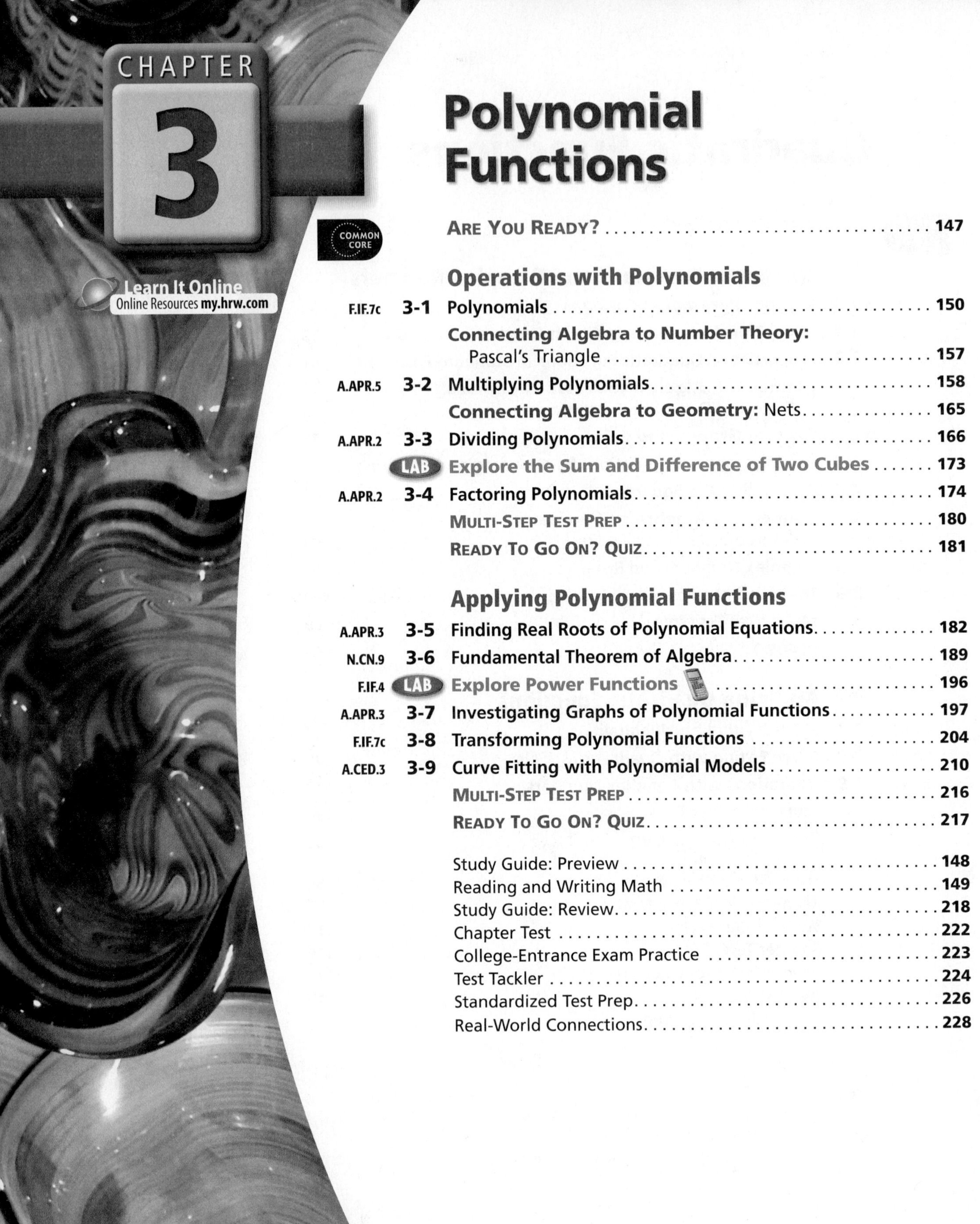

Polynomial Functions

Exponential and Logarithmic Functions

CHAPTER 4

COMMON CORE

Learn It Online
Online Resources my.hrw.com

CHAPTER 5

Rational and Radical Functions

COMMON CORE

Learn It Online
Online Resources my.hrw.com

Letser Lefkowitz/CORBIS

CHAPTER 6

Properties and Attributes of Functions

COMMON CORE

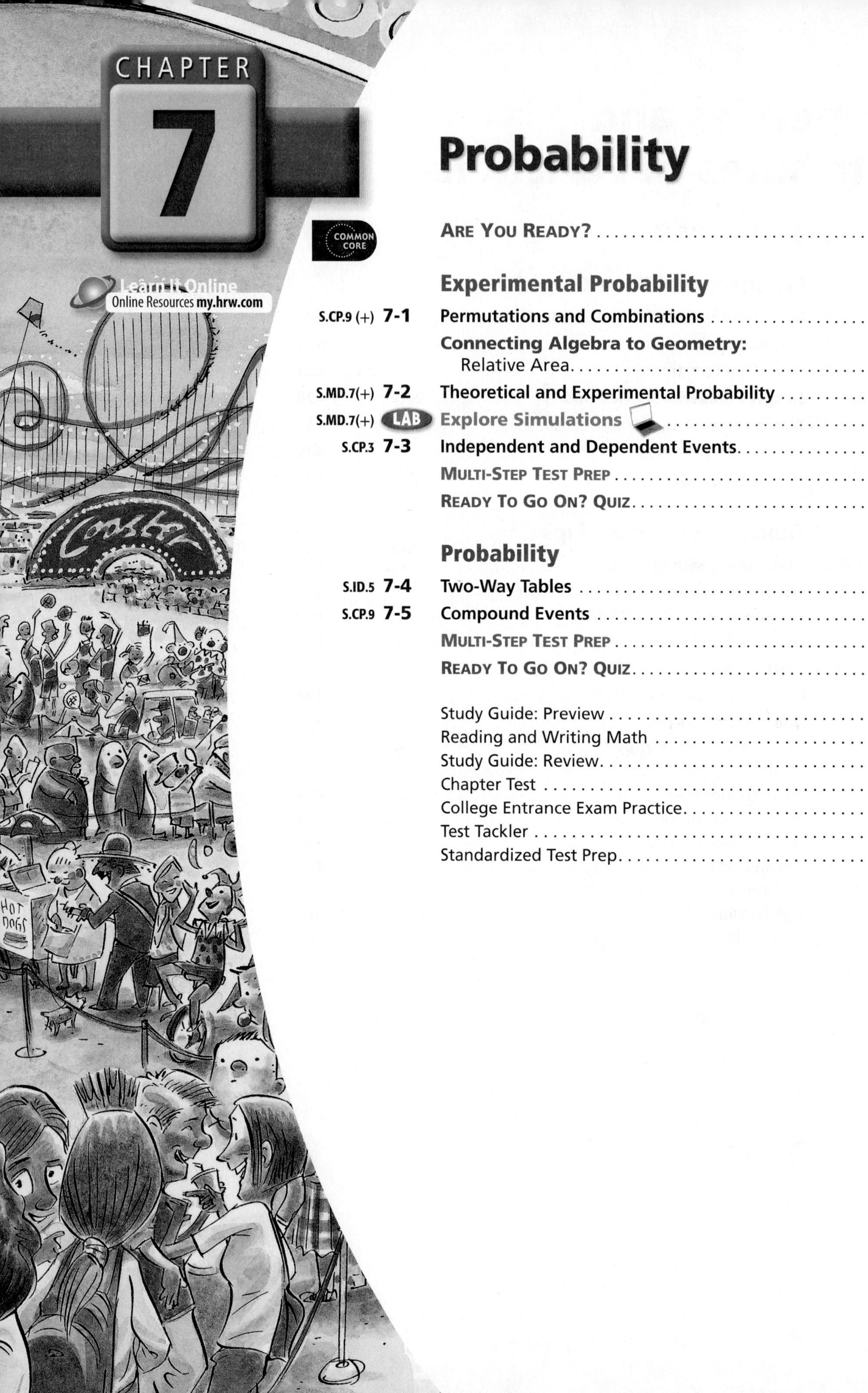

Probability

Data Analysis and Statistics

COMMON CORE

Learn It Online
Online Resources **my.hrw.com**

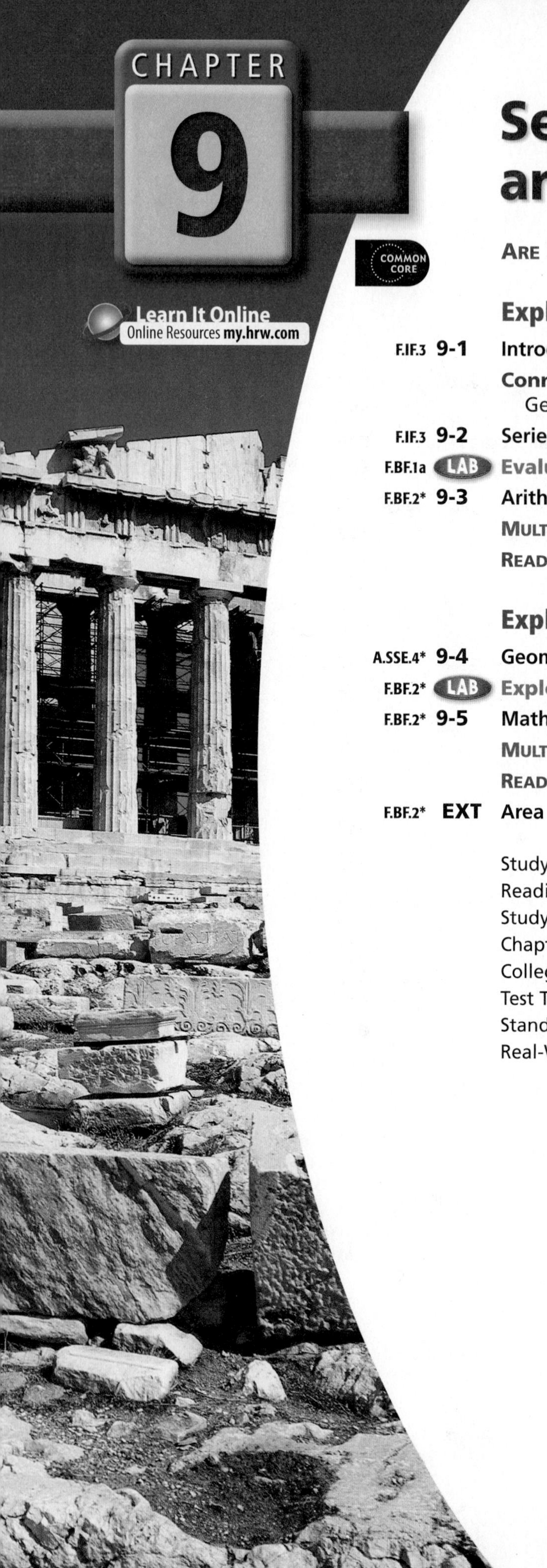

Sequences and Series

Trigonometric Functions

CHAPTER 10

Learn It Online
Online Resources **my.hrw.com**

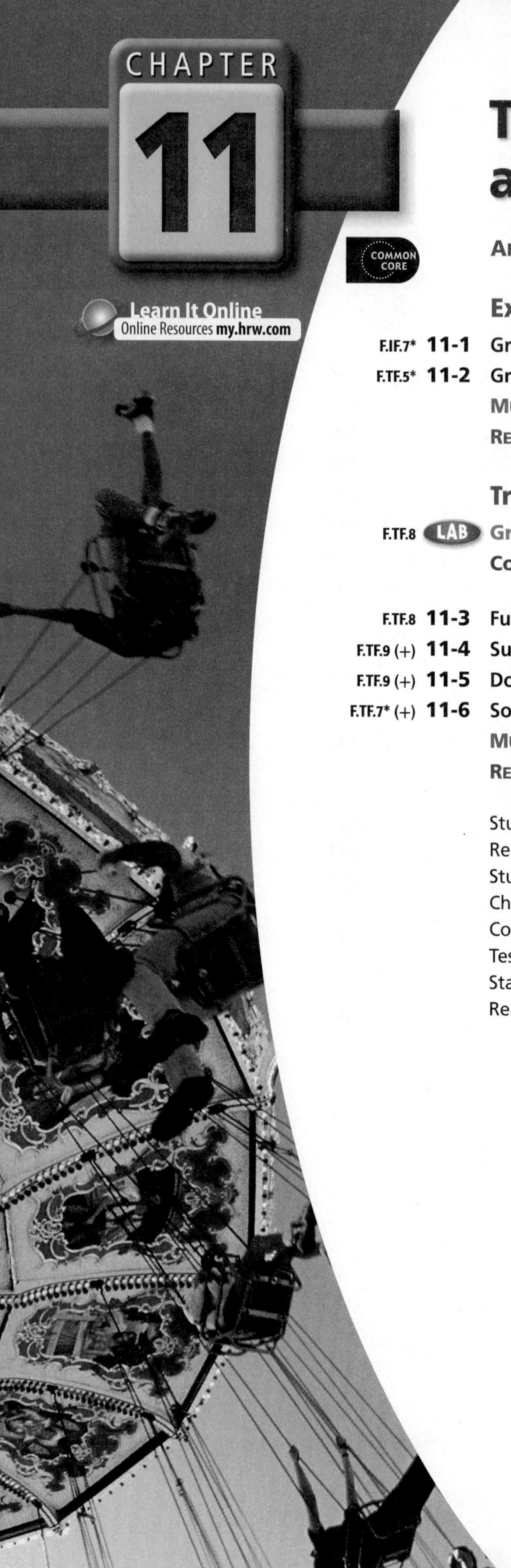

Trigonometric Graphs and Identities

Conic Sections

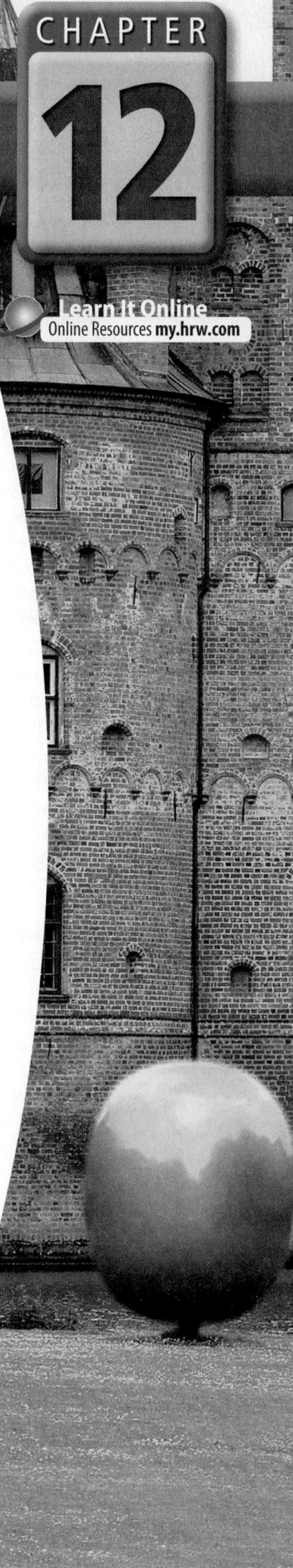

COMMON CORE

Standards for Mathematical Content

Correlation for Holt McDougal Algebra 1, Geometry, and Algebra 2

Standards	Descriptor	Algebra 1	Geometry	Algebra 2
Standards for Mathematical Content				
(+ = advanced; * = also a Modeling Standard)				
Number and Quantity				
CC.9-12.N.RN.1	Explain how the definition of the meaning of rational exponents follows from extending the properties of integer exponents to those values, allowing for a notation for radicals in terms of rational exponents.	SE: 392–393, 398–402		SE: 358–360, 395
CC.9-12.N.RN.2	Rewrite expressions involving radicals and rational exponents using the properties of exponents.	SE: 400–402	SE: 358	SE: 358–365, 392, 394, 398
CC.9-12.N.RN.3	Explain why the sum or product of two rational numbers is rational; that the sum of a rational number and an irrational number is irrational; and that the product of a nonzero rational number and an irrational number is irrational.	SE: 431–432		
CC.9-12.N.Q.1	Use units as a way to understand problems and to guide the solution of multi-step problems; choose and interpret units consistently in formulas; choose and interpret the scale and the origin in graphs and data displays.*	SE: 10, 26–30, 43–45, 53, 56–58, 59, 61, 62–68, 70–74, 83, 85–86, 88, 93, 108, 110, 115, 118, 122–124, 144, 159, 176, 184–185, 189–191, 194, 202, 208–209, 212, 213, 223, 265, 271–273, 279–281, 284, 488, 534, 536–537, 539–542, 549–550, 553, 556–558, 564–566, 572, 577–578, 598, 603, 628, 639–641	SE: 105, 108, 140, 186, 193–195, 197, 200, 211, 273, 445, 461, 528, 586, 593, 657, 671, 684–685, 695, 697–698, 703, 708, 713, 715, 727, 750, 753–756, 777, 786, 800, 865	SE: 12, 39, 90, 122, 229, 265, 293–294, 325, 340, 345–348, 363–364, 373, 381, 383, 437, 506, 650, 713, 732

SE = Student Edition

Standards	Descriptor	Algebra 1	Geometry	Algebra 2
Standards for Mathematical Content				
(+ = advanced; * = also a Modeling Standard)				
Number and Quantity				
CC.9-12.N.Q.2	Define appropriate quantities for the purpose of descriptive modeling.*	SE: 62–68, 75–81, 686–694, 695–701		
CC.9-12.N.Q.3	Choose a level of accuracy appropriate to limitations on measurement when reporting quantities.*	SE: 75–81		
CC.9-12.N.CN.1	Know there is a complex number i such that $i^2 = -1$, and every complex number has the form $a + bi$ with a and b real.			SE: 94–95, 138
CC.9-12.N.CN.2	Use the relation $i^2 = -1$ and the commutative, associative, and distributive properties to add, subtract, and multiply complex numbers.			SE: 128–131, 139, 141, 477
CC.9-12.N.CN.3	(+) Find the conjugate of a complex number; use conjugates to find moduli and quotients of complex numbers.			SE: 96–99, 126–133, 138, 145, 226
CC.9-12.N.CN.4	(+) Represent complex numbers on the complex plane in rectangular and polar form (including real and imaginary numbers), and explain why the rectangular and polar forms of a given complex number represent the same number.			*Opportunities to address this standard can be found on the following pages:* SE: 126–128, 139
CC.9-12.N.CN.5	(+) Represent addition, subtraction, multiplication, and conjugation of complex numbers geometrically on the complex plane; use properties of this representation for computation.			*Opportunities to address this standard can be found on the following pages:* SE: 126–133

SE = Student Edition

Standards	Descriptor	Algebra 1	Geometry	Algebra 2
Standards for Mathematical Content				
(+ = advanced; * = also a Modeling Standard)				
Number and Quantity				
CC.9-12.N.CN.6	(+) Calculate the distance between numbers in the complex plane as the modulus of the difference, and the midpoint of a segment as the average of the numbers at its endpoints.	*This standard is outside the scope of the Holt McDougal AGA series.*		
CC.9-12.N.CN.7	Solve quadratic equations with real coefficients that have complex solutions.			SE: 96–99, 101–107, 109, 138, 140, 190–195, 221
CC.9-12.N.CN.8	(+) Extend polynomial identities to the complex numbers.			SE: 189–195, 221
CC.9-12.N.CN.9	(+) Know the Fundamental Theorem of Algebra; show that it is true for quadratic polynomials.			SE: 189–195, 221, 222
CC.9-12.N.VM.1	(+) Recognize vector quantities as having both magnitude and direction. Represent vector quantities by directed line segments, and use appropriate symbols for vectors and their magnitudes (e.g., ***v***, |***v***|, ||***v***||, *v*).		SE: 577–585	
CC.9-12.N.VM.2	(+) Find the components of a vector by subtracting the coordinates of an initial point from the coordinates of a terminal point.		SE: 577	
CC.9-12.N.VM.3	(+) Solve problems involving velocity and other quantities that can be represented by vectors.		SE: 577–585, 586, 587, 591, 592, 593, 595	

SE = Student Edition

Standards	Descriptor	Algebra 1	Geometry	Algebra 2
Standards for Mathematical Content				
(+ = advanced; * = also a Modeling Standard)				
Number and Quantity				
CC.9-12.N.VM.4	(+) Add and subtract vectors. a. Add vectors end-to-end, component-wise, and by the parallelogram rule. Understand that the magnitude of a sum of two vectors is typically not the sum of the magnitudes. b. Given two vectors in magnitude and direction form, determine the magnitude and direction of their sum. c. Understand vector subtraction $\boldsymbol{v} - \boldsymbol{w}$ as $\boldsymbol{v} + (-\boldsymbol{w})$, where $-\boldsymbol{w}$ is the additive inverse of $\boldsymbol{w}$, with the same magnitude as $\boldsymbol{w}$ and pointing in the opposite direction. Represent vector subtraction graphically by connecting the tips in the appropriate order, and perform vector subtraction component-wise.		SE: 577–585, 586, 587, 591, 596, 785	
CC.9-12.N.VM.5	(+) Multiply a vector by a scalar. a. Represent scalar multiplication graphically by scaling vectors and possibly reversing their direction; perform scalar multiplication component-wise, e.g., as $c(v_x, v_y) = (cv_x, cv_y)$. b. Compute the magnitude of a scalar multiple $c\boldsymbol{v}$ using $\lVert c\boldsymbol{v} \rVert = \lvert c \rvert \boldsymbol{v}$. Compute the direction of $c\boldsymbol{v}$ knowing that when $\lvert c \rvert \boldsymbol{v} \neq 0$, the direction of $c\boldsymbol{v}$ is either along $\boldsymbol{v}$ (for $c > 0$) or against $\boldsymbol{v}$ (for $c < 0$).		SE: 577–585	
CC.9-12.N.VM.6	(+) Use matrices to represent and manipulate data, e.g., to represent payoffs or incidence relationships in a network.	*This standard is outside the scope of the Holt McDougal AGA series.*		

SE = Student Edition

Standards	Descriptor	Algebra 1	Geometry	Algebra 2
Standards for Mathematical Content				
(+ = advanced; * = also a Modeling Standard)				
Number and Quantity				
CC.9-12.N.VM.7	(+) Multiply matrices by scalars to produce new matrices, e.g., as when all of the payoffs in a game are doubled.	*This standard is outside the scope of the Holt McDougal AGA series.*		
CC.9-12.N.VM.8	(+) Add, subtract, and multiply matrices of appropriate dimensions.			SE: 144
CC.9-12.N.VM.9	(+) Understand that, unlike multiplication of numbers, matrix multiplication for square matrices is not a commutative operation, but still satisfies the associative and distributive properties.	*This standard is outside the scope of the Holt McDougal AGA series.*		
CC.9-12.N.VM.10	(+) Understand that the zero and identity matrices play a role in matrix addition and multiplication similar to the role of 0 and 1 in the real numbers. The determinant of a square matrix is nonzero if and only if the matrix has a multiplicative inverse.	*This standard is outside the scope of the Holt McDougal AGA series.*		
CC.9-12.N.VM.11	(+) Multiply a vector (regarded as a matrix with one column) by a matrix of suitable dimensions to produce another vector. Work with matrices as transformations of vectors.	*This standard is outside the scope of the Holt McDougal AGA series.*		
CC.9-12.N.VM.12	(+) Work with 2×2 matrices as a transformations of the plane, and interpret the absolute value of the determinant in terms of area.	*This standard is outside the scope of the Holt McDougal AGA series.*		

SE = Student Edition

Standards	Descriptor	Algebra 1	Geometry	Algebra 2
Standards for Mathematical Content				
(+ = advanced; * = also a Modeling Standard)				
Algebra				
CC.9-12.A.SSE.1	Interpret expressions that represent a quantity in terms of its context.* a. Interpret parts of an expression, such as terms, factors, and coefficients. b. Interpret complicated expressions by viewing one or more of their parts as a single entity.	SE: 10–11, 512, 514	SE: 36–41, 312–318, 689, 751, 757, 759	SE: 75, 234–240
CC.9-12.A.SSE.2	Use the structure of an expression to identify ways to rewrite it.	SE: 462, 463–469, 470–471, 472–479, 480–486, 487, 488, 489, 490–496, 498–503, 504, 505, 507–509, 510, 511, 514–515, 739	SE: 13–19	SE: 75, 141, 174–179, 219
CC.9-12.A.SSE.3	Choose and produce an equivalent form of an expression to reveal and explain properties of the quantity represented by the expression. a. Factor a quadratic expression to reveal the zeros of the function it defines. b. Complete the square in a quadratic expression to reveal the maximum or minimum value of the function it defines. c. Use the properties of exponents to transform expressions for exponential functions.	SE: a. & b.) 470–471, 472–479, 480–486, 487, 488, 489, 490–496, 499–503, 504, 505, 508–509, 510, 511, 514, 739 a.) 562–563, 636–641		SE: a. & b.) 75, 76, 77–84, 86–93, 137, 307 c.) 239
CC.9-12.A.SSE.4	Derive the formula for the sum of a finite geometric series (when the common ratio is not 1), and use the formula to solve problems.			SE: 658, 660–661, 678, 680

SE = Student Edition

Standards	Descriptor	Algebra 1	Geometry	Algebra 2
Standards for Mathematical Content				
(+ = advanced; * = also a Modeling Standard)				
Algebra				
CC.9-12.A.APR.1	Understand that polynomials form a system analogous to the integers, namely, they are closed under the operations of addition, subtraction, and multiplication; add, subtract, and multiply polynomials.	SE: 414–419, 422–429, 433–439		SE: 150–156, 158–164, 181, 218, 219, 222, 223, 224, 227, 307, 309, 335–338, 399, 403, 751
CC.9-12.A.APR.2	Know and apply the Remainder Theorem: For a polynomial $p(x)$ and a number a, the remainder on division by $x - a$ is $p(a)$, so $p(a) = 0$ if and only if $(x - a)$ is a factor of $p(x)$.			SE: 166–172, 174–179, 189–195, 220, 222
CC.9-12.A.APR.3	Identify zeros of polynomials when suitable factorizations are available, and use the zeros to construct a rough graph of the function defined by the polynomial.	SE: 562–567, 600–601		SE: 176–179, 181, 182–188, 219, 220, 223, 880
CC.9-12.A.APR.4	Prove polynomial identities and use them to describe numerical relationships.	SE: 433–439, 490–496, 497		SE: 158–161, 174–179
CC.9-12.A.APR.5	(+) Know and apply the Binomial Theorem for the expansion of $(x + y)^n$ in powers of x and y for a positive integer n, where x and y are any numbers, with coefficients determined for example by Pascal's Triangle. (The Binomial Theorem can be proved by mathematical induction or by a combinatorial argument.)			SE: 157, 158–164, 531, 532, 587, 590, 684
CC.9-12.A.APR.6	Rewrite simple rational expressions in different forms; write $a(x)/b(x)$ in the form $q(x) + r(x)/b(x)$, where $a(x)$, $b(x)$, $q(x)$, and $r(x)$ are polynomials with the degree of $r(x)$ less than the degree of $b(x)$, using inspection, long division, or, for the more complicated examples, a computer algebra system.		SE: 682, 685	SE: 166–172, 219, 222, 224, 537

SE = Student Edition

Standards	Descriptor	Algebra 1	Geometry	Algebra 2
Standards for Mathematical Content				
(+ = advanced; * = also a Modeling Standard)				
Algebra				
CC.9-12.A.APR.7	(+) Understand that rational expressions form a system analogous to the rational numbers, closed under addition, subtraction, multiplication, and division by a nonzero rational expression; add, subtract, multiply, and divide rational expressions.			SE: 321–326, 327–334, 335–338, 357, 391, 394, 395, 881
CC.9-12.A.CED.1	Create equations and inequalities in one variable and use them to solve problems. Include equations arising from linear and quadratic functions, and simple rational and exponential functions.*	SE: 19–22, 26–29, 34–38, 42–46, 54–59, 100–105, 107–111, 114–117, 118, 119, 122–125, 127–132, 144–147, 148, 149, 150–153, 154, 156–157, 158–159, 562–567, 568–573, 575–581, 582–589, 624–630		SE: 42, 46, 77–84, 85–92, 94–99, 100–107, 110–117, 144, 182–188, 189–195, 266–272, 348–355, 376–383, 474, 785–797
CC.9-12.A.CED.2	Create equations in two or more variables to represent relationships between quantities; graph equations on coordinate axes with labels and scales.*	SE: 179–185, 186–192, 230–236, 237–242, 244–251, 254–259, 260–265, 268–274, 275–282, 293–299, 301–307, 329–334, 336–342, 343–349, 352–357, 538–543, 545–551, 554–559, 582–589, 635–642, 649–655	SE: 182–187, 190–197, 201, 205, 206, 517	SE: 15–21, 24–30, 32–39, 44, 46, 59–66, 67–74, 118–125, 150–156, 197–203, 204–209, 210–215, 226, 234–240, 242–248, 249–255, 275–280, 281–288, 289–295, 313–320, 340–347, 367–375, 422–429, 432–439, 442–448, 450–456, 458–465, 536, 749, 754–761, 767

SE = Student Edition

Standards	Descriptor	Algebra 1	Geometry	Algebra 2
Standards for Mathematical Content				
(+ = advanced; * = also a Modeling Standard)				
Algebra				
CC.9-12.A.CED.3	Represent constraints by equations or inequalities, and by systems of equations and/or inequalities, and interpret solutions as viable or nonviable options in a modeling context.*	SE: 179–185, 230–236, 237–242, 260–265, 268–274, 275–282, 301–307, 331–334, 339–342, 346–349, 350–351, 354–356, 358, 359, 369–371, 374, 375, 376–378, 380, 381, 384–385, 451, 538–543, 554–559, 562–567, 568–573, 575–581, 582–589, 613, 635–642, 649–655		SE: 15–21, 24–30, 32–39, 59–66, 67–74, 110–117, 118–125, 150–156, 197–203, 204–209, 210–215, 234–240, 242–248, 249–255, 275–280, 281–288, 289–295, 313–320, 340–347, 367–375, 422–429, 432–439, 442–448, 450–456, 458–465, 749, 754–761, 762–767
CC.9-12.A.CED.4	Rearrange formulas to highlight a quantity of interest, using the same reasoning as in solving equations.*	SE: 49–53, 59, 68, 85, 88, 161	SE: 41, 673, 674, 676, 685	SE: 449
CC.9-12.A.REI.1	Explain each step in solving a simple equation as following from the equality of numbers asserted at the previous step, starting from the assumption that the original equation has a solution. Construct a viable argument to justify a solution method.	SE: 17–22, 24–30, 32–38, 40–46, 54–59, 61, 84–85	SE: 104–109, 127, 132, 134	SE: 77–84, 85–92, 100–107, 182–188, 266–272, 348–355, 376–383
CC.9-12.A.REI.2	Solve simple rational and radical equations in one variable, and give examples showing how extraneous solutions may arise.	SE: 669, 673, 674	SE: 466–471, 482–489, 493, 495–501, 520	SE: 348–355, 357, 376–383, 388, 389, 392, 393, 394, 395, 398, 399, 476, 809

SE = Student Edition

Standards	Descriptor	Algebra 1	Geometry	Algebra 2
Standards for Mathematical Content				
(+ = advanced; * = also a Modeling Standard)				
Algebra				
CC.9-12.A.REI.3	Solve linear equations and inequalities in one variable, including equations with coefficients represented by letters.	SE: 16, 17–22, 24–30, 31, 32–38, 39, 40–46, 53, 59, 60, 61, 68, 84–85, 88, 89, 92–93, 97, 106–111, 112–117, 118, 119, 120–125, 126–132, 140, 147, 148, 149, 151–152, 154, 155, 158–159, 161, 169, 185, 192, 203, 211, 222, 223, 236, 274, 299, 325, 334, 397, 403, 419, 450, 469, 519, 612, 623, 630, 679, 701, 721, 760		SE: 43, 46, 47, 48
CC.9-12.A.REI.4	Solve quadratic equations in one variable. a. Use the method of completing the square to transform any quadratic equation in x into an equation of the form $(x - p)^2 = q$ that has the same solutions. Derive the quadratic formula from this form. b. Solve quadratic equations by inspection (e.g., for $x^2 = 49$), taking square roots, completing the square, the quadratic formula and factoring, as appropriate to the initial form of the equation. Recognize when the quadratic formula gives complex solutions and write them as $a \pm bi$ for real numbers a and b.	SE: 554–559, 560–561, 562–567, 568–573, 576–581, 582–583, 585–589, 598, 599, 606–607, 608, 609, 613, 655	SE: 27, 45, 47–48, 55, 59, 63, 243, 245, 289, 338, 361–367, 377, 381, 382, 400, 427, 442, 444–446, 508, 798, 842, 844–846	SE: 77–84, 85–92, 96–99, 100–107, 108, 109, 137, 140, 143, 145, 307, 309, 684, 749
CC.9-12.A.REI.5	Prove that, given a system of two equations in two variables, replacing one equation by the sum of that equation and a multiple of the other produces a system with the same solutions.	SE: 343–349		

SE = Student Edition

Standards	Descriptor	Algebra 1	Geometry	Algebra 2
Standards for Mathematical Content				
(+ = advanced; * = also a Modeling Standard)				
Algebra				
CC.9-12.A.REI.6	Solve systems of linear equations exactly and approximately (e.g., with graphs), focusing on pairs of linear equations in two variables.	SE: 329–334, 336–342, 343–349, 350–351, 352–357, 358, 359, 376–378, 380, 381, 383, 384	SE: 152–153, 158–160, 161, 176, 194, 195, 328, 329–330	SE: 684
CC.9-12.A.REI.7	Solve a simple system consisting of a linear equation and a quadratic equation in two variables algebraically and graphically.	SE: 590–597	SE: 853	SE: 809, 862–869, 871, 872, 876, 877
CC.9-12.A.REI.8	(+) Represent a system of linear equations as a single matrix equation in a vector variable.	*This standard is outside the scope of the Holt McDougal AGA series.*		
CC.9-12.A.REI.9	(+) Find the inverse of a matrix if it exists and use it to solve systems of linear equations (using technology for matrices of dimension 3×3 or greater).	*This standard is outside the scope of the Holt McDougal AGA series.*		
CC.9-12.A.REI.10	Understand that the graph of an equation in two variables is the set of all its solutions plotted in the coordinate plane, often forming a curve (which could be a line).	SE: 186–192, 193, 216		SE: 43, 46
CC.9-12.A.REI.11	Explain why the x-coordinates of the points where the graphs of the equations $y = f(x)$ and $y = g(x)$ intersect are the solutions of the equation $f(x) = g(x)$; find the solutions approximately, e.g., using technology to graph the functions, make tables of values, or find successive approximations. Include cases where $f(x)$ and/or $g(x)$ are linear, polynomial, rational, absolute value, exponential, and logarithmic functions.*	SE: 47–48, 554–559, 560–561, 628, 629		SE: 79–80, 182–186, 191–192, 268–269, 351–352, 384–387

SE = Student Edition

Standards	Descriptor	Algebra 1	Geometry	Algebra 2
Standards for Mathematical Content				
(+ = advanced; * = also a Modeling Standard)				
Algebra				
CC.9-12.A.REI.12	Graph the solutions to a linear inequality in two variables as a half-plane (excluding the boundary in the case of a strict inequality), and graph the solution set to a system of linear inequalities in two variables as the intersection of the corresponding half-planes.	SE: 360–366, 368–372, 373, 374, 375, 379, 380, 381, 486		SE: 44, 46, 47, 50, 307, 880
CC.9-12.F.IF.1	Understand that a function from one set (called the domain) to another set (called the range) assigns to each element of the domain exactly one element of the range. If *f* is a function and *x* is an element of its domain, then $f(x)$ denotes the output of *f* corresponding to the input *x*. The graph of *f* is the graph of the equation $y = f(x)$.	SE: 170–176, 177, 179–186, 187–192, 193, 195, 215, 219, 222		
CC.9-12.F.IF.2	Use function notation, evaluate functions for inputs in their domains, and interpret statements that use function notation in terms of a context.	SE: 180–185, 192, 195, 216, 218, 219, 223, 322, 397, 629		SE: 50
CC.9-12.F.IF.3	Recognize that sequences are functions, sometimes defined recursively, whose domain is a subset of the integers.	SE: 206–211, 618–623		SE: 626–632
CC.9-12.F.IF.4	For a function that models a relationship between two quantities, interpret key features of graphs and tables in terms of the quantities, and sketch graphs showing key features given a verbal description of the relationship. Key features include: intercepts; intervals where the function is increasing, decreasing, positive, or negative; relative maximums and minimums; symmetries; end behavior; and periodicity.*	SE: 165, 167–168, 195, 214, 230, 234–235, 237–238, 240–242, 266, 267, 271–273, 309, 310–313, 315, 318, 531–532, 535–537, 541–543, 545–551, 552, 553, 554–559, 600–601, 603, 604–605, 608, 613, 630, 641, 644–647, 649–655, 565–659		SE: 7–14, 24–30, 43, 59–66, 67–74, 77–84, 109, 137, 140, 153–156, 183–188, 197–203, 204–209, 218, 220, 221, 222, 223, 236–240, 251–255, 275–280, 281–288, 313–320, 340–347, 367–375, 399, 406–413, 422–429, 432–439, 457, 476, 754–761, 762–767

SE = Student Edition

Standards	Descriptor	Algebra 1	Geometry	Algebra 2
Standards for Mathematical Content				
(+ = advanced; * = also a Modeling Standard)				
Functions				
CC.9-12.F.IF.5	Relate the domain of a function to its graph and, where applicable, to the quantitative relationship it describes.*	SE: 170–176, 182–184, 186–192, 194, 195, 218, 223, 233–235, 241, 260–265, 310–311, 313, 314, 323, 486, 525–529, 542–543, 545–551, 553, 600–601, 603, 669, 672, 674, 675	SE: 401, 685	SE: 14, 19–21, 65, 70, 72–73, 134, 172, 196, 226, 240, 241, 242, 245, 247, 253, 263, 280, 285–286, 288, 299, 302, 341, 345, 367–368, 371–372, 375, 388, 389, 392–393, 394, 413, 428–429, 439, 441, 453–454, 467, 470, 472, 685, 713, 719, 749, 754–761, 767, 851
CC.9-12.F.IF.6	Calculate and interpret the average rate of change of a function (presented symbolically or as a table) over a specified interval. Estimate the rate of change from a graph.*	SE: 244–245, 248–251, 254–259, 267, 268–274, 308, 315, 318, 323, 469, 656–659, 660–667, 739		SE: 44, 210–215, 408–413, 414–421, 468

SE = Student Edition

Standards	Descriptor	Algebra 1	Geometry	Algebra 2
Standards for Mathematical Content				
(+ = advanced; * = also a Modeling Standard)				
Functions				
CC.9-12.F.IF.7	Graph functions expressed symbolically and show key features of the graph, by hand in simple cases and using technology for more complicated cases.* a. Graph linear and quadratic functions and show intercepts, maxima, and minima. b. Graph square root, cube root, and piecewise-defined functions, including step functions and absolute value functions. c. Graph polynomial functions, identifying zeros when suitable factorizations are available, and showing end behavior. d. (+) Graph rational functions, identifying zeros and asymptotes when suitable factorizations are available, and showing end behavior. e. Graph exponential and logarithmic functions, showing intercepts and end behavior, and trigonometric functions, showing period, midline, and amplitude.	SE: a.) 186–192, 193, 195, 216, 218, 219, 220, 230–236, 237–242, 260–265, 266, 267, 268–274, 275–282, 283, 301–307, 309, 314–317, 318, 320, 321, 522–529, 531–537, 538–543, 553, 554–559, 605, 608, 609, 649–655 b.) 310–313 c.) 544, 545–551, 600–603 e.) 624–630		SE: a.) 24–30, 43, 46, 59–66, 67–74, 76, 77–84, 109, 137, 140, 144, 226, 476 b.) 45, 46, 367–375, 388, 389, 393, 394, 398, 422–429, 430–431, 441, 469, 685 c.) 153–156, 182–188, 196, 197–203, 204–209, 218, 220, 221 d.) 339, 340–347, 357, 392, 395, 399 e.) 234–240, 251–255, 275–280, 297, 298, 302, 754–755, 762–767, 768, 769, 800, 801, 804, 807
CC.9–12.F.IF.8	Write a function defined by an expression in different but equivalent forms to reveal and explain different properties of the function. a. Use the process of factoring and completing the square in a quadratic function to show zeros, extreme values, and symmetry of the graph, and interpret these in terms of a context. b. Use the properties of exponents to interpret expressions for exponential functions.	SE: 530, 533–534, 536–537, 541, 543, 553, 605, 608, 624–630		SE: a.) 67–74, 77–84, 85–92, 109, 881 b.) 234–240, 265, 302, 684

SE = Student Edition

Standards	Descriptor	Algebra 1	Geometry	Algebra 2
Standards for Mathematical Content				
(+ = advanced; * = also a Modeling Standard)				
Functions				
CC.9-12.F.IF.9	Compare properties of two functions each represented in a different way (algebraically, graphically, numerically in tables, or by verbal descriptions).	SE: 230–236, 310–313, 531–537, 538–543, 600–601, 624–630, 660–667		SE: 414–421
CC.9-12.F.BF.1	Write a function that describes a relationship between two quantities.* a. Determine an explicit expression, a recursive process, or steps for calculation from a context. b. Combine standard function types using arithmetic operations. c. (+) Compose functions.	SE: 179–185, 230–236, 268–274, 275–282, 545–551, 568–573, 635–642, 644–647, 649–655		SE: 32–39, 118–125, 159–163, 169–171, 180, 181, 206–209, 210–215, 219, 221, 222, 278, 289–295, 425–429, 434–438, 442–448, 450–456, 458–465, 470, 472, 475, 476, 881
CC.9-12.F.BF.2	Write arithmetic and geometric sequences both recursively and with an explicit formula, use them to model situations, and translate between the two forms.*	SE: 206–210, 622–623, 644–647		SE: 626–632, 647–650, 653, 654–663, 676, 677, 678, 680, 681, 684, 685, 749
CC.9-12.F.BF.3	Identify the effect on the graph of replacing $f(x)$ by $f(x) + k$, $k f(x)$, $f(kx)$, and $f(x + k)$ for specific values of k (both positive and negative); find the value of k given the graphs. Experiment with cases and illustrate an explanation of the effects on the graph using technology. Include recognizing even and odd functions from their graphs and algebraic expressions for them.	SE: 300, 301–307, 309, 310–313, 317, 318, 544, 545–551, 553, 559, 606, 608, 732, 747	SE: 101, 374, 618, 638, 640, 748	SE: 7–14, 15–21, 22, 23, 24–30, 44, 46, 51, 59–66, 109, 136, 204–209, 221, 222, 223, 225, 227, 281–288, 301, 302, 306, 368–375, 388, 389, 432–439, 469, 472, 473, 684, 748, 756–761, 762–767

SE = Student Edition

Standards	Descriptor	Algebra 1	Geometry	Algebra 2
Standards for Mathematical Content				
(+ = advanced; * = also a Modeling Standard)				
Functions				
CC.9-12.F.BF.4	Find inverse functions. a. Solve an equation of the form $f(x) = c$ for a simple function f that has an inverse and write an expression for the inverse. b. (+) Verify by composition that one function is the inverse of another. c. (+) Read values of an inverse function from a graph or a table, given that the function has an inverse. d. (+) Produce an invertible function from a non-invertible function by restricting the domain.		SE: 551, 558	SE: a.–c.) 241, 242–248, 251–255, 265, 299, 302, 303, 306, 450–456, 470, 472, 473, 684, 881 c.) 367
CC.9-12.F.BF.5	(+) Understand the inverse relationship between exponents and logarithms and use this relationship to solve problems involving logarithms and exponents.			SE: 249–255, 256–263, 264, 265, 266–272, 275–280, 297, 300, 302, 303, 306, 399, 881
CC.9-12.F.LE.1	Distinguish between situations that can be modeled with linear functions and with exponential functions.* a. Prove that linear functions grow by equal differences over equal intervals, and that exponential functions grow by equal factors over equal intervals. b. Recognize situations in which one quantity changes at a constant rate per unit interval relative to another. c. Recognize situations in which a quantity grows or decays by a constant percent rate per unit interval relative to another.	SE: 625–628, 649–655		SE: a.) 210–215, 406–413, 458–465 b.) 406–413, 441, 458–465, 471, 472 c.) 234–240, 458–465, 471, 472

SE = Student Edition

Standards	Descriptor	Algebra 1	Geometry	Algebra 2
Standards for Mathematical Content				
(+ = advanced; * = also a Modeling Standard)				
Functions				
CC.9-12.F.LE.2	Construct linear and exponential functions, including arithmetic and geometric sequences, given a graph, a description of a relationship, or two input-output pairs (include reading these from a table).*	SE: 206–211, 213, 216–217, 218, 219, 220, 230–236, 237–242, 260–265, 268–274, 275–282, 309, 314–317, 318, 320, 321, 618–623, 633, 635–642, 644–647, 649–655		SE: 44, 46, 234–240, 305, 398, 406–413, 441, 458–465, 468, 471, 472, 537, 643–651, 654–753, 880
CC.9-12.F.LE.3	Observe using graphs and tables that a quantity increasing exponentially eventually exceeds a quantity increasing linearly, quadratically, or (more generally) as a polynomial function.*	SE: 630, 660–667		SE: 234–240, 458–465
CC.9-12.F.LE.4	For exponential models, express as *a* logarithm the solution to $ab^{ct} = d$ where *a*, *c*, and *d* are numbers and the base *b* is 2, 10, or *e*; evaluate the logarithm using technology.*			SE: 249–255, 268–272, 274, 275–280
CC.9-12.F.LE.5	Interpret the parameters in a linear or exponential function in terms of a context.*	SE: 268–274, 635–642		SE: 234–240, 299
CC.9-12.F.TF.1	Understand radian measure of an angle as the length of the arc on the unit circle subtended by the angle.			SE: 707–713
CC.9-12.F.TF.2	Explain how the unit circle in the coordinate plane enables the extension of trigonometric functions to all real numbers, interpreted as radian measures of angles traversed counterclockwise around the unit circle.			SE: 700–702, 706–709

SE = Student Edition

Standards	Descriptor	Algebra 1	Geometry	Algebra 2
Standards for Mathematical Content				
(+ = advanced; * = also a Modeling Standard)				
Functions				
CC.9-12.F.TF.3	(+) Use special triangles to determine geometrically the values of sine, cosine, tangent for $\pi/3$, $\pi/4$ and $\pi/6$, and use the unit circle to express the values of sine, cosines, and tangent for x, $\pi + x$, and $2\pi - x$ in terms of their values for x, where x is any real number.			SE: 693–699, 706–713, 721, 741, 744, 745
CC.9-12.F.TF.4	(+) Use the unit circle to explain symmetry (odd and even) and periodicity of trigonometric functions.			*Opportunities to address this standard can be found on the following pages:* SE: 707–713, 754–761
CC.9-12.F.TF.5	Choose trigonometric functions to model periodic phenomena with specified amplitude, frequency, and midline.*			SE: 756–760, 762–767
CC.9-12.F.TF.6	(+) Understand that restricting a trigonometric function to a domain on which it is always increasing or always decreasing allows its inverse to be constructed.			SE: 714–719
CC.9-12.F.TF.7	(+) Use inverse functions to solve trigonometric equations that arise in modeling contexts; evaluate the solutions using technology, and interpret them in terms of the context.*		SE: 551, 552–559	SE: 716–719, 721, 742, 744, 745, 748, 791–797
CC.9-12.F.TF.8	Prove the Pythagorean identity $\sin^2(\theta) + \cos^2(\theta) = 1$ and use it to calculate trigonometric ratios.			SE: 772–777, 801, 804, 807
CC.9-12.F.TF.9	(+) Prove the addition and subtraction formulas for sine, cosine, and tangent and use them to solve problems.			SE: 778–783, 799, 802, 804, 805, 808

SE = Student Edition

Standards	Descriptor	Algebra 1	Geometry	Algebra 2
Standards for Mathematical Content				
(+ = advanced; * = also a Modeling Standard)				
Geometry				
CC.9-12.G.CO.1	Know precise definitions of angle, circle, perpendicular line, parallel line, and line segment, based on the undefined notions of point, line, distance along a line, and distance around a circular arc.		SE: 6–11, 20–27, 35, 64, 68, 69, 146–151, 688–693	SE: 700–705, 707–713
CC.9-12.G.CO.2	Represent transformations in the plane using, e.g., transparencies and geometry software; describe transformations as functions that take points in the plane as inputs and give other points as outputs. Compare transformations that preserve distance and angle to those that do not (e.g., translation versus horizontal stretch).		SE: 50–55, 56–57, 509–514, 523, 529, 596, 604–610, 611–617, 619–625, 626–631, 633, 650–657, 660–663, 664, 668, 669, 785	
CC.9-12.G.CO.3	Given a rectangle, parallelogram, trapezoid, or regular polygon, describe the rotations and reflections that carry it onto itself.		SE: 604–610, 611–617, 619–625, 626–631, 633, 634–640, 660–663, 664, 665	
CC.9-12.G.CO.4	Develop definitions of rotations, reflections, and translations in terms of angles, circles, perpendicular lines, parallel lines, and line segments.		SE: 50–55, 604–610, 611–617, 619–625, 633, 660, 661, 664	
CC.9-12.G.CO.5	Given a geometric figure and a rotation, reflection, or translation, draw the transformed figure using, e.g., graph paper, tracing paper, or geometry software. Specify a sequence of transformations that will carry a given figure onto another.		SE: 50–55, 56–57, 59, 63, 64, 604–610, 611–617, 619–625, 626–631, 633, 660–663, 664, 665, 668, 669, 785	

SE = Student Edition

Standards	Descriptor	Algebra 1	Geometry	Algebra 2
Standards for Mathematical Content				
(+ = advanced; * = also a Modeling Standard)				
Geometry				
CC.9-12.G.CO.6	Use geometric descriptions of rigid motions to transform figures and to predict the effect of a given rigid motion on a given figure; given two figures, use the definition of congruence in terms of rigid motions to decide if they are congruent.		SE: 220–223, 258–267, 274–277, 293, 298, 300, 604–610, 611–617, 619–625	
CC.9-12.G.CO.7	Use the definition of congruence in terms of rigid motions to show that two triangles are congruent if and only if corresponding pairs of sides and corresponding pairs of angles are congruent.	SE: 69–74	SE: 220–223, 268–273, 274–277, 293, 294–295, 298, 300	
CC.9-12.G.CO.8	Explain how the criteria for triangle congruence (ASA, SAS, and SSS) follow from the definition of congruence in terms of rigid motions.		SE: 248–249, 250–257, 260–267, 293, 297, 300, 302, 304, 387	
CC.9-12.G.CO.9	Prove geometric theorems about lines and angles. Theorems include: vertical angles are congruent; when a transversal crosses parallel lines, alternate interior angles are congruent and corresponding angles are congruent; points on a perpendicular bisector of a line segment are exactly those equidistant from the segment's endpoints.		SE: 118–125, 155–159, 162, 169, 181, 203–204, 206, 312–318	

SE = Student Edition

Standards	Descriptor	Algebra 1	Geometry	Algebra 2
Standards for Mathematical Content				
(+ = advanced; * = also a Modeling Standard)				
Geometry				
CC.9-12.G.CO.10	Prove theorems about triangles. Theorems include: measures of interior angles of a triangle sum to 180°; base angles of isosceles triangles are congruent; the segment joining midpoints of two sides of a triangle is parallel to the third side and half the length; the medians of a triangle meet at a point.		SE: 231–238, 247, 285–291, 293, 296, 299, 300, 326–331, 334–339, 341, 379, 380	
CC.9-12.G.CO.11	Prove theorems about parallelograms. Theorems include: opposite sides are congruent, the diagonals of a parallelogram bisect each other, and conversely, rectangles are parallelograms with congruent diagonals.	SE: 294, 297, 299	SE: 403–404, 419, 420–427, 451, 454	
CC.9-12.G.CO.12	Make formal geometric constructions with a variety of tools and methods (compass and straightedge, string, reflective devices, paper folding, dynamic geometry software, etc.). Copying a segment; copying an angle; bisecting a segment; bisecting an angle; constructing perpendicular lines, including the perpendicular bisector of a line segment; and constructing a line parallel to a given line through a point not on the line.		SE: 14, 16, 17-18, 22–27, 35, 61, 170–171, 172, 177, 179	
CC.9-12.G.CO.13	Construct an equilateral triangle, a square, and a regular hexagon inscribed in a circle.		SE: 392–393, 826	

SE = Student Edition

Standards	Descriptor	Algebra 1	Geometry	Algebra 2
Standards for Mathematical Content				
(+ = advanced; * = also a Modeling Standard)				
Geometry				
CC.9-12.G.SRT.1	Verify experimentally the properties of dilations given by a center and a scale factor: a. A dilation takes a line not passing through the center of the dilation to a parallel line, and leaves a line passing through the center unchanged. b. The dilation of a line segment is longer or shorter in the ratio given by the scale factor.		SE: 472–479, 509–514, 650–657, 659, 663, 664	
CC.9-12.G.SRT.2	Given two figures, use the definition of similarity in terms of similarity transformations to decide if they are similar; explain using similarity transformations the meaning of similarity for triangles as the equality of all corresponding angles and the proportionality of all corresponding pairs of sides.		SE: 466–471, 472–479, 480–481, 482–489, 493, 495–501, 519, 521, 524, 525, 526, 527, 531, 597	
CC.9-12.G.SRT.3	Use the properties of similarity transformations to establish the AA criterion for two triangles to be similar.		SE: 482–489, 521, 524	
CC.9-12.G.SRT.4	Prove theorems about triangles. Theorems include: a line parallel to one side of a triangle divides the other two proportionally, and conversely; the Pythagorean Theorem proved using triangle similarity.	SE: 69–70, 72–74, 83, 86, 88, 89, 185, 236, 323	SE: 312–318, 341, 359, 360–367, 377, 378, 490–491, 495, 501, 522, 696	
CC.9-12.G.SRT.5	Use congruence and similarity criteria for triangles to solve problems and prove relationships in geometric figures.		SE: 250–257, 258–267, 268–273, 293, 297–298, 300, 302, 304, 482–489, 493, 495–501, 519, 521, 524	

SE = Student Edition

Standards	Descriptor	Algebra 1	Geometry	Algebra 2
Standards for Mathematical Content				
(+ = advanced; * = also a Modeling Standard)				
Geometry				
CC.9-12.G.SRT.6	Understand that by similarity, side ratios in right triangles are properties of the angles in the triangle, leading to definitions of trigonometric ratios for acute angles.		SE: 534–539, 540, 541–548, 561, 588, 589, 592	SE: 693
CC.9-12.G.SRT.7	Explain and use the relationship between the sine and cosine of complementary angles.		SE: 549–550	
CC.9-12.G.SRT.8	Use trigonometric ratios and the Pythagorean Theorem to solve right triangles in applied problems.		SE: 360–371, 377, 381, 382, 383, 385, 552–559, 560, 561, 562–567, 568, 587, 589, 590, 592, 594, 596, 865	SE: 689, 693–699, 721, 740, 744, 745, 749, 809
CC.9-12.G.SRT.9	(+) Derive the formula $A = \frac{1}{2} ab \sin(C)$ for the area of a triangle by drawing an auxiliary line from a vertex perpendicular to the opposite side.		SE: 701	SE: 722
CC.9-12.G.SRT.10	(+) Prove the Laws of Sines and Cosines and use them to solve problems.		SE: 569–576, 587, 590, 592, 593	SE: 722–729, 730–737, 739, 742–743, 744, 745, 748
CC.9-12.G.SRT.11	(+) Understand and apply the Law of Sines and the Law of Cosines to find unknown measurements in right and non-right triangles (e.g., surveying problems, resultant forces).		SE: 569–576, 587, 590, 592, 593	SE: 725–729, 733–737, 739, 742–743, 744
CC.9-12.G.C.1	Prove that all circles are similar.		SE: 472–479	

SE = Student Edition

Standards	Descriptor	Algebra 1	Geometry	Algebra 2
Standards for Mathematical Content				
(+ = advanced; * = also a Modeling Standard)				
Geometry				
CC.9-12.G.C.2	Identify and describe relationships among inscribed angles, radii, and chords. Include the relationship between central, inscribed, and circumscribed angles; inscribed angles on a diameter are right angles; the radius of a circle is perpendicular to the tangent where the radius intersects the circle.		SE: 820–827, 830–837, 840–846, 855, 856, 860, 863, 864	
CC.9-12.G.C.3	Construct the inscribed and circumscribed circles of a triangle, and prove properties of angles for a quadrilateral inscribed in a circle.		SE: 319, 325, 823–827, 855, 858, 865	
CC.9-12.G.C.4	(+) Construct a tangent line from a point outside a given circle to the circle.		SE: 827	
CC.9-12.G.C.5	Derive using similarity the fact that the length of the arc intercepted by an angle is proportional to the radius, and define the radian measure of the angle as the constant of proportionality; derive the formula for the area of a sector.		SE: 810–815, 816–817	SE: 707–713
CC.9-12.G.GPE.1	Derive the equation of a circle of given center and radius using the Pythagorean Theorem; complete the square to find the center and radius of a circle given by an equation.		SE: 847–853, 859, 860	SE: 823–828, 858–860, 870, 871
CC.9-12.G.GPE.2	Derive the equation of a parabola given a focus and directrix.			SE: 845–851, 853, 871, 874, 876, 880

SE = Student Edition

Standards	Descriptor	Algebra 1	Geometry	Algebra 2
Standards for Mathematical Content				
(+ = advanced; * = also a Modeling Standard)				
Geometry				
CC.9–12.G.GPE.3	(+) Derive the equations of ellipses and hyperbolas given foci and directrices.			SE: 748, 830–836, 837, 838–844, 852, 853, 871, 873–874, 876, 881
CC.9-12.G.GPE.4	Use coordinates to prove simple geometric theorems algebraically.		SE: 279–284	SE: 820, 821
CC.9-12.G.GPE.5	Prove the slope criteria for parallel and perpendicular lines and use them to solve geometric problems (e.g., find the equation of line parallel or perpendicular to a given line that passes through a given point).	SE: 293–299, 307, 309, 317, 318, 323, 384, 450, 573, 761	SE: 190–197, 216–219, 412–417, 419, 426–427, 452, 454, 669	
CC.9-12.G.GPE.6	Find the point on a directed line segment between two given points that partitions the segment in a given ratio.	SE: 267, 316	SE: 515–516, 704–709	
CC.9-12.G.GPE.7	Use coordinates to compute perimeters of polygons and areas of triangles and rectangles, e.g., using the distance formula.*		SE: 704–705, 706–709, 727, 730, 732, 737	
CC.9-12.G.GMD.1	Give an informal argument for the formulas for the circumference of a circle, area of a circle, volume of a cylinder, pyramid, and cone. Use dissection arguments, Cavalieri's principle, and informal limit arguments.		SE: 688–693, 749–751, 757	
CC.9-12.G.GMD.2	(+) Give an informal argument using Cavalieri's principle for the formulas for the volume of a sphere and other solid figures.		SE: 749–756, 757–763, 765–772	

SE = Student Edition

Standards	Descriptor	Algebra 1	Geometry	Algebra 2
Standards for Mathematical Content				
(+ = advanced; * = also a Modeling Standard)				
Geometry				
CC.9-12.G.GMD.3	Use volume formulas for cylinders, pyramids, cones, and spheres to solve problems.*	SE: 402–403, 429, 430, 503, 573, 631	SE: 668, 749–756, 757–764, 766–773, 777, 779, 781, 784, 785, 864	SE: 172, 191–192, 325, 366, 816, 829
CC.9-12.G.GMD.4	Identify the shapes of two-dimensional cross-sections of three-dimensional objects, and identify three-dimensional objects generated by rotations of two-dimensional objects.		SE: 742–748, 778	
CC.9-12.G.MG.1	Use geometric shapes, their measures, and their properties to describe objects (e.g., modeling a tree trunk or a human torso as a cylinder).*	SE: 365, 410, 417, 428, 441, 477, 479, 485, 495, 577–578, 580	SE: 226–228, 235–237, 243–244, 253, 256, 266, 290, 291, 300, 316–317, 322–323, 336–337, 440, 444–446, 448, 449, 453, 544–547, 560, 750, 753–755, 758, 761–763, 797–799, 808, 813–814, 841, 843–845	
CC.9-12.G.MG.2	Apply concepts of density based on area and volume in modeling situations (e.g., persons per square mile, BTUs per cubic foot).*	SE: 68	SE: 750, 753, 755, 777	
CC.9-12.G.MG.3	Apply geometric methods to solve design problems (e.g., designing an object or structure to satisfy physical constraints or minimize cost; working with typographic grid systems based on ratios).*		SE: 105, 264, 268, 283, 323, 325, 329–330, 348, 372, 415, 445, 460–461, 471, 512–513, 605, 627, 695, 724, 748	

SE = Student Edition

Standards	Descriptor	Algebra 1	Geometry	Algebra 2
Standards for Mathematical Content				
(+ = advanced; * = also a Modeling Standard)				
Statistics and Probability				
CC.9-12.S.ID.1	Represent data with plots on the real number line (dot plots, histograms, and box plots).*	SE: 686–694, 695–701, 704–709, 710–713, 752, 753, 756		SE: 531, 532, 543–544, 547–548, 749
CC.9-12.S.ID.2	Use statistics appropriate to the shape of the data distribution to compare center (median, mean) and spread (interquartile range, standard deviation) of two or more different data sets.*	SE: 702–709		SE: 548, 576
CC.9-12.S.ID.3	Interpret differences in shape, center, and spread in the context of the data sets, accounting for possible effects of extreme data points (outliers).*	SE: 702–709, 710–713		SE: 527, 543–548
CC.9-12.S.ID.4	Use the mean and standard deviation of a data set to fit it to a normal distribution and to estimate population percentages. Recognize that there are data sets for which such a procedure is not appropriate. Use calculators, spreadsheets, and tables to estimate areas under the normal curve.*			SE: 594–595, 596–603
CC.9-12.S.ID.5	Summarize categorical data for two categories in two-way frequency tables. Interpret relative frequencies in the context of the data (including joint, marginal, and conditional relative frequencies). Recognize possible associations and trends in the data.*			SE: 501, 503–506, 509, 511–518, 530, 536

SE = Student Edition

Standards	Descriptor	Algebra 1	Geometry	Algebra 2
Standards for Mathematical Content				
(+ = advanced; * = also a Modeling Standard)				
Statistics and Probability				
CC.9-12.S.ID.6	Represent data on two quantitative variables on a scatter plot, and describe how the variables are related.* a. Fit a function to the data; use functions fitted to data to solve problems in the context of the data. Use given functions or choose a function suggested by the context. Emphasize linear and exponential models. b. Informally assess the fit of a function by plotting and analyzing residuals. c. Fit a linear function for a scatter plot that suggests a linear association.	SE: 196–198, 200–203, 204, 205, 211, 212, 213, 217, 218, 284, 285–292, 551, 649–655		SE: 32–39, 45, 46, 120–125, 135, 140, 210–215, 289–295, 296, 297, 301, 307, 458–465
CC.9-12.S.ID.7	Interpret the slope (rate of change) and the intercept (constant term) of a linear model in the context of the data.*	SE: 284, 285–292	SE: 183, 186, 193, 194, 195	SE: 32–39, 45
CC.9-12.S.ID.8	Compute (using technology) and interpret the correlation coefficient of a linear fit.*	SE: 285–292		SE: 32–39, 45, 46, 306
CC.9-12.S.ID.9	Distinguish between correlation and causation.*	SE: 285–292		
CC.9-12.S.IC.1	Understand statistics as a process for making inferences about population parameters based on a random sample from that population.*	SE: 716–721		SE: 551–558
CC.9-12.S.IC.2	Decide if a specified model is consistent with results from a given data-generating process, e.g., using simulation.*			SE: 505

SE = Student Edition

Standards	Descriptor	Algebra 1	Geometry	Algebra 2
Standards for Mathematical Content				
(+ = advanced; * = also a Modeling Standard)				
Statistics and Probability				
CC.9-12.S.IC.3	Recognize the purposes of and differences among sample surveys, experiments, and observational studies; explain how randomization relates to each.*	SE: 722–723		SE: 559–566
CC.9-12.S.IC.4	Use data from a sample survey to estimate a population mean or proportion; develop a margin of error through the use of simulation models for random sampling.*			SE: 579–586
CC.9-12.S.IC.5	Use data from a randomized experiment to compare two treatments; use simulations to decide if differences between parameters are significant.*			SE: 567–574
CC.9-12.S.IC.6	Evaluate reports based on data.*	SE: 716–721, 725, 754, 756		SE: 579–586
CC.9-12.S.CP.1	Describe events as subsets of a sample space (the set of outcomes) using characteristics (or categories) of the outcomes, or as unions, intersections, or complements of other events ("or," "and," "not").*	SE: 727–732, 734–739, 740–747		SE: 490–497, 509, 519–525, 530, 533, 534
CC.9-12.S.CP.2	Understand that two events *A* and *B* are independent if the probability of *A* and *B* occurring together is the product of their probabilities, and use this characterization to determine if they are independent.*	SE: 741–746, 755, 756	SE: 238	SE: 499–506, 509, 530, 532, 533

SE = Student Edition

Standards	Descriptor	Algebra 1	Geometry	Algebra 2
Standards for Mathematical Content				
(+ = advanced; * = also a Modeling Standard)				
Statistics and Probability				
CC.9-12.S.CP.3	Understand the conditional probability of *A* given *B* as *P*(*A* and *B*)/*P*(*B*), and interpret independence of *A* and *B* as saying that the conditional probability of *A* given *B* is the same as the probability of *A*, and the conditional probability of *B* given *A* is the same as the probability of *B*.*	SE: 740–747	SE: 351, 583	SE: 499–506, 530, 685
CC.9-12.S.CP.4	Construct and interpret two-way frequency tables of data when two categories are associated with each object being classified. Use the two-way table as a sample space to decide if events are independent and to approximate conditional probabilities.*			SE: 493–500, 511–518
CC.9-12.S.CP.5	Recognize and explain the concepts of conditional probability and independence in everyday language and everyday situations.*	SE: 740–741, 744–746		SE: 511–518
CC.9-12.S.CP.6	Find the conditional probability of *A* given *B* as the fraction of *B*'s outcomes that also belong to *A*, and interpret the answer in terms of the model.*	SE: 740–747		SE: 499–506, 530
CC.9-12.S.CP.7	Apply the Addition Rule, $P(A \text{ or } B) = P(A) + P(B) - P(A \text{ and } B)$, and interpret the answer in terms of the model.*	SE: 748–749		SE: 509, 519–525, 530, 535

SE = Student Edition

Standards	Descriptor	Algebra 1	Geometry	Algebra 2
Standards for Mathematical Content				
(+ = advanced; * = also a Modeling Standard)				
Statistics and Probability				
CC.9-12.S.CP.8	(+) Apply the general Multiplication Rule in a uniform probability model, $P(A \text{ and } B) = P(A)P(B\|A) = P(B)P(A\|B)$, and interpret the answer in terms of the model.*	SE: 740–747		SE: 499–506, 509, 530, 533
CC.9-12.S.CP.9	(+) Use permutations and combinations to compute probabilities of compound events and solve problems.*			SE: 482–488, 490–497, 509, 519–525, 528, 532, 534, 536, 809
CC.9-12.S.MD.1	(+) Define a random variable for a quantity of interest by assigning a numerical value to each event in a sample space; graph the corresponding probability distribution using the same graphical displays as for data distributions.*			SE: 592, 594
CC.9-12.S.MD.2	(+) Calculate the expected value of a random variable; interpret it as the mean of the probability distribution.*			SE: 527, 531, 532, 533, 545, 547
CC.9-12.S.MD.3	(+) Develop a probability distribution for a random variable defined for a sample space in which theoretical probabilities can be calculated; find the expected value. *			SE: 550

SE = Student Edition

Standards	Descriptor	Algebra 1	Geometry	Algebra 2
Standards for Mathematical Content				
(+ = advanced; * = also a Modeling Standard)				
Statistics and Probability				
CC.9-12.S.MD.4	(+) Develop a probability distribution for a random variable defined for a sample space in which probabilities are assigned empirically; find the expected value.*			SE: 527, 531, 532, 588–593
CC.9-12.S.MD.5	(+) Weigh the possible outcomes of a decision by assigning probabilities to payoff values and finding expected values.* a. Find the expected payoff for a game of chance. b. Evaluate and compare strategies on the basis of expected values.			SE: 509, 522–526
CC.9-12.S.MD.6	(+) Use probabilities to make fair decisions (e.g., drawing by lots, using a random number generator).*			SE: 551–558
CC.9-12.S.MD.7	(+) Analyze decisions and strategies using probability concepts (e.g., product testing, medical testing, pulling a hockey goalie at the end of a game).*	SE: 729, 731, 746, 748–749, 750, 754, 756		SE: 495–496, 504, 524, 526, 604–609

SE = Student Edition

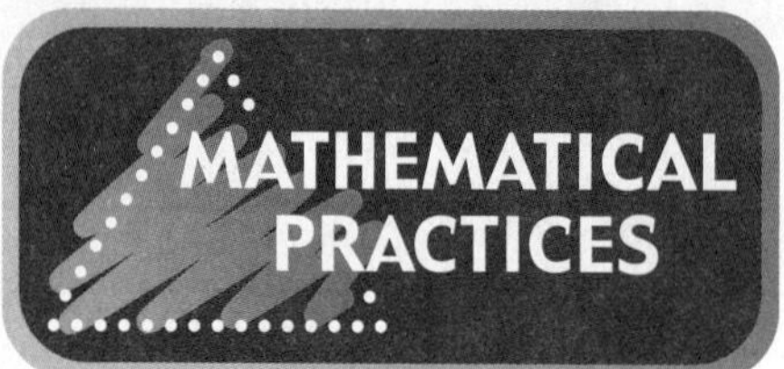

Mastering the Standards

for Mathematical Practice

The topics described in the Standards for Mathematical Content will vary from year to year. However, the *way* in which you learn, study, and think about mathematics will not. The Standards for Mathematical Practice describe skills that you will use in all of your math courses. These pages show some features of your book that will help you gain these skills and use them to master this year's topics.

1 Make sense of problems and persevere in solving them.

Mathematically proficient students start by explaining to themselves the meaning of a problem... They analyze givens, constraints, relationships, and goals. They make conjectures about the form... of the solution and plan a solution pathway...

In your book

Focus on Problem Solving describes a four-step plan for problem solving. The plan is introduced at the beginning of your book, and practice appears throughout.

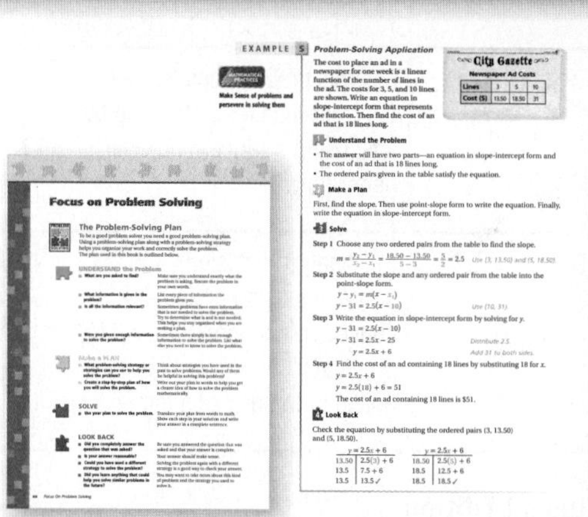

Focus on Problem Solving

The Problem-Solving Plan

EXAMPLE 5 *Problem-Solving Application*

Make Sense of problems and persevere in solving them

The cost to place an ad in a newspaper for one week is a linear function of the number of lines in the ad. The costs for 3, 5, and 10 lines are shown. Write an equation in slope-intercept form that represents the function. Then find the cost of an ad that is 18 lines long.

City Gazette

Newspaper Ad Costs

Lines	3	5	10
Cost ($)	13.50	18.50	31

1 Understand the Problem

- The **answer** will have two parts—an equation in slope-intercept form and the cost of an ad that is 18 lines long.
- The ordered pairs given in the table satisfy the equation.

2 Make a Plan

First, find the slope. Then use point-slope form to write the equation. Finally, write the equation in slope-intercept form.

3 Solve

Step 1 Choose any two ordered pairs from the table to find the slope.

$m = \frac{y_2 - y_1}{x_2 - x_1} = \frac{18.50 - 13.50}{5 - 3} = \frac{5}{2} = 2.5$ *Use (3, 13.50) and (5, 18.50).*

Step 2 Substitute the slope and any ordered pair from the table into the point-slope form.

$y - y_1 = m(x - x_1)$

$y - 31 = 2.5(x - 10)$ *Use (10, 31).*

Step 3 Write the equation in slope-intercept form by solving for y.

$y - 31 = 2.5(x - 10)$

$y - 31 = 2.5x - 25$ *Distribute 2.5.*

$y = 2.5x + 6$ *Add 31 to both sides.*

Step 4 Find the cost of an ad containing 18 lines by substituting 18 for x.

$y = 2.5x + 6$

$y = 2.5(18) + 6 = 51$

The cost of an ad containing 18 lines is $51.

4 Look Back

Check the equation by substituting the ordered pairs (3, 13.50) and (5, 18.50).

$y = 2.5x + 6$	
13.50	2.5(3) + 6
13.5	7.5 + 6
13.5	13.5 ✓

$y = 2.5x + 6$	
18.50	2.5(5) + 6
18.5	12.5 + 6
18.5	18.5 ✓

2 Reason abstractly and quantitatively.
3 Construct viable arguments and critique the reasoning of others.

Mathematically proficient students... justify their conclusions, [and]... distinguish correct... reasoning from that which is flawed.

In your book

Think and Discuss asks you to evaluate statements, explain relationships, apply mathematical principles, and justify your reasoning.

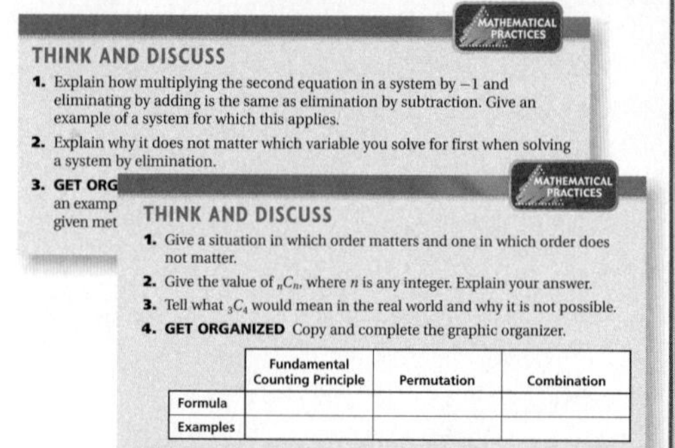

MATHEMATICAL PRACTICES

THINK AND DISCUSS

1. Explain how multiplying the second equation in a system by −1 and eliminating by adding is the same as elimination by subtraction. Give an example of a system for which this applies.
2. Explain why it does not matter which variable you solve for first when solving a system by elimination.
3. GET ORG... an examp... given met...

MATHEMATICAL PRACTICES

THINK AND DISCUSS

1. Give a situation in which order matters and one in which order does not matter.
2. Give the value of ${}_nC_n$, where n is any integer. Explain your answer.
3. Tell what ${}_3C_4$ would mean in the real world and why it is not possible.
4. **GET ORGANIZED** Copy and complete the graphic organizer.

	Fundamental Counting Principle	Permutation	Combination
Formula			
Examples			

Getty Images/PhotoDisc

④ Model with mathematics.

Mathematically proficient students can apply... mathematics... to... problems... in everyday life, society, and the workplace...

In your book

Multi-Step Test Prep and **Real-World Connections** apply mathematics to other disciplines and in real-world scenarios.

⑤ Use appropriate tools strategically.

Mathematically proficient students consider the available tools when solving a... problem... [and] are... able to use technological tools to explore and deepen their understanding...

In your book

Algebra Labs and **Technology Labs** use concrete and technological tools to explore mathematical concepts.

⑥ Attend to precision.

Mathematically proficient students... communicate precisely... with others and in their own reasoning... [They] give carefully formulated explanations...

In your book

Reading and Writing Math and **Write About It** help you learn and use the language of math to communicate mathematics precisely.

⑦ Look for and make use of structure.
⑧ Look for and express regularity in repeated reasoning.

Mathematically proficient students... look both for general methods and for shortcuts...

In your book

Lesson examples group similar types of problems together, and the solutions are carefully stepped out. This allows you to make generalizations about—and notice variations in—the underlying structures.

EXAMPLE 3 **Finding Products in the Form $(a+b)(a-b)$**

Multiply.

A $(x+6)(x-6)$

$(a+b)(a-b) = a^2 - b^2$ *Use the rule for $(a+b)(a-b)$.*

$(x+6)(x-6) = x^2 - 6^2$ *Identify a and b: $a = x$ and $b = 6$.*

$= x^2 - 36$ *Simplify.*

B $(x^2+2y)(x^2-2y)$

$(a+b)(a-b) = a^2 - b^2$ *Use the rule for $(a+b)(a-b)$.*

$(x^2+2y)(x^2-2y) = (x^2)^2 - (2y)^2$ *Identify a and b: $a = x^2$ and $b = 2y$.*

$= x^4 - 4y^2$ *Simplify.*

C $(7+n)(7-n)$

$(a+b)(a-b) = a^2 - b^2$ *Use the rule for $(a+b)(a-b)$.*

$(7+n)(7-n) = 7^2 - n^2$ *Identify a and b: $a = 7$ and $b = n$.*

$= 49 - n^2$ *Simplify.*

Countdown to Mastery

WEEK 1

DAY 1

The figure shows a square within a square. Which expression represents the area of the shaded region of the figure in square units?

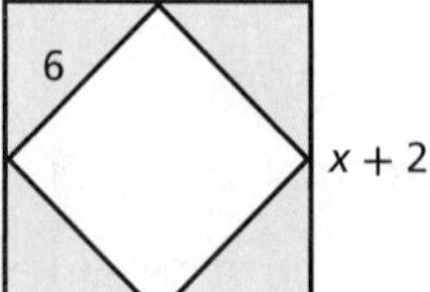

Ⓐ $(x + 2)^2 - 36$
Ⓑ $(x + 2) - 6$
Ⓒ $2(x + 2) - 12$
Ⓓ $(x + 2 - 6)^2$

DAY 2

If x is a nonzero real number, which expression is equivalent to $(x + 5) - 8$?

Ⓕ $-8x + 5$
Ⓖ $8 - (x + 5)$
Ⓗ $x + (5 - 8)$
Ⓙ $(x + 8) - 5$

DAY 3

If a, b, and c are positive integers, what is the greatest common factor of the expressions $18ab$ and $8abc$?

Ⓐ 18
Ⓑ ab
Ⓒ $2ab$
Ⓓ $72abc$

DAY 4

$\triangle ABC$ is a right triangle.

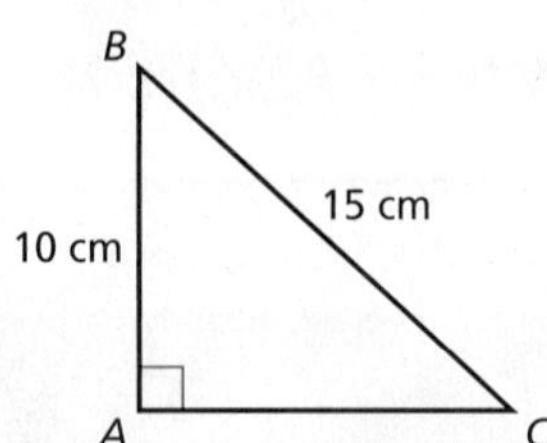

What is the length of $\overline{AC}$?

Ⓕ 5 cm
Ⓖ $5\sqrt{5}$ cm
Ⓗ $5\sqrt{13}$ cm
Ⓙ 25 cm

DAY 5

Simplify the expression $5(x^2 + 4x) + 3(x + 6)$.

Ⓐ $12x^2 + 6$
Ⓑ $12x^2 + 18$
Ⓒ $5x^2 + 7x + 6$
Ⓓ $5x^2 + 23x + 18$

Countdown to Mastery

WEEK 2

DAY 1

The figure shows a right triangle. Which equation can be solved for the unknown side length c?

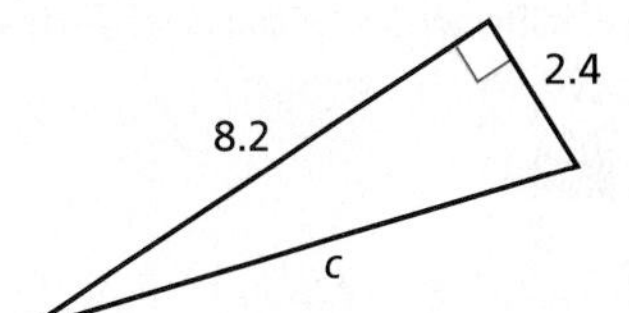

Ⓐ $\sqrt{8.2^2 + 2.4^2} = c$

Ⓑ $\sqrt{(8.2 + 2.4)^2} = c$

Ⓒ $\sqrt{8.2^2 - 2.4^2} = c$

Ⓓ $\sqrt{(8.2 - 2.4)^2} = c$

DAY 2

What is the perimeter in units of a rectangle with a length of $g + 8$ units and a width of $g - 6$ units?

Ⓕ $4g + 2$

Ⓖ $4g + 4$

Ⓗ $g^2 - 16$

Ⓙ $g^2 + 2g - 16$

DAY 3

Which expression is equivalent to $\frac{12x^4y^8}{9xy^4}$?

Ⓐ $\frac{4}{3}xy^2$

Ⓑ $\frac{4}{3}xy^4$

Ⓒ $\frac{4}{3}x^3y^4$

Ⓓ $\frac{4}{3}x^4y^2$

DAY 4

A particular hummingbird averages 60 wing beats per second. At this rate, how many times would the hummingbird beat its wings during an hour of flight?

Ⓕ 2.16×10^3

Ⓖ 2.16×10^4

Ⓗ 2.16×10^5

Ⓙ 2.16×10^6

DAY 5

A marathon is a 26.2-mile race. Kendra's average speed during marathons is 7.2 miles per hour. Which function d represents the distance in miles Kendra has left to run in a marathon t hours after the race begins?

Ⓐ $d(t) = \frac{t}{7.2} - 26.2$

Ⓑ $d(t) = 26.2 - \frac{t}{7.2}$

Ⓒ $d(t) = 7.2t - 26.2$

Ⓓ $d(t) = 26.2 - 7.2t$

Countdown to Mastery WEEK 3

DAY 1

Which of the following best represents the domain of the function shown in the graph?

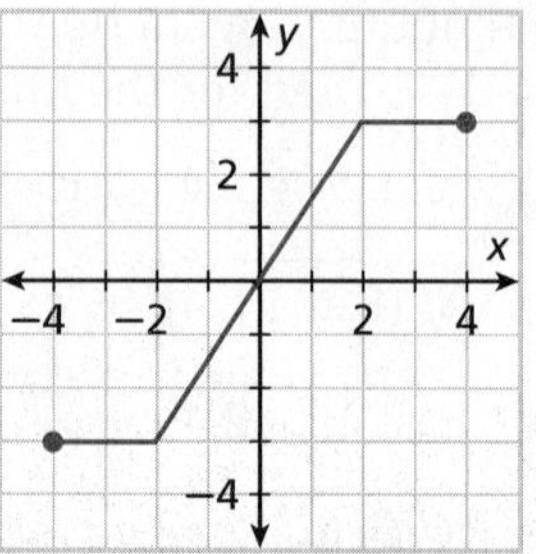

Ⓐ $-2 \le x \le 2$

Ⓑ $-3 \le x \le 3$

Ⓒ $-4 \le x \le 4$

Ⓓ $-5 \le x \le 5$

DAY 2

A diagonal of a rectangle measures 9 meters. The width of the rectangle is 6 meters. What is the length of the rectangle?

Ⓕ $3\sqrt{5}$ m

Ⓖ $9\sqrt{5}$ m

Ⓗ $\sqrt{15}$ m

Ⓙ $\sqrt{117}$ m

DAY 3

If a and b are integers, which expression is equivalent to $6^a \cdot 6^b$?

Ⓐ 6^{a+b}

Ⓑ $6^{a \cdot b}$

Ⓒ 36^{a+b}

Ⓓ $36^{a \cdot b}$

DAY 4

In the diagram, points W, X, Y, and Z are collinear, $WX = YZ$, and $XY = 25$. If WX is a whole number, which is NOT a possible value of WZ?

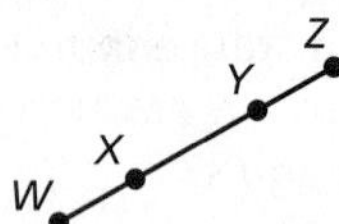

Ⓕ 27

Ⓖ 30

Ⓗ 35

Ⓙ 37

DAY 5

What is the parent function of the function shown in the graph?

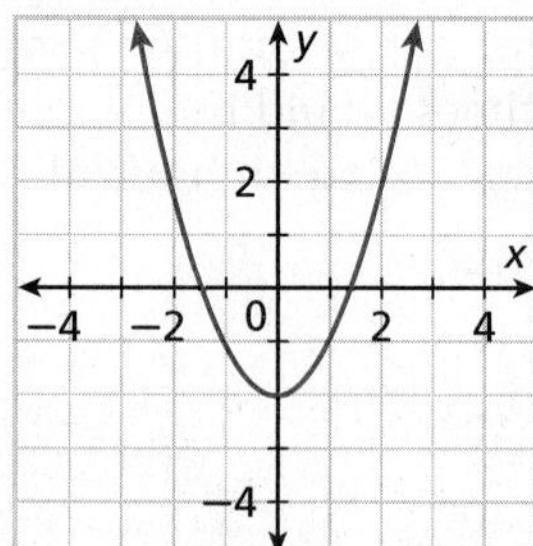

Ⓐ $f(x) = x$

Ⓑ $f(x) = x^2$

Ⓒ $f(x) = x^3$

Ⓓ $f(x) = \sqrt{x}$

Countdown to Mastery WEEK 4

DAY 1

Which graph best represents the function $f(x) = \frac{1}{2}x + 2$?

Ⓐ
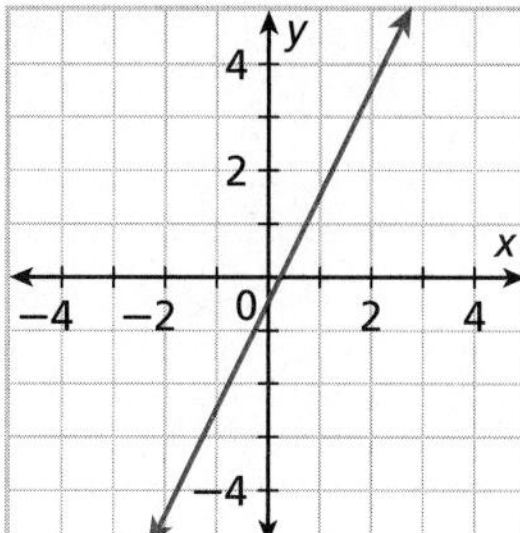

Ⓒ
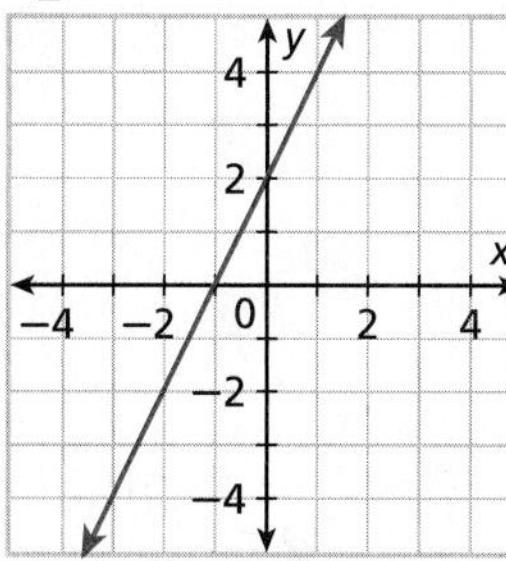

Ⓑ
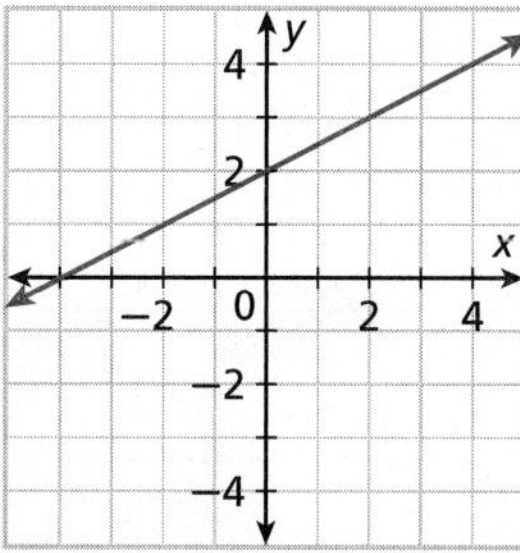

Ⓓ
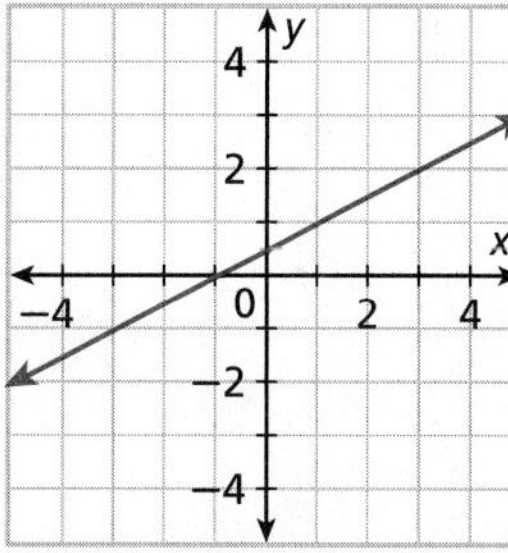

DAY 2

Given that $f(x) = -6x^2 - 12x + 3$, what is $f(-2)$?

Ⓕ −45

Ⓖ 0

Ⓗ 3

Ⓙ 51

DAY 3

What transformation is suggested by the spokes on a stationary bicycle tire?

Ⓐ Rotation

Ⓑ Reflection

Ⓒ Dilation

Ⓓ Translation

DAY 4

Which expression is equivalent to $\left(\frac{6x^2y^4}{x^4y^2}\right)^3$?

Ⓕ $216xy^5$

Ⓖ $216x^2y^{10}$

Ⓗ $216x^{-5}y^5$

Ⓙ $216x^{-6}y^6$

DAY 5

What is the parent function of the graph shown?

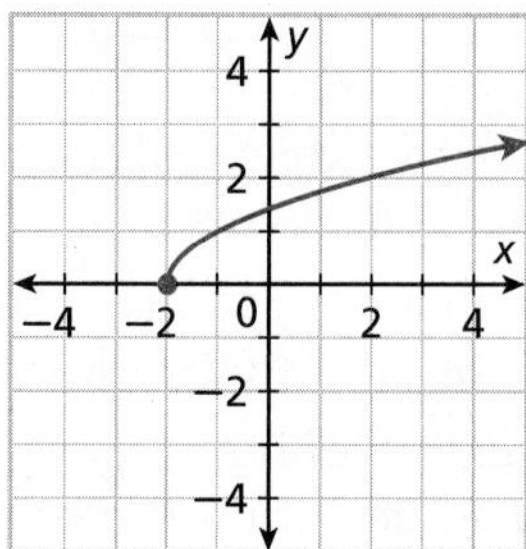

Ⓐ $f(x) = x$

Ⓑ $f(x) = x^2$

Ⓒ $f(x) = x^3$

Ⓓ $f(x) = \sqrt{x}$

Countdown to Mastery

WEEK 5

DAY 1

Which graph best represents the function $f(x) = x^2$?

Ⓐ
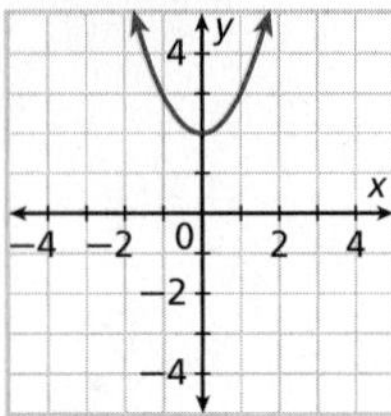

Ⓒ
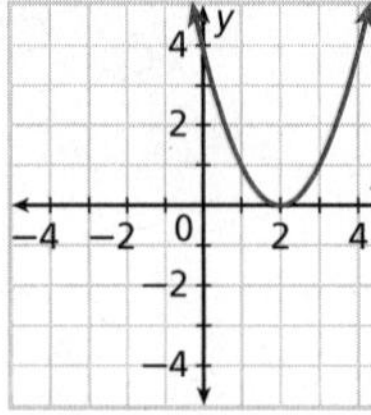

Ⓑ
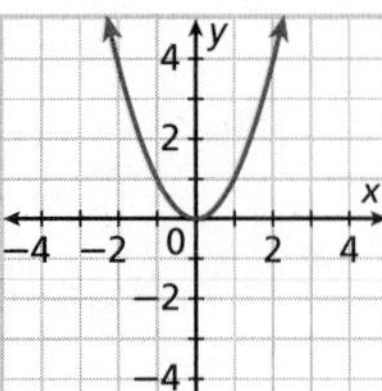

Ⓓ
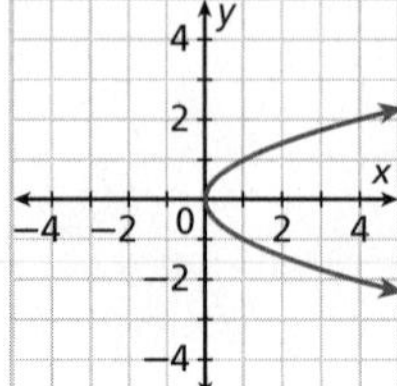

DAY 2

The graph of which function has the end behavior $f(x) \to -\infty$ as $x \to -\infty$ and $f(x) \to -\infty$ as $x \to +\infty$?

Ⓕ $y = x^4 + x^3 + x^2 + 1$

Ⓖ $y = 8x^5 + 2x^4 + 9$

Ⓗ $y = -x^5 - x^3 - 3x - 5$

Ⓙ $y = -9x^4 + 4x^3 + 16x$

DAY 3

Solve $4z + 16 - 3 = z - 7 + 5z$.

Ⓐ $z = 0$

Ⓑ $z = 2.5$

Ⓒ $z = 10$

Ⓓ $z = 20$

DAY 4

The scatter plot shown is most likely to represent which of the following sets of data?

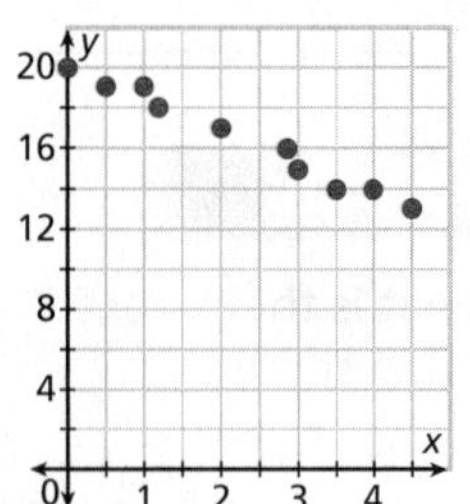

Ⓕ The age of a child and the number of toys he or she owns

Ⓖ The number of years in college and the amount of student loans

Ⓗ The number of hours spent practicing and the number of errors on a typing test

Ⓙ The duration of a movie and the cost in millions of dollars to produce it

DAY 5

What transformation of the graph of $f(x) = x$ is the graph of $g(x) = 4x$?

Ⓐ Vertical stretch by a factor of 4

Ⓑ Translation 4 units up

Ⓒ Horizontal stretch by a factor of 4

Ⓓ Translation 4 units right

Countdown to Mastery

WEEK 6

DAY 1

If $A = \frac{1}{2}bh$, what is the value of A when $b = 10x^3y^2$ and $h = 15x^{-2}y^4$?

Ⓐ $75x^{-1}y^6$
Ⓑ $75xy^6$
Ⓒ $3xy^8$
Ⓓ $150x^5y^2$

DAY 2

What are all the real-number solutions of the equation $3x^4 - x^3 = 12x^2 - 4x$?

Ⓕ $-2, 0, 2$
Ⓖ $-2, -\frac{1}{3}, 0, 2$
Ⓗ $-2, 0, 2, 3$
Ⓙ $-2, \frac{1}{3}, 0, 2$

DAY 3

The graph shows the number of survival kits s a company sells after d days. Which function can best be used to model the data?

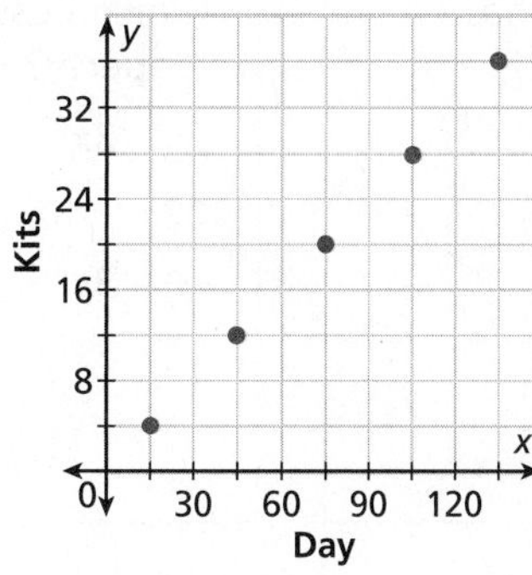

Ⓐ $s = \frac{1}{15}d + 4$
Ⓑ $s = \frac{1}{3}d - 1$
Ⓒ $s = \frac{4}{15}d$
Ⓓ $s = \frac{1}{5}d$

DAY 4

What is the equation of the graph shown?

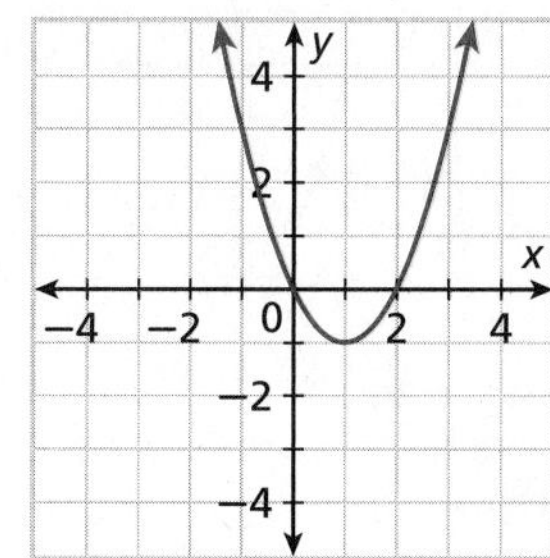

Ⓕ $y = (x - 1)^2 - 1$
Ⓖ $y = (x + 1)^2 - 1$
Ⓗ $y = (x - 1)^2 + 1$
Ⓙ $y = (x + 1)^2 + 1$

DAY 5

The graph represents which system of linear inequalities?

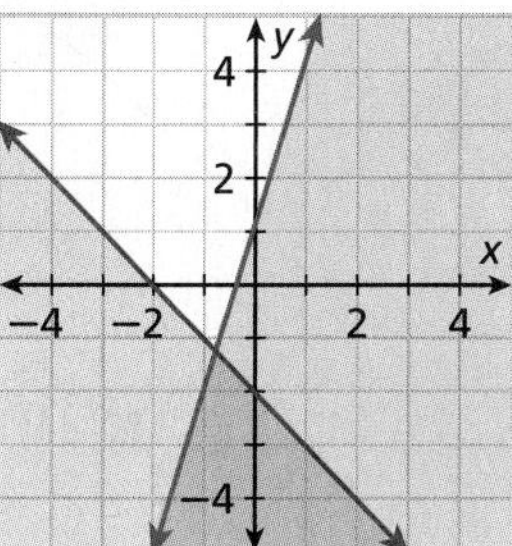

Ⓐ $\begin{cases} y \leq 3x + 1 \\ y \leq -x - 2 \end{cases}$
Ⓑ $\begin{cases} y \leq x + 3 \\ y \leq -2x - 1 \end{cases}$
Ⓒ $\begin{cases} y < 3x + 1 \\ y < -x - 2 \end{cases}$
Ⓓ $\begin{cases} y < x + 3 \\ y < -2x - 1 \end{cases}$

Countdown to Mastery

WEEK 7

DAY 1

Which equation fits the data in the table?

x	−3	−1	1	3	5
y	0.125	0.5	2	8	32

Ⓐ $y = 2x$ Ⓑ $y = x^2$ Ⓒ $y = 2^x$ Ⓓ $\log_2 x$

DAY 2

A polynomial function of degree 6 has roots -1, 4, $2 - \sqrt{3}$, and $1 + 3i$. Which of the following is an additional real root?

Ⓕ 1

Ⓖ -4

Ⓗ $2 + \sqrt{3}$

Ⓙ $1 - 3i$

DAY 3

Which best illustrates the Associative Property?

Ⓐ $3x^2 + 5x^2 - 6 = 3x^2 - 6 + 5x^2$

Ⓑ $x^2(3 + 5) - 6 = (3x^2 + 5x^2) - 6$

Ⓒ $3x^2 + (5x^2 - 6) = (3x^2 + 5x^2) - 6$

Ⓓ $3x^2 + (5x^2 - 6) = (-6 + 3x^2) + 5x^2$

DAY 4

The position of a moving dot on a computer screen over time is given by the graph. What is the domain of this function?

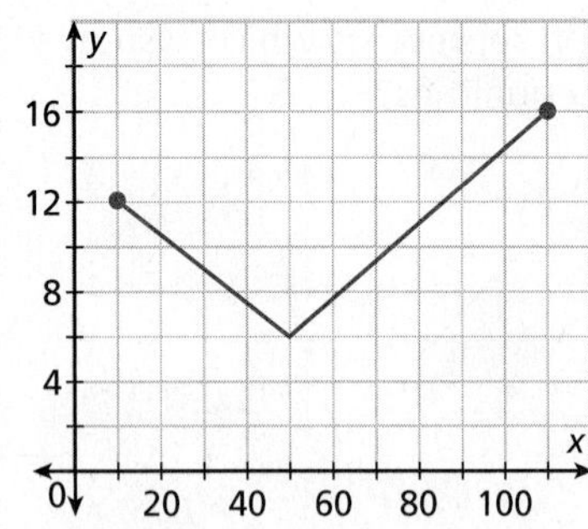

Ⓕ $\{x \mid 5 \le x \le 40\}$

Ⓖ $\{x \mid x \ge 10\}$

Ⓗ $\{x \mid 12 \le x \le 16\}$

Ⓙ $\{x \mid 10 \le x \le 110\}$

DAY 5

The graph shown represents which function?

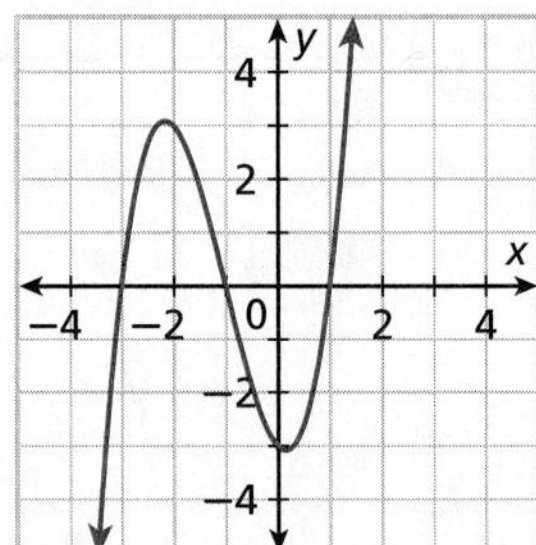

Ⓐ $(x^2 - 1)(x + 3)$

Ⓑ $(x^2 - 1)(x - 3)$

Ⓒ $(x^2 - 9)(x - 1)$

Ⓓ $(x^2 - 9)(x^2 - 1)$

Countdown to Mastery — WEEK 8

DAY 1

What is the range of the function $y = -(2x - 1)^2 + 3$?

Ⓐ $\{y \mid y \leq 3\}$

Ⓑ $\{y \mid y \geq 3\}$

Ⓒ all real numbers except $\frac{1}{2}$

Ⓓ all real numbers

DAY 2

By inspecting the polynomial function below, which of the following can you immediately rule out as a possible rational zero?

$$y = 3x^3 - 2x^2 + 2x + 3$$

Ⓕ 1

Ⓖ −3

Ⓗ $\frac{1}{3}$

Ⓙ $\frac{1}{2}$

DAY 3

Which is an extraneous solution obtained when you solve the radical equation $\sqrt{x - 3} + 2 = \sqrt{7 - x}$ by squaring?

Ⓐ 0

Ⓑ 3

Ⓒ 4

Ⓓ 7

DAY 4

Which ordered pair is the solution of the following system?

$$\begin{cases} 3x - 5y = 12 \\ 2x = 4 + 5y \end{cases}$$

Ⓕ $\left(8, 2\frac{2}{5}\right)$

Ⓖ $\left(3\frac{1}{5}, 2\frac{4}{5}\right)$

Ⓗ $\left(16, 7\frac{1}{5}\right)$

Ⓙ $\left(3\frac{2}{5}, \frac{12}{25}\right)$

DAY 5

Teresa has two identical CD binders that are partly filled with CDs.
How much does each binder weigh when empty, to the nearest ounce?

Ⓐ 1 oz

Ⓑ 2 oz

Ⓒ 24 oz

Ⓓ 26 oz

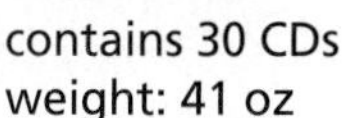

contains 30 CDs
weight: 41 oz

contains 75 CDs
weight: 66.5 oz

Countdown to Mastery — WEEK 9

DAY 1

What is the range of the function $f(x) = -2|x|$?

Ⓐ $y > 0$

Ⓑ $y \leq 0$

Ⓒ $y \leq -2$

Ⓓ All real numbers

DAY 2

What is the solution of the system?

$$\begin{cases} 0.5x + 2.5y = -6.4 \\ 2x - 5y = 19.4 \end{cases}$$

Ⓕ $(10.7, 2.1)$

Ⓖ $(4.\overline{3}, 2.15)$

Ⓗ $(2.2, -3)$

Ⓙ $(0.8, -3.56)$

DAY 3

The time to download a software update varies inversely with the speed of the Internet connection. An update downloads in 1 minute 20 seconds when the download speed is 1.5 megabytes per second. Which is the best prediction of the time that will be required for the update to download on a high-speed connection that has a speed of 24 megabytes per second?

Ⓐ 3.3 s

Ⓑ 5 s

Ⓒ 53 s

Ⓓ 21 min 20 s

DAY 4

What is the average rate of change over the domain interval [4, 6] of a set of data that can be modeled by the function $y = -16t^2 + 36t + 400$ over the interval?

Ⓕ 40

Ⓖ −124

Ⓗ −228

Ⓙ −248

DAY 5

What is the equation of the line through the origin that is perpendicular to $\overleftrightarrow{AB}$?

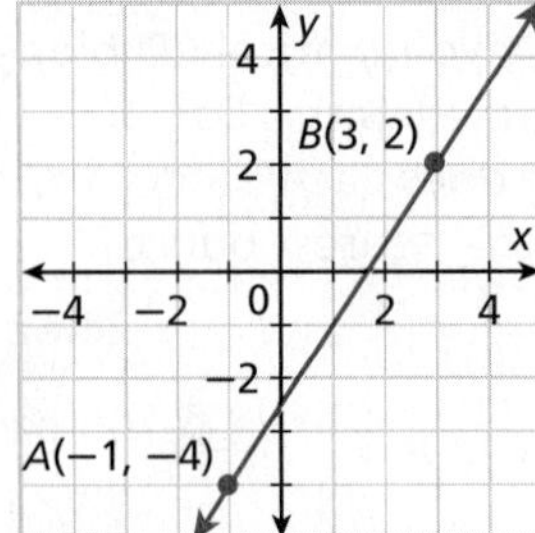

Ⓐ $y = \frac{2}{3}x$

Ⓑ $y = -\frac{2}{3}x$

Ⓒ $y = \frac{3}{2}x$

Ⓓ $y = -\frac{3}{2}x$

Countdown to Mastery

WEEK 10

DAY 1

Which function is shown in the graph?

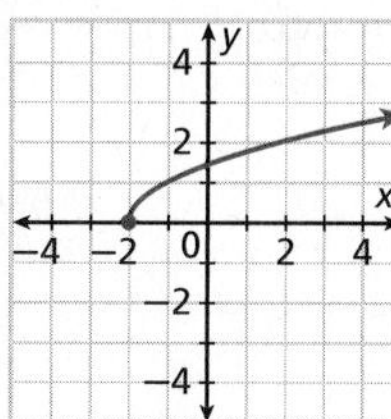

Ⓐ $f(x) = \sqrt{x} + 2$

Ⓑ $f(x) = \sqrt{x + 2}$

Ⓒ $f(x) = 2\sqrt{x}$

Ⓓ $f(x) = \sqrt{x - 2}$

DAY 2

Which equation represents the following relationship:

"p varies directly with q and inversely with r."

Ⓕ $p = \frac{kr}{q}$

Ⓖ $\frac{pq}{r} = k$

Ⓗ $\frac{pr}{q} = k$

Ⓙ $p = \frac{qr}{k}$

DAY 3

Which is the graph of $f(x) = 3x^2 - 1$?

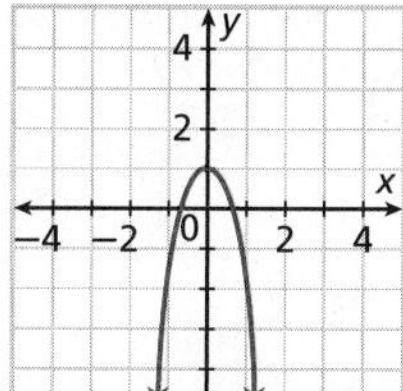

Ⓒ

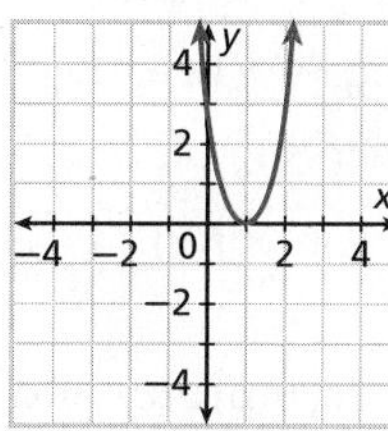

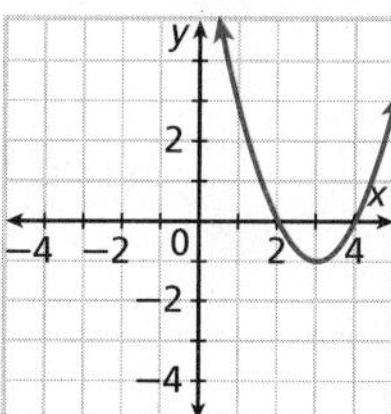

Ⓓ

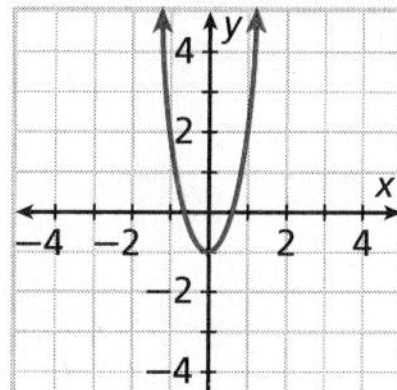

DAY 4

Between which two numbers does the polynomial function $2x^3 - 4x^2 + x - 5$ have a real zero?

Ⓕ $x = 0$ and $x = 1$

Ⓖ $x = 1$ and $x = 2$

Ⓗ $x = 2$ and $x = 3$

Ⓙ $x = 3$ and $x = 4$

DAY 5

The equation of a least-squares line is $y \approx 0.15x - 0.21$. Predict the x-value that corresponds to a y-value of 20.

Ⓐ 95.24

Ⓑ 131.93

Ⓒ 134.73

Ⓓ 175.13

Countdown to Mastery

WEEK 11

DAY 1

What is the range of the function $f(x) = -\frac{1}{4}|x - 2|$?

Ⓐ $y \leq 0$

Ⓑ $y > 0$

Ⓒ $y \leq -2$

Ⓓ $y > 2$

DAY 2

Which line is *not* an asymptote of the graph of the function $y = \frac{1.5\,(x - 1)(x + 3)}{x^2 - 4}$?

Ⓕ $x = 1$

Ⓖ $y = 1.5$

Ⓗ $x = -2$

Ⓙ $x = 2$

DAY 3

Which is a true statement about the rational function $f(x) = \frac{2x^3}{1 - x^2}$?

Ⓐ The function is an increasing function over all values of its domain.

Ⓑ The function is an even function.

Ⓒ The end behavior of the graph is $f(x) \to -\infty$ as $x \to -\infty$ and $f(x) \to +\infty$ as $x \to +\infty$.

Ⓓ The graph has two vertical asymptotes and one horizontal asymptote.

DAY 4

Which value is equivalent to $30 \div 2 + \sqrt{64} - 4^3(8 - 4)^{-2}$?

Ⓕ -1

Ⓖ 13

Ⓗ 19

Ⓙ 535

DAY 5

The graph shown represents which parent function?

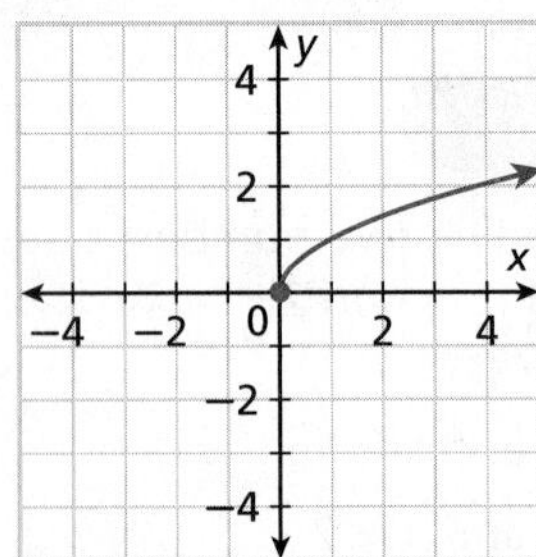

Ⓐ $f(x) = \sqrt{x}$

Ⓑ $f(x) = x^2$

Ⓒ $f(x) = 2$

Ⓓ $f(x) = x^3$

Countdown to Mastery

WEEK 12

DAY 1

How is the graph of $g(x) = |x| - 4$ transformed from the graph of $f(x) = |x|$?

Ⓐ The graph of f is translated 4 units up.

Ⓑ The graph of f is translated 4 units down.

Ⓒ The graph of f is translated 4 units right.

Ⓓ The graph of f is translated 4 units left.

DAY 2

Which expression represents the coefficient of the sixth term in the expansion of $(m + n)^9$?

Ⓕ ${}_9C_5$

Ⓖ ${}_9C_6$

Ⓗ ${}_9C_7$

Ⓙ ${}_6C_9$

DAY 3

The following graph represents which table of data?

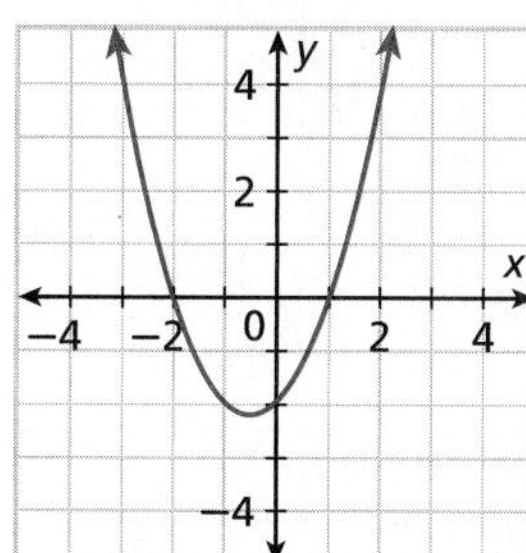

Ⓐ

x	−2	−1	0	1
$f(x)$	2	−2	2	1

Ⓑ

x	0	−2	−2	0
$f(x)$	−2	−1	0	1

Ⓒ

x	−2	−1	0	1
$f(x)$	0	−2	−2	0

Ⓓ

x	−2	−1	0	1
$f(x)$	−1	0	1	2

DAY 4

What is the domain of the function $f(x) = -\frac{1}{2}|x - 4|$?

Ⓕ All real numbers

Ⓖ $x < 0$

Ⓗ $x \geq -2$

Ⓙ $x > 4$

DAY 5

How is the graph of $g(x) = 2(x + 1)^2$ transformed from the graph of $f(x) = x^2$?

Ⓐ The graph of f is translated 2 units left and 1 unit up.

Ⓑ The graph of f is vertically compressed by a factor of $\frac{1}{2}$ and translated 1 unit left.

Ⓒ The graph of f is vertically stretched by a factor of 2 and translated 1 unit up.

Ⓓ The graph of f is vertically stretched by a factor of 2 and translated 1 unit left.

Countdown to Mastery

WEEK 13

DAY 1

Which of the following best describes the correlation found in the scatter plot?

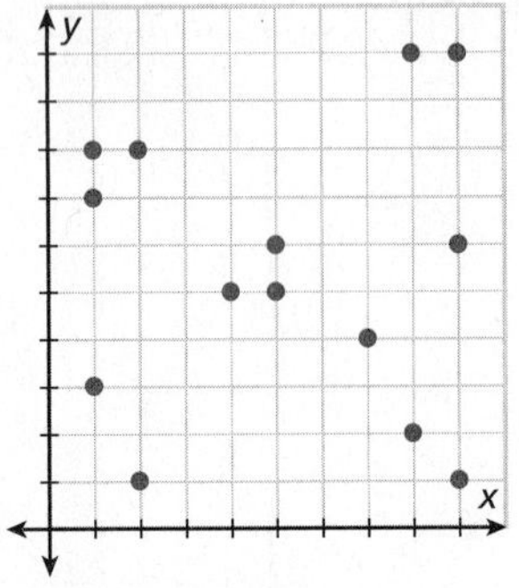

Ⓐ Strong positive correlation

Ⓑ Weak positive correlation

Ⓒ No correlation

Ⓓ Negative correlation

DAY 2

Which of the following best describes how to graph the function $f(x) = (x - 7)^2 + 3$?

Ⓕ Move the parent function to the right 7 units and up 3 units.

Ⓖ Move the parent function to the right 3 units and down 7 units.

Ⓗ Move the parent function to the left 7 units and up 3 units.

Ⓙ Move the parent function to the right 7 units and down 3 units.

DAY 3

Which situation is best represented by the data?

t	0	0.5	1	1.5	2	2.5
$f(t)$	112	108	96	76	48	12

Ⓐ The distance decreases by 4 miles for every 30 seconds traveled.

Ⓑ The height of an object above ground decreases nonlinearly over time.

Ⓒ As the time increases, the speed of a car increases at a constant rate.

Ⓓ As the time increases, the distance traveled decreases at a constant rate.

DAY 4

Which function is equivalent to $f(x) = 30x^2 + 2x - 56$?

Ⓕ $f(x) = (3x - 4)(5x + 14)$

Ⓖ $f(x) = 2(3x + 4)(5x - 7)$

Ⓗ $f(x) = (6x - 4)(5x + 7)$

Ⓙ $f(x) = 2(3x - 4)(5x + 7)$

DAY 5

The height h of a football t seconds after it is kicked is given by $h(t) = -16t^2 + 40t$. What is a reasonable real-world domain for the situation?

Ⓐ all positive real numbers

Ⓑ all real numbers between 0 and 3

Ⓒ all real numbers between 0 and 2.5

Ⓓ all real numbers between 0 and 1.25

Countdown to Mastery — WEEK 14

DAY 1

The length x of a rectangle is 6 feet longer than its width. What is a reasonable domain for the function that represents the area of the rectangle?

Ⓐ all real numbers

Ⓑ all positive numbers

Ⓒ $x > 6$

Ⓓ $0 \leq x \leq 6$

DAY 2

Which quadratic equation has no real-number solutions?

Ⓕ $x^2 - 8x + 16 = 0$

Ⓖ $4x^2 - 12x + 9 = 0$

Ⓗ $-x^2 + 4x - 5 = 0$

Ⓙ $x^2 - 3x - 7 = 0$

DAY 3

The function $P = (h - 3)^2 + 174$ models the power, in megawatts, generated between midnight and noon by a power plant, where h represents hours after midnight. How would the graph of the function change if the minimum power generated increased to 250 megawatts?

Ⓐ The vertex would change to (3, 250).

Ⓑ The vertex would change to (250, 174).

Ⓒ The graph of the function would be reflected over the x-axis.

Ⓓ The graph of the function would be horizontally compressed.

DAY 4

To solve the equation $0 = x^2 + 7x - 26$ by completing the square, the first step is to add 26 to both sides of the equation. Which statement best describes the second step?

Ⓕ Add $\frac{9}{4}$ to both sides.

Ⓖ Square the product of 7 and 2.

Ⓗ Take half of 7 and square it.

Ⓙ Rewrite the perfect square trinomial as a binomial squared.

DAY 5

Which quadratic inequality best represents the graph?

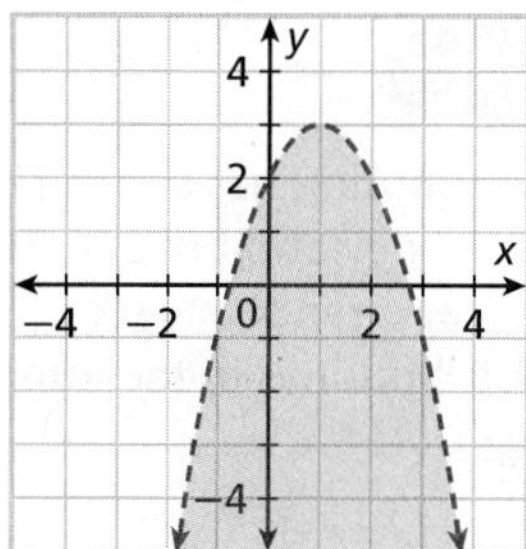

Ⓐ $y < -x^2 + 2x + 2$

Ⓑ $y > x^2 + 2x + 2$

Ⓒ $y \leq -x^2 + 2x + 2$

Ⓓ $y < x^2 - 2x + 2$

DAY 1

The equation of the graph shown has the form $y = a\sqrt[3]{x} + b$, where a and b are constants. Which is true?

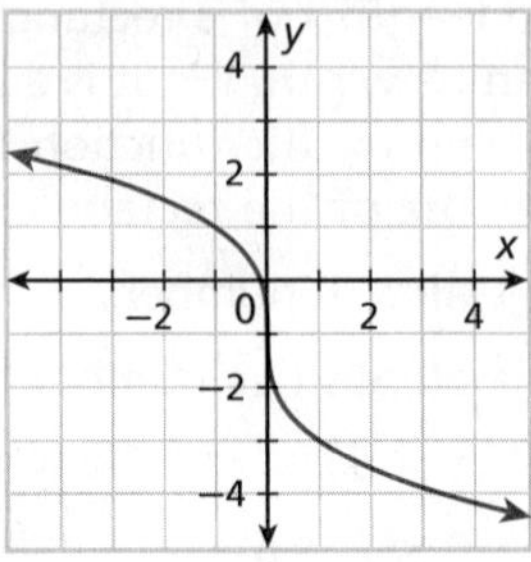

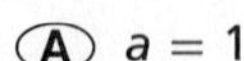

Ⓐ $a = 1$

Ⓑ $a < 0$

Ⓒ $b > 0$

Ⓓ $b = 0$

DAY 2

Which best describes $g(x) = \sqrt{2(x - 1)} + 4$ as a transformation of $f(x) = \sqrt{x}$?

Ⓕ g is f horizontally compressed by a factor of $\frac{1}{2}$ and translated left 1 unit and up 4 units.

Ⓖ g is f horizontally stretched by a factor of 2 and translated right 1 unit and up 4 units.

Ⓗ g is f horizontally compressed by a factor of $\frac{1}{2}$ and translated right 1 unit and up 4 units.

Ⓙ g is f horizontally stretched by a factor of 2 and translated left 1 unit and down 4 units.

DAY 3

Which statement is true of the function $f(x) = \frac{1}{5}x + 6$?

Ⓐ $f(x)$ is an odd function.

Ⓑ $f(x)$ is an always increasing function.

Ⓒ $f(x)$ is an always decreasing function.

Ⓓ $f(x)$ is always greater than x.

DAY 4

A normal distribution has a mean of 14 and a standard deviation of 2.5. What is the probability that a randomly-selected x-value from the distribution is in the interval [11.5, 19]?

Ⓕ 0.32

Ⓖ 0.68

Ⓗ 0.815

Ⓙ 0.95

DAY 5

A speaker wants to have a sample of the 400 people sitting in an audience answer a question. The speaker hands each of the 20 people in the first row a slip of paper with the question, and has them answer it and put the paper in a box. Which best describes the sample?

Ⓐ self-selected

Ⓑ random

Ⓒ convenience

Ⓓ systematic

Countdown to Mastery

WEEK 16

DAY 1

What are the solutions of the equation $3x^2 - 6x - 7 = 0$?

Ⓐ $x = \frac{3 \pm 2i\sqrt{3}}{3}$

Ⓑ $x \approx 2.8$ and $x \approx -0.8$

Ⓒ $x \approx 17$ and $x \approx -5$

Ⓓ $x \approx 3.2$ and $x \approx -0.6$

DAY 2

Which function best represents the data in the table?

x	−2	−1	0	1	2	3
$f(x)$	25	13	5	1	1	5

Ⓕ $f(x) = 2x^2 - 6x + 5$

Ⓖ $f(x) = -2x^2 - 6x + 8$

Ⓗ $f(x) = x^2 - 6x + 5$

Ⓙ $f(x) = 2x^2 - 9x + 5$

DAY 3

The graph can be used to determine the solutions to which quadratic equation?

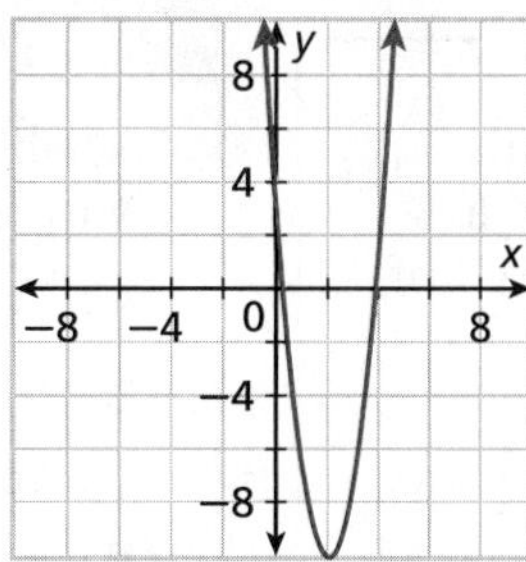

Ⓐ $x^2 - 5x + 4 = 0$

Ⓑ $3x^2 - 7x + 2 = 0$

Ⓒ $3x^2 - 13x + 4 = 0$

Ⓓ $3x^2 - 8x + 4 = 0$

DAY 4

At the beginning of a basketball game, the referee tosses the ball into the air with an initial vertical velocity of 24 feet per second. The ball's initial height is 5 feet above the floor. Which inequality can be used to find the time interval t for which the height of the ball is greater than 10 feet?

Ⓕ $-16t^2 + 24t + 5 < 10$

Ⓖ $-16t^2 + 24t + 5 > 10$

Ⓗ $24t^2 - 16t + 5 > 10$

Ⓙ $24t + 5 > 10$

DAY 5

The function $P = -16(c - 25)^2 + 10{,}000$ models the profit the student council makes from a dance, where c is the cost per ticket in dollars. How does the graph of the function change if the maximum profit is made by selling the tickets for $40?

Ⓐ The graph of the function would be reflected over the y-axis.

Ⓑ The vertex would change to (25, 40).

Ⓒ The vertex would change to(40, 10,000)
.

Ⓓ The graph of the function would not change.

Countdown to Mastery

WEEK 17

DAY 1

Which graph could represent a polynomial function of degree 5 whose leading coefficient is positive?

Ⓐ
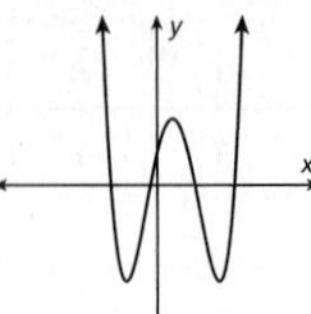

Ⓒ
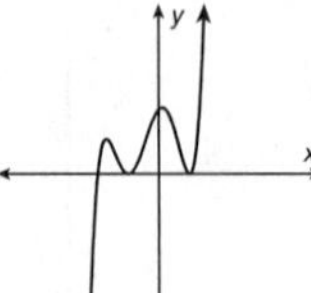

Ⓑ
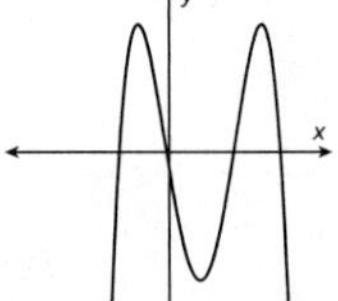

Ⓓ
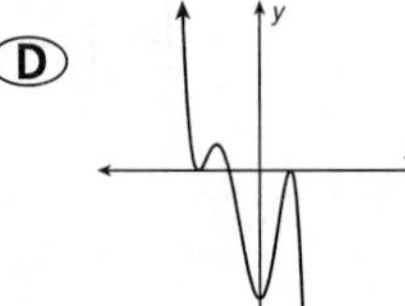

DAY 2

In chemistry, pH $= -\log[H^+]$, where $[H^+]$ is the hydrogen ion concentration of a solution in moles per liter. What is $[H^+]$ of a carbonated soda if its pH is 1.5?

Ⓕ $10^{-1.5}$

Ⓖ $10^{1.5}$

Ⓗ $-\log 1.5$

Ⓙ $-\log(-1.5)$

DAY 3

For which of the following functions does *y* vary inversely as *x*?

Ⓐ $y = \frac{x}{2}$

Ⓑ $y = -7x$

Ⓒ $10 = xy$

Ⓓ $y = x^0 - 15$

DAY 4

The distance a spring stretches varies directly as the amount of weight hanging from it. A weight of 60 pounds stretches the spring 15 centimeters. How heavy is the weight hanging on the spring when it stretches 12 centimeters?

Ⓕ 3 pounds

Ⓖ 12 pounds

Ⓗ 48 pounds

Ⓙ 52 pounds

DAY 5

The graph represents which parent function?

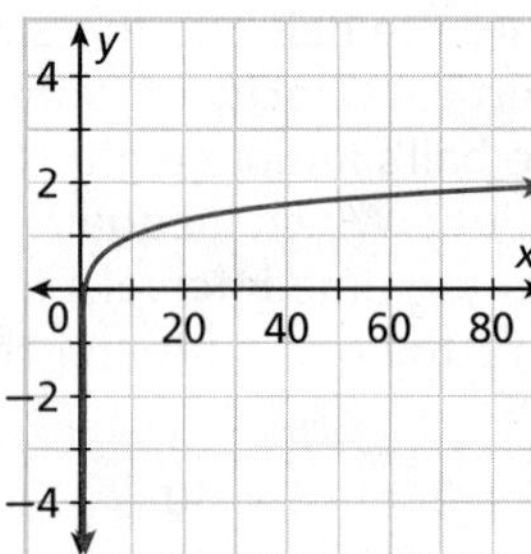

Ⓐ $y = x^2$

Ⓑ $y = x$

Ⓒ $y = \log x$

Ⓓ $y = e^x$

Countdown to Mastery

WEEK 18

DAY 1

The area of a rectangular parking lot with a length of 1500 feet can be no more than 3,000,000 square feet. Which is the most reasonable domain of the function representing the parking lot's area A in square feet in terms of its width w in feet?

Ⓐ $0 < w \leq 1500$

Ⓑ $0 < w \leq 2000$

Ⓒ $1500 < w \leq 2000$

Ⓓ $1500 < w \leq 3{,}000{,}000$

DAY 2

Which ordered pair is NOT a solution of the exponential inequality shown in the graph?

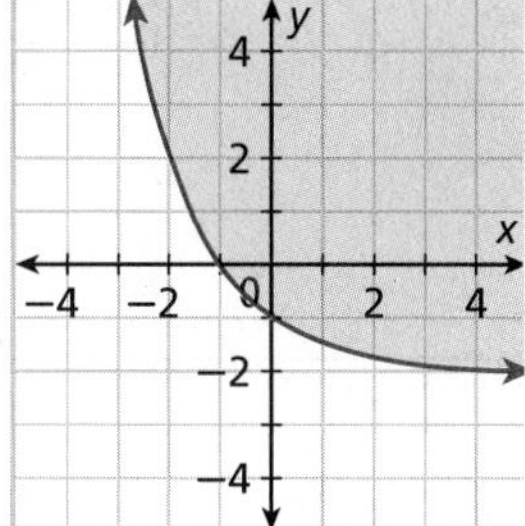

Ⓕ (2, −2)

Ⓖ (5, 1)

Ⓗ (3, 3)

Ⓙ (0, 4)

DAY 3

Which is *not* an essential characteristic of a randomized comparative experiment?

Ⓐ a statistical measure that can be tracked in a group over time

Ⓑ a randomly chosen control group composed of individuals to whom no treatment is applied

Ⓒ a randomly chosen experimental or treatment group composed of individuals to whom a treatment is applied

Ⓓ a statistical measure that can be compared between the control group and treatment group

DAY 4

Which function represents the graph of $f(x) = \ln x$ translated 2 units right and 5 units up?

Ⓕ $g(x) = \ln(x + 2) - 5$

Ⓖ $g(x) = \ln(x + 5) - 2$

Ⓗ $g(x) = \ln(x - 2) + 5$

Ⓙ $g(x) = \ln(x - 5) + 2$

DAY 5

Which ordered pair is a solution of the inequality $y > -(x - 3)^2 + 8$?

Ⓐ (5, 0)

Ⓑ (5, 1)

Ⓒ (5, 4)

Ⓓ (5, 6)

Countdown to Mastery

WEEK 19

DAY 1

The radius of a circle can be determined by dividing the area by π and taking the square root of the result. Which graph best shows the radius as a function of the area?

Ⓐ

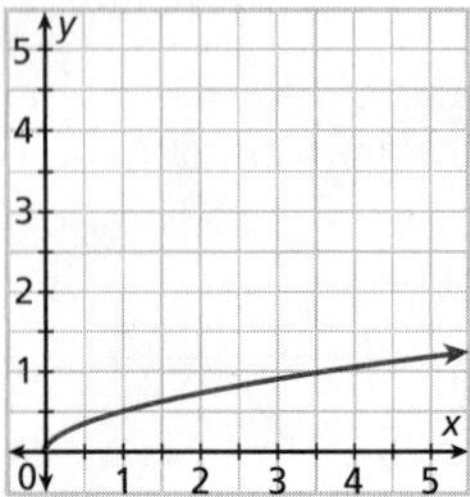

Ⓒ

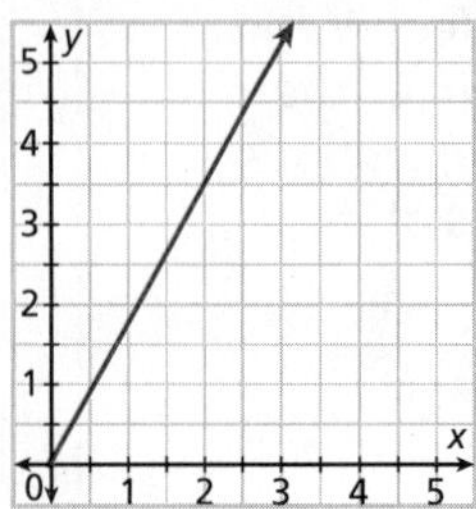

Ⓑ

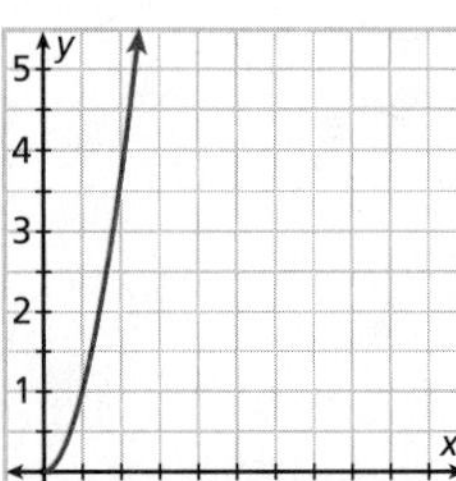

Ⓓ

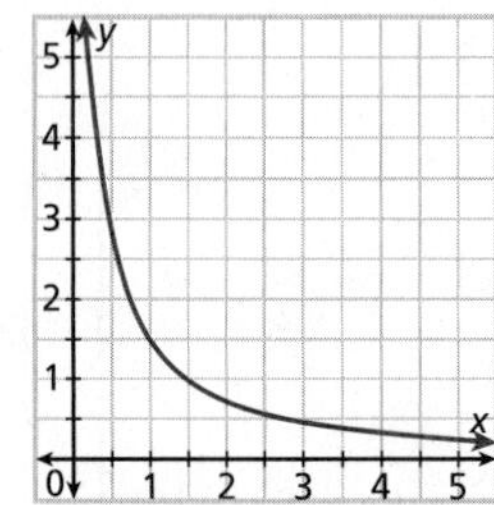

DAY 2

A section of seats in a stadium has 9 seats in the first row. With each successive row, the number of seats in the row increases by 2. There are 9 rows of seats in the section. How many seats are in the section in all?

Ⓕ 136

Ⓖ 153

Ⓗ 162

Ⓙ 180

DAY 3

What function best represents the data in the table?

x	$f(x)$
0	−2
1	−1
4	0
9	1
16	2

Ⓐ $f(x) = x - 2$

Ⓑ $f(x) = (x - 2)^2$

Ⓒ $f(x) = \sqrt{x - 2}$

Ⓓ $f(x) = \sqrt{x} - 2$

DAY 4

How does the graph of $g(x) = \sqrt{-x}$ differ from the graph of $f(x) = \sqrt{x}$?

Ⓕ The graph is reflected across the x-axis.

Ⓖ The graph is reflected across the y-axis.

Ⓗ The graph is rotated 180° about the origin.

Ⓙ The graph is shifted 4 units down.

DAY 5

Where does a hole occur in the graph of $f(x) = \dfrac{(x + 4)(x - 6)}{(x + 2)(x - 6)(x + 3)}$?

Ⓐ $x = 6$

Ⓑ $x = -2$

Ⓒ $x = -3$

Ⓓ $x = -4$

Countdown to Mastery

WEEK 20

DAY 1

The speed of a sound wave traveling through a thin rod is given by the formula $v = \sqrt{\frac{Y}{p}}$, where v is the speed of the waves in meters per second, Y is 8.0×10^{10} pascals, and p is the density of the rod in kilograms per cubic meter. If you know the value of v, which equation can you use to determine p?

Ⓐ $p = \sqrt{\frac{Y}{v}}$

Ⓑ $p = \frac{Y}{v^2}$

Ⓒ $p = \frac{\sqrt{Y}}{v}$

Ⓓ $p = (Yv)^2$

DAY 2

Martha invested \$12,000 and earned \$840 in interest in one year. She invested some of the money in an account that pays 8% per year and the rest of it in an account that pays 5% per year. Which system can be used to find the amount she invested at each rate?

Ⓕ $\begin{cases} x - y = 12{,}000 \\ 0.08x - 0.05y = 840 \end{cases}$

Ⓖ $\begin{cases} y = 12{,}000 - x \\ 0.08x + 0.05y = 12{,}000 - 840 \end{cases}$

Ⓗ $\begin{cases} xy = 12{,}000 \\ 0.08x - 0.05y = 840 \end{cases}$

Ⓙ $\begin{cases} y = 12{,}000 - x \\ 0.08x - 0.05y = 840 \end{cases}$

DAY 3

Which is the graph of $f(x) = \ln x$?

Ⓐ
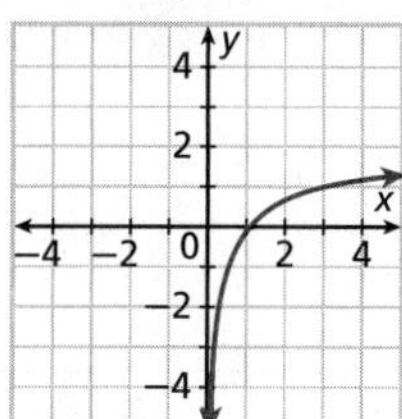

Ⓒ
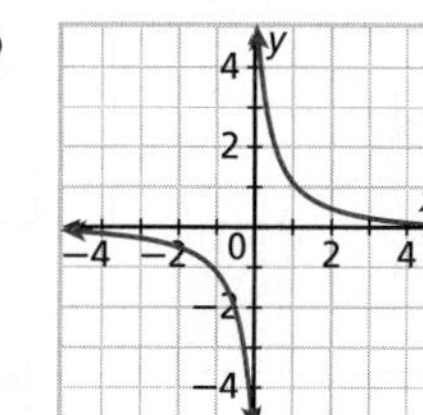

Ⓑ
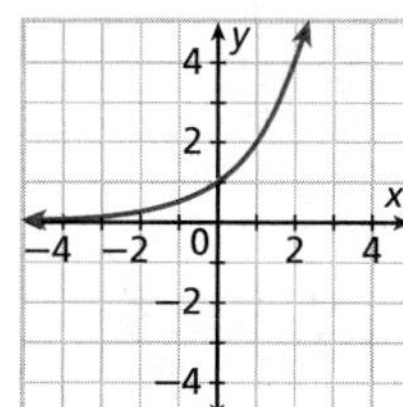

Ⓓ
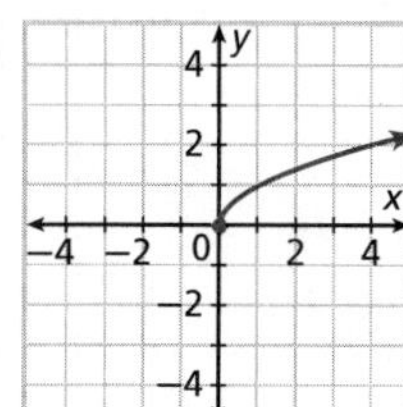

DAY 4

Which function represents a reflection of $f(x) = 2^x$ across the y-axis?

Ⓕ $g(x) = -2^x$

Ⓗ $g(x) = 2^{-x}$

Ⓖ $g(x) = \left(\frac{1}{2}\right)^x$

Ⓙ $g(x) = \left(\frac{1}{x}\right)^2$

DAY 5

Which equation is equivalent to $12^{-x} = 24$?

Ⓐ $\log_{24} 12 = x$

Ⓒ $\log_{12} 24 = -x$

Ⓑ $\log_x 24 = 12$

Ⓓ $\log_{-x} 12 = 24$

Countdown to Mastery

WEEK 21

DAY 1

The range of a quadratic function is $\{y|y \leq 4\}$. What is the range of the same function after a translation of 3 units up?

Ⓐ $\{y|y \leq 1\}$

Ⓑ $\{y|y \geq 1\}$

Ⓒ $\{y|y \leq 7\}$

Ⓓ $\{y|y \geq 7\}$

DAY 2

Which function represents a translation of $f(x) = 2^x$ six units right?

Ⓕ $g(x) = 2^x - 6$

Ⓖ $g(x) = 2^{x-x}$

Ⓗ $g(x) = 2^x + 6$

Ⓙ $g(x) = 2^{x+6}$

DAY 3

What is the domain of the function $f(x) = -\sqrt{7 - x}$?

Ⓐ $x \geq -7$

Ⓑ $x \leq -7$

Ⓒ $x \geq 7$

Ⓓ $x \leq 7$

DAY 4

Which transformation was NOT applied to the graph of $f(x) = \sqrt{x}$ to obtain $g(x) = -4\sqrt{6(x + 3)}$?

Ⓕ Vertical translation 3 units up

Ⓖ Reflection across the x-axis

Ⓗ Vertical stretch by a factor of 4

Ⓙ Horizontal compression by a factor of $\frac{1}{6}$.

DAY 5

Which quadratic function is represented by the graph?

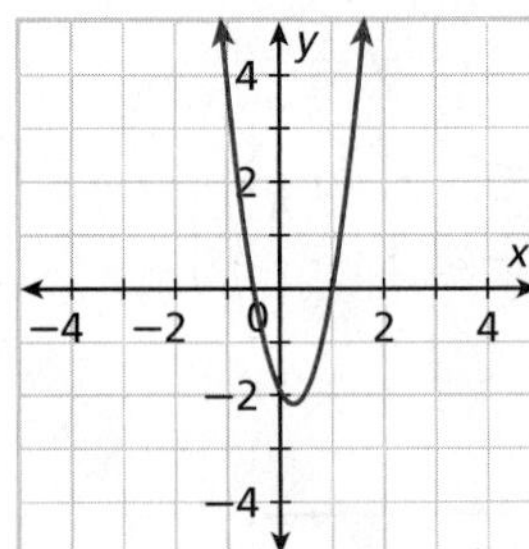

Ⓐ $f(x) = 4x^2 - 2x - 2$

Ⓑ $f(x) = x^2 - 2$

Ⓒ $f(x) = (x + 1)(x - 1)$

Ⓓ $f(x) = (x - 2)^2 - 2$

Countdown to Mastery

WEEK 22

DAY 1

Francisco wants to make a scatter plot to determine if there is a correlation between duration of a construction highway project and the number of managers assigned to the project. Which table would be best for Francisco to organize his findings?

Ⓐ

Duration of Project			
Manager Names			

Ⓑ

Number of Managers			
Project Number			

Ⓒ

Duration of Project			
Number of Managers			

Ⓓ

Project Number			
Manager Names			

DAY 2

Bobby is on a biking trip that consists of 55 miles on paved roads and 18 miles on unpaved roads. He is able to bike twice as fast on paved roads as on unpaved roads. Which function represents the total time T in hours that Bobby needs to complete the trip in terms of his average speed on unpaved roads x in miles per hour?

Ⓕ $T(x) = \frac{55}{x} + \frac{18}{2x}$

Ⓖ $T(x) = \frac{55}{2x} + \frac{18}{x}$

Ⓗ $T(x) = \frac{55}{x} - \frac{37}{2x}$

Ⓙ $T(x) = \frac{55}{x} - \frac{18}{2x}$

DAY 3

The graph of the inequality $y \geq -(x - 3)^2 + 8$ is shown below. Which of the given points is not in the solution region?

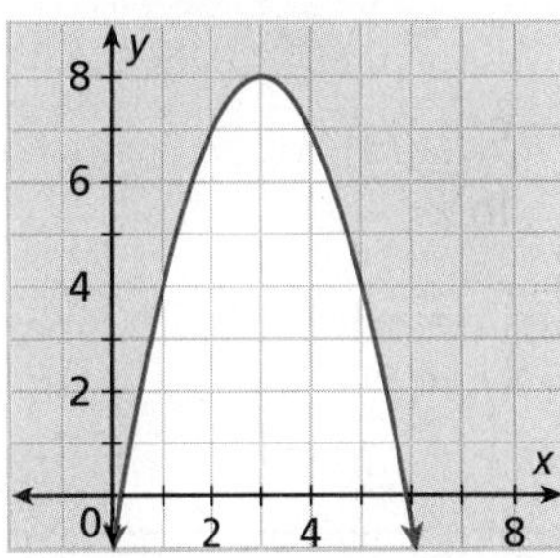

Ⓐ $(-2, -3)$

Ⓑ $(1, 7)$

Ⓒ $(3, 4)$

Ⓓ $(6, 5)$

DAY 4

Solve $\sqrt{x + 14} \leq x - 16$.

Ⓕ $x \geq 16$

Ⓖ $-16 \leq x \leq 22$

Ⓗ $x \leq -22$

Ⓙ $x \geq 22$

DAY 5

What is the relationship between the graph of the function $y = x^2 - 4x$ and the graph of its inverse?

Ⓐ Reflection across the line $y = x$

Ⓑ Translation of 4 units down

Ⓒ 180° rotation about the origin

Ⓓ Vertical stretch by a factor of 4

Countdown to Mastery

WEEK 23

DAY 1

What is the domain of $f(x) = \dfrac{3x + 5}{x^2 + 3x - 18}$?

(A) All real numbers

(B) All real numbers except −6

(C) All real numbers except 3

(D) All real numbers except 3 and −6

DAY 2

Which is the sum of the geometric series represented by the expression

$\sum_{i=1}^{8} 3(2)^{i-1}$?

(F) 384

(G) 387

(H) 765

(J) 768

DAY 3

Which parent function is shown in the graph?

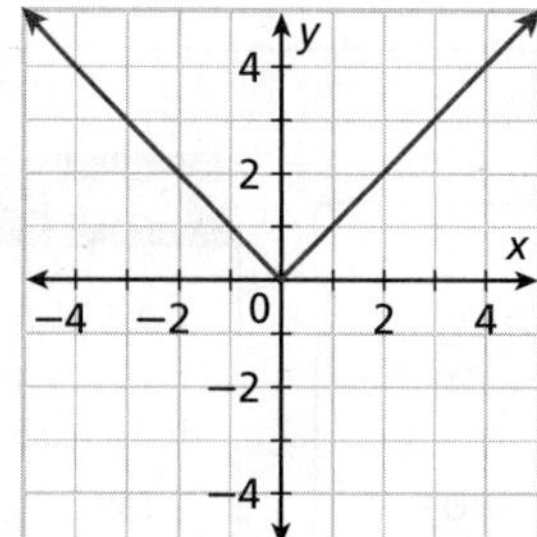

(A) $f(x) = e^x$

(B) $f(x) = \ln x$

(C) $f(x) = \sqrt{x}$

(D) $f(x) = |x|$

DAY 4

Which function does NOT include the values −2, 4, 8, and 12 in the domain?

(F) $f(x) = \sqrt{12x + 24}$

(G) $f(x) = \sqrt{7(x - 4)}$

(H) $f(x) = \sqrt{x^2 + 5x + 6}$

(J) $f(x) = \sqrt{\dfrac{2}{x^2 + 1}}$

DAY 5

A parabola is a conic section formed by the intersection of a plane and a(n) ________.

(A) circle

(B) hyperbola

(C) double cone

(D) ellipse

Countdown to Mastery

WEEK 24

DAY 1

Which graph can be used to determine the solution of $x^2 = \sqrt{2x}$?

Ⓐ

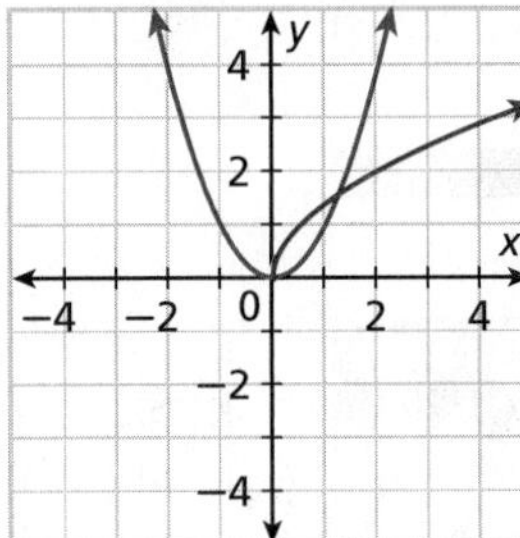

Ⓒ

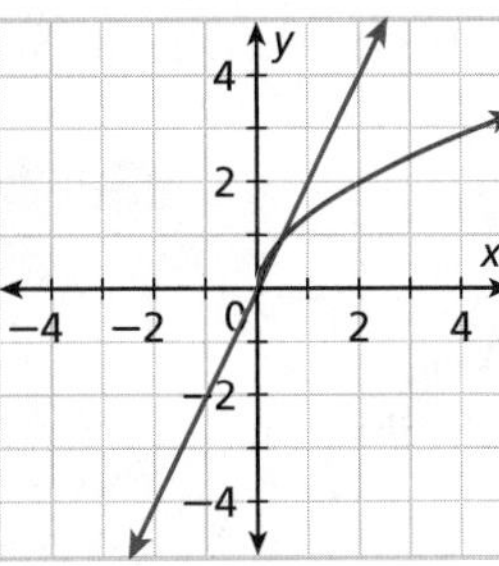

Ⓑ

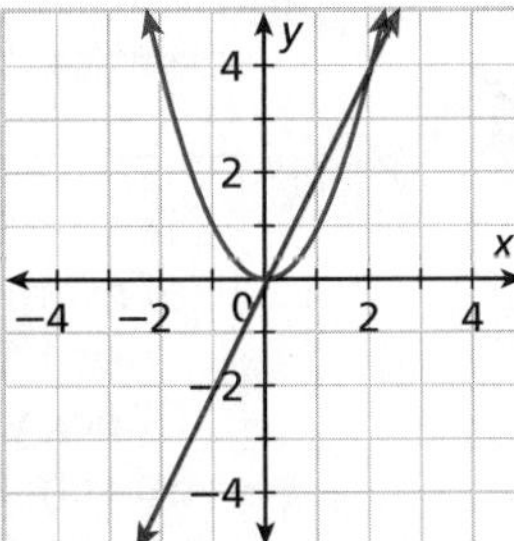

Ⓓ

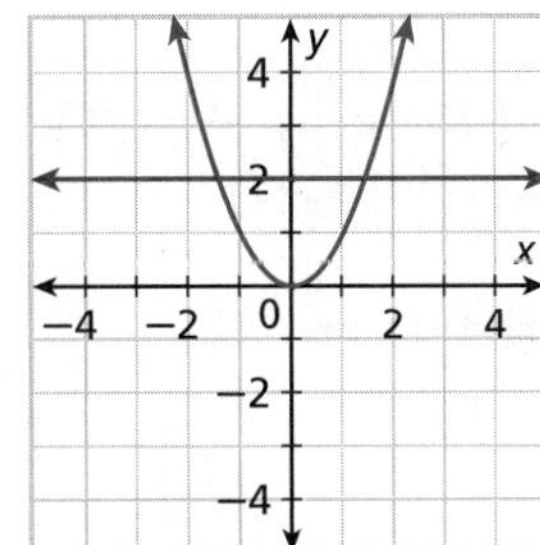

DAY 2

Solve $\frac{x}{x-2} = \frac{3x}{x+2}$.

Ⓕ $x = 2$ or $x = -2$

Ⓖ $x = 0$ or $x = 3$

Ⓗ $x = 0$ or $x = 4$

Ⓙ No real solution

DAY 3

The population of Warren County is 55,000 and is growing at a rate of 3.8% per decade. Which of the following expressions represents the population of Warren County after *n* decades?

Ⓐ $55{,}000(3.8)^n$

Ⓑ $55{,}000(1.38)^n$

Ⓒ $55{,}000(1.038)^n$

Ⓓ $55{,}000 + (3.8)^n$

DAY 4

What value of *x* makes the equation $3 = 1 + \log(2x)$ true?

Ⓕ 1

Ⓖ 10

Ⓗ 50

Ⓙ 100

DAY 5

The equation $\frac{x^2}{100} - \frac{y^2}{64} = 1$ represents which conic section?

Ⓐ Circle

Ⓑ Hyperbola

Ⓒ Parabola

Ⓓ Ellipse

HOW TO STUDY ALGEBRA 2

This book has many features designed to help you learn and study effectively. Becoming familiar with these features will prepare you for greater success on your exams.

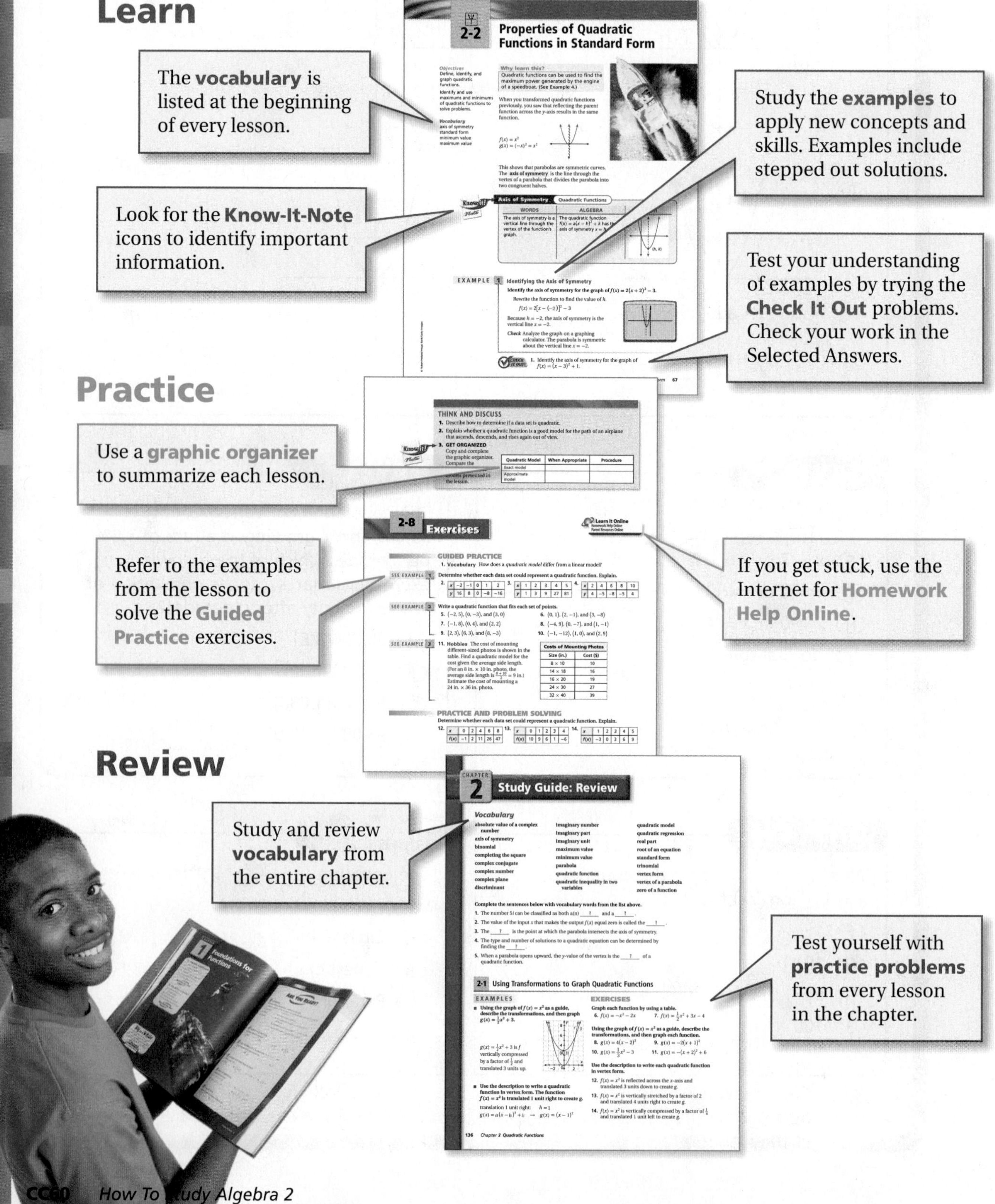

Learn
The vocabulary is listed at the beginning of every lesson.
Look for the Know-It-Note icons to identify important information.
Study the examples to apply new concepts and skills. Examples include stepped out solutions.
Test your understanding of examples by trying the Check It Out problems. Check your work in the Selected Answers.
2-2 Properties of Quadratic Functions in Standard Form
Practice
Use a graphic organizer to summarize each lesson.
Refer to the examples from the lesson to solve the Guided Practice exercises.
If you get stuck, use the Internet for Homework Help Online.
2-8 Exercises
Review
Study and review vocabulary from the entire chapter.
Test yourself with practice problems from every lesson in the chapter.
2 Study Guide: Review

Focus on Problem Solving

The Problem Solving Plan

Mathematical problems are a part of daily life. You need to use a good problem-solving plan to be a good problem solver. The plan used in this textbook is outlined below.

UNDERSTAND the Problem

First make sure you understand the problem you are asked to solve.

What are you asked to find?	Restate the question in your own words.
What information is given?	Identify the key facts given in the problem.
What information do you need?	Determine what information you need to solve the problem.
Do you have all the information needed?	Determine if you need more information.
Do you have too much information?	Determine if there is unnecessary information and eliminate it from your list of important facts.

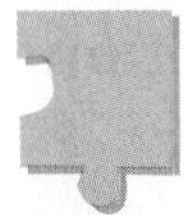

Make a PLAN

Plan how to use the information you are given.

Have you solved similar problems?	Think about similar problems you have solved successfully.
What problem solving strategy or strategies could you use to solve this problem?	Choose an appropriate problem solving strategy and decide how you will use it.

SOLVE

Use your plan to solve the problem. Show the steps in the solution, and write a final statement that gives the solution to the problem.

LOOK BACK

Check your answer against the original problem.

Have you answered the question?	Make sure you have answered the original question.
Is the answer reasonable?	The answer must make sense in relation to the question.
Are your calculations correct?	Check to make sure your calculations are accurate.
Can you use another strategy or solve the problem in another way?	Using another strategy is a good way to check your answer.
Did you learn anyting that could help you solve similar problems in the future?	Try to remember the types of problems you have solved and the strategies you applied.

ARE YOU READY?

Pre-Course Test

Fractions, Decimals, and Percents

Write the equivalent decimal and percent.

1. $\frac{63}{100}$ **2.** $\frac{11}{20}$

3. $\frac{3}{4}$ **4.** $\frac{5}{8}$

Graph Numbers on a Number Line

Graph each number on the same number line.

5. 2.5 **6.** -1.5

7. 1.3 **8.** -0.25

Compare and Order Real Numbers

Order the numbers from least to greatest.

9. $\frac{3}{10}$, 55%, $\frac{3}{4}$, 0.67

10. 160%, $1\frac{4}{5}$, 1.7, $\frac{9}{8}$

Order of Operations

Evaluate each expression.

11. $5 + 1 \cdot 4$ **12.** $(5 + 4)^2 - 9$

Connect Words and Algebra

13. Write an expression that represents a number x multiplied by 8.

14. Trevor has written 51 songs. Each week, he writes 3 more songs. Write an equation representing the number of songs s that Trevor has written at the end of w weeks.

Solve One-Step Equations

Solve.

15. $f + 6 = -6$ **16.** $\frac{h}{6} = 12$

Solve Multi-Step Equations

Solve.

17. $5c + 7 = 32$ **18.** $9 + \frac{k}{3} = 17$

Solve Equations with Variables on Both Sides

Solve.

19. $3g + 6 = 6g - 6$ **20.** $7h - 7 = 2h - 4$

Solve Equations with Fractions

Solve.

21. $b - \frac{11}{12} = \frac{5}{12}$ **22.** $\frac{3}{4}d + 7 = 19$

Convert Units of Measure

Convert each unit of measure.

23. 1.8 kilometers to meters

24. 3.5 pounds to ounces

Solve and Graph Inequalities

Solve and graph each inequality.

25. $j - 3 \geq 1$ **26.** $-3h < 12$

Graph Linear Functions

Graph each function.

27. $y = -3x + 5$ **28.** $y = \frac{2}{3}x - 4$

Slopes of Parallel and Perpendicular Lines

State whether the graphs of the linear equations in each pair are parallel, perpendicular, or neither.

29. $\begin{cases} y = \frac{1}{4}x - 4 \\ y = -4x + 8 \end{cases}$

30. $\begin{cases} 3y - 4x = 6 \\ 4y - 3x = -12 \end{cases}$

31. $\begin{cases} y = \frac{3}{4}x - 2 \\ 4y = 3x - 16 \end{cases}$

32. $\begin{cases} y = \frac{1}{3} \\ x = -3 \end{cases}$

Squares and Square Roots

Find each square root.

33. $\sqrt{169}$ **34.** $\sqrt{225}$

Simplify Radical Expressions

Simplify each expression.

35. $\sqrt{196} \cdot \sqrt{25}$ **36.** $\sqrt{\frac{16}{100}}$

Evaluate Powers

Find the value of each expression.

37. 2^6 **38.** $3^4 + 4^3$

Properties of Exponents

Simplify each expression.

39. $2a \cdot 5a^2$ **40.** $-3k^3 \cdot 4k$

41. $12e^2g \cdot 3eg$ **42.** $-8cd \cdot 2d \cdot 3c$

Multiply Binomials

Multiply.

43. $(x + 3)(x + 8)$

44. $(y - 2)(y + 7)$

45. $(2z + 5)(2z - 3)$

Graph Functions

Graph each function for the given domain.

46. $y = x^2 - 3$
D: $\{-2, -1, 0, 1, 2\}$

47. $y = (x + 4)^2$
D: $\{-6, -5, -4, -3, -2\}$

Solve Quadratic Equations

Solve each equation.

48. $3x^2 = 108$

49. $6x^2 = 324 + 2x^2$

50. $2x^2 - 50 = 192$

CHAPTER 1

Foundations for Functions

COMMON CORE

Chapter Focus

- Apply transformations to different families of functions.
- Fit data to linear models.

Big as a Whale

Humpback whales are among the world's largest animals. You can use expressions and functions to compare the sizes of whales to various objects.

Learn It Online
Chapter Project Online

Vocabulary

Match each term on the left with a definition on the right.

1. algebraic expression
2. opposites
3. origin
4. variable

A. the point in the coordinate plane where the x-axis and the y-axis intersect
B. a value that does not change
C. two numbers that are equal distances from zero on a number line
D. a mathematical phrase that contains one or more variables
E. a symbol that represents a quantity that can change

Fractions and Decimals

Write each fraction as a decimal.

5. $\frac{3}{10}$ **6.** $\frac{3}{5}$ **7.** $-\frac{4}{3}$ **8.** $5\frac{3}{4}$

Graph Numbers on a Number Line

Graph each number on the same number line.

9. 3.5 **10.** -4 **11.** $-\frac{12}{4}$ **12.** $3.\overline{3}$

Compare and Order Real Numbers

Compare using $<$ or $>$.

13. $\frac{5}{6}$ ■ $\frac{2}{3}$ **14.** $3\frac{7}{9}$ ■ $3\frac{10}{12}$ **15.** -0.38 ■ -0.3 **16.** $-\frac{15}{8}$ ■ -2

Order of Operations

Simplify each expression.

17. $14 \div 2(-3) + 1$ **18.** $8^2 - (-12) + 15 \div 3$

19. $-2(25 - 21)^2 + 11$ **20.** $3\left(\frac{21 - 9}{6} - 1\right) \div 2$

Ordered Pairs

Graph each point on the same coordinate plane.

21. $(0, 2)$ **22.** $(-3, 1)$ **23.** $(2, -1)$ **24.** $(-3, -2)$

CHAPTER 1

Study Guide: Preview

Where You've Been

Previously, you

- used properties of real numbers.
- graphed linear functions
- used variables, expressions, and equations to represent situations.

In This Chapter

You will study

- using parent functions to graph transformations finding a line of best fit to represent data
- using functions and their graphs to represent situations.

Where You've Been

You can use the skills in this chapter

- to build a foundation for calculus classes.
- to observe patterns and relationships in science and social studies.

Key Vocabulary/Vocabulario

correlation	correlación
parent function	función elemental
reflection	reflexión
regression	regresión
stretch	estiramiento
transformation	transformación

Vocabulary Connections

To become familiar with some of the vocabulary terms in the chapter, consider the following. You may refer to the chapter, the glossary, or a dictionary if you like.

1. When you look in the mirror, your reflection appears to be the same distance from the mirror, on the opposite side. Where might the **reflection** of the point (2, 5) appear if it is reflected over the y-axis?
2. What does the word *transform* mean? What do you think a mathematical **transformation** involves?

Study Strategy: Use Your Book for Success

Understanding how your textbook is organized will help you locate and use helpful information.

Pay attention to the **margin notes.** Know-It Note icons point out key information. Helpful Hints, Remember notes, and Caution notes help you understand concepts and avoid common mistakes.

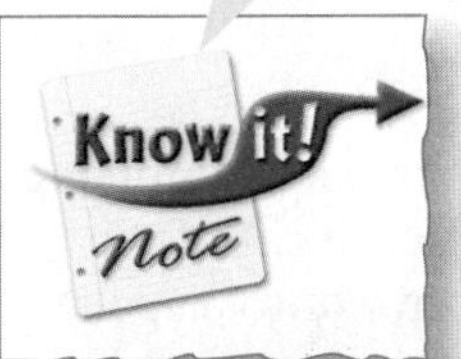

Helpful Hint
A replacement set
a set of numbers t
can be substitutec

Remember!
Terms that are
written without
a coefficient have

Caution!
In the expression
-5^2, 5 is the base
because the nega

The **Glossary** is found in the back of your textbook. Use it as a resource when you need the definition of an unfamiliar word or property.

The **Index** is located at the end of your textbook. Use it to locate the page where a particular concept is taught.

The **Problem Solving Handbook** is found in the back of your textbook. These pages review strategies that can help you solve real-world problems.

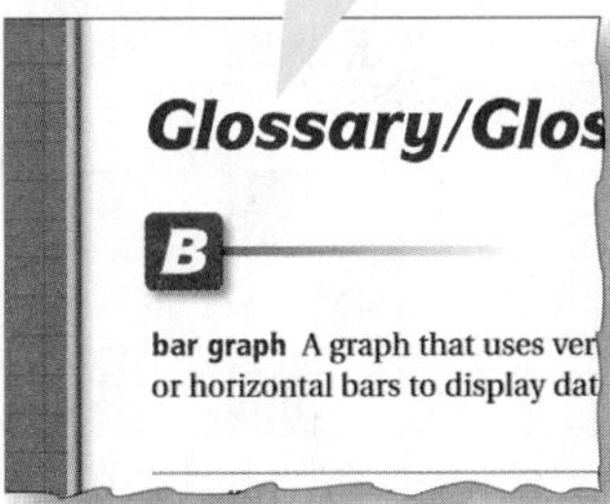

Glossary/Glos
B
bar graph A graph that uses ver
or horizontal bars to display dat

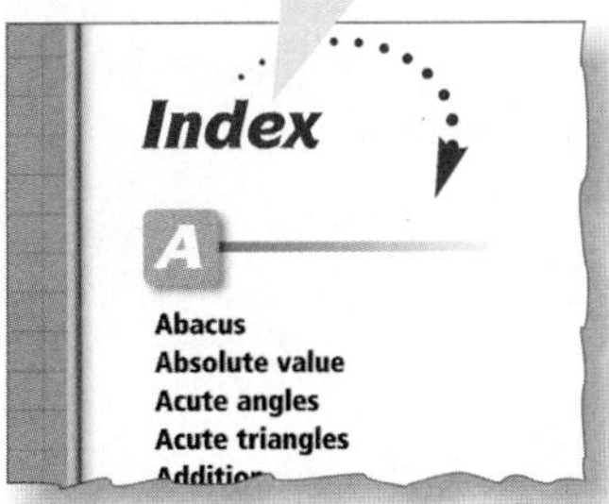

Index
A
Abacus
Absolute value
Acute angles
Acute triangles

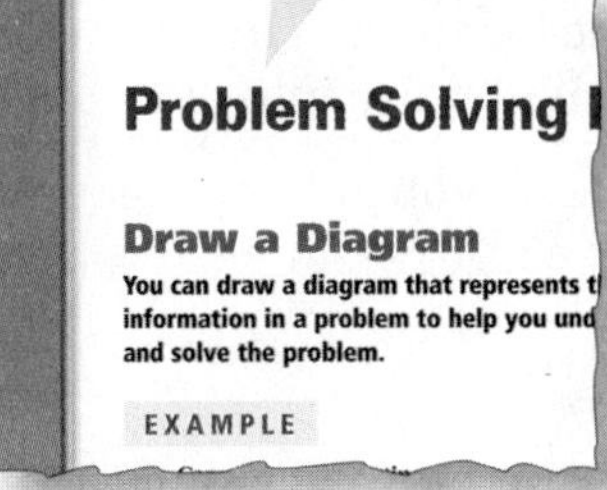

Problem Solving
Draw a Diagram
You can draw a diagram that represents t
information in a problem to help you und
and solve the problem.
EXAMPLE

Use your textbook for the following problems.

1. Use the index to find the page where a term from this chapter is defined.
2. Describe how a strategy from the Problem Solving Workbook can be used in this chapter.
3. Use the glossary to find the definition of a term from this chapter.

Use with Exploring Transformations

Chess Translations

You can use the game of chess to explore transformations.

A chessboard consists of 64 squares arranged into 8 rows (numbered 1 through 8) and 8 columns (lettered *a* through *h*). Each square is named by its column letter and row number. For instance, the square in the lower left corner is **a1.**

Chessboard Notation

Selected Rules of Movement		
♗	Bishop	Diagonally any number of squares
♔	King	One square in any direction
♘	Knight	L-shape: two squares horizontally or vertically and then one square perpendicularly
♖	Rook	Horizontally or vertically any number of squares

You move each chess piece by applying the rules of movement. Pieces of the same color cannot move onto a space occupied by another piece, and the knight is the only piece that can jump over other pieces.

Activity

Use the chessboard at right to name all possible locations of the bishop on f7 after one move.

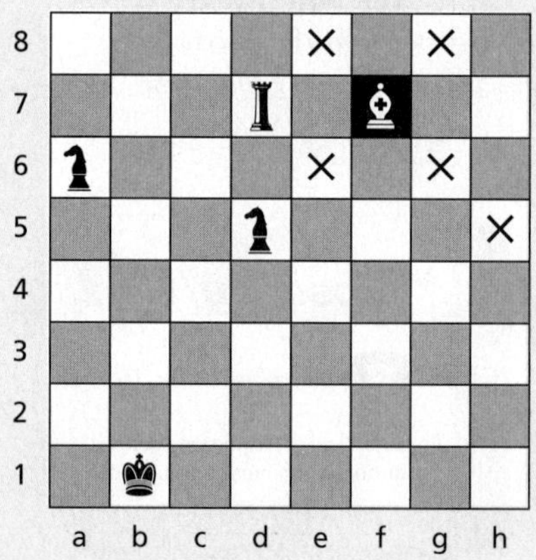

The bishop can move diagonally any number of spaces, but it cannot move into or through any other pieces.

The bishop at f7 can move to any of the marked spaces: e6, e8, g6, g8, or h5.

Try This

Use the chessboard from the activity to name all possible locations of each piece after one move.

1. the king on b1
2. the rook on d7
3. the knight on a6

Use the chessboard from the activity to name all possible locations of each piece after two moves.

4. the king on b1
5. the rook on d7
6. the knight on a6
7. **Critical Thinking** In the last move of a chess game a knight is moved to d5. What are the possible squares that it came from?
8. **Make a Conjecture** Explain the connection between the position labeling in chess and points in the coordinate plane.

1-1 Exploring Transformations

CC.9-12.F.BF.3 Identify the effect on the graph of replacing $f(x)$ by $f(x) + k$, $k\,f(x)$, $f(kx)$, and $f(x + k)$ … find the value of k given the graphs. … illustrate … using technology. *Also* **CC.9-12.F.IF.5**

Objectives

Apply transformations to points and sets of points.

Interpret transformations of real-world data.

Vocabulary

transformation
translation
reflection
stretch
compression

Why learn this?

Changes in recording studio fees can be modeled by transformations. (See Example 4.)

A **transformation** is a change in the position, size, or shape of a figure. A **translation**, or slide, is a transformation that moves each point in a figure the same distance in the same direction.

EXAMPLE 1 Translating Points

Perform the given translation on the point $(2, -1)$. Give the coordinates of the translated point.

4 units left

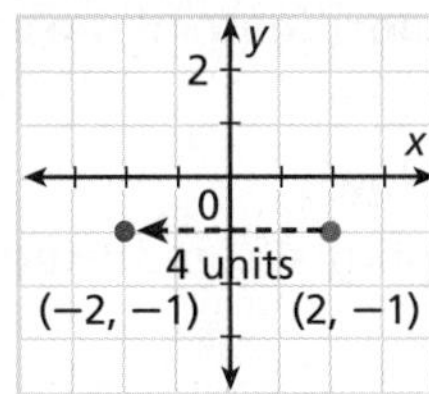

Translating $(2, -1)$ 4 units left results in the point $(-2, -1)$.

2 units right and 3 units up

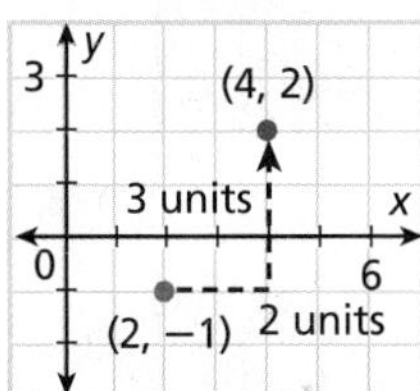

Translating $(2, -1)$ 2 units right and 3 units up results in the point $(4, 2)$.

Perform the given translation on the point $(-1, 3)$. Give the coordinates of the translated point.

1a. 4 units right

1b. 1 unit left and 2 units down

Notice that when you translate left or right, the x-coordinate changes, and when you translate up or down, the y-coordinate changes.

Translations	
Horizontal Translation	**Vertical Translation**
Each point shifts *right* or *left* by a number of units.	Each point shifts *up* or *down* by a number of units.
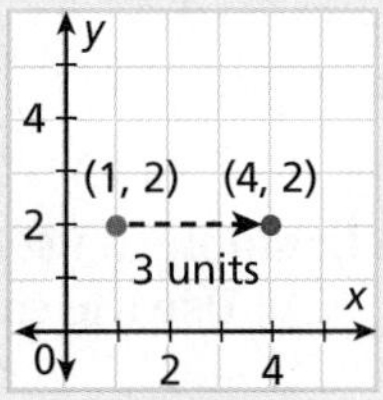 [Graph: (1, 2) → (4, 2), 3 units] The x-coordinate changes. $(1, 2) \rightarrow (1 + 3, 2)$ $(x, y) \rightarrow (x + h, y)$	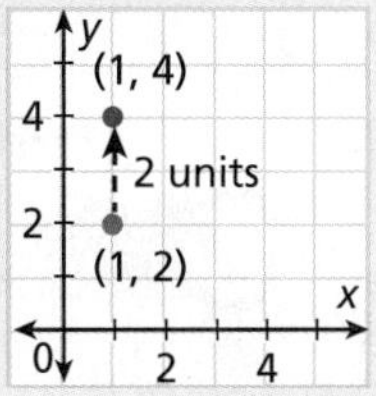 [Graph: (1, 2) → (1, 4), 2 units] The y-coordinate changes. $(1, 2) \rightarrow (1, 2 + 2)$ $(x, y) \rightarrow (x, y + k)$
left if $h < 0$ right if $h > 0$	down if $k < 0$ up if $k > 0$

A **reflection** is a transformation that flips a figure across a line called the line of reflection. Each reflected point is the same distance from the line of reflection, but on the opposite side of the line.

Know it! Note

Reflections	
Reflection Across y-axis	**Reflection Across x-axis**
Each point flips across the y-axis.	Each point flips across the x-axis.
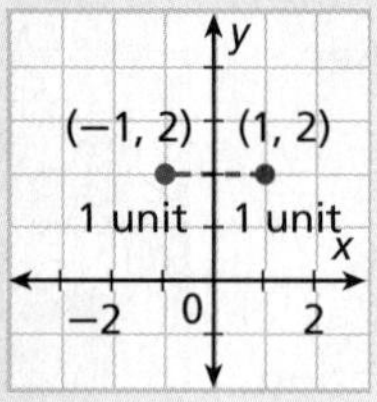 The x-coordinate changes. $(1, 2) \rightarrow (-1, 2)$ $(x, y) \rightarrow (-x, y)$	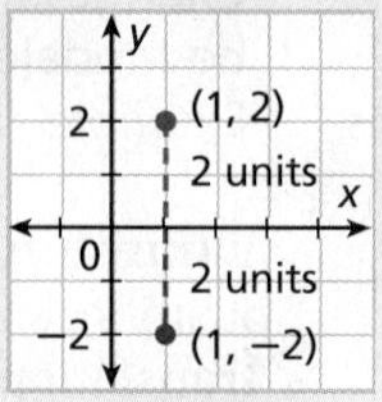 The y-coordinate changes. $(1, 2) \rightarrow (1, -2)$ $(x, y) \rightarrow (x, -y)$

You can transform a function by transforming its ordered pairs. When a function is translated or reflected, the original graph and the graph of the transformation are *congruent* because the size and shape of the graphs are the same.

EXAMPLE 2 Translating and Reflecting Functions

Use a table to perform each transformation of $y = f(x)$. Use the same coordinate plane as the original function.

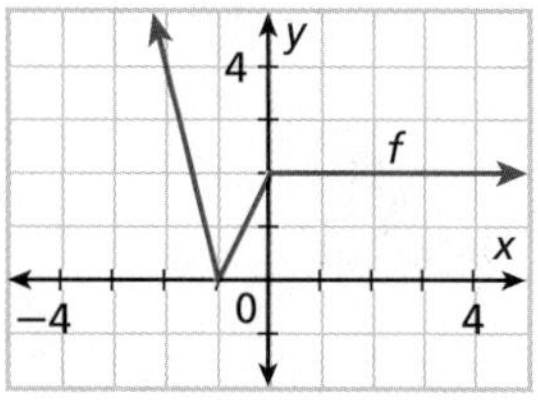

A translation 2 units down

Identify important points from the graph and make a table.

x	y	$y - 2$
−2	4	4 − 2 = 2
−1	0	0 − 2 = −2
0	2	2 − 2 = 0
2	2	2 − 2 = 0

The entire graph shifts 2 units down. Subtract 2 from each y-coordinate.

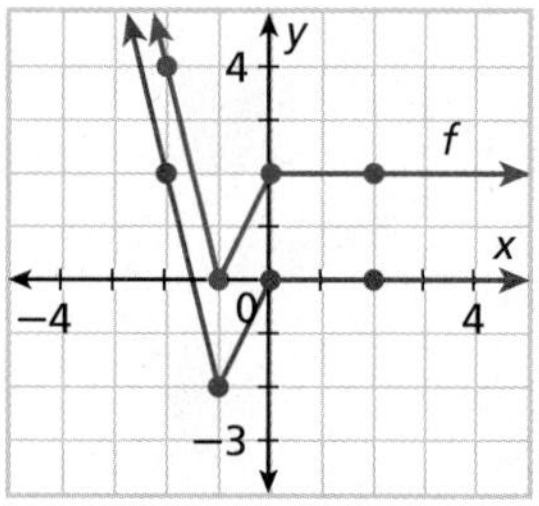

Helpful Hint

Transform x by adding a table column on the left side; transform y by adding a column on the right side.

B reflection across y-axis

Identify important points from the graph and make a table.

$-x$	x	y
−1(−2) = 2	−2	4
−1(−1) = 1	−1	0
−1(0) = 0	0	2
−1(2) = −2	2	2

Multiply each x-coordinate by −1. The entire graph flips across the y-axis.

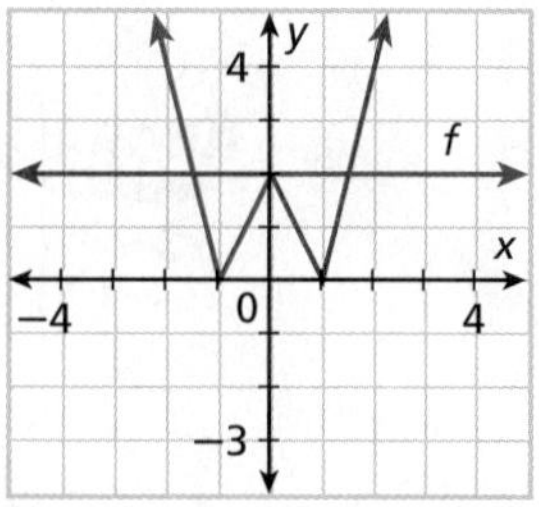

CHECK IT OUT! **For the function from Example 2, use a table to perform each transformation of $y = f(x)$. Use the same coordinate plane as the original function.**

2a. translation 3 units right **2b.** reflection across x-axis

Imagine grasping two points on the graph of a function that lie on opposite sides of the y-axis. If you pull the points away from the y-axis, you would create a horizontal **stretch** of the graph. If you push the points towards the y-axis, you would create a horizontal **compression**.

Stretches and compressions are not congruent to the original graph.

Know it! Note

Stretches and Compressions

	Horizontal	Vertical
Stretch	Each point is *pulled away* from the y-axis. The x-coordinate changes. $(4, 0) \rightarrow (2(4), 0)$ $(x, y) \rightarrow (bx, y)$ $\lvert b \rvert > 1$	Each point is *pulled away* from the x-axis. The y-coordinate changes. $(0, 4) \rightarrow (0, 2(4))$ $(x, y) \rightarrow (x, ay)$ $\lvert a \rvert > 1$
Compression	Each point is *pushed toward* the y-axis. The x-coordinate changes. $(4, 0) \rightarrow \left(\frac{1}{2}(4), 0\right)$ $(x, y) \rightarrow (bx, y)$ $0 < \lvert b \rvert < 1$	Each point is *pushed toward* the x-axis. The y-coordinate changes. $(0, 4) \rightarrow \left(0, \frac{1}{2}(4)\right)$ $(x, y) \rightarrow (x, ay)$ $0 < \lvert a \rvert < 1$

EXAMPLE 3 Stretching and Compressing Functions

Use a table to perform a horizontal compression of $y = f(x)$ by a factor of $\frac{1}{2}$. Use the same coordinate plane as the original function.

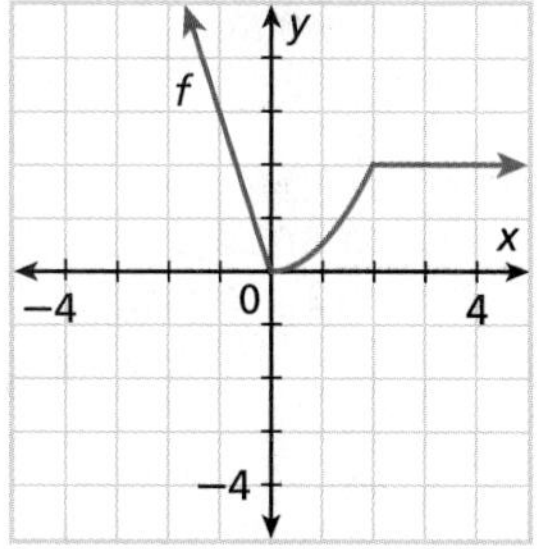

Identify important points from the graph and make a table.

$\frac{1}{2}x$	x	y
$\frac{1}{2}(-1) = -\frac{1}{2}$	−1	3
$\frac{1}{2}(0) = 0$	0	0
$\frac{1}{2}(2) = 1$	2	2
$\frac{1}{2}(4) = 2$	4	2

Multiply each x-coordinate by $\frac{1}{2}$.

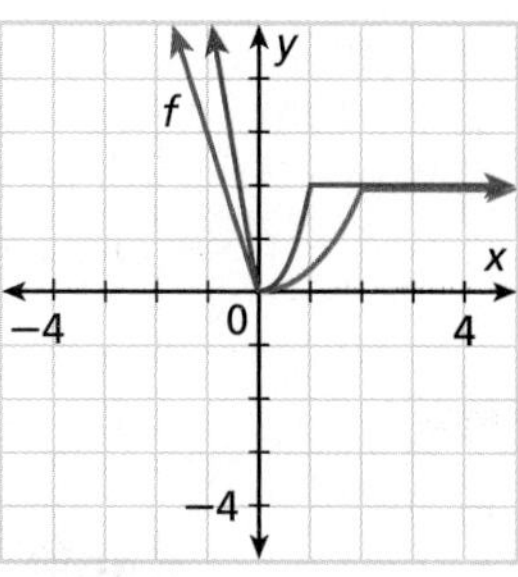

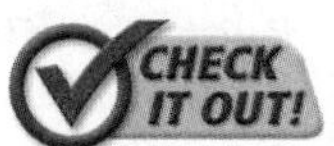

3. For the function from Example 3, use a table to perform a vertical stretch of $y = f(x)$ by a factor of 2. Graph the transformed function on the same coordinate plane as the original function.

EXAMPLE 4 *Business Application*

Recording studio fees are usually based on an hourly rate, but the rate can be modified due to various options. The graph shows a basic hourly studio rate. Sketch a graph to represent each situation below and identify the transformation of the original graph that it represents.

A **The engineer's time is needed, so the hourly rate is 1.5 times the original rate.**

If the fees are 1.5 times the basic hourly rate, the value of each y-coordinate would be multiplied by 1.5. This represents a vertical stretch by a factor of 1.5.

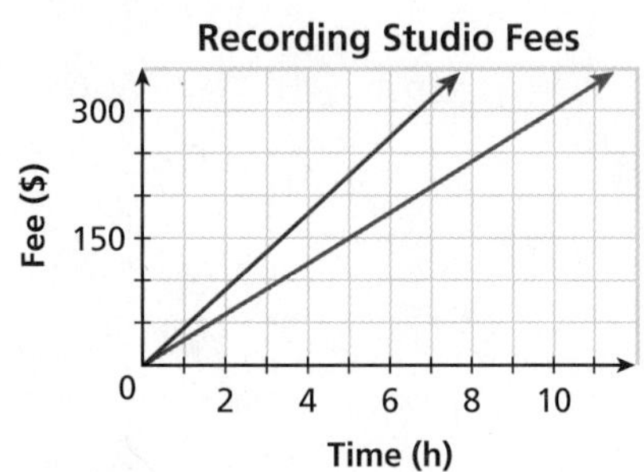

B **A $20 setup fee is added to the basic hourly rate.**

If the prices are $20 more than the original estimate, the value of each y-coordinate would increase by 20. This represents a vertical translation up 20 units.

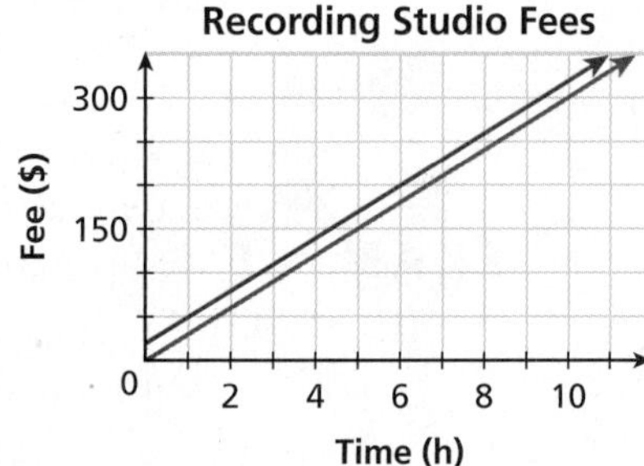

4. **What if...?** Suppose that a discounted rate is $\frac{3}{4}$ of the original rate. Sketch a graph to represent the situation and identify the transformation of the original graph that it represents.

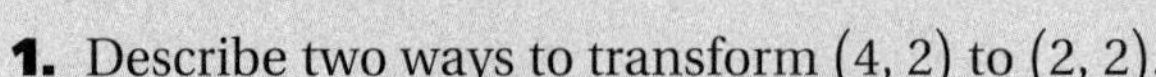

THINK AND DISCUSS

1. Describe two ways to transform $(4, 2)$ to $(2, 2)$.
2. Compare a vertical stretch with a horizontal compression.

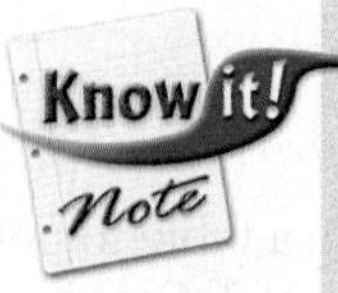

3. **GET ORGANIZED** Copy and complete the graphic organizer. In each box, describe the transformations indicated by the given rule.

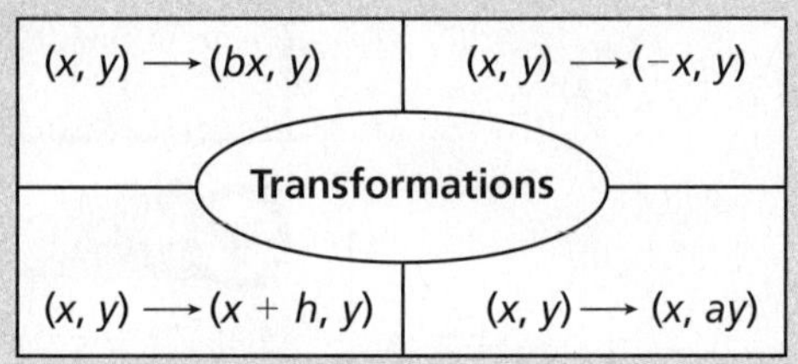

1-1 Exercises

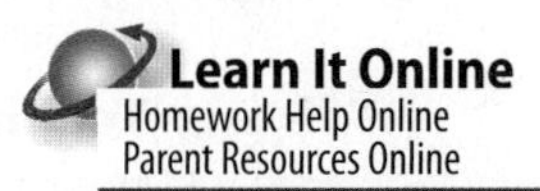

GUIDED PRACTICE

1. **Vocabulary** A transformation that pushes a graph toward the x-axis is a __?__. (*reflection* or *compression*)

SEE EXAMPLE 1

Perform the given translation on the point $(4, 2)$ and give the coordinates of the translated point.

2. 5 units left
3. 3 units down
4. 1 unit right, 6 units up

SEE EXAMPLE 2

Use a table to perform each transformation of $y = f(x)$. Use the same coordinate plane as the original function.

5. translation 2 units up
6. reflection across the y-axis
7. reflection across the x-axis

SEE EXAMPLE 3

Use a table to perform each transformation of $y = f(x)$. Use the same coordinate plane as the original function.

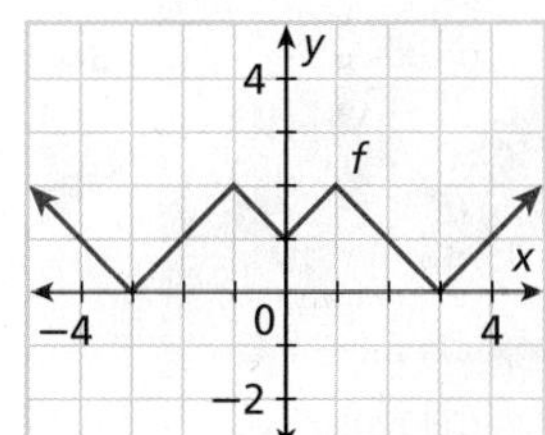

8. horizontal stretch by a factor of 3
9. vertical stretch by a factor of 3
10. vertical compression by a factor of $\frac{1}{3}$

SEE EXAMPLE 4

Recreation **The graph shows the price for admission by age at a local zoo. Sketch a graph to represent each situation and identify the transformation of the original graph that it represents.**

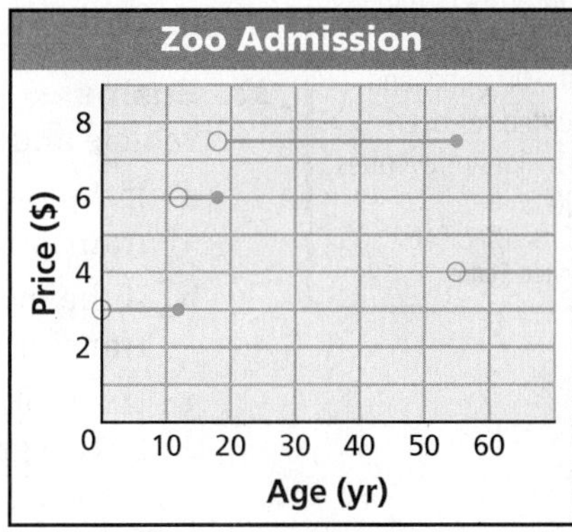

11. Admission is half price on Wednesdays.
12. To raise funds for endangered species, the zoo charges $1.50 extra per ticket.
13. The maximum age for each ticket price is increased by 5 years.

PRACTICE AND PROBLEM SOLVING

Independent Practice

For Exercises	See Example
14–16	1
17–20	2
21–24	3
25–27	4

Extra Practice

See Extra Practice for more Skills Practice and Applications Practice exercises.

Perform the given translation on $(3, 1)$. Give the coordinates of the translated point.

14. 2 units right
15. 4 units up
16. 5 units left, 4 units down

Use a table to perform each transformation of $y = f(x)$. Use the same coordinate plane as the original function.

17. translation 2 units down
18. reflection across the x-axis
19. translation 3 units right
20. reflection across the y-axis
21. vertical compression by a factor of $\frac{2}{3}$
22. horizontal compression by a factor of $\frac{1}{2}$
23. horizontal stretch by a factor of $\frac{3}{2}$
24. vertical stretch by a factor of 2

Technology **The graph shows the cost of Web page hosting depending on the Web space used. Sketch a graph to represent each situation and identify the transformation of the original graph that it represents.**

Web Page Hosting

25. The prices are reduced by $5.

26. The prices are discounted by 25%.

27. A special is offered for double the amount of Web space for the same price.

Estimation **The table gives the coordinates for the vertices of a triangle. Estimate the area of each transformed triangle by graphing it and counting the number of squares it covers on the coordinate plane. How does the area of each transformed triangle compare with the area of the original triangle?**

x	y
−2	2
2	−4
4	−2

28. reflection across the y-axis

29. 5 units left, 3 units up

30. horizontal stretch by a factor of 2

31. horizontal compression by a factor of $\frac{2}{3}$

32. vertical compression by a factor of $\frac{2}{3}$

33. reflection across the x-axis

34. 1 unit left, 6 units down

35. vertical stretch by a factor of 3

LINK

Entertainment

The amusement park industry in the United States includes about 700 parks and accounted for over $8.5 billion in revenues in 2001.
Source: Statistical Abstract of the United States

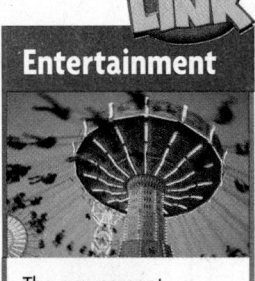

36. Entertainment The revenue from an amusement park ride is given by the admission price of $3 times the number of riders. As part of a promotion, the first 10 riders ride for free.

a. What kind of transformation describes the change in the revenue based on the promotion?

b. Write a function rule for this transformation.

37. Business An automotive mechanic charges $50 to diagnose the problem in a vehicle and $65 per hour for labor to fix it.

a. If the mechanic increases his diagnostic fee to $60, what kind of transformation is this to the graph of the total repair bill?

b. If the mechanic increases his labor rate to $75 per hour, what kind of transformation is this to the graph of the total repair bill?

c. If it took 3 hours to repair your car, which of the two rate increases would have a greater effect on your total bill?

MULTI-STEP TEST PREP

38. The student council wants to buy vases for the flowers for the school prom. A florist charges a $20 delivery fee plus $1.25 per vase. A home-decorating store charges a $10 delivery fee plus $1.25 per vase.

a. The function $f(x) = 20 + 1.25x$ models the cost of ordering x vases from the florist, and the function $g(x) = 10 + 1.25x$ models the cost of ordering x vases from the home-decorating store. What do the graphs of these functions look like?

b. How are the graphs related to each other?

c. How could you modify these functions so that their graphs are identical?

d. If the florist decided to waive the $20 delivery fee as long as the number of vases ordered was more than 150, how would the graph of f change? How would it compare with the graph of the other function?

Transportation Use the graph and the following information for Exercises 39–43.

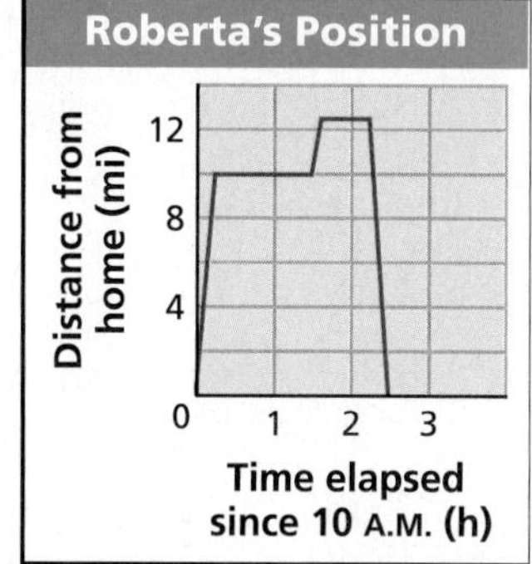

Roberta left her house at 10:00 A.M. and drove to the library. She was at the library studying until 11:30 A.M. Then she drove to the grocery store. At 12:15 P.M. Roberta left the grocery store and drove home. The graph shows Roberta's position with respect to time.

Sketch a graph to reflect each change to the original story. Assume the time Roberta spends inside each building remains the same.

39. Roberta drove at half the speed from her house to the library.

40. The grocery store she went to is twice as far from the library.

41. The grocery store is 2.5 miles closer to the house than the library is.

Change the original story about Roberta to match each graph.

42.

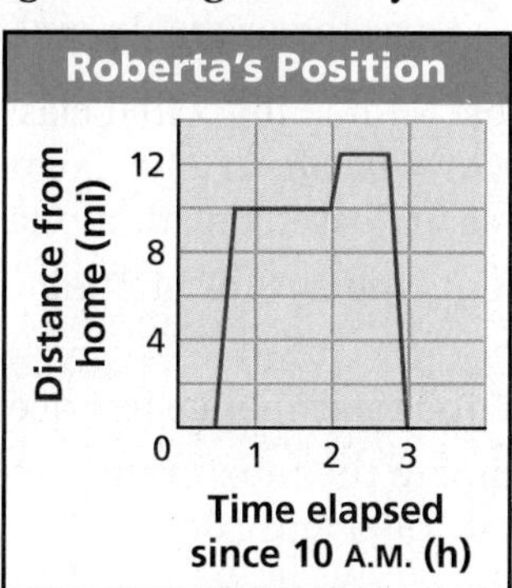

43.

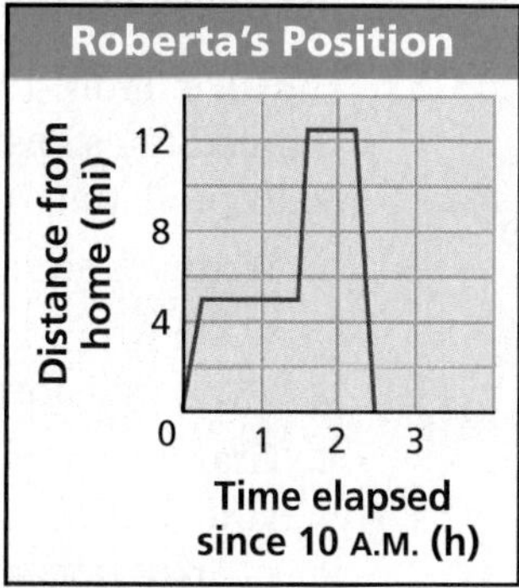

44. Critical Thinking Suppose two transformations are performed on a single point: a translation and a reflection. Does the order in which the transformations are performed make a difference? Does the type of translation or reflection matter? Explain your reasoning.

45. Write About It Describe how transformations might make graphing easier.

TEST PREP

46. The function $c(p) = 0.99p$ represents the cost in dollars of p pounds of peaches. If the cost per pound increases by 10%, how will the graph of the function change?

Ⓐ Translation 0.1 unit up
Ⓑ Translation 0.1 unit right
Ⓒ Horizontal stretch by a factor of 1.1
Ⓓ Vertical stretch by a factor of 1.1

47. Which transformation would change the point $(5, 3)$ into $(-5, 3)$?

Ⓕ Reflection across the x-axis
Ⓖ Translation 5 units down
Ⓗ Reflection across the y-axis
Ⓙ Translation 5 units left

48. The graph of the function f is a line that intersects the y-axis at the point $(0, 3)$ and the x-axis at the point $(3, 0)$. Which transformation of f does NOT intersect the y-axis at the point $(0, 6)$?

Ⓐ Translation 3 units up
Ⓑ Translation 3 units right
Ⓒ Vertical stretch by a factor of 2
Ⓓ Horizontal compression by a factor of $\frac{1}{2}$

49. Which transformation is displayed in the graph?

Ⓕ Reflection across the x-axis

Ⓖ Translation 5 units down

Ⓗ Reflection across the y-axis

Ⓙ Translation 5 units left

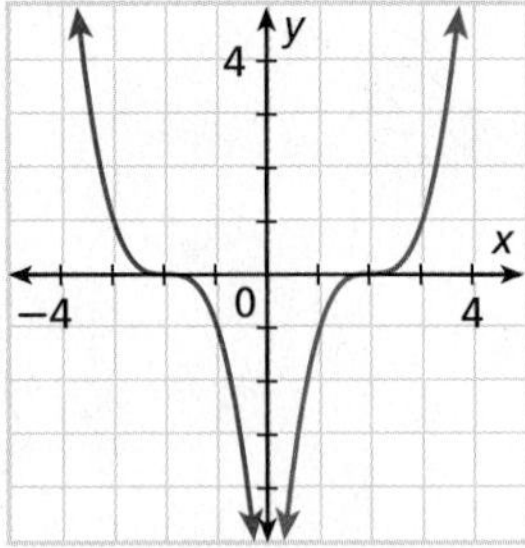

50. Which represents a translation 4 units right and 2 units down?

Ⓐ From (4, 2) to (0, 0)

Ⓑ From (4, −2) to (0, 0)

Ⓒ From (−4, −2) to (0, 0)

Ⓓ From (−4, 2) to (0, 0)

51. **Short Response** Graph the points (−1, 3) and (−1, −3). Describe two different transformations that would transform (−1, 3) to (−1, −3).

CHALLENGE AND EXTEND

52. Suppose the rule $(x, y) \rightarrow (2x, y - 3)$ is used to translate a point. If the coordinates of the translated point are (22, 7), what was the original point?

53. **History** From 1999 to 2001 the cost for mailing n first class letters through the United States Postal Service was $c(n) = 0.33n$. In 2001 the rate was increased by \$0.01 per letter. In 2002 the rate was increased an additional \$0.03 per letter.

    a. Write an equation that represents the cost of mailing n first class letters in 2002.

    b. What transformation describes the total change in price?

    c. Graph both functions and estimate the maximum number of first class letters you could mail for \$5.00 in both 1999 and 2002.

    d. Explain the effect of the reasonable domain and range for these functions on your answer for part **c**.

54. Name a point that when reflected across the x-axis has the same coordinates as if it were reflected across the y-axis. How many points are there that satisfy this condition?

COMMON CORE

1-2 Introduction to Parent Functions

CC.9-12.F.BF.3 Identify the effect on the graph of replacing $f(x)$ by $f(x) + k$, $k\,f(x)$, $f(kx)$, and $f(x + k)$ … find the value of k given the graphs. *Also* **CC.9-12.A.CED.2, CC.9-12.A.CED.3, CC.9-12.F.IF.5**

Objectives

Identify parent functions from graphs and equations.

Use parent functions to model real-world data and make estimates for unknown values.

Vocabulary

parent function

Who uses this?

Oceanographers use transformations of parent functions to approximate data sets such as wave height versus wind speed. (See Example 3.)

Similar to the way that numbers are classified into sets based on common characteristics, functions can be classified into *families of functions*. The **parent function** is the simplest function with the defining characteristics of the family. Functions in the same family are transformations of their parent function.

Parent Functions

Family	Constant	Linear	Quadratic	Cubic	Square root
Rule	$f(x) = c$	$f(x) = x$	$f(x) = x^2$	$f(x) = x^3$	$f(x) = \sqrt{x}$
Graph					
Domain	$\mathbb{R}$	$\mathbb{R}$	$\mathbb{R}$	$\mathbb{R}$	$x \geq 0$
Range	$y = c$	$\mathbb{R}$	$y \geq 0$	$\mathbb{R}$	$y \geq 0$
Intersects y-axis	$(0, c)$	$(0, 0)$	$(0, 0)$	$(0, 0)$	$(0, 0)$

EXAMPLE 1 Identifying Transformations of Parent Functions

Identify the parent function for g from its function rule. Then graph g on your calculator and describe what transformation of the parent function it represents.

A $g(x) = x + 5$

$g(x) = x + 5$ is linear. *x has a power of 1.*

The linear parent function $f(x) = x$ intersects the y-axis at the point $(0, 0)$.

Graph $\mathbf{Y_1 = X + 5}$ on a graphing calculator. The function $g(x) = x + 5$ intersects the y-axis at the point $(0, 5)$.

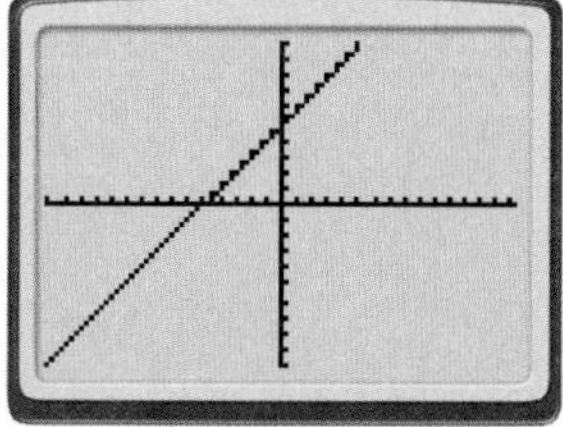

So $g(x) = x + 5$ represents a vertical translation of the linear parent function 5 units up.

Helpful Hint

To make graphs appear accurate on a graphing calculator, use the standard square window. Press ZOOM, choose **6:ZStandard,** press ZOOM again, and choose **5:ZSquare.**

Identify the parent function for *g* from its function rule. Then graph *g* on your calculator and describe what transformation of the parent function it represents.

B $g(x) = (x - 3)^2$

$g(x) = (x - 3)^2$ is quadratic. *$x - 3$ has a power of 2.*

The quadratic parent function $f(x) = x^2$ intersects the x-axis at the point $(0, 0)$.

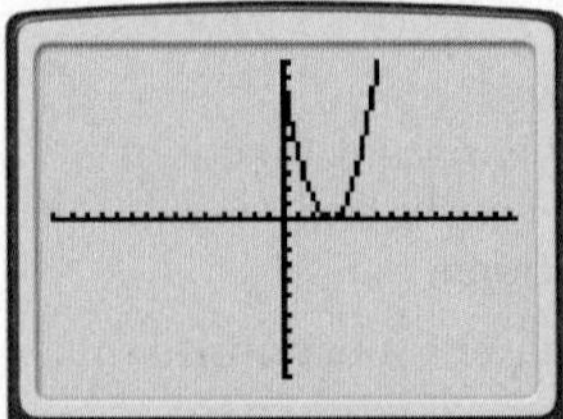

Graph $\mathbf{Y_1 = (X - 3)^2}$ on a graphing calculator. The function $g(x) = (x - 3)^2$ intersects the x-axis at the point $(3, 0)$.

So $g(x) = (x - 3)^2$ represents a horizontal translation of the quadratic parent function 3 units right.

Identify the parent function for *g* from its function rule. Then graph *g* on your calculator and describe what transformation of the parent function it represents.

1a. $g(x) = x^3 + 2$

1b. $g(x) = (-x)^2$

It is often necessary to work with a set of data points like the ones represented by the table at right.

x	−4	−2	0	2	4
y	8	2	0	2	8

With only the information in the table, it is impossible to know the exact behavior of the data between and beyond the given points. However, a working knowledge of the parent functions can allow you to sketch a curve to approximate those values not found in the table.

EXAMPLE 2 Identifying Parent Functions to Model Data Sets

Graph the data from the table. Describe the parent function and the transformation that best approximates the data set.

x	−4	−2	0	2	4
y	8	2	0	2	8

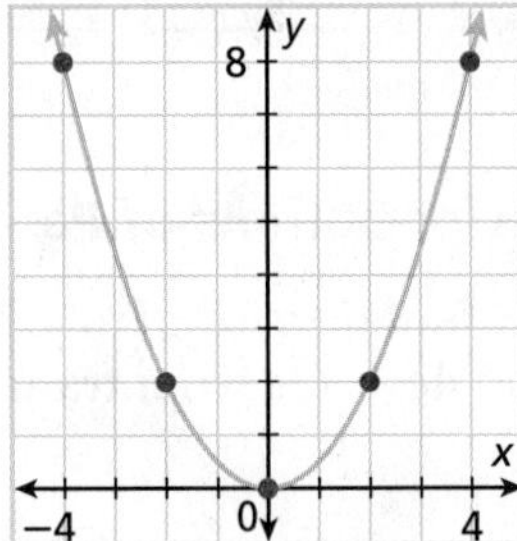

The graph of the data points resembles the shape of the quadratic parent function $f(x) = x^2$.

The quadratic parent function passes through the points $(2, 4)$ and $(4, 16)$. The data set contains the points

$$(2, 2) = \left(2, \frac{1}{2}(4)\right) \text{ and } (4, 8) = \left(2, \frac{1}{2}(16)\right).$$

The data set seems to represent a vertical compression of the quadratic parent function by a factor of $\frac{1}{2}$.

2. Graph the data from the table. Describe the parent function and the transformation that best approximates the data set.

x	−4	−2	0	2	4
y	−12	−6	0	6	12

Consider the two data points $(0, 0)$ and $(1, 1)$. If you plot them on a coordinate plane you might very well think that they are part of a linear function. In fact they belong to each of the parent functions below.

Linear	**Quadratic**	**Cubic**	**Square Root**
$f(x) = x$	$f(x) = x^2$	$f(x) = x^3$	$f(x) = \sqrt{x}$

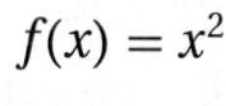

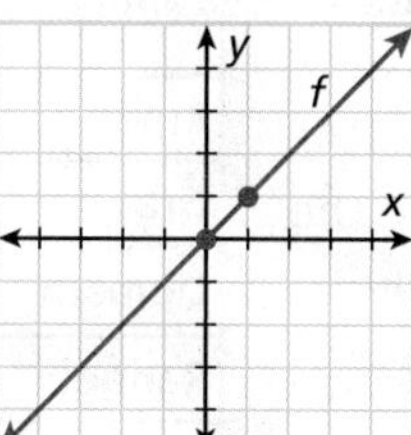

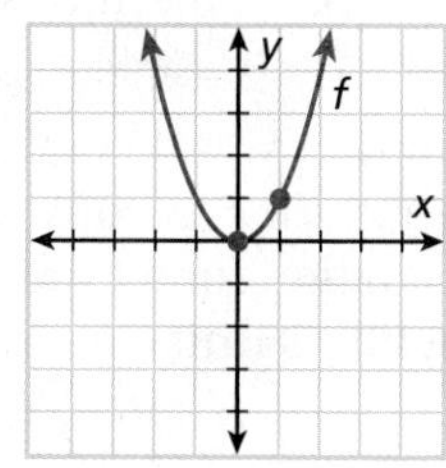

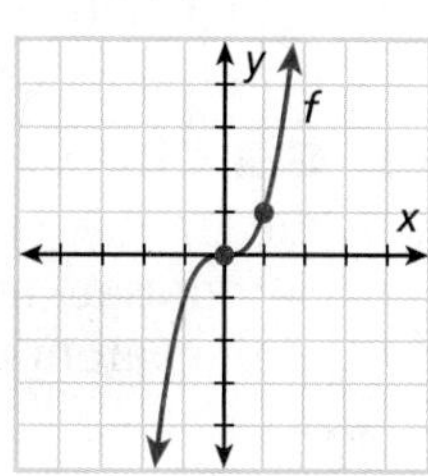

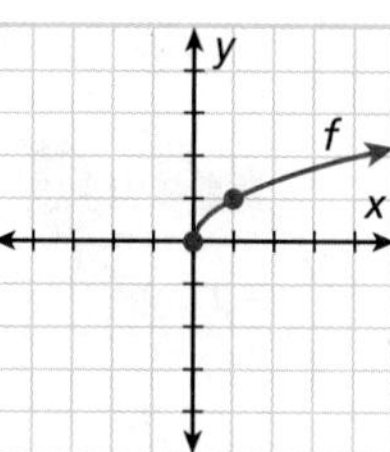

Helpful Hint

A greater number of data points increases your chances of correctly identifying the parent function that best describes the data.

Remember that any parent function you use to approximate a set of data should never be considered exact. However, these function approximations are often useful for estimating unknown values.

EXAMPLE 3 *Oceanography Application*

An oceanographer wants to determine a model that can be used to estimate wind speed based upon wave height. Graph the relationship from wave height to wind speed and identify which parent function best describes it. Then use the graph to estimate the wave height when the wind speed is 10 knots.

Ocean Waves	
Wave Height (ft)	**Wind Speed (knots)**
2	8.8
4	12.4
6	15.2
8	17.5
10	19.6

Step 1 Graph the relation.

Graph the points given in the table. Draw a smooth curve through them to help you see the shape.

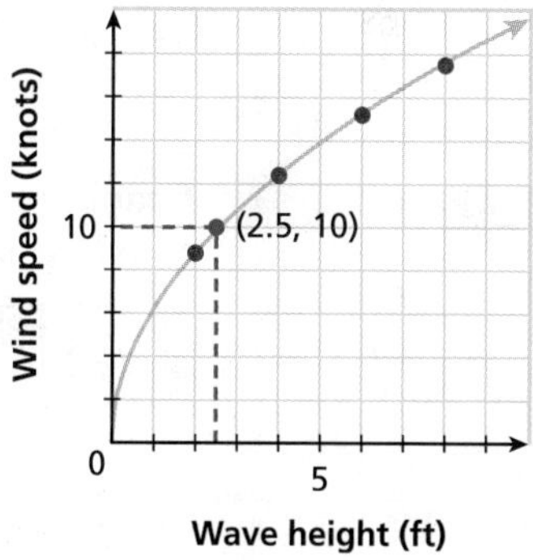

Step 2 Identify the parent function.

The graph of the data set resembles the shape of the square-root parent function $f(x) = \sqrt{x}$.

Step 3 Estimate the wave height when the wind speed is 10 knots.

The curve indicates that a wind speed of 10 knots would create a wave that is approximately 2.5 feet high.

3. The cost of playing an online video game depends on the number of months for which the online service is used. Graph the relationship from number of months to cost, and identify which parent function best describes the data. Then use the graph to estimate the cost for 5 months of online service.

Cost of Online Video Game					
Time (mo)	1	3	6	9	12
Cost ($)	40	56	80	104	128

THINK AND DISCUSS

1. Explain how to determine the parent function for a given equation.
2. Explain why recognizing parent functions is useful for graphing.

3. **GET ORGANIZED** Copy and complete the graphic organizer. In each box, give the appropriate information for a translation of the parent function 3 units up.

Transformed Parent Functions			
Family	Linear	Quadratic	Square root
Rule			
Graph			
Domain			
Range			
Intersects *y*-axis			

1-2 Exercises

GUIDED PRACTICE

1. **Vocabulary** Explain how transformations, families of functions, and *parent functions* are related.

SEE EXAMPLE 1

Identify the parent function for g from its function rule. Then graph g on your calculator and describe what transformation of the parent function it represents.

2. $g(x) = (x - 1)^3$
3. $g(x) = (x + 1)^2$
4. $g(x) = -x$
5. $g(x) = \sqrt{x + 3}$
6. $g(x) = x^2 + 4$
7. $g(x) = x - \sqrt{2}$

SEE EXAMPLE 2

Graph the data from the table. Describe the parent function and the transformation that best approximates the data set.

8.

x	−3	−1	0	1	3
y	−15	−5	0	5	15

9.

x	−3	−1	0	1	3
y	−1	$-\frac{1}{27}$	0	$\frac{1}{27}$	1

SEE EXAMPLE 3

10. **Physics** The time it takes a pendulum to make one complete swing back and forth depends on its string length.
    a. Graph the relationship from string length to time.
    b. Identify which parent function best describes the data.
    c. Use your graph to estimate the string length of a pendulum that takes 4.5 seconds to make one complete swing.
    d. Use your graph to estimate the time it takes to make a complete swing for a string of length 14 meters.

Pendulum Swing	
String Length (m)	**Time (s)**
2	2.8
4	4.0
6	4.9
8	5.7
10	6.3

PRACTICE AND PROBLEM SOLVING

Independent Practice	
For Exercises	See Example
11–13	1
14–15	2
16	3

Extra Practice

See Extra Practice for more Skills Practice and Applications Practice exercises.

Identify the parent function for g from its function rule. Then graph g on your calculator and describe what transformation of the parent function it represents.

11. $g(x) = x^2 - 1$ **12.** $g(x) = \sqrt{x - 2}$ **13.** $g(x) = x^3 + 3$

Graph the data from the table. Describe the parent function and the transformation that best approximates the data set.

14.

x	-3	-1	0	1	3
y	3	$\frac{1}{3}$	0	$\frac{1}{3}$	3

15.

x	0	1	4	9	16
y	0	2	4	6	8

16. Geometry The number of segments required to connect a given number of points is shown in the table.

a. Graph the relationship from the number of points to the number of segments.

b. Identify which parent function best describes the data.

c. Use your graph to estimate the number of points if there are 45 segments.

d. Use your graph to estimate the number of segments if there are 7 points.

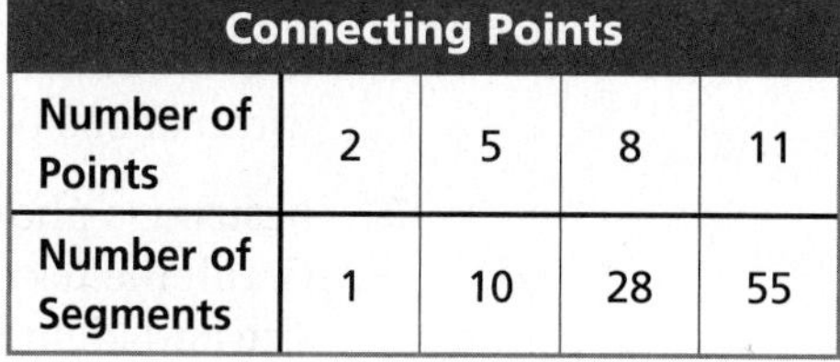

Connecting Points				
Number of Points	2	5	8	11
Number of Segments	1	10	28	55

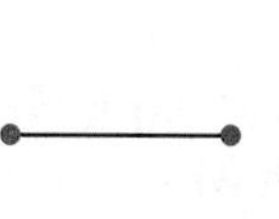

2 points
1 segment

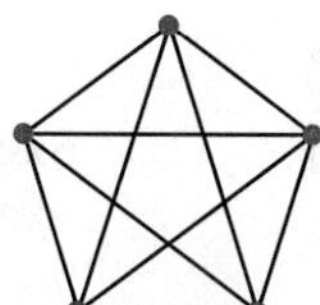

5 points
10 segments

Graphing Calculator Graph each function with a graphing calculator. Identify the domain and range of the function, and describe the transformation from its parent function.

17. $g(x) = 3\sqrt{x}$ **18.** $g(x) = \frac{2}{3}x$ **19.** $g(x) = -\sqrt{x}$

20. $g(x) = -(x - 2)^2$ **21.** $g(x) = -x^2 + 1$ **22.** $g(x) = -\frac{1}{2}x^3$

23. Sports Based on the information in the table, what is the total cost of 15 tickets to the hockey game? Explain how you determined your answer.

Hockey Tickets				
Number of Tickets	1	5	8	12
Total Cost ($)	13	65	104	156

Graph each function. Identify the parent function that best describes the set of points, and describe the transformation from the parent function.

24. $\{(-2, 8), (-1, 1), (0, 0), (1, -1), (2, -8)\}$ **25.** $\{(5, 4), (7, 0), (9, 4), (10, 9), (11, 16)\}$

26. $\{(0, 0), (-1, 1), (-4, 2), (-9, 3), (-16, 4)\}$ **27.** $\{(-4, 3), (-2, 1), (0, -1), (2, -3), (4, -5)\}$

MULTI-STEP TEST PREP

28. a. One function used in the Multi-Step Test Prep in the lesson *Exploring Transformations* was $f(x) = 20 + 1.25x$. What is its parent function?

b. The graph for a given function has a U shape. What could be the parent function?

c. Plot the data set $\{(0, 0), (1, 2), (4, 4), (9, 6), (16, 8), (25, 10)\}$. Which parent function best models the data set?

Photography When resizing a digital photo, it is often important to preserve its *aspect ratio*, the ratio of its width to its height. Use the table for Exercises 29–31.

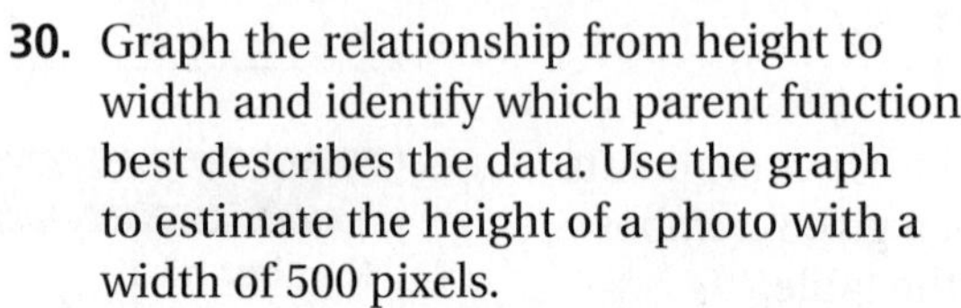

29. Graph the relationship from width to height and identify which parent function best describes the data. Use the graph to estimate the width of a photo with a height of 1000 pixels.

30. Graph the relationship from height to width and identify which parent function best describes the data. Use the graph to estimate the height of a photo with a width of 500 pixels.

31. Resizing a photo changes the file size. Graph the relationship from width to file size and identify which parent function best describes the data. Use the graph to estimate the width of a photo with a file size of 1000 KB.

Digital Photos with Aspect Ratio 3:2

Width (pixels)	Height (pixels)	File Size (KB)
640	427	220
800	533	254
1024	683	413
1280	853	750

Sketch a graph for each situation and identify the related parent function. Then explain what the reasonable domain and range for the function is and compare it with the domain and range of the parent function.

32. distance traveled after h hours at a speed of 55 mi/h

33. volume of a cube with side length ℓ

34. area of a room with width w and a length of 15 feet

35. cost to wash n loads of laundry at $1.00 per load

36. cost of an item with original price p after a 15% discount

37. side length of a square with area A

38. Chemistry The table shows properties of aerogel. Graph the relationship from mass to volume, and then estimate the volume of 1 gram of aerogel.

Aerogel Properties

Mass (mg)	30	90	300	450
Volume (cm^3)	10	30	100	150

LINK Chemistry

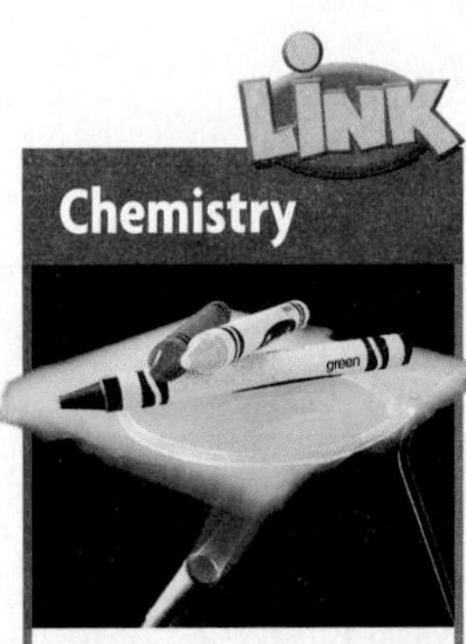

Aerogel has been called the world's lowest density solid. It is 99.8% air and is an excellent heat insulator. As shown above, a layer of aerogel can prevent a flame from melting crayons.

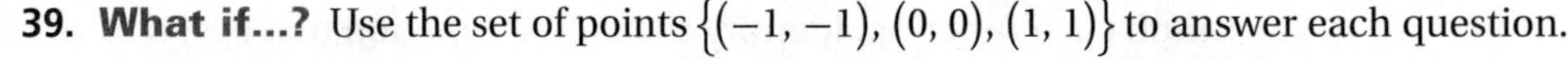

39. What if...? Use the set of points $\{(-1, -1), (0, 0), (1, 1)\}$ to answer each question.

a. What parent function best describes the set of points?

b. If the points $(-2, 8)$ and $(2, 8)$ were added, what parent function would best describe the set?

c. If the point $(1, 1)$ were replaced with $(1, -1)$, what parent function would best describe the set?

d. If the point $(-1, -1)$ were replaced with $(4, 2)$, what parent function would best describe the set?

e. **Multi-Step** If the x-coordinate of each point were doubled and 3 were added to each y-coordinate, what parent function would best describe the set? What transformation of the parent function would the set represent?

40. Critical Thinking Explain any relationship you have noticed between the quadratic parent function and a function rule that represents a horizontal translation, a vertical translation, or a reflection across the x-axis.

(tc), (tr) Photodisc/Getty Images; (bl) NASA

41. Write About It Order the parent functions covered in this lesson from least to greatest by the rate at which $f(x)$ increases as x increases for $x > 1$. Explain your answer.

TEST PREP

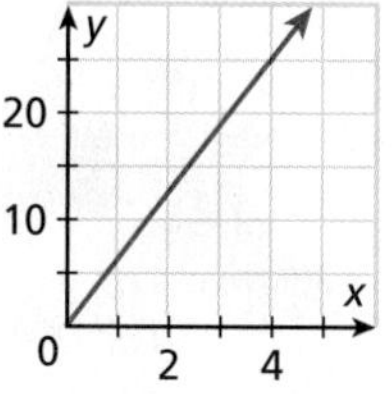

42. Which situation could be represented by the graph?

Ⓐ The area of a circle based on its radius

Ⓑ The volume of a sphere based on its radius

Ⓒ The surface area of a sphere based on its radius

Ⓓ The circumference of a circle based on its radius

43. Which graph best represents the function $f(x) = 2x^2 - 2$?

Ⓕ 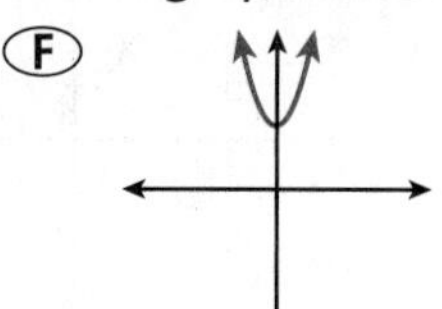

Ⓖ 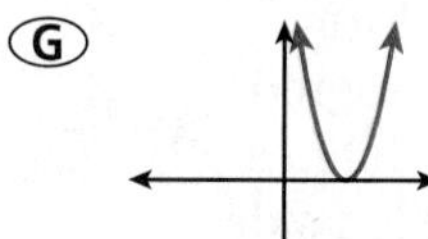

Ⓗ 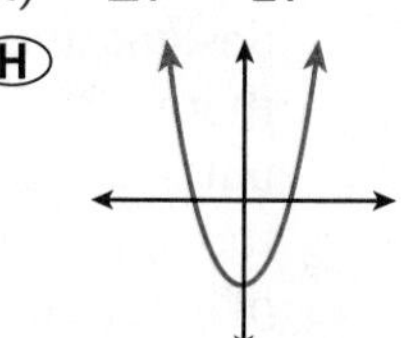

Ⓙ 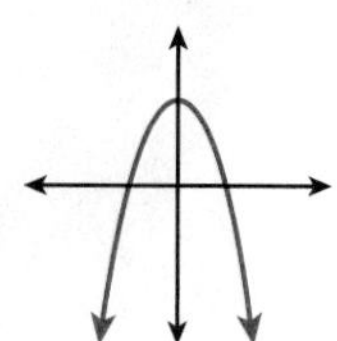

44. Which equation describes a relationship in which every nonzero real number x corresponds to a negative real number y?

Ⓐ $y = -x^3$ Ⓑ $y = -x^2$ Ⓒ $y = (-x)^2$ Ⓓ $y = -x$

45. For which function is -1 NOT an element of the range?

Ⓕ $y = -1$ Ⓖ $y = (-x)^2$ Ⓗ $y = -x$ Ⓙ $y = x^3$

46. What type of function can be used to determine the side length of a square if the independent variable is the square's area?

Ⓐ Cubic Ⓑ Linear Ⓒ Quadratic Ⓓ Square root

CHALLENGE AND EXTEND

Identify the parent function for each function.

47. $g(x) = 3(x - 1)^2 - 6$ **48.** $h(x) = \left(4x^3\right)^0 + 2$ **49.** $g(x) = 5(3x - 2) - 11x$

50. Another parent function is an exponential function of the form $f(x) = a^x$.

a. Graph $f(x) = 2^x$.

b. Find the domain and range of the function.

c. Identify the point where the function crosses the y-axis.

d. Predict where $f(x) = 3^x$ crosses the y-axis and explain your answer.

CHAPTER 1

SECTION 1A

MATHEMATICAL PRACTICES **Model with mathematics.**

Introduction to Functions

Native American Art Much of Native American art, in particular Navajo and Cherokee, displays symmetrical designs.

To reproduce these designs, artists can determine the points that make up the designs and transform them. The set of ordered pairs in the table defines the outline of the left side of a handmade Navajo vase. The graph shows the plotted points.

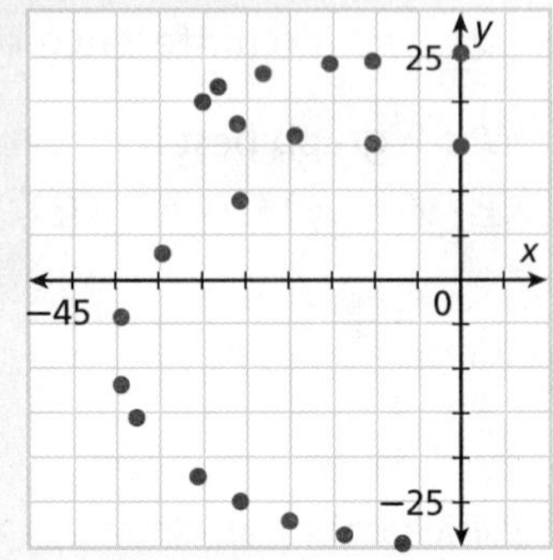

Vase Outline

x	y
0	25.5
−10.3	24.6
−15.3	24.3
−23.0	23.2
−28.2	21.7
−30.0	20.0
−26.0	17.5
−19.3	16.2
−10.3	15.3
0	15.0
−25.7	8.9
−34.6	3.0
−39.4	−4.2
−39.4	−11.8
−37.6	−15.5
−30.6	−22.1
−25.7	−24.9
−20.0	−27.1
−13.7	−28.7
−6.9	−29.7

1. What is the domain of this relation?

2. What is the range of this relation?

3. Is this relation a function?

4. If the coordinates were plotted such that the vase appears to be on its side (that is, the x- and y-coordinates switched places), would the relation be a function? Explain why or why not.

5. If the vase appears to be on its side, which parent function would best represent the bottom of the vase?

6. What transformation would create the right side of the upright vase?

7. What kind of transformation could be done on the relation in the table to make the vase shorter?

8. What kind of transformation could be done on the relation in the table to make the vase narrower?

READY TO GO ON?

CHAPTER 1

SECTION 1A

Quiz for Lessons 1-1 and 1-2

1-1 Exploring Transformations

Perform the given translation on the point (−3, 1) and give the coordinates of the translated point.

1. 7 units right
2. 1unit up, 2 units left
3. 4 units down

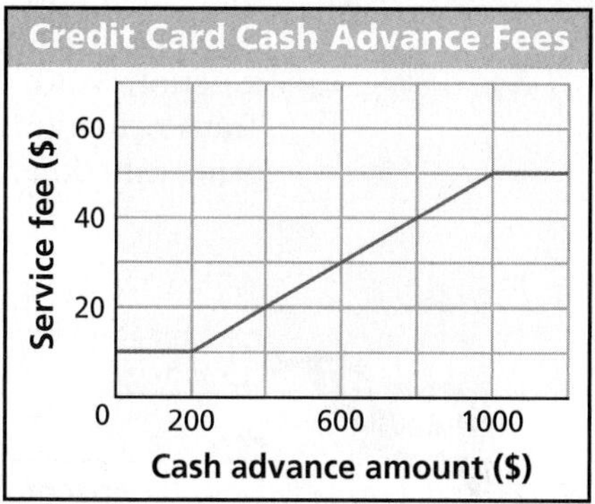

The graph shows some credit card fees for cash advances. Sketch a graph to represent each situation and identify the transformation of the original graph that it represents.

4. Each fee is increased by $15.
5. Each fee is decreased by 40%.

1-2 Introduction to Parent Functions

Identify the parent function for *g* from its equation. Then graph *g* on your calculator and describe what transformation of the parent function it represents.

6. $g(x) = -x^2$
7. $g(x) = \sqrt{x - 3}$
8. $g(x) = 1.5x$
9. The table lists the maximum load of a three-strand nylon rope based on its diameter. Graph the relationship from diameter to maximum load and identify which parent function best describes the data. Then use your graph to estimate the diameter of a three-strand nylon rope that has a maximum load of 7920 kilograms.

Nylon Rope Maximum Load					
Diameter (mm)	8	10	12	14	16
Maximum Load (kg)	1920	2720	3750	5100	6640

1-3 Transforming Linear Functions

CC.9-12.F.BF.3 Identify the effect on the graph of replacing $f(x)$ by $f(x) + k$, $k\,f(x)$, $f(kx)$, and $f(x + k)$ … find the value of k given the graphs. … illustrate … using technology. *Also* **CC.9-12.A.CED.2, CC.9-12.A.CED.3**

Objectives

Transform linear functions.

Solve problems involving linear transformations.

Why learn this?

Transformations allow you to visualize and compare many different functions at once.

You have learned to transform functions by transforming each point. Transformations can also be expressed by using function notation.

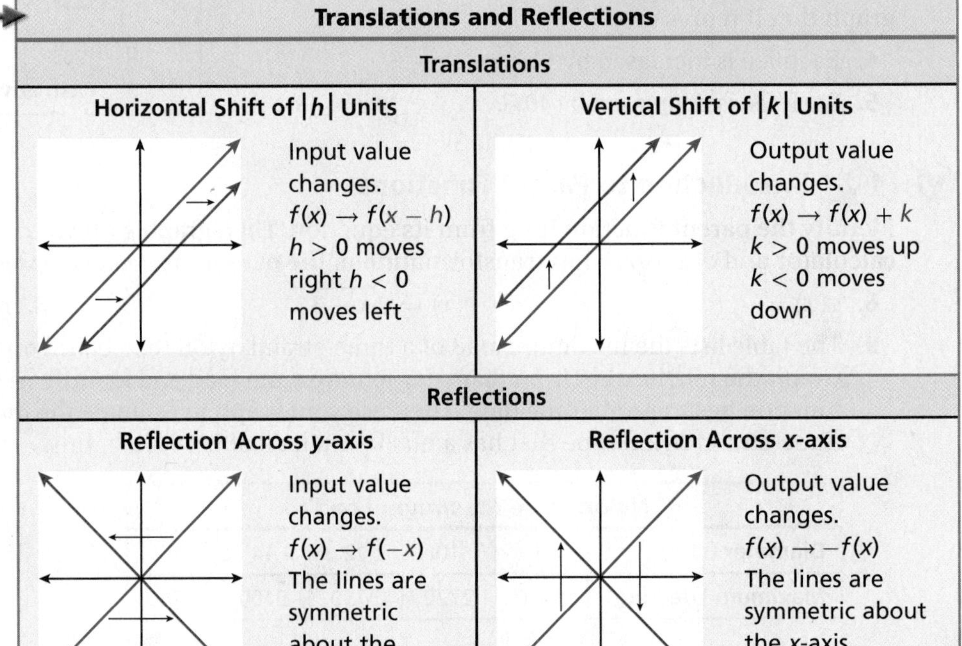

Translations and Reflections

Translations

Horizontal Shift of $\lvert h \rvert$ Units	Vertical Shift of $\lvert k \rvert$ Units
Input value changes. $f(x) \rightarrow f(x - h)$ $h > 0$ moves right $h < 0$ moves left	Output value changes. $f(x) \rightarrow f(x) + k$ $k > 0$ moves up $k < 0$ moves down

Reflections

Reflection Across *y*-axis	Reflection Across *x*-axis
Input value changes. $f(x) \rightarrow f(-x)$ The lines are symmetric about the *y*-axis.	Output value changes. $f(x) \rightarrow -f(x)$ The lines are symmetric about the *x*-axis.

Helpful Hint

To remember the difference between vertical and horizontal translations, think: "Add to *y*, go high." "Add to *x*, go left."

EXAMPLE 1 Translating and Reflecting Linear Functions

Let $g(x)$ be the indicated transformation of $f(x)$. Write the rule for $g(x)$.

A $f(x) = 2x + 3$; **vertical translation 4 units up**

Translating $f(x)$ 4 units up adds 4 to each output value.

$g(x) = f(x) + 4$ *Add 4 to $f(x)$.*

$g(x) = (2x + 3) + 4$ *Substitute $2x + 3$ for $f(x)$.*

$g(x) = 2x + 7$ *Simplify.*

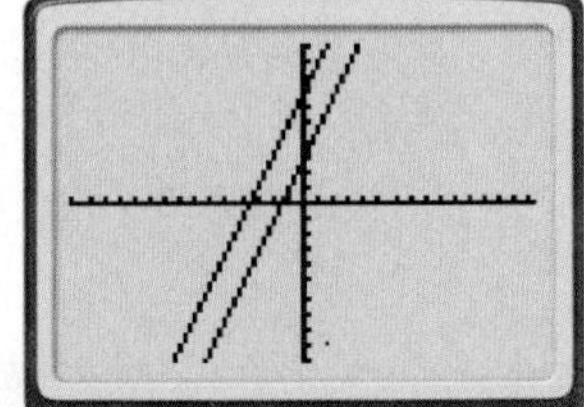

Check Graph $f(x)$ and $g(x)$ on a graphing calculator. The slopes are the same, but the y-intercept has moved 4 units up from 3 to 7. ✔

Let $g(x)$ be the indicated transformation of $f(x)$. Write the rule for $g(x)$.

x	$f(x)$
−1	0
0	2
1	4

B **linear function defined in the table; reflection across y-axis**

Step 1 Write the rule for $f(x)$ in slope-intercept form.

The y-intercept is 2. *The table contains (0, 2).*

Find the slope:

$m = \dfrac{2-0}{0-(-1)} = \dfrac{2}{1} = 2$ *Use (−1, 0) and (0, 2).*

$y = mx + b$ *Slope-intercept form*

$y = 2x + 2$ *Substitute 2 for m and 2 for b.*

$f(x) = 2x + 2$ *Replace y with f(x).*

Step 2 Write the rule for $g(x)$. Reflecting $f(x)$ across the y-axis replaces each x with $-x$.

$g(x) = 2(-x) + 2$ *$g(x) = f(-x)$*

$g(x) = -2x + 2$

Check Graph $f(x)$ and $g(x)$ on a graphing calculator. The graphs are symmetric about the y-axis. ✔

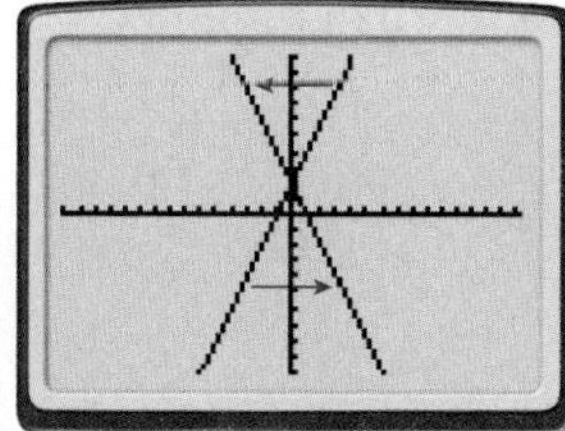

Let $g(x)$ be the indicated transformation of $f(x)$. Write the rule for $g(x)$.

1a. $f(x) = 3x + 1$; translation 2 units right

1b. linear function defined in the table; a reflection across the x-axis

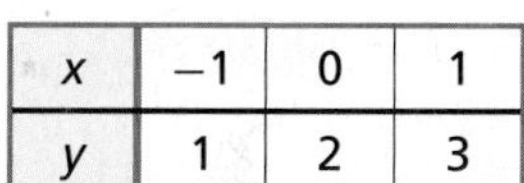

x	−1	0	1
y	1	2	3

Stretches and compressions change the slope of a linear function. If the line becomes steeper, the function has been stretched vertically or compressed horizontally. If the line becomes flatter, the function has been compressed vertically or stretched horizontally.

Stretches and Compressions

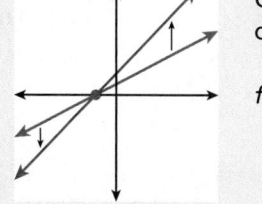

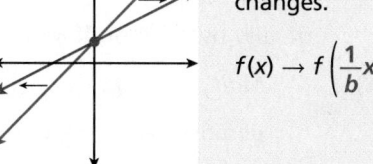

Horizontal	Vertical
Horizontal Stretch/Compression by a Factor of b	**Vertical Stretch/Compression by a Factor of a**
Input value changes. $f(x) \rightarrow f\left(\frac{1}{b}x\right)$	Output value changes. $f(x) \rightarrow a \cdot f(x)$
$b > 1$ stretches away from the y-axis. $0 < \lvert b \rvert < 1$ compresses toward the y-axis.	$a > 1$ stretches away from the x-axis. $0 < \lvert a \rvert < 1$ compresses toward the x-axis.

EXAMPLE 2 Stretching and Compressing Linear Functions

Let $g(x)$ be a horizontal compression of $f(x) = 2x - 1$ by a factor of $\frac{1}{3}$. Write the rule for $g(x)$, and graph the function.

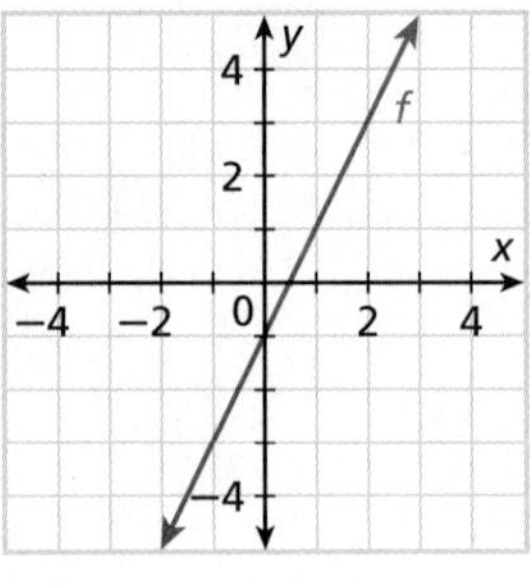

Horizontally compressing $f(x)$ by a factor of $\frac{1}{3}$ replaces each x with $\frac{1}{b}x$ where $b = \frac{1}{3}$.

$g(x) = 2\left(\frac{1}{b}\right)x - 1$ *For horizontal compression, use $\frac{1}{b}$.*

$= 2\left(\frac{1}{\frac{1}{3}}\right)x - 1$ *Substitute $\frac{1}{3}$ for b.*

$= 2(3x) - 1$ *Replace x with 3x.*

$g(x) = 6x - 1$ *Simplify.*

Check Graph both functions on the same coordinate plane. The graph of $g(x)$ is steeper than $f(x)$, which indicates that $g(x)$ has been horizontally compressed from $f(x)$, or pushed toward the y-axis.

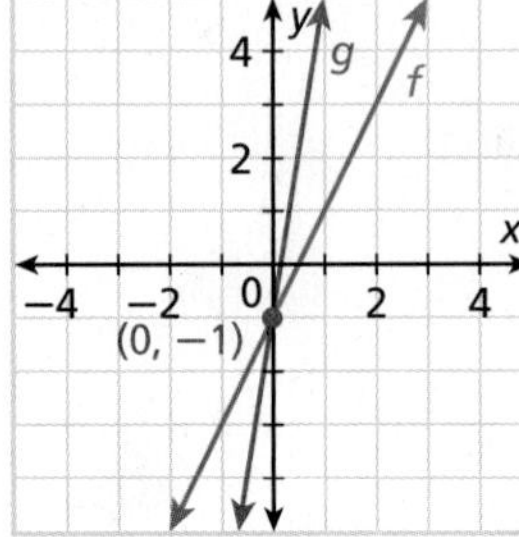

Helpful Hint

These don't change!
- y-intercepts in a horizontal stretch or compression
- x-intercepts in a vertical stretch or compression

2. Let $g(x)$ be a vertical compression of $f(x) = 3x + 2$ by a factor of $\frac{1}{4}$. Write the rule for $g(x)$.

Some linear functions involve more than one transformation. Combine transformations by applying individual transformations one at a time in the order in which they are given.

For multiple transformations, create a temporary function—such as $h(x)$ in Example 3 below—to represent the first transformation, and then transform it to find the combined transformation.

EXAMPLE 3 Combining Transformations of Linear Functions

Let $g(x)$ be a vertical shift of $f(x) = x$ down 2 units followed by a vertical stretch by a factor of 5. Write the rule for $g(x)$.

Step 1 First perform the translation.

Translating $f(x) = x$ down 2 units subtracts 2 from the function. You can use $h(x)$ to represent the translated function.

$h(x) = f(x) - 2$ *Subtract 2 from the function.*

$h(x) = x - 2$ *Substitute x for f(x).*

Step 2 Then perform the stretch.

Stretching $h(x)$ vertically by a factor of 5 multiplies the function by 5.

$g(x) = 5 \cdot h(x)$ *Multiply the function by 5.*

$g(x) = 5(x - 2)$ *Because $h(x) = x - 2$, substitute $x - 2$ for $h(x)$.*

$g(x) = 5x - 10$ *Simplify.*

3. Let $g(x)$ be a vertical compression of $f(x) = x$ by a factor of $\frac{1}{2}$ followed by a horizontal shift 8 units left. Write the rule for $g(x)$.

EXAMPLE 4 Fund-raising Application

The Dance Club is selling beaded purses as a fund-raiser. The function $R(n) = 12.5n$ represents the club's revenue in dollars where n is the number of purses sold.

a. The club paid \$75 for the materials needed to make the purses. Write a new function $P(n)$ for the club's profit.

The initial costs must be subtracted from the revenue.

$R(n) = 12.5n$	*Original function*
$P(n) = 12.5n - 75$	*Subtract the expenses.*

b. Graph $P(n)$ and $R(n)$ on the same coordinate plane.

Graph both functions. The lines have the same slope but different y-intercepts.

Note that the profit can be negative but the number of purses sold cannot be less than 0.

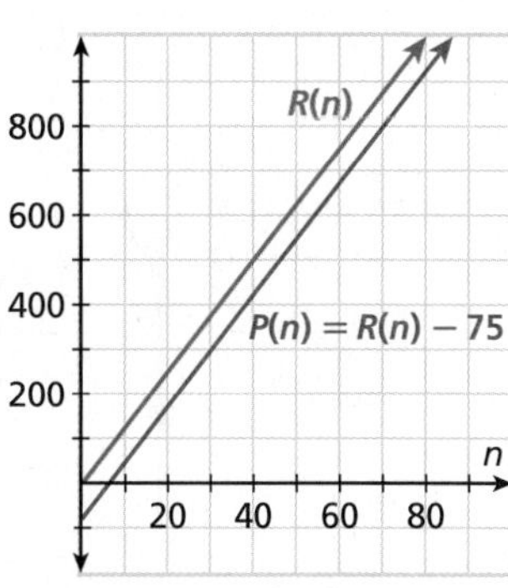

c. Describe the transformation(s) that have been applied.

The graphs indicate that $P(n)$ is a translation of $R(n)$. Because 75 was subtracted, $P(n) = R(n) - 75$. This indicates a vertical shift 75 units down.

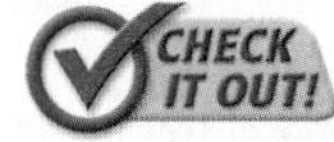

4. **What if...?** The club members decided to double the price of each purse.
   a. Write a new profit function $S(n)$ for the club.
   b. Graph $S(n)$ and $P(n)$ on the same coordinate plane.
   c. Describe the transformation(s) that have been applied.

MATHEMATICAL PRACTICES

THINK AND DISCUSS

1. Identify the horizontal translation that would have the same effect on the graph of $f(x) = x$ as a vertical translation of 6 units.

2. Give an example of two different transformations of $f(x) = 2x$ that would result in $g(x) = 2x - 6$.

3. Describe the transformation that would cause all of the function values to double.

4. GET ORGANIZED Copy and complete the graphic organizer. In each box, give an example of the indicated transformation of the parent function $f(x) = x$. Include an equation and a graph.

Translation	Reflection
Stretch	Compression

Center: $f(x) = x$

1-3 Exercises

GUIDED PRACTICE

SEE EXAMPLE 1

Let $g(x)$ be the indicated transformation of $f(x)$. Write the rule for $g(x)$.

1. linear function defined by the table; vertical translation 1.5 units up

x	−2	−1	0
$f(x)$	3.5	2	0.5

SEE EXAMPLE 2

2. $f(x) = -x + 5$; horizontal translation 2 units left

3. $f(x) = \frac{1}{3}x - 2$; vertical stretch by a factor of 3

4. $f(x) = -2x + 0.5$; horizontal stretch by a factor of $\frac{4}{3}$.

SEE EXAMPLE 3

Let $g(x)$ be the indicated combined transformation of $f(x) = x$. Write the rule for $g(x)$.

5. vertical compression by a factor of $\frac{2}{3}$ followed by a vertical shift 6 units down

6. horizontal shift right 4 units followed by a horizontal stretch by a factor of $\frac{3}{2}$

SEE EXAMPLE 4

7. Advertising An electronics company is changing its Internet ad from a banner ad to a pop-up ad. The cost of the banner ad in dollars is represented by $C(n) = 0.30n + 5.00$ where n is the average number of hits per hour. The cost of the pop-up ad will double the cost per hit.

a. Write a new cost function $D(n)$ for the ads.

b. Graph $C(n)$ and $D(n)$ on the same coordinate plane.

c. Describe the transformation(s) that have been applied.

PRACTICE AND PROBLEM SOLVING

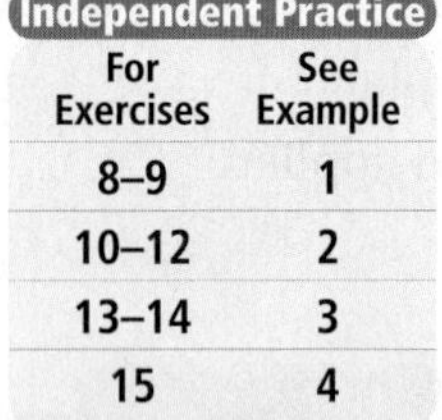

For Exercises	See Example
8–9	1
10–12	2
13–14	3
15	4

Extra Practice

See Extra Practice for more Skills Practice and Applications Practice exercises.

Let $g(x)$ be the indicated transformation of $f(x)$. Write the rule for $g(x)$.

8.

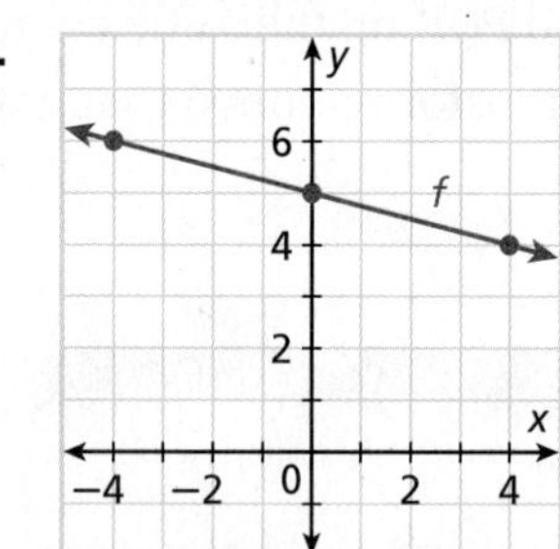

Reflection across the x-axis

9.

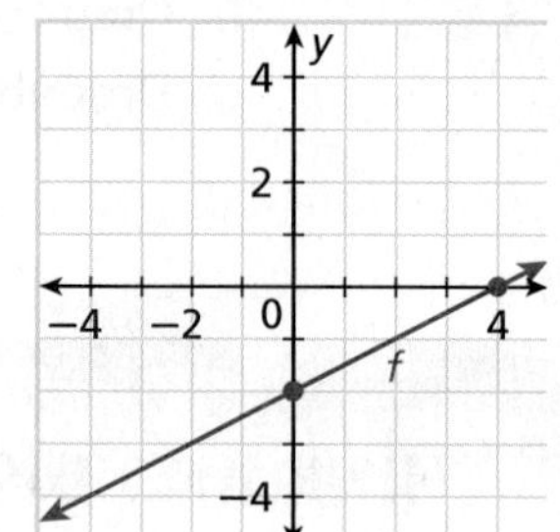

Vertical translation 2 units down

10.

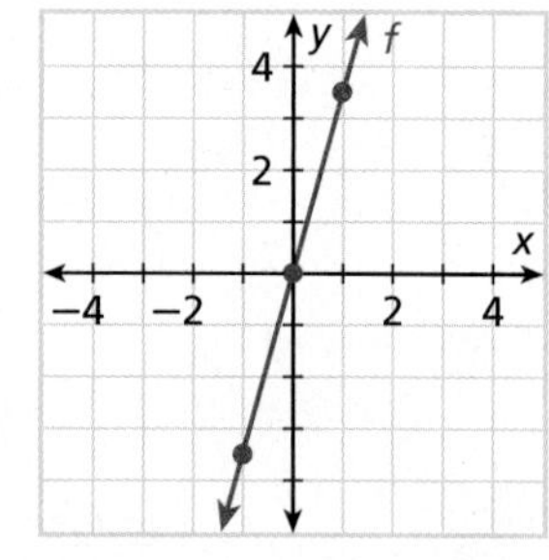

Horizontal compression by a factor of 0.5

11. linear function defined by the table; vertical stretch by a factor of 1.2 units

x	1	5	9
$f(x)$	0	−2	−4

12. $f(x) = -3x + 7$; vertical compression by a factor of $\frac{3}{4}$

Let $g(x)$ be the indicated combined transformation of $f(x) = x$. Write the rule for $g(x)$.

13. horizontal stretch by a factor of 2.75 followed by a horizontal shift 1 unit left

14. vertical shift 6 units down followed by a vertical compression by a factor of $\frac{2}{3}$

15. **Consumer Economics** In 1997, Southwestern Bell increased the price for local pay-phone calls. Before then, the price of a call could be determined by $f(x) = 0.15x + 0.25$, where x was the number of minutes after the *first* minute. The company increased the cost of the first minute by 10 cents.
    a. Write a new price function $g(x)$ for a phone call.
    b. Graph $f(x)$ and $g(x)$ on the same coordinate plane.
    c. Describe the transformation(s) that have been applied.

Write the rule for the transformed function $g(x)$ and graph.

16. 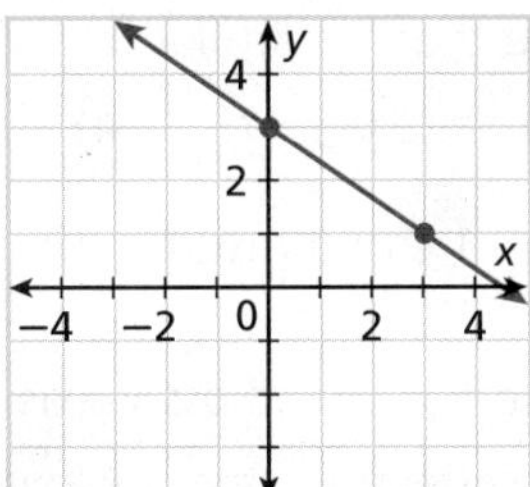

Reflection across the y-axis

17. 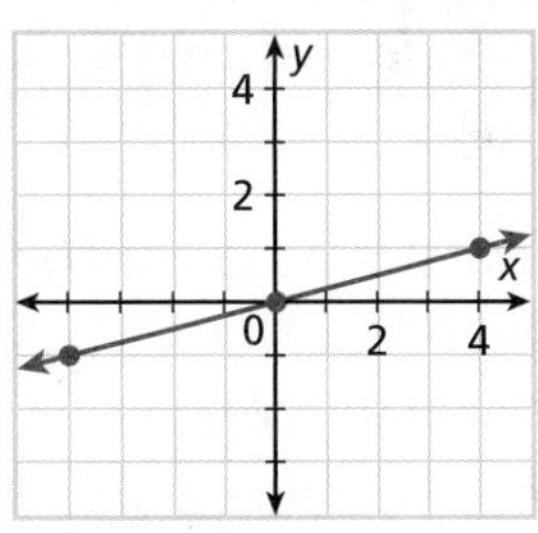

Vertical stretch by a factor of 8

18. 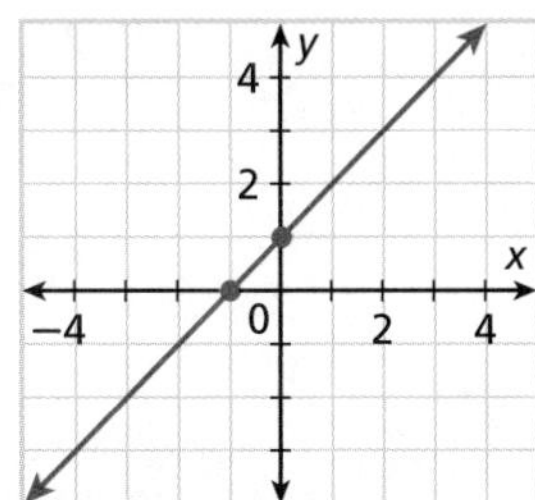

Horizontal stretch by a factor of 3

History **Historic tolls for traveling on the Cumberland Road in Pennsylvania are shown on the sign. Toll was paid every 15 miles.**

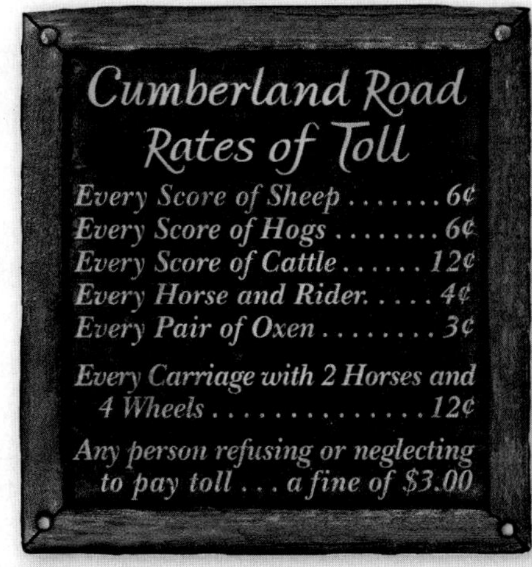

Cumberland Road
Rates of Toll
Every Score of Sheep . . . . 6¢
Every Score of Hogs . . . . 6¢
Every Score of Cattle . . . . . . 12¢
Every Horse and Rider. . . . . 4¢
Every Pair of Oxen . . . . 3¢
Every Carriage with 2 Horses and 4 Wheels . . . . 12¢
Any person refusing or neglecting to pay toll . . . a fine of $3.00

19. Write a function to represent the cost for 1 horse and rider to travel n miles with a score of sheep. What transformation describes the change in cost if the sheep were replaced by cattle?

20. Write a function to represent the cost for a carriage with 2 horses and 4 wheels to travel n miles. Name two different transformations that would represent a 6¢ increase in the toll rate.

21. **Critical Thinking** Consider the linear function $f(x) = x$.
    a. Shift $f(x)$ 2 units up and then reflect it over the x-axis.
    b. Perform the same transformations on $f(x)$ again but in reverse order.
    c. Make a conjecture about the order in which transformations are performed.

22. **Write About It** Which transformations affect the slope of a linear function, and which transformations affect the y-intercept? Support your answers.

MULTI-STEP TEST PREP

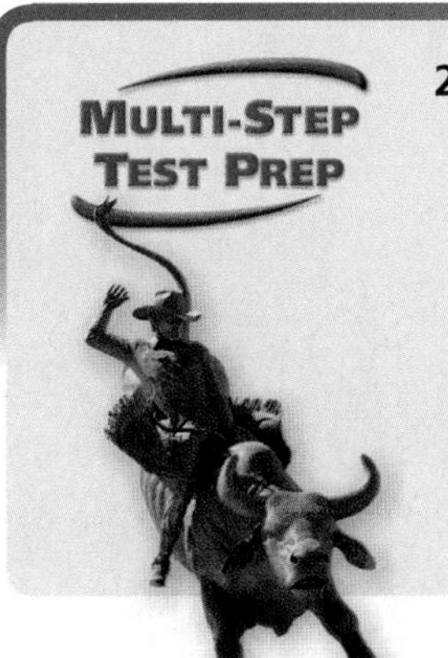

23. Use the data set $\{1, 5, 10, 17, 23, 23, 38, 60\}$.
    a. Find the mean, median, mode, and range.
    b. How does adding 7 to each number affect the mean, median, mode, and range?
    c. How does multiplying each number by 4 affect the mean, median, mode, and range?
    d. How does multiplying each number by 2 and then adding 5 affect the mean, median, mode, and range?

24. The cost function C of rent at an apartment complex increased \$50 last year and another \$60 this year. Which function accurately reflects these changes?

Ⓐ $60(C + 50)$ Ⓑ $60(50C)$ Ⓒ $(C + 50) + 60$ Ⓓ $50C + 60$

25. Given $f(x) = 28.5x + 45.6$, which function decreases the y-intercept by 20.3?

Ⓕ $g(x) = 8.2x + 45.6$ Ⓗ $g(x) = 28.5x + 25.3$

Ⓖ $g(x) = 8.2x + 66.1$ Ⓙ $g(x) = 28.5x + 66.1$

26. Which transformation describes a line that is parallel to $f(x)$?

Ⓐ $f(3x)$ Ⓑ $f\left(\frac{x}{2}\right)$ Ⓒ $f(x - 4)$ Ⓓ $f(-2x)$

27. Which transformation of $f(x) = \frac{1}{2}x - 1$ could result in the graph shown?

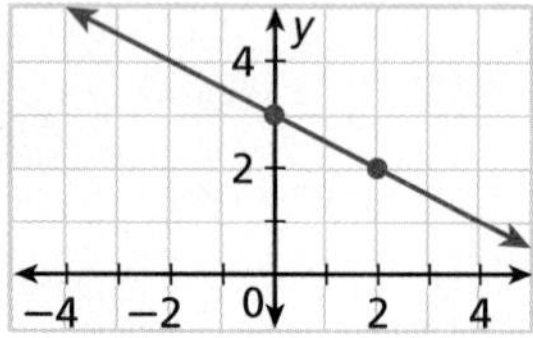

Ⓕ vertical shift 2 units down and reflection across x-axis

Ⓖ horizontal shift 2 units left and reflection across x-axis

Ⓗ vertical shift 2 units up and reflection across x-axis

Ⓙ horizontal shift 2 units right and reflection across x-axis

CHALLENGE AND EXTEND

28. Give two different combinations of transformations that would transform $f(x) = 3x + 4$ into $g(x) = 15x - 10$.

29. Give an example of two transformations of $f(x) = x$ that can be performed in any order and result in the same transformed function.

30. Education The graph shows the tuition at a university based on the number of credit hours taken. The rate per credit hour varies according to the number of hours taken: less than 12 hours, 12 to 18 hours, and greater than 18 hours.

a. Write the linear function that represents each segment of the graph.

b. Write the linear functions that would reflect a 12% increase in all tuition costs.

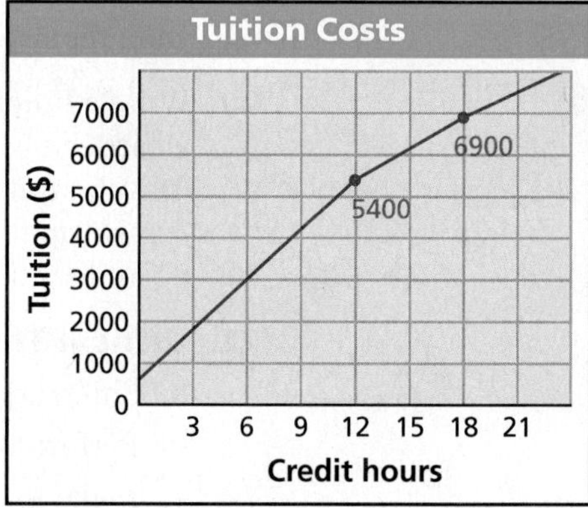

Statistical Graphs

Statistical data may be displayed in bar graphs or circle graphs. Use a bar graph to compare numerical amounts. Use a circle graph to compare parts of a whole.

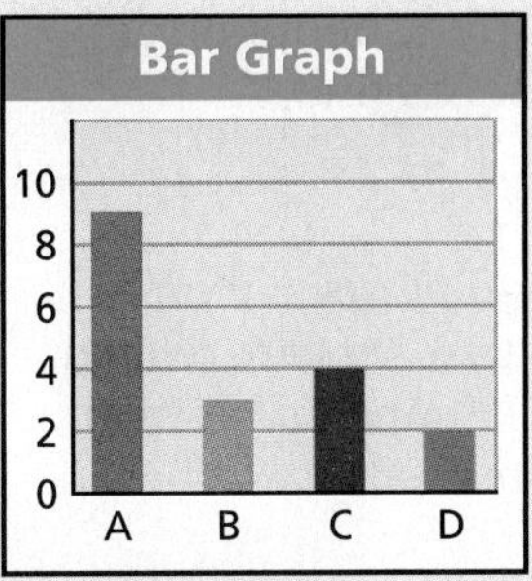

A bar graph compares numerical amounts.

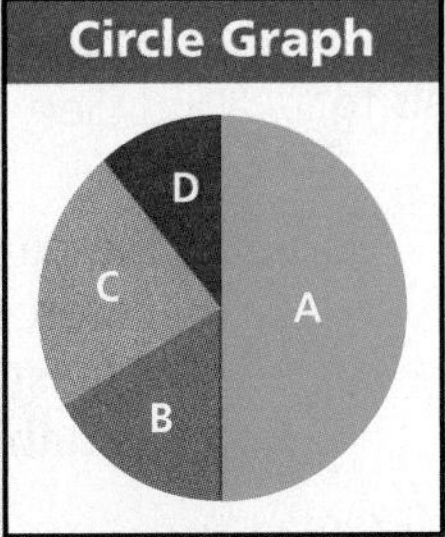

A circle graph compares parts of a whole.

The bar graph shows the numbers of pets owned by a group of students in a pet owners club.

Example

Use the bar graph. Find the central angle measure for the named category in a related circle graph, to the nearest degree.

Pet Ownership

Type of pet: Dogs, Cats, Fish, Birds, Reptiles

Pets owned: 0, 10, 20, 30, 40, 50, 60

Category: birds

1. Compute the total number of pets.
   Add the number of dogs, cats, fish, birds, and reptiles.
   $43 + 35 + 13 + 11 + 6 = 108$
2. Find the number of pets in the category.
   11 birds
3. A circle consists of 360°. Write and solve a proportion.
   $$\begin{matrix}\text{Part} \rightarrow \\ \text{Whole} \rightarrow\end{matrix} \frac{11}{108} = \frac{n}{360} \begin{matrix}\leftarrow \text{Circle part} \\ \leftarrow \text{Circle whole}\end{matrix}$$
4. Solve for the measure of the central angle.
   $11 \cdot 360 = 108n$
   $37° \approx n$

Try This

Find the central angle measure for each category, to the nearest degree.

1. fish **2.** reptiles **3.** dogs **4.** cats **5.** fish, birds, and reptiles combined

6. What categories combined give a central angle of approximately 207°?

1-4 Curve Fitting with Linear Models

CC.9-12.A.CED.3 Represent constraints by equations or inequalities, … and interpret solutions as viable or nonviable options in a modeling context. *Also* **CC.9-12.A.CED.2**

Objectives
Fit scatter plot data using linear models with and without technology.

Use linear models to make predictions.

Vocabulary
regression
correlation
line of best fit
correlation coefficient

Who uses this?
Anthropologists can use linear models to estimate the heights of ancient people from bones that the anthropologists find. (See Example 2.)

Researchers, such as anthropologists, are often interested in how two measurements are related. The statistical study of the relationship between variables is called **regression**.

A *scatter plot* is helpful in understanding the form, direction, and strength of the relationship between two variables. **Correlation** is the strength and direction of the linear relationship between the two variables.

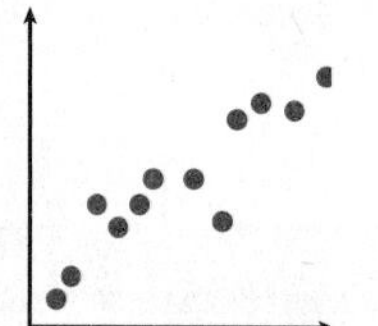

Positive correlation, positive slope

Negative correlation, negative slope

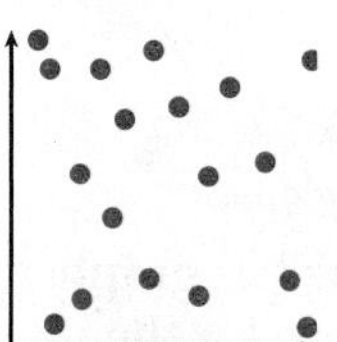

Relatively no correlation

If there is a strong linear relationship between two variables, a **line of best fit**, or a line that best fits the data, can be used to make predictions.

EXAMPLE 1 ***Meteorology Application***

Akron, Ohio, and Wellington, New Zealand, are about the same distance from the equator. Make a scatter plot for the temperature data, identify the correlation, and then sketch a line of best fit and find its equation.

Average High Temperatures (°F)

	Jan	Feb	Mar	Apr	May	Jun	Jul	Aug	Sep	Oct	Nov	Dec
Akron	33	37	48	59	70	78	82	80	73	61	49	38
Wellington	67	67	65	61	56	53	51	52	55	57	60	64

Step 1 Plot the data points.

Step 2 Identify the correlation.

Notice that the data set is negatively correlated—as the temperature rises in Akron, it falls in Wellington.

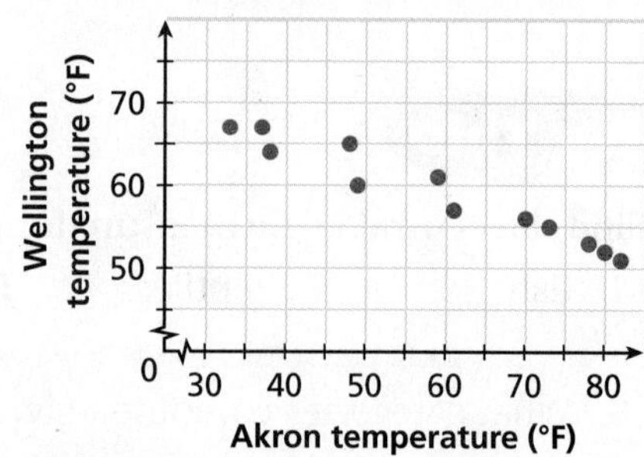

Reading Math

In a set of *bivariate* data, there are two variables for each observation. A set of data displayed in a scatter plot represents bivariate data.

Step 3 Sketch a line of best fit.

Draw a line that splits the data evenly above and below.

Step 4 Identify two points on the line.

For this data, you might select (30, 70) and (80, 52).

Step 5 Find the slope of the line that models the data.

$$m = \frac{70 - 52}{30 - 80} = \frac{18}{-50} = -0.36$$

Use the point-slope form.

$y - y_1 = m(x - x_1)$ *Point-slope form*

$y - 70 = -0.36(x - 30)$ *Substitute.*

$y = -0.36x + 80.8$ *Simplify.*

An equation that models the data is $y = -0.36x + 80.8$.

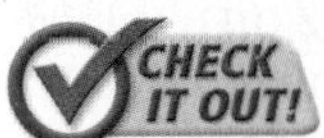

1. Basketball Make a scatter plot for this set of data. Identify the correlation, sketch a line of best fit, and find its equation.

Points Scored in Ten Games										
Minutes Played	28	35	8	20	39	23	19	27	15	30
Points Scored	16	13	2	12	31	10	9	15	4	19

The **correlation coefficient** r is a measure of how well the data set is fit by a model.

Caution!

Don't confuse slope with the *value* of r. Whether a line has a slope of 10 or a slope of $\frac{1}{10}$, it can have an r-value of 1. The r-value and the slope have the same sign.

Properties of the Correlation Coefficient r

r is a value in the range $-1 \le r \le 1$.

If $r = 1$, the data set forms a straight line with a positive slope.

If $r = 0$, the data set has no correlation.

If $r = -1$, the data set forms a straight line with a negative slope.

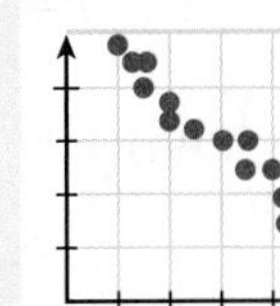

$r \approx -0.95$

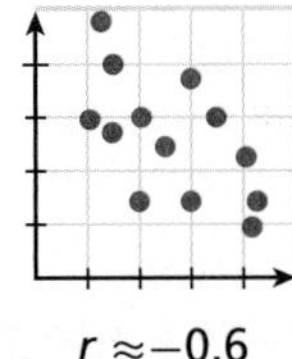

$r \approx -0.6$

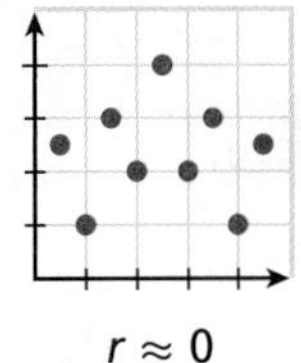

$r \approx 0$

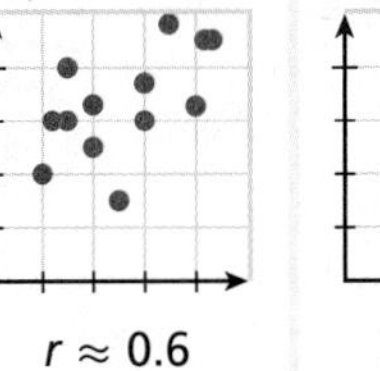

$r \approx 0.6$

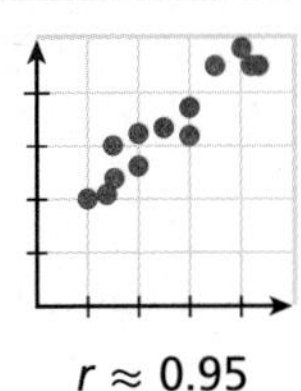

$r \approx 0.95$

You can use a graphing calculator to perform a linear regression and find the correlation coefficient r. To display the correlation coefficient, you may have to turn on the diagnostic mode. To do this, press 2nd 0 (CATALOG), and choose the **DiagnosticOn** mode.

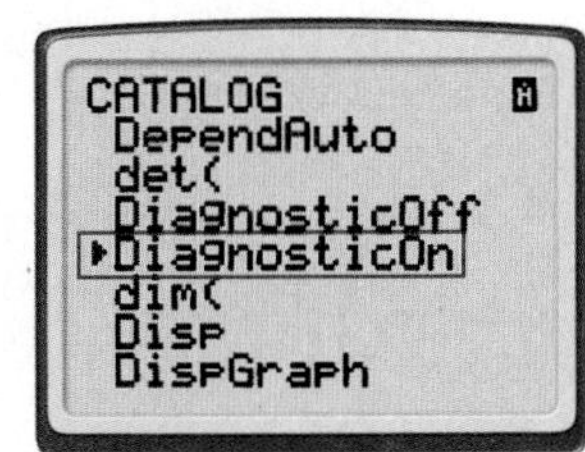

EXAMPLE 2 Anthropology Application

Anthropologists use known relationships between the height and length of a woman's humerus bone, the bone between the elbow and the shoulder, to estimate a woman's height. Some samples are shown in the table.

Bone Length and Height in Women								
Humerus Length (cm)	35	27	30	33	25	39	27	31
Height (cm)	167	146	154	165	140	180	149	155

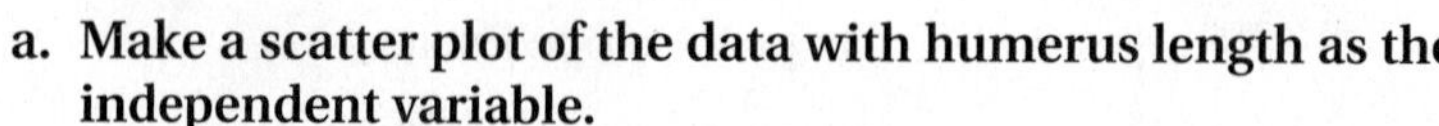

a. Make a scatter plot of the data with humerus length as the independent variable.

The scatter plot is shown at right.

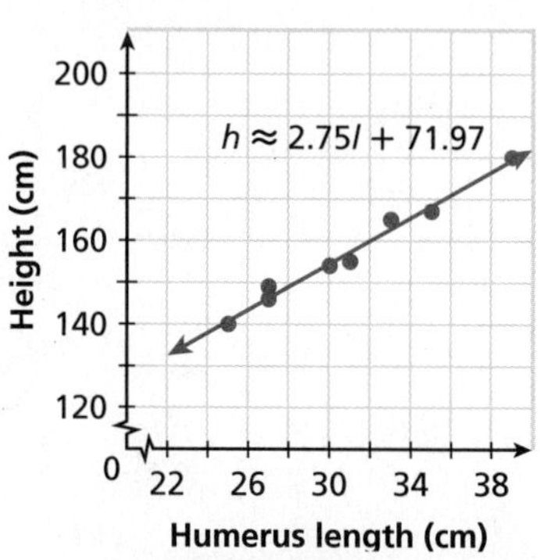

b. Find the correlation coefficient r and the line of best fit. Interpret the slope of the line of best fit in the context of the problem.

Enter the data into lists **L1** and **L2** on a graphing calculator. Use the linear regression feature by pressing STAT, choosing **CALC**, and selecting **4:LinReg**. The equation of the line of best fit is $h \approx 2.75\ell + 71.97$.

The slope is about 2.75, so for each 1 cm increase in humerus length, the predicted increase in a woman's height is 2.75 cm.

The correlation coefficient is $r \approx 0.991$, which indicates a strong positive correlation.

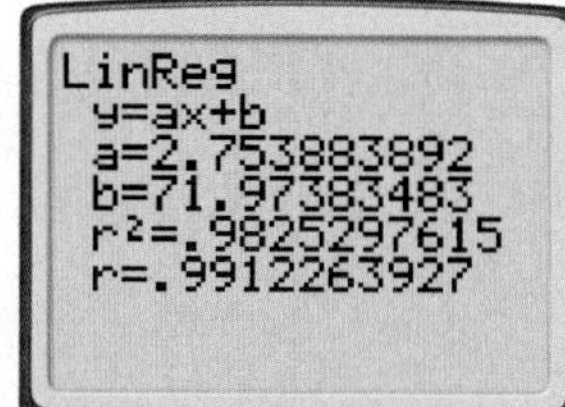

c. A humerus 32 cm long was found. Predict the woman's height.

The equation of the line of best fit is $h \approx 2.75\ell + 71.97$. Use the equation to predict the woman's height. For a 32-cm-long humerus,

$h \approx 2.75(32) + 71.97$ *Substitute 32 for ℓ.*

$h \approx 159.97$

The height of a woman with a 32-cm-long humerus would be about 160 cm.

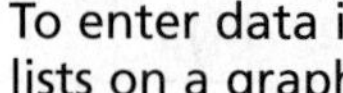

Helpful Hint

To enter data into lists on a graphing calculator, press STAT and select **1:Edit**. Enter the *x*-values in the **L1** column and the *y*-values in the **L2** column.

2. The gas mileage for randomly selected cars based upon engine horsepower is given in the table.

Gas Mileage and Horsepower of Cars										
Horsepower	175	255	140	165	115	120	190	180	110	125
Mileage (mi/gal)	22	13	25	18	32	28	15	21	35	30

a. Make a scatter plot of the data with horsepower as the independent variable.

b. Find the correlation coefficient r and the line of best fit. Interpret the slope of the line in the context of the problem.

c. Predict the gas mileage for a 210-horsepower engine.

EXAMPLE 3 Nutrition Application

Find the following information for this data set on the number of grams of fat and the number of calories in sandwiches served at Dave's Deli.

Dave's Deli Sandwiches Nutritional Information								
Fat (g)	5	9	12	15	12	10	21	14
Calories	360	455	460	420	530	375	580	390

Reading Math

A line of best fit may also be referred to as a *trend line*.

a. Make a scatter plot of the data with fat as the independent variable.

The scatter plot is shown below.

b. Find the correlation coefficient and the equation of the line of best fit. Draw the line of best fit on your scatter plot.

The correlation coefficient is $r = 0.682$.
The equation of the line of best fit is
$y \approx 11.1x + 309.8$.

c. Predict the amount of fat in a sandwich with 500 Calories. How accurate do you think your prediction is?

$500 \approx 11.1x + 309.8$ *Calories is the dependent variable.*

$190.2 \approx 11.1x$

$17.1 \approx x$

The line predicts 17.1 grams of fat, but the scatter plot and the value of r show that fat content by itself is *not* a good predictor of the number of calories in a sandwich at Dave's.

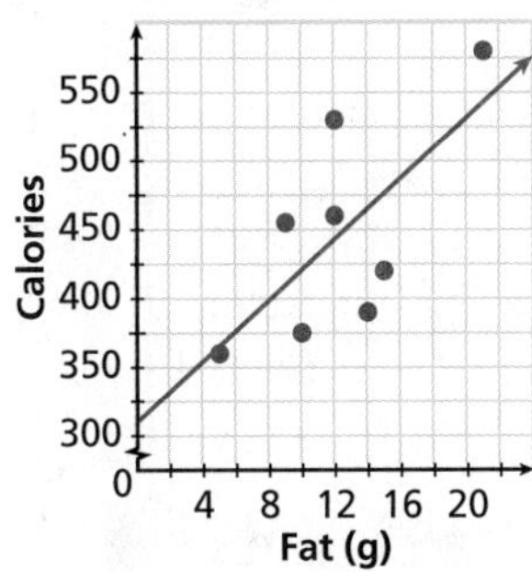

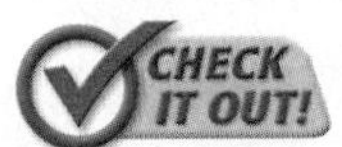

3. What If...? Use the equation of the line of best fit to predict the number of grams of fat in a sandwich with 420 Calories. How close is your answer to the value given in the table?

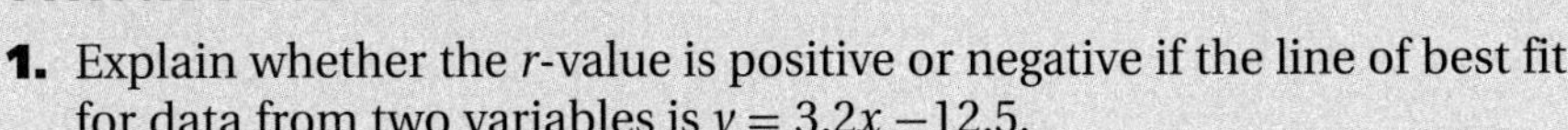

THINK AND DISCUSS

1. Explain whether the r-value is positive or negative if the line of best fit for data from two variables is $y = 3.2x - 12.5$.

2. Tell which correlation coefficient, $r = 0.65$ or $r = -0.75$, indicates a stronger linear relationship between two variables. Justify your answer.

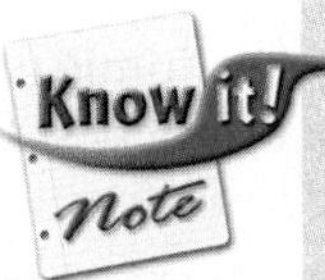

3. GET ORGANIZED Copy and complete the graphic organizer. Make a scatter plot for each type of correlation and estimate the r-value.

Correlation	Scatter Plot	Estimated r-value
Strong positive		
Weak positive		
No correlation		
Weak negative		
Strong negative		

1-4 Exercises

Learn It Online
Homework Help Online
Parent Resources Online

GUIDED PRACTICE

1. **Vocabulary** Explain what the following *correlation coefficients* tell you about two sets of data.

   a. $r = 0.4$ b. $r = -0.96$ c. $r = -0.02$

SEE EXAMPLE 1

2. **Driving** Make a scatter plot for this data set using gallons as the independent variable. Identify the correlation, sketch a line of best fit, and find its equation.

Distance Traveled							
Gallons	11.2	9.8	10.6	10.1	12.3	8.7	10.1
Distance (mi)	338	296	332	324	368	263	305

SEE EXAMPLE 2

3. **Home Economics** Use the data relating the average temperature in a month to the heating bill at Claire's house that month.

Claire's Heating Bills							
Mean Temperature (°F)	38	42	44	36	42	49	38
Heating Bill ($)	93	79	75	83	74	67	86

   a. Make a scatter plot using mean temperature as the independent variable.
   b. Find the correlation coefficient and the equation of the line of best fit. Draw the line of best fit on your scatter plot.
   c. Predict the heating bill for a month in which the average temperature is 40° F. How accurate do you think your prediction is?

SEE EXAMPLE 3

4. **School** Here are the number of teachers and the number of students at a randomly selected sample of high schools in a city.

Teachers and Students at Selected Schools								
Teachers	92	52	114	49	110	62	76	84
Students	1050	653	753	381	1312	813	496	910

   a. Make a scatter plot of the data using teachers as the independent variable.
   b. Find the correlation coefficient and the equation of the line of best fit. Draw the line of best fit on your scatter plot.
   c. Predict the number of teachers in a high school that has 600 students. How accurate do you think your prediction is?

PRACTICE AND PROBLEM SOLVING

5. **Chemistry** Make a scatter plot for this data set using the atomic number as the independent variable. Identify the correlation, sketch a line of best fit, and find its equation.

Selected Chemical Elements														
Atomic Number	89	13	95	51	18	33	85	56	97	4	83	107	5	35
Atomic Mass	227	27	243	122	40	75	210	137	247	9	209	264	11	80

Independent Practice	
For Exercises	See Example
5	1
6	2
7	3

Extra Practice

See Extra Practice for more Skills Practice and Applications Practice exercises.

6. **Biology** Hummingbird wing beat rates are much higher than those in other birds. Estimates for various species are given in the table.

Hummingbird Wing Beats							
Mass (g)	3.1	2.0	3.2	4.0	3.7	1.9	4.5
Wing Beats (per *s*)	60	85	50	45	55	90	40

a. Make a scatter plot of the data using mass as the independent variable.

b. Find the correlation coefficient and the equation of the line of best fit. Draw the line of best fit on your scatter plot.

c. Predict the wing beats rate for a Giant Hummingbird with a mass of 19 g. How accurate do you think your prediction is?

7. **Ticket Pricing** The manager of a band has kept track of the price of tickets and the attendance at the band's recent concerts.

Concert Attendance by Ticket Price									
Price ($)	6	5	8.5	8	10	5.50	7	7.5	8
Attendance	213	256	155	194	160	267	258	210	235

a. Make a scatter plot of the data using price as the independent variable.

b. Find the correlation coefficient and the equation of the line of best fit. Draw the line of best fit on your scatter plot.

c. Predict the attendance at a concert where the price of tickets is $9. How accurate do you think your prediction is?

8. Make a scatter plot for this data set. Estimate to find the equation of the line of best fit.

x	2	8	15	21	24	30	33	37
y	71	63	64	194	160	267	258	210

Estimation Estimate the value of r for each scatter plot.

9. 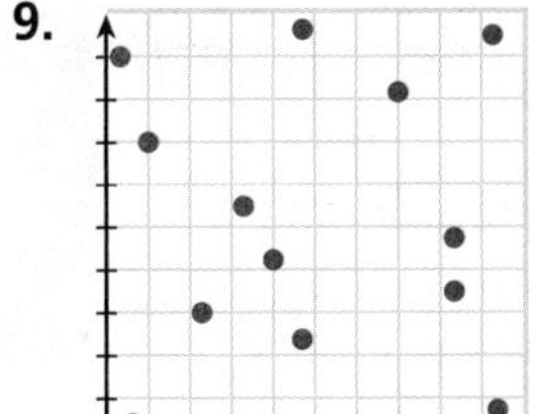

10. 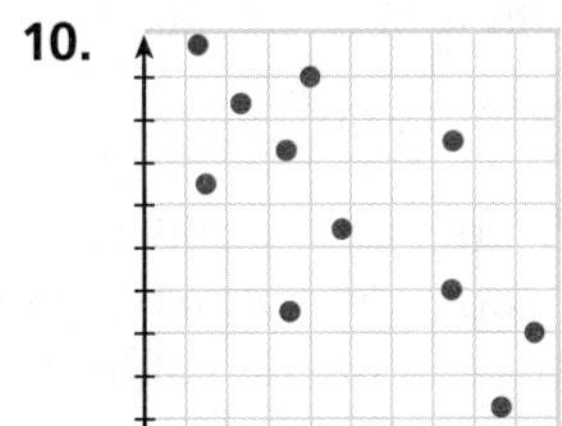

11. 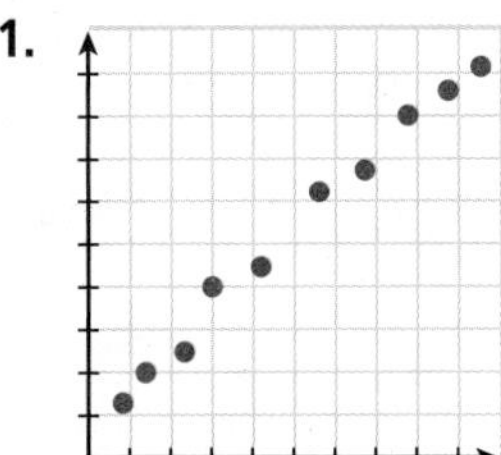

12. **Aviation** Make a scatter plot for the lengths and wingspans of planes in the American Airlines fleet. Sketch a line of best fit with length as the independent variable, and find its equation.

737	Super 80	757	767	A300	777
113 ft; 130 ft	108 ft; 148 ft	124 ft; 155 ft	147 ft; 178 ft	156 ft; 180 ft	200 ft; 209 ft

MULTI-STEP TEST PREP

13. The table gives the scores of the first 10 entries in a livestock show competition.
    a. What equation could you use to estimate the score from the place? Graph the equation.
    b. Suppose each score is increased by 5. How would this affect the equation and graph of the line?

Competition Results			
Place	Score	Place	Score
1	95	6	90
2	93	7	89
3	92	8	87
4	91	9	86
5	90	10	85

14. **Athletics** Use the data set relating the number of steps per second to speed for a group of top female runners at different speeds.

Steps Taken by Distance Runners							
Speed (ft/s)	15.86	16.88	17.5	18.62	19.97	21.06	22.11
Steps per second	3.05	3.12	3.17	3.25	3.36	3.46	3.55

Make a scatter plot of the data using speed as the independent variable. Find the correlation coefficient and the line of best fit, and draw it on your scatter plot. Use your equation to predict the number of steps per second taken by a runner going 18 feet per second. How accurate is your prediction? Explain.

15. **Paleontology** The table below shows the lengths of the femur, a leg bone, and the humerus, an arm bone, for five fossil specimens of the archaeopteryx, an extinct animal that had feathers and characteristics of a reptile.

Archaeopteryx Bone Lengths					
Femur Length (cm)	38	56	59	64	74
Humerus Length (cm)	41	63	70	72	84

a. Make a scatter plot of the data using femur length as the independent variable. Find the correlation coefficient and the line of best fit. Draw the line of best fit on your scatter plot.
b. What does the slope of your line mean for the archaeopteryx?
c. Use your equation to predict the length of the femur of an archaeopteryx whose humerus is 50 cm long. How accurate do you think your prediction is?

16. **Critical Thinking** Does a strong linear relationship between two variables mean that one causes the other (for example, if higher daily bee stings correspond to higher ice cream sales)? Explain.

17. **Data Collection** Use a graphing calculator and a motion detector. Stand in a doorway and measure the distance to a person as the person walks from the opposite side of the room toward the motion detector. Is a linear model a good model for distance versus time? Explain.

18. **Write About It** Describe the process of finding a line of best fit.

19. The equation of the line of best fit for a set of data is $y = 1.05x - 1.3$. Which of the following could be the correlation coefficient for the set of data?

Ⓐ $r = -1.3$ Ⓑ $r = -0.7$ Ⓒ $r = 0.8$ Ⓓ $r = 1.05$

20. Which of the following best describes the correlation shown?

Ⓕ Strong positive Ⓗ Strong negative

Ⓖ Weak positive Ⓙ Weak negative

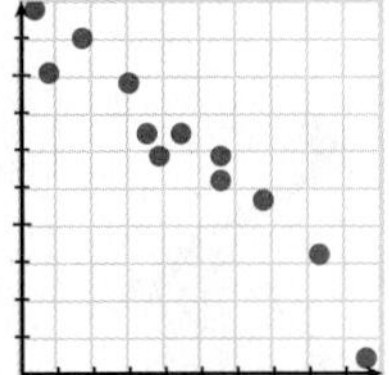

21. Which of the following relationships would likely have a negative correlation coefficient for an automobile?

Ⓐ Age and total miles Ⓒ Length and width

Ⓑ Age and resale value Ⓓ Highway mileage and city mileage

CHALLENGE AND EXTEND

Are the data linear? Are the data related? Explain.

22.

x	2	7	13	15	22
y	4	4	4	4	4

23.

x	35	45	55	65	75
y	30	34	36	34	30

24. The following data sets were developed by statistician Frank Anscombe. Make a scatter plot of each set of data, and find r and a line of best fit. Why is it important to plot the data before using a linear model to make predictions?

x	10	8	13	9	11	14	6	4	12	7	5
y	9.14	8.14	8.74	8.77	9.29	8.1	6.13	3.1	9.13	7.26	4.74

x	10	8	13	9	11	14	6	4	12	7	5
y	7.46	6.77	12.74	7.11	7.81	8.84	6.08	5.39	8.15	6.42	5.73

CHAPTER 1

MULTI-STEP TEST PREP

SECTION 1B

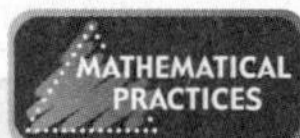

Model with mathematics.

Applying Linear Functions

Data Dilemma The Livestock Show and Rodeo School Art Program is an annual competition for students. Participants in grades ranging from kindergarten through 12 must submit an original art project based on Western culture, history, or heritage. Projects are judged by the show's School Art Committee. Each school district selects the top 20 students to compete in this annual citywide competition. The scores for the top entries in the East District are shown in the table.

The Art Committee guidelines state that the top score awarded in district competitions should be 100. The East District judges have decided to add 5 points to each score in order to comply with the competition guidelines.

Competition Results	
Entry	**Score**
1	95
2	93
3	92
4	91
5	90
6	90
7	89
8	87
9	86
10	85
11	84
12	83
13	82
14	81
15	80
16	79
17	77
18	74
19	71
20	65

1. Create a table to show the new scores. Compare the mean and median of the original scores with those of the modified scores.
2. Graph the original scores using the entry number as the x-coordinate and the score as the y-coordinate. Describe the parent function to which this graph belongs.
3. Predict how the graph of the modified scores will compare with the graph of the original scores. Graph the modified scores on the same graph as the original scores to check your prediction.
4. If $y = f(x)$ represents the function rule for the original scores, determine a function rule for the modified scores. Explain.
5. One judge suggested that the original scores should be multiplied by a factor that would make the highest score 100 points. What factor should be used?
6. Make a table showing the new scores. Compare the mean and median of the original scores with those of these new scores.
7. Graph the newest set of scores on the same graph as the original scores, and describe the transformation.
8. Which method do you think the judges should use to adjust the scores? Explain your answer.

(cl) Steve Vidler/SuperStock; (br) Kim Christensen

Quiz for Lessons 1-3 and 1-4

1-3 Transforming Linear Functions

Let $g(x)$ be the indicated transformation(s) of $f(x)$. Write the rule for $g(x)$.

1. $f(x) = x$; horizontal translation 5 units right
2. $f(x) = 2x$; vertical stretch by a factor of 5
3. $f(x) = x + 6$; vertical compression by a factor of $\frac{1}{3}$ followed by a horizontal translation left 4 units
4. $f(x) = 3x - 5$; vertical translation 6 units up followed by a horizontal stretch by a factor of $\frac{3}{2}$
5. Let $g(x)$ be the reflection of $f(x)$ across the y-axis. Write the rule for $g(x)$.

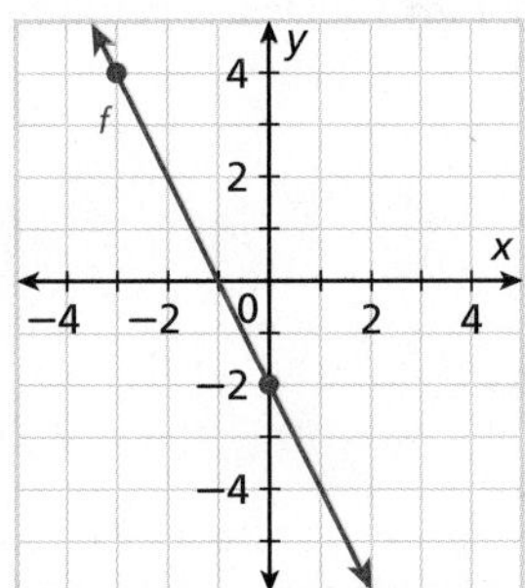

1-4 Curve Fitting with Linear Models

6. Lea keeps track of the number of hours she works in a week and her income for the week. Here are the results from a randomly selected sample of weeks.

Hours	8	23	18	30	12	28
Income ($)	152	465	315	530	240	525

   a. Draw a scatter plot of the data using hours as the independent variable.
   b. Use your graphing calculator to find the correlation coefficient and the equation of the line of best fit for the data. What does the slope of the line of best fit mean for Lea?
   c. Use your equation to predict how much Lea would make in a 40-hour week.

CHAPTER 1

Study Guide: Review

Vocabulary

compression

correlation

correlation coefficient

line of best fit

parent function

reflection

regression

stretch

translation

transformation

Complete the sentences below with vocabulary words from the list above.

1. The function $f(x) = x$ is the ___?___ of the function $g(x) = 3x - 5$.

2. A ___?___ is a transformation that moves each point in a figure the same distance in the same direction.

3. The statistical study of the relationship between variables is called ___?___ .

1-1 Exploring Transformations

EXAMPLE

- **The graph shows household alarm monitoring fees. Sketch a graph to represent a $\frac{1}{5}$ fee reduction on long-term contracts. Then identify the transformation of the original graph that the new graph represents.**

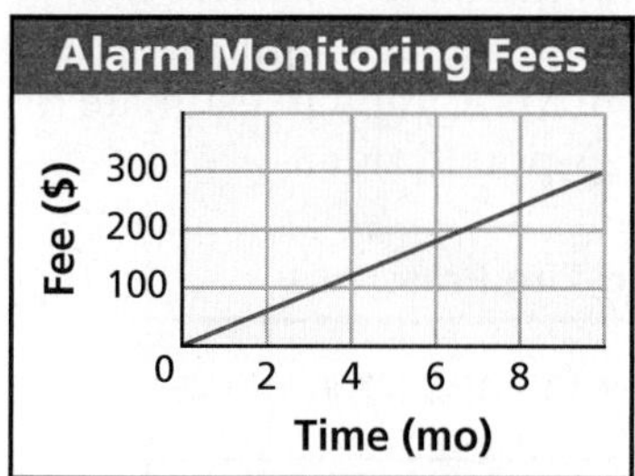

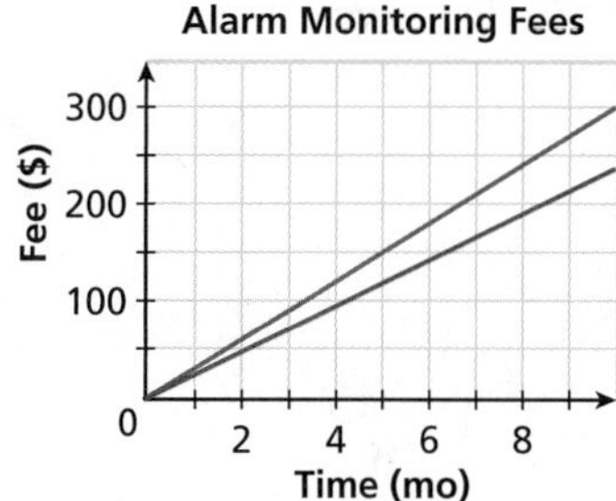

Each price is $\frac{4}{5}$ of the original price. This represents a vertical compression of the graph by a factor of $\frac{4}{5}$.

EXERCISES

Perform the given transformation to the point $(5, -1)$. Give the coordinates of the new point.

4. 5 units left, 4 units down
5. reflection across the x-axis

The graph shows parking garage fees. Sketch a graph to represent each situation and identify the transformation of the original graph that it represents.

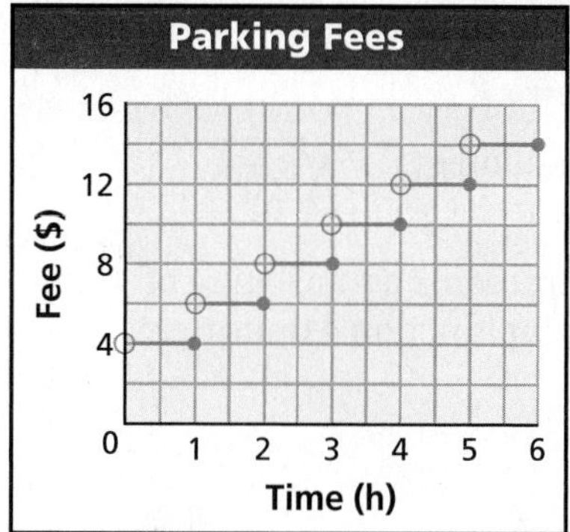

6. The fees are half price on weekends.
7. The fees are increased by 10%.
8. All fees are increased by $1.00.

1-2 Introduction to Parent Functions

EXAMPLE

- **Identify the parent function for $g(x) = \sqrt{x-4}$ from its equation. Then graph g on your calculator and describe what transformation of the parent function it represents.**

$g(x) = \sqrt{x-4}$ is a square-root function.

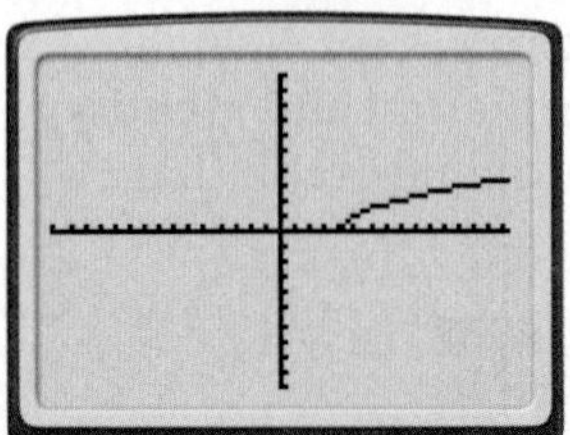

The graph of the square-root parent function intersects the x-axis at the point $(0, 0)$.

The graph of the function $g(x) = \sqrt{x-4}$ intersects the x-axis at the point $(4, 0)$.

So $g(x) = \sqrt{x-4}$ represents a translation of the square-root parent function 4 units right.

EXERCISES

Identify the parent function for g from its equation. Then graph g on your calculator and describe what transformation of the parent function it represents.

9. $g(x) = x^2 - 1$ **10.** $g(x) = -\sqrt{x}$

11. Graph the data from the table. Describe the parent function that would best approximate the data set. Then use the graph to estimate the tire pressure for a 95-pound rider.

Bicycle Road-Tire Pressures					
Weight of Rider (lb)	110	140	170	200	230
Pressure (psi)	95	105	115	125	135

1-3 Transforming Linear Functions

EXAMPLE

Let $g(x)$ be the indicated transformation of $f(x) = x$. Write the rule for $g(x)$.

- horizontal shift 5 units left followed by a horizontal stretch by a factor of 3

Translating $f(x)$ 5 units left replaces each x with $(x + 5)$.

Let $h(x) = f(x + 5)$

Replace each x with $\left(\frac{x}{3}\right)$.

$g(x) = h\left(\frac{x}{3}\right) = \frac{x}{3} + 5$

EXERCISES

Let $g(x)$ be the indicated transformation of $f(x) = x$. Write the rule for $g(x)$.

12. horizontal shift 8 units right

13. vertical shift 5 units up followed by a vertical stretch by a factor of 3

14. horizontal shift 3 units left followed by a vertical shift down 7 units

15. vertical shift 5 units up followed by a reflection across the x-axis

16. horizontal shift 12 units right followed by a reflection across the y-axis

1-4 Curve Fitting with Linear Models

EXAMPLE

■ **Make a scatter plot of the data. Find the correlation coefficient *r* and the equation of the line of best fit.**

x	2	5	9	13	16
y	8	10	24	16	29

The scatter plot is shown at right

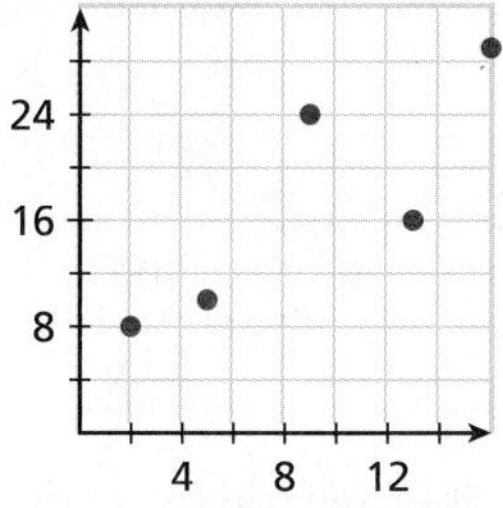

Use **LinReg** on your graphing calculator.

$r \approx 0.834$. The equation of the line of best fit is $y \approx 1.32x + 5.56$.

EXERCISES

17. Find the following for this set of data on median income and median home price.

a. Make a scatter plot of the data using median income as the independent variable.

b. Find the correlation coefficient *r* and the line of best fit for these data.

Median Income (thousands)	Median Home Price (thousands)
69.5	130.2
46.3	94.5
56.7	115.5
65.2	106.4
54.7	98.6
59.6	115.5

CHAPTER 1

CHAPTER TEST

1. The table shows how the distance from the top of a building to the horizon depends on the building's height. Graph the relationship from building height to horizon distance, and identify which parent function best describes the data. Then use your graph to estimate the distance to the horizon from the top of a building with a height of 80 m.

Horizon Distances					
Height of Building (m)	5	10	20	40	100
Distance to Horizon (km)	8.0	11.3	15.9	22.5	35.6

Let $g(x)$ be the indicated transformation(s) of $f(x) = x$. Write the rule for $g(x)$.

2. vertical stretch by a factor of 4

3. horizontal translation 6 units right

4. horizontal compression by a factor of $\frac{1}{6}$ followed by a vertical shift 4 units down

5. A consumer group is studying how hospitals are staffed. Here are the results from eight randomly selected hospitals in a state.

Full-Time Hospital Employees								
Hospital Beds	23	29	35	42	46	54	64	76
Full-Time Employees	69	95	118	126	123	178	156	176

   a. Make a scatter plot of the data with hospital beds as the independent variable.

   b. Find the correlation coefficient and the equation of the line of best fit. Draw the line of best fit on your scatter plot.

   c. Predict the number of beds in a hospital with 80 full-time employees.

6. Translate $f(x) = |x|$ so that its vertex is at $(4, -2)$. Then graph.

7. Find $g(x)$ if $f(x) = |2x| - 3$ is stretched horizontally by a factor of 3 and reflected across the x-axis.

FOCUS ON ACT

The ACT measures college-preparedness by testing skills in English, mathematics, reading, and science. The Mathematics Test is a 60-minute test with 60 multiple-choice questions. There is no penalty for incorrect answers.

All questions on the ACT Mathematics Test can be answered without using a calculator, but you are allowed to use one. If you bring a calculator to the test center, make sure it is one of the types of calculators approved for the test, as many types are prohibited.

You may want to time yourself as you take this practice test. It should take you about 5 minutes to complete.

---

1. In a school choir, the ratio of boys to girls is 3:5. If there are a total of 24 singers in the choir, how many girls are in the choir?

(A) 6

(B) 9

(C) 14

(D) 15

(E) 40

---

2. If $12 - 3(x + 2) = x + 8$, then what is the value of x?

(A) $-\frac{5}{2}$

(B) $-\frac{1}{2}$

(C) $\frac{1}{2}$

(D) $\frac{3}{2}$

(E) $\frac{5}{2}$

---

3. What are the values of x where $2|x + 4| < 6$?

(A) $x < -1$ and $x < -7$

(B) $x > -1$ or $x < -7$

(C) $x < -1$ or $x > -7$

(D) $x > -1$ and $x < -7$

(E) $x < -1$ and $x > -7$

---

4. Line ℓ passes through $(1, -3)$ and is perpendicular to $y = \frac{1}{5}x - 7$. What is the equation of line ℓ?

(A) $y = -5x + 2$

(B) $y = -5x - 2$

(C) $y = \frac{1}{5}x - \frac{14}{5}$

(D) $y = -\frac{1}{5}x - \frac{14}{5}$

(E) $y = 5x + 2$

---

5. Which of the following inequalities is equivalent to $-3y - 5x \leq 15$?

(A) $y \geq \frac{5}{3}x + 5$

(B) $y \leq -\frac{5}{3}x - 5$

(C) $y \geq -\frac{5}{3}x - 5$

(D) $y \geq \frac{5}{3}x - 5$

(E) $y \leq -\frac{5}{3}x + 5$

---

6. In a state park, any trout caught that weighs less than 10 oz or greater than 30 oz must be returned to the water. Which of the following represents the weights of trout that may be kept?

(A) $|x - 20| \leq 10$

(B) $|x - 10| \leq 10$

(C) $|x - 10| \geq 20$

(D) $|x - 30| \geq 10$

(E) $|x - 20| \leq 30$

CHAPTER 1

TEST TACKLER

Standardized Test Strategies

Gridded Response: Write Gridded Responses

To answer a gridded-response test item, you must write your answer correctly in the top of the provided grid and fill in the bubbles accurately, or the item will be marked as incorrect. Answers may be gridded using several correct formats.

The answer to a gridded-response item is always a *whole number,* a *fraction,* or a *decimal.* Non-numerical signs and symbols, such as units of measure, the percent sign, the degree sign, the negative sign, variables, and commas, cannot be gridded.

EXAMPLE 1

Gridded Response: Solve the equation. $25 - 3(5x - 4) = 32$

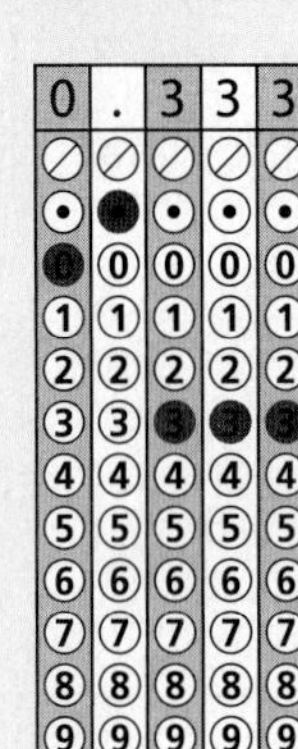

$$25 - 3(5x - 4) = 32$$
$$25 - 15x + 12 = 32$$
$$-15x = -5$$
$$x = \frac{5}{15} = \frac{1}{3}$$

Grid $\frac{1}{3}$ or its rounded decimal equivalent 0.333 or .3333:

Write your answer in the boxes at the top of the grid.
Put only a digit, the fraction bar, or the decimal point in each box.

Put the first digit of your answer in the box on the left OR put the last digit of your answer in the box on the right. Do not leave a blank box in the middle of an answer.

Shade the bubble of each digit or symbol in its corresponding column.

EXAMPLE 2

Gridded Response: Find the slope of the line that passes through $(-2, -5)$ and $(8, 10)$.

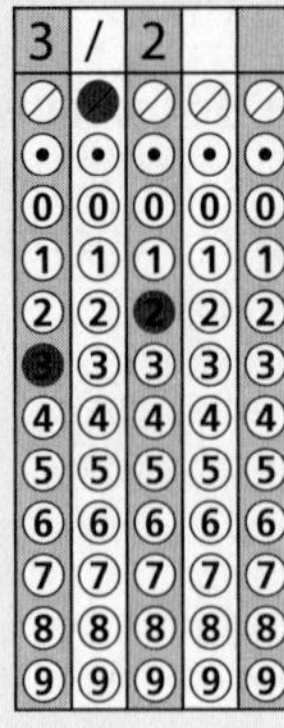

$$m = \frac{y_2 - y_1}{x_2 - x_1} = \frac{10-(-5)}{8-(-2)} = \frac{15}{10} = 1\frac{1}{2}$$

The slope of the line is $1\frac{1}{2}$, but a mixed number must be converted to either a decimal or an improper fraction before the answer can be written on the grid.

Grid the answer 1.5 or $\frac{3}{2}$ following the instructions in Example 1.

Read each statement, and then answer the questions that follow.

Sample A

A student solved a proportion for x and got $\frac{4}{5}$ as a result. He then gridded his answer as shown.

1. Is it possible to grid fractional answers? Explain.
2. If the student solved the proportion correctly, why was the answer marked as incorrect?
3. Describe one way to correctly grid the response $\frac{4}{5}$.

Sample B

What is the x-intercept of the linear function $6x + 9y = 18$?

Wyatt found that the x-intercept point occurs at $(3, 0)$, and then he filled out the grid.

4. Will Wyatt's answer be marked as correct? Explain.
5. Anita got the same answer as Wyatt, but her answer was marked as correct. She did not place the 3 in the last column. Describe Anita's grid.

When filling out a grid, be sure to completely fill in the bubbles, and be careful not to rip the paper.

Sample C

For a gridded-response test item, Jill had to determine the slope of a linear function. She correctly determined the slope to be $2\frac{1}{2}$ and then gridded her answer as shown.

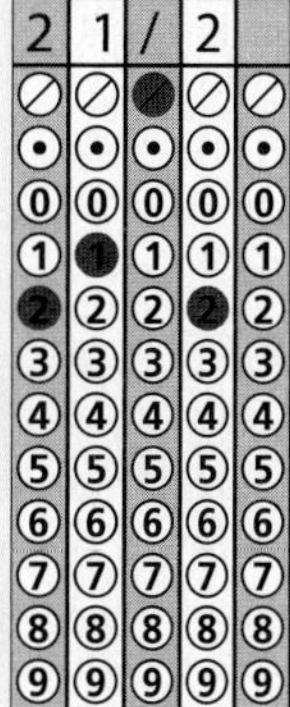

6. Read the number in the answer box grid. What number is recorded in the grid?
7. Why does gridding a mixed number result in an incorrect response?
8. Write a decimal equivalent for $2\frac{1}{2}$, and then write $2\frac{1}{2}$ as an improper fraction. Explain how to correctly grid these values.

Sample D

Daniel is taking an exam where he has to determine the y-intercept of the function shown below.

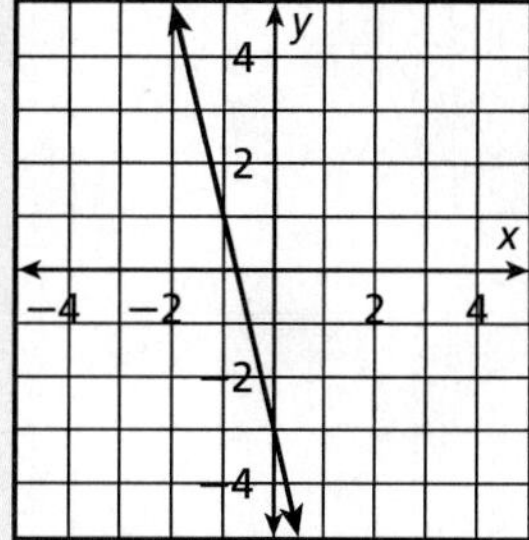

9. Is the y-intercept a positive or negative value?
10. Explain why the answer to this test item cannot be recorded on an answer grid.

CHAPTER 1

STANDARDIZED TEST PREP

CUMULATIVE ASSESSMENT

Multiple Choice

1. For which function is $g(-3) > g(5)$?

   (A) $g(x) = 5x - 9$
   (B) $g(x) = x^2 - 12$
   (C) $g(x) = (x + 5)^2$
   (D) $g(x) = (x - 9)^2$

2. A television commercial claims that 4 out of every 5 dentists surveyed preferred Freshen toothpaste to the leading brand. If 120 dentists in the survey preferred Freshen, how many dentists participated in the survey?

   (F) 30 (H) 150
   (G) 96 (J) 180

3. Which is an equation of a line with a slope of −3 that passes through (−2, 7)?

   (A) $y = -3x - 1$
   (B) $y = -3x + 1$
   (C) $y = -3x + 13$
   (D) $y = -\frac{1}{3}x + 1$

4. Which of the following shows the graph of $y + \frac{3}{4}x \geq 2$?

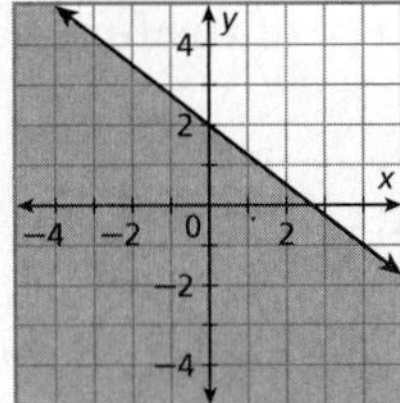
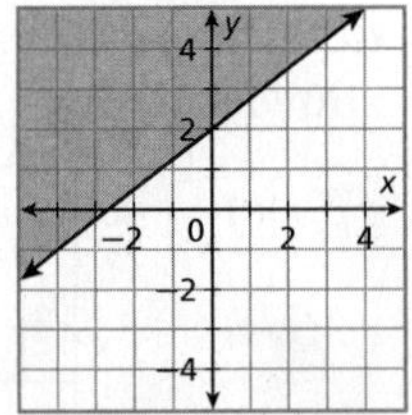

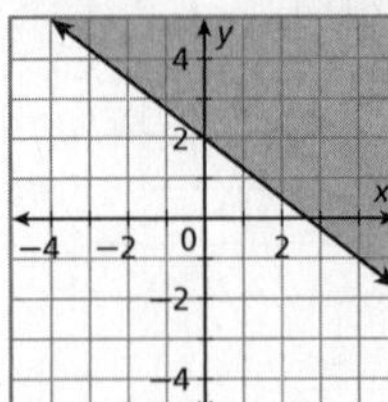
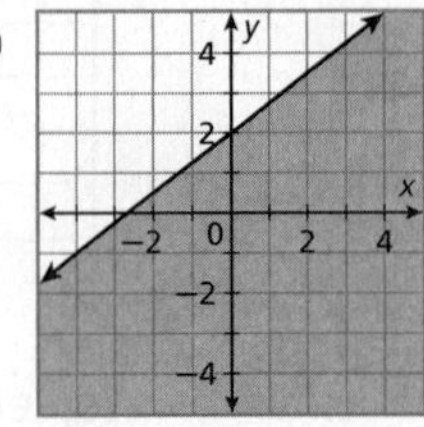

5. In which of the following number sets does −3 NOT belong?

   (A) Integers (C) Real numbers
   (B) Rational numbers (D) Whole numbers

6. What is a reasonable slope of the line of best fit of the salary data for teachers in a New York school district, as shown in the table below?

Salaries of Teachers	
Years of Experience	Salary
0	\$33,407
2	\$34,273
5	\$37,882
8	\$40,185
10	\$42,977
12	\$45,864
15	\$53,811

   (F) 450 (H) 1275
   (G) 750 (J) 2650

7. Which function has a range of all real numbers less than or equal to −3?

   (A) $y = -|x - 3|$ (C) $y = -|x| - 3$
   (B) $y = |x| - 3$ (D) $y = |x - 3|$

8. Simplify the expression $4\sqrt{50} + 3\sqrt{72}$.

   (F) $4\sqrt{7}$ (H) $12\sqrt{5}$
   (G) $7\sqrt{112}$ (J) $38\sqrt{2}$

9. Find the slope of the line $-3y = 6x + 12$.

   (A) −4 (C) $-\frac{1}{2}$
   (B) −2 (D) $-\frac{1}{4}$

When a word problem contains information about dimensions used to solve a problem, you might find it useful to draw a diagram. The diagram should be clearly labeled and sketched close to scale.

10. A lamppost casts a shadow that is 24 feet long. Tad, who is 6 feet tall, is standing directly next to the lamppost. His shadow is 15 feet long. About how tall is the lamppost?

(F) 10 feet

(G) 15 feet

(H) 33 feet

(J) 60 feet

11. What is the effect on the graph of $y = 2x + 2$ when it is changed to $y = 2x - 2$?

(A) The slope of the line becomes steeper.

(B) The line slants down and right instead of up and right.

(C) The y-intercept is translated 4 units down.

(D) The line is reflected across the y-axis.

12. The cost of renting a moving van is \$39.95 plus \$0.40 per mile. Which equation best represents the relationship between cost c and the number of miles driven m?

(F) $c = 39.95 + 0.40$

(G) $c = 39.95m + 0.40$

(H) $c = 39.95 + 0.40m$

(J) $c = 39.95m + 0.40m$

Gridded Response

13. The baseball statistic "total bases" is calculated by adding the number of singles, twice the number of doubles, three times the number of triples, and four times the number of home runs. In 2001, a player collected 411 total bases, including 49 singles, 32 doubles and 2 triples. How many home runs did the player hit that year?

14. The function $g(x)$ is the reflection across the y-axis of $f(x) = -\frac{2}{3}x - 5$. What is the slope, to the nearest hundredth, of $g(x)$?

15. Evaluate $h^2 - hk + 2k^3 - 2$ for $h = 4$ and $k = -1$.

16. Write the product of $(1.2 \times 10^{-8})(6.8 \times 10^{10})$ in standard form.

17. What is the y-intercept of $3x + 4y = 24$?

Short Response

18. Consider the inequality $|5x + 6| \geq 11$.

a. Solve the inequality.

b. Graph your solution on a number line.

19. The city would like to construct a community amphitheater in the park. The stage of the amphitheater should be 25 feet across and 12 feet deep. The production group that uses the facility has anticipated that at least 5 feet of space should be a sufficient amount for each row. The area allotted for placement of the amphitheater's stage and seating is 2000 ft^2.

a. Write an equation that can be used to determine the maximum number of rows that can be constructed.

b. Determine the maximum number of rows that can be constructed.

c. Suppose the city would like to construct a fence at least 200 feet away from the stage and all of the seats. Find the perimeter of fencing needed.

Extended Response

20. A container is filled with water at a constant rate. The water level over time is shown in the graph.

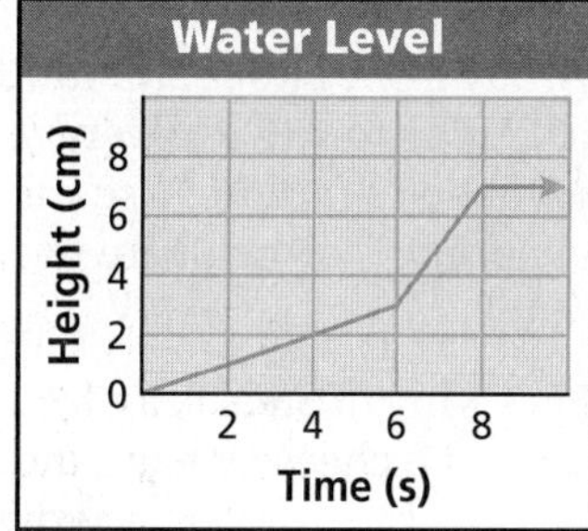

a. What does the flat portion of the graph represent?

b. Sketch a possible shape for the container.

c. Suppose the container is filled twice as fast. Sketch a graph to represent the situation, and identify the transformation of the original graph that it represents.

d. Suppose the container initially contains 2 cm of water. Would the new graph be a vertical translation of the original graph? Justify your answer.

Real-World CONNECTIONS

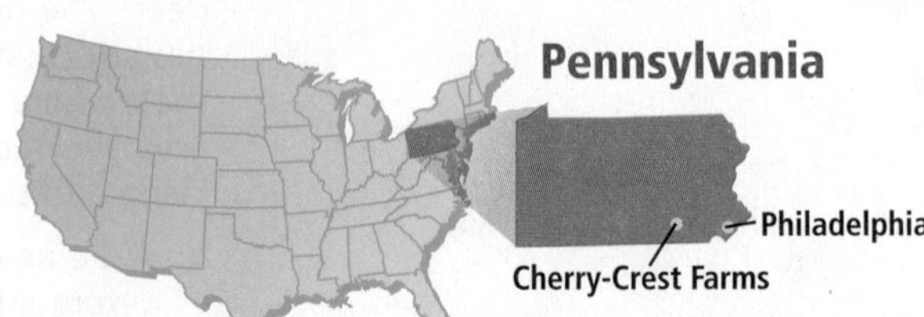

The Philly Cheese Steak Sandwich

Philadelphia's best-known sandwich was created in 1930 when a hot dog vendor tossed some steak and onions onto the grill and then served them on a hot dog bun. Cheese was soon added to the recipe, and the Philly cheese steak sandwich has been a local specialty ever since.

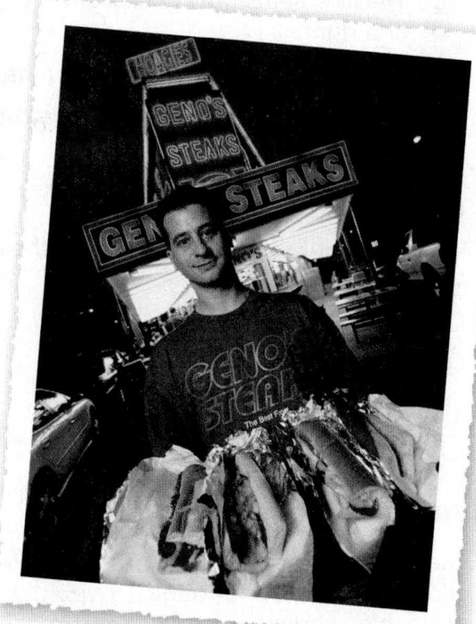

Choose one or more strategies to solve each problem.

1. At Geno's Steaks, the busiest shift of the week is on Saturday from 11:00 A.M. to 7:00 P.M. During that time Geno's makes an average of 1.5 cheese steak sandwiches a minute. Use the recipe below. How many pounds of steak are needed to get through this shift?
2. At Pat's King of Steaks, a plain steak sandwich costs $5.75 and a cheese steak sandwich costs $6.00. A tour group bought 32 sandwiches for a total of $189.00. How many of each type did they buy?
3. In 1930, the first steak sandwich sold for 2 cents. In 2004, a cheese steak sandwich cost $6. Assuming that cost is a linear function of time, predict the cost of a cheese steak sandwich in 2011.
4. You can expect to find a line at many cheese steak stands, but service is quick. Once an order is placed, the sandwich is made and served in 1 minute and 15 seconds. Suppose it takes 18 seconds for each person in line to place an order. What is the maximum number of people who can be in line ahead of you if you want to have your sandwich in less than 10 minutes from the time you get in line?

Philly Cheese Steak Recipe

5 oz steak
2 1/2 oz. American cheese
Fried onions
9 1/2 in. roll

Thinly slice steak and fry on grill. Just before it's done, cover with cheese and cook until melted. Serve on roll, topped with onions.

The Amazing Maize Maze

Cherry-Crest Farm, located in the heart of Pennsylvania Dutch Country, welcomes visitors by telling them to get lost—in an enormous cornfield maze! The design of the maze changes from year to year, but it always includes bridges and tunnels. There are also clues to discover along the way.

Choose one or more strategies to solve each problem.

1. Corn is usually planted at 30,000 plants per acre. The Amazing Maize Maze measures 360 feet by 660 feet. Assuming that 60% of that area is covered with corn plants, about how many plants form the maze? (*Hint:* 1 acre = 43,560 ft^2)
2. Admission to Cherry-Crest Farm is $11 for adults and $9 for children. One group of visitors paid $213 for admission, and there were more adults than children in the group. How many of each were in the group?

For 3, use the table.

3. Getting through the maze depends on two things: the speed at which you walk and your luck in choosing the right path. The table shows the average walking speeds of eight visitors and the time it took them to exit the maze. Predict the time it would take you to exit the maze if you walked at an average speed of 3.5 mi/h.

Average Walking Speed (mi/h)	2.5	3.0	4.0	3.1	2.8	3.9	4.0	2.7
Time to Exit Maze (min)	72	61	45	58	66	50	51	69

4. For most visitors, the time in minutes that it takes to exit the maze satisfies the inequality $|t - 60| \leq 15$.

   However, people who have already been through the maze usually improve their time by about 7 minutes. What are the minimum and maximum times it takes to exit the maze for repeat visitors?

CHAPTER 2

Quadratic Functions

COMMON CORE

Chapter Focus

- Make connections among representations of quadratic functions.
- Use various methods to solve quadratic equations and apply them to real-world problems.

Planetary Pass

How far could you throw a football if you were on Mars or Saturn? You can find the answer by using quadratic functions.

Learn It Online
Chapter Project Online

ARE YOU READY?

Vocabulary

Match each term on the left with a definition on the right.

1. linear equation
2. solution set
3. transformation
4. x-intercept

A. a change in a function rule and its graph

B. the x-coordinate of the point where a graph crosses the x-axis

C. the group of values that make an equation or inequality true

D. a letter or symbol that represents a number

E. an equation whose graph is a line

Squares and Square Roots

Simplify each expression.

5. 3.2^2
6. $\left(\frac{2}{5}\right)^2$
7. $\sqrt{121}$
8. $\sqrt{\frac{1}{16}}$

Simplify Radical Expressions

Simplify each expression.

9. $\sqrt{72}$
10. $2\left(\sqrt{144} - 4\right)$
11. $\sqrt{33} \cdot \sqrt{75}$
12. $\frac{\sqrt{54}}{\sqrt{3}}$

Multiply Binomials

Multiply.

13. $(x - 2)(x - 6)$
14. $(x + 9)(x - 9)$
15. $(x + 2)(x + 7)$
16. $(2x - 3)(5x + 1)$

Solve Multi-Step Equations

Solve each equation.

17. $2x + 10 = -32$
18. $2x - (1 - x) = 2$
19. $\frac{2}{3}(x - 1) = 11$
20. $2(x + 5) - 5x = 1$

Graph Linear Functions

Graph each function.

21. $y = -x$
22. $y = 2x - 1$
23. $y = -3x + 6$
24. $y = \frac{1}{3}x + 2$

CHAPTER 2

Study Guide: Preview

Where You've Been

Previously, you

- graphed and transformed linear functions.
- solved linear equations and inequalities.
- fit data using linear models.
- used and performed operations with real numbers.

In This Chapter

You will study

- graphing and transforming quadratic functions.
- solving quadratic equations and inequalities.
- fitting data to quadratic models.
- using and performing operations with imaginary and other complex numbers.

Where You're Going

You can use the skills in this chapter

- in advanced math classes, including Precalculus.
- in other classes, such as Chemistry, Physics, and Economics.
- outside of school to identify patterns and model data.

Key Vocabulary/Vocabulario

absolute value of a complex number	valor absoluto de un número complejo
complex conjugate	conjugado complejo
complex number	número complejo
imaginary number	número imaginario
maximum value	valor máximo
minimum value	valor mínimo
parabola	parábola
quadratic function	función cuadrática
vertex form	forma en vértice
zero of a function	cero de una función

Thinking About Vocabulary

To become familiar with some of the vocabulary terms in the chapter, consider the following. You may refer to the chapter, the glossary, or a dictionary if you like.

1. **Quadratic** is from the Latin *quadrum,* which means "square." A quadratic function always contains a *square* of the variable, such as x^2. What is a quadrilateral, and how does it relate to a square? What are some other words that use the root *quad-,* and what do they mean?
2. The word **conjugate** can mean "joined together, especially in pairs." Name some mathematical relationships that involve pairs.
3. What might the terms **maximum value** or **minimum value** of a function refer to?
4. The word *vertex* can mean "highest point." What might the **vertex form** of a quadratic function indicate about the function's graph?

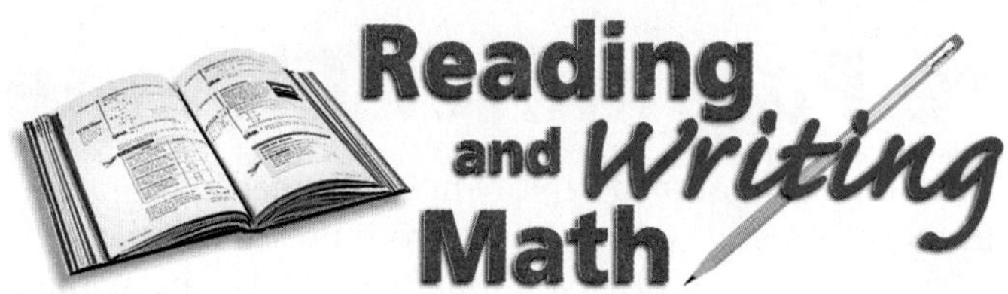

Study Strategy: Use Multiple Representations

The explanation and example problems used to introduce new math concepts often include various representations of information. Different representations of the same idea help you fully understand the material. As you study, take note of the tables, lists, graphs, diagrams, symbols, and/or words used to clarify a concept.

EXAMPLE 1 **Solving Linear Systems by Substitution**

Use substitution to solve each system of equations.

A $\begin{cases} y = x + 2 \\ x + y = 8 \end{cases}$

Symbols

Step 1 Solve one equation for one variable.
The first equation is already solved for y: $y = x + 2$.

Step 2 Substitute the expression into the other equation.

$x + y = 8$

$x + (x + 2) = 8$ *Substitute $(x + 2)$ for y in the other equation.*

$2x + 2 = 8$ *Combine like terms.*

$2x = 6$

$x = 3$

Step 3 Substitute the x-value into one of the original equations to solve for y.

$y = x + 2$

$y = (3) + 2$ *Substitute $x = 3$.*

$y = 5$

The solution is the ordered pair $(3, 5)$.

Caution!
The solution to an independent system of equations is an ordered pair. Do not stop working when you have found only one value.

Check A graph or table supports your answer.

Graph

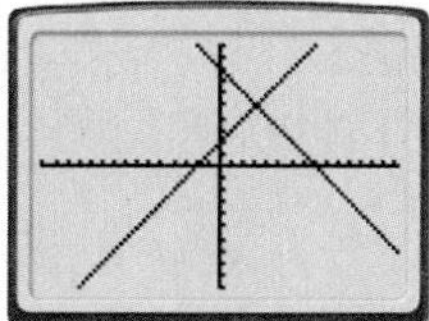

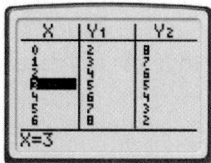

Table

X	Y1	Y2
0	2	8
1	3	7
2	4	6
3	5	5
4	6	4
5	7	3
6	8	2

X=3

Try This

Describe two representations you could use to solve each problem.

1. A triangle with coordinates $A(3, 5)$, $B(2, 2)$, and $C(3, -2)$ is translated 3 units left and 2 units up. Give the coordinates of the image.
2. A bottle of juice from a vending machine costs \$1.50. Hiroshi buys a bottle by inserting 8 coins in quarters and dimes. If Hiroshi receives 5 cents in change, how many quarters did he use? how many dimes?
3. What is the slope of the line that passes through the point $(6, 9)$ and has a y-intercept of 3?

Explore Parameter Changes

You can use a graphing calculator to explore how changes in the parameters of a quadratic function affect its graph. Recall from previous lessons that the quadratic parent function is $f(x) = x^2$ and that its graph is a parabola.

Use appropriate tools strategically.

Use with Using Transformations to Graph Quadratic Functions

CC.9-12.F.BF.3 Identify the effect on the graph of replacing $f(x)$ by $f(x) + k$, $k\,f(x)$, $f(kx)$, and $f(x + k)$ … find the value of k given the graphs. … illustrate … using technology.

Activity

Describe what happens when you change the value of k in the quadratic function $g(x) = x^2 + k$.

1. Choose three values for k. Use 0, −5 (a negative value), and 4 (a positive value). Press Y= , and enter $\mathbf{X^2}$ for **Y1**, $\mathbf{X^2 - 5}$ for **Y2**, and $\mathbf{X^2 + 4}$ for **Y3**.

2. Change the style of the graphs of **Y1** and **Y2** so that you can tell which graph represents which function. To do this, move the cursor to the graph style indicator next to **Y1**. Press ENTER to cycle through the options. For **Y1**, which represents the parent function, choose the thick line.

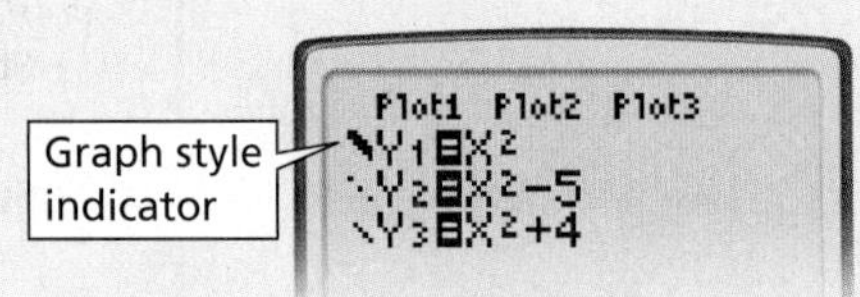

3. Next, change the line style for **Y2** to the dotted line.
4. Graph the functions in the square window by pressing ZOOM and choosing **5 : ZSquare**.

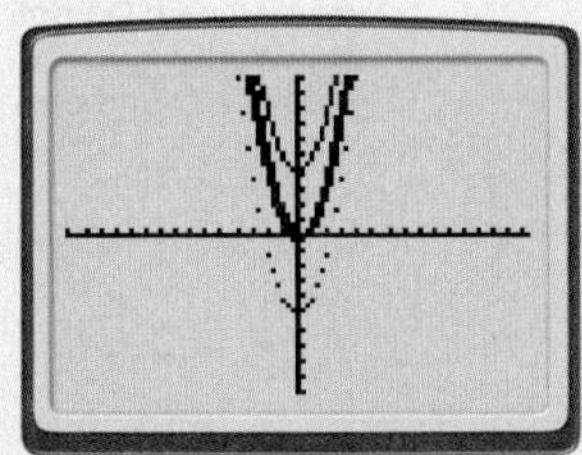

Notice that the graphs are identical except that the graph of **Y2** is shifted 5 units down and the graph of **Y3** has been shifted 4 units up from the graph of **Y1**.

You can conclude that the parameter k in the function $g(x) = x^2 + k$ has the effect of translating the parent function $f(x) = x^2$ k units up if k is positive and $|k|$ units down if k is negative.

Try This

Use your graphing calculator to compare the graph of each function to the graph of $f(x) = x^2$. Describe how the graphs differ.

1. $g(x) = (x - 4)^2$
2. $g(x) = (x + 3)^2$
3. $g(x) = -x^2$
4. **Make a Conjecture** Use your graphing calculator to determine what happens when you change the value of h in the quadratic function $g(x) = (x - h)^2$. Check both positive and negative values of h.
5. **Make a Conjecture** Use your graphing calculator to determine what happens when you change the value of a in the quadratic function $g(x) = ax^2$. Check values of a that are greater than 1 and values of a that are between 0 and 1.

COMMON CORE

2-1 Using Transformations to Graph Quadratic Functions

CC.9-12.F.IF.7a Graph linear and quadratic functions and show intercepts, maxima, and minima.* *Also* **CC.9-12.A.CED.2, CC.9-12.A.CED.3, CC.9-12.F.BF.3**

Objectives

Transform quadratic functions.

Describe the effects of changes in the coefficients of $y = a(x - h)^2 + k$.

Vocabulary

quadratic function
parabola
vertex of a parabola
vertex form

Why learn this?

You can use transformations of quadratic functions to analyze changes in braking distance. (See Example 5.)

You have studied linear functions of the form $f(x) = mx + b$. A **quadratic function** is a function that can be written in the form $f(x) = a(x - h)^2 + k$ $(a \neq 0)$. In a quadratic function, the variable is always squared. The table shows the linear and quadratic parent functions.

Linear and Quadratic Parent Functions

ALGEBRA	NUMBERS	GRAPH
Linear Parent Function $f(x) = x$	x: −2, −1, 0, 1, 2 f(x) = x: −2, −1, 0, 1, 2	
Quadratic Parent Function $f(x) = x^2$	x: −2, −1, 0, 1, 2 $f(x) = x^2$: 4, 1, 0, 1, 4	

x	−2	−1	0	1	2
$f(x) = x$	−2	−1	0	1	2

x	−2	−1	0	1	2
$f(x) = x^2$	4	1	0	1	4

Notice that the graph of the parent function $f(x) = x^2$ is a U-shaped curve called a **parabola**. As with other functions, you can graph a quadratic function by plotting points with coordinates that make the equation true.

EXAMPLE 1

Graphing Quadratic Functions Using a Table

Graph $f(x) = x^2 - 6x + 8$ by using a table.

Make a table. Plot enough ordered pairs to see both sides of the curve.

x	$f(x) = x^2 - 6x + 8$	$(x, f(x))$
1	$f(1) = 1^2 - 6(1) + 8 = 3$	$(1, 3)$
2	$f(2) = 2^2 - 6(2) + 8 = 0$	$(2, 0)$
3	$f(3) = 3^2 - 6(3) + 8 = -1$	$(3, -1)$
4	$f(4) = 4^2 - 6(4) + 8 = 0$	$(4, 0)$
5	$f(5) = 5^2 - 6(5) + 8 = 3$	$(5, 3)$

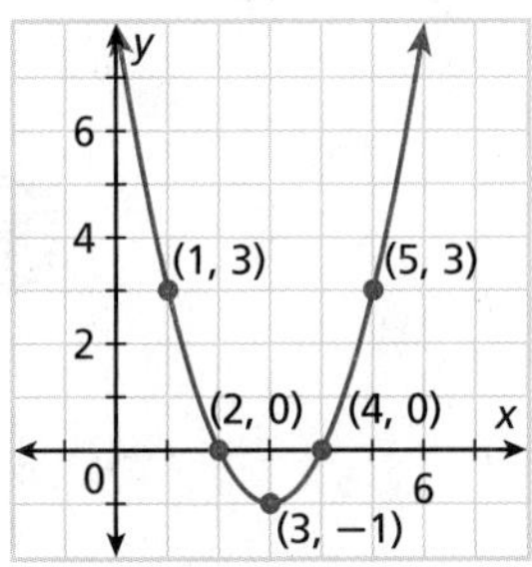

1. Graph $g(x) = -x^2 + 6x - 8$ by using a table.

You can also graph quadratic functions by applying transformations to the parent function $f(x) = x^2$. Transforming quadratic functions is similar to transforming linear functions.

Translations of Quadratic Functions	
Horizontal Translations	**Vertical Translations**
Horizontal Shift of $\lvert h \rvert$ Units	**Vertical Shift of $\lvert k \rvert$ Units**
$f(x) = x^2$ $f(x - h) = (x - h)^2$ Moves left for $h < 0$ Moves right for $h > 0$	$f(x) = x^2$ $f(x) + k = x^2 + k$ Moves down for $k < 0$ Moves up for $k > 0$

EXAMPLE 2 Translating Quadratic Functions

Using the graph of $f(x) = x^2$ as a guide, describe the transformations, and then graph each function.

A $g(x) = (x + 3)^2 + 1$

Identify h and k.

$$g(x) = \left(x - (-3)\right)^2 + 1$$

(-3 is h; 1 is k)

Because $h = -3$, the graph is translated **3 units left.**

Because $k = 1$, the graph is translated **1 unit up.**

Therefore, g is f translated 3 units left and 1 unit up.

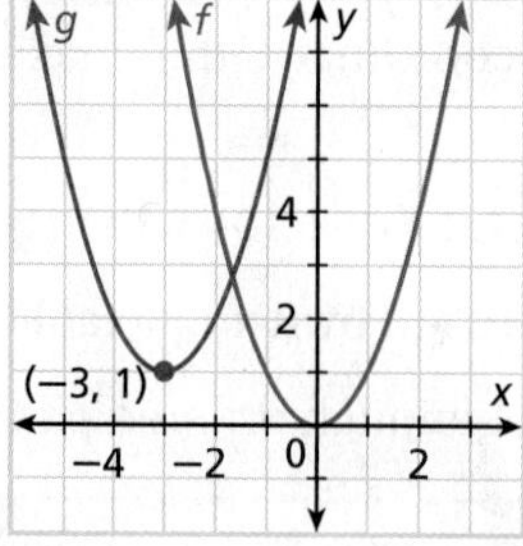

B $g(x) = (x - 2)^2 - 1$

Identify h and k.

$$g(x) = (x - 2)^2 + (-1)$$

(2 is h; -1 is k)

Because $h = 2$, the graph is translated **2 units right.**

Because $k = -1$, the graph is translated **1 unit down.**

Therefore, g is f translated 2 units right and 1 unit down.

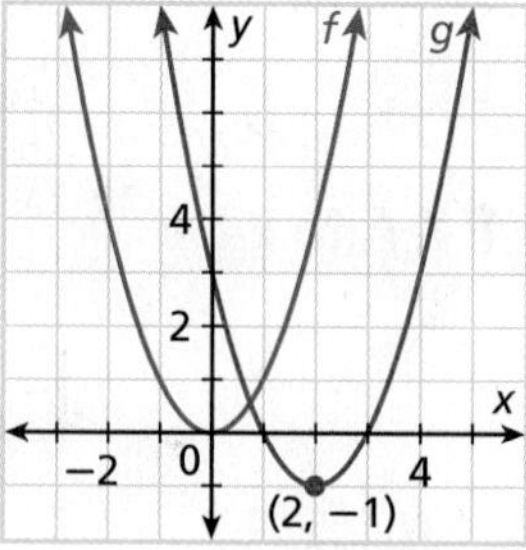

Using the graph of $f(x) = x^2$ as a guide, describe the transformations, and then graph each function.

2a. $g(x) = x^2 - 5$

2b. $g(x) = (x + 3)^2 - 2$

Recall that functions can also be reflected, stretched, or compressed.

Reflections, Stretches, and Compressions of Quadratic Functions

Reflections

Reflection Across y-axis	Reflection Across x-axis
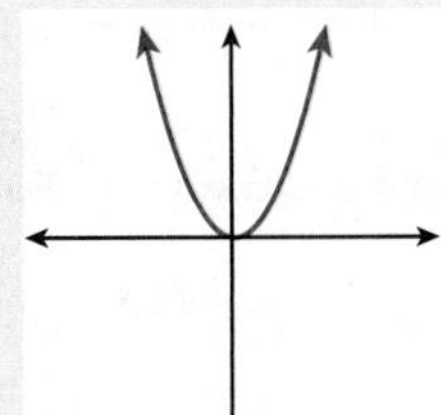 Input values change. $f(x) = x^2$ $f(-x) = (-x)^2 = x^2$ The function $f(x) = x^2$ is its own reflection across the y-axis.	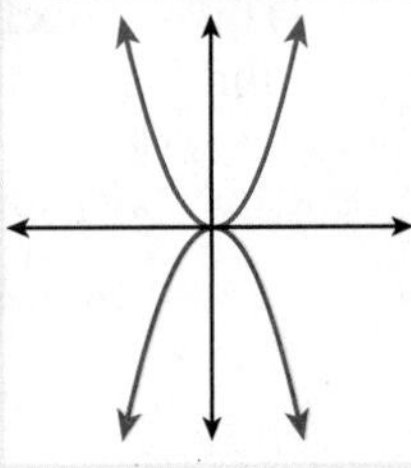 Output values change. $f(x) = x^2$ $-f(x) = -(x^2) = -x^2$ The function is flipped across the x-axis.

Stretches and Compressions

Horizontal Stretch/Compression by a Factor of $\|b\|$	Vertical Stretch/Compression by a Factor of $\|a\|$
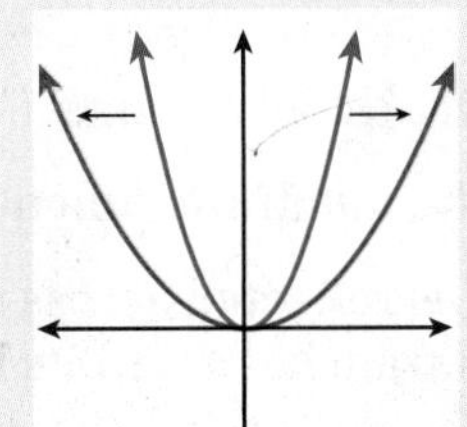 Input values change. $f(x) = x^2$ $f\left(\frac{1}{b}x\right) = \left(\frac{1}{b}x\right)^2$	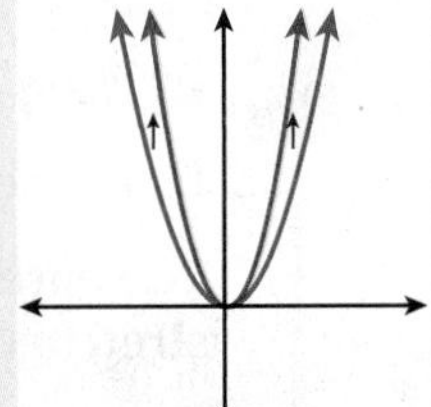 Output values change. $f(x) = x^2$ $a \cdot f(x) = ax^2$
$\|b\| > 1$ stretches away from the y-axis.	$\|a\| > 1$ stretches away from the x-axis.
$0 < \|b\| < 1$ compresses toward the y-axis.	$0 < \|a\| < 1$ compresses toward the x-axis.

EXAMPLE 3 Reflecting, Stretching, and Compressing Quadratic Functions

Using the graph of $f(x) = x^2$ as a guide, describe the transformations, and then graph each function.

A $g(x) = -4x^2$

Because a is negative, g is a reflection of f across the x-axis. Because $|a| = 4$, g is a vertical stretch of f by a factor of 4.

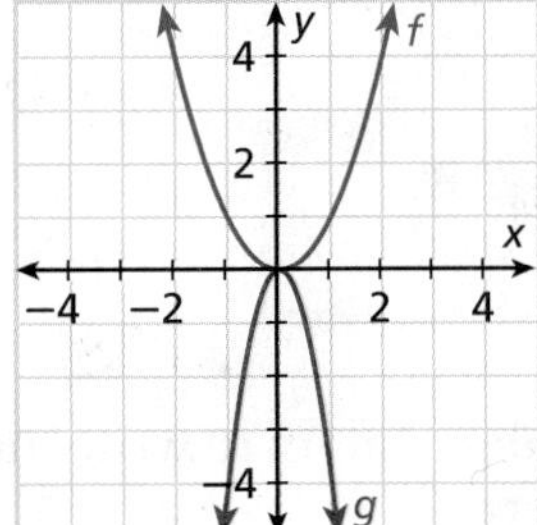

B $g(x) = \left(\frac{1}{2}x\right)^2$

Because $b = 2$, g is a horizontal stretch of f by a factor of 2.

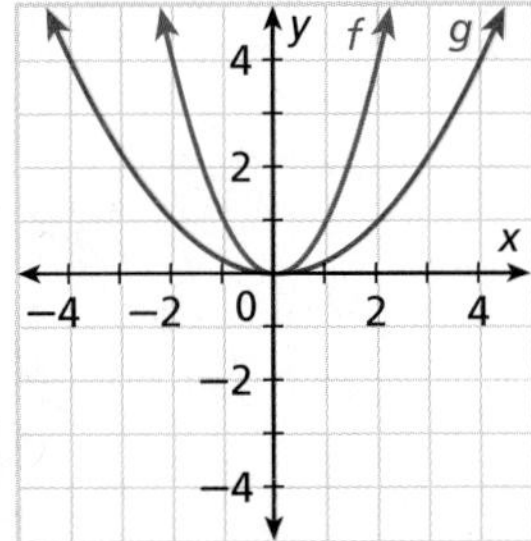

Using the graph of $f(x) = x^2$ as a guide, describe the transformations, and then graph each function.

3a. $g(x) = (2x)^2$

3b. $g(x) = -\frac{1}{2}x^2$

If a parabola opens upward, it has a lowest point. If a parabola opens downward, it has a highest point. This lowest or highest point is the **vertex of a parabola**.

The parent function $f(x) = x^2$ has its vertex at the origin. You can identify the vertex of other quadratic functions by analyzing the function in *vertex form.* The **vertex form** of a quadratic function is $f(x) = a(x - h)^2 + k$, where a, h, and k are constants.

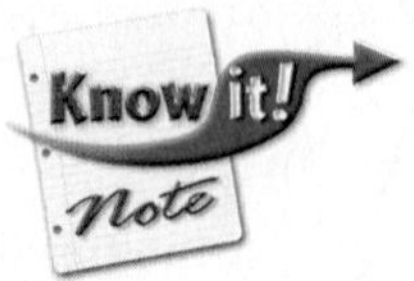

Vertex Form of a Quadratic Function

$$f(x) = a(x - h)^2 + k$$

a indicates a reflection across the *x*-axis and/or a vertical stretch or compression.

h indicates a horizontal translation.

k indicates a vertical translation.

Because the vertex is translated h horizontal units and k vertical units from the origin, the vertex of the parabola is at (h, k).

EXAMPLE 4 Writing Transformed Quadratic Functions

Use the description to write the quadratic function in vertex form.

The parent function $f(x) = x^2$ is reflected across the x-axis, vertically stretched by a factor of 6, and translated 3 units left to create g.

Step 1 Identify how each transformation affects the constants in vertex form.

reflection across x-axis: a is negative

vertical stretch by 6: $|a| = 6$

} $a = -6$

translation left 3 units: $h = -3$

Step 2 Write the transformed function.

$g(x) = a(x - h)^2 + k$ *Vertex form of a quadratic function*

$= -6(x - (-3))^2 + 0$ *Substitute −6 for a, −3 for h, and 0 for k.*

$= -6(x + 3)^2$ *Simplify.*

Check Graph both functions on a graphing calculator. Enter f as **Y1** and g as **Y2**. The graph indicates the identified transformations.

Helpful Hint

When the quadratic parent function $f(x) = x^2$ is written in vertex form, $y = a(x - h)^2 + k$, $a = 1$, $h = 0$, and $k = 0$.

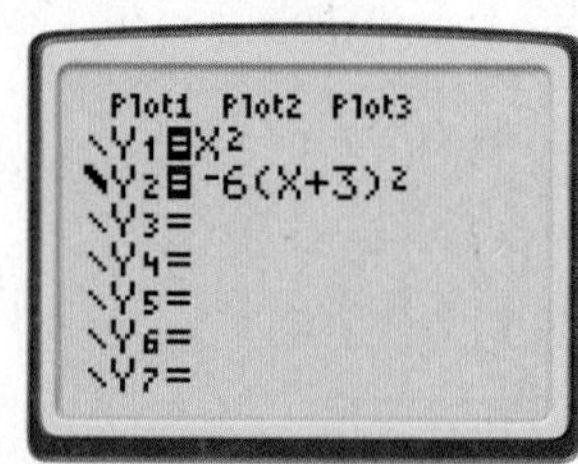

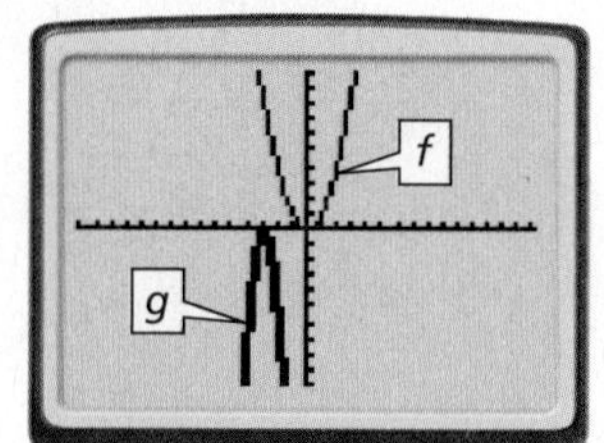

Use the description to write the quadratic function in vertex form.

4a. The parent function $f(x) = x^2$ is vertically compressed by a factor of $\frac{1}{3}$ and translated 2 units right and 4 units down to create g.

4b. The parent function $f(x) = x^2$ is reflected across the x-axis and translated 5 units left and 1 unit up to create g.

EXAMPLE 5 Automotive Application

The minimum braking distance d in feet for a vehicle on dry concrete is approximated by the function $d(v) = 0.045v^2$, where v is the vehicle's speed in miles per hour. If the vehicle's tires are in poor condition, the braking-distance function is $d_p(v) = 0.068v^2$. What kind of transformation describes this change, and what does the transformation mean?

Examine both functions in vertex form.

$$d(v) = 0.045(v - 0)^2 + 0 \qquad d_p(v) = 0.068(v - 0)^2 + 0$$

The value of a has increased from 0.045 to 0.068. The increase indicates a vertical stretch.

Find the stretch factor by comparing the new a-value to the old a-value:

$$\frac{a \text{ from } d_p(v)}{a \text{ from } d(v)} = \frac{0.068}{0.045} \approx 1.5$$

The function d_p represents a vertical stretch of d by a factor of approximately 1.5. Because the value of each function approximates braking distance, a vehicle with tires in poor condition takes about 1.5 times as many feet to stop as a vehicle with good tires does.

Check Graph both functions on a graphing calculator. The graph of d_p appears to be vertically stretched compared with the graph of d.

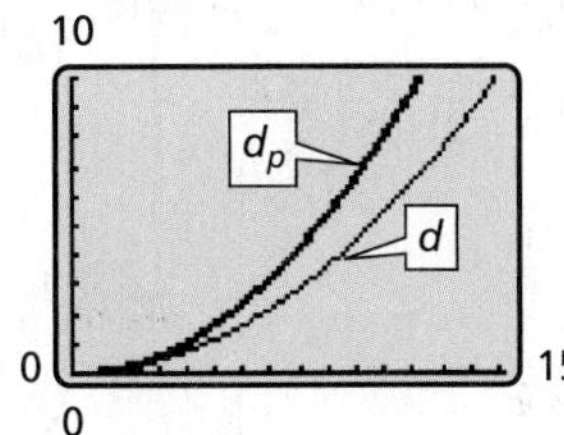

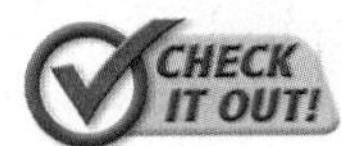

Use the information above to answer the following.

5. The minimum braking distance d_n in feet for a vehicle with new tires at optimal inflation is $d_n(v) = 0.039v^2$, where v is the vehicle's speed in miles per hour. What kind of transformation describes this change from $d(v) = 0.045v^2$, and what does this transformation mean?

THINK AND DISCUSS

1. Explain how the values of a, h, and k in the vertex form of a quadratic function affect the function's graph.
2. Explain how to determine which of two quadratic functions expressed in vertex form has a narrower graph.

3. **GET ORGANIZED** Copy and complete the graphic organizer. In each row, write an equation that represents the indicated transformation of the quadratic parent function, and show its graph.

Transformation	Equation	Graph
Vertical translation		
Horizontal translation		
Reflection		
Vertical stretch		
Vertical compression		

2-1 Exercises

Learn It Online
Homework Help Online
Parent Resources Online

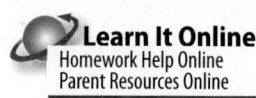

GUIDED PRACTICE

1. **Vocabulary** The highest or lowest point on the graph of a quadratic function is the ___?___. (*vertex* or *parabola*)

SEE EXAMPLE 1

Graph each function by using a table.

2. $f(x) = -2x^2 - 4$
3. $g(x) = -x^2 + 3x - 2$
4. $h(x) = x^2 + 2x$

SEE EXAMPLE 2

Using the graph of $f(x) = x^2$ as a guide, describe the transformations, and then graph each function.

5. $d(x) = (x - 4)^2$
6. $g(x) = (x - 3)^2 + 2$
7. $h(x) = (x + 1)^2 - 3$

SEE EXAMPLE 3

8. $g(x) = 3x^2$
9. $h(x) = \left(\frac{1}{8}x\right)^2$
10. $p(x) = 0.25x^2$
11. $h(x) = -(5x)^2$
12. $g(x) = 4.2x^2$
13. $d(x) = -\frac{2}{3}x^2$

SEE EXAMPLE 4

Use the description to write each quadratic function in vertex form.

14. The parent function $f(x) = x^2$ is vertically stretched by a factor of 2 and translated 3 units left to create g.

15. The parent function $f(x) = x^2$ is reflected across the x-axis and translated 6 units down to create h.

SEE EXAMPLE 5

16. **Physics** The safe working load L in pounds for a natural rope can be estimated by $L(r) = 5920r^2$, where r is the radius of the rope in inches. For an old rope, the function $L_o(r) = 4150r^2$ is used to estimate its safe working load. What kind of transformation describes this change, and what does this transformation mean?

PRACTICE AND PROBLEM SOLVING

Independent Practice

For Exercises	See Example
17–19	1
20–25	2
26–28	3
29–30	4
31	5

Extra Practice

See Extra Practice for more Skills Practice and Applications Practice exercises.

Graph each function by using a table.

17. $f(x) = -x^2 + 4$
18. $g(x) = x^2 - 2x + 1$
19. $h(x) = 2x^2 + 4x - 1$

Using the graph of $f(x) = x^2$ as a guide, describe the transformations, and then graph each function.

20. $g(x) = x^2 - 2$
21. $h(x) = (x + 5)^2$
22. $j(x) = (x - 1)^2$
23. $g(x) = (x + 4)^2 - 3$
24. $h(x) = (x + 2)^2 + 2$
25. $j(x) = (x - 4)^2 - 9$
26. $g(x) = \frac{4}{7}x^2$
27. $h(x) = -20x^2$
28. $j(x) = \left(\frac{1}{3}x\right)^2$

Use the description to write each quadratic function in vertex form.

29. The parent function $f(x) = x^2$ is reflected across the x-axis, vertically compressed by a factor of $\frac{1}{2}$, and translated 1 unit right to create g.

30. The parent function $f(x) = x^2$ is vertically stretched by a factor of 2.5 and translated 2 units left and 1 unit up to create h.

31. **Consumer Economics** The average gas mileage m in miles per gallon for a compact car is modeled by $m(s) = -0.015(s - 47)^2 + 33$, where s is the car's speed in miles per hour. The average gas mileage for an SUV is modeled by $m_u(s) = -0.015(s - 47)^2 + 15$. What kind of transformation describes this change, and what does this transformation mean?

32. **Pets** Keille is building a rectangular pen for a pet rabbit. She can buy wire fencing in a roll of 40 ft or a roll of 80 ft. The graph shows the area of pens she can build with each type of roll.

a. Describe the function for an 80 ft roll of fencing as a transformation of the function for a 40 ft roll of fencing.

b. Is the largest pen Keille can build with an 80 ft roll of fencing twice as large as the largest pen she can build with a 40 ft roll of fencing? Explain.

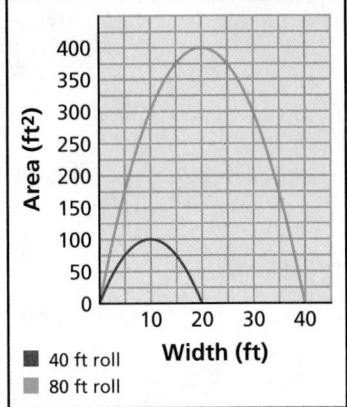

Possible Area of Pen

Area (ft²)
400
350
300
250
200
150
100
50
0
10 20 30 40
Width (ft)
40 ft roll
80 ft roll

Using $f(x) = x^2$ as a guide, describe the transformations for each function.

33. $p(x) = -(x-4)^2$

34. $g(x) = 8(x+2)^2$

35. $h(x) = 4x^2 - 2$

36. $p(x) = \frac{1}{4}x^2 + 2$

37. $g(x) = (3x)^2 + 1$

38. $h(x) = -\left(\frac{1}{3}x\right)^2$

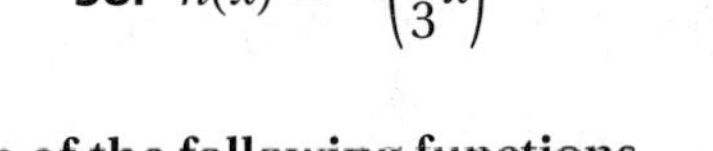

Match each graph with one of the following functions.

A. $a(x) = 4(x+8)^2 - 3$

B. $b(x) = -2(x-8)^2 + 3$

C. $c(x) = -\frac{1}{2}(x+3)^2 + 8$

39.

(−3, 8)
8
y
4
(1, 0)
x
−8
−4
0
4
−4

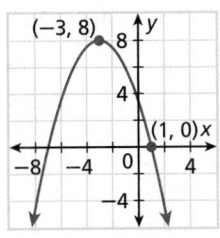

40.

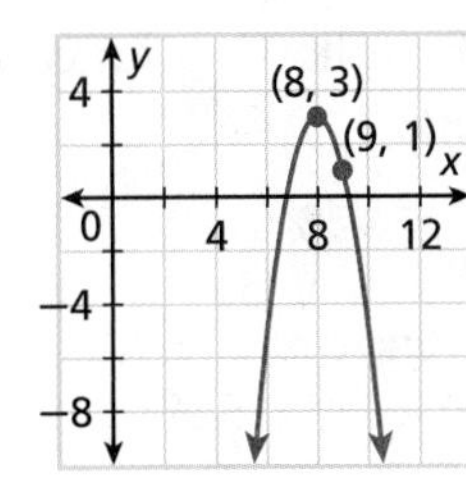

41.

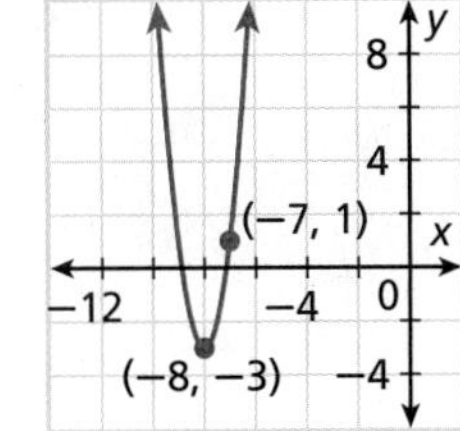

42. **Geometry** The area A of the circle in the figure can be represented by $A(r) = \pi r^2$, where r is the radius.

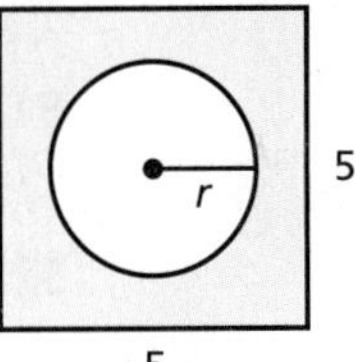

a. Write a function B in terms of r that represents the area of the shaded portion of the figure.

b. Describe B as a transformation of A.

c. What are the reasonable domain and range for each function? Explain.

43. **Critical Thinking** What type of graph would a function of the form $f(x) = a(x-h)^2 + k$ have if $a = 0$? What type of function would it be?

44. **Write About It** Describe the graph of $f(x) = 999{,}999(x+5)^2 + 5$ without graphing it.

45. The height h in feet of a baseball on Earth after t seconds can be modeled by the function $h(t) = -16(t-1.5)^2 + 36$, where -16 is a constant in ft/s^2 due to Earth's gravity.

a. **What if...?** The gravity on Mars is only 0.38 times that on Earth. If the same baseball were thrown on Mars, it would reach a maximum height 59 feet higher and 2.5 seconds later than on Earth. Describe the transformations that must be applied to make the function model the height of the baseball on Mars.

b. Write a height function for the baseball thrown on Mars.

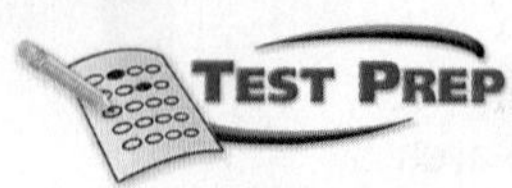

TEST PREP

Use the graph for Exercises 46 and 47.

46. Which best describes how the graph of the function $y = -x^2$ was transformed to produce the graph shown?

Ⓐ Translation 2 units right and 2 units up

Ⓑ Translation 2 units right and 2 units down

Ⓒ Translation 2 units left and 2 units up

Ⓓ Translation 2 units left and 2 units down

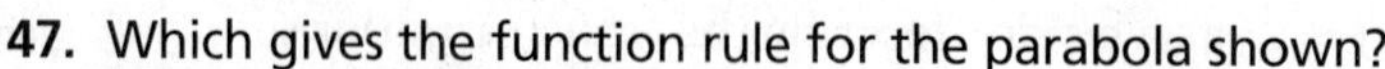

47. Which gives the function rule for the parabola shown?

Ⓕ $f(x) = (x + 2)^2 - 2$

Ⓖ $f(x) = -(x + 2)^2 - 2$

Ⓗ $f(x) = (x - 2)^2 - 2$

Ⓙ $f(x) = -(x - 2)^2 - 2$

48. Which shows the functions below in order from widest to narrowest of their corresponding graphs?

$m(x) = \frac{1}{6}x^2$ $\quad n(x) = 4x^2$ $\quad p(x) = 6x^2$ $\quad q(x) = -\frac{1}{2}x^2$

Ⓐ m, n, p, q

Ⓑ q, m, n, p

Ⓒ m, q, n, p

Ⓓ q, p, n, m

49. Which of the following functions has its vertex below the x-axis?

Ⓕ $f(x) = (x - 7)^2$

Ⓖ $f(x) = x^2 - 8$

Ⓗ $f(x) = -2x^2$

Ⓙ $f(x) = -(x + 3)^2$

50. Gridded Response What is the y-coordinate of the vertex of the graph of $f(x) = -3(x - 1)^2 + 5$?

CHALLENGE AND EXTEND

51. Identify the transformations of the graph of $f(x) = -3(x + 3)^2 - 3$ that would cause the graph's image to have a vertex at $(3, 3)$. Then write the transformed function.

52. Consider the functions $f(x) = (2x)^2 - 2$ and $g(x) = 4x^2 - 2$.

a. Describe each function as a transformation of the quadratic parent function.

b. Graph both functions on the coordinate plane.

c. Make a conjecture about the relationship between the two functions.

d. Write the rule for a horizontal compression of the parent function that would give the same graph as $f(x) = 9x^2$.

COMMON CORE

2-2 Properties of Quadratic Functions in Standard Form

CC.9-12.A.CED.2 Create equations in two or more variables to represent relationships between quantities; graph equations on coordinate axes with labels and scales. *Also* **CC.9-12.A.CED.3, CC.9-12.F.IF.5, CC.9-12.F.IF.7a*, CC.9-12.F.IF.8a**

Objectives

Define, identify, and graph quadratic functions.

Identify and use maximums and minimums of quadratic functions to solve problems.

Vocabulary

axis of symmetry
standard form
minimum value
maximum value

Why learn this?

Quadratic functions can be used to find the maximum power generated by the engine of a speedboat. (See Example 4.)

When you transformed quadratic functions previously, you saw that reflecting the parent function across the y-axis results in the same function.

$f(x) = x^2$
$g(x) = (-x)^2 = x^2$

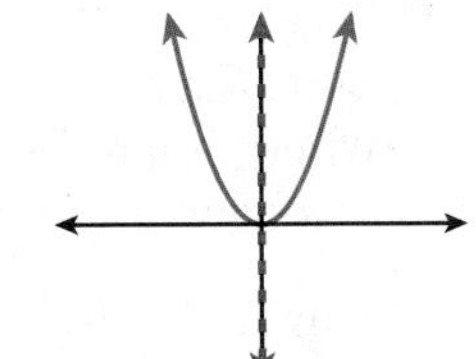

This shows that parabolas are symmetric curves. The **axis of symmetry** is the line through the vertex of a parabola that divides the parabola into two congruent halves.

Know it! Note

Axis of Symmetry — Quadratic Functions

WORDS	ALGEBRA	GRAPH
The axis of symmetry is a vertical line through the vertex of the function's graph.	The quadratic function $f(x) = a(x - h)^2 + k$ has the axis of symmetry $x = h$.	(h, k)

EXAMPLE 1 Identifying the Axis of Symmetry

Identify the axis of symmetry for the graph of $f(x) = 2(x + 2)^2 - 3$.

Rewrite the function to find the value of h.

$f(x) = 2[x - (-2)]^2 - 3$

Because $h = -2$, the axis of symmetry is the vertical line $x = -2$.

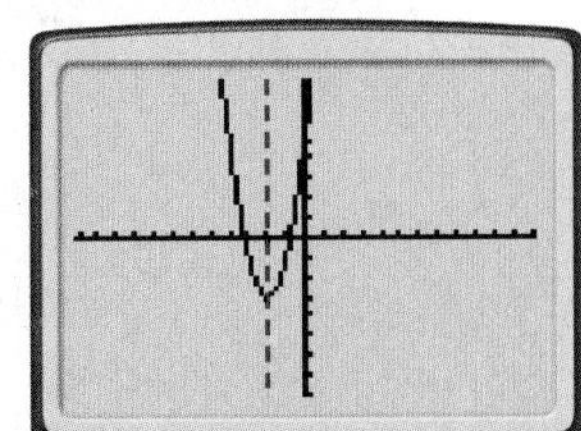

Check Analyze the graph on a graphing calculator. The parabola is symmetric about the vertical line $x = -2$.

CHECK IT OUT!

1. Identify the axis of symmetry for the graph of $f(x) = (x - 3)^2 + 1$.

Another useful form of writing quadratic functions is the *standard form.* The **standard form** of a quadratic function is $f(x) = ax^2 + bx + c$, where $a \neq 0$.

The coefficients a, b, and c can show properties of the graph of the function. You can determine these properties by expanding the vertex form.

$$f(x) = a(x - h)^2 + k$$

$$f(x) = a(x^2 - 2xh + h^2) + k \quad \text{Multiply to expand } (x - h)^2.$$

$$f(x) = a(x^2) - a(2hx) + a(h^2) + k \quad \text{Distribute } a.$$

$$f(x) = ax^2 + (-2ah)x + (ah^2 + k) \quad \text{Simplify and group like terms.}$$

$a = a$ $\quad -2ah = b$ $\quad ah^2 + k = c$

$$f(x) = ax^2 + bx + c$$

$a = a$: a in standard form is the same as in vertex form. It indicates whether a reflection and/or vertical stretch or compression has been applied.

$b = -2ah$: Solving for h gives $h = \frac{b}{-2a} = -\frac{b}{2a}$. Therefore, the axis of symmetry, $x = h$, for a quadratic function in standard form is $x = -\frac{b}{2a}$.

$c = ah^2 + k$: Notice that the value of c is the same value given by the vertex form of f when $x = 0$: $f(0) = a(0 - h)^2 + k = ah^2 + k$. So c is the y-intercept.

These properties can be generalized to help you graph quadratic functions.

Properties of a Parabola

For $f(x) = ax^2 + bx + c$, where a, b, and c are real numbers and $a \neq 0$, the parabola has these properties:

The parabola **opens upward** if $a > 0$ and **downward** if $a < 0$.

The **axis of symmetry** is the vertical line $x = -\frac{b}{2a}$.

The **vertex** is the point $\left(-\frac{b}{2a}, f\left(-\frac{b}{2a}\right)\right)$.

The **y-intercept** is c.

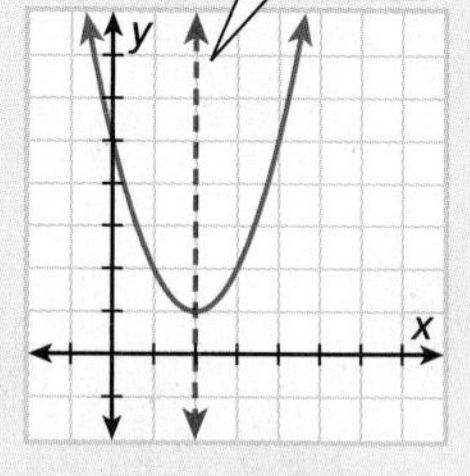

EXAMPLE 2 Graphing Quadratic Functions in Standard Form

A **Consider the function $f(x) = x^2 - 4x + 6$.**

a. Determine whether the graph opens upward or downward.

Because a is positive, the parabola opens upward.

b. Find the axis of symmetry.

The axis of symmetry is given by $x = -\frac{b}{2a}$.

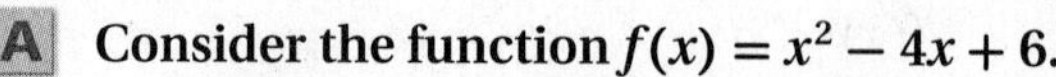

$$x = -\frac{(-4)}{2(1)} = 2 \quad \text{Substitute } -4 \text{ for } b \text{ and } 1 \text{ for } a.$$

The axis of symmetry is the line $x = 2$.

c. Find the vertex.

The vertex lies on the axis of symmetry, so the x-coordinate is 2. The y-coordinate is the value of the function at this x-value, or $f(2)$.

$$f(2) = (2)^2 - 4(2) + 6 = 2$$

The vertex is $(2, 2)$.

d. Find the y-intercept.

Because $c = 6$, the y-intercept is 6.

e. Graph the function.

Graph by sketching the axis of symmetry and then plotting the vertex and the intercept point, $(0, 6)$. Use the axis of symmetry to find another point on the parabola. Notice that $(0, 6)$ is 2 units left of the axis of symmetry. The point on the parabola symmetrical to $(0, 6)$ is 2 units right of the axis at $(4, 6)$.

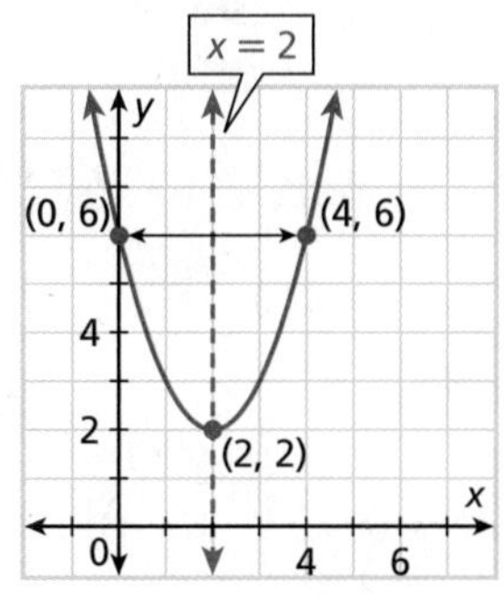

B **Consider the function $f(x) = -4x^2 - 12x - 3$.**

a. Determine whether the graph opens upward or downward.

Because a is negative, the parabola opens downward.

Helpful Hint

When a is positive, the parabola is happy (∪). When a is negative, the parabola is sad (∩).

b. Find the axis of symmetry.

The axis of symmetry is given by $x = -\frac{b}{2a}$.

$$x = -\frac{(-12)}{2(-4)} = -\frac{3}{2} \quad \textit{Substitute } -12 \textit{ for } b \textit{ and } -4 \textit{ for } a.$$

The axis of symmetry is the line $x = -\frac{3}{2}$, or $x = -1.5$.

c. Find the vertex.

The vertex lies on the axis of symmetry, so the x-coordinate is -1.5. The y-coordinate is the value of the function at this x-value, or $f(-1.5)$.

$$f(-1.5) = -4(-1.5)^2 - 12(-1.5) - 3 = 6$$

The vertex is $(-1.5, 6)$.

d. Find the y-intercept.

Because $c = -3$, the y-intercept is -3.

e. Graph the function.

Graph by sketching the axis of symmetry and then plotting the vertex and the intercept point, $(0, -3)$. Use the axis of symmetry to find another point on the parabola. Notice that $(0, -3)$ is 1.5 units right of the axis of symmetry. The point on the parabola symmetrical to $(0, -3)$ is 1.5 units left of the axis at $(-3, -3)$.

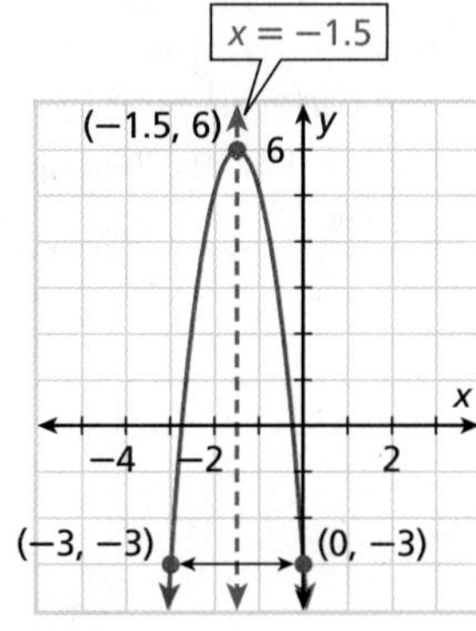

For each function, (a) determine whether the graph opens upward or downward, (b) find the axis of symmetry, (c) find the vertex, (d) find the y-intercept, and (e) graph the function.

2a. $f(x) = -2x^2 - 4x$ **2b.** $g(x) = x^2 + 3x - 1$

Substituting any real value of x into a quadratic equation results in a real number. Therefore, the domain of any quadratic function is all real numbers, $\mathbb{R}$. The range of a quadratic function depends on its vertex and the direction that the parabola opens.

Minimum and Maximum Values

OPENS UPWARD	OPENS DOWNWARD
When a parabola opens upward, the *y*-value of the vertex is the **minimum value.**	When a parabola opens downward, the *y*-value of the vertex is the **maximum value.**
D: $\{x \mid x \in \mathbb{R}\}$ R: $\{y \mid y \geq k\}$ 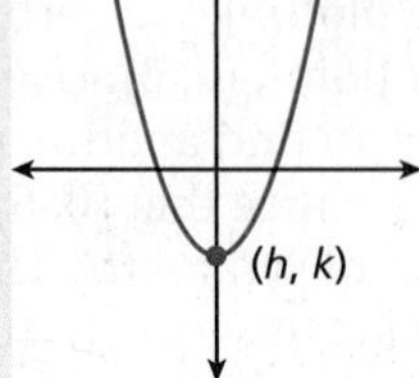	D: $\{x \mid x \in \mathbb{R}\}$ R: $\{y \mid y \leq k\}$ 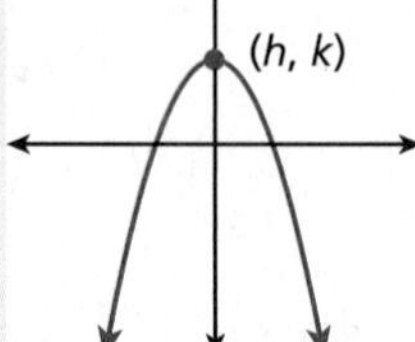
The domain is all real numbers, $\mathbb{R}$. The range is all values greater than or equal to the minimum.	The domain is all real numbers, $\mathbb{R}$. The range is all values less than or equal to the maximum.

EXAMPLE 3 Finding Minimum or Maximum Values

Find the minimum or maximum value of $f(x) = 2x^2 - 2x + 5$. Then state the domain and range of the function.

Step 1 Determine whether the function has a minimum or maximum value. Because a is positive, the graph opens upward and has a minimum value.

Step 2 Find the x-value of the vertex.

$$x = -\frac{b}{2a} = -\frac{(-2)}{2(2)} = \frac{2}{4} = \frac{1}{2}$$ *Substitute −2 for b and 2 for a.*

Caution!

The minimum (or maximum) value is the *y-value* of the vertex. It is *not* the ordered pair representing the vertex.

Step 3 Then find the y-value of the vertex, $f\left(-\frac{b}{2a}\right)$.

$$f\left(\frac{1}{2}\right) = 2\left(\frac{1}{2}\right)^2 - 2\left(\frac{1}{2}\right) + 5 = 4\frac{1}{2}$$

The minimum value is $4\frac{1}{2}$, or 4.5. The domain is all real numbers, $\mathbb{R}$. The range is all real numbers greater than or equal to 4.5, or $\{y \mid y \geq 4.5\}$.

Check Graph $f(x) = 2x^2 - 2x + 5$ on a graphing calculator. The graph and table support the answer.

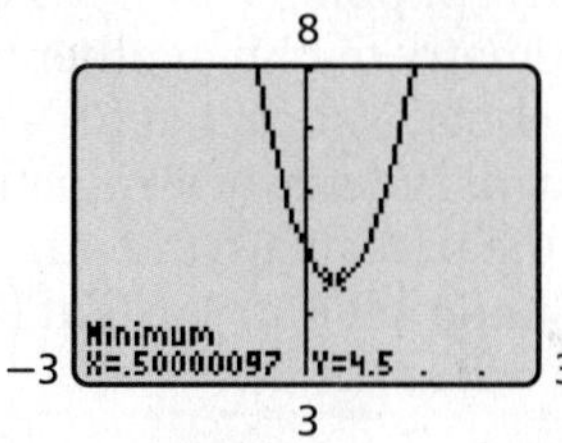

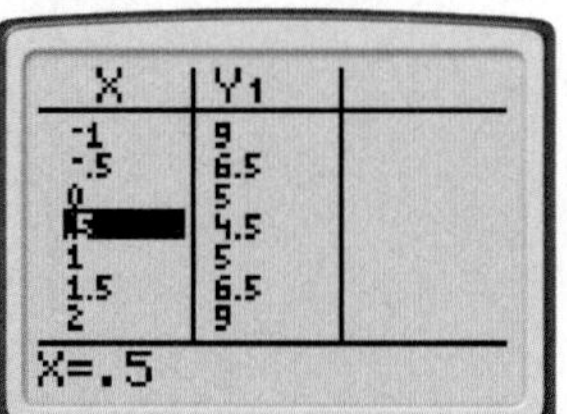

Find the minimum or maximum value of each function. Then state the domain and range of the function.

3a. $f(x) = x^2 - 6x + 3$ **3b.** $g(x) = -2x^2 - 4$

EXAMPLE 4 Transportation Application

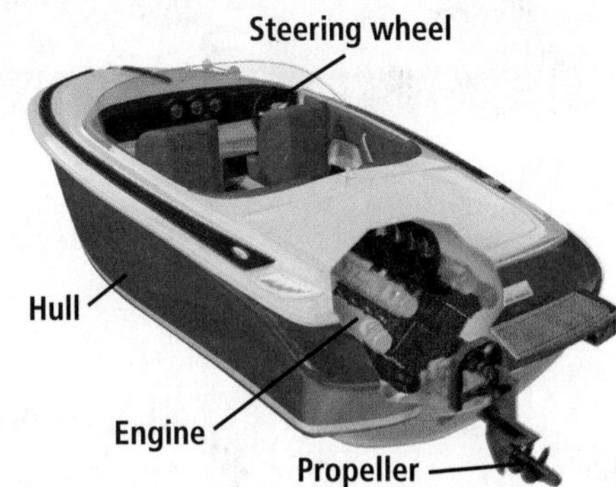

The power p in horsepower (hp) generated by a high-performance speedboat engine operating at r revolutions per minute (rpm) can be modeled by the function $p(r) = -0.0000147r^2 + 0.18r - 251$. What is the maximum power of this engine to the nearest horsepower? At how many revolutions per minute must the engine be operating to achieve this power?

The maximum value will be at the vertex $(r, p(r))$.

Step 1 Find the r-value of the vertex using $a = -0.0000147$ and $b = 0.18$.

$$r = -\frac{b}{2a} = -\frac{0.18}{2(-0.0000147)} \approx 6122$$

Step 2 Substitute this r-value into p to find the corresponding maximum, $p(r)$.

$$p(r) = -0.0000147r^2 + 0.18r - 251$$

$$p(6122) = -0.0000147(6122)^2 + 0.18(6122) - 251$$ *Substitute 6122 for r.*

$$p(6122) \approx 300$$ *Use a calculator.*

The maximum power is about 300 hp at 6122 rpm.

Check Graph the function on a graphing calculator. Use the **maximum** feature under the **CALCULATE** menu to approximate the maximum. The graph supports your answer.

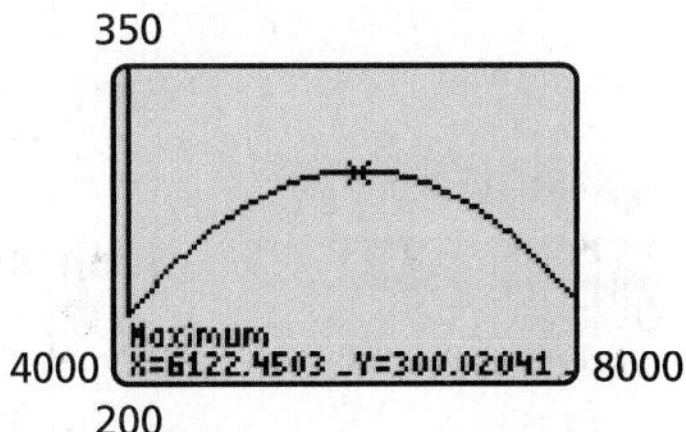

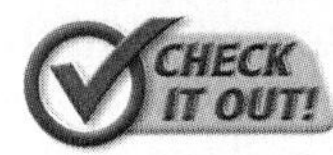

4. The highway mileage m in miles per gallon for a compact car is approximated by $m(s) = -0.025s^2 + 2.45s - 30$, where s is the speed in miles per hour. What is the maximum mileage for this compact car to the nearest tenth of a mile per gallon? What speed results in this mileage?

MATHEMATICAL PRACTICES

THINK AND DISCUSS

1. Explain whether a quadratic function can have both a maximum value and a minimum value.
2. Explain why the value of $f(x) = x^2 + 2x - 1$ increases as the value of x decreases from -1 to -10.
3. **GET ORGANIZED** Copy and complete the graphic organizer. In each box, write the criteria or equation to find each property of the parabola for $f(x) = ax^2 + bx + c$.

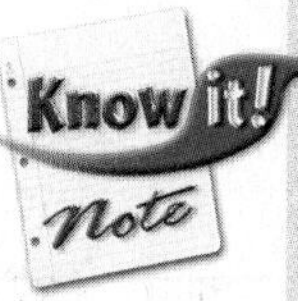

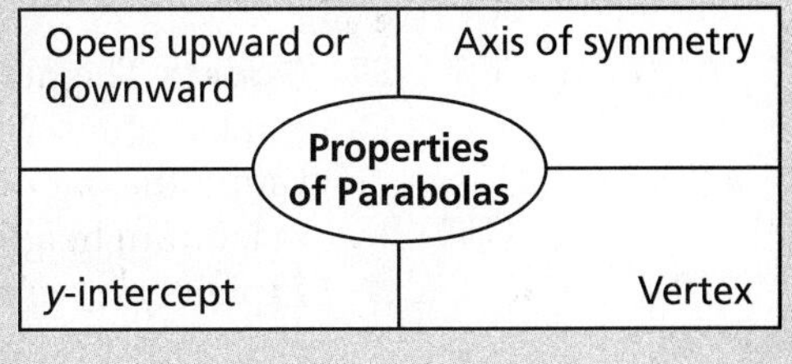

2-2 Exercises

Learn It Online
Homework Help Online
Parent Resources Online

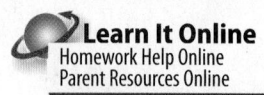

GUIDED PRACTICE

1. **Vocabulary** If the graph of a quadratic function opens upward, the y-value of the vertex is a __?__ value. (*maximum* or *minimum*)

SEE EXAMPLE 1

Identify the axis of symmetry for the graph of each function.

2. $f(x) = -2(x-2)^2 - 4$
3. $g(x) = 3x^2 + 4$
4. $h(x) = (x+5)^2$

SEE EXAMPLE 2

For each function, (a) determine whether the graph opens upward or downward, (b) find the axis of symmetry, (c) find the vertex, (d) find the y-intercept, and (e) graph the function.

5. $f(x) = -x^2 - 2x - 8$
6. $g(x) = x^2 - 3x + 2$
7. $h(x) = 4x - x^2 - 1$

SEE EXAMPLE 3

Find the minimum or maximum value of each function. Then state the domain and range of the function.

8. $f(x) = x^2 - 1$
9. $g(x) = -x^2 + 3x - 2$
10. $h(x) = -16x^2 + 32x + 4$

SEE EXAMPLE 4

11. **Sports** The path of a soccer ball is modeled by the function $h(x) = -0.005x^2 + 0.25x$, where h is the height in meters and x is the horizontal distance that the ball travels in meters. What is the maximum height that the ball reaches?

PRACTICE AND PROBLEM SOLVING

Independent Practice

For Exercises	See Example
12–14	1
15–23	2
24–29	3
30	4

Extra Practice

See Extra Practice for more Skills Practice and Applications Practice exercises.

Identify the axis of symmetry for the graph of each function.

12. $f(x) = -x^2 + 4$
13. $g(x) = (x-1)^2$
14. $h(x) = 2(x+1)^2 - 3$

For each function, (a) determine whether the graph opens upward or downward, (b) find the axis of symmetry, (c) find the vertex, (d) find the y-intercept, and (e) graph the function.

15. $f(x) = x^2 + x - 2$
16. $g(x) = -3x^2 + 6x$
17. $h(x) = 0.5x^2 - 2x - 4$
18. $f(x) = -2x^2 + 8x + 5$
19. $g(x) = 3x^2 + 2x - 8$
20. $h(x) = 2x - 1 + x^2$
21. $f(x) = -(2 + x^2)$
22. $g(x) = 0.5x^2 + 3x - 5$
23. $h(x) = \frac{1}{4}x^2 + x + 2$

Find the minimum or maximum value of each function. Then state the domain and range of the function.

24. $f(x) = -2x^2 + 7x - 3$
25. $g(x) = 6x - x^2$
26. $h(x) = x^2 - 4x + 3$
27. $f(x) = -\frac{1}{2}x^2 - 4$
28. $g(x) = -x^2 - 6x + 1$
29. $h(x) = x^2 + 8x + 16$

30. **Weather** The daily high temperature in Death Valley, California, in 2003 can be modeled by $T(d) = -0.0018d^2 + 0.657d + 50.95$, where T is temperature in degrees Fahrenheit and d is the day of the year. What was the maximum temperature in 2003 to the nearest degree?

31. **Sports** The height of a golf ball over time can be represented by a quadratic function. Graph the data in the table. What is the maximum height that the ball will reach? Explain your answer in terms of the axis of symmetry and vertex of the graph.

Golf Ball Height

Time (s)	0	0.5	1	2	3
Height (ft)	0	28	48	64	48

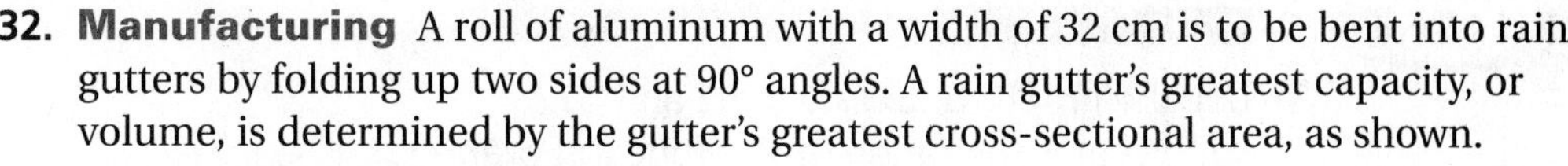

32. Manufacturing A roll of aluminum with a width of 32 cm is to be bent into rain gutters by folding up two sides at 90° angles. A rain gutter's greatest capacity, or volume, is determined by the gutter's greatest cross-sectional area, as shown.

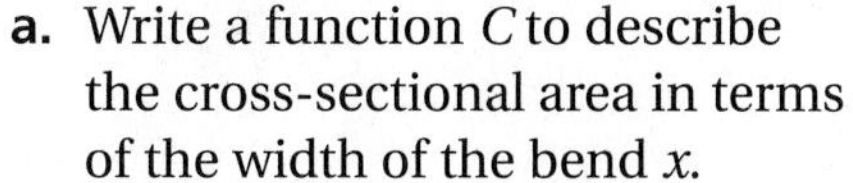

a. Write a function C to describe the cross-sectional area in terms of the width of the bend x.

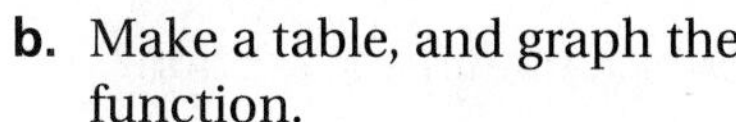

b. Make a table, and graph the function.

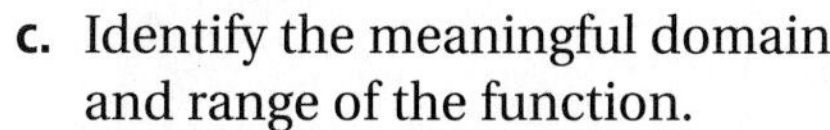

c. Identify the meaningful domain and range of the function.

d. Find the value of x that maximizes the cross-sectional area.

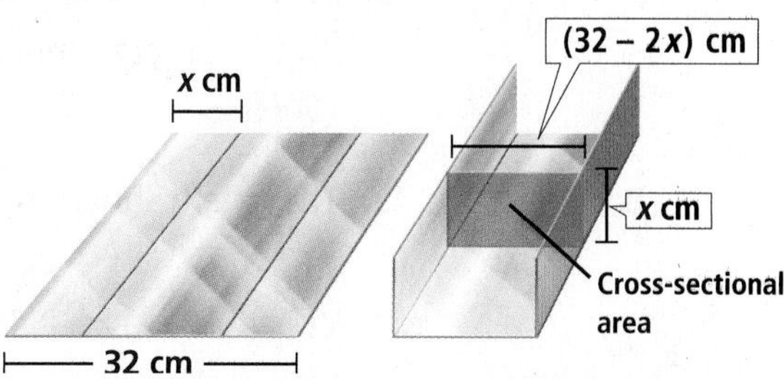

Biology

Spittlebugs are insects that feed on the sap of plants. Young spittlebug larvae use sap to produce a layer of bubbles around themselves. The bubbles help to keep the larvae from drying out and may protect them from predators.

33. Biology The spittlebug is the world's highest jumping animal relative to its body length of about 6 mm. The height h of a spittlebug's jump in millimeters can be modeled by the function $h(t) = -4000t^2 + 3000t$, where t is the time in seconds.

a. What is the maximum height that the spittlebug will reach?

b. What is the ratio of a spittlebug's maximum jumping height to its body length? In the best human jumpers, this ratio is about 1.38. Compare the ratio for spittlebugs with the ratio for the best human jumpers.

c. **What if...?** Suppose humans had the same ratio of maximum jumping height to body length as spittlebugs. How high would a person with a height of 1.8 m be able to jump?

34. Gardening The function $A(x) = x(10 - x)$ describes the area A of a rectangular flower garden, where x is its width in yards. What is the maximum area of the garden?

Graphing Calculator Once you have graphed a function, the graphing calculator can automatically find the minimum or maximum value. From the **CALC** menu, choose the **minimum** or **maximum** feature.

Use a graphing calculator to find the approximate minimum or maximum value of each function.

35. $f(x) = 5.23x^2 - 4.84x - 1.91$

36. $g(x) = -12.8x^2 + 8.73x + 11.69$

37. $h(x) = \frac{1}{12}x^2 - \frac{4}{5}x + \frac{2}{3}$

38. $j(x) = -\frac{5}{3}x^2 + \frac{9}{10}x + \frac{21}{4}$

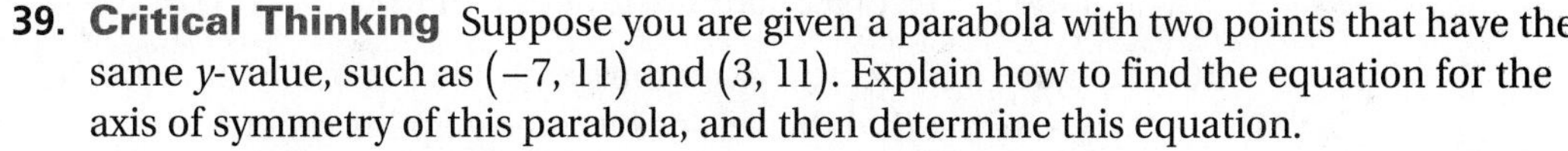

39. Critical Thinking Suppose you are given a parabola with two points that have the same y-value, such as $(-7, 11)$ and $(3, 11)$. Explain how to find the equation for the axis of symmetry of this parabola, and then determine this equation.

40. Write About It Can a maximum value for a quadratic function be negative? Can a minimum value for a quadratic function be positive? Explain by using examples.

MULTI-STEP TEST PREP

41. A baseball is thrown with a vertical velocity of 50 ft/s from an initial height of 6 ft. The height h in feet of the baseball can be modeled by $h(t) = -16t^2 + 50t + 6$, where t is the time in seconds since the ball was thrown.

a. Approximately how many seconds does it take the ball to reach its maximum height?

b. What is the maximum height that the ball reaches?

Use the graph for exercises 42 and 43.

42. What is the range of the function graphed?

Ⓐ All real numbers
Ⓑ $y \geq -2$
Ⓒ $y \leq 2$
Ⓓ $-2 \leq y \leq 2$

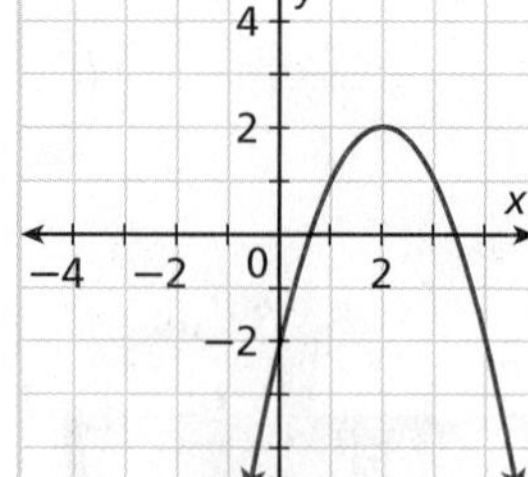

43. The graph shown represents which quadratic function?

Ⓕ $f(x) = x^2 + 2x - 2$
Ⓖ $f(x) = -x^2 + 4x - 2$
Ⓗ $f(x) = x^2 - 4x - 2$
Ⓙ $f(x) = -x^2 - 2x + 2$

44. Which of the following is NOT true of the graph of the function $f(x) = -x^2 - 6x + 5$?

Ⓐ Its vertex is at $(-3, 14)$.
Ⓑ Its axis of symmetry is $x = 14$.
Ⓒ Its maximum value is 14.
Ⓓ Its y-intercept is 5.

45. Which equation represents the axis of symmetry for $f(x) = 2x^2 - 4x + 5$?

Ⓕ $x = -4$ Ⓖ $x = 1$ Ⓗ $x = 2$ Ⓙ $x = 5$

46. **Short Response** Explain how to find the maximum value or minimum value of a quadratic function such as $f(x) = -x^2 - 8x + 4$.

CHALLENGE AND EXTEND

47. Write the equations in standard form for two quadratic functions that have the same vertex but open in different directions.

48. The graph of a quadratic function passes through the point $(-5, 8)$, and its axis of symmetry is $x = 3$.

a. What are the coordinates of another point on the graph of the function? Explain how you determined your answer.

b. Can you determine whether the graph of the function opens upward or downward? Explain.

49. **Critical Thinking** What conclusions can you make about the axis of symmetry and the vertex of a quadratic function of the form $f(x) = ax^2 + c$?

50. **Critical Thinking** Given the quadratic function f and the fact that $f(-1) = f(2)$, how can you find the axis of symmetry of this function?

Factoring Quadratic Expressions

Review the methods of factoring quadratic expressions in the examples below. Recall that the standard form of a quadratic expression is $ax^2 + bx + c$.

Examples

Factor each expression.

1 $x^2 - 3x - 10$

Because $a = 1$, use a table to find the factors of -10 that have a sum of -3. These factors are 2 and -5.

Factors of −10	Sum
−2 and 5	3 ✗
−1 and 10	9 ✗
1 and −10	−9 ✗
2 and −5	−3 ✔

Rewrite the expression as a product of binomial factors with 2 and -5 as constants.

$$x^2 - 3x - 10 = (x + 2)(x - 5)$$

Check your answer by multiplying.

$$(x + 2)(x - 5) = x^2 - 5x + 2x - 10$$
$$= x^2 - 3x - 10 \checkmark$$

2 $6x^2 - 15x$

Find the greatest common factor (GCF) of the terms.

$$6x^2 = 2 \cdot 3 \cdot x \cdot x$$
$$15x = 3 \cdot 5 \cdot x$$ *The GCF is 3x.*

Factor $3x$ from both terms.

$$6x^2 - 15x = 3x(2x - 5)$$

Check your answer by multiplying.

$$3x(2x - 5) = 3x(2x) - 3x(5)$$
$$= 6x^2 - 15x \checkmark$$

3 $-x^2 + 3x + 4$

Because a is negative, factor out -1.

$$-x^2 + 3x + 4 = -1(x^2 - 3x - 4)$$

Use the method from Example 1 to factor the expression in parentheses.

$$-(x^2 - 3x - 4) = -(x + 1)(x - 4)$$

Check your answer by multiplying.

$$-(x + 1)(x - 4) = -(x^2 - 3x - 4)$$
$$= -x^2 + 3x + 4 \checkmark$$

Try This

Factor each expression.

1. $4x^2 + 10x$ **2.** $16x - 2x^2$ **3.** $x^2 - 6x + 8$

4. $x^2 + 4x + 3$ **5.** $x^2 - 8x + 15$ **6.** $x^2 + 10x - 24$

7. $x^2 - x - 56$ **8.** $x^2 - 6x + 9$ **9.** $x^2 + 48x - 100$

10. $-x^2 + 12x - 32$ **11.** $-x^2 + x + 20$ **12.** $-x^2 - 14x - 13$

13. $4x^2 + 6x$ **14.** $x^2 + 14x + 24$ **15.** $x^2 - 16$

16. $2x^2 - x - 3$ **17.** $3x^2 + 16x + 5$ **18.** $2x^2 - 9x + 7$

Explore Graphs and Factors

You can use graphs and linear factors to find the x-intercepts of a parabola.

Use appropriate tools strategically.

Use with Solving Quadratic Equations by Graphing and Factoring

Graph the lines $y = x + 4$ and $y = x - 2$.

1. Press **Y=**, and enter **X + 4** for **Y1** and **X − 2** for **Y2**. Graph the functions in the square window by pressing **ZOOM** and choosing **5 : ZSquare**.
2. Identify the x-intercept of each line. The x-intercepts are -4 and 2.
3. Find the x-value halfway between the two x-intercepts. This x-value is the average of the x-intercepts: $\frac{-4+2}{2} = -1$.

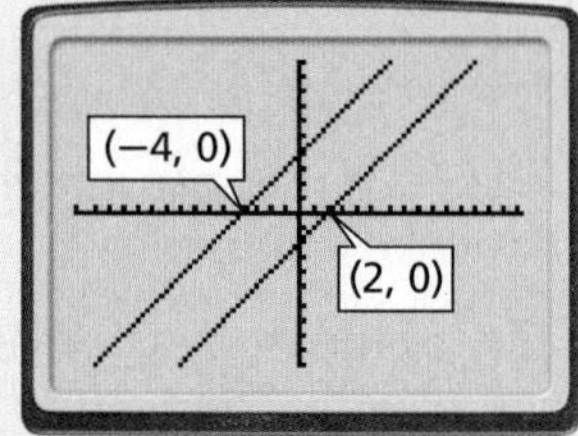

Graph the quadratic function $y = (x + 4)(x - 2)$, which is the product of the two linear factors graphed above.

4. Press **Y=** and enter **(X + 4)(X − 2)** for **Y3**. Press **GRAPH**.
5. Identify the x-intercepts of the parabola. The x-intercepts are -4 and 2. Notice that they are the same as those of the two linear factors.
6. Examine the parabola at $x = -1$ (the x-value that is halfway between the x-intercepts). The axis of symmetry and the vertex of the parabola occur at this x-value.

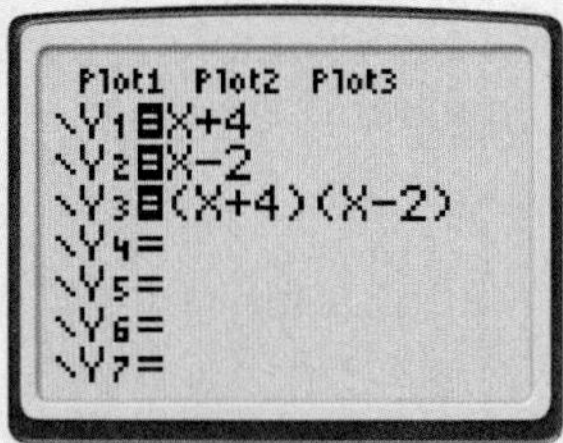

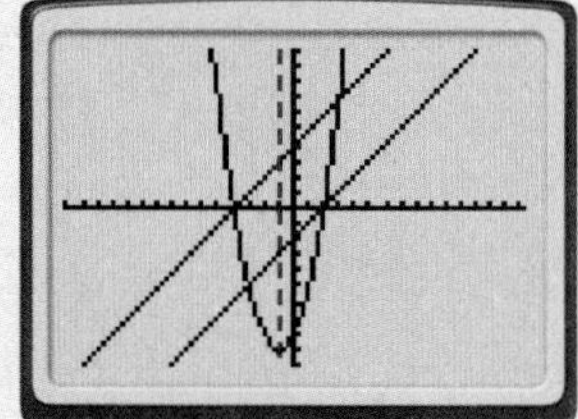

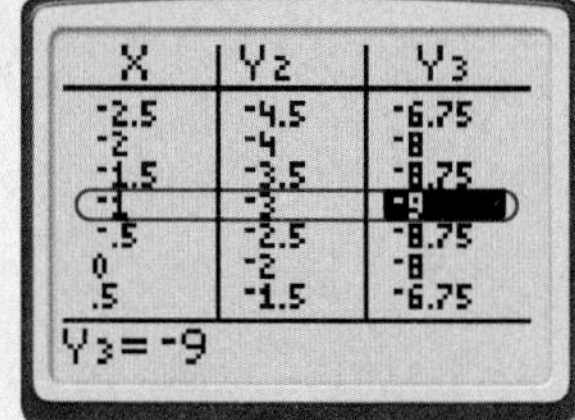

Try This

Graph each quadratic function and each of its linear factors. Then identify the x-intercepts and the axis of symmetry of each parabola.

1. $y = (x - 2)(x - 6)$
2. $y = (x + 3)(x - 1)$
3. $y = (x - 5)(x + 2)$
4. $y = (x + 4)(x - 4)$
5. $y = (x - 5)(x - 5)$
6. $y = (2x - 1)(2x + 3)$
7. **Critical Thinking** Use a graph to determine whether the quadratic function $y = 2x^2 + 5x - 12$ is the product of the linear factors $2x - 3$ and $x + 4$.
8. **Make a Conjecture** Make a conjecture about the linear factors, x-intercepts, and axis of symmetry of a quadratic function.

2-3 Solving Quadratic Equations by Graphing and Factoring

CC.9-12.F.IF.8a Use the process of factoring … to show zeros, extreme values, and symmetry of the graph, and interpret these in terms of a context. *Also* **CC.9-12.A.CED.1, CC.9-12.F.IF.7a*, CC.9-12.A.REI.11**

Objectives

Solve quadratic equations by graphing or factoring.

Determine a quadratic function from its roots.

Vocabulary

zero of a function
root of an equation
binomial
trinomial

Why learn this?

You can use quadratic functions to model the height of a football, baseball, or soccer ball. (See Example 3.)

When a soccer ball is kicked into the air, how long will the ball take to hit the ground? The height h in feet of the ball after t seconds can be modeled by the quadratic function $h(t) = -16t^2 + 32t$. In this situation, the value of the function represents the height of the soccer ball. When the ball hits the ground, the value of the function is zero.

A **zero of a function** is a value of the input x that makes the output $f(x)$ equal zero. The zeros of a function are the x-intercepts.

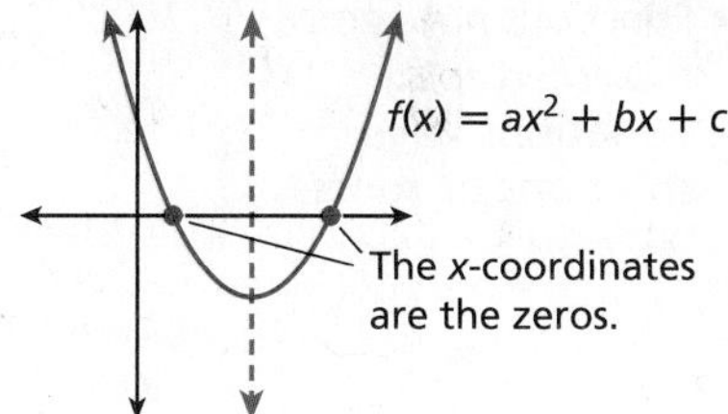

Unlike linear functions, which have no more than one zero, quadratic functions can have two zeros, as shown at right. These zeros are always symmetric about the axis of symmetry.

EXAMPLE 1 Finding Zeros by Using a Graph or Table

Find the zeros of $f(x) = x^2 + 2x - 3$ by using a graph and table.

Method 1 Graph the function $f(x) = x^2 + 2x - 3$.

The graph opens upward because $a > 0$. The y-intercept is -3 because $c = -3$.

Find the vertex: $x = -\frac{b}{2a} = -\frac{2}{2(1)} = -1$ *The x-coordinate of the vertex is $-\frac{b}{2a}$.*

Find $f(-1)$: $f(x) = x^2 + 2x - 3$

$f(-1) = (-1)^2 + 2(-1) - 3$ *Substitute −1 for x.*

$f(-1) = -4$

The vertex is $(-1, -4)$.

Plot the vertex and the y-intercept. Use symmetry and a table of values to find additional points.

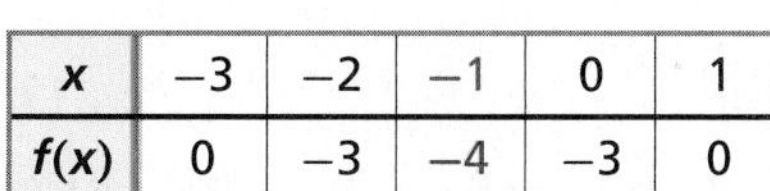

x	−3	−2	−1	0	1
$f(x)$	0	−3	−4	−3	0

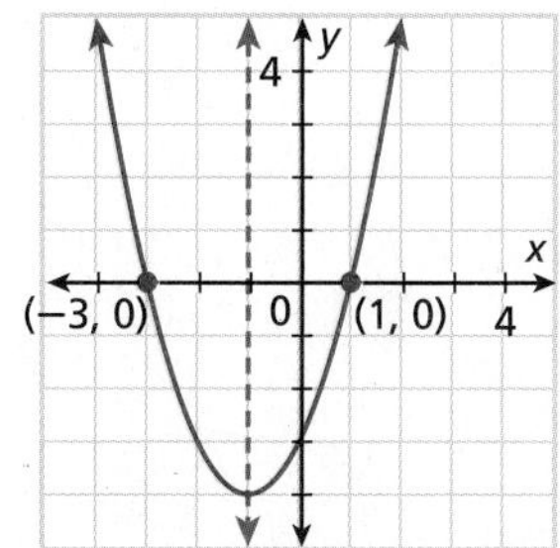

The table and the graph indicate that the zeros are −3 and 1.

Helpful Hint

Recall that for the graph of a quadratic function, *any* pair of points with the same *y*-value are symmetric about the axis of symmetry.

Find the zeros of $f(x) = x^2 + 2x - 3$ by using a graph and table.

Method 2 Use a calculator.

Enter $y = x^2 + 2x - 3$ into a graphing calculator.

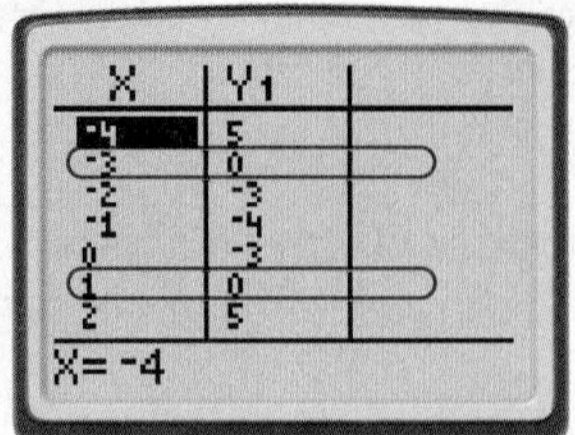

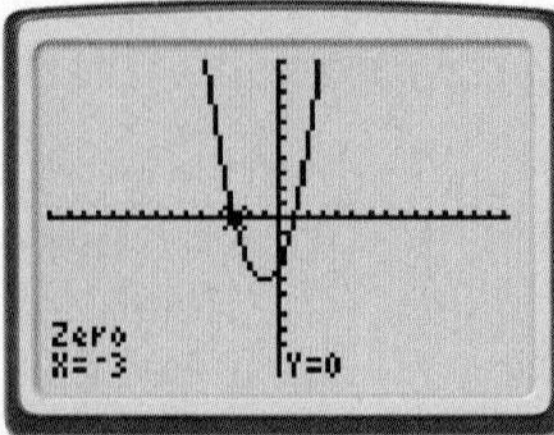

Both the table and the graph show that $y = 0$ at $x = -3$ and $x = 1$. These are the zeros of the function.

1. Find the zeros of $g(x) = -x^2 - 2x + 3$ by using a graph and a table.

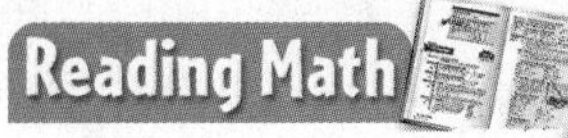

- Functions have *zeros* or *x-intercepts*.
- Equations have *solutions* or *roots*.

You can also find zeros by using algebra. For example, to find the zeros of $f(x) = x^2 + 2x - 3$, you can set the function equal to zero. The solutions to the related equation $x^2 + 2x - 3 = 0$ represent the zeros of the function.

The solutions to a quadratic equation of the form $ax^2 + bx + c = 0$ are *roots*. The **roots of an equation** are the values of the variable that make the equation true.

You can find the roots of some quadratic equations by factoring and applying the Zero Product Property.

Zero Product Property

For all real numbers *a* and *b*,

WORDS	NUMBERS	ALGEBRA
If the product of two quantities equals zero, at least one of the quantities equals zero.	$3(0) = 0$ $0(4) = 0$	If $ab = 0$, then $a = 0$ or $b = 0$.

EXAMPLE 2 Finding Zeros by Factoring

Find the zeros of each function by factoring.

A $f(x) = x^2 - 8x + 12$

$x^2 - 8x + 12 = 0$ *Set the function equal to 0.*

$(x - 2)(x - 6) = 0$ *Factor: Find factors of 12 that add to −8.*

$x - 2 = 0$ or $x - 6 = 0$ *Apply the Zero Product Property.*

$x = 2$ or $x = 6$ *Solve each equation.*

Check

$x^2 - 8x + 12$	$= 0$
$(2)^2 - 8(2) + 12$	0
$4 - 16 + 12$	0
0	0 ✔

$x^2 - 8x + 12$	$= 0$
$(6)^2 - 8(6) + 12$	0
$36 - 48 + 12$	0
0	0 ✔

Substitute each value into the original equation.

Find the zeros of each function by factoring.

B $g(x) = 3x^2 + 12x$

$3x^2 + 12x = 0$	*Set the function equal to 0.*
$3x(x + 4) = 0$	*Factor: The GCF is 3x.*
$3x = 0 \text{ or } x + 4 = 0$	*Apply the Zero Product Property.*
$x = 0 \text{ or } x = -4$	*Solve each equation.*

Check Check algebraically and by graphing.

$3x^2 + 12x = 0$		$3x^2 + 12x = 0$	
$3(0)^2 + 12(0)$	0	$3(-4)^2 + 12(-4)$	0
$0 + 0$	0 ✔	$48 - 48$	0 ✔

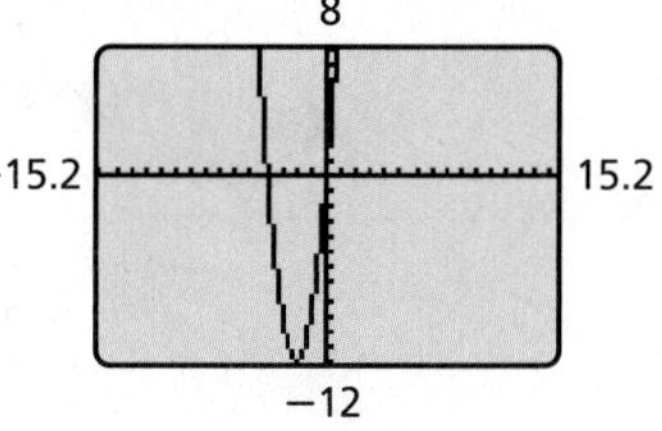

Find the zeros of each function by factoring.

2a. $f(x) = x^2 - 5x - 6$

2b. $g(x) = x^2 - 8x$

Any object that is thrown or launched into the air, such as a baseball, basketball, or soccer ball, is a *projectile*. The general function that approximates the height h in feet of a projectile on Earth after t seconds is given below.

$$h(t) = -16t^2 + v_0t + h_0$$

Constant due to Earth's gravity in ft/s² (−16) — **Initial vertical velocity in ft/s (at $t = 0$)** (v_0) — **Initial height in ft (at $t = 0$)** (h_0)

Note that this model has limitations because it does not account for air resistance, wind, and other real-world factors.

EXAMPLE 3 *Sports Application*

A soccer ball is kicked from ground level with an initial vertical velocity of 32 ft/s. After how many seconds will the ball hit the ground?

$h(t) = -16t^2 + v_0t + h_0$	*Write the general projectile function.*
$h(t) = -16t^2 + 32t + 0$	*Substitute 32 for v_0 and 0 for h_0.*

The ball will hit the ground when its height is zero.

$-16t^2 + 32t = 0$	*Set $h(t)$ equal to 0.*
$-16t(t - 2) = 0$	*Factor: The GCF is −16t.*
$-16t = 0 \text{ or } (t - 2) = 0$	*Apply the Zero Product Property.*
$t = 0 \text{ or } t = 2$	*Solve each equation.*

The ball will hit the ground in 2 seconds. Notice that the height is also zero when $t = 0$, the instant that the ball is kicked.

Check The graph of the function $h(t) = -16t^2 + 32t$ shows its zeros at 0 and 2.

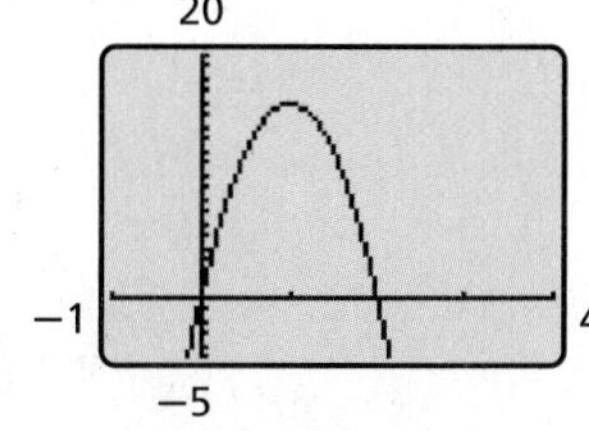

3. A football is kicked from ground level with an initial vertical velocity of 48 ft/s. How long is the ball in the air?

Quadratic expressions can have one, two, or three terms, such as $-16t^2$, $-16t^2 + 25t$, or $-16t^2 + 25t + 6$. Quadratic expressions with two terms are **binomials**. Quadratic expressions with three terms are **trinomials**. Some quadratic expressions with perfect squares have special factoring rules.

Special Products and Factors	
Difference of Two Squares	**Perfect-Square Trinomial**
$a^2 - b^2 = (a + b)(a - b)$	$a^2 - 2ab + b^2 = (a - b)^2$ $a^2 + 2ab + b^2 = (a + b)^2$

EXAMPLE 4 **Finding Roots by Using Special Factors**

Find the roots of each equation by factoring.

A $9x^2 = 1$

$9x^2 - 1 = 0$ — *Rewrite in standard form.*

$(3x)^2 - (1)^2 = 0$ — *Write the left side as $a^2 - b^2$.*

$(3x + 1)(3x - 1) = 0$ — *Factor the difference of squares.*

$3x + 1 = 0$ or $3x - 1 = 0$ — *Apply the Zero Product Property.*

$x = -\frac{1}{3}$ or $x = \frac{1}{3}$ — *Solve each equation.*

Check Graph each side of the equation on a graphing calculator. Let **Y1** equal $9x^2$, and let **Y2** equal 1. The graphs appear to intersect at $x = -\frac{1}{3}$ and at $x = \frac{1}{3}$.

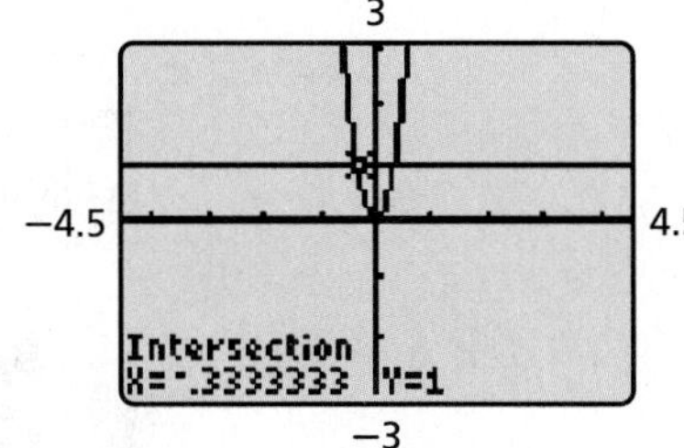

B $40x = 8x^2 + 50$

$8x^2 - 40x + 50 = 0$ — *Rewrite in standard form.*

$2(4x^2 - 20x + 25) = 0$ — *Factor. The GCF is 2.*

$4x^2 - 20x + 25 = 0$ — *Divide both sides by 2.*

$(2x)^2 - 2(2x)(5) + (5)^2 = 0$ — *Write the left side as $a^2 - 2ab + b^2$.*

$(2x - 5)^2 = 0$ — *Factor the perfect-square trinomial: $(a - b)^2$.*

$2x - 5 = 0$ or $2x - 5 = 0$ — *Apply the Zero Product Property.*

$x = \frac{5}{2}$ or $x = \frac{5}{2}$ — *Solve each equation.*

Check Substitute the root $\frac{5}{2}$ into the original equation.

$40x$	$= 8x^2 + 50$
$40\left(\frac{5}{2}\right)$	$8\left(\frac{5}{2}\right)^2 + 50$
100	100 ✓

Helpful Hint

A quadratic equation can have two roots that are equal, such as $x = \frac{5}{2}$ and $x = \frac{5}{2}$. Two equal roots are sometimes called a double root.

Find the roots of each equation by factoring.

4a. $x^2 - 4x = -4$

4b. $25x^2 = 9$

If you know the zeros of a function, you can work backward to write a rule for the function.

EXAMPLE  5 Using Zeros to Write Function Rules

Write a quadratic function in standard form with zeros 2 and −1.

$x = 2$ or $x = -1$	*Write the zeros as solutions for two equations.*
$x - 2 = 0$ or $x + 1 = 0$	*Rewrite each equation so that it equals 0.*
$(x - 2)(x + 1) = 0$	*Apply the converse of the Zero Product Property to write a product that equals 0.*
$x^2 - x - 2 = 0$	*Multiply the binomials.*
$f(x) = x^2 - x - 2$	*Replace 0 with $f(x)$.*

Check Graph the function $f(x) = x^2 - x - 2$ on a calculator. The graph shows the original zeros of 2 and −1.

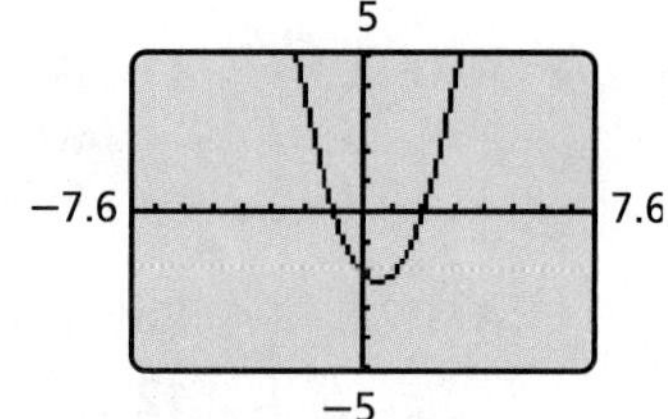

5. Write a quadratic function in standard form with zeros 5 and −5.

Note that there are many quadratic functions with the same zeros. For example, the functions $f(x) = x^2 - x - 2$, $g(x) = -x^2 + x + 2$, and $h(x) = 2x^2 - 2x - 4$ all have zeros at 2 and −1.

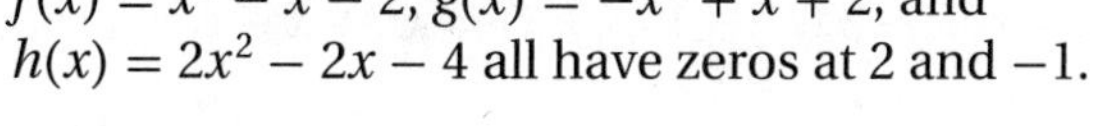

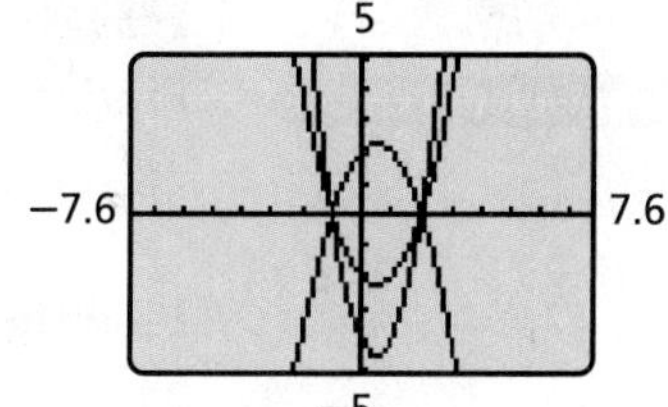

MATHEMATICAL PRACTICES

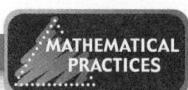

THINK AND DISCUSS

1. Describe the zeros of a function whose terms form a perfect square trinomial.

2. Compare the x- and y-intercepts of a quadratic function with those of a linear function.

3. A quadratic equation has no real solutions. Describe the graph of the related quadratic function.

4. GET ORGANIZED Copy and complete the graphic organizer. In each box, give information about special products and factors.

Name	Rule	Example	Graph
Difference of Two Squares			
Perfect-Square Trinomial			

2-3 Exercises

Learn It Online
Homework Help Online
Parent Resources Online

GUIDED PRACTICE

1. **Vocabulary** The solutions of the equation $3x^2 + 2x + 5 = 0$ are its __?__ . (*roots* or *zeros*)

SEE EXAMPLE 1

Find the zeros of each function by using a graph and table.

2. $f(x) = x^2 + 4x - 5$
3. $g(x) = -x^2 + 6x - 8$
4. $f(x) = x^2 - 1$

SEE EXAMPLE 2

Find the zeros of each function by factoring.

5. $f(x) = x^2 - 7x + 6$
6. $g(x) = 2x^2 - 5x + 2$
7. $h(x) = x^2 + 4x$
8. $f(x) = x^2 + 9x + 20$
9. $g(x) = x^2 - 6x - 16$
10. $h(x) = 3x^2 + 13x + 4$

SEE EXAMPLE 3

11. **Archery** The height h of an arrow in feet is modeled by $h(t) = -16t^2 + 63t + 4$, where t is the time in seconds since the arrow was shot. How long is the arrow in the air?

SEE EXAMPLE 4

Find the roots of each equation by factoring.

12. $x^2 - 6x = -9$
13. $5x^2 + 20 = 20x$
14. $x^2 = 49$

SEE EXAMPLE 5

Write a quadratic function in standard form for each given set of zeros.

15. 3 and 4
16. −4 and −4
17. 3 and 0

PRACTICE AND PROBLEM SOLVING

Independent Practice

For Exercises	See Example
18–20	1
21–26	2
27	3
28–33	4
34–36	5

Extra Practice

See Extra Practice for more Skills Practice and Applications Practice exercises.

Find the zeros of each function by using a graph and table.

18. $f(x) = -x^2 + 4x - 3$
19. $g(x) = x^2 + x - 6$
20. $f(x) = x^2 - 9$

Find the zeros of each function by factoring.

21. $f(x) = x^2 + 11x + 24$
22. $g(x) = 2x^2 + x - 10$
23. $h(x) = -x^2 + 9x$
24. $f(x) = x^2 - 15x + 54$
25. $g(x) = x^2 + 7x - 8$
26. $h(x) = 2x^2 - 12x + 18$
27. **Biology** A bald eagle snatches a fish from a lake and flies to an altitude of 256 ft. The fish manages to squirm free and falls back down into the lake. Its height h in feet can be modeled by $h(t) = 256 - 16t^2$, where t is the time in seconds. How many seconds will the fish fall before hitting the water?

Find the roots of each equation by factoring.

28. $x^2 + 8x = -16$
29. $4x^2 = 81$
30. $9x^2 + 12x + 4 = 0$
31. $36x^2 - 9 = 0$
32. $x^2 - 10x + 25 = 0$
33. $49x^2 = 28x - 4$

Write a quadratic function in standard form for each given set of zeros.

34. 5 and −1
35. 6 and 2
36. 3 and 3

Find the zeros of each function.

37. $f(x) = 6x - x^2$
38. $g(x) = x^2 - 25$
39. $h(x) = x^2 - 12x + 36$
40. $f(x) = 3x^2 - 12$
41. $g(x) = x^2 - 22x + 121$
42. $h(x) = 30 + x - x^2$
43. $f(x) = x^2 - 11x + 30$
44. $g(x) = x^2 - 8x - 20$
45. $h(x) = 2x^2 + 18x + 28$

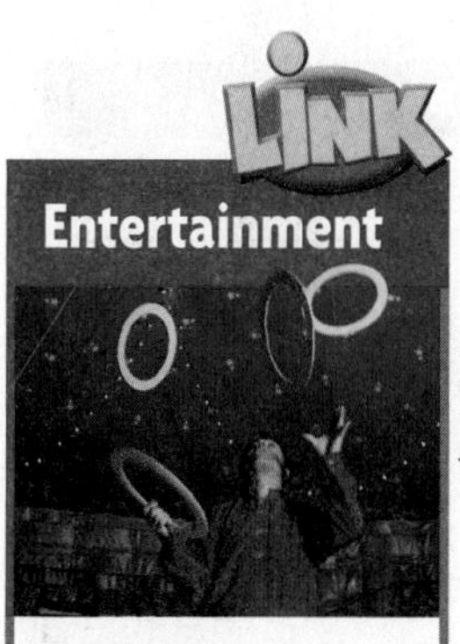

The Guinness world record for the greatest number of people juggling at one time was set in 1998 by 1508 people, each of whom juggled at least 3 objects for 10 seconds.

46. **Movies** A stuntwoman jumps from a building 73 ft high and lands on an air bag that is 9 ft tall. Her height above ground h in feet can be modeled by $h(t) = 73 - 16t^2$, where t is the time in seconds.

 a. **Multi-Step** How many seconds will the stuntwoman fall before touching the air bag? (*Hint:* Find the time t when the stuntwoman's height above ground is 9 ft.)

 b. **What if...?** Suppose the stuntwoman jumps from a building that is half as tall. Will she be in the air for half as long? Explain.

47. **Entertainment** A juggler throws a ball into the air from a height of 5 ft with an initial vertical velocity of 16 ft/s.

 a. Write a function that can be used to model the height h of the ball in feet t seconds after the ball is thrown.

 b. How long does the juggler have to catch the ball before it hits the ground?

Find the roots of each equation.

48. $x^2 - 2x + 1 = 0$
49. $x^2 + 6x = -5$
50. $25x^2 + 40x = -16$
51. $9x^2 + 6x = -1$
52. $5x^2 = 45$
53. $x^2 - 6 = x$

For each function, (a) find its vertex, (b) find its y-intercept, (c) find its zeros, and (d) graph it.

54. $f(x) = x^2 + 2x - 8$
55. $g(x) = x^2 - 16$
56. $h(x) = x^2 - x - 12$
57. $f(x) = -2x^2 + 4x$
58. $g(x) = x^2 - 5x - 6$
59. $h(x) = 3x^2 + x - 4$

60. **Geometry** The hypotenuse of a right triangle is 2 cm longer than one leg and 4 cm longer than the other leg.

 a. Let x represent the length of the hypotenuse. Use the Pythagorean Theorem to write an equation that can be solved for x.

 b. Find the solutions of the equation from part **a**.

 c. Are both solutions reasonable in the context of the problem situation? Explain.

Geometry Find the dimensions of each rectangle.

61. Rectangle: $A = 80\text{ ft}^2$; sides x and $x + 16$

62. Rectangle: $A = 210\text{ cm}^2$; sides x and $x + 1$

63. Rectangle: $A = 50\text{ m}^2$; sides $x - 3$ and $x + 2$

64. **Critical Thinking** Will a function whose rule can be factored as a binomial squared ever have two different zeros? Explain.

65. **Write About It** Explain how the Zero Product Property can be used to help determine the zeros of quadratic functions.

MULTI-STEP TEST PREP

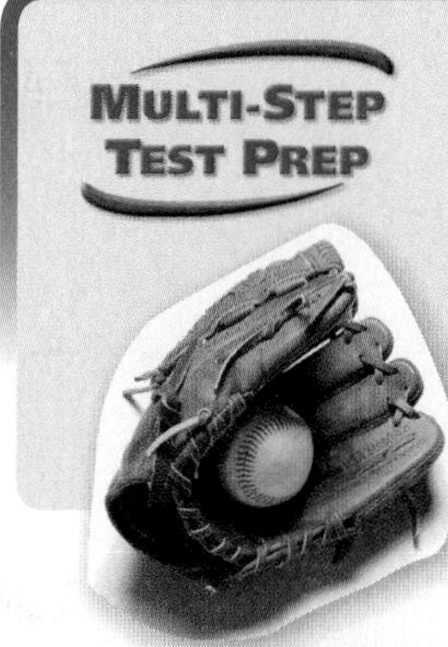

66. A baseball player hits a ball toward the outfield. The height h of the ball in feet is modeled by $h(t) = -16t^2 + 22t + 3$, where t is the time in seconds. In addition, the function $d(t) = 85t$ models the horizontal distance d traveled by the ball.

 a. If no one catches the ball, how long will it stay in the air?

 b. What is the horizontal distance that the ball travels before it hits the ground?

67. Use the graph provided to choose the best description of what the graph represents.

Ⓐ A ball is dropped from a height of 42 feet and lands on the ground after 3 seconds.

Ⓑ A ball is dropped from a height of 42 feet and lands on the ground after 1.5 seconds.

Ⓒ A ball is shot up in the air and reaches a height of 42 feet after 1 second.

Ⓓ A ball is shot up in the air, reaches a height of 42 feet, and lands on the ground after 1.5 seconds.

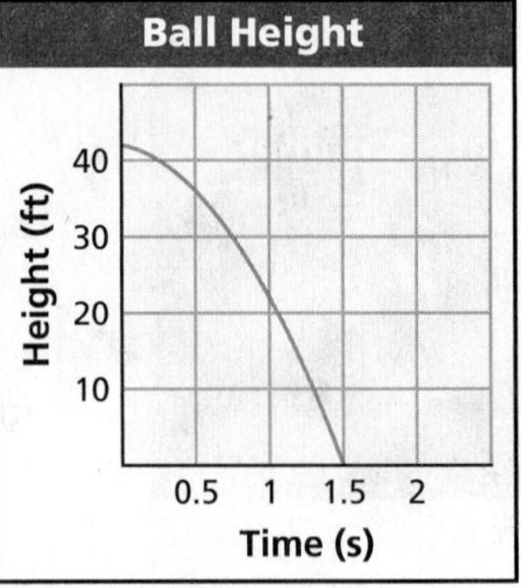

68. Which function has –7 as its only zero?

Ⓕ $f(x) = x(x - 7)$

Ⓖ $h(x) = (x - 7)^2$

Ⓗ $g(x) = (x + 1)(x + 7)$

Ⓙ $j(x) = (x + 7)^2$

69. Which expression is a perfect square trinomial?

Ⓐ $25y^2 - 16$

Ⓑ $25y^2 - 20y + 16$

Ⓒ $25y^2 - 40y + 16$

Ⓓ $25y^2 - 10y + 16$

70. **Gridded Response** Find the positive root of $x^2 + 4x - 21 = 0$.

CHALLENGE AND EXTEND

Find the roots of each equation by factoring.

71. $3(x^2 - x) = x^2$

72. $x^2 = \frac{1}{3}x$

73. $x^2 - \frac{3}{4}x + \frac{1}{8} = 0$

74. $x^2 + x + 0.21 = 0$

75. Another special factoring case involves perfect cubes. The sum of two cubes can be factored by using the formula $a^3 + b^3 = (a + b)(a^2 - ab + b^2)$.

a. Verify the formula by multiplying the right side of the equation.

b. Factor the expression $8x^3 + 27$.

c. Use multiplication and guess and check to find the factors of $a^3 - b^3$.

d. Factor the expression $x^3 - 1$.

2-4 Completing the Square

CC.9-12.F.IF.8a Use the process of … completing the square … to show zeros, extreme values, and symmetry of the graph, and interpret these in terms of a context. *Also* **CC.9-12.A.CED.1**

Objectives

Solve quadratic equations by completing the square.

Write quadratic equations in vertex form.

Vocabulary

completing the square

Why learn this?

You can solve quadratic equations to find how long water takes to fall from the top to the bottom of a waterfall. (See Exercise 39.)

Many quadratic equations contain expressions that cannot be easily factored. For equations containing these types of expressions, you can use square roots to find roots.

Square-Root Property

WORDS	NUMBERS	ALGEBRA
To solve a quadratic equation, you can take the square root of both sides. Be sure to consider the positive and negative square roots.	$x^2 = 15$ $\lvert x \rvert = \sqrt{15}$ $x = \pm\sqrt{15}$	If $x^2 = a$ and a is a nonnegative real number, then $x = \pm\sqrt{a}$.

EXAMPLE 1 Solving Equations by Using the Square Root Property

Solve each equation.

A $3x^2 - 4 = 68$

$3x^2 = 72$ — *Add 4 to both sides.*

$x^2 = 24$ — *Divide both sides by 3 to isolate the squared term.*

$x = \pm\sqrt{24}$ — *Take the square root of both sides.*

$x = \pm 2\sqrt{6}$ — *Simplify.*

Check Use a graphing calculator.

```
3*(2√(6))²-4
                68
3*(-2√(6))²-4
                68
```

Reading Math

Read $\pm\sqrt{a}$ as "plus or minus square root of a."

B $x^2 - 10x + 25 = 27$

$(x - 5)^2 = 27$ — *Factor the perfect square trinomial.*

$x - 5 = \pm\sqrt{27}$ — *Take the square root of both sides.*

$x = 5 \pm \sqrt{27}$ — *Add 5 to both sides.*

$x = 5 \pm 3\sqrt{3}$ — *Simplify.*

Check Use a graphing calculator.

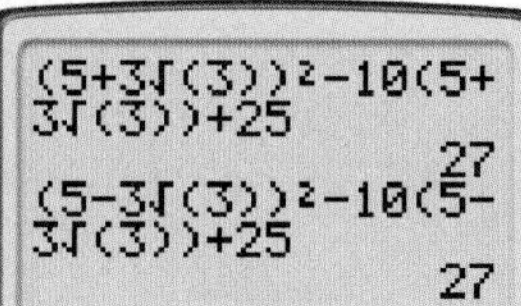

Solve each equation.

1a. $4x^2 - 20 = 5$

1b. $x^2 + 8x + 16 = 49$

The methods in the previous examples can be used only for expressions that are perfect squares. However, you can use algebra to rewrite any quadratic expression as a perfect square.

You can use algebra tiles to model a perfect square trinomial as a perfect square. The area of the square at right is $x^2 + 2x + 1$. Because each side of the square measures $x + 1$ units, the area is also $(x + 1)(x + 1)$, or $(x + 1)^2$. This shows that $(x + 1)^2 = x^2 + 2x + 1$.

If a quadratic expression of the form $x^2 + bx$ *cannot* model a square, you can add a term to form a perfect square trinomial. This is called **completing the square**.

Completing the Square

WORDS	NUMBERS	ALGEBRA
To complete the square of $x^2 + bx$, add $\left(\frac{b}{2}\right)^2$.	$x^2 + 6x + ■$ $x^2 + 6x + \left(\frac{6}{2}\right)^2$ $x^2 + 6x + 9$ $(x + 3)^2$	$x^2 + bx + ■$ $x^2 + bx + \left(\frac{b}{2}\right)^2$ $\left(x + \frac{b}{2}\right)^2$

The model shows completing the square for $x^2 + 6x$ by adding 9 unit tiles. The resulting perfect square trinomial is $x^2 + 6x + 9$. Note that completing the square does not produce an equivalent expression.

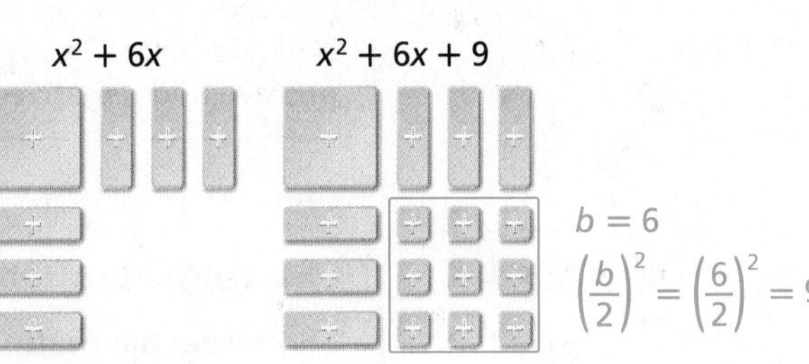

EXAMPLE 2 Completing the Square

Complete the square for each expression. Write the resulting expression as a binomial squared.

A $x^2 - 2x + ■$

$\left(\frac{-2}{2}\right)^2 = (-1)^2 = 1$ *Find $\left(\frac{b}{2}\right)^2$.*

$x^2 - 2x + 1$ *Add.*

$(x - 1)^2$ *Factor.*

Check Find the square of the binomial.

$$(x - 1)^2 = (x - 1)(x - 1)$$
$$= x^2 - 2x + 1$$

B $x^2 + 5x + ■$

$\left(\frac{5}{2}\right)^2 = \frac{25}{4}$ *Find $\left(\frac{b}{2}\right)^2$.*

$x^2 + 5x + \frac{25}{4}$ *Add.*

$\left(x + \frac{5}{2}\right)^2$ *Factor.*

Check Find the square of the binomial.

$$\left(x + \frac{5}{2}\right)^2 = \left(x + \frac{5}{2}\right)\left(x + \frac{5}{2}\right)$$
$$= x^2 + 5x + \frac{25}{4}$$

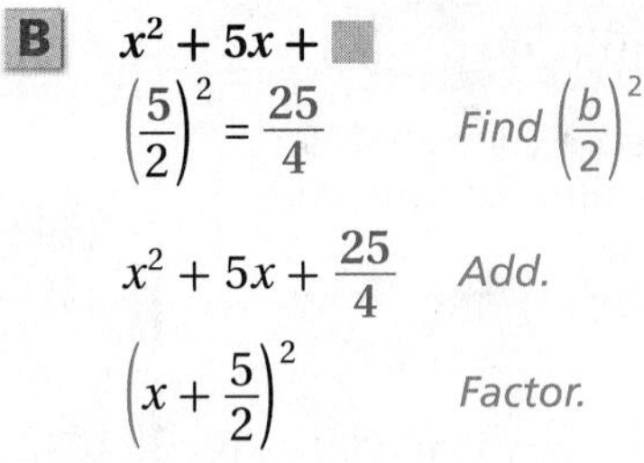

Complete the square for each expression. Write the resulting expression as a binomial squared.

2a. $x^2 + 4x + ■$ **2b.** $x^2 - 4x + ■$ **2c.** $x^2 + 3x + ■$

You can complete the square to solve quadratic equations.

Solving Quadratic Equations $ax^2 + bx + c = 0$ by Completing the Square

1. Collect variable terms on one side of the equation and constants on the other.
2. As needed, divide both sides by a to make the coefficient of the x^2-term 1.
3. Complete the square by adding $\left(\frac{b}{2}\right)^2$ to both sides of the equation.
4. Factor the variable expression as a perfect square.
5. Take the square root of both sides of the equation.
6. Solve for the values of the variable.

EXAMPLE 3 Solving a Quadratic Equation by Completing the Square

Solve each equation by completing the square.

A $x^2 = 27 - 6x$

$x^2 + 6x = 27$	*Collect variable terms on one side.*
$x^2 + 6x + \blacksquare = 27 + \blacksquare$	*Set up to complete the square.*
$x^2 + 6x + \left(\frac{6}{2}\right)^2 = 27 + \left(\frac{6}{2}\right)^2$	*Add $\left(\frac{b}{2}\right)^2$ to both sides.*
$x^2 + 6x + 9 = 27 + 9$	*Simplify.*
$(x + 3)^2 = 36$	*Factor.*
$x + 3 = \pm\sqrt{36}$	*Take the square root of both sides.*
$x + 3 = \pm 6$	*Simplify.*
$x + 3 = 6$ or $x + 3 = -6$	*Solve for x.*
$x = 3$ or $x = -9$	

Caution!

To keep the equation balanced, you must add $\left(\frac{b}{2}\right)^2$ to both sides of the equation.

B $2x^2 + 8x = 12$

$x^2 + 4x = 6$	*Divide both sides by 2.*
$x^2 + 4x + \blacksquare = 6 + \blacksquare$	*Set up to complete the square.*
$x^2 + 4x + \left(\frac{4}{2}\right)^2 = 6 + \left(\frac{4}{2}\right)^2$	*Add $\left(\frac{b}{2}\right)^2$ to both sides.*
$x^2 + 4x + 4 = 6 + 4$	*Simplify.*
$(x + 2)^2 = 10$	*Factor.*
$x + 2 = \pm\sqrt{10}$	*Take the square root of both sides.*
$x = -2 \pm \sqrt{10}$	*Solve for x.*

Solve each equation by completing the square.

3a. $x^2 - 2 = 9x$ **3b.** $3x^2 - 24x = 27$

Recall the vertex form of a quadratic function: $f(x) = a(x - h)^2 + k$, where the vertex is (h, k).

You can complete the square to rewrite any quadratic function in vertex form.

EXAMPLE 4 Writing a Quadratic Function in Vertex Form

Helpful Hint

In Example 3, the equation was balanced by adding $\left(\frac{b}{2}\right)^2$ to *both* sides. Here, the equation is balanced by adding and subtracting $\left(\frac{b}{2}\right)^2$ on *one* side.

Write each function in vertex form, and identify its vertex.

A $f(x) = x^2 + 10x - 13$

$f(x) = (x^2 + 10x + \blacksquare) - 13 - \blacksquare$ *Set up to complete the square.*

$f(x) = \left[x^2 + 10x + \left(\frac{10}{2}\right)^2\right] - 13 - \left(\frac{10}{2}\right)^2$ *Add and subtract* $\left(\frac{b}{2}\right)^2$.

$f(x) = (x + 5)^2 - 38$ *Simplify and factor.*

Because $h = -5$ and $k = -38$, the vertex is $(-5, -38)$.

Check Use the axis of symmetry formula to confirm the vertex.

$x = -\frac{b}{2a} = -\frac{10}{2(1)} = -5 \qquad y = f(-5) = (-5)^2 + 10(-5) - 13 = -38$ ✔

B $g(x) = 2x^2 - 8x + 3$

$g(x) = 2(x^2 - 4x) + 3$ *Factor so the coefficient of* x^2 *is 1.*

$g(x) = 2(x^2 - 4x + \blacksquare) + 3 - \blacksquare$ *Set up to complete the square.*

$g(x) = 2\left(x^2 - 4x + \left(\frac{-4}{2}\right)^2\right) + 3 - 2\left(\frac{-4}{2}\right)^2$ *Add* $\left(\frac{b}{2}\right)^2$. *Because* $\left(\frac{b}{2}\right)^2$ *is multiplied by 2, you must subtract* $2\left(\frac{b}{2}\right)^2$.

$g(x) = 2(x^2 - 4x + 4) - 5$ *Simplify.*

$g(x) = 2(x - 2)^2 - 5$ *Factor.*

Because $h = 2$ and $k = -5$, the vertex is $(2, -5)$.

Check A graph of the function on a graphing calculator supports your answer.

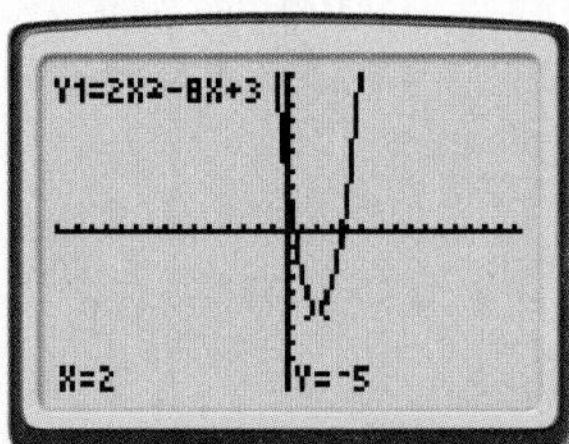

Write each function in vertex form, and identify its vertex.

4a. $f(x) = x^2 + 24x + 145$ **4b.** $g(x) = 5x^2 - 50x + 128$

MATHEMATICAL PRACTICES

THINK AND DISCUSS

1. Explain two ways to solve $x^2 = 25$.
2. Describe how to change a quadratic function from standard form to vertex form by completing the square.

3. **GET ORGANIZED** Copy and complete the graphic organizer. Compare and contrast two methods of solving quadratic equations.

Using Square-Root Property vs. Completing the Square
- Similarities
- Differences

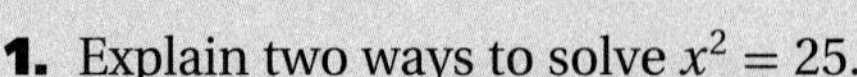

2-4 Exercises

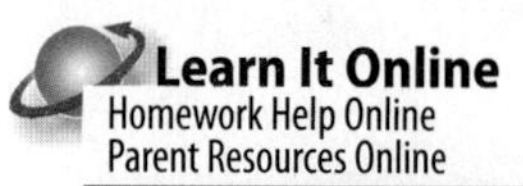

GUIDED PRACTICE

1. **Vocabulary** What must you add to the expression $x^2 + bx$ to *complete the square*?

SEE EXAMPLE 1 **Solve each equation.**

2. $(x - 2)^2 = 16$
3. $x^2 - 10x + 25 = 16$
4. $x^2 - 2x + 1 = 3$

SEE EXAMPLE 2 **Complete the square for each expression. Write the resulting expression as a binomial squared.**

5. $x^2 + 14x + \blacksquare$
6. $x^2 - 12x + \blacksquare$
7. $x^2 - 9x + \blacksquare$

SEE EXAMPLE 3 **Solve each equation by completing the square.**

8. $x^2 - 6x = -4$
9. $x^2 + 8 = 6x$
10. $2x^2 - 20x = 8$
11. $x^2 = 24 - 4x$
12. $10x + x^2 = 42$
13. $2x^2 + 8x - 15 = 0$

SEE EXAMPLE 4 **Write each function in vertex form, and identify its vertex.**

14. $f(x) = x^2 + 6x - 3$
15. $g(x) = x^2 - 10x + 11$
16. $h(x) = 3x^2 - 24x + 53$
17. $f(x) = x^2 + 8x - 10$
18. $g(x) = x^2 - 3x + 16$
19. $h(x) = 3x^2 - 12x - 4$

PRACTICE AND PROBLEM SOLVING

Independent Practice

For Exercises	See Example
20–22	1
23–25	2
26–31	3
32–37	4

Extra Practice

See Extra Practice for more Skills Practice and Applications Practice exercises.

Solve each equation.

20. $(x + 2)^2 = 36$
21. $x^2 - 6x + 9 = 100$
22. $(x - 3)^2 = 5$

Complete the square for each expression. Write the resulting expression as a binomial squared.

23. $x^2 - 18x + \blacksquare$
24. $x^2 + 10x + \blacksquare$
25. $x^2 - \frac{1}{2}x + \blacksquare$

Solve each equation by completing the square.

26. $x^2 + 2x = 7$
27. $x^2 - 4x = -1$
28. $2x^2 - 8x = 22$
29. $8x = x^2 + 12$
30. $x^2 + 3x - 5 = 0$
31. $3x^2 + 6x = 1$

Write each function in vertex form, and identify its vertex.

32. $f(x) = x^2 - 4x + 13$
33. $g(x) = x^2 + 14x + 71$
34. $h(x) = 9x^2 + 18x - 3$
35. $f(x) = x^2 + 4x - 7$
36. $g(x) = x^2 - 16x + 2$
37. $h(x) = 2x^2 + 6x + 25$

38. **Engineering** The height h above the roadway of the main cable of the Golden Gate Bridge can be modeled by the function $h(x) = \frac{1}{9000}x^2 - \frac{7}{15}x + 500$, where x is the distance in feet from the left tower.

a. Complete the square, and write the function in vertex form.

b. What is the vertex, and what does it represent?

c. **Multi-Step** The left and right towers have the same height. What is the distance in feet between them?

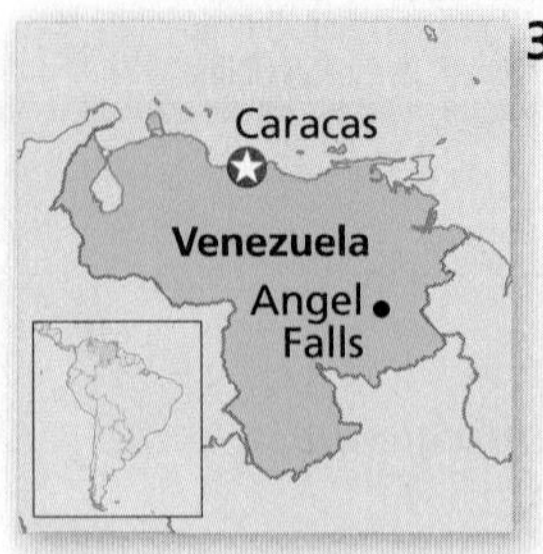

39. **Waterfalls** Angel Falls in Venezuela is the tallest waterfall in the world. Water falls uninterrupted for 2421 feet before entering the river below. The height h above the river in feet of water going over the edge of the waterfall is modeled by $h(t) = -16t^2 + 2421$, where t is the time in seconds after the initial fall.
    a. Estimate the time it takes for the water to reach the river.
    b. **Multi-Step** Ribbon Falls in California has a height of 1612 ft. Approximately how much longer does it take water to reach the bottom when going over Angel Falls than when going over Ribbon Falls?

40. **Sports** A basketball is shot with an initial vertical velocity of 24 ft/s from 6 ft above the ground. The ball's height h in feet is modeled by $h(t) = -16t^2 + 24t + 6$, where t is the time in seconds after the ball is shot. What is the maximum height of the ball, and when does the ball reach this height?

Solve each equation using square roots.

41. $x^2 - 1 = 2$
42. $25x^2 = 0$
43. $8x^2 - 200 = 0$
44. $-3x^2 + 6 = -1$
45. $(x + 13)^2 = 7$
46. $\left(x + \frac{1}{4}\right)^2 - \frac{9}{16} = 0$
47. $\left(x + \frac{3}{2}\right)^2 = \frac{25}{2}$
48. $x^2 + 14x + 49 = 64$
49. $9x^2 + 18x + 9 = 5$

50. **ERROR ANALYSIS** Two attempts to write $f(x) = 2x^2 - 8x$ in vertex form are shown. Which is incorrect? Explain the error.

A

$f(x) = 2x^2 - 8x$
$f(x) = 2(x^2 - 4x)$
$f(x) = 2(x^2 - 4x + 4) - 4$
$f(x) = 2(x - 2)^2 - 4$

B

$f(x) = 2x^2 - 8x$
$f(x) = 2(x^2 - 4x)$
$f(x) = 2(x^2 - 4x + 4) - 8$
$f(x) = 2(x - 2)^2 - 8$

Solve each equation by completing the square.

51. $x^2 + 8x = -15$
52. $x^2 + 22x = -21$
53. $3x^2 + 4x = 1$
54. $2x^2 = 5x + 12$
55. $x^2 - 7x - 2 = 0$
56. $x^2 = 4x + 11$
57. $x^2 + 6x + 4 = 0$
58. $5x^2 + 10x - 7 = 0$
59. $x^2 - 8x = 24$

LINK

Sports

Acapulco, Mexico, is famous for its cliff-diving shows. Divers perform complicated acrobatic dives from heights of up to 80 feet.

60. **Sports** A diver's height h in meters above the water is approximated by $h(t) = h_0 - 5t^2$, where h_0 is the initial height in meters, -5 is a constant based on the acceleration due to gravity in m/s^2, and t is the time in seconds that the diver falls through the air.
    a. Find the total time that the diver falls through the air for each type of dive in the table.
    b. How high is a dive that keeps the diver in the air twice as long as a 5-meter dive?
    c. The speed of a diver entering the water can be approximated by $s = 18t$, where s is the speed in kilometers per hour and t is the time in seconds. Using your results from part **a**, find the speed of the diver entering the water for each dive height.
    d. How many times as high is a dive that results in a speed that is twice as fast?

Dive Heights

Type	Height (m)
Platform	5
Platform	10
Cliff	20
Cliff	30

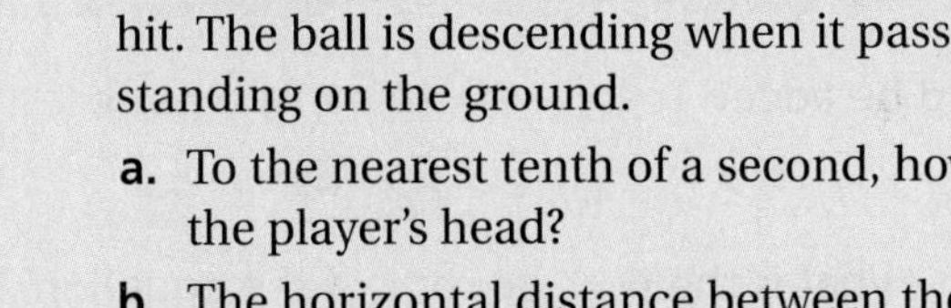

61. The height h in feet of a baseball hit from home plate can be modeled by the function $h(t) = -16t^2 + 32t + 5.5$, where t is the time in seconds since the ball was hit. The ball is descending when it passes 7.5 ft over the head of a 6 ft player standing on the ground.

a. To the nearest tenth of a second, how long after the ball is hit does it pass over the player's head?

b. The horizontal distance between the player and home plate is 120 ft. Use your answer from part **a** to determine the horizontal speed of the ball to the nearest foot per second.

62. Estimation A bag of grass seed will cover 525 square feet. Twenty bags of seed are used to cover an area shaped like a square. Estimate the side length of the square. Check your answer with a calculator.

63. Critical Thinking The functions f and g are defined by $f(x) = x^2 + 2x - 2$ and $g(x) = (x + 1)^2 - 3$. Use algebra to prove that f and g represent the same function.

64. Sports A player bumps a volleyball with an initial vertical velocity of 20 ft/s.

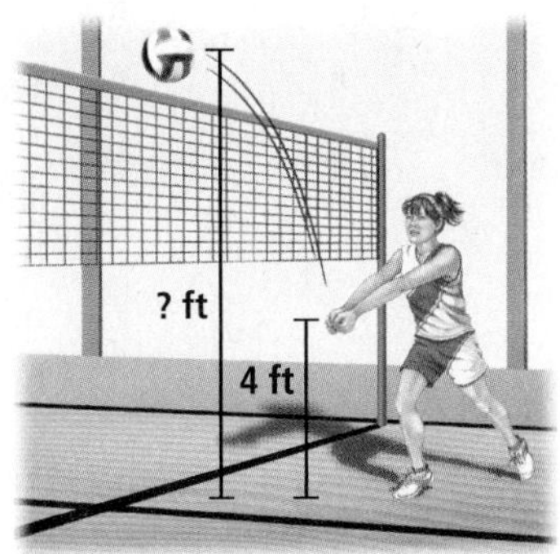

a. Write a function h in standard form for the ball's height in feet in terms of the time t in seconds after the ball is hit.

b. Complete the square to rewrite h in vertex form.

c. What is the maximum height of the ball?

d. What if...? Suppose the volleyball were hit under the same conditions, but with an initial velocity of 32 ft/s. How much higher would the ball go?

Graphing Calculator Use a graphing calculator to approximate the roots of each equation to the nearest thousandth.

65. $x^2 - 15 = 40$

66. $x^2 = 2.85$

67. $1.4x^2 = 24.6$

68. $(x + 0.6)^2 = 7.4$

69. $\frac{x^2}{7} = \frac{1}{3}$

70. $\left(x + \frac{1}{4}\right)^2 = \frac{5}{6}$

71. Critical Thinking Why do equations of the form $x^2 = k$ have no real solution when $k < 0$?

72. Write About It Compare the methods of factoring and completing the square for solving quadratic equations.

73. Which gives the solution to $3x^2 = 33$?

Ⓐ $\pm\sqrt{3}$ Ⓑ $\pm\sqrt{11}$ Ⓒ 11 Ⓓ 121

74. Which equation represents the graph at right?

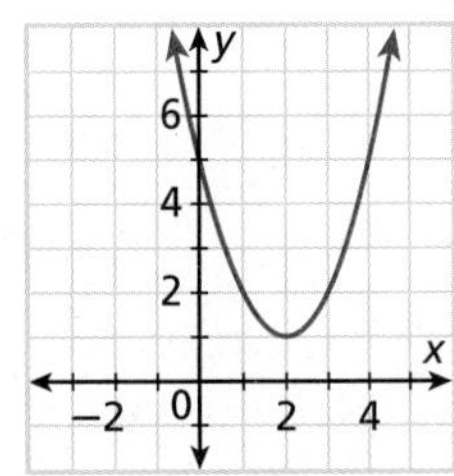

Ⓕ $y = (x - 2)^2 + 1$

Ⓖ $y = (x - 2)^2 - 1$

Ⓗ $y = (x + 2)^2 + 1$

Ⓙ $y = (x + 2)^2 - 1$

75. Which gives the vertex of the graph of $y = 3(x - 1)^2 - 22$?

Ⓐ $(1, -22)$ Ⓑ $(-1, -22)$ Ⓒ $(3, -22)$ Ⓓ $(-3, -22)$

76. Which number should be added to $x^2 + 14x$ to make a perfect square trinomial?

Ⓕ 7 Ⓖ 14 Ⓗ 49 Ⓙ 196

77. **Gridded Response** What is the positive root of the equation $2x^2 - x = 10$?

78. **Extended Response** Solve the quadratic equation $x^2 - 6x = 16$ by completing the square. Explain each step of the solution process, and check your answer.

CHALLENGE AND EXTEND

Find the value of *b* in each perfect square trinomial.

79. $x^2 - bx + 144$

80. $4x^2 - bx + 16$

81. $3x^2 + bx + 27$

82. $ax^2 + bx + c$

Find the zeros of each function.

83. $f(x) = x^2 - 4x\sqrt{5} + 19$

84. $f(x) = x^2 + 6x\sqrt{3} + 23$

85. **Farming** To create a temporary grazing area, a farmer is using 1800 feet of electric fencing to enclose a rectangular field and then to subdivide the field into two plots. The fence that divides the field into two plots is parallel to the field's shorter sides.

a. What is the largest area of the field that the farmer can enclose?

b. What are the dimensions of the field with the largest area?

c. **What if...?** What would be the largest area of a square field that the farmer could enclose and divide into two plots?

Plot 1

Plot 2

Areas of Composite Figures

Quadratic equations can be used to solve problems involving the areas of composite figures. Write an equation that represents the information given in the problem. Then solve the equation.

Example

The diagram shows a rectangular garden surrounded by a walkway. The garden measures 10 m by 34 m. The total area of the garden and walkway is 640 m^2. What is the width x of the walkway?

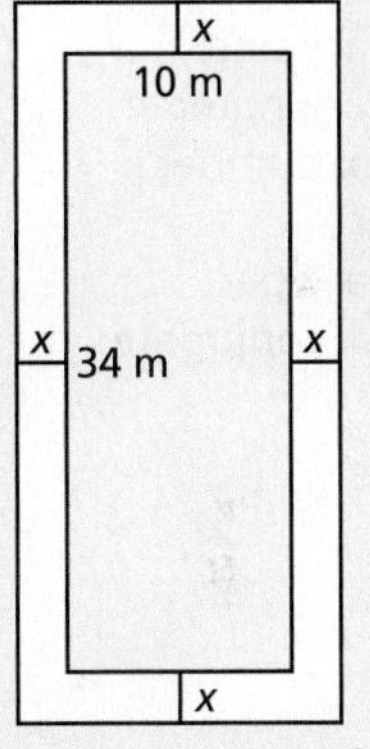

Total area = 640 m^2

The total area is equal to the total length multiplied by the total width. The total length is $2x + 34$ m, and the total width is $2x + 10$ m.

$A = \ell \times w$	*Write the formula for total area.*
$640 = (2x + 34)(2x + 10)$	*Substitute.*
$640 = 4x^2 + 88x + 340$	*Multiply the binomials.*
$0 = 4x^2 + 88x - 300$	*Subtract 640 from both sides.*
$0 = x^2 + 22x - 75$	*Divide both sides by 4.*
$0 = (x - 3)(x + 25)$	*Factor.*
$x - 3 = 0$ or $x + 25 = 0$	*Use the Zero Product Property.*
$x = 3$ or $x = -25$	*Solve for x.*

The width cannot be negative. Therefore, the width of the walkway is 3 m.

Try This

Write an equation that represents each problem. Then solve.

1. Use figure 1 below. A ring of grass with an area of 314 yd^2 surrounds a circular flower bed. Find the width x of the ring of grass.
2. Use figure 2 below. Sid cuts four congruent squares from the corners of a 30-in.-by-50-in. rectangular piece of cardboard so that it can be folded to make a box. Find the side length s of the squares, given that the area of the bottom of the box is 200 in^2.
3. Use figure 3 below. Harriet has 80 m of fencing materials to enclose three sides of a rectangular garden. She will use the side of her garage as a border for the fourth side. Find the width x of the garden if its area is to be 700 m^2.

Figure 1

x
10 yd

Grass area = 314 yd^2

Figure 2

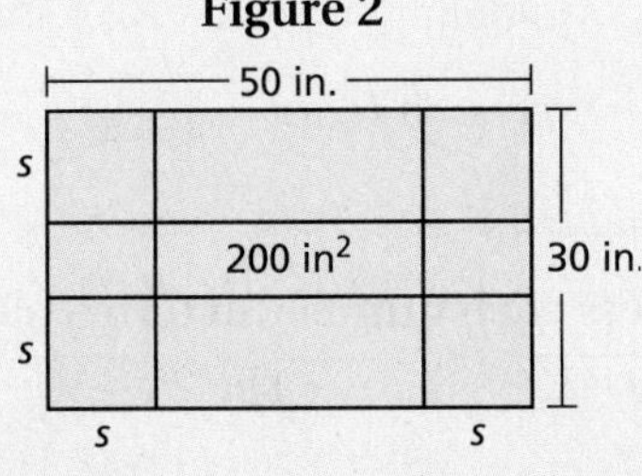

Figure 3

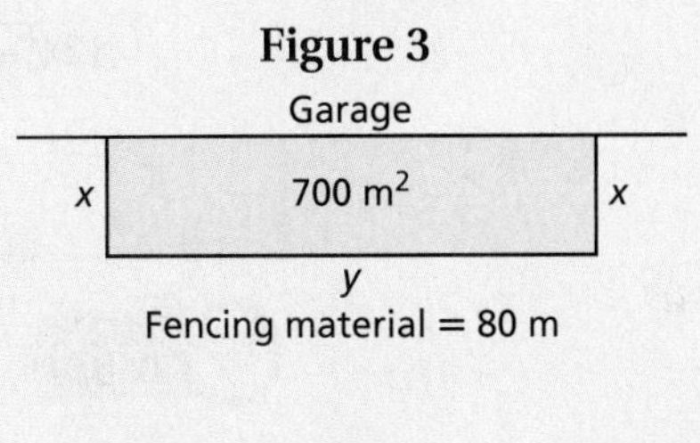

Fencing material = 80 m

COMMON CORE

2-5 Complex Numbers and Roots

CC.9-12.N.CN.1 Know there is a complex number i such that $i^2 = -1$, and every complex number has the form $a + bi$ with a and b real. *Also* **CC.9-12.N.CN.2, CC.9-12.N.CN.7, CC.9-12.A.CED.1**

Andrew Toos/CartoonResource.com

Objectives

Define and use imaginary and complex numbers.

Solve quadratic equations with complex roots.

Vocabulary

imaginary unit
imaginary number
complex number
real part
imaginary part
complex conjugate

Why learn this?

Complex numbers can be used to describe the zeros of quadratic functions that have no real zeros. (See Example 4.)

You can see in the graph of $f(x) = x^2 + 1$ below that f has no real zeros. If you solve the corresponding equation $0 = x^2 + 1$, you find that $x = \pm\sqrt{-1}$, which has no *real* solutions.

However, you can find solutions if you define the square root of negative numbers, which is why *imaginary numbers* were invented. The **imaginary unit** i is defined as $\sqrt{-1}$. You can use the imaginary unit to write the square root of any negative number.

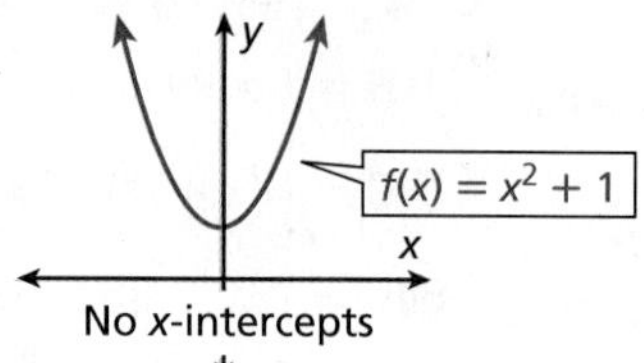

Know it! Note

Imaginary Numbers

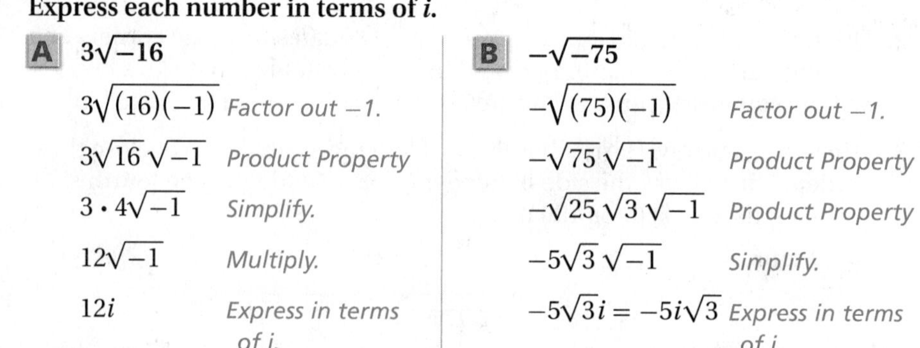

WORDS	NUMBERS	ALGEBRA
An **imaginary number** is the square root of a negative number.	$\sqrt{-1} = i$	If b is a positive real number,
Imaginary numbers can be written in the form bi, where b is a real number and i is the imaginary unit.	$\sqrt{-2} = \sqrt{-1}\sqrt{2} = i\sqrt{2}$ $\sqrt{-4} = \sqrt{-1}\sqrt{4} = 2i$	then $\sqrt{-b} = i\sqrt{b}$ and $\sqrt{-b^2} = bi$.
The square of an imaginary number is the original negative number.	$\left(\sqrt{-1}\right)^2 = i^2 = -1$	$\left(\sqrt{-b}\right)^2 = -b$

EXAMPLE 1 Simplifying Square Roots of Negative Numbers

Express each number in terms of *i*.

A $3\sqrt{-16}$

$3\sqrt{(16)(-1)}$	*Factor out −1.*
$3\sqrt{16}\sqrt{-1}$	*Product Property*
$3 \cdot 4\sqrt{-1}$	*Simplify.*
$12\sqrt{-1}$	*Multiply.*
$12i$	*Express in terms of i.*

B $-\sqrt{-75}$

$-\sqrt{(75)(-1)}$	*Factor out −1.*
$-\sqrt{75}\sqrt{-1}$	*Product Property*
$-\sqrt{25}\sqrt{3}\sqrt{-1}$	*Product Property*
$-5\sqrt{3}\sqrt{-1}$	*Simplify.*
$-5\sqrt{3}i = -5i\sqrt{3}$	*Express in terms of i.*

Express each number in terms of *i*.

1a. $\sqrt{-12}$ **1b.** $2\sqrt{-36}$ **1c.** $-\frac{1}{3}\sqrt{-63}$

EXAMPLE 2 Solving a Quadratic Equation with Imaginary Solutions

Solve each equation.

A $x^2 = -81$

$x = \pm\sqrt{-81}$ *Take square roots.*

$x = \pm 9i$ *Express in terms of i.*

Check

$x^2 = -81$	
$(9i)^2$	-81
$81i^2$	-81
$81(-1)$	-81 ✔

$x^2 = -81$	
$(-9i)^2$	-81
$81i^2$	-81
$81(-1)$	-81 ✔

B $3x^2 + 75 = 0$

$3x^2 = -75$ *Add −75 to both sides.*

$x^2 = -25$ *Divide both sides by 3.*

$x = \pm\sqrt{-25}$ *Take square roots.*

$x = \pm 5i$ *Express in terms of i.*

Check

$3x^2 + 75 = 0$	
$3(\pm 5i)^2 + 75$	0
$3(25)i^2 + 75$	0
$75(-1) + 75$	0 ✔

Solve each equation.

2a. $x^2 = -36$ **2b.** $x^2 + 48 = 0$ **2c.** $9x^2 + 25 = 0$

A **complex number** is a number that can be written in the form $a + bi$, where a and b are real numbers and $i = \sqrt{-1}$. The set of real numbers is a subset of the set of complex numbers $\mathbb{C}$.

Every complex number has a **real part** a and an **imaginary part** b.

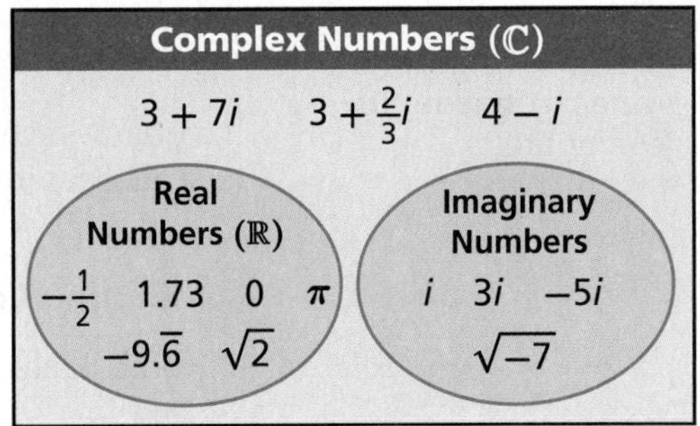

Real part Imaginary part

$$a + bi$$

Real numbers are complex numbers where $b = 0$. Imaginary numbers are complex numbers where $a = 0$ and $b \neq 0$. These are sometimes called *pure imaginary numbers.*

Two complex numbers are equal if and only if their real parts are equal and their imaginary parts are equal.

EXAMPLE 3 Equating Two Complex Numbers

Find the values of x and y that make the equation $3x - 5i = 6 - (10y)i$ true.

Real parts

$$3x - 5i = 6 - (10y)i$$

Imaginary parts

$3x = 6$ *Equate the real parts.*

$x = 2$ *Solve for x.*

$-5 = -(10y)$ *Equate the imaginary parts.*

$\frac{1}{2} = y$ *Solve for y.*

Find the values of x and y that make each equation true.

3a. $2x - 6i = -8 + (20y)i$ **3b.** $-8 + (6y)i = 5x - i\sqrt{6}$

EXAMPLE 4 Finding Complex Zeros of Quadratic Functions

Find the zeros of each function.

A $f(x) = x^2 - 2x + 5$

$x^2 - 2x + 5 = 0$	*Set equal to 0.*
$x^2 - 2x + \blacksquare = -5 + \blacksquare$	*Rewrite.*
$x^2 - 2x + 1 = -5 + 1$	*Add* $\left(\frac{b}{2}\right)^2$.
$(x - 1)^2 = -4$	*Factor.*
$x - 1 = \pm\sqrt{-4}$	*Take square roots.*
$x = 1 \pm 2i$	*Simplify.*

B $g(x) = x^2 + 10x + 35$

$x^2 + 10x + 35 = 0$

$x^2 + 10x + \blacksquare = -35 + \blacksquare$

$x^2 + 10x + 25 = -35 + 25$

$(x + 5)^2 = -10$

$x + 5 = \pm\sqrt{-10}$

$x = -5 \pm i\sqrt{10}$

Find the zeros of each function.

4a. $f(x) = x^2 + 4x + 13$ **4b.** $g(x) = x^2 - 8x + 18$

Helpful Hint

When given one complex root, you can always find the other by finding its conjugate.

The solutions $-5 + i\sqrt{10}$ and $-5 - i\sqrt{10}$ in Example 4B are related. These solutions are a *complex conjugate* pair. Their real parts are equal and their imaginary parts are opposites. The **complex conjugate** of any complex number $a + bi$ is the complex number $a - bi$.

If a quadratic equation with real coefficients has nonreal roots, those roots are complex conjugates.

EXAMPLE 5 Finding Complex Conjugates

Find each complex conjugate.

A $2i - 15$

$-15 + 2i$	*Write as a + bi.*
$-15 - 2i$	*Find a − bi.*

B $-4i$

$0 + (-4)i$	*Write as a + bi.*
$0 - (-4)i$	*Find a − bi.*
$4i$	*Simplify.*

Find each complex conjugate.

5a. $9 - i$ **5b.** $i + \sqrt{3}$ **5c.** $-8i$

THINK AND DISCUSS

1. Given that one solution of a quadratic equation is $3 + i$, explain how to determine the other solution.
2. Describe a number of the form $a + bi$ in which $a \neq 0$ and $b = 0$. Then describe a number in which $a = 0$ and $b \neq 0$. Are both numbers complex? Explain.

3. **GET ORGANIZED** Copy and complete the graphic organizer. In each box or oval, give a definition and examples of each type of number.

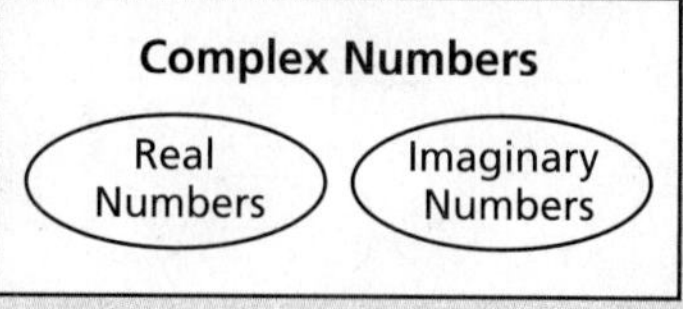

2-5 Exercises

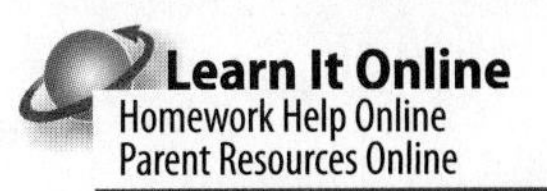

GUIDED PRACTICE

1. **Vocabulary** The number 7 is the __?__ part of the complex number $\sqrt{5} + 7i$. (*real* or *imaginary*)

SEE EXAMPLE 1 — **Express each number in terms of i.**

2. $5\sqrt{-100}$ 3. $\frac{1}{2}\sqrt{-16}$ 4. $-\sqrt{-32}$ 5. $\sqrt{-144}$

SEE EXAMPLE 2 — **Solve each equation.**

6. $x^2 = -9$ 7. $2x^2 + 72 = 0$ 8. $4x^2 = -16$ 9. $x^2 + 121 = 0$

SEE EXAMPLE 3 — **Find the values of x and y that make each equation true.**

10. $-2x + 6i = (-24y)i - 14$ 11. $-4 + (y)i = -12x - i + 8$

SEE EXAMPLE 4 — **Find the zeros of each function.**

12. $f(x) = x^2 - 12x + 45$ 13. $g(x) = x^2 + 6x + 34$

SEE EXAMPLE 5 — **Find each complex conjugate.**

14. $-9i$ 15. $\sqrt{5} + 5i$ 16. $8i - 3$ 17. $6 + i\sqrt{2}$

PRACTICE AND PROBLEM SOLVING

Independent Practice

For Exercises	See Example
18–21	1
22–25	2
26–27	3
28–31	4
32–35	5

Extra Practice

See Extra Practice for more Skills Practice and Applications Practice exercises.

Express each number in terms of i.

18. $8\sqrt{-4}$ 19. $-\frac{1}{3}\sqrt{-90}$ 20. $6\sqrt{-12}$ 21. $\sqrt{-50}$

Solve each equation.

22. $x^2 + 49 = 0$ 23. $5x^2 = -80$ 24. $3x^2 + 27 = 0$ 25. $\frac{1}{2}x^2 = -32$

Find the values of x and y that make each equation true.

26. $9x + (y)i - 5 = -12i + 4$ 27. $5(x - 1) + (3y)i = -15i - 20$

Find the zeros of each function.

28. $f(x) = x^2 + 2x + 3$ 29. $g(x) = 4x^2 - 3x + 1$

30. $f(x) = x^2 + 4x + 8$ 31. $g(x) = 3x^2 - 6x + 10$

Find each complex conjugate.

32. i 33. $-\frac{\sqrt{3}}{2} - 2i$ 34. $-2.5i + 1$ 35. $\frac{i}{10} - 1$

36. **What if...?** A carnival game asks participants to strike a spring with a hammer. The spring shoots a puck upward toward a bell. If the puck strikes the bell, the participant wins a prize. Suppose that a participant strikes the spring and shoots the puck according to the model $d(t) = 16t^2 - 32t + 18$, where d is the distance in feet between the puck and the bell and t is the time in seconds since the puck was struck. Is it possible for the participant to win a prize? Explain your answer.

18 ft

Given each solution to a quadratic equation, find the other solution.

37. $1 + 14i$

38. $\frac{5}{7}i$

39. $4i - 2\sqrt{5}$

40. $-12 - i$

41. $9 - i\sqrt{2}$

42. $-\frac{17i}{3}$

Find the values of c and d that make each equation true.

43. $2ci + 1 = -d + 6 - ci$

44. $c + 3ci = 4 + di$

45. $c^2 + 4i = d + di$

Solve each equation.

46. $8x^2 = -8$

47. $\frac{1}{3}x^2 = -27$

48. $2x^2 + 12.5 = 0$

49. $\frac{1}{2}x^2 + 72 = 0$

50. $x^2 = -30$

51. $2x^2 + 16 = 0$

52. $x^2 - 4x + 8 = 0$

53. $x^2 + 10x + 29 = 0$

54. $x^2 - 12x + 44 = 0$

55. $x^2 + 2x = -5$

56. $x^2 + 18 = -6x$

57. $-149 = x^2 - 24x$

LINK

Math History

The Swiss mathematician Leonhard Euler (1707–1783) was the first to use the notation i to represent $\sqrt{-1}$. He also introduced the notation $f(x)$ to represent the value of a function f at x.

Tell whether each statement is always, sometimes, or never true. If sometimes true, give examples to support your answer.

58. A real number is an imaginary number.

59. An imaginary number is a complex number.

60. A rational number is a complex number.

61. A complex number is an imaginary number.

62. An integer is a complex number.

63. Quadratic equations have no real solutions.

64. Quadratic equations have roots that are real and complex.

65. Roots of quadratic equations are conjugate pairs.

Find the zeros of each function.

66. $f(x) = x^2 - 10x + 26$

67. $g(x) = x^2 + 2x + 17$

68. $h(x) = x^2 - 10x + 50$

69. $f(x) = x^2 + 16x + 73$

70. $g(x) = x^2 - 10x + 37$

71. $h(x) = x^2 - 16x + 68$

72. **Critical Thinking** Can you determine the zeros of $f(x) = x^2 + 64$ by using a graph? Explain why or why not.

73. **Critical Thinking** What is the complex conjugate of a real number?

74. **Write About It** Explain the procedures you can use to solve for nonreal complex roots.

MULTI-STEP TEST PREP

75. A player throws a ball straight up toward the roof of an indoor baseball stadium. The height h in feet of the ball after t seconds can be modeled by the function $h(t) = -16t^2 + 112t$.

   a. The height of the roof is 208 ft. Solve the equation $208 = -16t^2 + 112t$.

   b. Based on your answer to part **a**, does the ball hit the roof? Explain your answer.

   c. Based on the function model, what is the maximum height that the ball will reach?

76. What is the complex conjugate of $-2 + i$?

Ⓐ $2 + i$ Ⓑ $2 - i$ Ⓒ $i - 2$ Ⓓ $-2 - i$

77. Express $\sqrt{-225}$ in terms of i.

Ⓕ $15i$ Ⓖ $-15i$ Ⓗ $i\sqrt{15}$ Ⓙ $-i\sqrt{15}$

78. Find the zeros of $f(x) = x^2 - 2x + 17$.

Ⓐ $1 \pm 4i$ Ⓑ $4 \pm i$ Ⓒ $-1 \pm 4i$ Ⓓ $-4 \pm i$

79. What value of c makes the equation $3 - 4i - 5 = (9 + ci) - 11$ true?

Ⓕ -2 Ⓖ -4 Ⓗ 2 Ⓙ 4

80. Which of the following equations has roots of $-6i$ and $6i$?

Ⓐ $-\frac{1}{6}x^2 = 6$ Ⓒ $\frac{1}{4}x^2 = 9$

Ⓑ $x^2 - 30 = 6$ Ⓓ $20 - x^2 = -16$

81. **Short Response** Explain the types of solutions that equations of the form $x^2 = a$ have when $a < 0$ and when $a > 0$.

CHALLENGE AND EXTEND

82. Find the complex number $a + bi$ such that $5a + 3b = 1$ and $-5b = 7 + 4a$.

83. Can a quadratic equation have only one real number root? only one imaginary root? only one complex root? Explain.

84. Given the general form of a quadratic equation $x^2 + bx + c = 0$, determine the effect of each condition on the solutions.

a. $b = 0$ **b.** $c \leq 0$ **c.** $c > 0$

d. What is needed for the solutions to have imaginary parts?

COMMON CORE

2-6 The Quadratic Formula

CC.9-12.N.CN.7 Solve quadratic equations with real coefficients that have complex solutions. *Also* **CC.9-12.A.CED.1**

Objectives

Solve quadratic equations using the Quadratic Formula.

Classify roots using the discriminant.

Vocabulary

discriminant

Who uses this?

Firefighting pilots can use the Quadratic Formula to estimate when to release water on a fire. (See Example 4.)

You have learned several methods for solving quadratic equations: graphing, making tables, factoring, using square roots, and completing the square. Another method is to use the *Quadratic Formula,* which allows you to solve a quadratic equation in standard form.

By completing the square on the standard form of a quadratic equation, you can determine the Quadratic Formula.

Numbers		Algebra
$3x^2 + 5x + 1 = 0$		$ax^2 + bx + c = 0\ (a \neq 0)$
$x^2 + \frac{5}{3}x + \frac{1}{3} = 0$	*Divide by a.*	$x^2 + \frac{b}{a}x + \frac{c}{a} = 0$
$x^2 + \frac{5}{3}x = -\frac{1}{3}$	*Subtract $\frac{c}{a}$.*	$x^2 + \frac{b}{a}x = -\frac{c}{a}$
$x^2 + \frac{5}{3}x + \left(\frac{5}{2(3)}\right)^2 = -\frac{1}{3} + \left(\frac{5}{2(3)}\right)^2$	*Complete the square.*	$x^2 + \frac{b}{a}x + \left(\frac{b}{2a}\right)^2 = -\frac{c}{a} + \left(\frac{b}{2a}\right)^2$
$\left(x + \frac{5}{6}\right)^2 = \frac{25}{36} - \frac{1}{3}$	*Factor.*	$\left(x + \frac{b}{2a}\right)^2 = \frac{b^2}{4a^2} - \frac{c}{a}$
$x + \frac{5}{6} = \pm\sqrt{\frac{13}{36}}$	*Take square roots.*	$x + \frac{b}{2a} = \pm\sqrt{\frac{b^2 - 4ac}{4a^2}}$
$x = -\frac{5}{6} \pm \frac{\sqrt{13}}{6}$	*Subtract $\frac{b}{2a}$.*	$x = -\frac{b}{2a} \pm \frac{\sqrt{b^2 - 4ac}}{2a}$
$x = \frac{-5 \pm \sqrt{13}}{6}$	*Simplify.*	$x = \frac{-b \pm \sqrt{b^2 - 4ac}}{2a}$

To subtract fractions, you need a common denominator.

$$\frac{b^2}{4a^2} - \frac{c}{a}$$

$$\frac{b^2}{4a^2} - \frac{c}{a}\left(\frac{4a}{4a}\right)$$

$$\frac{b^2 - 4ac}{4a^2}$$

The symmetry of a quadratic function is evident in the next to last step, $x = -\frac{b}{2a} \pm \frac{\sqrt{b^2 - 4ac}}{2a}$. These two zeros are the same distance, $\frac{\sqrt{b^2 - 4ac}}{2a}$, away from the axis of symmetry, $x = -\frac{b}{2a}$, with one zero on either side of the vertex.

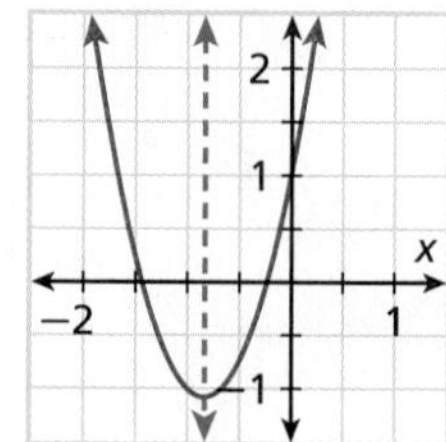

The Quadratic Formula

If $ax^2 + bx + c = 0\ (a \neq 0)$, then the solutions, or roots, are

$$x = \frac{-b \pm \sqrt{b^2 - 4ac}}{2a}.$$

You can use the Quadratic Formula to solve any quadratic equation that is written in standard form, including equations with real solutions or complex solutions.

EXAMPLE 1 **Quadratic Functions with Real Zeros**

Find the zeros of $f(x) = x^2 + 10x + 2$ by using the Quadratic Formula.

$x^2 + 10x + 2 = 0$ *Set f(x) = 0.*

$x = \frac{-b \pm \sqrt{b^2 - 4ac}}{2a}$ *Write the Quadratic Formula.*

$x = \frac{-10 \pm \sqrt{(10)^2 - 4(1)(2)}}{2(1)}$ *Substitute 1 for a, 10 for b, and 2 for c.*

$x = \frac{-10 \pm \sqrt{100 - 8}}{2} = \frac{-10 \pm \sqrt{92}}{2}$ *Simplify.*

$x = \frac{-10 \pm 2\sqrt{23}}{2} = -5 \pm \sqrt{23}$ *Write in simplest form.*

Check Solve by completing the square.

$$x^2 + 10x + 2 = 0$$
$$x^2 + 10x = -2$$
$$x^2 + 10x + 25 = -2 + 25$$
$$(x + 5)^2 = 23$$
$$x = -5 \pm \sqrt{23} \checkmark$$

Find the zeros of each function by using the Quadratic Formula.

1a. $f(x) = x^2 + 3x - 7$ **1b.** $g(x) = x^2 - 8x + 10$

EXAMPLE 2 **Quadratic Functions with Complex Zeros**

Find the zeros of $f(x) = 2x^2 - x + 2$ by using the Quadratic Formula.

$2x^2 - x + 2 = 0$ *Set f(x) = 0.*

$x = \frac{-b \pm \sqrt{b^2 - 4ac}}{2a}$ *Write the Quadratic Formula.*

$x = \frac{-(-1) \pm \sqrt{(-1)^2 - 4(2)(2)}}{2(2)}$ *Substitute 2 for a, −1 for b, and 2 for c.*

$x = \frac{1 \pm \sqrt{1 - 16}}{4} = \frac{1 \pm \sqrt{-15}}{4}$ *Simplify.*

$x = \frac{1 \pm i\sqrt{15}}{4} = \frac{1}{4} \pm \frac{\sqrt{15}}{4}i$ *Write in terms of i.*

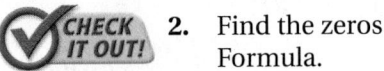

2. Find the zeros of $g(x) = 3x^2 - x + 8$ by using the Quadratic Formula.

The **discriminant** is part of the Quadratic Formula that you can use to determine the number of real roots of a quadratic equation.

$x = \frac{-b \pm \sqrt{b^2 - 4ac}}{2a}$ ← **Discriminant**

Discriminant

The discriminant of the quadratic equation $ax^2 + bx + c = 0$ $(a \neq 0)$ is $b^2 - 4ac$.

$b^2 - 4ac > 0$	$b^2 - 4ac = 0$	$b^2 - 4ac < 0$
two distinct real solutions	one distinct real solution	two distinct nonreal complex solutions

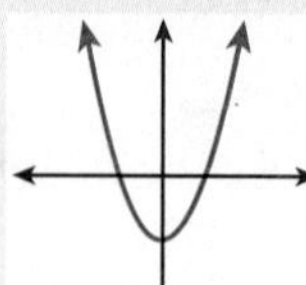

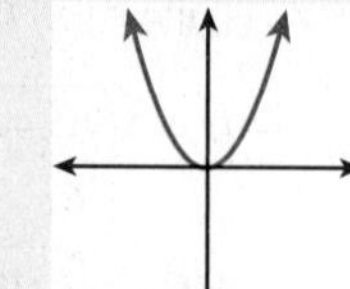

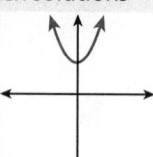

EXAMPLE 3 Analyzing Quadratic Equations by Using the Discriminant

Find the type and number of solutions for each equation.

Caution!

Make sure the equation is in standard form before you evaluate the discriminant, $b^2 - 4ac$.

A $x^2 - 6x = -7$

$x^2 - 6x + 7 = 0$

$b^2 - 4ac$

$(-6)^2 - 4(1)(7)$

$36 - 28 = 8$

$b^2 - 4ac > 0$; the equation has two distinct real solutions.

B $x^2 - 6x = -9$

$x^2 - 6x + 9 = 0$

$b^2 - 4ac$

$(-6)^2 - 4(1)(9)$

$36 - 36 = 0$

$b^2 - 4ac = 0$; the equation has one distinct real solution.

C $x^2 - 6x = -11$

$x^2 - 6x + 11 = 0$

$b^2 - 4ac$

$(-6)^2 - 4(1)(11)$

$36 - 44 = -8$

$b^2 - 4ac < 0$; the equation has two distinct nonreal complex solutions.

CHECK IT OUT! **Find the type and number of solutions for each equation.**

3a. $x^2 - 4x = -4$ **3b.** $x^2 - 4x = -8$ **3c.** $x^2 - 4x = 2$

The graph shows the related functions for Example 3. Notice that the number of real solutions for the equation can be changed by changing the value of the constant c.

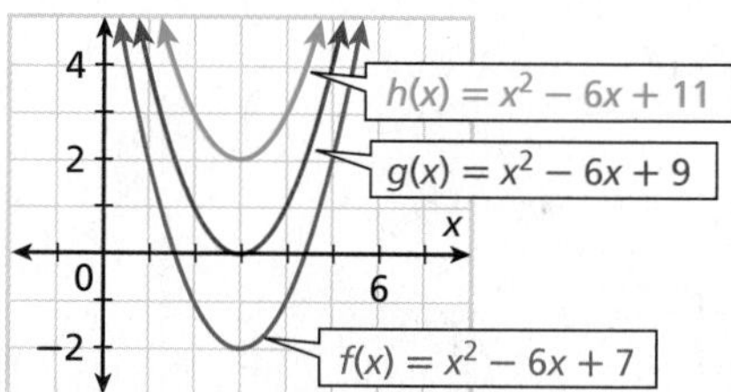

Student to Student

Double-Checking Roots

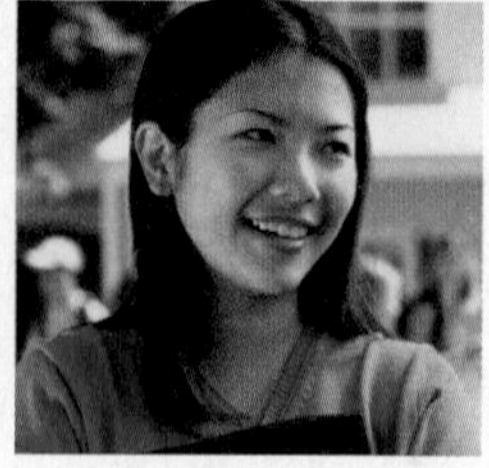

Terry Cannon, Carver High School

If I get integer roots when I use the Quadratic Formula, I know that I can quickly factor to check the roots. Look at my work for the equation $x^2 - 7x + 10 = 0$.

Quadratic Formula:

$$x = \frac{-(-7) \pm \sqrt{(-7)^2 - 4(1)(10)}}{2(1)}$$

$$= \frac{7 \pm \sqrt{9}}{2} = \frac{10}{2} \text{ or } \frac{4}{2} = 5 \text{ or } 2$$

Factoring:

$x^2 - 7x + 10 = 0$

$(x - 5)(x - 2) = 0$

$x = 5$ or $x = 2$

EXAMPLE 4 Aviation Application

The pilot of a helicopter plans to release a bucket of water on a forest fire. The height y in feet of the water t seconds after its release is modeled by $y = -16t^2 - 2t + 500$. The horizontal distance x in feet between the water and its point of release is modeled by $x = 91t$. At what horizontal distance from the fire should the pilot start releasing the water in order to hit the target?

Step 1 Use the first equation to determine how long it will take the water to hit the ground. Set the height of the water equal to 0 feet, and use the quadratic formula to solve for t.

$$y = -16t^2 - 2t + 500$$

$$0 = -16t^2 - 2t + 500 \quad \textit{Set y equal to 0.}$$

$$t = \frac{-b \pm \sqrt{b^2 - 4ac}}{2a} \quad \textit{Use the Quadratic Formula.}$$

$$t = \frac{-(-2) \pm \sqrt{(-2)^2 - 4(-16)(500)}}{2(-16)} \quad \textit{Substitute for a, b, and c.}$$

$$t = \frac{2 \pm \sqrt{32{,}004}}{-32} \quad \textit{Simplify.}$$

$$t \approx -5.65 \text{ or } t \approx 5.53$$

The time cannot be negative, so the water lands on the target about 5.5 seconds after it is released.

Step 2 Find the horizontal distance that the water will have traveled in this time.

$$x = 91t$$

$$x = 91(5.5) \quad \textit{Substitute 5.5 for t.}$$

$$x = 500.5 \quad \textit{Simplify.}$$

The water will have traveled a horizontal distance of about 500 feet. Therefore, the pilot should start releasing the water when the horizontal distance between the helicopter and the fire is 500 feet.

Check Use substitution to check that the water hits the ground after about 5.53 seconds.

$$y = -16t^2 - 2t + 500$$

$$y = -16(5.53)^2 - 2(5.53) + 500$$

$$y \approx -0.3544 \checkmark \quad \textit{The height is approximately equal to 0 when } t = 5.53.$$

Caution!

Once you have found the value of t, you have solved only part of the problem. You will use this value to find the answer you are looking for.

Use the information given above to answer the following.

4. The pilot's altitude decreases, which changes the function describing the water's height to $y = -16t^2 - 2t + 400$. To the nearest foot, at what horizontal distance from the target should the pilot begin releasing the water?

Summary of Solving Quadratic Equations		
Method	**When to Use**	**Examples**
Graphing	Only approximate solutions or the number of real solutions is needed.	$2x^2 + 5x - 14 = 0$ $x \approx -4.2$ or $x \approx 1.7$
Factoring	$c = 0$ or the expression is easily factorable.	$x^2 + 4x + 3 = 0$ $(x + 3)(x + 1) = 0$ $x = -3$ or $x = -1$
Square roots	The variable side of the equation is a perfect square.	$(x - 5)^2 = 24$ $\sqrt{(x - 5)^2} = \pm\sqrt{24}$ $x - 5 = \pm 2\sqrt{6}$ $x = 5 \pm 2\sqrt{6}$
Completing the square	$a = 1$ and b is an even number.	$x^2 + 6x = 10$ $x^2 + 6x + \square = 10 + \square$ $x^2 + 6x + \left(\frac{6}{2}\right)^2 = 10 + \left(\frac{6}{2}\right)^2$ $(x + 3)^2 = 19$ $x = -3 \pm \sqrt{19}$
Quadratic Formula	Numbers are large or complicated, and the expression does not factor easily.	$5x^2 - 7x - 8 = 0$ $x = \frac{-(-7) \pm \sqrt{(-7)^2 - 4(5)(-8)}}{2(5)}$ $x = \frac{7 \pm \sqrt{209}}{10}$

Helpful Hint

No matter which method you use to solve a quadratic equation, you should get the same answer.

THINK AND DISCUSS

1. Describe how the graphs of quadratic functions illustrate the type and number of zeros.

2. Describe the values of c for which the equation $x^2 + 8x + c = 0$ will have zero, one, or two distinct solutions.

3. GET ORGANIZED Copy and complete the graphic organizer. Describe the possible solution methods for each value of the discriminant.

Value of Discriminant	Type of Solutions	Possible Solution Methods
Negative		
Zero		
Positive		

2-6 Exercises

Learn It Online
Homework Help Online
Parent Resources Online

GUIDED PRACTICE

1. **Vocabulary** What information does the value of the *discriminant* give about a quadratic equation?

SEE EXAMPLE 1

Find the zeros of each function by using the Quadratic Formula.

2. $f(x) = x^2 + 7x + 10$
3. $g(x) = 3x^2 - 4x - 1$
4. $h(x) = 3x^2 - 5x$
5. $g(x) = -x^2 - 5x + 6$
6. $h(x) = 4x^2 - 5x - 6$
7. $f(x) = 2x^2 - 19$

SEE EXAMPLE 2

8. $f(x) = 2x^2 - 2x + 3$
9. $r(x) = x^2 + 6x + 12$
10. $h(x) = 3x^2 + 4x + 3$
11. $p(x) = x^2 + 4x + 10$
12. $g(x) = -5x^2 + 7x - 3$
13. $f(x) = 10x^2 + 7x + 4$

SEE EXAMPLE 3

Find the type and number of solutions for each equation.

14. $4x^2 + 1 = 4x$
15. $x^2 + 2x = 10$
16. $2x - x^2 = 4$

SEE EXAMPLE 4

17. **Geometry** One leg of a right triangle is 6 in. longer than the other leg. The hypotenuse of the triangle is 25 in. What is the length of each leg to the nearest inch?

PRACTICE AND PROBLEM SOLVING

Independent Practice

For Exercises	See Example
18–23	1
24–29	2
30–35	3
36	4

Extra Practice

See Extra Practice for more Skills Practice and Applications Practice exercises.

Find the zeros of each function by using the Quadratic Formula.

18. $f(x) = 3x^2 - 10x + 3$
19. $g(x) = x^2 + 6x$
20. $h(x) = x(x - 3) - 4$
21. $g(x) = -x^2 - 2x + 9$
22. $p(x) = 2x^2 - 7x - 8$
23. $f(x) = 7x^2 - 3$
24. $r(x) = x^2 + x + 1$
25. $h(x) = -x^2 - x - 1$
26. $f(x) = 2x^2 + 8$
27. $f(x) = 2x^2 + 7x - 13$
28. $g(x) = x^2 - x - 5$
29. $h(x) = -3x^2 + 4x - 4$

Find the type and number of solutions for each equation.

30. $2x^2 + 5 = 2x$
31. $2x^2 - 3x = 8$
32. $2x^2 - 16x = -32$
33. $4x^2 - 28x = -49$
34. $3x^2 - 8x + 8 = 0$
35. $3.2x^2 - 8.5x + 1.3 = 0$

36. **Safety** If a tightrope walker falls, he will land on a safety net. His height h in feet after a fall can be modeled by $h(t) = 60 - 16t^2$, where t is the time in seconds. How many seconds will the tightrope walker fall before landing on the safety net?

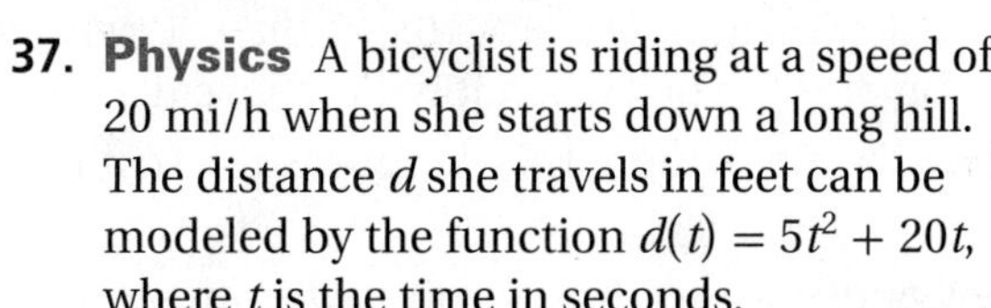

37. **Physics** A bicyclist is riding at a speed of 20 mi/h when she starts down a long hill. The distance d she travels in feet can be modeled by the function $d(t) = 5t^2 + 20t$, where t is the time in seconds.
    a. The hill is 585 ft long. To the nearest second, how long will it take her to reach the bottom?
    b. **What if...?** Suppose the hill were only half as long. To the nearest second, how long would it take the bicyclist to reach the bottom?

Aerospace

SpaceShipOne was the winner of the Ansari X Prize competition. The X Prize was awarded to the first nongovernmental spacecraft to reach an altitude of at least 100 km twice within a 2 week period.

Find the zeros of each function. Then graph the function.

38. $f(x) = 3x^2 - 4x - 2$ **39.** $g(x) = 2x^2 - 2x - 1$ **40.** $h(x) = 2x^2 + 6x + 5$

41. $p(x) = 2x^2 + 3x - 1$ **42.** $h(x) = 3x^2 - 5x - 4$ **43.** $r(x) = x^2 - x + 22$

44. Aerospace In 2004, the highest spaceplane flight was made by Brian Binnie in *SpaceShipOne*. A flight with this altitude can be modeled by the function $h(t) = -0.17t^2 + 187t + 61{,}000$, where h is the altitude in meters and t is flight time in seconds.

a. Approximately how long did the flight last?

b. What was the highest altitude to the nearest thousand meters?

c. The table shows the altitudes of layers of Earth's atmosphere. According to the model, which of these layers did *SpaceShipOne* enter, and at what time(s) did the spaceplane enter them?

Earth's Atmosphere

Layer	Altitude (in km)
Troposphere	0 to 10
Stratosphere	10 to 50
Mesosphere	50 to 85
Thermosphere	85 to 600

Solve each equation by any method.

45. $x^2 - 3x = 10$ **46.** $x^2 - 16 = 0$ **47.** $4x^2 + 4x = 15$

48. $x^2 + 2x - 2 = 0$ **49.** $x^2 - 4x - 21 = 0$ **50.** $4x^2 - 4x - 1 = 0$

51. $6x^2 = 150$ **52.** $x^2 = 7$ **53.** $x^2 - 16x + 64 = 0$

54. Critical Thinking If you are solving a real-world problem involving a quadratic equation, and the discriminant is negative, what can you conclude?

55. Multi-Step The outer dimensions of a picture frame are 25 inches by 20 inches. If the area inside the picture frame is 266 square inches, what is the width w of the frame?

Critical Thinking Find the values of c that make each equation have one real solution.

56. $x^2 + 8x + c = 0$ **57.** $x^2 + 12x = c$ **58.** $x^2 + 2cx + 49 = 0$

59. Write About It What method would you use to solve the equation $-14x^2 + 6x = 2.7$? Why would this method be easier to use than the other methods?

MULTI-STEP TEST PREP

60. An outfielder throws a baseball to the player on third base. The height h of the ball in feet is modeled by the function $h(t) = -16t^2 + 19t + 5$, where t is time in seconds. The third baseman catches the ball when it is 4 ft above the ground.

a. To the nearest tenth of a second, how long was the ball in the air before it was caught?

b. A player on the opposing team starts running from second base to third base 1.2 s before the outfielder throws the ball. The distance between the bases is 90 ft, and the runner's average speed is 27 ft/s. Will the runner reach third base before the ball does? Explain.

TEST PREP

61. Which best describes the graph of a quadratic function with a discriminant of −3?

    (A) Parabola with two x-intercepts
    (B) Parabola with no x-intercepts
    (C) Parabola that opens upward
    (D) Parabola that opens downward

62. What is the discriminant of the equation $2x^2 - 8x = 14$?

    (F) 48 (H) 176
    (G) −48 (J) −176

63. Which function has zeros of $3 \pm i$?

    (A) $f(x) = x^2 + 6x + 10$ (C) $g(x) = x^2 - 6x + 10$
    (B) $f(x) = x^2 + 6x - 10$ (D) $h(x) = x^2 - 6x - 10$

64. Which best describes the discriminant of the function whose graph is shown?

    (F) Positive (H) Negative
    (G) Zero (J) Undefined

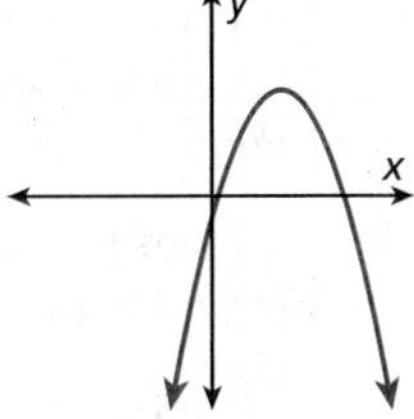

CHALLENGE AND EXTEND

65. **Geometry** The perimeter of a right triangle is 40 cm, and its hypotenuse measures 17 cm. Find the length of each leg.

66. **Geometry** The perimeter of a rectangle is 88 cm.
    a. Find the least possible value of the length of the diagonal. Round to the nearest tenth of a centimeter.
    b. What are the dimensions of the rectangle with this diagonal?

Write a quadratic equation whose solutions belong to the indicated sets.

67. integers 68. irrational real numbers 69. complex numbers

70. A quadratic equation has the form $ax^2 + bx + c = 0\ (a \neq 0)$.
    a. What is the sum of the roots of the equation? the product of the roots?
    b. Determine the standard form of a quadratic equation whose roots have a sum of 2 and a product of −15.

71. Describe the solutions to a quadratic equation for which $a = b = c$.

CHAPTER 2

MULTI-STEP TEST PREP

SECTION 2A

MATHEMATICAL PRACTICES Model with mathematics.

Quadratic Functions and Complex Numbers

Ballpark Figures When a baseball is thrown or hit into the air, its height h in feet after t seconds can be modeled by $h(t) = -16t^2 + v_y t + h_0$, where v_y is the initial vertical velocity of the ball in feet per second and h_0 is the ball's initial height. The horizontal distance d in feet that the ball travels in t seconds can be modeled by $d(t) = v_x t$, where v_x is the ball's initial horizontal velocity in feet per second.

1. A short stop makes an error by dropping the ball. As the ball drops, its height h in feet is modeled by $h(t) = -16t^2 + 3$. A slow-motion replay of the error shows the play at half speed. What function describes the height of the ball in the replay?
2. A player hits a foul ball with an initial vertical velocity of 70 ft/s and an initial height of 5 ft. To the nearest foot, what is the maximum height reached by the ball?
3. A pitch will be a strike if its height is between 2.5 ft and 5 ft when it crosses home plate. The pitcher throws the ball from a height of 6 ft with an initial vertical velocity of 5 ft/s and a horizontal velocity of 116 ft/s. Could this pitch be a strike? Explain.
4. The next pitch crosses home plate 1 ft too high to be a strike. The pitch is thrown from a height of 6 ft with an initial vertical velocity of 8 ft/s. What is the initial horizontal velocity of this pitch?
5. A player throws the ball home from a height of 5.5 ft with an initial vertical velocity of 28 ft/s. The ball is caught at home plate at a height of 5 ft. Three seconds before the ball is thrown, a runner on third base starts toward home plate at an average speed of 25 ft/s. Does the runner reach home plate before the ball does? Explain.

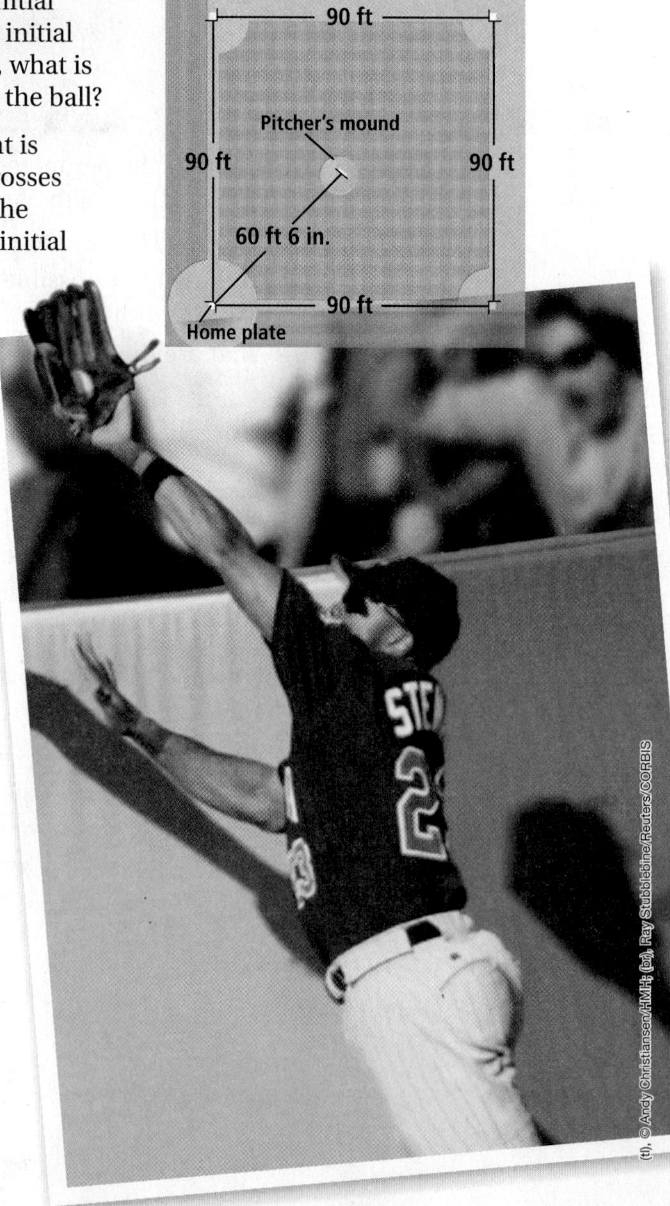

READY TO GO ON?

CHAPTER 2

SECTION 2A

Quiz for Lessons 2-1 Through 2-6

2-1 Using Transformations to Graph Quadratic Functions

Using the graph of $f(x) = x^2$ as a guide, describe the transformations, and then graph each function.

1. $g(x) = (x + 2)^2 - 4$ **2.** $g(x) = -4(x - 1)^2$ **3.** $g(x) = \frac{1}{2}x^2 + 1$

Use the description to write each quadratic function in vertex form.

4. $f(x) = x^2$ is vertically stretched by a factor of 9 and translated 2 units left to create g.

5. $f(x) = x^2$ is reflected across the x-axis and translated 4 units up to create g.

2-2 Properties of Quadratic Functions in Standard Form

For each function, (a) determine whether the graph opens upward or downward, (b) find the axis of symmetry, (c) find the vertex, (d) find the y-intercept, and (e) graph the function.

6. $f(x)= x^2 - 4x + 3$ **7.** $g(x) = -x^2 + 2x - 1$ **8.** $h(x) = x^2 - 6x$

9. A football kick is modeled by the function $h(x) = -0.0075x^2 + 0.5x + 5$, where h is the height of the ball in feet and x is the horizontal distance in feet that the ball travels. Find the maximum height of the ball to the nearest foot.

2-3 Solving Quadratic Equations by Graphing and Factoring

Find the roots of each equation by factoring.

10. $x^2 - 100 = 0$ **11.** $x^2 + 5x = 24$ **12.** $4x^2 + 8x = 0$

2-4 Completing the Square

Solve each equation by completing the square.

13. $x^2 - 6x = 40$ **14.** $x^2 + 18x = 15$ **15.** $x^2 + 14x = 8$

Write each function in vertex form, and identify its vertex.

16. $f(x) = x^2 + 24x + 138$ **17.** $g(x) = x^2 - 12x + 39$ **18.** $h(x) = 5x^2 - 20x + 9$

2-5 Complex Numbers and Roots

Solve each equation.

19. $3x^2 = -48$ **20.** $x^2 - 20x = -125$ **21.** $x^2 - 8x + 30 = 0$

2-6 The Quadratic Formula

Find the zeros of each function by using the Quadratic Formula.

22. $f(x) = (x + 6)^2 + 2$ **23.** $g(x) = x^2 + 7x + 15$ **24.** $h(x) = 2x^2 - 5x + 3$

25. A bicyclist is riding at a speed of 18 mi/h when she starts down a long hill. The distance d she travels in feet can be modeled by $d(t) = 4t^2 + 18t$, where t is the time in seconds. How long will it take her to reach the bottom of a 400-foot-long hill?

2-7 Solving Quadratic Inequalities

CC.9-12.A.CED.1 Create equations and inequalities in one variable and use them to solve problems. *Also* **CC.9-12.A.CED.3**

Objectives

Solve quadratic inequalities by using tables and graphs.

Solve quadratic inequalities by using algebra.

Vocabulary

quadratic inequality in two variables

Who uses this?

Tour companies and other businesses use quadratic inequalities to make predictions of profits. (See Example 4.)

Many business profits can be modeled by quadratic functions. To ensure that the profit is above a certain level, financial planners may need to graph and solve *quadratic inequalities.*

A **quadratic inequality in two variables** can be written in one of the following forms, where a, b, and c are real numbers and $a \neq 0$. Its solution set is a set of ordered pairs (x, y).

$$y < ax^2 + bx + c \qquad y > ax^2 + bx + c$$
$$y \leq ax^2 + bx + c \qquad y \geq ax^2 + bx + c$$

Previously, you solved linear inequalities in two variables by graphing. You can use a similar procedure to graph quadratic inequalities.

Graphing Quadratic Inequalities

To graph a quadratic inequality
1. Graph the parabola that defines the boundary.
2. Use a solid parabola for $y \leq$ and $y \geq$ and a dashed parabola for $y <$ and $y >$.
3. Shade above the parabola for $y >$ or $\geq$ and below the parabola for $y \leq$ or $<$.

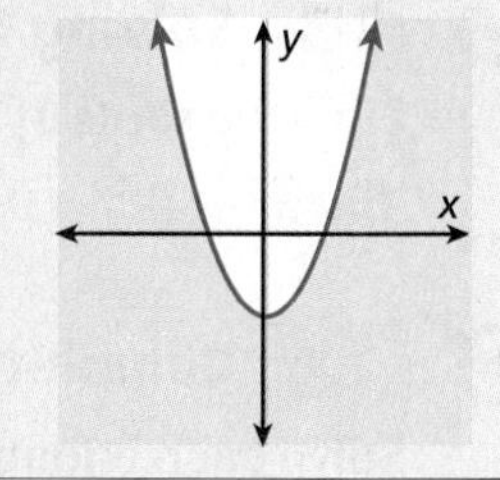

EXAMPLE 1 Graphing Quadratic Inequalities in Two Variables

Graph $y < -2x^2 - 4x + 6$.

Step 1 Graph the boundary of the related parabola $y = -2x^2 - 4x + 6$ with a dashed curve.

Its y-intercept is 6, its vertex is $(-1, 8)$, and its x-intercepts are -3 and 1.

Step 2 Shade below the parabola because the solution consists of y-values less than those on the parabola for corresponding x-values.

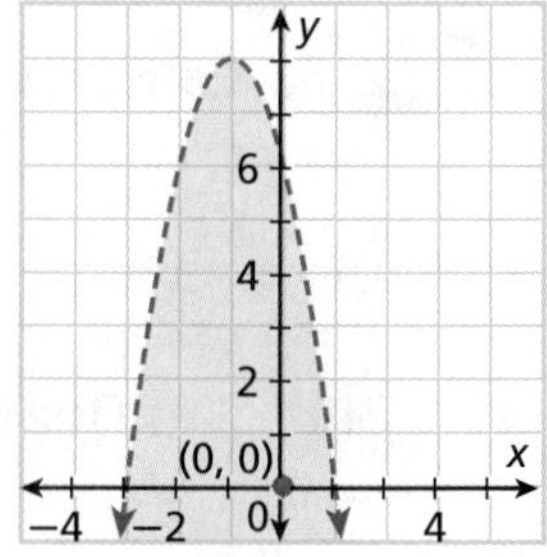

Check Use a test point to verify the solution region.

$$y < -2x^2 - 4x + 6$$
$$0 < -2(0)^2 - 4(0) + 6 \qquad \textit{Try } (0, 0).$$
$$0 < 6 \checkmark$$

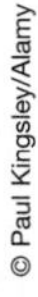

CHECK IT OUT! **Graph each inequality.**

1a. $y \geq 2x^2 - 5x - 2$ **1b.** $y < -3x^2 - 6x - 7$

Quadratic inequalities in one variable, such as $ax^2 + bx + c > 0\ (a \neq 0)$, have solutions in one variable that are graphed on a number line.

EXAMPLE 2 Solving Quadratic Inequalities by Using Tables and Graphs

Solve each inequality by using tables or graphs.

A $x^2 - 6x + 8 \leq 3$

Use a graphing calculator to graph each side of the inequality. Set **Y1** equal to $x^2 - 6x + 8$ and **Y2** equal to 3. Identify the values of x for which **Y1** $\leq$ **Y2**.

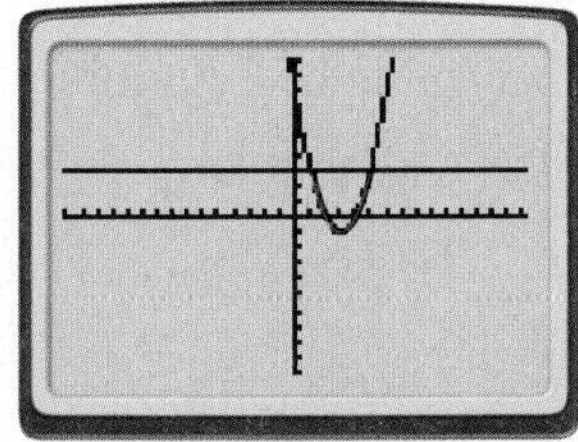

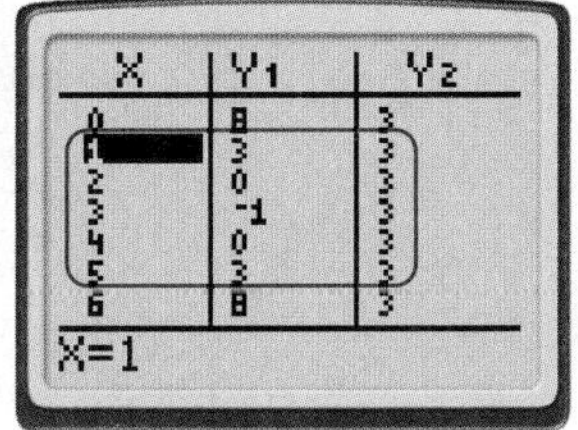

X	Y1	Y2
0	8	3
1	3	3
2	0	3
3	-1	3
4	0	3
5	3	3
6	8	3

X=1

The parabola is at or below the line when x is between 1 and 5 inclusive. So, the solution set is $1 \leq x \leq 5$, or $[1, 5]$. The table supports your answer.

The number line shows the solution set.

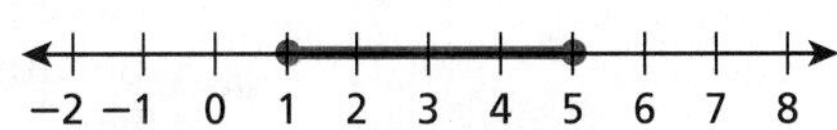

B $x^2 - 6x + 8 > 3$

Use a graphing calculator to graph each side of the inequality. Set **Y1** equal to $x^2 - 6x + 8$ and **Y2** equal to 3. Identify the values of x for which **Y1** $>$ **Y2**.

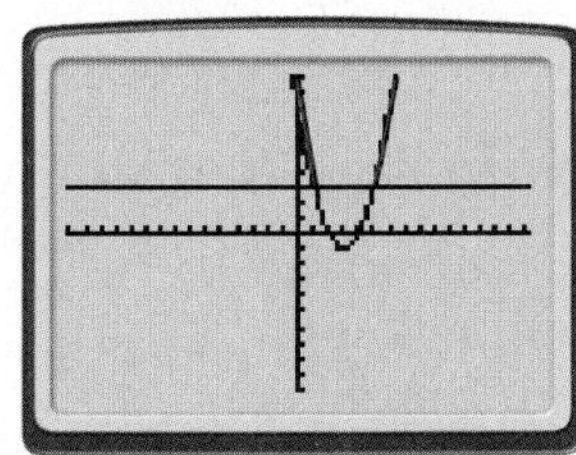

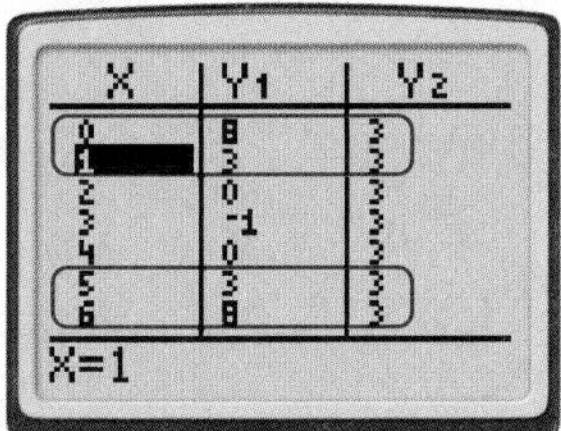

X	Y1	Y2
0	8	3
1	3	3
2	0	3
3	-1	3
4	0	3
5	3	3
6	8	3

X=1

The parabola is above the line $y = 3$ when x is less than 1 or greater than 5. So the solution set is $x < 1$ or $x > 5$, or $(-\infty, 1) \cup (5, \infty)$.

The number line shows the solution set.

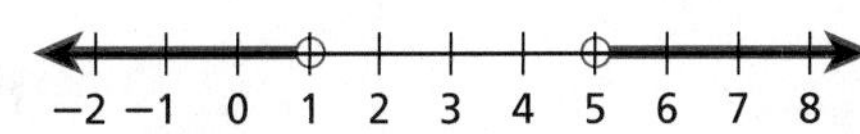

Reading Math

For *and* statements, *both* of the conditions must be true. For *or* statements, *at least one* of the conditions must be true.

CHECK IT OUT! **Solve each inequality by using tables or graphs.**

2a. $x^2 - x + 5 < 7$ **2b.** $2x^2 - 5x + 1 \geq 1$

The number lines showing the solution sets in Example 2 are divided into three distinct regions by the points 1 and 5. These points are called *critical values.* By finding the critical values, you can solve quadratic inequalities algebraically.

EXAMPLE 3 Solving Quadratic Inequalities by Using Algebra

Solve the inequality $x^2 - 4x + 1 > 6$ by using algebra.

Step 1 Write the related equation.

$$x^2 - 4x + 1 = 6$$

Step 2 Solve the equation for x to find the critical values.

$$x^2 - 4x - 5 = 0 \quad \textit{Write in standard form.}$$

$$(x - 5)(x + 1) = 0 \quad \textit{Factor.}$$

$$x - 5 = 0 \text{ or } x + 1 = 0 \quad \textit{Zero Product Property}$$

$$x = 5 \text{ or } x = -1 \quad \textit{Solve for x.}$$

The critical values are 5 and -1. The critical values divide the number line into three intervals: $x < -1$, $-1 < x < 5$, and $x > 5$.

Step 3 Test an x-value in each interval.

$$x^2 - 4x + 1 > 6$$

$(-2)^2 - 4(-2) + 1 > 6$ ✔ *Try $x = -2$.*

$(0)^2 - 4(0) + 1 > 6$ ✘ *Try $x = 0$.*

$(6)^2 - 4(6) + 1 > 6$ ✔ *Try $x = 6$.*

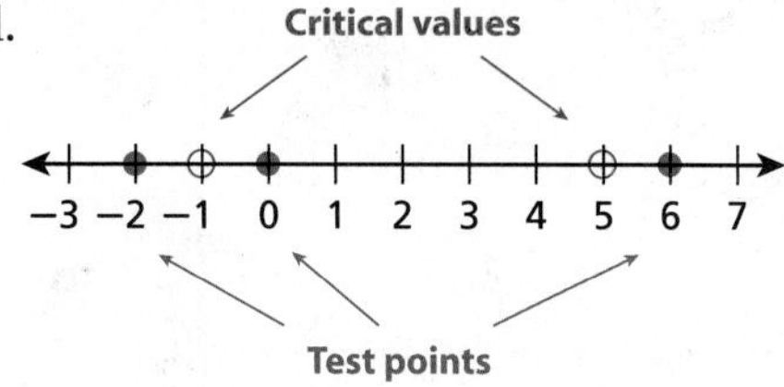

Shade the solution regions on the number line. Use open circles for the critical values because the inequality does not contain *or equal to*.

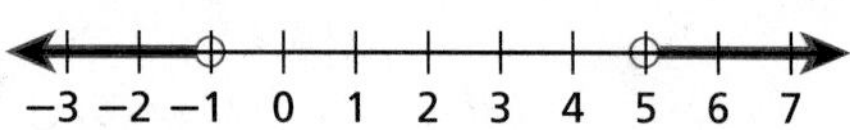

The solution is $x < -1$ or $x > 5$, or $(-\infty, -1) \cup (5, \infty)$.

Solve each inequality by using algebra.

3a. $x^2 - 6x + 10 \geq 2$ **3b.** $-2x^2 + 3x + 7 < 2$

EXAMPLE 4 *Problem-Solving Application*

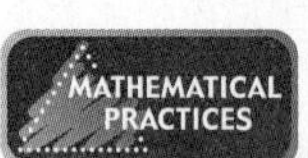

Make sense of problems and persevere in solving them.

A business offers tours to the Amazon. The profit P that the company earns for x number of tourists can be modeled by $P(x) = -25x^2 + 1000x - 3000$. How many people are needed for a profit of at least \$5000?

1 Understand the Problem

The **answer** will be the number of people required for a profit that is greater than or equal to \$5000.

List the important information:

- The profit must be at least \$5000.
- The function for the profit is $P(x) = -25x^2 + 1000x - 3000$.

2 Make a Plan

Write an inequality showing profit greater than or equal to \$5000. Then solve the inequality by using algebra.

3 Solve

Write the inequality.

$$-25x^2 + 1000x - 3000 \geq 5000$$

Find the critical values by solving the related equation.

$$-25x^2 + 1000x - 3000 = 5000 \quad \textit{Write as an equation.}$$

$$-25x^2 + 1000x - \mathbf{8000} = 0 \quad \textit{Write in standard form.}$$

$$-25\left(x^2 - 40x + 320\right) = 0 \quad \textit{Factor out } -25 \textit{ to simplify.}$$

$$x = \frac{-b \pm \sqrt{b^2 - 4ac}}{2a} = \frac{-(-40) \pm \sqrt{(-40)^2 - 4(1)(320)}}{2(1)} \quad \textit{Use the Quadratic Formula.}$$

$$= \frac{40 \pm \sqrt{320}}{2} \quad \textit{Simplify.}$$

$$x \approx 28.94 \text{ or } x \approx 11.06$$

Test an x-value in each of the three regions formed by the critical x-values.

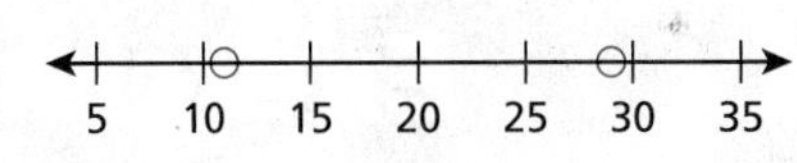

$$-25(10)^2 + 1000(10) - 3000 \overset{?}{\geq} 5000 \quad \textit{Try } x = 10.$$

$$4500 \geq 5000 \; ✗$$

$$-25(20)^2 + 1000(20) - 3000 \overset{?}{\geq} 5000 \quad \textit{Try } x = 20.$$

$$7000 \geq 5000 \; ✓$$

$$-25(30)^2 + 1000(30) - 3000 \overset{?}{\geq} 5000 \quad \textit{Try } x = 30.$$

$$4500 \geq 5000 \; ✗$$

Write the solution as an inequality. The solution is approximately $11.06 \leq x \leq 28.94$. Because you cannot have a fraction of a person, round each critical value to the appropriate whole number.

$$12 \leq x \leq 28$$

For a profit of at least \$5000, from 12 to 28 people are needed.

Remember!

A compound inequality such as $12 \leq x \leq 28$ can be written as $\{x \mid x \geq 12 \cup x \leq 28\}$, or $x \geq 12$ and $x \leq 28$.

4 Look Back

Enter $y = -25x^2 + 1000x - 3000$ into a graphing calculator, and create a table of values. The table shows that integer values of x between 12 and 28 inclusive result in y-values greater than or equal to 5000.

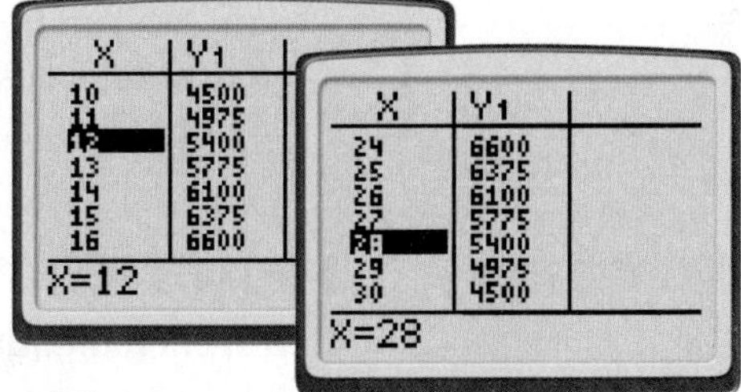

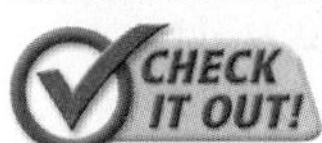

4. The business also offers educational tours to Patagonia, a region of South America that includes parts of Chile and Argentina. The profit P for x number of persons is $P(x) = -25x^2 + 1250x - 5000$. The trip will be rescheduled if the profit is less than \$7500. How many people must have signed up if the trip is rescheduled?

THINK AND DISCUSS

1. Compare graphing a quadratic inequality with graphing a linear inequality.
2. Explain how to determine if the intersection point(s) is/are included in the solution set when you solve a quadratic inequality by graphing.

3. **GET ORGANIZED** Copy and complete the graphic organizer. Compare the solutions of quadratic equations and inequalities.

	Equation (=)	"Less Than" Inequality (< or ≤)	"Greater Than" Inequality (> or ≥)
Example			
Graph			
Solution Set			

2-7 Exercises

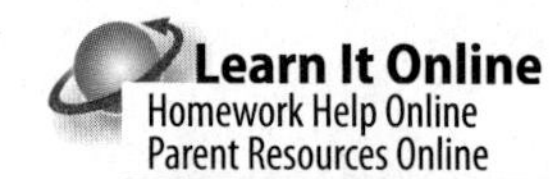

Learn It Online
Homework Help Online
Parent Resources Online

GUIDED PRACTICE

1. **Vocabulary** Give an example of a *quadratic inequality in two variables*.

SEE EXAMPLE 1

Graph each inequality.

2. $y > -(x + 1)^2 + 5$
3. $y \leq 2x^2 - 4x - 1$
4. $y \leq -3x^2 + x + 3$

SEE EXAMPLE 2

Solve each inequality by using tables or graphs.

5. $x^2 - 5x + 3 \leq 3$
6. $3x^2 - 3x - 1 > -1$
7. $2x^2 - 9x + 5 \leq -4$

SEE EXAMPLE 3

Solve each inequality by using algebra.

8. $x^2 + 10x + 1 \geq 12$
9. $x^2 + 13x + 45 < 5$
10. $-2x^2 + 3x + 12 > 10$

SEE EXAMPLE 4

11. **Business** A consultant advises the owners of a beauty salon that their profit p each month can be modeled by $p(x) = -50x^2 + 3500x - 2500$, where x is the average cost that a customer is charged. What range of costs will bring in a profit of at least $50,000?

PRACTICE AND PROBLEM SOLVING

Graph each inequality.

12. $y < x^2 + 2x - 5$
13. $y > -\frac{1}{2}x^2 + 3$
14. $y \leq 2(x - 1)^2 - 3$
15. $y \geq x^2 + 6$
16. $y < (x + 1)(x + 4)$
17. $y \leq x^2 - 2x + 6$

Solve each inequality by using tables or graphs.

18. $x^2 - x + 5 < 11$
19. $2x^2 + 3x + 6 \geq 5$
20. $x^2 - 5x + 12 > 6$
21. $x^2 - 2x - 8 > 0$
22. $x^2 + 7x + 6 \leq 6$
23. $x^2 - 12x + 32 < 12$

Independent Practice

For Exercises	See Example
12–17	1
18–23	2
24–26	3
27	4

Extra Practice

See Extra Practice for more Skills Practice and Applications Practice exercises.

Solve each inequality by using algebra.

24. $x^2 - 11x + 13 \leq 25$ **25.** $-2x^2 + 3x + 4 \geq -1$ **26.** $x^2 - 5x - 4 < -9$

27. Sports A football thrown by a quarterback follows a path given by $h(x) = -0.0095x^2 + x + 7$, where h is the height of the ball in feet and x is the horizontal distance the ball has traveled in feet. If any height less than 10 feet can be caught or knocked down, at what distances from the quarterback can the ball be knocked down?

Graph each quadratic inequality.

28. $y \leq 2x^2 + 4x - 3$ **29.** $y < 3x^2 - 12x - 4$ **30.** $y \geq -3x^2 + 4x$

31. $y > -2(x + 3)^2 + 1$ **32.** $y > -x^2 - 2x - 1$ **33.** $y \leq \frac{1}{3}x^2 + 2x - 1$

34. Circus The human cannonball is an act where a performer is launched through the air. The height of the performer can be modeled by $h(x) = -0.007x^2 + x + 20$, where h is the height in feet and x is the horizontal distance traveled in feet. The circus act is considering a flight path directly over the main tent.

a. If the performer wants at least 5 ft of vertical height clearance, how tall can the tent be?

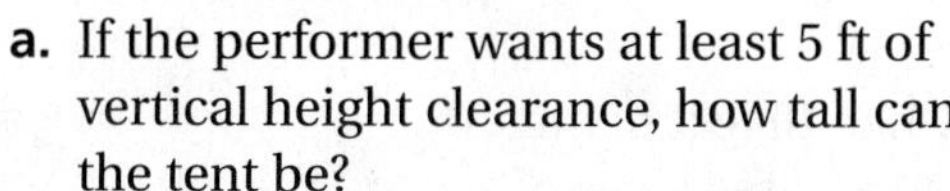

b. How far from the central pole should the "cannon" be placed?

Solve each inequality by using any method.

35. $x^2 - 5x - 24 \leq 0$ **36.** $x^2 - 14 \geq 2$ **37.** $-2x^2 - x + 8 > 6$

38. $x^2 - 4x - 5 \leq -9$ **39.** $3x^2 + 6x + 11 < 10$ **40.** $4x^2 - 9 > 0$

41. $3x^2 + 5x + 13 \leq 16$ **42.** $-2x^2 + 3x + 17 \geq 11$ **43.** $5x^2 - 2x - 1 \geq 0$

44. $(x - 2)(x + 11) \geq 2$ **45.** $x^2 + 27 > 12x$ **46.** $-2x^2 + 3x + 6 > 0$

47. Multi-Step A medical office has a rectangular parking lot that measures 120 ft by 200 ft. The owner wants to expand the size of the parking lot by adding an equal distance to two sides as shown. If zoning restrictions limit the total size of the parking lot to 35,000 ft², what range of distances can be added?

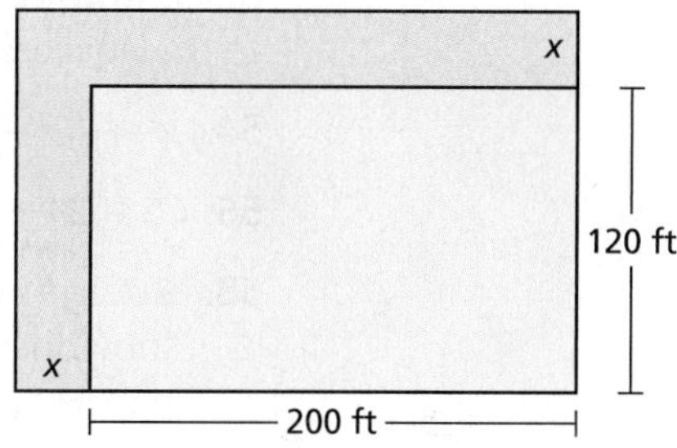

Match each graph with one of the following inequalities.

A. $y < x^2 + 2x - 3$ **B.** $y > -x^2 - 2x + 3$ **C.** $y < x^2 - 2x + 3$

48.

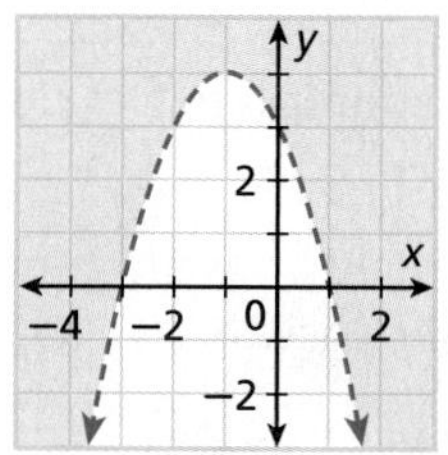

49.

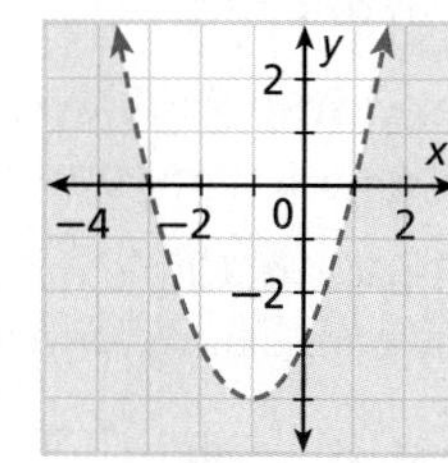

50.

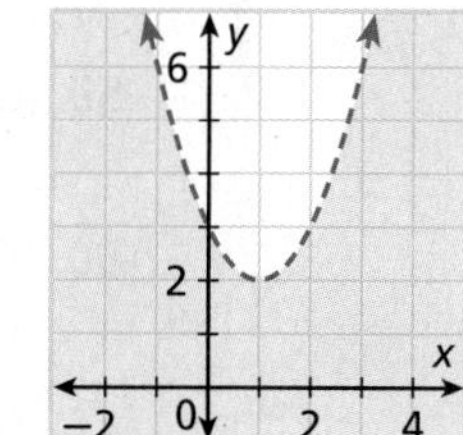

51. A small square tile is placed on top of a larger square tile as shown. This creates four congruent triangular regions.

   a. Write a function for the area A of one of the triangular regions in terms of x.

   b. For what values of x, to the nearest tenth, is the area of each triangular region at least 30 cm^2?

   c. For what values of x, to the nearest tenth, is the area of each triangular region less than 40 cm^2?

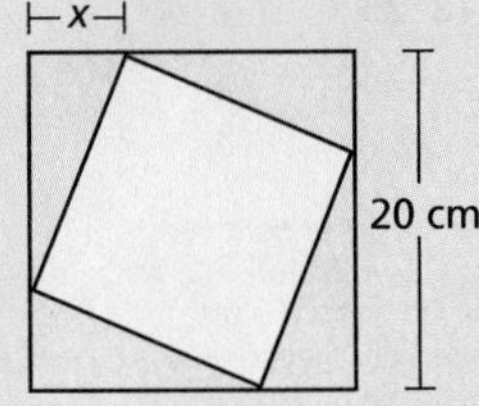

52. **Music** A manager estimates a band's profit p for a concert by using the function $p(t) = -200t^2 + 2500t - c$, where t is the price per ticket and c is the band's operating cost. The table shows the band's operating cost at three different concert locations. What range of ticket prices should the band charge at each location in order to make a profit of at least \$1000 at each concert?

Band's Costs

Location	Operating Cost
Freemont Park	\$900
Saltillo Plaza	\$1500
Riverside Walk	\$2500

53. **Gardening** Lindsey has 40 feet of metal fencing material to fence three sides of a rectangular garden. A tall wooden fence serves as her fourth side.

   a. Write a function for the area of the garden A in terms of x, the width in feet.

   b. What measures for the width will give an area of at least 150 square feet?

   c. What measures for the width will give an area of at least 200 square feet?

x

Graphing Calculator Use the intersect feature of a graphing calculator to solve each inequality to the nearest tenth.

54. $x^2 + 6x - 13 > 4$

55. $x^2 - 15x + 20 \leq 7$

56. $x^2 - 24 < 28$

57. $2x^2 + 3x + 5 \geq 8$

58. **Business** A wholesaler sells snowboards to sporting-good stores. The price per snowboard varies based on the number purchased in each order. The function $r(x) = -x^2 + 125x$ models the wholesaler's revenue r in dollars for an order of x snowboards.

   a. To the nearest dollar, what is the maximum revenue per order?

   b. How many snowboards must the wholesaler sell to make at least \$1500 in revenue in one order?

59. **Critical Thinking** Explain whether the solution to a quadratic inequality in one variable is always a compound inequality.

60. **Critical Thinking** Can a quadratic inequality have a solution set that is all real numbers? Give an example to support your answer.

61. **Write About It** Explain how the solutions of $x^2 - 3x - 4 \leq 6$ differ from the solutions of $x^2 - 3x - 4 = 6$.

62. Which is the solution set of $x^2 - 9 < 0$?

Ⓐ $-3 < x < 3$

Ⓑ $-9 < x < 9$

Ⓒ $x < -3$ or $x > 3$

Ⓓ $x < -9$ or $x > 9$

63. Which is the graph of the solution to $x^2 - 7x + 10 \geq 0$?

Ⓕ −6 −5 −4 −3 −2 −1 0

Ⓗ 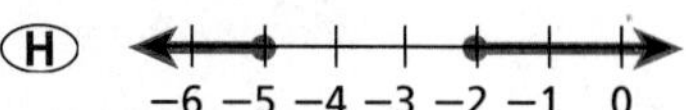

Ⓖ 0 1 2 3 4 5 6

Ⓙ 0 1 2 3 4 5 6

64. Which is the solution set of $x^2 - 7x \leq 0$?

Ⓐ $0 < x < 7$

Ⓑ $0 \leq x \leq 7$

Ⓒ $x < 0$ or $x > 7$

Ⓓ $x \leq 0$ or $x \geq 7$

65. **Short Response** Demonstrate the process for solving $x^2 + 4x + 4 > 1$ algebraically. Justify each step in the solution process.

CHALLENGE AND EXTEND

Graph each system of inequalities.

66. $\begin{cases} y \leq x^2 \\ y \geq -x^2 + 5 \end{cases}$

67. $\begin{cases} y \geq x^2 - 3 \\ y \leq -x^2 - 2x + 9 \end{cases}$

68. $\begin{cases} y \geq 2x^2 - 12x + 20 \\ y \geq \frac{1}{3}x^2 - 2x + 8 \end{cases}$

Geometry The area inside a parabola bounded from above or below by a horizontal line segment is $\frac{2}{3}bh$, where b is the length of the line segment and h is the vertical distance from the vertex of the parabola to the line segment. Find the area bounded by the graphs of each pair of inequalities.

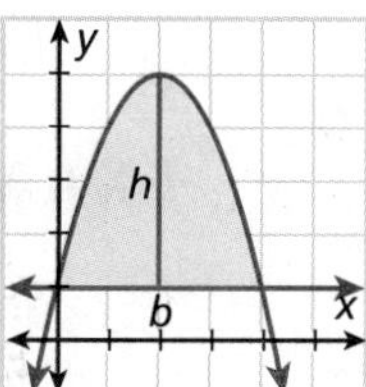

69. $y > x^2 + 5x - 6$; $y < 8$

70. $y < -2x^2 + 3x + 9$; $y > -5$

2-8 Curve Fitting with Quadratic Models

CC.9-12.A.CED.2 Create equations in two or more variables to represent relationships between quantities; graph equations on coordinate axes with labels and scales. *Also* **CC.9-12.A.CED.3**

Objectives
Use quadratic functions to model data.

Use quadratic models to analyze and predict.

Vocabulary
quadratic model
quadratic regression

Who uses this?
Film preservationists use quadratic relationships to estimate film run times. (See Example 3.)

The Granger Collection, New York

Recall that you can use differences to analyze patterns in data. For a set of ordered pairs with equally spaced x-values, a quadratic function has constant nonzero second differences, as shown below.

Equally spaced x-values

x	−3	−2	−1	0	1	2	3
$f(x) = x^2$	9	4	1	0	1	4	9

1st differences: −5, −3, −1, 1, 3, 5
2nd differences: 2, 2, 2, 2, 2

Constant 2nd differences

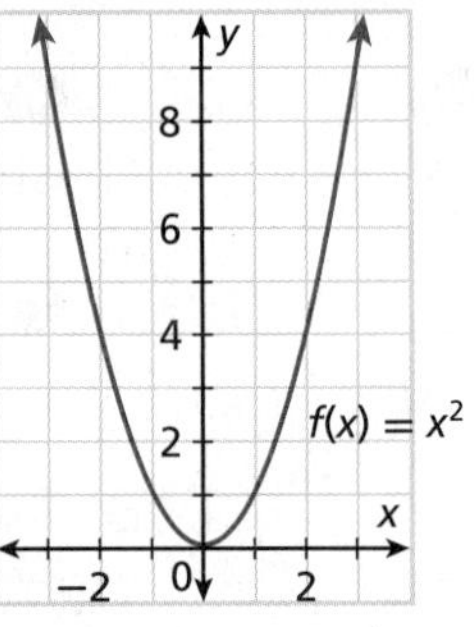

EXAMPLE **1**

Identifying Quadratic Data

Determine whether each data set could represent a quadratic function. Explain.

A

x	0	2	4	6	8
y	12	10	9	9	10

Find the first and second differences.

Equally spaced x-values

x	0	2	4	6	8
y	12	10	9	9	10

1st: −2, −1, 0, 1
2nd: 1, 1, 1

Quadratic function; second differences are constant for equally spaced x-values.

B

x	−2	−1	0	1	2
y	1	2	4	8	16

Find the first and second differences.

Equally spaced x-values

x	−2	−1	0	1	2
y	1	2	4	8	16

1st: 1, 2, 4, 8
2nd: 1, 2, 4

Not a quadratic function; second differences are not constant for equally spaced x-values.

Determine whether each data set could represent a quadratic function. Explain.

1a.

x	3	4	5	6	7
y	11	21	35	53	75

1b.

x	10	9	8	7	6
y	6	8	10	12	14

Just as two points define a linear function, three noncollinear points define a quadratic function. You can find the three coefficients, *a*, *b*, and *c*, of $f(x) = ax^2 + bx + c$ by using a system of three equations, one for each point. The points do not need to have equally spaced *x*-values.

Reading Math

Collinear points lie on the same line. *Noncollinear* points *do not* all lie on the same line.

EXAMPLE 2 Writing a Quadratic Function from Data

Write a quadratic function that fits the points (0, 5), (2, 1), and (3, 2).

Use each point to write a system of equations to find *a*, *b*, and *c* in $f(x) = ax^2 + bx + c$.

(x, y)	$f(x) = ax^2 + bx + c$	System in *a*, *b*, *c*
(0, 5)	$5 = a(0)^2 + b(0) + c$	$c = 5$ ❶
(2, 1)	$1 = a(2)^2 + b(2) + c$	$4a + 2b + c = 1$ ❷
(3, 2)	$2 = a(3)^2 + b(3) + c$	$9a + 3b + c = 2$ ❸

Substitute $c = 5$ from equation ❶ into both equation ❷ and equation ❸.

❷ $4a + 2b + c = 1$ ❸ $9a + 3b + c = 2$

$4a + 2b + 5 = 1$ $9a + 3b + 5 = 2$

$4a + 2b = -4$ ❹ $9a + 3b = -3$ ❺

Solve equation ❹ and equation ❺ for *a* and *b* using elimination.

❹ $3(4a + 2b) = 3(-4) \rightarrow 12a + 6b = -12$ *Multiply by 3.*

❺ $-2(9a + 3b) = -2(-3) \rightarrow -18a - 6b = 6$ *Multiply by −2.*

$-6a = -6$ *Add the equations.*

$a = 1$

Substitute 1 for *a* into equation ❹ or equation ❺ to find *b*.

❹ $4a + 2b = -4 \rightarrow 4(1) + 2b = -4$

$2b = -8$

$b = -4$

Write the function using $a = 1$, $b = -4$, and $c = 5$.

$$f(x) = ax^2 + bx + c \rightarrow f(x) = 1x^2 - 4x + 5, \text{ or } f(x) = x^2 - 4x + 5$$

Check Substitute or create a table to verify that (0, 5), (2, 1), and (3, 2) satisfy the function rule.

```
0²-4(0)+5
                5
2²-4(2)+5
                1
3²-4(3)+5
                2
```

2. Write a quadratic function that fits the points (0, −3), (1, 0), and (2, 1).

You may use any method that you studied to solve the system of three equations in three variables. For example, you can use a matrix equation as shown.

$$\begin{cases} c = 5 \\ 4a + 2b + c = 1 \\ 9a + 3b + c = 2 \end{cases} \rightarrow \begin{bmatrix} 0 & 0 & 1 \\ 4 & 2 & 1 \\ 9 & 3 & 1 \end{bmatrix}\begin{bmatrix} a \\ b \\ c \end{bmatrix} = \begin{bmatrix} 5 \\ 1 \\ 2 \end{bmatrix} \rightarrow \begin{bmatrix} a \\ b \\ c \end{bmatrix} = \begin{bmatrix} 1 \\ -4 \\ 5 \end{bmatrix}$$

```
[A]⁻¹[B]
            [[1 ]
             [-4]
             [5 ]]
```

A **quadratic model** is a quadratic function that represents a real data set. Models are useful for making estimates.

You have used a graphing calculator to perform a *linear regression* and make predictions. You can apply a similar statistical method to make a quadratic model for a given data set using **quadratic regression.**

EXAMPLE 3 *Film Application*

The table shows approximate run times for 16 mm films, given the diameter of the film on the reel. Find a quadratic model for the run time given the diameter. Use the model to estimate the run time for a reel of film with a diameter of 15 in.

Film Run Times (16 mm)

Diameter (in.)	Reel Length (ft)	Run Time (min)
5	200	5.55
7	400	11.12
9.25	600	16.67
10.5	800	22.22
12.25	1200	33.33
13.75	1600	44.45

Helpful Hint

The coefficient of determination R^2 shows how well a quadratic model fits the data. The closer R^2 is to 1, the better the fit. In this model, $R^2 \approx 0.996$, which is very close to 1, so the quadratic model is a good fit.

Step 1 Enter the data into two lists in a graphing calculator.

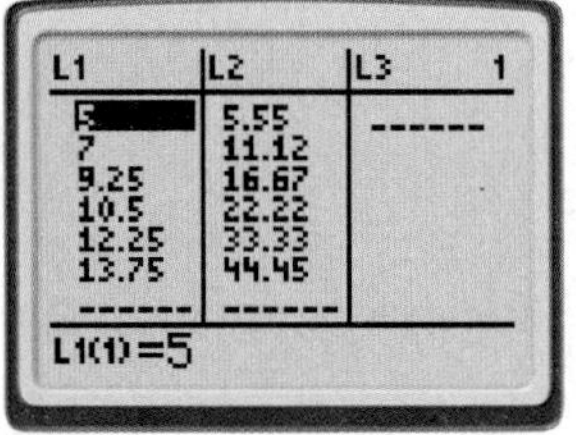

Step 2 Use the quadratic regression feature.

Step 3 Graph the data and function model to verify that the model fits the data.

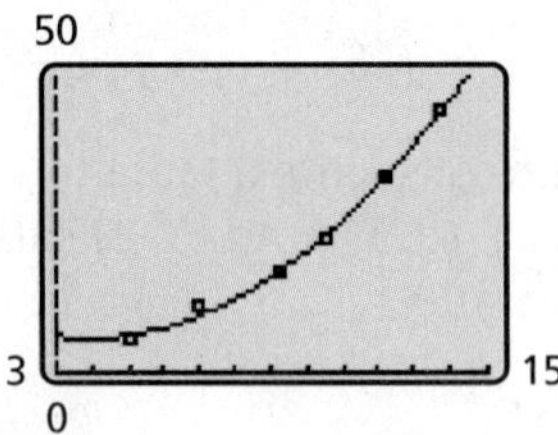

Step 4 Use the table feature to find the function value at $x = 15$.

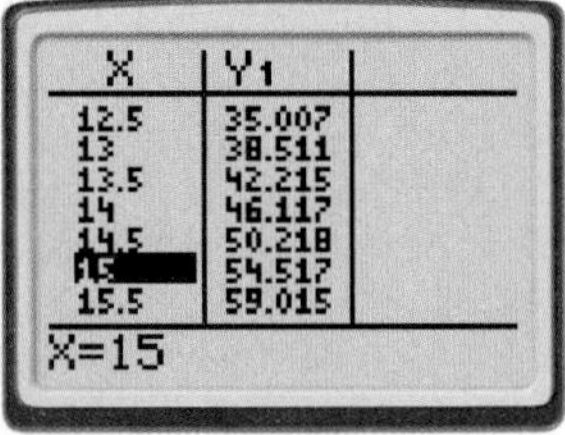

A quadratic model is $T(d) \approx 0.397d^2 - 3.12d + 11.94$, where T is the run time in minutes and d is the film diameter in inches.

For a 15 in. diameter, the model predicts a run time of about 54.5 min, or 54 min 30 s.

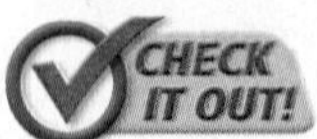

Use the information given above to answer the following.

3. Find a quadratic model for the reel length given the diameter of the film. Use the model to estimate the reel length for an 8-inch-diameter film.

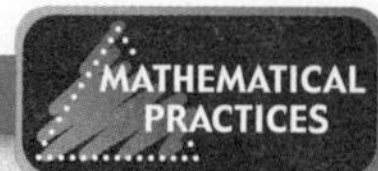

THINK AND DISCUSS

1. Describe how to determine if a data set is quadratic.
2. Explain whether a quadratic function is a good model for the path of an airplane that ascends, descends, and rises again out of view.

3. **GET ORGANIZED** Copy and complete the graphic organizer. Compare the different quadratic models presented in the lesson.

Quadratic Model	When Appropriate	Procedure
Exact model		
Approximate model		

2-8 Exercises

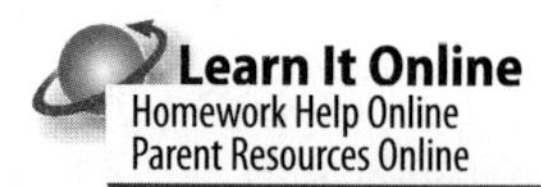

Learn It Online
Homework Help Online
Parent Resources Online

GUIDED PRACTICE

1. **Vocabulary** How does a *quadratic model* differ from a linear model?

SEE EXAMPLE 1

Determine whether each data set could represent a quadratic function. Explain.

2.

x	−2	−1	0	1	2
y	16	8	0	−8	−16

3.

x	1	2	3	4	5
y	1	3	9	27	81

4.

x	2	4	6	8	10
y	4	−5	−8	−5	4

SEE EXAMPLE 2

Write a quadratic function that fits each set of points.

5. $(-2, 5)$, $(0, -3)$, and $(3, 0)$
6. $(0, 1)$, $(2, -1)$, and $(3, -8)$
7. $(-1, 8)$, $(0, 4)$, and $(2, 2)$
8. $(-4, 9)$, $(0, -7)$, and $(1, -1)$
9. $(2, 3)$, $(6, 3)$, and $(8, -3)$
10. $(-1, -12)$, $(1, 0)$, and $(2, 9)$

SEE EXAMPLE 3

11. **Hobbies** The cost of mounting different-sized photos is shown in the table. Find a quadratic model for the cost given the average side length. (For an 8 in. × 10 in. photo, the average side length is $\frac{8+10}{2} = 9$ in.) Estimate the cost of mounting a 24 in. × 36 in. photo.

Costs of Mounting Photos

Size (in.)	Cost ($)
8 × 10	10
14 × 18	16
16 × 20	19
24 × 30	27
32 × 40	39

PRACTICE AND PROBLEM SOLVING

Determine whether each data set could represent a quadratic function. Explain.

12.

x	0	2	4	6	8
$f(x)$	−1	2	11	26	47

13.

x	0	1	2	3	4
$f(x)$	10	9	6	1	−6

14.

x	1	2	3	4	5
$f(x)$	−3	0	3	6	9

Independent Practice	
For Exercises	See Example
12–14	1
15–18	2
19	3

Extra Practice

See Extra Practice for more Skills Practice and Applications Practice exercises.

Write a quadratic function that fits each set of points.

15. $(-2, 5)$, $(-1, 0)$, and $(1, -2)$

16. $(1, 2)$, $(2, -1)$, and $(5, 2)$

17. $(-4, 12)$, $(-2, 0)$, and $(2, -12)$

18. $(-1, 2.6)$, $(1, 4.2)$, and $(2, 14)$

19. Gardening The table shows the amount spent on water gardening in the United States between 1999 and 2003. Find a quadratic model for the annual amount in millions of dollars spent on water gardening based on number of years since 1999. Estimate the amount that people in the United States will spend on water gardening in 2015.

Water Gardening	
Year	Amount Spent (million $)
1999	806
2000	943
2001	1205
2002	1441
2003	1565

Write a function rule for each situation, and identify each relationship as linear, quadratic, or neither.

20. the circumference C of a bicycle wheel, given its radius r

21. the area of a triangle A with a constant height, given its base length b

22. the population of bacteria P in a petri dish doubling every hour t

23. the area of carpet A needed for square rooms of length s

24. Physics In the past, different mathematical descriptions of falling objects were proposed.

Relative Distance Fallen (units)			
Time Interval (s)	Aristotle's Rule	da Vinci's Rule	Galileo's Rule
0	0	0	0
1	1	1	1
2	2	3	4
3	3	6	9
4	4	10	16

a. Which rule shows the greatest increase in the distance fallen per second and thus the greatest rate of increase in speed?

b. Identify each rule as linear, quadratic, or neither.

c. Describe the differences in da Vinci's rule, and compare it with the differences in Galileo's.

d. The most accurate rule is sometimes described as the odd-number law. Which rule shows an odd-number pattern of first differences and correctly describes the distance for falling objects?

Find the missing value for each quadratic function.

25.

x	−1	0	1	2	3
$f(x)$	0	1	0	■	−8

26.

x	−3	−2	−1	0	1
$f(x)$	12	2	■	0	8

27.

x	−2	0	2	4	6
$f(x)$	−2	■	2	7	14

28. A home-improvement store sells several sizes of rectangular tiles, as shown in the table.

a. Find a quadratic model for the area of a tile based on its length.

b. The store begins selling a new size of tile with a length of 9 in. Based on your model, estimate the area of a tile of this size.

Length (in.)	Area (in^2)
4	28
6	54
8	88
10	130

29. **Food** The pizza prices for DeAngelo's pizza parlor are shown at right.

a. Find a quadratic model for the price of a pizza based upon the size (diameter).

b. Use the quadratic model to find the price of a pizza with an 18 in. diameter.

c. Graph the quadratic function. Does the function have a minimum or maximum point? What does this point represent?

d. **What if...?** According to the model, how much should a 30 in. pizza cost? How much should an 8 in. pizza cost?

e. Is the quadratic function a good model for the price of DeAngelo's pizza? Explain your reasoning.

Determine whether each data set could represent a quadratic function. If so, find a quadratic function rule.

30.

x	0	1	2	3	4
y	−1	0	−1	−4	−9

31.

x	1	2	3	4	5
y	10	20	40	60	80

32.

x	2	4	6	8	10
y	−1	0	1	3	5

33.

x	−2	−1	0	1	2
y	16	3	0	7	24

34.

x	0	1	2	3	4
y	9	5	3	1	0

35.

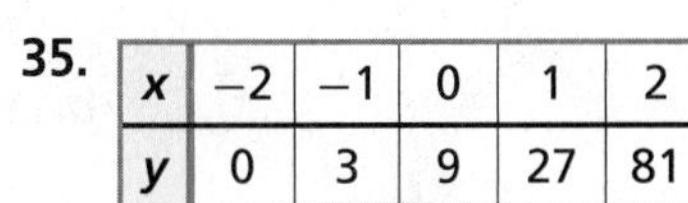

x	−2	−1	0	1	2
y	0	3	9	27	81

36. **Winter Sports** The diagram shows the motion of a skier following a jump. Find a quadratic model of the skier's height h in meters based on time t in seconds. Estimate the skier's height after 2 s.

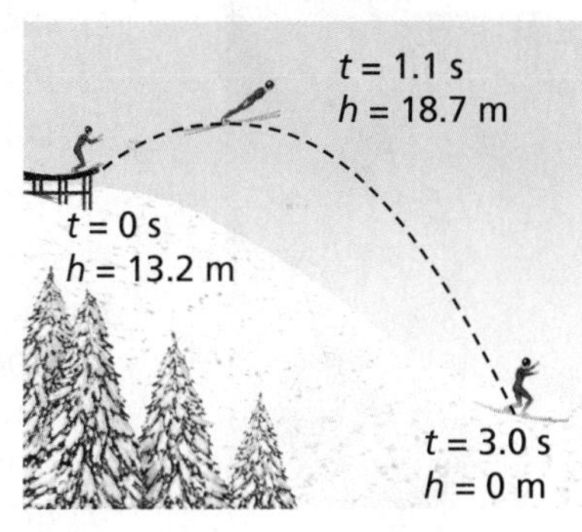

37. **Data Collection** Use a graphing calculator and a motion detector to measure the height of a basketball over time. Drop the ball from a height of 1 m, and let it bounce several times. Position the motion detector 0.5 m above the release point of the ball.

a. What is the greatest height the ball reaches during its first bounce?

b. Find an appropriate model for the height of the ball as a function of time during its first bounce.

38. **Safety** The light produced by high-pressure sodium vapor streetlamps for different energy usages is shown in the table.

High-Pressure Sodium Vapor Streetlamps

Energy Use (watts)	35	50	70	100	150
Light Output (lumens)	2250	4000	5800	9500	16,000

a. Find a quadratic model for the light output with respect to energy use.

b. Find a linear model for the light output with respect to energy use.

c. Apply each model to estimate the light output in lumens of a 200-watt bulb.

d. Which model gives the better estimate? Explain.

39. **Sports** The table lists the average distance that a normal shot travels for different golf clubs.

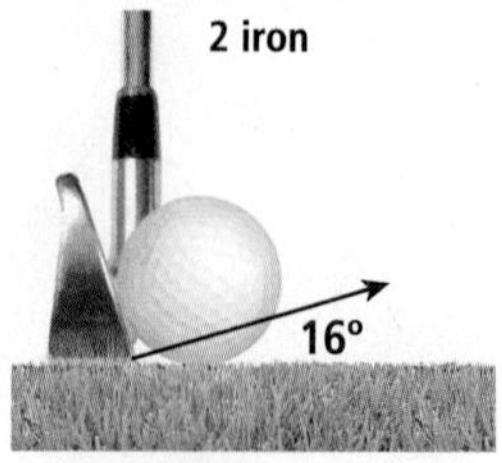

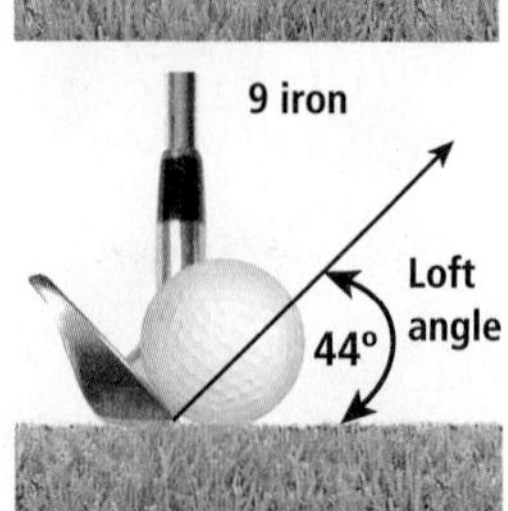

Average Distance for Normal Shot								
Club Iron (no.)	2	3	4	5	6	7	8	9
Loft Angle	16°	20°	24°	28°	32°	36°	40°	44°
Distance (yd)	186	176	166	155	143	132	122	112

a. Select three data values (club number, distance), and use a system of equations to find a quadratic model. Check your model by using a quadratic regression.

b. Is there a quadratic relationship between club number and average distance of a normal shot? Explain.

c. Is the relationship between club number and loft angle quadratic or linear? Find a model of this relationship.

40. **Multi-Step** Use the table of alloy-steel chain data.

a. Do each of the last two columns appear to be quadratic functions with respect to the nominal chain size? Explain.

b. Verify your response in part **a** by finding each of the quadratic regression equations. Do the models fit the data well? Explain.

c. Predict the values for the last two columns for a chain with a nominal size of $\frac{5}{8}$ in.

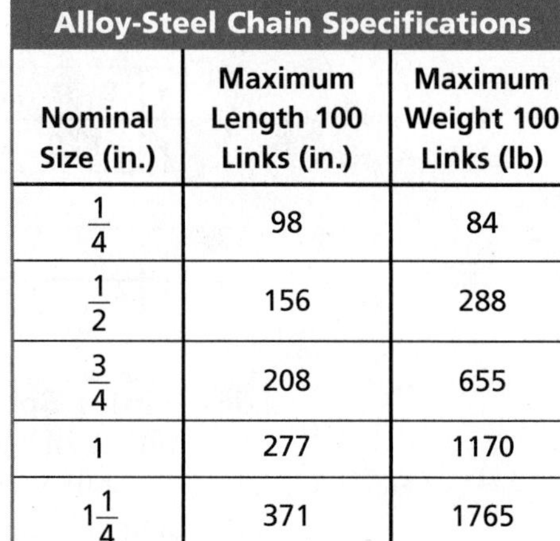

Alloy-Steel Chain Specifications		
Nominal Size (in.)	Maximum Length 100 Links (in.)	Maximum Weight 100 Links (lb)
$\frac{1}{4}$	98	84
$\frac{1}{2}$	156	288
$\frac{3}{4}$	208	655
1	277	1170
$1\frac{1}{4}$	371	1765

LINK

Math History

Pythagoras made numerous contributions to mathematics, including the Pythagorean Theorem, which bears his name.

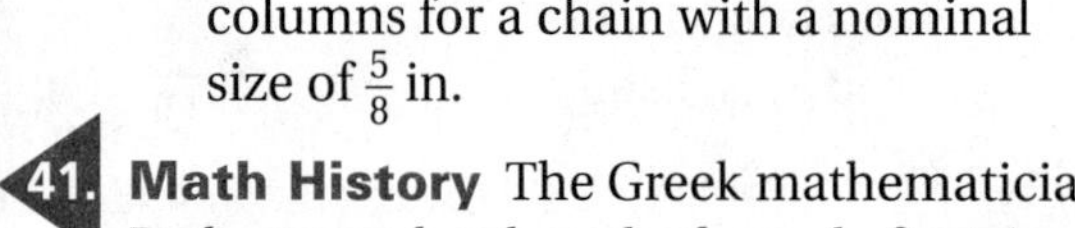

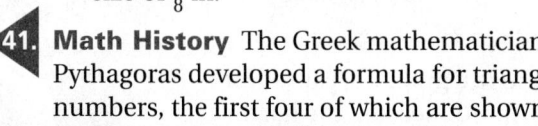

41. **Math History** The Greek mathematician Pythagoras developed a formula for triangular numbers, the first four of which are shown. Write a quadratic function that determines a triangular number t in terms of its place in the sequence n. (*Hint:* The fourth triangular number has $n = 4$.)

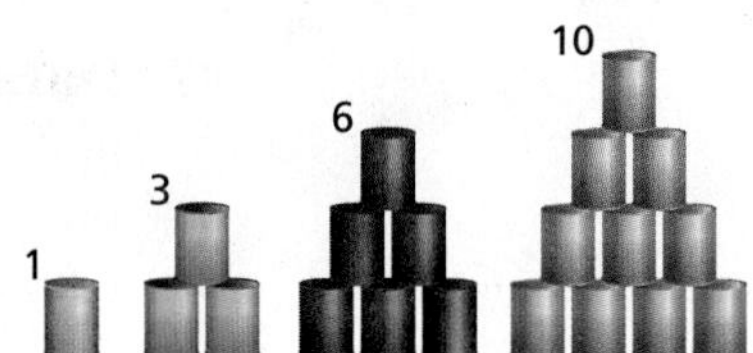

42. **Critical Thinking** Two points define a unique line. How many points define a unique parabola, and what restriction applies to the points?

43. **Critical Thinking** Consider the following data set.

x	10	8	13	9	11	14	6	4	12	7	5
y	9.14	8.14	8.74	8.77	9.29	8.1	6.13	3.1	9.13	7.26	4.74

a. Create a scatter plot of the data.

b. Perform a linear regression on the data.

c. Perform a quadratic regression on the data.

d. Which model best describes the data set? Explain your answer.

44. **Write About It** What does it mean when the coefficient a in a quadratic regression model is zero?

45. Which of the following would best be modeled by a quadratic function?

(A) Relationship between circumference and diameter

(B) Relationship between area of a square and side length

(C) Relationship between diagonal of a square and side length

(D) Relationship between volume of a cube and side length

46. If (7, 11) and (3, 11) are two points on a parabola, what is the x-value of the vertex of this parabola?

(F) 3 (G) 5 (H) 7 (J) 11

47. If y is a quadratic function of x, which value completes the table?

x	-2	0	2	4	6
y	-8	0	12	28	■

(A) 12 (B) 20 (C) 44 (D) 48

48. The graph of a quadratic function having the form $f(x) = ax^2 + bx + c$ passes through the points $(0, -8)$, $(3, 10)$, and $(6, 34)$. What is the value of the function when $x = -3$?

(F) -32 (G) -26 (H) -20 (J) 10

49. **Extended Response** Write a quadratic function in standard form that fits the data points $(0, -5)$, $(1, -3)$, and $(2, 3)$. Use a system of equations, and show all of your work.

CHALLENGE AND EXTEND

50. Three points defining a quadratic function are $(1, 2)$, $(4, 6)$, and $(7, w)$.
   a. If $w = 9$, what is the quadratic function? Does it have a maximum value or a minimum value? What is the vertex?
   b. If $w = 11$, what is the quadratic function? Does it have a maximum value or a minimum value? What is the vertex?
   c. If $w = 10$, what function best fits the points?

51. Explain how you can determine from three points whether the parabola that fits the points opens upward or downward.

2-9 Operations with Complex Numbers

CC.9-12.N.CN.2 Use the relation $i^2 = -1$ and the commutative, associate, and distributive properties to add, subtract, and multiply complex numbers.

Objective
Perform operations with complex numbers.

Vocabulary
complex plane
absolute value of a complex number

Why learn this?
Complex numbers can be used in formulas to create patterns called fractals. (See Exercise 84.)

Just as you can represent real numbers graphically as points on a number line, you can represent complex numbers in a special coordinate plane.

The **complex plane** is a set of coordinate axes in which the horizontal axis represents real numbers and the vertical axis represents imaginary numbers.

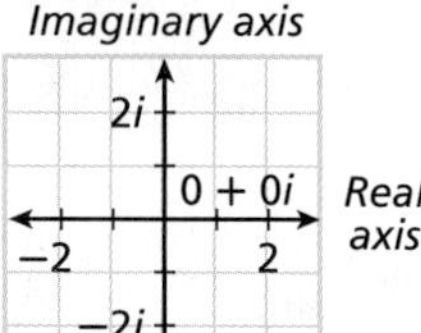

EXAMPLE 1 Graphing Complex Numbers

Helpful Hint
The real axis corresponds to the *x*-axis, and the imaginary axis corresponds to the *y*-axis. Think of $a + bi$ as $x + yi$.

Graph each complex number.

A $-3 + 0i$

B $-3i$

C $4 + 3i$

D $-2 + 4i$

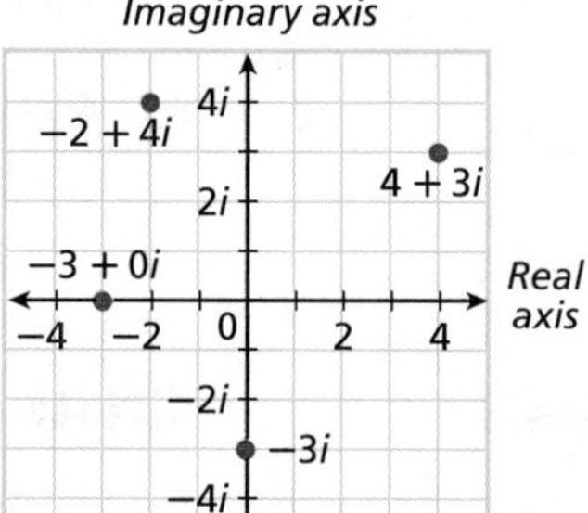

Graph each complex number.

1a. $3 + 0i$ **1b.** $2i$ **1c.** $-2 - i$ **1d.** $3 + 2i$

Recall that the absolute value of a real number is its distance from 0 on the real axis, which is also a number line. Similarly, the absolute value of an imaginary number is its distance from 0 along the imaginary axis.

Absolute Value of a Complex Number

WORDS	ALGEBRA	EXAMPLE
The **absolute value of a complex number** $a + bi$ is the distance from the origin to the point (a, b) in the complex plane, and is denoted $\lvert a + bi \rvert$.	$\lvert a + bi \rvert = \sqrt{a^2 + b^2}$	Imaginary axis; 4i; 3 + 4i; $\lvert 3 + 4i \rvert$; 4; 3; 0; 2; 4; Real axis $\lvert 3 + 4i \rvert = \sqrt{3^2 + 4^2}$ $= \sqrt{9 + 16}$ $= 5$

EXAMPLE 2 Determining the Absolute Value of Complex Numbers

Find each absolute value.

A $|-9 + i|$

$|-9 + 1i|$

$\sqrt{(-9)^2 + 1^2}$

$\sqrt{81 + 1}$

$\sqrt{82}$

B $|6|$

$|6 + 0i|$

$\sqrt{6^2 + 0^2}$

$\sqrt{36}$

6

C $|-4i|$

$|0 + (-4)i|$

$\sqrt{0^2 + (-4)^2}$

$\sqrt{16}$

4

Find each absolute value.

2a. $|1 - 2i|$ **2b.** $\left|-\frac{1}{2}\right|$ **2c.** $|23i|$

Adding and subtracting complex numbers is similar to adding and subtracting variable expressions with like terms. Simply combine the real parts, and combine the imaginary parts.

The set of complex numbers has all the properties of the set of real numbers. So you can use the Commutative, Associative, and Distributive Properties to simplify complex number expressions.

EXAMPLE 3 Adding and Subtracting Complex Numbers

Add or subtract. Write the result in the form $a + bi$.

A $(-2 + 4i) + (3 - 11i)$

$(-2 + 3) + (4i - 11i)$ *Associative and Commutative Properties*

$1 - 7i$ *Add real parts and imaginary parts.*

B $(4 - i) - (5 + 8i)$

$(4 - i) - 5 - 8i$ *Distributive Property*

$(4 - 5) + (-i - 8i)$ *Associative and Commutative Properties*

$-1 - 9i$ *Add real parts and imaginary parts.*

C $(6 - 2i) + (-6 + 2i)$

$(6 - 6) + (-2i + 2i)$ *Associative and Commutative Properties*

$0 + 0i$ *Add real parts and imaginary parts.*

0

D $(10 + 3i) - (10 - 4i)$

$(10 + 3i) - 10 - (-4i)$ *Distributive Property*

$(10 - 10) + (3i + 4i)$ *Associative and Commutative Properties*

$0 + 7i$ *Add real parts and imaginary parts.*

$7i$

Helpful Hint

Complex numbers also have additive inverses. The additive inverse of $a + bi$ is $-(a + bi)$, or $-a - bi$.

Add or subtract. Write the result in the form $a + bi$.

3a. $(-3 + 5i) + (-6i)$ **3b.** $2i - (3 + 5i)$ **3c.** $(4 + 3i) + (4 - 3i)$

You can also add complex numbers by using coordinate geometry.

EXAMPLE 4 Adding Complex Numbers on the Complex Plane

Find $(4 + 3i) + (-2 + i)$ by graphing on the complex plane.

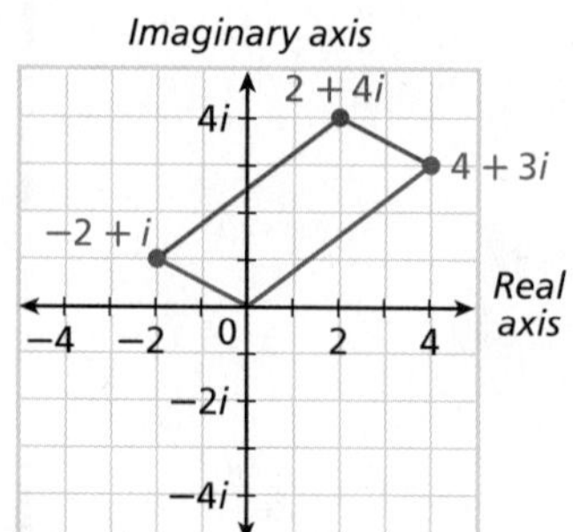

Step 1 Graph $4 + 3i$ and $-2 + i$ on the complex plane. Connect each of these numbers to the origin with a line segment.

Step 2 Draw a parallelogram that has these two line segments as sides. The vertex that is opposite the origin represents the sum of the two complex numbers, $2 + 4i$. Therefore, $(4 + 3i) + (-2 + i) = 2 + 4i$.

Check Add by combining the real parts and combining the imaginary parts.

$$(4 + 3i) + (-2 + i) = [4 + (-2)] + (3i + i) = 2 + 4i$$

Find each sum by graphing on the complex plane.

4a. $(3 + 4i) + (1 - 3i)$ **4b.** $(-4 - i) + (2 - 2i)$

You can multiply complex numbers by using the Distributive Property and treating the imaginary parts as like terms. Simplify by using the fact $i^2 = -1$.

EXAMPLE 5 Multiplying Complex Numbers

Multiply. Write the result in the form $a + bi$.

A $2i(3 - 5i)$

$6i - 10i^2$ *Distribute.*

$6i - 10(-1)$ *Use $i^2 = -1$.*

$10 + 6i$ *Write in a + bi form.*

B $(5 - 6i)(4 - 3i)$

$20 - 15i - 24i + 18i^2$ *Multiply.*

$20 - 39i + 18(-1)$ *Use $i^2 = -1$.*

$2 - 39i$

C $(7 + 2i)(7 - 2i)$

$49 - 14i + 14i - 4i^2$ *Multiply.*

$49 - 4(-1)$ *Use $i^2 = -1$.*

53

D $(6i)(6i)$

$36i^2$

$36(-1)$ *Use $i^2 = -1$.*

-36

Multiply. Write the result in the form $a + bi$.

5a. $2i(3 - 5i)$ **5b.** $(4 - 4i)(6 - i)$ **5c.** $(3 + 2i)(3 - 2i)$

Helpful Hint

Notice the repeating pattern in each row of the table. The pattern allows you to express any power of i as one of four possible values: i, -1, $-i$, or 1.

The imaginary unit i can be raised to higher powers as shown below.

Powers of i		
$i^1 = i$	$i^5 = i^4 \cdot i = 1 \cdot i = i$	$i^9 = i$
$i^2 = -1$	$i^6 = i^4 \cdot i^2 = 1 \cdot (-1) = -1$	$i^{10} = -1$
$i^3 = i^2 \cdot i = -1 \cdot i = -i$	$i^7 = i^4 \cdot i^3 = 1 \cdot (-i) = -i$	$i^{11} = -i$
$i^4 = i^2 \cdot i^2 = -1 \cdot (-1) = 1$	$i^8 = i^4 \cdot i^4 = 1 \cdot 1 = 1$	$i^{12} = 1$

EXAMPLE 6 Evaluating Powers of i

A **Simplify $-3i^{12}$.**

$-3i^{12} = -3(i^2)^6$ — *Rewrite i^{12} as a power of i^2.*

$= -3(-1)^6 = -3(1) = -3$ — *Simplify.*

B **Simplify i^{25}.**

$i^{25} = i \cdot i^{24}$ — *Rewrite as a product of i and an even power of i.*

$= i \cdot (i^2)^{12}$ — *Rewrite i^{24} as a power of i^2.*

$= i \cdot (-1)^{12} = i \cdot 1 = i$ — *Simplify.*

CHECK IT OUT! **6a.** Simplify $\frac{1}{2}i^7$. **6b.** Simplify i^{42}.

Remember!

The complex conjugate of a complex number $a + bi$ is $a - bi$.

Recall that expressions in simplest form cannot have square roots in the denominator. Because the imaginary unit represents a square root, you must rationalize any denominator that contains an imaginary unit. To do this, multiply the numerator and denominator by the complex conjugate of the denominator.

EXAMPLE 7 Dividing Complex Numbers

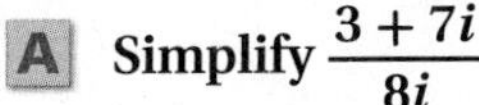

A **Simplify $\frac{3 + 7i}{8i}$.**

$\frac{3 + 7i}{8i}\left(\frac{-8i}{-8i}\right)$ — *Multiply by the conjugate.*

$\frac{-24i - 56i^2}{-64i^2}$ — *Distribute.*

$\frac{-24i + 56}{64}$ — *Use $i^2 = -1$.*

$\frac{-3i + 7}{8} = \frac{7}{8} - \frac{3}{8}i$ — *Simplify.*

B **Simplify $\frac{5 + i}{2 - 4i}$.**

$\frac{5 + i}{2 - 4i}\left(\frac{2 + 4i}{2 + 4i}\right)$

$\frac{10 + 20i + 2i + 4i^2}{4 + 8i - 8i - 16i^2}$

$\frac{10 + 22i - 4}{4 + 16}$

$\frac{6 + 22i}{20} = \frac{3}{10} + \frac{11}{10}i$

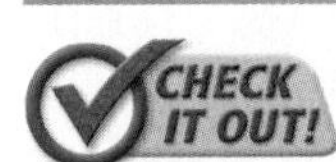

CHECK IT OUT! **7a.** Simplify $\frac{3 + 8i}{-i}$. **7b.** Simplify $\frac{3 - i}{2 - i}$.

THINK AND DISCUSS

1. Explain when a complex number $a + bi$ and its conjugate are equal.
2. Find the product $(a + bi)(c + di)$, and identify which terms in the product are real and which are imaginary.

3. **GET ORGANIZED** Copy and complete the graphic organizer. In each box, give an example.

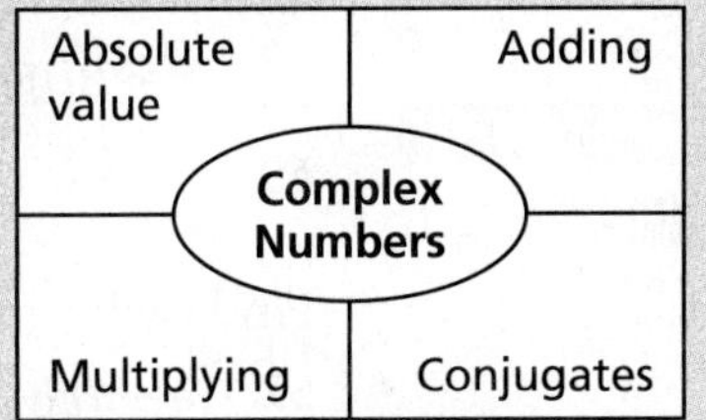

2-9 Exercises

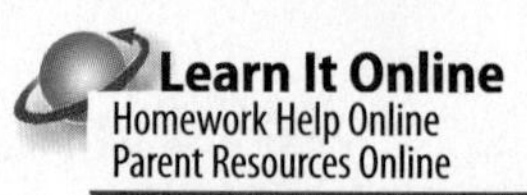

GUIDED PRACTICE

1. **Vocabulary** In the complex number plane, the horizontal axis represents __?__ numbers, and the vertical axis represents __?__ numbers. (*real, irrational,* or *imaginary*)

SEE EXAMPLE 1 **Graph each complex number.**

2. 4 3. $-i$ 4. $3 + 2i$ 5. $-2 - 3i$

SEE EXAMPLE 2 **Find each absolute value.**

6. $|4 - 5i|$ 7. $|-33.3|$ 8. $|-9i|$
9. $|5 + 12i|$ 10. $|-1 + i|$ 11. $|15i|$

SEE EXAMPLE 3 **Add or subtract. Write the result in the form $a + bi$.**

12. $(2 + 5i) + (-2 + 5i)$ 13. $(-1 - 8i) + (4 + 3i)$ 14. $(1 - 3i) - (7 + i)$
15. $(4 - 8i) + (-13 + 23i)$ 16. $(6 + 17i) - (18 - 9i)$ 17. $(-30 + i) - (-2 + 20i)$

SEE EXAMPLE 4 **Find each sum by graphing on the complex plane.**

18. $(3 + 4i) + (-2 - 4i)$ 19. $(-2 - 5i) + (-1 + 4i)$ 20. $(-4 - 4i) + (4 + 2i)$

SEE EXAMPLE 5 **Multiply. Write the result in the form $a + bi$.**

21. $(1 - 2i)(1 + 2i)$ 22. $3i(5 + 2i)$ 23. $(9 + i)(4 - i)$
24. $(6 + 8i)(5 - 4i)$ 25. $(3 + i)^2$ 26. $(-4 - 5i)(2 + 10i)$

SEE EXAMPLE 6 **Simplify.**

27. $-i^9$ 28. $2i^{15}$ 29. i^{30}

SEE EXAMPLE 7

30. $\frac{5 - 4i}{i}$ 31. $\frac{11 - 5i}{2 - 4i}$ 32. $\frac{8 + 2i}{5 + i}$
33. $\frac{17}{4 + i}$ 34. $\frac{45 - 3i}{7 - 8i}$ 35. $\frac{-3 - 12i}{6i}$

PRACTICE AND PROBLEM SOLVING

Independent Practice

For Exercises	See Example
36–39	1
40–45	2
46–51	3
52–54	4
55–60	5
61–63	6
64–69	7

Extra Practice

See Extra Practice for more Skills Practice and Applications Practice exercises.

Graph each complex number.

36. -3 37. $-2.5i$ 38. $1 + i$ 39. $4 - 3i$

Find each absolute value.

40. $|2 + 3i|$ 41. $|-18|$ 42. $\left|\frac{4}{5}i\right|$
43. $|6 - 8i|$ 44. $|-0.5i|$ 45. $|10 - 4i|$

Add or subtract. Write the result in the form $a + bi$.

46. $(8 - 9i) - (-2 - i)$ 47. $4i - (11 - 3i)$ 48. $(4 - 2i) + (-9 - 5i)$
49. $(13 + 6i) + (15 + 35i)$ 50. $(3 - i) - (-3 + i)$ 51. $-16 + (12 + 9i)$

Find each sum by graphing on the complex plane.

52. $(4 + i) + (-3i)$ 53. $(5 + 4i) + (-1 + 2i)$ 54. $(-3 - 3i) + (4 - 3i)$

Multiply. Write the result in the form $a + bi$.

55. $-12i(-1 + 4i)$ **56.** $(3 - 5i)(2 + 9i)$ **57.** $(7 + 2i)(7 - 2i)$

58. $(5 + 6i)^2$ **59.** $(7 - 5i)(-3 + 9i)$ **60.** $-4(8 + 12i)$

Simplify.

61. i^{27} **62.** $-i^{11}$ **63.** $5i^{10}$

64. $\dfrac{2 - 3i}{i}$ **65.** $\dfrac{5 - 2i}{3 + i}$ **66.** $\dfrac{3}{-1 - 5i}$

67. $\dfrac{19 + 9i}{5 + i}$ **68.** $\dfrac{8 + 4i}{7 + i}$ **69.** $\dfrac{6 + 3i}{2 - 2i}$

Write the complex number represented by each point on the graph.

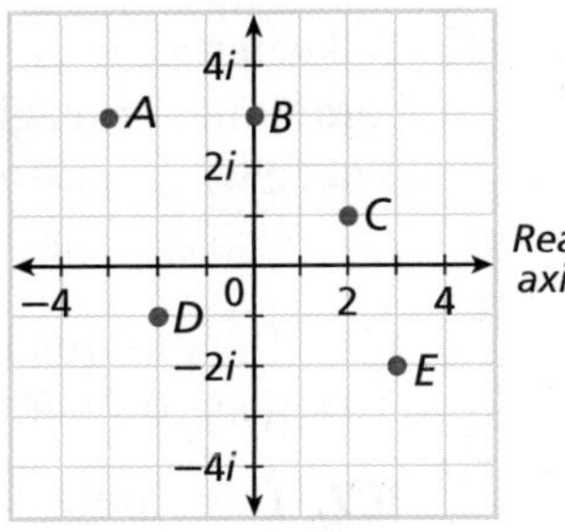

70. A

71. B

72. C

73. D

74. E

Find the absolute value of each complex number.

75. $3 - i$ **76.** $7i$ **77.** $-2 - 6i$

78. $-1 - 8i$ **79.** 0 **80.** $5 + 4i$

81. $\frac{3}{2} - \frac{1}{2}i$ **82.** $5 - i\sqrt{3}$ **83.** $2\sqrt{2} - i\sqrt{3}$

Fractals

Fractals are self-similar, which means that smaller parts of a fractal are similar to the fractal as a whole. Many objects in nature, such as the veins of leaves and snow crystals, also exhibit self-similarity. As a result, scientists can use fractals to model these objects.

84. Fractals Fractals are patterns produced using complex numbers and the repetition of a mathematical formula. Substitute the first number into the formula. Then take the result, put it back into the formula, and so on. Each complex number produced by the formula can be used to assign a color to a pixel on a computer screen. The result is an image such as the one at right. Many common fractals are based on the Julia Set, whose formula is $Z_{n+1} = (Z_n)^2 + c$, where c is a constant.

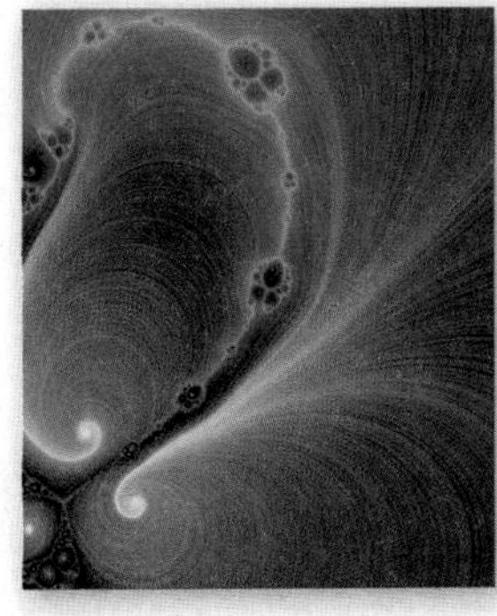

a. Find Z_2 using $Z_2 = (Z_1)^2 + 0.25$. Let $Z_1 = 0.5 + 0.6i$.

b. Find Z_3 using $Z_3 = (Z_2)^2 + 0.25$. Use Z_2 that you obtained in part **a.**

c. Find Z_4 using $Z_4 = (Z_3)^2 + 0.25$. Use Z_3 that you obtained in part **b.**

Simplify. Write the result in the form $a + bi$.

85. $(3.5 + 5.2i) + (6 - 2.3i)$ **86.** $6i - (4 + 5i)$ **87.** $(-2.3 + i) - (7.4 - 0.3i)$

88. $(-8 - 11i) + (-1 + i)$ **89.** $i(4 + i)$ **90.** $(6 - 5i)^2$

91. $(-2 - 3i)^2$ **92.** $(5 + 7i)(5 - 7i)$ **93.** $(2 - i)(2 + i)(2 - i)$

94. $3 - i^{11}$ **95.** $i^{52} - i^{48}$ **96.** $i^{35} - i^{24} + i^{18}$

97. $\dfrac{12 + i}{i}$ **98.** $\dfrac{18 - 3i}{i}$ **99.** $\dfrac{4 + 2i}{6 + i}$

100. $\dfrac{1 + i}{-2 + 4i}$ **101.** $\dfrac{4}{2 - 3i}$ **102.** $\dfrac{6}{\sqrt{2} - i}$

Multi-Step *Impedance* **is a measure of the opposition of a circuit to an electric current. Electrical engineers find it convenient to model impedance Z with complex numbers. In a parallel AC circuit with two impedances Z_1 and Z_2, the** ***equivalent*** **or total impedance in ohms can be determined by using the formula $Z_{eq} = \frac{Z_1 Z_2}{Z_1 + Z_2}$.**

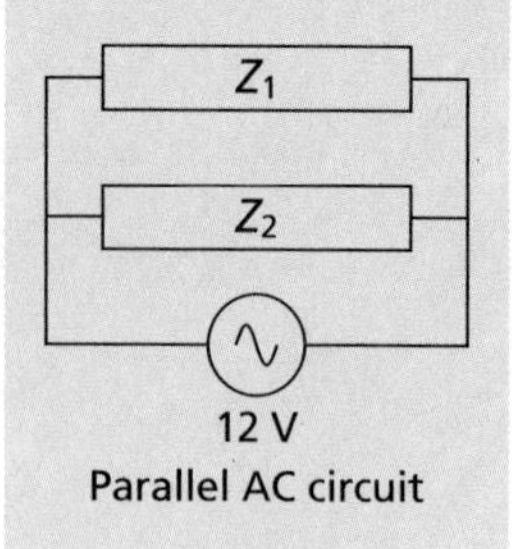

Parallel AC circuit

103. Find the equivalent impedance Z_{eq} for $Z_1 = 3 + 2i$ and $Z_2 = 1 - 2i$ arranged in a parallel AC circuit.

104. Find the equivalent impedance Z_{eq} for $Z_1 = 2 + 2i$ and $Z_2 = 4 - i$ arranged in a parallel AC circuit.

Tell whether each statement is sometimes, always, or never true. If the statement is sometimes true, give an example and a counterexample. If the statement is never true, give a counterexample.

105. The sum of any complex number $a + bi$ and its conjugate is a real number.

106. The difference between any complex number $a + bi\ (b \neq 0)$ and its conjugate is a real number.

107. The product of any complex number $a + bi\ (a \neq 0)$ and its conjugate is a positive real number.

108. The product of any two imaginary numbers $bi\ (b \neq 0)$ and $di\ (d \neq 0)$ is a positive real number.

109. ///ERROR ANALYSIS/// Two attempts to simplify $\frac{3}{2 + i}$ are shown. Which is incorrect? Explain the error.

A

$$\frac{3}{2+i} = \frac{3}{2+i}\left(\frac{2+i}{2+i}\right) = \frac{6+3i}{4+i^2} = \frac{6+3i}{3} = 2 + i$$

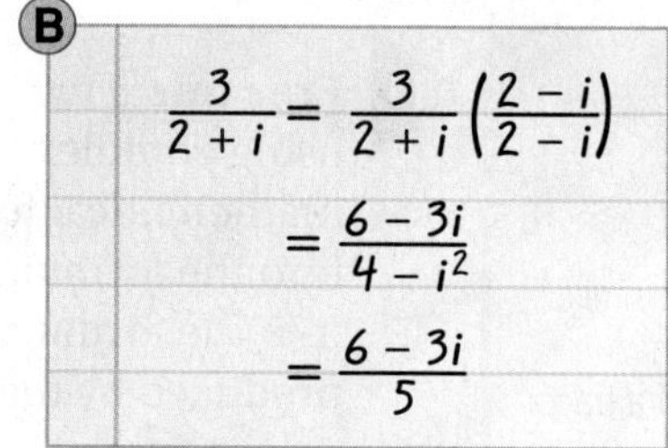

110. Critical Thinking Why are the absolute value of a complex number and the absolute value of its conjugate equal? Use a graph to justify your answer.

111. Write About It Discuss how the difference of two squares, $a^2 - b^2 = (a + b)(a - b)$, relates to the product of a complex number and its conjugate.

MULTI-STEP TEST PREP

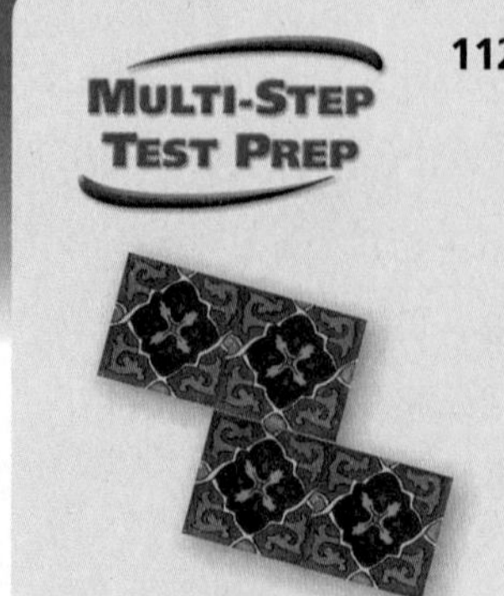

112. You have seen how to graph sums of complex numbers on the complex plane.

a. Find three pairs of complex numbers whose sum is $4 + 4i$.

b. Graph each of the sums on the same complex plane.

c. Describe the results of your graph.

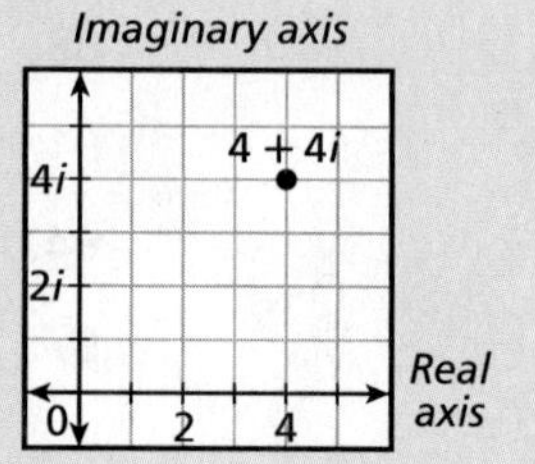

Use the graph for Exercises 113–114.

113. Which point on the graph represents $1 - 2i$?

Ⓐ A Ⓒ C

Ⓑ B Ⓓ D

114. What is the value of the complex number represented in the graph by E?

Ⓕ -2 Ⓗ $-2i$

Ⓖ 2 Ⓙ $2i$

115. Which expression is equivalent to $(2 - 5i) - (2 + 5i)$?

Ⓐ $10i$ Ⓑ $4 + 10i$ Ⓒ $-10i$ Ⓓ $4 - 10i$

116. Which expression is equivalent to $(-5 + 3i)^2$?

Ⓕ $16 - 15i$ Ⓖ $16 - 30i$ Ⓗ $34 - 15i$ Ⓙ $34 - 30i$

CHALLENGE AND EXTEND

117. Consider the powers of i.

a. Complete the table, and look for a pattern.

$i^1 = $ ■	$i^0 = $ ■	$i^{-1} = $ ■	$i^{-2} = $ ■	$i^{-3} = $ ■	$i^{-4} = $ ■	$i^{-5} = $ ■

b. Explain the pattern that you observed for i raised to negative powers. What are the only possible values of i raised to a negative integer power?

c. Simplify i^{-12}, i^{-37}, and i^{-90}.

Find the general form of the result for each complex operation.

118. $(a + bi)(c + di)$

119. $\dfrac{a + bi}{c + di}$

CHAPTER 2

MULTI-STEP TEST PREP

SECTION 2B

Model with mathematics.

Applying Quadratic Functions

Tilted Tiles Mitch and Jacob are making mosaics in an art class. To make one mosaic, Mitch first divides a wall into a grid made up of squares with a side length of 20 cm. Then Jacob glues a tile on each square, making sure that each corner of the tile touches a side of the grid square.

They measure the side length of each tile as well as the distance x from the upper right corner of the grid square to a corner of the tile. They find that for each tile there are two possible values of x, as shown.

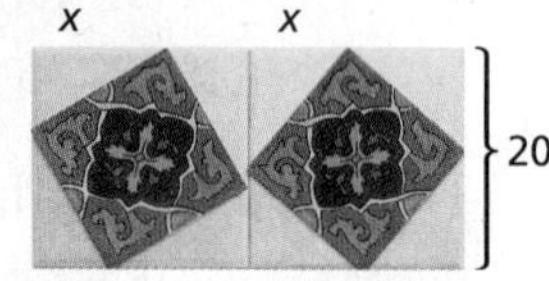

1. Complete the table by finding the area of each tile and the ratio y of the area of each tile to the area of the grid square.
2. Make a scatterplot of the ordered pairs (x, y). Find and graph a quadratic model for the data. Is the model a reasonable representation of the data? Explain.
3. Describe the domain for the problem situation. Explain why the domain of the problem situation is different from the domain of the model.
4. Use your model to determine the value of y when $x = 3.8$. Explain the meaning of your answer in the context of the problem.
5. For what values of x does a tile cover at least 75% of the grid square? Round to the nearest tenth.

Side Length of Tile (cm)	x (cm)	Area of Tile (cm^2)	y
15	6.4		
15	13.6		
15.5	5.5		
15.5	14.5		
16	4.7		
16	15.3		
17	3.3		
17	16.7		
18	2.1		
18	17.9		
19	1.1		
19	18.9		
20	0		

READY TO GO ON?

CHAPTER 2

SECTION 2B

Quiz for Lessons 2-7 Through 2-9

2-7 Solving Quadratic Inequalities

Graph each inequality.

1. $y > -x^2 + 6x$
2. $y \le -x^2 - x + 2$

Solve each inequality by using tables or graphs.

3. $x^2 - 4x + 1 > 6$
4. $2x^2 + 2x - 10 \le 2$

Solve each inequality by using algebra.

5. $x^2 + 4x - 7 \ge 5$
6. $x^2 - 8x < 0$
7. The function $p(r) = -1000r^2 + 6400r - 4400$ models the monthly profit p of a small DVD-rental store, where r is the rental price of a DVD. For what range of rental prices does the store earn a monthly profit of at least \$5000?

2-8 Curve Fitting with Quadratic Models

Determine whether each data set could represent a quadratic function. Explain.

8.

x	5	6	7	8	9
y	13	11	7	1	−7

9.

x	−4	−2	0	2	4
y	10	8	4	8	10

Write a quadratic function that fits each set of points.

10. $(0, 4)$, $(2, 0)$, and $(3, 1)$
11. $(1, 3)$, $(2, 5)$, and $(4, 3)$

For Exercises 12–14, use the table of maximum load allowances for various heights of spruce columns.

Maximum Load Allowance No. 1 Common Spruce	
Height of Column (ft)	Maximum Load (lb)
4	7280
5	7100
6	6650
7	5960

12. Find a quadratic regression equation to model the maximum load given the height.
13. Use your model to predict the maximum load allowed for a 6.5 ft spruce column.
14. Use your model to predict the maximum load allowed for an 8 ft spruce column.

2-9 Operations with Complex Numbers

Find each absolute value.

15. $|-6i|$
16. $|3 + 4i|$
17. $|2 - i|$

Perform each indicated operation, and write the result in the form $a + bi$.

18. $(3 - 5i) - (6 - i)$
19. $(-6 + 4i) + (7 - 2i)$
20. $3i(4 + i)$
21. $(3 + i)(5 - i)$
22. $(1 - 4i)(1 + 4i)$
23. $3i^{15}$
24. $\dfrac{2 - 7i}{-i}$
25. $\dfrac{3 - i}{4 - 2i}$

CHAPTER 2

Study Guide: Review

Vocabulary

absolute value of a complex number
axis of symmetry
binomial
completing the square
complex conjugate
complex number
complex plane
discriminant
imaginary number
imaginary part
imaginary unit
maximum value
minimum value
parabola
quadratic function
quadratic inequality in two variables
quadratic model
quadratic regression
real part
root of an equation
standard form
trinomial
vertex form
vertex of a parabola
zero of a function

Complete the sentences below with vocabulary words from the list above.

1. The number $5i$ can be classified as both a(n) __?__ and a __?__.
2. The value of the input x that makes the output $f(x)$ equal zero is called the __?__.
3. The __?__ is the point at which the parabola intersects the axis of symmetry.
4. The type and number of solutions to a quadratic equation can be determined by finding the __?__.
5. When a parabola opens upward, the y-value of the vertex is the __?__ of a quadratic function.

2-1 Using Transformations to Graph Quadratic Functions

EXAMPLES

■ **Using the graph of $f(x) = x^2$ as a guide, describe the transformations, and then graph $g(x) = \frac{1}{2}x^2 + 3$.**

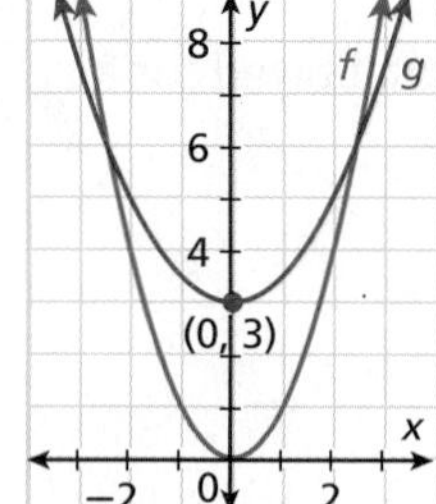

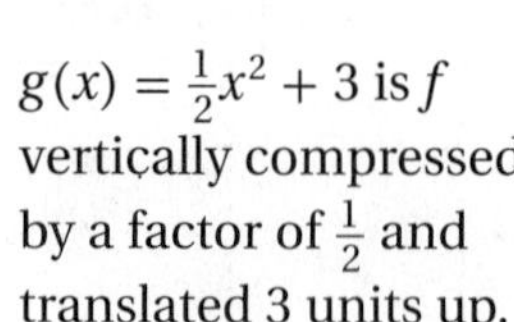

$g(x) = \frac{1}{2}x^2 + 3$ is f vertically compressed by a factor of $\frac{1}{2}$ and translated 3 units up.

■ **Use the description to write a quadratic function in vertex form. The function $f(x) = x^2$ is translated 1 unit right to create g.**

translation 1 unit right: $h = 1$

$g(x) = a(x - h)^2 + k \rightarrow g(x) = (x - 1)^2$

EXERCISES

Graph each function by using a table.

6. $f(x) = -x^2 - 2x$
7. $f(x) = \frac{1}{2}x^2 + 3x - 4$

Using the graph of $f(x) = x^2$ as a guide, describe the transformations, and then graph each function.

8. $g(x) = 4(x - 2)^2$
9. $g(x) = -2(x + 1)^2$
10. $g(x) = \frac{1}{3}x^2 - 3$
11. $g(x) = -(x + 2)^2 + 6$

Use the description to write each quadratic function in vertex form.

12. $f(x) = x^2$ is reflected across the x-axis and translated 3 units down to create g.
13. $f(x) = x^2$ is vertically stretched by a factor of 2 and translated 4 units right to create g.
14. $f(x) = x^2$ is vertically compressed by a factor of $\frac{1}{4}$ and translated 1 unit left to create g.

2-2 Properties of Quadratic Functions in Standard Form

EXAMPLE

- **For $f(x) = -x^2 + 2x + 3$, (a) determine whether the graph opens upward or downward, (b) find the axis of symmetry, (c) find the vertex, (d) find the y–intercept, and (e) graph the function.**

a. Because $a < 0$, the parabola opens downward.

b. axis of symmetry: $x = -\frac{b}{2a} = -\frac{2}{2(-1)} = 1$

c. $f(1) = -1^2 + 2(1) + 3 = 4$
The vertex is $(1, 4)$.

d. Because $c = 3$, the y-intercept is 3.

e.
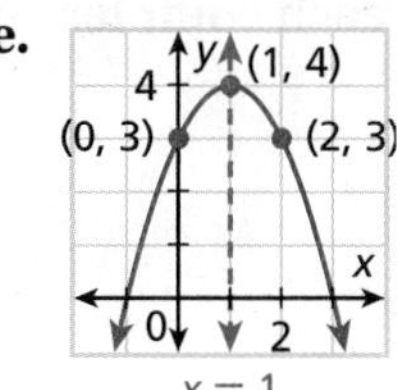

EXERCISES

For each function, (a) determine whether the graph opens upward or downward, (b) find the axis of symmetry, (c) find the vertex, (d) find the y–intercept, and (e) graph the function.

15. $f(x) = x^2 - 4x + 3$ **16.** $g(x) = x^2 + 2x + 3$

17. $h(x) = x^2 - 3x$ **18.** $j(x) = \frac{1}{2}x^2 - 2x + 4$

Find the minimum or maximum value of each function.

19. $f(x) = x^2 + 2x + 6$ **20.** $g(x) = 6x - 2x^2$

21. $f(x) = x^2 - 5x + 1$ **22.** $g(x) = -2x^2 - 8x + 10$

23. $f(x) = -x^2 - 4x + 8$ **24.** $g(x) = 3x^2 + 7$

2-3 Solving Quadratic Equations by Graphing and Factoring

EXAMPLES

- **Find the roots of $x^2 + x = 30$ by factoring.**

$x^2 + x - 30 = 0$ *Rewrite in standard form.*
$(x - 5)(x + 6) = 0$ *Factor.*
$x - 5 = 0$ or $x + 6 = 0$ *Zero Product Property.*
$x = 5$ or $x = -6$ *Solve each equation.*

- **Write a quadratic function with zeros 8 and –8.**

$x = 8$ or $x = -8$ *Write zeros as solutions.*
$x - 8 = 0$ or $x + 8 = 0$ *Set equations equal to 0.*
$(x - 8)(x + 8) = 0$ *Converse Zero Product Property*
$f(x) = x^2 - 64$ *Replace 0 with f(x).*

EXERCISES

Find the roots of each equation by factoring.

25. $x^2 - 7x - 8 = 0$ **26.** $x^2 - 5x + 6 = 0$

27. $x^2 = 144$ **28.** $x^2 - 21x = 0$

29. $4x^2 - 16x + 16 = 0$ **30.** $2x^2 + 8x + 6 = 0$

31. $x^2 + 14x = 32$ **32.** $9x^2 + 6x + 1 = 0$

Write a quadratic function in standard form for each given set of zeros.

33. 2 and –3 **34.** 1 and –1

35. 4 and 5 **36.** –2 and –3

37. –5 and –5 **38.** 9 and 0

2-4 Completing the Square

EXAMPLE

- **Solve $x^2 - 8x = 12$ by completing the square.**

$x^2 - 8x + \blacksquare = 12 + \blacksquare$ *Set up equation.*
$x^2 - 8x + 16 = 12 + 16$ *Add $\left(\frac{b}{2}\right)^2$.*
$(x - 4)^2 = 28$ *Factor.*
$x - 4 = \pm\sqrt{28}$ *Take square roots.*
$x = 4 \pm 2\sqrt{7}$ *Solve for x.*

EXERCISES

Solve each equation by completing the square.

39. $x^2 - 16x + 48 = 0$ **40.** $x^2 + 20x + 84 = 0$

41. $x^2 - 6x = 16$ **42.** $x^2 - 14x = 13$

Write each function in vertex form, and identify its vertex.

43. $f(x) = x^2 - 4x + 9$ **44.** $g(x) = x^2 + 2x - 7$

2-5 Complex Numbers and Roots

EXAMPLE

■ **Solve $x^2 - 22x + 133 = 0$.**

$x^2 - 22x + \blacksquare = -133 + \blacksquare$ — *Rewrite.*

$x^2 - 22x + 121 = -133 + 121$ — *Add $\left(\frac{b}{2}\right)^2$.*

$(x - 11)^2 = -12$ — *Factor.*

$x - 11 = \pm\sqrt{-12}$ — *Take square roots.*

$x = 11 \pm 2i\sqrt{3}$ — *Solve.*

EXERCISES

Solve each equation.

45. $x^2 = -81$

46. $6x^2 + 150 = 0$

47. $x^2 + 6x + 10 = 0$

48. $x^2 + 12x + 45 = 0$

49. $x^2 - 14x + 75 = 0$

50. $x^2 - 22x + 133 = 0$

Find each complex conjugate.

51. $5i - 4$

52. $3 + i\sqrt{5}$

2-6 The Quadratic Formula

EXAMPLES

■ **Find the zeros of $f(x) = 3x^2 - 5x + 3$ by using the Quadratic Formula.**

$x = \dfrac{-b \pm \sqrt{b^2 - 4ac}}{2a}$ — *Quadratic Formula*

$x = \dfrac{-(-5) \pm \sqrt{(-5)^2 - 4(3)(3)}}{2(3)}$ — *Substitute.*

$= \dfrac{5 \pm \sqrt{-11}}{6} = \dfrac{5}{6} \pm i\dfrac{\sqrt{11}}{6}$ — *Simplify.*

■ **Find the type and number of solutions for $x^2 + 9x + 20 = 0$.**

$b^2 - 4ac = 9^2 - 4(1)(20)$
$= 81 - 80 = 1$

There are two distinct real roots because the discriminant is positive.

EXERCISES

Find the zeros of each function by using the Quadratic Formula.

53. $f(x) = x^2 - 3x - 8$

54. $h(x) = (x - 5)^2 + 12$

55. $f(x) = 2x^2 - 10x + 18$

56. $g(x) = x^2 + 3x + 3$

57. $h(x) = x^2 - 5x + 10$

Find the type and number of solutions for each equation.

58. $2x^2 - 16x + 32 = 0$

59. $x^2 - 6x = -5$

60. $x^2 + 3x + 8 = 0$

61. $x^2 - 246x = -144$

62. $x^2 + 5x = -12$

63. $3x^2 - 5x + 3 = 0$

2-7 Solving Quadratic Inequalities

EXAMPLE

■ **Solve $x^2 - 4x - 9 \geq 3$ by using algebra.**

Write and solve the related equation.

$x^2 - 4x - 12 = 0$ — *Write in standard form.*

$(x + 2)(x - 6) = 0$ — *Factor.*

$x = -2$ or $x = 6$ — *Solve.*

The critical values are −2 and 6. These values divide the number line into three intervals: $x \leq -2$, $-2 \leq x \leq 6$, and $x \geq 6$.

Testing an x-value in each interval gives the solution of $x \leq -2$ or $x \geq 6$.

EXERCISES

Graph each inequality.

64. $y > x^2 + 3x + 4$

65. $y \leq 2x^2 - x - 5$

Solve each inequality by using tables or graphs.

66. $x^2 + 2x - 4 \geq -1$

67. $-x^2 - 5x > 4$

Solve each inequality by using algebra.

68. $-x^2 + 6x < 5$

69. $3x^2 - 25 \leq 2$

70. $x^2 - 3 < 0$

71. $3x^2 + 4x - 3 \leq 1$

2-8 Curve Fitting with Quadratic Models

EXAMPLE

- **Find a quadratic model for the wattage of fluorescent bulbs F given the comparable incandescent bulb wattage I. Use the model to estimate the wattage of a fluorescent bulb that produces the same amount of light as a 120–watt incandescent bulb.**

Wattage Comparison					
Incandescent (watts)	40	60	75	90	100
Fluorescent (watts)	11	15	20	23	28

Enter the data into two lists in a graphing calculator. Use the quadratic regression feature.

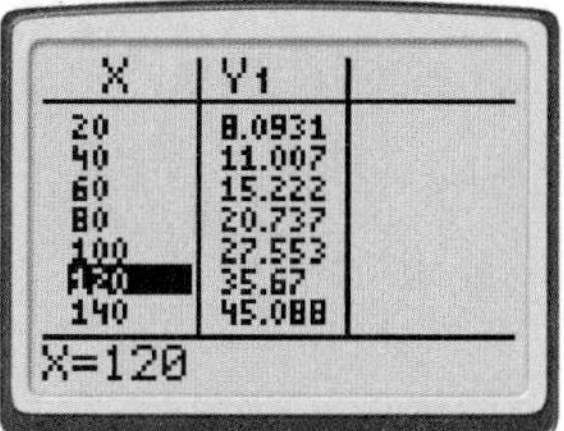

The model is $F(I) \approx 0.0016I^2 + 0.0481I + 6.48$. A 36-watt fluorescent bulb produces about the same amount of light as a 120-watt incandescent bulb.

EXERCISES

Write a quadratic function that fits each set of points.

72. $(-1, 8)$, $(0, 6)$, and $(1, 2)$

73. $(0, 0)$, $(1, -1)$, and $(2, -6)$

Construction For Exercises 74–77, use the table of copper wire gauges.

Common U.S. Copper Wire Gauges		
Gauge	Diameter (in.)	Resistance per 1000 ft (ohms)
24	0.0201	25.67
22	0.0254	16.14
20	0.0320	10.15
18	0.0403	6.385

74. Find a quadratic regression equation to model the diameter given the wire gauge.

75. Use your model to predict the diameter for a 12-gauge copper wire.

76. Find a quadratic regression equation to model the resistance given the wire gauge.

77. Use your model to predict the resistance for a 26-gauge copper wire.

2-9 Operations with Complex Numbers

EXAMPLES

Perform each indicated operation, and write the result in the form $a + bi$.

- $|-2 + 4i|$

$$\sqrt{(-2)^2 + 4^2} = \sqrt{4 + 16} = \sqrt{20} = 2\sqrt{5}$$

- $(3 + 2i)(4 - 5i)$

$$12 - 15i + 8i - 10i^2$$
$$12 - 7i - 10(-1) = 22 - 7i$$

- $\dfrac{-5 + 3i}{1 - 2i}$

$$\frac{-5 + 3i}{1 - 2i}\left(\frac{1 + 2i}{1 + 2i}\right) = \frac{-5 - 7i + 6i^2}{1 - 4i^2}$$
$$= \frac{-11 - 7i}{1 + 4} = -\frac{11}{5} - \frac{7}{5}i$$

EXERCISES

Perform each indicated operation, and write the result in the form $a + bi$.

78. $|-3i|$

79. $|4 - 2i|$

80. $|12 - 16i|$

81. $|7i|$

82. $(1 + 5i) + (6 - i)$

83. $(9 + 4i) - (3 + 2i)$

84. $(5 - i) - (11 - i)$

85. $-5i(3 - 4i)$

86. $(5 - 2i)(6 + 8i)$

87. $(3 + 2i)(3 - 2i)$

88. $(4 + i)(1 - 5i)$

89. $(-7 + 4i)(3 + 9i)$

90. i^{32}

91. $-5i^{21}$

92. $\dfrac{2 + 9i}{-2i}$

93. $\dfrac{5 + 2i}{3 - 4i}$

94. $\dfrac{8 - 4i}{1 + \mathrm{i}}$

95. $\dfrac{-12 + 26i}{2 + 4i}$

CHAPTER 2

CHAPTER TEST

Using the graph of $f(x) = x^2$ as a guide, describe the transformations, and then graph each function.

1. $g(x) = (x + 1)^2 - 2$

2. $h(x) = -\frac{1}{2}x^2 + 2$

3. Use the following description to write a quadratic function in vertex form: $f(x) = x^2$ is vertically compressed by a factor of $\frac{1}{2}$ and translated 6 units right to create g.

For each function, (a) determine whether the graph opens upward or downward, (b) find the axis of symmetry, (c) find the vertex, (d) find the *y*-intercept, and (e) graph the function.

4. $f(x) = -x^2 + 4x + 1$

5. $g(x) = x^2 - 2x + 3$

6. The area A of a rectangle with a perimeter of 32 cm is modeled by the function $A(x) = -x^2 + 16x$, where x is the width of the rectangle in centimeters. What is the maximum area of the rectangle?

Find the roots of each equation by using factoring.

7. $x^2 - 2x + 1 = 0$

8. $x^2 + 10x = -21$

Solve each equation.

9. $x^2 + 4x = 12$

10. $x^2 - 12x = 25$

11. $x^2 + 25 = 0$

12. $x^2 + 12x = -40$

Write each function in vertex form, and identify its vertex.

13. $f(x) = x^2 - 4x + 9$

14. $g(x) = x^2 - 18x + 92$

Find the zeros of each function by using the Quadratic Formula.

15. $f(x) = (x - 1)^2 + 7$

16. $g(x) = 2x^2 - x + 5$

17. The height h in feet of a person on a waterslide is modeled by the function $h(t) = -0.025t^2 - 0.5t + 50$, where t is the time in seconds. At the bottom of the slide, the person lands in a swimming pool. To the nearest tenth of a second, how long does the ride last?

18. Graph the inequality $y < x^2 - 3x - 4$.

Solve each inequality.

19. $-x^2 + 3x + 5 \geq 7$

20. $x^2 - 4x + 1 > 1$

For Exercises 21 and 22, use the table showing the average cost of LCD televisions at one store.

Costs of LCD Televisions

Size (in.)	15	17	23	30
Cost ($)	550	700	1500	2500

21. Find a quadratic model for the cost of a television given its size.

22. Use the model to estimate the cost of a 42 in. LCD television.

Perform the indicated operation, and write the result in the form $a + bi$.

23. $(12 - i) - (5 + 2i)$

24. $(6 - 2i)(2 - 2i)$

25. $-2i^{18}$

26. $\frac{1 - 8i}{4i}$

College Entrance Exam Practice

FOCUS ON SAT MATHEMATICS SUBJECT TESTS

The SAT Mathematics Subject Tests assess knowledge from course work rather than ability to learn. The Level 1 test is meant to be taken by students who have completed two years of algebra and one year of geometry, and it tests more elementary topics than the Level 2 test.

You will need to use a calculator for some of the problems on the SAT Mathematics Subject Tests. Before test day, make sure that you are familiar with the features of the calculator that you will be using.

You may want to time yourself as you take this practice test. It should take you about 8 minutes to complete.

---

1. For what value of c will $3x^2 - 2x + c = 0$ have exactly one distinct real root?

(A) $-\frac{2}{3}$

(B) $-\frac{1}{3}$

(C) 0

(D) $\frac{1}{3}$

(E) $\frac{2}{3}$

---

2. If m and n are real numbers, $i^2 = -1$, and $(m - n) - 4i = 7 + ni$, what is the value of m?

(A) -4

(B) -3

(C) 1

(D) 3

(E) 4

---

3. If $x^2 - 5x + 6 = (x - h)^2 + k$, what is the value of k?

(A) $-\frac{25}{4}$

(B) $-\frac{5}{2}$

(C) $-\frac{1}{4}$

(D) 0

(E) 6

---

4. What is the solution set of $y^2 - 2y \leq 3y + 14$?

(A) $y \geq -2$

(B) $y \leq 7$

(C) $y \leq -2$ or $y \geq 7$

(D) $-7 \leq y \leq 2$

(E) $-2 \leq y \leq 7$

---

5. Which of the following is a factor of $(a - 1)^2 - b^2$?

(A) $a + b - 1$

(B) $a - b$

(C) $a - 1$

(D) $a - b + 1$

(E) $1 - b$

---

6. If $z = 5 - 4i$ and $i^2 = -1$, what is $|z|$?

(A) 1

(B) 3

(C) 9

(D) $\sqrt{41}$

(E) $\sqrt{42}$

CHAPTER 2

TEST TACKLER

Standardized Test Strategies

Multiple Choice: Work Backward

When taking a multiple-choice test, you can sometimes work backward to determine which answer is correct. Because this method can be time consuming, it is best used only when you cannot solve a problem in any other way.

EXAMPLE 1

Which expression is equivalent to $2x^2 - 3x - 14$?

Ⓐ $(2x + 7)(x + 2)$

Ⓑ $(2x - 7)(x - 2)$

Ⓒ $(2x - 7)(x + 2)$

Ⓓ $(2x + 7)(x - 2)$

If you have trouble factoring the quadratic expression given in the question, you can multiply the binomials in the answer choices to find the product that is the same as $2x^2 - 3x - 14$.

Try Choice A: $(2x + 7)(x + 2) = 2x^2 + 11x + 14$

Try Choice B: $(2x - 7)(x - 2) = 2x^2 - 11x + 14$

Try Choice C: $(2x - 7)(x + 2) = \mathbf{2x^2 - 3x - 14}$

Choice C is the answer.

***Note:** Trying choice D can help you check your work.*

EXAMPLE 2

What is the solution set of $x^2 - 36 < 0$?

Ⓕ $x < -6$ or $x > 6$

Ⓖ $-6 < x < 6$

Ⓗ $-36 < x < 36$

Ⓙ $x < -36$ or $x > 36$

If you have trouble determining the solution set, substitute values of x into the inequality. Based on whether the values make the inequality true or false, you may be able to eliminate one or more of the answer choices.

Substitute 0 for x: $x^2 - 36 < 0 \rightarrow (\mathbf{0})^2 - 36 \overset{?}{<} 0 \rightarrow -36 < 0$ ✔

When $x = 0$, the inequality is true. Therefore, the solution set must include $x = 0$. Because choices F and J do not include $x = 0$, they can be eliminated.

Substitute 10 for x: $x^2 - 36 < 0 \rightarrow (\mathbf{10})^2 - 36 \overset{?}{<} 0 \rightarrow 64 \overset{?}{<} 0$ ✘

When $x = 10$, the inequality is false. Therefore, the solution set does not include $x = 10$. Because choice H includes $x = 10$, it can be eliminated.

The only remaining choice is choice G. Therefore, choice G must be correct.

You can also work backward to check whether the answer you found by another method is correct or reasonable.

Read each test item, and answer the questions that follow.

Item A

What are the zeros of the function $g(x) = 6x^2 - 8x - 4$, rounded to the nearest hundredth?

Ⓐ -10.32 and 2.32
Ⓑ -1.72 and 0.39
Ⓒ 1.72 and -0.39
Ⓓ 10.32 and -2.32

1. Rachel cannot remember how to determine the zeros of a quadratic function, so she plans to pick one of the answer choices at random. What could Rachel do to make a more educated guess?

2. Describe how to find the correct answer by working backward.

Item B

A portable television has a screen with a diagonal of 4 inches. The length of the screen is 1 inch greater than its width. What are the dimensions of the screen to the nearest hundredth?

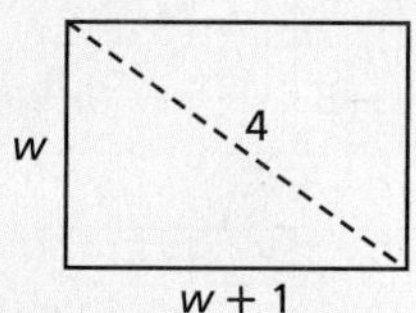

Ⓕ 1.28 inches by 2.28 inches
Ⓖ 1.28 inches by 3.28 inches
Ⓗ 2.28 inches by 2.28 inches
Ⓙ 2.28 inches by 3.28 inches

3. Can any of the answer choices be eliminated immediately? If so, which choices and why?

4. Describe how you can determine the correct answer by using the Pythagorean Theorem and working backward.

Item C

Which of the following is a solution of $(x + 4)^2 = 25$?

Ⓐ $x = -9$
Ⓑ $x = -1$
Ⓒ $x = 0$
Ⓓ $x = 9$

5. Explain how to use substitution to determine the correct answer.

6. Check whether choice A is correct by working backward. Explain your findings. What should you do next?

Item D

The height h of a golf ball in feet t seconds after it is hit into the air is modeled by $h(t) = -16t^2 + 64t$. How long is the ball in the air?

Ⓕ 2 seconds
Ⓖ 4 seconds
Ⓗ 12 seconds
Ⓙ 16 seconds

7. The measurements given in the answer choices represent possible values of which variable in the function?

8. Describe how you can work backward to determine that choice F is not correct.

Item E

The base of a triangle is 4 in. longer than twice its height. If the triangle has an area of 24 in^2, what is its height?

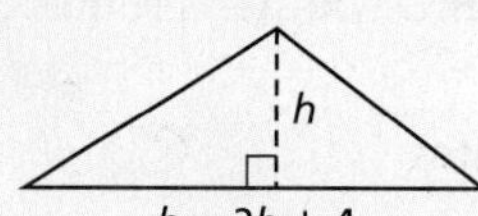

Ⓐ 2 in.
Ⓑ 4 in.
Ⓒ 6 in.
Ⓓ 8 in.

9. What equation do you need to solve to find the value of h?

10. Try choice A by working backward. Explain your findings. What should you do next?

CHAPTER 2

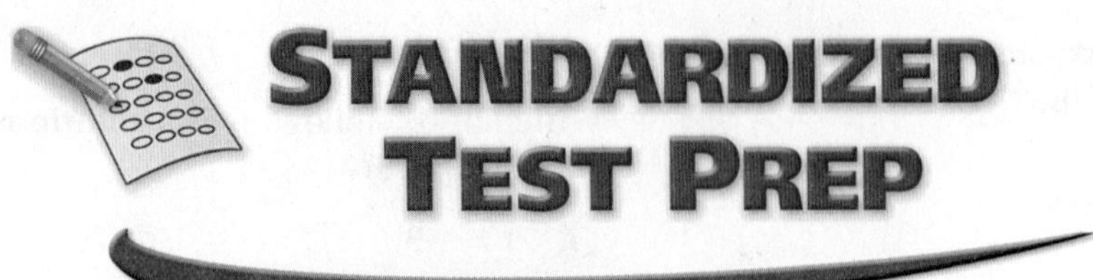

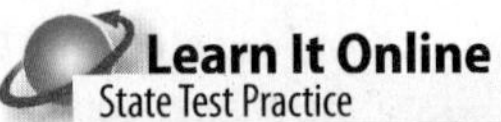

CUMULATIVE ASSESSMENT

Multiple Choice

1. Which of the following is true of the graph of the function $f(x) = x^2 + 2x + 3$?
Statement 1: Its y-intercept is 3.
Statement 2: The vertex is at $(-1, 2)$.
Statement 3: Its x-intercept is -1.
   - (A) Statement 1 and statement 2.
   - (B) Statement 1 only.
   - (C) Statement 1 and statement 3.
   - (D) All three statements are true.

2. Which of these functions does NOT have zeros at -1 and 4?
   - (F) $f(x) = x^2 - 3x - 4$
   - (G) $f(x) = 2x^2 + 6x - 8$
   - (H) $f(x) = -x^2 + 3x + 4$
   - (J) $f(x) = 2x^2 - 6x - 8$

3. Dawn and Julia are running on a jogging trail. Dawn starts running 5 minutes after Julia does. If Julia runs at an average speed of 8 ft/s and Dawn runs at an average speed of 9 ft/s, how many minutes after Dawn starts running will she catch up with Julia?
   - (A) 5 minutes
   - (B) 27 minutes
   - (C) 40 minutes
   - (D) 45 minutes

4. Which equation has intercepts at (20, 0, 0), (0, 40, 0), and (0, 0, 5)?
   - (F) $20x + 40y + 5z = 0$
   - (G) $20x + 40y + 5z = 1$
   - (H) $4x + 8y + z = 5$
   - (J) $2x + y + 8z = 40$

5. Which graph represents the function $f(x) = -\frac{1}{2}(x - 3) - 4$?

(A)

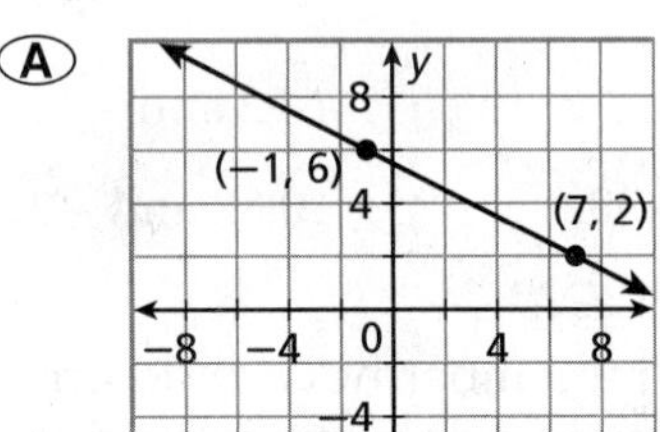

(B)

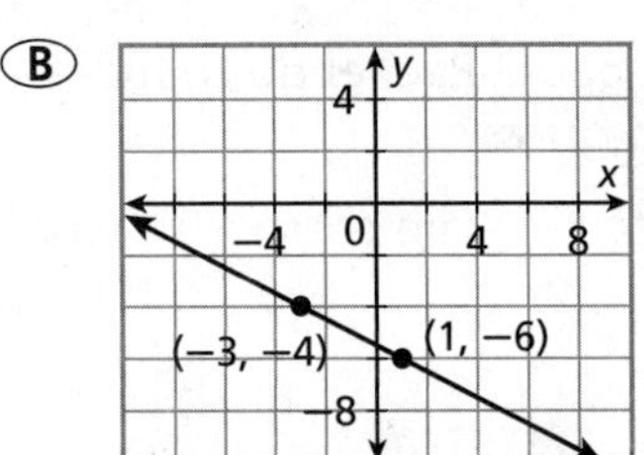

(C)

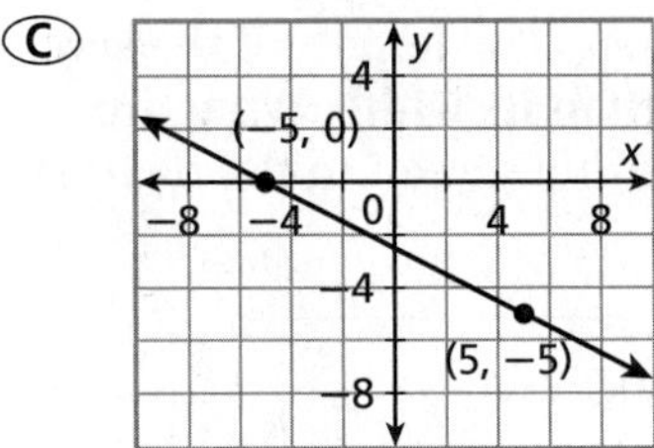

(D)

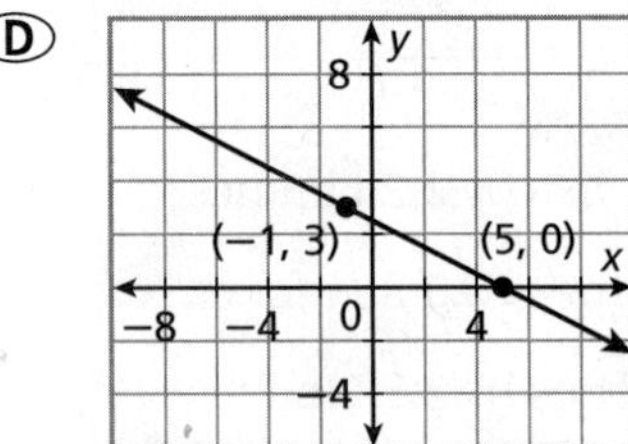

6. What is the equation of the function graphed below?

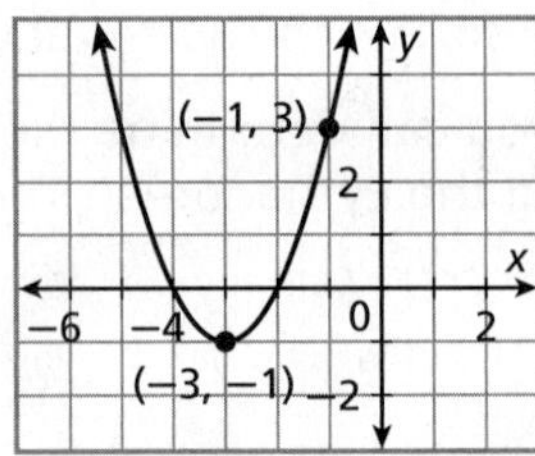

   - (F) $y = (x - 3)^2 - 1$
   - (G) $y = (x + 3)^2 - 1$
   - (H) $y = (x - 1)^2 - 3$
   - (J) $y = (x + 1)^2 - 3$

7. If the relationship between x and y is quadratic, which value of y completes the table?

x	−3	−1	1	3	5
y	21	7	■	27	61

Ⓐ 3
Ⓑ 7
Ⓒ 9
Ⓓ 17

8. Which is equivalent to the expression $\frac{5(6-8i)}{2-i}$?

Ⓕ $-20 + 10i$
Ⓖ $15 - 8i$
Ⓗ $15 - 40i$
Ⓙ $20 - 10i$

9. Solve the inequality $-x^2 + 4x - 6 < -2$.

Ⓐ $x < -2$
Ⓑ $x \neq 2$
Ⓒ $x < 2$
Ⓓ $x > 2$

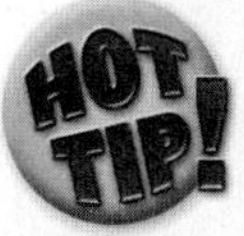

In nearly all standardized tests, you cannot enter a negative value as the answer to a gridded-response question. If you get a negative value as an answer to one of these questions, you have probably made a mistake in your calculations.

Gridded Response

10. What value of x makes the equation $x^2 + 64 = 16x$ true?

11. The table shows the fees that are charged at an airport parking lot for various lengths of time. What is the slope of the linear function that models the parking fee f in dollars for h number of hours?

Time (h)	1	3	5	7
Parking Fee ($)	3.35	5.05	6.75	8.45

12. What is the x-value of the vertex of $f(x) = 2x^2 - 15x + 5$?

13. What is the value of c given that the following system is dependent?

$$\begin{cases} 2y - x + 10 = 0 \\ 3x - 6y - c = 16 \end{cases}$$

Short Response

14. Determine whether the data set could represent a quadratic function. Explain.

x	−90	−75	−60	−45	−30
y	3	1	2	6	13

15. The graph below shows a feasible region for a set of constraints.

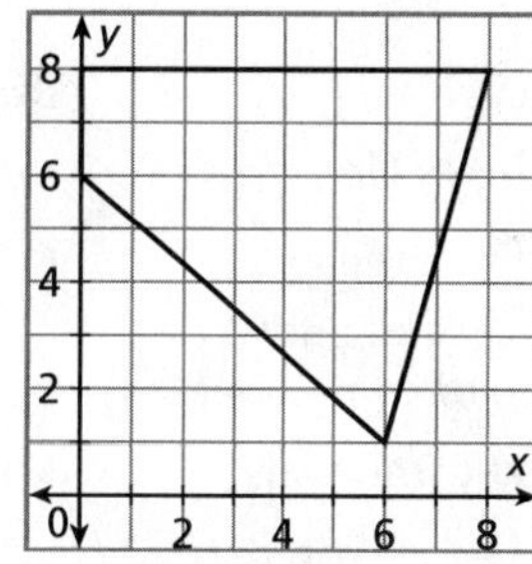

a. Write the constraints for the feasible region.

b. Maximize the objective function $P = 3x - 4y$ under these constraints.

16. Consider the function $f(x) = x^2 - 2x - 48$.

a. Determine the roots of the function. Show your work.

b. The function f is translated to produce the function g. The vertex of g is the point $(3, 30)$. Write the function rule for g in vertex form, and explain how you determined your answer.

Extended Response

17. A small alteration store charges $15.00 per hour plus a $12.50 consulting fee for alterations. A competing store charges $20.00 per hour but does not charge a consulting fee.

a. For each store, write a linear function c that can be used to find the total cost of an alteration that takes h hours.

b. For which values of h is the small alteration store less expensive than the competing store? Explain how you determined your answer.

c. The small store wants to adjust its pricing so that it is less expensive than the competing store for any alteration job that takes an hour or more. By how much should the small store lower its consulting fee in order to make this adjustment?

CHAPTER 3

Polynomial Functions

COMMON CORE

Chapter Focus

- Solve problems with polynomials.
- Identify characteristics of polynomial functions.

FILL IT UP!

You can use polynomials to predict the shape of containers.

Learn It Online
Chapter Project Online

Vocabulary

Match each term on the left with a definition on the right.

1. coefficient
2. like terms
3. root of an equation
4. x-intercept
5. maximum of a function

A. the y-value of the highest point on the graph of the function
B. the horizontal number line that divides the coordinate plane
C. the numerical factor in a term
D. a value of the variable that makes the equation true
E. terms that contain the same variables raised to the same powers
F. the x-coordinate of a point where a graph intersects the x-axis

Evaluate Powers

Evaluate each expression.

6. 6^4
7. -5^4
8. $(-1)^5$
9. $\left(-\frac{2}{3}\right)^2$

Evaluate Expressions

Evaluate each expression for the given value of the variable.

10. $x^4 - 5x^2 - 6x - 8$ for $x = 3$
11. $2x^3 - 3x^2 - 29x - 30$ for $x = -2$
12. $2x^3 - x^2 - 8x + 4$ for $x = \frac{1}{2}$
13. $3x^4 + 5x^3 + 6x^2 + 4x - 1$ for $x = -1$

Multiply and Divide Monomials

Multiply or divide.

14. $2x^3y \cdot 4x^2$
15. $-5a^2b \cdot ab^4$
16. $\frac{-7t^4}{3t^2}$
17. $\frac{3p^3q^2r}{12pr^4}$

Surface Area

Find the surface area of each solid.

18. cube with side length 4 cm
19. rectangular prism with height 3 ft, width 1.5 ft, and length 8 ft

Volume

Find the volume of each solid.

20. rectangular prism with height 1 in., width 6 in., and length $\frac{2}{3}$ in.
21. rectangular prism with height 5 cm and a square base with side length 2 cm

CHAPTER 3

Study Guide: Preview

Where You've Been

Previously, you

- used transformations to graph quadratic functions.
- solved quadratic equations.
- used the Zero Product Property to find the zeros of quadratic functions.
- modeled data with quadratic models.

In This Chapter

You will study

- using transformations to graph polynomial functions.
- solving polynomial equations.
- the zeros of polynomial functions.
- modeling data with polynomial models.

Where You're Going

You can use the skills in this chapter

- to solve problems in future math classes, including College Algebra and Trigonometry.
- to solve real-life problems in physics and graphic arts.
- to predict the value of stocks.
- to maximize or minimize volume and area.

Key Vocabulary/Vocabulario

end behavior	comportamiento extremo
leading coefficient	coeficiente principal
local maximum	máximo local
local minimum	mínimo local
monomial	monomio
multiplicity	multiplicidad
polynomial	polinomio
polynomial function	función polinomial
synthetic division	división sintética
turning point	punto de inflexión

Vocabulary Connections

To become familiar with some of the vocabulary terms in the chapter, consider the following. You may refer to the chapter, the glossary, or a dictionary if you like.

1. In what position would you find the *leading* runner in a race? In what position do you suppose you would find the **leading coefficient** in a polynomial?
2. A **local minimum** of a function is a value less than any other value in the region around it. Which of the vocabulary terms do you think describes the value of a function that is greater than any other value in the region around it?
3. The word **monomial** begins with the root *mono-*. List some other words that begin with *mono-*. What do all of these words have in common?
4. The everyday meaning of **turning point** is "a point at which a change takes place." What might happen at a *turning point* on the graph of a polynomial function?

Study Strategy: Remember Theorems and Formulas

In math, there are many formulas, properties, theorems, and rules that you must commit to memory. To help you remember an important rule, write it on an index card. Include a diagram or an example, and add notes about the important details. Study your index cards on a regular basis.

The Quadratic Formula

If $ax^2 + bx + c = 0$ $(a \neq 0)$, then the solutions, or roots, are

$$x = \frac{-b \pm \sqrt{b^2 - 4ac}}{2a}.$$

Sample Index Card

Quadratic Formula

If $ax^2 + bx + c = 0$ $(a \neq 0)$, then the roots are

$$x = \frac{-b \pm \sqrt{b^2 - 4ac}}{2a}.$$

- This can be used to solve any quadratic equation.
- Before using the formula, make sure the equation is written in standard form.
- $f(x) = x^2 + 2x - 24 \rightarrow x = \frac{-(2) \pm \sqrt{(2)^2 - 4(1)(-24)}}{2(1)}$

Try This

1. Create index cards for the discriminant formulas shown in the table below.
2. Explain why you need to understand the principles and concepts of the quadratic formula prior to memorizing the discriminant properties.
3. Describe a plan to help you memorize the quadratic formula and the discriminant formulas.

Discriminant

The discriminant of the quadratic equation $ax^2 + bx + c = 0$ $(a \neq 0)$ is $b^2 - 4ac$.

If $b^2 - 4ac > 0$, the equation has two distinct real solutions.	If $b^2 - 4ac = 0$, the equation has one distinct real solution.	If $b^2 - 4ac < 0$, the equation has two distinct nonreal complex solutions.
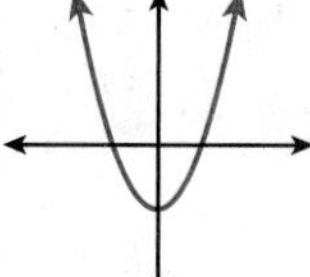	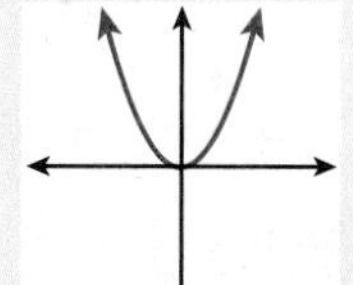	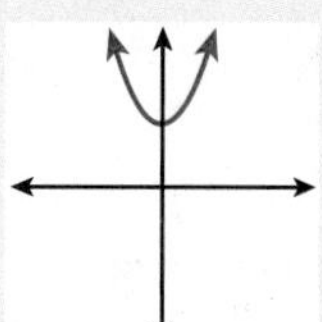

COMMON CORE

3-1 Polynomials

CC.9-12.F.IF.7c Graph polynomial functions, identifying zeros when suitable factorizations are available, and showing end behavior.* *Also* **CC.9-12.A.APR.1, CC.9-12.A.CED.2, CC.9-12.A.CED.3**

Objectives

Identify, evaluate, add, and subtract polynomials.

Classify and graph polynomials.

Vocabulary

monomial
polynomial
degree of a monomial
degree of a polynomial
leading coefficient
binomial
trinomial
polynomial function

Who uses this?

Doctors can use polynomials to model blood flow. (See Example 4.)

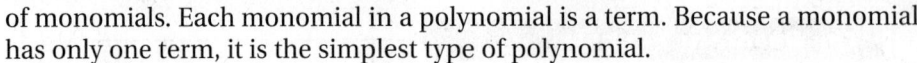

A **monomial** is a number or a product of numbers and variables with whole number exponents. A **polynomial** is a monomial or a sum or difference of monomials. Each monomial in a polynomial is a term. Because a monomial has only one term, it is the simplest type of polynomial.

Polynomials have no variables in denominators or exponents, no roots or absolute values of variables, and all variables have whole number exponents.

Polynomials: $3x^4$ $\quad 2z^{12} + 9z^3$ $\quad \frac{1}{2}a^7$ $\quad 0.15x^{101}$ $\quad 3t^2 - t^3$

Not polynomials: 3^x $\quad |2b^3 - 6b|$ $\quad \frac{8}{5y^2}$ $\quad \frac{1}{2}\sqrt{x}$ $\quad m^{0.75} - m$

The **degree of a monomial** is the sum of the exponents of the variables.

EXAMPLE  Identifying the Degree of a Monomial

Identify the degree of each monomial.

A x^4

x^4 *Identify the exponent.*

The degree is 4.

B 12

$12 = 12x^0$ *Identify the exponent.*

The degree is 0.

C $4a^2b$

$4a^2b^1$ *Add the exponents.*

The degree is 3.

D x^3y^4z

$x^3y^4z^1$ *Add the exponents.*

The degree is 8.

Identify the degree of each monomial.

1a. x^3 **1b.** 7 **1c.** $5x^3y^2$ **1d.** a^6bc^2

The **degree of a polynomial** is given by the term with the greatest degree. A polynomial with one variable is in standard form when its terms are written in descending order by degree. So, in standard form, the degree of the first term indicates the degree of the polynomial, and the **leading coefficient** is the coefficient of the first term.

Standard Form

Leading coefficient ↘ ↙ Degree of polynomial

$$5x^3 + 8x^2 + 3x - 17$$

Degree of term: 3 2 1 0

A polynomial can be classified by its number of terms. A polynomial with two terms is called a **binomial**, and a polynomial with three terms is called a **trinomial**. A polynomial can also be classified by its degree.

Classifying Polynomials by Degree

Name	Degree	Example
Constant	0	-9
Linear	1	$x - 4$
Quadratic	2	$x^2 + 3x - 1$
Cubic	3	$x^3 + 2x^2 + x + 1$
Quartic	4	$2x^4 + x^3 + 3x^2 + 4x - 1$
Quintic	5	$7x^5 + x^4 - x^3 + 3x^2 + 2x - 1$

EXAMPLE 2 Classifying Polynomials

Rewrite each polynomial in standard form. Then identify the leading coefficient, degree, and number of terms. Name the polynomial.

A $2x + 4x^3 - 1$

Write terms in descending order by degree.

$4x^3 + 2x - 1$

Leading coefficient: 4

Degree: 3

Terms: 3

Name: cubic trinomial

B $7x^3 - 11x + x^5 - 2$

Write terms in descending order by degree.

$1x^5 + 7x^3 - 11x - 2$

Leading coefficient: 1

Degree: 5

Terms: 4

Name: quintic polynomial with four terms

Rewrite each polynomial in standard form. Then identify the leading coefficient, degree, and number of terms. Name the polynomial.

2a. $4x - 2x^2 + 2$

2b. $-18x^2 + x^3 - 5 + 2x$

To add or subtract polynomials, combine like terms. You can add or subtract horizontally or vertically.

EXAMPLE 3 Adding and Subtracting Polynomials

Add or subtract. Write your answer in standard form.

A $(3x^2 + 7 + x) + (14x^3 + 2 + x^2 - x)$

Add vertically.

$(3x^2 + 7 + x) + (14x^3 + 2 + x^2 - x)$

$3x^2 + x + 7$ *Write in standard form.*

$+ 14x^3 + x^2 - x + 2$ *Align like terms.*

$14x^3 + 4x^2 + 0x + 9$ *Add.*

$14x^3 + 4x^2 + 9$ *Combine like terms.*

Add or subtract. Write your answer in standard form.

B $(1 - x^2) - (3x^2 + 2x - 5)$

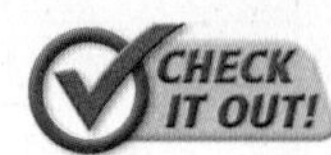

Remember!

To subtract a polynomial, distribute the negative to all terms.

Add the opposite horizontally.

$(1 - x^2) - (3x^2 + 2x - 5)$

$(-x^2 + 1) + (-3x^2 - 2x + 5)$ *Write in standard form.*

$(-x^2 - 3x^2) + (-2x) + (1 + 5)$ *Group like terms.*

$-4x^2 - 2x + 6$ *Add.*

CHECK IT OUT! **Add or subtract. Write your answer in standard form.**

3a. $(-36x^2 + 6x - 11) + (6x^2 + 16x^3 - 5)$

3b. $(5x^3 + 12 + 6x^2) - (15x^2 + 3x - 2)$

A **polynomial function** is a function whose rule is a polynomial. In this course, you will study only polynomial functions with one variable.

EXAMPLE 4 *Medical Application*

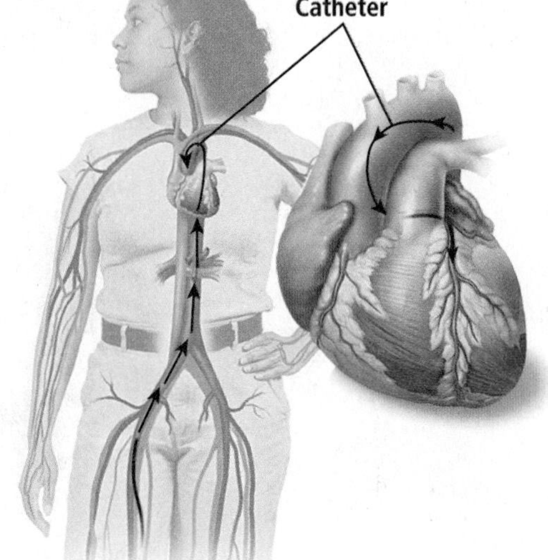

Cardiac output is the amount of blood pumped through the heart. The output is measured by a technique called dye dilution. A doctor injects dye into a vein near the heart and measures the amount of dye in the arteries over time.

The cardiac output of a particular patient can be approximated by the function $f(t) = 0.0056t^3 - 0.22t^2 + 2.33t$, where t represents time (in seconds after injection, $0 \le t \le 23$) and $f(t)$ represents the concentration of dye (in milligrams per liter).

a. Evaluate $f(t)$ for $t = 0$ and $t = 3$.

$f(0) = 0.0056(0)^3 - 0.22(0)^2 + 2.33(0) = 0$

$f(3) = 0.0056(3)^3 - 0.22(3)^2 + 2.33(3) = 5.1612$

b. Describe what the values of the function from part a represent.

$f(0)$ represents the concentration of dye, 0 mg/L, in the artery at the start of the dye dilution process.

$f(3)$ represents the concentration of dye, 5.1612 mg/L, in the artery after 3 seconds.

CHECK IT OUT! **4.** For a different patient, the dye dilution can be modeled by the function $f(t) = 0.000468x^4 - 0.016x^3 + 0.095x^2 + 0.806x$. Evaluate $f(t)$ for $t = 4$ and $t = 17$, and describe what the values of the function represent.

Graphing polynomial functions can be a challenge. Throughout this chapter, you will learn skills for analyzing, describing, and graphing higher-degree polynomials. Until then, the graphing calculator will be a useful tool.

EXAMPLE 5 Graphing Higher-Degree Polynomials on a Calculator

Graph each polynomial function on a calculator. Describe the graph, and identify the number of real zeros.

> **Caution!**
> Depending on your viewing window, a calculator may not show all of the important features of a graph. Watch out for hidden behavior.

A $f(x) = x^3 - x$

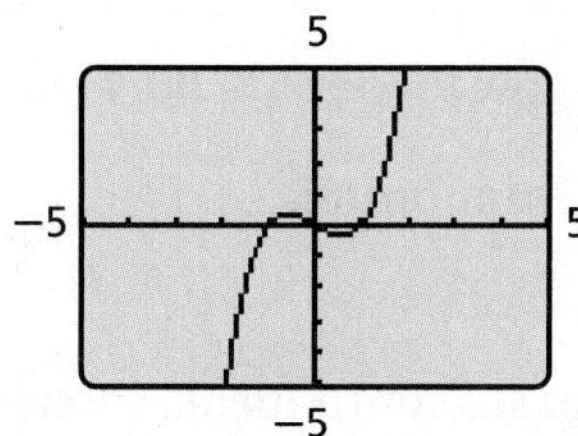

From left to right, the graph increases, decreases slightly, and then increases again. It crosses the x-axis three times, so there appear to be three real zeros.

B $f(x) = 3x^3 + 2x + 1$

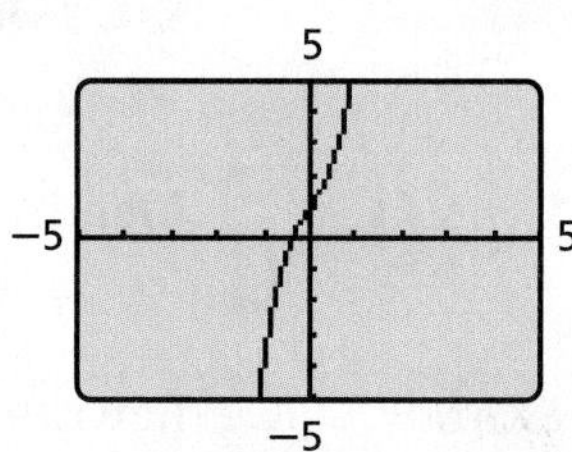

From left to right, the graph increases. It crosses the x-axis once, so there appears to be one real zero.

C $h(x) = x^4 - 8x^2 + 1$

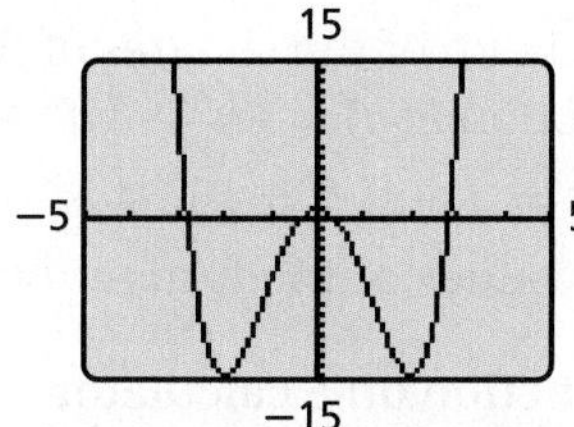

From left to right, the graph alternately decreases and increases, changing direction three times. It crosses the x-axis four times, so there appear to be four real zeros.

D $k(x) = x^4 + x^3 - x^2 + 2x - 3$

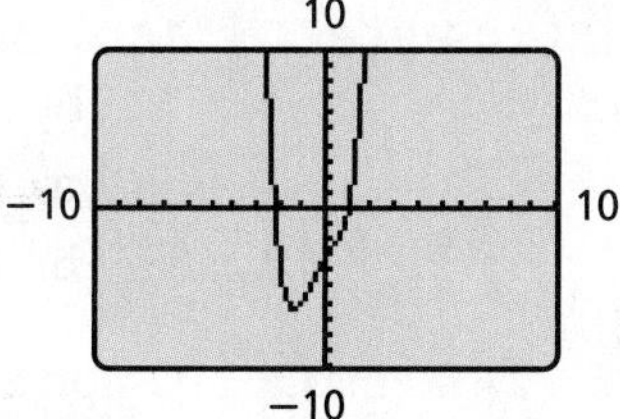

From left to right, the graph decreases and then increases. It crosses the x-axis twice, so there appear to be two real zeros.

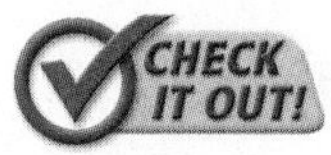

Graph each polynomial on a calculator. Describe the graph, and identify the number of real zeros.

5a. $f(x) = 6x^3 + x^2 - 5x + 1$ **5b.** $f(x) = 3x^2 - 2x + 2$

5c. $g(x) = x^4 - 3$ **5d.** $h(x) = 4x^4 - 16x^2 + 5$

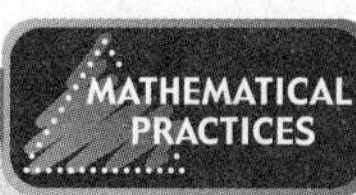

THINK AND DISCUSS

1. Can a polynomial have a leading coefficient of $\sqrt{3}$? Explain.
2. What is the degree of the sum of a quartic polynomial and a cubic polynomial? Explain.
3. Is the sum of two trinomial polynomials always a trinomial? Explain.
4. **GET ORGANIZED** Copy and complete the graphic organizer.

Know it! Note

Characteristics	Definition
Polynomial	
Examples	Nonexamples

3-1 Exercises

Learn It Online
Homework Help Online
Parent Resources Online

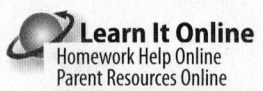

GUIDED PRACTICE

1. **Vocabulary** Explain how to identify the leading coefficient of a polynomial.

SEE EXAMPLE 1

Identify the degree of each monomial.

2. $-7x$
3. $4x^2y^3$
4. 13
5. m^3n^2p

SEE EXAMPLE 2

Rewrite each polynomial in standard form. Then identify the leading coefficient, degree, and number of terms. Name the polynomial.

6. $4x + 2x^2 - 7 + x^3$
7. $3x^2 + 5x - 4$
8. $5x^2 - 4x^3$
9. $4x^4 + 8x^2 + 1 - 3x$

SEE EXAMPLE 3

Add or subtract. Write your answer in standard form.

10. $(15x^2 - 3x + 11) + (2x^3 - x^2 + 6x + 1)$
11. $(12x - 1 + 2x^2) + (x^2 + 4)$
12. $(3x^2 - 5x) - (-4 + x^2 + x)$
13. $(x^2 - 3x + 7) - (6x^2 + 4x + 12)$

SEE EXAMPLE 4

14. **Number Theory** The sum of the squares of the first n natural numbers is given by the polynomial function $F(n) = \frac{1}{3}n^3 + \frac{1}{2}n^2 + \frac{1}{6}n$.
    a. Evaluate $F(n)$ for $n = 5$ and $n = 10$.
    b. Describe what the values of the function from part **a** represent.

SEE EXAMPLE 5

Graph each polynomial function on a calculator. Describe the graph, and identify the number of real zeros.

15. $f(x) = 4x^3 + 2x + 1$
16. $g(x) = \frac{1}{4}x^4 - 3x^2$
17. $h(x) = -3x^3 - 6$
18. $p(x) = -4x^4 + 6x^3 - 3x^2$

PRACTICE AND PROBLEM SOLVING

Independent Practice

For Exercises	See Example
19–22	1
23–26	2
27–30	3
31	4
32–35	5

Extra Practice

See Extra Practice for more Skills Practice and Applications Practice exercises.

Identify the degree of each monomial.

19. x^8
20. $6x^3y$
21. 8
22. $a^4b^6c^3$

Rewrite each polynomial in standard form. Then identify the leading coefficient, degree, and number of terms. Name the polynomial.

23. $3x^3 + 2x^4 - 7x + x^2$
24. $6x - 4x^4 + 5^7$
25. $2x^3 + 10x - 9$
26. $3x^2 + 2x^6 - 4x^4 - 1$

Add or subtract. Write your answer in standard form.

27. $(x^2 - 3x + 4) + (x^3 + 3x - 4)$
28. $(x^2 - 3x + 4) - (3x + x^3 - 4)$
29. $(5y^3 - 2y^2 - 1) - (y^2 - 2y - 3)$
30. $(2y^2 - 5y + 3) + (y^2 - 2y - 5)$

31. **Recreation** The distance d, in centimeters, that a diving board bends below its resting position when you stand at its end is dependent on your distance x, in meters, from the stabilized point. This relationship can be modeled by the function $d(x) = -4x^3 + x^2$.
    a. Evaluate $d(x)$ for $x = 1$ and $x = 2$.
    b. Describe what the values of the function from part **a** represent.

Graph each polynomial function on a calculator. Describe the graph, and identify the number of real zeros.

32. $f(x) = -2x^2 + x - 1$

33. $g(x) = x^3 + 1$

34. $h(x) = x^4 - 6x^2 + 10$

35. $p(x) = -x^5 + x - 1$

Complete the table.

	Polynomial	Standard Form	Leading Coefficient	Degree
36.	$8x + 3x^2 - 5$	■	■	■
37.	$3x^2 + x^4 - 2$	■	■	■
38.	$x^3 - x^4 + x - 1$	■	■	■
39.	$64 + x^2$	■	■	■

40. Critical Thinking Write a quartic trinomial with a leading coefficient of 2.

Geometry **Find a polynomial expression in terms of x for the surface area of each figure.**

41.

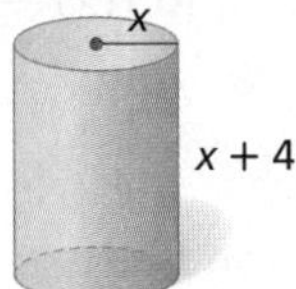

42.

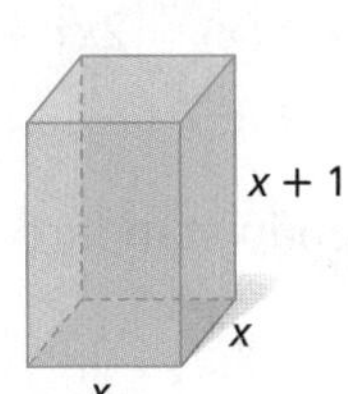

43.

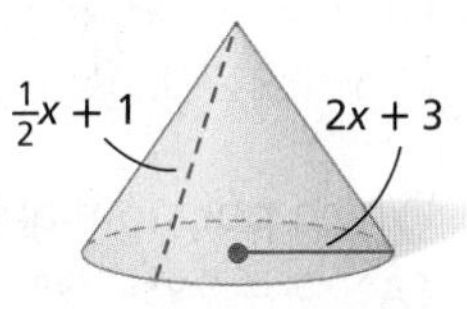

44.

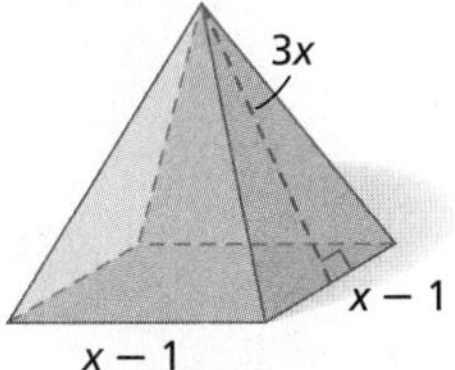

45. Business The manager of a gift-basket business will ship the baskets anywhere in the country. The cost to mail a basket based on its weight x, in pounds, is given by $C(x) = 0.03x^3 - 0.75x^2 + 4.5x + 7$.

a. What is the cost of shipping a 7-pound gift basket?

b. What is the cost of shipping a 19-pound gift basket?

46. Estimation Estimate the value of $P(x) = -2.03x^3 + \pi x^2 - x + 5.8$ for $P(-2.78)$.

Tell whether each statement is sometimes, always, or never true. If it is sometimes true, give examples to support your answer.

47. A quadratic polynomial is a trinomial.

48. The degree of a polynomial in standard form is equal to the degree of the first term.

49. The leading coefficient of a polynomial is the greatest coefficient of any term.

MULTI-STEP TEST PREP

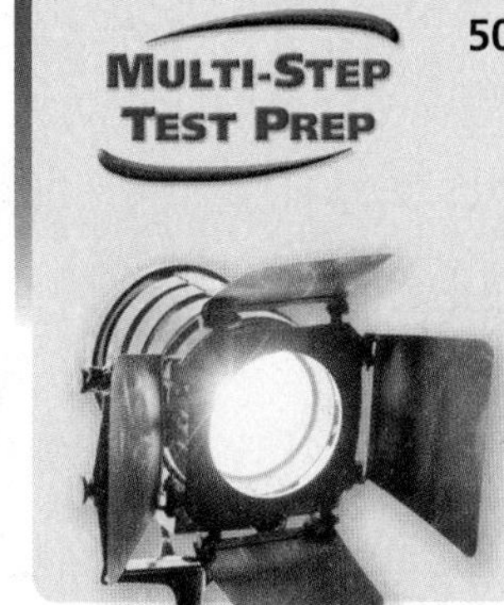

50. The total number of lights in a triangular lighting rig is related to the triangular numbers, as shown at right. The nth triangular number is given by $T(n) = \frac{1}{2}n^2 + \frac{1}{2}n$.

a. Write a polynomial function that represents the $(n + 1)$th triangular number, $T(n + 1)$.

b. The difference between two consecutive triangular numbers is $T(n + 1) - T(n)$. Subtract these two polynomial functions, and state a conclusion about the difference between consecutive triangular numbers.

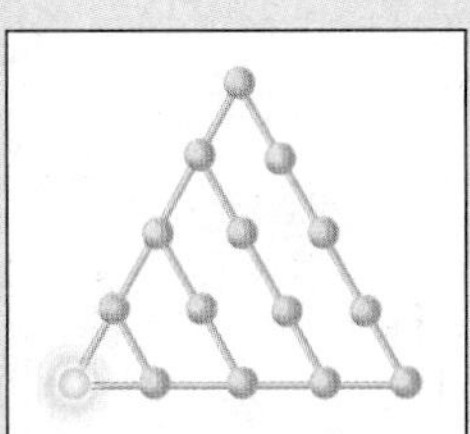

Triangular numbers: 1, 3, 6, 10, 15, . . .

51. Graphing Calculator The functions below are polynomials in factored form. Graph each function. Identify the x-intercepts. What can you say about the x-intercepts and the linear binomial factors in the functions?

a. $f(x) = (x + 3)(x - 1)(x - 4)$

b. $g(x) = (x + 1)(x + 2)(x - 3)(x - 1)$

c. $h(x) = x(x + 1)(x - 2)$

d. $k(x) = (x + 2)(x - 3)$

e. $j(x) = x\left(x + \frac{1}{2}\right)\left(x - \frac{1}{2}\right)$

Write About It **Recall the properties of real numbers.**

52. Is the addition of polynomial functions commutative? Explain.

53. Is the addition of polynomial functions associative? Explain.

TEST PREP

54. What is the degree of the monomial $5xy^4z$?

Ⓐ 6 Ⓑ 1 Ⓒ 4 Ⓓ 5

55. For $f(x) = 2x^2 + 4x - 6$ and $g(x) = 2x^2 + 2x + 8$, find $f(x) - g(x)$.

Ⓕ $-4x^2 - 2x + 2$ Ⓖ $2x + 2$ Ⓗ $4x^2 + 6x + 2$ Ⓙ $2x - 14$

56. Which polynomial is written in standard form?

Ⓐ $7 + 2x^4 - x^6$ Ⓑ $3x^3 - x^5$ Ⓒ x^4 Ⓓ $x^2 + 3 - 2x$

57. What is the degree of the polynomial function $h(x) = 7x^3 - x^6 + x$?

Ⓕ 10 Ⓖ 3 Ⓗ -1 Ⓙ 6

58. Short Response Evaluate $P(x) = \frac{1}{2}x^3 - x^2 + 8$ for $x = -2$.

CHALLENGE AND EXTEND

$P(x)$ and $R(x)$ are polynomials. $P(x)$ is a trinomial. Give examples of $P(x)$ and $R(x)$ that meet the given conditions.

59. $P(x) - R(x)$ is a binomial.

60. $P(x) - R(x)$ is a trinomial.

61. $P(x) - R(x)$ is a polynomial with four terms.

62. $P(x) - R(x)$ is a quartic.

63. $P(x) - R(x)$ is a quintic.

Pascal's Triangle

Each number in Pascal's triangle is the sum of the two numbers diagonally above it. All of the outside numbers are 1.

Many interesting number patterns can be found in Pascal's triangle, such as Fibonnacci's sequence and powers of 2.

Pascal's Triangle is useful for many different mathematical situations, such as expanding binomials and probability.

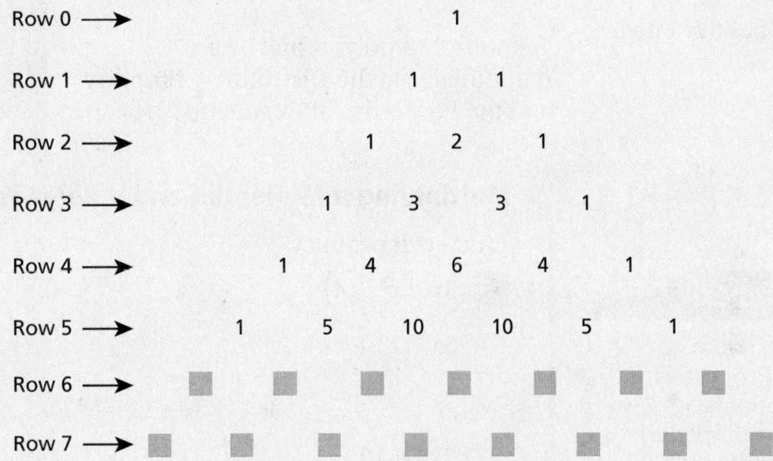

Activity

Find rows 6 and 7 of Pascal's triangle.

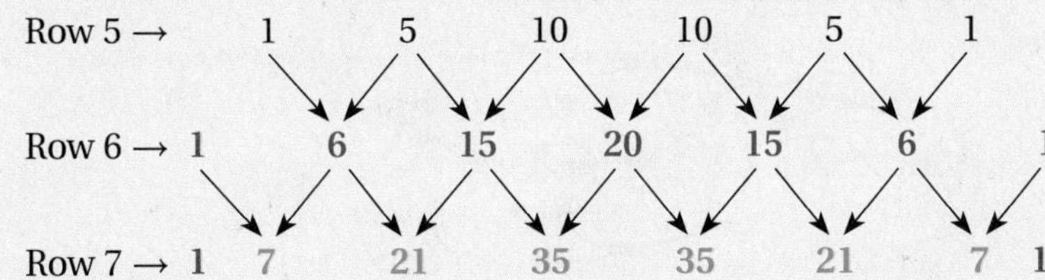

All of the outside numbers are 1. Fill in values by adding the numbers in row 5 that are diagonally above the new values.

Repeat the process for row 7.

Try This

1. Find rows 8, 9, and 10 of Pascal's triangle.
2. **Make a Conjecture** What can you say about the relationship between the row number and the number of terms in a row?
3. **Make a Conjecture** What can you say about the relationship between the row number and the second term in each row?
4. **Make a Conjecture** Expand $(x + 1)(x + 1)$ *and* $(x + 1)(x + 1)(x + 1)$, and use your answers to make a conjecture about the relationship between Pascal's triangle and the multiplication of binomials.
5. Test your conjecture from Problem 4 by expanding $(x + 1)(x + 1)(x + 1)(x + 1)$ with multiplication and by using Pascal's triangle.

3-2 Multiplying Polynomials

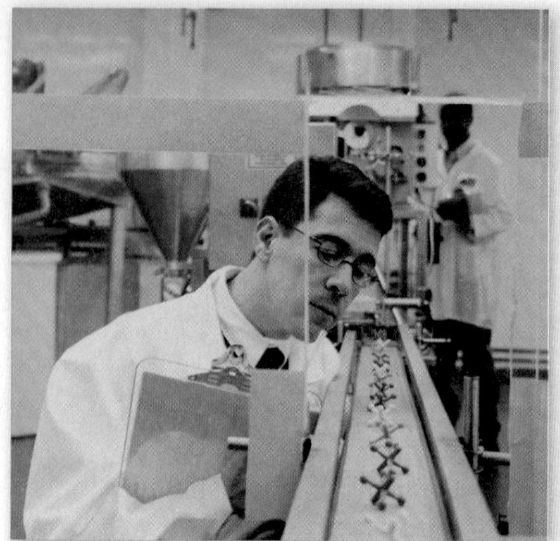

CC.9-12.A.APR.5 Know and apply the Binomial Theorem for the expansion of $(x + y)^n$ ... with coefficients determined for example by Pascal's Triangle. *Also* **CC.9-12.A.APR.1, CC.9-12.A.APR.4**

Objectives

Multiply polynomials.

Use binomial expansion to expand binomial expressions that are raised to positive integer powers.

Who uses this?

Business managers can multiply polynomials when modeling total manufacturing costs. (See Example 3.)

To multiply a polynomial by a monomial, use the Distributive Property and the Properties of Exponents.

EXAMPLE 1 Multiplying a Monomial and a Polynomial

Remember!

You may want to review Properties of Exponents before multiplying a monomial by a polynomial.

Find each product.

A $3x^2(x^3 + 4)$

$3x^2(x^3 + 4)$

$3x^2 \cdot x^3 + 3x^2 \cdot 4$ *Distribute.*

$3x^5 + 12x^2$ *Multiply.*

B $ab(a^3 + 3ab^2 - b^3)$

$ab(a^3 + 3ab^2 - b^3)$

$ab(a^3) + ab(3ab^2) + ab(-b^3)$

$a^4b + 3a^2b^3 - ab^4$

CHECK IT OUT! **Find each product.**

1a. $3cd^2(4c^2d - 6cd + 14cd^2)$ **1b.** $x^2y(6y^3 + y^2 - 28y + 30)$

To multiply any two polynomials, use the Distributive Property and multiply each term in the second polynomial by each term in the first.

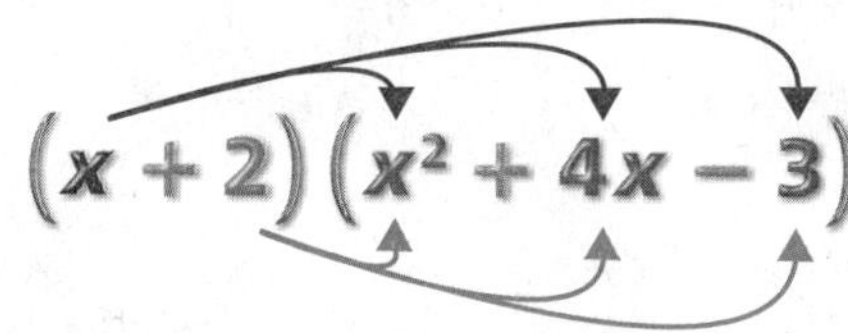

Keep in mind that if one polynomial has m terms and the other has n terms, then the product has mn terms before it is simplified.

EXAMPLE 2 Multiplying Polynomials

Find each product.

A $(x - 2)(1 + 3x - x^2)$

Method 1 Multiply horizontally.

$(x - 2)(-x^2 + 3x + 1)$ *Write polynomials in standard form.*

$x(-x^2) + x(3x) + x(1) - 2(-x^2) - 2(3x) - 2(1)$ *Distribute x and then −2.*

$-x^3 + 3x^2 + x + 2x^2 - 6x - 2$ *Multiply. Add exponents.*

$-x^3 + 5x^2 - 5x - 2$ *Combine like terms.*

Method 2 Multiply vertically.

$$\begin{array}{r} -x^2 + 3x + 1 \\ x - 2 \\ \hline 2x^2 - 6x - 2 \\ -x^3 + 3x^2 + x \qquad \\ \hline -x^3 + 5x^2 - 5x - 2 \end{array}$$

Write each polynomial in standard form.

Multiply $(-x^2 + 3x + 1)$ by -2.

Multiply $(-x^2 + 3x + 1)$ by x, and align like terms.

Combine like terms.

Find each product.

B $(x^2 + 3x - 5)(x^2 - x + 1)$

Multiply each term of one polynomial by each term of the other. Use a table to organize the products.

	x^2	$-x$	$+1$
x^2	x^4	$-x^3$	$+x^2$
$+3x$	$+3x^3$	$-3x^2$	$+3x$
-5	$-5x^2$	$+5x$	-5

The top left corner is the first term in the product. Combine terms along diagonals to get the middle terms. The bottom right corner is the last term in the product.

$x^4 + (3x^3 - x^3) + (-5x^2 - 3x^2 + x^2) + (5x + 3x) + (-5)$

$x^4 + 2x^3 - 7x^2 + 8x - 5$

Helpful Hint

When using a table to multiply, the polynomials must be in standard form. Use a zero for any missing terms.

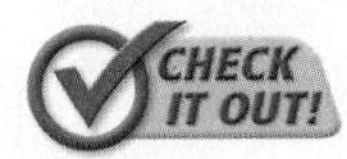

Find each product.

2a. $(3b - 2c)(3b^2 - bc - 2c^2)$ **2b.** $(x^2 - 4x + 1)(x^2 + 5x - 2)$

EXAMPLE 3 *Business Application*

Mr. Silva manages a manufacturing plant. From 1990 through 2005, the number of units produced (in thousands) can be modeled by $N(x) = 0.02x^2 + 0.2x + 3$. The average cost per unit (in dollars) can be modeled by $C(x) = -0.002x^2 - 0.1x + 2$, where x is the number of years since 1990. Write a polynomial $T(x)$ that can be used to model Mr. Silva's total manufacturing costs.

Total cost is the product of the number of units and the cost per unit.

$T(x) = N(x) \cdot C(x)$.

Multiply the two polynomials.

$$\begin{array}{r} 0.02x^2 + 0.2x + 3 \\ \times\ -0.002x^2 - 0.1x + 2 \\ \hline 0.04x^2 + 0.4x + 6 \\ -0.002x^3 - 0.02x^2 - 0.3x \qquad \\ -0.00004x^4 - 0.0004x^3 - 0.006x^2 \qquad\qquad \\ \hline -0.00004x^4 - 0.0024x^3 + 0.014x^2 + 0.1x + 6 \end{array}$$

Mr. Silva's total manufacturing costs, in thousands of dollars, can be modeled by $T(x) = -0.00004x^4 - 0.0024x^3 + 0.014x^2 + 0.1x + 6$.

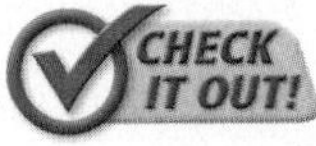

3. What if...? Suppose that in 2005 the cost of raw materials increases and the new average cost per unit is modeled by $C(x) = -0.004x^2 - 0.1x + 3$. Write a polynomial $T(x)$ that can be used to model the total costs.

You can also raise polynomials to powers.

EXAMPLE 4 Expanding a Power of a Binomial

Find the product.

$(x + y)^3$

$(x + y)(x + y)(x + y)$	*Write in expanded form.*
$(x + y)(x^2 + 2xy + y^2)$	*Multiply the last two binomial factors.*
$x(x^2) + x(2xy) + x(y^2) + y(x^2) + y(2xy) + y(y^2)$	*Distribute x and then y.*
$x^3 + 2x^2y + xy^2 + x^2y + 2xy^2 + y^3$	*Multiply.*
$x^3 + 3x^2y + 3xy^2 + y^3$	*Combine like terms.*

Find each product.

4a. $(x + 4)^4$

4b. $(2x - 1)^3$

Notice the coefficients of the variables in the final product of $(x + y)^3$. These coefficients are the numbers from the third row of Pascal's triangle.

Binomial Expansion		Pascal's Triangle (Coefficients)
$(a + b)^0 =$	1	1
$(a + b)^1 =$	$a + b$	1 1
$(a + b)^2 =$	$a^2 + 2ab + b^2$	1 2 1
$(a + b)^3 =$	$a^3 + 3a^2b + 3ab^2 + b^3$	1 3 3 1
$(a + b)^4 =$	$a^4 + 4a^3b + 6a^2b^2 + 4ab^3 + b^4$	1 4 6 4 1
$(a + b)^5 =$	$a^5 + 5a^4b + 10a^3b^2 + 10a^2b^3 + 5ab^4 + b^5$	1 5 10 10 5 1

Each row of Pascal's triangle gives the coefficients of the corresponding binomial expansion. The pattern in the table can be extended to apply to the expansion of any binomial of the form $(a + b)^n$, where n is a whole number.

Binomial Expansion

For a binomial expansion of the form $(a + b)^n$, the following statements are true.

1. There are $n + 1$ terms.
2. The coefficients are the numbers from the nth row of Pascal's triangle.
3. The exponent of a is n in the first term, and the exponent decreases by 1 in each successive term.
4. The exponent of b is 0 in the first term, and the exponent increases by 1 in each successive term.
5. The sum of the exponents in any term is n.

This information is formalized by the *Binomial Theorem*.

Student to Student: *Expanding Binomials*

Caitlin Humphrey
Hillcrest High School

I like to use a chart to expand binomials. I will use the binomial $(x + 2)^4$ as an example.

I write the coefficients from Pascal's triangle in the top row. I write the decreasing powers in the second row.

Then I shift one column to the right and write the increasing powers in the third row.

1	4	6	4	1
x^4	x^3	x^2	x	
	2	4	8	16

Finally, I multiply vertically to get $x^4 + 8x^3 + 24x^2 + 32x + 16$.

EXAMPLE 5 Using Pascal's Triangle to Expand Binomial Expressions

Expand each expression.

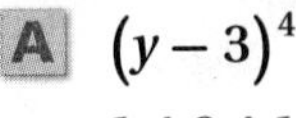

A $(y - 3)^4$

1 4 6 4 1 *Identify the coefficients for n = 4, or row 4.*

$$\left[1y^4(-3)^0\right] + \left[4y^3(-3)^1\right] + \left[6y^2(-3)^2\right] + \left[4y^1(-3)^3\right] + \left[1y^0(-3)^4\right]$$

$$y^4 - 12y^3 + 54y^2 - 108y + 81$$

B $(4z + 5)^3$

1 3 3 1 *Identify the coefficients for n = 3, or row 3.*

$$\left[1(4z)^3 5^0\right] + \left[3(4z)^2 5^1\right] + \left[3(4z)^1 5^2\right] + \left[1(4z)^0 5^3\right]$$

$$64z^3 + 240z^2 + 300z + 125$$

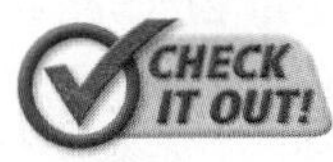

Expand each expression.

5a. $(x + 2)^3$ **5b.** $(x - 4)^5$ **5c.** $(3x + 1)^4$

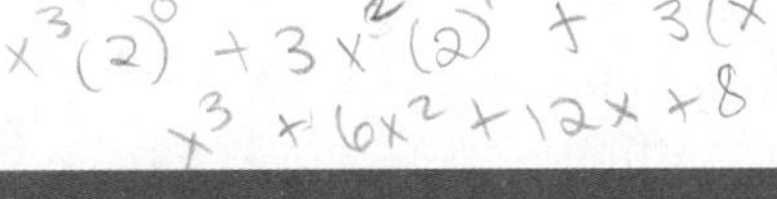

MATHEMATICAL PRACTICES

THINK AND DISCUSS

1. The product of $(3x^4 - 2x^2 - 1)$ and a polynomial $P(x)$ results in a polynomial of degree 9. What is the degree of $P(x)$? Explain.
2. After $(2x + 8)^7$ is expanded, what is the degree of the result, and how many terms does the result have? Explain.
3. **GET ORGANIZED** Copy and complete the graphic organizer. In each box, write an example and find the product.

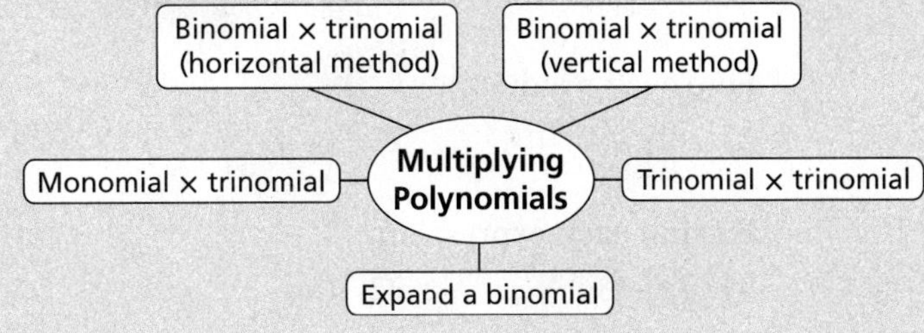

3-2 Exercises

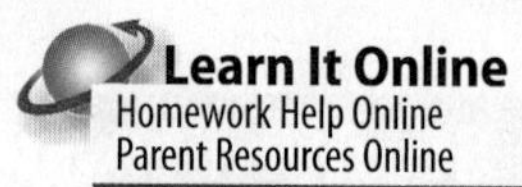

GUIDED PRACTICE

Find each product.

SEE EXAMPLE 1

1. $-4c^2d^3(5cd^2 + 3c^2d)$
2. $3x^2(2y + 5x)$
3. $xy(5x^2 + 8x - 7)$
4. $2xy(3x^2 - xy + 7)$

SEE EXAMPLE 2

5. $(x - y)(x^2 + 2xy - y^2)$
6. $(3x - 2)(2x^2 + 3x - 1)$
7. $(x^3 + 3x^2 + 1)(3x^2 + 6x - 2)$
8. $(x^2 + 9x + 7)(3x^2 + 9x + 5)$

SEE EXAMPLE 3

9. **Business** A businessman models the number of items (in thousands) that his company sold from 1998 through 2004 as $N(x) = -0.1x^3 + x^2 - 3x + 4$ and the average price per item (in dollars) as $P(x) = 0.2x + 5$, where x represents the number of years since 1998. Write a polynomial $R(x)$ that can be used to model the total revenue for this company.

SEE EXAMPLE 4

Find each product.

10. $(x + 2)^3$
11. $(x + y)^4$
12. $(x + 1)^4$
13. $(x - 3y)^3$

SEE EXAMPLE 5

Expand each expression.

14. $(x - 2)^4$
15. $(2x + y)^4$
16. $(x + 2y)^3$
17. $(2x - y)^5$

PRACTICE AND PROBLEM SOLVING

Independent Practice

For Exercises	See Example
18–21	1
22–25	2
26	3
27–30	4
31–34	5

Extra Practice

See Extra Practice for more Skills Practice and Applications Practice exercises.

Find each product.

18. $7x^3(2x + 3)$
19. $3x^2(2x^2 + 9x - 6)$
20. $xy^2(x^2 + 3xy + 9)$
21. $2r^2(6r^3 + 14r^2 - 30r + 14)$
22. $(x - y)(x^2 - xy + y^2)$
23. $(2x + 5y)(3x^2 - 4xy + 2y^2)$
24. $(x^3 + x^2 + 1)(x^2 - x - 5)$
25. $(4x^2 + 3x + 2)(3x^2 + 2x - 1)$
26. **Measurement** A bottom for a box can be made by cutting congruent squares from each of the four corners of a piece of cardboard. The volume of a box made from an 8.5-by-11-inch piece of cardboard would be represented by $V(x) = x(11 - 2x)(8.5 - 2x)$, where x is the side length of one square.

   a. Express the volume as a sum of monomials.
   b. Find the volume when $x = 1$ inch.

Find each product.

27. $(2x - 2)^3$
28. $\left(x + \frac{1}{3}\right)^4$
29. $(x - y)^4$
30. $(4 + y)^3$

Expand each expression.

31. $(x - 3y)^4$
32. $(x - 2)^5$
33. $(x + y)^5$
34. $(2x - 3y)^4$

Graphing Calculator Compare each pair of expressions with your graphing calculator. Use the table feature to make a conjecture about whether the expressions are equivalent.

35. $(x-6)^3$; $x^3 - 18x^2 + 108x - 216$

36. $(11x+10)(11x+1)$; $121x^2 + 121x + 10$

37. $(3x^2+2x)(3x+2)$; $9x^3 + 12x^2 + 4$

38. $(2x+1)^4$; $16x^4 + 32x^3 + 24x^2 + 8x + 1$

39. Business Ms. Liao runs a small dress company. From 1995 through 2005, the number of dresses she made can be modeled by $N(x) = 0.3x^2 - 1.6x + 14$ and the average cost to make each dress can be modeled by $C(x) = -0.001x^2 - 0.06x + 8.3$, where x is the number of years since 1995. Write a polynomial that can be used to model Ms. Liao's total dressmaking costs, $T(x)$, for those years.

LINK

Math History

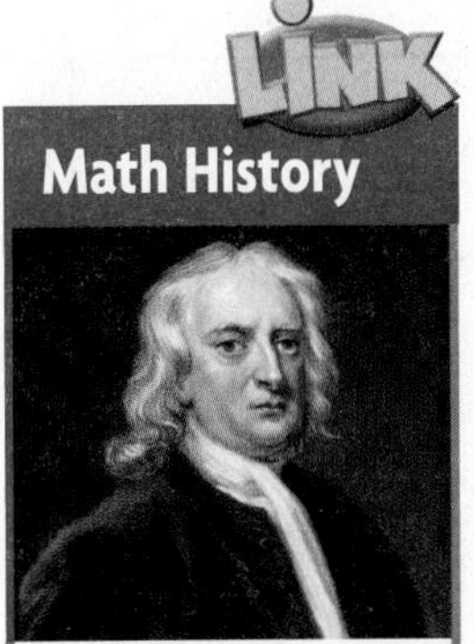

The Binomial Theorem was discovered by Sir Isaac Newton in 1665 or 1666. At this time, Trinity College, in Cambridge, England, was closed because of the plague, and Newton, working in solitude, was able to focus solely on his mathematical studies.

Multiply.

40. $-6x^3(15y^4 - 7xy^3 + 2)$

41. $(p-2q)^3$

42. $(x^2 - 2yz - y^2)(y^2 + x)$

43. $(x^4 + xy^3)(x^2 + y^3)$

44. $(3-3y)^4$

45. $(5x^3 + x^2 - 9x)(y+2)$

46. $(3 + x - 2x^2)(x-1)$

47. $3(x-2)^4$

48. $(x-6)(x^4 - 2x^3 + x^2 + 1)$

49. $(30 + x^3 + x^2)(x - 15 - x^2)$

50. $\left(\frac{1}{2} + z\right)^4$

51. $(2x-3)(x^5 - 4x^3 + 7)$

52. Generate the coefficients that would be used to expand $(a+b)^7$ by using binomial expansion.

53. Physics An object t seconds after it is thrown in the air has a velocity that can be described by $v(t) = -9.8t + 24$ (in meters/second) and a height $h(t) = -4.9t^2 + 24t + 60$ (in meters). The object has mass $m = 2$ kilograms. The kinetic energy of the object is given by $K = \frac{1}{2}mv^2$, and the potential energy is given by $U = 9.8mh$. Can you find a polynomial expression for the total kinetic and potential energy $K + U$ as a function of time, t? Explain.

54. ///ERROR ANALYSIS/// Two students used binomial expansion to expand $(a+b)^2$. Which answer is incorrect? Identify the error.

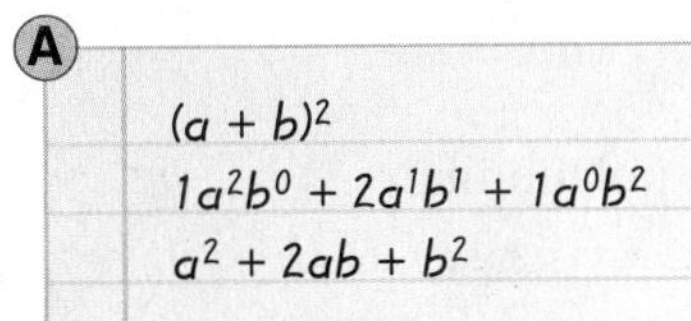

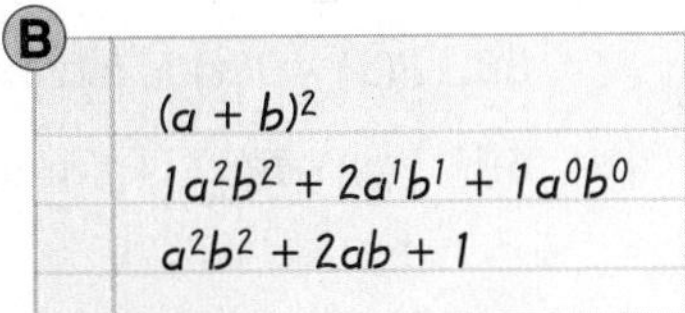

55. The total number of lights in a triangular lighting rig is related to the triangular numbers, as shown at right. The product of the nth triangular number and the $(n+1)$th triangular number is given by $f(n) = \frac{n(n+1)^2(n+2)}{4}$.

a. Write $f(n)$ as a polynomial function.

b. Find the product of the twelfth and thirteenth triangular numbers.

c. Evaluate $f(n)$ for $n = 20$ and describe what this value represents.

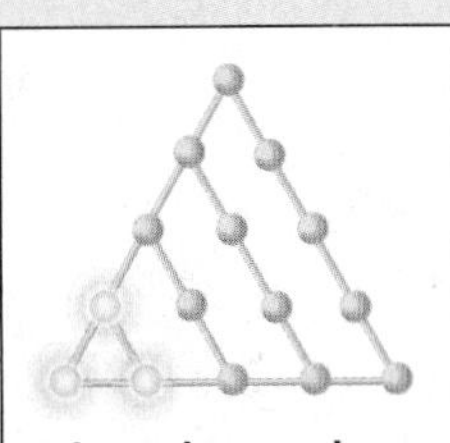

Triangular numbers:
1, 3, 6, 10, 15, . . .

56. **Critical Thinking** Using binomial expansion, explain why every other term of the resulting polynomial for $(x - y)^5$ is negative.

57. **Write About It** Explain how to expand a binomial raised to a power by using Pascal's Triangle.

TEST PREP

58. Multiply $(y - 3)(y^2 - 6y - 9)$.
   - Ⓐ $y^3 + 18y - 9$
   - Ⓑ $y^3 - 3y^2 + 3y + 27$
   - Ⓒ $y^3 + 9y^2 + 27y + 27$
   - Ⓓ $y^3 - 9y^2 + 9y + 27$

59. The rectangle shown is enlarged such that each side is multiplied by the value of the width, $2x$. Which expression represents the perimeter of the enlarged rectangle?

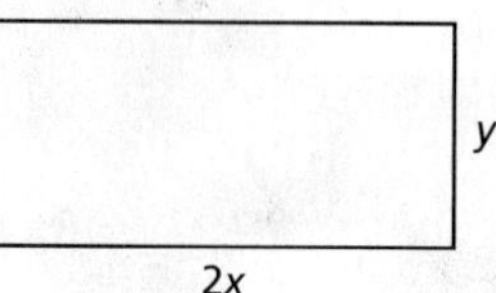

   - Ⓕ $4x + 2y$
   - Ⓖ $6x + 4xy$
   - Ⓗ $8x^2 + 2y$
   - Ⓙ $8x^2 + 4xy$

60. What is the third term of the binomial expansion of $(x - 4)^6$?
   - Ⓐ $240x^4$
   - Ⓑ $15x^4$
   - Ⓒ $160x^3$
   - Ⓓ $8x^3$

61. Find the product $a^2b(2a^3b - 5ab^4)$.
   - Ⓕ $-3a^4b^{-2}$
   - Ⓖ $2a^6b - 5a^2b^4$
   - Ⓗ $2a^5b^2 - 5a^3b^5$
   - Ⓙ $2a^5b^2 - 5ab^4$

62. **Short Response** Expand $(4 - x)^4$ by using binomial expansion.

CHALLENGE AND EXTEND

Find the product.

63. $(x - 1)^{10}$ 64. $(14 + y)^5$ 65. $(m - n)^3(m + n)^3$ 66. $(ab + 2c)^4$

Suppose $P(x) = x + 3$. Find a binomial $B(x)$ that satisfies the given condition.

67. $P(x) \cdot B(x)$ is a binomial.

68. $P(x) \cdot B(x)$ is a trinomial.

69. $P(x) \cdot B(x)$ is a quartic polynomial.

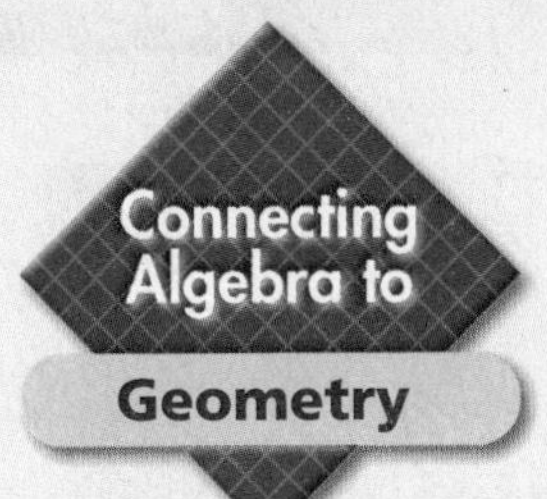

Nets

For a prism, volume equals the area of the base times the height. For a pyramid, volume equals $\frac{1}{3}$ the area of the base times the height. To find the surface area of a solid, add the areas of all of the faces.

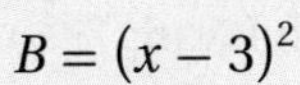

Find the volume and surface area of the square pyramid shown by this net.

For the volume, multiply the area of the square base by the height and then multiply by $\frac{1}{3}$.

$B = (x-3)^2$ *Find the area of the square base.*

$V = \frac{1}{3}(x-3)^2\,x$ *The height of the pyramid is x.*

$V = \frac{x^3}{3} - 2x^2 + 3x$ *Multiply the polynomials, and simplify.*

For the surface area, add the area of the square base to the area of the four triangular faces.

$B = (x-3)^2$ *Find the area of the square base.*

$A = \frac{1}{2}(x-3) \cdot 2x$ *Find the area of 1 triangular face.*

$L = 4A = 4 \cdot \frac{1}{2}(x-3) \cdot 2x$ *Find the area of 4 triangular faces.*

$SA = (x-3)^2 + 4 \cdot \frac{1}{2}(x-3) \cdot 2x$ *Add the area of the base to the area of the four triangular faces.*

$SA = (x^2 - 6x + 9) + (4x^2 - 12x)$ *Multiply.*

$SA = 5x^2 - 18x + 9$ *Add.*

Try This

Find the volume and surface area of the solid shown by each net.

1.

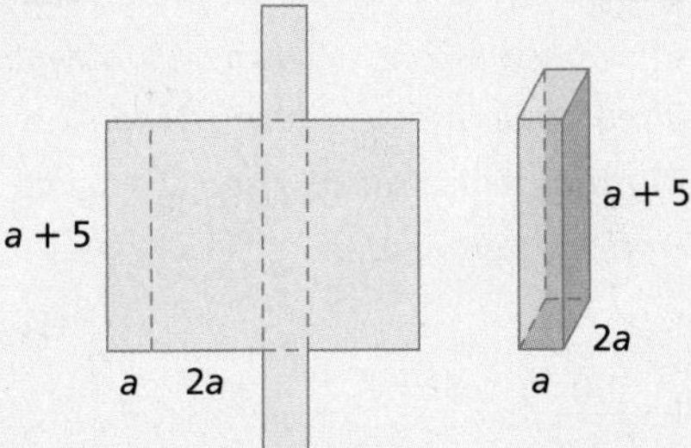

2.

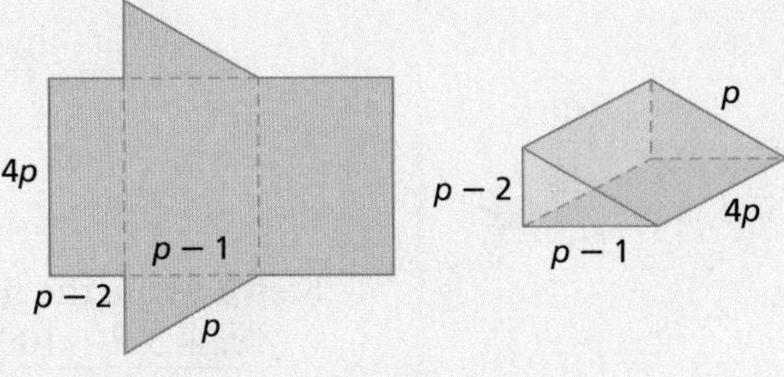

3. The volume of a rectangular prism is $6c^3 - 22c^2 - 8c$. Find the length and width of this prism if the height is $2c$.

3-3 Dividing Polynomials

CC.9-12.A.APR.2 Know and apply the Remainder Theorem ... *Also* CC.9-12.A.APR.6

Objective
Use long division and synthetic division to divide polynomials.

Vocabulary
synthetic division

Who uses this?
Electricians can divide polynomials in order to find the voltage in an electrical system. (See Example 4.)

"Okay, Copper—what's the charge? Assault and Battery? I have contacts, you know"

Polynomial long division is a method for dividing a polynomial by another polynomial of a lower degree. It is very similar to dividing numbers.

Arithmetic Long Division

Divisor 12; Quotient 23; Dividend 277

$$\begin{array}{r} 23 \\ 12\overline{)277} \\ \underline{24} \\ 37 \\ \underline{36} \\ 1 \end{array}$$

Remainder 1

Polynomial Long Division

Divisor $x + 2$; Quotient $2x + 3$; Dividend $2x^2 + 7x + 7$

$$\begin{array}{r} 2x + 3 \\ x + 2\overline{)2x^2 + 7x + 7} \\ \underline{2x^2 + 4x} \\ 3x + 7 \\ \underline{3x + 6} \\ 1 \end{array}$$

Remainder 1

EXAMPLE 1 Using Long Division to Divide Polynomials

Divide by using long division.

$(4x^2 + 3x^3 + 10) \div (x - 2)$

Step 1 Write the dividend in standard form, including terms with a coefficient of 0.

$3x^3 + 4x^2 + 0x + 10$

Step 2 Write division in the same way as you would when dividing numbers.

$x - 2\overline{)3x^3 + 4x^2 + 0x + 10}$

Step 3 Divide.

$$\begin{array}{r} 3x^2 + 10x + 20 \\ x - 2\overline{)3x^3 + 4x^2 + 0x + 10} \\ \underline{-(3x^3 - 6x^2)} \\ 10x^2 + 0x \\ \underline{-(10x^2 - 20x)} \\ 20x + 10 \\ \underline{-(20x - 40)} \\ 50 \end{array}$$

Notice that x times $3x^2$ is $3x^3$. Write $3x^2$ above $3x^3$.
Multiply $x - 2$ by $3x^2$. Then subtract.
Bring down the next term. Divide $10x^2$ by x.
Multiply $x - 2$ by 10x, then subtract.
Bring down the next term. Divide 20x by x.
Multiply $x - 2$ by 20, then subtract.
Find the remainder.

Step 4 Write the final answer.

$$\frac{4x^2 + 3x^3 + 10}{x - 2} = 3x^2 + 10x + 20 + \frac{50}{x - 2}$$

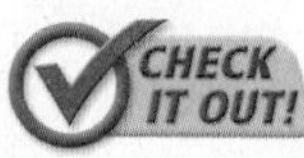

Divide by using long division.

1a. $(15x^2 + 8x - 12) \div (3x + 1)$ **1b.** $(x^2 + 5x - 28) \div (x - 3)$

Synthetic division is a shorthand method of dividing a polynomial by a linear binomial by using only the coefficients. For synthetic division to work, the polynomial must be written in standard form, using 0 as a coefficient for any missing terms, and the divisor must be in the form $(x - a)$.

Synthetic Division Method

Divide $(2x^2 + 7x + 9) \div (x + 2)$ by using synthetic division.

WORDS	NUMBERS
Step 1 Write the coefficients of the dividend, 2, 7, and 9. In the upper left corner, write the value of *a* for the divisor $(x - a)$. So $a = -2$. Copy the first coefficient in the dividend below the horizontal bar.	$\begin{array}{r|rrr} -2 & 2 & 7 & 9 \\ \hline & 2 & & \end{array}$
Step 2 Multiply the first coefficient by the divisor, and write the product under the next coefficient. Add the numbers in the new column.	$\begin{array}{r|rrr} -2 & 2 & 7 & 9 \\ & & -4 & \\ \hline & 2 & 3 & \end{array}$
Repeat Step 2 until additions have been completed in all columns. Draw a box around the last sum.	$\begin{array}{r|rrr} -2 & 2 & 7 & 9 \\ & & -4 & -6 \\ \hline & 2 & 3 & \boxed{3} \end{array}$
Step 3 The quotient is represented by the numbers below the horizontal bar. The boxed number is the remainder. The others are the coefficients of the polynomial quotient, in order of decreasing degree.	$= 2x + 3 + \frac{3}{x + 2}$

EXAMPLE 2 Using Synthetic Division to Divide by a Linear Binomial

Divide by using synthetic division.

A $(4x^2 - 12x + 9) \div \left(x + \frac{1}{2}\right)$

Step 1 Find *a*. Then write the coefficients and *a* in the synthetic division format.

$a = -\frac{1}{2}$ *For $\left(x + \frac{1}{2}\right)$, $a = -\frac{1}{2}$.*

$$\begin{array}{r|rrr} -\frac{1}{2} & 4 & -12 & 9 \\ \hline & & & \boxed{} \end{array}$$

Write the coefficients of $4x^2 - 12x + 9$.

Step 2 Bring down the first coefficient. Then multiply and add for each column.

$$\begin{array}{r|rrr} -\frac{1}{2} & 4 & -12 & 9 \\ & & -2 & 7 \\ \hline & 4 & -14 & \boxed{16} \end{array}$$

Draw a box around the remainder, 16.

Step 3 Write the quotient.

$4x - 14 + \frac{16}{x + \frac{1}{2}}$ *Write the remainder over the divisor.*

Check Multiply $\left(x + \frac{1}{2}\right)\left(4x - 14 + \frac{16}{x + \frac{1}{2}}\right)$.

$$4x\left(x + \frac{1}{2}\right) - 14\left(x + \frac{1}{2}\right) + \frac{16}{x + \frac{1}{2}}\left(x + \frac{1}{2}\right) = 4x^2 - 12x + 9$$

Caution!

Be careful to use the correct *a* value when doing synthetic division. If the divisor is $(x - a)$, use *a*. If the divisor is $(x + a)$, use $-a$.

Divide by using synthetic division.

B $(x^4 - 2x^3 + 3x + 1) \div (x - 3)$

Step 1 Find a.

$a = 3$ *For $(x - 3)$, $a = 3$.*

Step 2 Write the coefficients and a in the synthetic division format.

$$\begin{array}{r|rrrrr} 3 & 1 & -2 & 0 & 3 & 1 \\ & & & & & \\ \hline & & & & & \end{array}$$

Use 0 for the coefficient of x^2.

Step 3 Bring down the first coefficient. Then multiply and add for each column.

$$\begin{array}{r|rrrrr} 3 & 1 & -2 & 0 & 3 & 1 \\ & & 3 & 3 & 9 & 36 \\ \hline & 1 & 1 & 3 & 12 & \boxed{37} \end{array}$$

Draw a box around the remainder, 37.

Step 4 Write the quotient.

$x^3 + x^2 + 3x + 12 + \frac{37}{x-x}$ *Write the remainder over the divisor.*

Divide by using synthetic division.

2a. $(6x^2 - 5x - 6) \div (x + 3)$ **2b.** $(x^2 - 3x - 18) \div (x - 6)$

You can use synthetic division to evaluate polynomials. This process is called synthetic substitution. The process of synthetic substitution is exactly the same as the process of synthetic division, but the final answer is interpreted differently, as described by the Remainder Theorem.

Remainder Theorem

THEOREM	EXAMPLE
If the polynomial function $P(x)$ is divided by $x - a$, then the remainder r is $P(a)$.	Divide $x^3 - 4x^2 + 5x + 1$ by $x - 3$. $\begin{array}{r\|rrrr} 3 & 1 & -4 & 5 & 1 \\ & & 3 & -3 & 6 \\ \hline & 1 & -1 & 2 & \boxed{7} \end{array}$ $P(3) = 7$

EXAMPLE 3 Using Synthetic Substitution

Use synthetic substitution to evaluate the polynomial for the given value.

A $P(x) = x^3 - 4x^2 + 3x - 5$ **for** $x = 4$

$$\begin{array}{r|rrrr} 4 & 1 & -4 & 3 & -5 \\ & & 4 & 0 & 12 \\ \hline & 1 & 0 & 3 & \boxed{7} \end{array}$$

Write the coefficients of the dividend. Use $a = 4$.

$P(4) = 7$

Check Substitute 4 for x in $P(x) = x^3 - 4x^2 + 3x - 5$.

$P(4) = 4^3 - 4(4)^2 + 3(4) - 5$

$P(4) = 64 - 64 + 12 - 5$

$P(4) = 7$

Use synthetic substitution to evaluate the polynomial for the given value.

B $P(x) = 4x^4 + 2x^3 + 3x + 5$ for $x = -\frac{1}{2}$

$$\begin{array}{r|rrrrr} -\frac{1}{2} & 4 & 2 & 0 & 3 & 5 \\ & & -2 & 0 & 0 & -\frac{3}{2} \\ \hline & 4 & 0 & 0 & 3 & \boxed{3\frac{1}{2}} \end{array}$$

Write the coefficients of the dividend. Use 0 for the coefficient of x^2 and $a = -\frac{1}{2}$.

$P\left(-\frac{1}{2}\right) = 3\frac{1}{2}$

Use synthetic substitution to evaluate the polynomial for the given value.

3a. $P(x) = x^3 + 3x^2 + 4$ for $x = -3$

3b. $P(x) = 5x^2 + 9x + 3$ for $x = \frac{1}{5}$

EXAMPLE  4

Physics Application

A Van de Graaff generator is a machine that produces very high voltages by using small, safe levels of electric current. One machine has a current that can be modeled by $I(t) = t + 2$, where $t > 0$ represents time in seconds. The power of the system can be modeled by $P(t) = 0.5t^3 + 6t^2 + 10t$. Write an expression that represents the voltage of the system.

The voltage V is related to current I and power P by the equation $V = \frac{P}{I}$.

$V(t) = \frac{0.5t^3 + 6t^2 + 10t}{t + 2}$ *Substitute.*

$$\begin{array}{r|rrrr} -2 & 0.5 & 6 & 10 & 0 \\ & & -1 & -10 & 0 \\ \hline & 0.5 & 5 & 0 & \boxed{0} \end{array}$$

Use synthetic division.

The voltage can be represented by $V(t) = 0.5t^2 + 5t$.

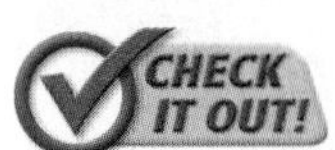

4. Write an expression for the length of a rectangle with width $y - 9$ and area $y^2 - 14y + 45$.

THINK AND DISCUSS

1. Can you use synthetic division to divide a polynomial by $x^2 + 3$? Explain.

2. Explain how to quickly find $P(6)$ for the function $P(x) = 2x^3 - 11x^2 - 5x + 2$ without using a calculator. Find $P(6)$.

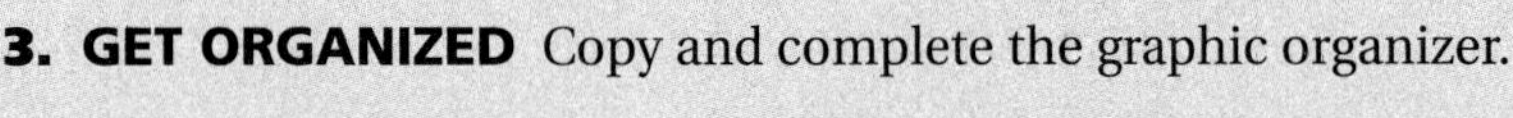

3. GET ORGANIZED Copy and complete the graphic organizer.

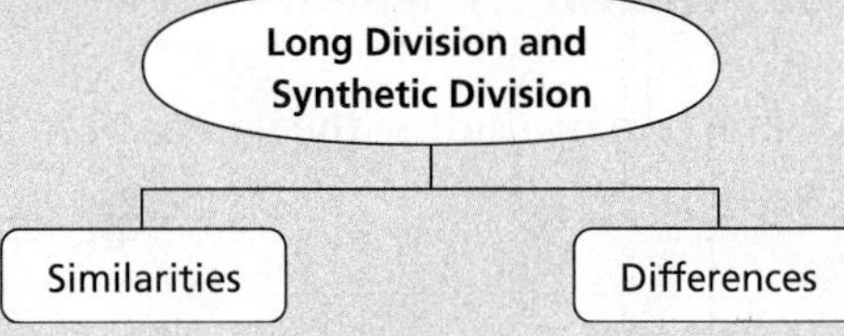

3-3 Exercises

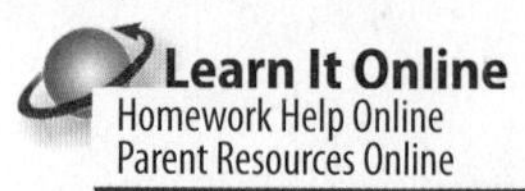

GUIDED PRACTICE

1. **Vocabulary** Describe *synthetic division* in your own words.

SEE EXAMPLE 1

Divide by using long division.

2. $(20x^2 - 13x + 2) \div (4x - 1)$
3. $(x^2 + x - 1) \div (x - 1)$
4. $(x^2 - 2x + 3) \div (x + 5)$

SEE EXAMPLE 2

Divide by using synthetic division.

5. $(7x^2 - 23x + 6) \div (x - 3)$
6. $(x^4 - 5x + 10) \div (x + 3)$
7. $(x^2 + x - x) \div (x + 7)$

SEE EXAMPLE 3

Use synthetic substitution to evaluate the polynomial for the given value.

8. $P(x) = 2x^3 - 9x^2 + 27$ for $x = 2$
9. $P(x) = x^2 - x - 30$ for $x = -8$
10. $P(x) = 3x^3 + 5x^2 + 4x + 2$ for $x = \frac{1}{3}$
11. $P(x) = 3x^5 + 4x^2 + x + 6$ for $x = -1$

SEE EXAMPLE 4

12. **Geometry** Find an expression for the width of a rectangle whose length is represented by $x - 2$ and whose area is represented by $2x^3 - 8x^2 + 2x + 12$.

PRACTICE AND PROBLEM SOLVING

Independent Practice

For Exercises	See Example
13–18	1
19–24	2
25–28	3
29	4

Extra Practice

See Extra Practice for more Skills Practice and Applications Practice exercises.

Divide by using long division.

13. $(2x^2 + 10x + 8) \div (2x + 2)$
14. $(9x^2 - 18x) \div (3x)$
15. $(x^3 + 2x^2 - x - 2) \div (x + 2)$
16. $(x^4 - 3x^3 - 7x - 14) \div (x - 4)$
17. $(x^6 - 4x^5 - 7x^3) \div (2x^3)$
18. $(6x^2 - 7x - 5) \div (3x - 5)$

Divide by using synthetic division.

19. $(x^2 + 5x + 6) \div (x + 1)$
20. $(x^4 + 6x^3 + 6x^2) \div (x + 5)$
21. $(x^2 + 9x + 6) \div (x + 8)$
22. $(2x^2 + 3x - 20) \div (x - 2)$
23. $(2x^2 + 13x - 8) \div \left(x - \frac{1}{2}\right)$
24. $(4x^2 + 5x + 1) \div (x + 1)$

Use synthetic substitution to evaluate the polynomial for the given value.

25. $P(x) = 2x^2 - 5x - 3$ for $x = 4$
26. $P(x) = 4x^3 - 5x^2 + 3$ for $x = -1$
27. $P(x) = 3x^3 - 5x^2 - x + 2$ for $x = -\frac{1}{3}$
28. $P(x) = 25x^2 - 16$ for $x = \frac{4}{5}$
29. **Physics** An experimental electrical system has a voltage that can be modeled by $V(t) = 0.5t^3 + 4.5t^2 + 4t$, where t represents time in seconds. The resistance in the system also varies and can be modeled by $R(t) = t + 1$. The current I is related to voltage and resistance by the equation $I = \frac{V}{R}$. Write an expression that represents the current in the system.
30. **What if...?** If the remainder of polynomial division is 0, what does it mean?

Complete by finding the values of *a*, *b*, and *c*.

31.
$$\begin{array}{r|rrrrr} 2 & 3 & -4 & 0 & 7 & -1 \\ & & 6 & 4 & b & 30 \\ \hline & 3 & a & 4 & 15 & c \end{array}$$

32.
$$\begin{array}{r|rrr} -2 & 1 & 5 & 6 \\ & & a & c \\ \hline & 1 & b & 0 \end{array}$$

33.
$$\begin{array}{r|rrrr} 3 & a & -2 & 3 & c \\ & & b & 21 & 72 \\ \hline & 3 & 7 & 24 & 68 \end{array}$$

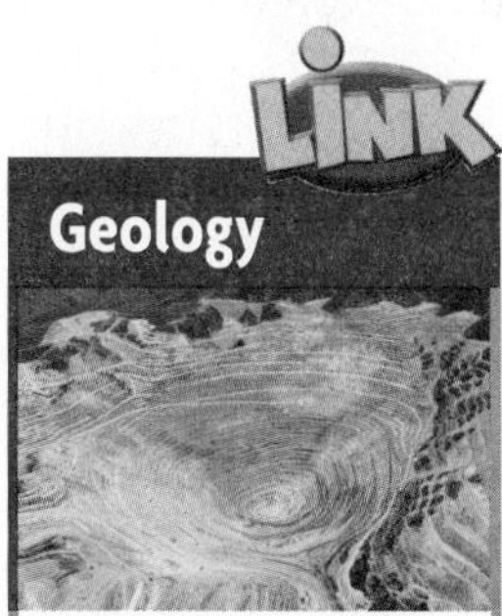

Bingham Canyon copper mine in Utah is the largest copper mine in the world in terms of both total metal production and size. Nicknamed "the richest hole on Earth," the mine has produced more than 14.5 million tons of copper.

Fill in each box to illustrate the Remainder Theorem for $P(x) = x^2 + 3x - 7$ and divisor $x - 2$.

34. Divide $P(x)$ by $(x - 2)$: $\frac{P(x)}{x-2} = \square$

35. Multiply both sides by $\square$: $P(x) = (x + 5)(x - 2) + 3$

36. Evaluate $P(2)$: $P(2) = \square$

37. **Geology** Geologists have taken a collection of samples of a substance from a proposed mining site and must identify the substance. Each sample is roughly cylindrical, and the volume of each sample as a function of cylinder height (in centimeters) is $V(h) = \frac{1}{4}\pi h^3$. The mass (in grams) of each sample in terms of height can be modeled by $M(h) = \frac{1}{4}h^3 - h^2 + 5h$. Write an expression that represents the density of the samples. (*Hint:* $D = \frac{M}{V}$)

38. **Geometry** The volume of a hexagonal pyramid is modeled by the function $V(x) = \frac{1}{3}x^3 + \frac{4}{3}x^2 + \frac{2}{3}x - \frac{1}{3}$. Use polynomial division to find an expression for the area of the base. (*Hint:* For a pyramid, $V = \frac{1}{3}Bh$.)

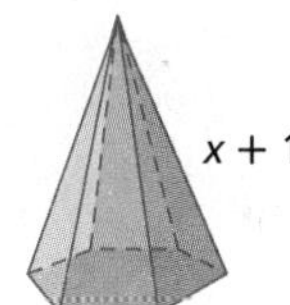

Divide.

39. $(y^4 + 9y^2 + 20) \div (y^2 + 4)$

40. $(2x^2 - 5x + 2) \div \left(x - \frac{1}{2}\right)$

41. $(3x^3 - 11x^2 - 56x - 48) \div (3x + 4)$

42. $(60 - 16y^2 + y^4) \div (10 - y^2)$

43. $(t^3 - 7t^2 + 12t) \div (t^2 - 3t)$

44. $(y^2 - 18y + 14) \div (y - 1)$

45. $(x^4 - 3x^3 - 28x^2 + 59x + 6) \div (x - 6)$

46. $(2d^2 + 10d + 8) \div (2d + 2)$

47. $(x^4 - 7x^3 + 9x^2 - 22x + 25) \div (x - 6)$

48. $(6x^3 - 14x^2 + 10x - 4) \div (x - 1)$

49. **/// ERROR ANALYSIS ///** Two students used synthetic division to divide $x^3 - 2x - 8$ by $x - 2$. Determine which solution is correct. Find the error in the other solution.

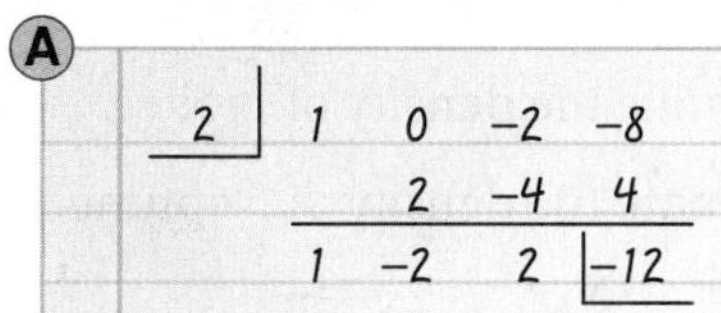

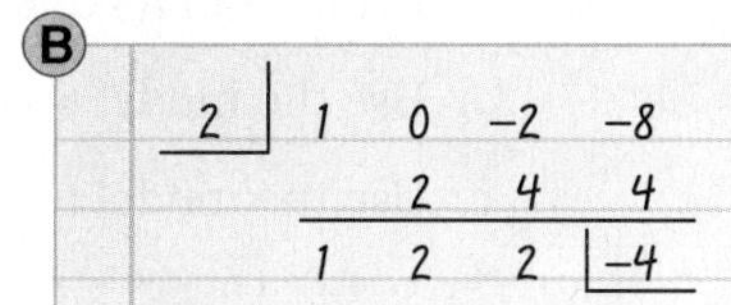

50. **Critical Thinking** Is $x + 3$ a factor of $3x^3 + 5x^2 + 2x - 12$? Explain.

51. **Write About It** What conditions must be met in order to use synthetic division?

52. The total number of lights in a triangular lighting rig is related to the triangular numbers, as shown at right. The sum of the first n triangular numbers is given by the polynomial function $g(n) = \frac{1}{6}n^3 + \frac{1}{2}n^2 + \frac{1}{3}n$.

a. Find the sum of the first five triangular numbers in the figure at right, and verify that the formula works when $n = 5$.

b. Use synthetic substitution to find the sum of the first 24 triangular numbers.

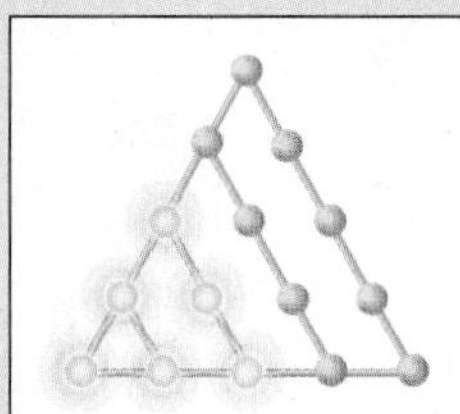

Triangular numbers: 1, 3, 6, 10, 15, . . .

53. What is the remainder when $2x^2 + 6x + 3$ is divided by $x + 3$?

Ⓐ 39 Ⓑ 3 Ⓒ 1 Ⓓ 0

54. Which expression is equivalent to $\frac{6a^2b + 9b^2}{3a^2}$?

Ⓕ $6b + \frac{9b^2}{a^2}$ Ⓖ $\frac{3a^2}{6a^2b + 9b^2}$ Ⓗ $2b + \frac{3b^2}{a^2}$ Ⓙ $\frac{2a^2b + 3b^2}{3a^2}$

55. Which expression is equivalent to $(x^2 + 3x - 28) \div (x - 4)$?

Ⓐ $x + 7 + \frac{3}{x - 4}$ Ⓑ $x - 7$ Ⓒ $28 + \frac{4}{x - 7}$ Ⓓ $x + 7$

56. **Gridded Response** Use synthetic substitution to evaluate $f(x) = 3x^4 - 6x^2 + 12$ for $x = -2$.

CHALLENGE AND EXTEND

Evaluate $P(x) = 4x^9 + 7x^7 - 6x^6 - 5x^4 - x^2 + 3x - 2$ for the given value of x.

57. $x = -4$ 58. $x = -1$ 59. $x = 1$ 60. $x = 3$

61. If -3 is a zero of $P(x) = 2x^3 + 3x^2 - kx - 27$, find the value of k.

62. Divide $(5a^2b - 3ab^2 - 2b^3)$ by $(ab - b^2)$

63. **Astronomy** The volumes of several planets in cubic kilometers can be modeled by $V(d) = \frac{1}{6}\pi d^3$, where d is the diameter of the planet in kilometers. The mass of each planet in kilograms in terms of diameter d can be modeled by $M(d) = (3.96 \times 10^{12})d^3 - (6.50 \times 10^{17})d^2 + (2.56 \times 10^{22})d - 5.56 \times 10^{25}$.

a. The density of a planet in kilograms per cubic kilometer can be found by dividing the planet's mass by its volume. Use polynomial division to find a model for the density of a planet in terms of its diameter.

b. Use the model to estimate the density of Jupiter.

c. Use the model to estimate the density of Neptune.

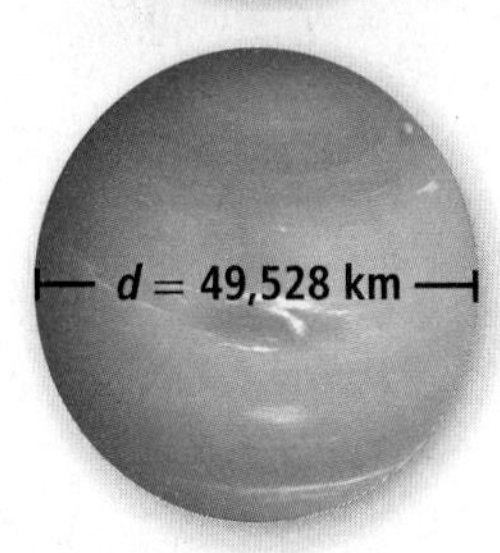

Use with Factoring Polynomials

Explore the Sum and Difference of Two Cubes

You can use a diagram of a cube with a corner removed to discover how to factor the difference of two cubes. You can use a similar diagram to discover how to factor the sum of two cubes.

Model with mathematics.

Activity

The figure shown is a large cube with a small cube removed from one corner.

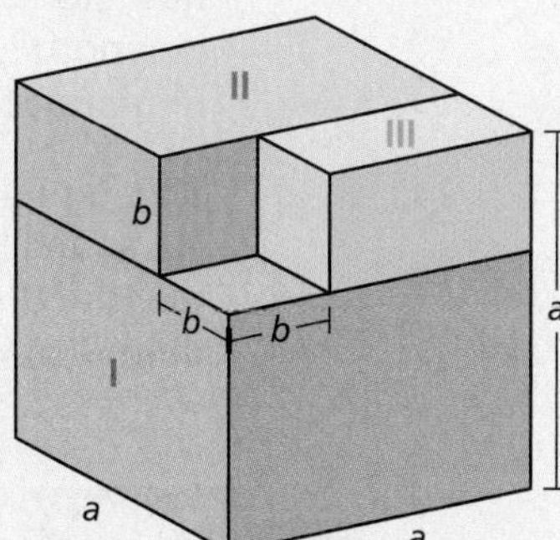

1 Explain why the volume of the figure is $a^3 - b^3$. How is this related to the volumes of the rectangular prisms labeled I, II, and III?

The volume of the complete cube is a^3, and the volume of the cube removed from the corner is b^3. The volume of the figure with the corner removed is $a^3 - b^3$ and can be expressed as the sum of the volumes of the rectangular prisms I, II, and III: $a^3 - b^3 = V_I + V_{II} + V_{III}$.

2 Use the diagram to write an algebraic expression for the volume of each rectangular prism.

$V_I = a^2(a - b)$ $\quad$ $V_{II} = ab(a - b)$ $\quad$ $V_{III} = b^2(a - b)$

3 Write the equation for $a^3 - b^3$ by using the expressions for the rectangular prisms labeled I, II, and III from Problem 2. Factor to get the factored form of $a^3 - b^3$.

$a^3 - b^3 = V_I + V_{II} + V_{III}$

$a^3 - b^3 = a^2(a - b) + ab(a - b) + b^2(a - b)$

$a^3 - b^3 = (a - b)(a^2 + ab + b^2)$

Try This

The figure shown is a large cube with a small cube added to one corner.

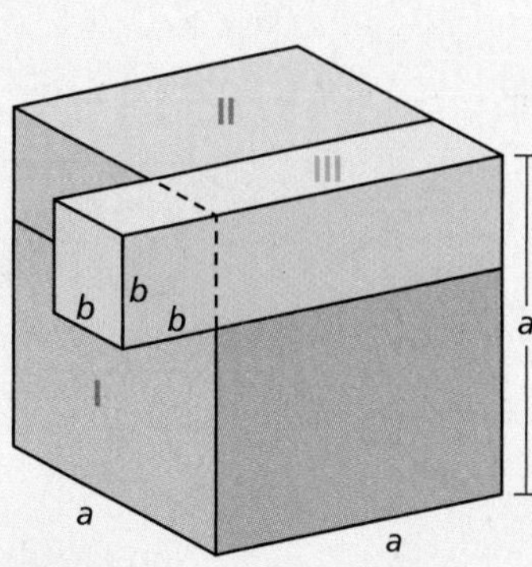

1. Explain why the volume of the figure is $a^3 + b^3$. How is this related to the volumes of the rectangular prisms labeled I, II, and III?
2. Use the diagram to write an algebraic expression for the volume of each rectangular prism.
3. Write the equation for $a^3 + b^3$ by using the expressions for the rectangular prisms labeled I, II, and III from Problem 2. Factor to get the factored form of $a^3 + b^3$. (*Hint:* Factor the expressions for I and II before adding the expression for III.)

3-4 Factoring Polynomials

CC.9-12.A.APR.2 Know and apply the Remainder Theorem ... *Also* **CC.9-12.A.SSE.2, CC.9-12.A.APR.3, CC.9-12.A.APR.4**

Objectives

Use the Factor Theorem to determine factors of a polynomial.

Factor the sum and difference of two cubes.

Who uses this?

Ecologists may use factoring polynomials to determine when species might become extinct. (See Example 4.)

Recall that if a number is divided by any of its factors, the remainder is 0. Likewise, if a polynomial is divided by any of its factors, the remainder is 0.

The Remainder Theorem states that if a polynomial is divided by $(x - a)$, the remainder is the value of the function at a. So, if $(x - a)$ is a factor of $P(x)$, then $P(a) = 0$.

Know it! Note

Factor Theorem

THEOREM	EXAMPLE
For any polynomial $P(x)$, $(x - a)$ is a factor of $P(x)$ if and only if $P(a) = 0$.	Because $P(1) = 1^2 - 1 = 0$, $(x - 1)$ is a factor of $P(x) = x^2 - 1$.

EXAMPLE 1 **Determining Whether a Linear Binomial is a Factor**

Determine whether the given binomial is a factor of the polynomial $P(x)$.

A $(x - 3); P(x) = x^2 + 2x - 3$

Find $P(3)$ by synthetic substitution.

$$\begin{array}{r|rrr} 3 & 1 & 2 & -3 \\ & & 3 & 15 \\ \hline & 1 & 5 & \boxed{12} \end{array}$$

$P(3) = 12$

$P(3) \neq 0$, so $(x - 3)$ is not a factor of $P(x) = x^2 + 2x - 3$.

B $(x + 4); P(x) = 2x^4 + 8x^3 + 2x + 8$

Find $P(-4)$ by synthetic substitution.

$$\begin{array}{r|rrrrr} -4 & 2 & 8 & 0 & 2 & 8 \\ & & -8 & 0 & 0 & -8 \\ \hline & 2 & 0 & 0 & 2 & \boxed{0} \end{array}$$

$P(-4) = 0$, so $(x + 4)$ is a factor of $P(x) = 2x^4 + 8x^3 + 2x + 8$.

Determine whether the given binomial is a factor of the polynomial $P(x)$.

1a. $(x + 2); P(x) = 4x^2 - 2x + 5$

1b. $(3x - 6); P(x) = 3x^4 - 6x^3 + 6x^2 + 3x - 30$

You are already familiar with methods for factoring quadratic expressions. You can factor polynomials of higher degrees using many of the same methods you previously learned.

EXAMPLE 2 Factoring by Grouping

Factor $x^3 + 3x^2 - 4x - 12$.

$(x^3 + 3x^2) + (-4x - 12)$	*Group terms.*
$x^2(x + 3) - 4(x + 3)$	*Factor common monomials from each group.*
$(x + 3)(x^2 - 4)$	*Factor out the common binomial $(x + 3)$.*
$(x + 3)(x + 2)(x - 2)$	*Factor the difference of squares.*

Check Use the table feature of your calculator to compare the original expression and the factored form.

```
Plot1 Plot2 Plot3
\Y1■X³+3X²-4X-12

\Y2■(X+3)(X+2)(X
-2)
```

X	Y1	Y2
-3	0	0
-2	0	0
-1	-6	-6
0	-12	-12
1	-12	-12
2	0	0
3	30	30

The table shows that the original function and the factored form have the same function values.

Factor each expression.

2a. $x^3 - 2x^2 - 9x + 18$ **2b.** $2x^3 + x^2 + 8x + 4$

Just as there is a special rule for factoring the difference of two squares, there are special rules for factoring the sum or difference of two cubes.

Factoring the Sum and the Difference of Two Cubes

METHOD	ALGEBRA
Sum of two cubes	$a^3 + b^3 = (a + b)(a^2 - ab + b^2)$
Difference of two cubes	$a^3 - b^3 = (a - b)(a^2 + ab + b^2)$

EXAMPLE 3 Factoring the Sum or Difference of Two Cubes

Factor each expression.

A $5x^4 + 40x$

$5x(x^3 + 8)$	*Factor out the GCF, 5x.*
$5x(x^3 + 2^3)$	*Rewrite as the sum of cubes.*
$5x(x + 2)(x^2 - x \cdot 2 + 2^2)$	*Use the rule $a^3 + b^3 = (a + b)(a^2 - ab + b^2)$.*
$5x(x + 2)(x^2 - 2x + 4)$	

Remember!

GCF stands for "greatest common factor." Always factor out the GCF before using other methods.

B $8y^3 - 27$

$(2y)^3 - 3^3$	*Rewrite as the difference of cubes.*
$(2y - 3)\left[(2y)^2 + 2y \cdot 3 + 3^2\right]$	*Use the rule $a^3 - b^3 = (a - b)(a^2 + ab + b^2)$.*
$(2y - 3)(4y^2 + 6y + 9)$	

Factor each expression.

3a. $8 + z^6$ **3b.** $2x^5 - 16x^2$

You can also use a graph to help you factor a polynomial. Recall that the real zeros of a function appear as x-intercepts on its graph. By the Factor Theorem, if you can determine the zeros of a polynomial function from its graph, you can determine the corresponding factors of the polynomial.

EXAMPLE 4 *Ecology Application*

The population of an endangered species of bird in the years since 1990 can be modeled by the function $P(x) = -x^3 + 32x^2 - 224x + 768$. Identify the year that the bird will become extinct if the model is accurate and no protective measures are taken. Use the graph to factor $P(x)$.

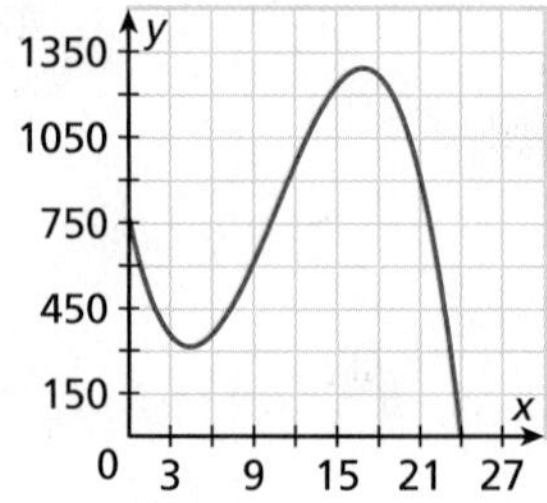

Because $P(x)$ represents the population, the real zero of $P(x)$ represents a population of zero, meaning extinction. $P(x)$ has only one real zero at $x = 24$, which corresponds to the year 2014.

If the model is accurate, the bird will become extinct in 2014.

The corresponding factor is $(x - 24)$.

$$\begin{array}{r|rrrr} 24 & -1 & 32 & -224 & 768 \\ & & -24 & 192 & -768 \\ \hline & -1 & 8 & -32 & \boxed{0} \end{array}$$

Use synthetic division to factor the polynomial.

$P(x) = (x - 24)(-x^2 + 8x - 32)$ *Write P(x) as a product.*

$P(x) = -(x - 24)(x^2 - 8x + 32)$ *Factor out −1 from the quadratic.*

4. The volume of a rectangular prism is modeled by the function $V(x) = x^3 - 8x^2 + 19x - 12$, which is graphed at right. Identify the values of x for which $V(x) = 0$, and use the graph to factor $V(x)$.

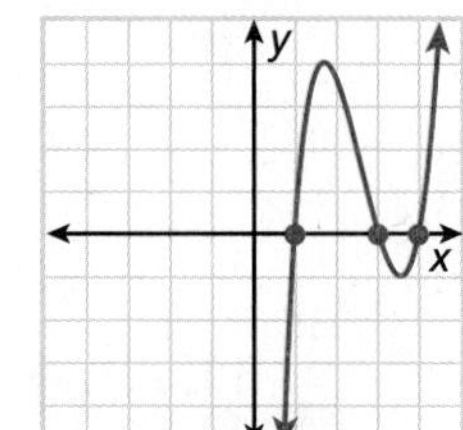

THINK AND DISCUSS

1. Explain how to use the Factor Theorem to determine whether a linear binomial is a factor of a polynomial.

2. Explain how you know when to use the sum or difference of cubes to factor a binomial.

3. GET ORGANIZED Copy and complete the graphic organizer. For each method, give an example of a polynomial and its factored form.

Method	Polynomial	Factored Form
Difference of Two Squares		
Difference of Two Cubes		
Sum of Two Cubes		

3-4 Exercises

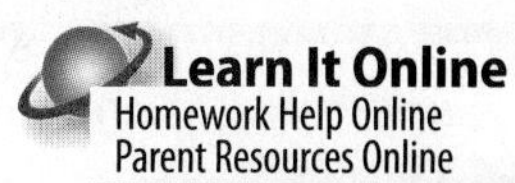

GUIDED PRACTICE

SEE EXAMPLE 1

Determine whether the given binomial is a factor of the polynomial $P(x)$.

1. $(x + 1)$; $P(x) = 2x^4 + 2x^3 - x^2 - 5x - 4$

2. $(x - 2)$; $P(x) = 5x^3 + x^2 - 7$

3. $(2x - 4)$; $P(x) = 2x^5 - 4x^4 + 2x^2 - 2x - 4$

SEE EXAMPLE 2

Factor each expression.

4. $x^3 + x^2 - x - 1$ **5.** $x^3 + 5x^2 - 4x - 20$ **6.** $8x^3 + 4x^2 - 2x - 1$

7. $2x^3 - 2x^2 - 8x + 8$ **8.** $2x^3 - 3x^2 - 2x + 3$ **9.** $12x^2 + 3x - 24x - 6$

SEE EXAMPLE 3

10. $8 - m^6$ **11.** $2t^7 + 54t^4$ **12.** $x^3 + 64$

13. $27 + x^3$ **14.** $4t^5 - 32t^2$ **15.** $y^3 - 125$

SEE EXAMPLE 4

16. The volume of a cargo container is modeled by the function $V(x) = x^3 - 39x - 70$. Identify the values of x for which $V(x) = 0$, and use the graph to factor $V(x)$.

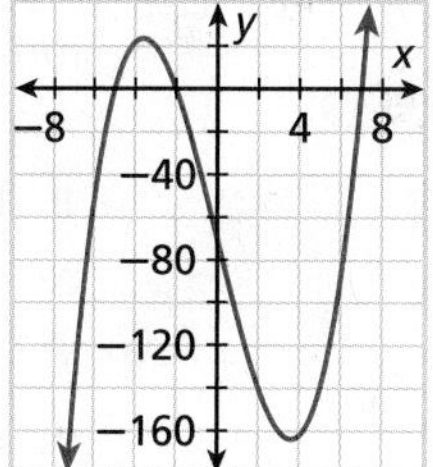

PRACTICE AND PROBLEM SOLVING

Independent Practice	
For Exercises	See Example
17–19	1
20–25	2
26–31	3
32	4

Extra Practice
See Extra Practice for more Skills Practice and Applications Practice exercises.

Determine whether the given binomial is a factor of the polynomial $P(x)$.

17. $(x - 3)$; $P(x) = 4x^6 - 12x^5 + 2x^3 - 6x^2 - 5x + 10$

18. $(x - 8)$; $P(x) = x^5 - 8x^4 + 8x - 64$

19. $(3x + 12)$; $P(x) = 3x^4 + 12x^3 + 6x + 24$

Factor each expression.

20. $8y^3 - 4y^2 - 50y + 25$ **21.** $4b^3 + 3b^2 - 16b - 12$ **22.** $3p^3 - 21p^2 - p + 7$

23. $3x^3 + x^2 - 27x - 9$ **24.** $8z^2 - 4z + 10z - 5$ **25.** $5x^3 - x^2 - 20x + 4$

26. $125 + z^3$ **27.** $s^6 - 1$ **28.** $24n^2 + 3n^5$

29. $6x^4 - 162x$ **30.** $40 - 5t^3$ **31.** $y^5 + 27y^2$

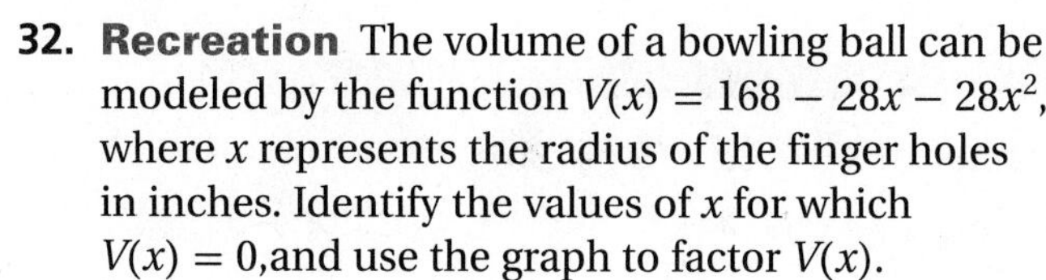

32. Recreation The volume of a bowling ball can be modeled by the function $V(x) = 168 - 28x - 28x^2$, where x represents the radius of the finger holes in inches. Identify the values of x for which $V(x) = 0$,and use the graph to factor $V(x)$.

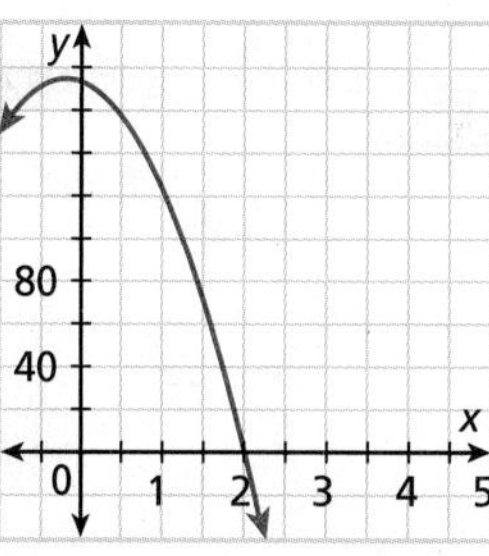

Factor completely.

33. $x^6 - 14x^4 + 49x^2$ **34.** $2x^3 + x^2 - 72x - 36$ **35.** $4x^3 + x^2 - 16x - 4$

36. $9x^9 - 16x^7 + 9x^6 - 16x^4$ **37.** $8x^7 - 4x^5 - 18x^3 + 9x$ **38.** $x^{13} - 15x^9 - 16x^5$

39. Critical Thinking The polynomial $ax^3 + bx^2 + cx + d$ is factored as $3(x - 2)(x + 3)(x - 4)$. What are the values of a and d? Explain.

40. The total number of lights in a triangular lighting rig is related to the triangular numbers, as shown at right. The sum of the first n triangular numbers is given by the polynomial function $g(n) = \frac{1}{6}n^3 + \frac{1}{2}n^2 + \frac{1}{3}n$.

a. Find the sum of the first seven triangular numbers.

b. Explain why $n - 7$ must be a factor of $n^3 + 3n^2 + 2n - 504$.

c. Factor $n^3 + 3n^2 + 2n - 504$.

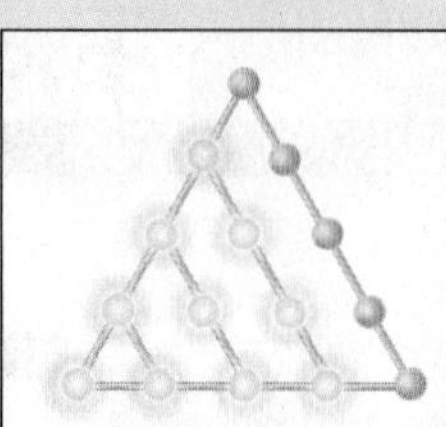

Triangular numbers: 1, 3, 6, 10, 15, . . .

Use the Factor Theorem to verify that each linear binomial is a factor of the given polynomial. Then use synthetic division to write the polynomial as a product.

41. $(x - 2)$; $P(x) = x^4 - 2x^3 + 5x^2 - 9x - 2$.

42. $(x - 1)$; $P(x) = 4x^6 - 4x^5 - 2x^4 + 3x^3 - x^2 - 7x + 7$.

43. $(x + 2)$; $P(x) = 2x^5 + 4x^4 - 6x^2 - 9x + 6$.

44. $(x - 4)$; $P(x) = 2x^4 - 9x^3 + 7x^2 - 14x + 8$.

45. Business The profit of a small business (in thousands of dollars) since it was founded can be modeled by the polynomial $f(t) = -t^4 + 44t^3 - 612t^2 + 2592t$, where t represents the number of years since 1980.

a. Factor $f(t)$ completely.

b. What was the company's profit in 1985?

c. Find and interpret $f(15)$.

d. What can you say about the company's long-term prospects?

Geometry Given the volume and height, find a polynomial expression for the area of the base in terms of x for each figure. (*Hint:* $V = Bh$)

46. $V(x) = 2x^3 - 17x^2 + 27x + 18$

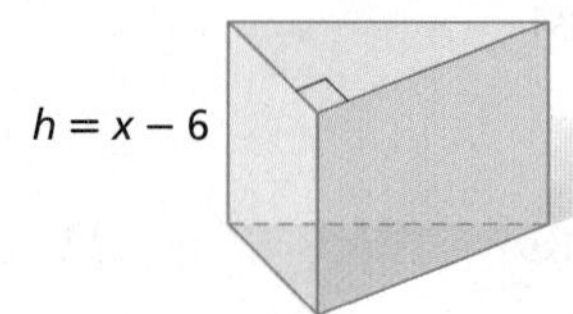

47. $V(x) = x^4 - 16$

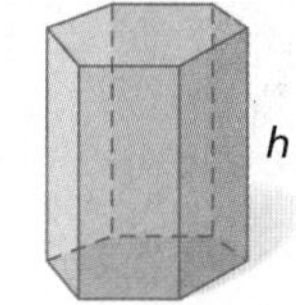

48. $V(x) = 3x^6 + 3x^3$

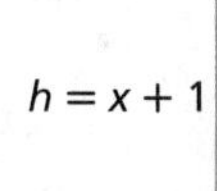

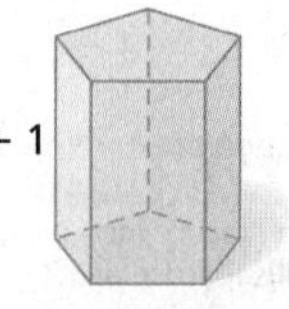

49. Write About It Describe how synthetic division can be used to factor a polynomial.

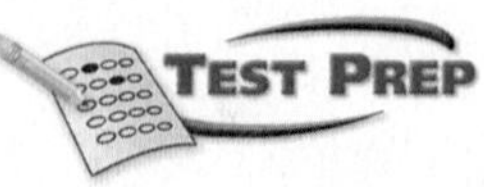

50. Which is a factor of $x^3 + 2x^2 - 9x + 30$?

Ⓐ $x + 2$ Ⓑ $x - 3$ Ⓒ $x + 5$ Ⓓ $x - 6$

51. $P(x)$ is a polynomial, and $P(4) = P(-2) = P(-1) = 0$. Which of the following could be $P(x)$?

Ⓕ $x^3 + 7x^2 + 14x + 8$ Ⓗ $x^2 + 3x + 2$

Ⓖ $-x^2 + 2x + 8$ Ⓙ $x^3 - x^2 - 10x - 8$

52. Short Response Factor $4p^5 - 16p^3 - 20p$ completely.

CHALLENGE AND EXTEND

53. Factor $(x-3)^3+8$ as the sum of two cubes. Then simplify each factor.

54. Factor $(2a+b)^3-b^3$ as the difference of two cubes. Then simplify each factor.

55. Divide (x^2-1), (x^3-1), and (x^4-1) by $(x-1)$ using synthetic division. Use the pattern you observe to find a formula for (x^n-1) divided by $(x-1)$.

The polynomial au^2+bu+c is in quadratic form when u is any function of x. Identify u, and factor each expression, simplifying the factors if possible.

56. $x+3\sqrt{x}+2$

57. $(3x-8)^2+6(3x-8)+9$

58. $2x^{\frac{1}{2}}-2x^{\frac{1}{4}}-12$

59. $\frac{1}{2}\left(x-\frac{1}{3}\right)^2+\frac{5}{2}\left(x-\frac{1}{3}\right)-42$

Career Path

Learn It Online
Career Resources Online

Katherine Shields
Nuclear propulsion officer candidate

Q: What math classes did you take in high school?

A: I took Algebra 1 and 2, Geometry, Trigonometry, and Precalculus.

Q: What math classes are you taking now?

A: I've taken two calculus classes. Right now, I'm taking Physics and an engineering class, both of which use a lot of math.

Q: How do you use math in the navy?

A: Nuclear propulsion officers operate aircraft carriers and nuclear-propelled submarines. It's amazing how much math is behind the theory and mechanics of nuclear propulsion.

Q: What are your future plans?

A: There are many options available after my nuclear officer training. While serving as an officer, I'd like to go to graduate school for an advanced degree in nuclear engineering.

CHAPTER 3

MULTI-STEP TEST PREP

SECTION 3A

Reason abstractly and quantitatively.

Operations with Polynomials

In the Spotlight A lighting rig is a large bank of lights that is used to create lighting effects at concerts and sporting events. A company makes rigs with lights arranged in polygonal patterns. The number of lights in a rig depends on the shape of the rig and the number of rows of lights. For example, a triangular rig may have 1, 3, 6, 10, or 15 lights, depending on the number of rows. The figures show the number of lights in a variety of rigs.

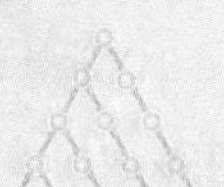

Triangular rig
Number of lights:
1, 3, 6, 10, 15, . . .

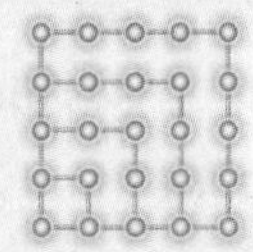

Square rig
Number of lights:
1, 4, 9, 16, 25, . . .

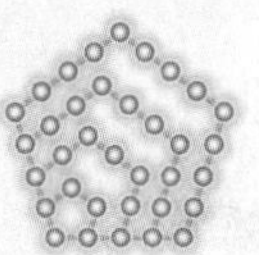

Pentagonal rig
Number of lights:
1, 5, 12, 22, 35, . . .

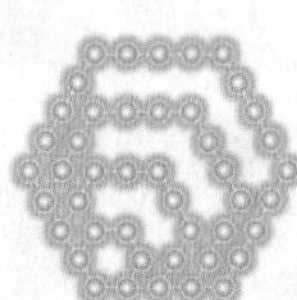

Hexagonal rig
Number of lights:
1, 6, 15, 28, 45, . . .

1. The number of lights in a triangular rig with n rows is given by $T(n) = \frac{1}{2}n^2 + \frac{1}{2}n$. Find the number of lights in triangular rigs with 1 to 10 rows.
2. The number of lights in a square rig with n rows is given by $S(n) = n^2$. Find the number of lights in square rigs with 1 to 10 rows.
3. The number of lights in a pentagonal rig with n rows is given by $P(n) = \frac{3}{2}n^2 - \frac{1}{2}n$. Find the number of lights in pentagonal rigs with 1 to 10 rows.
4. Write a polynomial function, $H(n)$, that gives the number of lights in a hexagonal rig with n rows. (*Hint:* Look for a pattern in the coefficients of the polynomial functions in parts **a**–**c**.)
5. Find $T(n) + P(n)$. What do you notice about this sum?
6. Find $H(n) \div S(n)$. What can you say about the ratio of the number of lights in a hexagonal rig with n rows to the number of lights in a square rig with n rows as n gets larger and larger?

READY TO GO ON?

CHAPTER 3

SECTION 3A

Quiz for Lesson 3-1 Through 3-4

3-1 Polynomials

Rewrite each polynomial in standard form. Then identify the leading coefficient, degree, and number of terms. Name the polynomial.

1. $4x^2 + 3x^5 - 5$ **2.** $7 + 13x$ **3.** $1 + 5x^3 + x^2 - 3x$ **4.** $8x + 2x^4 - 5x^3$

Add or subtract. Write your answer in standard form.

5. $(3x^2 + 1) + (4x^2 + 3)$

6. $(9x^3 - 6x^2) - (2x^3 + x^2 + 2)$

7. $(11x^2 + x^3 + 7) + (5x^3 + 4x^2 - 2x)$

8. $(x^5 - 4x^4 + 1) - (-7x^4 + 11)$

9. The cost of manufacturing x units of a product can be modeled by $C(x) = x^3 - 15x + 15$. Evaluate $C(x)$ for $x = 100$, and describe what the value represents.

Graph each polynomial function on a calculator. Describe the graph, and identify the number of real zeros.

10. $f(x) = -\frac{1}{4}x^5 - x^2$ **11.** $h(x) = \frac{1}{5}x^3 + x^2 - 2$ **12.** $f(x) = -2x^6 - 1$

3-2 Multiplying Polynomials

Find each product.

13. $2y(4x^2 + 7xy)$

14. $(a + b)(3ab + b^2)$

15. $\left(2x + \frac{1}{3}\right)^2$

16. $(2x - 3)(x^3 - x^2 + 3x + 5)$

Expand each expression.

17. $(x - 3)^4$ **18.** $(x + 2y)^3$ **19.** $(4x - 1)^4$

20. Find a polynomial expression in terms of x for the volume of the rectangular prism shown.

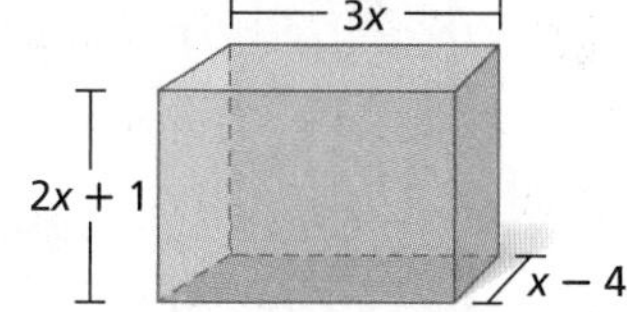

3-3 Dividing Polynomials

Divide.

21. $(6y^2 + 13y - 8) \div (2y - 1)$

22. $(3x^3 + 11x^2 + 11x + 15) \div (x + 3)$

Use synthetic substitution to evaluate the polynomial for the given value.

23. $P(x) = x^3 + 2x^2 - 5x + 6$ for $x = -1$

24. $P(x) = x^4 + x^2 + x - 6$ for $x = 2$

3-4 Factoring Polynomials

Factor each expression.

25. $3t^3 - 21t^2 - 12t$ **26.** $16y^2 - 49$

27. $y^3 + 7y^2 + 2y + 14$ **28.** $a^6 + 125$

29. The volume of a box is modeled by the function $V(x) = x^3 + 2x^2 - 11x - 12$. Identify the values of x for which the volume is 0 and use the graph to factor $V(x)$.

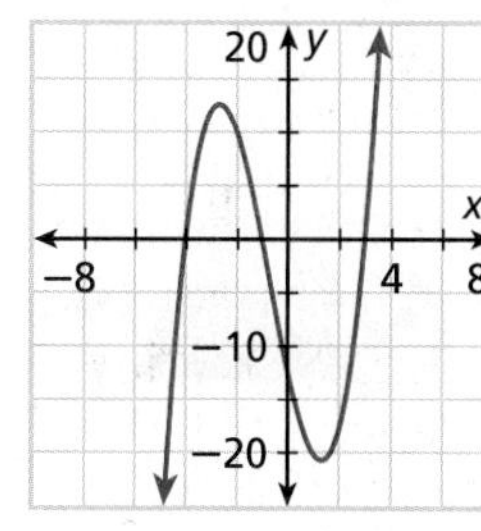

COMMON CORE

3-5 Finding Real Roots of Polynomial Equations

CC.9-12.A.APR.3 Identify zeros of polynomials ... and use the zeros to construct a rough graph of the function defined by the polynomial. *Also* **CC.9-12.A.CED.1, CC.9-12.A.REI.11***

Objectives

Identify the multiplicity of roots.

Use the Rational Root Theorem and the Irrational Root Theorem to solve polynomial equations.

Vocabulary

multiplicity

Who uses this?

Package designers can use roots of polynomial equations to set production specifications. (See Example 3.)

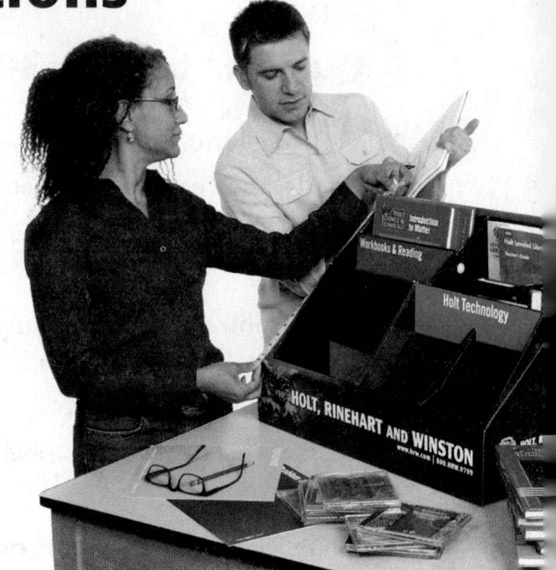

Previously, you have learned several methods for factoring polynomials. As with some quadratic equations, factoring a polynomial equation is one way to find its real roots.

Recall the Zero Product Property. You can find the *roots,* or *solutions,* of the polynomial equation $P(x) = 0$ by setting each factor equal to 0 and solving for x.

EXAMPLE 1 Using Factoring to Solve Polynomial Equations

Solve each polynomial equation by factoring.

A $3x^5 + 18x^4 + 27x^3 = 0$

$3x^3(x^2 + 6x + 9) = 0$ — *Factor out the GCF, $3x^3$.*

$3x^3(x + 3)(x + 3) = 0$ — *Factor the quadratic.*

$3x^3 = 0, x + 3 = 0, \text{ or } x + 3 = 0$ — *Set each factor equal to 0.*

$x = 0, x = -3, \text{ or } x = -3$ — *Solve for x.*

The roots are 0 and −3.

Check Use a graph. The roots appear to be located at $x = 0$ and $x = -3$. ✔

30, −5, 5, −30

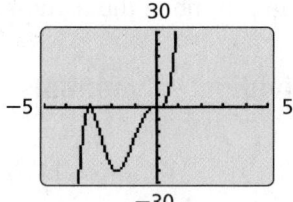

B $x^4 - 13x^2 = -36$

$x^4 - 13x^2 + 36 = 0$ — *Set the equation equal to 0.*

$(x^2 - 4)(x^2 - 9) = 0$ — *Factor the trinomial in quadratic form.*

$(x + 2)(x - 2)(x + 3)(x - 3) = 0$ — *Factor the difference of two squares.*

$x + 2 = 0, x - 2 = 0, x + 3 = 0, \text{ or } x - 3 = 0$

$x = -2, x = 2, x = -3, \text{ or } x = 3$

The roots are −2, 2, −3, and 3.

Solve each polynomial equation by factoring.

1a. $2x^6 - 10x^5 - 12x^4 = 0$ **1b.** $x^3 - 2x^2 - 25x = -50$

Sometimes a polynomial equation has a factor that appears more than once. This creates a *multiple root*. In Example 1A, $3x^5 + 18x^4 + 27x^3 = 0$ has two multiple roots, 0 and −3. For example, the root 0 is a factor three times because $3x^3 = 0$.

The **multiplicity** of root r is the number of times that $x - r$ is a factor of $P(x)$. When a real root has even multiplicity, the graph of $y = P(x)$ touches the x-axis but does not cross it. When a real root has odd multiplicity greater than 1, the graph "bends" as it crosses the x-axis.

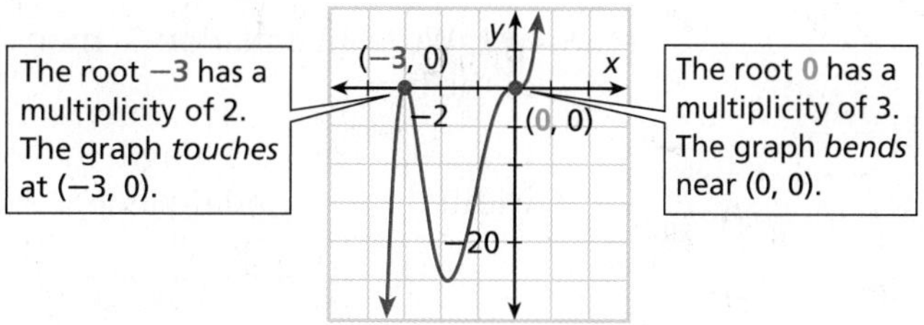

You cannot always determine the multiplicity of a root from a graph. It is easiest to determine multiplicity when the polynomial is in factored form.

EXAMPLE 2 Identifying Multiplicity

Identify the roots of each equation. State the multiplicity of each root.

A $x^3 - 9x^2 + 27x - 27 = 0$

$x^3 - 9x^2 + 27x - 27 = (x - 3)(x - 3)(x - 3)$

$x - 3$ is a factor three times.

The root 3 has a multiplicity of 3.

Check Use a graph. A calculator graph shows a bend near $(3, 0)$. ✔

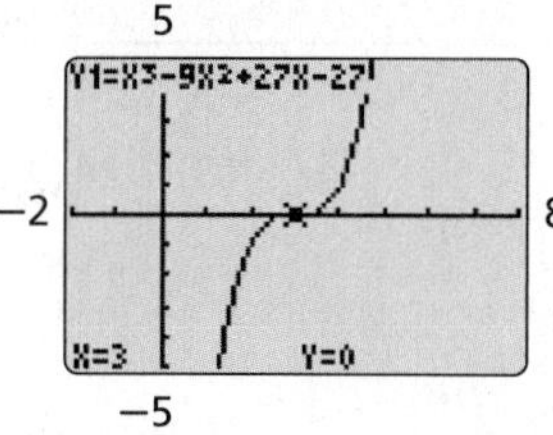

B $-2x^3 - 12x^2 + 30x + 200 = 0$

$-2x^3 - 12x^2 + 30x + 200 = -2(x - 4)(x + 5)(x + 5)$

$x - 4$ is a factor once, and $x + 5$ is a factor twice.

The root 4 has a multiplicity of 1.

The root −5 has a multiplicity of 2.

Check Use a graph. The graph crosses at $(4, 0)$ and touches at $(-5, 0)$. ✔

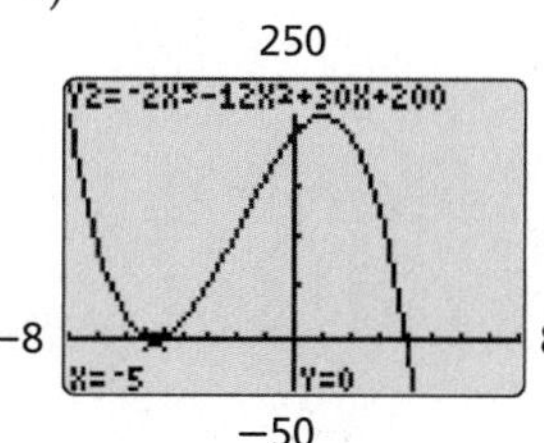

Identify the roots of each equation. State the multiplicity of each root.

2a. $x^4 - 8x^3 + 24x^2 - 32x + 16 = 0$

2b. $2x^6 - 22x^5 + 48x^4 + 72x^3 = 0$

Not all polynomials are factorable, but the Rational Root Theorem can help you find all possible rational roots of a polynomial equation.

Rational Root Theorem

If the polynomial $P(x)$ has integer coefficients, then every rational root of the polynomial equation $P(x) = 0$ can be written in the form $\frac{p}{q}$, where p is a factor of the constant term of $P(x)$ and q is a factor of the leading coefficient of $P(x)$.

EXAMPLE 3 Marketing Application

A popcorn producer is designing a new box for the popcorn. The marketing department has designed a box with the width 2 inches less than the length and with the height 5 inches greater than the length. The volume of each box must be 24 cubic inches. What is the length of the box?

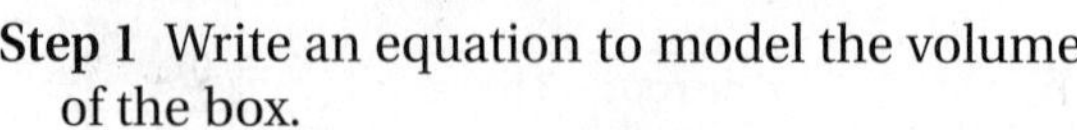

Step 1 Write an equation to model the volume of the box.

Let x represent the length in inches. Then the width is $x - 2$, and the height is $x + 5$.

$x(x-2)(x+5) = 24$	*$V = \ell wh$.*
$x^3 + 3x^2 - 10x = 24$	*Multiply the left side.*
$x^3 + 3x^2 - 10x - 24 = 0$	*Set the equation equal to 0.*

Step 2 Use the Rational Root Theorem to identify all possible rational roots.

Factors of -24: $\pm 1, \pm 2, \pm 3, \pm 4, \pm 6, \pm 8, \pm 12, \pm 24$

Step 3 Test the possible roots to find one that is actually a root. The length must be positive, so try only positive rational roots.

Use a synthetic substitution table to organize your work. The first row represents the coefficients of the polynomial. The first column represents the divisors and the last column represents the remainders. Test divisors to identify at least one root.

$\frac{p}{q}$	1	3	−10	−24
1	1	4	−6	−30
2	1	5	x	−24
3	1	6	x	x
4	1	7	x	x

Step 4 Factor the polynomial. The synthetic substitution of 3 results in a remainder of 0, so 3 is a root and the polynomial in factored form is $(x-3)(x^2 + 6x + 8)$.

$(x-3)(x^2 + 6x + 8) = 0$	*Set the equation equal to 0.*
$(x-3)(x+2)(x+4) = 0$	*Factor $x^2 + 6x + 8$.*
$x = 3, x = -2, \text{ or } x = -4$	*Set each factor equal to 0, and solve.*

The length must be positive, so the length should be 3 inches.

Check Substitute 3 for x in the formula for volume.

$$x(x-2)(x+5) = 24$$
$$3(3-2)(3+5) = 24$$
$$24 = 24 \checkmark$$

Helpful Hint

In Example 3, substitute 3 for x to check your (answer).

$x(x-2)(x+5) = 24$	
$3(3-2)(3+5)$	24
$3(1)(8)$	24
24	24 ✓

3. A shipping crate must hold 12 cubic feet. The width should be 1 foot less than the length, and the height should be 4 feet greater than the length. What should the length of the crate be?

Polynomial equations may also have irrational roots.

Irrational Root Theorem

If the polynomial $P(x)$ has rational coefficients and $a + b\sqrt{c}$ is a root of the polynomial equation $P(x) = 0$, where a and b are rational and $\sqrt{c}$ is irrational, then $a - b\sqrt{c}$ is also a root of $P(x) = 0$.

The Irrational Root Theorem says that irrational roots of the form $a + b\sqrt{c}$ come in conjugate pairs. For example, if you know that $1 + \sqrt{2}$ is a root of $x^3 - x^2 - 3x - 1 = 0$, then you know that $1 - \sqrt{2}$ is also a root.

Recall that the real numbers are made up of the rational and the irrational numbers. You can use the Rational Root Theorem and the Irrational Root Theorem together to find *all* of the real roots of $P(x) = 0$.

EXAMPLE 4 Identifying All of the Real Roots of a Polynomial Equation

Identify all of the real roots of $4x^4 - 21x^3 + 18x^2 + 19x - 6 = 0$.

Step 1 Use the Rational Root Theorem to identify possible rational roots.

$$\frac{\pm 1, \pm 2, \pm 3, \pm 6}{\pm 1, \pm 2, \pm 4} = \pm 1, \pm 2, \pm 3, \pm 6, \pm \frac{1}{2}, \pm \frac{3}{2}, \pm \frac{1}{4}, \pm \frac{3}{4}$$ *$p = -6$ and $q = 4$*

Step 2 Graph $y = 4x^4 - 21x^3 + 18x^2 + 19x - 6$ to find the x-intercepts.

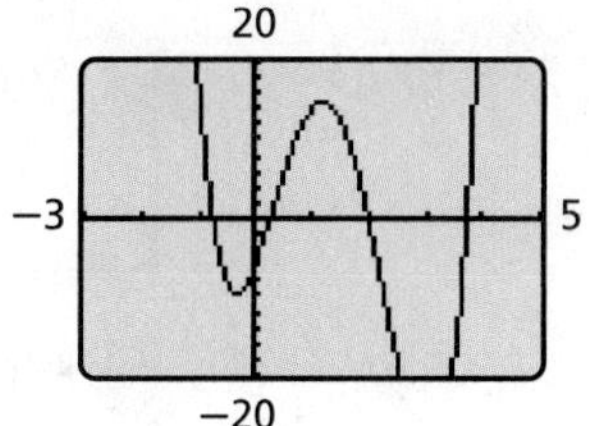

The x-intercepts are located at or near -0.75, 0.27, 2, and 3.73. The x-intercepts 0.27 and 3.73 do not correspond to any of the possible rational roots.

Helpful Hint

In Example 4, the x-intercepts 0.27 and 3.73 correspond to the irrational roots $2 - \sqrt{3}$ and $2 + \sqrt{3}$.

Step 3 Test the possible rational roots 2 and $-\frac{3}{4}$.

$$\begin{array}{r|rrrrr} 2 & 4 & -21 & 18 & 19 & -6 \\ & & 8 & -26 & -16 & 6 \\ \hline & 4 & -13 & -8 & 3 & \boxed{0} \end{array}$$

Test 2. The remainder is 0, so $(x - 2)$ is a factor.

The polynomial factors into $(x - 2)(4x^3 - 13x^2 - 8x + 3)$.

$$\begin{array}{r|rrrr} -\frac{3}{4} & 4 & -13 & -8 & 3 \\ & & -3 & 12 & -3 \\ \hline & 4 & -16 & 4 & \boxed{0} \end{array}$$

Test $-\frac{3}{4}$ in the cubic polynomial. The remainder is 0, so $\left(x + \frac{3}{4}\right)$ is a factor.

The polynomial factors into $(x - 2)\left(x + \frac{3}{4}\right)(4x^2 - 16x + 4)$.

Step 4 Solve $4x^2 - 16x + 4 = 0$ to find the remaining roots.

$4(x^2 - 4x + 1) = 0$ *Factor out the GCF of 4.*

$x = \dfrac{4 \pm \sqrt{16 - 4}}{2} = 2 \pm \sqrt{3}$ *Use the quadratic formula to identify the irrational roots.*

The fully factored equation is $4(x - 2)\left(x + \frac{3}{4}\right)\left[x - \left(2 + \sqrt{3}\right)\right]\left[x - \left(2 - \sqrt{3}\right)\right] = 0$.

The roots are 2, $-\frac{3}{4}$, $2 + \sqrt{3}$, and $2 - \sqrt{3}$.

4. Identify all of the real roots of $2x^3 - 3x^2 - 10x - 4 = 0$.

THINK AND DISCUSS

1. Explain how to recognize the multiplicity of a root of a polynomial in factored form.

2. **GET ORGANIZED** Copy and complete the graphic organizer. Give roots that satisfy each theorem and write a polynomial equation that has those roots.

Theorem	Roots	Polynomial
Rational Root Theorem		
Irrational Root Theorem		

3-5 Exercises

GUIDED PRACTICE

1. **Vocabulary** Explain how *multiplicity* is related to the word *multiple*.

SEE EXAMPLE 1

Solve each polynomial equation by factoring.

2. $2x^4 + 16x^3 + 32x^2 = 0$
3. $x^4 - 37x^2 + 36 = 0$
4. $4x^7 - 28x^6 = -48x^5$
5. $3x^4 + 11x^3 = 4x^2$
6. $2x^3 - 12x^2 = 32x - 192$
7. $x^4 + 100 = 29x^2$

SEE EXAMPLE 2

Identify the roots of each equation. State the multiplicity of each root.

8. $2x^5 + 12x^4 + 16x^3 - 12x^2 - 18x = 0$
9. $x^6 - 12x^4 + 48x^2 - 64 = 0$

SEE EXAMPLE 3

10. **Storage** A cedar chest has a length that is 3 feet longer than its width and a height that is 1 foot longer than its width. The volume of the chest is 30 cubic feet. What is the width?

SEE EXAMPLE 4

Identify all of the real roots of each equation.

11. $x^3 + 6x^2 - 5x - 30 = 0$
12. $3x^3 - 18x^2 - 9x + 132 = 0$
13. $2x^3 - 42x + 40 = 0$
14. $x^4 - 9x^2 + 20 = 0$

PRACTICE AND PROBLEM SOLVING

Independent Practice

For Exercises	See Example
15–20	1
21–22	2
23	3
24–26	4

Extra Practice

See Extra Practice for more Skills Practice and Applications Practice exercises.

Solve each polynomial equation by factoring.

15. $x^3 + 3x^2 - 9x = 27$
16. $4x^5 - 8x^3 + 4x = 0$
17. $10x^3 - 640x = 0$
18. $x^4 - 12x^2 = -36$
19. $2x^3 - 5x^2 - 4x + 10 = 0$
20. $4x^3 + 7x^2 - 5x = 6$

Identify the roots of each equation. State the multiplicity of each root.

21. $8x^5 - 192x^4 + 1536x^3 - 4096x^2 = 0$
22. $x^4 + 2x^3 - 11x^2 - 12x + 36 = 0$

23. **Measurement** An open box is to be made from a square piece of material with a side length of 10 inches by cutting equal squares from the corners and turning up the sides. What size of square would you cut out if the volume of the box must be 48 cubic inches?

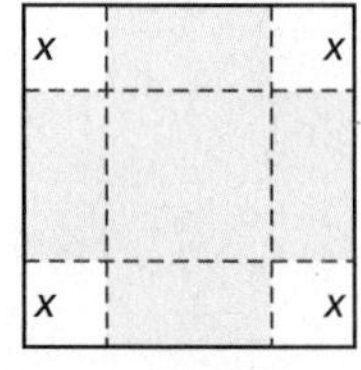

Identify all of the real roots of each equation.

24. $x^4 - 3x^2 - 4 = 0$ **25.** $3x^3 + 4x^2 - 6x - 8 = 0$ **26.** $x^4 - 2x^3 - 2x^2 = 0$

27. Graphing Calculator Consider the polynomial function $f(x) = x^4 + 3x^3 - 3x^2 - 12x - 4$.

a. Use the Rational Root Theorem to list the possible rational roots of this equation.

b. Graph the polynomial on a graphing calculator. Which possible rational roots are zeros of $f(x)$?

c. According to the graph, how many other real zeros does the function have?

d. Approximate these zeros to the nearest hundredth by using the zero feature.

28. Multi-Step A manufacturing company must design a box in the shape of a cube.

a. Let the side length of the box in inches equal x. Write a polynomial equation to represent the volume V of the box in cubic inches.

b. The box must have a volume of 125 cubic inches. Identify all possible rational roots of the resulting equation.

c. Identify the real roots of the equation, and state the multiplicity of each root.

d. What is the side length of the box?

e. Assuming no overlap of the sides, how many square inches of cardboard are needed to make each box?

Identify all of the real roots of each equation.

29. $x^3 - 7x^2 + 14x - 6 = 0$ **30.** $\frac{5}{3}x^3 + \frac{8}{3}x^2 - \frac{4}{3}x = 0$

31. $x^4 - x^3 - 31x^2 + 25x + 150 = 0$ **32.** $3x^4 + 19x^2 + 27x + 6 = 23x^3$

33. $x^5 - 4x^4 - 2x^3 + 4x^2 + x = 0$ **34.** $x^3 + 9 - 6x^2 = -4(11x - 2x^2)$

LINK **Entertainment**

The SheiKra roller coaster at Busch Gardens in Tampa is Florida's tallest roller coaster and includes a 138 ft dive into an underground tunnel.

35. Entertainment The paths of some roller coasters may be modeled by a polynomial function, where t is the time, in tens of seconds, after the ride has started and $h(t)$ is the height, in feet. Some roller coasters go underground as well as above the ground. In factored form, the beginning part of one roller-coaster ride can be modeled by the function $h(t) = \frac{1}{4}(t - 2)(t - 4)(t - 7)(t - 9)$.

a. What is the starting height of this roller coaster?

b. Graph this function on your graphing calculator, and describe the path of the roller coaster for the first 100 seconds.

c. Write an equation of a polynomial function that can be used to model a portion of a roller-coaster ride when the coaster starts 45 feet above the ground, enters an underground tunnel after 30 seconds, and then emerges from underground 20 seconds later.

MULTI-STEP TEST PREP

36. A type of cheese is packaged in a cardboard box shaped like a pyramid. As shown in the figure, the height is 2 cm greater than the length of the base.

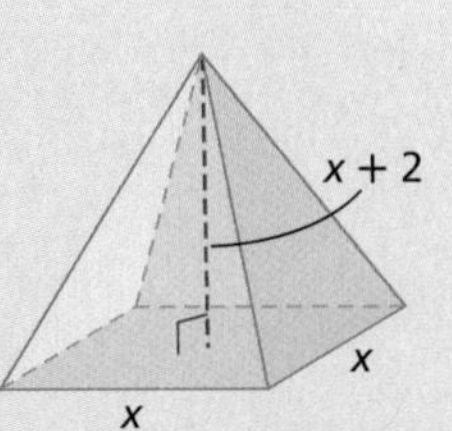

a. Write a polynomial function for the volume of the box.

b. The volume of the box must be 147 cm^3. Write a polynomial equation with integer coefficients that you can solve in order to find the length of the base.

c. What are the dimensions of the box?

37. **Critical Thinking** Suppose you are looking at a graph to identify which possible rational roots correspond to zeros. You see an x-intercept near 4. You have 4 as a possible rational root, but $P(4) \neq 0$. What can you say about the zero that you located on the graph?

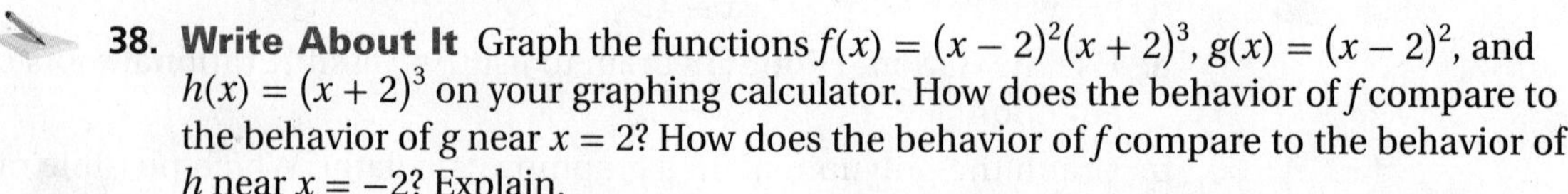

38. **Write About It** Graph the functions $f(x) = (x - 2)^2(x + 2)^3$, $g(x) = (x - 2)^2$, and $h(x) = (x + 2)^3$ on your graphing calculator. How does the behavior of f compare to the behavior of g near $x = 2$? How does the behavior of f compare to the behavior of h near $x = -2$? Explain.

39. **Write About It** How does the graph of $5x^4 - 20x^3$ behave near $(0, 0)$? How can you determine the behavior by factoring the expression?

TEST PREP

40. Find the solutions to the equation $8x^3 - 2x^2 - 43x + 30 = 0$.

   Ⓐ 2 and $\frac{-7 \pm \sqrt{42}}{8}$
   Ⓑ 2, $-\frac{5}{2}$, and $\frac{3}{4}$
   Ⓒ 2, 15, and 1
   Ⓓ 1, 2, and −3

41. How many real zeros does the polynomial $f(x) = 4x^2 - 3x + 2x^4 - 5x^3 - 7$ have?

   Ⓕ 2 Ⓖ 3 Ⓗ 4 Ⓙ 5

42. Which of the following is NOT a factor of $g(x) = 6x^3 + 13x^2 - 4$?

   Ⓐ $x + 2$ Ⓑ $2x - 1$ Ⓒ $x - 3$ Ⓓ $3x + 2$

43. Use the graph shown at right to identify the multiplicity of the roots of $f(x) = 0$.

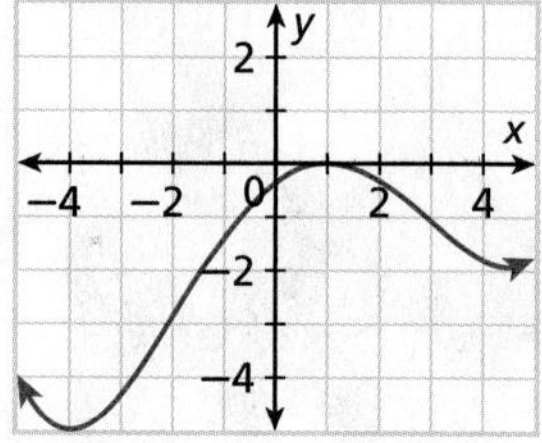

   Ⓕ Root 2 with a multiplicity of 1
   Ⓖ Root 2 with a multiplicity of 2
   Ⓗ Root 1 with a multiplicity of 2
   Ⓙ Root 1 with a multiplicity of 3

CHALLENGE AND EXTEND

44. Give a polynomial function that has the zeros 0, 1, and $3 - \sqrt{5}$.

Identify the value of k that makes the x-value a solution to the cubic equation.

45. $x^3 + 3x^2 - x + k = 0$; $x = 2$

46. $kx^3 - 2x^2 + x - 6 = 0$; $x = -3$

47. $6x^3 - 23x^2 - kx + 8 = 0$; $x = 4$

3-6 Fundamental Theorem of Algebra

CC.9-12.N.CN.9 Know the Fundamental Theorem of Algebra; show that it is true for quadratic polynomials.
Also **CC.9-12.N.CN.7, CC.9-12.N.CN.8, CC.9-12.A.APR.2, CC.9-12.A.CED.1, CC.9-12.A.REI.11***

Objectives

Use the Fundamental Theorem of Algebra and its corollary to write a polynomial equation of least degree with given roots.

Identify all of the roots of a polynomial equation.

Who uses this?

Aerospace engineers may find roots of polynomial equations to determine dimensions of rockets. (See Example 4.)

You have learned several important properties about real roots of polynomial equations.

The following statements are equivalent:
A real number r is a root of the polynomial equation $P(x) = 0$.
$P(r) = 0$
r is an x-intercept of the graph of $P(x)$.
$x - r$ is a factor of $P(x)$.
When you divide the rule for $P(x)$ by $x - r$, the remainder is 0.
r is a zero of $P(x)$.

You can use this information to write a polynomial function when given its zeros.

EXAMPLE 1 **Writing Polynomial Functions Given Zeros**

Write the simplest polynomial function with zeros $-3, \frac{1}{2}$, and 1.

$P(x) = (x + 3)\left(x - \frac{1}{2}\right)(x - 1)$ *If r is a zero of P(x), then x − r is a factor of P(x).*

$P(x) = \left(x^2 + \frac{5}{2}x - \frac{3}{2}\right)(x - 1)$ *Multiply the first two binomials.*

$P(x) = x^3 + \frac{3}{2}x^2 - 4x + \frac{3}{2}$ *Multiply the trinomial by the binomial.*

$P(x) = x^3 + \frac{3}{2}x^2 - 4x + \frac{3}{2}$

Write the simplest polynomial function with the given zeros.

1a. $-2, 2, 4$

1b. $0, \frac{2}{3}, 3$

Notice that the degree of the function in Example 1 is the same as the number of zeros. This is true for all polynomial functions. However, all of the zeros are not necessarily real zeros. Polynomial functions, like quadratic functions, may have complex zeros that are not real numbers.

The Fundamental Theorem of Algebra

Every polynomial function of degree $n \geq 1$ has at least one zero, where a zero may be a complex number.

Corollary: Every polynomial function of degree $n \geq 1$ has exactly n zeros, including multiplicities.

Using this theorem, you can write any polynomial function in factored form.

To find all roots of a polynomial equation, you can use a combination of the Rational Root Theorem, the Irrational Root Theorem, and methods for finding complex roots, such as the quadratic formula.

EXAMPLE 2 Finding All Roots of a Polynomial Equation

Solve $x^4 + x^3 + 2x^2 + 4x - 8 = 0$ by finding all roots.

The polynomial is of degree 4, so there are exactly four roots for the equation.

Step 1 Use the Rational Root Theorem to identify possible rational roots.

$$\frac{\pm1, \pm2, \pm4, \pm8}{\pm1} = \pm1, \pm2, \pm4, \pm8$$ *$p = -8$ and $q = 1$*

Step 2 Graph $y = x^4 + x^3 + 2x^2 + 4x - 8$ to find the real roots.

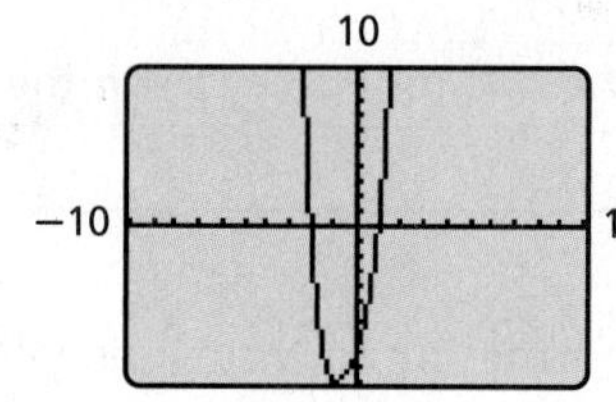

Find the real roots at or near −2 and 1.

Step 3 Test the possible real roots.

$$\begin{array}{r|rrrrr} 1 & 1 & 1 & 2 & 4 & -8 \\ & & 1 & 2 & 4 & 8 \\ \hline & 1 & 2 & 4 & 8 & \boxed{0} \end{array}$$

Test 1. The remainder is 0, so $(x - 1)$ is a factor.

The polynomial factors into $(x - 1)(x^3 + 2x^2 + 4x + 8) = 0$.

$$\begin{array}{r|rrrr} -2 & 1 & 2 & 4 & 8 \\ & & -2 & 0 & -8 \\ \hline & 1 & 0 & 4 & \boxed{0} \end{array}$$

Test −2 in the cubic polynomial. The remainder is 0, so $(x + 2)$ is a factor.

The polynomial factors into $(x - 1)(x + 2)(x^2 + 4) = 0$.

Step 4 Solve $x^2 + 4 = 0$ to find the remaining roots.

$$x^2 + 4 = 0$$
$$x^2 = -4$$
$$x = \pm 2i$$

The fully factored form of the equation is $(x - 1)(x + 2)(x + 2i)(x - 2i) = 0$.

The solutions are 1, −2, $2i$, and $-2i$.

2. Solve $x^4 + 4x^3 - x^2 + 16x - 20 = 0$ by finding all roots.

The real numbers are a subset of the complex numbers, so a real number a can be thought of as the complex number $a + 0i$. But here the term *complex root* will only refer to a root of the form $a + bi$, where $b \neq 0$. Complex roots, like irrational roots, come in conjugate pairs. Recall that the complex conjugate of $a + bi$ is $a - bi$.

Complex Conjugate Root Theorem

If $a + bi$ is a root of a polynomial equation with real-number coefficients, then $a - bi$ is also a root.

EXAMPLE 3 Writing a Polynomial Function with Complex Zeros

Write the simplest polynomial function with zeros $1 + i$, $\sqrt{2}$, and -3.

Step 1 Identify all roots.

By the Irrational Root Theorem and the Complex Conjugate Root Theorem, the irrational roots and complex roots come in conjugate pairs. There are five roots: $1 + i$, $1 - i$, $\sqrt{2}$, $-\sqrt{2}$, and -3. The polynomial must have degree 5.

Step 2 Write the equation in factored form.

$$P(x) = [x - (1 + i)][x - (1 - i)](x - \sqrt{2})[x - (-\sqrt{2})][x - (-3)]$$

Step 3 Multiply.

$$P(x) = (x^2 - 2x + 2)(x^2 - 2)(x + 3)$$
$$= (x^4 - 2x^3 + 4x - 4)(x + 3)$$
$$P(x) = x^5 + x^4 - 6x^3 + 4x^2 + 8x - 12$$

3. Write the simplest polynomial function with zeros $2i$, $1 + \sqrt{2}$, and 3.

EXAMPLE 4 *Problem-Solving Application*

An engineering class is designing model rockets for a competition. The body of the rocket must be cylindrical with a cone-shaped top. The cylinder part must be 60 cm tall, and the height of the cone must be twice the radius. The volume of the payload region must be 558π cm^3 in order to hold the cargo. Find the radius of the rocket.

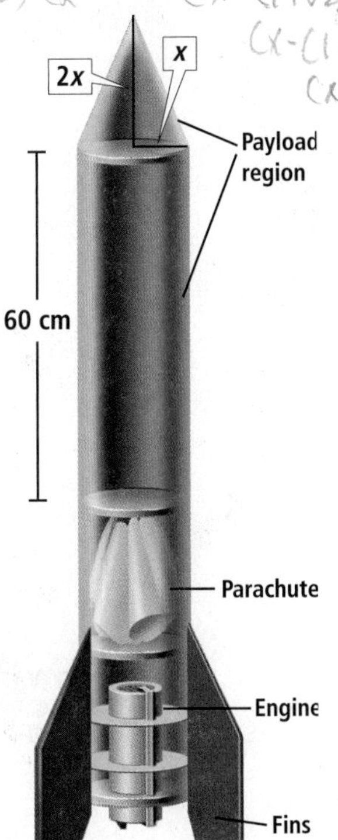

Make sense of problems and persevere in solving them.

1 Understand the Problem

The cylinder and the cone have the same radius, x. The answer will be the value of x.

List the important information:

- The cylinder is 60 cm tall.
- The height of the cone part is twice the radius, $2x$.
- The volume of the payload region is 558π cm^3.

2 Make a Plan

Write an equation to represent the volume of the body of the rocket.

$V = V_{\text{cone}} + V_{\text{cylinder}}$

$V(x) = \frac{2}{3}\pi x^3 + 60\pi x^2$ *$V_{cone} = \frac{1}{3}\pi x^2 h$ and $V_{cylinder} = \pi x^2 h$*

Set the volume equal to 558π.

$\frac{2}{3}\pi x^3 + 60\pi x^2 = 558\pi$

3 Solve

$\frac{2}{3}x^3 + 60x^2 = 558$ *Divide both sides by π.*

$\frac{2}{3}x^3 + 60x^2 - 558 = 0$ *Write in standard form.*

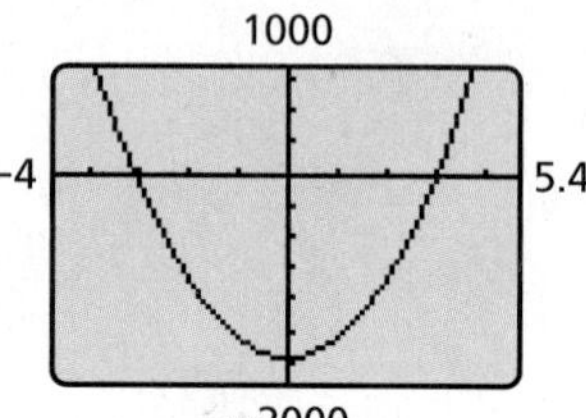

The graph indicates a possible positive root of 3. Use synthetic division to verify that 3 is a root, and write the equation as $(x-3)\left(\frac{2}{3}x^2 + 62x + 186\right) = 0$. By the quadratic formula, you can find that −3.1 and −89.9 are approximate roots of $\frac{2}{3}x^2 + 62x + 186 = 0$. The radius must be a positive number, so the radius of the rocket is 3 cm.

$$\begin{array}{r|rrrr} 3 & \frac{2}{3} & 60 & 0 & -558 \\ & & 2 & 186 & 558 \\ \hline & \frac{2}{3} & 62 & 186 & \boxed{0} \end{array}$$

4 Look Back

Substitute 3 cm into the original equation for the volume of the rocket.

$V(3) = \frac{2}{3}\pi(3)^3 + 60\pi(3)^2$

$V(3) = 558\pi$ ✔

4. A grain silo is in the shape of a cylinder with a hemisphere top. The cylinder is 20 feet tall. The volume of the silo is 2106π cubic feet. Find the radius of the silo.

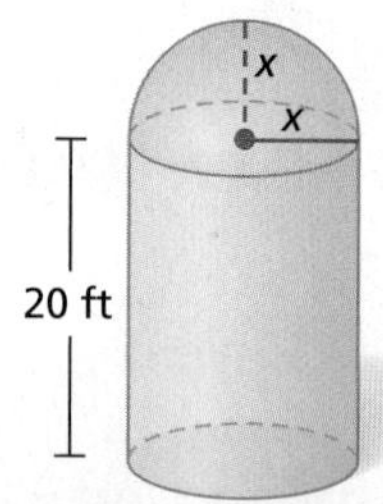

THINK AND DISCUSS

1. Explain why a polynomial equation with real coefficients and root $1 - i$ must be of degree two or greater.

2. If $P(x)$ is the product of a linear polynomial and a cubic polynomial, how many roots does $P(x) = 0$ have? Explain.

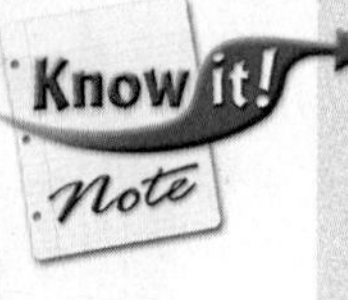

3. GET ORGANIZED Copy and complete the graphic organizer. Give an example of a polynomial with each type of root.

Rational	Irrational
Polynomial Roots	
Real	Complex

3-6 Exercises

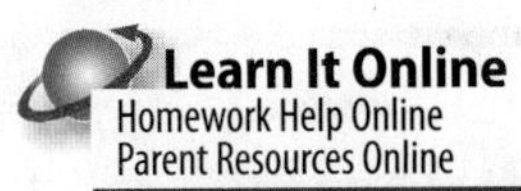

GUIDED PRACTICE

SEE EXAMPLE 1 — Write the simplest polynomial function with the given zeros.

1. $\frac{1}{3}, 1, 2$
2. $-2, 2, 3$
3. $-2, \frac{1}{2}, 2$

SEE EXAMPLE 2 — Solve each equation by finding all roots.

4. $x^4 - 81 = 0$
5. $3x^3 - 10x^2 + 10x - 4 = 0$
6. $x^3 - 3x^2 + 4x - 12 = 0$

SEE EXAMPLE 3 — Write the simplest polynomial function with the given zeros.

7. $1 - i$ and 2
8. $1 + \sqrt{5}$ and 3
9. $2i, \sqrt{2}$, and 2

SEE EXAMPLE 4

10. **Farming** A grain silo is shaped like a cylinder with a cone-shaped top. The cylinder is 30 feet tall. The volume of the silo is 1152π cubic feet. Find the radius of the silo.

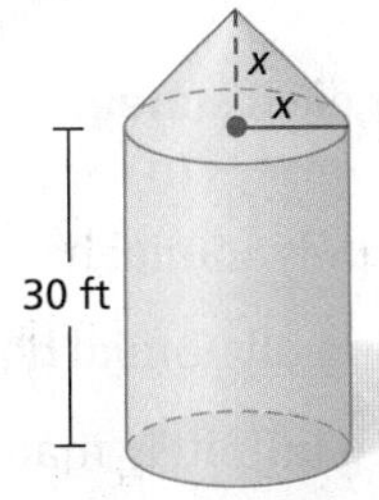

PRACTICE AND PROBLEM SOLVING

Independent Practice

For Exercises	See Example
11–13	1
14–19	2
20–22	3
23	4

Extra Practice

See Extra Practice for more Skills Practice and Applications Practice exercises.

Write the simplest polynomial function with the given zeros.

11. $-1, -1, 2$
12. $2, 1, \frac{2}{3}$
13. $-4, -1, 2$

Solve each equation by finding all roots.

14. $x^4 - 16 = 0$
15. $x^3 - 7x^2 + 15x - 9 = 0$
16. $x^4 + 5x^2 - 36 = 0$
17. $2x^3 - 3x^2 + 8x - 12 = 0$
18. $x^4 - 5x^3 + 3x^2 + x = 0$
19. $x^4 - 4x^2 + 3 = 0$

Write the simplest polynomial function with the given zeros.

20. $2 - i, \sqrt{3}$, and 2
21. $2\sqrt{2}, \sqrt{5}$, and -3
22. $-2i$ and $1 + i$
23. **Storage** A storage bin is shaped like a cylinder with a hemisphere-shaped top. The cylinder is 45 inches tall. The volume of the bin is 4131π cubic inches. Find the radius of the bin.

Solve each equation by finding all roots.

24. $x^4 - 3x^3 + 5x^2 - 27x - 36 = 0$
25. $x^4 + 4x^3 - 3x^2 - 14x - 8 = 0$
26. $x^3 + 3x^2 + 3x + 1 = 0$
27. $x^4 + 4x^3 + 6x^2 + 4x + 1 = 0$
28. $6x^3 + 11x^2 - 3x - 2 = 0$
29. $x^3 - 2x^2 - 2x - 3 = 0$
30. $x^3 - 6x^2 + 11x - 6 = 0$
31. $x^4 - 13x^3 + 55x^2 - 91x = 0$
32. $x^4 + x^2 - 12 = 0$
33. $x^4 + 14x^2 + 45 = 0$
34. $x^3 + 13x - 85 = 31$
35. $x^3 - 4x^2 + x + 14 = 8$
36. **Geometry** The volume of the rectangular prism is 105 cubic units. Find the dimensions of the prism.

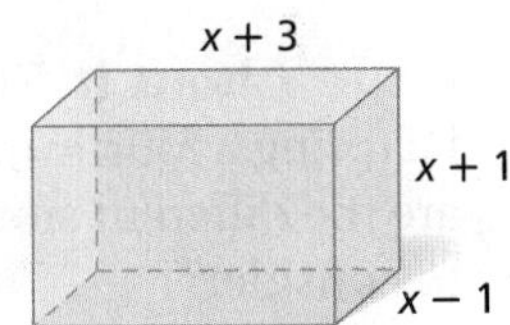

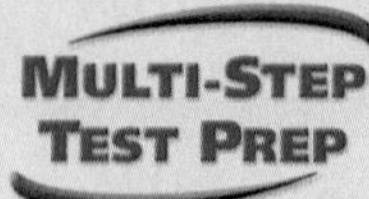

37. The volume of a pyramid-shaped tent with a square base can be represented by the function $V(x) = \frac{1}{3}x^3 - 2x^2$, where x is the length of the base in meters.
   a. The volume of the tent is 81 m^3. Write a polynomial equation with integer coefficients that you can solve in order to find the length of the base.
   b. Find the length of the base.
   c. What can you say about the other roots of the polynomial equation? Why?

Write the simplest polynomial function with the given zeros.

38. 0, $\sqrt{5}$, and 2
39. $4i$, 2, and -2
40. 1, -1 (multiplicity of 3), and $3i$
41. 1, 1, and 2
42. $1 - \sqrt{2}$, and $2i$
43. 3 (multiplicity of 2), and $3i$

Tell whether each statement is sometimes, always, or never true. If it is sometimes true, give examples to support your answer.

44. A cubic polynomial has no real zeros.
45. A quartic polynomial has an odd number of real zeros.
46. There are infinitely many polynomials with zeros a, b, and c.
47. The multiplicity of a root is equal to the degree of the polynomial.

Use your graphing calculator to approximate the solutions of each equation by finding all roots. Round your answer to the nearest thousandth.

48. $3x^4 - x = 6x^2 + \sqrt{2}$
49. $2\sqrt{3}x^4 - x^2 = 0$
50. $-6x^3 = -5\sqrt{3}x + \sqrt{2}$
51. $\sqrt{7}x^3 - 11x^2 + 8 = 0$

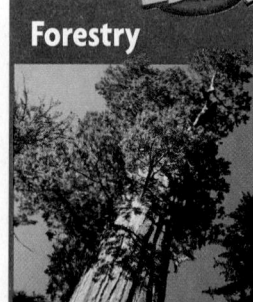

LINK

Forestry

The sequoias in Sequoia National Park in California are among the largest trees in the world. Many are as tall as a 26-story building and wider than some city streets.

52. **Forestry** The volume of a giant sequoia can be modeled by $V(h) = 0.485h^3 - 362h^2 + 89889h - 7379874$, where h represents the height of a tree in feet and $220 \le h \le 280$.
   a. Find the height of a tree with volume 39,186 cubic feet.
   b. The Lincoln tree in the Giant Forest in Sequoia National Park has a volume of 44,471 cubic feet. What are its possible heights?
   c. The actual height of the Lincoln tree is 255.8 feet. What is the difference between the true volume of the tree and the volume given by the model?

53. The volume of a cylindrical propane tank with a hemispherical top and bottom can be represented by the function $V(r) = 33\pi r^2 + \frac{4}{3}\pi r^3$, where V is the volume in cubic inches and r is the radius in inches. What is the radius if the volume of the tank is 1476π cubic inches?

54. **Critical Thinking** What is the least degree of a polynomial equation that has $3i$ as a root with a multiplicity of 3? Explain.

55. **Estimation** Use the graph to estimate the roots of $y = 3x^3 - 2x^2 - 15x + 10$. Then find the exact roots. (*Hint:* Factor by grouping.)

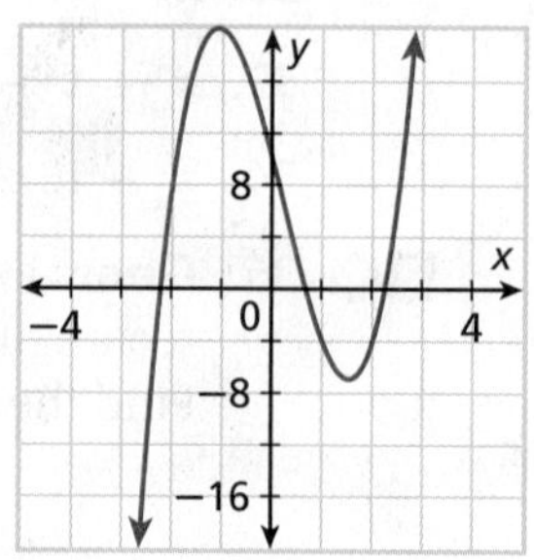

56. **Write About It** Describe your method for factoring a fourth-degree polynomial. What are the different situations that you need to consider?

57. What is the multiplicity of the root -1 in the equation $y = x^4 - 2x^3 - 3x^2 + 4x + 4$?

Ⓐ 1 Ⓑ 2 Ⓒ 3 Ⓓ 4

58. What is the conjugate of $-6 - 5i$?

Ⓕ $-6 - 5i$ Ⓖ $-6 + 5i$ Ⓗ $6 - 5i$ Ⓙ $6 + 5i$

59. Which polynomial function has zeros 0, i, and $-i$?

Ⓐ $P(x) = x^3 + 2x^2 + 1$
Ⓑ $P(x) = x^3 + x^2$
Ⓒ $P(x) = x^3 + 2x^2 + x$
Ⓓ $P(x) = x^3 + x$

60. A polynomial has zeros $3 - \sqrt{2}$, 4, and $6i$. What is the minimum degree of the polynomial?

Ⓕ 3 Ⓖ 4 Ⓗ 5 Ⓙ 6

61. Which polynomial function has zeros $1 + \sqrt{3}$ and $1 - \sqrt{3}$?

Ⓐ $f(x) = x^2 + 8$
Ⓑ $f(x) = x^2 - 3x + 9$
Ⓒ $f(x) = x^2 - x + \sqrt{3}$
Ⓓ $f(x) = x^2 - 2x - 2$

62. **Short Response** Solve the equation $2x^3 - 6x^2 + 8x - 24 = 0$ by finding all roots.

CHALLENGE AND EXTEND

63. Use synthetic substitution to evaluate $f(x) = x^3 - 3x^2 + 9x - 27$ for $x = 3i$ and $x = -\sqrt{3}$. Is either $x = 3i$ or $x = -\sqrt{3}$ a zero of f?

64. $2i$ is a zero of $P(x) = x^3 - 2ix^2 - 4x + 8i$. Find the other zeros of P.

65. One zero of $Q(x) = x^3 - \sqrt{2}x^2 + 9x - 9\sqrt{2}$ is $\sqrt{2}$. Find the other zeros of Q.

66. **Critical Thinking** Based on your answers to Exercises 64 and 65, what can you say about a polynomial function with nonreal or irrational coefficients?

67. Factor the sum $a^2 + b^2$.

68. Factor the sum $a^4 + b^4$.

69. Factor the sum $a^6 + b^6$.

70. **Critical Thinking** Does your answer to Exercise 67 help you answer Exercises 68 or 69? Explain.

71. **Critical Thinking** Give an example of a fourth-degree polynomial equation that has no real zeros. What are the roots of your example?

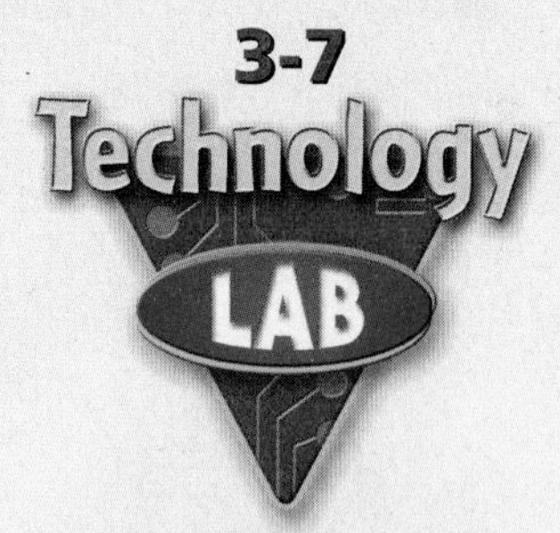

Explore Power Functions

A power function can be written in the form $f(x) = ax^n$, where a and n are real numbers and $a \neq 0$. When n is a positive integer, a power function is also a polynomial function.

End behavior is a description of the values of a function as x approaches positive infinity ($x \to +\infty$) or negative infinity ($x \to -\infty$).

Use with Investigating Graphs of Polynomial Functions

Reason abstractly and quantitatively.

CC.9-12.F.IF.4 For a function that models a relationship ..., interpret key features of graphs and tables ..., and sketch graphs showing key features ....

Describe the end behavior of $f(x) = \frac{1}{5}x^4$, and give the function's domain and range.

1. Enter the function as **Y1**, and graph it in a friendly window.

2. Examine the end behavior. As x increases for positive values of x, the values of f appear to increase. As x decreases for negative values of x, the values of f also appear to increase.

3. Find the domain and range. Substituting any real value of x into the function results in a real number, so the domain is $\mathbb{R}$.

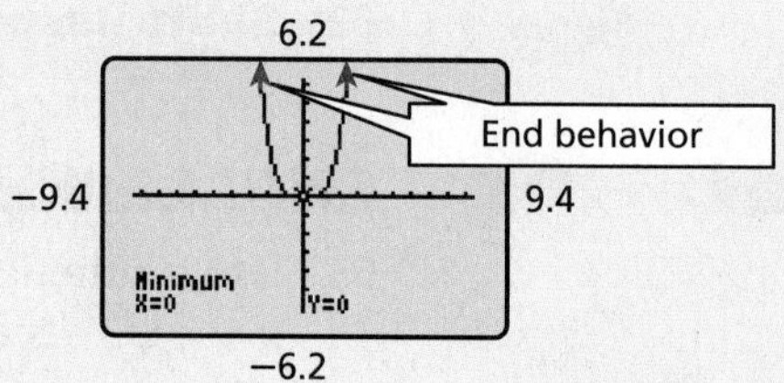

The function has a minimum value, so the minimum determines the range. To find the minimum, press 2nd CALC TRACE and select **3:minimum.**

Move the cursor to the left of the point containing the minimum; press ENTER. Repeat on the right. Then move the cursor close to the point containing the minimum. Press ENTER to display its coordinates.

The minimum is 0, so the range is $\{y \mid y \geq 0\}$ or $[0, \infty)$.

Try This

Describe the end behavior of each function, and give the function's domain and range.

1. $f(x) = \frac{1}{2}x^3$
2. $f(x) = -5x^2$
3. $f(x) = -2x^3$
4. $f(x) = \frac{1}{10}x^3$
5. $f(x) = x^5$
6. $f(x) = -3x^4$
7. **Make a Conjecture** Make a conjecture about the domain and range of polynomial power functions that meet each given condition. Graph as many functions as needed in order to make the conjecture.
   a. n is odd.
   b. a is positive, and n is even.
   c. a is negative, and n is even.
8. **Make a Conjecture** Make a conjecture about the end behavior of polynomial power functions that meet each given condition. Graph as many functions as needed in order to make the conjecture.
   a. a is positive, and n is odd.
   b. a is negative, and n is odd.
   c. a is positive, and n is even.
   d. a is negative, and n is even.

3-7 Investigating Graphs of Polynomial Functions

CC.9-12.A.APR.3 Identify zeros of polynomials … and use the zeros to construct a rough graph of the function defined by the polynomial. *Also* **CC.9-12.F.IF.7c*, CC.9-12.A.CED.2, CC.9-12.A.CED.3**

Objectives

Use properties of end behavior to analyze, describe, and graph polynomial functions.

Identify and use maxima and minima of polynomial functions to solve problems.

Vocabulary

end behavior
turning point
local maximum
local minimum

Who uses this?

Welders can use graphs of polynomial functions to optimize the use of construction materials. (See Example 5.)

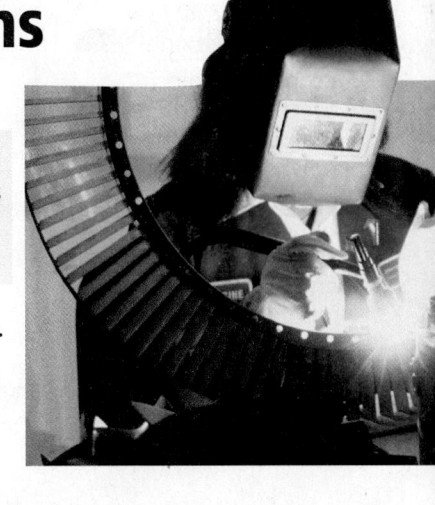

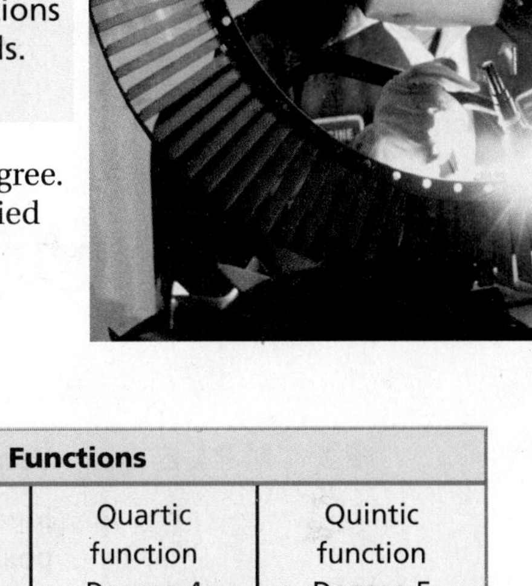

Polynomial functions are classified by their degree. The graphs of polynomial functions are classified by the degree of the polynomial. Each graph, based on the degree, has a distinctive shape and characteristics.

Graphs of Polynomial Functions

Linear function Degree 1	Quadratic function Degree 2	Cubic function Degree 3	Quartic function Degree 4	Quintic function Degree 5

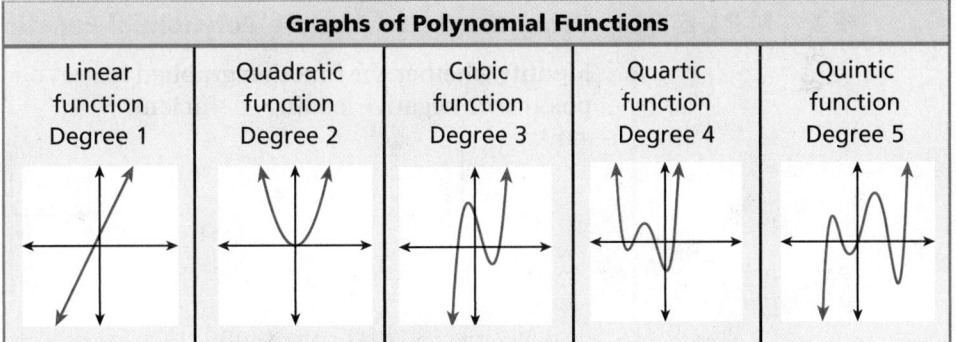

End behavior is a description of the values of the function as x approaches positive infinity ($x \to +\infty$) or negative infinity ($x \to -\infty$). The degree and leading coefficient of a polynomial function determine its end behavior. It is helpful when you are graphing a polynomial function to know about the end behavior of the function.

Know it! Note

Polynomial End Behavior

$P(x)$ has...	Odd Degree	Even Degree
Leading coefficient $a > 0$	As $x \to +\infty$, $P(x) \to +\infty$ As $x \to -\infty$, $P(x) \to -\infty$ Domain: $\mathbb{R}$ Range: $\mathbb{R}$	As $x \to -\infty$, $P(x) \to +\infty$ As $x \to +\infty$, $P(x) \to +\infty$ Domain: $\mathbb{R}$ Range: all values $\geq$ minimum
Leading coefficient $a < 0$	As $x \to -\infty$, $P(x) \to +\infty$ As $x \to +\infty$, $P(x) \to -\infty$ Domain: $\mathbb{R}$ Range: $\mathbb{R}$	As $x \to -\infty$, $P(x) \to -\infty$ As $x \to +\infty$, $P(x) \to -\infty$ Domain: $\mathbb{R}$ Range: all values $\leq$ maximum

EXAMPLE 1 Determining End Behavior of Polynomial Functions

Helpful Hint

Both the leading coefficient and the degree of the polynomial are contained in the term of greatest degree. When determining end behavior, you can ignore all other terms.

Identify the leading coefficient, degree, and end behavior.

A $P(x) = -4x^3 - 3x^2 + 5x + 6$

The leading coefficient is -4, which is negative.

The degree is 3, which is odd.

As $x \to -\infty$, $P(x) \to +\infty$, and as $x \to +\infty$, $P(x) \to -\infty$.

B $R(x) = x^6 - 7x^5 + x^3 - 2$

The leading coefficient is 1, which is positive.

The degree is 6, which is even.

As $x \to -\infty$, $P(x) \to +\infty$, and as $x \to +\infty$, $P(x) \to +\infty$.

Identify the leading coefficient, degree, and end behavior.

1a. $P(x) = 2x^5 + 3x^2 - 4x - 1$

1b. $S(x) = -3x^2 + x + 1$

EXAMPLE 2 Using Graphs to Analyze Polynomial Functions

Identify whether the function graphed has an odd or even degree and a positive or negative leading coefficient.

A

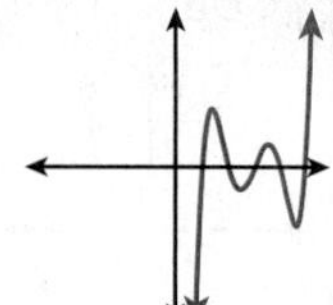

As $x \to -\infty$, $P(x) \to -\infty$, and as $x \to +\infty$, $P(x) \to +\infty$.

$P(x)$ is of odd degree with a positive leading coefficient.

B

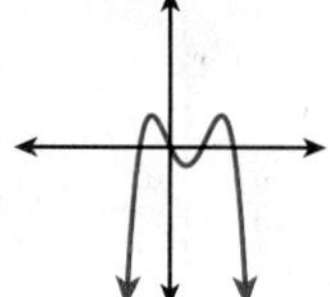

As $x \to -\infty$, $P(x) \to -\infty$, and as $x \to +\infty$, $P(x) \to -\infty$.

$P(x)$ is of even degree with a negative leading coefficient.

Identify whether the function graphed has an odd or even degree and a positive or negative leading coefficient.

2a.

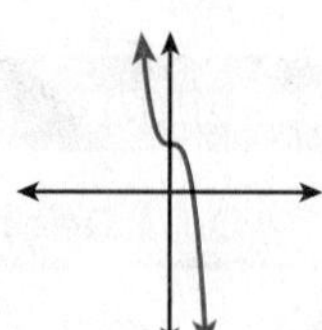

2b.

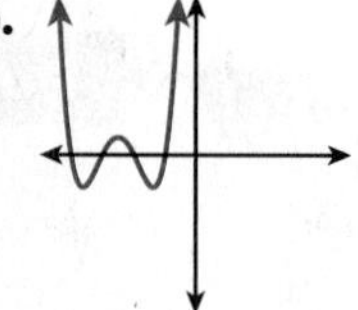

Now that you have studied factoring, solving polynomial equations, and end behavior, you can graph a polynomial function.

Steps for Graphing a Polynomial Function
1. Find the real zeros and *y*-intercept of the function.
2. Plot the *x*- and *y*-intercepts.
3. Make a table for several *x*-values that lie between the real zeros.
4. Plot the points from your table.
5. Determine the end behavior of the graph.
6. Sketch the graph.

EXAMPLE 3 Graphing Polynomial Functions

Graph the function.

$f(x) = x^3 + 3x^2 - 6x - 8$

Step 1 Identify the possible rational roots by using the Rational Root Theorem.

$\pm1, \pm2, \pm4, \pm8$ *p = −8 and q = 1*

Step 2 Test possible rational zeros until a zero is identified.

Test $x = 1$.

$$\begin{array}{r|rrrr} 1 & 1 & 3 & -6 & -8 \\ & & 1 & 4 & -2 \\ \hline & 1 & 4 & -2 & -10 \end{array}$$

Test $x = -1$.

$$\begin{array}{r|rrrr} -1 & 1 & 3 & -6 & -8 \\ & & -1 & -2 & 8 \\ \hline & 1 & 2 & -8 & 0 \end{array}$$

$x = -1$ is a zero, and $f(x) = (x + 1)(x^2 + 2x - 8)$.

Step 3 Factor: $f(x) = (x + 1)(x - 2)(x + 4)$.
The zeros are -1, 2, and -4.

Step 4 Plot other points as guidelines.
$f(0) = -8$, so the y-intercept is -8.

Plot points between the zeros. Choose $x = -3$ and $x = 1$ for simple calculations.
$f(-3) = 10$ and $f(1) = -10$

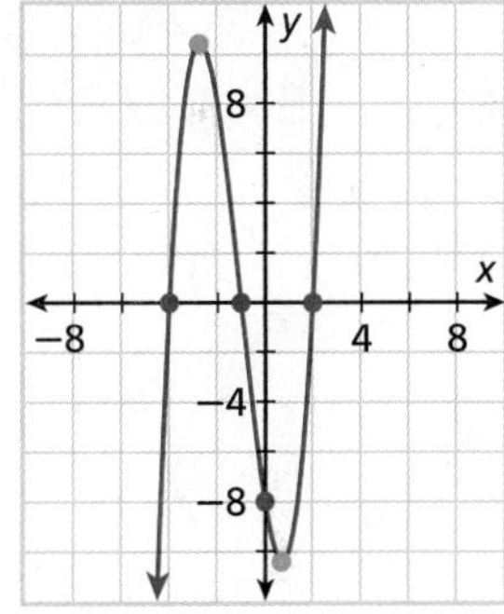

Step 5 Identify end behavior.
The degree is odd and the leading coefficient is positive so as $x \to -\infty$, $P(x) \to -\infty$, and as $x \to +\infty$, $P(x) \to +\infty$.

Step 6 Sketch the graph of $f(x) = x^3 + 3x^2 - 6x - 8$ by using all of the information about $f(x)$.

Graph each function.

3a. $f(x) = x^3 - 2x^2 - 5x + 6$ **3b.** $f(x) = -2x^2 - x + 6$

A **turning point** is where a graph changes from increasing to decreasing or from decreasing to increasing. A turning point corresponds to a *local maximum* or *minimum*.

Local Maxima and Minima

For a function $f(x)$, $f(a)$ is a **local maximum** if there is an interval around a such that $f(x) < f(a)$ for every x-value in the interval except a.

For a function $f(x)$, $f(a)$ is a **local minimum** if there is an interval around a such that $f(x) > f(a)$ for every x-value in the interval except a.

A polynomial function of degree n has at most $n - 1$ turning points and at most n x-intercepts. If the function has n distinct real roots, then it has exactly $n - 1$ turning points and exactly n x-intercepts. You can use a graphing calculator to graph and estimate maximum and minimum values.

EXAMPLE 4 Determine Maxima and Minima with a Calculator

Graph $g(x) = 2x^3 - 12x + 6$ on a calculator, and estimate the local maxima and minima.

Step 1 Graph.

The graph appears to have one local maximum and one local minimum.

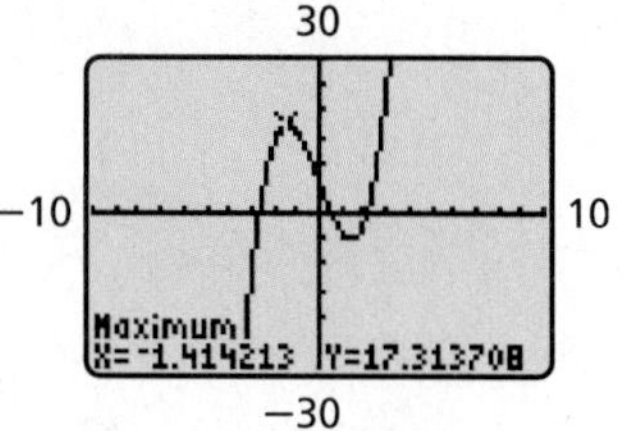

Step 2 Find the maximum.

Press 2nd TRACE (CALC) to access the **CALC** menu. Choose **4:maximum**.

The local maximum is approximately 17.3137.

Step 3 Find the minimum.

Press 2nd TRACE (CALC) to access the **CALC** menu. Choose **3:mininum**.

The local minimum is approximately −5.3137.

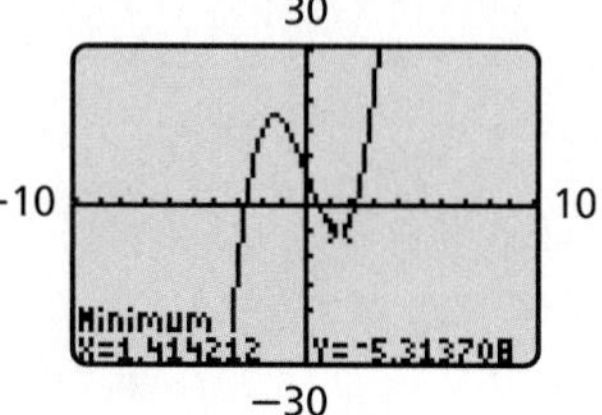

> **Reading Math**
> *Maxima* is the plural form of *maximum*. *Minima* is the plural form of *minimum*.

Graph each function on a calculator, and estimate the local maxima and minima.

4a. $g(x) = x^3 - 2x - 3$ **4b.** $h(x) = x^4 + 4x^2 - 6$

EXAMPLE 5 *Industrial Application*

A welder plans to construct an open box from an 18.5 ft by 24.5 ft sheet of metal by cutting squares from the corners and folding up the sides. Find the maximum volume of the box and the corresponding dimensions.

Find a formula to represent volume.

$V(x) = x(18.5 - 2x)(24.5 - 2x)$ $V = \ell wh$

Graph $V(x)$. Note that values of x greater than 9.25 or less than 0 do not make sense for this problem.

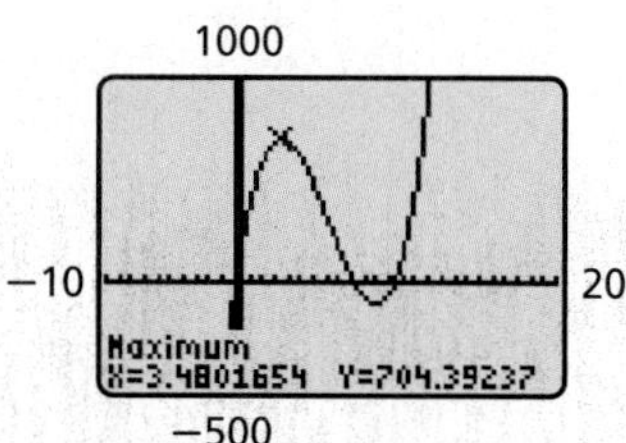

The graph has a local maximum of about 704.4 when $x \approx 3.48$. So, the largest open box will have a volume of 704.4 ft^3.

5. What is the maximum volume of a box made from a 16 ft by 20 ft sheet of metal?

THINK AND DISCUSS

1. Explain why a polynomial function that has exactly n distinct real roots must have $n - 1$ turning points.

2. GET ORGANIZED Copy and complete the graphic organizer. In each box, sketch a graph that fits the description.

Leading Coefficient	Odd Degree	Even Degree
Positive		
Negative		

3-7 Exercises

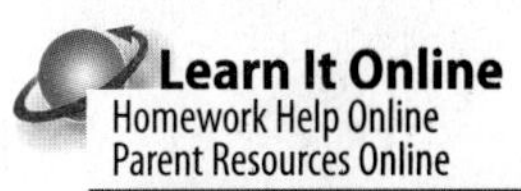

GUIDED PRACTICE

1. **Vocabulary** Explain why a *turning point* is appropriately named.

SEE EXAMPLE 1

Identify the leading coefficient, degree, and end behavior.

2. $P(x) = -4x^4 - 3x^3 + x^2 + 4$
3. $Q(x) = -2x^7 + 6x^5 + 2x^3$
4. $R(x) = x^5 - 4x^2 + 3x - 1$
5. $S(x) = 3x^2 + 6x - 10$

SEE EXAMPLE 2

Identify whether the function graphed has an odd or even degree and a positive or negative leading coefficient.

6. 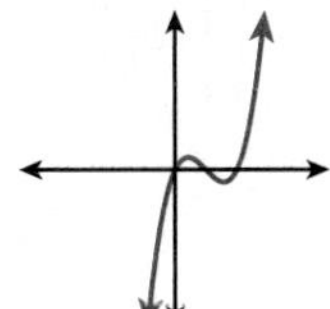
7. 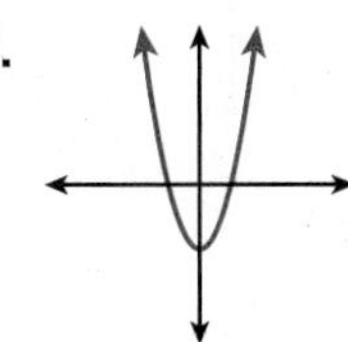
8. 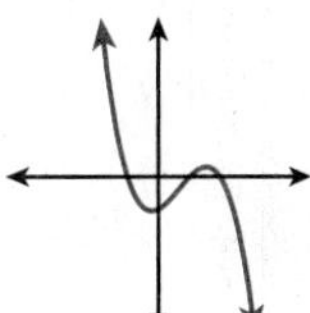
9. 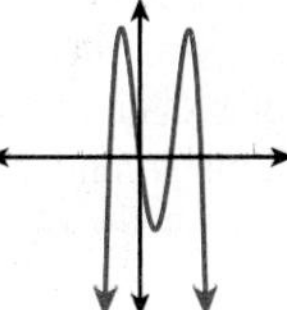

SEE EXAMPLE 3

Graph each function.

10. $f(x) = x^2 - 5x - 50$
11. $f(x) = -x^3 + \frac{3}{2}x^2 + 25x + 12$

SEE EXAMPLE 4

Graph each function on a calculator, and estimate the local maxima and minima.

12. $f(x) = x^4 - 4x^3 + 3x + 5$
13. $f(x) = 2x^3 - 3x^2 - 6x - 5$

SEE EXAMPLE 5

14. **Landscape Design** Vera has 60 ft of fencing and wants to enclose a patio, using an existing wall for one side as shown. The area of the patio can be modeled by $A(x) = 60x - 3x^2$, where x is in feet. Find the maximum area of the patio.

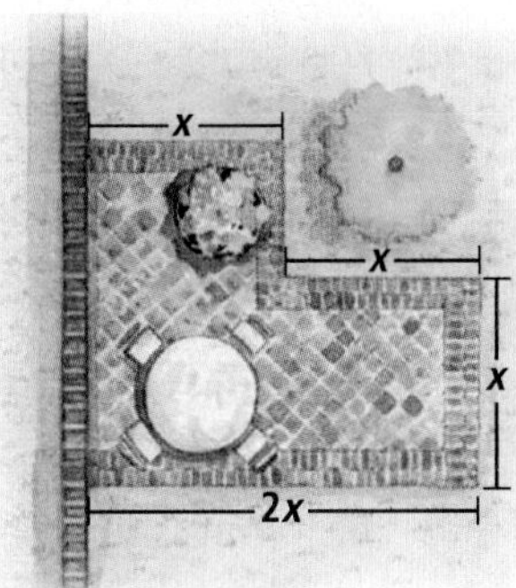

PRACTICE AND PROBLEM SOLVING

Independent Practice

For Exercises	See Example
15–18	1
19–22	2
23–26	3
27–30	4
31	5

Extra Practice

See Extra Practice for more Skills Practice and Applications Practice exercises.

Identify the leading coefficient, degree, and end behavior.

15. $P(x) = 2x^3 + 3x^2 - 4x$
16. $Q(x) = -3x^4 - 8x^2$
17. $R(x) = -x^5 + 5x^4 + 1$
18. $S(x) = 5.5x^8 + 7.5x^4$

Identify whether the function graphed has an odd or even degree and a positive or negative leading coefficient.

19. 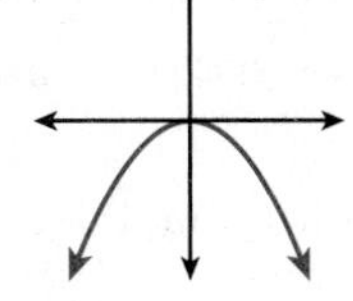
20. 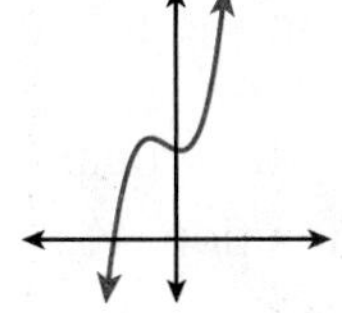
21. 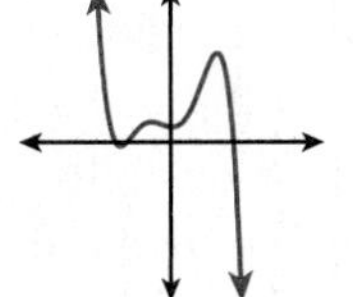
22. 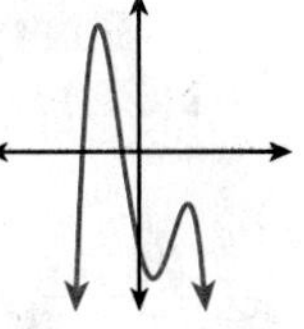

Graph each function.

23. $f(x) = x^3 - \frac{7}{3}x^2 - \frac{43}{3}x + 5$
24. $f(x) = 25x^2 - 4$
25. $f(x) = x^4 + x^3 - 28x^2 + 20x + 48$
26. $f(x) = x^3 + \frac{13}{2}x^2 + 11x + 4$

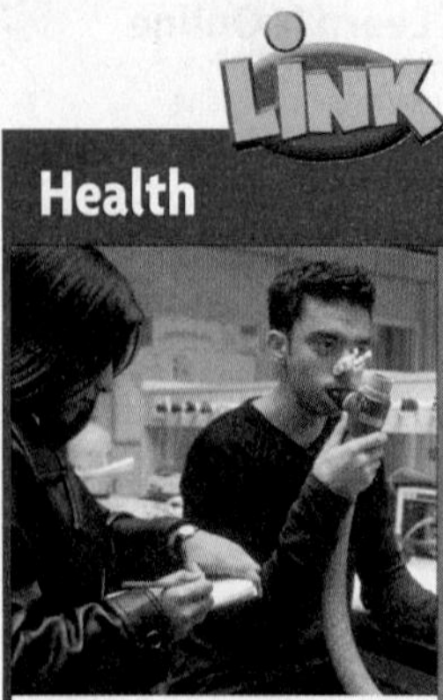

Health

A person's total lung capacity depends on many factors. Typically, age, weight, gender, and physical fitness affect the volume of air that a person's lungs can hold.

Graph each function on a calculator, and estimate the local maxima and minima.

27. $f(x) = 9x^6 + 20$

28. $f(x) = x^3 - 4x^2 + x + 1$

29. $f(x) = -x^2 + 6x - 10$

30. $f(x) = -5x^2 + 7$

31. Health The volume of air (in liters) in the human lung during one normal breath can be modeled by the function $V(t) = -1.7t^2 + 1.7t + 3$, for $0 \leq t \leq 1$. What is the maximum volume of air in the lungs during a normal breath, and at what time does it occur?

Use the degree and end behavior to match each polynomial function to its graph.

A. 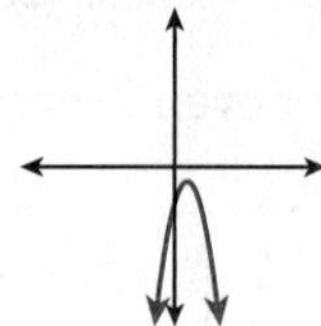

B. 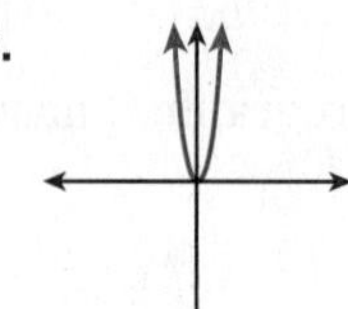

C. 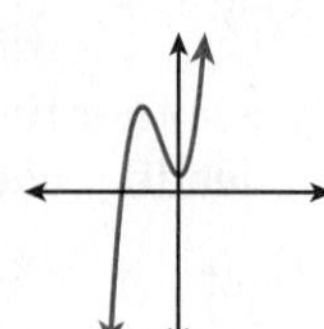

D. 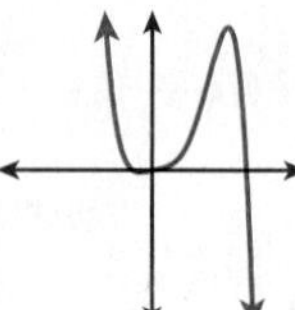

32. $f(x) = 5x^3 + 9x^2 + 1$

33. $f(x) = 2x^6 + 3x^4 + 5x^2$

34. $f(x) = 3x^4 - x^5 + x$

35. $f(x) = -4x^2 + 3x - 1$

Describe the end behavior of each function by completing the statements $f(x) \to$ _______ as $x \to -\infty$, and $f(x) \to$ _______ as $x \to +\infty$.

36. $f(x) = 2x^5 - x^2 + 75$

37. $f(x) = 10x^4 + 9x^2$

38. $f(x) = -5x^3 + x - 8$

39. $f(x) = 1000x^4 - 0.0002x^8$

40. $f(x) = x^{13} - x^7 + 12x$

41. $f(x) = -331x^{44} + 98$

42. Retail Hiromi sells 12 T-shirts each week at a price of \$13.00. Past sales have shown that for every \$0.25 decrease in price, 4 more T-shirts are sold. Knowing that revenue is a product of price and quantity, Hiromi models his revenue by $R(x) = (13 - 0.25x)(12 + 4x)$, where x represents the number of times there is a reduction in price.

a. Graph the function on a graphing calculator.

b. What is the maximum revenue Hiromi can generate each week?

c. How many \$0.25 reductions will maximize Hiromi's revenue? What would be the price per T-shirt, given the price is $13 - 0.25x$?

43. Critical Thinking Why are the leading coefficient and degree of the first term of the polynomial the only characteristics that determine end behavior?

44. Which of the following has a range that is different from the others? Explain.

$f(x) = 2x^3 - 6$ $\quad g(x) = x^4 + x - 7$ $\quad h(x) = 3x^5 + x^2$

MULTI-STEP TEST PREP

45. A packaging company wants to manufacture a pyramid-shaped gift box with a rectangular base. The base must have a perimeter of 20 in., and the height of the box must be equal to the length of the base.

a. Write a polynomial function, $V(x)$, for the volume of the box, where x is the length of the base.

b. Find the maximum volume of the box.

c. What dimensions result in a box with the maximum volume?

46. **Critical Thinking** Is there always an x-intercept between two turning points? Explain.

47. **Write About It** Describe the steps for graphing a polynomial by hand.

48. How many turning points will a quartic function with four real zeros have?

Ⓐ 1　　Ⓑ 2　　Ⓒ 3　　Ⓓ 4

49. Which function could describe the graph?

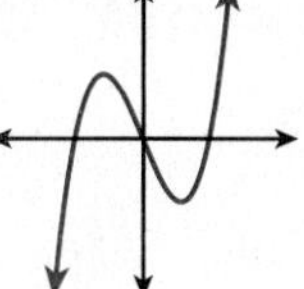

Ⓕ $f(x) = -2x^5 + x - 4$　　Ⓗ $f(x) = 3x^3 - 9x$

Ⓖ $f(x) = -x^3 + 5x^2 + 4x + 3$　　Ⓙ $f(x) = \frac{1}{4}x^2 + \frac{1}{2}x + 1$

50. **Extended Response** Consider the polynomial function $f(x) = 2x^4 + 12x^3 + 24x^2 + 16x$.

  a. Find all solutions to the equation $f(x) = 0$.

  b. Describe the end behavior of $f(x)$. Explain your reasoning.

  c. Sketch a graph of $f(x)$ by using your answers to part **a** and part **b**.

CHALLENGE AND EXTEND

Graph each function without using a graphing calculator.

51. $3x^6 - 57x^4 + 6x^3 + 144x^2 - 96x$　　52. $-2x^5 - 14x^4 - 30x^3 - 18x^2$

Examine the behavior of the cubic polynomials $f(x) = x^3$ and $g(x) = x^3 - 6x^2 + 4x - 20$ for the given values of x by using a spreadsheet or graphing calculator.

53. Complete the table.

54. Use your answer to Exercise 50 to complete this statement.

  As $x \to +\infty$, $\frac{f(x)}{g(x)} \to$ ______.

55. Explain what the statement in Exercise 54 implies about the end behavior of $f(x)$ and $g(x)$.

x	$f(x)$	$g(x)$	$\frac{f(x)}{g(x)}$
5			
10			
50			
100			
500			
1000			
5000			

COMMON CORE

3-8 Transforming Polynomial Functions

CC.9-12.F.IF.7c Graph polynomial functions, identifying zeros when suitable factorizations are available, and showing end behavior.* *Also* **CC.9-12.F.BF.3, CC.9-12.A.CED.2, CC.9-12.A.CED.3**

Objective
Transform polynomial functions.

Why learn this?
Transformations can be used in business to model sales. (See Example 5.)

You can perform the same transformations on polynomial functions that you performed on quadratic and linear functions.

Transformations of $f(x)$

Transformation	$f(x)$ Notation	Examples	
Vertical translation	$f(x) + k$	$g(x) = x^3 + 3$	3 units up
		$g(x) = x^3 - 4$	4 units down
Horizontal translation	$f(x - h)$	$g(x) = (x - 2)^3$	2 units right
		$g(x) = (x + 1)^3$	1 unit left
Vertical stretch/compression	$af(x)$	$g(x) = 6x^3$	stretch by 6
		$g(x) = \frac{1}{2}x^3$	compression by $\frac{1}{2}$
Horizontal stretch/compression	$f\left(\frac{1}{b}x\right)$	$g(x) = \left(\frac{1}{5}x\right)^3$	stretch by 5
		$g(x) = (3x)^3$	compression by $\frac{1}{3}$
Reflection	$-f(x)$	$g(x) = -x^3$	across x-axis
	$f(-x)$	$g(x) = (-x)^3$	across y-axis

EXAMPLE 1 Translating a Polynomial Function

For $f(x) = x^3 + 4$, write the rule for each function and sketch its graph.

A $g(x) = f(x) + 3$

$g(x) = (x^3 + 4) + 3$

$g(x) = x^3 + 7$

To graph $g(x) = f(x) + 3$, translate the graph of $f(x)$ 3 units up.

This is a vertical translation.

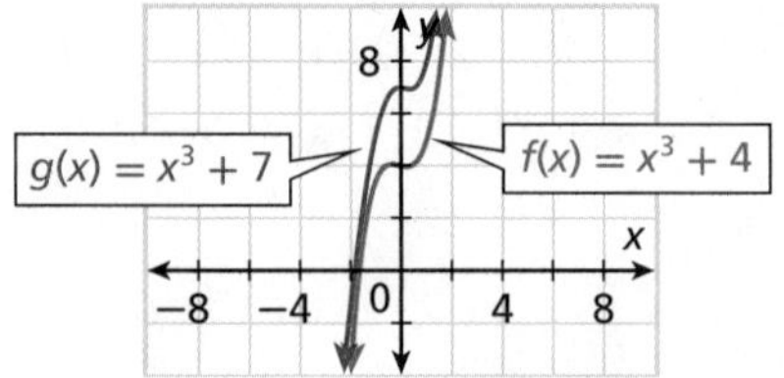

Helpful Hint
You can use a calculator to check your graph.

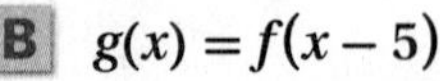

B $g(x) = f(x - 5)$

$g(x) = (x - 5)^3 + 4$

$g(x) = (x - 5)^3 + 4$

To graph $g(x) = f(x - 5)$, translate the graph of $f(x)$ 5 units right.

This is a horizontal translation.

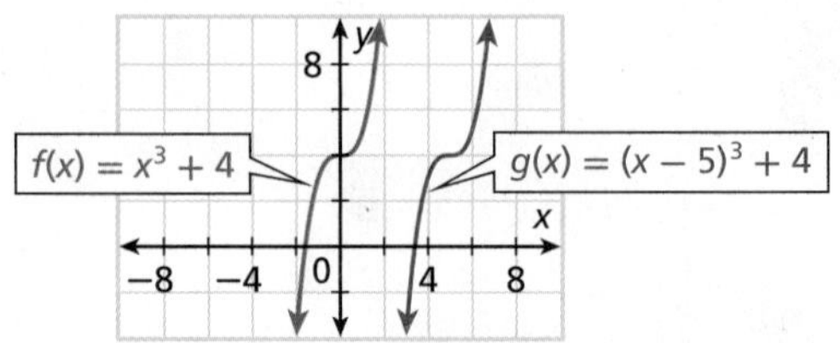

For $f(x) = x^3 + 4$, write the rule for each function and sketch its graph.

1a. $g(x) = f(x) - 5$

1b. $g(x) = f(x + 2)$

EXAMPLE 2 Reflecting Polynomial Functions

Let $f(x) = x^3 - 7x^2 + 6x - 5$. Write a function g that performs each transformation.

A **Reflect $f(x)$ across the x-axis.**

$g(x) = -f(x)$

$g(x) = -(x^3 - 7x^2 + 6x - 5)$

$g(x) = -x^3 + 7x^2 - 6x + 5$

Check Graph both functions. The graph appears to be a reflection. ✔

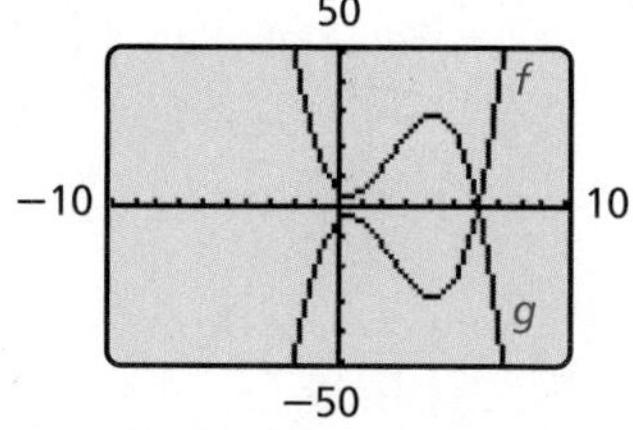

B **Reflect $f(x)$ across the y-axis.**

$g(x) = f(-x)$

$g(x) = (-x)^3 - 7(-x)^2 + 6(-x) - 5$

$g(x) = -x^3 - 7x^2 - 6x - 5$

Check Graph both functions. The graph appears to be a reflection. ✔

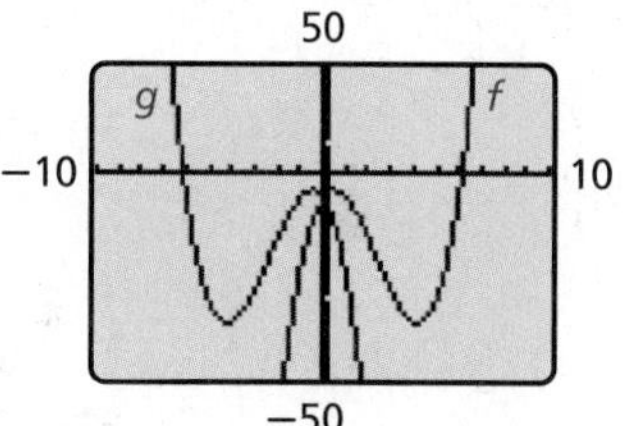

Let $f(x) = x^3 - 2x^2 - x + 2$. Write a function $g(x)$ that performs each transformation.

2a. Reflect $f(x)$ across the x-axis.

2b. Reflect $f(x)$ across the y-axis.

EXAMPLE 3 Compressing and Stretching Polynomial Functions

Let $f(x) = x^4 - 4x^2 + 2$. Graph f and g on the same coordinate plane. Describe g as a transformation of f.

A $g(x) = 2f(x)$

$g(x) = 2(x^4 - 4x^2 + 2)$

$g(x) = 2x^4 - 8x^2 + 4$

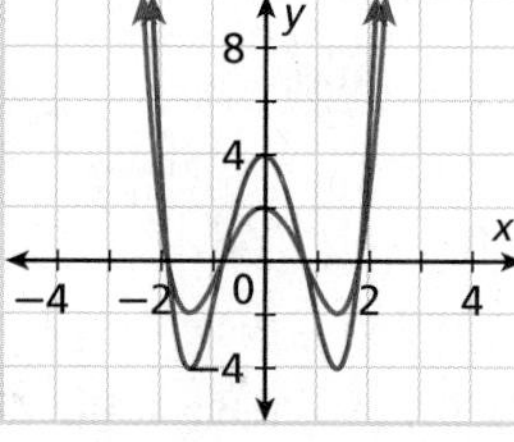

$g(x)$ is a vertical stretch of $f(x)$.

B $g(x) = f(3x)$

$g(x) = (3x)^4 - 4(3x)^2 + 2$

$g(x) = 81x^4 - 36x^2 + 2$

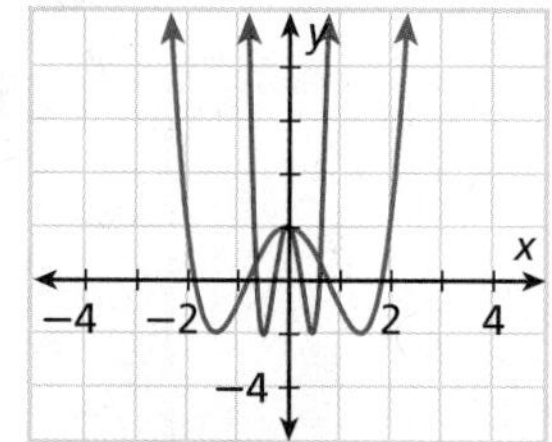

$g(x)$ is a horizontal compression of $f(x)$.

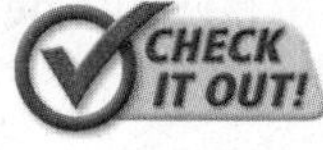

Let $f(x) = 16x^4 - 24x^2 + 4$. Graph f and g on the same coordinate plane. Describe g as a transformation of f.

3a. $g(x) = \frac{1}{4}f(x)$

3b. $g(x) = f\left(\frac{1}{2}x\right)$

EXAMPLE 4 Combining Transformations

Write a function that transforms $f(x) = 3x^3 + 6$ in each of the following ways. Support your solution by using a graphing calculator.

A **Stretch vertically by a factor of 2, and shift 3 units left.**

A vertical stretch is represented by $af(x)$, and a horizontal shift is represented by $f(x - h)$. Combining the two transformations gives $g(x) = af(x - h)$.

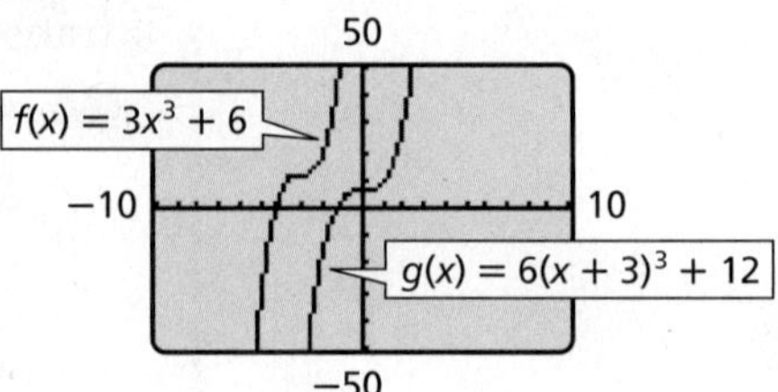

Substitute 2 for a and 3 for h.

$$g(x) = 2f(x + 3)$$

$$g(x) = 2\left(3(x + 3)^3 + 6\right)$$

$$g(x) = 6(x + 3)^3 + 12$$

B **Reflect across the x-axis and shift 3 units up.**

A reflection across the x-axis is represented by $-f(x)$, and a vertical shift is represented by $f(x) + k$. Combining the two transformations gives $h(x) = -f(x) + k$.

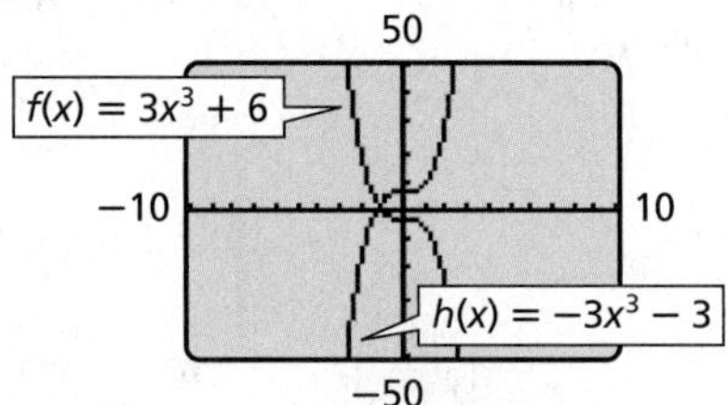

Substitute 3 for k.

$$h(x) = -f(x) + 3$$

$$h(x) = -\left(3x^3 + 6\right) + 3$$

$$h(x) = -3x^3 - 3$$

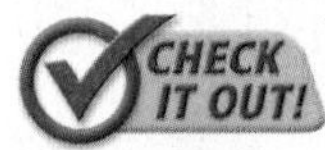

Write a function that transforms $f(x) = 8x^3 - 2$ in each of the following ways. Support your solution by using a graphing calculator.

4a. Compress vertically by a factor of $\frac{1}{2}$, and move the x-intercept 3 units right.

4b. Reflect across the x-axis, and move the x-intercept 4 units left.

EXAMPLE 5 *Bicycle Sales*

The number of bicycles sold per month by a business can be modeled by $f(x) = 0.01x^3 + 0.7x^2 + 0.4x + 120$, where x represents the number of months since January. Let $g(x) = f(x) - 30$. Find the rule for g, and explain the meaning of the transformation in terms of monthly bicycle sales.

Step 1 Write the new rule.

The new rule is $g(x) = f(x) - 30$.

$$g(x) = f(x) - 30$$

$$g(x) = 0.01x^3 + 0.7x^2 + 0.4x + 120 - 30$$

$$g(x) = 0.01x^3 + 0.7x^2 + 0.4x + 90$$

Step 2 Interpret the transformation.

The transformation represents a vertical shift 30 units down, which corresponds to a decrease in sales of 30 units per month.

5. Let $g(x) = f(x - 5)$. Find the rule for g, and explain the meaning of the transformation in terms of monthly bicycle sales.

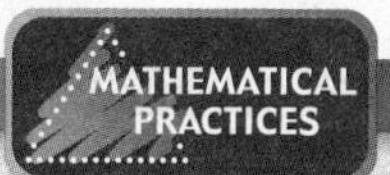

THINK AND DISCUSS

1. How does shifting $f(x) = x^4 - 4$ up 5 units affect the number of real zeros? What if $f(x)$ is shifted 5 units down?
2. Does a horizontal shift affect the number of real zeros of a function? Explain.

3. **GET ORGANIZED** Copy and complete the graphic organizer.

Transformation	Vertical shift	Horizontal shift	Vertical stretch	Horizontal compression
Example				

3-8 Exercises

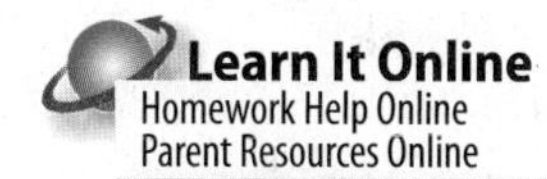

GUIDED PRACTICE

SEE EXAMPLE 1

For $f(x) = x^4 - 8$, write the rule for each function, and sketch its graph.

1. $g(x) = f(x) + 4$
2. $h(x) = f(x - 2)$
3. $j(x) = f(3x)$
4. $k(x) = f(x) - \frac{1}{2}$

SEE EXAMPLE 2

Let $f(x) = -x^3 + 3x^2 - 2x + 1$. Write a function g that performs each transformation.

5. Reflect $f(x)$ across the y-axis.
6. Reflect $f(x)$ across the x-axis.

SEE EXAMPLE 3

Let $f(x) = x^3 - 4x^2 + 2$. Graph f and g on the same coordinate plane. Describe g as a transformation of f.

7. $g(x) = f\left(\frac{1}{2}x\right)$
8. $g(x) = 3f(x)$
9. $g(x) = f(2x) + 4$

SEE EXAMPLE 4

Write a function that transforms $f(x) = 4x^3 + 2$ in each of the following ways. Support your solution by using a graphing calculator.

10. Compress vertically by a factor of $\frac{1}{2}$, and move the y-intercept 2 units down.
11. Reflect across the y-axis, and compress horizontally by a factor of $\frac{1}{2}$.
12. Move 2 units right, move 3 units down, and reflect across the x-axis.

SEE EXAMPLE 5

13. **Manufacturing** The cost to manufacture x units of a product can be modeled by the function $C(x) = 2x^3 - 3x + 30$, where the cost is in thousands of dollars. Describe the transformation $2C(x)$ by writing the new rule and explaining the change in the context of the problem.

PRACTICE AND PROBLEM SOLVING

For $f(x) = x^3 - 4$, write the rule for each function and sketch its graph.

14. $g(x) = f(x) - 3$
15. $h(x) = f(x - 3)$
16. $j(x) = f(x) + 5$

Let $f(x) = x^3 - 2x^2 + 5x - 3$. Write a function g that performs each transformation.

17. Reflect $f(x)$ across the x-axis.
18. Reflect $f(x)$ across the y-axis.

Independent Practice	
For Exercises	See Example
14–16	1
17–18	2
19–21	3
22–24	4
25	5

Extra Practice

See Extra Practice for more Skills Practice and Applications Practice exercises.

Let $f(x) = 2x^4 - 8x^2 - 2$. Graph f and g on the same coordinate plane. Describe g as a transformation of f.

19. $g(x) = 2f(x)$

20. $g(x) = \frac{1}{2}f(x)$

21. $g(x) = f\left(\frac{1}{2}x\right)$

Write a function that transforms $f(x) = x^4 - 6$ in each of the following ways. Support your solution by using a graphing calculator.

22. Reflect across the x-axis, and move the x-intercept 3 units left.

23. Compress vertically by a factor of $\frac{1}{3}$, and move 1 unit up.

24. Stretch horizontally by a factor of 2, move 4 units down, and reflect across the y-axis.

25. **Geometry** The volume of a rectangular prism can be modeled by the function $V(x) = x^3 + 3x^2 + x + 8$, where V is the volume in cubic meters and x represents length in meters. Describe the transformation $V\left(\frac{2}{3}x\right)$ by writing the new rule and explaining the change in the context of the problem.

26. **///ERROR ANALYSIS///** Students were asked to write a function g that translates f 3 units to the right. Which answer is incorrect? Identify and explain the error.

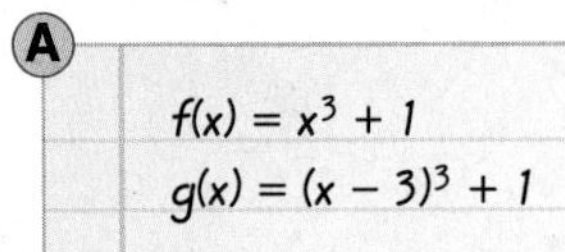
A
$f(x) = x^3 + 1$
$g(x) = (x - 3)^3 + 1$

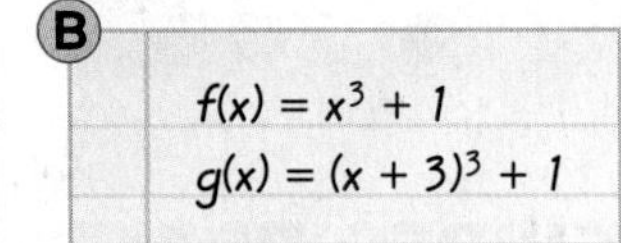
B
$f(x) = x^3 + 1$
$g(x) = (x + 3)^3 + 1$

27. **Fish** Some flying fish travel in the air up to a quarter of a mile by using a lift force F to overcome their weight W while in the air. The lift force is modeled by $F(v) = 0.24v^2$, where $v \geq 0$ is the initial air speed in meters per second.
    a. Graph $F(v) = 0.24v^2$. For $W = 1$, find the values of v such that $F > W$.
    b. A flying fish swimming with a current leaps out of the water with a speed that is 5 units greater than normal. Write a function $G(v)$ for the lift force. What transformation does this represent?
    c. Find the values of v for which $G > W$.
    d. $H(v) = 20v^2$ represents the underwater lift force. What transformation of $F(v)$ does this represent?

28. **Critical Thinking** In the function $f(x) = (x + 5)^4 + k$, for which values of k does the function have two real solutions? no real solutions? Explain.

29. **Write About It** Explain in your own words what happens to the graph of a function when you reflect it across the x-axis.

MULTI-STEP TEST PREP

30. The volume of a pyramid with a square base is modeled by the function $V(x) = \frac{1}{3}x^3 + x^2$, where x is the length of the base in inches.
    a. Write a new function, $W(x)$, that gives the volume of the pyramid in cubic inches when the length of the base is expressed in feet.
    b. Write $W(x)$ in terms of $V(x)$.
    c. Graph W and V on the same coordinate plane. How is the graph of W related to the graph of V?
    d. How would your answer to part **c** be different if the length of the base were expressed in centimeters?

31. Which graph represents a vertical shift of $f(x) = x^3 - 3x^2 - x + 3$ up 3 units?

Ⓐ 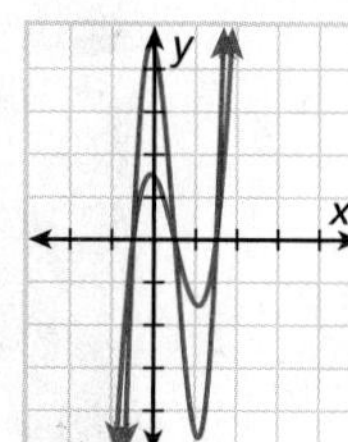

Ⓑ 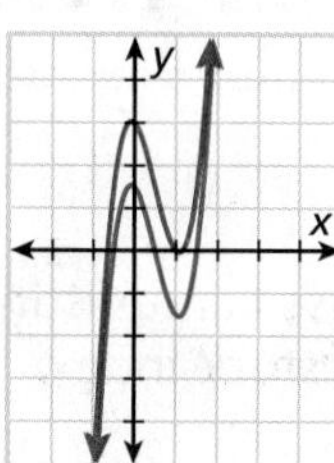

Ⓒ 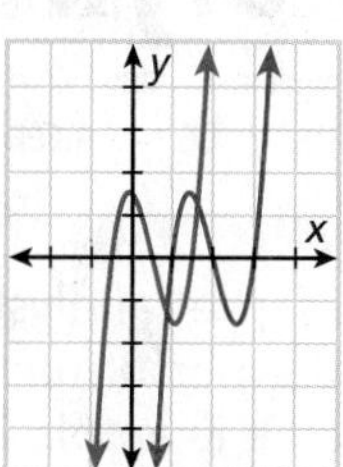

Ⓓ 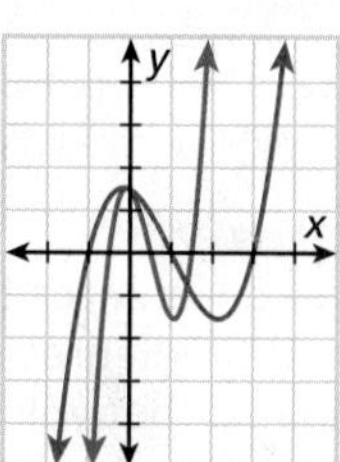

32. Which description matches the transformation from $f(x)$ to $g(x)$ shown?

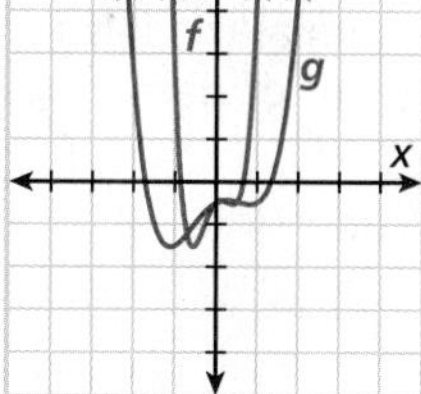

Ⓕ Vertical shift
Ⓗ Horizontal shift
Ⓖ Vertical stretch
Ⓙ Horizontal stretch

33. $f(x) = x^3 - 6x^2 + 6x + 1$ has three real zeros. How many real zeros does $f(x) - 6$ have?

Ⓐ 0
Ⓒ 2
Ⓑ 1
Ⓓ 3

34. **Extended Response** Consider the function $f(x) = 3x^3 - 9x^2 - 3x + 9$.
   a. Use the leading coefficient and degree of $f_{(x)}$ to describe the end behavior.
   b. Write the rule for the function $g_{(x)} = f_{(-x)}$, and describe the transformation.
   c. Describe the end behavior of $g(x)$. How does the end behavior of $g(x)$ relate to the transformation of $f(x)$?

CHALLENGE AND EXTEND

Identify the transformation(s) that would take $f(x) = (x + 2)^3 - 6$ to $g(x)$.

35. $g(x) = x^3 - 6$
36. $g(x) = (x + 2)^3$
37. $g(x) = (x - 1)^3 + 2$

38. For $f(x) = x^4 - x^2 - 9x + 9$, describe three different transformations that could be performed to obtain a function with a y-intercept of 3.

3-9 Curve Fitting with Polynomial Models

CC.9-12.A.CED.3 Represent constraints by equations ... and interpret solutions as viable or nonviable options in a modeling context. *Also* **CC.9-12.F.IF.7c*, CC.9-12.A.CED.2**

Objectives

Use finite differences to determine the degree of a polynomial that will fit a given set of data.

Use technology to find polynomial models for a given set of data.

Who uses this?

Market analysts can use curve fitting to predict the performance of a stock index. (See Example 3.)

The table shows the closing value of a stock index on the first day of trading for various years.

Year	1994	1995	1996	1997	2000	2001	2003	2004
Price ($)	774	751	1053	1293	4186	2474	1347	2011

To create a mathematical model for the data, you will need to determine what type of function is most appropriate. You have learned that a set of data that has constant second differences can be modeled by a quadratic function. Finite differences can be used to identify the degree of any polynomial data.

Finite Differences of Polynomials		
Function Type	**Degree**	**Constant Finite Differences**
Linear	1	First
Quadratic	2	Second
Cubic	3	Third
Quartic	4	Fourth
Quintic	5	Fifth

EXAMPLE 1 **Using Finite Differences to Determine Degree**

Use finite differences to determine the degree of the polynomial that best describes the data.

Remember!

To find the differences in the y-values, subtract each y-value from the y-value that follows it. For the first differences,
$-4 - (-10) = 6$
$-1.4 - (-4) = 2.6$
$0 - (-1.4) = 1.4$
and so on.

A

x	−2	−1	0	1	2	3
y	−10	−4	−1.4	0	2.4	8

The x-values increase by a constant 1. Find the differences of the y-values.

y	−10	−4	−1.4	0	2.4	8

First differences: 6 2.6 1.4 2.4 5.6 **Not constant**
Second differences: −3.4 −1.2 1 3.2 **Not constant**
Third differences: 2.2 2.2 2.2 **Constant**

The third differences are constant. A cubic polynomial best describes the data.

Scott Olson/Getty Images

Use finite differences to determine the degree of the polynomial that best describes the data.

B

x	−6	−4	−2	0	2	4
y	−30	15	30	34	41	60

The x-values increase by a constant, 2. Find the differences of the y-values.

First differences:	45	15	4	7	19	**Not constant**
Second differences:	−30	−11	3	12		**Not constant**
Third differences:	19	14	9			**Not Constant**
Fourth differences:	−5	−5				**Constant**

The fourth differences are constant. A quartic polynomial best describes the data.

1. Use finite differences to determine the degree of the polynomial that best describes the data.

x	12	15	18	21	24	27
y	3	23	29	29	31	43

Once you have determined the degree of the polynomial that best describes the data, you can use your calculator to create the function.

EXAMPLE 2 Using Finite Differences to Write a Function

The table below shows the population of a city from 1950 to 2000. Write a polynomial function for the data.

Year	1950	1960	1970	1980	1990	2000
Population (thousands)	2853	4011	5065	6720	9704	14,759

Helpful Hint

Keep the scale of the original data in mind. In Example 2, the population ranges from 2853 to 14,759. The gap between 705 and 728 is small in comparison.

Step 1 Find the finite differences of the y-values.

Let x represent the number of years since 1950. The years increase by a constant amount of 10. The populations are the y-values.

First differences:	1158	1054	1655	2984	5055	
Second differences:	−104	601	1329	2071		
Third differences:	705	728	742			**Close**

Step 2 Determine the degree of the polynomial.

Because the third differences are relatively close, a cubic function should be a good model.

Step 3 Use the cubic regression feature on your calculator.

$f(x) \approx 0.12x^3 - 4.21x^2 + 146.37x + 2851.64$

2. The table below shows the gas consumption of a compact car driven a constant distance at various speeds. Write a polynomial function for the data.

Speed	25	30	35	40	45	50	55	60
Gas (gal)	23.8	25	25.2	25	25.4	27	30.6	37

Often, real-world data can be too irregular for you to use finite differences or find a polynomial function that fits perfectly. In these situations, you can use the regression feature of your graphing calculator. Remember that the closer the R^2-value is to 1, the better the function fits the data.

EXAMPLE 3 *Finance Application*

The table shows the opening value of a stock index on the first day of trading in various years. Use a polynomial model to estimate the value on the first day of trading in 2002.

Year	Price ($)	Year	Price ($)
1994	774	2000	4186
1995	751	2001	2474
1996	1053	2003	1347
1997	1293	2004	2011

Step 1 Choose the degree of the polynomial model.

Let x represent the number of years since 1994. Make a scatter plot of the data.

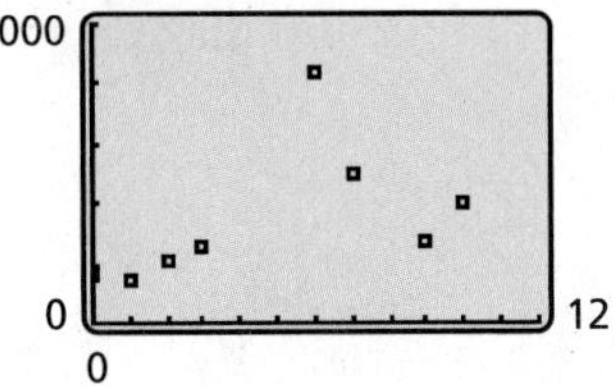

The function appears to be cubic or quartic. Use the regression feature to check the R^2-values.

cubic: $R^2 \approx 0.6279$ quartic: $R^2 \approx 0.8432$

The quartic function is a more appropriate choice.

Step 2 Write the polynomial model.

The data can be modeled by
$f(x) = 9.27x^4 - 191.56x^3 + 1168.22x^2 - 1702.58x + 999.60$

Step 3 Find the value of the model corresponding to 2002.

2002 is 8 years after 1994. Substitute 8 for x in the quartic model.

$f(x) = 9.27(8)^4 - 191.56(8)^3 + 1168.22(8)^2 - 1702.58(8) + 999.60 =$ 2036.24

Based on the model, the opening value was about $2036.24 in 2002.

3. Use a polynomial model to estimate the value of the index in 1999.

Year	1994	1995	1996	2000	2003	2004
Price ($)	3754	3835	5117	11,497	8342	10,454

THINK AND DISCUSS

1. Suppose that finite differences are used to determine that a quartic polynomial best describes a particular data set. What is the minimum number of data pairs in the data set? Explain.

2. GET ORGANIZED Copy and complete the graphic organizer. For each type of function, indicate the degree and the constant differences and give an example of a data set.

Linear	Quadratic
Polynomial Models	
Cubic	Quartic

3-9 Exercises

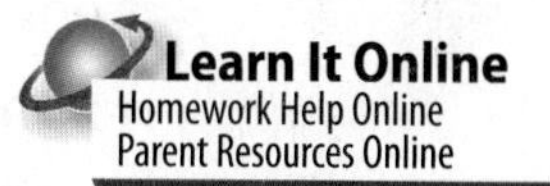

GUIDED PRACTICE

SEE EXAMPLE 1

Use finite differences to determine the degree of the polynomial that best describes the data.

1.

x	y
−2	22
−1	16
0	10
1	4
2	−2
3	−8

2.

x	y
−2	0
−1	−5
0	−3
1	5
2	18
3	35

3.

x	y
−2	23
−1	−2
0	1
1	2
2	−5
3	−2

SEE EXAMPLE 2

4. **Business** The table below shows the number of square feet of retail space available for rent in various years. Write a polynomial function for the data.

Year	1957	1967	1977	1987	1997	2007
Retail Space (billion ft^2)	2.8	6.7	14.7	27.3	44.9	67.9

SEE EXAMPLE 3

5. **Health** The table below shows the number of infected patients at various stages of a flu outbreak. Use a polynomial model to estimate the number of infected patients after 120 hours.

Time (h)	12	24	48	96	144	240
Patients	21	301	679	973	562	320

PRACTICE AND PROBLEM SOLVING

Independent Practice

For Exercises	See Example
6–8	1
9	2
10–11	3

Extra Practice

See Extra Practice for more Skills Practice and Applications Practice exercises.

Use finite differences to determine the degree of the polynomial that best describes the data.

6.

x	y
−5	−20
−4	−19
−3	−9
−2	5.5
−1	20
0	30

7.

x	y
−2	−2
−1	−6
0	0
1	10
2	20
3	28

8.

x	y
−2	−3
−1	1
0	4.3
1	6.9
2	8.8
3	10

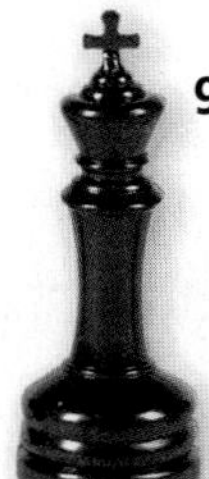

9. **Hobbies** The table below shows the number of Chess Club members in various years. Write a polynomial function for the data.

Year	2002	2003	2004	2005	2006	2007
Members	23	23	23	25	29	35

10. **Tourism** The table below shows the number of Canadian visitors to the United States. Use a polynomial model to predict the number of visitors in 2005.

Year	1996	1998	2000	2001	2002	2003
Visitors (millions)	15.3	13.4	14.6	13.5	13.0	12.7

11. **Education** The table shows the total high school graduates in the United States. Use a polynomial model to estimate the total graduates in 1999.

Year	1989	1991	1995	1996	1998	2000
Graduates (thousands)	59,336	61,272	56,450	56,559	58,174	58,086

12. **Weather** The figure shows the latitude, longitude, and average January minimum temperature of various locations.

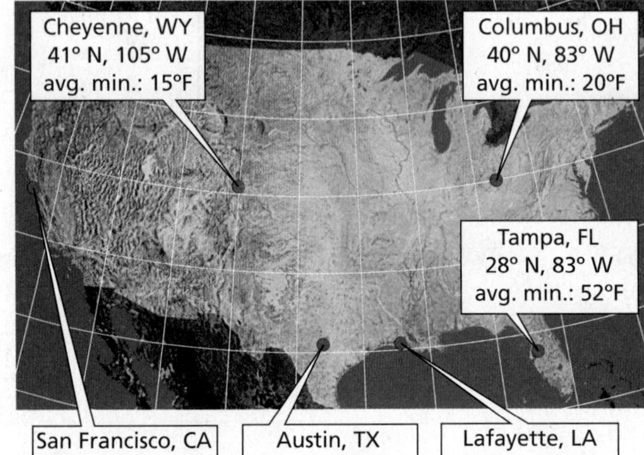

a. Which pair of variables has a closer polynomial relationship: latitude and temperature or longitude and temperature? Give numerical data to support your answer.

b. Is the relationship between latitude and temperature a function? Explain.

c. Is a polynomial model relating longitude and temperature a function? Explain.

13. **Multi-Step** The table shows the total December clothing sales in the United States in billions of dollars.

Year	1997	1998	1999	2001	2002	2003
Sales (billions of $)	12.1	12.7	13.5	14.1	14.6	15.3

a. Write a cubic polynomial to model the data. What is the R^2-value?

b. Write a quartic polynomial to model the data. What is the R^2-value?

c. Is the difference in R^2-values significant?

d. What do the R^2-values say about your answers to part **a** and part **b**?

14. You can make a pyramid by stacking balls in triangular layers. For example, three balls can be arranged as a triangle with a fourth ball on top of the other three.

Number of Balls on One Side of the Bottom Layer	1	2	3	4	5
Total Number of Balls in the Pyramid	1	4	10	20	35

a. Use finite differences to determine the degree of the polynomial that best describes the data.

b. Write a polynomial function for the data.

c. How many balls are in a pyramid that has 12 balls on one side of the bottom layer?

15. **Critical Thinking** The fourth differences of a given data set are 0.01, 0, 0, and −0.01. Is a cubic polynomial appropriate to model the data? Explain.

16. **Write About It** Describe the process you would use to determine the appropriate type of polynomial for a given data set.

TEST PREP

17. What type of polynomial best models the data below?
$\{(0, 1), (1, 21), (2, 27), (3, 27), (4, 29), (5, 41)\}$

Ⓐ Linear　Ⓑ Quadratic　Ⓒ Cubic　Ⓓ Quartic

18. Which cubic function represents the graph?

Ⓕ $f(x) = -(x + 2)(x - 1)(x - 3)$
Ⓖ $f(x) = (x + 2)(x - 1)(x - 3)$
Ⓗ $f(x) = -(x - 2)(x + 1)(x + 3)$
Ⓙ $f(x) = (x - 2)(x + 1)(x + 3)$

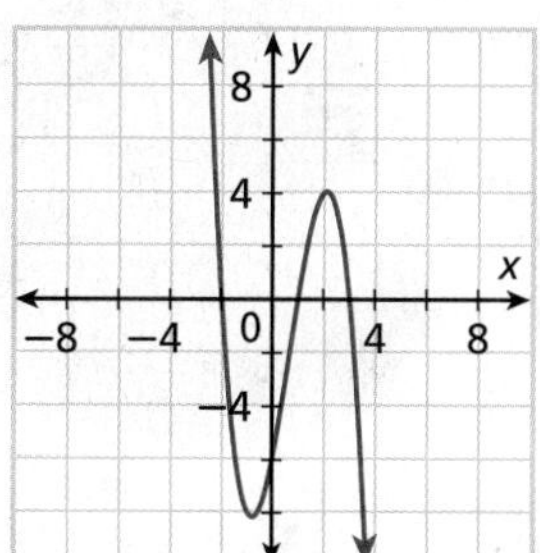

19. **Short Response** Give a cubic polynomial that can be used to model the data below.
$\{(0, 4), (-1, 8), (1, 0), (-2, 6), (2, 2)\}$

CHALLENGE AND EXTEND

The *average slope* of the graph of $f(x)$ between $x = a$ and $x = b$ is the slope of the line through $(a, f(a))$ and $(b, f(b))$. Use the table to complete Exercises 20–22.

x	$f(x)$
−3	−5.5
−2	−1
−1	1.5
0	2
1	0.5
2	−3

20. What is the average slope between $x = -2$ and $x = 2$?

21. How can you use first differences to find the average slope between each pair of points on the graph?

22. What happens to the average slope of the graph as the chosen points get closer to the maximum point?

23. Use finite differences to create a data set that could be modeled by a quartic polynomial.

CHAPTER 3

SECTION 3B

MULTI-STEP TEST PREP

MATHEMATICAL PRACTICES **Reason abstractly and quantitatively.**

Applying Polynomial Functions

Pyramid Pile-Up You can build a pyramid by stacking blocks in layers. The blocks in each layer are arranged in a square, and the layers grow successively larger as shown below.

1. The figure shows the relationship between the number of layers and the total number of blocks in the pyramid. Make a table that shows the relationship for the first five layers.

1 layer
1 block

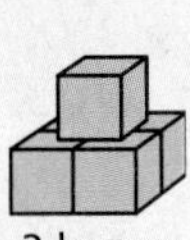
2 layers
5 blocks

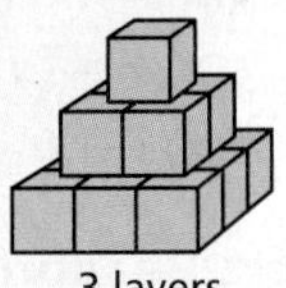
3 layers
14 blocks

2. Use finite differences to determine the degree of the polynomial that best describes the data.
3. Write a polynomial function for the data.
4. The Great Pyramid in Giza, Egypt, has 201 layers. Use your function to estimate the number of blocks in the pyramid.
5. A pyramid contains a total of 285 blocks. How many layers are in the pyramid?
6. Is it possible to build a pyramid that uses exactly 811 blocks? Why or why not? Give an explanation in terms of the solutions to a polynomial equation.
7. A pyramid is known to contain at least 10,000 blocks. What is the minimum number of layers in the pyramid?

READY TO GO ON?

CHAPTER 3

SECTION 3B

Quiz for Lessons 3-5 Through 3-9

3-5 Finding Real Roots of Polynomial Equations

1. The yearly profit of a company in thousands of dollars can be modeled by $P(t) = t^4 - 10t^2 + 9$, where t is the number of years since 2000. Factor to find the years in which the profit was 0.

Identify the roots of each equation. State the multiplicity of each root.

2. $x^3 + 6x^2 + 12x + 8 = 0$
3. $2x^3 + 8x^2 - 32x - 128 = 0$
4. $x^4 - 6x^3 + 9x^2 = 0$

3-6 Fundamental Theorem of Algebra

Write the simplest polynomial function with the given roots.

5. 1, 1, 2
6. $i, -1, 0$
7. Solve $x^4 - 2x^3 + 6x^2 - 18x - 27 = 0$ by finding all roots.

3-7 Investigating Graphs of Polynomial Functions

Graph each function.

8. $f(x) = x^4 - 13x^2 + 36$
9. $f(x) = x^3 - 4x^2 - 15x + 18$

Identify whether the function graphed has an odd or even degree and a positive or negative leading coefficient.

10. 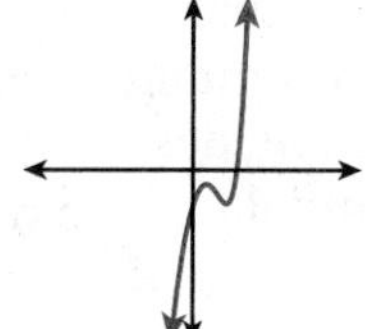

11. 

12. 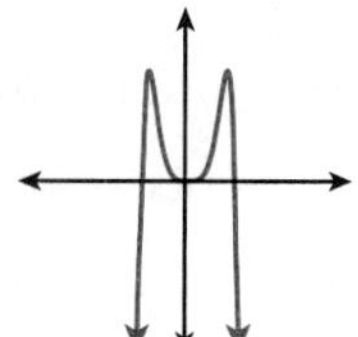

3-8 Transforming Polynomial Functions

Let $f(x) = x^4 - 3x^2 + 6$. Write a function $g(x)$ that performs each transformation.

13. Reflect $f(x)$ across the x-axis.
14. Reflect $f(x)$ across the y-axis.

Let $f(x) = 8x^4 - 12x^2 + 2$. Graph $f(x)$ and $g(x)$ on the same coordinate plane. Describe $g(x)$ as a transformation of $f(x)$.

15. $g(x) = 3f(x)$
16. $g(x) = f\left(\frac{1}{2}x\right)$
17. $g(x) = f(x - 4)$

3-9 Curve Fitting with Polynomial Models

18. The table shows the population of a bacteria colony over time. Write a polynomial function for the data.

Time (*h*)	1	2	3	4	5
Bacteria	44	112	252	515	949

CHAPTER 3

Study Guide: Review

Vocabulary

degree of a monomial
degree of a polynomial
end behavior
leading coefficient
local maximum
local minimum
monomial
multiplicity
polynomial
polynomial function
synthetic division
turning point

Complete the sentences below with vocabulary words from the list above.

1. A(n) ___?___ is a number or product of numbers and variables with whole number exponents.
2. A method of dividing a polynomial by a linear binomial of the form $x - a$ by using only the coefficients is ___?___ .
3. The number of times $x - r$ is a factor of $P(x)$ is the ___?___ of r.
4. The ___?___ of a function is a description of the function values as x approaches positive infinity or negative infinity.

3-1 Polynomials

EXAMPLES

- **Subtract. Write your answer in standard form.**

$(6x - 2x^2 + 1) - (4x - 5x^2)$

$(-2x^2 + 6x + 1) + (5x^2 - 4x)$ *Add the opposite.*

$(-2x^2 + 5x^2) + (6x - 4x) + 1$ *Combine like terms.*

$3x^2 + 2x + 1$

- **Graph $f(x) = -x^3 + 4x + 1$ on a calculator. Describe the graph, and identify the number of real zeros.**

From left to right, the function decreases, increases, and then decreases again. It crosses the x-axis three times. There appear to be three real zeros.

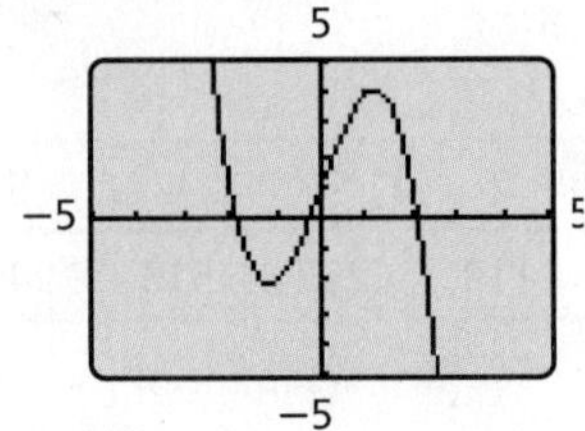

EXERCISES

Rewrite each polynomial in standard form. Then identify the leading coefficient, degree, and number of terms. Name the polynomial.

5. $4x^2 - 3x^3 + 6x + 7$
6. $5x^3 - x^5 + 8x + 2x^4$
7. $1 - 11x + 9x^2$
8. $-6x^2 + x^4$

Add or subtract. Write your answer in standard form.

9. $(8x^3 - 4x^2 - 3x + 1) - (1 - 5x^2 + x)$
10. $(6x^2 + 7x - 2) + (1 - 5x^3 + 3x)$
11. $(5x - 2x^2) - (4x^2 + 6x - 9)$
12. $(x^4 - x^2 + 4) + (x^2 - x^3 - 5x^4 - 7)$

Graph each polynomial function on a calculator. Describe the graph, and identify the number of real zeros.

13. $f(x) = -x^4 + 4x^2 + 1$
14. $f(x) = x^3 + 2x^2 + 1$
15. $f(x) = x^4 - 5x^2 + 2$
16. $f(x) = x^3 - 3x^2 + 2$

3-2 Multiplying Polynomials

EXAMPLE

■ **Find the product.**

$(x-3)(5-x-2x^2)$

Multiply horizontally.

$(x-3)(-2x^2-x+5)$ *Write in standard form.*

$x(-2x^2)+x(-x)+x(5)-3(-2x^2)-3(-x)-3(5)$

$-2x^3-x^2+5x+6x^2+3x-15$ *Multiply.*

$-2x^3+5x^2+8x-15$ *Combine like terms.*

EXERCISES

Find each product.

17. $5x^2(3x-2)$ **18.** $-3t(2t^2-6t+1)$

19. $ab^2(a^2-a+ab)$ **20.** $(x-2)(x^2-2x-3)$

21. $(2x+5)(x^3-x^2+1)$ **22.** $(x-3)^3$

23. $(x+4)(x^4-3x^2+x)$ **24.** $(2x+1)^4$

25. A cylinder has a height of x^2-x-3 and a radius of $2x$ as shown. Express the volume of the cylinder as a sum of monomials.

2x

x^2-x-3

3-3 Dividing Polynomials

EXAMPLE

■ **Divide by using synthetic division.**

$(x^3-3x^2+8)\div(x+2)$

$a=-2$

x^3-3x^2+0x+8 *Write in standard form.*

-2	1	-3	0	8
		-2	10	-20
	1	-5	10	-12

Write the coefficients of the terms.

$$\frac{x^3-3x^2+8}{x+2}=x^2-5x+10+\frac{-12}{x+2}$$

EXERCISES

Divide by using long division.

26. $(x^3-5x^2+2x-7)\div(x+2)$

27. $(8x^4+6x^2-2x+4)\div(2x-1)$

Divide by using synthetic division.

28. $(x^3-4x^2+3x+2)\div(x-3)$

29. $(x^3+2x-1)\div(x-2)$

30. A spool of ribbon has a length of x^3+x^2 inches. Write an expression that represents the number of strips of ribbon with a length of $x-1$ inches that can be cut from one spool.

3-4 Factoring Polynomials

EXAMPLES

Determine whether each binomial is a factor of the polynomial $P(x)=2x^2+x-10$.

■ $(x+5)$

-5	2	1	-10
		-10	45
	2	-9	35

$x+5$ is not a factor of $P(x)$.

■ $(x-2)$

2	2	1	-10
		4	10
	2	5	0

$x-2$ is a factor of $P(x)$.

EXERCISES

Determine whether the given binomial is a factor of the polynomial $P(x)$.

31. $(x+3)$; $P(x)=x^3+2x^2-5$

32. $(x-1)$; $P(x)=4x^4-5x^2+3x-2$

33. $(x–x)$; $P(x)=2x^3-3x^2+x-6$

Factor each expression.

34. $x^3-x^2-16x+16$ **35.** $4x^3-8x^2-x+2$

36. $3x^3+81$ **37.** $16x^3-2$

3-5 Finding Real Roots of Polynomial Equations

EXAMPLE

■ **Identify all of the real roots of $x^4 - 4x^3 + 4x^2 - 1 = 0$.**

By the Rational Root Theorem, possible roots are ± 1.

$$\begin{array}{r|rrrrr} 1 & 1 & -4 & 4 & 0 & -1 \\ & & 1 & -3 & 1 & 1 \\ \hline & 1 & -3 & 1 & 1 & \boxed{0} \end{array}$$

Try 1.

$$\begin{array}{r|rrrr} 1 & 1 & -3 & 1 & 1 \\ & & 1 & -2 & -1 \\ \hline & 1 & -2 & -1 & \boxed{0} \end{array}$$

Try 1 again.

Factor $x^2 - 2x - 1$ by using the quadratic formula.

$$x = \frac{-(-2) \pm \sqrt{(-2)^2 - 4(1)(-1)}}{2(1)} = 1 \pm \sqrt{2}$$

The roots are 1 with a multiplicity of 2, and $1 \pm \sqrt{2}$.

EXERCISES

Identify all of the real roots of each equation.

38. $x^3 - 5x^2 + 8x - 4 = 0$

39. $x^3 + 6x^2 + 9x + 2 = 0$

40. $x^3 + 3x^2 + 3x + 1 = 0$

41. $x^4 - 12x^2 + 27 = 0$

42. $x^3 + x^2 - 2x - 2 = 0$

43. $x^3 - 5x^2 + 4 = 0$

44. A rectangular prism has length that is twice its width and height that is 4 meters longer than its width. The volume of the rectangular prism is 48 cubic meters. What is the width of the rectangular prism?

3-6 Fundamental Theorem of Algebra

EXAMPLES

■ **Write the simplest polynomial function with roots −2, −1, and 4.**

$P(x) = 0$ — *If r is a root of P(x), then x − r is a factor of P(x).*

$a(x + 2)(x + 1)(x - 4) = 0$

$a(x^3 - x^2 - 10x - 8) = 0$ — *Multiply. For the simplest equation, let a = 1.*

$x^3 - x^2 - 10x - 8 = 0$

■ **Solve $x^3 + 2x^2 + x + 2 = 0$ by finding all roots.**

The graphing calculator shows −2 as a root. Use synthetic division to write the equation as $(x + 2)(x^2 + 1) = 0$. Solve $x^2 + 1 = 0$ to find the remaining roots. The solutions are −2, i, and $-i$.

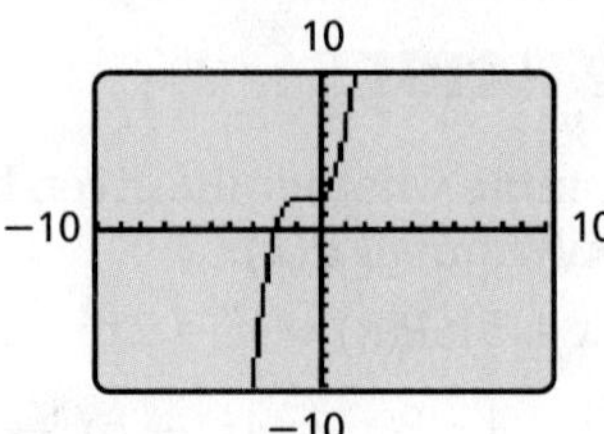

EXERCISES

Write the simplest polynomial function with the given roots.

45. −3, 2, 4

46. $-\frac{1}{2}$, −2, 3

47. $-\sqrt{2}$, −1

48. −3, i

49. $\sqrt{2}$, $\sqrt{3}$

50. $1 + \sqrt{3}$, $2i$

Solve the equation by finding all roots.

51. $x^3 - x^2 + 4x - 4 = 0$

52. $x^4 - x^2 - 2 = 0$

53. $x^4 - \frac{63}{4}x^2 - 4 = 0$

54. $x^3 + 3x^2 - 5x - 15 = 0$

3-7 Investigating Graphs of Polynomial Functions

EXAMPLE

■ **Graph the function $f(x) = x^3 + 2x^2 - 5x - 6$.**

Leading coefficient: 1; Degree: 3;
End behavior: $x \to -\infty, f(x) \to -\infty$
$x \to +\infty, f(x) \to +\infty$

The zeros are $-3, -1, 2$. *Factor to find the zeros.*

$f(0) = -6; f(-2) = 4; f(1) = -8$ *Evaluate f(x) at values between the roots. Plot these points.*

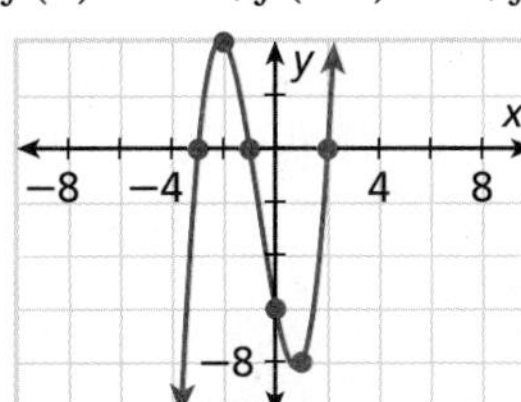

EXERCISES

Identify the leading coefficient, degree, and end behavior.

55. $-2x^3 + 5x^2 + 3$
56. $x^4 + 2x^3 - 3x + 1$
57. $-3x^6 + 9x^3 - 2x - 9$
58. $7x^5 + x^4 - 2x^2 + 5$

Graph each function.

59. $f(x) = x^3 - x^2 - 5x + 6$
60. $f(x) = x^4 - 10x^2 + 9$
61. $f(x) = -x^3 + 5x^2 + x - 5$

3-8 Transforming Polynomial Functions

EXAMPLE

■ **Write a function that transforms $f(x) = x^3 + 5$ by reflecting it across the x-axis and shifting it 2 units right. Support your solution by using a graphing calculator.**

$g(x) = -f(x - 2)$

$g(x) = -(x - 2)^3 - 5$

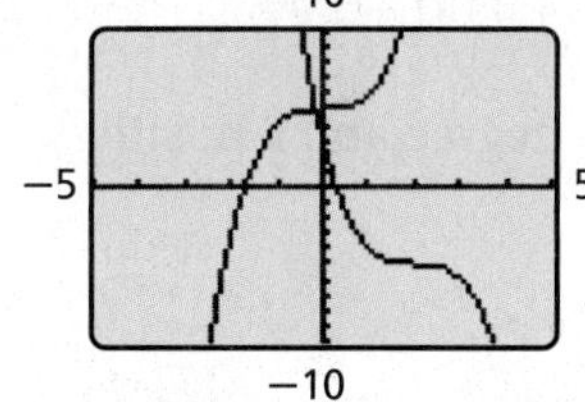

EXERCISES

Write a function that transforms $f(x) = x^4 - 6x^2 - 4$ in each of the following ways. Support your solution by using a graphing calculator.

62. Stretch vertically by a factor of 2, and move 9 units up.
63. Move 2 units down, and reflect across the x-axis.
64. Move 3 units right, and reflect across the y-axis.

3-9 Curve Fitting with Polynomial Models

EXAMPLE

■ **The table shows the profit for a company in thousands of dollars for the years shown. Write a polynomial function for the data.**

Year	1999	2000	2001	2002	2003
Profits	\$286	\$401	\$507	\$671	\$960

First differences: 115 106 164 289
Second differences: −9 58 125
Third differences: 67 67 *Constant*
A cubic polynomial best describes the data. Use the cubic regression feature on your graphing calculator.

$f(x) = 11.17x^3 - 38x^2 + 141.3x + 286$

EXERCISES

65. The chart shows the attendance for a new movie theater over five days. Write a polynomial function for the data.

Day	1	2	3	4	5
Attendance	248	298	318	388	428

66. The chart shows the population of a city for five years. Write a polynomial function for the data.

Year	1	2	3	4	5
Population (thousands)	1891	2674	3376	4480	6469

CHAPTER 3

CHAPTER TEST

Add or subtract. Write your answer in standard form.

1. $(3x^2 - x + 1) + (x)$
2. $(6x^3 - 3x + 2) - (7x^3 + 3x + 7)$
3. $(y^2 + 3y^2 + 2) + (y^4 + y^3 - y^2 + 5)$
4. $(4x^4 + x^2) - (x^3 - x^2 - 1)$
5. The cost of producing x units of a product can be modeled by $C(x) = \frac{1}{10}x^3 - x^2 + 25$. Evaluate $C(x)$ for $x = 15$, and describe what the value represents.

Find each product.

6. $xy(2x^4y + x^2y^2 - 3xy^3)$
7. $(t + 3)(2t^2 - t + 3)$
8. $(x + 5)^3$
9. $(2y + 3)^4$

Divide.

10. $(5x^2 - 6x - 8) \div (x - 2)$
11. $(2x^3 - 7x^2 + 9x - 4) \div (2x - 1)$
12. Use synthetic substitution to evaluate $x^4 + 3x^3 - x^2 + 2x - 6$ for $x = 3$.

Factor each expression.

13. $-2x^2 - 6x + 56$
14. $m^5 + m^4 - 625m - 625$
15. $4x^3 - 32$
16. Identify the roots of the equation $2x^4 - 9x^3 + 7x^2 + 2x - 2 = 0$. State the multiplicity of each root.
17. Write the simplest polynomial function with roots of 1, 4, and -5.

Identify whether the function graphed has an odd or even degree and a positive or negative leading coefficient.

18. 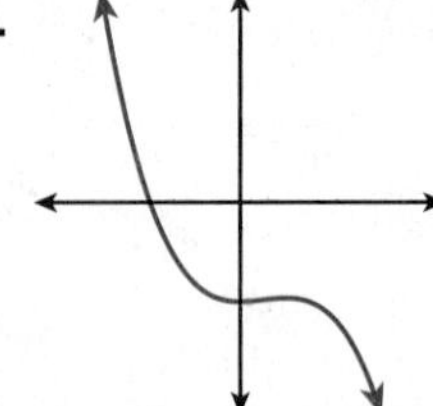

19. 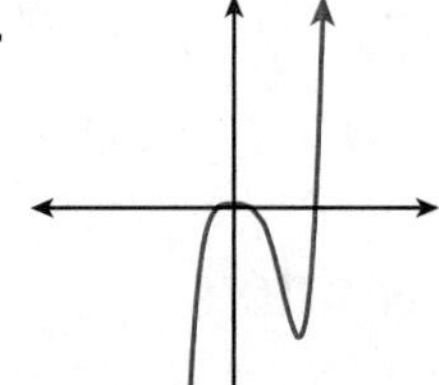

20. 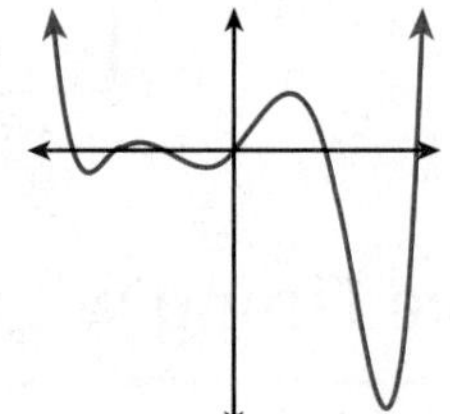

Let $f(x) = 12x^3 + 4$. Graph $f(x)$ and $g(x)$ on the same coordinate plane. Describe $g(x)$ as a transformation of $f(x)$.

21. $g(x) = f(-x)$
22. $g(x) = \frac{1}{2}f(x)$
23. $g(x) = -f(x) + 3$
24. The table shows the number of bracelets Carly can make over time. Write a polynomial function for the data.

Time (h)	1	2	3	4	5	6
Bracelets	3	5	11	21	35	53

25. The table shows the number of sandwiches sold each day at a deli over 5 days. Write a polynomial function for the data.

Day	1	2	3	4	5
Sandwiches	57	72	101	89	66

College Entrance Exam Practice

FOCUS ON SAT MATHEMATICS SUBJECT TESTS

SAT Mathematics Subject Test results include scaled scores and percentiles. Your scaled score is a number from 200 to 800, calculated by using a formula that varies. The percentile indicates the percentage of people who took the same test and scored lower than you did.

The questions are written so that you should not need to do any lengthy calculations. If you find yourself getting involved in a long calculation, think again about all of the information in the problem to see if you might have missed something helpful.

You may want to time yourself as you take this practice test. It should take you about 7 minutes to complete.

1. If $x^4 - 7x^3 - 24x^2 + 112x + 128$ has a rational root a. Which could NOT be the value of a?

(A) 0

(B) 16

(C) 24

(D) 32

(E) 64

2. If there is a remainder of 3 when you divide $p(x) = x^3 + 4x^2 - hx + 30$ by $x - 3$, what is the value of h?

(A) -90

(B) 4

(C) 12

(D) 27

(E) 30

3. The graph of $q(x) = ax^4 + bx^3 + cx^2 + dx + f$ is shown below. Which of the following is true?

(A) $q(x)$ has an odd degree.

(B) $q(x) = (x + 3)h(x)$ for some polynomial $h(x)$.

(C) $f > 0$

(D) $q(0)$ is a local minimum.

(E) $q(x) \to \infty$ as $x \to \infty$

4. Which of the following is the expanded form of $(3x + 2)^3$?

(A) $9x + 6$

(B) $27x^3 + 8$

(C) $27x^3 + 90x + 8$

(D) $27x^3 + 60x^2 + 30x + 8$

(E) $27x^3 + 54x^2 + 36x + 8$

5. If $f(x)$ is a polynomial, which of the following transformations may affect the number of zeros of $f(x)$?

(A) Reflecting $f(x)$ across the y-axis

(B) Reflecting $f(x)$ across the x-axis

(C) Translating $f(x)$ 2 units to the right

(D) Translating $f(x)$ 6 units down

(E) Vertically stretching by a factor of 2

6. Which of the following is a possible root of the polynomial $16x^4 + 80x^3 - 191x^2 + 8x + 15$?

(A) $\frac{1}{12}$

(B) $\frac{1}{5}$

(C) $\frac{3}{8}$

(D) $\frac{3}{5}$

(E) $\frac{8}{3}$

CHAPTER 3

TEST TACKLER

Standardized Test Strategies

Any Question Type: Identify Key Words and Context Clues

When reading a test item, you should pay attention to key words and context clues in the problem statement. These clues will help you provide a correct response.

EXAMPLE 1

Short Response

Write a polynomial in standard form for the volume of the rectangular prism. Find the volume when $x = 5$ inches.

Look *for key words and context clues. Identify what they mean.*

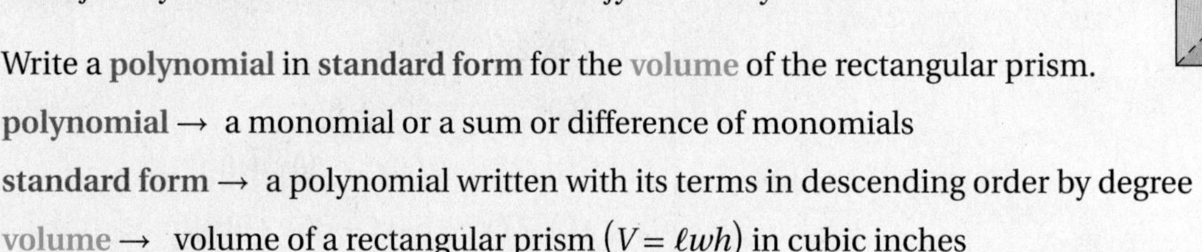

Write a **polynomial** in **standard form** for the **volume** of the rectangular prism.

polynomial → a monomial or a sum or difference of monomials

standard form → a polynomial written with its terms in descending order by degree

volume → volume of a rectangular prism ($V = \ell wh$) in cubic inches

$V(x) = x(x+1)(x+2) = x^3 + 3x^2 + 2x$ ← Standard form

$V(5) = 5^3 + 3(5^2) + 2(5) = 125 + 75 + 10 = 210$ cubic inches

The volume of the prism can be represented by $V(x) = x^3 + 3x^2 + 2x$, and when $x = 5$, $V = 210$ cubic inches.

EXAMPLE 2

Multiple Choice

Paige runs a small jewelry business. From 2000 through 2005, the number of items she created can be modeled by $24x + 12$, and the average cost to make each item can be modeled by $-0.05x^2 + 10$, where x is the number of years since 2000. Which polynomial can be used to model Paige's total jewelry-making costs for those years?

Ⓐ $-0.05x^2 + 24x + 22$

Ⓑ $0.05x^2 + 24x + 2$

Ⓒ $-12x^3 - 6x^2 + 240x + 120$

Ⓓ $-1.2x^3 - 0.6x^2 + 240x + 120$

The key words in this test item are **total cost.**

total cost → average cost per unit times the number of units

$= -0.05x^2 + 10 \quad \times \quad 24x + 12$

$= -1.2x^3 - 0.6x^2 + 240x + 120$

The correct answer is choice D.

If you do not understand what a word means, reread the sentences around the word and make a logical guess.

Read each test item and answer the questions that follow.

Item A

Short Response **A box can be made by cutting squares from each of the four corners of a piece of cardboard. The volume of a box made from a 27.5-by-40-centimeter piece of cardboard can be modeled by $x(27.5 - 2x)(40 - 2x)$, where x is the length of one side of the square. Write the volume as a sum of monomials, and find the volume when $x = 5$ centimeters.**

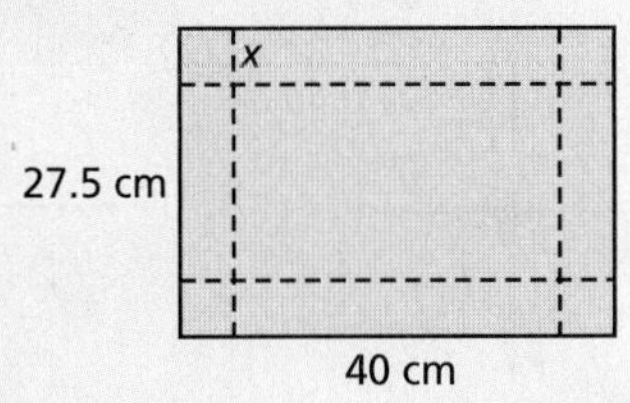

1. What do $(27.5 - 2x)$ and $(40 - 2x)$ represent in the model?
2. Describe what "sum of monomials" means.
3. When you calculate the volume for $x = 5$, in what units should you give your response?

Item B

Short Response **The volume of a cylindrical tank with a hemispherical top and bottom can be represented by the function $V(r) = 24\pi r^2 + \frac{4}{3}\pi r^3$, where V is the volume in cubic meters and r is the radius in meters. What is the radius if the volume of the tank is 5760π cubic meters?**

4. Which word(s) in the problem statement tells you that the volume of a sphere is part of the function?
5. What does the term $24\pi r^2$ in the function represent?
6. Describe how to find the radius given the volume of the tank.

Item C

Multiple Choice **Which description matches the transformation from f to g shown?**

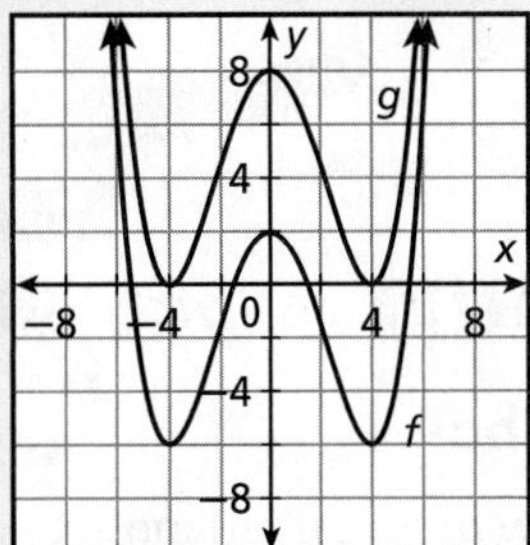

Ⓐ Vertical shift of 3 units

Ⓑ Vertical stretch by a factor of 3

Ⓒ Horizontal shift of 3 units

Ⓓ Horizontal stretch by a factor of 3

7. How do you know which is the original function and which is the image of the function?
8. Because the graphs are shown with an x- and y-scale of 1, how can you use the grid to identify a shift of 3 units?

Item D

Gridded Response **A rectangular storage compartment has a length equal to its width and a height that is 5 feet greater than its width. The volume of the compartment is 72 cubic feet. What is the width?**

9. Make a list of the key words given in the problem statement, and link each word to its mathematical meaning.
10. Write expressions representing the length and height of the compartment in terms of width.
11. Write an expression for the volume of the compartment.

CHAPTER 3

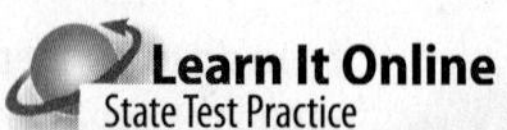

CUMULATIVE ASSESSMENT

Multiple Choice

1. Which row of Pascal's triangle gives the coefficients for the binomial expansion of $(a + b)^4$?

(A) 1 2 1

(B) 1 3 3 1

(C) 1 4 6 4 1

(D) 1 5 10 10 5 1

2. Which binomial is a factor of $2x^4 - 11x^3 + 19x^2 - 13x + 3$?

(F) $x - 2$

(G) $x - 3$

(H) $x + 1$

(J) $x + 2$

3. Which graph shows the ordered triple $(-3, 3, -4)$ graphed in a three-dimensional coordinate plane?

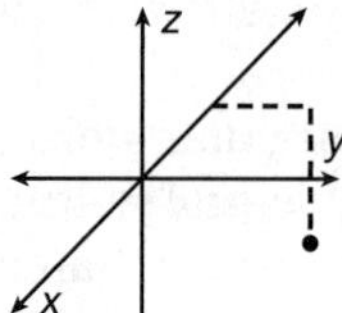

(B)
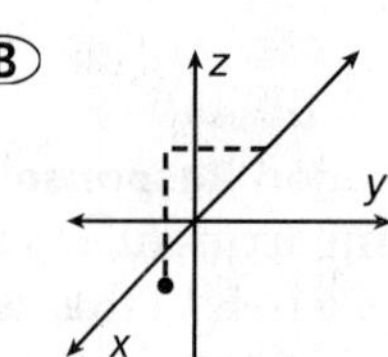

(C)
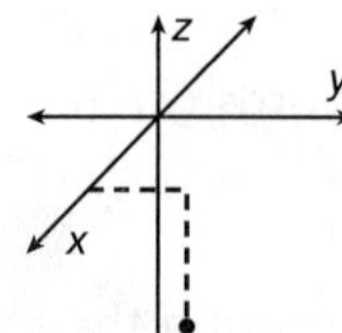

(D)
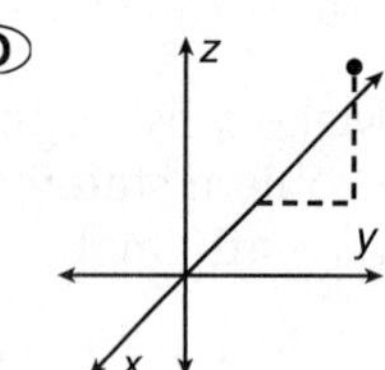

4. What is the value of the y-intercept of $2x + 4y = 1$?

(F) $\frac{1}{4}$

(G) $-\frac{1}{2}$

(H) 1

(J) -2

5. Simplify $\frac{4 - i}{1 + 3i}$.

(A) $\frac{2}{5} - \frac{1}{10}i$

(B) $\frac{1}{10} - \frac{13}{10}i$

(C) $\frac{7}{10} + \frac{11}{10}i$

(D) $4 - \frac{1}{3}i$

6. Which graph represents an odd degree polynomial function with a positive leading coefficient?

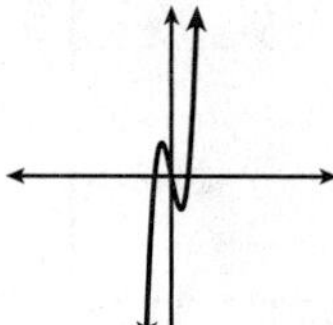

(G)
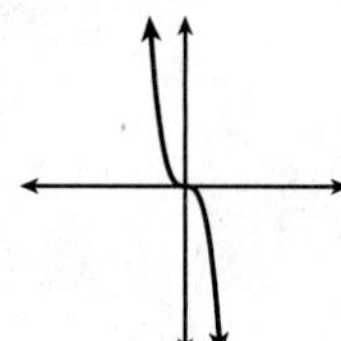

(H)
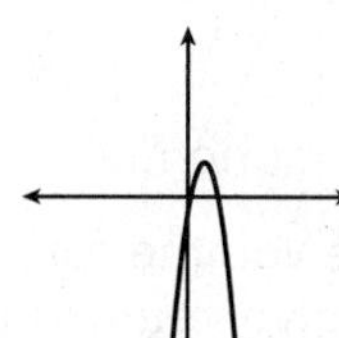

(J)
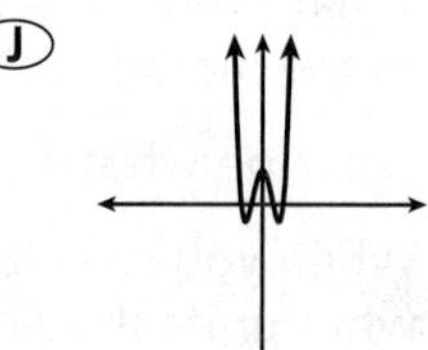

7. What are the domain and range of the polynomial function shown in the graph?

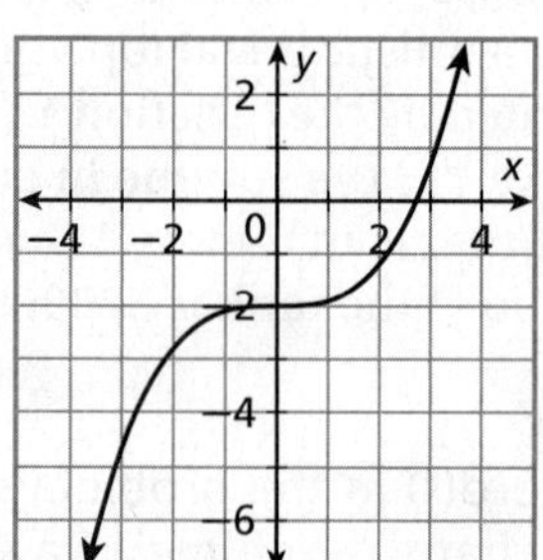

(A) D: $\mathbb{R}$; R: $\mathbb{R}$

(B) D: $\mathbb{R}$; R: $\{y \mid y \geq -2\}$

(C) D: $\{x \mid x \geq -4\}$; R: $\mathbb{R}$

(D) D: $\{x \mid x \geq 4\}$; R: $\{y \mid y \geq -2\}$

8. What is the third term of the expansion of $(g^2 - 2g)^4$?

Ⓕ $6g^4$

Ⓖ $24g^4$

Ⓗ $24g^6$

Ⓙ $4g^6$

9. Multiply: $(-2z - z^2)(4z^2 - 2z^3 + z^4)$.

Ⓐ $-8z^3 + 4z^4 - 2z^5$

Ⓑ $-4z^4 + 2z^5 - z^6$

Ⓒ $4z^3 + 6z^4 - 3z^5$

Ⓓ $-8z^3 - z^6$

In Item 10, use the end behavior of the graph to identify the sign of the leading coefficent and eliminate answer choices. Then use the *y*-intercept to choose the correct response.

10. What is the equation of the parabola shown?

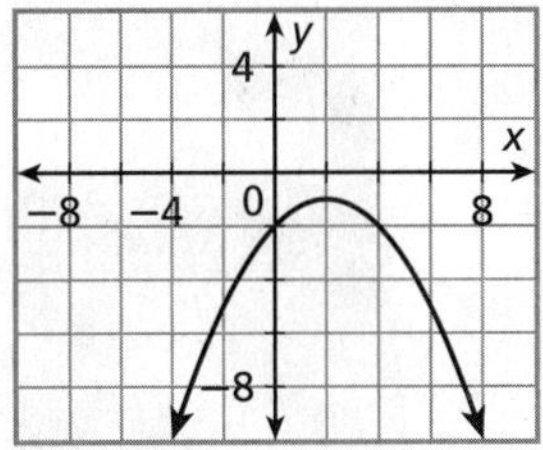

Ⓕ $f(x) = 0.25x^2 + x - 2$

Ⓖ $f(x) = 0.25x^2 - x - 2$

Ⓗ $f(x) = -0.25x^2 + x + 2$

Ⓙ $f(x) = -0.25x^2 + x - 2$

Gridded Response

11. What is the degree of the polynomial $7x^4 + 3x^2 - x^6 + 4$?

12. Divide by using long division. Identify the numerator of the remainder.

$$(2x^5 + 6x^4 - 10x^3 - 2x^2 + 54x + 14) \div (x - 4)$$

13. Complete the square for the expression $x^2 - 3x + ■$.

Short Response

14. The table below shows the number of spyware traces detected and removed from Larry's computer from January to June.

Jan	Feb	Mar	Apr	May	Jun
120	395	545	220	145	130

a. Write a cubic function for the data.

b. Using your answer to part **a**, about how many traces can Larry expect to find in July?

15. Consider $5x^3 + 5x^2 - 40x - 60 = 0$.

a. Identify the roots of the equation.

b. State the multiplicity of each root. Explain what the multiplicity means in terms of the graph.

16. Write the simplest polynomial function with zeros −1, 3, and 4.

17. Use synthetic substitution to evaluate $f(x) = x^3 + 5x^2 - 4x - 20$ for $x = -2$ and $x = 3$.

Extended Response

18. The functions g and h are the result of transformations of the function f.

a. $f(x) = x^3 - 5x^2 + 8x - 1$ is reflected across the x-axis to produce $g(x)$. Write the equation for $g(x)$.

b. Use a graphing calculator to graph f and g. Explain how the graph supports your answer to part **a**.

c. $f(x) = 4(x + 1)^3 + 4$ is translated 1 unit to the right and 3 units down to produce $h(x)$. Write the equation for $h(x)$.

d. Use a graphing calculator to graph f and h. Explain how the graph supports your answer to part **c**.

Real-World CONNECTIONS

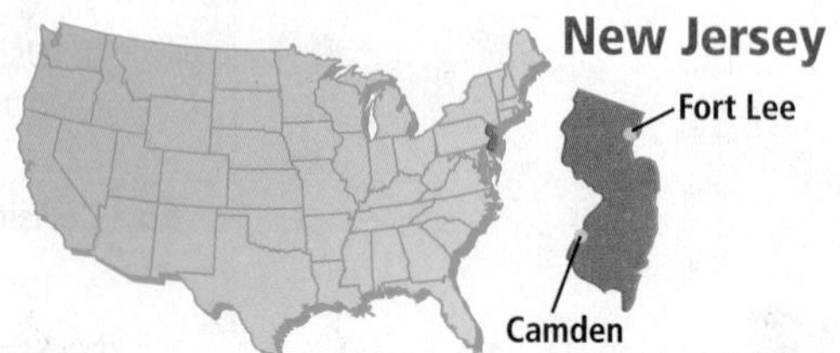

The Camden Waterfront

Located along the Delaware River, the Camden Waterfront offers a variety of attractions, including the Camden Riversharks minor league baseball team and the former home of poet Walt Whitman. The waterfront's most popular destination is the interactive Adventure Aquarium, which features two huge tanks: a 760,000-gallon open tank and a two-story, 550,000-gallon shark tank.

Choose one or more strategies to solve each problem. For 1 and 2, use the table.

Adventure Aquarium		
Tank	Volume (gal)	Volume (m^3)
Open Ocean	760,000	2877
Shark Realm	550,000	2082

1. The volume of a cylindrical tank can be modeled by the function $V(h) = \pi(h^3 + 6h^2 + 9h)$, where h is the tank's height in meters. Use this model to find the height of the Open Ocean tank.
2. The Shark Realm tank has a viewing tunnel along its length. The volume of the tank can be modeled by $V(\ell) = \ell(\ell - 3.2)(\ell + 6.8)$, where ℓ is the tank's length in meters. What is the length of the viewing tunnel?
3. The children's garden at the Camden Waterfront includes a 1200-square-foot room where visitors can walk among hundreds of flying butterflies. During one month of the year, the population of butterflies is modeled by $P(x) = 0.026x^3 - 1.3x^2 + 15.3x + 200$, where x is the number of days since the beginning of the month. What is the maximum population of butterflies during the month?

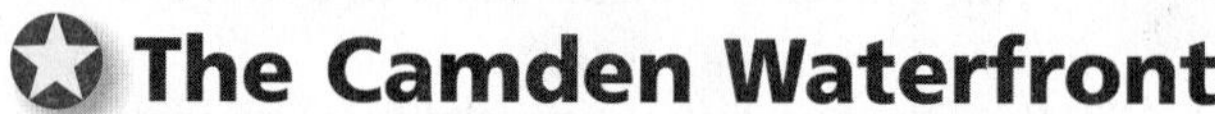

(cr) Courtesy Adventure Aquarium; (b) Grace Davies/Omni-Photo Communications

The George Washington Bridge

When the George Washington Bridge opened to traffic in 1931, it was the world's longest suspension bridge. Since then, it has been eclipsed by longer spans, but it remains one of the world's busiest bridges. On a typical day, more than 300,000 vehicles use the bridge to cross the Hudson River between Upper Manhattan and Fort Lee, New Jersey.

Choose one or more strategies to solve each problem.

1. The height in feet of the main cable above the roadway can be modeled by the equation $h = \frac{2}{15625}(x - 1750)^2$, where x is the distance in feet from the west tower. Find the height of the west tower.
2. The cable touches the roadway at the midpoint between the two towers. What is the length of the span between the towers?
3. The distance d traveled by a vehicle moving at an initial velocity of v_0 mi/h with a constant acceleration of a mi/h^2 is given by $d = \frac{1}{2}at^2 + v_0t$, where t is the time in hours. Given that the George Washington Bridge is 0.9 mi long, how long does it take a motorist to cross the bridge if she enters the bridge at 50 mi/h and accelerates at 10 mi/h^2?

(cr), Bettman/Corbis; (b), Rafael Macia/Photo Researchers, Inc.

For 4, use the table.

4. The table shows the average hourly volume of eastbound traffic into Manhattan. Use a quadratic model to predict the hourly volume of traffic during the rush-hour peak from 6:00 A.M. to 7:00 A.M.

George Washington Bridge, Eastbound

Hour	Average Vehicular Volume
3:00 A.M. to 4:00 A.M.	1274
4:00 A.M. to 5:00 A.M.	2035
5:00 A.M. to 6:00 A.M.	5581

Real-World Connections

CHAPTER 4

Exponential and Logarithmic Functions

COMMON CORE

Chapter

- Communicate the relationship between exponential and logarithmic functions.
- Solve problems using exponential and logarithmic functions.

MEET "e" IN ST. LOUIS

The Gateway Arch is the tallest national monument. Its shape is a *catenary*. You will examine features of catenaries in this chapter project.

Learn It Online
Chapter Project Online

Vocabulary

Match each term on the left with a definition on the right.

1. exponent
2. function
3. relation
4. variable

A. a symbol used to represent one or more numbers
B. the set of counting numbers and their opposites
C. a relation with at most one y-value for each x-value
D. the number of times the base of a power is used as a factor
E. a set of ordered pairs

Properties of Exponents

Simplify each expression. Assume all variables are positive.

5. $x^2(x^3)(x)$
6. $3y^{-1}(5x^2y^2)$
7. $\frac{a^8}{a^2}$
8. $y^{15} \div y^{10}$
9. $\frac{x^2y^5}{xy^6}$
10. $\left(\frac{x}{3}\right)^{-3}$
11. $(3x)^2(4x^3)$
12. $\frac{a^{-2}b^3}{a^4b^{-1}}$

Simple Interest

Use the simple interest formula, $I = Prt$, where I is the interest, P is the initial amount (the principal), and r is the interest rate for Problems 13–15.

13. Find the simple interest on an investment of $3000 at 3% for 2 years.
14. A savings account of $2000 earned $90 simple interest in 3 years. Find the interest rate.
15. Jeri got a loan at 6% simple interest for 3 years. She paid back a total of $5310. How much was the loan?

Solve for a Variable

Solve each equation for x.

16. $3x - y = 4$
17. $y = -7x + 3$
18. $\frac{x}{2} = 3y - 4$
19. $y = \frac{3}{4}x - \frac{1}{2}$

Symmetry

20. Copy the graph, and use the line of symmetry to complete the figure.

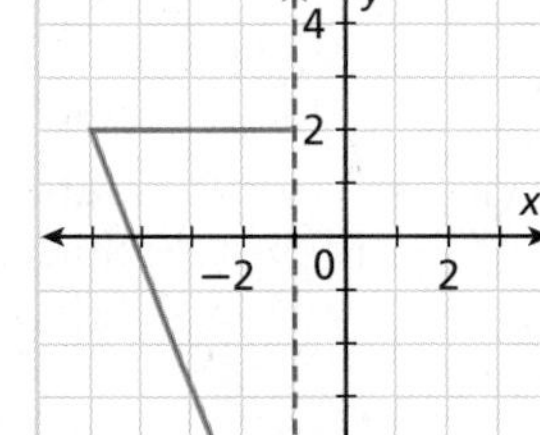

Scientific Notation

Write in scientific notation.

21. 7,000,000,000
22. 0.0000000093
23. 16.75

Write in standard notation.

24. 9.4×10^{-6}
25. 4.7×10^5
26. 7.8×10^4

CHAPTER 4

Study Guide: Preview

Where You've Been

Previously, you

- used the properties of exponents to simplify expressions.
- performed inverse operations.
- solved problems involving linear, quadratic, and polynomial functions.

In This Chapter

You will study

- exponential functions.
- logarithms, the inverse of exponents, and logarithmic functions.
- solving problems involving exponents and logarithms.

Where You're Going

You can use the skills in this chapter

- to solve problems involving compound interest.
- in scientific fields such as biology and sociology where you collect, organize, and analyze data.
- in future math classes, including Statistics and Business Calculus.

Key Vocabulary/Vocabulario

asymptote	asíntota
base	base
common logarithm	logaritmo común
exponential equation	ecuación exponencial
inverse function	función inversa
logarithmic equation	ecuación logarítmica
logarithmic function	función logarítmica
natural logarithm	logaritmo natural

Vocabulary Connections

To become familiar with some of the vocabulary terms in the chapter, consider the following. You may refer to the chapter, the glossary, or a dictionary if you like.

1. You can think of the **base** as carrying its exponent. Which number in $10^3 = 1000$ is the base?
2. A logarithm is an exponent. The base for common logarithms is 10. What would you think would be the **common logarithm** of 1000?
3. Where would you expect to find the variable x in an **exponential equation**?
4. Multiplication and division are *inverse functions.* What would you expect an **inverse function** to do to its corresponding function?
5. The base of a **natural logarithm** is the number e. What are other constant values that are often named by a letter or symbol?
6. The Greek word *asymptōtos* means "not meeting." How do you think a line on a graph called an **asymptote** would relate to a curve on a graph?

Writing Strategy: Use Your Own Words

When studying a difficult mathematical concept, rewrite the concept using your own words so that you can better comprehend the material. You may also find it helpful to provide your own example.

The **degree of a polynomial** is given by the term with the greatest degree. A polynomial with one variable is in standard form when its terms are written in descending order by degree. So, in standard form, the degree of the first term indicates the degree of the polynomial, and the **leading coefficient** is the coefficient of the first term.

REWRITE the above paragraph with short phrases and sentences to clarify important concepts about polynomials.

Polynomials:

1. The term with the highest degree gives the degree of the polynomial.
2. Standard form—terms are in decreasing order of degree.
3. In standard form, the degree of the first term is the degree of the polynomial.
4. The coefficient of the first term is called the leading coefficient.

INCLUDE an example to connect the words and the mathematics.

Example:

Standard form: $2x^4 - 5x^3 + 3x^2 - 9x + 10$

Leading coefficient: 2

Degree of polynomial: 4

Read the following paragraph and rewrite it using your own words.

The Irrational Root Theorem states that irrational roots come in conjugate pairs. For example, if you know that $1 + \sqrt{2}$ is a root of $x^3 - x^2 - 3x - 1 = 0$, then you know that $1 - \sqrt{2}$ is also a root.

Recall that the real numbers are made up of the rational and the irrational numbers. You can use the Rational Root Theorem and the Irrational Root Theorem together to find *all* of the real roots of $P(x) = 0$.

COMMON CORE

4-1 Exponential Functions, Growth, and Decay

CC.9-12.F.IF.7e Graph exponential … functions, showing intercepts and end behavior….* *Also* **CC.9-12.F.IF.5, CC.9-12.F.IF.8b, CC.9-12.A.SSE.1*, CC.9-12.A.CED.2, CC.9-12.A.CED.3**

Objectives
Write and evaluate exponential expressions to model growth and decay situations.

Vocabulary
exponential function
base
asymptote
exponential growth
exponential decay

Who uses this?
Collectors can use exponential functions to model the value of rare musical instruments. (See Example 2.)

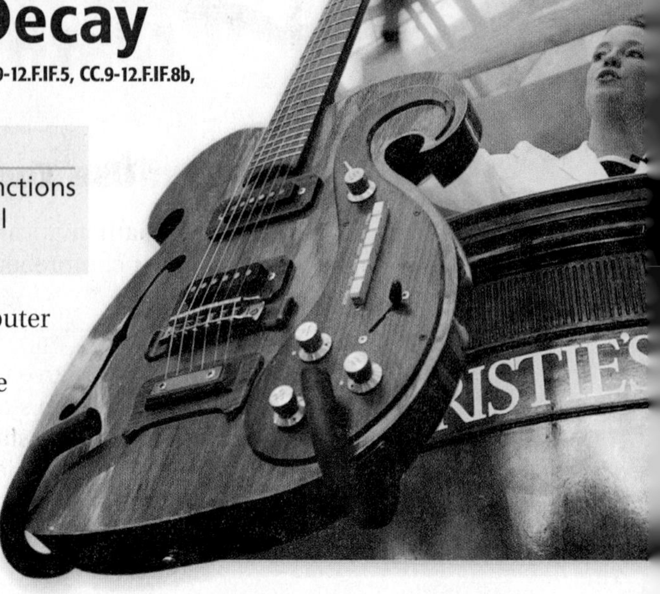

Moore's law, a rule used in the computer industry, states that the number of transistors per integrated circuit (the processing power) doubles every year. Beginning in the early days of integrated circuits, the growth in capacity may be approximated by this table.

Transistors per Integrated Chip

Year	1965	1966	1967	1968	1969	1970	1971
Transistors	60	120	240	480	960	1920	3840

×2 ×2 ×2 ×2 ×2 ×2

Remember!
In the function $y = b^x$, y is a function of x because the value of y *depends* on the value of x.

Growth that doubles every year can be modeled by using a function with a variable as an exponent. This function is known as an *exponential function.* The parent **exponential function** is $f(x) = b^x$, where the **base** b is a constant and the exponent x is the independent variable.

Base Exponent

$$f(x) = b^x, \text{ where } b > 0, b \neq 1$$

The graph of the parent function $f(x) = 2^x$ is shown. The domain is all real numbers and the range is $\{y \mid y > 0\}$.

x	−2	−1	0	1	2	3
$f(x) = 2^x$	$\frac{1}{4}$	$\frac{1}{2}$	1	2	4	8

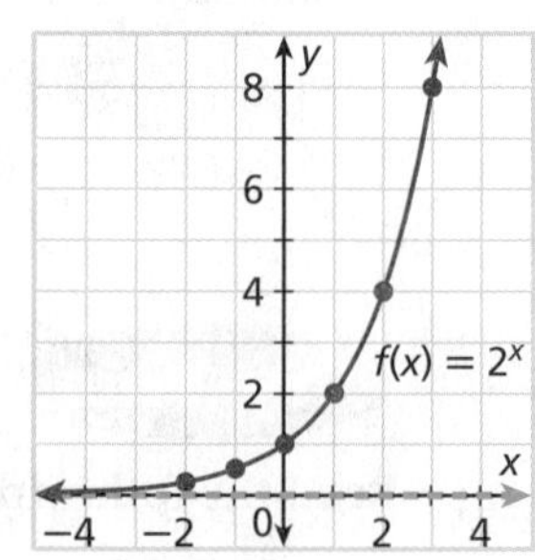

Notice that as the x-values decrease, the graph of the function gets closer and closer to the x-axis. The function never reaches the x-axis because the value of 2^x cannot be zero. In this case, the x-axis is an *asymptote.* An **asymptote** is a line that a graphed function approaches as the value of x gets very large or very small.

A function of the form $f(x) = ab^x$, with $a > 0$ and $b > 1$, is an **exponential growth** function, which increases as x increases. When $0 < b < 1$, the function is called an **exponential decay** function, which decreases as x increases.

Richard Lewis/AP/Wide World Photos

EXAMPLE 1 Graphing Exponential Functions

Tell whether the function shows growth or decay. Then graph.

A $f(x) = 1.5^x$

Step 1 Find the value of the base.

$f(x) = 1.5^x$ *The base, 1.5, is greater than 1. This is an exponential growth function.*

Step 2 Graph the function by using a table of values.

x	−2	−1	0	1	2	3	4
$f(x)$	0.4	0.7	1	1.5	2.3	3.4	5.1

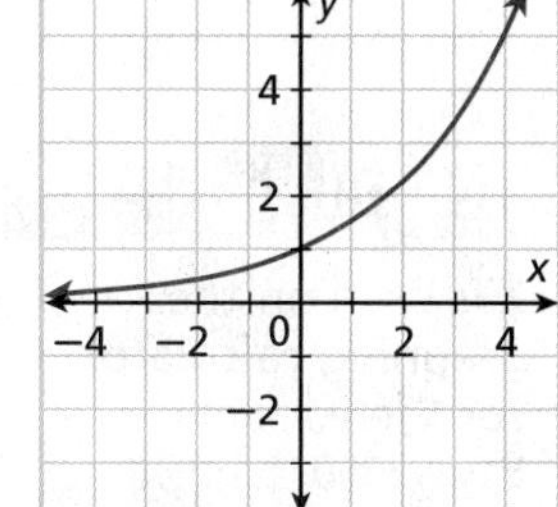

Remember!

Negative exponents indicate a reciprocal. For example:

$x^{-2} = \frac{1}{x^2}$

B $g(x) = 30(0.8^x)$

Step 1 Find the value of the base.

$g(x) = 30(0.8^x)$ *The base, 0.8, is less than 1. This is an exponential decay function.*

Step 2 Graph the function by using a graphing calculator.

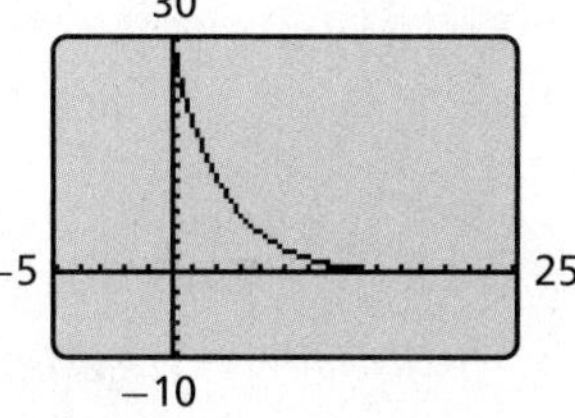

CHECK IT OUT! **1.** Tell whether the function $p(x) = 5(1.2^x)$ shows growth or decay. Then graph.

You can model growth or decay by a constant percent increase or decrease with the following formula:

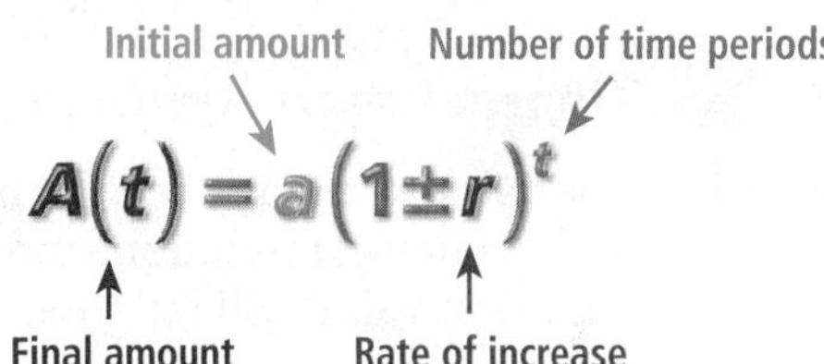

In the formula, the base of the exponential expression, $1 + r$, is called the *growth factor*. Similarly, $1 - r$ is the *decay factor*.

Student to Student *Growth and Decay*

Angela Jones, Independence High School

*When a function **increases** by a constant rate, such as 7%, this is the same as multiplying by 100% + 7%, or 107% .*

In decimal form, I would multiply by 1 + 0.07, or 1.07.

*When a function **decreases** by a constant rate, such as 12%, this is the same as multiplying by 100% – 12%, or 88% .*

In decimal form, it's (1 – 0.12), or 0.88.

EXAMPLE 2 Economics Application

Tony purchased a rare 1959 Gibson Les Paul guitar in 2000 for $12,000. Experts estimate that its value will increase by 14% per year. Use a graph to find when the value of the guitar will be $60,000.

Step 1 Write a function to model the growth in value for this guitar.

$f(t) = a(1 + r)^t$ *Exponential growth function*

$= \mathbf{12,000(1 + 0.14)^t}$ *Substitute 12,000 for a and 0.14 for r.*

$= 12,000(1.14)^t$

Helpful Hint

X is used on the graphing calculator for the variable t:
Y1=12000*1.14^X

Step 2 Graph the function.

When graphing exponential functions in an appropriate domain, you may need to adjust the range a few times to show the key points.

Step 3 Use the graph to predict when the value of the guitar will reach $60,000.

Use the TRACE feature to find the t-value where $f(t) \approx 60,000$.

The function value is approximately 60,000 when $t \approx 12.29$. The guitar will be worth $60,000 about 12.29 years after it is purchased, or sometime in 2012.

100,000

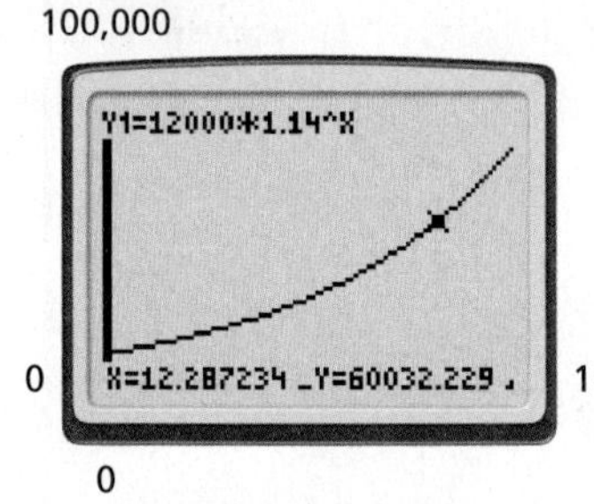

0 15

0

2. In 1981, the Australian humpback whale population was 350 and has increased at a rate of about 14% each year since then. Write a function to model population growth. Use a graph to predict when the population will reach 20,000.

EXAMPLE 3 Depreciation Application

The value of a truck bought new for $28,000 decreases 9.5% each year. Write an exponential function, and graph the function. Use the graph to predict when the value will fall to $5000.

Write a function to model the growth in value for this truck.

$f(x) = a(1 - r)^t$ *Exponential decay function*

$= \mathbf{28,000(1 - 0.095)^t}$ *Substitute 28,000 for a and 0.095 for r.*

$= 28,000(0.905)^t$ *Simplify.*

Graph the function. Use TRACE to find when the value of the truck will fall below $5000.

It will take about 17.3 years for the value to drop to $5000.

30,000

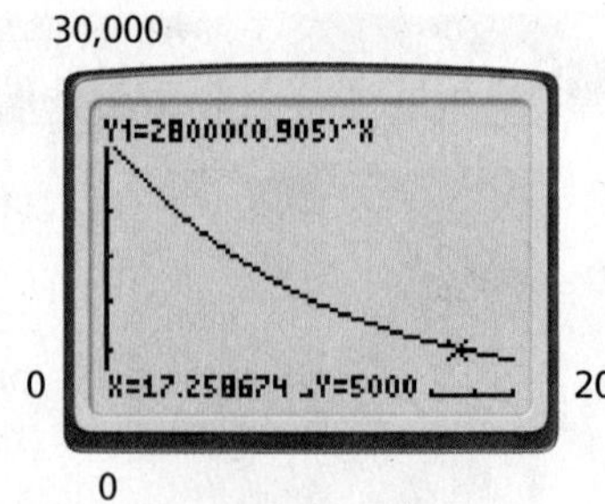

0 20

0

3. A motor scooter purchased for $1000 depreciates at an annual rate of 15%. Write an exponential function, and graph the function. Use the graph to predict when the value will fall below $100.

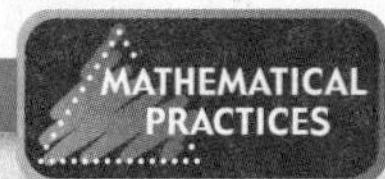

THINK AND DISCUSS

1. Tell how you can determine, without graphing the function or performing any calculations, whether $f(x) = \left(\frac{2}{3}\right)^x$ increases or decreases over the interval $-16 \le x \le -4$.
2. Discuss the differences between the graph of $f(x) = 1.1^x$ and the graph of $g(x) = 0.9^x$. What happens in each when $x = 0$?
3. Describe the function $f(t) = a(1 - r)^t$ when $0 < r < 1$ and $t > 0$. Describe the function when $-1 < r < 0$ and $t > 0$.

4. **GET ORGANIZED** Copy and complete the graphic organizer. Compare exponential growth and decay.

$f(x) = ab^x$, where $a > 0$	Growth	Decay
Value of b		
General shape of the graph		
What happens to $f(x)$ as x increases?		
What happens to $f(x)$ as x decreases?		

4-1 Exercises

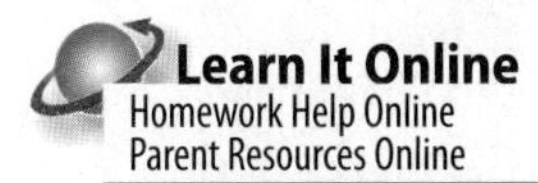

GUIDED PRACTICE

1. **Vocabulary** When the base in an exponential function is between 0 and 1, the function shows __?__. (*exponential growth* or *exponential decay*)

SEE EXAMPLE 1

Tell whether the function shows growth or decay. Then graph.

2. $f(x) = 32(0.5^x)$
3. $f(x) = 0.5(1.2^x)$
4. $f(x) = 0.4\left(\frac{3}{4}\right)^x$

SEE EXAMPLE 2

5. **Biology** An acidophilus culture containing 150 bacteria doubles in population every hour. Predict the number of bacteria after 12 hours.
   a. Write a function representing the bacteria population for every hour that passes.
   b. Graph the function.
   c. Use the graph to predict the number of bacteria after 12 hours.

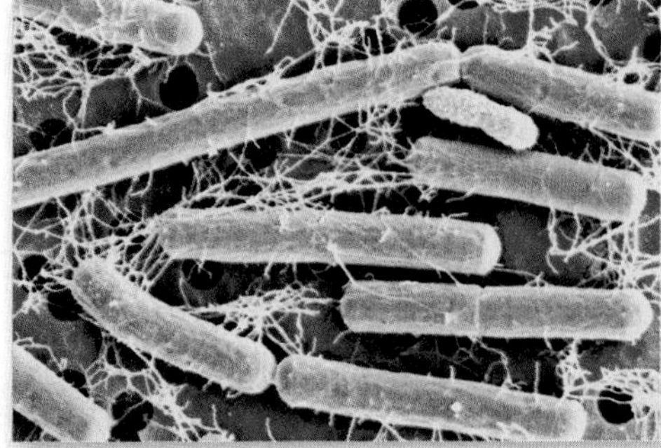

SEE EXAMPLE 3

6. **Physics** A new softball dropped onto a hard surface from a height of 25 inches rebounds to about $\frac{2}{5}$ the height on each successive bounce.
   a. Write a function representing the rebound height for each bounce.
   b. Graph the function.
   c. After how many bounces would a new softball rebound less than 1 inch?

PRACTICE AND PROBLEM SOLVING

Independent Practice

For Exercises	See Example
7–9	1
10	2
11	3

Extra Practice

See Extra Practice for more Skills Practice and Applications Practice exercises.

Tell whether the function shows growth or decay. Then graph.

7. $f(x) = \left(\frac{1}{3}\right)^x$ **8.** $f(x) = \left(\frac{1}{3}\right)(1.3)^x$ **9.** $f(x) = 10(2.7)^x$

10. Railroads The amount of freight transported by rail in the United States was about 580 billion *ton-miles* in 1960 and has been increasing at a rate of 2.32% per year since then.

a. Write a function representing the amount of freight, in billions of ton-miles, transported annually $(1960 = \text{year } 0)$.

b. Graph the function.

c. In what year would you predict that the number of ton-miles would have exceeded or would exceed 1 trillion (1000 billion)?

11. Medicine A quantity of insulin used to regulate sugar in the bloodstream breaks down by about 5% each minute. A body-weight adjusted dose is generally 10 units.

a. Write a function representing the amount of the dose that remains.

b. Use a calculator to graph the function.

c. About how much insulin remains after 10 minutes?

d. About how long does it take for half of the dose to remain?

History

The name *Manhattan* is probably a combination of two Native American words, the Delaware word *mannah,* "island," and the Algonquian word *hatin,* "hills." So the name *Manhattan* means "hilly island."

Explain whether each function is exponential.

12. $f(x) = 2x^{10}$ **13.** $f(x) = 0^x$ **14.** $f(x) = 1 \cdot 0.5^x$

15. History In 1626, the Dutch bought Manhattan Island, now part of New York City, for $24 worth of merchandise. Suppose that, instead, $24 had been invested in an account that paid 3.5% interest each year. Find the balance in 2008.

16. Technology The quantity of new information stored electronically in 2002 was about 5 *exabytes,* or 5×10^{18} bytes. Researchers estimate that this is double what was stored in 1999. Suppose this trend continues. Write and graph a function to predict the pattern of growth beginning in 1999.

17. Business On federal income tax returns, self-employed people can depreciate the value of business equipment. Suppose a computer valued at $2765 depreciates at a rate of 30% per year. Estimate the number of years it will take for the computer's value to be less than $350.

Complete the table for each function. Round each value to the nearest hundredth.

	x	−3	−2	−1	0	1	2	3	4	5
18.	$f(x) = 2.2^x$	■	■	■	■	■	■	■	■	■
19.	$g(x) = 0.4^x$	■	■	■	■	■	■	■	■	■

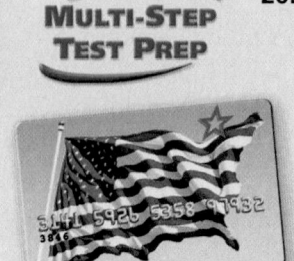

MULTI-STEP TEST PREP

20. For a certain credit card, the total amount A that you owe after n months is given by $A = P(1.015)^n$, where P is the starting balance.

a. Suppose that you begin with a debt of $1000. Graph the function for the amount that you owe.

b. How much will you owe after one year?

c. How long will it take for the total amount that you owe to reach $1300?

Bettmann/CORBIS

21. **Collectibles** At the peak of a beanbag animal fad, one sales representative sold 12,000 of the animals in one month. Each month after that, the rep sold about 20% fewer animals.

   a. About how many beanbag animals did the rep sell in the 6th month after the peak?

   b. In which month did the rep first sell fewer than 1000 animals?

22. **Banking** The compound interest formula is $A = P\left(1 + \frac{r}{n}\right)^{nt}$, where A is the amount earned, P is the principal, r is the annual interest rate, t is the time in years, and n is the number of compounding periods per year. Harry invested \$5000 at 5% interest compounded quarterly (4 times per year).

   a. How much will the investment be worth after 5 years?

   b. When will the investment be worth more than \$10,000?

   c. **What if...?** Harry could have invested the same amount in an account that paid 5% interest compounded monthly (12 times per year). How much more would his investment have been worth after 5 years?

23. **Critical Thinking** What are the coordinates of the point that is common to the graph of $f(x) = \left(\frac{2}{3}\right)^x$ and the graph of $f(x) = \left(\frac{3}{2}\right)^x$?

Find the range of each function for the domain $(0, 10]$.

24. $f(x) = 3^x - 2^x$

25. $f(x) = 100(0.9)^x$

26. $f(x) = \frac{3}{4}(2)^x$

27. **Geology** Radon-222 is a gas that escapes from rocks and soil. It can accumulate in buildings and can be dangerous for people who breathe it. Radon-222 decays to polonium and eventually to lead.

   a. Find the percent decrease in the amount of radon-222 each day.

   b. Write an exponential decay function for the amount of a 500 mg sample of radon-222 remaining after t days.

   c. How much of the radon-222 sample would remain after 14 days?

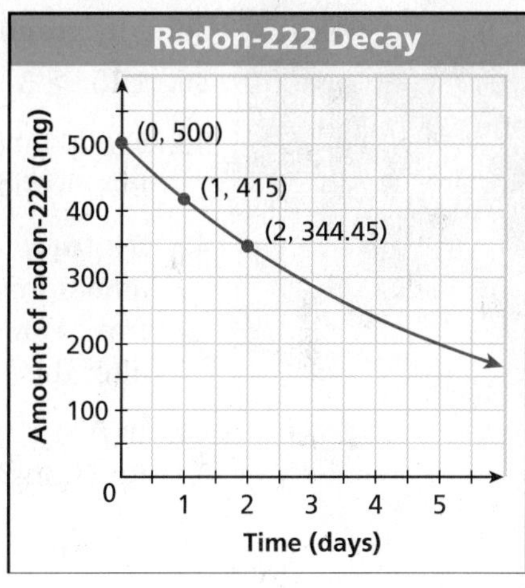

28. **Estimation** According to the Population Reference Bureau, the world population in 2000 was 6.1 billion and increasing at an annual rate of 1.4%. Estimate the world population in 2020. Then write and evaluate an exponential function to predict the actual population, and compare it to your estimate.

29. **Critical Thinking** Which grows faster as x increases, x^3 or 3^x? Explain.

30. **Write About It** Describe a situation that could be modeled by an exponential function. Give the function and describe the meanings of several function values.

TEST PREP

31. Which function represents exponential decay?

   (A) $f(x) = 0.9(1.001^x)$

   (B) $f(x) = 1.5\left(\frac{10}{11}\right)^x$

   (C) $f(x) = 0.5(2^x)$

   (D) $f(x) = \left(\frac{1}{0.5}\right)^x$

32. Which number line represents the values of b in $y = ab^x$ for an exponential decay function?

(F) 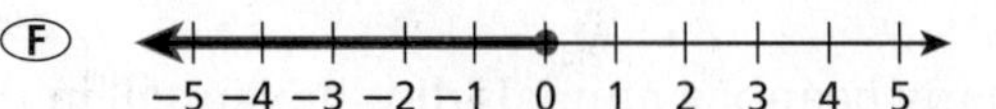

(H) 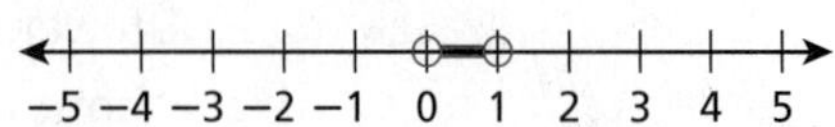

(G) 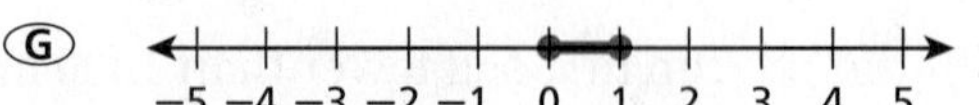

(J) 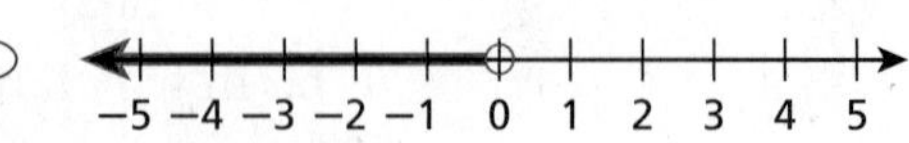

33. Short Response What are the values of a and b in $f(x) = ab^x$ for the graph shown?

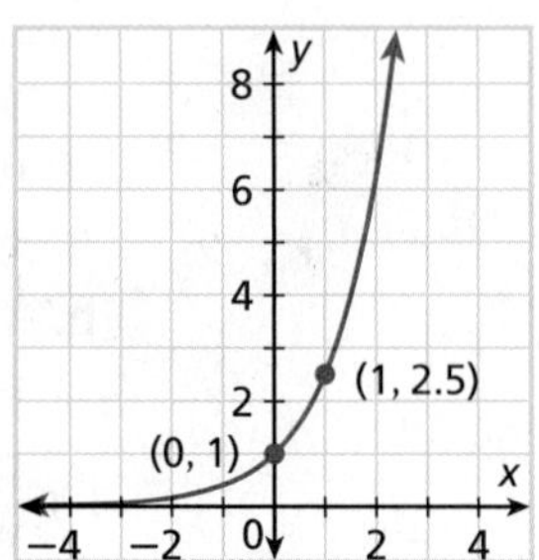

34. The population of a town was 89,443 in 1990 and has increased at a rate of 0.6% per year since then. Which function represents the town's population t years after 1990?

(A) $89{,}443(1.6)^t$ (C) $89{,}443(1.06)^t$

(B) $89{,}443(1.006)^t$ (D) $89{,}443(1.0006)^t$

CHALLENGE AND EXTEND

35. Critical Thinking Recall that polynomials are classified by degree. Why doesn't an exponential function have a degree?

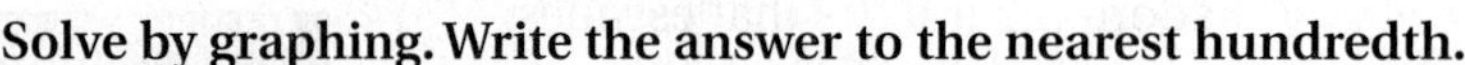

Solve by graphing. Write the answer to the nearest hundredth.

36. $1.15^x \geq 3$ **37.** $0.97^x < 0.5$ **38.** $5 < 1.5^x < 6$

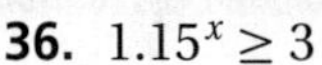

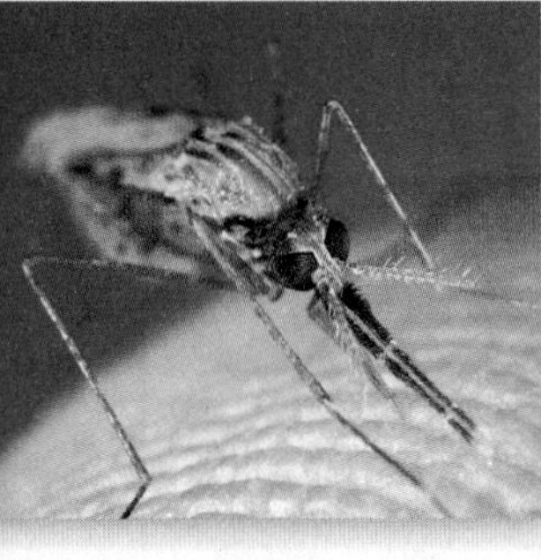

39. Compare the graphs of $y = 2^x$ and $y = x^2$, where $-10 < x < 10$. How many points of intersection are there? Give the coordinates of these points.

40. Biology Researchers found that the number of mosquitoes per acre of wetland after a frost is about 10 to the power $\frac{1}{2}d + 2$, where d is the number of days since the frost. How many mosquitoes per acre are there at the time of the frost? How long after the frost does it take for the population to quadruple?

41. In $f(x) = b^x$, why is the domain of b restricted $(b > 0, b \neq 1)$ for exponential functions?

CDC/PHIL/CORBIS

Explore Inverses of Functions

You can use a graphing calculator to explore inverse functions and their relationship to the linear parent function $f(x) = x$.

Use with Inverses of Relations and Functions

Use appropriate tools strategically

CC.9-12.F.BF.4 Find inverse functions. *Also* **CC.9-12.A.CED.2, CC.9-12.A.CED.3**

Activity

Graph the function $f(x) = 2^x$ and its inverse.

1. Graph the function $f(x) = 2^x$ and the linear parent $f(x) = x$ in the decimal window. Enter the functions, and then press ZOOM and select **4:ZDecimal**.

2. Use the **DrawInv** feature to graph the inverse of **Y1**. Enter the DRAW menu by pressing 2nd PRGM (DRAW). Then select **8:DrawInv**.

   To select **Y1**, press VARS. Use the arrow keys to move to the **Y-VARS** submenu. Select **1:Function**, and then select **1:Y1** and press ENTER.

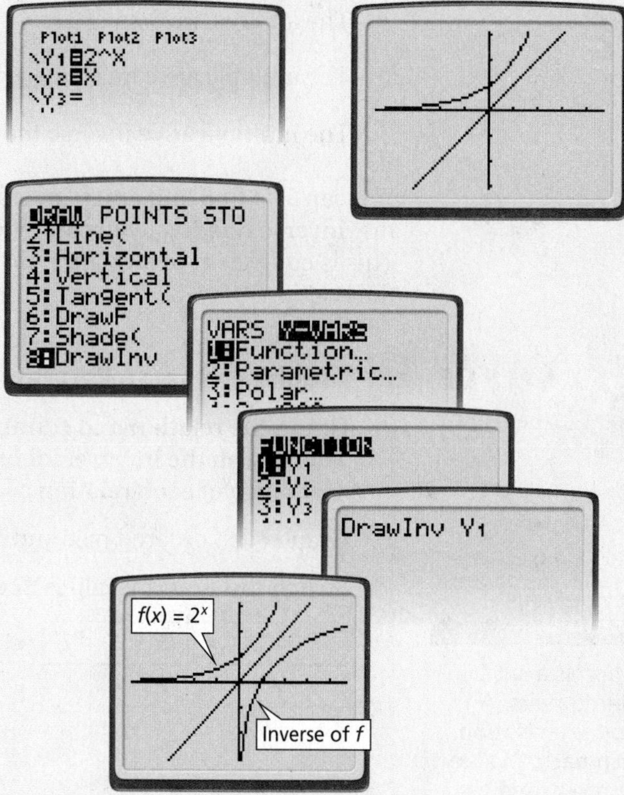

The graph shows the original function $f(x) = 2^x$, its inverse, and the linear parent $f(x) = x$. Notice that the inverse appears to be a function. Its domain is $\{x \mid x > 0\}$, and its range is $\mathbb{R}$.

Try This

Graph $f(x) = x^2$, its inverse, and $f(x) = x$.

1. Compare the domain and range of $f(x) = x^2$ with the domain and range of its inverse. Is the inverse of $f(x) = x^2$ a function? Explain why or why not.

Graph $f(x) = x^3$, its inverse, and $f(x) = x$.

2. Compare the domain and range of $f(x) = x^3$ with the domain and range of its inverse. Is the inverse of $f(x) = x^3$ a function? Explain why or why not.

3. **Make a Conjecture** Make a conjecture about the relationship between the domain and range of a function and its inverse.

4. **Make a Conjecture** Make a conjecture about the relationship of a function and its inverse to the line $f(x) = x$.

4-2 Inverses of Relations and Functions

CC.9-12.F.BF.4c (+) Read values of an inverse function from a graph or a table, given that the function has an inverse. *Also* **CC.9-12.F.IF.5, CC.9-12.A.CED.2, CC.9-12.A.CED.3**

Objectives
Graph and recognize inverses of relations and functions.
Find inverses of functions.

Vocabulary
inverse relation
inverse function

Who uses this?
Scuba divers can use an inverse function to determine their depth based on the water pressure. (See Exercise 47.)

You have seen the word *inverse* used in various ways.

The additive inverse of 3 is −3.

The multiplicative inverse of 5 is $\frac{1}{5}$.

The multiplicative inverse matrix of $A = \begin{bmatrix} 3 & 1 \\ 4 & 2 \end{bmatrix}$ is $A^{-1} = \begin{bmatrix} 1 & -0.5 \\ -2 & 1.5 \end{bmatrix}$.

You can also find and apply inverses to relations and functions. To graph the **inverse relation**, you can reflect each point across the line $y = x$. This is equivalent to switching the x- and y-values in each ordered pair of the relation.

EXAMPLE 1 Graphing Inverse Relations

Graph the relation and connect the points. Then graph the inverse. Identify the domain and range of each relation.

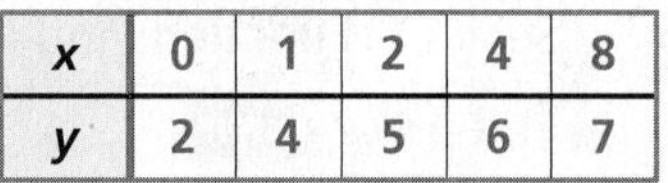

x	0	1	2	4	8
y	2	4	5	6	7

Graph each ordered pair and connect them.

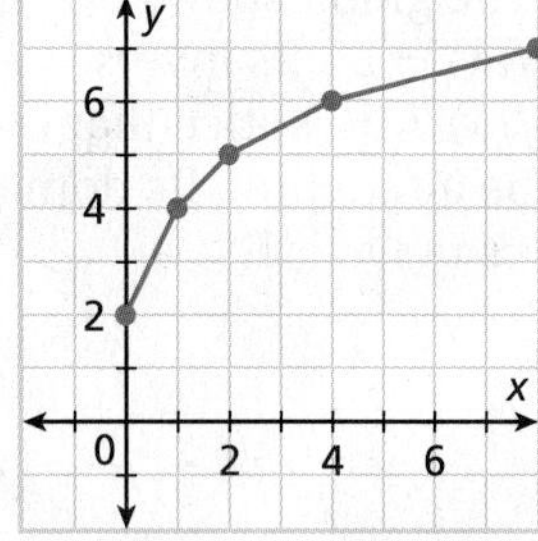

Switch the x- and y-values in each ordered pair.

x	2	4	5	6	7
y	0	1	2	4	8

Remember!
A *relation* is a set of ordered pairs. A *function* is a relation in which each x-value has, at most, one y-value paired with it.

Reflect each point across $y = x$, and connect them. Make sure the points match those in the table.

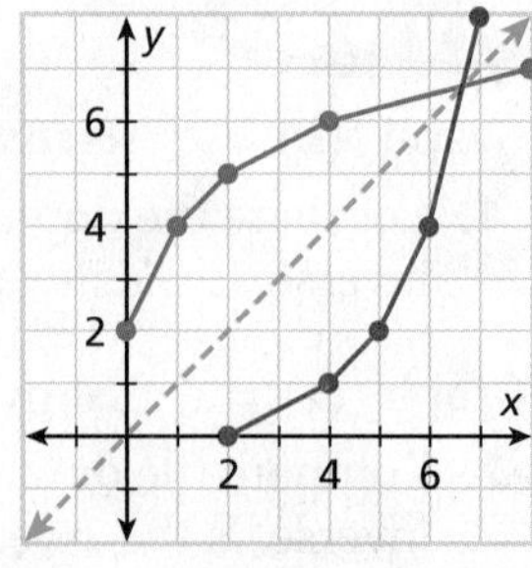

Domain: $\{x \mid 0 \le x \le 8\}$ Range: $\{y \mid 2 \le y \le 7\}$

Domain: $\{x \mid 2 \le x \le 7\}$ Range: $\{y \mid 0 \le y \le 8\}$

1. Graph the relation and connect the points. Then graph the inverse. Identify the domain and range of each relation.

x	1	3	4	5	6
y	0	1	2	3	5

Wolfgang Polzer/Alamy

When the relation is also a function, you can write the inverse of the function $f(x)$ as $f^{-1}(x)$. This notation does *not* indicate a reciprocal.

Functions that undo each other are **inverse functions**.

Input		Function		Output
3	→	$f(x) = x + 6$	→	9

Input		Inverse function		Output
9	→	$f^{-1}(x) = x - 6$	→	3

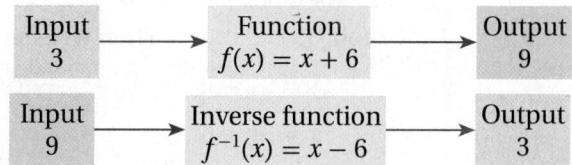

To find the inverse function, use the inverse operation. In the example above, 6 is added to x in $f(x)$, so 6 is subtracted to find $f^{-1}(x)$.

EXAMPLE 2 Writing Inverse Functions by Using Inverse Operations

Use inverse operations to write the inverse of $f(x) = 2x$.

$f(x) = 2x$ *The variable, x, is multiplied by 2.*

$f^{-1}(x) = \frac{x}{2}$ *Divide x by 2 to write the inverse.*

Check Use the input $x = 7$ in $f(x)$.

$f(x) = 2x$

$f(7) = 2(7)$ *Substitute 7 for x.*

$= 14$

Substitute the result into $f^{-1}(x)$.

$f^{-1}(x) = \frac{x}{2}$

$f^{-1}(14) = \frac{14}{2}$ *Substitute 14 for x.*

$= 7$

The inverse function *does* undo the original function. ✔

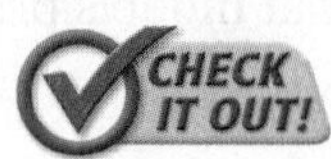

Use inverse operations to write the inverse of each function.

2a. $f(x) = \frac{x}{3}$ **2b.** $f(x) = x + \frac{2}{3}$

Undo operations in the opposite order of the order of operations.

EXAMPLE 3 Writing Inverses of Multi-Step Functions

Use inverse operations to write the inverse of $f(x) = \frac{x}{4} - 5$.

$f(x) = \frac{x}{4} - 5$ *The variable x is divided by 4, then 5 is subtracted.*

$f^{-1}(x) = 4(x + 5)$ *First, undo the subtraction by adding 5 to x. Then, undo the division by multiplying by 4.*

Check Use a sample input.

$f(40) = \frac{40}{4} - 5 = 10 - 5 = 5$ $f^{-1}(5) = 4(5 + 5) = 4(10) = 40$ ✔

Helpful Hint

The *reverse* order of operations:
Addition or Subtraction
Multiplication or Division
Exponents
Parentheses

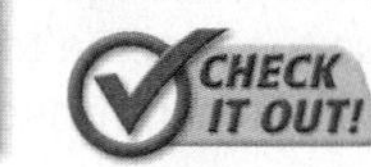

3. Use inverse operations to write the inverse of $f(x) = 5x - 7$.

You can also find the inverse function by writing the original function with x and y switched and then solving for y.

EXAMPLE 4 Writing and Graphing Inverse Functions

Graph $f(x) = 3x + 6$. Then write and graph the inverse.

$y = 3x + 6$	*Set $y = f(x)$ and graph f.*
$x = 3y + 6$	*Switch x and y.*
$x - 6 = 3y$	*Solve for y.*
$\frac{x-6}{3} = y$	
$y = \frac{x-6}{3}$	*Write in $y =$ format.*
$f^{-1}(x) = \frac{x-6}{3}$	*Set $y = f(x)$.*
$= \frac{1}{3}x - 2$	*Simplify. Then graph f^{-1}.*

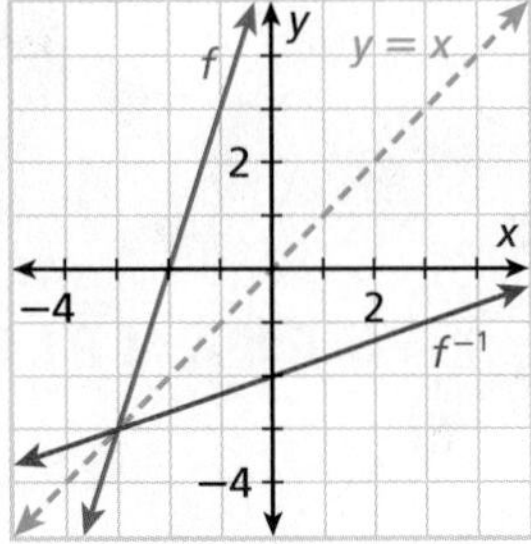

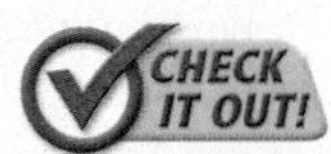

4. Graph $f(x) = \frac{2}{3}x + 2$. Then write the inverse and graph.

Any time you need to undo an operation or work backward from a result to the original input, you can apply inverse functions.

EXAMPLE 5 Retailing Application

A clerk needs to price a digital camera returned by a customer. The customer paid a total of \$103.14, which included a gift-wrapping charge of \$3 and 8% sales tax. What price should the clerk mark on the tag?

Step 1 Write an equation for the total cost as a function of price.

$c = 1.08(p + 3)$ *Cost c is a function of price p.*

Step 2 Find the inverse function that models price as a function of cost.

$c = 1.08(p + 3)$

$c = 1.08p + 3.24$ *Distribute.*

$c - 3.24 = 1.08p$ *Subtract 3.24 from both sides.*

$\frac{c - 3.24}{1.08} = p$ *Divide to isolate p.*

Step 3 Evaluate the inverse function for $c = \$103.14$.

$$p = \frac{103.14 - 3.24}{1.08} = 92.50$$

The clerk should mark the tag as \$92.50.

Check $c = 1.08(92.50 + 3)$ *Substitute.*

$= 1.08(95.50)$

$= 103.14$ ✔

Remember!

In a real-world situation, don't switch the variables, because they are named for specific quantities.

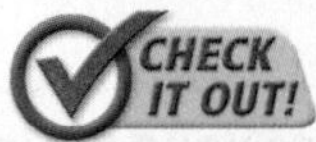

5. To make tea, use $\frac{1}{6}$ teaspoon of tea per ounce of water plus a teaspoon for the pot. Use the inverse to find the number of ounces of water needed if 7 teaspoons of tea are used.

THINK AND DISCUSS

1. Explain the result of interchanging x and y to find the inverse function of $f(x) = x$. How could you have predicted this from the graph of $f(x)$?
2. Give an example of a function whose inverse is a function. Give an example of a function whose inverse is not a function.
3. Tell what happens when you take the inverse of the inverse of a function. Is the result necessarily a function? Explain.

4. **GET ORGANIZED** Copy and complete the graphic organizer. Show a possible input value, inverse function, and output value for a function $f(x)$.

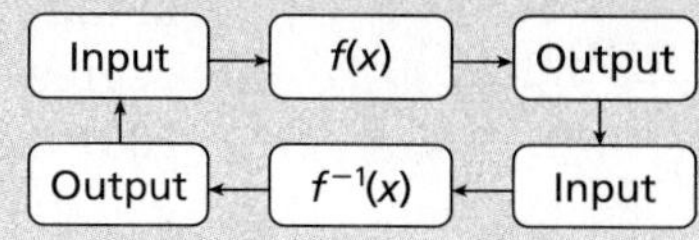

4-2 Exercises

GUIDED PRACTICE

1. **Vocabulary** When switching x and y, the result is always an *inverse* ___?___. (*relation* or *function*)

SEE EXAMPLE 1

Graph the relation and connect the points. Then graph the inverse. Identify the domain and range of each relation.

2.

x	1	2	3	4
y	1	2	4	8

3.

x	3	4	1	−1
y	−1	−2	−4	−4

SEE EXAMPLE 2

Use inverse operations to write the inverse of each function.

4. $f(x) = x + 3$
5. $f(x) = 4x$
6. $f(x) = \frac{x}{2}$
7. $f(x) = x - 2\frac{1}{2}$

SEE EXAMPLE 3

8. $f(x) = 5x - 1$
9. $f(x) = \frac{x}{2} + 3$
10. $f(x) = 3 - \frac{1}{2}x$
11. $f(x) = \frac{1}{2}(3 - 3x)$
12. $f(x) = 4(x + 1)$
13. $f(x) = \frac{3x - 5}{2}$

SEE EXAMPLE 4

Graph each function. Then write and graph its inverse.

14. $f(x) = 5 - 2x$
15. $f(x) = \frac{x}{4} + 2$
16. $f(x) = 10 + 0.6x$

SEE EXAMPLE 5

17. **Meteorology** The formula $C = \frac{5}{9}(F - 32)$ gives degrees Celsius as a function of degrees Fahrenheit. Find the inverse of this function to convert degrees Celsius to Fahrenheit and use it to find 16°C in degrees Fahrenheit.

PRACTICE AND PROBLEM SOLVING

Graph the relation and connect the points. Then graph the inverse. Identify the domain and range of each relation.

18.

x	−1	2	3	5
y	1	3	5	5

19.

x	−4	−2	0	2	4
y	−2	−1	0	1	2

Independent Practice

For Exercises	See Example
18–19	1
20–22	2
23–25	3
26–28	4
29	5

Extra Practice

See Extra Practice for more Skills Practice and Applications Practice exercises.

Use inverse operations to write the inverse of each function.

20. $f(x) = 0.825x$
21. $f(x) = x - 1\frac{3}{4}$
22. $f(x) = \frac{x}{0.25}$
23. $f(x) = 21 - 32x$
24. $f(x) = 145 + 12.5x$
25. $f(x) = \frac{1}{5}x + 12$

Graph each function. Then write and graph its inverse.

26. $f(x) = \frac{4}{5}(x - 15)$
27. $f(x) = 2 - \frac{x}{3}$
28. $f(x) = 1.21x$

29. **Education** A linear model projects that the number of bachelor's degrees awarded in the United States will increase by 19,500 each year. In 2001, 1.28 million bachelor's degrees were awarded. Use the inverse function to predict the number of years after 2001 that 1.7 million bachelor's degrees will be awarded. *Source:* nces.ed.gov

30. **Critical Thinking** Graph the line that passes through (2, 9) and (3, 4).
    a. What is the slope of this line?
    b. What is the slope of the line that is the inverse of the original line?

LINK

Physics

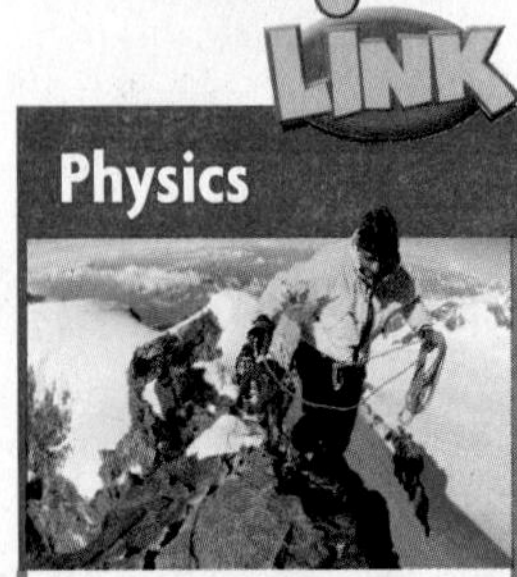

Mountain climbers at very high altitudes can drink tea while it's boiling with bubbles because it's cool enough not to burn them.

31. **Physics** At sea level, the boiling point of water is 212°F. At x thousand feet, the boiling point of water is given by the function $f(x) = 212 - 1.85x$.
    a. Write the inverse function.
    b. Above what altitude, to the nearest 500 feet, does the boiling point of water fall below 200°F?
    c. At the summit of Nepal's Lhotse Mountain, water boils at 160.3°F. What is the mountain peak's altitude?

Geometry Find the coordinates of the vertices of the inverse for each figure.

32.

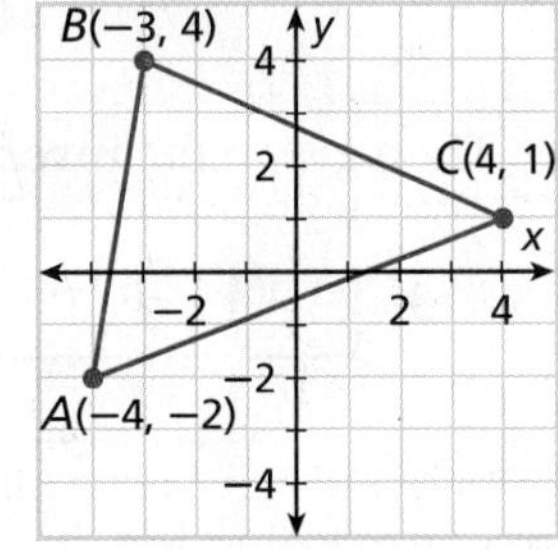

33.

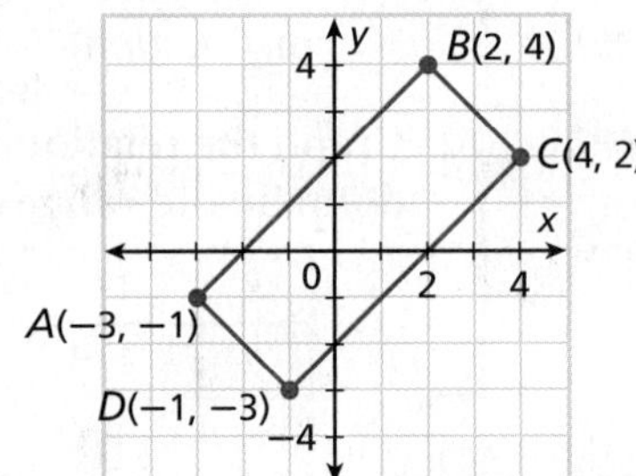

34. **Critical Thinking** What is the inverse of $f(x) = 3$? (Hint: Write this function as $y = 0x + 3$.) Is the inverse a function? Explain.

35. **Animals** In 1999, Warhol the albino ferret ran a 10 m tube race in 12.59 s. Assume that he ran at a constant rate. Write a function that gives distance as a function of time. Write and use the inverse function to find the time it would take Warhol to complete a 25 m race at the same speed.

MULTI-STEP TEST PREP

36. A theater sells tickets for \$22. If you pay by credit card, the theater adds a service charge of \$3.50 to the entire order.
    a. Write a function that gives the amount billed to the credit card as a function of the number of tickets purchased.
    b. Write the inverse function, and use it to find the number of tickets purchased when the credit card bill is \$157.50.
    c. Is it possible to have a total of \$332.50 billed to your credit card for these tickets? Why or why not?

37. **ERROR ANALYSIS** Two students found the inverse of $f(x) = \frac{1}{2}x + 1$. Which is incorrect? Explain the error.

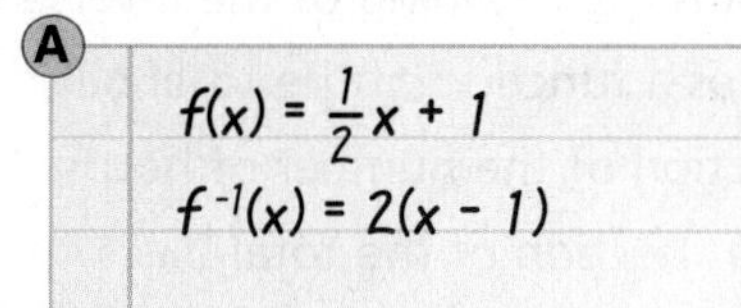

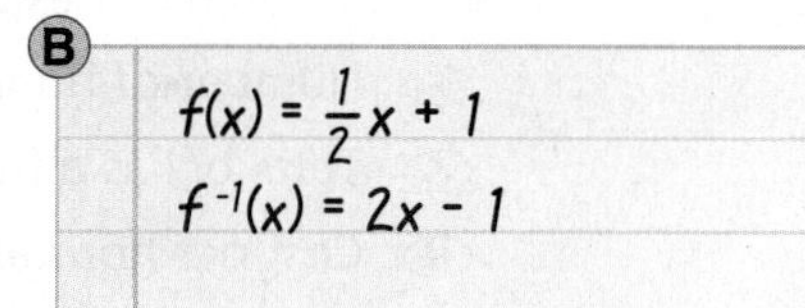

38. **Write About It** Explain the effect on a function and its graph when you switch the coordinates of the ordered pairs.

39. **Critical Thinking** Can the inverse of a relation that is not a function be a function itself? Explain your answer by using an example.

40. **Clothing** Hat size is a linear function of head circumference. A person with a head circumference of $21\frac{1}{2}$ in. has a hat size of $6\frac{7}{8}$, while a person with a head circumference of $21\frac{7}{8}$ in. has a hat size of 7.
   a. Find hat size as a function of head circumference.
   b. Find the inverse. Is it a function? What does the inverse represent?
   c. A hat was found with a size of $7\frac{3}{8}$. What is the head circumference of the owner?

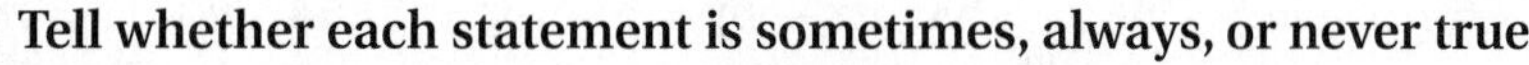

Tell whether each statement is sometimes, always, or never true.

41. The inverse of an ordered pair on a graph is its reflection across the line $y = x$.

42. The inverse of a linear function is a linear function.

43. The inverse of a line with positive slope is a line with negative slope.

44. The inverse of a line with a slope greater than 1 is a line with slope less than 1.

45. The inverse of the inverse of a point (x, y) is the original point.

46. The line $y = k$, where k is a constant, has an inverse.

47. **Diving** Scuba divers must know that the deeper the dive, the greater the water pressure in pounds per square inch (psi) for fresh water diving, as shown in the diagram.
   a. Write the pressure as a function of depth.
   b. Identify a reasonable domain and range of the pressure function.
   c. Find the inverse of the function from part **a.** What does the inverse function represent?
   d. The point $(25.9, 25.9)$ is an approximate solution to both the function from part **a** and its inverse. What does this point mean in the context of the problem?

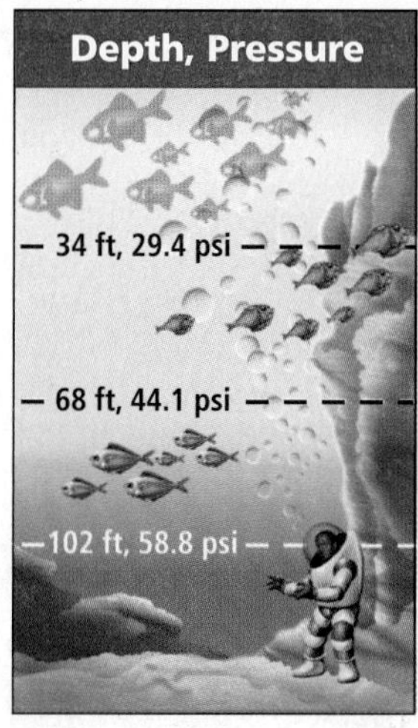

TEST PREP

48. Which function is the inverse of $f(x) = 4x - \frac{3}{4}$?

Ⓐ $f^{-1}(x) = \frac{1}{4}x + \frac{3}{16}$

Ⓑ $f^{-1}(x) = -\frac{1}{4}x + 3$

Ⓒ $f^{-1}(x) = \frac{1}{4}x + 3$

Ⓓ $f^{-1}(x) = -\frac{1}{4}x + \frac{3}{16}$

49. Eliza's auto repair bill includes $175 for parts and $35 per hour for labor. The bill can be expressed as a function of hours x with the function $f(x) = 175 + 35x$. Which statement explains the meaning of the inverse of the function?

(F) Number of hours as a function of the total bill

(G) Total bill as a function of the number of hours

(H) Cost per hour as a function of the total bill

(J) Total bill as a function of the cost per hour

50. The inverse of a point is (5, –2). What point is this the inverse of?

(A) (–5, 2) (B) (5, 2) (C) (–2, 5) (D) (2, –5)

51. Short Response Make a table to show the inverse of the relation shown in the graph.

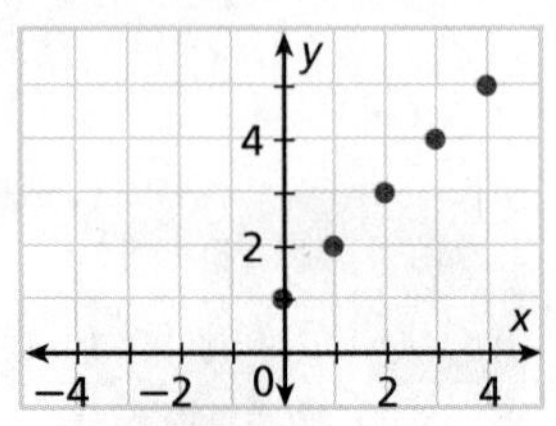

CHALLENGE AND EXTEND

Give the inverse of each linear function, where $y = f(x)$.

52. $y = mx + b$ **53.** $ax + by = c$ **54.** $y - y_1 = m(x - x_1)$

55. Graph the relation given by the points in the table. Then reflect each point across the line $y = x$ to see the graph of the inverse relation. If the equation of the relation is $f(x) = x^2$, verify algebraically that the equation of the inverse relation is $x = y^2$.

x	y
–3	9
–2	4
–1	1
0	0
1	1
2	4
3	9

56. Critical Thinking A linear function and its inverse have the same slope. What must be true of these functions?

Graph each function and its inverse.

57. $y = 3$ **58.** $y = x^3$ **59.** $y = 2^x$

4-3 Logarithmic Functions

CC.9-12.F.BF.5 (+) Understand the inverse relationship between exponents and logarithms and use this relationship to solve problems .... *Also* **CC.9-12.F.IF.7e*, CC.9-12.A.CED.2, CC.9-12.A.CED.3**

Objectives

Write equivalent forms for exponential and logarithmic functions.

Write, evaluate, and graph logarithmic functions.

Vocabulary

logarithm
common logarithm
logarithmic function

Why learn this?

A logarithmic scale is used to measure the acidity, or pH, of water. (See Example 5.)

How many times would you have to double \$1 before you had \$8? You could use an exponential equation to model this situation. $1(2^x) = 8$. You may be able to solve this equation by using mental math if you know that $2^3 = 8$. So you would have to double the dollar 3 times to have \$8.

How many times would you have to double \$1 to have \$512? You could solve this problem if you could solve $2^x = 8$ by using an inverse operation that undoes raising a base to an exponent. This operation is called finding the logarithm. A **logarithm** is the exponent to which a specified base is raised to obtain a given value.

Reading Math

Read $\log_b a = x$, as "the log base b of a is x." Notice that the log is the exponent.

You can write an exponential equation as a logarithmic equation and vice versa.

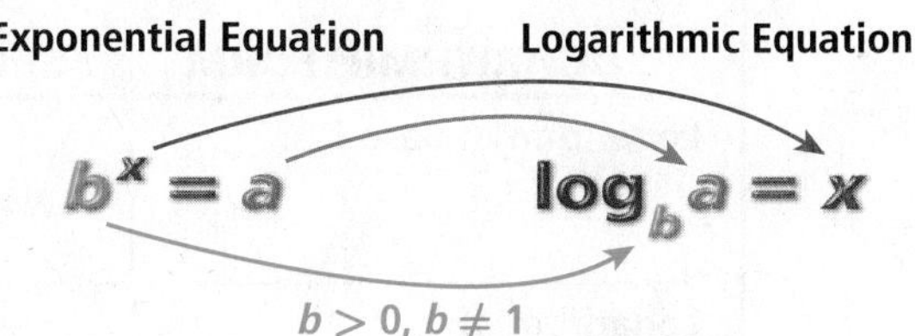

EXAMPLE 1 Converting from Exponential to Logarithmic Form

Write each exponential equation in logarithmic form.

	Exponential Equation	Logarithmic Form	
a.	$2^6 = 64$	$\log_2 64 = 6$	*The base of the exponent becomes the base of the logarithm.*
b.	$4^1 = 4$	$\log_4 4 = 1$	*The exponent is the logarithm.*
c.	$5^0 = 1$	$\log_5 1 = 0$	*Any nonzero base to the 0 power is 1.*
d.	$5^{-2} = 0.04$	$\log_5 0.04 = -2$	*An exponent (or log) can be negative.*
e.	$3^x = 81$	$\log_3 81 = x$	*The log (and the exponent) can be a variable.*

Write each exponential equation in logarithmic form.

1a. $9^2 = 81$ **1b.** $3^3 = 27$ **1c.** $x^0 = 1(x \neq 0)$

EXAMPLE 2 Converting from Logarithmic to Exponential Form

Write each logarithmic equation in exponential form.

	Logarithmic Equation	Exponential Form	
a.	$\log_{10} 100 = 2$	$10^2 = 100$	*The base of the logarithm becomes the base of the power.*
b.	$\log_7 49 = 2$	$7^2 = 49$	*The logarithm is the exponent.*
c.	$\log_8 0.125 = -1$	$8^{-1} = 0.125$	*A logarithm can be a negative number.*
d.	$\log_5 5 = 1$	$5^1 = 5$	
e.	$\log_{12} 1 = 0$	$12^0 = 1$	

Write each logarithmic equation in exponential form.

2a. $\log_{10} 10 = 1$ **2b.** $\log_{12} 144 = 2$ **2c.** $\log_{\frac{1}{2}} 8 = -3$

A logarithm is an exponent, so the rules for exponents also apply to logarithms. You may have noticed the following properties in the last example.

Special Properties of Logarithms

For any base b such that $b > 0$ and $b \neq 1$,

LOGARITHMIC FORM	EXPONENTIAL FORM	EXAMPLE
Logarithm of Base b $\log_b b = 1$	$b^1 = b$	$\log_{10} 10 = 1$ $10^1 = 10$
Logarithm of 1 $\log_b 1 = 0$	$b^0 = 1$	$\log_{10} 1 = 0$ $10^0 = 1$

A logarithm with base 10 is called a **common logarithm**. If no base is written for a logarithm, the base is assumed to be 10. For example, $\log 5 = \log_{10} 5$.

You can use mental math to evaluate some logarithms.

EXAMPLE 3 Evaluating Logarithms by Using Mental Math

Evaluate by using mental math.

A $\log 1000$

$10^? = 1000$ *The log is the exponent.*

$10^3 = 1000$ *Think: What power of the base is the value?*

$\log 1000 = 3$

B $\log_4 \frac{1}{4}$

$4^? = \frac{1}{4}$

$4^{-1} = \frac{1}{4}$

$\log_4 \frac{1}{4} = -1$

CHECK IT OUT! **Evaluate by using mental math.**

3a. $\log 0.00001$ **3b.** $\log_{25} 0.04$

Because logarithms are the inverses of exponents, the inverse of an exponential function, such as $y = 2^x$, is a **logarithmic function**, such as $y = \log_2 x$.

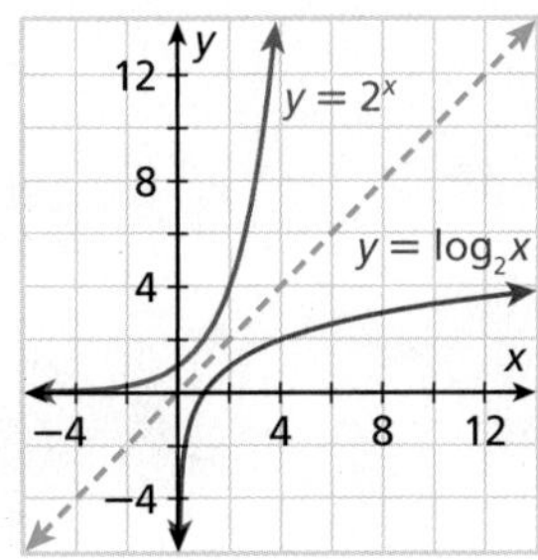

You may notice that the domain and range of each function are switched.

The domain of $y = 2^x$ is all real numbers ($\mathbb{R}$), and the range is $\{y \mid y > 0\}$. The domain of $y = \log_2 x$ is $\{x \mid x > 0\}$, and the range is all real numbers ($\mathbb{R}$).

EXAMPLE 4 Graphing Logarithmic Functions

Use the given *x*-values to graph each function. Then graph its inverse. Describe the domain and range of the inverse function.

A $f(x) = 3^x$; $x = -2, -1, 0, 1,$ and 2

Graph $f(x) = 3^x$ by using a table of values.

x	-2	-1	0	1	2
$f(x) = 3^x$	$\frac{1}{9}$	$\frac{1}{3}$	1	3	9

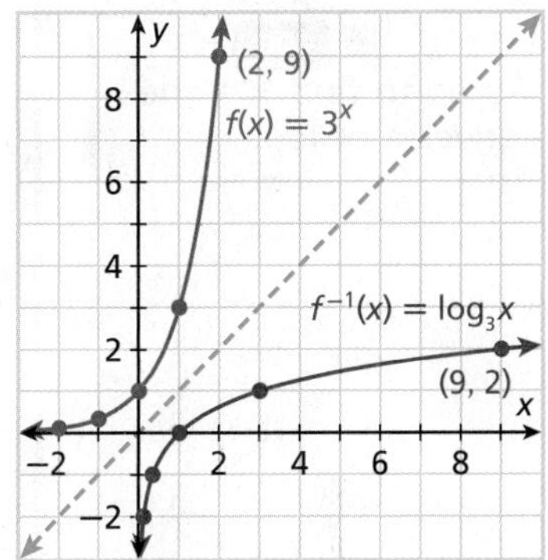

To graph the inverse, $f^{-1}(x) = \log_3 x$, reverse each ordered pair.

x	$\frac{1}{9}$	$\frac{1}{3}$	1	3	9
$f^{-1}(x) = \log_3 x$	-2	-1	0	1	2

The domain of $f^{-1}(x)$ is $\{x \mid x > 0\}$, and the range is $\mathbb{R}$.

B $f(x) = 0.8^x$; $x = -3, 0, 1, 4,$ and 7

Graph $f(x) = 0.8^x$ by using a table of values. Round the output values to the nearest tenth, if necessary.

x	-3	0	1	4	7
$f(x) = 0.8^x$	2	1	0.8	0.4	0.2

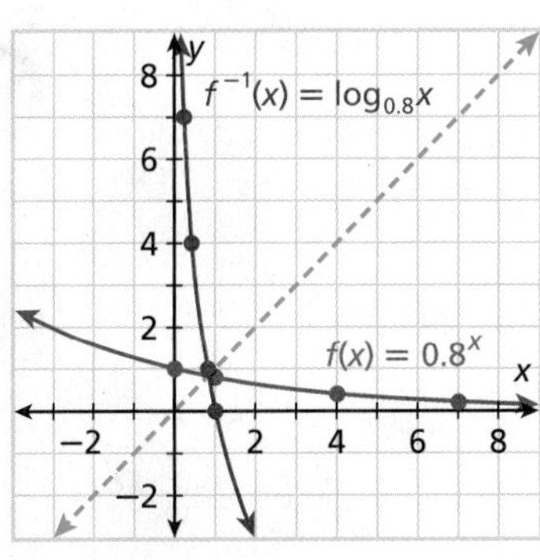

To graph $f^{-1}(x) = \log_{0.8} x$, reverse each ordered pair.

x	2	1	0.8	0.4	0.2
$f^{-1}(x) = \log_{0.8} x$	-3	0	1	4	7

The domain of $f^{-1}(x)$ is $\{x \mid x > 0\}$, and the range is $\mathbb{R}$.

4. Use $x = -2, -1, 1, 2,$ and 3 to graph $f(x) = \left(\frac{3}{4}\right)^x$. Then graph its inverse. Describe the domain and range of the inverse function.

EXAMPLE 5 Environmental Application

Chemists regularly test rain samples to determine the rain's acidity, or concentration of hydrogen ions (H^+). Acidity is measured in pH, as given by the function $pH = -\log[H^+]$, where $[H^+]$ represents the hydrogen ion concentration in moles per liter.

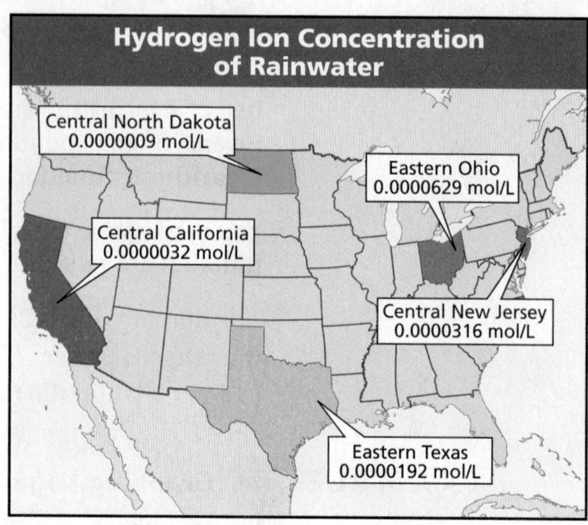

Find the pH of rainwater from each location.

Helpful Hint

The LOG key is used to evaluate logarithms in base 10. 2nd LOG (10^x) is used to find 10^x, the inverse of log.

A **Central New Jersey**

The hydrogen ion concentration is 0.0000316 moles per liter.

$pH = -\log[H^+]$

$pH = -\log(0.0000316)$ *Substitute the known values in the function.*

Use a calculator to find the value of the logarithm in base 10. Press the LOG key.

The rainwater has a pH of about 4.5.

B **Central North Dakota**

The hydrogen ion concentration is 0.0000009 moles per liter.

$pH = -\log[H^+]$

$pH = -\log(0.0000009)$ *Substitute the known values in the function.*

Use a calculator to find the value of the logarithm in base 10. Press the LOG key.

The rainwater has a pH of about 6.0.

5. What is the pH of iced tea with a hydrogen ion concentration of 0.000158 moles per liter?

THINK AND DISCUSS

1. Contrast exponential functions with logarithmic functions.
2. Explain whether $\log_b a$ is the same as $\log_a b$. Support your answer.

3. **GET ORGANIZED** Copy and complete the graphic organizer. Use your own words to explain a logarithmic function.

Definition	Characteristics
Logarithmic Function	
Examples	Nonexamples

4-3 Exercises

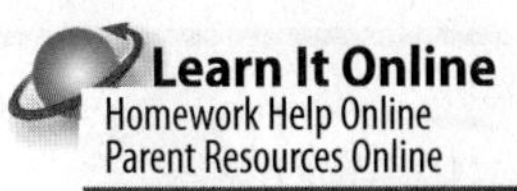

GUIDED PRACTICE

1. **Vocabulary** In the exponential equation $a^x = b$, the logarithm is ___?___. (a, x, or b)

SEE EXAMPLE 1

Write each exponential equation in logarithmic form.

2. $2.4^0 = 1$
3. $4^{1.5} = 8$
4. $10^{-2} = 0.01$
5. $3^x = 243$

SEE EXAMPLE 2

Write each logarithmic equation in exponential form.

6. $\log_4 0.0625 = -2$
7. $\log_x (-16) = 3$
8. $\log_{0.9} 0.81 = 2$
9. $\log_6 x = 3$

SEE EXAMPLE 3

Evaluate by using mental math.

10. $\log_7 343$
11. $\log_3 \left(\frac{1}{9}\right)$
12. $\log_{0.5} 0.25$
13. $\log_{1.2} 1.44$

SEE EXAMPLE 4

Use the given x-values to graph each function. Then graph its inverse. Describe the domain and range of each function.

14. $f(x) = 5^x$; $x = -2, -1, 0, 1, 1.5$
15. $f(x) = 0.5^x$; $x = -2, -1, 0, 1, 2$

SEE EXAMPLE 5

16. **Chemistry** The acid potential of a solution is given by pOH, where $\text{pOH} = -\log\left[\text{OH}^-\right]$, and OH^- represents the concentration of hydroxide ions in moles per liter. The water in one sample contains a hydroxide ion concentration of 0.000000004. What is the pOH of the water?

PRACTICE AND PROBLEM SOLVING

Independent Practice	
For Exercises	See Example
17–20	1
21–24	2
25–28	3
29–30	4
31	5

Extra Practice

See Extra Practice for more Skills Practice and Applications Practice exercises.

Write each exponential equation in logarithmic form.

17. $x^{2.5} = 32$
18. $6^x = 216$
19. $1.2^0 = 1$
20. $4^{-1} = 0.25$

Write each logarithmic equation in exponential form.

21. $\log_5 625 = 4$
22. $\log_2 x = 6$
23. $\log_{4.5} 1 = 0$
24. $\log_\pi \pi = 1$

Evaluate by using mental math.

25. $\log_2 1$
26. $\log 0.001$
27. $\log_4 64$
28. $\log_{0.1} 100$

Use the given x-values to graph each function. Then graph its inverse. Describe the domain and range of each function.

29. $f(x) = \left(\frac{4}{5}\right)^x$; $x = -2, -1, 0, 1, 2, 3$
30. $f(x) = \left(\frac{4}{3}\right)^x$; $x = -2, -1, 0, 1, 2, 3$

31. **Gardening** The flower color of bigleaf hydrangeas is determined by the soil pH. A gardener growing blue hydrangeas believes that lime may be leaching out of a nearby sidewalk and increasing the pH of the soil. The gardener measures the hydrogen ion concentration and finds it to be 0.0000006 moles per liter. Is the soil still good for growing blue flowers? Explain.

5 < pH < 5.5

5.5 < pH < 6

6 < pH < 6.5

32. For a certain credit card, given a starting balance of P and an ending balance of A, the function $n = \frac{\log A - \log P}{\log(1.0175)}$ gives the number of months that have passed, assuming that there were no payments or additional purchases during that time.
   a. You started with a debt of \$1000 and now owe \$1210.26. For how many months has the debt been building? Use a calculator.
   b. How many additional months will it take until the debt exceeds \$1420?
   c. What do you notice from the results of parts **a** and **b**?

33. **Critical Thinking** If $\log_a b = 0$, what is the value of b? Explain.

34. **Sound** The loudness of sound is measured on a logarithmic scale according to the formula $L = 10\log\left(\frac{I}{I_0}\right)$, where L is the loudness of sound in decibels (dB), I is the intensity of sound, and I_0 is the intensity of the softest audible sound.
   a. Find the loudness in decibels of each sound listed in the table.
   b. The sound at a rock concert is found to have a loudness of 110 decibels. Where should this sound be placed in the table in order to keep the sound intensities in order from least to greatest?
   c. **What if...?** A decibel is $\frac{1}{10}$ of a *bel*. Is a jet plane louder than a sound that measures 20 *bels*? Explain.

Sound	Intensity
Jet takeoff	$10^{15}I_0$
Jackhammer	$10^{12}I_0$
Hair dryer	$10^{7}I_0$
Whisper	$10^{3}I_0$
Leaves rustling	$10^{2}I_0$
Softest audible sound	I_0

35. **Critical Thinking** If n is an integer, and 10^n is written in expanded form, can you find $\log 10^n$ by counting the number of zeros in 10^n? Support your answer with an example or counterexample.

36. **Estimation** Given that $\log 100 = 2$ and $\log 1000 = 3$, estimate the values of log 200 and log 500.

37. **Food** The hydrogen ion concentrations of three juice samples are given. Identify the type of juice in each sample.
   a. 0.00014 moles per liter
   b. 0.0081 moles per liter
   c. 0.00074 moles per liter

Juice	pH Range
Lemon	2.0–2.6
Grapefruit	2.9–3.2
Orange	3.3–4.1
Tomato	4.1–4.6

38. **Write About It** Explain why $\log_0 3$ and $\log_1 3$ do not exist.

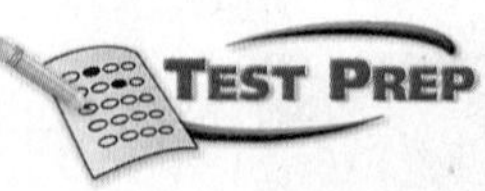

39. The graph of which function is shown?
   Ⓐ $f(x) = \log x$
   Ⓑ $f(x) = \log_2 x$
   Ⓒ $f(x) = \log_4 x$
   Ⓓ $f(x) = 2^x$

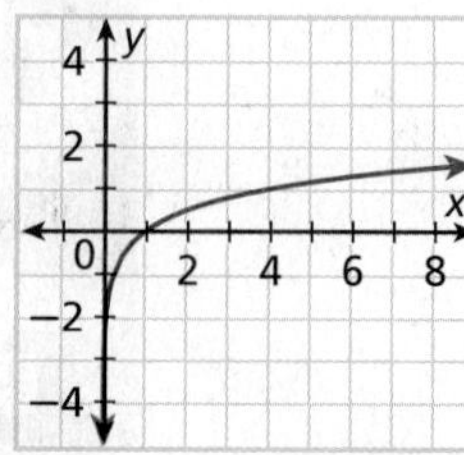

40. Which logarithmic equation is equivalent to $2^7 = 128$?

Ⓕ $\log_7 2 = 128$ Ⓗ $\log_2 7 = 128$

Ⓖ $\log_2 128 = 7$ Ⓙ $\log_7 128 = 2$

41. Which is the best estimate of $\log 50$?

Ⓐ 1.7 Ⓑ 2.5 Ⓒ 5 Ⓓ 10

42. Which graph is the best representation of $f(x) = \log_{0.5} x$?

Ⓕ 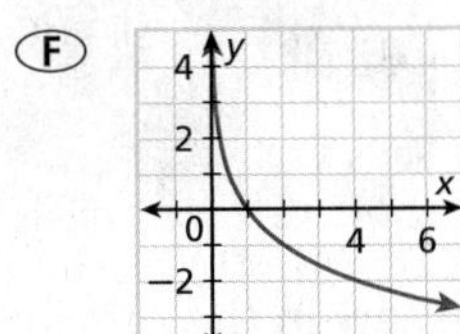

Ⓖ

Ⓗ 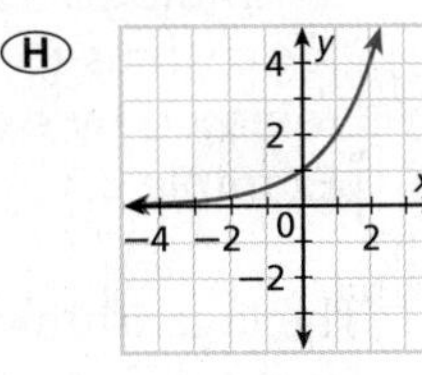

Ⓙ 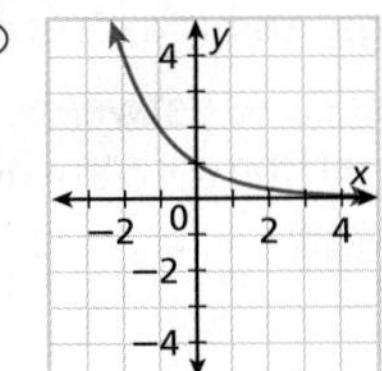

43. Gridded Response Evaluate $\log_2 64$.

CHALLENGE AND EXTEND

44. Graph $\log_7 x$ and $\log_{0.7} x$. Describe the difference between the two functions in terms of their graphs.

45. Evaluate $\log_3 9$, $\log_3 27$, and $\log_3 243$. Make a statement about the relationship between the three logarithms. Generalize the result by using variables.

46. Prove that $\log_7 7^{2x+1} = 2x + 1$, giving a reason for each step.

47. Music Musical scales are logarithmic. One scale uses a pitch standard called "scientific pitch." In this scale, the frequency of each C note, in vibrations per second, or Hz, can be expressed as a power of 2, as shown.

a. Express the frequency of the note C_7 in exponential form and in logarithmic form.

b. If the frequency of one note C is 32 vibrations per second, how many octaves higher or lower than middle C is this note? Explain by using logarithms.

4-4 Properties of Logarithms

CC.9-12.A.CED.2 Create equations in two or more variables to represent relationships between quantities; graph equations on coordinate axes with labels and scales. *Also* CC.9-12.A.CED.3, CC.9-12.F.IF.7*, CC.9-12.F.BF.4

Objectives

Use properties to simplify logarithmic expressions.

Translate between logarithms in any base.

Who uses this?

Seismologists use properties of logarithms to calculate the energy released by earthquakes. (See Example 6.)

The logarithmic function for pH that you saw in the previous lesson, $\text{pH} = -\log[\text{H}^+]$, can also be expressed in exponential form, as $10^{-\text{pH}} = [\text{H}^+]$. Because logarithms are exponents, you can derive the properties of logarithms from the properties of exponents.

Remember that to *multiply* powers with the same base, you *add* exponents.

$$b^m b^n = b^{m+n}$$

Product Property of Logarithms

For any positive numbers m, n, and b $(b \neq 1)$,

WORDS	NUMBERS	ALGEBRA
The logarithm of a product is equal to the sum of the logarithms of its factors.	$\log_3 1000 = \log_3(10 \cdot 100)$ $= \log_3 10 + \log_3 100$	$\log_b mn = \log_b m + \log_b n$

Helpful Hint

Think:
$\log j + \log a + \log m = \log jam$

The property above can be used in reverse to write a sum of logarithms (exponents) as a single logarithm, which can often be simplified.

EXAMPLE 1 Adding Logarithms

Express as a single logarithm. Simplify, if possible.

A $\log_4 2 + \log_4 32$

$\log_4 (2 \cdot 32)$ — *To add the logarithms, multiply the numbers.*

$\log_4 64$ — *Simplify.*

3 — *Think:* $4^? = 64$

Express as a single logarithm. Simplify, if possible.

1a. $\log_5 625 + \log_5 25$ **1b.** $\log_{\frac{1}{3}} 27 + \log_{\frac{1}{3}} \frac{1}{9}$

Remember that to *divide* powers with the same base, you *subtract* exponents.

$$\frac{b^m}{b^n} = b^{m-n}$$

Because logarithms are exponents, subtracting logarithms with the same base is the same as finding the logarithm of the quotient with that base.

Quotient Property of Logarithms

For any positive numbers m, n, and $b\ (b \neq 1)$,

WORDS	NUMBERS	ALGEBRA
The logarithm of a quotient is the logarithm of the dividend minus the logarithm of the divisor.	$\log_5\left(\frac{16}{2}\right) = \log_5 16 - \log_5 2$	$\log_b \frac{m}{n} = \log_b m - \log_b n$

Caution!

Just as a^5b^3 cannot be simplified, logarithms must have the *same* base to be simplified.

The property above can also be used in reverse.

EXAMPLE 2 **Subtracting Logarithms**

Express $\log_2 32 - \log_2 4$ as a single logarithm. Simplify, if possible.

$\log_2 32 - \log_2 4$

$\log_2 (32 \div 4)$ — *To subtract the logarithms, divide the numbers.*

$\log_2 8$ — *Simplify.*

3 — *Think: $2^? = 8$*

2. Express $\log_7 49 - \log_7 7$ as a single logarithm. Simplify, if possible.

Because you can multiply logarithms, you can also take powers of logarithms.

Power Property of Logarithms

For any real number p and positive numbers a and $b\ (b \neq 1)$,

WORDS	NUMBERS	ALGEBRA
The logarithm of a power is the product of the exponent and the logarithm of the base.	$\log 10^3$ $\log (10 \cdot 10 \cdot 10)$ $\log 10 + \log 10 + \log 10$ $3 \log 10$	$\log_b a^p = p \log_b a$

EXAMPLE 3 **Simplifying Logarithms with Exponents**

Express as a product. Simplify, if possible.

A $\log_3 81^2$

$2 \log_3 81$

$2(4) = 8$ — *Because $3^4 = 81$, $\log_3 81 = 4$.*

B $\log_5 \left(\frac{1}{5}\right)^3$

$3 \log_5 \frac{1}{5}$

$3(-1) = -3$ — *$5^{-1} = \frac{1}{5}$*

Express as a product. Simplify, if possible.

3a. $\log 10^4$ **3b.** $\log_5 25^2$ **3c.** $\log_2 \left(\frac{1}{2}\right)^5$

Exponential and logarithmic operations undo each other since they are inverse operations.

Inverse Properties of Logarithms and Exponents

For any base b such that $b > 0$ and $b \neq 1$,

ALGEBRA	EXAMPLE
$\log_b b^x = x$	$\log_{10} 10^7 = 7$
$b^{\log_b x} = x$	$10^{\log_{10} 2} = 2$

EXAMPLE 4 Recognizing Inverses

Simplify each expression.

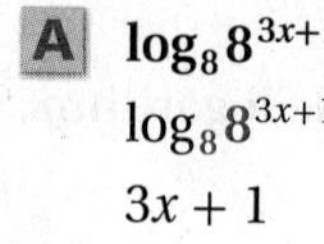

A $\log_8 8^{3x+1}$

$\log_8 8^{3x+1}$

$3x + 1$

B $\log_5 125$

$\log_5 (5 \cdot 5 \cdot 5)$

$\log_5 5^3$

3

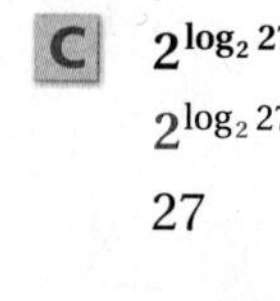

C $2^{\log_2 27}$

$2^{\log_2 27}$

27

CHECK IT OUT! **4a.** Simplify $\log 10^{0.9}$. **4b.** Simplify $2^{\log_2 (8x)}$.

Most calculators calculate logarithms only in base 10 or base e. You can change a logarithm in one base to a logarithm in another base with the following formula.

Change of Base Formula

For $a > 0$ and $a \neq 1$ and any base b such that $b > 0$ and $b \neq 1$,

ALGEBRA	EXAMPLE
$\log_b x = \dfrac{\log_a x}{\log_a b}$	$\log_4 8 = \dfrac{\log_2 8}{\log_2 4}$

EXAMPLE 5 Changing the Base of a Logarithm

Evaluate $\log_4 8$.

Method 1 Change to base 10.

$$\log_4 8 = \frac{\log 8}{\log 4}$$

$$\approx \frac{0.9030}{0.602} \quad \textit{Use a calculator.}$$

$$= 1.5 \quad \textit{Divide.}$$

Method 2 Change to base 2, because both 4 and 8 are powers of 2.

$$\log_4 8 = \frac{\log_2 8}{\log_2 4} = \frac{3}{2}$$

$$= 1.5$$

CHECK IT OUT! **5a.** Evaluate $\log_9 27$. **5b.** Evaluate $\log_8 16$.

Logarithmic scales are useful for measuring quantities that have a very wide range of values, such as the intensity (loudness) of a sound or the energy released by an earthquake.

EXAMPLE 6 Geology Application

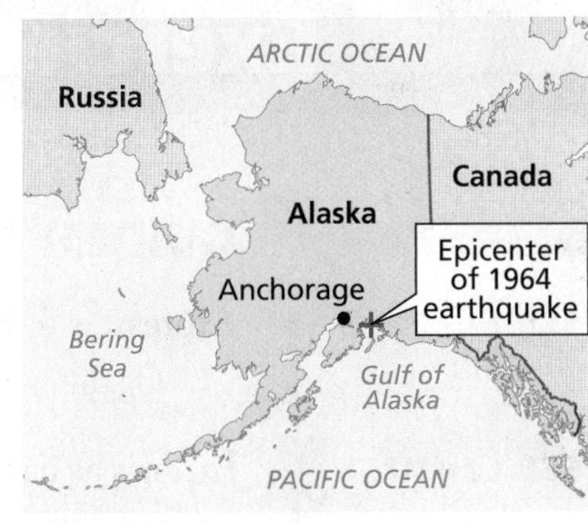

Seismologists use the Richter scale to express the energy, or magnitude, of an earthquake. The Richter magnitude of an earthquake, M, is related to the energy released in ergs E shown by the formula $M = \frac{2}{3}\log\left(\frac{E}{10^{11.8}}\right)$.

In 1964, an earthquake centered at Prince William Sound, Alaska, registered a magnitude of 9.2 on the Richter scale. Find the energy released by the earthquake.

Helpful Hint

The Richter scale is logarithmic, so an increase of 1 corresponds to a release of 10 times as much energy.

$9.2 = \frac{2}{3}\log\left(\frac{E}{10^{11.8}}\right)$	*Substitute 9.2 for M.*
$\left(\frac{3}{2}\right)9.2 = \log\left(\frac{E}{10^{11.8}}\right)$	*Multiply both sides by $\frac{3}{2}$.*
$13.8 = \log\left(\frac{E}{10^{11.8}}\right)$	*Simplify.*
$13.8 = \log E - \log 10^{11.8}$	*Apply the Quotient Property of Logarithms.*
$13.8 = \log E - 11.8$	*Apply the Inverse Properties of Logarithms and Exponents.*
$25.6 = \log E$	
$10^{25.6} = E$	*Given the definition of a logarithm, the logarithm is the exponent.*
$3.98 \times 10^{25} = E$	*Use a calculator to evaluate.*

The energy released by an earthquake with a magnitude of 9.2 is 3.98×10^{25} ergs.

6. How many times as much energy is released by an earthquake with a magnitude of 9.2 than by an earthquake with a magnitude of 8?

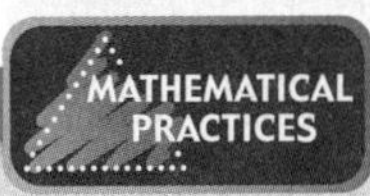

THINK AND DISCUSS

1. Explain how to graph $y = \log_5 x$ on a calculator.
2. Tell how you could find $10^{25.6}$ in Example 6 by applying a law of exponents.
3. Describe what happens when you use the change-of-base formula, $\log_b x = \frac{\log_a x}{\log_a b}$, when $x = a$.

4. **GET ORGANIZED** Copy and complete the graphic organizer. Use your own words to show related properties of exponents and logarithms.

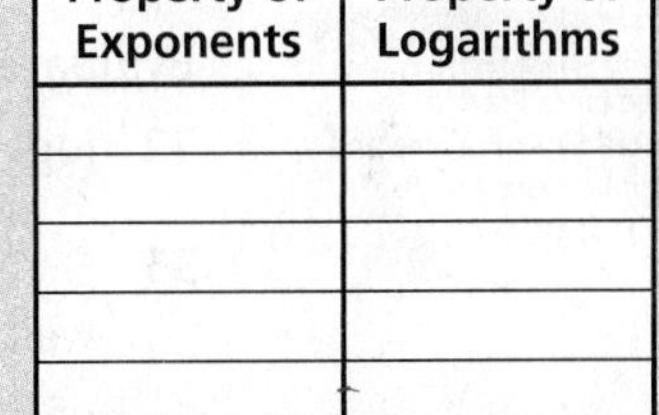

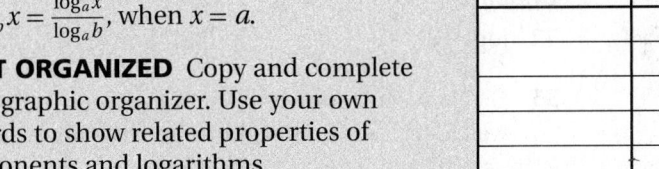

Property of Exponents	Property of Logarithms

4-4 Exercises

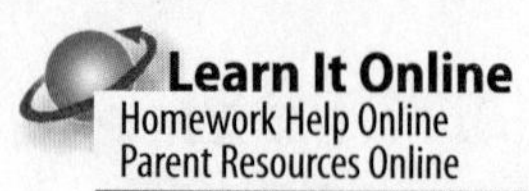

GUIDED PRACTICE

SEE EXAMPLE 1

Express as a single logarithm. Simplify, if possible.

1. $\log_5 50 + \log_5 62.5$
2. $\log 100 + \log 1000$
3. $\log_3 3 + \log_3 27$

SEE EXAMPLE 2

Express as a single logarithm. Simplify, if possible.

4. $\log_4 320 - \log_4 5$
5. $\log 5.4 - \log 0.054$
6. $\log_6 496.8 - \log_6 2.3$

SEE EXAMPLE 3

Simplify, if possible.

7. $\log_8 8^2$
8. $\log_3 3^5$
9. $\log_7 49^3$
10. $\log_{\frac{1}{2}}(0.25)^4$

SEE EXAMPLE 4

11. $\log_2 2^{\frac{x}{2}+5}$
12. $2.5^{\log_{2.5} 19}$
13. $\log_4 1024$
14. $\log_2(0.5)^4$

SEE EXAMPLE 5

Evaluate.

15. $\log_9\left(\frac{1}{27}\right)$
16. $\log_8 32$
17. $\log_5 10$
18. $\log_2 27$

SEE EXAMPLE 6

19. **Geology** The Richter magnitude M of an earthquake is related to the energy released in ergs E shown by the formula $M = \frac{2}{3}\log\left(\frac{E}{10^{11.8}}\right)$. How many times as much energy was released by the 1811 New Madrid, Missouri, earthquake than by the Fort Tejon, California, earthquake?

Largest Earthquakes in Continental U.S.

Location	Year	*M*
New Madrid, MO	1811	8.1
New Madrid, MO	1812	8.0
Fort Tejon, CA	1957	7.9
San Francisco, CA	1906	7.8
Imperial Valley, CA	1892	7.8

PRACTICE AND PROBLEM SOLVING

Independent Practice

For Exercises	See Example
20–22	1
23–25	2
26–28	3
29–31	4
32–34	5
35	6

Extra Practice

See Extra Practice for more Skills Practice and Applications Practice exercises.

Express as a single logarithm. Simplify, if possible.

20. $\log_8 4 + \log_8 16$
21. $\log 2 + \log 5$
22. $\log_{2.5} 3.125 + \log_{2.5} 5$
23. $\log 1000 - \log 100$
24. $\log_2 16 - \log_2 2$
25. $\log_{1.5} 6.75 - \log_{1.5} 2$

Simplify, if possible.

26. $\log_2 16^3$
27. $\log(100)^{0.1}$
28. $\log_5 125^{\frac{1}{3}}$
29. $\log_3 3^{7+x}$
30. $3^{\log_3 4.52}$
31. $\log_9 6561$

Evaluate.

32. $\log_{\frac{1}{2}} 16$
33. $\log_{25} 125$
34. $\log_4 9$

35. **Sound** After some complaints, it was found that the music from an outdoor concert was 5 decibels louder than the city's allowable level of 100 decibels. The loudness L of sound in decibels is given by $L = 10\log\left(\frac{I}{I_0}\right)$, where I is the intensity of sound and I_0 is the intensity of the softest audible sound. How many times more intense is the concert sound than the allowable level?

36. **Astronomy** The difference between the apparent magnitude (brightness) m of a star, and its absolute magnitude M is given by the formula $m - M = 5 \log \frac{d}{10}$, where d is the distance of the star from Earth, measured in parsecs.

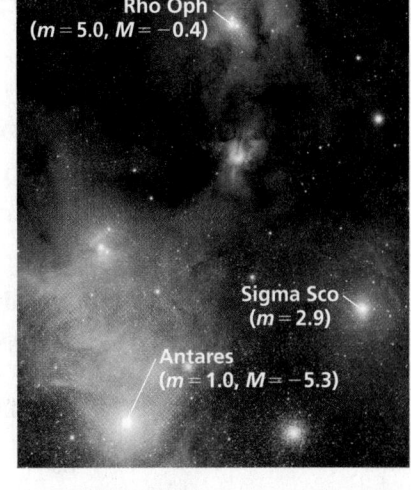

   a. Find the distance d of Antares from Earth.

   b. Sigma Sco is 225 parsecs from Earth. Find its absolute magnitude.

   c. How many times as great is the distance to Antares as the distance to Rho Oph?

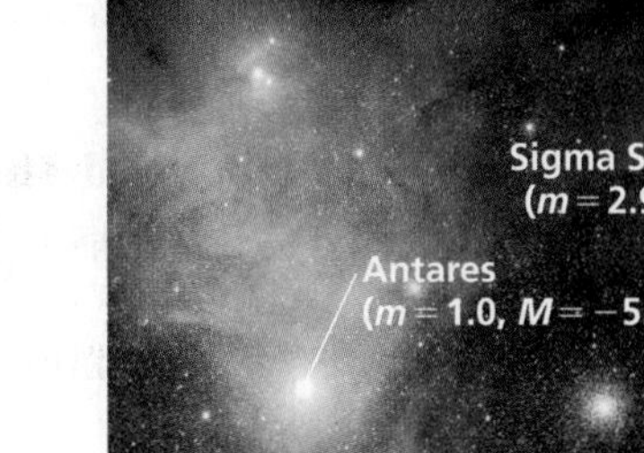

Write the equivalent logarithmic form for each equation.

37. $b^{m+n} = b^m b^n$

38. $b^{m-n} = \frac{b^m}{b^n}$

39. $(b^m)^n = b^{mn}$

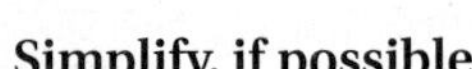

Math History

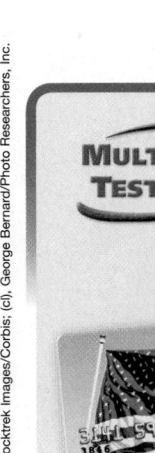

Scottish mathematician John Napier (1550–1617) invented logarithms and named them by joining the Greek words *logos* (ratio) and *arithmos* (number).

Simplify, if possible.

40. $\log_2 32 - \log_2 128$

41. $\log 0.1 + \log 1 + \log 10$

42. $2 - \log_{11} 121$

43. $\log_{\frac{1}{2}} 2 + \log_{\frac{1}{2}} 2^{\frac{1}{2}}$

44. $7^{\log_7 7} - \log_7 7^7$

45. $\frac{10^{\log 10}}{\log 10^{10}}$

46. **Critical Thinking** Use the properties of logarithms with the fact that $\log 2 \approx 0.301$ to evaluate.

   a. $\log 20$

   b. $\log 200$

   c. $\log 2000$

47. **Chemistry** Most swimming pool experts recommend a pH of between 7.0 and 7.6 for water in a swimming pool. Use $\text{pH} = -\log[H^+]$, and write an expression for the difference in hydrogen ion concentration over this pH range.

48. **Multi-Step** Suppose that the population of one endangered species decreases at a rate of 4% per year. In one habitat, the current population of the species is 143.

   a. Write an exponential function for the population by year.

   b. Write a logarithmic function for the time based upon population.

   c. Write the keystrokes necessary to enter the logarithmic function on a calculator.

   d. After how long will the population drop below 30, to the nearest year?

49. **Finance** A stock priced at \$40 increases at a rate of 8% per year. Write and evaluate a logarithmic expression for the number of years that it will take for the value of the stock to reach \$50. (*Hint:* Write the expression in exponential form first.)

MULTI-STEP TEST PREP

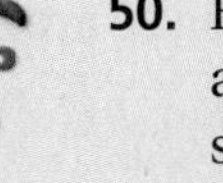

50. For a certain credit card with 19.2% annual interest compounded monthly, the total amount A that you owe after n months is given by $A = P(1.016)^n$, where P is the starting balance.

   a. You start with a balance of \$500. Write and solve a logarithmic expression for the number of months it will take for the debt to double.

   b. How many additional months will it take for the debt to double again?

   c. Does the amount of time that it takes the debt to double depend on the starting balance?

Graphing Calculator Use the change of base formula and a graphing calculator to graph.

51. $y = \log_3 x$ **52.** $y = 2\log_5 x$ **53.** $y = \dfrac{\log_{12} x}{3}$

54. Write About It Explain how to graph a logarithm in a base other than 10 on a calculator.

55. Critical Thinking Given $\log_{12} 20 \approx 1.2$ and $\log_{12} 33 \approx 1.4$, find each approximate value.

a. $\log_{12} 1.65$ **b.** $\log_{12} 660$ **c.** $\log_{12} 400$

56. Critical Thinking There is an interesting relationship between logarithms and scientific notation.

a. Find the logarithm of 2.5.

b. Find the logarithm of the mass of the *Titanic*. Compare it to your answer from part **a.**

c. Make a Conjecture A lion has a mass of 2.5×10^2 kg. Find the logarithm of this number. Use your answers and the answers to parts **a** and **b,** to explain how to find the base 10 logarithm of a number written in scientific notation.

d. Use your conjecture to find the logarithm of the mass of a dime. Does your conjecture hold for scientific notation with negative exponents?

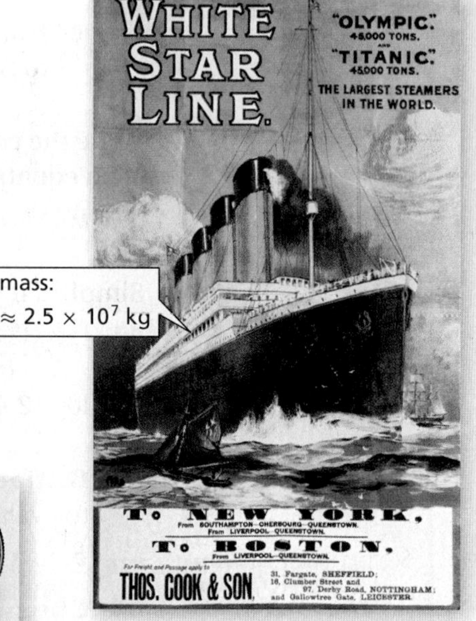

mass: $\approx 2.5 \times 10^7$ kg

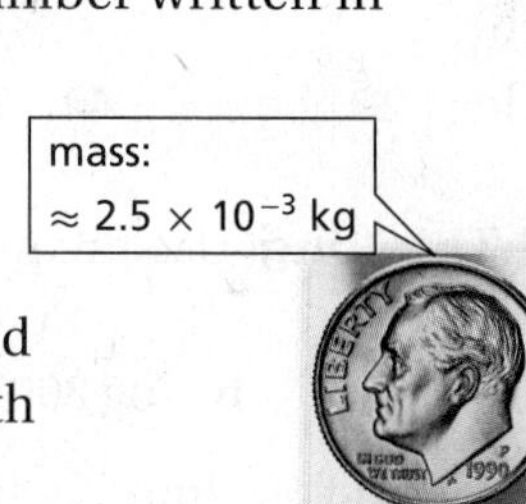

mass: $\approx 2.5 \times 10^{-3}$ kg

Assume $b > 0$ and $b \neq 1$. Tell whether each statement is sometimes, always, or never true.

57. A logarithm with base b can be changed to another rational-number base.

58. The logarithm with base 6 of 6 raised to an expression is equal to the expression.

59. Subtracting log base b of 1 from a number is just the number itself.

60. The base of a logarithm can be a negative number.

61. The logarithm of the square of a number is equal to twice the logarithm of the number.

62. Logarithms with different bases can be added without changing a base.

63. $\dfrac{\log_b 16}{\log_b 8}$ can be simplified.

64. A logarithm of a logarithm of a number is the number.

65. ////ERROR ANALYSIS//// Two simplifications of $\log 80 + \log 20$ are shown. Which of these is incorrect? Explain.

A

$$\begin{aligned} \log 80 + \log 20 &= \log(80 \cdot 20) \\ &= \log(1600) \\ &= \log(16 \cdot 10^2) \\ &= \log 16 + \log 10^2 \\ &= \log 16 + 2 \end{aligned}$$

B

$$\begin{aligned} \log 80 + \log 20 &= \log(80 + 20) \\ &= \log 100 \\ &= \log 10^2 \\ &= 2\log 10 \\ &= 2 \end{aligned}$$

66. Which statement is NOT true?

Ⓐ $\log 140 - \log 35 = \log 4$

Ⓑ $\dfrac{\log 140}{\log 35} = \log 4$

Ⓒ $\log 35 + \log 4 = \log 140$

Ⓓ $\log \dfrac{140}{35} = \log 4$

67. Simplify $\log_9 x^2 + \log_9 x$.

Ⓕ $\log_9 (x^2 + x)$ Ⓖ $\log_9 3x$ Ⓗ $3\log_9 x$ Ⓙ $3(x^2 + x)$

68. Which logarithmic expression is equal to $\log 6$?

Ⓐ $\log 3 + \log 2$ Ⓑ $\log 3 + \log 3$ Ⓒ $(\log 3)(\log 2)$ Ⓓ $(\log 3)(\log 3)$

CHALLENGE AND EXTEND

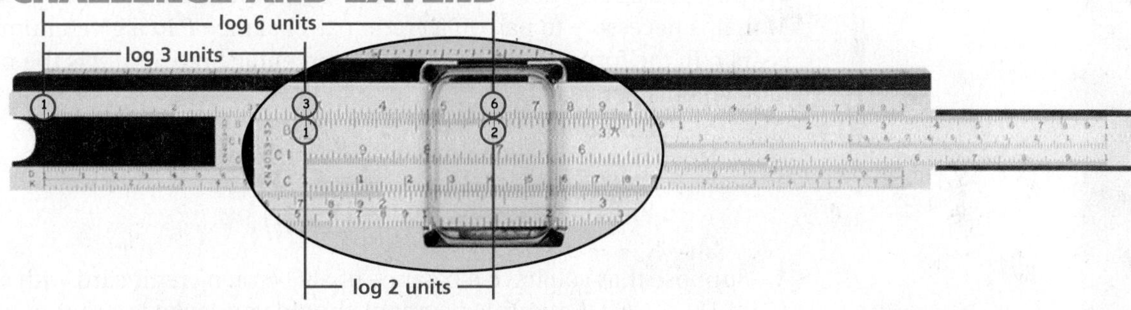

69. **Math History** The slide rule used two number lines that slid against each other. The scale on each was logarithmic, so the properties of logarithms could be applied to multiply and divide numbers.

a. Explain how the product of 2 and 3 is shown on the slide rule.

b. How does this show the product property of logarithms?

Find the domain of each function.

70. $f(x) = \log(x^2 - 4)$

71. $f(x) = \log x - \log(x - 1)$

72. $f(x) = \log\left(\dfrac{x}{x^2 - 1}\right)$

73. $f(x) = \log\left(\dfrac{1}{x}\right)^2$

74. $f(x) = -\sqrt{\log(x + 1)}$

75. $f(x) = \sqrt{-2\log(-x)}$

76. Prove: $\log_b a^p = p\log_b a$.

77. Simplify $\log_9 3^{2x}$.

Solve.

78. $\log_x 25 = 2$

79. $\log_x(-8) = 3$

80. $0 = \log_x 1$

Sam Dudgeon/HMH

CHAPTER 4

MULTI-STEP TEST PREP

SECTION 4A

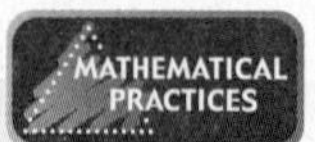

Make sense of problems and persevere in solving them

Exponential Functions and Logarithms

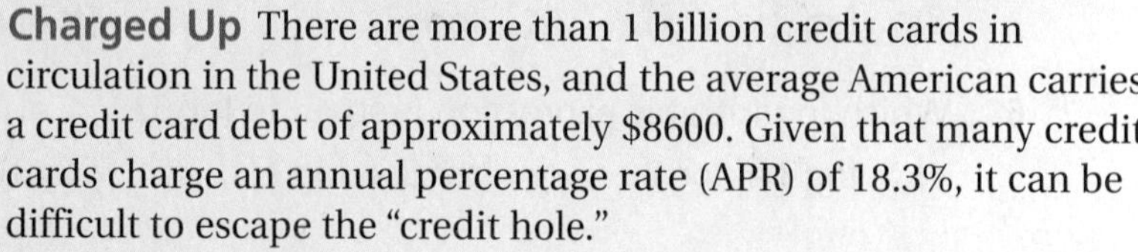

Charged Up There are more than 1 billion credit cards in circulation in the United States, and the average American carries a credit card debt of approximately \$8600. Given that many credit cards charge an annual percentage rate (APR) of 18.3%, it can be difficult to escape the "credit hole."

The formula shown below can be used to compute the monthly payment M that is necessary to pay off a credit card balance P in a given number of years t. In the formula, r is the annual percentage rate and n is the number of payments per year.

$$M = \frac{P\left(\frac{r}{n}\right)}{1 - \left(1 + \frac{r}{n}\right)^{-nt}}$$

1. Suppose that you have a balance of \$8600 on a credit card with an APR of 18.3%. What monthly payment should you make in order to pay off the debt in exactly five years?

2. How much money do you end up paying altogether over the five years?

In order to calculate the number of years necessary for a given payment schedule, the formula can be written as shown.

$$t = \frac{\log\left(1 - \frac{Pr}{Mn}\right)}{-n\log\left(1 + \frac{r}{n}\right)}$$

3. If you can afford only a monthly payment of \$160, how long will it take to pay off the credit card debt?

4. Suppose you can afford a monthly payment of \$130. Will you be able to pay off the debt? If so, how long will it take? If not, why not?

5. What is the minimum monthly payment that will work toward paying off the debt?

"I didn't have time to mow the lawn, so I used your credit card to have it carpeted."

CHAPTER 4

SECTION 4A

Quiz for Lesson 4-1 Through 4-4

4-1 Exponential Functions, Growth, and Decay

Tell whether the function shows growth or decay. Then graph.

1. $f(x) = \left(\frac{1}{4}\right)^x$
2. $f(x) = \frac{1}{5}(0.2)^x$
3. $f(x) = 14(1.4^x)$
4. $f(x) = 6.4\left(1\frac{3}{8}\right)^x$
5. Suppose that the number of bacteria in a culture was 1000 on Monday and the number has been increasing at a rate of 50% per day since then.
   a. Write a function representing the growth of the culture per day.
   b. Graph the function, and use the graph to predict the number of bacteria in the culture the following Monday.

4-2 Inverses of Relations and Functions

Graph each relation. Then graph its inverse.

6.

x	−1	0	1	2	3
y	0	4	8	12	16

7.

x	0	1	2	3	4
y	−1	$-\frac{1}{3}$	$\frac{1}{3}$	1	$1\frac{2}{3}$

Graph each function. Then write and graph the inverse.

8. $f(x) = x + 2.1$
9. $f(x) = \frac{3}{4} - x$
10. $f(x) = 5x + 4$
11. $f(x) = 0.4\left(\frac{x}{2} + 1.5\right)$
12. Rebekah's computer repair bill includes $210 for parts and $55 per hour for labor. Her bill can be expressed as a function of hours x by $f(x) = 210 + 55x$. Find the inverse function. Use it to find the number of hours of labor if her bill was $402.50.

4-3 Logarithmic Functions

Write the exponential equation in logarithmic form.

13. $3^2 = 9$
14. $17.6^0 = 1$
15. $2^{-2} = 0.25$
16. $0.5^x = 0.0625$

Write the logarithmic equation in exponential form.

17. $\log_4 64 = 3$
18. $\log_{\frac{1}{5}} 25 = -2$
19. $\log_{0.99} 1 = 0$
20. $\log_e x = 5$
21. Use the given x-values to graph $f(x) = \left(\frac{5}{6}\right)^x$; $x = -1, 0, 1, 2, 3$. Then graph the inverse function.

4-4 Properties of Logarithms

Express as a single logarithm. Simplify, if possible.

22. $\log_3 81 + \log_3 9$
23. $\log_{\frac{1}{5}} 25 + \log_{\frac{1}{5}} 5$
24. $\log_{1.2} 2.16 - \log_{1.2} 1.5$

Simplify each expression.

25. $\log_4 256^2$
26. $\log_7 343$
27. $17^{\log_{17} 0.73}$

Evaluate.

28. $\log_{27} 243$
29. $\log_{10} 0.01$
30. $\log_5 625$

4-5 Exponential and Logarithmic Equations and Inequalities

CC.9-12.F.LE.4 For exponential models, express as a logarithm the solution to $ab^{ct} = d$ ... evaluate the logarithm using technology. *Also* CC.9-12.A.CED.1, CC.9-12.A.REI.11

Objectives

Solve exponential and logarithmic equations and inequalities.

Solve problems involving exponential and logarithmic equations.

Vocabulary

exponential equation
logarithmic equation

Who uses this?

Exponential scales are used to measure light in photography. (See Exercise 40.)

An **exponential equation** is an equation containing one or more expressions that have a variable as an exponent. To solve exponential equations:

- Try writing them so that the bases are all the same. If $b^x = b^y$, then $x = y$ $(b \neq 0, b \neq 1)$.
- Take the logarithm of both sides. If $a = b$, then $\log a = \log b$ $(a > 0, b > 0)$.

EXAMPLE 1 Solving Exponential Equations

Solve and check.

A $8^x = 2^{x+6}$

$(2^3)^x = 2^{x+6}$ — *Rewrite each side with the same base; 8 is a power of 2.*

$2^{3x} = 2^{x+6}$ — *To raise a power to a power, multiply exponents.*

$3x = x + 6$ — *Bases are the same, so the exponents must be equal.*

$x = 3$ — *Solve for x.*

Check

8^x	2^{x+6}
8^3	2^{3+6}
8^3	2^9
512	512 ✔

The solution is $x = 3$.

B $5^{x-2} = 200$

$\log 5^{x-2} = \log 200$ — *200 is not a power of 5, so take the log of both sides.*

$(x-2)\log 5 = \log 200$ — *Apply the Power Property of Logarithms.*

$x - 2 = \dfrac{\log 200}{\log 5}$ — *Divide both sides by log 5.*

$x = 2 + \dfrac{\log 200}{\log 5} \approx 5.292$

Check Use a calculator.

```
5^(5.292-2)
       199.9904485
```

The solution is $x \approx 5.292$.

Helpful Hint

When you use a rounded number in a check, the result will not be exact, but it should be reasonable.

Solve and check.

1a. $3^{2x} = 27$ **1b.** $7^{-x} = 21$ **1c.** $2^{3x} = 15$

Philippe Petit-Mars/CORBIS

EXAMPLE 2 Money Application

You can choose a prize of either a \$20,000 car or one penny on the first day, double that (2 cents) on the second day, and so on for a month. On what day would you receive more than the value of the car?

\$20,000 is 2,000,000 cents. On day 1, you would receive 1 cent, or 2^0 cents. On day 2, you would receive 2 cents, or 2^1 cents, and so on. So, on day n you would receive 2^{n-1} cents.

Solve $2^{n-1} > 2 \times 10^6$. *Write 2,000,000 in scientific notation.*

$\log 2^{n-1} > \log\left(2 \times 10^6\right)$ *Take the log of both sides.*

$(n-1)\log 2 > \log 2 + \log 10^6$ *Use the Power Property and Product Property.*

$(n-1)\log 2 > \log 2 + 6$ *$\log 10^6$ is 6.*

$n - 1 > \dfrac{\log 2 + 6}{\log 2}$ *Divide both sides by $\log 2$.*

$n > \approx \dfrac{0.301 + 6}{0.301} + 1$ *Evaluate by using a calculator.*

$n > \approx 21.93$ *Round this up to the next whole number.*

Beginning on day 22, you would receive more than the value of the car.

Check On day 22, you would receive 2^{22-1} cents.

$2^{22-1} = 2^{21} = 2{,}097{,}152$ cents, or \$20,971.52.

2. In Example 2, suppose that you receive triple the amount each day. On what day would you receive at least a million dollars?

A **logarithmic equation** is an equation with a logarithmic expression that contains a variable. You can solve logarithmic equations by using the properties of logarithms.

$$\text{If } \log_b x = \log_b y \text{ then } x = y$$

EXAMPLE 3 Solving Logarithmic Equations

Solve.

A $\log_3(x-5) = 2$

$3^{\log_3(x-5)} = 3^2$ *Use 3 as the base for both sides.*

$x - 5 = 9$ *Use inverse properties to remove 3 to the log base 3.*

$x = 14$ *Simplify.*

Remember!

Review the properties of logarithms from the previous lesson.

B $\log 45x - \log 3 = 1$

$\log\left(\dfrac{45x}{3}\right) = 1$ *Write as a quotient.*

$\log(15x) = 1$ *Divide.*

$10^{\log 15x} = 10^1$ *Use 10 as a base for both sides.*

$15x = 10$ *Use inverse properties on the left side.*

$x = \dfrac{2}{3}$

Solve.

C $\log_4 x^2 = 7$

$2\log_4 x = 7$	*Power Property of Logarithms*
$\log_4 x = \frac{7}{2}$	*Divide both sides by 2 to isolate $\log_4 x$.*
$x = 4^{\frac{7}{2}}$	*Definition of a logarithm*
$x = (2^2)^{\frac{7}{2}}$	*4 is a power of 2.*
$x = 2^7$, or 128	

D $\log x + \log(x + 9) = 1$

$\log x(x + 9) = 1$	*Product Property of Logarithms.*
$10^{\log x(x+9)} = 10^1$	*Exponential form*
$x(x + 9) = 10$	*Use the inverse properties.*
$x^2 + 9x - 10 = 0$	*Multiply and collect terms.*
$(x - 1)(x + 10) = 0$	*Factor.*
$x - 1 = 0$ or $x + 10 = 0$	*Set each of the factors equal to zero.*
$x = 1$ or $x = -10$	*Solve.*

Caution!

Watch out for calculated solutions that are not solutions of the original equation.

Check Check both solutions in the original equation.

$\log x + \log(x + 9)$	1
$\log 1 + \log(1 + 9)$	1
$\log 1 + \log 10$	1
$0 + 1$	1
1	1 ✔

$\log x + \log(x + 9)$	1
$\log(-10) + \log(-10 + 9)$	1 ✘

$\log(-10)$ is undefined.

The solution is $x = 1$.

3a. Solve $3 = \log 8 + 3\log x$. **3b.** Solve $2\log x - \log 4 = 0$.

EXAMPLE 4 Using Tables and Graphs to Solve Exponential and Logarithmic Equations and Inequalities

Use a table and graph to solve.

A $2^{2x} = 1024$

Use a graphing calculator. Enter **2^(2X)** as **Y1** and **1024** as **Y2**.

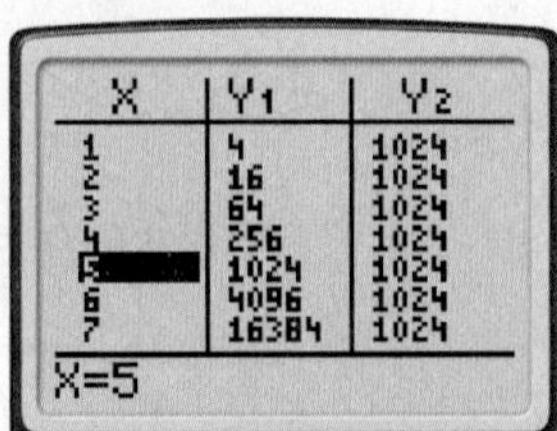

X	Y1	Y2
1	4	1024
2	16	1024
3	64	1024
4	256	1024
5	1024	1024
6	4096	1024
7	16384	1024

X=5

In the table, find the x-value where Y1 and Y2 are equal.

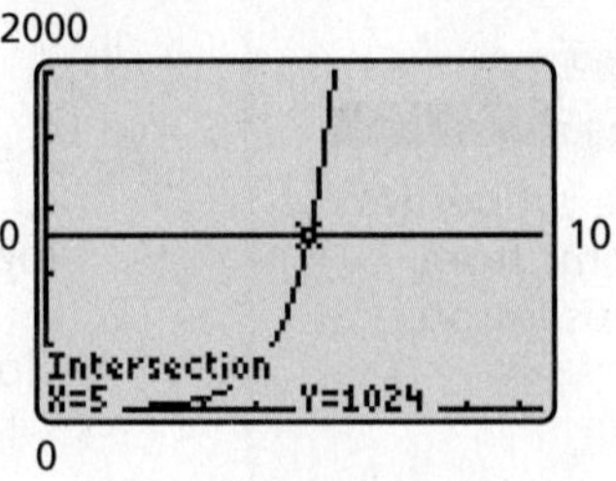

In the graph, find the x-value at the point of intersection.

The solution is $x = 5$.

Use a table and graph to solve.

B $\log x - \log 2 \le \log 75$

Use a graphing calculator. Enter $\log x - \log 2$ as **Y1** and $\log 75$ as **Y2**.

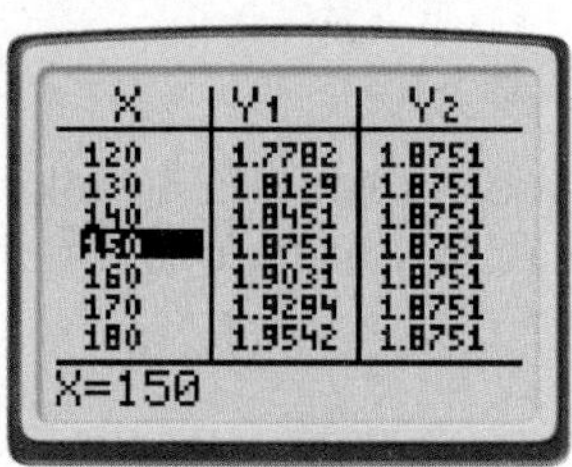

X	Y1	Y2
120	1.7782	1.8751
130	1.8129	1.8751
140	1.8451	1.8751
150	1.8751	1.8751
160	1.9031	1.8751
170	1.9294	1.8751
180	1.9542	1.8751

X=150

In the table, find the x-values where Y1 is less than or equal to Y2.

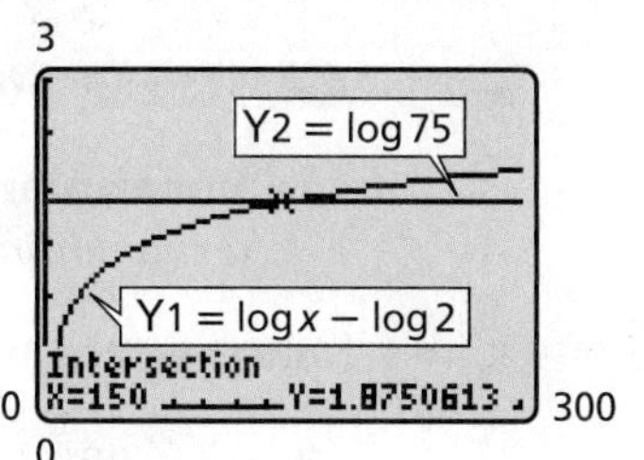

In the graph, find the x-value at the point of intersection.

The solution set is $\{x \mid 0 < x \le 150\}$.

Check Use algebra.

$$\log x - \log 2 \le \log 75$$

$$\log\left(\frac{x}{2}\right) \le \log 75 \qquad \textit{Quotient Property of Logarithms}$$

$$10^{\log\left(\frac{x}{2}\right)} \le 10^{\log 75} \qquad \textit{Use 10 as a base for both sides.}$$

$$\frac{x}{2} \le 75 \qquad \textit{Inverse Property}$$

$$x \le 150 \checkmark \qquad \textit{log x is only defined for } x > 0.$$

CHECK IT OUT! **Use a table and graph to solve.**

4a. $2^x = 4^{x-1}$ **4b.** $2^x > 4^{x-1}$ **4c.** $\log x^2 = 6$

MATHEMATICAL PRACTICES

THINK AND DISCUSS

1. Explain why a and b must be equal if $\log a = \log b\ (a > 0, b > 0)$.
2. Give only the first step you would use to solve each equation.
   - **a.** $\log x^5 = 10$
   - **b.** $\log 2x + \log 2 = 1$
   - **c.** $x^4 = 100$
   - **d.** $\log(x + 1000) = 2$
   - **e.** $\log(x + 4) + \log x = 2$
   - **f.** $\log_6(x + 6) = 3$
3. Explain whether a logarithmic equation can have a negative number as a solution. Justify your answer. Give an example, if possible.

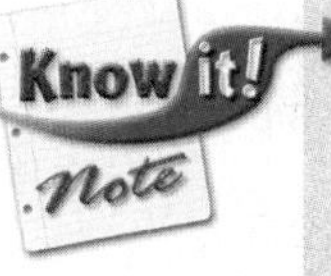

Know it! Note

4. **GET ORGANIZED** Copy and complete the graphic organizer. Write the strategies and points to remember in your own words for both exponential and logarithmic equations.

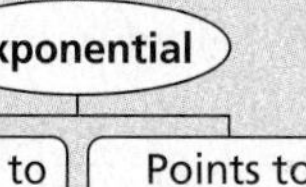

Equation
- Exponential
  - Strategies to solve
  - Points to remember
- Logarithmic
  - Strategies to solve
  - Points to remember

4-5 Exercises

GUIDED PRACTICE

1. **Vocabulary** You can solve a(n) __?__ by taking the logarithm of both sides. (*exponential equation* or *logarithmic equation*)

SEE EXAMPLE 1

Solve and check.

2. $4^{2x} = 32^{\frac{1}{2}}$
3. $9^x = 3^{x-2}$
4. $2^x = 4^{x+1}$
5. $4^x = 10$
6. $\left(\frac{1}{4}\right)^{2x} = \left(\frac{1}{2}\right)^x$
7. $2.4^{3x+1} = 9$

SEE EXAMPLE 2

8. **Population** The population of a small coastal resort town, currently 3400, grows at a rate of 3% per year. This growth can be expressed by the exponential equation $P = 3400(1 + 0.03)^t$, where P is the population after t years. Find the number of years it will take for the population to exceed 10,000.

SEE EXAMPLE 3

Solve.

9. $\log_2(7x + 1) = \log_2(2 - x)$
10. $\log_6(2x + 3) = 3$
11. $\log 72 - \log\left(\frac{2x}{3}\right) = 0$
12. $\log_3 x^9 = 12$
13. $\log_7(3 - 4x) = \log_7\left(\frac{x}{3}\right)$
14. $\log 50 + \log\left(\frac{x}{2}\right) = 2$
15. $\log x + \log(x + 48) = 2$
16. $\log\left(x + \frac{3}{10}\right) + \log x + 1 = 0$

SEE EXAMPLE 4

Use a table and graph to solve.

17. $2^{2x+1} = 256$
18. $2^x 3^x \leq 7776$
19. $2\log x^4 = 16$
20. $x > 10\log x$

PRACTICE AND PROBLEM SOLVING

Independent Practice

For Exercises	See Example
21–26	1
27	2
28–33	3
34–36	4

Extra Practice

See Extra Practice for more Skills Practice and Applications Practice exercises.

Solve and check.

21. $2^{x-1} = \frac{1}{64}$
22. $\left(\frac{1}{4}\right)^x = 8^{x-1}$
23. $\left(\frac{1}{5}\right)^{x-2} = 125^{\frac{x}{2}}$
24. $\left(\frac{1}{2}\right)^{-x} = 1.6$
25. $(1.5)^{x-1} = 14.5$
26. $3^{\frac{x}{2}+1} = 12.2$

27. **Pets** A veterinarian has instructed Harrison to give his 75 lb dog one 325 mg aspirin tablet for arthritis. The amount of aspirin A remaining in the dog's body after t minutes can be expressed by $A = 325\left(\frac{1}{2}\right)^{\frac{t}{15}}$. Write and solve a logarithmic inequality to find the time it takes for the amount of aspirin to drop below 50 mg.

Solve.

28. $\log_3(7x) = \log_3(2x + 0.5)$
29. $\log_2\left(1 + \frac{x}{2}\right) = 4$
30. $\log 5x - \log(15.5) = 2$
31. $\log_5 x^4 = 2.5$
32. $\log x - \log\left(\frac{x}{100}\right) = x$
33. $2 - \log 3x = \log\left(\frac{x}{12}\right)$

Use a table and graph to solve.

34. $2 \cdot 3^{x-1} = 162$
35. $4x < 2^{x+1}$
36. $\log(2x - 17) + \log x \geq 2$

37. Solve $\log x = \log(x^2 - 12)$. Explain your answer.

38. Solve $5^{2x} = 100$ to the nearest hundredth.

39. Solve $2^{x+2} = 64$ using more than one method.

40. **Photography** On many cameras, the amount of light admitted through the lens can be controlled by changing the size of the opening, or *aperture*. The size of the aperture is measured as an f-stop setting. The relationship between the f-stop and the amount of light admitted can be represented by the equation $n = \log_2 \frac{1}{\ell}$, where n is the change in f-stop setting from the starting value, f/5.6.

F-stop Setting	f/2	f/2.8	f/4	f/5.6	f/8	f/11	f/16
Change in F-stop Setting	−3	−2	−1	0	1	2	3

a. Solve the equation for ℓ when the f-stop setting is increased to f/16.

b. Solve the equation for n when the light admitted through the lens is twice the amount at f/5.6. What is the f-stop setting? Use a calculator to verify the solution.

LINK

Music

Pianos could be considered both percussion and stringed instruments, with hammers that hit each string. Pianos are usually located near the drums in an orchestra.

41. **Music** The frequency of a note on the piano, in Hz, is related to its position on the keyboard by the function $f(n) = 440 \cdot 2^{\frac{n}{12}}$, where n is the number of keys above or below the note concert A. (A negative value for n means that the key is to the left of, or lower on the keyboard than, concert A.) Find the position n of the key that has a frequency of 110 Hz.

42. **Finance** Suppose that \$250 is deposited into an account that pays 4.5% compounded quarterly. The equation $A = P\left(1 + \frac{r}{4}\right)^n$ gives the amount A in the account after n quarters for an initial investment P that earns interest at a rate r. Solve for n to find how long it will take for the account to contain at least \$500. (*Hint:* Divide both sides by P first.)

43. **Critical Thinking** How many real-number solutions are there for $\log x^2 < 2\log x$? Use a calculator to graph and verify the answer. Explain what the graph indicates about the answer.

44. **/// ERROR ANALYSIS ///** When a student solved $\log x + 4 = 8$, he arrived at 99,999,996. Give a possible reason for the error.

45. **Write About It** Describe two methods you can use to solve an exponential equation. Give an example of when you would use each method.

MULTI-STEP TEST PREP

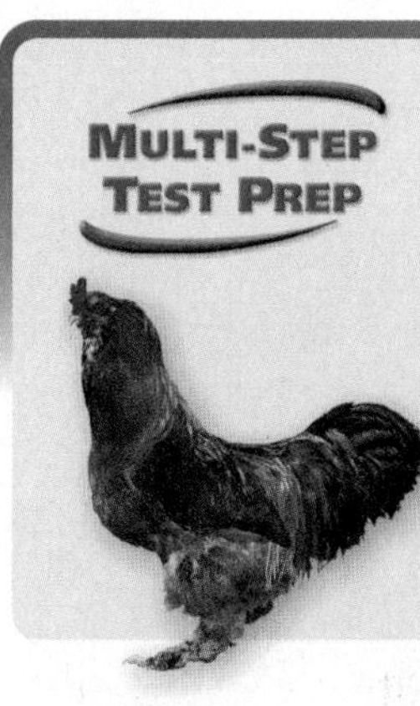

46. The number of farms in Iowa (in thousands) can be modeled by $N(t) = 119(0.987)^t$, where t is the number of years since 1980.

a. Has the number of farms in Iowa been increasing or decreasing since 1980? How can you tell?

b. Find the number of farms in Iowa in 1980 and 2000.

c. According to the model, when will be the number of farms in Iowa be about 80,000?

47. **Meteorology** In one part of the atmosphere where the temperature is a constant –70°F, pressure can be expressed as a function of altitude by the equation $P(h) = 128(10)^{-0.0682h}$, where P is the atmospheric pressure in kilopascals (kPa) and h is the altitude in kilometers above sea level. The pressure ranges from 2.55 kPa to 22.9 kPa in this region.

a. What are the lowest and highest altitudes where this model is appropriate? In what part of the atmosphere is the model useful?

b. **What if...?** A kilopascal is 0.145 psi. Would the model predict a sea-level pressure less than or greater than the actual sea-level pressure, 14.7 psi? Explain.

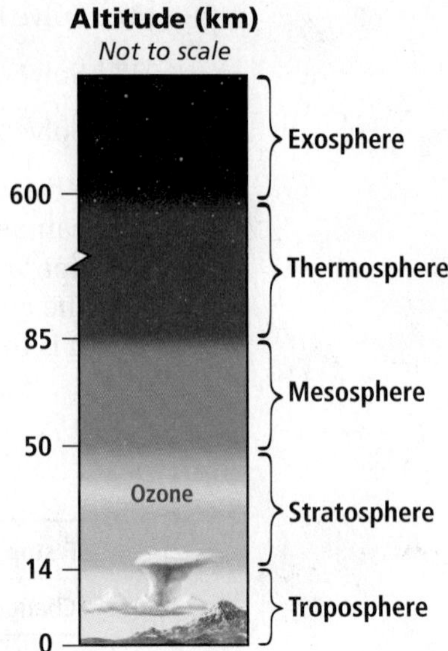

Test Prep

48. What is the solution of the equation $b^x = c$?

Ⓐ $x = \dfrac{\log b}{\log c}$ Ⓑ $x = \dfrac{\log c}{\log b}$ Ⓒ $x = \dfrac{\log b}{c}$ Ⓓ $x = \dfrac{\log c}{b}$

49. What is the solution of $\log(x - 21) = 2 - \log x$?

Ⓕ $x = 4$ Ⓖ $x = \dfrac{25}{4}$ Ⓗ $x = \dfrac{21}{2}$ Ⓙ $x = 25$

50. Which expression has the greatest value when $p = 5$ and $q = 2$?

Ⓐ $\log 2p - \log 3q$

Ⓑ $\log p^2 - \log q^3$

Ⓒ $2\log q - 3\log p$

Ⓓ $\log p - \log q$

Challenge and Extend

51. If $\log_x x = x$, can the equation be solved for x? Explain.

52. Solve $x = 0.125^{\log_2 5}$ algebraically.

53. For what domain is $\log_3 36 - \log_3 x > 1$? Use a calculator to graph and support your solution.

Exponents in Probability

You can use exponents to determine a probability when a certain experiment is repeated.

Recall that the probability P of an event is $P(\text{Event } E) = \dfrac{\text{number of favorable outcomes}}{\text{total number of outcomes}}$.

For example, when rolling a number cube with six possible outcomes, the probability of rolling an odd prime number, 3 or 5, is $\frac{2}{6}$, or $\frac{1}{3}$. The probability of rolling an odd prime number two rolls in a row is $\frac{1}{3} \cdot \frac{1}{3}$. If the probability of an event is r and the events are independent, then the probability of getting the same result when the event is repeated n times is $P(\text{Event } E \text{ occurring } n \text{ times in succession}) = r^n$

Examples

A machine on an assembly line makes an acceptable product 90% of the time. The machine makes 10 samples of the product.

1 What is the probability that all 10 samples are acceptable, to the nearest percent?

$P(\text{All 10 samples are acceptable}) = 0.9^{10}$ *Substitute 0.9 for r and 10 for n in r^n.*

≈ 0.35 *Use a calculator.*

The probability that all 10 samples are acceptable is about 35%.

2 At what number of samples does the probability fall below 10%?

You can solve an inequality.

$0.9^n < 0.1$

$\log 0.9^n < \log 0.1$ *Take the log of both sides.*

$n \log 0.9 < \log 0.1$ *Use the Power Property of Logarithms.*

$n > \dfrac{\log 0.1}{\log 0.9}$ ← $= -1$ (numerator), ← ≈ -0.0458 (denominator)

$n > \approx 21.85$

For 22 or more samples, the probability that all are acceptable drops below 10%.

Try This

1. You toss a coin 6 times. Find the probability of getting heads every time.
2. You toss a number cube 10 times. Find the probability that no roll is a six.
3. A basketball player has a 70% chance of making each free throw. For what number of free throws does the probability of making them all drop below 10%?
4. A test contains multiple-choice questions with 4 choices for each question. For what number of questions does the probability of guessing all of them correctly drop below 0.01%?

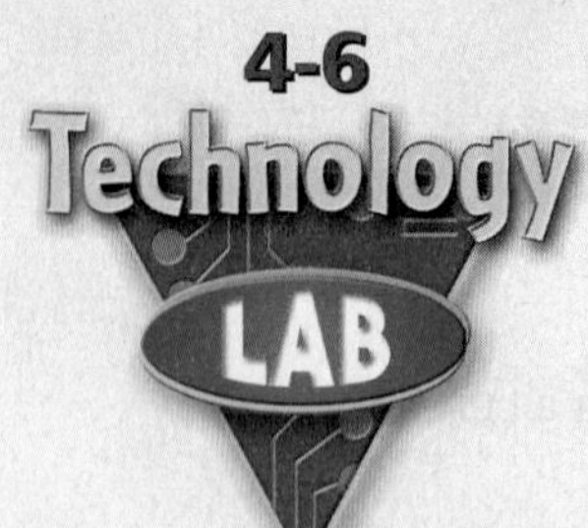

Explore the Rule of 72

You can use a spreadsheet to discover a rule to estimate the time needed to double an investment at different interest rates.

Use with The Natural Base, e

Activity

Use a spreadsheet to find the number of years it will take for an investment to double at 3% annual interest. Find the product of the interest rate and the doubling time.

Find a formula for doubling time as a function of interest rate. Use the compound interest formula.

$A = P\left(1 + \frac{r}{n}\right)^{nt}$ — *A is the total amount, P is the principal, r is the interest rate, n is the number of compounding periods, and t is the time in years.*

$2 = 1(1 + r)^t$ — *Substitute 2 for A, 1 for P, and 1 for n. Then solve for t.*

$\log 2 = \log(1 + r)^t$ — *Take the log of both sides.*

$\log 2 = t\log(1 + r)$ — *Power Property of Logarithms*

$t = \frac{\log 2}{\log(1 + r)}$ — *Divide both sides by log(1 + r) to solve for t.*

1. In cells A1 through C1, enter column headings for rate, doubling time, and their product. Enter **3%** in cell A2.

2. In cell B2, enter the formula derived above as shown in the screenshot.

	A	B	C
1	Rate	Doubling Time	Product
2	3%	=LOG(2)/LOG(1+A2)	

3. In cell C2, enter the formula for the product as shown.

	A	B	C
1	Rate	Doubling Time	Product
2	3%	23.44977225	=A2*B2

The spreadsheet shows that at 3% annual interest, an investment will double in about 23.4 years. The product of the interest rate and the doubling time is about 70.

	A	B	C
1	Rate	Doubling Time	Product
2	3%	23.44977225	0.703493168

Try This

1. Complete cells A3 through A20 with interest rates from 3.5% to 12%.
2. Copy and paste the formula from cell B2 into cells B3 through B20.
3. Copy and paste the formula from cell C2 into cells C3 through C20.
4. What is the lowest interest rate that gives you a doubling time less than 9 years?
5. **Make a Conjecture** The rule of 72 is a rule used by investors to estimate the time it will take for an investment to double at a certain rate. Explain why.
6. **Critical Thinking** Write an equation for the rule of 72.

4-6 The Natural Base, e

CC.9-12.F.LE.4 For exponential models, express as a logarithm the solution to $ab^{ct} = d$ ... evaluate the logarithm using technology. *Also* CC.9-12.F.IF.7e*, CC.9-12.A.CED.2, CC.9-12.A.CED.3, CC.9-12.F.IF.5

Objectives

Use the number e to write and graph exponential functions representing real-world situations.

Solve equations and problems involving e or natural logarithms.

Vocabulary

natural logarithm
natural logarithmic function

Why learn this?

Scientists use natural logarithms and carbon dating to determine the ages of ancient bones and fossils. (See Example 4.)

Recall the *compound interest formula* $A = P\left(1 + \frac{r}{n}\right)^{nt}$, where A is the total amount, P is the principal, r is the annual interest rate, n is the number of times the interest is compounded per year, and t is the time in years.

Suppose that \$1 is invested at 100% interest $(r = 1)$ compounded n times for one year as represented by the function $f(n) = \left(1 + \frac{1}{n}\right)^n$.

As n gets very large, interest is *continuously compounded*. Examine the graph of $f(n) = \left(1 + \frac{1}{n}\right)^n$. The function has a horizontal asymptote. As n becomes infinitely large, the value of the function approaches approximately 2.7182818.... This number is called *e*. Like π, the constant *e* is an irrational number.

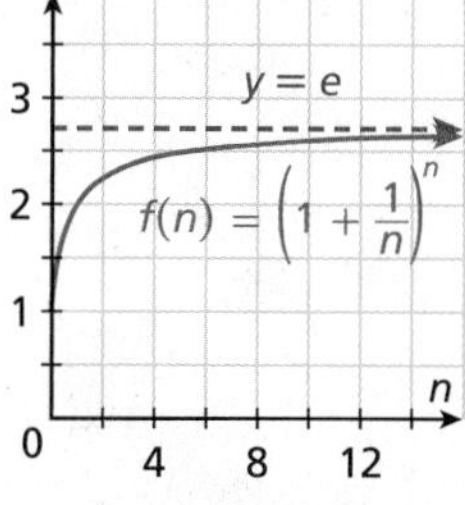

Caution!

The decimal value of e looks like it repeats: 2.718281828.... The value is actually 2.7182818284590.... There is no repeating portion.

Exponential functions with *e* as a base have the same properties as the functions you have studied. The graph of $f(x) = e^x$ is like other graphs of exponential functions, such as $f(x) = 3^x$.

The domain of $f(x) = e^x$ is all real numbers. The range is $\{y \mid y > 0\}$.

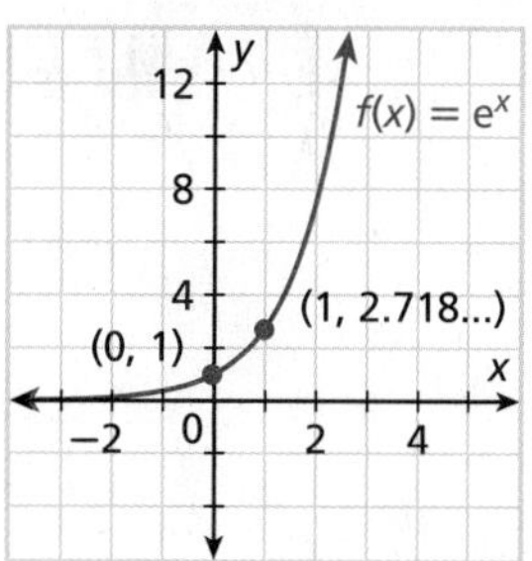

EXAMPLE 1 Graphing Exponential Functions

Graph $f(x) = e^x + 2$.

Make a table. Because *e* is irrational, the table values are rounded to the nearest tenth.

x	−3	−2	−1	0	1	2	3
$f(x) = e^x + 2$	2.0	2.1	2.4	3	4.7	9.4	22.1

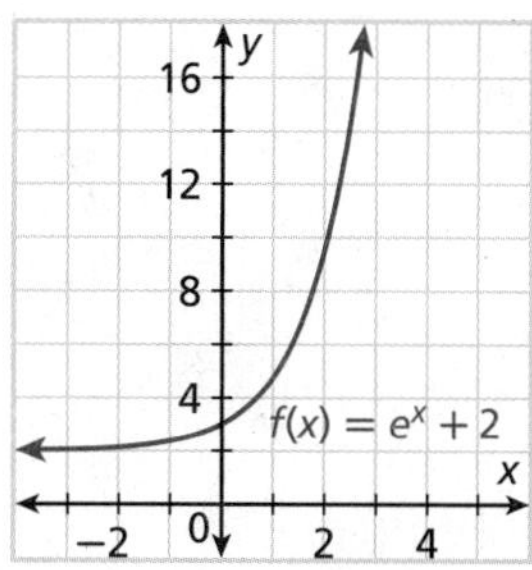

1. Graph $f(x) = e^x - 3$.

A logarithm with a base of e is called a **natural logarithm** and is abbreviated as "ln" (rather than as $\log_e$). Natural logarithms have the same properties as log base 10 and logarithms with other bases.

The **natural logarithmic function** $f(x) = \ln x$ is the inverse of the natural exponential function $f(x) = e^x$.

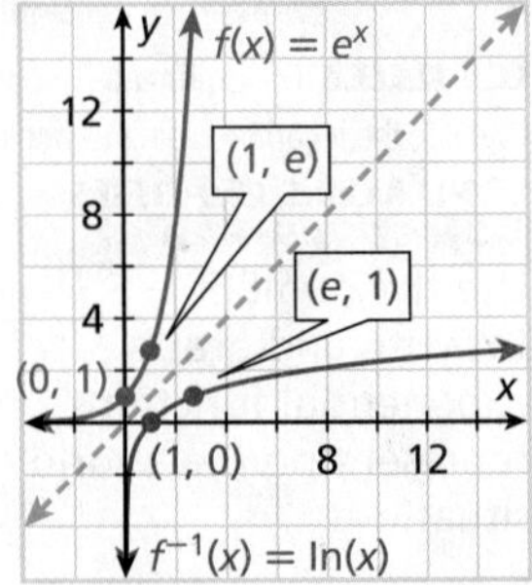

The domain of $f(x) = \ln x$ is $\{x \mid x > 0\}$.
The range of $f(x) = \ln x$ is all real numbers.
All of the properties of logarithms also apply to natural logarithms.

EXAMPLE 2 Simplifying Expressions with e or ln

Simplify.

A $\ln e^{-2t}$

$\ln e^{-2t} = -2t$

B $e^{\ln(t-1)}$

$e^{\ln(t-1)} = t - 1$

C $e^{5\ln x}$

$e^{5\ln x} = e^{\ln x^5} = x^5$

Simplify.

2a. $\ln e^{3.2}$ **2b.** $e^{2\ln x}$ **2c.** $\ln e^{x+4y}$

The formula for continuously compounded interest is $A = Pe^{rt}$, where A is the total amount, P is the principal, r is the annual interest rate, and t is the time in years.

EXAMPLE 3 *Economics Application*

What is the total amount for an investment of \$1000 invested at 5% for 10 years compounded continuously?

$A = Pe^{rt}$ *Substitute 1000 for P, 0.05 for r, and 10 for t.*

$A = 1000e^{0.05(10)}$

$A \approx 1648.72$ *Use the e^x key on a calculator.*

The total amount is \$1648.72.

3. What is the total amount for an investment of \$100 invested at 3.5% for 8 years and compounded continuously?

The *half-life* of a substance is the time it takes for half of the substance to breakdown or convert to another substance during the process of decay. Natural decay is modeled by the function below.

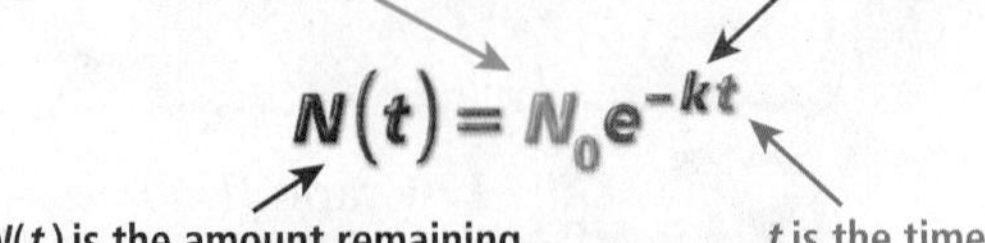

EXAMPLE 4 *Paleontology Application*

A paleontologist uncovers a fossil of a saber-toothed cat in California. He analyzes the fossil and concludes that the specimen contains 15% of its original carbon-14. Carbon-14 has a half-life of 5730 years. Use carbon-14 dating to determine the age of the fossil.

Step 1 Find the decay constant for carbon-14.

$N(t) = N_0 e^{-kt}$	*Use the natural decay function.*
$\frac{1}{2} = 1e^{-k(5730)}$	*Substitute 1 for N_0, 5730 for t, and $\frac{1}{2}$ for N(t), because half of the initial quantity will remain.*
$\ln\frac{1}{2} = \ln e^{-5730k}$	*Simplify and take the ln of both sides.*
$\ln 2^{-1} = -5730k$	*Write $\frac{1}{2}$ as 2^{-1}, and simplify the right side.*
$-\ln 2 = -5730k$	*$\ln 2^{-1} = -1\ln 2 = -\ln 2$*
$k = \frac{\ln 2}{5730} \approx 0.00012$	

Step 2 Write the decay function and solve for *t*.

$N(t) = N_0 e^{-0.00012t}$	*Substitute 0.00012 for k.*
$15 = 100e^{-0.00012t}$	*Substitute 100 for N_0 and 15 for N(t), since N(t) is 15% of N_0.*
$0.15 = e^{-0.00012t}$	*Divide both sides by 100.*
$\ln 0.15 = \ln e^{-0.00012t}$	*Take the ln of both sides.*
$\ln 0.15 = -0.00012t$	*Simplify.*
$t = -\frac{\ln 0.15}{0.00012} \approx 15{,}809$	

The fossil is approximately 15,800 years old.

4. Determine how long it will take for 650 mg of a sample of chromium-51, which has a half-life of about 28 days, to decay to 200 mg.

THINK AND DISCUSS

1. Tell how *e* and π are alike. Tell how they are different.

2. Explain how *e* and ln are related.

3. GET ORGANIZED Copy and complete the graphic organizer. Fill in each box to compare and contrast the two kinds of logarithms. Give general forms and examples. Simplify, if appropriate.

	Common Logarithms	Natural Logarithms
Base		
Logarithmic Form		
Exponential Form		
$\log_b 1$		
$\log_b b$		
$\log_b b^x$		
$b^{\log_b x}$		

R.A. Mittermeir/Bruce Coleman, Inc.

4-6 Exercises

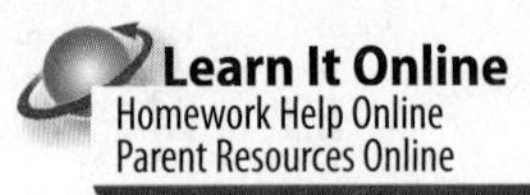

GUIDED PRACTICE

1. **Vocabulary** Write the logarithm of a number x to the natural base e as a function of x. This function is called the ___?___.

SEE EXAMPLE 1

Graph.

2. $f(x) = e^x - 4$
3. $f(x) = -e^x$
4. $f(x) = 4 - e^x$
5. $f(x) = e^{1-x}$

SEE EXAMPLE 2

Simplify.

6. $\ln e^1$
7. $\ln e^{x-y}$
8. $\ln e^{\left(-\frac{x}{3}\right)}$
9. $e^{\ln 2x}$
10. $e^{3\ln x}$

SEE EXAMPLE 3

11. **Economics** Emma receives \$7750 and invests it in an account that earns 4% interest compounded continuously. What is the total amount of her investment after 5 years?

SEE EXAMPLE 4

12. **Physics** Technetium-99m, a radioisotope used to image the skeleton and the heart muscle, has a half-life of about 6 hours. Find the decay constant. Use the decay function $N(t) = N_0e^{-kt}$ to determine the amount of a 250 mg dose that remains after 24 hours.

PRACTICE AND PROBLEM SOLVING

Independent Practice

For Exercises	See Example
13–16	1
17–20	2
21	3
22	4

Extra Practice

See Extra Practice for more Skills Practice and Applications Practice exercises.

Graph.

13. $f(x) = e^x + 1$
14. $f(x) = e^x - 1$
15. $f(x) = 1 - e^x$
16. $f(x) = 10 - e^x$

Simplify.

17. $\ln e^0$
18. $\ln e^{2a}$
19. $e^{\ln(c+2)}$
20. $e^{4\ln x}$

21. **Economics** Aidan has \$7565 in his checking account. He invests \$5000 of it in an account that earns 3.5% interest compounded continuously. What is the total amount of his investment after 3 years?

22. **Environment** An accident in 1986 at the Chernobyl nuclear plant in the Ukraine released a large amount of plutonium (Pu-239) into the atmosphere. The half-life of Pu-239 is about 24,110 years. Find the decay constant. Use the function $N(t) = N_0e^{-kt}$ to find what remains of an initial 20 grams of Pu-239 after 5000 years. How long will it take for these 20 grams to decay to 1 gram?

23. **Calculator** Find the approximate values of $\ln 10$ and $\log e$.
    a. How are these numbers related?
    b. How can you use the change of base formula to support your answer?

24. Show that $\ln x = \ln 10 \times \log x$.

25. **Multi-Step** Newton's law of cooling states that the temperature of an object decreases exponentially as a function of time, according to $T = T_s + (T_0 - T_s)e^{-kt}$, where T_0 is the initial temperature of the liquid, T_s is the surrounding temperature, and k is a constant. For a time in minutes, the constant for coffee is approximately 0.283. The corner coffee shop has an air temperature of 70°F and serves coffee at 206°F. Coffee experts say coffee tastes best at 140°F.
    a. How long does it take for the coffee to reach its best temperature?
    b. The air temperature on the patio is 86°F. How long does it take for coffee to reach its best temperature there?
    c. Graph the cooling functions from parts **a** and **b.** Use the graph to find the time it takes for the coffee to cool to 71°F.

26. Graph the functions $y = \frac{\ln x}{\ln 6}$ and $y = \frac{\log x}{\log 6}$. Explain how the graphs compare with each other and with the graph of $y = \log_6 x$.

Match each transformation of $f(x) = \ln x$ with one of the following graphs.

A. 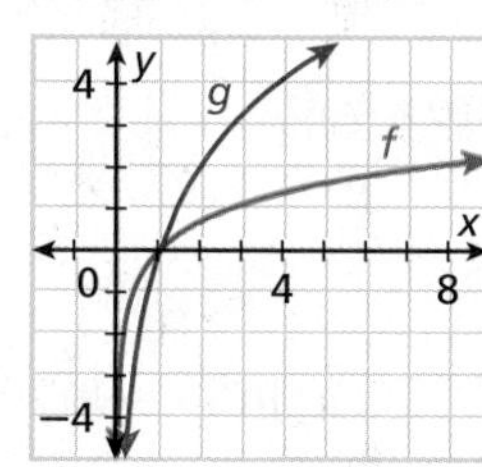

B. 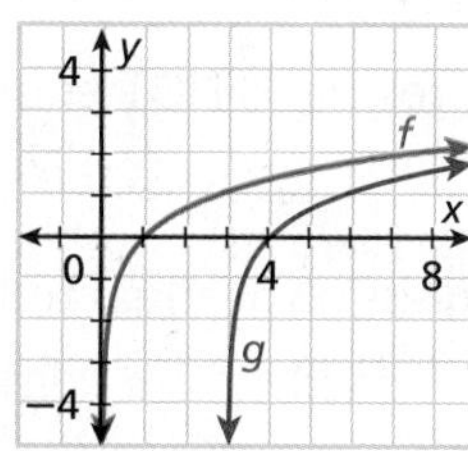

C. 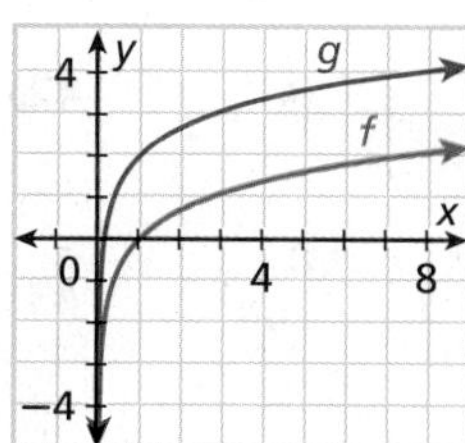

27. $g(x) = \ln(x - 3)$

28. $g(x) = 3\ln x$

29. $g(x) = \ln x + 3$

LINK

Ecology

The George River herd, the largest caribou herd in the world, reached its peak population in 1993 at about 776,000.

30. **Ecology** The George River herd of caribou in Canada was estimated to be about 4700 in 1954 and grew at an exponential rate to about 472,000 in 1984.
  a. Use the exponential growth function $P(t) = P_0e^{kt}$, where P_0 is the initial population and $P(t)$ is the population at time t, to determine the growth factor k.
  b. **What if...?** If the herd had continued to grow at the same rate, what would its population be in 2010?

Solve.

31. $\ln 5 + \ln x = 1$

32. $\ln 5 - \ln x = 3$

33. $\ln 10 + \ln x^2 = 10$

34. $2\ln x - 2 = 0$

35. $4\ln x - \ln x^4 = 0$

36. $e^{\ln x^3} = 8$

37. **Logistics** A *logistic function*, such as $f(x) = \frac{1}{(1 + e^{-x})}$, can be used to describe the spread of an epidemic in a population.
  a. Graph the function.
  b. How many asymptotes does the function have?
  c. Describe the function in the context of the real-world situation of an epidemic.

38. **Critical Thinking** The graphs of $f(x) = 2^x$, $f(x) = 10^x$, and $f(x) = e^x$ are shown.
  a. Identify the graph of each function.
  b. Name the coordinates of the point that all three functions have in common.
  c. Explain why this point is common to all three functions.

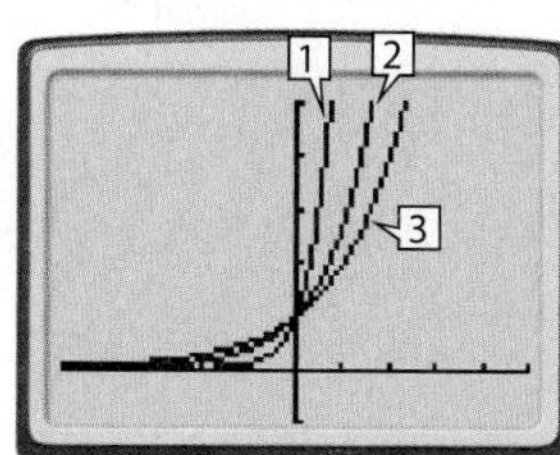

39. **Write About It** Compare compounding interest continuously with compounding daily. How much more is an investment worth when compounding interest continuously? Include an example.

MULTI-STEP TEST PREP

40. In 1990, there were 33,500 farms in North Dakota. In 2000, there were 30,800.
  a. Find the value of k for the exponential function $N(t) = N_0e^{kt}$ to model the number of farms.
  b. Use your model to predict the number of farms in North Dakota in 2010.
  c. From 1990 to 2000, the average farm increased from 1209 acres to 1279 acres. Use an exponential model to predict the average farm size in 2010.

TEST PREP

41. Which group shows values in the order from least to greatest?

Ⓐ $\log e, \ln 10, \log 10, \ln 1$
Ⓑ $\ln 1, \log e, \ln 10, \log 10$
Ⓒ $\ln 1, \log e, \log 10, \ln 10$
Ⓓ $\ln 1, \log 10, \ln 10, \log e$

42. Which expression is NOT equal to x where $x \neq 0$?

Ⓕ $e^{\ln x}$ Ⓖ $\ln e^x$ Ⓗ $x \ln e$ Ⓙ $x + \ln e$

43. Which expression is equal to $\log 50$?

Ⓐ $\ln 50 \div \ln 10$ Ⓑ $\ln(50 \div 10)$ Ⓒ $\ln 50 + \ln 10$ Ⓓ $\ln 50(\ln 10)$

44. **Short Response** Write an expression that is equivalent to $-\ln x$ without using a negative sign.

CHALLENGE AND EXTEND

45. **Finance** For how many compounding periods in a year would the yield of an investment after 1 year at 8% interest be at least 99.9% of the yield if interest were compounded continuously? Does changing the interest rate change the answer? Explain.

46. Graph the function $f(x) = \frac{1}{\sqrt{2\pi}} e^{-\left(\frac{x^2}{2}\right)}$. Describe the graph, the domain, and the range.

47. Consider the graph of $f(x) = \ln x$.
 a. What function represents the reflection of f across the y-axis?
 b. What function represents the reflection of f across the x-axis?
 c. What function represents the reflection of f across both axes?
 d. Graph the function and the three reflections. Name any asymptotes that the four graphs have in common.

4-7 Transforming Exponential and Logarithmic Functions

CC.9-12.F.BF.3 Identify the effect on the graph of replacing $f(x)$ by $f(x) + k$, $k\,f(x)$, $f(kx)$, and $f(x + k)$ … find the value of k given the graphs. … illustrate … using technology. *Also* **CC.9-12.A.CED.2, CC.9-12.A.CED.3, CC.9-12.F.IF.5**

Objectives

Transform exponential and logarithmic functions by changing parameters.

Describe the effects of changes in the coefficients of exponential and logarithmic functions.

Who uses this?

Psychologists can use transformations of exponential functions to describe knowledge retention rates over time. (See Example 5.)

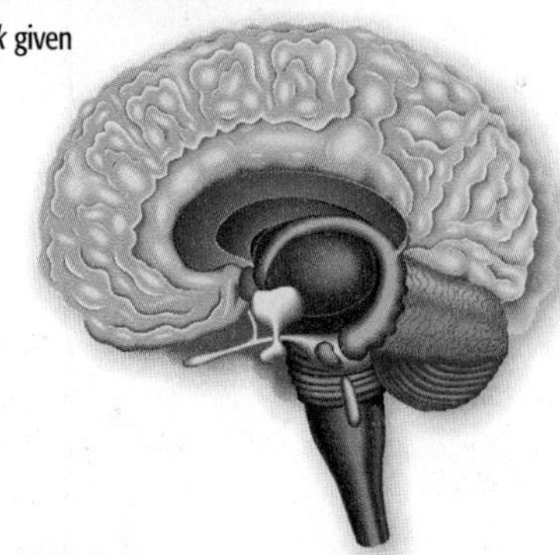

The hippocampus, in orange, directs the storage of memory in the brain.

You can perform the same transformations on exponential functions that you performed on polynomial, quadratic, and linear functions.

Helpful Hint

It may help you remember the direction of the shift if you think of "*h* is for horizontal."

Transformations of Exponential Functions

Transformation	$f(x)$ Notation	Examples	
Vertical translation	$f(x) + k$	$y = 2^x + 3$	3 units up
		$y = 2^x - 6$	6 units down
Horizontal translation	$f(x - h)$	$y = 2^{x-2}$	2 units right
		$y = 2^{x+1}$	1 unit left
Vertical stretch or compression	$af(x)$	$y = 6(2^x)$	stretch by 6
		$y = \frac{1}{2}(2^x)$	compression by $\frac{1}{2}$
Horizontal stretch or compression	$f\left(\frac{1}{b}x\right)$	$y = 2^{\left(\frac{1}{5}x\right)}$	stretch by 5
		$y = 2^{3x}$	compression by $\frac{1}{3}$
Reflection	$-f(x)$	$y = -2^x$	across x-axis
	$f(-x)$	$y = 2^{-x}$	across y-axis

EXAMPLE 1 **Translating Exponential Functions**

Make a table of values, and graph the function $g(x) = 2^x - 4$. Describe the asymptote. Tell how the graph is transformed from the graph of $f(x) = 2^x$.

x	−2	−1	0	1	2	3
$g(x)$	−3.75	−3.5	−3	−2	0	4

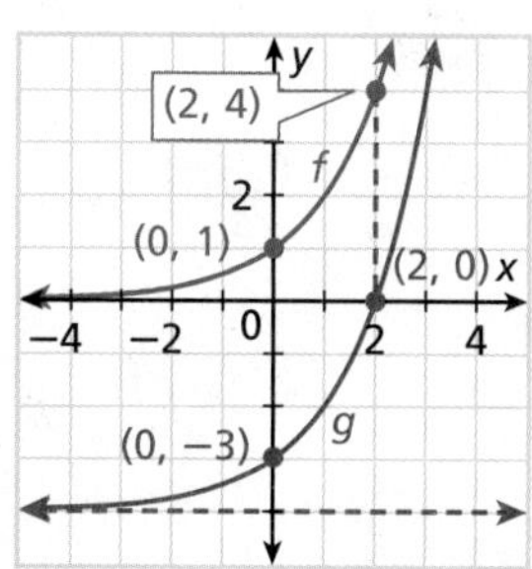

The asymptote is $y = -4$, and the graph approaches this line as the value of x decreases. The transformation moves the graph of $f(x) = 2^x$ down 4 units. The range changes to $\{y \mid y > -4\}$.

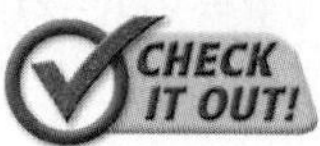

1. Make a table of values, and graph $j(x) = 2^{x-2}$. Describe the asymptote. Tell how the graph is transformed from the graph of $f(x) = 2^x$.

doc-stock/Alamy

EXAMPLE 2 Stretching, Compressing, and Reflecting Exponential Functions

Graph the exponential function. Find the y-intercept and the asymptote. Describe how the graph is transformed from the graph of its parent function.

A $g(x) = 2(3^x)$

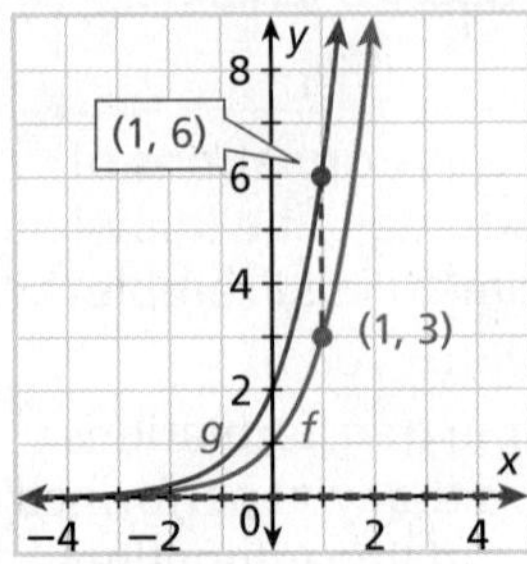

parent function: $f(x) = 3^x$

y-intercept: 2, asymptote: $y = 0$

The graph of $g(x)$ is a vertical stretch of the parent function $f(x) = 3^x$ by a factor of 2.

B $h(x) = -\frac{1}{4}(2^x)$

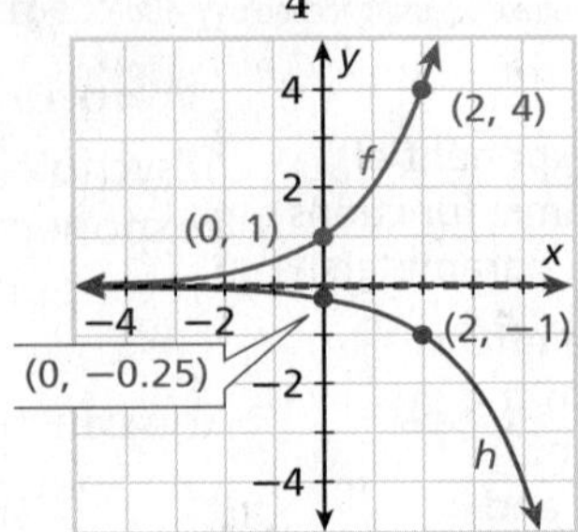

parent function: $f(x) = 2^x$

y-intercept: $-\frac{1}{4}$, asymptote: $y = 0$

The graph of $h(x)$ is a reflection of the parent function $f(x) = 2^x$ across the x-axis and a vertical compression by a factor of $\frac{1}{4}$. The range is $\{y \mid y < 0\}$.

Graph the exponential function. Find the y-intercept and the asymptote. Describe how the graph is transformed from the graph of its parent function.

2a. $h(x) = \frac{1}{3}(5^x)$

2b. $g(x) = 2(2^{-x})$

Remember!

Transformations of $\ln x$ work the same way because $\ln x$ means $\log_e x$.

Because a log is an exponent, transformations of logarithmic functions are similar to transformations of exponential functions. You can stretch, reflect, and translate the graph of the parent logarithmic function $f(x) = \log_b x$.

Examples are given in the table below for $f(x) = \log x$.

Transformations of Logarithmic Functions

Transformation	$f(x)$ Notation	Examples	
Vertical translation	$f(x) + k$	$y = \log x + 3$	3 units up
		$y = \log x - 4$	4 units down
Horizontal translation	$f(x - h)$	$y = \log(x - 2)$	2 units right
		$y = \log(x + 1)$	1 unit left
Vertical stretch or compression	$af(x)$	$y = 6\log x$	stretch by 6
		$y = \frac{1}{2}\log x$	compression by $\frac{1}{2}$
Horizontal stretch or compression	$f\left(\frac{1}{b}x\right)$	$y = \log\left(\frac{1}{5}x\right)$	stretch by 5
		$y = \log(3x)$	compression by $\frac{1}{3}$
Reflection	$-f(x)$	$y = -\log x$	across x-axis
	$f(-x)$	$y = \log(-x)$	across y-axis

EXAMPLE 3 Transforming Logarithmic Functions

Graph each logarithmic function. Find the asymptote. Then describe how the graph is transformed from the graph of its parent function.

A $q(x) = -\ln(x - 4)$

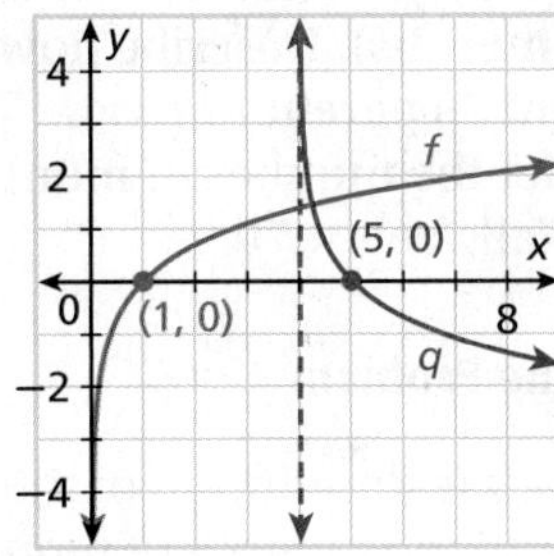

asymptote: $x = 4$

The graph of $q(x)$ is a translation of the parent function $f(x) = \ln x$ 4 units right and a reflection across the x-axis. The domain is $\{x \mid x > 4\}$.

B $p(x) = 3\log x + 5$

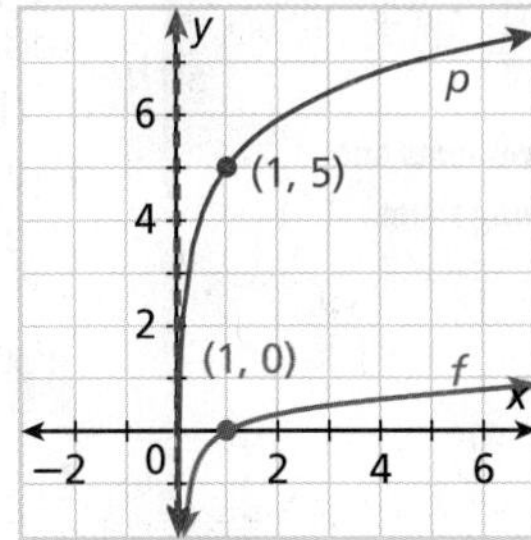

asymptote: $x = 0$

The graph of $p(x)$ is a vertical stretch of the parent function $f(x) = \log x$ by a factor of 3 and a translation 5 units up.

3. Graph the logarithmic function $p(x) = -\ln(x + 1) - 2$. Find the asymptote. Then describe how the graph is transformed from the graph of its parent function.

EXAMPLE 4 Writing Transformed Functions

Write each transformed function.

A $f(x) = 0.2^x$ is translated 2 units right, compressed vertically by a factor of $\frac{1}{3}$, and reflected across the x-axis.

0.2^x	*Begin with the rule for the parent function.*
0.2^{x-2}	*To translate 2 units right, replace x with x − 2.*
$g(x) = \left(-\dfrac{1}{3}\right)0.2^{x-2}$	*Compress vertically by $\frac{1}{3}$ and reflect across the x-axis.*

B $f(x) = \ln x$ is translated 1 unit left and 3 units up and horizontally stretched by a factor of 5.

$$g(x) = \ln\left(\frac{x}{5} + 1\right) + 3$$

When you write a transformed function, you many want to graph it as a check.

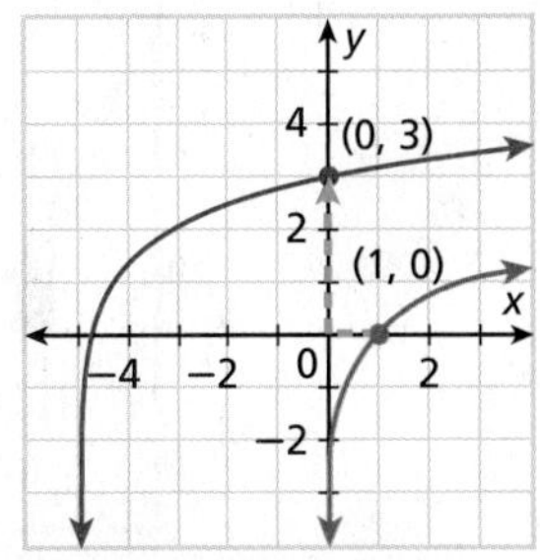

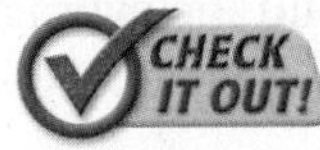

4. Write the transformed function when $f(x) = \log x$ is translated 3 units left and stretched vertically by a factor of 2.

EXAMPLE 5 Problem-Solving Application

MATHEMATICAL PRACTICES

Make sense of problems and persevere in solving them.

A group of students retake the written portion of a driver's test after several months without reviewing the material. A model used by psychologists describes retention of the material by the function $a(t) = 85 - 15\log(t + 1)$, where a is the average score at time t (in months). Describe how the model is transformed from its parent function. Then use the model to predict the number of months when the average score falls below 70.

1 Understand the Problem

The **answers** will be the description of the transformations in $a(t) = 85 - 15\log(t + 1)$ and the number of months when the score falls below 70.

List the important information:

- The model is the function $a(t) = 85 - 15\log(t + 1)$.
- The function is a transformation of $f(t) = \log(t)$.
- The problem asks for t when $a < 70$.

2 Make a Plan

Rewrite the function in a more familiar form, and then use what you know about the effect of changing the parent function to describe the transformations. Substitute known values into $a(t) = 85 - 15\log(t + 1)$, and solve for the unknown.

3 Solve

Rewrite the function, and describe the transformations.

$a(t) = 85 - 15\log(t + 1)$

$a(t) = -15\log(t + 1) + 85$ *Commutative Property*

The graph of $f(t) = \log(t)$ is reflected across the x-axis, vertically stretched by a factor of 15, and translated 85 units up and 1 unit left. The domain $\{t \mid t \geq 0\}$ makes sense in the problem.

Find the time when the average score drops below 70.

$70 > -15\log(t + 1) + 85$ *Substitute 70 for a(t) and replace = with >.*

$-15 > -15\log(t + 1)$ *Subtract 85 from both sides.*

$1 < \log(t + 1)$ *Divide by −15, and reverse the inequality symbol.*

$10^1 < t + 1$ *Change to exponential form.*

$9 < t$

The model predicts a score below 70 after 9 months.

4 Look Back

It is reasonable that scores would drop from 85 to below 70 nine months after the students take the test without reviewing the material.

5. **What if...?** When would the average score drop to 0? Is your answer reasonable?

THINK AND DISCUSS

1. Describe the domain of $f(x) = \log_b(-x)$.
2. Explain how the process of transforming exponential and logarithmic functions is similar to transforming quadratic functions.
3. Tell which transformations of $f(x) = a^x$ change the domain or range. Tell which transformations of $f(x) = \log_b x$ change the domain or range. Are these transformations the same?

4. **GET ORGANIZED** Copy and complete the graphic organizer. Give an example of an indicated transformation for both types of exponential and logarithmic functions. Remember, *e* is a constant.

Transformation	$f(x) = 5^x$ $f(x) = e^x$	$f(x) = \log_b x$ $f(x) = \ln x$
Vertical translation		
Horizontal translation		
Reflection		
Vertical stretch		
Vertical compression		

4-7 Exercises

GUIDED PRACTICE

SEE EXAMPLE 1

Make a table of values, and graph each function. Describe the asymptote. Tell how the graph is transformed from the graph of $f(x) = 3^x$.

1. $g(x) = 3^x + 2$
2. $h(x) = 3^x - 2$
3. $j(x) = 3^{x+1}$

SEE EXAMPLE 2

Graph each exponential function. Find the *y*-intercept and the asymptote. Describe how the graph is transformed from the graph of its parent function.

4. $g(x) = 3(4^x)$
5. $h(x) = \frac{1}{3}(4^x)$
6. $j(x) = -\frac{1}{3}(4^x)$
7. $k(x) = -2(4^x)$
8. $m(x) = -(4^{-x})$
9. $n(x) = e^{2x}$

SEE EXAMPLE 3

Graph each logarithmic function. Find the asymptote. Then describe how the graph is transformed from the graph of its parent function.

10. $g(x) = 2.5\log x$
11. $h(x) = 2.5\log(x + 3)$
12. $j(x) = -\frac{1}{3}\ln x + 1.5$

SEE EXAMPLE 4

Write each transformed function by using the given parent function and the indicated transformations.

13. The parent exponential function $f(x) = 0.7^x$ is horizontally stretched by a factor of 3, reflected across the *x*-axis, and translated 2 units left.
14. The parent logarithmic function $f(x) = \log x$ is translated 12 units right, vertically compressed by a factor of $\frac{1}{2}$, and translated 25 units up.

SEE EXAMPLE 5

15. **Forestry** The height of a poplar tree in feet, at age *t* years can be modeled by the function $h(t) = 6 + 3\ln(t + 1)$. Describe how the model is transformed from its parent function. Then use the model to predict the number of years when the height will exceed 17 feet.

PRACTICE AND PROBLEM SOLVING

Independent Practice

For Exercises	See Example
16–18	1
19–24	2
25–27	3
28–30	4
31	5

Extra Practice

See Extra Practice for more Skills Practice and Applications Practice exercises.

Make a table of values, and graph each function. Describe the asymptote. Tell how the graph is transformed from the graph of $f(x) = 5^x$.

16. $g(x) = 5^x - 1$ **17.** $h(x) = 5^{x+2}$ **18.** $j(x) = 5^{x-x} - 1$

Graph each exponential function. Find the y-intercept and the asymptote. Describe how the graph is transformed from the graph of its parent function.

19. $g(x) = 4\left(\frac{1}{2}\right)^x$ **20.** $h(x) = 0.25\left(\frac{1}{2}\right)^x$ **21.** $j(x) = -0.25\left(\frac{1}{2}\right)^x$

22. $k(x) = -\left(\frac{1}{2}\right)^{\frac{x}{2}}$ **23.** $m(x) = 4\left(\frac{1}{2}\right)^{-x}$ **24.** $n(x) = -4\left(\frac{1}{2}\right)^{-x}$

Graph each logarithmic function. Find the asymptote. Describe how the graph is transformed from the graph of its parent function.

25. $g(x) = \ln(x - 5)$ **26.** $h(x) = \frac{4}{5}\log(x + 3) - 2$ **27.** $m(x) = -4\log x$

Write each transformed function.

28. The function $f(x) = \left(\frac{1}{2}\right)^x$ is translated 4 units right, reflected across the x-axis, and vertically stretched by a factor of 1.5.

29. The function $f(x) = \ln x$ is translated 3 units left, horizontally compressed by a factor of $\frac{1}{4}$ and translated 0.5 units down.

30. The function $f(x) = e^x$ is horizontally stretched by a factor of 3, reflected across the y-axis, and translated 1 unit right.

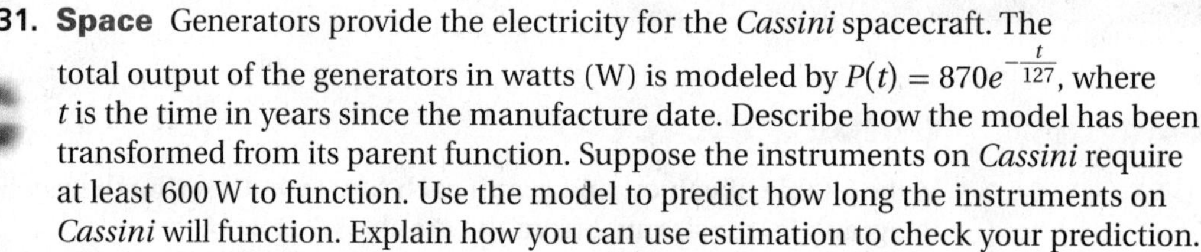

31. Space Generators provide the electricity for the *Cassini* spacecraft. The total output of the generators in watts (W) is modeled by $P(t) = 870e^{-\frac{t}{127}}$, where t is the time in years since the manufacture date. Describe how the model has been transformed from its parent function. Suppose the instruments on *Cassini* require at least 600 W to function. Use the model to predict how long the instruments on *Cassini* will function. Explain how you can use estimation to check your prediction.

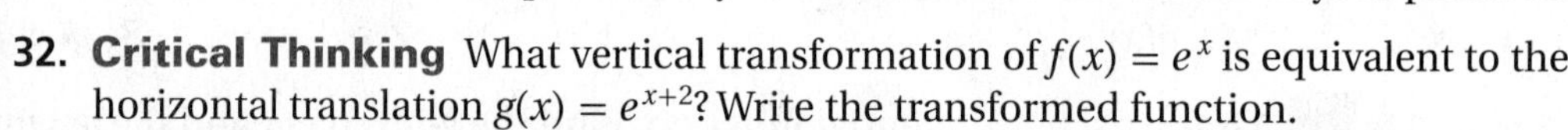

32. Critical Thinking What vertical transformation of $f(x) = e^x$ is equivalent to the horizontal translation $g(x) = e^{x+2}$? Write the transformed function.

For Exercises 33–37, match each order of transformation of $f(x) = e^x$ with its transformed function.

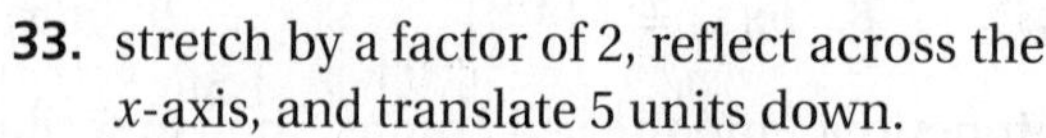

33. stretch by a factor of 2, reflect across the x-axis, and translate 5 units down.

34. stretch by a factor of 2, translate 5 units down, and reflect across the x-axis

35. reflect across the x-axis, stretch by a factor of 2, and translate 5 units down.

36. reflect across the x-axis, translate 5 units down, and stretch by a factor of 2.

37. translate 5 units down, stretch by a factor of 2, and reflect across the x-axis.

A. $g(x) = -2e^x - 5$

B. $g(x) = 2[-(e^x - 5)]$

C. $g(x) = 2(-e^x - 5)$

D. $g(x) = 2(-e^x) - 5$

E. $g(x) = -(2e^x - 5)$

F. $g(x) = -2(e^x - 5)$

State the domain and range of each function. Then find the intercepts. If necessary, round to the nearest hundredth.

38. $f(x) = 2^{x-2} + 4$ **39.** $g(x) = 5\log(x + 3)$

Tell whether each statement is sometimes, always, or never true.

40. A vertical translation of $f(x) = \log x$ changes its asymptote.

41. A vertical translation of $f(x) = e^x$ changes its asymptote.

42. A horizontal translation of $f(x) = \log x$ has a range of $\mathbb{R}$.

43. The graph of a transformation of $f(x) = \ln x$ intersects the graph of $f(x)$.

44. Banking The function $A(t) = 1000\left(1 + \frac{r}{n}\right)^{nt}$ can be used to calculate the growth of an investment of \$1000 in an account where the interest is compounded n times per year at an annual rate r. Suppose that you invest \$1000 in such an account compounded quarterly (4 times per year).

- **a.** What annual rate would double your investment in 5 years?
- **b.** At an annual rate of 3.5%, how long (to the nearest year) would it take for your investment to double?
- **c.** What does the model predict for the amount in the account after 10 years if the investment continues to grow at an annual rate of 3.5%?

Match each equation with one of the following graphs.

A.

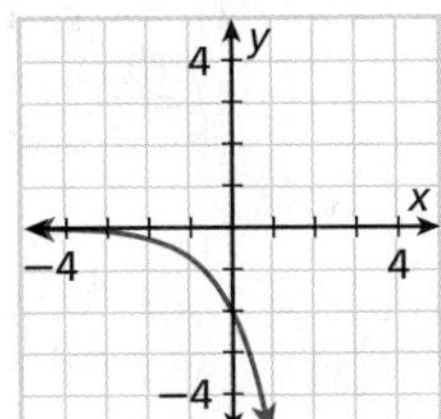

B.

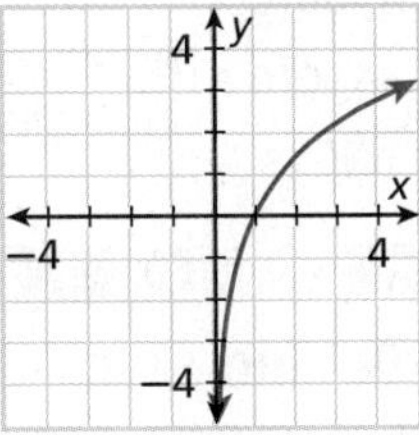

C.

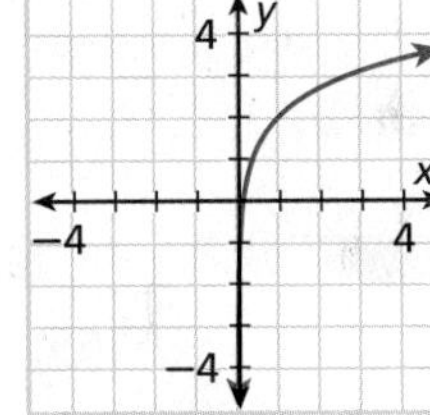

45. $f(x) = \ln x + 2$ **46.** $f(x) = -2e^x$ **47.** $f(x) = 2\ln x$

LINK

Medicine

Insulin is a hormone that allows the body's cells, including red blood cells, to absorb glucose. Synthetic insulin can help diabetics maintain a healthy level of blood sugar.

48. Medicine A dose of synthetic insulin breaks down in the bloodstream over time. The amount of insulin in the blood with an initial dose of A_0 mg, under some conditions, is given by $A = A_0 0.97^t$, where t is the time in minutes. The standard dose is 10 mg. Describe each transformation.

- **a.** The initial dose is changed from 10 mg to 20 mg.
- **b.** The breakdown of the medicine does not begin for 5 minutes.
- **c.** The breakdown time period is increased from one-minute intervals to two-minute intervals.
- **d. What if...?** The breakdown rate of 0.97 is reduced to 0.95. Is this a transformation of A?

49. Critical Thinking Describe how changing the value of h and changing the value of k differ in the effect on the graph of $f(x) = a\left(b^{x-h}\right) + k$.

50. Write About It Explain how to translate, reflect, stretch, and compress the graph of $f(x) = b^x$.

MULTI-STEP TEST PREP

51. The number of farms in a county is modeled by $N(t) = 1257(0.99)^t$, where t is the number of years since 1990.

- **a.** One-third of the farms in the county always produce soybeans. Write a new function that models the number of soybean farms.
- **b.** Write a new function that gives the number of soybean farms m months after January 1, 1990.
- **c.** How many soybean farms were there at the end of May 1991?

52. Which function is vertically stretched by a factor of 3 and translated 2 units left from its parent function?

Ⓐ $f(x) = 3(2^{x+2})$

Ⓑ $f(x) = 2^{3x} - 2$

Ⓒ $f(x) = 3\log(x - 2)$

Ⓓ $f(x) = \log(3x + 2)$

53. Which list shows the functions in order from the most compressed horizontally from $f(x) = \log x$ to the most stretched?

Ⓕ $f(x) = \log(x - 10)$, $f(x) = \log(10x)$, $f(x) = \log\left(\frac{x}{10}\right)$

Ⓖ $f(x) = \log\left(\frac{x}{10}\right)$, $f(x) = \log(x - 10)$, $f(x) = \log(10x)$

Ⓗ $f(x) = \log(10x)$, $f(x) = \log(x - 10)$, $f(x) = \log\left(\frac{x}{10}\right)$

Ⓙ $f(x) = \log\left(\frac{x}{10}\right)$, $f(x) = \log(10x)$, $f(x) = \log(x - 10)$

54. The trade-in value of Cindy's car is $4500 and decreases by about 40% per year. Which choice represents the trade-in value as a function of time?

Ⓐ $f(t) = 4500(0.4)^t$

Ⓑ $f(t) = 4500(0.6)^t$

Ⓒ $f(t) = 0.6(4500)^t$

Ⓓ $f(t) = 0.4(4500)^t$

CHALLENGE AND EXTEND

55. **Critical Thinking** Consider the function $f(x) = \log x$.

a. Identify the transformation applied to $f(x)$ to create $g(x) = \log x + 1$.

b. Identify the transformation applied to $f(x)$ to create $h(x) = \log(10x)$.

c. Use a graphing calculator to compare the graphs and tables of both functions. What do you notice?

d. Use the properties of logarithms to explain your answer to part **c.**

56. **Graphing Calculator** Graph the function $y = -\ln(x + 2)$ in the standard window. Make a conjecture explaining why the calculator screen appears to show that the graph stops abruptly and does not extend infinitely in two directions.

57. What can you say about the value of $f(x)$ as the value of x gets closer and closer to h in the standard equation for a logarithmic function, $f(x) = a\log(x - h) + k$, given that a, h, and $k \geq 0$?

COMMON CORE

4-8 Curve Fitting with Exponential and Logarithmic Models

CC.9-12.A.CED.3 Represent constraints by equations or inequalities, ... and interpret solutions as viable or nonviable options in a modeling context. *Also* CC.9-12.A.CED.2

Objectives
Model data by using exponential and logarithmic functions.

Use exponential and logarithmic models to analyze and predict.

Vocabulary
exponential regression
logarithmic regression

Who uses this?
Gem cutters know that values of precious stones of similar quality are exponentially related to the gems' weights. (See Example 2.)

Analyzing data values can identify a pattern, or repeated relationship, between two quantities.

Look at this table of values for the exponential function $f(x) = 2(3^x)$.

Remember!
For linear functions (first degree), first differences are constant. For quadratic functions, second differences are constant, and so on.

x	−1	0	1	2	3
f(x)	$\frac{2}{3}$	2	6	18	54

$\times 3 \quad \times 3 \quad \times 3 \quad \times 3$

Notice that the *ratio* of each *y*-value and the previous one is constant. Each value is three times the one before it, so the ratio of function values is constant for equally spaced *x*-values. This data can be fit by an exponential function of the form $f(x) = ab^x$.

EXAMPLE 1 **Identifying Exponential Data**

Determine whether *f* is an exponential function of *x* of the form $f(x) = ab^x$. If so, find the constant ratio.

A

x	−1	0	1	2	3
f(x)	−3	−1	1	3	5

$+2 \quad +2 \quad +2 \quad +2$ *First differences*

y is a linear function of *x*.

B

x	−1	0	1	2	3
f(x)	$\frac{1}{2}$	1	2	4	8

$+\frac{1}{2} \quad +1 \quad +2 \quad +4$

Ratios $\frac{1}{\frac{1}{2}} = \frac{2}{1} = \frac{4}{2} = \frac{8}{4} = 2$

This data set is exponential, with a constant ratio of 2.

CHECK IT OUT! **Determine whether *y* is an exponential function of *x* of the form $f(x) = ab^x$. If so, find the constant ratio.**

1a.

x	−1	0	1	2	3
f(x)	$2.\overline{6}$	4	6	9	13.5

1b.

x	−1	0	1	2	3
f(x)	−3	2	7	12	17

Steve Taylor/Getty Images

You have used a graphing calculator to perform *linear regressions* and *quadratic regressions* to make predictions. You can also use an *exponential model,* which is an exponential function that represents a real data set.

Once you know that data are exponential, you can use **ExpReg** (exponential regression) on your calculator to find a function that fits. This method of using data to find an exponential model is called an **exponential regression**. The calculator fits exponential functions to ab^x, so translations cannot be modeled.

EXAMPLE 2 ***Gemology Application***

The table gives the approximate values of diamonds of the same quality. Find an exponential model for the data. Use the model to estimate the weight of a diamond worth $2325.

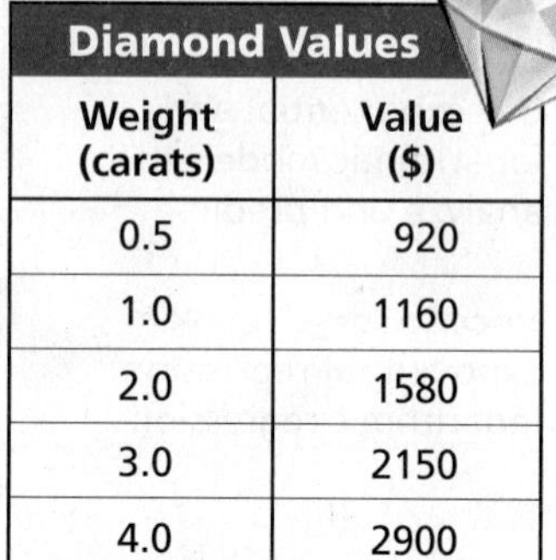

Diamond Values	
Weight (carats)	Value ($)
0.5	920
1.0	1160
2.0	1580
3.0	2150
4.0	2900

Step 1 Enter the data into two lists in a graphing calculator. Use the exponential regression feature.

An exponential model is $V(w) \approx 814.96(1.38)^w$, where V is the diamond value and w is the weight in carats.

Remember!

If you do not see r^2 and **r** when you calculate regression, use

CATALOG
2nd 0 and turn these features on by selecting **DiagnosticOn**.

Step 2 Graph the data and the function model to verify that it fits the data.

To enter the regression equation as **Y1** from the Y= screen, press VARS, choose **5:Statistics**, press ENTER, scroll to the **EQ** menu and select **1:RegEQ.**

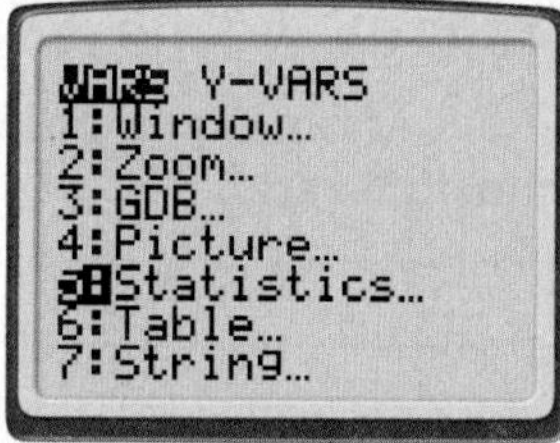

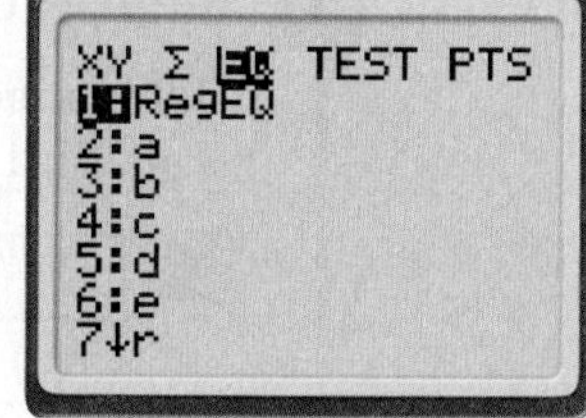

Enter 2325 as **Y2**. Use the intersection feature. You may need to adjust the window dimensions to find the intersection.

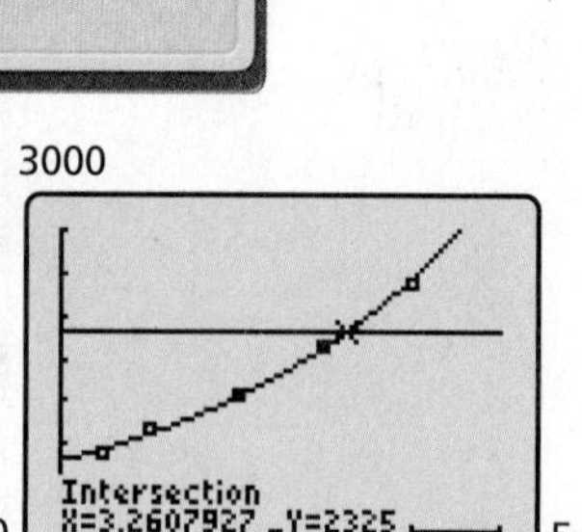

A diamond weighing about 3.26 carats will have a value of $2325.

2. Use exponential regression to find a function that models this data. When will the number of bacteria reach 2000?

Time (min)	0	1	2	3	4	5
Bacteria	200	248	312	390	489	610

Many natural phenomena can be modeled by natural log functions. You can use a **logarithmic regression** to find a function.

EXAMPLE 3 ***Physics Application***

The table gives the Richter scale equivalent for an explosion involving a quantity of TNT. Find a natural log model for the data. Use the model to estimate the number of tons of TNT that would be the equivalent of an earthquake measuring 6.5 on the Richter scale.

Richter Scale TNT Equivalence

TNT (tons)	Magnitude
1 TON	2.0
10 TONS (×3)	3.0
1000 TONS	4.0
10,000 TONS (×3)	5.0

Helpful Hint

Most calculators that perform logarithmic regression use ln rather than log.

Enter the data into two lists in a graphing calculator. Then use the logarithmic regression feature. Press STAT **CALC 9:LnReg.** A logarithmic model is $R(t) \approx 2 + 0.29 \ln t$, where R is the Richter scale reading and t is the equivalent number of tons of TNT.

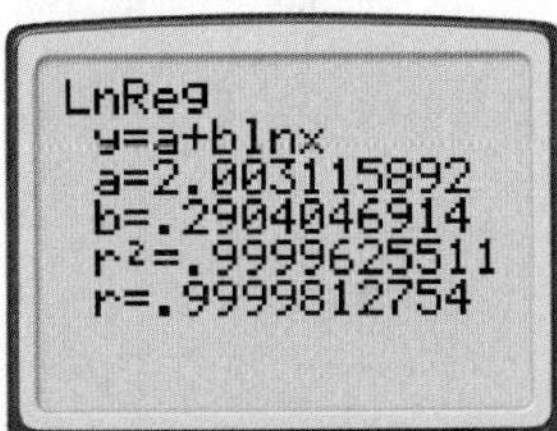

The calculated value of r^2 shows that the function fits the data.

Graph the data and function model to verify that it fits the data.

Use the intersection feature to find x when y is 6.5. The TNT equivalent of an earthquake measuring 6.5 on the Richter scale is about 5.3 million tons.

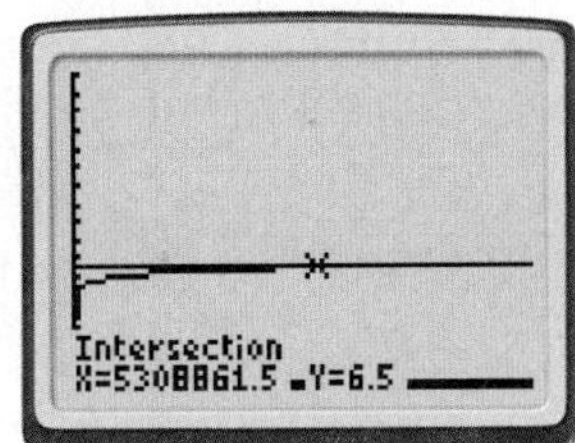

3. Use logarithmic regression to find a function that models this data. When will the speed reach 8.0 m/s?

Time (min)	1	2	3	4	5	6	7
Speed (m/s)	0.5	2.5	3.5	4.3	4.9	5.3	5.6

THINK AND DISCUSS

1. Explain how you can determine whether or not a data set can be fit by an exponential function of the form $f(x) = ab^x$.

2. Explain why having only two data points is not enough to tell you whether the data set is exponential or logarithmic.

3. GET ORGANIZED Copy and complete the graphic organizer. Show the procedures and tools for finding an exponential or logarithmic model.

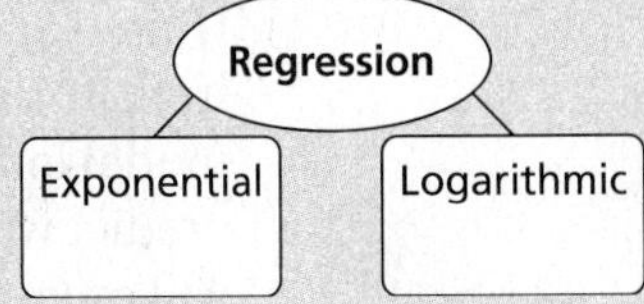

4-8 Exercises

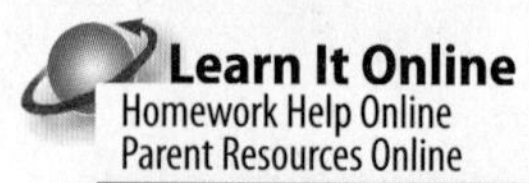

GUIDED PRACTICE

1. **Vocabulary** __?__ is useful when data can be modeled by a function of the form $f(x) = ab^x$. (*Exponential regression* or *Logarithmic regression*)

SEE EXAMPLE 1

Determine whether f is an exponential function of x of the form $f(x) = ab^x$. If so, find the constant ratio.

2.

x	−1	0	1	2	3
$f(x)$	$-2\frac{5}{7}$	−1	11	95	683

3.

x	−1	0	1	2	3
$f(x)$	27	18	12	8	$5\frac{1}{3}$

4.

x	−1	0	1	2	3
$f(x)$	5	1	−3	−7	−11

5.

x	−1	0	1	2	3
$f(x)$	$2\frac{1}{4}$	3	4	$5\frac{1}{3}$	$7\frac{1}{9}$

SEE EXAMPLE 2

6. **Physics** The table gives the approximate number of degrees Fahrenheit above room temperature of a cup of tea as it cools. Find an exponential model for the data. Use the model to estimate how long it will take the tea to reach a temperature that is less than 40 degrees above room temperature.

Cooling Tea					
Time (min)	0	1	2	3	4
Degrees above room temperature (°F)	132	120	110	101	93

SEE EXAMPLE 3

7. **Community** The table shows the population milestones for a small town following its incorporation. Find a natural log model for the data. Use the model to predict how long it will take for the population to reach 8000.

Town Population Milestones					
Time (mo)	6	18	42	90	150
Population	3000	4000	5000	6000	7000

PRACTICE AND PROBLEM SOLVING

Independent Practice

For Exercises	See Example
8–11	1
12	2
13	3

Extra Practice

See Extra Practice for more Skills Practice and Applications Practice exercises.

Determine whether f is an exponential function of x of the form $f(x) = ab^x$. If so, find the constant ratio.

8.

x	−1	0	1	2	3
$f(x)$	1.25	1	0.75	0.5	0.25

9.

x	−5	−3	1	3	5
$f(x)$	20	6	2	12	30

10.

x	−1	0	1	2	3
$f(x)$	0.667	1	1.5	2.25	3.375

11.

x	−1	0	1	2	3
$f(x)$	−16	−8	−4	−2	−1

12. **Social Studies** The table gives the United States Hispanic population from 1980 to 2000. Find an exponential model for the data. Use the model to predict when the Hispanic population will exceed 120 million.

United States Hispanic Population			
Years After 1970	10	20	30
Population (millions)	14.6	22.5	35.3

Source: Census 2000

13. **Telecommunication** The table gives the number of telecommuters in the United States from 1990 to 2000. Find an exponential model for the data. Use the model to estimate when the number of telecommuters will exceed 100 million.

U.S. Telecommuters											
Years After 1990	0	1	2	3	4	5	6	7	8	9	10
Telecommuters (millions)	4.4	5.5	6.6	7.3	9.1	8.5	8.7	11.1	15.7	19.6	23.6

Source: Federal Highway Administration

14. **Ecology** Data on an endangered crane species indicate that their numbers are increasing. The table shows the population size over the last 55 years. Find a logarithmic model for the data. Predict the year when the population will reach 500.

Crane Population					
Population Size	18	40	85	120	185
Years Since 1940	5	22	40	47	57

Decide whether the data set is exponential, and if it is, use exponential regression to find a function that models the data.

15.

x	1	2	3	4
$f(x)$	11	95	683	4799

16.

x	−1	0	2	3
$f(x)$	4	2	0.5	0.25

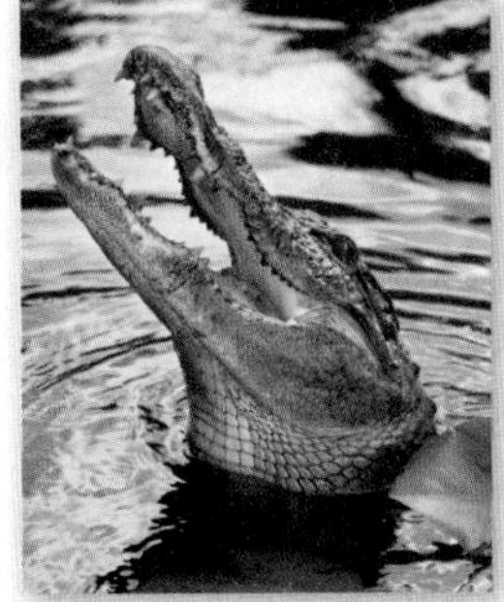
American alligator, Everglades National Park

17. **Critical Thinking** According to one source, the population of nesting wading birds in the wetlands of the Florida Everglades Park System has decreased from more than a half-million in the 1930s to less than 15,000 today. What do you need to know to determine whether this decrease in numbers is exponential? Explain.

18. **Ecology** One research study showed that the rate of calf survival in Yellowstone elk herds depends on spring snow depths. At snow depths of about 5000 mm, the rate of survival is about 0.9 per hundred cows; at 6700 mm it is about 0.3; and at 8250 mm, it is about 0.17. Find an exponential function to model the data. Use the model to predict the calf survival rate per hundred cows at snow depths of 4000 mm.

19. **Technology** Holiday season sales of a portable digital music player are shown in the graph. Assume that growth rate continues in the same way. Write an exponential function to model the data. Use the model to predict sales in three years.

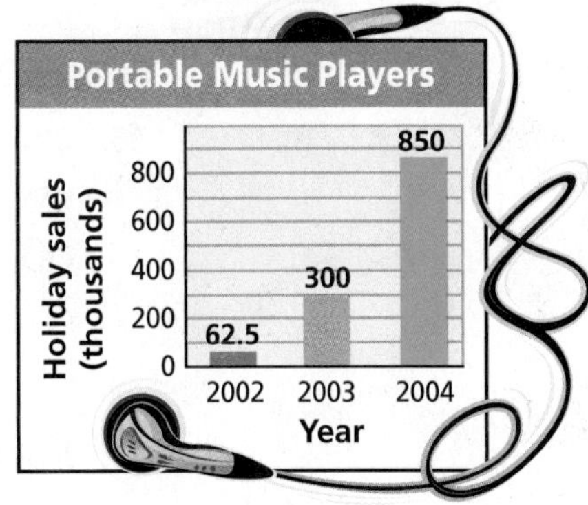

20. **Data Collection** Use a graphing calculator and a temperature probe to measure the temperature of a refrigerated liquid from the time it is taken from refrigeration. Use the list feature to subtract the temperatures from room temperature. Find a model for the difference from room temperature over time. Describe the model and explain why you chose it.

21. **Make a Conjecture** Make a table of values for an exponential function with $x = 1, 2, 3, \ldots 8$. Find the first differences, second differences, and third differences. Make a conjecture about the nth differences, assuming that the domain of the function is all natural numbers.

22. The table shows the total amount of farmland in Vermont since 1970.
   a. Use exponential regression to find a function that models the data.
   b. According to the model, by what percent does the amount of farmland decrease each year?
   c. Predict the amount of farmland in 2010.

Farmland in Vermont	
Year	Farmland (thousands of acres)
1970	2010
1980	1740
1990	1440
2000	1270

23. **Recreation** At the Autosport Show in Birmingham, England, in January 2001, karting champion Stuart Ziemelis demonstrated an electric race kart with a top speed of over 100 mi/h and acceleration from 0-to-60 mi/h in less than 4 s. The *difference* between the race kart's speed S and its top speed can be modeled by $(100 - S) = 100(0.795)^t$, where t is the time in seconds after the start.
   a. Predict the electric race kart's speed at 1, 2, and 8 s.
   b. Use your answers to part **a** to verify that the speed is an exponential function of time. Use exponential regression to find the function that models the speed.

24. **Write About It** Describe how to tell whether data is exponential rather than linear, quadratic, or cubic.

25. **Biology** The number of fronds of duckweed present during an experiment are given in the table.

Day	0	2	3	4	5	6
Fronds	18	32	43	57	76	101

   a. Which fits the data better, an exponential function or a linear function?
   b. Enter the day numbers in L1 and the logarithm of each number of fronds in L2 (use either log or ln). Which fits this data better, an exponential function or a linear function? Why?

26. Which situation can be modeled by an exponential function?
   Ⓐ A cost that increases by $100 each month
   Ⓑ The area of a square as the length increases by increments of 10 cm
   Ⓒ The radius of a spiral that gets 10% larger with each rotation
   Ⓓ A population that doubles as the time doubles

27. Which data set is exponential?
   Ⓕ (0, 0.1), (1, 0.5), (2, 2.5), (3, 12.5)
   Ⓗ (0, −1), (1, 0.5), (2, 2), (3, 3.5)
   Ⓖ (0, −1), (1, 0), (2, 7), (3, 20)
   Ⓙ (0, −1), (1, 2), (2, 11), (3, 26)

28. **Gridded Response** Find the missing value if f is an exponential function.

x	0	1	2	3
y	2	3.5	■	10.71875

CHALLENGE AND EXTEND

29. Find an exponential function that goes through the points $(2, 48)$ and $(4, 300)$. Show your work.

30. **Environment** Helena works in a chemistry laboratory. Due to equipment failure, she may have inhaled toxic fumes. Five hours after the incident, a blood sample shows a toxin concentration of 0.01006 mg/cm^3. Two hours later, another sample detects a concentration of 0.00881 mg/cm^3. Assume that concentration varies exponentially with time.
    a. Write an exponential function to model the data.
    b. There is a health risk if the toxin concentration was as high as 0.015 mg/cm^3. Was the initial concentration above this level?
    c. Helena can return to work when the concentration drops below 0.00010 mg/cm^3. How many hours (to the nearest hour) after the incident will this be?

31. The calculator uses logarithms to fit data to exponential and logarithmic functions. Determine what domains or ranges of data cause the calculator to get an error when using the exponential regression and logarithmic regression functions.

Career Path

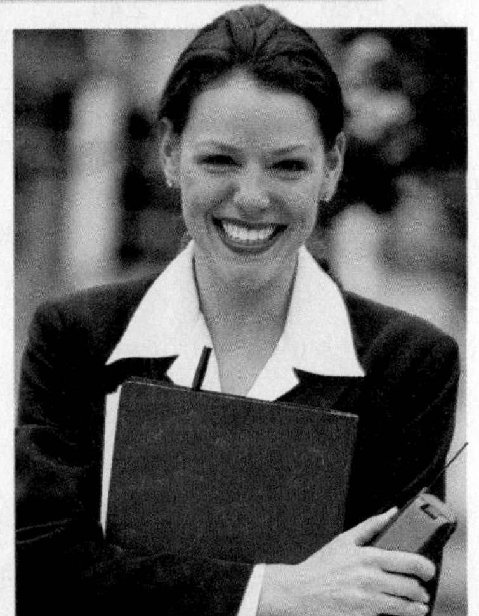

Colleen Murray
Real estate agent

Q: What high school math classes did you take?
A: Algebra 1, Geometry, Business Math, and Algebra 2.

Q: How did you become a real estate agent?
A: After high school, I took an online training course in real estate. Then I had to pass a state license exam.

Q: How is math used in real estate?
A: We calculate house prices, interest rates, payments, taxes, closing costs, commissions, and other fees. I use geometry to calculate areas and formulas to convert between units of measurement, such as square feet to acres.

Q: What are your future plans?
A: I may look into becoming a broker. Then I can supervise other agents and manage my own office.

CHAPTER 4

MULTI-STEP TEST PREP

SECTION 4B

Model with mathematics.

Applying Exponential and Logarithmic Functions

Down on the Farm According to data from the U.S. Department of Agriculture, the number of farms in the United States has been decreasing over the past several decades. During this time, however, the average size of each farm has increased.

1. From 1940 to 1980, the average size A of a U.S. farm can be modeled by the function $A(t) = 174e^{0.022t}$, where t is the number of years since 1940. What was the average farm size in 1940? in 1980?
2. In what year did the average farm size reach 250 acres?
3. During the period from 1940 to 1980, how many years did it take for the average farm size to double?
4. The table shows the number of farms in the United States since 1940. Find an exponential model for the data.
5. Predict the number of farms in the United States in 2010.
6. According to your model, how many years does it take for the number of farms to decrease by 50%?
7. According to your model, when will the number of farms in the United States fall below 1 million?

Farms in the United States

Year	Number of Farms (millions)
1940	6.35
1950	5.65
1960	3.96
1970	2.95
1980	2.44
1990	2.15
2000	2.17

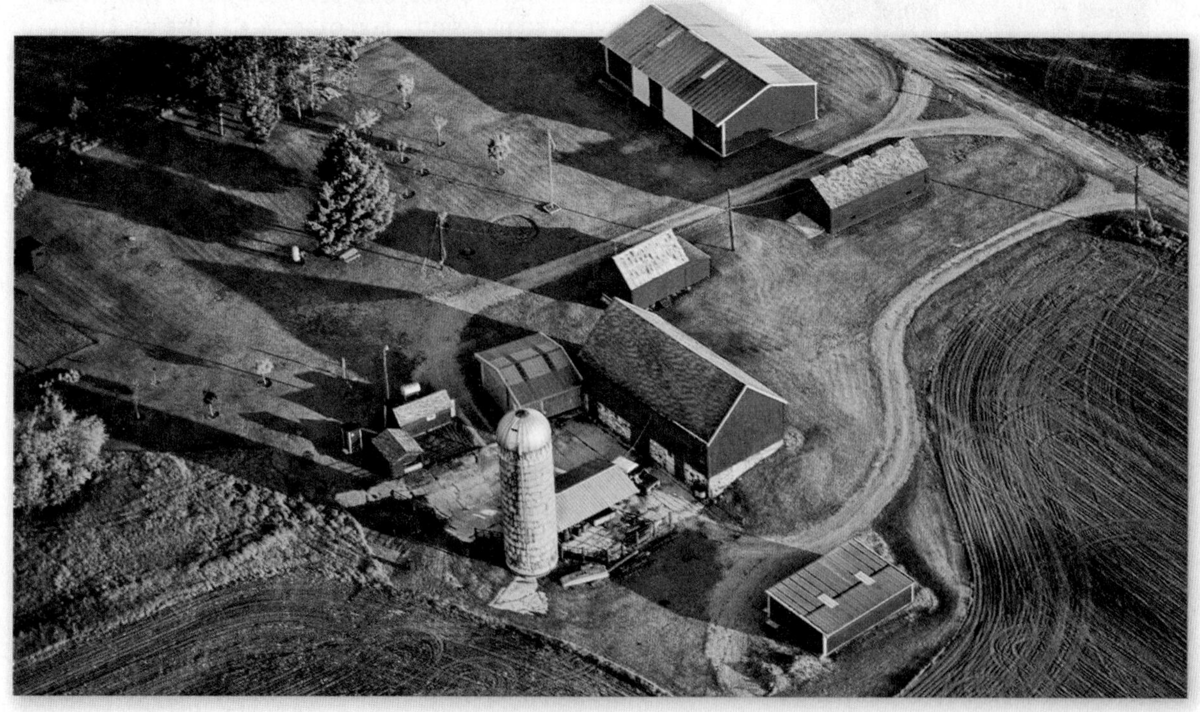

(tl) Photodisc/Getty Images; (b) Jim Wark/Airphoto

READY TO GO ON?

CHAPTER 4

SECTION 4B

Quiz for Lessons 4-5 Through 4-8

4-5 Exponential and Logarithmic Equations and Inequalities

Solve.

1. $3^x = \frac{1}{27}$ **2.** $49^{x+4} < 7^{\frac{x}{2}}$ **3.** $13^{3x-x} = 91$ **4.** $2^{x+4} = 20$

5. $\log_4(x - 1) \geq 3$ **6.** $\log_2 x^{\frac{1}{3}} = 5$ **7.** $\log 16x - \log 4 = 2$

8. $\log x + \log(x + 3) = 1$

9. Suppose that you deposit \$500 into an account that pays 3.5% compounded quarterly. The equation $A = P(1 + r)^n$ gives the amount A in the account after n quarters for an initial investment of P that earns interest at a rate of r. Use logarithms to solve for n to find how long it will take for the account to contain at least \$2000.

4-6 The Natural Base, *e*

Graph.

10. $f(x) = e^x + 3$ **11.** $f(x) = 3 - e^x$ **12.** $f(x) = \frac{e^x}{3}$ **13.** $f(x) = 3(e^x - 1)$

Simplify.

14. $\ln e^2$ **15.** $\ln e^{\frac{x}{2}}$ **16.** $e^{\ln(1-3a)}$ **17.** $\ln e^{b+5}$

18. Carbon-14 is a useful dating tool for specimens between 500 and 25,000 years old, such as ancient manuscripts and artifacts. Carbon-14's half-life is 5730 years.

a. Use the formula $\frac{1}{2} = e^{-kt}$ to find the value of the decay constant for carbon-14.

b. Use the decay function $N_t = N_0 e^{-kt}$ to determine how much of 10 grams of carbon-14 will remain after 1000 years.

4-7 Transforming Exponential and Logarithmic Functions

Graph the function. Find the *y*-intercept and asymptote. Describe how the graph is transformed from the graph of the parent function.

19. $g(x) = 1.5(3^x)$ **20.** $k(x) = e^{\frac{x}{2}}$

Graph the function. Find the *x*-intercept and asymptote. Describe how the graph is transformed from the graph of the parent function.

21. $n(x) = 3.5 \log(x + 1)$ **22.** $p(x) = -\ln(x + 2)$

Write the transformed function.

23. $f(x) = 0.5^x$ is horizontally compressed by a factor of $\frac{1}{2}$ and reflected across the *x*-axis.

4-8 Curve Fitting with Exponential and Logarithmic Models

Determine whether *y* is an exponential function of *x*. If so, find the constant ratio. Then use exponential regression to find a function that models the data.

24.

x	0	1	2	3	4	5
y	1.5	3	6	12	24	48

25.

x	0	1	2	3	4	5
y	1.5	2.4	3.3	4.2	5.1	6.0

CHAPTER 4

Study Guide: Review

Vocabulary

asymptote
base
common logarithm
exponential decay
exponential equation
exponential function
exponential growth
exponential regression
inverse function
inverse relation
logarithm
logarithmic equation
logarithmic function
logarithmic regression
natural logarithm
natural logarithmic function

Complete the sentences below with vocabulary words from the list above.

1. A(n) ___?___ has a base of e.

2. A(n) ___?___ is a line that a graphed function approaches but does not touch.

3. To graph a(n) ___?___, reflect each point in the relation across the line $y = x$.

4-1 Exponential Functions, Growth, and Decay

EXAMPLE

A quantity of a certain vitamin is eliminated from the bloodstream at about 15% per hour.

- Will the function that represents this situation show growth or decay?

  It will show decay because the quantity decreases.

- Write a function to show the amount of the vitamin that remains t hours after the peak level of 400 mg.

  $f(x) = 400(0.85)^t$

- Graph the function. Use the graph to predict the amount remaining after 7 hours.

  After 7 hours, about 130 mg are left.

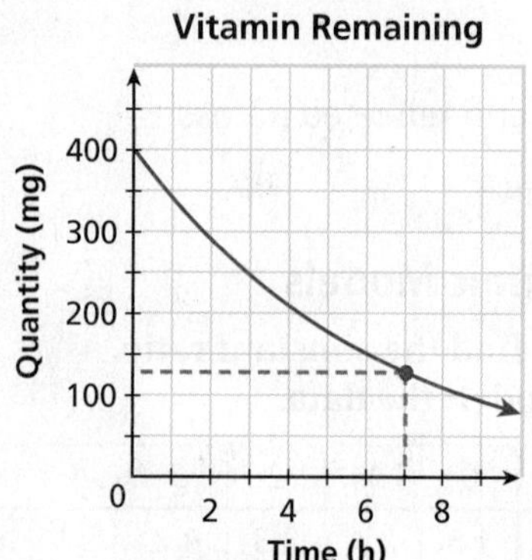

EXERCISES

Tell whether the function shows growth or decay. Then graph.

4. $f(x) = 0.5(1.25)^x$

5. $f(x) = 0.5\left(\frac{3}{2}\right)^x$

6. $f(x) = 2.5(0.25)^x$

7. $f(x) = 2(1 + 0.25)^x$

Use the following data to answer the questions.

The student population in a small resort town has increased by 2% per year for the last 5 years. This year's population is 765 students.

8. Will the function that represents this situation show growth or decay?

9. Suppose that the student population continues to follow the same trend. Write a function to show the number of students as a function of the year, starting with the current year.

10. Graph the function.

11. Use the graph to predict the number of students in 5 years.

12. When will the population exceed 1000 students?

4-2 Inverses of Relations and Functions

EXAMPLE

■ **Graph the function $f(x) = \frac{4}{5} - 3x$. Then write its inverse and graph.**

$y = -3x + \frac{4}{5}$ *Set y = f(x) and graph*

$x = -3y + \frac{4}{5}$ *Interchange x and y.*

$3y = -x + \frac{4}{5}$ *Solve for y.*

$y = -\frac{1}{3}x + \frac{4}{15}$

Write the inverse and graph.

$f^{-1}(x) = -\frac{1}{3}x + \frac{4}{15}$

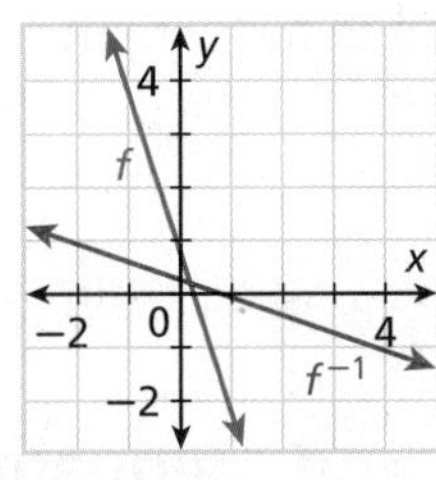

EXERCISES

13. Graph the relation and connect the points. Then graph and write the inverse.

x	−1	0	1	2	3
y	1	0.2	0.04	0.008	0.001

This year the population of a species decreased by 3% from last year.

14. Write an expression for the size of the population this year P_T as a function of last year's population P_L.

15. Write an expression for the year as a function of the size of the population.

16. The formula $M = \frac{5}{8}K$ gives the approximate distance in miles as a function of kilometers. Write and use the inverse of this function to express 25 miles in kilometers.

4-3 Logarithmic Functions

EXAMPLES

■ **Write the exponential equation $9^{1.5} = 27$ in logarithmic form.**

$9^{1.5} = 27$

$\log_9 27 = 1.5$ *A logarithm is an exponent.*

■ **Evaluate $\log_4 64$.**

Because $4^3 = 64$, $\log_4 64 = 3$.

■ **Graph $f(x) = 0.6^x$. Then graph its inverse. Describe the domain and range of the inverse function.**

x	−2	−1	0	1	2
f(x)	2.8	1.7	1	0.6	0.4

To graph the inverse, reverse each ordered pair.

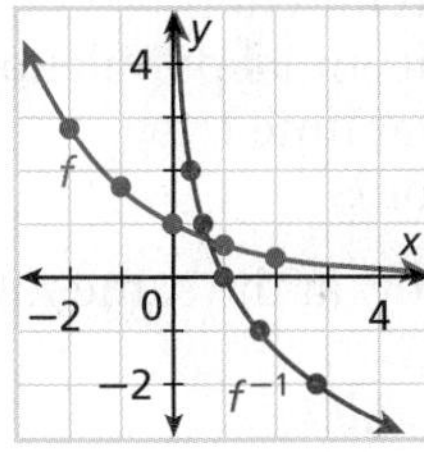

For the inverse function, the domain is $\{x \mid x > 0\}$, and the range is $\mathbb{R}$.

EXERCISES

Write each exponential equation in logarithmic form.

17. $3^5 = 243$ **18.** $1 = 9^0$ **19.** $\left(\frac{1}{3}\right)^{-3} = 27$

Write each logarithmic equation in exponential form.

20. $\log_2 16 = 4$ **21.** $\log 10 = 1$ **22.** $2 = \log_{0.6} 0.36$

Evaluate by using mental math.

23. $\log_7 49$ **24.** $\log_{0.5} 0.25$

25. $\log_{12}\left(\frac{1}{12}\right)$ **26.** $\log 0.01$ **27.** $\log_2 1$

28. Make a table of ordered pairs for $f(x) = \left(\frac{1}{2}\right)^x$. Graph the function and its inverse. Describe the domain and range of the inverse function.

4-4 Properties of Logarithms

EXAMPLES

Express as a single logarithm and simplify.

- $\log 25 + \log 40$
  $= \log(25 \cdot 40) = \log 1000 = 3$
- $\log_5 125 - \log_5 25$
  $= \log_5\left(\frac{125}{25}\right) = \log_5 5 = 1$
- $\log_3 8^2$
  $= 2\log_3 8 = 2 \cdot 2 = 4$
- **Evaluate $\log_5 16$.**

$= \frac{\log 16}{\log 5}$ *Use the change of base formula.*

$\approx \frac{1.2}{0.7} \approx 1.72$ *Use a calculator to evaluate.*

EXERCISES

Express as a single logarithm and simplify.

29. $\log_2 8 + \log_2 16$
30. $\log 100 + \log 10{,}000$
31. $\log_2 128 - \log_2 2$
32. $\log 10 - \log 0.1$
33. $\log_5 25^2$
34. $\log 10^5 + \log 10^4$
35. The apparent loudness of the music today at Sam's Café was 10 decibels greater than the loudness yesterday. Apparent loudness L is given by $L = 10\log\frac{I}{I_0}$, where I is the intensity of sound, in W/m^2 and I_0 is the lowest intensity that the ear can detect. How many times more intense was the sound today than yesterday?

4-5 Exponential and Logarithmic Equations and Inequalities

EXAMPLES

Solve.

- $5^x = 50$

$\log 5^x = \log 50$

$x\log 5 = \log 50$

$x = \frac{\log 50}{\log 5} \approx 2.43$

- $\log_9 x^2 = 5$

$2\log_9 x = 5$

$\log_9 x = \frac{5}{2}$

$x = 9^{\frac{5}{2}}$

$x = (3^2)^{\frac{5}{2}} = 3^5 = 243$

EXERCISES

Solve and check.

36. $3^{x-x} = \frac{1}{9}$
37. $\left(\frac{1}{2}\right)^x \le 64$
38. $\log x^{\frac{5}{2}} > 2.5$
39. $A = P(1 + r)^n$ gives amount A in an account after n years for an initial investment P that earns interest at an annual rate r. How long will it take for \$250 to increase to \$500 at 4% annual interest?

4-6 The Natural Base, *e*

EXAMPLE

- **Simplify $e^{\ln(2s+1)}$.**
  $e^{\ln(2s+1)} = 2s + 1$ *e to the ln of a number is just the number.*
- **What is the total value of an investment of \$5000 that earned 6% interest compounded continuously for 5 years?**

$A = 5000e^{0.06(5)}$ *Substitute in $A = Pe^{rt}$.*

$A \approx 6749.29$ *Use a calculator.*

The value is \$6749.29.

EXERCISES

40. The population of whooping cranes was about 22 in 1940 and grew at an exponential rate to about 194 in 2003.

a. Use the exponential growth function $P(t) = P_0e^{kt}$, where P_0 is the initial population and $P(t)$ is the population at time t, to determine the growth factor k.

b. If the flock continues to grow at the same rate, how large will it be in 2020?

4-7 Transforming Exponential and Logarithmic Functions

EXAMPLES

Write each transformed function.

- $f(x) = \left(\frac{1}{3}\right)^x$ is shifted 1 unit left, stretched vertically by a factor of 2, and reflected across the y-axis.

$\left(\frac{1}{3}\right)^x$ *Begin with the rule for the parent function.*

$\left(\frac{1}{3}\right)^{x+1}$ *To shift 1 unit left, replace x with x + 1.*

$2\left(\frac{1}{3}\right)^{x+1}$ *Stretch vertically by 2.*

$g(x) = 2\left(\frac{1}{3}\right)^{-x+1}$ *Reflect across the y-axis.*

- $f(x) = \log x$ is shifted 2 units right and 1 unit down and is compressed vertically by a factor of 0.3.

$g(x) = \log\left(\frac{x}{0.3} - 2\right) - 1$

EXERCISES

Write the transformed function.

41. $f(x) = e^x$ is reflected across the x-axis, stretched vertically by a factor of 3, and shifted 2 units down.

Graph each function. Find the intercept and asymptote. Describe how the graph is transformed from the graph of the parent function.

42. $k(x) = \frac{3}{5}(1.5)^{6x}$

43. $m(x) = 2\log\left(x + \frac{1}{2}\right)$

The trade-in value of Marc's truck is \$5300. A truck dealer tells him that the trade-in value of a truck decreases by about 35% each year.

44. Write an equation for the trade-in value as a function of time.

45. Describe how the graph of this function is transformed from the graph of the parent function.

4-8 Curve Fitting with Exponential and Logarithmic Models

EXAMPLES

- **Use logarithmic regression to find a function that models the increase in the number of pepper trees in a wilderness preserve over six years. Predict the year when the number of trees will reach 70.**

Year	1	2	3	4	5	6
Trees	14	30	40	46	53	55

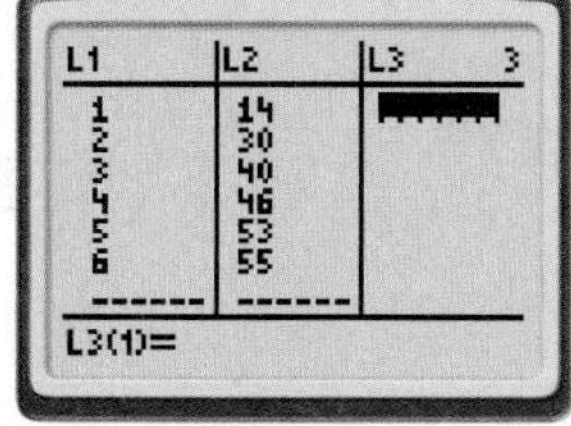

$y \approx 14 + 23.4 \ln x$ *Write the model.*

$\ln x \approx \frac{70 - 14}{23.4} \approx 2.39$ *Substitute 70 for y. Then solve for ln x.*

$x \approx e^{2.39} \approx 10.9$ *Solve for x.*

There will be 70 trees in about 11 years.

EXERCISES

The table gives the population size of a flock of birds in one habitat over the last 57 years.

Years Since Data Was First Collected	Population Size
5	18
22	22
40	85
57	185

46. Use exponential regression, **ExpReg**, to find an exponential function that models the data.

47. Use logarithmic regression, **LnReg**, to find a logarithmic function that models the data.

48. Compare r^2-values of the two functions. Tell which function best models the data and why.

CHAPTER 4

CHAPTER TEST

Tell whether the function shows growth or decay. Then graph.

1. $f(x) = 0.4^x$

2. $f(x) = 1.3\left(\frac{2}{5}\right)^x$

3. $f(x) = \frac{7}{8}(1.1)^x$

4. $f(x) = 50(1 + 0.04)^x$

5. Gina buys a car for $13,500. Assume that its value will decrease by about 15% per year. Write an exponential function to model the value of the car. Graph the function. When will the value fall below $3000?

Graph each function. Then write its inverse and graph.

6. $f(x) = x - 1.06$

7. $f(x) = \frac{5}{6}x - 1.06$

8. $f(x) = 1.06 - \frac{5}{6}x$

9. $f(x) = \frac{1}{4}\left(1.06 - \frac{5}{6}x\right)$

Write in the alternative form (exponential or logarithmic).

10. $16^{\frac{1}{4}} = 2$

11. $16^{-0.5} = \frac{1}{4}$

12. $\log_{\frac{1}{4}} 64 = -3$

13. $\log_{81} \frac{1}{3} = -\frac{1}{4}$

Use the given x-values to graph each function. Then write and graph its inverse. Describe the domain and range of the inverse function.

14. $f(x) = \left(\frac{1}{4}\right)^x$; $x = -1, 0, 2, 4$

15. $f(x) = 2.5^x$; $x = -1, 0, 1, 2, 3$

16. $f(x) = 5^{-x}$; $x = -1, 0, 1, 2, 3$

Simplify.

17. $\log_4 128 - \log_4 8$

18. $\log_2 12.8 + \log_2 5$

19. $\log_3 243^2$

20. $5^{\log_5 x}$

Solve.

21. $3^{x-x} = 729^{\frac{x}{2}}$

22. $5^{1.5-x} \leq 25$

23. $\log_4(x + 48) = 3$

24. $\log(6x^2) - \log 2x = 1$

25. The rate at which a liquid vitamin breaks down in the average human body can be modeled by $y = D(0.95)^x$, where y ml of the original dose D remains after x minutes. How long will it take for an original dose of 15 ml to be reduced to less than 5 ml?

26. Plutonium Pu-239 has a half-life of about 24,000 years. The formula $\frac{1}{2} = e^{-kt}$ relates the half-life t to the decay constant k for a given substance. How much of a 100-gram quantity of plutonium will remain after 5 years?

27. $f(x) = \ln x$ is shifted 2 units left and 1 unit up and is vertically stretched by a factor of 3. Write the transformed function.

28. Use logarithmic regression to find the function that models the population data in the table. In what year will the population exceed 100?

Population	50	62	78
Year	1	2	3

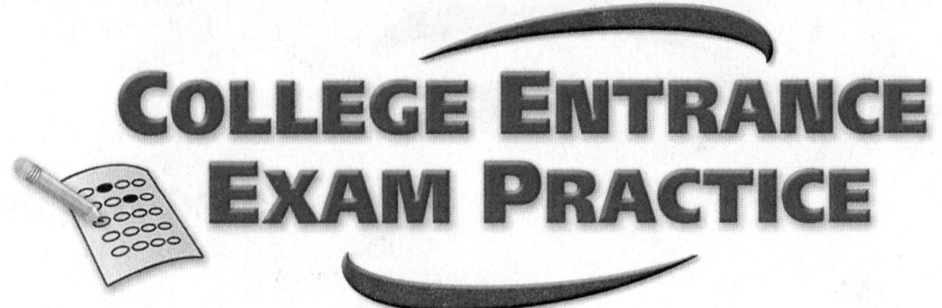

CHAPTER 4

COLLEGE ENTRANCE EXAM PRACTICE

FOCUS ON SAT SUBJECT TESTS

The SAT Mathematics Subject Test Level 2 test is meant to be taken by students who have completed two years of algebra and one year of geometry and have studied elementary functions, trigonometry, and some precalculus topics, such as limits.

The questions are placed in an order of increasing difficulty. Because each question is worth the same amount of points, answer as many of the less difficult questions as you can before tackling the more difficult ones.

You may want to time yourself as you take this practice test. It should take you about 6 minutes to complete.

1. If $f^{-1}(x) = \frac{4}{3}x + 8$, what is $f(x)$?

(A) $f(x) = \frac{3}{4}(x - 8)$

(B) $f(x) = \frac{3}{4}x - 8$

(C) $f(x) = \frac{3}{4}(x + 6)$

(D) $f(x) = \frac{4}{3}(x - 8)$

(E) $f(x) = \frac{4}{3}x - 6$

2. If $f(x) = e^x$, then which of the following is $f^{-1}(7)$?

(A) e^7

(B) 7

(C) log 7

(D) ln 7

(E) $\ln\left(e^7\right)$

3. If $e^x e^{2.5} = e^{2.5x}$, what is the vaue of x?

(A) 0

(B) 1

(C) $\frac{5}{3}$

(D) $\mathbb{R}$

(E) $\varnothing$

4. What is $\log_{27} 9$?

(A) $\frac{1}{2}$

(B) $\frac{2}{3}$

(C) $\frac{3}{2}$

(D) 2

(E) 3

5. What is the y-coordinate of the point where the graphs of $y = \log_2\left(\frac{3}{4}x - \frac{23}{4}\right)$ and $y = \log_2\left(-2x + \frac{65}{4}\right)$ intersect?

(A) -2

(B) $\frac{1}{4}$

(C) $\frac{1}{2}$

(D) 2

(E) 8

6. If $\log_9\left\{\log_2\left[\log_4(x)\right]\right\} = \frac{1}{2}$, then what is x?

(A) 1.73

(B) 8

(C) 81

(D) 6561

(E) 65,536

CHAPTER 4

TEST TACKLER

Standardized Test Strategies

Any Question Type: Read a Test Item for Understanding

Test items given on a standardized test may vary in type from multiple choice to gridded response to short and extended response. All test items should be read thoroughly so that you recognize important information and have a complete understanding of what is being asked.

EXAMPLE 1

Extended Response The value of a computer purchased new for \$2300 goes down by 15.5% each year. Write and graph an exponential function to estimate the value of the computer after 3 years. When will the value of the computer fall below \$500?

READ the problem again.

RESTATE the important parts of the test item by using your own words:

What information are you given? The cost of the computer: \$2300
The annual percent decrease: 15.5%

What are you asked to do?
1. Write an exponential function.
2. Graph the exponential function.
3. Estimate the computer's value after 3 years.
4. Find when the value will fall below \$500.

What should your response include?
1. An exponential function
2. A graph
3. An estimated value, in dollars
4. The time in years

NOTE: Your response should include four parts.

EXAMPLE 2

Short Response Two samples of water taken Monday from a wastewater treatment holding tank have a pH of 4.2 and 4.9. To record the pH for the day, a technician finds the average pH for the two samples. What is the difference in the average pH for Monday and the sample that is most acidic?

READ the problem again.

RESTATE the important parts of the test item by using your own words:

What information are you given? The pH of two samples: 4.2, 4.9

What are you asked to do? Subtract: $pH_{\text{average}} - pH_{\text{most acidic sample}}$

Make a plan for your response. Calculate the average pH.
Identify the most acidic sample.
Find the difference.

NOTE: The question requires an intermediate step.

Break a test item into parts to help you organize your approach to the problem.

Read each test item, and answer the questions that follow.

Item A

Gridded Response What is the total amount, to the nearest whole dollar, for an investment of $800 invested at 3.5% for 15 years and compounded continuously?

1. What information are you given?
2. What are you asked to find?
3. Antonio solved this problem and got an incorrect answer of $1220 after using the formula $I = Prt$. What important word(s) did Antonio overlook that may have led him to the correct formula? Explain.
4. Cleo solved this problem by using the formula $800(1 + 0.035)^{15}$ and got an answer of $1340. Did Cleo solve the problem correctly? Explain.

Item B

Gridded Response A doctor prescribed a daily 15-milligram dose of vitamin D to a 55-year-old man. The man weighs 225 pounds. The half-life of vitamin D is about 25 days. The amount A of vitamin D left after t days can be expressed by the exponential function $A = 15\left(\frac{1}{2}\right)^{\frac{t}{25}}$. Find the number of days (to the nearest day) that it takes for the initial dose of vitamin D to drop below 9 milligrams.

5. What information are you given?
6. Identify any information not necessary for your calculations. Explain.
7. Describe a plan that you can use to solve this problem.
8. A student gridded a decimal answer for his response. What part of the problem statement did he overlook?

Item C

Short Response Martha has $6435 in her home safe. She decides to take two-thirds of this amount and invest it in an account that earns 4.25% interest, compounded continuously. What is the total amount of money that Martha has in 3 years?

9. List the information given and what you are being asked to find.
10. Are there intermediate steps that you need to perform to solve the problem? If so, describe the steps.

Item D

Extended Response A runner ran a 3000 m race in 12 minutes and 48 seconds. Write a function that gives distance as a function of time. Write and use the inverse function to find the time it would take the runner to complete a 10,000 m race at the same speed.

11. How many parts are there to this question? Make a list of what needs to be included in your response.
12. What question are you to answer? What units would be acceptable for your answer?

Item E

Short Response Which data set is best represented by using a logarithmic model? Explain your reasoning, and give the function of the logarithmic model.

A)

x	1	20	40	60	80
y	88	218	341	647	980

B)

x	5	15	25	35	45
y	26	43	52	59	61

13. To determine which data set *best* represents a logarithmic model, what intermediate step must you perform to make a comparison?
14. Make a plan for your response.

STANDARDIZED TEST PREP

CUMULATIVE ASSESSMENT

Multiple Choice

1. Which graph is the inverse of $f(x) = -3x + 6$?

Ⓐ
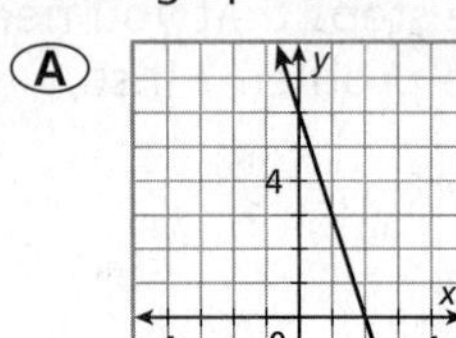

Ⓒ
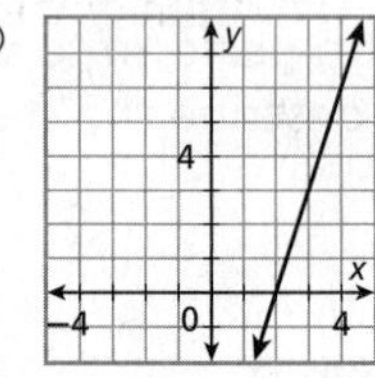

Ⓑ
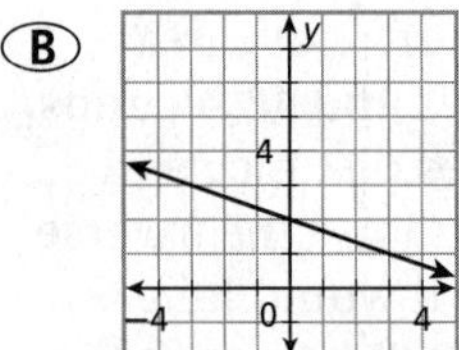

Ⓓ
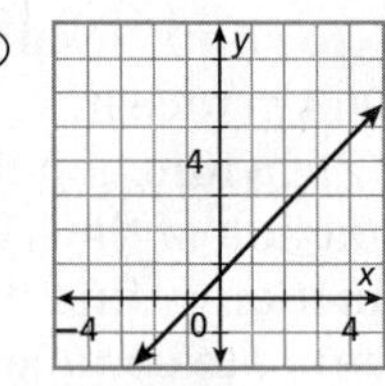

2. Which is equivalent to $\log_5 12 - \log_5 4$?

Ⓕ $\log_5 48$

Ⓖ $\log_5 8$

Ⓗ $\log_5 16$

Ⓙ $\log_5 3$

3. What is the value of x in the equation $\log_4(x-1)^3 = 9$?

Ⓐ $x = 27$

Ⓑ $x = 64$

Ⓒ $x = 65$

Ⓓ $x = 81$

4. The parent logarithmic function $f(x) = \ln x$ is shifted 2 units to the right and 7 units down and is horizontally stretched by a factor of 6. Which is the transformed function?

Ⓕ $f(x) = 6\ln(x-2) - 7$

Ⓖ $f(x) = \ln\left(\frac{x}{6} - 2\right) - 7$

Ⓗ $f(x) = 6\ln(x+2) + 7$

Ⓙ $f(x) = 6\ln\left(\frac{x}{6} + 2\right) + 7$

5. Which equation best fits the data in the scatter plot?

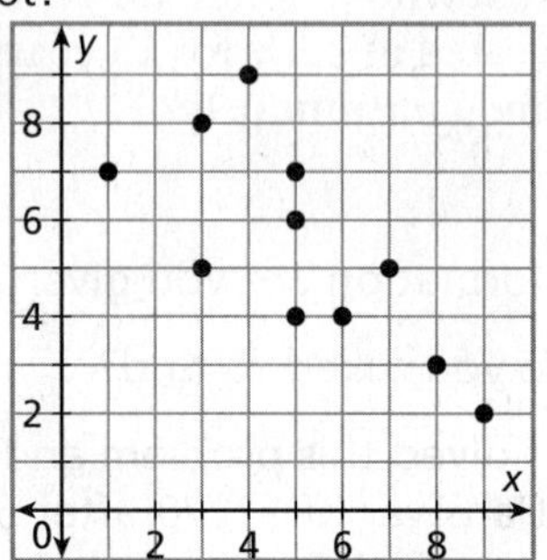

Ⓐ $y = -\frac{10}{11}x + 10$

Ⓑ $y = \frac{10}{11}x + 10$

Ⓒ $y = -\frac{11}{10}x + 1$

Ⓓ $y = \frac{11}{10}x + 1$

6. Which is a factor of $P(x) = 8x^3 - 26x^2 + 17x + 6$?

Ⓕ $4x - 1$

Ⓖ $x + 2$

Ⓗ $2x + 3$

Ⓙ $2x - 3$

7. Which function has a zero of 1?

Ⓐ $f(x) = 2^x - 2$

Ⓑ $f(x) = 2^x + 2$

Ⓒ $f(x) = 2^{x-2}$

Ⓓ $f(x) = 2^{x+2}$

8. The linear correlation coefficient r relating two sets of data is found to be -0.24, and the line of best fit has a y-intercept of 10. Which of the following is NOT necessarily true?

Ⓕ As the values of one set of data increase, the values of the other set decrease.

Ⓖ For positive values of x, the y-value of the line of best fit is less than 10.

Ⓗ The line of best fit is a good model for the data.

Ⓙ The line of best fit has a negative slope.

9. Which has a vertex at $(-2, -3)$?

Ⓐ $y = x^2 + 4x + 1$

Ⓑ $y = x^2 + 4x - 1$

Ⓒ $y = x^2 - 4x + 1$

Ⓓ $y = x^2 - 4x - 1$

10. What is the product $3(x + y)^4$?

Ⓕ $x^4 + 4x^3y + 6x^2y^2 + 4xy^3 + y^4$

Ⓖ $3x^4 + 12x^3y + 18x^2y^2 + 12xy^3 + 3y^4$

Ⓗ $81x^4 + y^4$

Ⓙ $3x^4 + 3y^4$

11. A line in $y = mx + b$ form has a positive slope and a y-intercept of 5. The slope of the line is decreased. Which of the following must be true?

Ⓐ The x-intercept of the new line is less than the x-intercept of the original line.

Ⓑ The original line and the new line intersect only at $(0, 5)$.

Ⓒ The slope of the new line is greater than 0.

Ⓓ The new line is parallel to the original line.

In Item 12, you can replace a missing number with a variable, such as *x*. Choose a different variable if there is already an *x* in the problem.

Gridded Response

12. Simplify the expression
$\log_2 256 - \log_5 625 + \ln e$.

13. Evaluate $\log_{6.25} 2.5$.

14. Find the positive zero of the equation $f(x) = x^2 + 2.6x - 7.31$ by using the Quadratic Formula.

15. What is the multiplicity of the root 2 in the equation $x^3 - 8x^2 + 20x - 16 = 0$?

16. Use the parent function $f(x) = x^2$. What is the horizontal compression factor of the function $g(x) = \frac{1}{2}(5x)^2 - 4$?

17. What power of 2 has a value of 268,435,456?

Short Response

18. A school is selling used computers and printers. The school sells the computers for \$500 each and the printers for \$50 each. The goal is for the school to make at least \$5200. The school expects to sell at least five computers for every two printers.

a. Write a system of inequalities that models this situation, where x is the number of computers sold, and y is the number of printers sold.

b. Graph the system of inequalities.

19. Radium-226, which has a half-life of 1620 years, is used in medicine for treatment of disease.

a. Find the value of k for radium-226.

b. How much of a 100-gram dose of radium-226 will remain after 3240 years? Round to the nearest gram.

20. Twenty equally spaced points along a 6-foot board are marked for drilling. The distance from the first and last point to the ends is equal to the space between points. What is the distance between consecutive points, to the nearest hundredth of an inch?

Extended Response

21. The chart below shows how many hours students in different grades study each night.

Grade (x)	4	6	8	10	12
Hours (y)	$\frac{1}{4}$	$\frac{1}{2}$	1	2	4

a. Determine if the data set is exponential or logarithmic.

b. Graph the points.

c. Find a function to model the data. Round to the nearest ten thousandth.

d. In which grade do students study 45 minutes each night? Round to the nearest grade.

e. How long do third graders study each night? Round to the nearest half minute.

CHAPTER 5

Rational and Radical Functions

COMMON CORE

Chapter Focus

- Apply algebraic reasoning to solve problems with rational and radical expressions.
- Make connections among multiple representations of rational and radical functions.

Race to the Finish

You can use rational expressions and functions to determine a bicyclist's average speed in a race with multiple stages.

Learn It Online
Chapter Project Online

Vocabulary

Match each term on the left with a definition on the right.

1. asymptote
2. rational number
3. reflection
4. translation
5. zero of a function

A. any number that can be expressed as a quotient of two integers, where the denominator is not zero
B. a transformation that flips a figure across a line
C. any number x such that $f(x) = 0$
D. a line that a curve approaches as the value of x or y becomes very large or very small
E. a whole number or its opposite
F. a transformation that moves each point in a figure the same distance in the same direction

Properties of Exponents

Simplify each expression. Assume that all variables are nonzero.

6. $\dfrac{x^{11}y^5}{x^4y^7}$
7. $\left(\dfrac{3x^2y}{z}\right)^4$
8. $(x^3)^{-2}$
9. $(3x^3y)(6xy^5)$
10. $(2x^{-4})^3$
11. $12x^0$

Combine Like Terms

Simplify each expression.

12. $5x^2 + 10x - 4x + 6$
13. $3x + 12 - 10x$
14. $x^2 + x + 3x^2 - 4x$

Greatest Common Factor

Find the greatest common factor of each pair of expressions.

15. $3a^2$ and $12a$
16. c^2d and cd^2
17. $16x^4$ and $40x^3$

Factor Trinomials

Factor each trinomial.

18. $x^2 - 4x - 5$
19. $x^2 + 2x - 24$
20. $x^2 + 12x + 32$
21. $x^2 + 9x + 18$
22. $x^2 - 6x + 9$
23. $x^2 - 8x - 20$

Solve Quadratic Equations

Solve.

24. $5x^2 = 45$
25. $4x^2 - 7 = 93$
26. $2(x - 2)^2 = 32$

CHAPTER 5

Study Guide: Preview

Where You've Been

Previously, you

- solved problems with linear functions.
- simplified polynomial expressions.
- graphed functions with asymptotes.
- solved quadratic equations and inequalities.

In This Chapter

You will study

- solving problems with variation functions.
- simplifying rational and radical expressions.
- graphing rational and radical functions.
- solving rational and radical equations and inequalities.

Where You're Going

You can use the skills in this chapter

- in future math classes, including Precalculus.
- to solve problems in other classes, such as Chemistry, Physics, and Biology.
- outside of school to make predictions involving time, money, or speed.

Key Vocabulary/Vocabulario

complex fraction	fracción compleja
constant of variation	constante de variación
continuous function	función continua
direct variation	variación directa
discontinuous function	función discontinua
extraneous solutions	soluciones extrañas
hole (in a graph)	hoyo (en una gráfica)
inverse variation	variación inversa
radical equation	ecuación radical
radical function	función radical
rational equation	ecuación racional
rational exponent	exponente racional
rational function	función racional

Vocabulary Connections

To become familiar with some of the vocabulary terms in the chapter, consider the following. You may refer to the chapter, the glossary, or a dictionary if you like.

1. The word *extraneous* contains the word *extra*. What does *extra* mean? What do you think an **extraneous solution** is?
2. The graph of a **continuous function** has no gaps or breaks. How do you think a **discontinuous function** differs from a continuous function?
3. Do you think a **hole** could occur in the graph of a *continuous function* or a *discontinuous function*? Why?
4. A rational number can be written as a ratio of two integers. What do you think a **rational exponent** is?

Study Strategy: Make Flash Cards

You can use flash cards to help you remember a sequence of steps, the definitions of vocabulary words, or important formulas and properties.

Use these hints to make useful flash cards:

- Write a vocabulary word or the name of a formula or property on one side of a card and the meaning on the other.
- When memorizing a sequence of steps, make a flash card for each step.
- Use examples or diagrams if needed.

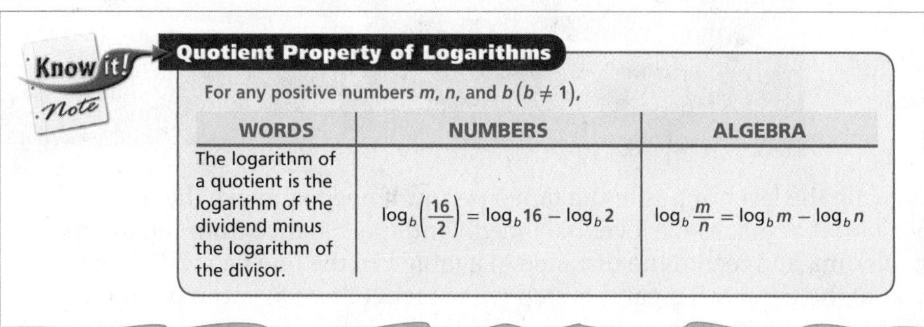

Know it! Note

Quotient Property of Logarithms

For any positive numbers m, n, and $b \left(b \neq 1\right)$,

WORDS	NUMBERS	ALGEBRA
The logarithm of a quotient is the logarithm of the dividend minus the logarithm of the divisor.	$\log_b\left(\frac{16}{2}\right) = \log_b 16 - \log_b 2$	$\log_b \frac{m}{n} = \log_b m - \log_b n$

Sample Flash Card

Quotient Property of Logarithms

$\log_b \frac{m}{n} = ?$

Front

$\log_b \frac{m}{n} = \log_b m - \log_b n$

example:

$\log_2\left(\frac{16}{2}\right) = \log_2 16 - \log_2 2$

Back

Try This

Make flash cards that can help you remember each piece of information.

1. The Product of Powers Property states that to multiply powers with the same base, add the exponents.
2. The quadratic formula, $x = \frac{-b \pm \sqrt{b^2 - 4ac}}{2a}$, can be used to find the roots of an equation with the form $ax^2 + bx + c = 0 \left(a \neq 0\right)$.

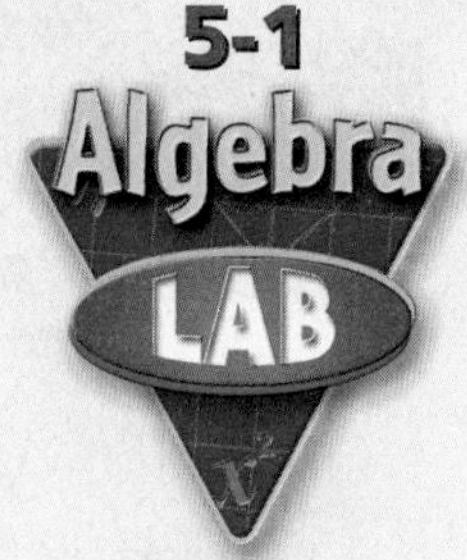

Model Inverse Variation

In this activity, you will explore the relationship between the mass of an object and the object's distance from the pivot point, or fulcrum, of a balanced lever.

MATHEMATICAL PRACTICES **Model with mathematics.**

Use with Variation Functions

Activity

1. Secure a pencil to a tabletop with tape. The pencil will be the *fulcrum.*

2. Draw an arrow on a piece of tape, and use the arrow to mark the midpoint of a ruler. Then tape a penny to the end of the ruler.

3. Place the midpoint of the ruler on top of the pencil. The ruler is the *lever.*

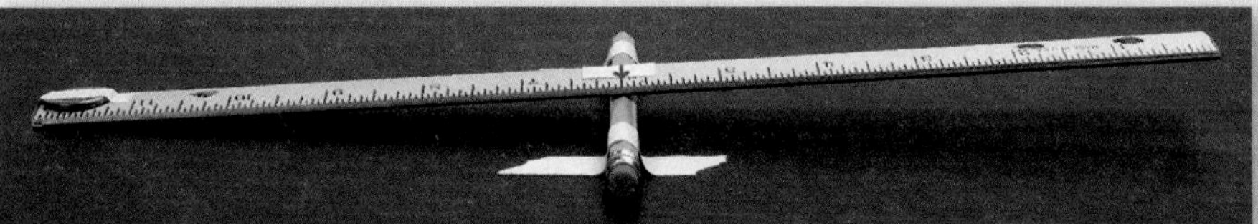

4. Place one penny on the lever opposite the taped penny. If needed, move the untaped penny to a position that makes the lever balanced. Find the distance from the untaped penny to the fulcrum, and record the distance in a table like the one below. (Measure from the center of the penny.) Repeat this step with stacks of two to seven pennies.

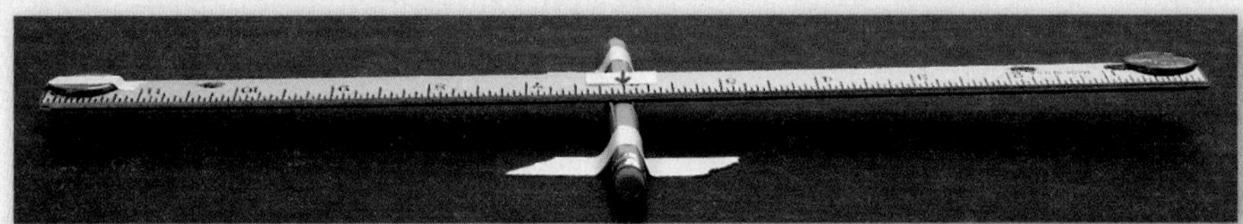

Let x be the number of pennies and y be the distance from the fulcrum. Plot the points from your table on a graph. Then draw a smooth curve through the points.

Number of Pennies	1	2	3	4	5	6	7
Distance from Fulcrum (cm)	■	■	■	■	■	■	■

Try This

1. Multiply the corresponding x- and y-values together. What do you notice?
2. Use your answer to Problem 1 to write an equation relating distance from the fulcrum to the number of pennies.
3. Would it be possible to balance a stack of 20 pennies on the lever? Use your equation from Problem 2 to justify your answer.
4. **Make a Conjecture** The relationship between the mass of an object on a balanced lever and the object's distance from the fulcrum can be modeled by an *inverse variation* function. Based on your data and graph, how are the variables in an inverse variation related?

5-1 Variation Functions

CC.9-12.A.CED.2 Create equations in two or more variables to represent relationships between quantities; graph equations on coordinate axes with labels and scales. *Also* **CC.9-12.A.CED.3**

Objective
Solve problems involving direct, inverse, joint, and combined variation.

Vocabulary
direct variation
constant of variation
joint variation
inverse variation
combined variation

Why learn this?
You can use variation functions to determine how many people are needed to complete a task, such as building a home, in a given time. (See Example 5.)

You have studied many types of linear functions. One special type of linear function is called *direct variation.* A **direct variation** is a relationship between two variables x and y that can be written in the form $y = kx$, where $k \neq 0$. In this relationship, k is the **constant of variation**. For the equation $y = kx$, y varies directly as x.

A direct variation equation is a linear equation in the form $y = mx + b$, where $b = 0$ and the constant of variation k is the slope. Because $b = 0$, the graph of a direct variation always passes through the origin.

EXAMPLE 1 Writing and Graphing Direct Variation

Given: y varies directly as x, and $y = 14$ when $x = 3.5$. Write and graph the direct variation function.

$y = kx$ — *y varies directly as x.*

$14 = k(3.5)$ — *Substitute 14 for y and 3.5 for x.*

$4 = k$ — *Solve for the constant of variation k.*

$y = 4x$ — *Write the variation function by using the value of k.*

Graph the direct variation function.

The y-intercept is 0, and the slope is 4.

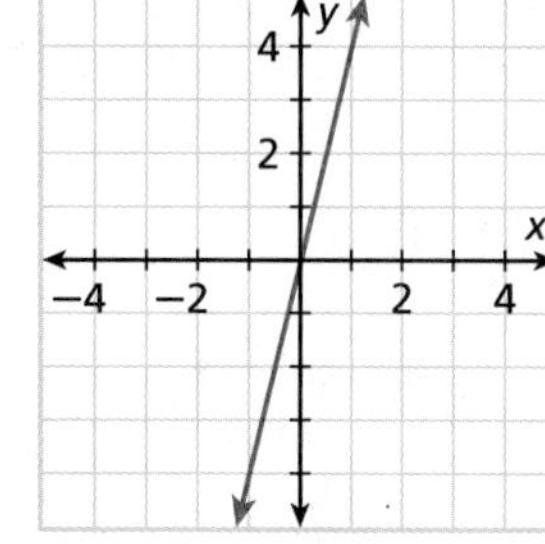

Check Substitute the original values of x and y into the equation.

$y = 4x$	
14	4(3.5)
14	14 ✓

Helpful Hint
If k is positive in a direct variation, the value of y increases as the value of x increases.

1. Given: y varies directly as x, and $y = 6.5$ when $x = 13$. Write and graph the direct variation function.

When you want to find specific values in a direct variation problem, you can solve for k and then use substitution or you can use the proportion derived below.

$$y_1 = kx_1 \rightarrow \frac{y_1}{x_1} = k \quad \text{and} \quad y_2 = kx_2 \rightarrow \frac{y_2}{x_2} = k \quad \text{so,} \quad \frac{y_1}{x_1} = \frac{y_2}{x_2}.$$

Steve Gates/AP/Wide World Photos

EXAMPLE 2 Solving Direct Variation Problems

Geometry

The circumference of a circle C varies directly as the radius r, and $C = 7\pi$ ft when $r = 3.5$ ft. Find r when $C = 4.5\pi$ ft.

Method 1 Find k.

$C = kr$

$7\pi = k(3.5)$ *Substitute.*

$2\pi = k$ *Solve for k.*

Write the variation function.

$C = (2\pi)r$ *Use 2π for k.*

$4.5\pi = (2\pi)r$ *Substitute 4.5π for C.*

$2.25 = r$ *Solve for r.*

Method 2 Use a proportion.

$\frac{C_1}{r_1} = \frac{C_2}{r_2}$

$\frac{7\pi}{3.5} = \frac{4.5\pi}{r}$ *Substitute.*

$7\pi r = 15.75\pi$ *Find the cross products.*

$r = 2.25$ *Solve for r.*

The radius r is 2.25 ft.

Reading Math

The phrases "y varies directly as x" and "y is directly proportional to x" have the same meaning.

CHECK IT OUT! **2.** The perimeter P of a regular dodecagon varies directly as the side length s, and $P = 18$ in. when $s = 1.5$ in. Find s when $P = 75$ in.

A **joint variation** is a relationship among three variables that can be written in the form $y = kxz$, where k is the constant of variation. For the equation $y = kxz$, y varies jointly as x and z.

EXAMPLE 3 Solving Joint Variation Problems

Geometry

The area A of a triangle varies jointly as the base b and the height h, and $A = 12$ m^2 when $b = 6$ m and $h = 4$ m. Find b when $A = 36$ m^2 and $h = 8$ m.

Step 1 Find k.

$A = kbh$ *Joint variation*

$12 = k(6)(4)$ *Substitute.*

$\frac{1}{2} = k$ *Solve for k.*

Step 2 Use the variation function.

$A = \frac{1}{2}bh$ *Use $\frac{1}{2}$ for k.*

$36 = \frac{1}{2}b(8)$ *Substitute.*

$9 = b$ *Solve for b.*

The base b is 9 m.

CHECK IT OUT! **3.** The lateral surface area L of a cone varies jointly as the base radius r and the slant height ℓ, and $L = 63\pi$ m^2 when $r = 3.5$ m and $\ell = 18$ m. Find r to the nearest tenth when $L = 8\pi$ m^2 and $\ell = 5$ m.

A third type of variation describes a situation in which one quantity increases and the other decreases. For example, the table shows that the time needed to drive 600 miles decreases as speed increases.

Speed (mi/h)	Time (h)	Distance (mi)
30	20	600
40	15	600
50	12	600

This type of variation is an inverse variation. An **inverse variation** is a relationship between two variables x and y that can be written in the form $y = \frac{k}{x}$, where $k \neq 0$. For the equation $y = \frac{k}{x}$, y varies inversely as x.

EXAMPLE 4 Writing and Graphing Inverse Variation

Given: y varies inversely as x, and $y = 3$ when $x = 8$. Write and graph the inverse variation function.

$y = \frac{k}{x}$ *y varies inversely as x.*

$3 = \frac{k}{8}$ *Substitute 3 for y and 8 for x.*

$k = 24$ *Solve for k.*

$y = \frac{24}{x}$ *Write the variation function.*

> **Helpful Hint**
> When graphing an inverse variation function, use values of x that are factors of k so that the y-values will be integers.

To graph, make a table of values for both positive and negative values of x. Plot the points, and connect them with two smooth curves. Because division by 0 is undefined, the function is undefined when $x = 0$.

x	y
−3	−8
−4	−6
−8	−3
−12	−2

x	y
3	8
4	6
8	3
12	2

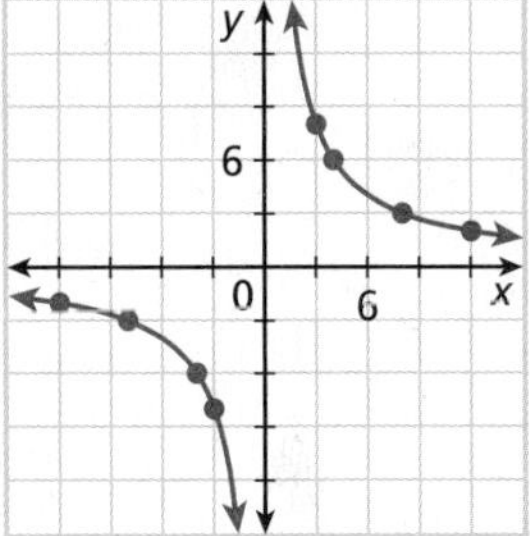

4. Given: y varies inversely as x, and $y = 4$ when $x = 10$. Write and graph the inverse variation function.

When you want to find specific values in an inverse variation problem, you can solve for k and then use substitution or you can use the equation derived below.

$$y_1 = \frac{k}{x_1} \rightarrow y_1x_1 = k \quad \text{and} \quad y_2 = \frac{k}{x_2} \rightarrow y_2x_2 = k \quad \text{so,} \quad y_1x_1 = y_2x_2.$$

EXAMPLE 5 *Community Service Application*

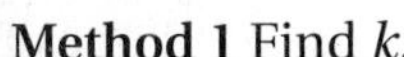

The time t that it takes for a group of volunteers to construct a house varies inversely as the number of volunteers v. If 20 volunteers can build a house in 62.5 working hours, how many volunteers would be needed to build a house in 50 working hours?

Method 1 Find k.

$t = \frac{k}{v}$

$62.5 = \frac{k}{20}$ *Substitute.*

$1250 = k$ *Solve for k.*

$t = \frac{1250}{v}$ *Use 1250 for k.*

$50 = \frac{1250}{v}$ *Substitute 50 for t.*

$v = 25$ *Solve for v.*

Method 2 Use $t_1v_1 = t_2v_2$.

$t_1v_1 = t_2v_2$

$62.5(20) = 50v$ *Substitute.*

$1250 = 50v$ *Simplify.*

$25 = v$ *Solve for v.*

So 25 volunteers would be needed to build a home in 50 working hours.

5. What if...? How many working hours would it take 15 volunteers to build a house?

Andy Christiansen/HMH

You can use algebra to rewrite variation functions in terms of k.

Direct Variation

$$y = kx \rightarrow k = \frac{y}{x}$$

Constant ratio

Inverse Variation

$$y = \frac{k}{x} \rightarrow k = xy$$

Constant product

Notice that in direct variation, the *ratio* of the two quantities is constant. In inverse variation, the *product* of the two quantities is constant.

EXAMPLE 6 Identifying Direct and Inverse Variation

Determine whether each data set represents a direct variation, an inverse variation, or neither.

A

x	3	8	10
y	9	24	30

In each case, $\frac{y}{x} = 3$. The ratio is constant, so this represents a direct variation.

B

x	4.5	12	2
y	8	3	18

In each case, $xy = 36$. The product is constant, so this represents an inverse variation.

CHECK IT OUT! **Determine whether each data set represents a direct variation, an inverse variation, or neither.**

6a.

x	3.75	15	5
y	12	3	9

6b.

x	1	40	26
y	0.2	8	5.2

A **combined variation** is a relationship that contains both direct and inverse variation. Quantities that vary directly appear in the numerator, and quantities that vary inversely appear in the denominator.

EXAMPLE 7 *Chemistry Application*

Helpful Hint

A kelvin (K) is a unit of temperature that is often used by chemists.
0°C = 273.15 K
100°C = 373.15 K

The volume V of a gas varies inversely as the pressure P and directly as the temperature T. A certain gas has a volume of 10 liters (L), a temperature of 300 kelvins (K), and a pressure of 1.5 atmospheres (atm). If the gas is compressed to a volume of 7.5 L and is heated to 350 K, what will the new pressure be?

Step 1 Find k.

$V = \frac{kT}{P}$ *Combined variation*

$10 = \frac{k(300)}{1.5}$ *Substitute.*

$0.05 = k$ *Solve for k.*

Step 2 Use the variation function.

$V = \frac{0.05T}{P}$ *Use 0.05 for k.*

$7.5 = \frac{0.05(350)}{P}$ *Substitute.*

$P = 2.\overline{3}$ *Solve for P.*

The new pressure will be $2.\overline{3}$, or $2\frac{1}{3}$, atm.

CHECK IT OUT! **7.** If the gas is heated to 400 K and has a pressure of 1 atm, what is its volume?

THINK AND DISCUSS

1. Explain why the graph of a direct variation is a line.
2. Describe the type of variation between the length and the width of a rectangular room with an area of 400 ft^2.

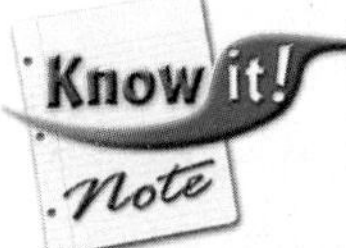

3. **GET ORGANIZED** Copy and complete the graphic organizer. In each box, write the general variation equation, draw a graph, or give an example.

Type of Variation	Equation	Graph	Example
Direct			
Joint			
Inverse			

5-1 Exercises

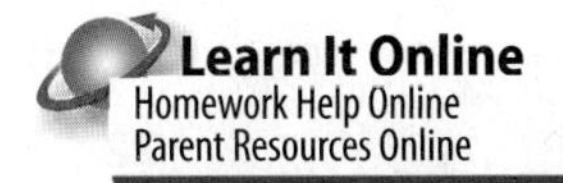

GUIDED PRACTICE

1. **Vocabulary** A variation function in which k is positive and one quantity decreases when the other increases is a(n) __?__. (*direct variation* or *indirect variation*)

SEE EXAMPLE 1

Given: y varies directly as x. Write and graph each direct variation function.

2. $y = 6$ when $x = 3$
3. $y = 45$ when $x = -5$
4. $y = 54$ when $x = 4.5$

SEE EXAMPLE 2

5. **Physics** The wavelength λ of a wave of a certain frequency varies directly as the velocity v of the wave, and $\lambda = 60$ ft when $v = 15$ ft/s. Find λ when $v = 3$ ft/s.
6. **Work** The dollar amount d that Julia earns varies directly as the number of hours t that she works, and $d = \$116.25$ when $t = 15$ h. Find t when $d = \$178.25$.

SEE EXAMPLE 3

7. **Geometry** The volume V of a rectangular prism of a particular height varies jointly as the length ℓ and the width w, and $V = 224$ ft^3 when $\ell = 8$ ft and $w = 4$ ft. Find ℓ when $V = 210$ ft^3 and $w = 5$ ft.
8. **Economics** The total cost C of electricity for a particular light bulb varies jointly as the time t that the light bulb is used and the cost k per kilowatt-hour, and $C = 12¢$ when $t = 50$ h and $k = 6¢$ per kilowatt-hour. Find C to the nearest cent when $t = 30$ h and $k = 8¢$ per kilowatt-hour.

SEE EXAMPLE 4

Given: y varies inversely as x. Write and graph each inverse variation function.

9. $y = 2$ when $x = 7$
10. $y = 8$ when $x = 4$
11. $y = \frac{1}{2}$ when $x = -10$

SEE EXAMPLE 5

12. **Travel** The time t that it takes for a salesman to drive a certain distance d varies inversely as the average speed r. It takes the salesman 4.75 h to travel between two cities at 60 mi/h. How long would the drive take at 50 mi/h?

SEE EXAMPLE 6

Determine whether each data set represents a direct variation, an inverse variation, or neither.

13.

x	2	5	9
y	3	6	4

14.

x	6	4	1
y	2	3	12

15.

x	24	4	12
y	30	5	15

SEE EXAMPLE 7

16. **Cars** The power P that must be delivered by a car engine varies directly as the distance d that the car moves and inversely as the time t required to move that distance. To move the car 500 m in 50 s, the engine must deliver 147 kilowatts (kW) of power. How many kilowatts must the engine deliver to move the car 700 m in 30 s?

PRACTICE AND PROBLEM SOLVING

Independent Practice

For Exercises	See Example
17–19	1
20–21	2
22–23	3
24–26	4
27	5
28–30	6
31	7

Extra Practice

See Extra Practice for more Skills Practice and Applications Practice exercises.

Given: y varies directly as x. Write and graph each direct variation function.

17. $y = 4$ when $x = 8$
18. $y = 12$ when $x = 2$
19. $y = -15$ when $x = 5$

20. **Medicine** The dosage d of a drug that a physician prescribes varies directly as the patient's mass m, and $d = 100$ mg when $m = 55$ kg. Find d to the nearest milligram when $m = 70$ kg.

21. **Nutrition** The number of Calories C in a horned melon varies directly as its weight w, and $C = 25$ Cal when $w = 3.5$ oz. How many Calories are in the horned melon shown on the scale? Round to the nearest Calorie.

22. **Agriculture** The number of bags of soybean seeds N that a farmer needs varies jointly as the number of acres a to be planted and the pounds of seed needed per acre p, and $N = 980$ when $a = 700$ acres and $p = 70$ lb/acre. Find N when $a = 1000$ acres and $p = 75$ lb/acre.

23. **Physics** The heat Q required to raise the temperature of water varies jointly as the mass m of the water and the amount of temperature change T, and $Q = 20{,}930$ joules (J) when $m = 1$ kg and $T = 5$°C. Find m when $Q = 8372$ J and $T = 10$°C.

LINK Entertainment

Broadway shows are plays or musicals presented in larger theaters near New York City's Times Square. In 2004, 11.3 million tickets were sold to Broadway shows for a total of almost $750 million.

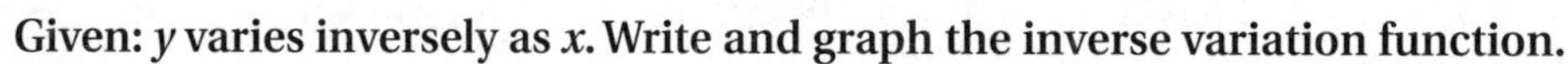

Given: y varies inversely as x. Write and graph the inverse variation function.

24. $y = 1$ when $x = 0.8$
25. $y = 1.75$ when $x = 6$
26. $y = -2$ when $x = 3$

27. **Entertainment** The number of days it takes a theater crew to set up a stage for a musical varies inversely as the number of workers. If the stage can be set up in 3 days by 20 workers, how many days would it take if only 12 workers were available?

Determine whether each data set represents a direct variation, an inverse variation, or neither.

28.

x	5	6.25	10
y	5	4	2.5

29.

x	5	7	9
y	3	5	7

30.

x	8	14	24
y	12	21	36

31. **Chemistry** The volume V of a gas varies inversely as the pressure P and directly as the temperature T. A certain gas has a volume of 20 L, a temperature of 320 K, and a pressure of 1 atm. If the gas is compressed to a volume of 15 L and is heated to 330 K, what will the new pressure be?

Tell whether each statement is sometimes, always, or never true.

32. Direct variation is a linear function.

33. A linear function is a direct variation.

34. An inverse variation is a linear function.

35. In a direct variation, $x = 0$ when $y = 0$.

36. The graph of an inverse variation passes through the origin.

37. In an auto race, a car with an average speed of 200 mi/h takes an average of 31.5 s to complete one lap of the track.
   a. Write an inverse variation function that gives the average speed s of a car in miles per hour as a function of the time t in seconds needed to complete one lap.
   b. How many seconds does it take the car to complete one lap at an average speed of 210 mi/h?

38. **Data Collection** Use a graphing calculator, a motion detector, and a light detector to measure the intensity of light as distance from the light source increases. Position the detectors next to each other. Place a flashlight in front of the detectors, and then pull the flashlight away from them. Find an appropriate model for the intensity of the light as a function of the square of the distance from the light source.

39. **Multi-Step** Interest earned on a certificate of deposit (CD) at a certain rate varies jointly as the principal in dollars and the time in years.
   a. Diane purchased a CD for $2500 that earned $12.50 simple interest in 3 months. Write a variation function for this data.
   b. At which bank did Diane buy her CD?
   c. How much interest would Diane earn in 6 months on a $3000 CD bought from the same bank?

Complete each table.

40. y varies jointly as x and z.

x	y	z
2		4
5	52.5	7
1.5	−36	
	1.38	23

41. y varies directly as x and inversely as z.

x	y	z
25	13.75	4
	1	11
17	18.7	
10		5

42. **Estimation** Shane swims 42 laps in 26 min 19 s. Without using a calculator, estimate how many minutes it would take Shane to swim 15 laps at the same average speed.

43. **Critical Thinking** Explain why only one point (x, y) is needed to write a direct variation function whose graph passes through this point.

44. **Write About It** Explain how to identify the type of variation from a list of ordered pairs.

45. Which of the following would best be represented by an inverse variation function?
   (A) The distance traveled as a function of speed
   (B) The total cost as a function of the number of items purchased
   (C) The area of a circular swimming pool as a function of its radius
   (D) The number of posts in a 20-ft fence as a function of distance between posts

Stockdisc/gettyimages

46. Which statement is best represented by the graph?

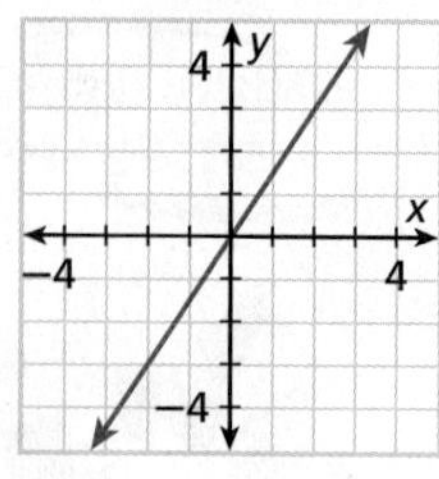

Ⓕ y varies directly as x^2.

Ⓖ y varies inversely as x.

Ⓗ y varies directly as x.

Ⓙ x varies inversely as y.

47. Which equation is best represented by the following statement: y varies directly as the square root of x?

Ⓐ $y = \frac{k}{\sqrt{x}}$ Ⓑ $y = \frac{k}{x^2}$ Ⓒ $k = \sqrt{xy}$ Ⓓ $y = k\sqrt{x}$

48. **Gridded Response** The cost per student of a ski trip varies inversely as the number of students who attend. It will cost each student \$250 if 24 students attend. How many students would have to attend to get the cost down to \$200?

CHALLENGE AND EXTEND

49. Given: y varies jointly as x and the square of z, and $y = 189$ when $x = 7$ and $z = 9$. Find y when $x = 2$ and $z = 6$.

50. **Government** The number of U.S. Representatives that each state receives can be approximated with a direct variation function where the number of representatives (rounded to the nearest whole number) varies directly with the state's population.

   a. Given that Pennsylvania has 19 representatives, find k to eight decimal places and write the direct variation function.

   b. Find the number of representatives for each state shown.

   c. Given that Texas had 32 U.S. representatives in the year 2000, estimate the state's population in that year.

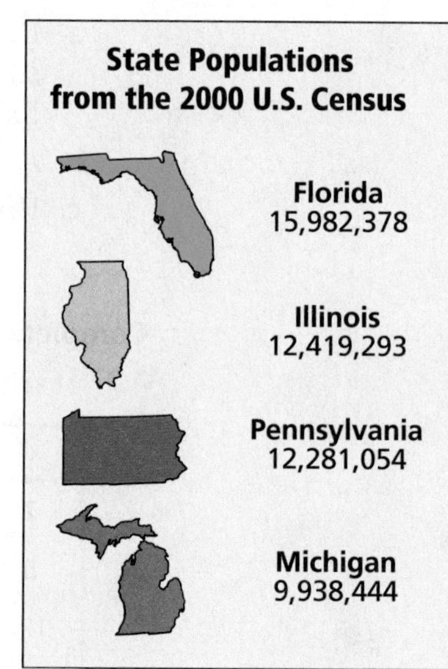

State Populations
from the 2000 U.S. Census
Florida
15,982,378
Illinois
12,419,293
Pennsylvania
12,281,054
Michigan
9,938,444

51. **Estimation** Given: y is inversely proportional to x, directly proportional to z^2, and the constant of variation is 7π. Estimate the value of y when $x = 12$ and $z = 2$.

5-2 Multiplying and Dividing Rational Expressions

CC.9-12.A.APR.7 Understand that rational expressions form a system analogous to the rational numbers … add, subtract, multiply, and divide rational expressions.

Objectives
Simplify rational expressions.

Multiply and divide rational expressions.

Vocabulary
rational expression

Why learn this?
You can simplify rational expressions to determine the probability of hitting an archery target. (See Exercise 35.)

You have worked with inverse variation functions such as $y = \frac{5}{x}$. The expression on the right side of this equation is a *rational expression.* A **rational expression** is a quotient of two polynomials. Other examples of rational expressions include the following:

$$\frac{x^2 - 4}{x + 2} \qquad \frac{10}{x^2 - 6} \qquad \frac{x + 3}{x - 7}$$

Because rational expressions are ratios of polynomials, you can simplify them the same way as you simplify fractions. Recall that to write a fraction in simplest form, you can divide out common factors in the numerator and denominator.

$$\frac{9}{24} = \frac{3 \cdot \cancel{3}}{8 \cdot \cancel{3}} = \frac{3}{8}$$

EXAMPLE 1 Simplifying Rational Expressions

Simplify. Identify any x-values for which the expression is undefined.

A $\dfrac{3x^7}{2x^4}$

$\frac{3}{2}x^{7-4} = \frac{3}{2}x^3$ *Quotient of Powers Property*

The expression is undefined at $x = 0$ because this value of x makes $2x^4$ equal 0.

Caution!
When identifying values for which a rational expression is undefined, identify the values of the variable that make the original denominator equal to 0.

B $\dfrac{x^2 - 2x - 3}{x^2 + 5x + 4}$

$\dfrac{(x-3)\cancel{(x+1)}}{\cancel{(x+1)}(x+4)} = \dfrac{(x-3)}{(x+4)}$ *Factor; then divide out common factors.*

The expression is undefined at $x = -1$ and $x = -4$ because these values of x make the factors $(x + 1)$ and $(x + 4)$ equal 0.

Check Substitute $x = -1$ and $x = -4$ into the original expression.

$$\frac{(-1)^2 - 2(-1) - 3}{(-1)^2 + 5(-1) + 4} = \frac{0}{0} \qquad \frac{(-4)^2 - 2(-4) - 3}{(-4)^2 + 5(-4) + 4} = \frac{21}{0}$$

Both values of x result in division by 0, which is undefined.

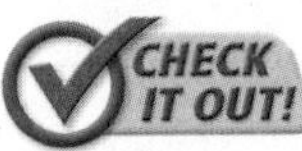

Simplify. Identify any x-values for which the expression is undefined.

1a. $\dfrac{16x^{11}}{8x^2}$ **1b.** $\dfrac{3x + 4}{3x^2 + x - 4}$ **1c.** $\dfrac{6x^2 + 7x + 2}{6x^2 - 5x - 6}$

Design Pics Inc/Alamy

EXAMPLE 2 Simplifying by Factoring −1

Simplify $\frac{2x - x^2}{x^2 - x - 2}$. Identify any x-values for which the expression is undefined.

$\frac{-1(x^2 - 2x)}{x^2 - x - 2}$ *Factor out −1 in the numerator so that x^2 is positive, and reorder the terms.*

$\frac{-1(x)\cancel{(x-2)}}{\cancel{(x-2)}(x+1)}$ *Factor the numerator and denominator. Divide out common factors.*

$\frac{-x}{x+1}$ *Simplify.*

The expression is undefined at $x = 2$ and $x = -1$.

Check The calculator screens suggest that $\frac{2x - x^2}{x^2 - x - 2} = \frac{-x}{x+1}$ except when $x = 2$ or $x = -1$.

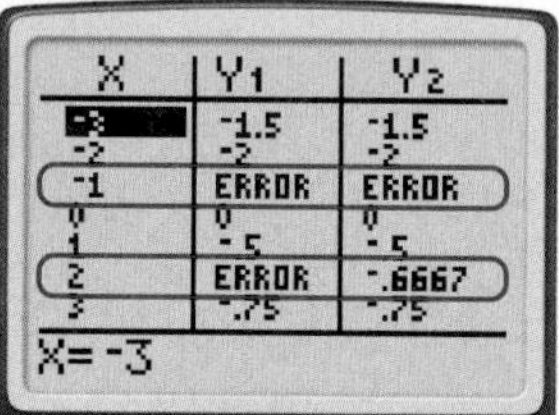

Simplify. Identify any x-values for which the expression is undefined.

2a. $\frac{10 - 2x}{x - 5}$ **2b.** $\frac{-x^2 + 3x}{2x^2 - 7x + 3}$

You can multiply rational expressions the same way that you multiply fractions.

Multiplying Rational Expressions
1. Factor all numerators and denominators completely.
2. Divide out common factors of the numerators and denominators.
3. Multiply numerators. Then multiply denominators.
4. Be sure the numerator and denominator have no common factors other than 1.

EXAMPLE 3 Multiplying Rational Expressions

Multiply. Assume that all expressions are defined.

A $\frac{2x^4y^5}{3x^2} \cdot \frac{15x^2}{8x^3y^2}$

$\frac{\cancel{2}x^{\cancel{4}1}y^{\cancel{5}3}}{\cancel{3}\cancel{x^2}} \cdot \frac{{}^5\cancel{15}\cancel{x^2}}{{}_4\cancel{8}\cancel{x^3}\cancel{y^2}}$

$\frac{5xy^3}{4}$

B $\frac{x+2}{3x+12} \cdot \frac{x+4}{x^2 - 4}$

$\frac{\cancel{x+2}}{3\cancel{(x+4)}} \cdot \frac{\cancel{x+4}}{\cancel{(x+2)}(x-2)}$

$\frac{1}{3(x-2)}$ or $\frac{1}{3x-6}$

Multiply. Assume that all expressions are defined.

3a. $\frac{x}{15} \cdot \frac{x^7}{2x} \cdot \frac{20}{x^4}$ **3b.** $\frac{10x - 40}{x^2 - 6x + 8} \cdot \frac{x + 3}{5x + 15}$

You can also divide rational expressions. Recall that to divide by a fraction, you multiply by its reciprocal.

$$\frac{1}{2} \div \frac{3}{4} = \frac{1}{\cancel{2}} \cdot \frac{\cancel{4}^2}{3} = \frac{2}{3}$$

EXAMPLE 4 Dividing Rational Expressions

Divide. Assume that all expressions are defined.

A $\frac{4x^3}{9x^2y} \div \frac{16}{9y^5}$

$\frac{4x^3}{9x^2y} \cdot \frac{9y^5}{16}$ *Rewrite as multiplication by the reciprocal.*

$\frac{\cancel{4}x^{\cancel{3}1}}{\cancel{9}\cancel{x^2}y} \cdot \frac{\cancel{9}y^{\cancel{5}4}}{\cancel{16}_4}$

$\frac{xy^4}{4}$

B $\frac{x^5 - 4x^3}{x^2 - x - 2} \div \frac{x^5 - x^4 - 2x^3}{x^2 - 1}$

$\frac{x^5 - 4x^3}{x^2 - x - 2} \cdot \frac{x^2 - 1}{x^5 - x^4 - 2x^3}$

$\frac{x^3(x^2 - 4)}{x^2 - x - 2} \cdot \frac{x^2 - 1}{x^3(x^2 - x - 2)}$

$\frac{\cancel{x^3}\cancel{(x-2)}(x+2)}{\cancel{(x-2)}(x+1)} \cdot \frac{(x-1)\cancel{(x+1)}}{\cancel{x^3}(x-2)\cancel{(x+1)}}$

$\frac{(x+2)(x-1)}{(x+1)(x-2)}$ or $\frac{x^2 + x - 2}{x^2 - x - 2}$

Divide. Assume that all expressions are defined.

4a. $\frac{x^2}{4} \div \frac{x^4y}{12y^2}$

4b. $\frac{2x^2 - 7x - 4}{x^2 - 9} \div \frac{4x^2 - 1}{8x^2 - 28x + 12}$

EXAMPLE 5 Solving Simple Rational Equations

Solve. Check your solution.

A $\frac{x^2 - 9}{x + 3} = 7$

$\frac{(x-3)\cancel{(x+3)}}{\cancel{x+3}} = 7$ *Note that $x \neq -3$.*

$x - 3 = 7$

$x = 10$

Check

$\frac{x^2 - 9}{x + 3}$	$= 7$
$\frac{(10)^2 - 9}{10 + 3}$	7
$\frac{91}{13}$	7
7	7 ✔

B $\frac{x^2 + 3x - 4}{x - 1} = 5$

$\frac{\cancel{(x-1)}(x+4)}{\cancel{x-1}} = 5$ *Note that $x \neq 1$.*

$x + 4 = 5$

$x = 1$

Because the left side of the original equation is undefined when $x = 1$, there is no solution.

Check A graphing calculator shows that 1 is not a solution.

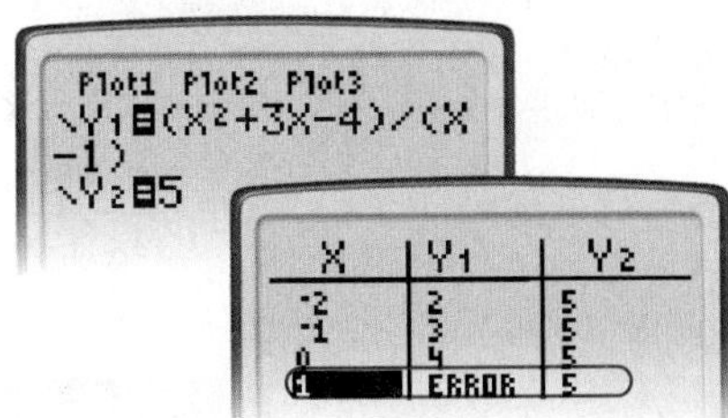

Caution!

As you simplify a rational expression, take note of values that must be excluded. The excluded values are those that make the rational expression undefined.

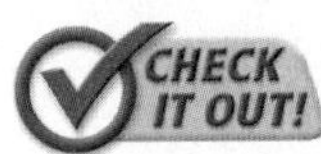

Solve. Check your solution.

5a. $\frac{x^2 + x - 12}{x + 4} = -7$

5b. $\frac{4x^2 - 9}{(2x + 3)} = 5$

THINK AND DISCUSS

MATHEMATICAL PRACTICES

1. Explain how you find undefined values for a rational expression.
2. Explain why it is important to check solutions to rational equations.

3. **GET ORGANIZED** Copy and complete the graphic organizer. In each box, write a worked-out example.

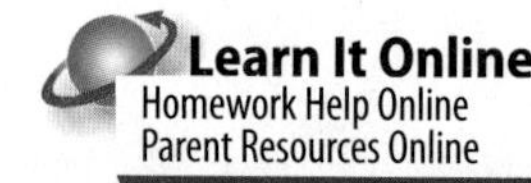

	Numerical Fractions	Rational Expressions
Simplifying		
Multiplying		
Dividing		

5-2 Exercises

Learn It Online
Homework Help Online
Parent Resources Online

GUIDED PRACTICE

1. **Vocabulary** How can you tell if an algebraic expression is a *rational expression*?

SEE EXAMPLE 1

Simplify. Identify any x-values for which the expression is undefined.

2. $\dfrac{4x^6}{2x-6}$
3. $\dfrac{6x^2+13x-5}{6x^2-23x+7}$
4. $\dfrac{x+4}{3x^2+11x-4}$

SEE EXAMPLE 2

5. $\dfrac{-x-4}{x^2-x-20}$
6. $\dfrac{6x^2+7x-3}{-3x^2+x}$
7. $\dfrac{6x^3+6x}{x^2+1}$

SEE EXAMPLE 3

Multiply. Assume that all expressions are defined.

8. $\dfrac{x-2}{2x-3}\cdot\dfrac{4x-6}{x^2-4}$
9. $\dfrac{x-2}{x-3}\cdot\dfrac{2x-6}{x+5}$
10. $\dfrac{x^2-16}{x^2-4x+4}\cdot\dfrac{x-2}{x^2+6x+8}$

SEE EXAMPLE 4

Divide. Assume that all expressions are defined.

11. $\dfrac{x^5y^4}{3xy}\div\dfrac{1}{x^3y}$
12. $\dfrac{x+3}{x^2-2x+1}\div\dfrac{x+3}{x-1}$
13. $\dfrac{x^2-25}{2x^2+5x-12}\div\dfrac{x^2-3x-10}{x^2+9x+20}$
14. $\dfrac{x^2+2x+1}{x^2-3x-18}\div\dfrac{x^2-1}{x^2-7x+6}$

SEE EXAMPLE 5

Solve. Check your solution.

15. $\dfrac{16x^2-9}{4x+3}=-6$
16. $\dfrac{2x^2+7x-15}{2x-3}=10$
17. $\dfrac{x^2-4}{x-2}=1$

PRACTICE AND PROBLEM SOLVING

Simplify. Identify any x-values for which the expression is undefined.

18. $\dfrac{4x-8}{x^2-2x}$
19. $\dfrac{8x-4}{2x^2+9x-5}$
20. $\dfrac{x^2-36}{x^2-12x+36}$
21. $\dfrac{3x+18}{24-2x-x^2}$
22. $\dfrac{-2x^2-9x}{4x^2-81}$
23. $\dfrac{4x+20}{-5-x}$

Independent Practice

For Exercises	See Example
18–20	1
21–23	2
24–27	3
28–31	4
32–34	5

Extra Practice

See Extra Practice for more Skills Practice and Applications Practice exercises.

Multiply. Assume that all expressions are defined.

24. $\dfrac{x^2y}{4xy} \cdot \dfrac{x}{6} \cdot \dfrac{3y^5}{x^4}$

25. $\dfrac{x-4}{x-3} \cdot \dfrac{2x-1}{x+4}$

26. $\dfrac{x^2-2x-8}{9x^2-16} \cdot \dfrac{3x^2+10x+8}{x^2-16}$

27. $\dfrac{4x^2-20x+25}{x^2-4x} \cdot \dfrac{3x-12}{2x-5}$

Divide. Assume that all expressions are defined.

28. $\dfrac{4x^2+15x+9}{8x^2+10x+3} \div \dfrac{x^2+4x}{2x+1}$

29. $\dfrac{x^2-4x-5}{x^2-3x+2} \div \dfrac{x^2-3x-10}{x^2-4}$

30. $\dfrac{x+2}{x-4} \div \dfrac{1}{3x-12}$

31. $\dfrac{x^2-2x-3}{x^2-x-2} \div \dfrac{x^2+2x-15}{x^2+x-6}$

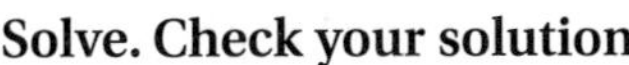

Solve. Check your solution.

32. $\dfrac{3x^2+10x+8}{-x-2} = -2$

33. $\dfrac{x^2-9}{x-3} = 5$

34. $\dfrac{x^2+3x-28}{(x+7)(x-4)} = -11$

LINK

Archery

Archery was practiced in ancient times on every inhabited continent except Australia. The painting in the photo above dates from about 1400 B.C.E. and shows archers from ancient Egypt.

35. **Archery** An archery target consists of an inner circle and four concentric rings. The width of each ring is equal to the radius r of the inner circle. Write a rational expression in terms of r that represents the probability that an arrow hitting the target at random will land in the inner circle. Then simplify the expression.

Multiply or divide. Assume that all expressions are defined.

36. $\dfrac{2x}{3} \cdot \dfrac{x^3}{6x-8}$

37. $\dfrac{4x^2-3x}{4x^2-1} \cdot \dfrac{2x+1}{x}$

38. $\dfrac{1}{25x^2-49} \div \dfrac{x}{10x-14}$

39. $2xy \cdot \dfrac{2x^2}{y} \cdot \dfrac{y^2}{2x}$

40. $\dfrac{14x^4}{xy} \cdot \dfrac{x^3}{6y^3} \div \dfrac{5x^2}{12y^5}$

41. $(y+4) \div \dfrac{4x+4+xy+y}{3}$

42. **Critical Thinking** What polynomial completes the equation $\dfrac{x-5}{x-2} \cdot \dfrac{■}{x-5} = x+1$?

43. **Geometry** Use the table to determine the following.

	Square Prism	Cylinder
Area of Base	s^2	πr^2
Volume	s^2h	πr^2h
Surface Area	$2s^2 + 4sh$	$2\pi r^2 + 2\pi rh$

a. For each figure, find the ratio of the volume to the area of the base.

b. For each figure, find the ratio of the surface area to the volume.

c. **What if...?** If the radius and the height of a cylinder were doubled, what effect would this have on the ratio of the cylinder's surface area to its volume?

MULTI-STEP TEST PREP

44. For a car moving with initial speed v_0 and acceleration a, the distance d that the car travels in time t is given by $d = v_0t + \frac{1}{2}at^2$.

a. Write a rational expression in terms of t for the average speed of the car during a period of acceleration. Simplify the expression.

b. During a race, a driver accelerates for 3 s at a rate of 10 ft/s^2 in order to pass another car. The driver's initial speed was 264 ft/s. What was the driver's average speed during the acceleration?

45. **ERROR ANALYSIS** Two students simplified the same expression. Which is incorrect? Explain the error.

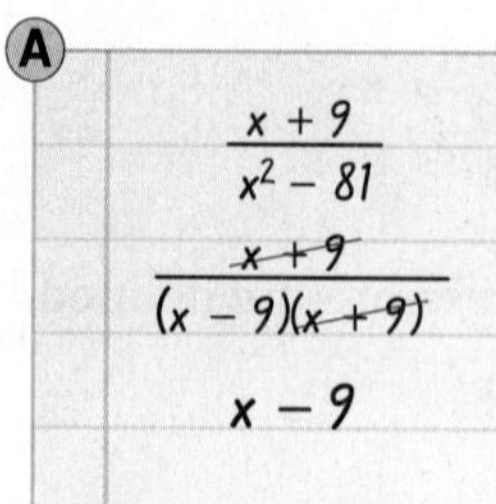

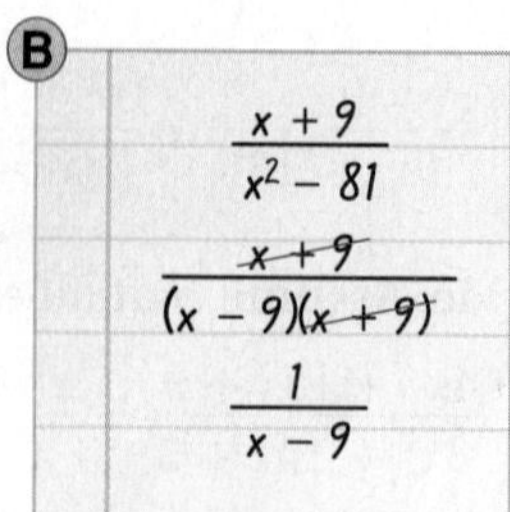

46. **Write About It** You can use polynomial division to find that $\frac{x^3 - 7x + 6}{x - 2} = x^2 + 2x - 3$. Is this equation true for all values of x? Explain.

TEST PREP

47. For which values of x is the expression $\frac{x^2 - x - 12}{x^2 + x - 2}$ undefined?

Ⓐ 0 and 1 Ⓑ 1 and 2 Ⓒ −1 and 2 Ⓓ −2 and 1

48. Assume that all expressions are defined. Which expression is equivalent to $\frac{x^2 + 7x + 10}{x^2 - 6x} \div \frac{x^3 - 4x}{x^2 - 8x + 12}$?

Ⓕ $\frac{x + 5}{x^2}$ Ⓖ $\frac{x^2}{x + 5}$ Ⓗ $\frac{(x + 5)(x + 2)^2}{(x - 6)^2}$ Ⓙ $\frac{(x - 6)^2}{(x + 5)(x + 2)^2}$

49. The area of a rectangle is equal to $x^2 + 13x + 36$ square units. If the length of the rectangle is equal to $x + 9$ units, which expression represents its width?

Ⓐ $x + 4$ Ⓑ $x + 27$ Ⓒ $x^2 + 4$ Ⓓ $x^2 + 27$

CHALLENGE AND EXTEND

Multiply or divide. Assume that all expressions are defined.

50. $\frac{8x^3 - 1}{x + 2} \cdot \frac{x^2 - 4}{2x^2 - 5x + 2}$

51. $\frac{2x^2 - 50}{x^3 + 125} \cdot \frac{x^3 - 125}{x^2 - 10x + 25}$

52. $\frac{x^2 - 16}{x - 3} \div \left(\frac{x^2 - 9}{x + 4}\right)^{-1}$

53. $\frac{x^5 - 4x^3 - x^2 + 4}{x^3 - 2x^2 + x - 2} \div \frac{3x^3 + 3x^2 + 3x}{x^2 - 1} \cdot \frac{6x}{x^2 - 2x + 1}$

5-3 Adding and Subtracting Rational Expressions

CC.9-12.A.APR.7 Understand that rational expressions form a system analogous to the rational numbers … add, subtract, multiply, and divide rational expressions.

Objectives

Add and subtract rational expressions.

Simplify complex fractions.

Vocabulary

complex fraction

Why learn this?

You can add and subtract rational expressions to estimate a train's average speed. (See Example 6.)

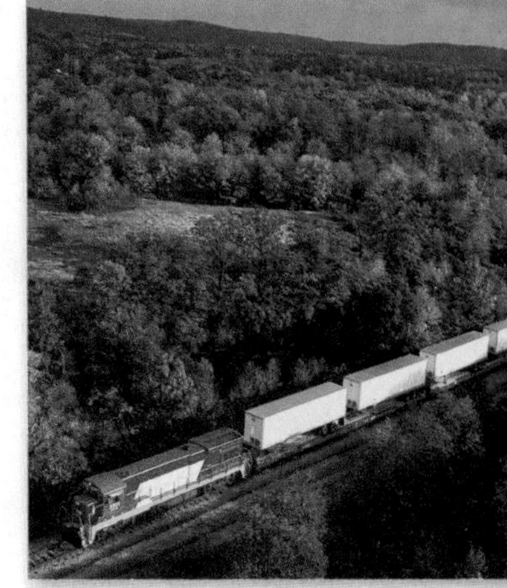

Adding and subtracting rational expressions is similar to adding and subtracting fractions. To add or subtract rational expressions with like denominators, add or subtract the numerators and use the same denominator.

$$\frac{1}{5} + \frac{3}{5} = \frac{4}{5} \qquad \frac{6}{7} - \frac{4}{7} = \frac{2}{7}$$

EXAMPLE 1 Adding and Subtracting Rational Expressions with Like Denominators

Add or subtract. Identify any x-values for which the expression is undefined.

A $\dfrac{3x-4}{x+3} + \dfrac{2x+5}{x+3}$

$\dfrac{3x-4+2x+5}{x+3}$ *Add the numerators.*

$\dfrac{5x+1}{x+3}$ *Combine like terms.*

The expression is undefined at $x = -3$ because this value makes $x + 3$ equal 0.

B $\dfrac{2x-1}{x^2+2} - \dfrac{4x+4}{x^2+2}$

$\dfrac{2x-1-(4x+4)}{x^2+2}$ *Subtract the numerators.*

$\dfrac{2x-1-4x-4}{x^2+2}$ *Distribute the negative sign.*

$\dfrac{-2x-5}{x^2+2}$ *Combine like terms.*

There is no real value of x for which $x^2 + 2 = 0$; the expression is always defined.

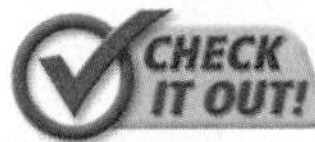

Add or subtract. Identify any x-values for which the expression is undefined.

1a. $\dfrac{6x+5}{x^2-3} + \dfrac{3x-1}{x^2-3}$ **1b.** $\dfrac{3x^2-5}{3x-1} - \dfrac{2x^2-3x-2}{3x-1}$

To add or subtract rational expressions with unlike denominators, first find the least common denominator (LCD). The LCD is the least common multiple of the polynomials in the denominators.

Least Common Multiple (LCM) of Polynomials
To find the LCM of polynomials:
1. Factor each polynomial completely. Write any repeated factors as powers. For example, $x^3 + 6x^2 + 9x = x(x + 3)^2$.
2. List the different factors. If the polynomials have common factors, use the highest power of each common factor.

EXAMPLE 2 Finding the Least Common Multiple of Polynomials

Find the least common multiple for each pair.

A $2x^3y^4$ **and** $3x^5y^3$

$$2x^3y^4 = 2 \cdot x^3 \cdot y^4$$

$$3x^5y^3 = 3 \cdot x^5 \cdot y^3$$

The LCM is $2 \cdot 3 \cdot x^5 \cdot y^4$, or $6x^5y^4$.

B $x^2 + 3x - 4$ **and** $x^2 - 3x + 2$

$$x^2 + 3x - 4 = (x + 4)(x - 1)$$

$$x^2 - 3x + 2 = (x - 2)(x - 1)$$

The LCM is $(x + 4)(x - 1)(x - 2)$.

Find the least common multiple for each pair.

2a. $4x^3y^7$ and $3x^5y^4$

2b. $x^2 - 4$ and $x^2 + 5x + 6$

To add rational expressions with unlike denominators, rewrite both expressions with the LCD. This process is similar to adding fractions.

$$\frac{2}{6} + \frac{3}{10} = \frac{2}{2 \cdot 3}\left(\frac{5}{5}\right) + \frac{3}{2 \cdot 5}\left(\frac{3}{3}\right) = \frac{10}{30} + \frac{9}{30} = \frac{19}{30}$$

EXAMPLE 3 Adding Rational Expressions

Add. Identify any *x*-values for which the expression is undefined.

A $\dfrac{x - 1}{x^2 + 3x + 2} + \dfrac{x}{x + 1}$

$$\frac{x - 1}{(x + 2)(x + 1)} + \frac{x}{x + 1}$$ *Factor the denominators.*

$$\frac{x - 1}{(x + 2)(x + 1)} + \frac{x}{x + 1}\left(\frac{x + 2}{x + 2}\right)$$ *The LCD is $(x + 2)(x + 1)$, so multiply $\frac{x}{x+1}$ by $\frac{x+2}{x+2}$.*

$$\frac{x - 1 + x(x + 2)}{(x + 2)(x + 1)}$$ *Add the numerators.*

$$\frac{x^2 + 3x - 1}{(x + 2)(x + 1)}$$ *Simplify the numerator.*

$$\frac{x^2 + 3x - 1}{(x + 2)(x + 1)} \text{ or } \frac{x^2 + 3x - 1}{x^2 + 3x + 2}$$ *Write the sum in factored or expanded form.*

The expression is undefined at $x = -2$ and $x = -1$ because these values of x make the factors $(x + 2)$ and $(x + 1)$ equal 0.

Remember!

Multiplying by 1 or a form of 1, such as $\frac{x+2}{x+2}$, does not change the value of an expression.

Add. Identify any x-values for which the expression is undefined.

B $\dfrac{x}{x+3} + \dfrac{-18}{x^2-9}$

$\dfrac{x}{x+3} + \dfrac{-18}{(x+3)(x-3)}$ *Factor the denominators.*

$\dfrac{x}{x+3}\left(\dfrac{x-3}{x-3}\right) + \dfrac{-18}{(x+3)(x-3)}$ *The LCD is $(x+3)(x-3)$, so multiply $\frac{x}{x+3}$ by $\frac{x-3}{x-3}$.*

$\dfrac{x(x-3)+(-18)}{(x+3)(x-3)}$ *Add the numerators.*

$\dfrac{x^2-3x-18}{(x+3)(x-3)}$ *Write the numerator in standard form.*

$\dfrac{\cancel{(x+3)}(x-6)}{\cancel{(x+3)}(x-3)}$ *Factor the numerator.*

$\dfrac{x-6}{x-3}$ *Divide out common factors.*

The expression is undefined at $x = -3$ and $x = 3$ because these values of x make the factors $(x+3)$ and $(x-3)$ equal 0.

Helpful Hint

Always simplify the sum or difference of rational expressions. A rational expression can be simplified if its numerator and denominator contain the same factor.

CHECK IT OUT! Add. Identify any x-values for which the expression is undefined.

3a. $\dfrac{3x}{2x-2} + \dfrac{3x-2}{3x-3}$ **3b.** $\dfrac{x}{x+3} + \dfrac{2x+6}{x^2+6x+9}$

EXAMPLE 4 Subtracting Rational Expressions

Subtract $\dfrac{2x^2-16}{x^2-4} - \dfrac{x+4}{x+2}$. Identify any x-values for which the expression is undefined.

$\dfrac{2x^2-16}{(x-2)(x+2)} - \dfrac{x+4}{x+2}$ *Factor the denominators.*

$\dfrac{2x^2-16}{(x-2)(x+2)} - \dfrac{x+4}{x+2}\left(\dfrac{x-2}{x-2}\right)$ *The LCD is $(x-2)(x+2)$, so multiply $\frac{x+4}{x+2}$ by $\frac{x-2}{x-2}$.*

$\dfrac{2x^2-16-(x+4)(x-2)}{(x-2)(x+2)}$ *Subtract the numerators.*

$\dfrac{2x^2-16-(x^2+2x-8)}{(x-2)(x+2)}$ *Multiply the binomials in the numerator.*

$\dfrac{2x^2-16-x^2-2x+8}{(x-2)(x+2)}$ *Distribute the negative sign.*

$\dfrac{x^2-2x-8}{(x-2)(x+2)}$ *Write the numerator in standard form.*

$\dfrac{(x-4)\cancel{(x+2)}}{(x-2)\cancel{(x+2)}}$ *Factor the numerator.*

$\dfrac{x-4}{x-2}$ *Divide out common factors.*

The expression is undefined at $x = 2$ and $x = -2$ because these values of x make the factors $(x-2)$ and $(x+2)$ equal 0.

Subtract. Identify any x-values for which the expression is undefined.

4a. $\dfrac{3x-2}{2x+5} - \dfrac{2}{5x-2}$

4b. $\dfrac{2x^2+64}{x^2-64} - \dfrac{x-4}{x+8}$

Some rational expressions are *complex fractions*. A **complex fraction** contains one or more fractions in its numerator, its denominator, or both. Examples of complex fractions are shown below.

$$\frac{x+2}{\frac{3}{x}} \qquad \frac{1+\frac{1}{x}}{4x+5} \qquad \frac{\frac{x+3}{x}}{\frac{x+4}{7x}}$$

Recall that the bar in a fraction represents division. Therefore, you can rewrite a complex fraction as a division problem and then simplify. You can also simplify complex fractions by using the LCD of the fractions in the numerator and denominator.

EXAMPLE 5 Simplifying Complex Fractions

Simplify $\dfrac{\frac{2}{x}+\frac{x}{4}}{\frac{x+1}{x}}$. Assume that all expressions are defined.

Method 1 Write the complex fraction as division.

$\left(\frac{2}{x}+\frac{x}{4}\right) \div \frac{x+1}{x}$ *Write as division.*

$\left(\frac{2}{x}+\frac{x}{4}\right) \cdot \frac{x}{x+1}$ *Multiply by the reciprocal.*

$\left[\frac{2}{x}\left(\frac{4}{4}\right)+\frac{x}{4}\left(\frac{x}{x}\right)\right] \cdot \frac{x}{x+1}$ *The LCD is 4x.*

$\left[\frac{2(4)+x(x)}{4x}\right] \cdot \frac{x}{x+1}$ *Add the numerators.*

$\frac{8+x^2}{4\cancel{x}} \cdot \frac{\cancel{x}}{x+1}$ *Simplify and divide out common factors.*

$\frac{8+x^2}{4(x+1)}$ or $\frac{x^2+8}{4x+4}$ *Multiply.*

Method 2 Multiply the numerator and denominator of the complex fraction by the LCD of the fractions in the numerator and denominator.

$\dfrac{\frac{2}{\cancel{x}}(4\cancel{x})+\frac{x}{\cancel{4}}(\cancel{4}x)}{\frac{x+1}{\cancel{x}}(4\cancel{x})}$ *The LCD is 4x.*

$\dfrac{(2)(4)+(x)(x)}{(x+1)(4)}$ *Divide out common factors.*

$\dfrac{8+x^2}{(x+1)(4)}$ or $\dfrac{x^2+8}{4x+4}$ *Simplify.*

Simplify. Assume that all expressions are defined.

5a. $\dfrac{\frac{x+1}{x^2-1}}{\frac{x}{x-1}}$

5b. $\dfrac{\frac{20}{x-1}}{\frac{6}{3x-3}}$

5c. $\dfrac{\frac{1}{x}+\frac{1}{2x}}{\frac{x+4}{x-2}}$

Student to Student

Simplifying Complex Fractions

Brian Carr
Riverside High School

When I simplify complex fractions, I draw arrows connecting the outermost and innermost numbers.

Then I make a new fraction by writing the product of the outermost numbers as the numerator and the product of the innermost numbers as the denominator.

$$\frac{\frac{3}{5}}{\frac{1}{2}} = \frac{6}{5} = 1\frac{1}{5}$$

It also works for rational expressions.

$$\frac{\frac{x^2}{x+1}}{\frac{x}{2}} = \frac{2x^2}{x(x+1)} = \frac{2x}{x+1}$$

EXAMPLE 6 ***Transportation Application***

A freight train averages 30 mi/h traveling to its destination with full cars and 40 mi/h on the return trip with empty cars. What is the train's average speed for the entire trip? Round to the nearest tenth.

Total distance: $2d$ — *Let d represent the one-way distance.*

Total time: $\frac{d}{30} + \frac{d}{40}$ — *Use the formula $t = \frac{d}{r}$.*

Average speed: $\dfrac{2d}{\frac{d}{30} + \frac{d}{40}}$ — *The average speed is $\frac{\text{total distance}}{\text{total time}}$.*

$\dfrac{2d(120)}{\frac{d}{30}(120) + \frac{d}{40}(120)}$ — *The LCD of the fractions in the denominator is 120.*

$\dfrac{240d}{4d + 3d}$ — *Simplify.*

$\dfrac{240\cancel{d}}{7\cancel{d}} \approx 34.3$ — *Combine like terms and divide out common factors.*

The train's average speed is 34.3 mi/h.

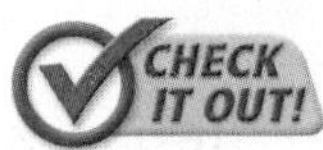

CHECK IT OUT! **6.** Justin's average speed on his way to school is 40 mi/h, and his average speed on the way home is 45 mi/h. What is Justin's average speed for the entire trip? Round to the nearest tenth.

MATHEMATICAL PRACTICES

THINK AND DISCUSS

1. Explain how to find the LCD of two rational expressions.

2. GET ORGANIZED Copy and complete the graphic organizer. In each box, write an example and show how to simplify it.

Rational Expressions
- Adding (like denominators)
- Subtracting (unlike denominators)
- Simplifying a complex fraction

5-3 Exercises

Learn It Online
Homework Help Online
Parent Resources Online

GUIDED PRACTICE

1. **Vocabulary** How does a *complex fraction* differ from other types of fractions?

SEE EXAMPLE 1

Add or subtract. Identify any x-values for which the expression is undefined.

2. $\frac{2x-3}{4x-1}+\frac{3x+4}{4x-1}$
3. $\frac{3x-4}{4x+5}-\frac{5x+3}{4x+5}$
4. $\frac{4x-3}{2x-5}-\frac{4x+3}{2x-5}$

SEE EXAMPLE 2

Find the least common multiple for each pair.

5. $4x^2y^3$ and $16x^4y$
6. x^2-25 and $x^2+10x+25$

SEE EXAMPLE 3

Add or subtract. Identify any x-values for which the expression is undefined.

7. $\frac{3x-2}{x+6}+\frac{2x-3}{2x-1}$
8. $\frac{4x-5}{12x+4}+\frac{3x-1}{3x+1}$
9. $\frac{3x-4}{x^2-9}+\frac{2x-1}{x+3}$

SEE EXAMPLE 4

10. $\frac{3x-5}{2x-5}-\frac{2x-5}{3x+1}$
11. $\frac{2x+8}{x^2-16}-\frac{3}{x-4}$
12. $\frac{x+2}{x^2+4x+3}-\frac{x+1}{x+3}$

SEE EXAMPLE 5

Simplify. Assume that all expressions are defined.

13. $\frac{\frac{2x-3}{x-2}}{\frac{4x-3}{x^2-4}}$
14. $\frac{\frac{3x-7}{4x+5}}{\frac{6x-1}{5x-6}}$
15. $\frac{\frac{2}{x}+\frac{1}{x}}{\frac{2x}{x+2}}$

SEE EXAMPLE 6

16. **Track** Yvette ran at an average speed of 6.20 ft/s during the first two laps of a race and an average speed of 7.75 ft/s during the second two laps of a race. What was Yvette's average speed for the entire race? Round to the nearest tenth.

PRACTICE AND PROBLEM SOLVING

Independent Practice

For Exercises	See Example
17–19	1
20–21	2
22–24	3
25–27	4
28–30	5
31	6

Extra Practice
See Extra Practice for more Skills Practice and Applications Practice exercises.

Add or subtract. Identify any x-values for which the expression is undefined.

17. $\frac{2x-3}{4x-7}+\frac{2x-3}{4x-7}$
18. $\frac{x-5}{3x+4}-\frac{3x-5}{3x+4}$
19. $\frac{x^2-3}{2x+7}-\frac{2x-5}{2x+7}$

Find the least common multiple for each pair.

20. $12x^2y^3$ and $14x^3y^2$
21. $16x^2-25$ and $4x^2-x-5$

Add or subtract. Identify any x-values for which the expression is undefined.

22. $\frac{3x-2}{x+2}+\frac{2x}{4x-1}$
23. $\frac{2x-7}{x-2}+\frac{8x}{3x-6}$
24. $\frac{5x}{4x^2}+\frac{7}{x+1}$
25. $\frac{4x-3}{x^2-9}-\frac{2x-3}{x-3}$
26. $\frac{x}{2x+3}-\frac{2x+1}{2x-3}$
27. $\frac{1}{x-4}-\frac{2}{x^2-6x+8}$

Simplify. Assume that all expressions are defined.

28. $\frac{\frac{2x-5}{x^2-9}}{\frac{3x-1}{x+3}}$
29. $\frac{\frac{3x-2}{x^2-4}}{\frac{5x+1}{x^2+x-6}}$
30. $\frac{\frac{x}{x+1}}{x+\frac{x}{3}}$

31. **Chemistry** A solution is heated from 0°C to 100°C. Between 0°C and 50°C, the rate of temperature increase is 1.5°C/min. Between 50°C and 100°C, the rate of temperature increase is 0.4°C/min. What is the average rate of temperature increase during the entire heating process? Round to the nearest tenth.

32. An auto race consists of 8 laps. A driver completes the first 3 laps at an average speed of 185 mi/h and the remaining laps at an average speed of 200 mi/h.

a. Let d represent the length of one lap. Write an expression in terms of d that represents the time in hours that it takes the driver to complete the race.

b. What is the driver's average speed during the race to the nearest mile per hour?

Add or subtract. Identify any x-values for which the expression is undefined.

33. $\frac{2}{x+4} + \frac{x}{x-3}$ 34. $\frac{2x}{x^2-36} + \frac{x+4}{x+6}$ 35. $\frac{2}{x^2-x-20} + \frac{3}{x^2+7x+12}$

36. $\frac{7x}{x^2-5x} + \frac{x^2}{x-5}$ 37. $\frac{2x}{x-1} - \frac{9}{x-2}$ 38. $\frac{2x+3}{3x+4} - \frac{x}{9x+12}$

39. $\frac{4x^2}{3x+4} - \frac{2}{2x-3}$ 40. $\frac{6}{x^2+4x-32} - \frac{x-5}{x-4}$ 41. $\frac{x+7}{x^2+13x+42} - \frac{10x}{x^2+8x+7}$

42. **Environment** The junior and senior classes of a high school are cleaning up a beach. Each class has pledged to clean 1600 m of shoreline. The junior class has 12 more students than the senior class.

a. Let s represent the number of students in the senior class. Write and simplify an expression in terms of s that represents the difference between the number of meters of shoreline each senior must clean and the number each junior must clean.

b. If there are 48 seniors, how many more meters of shoreline must each senior clean than the number each junior must clean? Round to the nearest tenth of a meter.

c. **Multi-Step** If it takes each student about 10 min to clean 15 m of shoreline, approximately how much sooner will the junior class finish than the senior class?

Simplify. Assume that all expressions are defined.

43. $\dfrac{\frac{4}{x+2}}{\frac{x+2}{6}}$ 44. $\dfrac{\frac{2}{3x-4}}{5x+3}$ 45. $\dfrac{\frac{1}{2x}+\frac{2}{3x}}{\frac{x-1}{x-3}}$

Architecture

Andrea Palladio stated that his preferred room shapes were squares, circles, and rectangles with precise length-to-width ratios. Some of these shapes can be seen above in Il Redentore church that Palladio designed.

46. **Architecture** The Renaissance architect Andrea Palladio preferred that the length and width of rectangular rooms be limited to certain ratios. These ratios are listed in the table. Palladio also believed that the height of a room with vaulted ceilings should be the harmonic mean of the length and width.

a. The harmonic mean of two positive numbers a and b is equal to $\frac{2}{\frac{1}{a}+\frac{1}{b}}$. Simplify this expression.

b. Complete the table for a rectangular room with a width of 30 feet that meets Palladio's requirements for its length and height. If necessary, round to the nearest tenth.

c. **What if...?** A Palladian room has a length-to-width ratio of 4:3. If the length of this room is doubled, what effect should this change have on the room's width and height, according to Palladio's principles?

Rooms with a Width of 30 ft

Length-to-Width Ratio	Length (ft)	Height (ft)
2:1		
3:2		
4:3		
5:3		
$\sqrt{2}$:1		

47. **Critical Thinking** Write two expressions whose sum is $\frac{x-3}{x+2}$.

48. **Write About It** The first step in adding rational expressions is to write them with a common denominator. This denominator does not necessarily need to be the least common denominator (LCD). Why is it often easier to use the LCD than it is to use other common denominators?

TEST PREP

49. Which best represents $\frac{3}{3x} + \frac{5}{9x}$?

Ⓐ $\frac{2}{3x}$ Ⓑ $\frac{7}{2x}$ Ⓒ $\frac{8}{9x}$ Ⓓ $\frac{14}{9x}$

50. Which of the following is equivalent to $\frac{5}{x+2} - \frac{8}{x+4}$?

Ⓕ $\frac{-3x+4}{x^2+8}$ Ⓖ $\frac{-5}{x+4}$ Ⓗ $\frac{-3x+4}{x^2+6x+8}$ Ⓙ $\frac{-3x+36}{x^2+6x+8}$

51. Which of the following is equivalent to $\frac{\frac{8}{7x}}{\frac{-4}{x+1}}$?

Ⓐ $-\frac{2x+2}{7x}$ Ⓑ $-\frac{32}{7x^2+7}$ Ⓒ $-\frac{2}{7x^2+7}$ Ⓓ $-\frac{7x}{2x+2}$

52. A three-day bicycle race has 3 stages of equal length. The table shows a rider's average speed in each of the stages. What is the rider's average speed for the entire race, rounded to the nearest tenth of a kilometer per hour?

Ⓕ 29.5 km/h Ⓗ 30.2 km/h

Ⓖ 29.7 km/h Ⓙ 30.7 km/h

Race Results

Stage	Speed (km/h)
1	35.5
2	31.1
3	25.6

CHALLENGE AND EXTEND

Simplify. Assume that all expressions are defined.

53. $\frac{x-1}{x+2} + \frac{4}{x^2-4} - \frac{6x}{x-2}$

54. $\frac{x^{-1}+y^{-1}}{x^{-1}-y^{-1}}$

55. $(x+2)^{-2} - (x^2-4)^{-1}$

56. $(x-y)^{-1} - (x+y)^{-1}$

57. What polynomial completes the equation $\frac{■}{x^3+4x^2-5x} - \frac{x+4}{x^2-x} = \frac{5}{x+5}$?

EXTENSION

Polynomials, Rational Expressions, and Closure

CC.9-12.A.APR.1 Understand that polynomials form a system analogous to the integers … add, subtract, and multiply polynomials. *Also* **CC.9-12.A.APR.7**

Objective
Understand under which operations rational expressions are closed.

A set of numbers is *closed*, or has closure, under a given operation if the result of the operation on any two numbers in the set is also in the set.

For example, the set of real numbers is closed under addition, because adding any two real numbers results in another real number. Likewise, the real numbers are closed under subtraction, multiplication and division (by a nonzero real number), because performing these operations on two real numbers always yields another real number.

Polynomials are closed under the same operations as integers. Rational expressions are closed under addition, subtraction, multiplication, and division by a nonzero rational expression.

EXAMPLE 1 Determining Closure of the Set of Integers Under Operations

Explain why the integers are closed under the stated operation or give a counterexample to explain why they are not closed under the stated operation.

Addition

For any two integers a and b, the sum of the integers would result in an integer. Looking at a number line and starting at any integer point a, the sum would indicate a move to point b to the left or right using b units, which are integers. The set of integers is closed under addition.

Subtraction

Subtraction can be rewritten as an addition, that is, $a - b = a + (-b)$. Because b is an integer, $-b$ is one too, so integer subtraction is also closed.

Multiplication

The product of a and b, where a and b are integers, will always result in an integer, since multiplication is repeated addition. For example, $2 \cdot 3$ can be written as $2 + 2 + 2$. Since integers are closed under addition, they are also closed under multiplication.

Division

Integers are not closed under division. A counterexample to demonstrate this is $a = 5$ and $b = -4$. The division $a \div b$ would result in the fraction, $-\frac{5}{4}$, which is not an integer.

1. Determine if the set of positive integers is closed under addition, subtraction, multiplication, and division. Explain.

A rational number is any number that can be written as a ratio of two integers. All rational numbers can be written in the form $\frac{a}{b}$, where a and b are integers.

EXAMPLE 2 Determining Closure of the Set of Rational Numbers Under Operations

Explain why the rational numbers are closed under the stated operation or give a counterexample to explain why they are not closed under the stated operation.

Addition

If $\frac{a}{b}$ and $\frac{c}{d}$ are nonzero and *a, b, c,* and *d* are integers, then $\frac{a}{b} + \frac{c}{d} = \frac{(ad + bc)}{bd}$. Since integers are closed under addition and the products *ad, bc, bd,* and $(ad + bc)$ are integers, then the sum of two nonzero rational numbers is a rational number. Therefore the rational numbers are closed under addition.

Subtraction

Since subtraction can be rewritten as an addition, that is, $\frac{a}{b} - \frac{c}{d} = \frac{a}{b} + \left(-\frac{c}{d}\right)$, then rational numbers are also closed under subtraction.

Multiplication

If $\frac{a}{b}$ and $\frac{c}{d}$ are nonzero and *a, b, c,* and *d* are integers, then $\frac{a}{b} \cdot \frac{c}{d} = \frac{ac}{bd}$. Since integers are closed under multiplication, then *ac* and *bd* are also integers and the fraction is a rational number. Therefore the rational numbers are closed under multiplication.

Division (nonzero)

Since division of two fractions can be rewritten as a multiplication, rational numbers are closed under division. Let $\frac{a}{b}$ and $\frac{c}{d}$ be nonzero and *a, b, c,* and *d* be integers, then $\frac{a}{b} \div \frac{c}{d} = \frac{a}{b} \cdot \frac{d}{c} = \frac{ad}{bc}$. Since integers are closed under multiplication, then *ad* and *bc* are also integers and the fraction is a rational number. Therefore the rational numbers are closed under (nonzero) division.

2. Determine if the set of negative rational numbers is closed under addition, subtraction, multiplication, and division. Explain.

The operations of polynomials are similar to operations with real numbers. Examples of operations with polynomials are shown below.

Addition

$4t + 6r$

$+[2t - 4r]$

$(4 + 2)t + [6 + (-4)]r$

$6t + 2r$

Combine like terms.

Subtraction

$-4t + 2r$

$-[2t - 4r]$

$(-4 - 2)t + [2 - (-4)]r$

$-6t + 6r$

Combine like terms.

Multiplication

$(x^3 + 3)(-x^2 + x)$

$x^3(-x^2 + x) + 3(-x^2 + x)$

$-x^5 + x^4 - 3x^2 + 3x$

Use the distributive property or FOIL.

Division

$$\begin{array}{r} x + 2 \\ x + 1\overline{)x^2 + 3x + 2} \\ -(x^2 + x) \\ \hline 2x + 2 \\ -(2x + 2) \\ \hline 0 \end{array}$$

EXAMPLE 3 Determining Closure of Polynomials

Explain why polynomials are closed under the stated operation or give a counterexample to explain why they are not closed under the stated operation.

Addition

When combining like terms, real numbers are added. The coefficients are sums of real numbers and the result is therefore real. The powers of variables do not change in addition of polynomials, so the exponents remain whole numbers. Therefore, the set of polynomials is closed under addition with real-number coefficients.

Multiplication

The distributive property is used to multiply each of the terms in each polynomial multiplied. Since the coefficients are multiplied and they are real numbers, their products will also be real numbers. The product of variables with whole number exponents m and n results in the same variable with exponent $m + n$: $x^m \cdot x^n = x^{m+n}$. The exponents are whole numbers, so the multiplication of polynomials is closed with real-number coefficients and whole-number exponents.

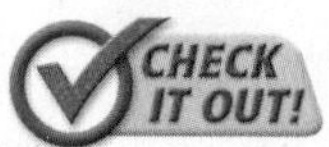

3. Determine if the set of polynomials is closed under subtraction with real-number coefficients.

A rational expression is the ratio of two polynomial expressions. The denominator of a rational expression cannot equal 0, as division by 0 is undefined.

Closure properties for rational expressions can be derived using the closure properties of polynomial expressions, as rational expressions are composed of polynomial expressions.

EXAMPLE 4 Determining Closure of Rational Expressions

Show that rational expressions are closed under addition.

We can consider generic rational expressions $\frac{f(x)}{g(x)}$ and $\frac{p(x)}{q(x)}$, where $f(x)$, $g(x)$, $p(x)$, and $q(x)$ represent polynomials. To add the functions, use a common denominator.

$$\frac{f(x)}{g(x)} + \frac{p(x)}{q(x)} = \left(\frac{f(x)}{g(x)} \cdot \frac{q(x)}{q(x)}\right) + \left(\frac{p(x)}{q(x)} \cdot \frac{g(x)}{g(x)}\right)$$

$$= \left(\frac{f(x) \cdot q(x)}{g(x) \cdot q(x)}\right) + \left(\frac{p(x) \cdot g(x)}{g(x) \cdot q(x)}\right)$$

$$= \frac{\big(f(x) \cdot q(x)\big) + \big(p(x) \cdot g(x)\big)}{\big(g(x) \cdot q(x)\big)}$$

Since the product of two polynomials is a polynomial and the sum of two polynomials is a polynomial, then the sum of two rational expressions is a rational expression.

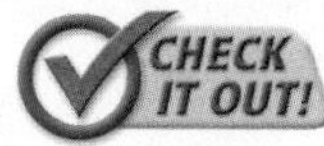

4. Determine if the set of rational numbers is closed under multiplication.

EXTENSION

Exercises

Determine if each set is closed under the given operation. Explain why the set is closed or provide a counterexample to show the set is not closed.

1. The set of whole numbers; division
2. The set of odd numbers; addition
3. The set of positive even numbers; subtraction
4. The set of multiples of 5; multiplication
5. The set of even integers; addition
6. The set of multiples of 2; division

7. **Challenge** Show that the set of numbers {$a + b\sqrt{2}$, a and b are positive integers} is closed under multiplication.
8. **Challenge** Show that rational expressions are closed under division. Explain all steps in your response.
9. **///ERROR ANALYSIS///** David used the following logic to show that the set of integers is closed under division. What is wrong with his logic?

1, 3, and 9 integers.

$\frac{9}{1} = 9$, *which is an integer.*

$\frac{9}{3} = 3$, *which is an integer.*

$\frac{9}{9} = 1$, *which is an integer.*

Since each division results in an integer, the set of integers is closed under division.

10. Show that the set {–1, 1} is closed under division.
11. Show that the set {–1, 1} is closed under multiplication.
12. Is the set {–1, 1} closed under addition and/or subtraction? If yes, show it. If no, provide a counterexample.
13. What is the smallest subset of the integers that is closed under addition?
14. Under how many and which of the four operations discussed in this extension (addition, subtraction, multiplication, and nonzero division) is the set of natural numbers closed?
15. **Challenge** Modular arithmetic is a system of arithmetic where the numbers 'wrap around' after a certain value, called the *modulus*. As an example, think of the 'hour' numbers on a clock: – 12 is considered the same as 0, and after 12, the time wraps back around to 1. Twenty hours after 10:00 is 6:00, not 30:00.
    a. What is the modulus on a clock?
    b. Is the set of 'clock numbers' closed under addition? Explain.

Explore Holes in Graphs

You can use a graphing calculator to explore the relationship between the graphs of rational functions and their simplified forms.

Use with Rational Functions

Use appropriate tools strategically.

CC.9-12.F.IF.5 Relate the domain of a function to its graph and, where applicable, to the quantitative relationship it describes.

Activity

Use a graph and a table to identify holes in the graph of $f(x) = \dfrac{(x+1)(x-1)}{(x-1)}$.

1 Graph the function $f(x) = \dfrac{(x+1)(x-1)}{(x-1)}$ in the square window.

The graph appears to be identical to the graph of the function in simplified form, $f(x) = x + 1$.

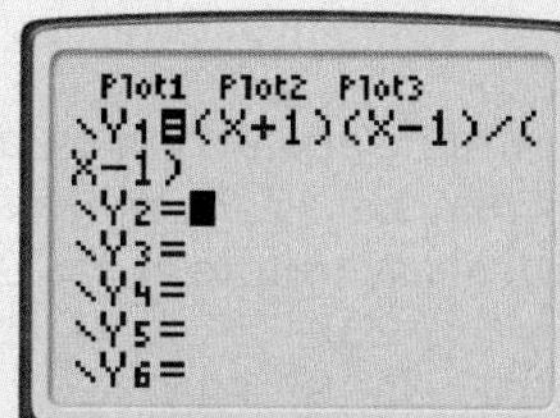

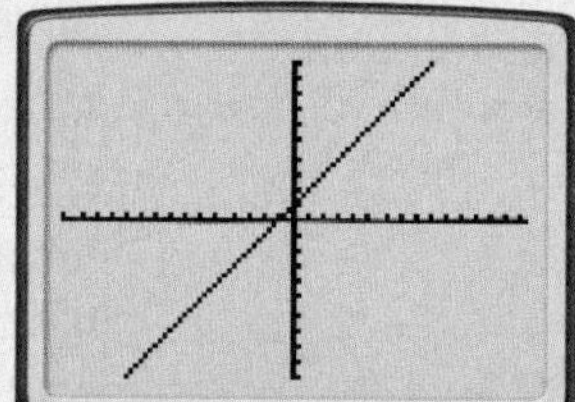

2 Change the window on your graph to the decimal window by pressing ZOOM and selecting **4:ZDecimal.**

Notice that there is a break, or *hole*, in the graph when $x = 1$ because the function is undefined at that x-value.

The hole appears only if you are in a friendly window that allows the calculator to evaluate the function exactly at that point.

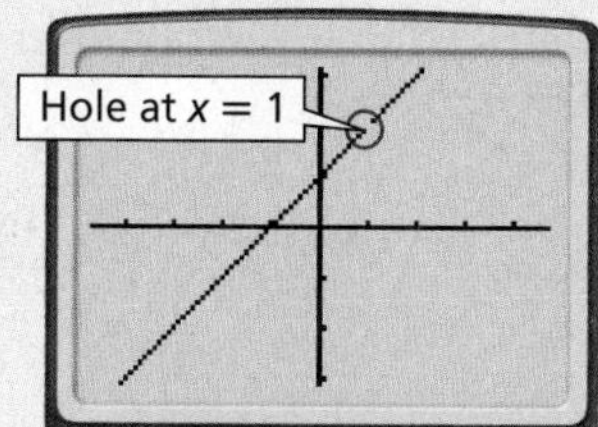

3 Use a table to compare the function $f(x) = \dfrac{(x+1)(x-1)}{(x-1)}$ to the linear function $f(x) = x + 1$. The table suggests that the graphs are identical except when $x = 1$.

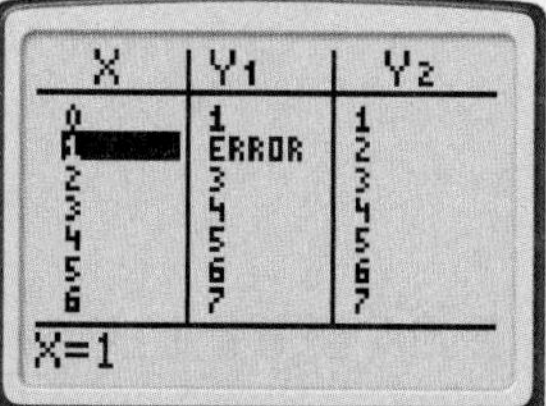

Try This

Use a graph and a table to identify the hole in the graph of each function.

1. $f(x) = \dfrac{(x-2)(x+3)}{x+3}$

2. $g(x) = \dfrac{(x+1)(x+3)}{x+1}$

3. $h(x) = \dfrac{x(x+2)}{x+2}$

4. Make a Conjecture Make a conjecture about where the holes in the graph of a rational function appear, based on the factors of the numerator and the denominator.

Use a graph and a table to identify the hole(s) in the graph of each function. Confirm your answer by factoring.

5. $f(x) = \dfrac{x^2 - 4x + 3}{x - 3}$

6. $g(x) = \dfrac{x^2 + x - 2}{x - 1}$

7. $h(x) = \dfrac{x^3 - x}{x^2 - 1}$

5-4 Rational Functions

CC.9-12.A.CED.2 Create equations in two or more variables to represent relationships between quantities; graph equations on coordinate axes with labels and scales. *Also* **CC.9-12.A.CED.3**

Objectives

Graph rational functions.

Transform rational functions by changing parameters.

Vocabulary

rational function
discontinuous function
continuous function
hole (in a graph)

Why learn this?

Rational functions can be used to model the cost per person for group events, such as a band trip to a bowl game. (See Exercise 32.)

A **rational function** is a function whose rule can be written as a ratio of two polynomials. The parent rational function is $f(x) = \frac{1}{x}$. Its graph is a *hyperbola,* which has two separate branches.

Like logarithmic and exponential functions, rational functions may have asymptotes. The function $f(x) = \frac{1}{x}$ has a vertical asymptote at $x = 0$ and a horizontal asymptote at $y = 0$.

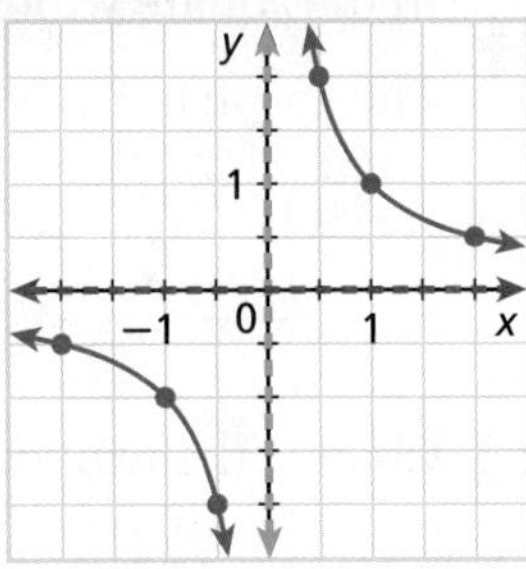

The rational function $f(x) = \frac{1}{x}$ can be transformed by using methods similar to those used to transform other types of functions.

Know it! Note

$$f(x) = \frac{a}{x - h} + k$$

- $|a|$ → vertical stretch or compression factor; $a < 0$ → reflection across the x-axis
- k → vertical translation down for $k < 0$; up for $k > 0$
- h → horizontal translation left for $h < 0$; right for $h > 0$

EXAMPLE 1 Transforming Rational Functions

Using the graph of $f(x) = \frac{1}{x}$ as a guide, describe the transformation and graph each function.

A $g(x) = \frac{1}{x - 3}$

Because $h = 3$, translate f 3 units right.

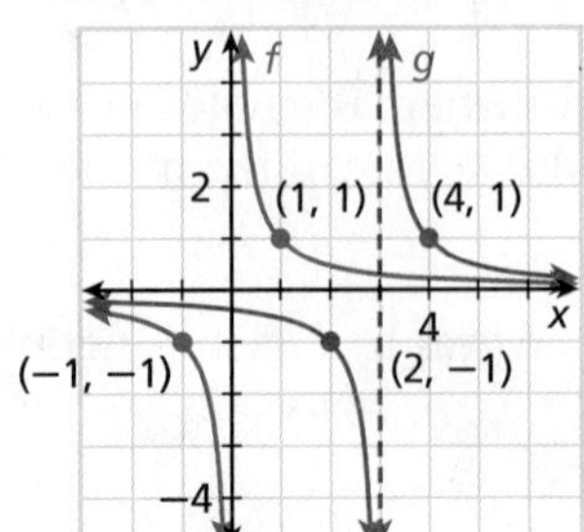

B $g(x) = \frac{1}{x} - 2$

Because $k = -2$, translate f 2 units down.

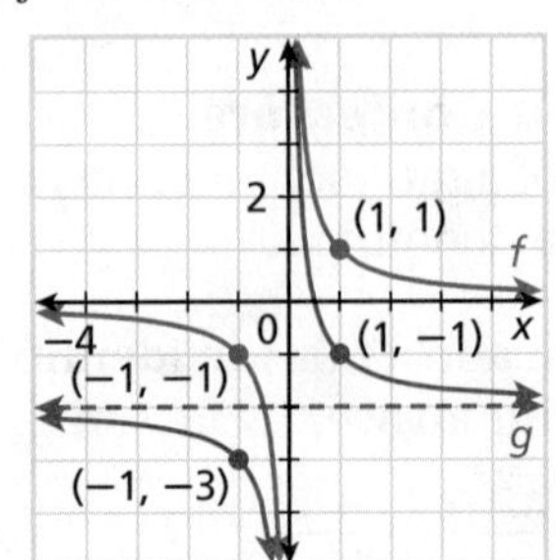

Simon Hayter/Toronto Star/NewsCom

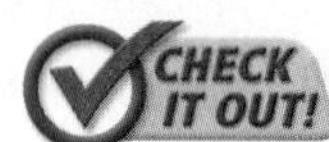

Using the graph of $f(x) = \frac{1}{x}$ as a guide, describe the transformation and graph each function.

1a. $g(x) = \frac{1}{x + 4}$ **1b.** $g(x) = \frac{1}{x} + 1$

The values of h and k affect the locations of the asymptotes, the domain, and the range of rational functions whose graphs are hyperbolas.

Rational Functions

For a rational function of the form $f(x) = \frac{a}{x - h} + k$,
- the graph is a hyperbola.
- there is a vertical asymptote at the line $x = h$, and the domain is $\{x \mid x \neq h\}$.
- there is a horizontal asymptote at the line $y = k$, and the range is $\{y \mid y \neq k\}$.

EXAMPLE 2 **Determining Properties of Hyperbolas**

Identify the asymptotes, domain, and range of the function $g(x) = \frac{1}{x + 2} + 4$.

$g(x) = \frac{1}{x - (-2)} + 4$ *$h = -2$, $k = 4$*

Vertical asymptote: $x = -2$ *The value of h is -2.*

Domain: $\{x \mid x \neq -2\}$

Horizontal asymptote: $y = 4$ *The value of k is 4.*

Range: $\{y \mid y \neq 4\}$

Check Graph the function on a graphing calculator. The graph suggests that the function has asymptotes at $x = -2$ and $y = 4$.

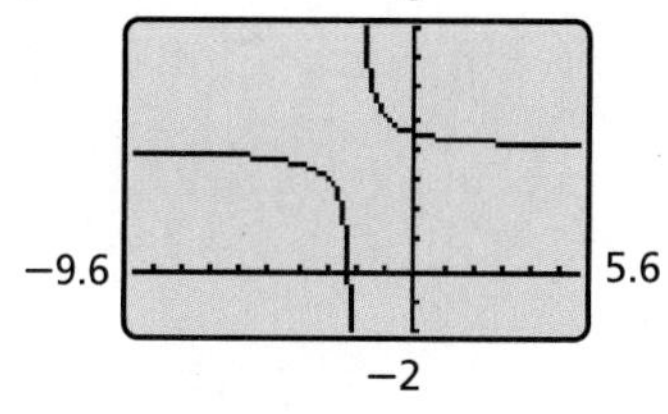

Caution!

Graphing calculators may incorrectly connect two branches of the graph of a rational function with a nearly vertical segment that looks like an asymptote.

2. Identify the asymptotes, domain, and range of the function $g(x) = \frac{1}{x - 3} - 5$.

A **discontinuous function** is a function whose graph has one or more gaps or breaks. The hyperbola graphed above and many other rational functions are discontinuous functions.

A **continuous function** is a function whose graph has no gaps or breaks. The functions you have studied before this, including linear, quadratic, polynomial, exponential, and logarithmic functions, are continuous functions.

The graphs of some rational functions are not hyperbolas. Consider the rational function $f(x) = \frac{(x - 3)(x + 2)}{x + 1}$ and its graph. The numerator of this function is 0 when $x = 3$ or $x = -2$. Therefore, the function has x-intercepts at -2 and 3. The denominator of this function is 0 when $x = -1$. As a result, the graph of the function has a vertical asymptote at the line $x = -1$.

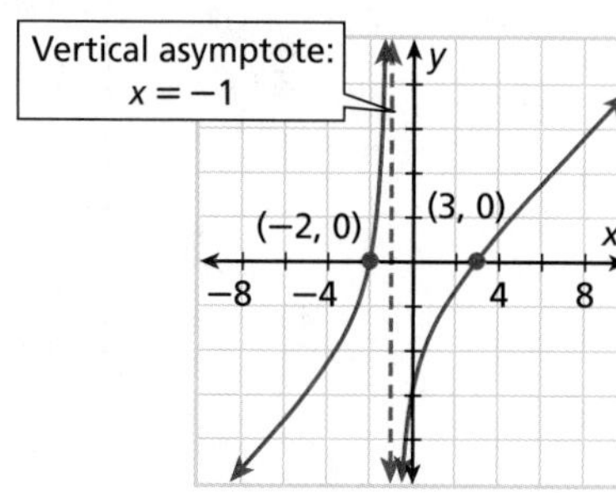

Zeros and Vertical Asymptotes — Rational Functions

If $f(x) = \frac{p(x)}{q(x)}$, where p and q are polynomial functions in standard form with no common factors other than 1, then the function f has

- zeros at each real value of x for which $p(x) = 0$.
- a vertical asymptote at each real value of x for which $q(x) = 0$.

EXAMPLE 3 Graphing Rational Functions with Vertical Asymptotes

Identify the zeros and vertical asymptotes of $f(x) = \frac{x^2 - 2x - 3}{x - 2}$. Then graph.

Step 1 Find the zeros and vertical asymptotes.

$f(x) = \frac{(x + 1)(x - 3)}{x - 2}$ — *Factor the numerator.*

Zeros: -1 and 3 — *The numerator is 0 when $x = -1$ or $x = 3$.*

Vertical asymptote: $x = 2$ — *The denominator is 0 when $x = 2$.*

Remember!

You may want to review factoring and finding zeros of polynomial functions before graphing rational functions.

Step 2 Graph the function.

Plot the zeros and draw the asymptote. Then make a table of values to fill in missing points.

x	-4	-1	0	1.5	2.5	3	5
y	-3.5	0	1.5	7.5	-3.5	0	4

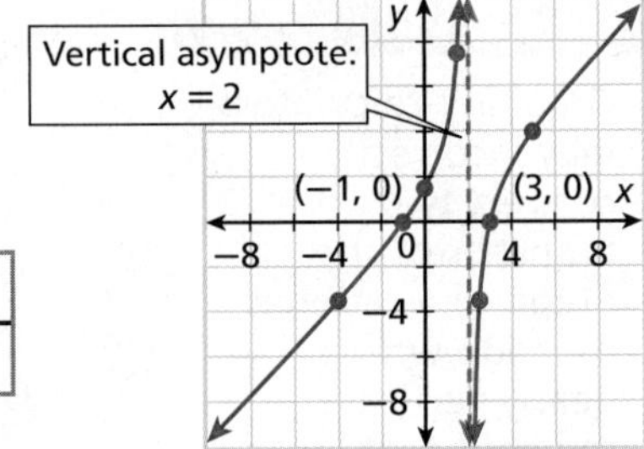

3. Identify the zeros and vertical asymptotes of $f(x) = \frac{x^2 + 7x + 6}{x + 3}$. Then graph.

Some rational functions, including those whose graphs are hyperbolas, have a horizontal asymptote. The existence and location of a horizontal asymptote depends on the degrees of the polynomials that make up the rational function.

Note that the graph of a rational function can sometimes cross a horizontal asymptote. However, the graph will approach the asymptote when $|x|$ is large.

Horizontal Asymptotes — Rational Functions

Let $f(x) = \frac{p(x)}{q(x)}$, where p and q are polynomial functions in standard form with no common factors other than 1. The graph of f has at most one horizontal asymptote.

- If degree of $p >$ degree of q, there is no horizontal asymptote.
- If degree of $p <$ degree of q, the horizontal asymptote is the line $y = 0$.
- If degree of $p =$ degree of q, the horizontal asymptote is the line $y = \frac{\text{leading coefficient of } p}{\text{leading coefficient of } q}$.

EXAMPLE 4 Graphing Rational Functions with Vertical and Horizontal Asymptotes

Identify the zeros and asymptotes of each function. Then graph.

A $f(x) = \dfrac{x^2 + x - 6}{x}$

$f(x) = \dfrac{(x + 3)(x - 2)}{x}$ *Factor the numerator.*

Zeros: -3 and 2 *The numerator is 0 when $x = -3$ or $x = 2$.*

Vertical asymptote: $x = 0$ *The denominator is 0 when $x = 0$.*

Horizontal asymptote: none *Degree of $p >$ degree of q*

Graph with a graphing calculator or by using a table of values.

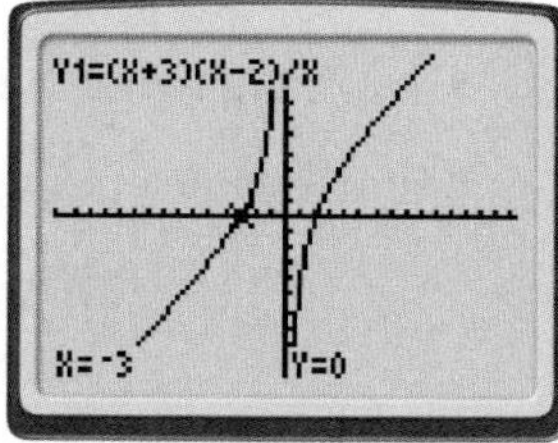

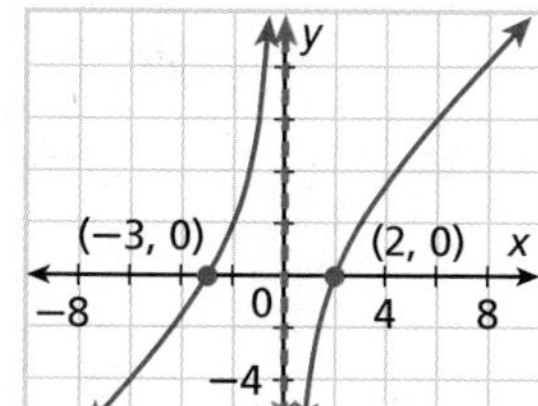

B $f(x) = \dfrac{x - 1}{x^2}$

Zero: 1 *The numerator is 0 when $x = 1$.*

Vertical asymptote: $x = 0$ *The denominator is 0 when $x = 0$.*

Horizontal asymptote: $y = 0$ *Degree of $p <$ degree of q*

1

−4 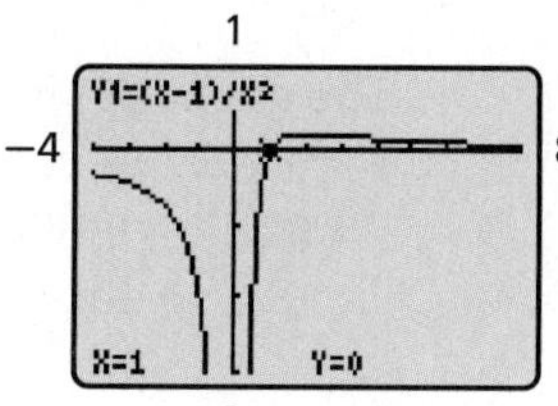 8

−3

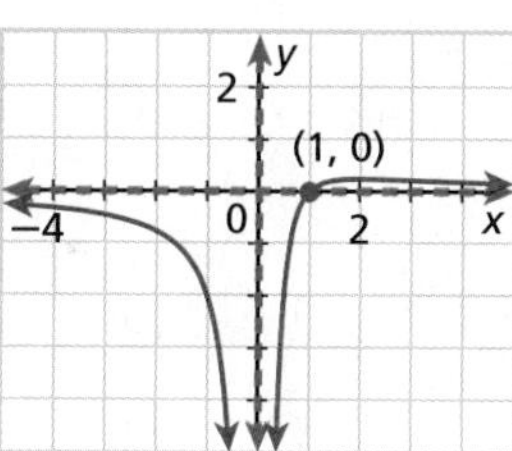

> **Remember!**
> The leading coefficient of a polynomial is the coefficient of the first term when the polynomial is written in standard form.

C $f(x) = \dfrac{2x^2 - 2}{x^2 - 4}$

$f(x) = \dfrac{2(x + 1)(x - 1)}{(x + 2)(x - 2)}$ *Factor the numerator and denominator.*

Zeros: -1 and 1 *The numerator is 0 when $x = -1$ or $x = 1$.*

Vertical asymptotes: $x = -2$, $x = 2$ *The denominator is 0 when $x = \pm 2$.*

Horizontal asymptote: $y = 2$ *The horizontal asymptote is* $y = \dfrac{\text{leading coefficient of } p}{\text{leading coefficient of } q} = \dfrac{2}{1} = 2.$

6.2

−9.4 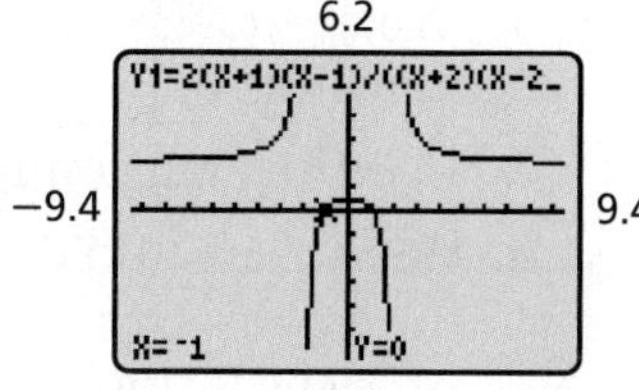 9.4

−6.2

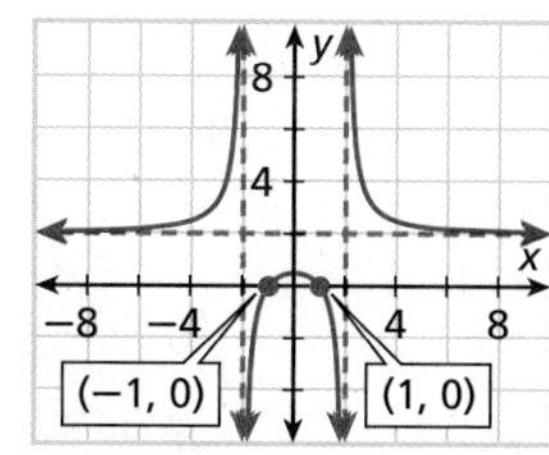

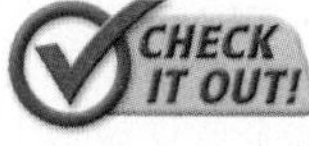

Identify the zeros and asymptotes of each function. Then graph.

4a. $f(x) = \dfrac{x^2 + 2x - 15}{x - 1}$ **4b.** $f(x) = \dfrac{x - 2}{x^2 + x}$ **4c.** $f(x) = \dfrac{3x^2 + x}{x^2 - 9}$

In some cases, both the numerator and the denominator of a rational function will equal 0 for a particular value of x. As a result, the function will be undefined at this x-value. If this is the case, the graph of the function may have a *hole.* A **hole** is an omitted point in a graph.

Holes in Graphs **Rational Functions**

If a rational function has the same factor $x - b$ in both the numerator and the denominator, then there is a hole in the graph at the point where $x = b$, unless the line $x = b$ is a vertical asymptote.

EXAMPLE 5 Graphing Rational Functions with Holes

Identify holes in the graph of $f(x) = \frac{x^2 - 4}{x + 2}$. Then graph.

$$f(x) = \frac{(x - 2)(x + 2)}{(x + 2)}$$ *Factor the numerator.*

There is a hole in the graph at $x = -2$. *The expression $x + 2$ is a factor of both the numerator and the denominator.*

For $x \neq -2$, $f(x) = \frac{(x - 2)\cancel{(x + 2)}}{\cancel{(x + 2)}} = x - 2$ *Divide out common factors.*

The graph of f is the same as the graph of $y = x - 2$, except for the hole at $x = -2$. On the graph, indicate the hole with an open circle. The domain of f is $\{x \mid x \neq -2\}$.

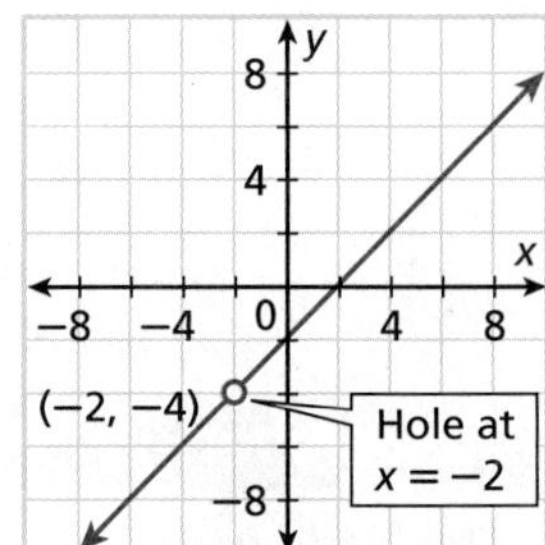

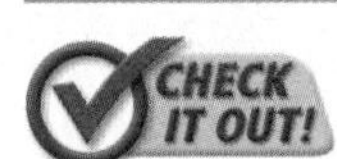

5. Identify holes in the graph of $f(x) = \frac{x^2 + x - 6}{x - 2}$. Then graph.

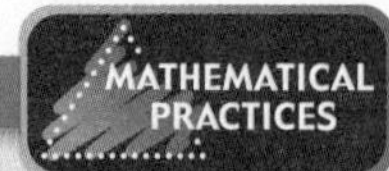

THINK AND DISCUSS

1. Explain how vertical asymptotes relate to the domain of a rational function.

2. Compare and contrast rational functions and polynomial functions.

3. GET ORGANIZED Copy and complete the graphic organizer. In each box, write the formula or method for identifying the characteristic of graphs of rational functions.

Zeros	Vertical asymptotes
Horizontal asymptotes	Holes

Center: $f(x) = \frac{p(x)}{q(x)}$

5-4 Exercises

GUIDED PRACTICE

1. **Vocabulary** A function with a hole in its graph is __?__. (*continuous* or *discontinuous*)

SEE EXAMPLE 1

Using the graph of $f(x) = \frac{1}{x}$ as a guide, describe the transformation and graph each function.

2. $g(x) = \frac{1}{x} - 2$
3. $g(x) = \frac{1}{x+5}$
4. $g(x) = \frac{1}{x-1} + 4$

SEE EXAMPLE 2

Identify the asymptotes, domain, and range of each function.

5. $f(x) = \frac{1}{x} - 1$
6. $f(x) = \frac{1}{x+4} + 3$
7. $f(x) = \frac{2}{x-2} - 8$

SEE EXAMPLE 3

Identify the zeros and vertical asymptotes of each function. Then graph.

8. $f(x) = \frac{x^2 - x - 12}{x}$
9. $f(x) = \frac{x^2 - 5x}{x-2}$
10. $f(x) = \frac{x^2}{x-1}$

SEE EXAMPLE 4

Identify the zeros and asymptotes of each function. Then graph.

11. $f(x) = \frac{x^2 + 3x + 2}{3 - x}$
12. $f(x) = \frac{x-2}{x^2 + 6x}$
13. $f(x) = \frac{5x+2}{x+1}$

SEE EXAMPLE 5

Identify holes in the graph of each function. Then graph.

14. $f(x) = \frac{x^2 - 5x + 6}{x^2 - 4x + 3}$
15. $f(x) = \frac{x^2 - 4x + 4}{x - 2}$
16. $f(x) = \frac{4x + 20}{2x + 10}$

PRACTICE AND PROBLEM SOLVING

Independent Practice

For Exercises	See Example
17–19	1
20–22	2
23–25	3
26–28	4
29–31	5

Extra Practice

See Extra Practice for more Skills Practice and Applications Practice exercises.

Using the graph of $f(x) = \frac{1}{x}$ as a guide, describe the transformation and graph each function.

17. $g(x) = \frac{1}{x} - 5$
18. $g(x) = \frac{1}{x+3}$
19. $g(x) = \frac{2}{x}$

Identify the asymptotes, domain, and range of each function.

20. $f(x) = \frac{1}{x+6}$
21. $f(x) = \frac{4}{x} + 5$
22. $f(x) = \frac{3}{x-4} - 1$

Identify the zeros and vertical asymptotes of each function. Then graph.

23. $f(x) = \frac{(x+2)(x-5)}{(x-2)}$
24. $f(x) = \frac{(2-x)(4+x)}{(x-1)}$
25. $h(x) = \frac{x^2 - 4}{x + 3}$

Identify the zeros and asymptotes of each function. Then graph.

26. $f(x) = \frac{x^2 - x - 2}{1 - x}$
27. $f(x) = \frac{x-3}{x^2 - 4}$
28. $f(x) = \frac{2x^2 + x}{1 - x^2}$

Identify holes in the graph of each function. Then graph.

29. $f(x) = \frac{x^4}{x}$
30. $f(x) = \frac{-x^2 + x}{x - 1}$
31. $f(x) = \frac{x^2 - 14x + 49}{x - 7}$

32. **Band** Members of a high school band plan to play at a college bowl game. The trip will cost \$350 per band member plus a \$2000 deposit.
    a. Write a function to represent the total average cost of the trip per band member.
    b. Graph the function.
    c. **What if...?** Find the total average cost per person if 40 band members attend the bowl game.

Identify all zeros, asymptotes, and holes in the graph of each function.

33. $f(x) = \dfrac{x^2 - 2x - 3}{x^2 - 3x}$

34. $f(x) = \dfrac{x^3 - 1}{x - 1}$

35. $f(x) = \dfrac{6x - 5}{2 - 3x}$

36. $f(x) = \dfrac{x^2 + 6x + 8}{x^2}$

37. $f(x) = \dfrac{x}{x^2 - 9}$

38. $f(x) = \dfrac{x^2 - 9}{x^2 - 4}$

Math History

The Agnesi curve is named for Maria Agnesi (1718–1799), a mathematician from Milan who wrote one of the earliest surviving mathematical works composed by a woman.

The Granger Collection, New York

Write a rational function with the given characteristics.

39. zeros at -1 and 3 and vertical asymptote at $x = 0$

40. zero at 2, vertical asymptotes at $x = -2$ and $x = 0$, and horizontal asymptote at $y = 0$

41. zero at 2, vertical asymptote at $x = -1$, horizontal asymptote at $y = 1$, and hole at $x = -3$

42. **Math History** The *Agnesi curve* is the graph of the function $y = \dfrac{a^3}{x^2 + a^2}$.
   a. Graph the Agnesi curve for $a = 3$.
   b. What are the domain and the range of the function?
   c. Identify all asymptotes of the function.

43. **Chemistry** A chemist has 100 g of a 12% saline solution that she wants to strengthen to 25%. The percentage P of salt in the solution by mass can be modeled by $P(x) = \frac{100(12 + x)}{100 + x}$, where x is the number of grams of salt added.
   a. Graph the function for $0 \le x \le 100$.
   b. Use your graph to estimate how much salt the chemist must add to create a 25% solution.

44. **Multi-Step** The average cost per DVD purchased from a movie club is a function of the number of DVDs a member buys.
   a. Graph the data in the table.
   b. The function that describes the data in the table has the form $f(x) = \frac{40}{x} + k$, where k is a constant. What is the value of k?
   c. What is the total cost of buying 15 DVDs from the club?

Number of DVDs	Average Cost ($)
1	55
2	35
4	25
5	23
10	19
20	17

45. **///ERROR ANALYSIS///** A student wrote the following description for the graph of $f(x) = \frac{(x - 1)(2x - 3)}{(x + 1)(x - 1)}$. Explain the error. Write a correct description.
   The graph has vertical asymptotes at $x = 1$ and $x = -1$ and a horizontal asymptote at $y = 2$.

46. **Critical Thinking** Is it possible to have a rational function with no vertical asymptotes? Explain.

MULTI-STEP TEST PREP

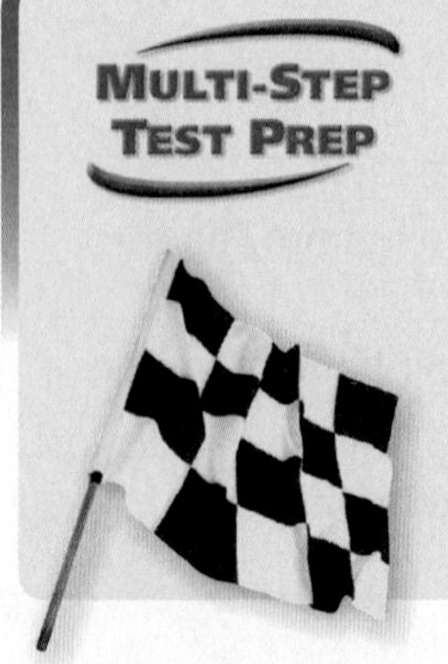

47. A race car driver makes a pit stop at the beginning of a lap. The time t in seconds that it takes the driver to complete the lap, including the pit stop, can be modeled by $t(r) = \frac{12r + 9000}{r}$, where r is the driver's average speed in miles per hour after the pit stop.
   a. Graph the function.
   b. What is the horizontal asymptote of the function, and what does it represent?
   c. The driver's average speed after the pit stop is 200 mi/h. How long does it take the driver to complete the lap, including the pit stop?

(tl), The Granger Collection, New York; (bl), Stockdisc/gettyimages

48. **Critical Thinking** For what value(s) of x is $\frac{x^2 - 9}{x + 3} = x - 3$ a false statement? Explain.

49. **Write About It** Explain how to identify the domain of a rational function.

TEST PREP

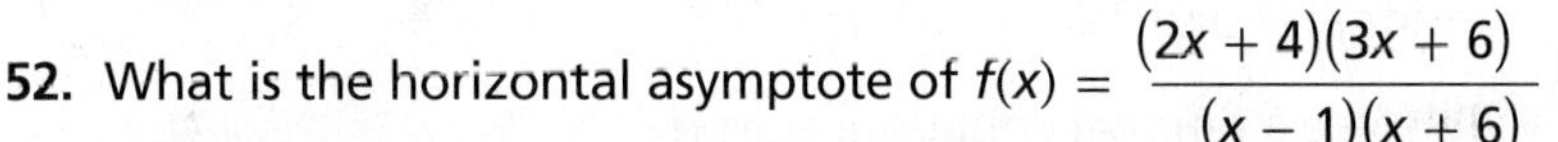

50. The graph of which of the following rational functions has a hole?

Ⓐ $f(x) = \frac{x^2 + 5x + 4}{x^2 + x - 12}$

Ⓑ $f(x) = \frac{x^2 - 2x + 1}{x^2 + 7x - 15}$

Ⓒ $f(x) = \frac{x^2 - 9}{x^2 - 2x - 7}$

Ⓓ $f(x) = \frac{x^2 + x - 30}{x^2 + 5x - 14}$

51. Which function is shown in the graph?

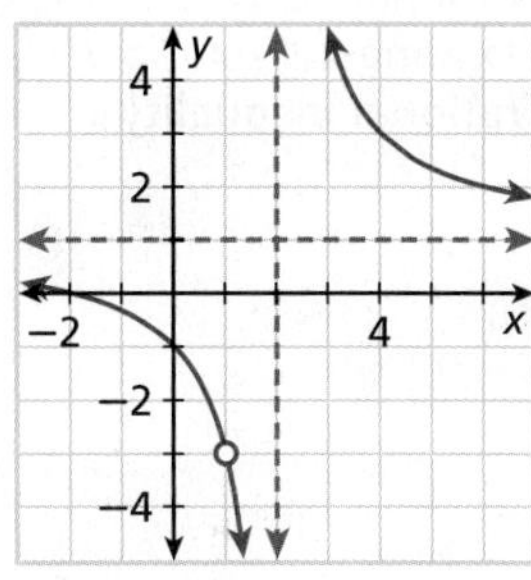

Ⓕ $f(x) = \frac{x^2 + x - 2}{x^2 - 3x + 2}$

Ⓖ $f(x) = \frac{x^2 + 3x + 2}{x^2 - x - 2}$

Ⓗ $f(x) = \frac{x^2 + x - 2}{x^2 + 3x + 2}$

Ⓙ $f(x) = \frac{x^2 - 3x + 2}{x^2 + x - 2}$

52. What is the horizontal asymptote of $f(x) = \frac{(2x + 4)(3x + 6)}{(x - 1)(x + 6)}$?

Ⓐ $y = -6$

Ⓑ $y = -2$

Ⓒ $y = 2$

Ⓓ $y = 6$

CHALLENGE AND EXTEND

Identify all zeros, asymptotes, and holes in the graph of each function. Then graph.

53. $f(x) = \frac{(x^2 - 3x + 2)(x - 3)}{(x - 1)(x^2 - 5x + 6)}$

54. $f(x) = \frac{(x^2 - 9)(3x + 2)}{(x^2 - 4)(x - 3)}$

55. Let $f(x) = \frac{1}{x^2 - 2x + c}$. Find c such that the graph of f has the given number of vertical asymptotes.

a. none **b.** one **c.** two

Write a rational function with the given characteristics.

56. no zeros, no vertical asymptotes, and a horizontal asymptote at $y = 1$

57. zero at 0, vertical asymptotes at $x = -3$ and $x = 3$, and holes at $x = -1$ and $x = 1$

5-5 Solving Rational Equations and Inequalities

CC.9-12.F.IF.5 Relate the domain of a function to its graph and, where applicable, to the quantitative relationship it describes.

Objective
Solve rational equations and inequalities.

Vocabulary
rational equation
extraneous solution
rational inequality

Who uses this?

Kayakers can use rational equations to determine how fast a river is moving. (See Example 3.)

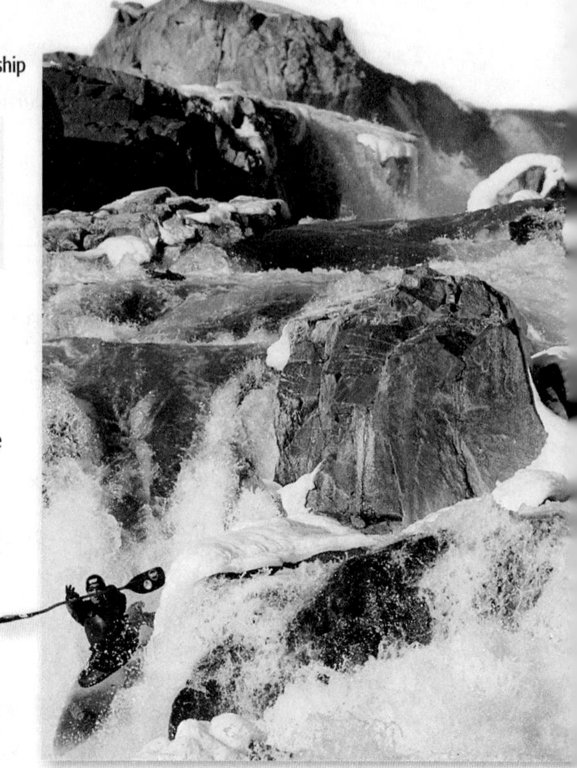

A **rational equation** is an equation that contains one or more rational expressions. The time t in hours that it takes to travel d miles can be determined by using the equation $t = \frac{d}{r}$, where r is the average rate of speed. This equation is a rational equation.

To solve a rational equation, start by multiplying each term of the equation by the least common denominator (LCD) of all of the expressions in the equation. This step eliminates the denominators of the rational expressions and results in an equation you can solve by using algebra.

EXAMPLE 1 Solving Rational Equations

Solve the equation $x + \frac{8}{x} = 6$.

$x(x) + \frac{8}{x}(x) = 6(x)$ *Multiply each term by the LCD, x.*

$x^2 + 8 = 6x$ *Simplify. Note that $x \neq 0$.*

$x^2 - 6x + 8 = 0$ *Write in standard form.*

$(x - 2)(x - 4) = 0$ *Factor.*

$x - 2 = 0$ or $x - 4 = 0$ *Apply the Zero Product Property.*

$x = 2$ or $x = 4$ *Solve for x.*

Check

$x + \frac{8}{x} = 6$	
$2 + \frac{8}{2}$	6
6	6 ✓

$x + \frac{8}{x} = 6$	
$4 + \frac{8}{4}$	6
6	6 ✓

Remember!

Factoring is not the only method of solving the quadratic equation that results in Example 1. You could also complete the square or use the Quadratic Formula.

CHECK IT OUT! **Solve each equation.**

1a. $\frac{10}{3} = \frac{4}{x} + 2$ **1b.** $\frac{6}{x} + \frac{5}{4} = -\frac{7}{4}$ **1c.** $x = \frac{6}{x} - 1$

An **extraneous solution** is a solution of an equation derived from an original equation that is not a solution of the original equation. When you solve a rational equation, it is possible to get extraneous solutions. These values should be eliminated from the solution set. Always check your solutions by substituting them into the original equation.

EXAMPLE 2 Extraneous Solutions

Solve each equation.

A $\dfrac{3x}{x-3} = \dfrac{2x+3}{x-3}$

$$\frac{3x}{x-3}(x-3) = \frac{2x+3}{x-3}(x-3)$$ *Multiply each term by the LCD, x − 3.*

$$\frac{3x}{\cancel{x-3}}\cancel{(x-3)} = \frac{2x+3}{\cancel{x-3}}\cancel{(x-3)}$$ *Divide out common factors.*

$$3x = 2x + 3$$ *Simplify. Note that $x \neq 3$.*

$$x = 3$$ *Solve for x.*

> **Remember!**
> A rational expression is undefined for any value of a variable that makes a denominator in the expression equal to 0.

The solution $x = 3$ is extraneous because it makes the denominators of the original equation equal to 0. Therefore, the equation has no solution.

Check Substitute 3 for x in the original equation.

$$\frac{3(3)}{3-3} = \frac{2(3)+3}{3-3}$$

$$\frac{9}{0} \quad \Big| \quad \frac{9}{0}$$ *Division by 0 is undefined.*

B $\dfrac{2x-9}{x-7} + \dfrac{x}{2} = \dfrac{5}{x-7}$

$$\frac{2x-9}{x-7}\cdot 2(x-7) + \frac{x}{2}\cdot 2(x-7) = \frac{5}{x-7}\cdot 2(x-7)$$ *Multiply each term by the LCD, 2(x − 7).*

$$\frac{2x-9}{\cancel{x-7}}\cdot 2\cancel{(x-7)} + \frac{x}{\cancel{2}}\cdot\cancel{2}(x-7) = \frac{5}{\cancel{x-7}}\cdot 2\cancel{(x-7)}$$ *Divide out common factors.*

$$2(2x-9) + x(x-7) = 5(2)$$ *Simplify. Note that $x \neq 7$.*

$$4x - 18 + x^2 - 7x = 10$$ *Use the Distributive Property.*

$$x^2 - 3x - 28 = 0$$ *Write in standard form.*

$$(x-7)(x+4) = 0$$ *Factor.*

$$x - 7 = 0 \text{ or } x + 4 = 0$$ *Use the Zero Product Property.*

$$x = 7 \text{ or } x = -4$$ *Solve for x.*

The solution $x = 7$ is extraneous because it makes the denominators of the original equation equal to 0. The only solution is $x = -4$.

Check Write $\frac{2x-9}{x-7} + \frac{x}{2} = \frac{5}{x-7}$ as $\frac{2x-9}{x-7} + \frac{x}{2} - \frac{5}{x-7} = 0$. Graph the left side of the equation as **Y1** and identify the values of x for which **Y1** $= 0$.

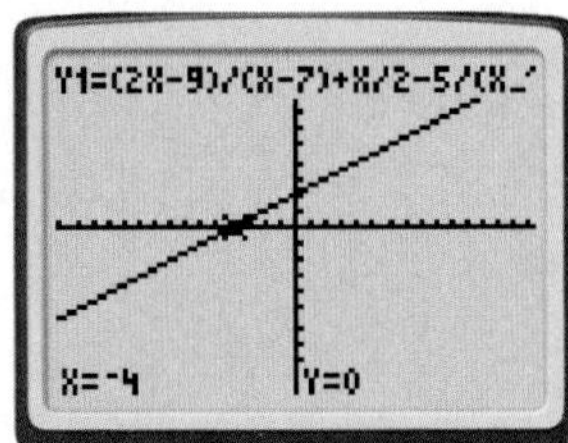

The graph intersects the x-axis only when $x = -4$. Therefore, $x = -4$ is the only solution.

Solve each equation.

2a. $\dfrac{16}{x^2-16} = \dfrac{2}{x-4}$

2b. $\dfrac{1}{x-1} = \dfrac{x}{x-1} + \dfrac{x}{6}$

EXAMPLE 3 Problem-Solving Application

A kayaker spends an afternoon paddling on a river. She travels 3 mi upstream and 3 mi downstream in a total of 4 h. In still water, the kayaker can travel at an average speed of 2 mi/h. Based on this information, what is the average speed of the river's current? Is your answer reasonable?

Make sense of problems and persevere in solving them.

1 Understand the Problem

The **answer** will be the average speed of the current.
List the **important information:**

- The kayaker spent 4 hours kayaking.
- She went 3 mi upstream and 3 mi downstream.
- Her average speed in still water is 2 mi/h.

2 Make a Plan

Let c represent the speed of the current. When the kayaker is going upstream, her speed is equal to her speed in still water minus c. When the kayaker is going downstream, her speed is equal to her speed in still water plus c.

	Distance (mi)	Average Speed (mi/h)	Time (h)
Up	3	$2 - c$	$\frac{3}{2-c}$
Down	3	$2 + c$	$\frac{3}{2+c}$

Helpful Hint

distance = rate × time
Therefore,
time = $\frac{\text{distance}}{\text{rate}}$.

total time = time upstream + time downstream

$$4 = \frac{3}{2-c} + \frac{3}{2+c}$$

3 Solve

$$4(2-c)(2+c) = \frac{3}{2-c}(2-c)(2+c) + \frac{3}{2+c}(2-c)(2+c)$$ *The LCD is $(2-c)(2+c)$.*

$$4(2-c)(2+c) = 3(2+c) + 3(2-c)$$ *Simplify. Note that $c \neq \pm 2$.*

$$16 - 4c^2 = 6 + 3c + 6 - 3c$$ *Use the Distributive Property.*

$$16 - 4c^2 = 12$$ *Combine like terms.*

$$-4c^2 = -4$$ *Solve for c.*

$$c = \pm 1$$

The speed of the current cannot be negative. Therefore, the average speed of the current is 1 mi/h.

4 Look Back

If the speed of the current is 1 mi/h, the kayaker's speed when going upstream is $2 - 1 = 1$ mi/h. It will take her 3 h to travel 3 mi upstream. Her speed when going downstream is $2 + 1 = 3$ mi/h. It will take her 1 hour to travel 3 mi downstream. The total trip will take 4 h, which is the given time.

Use the information given above to answer the following.

3. On a different river, the kayaker travels 2 mi upstream and 2 mi downstream in a total of 5 h. What is the average speed of the current of this river? Round to the nearest tenth.

EXAMPLE 4 Work Application

Jason can clean a large tank at an aquarium in about 6 hours. When Jason and Lacy work together, they can clean the tank in about 3.5 hours. About how long would it take Lacy to clean the tank if she works by herself?

Jason's rate: $\frac{1}{6}$ of the tank per hour

Lacy's rate: $\frac{1}{h}$ of the tank per hour, where h is the number of hours needed to clean the tank by herself

Jason's rate × hours worked	+	Lacy's rate × hours worked	=	1 complete job
$\frac{1}{6}(3.5)$	+	$\frac{1}{h}(3.5)$	=	1

$\frac{1}{6}(3.5)(6h) + \frac{1}{h}(3.5)(6h) = 1(6h)$ *Multiply by the LCD, 6h.*

$3.5h + 21 = 6h$ *Simplify.*

$21 = 2.5h$ *Solve for h.*

$8.4 = h$

It will take Lacy about 8.4 hours, or 8 hours 24 minutes, to clean the tank when working by herself.

4. Julien can mulch a garden in 20 minutes. Together, Julien and Remy can mulch the same garden in 11 minutes. How long will it take Remy to mulch the garden when working alone?

A **rational inequality** is an inequality that contains one or more rational expressions. One way to solve rational inequalities is by using graphs and tables.

EXAMPLE 5 Using Graphs and Tables to Solve Rational Equations and Inequalities

Solve $\frac{x}{x-4} \leq 2$ by using a graph and a table.

Use a graph. On a graphing calculator, let **Y1** $= \frac{x}{x-4}$ and **Y2** $= 2$.

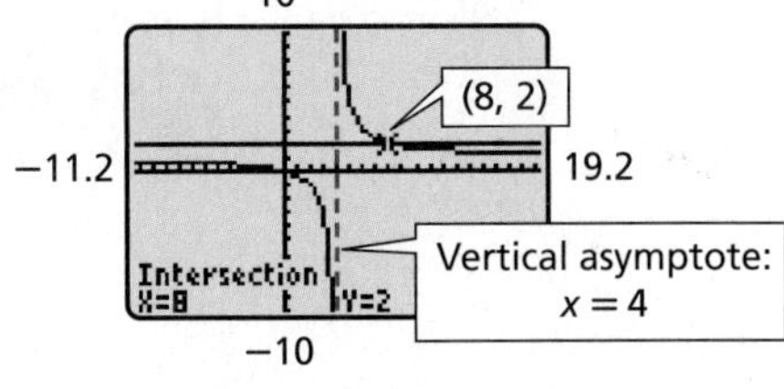

The graph of **Y1** is at or below the graph of **Y2** when $x < 4$ or when $x \geq 8$.

Remember!

The solution $x < 4$ or $x \geq 8$ can be written in set-builder notation as $\{x \mid x < 4 \cup x \geq 8\}$

Use a table. The table shows that **Y1** is undefined when $x = 4$ and that **Y1** $\leq$ **Y2** when $x < 4$ or when $x \geq 8$.

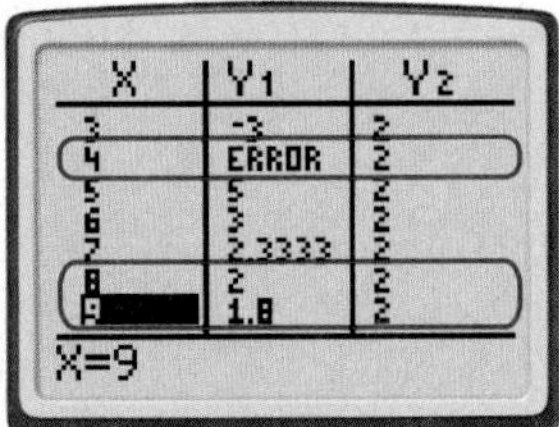

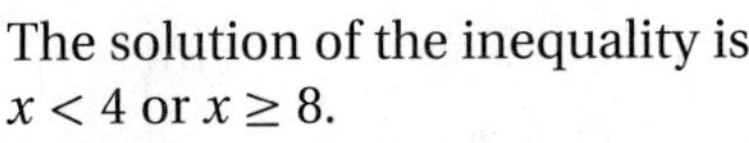

The solution of the inequality is $x < 4$ or $x \geq 8$.

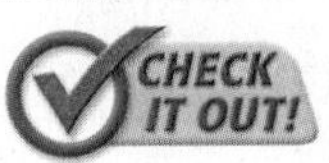

Solve by using a graph and a table.

5a. $\frac{x}{x-3} \geq 4$

5b. $\frac{8}{x+1} = -2$

You can also solve rational inequalities algebraically. You start by multiplying each term by the least common denominator (LCD) of all the expressions in the inequality. However, you must consider two cases: the LCD is positive or the LCD is negative.

EXAMPLE 6 Solving Rational Inequalities Algebraically

Solve the inequality $\frac{8}{x+5} \le 4$ algebraically. Check your answer for reasonableness.

Remember!

If you multiply or divide both sides of an inequality by a negative value, you must reverse the inequality symbol.

Case 1 LCD is positive.

Step 1 Solve for x.

$\frac{8}{x+5}(x+5) \le 4(x+5)$ *Multiply by the LCD.*

$8 \le 4x + 20$ *Simplify. Note that $x \ne -5$.*

$-12 \le 4x$ *Solve for x.*

$-3 \le x$

Step 2 Consider the sign of the LCD.

$x + 5 > 0$ *LCD is positive.*

$x > -5$ *Solve for x.*

For Case 1, the solution must satisfy $x \ge -3$ *and* $x > -5$, which simplifies to $x \ge -3$.

Case 2 LCD is negative.

Step 1 Solve for x.

$\frac{8}{x+5}(x+5) \ge 4(x+5)$ *Multiply by the LCD. Reverse the inequality.*

$8 \ge 4x + 20$ *Simplify. Note that $x \ne -5$.*

$-12 \ge 4x$ *Solve for x.*

$-3 \ge x$

Step 2 Consider the sign of the LCD.

$x + 5 < 0$ *LCD is negative.*

$x < -5$ *Solve for x.*

For Case 2, the solution must satisfy $x \le -3$ *and* $x < -5$, which simplifies to $x < -5$.

The solution set of the original inequality is the union of the solutions to both Case 1 and Case 2. The solution to the inequality $\frac{8}{x+5} \le 4$ is $x < -5$ or $x \ge -3$, or $\{x \mid x < -5 \cup x \ge -3\}$. The expression will be less than 4 when the denominator is negative or is very large, so the answer is reasonable.

Solve each inequality algebraically.

6a. $\frac{6}{x-2} \ge -4$

6b. $\frac{9}{x+3} < 6$

THINK AND DISCUSS

1. Explain why multiplying both sides of a rational equation by the LCD eliminates all of the denominators.
2. Explain why rational equations may have extraneous solutions.
3. Describe two methods for solving the inequality $\frac{12}{x} > 3$.

4. **GET ORGANIZED** Copy and complete the graphic organizer. In each box, write the appropriate information related to rational equations.

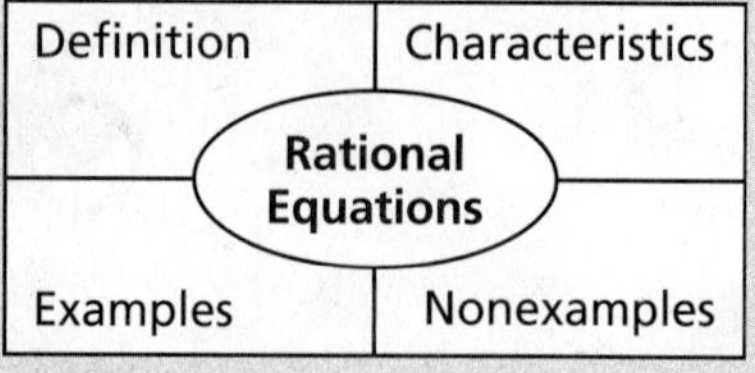

5-5 Exercises

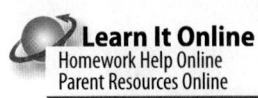

Learn It Online
Homework Help Online
Parent Resources Online

GUIDED PRACTICE

1. **Vocabulary** How does a *rational expression* differ from a *rational equation*?

SEE EXAMPLE 1

Solve each equation.

2. $\frac{1}{8} + \frac{2}{t} = \frac{17}{8t}$
3. $7 = \frac{1}{w} - 4$
4. $\frac{1}{r-5} = \frac{7}{2r}$
5. $\frac{1}{x} = \frac{x}{6} - \frac{5}{6}$
6. $m + \frac{12}{m} = 7$
7. $k + \frac{1}{k} = 2$

SEE EXAMPLE 2

8. $\frac{-2x}{x+2} + \frac{x}{3} = \frac{4}{x+2}$
9. $\frac{x}{x-3} + \frac{x}{2} = \frac{6x}{2x-6}$
10. $\frac{3}{x(x+1)} - 1 = \frac{3}{x^2+x}$

SEE EXAMPLE 3

11. **Transportation** A river barge travels at an average of 8 mi/h in still water. The barge travels 60 mi up the Mississippi River and 60 mi down the river in a total of 16.5 h. What is the average speed of the current in this section of the Mississippi River? Round to the nearest tenth. Is your answer reasonable?

SEE EXAMPLE 4

12. **Work** Each month Leo must make copies of a budget report. When he uses both the large and the small copier, the job takes 30 min. If the small copier is broken, the job takes him 50 min. How long will the job take if the large copier is broken?

SEE EXAMPLE 5

Solve by using a graph and a table.

13. $\frac{x-5}{x} > 2$
14. $\frac{3}{x+6} = 3$
15. $\frac{x+3}{2x} < 2$

SEE EXAMPLE 6

Solve each inequality algebraically.

16. $\frac{4}{x+1} < 4$
17. $\frac{12}{x-4} \leq 3$
18. $\frac{10}{x+8} > 2$

PRACTICE AND PROBLEM SOLVING

Independent Practice

For Exercises	See Example
19–24	1
25–27	2
28	3
29	4
30–32	5
33–35	6

Extra Practice

See Extra Practice for more Skills Practice and Applications Practice exercises.

Solve each equation.

19. $4 + \frac{1}{x} = \frac{10}{2x}$
20. $\frac{5}{4} = \frac{n-3}{n-4}$
21. $\frac{1}{a-7} = 3$
22. $\frac{1}{x} - \frac{3}{4} = \frac{x}{4}$
23. $\frac{14}{z} = 9 - z$
24. $x + \frac{4}{x} = 4$
25. $\frac{4x}{x-3} + \frac{x}{2} = \frac{12}{x-3}$
26. $\frac{3x}{x+1} = \frac{2x-1}{x+1}$
27. $\frac{2}{x(x-1)} = 1 + \frac{2}{x-1}$
28. **Multi-Step** A passenger jet travels from Los Angeles to Mumbai, India, in 22 h. The return flight takes 17 h. The difference in flight times is caused by winds over the Pacific Ocean that blow primarily from west to east. If the jet's average speed in still air is 550 mi/h, what is the average speed of the wind during the round-trip flight? Round to the nearest mile per hour. Is your answer reasonable?
29. **Art** A glassblower can produce a set of simple glasses in about 2 h. When the glassblower works with an apprentice, the job takes about 1.5 h. How long would it take the apprentice to make a set of glasses when working alone?

Solve by using a graph and a table.

30. $\frac{1}{x} > 1$
31. $\frac{x+1}{x+2} = 2$
32. $\frac{x}{x-5} \leq 0$

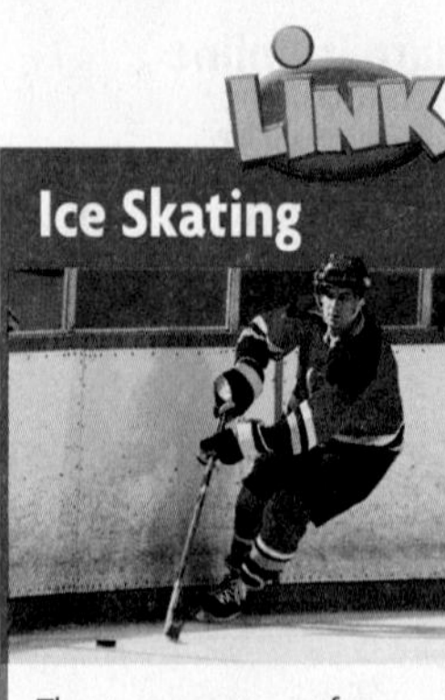

The temperature of the ice in many indoor skating rinks is kept between 24°F and 28°F. Ice that is colder than these temperatures may chip too easily, and ice that is warmer may result in too much friction as skate blades pass over it.

Solve each inequality algebraically.

33. $\frac{1}{3x} < 2$ **34.** $\frac{9}{x-4} \geq -6$ **35.** $\frac{9}{x+10} > 3$

36. Ice Skating A new skating rink will be approximately rectangular in shape and will have an area of no more than 17,000 square feet.

a. Write an inequality expressing the possible perimeter P of the skating rink in feet in terms of its width w.

b. Is 400 feet a reasonable value for the perimeter? Explain.

37. Baseball The baseball card shows statistics for a professional player during four seasons.

a. A player's batting average is equal to his number of hits divided by his number of at bats. For which year listed on the card did Derek Jeter have the greatest batting average?

b. Write and solve an equation to find how many additional consecutive hits h Jeter would have needed to raise his batting average in 2004 to that of his average in 2001.

c. What if...? How many additional hits in a row would Jeter have needed to raise his batting average in 2003 to .500? Check your answer for reasonableness.

DEREK JETER
SHORTSTOP
YEAR HITS AT BATS
2001 191 614
2002 191 644
2003 156 482
2004 188 643

Solve each equation or inequality.

38. $\frac{15n}{n-3} = \frac{5}{n-3} - 8$ **39.** $\frac{z}{z+1} = \frac{z}{z-4}$ **40.** $\frac{4}{x} + 6 = \frac{1}{x^2}$

41. $\frac{8}{x} - \frac{3}{x} = \frac{6}{x-1}$ **42.** $\frac{2(x+4)}{x-4} = \frac{3x}{x-4}$ **43.** $\frac{1}{a-1} + \frac{4}{a+1} = \frac{7}{a^2-1}$

44. $\frac{6}{r} \geq \frac{5}{2}$ **45.** $\frac{8}{x+1} > 4$ **46.** $x \geq \frac{4}{x}$

Use a graphing calculator to solve each rational equation. Round your answers to the nearest hundredth.

47. $\frac{1}{x^2} = 5$ **48.** $\frac{1}{x^2} = x^2 - 1$ **49.** $\frac{1}{x-1} = x - 1$

50. Critical Thinking The reciprocal of a number plus $\frac{7}{2}$ equals 2. Find the number.

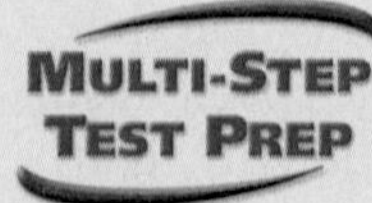

51. The average speed for the winner of the 2002 Indy 500 was 25 mi/h greater than the average speed for the 2001 winner. In addition, the 2002 winner completed the 500 mi race 32 min faster than the 2001 winner.

a. Let s represent the average speed of the 2001 winner in miles per hour. Write expressions in terms of s for the time in hours that it took the 2001 and 2002 winners to complete the race.

b. Write a rational equation that can be used to determine s. Solve your equation to find the average speed of the 2001 winner to the nearest mile per hour.

(r), Ezra Shaw/Getty Images; (b), Stockdisc/gettyimages; (tl), © William Sallaz/Duomo/CORBIS

52. **Critical Thinking** An equation has the form $\frac{a}{x} + \frac{x}{b} = c$, where a, b, and c are constants and $b \neq 0$. How many values of x could make this equation true?

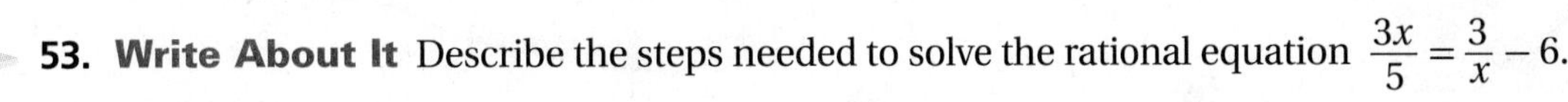

53. **Write About It** Describe the steps needed to solve the rational equation $\frac{3x}{5} = \frac{3}{x} - 6$.

TEST PREP

54. What value of x makes the equation $\frac{1}{x} + \frac{3}{x+3} = \frac{6}{x}$ true?

Ⓐ $-\frac{15}{2}$ Ⓑ $-\frac{12}{5}$ Ⓒ $-\frac{3}{2}$ Ⓓ $-\frac{6}{7}$

55. How many solutions does the equation $\frac{x+2}{x-4} - \frac{1}{x} = \frac{4}{x^2 - 4x}$ have?

Ⓕ 0 Ⓖ 1 Ⓗ 2 Ⓙ 3

56. If $x \neq -2$, which is equivalent to $\frac{4x}{x-2} = 6 + \frac{10}{x-2}$?

Ⓐ $\frac{4x}{x-2} = \frac{16}{x-2}$

Ⓒ $4x = 6 + 10$

Ⓑ $4x = 6(x-2) + 10$

Ⓓ $\frac{4}{-2} = 6 + \frac{5}{x-1}$

57. **Short Response** Water flowing through both a small pipe and a large pipe can fill a water tank in 7 h. Water flowing through the small pipe alone can fill the tank in 15 h.

a. Write an equation that can be used to find the number of hours it would take to fill the tank using only the large pipe.

b. How many hours would it take to fill the tank using only the large pipe? Show your work, or explain how you determined your answer.

CHALLENGE AND EXTEND

Solve each equation or inequality.

58. $\frac{4x}{x^2 + x - 6} = \frac{7x}{x^2 - 5x - 24}$

59. $\frac{1 - 4x^{-1} + 3x^{-2}}{1 - 9x^{-2}} = \frac{x-1}{x+3}$

60. $\frac{3x}{x+2} - \frac{2}{x+4} \geq 7$

61. $\frac{6}{x-3} > \frac{x}{4} + 5$

62. Marcus and Will are painting a barn. Marcus paints about twice as fast as Will. On the first day, they have worked for 6 h and completed about $\frac{1}{3}$ of the job when Will gets injured. If Marcus has to complete the rest of the job by himself, about how many additional hours will it take him?

CHAPTER 5

SECTION 5A

MULTI-STEP TEST PREP

Model with mathematics.

Rational Functions

Math in the Fast Lane The Indianapolis 500 is one of the most exciting events in sports. Each spring, 33 drivers compete in the 500 mi race, sometimes hitting speeds of more than 220 mi/h.

Year	Winner	Winning Time
1911	Roy Harroun	6 h 42 min
1990	Arie Luyendyk	2 h 41 min 18 s
2004	Buddy Rice	3 h 15 s

Winners of the Indianapolis 500

1. Write a rational function that can be used to model the race, where the independent variable represents the average speed in miles per hour and the dependent variable represents the time in hours it takes to complete the race. What type of variation function is it?

2. To the nearest mile per hour, how much faster was the average winning speed in 2004 than in 1911?

3. In 1990, Arie Luyendyk set the record for the fastest Indy 500 average speed, about 186 mi/h. The time in hours to finish the race based on Arie Luyendyk's record can be modeled by the function $t = \frac{500}{186 + s}$, where s is the speed above 186 in miles per hour. Graph the function, and evaluate it for $s = 10$. What does this value of the function represent?

4. During the race, a driver completes one lap with an average speed of 200 mi/h and then completes the following lap at an average speed of 210 mi/h. What is the driver's average speed for the two laps, to the nearest tenth of a mile per hour?

5. Each lap in the Indy 500 is 2.5 mi. A driver completes two laps in 1.5 min. The average speed during the second lap is 8 mi/h faster than the average speed during the first lap. Find the driver's average speed for each of the two laps, to the nearest mile per hour.

READY TO GO ON?

CHAPTER 5

SECTION 5A

Quiz for Lessons 5-1 Through 5-5

5-1 Variation Functions

1. The mass m in kilograms of a bronze statue varies directly as its volume V in cubic centimeters. If a statue made from 1000 cm^3 of bronze has a mass of 8.7 kg, what is the mass of a statue made from 4500 cm^3 of bronze?
2. The time t in hours needed to clean the rides at an amusement park varies inversely with the number of workers n. If 6 workers can clean the rides in 6 hours, how many hours will it take 10 workers to clean the rides?

5-2 Multiplying and Dividing Rational Expressions

Simplify. Identify any x-values for which the expression is undefined.

3. $\dfrac{5x^3}{10x^2 + 5x}$
4. $\dfrac{x^2 - 2x - 3}{x^2 + 5x + 4}$
5. $\dfrac{-x + 6}{x^2 - 3x - 18}$

Multiply or divide. Assume that all expressions are defined.

6. $\dfrac{x + 3}{x + 2} \cdot \dfrac{2x - 4}{x^2 - 9}$
7. $\dfrac{9x^6 y}{27x^2 y^5} \div \dfrac{x}{6y^2}$
8. $\dfrac{2x^3 - 18x}{x^2 - 2x - 8} \div \dfrac{x^2 + x - 12}{x^2 - 16}$

5-3 Adding and Subtracting Rational Expressions

Add or subtract. Identify any x-values for which the expression is undefined.

9. $\dfrac{3x + 2}{x - 2} - \dfrac{x + 5}{x - 2}$
10. $\dfrac{x^2 - x}{x^2 - 25} + \dfrac{3}{x + 5}$
11. $\dfrac{x}{x - 3} - \dfrac{1}{x + 3}$
12. A plane's average speed when flying from one city to another is 550 mi/h and is 430 mi/h on the return flight. To the nearest mile per hour, what is the plane's average speed for the entire trip?

5-4 Rational Functions

Using the graph of $f(x) = \frac{1}{x}$ as a guide, describe the transformations and graph each function.

13. $g(x) = \dfrac{1}{x - 4}$
14. $g(x) = \dfrac{1}{x + 1} + 2$

Identify the zeros and asymptotes of each function. Then graph.

15. $f(x) = \dfrac{x^2 - 16}{x - 3}$
16. $f(x) = \dfrac{2x}{x^2 - 4}$

5-5 Solving Rational Equations and Inequalities

Solve each equation.

17. $y - \dfrac{10}{y} = 3$
18. $\dfrac{x}{x - 8} = \dfrac{24 - 2x}{x - 8}$
19. $\dfrac{-3x}{3} - \dfrac{x + 15}{x + 9} = 1$
20. A restaurant has two pastry ovens. When both ovens are used, it takes about 3 hours to bake the bread needed for one day. When only the large oven is used, it takes about 4 hours to bake the bread for one day. Approximately how long would it take to bake the bread for one day if only the small oven were used?

5-6 Radical Expressions and Rational Exponents

CC.9-12.A.REI.12 Graph the solutions to a linear inequality in two variables as a half-plane … and graph the solution set to a system of linear inequalities in two variables as the intersection of the corresponding half-planes.

Objectives

Rewrite radical expressions by using rational exponents.

Simplify and evaluate radical expressions and expressions containing rational exponents.

Vocabulary

index

rational exponent

Who uses this?

Guitar makers use radical expressions to ensure that the strings produce the correct notes. (See Example 6.)

You are probably familiar with finding the square and square root of a number. These two operations are inverses of each other. Similarly, there are roots that correspond to larger powers.

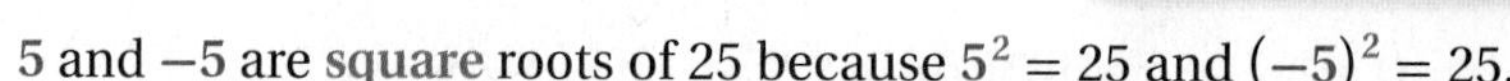

5 and -5 are **square** roots of 25 because $5^2 = 25$ and $(-5)^2 = 25$.

2 is the **cube** root of 8 because $2^3 = 8$.

2 and -2 are **fourth** roots of 16 because $2^4 = 16$ and $(-2)^4 = 16$.

a is the **nth** root of b if $a^n = b$.

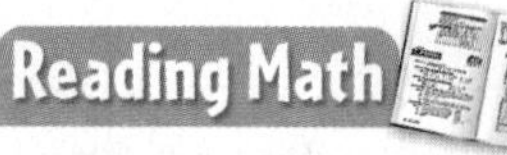

Reading Math

When a radical sign shows no index, it represents a square root.

The nth root of a real number a can be written as the radical expression $\sqrt[n]{a}$, where n is the **index** (plural: *indices*) of the radical and a is the radicand. When a number has more than one real root, the radical sign indicates only the principal, or positive, root.

Numbers and Types of Real Roots

Case	Roots	Example
Odd index	1 real root	The real 3rd root of 8 is 2.
Even index; positive radicand	2 real roots	The real 4th roots of 16 are ± 2.
Even index; negative radicand	0 real roots	-16 has no real 4th roots.
Radicand of 0	1 root of 0	The 3rd root of 0 is 0.

EXAMPLE 1 Finding Real Roots

Find all real roots.

A **fourth roots of 81**

A positive number has two real fourth roots. Because $3^4 = 81$ and $(-3)^4 = 81$, the roots are 3 and -3.

B **cube roots of -125**

A negative number has one real cube root. Because $(-5)^3 = -125$, the root is -5.

C **sixth roots of -729**

A negative number has no real sixth roots.

Find all real roots.

1a. fourth roots of -256 **1b.** sixth roots of 1 **1c.** cube roots of 125

Paul Sancya/AP/Wide World Photos

The properties of square roots also apply to nth roots.

Properties of nth Roots

For $a > 0$ and $b > 0$,

WORDS	NUMBERS	ALGEBRA
Product Property of Roots The nth root of a product is equal to the product of the nth roots.	$\sqrt[3]{16} = \sqrt[3]{8} \cdot \sqrt[3]{2} = 2\sqrt[3]{2}$	$\sqrt[n]{ab} = \sqrt[n]{a} \cdot \sqrt[n]{b}$
Quotient Property of Roots The nth root of a quotient is equal to the quotient of the nth roots.	$\sqrt{\frac{25}{16}} = \frac{\sqrt{25}}{\sqrt{16}} = \frac{5}{4}$	$\sqrt[n]{\frac{a}{b}} = \frac{\sqrt[n]{a}}{\sqrt[n]{b}}$

EXAMPLE 2 Simplifying Radical Expressions

Simplify each expression. Assume that all variables are positive.

A $\sqrt[3]{27x^6}$

$\sqrt[3]{3^3 \cdot x^3 \cdot x^3}$ *Factor into perfect cubes.*

$\sqrt[3]{3^3} \cdot \sqrt[3]{x^3} \cdot \sqrt[3]{x^3}$ *Product Property*

$3 \cdot x \cdot x$ *Simplify.*

$3x^2$

B $\sqrt[3]{\frac{x^3}{7}}$

$\frac{\sqrt[3]{x^3}}{\sqrt[3]{7}}$ *Quotient Property*

$\frac{x}{\sqrt[3]{7}}$ *Simplify the numerator.*

$\frac{x}{\sqrt[3]{7}} \cdot \frac{\sqrt[3]{7}}{\sqrt[3]{7}} \cdot \frac{\sqrt[3]{7}}{\sqrt[3]{7}}$ *Rationalize the denominator.*

$\frac{x\sqrt[3]{7^2}}{\sqrt[3]{7^3}}$ *Product Property*

$\frac{x\sqrt[3]{49}}{7}$ *Simplify.*

Remember!

When an expression contains a radical in the denominator, you must rationalize the denominator. To do so, rewrite the expression so that the denominator contains no radicals.

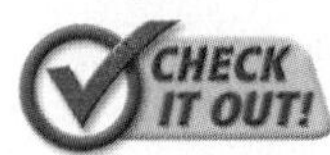

Simplify each expression. Assume that all variables are positive.

2a. $\sqrt[4]{16x^4}$ **2b.** $\sqrt[4]{\frac{x^8}{3}}$ **2c.** $\sqrt[3]{x^7} \cdot \sqrt[3]{x^2}$

A **rational exponent** is an exponent that can be expressed as $\frac{m}{n}$, where m and n are integers and $n \neq 0$. Radical expressions can be written by using rational exponents.

Rational Exponents

For any natural number n and integer m,

WORDS	NUMBERS	ALGEBRA
The exponent $\frac{1}{n}$ indicates the nth root.	$16^{\frac{1}{4}} = \sqrt[4]{16} = 2$	$a^{\frac{1}{n}} = \sqrt[n]{a}$
The exponent $\frac{m}{n}$ indicates the nth root raised to the mth power.	$8^{\frac{2}{3}} = (\sqrt[3]{8})^2 = 2^2 = 4$	$a^{\frac{m}{n}} = (\sqrt[n]{a})^m = \sqrt[n]{a^m}$

EXAMPLE 3 **Writing Expressions in Radical Form**

Write the expression $(-125)^{\frac{2}{3}}$ in radical form, and simplify.

Writing Math

The denominator of a rational exponent becomes the index of the radical.

Method 1 Evaluate the root first.

$(\sqrt[3]{-125})^2$	*Write with a radical.*
$(-5)^2$	*Evaluate the root.*
25	*Evaluate the power.*

Method 2 Evaluate the power first.

$\sqrt[3]{(-125)^2}$	*Write with a radical.*
$\sqrt[3]{15{,}625}$	*Evaluate the power.*
25	*Evaluate the root.*

Write each expression in radical form, and simplify.

3a. $64^{\frac{1}{3}}$ **3b.** $4^{\frac{5}{2}}$ **3c.** $625^{\frac{3}{4}}$

EXAMPLE 4 **Writing Expressions by Using Rational Exponents**

Write each expression by using rational exponents.

A $\sqrt[4]{7^3}$

$7^{\frac{3}{4}}$ $\quad \sqrt[n]{a^m} = a^{\frac{m}{n}}$

B $\sqrt[3]{11^6}$

$11^{\frac{6}{3}}$ $\quad \sqrt[n]{a^m} = a^{\frac{m}{n}}$

$11^2 = 121$ *Simplify.*

Write each expression by using rational exponents.

4a. $(\sqrt[4]{81})^3$ **4b.** $\sqrt[3]{10^9}$ **4c.** $\sqrt[4]{5^2}$

Rational exponents have the same properties as integer exponents.

Properties of Rational Exponents

For all nonzero real numbers *a* and *b* and rational numbers *m* and *n*,

WORDS	NUMBERS	ALGEBRA
Product of Powers Property To multiply powers with the same base, add the exponents.	$12^{\frac{1}{2}} \cdot 12^{\frac{3}{2}} = 12^{\frac{1}{2}+\frac{3}{2}} = 12^2 = 144$	$a^m \cdot a^n = a^{m+n}$
Quotient of Powers Property To divide powers with the same base, subtract the exponents.	$\frac{125^{\frac{2}{3}}}{125^{\frac{1}{3}}} = 125^{\frac{2}{3}-\frac{1}{3}} = 125^{\frac{1}{3}} = 5$	$\frac{a^m}{a^n} = a^{m-n}$
Power of a Power Property To raise one power to another, multiply the exponents.	$\left(8^{\frac{2}{3}}\right)^3 = 8^{\frac{2}{3}\cdot 3} = 8^2 = 64$	$(a^m)^n = a^{m \cdot n}$
Power of a Product Property To find the power of a product, distribute the exponent.	$(16 \cdot 25)^{\frac{1}{2}} = 16^{\frac{1}{2}} \cdot 25^{\frac{1}{2}} = 4 \cdot 5 = 20$	$(ab)^m = a^m b^m$
Power of a Quotient Property To find the power of a quotient, distribute the exponent.	$\left(\frac{16}{81}\right)^{\frac{1}{4}} = \frac{16^{\frac{1}{4}}}{81^{\frac{1}{4}}} = \frac{2}{3}$	$\left(\frac{a}{b}\right)^m = \frac{a^m}{b^m}$

EXAMPLE 5 Simplifying Expressions with Rational Exponents

Simplify each expression.

A $25^{\frac{3}{5}} \cdot 25^{\frac{2}{5}}$

$25^{\frac{3}{5}+\frac{2}{5}}$	*Product of Powers*
25^1	*Simplify.*
25	*Evaluate the power.*

Check Enter the expression in a graphing calculator.

```
25^(3/5)*25^(2/5
)
                25
```

B $\dfrac{8^{\frac{1}{3}}}{8^{\frac{2}{3}}}$

$8^{\frac{1}{3}-\frac{2}{3}}$	*Quotient of Powers*
$8^{-\frac{1}{3}}$	*Simplify.*
$\dfrac{1}{8^{\frac{1}{3}}}$	*Negative Exponent Property*
$\dfrac{1}{2}$	*Evaluate the power.*

Check Enter the expression in a graphing calculator.

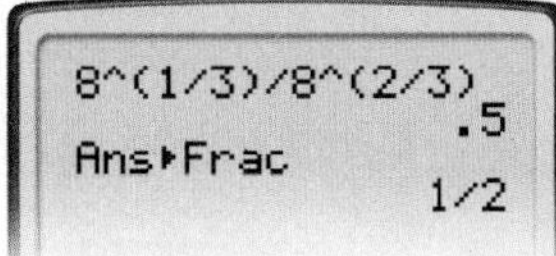

Simplify each expression.

5a. $36^{\frac{3}{8}} \cdot 36^{\frac{1}{8}}$ **5b.** $(-8)^{-\frac{1}{3}}$ **5c.** $\dfrac{5^{\frac{9}{4}}}{5^{\frac{1}{4}}}$

EXAMPLE 6 *Music Application*

Frets are small metal bars positioned across the neck of a guitar so that the guitar can produce the notes of a specific scale.

To find the distance a fret should be placed from the bridge, multiply the length of the string by $2^{-\frac{n}{12}}$, where n is the number of notes higher than the string's root note. Where should a fret be placed to produce a G note on the E string (3 notes higher)?

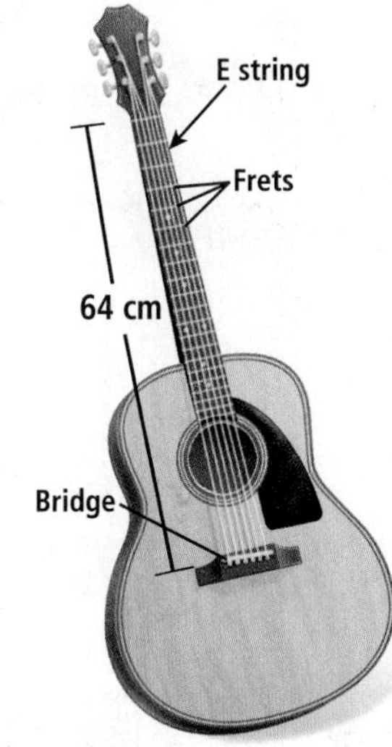

$64\left(2^{-\frac{n}{12}}\right) = 64\left(2^{-\frac{3}{12}}\right)$	*Use 64 cm for the length of the string, and substitute 3 for n.*
$= 64\left(2^{-\frac{1}{4}}\right)$	*Simplify.*
$= 64\left(\dfrac{1}{2^{\frac{1}{4}}}\right)$	*Negative Exponent Property*
$= \dfrac{64}{2^{\frac{1}{4}}}$	*Simplify.*
≈ 53.82	*Use a calculator.*

```
64/(2^(1/4))
      53.81737058
```

The fret should be placed about 53.82 cm from the bridge.

6. Where should a fret be placed to produce the E note that is one octave higher on the E string (12 notes higher)?

THINK AND DISCUSS

1. Explain why $\sqrt[n]{a^n}$ is equal to a for all natural numbers a and n.

2. **GET ORGANIZED** Copy and complete the graphic organizer. In each box, give a numeric and an algebraic example of the given property of rational exponents.

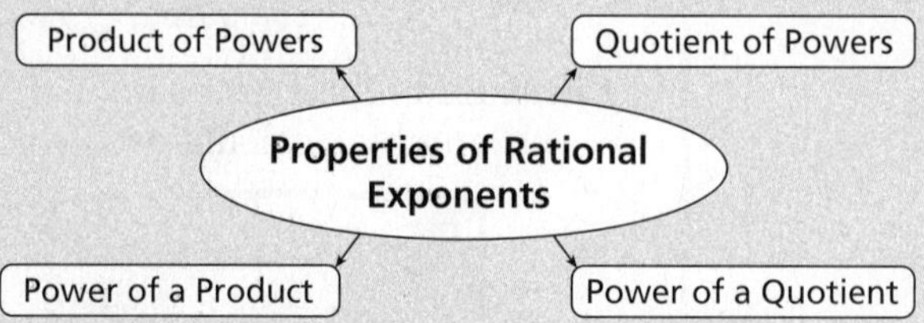

5-6 Exercises

GUIDED PRACTICE

1. **Vocabulary** The *index* of the expression $\sqrt[3]{4^2}$ is ___?___. (2, 3, or 4)

SEE EXAMPLE 1 **Find all real roots.**

2. cube roots of 27
3. fourth roots of 625
4. cube roots of 0

SEE EXAMPLE 2 **Simplify each expression. Assume that all variables are positive.**

5. $\sqrt[3]{8x^3}$
6. $\sqrt[4]{\dfrac{32}{x^4}}$
7. $\sqrt[3]{\dfrac{125x^6}{6}}$
8. $\sqrt{50x^3}$
9. $\sqrt[4]{x^8} \cdot \sqrt[3]{x^4}$
10. $\sqrt[3]{\dfrac{x^5}{4}}$
11. $\dfrac{\sqrt{40x^4}}{\sqrt[3]{-x^3}}$
12. $\sqrt[4]{\dfrac{x^{12}y^4}{3}}$

SEE EXAMPLE 3 **Write each expression in radical form, and simplify.**

13. $36^{\frac{3}{2}}$
14. $32^{\frac{3}{5}}$
15. $(-27)^{\frac{1}{3}}$
16. $8^{\frac{2}{3}}$

SEE EXAMPLE 4 **Write each expression by using rational exponents.**

17. $\sqrt[5]{9^{10}}$
18. $\sqrt{8^3}$
19. $(\sqrt[6]{5})^3$
20. $(\sqrt[3]{27})^2$

SEE EXAMPLE 5 **Simplify each expression.**

21. $13^{\frac{1}{2}} \cdot 13^{\frac{3}{2}}$
22. $\dfrac{9^{\frac{4}{3}}}{9^{\frac{2}{3}}}$
23. $\left(64^{\frac{1}{2}}\right)^{\frac{1}{3}}$
24. $\left(\dfrac{8}{27}\right)^{\frac{1}{3}}$
25. $25^{-\frac{1}{2}}$
26. $7^{\frac{1}{4}} \cdot 7^{-\frac{3}{4}}$
27. $(-125)^{-\frac{1}{3}}$
28. $\left(6^{\frac{1}{2}}\right)^6$

SEE EXAMPLE 6

29. **Geometry** The side length of a cube can be determined by finding the cube root of the volume. What is the side length to the nearest *inch* of the cube shown?

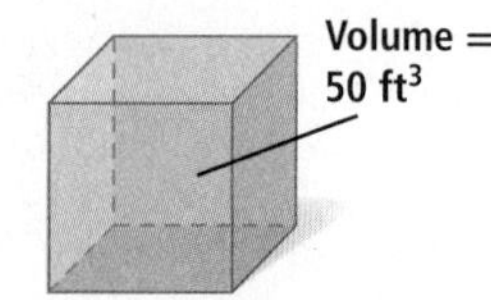

PRACTICE AND PROBLEM SOLVING

Independent Practice

For Exercises	See Example
30–32	1
33–40	2
41–44	3
45–48	4
49–56	5
57	6

Extra Practice

See Extra Practice for more Skills Practice and Applications Practice exercises.

Find all real roots.

30. cube roots of −64 **31.** fifth roots of 32 **32.** fourth roots of −16

Simplify each expression. Assume that all variables are positive.

33. $\sqrt[3]{9x} \cdot \sqrt[3]{3x^2}$ **34.** $\sqrt[4]{324x^8}$ **35.** $\sqrt[3]{\frac{x^6}{250}}$ **36.** $\sqrt{\frac{x^5}{45}}$

37. $\sqrt[3]{56x^9}$ **38.** $\frac{\sqrt[4]{x^{10}}}{\sqrt[4]{x^4}}$ **39.** $\sqrt[5]{x^7} \cdot \sqrt[5]{x^6}$ **40.** $\sqrt[3]{-54x^9y^3}$

Write each expression in radical form, and simplify.

41. $64^{\frac{1}{2}}$ **42.** $216^{\frac{2}{3}}$ **43.** $(-1000)^{\frac{4}{3}}$ **44.** $6^{\frac{3}{2}}$

Write each expression by using rational exponents.

45. $\sqrt[3]{14^3}$ **46.** $\left(\sqrt[5]{-8}\right)^4$ **47.** $\left(\sqrt[4]{144}\right)^2$ **48.** $\sqrt{48^3}$

Simplify each expression.

49. $(8 \cdot 64)^{\frac{2}{3}}$ **50.** $144^{-\frac{1}{2}}$ **51.** $\left(\frac{2^3}{27}\right)^{\frac{1}{3}}$ **52.** $2^{\frac{1}{2}} \cdot 2^{\frac{1}{4}}$

53. $\left(\frac{49}{81}\right)^{-\frac{1}{2}}$ **54.** $\frac{12^{\frac{1}{4}}}{12^{\frac{3}{4}}}$ **55.** $\left(5^{\frac{1}{3}}\right)^{\frac{1}{3}}$ **56.** $\left(\frac{27}{27^{\frac{1}{3}}}\right)^{\frac{1}{2}}$

57. Banking The initial amount deposited in a savings account is \$1000. The amount a in dollars in the account after t years can be represented by the function $a(t) = 1000\left(2^{\frac{t}{24}}\right)$. To the nearest dollar, what will the amount in the account be after 6 years?

LINK

Biology

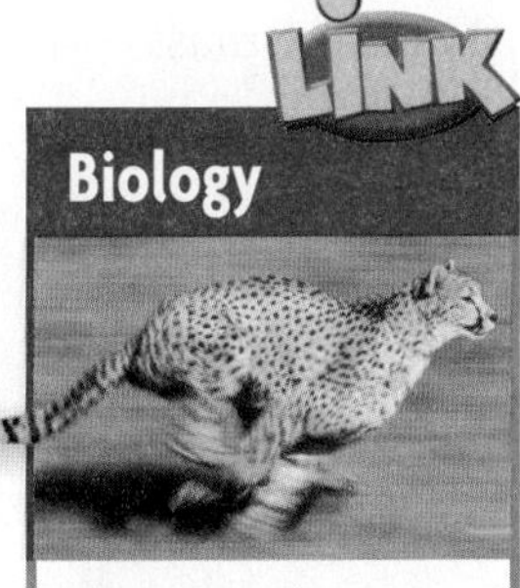

Suppose that a cheetah, a lion, a house cat, and the fastest human runner competed in a 100 m race. At top speed, the cheetah would finish in 3.20 s, the lion in 4.47 s, the house cat in 7.46 s, and the human in 9.77 s.

58. Biology The formula $P = 73.3\sqrt[4]{m^3}$, known as Kleiber's law, relates the metabolism rate P of an organism in Calories per day and the body mass m of the organism in kilograms. The table shows the typical body mass of several members of the cat family.

Typical Body Mass

Animal	Mass (kg)
House cat	4.5
Cheetah	55.0
Lion	170.0

a. What is the metabolism rate of a cheetah to the nearest Calorie per day?

b. **Multi-Step** Approximately how many more Calories of food does a lion need to consume each day than a house cat does?

59. Medicine Iodine-131 is a radioactive material used to treat certain types of cancer. Iodine-131 has a half-life of 8 days, which means that it takes 8 days for half of an initial sample to decay. The percent of radioactive material that remains after t days can be determined from the expression $100\left(\frac{1}{2}\right)^{\frac{t}{h}}$, where h is the half-life in days.

a. What percent of a sample of iodine-131 will remain after 20 days?

b. **What if...?** Another form of radioactive iodine used in cancer treatment is iodine-125. Iodine-125 has a half-life of 59 days. A hospital has 20 g of iodine-125 and 20 g of iodine-131 left over from treating patients. How much more iodine-125 than iodine-131 will remain after a period of 30 days?

60. Meteorology The formula $W = 35.74 + 0.6215T - 35.75V^{\frac{4}{25}} + 0.4275TV^{\frac{4}{25}}$ relates the wind chill temperature W to the air temperature T in degrees Fahrenheit and the wind speed V in miles per hour. Use a calculator to find the wind chill to the nearest degree when the air temperature is 40°F and the wind speed is 35 mi/h.

MULTI-STEP TEST PREP

61. This problem will prepare you for the Multi-Step Test Prep.

For a pendulum with a length L in meters, the expression $2\pi\sqrt{\frac{L}{g}}$ models the time in seconds for the pendulum to complete one back-and-forth swing. In this expression, g is the acceleration due to gravity, 9.8 m/s^2.

a. Simplify the expression by rationalizing the denominator.

b. To the nearest tenth of a second, how long does it take a pendulum with a length of 0.35 m to complete one back-and-forth swing?

Write each expression by using rational exponents. Assume that all variables are positive.

62. $\sqrt[4]{20x^3}$ **63.** $\sqrt{(5x)^7}$ **64.** $\left(\sqrt[5]{-9}\sqrt[3]{x}\right)^4$ **65.** $\left(\sqrt[4]{11x^8}\right)^6$

Simplify each expression, and write it by using a radical. Assume that all variables are positive.

66. $\left(-8x^{12}\right)^{\frac{2}{3}}$ **67.** $5^{\frac{7}{4}}x^{\frac{3}{4}}$ **68.** $\left(-12x^{15}\right)^{\frac{3}{5}}$

69. $\left(a^2b^4\right)^{\frac{1}{3}}$ **70.** $\left(\frac{a^4}{b}\right)^{\frac{1}{4}}$ **71.** $a^{\frac{3}{4}}\left(4b^6\right)^{\frac{1}{4}}$

72. Botany Duckweed is a quickly growing plant that floats on the surface of lakes and ponds. The initial mass of a population of duckweed plants is 100 kg. The mass of the population doubles every 60 h and can be represented by the function $m(t) = 100 \cdot 2^{\frac{t}{60}}$, where t is time in hours. To the nearest kilogram, what is the mass of the plants after 24 h?

Explain whether each statement is sometimes, always, or never true for nonzero values of the variable.

73. $\sqrt[3]{x^6} = x^2$ **74.** $(x)^{\frac{1}{3}} = (-x)^{\frac{1}{3}}$ **75.** $-\sqrt[4]{x^8} = x^{-2}$ **76.** $-\sqrt[3]{x} < 0$

Estimation Identify the pair of consecutive integers that each value is between. Then use a calculator to check your answer.

77. $\sqrt[3]{18}$ **78.** $\sqrt[4]{200}$ **79.** $\sqrt[3]{-80}$

80. Physics Air pressure decreases with altitude according to the formula $P = 14.7(10)^{-0.000014a}$, where P is the air pressure in pounds per square inch and a is the altitude in feet above sea level.

a. Use the formula to estimate the air pressure in Denver, Colorado, which is 5280 ft above sea level.

b. Use the formula to estimate the air pressure at the top of Mount Everest, which is 29,028 ft above sea level.

81. ERROR ANALYSIS Below are two methods of simplifying an expression. Which is incorrect? Explain the error.

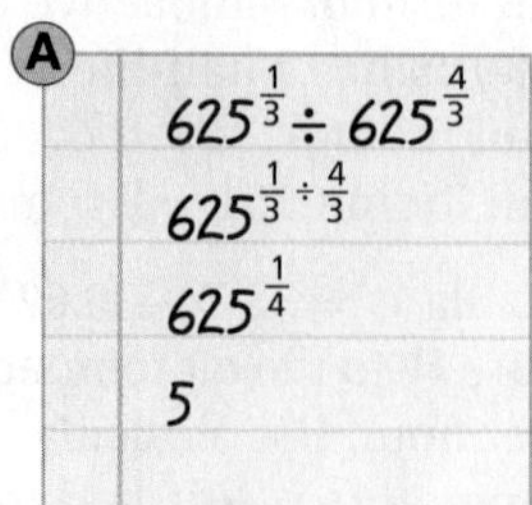

A
$625^{\frac{1}{3}} \div 625^{\frac{4}{3}}$
$625^{\frac{1}{3} \div \frac{4}{3}}$
$625^{\frac{1}{4}}$
5

B

$625^{\frac{1}{3}} \div 625^{\frac{4}{3}}$

$625^{\frac{1}{3} - \frac{4}{3}}$

625^{-1}

$\frac{1}{625}$

(cl), David Davis Photoproductions/Alamy; (tl), Comstock Images/Alamy

82. How many different positive integer values of n result in a whole number nth root of 64? What are these values?

83. Critical Thinking Describe two ways to find the sixth root of 10 on a calculator.

84. Write About It Explain whether the expression $x^{2.4}$ contains a rational exponent.

TEST PREP

85. Which of the following represents a real number?

Ⓐ $6^{-\frac{4}{3}}$ Ⓑ $(-9)^{\frac{3}{2}}$ Ⓒ $\sqrt[4]{-11}$ Ⓓ $\left(\sqrt[4]{-14}\right)^3$

86. The surface area S of a sphere with volume V is $S = (4\pi)^{\frac{1}{3}}(3V)^{\frac{2}{3}}$. What effect does increasing the volume of a sphere by a factor of 8 have on its surface area?

Ⓕ The surface area doubles.

Ⓖ The surface area triples.

Ⓗ The surface area increases by a factor of 4.

Ⓙ The surface area increases by a factor of 8.

87. If $a = x^6$, what is $\sqrt[4]{a}$?

Ⓐ $\left(\sqrt{x}\right)^3$ Ⓑ x^2 Ⓒ $x^2\sqrt{x}$ Ⓓ $x^{\frac{2}{3}}$

88. Which expression is equivalent to $\sqrt[3]{\frac{56a^6}{7}}$?

Ⓕ $2a^2$ Ⓖ $8a^2$ Ⓗ $2a^3$ Ⓙ $8a^3$

CHALLENGE AND EXTEND

89. Write an expression by using rational exponents for the square root of the square root of the square root of 20.

90. Simplify the expression $2^{\frac{1}{3}} \cdot 4^{\frac{1}{6}} \cdot 8^{\frac{1}{9}}$.

91. Critical Thinking For what real values of a is $\sqrt[3]{a}$ greater than a?

92. Any nonzero real number has three cube roots, only one of which is real. Show that the cube roots of 1 are 1, $\frac{-1 + i\sqrt{3}}{2}$, and $\frac{-1 - i\sqrt{3}}{2}$.

Area and Volume Relationships

When you change the linear dimensions of a solid figure, its surface area and volume may change in different ways.

Recall that when you multiply the side length of a cube by a constant a, the surface area increases by a factor of a^2 and the volume increases by a factor of a^3, as shown.

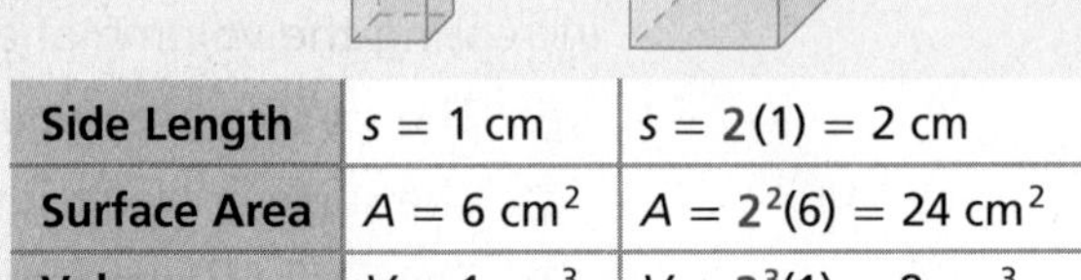

Side Length	$s = 1$ cm	$s = 2(1) = 2$ cm
Surface Area	$A = 6$ cm^2	$A = 2^2(6) = 24$ cm^2
Volume	$V = 1$ cm^3	$V = 2^3(1) = 8$ cm^3

When you want to change the surface area or volume of a figure but maintain the same linear proportions, you can use the reverse process. If the surface area increases by a factor of a, the linear dimensions increase by a factor of $\sqrt{a}$. If the volume increases by a factor of a, the linear dimensions increase by a factor of $\sqrt[3]{a}$.

Example

A cylindrical water storage tank has a radius of 5 ft and a height of 10 ft. A new tank similar to the first is constructed with 20% more capacity. What are the radius and height of the new tank?

The capacity of the larger tank is 120% of the smaller tank. So, the volume is increased by a factor of 1.2.

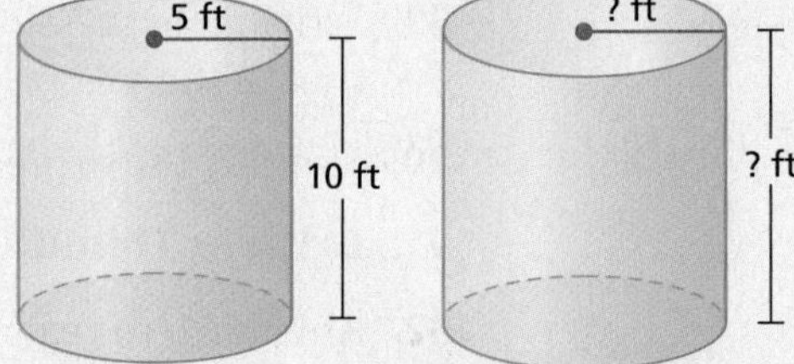

Step 1 Find the scale factor for the linear dimensions.

$\sqrt[3]{1.2} \approx 1.0627$ *Take the cube root.*

Step 2 Find the new dimensions.

$1.0627(5) \approx 5.31$

$1.0627(10) \approx 10.63$

Multiply the original dimensions by the scale factor.

The radius is about 5.31 ft, and the height is about 10.63 ft.

Try This

Solve each problem. If necessary, round your answers to the nearest thousandth.

1. Marsha wants to double the surface area of a circular pond. How should she change the radius? the diameter?
2. The volume of a sphere is increased by a factor of 100. The new radius is 30 cm. What was the radius of the original sphere?
3. The surface area of a cube is decreased from 150 cm^2 to 96 cm^2. By what factor has the volume changed?
4. A store owner wants to create giant ice-cream cones that contain 3 times the volume of a traditional cone. How should he change the radius and height of the traditional cone?

5-7 Radical Functions

CC.9-12.F.IF.7b Graph square root, cube root, and piecewise-defined functions, including step functions and absolute value functions.* *Also* **CC.9-12.F.BF.3, CC.9-12.F.IF.5, CC.9-12.A.CED.2, CC.9-12.A.CED.3**

Objectives
Graph radical functions and inequalities.

Transform radical functions by changing parameters.

Vocabulary
radical function
square-root function

Who uses this?

Aerospace engineers use transformations of radical functions to adjust for gravitational changes on other planets. (See Example 5.)

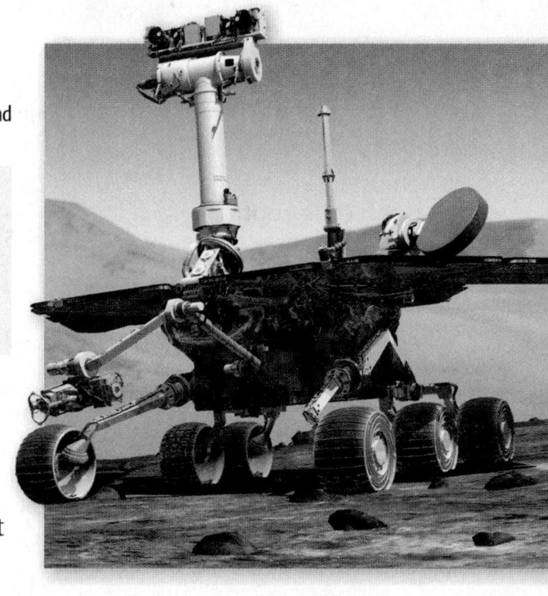

Recall that exponential and logarithmic functions are inverse functions. Quadratic and cubic functions have inverses as well. The graphs below show the inverses of the quadratic parent function and the cubic parent function.

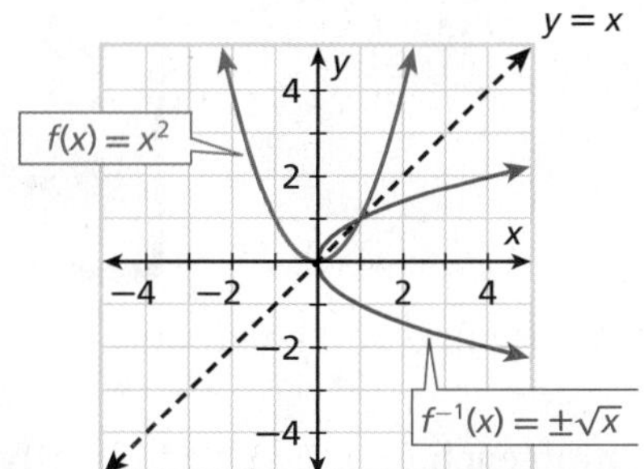

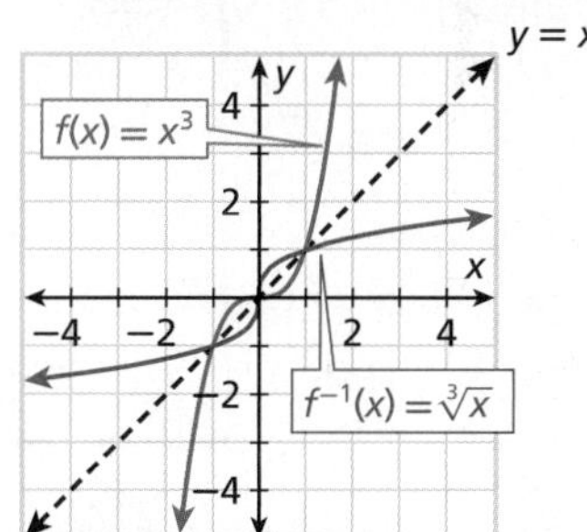

Notice that the inverse of $f(x) = x^2$ is not a function because it fails the vertical line test. However, if we limit the domain of $f(x) = x^2$ to $x \geq 0$, its inverse is the function $f^{-1}(x) = \sqrt{x}$.

A **radical function** is a function whose rule is a radical expression. A **square-root function** is a radical function involving $\sqrt{x}$. The square-root parent function is $f(x) = \sqrt{x}$. The cube-root parent function is $f(x) = \sqrt[3]{x}$.

EXAMPLE 1 Graphing Radical Functions

Graph the function, and identify its domain and range.

A $f(x) = \sqrt{x}$

Make a table of values. Plot enough ordered pairs to see the shape of the curve. Because the square root of a negative number is imaginary, choose only nonnegative values for x.

x	$f(x) = \sqrt{x}$	$(x, f(x))$
0	$f(0) = \sqrt{0} = 0$	(0, 0)
1	$f(1) = \sqrt{1} = 1$	(1, 1)
4	$f(4) = \sqrt{4} = 2$	(4, 2)
9	$f(9) = \sqrt{9} = 3$	(9, 3)

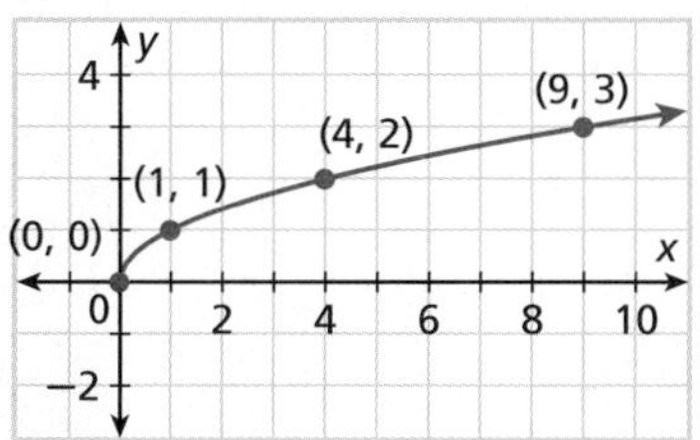

The domain is $\{x \mid x \geq 0\}$, and the range is $\{y \mid y \geq 0\}$.

Helpful Hint

When using a table to graph square-root functions, choose x-values that make the radicands perfect squares.

NASA

Graph the function, and identify its domain and range.

B $f(x) = 4\sqrt[3]{x+4}$

Make a table of values. Plot enough ordered pairs to see the shape of the curve. Choose both negative and positive values for x.

> **Helpful Hint**
>
> When using a table to graph cube-root functions, choose x-values that make the radicands perfect cubes.

x	$4\sqrt[3]{x+4}$	$(x, f(x))$
-12	$4\sqrt[3]{-12+4} = 4\sqrt[3]{-8} = -8$	$(-12, -8)$
-5	$4\sqrt[3]{-5+4} = 4\sqrt[3]{-1} = -4$	$(-5, -4)$
-4	$4\sqrt[3]{-4+4} = 4\sqrt[3]{0} = 0$	$(-4, 0)$
-3	$4\sqrt[3]{-3+4} = 4\sqrt[3]{1} = 4$	$(-3, 4)$
4	$4\sqrt[3]{4+4} = 4\sqrt[3]{8} = 8$	$(4, 8)$

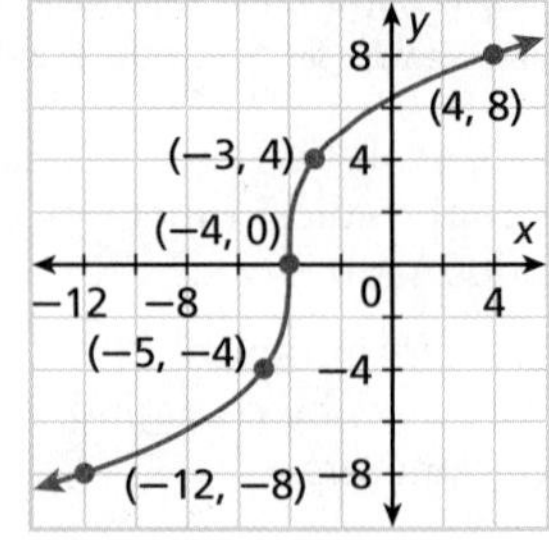

The domain is the set of all real numbers. The range is also the set of all real numbers.

Check Graph the function on a graphing calculator.

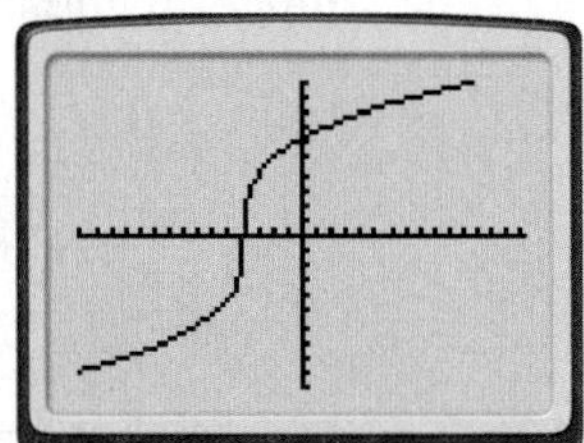

The graphs appear to be identical.

Graph each function, and identify its domain and range.

1a. $f(x) = \sqrt[3]{x}$ **1b.** $f(x) = \sqrt{x+1}$

The graphs of radical functions can be transformed by using methods similar to those used to transform linear, quadratic, polynomial, and exponential functions. This lesson will focus on transformations of square-root functions.

Transformations of the Square-Root Parent Function $f(x) = \sqrt{x}$

Transformation	$f(x)$ Notation	Examples
Vertical translation	$f(x) + k$	$y = \sqrt{x} + 3$ 3 units up $y = \sqrt{x} - 4$ 4 units down
Horizontal translation	$f(x - h)$	$y = \sqrt{x-2}$ 2 units right $y = \sqrt{x+1}$ 1 unit left
Vertical stretch/compression	$af(x)$	$y = 6\sqrt{x}$ vertical stretch by 6 $y = \frac{1}{2}\sqrt{x}$ vertical compression by $\frac{1}{2}$
Horizontal stretch/ compression	$f\left(\frac{1}{b}x\right)$	$y = \sqrt{\frac{1}{5}x}$ horizontal stretch by 5 $y = \sqrt{3x}$ horizontal compression by $\frac{1}{3}$
Reflection	$-f(x)$ $f(-x)$	$y = -\sqrt{x}$ across x-axis $y = \sqrt{-x}$ across y-axis

EXAMPLE 2 Transforming Square-Root Functions

Using the graph of $f(x) = \sqrt{x}$ as a guide, describe the transformation and graph each function.

A $g(x) = \sqrt{x} - 2$

$g(x) = f(x) - 2$

Translate f 2 units down.

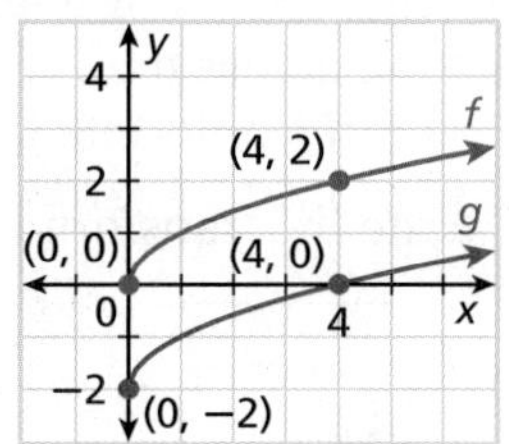

B $g(x) = 3\sqrt{x}$

$g(x) = 3 \cdot f(x)$

Stretch f vertically by a factor of 3.

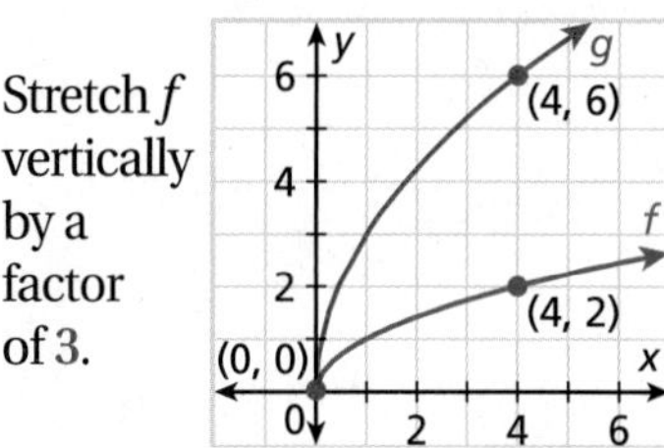

Using the graph of $f(x) = \sqrt{x}$ as a guide, describe the transformation and graph each function.

2a. $g(x) = \sqrt{x} + 1$

2b. $g(x) = \frac{1}{2}\sqrt{x}$

Transformations of square-root functions are summarized below.

$$f(x) = a\sqrt{\frac{1}{b}(x - h)} + k$$

$|a| \rightarrow$ vertical stretch or compression factor
$a < 0 \rightarrow$ reflection across the x-axis

$h \rightarrow$ horizontal translation

$|b| \rightarrow$ horizontal stretch or compression factor
$b < 0 \rightarrow$ reflection across the y-axis

$k \rightarrow$ vertical translation

EXAMPLE 3 Applying Multiple Transformations

Using the graph of $f(x) = \sqrt{x}$ as a guide, describe the transformation and graph each function.

A $g(x) = 2\sqrt{x + 3}$

Stretch f vertically by a factor of 2, and translate it 3 units left.

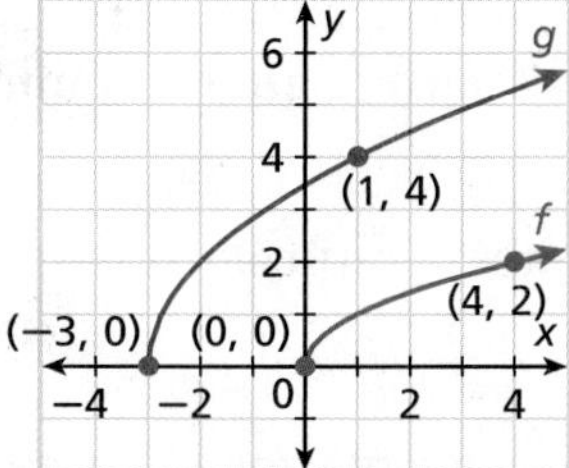

B $g(x) = \sqrt{-x} - 2$

Reflect f across the y-axis, and translate it 2 units down.

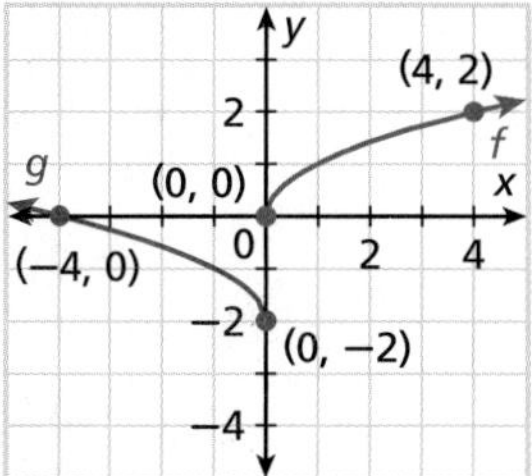

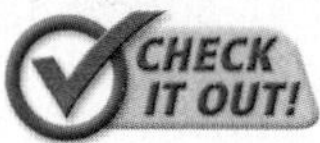

Using the graph of $f(x) = \sqrt{x}$ as a guide, describe the transformation and graph each function.

3a. $g(x) = \sqrt{-x} + 3$

3b. $g(x) = -3\sqrt{x} - 1$

EXAMPLE 4 Writing Transformed Square-Root Functions

Use the description to write the square-root function *g*.

The parent function $f(x) = \sqrt{x}$ is stretched horizontally by a factor of 2, reflected across the *y*-axis, and translated 3 units left.

Step 1 Identify how each transformation affects the function.

Horizontal stretch by a factor of 2: $|b| = 2$
Reflection across the *y*-axis: *b* is negative
} $b = -2$
Translation 3 units left: $h = -3$

Step 2 Write the transformed function.

$$g(x) = \sqrt{\frac{1}{b}(x - h)}$$

$$g(x) = \sqrt{\frac{1}{-2}\left[x-(-3)\right]} \qquad \textit{Substitute } -2 \textit{ for } b \textit{ and } -3 \textit{ for } h.$$

$$g(x) = \sqrt{-\frac{1}{2}(x + 3)} \qquad \textit{Simplify.}$$

Check Graph both functions on a graphing calculator. The graph of *g* indicates the given transformations of *f*.

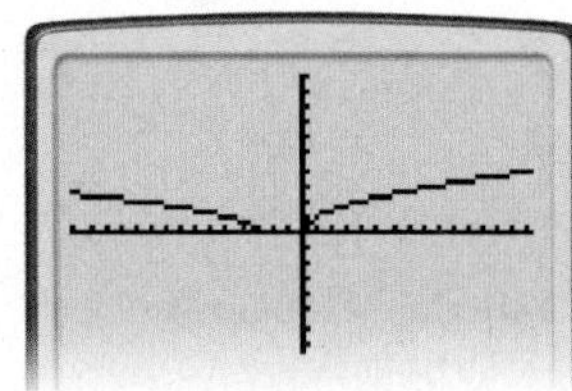

Use the description to write the square-root function *g*.

4. The parent function $f(x) = \sqrt{x}$ is reflected across the *x*-axis, stretched vertically by a factor of 2, and translated 1 unit up.

EXAMPLE 5 *Space Exploration Application*

Special airbags are used to protect scientific equipment when a rover lands on the surface of Mars. On Earth, the function $f(x) = \sqrt{64x}$ approximates an object's downward velocity in feet per second as the object hits the ground after bouncing *x* ft in height.

The corresponding function for Mars is compressed vertically by a factor of about $\frac{3}{5}$. Write the corresponding function *g* for Mars, and use it to estimate how fast a rover will hit Mars's surface after a bounce of 45 ft in height.

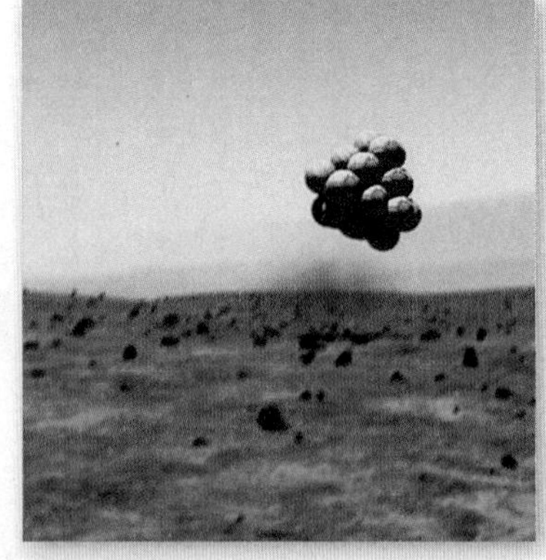

Step 1 To compress *f* vertically by a factor of $\frac{3}{5}$, multiply *f* by $\frac{3}{5}$.

$$g(x) = \frac{3}{5}f(x) = \frac{3}{5}\sqrt{64x}$$

Step 2 Find the value of *g* for a bounce height of 45 ft.

$$g(45) = \frac{3}{5}\sqrt{64(45)} \approx 32 \qquad \textit{Substitute 45 for x and simplify.}$$

The rover will hit Mars's surface with a downward velocity of about 32 ft/s at the end of the bounce.

NASA

Use the information on the previous page to answer the following.

5. The downward velocity function for the Moon is a horizontal stretch of f by a factor of about $\frac{25}{4}$. Write the velocity function h for the Moon, and use it to estimate the downward velocity of a landing craft at the end of a bounce 50 ft in height.

In addition to graphing radical functions, you can also graph radical inequalities. Use the same procedure you used for graphing linear and quadratic inequalities.

EXAMPLE 6 Graphing Radical Inequalities

Graph the inequality $y < \sqrt{x} + 2$.

Step 1 Use the related equation $y = \sqrt{x} + 2$ to make a table of values.

x	0	1	4	9
y	2	3	4	5

Step 2 Use the table to graph the boundary curve. The inequality sign is <, so use a dashed curve and shade the area below it.

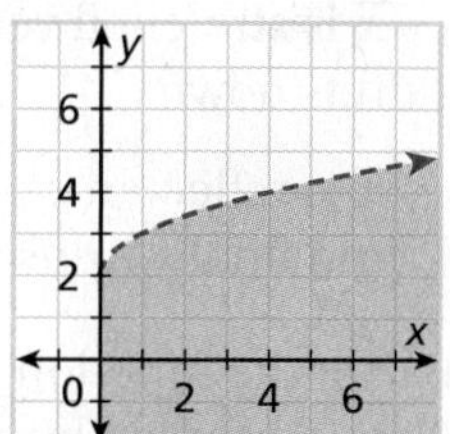

Because the value of x cannot be negative, do not shade left of the y-axis.

Check Choose a point in the solution region, such as $(1, 0)$, and test it in the inequality.

$$y < \sqrt{x} + 2$$
$$0 \overset{?}{<} \sqrt{1} + 2$$
$$0 < 3 \checkmark$$

Graph each inequality.

6a. $y > \sqrt{x + 4}$ **6b.** $y \geq \sqrt[3]{x - 3}$

THINK AND DISCUSS

1. Explain whether radical functions have asymptotes.

2. Explain how to determine the domain of the function $f(x) = \sqrt{2x + 2}$.

3. GET ORGANIZED Copy and complete the graphic organizer. In each box, give an example of the transformation of the square-root function $f(x) = \sqrt{x}$.

Transformation	Equation	Graph
Vertical translation		
Horizontal translation		
Reflection		
Vertical stretch		

5-7 Exercises

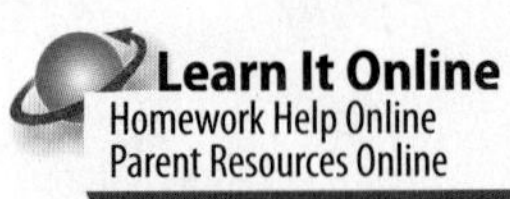

GUIDED PRACTICE

1. **Vocabulary** Explain why $f(x) = \sqrt{3x} + 4$ is a radical function.

SEE EXAMPLE 1

Graph each function, and identify its domain and range.

2. $f(x) = \sqrt{x+6}$
3. $f(x) = \sqrt{x} - 1$
4. $f(x) = 2\sqrt{x-3}$
5. $f(x) = 3\sqrt[3]{x}$
6. $f(x) = \sqrt[3]{x} + 2$
7. $f(x) = \sqrt[3]{x-2}$

SEE EXAMPLE 2

Using the graph of $f(x) = \sqrt{x}$ as a guide, describe the transformation and graph each function.

8. $g(x) = \sqrt{x} - 7$
9. $h(x) = 3\sqrt{x}$
10. $j(x) = \sqrt{x-5}$

SEE EXAMPLE 3

11. $g(x) = \frac{1}{2}\sqrt{x} - 1$
12. $h(x) = \sqrt{\frac{1}{3}(x+4)}$
13. $j(x) = \sqrt{-(x-3)}$
14. $g(x) = -2\sqrt{x} - 4$
15. $h(x) = \sqrt{-2(x+2)}$
16. $j(x) = 3\sqrt{x+3} + 3$

SEE EXAMPLE 4

Use the description to write the square-root function g.

17. The parent function $f(x) = \sqrt{x}$ is stretched vertically by a factor of 4 and then translated 5 units left and 2 units down.
18. The parent function $f(x) = \sqrt{x}$ is reflected across the y-axis, then compressed horizontally by a factor of $\frac{1}{2}$, and finally translated 7 units right.

SEE EXAMPLE 5

19. **Space Exploration** On Earth, the function $f(x) = \frac{6}{5}\sqrt{x}$ approximates the distance in miles to the horizon observed by a person whose eye level is x feet above the ground. The graph of the corresponding function for Mars is a horizontal stretch of f by a factor of about $\frac{9}{5}$. Write the corresponding function g for Mars, and use it to estimate the distance to the horizon for an astronaut whose eyes are 6 ft above Mars's surface.

SEE EXAMPLE 6

Graph each inequality.

20. $y \geq \sqrt{x}$
21. $y \leq \sqrt{x-4}$
22. $y < \sqrt{x} - 3$
23. $y > \sqrt[3]{x}$

PRACTICE AND PROBLEM SOLVING

Independent Practice

For Exercises	See Example
24–29	1
30–32	2
33–38	3
39–41	4
42	5
43–46	6

Extra Practice

See Extra Practice for more Skills Practice and Applications Practice exercises.

Graph each function, and identify its domain and range.

24. $f(x) = \sqrt{x-2}$
25. $f(x) = -3\sqrt{x}$
26. $f(x) = 2\sqrt{x+1} - 3$
27. $f(x) = \sqrt[3]{x+1}$
28. $f(x) = \sqrt[3]{x} - 4$
29. $f(x) = -2\sqrt[3]{x-3}$

Using the graph of $f(x) = \sqrt{x}$ as a guide, describe the transformation and graph each function.

30. $g(x) = \sqrt{x} + 2$
31. $h(x) = \sqrt{x-4}$
32. $j(x) = 0.5\sqrt{x}$
33. $g(x) = \sqrt{3(x+5)}$
34. $h(x) = \frac{1}{4}\sqrt{-x}$
35. $j(x) = \sqrt{x+4} - 1$
36. $g(x) = -4\sqrt{x} + 1$
37. $h(x) = 3\sqrt{-x} + 2$
38. $j(x) = \frac{1}{3}\sqrt{-(x+2)}$

Use the description to write the square-root function g.

39. The parent function $f(x) = \sqrt{x}$ is compressed vertically by a factor of $\frac{1}{3}$ and then translated 3 units left.
40. The parent function $f(x) = \sqrt{x}$ is reflected across the y-axis, stretched horizontally by a factor of 6, and then translated 2 units right.

41. The parent function $f(x) = \sqrt{x}$ is reflected across the x-axis and then translated 1 unit left and 4 units down.

42. **Manufacturing** A company manufactures cans for pet food. The function $f(x) = \sqrt{\frac{x}{40}}$ models the radius in centimeters of a can holding x cm^3 of dog food. The graph of the corresponding function for cans of cat food is a horizontal compression of f by a factor of about $\frac{3}{5}$. Write the corresponding function g for cans of cat food, and use it to estimate the radius of a can holding 216 cm^3 of cat food.

Okapi

Graph each inequality.

43. $y < \sqrt{x+5}$ 44. $y \geq \sqrt{x-1}$ 45. $y > \sqrt[3]{x} + 2$ 46. $y \leq \sqrt[3]{x+3}$

47. **Biology** The function $h(m) = 241m^{-\frac{1}{4}}$ can be used to approximate an animal's resting heart rate h in beats per minute, given its mass m in kilograms.

a. A common shrew is one of the world's smallest mammals. What is the resting heart rate of a common shrew with a mass of 0.01 kg?

b. An okapi is an African animal related to the giraffe. What is the resting heart rate of an okapi with a mass of 300 kg?

Describe how $f(x) = \sqrt{x}$ was transformed to produce each function.

48. $g(x) = 6\sqrt{x+1}$ 49. $h(x) = 3\sqrt{x-1} - 9$ 50. $j(x) = -\sqrt{x-3} - 7$

Match each function to its graph.

51. $f(x) = \sqrt{x+2} - 2$ 52. $g(x) = \sqrt{x-2} + 2$

53. $h(x) = \sqrt{-(x+2)} + 2$ 54. $j(x) = -\sqrt{x-2} - 2$

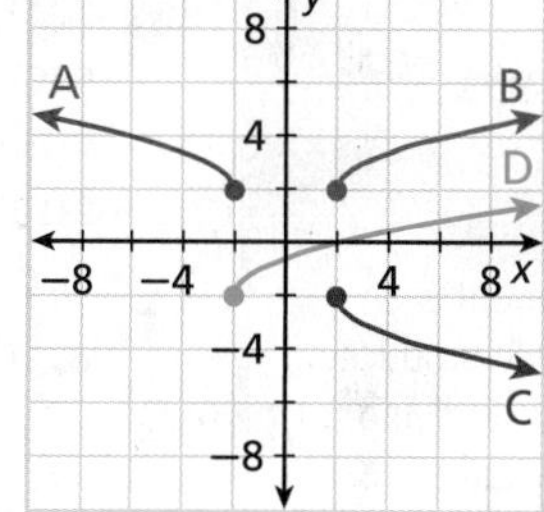

55. **Aviation** Pilots use the function $D(A) = 3.56\sqrt{A}$ to approximate the distance D in kilometers to the horizon from an altitude A in meters.

a. What is the approximate distance to the horizon observed by a pilot flying at an altitude of 11,000 m?

b. **What if...?** How will the approximate distance to the horizon appear to change if the pilot descends by 4000 m?

56. **Earth Science** The speed in miles per hour of a tsunami can be modeled by the function $s(d) = 3.86\sqrt{d}$, where d is the average depth in feet of the water over which the tsunami travels. Graph this function. Use the graph to predict the speed of a tsunami over water with a depth of 1500 feet.

57. **Astrophysics** New stars can form inside an interstellar cloud of gas when a cloud fragment, called a clump, has a mass M that is greater than what is known as the Jean's mass. The Jean's mass M_J is given by $M_J = 100\sqrt{\frac{(T+273)^3}{n}}$, where T is the temperature of the gas in degrees Celsius and n is the density of the gas in molecules per cubic centimeter. An astronomer discovers a gas clump with $M = 137$, $T = -263$, and $n = 1000$. Will the clump form a star? Justify your answer.

58. **Multi-Step** The formula $v = \sqrt{4909gR}$ approximates the velocity in miles per hour necessary to escape the gravity of a planet with acceleration due to gravity g in ft/s^2 and radius R in miles. On Earth, which has a radius of 3960 mi, the acceleration due to gravity is 32 ft/s^2. On the Moon, which has a radius of 1080 mi, the acceleration due to gravity is about $\frac{1}{6}$ that on Earth. How much faster would a vehicle need to be traveling to escape Earth's gravity than to escape the Moon's gravity?

MULTI-STEP TEST PREP

59. For a pendulum with length x in meters, the function $T(x) = 2\pi\sqrt{\frac{x}{9.8}}$ gives the period of the pendulum in seconds. The period of a pendulum is the time it takes the pendulum to complete one back-and-forth swing.

a. Graph the function.

b. Describe the graph of T as a transformation of $f(x) = \sqrt{x}$.

c. By what factor must the length of a pendulum be increased to double its period?

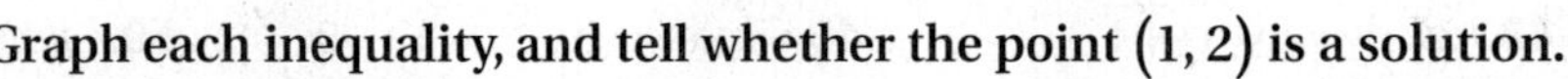

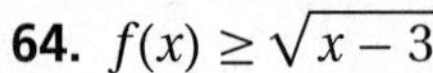

Tell whether each statement is sometimes, always, or never true.

60. For $n > 0$, the value of $\sqrt{n}$ is greater than the value of $\sqrt[3]{n}$.

61. The domain of a radical function is all real numbers.

62. The range of $f(x) = a\sqrt[3]{x - h}$, where a and h are nonzero real numbers, is all real numbers.

63. The range of $f(x) = a\sqrt{x} + k$, where a and k are nonzero real numbers, is all real numbers.

Graph each inequality, and tell whether the point $(1, 2)$ is a solution.

64. $f(x) \geq \sqrt{x - 3}$ **65.** $f(x) \leq \sqrt{x + 5}$ **66.** $f(x) > \sqrt[3]{x} - 3$

LINK Physics

A sonic boom is a shock wave produced by an aircraft flying at or above the speed of sound in air. Occasionally, an unusual cone-shaped cloud forms around a plane when the plane's speed is near that of sound, as shown above.

67. Physics The speed s of sound in air in meters per second is given by the function $s = \sqrt{k(T + 273.15)}$, where T is the air temperature in degrees Celsius and k is a positive constant. The table shows the speed of sound in air at a pressure of 1 atmosphere.

Temperature (°C)	Speed of Sound in Air (m/s)
0	331
10	337
20	343
30	348
40	354

a. Graph the data in the table.

b. Use your graph to predict the speed of sound in air at 25°C.

c. Based on the function above, at what temperature would the speed of sound in air be 0 m/s? Explain.

68. Medicine A pharmaceutical company samples the raw materials it receives before they are used in the manufacture of drugs. For inactive ingredients, the company uses the function $s(x) = \sqrt{x} + 1$ to determine the number of samples s that should be taken from a shipment of x containers.

a. Describe the graph of s as a transformation of $f(x) = \sqrt{x}$. Then graph the function.

b. How many samples should be taken from a shipment of 45 containers of an inactive ingredient?

69. Multi-Step The time t in seconds required for an object to fall from a certain height can be modeled by the function $t = \frac{\sqrt{h}}{4}$, where h is the initial height of the object in feet. To the nearest tenth of a second, how much longer will it take for a piece of an iceberg to fall to the ocean from a height of 240 ft than from a height of 100 ft?

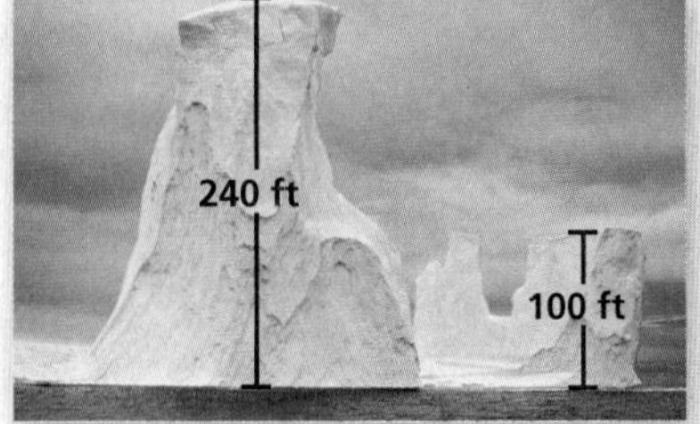

70. Critical Thinking Explain why a vertical compression of a square-root function by a factor of $\frac{1}{2}$ is equivalent to a horizontal stretch of a square-root function by a factor of 4.

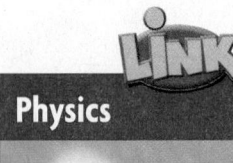

71. **Critical Thinking** Why does the square-root function have a limited domain but the cube-root function does not?

72. **Write About It** Describe how a horizontal translation and a vertical translation of the function $f(x) = \sqrt{x}$ each affects the function's domain and range.

TEST PREP

73. What is the domain of the function $f(x) = \sqrt{x - 9}$?

    (A) All real numbers
    (B) $x \geq -9$
    (C) $x \geq 0$
    (D) $x \geq 9$

74. Which situation could best be modeled by a cube-root function?

    (F) The volume of a cube as a function of its edge length
    (G) The diameter of a circle as a function of its area
    (H) The edge length of a cube as a function of its surface area
    (J) The radius of a sphere as a function of its volume

75. The function g is a translation 2 units left and 5 units up of $f(x) = \sqrt{x}$. Which of the following represents g?

    (A) $g(x) = \sqrt{x + 2} + 5$
    (B) $g(x) = 2\sqrt{x} + 5$
    (C) $g(x) = \sqrt{x + 5} + 2$
    (D) $g(x) = 5\sqrt{x - 2}$

76. Which function has a range of $\{y \mid y \leq -2\}$?

    (F) $f(x) = \sqrt{x} - 2$
    (G) $f(x) = \sqrt{x - 2}$
    (H) $f(x) = \sqrt{-x} - 2$
    (J) $f(x) = -\sqrt{x} - 2$

77. **Short Response** Describe how the graph of $f(x) = \sqrt{x}$ was transformed to produce the graph shown. Then write the equation of the graphed function.

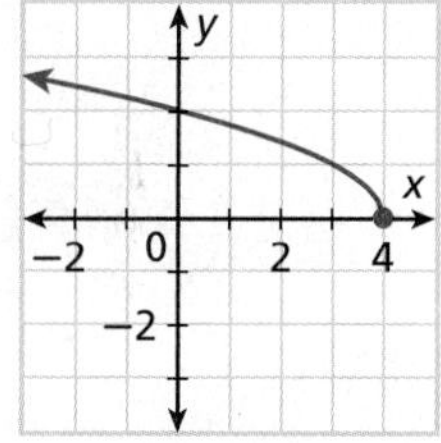

CHALLENGE AND EXTEND

78. The function $f(x) = \sqrt{x}$ is transformed solely by using translations and reflections to produce g. The domain of g is all real numbers greater than or equal to 3, and the range is all real numbers less than or equal to 2. What is the equation that represents g?

79. Write the equation of a square-root function whose graph has its endpoint at $(-3, 4)$ and passes through the point $(2, 2)$.

COMMON CORE

5-8 Solving Radical Equations and Inequalities

CC.9-12.A.CED.1 Create equations and inequalities in one variable and use them to solve problems.

Objective
Solve radical equations and inequalities.

Vocabulary
radical equation
radical inequality

Who uses this?
Police officers can use radical equations to determine whether a car is speeding. (See Example 6.)

A **radical equation** contains a variable within a radical. Recall that you can solve quadratic equations by taking the square root of both sides. Similarly, radical equations can be solved by raising both sides to a power.

IT'S AMAZING HOW PEOPLE SLOW DOWN WHEN YOU POINT A HAIR DRYER AT THEM.

Solving Radical Equations	
Steps	**Example**
1. Isolate the radical.	$\sqrt[3]{x} - 2 = 0$ $\sqrt[3]{x} = 2$
2. Raise both sides of the equation to the power equal to the index of the radical.	$(\sqrt[3]{x})^3 = (2)^3$
3. Simplify and solve.	$x = 8$

EXAMPLE 1 Solving Equations Containing One Radical

Solve each equation.

A $2\sqrt{x+1} = 14$

$\frac{2\sqrt{x+1}}{2} = \frac{14}{2}$ *Divide by 2.*

$\sqrt{x+1} = 7$ *Simplify.*

$\left(\sqrt{x+1}\right)^2 = 7^2$ *Square both sides.*

$x + 1 = 49$ *Simplify.*

$x = 48$ *Solve for x.*

Check $2\sqrt{x+1} = 14$

$2\sqrt{48+1}$	14
$2\sqrt{49}$	14
$2(7)$	14 ✓

B $5\sqrt[3]{4x+3} = 15$

$\frac{5\sqrt[3]{4x+3}}{5} = \frac{15}{5}$ *Divide by 5.*

$\sqrt[3]{4x+3} = 3$ *Simplify.*

$\left(\sqrt[3]{4x+3}\right)^3 = 3^3$ *Cube both sides.*

$4x + 3 = 27$ *Simplify.*

$4x = 24$ *Solve for x.*

$x = 6$

Check $5\sqrt[3]{4x+3} = 15$

$5\sqrt[3]{4(6)+3}$	15
$5\sqrt[3]{27}$	15
$5(3)$	15 ✓

Remember!
For a square root, the index of the radical is 2.
$\sqrt{x+1} = \sqrt[2]{x+1}$

Solve each equation.

1a. $4 + \sqrt{x-1} = 5$ **1b.** $\sqrt[3]{3x-4} = 2$ **1c.** $6\sqrt{x+10} = 42$

EXAMPLE 2 Solving Equations Containing Two Radicals

Solve $\sqrt{35x} = 5\sqrt{x+2}$.

$$\left(\sqrt{35x}\right)^2 = \left(5\sqrt{x+2}\right)^2 \qquad \textit{Square both sides.}$$

$$35x = 25(x+2) \qquad \textit{Simplify.}$$

$$35x = 25x + 50 \qquad \textit{Distribute 25.}$$

$$10x = 50 \qquad \textit{Solve for x.}$$

$$x = 5$$

Check

$$\begin{array}{c|l} \multicolumn{2}{c}{\sqrt{35x} = 5\sqrt{x+2}} \\ \hline \sqrt{35 \cdot 5} & 5\sqrt{5+2} \\ 5\sqrt{7} & 5\sqrt{7}\ \checkmark \end{array}$$

Solve each equation.

2a. $\sqrt{8x+6} = 3\sqrt{x}$

2b. $\sqrt[3]{x+6} = 2\sqrt[3]{x-1}$

Raising each side of an equation to an even power may introduce extraneous solutions.

EXAMPLE 3 Solving Equations with Extraneous Solutions

Solve $\sqrt{x+18} = x - 2$.

> **Helpful Hint**
>
> You can also use the intersect feature on a graphing calculator to find the point where the two curves intersect.

Method 1 Use a graphing calculator. Let **Y1** $= \sqrt{x+18}$ and **Y2** $= x - 2$.

The graphs intersect in only one point, so there is exactly one solution.

The solution is $x = 7$.

Intersection X=7 Y=5

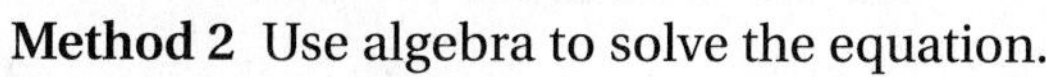

Method 2 Use algebra to solve the equation.

Step 1 Solve for x.

$$\sqrt{x+18} = x - 2$$

$$\left(\sqrt{x+18}\right)^2 = (x-2)^2 \qquad \textit{Square both sides.}$$

$$x + 18 = x^2 - 4x + 4 \qquad \textit{Simplify.}$$

$$0 = x^2 - 5x - 14 \qquad \textit{Write in standard form.}$$

$$0 = (x+2)(x-7) \qquad \textit{Factor.}$$

$$x + 2 = 0 \text{ or } x - 7 = 0 \qquad \textit{Solve for x.}$$

$$x = -2 \text{ or } x = 7$$

Step 2 Use substitution to check for extraneous solutions.

$$\begin{array}{r|l} \multicolumn{2}{c}{\sqrt{x+18} = x - 2} \\ \hline \sqrt{-2+18} & -2-2 \\ \sqrt{16} & -4 \\ 4 & -4\ \times \end{array} \qquad \begin{array}{r|l} \multicolumn{2}{c}{\sqrt{x+18} = x - 2} \\ \hline \sqrt{7+18} & 7-2 \\ \sqrt{25} & 5 \\ 5 & 5\ \checkmark \end{array}$$

Because $x = -2$ is extraneous, the only solution is $x = 7$.

Solve each equation.

3a. $\sqrt{2x+14} = x + 3$

3b. $\sqrt{-9x+28} = -x + 4$

You can use similar methods to solve equations containing rational exponents. You raise both sides of the equation to the reciprocal of the exponent. You can also rewrite any expressions with rational exponents in radical form and solve as you would other radical equations.

EXAMPLE 4 Solving Equations with Rational Exponents

Solve each equation.

A $(3x-1)^{\frac{1}{5}}=2$

$\sqrt[5]{3x-1}=2$ *Write in radical form.*

$\left(\sqrt[5]{3x-1}\right)^5=2^5$ *Raise both sides to the fifth power.*

$3x-1=32$ *Simplify.*

$3x=33$ *Solve for x.*

$x=11$

Remember!

To find a power of a power, multiply the exponents.

$\left[(x+12)^{\frac{1}{2}}\right]^2$

$(x+12)^{\frac{1}{2}\cdot 2}$

$x+12$

B $x=(x+12)^{\frac{1}{2}}$

Step 1 Solve for x.

$x^2=\left[(x+12)^{\frac{1}{2}}\right]^2$ *Raise both sides to the reciprocal power.*

$x^2=x+12$ *Simplify.*

$x^2-x-12=0$ *Write in standard form.*

$(x+3)(x-4)=0$ *Factor.*

$x+3=0$ or $x-4=0$ *Solve for x.*

$x=-3$ or $x=4$

Step 2 Use substitution to check for extraneous solutions.

x	$(x+12)^{\frac{1}{2}}$
-3	$(-3+12)^{\frac{1}{2}}$
-3	$9^{\frac{1}{2}}$
-3	3 ✗

x	$(x+12)^{\frac{1}{2}}$
4	$(4+12)^{\frac{1}{2}}$
4	$16^{\frac{1}{2}}$
4	4 ✓

The only solution is $x=4$.

CHECK IT OUT! **Solve each equation.**

4a. $(x+5)^{\frac{1}{3}}=3$ **4b.** $(2x+15)^{\frac{1}{2}}=x$ **4c.** $3(x+6)^{\frac{1}{2}}=9$

A **radical inequality** is an inequality that contains a variable within a radical. You can solve radical inequalities by graphing or by using algebra.

EXAMPLE 5 Solving Radical Inequalities

Solve $\sqrt{2x+4}\le 4$.

Method 1 Use a graph and a table.

On a graphing calculator, let **Y1** $=\sqrt{2x+4}$ and **Y2** $=4$. The graph of **Y1** is at or below the graph of **Y2** for values of x between -2 and 6. Notice that **Y1** is undefined when $x<-2$.

The solution is $-2\le x\le 6$.

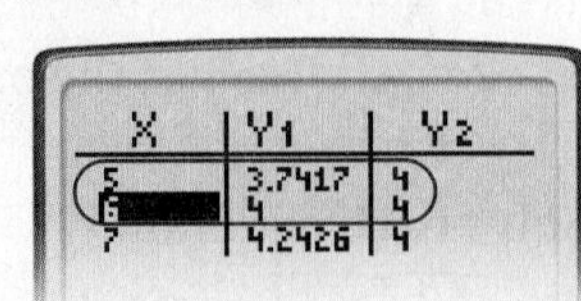

X	Y1	Y2
5	3.7417	4
6	4	4
7	4.2426	4

Method 2 Use algebra to solve the inequality.

Step 1 Solve for x.

$$\sqrt{2x+4} \le 4$$

$$\left(\sqrt{2x+4}\right)^2 \le (4)^2 \quad \textit{Square both sides.}$$

$$2x + 4 \le 16 \quad \textit{Simplify.}$$

$$2x \le 12 \quad \textit{Solve for x.}$$

$$x \le 6$$

Remember!

A radical expression with an even index and a negative radicand has no real roots.

Step 2 Consider the radicand.

$$2x + 4 \ge 0 \quad \textit{The radicand cannot be negative.}$$

$$2x \ge -4 \quad \textit{Solve for x.}$$

$$x \ge -2$$

The solution of $\sqrt{2x+4} \le 4$ is $x \ge -2$ and $x \le 6$, or $-2 \le x \le 6$.

Solve each inequality.

5a. $\sqrt{x-3} + 2 \le 5$

5b. $\sqrt[3]{x+2} \ge 1$

EXAMPLE 6 *Automobile Application*

The speed s in miles per hour that a car is traveling when it goes into a skid can be estimated by using the formula $s = \sqrt{30fd}$, where f is the coefficient of friction and d is the length of the skid marks in feet.

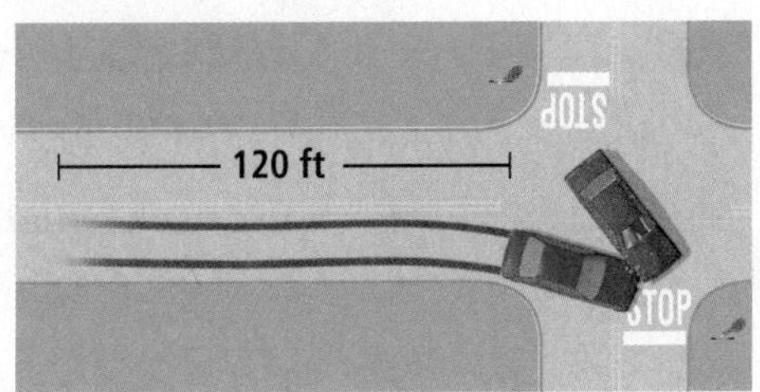

After an accident, a driver claims to have been traveling the speed limit of 45 mi/h. The coefficient of friction under accident conditions was 0.7. Is the driver telling the truth about his speed? Explain.

Use the formula to determine the greatest possible length of the driver's skid marks if he were traveling 45 mi/h.

$$s = \sqrt{30fd}$$

$$45 = \sqrt{30(0.7)d} \quad \textit{Substitute 45 for s and 0.7 for f.}$$

$$45 = \sqrt{21d} \quad \textit{Simplify.}$$

$$(45)^2 = \left(\sqrt{21d}\right)^2 \quad \textit{Square both sides.}$$

$$2025 = 21d \quad \textit{Simplify.}$$

$$96 \approx d \quad \textit{Solve for d.}$$

If the driver were traveling 45 mi/h, the skid marks would measure about 96 ft. Because the skid marks actually measure 120 ft, the driver must have been driving faster than 45 mi/h.

6. A car skids to a stop on a street with a speed limit of 30 mi/h. The skid marks measure 35 ft, and the coefficient of friction was 0.7. Was the car speeding? Explain.

THINK AND DISCUSS

MATHEMATICAL PRACTICES

1. Describe two methods that can be used to solve $\sqrt{x+2} = 6$.
2. Explain the relationship between solving a quadratic equation of the form $x^2 = a$ and a square-root equation of the form $\sqrt{x} = b$, where a and b are real numbers.

3. **GET ORGANIZED** Copy and complete the graphic organizer. In each box, write a step needed to solve a radical equation with extraneous solutions.

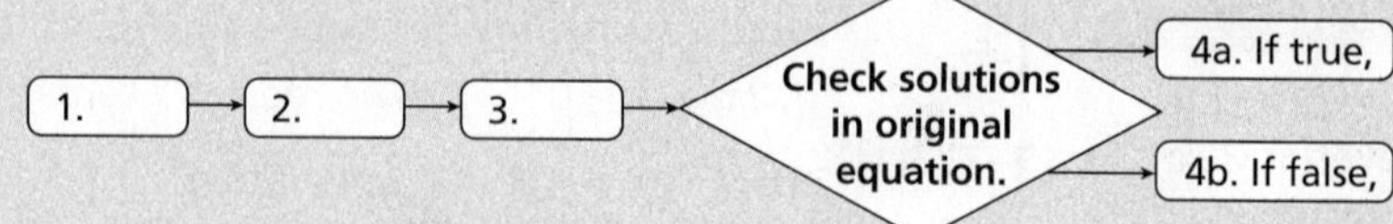

5-8 Exercises

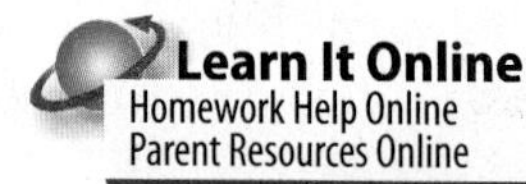

GUIDED PRACTICE

1. **Vocabulary** Is $4x + \sqrt{9} = 5$ a *radical equation*? Explain.

SEE EXAMPLE 1

Solve each equation.

2. $\sqrt{x-9} = 5$
3. $\sqrt{3x} = 6$
4. $\sqrt[3]{x-2} = 2$

SEE EXAMPLE 2

5. $\sqrt{3x-1} = \sqrt{2x+4}$
6. $2\sqrt{x} = \sqrt{x+9}$
7. $\sqrt[5]{x+4} = \sqrt[5]{3x-2}$
8. $2\sqrt[3]{x} = \sqrt[3]{x+7}$
9. $\sqrt{x+6} - \sqrt{2x-4} = 0$
10. $4\sqrt{x+1} = 3\sqrt{x+2}$

SEE EXAMPLE 3

11. $\sqrt{x+56} = x$
12. $\sqrt{x+18} = x-2$
13. $\sqrt{3x-11} = x-3$
14. $\sqrt{x+6} - x = 4$
15. $\sqrt{-x-1} = x+1$
16. $\sqrt{15x+10} = 2x+3$

SEE EXAMPLE 4

17. $(x-5)^{\frac{1}{2}} = 3$
18. $(2x+1)^{\frac{1}{3}} = 2$
19. $(4x+5)^{\frac{1}{2}} = x$
20. $2(x-50)^{\frac{1}{3}} = -10$
21. $2(x+1)^{\frac{1}{2}} = 1$
22. $(45-9x)^{\frac{1}{2}} = x-5$

SEE EXAMPLE 5

Solve each inequality.

23. $\sqrt{x+5} - 1 \le 4$
24. $\sqrt{2x} + 6 \le 10$
25. $\sqrt{2x+5} < 5$

SEE EXAMPLE 6

26. **Stunts** The formula $s = \sqrt{21d}$ relates a stunt car's speed s in miles per hour at the beginning of a skid to the length d of the skid in feet. A stunt driver must skid her car to a stop just in front of a wall. When the driver starts her skid, she is traveling at 64 mi/h. When the driver comes to a stop, how many feet will be between her car and the wall? Round to the nearest foot.

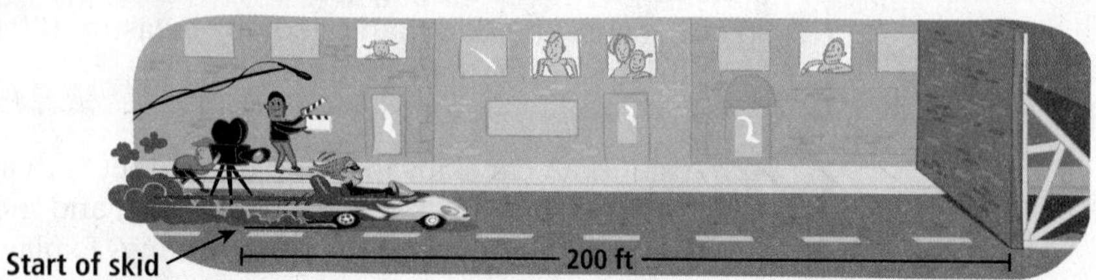

PRACTICE AND PROBLEM SOLVING

Independent Practice

For Exercises	See Example
27–32	1
33–35	2
36–38	3
39–41	4
42–44	5
45	6

Extra Practice

See Extra Practice for more Skills Practice and Applications Practice exercises.

Solve each equation.

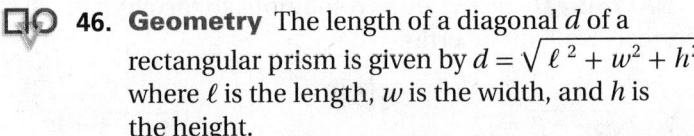

27. $\sqrt{x-12}=9$ **28.** $\sqrt[3]{2x+1}-3=0$ **29.** $5\sqrt{x+7}=25$

30. $\sqrt[4]{2x+6}=2$ **31.** $3=\frac{1}{4}\sqrt{3x+30}$ **32.** $-3=2\sqrt{x-7}-7$

33. $\sqrt{4x+12}=\sqrt{6x}$ **34.** $5\sqrt{x-1}=\sqrt{x+1}$ **35.** $\sqrt[3]{4x}=\sqrt[3]{x+7}$

36. $x+3=\sqrt{x+5}$ **37.** $\sqrt{3x+13}+3=2x$ **38.** $\sqrt{x+8}-x=-4$

39. $(x-9)^{\frac{1}{2}}=4$ **40.** $(5x+1)^{\frac{1}{4}}=4$ **41.** $(3x+28)^{\frac{1}{2}}=x$

Solve each inequality.

42. $\sqrt{3x+3}\le 6$ **43.** $\sqrt{x-3}\le 4$ **44.** $\sqrt{8x+1}\ge 7$

45. Construction The diameter d in inches of a rope needed to lift a weight of w tons is given by the formula $d=\frac{\sqrt{15w}}{\pi}$. How much weight can be lifted with a rope with a diameter of 1.5 in.?

46. Geometry The length of a diagonal d of a rectangular prism is given by $d=\sqrt{\ell^2+w^2+h^2}$, where ℓ is the length, w is the width, and h is the height.

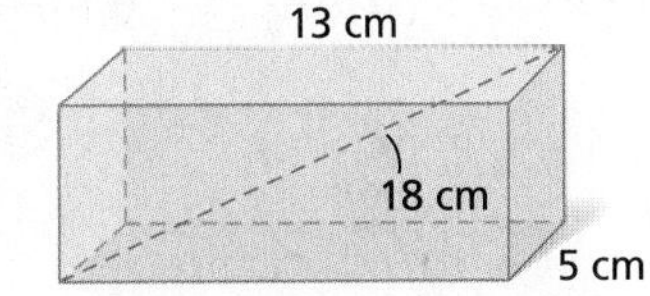

a. What is the height of the prism shown? Round to the nearest tenth.

b. What if...? Suppose that the length, width, and height of the prism are doubled. What effect will this change have on the length of the diagonal?

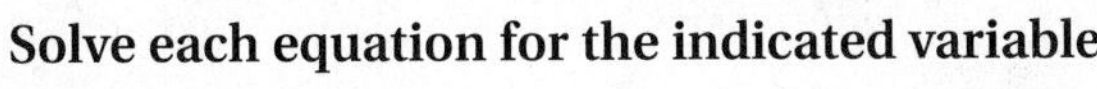

Solve each equation for the indicated variable.

47. $r=\sqrt{\frac{A}{\pi}}$ for A **48.** $r=\sqrt[3]{\frac{3V}{4\pi}}$ for V **49.** $v=\sqrt{\frac{2E}{m}}$ for E

Tornadoes

The Fujita Tornado Scale goes up to category F12, even though scientists expect that Earth's most powerful tornadoes will reach wind speeds of no higher than those of category F5.

50. Tornadoes The Fujita Tornado Scale is used to estimate the wind velocity of a tornado based on the damage that the tornado causes. The equation $V=k(F+2)^{\frac{3}{2}}$ can be used to determine a tornado's minimum wind velocity V in miles per hour, where k is a constant and F is the tornado's category number on the Fujita Scale.

Fujita Tornado Scale

Damage Level	Category	Minimum Wind Velocity (mi/h)
Moderate	F1	73
Significant	F2	113
Severe	F3	158
Devastating	F4	207
Incredible	F5	261

a. Based on the information in the table, what is the value of the constant k?

b. What would be the minimum wind velocity of an F6 tornado?

c. Winds on Neptune can reach velocities of more than 600 mi/h. Use the equation given above to determine the Fujita category of this wind velocity.

51. Amusement Parks For a spinning amusement park ride, the velocity v in meters per second of a car moving around a curve with a radius r meters is given by $v=\sqrt{ar}$, where a is the car's acceleration in m/s^2.

a. For safety reasons, a ride has a maximum acceleration of $39.2\ \text{m/s}^2$. If the cars on the ride have a velocity of 14 m/s, what is the smallest radius that any curve on the ride may have?

b. What is the acceleration of a car moving at 8 m/s around a curve with a radius of 2.5 m?

52. The time T in seconds for a pendulum to complete one back-and-forth swing is given by $T = 2\pi\sqrt{\frac{L}{9.8}}$, where L is the length of the pendulum in meters.
   a. Find the length of a pendulum that completes one back-and-forth swing in 2.2 s. Round to the nearest hundredth of a meter.
   b. A clockmaker needs a pendulum that will complete 120 back-and-forth swings in one minute. To the nearest hundredth of a meter, how long should the pendulum be?

53. **Art** Gabriel plans to cover a circular area on a mural with yellow paint.
   a. Write a radical inequality that can be used to determine the possible radius r of the circle given that Gabriel has enough paint to cover at most A ft^2.
   b. If Gabriel can cover up to 80 ft^2, is 20 a reasonable value of r? Explain.

54. **/// ERROR ANALYSIS ///** Below are two solutions to the equation $2\sqrt{3x + 3} = 12$. Which is incorrect? Explain the error.

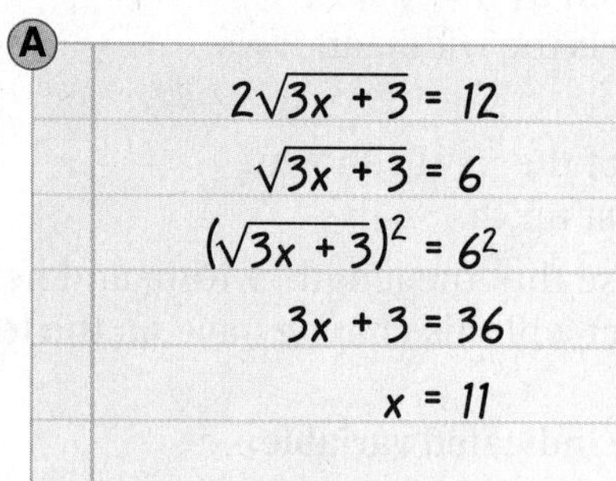

(A)

$2\sqrt{3x + 3} = 12$

$\sqrt{3x + 3} = 6$

$(\sqrt{3x + 3})^2 = 6^2$

$3x + 3 = 36$

$x = 11$

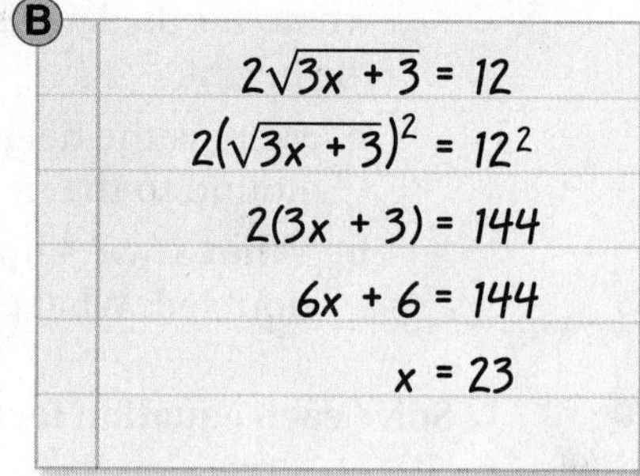

(B)

$2\sqrt{3x + 3} = 12$

$2(\sqrt{3x + 3})^2 = 12^2$

$2(3x + 3) = 144$

$6x + 6 = 144$

$x = 23$

Graphing Calculator **Use a graphing calculator to solve each equation. Graph each side of the equation on the same screen, and find the point(s) of intersection.**

55. $1.6x - 4 = 1.4\sqrt{x + 8.7}$ 56. $3(x + 7.4)^{\frac{2}{3}} = 8.8$ 57. $\sqrt[3]{x^2 + 4.2} = 2.7x - 4.2$

58. **Multi-Step** On a clear day, the approximate distance d in miles that a person can see is given by $d = 1.2116\sqrt{h}$, where h is the person's height in feet above the ocean.
   a. To the nearest tenth of a mile, how far can the captain on the clipper ship see?
   b. How much farther, to the nearest tenth of a mile, will the sailor be able to see than will the captain?
   c. A pirate ship is approaching the clipper ship at a relative speed of 10 mi/h. Approximately how many minutes sooner will the sailor be able to see the pirate ship than will the captain?

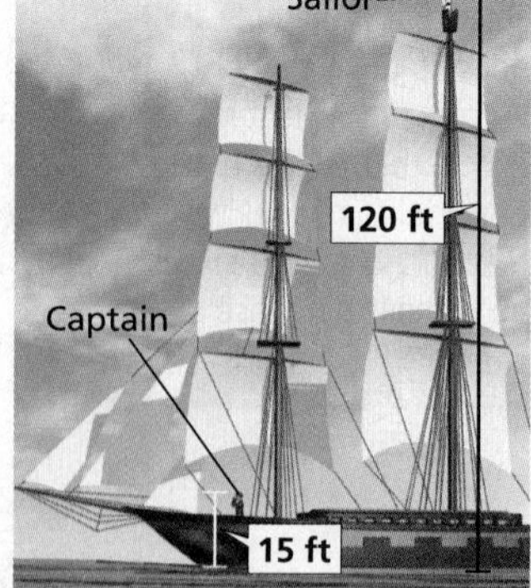

59. **Chemistry** The formula $s = \sqrt[3]{\frac{m}{\rho}}$ relates the side length s of a metal cube to its mass m and its density ρ. The density of gold is 19.30 g/cm^3, and the density of lead is 11.34 g/cm^3. How much greater is the mass of a cube of gold than the mass of a cube of lead if both cubes have a side length of 5 cm?

60. **Critical Thinking** Without solving the equation, how can you tell that $\sqrt{5x + 17} + 5 = 2$ has no real solutions?

61. **Write About It** Describe how solving a radical equation is similar to solving a rational equation.

62. Solve $\sqrt[3]{2x+4} = 3$.

Ⓐ -0.5 Ⓑ -1.5 Ⓒ 2.5 Ⓓ 11.5

63. How many solutions does $x - 1 = \sqrt{5x - 9}$ have?

Ⓕ 0 Ⓖ 1 Ⓗ 2 Ⓙ 3

64. The surface area S of a cone is given by the formula $S = \pi\sqrt{r^2 + h^2}$, where r is the radius of the base and h is the height. What is the approximate height of a cone with a surface area of 40 square inches and a base radius of 8 inches?

Ⓐ 5 inches Ⓒ 15 inches

Ⓑ 10 inches Ⓓ 20 inches

65. The equation $V = \left(\frac{A}{6}\right)^{\frac{3}{2}}$ relates the volume V of a cube to its surface area A. Which of the following is equivalent to this equation?

Ⓕ $A = 6V^{\frac{2}{3}}$ Ⓖ $A = (6V)^{\frac{2}{3}}$ Ⓗ $A = 36V^{\frac{1}{3}}$ Ⓙ $A = (216V)^{\frac{1}{2}}$

66. **Gridded Response** What value of x makes $(2x - 3)^{\frac{1}{4}} = 3$ a true statement?

CHALLENGE AND EXTEND

Indicate whether each of the following statements is sometimes, always, or never true. Equations of the form $\sqrt{x + a} = b$ have at least one real solution when

67. Both a and b are positive.

68. Both a and b are negative.

69. a is negative and b is positive.

70. a is positive and b is negative.

Solve each equation.

71. $\sqrt{x} = \frac{9}{\sqrt{x}}$

72. $\sqrt{\sqrt{x+2}} = 4$

73. $\sqrt{x^2 - 64} = x - 4$

74. **Biology** The surface area S of a human body in square meters can be approximated by $S = \sqrt{\frac{hm}{36}}$, where h is height in meters and m is mass in kilograms. Between the ages of 4 and 17, an athlete's height increased by 75% and mass increased by 350%. By approximately what percent did the surface area of the athlete's skin increase?

EXTENSION Solving Equations Graphically

CC.9-12.A.REI.11 Explain why the … points where the graphs of … equations … intersect are the solutions of the equation $f(x) = g(x)$; find the solutions approximately ….*

Objective
Solve equations graphically.

Equations can be solved graphically, using the intersection of functions to find the solutions. Each side of the equal sign is graphed as a separate function, where $f(x) = g(x)$ and the intersection represents the solution.

EXAMPLE 1 Solving Equations Algebraically and Graphically

Solve the equation $5x + 10 = 2x + 31$ algebraically and graphically.

Method 1 Solve the equation algebraically.

$$5x + 10 = 2x + 31$$
$$5x - 2x + 10 = 2x - 2x + 31$$
$$3x + 10 - 10 = 31 - 10$$
$$3x = 21$$
$$x = 7$$

Method 2 Solve the equation graphically. Divide the equation into two equations:

Let $y_1 = 5x + 10$ and $y_2 = 2x + 31$. Graph each equation.

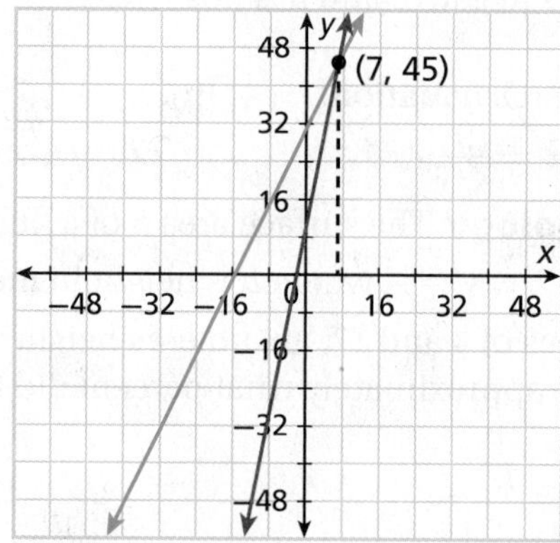

The x-coordinate of the point where the lines intersect is the solution to the equation.

In this case, the solution is $x = 7$. Compare the solution found through graphing to the solution found algebraically. Notice that the solutions are the same, so the solution to the equation $5x + 10 = 2x + 31$.

1. Solve the equation $-3x + 10 = 2x + 5$ algebraically and graphically.

The solutions of the equation $f(x) = g(x)$ are the x-coordinates of the intersections of $y = f(x)$ and $y = g(x)$.

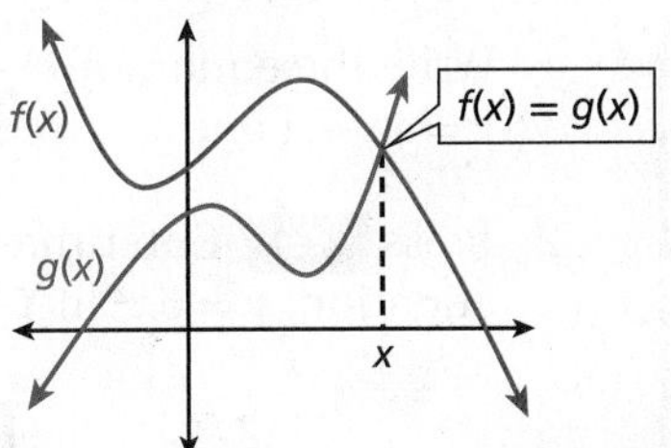

If the graphs do not intersect, there is no solution. If the graphs share every point in common, there are an infinite number of solutions.

EXAMPLE 2 Solving Equations Graphically with the Use of Technology

Solve the equation $x + 2 = -4x + 7$ graphically using technology.

1. Write the equation $x + 2 = -4x + 7$ as two separate equations: $y_1 = x + 2$ and $y_2 = -4x + 7$. Enter each equation into a calculator to graph.
2. Press GRAPH to display the functions.
3. Press TRACE and use the ◀ and ▶ to locate the point of intersection. The X value is the solution to the equation.

Alternatively, you can follow the steps below:

1. Write the equation $x + 2 = -4x + 7$ as two separate equations: $y_1 = x + 2$ and $y_2 = -4x + 7$. Enter each equation into the calculator to graph.
2. Press 2nd TRACE (CALC) and choose Intersect (#5).
3. Select the first line and press ENTER, then select the second line and press ENTER.
4. Arrow to the intersection and press ENTER. The calculator will display the intersection.

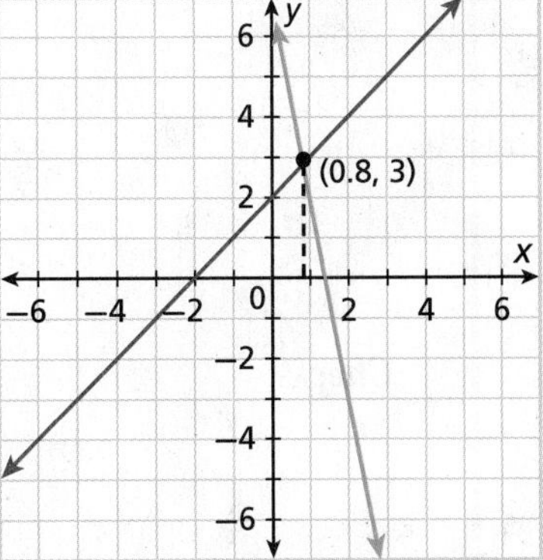

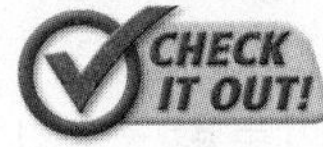

2. Solve the equation $5x + 1 = 2x - 9$ using technology.

EXAMPLE 3 **Using a Graphing Calculator Table to Solve**

Solve the equation $x^4 + 4 = 5x^2$ graphically using tables.

1. Write the equation $x^4 + 4 = 5x^2$ as two separate equations: $y = x^4 + 4$ and $y = 5x^2$.

2. Press Y=. Enter the first equation, $y = x^4 + 4$, in $\mathbf{Y_1}$ and the second equation, $y = 5x^2$ in $\mathbf{Y_2}$.

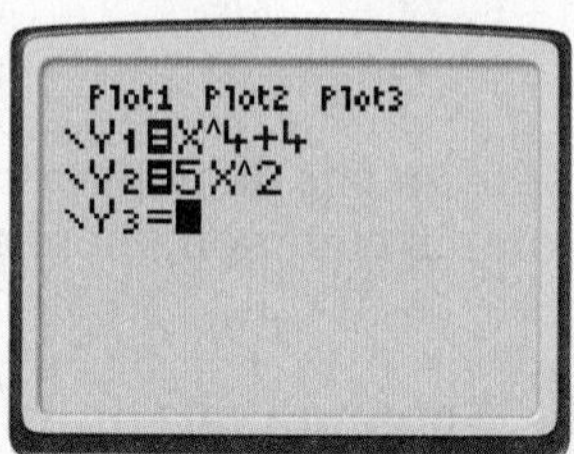

Helpful Hint

Press 2nd WINDOW (TBLSET) to change the starting value of the table and the difference between *x*-values. If the graphs intersect between *x*-values in the table, you may not find every solution.

3. Press 2nd GRAPH (TABLE) to use the **TABLE** function.

4. Scroll through the values using ▲ and ▼. Look for values where Y_1 and Y_2 are equal, then find the corresponding X value. The X value is the solution to the equation. Make sure you continue to verify all values to find all possible solutions to the equation.

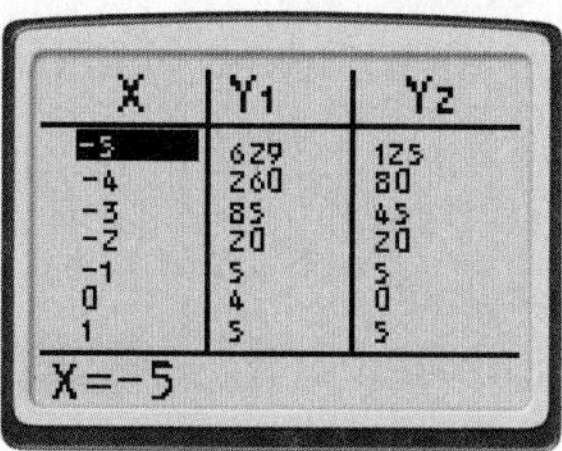

X	Y1	Y2
-5	629	125
-4	260	80
-3	85	45
-2	20	20
-1	5	5
0	4	0
1	5	5

X=-5

5. Press GRAPH and verify where your lines intersect. The solutions are $x = -2, -1, 1$, and 2.

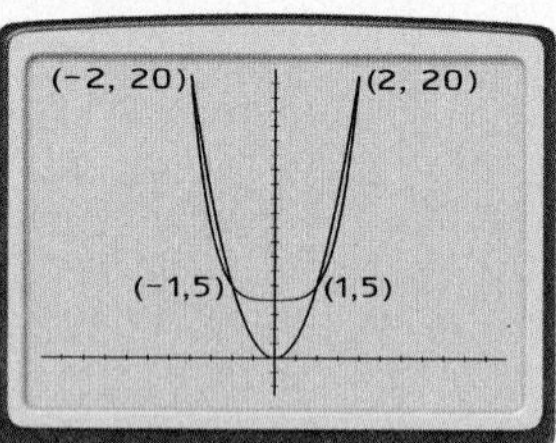

Check

$$x^4 + 4 = 5x^2$$

$$x^4 - 5x^2 + 4 = 0$$

$$(x^2 - 4)(x^2 - 1) = 0$$

$$(x + 2)(x - 2)(x + 1)(x - 1) = 0$$

3. Solve the equation $x^2 + 8 = 3x + 6$ graphically using technology.

EXAMPLE 4 Verifying Special Cases Graphically

Use technology to verify graphically that the equation $x^2 - 2x + 3 = -x^2 + 1$ has no solution.

Write the equation as two separate equations: $y_1 = x^2 - 2x + 3$ and $y_2 = -x^2 + 1$. Graph using technology.

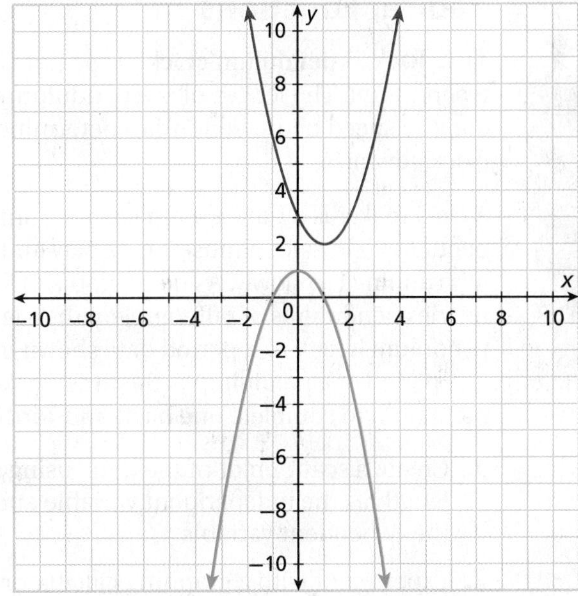

Notice that the graphs don't intersect. Since the graphs will never intersect, regardless of the window chosen to display the graphs, the equation has no solution.

4. Use technology to verify graphically that the equation $4(x^3 - 3) = 4x^3 - 12$ has infinitely many solutions.

EXTENSION Exercises

Solve each equation graphically.

1. $-\frac{1}{2}x + 5 = 3x + 9$

2. $x^5 + 1 = 2x^2 + x - 10$

3. $|x + 2| = x^2$

4. $\frac{1}{x - 8} = x$

5. $\log(x + 1) = -4\log(x)$

6. $e^x = 2e^{3x}$

7. $x^2 = -x^4 - 2$

8. $|x^2 + 1| = |x - 2|$

9. $3x^2 + 6 = 3(x^2 + 2)$

10. $-x^4 - 5x + 2 = x^2 + 7$

11. Write About It How do you determine if an equation has undefined values? What should be done if a calculator shows an intersection in a value that should be undefined?

MULTI-STEP TEST PREP

MATHEMATICAL PRACTICES **Model with mathematics.**

Radical Functions

Tick Tock A pendulum clock keeps time by using weights, gears, and a pendulum. The length of the pendulum determines how fast it swings, and the speed of the pendulum determines how fast the hands of the clock advance.

A clockmaker is building a replica of an antique pendulum clock for a museum display and finds that it is running too slowly. As he attempts to fix the clock, he tries pendulums of different lengths. He records the pendulum length and period data shown in the table. The period of a pendulum is the time it takes for the pendulum to complete one back-and-forth swing.

Pendulum Swings

Length (cm)	Period (s)
10	0.6
20	0.9
30	1.1
40	1.3
50	1.4
60	1.6

1. Create a scatter plot of the data, using pendulum length as the independent variable and period as the dependent variable.
2. Experiment with a graphing calculator to find a function rule that models the data in the scatter plot. Describe your model as a transformation of $f(x) = \sqrt{x}$.
3. What is a reasonable domain for this situation? Explain.
4. Use your model to determine the period of a pendulum that has a length of 16 cm. Round to the nearest tenth of a second.
5. From his observations, the clockmaker concludes that the pendulum needs to have a period of 1 s. To the nearest centimeter, how long should the pendulum be?
6. The function $y = 2\pi\sqrt{\frac{x}{9.8}}$ gives the period y of a pendulum in seconds in terms of the pendulum's length x in meters. Graph this function with the data from the table and explain whether the function is a reasonable model for the data.

(t), Comstock Images/Alamy Photos; (b), Bob Krist/CORBIS

READY TO GO ON?

CHAPTER 5

SECTION 5B

Quiz for Lessons 5-6 Through 5-8

5-6 Radical Expressions and Rational Exponents

Simplify each expression. Assume that all variables are positive.

1. $\sqrt{32x^3}$ **2.** $\sqrt[3]{8y^{12}z^6}$ **3.** $\sqrt[4]{\frac{a^4}{9}}$

Write each expression in radical form, and simplify.

4. $4^{\frac{3}{2}}$ **5.** $16^{\frac{5}{4}}$ **6.** $(-27)^{\frac{2}{3}}$

Write each expression by using rational exponents.

7. $\sqrt[4]{8^3}$ **8.** $\left(\sqrt[5]{243}\right)^2$ **9.** $\left(\sqrt[3]{-1000}\right)^2$

10. In an experiment involving fruit flies, the initial population is 112. The growth of the population can be modeled by the function $n(t) = 112 \cdot 2^{\frac{t}{50}}$, where n is the number of fruit flies and t is the time in hours. Based on this model, what is the population of fruit flies after 1 week?

5-7 Radical Functions

Graph each function, and identify its domain and range.

11. $f(x) = -\sqrt{x} + 4$ **12.** $f(x) = \sqrt[3]{x+1}$

13. Water is draining from a tank connected to two pipes. The speed f in feet per second at which water drains through the first pipe can be modeled by $f(x) = \sqrt{64(x-2)}$, where x is the depth of the water in the tank in feet. The graph of the corresponding function for the second pipe is a translation of f 4 units right. Write the corresponding function g, and use it to estimate the speed at which water drains through the second pipe when the depth of the water is 10 ft.

14. Use the description to write the square-root function g. The parent function $f(x) = \sqrt{x}$ is reflected across the x-axis and then translated 2 units right and 3 units down.

Graph each inequality.

15. $y > \sqrt{x} + 4$ **16.** $y \leq \sqrt{x-2}$

5-8 Solving Radical Equations and Inequalities

Solve each equation.

17. $-2\sqrt[3]{5x-5} = -10$ **18.** $\sqrt{x+4} = x - 8$ **19.** $3\sqrt[3]{x-2} = \sqrt[3]{6x}$

20. The formula $d = \sqrt[3]{\frac{4w}{0.02847}}$ relates the average diameter d of a cultured pearl in millimeters to its weight w in carats. To the nearest tenth of a carat, what is the weight of a cultured pearl with an average diameter of 7 mm?

Solve each inequality.

21. $\sqrt{x+5} < 4$ **22.** $\sqrt[3]{2x} \geq -2$ **23.** $\sqrt{x-6} - 10 \leq 4$

CHAPTER 5

Study Guide: Review

Vocabulary

combined variation
complex fraction
constant of variation
continuous function
direct variation
discontinuous function
extraneous solution
hole (in a graph)
index
inverse variation
joint variation
radical equation
radical function
radical inequality
rational equation
rational exponent
rational expression
rational function
rational inequality
square-root function

Complete the sentences below with vocabulary words from the list above.

1. A(n) ____?____ is a function whose rule is a ratio of two polynomials.

2. A(n) ____?____ is a relationship that can be written in the form $y = kx$, where k is the ____?____.

5-1 Variation Functions

EXAMPLES

■ **The cost in dollars of apples a varies directly as the number of pounds p, and $a = 3.12$ when $p = 2.4$. Find p when $a = 1.04$.**

$\frac{a_1}{p_1} = \frac{a_2}{p_2}$ *Use a proportion.*

$\frac{3.12}{2.4} = \frac{1.04}{p_2}$ *Substitute.*

$3.12p = 2.4(1.04)$ *Find the cross products.*

$p = 0.8$ *Solve for p.*

Apples that cost $1.04 have a weight of 0.8 lb.

■ **The base b of a parallelogram with fixed area varies inversely as the height h, and $b = 12$ cm when $h = 8$ cm. Find b when $h = 3$ cm.**

$b = \frac{k}{h}$ *b varies inversely with h.*

$12 = \frac{k}{8}$ *Substitute.*

$k = 96$ *Solve for k.*

$b = \frac{96}{h}$ *Substitute 96 for k.*

$b = \frac{96}{3}$ *Substitute 3 for h.*

$b = 32$ *Solve for b.*

The base is 32 cm when the height is 3 cm.

EXERCISES

Given: y varies directly as x. Write and graph each direct variation function.

3. $y = 2$ when $x = 6$

4. $y = 4$ when $x = 1$

5. The number of tiles n needed to cover a floor varies directly as the area a of the floor, and $n = 180$ when $a = 20$ ft^2. Find n when $a = 34$ ft^2.

6. The simple interest I earned over a particular period of time varies jointly as the principal P and rate r, and $I = \$264$ when $P = \$1100$ and $r = 0.12$. Find P when $I = \$360$ and $r = 0.09$.

Given: y varies inversely as x. Write and graph each inverse variation function.

7. $y = 3$ when $x = 2$

8. $y = 4$ when $x = 1$

9. For a fixed voltage, the current I flowing in a wire varies inversely as the resistance R of the wire. If the current is 8 amperes when the resistance is 15 ohms, what will the resistance be when the current is 5 amperes?

10. Determine whether the data set represents a direct variation, an inverse variation, or neither.

x	2	5	10
y	25	10	5

5-2 Multiplying and Dividing Rational Expressions

EXAMPLES

- **Simplify $\frac{4-x}{x^2-x-20}$. Identify any x-values for which the expression is undefined.**

$$\frac{-1\cancel{(x+4)}}{(x-5)\cancel{(x+4)}}=\frac{-1}{x-5}$$

Factor. Then divide out common factors.

Undefined at $x = 5$ and $x = -4$

- **Divide. Assume that all expressions are defined.**

$$\frac{x^2-9}{x+2} \div \frac{x+3}{x^2+7x+10}$$

$$\frac{x^2-9}{x+2} \cdot \frac{x^2+7x+10}{x+3}$$

Rewrite as multiplication.

$$\frac{(x-3)\cancel{(x+3)}}{\cancel{x+2}} \cdot \frac{\cancel{(x+2)}(x+5)}{\cancel{x+3}} = (x-3)(x+5)$$

EXERCISES

Simplify. Identify any x-values for which the expression is undefined.

11. $\frac{24x^{14}}{9x^{16}}$ 12. $\frac{6x^3}{3x+12}$ 13. $\frac{x^2+x-12}{x^2+5x+4}$

Multiply. Assume that all expressions are defined.

14. $\frac{x+5}{3x+1} \cdot \frac{9x+3}{x^2-25}$ 15. $\frac{x}{x-4} \cdot \frac{-x+2}{x^2+x-6}$

16. $\frac{x^2+2x-3}{x^2-x-2} \cdot \frac{x-2}{x+3}$ 17. $\frac{9x^2-1}{x^2-9} \cdot \frac{x+3}{3x+1}$

Divide. Assume that all expressions are defined.

18. $\frac{x^3y}{4xy^4} \div \frac{x}{8y^2}$ 19. $\frac{x^2+2x-15}{x-2} \div \frac{x^2-9}{2x-4}$

20. $\frac{3x-21}{3x} \div \frac{x^2-49}{x^2+7x}$ 21. $\frac{x^2+4x+3}{x^2+2x-8} \div \frac{3x+3}{x-2}$

5-3 Adding and Subtracting Rational Expressions

EXAMPLES

- **Add. Identify any x-values for which the expression is undefined.**

$$\frac{6x-3}{x^2-x-12} + \frac{x}{x+3}$$

$$\frac{6x-3}{(x-4)(x+3)} + \frac{x}{x+3}\left(\frac{x-4}{x-4}\right)$$

$$\frac{6x-3+x(x-4)}{(x-4)(x+3)}$$

Add the numerators.

$$\frac{x^2+2x-3}{(x-4)(x+3)}$$

Simplify the numerator.

$$\frac{\cancel{(x+3)}(x-1)}{(x-4)\cancel{(x+3)}} = \frac{x-1}{x-4}$$

Factor the numerator.

Undefined at $x = 4$ and $x = -3$

- **Simplify. Assume that all expressions are defined.**

$$\frac{\frac{x+2}{6x}}{\frac{x}{x-4}} = \frac{\frac{x+2}{\cancel{6x}}\cancel{(6x)}(x-4)}{\frac{x}{\cancel{x-4}}(6x)\cancel{(x-4)}}$$

The LCD is $(6x)(x-4)$.

$$\frac{(x+2)(x-4)}{x(6x)} = \frac{(x+2)(x-4)}{6x^2}$$

EXERCISES

Add. Identify any x-values for which the expression is undefined.

22. $\frac{4}{x^2+4} + \frac{x^2+8}{x^2+4}$ 23. $\frac{1}{x+3} + \frac{1}{x-3}$

24. $\frac{x}{x^2-4} + \frac{1}{x-2}$ 25. $\frac{2x-3}{3x+7} + \frac{6}{4x-1}$

Find the least common multiple for each pair.

26. $x^2 - 9$ and $x^2 - 6x + 9$

27. $x^2 + 2x - 35$ and $x^2 + 9x + 14$

Subtract. Identify any x-values for which the expression is undefined.

28. $\frac{2x}{x+4} - \frac{3}{x+4}$ 29. $\frac{x}{x+5} - \frac{5}{x-5}$

30. $\frac{1}{x^2-x-6} - \frac{x}{x+2}$ 31. $\frac{2x}{2x+1} - \frac{7}{3x-1}$

Simplify. Assume that all expressions are defined.

32. $\frac{\frac{x-6}{5}}{\frac{x+2}{8}}$ 33. $\frac{\frac{x+3}{3x}}{\frac{x^2-9}{6x-9}}$ 34. $\frac{\frac{x}{4}-\frac{1}{x}}{\frac{x+2}{x-2}}$

35. A jet's average speed is 520 mi/h when flying from Dallas to Chicago and 580 mi/h on the return trip. What is the jet's average speed for the entire trip?

5-4 Rational Functions

EXAMPLES

- **Using the graph of $f(x) = \frac{1}{x}$ as a guide, describe the transformation and graph $g(x) = \frac{1}{x} - 3$.**

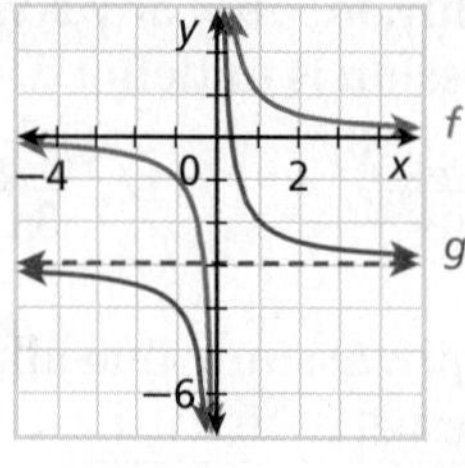

Because $k = -3$, translate f down 3 units.

- **Identify the zeros and asymptotes of $f(x) = \frac{2x-4}{x+3}$. Then graph.**

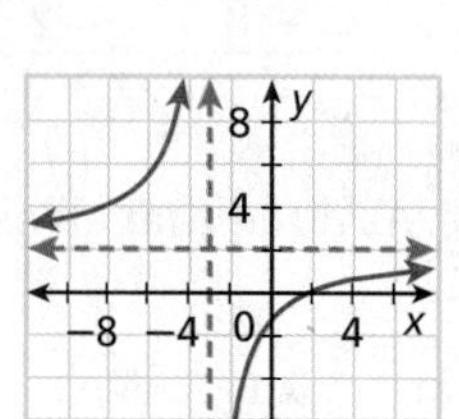

Zero: 2
Vertical asymptote: $x = -3$
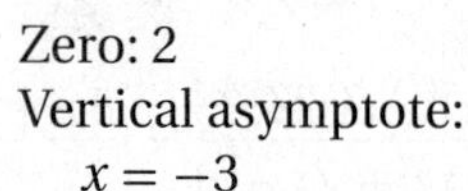
Horizontal asymptote: $y = 2$

EXERCISES

Using the graph of $f(x) = \frac{1}{x}$ as a guide, describe the transformation and graph each function.

36. $g(x) = \dfrac{1}{x-4}$ **37.** $g(x) = \dfrac{1}{x-2} + 3$

Identify the asymptotes, domain, and range of each function.

38. $f(x) = \dfrac{2}{x-1} - 3$ **39.** $f(x) = \dfrac{3}{x+2} + 1$

Identify the zeros and asymptotes of each function. Then graph.

40. $f(x) = \dfrac{x^2 - 3x}{x+4}$ **41.** $f(x) = \dfrac{x-3}{x^2 + 6x + 5}$

42. $f(x) = \dfrac{2x-4}{x+3}$ **43.** $f(x) = \dfrac{x^2 - 9}{x-2}$

44. Identify holes in the graph of $f(x) = \frac{x^2 - 3x - 18}{x+3}$. Then graph.

5-5 Solving Rational Equations and Inequalities

EXAMPLE

- **Solve the equation $\frac{30}{x+1} + x = 10$.**

$$\frac{30}{x+1}(x+1) + x(x+1) = 10(x+1)$$

$30 + x^2 + x = 10x + 10$ *Simplify. $x \neq -1$*

$x^2 - 9x + 20 = 0$ *Write in standard form.*

$(x-4)(x-5) = 0$ *Factor.*

$x = 4$ or $x = 5$ *Solve for x.*

EXERCISES

Solve each equation.

45. $x - \dfrac{6}{x} = 1$ **46.** $\dfrac{4x}{x-5} = \dfrac{3x+5}{x-5}$

47. $\dfrac{3x}{x+2} = \dfrac{2x+2}{x+2}$ **48.** $\dfrac{x}{x+4} + \dfrac{x}{2} = \dfrac{2x}{2x+8}$

Solve each inequality.

49. $\dfrac{x+4}{x} > -2$ **50.** $\dfrac{2}{x-3} < 4$

5-6 Radical Expressions and Rational Exponents

EXAMPLES

Simplify each expression. Assume that all variables are positive.

- $\sqrt[3]{-8x^9} = \sqrt[3]{(-2^3)} \cdot \sqrt[3]{x^3} \cdot \sqrt[3]{x^3} \cdot \sqrt[3]{x^3} = -2x^3$
- $\sqrt[4]{8x^6} \cdot \sqrt[4]{2x^2} = \sqrt[4]{16x^8} = \sqrt[4]{2^4} \cdot \sqrt[4]{x^4} \cdot \sqrt[4]{x^4} = 2x^2$
- **Write the expression $\left(\sqrt{16}\right)^3$ by using rational exponents.**

$16^{\frac{3}{2}}$ $\left(\sqrt[n]{a}\right)^m = a^{\frac{m}{n}}$

EXERCISES

Simplify each expression. Assume that all variables are positive.

51. $\sqrt[3]{27x^6}$ **52.** $\sqrt[4]{81x^{12}}$ **53.** $\sqrt[3]{\dfrac{8x^3}{3}}$

Write each expression by using rational exponents.

54. $\left(\sqrt[3]{-27}\right)^2$ **55.** $\sqrt[4]{16^3}$ **56.** $\left(\sqrt{9}\right)^3$

Simplify each expression.

57. $17^{\frac{1}{3}} \cdot 17^{\frac{2}{3}}$ **58.** $\left(9^4\right)^{\frac{1}{2}}$ **59.** $\left(\dfrac{1}{16}\right)^{\frac{1}{4}}$

5-7 Radical Functions

EXAMPLE

■ **Graph $f(x) = \frac{\sqrt{x+8}}{2}$, and identify its domain and range.**

Make a table of values. Then graph.

x	y
−8	0
−7	0.5
−4	1
1	1.5
8	2

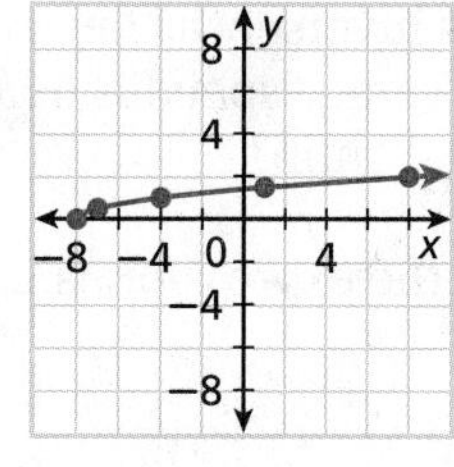

D: $\{x \mid x \geq -8\}$; R: $\{y \mid y \geq 0\}$

EXERCISES

Graph each function, and identify its domain and range.

60. $f(x) = \sqrt{x} + 5$

61. $f(x) = -4\sqrt[3]{x}$

Using the graph of $f(x) = \sqrt{x}$ as a guide, describe the transformation and graph each function.

62. $g(x) = -\sqrt{x} + 1$

63. $h(x) = \sqrt{4x}$

64. $j(x) = \sqrt{-(x-8)}$

65. $k(x) = -\frac{1}{2}\sqrt{x} + 1$

66. Use the description to write the square-root function g. The parent function $f(x) = \sqrt{x}$ is stretched vertically by a factor of 3 and translated 4 units left.

Graph each inequality.

67. $y < \sqrt{x}$

68. $y < \sqrt[3]{x+4}$

5-8 Solving Radical Equations and Inequalities

EXAMPLES

Solve each equation.

■ $4\sqrt[3]{x-4} = 12$

$\sqrt[3]{x-4} = 3$ *Divide by 4.*

$\left(\sqrt[3]{x-4}\right)^3 = 3^3$ *Cube both sides.*

$x - 4 = 27$ *Simplify.*

$x = 31$ *Solve for x.*

■ $\sqrt{x+15} = x - 5$

$\left(\sqrt{x+15}\right)^2 = (x-5)^2$ *Square both sides.*

$x + 15 = x^2 - 10x + 25$

$x^2 - 11x + 10 = 0$ *Write in standard form.*

$(x-10)(x-1) = 0$ *Factor.*

$x = 10$ or $x = 1$ *Solve for x.*

Use substitution to check for extraneous solutions.

$\sqrt{x+15}$	$= x - 5$
$\sqrt{10+15}$	$10 - 5$
5	5 ✔

$\sqrt{x+15}$	$= x - 5$
$\sqrt{1+15}$	$1 - 5$
4	−4 ✘

The solution $x = 1$ is extraneous. The only solution is $x = 10$.

EXERCISES

Solve each equation.

69. $\sqrt{x+6} - 7 = -2$

70. $\frac{\sqrt[3]{2x-2}}{6} = 1$

71. $\sqrt{10x} = 3\sqrt{x+1}$

72. $2\sqrt[5]{x} = \sqrt[5]{64}$

73. $\sqrt{6x-12} = x - 2$

74. $\sqrt{x+1} = x - 5$

75. $(4x+7)^{\frac{1}{2}} = 3$

76. $(x-4)^{\frac{1}{4}} = 3$

77. $x = (2x+35)^{\frac{1}{2}}$

78. $(x+3)^{\frac{1}{3}} = -6$

Solve each inequality.

79. $\sqrt{x-4} \leq 3$

80. $\sqrt{2x+7} - 6 > -1$

81. $\sqrt{3x} - 4 < 2$

82. $\sqrt[3]{x-1} > -2$

83. The time T in seconds required for a pendulum to complete one back-and-forth swing can be determined from the formula $T = 2\pi\sqrt{\frac{L}{9.8}}$, where L is the length of the pendulum in meters. Estimate the length of a pendulum that completes one back-and-forth swing in 2.5 s.

84. A tetrahedron is a triangular pyramid with four congruent faces. The side length s in meters of a tetrahedron is given by the formula $s = \left(6V\sqrt{2}\right)^{\frac{1}{3}}$, where V is the volume of the tetrahedron in cubic meters. What is the volume of a tetrahedron with a side length of 8 m? Round to the nearest tenth.

CHAPTER 5

CHAPTER TEST

1. The monthly minimum payment p due on a certain credit card with a fixed rate varies directly as the balance b, and $p = \$19.80$ when $b = \$1100$. Find p when $b = \$3000$.

2. The time t that it takes Hannah to bike to school varies inversely as her average speed s. If she can bike to school in 25 min when her average speed is 6 mi/h, what would her average speed need to be to get to school in 20 min?

3. Simplify $\frac{x^2 - x - 6}{x^2 - 4x + 3}$. Identify any x-values for which the expression is undefined.

Multiply or divide. Assume that all expressions are defined.

4. $\frac{x - 9}{2x - 10} \cdot \frac{x - 5}{x^2 - 81}$

5. $\frac{3x^3 - 9x^2}{x^2 - 16} \div \frac{2x - 6}{x^2 - 8x + 16}$

Add or subtract. Identify any x-values for which the expression is undefined.

6. $\frac{5}{x - 5} + \frac{x}{2x - 10}$

7. $\frac{5x}{x - 7} - \frac{9x - 6}{x + 3}$

8. Lorraine averaged 62 words per minute when typing the first 3 pages of a 6-page report. Her average typing speed for the last 3 pages was 45 words per minute. To the nearest word per minute, what was Lorraine's average typing speed for the entire report?

9. Identify the zeros and asymptotes of $f(x) = \frac{3x + 3}{x + 2}$. Then graph.

Solve each equation.

10. $2 + \frac{3}{x - 1} = 10$

11. $\frac{x}{x - 1} + \frac{x}{3} = \frac{5}{x - 1}$

12. Beth can tile a floor in about 6 h. When Beth and Mike work together, they can tile a floor in about 2.4 h. About how long would it take Mike to tile a floor if he works by himself?

Simplify each expression. Assume that all variables are positive.

13. $\sqrt[3]{-32x^6}$

14. $8^{-\frac{2}{3}}$

15. $\frac{27^{\frac{2}{3}}}{27^{\frac{1}{3}}}$

16. Write the expression $\sqrt[5]{x^2}$ by using a rational exponent.

17. Graph the function $f(x) = \sqrt{x + 2} - 4$ and identify its domain and range.

18. Graph the inequality $y \le \sqrt{x} - 2$.

Solve each equation.

19. $\sqrt{x + 7} = 5$

20. $\sqrt{2x + 1} = \sqrt{x + 9}$

21. $(3x + 1)^{\frac{1}{3}} = -2$

22. The formula $s = \sqrt{\frac{A}{4.828}}$ can be used to approximate the side length s of a regular octagon with area A. A stop sign is shaped like a regular octagon with a side length of 12.4 in. To the nearest square inch, what is the area of the stop sign?

23. Solve the inequality $\sqrt{2x + 1} > 3$.

FOCUS ON SAT

There is a set of criteria that your calculator must meet in order for it to be allowed in the testing facility when you take the SAT. For example, calculators that make noise or have QWERTY keypads are not allowed. For complete guidelines, check www.collegeboard.com.

If you do not already have a graphing calculator, consider purchasing or borrowing one because it may give you an advantage when solving some problems on the SAT. Be sure to spend time getting used to any new calculator before test day.

You may want to time yourself as you take this practice test. It should take you about 6 minutes to complete.

1. Which of the following functions is graphed below?

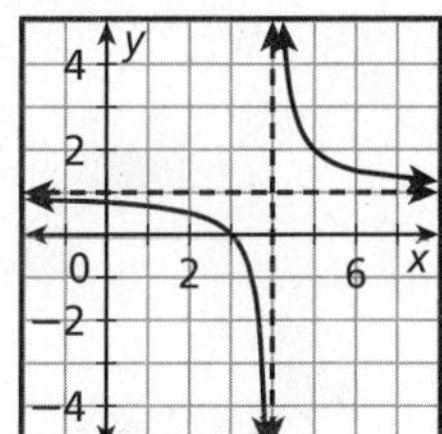

(A) $f(x) = (x + 3)(x - 4)$

(B) $f(x) = (x - 3)(x + 4)$

(C) $f(x) = \dfrac{x - 3}{x - 4}$

(D) $f(x) = \dfrac{x - 3}{x + 4}$

(E) $f(x) = \dfrac{x + 3}{x + 4}$

2. If each of the following expressions is defined, which is equivalent to $x - 1$?

(A) $\dfrac{(x + 1)(x - 1)}{x - 1}$

(B) $\dfrac{(x - 1)(x + 2)}{x + 1} \cdot \dfrac{x + 1}{x + 2}$

(C) $\dfrac{(x + 1)(x + 2)}{x - 2} \div \dfrac{x + 2}{x - 2}$

(D) $\dfrac{x + 1}{x + 2} + \dfrac{x - 1}{x + 2}$

(E) $\dfrac{2x - 2}{x - 2} - \dfrac{x - 1}{x - 2}$

3. The cube root of the square of a real number n is 16. What is the value of n?

(A) $\dfrac{4}{3}$

(B) $\dfrac{8}{3}$

(C) 4

(D) 12

(E) 64

4. If y varies inversely as the square of x and $y = 1$ when $x = 2$, what is the value of y when $x = -4$?

(A) -2

(B) $-\dfrac{1}{2}$

(C) $\dfrac{1}{4}$

(D) 4

(E) 16

5. If $\sqrt[3]{12x + 28} = 4$, what is the value of x^3?

(A) -8

(B) 3

(C) 12

(D) 27

(E) 64

CHAPTER 5

TEST TACKLER

Standardized Test Strategies

Any Question Type: Use a Diagram

Diagrams are often useful when you are solving problems. For some problems, a diagram is provided for you and you must correctly interpret it. In other situations, you can sketch your own diagram to help you visualize a problem.

EXAMPLE 1

Short Response The height h of a square pyramid can be determined from the equation $h = \sqrt{\ell^2 - \left(\frac{s}{2}\right)^2}$, where ℓ is the slant height of the pyramid and s is the side length of the square base. What is the slant height ℓ of the square pyramid shown? Show your work.

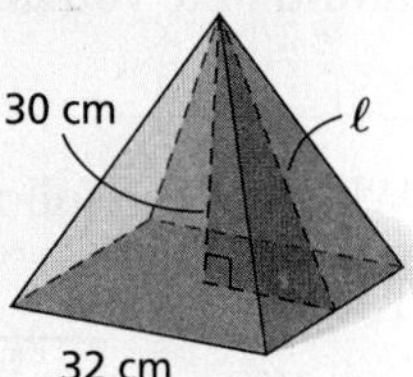

To solve this problem, you must use information from the diagram.

$30 = \sqrt{\ell^2 - \left(\frac{32}{2}\right)^2}$ — *Substitute 30 for h and 32 for s.*

$30 = \sqrt{\ell^2 - 16^2}$ — *Simplify.*

$900 = \ell^2 - 256$ — *Square both sides.*

$1156 = \ell^2$ — *Add 256 to both sides.*

$\pm 34 = \ell$ — *Solve for ℓ.*

The slant height of the pyramid is 34 centimeters.

EXAMPLE 2

Multiple Choice A circular fountain with radius r feet is built into a square base with a side length of $3r$ feet. What is the probability that a penny hitting the square base at random will land in the circular fountain?

(A) $\frac{\pi}{9}$ (B) $\frac{\pi}{3}$ (C) $\frac{1}{3}$ (D) $\frac{1}{9}$

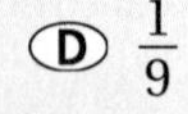

A diagram would be helpful with this problem. Sketch a square with side length 3r to represent the square base. Then sketch a circle inside it with radius r to represent the circular fountain.

$\frac{\pi r^2}{(3r)^2}$ — *The probability that the penny will land in the fountain is the ratio of the area of the fountain to the area of the base.*

$\frac{\pi r^2}{9r^2} = \frac{\pi}{9}$ — *Simplify.*

The correct answer is A.

If you sketch your own diagram to help you solve a problem, be sure to label it with any measurements you are given.

Read each test item and answer the questions that follow.

Item A

Multiple Choice What is the area of this composite figure?

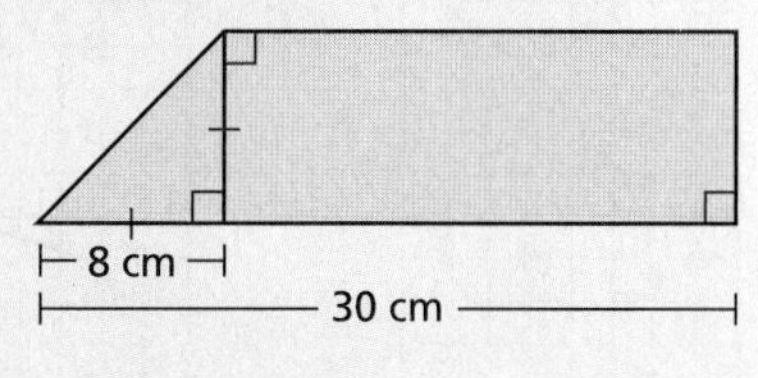

Ⓐ 176 cm^2 Ⓒ 240 cm^2

Ⓑ 208 cm^2 Ⓓ 272 cm^2

1. How can you use the information given in the diagram to determine the length of the rectangle?
2. Explain how you can use the diagram to determine the rectangle's width.
3. What is the area of the triangle? What is the area of the rectangle?

Item B

Multiple Choice A square courtyard has a perimeter of 200 meters. What is the approximate length of a sidewalk that lies along one of the courtyard's diagonals?

Ⓕ 50 meters   Ⓗ 71 meters

Ⓖ 57 meters   Ⓙ 87 meters

4. Sketch a diagram that can help you visualize the situation.
5. How can you use the information given in the problem to label each side of the courtyard in your diagram with its length?
6. Into what shapes does the diagonal sidewalk divide the courtyard?
7. What equation can you use to determine the length of the sidewalk?

Item C

Short Response What are the measures of the three numbered angles of this triangle? Explain how you determined your answer.

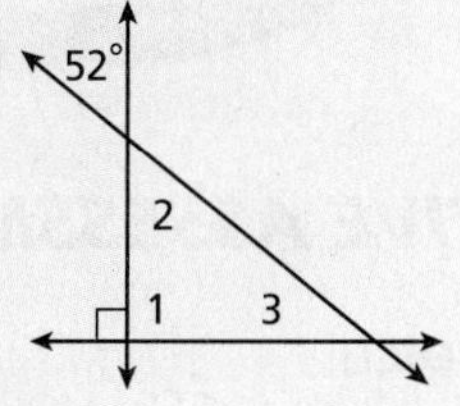

8. Based on the information in the diagram, what type of angle is $\angle 1$? What is its measure?
9. What is the relationship between the 52° angle and $\angle 2$? What is the measure of $\angle 2$?
10. How can you use the measures of $\angle 1$ and $\angle 2$ to determine the measure of $\angle 3$?

Item D

Extended Response A rectangular pool is surrounded on all four sides by a tiled lounging area. The length of the pool is 5 feet greater than the width. The width of the lounging area is 10 feet greater than twice the width of the pool. The length of the lounging area is 5 times the width of the pool.

a. Write a rational expression that represents the ratio of the area of the pool to the entire area of the pool and lounging area.

b. Determine the value of the ratio if the width of the pool is 30 feet.

11. Sketch a diagram that can help you visualize the situation.
12. Explain how you determined the labels for the dimensions of your diagram.
13. Is it necessary to draw your diagram to scale? Why or why not?
14. What expression represents the area of the pool? What expression represents the entire area of the pool and lounging area?

CHAPTER 5

STANDARDIZED TEST PREP

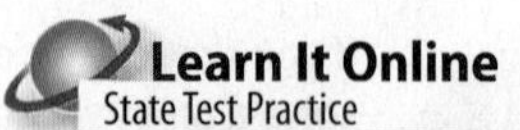

CUMULATIVE ASSESSMENT

Multiple Choice

1. Given: y varies jointly as x and z, and $y = 16$ when $x = \frac{1}{2}$ and $z = 8$. What equation represents the joint variation function?
   - (A) $y = \frac{4x}{z}$
   - (B) $y = 4x$
   - (C) $y = \frac{1}{4}xz$
   - (D) $y = 4xz$

2. What is the solution of the equation $\sqrt{3x + 2} = 3\sqrt{2x - 2}$?
   - (F) $x = \frac{4}{15}$
   - (G) $x = \frac{8}{15}$
   - (H) $x = \frac{4}{3}$
   - (J) $x = \frac{8}{3}$

3. Which is equivalent to $(3 - 5i)(2 + i)$?
   - (A) 11
   - (B) $11 - 7i$
   - (C) $11 + 7i$
   - (D) $1 - 7i$

4. Which is equivalent to $\frac{4x^2y^3}{5xy^2} \div \frac{2y}{10xy}$?
   - (F) $\frac{4y}{25}$
   - (G) $\frac{4x^2}{y}$
   - (H) $4x^2y$
   - (J) $4x^2y^5$

5. What is the slope of the line $3y = 2x + 9$?
   - (A) $\frac{2}{3}$
   - (B) $\frac{3}{2}$
   - (C) 3
   - (D) 9

6. Which expression can be simplified to a rational number?
   - (F) $\sqrt{1} + \sqrt{8}$
   - (G) $\sqrt{10} \cdot \sqrt{25}$
   - (H) $(\sqrt{15})^2$
   - (J) $\sqrt{\frac{20}{4}}$

7. Which is the graph of the function $f(x) = 4\sqrt{x + 2} - 3$?

   (A)
   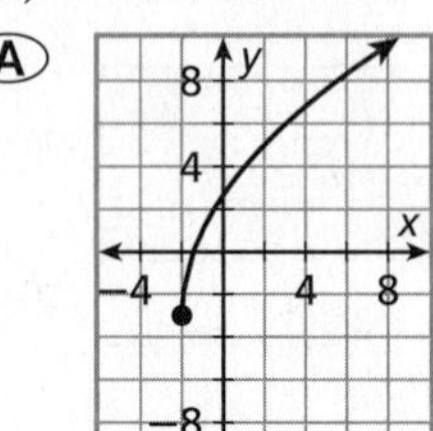

   (C)
   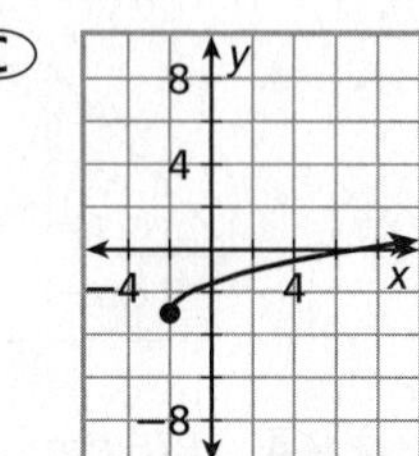

   (B)
   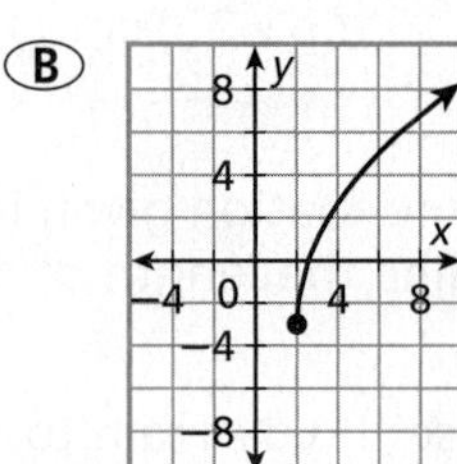

   (D)
   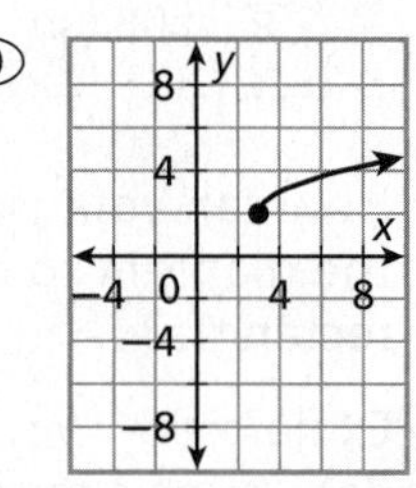

8. At track practice, Jamie ran 0.5 mile farther than twice the distance Rochelle ran. If x represents the distance in miles that Rochelle ran, which expression represents the distance that Jamie ran?
   - (F) $0.5(2x)$
   - (G) $0.5x + 2$
   - (H) $2(x + 0.5)$
   - (J) $2x + 0.5$

9. Which equation best describes the relationship between x and y shown in the table?

x	1	3	6	10	15
y	−1	5	14	26	41

   - (A) $y = -3x + 2$
   - (B) $y = -2x + 1$
   - (C) $y = 2x - 3$
   - (D) $y = 3x - 4$

10. A triangle with vertices at (1, 4), (−2, 3), and (5, 0) is translated 2 units right and 3 units down. Which are the coordinates of a vertex of the image?
    - (F) (−5, 5)
    - (G) (−1, 1)
    - (H) (0, 0)
    - (J) (3, 3)

If you have extra time at the end of a test, go back and check your answers. Remember that you can always check the solution to an equation by substituting your answer to see if it makes the equation true.

11. What is the standard form of the expression $(2x^2 - x + 4) - (3x^3 + x^2 - 2x)$?

Ⓐ $-3x^3 - x^2 - 3x + 4$

Ⓑ $-3x^3 + x^2 + x + 4$

Ⓒ $x^2 + x + 4 - 3x^3$

Ⓓ $3x^3 + 3x^2 + 3x + 4$

12. At what point does the graph of $f(x) = \frac{2x^2 - x - 3}{x + 1}$ have a hole?

Ⓕ $(-1, -5)$ Ⓗ $(1.5, 0)$

Ⓖ $(-1, 0)$ Ⓙ $(1.5, 2.5)$

13. What function is graphed below?

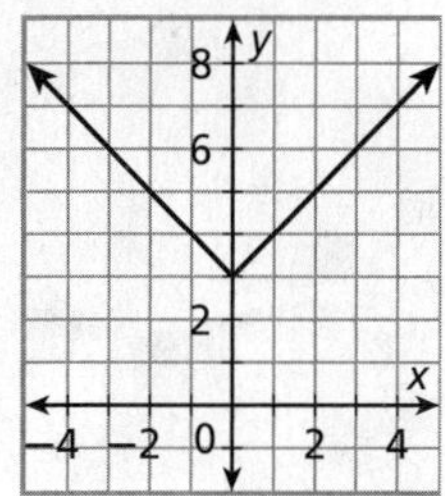

Ⓐ $f(x) = |3x|$ Ⓒ $f(x) = 3|x|$

Ⓑ $f(x) = |x + 3|$ Ⓓ $f(x) = |x| + 3$

Gridded Response

14. What value of x makes the equation true?

$\frac{7}{4} = \frac{3}{x} + 1$

15. What value completes the square for the expression below?

$x^2 - 3x + \blacksquare$

16. Simplify the expression.

$(\sqrt[3]{-8})^2$

17. What value of x makes the equation true?

$\log_5(x + 8) = 2$

18. Simplify the expression.

$\frac{5x}{x + \frac{1}{4}} - \frac{20x}{4x + 1}$

Short Response

19. The function $K = \frac{5}{9}(F - 32) + 273$ expresses temperature in kelvins K as a function of temperature in degrees Fahrenheit F.

a. Find the inverse of the function.

b. What does the inverse represent?

c. Use the inverse to find the temperature in degrees Fahrenheit that is equivalent to 300 kelvins.

20. The WNBA Most Valuable Player award is given to the player with the greatest number of total points, which are tallied based on the number of first-, second-, and third-place votes that the player receives. The table shows the number of votes for the top three nominees in 2004. Find the number of points awarded for each vote.

Player	First-Place Votes	Second-Place Votes	Third-Place Votes	Total Points
L. Leslie	33	0	19	425
L. Jackson	15	18	15	351
D. Taurasi	0	13	7	126

21. The graph of $f(x) = \frac{1}{2}x^2 + c$ is a parabola with its vertex at $(0, 3)$.

a. What is the value of c? Explain how you determined this value.

b. Graph the function f.

Extended Response

22. The information in the table describes a polynomial function.

Leading Coefficient	1
Degree	3
Zeros	$-1, 2, 4$
Local Minimum	≈ -4.1
Local Maximum	≈ 8.2
y-intercept	8

a. Describe the end behavior of the graph of the function. Justify your answer.

b. How many turning points does the graph of the function have? Justify your answer.

c. Sketch a graph of the function.

Real-World CONNECTIONS

The Return of the Trumpeter Swan

The majestic trumpeter swan was once abundant throughout Michigan, but by 1900, the species had been hunted almost to extinction. Since 1985, the Detroit Zoo has been working with Michigan State University to reintroduce the species to Michigan's wetlands. The program has been a great success—the population of trumpeter swans continues to grow every year.

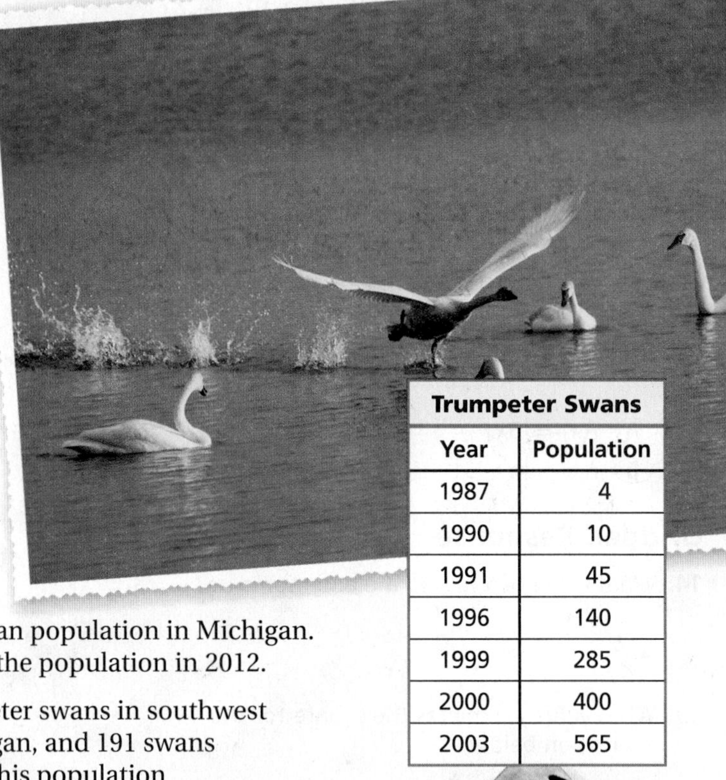

Trumpeter Swans	
Year	**Population**
1987	4
1990	10
1991	45
1996	140
1999	285
2000	400
2003	565

Choose one or more strategies to solve each problem. For 1–3, use the table.

1. The table shows the growth of the swan population in Michigan. Use an exponential model to predict the population in 2012.
2. In 2000, there were about 100 trumpeter swans in southwest Michigan, 50 swans in eastern Michigan, and 191 swans in Seney National Wildlife Refuge. If this population distribution continues, about how many swans will be in each region in 2012?
3. In what year do you predict that the total population of trumpeter swans in Michigan will exceed 6000? Justify your answer.
4. A cygnet is a young swan. In 1997, there were 60 trumpeter swan cygnets in Michigan. In each of the next 2 years, their population increased by 30% compared with the year before. If this rate of increase continues, in what year will the population of cygnets exceed 1500?

GENTLEMEN
OUR
COUNTRY
HENRY FORD AND HIS FIRST CAR.

The Motor City

In 1903, Henry Ford opened a small car company in Detroit that employed 10 people. Within a decade, Detroit had become the heart of America's automotive industry, earning it the nickname the "Motor City." Today, Detroit remains an important center for automotive research.

Choose one or more strategies to solve each problem. For 1–3, use the table.

Stopping Distances on Dry Pavement	
Speed (mi/h)	**Distance (ft)**
10	4.2
20	16.8
30	37.8
40	67.2

1. Automotive engineers use the equation $s = \sqrt{30fd}$ to study the relationship between a vehicle's speed s in miles per hour and its stopping distance d in feet once the brakes have been applied. In this equation, f is the coefficient of friction, which depends in part on the condition of the road.
   a. Determine the coefficient of friction to the nearest tenth for dry pavement.
   b. Predict the stopping distance to the nearest foot for a vehicle moving at 65 mi/h.
2. For a vehicle on wet pavement, the coefficient of friction is 0.4. How does driving on wet pavement affect the stopping distance for a given speed?
3. Engineers want to design brakes that will reduce stopping distances by 10%. How would this change the equation relating speed and stopping distance?
4. The equation $v_{\text{max}} = \sqrt{14.88fr}$ gives the maximum velocity in miles per hour that a vehicle can safely travel around a curve that has a radius of r feet. If the velocity is greater than v_{max}, the tires will slip. Engineers find that under snowy conditions, $v_{\text{max}} = 15$ mi/h for a freeway off-ramp that has a radius of 50 ft. To the nearest tenth, what is the coefficient of friction for the off-ramp in these conditions?

CHAPTER

6 Properties and Attributes of Functions

COMMON CORE

Chapter Focus

- Make connections among representations of various function families.
- Operate and solve problems with functions and their inverses.

COSMIC DEBRIS

Space missions have left more than 28,000 pieces of debris floating in space. You can analyze the debris trends by using functions and graphs.

Learn It Online
Chapter Project Online

(all) CORBIS

ARE YOU READY?

Vocabulary

Match each term on the left with a definition on the right.

1. translation
2. slope
3. regression
4. correlation

A. the statistical study of the relationship between variables
B. the constant rate of change of a linear function
C. the ratio between two sets of measurements
D. a transformation that moves each point in a figure or graph the same distance in the same direction
E. a measure of the strength and direction of the linear relationship between two variables

Connect Words and Algebra

Write an equation to represent each situation.

5. The cost of renting a recording studio is \$30 for the first hour and \$20 for each additional hour.
6. The volume of water in a tank is equal to 30 gallons plus 8 gallons for every minute the pump is on.

Line Graphs

Find each value for the graph of $f(x)$ shown.

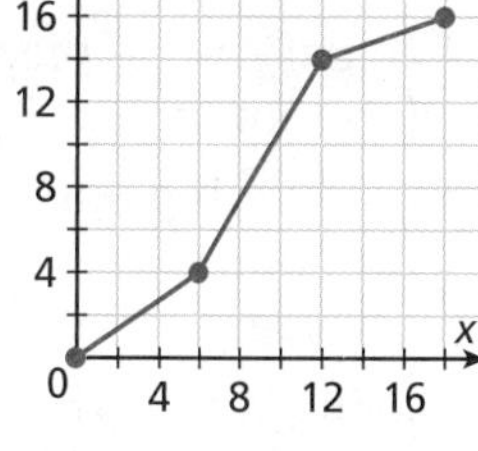

7. $f(6)$
8. $f(15)$
9. x such that $f(x) = 2$
10. x such that $f(x) = 9$
11. Find the slope of the line segment between $x = 6$ and $x = 12$.
12. Find the slope of the line segment between $x = 12$ and $x = 18$.

Multiply Binomials

Multiply. Then simplify.

13. $(x - 6)(x + 4)$
14. $(6 - x)(4 - x)$
15. $(5x + 8)(2x - 7)$
16. $(x^2 - 7)(4x + 5)$
17. $(3x^2 + 8)(7x^2 + 8)$
18. $(x - 8)(x + 8)$

Simplify Polynomial Expressions

Simplify.

19. $8(3x^5) - (2x)^3(5x^2)$
20. $5(x + 3)^2 - 6(x + 3)$
21. $3x(4 - x^3) - 6x^2(x + 4)$
22. $3x^3(x^2 + 4) - x(x^4 - 5)$

CHAPTER 6

Study Guide: Preview

Where You've Been

Previously, you

- studied different functions, graphs, and equations.
- transformed linear, quadratic, exponential, and radical functions.
- performed operations on many types of expressions.
- used linear, quadratic, and exponential functions to model real-world data.

In This Chapter

You will study

- multiple representations of functions.
- transforming piecewise functions.
- performing operations on functions and function inverses.
- using various functions to model real-world data.

Where You're Going

You can use the skills in this chapter

- in all of your future math classes, including Calculus and Statistics.
- in other classes, such as Health, Chemistry, Physics, and Economics.
- outside of school to model data and make predictions in sports, travel, and finance.

Key Vocabulary/Vocabulario

composition of functions	composición de funciones
one-to-one function	función uno a uno
piecewise function	función a trozos
step function	función escalón

Vocabulary Connections

To become familiar with some of the vocabulary terms in the chapter, consider the following. You may refer to the chapter, the glossary, or a dictionary if you like.

1. One definition of the word *composition* is "the act or process of putting together." How can you use this definition of *composition* to understand **composition of functions** in mathematics?
2. Imagine looking at a set of stairs from the side. Would a graph that looked like stairs represent a function? What might a **step function** look like?
3. Recall the definition of a function. What do you think a **one-to-one function** is? Give examples of functions from mathematics and from real life that are one-to-one functions and that are not one-to-one functions.

Reading Strategy: Read Problems for Understanding

Read a problem once to become aware of the concept being reviewed. Then read it again slowly and carefully to identify what the problem is asking. As you read, highlight key information given in the problem statement. When dealing with a multi-step problem, break the problem into parts and then make a plan to solve it.

19. Space Exploration On Earth, the function $f(x) = \frac{6}{5}\sqrt{x}$ approximates the distance in miles to the horizon observed by a person whose eye level is x feet above the ground. The graph of the corresponding function for Mars is a horizontal stretch of f by a factor of about $\frac{9}{5}$. Write the corresponding function g for Mars, and use it to estimate the distance to the horizon for an astronaut whose eyes are 6 ft above Mars's surface.

Step	Question	Answer
Step 1	What concept is being reviewed?	• transforming a rational function by changing its parameters
Step 2	What are you being asked to do?	• Rewrite the function to include the new parameter. • Evaluate the revised function for a given value.
Step 3	What is the key information needed to solve the problem?	• The function $f(x) = \frac{6}{5}\sqrt{x}$ represents the distance on Earth • The function for Mars is a horizontal stretch by a factor of $\frac{9}{5}$ • The astronaut's eye level on Mars is 6 ft.
Step 4	What is my plan to solve this multi-part problem?	• Revise the given function to account for horizontal stretch on Mars. • Evaluate the revised function for $x = 6$.

Try This

For each problem, complete each step in the four-step method described above.

1. A rectangle has a length of $(x + 5)$ units and a width of $(x + 4)$ units. Write and graph a rational function R to represent the ratio of the area to the perimeter. Identify a reasonable domain and range of the function.

2. The diameter d (in inches) of a rope needed to lift w tons is given by $d = \frac{\sqrt{15w}}{\pi}$. How much more can be lifted with a rope 1.25 inches in diameter than with a rope 0.75 inch in diameter?

COMMON CORE

6-1 Multiple Representations of Functions

CC.9-12.F.IF.7 Graph functions expressed symbolically and show key features of the graph…*

Objectives

Translate between the various representations of functions.

Solve problems by using the various representations of functions.

Who uses this?

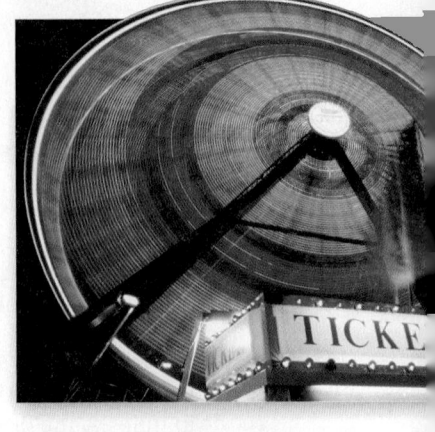

An amusement park manager can use representations of functions, such as graphs and tables, to analyze ticket sales. (See Example 1.)

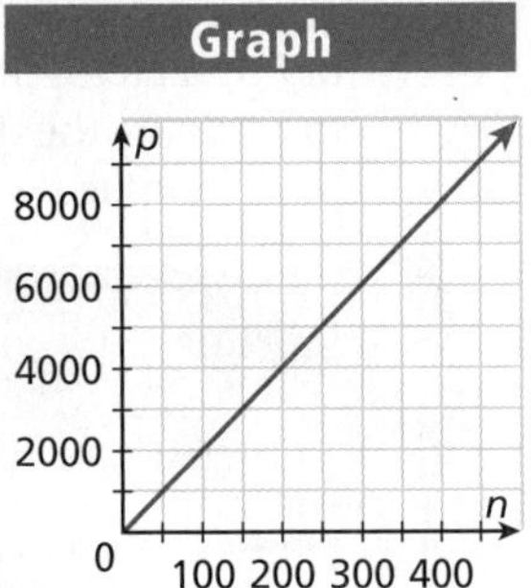

An amusement park manager estimates daily profits by multiplying the number of tickets sold by 20. This verbal description is useful, but other representations of the function may be more useful.

Equation

$p = 20n$

or

$p(n) = 20n$

Table

n	p
50	1000
100	2000
150	3000
200	4000

Graph

p: 8000, 6000, 4000, 2000; 0; n: 100 200 300 400

These different representations can help the manager set, compare, and predict prices.

EXAMPLE 1 ***Business Application***

A manager at an amusement park monitors the ticket sales at the park over a four-day weekend. Match each situation to one of the following graphs. Sketch a possible graph of the situation if the situation does not match any of the given graphs.

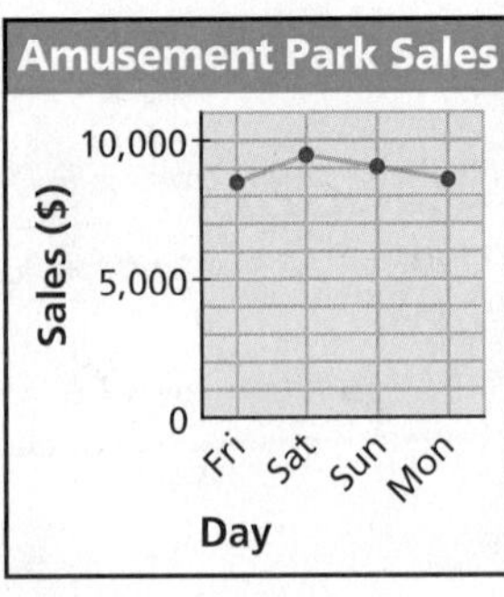

Graph 1

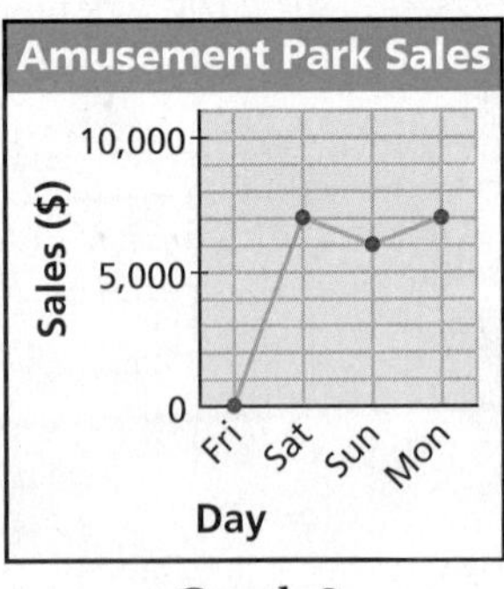

Graph 2

Graph 3

A **The park was closed on Friday for repairs.**

graph 2 *The graph shows no ticket sales on Friday.*

B **The park hosted a big concert on Saturday and a parade on Monday.**

graph 3 *The graph shows increased ticket sales on Saturday and Monday.*

C **The park was very busy during the holiday weekend.**

graph 1 *The graph shows high ticket sales every day.*

What if...? Sketch a possible graph to represent the following.

1a. The weather was beautiful on Friday and Saturday, but it rained all day on Sunday and Monday.

1b. Only $\frac{1}{2}$ of the rides were running on Friday and Sunday.

Because each representation of a function (words, equation, table, or graph) describes the same relationship, you can often use any representation to generate the others.

EXAMPLE 2 *Recreation Application*

Kurt is rappelling down a 500-foot cliff at a rate of 6 feet per second. Create a table, equation, and graph to represent Kurt's height from the ground with relation to time. When will Kurt reach the ground?

Step 1 Create a table.

Let t be the time in seconds and h be Kurt's height, in feet, from the ground.

Kurt begins at a height of 500 feet, and the height decreases by 6 feet each second.

t	h
0	500
1	494
2	488
3	482
4	476
5	470

500 − 6
500 − 6(2)
500 − 6(3)
500 − 6(4)
500 − 6(5)

Step 2 Write an equation.

Height	is equal to	500	minus	6 feet per second.
h	$=$	500	$-$	$6t$

Step 3 Find the intercepts and graph the equation.

h-intercept: 500

Solve for t when $h = 0$.

$$h = 500 - 6t$$
$$0 = 500 - 6t$$
$$-500 = -6t$$

t-intercept: $83\frac{1}{3}$

Height (ft)
h
400
300
200
100
0
20 40 60 80
t
Time (s)

Kurt will reach the ground after $83\frac{1}{3}$ seconds.

2. The table shows the height, in feet, of an arrow in relation to its horizontal distance from the archer. Create a graph, an equation, and a verbal description to represent the height of the arrow with relation to its horizontal distance from the archer.

Arrow Distance and Height						
Distance from Archer (ft)	0	75	150	225	300	375
Height (ft)	6.55	59.80	90.55	98.80	84.50	47.50

Translating Between Multiple Representations	
When given a(n)...	**Try to...**
Table	• Find finite differences or ratios to determine which parent function best describes the data. • Graph points as ordered pairs and look for a pattern. • Match the data to the related parent function, if applicable, and perform a regression.
Graph	• Identify which parent function the graph most resembles, and then use key points (intercepts, maxima, minima, and so on) from the graph to help write an equation. • Locate several points on the graph and write them in a table. • Use slope; increasing, decreasing, or constant intervals; and intercepts to write a verbal description.
Equation	• Make a table of values. You may use a graphing calculator. • Make a graph by using transformations of parent functions or a graphing calculator.
Verbal Description	• Identify dependent and independent variables, and write an algebraic equation. • Generate a table of values by using the pattern described. • Sketch a graph of the situation by using hints from the description about increasing, decreasing, or constant intervals, as well as intercepts.

EXAMPLE 3 Using Multiple Representations to Solve Problems

A **Stacy runs three days a week at a track. Stacy starts keeping time when she starts warming up and notes after every 2 laps how long she has been at the track. The table shows the times for several laps. Use a graph and an equation to find the time it will take Stacy to run 20 laps.**

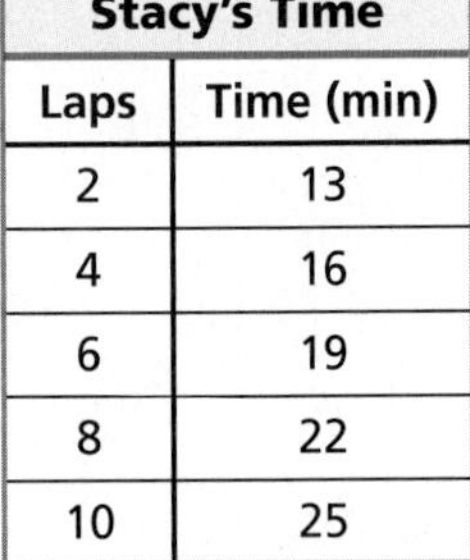

Stacy's Time	
Laps	Time (min)
2	13
4	16
6	19
8	22
10	25

Step 1 Graph the data.

The data appear to be linear.

Step 2 Write a linear equation.

Let x = the number of laps and y = the time in minutes.

$m = \frac{y_2 - y_1}{x_2 - x_1} = \frac{16 - 13}{4 - 2} = \frac{3}{2}$ *Find the slope. Use any two points.*

$y - y_1 = m(x - x_1)$ *Point-slope form*

$y - 13 = \frac{3}{2}(x - 2)$ *Use (2, 13) and slope $\frac{3}{2}$.*

$y = \frac{3}{2}x + 10$ *Simplify.*

Step 3 Evaluate the function for 20 laps.

$y = \frac{3}{2}(20) + 10 = 40.$

It will take Stacy 40 minutes to complete 20 laps.

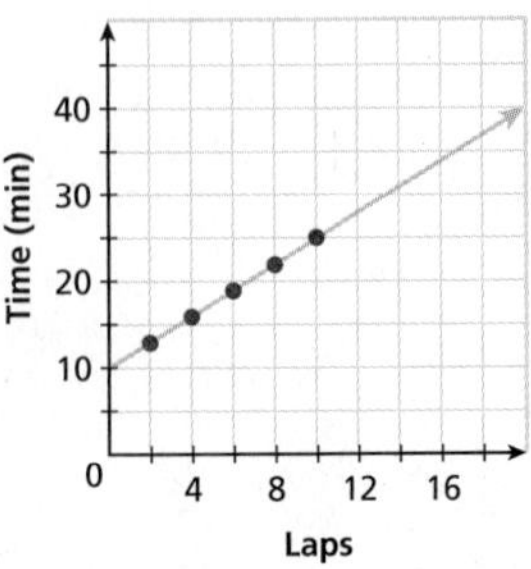

Remember!

The point-slope form of the equation of a line is $y - y_1 = m(x - x_1)$, where m is the slope and (x_1, y_1) is a point on the line.

B **The owner of an orange grove finds that if 26 trees are planted per acre, each mature tree yields about 576 oranges per year. For each additional tree planted per acre, the number of oranges produced annually by each tree decreases by 12. Use a table, a graph, and an equation to find how many trees per acre should be planted to maximize the yield per acre.**

Make a table for an acre of orange trees. Because the orchard owner is interested in the total number of oranges, make a graph by using trees t as the independent variable and total oranges as the dependent variable.

Orange Tree Yield

Trees	Oranges per Tree	Total Oranges
26	576	14,976
27	564	15,228
28	552	15,456
29	540	15,660
30	528	15,840
31	516	15,996
32	504	16,128

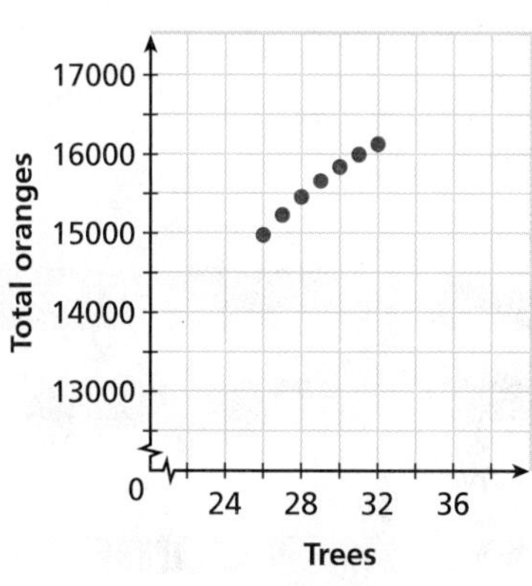

The data do not appear to be linear, so check finite differences.

Total oranges	14,976	15,228	15,456	15,660	15,840	15,996	16,128
First differences	252	228	204	180	156	132	
Second differences	−24	−24	−24	−24	−24		

Remember!

First differences are constant in linear functions. Second differences are constant in quadratic functions.

Because the second differences are constant, a quadratic model is appropriate. Use a graphing calculator to perform a quadratic regression on the data.

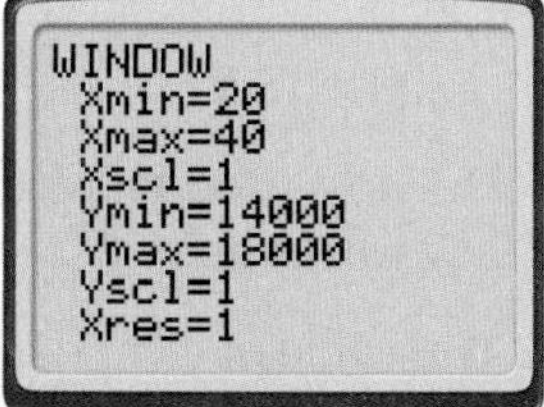

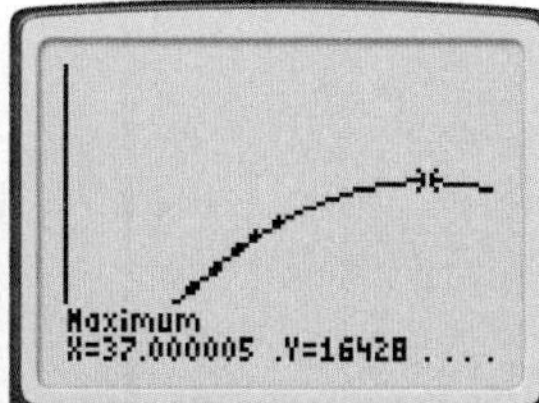

The equation $y = -12x^2 + 888x$ models the data, and the graph appears to fit. Use the **TRACE** or **MAXIMUM** feature to identify the maximum orange yield.

The maximum occurs when 37 trees are planted on each acre.

3. Bartolo opened a new sporting goods business and has recorded his sales each week. To break even, Bartolo needs to sell $48,000 worth of merchandise in a week. Assuming the sales trend continues, use a graph and an equation to find the number of weeks before Bartolo breaks even.

Bartolo's Sales

Week	Sales ($)
1	25,000
2	27,500
3	30,250
4	33,275
5	36,603

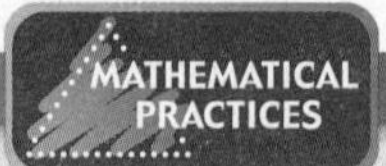

THINK AND DISCUSS

1. Explain how to use a table to help create an equation for a set of data.
2. Give an example of a real-world situation where a graph might be the most useful representation of a set of data.
3. **GET ORGANIZED** Copy and complete the graphic organizer. In each box give an example.

Know it! Note

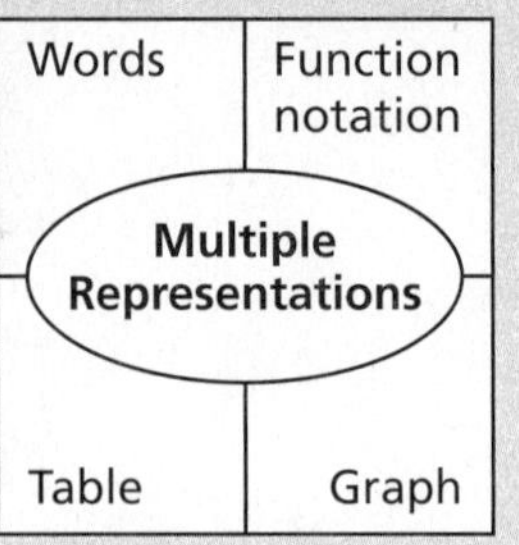

6-1 Exercises

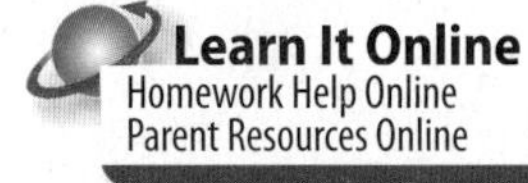

GUIDED PRACTICE

SEE EXAMPLE 1

Match each situation to its corresponding graph. Sketch a possible graph of the situation if the situation does not match any of the given graphs.

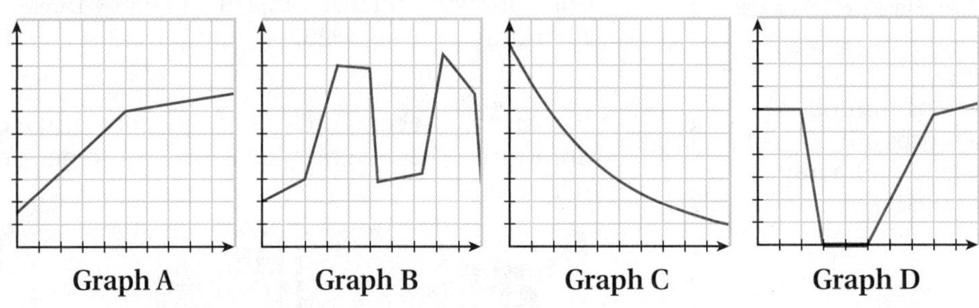

1. Due to a product recall, a company's profits drop sharply into a loss but rebound a few weeks later.
2. The value of a car declines as the car gets older.
3. A souvenir shop's sales are seasonal, with high sales in summer and winter and low sales in spring and fall.
4. An airplane ascends to a peak height of 30,000 feet and then descends to a cruising altitude of 24,000 feet.

SEE EXAMPLE 2

5. **Education** Part-time students at a university must pay an enrollment fee of $179.35, plus $218.40 per credit hour. Create a table, an equation, and a graph that give the total cost of enrollment as a function of credit hours.

SEE EXAMPLE 3

6. **Recreation** Claire is hiking up the South Kaibab Trail at the Grand Canyon. The table shows Claire's altitude above sea level every 15 minutes after she starts to hike. Use a graph and an equation to find how long it will take Claire to reach the rim of the canyon at 7260 feet.

Claire's Altitude

Time (min)	Altitude (ft)
15	2940
30	3240
45	3540
60	3840
75	4140

Independent Practice	
For Exercises	See Example
7–10	1
11–12	2
13–14	3

Extra Practice

See Extra Practice for more Skills Practice and Applications Practice exercises.

PRACTICE AND PROBLEM SOLVING

Match each situation to its corresponding graph. Sketch a possible graph of the situation if the situation does not match any of the given graphs.

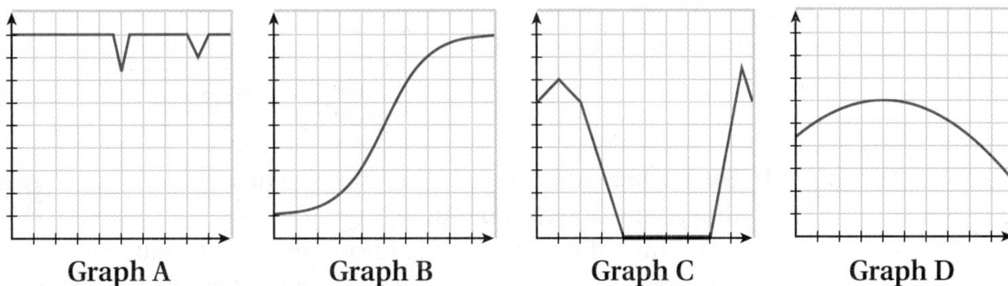

Graph A Graph B Graph C Graph D

7. The sales of lift tickets at a ski resort are highest at the beginning and end of the year.
8. The attendance at a pop singer's concerts is steadily high except on two nights.
9. The population of a city peaked in the 1980s and has been decreasing slowly but steadily in the years since.
10. Sales of a new type of cell phone increase rapidly and then level off.
11. **Health** Carl has a severe fever, so his doctor advises him to take his temperature every 4 hours until it falls below 100°F. The table shows Carl's temperature with relation to time. Create a graph, an equation, and a verbal description to represent Carl's temperature with relation to time. When will Carl's temperature drop below 100°F?

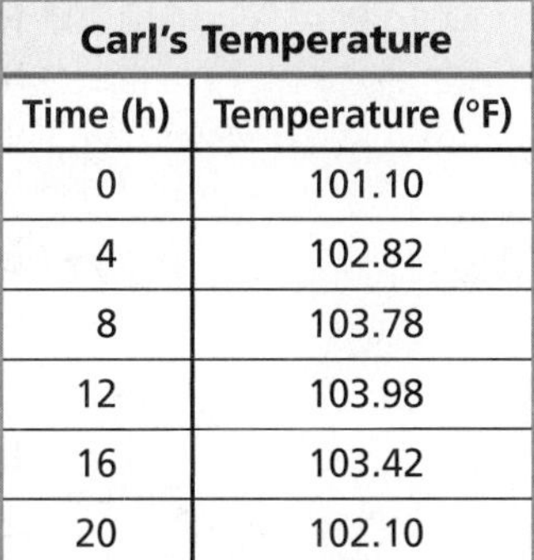

Carl's Temperature

Time (h)	Temperature (°F)
0	101.10
4	102.82
8	103.78
12	103.98
16	103.42
20	102.10

12. **Transportation** A truck begins a trip of 1675 miles. The truck averages 55 miles per hour, including stops. Create a table, a graph, and an equation to represent the distance that the truck has left to travel with relation to time.

LINK

Whales

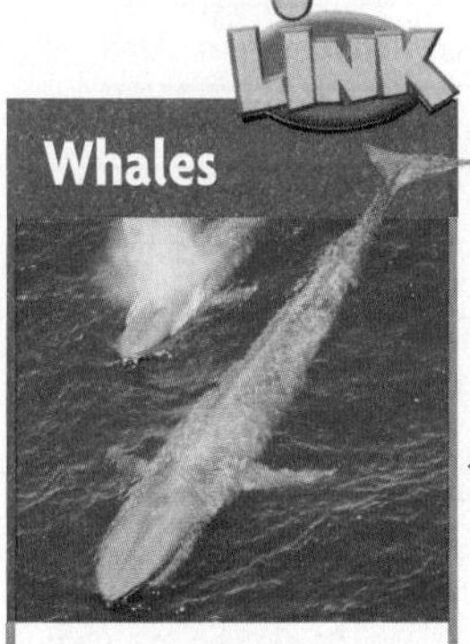

Blue whales are the largest and loudest animals on Earth. Their calls can reach intensity levels of 180 decibels, louder than a jet airplane.

13. **Whales** Researchers are studying the growth of a young blue whale. The graph shows the approximate weight of the whale from birth to 8 months.
    a. Find an equation for the weight of the whale as a function of time, and describe the relationship in words.
    b. Will the weight of the whale continue to increase by the same amount each month? Explain your answer.

Weight of a Blue Whale from Birth

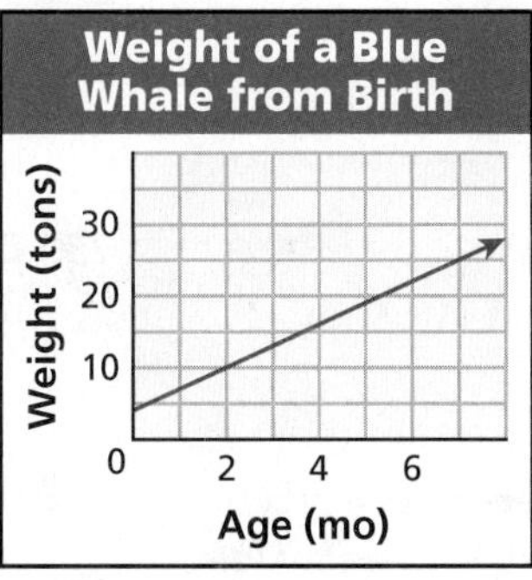

14. **Business** Alex is painting a house. When Alex starts work on Monday morning, there are 2452 square feet of surface area that remain to be painted. Alex can paint 64 square feet of surface area in an hour.
    a. Write an equation for the amount of surface area that Alex has left to paint after t hours.
    b. If Alex works for 40 hours a week, will he be able to finish painting the house in a week?
15. **Sports** The owners of a minor league hockey team have found that when they charge \$12 for a lower-level seat, they average 800 fans per game. For every \$1 increase in ticket price, the attendance decreases by an average of 50 people. Find the ticket price that will maximize revenue for the team's owners.

Classify each function as linear, absolute-value, quadratic, exponential, or rational, and justify your choice.

16. 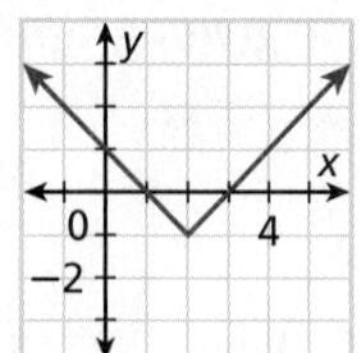

17. 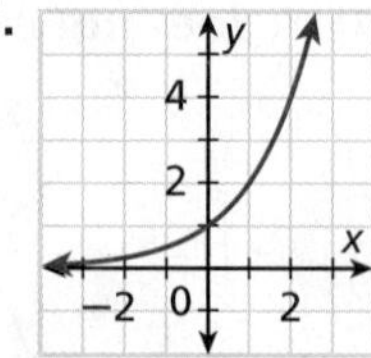

18. 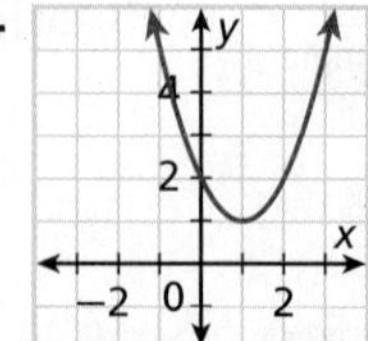

19. Bu siness In order to better manage her restaurant, Rita counts the number of people who are in the restaurant at the end of every hour after the restaurant is opened. The results are shown in the graph.

a. Write a function for the graph.

b. According to your function, what was the maximum number of customers in Rita's restaurant on this evening?

c. Based on the function, when will there be no customers in Rita's restaurant?

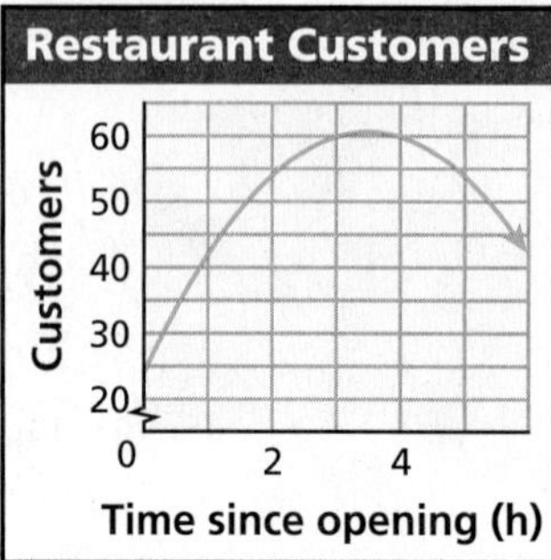

20. Hobbies Susan collects antique dolls. In 2005, her collection contained 6 dolls. She plans to double the number of dolls in her collection every year. Use a table, a graph, and an equation to determine when Susan will have more than 100 dolls in her collection.

21. Forestry The *Sorbus aucuparia*, or mountain ash tree, typically grows to the heights shown in the table.

a. Create a graph of height versus time.

b. Write a function that models the height.

c. During which year would you expect the height to reach 18 ft?

Growth of Mountain Ash

Year	Height (ft)
1	4
3	7
6	10
10	13

22. Write About It Describe a different situation in which you would find each representation of a function, including a table, a graph, and an equation, useful.

23. Critical Thinking When would a graph give you more evidence about a relationship than a table would? When would a table give more evidence than a graph would?

24. A group of people stand in a circle and hold hands. One person squeezes the hand of the person on her left, who then squeezes the hand of the next person, and so on. The table shows the time that it takes the signal to go all the way around the circle.

a. Create a graph of time versus the number of participants.

b. Write a function that models the situation.

c. Suppose the signal takes about a minute to go around the circle. How many participants are there?

Time for Hand Squeeze to Complete a Cycle

People	Time (s)
5	2.10
8	3.36
14	5.88
23	9.66

TEST PREP

25. **Business** This graph shows data on the number of olive slices on pizzas of different radii. Let r represent the radius of the pizza and n represent the number of olive slices. Identify the equation that best represents the relationship between the radius and the number of olive slices.

Number of Olive Slices on Pizzas

Olive slices: 0, 30, 60, 90, 120

Radius (in.): 2, 4, 6, 8

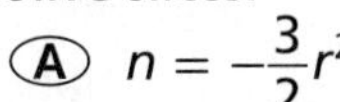

Ⓐ $n = -\frac{3}{2}r^2$ Ⓒ $n = \frac{3}{2}r^2$

Ⓑ $n = -6r$ Ⓓ $n = 6r$

26. A charity is selling American flags to celebrate Independence Day. The charity's profit in dollars is modeled by $p = \frac{1}{2}n$, where n is the number of flags sold. Which of the following choices identifies the same function?

Ⓐ The profit is \$2 per flag.

Ⓑ

n	1	2	3
p	2	4	6

Ⓒ For every 2 flags sold, the profit is \$1.

Ⓓ

n	1	2	3	4
p	0.5	1.5	2.5	3.5

27. **Short Response** Which type of function would best model the cost for carpeting a square room as a function of the room's width? Explain your answer.

CHALLENGE AND EXTEND

Write an equation and create a graph for each situation described.

28. The volume of a box for a glass decoration is found by doubling the radius of the decoration, raising it to the third power, and then adding 10.

29. The total cost of an item at a sale is found by taking off a 20% discount, subtracting a \$10-off coupon, and adding 6.5% sales tax.

30. **Finance** Sharmila was able to save \$500 from her summer job. She put the money into a mutual fund. This table shows how the value of Sharmila's money has grown.

Sharmila's Mutual Fund

Year	Value (\$)
1	545.00
2	594.00
3	647.51
4	705.79
5	769.31

   a. Write an appropriate model for the amount that Sharmila will have in this mutual fund after t years.

   b. Use your model to predict when Sharmila will have \$2000 in the mutual fund.

6-2 Comparing Functions

CC.9-12.F.IF.9 Compare properties of two functions each represented in a different way… *Also* **CC.9-12.F.IF.6***

Objective
Compare properties of two functions. Estimate and compare rates of change.

Who uses this?
A real estate developer may use graphs of exponential population growth to decide when and where to invest.

The graph of the exponential function $y = 0.2491e^{0.0081x}$ approximates the population growth in Baltimore, Maryland.

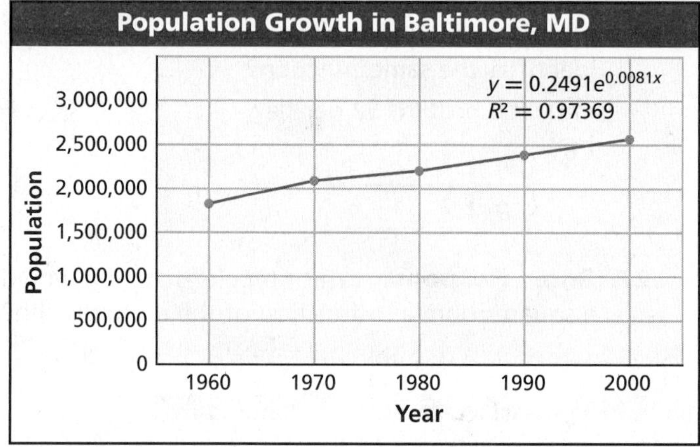

The graph of the exponential function $y = 0.0023e^{0.0089x}$ approximates the population growth in Hagerstown, Maryland. The trends can be used to predict what the population will be in the future in each city.

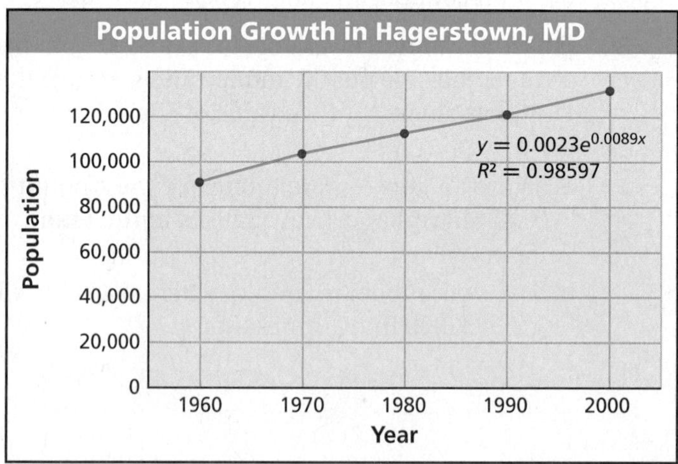

In this lesson, you will compare the graphs of linear, quadratic, and exponential functions.

Minimum and Maximum

A **linear function** will not have a minimum or maximum. A **quadratic function** will have either an absolute minimum or an absolute maximum. Polynomials of degree 3 or higher may have both local and absolute minimum or maximum values.

EXAMPLE 1 Comparing the Average Rates of Change of Two Functions

Katie and Jackie swim laps every day. They each keep track of the time it takes to complete their laps. Jackie's times are shown in the graph, and Katie's times are shown in the table. Compare the average rates and explain what the difference in rate of change represents.

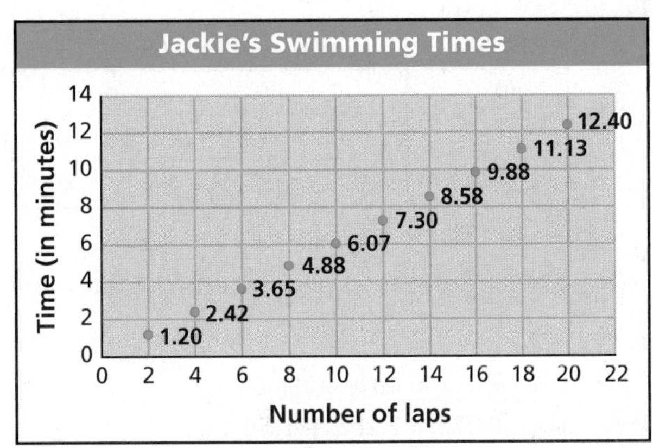

Katie's Swimming Times

Number of Laps	Time Elapsed (in minutes)
2	1.08
4	2.22
6	3.43
8	4.70
10	5.98
12	7.13
14	8.23
16	9.40
18	10.60
20	11.77

Helpful Hint

Remember, to find the average rate of change over a data set, find the slope between the first and last data point.

Step 1 Find the average rate of change for each of the data sets.

Rate of change for Jackie's data: $m = \frac{y_2 - y_1}{x_2 - x_1} = \frac{12.40 - 1.2}{20 - 2} \approx 0.62$

Rate of change for Katie's data: $m = \frac{y_2 - y_1}{x_2 - x_1} = \frac{11.77 - 1.08}{20 - 2} \approx 0.59$

Step 2 Compare the rates and interpret the data.

Katie's rate of change is less than Jackie's rate of change. In this case, the rate of change represents the average time per lap, so Jackie has a faster average speed per lap than Katie.

1. John and Mike opened savings accounts on the same day. They did not deposit any money initially, but deposited each week as shown by the graph and the table. Compare the average rates of change and explain what the rates represent in this situation.

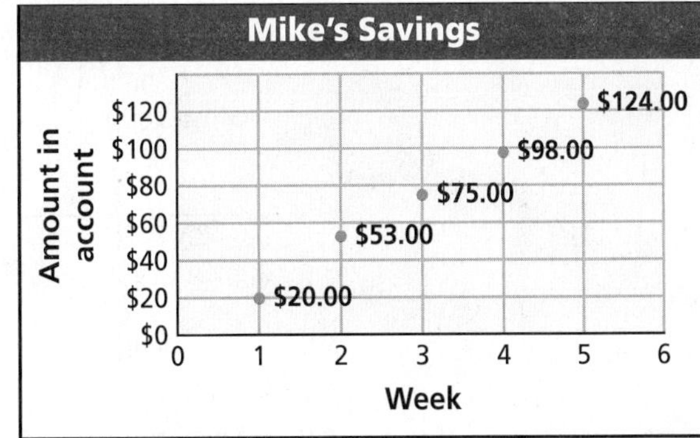

John's Savings

Week	Amount in Account
1	$25.00
3	$86.00
4	$106.00
5	$130.00
8	$204.00

EXAMPLE 2 Sketching Graphs of Functions Given Key Features

Saul launched an object from the ground. The graph for the height of the object, $h(t)$, in meters after t seconds passes through the points (0, 0), (2, 3.2), and (1.5, 6.075). Sketch a graph of the quadratic equation that models the situation. Find the point that represents the maximum height of the object.

Step 1 Use the points to find the values of a, b, and c in the function $h(t) = at^2 + bt + c$.

$(t, h(t))$	$h(t) = at^2 + bt + c$	System in a, b, c
(0, 0)	$0 = a(0)^2 + b(0) + c$	$0 = c$
(2, 3.2)	$3.2 = a(2)^2 + b(2) + c$	$3.2 = 4a + 2b + c$
(1.5, 6.075)	$6.075 = a(1.5)^2 + b(1.5) + c$	$6.075 = 2.25a + 1.5b + c$

Step 2 Solve the system found in Step 1 and write the equation.

$$\begin{cases} 0 = c \\ 3.2 = 4a + 2b + c \\ 6.075 = 2.25a + 1.5b + c \end{cases}$$

$$\begin{cases} 3.2 = 4a + 2b + 0 \\ 6.075 = 2.25a + 1.5b + 0 \end{cases}$$

Substitute $c = 0$ in 2nd and 3rd equation.

$$\begin{cases} 4.8 = 6a + 3b \\ -12.15 = -4.5a - 3b \end{cases}$$

Multiply the first equation by 1.5 and the second equation by –2 in order to use elimination.

$$-7.35 = 1.5a$$

Add equations and solve.

$$-4.9 = a$$

$$3.2 = 4(-4.9) + 2b + 0$$

$$3.2 = -19.6 + 2b$$

$$11.4 = b$$

$$h(t) = -4.9t^2 + 11.4t$$

Helpful Hint

Remember, in the equation $f(x) = a(x - h)^2 + k$, the point (h, k) represents the vertex.

Step 3 Find the maximum height of the function by finding the vertex. Graph the function and approximate the vertex.

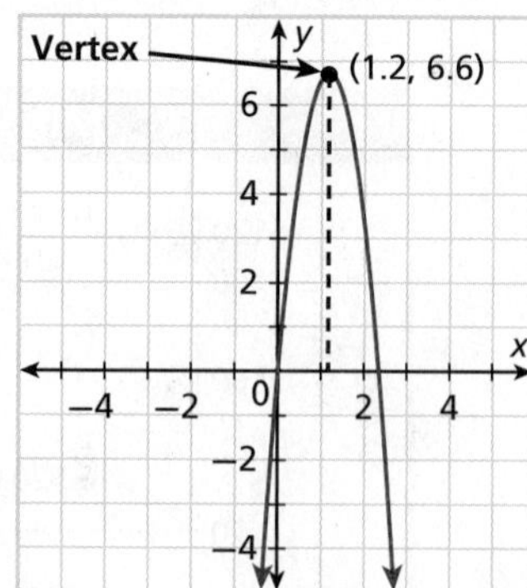

The maximum height of the object is approximately 6.6 meters.

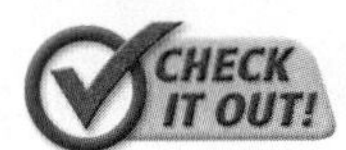

2. The height of a model rocket after launch is tracked in the table. Find and graph a quadratic function that describes the data.

Time (s)	0.5	1.5	2.5
Height (ft)	31	59	55

EXAMPLE 3

Comparing Exponential and Polynomial Functions

Compare the end behavior of the functions $f(x) = 3^x$ and $g(x) = x^4$.

Graph each of the functions.

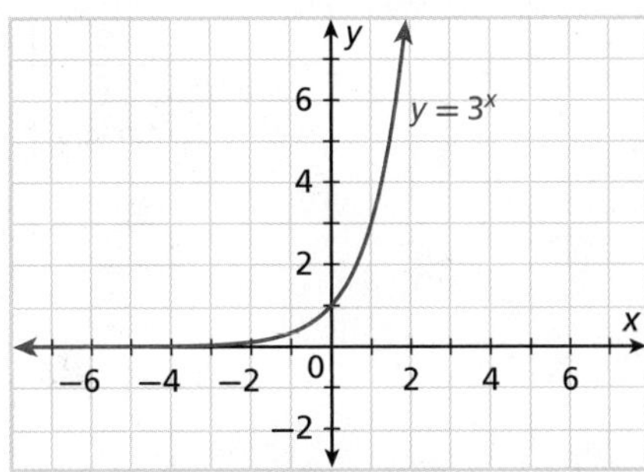

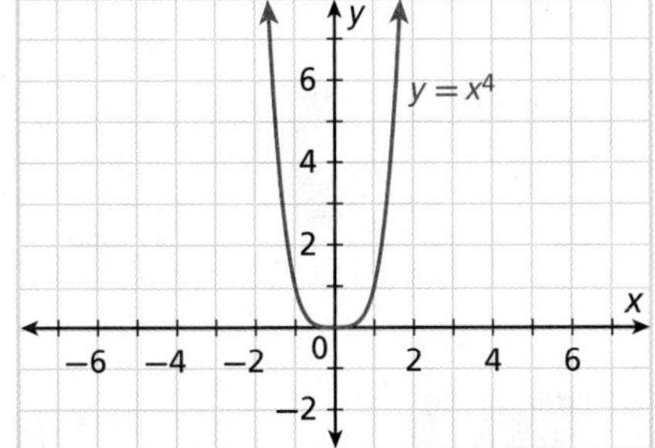

The end behavior for the graph of $f(x) = 3^x$:

As x approaches positive infinity, $f(x)$ approaches positive infinity. As x approaches negative infinity, $f(x)$ approaches 0.

The end behavior for the graph of $g(x) = x^4$:

As x approaches positive infinity, $f(x)$ approaches positive infinity. As x approaches negative infinity, $f(x)$ approaches positive infinity.

3. Compare the end behavior of the functions $f(x) = 4x^2$ and $g(x) = x^3$.

Exponential Function End Behavior

For a function of the form $f(x) = ab^x$, $a > 0$		For a function of the form $f(x) = ab^x$, $a < 0$	
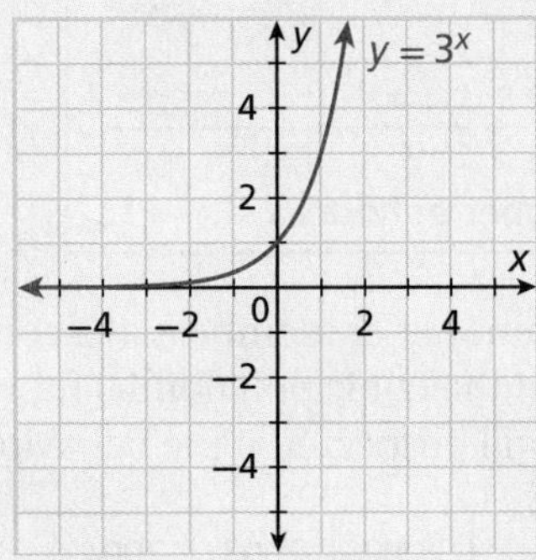		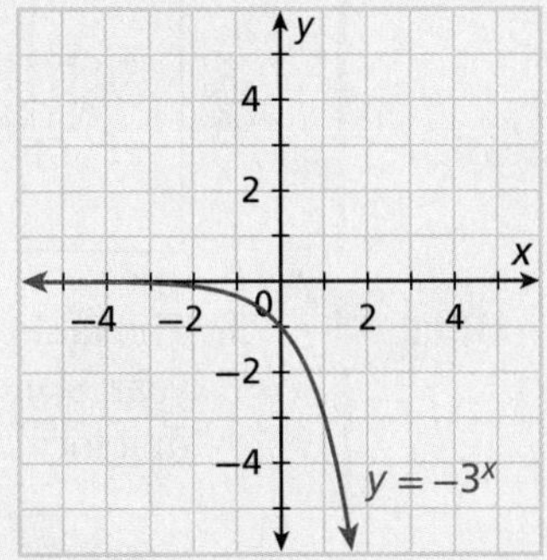	
As $x \to +\infty$ $f(x) \to +\infty$	As $x \to -\infty$ $f(x) \to 0$	As $x \to +\infty$ $f(x) \to -\infty$	As $x \to -\infty$ $f(x) \to 0$

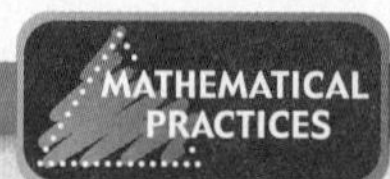

THINK AND DISCUSS

1. Explain how to find the average rate of change over an interval for a polynomial function.
2. Describe a situation that could be modeled by the function $f(x) = 5x + 25.50$.
3. **GET ORGANIZED** Copy and complete the graphic organizer at right. In each cell, write an example of an equation that satisfies the given end behavior.

		Type of Function
Leading Coefficient $a > 0$	As $x \to +\infty$ $f(x) \to +\infty$ As $x \to -\infty$ $f(x) \to -\infty$	
Leading Coefficient $a < 0$	As $x \to -\infty$ $f(x) \to -\infty$ As $x \to +\infty$ $f(x) \to -\infty$	

6-2 Exercises

GUIDED PRACTICE

1. **Vocabulary** Does the *slope* always represent a rate of change? Explain.

SEE EXAMPLE 1

2. The cost of renting a pedal boat is shown for Company A and Company B below. Compare the y-intercept and hourly rates of each function. Explain what the y-intercept represents in this situation.

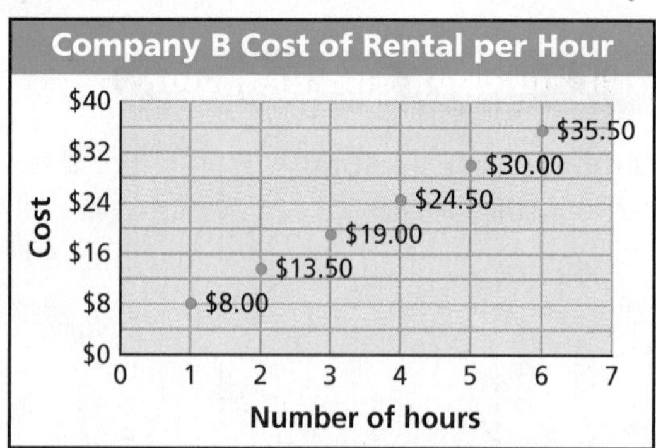

Company A	
Number of Hours	Cost
0.5	$7.25
1.0	$8.50
1.5	$9.75
2.0	$11.00
2.5	$12.25
3.0	$13.50

SEE EXAMPLE 2

3. The table shows the number of members of a community volunteer group per year. Sketch a graph of the cubic polynomial function. Find the year where the first local maximum will be located if the behavior of the graph remains the same.

Year	2002	2003	2004	2005	2006	2007
Number of Members	12	45	69	85	94	97

SEE EXAMPLE 3

4. Compare the end behavior of the functions $f(x) = -2^x$ and $g(x) = e^x$.

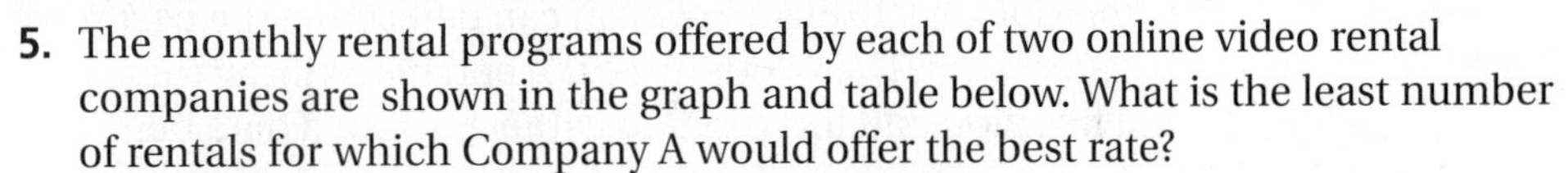

PRACTICE AND PROBLEM SOLVING

Independent Practice

For Exercises	See Example
5	1
6	2
7–10	3

Extra Practice

See Extra Practice for more Skills Practice and Applications Practice exercises.

5. The monthly rental programs offered by each of two online video rental companies are shown in the graph and table below. What is the least number of rentals for which Company A would offer the best rate?

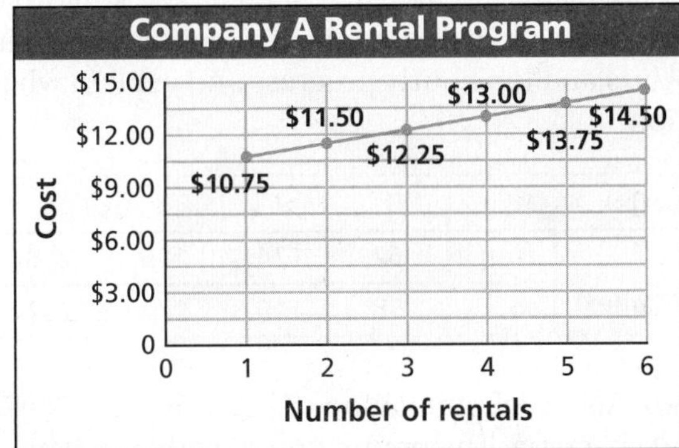

Company B

Number of Rentals	Cost
2	$8.00
4	$11.00
6	$14.00
8	$17.00
10	$20.00
12	$23.00

6. **Estimation** The table shows the height of an object, $h(t)$, in meters after t seconds. Sketch a graph of the quadratic polynomial function. Using the graph, find the approximate time, to the nearest hundredth of a second, after which the object will reach its maximum height.

t	1	2	3	4	5	6
$h(t)$	138.5	147.2	146.1	135.2	114.5	84

Compare the end behavior for each pair of functions.

7. $f(x) = -3x + 4$ and $g(x) = \log_3 x$

8. $f(x) = \sqrt{x}$ and $g(x) = x^2$

9. $f(x) = -e^{2x}$ and $g(x) = 2\log x$

10. $f(x) = -x^3$ and $g(x) = -x^4$

Find the function which matches the graphical representation shown.

11.

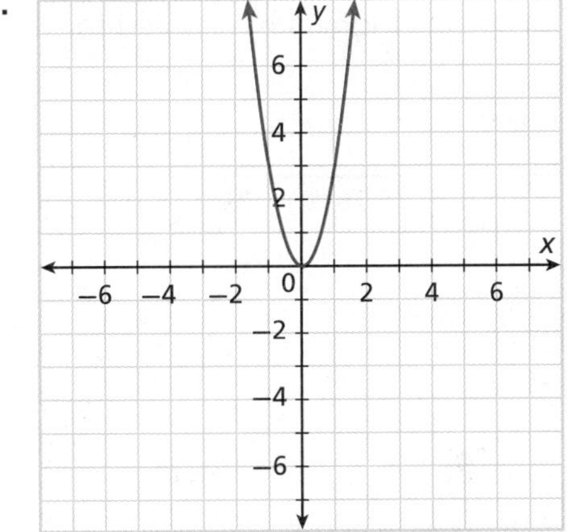

12.

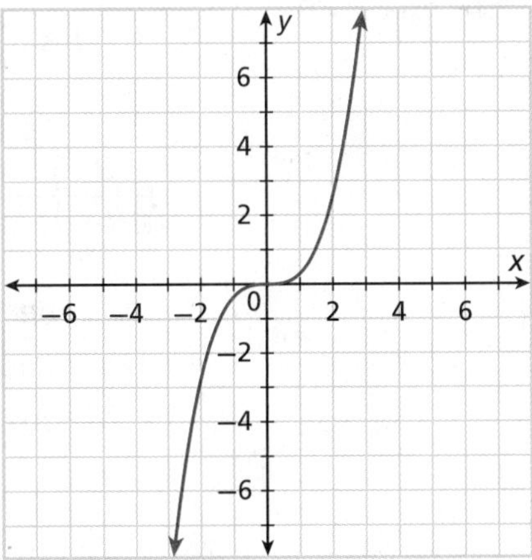

13. Below are two equations. Find the maximum of each, and classify each maximum as absolute maximum or local maximum.

$$f(x) = 3 - (x + 5)^2 \qquad g(x) = x^3 - x^2$$

Find the end behavior of the function.

14. $f(x) = \frac{1}{2}x^5$

15. $f(x) = -e^x$

16. $f(x) = -6^x$

17. $f(x) = 4x^4 + 3$

18. **Write About It** Polynomial function graphs have similarities depending on their degree. Explain how you can determine the best regression for using finite differences. Then determine the end behavior of the graph based on the degree of a function and information gathered from a data table.

19. Ann and Jo are taking a road trip. The first day, Ann drives. The second day, Jo drives. Their hourly progress for the two days is shown in the table. Use a graph to compare Ann's and Jo's hourly progress and explain what the slope represents in this situation.

Time (hours)		1	2	3	4	5	6
Distance traveled (miles)	Ann	62	124	186	248	310	372
	Jo	58	116	174	232	290	348

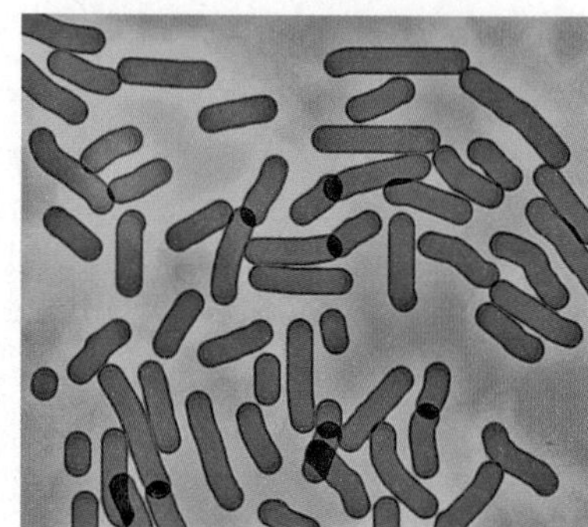

20. **Multi-Step** An initial population of bacteria contains 500 bacteria. The population growth rate is 3.5%. The function $N(t) = 500e^{0.035t}$ gives the population N at time t.
    a. Graph the function for the population growth.
    b. What does the y-intercept represent for this function?

21. **Critical Thinking** Compare the end behavior of the logarithmic functions $f(x) = 3\log x$, $g(x) = \log(3x)$, and $h(x) = \log\left(x^3\right)$.

22. **///ERROR ANALYSIS///** John determined that the average rate of change for the functions $f(x) = 3(x+5)$ and $h(x) = 3\left(\frac{1}{3}x-2\right)$ are the same. Explain the error.

TEST PREP

23. What is the degree of the polynomial best suited for the data below, based on finite differences?

x	4	5	6	7	8
f(x)	5	11	18	26	35

Ⓐ linear
Ⓑ quadratic
Ⓒ cubic
Ⓓ quartic

24. Which of the following describes the end behavior of the function $f(x) = 0.2x^5 + 5$?

Ⓐ As $x \to +\infty$, $f(x) \to +\infty$ and as $x \to -\infty$, $f(x) \to -\infty$
Ⓑ As $x \to +\infty$, $f(x) \to -\infty$ and as $x \to -\infty$, $f(x) \to +\infty$
Ⓒ As $x \to +\infty$, $f(x) \to +\infty$ and as $x \to -\infty$, $f(x) \to +\infty$
Ⓓ As $x \to +\infty$, $f(x) \to -\infty$ and as $x \to -\infty$, $f(x) \to -\infty$

25. Which of the following functions has the greatest rate of change?

Ⓐ $4y + x = 1$

Ⓑ $y + x = -\frac{1}{3}x + 8$

Ⓒ $5y - 10x = 3$

Ⓓ $2y + x = 10$

CHALLENGE AND EXTEND

26. Two car rental companies use different rates per week. The table shows the data for Company A and the graph shows the data for Company B. Compare the *y*-intercepts and the rates per week for each of the companies. Which company would you choose if you were renting a car for 1 week? Which would you choose for 4 weeks? Explain your response.

Company A	
Number of Weeks	Cost
1	$79.00
2	$158.00
3	$237.00
4	$316.00
5	$395.00
6	$474.00

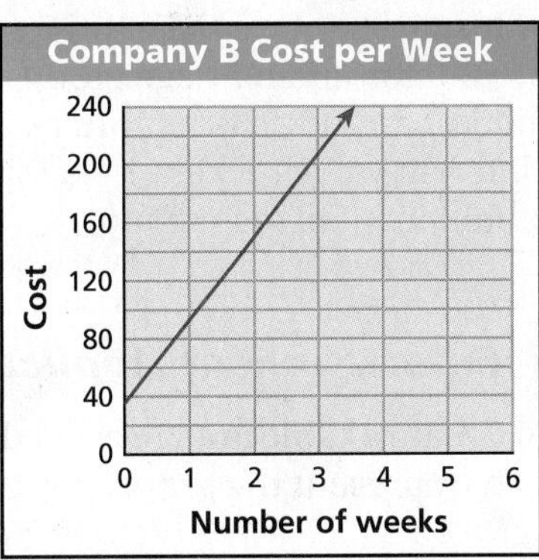

6-3 Piecewise Functions

CC.9-12.A.CED.2 Create equations in two or more variables to represent relationships between quantities; graph equations on coordinate axes with labels and scales. *Also* **CC.9-12.A.CED.3**

Objectives

Write and graph piecewise functions.

Use piecewise functions to describe real-world situations.

Vocabulary

piecewise function
step function

Why learn this?

You can use piecewise functions to model an athlete's performance in a triathlon. (See Example 4.)

A **piecewise function** is a function that is a combination of one or more functions. The rule for a piecewise function is different for different parts, or pieces, of the domain. For instance, movie ticket prices are often different for different age groups. So the function for movie ticket prices would assign a different value (ticket price) for each domain interval (age group).

EXAMPLE 1 *Entertainment Application*

Create a table and a verbal description to represent the graph.

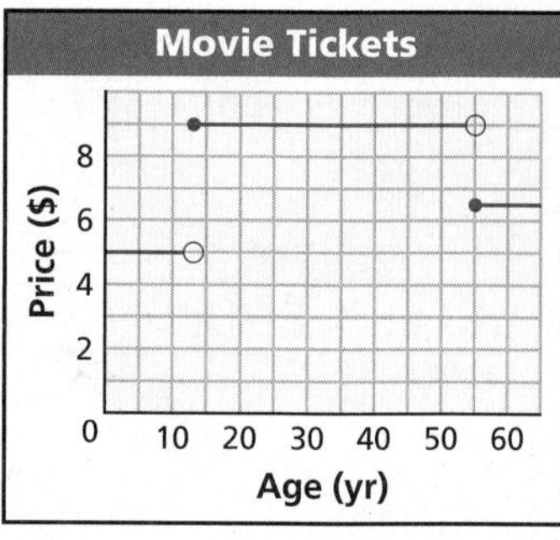

Step 1 Create a table.

Because the endpoints of each segment of the graph identify the intervals of the domain, use the endpoints and points close to them as the domain values in the table.

Remember!

When using interval notation, square brackets [ ] indicate an included endpoint, and parentheses ( ) indicate an excluded endpoint.

Movie Tickets

Age	Price ($)
0–12	5.00
13–54	9.00
55+	6.50

The domain of the function is divided into three intervals:

Ages 12 and under ⟶ $[0, 13)$

Ages 13 and under 55 ⟶ $[13, 55)$

Ages 55 and over ⟶ $[55, \infty)$

Step 2 Write a verbal description.

Use the domain intervals and the prices from the table.

Movie tickets are $5.00 for children ages 12 and under, $9.00 for people ages 13 through 54, and $6.50 for seniors ages 55 years and older.

1. Create a table and a verbal description to represent the graph.

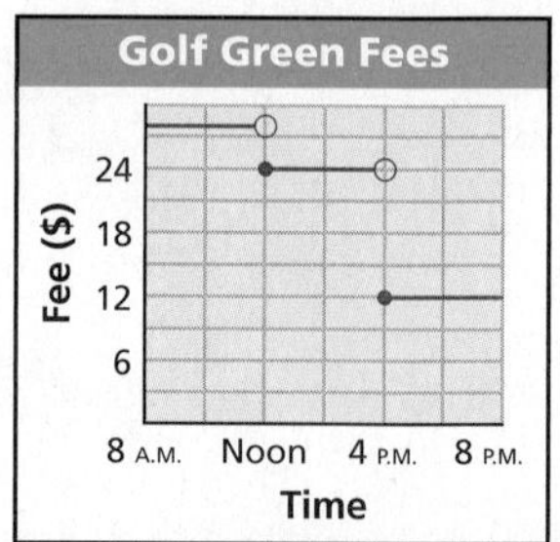

A piecewise function that is constant for each interval of its domain, such as the ticket price function, is called a **step function**. You can describe piecewise functions with a function rule. The rule for the movie ticket prices from Example 1 is shown.

$$f(x) = \begin{cases} 5 & \text{if } 0 < x < 13 \\ 9 & \text{if } 13 \le x < 55 \\ 6.5 & \text{if } x \ge 55 \end{cases}$$

Read this as "*f* of *x* is 5 if *x* is greater than 0 and less than 13, 9 if *x* is greater than or equal to 13 and less than 55, and 6.5 if *x* is greater than or equal to 55."

To evaluate any piecewise function for a specific input, find the interval of the domain that contains that input and then use the rule for that interval.

EXAMPLE 2 Evaluating a Piecewise Function

Evaluate each piecewise function for $x = -2$ and $x = 5$.

A $f(x) = \begin{cases} -5 & \text{if } x \le 0 \\ 4 & \text{if } 0 < x \le 3 \\ 12 & \text{if } x > 3 \end{cases}$

$f(-2) = -5$ *Because $-2 \le 0$, use the rule for $x \le 0$.*

$f(5) = 12$ *Because $5 > 3$, use the rule for $x > 3$.*

B $g(x) = \begin{cases} 3x + 4 & \text{if } x < 5 \\ x^2 - 3 & \text{if } x \ge 5 \end{cases}$

$g(-2) = 3(-2) + 4 = -2$ *Because $-2 < 5$, use the rule for $x < 5$.*

$g(5) = 5^2 - 3 = 22$ *Because $5 \ge 5$, use the rule for $x \ge 5$.*

Evaluate each piecewise function for $x = -1$ and $x = 3$.

2a. $f(x) = \begin{cases} 12 & \text{if } x < -3 \\ 15 & \text{if } -3 \le x < 6 \\ 20 & \text{if } x \ge 6 \end{cases}$ **2b.** $g(x) = \begin{cases} 3x^2 + 1 & \text{if } x < 0 \\ 5x - 2 & \text{if } x \ge 0 \end{cases}$

You can graph a piecewise function by graphing each piece of the function.

EXAMPLE 3 Graphing Piecewise Functions

Graph each function.

A $f(x) = \begin{cases} -4 & \text{if } x < 2 \\ 4 & \text{if } x \ge 2 \end{cases}$

The function is composed of two constant pieces that will be represented by horizontal rays. Because the domain is divided at $x = 2$, evaluate both branches of the function at $x = 2$. The function is -4 when $x < 2$, so plot the point $(2, -4)$ with an open circle and draw a horizontal ray to the left. The function is 4 when $x \ge 2$, so plot the point $(2, 4)$ with a solid dot and draw a horizontal ray to the right.

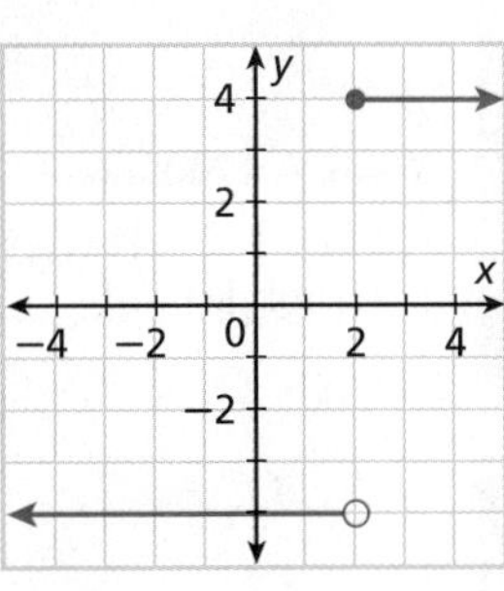

Graph each function.

B $g(x) = \begin{cases} 3x + 8 & \text{if } x \leq -3 \\ -2x & \text{if } -3 < x < 1 \\ x^2 - 3 & \text{if } x \geq 1 \end{cases}$

The function is composed of two linear pieces and a quadratic piece. The domain is divided at $x = -3$ and $x = 1$.

Use a table of values to graph each piece.

x	$g(x) = 3x + 8$	$g(x) = -2x$	$g(x) = x^2 - 3$
−4	−4		
−3	−1	6	
−2		4	
−1		2	
0		0	
1		−2	−2
2			1
3			6

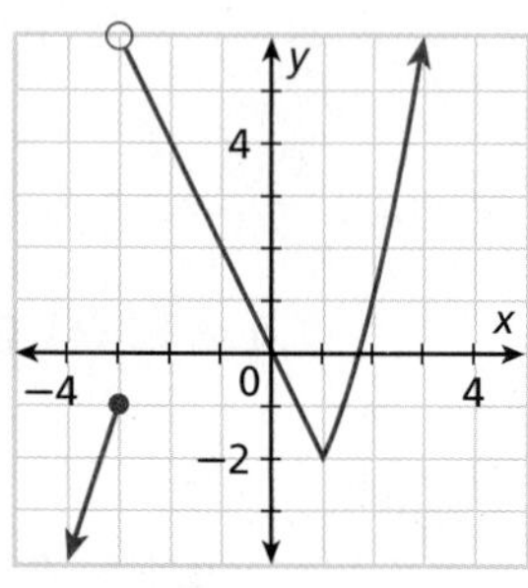

Add a closed circle at $(-3, -1)$ and an open circle at $(-3, 6)$ so that the graph clearly shows the function value when $x = -3$.

No circle is required at $(1, -2)$ because the function is connected at that point.

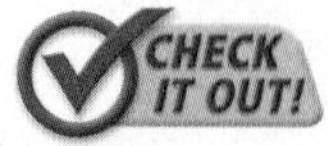

Graph each function.

3a. $f(x) = \begin{cases} 4 & \text{if } x \leq -1 \\ -2 & \text{if } x > -1 \end{cases}$

3b. $g(x) = \begin{cases} -3x & \text{if } x < 2 \\ x + 3 & \text{if } x \geq 2 \end{cases}$

Notice that piecewise functions are not necessarily *continuous*, meaning that the graph of the function may have breaks or gaps.

To write the rule for a piecewise function, determine where the domain is divided and write a separate rule for each piece. Combine the pieces by using the correct notation.

Student to Student

Graphing Piecewise Functions

Mateo Morales
Lee High School

When I graph a piecewise function, I like to graph each piece like it's a separate function. Then I go back and erase the parts that are outside of the restricted domain.

Example: $f(x) = \begin{cases} x + 4 & \text{if } x < -2 \\ -2x & \text{if } x \geq -2 \end{cases}$

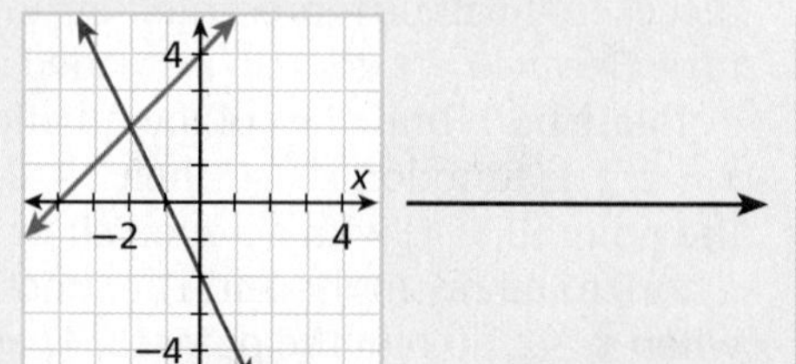

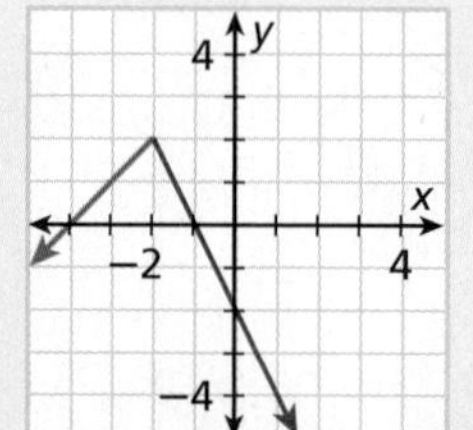

EXAMPLE 4 Sports Application

David is completing a 100-mile triathlon. He swims 2 miles in 1 hour, then bikes 80 miles in 4 hours, and finally he runs 18 miles in 3 hours. Sketch a graph of David's distance versus time. Then write a piecewise function for the graph.

> **Remember!**
> The distance formula $d = rt$ can be rearranged to find rates: $r = \frac{d}{t}$.

Step 1 Make a table to organize the data. Use the distance formula to find David's rate for each leg of the race.

David's Race

Activity	Time (h)	Distance (mi)	Rate (mi/h)
Swimming	1	2	2
Biking	4	80	20
Running	3	18	6

Step 2 Because time is the independent variable, determine the intervals for the function.

Swimming: $0 \leq t \leq 1$ — *He swims for 1 hour.*
Biking: $1 < t \leq 5$ — *He bikes for the next 4 hours.*
Running: $5 < t \leq 8$ — *He runs the final 3 hours.*

Step 3 Graph the function.

After 1 hour, David has covered 2 miles. On the next leg, he reaches a distance of 82 total miles after 5 total hours. Finally, he completes the 100 miles after 8 hours.

Triathlon Distance Covered

Distance (mi) vs. Time (h)

Step 4 Write a linear function for each leg.

Use point-slope form: $y - y_1 = m(x - x_1)$.

Swimming: $d = 2t$ — *Use $m = 2$ and $(0, 0)$.*
Biking: $d = 20t - 18$ — *Use $m = 20$ and $(5, 82)$.*
Running: $d = 6t + 52$ — *Use $m = 6$ and $(8, 100)$.*

The function rule is $d(t) = \begin{cases} 2t & \text{if } 0 \leq t \leq 1 \\ 20t - 18 & \text{if } 1 < t \leq 5 \\ 6t + 52 & \text{if } 5 < t \leq 8 \end{cases}$.

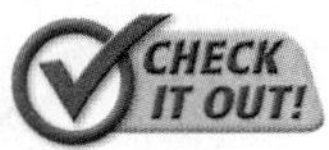

4. Shelly earns \$8 an hour. She earns \$12 an hour for each hour over 40 that she works. Sketch a graph of Shelly's earnings versus the number of hours that she works up to 60 hours. Then write a piecewise function for the graph.

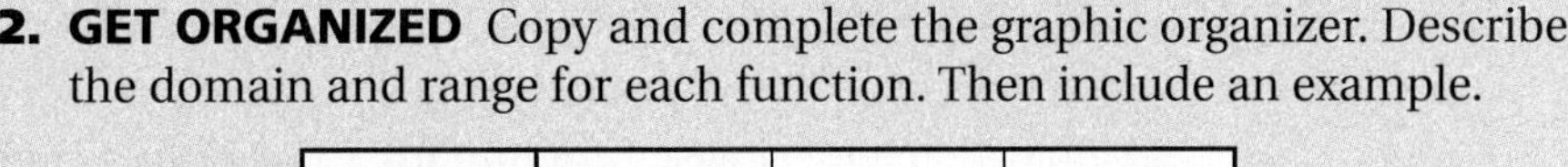

THINK AND DISCUSS

1. Tell whether it is possible to have a continuous step function.

2. GET ORGANIZED Copy and complete the graphic organizer. Describe the domain and range for each function. Then include an example.

Function	Domain	Range	Example
Piecewise			
Step			

6-3 Exercises

GUIDED PRACTICE

1. **Vocabulary** How are step functions related to piecewise functions?

Create a table and a verbal description to represent each graph.

SEE EXAMPLE 1

2. 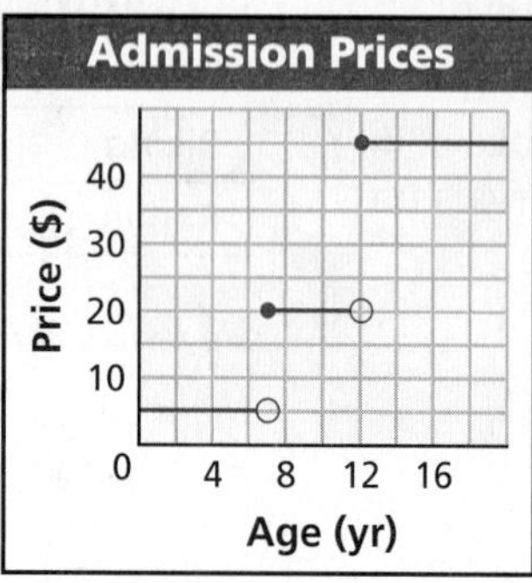

3. 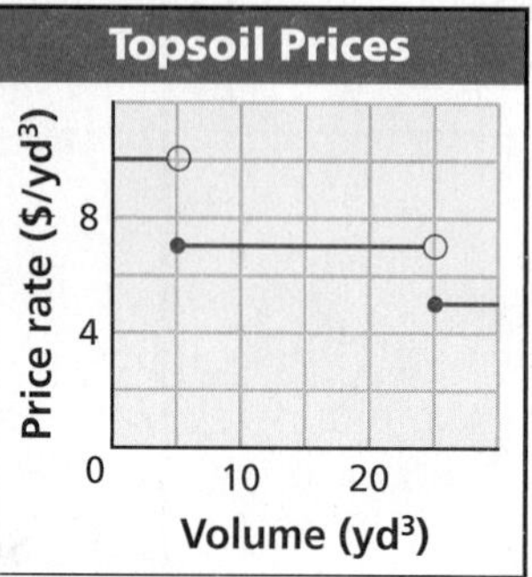

SEE EXAMPLE 2

Evaluate each piecewise function for $x = -6$ and $x = 3$.

4. $f(x) = \begin{cases} -8 & \text{if } x \leq -5 \\ 0 & \text{if } -5 < x < 5 \\ 5 & \text{if } x \geq 5 \end{cases}$

5. $g(x) = \begin{cases} 5x - 9 & \text{if } x < 2 \\ 4 - x^2 & \text{if } x \geq 2 \end{cases}$

SEE EXAMPLE 3

Graph each function.

6. $f(x) = \begin{cases} 7 & \text{if } x < -2 \\ -2 & \text{if } x \geq -2 \end{cases}$

7. $g(x) = \begin{cases} -2x + 8 & \text{if } x \leq 4 \\ \frac{1}{2}x & \text{if } x > 4 \end{cases}$

SEE EXAMPLE 4

8. The cost of renting a canoe is $20 for the first 4 hours and $3 per hour for additional hours. Sketch a graph of the cost of renting a canoe from 0 to 8 hours. Then write a piecewise function for the graph.

PRACTICE AND PROBLEM SOLVING

Independent Practice

For Exercises	See Example
9–10	1
11–12	2
13–14	3
15	4

Extra Practice

See Extra Practice for more Skills Practice and Applications Practice exercises.

Create a table and a verbal description to represent each graph.

9. 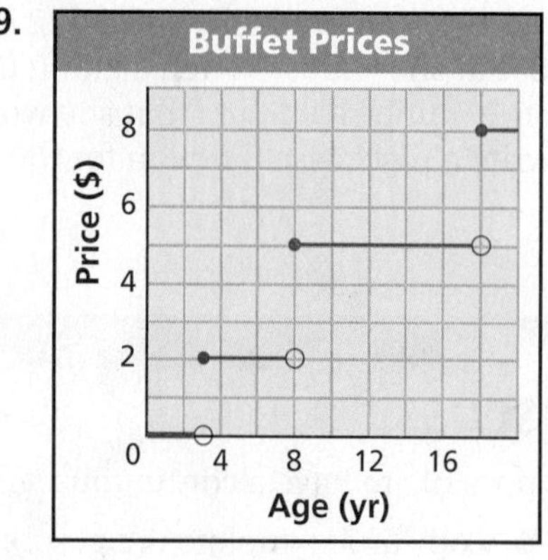

10. 

Evaluate each piecewise function for $x = -2$, $x = 2$, and $x = 6$.

11. $g(x) = \begin{cases} 9x - 2 & \text{if } x < -3 \\ x^2 - 3 & \text{if } -3 \leq x < 1 \\ 5 & \text{if } x \geq 1 \end{cases}$

12. $f(x) = \begin{cases} 12 - 9x & \text{if } x \leq 0 \\ x^2 + 3x & \text{if } 0 < x < 3 \\ 4^x & \text{if } x \geq 3 \end{cases}$

LINK

Pets

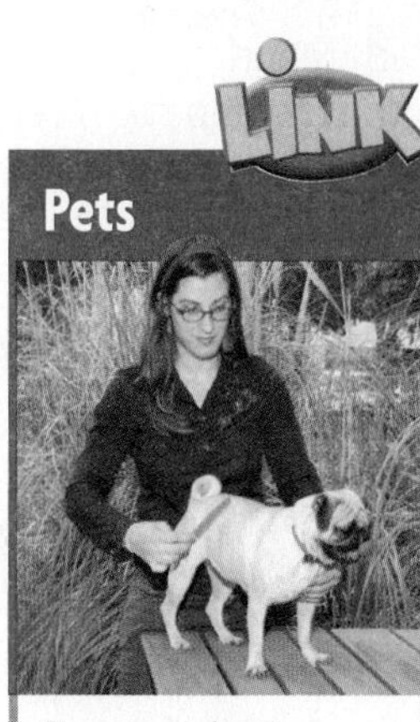

Dog grooming is a \$2 billion industry in the United States. There is evidence that there were dog-grooming parlors in France as early as the 1700s.

Graph each function.

13. $f(x) = \begin{cases} \frac{3}{4}x + 1 & \text{if } x < 4 \\ \frac{3}{4}x - 2 & \text{if } x \geq 4 \end{cases}$

14. $g(x) = \begin{cases} -2x - 5 & \text{if } x < -2 \\ x^2 - 3 & \text{if } x \geq -2 \end{cases}$

15. Pets A dog groomer charges different prices based on the weight of the dog. Sketch a graph of the cost of grooming a dog from 0 to 100 pounds. Then write a piecewise function for the graph.

Grooming Prices	
Weight (lb)	**Price (\$)**
15 and under	30
Over 15 and up to 50	50
Over 50	75

Write a piecewise function for each graph.

16.

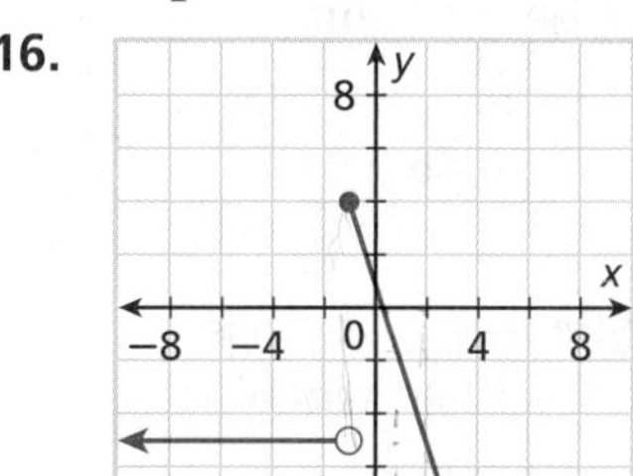

17.

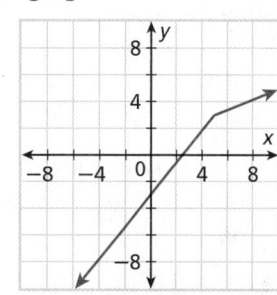

18.

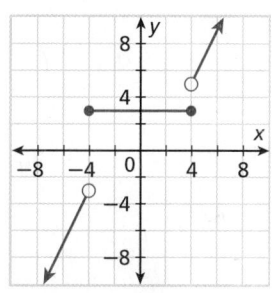

19. Parking A parking garage charges \$6 for the first 4 hours that a car is parked in the lot. After that, the garage charges an additional \$3 an hour. Write a piecewise function for the cost of parking a car in this garage for x hours.

20. Travel Derek and his friends drove from San Francisco to Lake Tahoe to go skiing. The average speed that they traveled during each leg of the trip is shown on the map. They drove 30 min in the city, 3 h on the highway, and 30 min up the mountain.

a. Write a piecewise function to represent the distance that Derek traveled during his 4 h trip.

b. Graph the function.

c. What if...? How much longer would the trip have taken if Derek had averaged 50 mi/h on the highway?

Average Speed

Write each absolute-value function as a piecewise function.

21. $f(x) = |x|$

22. $g(x) = |x - 4|$

23. $h(x) = 2|x| - 4$

24. Shipping An overnight delivery service charges \$11 for a package that weighs 2 pounds or less. The delivery service charges \$3 for each additional pound. Sketch a graph of the cost of shipping a package from 0 to 8 pounds. Then write a piecewise function for the graph.

Graph each function.

25. $h(x) = \begin{cases} \frac{1}{2}x^2 & \text{if } x \leq 0 \\ 2^x - 4 & \text{if } 0 < x \leq 3 \\ 2x - 2 & \text{if } x > 3 \end{cases}$

26. $h(x) = \begin{cases} -3 & \text{if } x \leq 0 \\ 3^x - 4 & \text{if } x > 0 \end{cases}$

27. A human chain is formed by 60 people standing with their arms outstretched, each holding the hand of the person on either side. The first 30 people in the chain have arm spans of 6 feet. The next 30 people have arm spans of 5.5 feet. At the word "go," the first person squeezes the hand of the second person, then the second person squeezes the hand of the third, and so on. Assume that each person takes $\frac{1}{3}$ second to pass along the signal.

a. Write a piecewise function for the distance that the signal travels in t seconds.

b. Does the signal travel faster in the first half of the chain or the second half? How is this shown in the function?

Find the domain and range of each piecewise function.

28. $f(x) = \begin{cases} -\frac{5}{2}x - 2 & \text{if } x \le -2 \\ -x - 5 & \text{if } x > -2 \end{cases}$

29. $g(x) = \begin{cases} x^2 - 2x - 3 & \text{if } x < 4 \\ 3x - 7 & \text{if } x \ge 4 \end{cases}$

30. **Sales** Mary works at a jewelry store. She receives a base salary every week plus a commission based on how much she sells. Mary's income function can be modeled by $P(x) = \begin{cases} 400 + 0.06x & \text{if } 0 \le x \le 5000 \\ 700 + 0.09(x - 5000) & \text{if } x > 5000 \end{cases}$, where $P(x)$ is her income and x is the amount of her sales in dollars.

a. Write a description of Mary's income function.

b. How much will Mary earn in a week in which she sells \$4000 worth of jewelry?

c. Find the value of the jewelry that Mary must sell in a week if she wants to earn \$900 for that week.

31. **Critical Thinking** Why would a piecewise function best describe the height of an elevator t seconds after it leaves the bottom floor of a building? Would the piecewise function also be a step function?

32. **Write About It** Explain why piecewise functions are often good for representing real-world situations. Include at least two examples.

33. A car rental agency charges \$15 a day for driving a car 200 miles or less. If a car is driven over 200 miles, the renter must pay \$0.05 for each mile over 200 driven. Which of the following functions represents the cost to drive a car from this agency x miles in a day?

Ⓐ $C(x) = \begin{cases} 15 & \text{if } 0 \le x \le 200 \\ 0.05x & \text{if } x > 200 \end{cases}$

Ⓑ $C(x) = \begin{cases} 0.05 & \text{if } 0 \le x \le 200 \\ 15x & \text{if } x > 200 \end{cases}$

Ⓒ $C(x) = \begin{cases} 15 & \text{if } 0 \le x \le 200 \\ 15 + 0.05(x - 200) & \text{if } x > 200 \end{cases}$

Ⓓ $C(x) = \begin{cases} 15 & \text{if } 0 \le x \le 200 \\ 15 + 0.05x & \text{if } x > 200 \end{cases}$

34. Which of the following is a continuous function?

Ⓕ $f(x) = \begin{cases} 3x - 4 & \text{if } x < 0 \\ -1 & \text{if } x \ge 0 \end{cases}$

Ⓖ $g(x) = \begin{cases} 5x - 4 & \text{if } x < 3 \\ 2x + 5 & \text{if } x \ge 3 \end{cases}$

Ⓗ $h(x) = \begin{cases} x^2 & \text{if } x < -2 \\ 2x & \text{if } x \ge -2 \end{cases}$

Ⓙ $j(x) = \begin{cases} 3x + 4 & \text{if } x \le -1 \\ 3^x + 4 & \text{if } x > -1 \end{cases}$

35. Let $f(x) = \begin{cases} 1 - 5x & \text{if } x < -5 \\ 3 - x^3 & \text{if } -5 \le x < -2 \\ 5 - x^2 & \text{if } x \ge -2 \end{cases}$. Find $f(-2)$.

Ⓐ -5 Ⓑ 1 Ⓒ 9 Ⓓ 11

CHALLENGE AND EXTEND

The *greatest integer function* returns the greatest integer less than or equal to a given number. The greatest integer function is written $f(x) = \lfloor x \rfloor$ and is often written as int(x) on graphing calculators. For example, if hamburgers cost \$1.79 each, the function $f(x) = \left\lfloor \frac{x}{1.79} \right\rfloor$ would return the number of hamburgers you could buy for x dollars.

36. Write a function for the number of orders of fries that can be bought with x dollars if an order of fries costs \$1.29. Then use your function to find the number of orders of fries that you can buy with \$10.

The *least integer function* returns the least integer greater than or equal to a given number. The least integer function is written $f(x) = \lceil x \rceil$. For example, $f(2.9) = \lceil 2.9 \rceil = 3$.

37. At a parking garage, parking costs \$4 for up to 1 hour. After that, it costs \$1.50 for each additional hour or fraction thereof. Write a function to represent the cost of parking for x hours. Then use the function to find the cost of parking for 5 hours and 23 minutes.

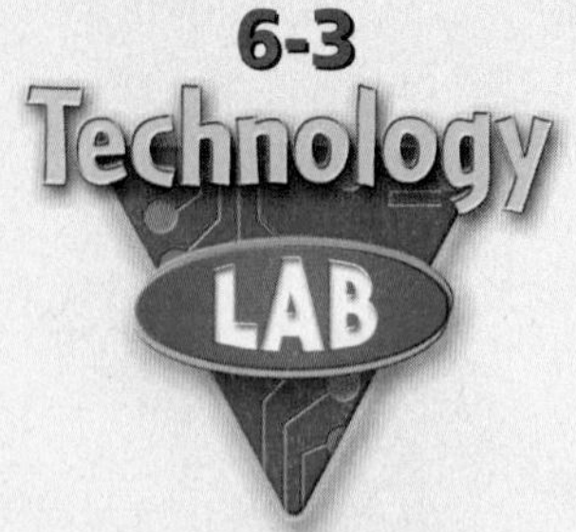

6-3 Technology LAB

Graph Piecewise Functions

You can graph piecewise functions on a graphing calculator by using logical tests to restrict the domain for each piece of the function.

Use with Piecewise Functions

Use appropriate tools strategically.

CC.9-12.F.IF.7b Graph square root, cube root, and piecewise-defined functions, including step functions and absolute value functions.

Activity 1

A graphing calculator can determine whether mathematical statements, such as $5 > 3$, are true. You can enter these statements by using the **TEST** menu. The calculator returns a value of 1 if the statement is true and a value of 0 if the statement is false.

Determine whether 5^7 is greater than or less than 50,000.

Enter the first expression. Access the **TEST** menu (as shown) by pressing 2nd MATH. Choose the less-than symbol (**5:<**), and then enter the second expression. Enter the second inequality using the greater-than symbol (**3:>**).

The first inequality returns a value of 0, so it is false. The second inequality returns a value of 1, so it is true. The expression 5^7 is greater than 50,000.

Try This

Use logical tests to determine whether each statement is true or false.

1. $4 - 3 \stackrel{?}{=} 3 - 4$
2. $(-6)^4 \stackrel{?}{\geq} 1000$
3. $\frac{3}{16} \stackrel{?}{<} 0.1875$
4. $\frac{3}{16} \stackrel{?}{>} 0.1875$
5. **Draw a Conclusion** What conclusion can you make about $\frac{3}{16}$ and 0.1875 based on the answers to Problems 3 and 4?

Activity 2

You can use the commands from the **LOGIC** submenu of the **TEST** menu to create compound logical tests.

Determine whether the statement $3.14 < \pi < \frac{22}{7}$ is true.

Recall that the compound inequality $3.14 < \pi < \frac{22}{7}$ can be written as $3.14 < \pi$ and $\pi < \frac{22}{7}$. Enter the first inequality, and then access the **LOGIC** submenu by pressing 2nd MATH ▶. Choose **1: and,** and then enter the second inequality.

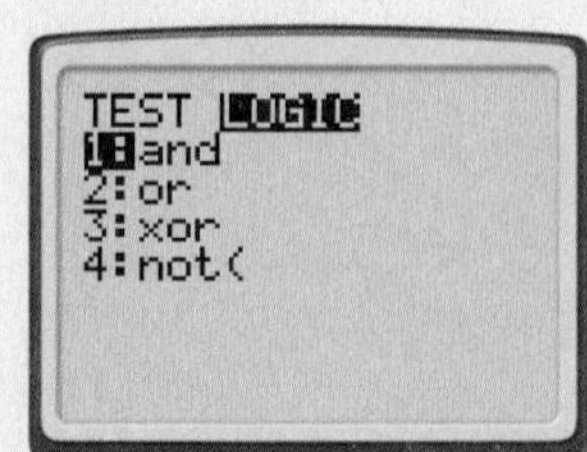

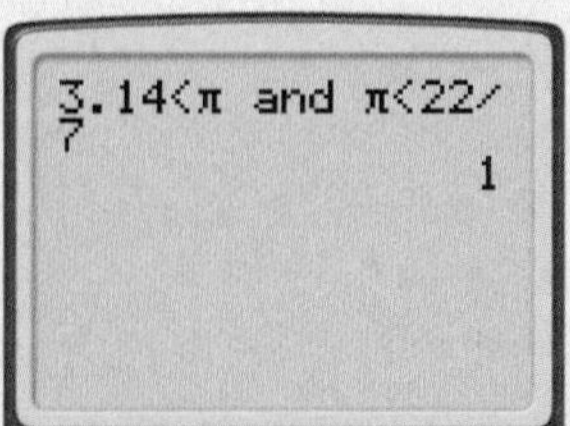

Because the statement returns a value of 1, the statement is true: $3.14 < \pi < \frac{22}{7}$. ✔

Try This

Use logical tests to determine whether each statement is true or false.

6. $-2^2 < -2 < (-2)^2$

7. $(-2)^1 < (-2)^2 < (-2)^3$

8. $\sqrt{2} < 2 < 2^2$

9. $\sqrt{\frac{1}{2}} < \frac{1}{2} < \left(\frac{1}{2}\right)^2$

10. Make a Conjecture What conjecture can you make about the relationship between a number, its square, and its square root if the number is greater than 1? What if the number is between 0 and 1?

Activity 3

Graph the piecewise function $f(x) = \begin{cases} 2x + 7 & \text{if } x \le -2 \\ 3 & \text{if } -2 < x \le 2 \\ x + 1 & \text{if } x > 2 \end{cases}$.

1 Enter the first part of the function rule as **Y1**. Then divide by the domain interval of the first part of the rule. Be sure to enclose both the first part of the rule and the domain interval in parentheses as shown.

The domain interval is a logical test. When the logical test is true, the calculator returns a value of 1, so **Y1** is equal to $2x + 7$. When the logical test is false, the calculator returns a value of 0, so **Y1** is undefined.

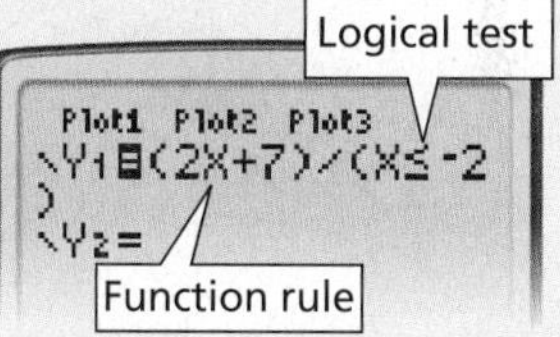

2 Use similar methods to enter the second part of the rule, divided by its domain interval, as **Y2**. Because the domain interval is a compound inequality, use the **and** command from the **LOGIC** menu.

```
Plot1 Plot2 Plot3
\Y1■(2X+7)/(X≤-2
)
\Y2■(3)/(X>-2 an
d X≤2)
\Y3■(X+1)/(X>2)
\Y4=
\Y5=
```

3 Finally, enter the third part of the rule, divided by its domain interval, as **Y3**, and graph in the standard square window.

4 The table shows values for each part of the rule. Notice that for each part, the value of y is undefined outside of the domain interval. (To see values of **Y3**, use the ▶ key to scroll to the right.)

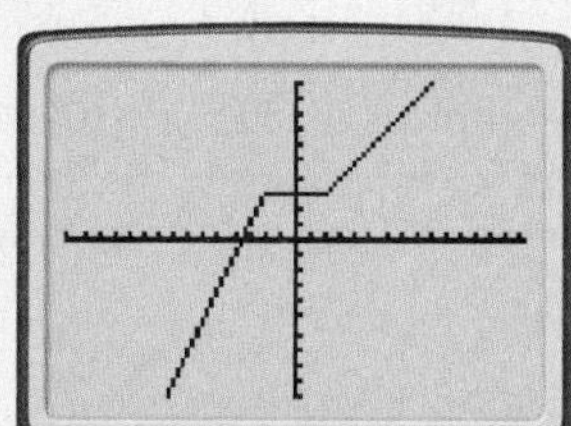

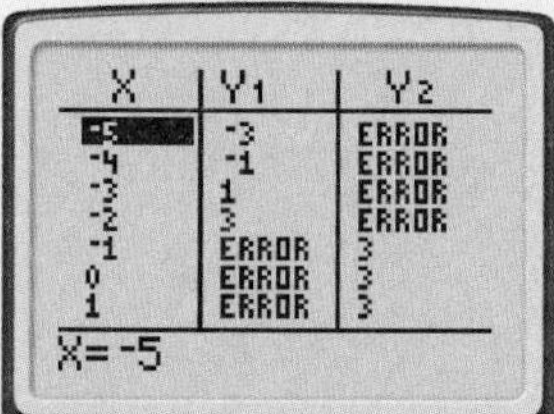

X	Y1	Y2
-5	-3	ERROR
-4	-1	ERROR
-3	1	ERROR
-2	3	ERROR
-1	ERROR	3
0	ERROR	3
1	ERROR	3

X=-5

Try This

Graph each piecewise function.

11. $g(x) = \begin{cases} x & \text{if } x < 0 \\ -x & \text{if } x \ge 0 \end{cases}$

12. $h(x) = \begin{cases} 2x + 8 & \text{if } x \le -2 \\ x^2 & \text{if } x > -2 \end{cases}$

13. $f(x) = \begin{cases} -3x & \text{if } x < 1 \\ x - 4 & \text{if } 1 \le x < 5 \\ -\frac{1}{2}x + \frac{7}{2} & \text{if } x \ge 5 \end{cases}$

14. Critical Thinking Explain how dividing the function by a logical test value visually restricts the domain of the function on your graph.

15. Critical Thinking Explain how you can use the table feature of a graphing calculator to evaluate a piecewise function.

COMMON CORE

6-4 Transforming Functions

CC.9-12.F.BF.3 Identify the effect on the graph of replacing $f(x)$ by $f(x) + k$, $k\,f(x)$, $f(kx)$, and $f(x + k)$... *Also* **CC.9-12.A.CED.2, CC.9-12.A.CED.3**

Objectives

Transform functions.

Recognize transformations of functions.

Why learn this?

Transformations can be used to describe changes in college tuition fees. (See Example 4.)

"If you miss a payment, we show up and embarrass you in front of your friends."

In previous lessons, you learned how to transform several types of functions. You can transform piecewise functions by applying transformations to each piece independently. Recall the rules for transforming functions given in the table.

Transformations of $f(x)$

Horizontal Translation	Vertical Translation
$f(x) \rightarrow f(x - h)$ left for $h < 0$ right for $h > 0$	$f(x) \rightarrow f(x) + k$ down for $k < 0$ up for $k > 0$
Reflection Across *y*-axis	**Reflection Across *x*-axis**
$f(x) \rightarrow f(-x)$ The graph is reflected across the *y*-axis.	$f(x) \rightarrow -f(x)$ The graph is reflected across the *x*-axis.
Horizontal Stretch/Compression	**Vertical Stretch/Compression**
$f(x) \rightarrow f\left(\frac{1}{b}x\right)$ stretch for $b > 1$ compression for $0 < b < 1$	$f(x) \rightarrow af(x)$ stretch for $a > 1$ compression for $0 < a < 1$

EXAMPLE 1 Transforming Piecewise Functions

Given $f(x) = \begin{cases} x + 3 & \text{if } x > 0 \\ 2x + 3 & \text{if } x \le 0 \end{cases}$, write the rule for $g(x)$, a horizontal translation of $f(x)$ 4 units right.

Each piece of $f(x)$ must be shifted 4 units right. Replace every x in the function with $(x - 4)$, and simplify.

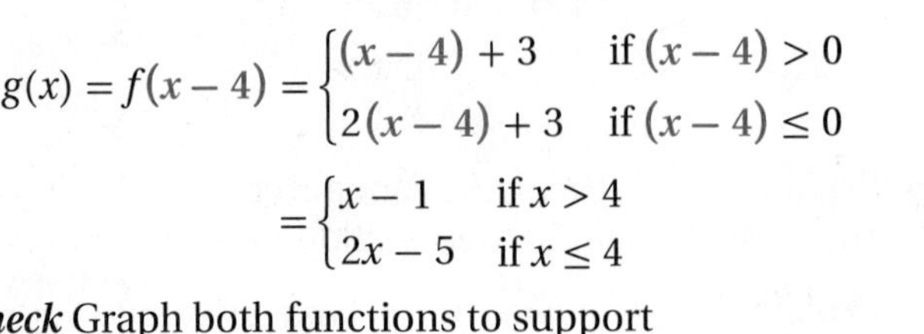

$$g(x) = f(x - 4) = \begin{cases} (x - 4) + 3 & \text{if } (x - 4) > 0 \\ 2(x - 4) + 3 & \text{if } (x - 4) \le 0 \end{cases}$$

$$= \begin{cases} x - 1 & \text{if } x > 4 \\ 2x - 5 & \text{if } x \le 4 \end{cases}$$

Check Graph both functions to support your answer.

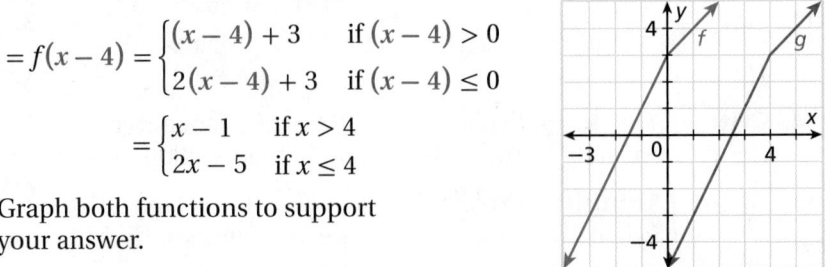

Caution!

Horizontal translations change both the rules and the intervals of piecewise functions. Vertical translations change only the rules.

1. Given $f(x) = \begin{cases} x^2 & \text{if } x \le 0 \\ x - 3 & \text{if } x > 0 \end{cases}$, write the rule for $g(x)$, a horizontal stretch of $f(x)$ by a factor of 2.

When functions are transformed, the intercepts may or may not change. By identifying the transformations, you can determine the intercepts, which can help you graph a transformed function.

Effects of Transformations on Intercepts of $f(x)$	
Horizontal Stretch or Compression by a Factor of b	**Vertical Stretch or Compression by a Factor of a**
x-intercepts are multiplied by b. y-intercept stays the same.	x-intercepts stay the same. y-intercept is multiplied by a.
Reflection Across y-axis	**Reflection Across x-axis**
x-intercepts are negated. y-intercept stays the same.	x-intercepts stay the same. y-intercept is negated.

EXAMPLE 2 Identifying Intercepts

Identify the x- and y-intercepts of $f(x)$. Without graphing $g(x)$, identify its x- and y-intercepts.

A $f(x) = \frac{1}{2}x - 3$ and $g(x) = 3f(x)$

Find the intercepts of the original function.

$f(0) = \frac{1}{2}(0) - 3 = -3$ $\quad\quad 0 = \frac{1}{2}x - 3$

$f(0) = -3$ $\quad\quad 6 = x$

The y-intercept is -3, and the x-intercept is 6. Note that $g(x)$ is a vertical stretch of $f(x)$ by a factor of 3. So the x-intercept of $g(x)$ is also 6. The y-intercept is $3(-3)$, or -9.

Check A graph supports your answer.

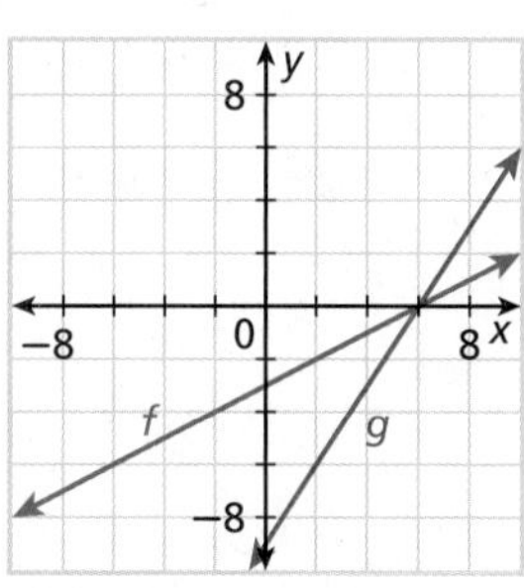

Identify the x- and y-intercepts of $f(x)$. Without graphing $g(x)$, identify its x- and y-intercepts.

B $f(x) = x^2 - 4$ **and** $g(x) = f(2x)$

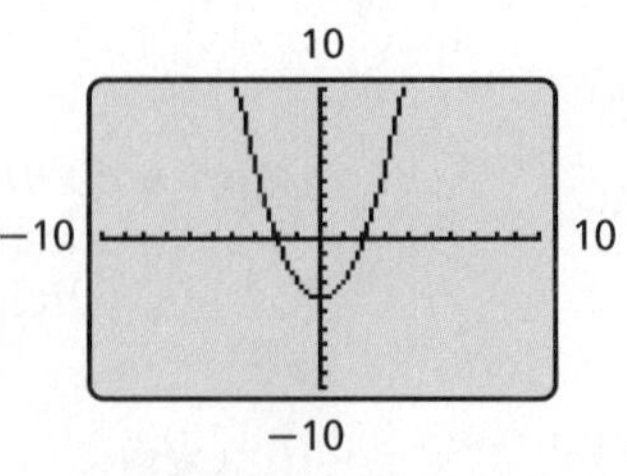

From the graph of $f(x)$, the y-intercept is -4 and the x-intercepts are -2 and 2.

Note that $g(x)$ is a horizontal compression by a factor of $\frac{1}{2}$. So the x-intercepts of $g(x)$ will be $\frac{1}{2}(-2)$ and $\frac{1}{2}(2)$, or -1 and 1. The y-intercept is unchanged at -4.

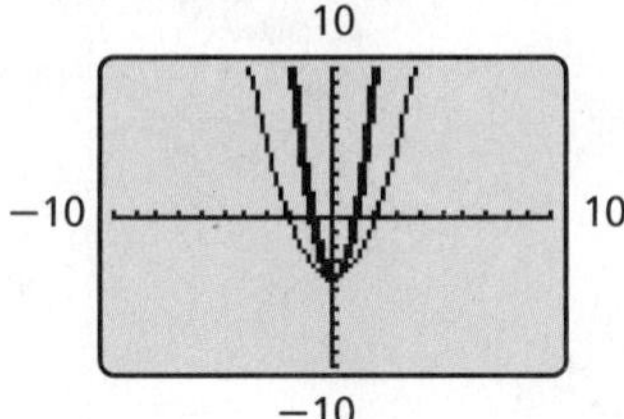

Check A graph supports your answer.

Identify the x- and y-intercepts of $f(x)$. Without graphing $g(x)$, identify its x- and y-intercepts.

2a. $f(x) = \frac{2}{3}x + 4$ and $g(x) = -f(x)$

2b. $f(x) = x^2 - 9$ and $g(x) = \frac{1}{3}f(x)$

EXAMPLE 3 Combining Transformations

Given $f(x) = -\frac{2}{3}x^2 + 6$ and $g(x) = f\left(\frac{3}{2}x\right) + 4$, graph $g(x)$.

> **Remember!**
>
> The factor for horizontal stretches and compressions is the reciprocal of the coefficient in the equation.
>
> $\frac{1}{\frac{3}{2}} = \frac{2}{3}$

Step 1 Graph $f(x)$. The graph of $f(x)$ has y-intercept $(0, 6)$ and x-intercepts $(-3, 0)$ and $(3, 0)$.

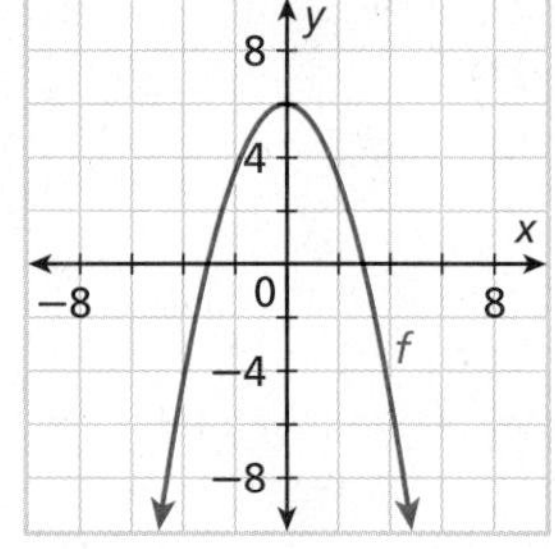

Step 2 Analyze each transformation one at a time.

The first transformation is a horizontal compression by a factor of $\frac{2}{3}$. After the horizontal compression, the x-intercepts will be -2 and 2, but the y-intercept will remain 6.

The second transformation is a vertical translation of 4 units up. Use a table to shift each identified point up 4 units.

Intercept Points	(−2, 0)	(2, 0)	(0, 6)
Shifted	(−2, 4)	(2, 4)	(0, 10)

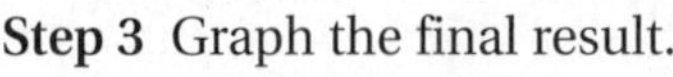

Step 3 Graph the final result.

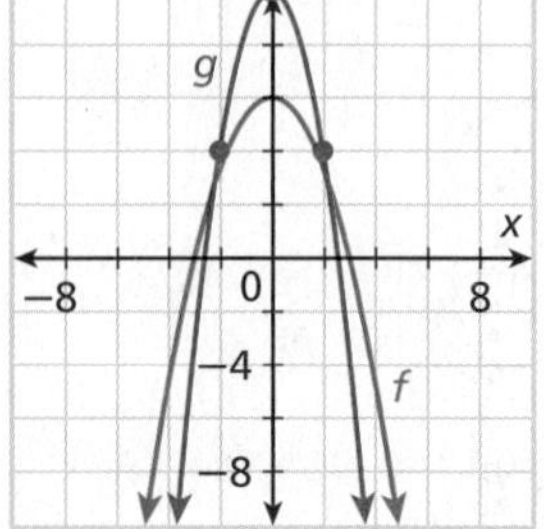

3. Given $f(x) = 2^x - 4$ and $g(x) = -\frac{1}{2}f(x)$, graph $g(x)$.

EXAMPLE 4 *Problem-Solving Application*

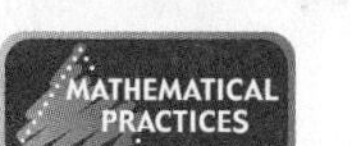

Make sense of problems and persevere in solving them.

A college charges different fees according to the number of credit hours in which students have enrolled. The fee scale is modeled by the piecewise function below, where x is the number of credit hours.

$$f(x) = \begin{cases} 110x & \text{if } 0 < x < 12 \\ 1320 & \text{if } 12 \le x \le 18 \\ 150(x - 18) + 1320 & \text{if } x > 18 \end{cases}$$

The college plans to increase all fees by 10% for the fall semester. In the spring semester, the college plans to add an administrative fee of \$75 to each enrollment. Write the rule for the fee function for the spring semester.

1 Understand the Problem

The new fee function will include two changes, a 10% increase and an additional fee of \$75. The 10% increase is equivalent to multiplying all of the parts of the function by 110%, or 1.1. This will be a vertical stretch by a factor of 1.1. The administrative fee will be a vertical translation of 75 units up.

2 Make a Plan

Perform each transformation, one at a time, and then write the new rule.

3 Solve

First find the fees for the fall semester.

$$f_{\text{fall}}(x) = (1.1)f(x) = \begin{cases} (1.1)110x & \text{if } 0 < x < 12 \\ (1.1)1320 & \text{if } 12 \le x \le 18 \\ (1.1)[150(x - 18) + 1320] & \text{if } x > 18 \end{cases}$$

Multiply all parts by 1.1.

$$= \begin{cases} 121x & \text{if } 0 < x < 12 \\ 1452 & \text{if } 12 \le x \le 18 \\ 165(x - 18) + 1452 & \text{if } x > 18 \end{cases}$$

Then find the fees for the spring semester.

$$f_{\text{spring}}(x) = f_{\text{fall}}(x) + 75 = \begin{cases} 121x + 75 & \text{if } 0 < x < 12 \\ 1452 + 75 & \text{if } 12 \le x \le 18 \\ 165(x - 18) + 1452 + 75 & \text{if } x > 18 \end{cases}$$

$$= \begin{cases} 121x + 75 & \text{if } 0 < x < 12 \\ 1527 & \text{if } 12 \le x \le 18 \\ 165(x - 18) + 1527 & \text{if } x > 18 \end{cases}$$

4 Look Back

Check your answer by trying a few values. For 20 hours, the original fee would have been \$1620. A 10% increase plus a \$75 fee would amount to \$1857. Evaluate the function for $x = 20$ to check.

$$f_{\text{spring}}(20) = \{165(20 - 18) + 1527 = 1857 \checkmark$$

Continue by checking each piece of the function.

4. A movie theater charges \$5 for children under 12 and \$7.50 for anyone 12 and over. The theater decides to increase its prices by 20%. It charges an additional \$0.50 fee for online ticket purchases. Write a function for the online ticket prices.

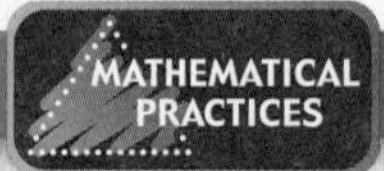

THINK AND DISCUSS

1. Identify the transformations that leave the y-intercept unchanged.
2. Explain why the point (0, 0) is unchanged under any stretch or compression.

3. **GET ORGANIZED** Copy and complete the graphic organizer. Identify the effects of each transformation on the intercepts.

Transformation	x-intercepts	y-intercept
Horizontal stretch or compression by a factor of b		
Vertical stretch or compression by a factor of a		
Reflection across y-axis		
Reflection across x-axis		

6-4 Exercises

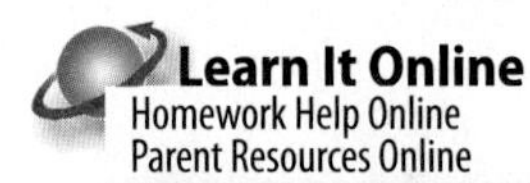

GUIDED PRACTICE

SEE EXAMPLE 1

Given $f(x) = \begin{cases} x - 3 & \text{if } x \leq 0 \\ 4x & \text{if } x > 0 \end{cases}$, write the rule for each function.

1. $g(x)$, a horizontal translation of $f(x)$ 6 units left
2. $h(x)$, a horizontal compression by a factor of $\frac{1}{4}$

SEE EXAMPLE 2

Identify the x- and y-intercepts of $f(x)$. Without graphing $g(x)$, identify its x- and y-intercepts.

3. $f(x) = 4x + 12$ and $g(x) = \frac{1}{6}f(x)$
4. $f(x) = -x^2 + 16$ and $g(x) = f(4x)$

SEE EXAMPLE 3

Given $f(x)$, graph $g(x)$.

5. $f(x) = -x^2 + 1$ and $g(x) = f(2x) - 1$
6. $f(x) = |x - 1| - 2$ and $g(x) = -2f(x)$

SEE EXAMPLE 4

7. **Taxes** The state income tax in Connecticut is modeled by the function $T(x) = \begin{cases} 0.02x & \text{if } 0 < x \leq 10{,}000 \\ 0.05x & \text{if } x > 10{,}000 \end{cases}$, where x is income in dollars. Suppose that Connecticut decided to increase its tax rates by 20% and add a filing fee of \$100 dollars. Write a function for the new state income tax.

PRACTICE AND PROBLEM SOLVING

Given $f(x) = \begin{cases} x^2 & \text{if } x < 1 \\ 4x & \text{if } x \geq 1 \end{cases}$, write the rule for each function.

8. $g(x)$, a vertical compression of $f(x)$ by a factor of $\frac{1}{4}$
9. $h(x)$, a horizontal stretch by a factor of 2
10. $p(x)$, a vertical translation 3 units down

Independent Practice	
For Exercises	See Example
8–10	1
11–16	2
17–18	3
19	4

Extra Practice

See Extra Practice for more Skills Practice and Applications Practice exercises.

Identify the x- and y-intercepts of $f(x)$. Without graphing $g(x)$, identify its x- and y-intercepts.

11. $f(x) = -\frac{3}{2}x + 9$ and $g(x) = \frac{2}{3}f(x)$

12. $f(x) = x^2 - 25$ and $g(x) = f\left(\frac{5}{3}x\right)$

13. $f(x) = -\frac{2}{5}x + 2$ and $g(x) = f(2x)$

14. $f(x) = x^2 - 3x - 4$ and $g(x) = -f\left(\frac{1}{3}x\right)$

15. $f(x) = 3^x - 1$ and $g(x) = 2f(x) - 4$

16. $f(x) = x^3 + 8$ and $g(x) = f\left(-\frac{1}{2}x\right)$

Given $f(x)$, graph $g(x)$.

17. $f(x) = \frac{1}{2}x + 4$ and $g(x) = 3f(-x)$

18. $f(x) = \left(\frac{1}{2}\right)^x - 2$ and $g(x) = -f(2x)$

19. Business The amount that a caterer charges to cater a party for n people is given by the function $C(n) = \begin{cases} 18n & \text{if } n \le 50 \\ 400 + 10n & \text{if } n > 50 \end{cases}$.

a. During a sale, the caterer reduces the amount charged by 10%. Find the function for how much the caterer will charge during the sale.

b. If the caterer then decides to take an additional $2 off per person, find the function for how much the caterer will charge.

In some cities, automatic cameras are used to identify and photograph vehicles that are speeding. The first stationary speed camera in Washington, D.C., detected more than 10,000 speeding drivers in its first 15 days of operation.

20. Safety Speeding fines in Washington, D.C., are shown in the table.

a. Write a function to represent speeding fines.

b. If the speeding offense occurs in a school zone, the city adds a fine of $50. Write a function for the increased fines in a school zone.

c. **What if...?** The city is considering increasing speeding fines by 15%. Write a new function for the increased speeding fines.

Speeding Fines in Washington, D.C.

Speed Over Limit (mi/h)	Fine ($)
1–10	30
11–15	50
16–20	100
21–25	150
26–30	200

21. Critical Thinking Suppose that the graph of $f(x)$ has n x-intercepts.

a. How many x-intercepts does the graph of $bf(ax)$ have? Explain.

b. Explain why you cannot tell how many x-intercepts the graph of $f(x - h) + k$ has.

22. Money A credit card company charges a person taking a cash advance on its credit card at an ATM a $6 transaction fee if $200 or less is withdrawn. For amounts over $200, the transaction fee is 3% of the amount withdrawn.

a. Write a function for the transaction fee to withdraw x dollars.

b. Suppose that the company wants to increase fees by 15% in order to reflect increased costs. Adjust your function to include the increase.

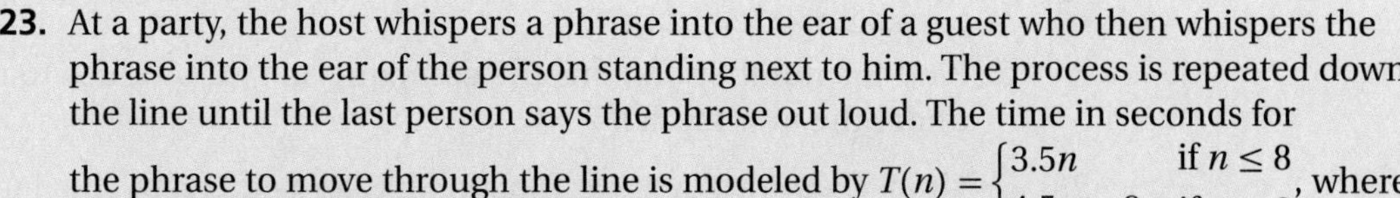

23. At a party, the host whispers a phrase into the ear of a guest who then whispers the phrase into the ear of the person standing next to him. The process is repeated down the line until the last person says the phrase out loud. The time in seconds for the phrase to move through the line is modeled by $T(n) = \begin{cases} 3.5n & \text{if } n \le 8 \\ 4.5n - 8 & \text{if } n > 8 \end{cases}$, where n is the number of guests in the line.

a. The second time that the game is played, each person's reaction time is 20% faster. Write a new function to model this situation.

b. Describe the effect of this improvement on the graph of $T(n)$.

24. **Technology** Morphing is a computerized technique for making one picture turn into another picture. Morphing is created by transforming specific points from one location to another.
   a. Graph the functions $f(x) = \left\{\frac{1}{2}x + 4 \text{ for } 1 \le x \le 2\right.$, $g(x) = \left\{-x^2 + 6x - 7 \text{ for } 2 \le x \le 4\right.$, and $h(x) = \left\{-\frac{1}{2}x + 7 \text{ for } 4 \le x \le 5\right.$ on the same coordinate grid.
   b. Graph the transformed functions $f_{new}(x) = -f(x) + 8$, $g_{new}(x) = -g(x) + 3$, and $h_{new}(x) = -h(x) + 8$.
   c. Describe the morph that you created.

For each function, give the new function rule after the given transformation.

25. $f(x) = \begin{cases} 2^x - 1 & \text{if } x \le -3 \\ -5x + 3 & \text{if } x > -3 \end{cases}$ after a translation of 7 units down

26. $f(x) = \begin{cases} 3x^2 & \text{if } x < 1 \\ -2x + 4 & \text{if } x \ge 1 \end{cases}$ after a vertical stretch by a factor of 5

27. **Food** A farmers' market sells fruits and vegetables at a flat rate with discounts for larger purchases.
   a. Sketch a graph of the cost of 0 to 10 pounds of produce.
   b. Write a piecewise function for the cost of x pounds of produce.
   c. **What if...?** During a sale, the market offers a buy-one-get-one-free sale. Graph the new cost function and describe the transformation from the original function.

28. **Business** A company's profit model is given by $P(n) = -0.002n^2 + 19n - 9000$, where $P(n)$ is the profit in dollars and n is the number of items produced. Based on some new data, the profit model for next year is predicted to be $R(n) = P(0.8n)$.
   a. How will the change affect the number of items the company should produce to maximize its profit?
   b. Find the number of items the company should produce to maximize profit under the new model.

29. **Critical Thinking** A linear function has an x-intercept equal to 2 and a y-intercept equal to 3. The function is stretched vertically by a factor of 2, then translated 3 units down, and then stretched horizontally by a factor of 2. What are the new intercepts?

30. **Critical Thinking** Why does a vertical translation not affect the domain of a function but a horizontal translation might? Explain.

31. **Write About It** Can a graph that is not continuous be transformed into a continuous graph by using stretches and compressions only? Explain.

32. For the graphs shown, which of the following is $g(x)$?

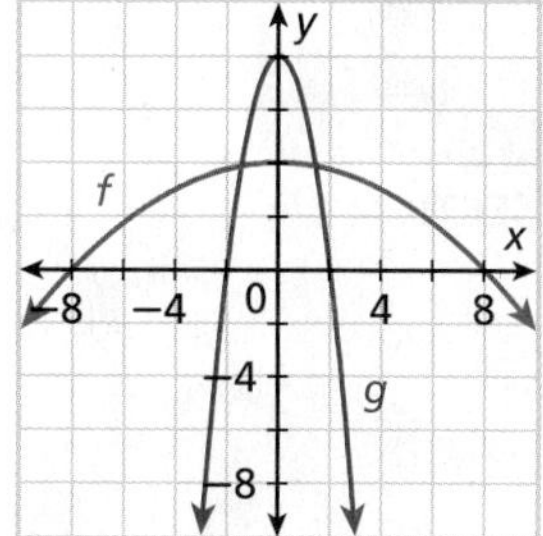

Ⓐ $g(x) = 2f\left(\frac{1}{4}x\right)$

Ⓑ $g(x) = \frac{1}{2}f\left(\frac{1}{4}x\right)$

Ⓒ $g(x) = 2f(4x)$

Ⓓ $g(x) = \frac{1}{2}f(4x)$

33. Suppose that $f(x) = \begin{cases} 2x & x > 8 \\ x^2 & x \le 8 \end{cases}$.

Which of the following is $g(x) = f(4x)$?

Ⓕ $g(x) = \begin{cases} \frac{x}{2} & \text{if } x > 2 \\ \frac{x^2}{16} & \text{if } x \le 2 \end{cases}$

Ⓗ $g(x) = \begin{cases} 8x & \text{if } x > 32 \\ 4x^2 & \text{if } x \le 32 \end{cases}$

Ⓖ $g(x) = \begin{cases} \frac{x}{2} & \text{if } x > 8 \\ \frac{x^2}{16} & \text{if } x \le 8 \end{cases}$

Ⓙ $g(x) = \begin{cases} 8x & \text{if } x > 2 \\ 16x^2 & \text{if } x \le 2 \end{cases}$

34. The y-intercept of $g(x) = \frac{3}{5}f(5x)$ is 15. Which of the following is the y-intercept of $f(x)$?

Ⓐ 3 Ⓑ 9 Ⓒ 25 Ⓓ 75

CHALLENGE AND EXTEND

35. **Geometry** Consider the function $f(x) = \begin{cases} \frac{2}{3}x + 4 & \text{if } x < 0 \\ -\frac{1}{2}x + 4 & \text{if } x \ge 0 \end{cases}$.

a. Graph the function, and find its intercepts. Then find the area bounded by the function and the x-axis.

b. Graph the transformation $g(x) = 4f(2x)$. Find the area bounded by $g(x)$ and the x-axis.

c. Write a function $h(x)$ that creates an area of 7 square units.

36. Consider the functions $f(x) = 2x^3 - 3x^2 - 11x + 6$, $g(x) = 3f\left(\frac{1}{2}x\right)$, and $h(x) = -g\left(\frac{1}{2}x\right)$.

a. Find the x- and y-intercepts of $g(x)$.

b. Find the x- and y-intercepts of $h(x)$.

CHAPTER 6

SECTION 6A

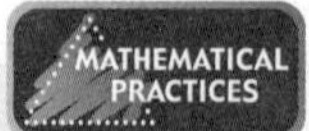

Model with mathematics.

Functions and Their Graphs

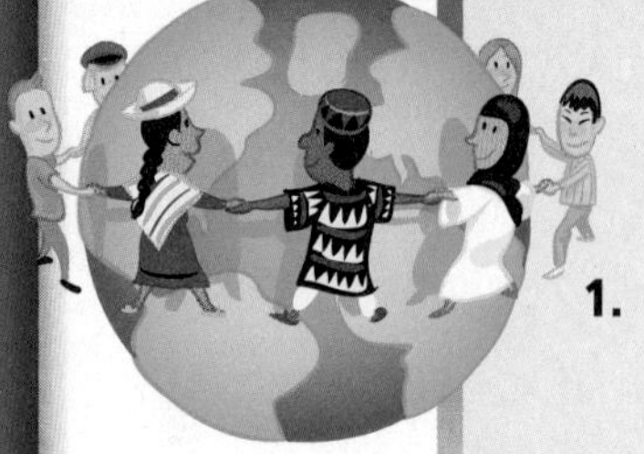

Hands Around the World Imagine a human chain of people holding hands. Assume that each person stands with his or her arms fully outstretched.

1. Suppose that the chain could go all the way around the planet. Then the chain's length would be equal to the circumference of the earth at the equator (about 24,000 miles). Assuming that the average adult arm span is 6 feet, how many people would it take to make this human chain?
2. At the word "go!" the first person in the chain squeezes the hand of the second person, who in turn immediately squeezes the hand of the third person, and so on. Given that it takes 20 seconds for the 60th person to react to having his or her hand squeezed, how many hours would it take the signal to travel all the way around the world?
3. Sketch a graph of the distance in feet that the signal travels in the span of 0 to 1000 seconds. Identify the slope of the line.
4. Researchers at the University of British Columbia have measured muscle reaction times of 0.1 second for Olympic sprinters. If the human chain consisted entirely of Olympic sprinters, how long would it take for the signal to travel all the way around the world?
5. Create a graph of the distance the signal travels in the chain of Olympic sprinters. How does the slope compare to the graph in Problem 3?
6. Suppose that the first half of a human chain is formed by 500 Olympic sprinters and the second half is formed by 500 people whose reaction time is 0.9 second. Write and graph a piecewise function that describes the distance traveled by the signal as a function of time.

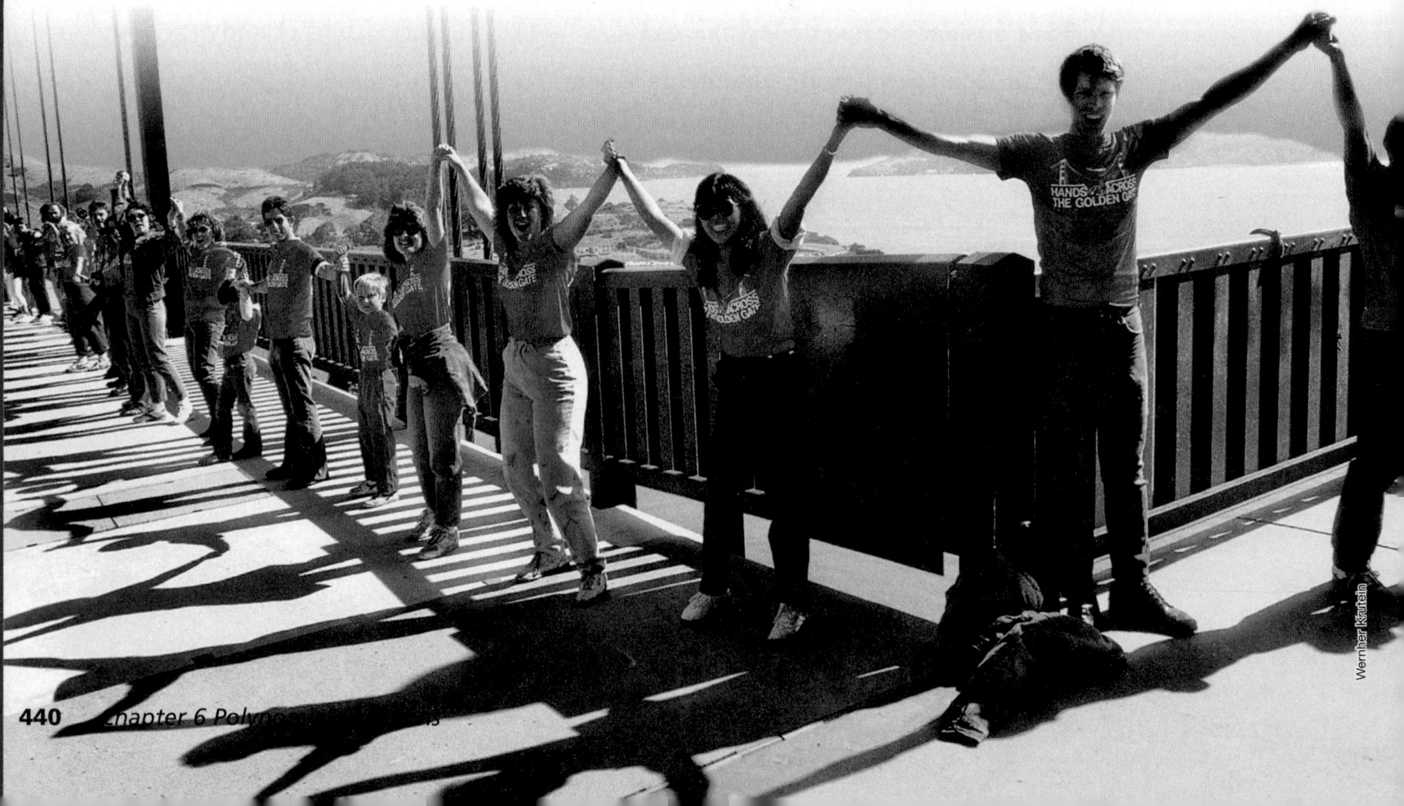

Wernher Krutein

READY TO GO ON?

CHAPTER 6

SECTION 6A

Quiz for Lessons 6-1 Through 6-4

6-1 Multiple Representations of Functions

1. Amanda must read a 294-page book for her history class over the next week. Amanda has found that she can read 42 pages in an hour. Create a table, a graph, and an equation to represent the number of pages that Amanda has left to read with relation to time.

2. The height of a rocket at different times after it was fired is shown in the table.

Time (s)	0	1	2	3	4	5
Height (m)	50.0	65.1	70.4	65.9	51.5	27.5

   a. Find an appropriate model for the height of the rocket.
   b. Find the maximum height of the rocket.
   c. How long will the rocket stay in the air?

6-2 Comparing Functions

Compare the end behavior of each pair of functions.

3. $p(x) = 3 - x$ and $q(x) = 3 - \frac{1}{x}$

4. $r(x) = e^x$ and $s(x) = e^{x^2}$

6-3 Piecewise Functions

5. The cost of renting a mountain bike is \$25 for the first 3 hours and \$5 for each additional hour. Sketch a graph of the cost of renting a mountain bike for 0 to 8 hours. Then write a piecewise function for the graph.

Write a piecewise function for each graph.

6. 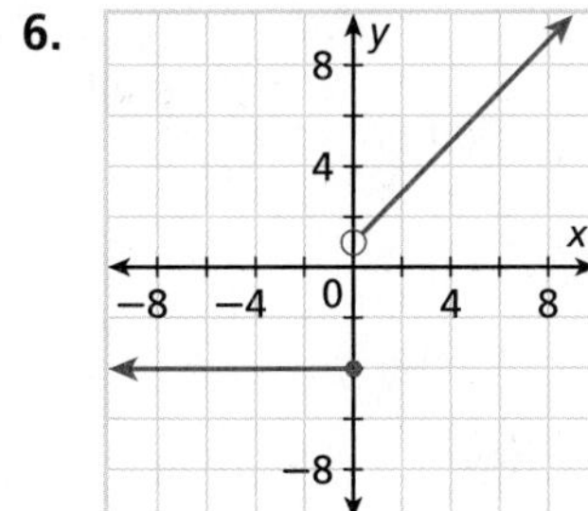

7. 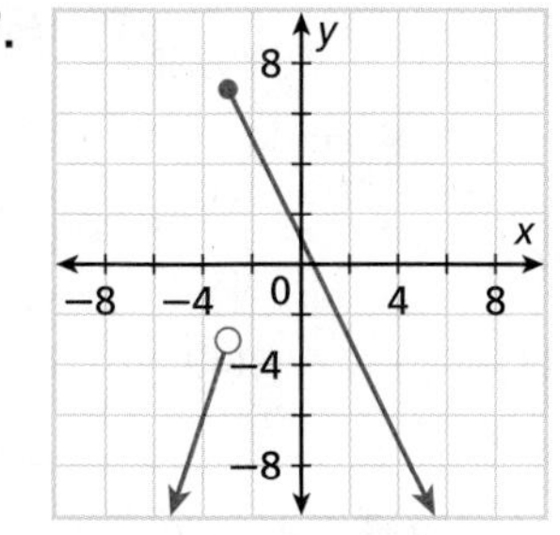

8. 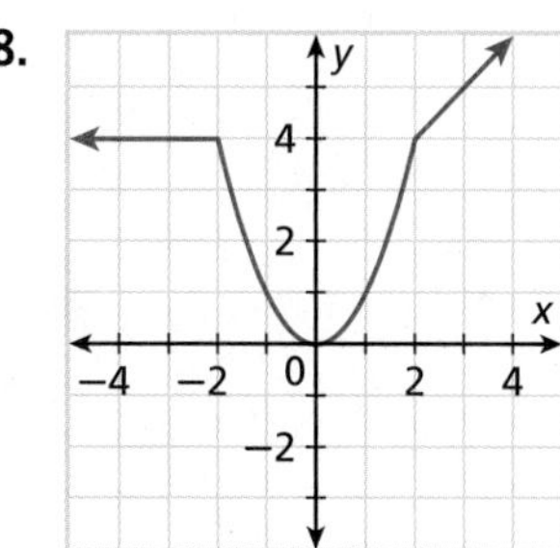

6-4 Transforming Functions

Identify the *x*- and *y*-intercepts of $f(x)$. Without graphing $g(x)$, identify its *x*- and *y*-intercepts.

9. $f(x) = 2x - 2$ and $g(x) = -f\left(\frac{1}{2}x\right)$

10. $f(x) = x^2 - 4$ and $g(x) = 2f(x)$

Given $f(x)$, graph $g(x)$.

11. $f(x) = |x| - 3$ and $g(x) = 2f(x) + 3$

12. $f(x) = x^2 + 1$ and $g(x) = -3f(x)$

6-5 Operations with Functions

CC.9-12.F.BF.1b Combine standard function types using arithmetic operations. *Also* **CC.9-12.F.BF.1c (+), CC.9-12.A.CED.2, CC.9-12.A.CED.3**

Objectives

Add, subtract, multiply, and divide functions.

Write and evaluate composite functions.

Vocabulary

composition of functions

Who uses this?

Importers can use function operations to determine the costs of items that are purchased in foreign currencies. (See Example 5.)

You can perform operations on functions in much the same way that you perform operations on numbers or expressions. You can add, subtract, multiply, or divide functions by operating on their rules.

Notation for Function Operations

Operation	Notation
Addition	$(f+g)(x) = f(x) + g(x)$
Subtraction	$(f-g)(x) = f(x) - g(x)$
Multiplication	$(fg)(x) = f(x) \cdot g(x)$
Division	$\left(\frac{f}{g}\right)(x) = \frac{f(x)}{g(x)}$, where $g(x) \neq 0$

EXAMPLE 1 Adding and Subtracting Functions

Given $f(x) = 2x^2 + 4x - 6$ and $g(x) = 2x - 2$, find each function.

A $(f+g)(x)$

$(f+g)(x) = f(x) + g(x)$

$= (2x^2 + 4x - 6) + (2x - 2)$ *Substitute function rules.*

$= 2x^2 + 6x - 8$ *Combine like terms.*

B $(f-g)(x)$

$(f-g)(x) = f(x) - g(x)$

$= (2x^2 + 4x - 6) - (2x - 2)$ *Substitute function rules.*

$= 2x^2 + 4x - 6 - 2x + 2$ *Distributive Property*

$= 2x^2 + 2x - 4$ *Combine like terms.*

Given $f(x) = 5x - 6$ and $g(x) = x^2 - 5x + 6$, find each function.

1a. $(f+g)(x)$ **1b.** $(f-g)(x)$

When you divide functions, be sure to note any domain restrictions that may arise.

EXAMPLE 2 Multiplying and Dividing Functions

Given $f(x) = 2x^2 + 4x - 6$ and $g(x) = 2x - 2$, find each function.

A $(gf)(x)$

$$(gf)(x) = g(x) \cdot f(x)$$

$= (2x - 2)(2x^2 + 4x - 6)$	*Substitute function rules.*
$= 2x(2x^2 + 4x - 6) - 2(2x^2 + 4x - 6)$	*Distributive Property*
$= 4x^3 + 8x^2 - 12x - 4x^2 - 8x + 12$	*Multiply.*
$= 4x^3 + 4x^2 - 20x + 12$	*Combine like terms.*

B $\left(\frac{f}{g}\right)(x)$

$$\left(\frac{f}{g}\right)(x) = \frac{f(x)}{g(x)}$$

$= \frac{2x^2 + 4x - 6}{2x - 2}$	*Set up the division as a rational expression.*
$= \frac{2(x - 1)(x + 3)}{2(x - 1)}$	*Factor completely. Note that $x \neq 1$.*
$= \frac{\cancel{2(x-1)}(x + 3)}{\cancel{2(x-1)}}$	*Divide out common factors.*
$= x + 3$, where $x \neq 1$	*Simplify.*

CHECK IT OUT! **Given $f(x) = x + 2$ and $g(x) = x^2 - 4$, find each function.**

2a. $(fg)(x)$ **2b.** $\left(\frac{g}{f}\right)(x)$

Another function operation uses the output from one function as the input for a second function. This operation is called the **composition of functions**.

Know it! Note

Composition of Functions

The composition of functions f and g is notated

$$(f \circ g)(x) = f(g(x)).$$

The domain of $(f \circ g)(x)$ is all values of x in the domain of g such that $g(x)$ is in the domain of f.

Reading Math

The composition $(f \circ g)(x)$ or $f(g(x))$ is read "f of g of x."

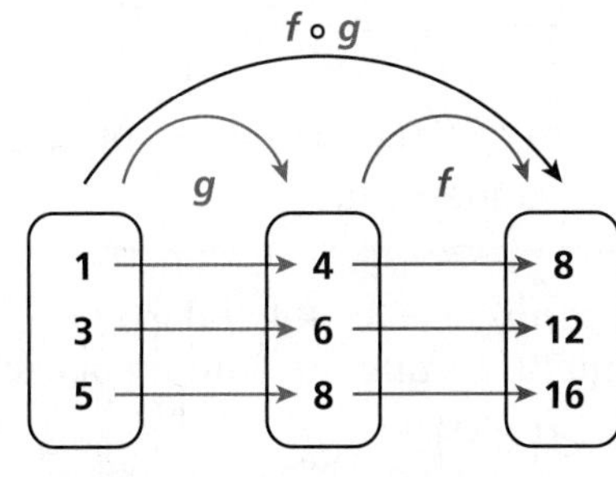

To find $(f \circ g)(1)$, first find $g(1)$.

$$g(1) = 4$$

Then use 4 as the input into f:

$$f(4) = 8$$

So $(f \circ g)(1) = f(g(1)) = 8$.

The order of function operations is the same as the order of operations for numbers and expressions. To find $f(g(3))$, evaluate $g(3)$ first and then substitute the result into f.

EXAMPLE 3 Evaluating Composite Functions

Given $f(x) = 3x + 1$ and $g(x) = x^3$, find each value.

Caution!

Be careful not to confuse the notation for multiplication of functions with composition.
$fg(x) \neq f(g(x))$

A $f(g(2))$

Step 1 Find $g(2)$.

$g(2) = 2^3$ *$g(x) = x^3$*

$= 8$

Step 2 Find $f(8)$.

$f(8) = 3(8) + 1$ *$f(x) = 3x + 1$*

$= 25$

So $f(g(2)) = 25$.

B $g(f(2))$

Step 1 Find $f(2)$.

$f(2) = 3(2) + 1$ *$f(x) = 3(x) + 1$*

$= 7$

Step 2 Find $g(7)$.

$g(7) = 7^3$ *$g(x) = x^3$*

$= 343$

So $g(f(2)) = 343$.

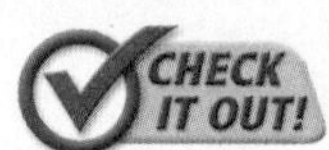

Given $f(x) = 2x - 3$ and $g(x) = x^2$, find each value.

3a. $f(g(3))$ **3b.** $g(f(3))$

You can use algebraic expressions as well as numbers as inputs into functions. To find a rule for $f(g(x))$, substitute the rule for g into f.

EXAMPLE 4 Writing Composite Functions

Given $f(x) = 5x + 2$ and $g(x) = \frac{2}{x-1}$, write each composite function. State the domain of each.

A $f(g(x))$

$f(g(x)) = f\left(\frac{2}{x-1}\right)$ *Substitute the rule for g into f.*

$= 5\left(\frac{2}{x-1}\right) + 2$ *Use the rule for f. Note that $x \neq 1$.*

$= \frac{10}{x-1} + 2, x \neq 1$ *Simplify.*

The domain of $f(g(x))$ is $x \neq 1$ or $\{x \mid x \neq 1\}$ because $g(1)$ is undefined.

B $g(f(x))$

$g(f(x)) = g(5x + 2)$ *Substitute the rule for f into g.*

$= \frac{2}{(5x+2) - 1}$ *Use the rule for g.*

$= \frac{2}{5x+1}, x \neq -\frac{1}{5}$ *Simplify. Note that $x \neq -\frac{1}{5}$.*

The domain of $g(f(x))$ is $x \neq -\frac{1}{5}$ or $\left\{x \mid x \neq -\frac{1}{5}\right\}$ because $f\left(-\frac{1}{5}\right) = 1$ and $g(1)$ is undefined.

Given $f(x) = 3x - 4$ and $g(x) = \sqrt{x} + 2$, write each composite function. State the domain of each.

4a. $f(g(x))$ **4b.** $g(f(x))$

Composite functions can be used to simplify a series of functions.

EXAMPLE 5 Business Application

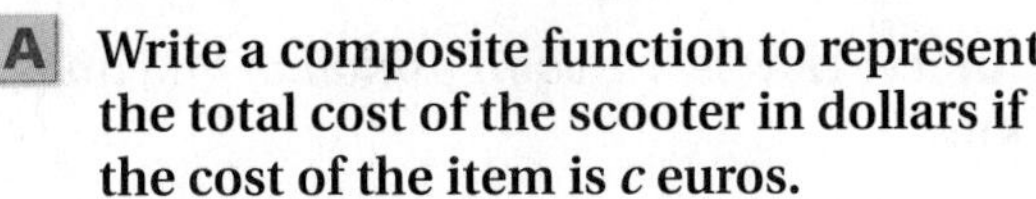

Lisa imports scooters from Italy. The cost of the scooters is given in euros. The total cost of each scooter includes a 10% service charge and 75 euros for shipping.

EXCHANGE RATES	
CURRENCY	UNITS PER U.S. DOLLAR
BRITISH POUND	0.53
EUROPEAN EURO	0.77
JAPANESE YEN	103.60
MEXICAN PESO	11.30

A Write a composite function to represent the total cost of the scooter in dollars if the cost of the item is c euros.

Step 1 Write a function for the total cost in euros.

$$E(c) = c + 0.1c + 75$$
$$= 1.1c + 75$$

Step 2 Write a function for the cost in dollars based on the cost in euros.

$$D(c) = \frac{c}{0.77}$$ *Use the exchange rate table.*

Step 3 Find the composition $D\big(E(c)\big)$.

$$D\big(E(c)\big) = \frac{E(c)}{0.77}$$ *Substitute $E(c)$ for c.*

$$= \frac{1.1c + 75}{0.77}$$ *Replace $E(c)$ with its rule.*

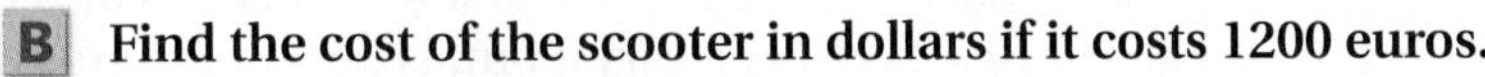

B Find the cost of the scooter in dollars if it costs 1200 euros.

Evaluate the composite function for $c = 1200$.

$$D\big(E(1200)\big) = \frac{1.1(1200) + 75}{0.77}$$
$$\approx 1811.69$$

The scooter would cost $1811.69, including all charges.

CHECK IT OUT! **During a sale, a music store is selling all drum kits for 20% off. Preferred customers also receive an additional 15% off.**

5a. Write a composite function to represent the final cost of a kit that originally cost c dollars.

5b. Find the cost of a drum kit priced at $248 that a preferred customer wants to buy.

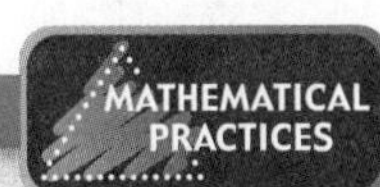

THINK AND DISCUSS

1. Explain why $(f + g)x = (g + f)x$ for any functions f and g.

2. Find two functions such that $f\big(g(x)\big) = g\big(f(x)\big)$.

3. GET ORGANIZED Copy and complete the graphic organizer. Write the correct notation for each function operation.

Operation	Notation
Addition	
Subtraction	
Multiplication	
Division	
Composition	

6-5 Exercises

Learn It Online
Homework Help Online
Parent Resources Online

GUIDED PRACTICE

1. **Vocabulary** How is the *composition of functions* different from the other function operations?

SEE EXAMPLE 1

Given $f(x) = 8x + 13$ and $g(x) = x^2 - 5x$, find each function.

2. $(f+g)(x)$
3. $(f-g)(x)$
4. $(g-f)(x)$

SEE EXAMPLE 2

Given $f(x) = 2x^2 + 2x$ and $g(x) = x + 1$, find each function.

5. $(fg)(x)$
6. $\left(\frac{f}{g}\right)(x)$
7. $\left(\frac{g}{f}\right)(x)$

SEE EXAMPLE 3

Given $f(x) = 3x^2$ and $g(x) = 7 - x$, find each value.

8. $f(g(5))$
9. $g(f(5))$
10. $f(g(-2))$

SEE EXAMPLE 4

Given $f(x) = x^2$, $g(x) = 2x - 3$, and $h(x) = \sqrt{x+1}$, write each composite function. State the domain of each.

11. $f(g(x))$
12. $g(f(x))$
13. $f(h(x))$

SEE EXAMPLE 5

14. **Consumer Economics** Ron is saving money for college. Each month he deposits 10% of his net income plus an additional \$50 into a savings account. His net income, after taxes have been taken out, is 80% of his gross income.
    a. Write a composite function for the amount that Ron saves each month if his gross income is *g*.
    b. Find the amount that Ron saves in a month when his gross income is \$2400.

PRACTICE AND PROBLEM SOLVING

Independent Practice

For Exercises	See Example
15–18	1
19–23	2
24–29	3
30–32	4
33	5

Extra Practice

See Extra Practice for more Skills Practice and Applications Practice exercises.

Given $f(x) = 2x^2 - 8$, $g(x) = x^2 + 5x + 6$, and $h(x) = 2x + 4$, find each function.

15. $(f+g)(x)$
16. $(f-g)(x)$
17. $(f+h)(x)$
18. $(g-h)(x)$
19. $(fg)(x)$
20. $\left(\frac{f}{g}\right)(x)$
21. $\left(\frac{h}{f}\right)(x)$
22. $(gh)(x)$
23. $\left(\frac{g}{h}\right)(x)$

Given $f(x) = 2\sqrt{x+3}$ and $g(x) = -3x + 1$, find each value.

24. $f(g(1))$
25. $g(f(1))$
26. $f(g(4))$
27. $g(f(6))$
28. $f\left(g\left(\frac{4}{3}\right)\right)$
29. $g(f(97))$

Given $f(x) = 4x + 3$, $g(x) = \frac{x}{x+3}$, and $h(x) = -x^2 - 2$, write each composite function. State the domain of each.

30. $f(g(x))$
31. $g(f(x))$
32. $f(h(x))$

33. **Business** The cost of carpeting a room is \$4 per square yard plus \$100. Each square yard is equal to 9 square feet.
    a. Write a composite function for the cost of carpeting a room that covers x square feet.
    b. Find the square footage of a room that costs \$380 to carpet.

34. When the air in a hot-air balloon is heated to 100°F, each cubic foot of air can lift about 7 g.
   a. Write a function $f(x)$ for the number of grams that can be lifted by a balloon containing x ft^3 of air.
   b. The equation $g(x) = \dfrac{x}{453.6}$ converts x grams to pounds. Write a composite function for the number of pounds that can be lifted by a balloon containing x ft^3 of air.
   c. Approximately how many cubic feet of air are needed to lift 1000 lb?

35. **Consumer Economics** Lanie has two coupons for a shoe store. One is for \$10 off, and the other is for 15% off.
   a. Write a function $f(p)$ for the final cost of an item of original price p if Lanie uses only the \$10-off coupon.
   b. Write a function $g(p)$ for the final cost of an item of original price p if Lanie uses only the 15%-off coupon.
   c. Find $f(g(p))$ and $g(f(p))$.
   d. Which coupon should Lanie apply first? Explain.
   e. Find the lowest price that Lanie could pay for a pair of shoes priced at \$49.

LINK

Earthquakes

Earthquakes are generally caused by movement along faults. Faults are cracks in Earth's crust, the largest of which occur at tectonic plate boundaries.

36. **Earthquakes** The shock waves created from an earthquake travel away from the epicenter at a rate of 9 km/s. As the radius of the circular waves increases, more and more area is affected by the earthquake.
   a. Find a function for the total area in square kilometers affected by the earthquake after t s.
   b. Geologists predict that the earthquake will be felt over an area of approximately 35,000 km^2. How long after the earthquake begins will this area be affected?

37. **Population** The population of Las Vegas, Nevada, can be approximated by the function $p(t) = 160{,}000 \cdot 1.05^t$, where t is the number of years since 1980. The number of doctors in Las Vegas can be approximated by the function $d(p) = 0.0044p$, where p is the population.
   a. Find a function for the number of doctors in Las Vegas as a function of the number of years t since 1980.
   b. **Estimation** Estimate the number of doctors in Las Vegas in 2010.
   c. Approximately when will the number of doctors in Las Vegas exceed 5000?

38. **Critical Thinking** Given $f(x) = x$ and given any function $g(x)$, is $f(g(x))$ always equal to $g(f(x))$? Explain.

Use the tables to find each value.

x	2	3	4	5
f(x)	0	1	2	3

x	1	2	3	4
g(x)	1	2	4	8

39. $(g \circ f)(5)$
40. $(f \circ g)(3)$
41. $g(f(4))$
42. $f(g(2))$

43. **Critical Thinking** Can you use the tables to find $f(g(4))$? Explain your answer.

44. **Write About It** Is the sum of two linear functions also a linear function? Is the product of two linear functions also a linear function? Explain.

45. If $(f \circ g)(x) = (3x + 4)^2$, which of the following could be true?

(A) $f(x) = 3x + 4$ and $g(x) = x^2$
(B) $f(x) = x^2$ and $g(x) = 3x + 4$
(C) $f(x) = (3x)^2$ and $g(x) = 4^2$
(D) $f(x) = 3x + 4$ and $g(x) = \sqrt{x}$

46. If $f(x) = 2x + 1$ and $g(x) = 5x - 2$, then which of the following is $(fg)(5)$?

(F) 253
(G) 53
(H) 47
(J) 13

47. Given $f(x) = 4 - x^2$ and $g(x) = \frac{1}{2}x - 2$, which of the following is $(f \circ g)(x)$?

(A) $(f \circ g)(x) = -\frac{1}{2}x^2$
(B) $(f \circ g)(x) = -\frac{1}{4}x^2 + 2x$
(C) $(f \circ g)(x) = -\frac{1}{2}x^3 + 2x^2 + 2x - 8$
(D) $(f \circ g)(x) = -x^2 + \frac{1}{2}x + 2$

48. **Gridded Response** Given that $f(x) = (x + 1)^2$ and $g(x) = 3x$, find $(f + g)(2)$.

CHALLENGE AND EXTEND

49. Given $f(x) = 2x - 6$ and $f(g(x)) = 3x^2 + 4$, find $g(x)$.

50. Given $f(x) = 3x + 8$ and $g(x) = \begin{cases} x^2 & \text{if } x < 0 \\ 5x + 2 & \text{if } x \geq 0 \end{cases}$, find $g(f(x))$.

51. **Physics** When a ball is thrown up a hill, the height y of the ball is given by the function $y = -0.12x^2 + 2.8x$, where x is the horizontal distance from the thrower. The hill is represented by the linear function $y = \frac{2}{5}x$.

a. Find the maximum height of the ball above the ground.

b. Find the height of the ball when it hits the ground.

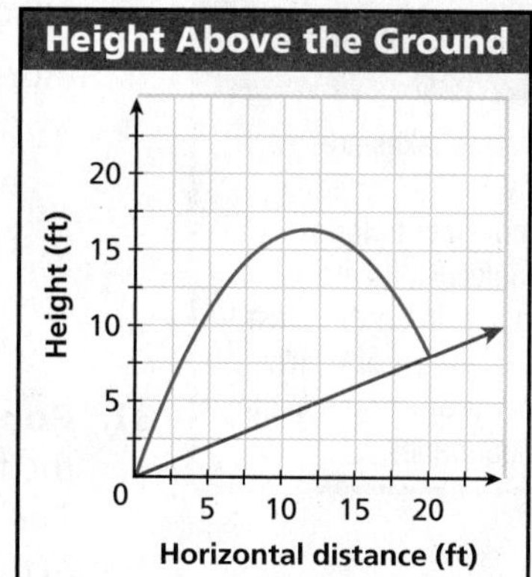

Using Geometric Formulas

Geometric formulas can be used to find lengths of sides or edges. Solve the formula for the variable that you need. In these formulas, s is the length of a side or an edge and r is the radius.

Regular Hexagon	Regular Octagon	Regular Tetrahedron	Regular Octahedron	Sphere
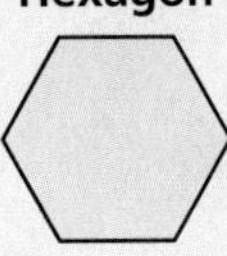	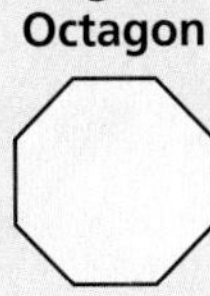	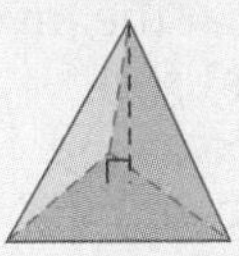	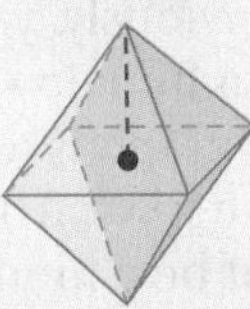	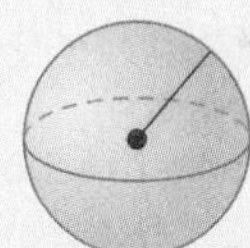
				$A = 4\pi r^2$
$A = \frac{3s^2}{2}\sqrt{3}$	$A = 2s^2(\sqrt{2} + 1)$	$V = \frac{s^3}{12}\sqrt{2}$	$V = \frac{s^3}{3}\sqrt{2}$	$V = \frac{4\pi r^3}{3}$

Example

A rectangle is 30 cm long and 10 cm wide. Find the length of the sides of a regular octagon that has the same area as this rectangle.

1 Find the area of the rectangle.

$30 \cdot 10 = 300$ *The area is 300 cm².*

2 Use the octagon formula. Solve for s, the length of one side.

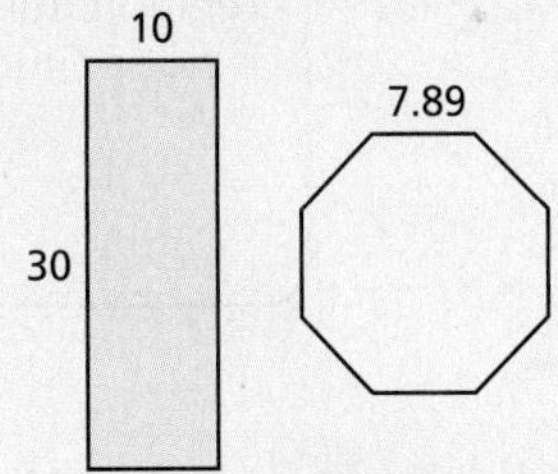

$$A = 2s^2\left(\sqrt{2} + 1\right)$$

$$\frac{A}{2\left(\sqrt{2} + 1\right)} = s^2$$ *Divide both sides by $2\left(\sqrt{2} + 1\right)$.*

$$s = \sqrt{\frac{A}{2\left(\sqrt{2} + 1\right)}}$$ *Take the square root of both sides.*

3 Substitute 300 for the area A, and solve for the side length.

$$s \approx \sqrt{\frac{300}{2(1.41 + 1)}} \approx \sqrt{\frac{300}{4.82}} \approx \sqrt{62.24} \approx 7.89$$ *Use 1.41 as an approximation for $\sqrt{2}$.*

Try This

Solve each problem. Start by solving the appropriate formula for s or r.

1. What is the radius of a sphere made with 1000 cubic feet of clay?
2. Jake used 540 square inches of mosaic tile to build a tabletop in the shape of a regular hexagon. How long is one edge of this tabletop?
3. A tent shaped like a tetrahedron has 30 cubic feet of air space. Describe the base of this tent.
4. Cyndi wants to construct an octahedron that has the same volume as a sphere with a radius of 9 cm. What length should she make each edge of the octahedron?

6-6 Functions and Their Inverses

CC.9-12.F.BF.1c (+) Compose functions. *Also* CC.9-12.A.CED.2, CC.9-12.A.CED.3

Objectives
Determine whether the inverse of a function is a function.

Write rules for the inverses of functions.

Vocabulary
one-to-one function

Who uses this?
Nurses can use inverse functions to approximate the ages of infants. (See Exercise 37.)

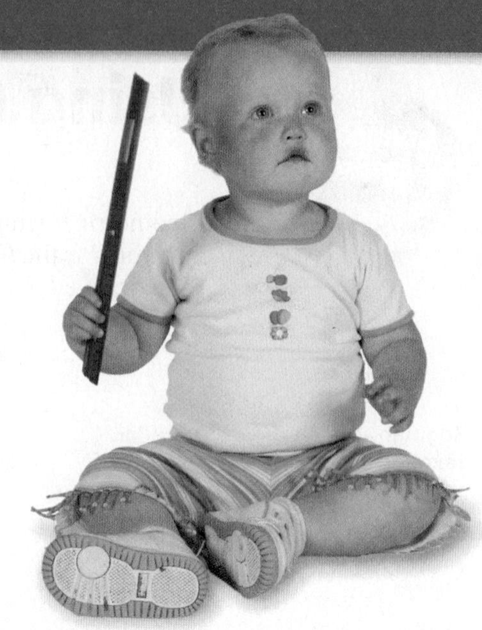

Previously, you learned that the inverse of a function $f(x)$ "undoes" $f(x)$. Its graph is a reflection across the line $y = x$. The inverse may or may not be a function.

Recall that the vertical-line test can help you determine whether a relation is a function. Similarly, the *horizontal-line test* can help you determine whether the inverse of a function is a function.

Know it! Note

Horizontal-line Test

WORDS	EXAMPLES	
If any horizontal line passes through more than one point on the graph of a relation, the inverse relation is not a function.	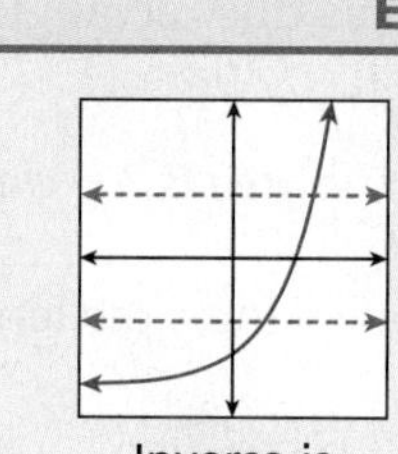 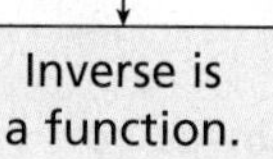 Inverse is a function.	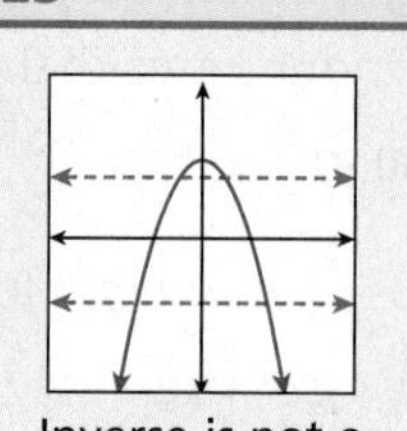 Inverse is not a function.

EXAMPLE 1 Using the Horizontal-Line Test

Use the horizontal-line test to determine whether the inverse of each relation is a function.

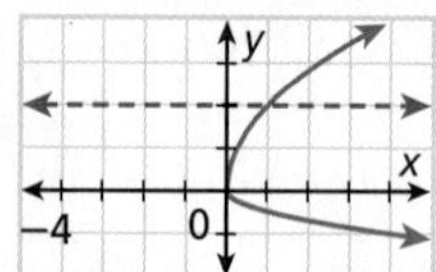

The inverse is a function because no horizontal line passes through two points on the graph.

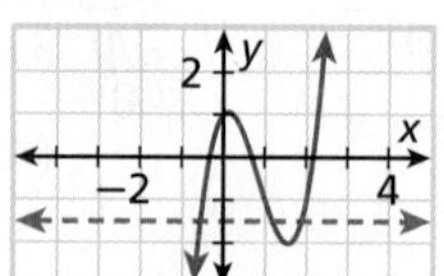

The inverse is not a function because a horizontal line passes through more than one point on the graph.

1. Use the horizontal-line test to determine whether the inverse of the relation is a function.

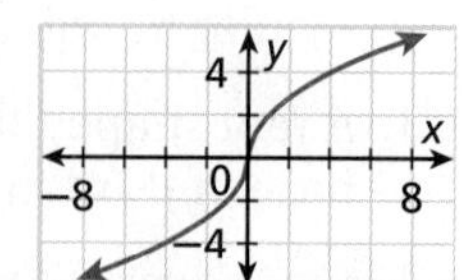

Recall that to write the rule for the inverse of a function, you can exchange x and y and solve the equation for y. Because the values of x and y are switched, the domain of the function will be the range of its inverse and vice versa.

EXAMPLE 2 Writing Rules for Inverses

Find the inverse of $f(x) = \left(\frac{1}{2}x + 2\right)^2$. Determine whether it is a function, and state its domain and range.

Step 1 Graph the function.

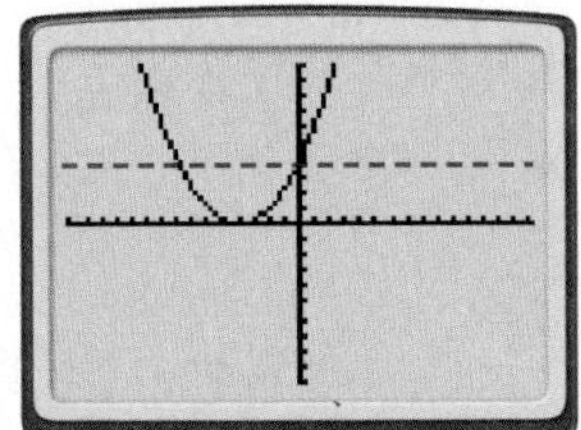

The horizontal-line test shows that the inverse is not a function. Note that the domain of f is all real numbers and the range is $\{y \mid y \geq 0\}$.

Step 2 Find the inverse.

$$y = \left(\frac{1}{2}x + 2\right)^2$$ *Rewrite the function using y instead of f(x).*

$$x = \left(\frac{1}{2}y + 2\right)^2$$ *Switch x and y in the equation.*

$$\sqrt{x} = \sqrt{\left(\frac{1}{2}y + 2\right)^2}$$ *Take the square root of both sides.*

$$\pm\sqrt{x} = \frac{1}{2}y + 2$$ *Note the domain restriction $x \geq 0$.*

$$\pm\sqrt{x} - 2 = \frac{1}{2}y$$ *Subtract 2 from each side.*

$$y = 2\left(\pm\sqrt{x} - 2\right)$$ *Isolate y.*

$$y = \pm 2\sqrt{x} - 4$$ *Simplify.*

Because of the $\pm$ symbol, there may be two y-values for an x-value. This confirms that the inverse is not a function. Because the inverse is not a function, you cannot use the notation $f^{-1}(x)$.

The domain of the inverse is the range of $f(x)$: $\{x \mid x \geq 0\}$. The range is the domain of $f(x)$: all real numbers.

Check Graph both relations to see that they are symmetric about $y = x$. To graph the inverse, you will have to graph the positive and negative cases separately.

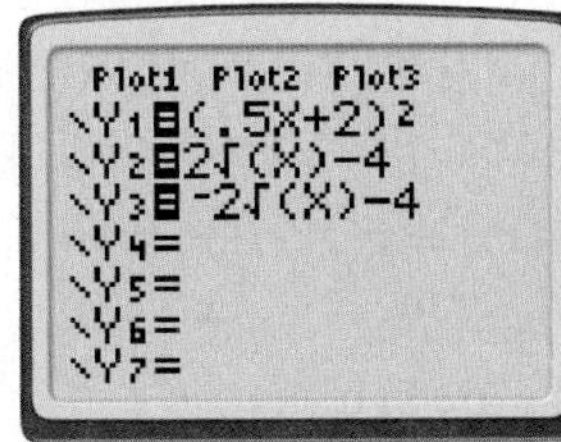

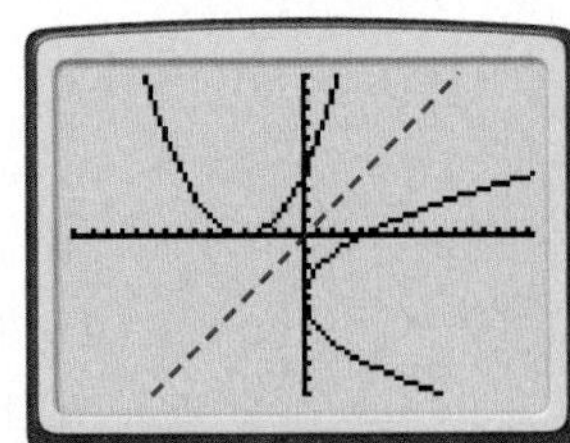

> **Caution!**
> When you take the square root of both sides of a quadratic equation be sure to add the $\pm$ symbol.

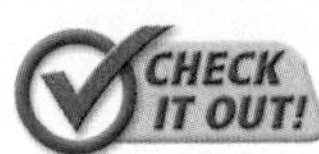

2. Find the inverse of $f(x) = x^3 - 2$. Determine whether it is a function, and state its domain and range.

You have seen that the inverses of functions are not necessarily functions. When both a relation and its inverse are functions, the relation is called a *one-to-one function*. In a **one-to-one function**, each y-value is paired with exactly one x-value.

You can use composition of functions to verify that two functions are inverses. Because inverse functions "undo" each other, when you compose two inverses the result is the input value x.

Identifying Inverse Functions

WORDS	ALGEBRA	EXAMPLE
If the compositions of two functions equal the input value, the functions are inverses.	If $f(g(x)) = g(f(x)) = x$, then $f(x)$ and $g(x)$ are inverse functions.	$f(x) = 3x$ and $g(x) = \frac{1}{3}x$ $f(g(x)) = 3\left(\frac{1}{3}x\right) = x$ $g(f(x)) = \frac{1}{3}(3x) = x$

EXAMPLE 3 Determining Whether Functions Are Inverses

Determine by composition whether each pair of functions are inverses.

A $f(x) = 2x + 4$ and $g(x) = \frac{1}{2}x - 4$

Find the composition $f(g(x))$.

$f(g(x)) = 2\left(\frac{1}{2}x - 4\right) + 4$ — *Substitute $\frac{1}{2}x - 4$ for x in f.*

$= (x - 8) + 4$ — *Use the Distributive Property.*

$= x - 4$ — *Simplify.*

Because $f(g(x)) \neq x$, f and g are not inverses. There is no need to check $g(f(x))$.

Check The graphs are not symmetric about the line $y = x$.

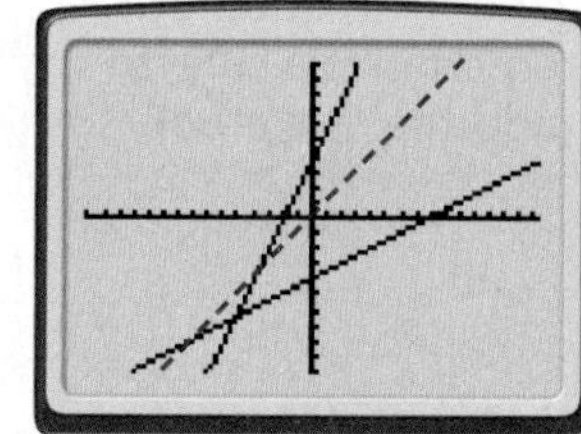

B For $x \geq 0$, $f(x) = \frac{1}{4}x^2$ and $g(x) = 2\sqrt{x}$.

Find the compositions $f(g(x))$ and $g(f(x))$.

$f(g(x)) = \frac{1}{4}(2\sqrt{x})^2$

$= \frac{1}{4}(4x)$

$= x, x \geq 0$

$g(f(x)) = 2\sqrt{\frac{1}{4}x^2}$

$= 2\left(\frac{1}{2}x\right)$

$= x$

Because $f(g(x)) = g(f(x)) = x$ for $x \geq 0$, f and g are inverses.

Check The graphs are symmetric about the line $y = x$ when $x \geq 0$.

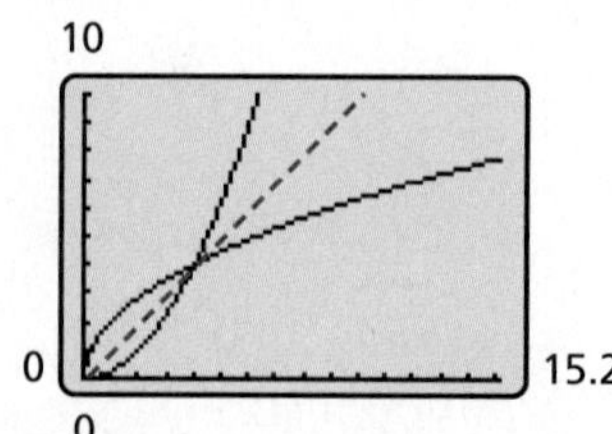

Determine by composition whether each pair of functions are inverses.

3a. $f(x) = \frac{2}{3}x + 6$ and $g(x) = \frac{3}{2}x - 9$

3b. $f(x) = x^2 + 5$ and $g(x) = \sqrt{x} - 5$ for $x \geq 0$

THINK AND DISCUSS

1. Explain why the horizontal-line test works.
2. Explain the relationship between the domain and range of a function and the domain and range of its inverse.

3. **GET ORGANIZED** Copy and complete the graphic organizer. Describe how each method or characteristic is used to find or verify inverses.

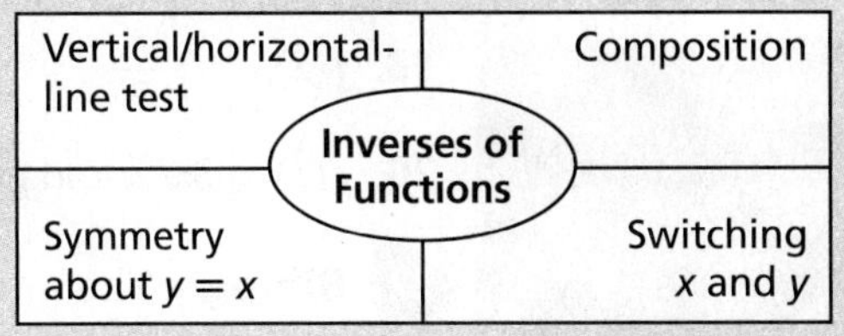

Vertical/horizontal-line test	Composition
Inverses of Functions	
Symmetry about $y = x$	Switching x and y

6-6 Exercises

GUIDED PRACTICE

SEE EXAMPLE 1

Use the horizontal-line test to determine whether the inverse of each relation is a function.

1. 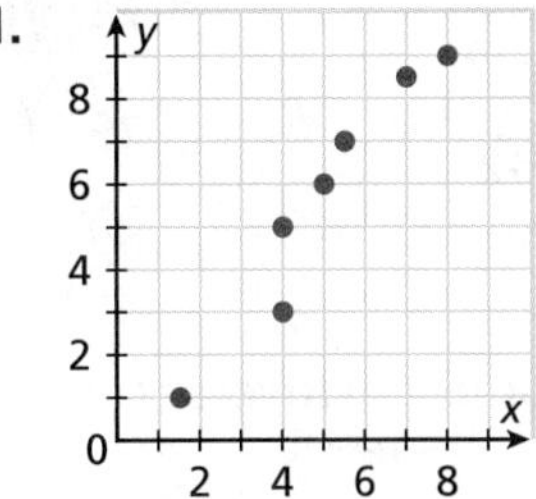

2. 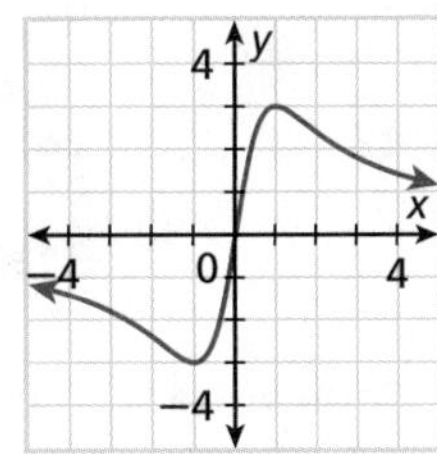

3. 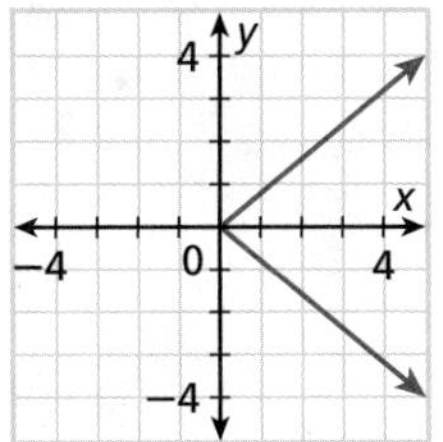

SEE EXAMPLE 2

Find the inverse of each function. Determine whether the inverse is a function, and state its domain and range.

4. $f(x) = -3x + 21$
5. $g(x) = x^2 - 9$
6. $h(x) = \dfrac{x + 5}{8}$

SEE EXAMPLE 3

Determine by composition whether each pair of functions are inverses.

7. $f(x) = 4x - 12$ and $g(x) = -4x + 8$
8. $f(x) = \sqrt{3x}$ and $g(x) = \dfrac{x^2}{3}$ for $x \geq 0$

PRACTICE AND PROBLEM SOLVING

Independent Practice

For Exercises	See Example
9–11	1
12–17	2
18–21	3

Extra Practice

See Extra Practice for more Skills Practice and Applications Practice exercises.

Use the horizontal-line test to determine whether the inverse of each relation is a function.

9. 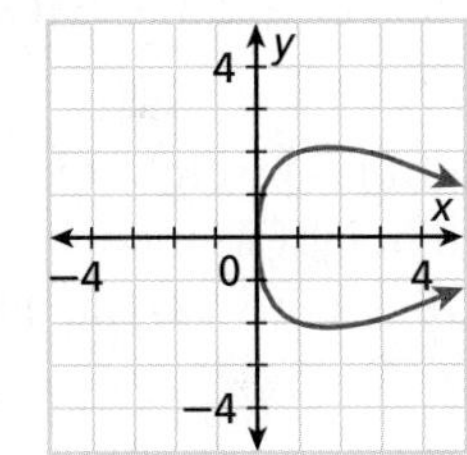

10. 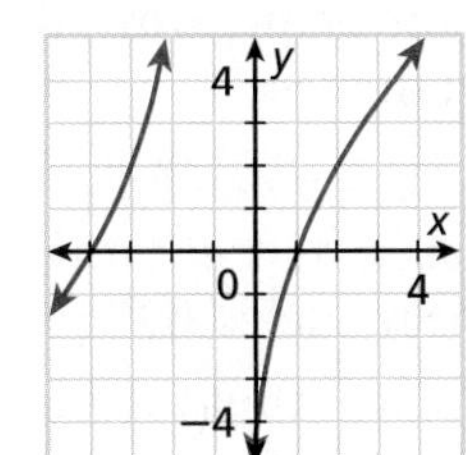

11. 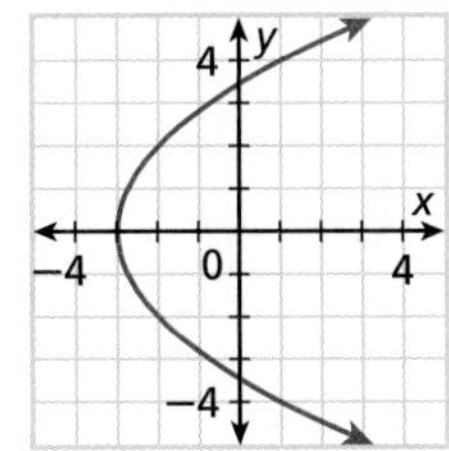

Find the inverse of each function. Determine whether the inverse is a function, and state its domain and range.

12. $f(x) = \frac{3}{5}x$ **13.** $f(x) = 8x^3$ **14.** $f(x) = \frac{x}{x+1}$

15. $f(x) = \frac{5x+9}{6}$ **16.** $f(x) = (x-4)^2$ **17.** $f(x) = 5 + \sqrt{x+8}$

Determine by composition whether each pair of functions are inverses.

18. $f(x) = \frac{5-2x}{9}$ and $g(x) = -\frac{9}{2}x + \frac{5}{2}$ **19.** $f(x) = \frac{5}{x+1}$ and $g(x) = \frac{x-1}{5}$ for $x \neq -1$

20. $f(x) = 3\sqrt{x}$ and $g(x) = \frac{1}{3}x^2$ for $x \geq 0$ **21.** $f(x) = \log \frac{x}{2}$ and $g(x) = 2(10^x)$ for $x > 0$

LINK

Biology

There are about 900 species of crickets worldwide. Many male crickets make chirping noises either by rubbing their wings together or by rubbing their wing cases against their hind legs.

22. Biology The number of times that a cricket chirps per minute can be found by using the function $N(F) = 4F - 160$, where F is the temperature in degrees Fahrenheit.

a. Find and interpret the inverse of $N(F)$.

b. What is the temperature when the cricket is chirping 60 times a minute?

c. How many times will the cricket chirp in 1 minute at a temperature of 80°F?

23. Business The managers of a pizza restaurant have found that the function $t(d) = 20 + 2.5d$ models the length of time in minutes, after it is ordered, for a pizza to be delivered a distance of d miles.

a. Write the inverse of $t(d)$, and explain what it represents.

b. How far away can a customer live and still get a pizza within 30 minutes of placing an order?

Write the rule for the inverse of each function. Then state its domain and range.

24. $f(x) = \frac{7-8x}{3}$ **25.** $f(x) = \frac{5}{x+4}$ **26.** $f(x) = 5(x+6)^2$

27. $f(x) = \sqrt[3]{x-12}$ **28.** $f(x) = \frac{x^3-5}{12}$ **29.** $f(x) = 7^x$

30. $f(x) = \ln(x+2)$ **31.** $f(x) = 3e^{x+5}$ **32.** $f(x) = \frac{\log(x+8)}{4}$

For each graph, determine which two functions are inverses.

33.

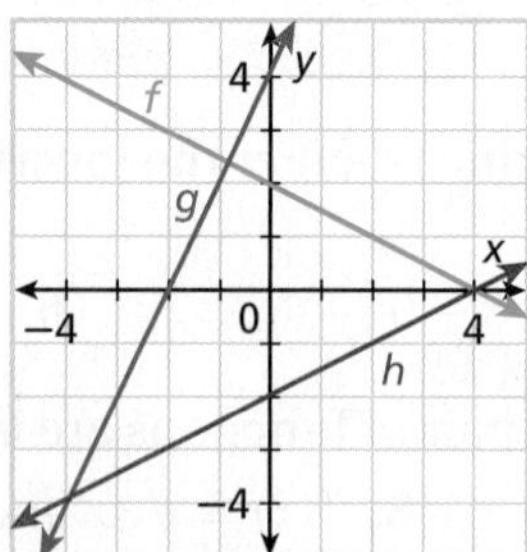

34.

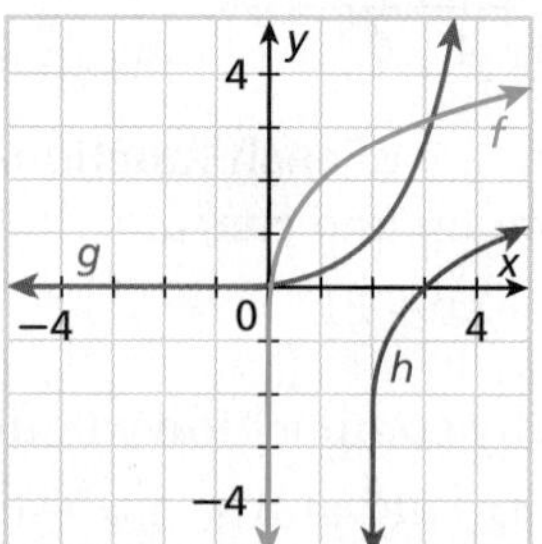

35.

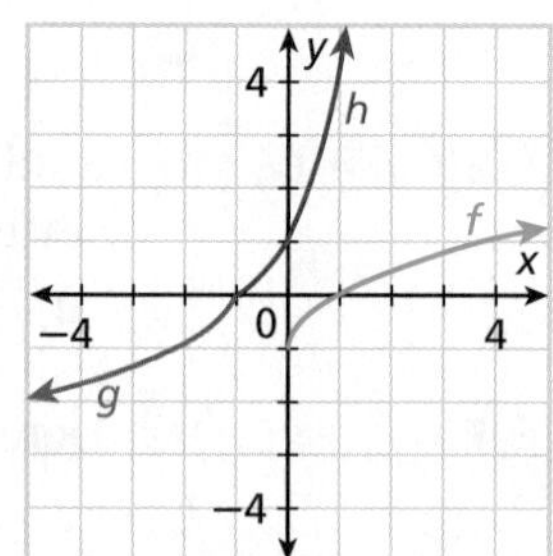

36. Statistics A person's standardized score on a test is given by the function $z(x) = \frac{x-250}{40}$, where x is the actual score on the test.

a. Find and interpret the inverse of $z(x)$.

b. If a person's standardized score on a test was 2.5, what was the person's actual score on the test?

37. Medicine Nurses carefully track the height and weight of infants to ensure that they are healthy as they grow. The average height in inches of a girl in the first 3 years of life can be modeled by $h(a) = 3\sqrt{a} + 19$, where a is the age of the girl in months.

a. Find and interpret the inverse of $h(a)$.

b. Estimation Estimate the age of a girl whose height is $32\frac{1}{2}$ inches.

38. If an object is dropped from a hot-air balloon at an altitude of 500 ft, the object's height after t seconds can be modeled by $h(t) = -16t^2 + 500$.
    a. Find and interpret the inverse of $h(t)$.
    b. How long does it take the object to hit the ground?
    c. How long does it take the object to fall if it lands on the roof of a building that is 128 ft tall?

39. **Conservation** As a brown bear with a radio collar walks along a river, the distance from the bear to an observation post after t seconds is given by the function $d(t) = \sqrt{1600 + 9t^2}$.
    a. Find and interpret the inverse of $d(t)$.
    b. If the tracking equipment has a range of 5500 feet, how long will a person in the observation post be able to track the bear before having to move?

40. **Photography** The cost in dollars of enlarging a photo is given by the function $c = 0.1\ell^2$, where ℓ is the length of the enlargement in inches.
    a. Write the inverse of the function, and explain what it represents.
    b. Determine the length of an enlargement that costs $25.60.

41. **Manufacturing** The surface area of an aluminum can is given by the function $S(h) = 18\pi + 6\pi h$.
    a. Find and interpret the inverse of $S(h)$.
    b. Find the height to the nearest hundredth of a centimeter of a can with a surface area of 500 cm^2.

42. **Critical Thinking** Identify two functions that are their own inverses.

43. **Geometry** The area of a square is $A = s^2$, where s is the length of a side.
    a. Find and interpret the inverse of the function.
    b. Explain how an architect or city planner might use the inverse.
    c. **Estimation** Estimate the side length of a square park that covers an area of 800,000 square feet.

44. **Critical Thinking** If a relation is not a function, can its inverse be a function? Use an example to illustrate your answer.

45. **Write About It** Describe two ways to determine whether two functions are inverses of each other. How would your methods apply to determining whether a function is its own inverse?

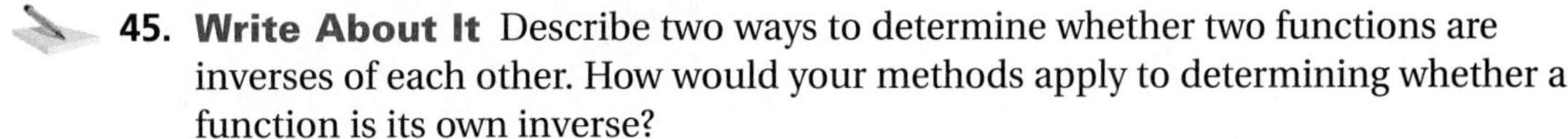

46. The formula for converting from degrees Celsius to degrees Fahrenheit is $F = \frac{9}{5}C + 32$. Which of the following formulas converts degrees Fahrenheit to degrees Celsius?

    Ⓐ $C = \frac{9}{5}F - 32$
    Ⓒ $C = \frac{5}{9}F + 32$
    Ⓑ $C = \frac{9}{5}(F - 32)$
    Ⓓ $C = \frac{5}{9}(F - 32)$

47. Which of the following is true about the relation graphed?

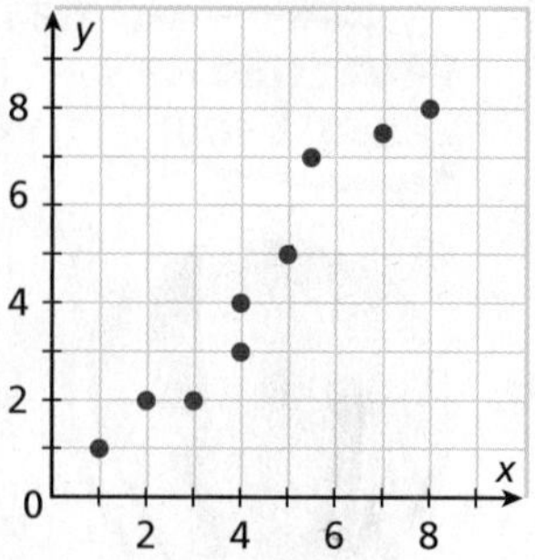

Ⓕ Both the relation and its inverse are functions.

Ⓖ The relation is a function, but its inverse is not a function.

Ⓗ The relation is not a function, but its inverse is a function.

Ⓙ Neither the relation nor its inverse is a function.

48. Which of the following is the inverse of $f(x) = \sqrt{x} + 1$?

Ⓐ $f^{-1}(x) = x^2 - 1, x \geq 0$

Ⓑ $f^{-1}(x) = (x - 1)^2, x \geq 0$

Ⓒ $f^{-1}(x) = x^2 + 1, x \geq 0$

Ⓓ $f^{-1}(x) = (x + 1)^2, x \geq 0$

49. For a certain function, $f(0) = 2$ and $f^{-1}(4) = 1$. Which of the following is also true?

Ⓕ $f^{-1}(0) = 2$

Ⓖ $f^{-1}(2) = 0$

Ⓗ $f(4) = 1$

Ⓙ $f(2) = 0$

50. Which function has an inverse that is NOT a function?

Ⓐ $f(x) = 2x^3 + 3$

Ⓑ $f(x) = \sqrt{2x} + 5$

Ⓒ $f(x) = x^2 - 1$

Ⓓ $f(x) = 3^x + 1$

51. **Short Response** Given that $f(x)$ is a quadratic function, is its inverse a function? Explain.

CHALLENGE AND EXTEND

52. Use the Quadratic Formula to find a rule for the inverse of $f(x) = 3x^2 - 6x - 9$.

Find a rule for the inverse of each function.

53. $f(x) = \dfrac{3 + \ln x}{3 - \ln x}$

54. $f(x) = \dfrac{5\log\left(x^3\right) - 3\log\left(x^2\right)}{3}$

55. Is $f^{-1}\left(g^{-1}(x)\right) = \left(f\left(g(x)\right)\right)^{-1}$ correct? Support your answer.

56. **Personal Finance** A financial manager predicts that if a person leaves \$1000 in his mutual fund, the value of the money after t years will be $V(t) = 1000\left(1.08^t\right)$.

a. Find and interpret the inverse of $V(t)$.

b. If a person puts \$1000 into this mutual fund, predict how much money the person will have in the fund in 10 years.

c. If a person puts \$1000 into this mutual fund, after how many years will the person have \$4000 in the fund?

Explore Symmetry

Use with Modeling Real-World Data

A graph is *symmetric with respect to the y-axis* if a reflection of the graph across the *y*-axis produces an identical graph. A graph is *symmetric with respect to the origin* if a 180° rotation of the graph about the origin produces an identical graph.

MATHEMATICAL PRACTICES **Use appropriate tools strategically.**

CC.9-12.A.CED.2 Create equations in two or more variables to represent relationships between quantities; graph equations on coordinate axes with labels and scales.

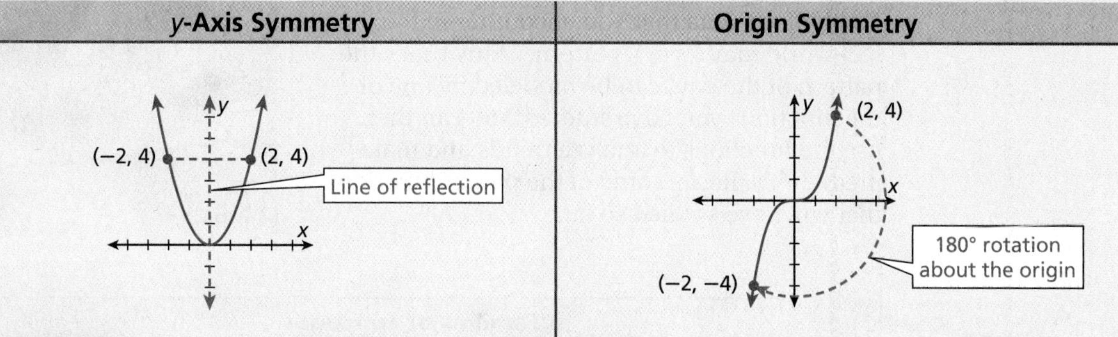

Activity

Graph and classify the function $f(x) = \frac{1}{2}x^4 - 4x^2$. Then describe the symmetry of the graph.

1 Enter the function rule for **Y1**, and view the graph in a friendly window.

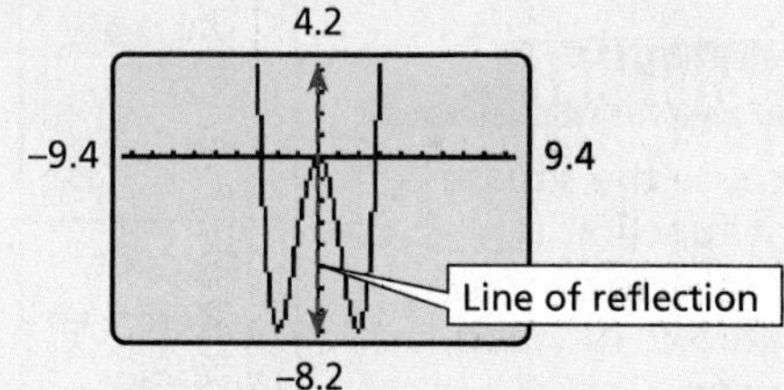

2 Classify the function. The expression $\frac{1}{2}x^4 - 4x^2$ is a polynomial, so $f(x) = \frac{1}{2}x^4 - 4x^2$ is a polynomial function.

3 Examine the symmetry of the graph. The *y*-axis divides the graph into two parts that appear to be reflections of each other, so the graph appears to have *y*-axis symmetry. The graph does not appear to have origin symmetry.

Confirm the symmetry of the graph by viewing a table of values. Except for the origin, the table includes only pairs of points that are reflections of each other across the *y*-axis.

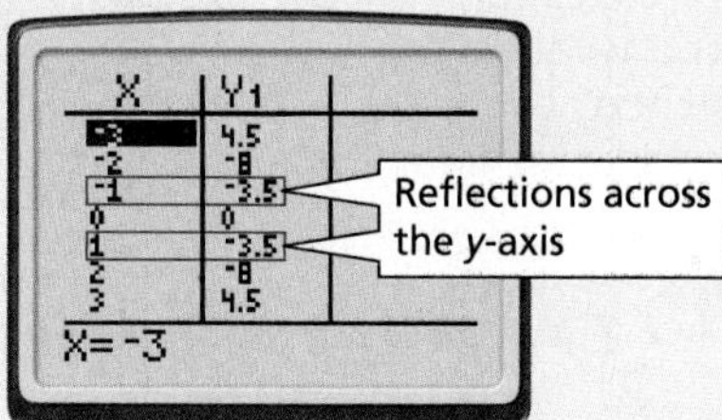

Try This

Graph and classify each function. Then describe the symmetry of the graph.

1. $f(x) = |x|$ **2.** $f(x) = -2x$ **3.** $f(x) = 3^x$

4. $f(x) = \frac{3}{x}$ **5.** $f(x) = x^3 - 5x$ **6.** $f(x) = x^2 + 4$

7. A power function can be written in the form $f(x) = ax^n$, where a and n are real numbers and $a \neq 0$. Graph several power functions with positive integer values of n.

a. Make a Conjecture Describe the symmetry of the graphs of power functions for which n is a positive odd integer.

b. Make a Conjecture Describe the symmetry of the graphs of power functions for which n is a positive even integer.

6-7 Modeling Real-World Data

CC.9-12.A.CED.3 Represent constraints by equations or inequalities,...and interpret solutions...in a modeling context. *Also* **CC.9-12.A.CED.2**

Objectives

Apply functions to problem situations.

Use mathematical models to make predictions.

Who uses this?

You can use mathematical models to analyze and predict the number of automated teller machines (ATMs) in use. (See Example 3.)

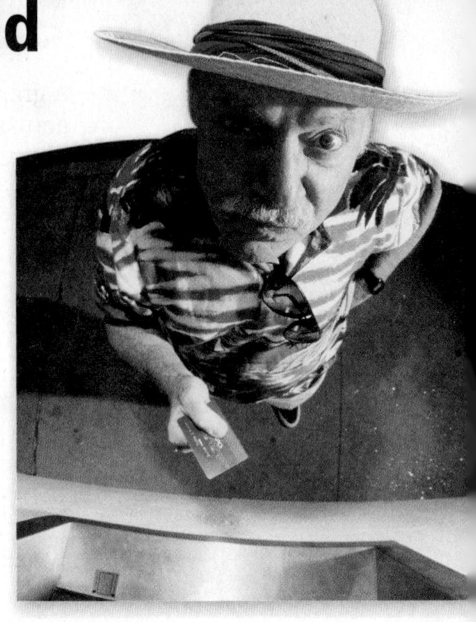

Much of the data that you encounter in the real world may form a pattern. Many times the pattern of the data can be modeled by one of the functions you have studied. You can then use the functions to analyze trends and make predictions. Recall some of the parent functions that you have studied so far.

Families of Functions

Family	Linear	Quadratic	Exponential	Square Root
Rule	$f(x) = x$	$f(x) = x^2$	$f(x) = b^x,\ b > 0$	$f(x) = \sqrt{x}$
Graph				
Constant Differences or Ratios	Constant first differences between y-values for evenly spaced x-values	Constant second differences between y-values for evenly spaced x-values	Constant ratios between y-values for evenly spaced x-values	Constant second differences between x-values for evenly spaced y-values

Helpful Hint

Because the square-root function is the inverse of the quadratic function, the constant differences for x- and y-values are switched.

EXAMPLE 

Identifying Models by Using Constant Differences or Ratios

Use constant differences or ratios to determine which parent function would best model the given data set.

 **The length of a spring depends on the mass attached.**

Mass (kg)	4	5	6	7	8	9	10
Length (cm)	30.6	32	33.4	34.8	36.2	37.6	39

Notice that the mass data are evenly spaced. Check the first differences between the lengths to see if the data set is linear.

Length (cm)	30.6	32	33.4	34.8	36.2	37.6	39

First differences 1.4 1.4 1.4 1.4 1.4 1.4

Because the first differences are a constant 1.4, a linear model will best model the data.

Use constant differences or ratios to determine which parent function would best model the given data set.

B **The age of a tree can be determined from its diameter.**

Diameter (cm)	1.6	3.6	6.4	10.0	14.4	19.6	25.6
Age (yr)	2	3	4	5	6	7	8

Notice that the age data are evenly spaced. Check the first differences between diameters.

Diameter (cm)	1.6	3.6	6.4	10.0	14.4	19.6	25.6

First differences 2 2.8 3.6 4.4 5.2 6

Second differences 0.8 0.8 0.8 0.8 0.8

Because the second differences of the independent variable are constant when the dependent variables are evenly spaced, a square-root function will best model the data.

Check A scatter plot reveals a shape similar to the square-root parent function $f(x) = \sqrt{x}$.

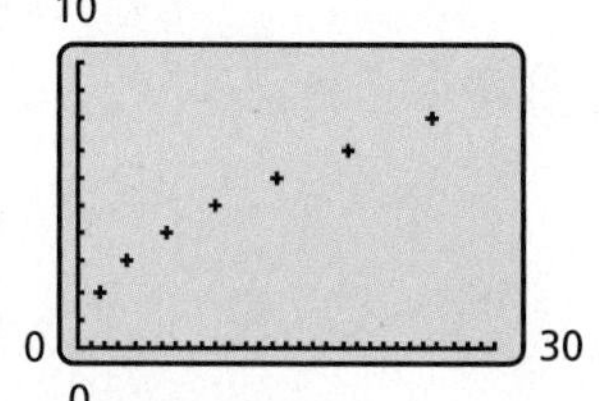

C **The volume of a liquid remaining after evaporation depends on the time elapsed.**

Time (h)	1	2	3	4	5	6
Volume (mL)	512	384	288	216	162	121.5

Because the time data are evenly spaced, check the differences between the volumes.

Volume (mL)	512	384	288	216	162	121.5

First differences −128 −96 −72 −54 −40.5

Second differences 32 24 18 13.5

Neither the first nor second differences are constant. Check ratios between the volumes.

$\frac{384}{512} = 0.75$, $\frac{288}{384} = 0.75$, $\frac{216}{288} = 0.75$, $\frac{162}{216} = 0.75$, and $\frac{121.5}{162} = 0.75$.

Because the ratios between the values of the dependent variable are constant, an exponential function would best model the data.

Check A scatter plot reveals a shape similar to an exponential decay function.

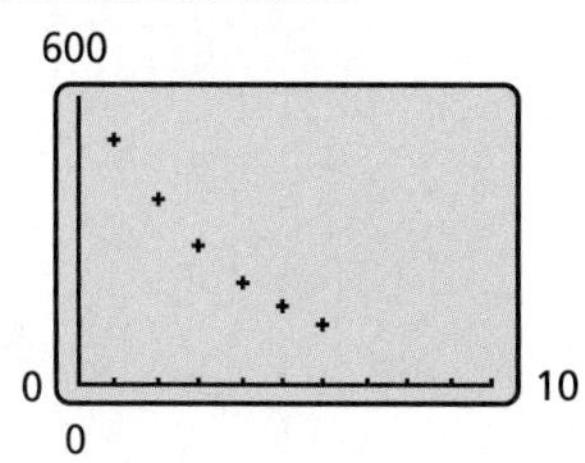

Use constant differences or ratios to determine which parent function would best model the given data set.

1a.

x	12	48	108	192	300
y	10	20	30	40	50

1b.

x	21	22	23	24
y	243	324	432	576

Real-world data rarely have differences or ratios that are mathematically constant, but you can analyze them to see if they are close to constant. You can also use a scatter plot to visually determine which model best suits a data set. Then you can perform a regression to find a function to model the data. Recall that the correlation coefficient *r* helps you see how well the model fits the data.

EXAMPLE 2 Conservation Application

A zoologist is monitoring the size of a herd of buffalo in the years since the herd was released into a wilderness area. Write a function that models the given data.

Time (yr)	5	6	7	8	9	10
Buffalo	124	150	185	213	261	322

Step 1 Make a scatter plot of the data.

The data appear to form a quadratic or an exponential pattern.

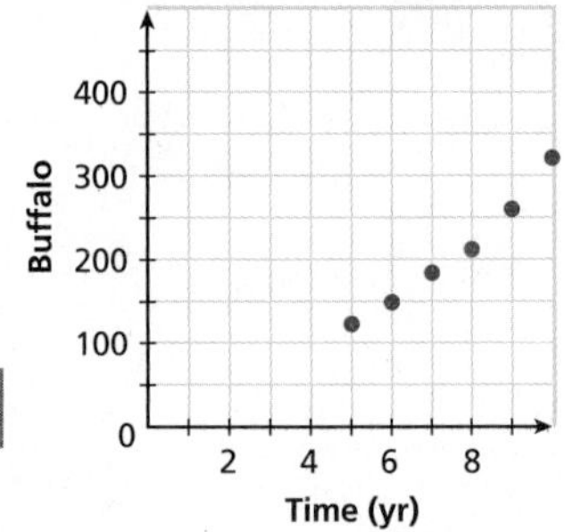

Step 2 Analyze differences.

Buffalo	124	150	185	213	261	322

First differences 26 35 28 48 61

Second differences 9 −7 20 13

Helpful Hint

To display the correlation coefficient *r* on some calculators, you must turn on the diagnostic mode.

Press 2nd CATALOG 0, and choose **DiagnosticOn.**

Step 3 Neither the first nor the second differences are close to constant, so analyze the ratios.

$$\frac{150}{124} = 1.210, \frac{185}{150} = 1.233, \frac{213}{185} = 1.151, \frac{261}{213} = 1.225, \text{ and } \frac{322}{261} = 1.234$$

The ratios are all close to 1.2, indicating that an exponential model would be appropriate.

Step 4 Use your graphing calculator to perform an exponential regression.

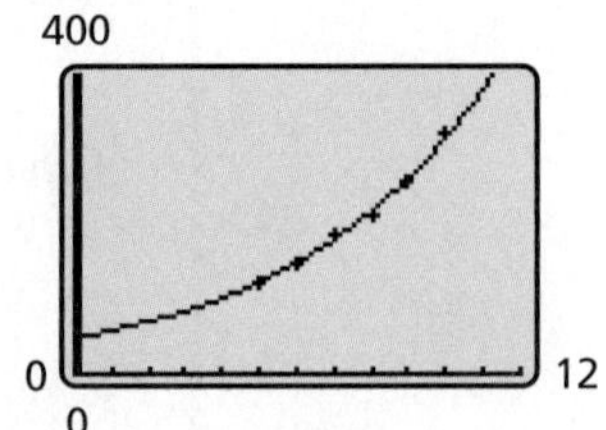

An exponential function that models the data is $f(x) = 48.581(1.207^x)$. The correlation coefficient *r* is very close to 1, which indicates a good fit.

2. Write a function that models the given data.

x	12	14	16	18	20	22	24
y	110	141	176	215	258	305	356

When data are not ordered or evenly spaced, you may have to try several models to determine which best approximates the data. Graphing calculators often indicate the value of the *coefficient of determination*, indicated by r^2 or R^2. The closer the coefficient is to 1, the better the model approximates the data.

EXAMPLE 3 *Banking Application*

The data set shows the approximate number of automated teller machines (ATMs) in operation in the United States. Using 1990 as a reference year, write a function that models the data.

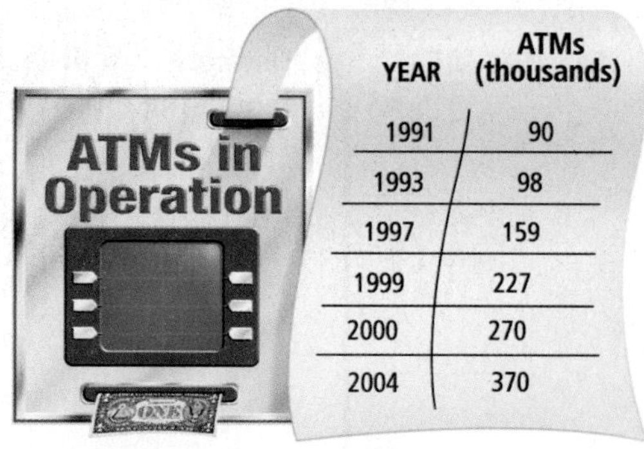

YEAR	ATMs (thousands)
1991	90
1993	98
1997	159
1999	227
2000	270
2004	370

The data are not evenly spaced, so you cannot analyze differences or ratios.

Create a scatter plot of the data. Use 1990 as year 0. The data appears to be quadratic, cubic, or exponential.

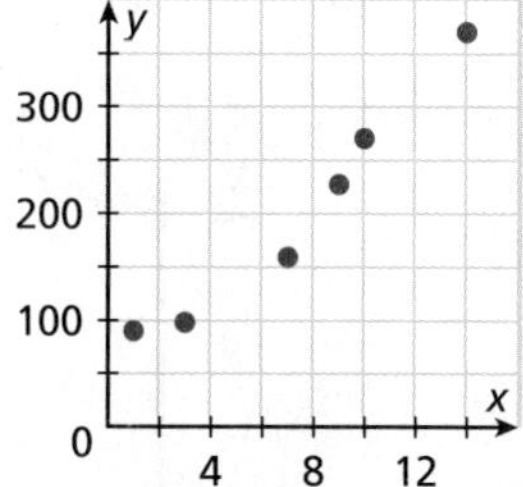

Use the calculator to perform each type of regression.

Compare the values of r^2. The cubic model seems to be the best fit. The function $f(x) \approx 0.2x^3 + 5.44x^2 - 22.13x + 110.07$ models the data.

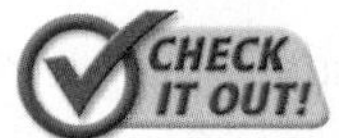

3. Write a function that models the data.

Fertilizer/Acre (lb)	11	14	25	31	40	50
Yield/Acre (bushels)	245	302	480	557	645	705

MATHEMATICAL PRACTICES

THINK AND DISCUSS

1. Explain the limitations of finding constant differences or ratios when working with real-world data.

2. GET ORGANIZED Copy and complete the graphic organizer. Explain how each method can help you determine which model best fits a data set.

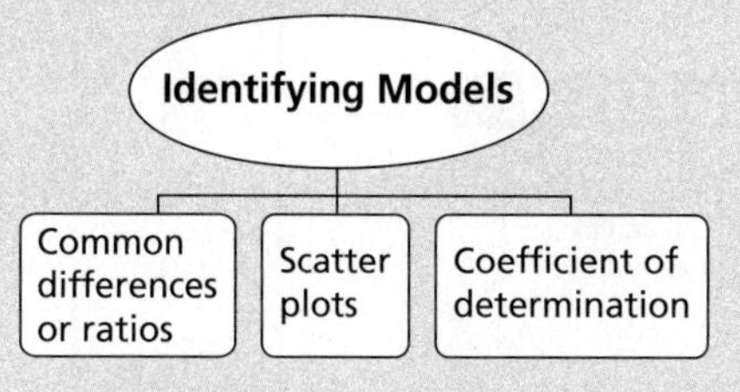

6-7 Exercises

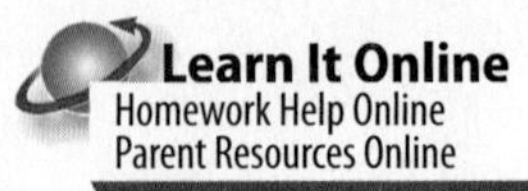

GUIDED PRACTICE

SEE EXAMPLE 1

Use constant differences or ratios to determine which parent function would best model the given data set.

1.

x	y
6	69.6
13	51.4
20	33.2
27	15
34	−3.2
41	−21.4

2.

x	y
11	2
47	6
99	10
167	14
251	18
351	22

3.

x	y
0	125
1	150
2	180
3	216
4	259.2
5	311.04

SEE EXAMPLE 2

4. This table shows the mass in grams m of the radioactive substance iodine-131 remaining in a container t days after the beginning of an experiment.

Time t (days)	0	1	2	3	4	5	6
Mass m (g)	1000	917.40	841.62	772.10	708.33	649.82	596.14

a. Write a function that models the data.

b. Use your model to predict the number of grams of iodine-131 that will be left after 20 days.

c. Use your model to predict when there will be less than 50 grams remaining.

SEE EXAMPLE 3

5. The table shows the value of a stock at various points in the past 24 months since Carla bought the stock.

Time t (months)	0	4	9	12	15	20	24
Stock Value v ($)	62	54	45	48	55	53	60

a. Write a function that models the data.

b. Use your model to predict the stock price 6 months after Carla bought it.

c. Would you recommend that Carla use your model to predict the value of her stock a year from now? Why or why not?

PRACTICE AND PROBLEM SOLVING

Independent Practice

For Exercises	See Example
6–8	1
9	2
10	3

Extra Practice

See Extra Practice for more Skills Practice and Applications Practice exercises.

Use constant differences or ratios to determine which parent function would best model the given data set.

6.

x	y
1	380
3	343
5	310
7	279
9	252
11	228

7.

x	y
2	97
8	202
14	253
20	250
26	193
32	82

8.

x	y
4	4
9	6
16	8
25	10
36	12

9. **Agriculture** A farmer is experimenting with the amount of fertilizer to put on his corn fields. Different amounts of fertilizer are applied to each field, and the resulting yields are measured. Write a function that models the given data.

Fertilizer/Acre (lb)	45	70	90	115	125	135	150
Yield/Acre (bushels)	29	60	70	88	84	86	76

10. **Biology** The table shows the estimated number of *E. coli* bacteria in a lab dish t minutes after the start of an experiment.

Time (min)	0	10	20	30	40	50	60
Bacteria	300	423	596	842	1188	1686	2354

Math History

In 1806, French mathematician Adrien-Marie Legendre (1752–1833) modeled the orbit of a comet by fitting a quadratic curve to location data.

a. Using t as the independent variable, find the model that best fits the data.

b. Use your model to predict the number of bacteria after 3 hours.

c. How long does it take the population of *E. coli* to triple?

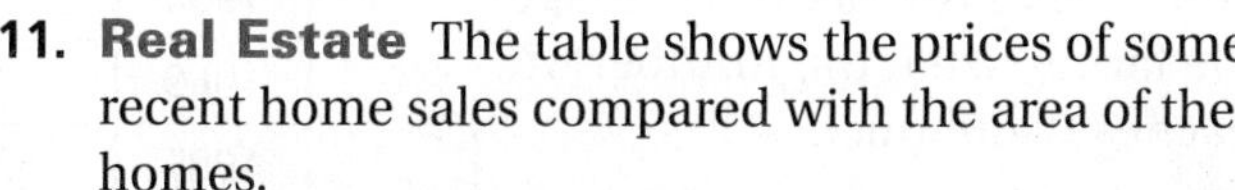

11. **Real Estate** The table shows the prices of some recent home sales compared with the area of the homes.

a. Using area as the independent variable, find a model for the data.

b. Use your model to predict the number of square feet in a house that is priced at $175,000.

c. How accurate do you think your answer to part **b** is?

Area of Homes Sold

Area (ft^2)	Price ($)
2675	179,000
1170	125,900
1486	136,750
2510	172,500
2444	169,900
2980	187,000

12. **Economics** An economist is studying the median yearly income of workers by their ages.

Age (yr)	18	28	38	48	58	68
Median Income ($)	17,480	30,650	37,440	41,230	37,570	21,390

a. Find an appropriate model for the data.

b. Use your model to predict the median income for a worker who is 43 years old.

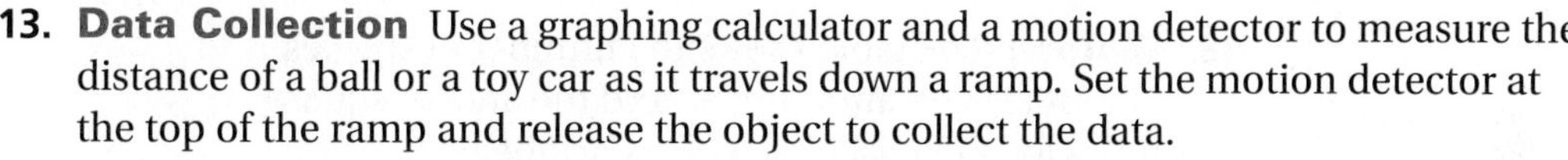

13. **Data Collection** Use a graphing calculator and a motion detector to measure the distance of a ball or a toy car as it travels down a ramp. Set the motion detector at the top of the ramp and release the object to collect the data.

a. Find an appropriate model for distance versus time.

b. Use your model to predict the distance the object would travel in 1 minute if the ramp continued indefinitely.

14. **Health** The table shows the mean age of mothers in the United States when they had their first child.

Year	1980	1985	1990	1995	2000
Mean Age of Mother at First Birth	22.7	23.7	24.2	24.5	24.9

a. Using 1980 as a reference year, find both a quadratic and cubic model for the data.

b. Use both models to predict the mean age of a mother at first birth in 2010.

c. Explain which prediction you think is more accurate.

MULTI-STEP TEST PREP

15. The table shows how the volume v of air in a hot-air balloon relates to the temperature t of the air.
    a. Find an exponential model for the data.
    b. Use your model to predict the volume of the air when its temperature is 109°F.
    c. Would your model be accurate for any air temperature greater than 118°F? Why or why not?

Temperature (°F)	Volume (ft^2)
100	30,000
106	33,000
112	36,300
118	39,930

16. **Agriculture** The table shows the number and the average area of farms in the United States in the last century.
    a. Using the number of farms as the independent variable, find a model for the average size of farms.
    b. Use your model to predict the average size of the farms when the number of farms reaches 1 million.
    c. Use your model to estimate the average size of the farms when there were 4.5 million farms.

Number and Size of U.S. Farms

Year	Farms (millions)	Average Area (acres)
1910	6.4	139
1930	6.3	157
1950	5.4	216
1969	2.7	390
1987	2.1	462
1997	1.9	487

17. **Baseball** The Fan Cost Index tracks the cost for a family of four to attend a Major League Baseball game.

Year	1991	1994	1997	2000	2003
FCI	\$79.41	\$96.41	\$107.26	\$132.44	\$151.19

    a. Find a model for the data. Use 1990 as year 0.
    b. How fast has the FCI been increasing according to your model?
    c. The FCI in 2004 was \$155.52. How close is the actual value to the value predicted by your model?
    d. Use your model to predict when the FCI will reach \$200.
    e. Because of inflation, something that cost \$1.00 in 1991 cost \$1.34 in 2003. How does the change in the FCI compare with inflation?

18. **Biology** The table shows the number of species of reptiles and amphibians and the area in square miles for some islands in the Caribbean.
    a. Using number of species as the independent variable, find an appropriate model for the data.
    b. Use your model to predict the area of an island with 75 species of reptiles and amphibians.
    c. How accurate do you think your prediction in part **b** is? Explain.

Species	Area (mi^2)
11	5
16	32
53	3,435
45	4,244
108	29,371
100	44,218

Green iguana

19. **Critical Thinking** Sometimes data that appear linear are better modeled by a quadratic function. What can you conclude about the value of a in the quadratic model of such a data set?

20. **Write About It** Suppose that a model can be found that provides a good fit for data on two variables. What evidence does the model give of a cause-and-effect relationship between the two variables? Use examples in your explanation.

TEST PREP

21. Which of the following is true for the data in the table?

Ⓐ The first differences of values of the dependent variable are constant.

Ⓑ The second differences of values of the dependent variable are constant.

Ⓒ The ratios of values of the dependent variable are constant.

Ⓓ The ratios of values of the independent variable are constant.

x	y
3	2
4	23
5	50
6	83
7	122
8	167

22. Find n so that an exponential model will fit the data exactly.

Ⓕ $n = 40$ Ⓗ $n = 45$

Ⓖ $n = 49$ Ⓙ $n = 52$

x	5	6	7
y	16	28	n

23. Find n so that a quadratic model will fit the data exactly.

Ⓐ $n = 60$ Ⓒ $n = 80$

Ⓑ $n = 70$ Ⓓ $n = 90$

x	5	6	7	8
y	12	32	58	n

CHALLENGE AND EXTEND

24. The function $P(t) = \frac{a}{1 + be^{-kt}}$, called a *logistic function*, is often used when there are factors such as food or space that limit a population's growth. The number of fish in a stocked pond can be modeled by the function $F(t) = \frac{4000}{1 + 5.7e^{-0.2t}}$, where t is the number of months after the pond is stocked.

   a. Predict the number of fish in the lake after 10 months.

   b. When will the population of fish reach 3000?

   c. Find the maximum number of fish that the pond can hold if the function is correct.

25. **Graphing Calculator** Another type of regression you can perform is a power regression. Use the **PwrReg** feature to find a model for the given data. Which parent function best fits the data?

x	1	24	41	74
y	1	4.9	6.4	8.6

MULTI-STEP TEST PREP

MATHEMATICAL PRACTICES **Model with mathematics.**

Functional Relationships

Full of Hot Air When you ride in a hot-air balloon that is rising vertically, the distance to the farthest object that you can see increases as the balloon's height increases. The table shows data that were collected on a hot-air balloon.

Balloon's Height (m)	7.8	31.3	70.5	125.4	196.0
Distance That You Can See (km)	10	20	30	40	50

1. Which is the independent variable? Why?
2. Which parent function best models the data set? Why?
3. Write a function $f(x)$ that models the data.
4. If you are in a hot-air balloon at a height of 100 m, how far would you expect to be able to see?
5. Write the inverse function of $f(x)$, and explain what it represents.
6. Find the approximate minimum height for a hot-air balloon if you want to be able to see objects that are 25 km away.
7. The function $g(x) = 0.3x$ converts distances in feet to approximate distances in meters. Write a composite function for the distance that you can see in kilometers from a height of x feet.

READY TO GO ON?

CHAPTER 6

SECTION 6B

Quiz for Lessons 6-5 Through 6-7

6-5 Operations with Functions

Given $f(x) = \dfrac{5}{x+3}$, $g(x) = x - 6$, and $h(x) = x^2 - 4x - 12$, find each function or value.

1. $(f - g)(2)$
2. $(g + h)(x)$
3. $\left(\dfrac{g}{h}\right)(8)$
4. $\left(\dfrac{h}{g}\right)(x)$
5. $(gh)(5)$
6. $(gf)(x)$
7. $g(f(-2))$
8. $h(g(x))$
9. Find $(f \circ g)(x)$. State the domain of the composite function.
10. Erin receives a 30% employee discount at the camera store where she works. During a sale, she receives an additional 20% off the discounted price. Write a composite function for the price Erin pays for an item with an original price of p dollars.

6-6 Functions and Their Inverses

State whether the inverse of each relation is a function.

11. 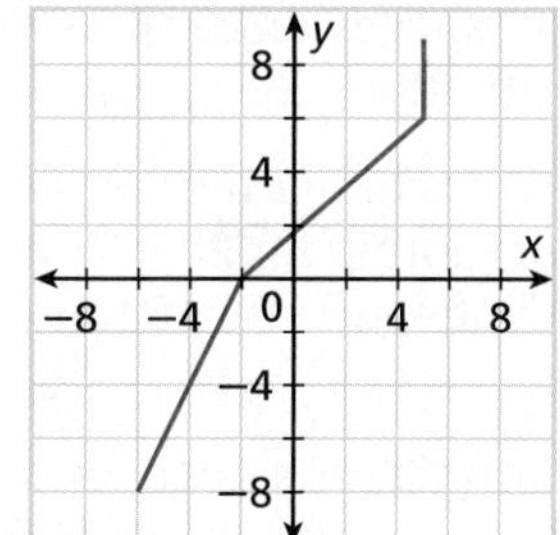

12. 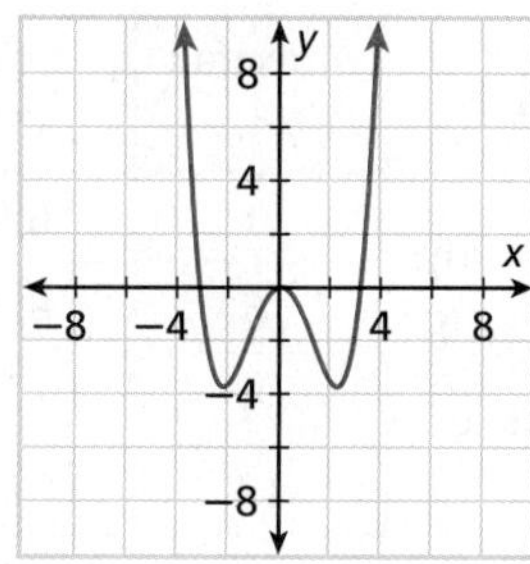

Write the rule for the inverse of each function. Then state the domain and range of the inverse.

13. $f(x) = \dfrac{2}{3}x - 12$
14. $g(x) = \dfrac{12}{x-5}$
15. $h(x) = x^2 - 4$
16. $n(x) = 3^x$

6-7 Modeling Real-World Data

17. Use finite differences or ratios to determine which parent function would best model this set of data.

x	0	1	2	3	4
y	625	375	225	135	81

18. The table shows the average temperature in degrees Fahrenheit and the average utility bill for the households in a town in recent months. Using average temperature as the independent variable, find a model for the average bill.

Average Monthly Temperature (°F)	Average Monthly Utility Bill ($)
61	108
80	103
46	148
72	89
50	125
88	132

CHAPTER 6

Study Guide: Review

Vocabulary

composition of functions

one-to-one function

piecewise function

step function

Complete the sentences below with vocabulary words from the list above.

1. In a(n) ___?___, each y-value is paired with exactly one x-value.
2. A(n) ___?___ is a piecewise function that is constant for each interval of its domain.
3. The function operation that uses the output from one function as the input for a second function is the ___?___.

6-1 Multiple Representations of Functions

EXAMPLE

■ **The managers of a town are interested in the cost of snow removal over the winter. The table shows the cost of removing various amounts of snow. Use a graph and an equation to find the cost to remove 24 inches of snow.**

Snowfall (in.)	Cost ($)
3	6,950
6	8,900
9	10,850
12	12,800

A scatter plot shows that the data is linear.

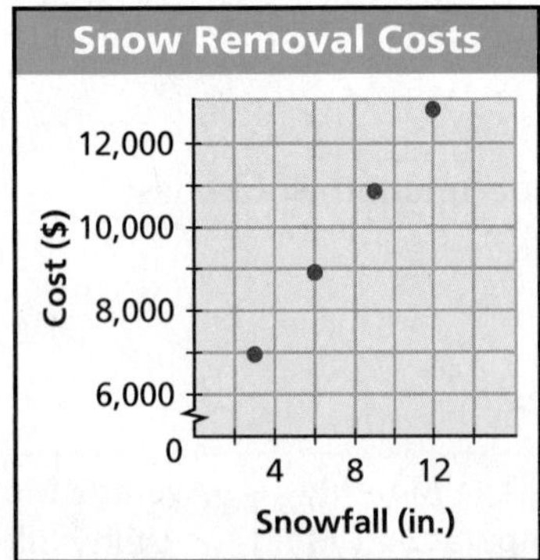

Find the slope of the line by using two points.

$$m = \frac{8900 - 6950}{6 - 3} = \frac{1950}{3} = 650$$

Write an equation by using one of the points.

$$y - 6950 = 650(x - 3)$$
$$y = 650x + 5000$$

The cost for removing 24 inches of snow is $y = 5000 + 650(24) = \$20{,}600$.

EXERCISES

4. Draw a graph of speed versus time that represents the following situation.

   Avery drove 5 miles to her mother's house and visited with her mother for 20 minutes. Then she drove on the freeway for 15 minutes before arriving home.

5. A caterer is planning for a large fund-raising dinner. He plans to have 4 trays of 30 appetizers each on the buffet. In addition, he will prepare an additional 4 appetizers per guest. Create a table, a graph, and an equation to represent the number of appetizers with relation to the number of guests.

6. The scatter plot shows how long it takes to fill various cylindrical containers of different radii.

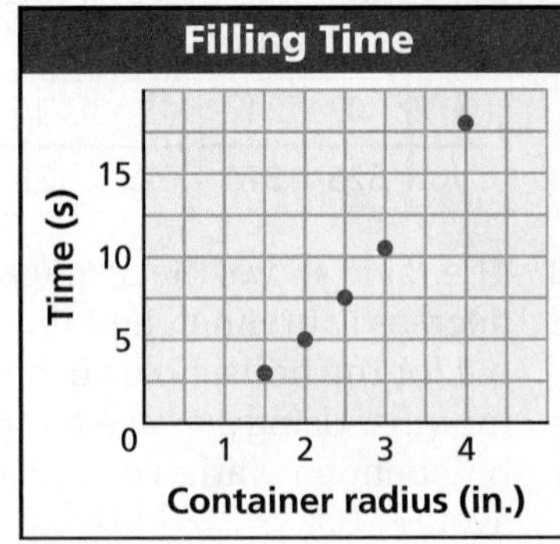

   a. Create a table and an equation for the data.

   b. Use your equation to predict the time that it would take to fill a cylindrical container with a radius of 7 inches.

6-2 Comparing Functions

EXAMPLE

Determine the end behavior of the function $f(x) = -2^{2x}$.

As x increases, $2x$ also increases. As $2x$ increases, 2^{2x} increases without bound. As 2^{2x} increases, $f(x)$ decreases: as $x \to +\infty$, $f(x) \to -\infty$.

As x decreases, $2x$ also decreases. As $2x$ decreases, 2^{2x} approaches 1. As 2^{2x} approaches 1, $f(x)$ approaches –1: as $x \to -\infty$, $f(x) \to -1$.

EXERCISES

Determine the end behavior of each function.

7. $g(x) = -2x^3$
8. $h(x) = \dfrac{e}{x^5}$

6-3 Piecewise Functions

EXAMPLE

- **Graph $g(x) = \begin{cases} 2x + 4 & \text{if } x < -2 \\ -3x + 2 & \text{if } x \geq -2 \end{cases}$.**

The domain of the function is split at $x = -2$.

Graph both pieces. Use an open circle at $(-2, 0)$ and a closed circle at $(-2, 8)$.

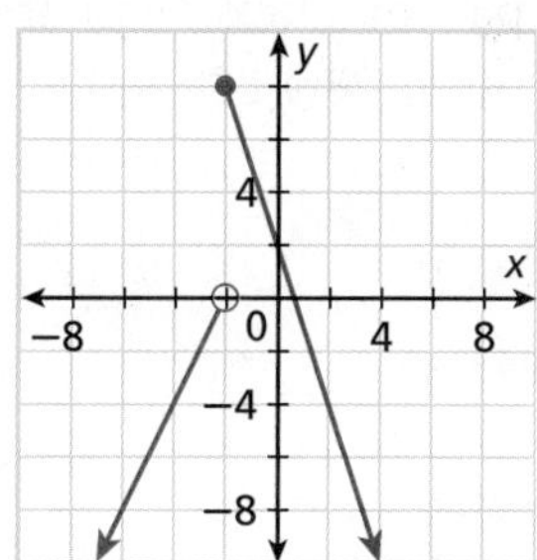

EXERCISES

Graph each function.

9. $f(x) = \begin{cases} 2x - 4 & \text{if } x < 0 \\ 5 & \text{if } x \geq 0 \end{cases}$
10. $g(x) = \begin{cases} \dfrac{3x - 1}{2} & \text{if } x \leq 2 \\ \sqrt{x + 2} & \text{if } x > 2 \end{cases}$
11. A bicycle delivery service charges \$6 to deliver a package that weighs 8 ounces or less. For each additional ounce, the service charges \$1.50 per ounce. Write a piecewise function for the amounts that this company charges to deliver packages that weigh 3 pounds or less.

6-4 Transforming Functions

EXAMPLE

- **Given $f(x) = \begin{cases} 2x - 2 & \text{if } x \leq 3 \\ -4x + 16 & \text{if } x > 3 \end{cases}$, write the rule for $g(x)$, a horizontal translation of $f(x)$ 5 units left.**

Each piece of $f(x)$ must be shifted 5 units left. Replace every x with $(x + 5)$, and simplify.

$$g(x) = f(x+5) = \begin{cases} 2(x+5) - 2 & \text{if } (x+5) \leq 3 \\ -4(x+5) + 16 & \text{if } (x+5) > 3 \end{cases}$$

$$= \begin{cases} 2x + 8 & \text{if } x \leq -2 \\ -4x - 4 & \text{if } x > -2 \end{cases}$$

EXERCISES

12. Given $f(x) = \begin{cases} 2x - 2 & \text{if } x \leq 3 \\ -4x + 16 & \text{if } x > 3 \end{cases}$, write the rule for $h(x)$, a vertical translation of $f(x)$ 2 units up.
13. Given $f(x) = \begin{cases} 3x + 2 & \text{if } x \leq 0 \\ x^2 & \text{if } x > 0 \end{cases}$, write the rule for $g(x)$, a horizontal translation of $f(x)$ 7 units right.
14. Given $f(x) = 2x^2 + 1$ and $g(x) = f\left(\frac{1}{2}x\right) + 1$, graph $g(x)$.

6-5 Operations with Functions

EXAMPLES

Given $f(x) = x + 3$ and $g(x) = x^2 - 9$, find each function.

■ $\left(\frac{g}{f}\right)(x)$

$$\left(\frac{g}{f}\right)(x) = \frac{g(x)}{f(x)} = \frac{x^2 - 9}{x + 3}$$

$$= \frac{(x + 3)(x - 3)}{x + 3} = x - 3, x \neq -3$$

■ **Given $f(x) = x + 6$ and $g(x) = \frac{18}{x + 4}$, find $g(f(x))$. State its domain.**

$g(f(x)) = g(x + 6)$ *Substitute the rule for f into g.*

$= \frac{18}{(x + 6) + 4}$ *Use the rule for g.*

$= \frac{18}{x + 10}$

The domain of $g(f(x))$ is $\{x | x \neq -10\}$ because the function is undefined at $x = -10$.

EXERCISES

Given $f(x) = x^2 - 5x - 14$ and $g(x) = x - 7$, find each function.

15. $(f + g)(x)$
16. $(f - g)(x)$
17. $(g - f)(x)$
18. $(fg)(x)$
19. $\left(\frac{f}{g}\right)(x)$
20. $\left(\frac{g}{f}\right)(x)$

Let $f(x) = x - 2$ and $g(x) = \frac{8}{x + 1}$.

21. Find $f(g(-2))$ and $g(f(-2))$.
22. Find $f(g(1))$, and $g(f(1))$.
23. Find $g(f(x))$, and state its domain.
24. Find $f(g(x))$ and state its domain.
25. Because of high fuel costs, an airline begins adding a fuel surcharge of \$30 to the price of each airline ticket the airline sells. Also, the airline must add 9% to the price for airport and sales taxes. Write a composite function for how much a person would pay for a ticket with this airline that is x dollars before surcharges and taxes.

6-6 Functions and Their Inverses

EXAMPLES

■ **Find the inverse of $f(x) = -3(x - 6)^2$. Determine whether it is a function, and state its domain and range.**

$y = -3(x - 6)^2$ *Rewrite the function by using y.*

$x = -3(y - 6)^2$ *Switch x and y in the equation.*

$-\frac{x}{3} = (y - 6)^2$ *Divide both sides by −3.*

$\pm\sqrt{-\frac{x}{3}} = y - 6$ *Take the square root of both sides.*

$y = \pm\sqrt{-\frac{x}{3}} + 6$ *Simplify.*

$f^{-1}(x) = \pm\sqrt{-\frac{x}{3}} + 6$ *Rewrite as $f^{-1}(x)$.*

Because there is a positive y-value and a negative y-value for any $x < 0$, the inverse is not a function. Because the radicand must be greater than or equal to 0, the domain is $\{x | x \leq 0\}$. The range is $\mathbb{R}$.

EXERCISES

26. Use the horizontal-line test to determine whether the inverse of the relation graphed is a function.

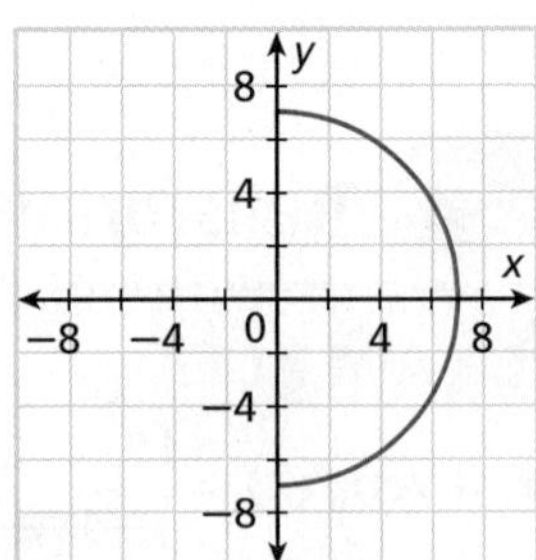

Find the inverse of each function. Determine whether the inverse is a function, and state its domain and range.

27. $f(x) = 5 - 8x$
28. $f(x) = \left(\frac{1}{3}x + 2\right)^2$
29. $f(x) = \frac{5}{2x + 8}$
30. $f(x) = 3 + \sqrt{x - 5}$

EXAMPLES

- **Determine by composition whether $f(x) = \frac{1}{3}x - 4$ and $g(x) = 12 + 3x$ are inverses.**

Find both compositions.

$f(g(x)) = \frac{1}{3}(12 + 3x) - 4 = 4 + x - 4 = x$

$g(f(x)) = 12 + 3\left(\frac{1}{3}x - 4\right) = 12 + x - 12 = x$

Because $f(g(x)) = g(f(x)) = x$, f and g are inverses.

EXERCISES

Determine by composition whether each pair of functions are inverses.

31. $f(x) = 3x - 5$ and $g(x) = \frac{x - 3}{5}$

32. $f(x) = \sqrt[3]{x - 5}$ and $g(x) = x^3 + 5$

33. The formula for the surface area of a sphere with radius r is $A(r) = 4\pi r^2$. Find and interpret the inverse of $A(r)$.

6-7 Modeling Real-World Data

EXAMPLE

- **The table shows the ticket prices to a minor league baseball game in relation to the number of years since the team began playing.**

Baseball Ticket Prices	
Year	**Price ($)**
1	9.50
2	10.25
3	11.10
4	12.00
5	12.92

Step 1 Check the first differences of the prices.

0.75 0.85 0.90 0.92

Because the first differences are not constant, a linear model is not a good fit.

Step 2 Check the second differences.

0.10 0.05 0.02

Because the second differences are not constant, a quadratic model is not a good fit.

Step 3 Check the ratios.

$\frac{10.25}{9.5} \approx 1.08$, $\frac{11.10}{10.25} \approx 1.08$, $\frac{12}{11.10} \approx 1.08$, $\frac{12.92}{12} \approx 1.08$

The ratios are close to 1.08. An exponential model is a good fit.

Step 4 Perform an exponential regression.

An appropriate model is $f(x) = 8.79(1.08)^x$.

EXERCISES

34. The table shows the city of Culver's water use in relation to daily high temperature.

Water Use in Culver	
Daily High Temperature (°F)	**Water Use (million gal)**
55	71.3
60	78.7
65	86.9
70	96
75	106
80	117

a. Find an appropriate model for this data. Use temperature t as the independent variable.

b. Use your model to predict the number of gallons that Culver will use when the high temperature is 85°F.

c. Use your model to predict the high temperature when the water use is 50 million gallons.

CHAPTER 6

Chapter Test

1. While standing at the top of a cliff, Kurt accidentally knocks a stone loose. The table shows the height of the stone in meters after t seconds.

   a. Create a graph and an equation for the data by using time t as the independent variable.

   b. How high is the cliff?

   c. Find the height of the stone after 10 seconds.

   d. When will the stone hit the ground?

Height of Falling Stone

Time (s)	Height (m)
1	615.1
2	600.4
3	575.9
4	541.6
5	497.5
6	443.6

2. An astronaut on the moon throws an object up and watches it fall down. The graph of the object's height in meters, relative to time in seconds, passes through the points (0.5, 2.595), (1, 3.38), and (2, 2.52). Find a quadratic equation that models the situation.

Graph each function.

3. $f(x) = \begin{cases} -x - 3 & \text{if } x < 1 \\ 2x - 6 & \text{if } x \geq 1 \end{cases}$

4. $g(x) = \begin{cases} 5 & \text{if } x \leq -2 \\ -x^2 - 4x & \text{if } x > -2 \end{cases}$

Given $f(x)$, graph $g(x)$.

5. $f(x) = 2x - 4$ and $g(x) = -\frac{1}{2} f(x) - 1$

6. $f(x) = x^2 - 2$ and $g(x) = -f(x + 2)$

Given $f(x) = 4x^2 - 9$ and $g(x) = 2x + 3$, find each function or value.

7. $(f - g)(4)$

8. $g(f(3))$

9. $(fg)(5)$

10. $\left(\frac{g}{f}\right)(x)$

11. Ramon pays a 10% insurance fee for each piece of jewelry in his store. He then prices the item for sale at 150% of his total cost. Write a composite function for the price of an item with an original cost of c dollars.

Write the rule for the inverse of each function. Determine whether the inverse is a function, and state its domain and range.

12. $f(x) = 12 - 5x$

13. $g(x) = \frac{10}{x + 4}$

14. $h(x) = \frac{(x + 5)^2}{2}$

15. The table shows the average sales prices of houses and the houses' distances from downtown.

    a. Find an appropriate model for the data by using distance d as the independent variable.

    b. Use your model to predict the average sales prices of houses that are 20 miles from downtown.

Sales Prices of Houses

Distance from Downtown (mi)	Average Sales Price ($)
2	118,496
4	109,016
6	100,295
8	92,271
10	84,890
12	78,098

CHAPTER 6

COLLEGE ENTRANCE EXAM PRACTICE

FOCUS ON SAT STUDENT-PRODUCED RESPONSES

Some questions on the SAT require you to enter your answer in a special grid. Your answers must be positive integers, fractions, or decimals. You cannot enter negative numbers or mixed numbers in the grid.

Some questions may have multiple answers; in these cases you may enter any one correct answer. If the solution is an inequality, be sure that you choose a number from the solution region.

You may want to time yourself as you take this practice test. It should take you about 9 minutes to complete.

1. If 5 less than 3 times a number is equal to 2 more than twice the number, what is the number?

2. The graph of $f(x)$ is shown.

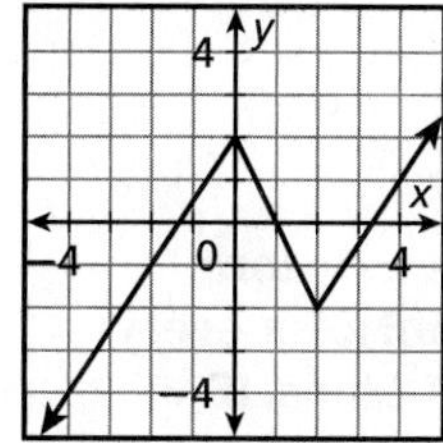

If $g(x) = -f(x) + 1$, what is $g(2)$?

3. Give a possible value for x in the inequality $-4(2x - 3) > 4x - 24$.

4. Let the operations ♦ and ♥ be defined for real numbers a and b as shown.

$a ♦ b = 2a - b$

$a ♥ b = \dfrac{a + b}{2}$

What is the value of $(4 ♥ 9) ♦ 3$?

5. Maria drove to her grandmother's house at an average speed of 60 miles per hour. On the way home, she averaged only 45 miles per hour due to traffic. If she spent a total of $3\frac{1}{2}$ hours driving, how many miles is the trip to her grandmother's house?

6. The table shows some values for the function f.

x	−2	0	2	4
$f(x)$	7	4	1	−2

What is the value of $f^{-1}(-2)$?

CHAPTER 6

TEST TACKLER

Standardized Test Strategies

Multiple Choice: Eliminate Answer Choices

With some multiple choice test items, you can use mental math or logic to quickly eliminate some of the answer choices before you begin solving the problem.

EXAMPLE 1

Tyler can install an air conditioning unit in 3 hours. If Laura helps him, the job is done in 2 hours. How many hours would it take Laura working alone?

Ⓐ 1 hour Ⓒ 6 hours

Ⓑ 2 hours Ⓓ 8 hours

*READ the question. Then try to **eliminate** some of the answer choices.*

Use logic:
When Tyler works alone, the job gets done in 3 hours. When working with Laura, the job takes only 2 hours. So, it is reasonable to assume that Laura working alone takes MORE THAN 2 hours to complete the job.

Based on this logic, **eliminate** choices A and B.
Set up and solve a rational equation to find the correct answer, C.

EXAMPLE 2

Ryanne swims six days a week. Her coach starts keeping time when Ryanne starts warming up and notes how long Ryanne has been at the pool after every 2 laps. The table shows the time that it takes for Ryanne to swim 12 laps. If Ryanne wants to swim 24 laps, how long will it take?

Laps	Time (min)
2	6
4	10
6	14
8	18
10	22
12	26

Ⓕ 28 minutes Ⓗ 48 minutes

Ⓖ 38 minutes Ⓙ 50 minutes

*LOOK at the data, and **eliminate** some answer choices.*

Use mental math and logic:
From the data in the table, you can tell that Ryanne swims 2 laps every 4 minutes. So it takes her 2 minutes to swim 1 lap.

So 24 laps would take $24(2) = 48$ minutes. You can eliminate any answer choice that is LESS THAN 48 minutes: choices F and G.

Before you select choice H as your answer, be careful. Look at the data in the table again. The first 2 laps that Ryanne swims take her **6** minutes, not 4 minutes, so your estimate of 48 laps is a bit low. Therefore, **eliminate** choice H. Choice J is the correct answer.

Try to eliminate unreasonable answer choices. Some choices may be too great or too small or may have incorrect units.

Read each test item and answer the questions that follow.

Item A

The width of a rectangle is 6 feet less than its length. Which of the following systems of equations can be used to find the dimensions of the rectangle if the perimeter of the rectangle is 56 feet?

Ⓐ $\ell = w - 6$
$2\ell + 2w = 56$

Ⓑ $w = \ell - 6$
$2(\ell + w) = 56$

Ⓒ $\ell = w - 6$
$\ell w = 56$

Ⓓ $w = \ell - 6$
$\ell w = \ell 6$

1. What is the perimeter formula for the area of a rectangle? Based on this formula, are there any choices that you can eliminate immediately? If so, which choices and why?
2. Read the first sentence of the test item again and write an expression. Are there any more answer choices that you can eliminate? Explain.

Item B

The volume *V* of a gas varies inversely with the pressure *P* and directly with the temperature *T*. A certain gas has a volume of 30 liters, a temperature of 345 kelvins, and a pressure of 1 atmosphere. If the gas is compressed to a volume of 20 liters and heated to 375 kelvins, what will the new pressure be?

Ⓕ 0.72 atmosphere

Ⓖ 0.72 liter

Ⓗ 1.5 atmospheres

Ⓙ 1.63 atmospheres

3. Are there any answer choices that logically do not make sense and can be eliminated? If so, which choices and why.
4. Because the volume of a gas varies inversely with the pressure, if the volume decreases, should the pressure increase or decrease? Can you eliminate any of the answer choices by using this information?

Item C

A moving truck company charges \$125 a day for driving its truck 50 miles or less. The company charges an additional \$0.05 per mile for all miles driven over 50 miles. Which of the following functions represents the fee for this moving truck for *x* miles in a day?

Ⓐ $C(x) = \begin{cases} 125 & \text{if } 0 \le x \le 50 \\ 2.5 & \text{if } x > 50 \end{cases}$

Ⓑ $C(x) = \begin{cases} 125 & \text{if } 0 \le x \le 50 \\ 125 + 0.05(x - 50) & \text{if } x > 50 \end{cases}$

Ⓒ $C(x) = \begin{cases} 50 & \text{if } 0 \le x \le 50 \\ 50 + 0.05x & \text{if } x > 50 \end{cases}$

Ⓓ $C(x) = \begin{cases} 0.05 & \text{if } 0 \le x \le 50 \\ 125x & \text{if } x > 50 \end{cases}$

5. Look at answer choice A. Why can it be eliminated immediately?
6. Sarah wants to eliminate choice C. Do you agree? Explain.

Item D

Which function corresponds to the graph?

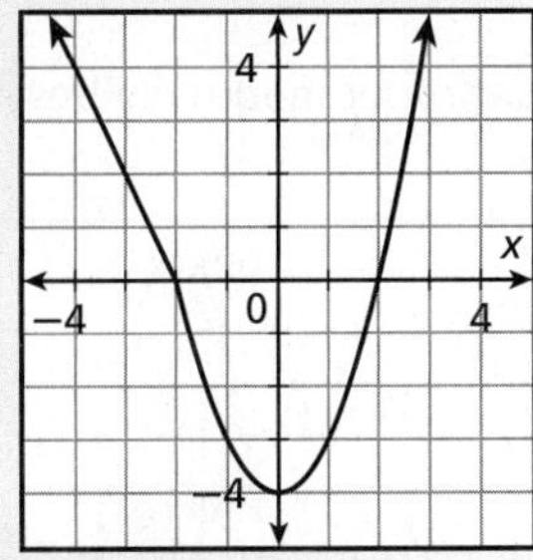

Ⓕ $g(x) = \begin{cases} x^2 - 4 & \text{if } x \ge 0 \\ -2x - 4 & \text{if } x < 0 \end{cases}$

Ⓖ $g(x) = \begin{cases} x - 4 & \text{if } x \ge -2 \\ -2x & \text{if } x < -2 \end{cases}$

Ⓗ $g(x) = \begin{cases} x^2 - 4 & \text{if } x \ge -2 \\ -2x - 4 & \text{if } x < -2 \end{cases}$

Ⓙ $g(x) = \begin{cases} x^2 & \text{if } x \ge -2 \\ -2x + 4 & \text{if } x < -2 \end{cases}$

7. Describe the functions on the graph. Which answer choice can be eliminated based on the shape of the function?
8. Kaye looked at the domain of the function and decided to eliminate choice F. Do you agree with Kaye's decision? Explain.

CHAPTER 6

STANDARDIZED TEST PREP

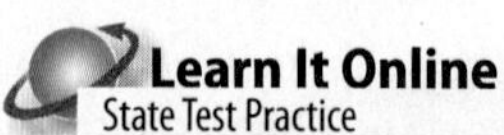

CUMULATIVE ASSESSMENT

Multiple Choice

1. Which is the graph of $f(x) = |x + 1| - 2$?

Ⓐ 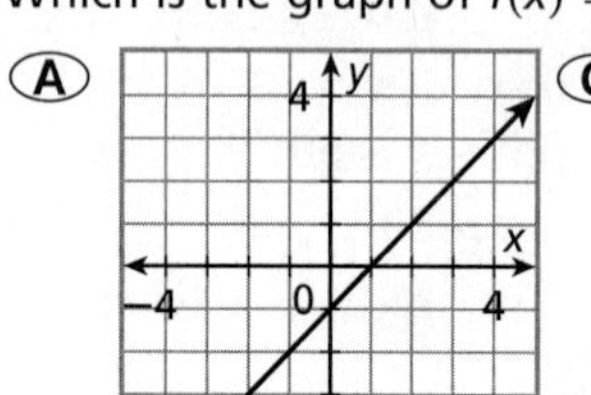

Ⓒ 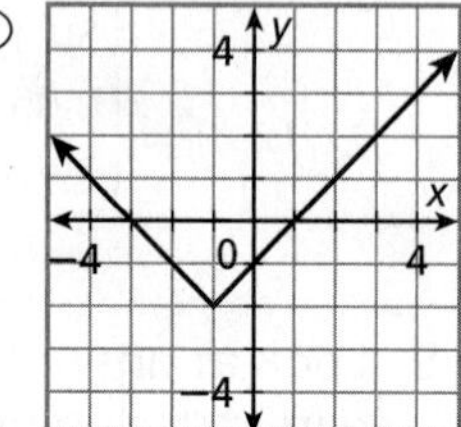

Ⓑ 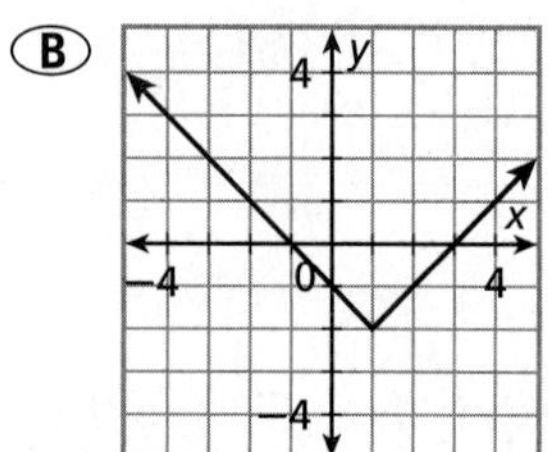

Ⓓ 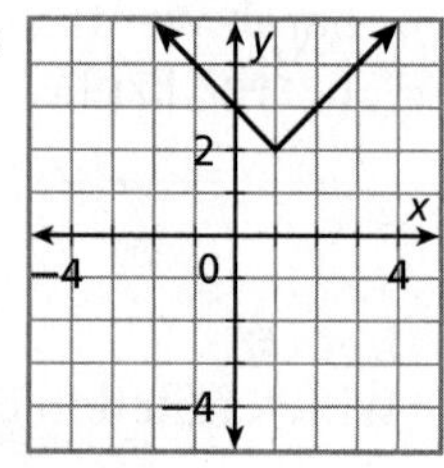

2. Which equation or inequality best represents the graph?

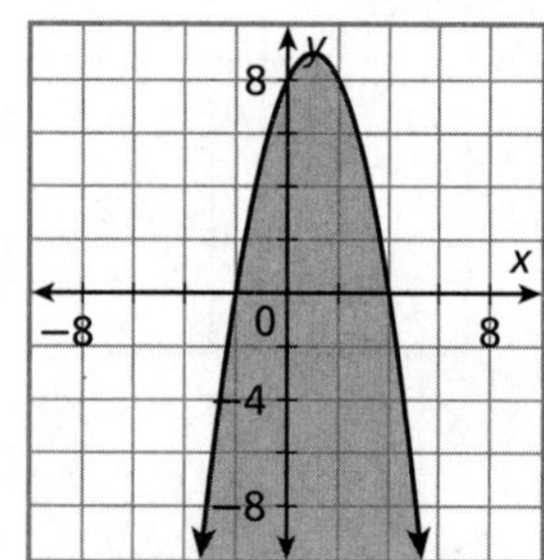

Ⓕ $y = x^2 + 2x + 8$

Ⓖ $y = -x^2 + 2x + 8$

Ⓗ $y \leq x^2 + 2x + 8$

Ⓙ $y \leq -x^2 + 2x + 8$

3. Which of the following describes the end behavior of the function $h(x) = -e^{x^2} + 3$?

Ⓐ As $x \to +\infty$, $h(x) \to +\infty$ and as $x \to -\infty$, $h(x) \to 3$

Ⓑ As $x \to +\infty$, $h(x) \to +\infty$ and as $x \to -\infty$, $h(x) \to 0$

Ⓒ As $x \to +\infty$, $h(x) \to +\infty$ and as $x \to -\infty$, $h(x) \to -\infty$

Ⓓ As $x \to +\infty$, $h(x) \to -\infty$ and as $x \to -\infty$, $h(x) \to -\infty$

4. Which description best reflects the graph shown?

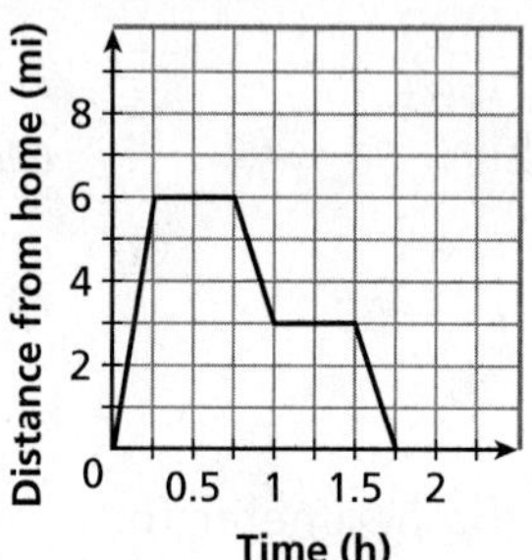

Ⓕ Lou drove 6 miles to the library, spent an hour there, and then drove straight home.

Ⓖ Lou drove 6 miles to the library, spent half an hour there, stopped by the video store for half an hour, and then drove home.

Ⓗ Lou drove 3 miles to the library, spent half an hour there, drove another 3 miles to the movie store, and then drove home.

Ⓙ Lou drove 6 miles to the library, spent half an hour there, drove another 3 miles to the video store, and spent an hour there.

5. Evaluate the piecewise function for $x = -1$.

$$f(x) = \begin{cases} x^2 + 4x - 8 & x < -1 \\ x^3 - x^2 + 5 & x \geq -1 \end{cases}$$

Ⓐ -13 Ⓒ 3

Ⓑ -11 Ⓓ 5

6. Solve for x.

$\sqrt{2x - 4} = x - 6$

Ⓕ $x = 10$ Ⓗ $x = 2$ and $x = 20$

Ⓖ $x = 4$ and $x = 10$ Ⓙ $x = 2$ and $x = 12$

7. Given $f(x) = 2x^2 - 7x - 30$ and $g(x) = x - 6$, find $\left(\frac{f}{g}\right)(x)$.

Ⓐ $2x - 5$ Ⓒ $\frac{(2x - 5)(x + 6)}{x - 6}$

Ⓑ $2x + 5$ Ⓓ $\frac{(2x - 10)(9x + 3)}{x - 6}$

8. Which transformation of triangle ABC creates an image with a vertex at $(-2, 1)$?

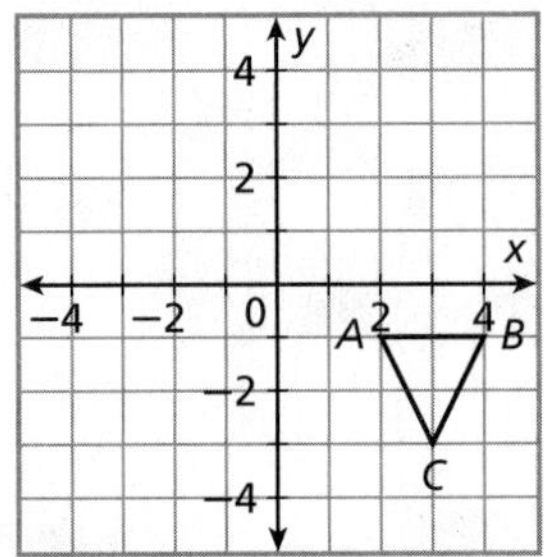

Ⓕ Reflect $\triangle ABC$ across the x-axis.

Ⓖ Reflect $\triangle ABC$ across the y-axis.

Ⓗ Translate $\triangle ABC$ 3 units left and 3 units up.

Ⓙ Rotate $\triangle ABC$ 180° about the origin.

In Item 9, examine one part of the function at a time, eliminating answer choices until you find a graph that matches all parts of the function.

9. Which is the graph of $f(x) = -\frac{1}{2}x^2 + 6$?

Ⓐ 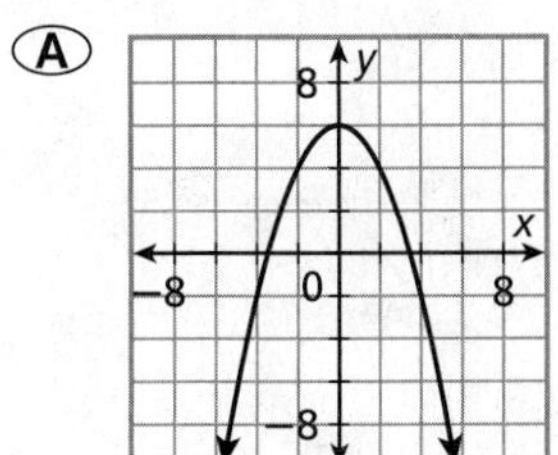

Ⓒ 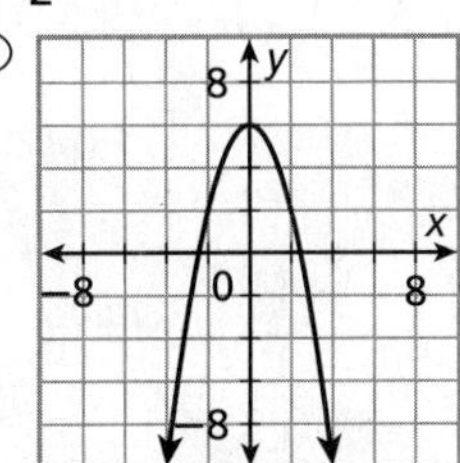

Ⓑ 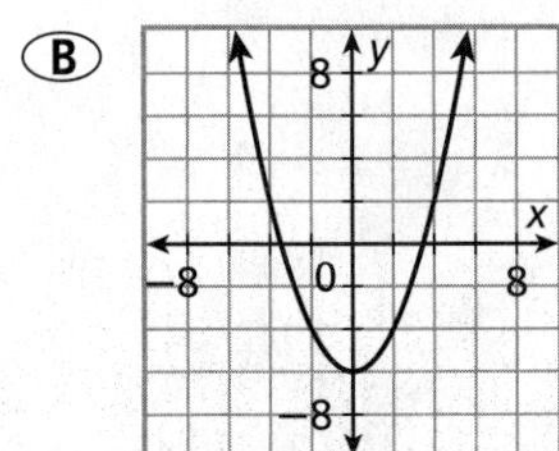

Ⓓ 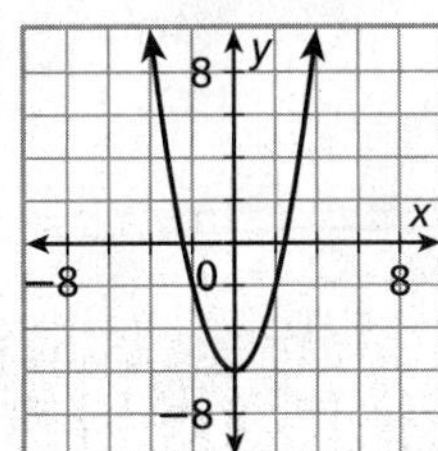

Gridded Response

10. Find the value of $\log_4 256^3$.

11. What is the value of c in the given equation?

$4(5i - 2) + 3 = 2(10i + c) - 7$

12. Find the value of the given expression when $x = 5$.

$$\left(\frac{x^2 + 5x - 36}{2x^2 - 10x + 8}\right)\left(\frac{x^2 + x - 2}{x^2 + 11x + 18}\right)$$

Short Response

13. The equation $f(x) = x^2 + 1$ is a function.
   a. Find the inverse of the function.
   b. Graph $f(x) = x^2 + 1$ and its inverse.
   c. Explain whether the inverse is a function.

14. Use the points below.
   $(0, 6)$, $(2, 2)$, and $(5, 11)$
   a. Write a quadratic function that fits the points.
   b. Check the quadratic function that you wrote by substituting the ordered pairs. Verify that each is a solution.
   c. Graph the equation.
   d. Find $f(7)$ and $f(-7)$.

15. Consider the function $f(x) = x^2 - 4$.
   a. Identify two different transformations of f so that the vertex would be $(1, 4)$.
   b. Identify two different transformations of f so that its graph would pass through $(0, 2)$ and $(-4, 2)$.

Extended Response

16. The volume of gas in a car depends on the number of miles that have been driven since the tank was last filled.

Distance driven (mi)	0	50	100	150	200
Gas (gal)	10	8	6	4	2

   a. Use constant differences or ratios to determine which parent function would best model the given data.
   b. Write the equation for the data.
   c. How many gallons are left after 75 miles?
   d. Can the car be driven for 300 miles? Why or why not?
   e. Find and interpret the inverse of the equation.

CHAPTER

7 Probability

COMMON CORE

Chapter Focus

- Apply concepts of probability to solve problems.
- Use tables and diagrams to find probabilities of compound events.

Wait a Second!

You can use probability and statistics to analyze *queuing,* the study of waiting in line.

Learn It Online
Chapter Project Online

APPROXIMATE WAIT
TIME FROM HERE
4872
MINUTES

Tree Diagrams

1. Natalie has three colors of wrapping paper (purple, blue, and yellow) and three colors of ribbon (gold, white, and red). Make a tree diagram showing all possible ways that she can wrap a present using one color of paper and one color of ribbon.

Ratios

For each circle, find the ratio of the shaded area to the entire area.

2.

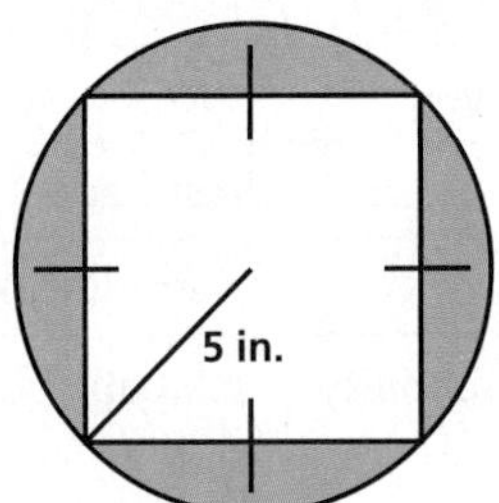

3.

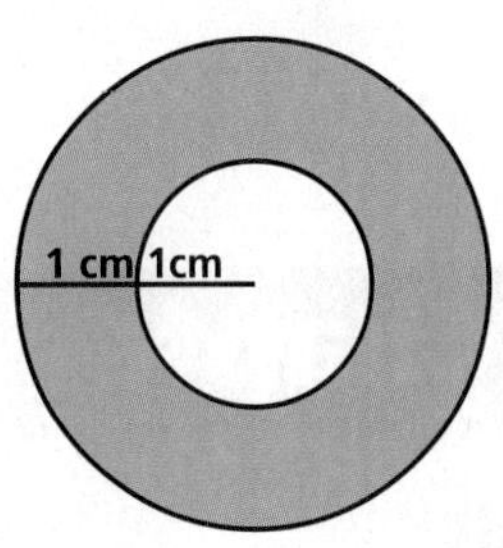

Add and Subtract Fractions

Add or subtract.

4. $1 - \frac{14}{20}$

5. $\frac{3}{8} + \frac{5}{6}$

6. $\frac{8}{15} - \frac{2}{5}$

7. $\frac{1}{12} + \frac{1}{10}$

Multiply and Divide Fractions

Multiply or divide.

8. $\frac{1}{2} \cdot \frac{3}{7}$

9. $2\frac{1}{3} \cdot \frac{1}{4}$

10. $\frac{4}{5} \div \frac{1}{2}$

11. $5\frac{1}{3} \div \frac{1}{4}$

Percent Problems

Solve.

12. What number is 7% of 150?

13. 90% of what number is 45?

14. A $24 item receives a price increase of 12%. How much was the price increased?

15. Twenty percent of the water in a large aquarium should be changed weekly. How much water should be changed each week if an aquarium holds 65 gallons of water?

CHAPTER 7

Study Guide: Preview

Where You've Been

Previously, you

- made tree diagrams to find the number of possible combinations of a group of objects.
- made lists to count and arrange objects.
- calculated measures of central tendency.

In This Chapter

You will study

- solving problems involving counting and arranging.
- finding theoretical, experimental, and binomial probabilities.
- two-way tables and conditional frequencies.

Where You're Going

You can use the skills in this chapter

- to find probabilities involved in games and events involving chance.
- to compare conditional probabilities.
- to make mathematically informed decisions.

Key Vocabulary/Vocabulario

combination	combinación
conditional probability	probabilidad condicional
dependent events	sucesos dependientes
experimental probability	probabilidad experimental
factorial	factorial
independent events	sucesos independientes
outcome	resultado
permutation	permutación
theoretical probability	probabilidad teórica

Vocabulary Connections

To become familiar with some of the vocabulary terms in the chapter, consider the following. You may refer to the chapter, the glossary, or a dictionary if you like.

1. A number is the product of its *factors*. What operation do you think is involved in finding a **factorial** ?
2. A *theory* can be described as a sound and rational explanation. An *experiment* can be described as a procedure carried out in a controlled environment. Knowing this, how do you think **theoretical probability** differs from **experimental probability** ?
3. A *conditional* is used to describe something that will be done only if another thing is done. Do you think **conditional probability** is used with **independent events** or **dependent events** ? Why?
4. Each possible result of an experiment is an **outcome** .

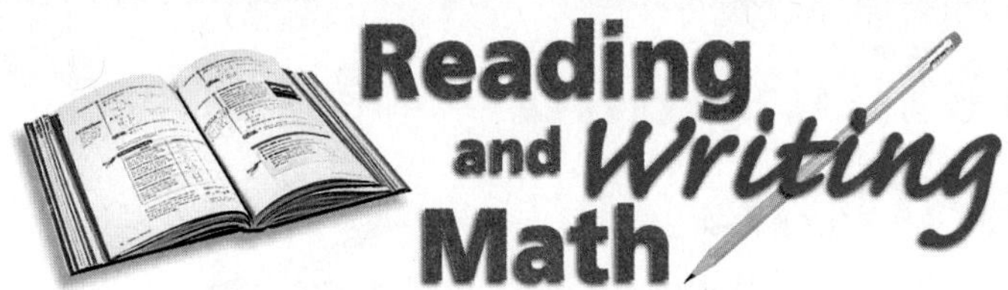

Writing Strategy: Translate Between Words and Math

It is important to correctly interpret the type of math being described by a verbal or written description. Listen/look for key words to help you translate between the words and the math.

15. In 1626, the Dutch bought Manhattan Island for $24 worth of merchandise. Suppose that, instead, $24 had been invested in an account that paid 3.5% interest compounded annually. Find the balance in 2008.

compounded: *Compounding indicates an exponential function.*

31. Gardeners check the pH level of soil to ensure a pH of 6 or 7. Soil is usually more acidic in areas where rainfall is high, whereas soil in dry areas is usually more alkaline. The pH level of a certain soil sample is 5.5. What is the difference in hydrogen ion concentration, or $[H^+]$, between the sample and an acceptable level?

pH

hydrogen ion concentration: *These terms indicate a logarithmic function.*

parabola: *A parabola indicates a quadratic function.*

27. You are given a parabola with two points that have the same y-value, $(-7, 11)$ and $(3, 11)$. Explain how to find the equation for the axis of symmetry of this parabola.

Try This

Identify the key word and the type of function being described.

1. Kelly invested $2000 in a savings account at a simple interest rate of 2.5%. How much money will she have in 8 months?

2. The diameter d in inches of a chain needed to move p pounds is given by the square root of $85p$, divided by pi. How much more can be lifted with a chain 2.5 inches in diameter than by a rope 0.5 inch in diameter?

3. A technician took a blood sample from a patient and detected a toxin concentration of 0.01006 mg/cm^3. Two hours later, the technician took another sample and detected a concentration of 0.00881 mg/cm^3. Assume that the concentration varies exponentially with time. Write a function to model the data.

4. Students found that the number of mosquitoes per acre of wetland grows by about 10 to the power $\frac{1}{2}d + 2$, where d is the number of days since the last frost. Write and graph the function representing the number of mosquitoes on each day.

COMMON CORE

7-1 Permutations and Combinations

CC.9-12.S.CP.9 (+) Use permutations and combinations to compute probabilities…and solve problems.
Also CC.9-12.S.CP.1

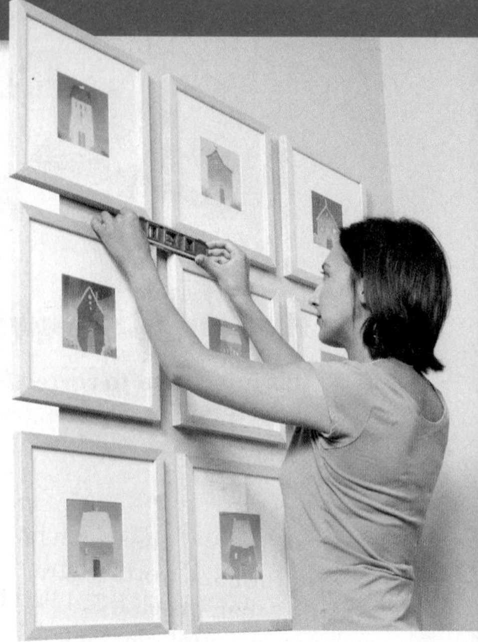

Objectives

Solve problems involving the Fundamental Counting Principle.

Solve problems involving permutations and combinations.

Vocabulary

Fundamental Counting Principle
permutation
factorial
combination

Why learn this?

Permutations can be used to determine the number of ways to select and arrange artwork so as to give a new look each day. (See Example 2B.)

You have previously used tree diagrams to find the number of possible combinations of a group of objects. In this lesson, you will learn to use the **Fundamental Counting Principle**.

Fundamental Counting Principle

If there are n items and m_1 ways to choose a first item, m_2 ways to choose a second item after the first item has been chosen, and so on, then there are $m_1 \cdot m_2 \cdot \ldots \cdot m_n$ ways to choose n items.

EXAMPLE 1 Using the Fundamental Counting Principle

A **For the lunch special, you can choose an entrée, a drink, and one side dish. How many meal choices are there?**

number of main dishes	times	number of beverages	times	number of sides	equals	number of choices
3	×	4	×	3	=	36

There are 36 meal choices.

B **In Utah, a license plate consists of 3 digits followed by 3 letters. The letters *I*, *O*, and *Q* are not used, and each digit or letter may be used more than once. How many different license plates are possible?**

digit		*digit*		*digit*		*letter*		*letter*		*letter*	
10	×	10	×	10	×	23	×	23	×	23	= 12,167,000

There are 12,167,000 possible license plates.

Helpful Hint

In Example 1B, there are 10 possible digits and $26 - 3 = 23$ possible letters.

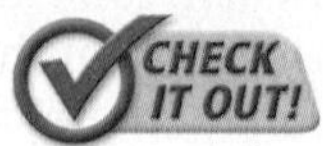

1a. A "make-your-own-adventure" story lets you choose 6 starting points, gives 4 plot choices, and then has 5 possible endings. How many adventures are there?

1b. A password is 4 letters followed by 1 digit. Uppercase letters (A) and lowercase letters (a) may be used and are considered different. How many passwords are possible?

A **permutation** is a selection of a group of objects in which order is important.

There is one way to arrange one item A.

A second item B can be placed first or second.

A third item C can be first, second, or third for each order above.

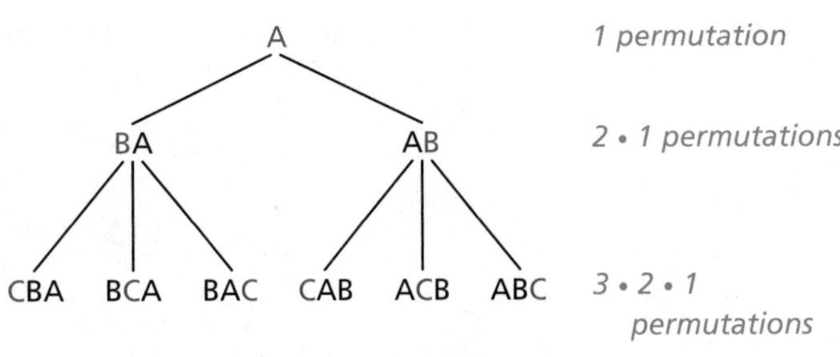

You can see that the number of permutations of 3 items is $3 \cdot 2 \cdot 1$. You can extend this to permutations of n items, which is $n \cdot (n-1) \cdot (n-2) \cdot (n-3) \cdot \ldots \cdot 1$. This expression is called *n factorial*, and is written as $n!$.

n Factorial

For any whole number n,

WORDS	NUMBERS	ALGEBRA
The **factorial** of a number is the product of the natural numbers less than or equal to the number. 0! is defined as 1.	$6! = 6 \cdot 5 \cdot 4 \cdot 3 \cdot 2 \cdot 1 = 720$	$n! = n \cdot (n-1) \cdot (n-2) \cdot (n-3) \cdot \ldots \cdot 1$

Sometimes you may not want to order an entire set of items. Suppose that you want to select and order 3 people from a group of 7. One way to find possible permutations is to use the Fundamental Counting Principle.

First Person		Second Person		Third Person		*There are 7 people. You are choosing 3 of them in order.*
7 choices	•	6 choices	•	5 choices	=	210 permutations

Another way to find the possible permutations is to use factorials. You can divide the total number of arrangements by the number of arrangements that are not used. In the example above, there are 7 total people and 4 whose arrangements do not matter.

$$\frac{\text{arrangements of 7 people}}{\text{arrangements of 4 people}} = \frac{7!}{4!} = \frac{7 \cdot 6 \cdot 5 \cdot \cancel{4} \cdot \cancel{3} \cdot \cancel{2} \cdot \cancel{1}}{\cancel{4} \cdot \cancel{3} \cdot \cancel{2} \cdot \cancel{1}} = 210$$

This can be generalized as a formula, which is useful for large numbers of items.

Permutations

NUMBERS	ALGEBRA
The number of permutations of 7 items taken 3 at a time is $_7P_3 = \frac{7!}{(7-3)!} = \frac{7!}{4!}$.	The number of permutations of n items taken r at a time is $_nP_r = \frac{n!}{(n-r)!}$.

EXAMPLE 2 Finding Permutations

A **How many ways can a club select a president, a vice president, and a secretary from a group of 5 people?**

This is the equivalent of selecting and arranging 3 items from 5.

$${}_5P_3 = \frac{5!}{(5-3)!} = \frac{5!}{2!}$$ *Substitute 5 for n and 3 for r in $\frac{n!}{(n-r)!}$.*

$$= \frac{5 \cdot 4 \cdot 3 \cdot \cancel{2 \cdot 1}}{\cancel{2 \cdot 1}}$$ *Divide out common factors.*

$$= 5 \cdot 4 \cdot 3 = 60$$

There are 60 ways to select the 3 people.

B **An art gallery has 9 fine-art photographs from an artist and will display 4 from left to right along a wall. In how many ways can the gallery select and display the 4 photographs?**

$${}_9P_4 = \frac{9!}{(9-4)!} = \frac{9!}{5!} = \frac{9 \cdot 8 \cdot 7 \cdot 6 \cdot \cancel{5 \cdot 4 \cdot 3 \cdot 2 \cdot 1}}{\cancel{5 \cdot 4 \cdot 3 \cdot 2 \cdot 1}}$$ *Divide out common factors.*

$$= 9 \cdot 8 \cdot 7 \cdot 6$$
$$= 3024$$

There are 3024 ways that the gallery can select and display the photographs.

Helpful Hint

The number of factors left after dividing is the number of items selected. In Example 2B, there are 4 photographs and 4 factors in $9 \cdot 8 \cdot 7 \cdot 6$.

2a. Awards are given out at a costume party. How many ways can "most creative," "silliest," and "best" costume be awarded to 8 contestants if no one gets more than one award?

2b. How many ways can a 2-digit number be formed by using only the digits 5–9 and by each digit being used only once?

A **combination** is a grouping of items in which order does not matter. There are generally fewer ways to select items when order does not matter. For example, there are 6 ways to order 3 items, but they are all the same combination:

6 permutations → {ABC, ACB, BAC, BCA, CAB, CBA}

1 combination → {ABC}

To find the number of combinations, the formula for permutations can be modified.

$$\text{number of permutations} = \frac{\text{ways to arrange all items}}{\text{ways to arrange items not selected}}$$

Because order does not matter, divide the number of permutations by the number of ways to arrange the selected items.

$$\text{number of combinations} = \frac{\text{ways to arrange all items}}{(\text{ways to arrange selected items})(\text{ways to arrange items not selected})}$$

(l), Main Ideas/Jupiter Images/Getty Images; (cl), Royalty-free/Corbis; (cr), Visions of America/Joe Sohm/Digital Vision/Getty Images; (r), Royalty-free/Corbis

Combinations

NUMBERS	ALGEBRA
The number of combinations of 7 items taken 3 at a time is $_7C_3 = \dfrac{7!}{3!(7-3)!}$.	The number of combinations of n items taken r at a time is $_nC_r = \dfrac{n!}{r!(n-r)!}$.

When deciding whether to use permutations or combinations, first decide whether order is important. Use a permutation if order matters and a combination if order does not matter.

EXAMPLE 3 *Pet Adoption Application*

Katie is going to adopt kittens from a litter of 11. How many ways can she choose a group of 3 kittens?

Step 1 Determine whether the problem represents a permutation or combination.

The order does not matter. The group Kitty, Smoky, and Tigger is the same as Tigger, Kitty, and Smoky. It is a combination.

Step 2 Use the formula for combinations.

$$_{11}C_3 = \frac{11!}{3!(11-3)!} = \frac{11!}{3!(8!)} \quad \textit{n = 11 and r = 3}$$

$$= \frac{11\cdot 10\cdot 9\cdot \cancel{8\cdot 7\cdot 6\cdot 5\cdot 4\cdot 3\cdot 2\cdot 1}}{3\cdot 2\cdot 1(\cancel{8\cdot 7\cdot 6\cdot 5\cdot 4\cdot 3\cdot 2\cdot 1})} \quad \textit{Divide out common factors.}$$

$$= \frac{11\cdot 10\cdot 9}{3\cdot 2\cdot 1} = \frac{11\cdot \cancel{10}^5\cdot \cancel{9}^3}{{}_1\cancel{3}\cdot {}_1\cancel{2}\cdot 1} = 165$$

There are 165 ways to select a group of 3 kittens from 11.

Helpful Hint

You can find permutations and combinations by using **nPr** and **nCr**, respectively, on scientific and graphing calculators.

CHECK IT OUT! 3. The swim team has 8 swimmers. Two swimmers will be selected to swim in the first heat. How many ways can the swimmers be selected?

MATHEMATICAL PRACTICES

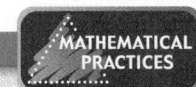

THINK AND DISCUSS

1. Give a situation in which order matters and one in which order does not matter.
2. Give the value of $_nC_n$, where n is any integer. Explain your answer.
3. Tell what $_3C_4$ would mean in the real world and why it is not possible.

4. **GET ORGANIZED** Copy and complete the graphic organizer.

	Fundamental Counting Principle	Permutation	Combination
Formula			
Examples			

Japack Photo Library/Photolibrary

7-1 Exercises

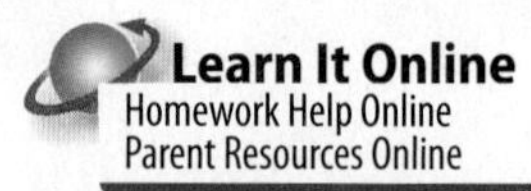

GUIDED PRACTICE

1. **Vocabulary** When you open a rotating combination lock, order is __?__ (*important* or *not important*), so this is a __?__ (*permutation* or *combination*).

SEE EXAMPLE 1

2. Jamie purchased 3 blouses, 3 jackets, and 2 skirts. How many different outfits using a blouse, a jacket, and a skirt are possible?
3. An Internet code consists of one digit followed by one letter. The number zero and the letter *O* are excluded. How many codes are possible?

SEE EXAMPLE 2

4. Nate is on a 7-day vacation. He plans to spend one day jet skiing and one day golfing. How many ways can Nate schedule the 2 activities?
5. How many ways can you listen to 3 songs from a CD that has 12 selections?
6. Members from 6 different school organizations decorated floats for the homecoming parade. How many different ways can first, second, and third prize be awarded?

SEE EXAMPLE 3

7. A teacher wants to send 4 students to the library each day. There are 21 students in the class. How many ways can he choose 4 students to go to the library on the first day?
8. Gregory has a coupon for $1 off the purchase of 3 boxes of Munchie brand cereal. The store has 5 different varieties of Munchie brand cereal. How many ways can Gregory choose 3 boxes of cereal so that each box is a different variety?

PRACTICE AND PROBLEM SOLVING

Independent Practice

For Exercises	See Example
9–10	1
11–13	2
14	3

Extra Practice

See Extra Practice for more Skills Practice and Applications Practice exercises.

9. **Hiking** A hiker can take 4 trails to the lake and then 3 trails from the lake to the cabins. How many routes are there from the lake to the cabins?
10. The cheerleading squad is making posters. They have 3 different colors of poster board and 4 different colors of markers. How many different posters can be made by using one poster board and one marker?
11. How many ways can you choose a manager and assistant from a 9-person task force?
12. How many identification codes are possible by using 3 letters if no letter may be repeated?
13. There are 5 airplanes ready to depart. Runway A and runway D are available. How many ways can 2 planes be assigned to runways without using the same runway?
14. **Food** How many choices of 3 hamburger toppings are possible?
15. **What if...?** In the United Kingdom's National Lottery, you must correctly select a group of 6 numbers from 49. Suppose that the contest were changed to selecting 7 numbers. How many more ways would there be to select the numbers?

Evaluate.

16. ${}_6P_6$
17. ${}_5C_5$
18. ${}_9P_1$
19. ${}_6C_1$
20. $\frac{2!}{6!}$
21. $\frac{4!3!}{2!}$
22. $\frac{9!}{7!}$
23. $\frac{8! - 5!}{(8-5)!}$

Geometry Find the number of ways that each selection can be made.

24. two marked points to determine slope

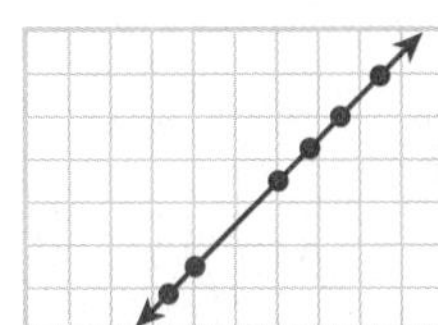

25. four points to form a quadrilateral

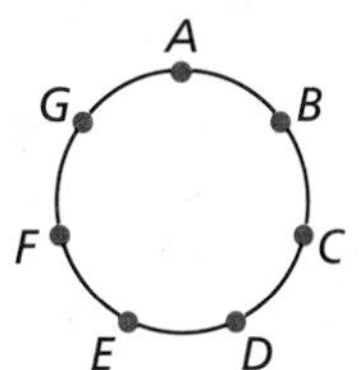

Compare. Write >, <, or =.

26. ${}_7P_3$ ■ ${}_7C_4$

27. ${}_7P_4$ ■ ${}_7P_3$

28. ${}_7C_3$ ■ ${}_7C_4$

29. ${}_{10}C_{10}$ ■ ${}_{10}P_{10}$

30. Copy and complete the table. Use the table to explain why 0! is defined as 1.

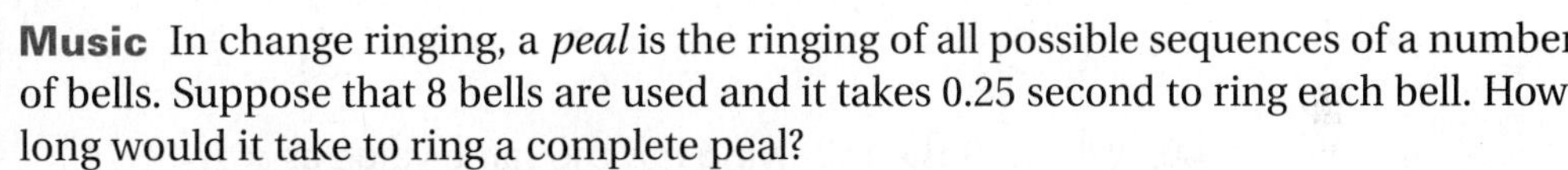

$n!$	4!	3!	2!	1!
$n(n-1)!$	$4(3!) = 24$	■	■	■

LINK

Music

There are many change-ringing societies and groups, especially in the United Kingdom. Bell ringers work together to follow patterns and called changes to avoid repeating sequences.

31. **Critical Thinking** Why are there more unique permutations of the letters in YOUNG than in GEESE?

32. **Music** In change ringing, a *peal* is the ringing of all possible sequences of a number of bells. Suppose that 8 bells are used and it takes 0.25 second to ring each bell. How long would it take to ring a complete peal?

33. **Multi-Step** Amy, Bob, Charles, Dena, and Esther are club officers.

a. Copy and complete the table to show the ways that a president, a vice president, and a secretary can be chosen if Amy is chosen president. (Use first initials for names.)

President	A	A	A	A	A	A	A	A	A	A	A	A
Vice President	B	B	B	C	C	C	■	■	■	■	■	■
Secretary	C	D	E	■	■	■	■	■	■	■	■	■

b. Extend the table to show the number of ways that the three officers can be chosen if Bob is chosen president. Make a conjecture as to the number of ways that a president, a vice president, and a secretary can be chosen.

c. Use a formula to find the number of different ways that a president, a vice president, and a secretary can be chosen. Compare your result with part **b.**

d. How many different ways can 3 club officers be chosen to form a committee? Compare this with the answer to part **c.** Which answer is a number of permutations? Which answer is a number of combinations?

34. **Critical Thinking** Use the formulas to divide ${}_nP_r$ by ${}_nC_r$. Predict the result of dividing ${}_6P_3$ by ${}_6C_3$. Check your prediction. What meaning does the result have?

35. **Write About It** Find ${}_9C_2$ and ${}_9C_7$. Find ${}_{10}C_6$ and ${}_{10}C_4$. Explain the results.

36. While playing the game of Yahtzee, Jen rolls 5 dice and gets the result shown at right.

a. How many different ways can she arrange the dice from left to right?

b. How many different ways can she choose 3 of the dice to reroll?

37. **ERROR ANALYSIS** Below are two solutions for "How many Internet codes can be made by using 3 digits if 0 is excluded and digits may not be repeated?" Which is incorrect? Explain the error.

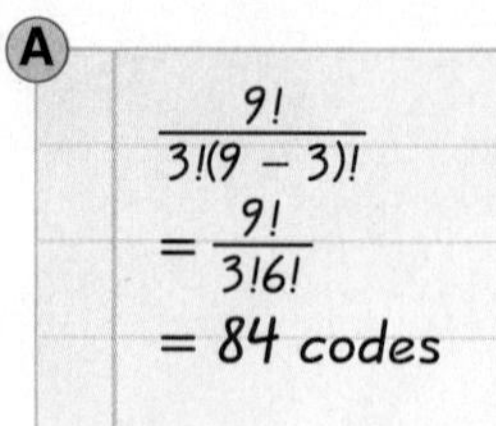

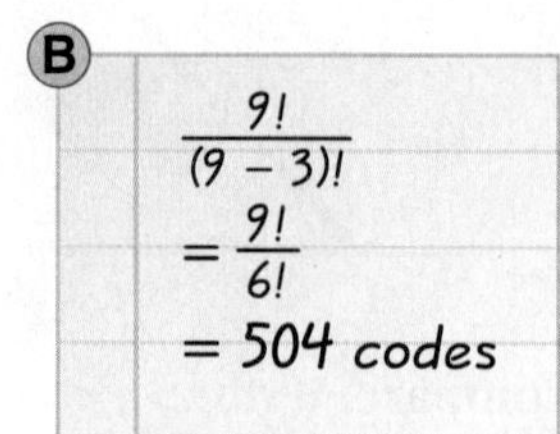

38. **Critical Thinking** Explain how to use the Fundamental Counting Principle to answer the question in Exercise 37.

39. There are 14 players on the team. Which of the following expressions models the number of ways that the coach can choose 5 players to start the game?

Ⓐ 5! Ⓑ $\frac{14!}{5!}$ Ⓒ $\frac{14!}{9!}$ Ⓓ $\frac{14!}{5!9!}$

40. Which of the following has the same value as ${}_9C_4$?

Ⓕ ${}_9P_4$ Ⓖ ${}_4C_9$ Ⓗ ${}_9P_5$ Ⓙ ${}_9C_5$

41. **Short Response** Rene can choose 1 elective each of the 4 years that she is in high school. There are 15 electives. How many ways can Rene choose her electives?

CHALLENGE AND EXTEND

42. **Geometry** Consider a circle with two points, A and B. You can form exactly 1 segment, $\overline{AB}$. If there are 3 points, you can form 3 segments as shown in the diagram.

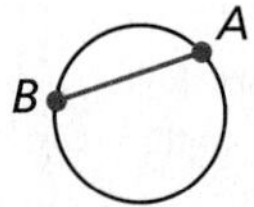

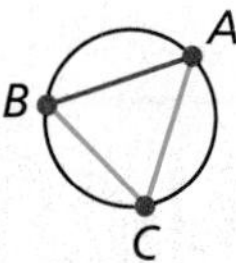

   a. How many segments can be formed from 4 points, 5 points, 6 points, and n points? Write your answer for n points as a permutation or combination.

   b. How many segments can be formed from 20 points?

43. **Government** How many ways can a jury of 12 and 2 alternate jurors be selected from a pool of 30 potential jurors? (*Hint:* Consider how order is both important and unimportant in selection.) Leave your answer in unexpanded notation.

Relative Area

In *geometric probability,* the probability of an event corresponds to ratios of the areas (or lengths or volumes) or parts of one or more figures.

In the spinners shown, the probability of landing on a color is based on relative area.

$\frac{1}{2}$ shaded $\frac{3}{8}$ shaded $\frac{1}{4}$ shaded

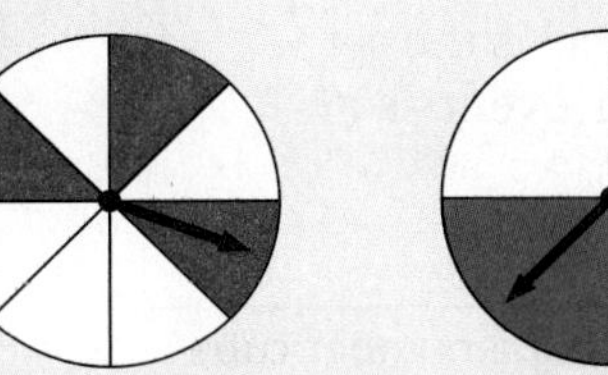

Use the area formulas at right to help you determine relative area.

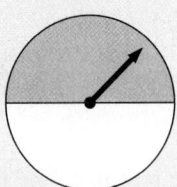

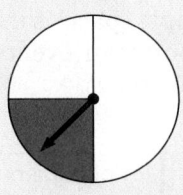

Area Formulas	
Figure	**Formula**
Rectangle	$A = bh$
Square	$A = s^2$
Triangle	$A = \frac{1}{2}bh$
Trapezoid	$A = \frac{1}{2}h(b_1 + b_2)$
Circle	$A = \pi r^2$

Example

What portion of the rectangle is shaded? Write the relative area as a fraction, a decimal, and a percent.

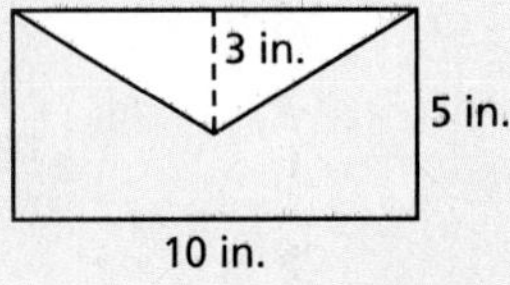

Find the ratio of the area of the shaded region to the area of the rectangle.

$A = 10(5) = 50 \text{ in}^2$ *Area of the rectangle: A = bh*

$A = \frac{1}{2}(3)(10) = 15 \text{ in}^2$ *Area of the unshaded triangle:* $A = \frac{1}{2}bh$

$$\frac{\text{area of shaded region}}{\text{area of the rectangle}} = \frac{50 - 15}{50} = \frac{35}{50} = \frac{7}{10} = 0.7, \text{ or } 70\%$$

Try This

What portion of each figure is shaded? Write the relative area as a fraction, a decimal, and a percent.

1.

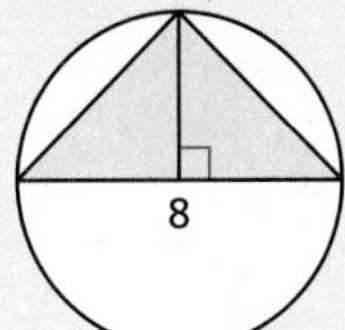

2.

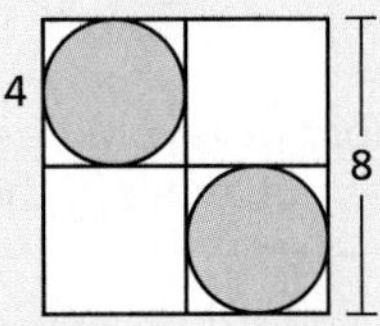

3.

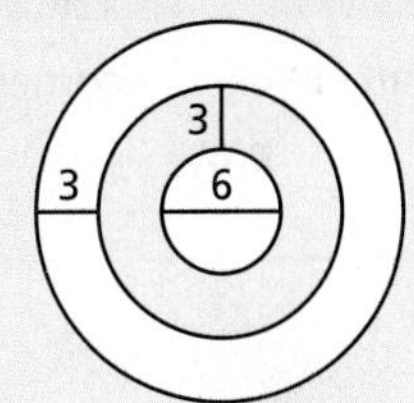

4.

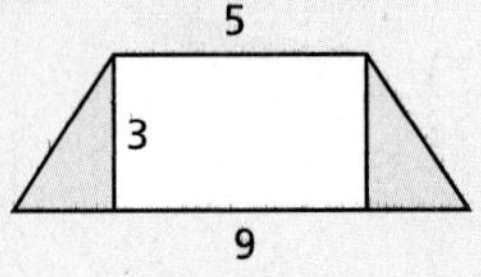

5. Write the relative area of each sector of the spinner as a fraction, decimal, and percent.

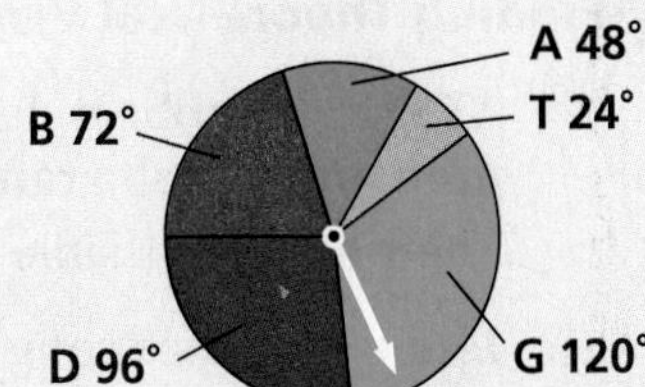

COMMON CORE

7-2 Theoretical and Experimental Probability

CC.9-12.S.MD.7 (+) Analyze decisions and strategies using probability concepts... *Also* CC.9-12.S.CP.9 (+)

Objectives

Find the theoretical probability of an event.

Find the experimental probability of an event.

Vocabulary

probability
outcome
sample space
event
equally likely outcomes
favorable outcomes
theoretical probability
complement
geometric probability
experiment
trial
experimental probability

Why learn this?

You can use probability to find the chances of hitting or missing a target in the game Battleship. (See Example 2.)

Probability is the measure of how likely an event is to occur. Each possible result of a probability experiment or situation is an **outcome**. The **sample space** is the set of all possible outcomes. An **event** is an outcome or set of outcomes.

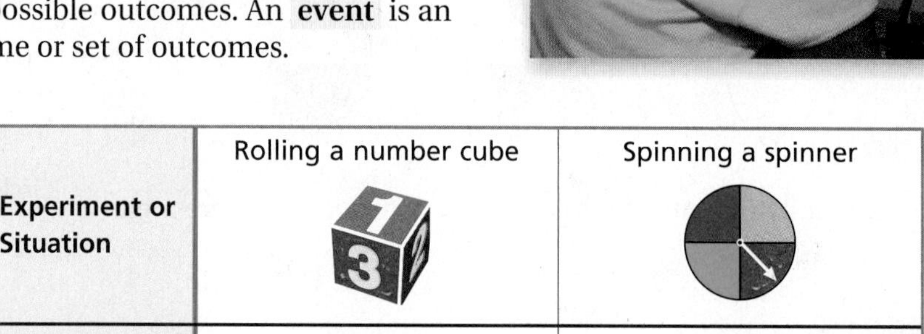

Experiment or Situation	Rolling a number cube	Spinning a spinner
Sample Space	{1, 2, 3, 4, 5, 6}	{red, blue, green, yellow}

Probabilities are written as fractions or decimals from 0 to 1, or as percents from 0% to 100%.

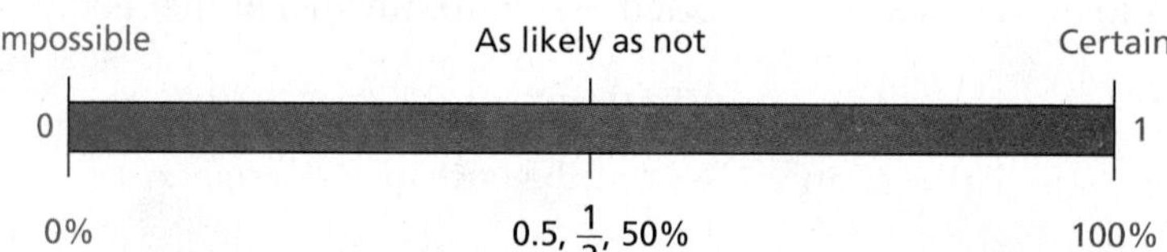

Equally likely outcomes have the same chance of occurring. When you toss a fair coin, heads and tails are equally likely outcomes. **Favorable outcomes** are outcomes in a specified event. For equally likely outcomes, the **theoretical probability** of an event is the ratio of the number of favorable outcomes to the total number of outcomes.

Theoretical Probability

For equally likely outcomes,

$$P(\text{event}) = \frac{\text{number of favorable outcomes}}{\text{number of outcomes in the sample space}}.$$

EXAMPLE 1 **Finding Theoretical Probability**

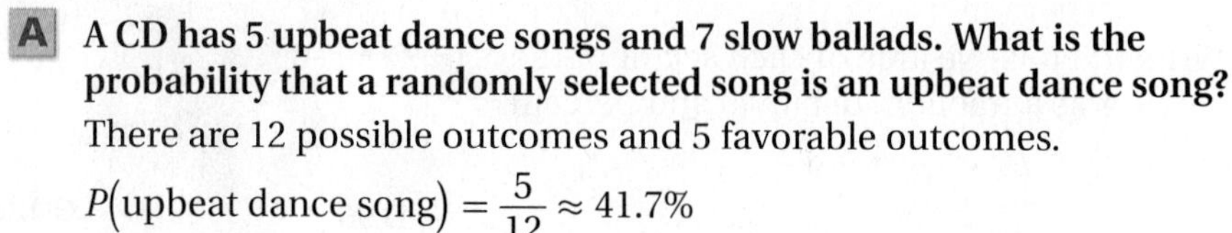

A **A CD has 5 upbeat dance songs and 7 slow ballads. What is the probability that a randomly selected song is an upbeat dance song?**

There are 12 possible outcomes and 5 favorable outcomes.

$P(\text{upbeat dance song}) = \frac{5}{12} \approx 41.7\%$

Sam Dudgeon/HMH

B **A red number cube and a blue number cube are rolled. If all numbers are equally likely, what is the probability that the sum is 10?**

There are 36 possible outcomes.

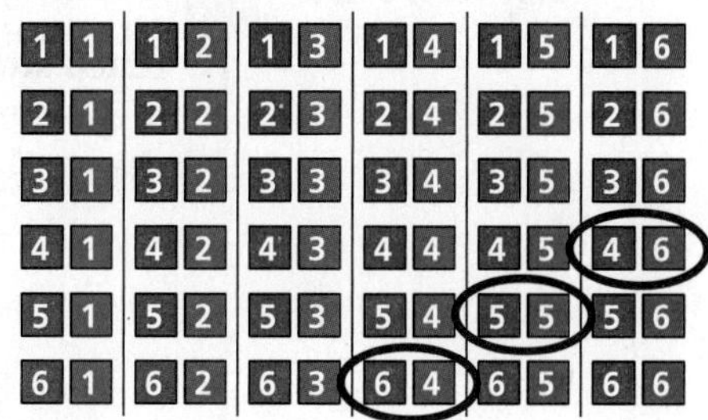

$P(\text{sum is } 10) = \frac{\text{number of outcomes with sum of } 10}{36}$

$P(\text{sum is } 10) = \frac{3}{36} = \frac{1}{12}$ *3 outcomes with a sum of 10: (4, 6) (5, 5), and (6, 4)*

A red number cube and a blue number cube are rolled. If all numbers are equally likely, what is the probability of each event?

1a. The sum is 6.

1b. The difference is 6.

1c. The red cube is greater.

The sum of all probabilities in the sample space is 1. The **complement** of an event E is the set of all outcomes in the sample space that are not in E.

Complement

The probability of the complement of event E is

$$P(\text{not } E) = 1 - P(E).$$

EXAMPLE 2 *Entertainment Application*

The game Battleship is played with 5 ships on a 100-hole grid. Players try to guess the locations of their opponent's ships and sink them. At the start of the game, what is the probability that the first shot misses all targets?

$P(\text{miss}) = 1 - P(\text{hit})$ *Use the complement.*

$P(\text{miss}) = 1 - \frac{17}{100}$ *There are 17 total holes covered by game pieces.*

$= \frac{83}{100}$, or 83%

There is an 83% chance of the first shot missing all targets.

Battleship Pieces

Game Piece	Number of Holes Covered
Destroyer	2
Cruiser	3
Submarine	3
Battleship	4
Carrier	5

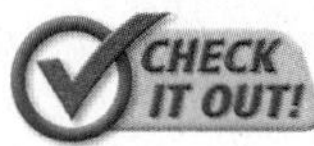

2. Two integers from 1 to 10 are randomly selected. The same number may be chosen twice. What is the probability that both numbers are less than 9?

EXAMPLE 3 Finding Probability with Permutations or Combinations

Each student received a 4-digit code to use the library computers, with no digit repeated. Manu received the code 7654. What was the probability that he would receive a code of consecutive numbers?

Step 1 Determine whether the code is a permutation or a combination.

Order is important, so it is a permutation.

Step 2 Find the number of outcomes in the sample space.

The sample space is the number of permutations of 4 of 10 digits.

$$_{10}P_4 = \frac{10!}{6!} = \frac{10 \cdot 9 \cdot 8 \cdot 7 \cdot \cancel{6 \cdot 5 \cdot 4 \cdot 3 \cdot 2 \cdot 1}}{\cancel{6 \cdot 5 \cdot 4 \cdot 3 \cdot 2 \cdot 1}} = 5040$$

Step 3 Find the favorable outcomes.

The favorable outcomes are the codes 0123, 1234, 2345, 3456, 4567, 5678, 6789, and the reverse of each of these numbers. There are 14 favorable outcomes.

Step 4 Find the probability.

$$P(\text{consecutive numbers}) = \frac{14}{5040} = \frac{1}{360}$$

The probability that Manu would receive a code of consecutive numbers was $\frac{1}{360}$.

3. A DJ randomly selects 2 of 8 ads to play before her show. Two of the ads are by a local retailer. What is the probability that she will play both of the retailer's ads before her show?

Geometric probability is a form of theoretical probability determined by a ratio of lengths, areas, or volumes.

EXAMPLE 4 Finding Geometric Probability

Three semicircles with diameters 2, 4, and 6 cm are arranged as shown in the figure. If a point inside the figure is chosen at random, what is the probability that the point is inside the shaded region?

4 cm 2 cm
6 cm

Find the ratio of the area of the shaded region to the area of the entire semicircle. The area of a semicircle is $\frac{1}{2}\pi r^2$.

First, find the area of the entire semicircle.

$$A_t = \frac{1}{2}\pi(3^2) = 4.5\pi$$ *Total area of largest semicircle*

Next, find the unshaded area.

$$A_u = \left[\frac{1}{2}\pi(2^2)\right] + \left[\frac{1}{2}\pi(1^2)\right] = 2\pi + 0.5\pi = 2.5\pi$$ *Sum of areas of the unshaded semicircles*

Subtract to find the shaded area.

$$A_s = 4.5\pi - 2.5\pi = 2\pi$$ *Area of shaded region*

$$\frac{A_s}{A_t} = \frac{2\pi}{4.5\pi} = \frac{2}{4.5} = \frac{4}{9}$$ *Ratio of shaded region to total area*

The probability that the point is in the shaded region is $\frac{4}{9}$.

4. Find the probability that a point chosen at random inside the large triangle is in the small triangle.

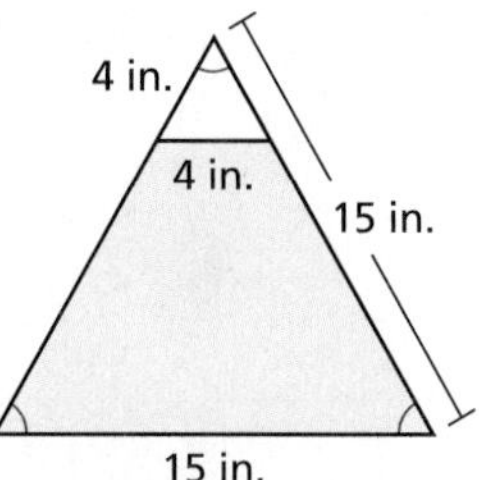

You can estimate the probability of an event by using data, or by **experiment**. For example, if a doctor states that an operation "has an 80% probability of success," 80% is an estimate of probability based on similar case histories.

Each repetition of an experiment is a **trial**. The sample space of an experiment is the set of all possible outcomes. The **experimental probability** of an event is the ratio of the number of times that the event occurs, the *frequency*, to the number of trials.

Experimental Probability

$$\text{experimental probability} = \frac{\text{number of times the event occurs}}{\text{number of trials}}$$

Experimental probability is often used to estimate theoretical probability and to make predictions.

EXAMPLE 5 Finding Experimental Probability

The bar graph shows the results of 100 tosses of an oddly shaped number cube. Find each experimental probability.

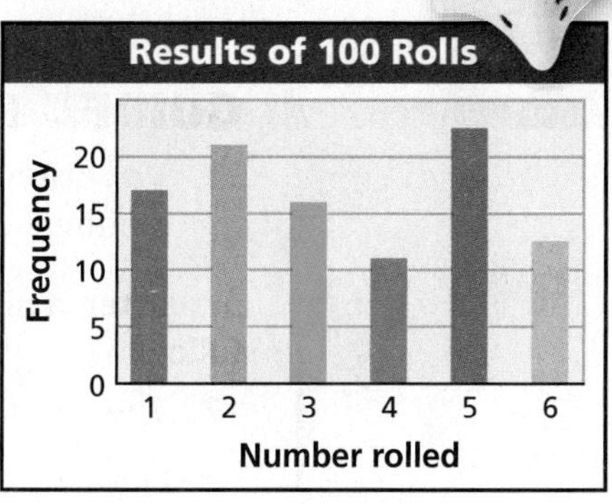

A rolling a 3

The outcome 3 occurred 16 times out of 100 trials.

$$P(3) = \frac{16}{100} = \frac{4}{25} = 0.16$$

B rolling a perfect square

$$P(\text{perfect square}) = \frac{17 + 11}{100}$$

$$= \frac{28}{100} = \frac{7}{25} = 0.28$$

The numbers 1 and 4 are perfect squares. 1 occurred 17 times and 4 occurred 11 times.

C rolling a number other than 5

Use the complement.

$$P(5) = \frac{22}{100}$$

5 occurred 22 times out of 100 trials.

$$1 - P(5) = 1 - \frac{22}{100} = \frac{78}{100} = \frac{39}{50} = 0.78$$

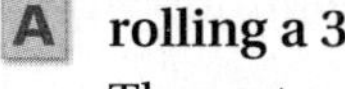

Helpful Hint

Frequencies must be whole numbers, so they can be easily read from the graph in Example 5.

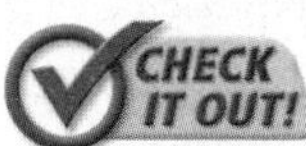

5. The table shows the results of choosing one card from a deck of cards, recording the suit, and then replacing the card.

Card Suit	Hearts	Diamonds	Clubs	Spades
Number	5	9	7	5

5a. Find the experimental probability of choosing a diamond.

5b. Find the experimental probability of choosing a card that is not a club.

THINK AND DISCUSS

1. Explain whether the probability of an event can be 1.5.
2. Tell which events have the same probability when two number cubes are tossed: sum of 7, sum of 5, sum of 9, and sum of 11.
3. Compare the theoretical and experimental probabilities of getting heads when tossing a coin if Joe got heads 8 times in 20 tosses of the coin.

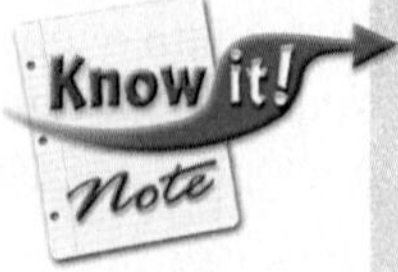

4. **GET ORGANIZED** Copy and complete the graphic organizer. Give an example of each probability concept.

Experimental	Theoretical
Probability	
Complement	Geometric

7-2 Exercises

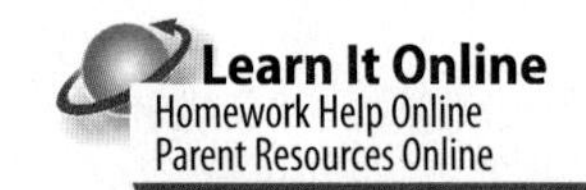

GUIDED PRACTICE

1. **Vocabulary** A fair coin is tossed 8 times and lands heads up 3 times. The __?__ of landing heads is $\frac{1}{2}$. (*theoretical probability* or *experimental probability*)

SEE EXAMPLE 1

A quarter, a nickel, and a penny are flipped. Find the probability of each of the following.

2. The quarter shows heads.
3. The penny and nickel show heads.
4. One coin shows heads.
5. All three coins land the same way.

SEE EXAMPLE 2

6. What is the probability that a random 2-digit number (00-99) does not end in 5?
7. What is the probability that a randomly selected date in one year is not in the month of December or January?

SEE EXAMPLE 3

8. A clerk has 4 different letters that need to go in 4 different envelopes. What is the probability that all 4 letters are placed in the correct envelopes?
9. There are 12 balloons in a bag: 3 each of blue, green, red, and yellow. Three balloons are chosen at random. Find the probability that all 3 of the balloons are green.

SEE EXAMPLE 4

Use the diagram for Exercises 10 and 11. Find each probability.

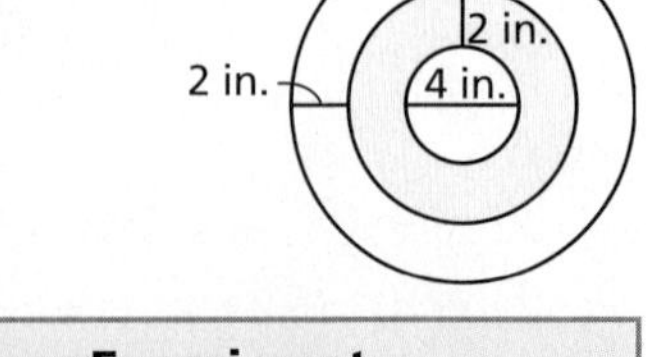

10. that a point chosen at random is in the shaded area
11. that a point chosen at random is in the smallest circle

SEE EXAMPLE 5

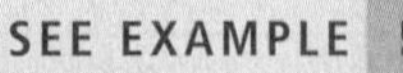

Use the table for Exercises 12 and 13.

12. Find the experimental probability of spinning red.
13. Find the experimental probability of spinning red or blue.

Spinner Experiment			
Color	Red	Green	Blue
Spins	5	8	7

PRACTICE AND PROBLEM SOLVING

Independent Practice

For Exercises	See Example
14–15	1
16	2
17–18	3
19	4
20	5

Extra Practice

See Extra Practice for more Skills Practice and Applications Practice exercises.

There are 3 green marbles, 7 red marbles, and 5 white marbles in a bag. Find the probability of each of the following.

14. The chosen marble is white.

15. The chosen marble is red or white.

16. Two integers from 1 to 8 are randomly selected. The same number can be chosen both times. What is the probability that both numbers are greater than 2?

17. Swimming The coach randomly selects 3 swimmers from a team of 8 to swim in a heat. What is the probability that she will choose the three strongest swimmers?

18. Books There are 7 books numbered 1–7 on the summer reading list. Peter randomly chooses 2 books. What is the probability that Peter chooses books numbered 1 and 2?

19. Games In the game of corntoss, players throw corn-filled bags at a hole in a wooden platform. If a bag that hits the platform can hit any location with an equal likelihood, find the probability that a tossed bag lands in the hole.

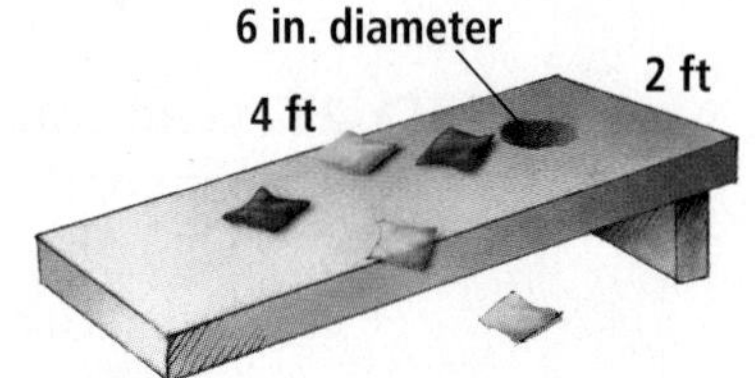

20. Cards An experiment consists of choosing one card from a standard deck and then replacing it. The experiment was done several times, and the results are: 8 hearts, 8 diamonds, 6 spades, and 6 clubs. Find the experimental probability that a card is red.

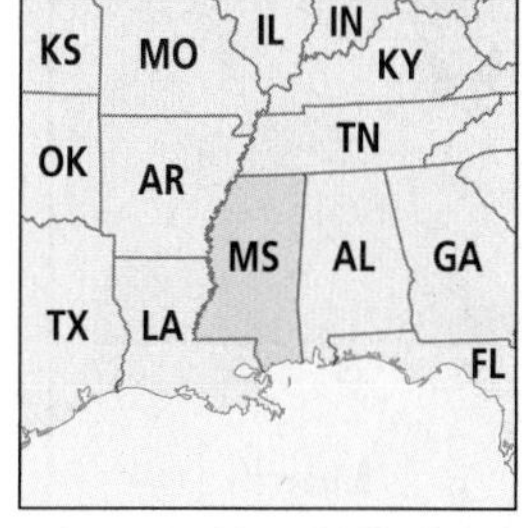

21. Critical Thinking Explain whether the experimental probability of tossing tails when a fair coin is tossed 25 times is always, sometimes, or never equal to the theoretical probability.

22. Games A radio station in Mississippi is giving away a trip to the Mississippi coast from any other state in the United States. Assuming an equally likely chance for a winner from any other state, what is the probability that the winner will be from a state that does not border Mississippi?

23. Geometry Use the figure.

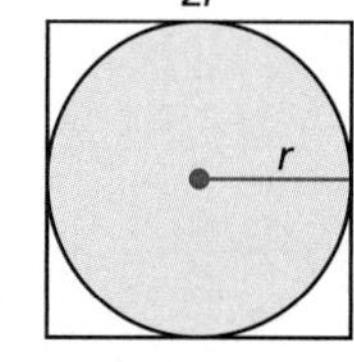

a. A circle with radius r is inscribed in a square with side length $2r$. What is the ratio of the area of the circle to the area of the square?

b. A square board has an inscribed circle with a 15 in. radius. A small button is dropped 10,000 times on the board, landing inside the circle 7852 times. How can you use this experiment to estimate a value for π?

24. Games The sides of a backgammon die are marked with the numbers 2, 4, 8, 16, 32, and 64. Describe an outcome that has a probability of $\frac{2}{3}$.

25. Computer A player in a computer basketball program has a constant probability of making each free throw. Jack notes the success rate over a period of time.

a. Find the experimental probability for each set of 25 attempts as a decimal.

b. Find the experimental probability for the entire experiment.

c. What is the best estimate of the theoretical probability? Justify your answer.

Free Throw Shooting

Attempts	Free Throws Made
1–25	17
26–50	21
51–75	19
76–100	16

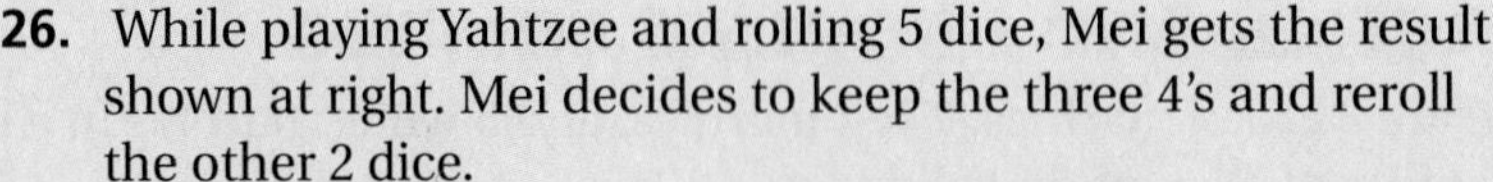

26. While playing Yahtzee and rolling 5 dice, Mei gets the result shown at right. Mei decides to keep the three 4's and reroll the other 2 dice.

a. What is the probability that Mei will have 5 of a kind?

b. What is the probability that she will have 4 of a kind (four 4's plus something else)?

c. What is the probability that she will have exactly three 4's?

d. How are the answers to parts **a, b,** and **c** related?

27. Geometry The points along $\overline{AF}$ are evenly spaced. A point is randomly chosen. Find the probability that the point lies on $\overline{BD}$.

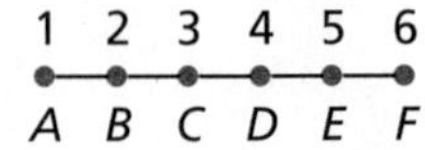

Weather **Use the graph and the following information for Exercises 28–30.**

The table shows the number of days that the maximum temperature was above 90°F in Death Valley National Park in 2002.

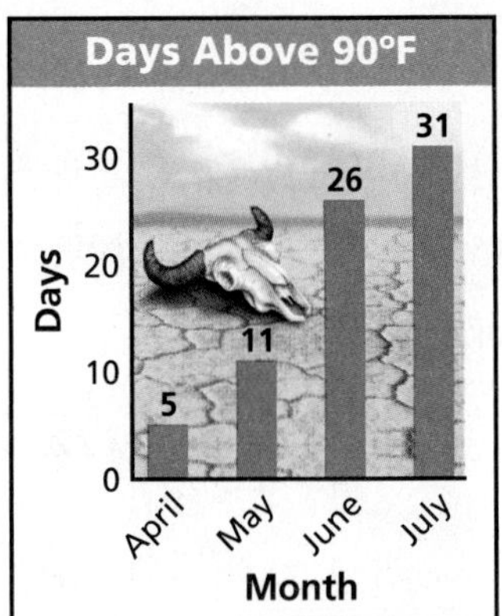

28. What is the experimental probability that the maximum temperature will be greater than 90°F on a given day in April?

29. For what month would you estimate the theoretical probability of a maximum temperature no greater than 90°F to be about 0.13? Explain.

30. May has 31 days. How would the experimental probability be affected if someone mistakenly used 30 days to calculate the experimental probability that the maximum temperature will not be greater than 90°F on a given day in May?

31. Critical Thinking Is it possible for the experimental probability of an event to be 0 if the theoretical probability is 1? Is it possible for the experimental probability of an event to be 0 if the theoretical probability is 0.99? Explain.

32 Geometry The two circles circumscribe and inscribe the square. Find the probability that a random point in the large circle is within the inner circle. (*Hint:* Use the Pythagorean Theorem.)

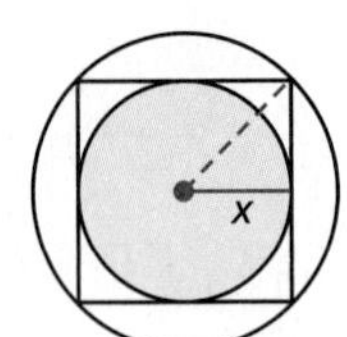

33. Critical Thinking Lexi tossed a fair coin 20 times, resulting in 12 heads and 8 tails. What is the theoretical probability that Lexi will get heads on the next toss? Explain.

34. Athletics Do male or female high school basketball players have a better chance of playing on college teams? on professional teams? Explain.

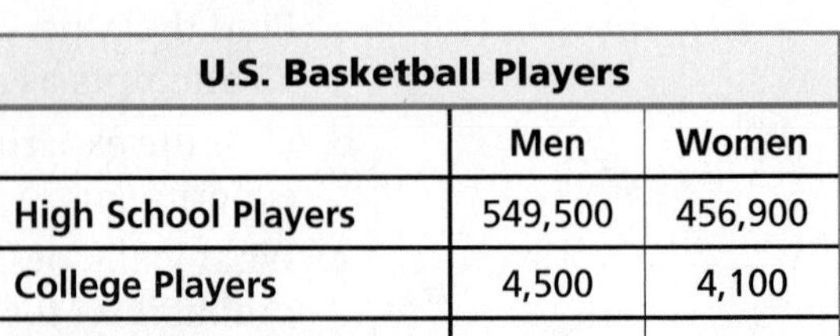

U.S. Basketball Players

	Men	Women
High School Players	549,500	456,900
College Players	4,500	4,100
College Players Drafted by Pro Leagues	44	32

Source: www.ncaa.org

35. Write About It Describe the difference between theoretical probability and experimental probability. Give an example in which they may differ.

36. A fair coin is tossed 25 times, landing tails up 14 times. What is the experimental probability of heads?

Ⓐ 0.44 Ⓑ 0.50 Ⓒ 0.56 Ⓓ 0.79

37. **Geometry** Find the probability that a point chosen at random in the large rectangle at right will lie in the shaded area, to the nearest percent.

16; 5; 14; 8

Ⓕ 18% Ⓖ 45% Ⓗ 55% Ⓙ 71%

38. How many outcomes are in the sample space when a quarter, a dime, and a nickel are tossed?

Ⓐ 3 Ⓑ 6 Ⓒ 8 Ⓓ 12

39. Two number cubes are rolled. What is the theoretical probability that the sum is 5?

Ⓕ $\frac{1}{3}$ Ⓖ $\frac{1}{6}$ Ⓗ $\frac{1}{9}$ Ⓙ $\frac{1}{12}$

40. **Short Response** Find the probability that a point chosen at random on the part of the number line shown will lie between points B and C.

4 8 12 24; A B C D

CHALLENGE AND EXTEND

41. The graph illustrates a statistical property known as the *law of large numbers.* Make a conjecture about the effect on probability as the number of trials gets very large. Give an example of how the probability might be affected for a real-world situation.

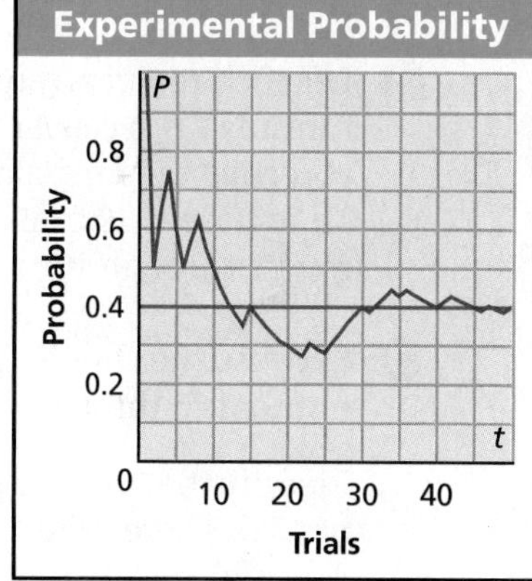

42. Four trumpet players' instruments are mixed up, and the trumpets are given to the players just before a concert. What is the probability that *no one* gets his or her trumpet back?

43. The table shows the data from a spinner experiment. Draw a reasonable spinner with 6 regions that may have been used for this experiment.

Spinner Experiment				
Color	Red	Blue	Green	Yellow
Occurrences	23	44	7	26

Use with Theoretical and Experimental Probability

Use appropriate tools strategically.

CC.9-12.S.MD.7 (+) Analyze decisions and strategies using probability concepts…

Explore Simulations

A *simulation* is a model that uses random numbers to approximate experimental probability. You can use a spreadsheet to perform simulations. The **RAND( )** function generates random decimal values greater than or equal to 0 and less than 1. The **INT** function gives the greatest integer less than or equal to the input value. The functions can be used together to generate random integers as shown in the table

Random Numbers		
Formula	**Output**	**Example**
=RAND()	Decimal values $0 \le n < 1$	0.279606096
=100*RAND()	Decimal values $0 \le n < 100$	27.9606096
=INT(100*RAND())	Integers $0 \le n \le 99$	27
=INT(100*RAND())+1	Integers $1 \le n \le 100$	28

Activity

Use a simulation to find the experimental probability that a 65% free throw shooter will make at least 4 of his next 5 attempts.

1. To represent a percent, enter the formula for random integers from 1 to 100 into cell A1.

A1 ▾ fx =INT(100*RAND())+1

	A	B	C	D	E
1	38				

2. Let each row represent a trial of 5 attempts. Copy the formula from cell A1 into cells B1 through E1. Each time you copy the formula, the random values will change. To represent 10 trials, copy the formulas from row 1 into rows 2 through 10.

A1 ▾ fx =INT(100*RAND())+1

	A	B	C	D	E
1	72	98	34	74	87

3. Because the shooter makes 65% of his attempts, let the numbers 1 through 65 represent a successful attempt.

	A	B	C	D	E
1	✓ 25	✓ 2	✓ 62	✓ 26	✓ 38
2	✓ 30	✓ 32	66	88	✓ 9
3	✓ 27	✓ 18	✓ 9	✓ 9	93
4	98	✓ 34	✓ 10	86	99
5	87	✓ 64	✓ 4	74	✓ 36
6	✓ 5	97	69	83	✓ 51
7	✓ 39	✓ 39	80	95	97
8	✓ 32	✓ 64	✓ 51	✓ 64	✓ 46
9	✓ 52	81	✓ 39	✓ 5	✓ 36
10	✓ 48	✓ 46	✓ 45	69	✓ 21

Identify the number of successful attempts in each row, or trial. There were 4 or more successes in trials 1, 3, 8, 9, and 10. So there is about a $\frac{5}{10}$, or 50%, experimental probability that the shooter will make at least 4 of his next 5 attempts.

Note that each time you run the simulation, you may get a different probability. The more trials you perform, the more reliable your estimate will be.

Try This

Use a simulation to find each experimental probability.

1. An energy drink game advertises a 25% chance of winning with each bottle cap. Find the experimental probability that a 6-pack will contain at least 3 winners.
2. In a game with a 40% chance of winning, your friend challenges you to win 4 times in a row. Find the experimental probability of this happening in the next 4 games.
3. **Critical Thinking** How would you design a simulation to find the probability that a baseball player with a .285 batting average will get a hit in 5 of his next 10 at bats?

COMMON CORE

7-3 Independent and Dependent Events

CC.9-12.S.CP.3 Understand the conditional probability of *A* given *B*...and interpret independence of *A* and *B*...
Also **CC.9-12.S.CP.2, CC.9-12.S.CP.4, CC.9-12.S.CP.6, CC.9-12.S.IC.2, CC.9-12.S.ID.5, CC.9-12.S.CP.8** (+)

Objectives

Determine whether events are independent or dependent.

Find the probability of independent and dependent events.

Vocabulary

independent events
dependent events
conditional probability

Who uses this?

Political analysts can use demographic information and probabilities to predict the results of elections. (See Example 3.)

Events are **independent events** if the occurrence of one event does not affect the probability of the other.

If a coin is tossed twice, its landing heads up on the first toss and landing heads up on the second toss are independent events. The outcome of one toss does not affect the probability of heads on the other toss. To find the probability of tossing heads twice, multiply the individual probabilities, $\frac{1}{2} \cdot \frac{1}{2}$, or $\frac{1}{4}$.

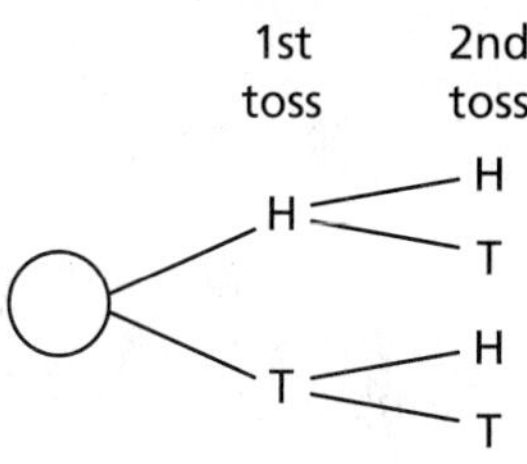

Know it! Note

Probability of Independent Events

If A and B are independent events, then $P(A \text{ and } B) = P(A) \cdot P(B)$.

EXAMPLE 1 Finding the Probability of Independent Events

Find each probability.

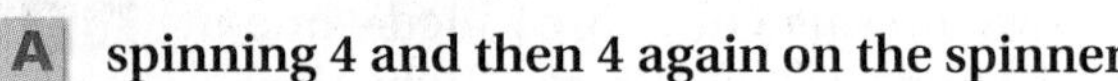

A spinning 4 and then 4 again on the spinner

Spinning a 4 once does not affect the probability of spinning a 4 again, so the events are independent.

$P(4 \text{ and then } 4) = P(4) \cdot P(4)$

$\frac{3}{8} \cdot \frac{3}{8} = \frac{9}{64}$ *3 of the 8 equal sectors are labeled 4.*

B spinning red, then green, and then red on the spinner

The result of any spin does not affect the probability of any other outcome.

$P(\text{red, then green, and then red}) = P(\text{red}) \cdot P(\text{green}) \cdot P(\text{red})$

$= \frac{1}{4} \cdot \frac{3}{8} \cdot \frac{1}{4} = \frac{3}{128}$ *2 of the 8 equal sectors are red; 3 are green.*

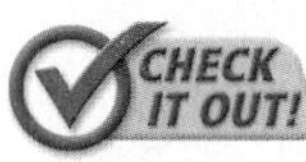

Find each probability.

1a. rolling a 6 on one number cube and a 6 on another number cube

1b. tossing heads, then heads, and then tails when tossing a coin 3 times

Events are **dependent events** if the occurrence of one event affects the probability of the other. For example, suppose that there are 2 lemons and 1 lime in a bag. If you pull out two pieces of fruit, the probabilities change depending on the outcome of the first.

The tree diagram shows the probabilities for choosing two pieces of fruit from a bag containing 2 lemons and 1 lime.

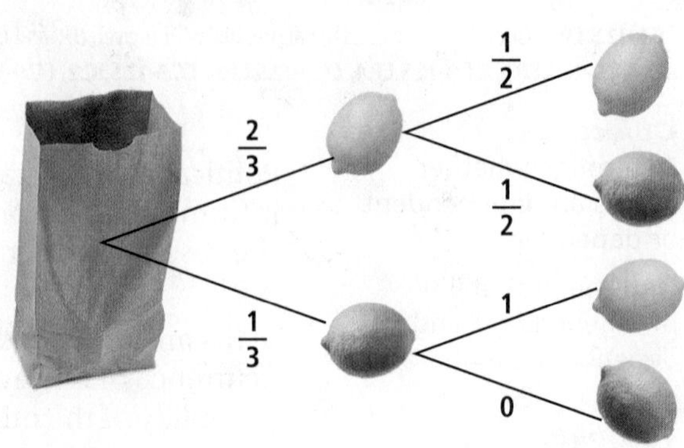

The probability of a specific event can be found by multiplying the probabilities on the branches that make up the event. For example, the probability of drawing two lemons is $\frac{2}{3} \cdot \frac{1}{2} = \frac{1}{3}$.

To find the probability of dependent events, you can use **conditional probability** $P(B \mid A)$, the probability of event B, given that event A has occurred.

Probability of Dependent Events

If A and B are dependent events, then $P(A \text{ and } B) = P(A) \cdot P(B \mid A)$, where $P(B \mid A)$ is the probability of B, given that A has occurred.

EXAMPLE 2 Finding the Probability of Dependent Events

Two number cubes are rolled—one red and one blue. Explain why the events are dependent. Then find the indicated probability.

1 1	1 2	1 3	1 4	1 5	1 6
2 1	2 2	2 3	2 4	2 5	2 6
3 1	3 2	3 3	3 4	3 5	3 6
4 1	4 2	4 3	4 4	4 5	4 6
5 1	5 2	5 3	5 4	5 5	5 6
6 1	6 2	6 3	6 4	6 5	6 6

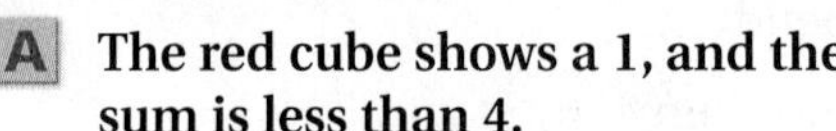

A The red cube shows a 1, and the sum is less than 4.

Step 1 Explain why the events are dependent.

$P(\text{red } 1) = \frac{6}{36} = \frac{1}{6}$ *Of 36 outcomes, 6 have a red 1.*

$P(\text{sum} < 4 \mid \text{red } 1) = \frac{2}{6} = \frac{1}{3}$ *Of 6 outcomes with a red 1, 2 have a sum less than 4.*

The events "the red cube shows a 1" and "the sum is less than 4" are dependent because $P(\text{sum} < 4)$ is different when it is known that a red 1 has occurred.

Step 2 Find the probability.

$$P(A \text{ and } B) = P(A) \cdot P(B \mid A)$$

$$P(\text{red } 1 \text{ and sum} < 4) = P(\text{red } 1) \cdot P(\text{sum} < 4 \mid \text{red } 1)$$

$$= \frac{1}{6} \cdot \frac{1}{3} = \frac{1}{18}$$

Helpful Hint

In Example 2A, you can check to see that 2 of the 36 outcomes, or $\frac{1}{18}$, have a red 1 and a sum less than 4: (1, 1) and (1, 2).

Explain why the events are dependent. Then find the indicated probability.

B **The blue cube shows a multiple of 3, and the sum is 8.**

The events are dependent because $P(\text{sum is } 8)$ is different when the blue cube shows a multiple of 3.

$P(\text{blue multiple of } 3) = \frac{2}{6} = \frac{1}{3}$ *Of 6 outcomes for blue, 2 have a multiple of 3.*

$P(\text{sum is } 8 \mid \text{blue multiple of } 3) = \frac{2}{12} = \frac{1}{6}$ *Of 12 outcomes that have a blue multiple of 3, 2 have a sum 8.*

$P(\text{blue multiple of 3 and sum is } 8) =$

$P(\text{blue multiple of } 3) \cdot P(\text{sum is } 8 \mid \text{blue multiple of } 3) = \left(\frac{1}{3}\right)\left(\frac{1}{6}\right) = \frac{1}{18}$

Two number cubes are rolled—one red and one black. Explain why the events are dependent, and then find the indicated probability.

2. The red cube shows a number greater than 4, and the sum is greater than 9.

Conditional probability often applies when data fall into categories.

EXAMPLE 3 Using a Table to Find Conditional Probability

Largest Texas Counties' Votes for President 2004 (thousands)			
County	**Bush**	**Kerry**	**Other**
Harris	581	472	5
Dallas	345	336	4
Tarrant	349	207	3
Bexar	260	210	3
Travis	148	197	5

The table shows the approximate distribution of votes in Texas' five largest counties in the 2004 presidential election. Find each probability.

A **that a voter from Tarrant County voted for George Bush**

$P(\text{Bush} \mid \text{Tarrant}) = \frac{349}{559} \approx 0.624$ *Use the Tarrant row. Of 559,000 Tarrant voters, 349,000 voted for Bush.*

B **that a voter voted for John Kerry and was from Dallas County**

$P(\text{Dallas} \mid \text{Kerry}) = \frac{336}{1422}$ *Of 1,422,000 who voted for Kerry, 336,000 were from Dallas County.*

$P(\text{Kerry and Dallas}) = \frac{1422}{3125} \cdot \frac{336}{1422}$ *There were 3,125,000 total voters.*

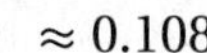

≈ 0.108

Find each probability.

3a. that a voter from Travis county voted for someone other than George Bush or John Kerry

3b. that a voter was from Harris county and voted for George Bush

In many cases involving random selection, events are independent when there is replacement and dependent when there is not replacement.

EXAMPLE 4 **Determining Whether Events Are Independent or Dependent**

Two cards are drawn from a deck of 52. Determine whether the events are independent or dependent. Find the probability.

 **A** **selecting two aces when the first card is replaced**

Replacing the first card means that the occurrence of the first selection will not affect the probability of the second selection, so the events are independent.

$P(\text{ace} \mid \text{ace on first draw}) = P(\text{ace}) \cdot P(\text{ace})$

$= \frac{4}{52} \cdot \frac{4}{52} = \frac{1}{169}$ *4 of the 52 cards are aces.*

> **Remember!**
> A standard card deck contains 4 suits of 13 cards each. The face cards are the jacks, queens, and kings.

 **B** **selecting a face card and then a 7 when the first card is not replaced**

Not replacing the first card means that there will be fewer cards to choose from, affecting the probability of the second selection, so the events are dependent.

$P(\text{face card}) \cdot P(7 \mid \text{first card was a face card})$

$= \frac{12}{52} \cdot \frac{4}{51} = \frac{4}{221}$ *There are 12 face cards, four 7's and 51 cards available for the second selection.*

A bag contains 10 beads—2 black, 3 white, and 5 red. A bead is selected at random. Determine whether the events are independent or dependent. Find the indicated probability.

4a. selecting a white bead, replacing it, and then selecting a red bead

4b. selecting a white bead, not replacing it, and then selecting a red bead

4c. selecting 3 nonred beads without replacement

THINK AND DISCUSS

1. Describe some independent events.

2. Extend the rule for the probability of independent events to more than two independent events. When might this be used?

3. GET ORGANIZED Copy and complete the graphic organizer. In each box, compare independent and dependent events and their related probabilities.

Probability of Independent Events vs. Probability of Dependent Events

Similarities	Differences

7-3 Exercises

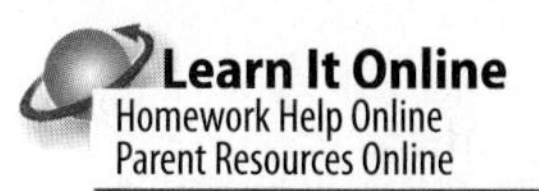

GUIDED PRACTICE

1. **Vocabulary** Two events are __?__ if the occurrence of one event does not affect the probability of the other event. (*independent* or *dependent*)

SEE EXAMPLE 1

Find each probability.

2. rolling a 1 and then another 1 when a number cube is rolled twice
3. a coin landing heads up on every toss when it is tossed 3 times

SEE EXAMPLE 2

Two number cubes are rolled—one blue and one yellow. Explain why the events are dependent. Then find the indicated probability.

4. The blue cube shows a 4 and the product is less than 20.
5. The yellow cube shows a multiple of 3, given that the product is 6.

SEE EXAMPLE 3

The table shows the results of a quality-control study of a lightbulb factory. A lightbulb from the factory is selected at random. Find each probability.

6. that a shipped bulb is not defective
7. that a bulb is defective and shipped

Lightbulb Quality		
	Shipped	Not Shipped
Defective	10	45
Not Defective	942	3

SEE EXAMPLE 4

A bag contains 20 checkers—10 red and 10 black. Determine whether the events are independent or dependent. Find the indicated probability.

8. selecting 2 black checkers when they are chosen at random with replacement
9. selecting 2 black checkers when they are chosen at random without replacement

PRACTICE AND PROBLEM SOLVING

Independent Practice

For Exercises	See Example
10–11	1
12–14	2
15–16	3
17–18	4

Extra Practice

See Extra Practice for more Skills Practice and Applications Practice exercises.

Find each probability.

10. choosing the same activity when two friends each randomly choose 1 of 4 extracurricular activities to participate in
11. rolling an even number and then rolling a 6 when a number cube is rolled twice

Two number cubes are rolled—one blue and one yellow. Explain why the events are dependent. Then find the indicated probability.

12. The yellow cube is greater than 5 and the product is greater than 24.
13. The blue cube is less than 3 and the product is 8.
14. The table shows immigration to the United States from three countries in three different years. A person is randomly selected. Find each probability.
    a. that a selected person is from Cuba, given that the person immigrated in 1990
    b. that a person came from Spain and immigrated in 2000
    c. that a selected person immigrated in 1995, given that the person was from Ghana.

Immigration to the United States			
Country	1990	1995	2000
Cuba	10,645	17,937	20,831
Ghana	4,466	3,152	4,344
Spain	1,886	1,321	1,264

Employment Find each probability.

15. that a person with an advanced degree is employed

16. that a person is not a high school graduate and is not employed

Employment by Education Level, Ages 21–24		
Education Level	Employed (millions)	Not employed (millions)
Not a high school graduate	1.060	0.834
High school graduate	2.793	1.157
Some college	4.172	1.634
Bachelor's degree	1.53	0.372
Advanced degree	0.104	0.041

A bag contains number slips numbered 1 to 9. Determine whether the events are independent or dependent, and find the indicated probability.

17. selecting 2 even numbers when 2 slips are chosen without replacement

18. selecting 2 even numbers when 2 slips are chosen with replacement

Determine whether the events are independent or dependent.

19. A coin comes up heads, and a number cube rolled at the same time comes up 6.

20. A 4 is drawn from a deck of cards, set aside, and then an ace is drawn.

21. A 1 is rolled on a number cube, and then a 4 is rolled on the same number cube.

22. A dart hits the bull's-eye, and a second dart also hits the bull's eye.

LINK

Tennis

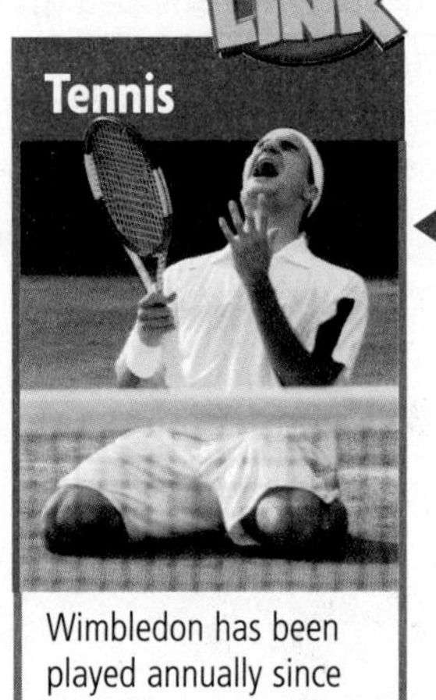

Wimbledon has been played annually since 1877 at the All England Lawn Tennis and Croquet Club.

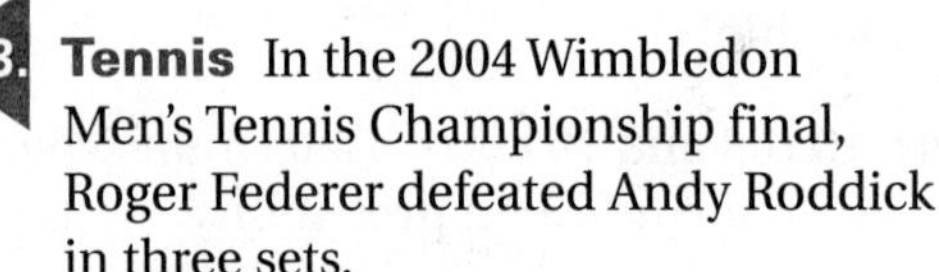

23. **Tennis** In the 2004 Wimbledon Men's Tennis Championship final, Roger Federer defeated Andy Roddick in three sets.

a. What was the probability that Federer won the point when his second serve was in?

b. When Federer lost a point, what was the probability that he *double faulted*?

Roger Federer's Service Points		
	Won	Lost
First Serve In	64	31
Second Serve In	34	22
Second Serve Out (Double Fault)	0	3

24. **Multi-Step** At one high school, the probability that a student is absent today, given that the student was absent yesterday, is 0.12. The probability that a student is absent today, given that the student was present yesterday, is 0.05. The probability that a student was absent yesterday is 0.1. Draw a tree diagram to represent the situation. What is the probability that a randomly selected student was present yesterday and today?

MULTI-STEP TEST PREP

25. While playing Yahtzee, Jake rolls 5 dice and gets the result shown at right. The rules allow him to reroll these dice 2 times. Jake decides to try for all 5's, so he rerolls the 2 and the 3.

a. What is the probability that Jake gets no additional 5's in either of the 2 rolls?

b. What is the probability that he gets all 5's on his first reroll of the 2 and the 3?

c. What is the probability that he gets all 5's on his first reroll, given that at least one of the dice is a 5?

Estimation **Use the graph to estimate each probability.**

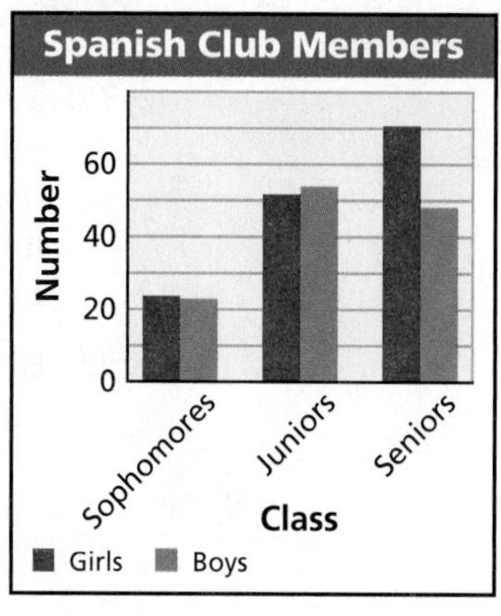

26. that a Spanish club member is a girl
27. that a senior Spanish club member is a girl
28. that a male Spanish club member is a senior
29. **Critical Thinking** A box contains 100 balloons. Eighty are yellow, and 20 are green. Fifty are marked "Happy Birthday!" and 50 are not. A balloon is randomly chosen from the box. How many yellow "Happy Birthday!" balloons must be in the box if the event "a balloon is yellow" and the event "a balloon is marked 'Happy Birthday!'" are independent?
30. **Travel** Airline information for three years is given in the table.
    a. Complete the table.
    b. What was the probability that a scheduled flight in 2004 was canceled?
    c. An on-time flight is selected randomly for study. What is the probability that it was a flight from 2005?

Scheduled Flights (thousands) January to July

	2003	2004	2005	Total
On Time	■	3197	3237	■
Delayed	598	■	877	2321
Canceled	61	68	■	■
Total	3761	■	4196	■

Source: Bureau of Transportation Statistics

31. **Write About It** The "law of averages" is a nonmathematical term that means that events eventually "average out." So, if a coin comes up heads 10 tosses in a row, there is a greater probability that it will come up tails on the eleventh toss. Explain the error in this thinking.

32. What is the probability that a person's birthday falls on a Saturday next year, given that it falls on a Saturday this year?

    Ⓐ 0　　Ⓑ $\frac{1}{7}$　　Ⓒ $\frac{1}{2}$　　Ⓓ 1

33. Which of the following has the same probability as rolling doubles on 2 number cubes 3 times in a row?

    Ⓕ A single number cube is rolled 3 times. The cube shows 5 each time.

    Ⓖ Two number cubes are rolled 3 times. Each time the sum is 6.

    Ⓗ Two number cubes are rolled 3 times. Each time the sum is greater than 2.

    Ⓙ Three number cubes are rolled twice. Each time all cubes show the same number (triples).

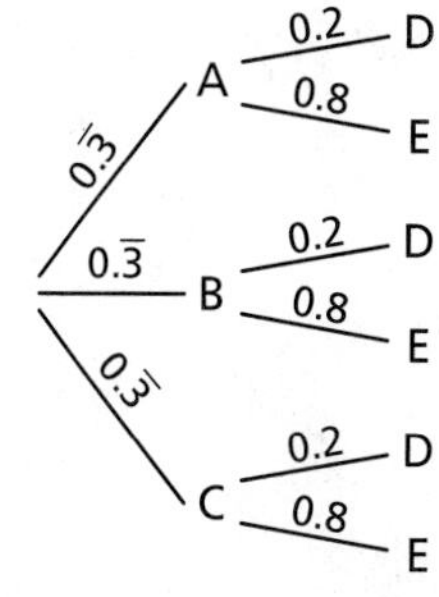

34. **Extended Response** **Use the tree diagram.**
    a. Find $P(D \mid A)$, $P(D \mid B)$, and $P(D \mid C)$.
    b. Does the tree diagram represent independent or dependent events? Explain your answer.
    c. Describe a scenario for which the tree diagram could be used to find probabilities.

CHALLENGE AND EXTEND

35. Two number cubes are rolled in succession and the numbers that they show are added together. What is the only sum for which the probability of the sum is independent of the number shown on the first roll? Explain.

36. **Birthdays** People born on February 29 have a birthday once every 4 years.
    a. What is the smallest group of people in which there is a greater than 50% chance that 2 people share a birthday? (Do not include February 29.)
    b. What is the probability that in a group of 150 people, none are born on February 29?
    c. What is the least number of people such that there is a greater than 50% chance that one of the people in the group has a birthday on February 29?

37. There are 150 people at a play. Ninety are women, and 60 are men. Half are sitting in the lower level, and half are sitting in the upper level. There are 35 women sitting in the upper level. A person is selected at random for a prize. What is the probability that the person is sitting in the lower level, given that the person is a woman? Is the event "person is sitting in the lower level" independent of the event "person is a woman"? Explain.

38. **Medicine** Suppose that strep throat affects 2% of the population and a test to detect it produces an accurate result 99% of the time.
    a. Complete the table.
    b. What is the probability that someone who tests positive actually has strep throat?

Per 10,000 People Tested			
	Have strep	Do not have strep	Total
Test Positive	■	■	■
Test Negative	■	■	■
Total	■	■	10,000

Mastering the *Standards*

for Mathematical Practice

The topics described in the Standards for Mathematical Content will vary from year to year. However, the *way* in which you learn, study, and think about mathematics will not. The Standards for Mathematical Practice describe skills that you will use in all of your math courses.

Mathematical Practices

1. *Make sense of problems and persevere in solving them.*
2. *Reason abstractly and quantitatively.*
3. *Construct viable arguments and critique the reasoning of others.*
4. *Model with mathematics.*
5. *Use appropriate tools strategically.*
6. *Attend to precision.*
7. *Look for and make use of structure.*
8. *Look for and express regularity in repeated reasoning.*

① Make sense of problems and persevere in solving them.

Mathematically proficient students start by explaining to themselves the meaning of a problem... They analyze givens, constraints, relationships, and goals. They make conjectures about the form... of the solution and plan a solution pathway...

In your book

Focus on Problem Solving describes a four-step plan for problem solving. The plan is introduced at the beginning of your book, and practice with the plan appears throughout the book.

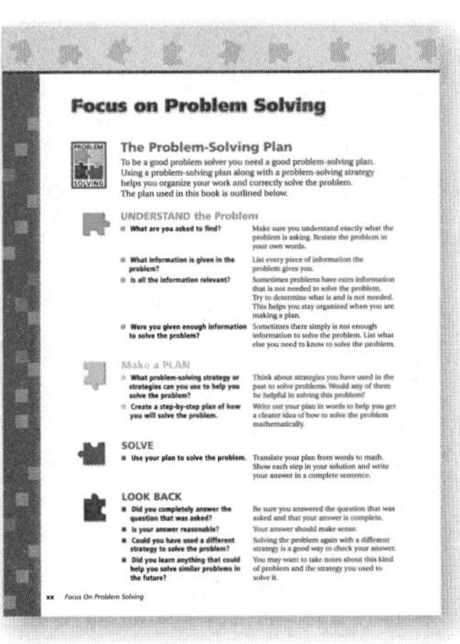

Focus on Problem Solving

The Problem-Solving Plan

To be a good problem solver you need a good problem-solving plan. Using a problem-solving plan along with a problem-solving strategy helps you organize your work and correctly solve the problem. The plan used in this book is outlined below.

UNDERSTAND the Problem

What are you asked to find?	Make sure you understand exactly what the problem is asking. Restate the problem in your own words.
What information is given in the problem?	List every piece of information the problem gives you.
Is all the information relevant?	Sometimes problems have extra information that is not needed to solve the problem. Try to determine what is and is not needed. This helps you stay organized when you are making a plan.
Were you given enough information to solve the problem?	Sometimes there simply is not enough information to solve the problem. List what else you need to know to solve the problem.

Make a PLAN

What problem-solving strategy or strategies can you use to help you solve the problem?	Think about strategies you have used in the past to solve problems. Would any of them be helpful in solving this problem?
Create a step-by-step plan of how you will solve the problem.	Write out your plan in words to help you get a clearer idea of how to solve the problem mathematically.

SOLVE

Use your plan to solve the problem.	Translate your plan from words to math. Show each step in your solution and write your answer in a complete sentence.

LOOK BACK

Did you completely answer the question that was asked?	Be sure you answered the question that was asked and that your answer is complete.
Is your answer reasonable?	Your answer should make sense.
Could you have used a different strategy to solve the problem?	Solving the problem again with a different strategy is a good way to check your answer.
Did you learn anything that could help you solve similar problems in the future?	You may want to take notes about this kind of problem and the strategy you used to solve it.

xx *Focus On Problem Solving*

EXAMPLE 5 PROBLEM SOLVING ***Problem-Solving Application***

The cost to place an ad in a newspaper for one week is a linear function of the number of lines in the ad. The costs for 3, 5, and 10 lines are shown. Write an equation in slope-intercept form that represents the function. Then find the cost of an ad that is 18 lines long.

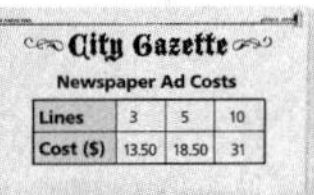
City Gazette

Newspaper Ad Costs

Lines	3	5	10
Cost ($)	13.50	18.50	31

1 Understand the Problem

- The **answer** will have two parts—an equation in slope-intercept form and the cost of an ad that is 18 lines long.
- The ordered pairs given in the table satisfy the equation.

2 Make a Plan

First, find the slope. Then use point-slope form to write the equation. Finally, write the equation in slope-intercept form.

3 Solve

Step 1 Choose any two ordered pairs from the table to find the slope.

$$m = \frac{y_2 - y_1}{x_2 - x_1} = \frac{18.50 - 13.50}{5 - 3} = \frac{5}{2} = 2.5 \quad \textit{Use (3, 13.50) and (5, 18.50).}$$

Step 2 Substitute the slope and any ordered pair from the table into the point-slope form.

$$y - y_1 = m(x - x_1)$$
$$y - 31 = 2.5(x - 10) \quad \textit{Use (10, 31).}$$

Step 3 Write the equation in slope-intercept form by solving for y.

$$y - 31 = 2.5(x - 10)$$
$$y - 31 = 2.5x - 25 \quad \textit{Distribute 2.5.}$$
$$y = 2.5x + 6 \quad \textit{Add 31 to both sides.}$$

Step 4 Find the cost of an ad containing 18 lines by substituting 18 for x.

$$y = 2.5x + 6$$
$$y = 2.5(18) + 6 = 51$$

The cost of an ad containing 18 lines is $51.

4 Look Back

Check the equation by substituting the ordered pairs (3, 13.50) and (5, 18.50).

y	$= 2.5x + 6$
13.50	2.5(3) + 6
13.5	7.5 + 6
13.5	13.5 ✓

y	$= 2.5x + 6$
18.50	2.5(5) + 6
18.5	12.5 + 6
18.5	18.5 ✓

Comstock/Getty Images

CHAPTER 7

MULTI-STEP TEST PREP

SECTION 7A

Reason abstractly and quantitatively.

Experimental Probability

You can use a spinner to examine the relationship between experimental and theoretical probability. Construct a spinner like the one shown below, and use it to answer the questions.

1. What is the theoretical probability of spinning yellow?

2. What is the theoretical probability of spinning red OR yellow?

3. Spin the spinner 10 times, then copy the table below and record your results.. What is the experimental probability of spinning yellow?

Spinner Experiment				
Blue	**Red**	**Yellow**	**Purple**	**Green**

4. Perform another 10 spins and record them. What is the new experimental probability of spinning yellow?

5. Share your results with the rest of the class. What is the experimental probability of the class's results as a whole?

READY TO GO ON?

Quiz for Lessons 7-1 Through 7-3

7-1 Permutations and Combinations

1. A security code consists of 5 digits (0–9), and a digit may not be used more than once. How many possible security codes are there?
2. Adric owns 8 pairs of shoes. How many ways can he choose 4 pairs of shoes to pack into his luggage?
3. A plumber received calls from 5 customers. There are 6 open slots on today's schedule. How many ways can the plumber schedule the customers?

7-2 Theoretical and Experimental Probability

4. A cooler contains 18 cans: 9 of lemonade, 3 of iced tea, and 6 of cola. Dee selects a can without looking. What is the probability that Dee selects iced tea?
5. Jordan has 9 pens in his desk; 2 are out of ink. If his mom selects 2 pens from his desk, what is the probability that both are out of ink?
6. Find the probability that a point chosen at random inside the figure shown is in the shaded area.

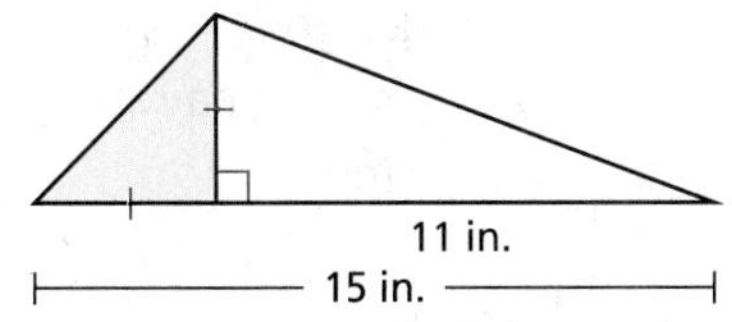

7. A number cube is tossed 50 times, and a 2 is rolled 12 times. Find the experimental probability of not rolling a 2.

7-3 Independent and Dependent Events

8. Explain why the events "getting tails, then tails, then tails, then tails, then heads when tossing a coin 5 times" are independent, and find the probability.
9. Two number cubes are rolled—one red and one black. Explain why the events "the red cube shows a 6" and "the sum is greater than or equal to 10" are dependent, and find the probability.
10. The table shows the breakdown of math students for one school year. Find the probability that a Geometry student is in the 11th grade.
11. A bag contains 25 checkers—15 red and 10 black. Determine whether the events "a red checker is selected, not replaced, and then a black checker is selected" are independent or dependent, and find the probability.

Math Students by Grade

	Geometry	Algebra 2
9th Grade	26	0
10th Grade	68	24
11th Grade	33	94

Mastering the Standards

for Mathematical Practice

The topics described in the Standards for Mathematical Content will vary from year to year. However, the *way* in which you learn, study, and think about mathematics will not. The Standards for Mathematical Practice describe skills that you will use in all of your math courses.

Mathematical Practices

1. *Make sense of problems and persevere in solving them.*
2. *Reason abstractly and quantitatively.*
3. *Construct viable arguments and critique the reasoning of others.*
4. *Model with mathematics.*
5. *Use appropriate tools strategically.*
6. *Attend to precision.*
7. *Look for and make use of structure.*
8. *Look for and express regularity in repeated reasoning.*

④ Model with mathematics.

Mathematically proficient students can apply... mathematics... to... problems... in everyday life, society, and the workplace...

In your book

Multi-Step Test Prep and **Real-World Connections** apply mathematics to other disciplines and in real-world scenarios.

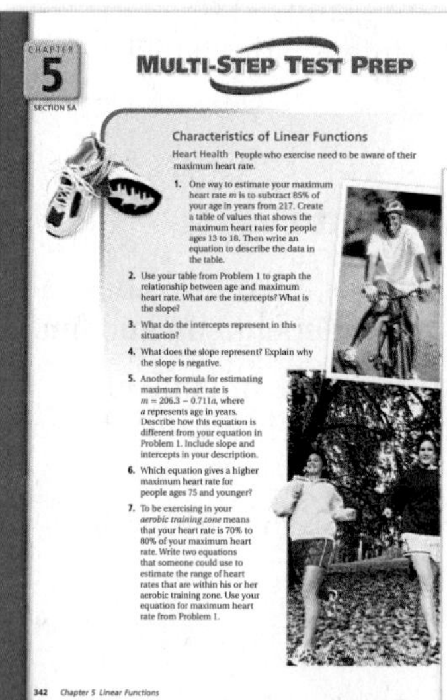
CHAPTER 5
SECTION 5A

MULTI-STEP TEST PREP

Characteristics of Linear Functions

Heart Health People who exercise need to be aware of their maximum heart rate.

1. One way to estimate your maximum heart rate m is to subtract 85% of your age in years from 217. Create a table of values that shows the maximum heart rates for people ages 13 to 18. Then write an equation to describe the data in the table.
2. Use your table from Problem 1 to graph the relationship between age and maximum heart rate. What are the intercepts? What is the slope?
3. What do the intercepts represent in this situation?
4. What does the slope represent? Explain why the slope is negative.
5. Another formula for estimating maximum heart rate is $m = 206.3 - 0.711a$, where a represents age in years. Describe how this equation is different from your equation in Problem 1. Include slope and intercepts in your description.
6. Which equation gives a higher maximum heart rate for people ages 75 and younger?
7. To be exercising in your *aerobic training zone* means that your heart rate is 70% to 80% of your maximum heart rate. Write two equations that someone could use to estimate the range of heart rates that are within his or her aerobic training zone. Use your equation for maximum heart rate from Problem 1.

342 *Chapter 5 Linear Functions*

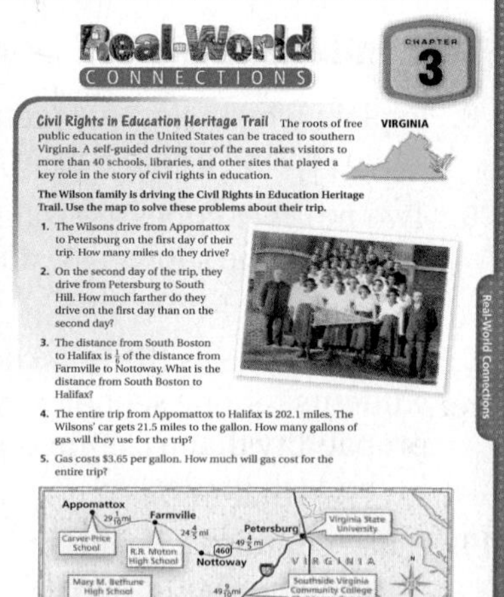
Real-World CONNECTIONS

CHAPTER 3

Civil Rights in Education Heritage Trail The roots of free public education in the United States can be traced to southern Virginia. A self-guided driving tour of the area takes visitors to more than 40 schools, libraries, and other sites that played a key role in the story of civil rights in education.

VIRGINIA

The Wilson family is driving the Civil Rights in Education Heritage Trail. Use the map to solve these problems about their trip.

1. The Wilsons drive from Appomattox to Petersburg on the first day of their trip. How many miles do they drive?
2. On the second day of the trip, they drive from Petersburg to South Hill. How much farther do they drive on the first day than on the second day?
3. The distance from South Boston to Halifax is $\frac{1}{6}$ of the distance from Farmville to Nottoway. What is the distance from South Boston to Halifax?
4. The entire trip from Appomattox to Halifax is 202.1 miles. The Wilsons' car gets 21.5 miles to the gallon. How many gallons of gas will they use for the trip?
5. Gas costs $3.65 per gallon. How much will gas cost for the entire trip?

Real-World Connections 199

PhotoDisc/Getty Images

7-4 Two-Way Tables

CC.9-12.S.ID.5 Summarize categorical data for two categories in two-way frequency tables. Interpret relative frequencies... Recognize possible associations and trends... *Also* **CC.9-12.S.CP.4, CC.9-12.S.CP.5**

Objectives
Construct and interpret two-way frequency tables of data when two categories are associated with each object being classified.

Vocabulary
joint relative frequency
marginal relative frequency
conditional relative frequency

Who uses this?
Commuters can use two-way tables to determine the best route to work. (See Example 3.)

A *two-way table* is a useful way to organize data that can be categorized by two variables. Suppose you asked 20 children and adults whether they liked broccoli. The table shows one way to arrange the data.

	Yes	No
Children	3	8
Adults	7	2

The **joint relative frequencies** are the values in each category divided by the total number of values, shown by the shaded cells in the table. Each value is divided by 20, the total number of individuals.

	Yes	No	Total
Children	0.15	0.4	0.55
Adults	0.35	0.1	0.45
Total	0.5	0.5	1

The **marginal relative frequencies** are found by adding the joint relative frequencies in each row and column.

EXAMPLE 1 Finding Joint and Marginal Relative Frequencies

The table shows the results of a poll of 80 randomly selected high school students who were asked if they prefer math or English. Make a table of the joint and marginal relative frequencies.

	9th grade	10th grade	11th grade	12th grade
Math	10	12	11	8
English	12	11	8	8

Divide each value by the total of 80 to find the joint relative frequencies, and add each row and column to find the marginal relative frequencies.

	9th grade	10th grade	11th grade	12th grade	Total
Math	0.125	0.15	0.1375	0.1	0.5125
English	0.15	0.1375	0.1	0.1	0.4875
Total	0.275	0.2875	0.2375	0.2	1

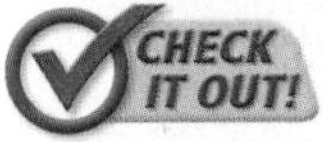

1. The table shows the number of books sold at a library sale. Make a table of the joint and marginal relative frequencies.

	Fiction	Nonfiction
Hardcover	28	52
Paperback	94	36

To find a **conditional relative frequency**, divide the joint relative frequency by the marginal relative frequency. Conditional relative frequencies can be used to find conditional probabilities.

EXAMPLE 2 Using Conditional Relative Frequency to Find Probability

A sociologist collected data on the types of pets in 100 randomly selected households, and summarized the results in a table.

		Owns a cat	
		Yes	No
Owns a dog	Yes	15	24
	No	18	43

A **Make a table of the joint and marginal relative frequencies.**

		Owns a cat		
		Yes	No	Total
Owns a dog	Yes	0.15	0.24	0.39
	No	0.18	0.43	0.61
	Total	0.33	0.67	1

Idamini/Alamy

B **If you are given that a household has a dog, what is the probability that the household also has a cat?**

Use the conditional relative frequency for the row with the condition "Owns a dog." The total for households with dogs is 0.39, or 39%. Out of these, 0.15, or 15%, also have cats. The conditional relative frequency is $\frac{0.15}{0.39} \approx 0.38$.

Given that a household has a dog, there is a probability of about 0.38 that the household also has a cat.

The classes at a dance academy include ballet and tap dancing. Enrollment in these classes is shown in the table.

		Ballet	
		Yes	No
Tap	Yes	38	52
	No	86	24

2a. Copy and complete the table of the joint relative frequencies and marginal relative frequencies.

		Ballet		
		Yes	No	Total
Tap	Yes			
	No			
	Total			1

2b. If you are given that a student is taking ballet, what is the probability that the student is not taking tap?

Notice that in Example 2, the conditional relative frequency could have been found from the original data:

$$\frac{0.15}{0.39} = \frac{15}{39} \approx 0.38$$

EXAMPLE 3 Comparing Conditional Probabilities

Tomas is trying to decide on the best possible route to drive to work. He has a choice of three possible routes. On each day, he randomly selects a route and keeps track of whether he is late. After a 40-day trial, his notes look like this.

	Late	Not Late
Route A	||||	𝍸 𝍸
Route B	|||	𝍸 ||
Route C	||||	𝍸 𝍸 ||

Use conditional probabilities to determine the best route for Tomas to take to work.

Create a table of joint and marginal relative frequencies. There are 40 data values, so divide each frequency by 40.

	Late	Not late	Total
Route A	0.1	0.25	0.35
Route B	0.075	0.175	0.25
Route C	0.1	0.3	0.4
Total	0.275	0.725	1

To find the conditional probabilities, divide the joint relative frequency of being late by the marginal relative frequency in each row.

$P(\text{being late if driving Route A}) = \frac{0.1}{0.35} \approx 0.29$

$P(\text{being late if driving Route B}) = \frac{0.075}{0.25} = 0.3$

$P(\text{being late if driving Route C}) = \frac{0.1}{0.4} = 0.25$

The probability of being late is least for Route C. Based on the sample, Tomas is least likely to be late if he takes Route C.

3. Francine is evaluating three driving schools. She asked 50 people who attended the schools whether they passed their driving tests on the first try.

Use conditional probabilities to determine which is the best school.

	Pass	Fail
Al's Driving	𝍸 𝍸 ||||	𝍸 |||
Drive Time	𝍸 𝍸 |	𝍸 ||
Crash Course	𝍸	𝍸

THINK AND DISCUSS

1. Describe the relationship between joint relative frequencies and marginal relative frequencies.

2. Explain how to find the conditional relative frequencies from a two-way table showing joint and marginal relative frequencies.

3. GET ORGANIZED Copy and complete the graphic organizer at right. In each column, explain how to find the relative frequency from a two-way table.

Relative Frequencies		
Joint	Marginal	Conditional

7-4 Exercises

GUIDED PRACTICE

Vocabulary **Apply the vocabulary from this lesson to answer each question.**

1. The ___?___ relative frequencies are the sums of each row and column in a two-way table. (*joint, marginal,* or *conditional*)

2. You can compare ___?___ probabilities to evaluate the best one out of a number of options. (*joint, marginal,* or *conditional*)

SEE EXAMPLE 1

3. The table shows the results of a poll of randomly selected high school students who were asked if they prefer to hear all-school announcements in the morning or afternoon.

	Underclassmen	Upperclassmen
Morning	8	14
Afternoon	18	10

Make a table of the joint and marginal relative frequencies.

4. **Customer Service** The table shows the results of a customer satisfaction survey for a cellular service provider, by location of the customer. In the survey, customers were asked whether they would recommend a plan with the provider to a friend.

	Arlington	Towson	Parkville
Yes	40	35	41
No	18	10	6

Make a table of the joint and marginal relative frequencies. Round to the nearest hundredth where appropriate.

SEE EXAMPLE 2

5. **School** Pamela has collected data on the number of students in the sophomore class who play a sport or play a musical instrument.

		Plays a sport	
		Yes	No
Plays an instrument	Yes	47	38
	No	51	67

Artville/Getty Images

a. Copy and complete the table of the joint and marginal relative frequencies. Round to the nearest hundredth where appropriate.

		Play Sport		
		Yes	No	Total
Play instrument	Yes			
	No			
	Total			

b. If you are given that a student plays an instrument, what is the probability that the student also plays a sport? Round your answer to the nearest hundredth.

c. If you are given that a student plays a sport, what is the probability that the student also plays an instrument? Round your answer to the nearest hundredth.

SEE EXAMPLE 3

6. **Business** Roberto is the owner of a car dealership. He is assessing the success rates of his top three salespeople in order to offer one of them a promotion. Over two months, for each attempted sale, he records whether the salesperson made a successful sale or not. The results are shown in the chart below.

	Successful	Unsuccessful
Becky	6	6
Raul	4	5
Darrell	6	9

a. Make a table of the joint relative frequencies and marginal relative frequencies. Round to the nearest hundredth where appropriate.

b. Find the probability that each salesperson will make a successful sale. Round to the nearest hundredth where appropriate.

c. Determine which salesperson has the highest success rate.

PRACTICE AND PROBLEM SOLVING

Independent Practice

For Exercises	See Example
7–8	1
9–12	2
13	3

Extra Practice

See Extra Practice for more Skills Practice and Applications Practice exercises.

7. **Fundraising** The table shows the number of T-shirts and sweatshirts sold at a fundraiser during parent visitation night at Preston High School.

	Students	Adults
T-Shirts	16	23
Sweatshirts	7	14

Make a table of the joint relative frequencies and marginal relative frequencies.

8. **Write About It** Describe in your own words the process you use to write marginal relative frequencies for data given in a two-way table.

9. **Customer Service** The claims handlers at a car insurance company help customers with insurance issues when there has been an accident, so their customer service skills are very important.

The claims handlers at the Trust Auto Insurance Company are divided into three teams. For one month, a customer satisfaction survey was given for each team. The results of the surveys are shown below.

	Satisfied	Dissatisfied
Team 1	20	8
Team 2	34	12
Team 3	34	10

a. Make a table of the joint relative frequencies and marginal relative frequencies. Round to the nearest hundredth where appropriate.

b. Find the probability that a customer will be satisfied after working with each team. Round to the nearest hundredth where appropriate.

c. Determine which team has the highest rate of customer satisfaction.

10. **Critical Thinking** What do you notice about the value that always falls in the cell to the lower right of a two-way table when marginal relative frequencies have been written in? What does this value represent?

11. ///ERROR ANALYSIS/// One hundred adults and children were randomly selected and asked whether they spoke more than one language fluently. The data were recorded in a two-way table. Maria and Brennan each used the data to make the tables of joint relative frequencies shown below, but their results are slightly different. The difference is shaded. Can you tell by looking at the tables which of them made an error? Explain.

Maria's table

	Yes	No
Children	0.15	0.25
Adults	0.1	0.6

Brennan's table

	Yes	No
Children	0.15	0.25
Adults	0.1	0.5

12. **Estimation** A total of 107 brownies and muffins was sold at a school bake sale. The joint relative frequency representing muffins sold to seniors was 0.48. Use mental math to find approximately how many muffins were sold to seniors.

13. **Public Transit** A town planning committee is considering a new system for public transit. Residents of the town were randomly selected to answer two questions: "Do you work less than 5 miles from home?" and "Would you use the new system to get to work, if it were available?"
The results are shown below.

		Work less than 5 miles from home?	
		Yes	No
Use new system?	Yes	24	32
	No	44	20

UpperCut Images/Getty Images

a. Make a table of the joint relative frequencies and marginal relative frequencies. Round to the nearest hundredth where appropriate.

b. If residents work less than 5 miles from home, what is the probability that they would use the new system? Round to the nearest hundredth.

c. If residents are willing to use the new system, what is the probability that they don't work less than 5 miles from home? Round to the nearest hundredth.

TEST PREP

14. Students and teachers at a school were polled to see if they were in favor of extending the parking lot into part of the athletic fields. The results of the poll are shown in the two-way table.

	In Favor	Not in Favor
Students	16	23
Teachers	9	14

Which of the following statements is false?

(A) Thirty-nine students were polled in all.

(B) Fourteen teachers were polled in all.

(C) Twenty-three students are not in favor of extending the parking lot.

(D) Nine teachers are in favor of extending the parking lot.

15. A group of students were polled to find out how many were planning to major in a scientific field of study in college. The results of the poll are shown in the two-way table.

		Majoring in a science field	
		Yes	No
Class	Junior	150	210
	Senior	112	200

Which of the following statements is true?

Ⓐ Three hundred sixty students were polled in all.

Ⓑ A student in the senior class is more likely to be planning on a scientific major than a nonscientific major.

Ⓒ A student planning on a scientific major is more likely to be a junior than a senior.

Ⓓ More seniors than juniors plan to enter a scientific field of study.

16. **Gridded Response** A group of children and adults were polled about whether they watch a particular TV show. The survey results, showing the joint relative frequencies and marginal relative frequencies, are shown in the two-way table.

	Yes	No	Total
Children	0.3	0.4	0.7
Adults	0.25	x	0.3
Total	0.55	0.45	1

What is the value of x?

CHALLENGE AND EXTEND

The table shows the joint relative frequencies for data on how many children and teenagers attended a fair in one evening, and whether each bought a booklet of tickets for rides at the entrance gate.

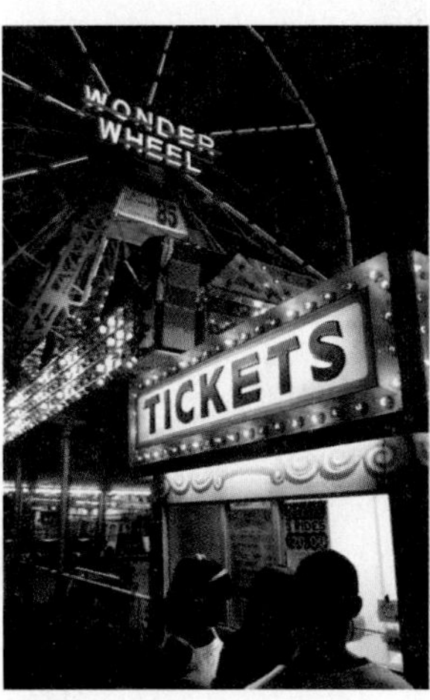

M. Scott Brauer/Alamy

	Yes	No
Children	0.125	0.1
Teenagers	0.725	0.05

Use the table to answer questions 17–20. Round answers to the nearest hundredth where appropriate.

17. Find the marginal relative frequencies for the data.

18. Based on this data, use a percentage to express how likely it is that tomorrow evening a teenager at the fair will buy a ticket booklet at the entrance. Round your answer to the nearest whole percent, if necessary.

19. If the data represent 80 teenagers and children altogether, how many children will have bought a ticket booklet at the entrance?

20. If 12 children did not buy ticket booklets at the entrance, then how many children and teenagers altogether does the data represent?

21. A poll with the options of 'yes' and 'no' was given. If the marginal relative frequency of 'yes' is 1.0, what was the marginal relative frequency of 'no'?

	Yes	No	Total
Group 1	0.24	?	?
Group 2	0.76	?	?
Total	1.0	?	?

22. **Short Response** What is the maximum a marginal relative frequency can be, and why?

7-5 Compound Events

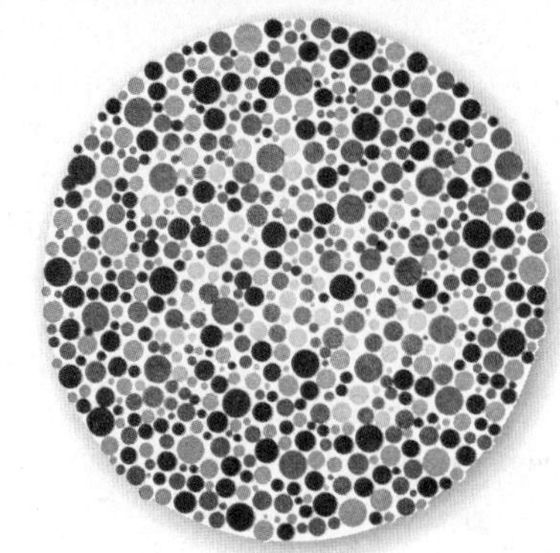

CC.9-12.S.CP.9 (+) Use permutations and combinations to compute probabilities...and solve problems.
Also **CC.9-12.S.CP.1, CC.9-12.S.CP.7**

Objectives

Find the probability of mutually exclusive events.

Find the probability of inclusive events.

Vocabulary

simple event
compound event
mutually exclusive events
inclusive events

Why learn this?

You can use the probability of compound events to determine the likelihood that a person of a specific gender is color-blind. (See Example 3.)

A **simple event** is an event that describes a single outcome. A **compound event** is an event made up of two or more simple events. **Mutually exclusive events** are events that cannot both occur in the same trial of an experiment. Rolling a 1 and rolling a 2 on the same roll of a number cube are mutually exclusive events.

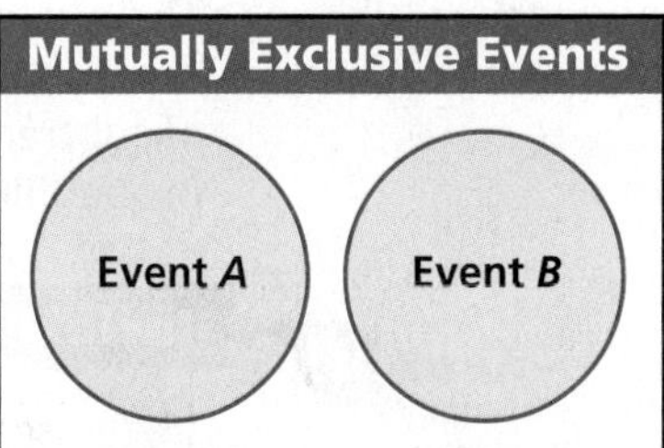

Mutually Exclusive Events

WORDS	ALGEBRA	EXAMPLE
The probability of two mutually exclusive events *A* or *B* occurring is the sum of their individual probabilities.	For two mutually exclusive events *A* and *B*, $P(A \cup B) = P(A) + P(B)$.	When a number cube is rolled, $P(\text{less than } 3) =$ $P(1 \text{ or } 2) =$ $P(1) + P(2) = \frac{1}{6} + \frac{1}{6} = \frac{1}{3}$.

Remember!

Recall that the union symbol ∪ means "or."

EXAMPLE 1 **Finding Probabilities of Mutually Exclusive Events**

A drink company applies one label to each bottle cap: "free drink," "free meal," or "try again." A bottle cap has a $\frac{1}{10}$ probability of being labeled "free drink" and a $\frac{1}{25}$ probability of being labeled "free meal."

a. Explain why the events "free drink" and "free meal" are mutually exclusive.

Each bottle cap has only one label applied to it.

b. What is the probability that a bottle cap is labeled "free drink" or "free meal"?

$$P(\text{free drink} \cup \text{free meal}) = P(\text{free drink}) + P(\text{free meal})$$
$$= \frac{1}{10} + \frac{1}{25} = \frac{5}{50} + \frac{2}{50} = \frac{7}{50}$$

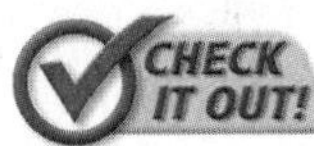

1. Each student cast one vote for senior class president. Of the students, 25% voted for Hunt, 20% for Kline, and 55% for Vila. A student from the senior class is selected at random.

a. Explain why the events "voted for Hunt," "voted for Kline," and "voted for Vila" are mutually exclusive.

b. What is the probability that a student voted for Kline or Vila?

Inclusive events are events that have one or more outcomes in common. When you roll a number cube, the outcomes "rolling an even number" and "rolling a prime number" are not mutually exclusive. The number 2 is both prime and even, so the events are inclusive.

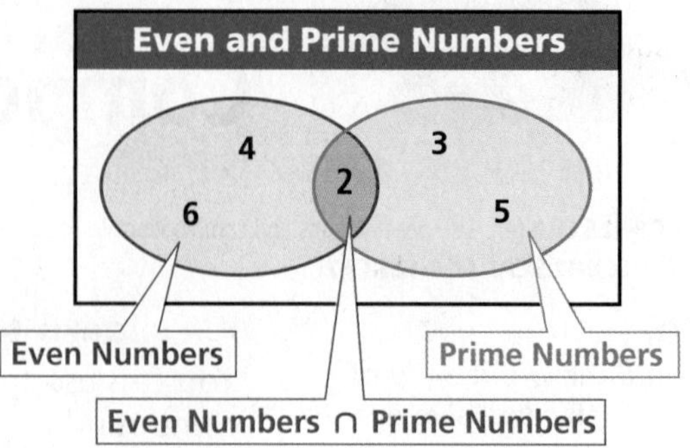

Remember!

Recall that the intersection symbol ∩ means "and."

There are 3 ways to roll an even number, $\{2, 4, 6\}$.

There are 3 ways to roll a prime number, $\{2, 3, 5\}$.

The outcome "2" is counted twice when outcomes are added $(3 + 3)$. The actual number of ways to roll an even number or a prime is $3 + 3 - 1 = 5$. The concept of subtracting the outcomes that are counted twice leads to the following probability formula.

Inclusive Events

WORDS	The probability of two inclusive events A or B occurring is the sum of their individual probabilities minus the probability of *both* occurring.
ALGEBRA	For two inclusive events A and B, $P(A \cup B) = P(A) + P(B) - P(A \cap B)$.
EXAMPLE	When you roll a number cube, $P(\text{even number or prime}) =$ $P(\text{even or prime}) = P(\text{even}) + P(\text{prime}) - P(\text{even and prime})$ $= \frac{3}{6} + \frac{3}{6} - \frac{1}{6} = \frac{5}{6}$.

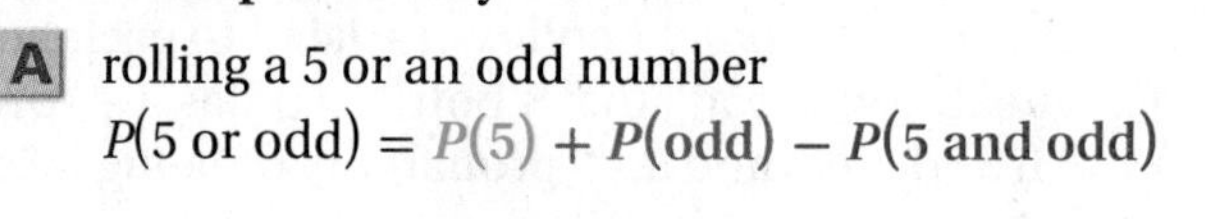

EXAMPLE 2 Finding Probabilities of Inclusive Events

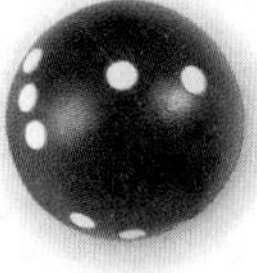

Find each probability on a die.

A rolling a 5 or an odd number

$P(5 \text{ or odd}) = P(5) + P(\text{odd}) - P(5 \text{ and odd})$

$= \frac{1}{6} + \frac{3}{6} - \frac{1}{6}$ *5 is also an odd number.*

$= \frac{1}{2}$

B rolling at least one 4 when rolling 2 dice

$P(4 \text{ or } 4) = P(4) + P(4) - P(4 \text{ and } 4)$

$= \frac{1}{6} + \frac{1}{6} - \frac{1}{36}$ *There is 1 outcome in 36 where both dice show 4.*

$= \frac{11}{36}$

A card is drawn from a deck of 52. Find the probability of each.

2a. drawing a king or a heart

2b. drawing a red card (hearts or diamonds) or a face card (jack, queen, or king)

EXAMPLE 3 ### *Health Application*

Of 3510 drivers surveyed, 1950 were male and 103 were color-blind. Only 6 of the color-blind drivers were female. What is the probability that a driver was male or was color-blind?

> **Helpful Hint**
>
> As you work through Example 3, fill in the Venn diagram with information as you find it.

Step 1 Use a Venn diagram.

Label as much information as you know. Being male and being color-blind are inclusive events.

3510 total drivers

male drivers	both	color-blind drivers
1853	97	6

Step 2 Find the number in the overlapping region.

Subtract 6 from 103. This is the number of color-blind males, **97**.

Step 3 Find the probability.

$= P(\text{male} \cup \text{color-blind}) =$

$= P(\textbf{male}) + P(\textbf{color-blind}) - P(\textbf{male} \cap \textbf{color-blind})$

$= \frac{\mathbf{1950}}{3510} + \frac{\mathbf{103}}{3510} - \frac{\mathbf{97}}{3510} = \frac{1956}{3510} \approx 0.557$

The probability that a driver was male or was color-blind is about 55.7%.

3. Of 160 beauty spa customers, 96 had a hair styling and 61 had a manicure. There were 28 customers who had only a manicure. What is the probability that a customer had a hair styling or a manicure?

Recall that the complement of an event with probability p, all outcomes that are not in the event, has a probability of $1 - p$. You can use the complement to find the probability of a compound event.

EXAMPLE 4 ### *Book Club Application*

There are 5 students in a book club. Each student randomly chooses a book from a list of 10 titles. What is the probability that at least 2 students in the group choose the same book?

$P(\text{at least 2 students choose same}) = 1 - P(\text{all choose different})$ *Use the complement.*

$$P(\text{all choose different}) = \frac{\textbf{number of ways 5 students can choose different books}}{\textbf{total number of ways 5 students can choose books}}$$

$$= \frac{{}_{10}P_5}{10^5}$$

$$= \frac{10 \cdot 9 \cdot 8 \cdot 7 \cdot 6}{10 \cdot 10 \cdot 10 \cdot 10 \cdot 10} = \frac{30{,}240}{100{,}000} = 0.3024$$

$P(\text{at least 2 students choose same}) = 1 - 0.3024 = 0.6976$

The probability that at least 2 students choose the same book is 0.6976, or 69.76%.

4. In one day, 5 different customers bought earrings from the same jewelry store. The store offers 62 different styles. Find the probability that at least 2 customers bought the same style.

THINK AND DISCUSS

1. Explain why the formula for inclusive events, $P(A \cup B) = P(A) + P(B) - P(A \cap B)$, also applies to mutually exclusive events.
2. Tell whether the probability of sharing a birthday with someone else in the room is the same whether your birthday is March 13 or February 29. Explain.

3. **GET ORGANIZED** Copy and complete the graphic organizer. Give at least one example for each.

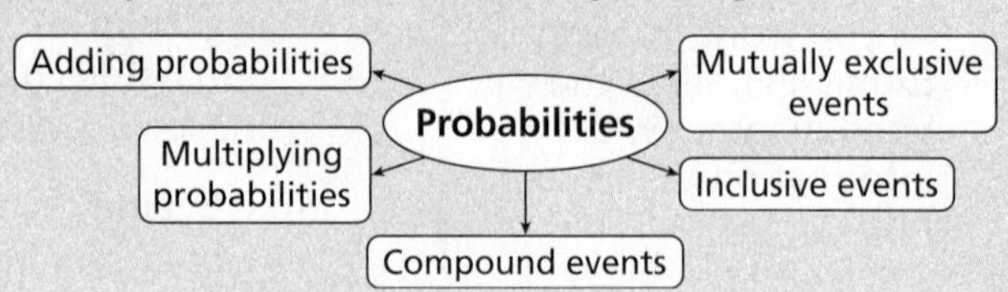

7-5 Exercises

GUIDED PRACTICE

1. **Vocabulary** A compound event where one outcome overlaps with another is made up of two __?__. (*inclusive event* or *mutually exclusive events*)

A bag contains 25 marbles: 10 black, 13 red, and 2 blue. A marble is drawn from the bag at random.

SEE EXAMPLE 1

2. Explain why the events "getting a black marble" and "getting a red marble" are mutually exclusive.
3. What is the probability of getting a red or a blue marble?
4. A car approaching an intersection has a 0.1 probability of turning left and a 0.2 probability of turning right. Explain why the events are mutually exclusive. What is the probability that the car will turn?

SEE EXAMPLE 2

Numbers 1–10 are written on cards and placed in a bag. Find each probability.

5. choosing a number greater than 5 or choosing an odd number
6. choosing an 8 or choosing a number less than 5
7. choosing at least one even number when selecting 2 cards from the bag

SEE EXAMPLE 3

Five years after 650 high school seniors graduated, 400 had a college degree and 310 were married. Half of the students with a college degree were married.

8. What is the probability that a student has a college degree or is married?
9. What is the probability that a student has a college degree or is not married?
10. What is the probability that a student does not have a college degree or is married?

SEE EXAMPLE 4

11. A vending machine offers 8 different drinks. One day, 6 employees each purchased a drink from the vending machine. Find the probability that at least 2 employees purchased the same drink.

PRACTICE AND PROBLEM SOLVING

Independent Practice

For Exercises	See Example
12–13	1
14–15	2
16–18	3
19	4

Extra Practice

See Extra Practice for more Skills Practice and Applications Practice exercises.

Jump ropes are given out during gym class. A student has a $\frac{1}{6}$ chance of getting a red jump rope and a $\frac{1}{3}$ chance of getting a green jump rope. Meg is given a jump rope.

12. Explain why the events "getting a red jump rope" and "getting a green jump rope" are mutually exclusive.

13. What is the probability that Meg gets a red or green jump rope?

The letters *A–P* are written on cards and placed in a bag. Find the probability of each outcome.

14. choosing an E or choosing a G

15. choosing an E or choosing a vowel

Lincoln High School has 98 teachers. Of the 42 female teachers, 8 teach math. One-seventh of all of the teachers teach math.

16. What is the probability that a teacher is a woman or teaches math?

17. What is the probability that a teacher is a man or teaches math?

18. What is the probability that a teacher is a man or does not teach math?

19. A card is drawn from a deck of 52 and recorded. Then the card is replaced, and the deck is shuffled. This process is repeated 13 times. What is the probability that at least one of the cards drawn is a heart?

LINK

Television

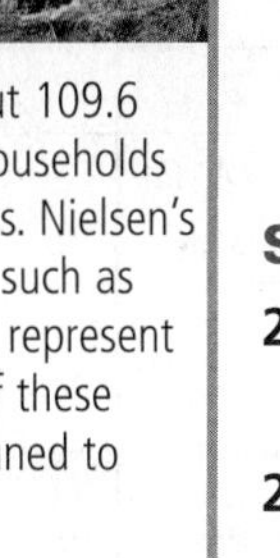

In 2004, about 109.6 million U.S. households had televisions. Nielsen's *rating points*, such as those for *CSI*, represent the percent of these households tuned to a show.

20. **Critical Thinking** Events A and B are mutually exclusive. Must the complements of events A and B be mutually exclusive? Explain by example.

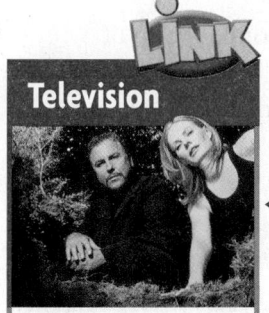

21. **Television** According to Nielsen Media Research, on June 21, 2005, from 9 to 10 P.M., the NBA Finals Game 7 between San Antonio and Detroit had a 22 *share* (was watched by 22% of television viewers), while *CSI* had a 15 share. What is the probability that someone who was watching television during this time watched the NBA Finals or *CSI*? Do you think that this is theoretical or experimental probability? Explain.

School Arts Use the table for Exercises 22 and 23.

22. What would you need to know to find the probability that a U.S. public school offers music or dance classes?

23. What is the minimum probability that a U.S. public school offers visual arts or drama? What is the maximum probability?

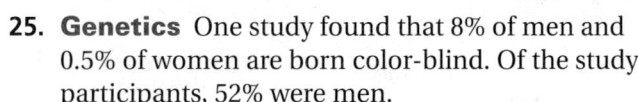

Arts Offered by U.S. Public Schools

Class Type	Music	Visual arts	Dance	Drama and theater
Percent of Schools	94%	87%	20%	19%

24. **Geometry** A square dartboard contains a red square and a blue square that overlap. A dart hits a random point on the board.
    a. Find $P(\text{red} \cap \text{blue})$.
    b. Find $P(\text{red})$.
    c. Find $P(\text{red} \cup \text{blue})$.
    d. Find $P(\text{yellow})$.

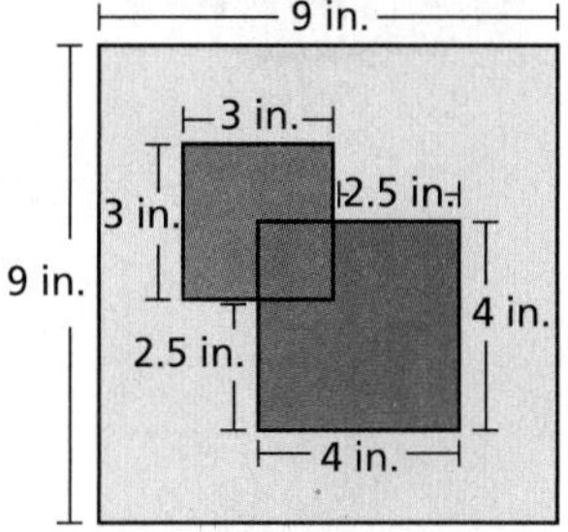

25. **Genetics** One study found that 8% of men and 0.5% of women are born color-blind. Of the study participants, 52% were men.
    a. Which probability would you expect to be greater: that a study participant is male *and* born color-blind or that a participant is male *or* born color-blind? Explain.
    b. What is the probability that a study participant is male and born color-blind? What is the probability that a study participant is male or born color-blind?

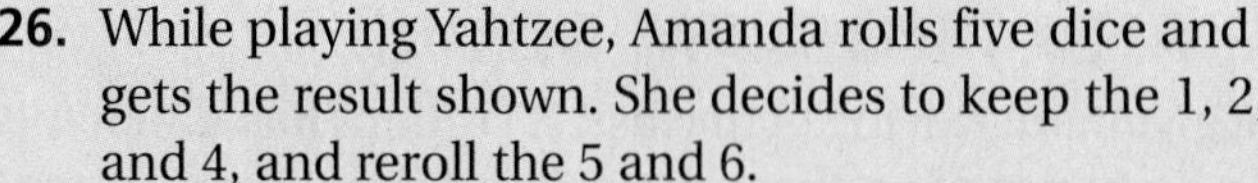

26. While playing Yahtzee, Amanda rolls five dice and gets the result shown. She decides to keep the 1, 2, and 4, and reroll the 5 and 6.

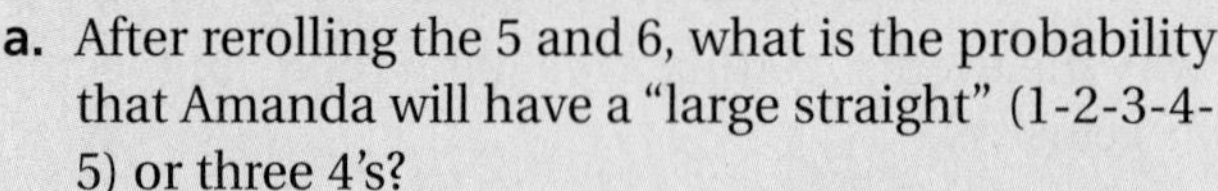

   a. After rerolling the 5 and 6, what is the probability that Amanda will have a "large straight" (1-2-3-4-5) or three 4's?

   b. After rerolling the 5 and 6, what is the probability that Amanda will have a "small straight" (1-2-3-4 plus anything else) or a pair of 3's?

27. **Public Safety** In a study of canine attacks, the probability that the victim was under 18 years of age was 0.8. The probability that the attack occurred on the dog owner's property was 0.64. The probability that the victim was under 18 years of age or the attack occurred on the owner's property was 0.95. What was the probability that the victim was under 18 years of age and the attack occurred on the owner's property?

28. **Politics** A 4-person leadership committee is randomly chosen from a group of 24 candidates. Ten of the candidates are men, and 14 are women.

   a. What is the probability that the committee is all male or all female?

   b. What is the probability that the committee has at least 1 man or at least 1 woman?

29. **Multi-Step** The game Scrabble contains letter tiles that occur in different numbers. Suppose that one tile is selected.

   a. What is the probability of choosing a vowel if Y is not included?

   b. What is the probability of choosing a Y?

   c. What is the probability of choosing a vowel if Y is included? How does this relate to the answer to parts **a** and **b**?

Distribution of Scrabble Tiles

Tiles	Frequency
J, K, Q, X, Z	1
B, C, F, H, M, P, V, W, Y, blank	2
G	3
D, L, S, U	4
N, R, T	6
O	8
A, I	9
E	12

30. **Write About It** Demonstrate two ways to find the probability of a coin's landing heads up at least once in 2 tosses of a coin.

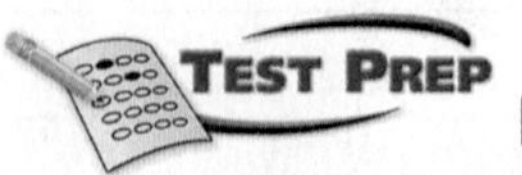

31. For a quilt raffle, 2500 tickets numbered 0001–2500 are sold. Jamie has number 1527. The winning raffle number is read one digit at a time. The first winning number begins "One...". After the first digit is called, Jamie's chances of winning do which of the following?

   Ⓐ Go to 0

   Ⓑ Stay the same

   Ⓒ Increase from $\frac{1}{2500}$ to $\frac{1}{1527}$

   Ⓓ Increase from $\frac{1}{2500}$ to $\frac{1}{1000}$

32. A fair coin is tossed 4 times. Given that each of the first 3 tosses land tails up, what is the probability that all 4 tosses land tails up?

   Ⓕ 0.5

   Ⓖ Greater than 0.5

   Ⓗ 0.5^4

   Ⓙ Between 0.5^4 and 0.5

Sam Dudgeon/HMH

33. If Travis rolls a 5 on a number cube, he lands on "roll again." If Travis rolls a number greater than 3, he'll pass "start" and collect $100. What is the probability that Travis rolls again or collects $100?

Ⓐ $\frac{1}{6}$ Ⓑ $\frac{1}{5}$ Ⓒ $\frac{1}{4}$ Ⓓ $\frac{1}{2}$

34. Short Response What is the probability of an event or its complement? Explain.

CHALLENGE AND EXTEND

35. What is the probability that at least 2 people in a group of 10 people have the same birthday? (Assume no one in the group was born on February 29th.)

Travel For Exercises 36–38, use the Venn diagram, which shows the transportation methods used by 162 travelers. Find each probability if a traveler is selected at random.

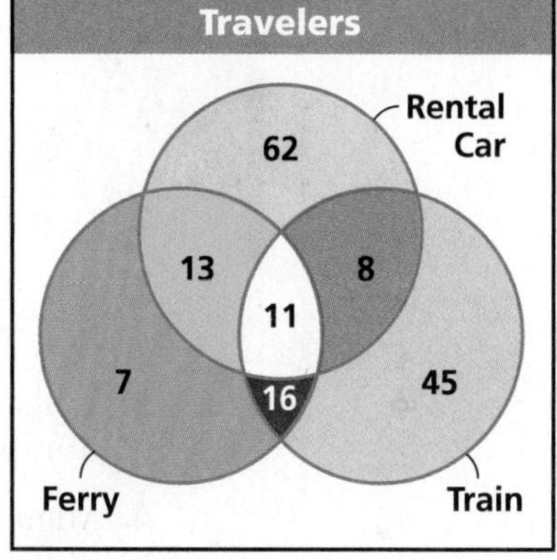

36. $P(\text{ferry or train})$

37. $P(\text{ferry or rental car})$

38. $P(\text{train and ferry, or train and rental car})$

Use the table of probabilities and the following information for Exercises 39–41. Hint: Draw a Venn diagram.

For any three events A, B, and C, $P(A \text{ or } B \text{ or } C) =$
$P(A) + P(B) + P(C) - P(A \cap B) - P(A \cap C) - P(B \cap C) + P(A \cap B \cap C)$

Event	$P(A)$	$P(B)$	$P(C)$	$P(A \cap B)$	$P(A \cap C)$	$P(B \cap C)$	$P(A \cap B \cap C)$
Probability	0.5	0.3	0.7	0.2	0.3	0.1	0.1

39. Find $P(B \cup C)$.

40. Find $P(A \cup B \cup C)$.

41. Find $P(B \cap (A \cup C))$.

CHAPTER 7

MULTI-STEP TEST PREP

SECTION 7B

Reason abstractly and quantitatively.

Probability

Roll Call Yahtzee is played with 5 dice. A player rolls all 5 dice and may choose to roll any or all of the dice a second time and then a third time. At that point, the player scores points for various combinations of dice, such as 3 of a kind, 4 of a kind, or 5 of a kind.

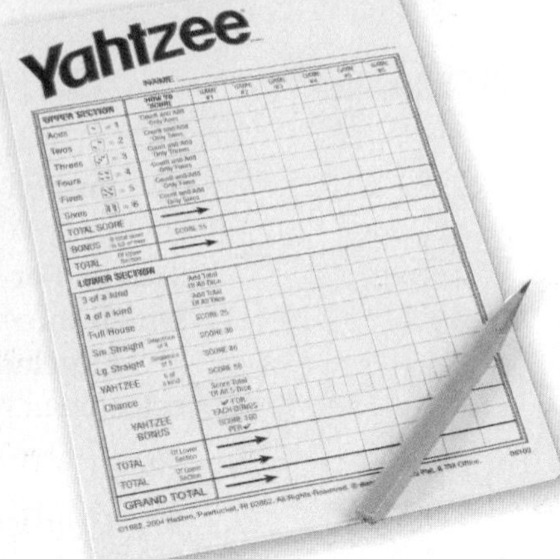

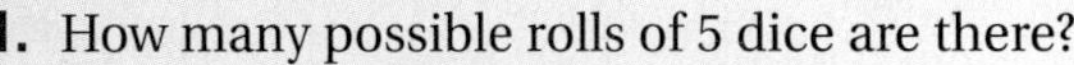

1. How many possible rolls of 5 dice are there?
2. What is the probability of rolling five 6's on the first roll of the dice?
3. What is the probability of rolling 5 of any one number on the first roll?
4. Miguel's first roll is shown at right. He decides to reroll the 6's. What is the probability that he has a 1, 2, 3, 4, and 5 after this roll?
5. What is the probability that Miguel has a 1, 2, 3, 4, and 5 after the roll, given that at least one of the dice comes up a 4?
6. What is the probability that Miguel has a 1, 2, 3, 4, and 5 or a pair of 2's after the roll in Problem 4?
7. What is the probability that Miguel has a 1, 2, 3, 4, and any other number or a pair of 4's after the roll in Problem 4?

Sam Dudgeon/HMH

Quiz for Lessons 7-4 and 7-5

7-4 Two-Way Tables

A bookshop surveys its customers about their magazine-buying habits, summarized in the table.

1. Make a table of the joint relative frequencies and the marginal relative frequencies.
2. Given that a customer reads *Super News,* what is the probability that he or she also reads *Look Around?*
3. Given that a customer reads *Look Around,* what is the probability that he or she also reads *Super News?*

		Reads *Look Around*	
		Yes	No
Reads *Super News*	Yes	62	15
	No	21	136

7-5 Compound Events

Numbers 1–30 are written on cards and placed in a bag. One card is drawn. Find each probability.

4. drawing an even number or a 1
5. drawing an even number or a multiple of 7
6. Of a company's 85 employees, 60 work full time and 40 are married. Half of the full-time workers are married. What is the probability that an employee works part time or is not married?

CHAPTER 7

Study Guide: Review

Vocabulary

combination
complement
compound event
conditional probability
conditional relative frequency
dependent events
equally likely outcomes
event
experiment
experimental probability
factorial
favorable outcomes
Fundamental Counting Principle
geometric probability
inclusive events
independent events
joint relative frequency
marginal relative frequency
mutually exclusive events
outcome
permutation
probability
sample space
simple event
theoretical probability
trial

Complete the sentences below with vocabulary words from the list above.

1. If the occurrence of one event affects the probability of the other, then the events are ___?___ .
2. When arranging items, order is important when using a(n) ___?___ .
3. The ___?___ is the joint relative frequency divided by the marginal relative frequency.

7-1 Permutations and Combinations

EXAMPLES

■ **If you have 8 vases to choose from, how many ways can you arrange 5 of them on a shelf?**

The order matters, so it is a permutation.

$${}_8P_5 = \frac{8!}{(8-5)!} = \frac{8 \cdot 7 \cdot 6 \cdot 5 \cdot 4 \cdot \cancel{3} \cdot \cancel{2} \cdot \cancel{1}}{\cancel{3} \cdot \cancel{2} \cdot \cancel{1}}$$
$$= 8 \cdot 7 \cdot 6 \cdot 5 = 6720$$

There are 6720 ways to arrange the vases.

■ **If 7 pizza toppings are available, how many ways can you choose 2 toppings?**

The order does not matter, so it is a combination.

$${}_7C_2 = \frac{7!}{2!(7-2)!} = \frac{7 \cdot 6 \cdot \cancel{5} \cdot \cancel{4} \cdot \cancel{3} \cdot \cancel{2} \cdot \cancel{1}}{2 \cdot 1(\cancel{5} \cdot \cancel{4} \cdot \cancel{3} \cdot \cancel{2} \cdot \cancel{1})}$$
$$= \frac{42}{2} = 21$$

There are 21 ways to choose the toppings.

EXERCISES

4. How many different 7-digit telephone numbers can be made if the first digit cannot be 7, 8, or 9?
5. From a group of 12 volunteers, a surveyor must choose 5 to complete an advanced survey. How many groups of 5 people can be chosen?
6. In one day, a salesman plans to visit 6 out of 14 companies that are in the neighborhood. How many ways can he plan the visits?
7. How many ways can 7 people arrange themselves inside a van that has 10 seats?
8. The caterer told Kathy that she can choose 3 entrées from the 6 listed on the menu. How many groups of 3 entrées can she choose?

7-2 Theoretical and Experimental Probability

EXAMPLES

A paper clip holder has 100 paper clips: 30 are red, 20 are yellow, 25 are green, 15 are pink, and 10 are black. A paper clip is randomly chosen. Find each probability.

- The paper clip is green.

$$P(\text{green}) = \frac{\text{number of green paper clips}}{\text{total number of paper clips}}$$

$$= \frac{25}{100} = \frac{1}{4}$$

- The paper clip is not pink.

$$P(\text{not pink}) = 1 - P(\text{pink}) = 1 - \frac{15}{100} = \frac{17}{20}$$

- **Carl and Pedro each put their names in a hat for a door prize. Two names will be selected, and there are a total of 40 names in the hat. What is the probability that Carl wins the first prize and Pedro wins the second?**

The number of outcomes in the sample space is the number of ways that 2 people can be selected from 40 and then ordered.

$$P(\text{Carl, then Pedro}) = \frac{1}{{}_{40}P_2} = \frac{1}{1560}$$

- **A dart is randomly thrown at the dartboard. What is the probability that it lands in the outer ring?**

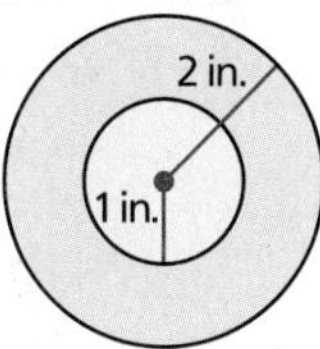

$$P(\text{outer ring}) = \frac{\text{area of outer ring}}{\text{area of dart board}}$$

$$= \frac{\text{area of large circle} - \text{area of inner circle}}{\text{area of large circle}}$$

$$= \frac{\pi(3)^2 - \pi(1)^2}{\pi(3)^2} = \frac{9\pi - 1\pi}{9\pi} = \frac{8\pi}{9\pi} = \frac{8}{9}$$

- **The table shows the results of 75 tosses of a number cube. Find the experimental probability of rolling a 4.**

1	2	3	4	5	6
10	12	16	15	9	13

$$P(4) = \frac{\text{number of times 4 occurred}}{\text{number of trials}} = \frac{15}{75}$$

$$= \frac{1}{5} = 0.2$$

EXERCISES

Two number cubes are rolled. What is the probability of each event?

9. Sum is 8.

10. Difference is 1.

11. Sum is even.

12. Product is less than 30.

13. The 10-member math team randomly selects 4 representatives to send to a meet. What is the probability that the 4 members chosen are the 4 with the lowest math grades?

14. A 5-digit code is given to all cashiers at a store to let them log onto the cash register. What is the probability that an employee receives a code with all 5 numbers the same?

15. Find the probability that a point chosen at random inside the rectangle is in the shaded area.

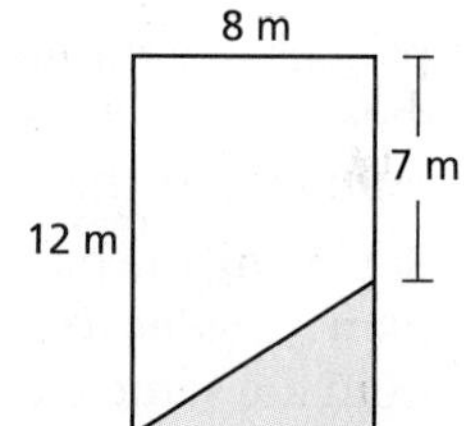

16. Find the probability that a point chosen at random inside the square is not inside the circle.

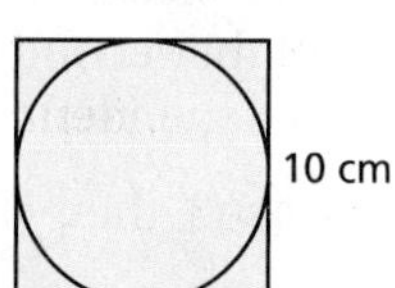

The bar graph shows the results of tossing two pennies 50 times. Find the experimental probability of each of the following.

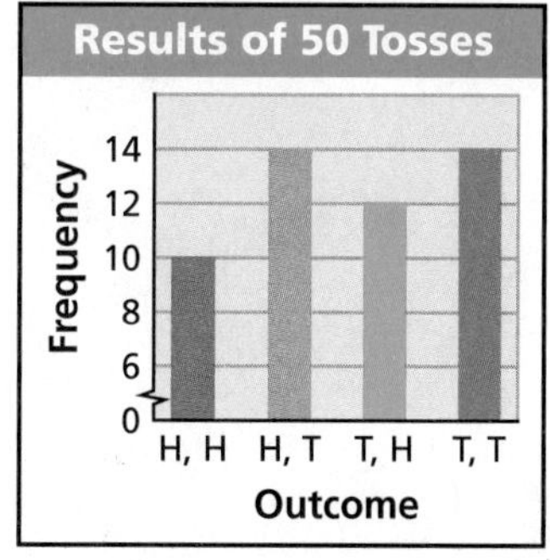

17. tossing 2 heads

18. tossing at least 1 tail

19. not tossing a head

20. tossing exactly 1 tail

Two pennies are tossed. Find the theoretical probability of each of the following.

21. tossing 2 heads

22. tossing at least 1 tail

23. not tossing a head

24. tossing exactly 1 tail

7-3 Independent and Dependent Events

EXAMPLES

A bag contains slips of papers with the following numbers: 2, 2, 3, 3, 4, 5, 6. Determine whether the events are independent or dependent, and find the indicated probability.

- You select a 3, keep the paper, and then your friend selects a 3.

  Keeping the paper with the first 3 changes the number of 3's left in the bag for your friend to choose from, so the events are dependent.

  $$P(3, \text{ then } 3) = P(3) \cdot P(3 \mid 3).$$
  $$= \frac{2}{7} \cdot \frac{1}{6} = \frac{2}{42} = \frac{1}{21}$$

- You select a number greater than 3, replace the paper, and then your friend selects a number less than 3.

  Replacing the paper with the number greater than 3 means that your friend will also select from the same papers, so the occurrence of the first selection does not affect the probability of the second selection. The events are independent.

  $$P(> 3, \text{ then } < 3) = P(> 3) \cdot P(< 3)$$
  $$= \frac{3}{7} \cdot \frac{2}{7} = \frac{6}{49}$$

EXERCISES

Explain why the events are independent, and find the probability.

25. rolling "doubles" 3 times in a row when rolling 2 number cubes

26. selecting a red pen and then a blue pen, when selecting 2 pens from a bag of 10 red and 15 blue pens with replacement

The table shows the age and marital status of the members of an environmental group. One person from the group is randomly selected. Find each probability.

Marital Status by Age				
	18–34	35–50	51–65	66+
Married	6	20	22	4
Single	14	22	11	0

27. that the selected person is single, given that he or she is in the 35–50 age group

28. that a married person is 66 or older

29. that a person aged 18–50 is married

30. that a person in the group is single and in the 18–34 age group

7-4 Two-Way Tables

EXAMPLES

A teacher collected data on the activities the class performed last weekend and summarized the data in a table.

		Went to Park	
		Yes	No
Saw a movie	Yes	4	10
	No	5	5

- **Make a table of the joint and marginal relative frequencies.**

  Divide each value by the total of 24 to find the joint relative frequencies, and add each row and column to find the marginal relative frequencies.

		Went to Park		
		Yes	No	Total
Saw a movie	Yes	0.167	0.417	0.583
	No	0.208	0.208	0.417
	Total	0.375	0.625	1

EXERCISES

A teacher collected data on the activities the class performed on their summer break and summarized the data in a table.

		Went to Beach	
		Yes	No
Joined a sports team	Yes	10	9
	No	11	6

31. Make a table of the joint and marginal relative frequencies.

32. Given that a student went to the beach, what is the probability he or she joined a sports team?

33. Given that a student did not go to the beach, what is the probability he or she did not join a sports team?

7-5 Compound Events

EXAMPLES

Andy is using his calculator to obtain a random number from 10 to 20. Find the probability that

- Andy gets a 15 or a multiple of 2.

  10 11 12 13 14 15 16 17 18 19 20

  $\frac{1}{11} + \frac{6}{11} = \frac{7}{11}$ *The events are mutually exclusive.*

- Andy gets a multiple of 3 or a multiple of 5.

  10 11 12 13 14 15 16 17 18 19 20

  $\frac{3}{11} + \frac{3}{11} - \frac{1}{11} = \frac{5}{11}$ *The events are inclusive.*

- Andy gets all different numbers if he has the calculator randomly select 5 numbers.

  $\frac{{}_{11}P_5}{11^5} = \frac{11 \cdot 10 \cdot 9 \cdot 8 \cdot 7}{11 \cdot 11 \cdot 11 \cdot 11 \cdot 11} = \frac{55{,}440}{161{,}051} \approx 0.3442$

EXERCISES

A store is handing out coupons. One-third of the coupons offer a 10% discount, half offer a 15% discount, and one-sixth offer a 20% discount. A customer is handed a coupon.

34. Explain why the events "10% discount" and "15% discount" are mutually exclusive.

35. What is the probability that the coupon offers a 10% discount or a 15% discount?

A card is drawn from a deck of 52. Find the probability of each outcome.

36. drawing a red card or drawing a 5

37. drawing a club or drawing a heart

38. Of 120 males and 180 females who took an eye exam, 170 passed. One-third of the males did not pass. What is the probability that a person who took the exam passed or was male?

CHAPTER 7

CHAPTER TEST

1. A mall employee is dressing a mannequin. There are 6 pairs of shoes, 4 types of jeans, and 8 sweaters. Using 1 of each, how many ways can the mannequin be dressed?
2. How many ways can you award first, second, and third place to 8 contestants?
3. How many ways can a group of 3 students be chosen from a class of 30?
4. Four cards are randomly selected from a standard deck of 52 playing cards. What is the probability that the cards are all jacks, all queens, or all kings?
5. The table shows the results of tossing 2 coins. Find the experimental probability of tossing 2 tails.

HH	HT	TH	TT
3	6	5	6

Each letter of the alphabet is written on a card. The cards are placed into a bag. Determine whether the events are independent or dependent, and find the indicated probability.

6. The letter *D* is drawn, replaced in the bag, and then the letter *J* is drawn.
7. Three vowels are drawn without replacement.

A card is drawn from a bag containing the 9 cards shown. Find each probability.

8. selecting a *C* or an even number
9. selecting an odd number or a multiple of 3
10. The probability distribution for the number of absent students on any given day for a certain class is given. Find the expected number of absent students.

Number of Students Absent *n*	0	1	2	3	4
Probability of *n* Absent Students	$\frac{7}{20}$	$\frac{5}{20}$	$\frac{4}{20}$	$\frac{3}{20}$	$\frac{1}{20}$

A school is voting on a new mascot. While voting, the student body also tracked whether each person played on one of the school's sports teams. The data are presented in the table.

		Plays a sport	
		Yes	No
Mascot	Aardvark	9	75
	Fruit bat	35	56
	Plankton	51	123

11. Make a table of the joint relative frequencies and marginal relative frequencies.
12. Given that a student voted for fruit bat, what is the probability they play a sport?
13. Given that a student plays a sport, what is the probability they voted for fruit bat?
14. Given that a student plays a sport, what is the probability they did not vote for fruit bat?

CHAPTER 7

FOCUS ON SAT MATHEMATICS SUBJECT TESTS

The reference information at the beginning of a test is usually the same each time the test is given. Memorize this information so that you won't have to refer back to it during the test. When you take the test, note whether any information is different from what you expected.

You may want to time yourself as you take this practice test. It should take you about 6 minutes to complete.

If you do not know how to solve a general problem, try working out a simple example or two to see if a general solution method becomes apparent. But do not spend too much time on examples. If you are still stuck after a while, move on to the next problem.

1. Two cards are drawn from a standard deck of 52 cards. What is the probability that a king and a queen are drawn?

(A) $\frac{1}{169}$

(B) $\frac{2}{169}$

(C) $\frac{8}{663}$

(D) $\frac{14}{663}$

(E) $\frac{4}{169}$

2. A poll with the options of 'yes' and 'no' was given. What is the maximum a marginal relative frequency can be for this poll, and why?

(A) The maximum is 2, because 2 is the number of options on the poll.

(B) The maximum is 0.5, because 0.5 equals one-half of the answer choices.

(C) The maximum is 1, because 1 represents 100% of the data.

(D) The maximum can't be determined from the information given.

(E) There is no maximum for the marginal relative frequencies.

3. A number cube is rolled twice. What is the probability of getting a 6 at least once?

(A) $\frac{1}{36}$

(B) $\frac{1}{6}$

(C) $\frac{11}{36}$

(D) $\frac{1}{3}$

(E) $\frac{5}{6}$

4. Your CD player can hold 6 CDs. You have 10 CDs to choose from, one of which is your favorite and is always in your player. How many ways can the player be filled if order does not matter?

(A) 126

(B) 210

(C) 720

(D) 15,120

(E) 151,200

5. Of 100 students, 37 play an instrument, 45 play sports, and 11 do both. What is the probability that a student neither plays an instrument nor plays sports?

(A) 0.145

(B) 0.18

(C) 0.29

(D) 0.40

(E) 0.82

CHAPTER 7

TEST TACKLER

Standardized Test Strategies

Multiple Choice: None of the Above or All of the Above

Given a multiple-choice test item where one of the answer choices is *none of the above* or *all of the above*, the correct response is the best, most-complete answer choice available.

To answer these types of test items, compare each answer choice with the question and determine if the answer is true or false. If you determine that more than one of the choices is true, then the correct choice is likely to be *all of the above.*

If you do not know how to solve the problem and have to guess at the answer, more often than not, *all of the above* is correct and *none of the above* is incorrect.

EXAMPLE 1

There are 8 players on the chess team. Which of the following models the number of ways that the coach can choose 2 players to start the game?

Ⓐ ${}_8C_2$

Ⓑ $\dfrac{8!}{2!(6!)}$

Ⓒ 28

Ⓓ All of the above

LOOK at each choice separately, and determine if it is true or false.

As you consider each choice, mark it "true" or "false."

Consider Choice A: *Because order does not matter, this is a combination problem. The number of combinations of 8 players, taken 2 at a time, is given by ${}_nC_r$, where $n = 8$ and $r = 2$. So, ${}_8C_2$ is a correct model of the combination.*

Choice A is *"true."* The answer could be choice A, but you need to check if choices B and C are also correct because the answer could be *all of the above.*

Consider Choice B: *The number of combinations of 8 players, taken two at a time, is given by ${}_nC_r = \frac{n!}{r!(n-r)!}$, where $n = 8$ and $r = 2$.*

$${}_nC_r = \frac{n!}{r!(n-r)!} = \frac{8!}{2!(8-2)!} = \frac{8!}{2!(6)!}$$

Choice B is also a correct model of the combination. Choice B is *"true."* The answer is likely to be choice D, *all of the above,* but you still should check to see if choice C is true.

Consider Choice C: *The number of combinations of 8 players, taken two at a time, is given by ${}_nC_r = \frac{n!}{r!(n-r)!}$, where $n = 8$ and $r = 2$.*

$${}_nC_r = \frac{n!}{r!(n-r)!} = \frac{8!}{2!(8-2)!} = \frac{8!}{2!(6)!} = 28$$

Choice C is also a correct model of the combination. Choice C is *"true."* Because choices A, B, and C are all *"true,"* the correct answer choice is choice D, *all of the above.*

Be careful of problems with double negatives. Read the problem statement and each answer choice twice before selecting an answer.

Read each test item and answer the questions that follow.

Item A

Some people were polled about their support for a community garden and whether or not they had any experience growing their own food. The results of the poll are shown in the two-way table.

	Support the garden	Do not support the garden
Have grown food	7	4
Have not grown food	19	16

Which of the following statements is not true?

Ⓐ A person that supports the garden is more likely than not to have not grown food.

Ⓑ A person that hasn't grown food is more likely than not to support the garden.

Ⓒ Both statements A and B

Ⓓ None of these.

1. Read the problem statement again. If an answer choice is true, is that the correct answer? Explain.
2. Willie determined that because choice B is the reverse of choice A, choice C couldn't be correct. Do you agree? If not, what would you have done differently?

Item B

For a number cube, what is the probability of rolling a 2 or a number greater than 4?

Ⓕ 50%

Ⓖ $P(\text{rolling a } 2 \cup \text{rolling 5 or 6}) =$
$P(\text{rolling a } 2) + P(\text{rolling 5 or 6})$

Ⓗ $\frac{1}{6} + \frac{2}{6}$

Ⓙ All of the above

3. Is this event mutually exclusive or inclusive? How do you know? Determine if choice G is a true or false statement.
4. If you roll a number cube, what is the probability of rolling a 2? What is the probability of rolling a 5 or 6?
5. Simplify choice H to find its value. Is this value equivalent to any other answer choices?
6. How many answer choices are correct? What is the correct response?

Item C

Suppose that a dart lands at a random point on the circular dartboard. Find the probability that the dart lands inside only the dark gray or white region. The radius of the dartboard is 3 inches.

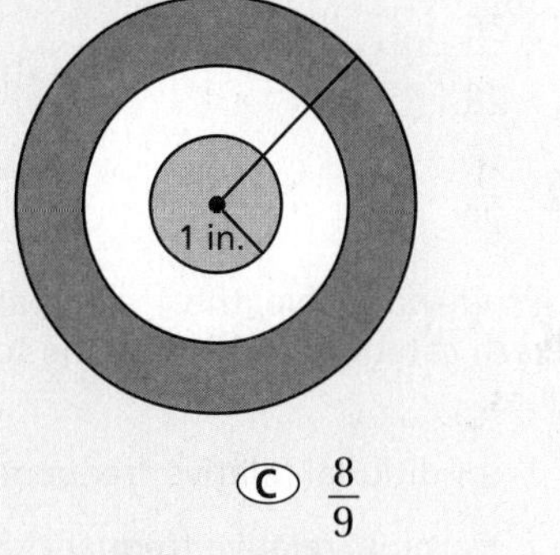

Ⓐ $\frac{1}{9}$

Ⓑ 8π

Ⓒ $\frac{8}{9}$

Ⓓ None of these

7. A student finds that both choice A and choice B are incorrect. To save time, he chooses choice D as his answer because he figures it is likely that choice C will also be incorrect. Do you think that this student made a wise decision? Explain.
8. What is the formula for the area of a circle? What is the area of this dartboard? How can you determine the area of the dark gray and white regions?
9. Find if choice A, B, or C is true, and determine the response to the test item.

Item D

Each gym member receives a 3-digit code to use for a locker combination with no digit repeated. Grace received the code 210. What was the probability that she would receive a code of consecutive numbers?

Ⓕ $1.\overline{6}\%$

Ⓖ $\frac{1}{45}$

Ⓗ $\frac{1}{{}_{10}P_3}$

Ⓙ All of the above

10. How can you determine if choice J is correct?
11. Are the values given in choices F, G, and H equivalent? What does this tell you about choice J?

CHAPTER 7

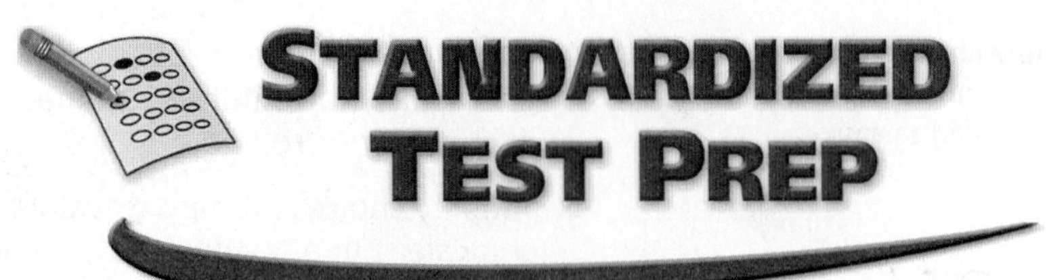

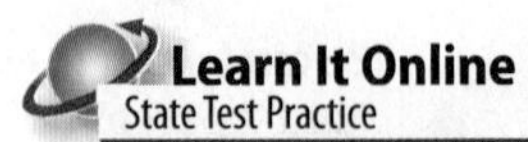

CUMULATIVE ASSESSMENT

Multiple Choice

1. There were 8 dogs in a litter. How many ways can Mike choose 2 dogs?

   Ⓐ 20,160

   Ⓑ 56

   Ⓒ 28

   Ⓓ $\frac{1}{28}$

2. In a two-way table, the _______ are the values in each category divided by the total number of values.

   Ⓕ conditional relative frequencies

   Ⓖ marginal relative frequencies

   Ⓗ joint relative frequencies

   Ⓙ conditional probabilities

3. The table shows the number of teachers, coaches, and students at a high school of each gender. What is the probability, to the nearest hundredth, that a coach is male?

School Population and Gender

	Male	Female
Teachers	12	24
Coaches	17	9
Students	429	453

   Ⓐ 0.65

   Ⓑ 0.35

   Ⓒ 0.04

   Ⓓ 0.02

4. For $f(x) = ab^x$, if x increases by 1, the value of $f(x)$ does which of the following?

   Ⓕ $f(x)$ increases by b.

   Ⓖ $f(x)$ is multiplied by b.

   Ⓗ $f(x)$ increases by a.

   Ⓙ $f(x)$ is multiplied by a.

5. A slice of an 18-inch diameter pizza that is cut into sixths sells for \$3.25. At this rate, how much should a slice that is one eighth of a 16-inch diameter pizza sell for, to the nearest \$0.05?

   Ⓐ \$1.75

   Ⓑ \$1.95

   Ⓒ \$2.15

   Ⓓ \$2.45

6. Which graph shows a line with a slope of $-\frac{4}{3}$ that passes through $(5, 2)$?

   Ⓕ 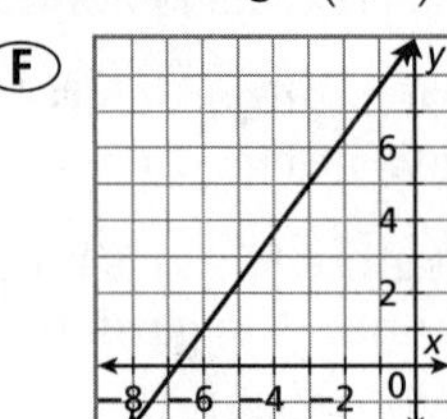

   Ⓗ 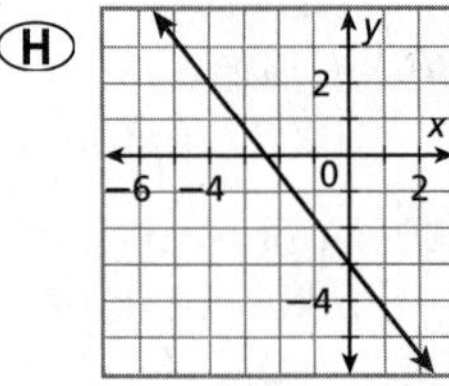

   Ⓖ 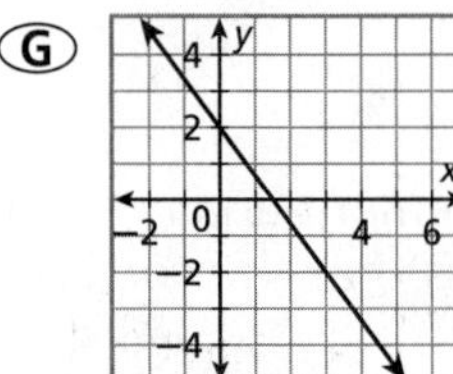

   Ⓙ 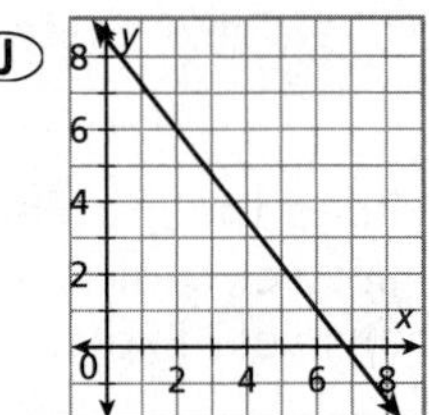

7. Which type of function is shown in the graph?

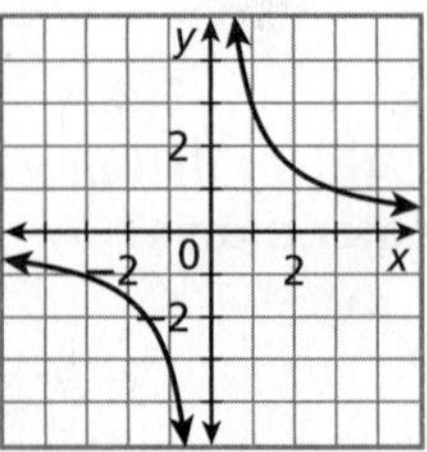

   Ⓐ exponential

   Ⓑ polynomial

   Ⓒ radical

   Ⓓ rational

8. Suppose y varies directly with x. If $y = 6$ when $x = -2$, find x when $y = -9$.

Ⓕ -3

Ⓖ 3

Ⓗ 6

Ⓙ 12

In item 9, remember that a real number with a 0 exponent is 1. You can use mental math to quickly evaluate each function and compare your result to the corresponding value in the graphed function.

9. Which is the equation of the graph below?

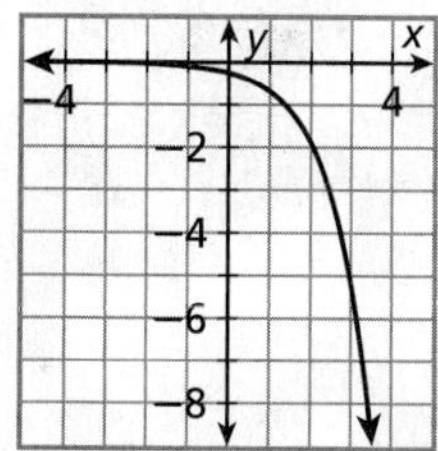

Ⓐ $f(x) = 0.25(2.75^x)$

Ⓑ $f(x) = -2.75(0.25^x)$

Ⓒ $f(x) = 2.75(0.25^x)$

Ⓓ $f(x) = -0.25(2.75^x)$

Gridded Response

10. What value of x makes the equation true?
$6(x - i) - 2i = (4 - i)^2$

11. Use long division to find the coefficient of the x term in the quotient.
$(2x^3 + 5x^2 + 10x + 7) \div (x + 1)$

Use the spinner for Items 12 and 13.

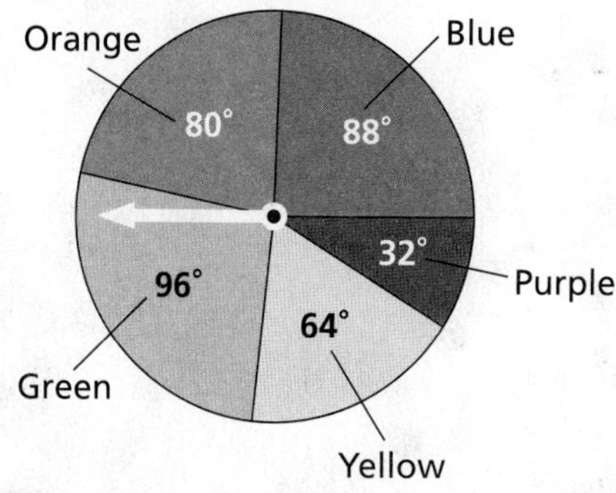

12. What is the probability of the spinner landing on the orange or purple sector, to the nearest hundredth?

13. What is the probability that the spinner will land on green in at least 2 of the next 3 spins? Write the answer to the nearest thousandth.

Short Response

14. Find the center and the radius of a circle that has a diameter with the endpoints $(-2, 8)$ and $(4, 2)$.
    a. What is the length of the diameter?
    b. The endpoints $(4, 8)$ and $(-2, y)$ are located on the circle. Find the missing value of y.

15. The table below shows the number of students that graduated from a high school from 1920 to 2000, measured every 20 years.

x	1920	1940	1960	1980	2000
y	9	59	159	409	909

    a. Write a polynomial function for the data. Let x be the number of years since 1920. Round your answer to the nearest thousandth.
    b. At this rate how many students will graduate in 2020? Round your answer to the nearest student.
    c. About how many students graduated in 1990? Round your answer to the nearest student.

16. The Badgers won 70% of their games this season. They won 5 of the 12 games they played during their last road trip. Before the road trip, the Badgers had won 75% of their games.
    a. How many wins and losses did the Badgers have during the season?
    b. How many wins and losses did the Badgers have before their last road trip?

Extended Response

17. Randy wants to collect 515 baseball cards. Each week Randy buys 15 baseball cards.
    a. Create a table to represent this situation where t is the amount of time in weeks and c is the number of cards that Randy still wants to buy.
    b. Write an equation to model the data in the table.
    c. Graph the equation.
    d. After how many weeks will Randy meet his goal?

CHAPTER 8

Data Analysis and Statistics

COMMON CORE

- Compare and contrast types of data collection.
- Examine different data distributions.

Eruption!

You can collect data about geysers to help determine the time between eruptions.

Learn It Online
Chapter Project Online

Stewart Smith/Alamy

Find Area in the Coordinate Plane

Use the figure for Exercises 1–3.

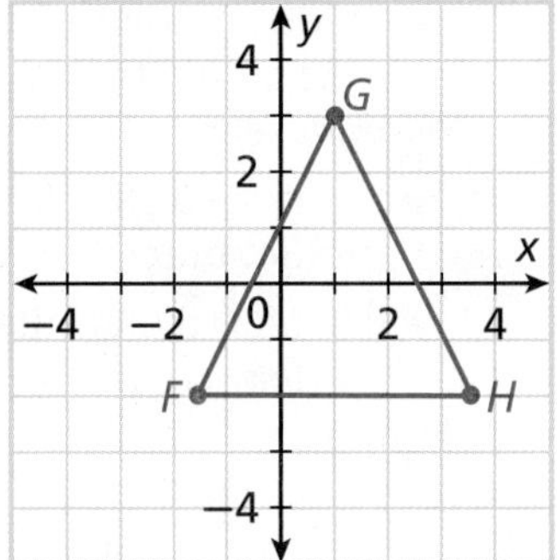

1. Estimate the area of the figure by counting squares. Use 0, $\frac{1}{2}$, or 1 for incomplete squares.
2. Suppose the figure represents an area to be painted, and each square represents 50 square feet. If Jo can paint 400 square feet per hour, how long will it take him to paint the area?
3. Point F has coordinates $(-1.5, -2)$ and point H has coordinates $(3.5, -2)$. What is the actual area of triangle FGH?

Multiply Monomials

Multiply.

4. $4a^3 \cdot 28b^2$
5. $3x^5y \cdot 21xy^2$
6. $-m^3n^4 \cdot 10m^2n^5$

Exponents

Simplify. Round to the nearest hundredth.

7. $(0.1)(0.9)^4$
8. $(0.6)^{4-4}$
9. $(0.25)^1(0.75)^3$
10. $(0.5)^{5-3}(0.5)$

Add Decimals

Add.

11. $0.343 + 0.601$
12. $0.403 + 0.084$
13. $0.555 + 0.191$
14. $0.756 + 0.129$

Find Measures of Central Tendency

Find the mean, median, and mode of each data set.

15. $\{9, 4, 2, 6, 4\}$
16. $\{1, 1, 1, 2, 2, 2\}$
17. $\{1, 2, 3, 4, 5, 6\}$
18. $\{18, 14, 20, 18, 14, 3, 18\}$

CHAPTER 8

Study Guide: Preview

Where You've Been

Previously, you

- made stem-and-leaf plots to examine the spread of a data set.
- performed simulations to predict outcomes.
- calculated measures of central tendency.

In This Chapter

You will study

- collecting data in appropriate ways.
- finding binomial probabilities.
- analyzing data to include expected value and variance.

Where You're Going

You can use the skills in this chapter

- to run experiments or conduct surveys.
- to calculate and report appropriate measures when analyzing data.
- to form a solid foundation for studies in advanced statistics.

Key Vocabulary/Vocabulario

binomial experiment	experimento binomial
census	censo
convenience sample	muestra de conveniencia
experiment	experimento
margin of error	margen de error
null hypothesis	hipótesis nula
observational study	estudio de observación
population	población
sample	muestra

Vocabulary Connections

To become familiar with some of the vocabulary terms in the chapter, consider the following. You may refer to the chapter, the glossary, or a dictionary if you like.

1. Something that is easy to get done is *convenient.* How do you think a survey for shoppers at a grocery may be done if a **convenience sample** is used?
2. A school principal wants to know how many students plan to attend college. He surveys a teacher's geometry class. What do you think the **population** in this situation is?
3. The words of a document are contained within the *margins.* If a calculated value has a **margin of error** of ±5%, what do you think this means?

CHAPTER 8

Reading Strategy: Read a Lesson for Understanding

As you read a lesson, read with a purpose. Lessons are centered on one or two specific objectives given at the top of the first page. Reading with the objectives in mind will help guide you through the lesson. You can use some of the following tips to help you follow the math as you read.

Reading Tips

Objective
Identify and use properties of real numbers.

Identify the **objectives** of the lesson. Then skim through the lesson to get a sense of where the objectives are covered.

"What is an inverse?"

"What is an integer?"

As you read through the lesson, list any questions, problems, or trouble spots you may have.

EXAMPLE:
Find the additive and multiplicative inverse of −9.

Additive inverse: 9 — *The opposite of −9 is $-(-9) = 9$*

Check $-9 + 9 = 0$ ✓ *The Additive Inverse Property holds.*

Multiplicative inverse: $\frac{1}{-9}$ — *The reciprocal of −9 is $\frac{1}{-9}$.*

Check $-9\left(\frac{1}{-9}\right) = 1$ ✓ *The Multiplicative Inverse Property holds.*

Work through each example, as the examples help demonstrate the objectives.

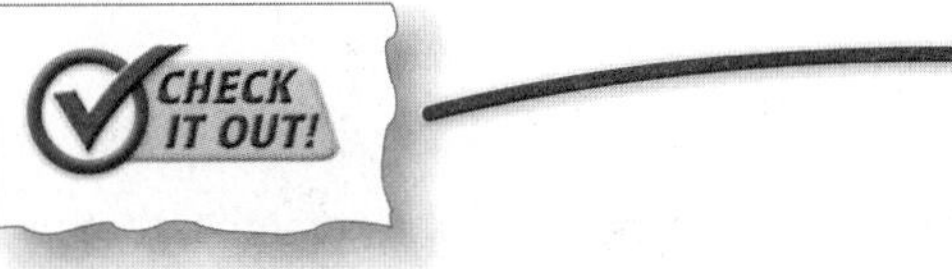

Practice your skills in the Check It Out sections to verify your understanding of the lesson.

Try This

Choose a lesson from your textbook to answer each question.

1. What is the objective of the lesson?
2. What new terms are defined in the lesson?
3. What skill is being practiced in the first Check It Out problem in the lesson?

COMMON CORE

8-1 Measures of Central Tendency and Variation

CC.9-12.S.ID.2 Use statistics...to compare center...and spread...of two or more...data sets. *Also* **CC.9-12.S.ID.1, CC.9-12.S.ID.3, CC.9-12.S.MD.5**

Objectives

Find measures of central tendency and measures of variation for statistical data.

Examine the effects of outliers on statistical data.

Vocabulary

expected value
probability distribution
variance
standard deviation
outlier

Who uses this?

Statisticians can use measures of central tendency and variation to analyze World Series results. (See Example 2.)

Recall that the *mean, median,* and *mode* are measures of central tendency—values that describe the center of a data set.

The *mean* is the sum of the values in the set divided by the number of values. It is often represented as $\bar{x}$. The *median* is the middle value or the mean of the two middle values when the set is ordered numerically. The *mode* is the value or values that occur most often. A data set may have one mode, no mode, or several modes.

EXAMPLE 1 Finding Measures of Central Tendency

Reading Math

A set of *univariate* data involves a single variable. The data set in Example 1 involves only one variable—number of days—so it is univariate.

Find the mean, median, and mode of the data.

Number of days from mailing to delivery: 6, 4, 3, 4, 2, 5, 3, 4, 5, 2, 3, 4

Mean: $\frac{6+4+3+4+2+5+3+4+5+2+3+4}{12} = \frac{45}{12} = 3.75$ days

Median: 2 2 3 3 3 4 ¦ 4 4 4 5 5 6 $\quad \frac{4+4}{2} = 4$ days

Mode: The most common result is 4 days.

CHECK IT OUT! **Find the mean, median, and mode of each data set.**

1a. $\{6, 9, 3, 8\}$ **1b.** $\{2, 5, 6, 2, 6\}$

A *weighted average* of a data set gives greater importance, or weight, to some values in the set than to others. To find a weighted average, multiply each value by its weight. Then divide the sum of these products by the sum of the weights.

Suppose a teacher grades students' work in a class by using a weighted average in which homework has a weight of 30%, tests have a weight of 40%, and the final exam has a weight of 30%. Mia has a homework score of 84, a test score of 88, and a final exam score of 91.

$$\text{Mia's weighted average} = \frac{84(0.30) + 88(0.40) + 91(0.30)}{0.30 + 0.40 + 0.30} = \frac{87.7}{1.00} = 87.7$$

For an experiment with numerical outcomes, the **expected value** is the weighted average of the possible outcomes. The weight for each outcome is its probability.

EXAMPLE 2 Finding Expected Value

The probability distribution for the number of games played in each World Series for the years 1923–2004 is given below. Find the expected number of games in a World Series.

> **Helpful Hint**
>
> The sum of all of the probabilities in a probability distribution is 1. In Example 2,
>
> $\frac{5}{27} + \frac{5}{27} + \frac{6}{27} + \frac{11}{27} = 1$

World Series Games				
Number of Games *n* in World Series	4	5	6	7
Probability of *n* Games	$\frac{5}{27}$	$\frac{5}{27}$	$\frac{6}{27}$	$\frac{11}{27}$

$$\text{expected value} = 4\left(\frac{5}{27}\right) + 5\left(\frac{5}{27}\right) + 6\left(\frac{6}{27}\right) + 7\left(\frac{11}{27}\right)$$ *Use the weighted average.*

$$= \frac{20}{27} + \frac{25}{27} + \frac{36}{27} + \frac{77}{27} = \frac{158}{27} \approx 5.85$$ *Simplify.*

The expected number of games in a World Series is about 5.85.

2. The probability distribution of the number of accidents in a week at an intersection, based on past data, is given below. Find the expected number of accidents for one week.

Number of accidents *n*	0	1	2	3
Probability of *n* accidents	0.75	0.15	0.08	0.02

A *box-and-whisker plot* shows the spread of a data set. It displays 5 key points: the **minimum** and **maximum** values, the **median**, and the **first** and **third quartiles**.

> **Reading Math**
>
> The first quartile is sometimes called the 25th percentile, and the third quartile is sometimes called the 75th percentile.

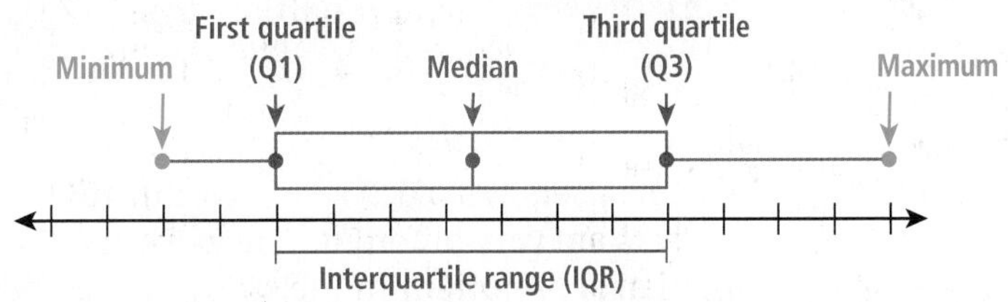

The quartiles are the medians of the lower and upper halves of the data set. If there are an odd number of data values, do not include the median in either half.

The *interquartile range*, or IQR, is the difference between the 1st and 3rd quartiles, or Q3 – Q1. It represents the middle 50% of the data.

Student to Student

Box-and-Whisker Plots

Jenny Rivera
Lincoln High School

I know I have to sort the data before I can make a box-and-whisker plot. I enter the data into my graphing calculator list. Then I use the STAT sort feature to sort the list in ascending order.

Other times, I'll use a spreadsheet and sort the data there.

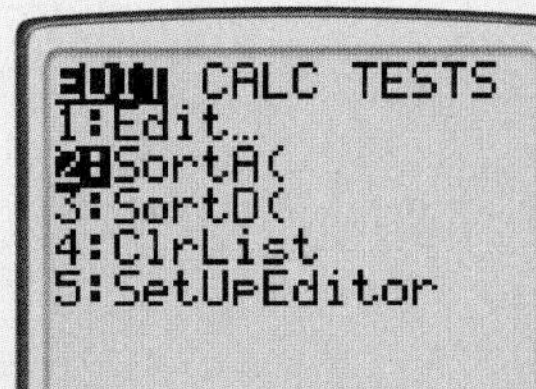

EXAMPLE 3 Making a Box-and-Whisker Plot and Finding the Interquartile Range

Make a box-and-whisker plot of the data. Find the interquartile range.
$\{5, 3, 9, 2, 14, 6, 8, 9, 5, 8, 13, 3, 15, 7, 4, 2, 12, 8\}$

Step 1 Order the data from least to greatest.

2, 2, 3, 3, 4, 5, 5, 6, 7, 8, 8, 8, 9, 9, 12, 13, 14, 15

Step 2 Find the minimum, maximum, median, and quartiles.

(2, 2, 3, 3, 4, 5, 5, 6, 7), (8, 8, 8, 9, 9, 12, 13, 14, 15)

Minimum	First quartile	Median 7.5	Third quartile	Maximum

Step 3 Draw a box-and-whisker plot.

Draw a number line, and plot a point above each of the five values. Then draw the box from the first quartile to the third quartile with a line segment through the median. Draw whiskers from the box to the minimum and maximum.

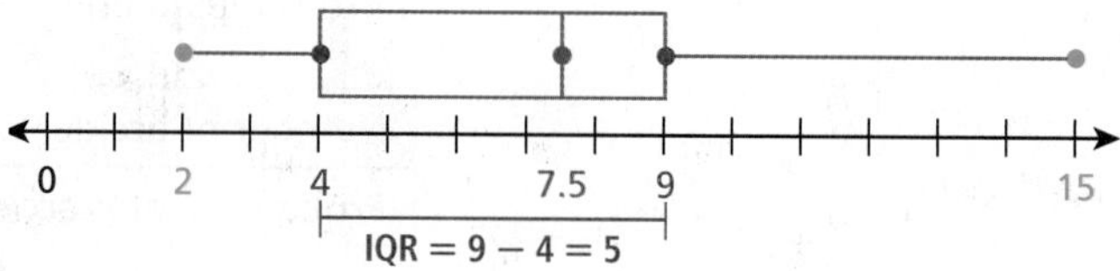

The interquartile range is 5, the length of the box in the diagram.

3. Make a box-and-whisker plot of the data. Find the interquartile range.
$\{13, 14, 18, 13, 12, 17, 15, 12, 13, 19, 11, 14, 14, 18, 22, 23\}$

The data sets $\{19, 20, 21\}$ and $\{0, 20, 40\}$ have the same mean and median, but the sets are very different. The way that data are spread out from the mean or median is important in the study of statistics.

Reading Math

The symbol commonly used to represent the mean is $\bar{x}$, or "*x* bar." The symbol for standard deviation is the lowercase Greek letter *sigma*, σ.

A *measure of variation* is a value that describes the spread of a data set. The most commonly used measures of variation are the *range*, the interquartile range, the *variance*, and the *standard deviation.*

The **variance**, denoted by σ^2, is the average of the squared differences from the mean. **Standard deviation**, denoted by σ, is the square root of the variance and is one of the most common and useful measures of variation.

Low standard deviations indicate data that are clustered near the measures of central tendency, whereas high standard deviations indicate data that are spread out from the center.

Finding Variance and Standard Deviation
Step 1. Find the mean of the data, $\bar{x}$.
Step 2. Find the difference between the mean and each data value, and square it.
Step 3. Find the variance, σ^2, by adding the squares of all of the differences from the mean and dividing by the number of data values.
Step 4. Find the standard deviation, σ, by taking the square root of the variance.

EXAMPLE 4 Finding the Mean and Standard Deviation

The data represent the number of milligrams of a substance in a patient's blood, found on consecutive doctor visits. Find the mean and the standard deviation of the data.

$\{14, 13, 16, 9, 3, 7, 11, 12, 11, 4\}$

Step 1 Find the mean.

$$\bar{x} = \frac{14 + 13 + 16 + 9 + 3 + 7 + 11 + 12 + 11 + 4}{10} = 10$$

Step 2 Find the difference between the mean and each data value, and square it.

Data Value x	14	13	16	9	3	7	11	12	11	4
$x - \bar{x}$	4	3	6	−1	−7	−3	1	2	1	−6
$(x - \bar{x})^2$	16	9	36	1	49	9	1	4	1	36

Step 3 Find the variance.

$$\sigma^2 = \frac{16 + 9 + 36 + 1 + 49 + 9 + 1 + 4 + 1 + 36}{10} = 16.2$$

Find the average of the last row of the table.

Step 4 Find the standard deviation.

$$\sigma = \sqrt{16.2} \approx 4.02$$

The standard deviation is the square root of the variance.

The mean is 10 mg, the standard deviation is about 4.02 mg.

4. Find the mean and standard deviation for the data set of the number of elevator stops for several rides.

$\{0, 3, 1, 1, 0, 5, 1, 0, 3, 0\}$

Remember!

Enter lists in the graphing calculator by pressing STAT and choosing **1:Edit...**

An **outlier** is an extreme value that is much less than or much greater than the other data values. Outliers have a strong effect on the mean and standard deviation. If an outlier is the result of measurement error or represents data from the wrong population, it is usually removed. There are different ways to determine whether a value is an outlier. One is to look for data values that are more than 3 standard deviations from the mean.

EXAMPLE 5 Examining Outliers

The number of electoral votes in 2004 for 11 western states are shown. Find the mean and the standard deviation of the data. Identify any outliers, and describe how they affect the mean and the standard deviation.

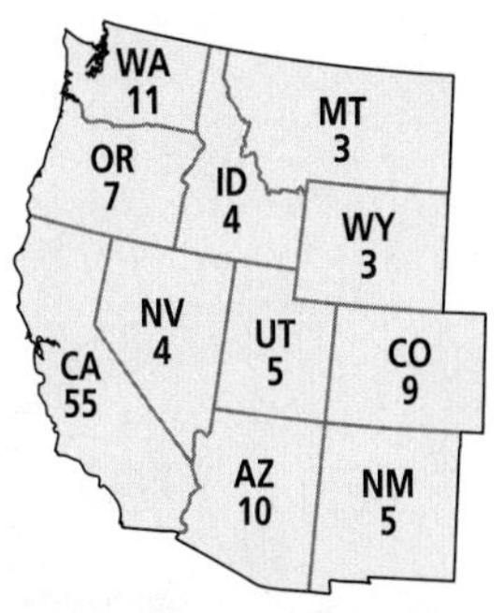

Step 1 Enter the data values into list **L1** on a graphing calculator.

Step 2 Find the mean and standard deviation.

On the graphing calculator, press STAT, scroll to the **CALC** menu, and select **1:1-Var Stats**.

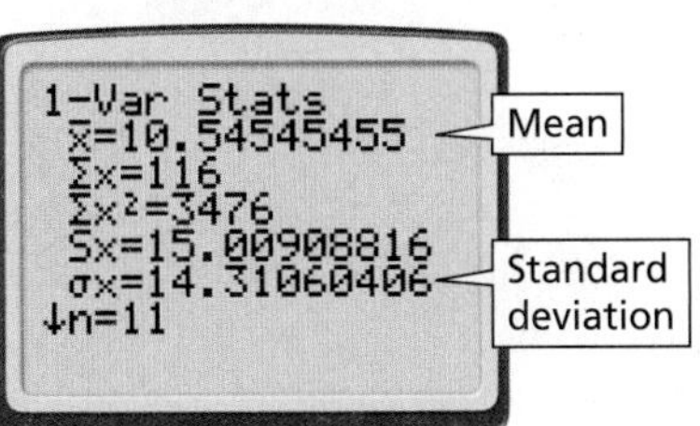

The mean is about 10.5, and the standard deviation is about 14.3.

Step 3 Identify the outliers.

Look for data values that are more than 3 standard deviations away from the mean in either direction.

Three standard deviations is about $3(14.3) = 42.9$.

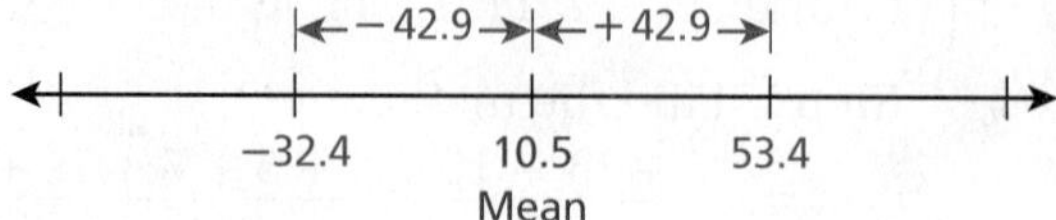

Values 42.9 units below the mean are negative and would not make sense in the problem (a state cannot have a negative number of electoral votes).

Values greater than 53.4 are outliers, so 55, the number of California electoral votes, is an outlier.

Check $\dfrac{|\text{value} - \text{mean}|}{\text{standard deviation}} = \dfrac{|55 - 10.5|}{14.3} \approx 3.1$ *55 is about 3.1 standard deviations from the mean, so it is an outlier.*

Step 4 Remove the outlier to see the effect that it has on the mean and standard deviation.

All data **Without outlier**

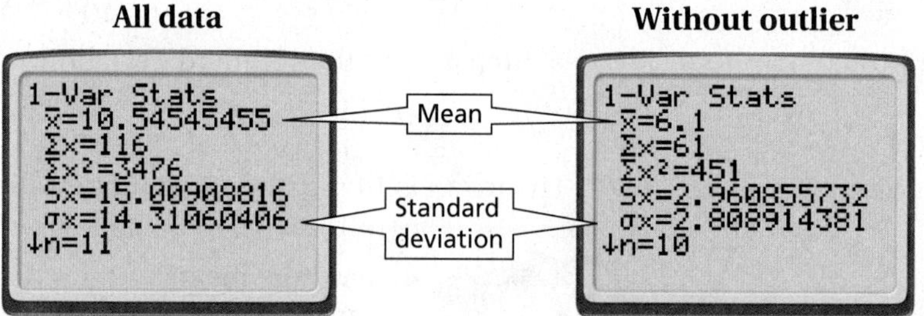

The outlier in the data set causes the mean to increase from 6.1 to ≈ 10.5 and the standard deviation to increase from ≈ 2.8 to ≈ 14.3.

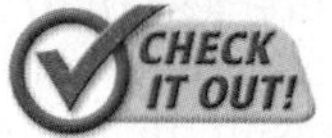

5. In the 2003 and 2004 American League Championship Series, the New York Yankees scored the following numbers of runs against the Boston Red Sox: 2, 6, 4, 2, 4, 6, 6, 10, 3, 19, 4, 4, 2, 3. Identify the outlier, and describe how it affects the mean and standard deviation.

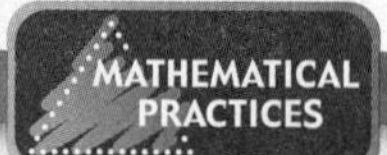

THINK AND DISCUSS

1. Describe the effect of adding a constant to each data value on the mean.
2. Describe the effect of adding a constant to each data value on the standard deviation.
3. What effect does doubling the variance have on the standard deviation?

4. **GET ORGANIZED** Copy and complete the graphic organizer. In each box, define and give an example of each measure.

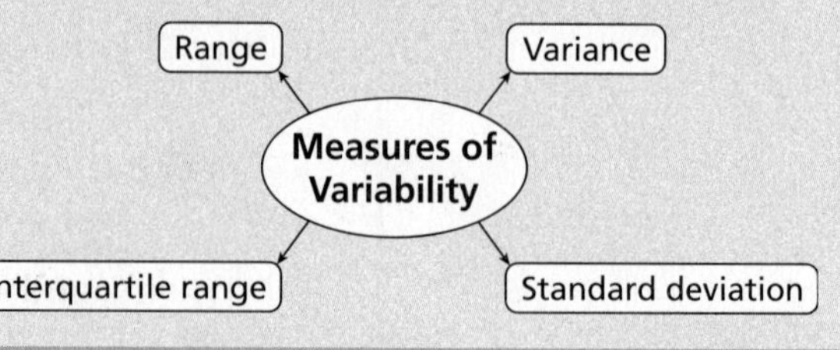

8-1 Exercises

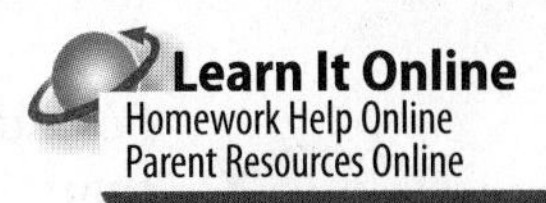

GUIDED PRACTICE

1. **Vocabulary** A measure of variation, or spread of a data set, is the __?__. (*variance* or *expected value*)

SEE EXAMPLE 1

Find the mean, median, and mode of each data set.

2. $\{5, 7, 4, 7, 6, 7\}$ 3. $\{2, 4, 4, 6, 6, 6, 7, 8\}$ 4. $\{10, 14, 18, 22, 26\}$

SEE EXAMPLE 2

5. Find the expected value of the prize.

Prize Giveaway						
Value	\$0	\$1	\$5	\$20	\$100	\$1000
Probability	0.9359	0.05	0.01	0.003	0.001	0.0001

SEE EXAMPLE 3

Make a box-and-whisker plot of the data. Find the interquartile range.

6. $\{3, 5, 2, 2, 8, 9, 1, 11\}$ 7. $\{2, 4, 1, 4, 2, 2, 7, 4\}$ 8. $\{33, 34, 31, 27, 22\}$

SEE EXAMPLE 4

Find the variance and standard deviation.

9. $\{3, 3, 4, 5, 5\}$ 10. $\{10, 12, 14, 15, 18, 20, 23\}$ 11. $\{7, 14, 21, 28, 35, 42\}$

SEE EXAMPLE 5

12. **Measurement** Students in a fourth-grade class were asked to measure the widths of their desks in centimeters. They recorded the following measures: 49, 50, 49, 48, 49, 19, 50, 49, 48, 50, 49, and 50. Identify the outlier, and describe how it affects the mean and the standard deviation.

PRACTICE AND PROBLEM SOLVING

Independent Practice

For Exercises	See Example
13–15	1
16	2
17–19	3
20–22	4
23	5

Extra Practice

See Extra Practice for more Skills Practice and Applications Practice exercises.

Find the mean, median, and mode of each data set.

13. $\{4, 16, 25, 9, 36, 49\}$ 14. $\{1, 7, 7, 2, 3, 14, 127, 8\}$ 15. $\{5, 10, 15, 20, 25\}$

16. Find the expected number of heads.

Three Coins Are Tossed				
Number of Heads	0	1	2	3
Probability	$\frac{1}{8}$	$\frac{3}{8}$	$\frac{3}{8}$	$\frac{1}{8}$

Make a box-and-whisker plot of the data. Find the interquartile range.

17. $\{12, 15, 12, 6, 18, 29\}$
18. $\{2, 2, 3, 8, 2, 8, 2, 42\}$
19. $\{3, 4, 3, 1, 2\}$

Find the variance and standard deviation.

20. $\{4, 4, 4, 4, 5\}$ 21. $\{8, 12, 30, 35, 48, 50, 62\}$ 22. $\{14, 26, 40, 52\}$

23. **Football** The 2004 Cincinnati Bengals scored 24, 16, 9, 17, 17, 23, 20, 26, 17, 14, 58, 27, and 28 points in their first 13 games. Find the mean and the standard deviation of the data. Identify the outlier, and describe how it affects the mean and the standard deviation.

24. **Critical Thinking** Write a set of data in which neither the mean nor the median are data values.

25. **Shopping** You are at a store and want to purchase an accurate room thermometer. One says 73°F, six say 75°F, eight say 76°F, and one says 37°F. Which measure of central tendency would you be least likely to use to pick a thermometer? Explain.

LINK

Geology

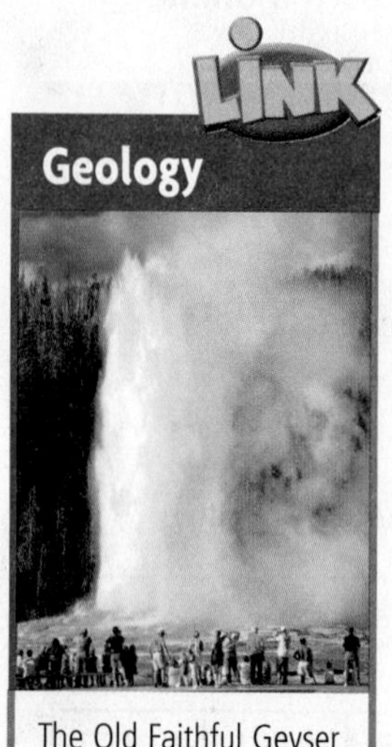

The Old Faithful Geyser at Yellowstone National Park can send 8500 gallons of boiling water to a height of 185 feet.

For a data set with a first quartile of Q1 and a third quartile of Q3, a value less than Q1 – 1.5(IQR) or greater than Q3 + 1.5(IQR) may be considered to be an outlier. Use this rule to identify any outliers in each data set. Show your work.

26. $\{2, 3, 4, 5, 5, 25\}$ **27.** $\{91, 90, 79, 15, 82, 90, 88\}$ **28.** $\{1, 36, 34, 33, 35, 92\}$

Geology **Use the graph of 222 eruptions of the Old Faithful Geyser for Exercises 29 and 30.**

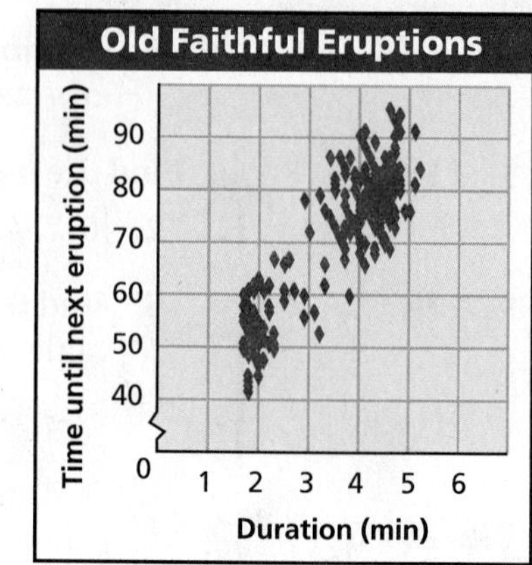

29. The duration has a mean of 3.6 min and a standard deviation of 1.1 min. What duration time intervals would be outliers? Describe any outliers for duration on the graph.

30. The time between eruptions has a mean of 71 min and a standard deviation of 12.8 min. What time intervals would be outliers? Describe any outliers for time intervals on the graph.

Estimation **Use the box-and-whisker plots for Exercises 31–34.**

Home Runs by Season

Babe Ruth

Hank Aaron

0 10 20 30 40 50 60

31. Which player hit the most home runs in a season? By approximately how many home runs did he do so?

32. Which player had the greater median number of home runs? Estimate how much greater.

33. Estimate the interquartile range for both players.

34. Which data set has the smaller standard deviation? Explain.

35. You have a 0.1% chance of winning \$500 and a 99.9% chance of losing \$1. What is the expected value of your gain? (*Hint*: The two possible outcomes for this "experiment" are + 500 and –1.)

36. Suppose that you have a 10% chance of winning \$100, a 30% chance of losing \$2, and a 60% chance of breaking even. What is the expected value?

37. **/// ERROR ANALYSIS ///** Two students attempt to find the standard deviation of 4, 6, 8, and 10. Which is incorrect? Explain the error.

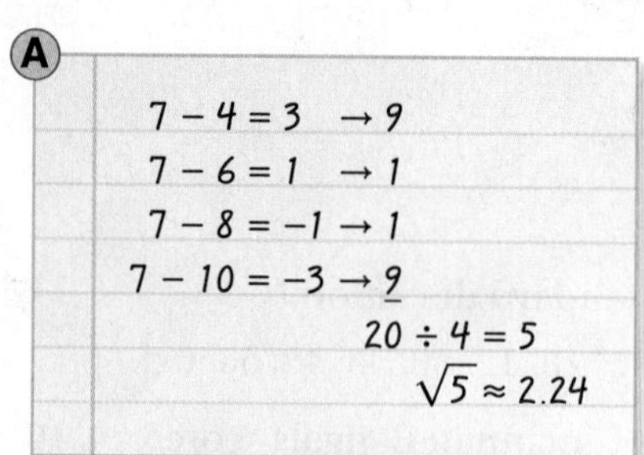

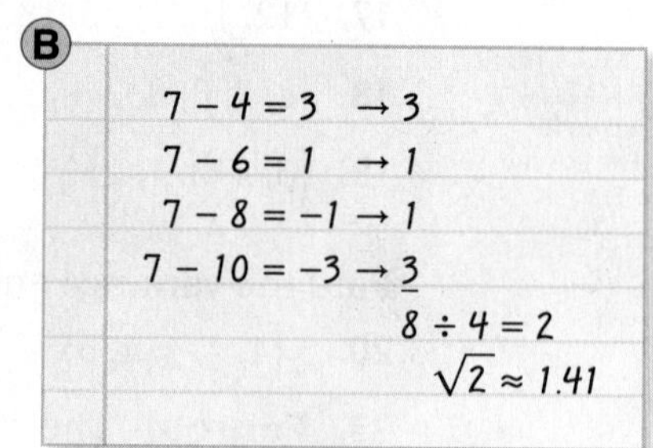

38. **Write About It** Is an expected value always, sometimes, or never a value in the data set? Give an example to justify your answer.

39. **Games** In a game, you multiply the values of two number cubes.

a. What is the expected value of this product?

b. What is the probability that a product is greater than the expected value?

c. What is the probability that a product is less than the expected value?

d. Are the answers to parts **b** and **c** equal? Explain.

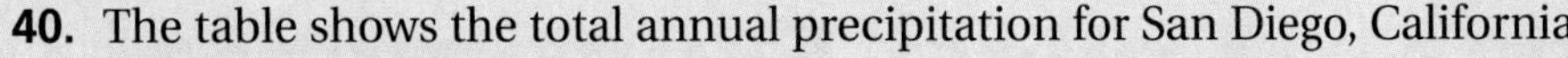

40. The table shows the total annual precipitation for San Diego, California.

Year	1994	1995	1996	1997	1998
Precipitation (in.)	9.4	17.0	7.3	7.0	16.1

Year	1999	2000	2001	2002	2003
Precipitation (in.)	5.4	6.9	8.5	4.2	9.2

a. Find the mean annual precipitation and the standard deviation.

b. In what years was the precipitation more than one standard deviation from the mean?

c. Find the median and interquartile range for the data.

41. Which data set would give the smallest standard deviation?

Ⓐ $\{1, 5, 7, 50\}$

Ⓑ $\{2, 10, 102, 110\}$

Ⓒ $\{100, 200, 300, 400\}$

Ⓓ $\{100, 101, 102, 105\}$

42. Which of the following is NOT true about the data sets $\{0, 48, 49, 50, 51, 52, 100\}$ and $\{0, 1, 2, 50, 98, 99, 100\}$?

Ⓕ The means are equal.

Ⓖ The ranges are equal.

Ⓗ The variances are equal.

Ⓙ The medians are equal.

43. The mean score on a test is 50. Which cannot be true?

Ⓐ Half the scores are 0, and half the scores are 100.

Ⓑ The range is 50.

Ⓒ Half the scores are 25, and half the scores are 50.

Ⓓ Every score is 50.

CHALLENGE AND EXTEND

44. A data set has a mean of 4, a median of 3, and a standard deviation of 1.6.

a. Suppose that every value of the data set is multiplied by 5. What is the mean, median, and standard deviation of the new data set?

b. Suppose that 5 is added to every value of the original data set. What is the mean, median, and standard deviation of the new data set?

45. A deck of cards is shuffled. What is the expected number of cards that will be in the same position that they were in originally? (*Hint:* Look at decks of 1, 2, 3, and 4 cards.)

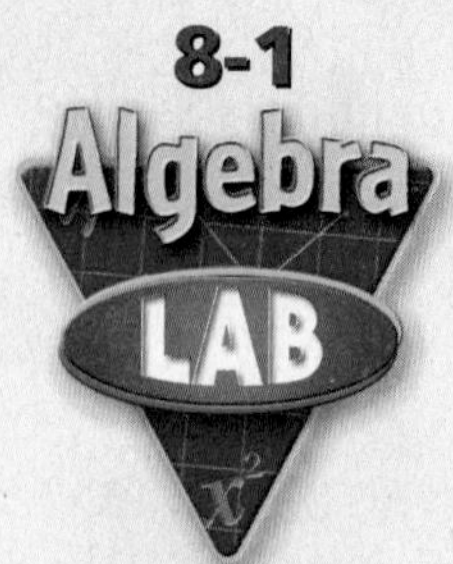

8-1 Algebra LAB

Collect Experimental Data

You can perform an experiment to generate, collect, organize, and analyze data in order to form mathematical conjectures.

Reason abstractly and quantitatively.

CC.9-12.S.IC.1 Understand statistics as a process for making inferences about population parameters based on a random sample from that population.

Use with Measures of Central Tendency and Variation.

Activity

Make a table of the sum of two number cubes.

Blue cube (columns), Red cube (rows)

	1	2	3	4	5	6
1	2	3	4	5	6	7
2	3	4	5	6	7	8
3	4	5	6	7	8	9
4	5	6	7	8	9	10
5	6	7	8	9	10	11
6	7	8	9	10	11	12

Try This

1. Describe any symmetry you notice in the table.
2. Make a probability distribution by using theoretical probabilities.

Sums	2	3	4	5	6	7	8	9	10	11	12
Probability	■	■	■	■	■	■	■	■	■	■	■

3. Find the expected value by using the theoretical probability distribution.
4. Which sum is most likely? least likely?
5. Do any two different sums have the same probability? If so, what are those sums?
6. Roll two number cubes 36 times. Record the results in a table.
7. Make a probability distribution of your data.
8. Find the expected value by using your probability distribution.

Answer the following questions based on your experiment.

9. Which sum was most likely? least likely?
10. Did any two different sums have the same probability? If so, what are those sums?
11. Compare your results with the theoretical results.
12. Combine the results of your experiment with those of other students. How do the experimental results of the group compare with your results? with the theoretical results?

8-2 Data Gathering

CC.9-12.S.IC.1 Understand statistics as a process for making inferences about population parameters based on a random sample from that population. *Also* **CC.9-12.S.MD.6, CC.9-12.S.MD.7**

Objectives

Explain how random samples can be used to make inferences about a population.

Use probability to analyze decisions and strategies.

Vocabulary

population
census
sample
random sample
biased sample
statistic
parameter

Who uses this?

Researchers can use surveys to make predictions about the population of fish in a lake.

Surveys are often conducted to gather data about a population. A **population** is the entire group of people or objects that you want information about. A **census** is a survey of an entire population. When it is too difficult, expensive, or time-consuming to conduct a census, a **sample**, or part of the population, is surveyed.

When every member of a population has an equal chance of being selected for a sample, the sample is called a **random sample**, or *probability sample.* Random samples are most likely to be representative of a population and are preferred over non-random samples such as *convenience samples* and *self-selected samples.*

EXAMPLE 1 Wildlife Application

A wildlife researcher is studying the effects of certain pollutants on different types of fish in a lake. Because it is difficult or impossible to catch every fish in the lake, the researcher decides to use a random sample. She catches 5 groups of 10 fish each from random spots in the lake, examines them, and returns them to the lake. The table shows the numbers of perch and walleye from each group.

	Perch	Walleye
Group 1	5	5
Group 2	6	4
Group 3	3	7
Group 4	5	5
Group 5	1	9

A **Identify the population and sample in the researcher's study.**

The population is the entire group being studied, so it is the total number of fish in the lake. The sample is the 50 fish that are caught as the representative of the entire population.

B **Use the table to estimate the ratio of perch to walleye in the lake.**

The sample included 20 perch and 30 walleye, so a good estimate of the ratio of perch to walleye in the lake is 2:3.

Identify the population and the sample.

1. A car factory just manufactured a load of 6,000 cars. The quality control team randomly chooses 60 cars and tests the air conditioners. They discover that 2 of the air conditioners do not work.

A non-random sample can result in a *biased sample.* A **biased sample** is a sample that may not be representative of a population. In a biased sample, the population can be underrepresented or overrepresented.

Underrepresented	One or more of the parts of a population are left out when choosing the sample.
Overrepresented	A greater emphasis is placed on one or more of the parts of a population when choosing the sample.

Random samples are less likely to be biased, while nonrandom samples are more likely to be biased. Bias in a sample is not always obvious at first glance.

EXAMPLE 2 Identifying Potentially Biased Samples

Decide whether the sampling method could result in a biased sample. Explain your reasoning.

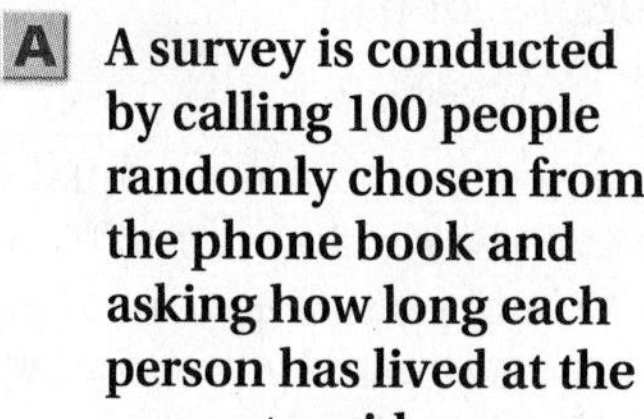

A **A survey is conducted by calling 100 people randomly chosen from the phone book and asking how long each person has lived at the current residence.**

Although the sample is chosen randomly from the phone book, the people who are listed in the phone book are not necessarily representative of the entire population of the city.

In particular, anyone who recently moved may not be listed yet under his or her current number. So people who have lived in their current residence for less than a year are underrepresented. The sample is biased.

B **A survey of students at a school is conducted by contacting every 10th student from the complete roster and asking whether he or she plans to go to college.**

The sample is selected from the entire school population, and there is no group that is overrepresented or underrepresented, so the sample is not likely to be biased.

Decide whether the sampling method could result in a biased sample. Explain your reasoning.

2. An online news site asks readers to take a brief survey about whether they subscribe to a daily newspaper.

Design Pics Inc./Alamy

EXAMPLE 3 Analyzing a Survey

The owner of a health club wants to determine the percent of adults in his area who exercise for at least 20 minutes three times a week. He asks the first 25 adults he sees at a mall on a weekday around 10:00 A.M. Are the results of the survey likely to be representative of the population? Explain.

Do you exercise for at least 20 minutes three times a week?
Yes 32%
No 68%

The sample chosen is a convenience sample, which is not likely to be representative of the population. Also, 25 adults make up a small sample for a large population. Finally, the sample underrepresents the adults who are not at the mall on a weekday around 10:00 A.M., such as those who are at work. No, the results are not likely to be representative of the population.

3. A restaurant owner wants to know how often families in his area go out for dinner. He surveys 25 families who eat at his restaurant on Tuesday night. Are his results likely to be representative of the population? Explain.

A **statistic** is a number that describes a sample. A **parameter** is a number that describes a population. You can use a statistic from a survey to estimate a parameter. In this way, surveys can be used to make predictions about a population.

EXAMPLE 4 Making Predictions

In a survey of 50 students at a high school, 32 students said that they plan to attend the homecoming dance. The school has 720 students.

A **Which of these numbers is a statistic, and which is a parameter?**

The statistic describes the sample: 32 out of 50 students said they plan to attend the homecoming dance. The parameter describes the population. The number of students in the school that plan to attend the dance is the parameter.

B **Predict the number of students who plan to attend the homecoming dance.**

Let x be the number of students who plan to attend the dance.

$$\frac{\text{students in sample to attend}}{\text{students in sample}} = \frac{\text{students in school to attend}}{\text{students in school}}$$

$\frac{32}{50} = \frac{x}{720}$ *Substitute.*

$32 \cdot 720 = 50x$ *Cross products property*

$460.8 = x$ *Solve for x.*

You can predict that about 461 students plan to attend the dance.

4. In a random sample of phone calls to a police station, 11 of the 25 calls were for emergencies. Suppose the police station receives 175 calls in one day. Predict the number of calls that will be for emergencies.

A strong understanding of statistics is important for decision-making. An understanding of the relative importance of statistical data allows for making good, informed decisions. A poor understanding of statistics can be costly.

EXAMPLE 5 Manufacturing

A production manager conducts a product inspection of a factory that has 10 machines, each assembling 1,000 widgets per day. She hires an inspector to choose a random time in the workday and check the next 25 widgets that are made at a random machine. The inspector finds that 5 of those widgets have defects. Since 20% is too high an error rate, the manager decides to shut the factory down until the problem can be fixed. Did the manager make a good decision? Why or why not?

The manager did not make a good decision. The sample chosen was very small compared to the factory's total output, so it might not have been a representative sample. Also, because the sample was taken from only one machine, the sample was not representative of the entire factory's output.

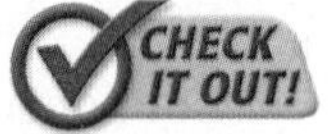

5. A promotion on a cereal box says that 1 in 4 boxes will have a prize inside. Marion has bought 5 boxes but hasn't opened a prize. He decides the advertised prize rate must be wrong. Is he justified in this evaluation? What are the chances, to the nearest percent, of not opening a prize in 5 boxes?

THINK AND DISCUSS

1. Explain why a census cannot be biased.
2. Give an example of a parameter that can be estimated by a statistic.
3. **GET ORGANIZED** Copy and complete the graphic organizer at right. Arrange the ovals to show which terms describe the population, and which terms describe the sample.

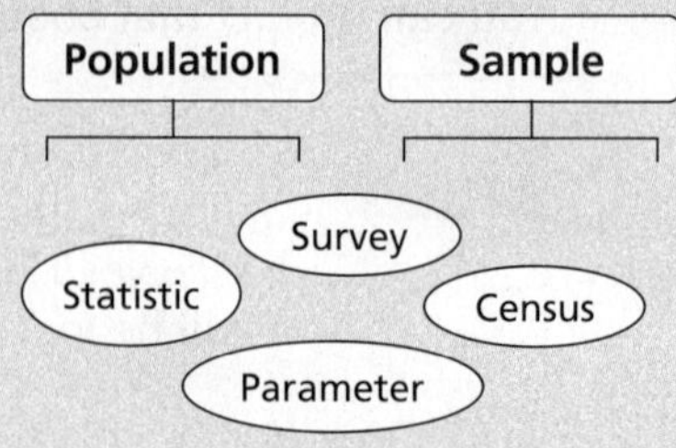

Photodisc/Getty Images

8-2 Exercises

GUIDED PRACTICE

Vocabulary **Apply the vocabulary from this lesson to answer each question.**

1. If a particular group in a population is underrepresented in a sample, the sample is ___?___. (*convenient*; *random*; *biased*)
2. A ___?___ is a measure of the population that is estimated by a statistic from a sample. (*census*; *parameter*; *survey*)

SEE EXAMPLE 1

Identify the population and the sample

3. A quality control inspector needs to estimate the number of defective computers in a group of 250 computers. He tests 25 randomly chosen computers.
4. The manager of the human resources department at a company wants to know if any of the company's 281 employees would take advantage of a reduced membership to a health club. The manager surveys 70 randomly chosen employees.

SEE EXAMPLE 2

Decide whether the sampling method could result in a biased sample. Explain your reasoning.

5. A survey of students at a school is taken by asking all the students that are still at the school at 5 PM whether they play sports.
6. A baker wants to know if her customers are satisfied with the selection of baked goods. She asks the first 20 people who make a purchase on a Saturday morning.

SEE EXAMPLE 3

For Exercises 7-9, determine whether the results of the survey are likely to be representative of the population. Explain.

The principal of a school wants to know if the students at the school would like to have wider selection of food available in the cafeteria for breakfast.

7. Survey the first 30 students who walk into the school.
8. Survey every 10th student who enters the cafeteria during the lunch period.
9. Survey every student who buys a meal in the cafeteria at least three times a week.

SEE EXAMPLE 4

10. In a survey of 20 sophomores at a high school, 8 students said that they would prefer a class field trip to an amusement park, rather than a museum. The sophomore class has 150 students. Predict the number of sophomores who would prefer a class trip to an amusement park.
11. In a survey of 30 employees at a company, 25 employees said that they were satisfied with their jobs. The company has 210 employees. Predict the number of employees at the company who are satisfied with their jobs.

SEE EXAMPLE 5

12. The manager of a radio station conducts a survey about people's favorite bands. The station plays announcements at regular intervals during the day and night asking listeners to call in and name their favorite band. After one week, the manager notices that 70% of his listeners name the same band as their favorite. The manager arranges for that band to play a concert to be advertised on air beforehand, in order to make a profit for the station from the ticket sales. Did the station manager make a good decision? Why or why not?

13. A chef at a restaurant that serves about 1200 customers a week introduces a dish at a special discounted price on a Wednesday night. Out of the 110 total customers that night, 45% order the dish. Because the dish sold so well, the chef decides to add it to the menu at full price. Did the chef make a good decision? Why or why not?

PRACTICE AND PROBLEM SOLVING

Independent Practice

For Exercises	See Example
14–15	1
16–21	2
22–25	3
27–31	4
33	5

Extra Practice

See Extra Practice for more Skills Practice and Applications Practice exercises.

Identify the population and the sample.

14. The manager of a department store wants to know how the shoppers at the store learned about the store's one-day sale. He asks 50 randomly chosen customers.

15. A family wants to know the average number of pieces of junk mail they receive each day. They count the pieces of junk mail that they receive each day for a week and find the average.

Decide whether the sampling method could result in a biased sample. Explain your reasoning.

16. On the first day of school, all of the incoming freshmen attend an orientation program. The principal wants to learn the opinions of the freshmen regarding the orientation program. He decides to ask the first 25 freshmen that he sees.

17. The manager of an apartment building wants to know if the residents are satisfied with his service. He writes each apartment number on a piece of paper and places the pieces of paper in a hat. Then he randomly chooses 10 apartment numbers and asks the residents of the 10 apartments about his service.

18. The members of the school drama club want to know how much students are willing to pay for a ticket to one of their productions. They decide that each member of the drama club should ask five of his or her friends what they are each willing to pay.

19. The manager of a city bus system wants to know if the people who ride the buses are satisfied with the service. She decides to post mail-in surveys on each of the city's buses.

20. A writer for a travel magazine wants to learn tourists' opinions about the nightlife in a city. She decides to visit some of the tourist attractions in the city on a Thursday morning. She plans to ask the first 50 tourists she meets for their opinions.

21. **Write About It** Administrators at your school want to know if more vegetarian items should be added to the lunch menu. They want to find out how many students are vegetarians. Give an example of one sampling method that could result in a biased sample, and one that is not likely to result in a biased sample. Explain your reasoning.

In exercises 22–25, determine whether the results of the survey are likely to be representative of the population in the following situation. Explain.

A marching band at a school is trying to decide whether having a bake sale or a raffle during a football game will earn more money for a field trip.

22. Ask every tenth person in the cafeteria at lunch on a school day whether he or she would be more likely to buy a baked good or a raffle ticket.

23. At the next football game, ask every fifth person if he or she would be more likely to buy a baked good or a raffle ticket.

24. Survey every member of the marching band.

25. Survey every customer at an upcoming bake sale that the art club is holding.

26. **ERROR ANALYSIS** The dance team wants to find out whether the student body at their school enjoyed their last production. They decide to have the dancers from the last production go around the school and randomly survey students by asking them the question "Did you like our last production?" Explain what is wrong with this method.

One hundred students out of 800 at a school were surveyed. The results are recorded in each problem below. Predict the number of students in the population that would answer similarly.

27. Twenty-five said they attended the fall play.

28. Seventy-eight said they rode the bus to school.

29. Eighty-two said they had taken an art class as an elective.

30. Sixty-four said they were members of an extracurricular club.

31. Sixty-five said they played a sport.

32. **Estimation** In a survey of 100 students, about 32 reported that they lived within walking distance of the school. The school has 893 students. Use mental math to estimate how many students in the school are within walking distance.

33. **Critical Thinking** A town recently passed a leash law for dogs. A survey asks whether the town should designate an off-leash area where dogs can roam freely in the town park. The results of the survey are shown below.

Should Spruce Park have an off-leash area?*
Yes 92%
No 8%
*From a survey of 100 dog owners

Based on the results of the survey, the town designates the off-leash area. Was this a good decision? Explain why it was a good decision or, if not, suggest a better way to gather information to make a better decision.

34. In a survey of 80 students, 25 said that they planned on attending the pep rally. The school has 550 students. Predict the number of students who plan to attend the pep rally.

Ⓐ 55 students

Ⓑ 80 students

Ⓒ 172 students

Ⓓ 378 students

DLILLC/Corbis

35. The principal of a school wants to know if the students at the school would like to have the morning announcements posted on the school's Web site. Which sampling method is most likely to yield an accurate predication about the population?

Ⓕ Survey every 10th student who enters the cafeteria during the lunch period.

Ⓖ Survey every 20th student who enters the cafeteria during the lunch period.

Ⓗ Survey only the students who report that they visit the school's Web site regularly.

Ⓙ Survey only the students who report that they do not visit the school's Web site regularly.

CHALLENGE AND EXTEND

36. A high school is made up of 19% freshmen, 27% sophomores, 29% juniors, and 25% seniors. The editor of the school newspaper wants to survey a sample of 100 students.

a. Suppose the sample includes 25 students from each class. Explain why the results may be biased.

b. Suggest a way to eliminate the bias.

37. Which sample is more likely to represent the population: 100 students randomly chosen from a school with 677 students, or 100 students randomly chosen from a school with 504 students? Explain.

38. A survey was taken in your school and the results showed that 646 of 760 students had performed some type of community service in the last two months. Out of a randomly chosen group of 20 students, how many would you expect to have done some type of community service in the past two months?

39. A manufacturer of compact discs will not sell a batch of discs if 3% or more of the discs in the batch are defective. A quality control inspector finds 2 defective discs in a sample of 50 discs. The sample was randomly chosen from a lot of 1000 discs. Will the manufacturer sell this batch? Explain.

40. Find the results of a survey published in a newspaper or magazine. Do you think that the results are representative of the population? Explain.

8-3 Surveys, Experiments, and Observational Studies

CC.9-12.S.IC.3 Recognize the purposes of and differences among sample surveys, experiments, and observational studies…

Objectives
Focus on the commonalities and differences between surveys, experiments, and observational studies.

Vocabulary
experiment
observational study
controlled experiment
control group
treatment group
randomized comparative experiment

Who uses this?
Researchers use observational studies to evaluate the effect of earphones on hearing loss. (See Example 3.)

You have already seen that a survey is one way to collect data. Although surveys are useful, different situations require different techniques for gathering data.

Individuals are people, animals, or objects that are described by data. If you collect data on the fuel efficiency of cars and trucks, the individuals are vehicles. Variables are used to describe individuals. Fuel efficiency, measured in miles per gallon, is an example of a variable.

Data Collection Methods

TERM	EXAMPLE
An **experiment** imposes a treatment on individuals to collect data on their response to the treatment.	A researcher adds acetone to gasoline to measure its effect on fuel efficiency.
An **observational study** observes individuals and measures variables without controlling the individuals or their environment in any way.	A researcher wants to find out if poor nutrition affects eyesight, but it would be unethical to deliberately subject some individuals to poor nutrition.

EXAMPLE 1 Identifying Experiments and Observational Studies

Explain whether each situation is an experiment or an observational study.

A **A researcher asks students the average number of hours of sleep they get per night and examines whether the amount of sleep affects students' grades.**

The researcher gathers data without controlling the individuals or applying a treatment. The situation is an example of an observational study.

B **A park employee wants to know if latex paint is more durable than non-latex paint. She paints 50 benches with latex paint, and 50 with non-latex paint.**

The employee applies a treatment (painting benches with latex paint) to some of the individuals (benches). The situation is an experiment.

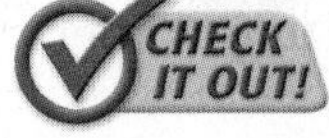

1. A scientist measures the height of 20 birds' nests, and counts the number of eggs to see if there is a relationship. Is this experiment or an observational study? Explain.

For data from an experiment to be useful, the experiment must be carefully designed. In a **controlled experiment**, two groups are studied under conditions that are identical except for one variable. The effects of the treatment are determined by comparing the *control group* and the *treatment group.*

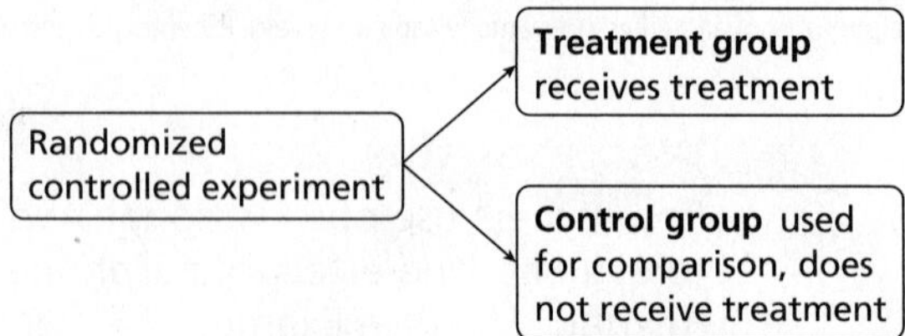

Often, to demonstrate a cause and effect hypothesis, an experiment must show two things. First, that a phenomenon occurs with the treatment; and second, that the phenomenon does not occur in the absence of the treatment.

In a **randomized comparative experiment**, the individuals are assigned to the control group or the treatment group at random, in order to minimize bias. An experiment that is not a randomized comparative experiment may be subject to bias, and any conclusions drawn from the experiment may not be valid.

EXAMPLE 2 Evaluating a Published Report

The study described in the report is a randomized comparative experiment. Describe the treatment, the treatment group, and the control group.

> **Milk Fights Cavities**
> At Ashland Middle School, fifty randomly chosen students were given milk at lunch every day for a year, and fifty other randomly chosen students were given other beverages. At the end of the year, students in the "milk" group had 15% fewer cavities than students in the other group.

The treatment in this study is *drinking milk at lunch.* The treatment group consists of the fifty students who drink milk, and the control group consists of the fifty students who were given other beverages.

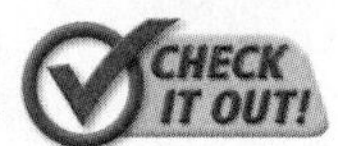

2. The study described in the report is a randomized comparative experiment. Describe the treatment, the treatment group, and the control group.

> **A Faster Web Site**
> To test the redesign of its Web site, an online bookseller assembled 96 users of the site and randomly divided them into two groups. One group used the new Web site to make an online purchase and one group used the old Web site to do the same transaction. Users of the new site were able to complete the purchase 22% faster.

A randomized comparative experiment should be used to gather data whenever feasible because this type of study makes it possible to draw valid cause-and-effect conclusions.

Such experiments are also *reliable.* That is, they can be repeated and can be expected to produce similar results each time. Experiments like these are often performed in duplicate or even triplicate simultaneously.

Randomization is an important feature of experiments. When conclusions are drawn from an experiment using randomization, the results can be counted on to be useful with another, different randomized sample. If the group wasn't chosen randomly, the results would likely not be valid for any other group. Randomization of the experiment allows generalization of the results.

Generally, a controlled, randomized experiment gives the most reliable results. In some situations, however, there may be ethical or practical reasons against using an experiment. If possible, the study should still be comparative.

For example, it would be unethical to ask some individuals to smoke in order to study the effects of nicotine on their health. Therefore, an observational study should be used. To make the study comparative, the researchers should randomly choose one group of people who already smoke and one group of people who do not smoke.

EXAMPLE 3 Designing an Experiment or Observational Study

Explain whether the research topic is best addressed through an experiment or an observational study. Then explain how you would set up the experiment or the observational study.

Does listening to an MP3 player with earphones for more than one hour per day affect a person's hearing?

The treatment (listening to an MP3 player with earphones for more than one hour per day) may negatively affect an individual's hearing, so it is not ethical to assign individuals to a treatment group. Use an observational study.

Randomly choose one group of people who already listen to an MP3 player with earphones for more than one hour per day.

Randomly choose another group of people who do not listen to an MP3 player with earphones for more than one hour per day.

Monitor the hearing of the individuals in both groups at regular intervals.

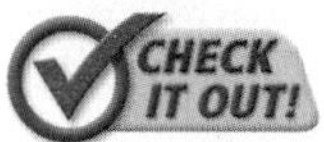

3. Explain whether the research topic is best addressed through an experiment or an observational study. Then explain how you would set up the experiment or the observational study.

Do people who consume 1000 milligrams of vitamin C each day as a dietary supplement have lower cholesterol levels than people who do not consume vitamin C supplements?

Another important feature distinguishing surveys from observational studies and experiments is that surveys are not comparative – they draw data from only one group, so they can't make conclusions about cause and effect. Well-designed studies and experiments compare data from two or more groups, allowing them to look for a relationship between variables.

It is possible to give the same survey to two or more groups and compare the results – but that is a type of observational study!

EXAMPLE 4 Evaluating Data Collection Methods

A researcher is considering three methods of evaluating two different cold medicines. Tell whether each method is a survey, an experiment or an observational study. Then explain which method would be most reliable.

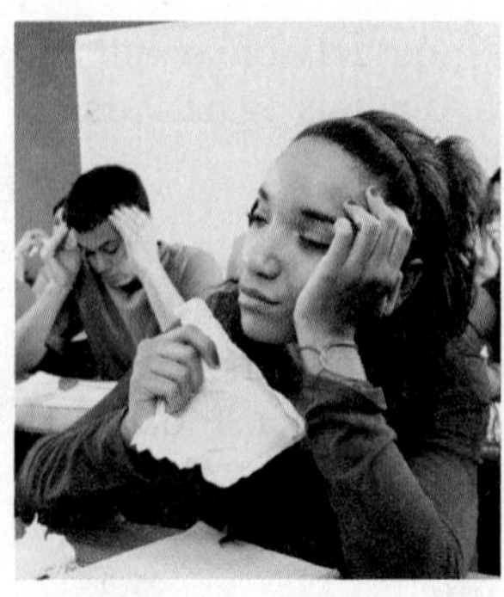

Method A	Method B	Method C
Choose 50 people at random. Ask which cold medicines they have taken in the past, and how effective they were.	Monitor 50 people with colds, and measure the length of the symptoms for the individuals who choose to take each type of medicine.	Randomly divide a group of 50 people with colds into two groups. Give each group a different medicine, and measure the length of the symptoms.

In method A, the researcher asks questions about cold medicines that people have taken. This method is a survey.

In method B, the researcher observes people who have chosen different cold medicines, but does not impose a treatment. This is an observational study.

In method C, the researcher gives each group a treatment, so the method is an experiment.

Method A is least reliable, because there is no basis for comparison. Method B has a comparison group, but the members are self-selected, which could lead to bias. In method C, the members of each group are randomly selected, which makes the two groups theoretically similar except for the variable, the different medicines. This method is most reliable.

4. Classify each method as a survey, an experiment, or an observational study, and explain which would be most reliable.

Method A	Method B	Method C
Randomly choose 50 people to exercise 3 hours a week, and 50 people to participate in another activity, and monitor their health.	Randomly choose 100 people. Ask how many hours a week they exercise, and how healthy they are.	Choose 50 people who exercise regularly and 50 who do not, and monitor their health.

THINK AND DISCUSS

1. Explain how an experiment is different from an observational study.
2. Describe a comparative experiment that would be considered unethical.
3. **GET ORGANIZED** Copy and complete the graphic organizer at right. In each column, describe the individuals in the group.

Experiment: A baker testing a new brand of yeast bakes 10 loaves with the old brand and 10 with the new brand.	
Control group:	**Treatment Group:**

Steve Hix/Somos Images/Corbis

8-3 Exercises

GUIDED PRACTICE

Vocabulary Apply the vocabulary from this lesson to answer each question.

1. A data-gathering technique that uses a treatment to influence individuals or aspects of the individuals' environment is a(n) ___?___. (*survey*; *observational study*; *experiment*)
2. Which is generally the more reliable data-gathering technique, a randomized comparative experiment or a survey?

SEE EXAMPLE 1

Explain whether each situation is an experiment or an observational study.

3. A caretaker at a zoo wants to study the effect of a new diet on the health of the zoo's elephants. She continues to feed half of the elephants their old food, switches the other half to a new diet, and then monitors the health of the elephants.
4. A school system wants to see if there is a correlation between students' standardized test scores and the amount of time they spend on extracurricular activities. The school board surveys students from each school in the system to gather data about the average number of hours per week spent on extracurricular activities and each student's most recent test scores.

SEE EXAMPLE 2

The studies described below are randomized comparative experiments. Describe the treatment, the treatment group, and the control group.

5. At Clara Barton High School, one hundred randomly chosen students were asked to stop drinking soft drinks for six months, and one hundred other randomly chosen students who were self-reported soft drink consumers were told to continue with their normal habits. At the end of six months, the students who did not drink soft drinks reported steadier energy levels throughout the school day.
6. A park service wants to determine whether reintroducing a particular species of underwater weed to their lakes would be beneficial to a particular species of fish. They plant the weed in the bed of one lake containing the species of fish. One year later, they study the health of the fish population in the lake where the weeds were reintroduced, as well as in an ecologically similar lake without the weeds.

SEE EXAMPLE 3

Explain whether each research topic is best addressed through an experiment or an observational study. Then explain how you would set up the experiment or the observational study.

7. Does second-hand smoke affect the health of pets?
8. Does a particular vitamin supplement make seasonal allergy symptoms less severe?
9. Does increasing the number of stoplights per mile on a road decrease the number of car accidents on the road?
10. Does a certain toothpaste prevent cavities in children better than another one?
11. Does eating chicken before playing a game of baseball increase the number of home runs scored?
12. Does eating ginger alleviate seasickness?

SEE EXAMPLE 4

13. A researcher is considering three methods of evaluating the effect of drinking coffee on sleep habits. Classify each method as a survey, an experiment or an observational study. Then explain which method would be most reliable.

Method A	Method B	Method C
Randomly choose 50 people to drink coffee every day. Choose another 50 people to cut all coffee out of their diet. Record the number of hours of sleep per night for each group.	Randomly choose 100 people. Ask whether they are coffee drinkers and how many hours of sleep they usually get each night.	Choose 50 people who drink coffee regularly and record how many hours of sleep they get each night. Choose another 50 who do not drink coffee, and record how many hours of sleep they get each night.

PRACTICE AND PROBLEM SOLVING

Independent Practice

For Exercises	See Example
14–18	1
19–22	2
24–29	3
31	4

Extra Practice

See Extra Practice for more Skills Practice and Applications Practice exercises.

Determine whether each situation is an experiment or an observational study.

14. A researcher wants to know whether babies born into homes with older siblings develop speech skills earlier than babies who are born as only children.

15. A bakery wants to know whether glaze or powdered sugar is a more enticing pastry topping. They make some pastries with each topping, and see which sells better.

16. A car dealer wants to know what color cars seem to sell the best, so she looks over the past year's sales records.

17. A cell phone manufacturer wants to investigate the user-friendliness of a new design, so the manufacturer gives the new phones to fifty people for a week and then gets their feedback.

18. A filmmaker wants to know the effect of eating fast food on his general health, so he eats fast food every day for four weeks and has doctors monitor his health.

In exercises 19–22, the study described in the report is a randomized comparative experiment. Describe the treatment, the treatment group, and the control group.

19. A pharmaceutical company wants to know about the side effects of a new blood pressure drug. Out of 200 randomly selected volunteers currently on blood pressure medication, it switches the old drug with the new drug for 100 of them, and continues to give the other 100 the old drug. It then monitors the two groups for side effects.

20. A research team wants to know whether a new laundry detergent is effective. The team washes variety of fabrics with a variety of stains in the new detergent, and washes the same pairings of fabrics and stains in just hot water, and compares the results.

21. A food company is testing a new recipe for a dinner entree. The company invites 100 people to a dinner to test the new recipe. Half the people are served the old recipe, and half are served the new recipe. They find that the people who were served the new recipe ate 15% more.

22. A battery manufacturer develops a new battery that it claims is an improvement on its existing product. A research group compares the battery life for 20 assorted devices on the new battery and the old battery, and finds that the devices run an average of 20% longer on the new battery.

23. **///ERROR ANALYSIS///** Consider the controlled experiment described below.

> Mr. Johnson wants to determine what the condition of his deck would be if he did not continue to reapply wood sealant to it once every spring to protect it. So, he conducts an experiment. This spring, he uses the sealant on the entire deck except for one board. He then observes how exposure to the weather affects that board in relation to the rest of the deck.

Lindsay claims that, in the experiment, the part of the deck to which the sealant is applied corresponds to the treatment group because that is the part that is actually 'treated'. Riley claims that the single board corresponds to the treatment group. Which person is correct? Explain your reasoning.

In exercises 24–29, explain whether the research topic is best addressed through an experiment or an observational study.

24. Does using a certain brand of cleaning product put people who use it frequently at greater risk of respiratory problems?

25. Does a certain shampoo work to reduce dandruff?

26. Do people who bite their nails get sick more often than people who don't?

27. Is a certain chemical effective at killing a certain bacteria commonly found in household kitchens and bathrooms?

28. Do dogs kept as pets live longer if they run in a yard every day?

29. Does working a job for which half or more of the tasks involve typing increase the risk of certain diseases?

30. **Write About It** Explain whether the research topic below is best addressed through an experiment or an observational study. Then explain how you would set up the experiment or the observational study.

> Will a car get better gas mileage if it uses Brand X motor oil?

31. A researcher is considering three methods of evaluating two different brands of first aid healing ointment for minor cuts. Classify each method as a survey, an experiment or an observational study. Then explain which method would be most reliable.

Method A	Method B	Method C
Randomly divide a group of 100 people with minor cuts into two groups. Have each group use a different ointment, and record how long it takes their cuts to heal.	Choose 100 people at random. Ask which ointments they have used in the past, and how quickly their cuts have healed with each ointment.	Monitor 100 people who are currently treating minor cuts with an ointment of their choosing, and record how long it takes for them to heal.

32. Which of the following is generally the most reliable data-gathering technique?
    (A) survey
    (B) randomized comparative experiment
    (C) observational study
    (D) treatment

33. Which is the control group in the study described below?

    > Out of a group of 100 subjects, 50 were randomly selected to receive a vitamin D supplement. All 100 subjects were monitored through the winter to see how many caught the flu.

    (F) the 100 subjects randomly selected for the study
    (G) subjects who caught the flu
    (H) the 50 subjects who received vitamin D supplements
    (J) the 50 subjects who did not receive vitamin D supplements

CHALLENGE AND EXTEND

34. Give an example of a question that could be better answered by gathering data in an observational study than it could by gathering data in an experiment. Explain why an observational study would be more appropriate. Then design an observational study that would answer the question.

35. Give an example of a question that could be better answered by gathering data in a survey than it could by gathering data in an observational study or an experiment. Explain why survey would be more appropriate. Then design a survey that would answer the question.

8-4 Significance of Experimental Results

CC.9-12.S.IC.5 Use data from a randomized experiment to compare two treatments; use simulations to decide if differences between parameters are significant.

Objective
Use simulations and hypothesis testing to compare treatments from a randomized experiment.

Vocabulary
hypothesis testing
null hypothesis

Who uses this?
Medical researchers use hypothesis testing to determine the effectiveness of new drugs. (See Example 1.)

Suppose you flipped a coin 20 times. Even if the coin were fair, you would not necessarily get exactly 10 heads and 10 tails. But what if you got 15 heads and 5 tails, or 20 heads and no tails? You might start to think that the coin was not a fair coin, after all.

Hypothesis testing is used to determine whether the difference in two groups is likely to be caused by chance. For example, when tossing a coin 20 times, 11 heads and 9 tails is likely to occur if the coin is fair, but if you tossed 19 heads and 1 tail, you could say it was not likely to be a fair coin. To understand why, calculate the number of possible ways each result could happen. There are 2^{20} possible sequences of flips. Of these, how many fit the description '19 heads, 1 tails' and how many fit the description, '11 heads, 9 tails'?

19 heads, 1 tails	Choose 1 flip to be tails	$\binom{20}{1} = \frac{20!}{(1!)\,(19!)} = 20$
11 heads, 9 tails	Choose 9 flips to be tails	$\binom{20}{9} = \frac{20!}{(9!)\,(11!)} = 167{,}960$

Since there are $\frac{167{,}960}{20} = 8398$ times as many sequences that fit the latter description as the first, the result '11 heads, 9 tails' is 8398 times as likely as the result of '19 heads, 1 tails'! Therefore, it is very unlikely that a coin that flipped 19 heads and only 1 tails was a fair coin.

However, that outcome, while unlikely, is still possible. Hypothesis testing cannot prove that a coin is unfair – it is still possible for a coin to come up with 19 heads by chance, it is just very unlikely. Therefore, you can only say how likely or unlikely a coin is to be biased.

Hypothesis testing begins with an assumption called the *null hypothesis*. The **null hypothesis** states that there is no difference between the two groups being tested. The purpose of hypothesis testing is to use experimental data to test the viability of the null hypothesis.

Helpful Hint
The word *null* means "zero," so the *null* hypothesis is that the difference between the two groups is zero.

The null hypothesis is often the reverse of what the experimenter believes; it is presented to allow the data to contradict it.

For a coin toss, the null hypothesis is that coin is *not* biased: the number of heads will equal the number of tails. The null hypothesis is *rejected* if the difference is too large, which in this case means that it is likely that the coin is not fair.

In a randomized controlled experiment, the null hypothesis is that there is no difference in the value of the variable for the control group and treatment group.

EXAMPLE 1 Analyzing a Controlled Experiment

A medical researcher is testing a new gel coating for a pill, and wants to know if it affects absorption. In a random trial, blood samples were taken from 12 patients in each group 30 minutes after ingesting the pill. The drug levels in micrograms per milliliter are shown below.

Control group	42	43	43	42	36	38	45	50	40	40	34	47
Treatment group	34	26	33	27	36	29	39	33	24	34	37	31

A **State the null hypothesis for the experiment.**

The null hypothesis is that the blood levels of the drug will be the same for the control group and the treatment group.

B **Compare the results for the control group and the treatment group. Do you think that the researcher has enough evidence to reject the null hypothesis?**

You can use box-and-whisker plots to compare the results for the control group and the treatment group.

First, arrange the data in order and find the median, quartiles, minimum, and maximum. Then draw a box-and-whisker plot for each group.

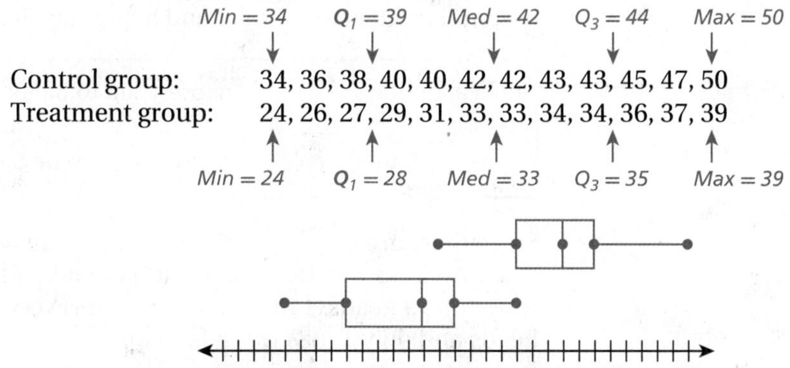

There is a large difference in the two groups that is unlikely to be caused by chance. The researcher should reject the null hypothesis, which means that the coating probably does affect absorption.

1. A teacher wants to know if students in her morning class do better on a test than students in her afternoon class. She compares the test scores of 10 randomly chosen students in each class.

   Morning class: 76, 81, 71, 80, 88, 66, 79, 67, 85, 68
   Afternoon class: 80, 91, 74, 92, 80, 80, 88, 67, 75, 78

   a. State the null hypothesis.

   b. Compare the results of the two groups. Does the teacher have enough evidence to reject the null hypothesis?

Hypothesis testing can be used to compare the mean from a sample to the mean of a population. If the sample contains at least 30 individuals, you can use the *z-test.* Suppose that the population mean is estimated to be μ, and a random sample has n individuals ($n \geq 30$). To find the z-value of a statistic, you need to know the sample mean $\overline{x}$ and standard deviation σ. The *z-value* is found using the following formula:

$$z = \frac{\overline{x} - \mu}{\frac{\sigma}{\sqrt{n}}}$$

The null hypothesis is that there is no difference in the two groups. If the sample mean is close to the population mean, then the z-value is close to 0. If the z-value is too large, you can reject the null hypothesis.

One common measure used in z-tests is known as a 95% confidence level:

- If $|z| > 1.96$, then you can reject the null hypothesis with 95% certainty.
- If $|z| < 1.96$, then you do not have enough evidence to reject the null hypothesis.

EXAMPLE 2 Using a z-Test

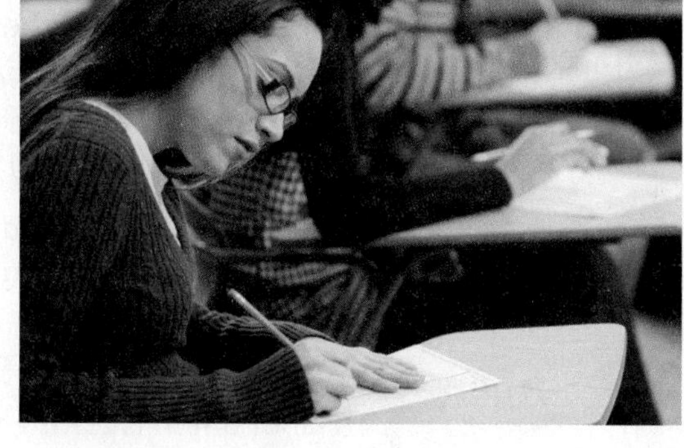

A test prep company claims it can boost SAT scores to an average of 1800. In a random sample of 36 students who took the course, the average was 1745, with a standard deviation of 210. Is there enough evidence to reject the claim?

First, state the null hypothesis. The sample mean is 1745, and the company claims that the population mean is 1800. The null hypothesis is that there is no difference in the sample and the population.

Next, find the z-value, using $\mu = 1800$, $\overline{x} = 1745$, $\sigma = 210$, and $n = 36$.

$$z = \frac{\overline{x} - \mu}{\frac{\sigma}{\sqrt{n}}}$$

$$z = \frac{1745 - 1800}{\frac{210}{\sqrt{36}}} = \frac{-55}{35} \approx -1.57$$

Because $|z| = 1.57 < 1.96$, you do not have enough evidence to reject the claim with 95% confidence. This does not necessarily mean that the claim is true, just that you cannot prove it is false.

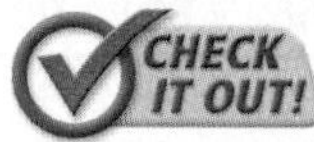

2. A tax preparer claims an average refund of $3000. In a random sample of 40 clients, the average refund was $2600, and the standard deviation was $300. Is there enough evidence to reject his claim?

Greg Hinsdale/Corbis

THINK AND DISCUSS

1. Give an example of a null hypothesis.
2. Explain what is true if you do not reject the null hypothesis.
3. **GET ORGANIZED** Copy and complete the graphic organizer at right. Arrange the steps of the z-test in the correct order.

If $|z| < 1.96$, do not reject the null hypothesis.

State the null hypothesis.

If $|z| > 1.96$, reject the null hypothesis.

Find the z-value.

8-4 Exercises

GUIDED PRACTICE

Vocabulary Apply the vocabulary from this lesson to answer each question.

1. If a difference between the treatment group and the control group in a randomized controlled experiment is caused by __?__, the z-value will be close to 0. (*chance*; *experimental error*)

2. The __?__ in randomized controlled experiment is that there is no difference between the treatment group and the control group. (*conclusion*; *null hypothesis*)

Use the following information to complete exercises 3–4.

A labor union is testing whether a professional development program in a certain industry has been successful in raising the scores of new employees on a standardized test. The given tables contain data for each of two companies in the industry. The data for each company show the scores of the new employees who have undergone the professional development program (the treatment group) and the scores of those who have not (the control group).

SEE EXAMPLE 1

3. The data for Company A is shown below.

Control group	82	77	82	78	90	72	80	87	70	68	88	85
Treatment group	92	84	88	95	89	84	79	85	94	90	85	92

   a. State the null hypothesis for the experiment.
   b. Compare the results for the control group and the treatment group. Do you think that the researcher has enough evidence to reject the null hypothesis?

4. The data for Company B is shown below.

Control group	77	89	75	91	68	82	80	89	74	78	83	80
Treatment group	88	87	79	82	90	87	92	85	84	88	94	76

   a. State the null hypothesis for the experiment.
   b. Compare the results for the control group and the treatment group. Do you think that the researcher has enough evidence to reject the null hypothesis?

SEE EXAMPLE 2

5. **Investment** An investment consultation firm claims that it will increase the returns on its clients' investments to an average of 20% of the original investments, with minimal risk involved. In a random sample of 50 clients of the firm, the average return on investments with minimal risk was 18.5% of the original investment, with a standard deviation of 4%. What is the z-value rounded to the nearest hundredth, and is there enough evidence to reject the firm's claim?

6. The publishers of a study guide claim that their book will increase average quarterly math grades of users to 85%. In a random sample of 20 students who have used the study guide, the math grade was 88%, with a standard deviation of 8%. What is the z-value rounded to the nearest hundredth, and is there enough evidence to reject the publishers' claim?

PRACTICE AND PROBLEM SOLVING

Independent Practice

For Exercises	See Example
7–9	1
10–13	2

Extra Practice

See Extra Practice for more Skills Practice and Applications Practice exercises.

7. **Water Quality** A city is conducting a water quality study. It is measuring trace levels of a certain substance in the blood of residents who live in a city with unknown water quality against the same substance in another city with water quality that is known to be high. The blood levels of the substance in micrograms per milliliter are shown in the chart.

Known quality	9	5	4	7	5	8	7	3	4	6	8	5
Unknown quality	2	4	8	5	9	7	9	5	4	10	5	2

a. State the null hypothesis for the experiment.

b. Compare the results for the control group and the treatment group. Do you think that the researcher has enough evidence to reject the null hypothesis?

Use the following information to complete exercises 8–9 below.

Botany A researcher is investigating the health of some plants that have been treated with a chemical to increase their rate of growth. In the problems below, there are data given about levels of two different elements in the plants. The data for each element show the levels of the element in the treated plants, and the levels of the element in untreated plants.

8. The nitrogen levels of the treated and untreated plants are given in parts per million in the chart below.

Untreated plants	140	100	120	110	130	100	130	150	120
Treated plants	120	180	130	150	220	150	170	160	130

a. State the null hypothesis about nitrogen for the experiment.

b. Compare the results for the control group and the treatment group. Do you think that the researcher has enough evidence to reject the null hypothesis?

9. The potassium levels of the treated and untreated plants are given in parts per million in the chart below.

Untreated plants	200	250	320	310	340	310	270	340	370
Treated plants	310	260	280	310	220	260	290	220	250

a. State the null hypothesis about potassium for the experiment.

b. Compare the results for the control group and the treatment group. Do you think that the researcher has enough evidence to reject the null hypothesis?

10. **Medicine** A pharmaceutical company has developed a new drug to treat high blood pressure. Blood pressure measures are given as two distinct numbers, known as the systolic and diastolic pressures, both measured in millimeters of mercury (mm Hg). The company claims that the drug will decrease systolic pressure to an average of 120 mm Hg, and diastolic to an average of 80 mm Hg.

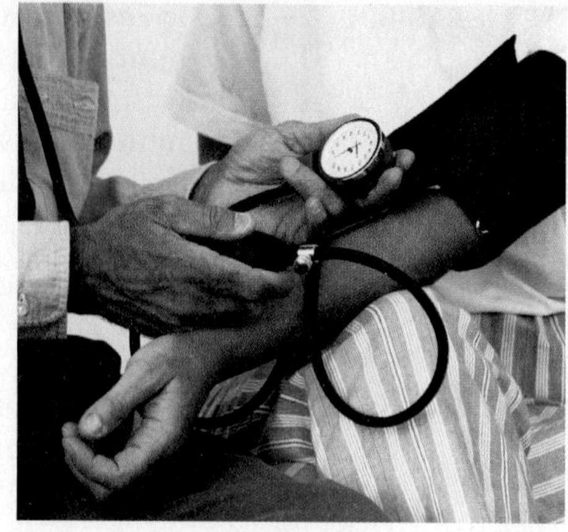

An independent trial is conducted by treating a random sample of 20 people with the drug. The findings are presented in the chart. Find the z-scores for the two trials, rounded to the nearest hundredth, and choose whether or not to reject the company's claims.

Company's Claims	Avg. systolic 120 mm Hg	Avg. diastolic 80 mm Hg
Trial results	Avg. 122 mm Hg	Avg. 85 mm Hg
Standard Dev.	10 mm Hg	8 mm Hg
z-score	a. ________	c. ________
Reject claim?	b. Yes / No	d. Yes / No

11. A math teacher claimed that the average grade of the students in her Algebra 2 classes this year would be equal to the average grade of the same students in Algebra 1 classes last year. The average grade of last year's Algebra 1 students was a 92%. In a random sample of 25 current Algebra 2 students, the average grade was 87%, with a standard deviation of 7%.
   a. Find the z-value, rounded to the nearest hundredth.
   b. Is there enough evidence to reject the teacher's claim?

12. A car insurance company claims that it will save new customers 15% of what they pay for their current plans with other companies. In a random sample of 30 new customers, the average amount saved was 8% with a standard deviation of 2%.
   a. Find the z-value, rounded to the nearest hundredth.
   b. Is there enough evidence to reject the insurance company's claim?

13. **Marketing** A marketing firm claims that its ad campaign will increase sales for a fast-food chain by 15%. In a random sample of 25 stores, the average increase in sales was 14% with a standard deviation of 5%.
   a. Find the z-value, rounded to the nearest hundredth.
   b. Is there enough evidence to reject the marketing firm's claim?

14. **Write About It** Translate the formula for calculating z-values into English instructions.

15. **Critical Thinking** Consider the two statements below:
   I. This drug raises insulin levels in the blood stream.
   II. It will rain tomorrow.

   Which of these claims is a candidate for hypothesis testing? Can each statement be proven either true or false with certainty today? Explain.

16. **Critical Thinking** What does a positive z-value indicate about the values of the mean in the entire population versus the value of the mean in the sample? What does a negative z-value indicate about the same two values?

17. **ERROR ANALYSIS** A claim is made that the mean of a data set will be 60. In a test of the claim, the mean among 16 trials is actually 58, with a standard deviation of 3. Shondell rejects the claim based on her calculation of the z-value, but Mandy says rejection is unjustified based on her calculation of the z-value. Whose work is correct? Explain the error.

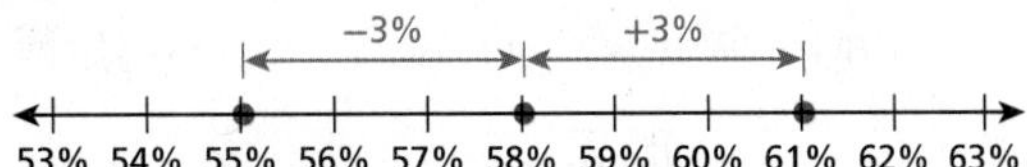

TEST PREP

18. Which measure is not needed for calculating a z-value, given data about a treatment group and a control group?
   - (A) standard deviation for the population
   - (B) standard deviation for the sample
   - (C) mean of the population
   - (D) mean of the sample

19. A claim is made that the mean of a data set will be 4.7. In a test of the claim, the mean among 49 trials is actually 5, with a standard deviation of 0.5. Which is the z-value of the given data, rounded to the nearest hundredth?
   - (F) 11.67
   - (G) 1.96
   - (H) 4.20
   - (J) 0.021

CHALLENGE AND EXTEND

20. A foreign language teacher wants to know whether strength of math skills is a good indicator of how a student will do in a foreign language. The class average among the students with average math skills is 87.6%. The teacher records the test scores of 5 students in her class with particularly strong math skills separately. The results are shown in the table.

Strong math student scores	89	78	90	85	92

   a. Find the mean and the standard deviation of the scores, rounded to the nearest percentage point, for the students with strong math skills.
   b. State the null hypothesis for the teacher's experiment.
   c. Find a z-value, rounded to the nearest hundredth, and use it to evaluate the null hypothesis.

21. **///ERROR ANALYSIS///** Thaddeus and Billy are analyzing the results of an experiment in science class. Their science teacher tells them they should expect to see a mean value of 54 in their data, if the experiment is performed correctly. After 15 trials, the mean value they actually measure is 50, with a standard deviation of 5. Thaddeus' and Billy's claims are presented below. Whose logic is correct, assuming the teacher is right about the expected results? Justify your answer.

Thaddeus	Billy
The mean we measured was far off from what was expected, so we can be sure that we performed the experiment incorrectly.	"It can't be proved that our results fall outside the expected range. It's possible that we got these results while performing the experiment correctly."

Mastering the Standards

for Mathematical Practice

The topics described in the Standards for Mathematical Content will vary from year to year. However, the *way* in which you learn, study, and think about mathematics will not. The Standards for Mathematical Practice describe skills that you will use in all of your math courses.

Mathematical Practices

1. *Make sense of problems and persevere in solving them.*
2. *Reason abstractly and quantitatively.*
3. *Construct viable arguments and critique the reasoning of others.*
4. *Model with mathematics.*
5. *Use appropriate tools strategically.*
6. *Attend to precision.*
7. *Look for and make use of structure.*
8. *Look for and express regularity in repeated reasoning.*

5 Use appropriate tools strategically.

Mathematically proficient students consider the available tools when solving a... problem... [and] are... able to use technological tools to explore and deepen their understanding...

In your book

Algebra Labs and **Technology Labs** use concrete and technological tools to explore mathematical concepts.

2-4 Algebra LAB
Model Equations with Variables on Both Sides

4-4 Technology LAB
Connect Function Rules, Tables, and Graphs

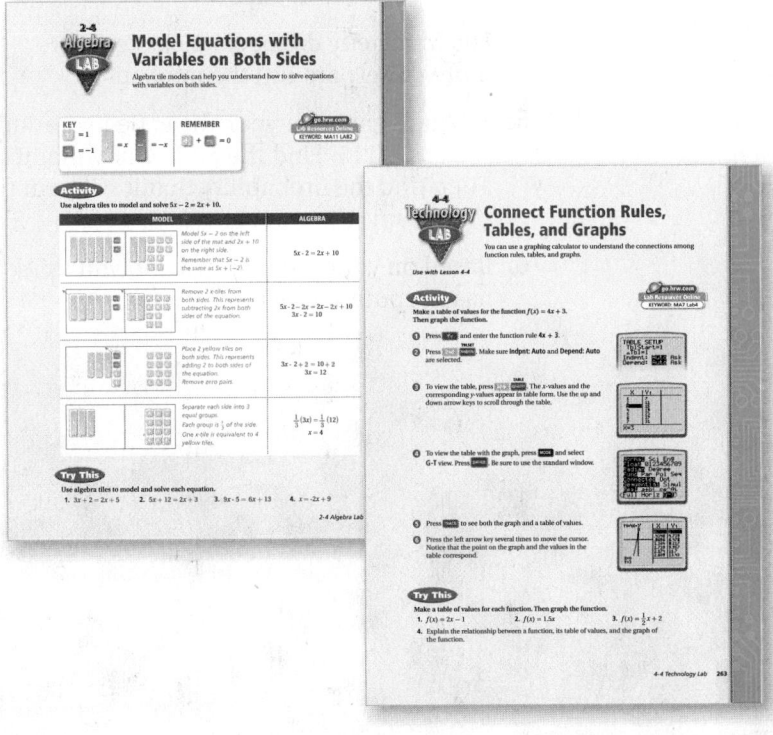

Getty Images/Image Source

CHAPTER 8

SECTION 8A

Multi-Step Test Prep

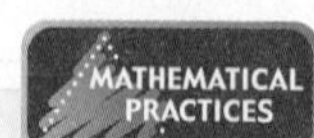

Reason abstractly and quantitatively.

Analyzing Data

Rain Reign Many people think of Seattle, Washington, as one of the rainiest cities in the United States. The table provides precipitation data for Seattle and Atlanta, Georgia, over a 10-year period. By analyzing this data set, you can decide for yourself whether Seattle deserves its soggy reputation.

Annual Precipitation (in.)		
Year	Seattle	Atlanta
1994	34.8	60.0
1995	42.6	52.8
1996	50.7	44.6
1997	43.3	51.7
1998	44.1	46.2
1999	42.1	38.9
2000	28.7	35.6
2001	37.6	38.4
2002	31.4	47.6
2003	41.5	52.9

1. Find the mean annual precipitation and the standard deviation for Seattle and for Atlanta.
2. For which city do the data cluster more closely around the mean?
3. Find the interquartile range for Seattle and for Atlanta.
4. For which city do the data cluster more closely around the median?
5. During a calendar year, the expected number of rainy days in Atlanta is 115. Find the probability that it will rain on any given day. Then find the probability that it will rain there on at least 2 days during any given week.
6. Based on your findings, why do you think Seattle, rather than Atlanta, has a reputation as a rainy city?

Steven Vidler/Eurasia Press/Corbis

Quiz for Lessons 8-1 Through 8-4

8-1 Measures of Central Tendency and Variation

1. The probability distribution for the number of defects in a shipment of alarm clocks, based on past data, is given below. Find the expected number of defects in a shipment of alarm clocks.

Number of Defects, n	0	1	2	3	4
Probability of n Defects	0.82	0.11	0.04	0.02	0.01

2. Make a box-and-whisker plot of the data. Find the interquartile range. Ages of employees at a movie theater: 17, 23, 18, 22, 45, 28, 21, 25

The data set shows the amount of money, rounded to the nearest dollar, spent by 20 consecutive shoppers at a home-improvement store.

35, 18, 49, 55, 280, 29, 42, 61, 19, 80, 33, 45, 67, 28, 71, 37, 48, 50, 31, 22

3. Find the mean and standard deviation of the data.
4. Identify the outlier, and describe how it affects the mean and standard deviation.

8-2 Data Gathering

Decide whether the sampling method could result in a biased sample. Explain your reasoning.

5. An online seller sends an e-mail message to its customers, asking them to fill out a short customer satisfaction survey.
6. In a survey of 30 randomly-chosen employees, 12 said they would prefer a company-sponsored lunch, while 18 said they would prefer a company-sponsored breakfast. If the company employs 250 people, predict the number of employees who would prefer a company-sponsored lunch.

8-3 Surveys, Experiments, and Observational Studies

Explain whether each research topic is best addressed through an experiment or an observational study. Then explain how you would set up the experiment or the observational study.

7. Does exposure to x-rays affect vision?
8. Does a particular gasoline additive improve fuel economy?

8-4 Significance of Experimental Results

9. A marketing firm claims that its ad campaign will increase sales for a fast-food chain by 9%. In a random sample of 35 stores, the average increase in sales was 8% with a standard deviation of 4%. Find the z-value, rounded to the nearest hundredth. Is there enough evidence to reject the marketing firm's claim?

COMMON CORE

Mastering the Standards

for Mathematical Practice

The topics described in the Standards for Mathematical Content will vary from year to year. However, the *way* in which you learn, study, and think about mathematics will not. The Standards for Mathematical Practice describe skills that you will use in all of your math courses.

Mathematical Practices

1. *Make sense of problems and persevere in solving them.*
2. *Reason abstractly and quantitatively.*
3. *Construct viable arguments and critique the reasoning of others.*
4. *Model with mathematics.*
5. *Use appropriate tools strategically.*
6. *Attend to precision.*
7. *Look for and make use of structure.*
8. *Look for and express regularity in repeated reasoning.*

1 Make sense of problems and persevere in solving them.

Mathematically proficient students start by explaining to themselves the meaning of a problem... They analyze givens, constraints, relationships, and goals. They make conjectures about the form... of the solution and plan a solution pathway...

In your book

Focus on Problem Solving describes a four-step plan for problem solving. The plan is introduced at the beginning of your book, and practice with the plan appears throughout the book.

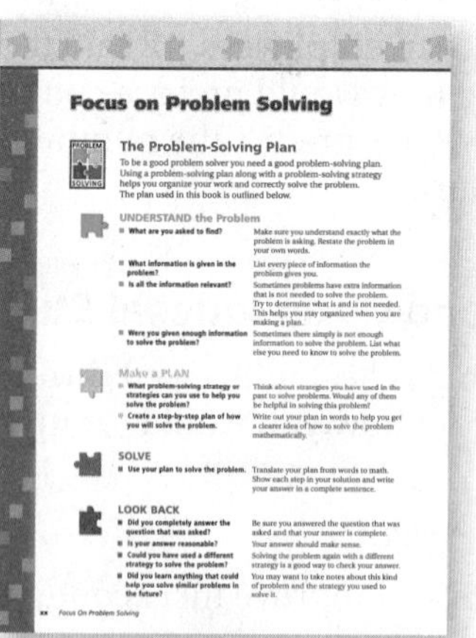

Focus on Problem Solving

The Problem-Solving Plan

To be a good problem solver you need a good problem-solving plan. Using a problem-solving plan along with a problem-solving strategy helps you organize your work and correctly solve the problem. The plan used in this book is outlined below.

UNDERSTAND the Problem

- **What are you asked to find?** Make sure you understand exactly what the problem is asking. Restate the problem in your own words.
- **What information is given in the problem?** List every piece of information the problem gives you.
- **Is all the information relevant?** Sometimes problems have extra information that is not needed to solve the problem. Try to determine what is and is not needed. This helps you stay organized when you are making a plan.
- **Were you given enough information to solve the problem?** Sometimes there simply is not enough information to solve the problem. List what else you need to know to solve the problem.

Make a PLAN

- **What problem-solving strategy or strategies can you use to help you solve the problem?** Think about strategies you have used in the past to solve problems. Would any of them be helpful in solving this problem?
- **Create a step-by-step plan of how you will solve the problem.** Write out your plan in words to help you get a clearer idea of how to solve the problem mathematically.

SOLVE

- **Use your plan to solve the problem.** Translate your plan from words to math. Show each step in your solution and write your answer in a complete sentence.

LOOK BACK

- **Did you completely answer the question that was asked?** Be sure you answered the question that was asked and that your answer is complete.
- **Is your answer reasonable?** Your answer should make sense.
- **Could you have used a different strategy to solve the problem?** Solving the problem again with a different strategy is a good way to check your answer.
- **Did you learn anything that could help you solve similar problems in the future?** You may want to take notes about this kind of problem and the strategy you used to solve it.

xx *Focus On Problem Solving*

EXAMPLE 5 ***Problem-Solving Application***

PROBLEM SOLVING

The cost to place an ad in a newspaper for one week is a linear function of the number of lines in the ad. The costs for 3, 5, and 10 lines are shown. Write an equation in slope-intercept form that represents the function. Then find the cost of an ad that is 18 lines long.

City Gazette

Newspaper Ad Costs

Lines	3	5	10
Cost ($)	13.50	18.50	31

1 Understand the Problem

- The **answer** will have two parts—an equation in slope-intercept form and the cost of an ad that is 18 lines long.
- The ordered pairs given in the table satisfy the equation.

2 Make a Plan

First, find the slope. Then use point-slope form to write the equation. Finally, write the equation in slope-intercept form.

3 Solve

Step 1 Choose any two ordered pairs from the table to find the slope.

$m = \frac{y_2 - y_1}{x_2 - x_1} = \frac{18.50 - 13.50}{5 - 3} = \frac{5}{2} = 2.5$ *Use (3, 13.50) and (5, 18.50).*

Step 2 Substitute the slope and any ordered pair from the table into the point-slope form.

$y - y_1 = m(x - x_1)$

$y - 31 = 2.5(x - 10)$ *Use (10, 31).*

Step 3 Write the equation in slope-intercept form by solving for y.

$y - 31 = 2.5(x - 10)$

$y - 31 = 2.5x - 25$ *Distribute 2.5.*

$y = 2.5x + 6$ *Add 31 to both sides.*

Step 4 Find the cost of an ad containing 18 lines by substituting 18 for x.

$y = 2.5x + 6$

$y = 2.5(18) + 6 = 51$

The cost of an ad containing 18 lines is $51.

4 Look Back

Check the equation by substituting the ordered pairs (3, 13.50) and (5, 18.50).

y	$= 2.5x + 6$
13.50	$2.5(3) + 6$
13.5	$7.5 + 6$
13.5	13.5 ✓

y	$= 2.5x + 6$
18.50	$2.5(5) + 6$
18.5	$12.5 + 6$
18.5	18.5 ✓

Comstock/Getty Images

8-5 Sampling Distributions

CC.9-12.S.IC.4 Use data…to estimate a population mean or proportion; develop a margin of error… *Also* **CC.9-12.S.IC.6**

Objective
Estimate population means and proportions and develop margin of error from simulations involving random sampling.

Analyze surveys, experiments, and observational studies to judge the validity of the conclusion.

Vocabulary
simple random sample
systematic sample
stratified sample
cluster sample
convenience sample
self-selected sample
probability sample
margin of error

Who uses this?
Pollsters use different survey methods to accurately reflect public opinion.

When a survey is used to gather data, it is important to consider how the sample is selected for the survey. If the sampling method is biased, the survey will not accurately reflect the population.

Most national polls that are reported in the news are conducted using careful sampling methods in order to minimize bias. Other polls, such as those where people phone in to express their opinion, are not usually reliable as a reflection of the general population.

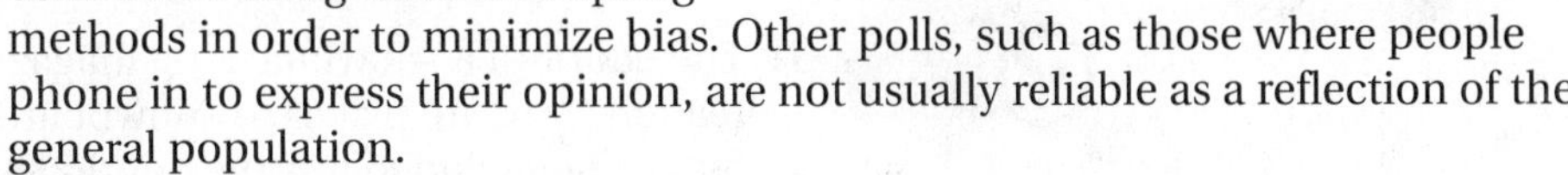

Remember that a random sample is one that involves chance. Six different types of samples are shown below.

Types of Samples
Simple Random Sample Members are chosen using a method that gives everyone an equally likely chance of being selected.
Systematic Sample Members are chosen using a pattern, such as selecting every other person.
Stratified Sample The population is first divided into groups. Then members are randomly chosen from each group.
Cluster Sample The population is first divided into groups. A sample of the groups is randomly chosen. All members of the chosen groups are surveyed.
Convenience Sample Members are chosen because they are easily accessible.
Self-Selected Sample Members volunteer to participate.

EXAMPLE 1 Classifying a Sample

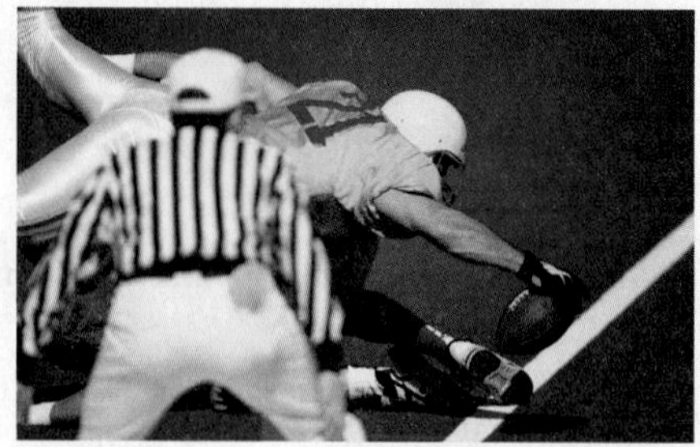

The officials of the National Football League (NFL) want to know how the players feel about some proposed changes to the NFL rules. They decide to ask a sample of about 100 players. Classify each sample.

A **The officials choose the first 100 players who volunteer their opinions.**

This is a self-selected sample because the players volunteer.

B **The officials randomly choose 3 players from each of the 32 teams in the NFL.**

This is a stratified sample because the players are separated by team and randomly chosen from each team.

C **The officials have a computer generate a list of 100 players from a database that includes all of the players in the NFL.**

This is a simple random sample because each player has an equally likely chance of being chosen.

1. The editor of a snowboarding magazine wants to know the readers' favorite places to snowboard. The latest issue of the magazine included a survey, and 238 readers completed and returned the survey. Classify the sample.

When choosing a sampling method, the most important concerns are usually accuracy and budget. The most accurate survey is a census, because it samples every individual in the population. However, a census is not always possible.

The sampling methods that are more accurate tend to be more difficult or expensive. For example, if you wanted a simple random sample of the entire United States, you would need a list of every person in the country to choose from.

A **probability sample** is a sample where every member of the population being sampled has a nonzero probability of being selected. Simple random samples, stratified samples, and cluster samples are all examples of probability sampling. However, not every sampling method performed is a probability sample. A convenience sampling is not a probability sample, because people in the population who are not convenient for the surveyor to survey have no chance of being surveyed.

Self-selected sampling is also not a probability sample, although the reason why is more subtle. This kind of sampling is not a probability sample because the members of the population that don't self-select have no chance of being surveyed.

These non-probability methods of sampling are usually the easiest to conduct, but also the least reliable.

Most Accurate	Very Accurate	Not Very Accurate
census	simple random sample stratified sample cluster sample	convenience sample self-selected sample

EXAMPLE 2 Evaluating Sampling Methods

A high school has 552 freshmen, 495 sophomores, 449 juniors, and 439 seniors enrolled. The student newspaper wants to take a survey of the school. Classify each sampling method. Which is most accurate? Which is least accurate? Explain your reasoning.

Method A Randomly select 50 freshmen, 50 sophomores, 50 juniors, and 50 seniors from the complete roster.

Method B Randomly select 200 students from the complete roster.

Method C Choose every 10th student who enters the cafeteria at lunchtime.

Method A is a stratified sample. The population is divided into groups, and a sample is randomly selected from each group. Method B is a simple random sample, and Method C is a convenience sample.

Method B is the most accurate, because every member of the population is equally likely to be in the sample. In Method A, the sample contains an equal number of freshmen and seniors, even though there are 552 freshmen and 439 seniors in the population. So seniors are overrepresented in the sample.

Method C is the least accurate, because some individuals may not have a chance of being included, such as those who do not eat in the cafeteria.

2. A small-town newspaper wants to report on public opinion about the new City Hall building. Classify each sampling method. Which is most accurate? Which is least accurate? Explain your reasoning.

Method A Ask readers to write in and give their opinion.

Method B Survey 10 randomly selected female students and 10 randomly selected male students in the cafeteria during the lunch period.

Method C Randomly choose 10 streets in the town and survey everyone who lives on each street.

Imagine a polling organization that surveys 1000 voters in a city to find out how they plan to vote in an upcoming mayoral election. The organization reports that 58% of city residents plan to vote for Smith, and that the survey has a *margin of error* of $\pm 3\%$. The margin of error expresses the amount of error in the survey results due to the nature of random sampling.

The **margin of error** of a random sample defines an interval, centered on the sample percent, in which the population percent is most likely to lie. In the above example, the margin of error of $\pm 3\%$ means that the percent of voters in the population who plan to vote for Smith is likely to lie within 3 percentage points of 58%. That is, it is likely that between 55% and 61% of city voters plan to vote for Smith.

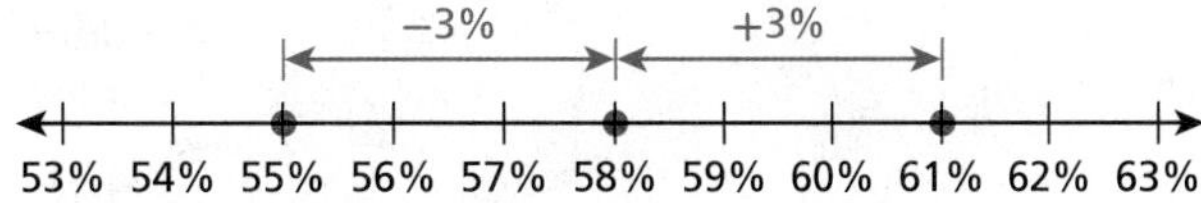

EXAMPLE 3 Interpreting a Margin of Error

Students at a high school will vote on a proposal to start classes later in the day. According to a survey of a random sample of students, 54% of the students agree with the proposal and 46% of the students disagree with the proposal. The survey's margin of error is ±5%. Does the survey clearly project the outcome of the voting?

Use the margin of error to find an interval in which the actual percent of students who agree with the proposal is likely to lie.

54% ± 5% represents the interval 54% – 5% = 49% to 54% + 5% = 59%.

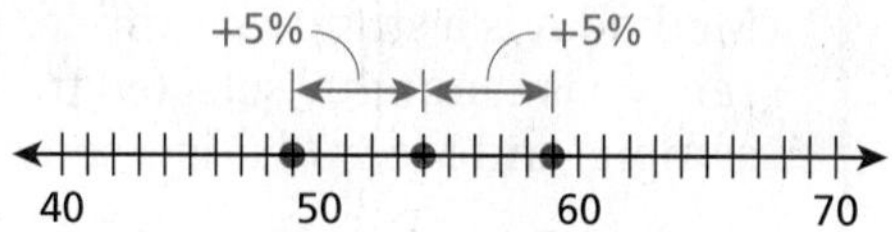

Use the margin of error to find an interval in which the actual percent of students who disagree with the proposal is likely to lie.

46% ± 5% represents the interval 46% – 5% = 41% to 46% + 5% = 51%.

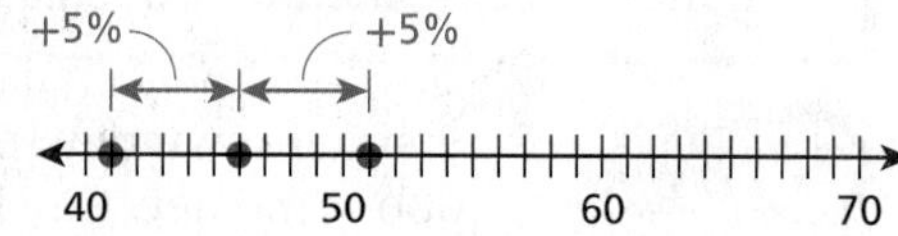

You can conclude that between 49% and 59% of all students agree with the proposal and between 41% and 51% of all students disagree with the proposal. Because the intervals overlap, the survey does not clearly project the outcome of the voting.

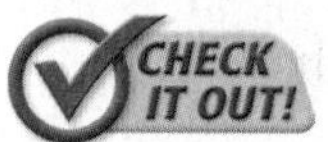

3. A survey of a random sample of voters shows that 38% of voters plan to vote for Gonzalez, 31% of voters plan to vote for Chang, and 31% plan to vote for Harris. The survey has a margin of error of ±3%. Does the survey clearly project the outcome of the voting? Explain.

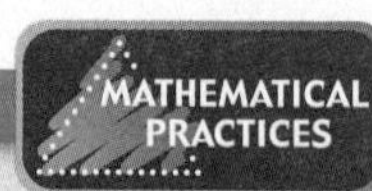

THINK AND DISCUSS

1. Explain the difference between a stratified sample and a cluster sample.
2. Describe how to find the interval that is likely to contain the actual percent of voters who favor a proposition, if a survey result is 63% and the margin of error is ±3%.
3. **GET ORGANIZED** Copy and complete the graphic organizer below. In each oval, write a sampling method.

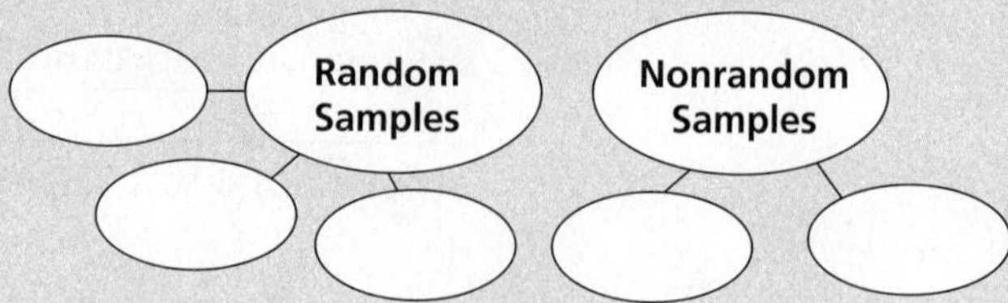

8-5 Exercises

GUIDED PRACTICE

1. **Vocabulary** Add and subtract the ___?___ from the reported percentage of people in favor of one response to find the interval in which the actual percentage lies. (*standard deviation; margin of error*)

SEE EXAMPLE 1

Classify each sample.

2. **Radio** The host of a radio show wants to know the listeners' favorite bands. He asks listeners to call the radio station and tell him their favorite bands.
3. **Customer Satisfaction** The owner of a lawn care company wants to know if his clients are satisfied with the company's service. He decides to ask 15 clients, randomly chosen from a list of his 32 clients, for their opinions of the company's service.
4. **Business** The general manager of a fast-food restaurant chain wants to determine the interest in a new food item that he is considering adding to the menu in the next month. He has the local manager at each of the 10 restaurants in the chain survey 20 randomly selected people throughout the day.

SEE EXAMPLE 2

5. **School Administration** A high school has 228 freshmen, 309 sophomores, 322 juniors, and 260 seniors enrolled. The principal of a school wants to know whether the students at the school would like to have a print-making class or a computer repair class offered as a spring elective. Classify each sampling method. Which is most accurate? Which is least accurate? Explain your reasoning.

   Method A Randomly choose 80 students who enter the cafeteria during the lunch period.

   Method B Randomly choose 20 freshmen, 20 sophomores, 20 juniors, and 20 seniors from the cafeteria during lunch period.

   Method C Survey every sophomore and senior.

For exercises 6–7, determine whether the survey clearly projects the winner. Explain your response.

SEE EXAMPLE 3

6. **Student Government** According to a survey of a random sample of students voting for student council president, 57% planned to vote for James and 43% plan to vote for Thea. The survey's margin of error is ±6%.
7. **Elections** A community association surveys its members about who they'd like to have as the next chairman, Hickory or Washington. In the survey, 36% preferred Hickory and 64% preferred Washington. The survey's margin of error is ±9%.

PRACTICE AND PROBLEM SOLVING

Independent Practice

For Exercises	See Example
8–15	1
17, 18	2
20, 21	3

Extra Practice

See Extra Practice for more Skills Practice and Applications Practice exercises.

Classify each sample.

8. **Television** The programming director of a local television station decides to conduct a survey to find out if the station's viewers prefer to watch the local news at 5:30 or 6:00. He asks each viewer to call a toll-free number and state his or her preference.
9. **Business** The manager of a credit union wants to know whether its members utilize the online services offered on the credit union's Web site. He randomly selects 20 members registered as local patrons of each at the five branches of the credit union to call and ask whether they use the online services.

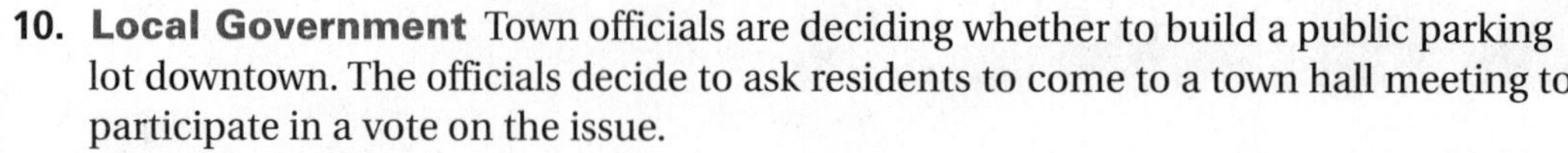

LINK

Optics

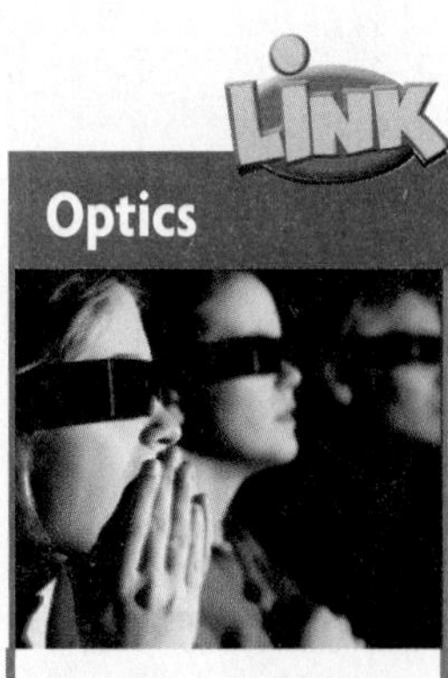

3D movies are shown by projecting two slightly different images on the screen. Each image is polarized, and each lens of the glasses permits only light that is polarized a certain way. In this way, the glasses control which of the two projections each eye is seeing, which your eyes combine to form a 3D image.

10. **Local Government** Town officials are deciding whether to build a public parking lot downtown. The officials decide to ask residents to come to a town hall meeting to participate in a vote on the issue.

11. **Human Resources** The human resources manager at a business wants to know how satisfied the company's employees are with their jobs. She surveys the 20 people who sit closest to her office.

12. **Scientific Research** The researchers at a hearing research center want to know if the music played during aerobics classes at health clubs is loud enough to cause hearing damage.They randomly choose 10 health clubs from the 150 health clubs in the area and measure the loudness of the music played during the aerobics classes.

13. **Customer Satisfaction** The manager of a movie theater wants to know how the movie viewers feel about the new 3D glasses at the theater. She asks every 30th person who exits the theater each Saturday night for a month.

14. **Journalism** A writer for a travel magazine wants to learn tourists' opinions about the nightlife in a city. She decides to visit a different tourist attraction every day for a week. She will have the magazine's interns, who are traveling with her, interview every tourist they see at each attraction.

15. **Student Government** Your class officers are planning a dance, and they want to know if they should hire a disc jockey or a live band. They decide to survey every tenth student as he or she leaves at the end of the school day.

16. **Write About It** Describe the difference between a simple random sample and a systematic sample.

17. **School Administration** A principal wants to know how teachers feel about changes to their schedule. He decides to ask a sample of 20 teachers. Classify each sampling method. Which is most accurate? Which is least accurate?

    Method A Randomly choose 2 teachers from each of the school's 10 departments of various sizes.

    Method B Survey the first 20 teachers who volunteer.

    Method C Randomly choose 20 teachers from an alphabetical list of the 60 teachers in the school.

18. **Quality Control** The manager of the produce department at a grocery store receives ten crates of oranges. She wants to examine the shipment to determine the quality of the fruit. Classify each sampling method. Which is most accurate? Which is least accurate?

    Method A Open the first crate and examine the fruit on the top.

    Method B Examine every fruit in a third of the crates.

    Method C Examine several randomly selected oranges from each of the ten crates.

19. **Critical Thinking** The editor of a school newspaper wants to survey students about which one of the following methods of communication they prefer: talking on the telephone, writing e-mail, or using text messaging.

   a. Describe a sampling method that can be used so that the sample will best represent the population.

   b. Write a question to ask the members of the sample.

20. **Local Government** Town officials in Lauraville want to build a new fire station on Northern Avenue. A local newspaper surveys residents about the new fire station. The results are shown below.

   Should the new fire station be on Northern Avenue?

   Yes 56%
   No 44%
   Margin of error: ±4%

   Does the survey clearly show the majority's preference? Explain your response.

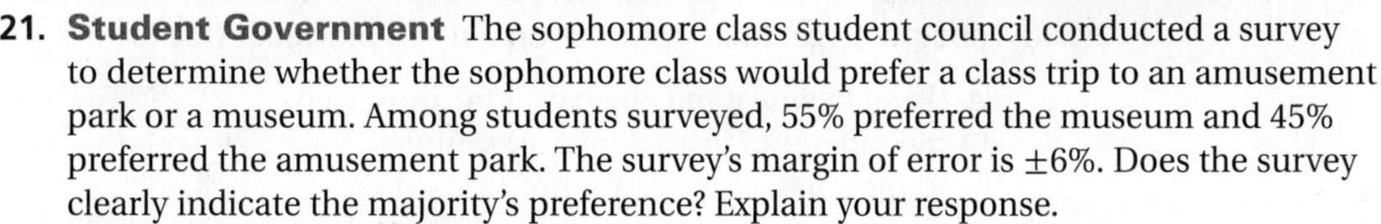

21. **Student Government** The sophomore class student council conducted a survey to determine whether the sophomore class would prefer a class trip to an amusement park or a museum. Among students surveyed, 55% preferred the museum and 45% preferred the amusement park. The survey's margin of error is ±6%. Does the survey clearly indicate the majority's preference? Explain your response.

22. **ERROR ANALYSIS** A reporter for a school newspaper surveys a random sample of students to find out for whom they plan to vote in an upcoming election for student body president. The survey's results are shown below.

   Diedrich 58%
   LeBlanc 42%
   Margin of error: ±12%

   Diedrich begins to celebrate his win based on the results of the survey. LeBlanc chides him and tells him not to be so sure he'll win in the actual election because even the survey is inconclusive. Who has a more accurate understanding of the results? Explain.

TEST PREP

23. The manager of a clothing store wants to know whether shoppers are satisfied with the store's products. She sends a survey to shoppers who signed up to be on the store's mailing list. Which type of sample is she gathering?

   Ⓐ convenience

   Ⓑ self-selected

   Ⓒ simple random

   Ⓓ systematic

Stockbyte/Getty Images

24. Every registered voter in Humboldt County receives a questionnaire in the mail they can fill out and return. What type of sample is this?

Ⓐ convenience Ⓒ simple random

Ⓑ self-selected Ⓓ systematic

25. Which of the following sampling types is not a probability sample?

Ⓐ stratified Ⓒ simple random

Ⓑ cluster Ⓓ convenience

26. Which tends to be the most reliable sampling technique?

Ⓕ stratified Ⓗ simple random

Ⓖ self-selected Ⓙ convenience

CHALLENGE AND EXTEND

27. **Local Government** City officials want to conduct a survey about an upcoming election. Describe how to generate a simple random sample, a systematic sample, and a stratified sample of the registered voters in the city.

28. **Medical Research** A medical conference has 500 participating doctors. The table lists the doctors' specialties. A researcher wants to survey a sample of 25 of the doctors to get their opinions on a new medical device.

Specialty	Number of Doctors
Dermatology	40
Oncology	140
Surgery	100
Geriatrics	120
Pediatrics	100

a. Explain why it may be better for the researcher to use a stratified sample rather than a simple random sample.

b. When a stratified sample is chosen using *proportionate allocation*, the size of each group in the sample is proportional to the size of the group in the population. Assuming the researcher uses proportionate allocation, how many dermatologists should be in the sample?

29. **///ERROR ANALYSIS///** Identify which of the following survey questions are likely to result in a biased sample. For each one you identify, revise the question to remove the tendency toward bias.

a. Do you favor the proposal to increase spending on technology in our schools?

b. Do you like the refreshing taste of sample A or the flat taste of sample B?

c. Would you rather read a boring book or watch an exciting movie?

d. Do you, like most people your age, enjoy watching music videos?

8-6 Binomial Distributions

CC.9-12.A.APR.6 Rewrite simple rational expressions in different forms... *Also* **CC.9-12.S.MD.4**

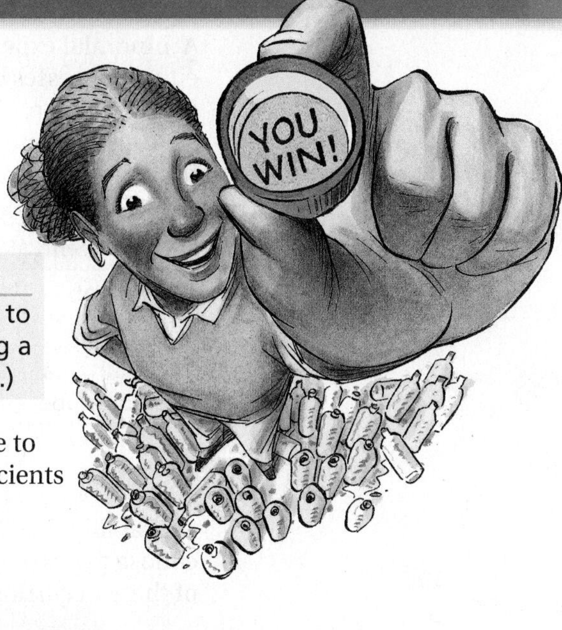

Objectives

Use the Binomial Theorem to expand a binomial raised to a power.

Find binomial probabilities and test hypotheses.

Vocabulary

Binomial Theorem
binomial experiment
binomial probability

Why learn this?

You can use binomial distributions to determine your chances of winning a marketing contest. (See Example 3.)

You know how to use Pascal's triangle to find binomial expansions. The coefficients of the expansion of $(x + y)^n$ are the numbers in Pascal's triangle, which are actually combinations.

Pascal's Triangle	Combinations (Binomial Coefficients)	Binomial Expansion
1	${}_0C_0$	$(x + y)^0 = 1$
1 1	${}_1C_0 \quad {}_1C_1$	$(x + y)^1 = x + y$
1 2 1	${}_2C_0 \quad {}_2C_1 \quad {}_2C_2$	$(x + y)^2 = x^2 + 2xy + y^2$
1 3 3 1	${}_3C_0 \quad {}_3C_1 \quad {}_3C_2 \quad {}_3C_3$	$(x + y)^3 = x^3 + 3x^2y + 3xy^2 + y^3$

The pattern in the table can help you expand any binomial by using the **Binomial Theorem**.

Binomial Theorem

For any whole number n,

$$(x + y)^n = {}_nC_0x^ny^0 + {}_nC_1x^{n-1}y^1 + {}_nC_2x^{n-2}y^2 + \cdots + {}_nC_{n-1}x^1y^{n-1} + {}_nC_nx^0y^n$$

EXAMPLE 1 Expanding Binomials

Use the Binomial Theorem to expand each binomial.

A $(x + y)^4$ *The sum of the exponents for each term is 4.*

$$(x + y)^4 = {}_4C_0x^4y^0 + {}_4C_1x^3y^1 + {}_4C_2x^2y^2 + {}_4C_3x^1y^3 + {}_4C_4x^0y^4$$
$$= 1x^4y^0 + 4x^3y^1 + 6x^2y^2 + 4x^1y^3 + 1x^0y^4$$
$$= x^4 + 4x^3y + 6x^2y^2 + 4xy^3 + y^4$$

B $(3p + q)^3$

$$(3p + q)^3 = {}_3C_0(3p)^3q^0 + {}_3C_1(3p)^2q^1 + {}_3C_2(3p)^1q^2 + {}_3C_3(3p)^0q^3$$
$$= 1 \cdot 27p^3 \cdot 1 + 3 \cdot 9p^2q + 3 \cdot 3pq^2 + 1 \cdot 1q^3$$
$$= 27p^3 + 27p^2q + 9pq^2 + q^3$$

Remember!

In the expansion of $(x + y)^n$, the powers of x decrease from n to 0 and the powers of y increase from 0 to n. Also, the sum of the exponents is n for each term.

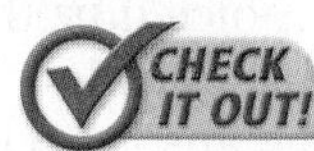

Use the Binomial Theorem to expand each binomial.

1a. $(x - y)^5$ **1b.** $(a + 2b)^3$

A **binomial experiment** consists of n independent trials whose outcomes are either successes or failures; the probability of success p is the same for each trial, and the probability of failure q is the same for each trial. Because there are only two outcomes, $p + q = 1$, or $q = 1 - p$. Below are some examples of binomial experiments:

Experiment	Success	Failure	P(success)	P(failure)
10 flips of a coin	Heads	Tails	$p = 0.5$	$q = 1 - p = 0.5$
100 rolls of a number cube	Roll a 3.	Roll any other number.	$p = \frac{1}{6}$	$q = \frac{5}{6}$

Suppose the probability of being left-handed is 0.1 and you want to find the probability that 2 out of 3 people will be left-handed. There are ${}_3C_2$ ways to choose the two left-handed people: LLR, LRL, and RLL. The probability of each of these occurring is $0.1(0.1)(0.9)$. This leads to the following formula.

Binomial Probability

If a binomial experiment has n trials in which p is the probability of success and q is the probability of failure in any given trial, then the **binomial probability** that there will be exactly r successes is:

$$P(r) = {}_nC_r\, p^r q^{n-r}$$

EXAMPLE 2 Finding Binomial Probabilities

One in 5 boats going through a *slough* at midday will bypass the harbor and head out to sea. Four boats are going through the slough.

A What is the probability that exactly 2 boats will head out to sea?

The probability that a boat will head out to sea is $\frac{1}{5}$, or 0.2.

$P(r) = {}_nC_r p^r q^{n-r}$

$P(2) = {}_4C_2(0.2)^2(0.8)^{4-2}$ *Substitute 4 for n, 2 for r, 0.2 for p, and 0.8 for q.*

$= 6(0.04)(0.64) = 0.1536$

The probability that exactly 2 of the boats will head out to sea is about 15.4%.

B What is the probability that at least 2 boats will head out to sea?

At least 2 boats is the same as exactly 2, 3, or 4 boats heading out to sea.

$P(2) + P(3) + P(4)$

$0.1536 + {}_4C_3(0.2)^3(0.8)^{4-3} + {}_4C_4(0.2)^4(0.8)^{4-4}$

$0.1536 + 0.0256 + 0.0016 = 0.1808$

The probability that at least 2 boats will head out to sea is about 18.1%.

2a. Students are assigned randomly to 1 of 3 guidance counselors. What is the probability that Counselor Jenkins will get 2 of the next 3 students assigned?

2b. Ellen takes a multiple-choice quiz that has 5 questions, with 4 answer choices for each question. What is the probability that she will get at least 2 answers correct by guessing?

EXAMPLE 3 Problem-Solving Application

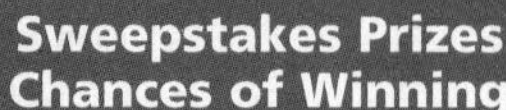

MATHEMATICAL PRACTICES

Make sense of problems and persevere in solving them.

Vince buys 10 juice drinks. What is the probability that he will get at least 2 prizes?

Sweepstakes Prizes Chances of Winning	
Free drink	1 in 5
Water bottle	1 in 22
T-shirt	1 in 250
Music player	1 in 100,000
Car	1 in 20,000,000
Any prize	1 in 4

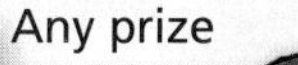

1 Understand the Problem

The **answer** will be the probability that Vince will get at least 2 prizes.

List the important information:

- Vince buys 10 juice drinks.
- The binomial probability that each bottle wins a prize is $\frac{1}{4}$.

2 Make a Plan

The direct way to solve the problem is to calculate $P(2) + P(3) + P(4) + \cdots + P(10)$.

An easier way is to use the complement. "Getting 0 or 1 prize" is the complement of "getting at least 2 prizes." Find this probability, and then subtract the result from 1.

3 Solve

Step 1 Find $P\big(0 \text{ or } 1 \text{ prize}\big)$.

$$P(0) \quad + \quad P(1)$$

$$= {}_{10}C_0\,(0.25)^0(0.75)^{10-0} + {}_{10}C_1\,(0.25)^1(0.75)^{10-1}$$

$$= 1(1)(0.75)^{10} + 10(0.25)(0.75)^9$$

$$\approx 0.0563 + 0.1877$$

$$\approx 0.2440$$

Step 2 Use the complement to find the probability.

$1 - 0.2440$ *Subtract from 1.*

≈ 0.7560

The probability that Vince will get at least 2 prizes is about 0.76.

4 Look Back

The answer is reasonable, as the expected number of winners is $\frac{1}{4}$ of 10, = 2.5, which is greater than 2. So the probability that Vince will get at least 2 prizes should be greater than 0.5.

3a. Wendy takes a multiple-choice quiz that has 20 questions. There are 4 answer choices for each question. What is the probability that she will get at least 2 answers correct by guessing?

3b. A machine has a 98% probability of producing a part within acceptable tolerance levels. The machine makes 25 parts an hour. What is the probability that there are 23 or fewer acceptable parts?

MATHEMATICAL PRACTICES

THINK AND DISCUSS

1. Describe and explain the sum of p and q for a binomial experiment.
2. Tell what three expressions are multiplied to find the probability that there will be r successes in a binomial experiment of n trials.

3. **GET ORGANIZED** Copy and complete the graphic organizer. Solve each problem that you include.

Binomial Experiments	
Probability	**Example**
Probability of r successes in n trials	
Probability of at least r successes	
Probability of at most r successes	
Probability using a complement	

8-6 Exercises

GUIDED PRACTICE

1. **Vocabulary** There are __?__ possible outcomes in each trial of a *binomial experiment.*

SEE EXAMPLE 1

Use the Binomial Theorem to expand each binomial.

2. $(x + 3)^4$
3. $(3x + 5)^3$
4. $(p - 2)^6$
5. $(x + y)^6$

SEE EXAMPLE 2

6. **School** The principal will randomly choose 6 students from a large school to represent the school in a newspaper photograph. The probability that a chosen student is an athlete is 30% (assume that this doesn't change). What is the probability that 4 athletes are chosen? What is the probability that at least 4 athletes are chosen?
7. **Shopping** Wilma bought 4 boxes of Crunch-A-Lot cereal. One out of every 5 boxes has a coupon for a free box of Crunch-A-Lot. What is the probability that Wilma got 3 coupons? What is the probability that Wilma got at least 2 coupons?

SEE EXAMPLE 3

8. **Manufacturing** In a manufacturing plant, there is a 2% chance that a stamp will be placed on a box upside down. The plant shipped 30 boxes today. What is the probability that at least 2 of the boxes have an upside-down stamp?

PRACTICE AND PROBLEM SOLVING

Use the Binomial Theorem to expand each binomial.

9. $(y + 5)^4$
10. $(2m - 1)^3$
11. $(4 + 3x)^5$
12. $(2a + 3c)^3$
13. **Civil Rights** In a survey of more than 100,000 high school students in 2004 by researchers at the University of Connecticut, 83% agreed with the statement "People should be allowed to express unpopular opinions." If 8 students are selected at random, what is the probability that at least 6 agree with the statement?

Independent Practice

For Exercises	See Example
9–12	1
13–14	2
15–16	3

Extra Practice

See Extra Practice for more Skills Practice and Applications Practice exercises.

14. Five marbles are randomly selected with replacement. The probability that a black marble is chosen is 15%. What is the probability that 2 marbles are black? What is the probability that at least 2 marbles are black?

15. Genetics A woman is expecting triplets. What is the probability that there are 2 girls and 1 boy? What is the probability that all 3 babies are girls?

16. Botany A tree has a 25% chance of flowering. In a random sample of 15 trees, what is the probability that at least 4 develop flowers?

Use the Binomial Theorem to expand each binomial.

17. $(x-y)^5$ **18.** $(c+6)^3$ **19.** $(4k-1)^4$ **20.** $(p+q)^7$

Evaluate $P(r) = {}_nC_r\, p^r q^{n-r}$, where $q = 1 - p$.

21. $p = 0.8, n = 3, r = 2$ **22.** $p = 0.5, n = 5, r = 1$ **23.** $p = \frac{1}{3}, n = 4, r = 2$

24. Travel A small airline overbooks flights on the assumption that several passengers will not show up. Suppose that the probability that a passenger shows up is 0.91. What is the probability that a 20-seat flight with 22 tickets sold will be able to seat all passengers who arrive?

25. Genetics A hedgehog has a litter of 4. What is the probability that all 4 are male? What is the probability that at least 3 are male?

Find each probability when a fair coin is tossed 10 times.

26. more than 7 heads **27.** at least 2 heads **28.** exactly 5 heads

29. Quality Control An auto part has a 95% chance of being made within its tolerance level and a 5% chance of being pulled as defective. What is the probability that in a box of 8 parts, no more than 1 is defective?

30. Graphing Calculator The **randBin** function simulates a binomial experiment and reports the number of successes. To simulate a binomial experiment with $n = 6$ and $p = 0.3$ five times, press MATH, move to **PRB**, select **randBin(** and enter 6, 0.3, and 5, separated by commas.

a. Simulate a binomial experiment with $n = 5$ and $p = 0.8$ five times.

b. Use the formula to find the probability of at least 4 successes.

c. How do your simulation results compare?

31. Multi-Step For $P = 0.8$ and $n = 10$, use a calculator to find the binomial probabilities for $r = 0$ to $r = 10$. Round to the nearest hundredth. Construct a bar graph of the probabilities. Describe the shape of the graph. How does the graph relate to the expected value?

32. Critical Thinking Which is more likely, a family with 4 children of 2 girls and 2 boys or a family of 4 children with 3 of one gender and 1 of the other? Explain.

MULTI-STEP TEST PREP

33. Based on historical data, the expected number of rainy days in San Antonio, Texas, during a calendar year is 82. Assume that rainy days are independent events.

a. What is the probability that there will be rain on any given day in San Antonio?

b. What is the probability that there will be exactly 3 rainy days during any given week?

c. What is the probability that there will be at least 3 rainy days during any given week?

34. There are 10 marbles in a bag. Half are striped, and half are not striped. Explain why choosing 3 marbles without replacement and noting whether they are striped does not fit the definition of a binomial experiment.

The trials in a binomial experiment are often called Bernoulli trials after Italian mathematician Jacob Bernoulli (1654–1705).

35. **Air Travel** In 2003, 20.46% of all direct flights from Dallas/Fort Worth to Los Angeles International Airport were delayed. Kelly flew that route 4 times and was on a delayed flight 3 times. What is the probability that she would have been on a delayed flight at least 3 times?

36. **Games** As the ball drops, it has an equal chance of making a left turn or right turn at each peg.
    a. What is the probability of a home run?
    b. What is the probability of an out?
    c. What is the probability of a hit (a single, double, triple, or home run)?
    d. How are the answers to parts **b** and **c** related?

37. **Pets** A survey showed that 45% of dog owners take their dog with them on vacation. If 5 dog owners go on vacation, what is the probability that fewer than 3 take their dog?

38. **Write About It** Describe a situation for which it would be beneficial to use the complement to find binomial probabilities.

Estimation **Use the graph for Exercises 39 and 40. The graph shows the probability of r successes in 10 trials of a binomial experiment.**

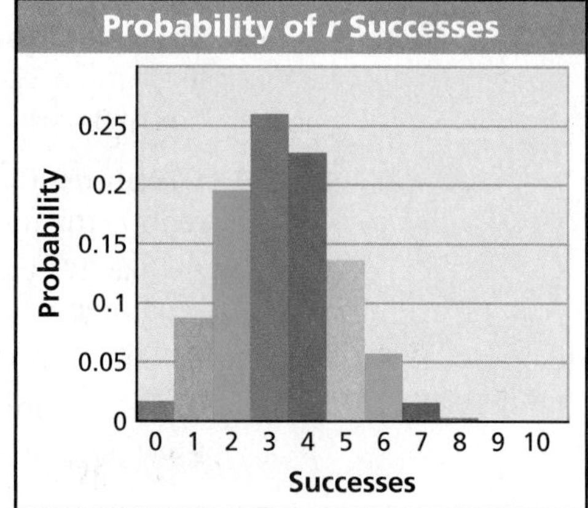

39. Estimate the probability of 2 or fewer successes.

40. Estimate the binomial probability p. Explain how you arrived at your answer.

41. Which of the following is NOT true about a binomial experiment?
    (A) The outcomes are either successes or failures.
    (B) The trials are dependent.
    (C) The probability of success is constant.
    (D) The trials are identical.

42. In a binomial experiment with 2 trials and a probability of success on each trial of 40%, what is the probability of exactly 1 success?
    (F) 16% (G) 36% (H) 48% (J) 52%

43. In a binomial experiment, the probability of success is 20%. Which gives the probability of 3 successes in 5 trials?
    (A) $3(0.2)^3(0.8)^2$ (B) $10(0.2)^3(0.8)^2$ (C) $3(0.2)^2(0.8)^3$ (D) $10(0.2)^2(0.8)^3$

44. **Gridded Response** A part has a 4% chance of being discarded for imperfections. Out of 10 randomly selected parts, what is the probability that no more than 1 has an imperfection? Round to the nearest whole percent.

45. **Short Response** About 18.8% of the people in the United States have one of the 100 most common last names. What is the probability that in a group of 10 randomly-selected people, 3 or more have one of these names?

CHALLENGE AND EXTEND

46. **Genetics** There is about a 0.1 probability that a person is left-handed. There are 650 people in an auditorium.
    a. What is the expected number of left-handed people in the auditorium? Explain.
    b. The standard deviation for a binomial experiment with n trials is given by $\sqrt{npq}$. Describe the number of left-handed people that you would expect in the auditorium as an interval within 1 standard deviation of the expected number.

47. Find each probability. Which is greater?
    a. rolling at least one 1 in 6 rolls of a die
    b. rolling at least two 1's in 12 rolls of a die

48. **Calculator** The **binomcdf** function, found in 2nd 0 (CATALOG), computes the cumulative probability of r successes in a binomial experiment of n trials with a probability of success p. To compute the probability of at most 3 successes in a binomial experiment with $n = 6$ and $p = 0.3$, use **binomcdf**, enter 6, 0.3, and 3, separated by commas, and press ENTER. Use the **binomcdf** function to find the probability of *at least* 4 successes in a binomial experiment of 20 trials with probability of success 0.4.

49. Show why any number ${}_{n+1}C_{r+1}$ in Pascal's triangle is the sum of the two numbers above it, ${}_nC_r$ and ${}_nC_{r+1}$ where r is not equal to 0 or n, and $n > 1$.

50. **Bowling** A bowler has a 0.4 probability of making exactly 1 strike in 2 frames, either in the first frame or the second frame. Assume that the bowler's probability p of getting a strike is the same for any frame.
    a. Write an equation and solve for p.
    b. Find the probability that the bowler makes strikes in both frames.

EXTENSION Normal Distributions

CC.9-12.S.ID.4 Use the mean and standard deviation of a data set to fit it to a normal distribution and to estimate population percentages…Estimate areas under the normal curve.

Objectives

Recognize normally distributed data.

Use the characteristics of the normal distribution to solve problems.

A *random variable* is associated with the possible outcomes of an experiment. For example, if the random variable X is associated with the possible outcomes of rolling a number cube, the possible values of X are 1, 2, 3, 4, 5, and 6.

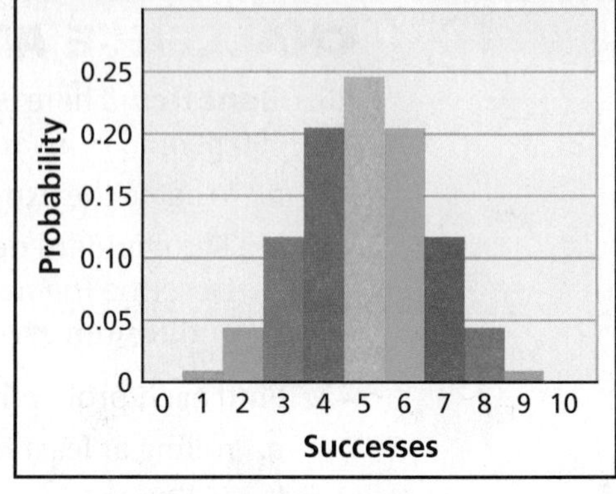

A *probability distribution* shows the probabilities that correspond to the possible values of a random variable. Probability distributions can be based on either discrete or continuous data.

The binomial distributions that you studied in were *discrete probability distributions* because there were a finite number of possible outcomes.

In a *continuous probability distribution,* the outcome can be any real number—for example, the time it takes to complete a task.

You may be familiar with the bell-shaped curve called the *normal curve.* A *normal distribution* is a function of the mean and standard deviation of a data set that assigns probabilities to intervals of real numbers associated with continuous random variables.

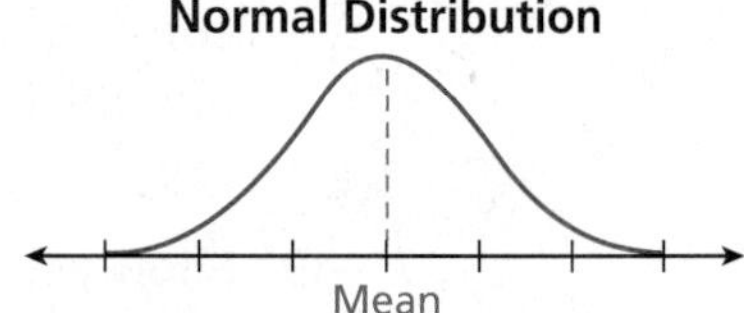

Normal Distributions
The probability assigned to a real-number interval is the area under the normal curve in that interval. Because the area under the curve represents probability, the total area under the curve is 1.
The maximum value of a normal curve occurs at the mean.
The normal curve is symmetric about a vertical line through the mean.
The normal curve has a horizontal asymptote at $y = 0$.

The figure shows the percent of data in a normal distribution that falls within a number of standard deviations from the mean.

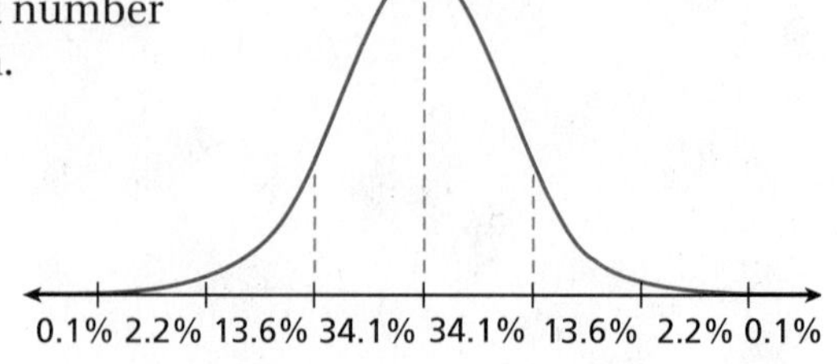

The diagram shows the following:

- About 68% lie within 1 standard deviation of the mean.
- About 95% lie within 2 standard deviations of the mean.
- More than 99.7% lie within 3 standard deviations of the mean.

EXAMPLE 1 Finding Normal Probabilities

The SAT is designed so that scores are normally distributed with a mean of 500 and a standard deviation of 100.

A **What percent of SAT scores are between 400 and 600?**

Both 400 and 600 are 1 standard deviation from the mean. Use the percents from the figure on the previous page.

34.1% + 34.1% = 68.2%

About 68.2% of the scores are between 400 and 600.

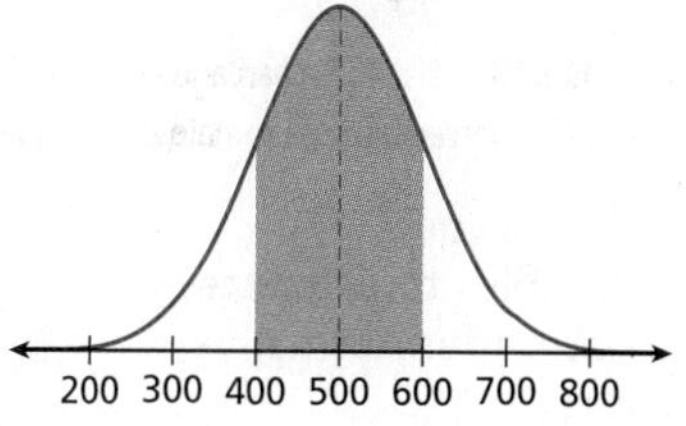

Reading Math

Each end of a normal distribution is called a *tail*.

B **What is the probability that an SAT score is above 600?**

Because the graph is symmetric, the right side of the graph shows 50% of the data.

50% − 34.1% = 15.9%

The probability that an SAT score is above 600 is about 0.159, or 15.9%.

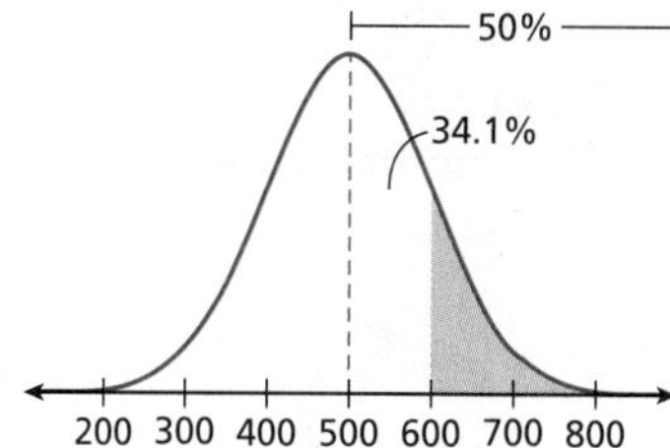

C **What is the probability that an SAT score is less than 300 or greater than 700?**

50% − (34.1% + 13.6%) = 2.3%

Because the curve is symmetric, the probability that an SAT score is less than 300 or greater than 700 is about 2(2.3%), or 4.6%.

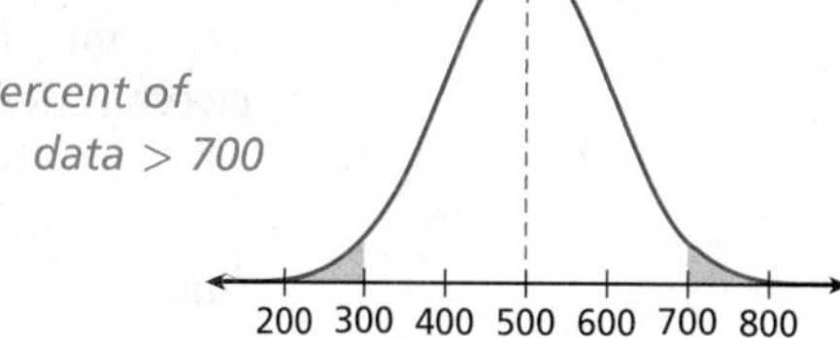

CHECK IT OUT!

Use the information above to answer the following.

1. What is the probability that an SAT score is above 300?

EXTENSION Exercises

A standardized test has a mean of 50 and a standard deviation of 4. Find the probability of test scores in the following ranges.

1. between 42 and 58
2. below 46
3. between 46 and 54

The amount of coffee in a can has a mean of 350 g and a standard deviation of 4 g.

4. What percent of cans have less than 338 g of coffee?
5. What is the probability that a can has between 342 g and 350 g of coffee?
6. What is the probability that a can has less than 342 g or more than 346 g of coffee?

Flight 202's arrival time is normally distributed with a mean arrival time of 4:30 P.M. and a standard deviation of 15 minutes.

7. Find the probability that an arrival time is after 4:45 P.M.
8. Find the probability that an arrival time is between 4:15 P.M. and 5:00 P.M.

8-7 Fitting to a Normal Distribution

CC.9-12.S.ID.4 Use the mean and standard deviation of a data set to fit it to a normal distribution and to estimate population percentages...Estimate areas under the normal curve.

Objectives
Use tables to estimate areas under normal curves.

Recognize data sets that are not normal.

Vocabulary
standard normal value

Who uses this?
Biologists can use standard normal values to study animal populations. (See Example 3.)

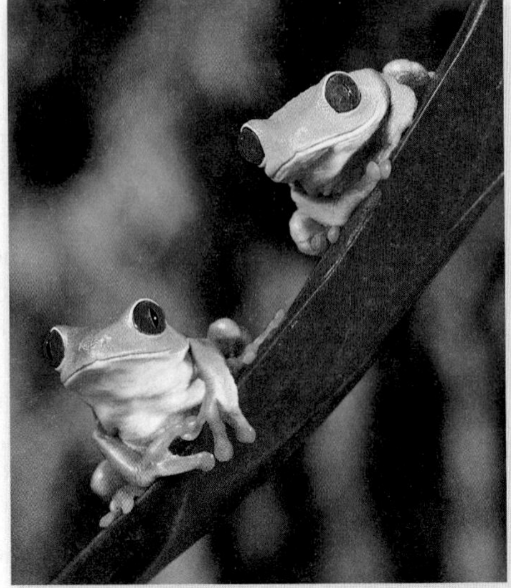

Normal curves are used in a wide variety of situations to estimate probabilities. Remember that the maximum value of the curve occurs at the mean, and that the curve is symmetric about a vertical line through the mean. If a random variable x has a mean of μ, and standard deviation of σ, then nearly all of the area under the curve (99.7%) is within three standard deviations from the mean (between $\mu - 3\sigma$ and $\mu + 3\sigma$).

The total area under a normal curve is always 1. The area under the curve between two x-values corresponds to the probability that x is between those values.

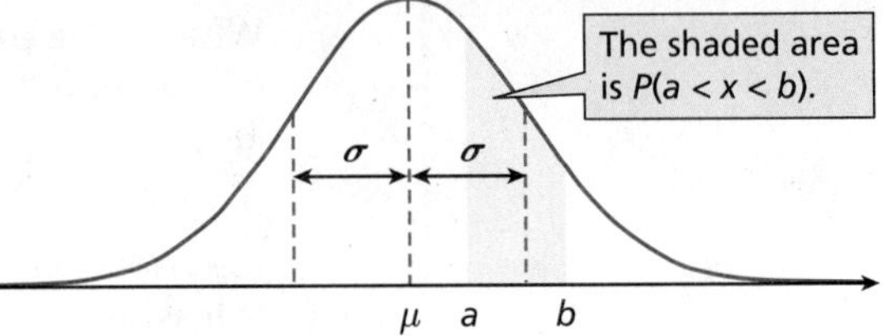

EXAMPLE 1 Estimating Probabilities Using a Normal Curve

Jamie can drive her car an average of 432 gallons per tank of gas, with a standard deviation of 36 miles. Use the graph to estimate the probability that Jamie will be able to drive more than 450 miles on her next tank of gas.

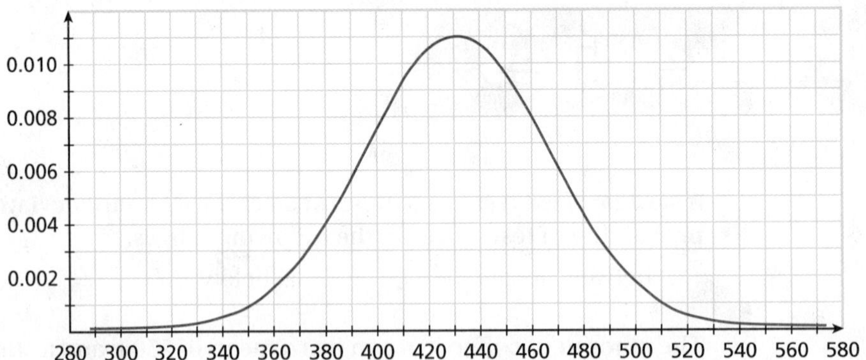

The area under the normal curve is always equal to 1. Each square on the grid has an area of $10(0.001) = 0.01$. Count the number of grid squares under the curve for values of x greater than 450. There are about 31 squares under the graph, so the probability is about $31(0.01) = 0.31$ that she will be able to drive more than 450 miles on her next tank of gas.

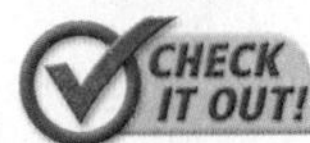

1. Using the graph above, estimate the probability that Jamie will be able to drive less than 400 miles on her next tank of gas.

All normal curves have the same basic shape. If μ is changed, the curve shifts left or right. If σ is changed, the curve is stretched vertically and compressed vertically, or vice versa. The *standard normal curve* has a mean of $\mu = 0$ and standard deviation of $\sigma = 1$, and is found by adjusting the variable in question, x, to match the standard normal curve.

Standard Normal Values

If a random variable x is normally distributed with mean μ and standard deviation σ, then the **standard normal value** of x is given by the following formula:

$$z = \frac{x - \mu}{\sigma}$$

The area under the normal curve between $x = a$ and $x = b$ is equal to the area between the standard normal values of a and b.

The table shows the approximate area under the standard normal curve for all values less than z for selected values of z.

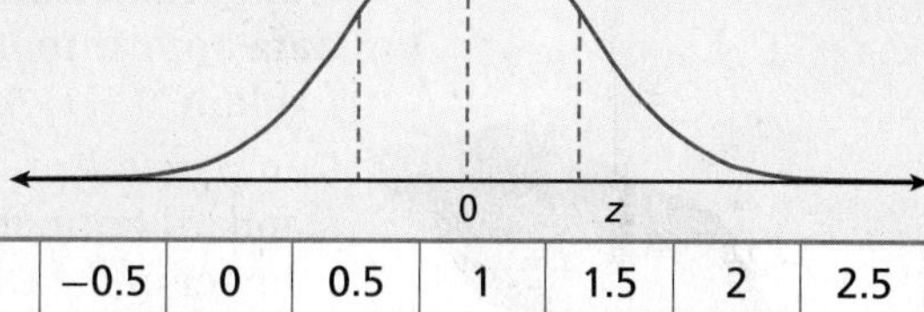

z	−2.5	−2	−1.5	−1	−0.5	0	0.5	1	1.5	2	2.5
Area	0.01	0.02	0.07	0.16	0.31	0.5	0.69	0.84	0.93	0.98	0.99

EXAMPLE 2 Using Standard Normal Values

Scores on a test are normally distributed with a mean of 75 and a standard deviation of 8.

A Estimate the probability that a randomly selected student scored less than 87.

First, find the standard normal value of 87, using $\mu = 75$ and $\sigma = 8$.

$$z = \frac{x - \mu}{\sigma} = \frac{87 - 75}{8} = \frac{12}{8} = 1.5$$

Use the table to find the area under the curve for all values less than 1.5, which is 0.93. The probability of scoring less than 87 is about 0.93.

B Estimate the probability that a randomly selected student scored between 71 and 75.

Find the standard normal values of 71 and 75. Use the table to find the areas under the curve for all values less than z.

$$z = \frac{71 - 75}{8} = \frac{-4}{8} = -0.5 \quad \text{Area} \approx 0.31 \qquad z = \frac{75 - 75}{8} = 0 \quad \text{Area} = 0.5$$

Subtract the areas to eliminate where the regions overlap. The probability of scoring between 71 and 75 is about $0.5 - 0.31 = 0.19$.

2. Scores on a test are normally distributed with a mean of 142 and a standard deviation of 18. Estimate the probability of scoring above 106.

There are many data sets in a variety of situations that can be modeled by using a normal curve. However, not all data is normally distributed. Sometimes the "tail" is longer on one side than the other, resulting in a skewed distribution.

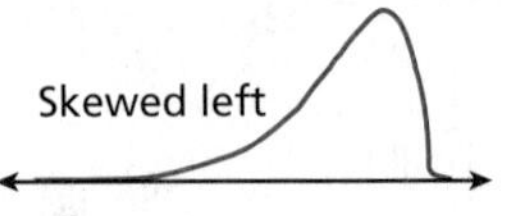

You can compare the data to the areas under the curve to determine whether the normal curve is a good fit for a data set. For example, about half of the values should be less than the mean.

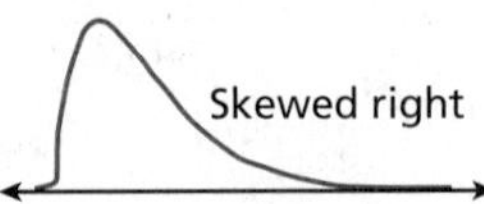

EXAMPLE 3 Determining Whether Data May Be Normally Distributed

A biologist is measuring the lengths of frogs in a certain location. The lengths of 20 frogs randomly chosen from the sample are shown. If the mean is 7.4 cm and the standard deviation is 0.8 cm, does the data appear to be normally distributed? Explain.

Length (cm)				
7.6	5.8	7.9	7.6	8.1
7.9	7.1	5.9	8.4	7.3
7.1	6.4	8.3	8.4	6.7
8.2	7.8	5.9	6.8	8.1

Compare the areas under the standard normal curve to the number of data values.

The projected number of values that corresponds to each value of z is close to the actual number of data values. The data appears to be normally distributed.

z	Area below z	x	Values below x	
			Projected	Actual
−2	0.02	5.8	0	0
−1	0.16	6.6	3	4
0	0.5	7.4	10	9
1	0.84	8.2	17	17
2	0.98	9	20	20

3. A random sample of salaries at a company is shown. If the mean is $37,000 and the standard deviation is $16,000, does the data appear to be normally distributed?

Salaries (thousands $)					
61	33	29	28	32	43
29	35	34	22	64	35
32	25	28	29	25	84

MATHEMATICAL PRACTICES

THINK AND DISCUSS

1. Explain how to find the standard normal value of the random variable x if the mean is 50 and the standard deviation is 5.
2. Describe the relationship between the areas under the normal curve for all x-values less than a and for all x-values greater than a.
3. **GET ORGANIZED** Copy the normal curve at right. Write the area in each section of the graph.

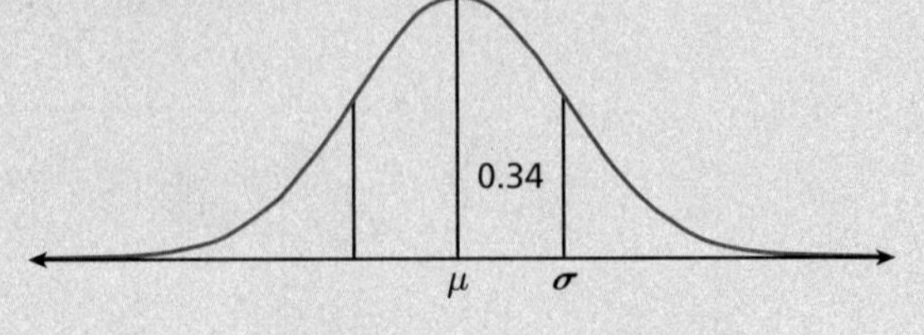

www.lifeonwhite.eu/Alamy

8-7 Exercises

GUIDED PRACTICE

1. **Vocabulary** How is the *standard normal value* of a statistic related to the mean and standard deviation of the random variable?

SEE EXAMPLE 1

2. In Ms. Bartholomew's class, the average amount of time spent studying for the test was 7.5 hours, with a standard deviation of 1.6 hours. Use the graph to estimate the probability that a randomly selected student spent more than 6 hours studying for the test.

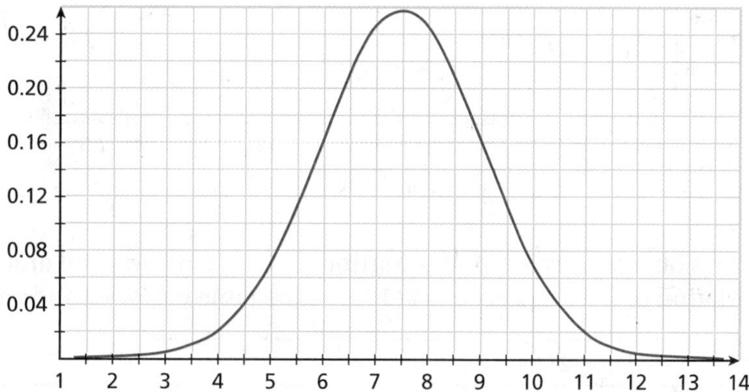

SEE EXAMPLE 2

Scores on a test are normally distributed with a mean of 70 and a standard deviation of 10. For questions 3–6, use the table below to find each probability.

z	−2.5	−2	−1.5	−1	−0.5	0	0.5	1	1.5	2	2.5
Area	0.01	0.02	0.07	0.16	0.31	0.5	0.69	0.84	0.93	0.98	0.99

3. A randomly selected student scored below 65.
4. A randomly selected student scored above 80.
5. A randomly selected student scored between 50 and 60.
6. A randomly selected student scored between 70 and 90.

SEE EXAMPLE 3

7. The weights of a sample of 30 potatoes from a farm are given below. If the mean is 0.5 lb and the standard deviation is 0.1 lb, does the data appear to be normally distributed? Explain.

0.55	0.45	0.50	0.44	0.61
0.45	0.49	0.53	0.75	0.49
0.44	0.46	0.35	0.45	0.48
0.66	0.33	0.60	0.49	0.66
0.41	0.52	0.58	0.41	0.64
0.39	0.54	0.48	0.57	0.43

PRACTICE AND PROBLEM SOLVING

Independent Practice

For Exercises	See Example
8	1
9–12	2
13	3

Extra Practice

See Extra Practice for more Skills Practice and Applications Practice exercises.

8. At a bottling plant, the amount of liquid in 12-ounce bottles is normally distributed with a mean of 12 ounces and a standard deviation of 0.15 ounces. If an inspector chooses a bottle at random, use the graph to estimate the probability that it will contain between 11.9 and 12.1 ounces.

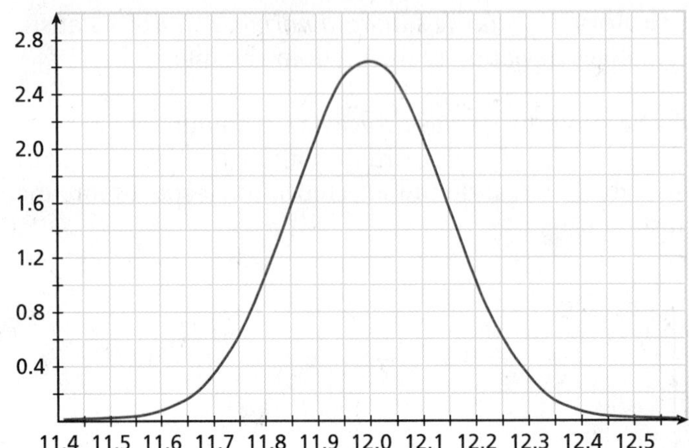

Scores on a test are normally distributed with a mean of 76 and a standard deviation of 6. For questions 9–12, use the table below to find each probability.

z	−2.5	−2	−1.5	−1	−0.5	0	0.5	1	1.5	2	2.5
Area	0.01	0.02	0.07	0.16	0.31	0.5	0.69	0.84	0.93	0.98	0.99

9. A randomly selected student scored below 64.

10. A randomly selected student scored above 70.

11. A randomly selected student scored between 85 and 91.

12. A randomly selected student scored between 73 and 79.

13. The heights of 24 children on a merry-go-round in a park are given below. If the mean of all the children at the park is 45 inches and the standard deviation is 6 inches, does the data appear to be normally distributed? Explain.

50	44	51	52	53	51	51	48
53	53	46	51	45	54	48	51
47	50	45	48	46	52	50	52

For a normally distributed random variable x with $\mu = 100$ and $\sigma = 16$, find each probability.

14. $x > 100$

15. $x < 140$

16. $92 < x < 108$

17. $x < 84$

18. $60 < x < 124$

19. $x < 68$ or $x > 132$

20. **Write About It** Apples at an orchard are packaged in approximately 5-lb bags. Each bag contains a whole number of apples. The weights are normally distributed with a mean of 5 lb and a standard deviation of 0.25 lb. An inspector weighs each bag, and rejects all bags that weigh less than 5 lb. Describe the shape of the distribution of the weights of the bags that are not rejected.

TEST PREP

21. If x is a normally distributed random variable with mean μ and standard deviation σ, then what is the probability that $x < \mu$?

   (A) 0.16
   (B) 0.5
   (C) 0.84
   (D) 0.99

22. Scores on a test are normally distributed with a mean of 78 and a standard deviation of 6. A student is selected at random. Which has the greatest probability?

   (F) The student's score is greater than 90.
   (G) The student's score is less than 69.
   (H) The student's score is between 78 and 81.
   (J) The student's score is between 63 and 72.

CHALLENGE AND EXTEND

Suppose that x is a normally distributed random variable with mean μ and standard deviation σ.

23. If $\mu = 65$ and $P(x > 70) = 0.31$, what is σ?

24. If $\sigma = 12$ and $P(x < 30) = 0.07$, what is μ?

25. If $P(x < 16) = 0.16$ and $P(x > 26) = 0.93$, what are μ and σ?

26. **Critical Thinking** Suppose that $f(x)$ is the equation of a normal curve with mean μ and standard deviation σ.

   a. What is the effect of the transformation $f(x - \mu)$?
   b. What is the effect of the transformation $f\left(\frac{x}{\sigma}\right)$?
   c. If $z = \frac{x - \mu}{\sigma}$, describe the relationship of $f(x)$ and $f(z)$.

Image Source/Getty Images

8-8 Analyzing Decisions

CC.9-12.S.MD.5 Weigh the possible outcomes...by...finding expected values... *Also* **CC.9-12.S.MD.7** (+)

Objectives
Explain that probability can be used to help determine if good decisions are made. Use probabilities to analyze decisions and strategies.

Who uses this?
Insurance policies use the probability of certain outcomes to calculate the premiums they will charge individuals. The individuals who examine the data are called actuaries.

In experiments with numerical outcomes, the **expected value (EV)** is the weighted average of the numerical outcomes of a probability experiment. To find the expected value of an event, multiply each possible outcome of the event by the likelihood of that outcome. The expected value of an event with k potential outcomes $n_1, n_2, n_3, \dots n_k$ each with probability $p_1, p_2, p_3 \dots p_k$ is given by $EV = n_1p_1 + n_2p_2 + n_3p_3 + \dots + n_kp_k$.

Probability

The probability *P* of an event *A* can be found by using

$$P(A) = \frac{\text{number of ways event occurs}}{\text{total number of outcomes}}$$

In addition, when conducting an experiment, the sum of the probabilities is equal to 1.

That is, for an experiment with events *A*, *B*, *C*, and *D* in an experiment,

$$P(A) + P(B) + P(C) + P(D) = 1$$

EXAMPLE 1 Finding Expected Value

A **What is the expected value of a six-sided number cube with sides labeled 1–6?**

The probability for each number is listed in the table below.

Value of Side	1	2	3	4	5	6
Probability	$\frac{1}{6}$	$\frac{1}{6}$	$\frac{1}{6}$	$\frac{1}{6}$	$\frac{1}{6}$	$\frac{1}{6}$

$$EV = 1\left(\frac{1}{6}\right) + 2\left(\frac{1}{6}\right) + 3\left(\frac{1}{6}\right) + 4\left(\frac{1}{6}\right) + 5\left(\frac{1}{6}\right) + 6\left(\frac{1}{6}\right)$$

$$EV = \frac{1 + 2 + 3 + 4 + 5 + 6}{6} = \frac{21}{6} = 3.5$$

Notice that the expected value of rolling the cube (3.5) is *not* one of the possible outcomes.

Brand X Pictures/Getty Images

B **What is the expected value of the sum of rolling two six-sided number cubes with sides labeled 1 through 6?**

Let $EV(X)$ represent the expected value of the first number cube and $EV(Y)$ represent the expected value of the second number cube.

$EV(X + Y) = EV(X) + EV(Y)$

Since both number cubes are labeled in the same way, use the information from part A to solve:

$EV(X) = 3.5$ and $EV(Y) = 3.5$

So, $EV(X) + EV(Y) = 7$.

The expected value of rolling two six-sided number cubes is 7.

1. What is the expected value of rolling the six-sided number cube as shown in the net below?

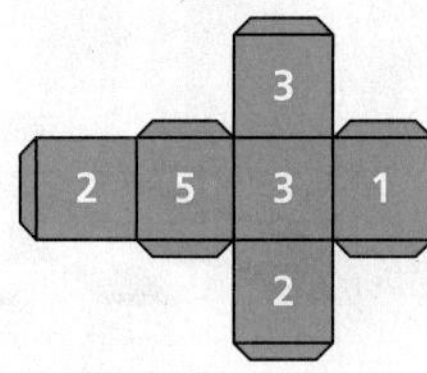

Expected value can be used to make decisions in business, insurance settings, traffic, games, and other situations. For example, if two people want to end a game early, they can use the expected value to verify who was the most likely to win.

EXAMPLE 2 Using Expected Value in Real-World Situations

Lisa has two choices of route when she goes to school. Route A always takes 15 minutes. Route B takes 12 minutes, unless there is a traffic jam, in which case that route will take 20 minutes. If the chance of a traffic jam is 15%, which route should she take?

To find the best route, compare the expected value for each route.

$EV(A) = 1(15) = 15$ minutes

$EV(B) = 0.15(20) + 0.85(12) = 3 + 10.2 = 13.2$ minutes

Since the expected value for Route B is lower than the estimated value of Route A, Lisa should take Route B.

2. Jack can take one of three routes to work each day. Route A takes 16 minutes, Route B takes 10 minutes, and Route C takes 20 minutes. There is a 40% chance he will encounter an accident in Route A, which increases travel time to 25 minutes. There is also a 20% chance he will encounter a traffic jam if he takes Route B, which increases his travel time to 40 minutes. He has a 10% chance of experiencing a delay in Route C, which increases his travel time to 32 minutes. Which route should Jack take to work each day?

EXAMPLE 3 The Monty Hall Problem

The Monty Hall problem is a problem derived from a TV game show. On the show, the contestant is challenged to choose from one of the three closed doors.

Two of the doors hide goats, while the third door hides a prize. Once the contestant picks a door, the host, who knows the contents behind each door, opens one of the other doors to reveal a goat. If both remaining doors contain a goat, the host chooses randomly which door to reveal. The host then offers the contestant a chance to stay with their original choice of door or switch his choice to the other remaining door. What should the contestant do?

The Monty Hall problem is a tricky problem. Many assume changing doors either does not matter or that each door has the same probability of containing the prize. They reason that since there is one prize and two doors, there is a 50% chance each of the two remaining doors will contain the prize. But that is incorrect! Let's examine at all the possibilities.

Assume the contestant picks door A initially.

Contents Behind Each Door			Results	
Door A	Door B	Door C	Result if door is switched	Result if door is not switched
Car	Goat	Goat	Goat	Car
Goat	Car	Goat	Car	Goat
Goat	Goat	Car	Car	Goat

Notice that if the contestant switches doors, they have a $\frac{2}{3}$ chance of winning the prize while they only have a $\frac{1}{3}$ chance of winning the car if they keep the door they initially chose. The expected value of switching is twice that of staying with the original choice!

If you were in the game show, would you switch doors?

Photodisc/Getty Images

3. Mikayla is applying to 3 colleges. She makes estimates of her chances of being accepted, and estimates of her chances of receiving financial aid from each, presented below:

	% chance of acceptance	% chance of financial aid
College A	75%	30%
College B	65%	40%
College C	70%	45%

At which college is she most likely to be both accepted and receive financial aid?

Expected Value

In an experiment with k events, n_k represents the value of each individual event, and $P(n_k)$ represents the probability of n_k.

Outcome	1	2	...	k
Value	n_1	n_2	...	n_k
Probability	$P(n_1)$	$P(n_2)$	...	$P(n_k)$
	$n_1P(n_1)$	$n_2P(n_2)$		$n_kP(n_k)$

The expected value is

$EV = n_1P(n_1) + n_2P(n_2) + \cdots + n_kP(n_k)$

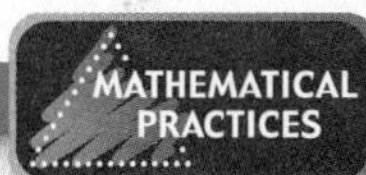

THINK AND DISCUSS

1. Explain how the expected value in an experiment is different from the individual probabilities.
2. Give an example of a situation where you could use expected value in your everyday life. Describe how you could use expected value to help you make a decision.
3. **GET ORGANIZED** Copy and complete the graphic organizer. Use the table to find the expected value of the experiment with the given probability distribution.

Outcome	A	B	C	
Value	10	5	1	
Probability	0.05	0.2	0.75	Expected Value

8-8 Exercises

GUIDED PRACTICE

1. **Vocabulary** The weighted average of the outcomes in an experiment is its __?__ (*expected value* or *probability*).

SEE EXAMPLE 1

Find the expected value for each of the number cubes with the given sides.

2.
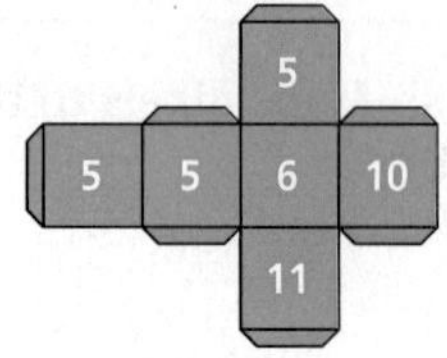

3.
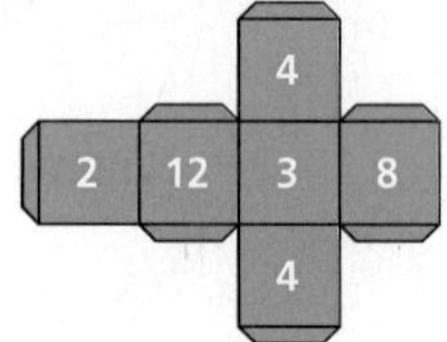

4.
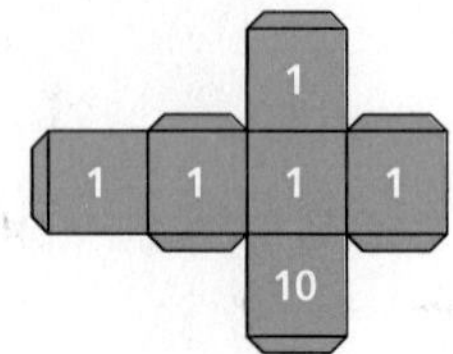

5. Find the expected value for the sum of the number cubes in exercises 2 and 3.

SEE EXAMPLE 2

6. Gloria can take two routes to get to work. Route A takes 14 minutes without traffic, but 25 minutes with traffic. Route B takes 10 minutes without traffic, and 30 minutes with traffic. She estimates a 20% chance of encountering traffic on Route A and a 40% chance of encountering traffic on Route B. Which route would you recommend Gloria take? Explain.

SEE EXAMPLE 3

7. In a game show, a contestant must choose a question from one of three categories. Questions in category A are worth \$500, but there is a penalty of \$100 for each incorrect answer. Questions in category B are worth \$100, with a \$20 penalty for incorrect answers. Questions in category C are worth \$50, with no penalty for incorrect answers. The probability of answering correctly is 0.1 for category A, 0.3 for category B, and 0.6 for category C. Which category has the highest expected value?

PRACTICE AND PROBLEM SOLVING

Independent Practice

For Exercises	See Example
8–11	1
12–13	2
23	3

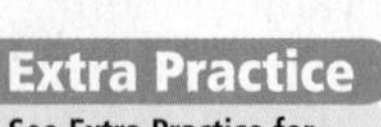

See Extra Practice for more Skills Practice and Applications Practice exercises.

Find the expected value for each of the number cubes with the given sides.

8.
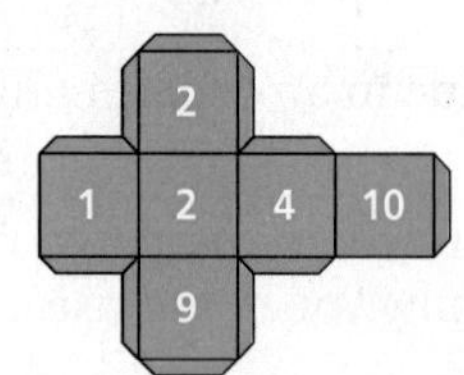

9.
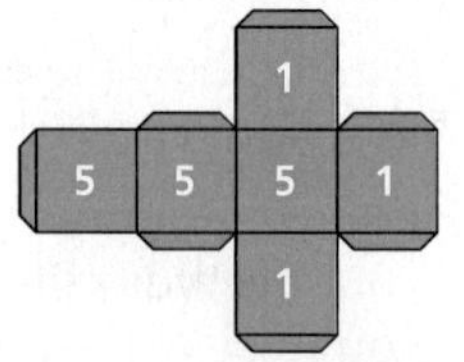

10.
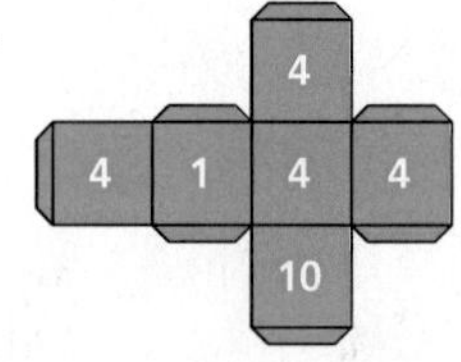

11. Find the expected value for the sum of the number cubes in exercises 9 and 10.

12. Tristan is buying a new camera, and is deciding whether to purchase a 1-year warranty. The warranty costs \$50, and covers all repairs. If he does not get the warranty, then within the first year he estimates there is a 5% chance he will have to replace the camera for \$180, and a 15% chance that he will need a repair costing \$60. Should he buy the warranty? Explain.

CreativeAct-Technology series/Alamy

13. A high school is having a raffle to raise funds. The top prize is worth \$2,000 and the probability of winning is 0.1%. The second prize is worth \$150 and the probability of winning is 2%. Using expected value, find the expected value of a raffle ticket.

Find the expected value for each of the spinners shown.

14.

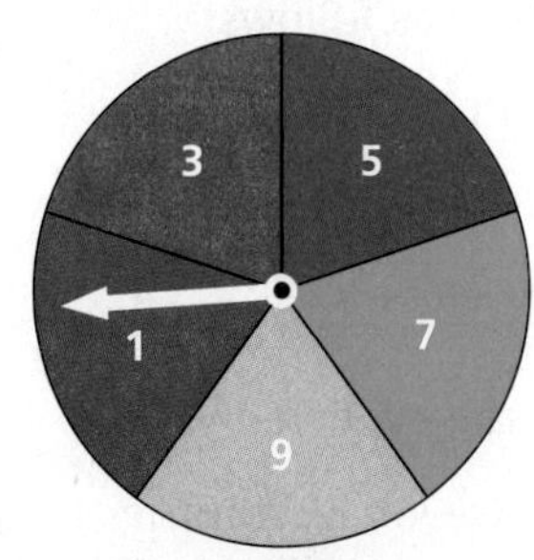

15.

16.

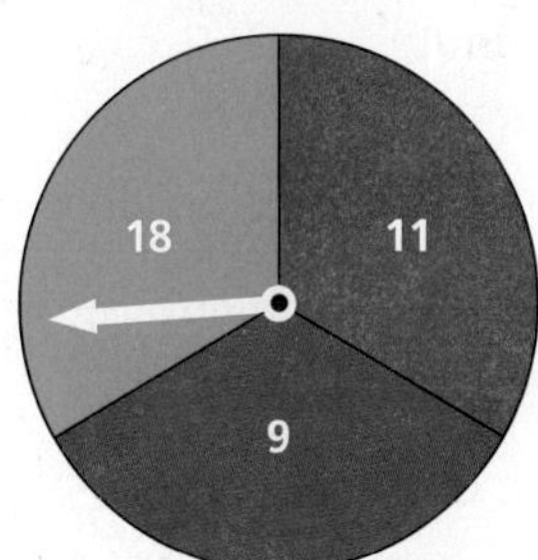

17.

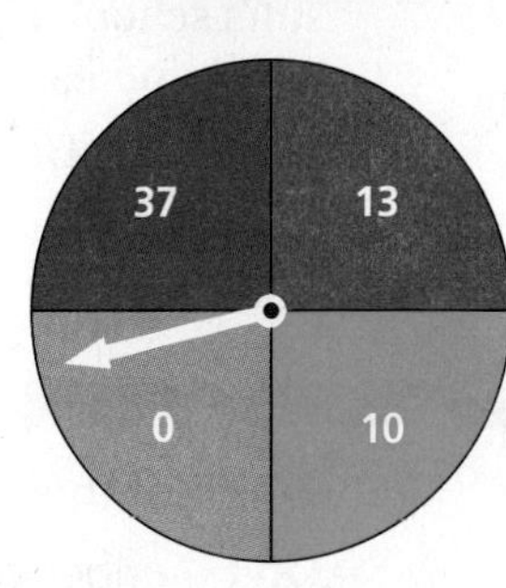

Find the expected value for each of the unequal spinners shown.

18.

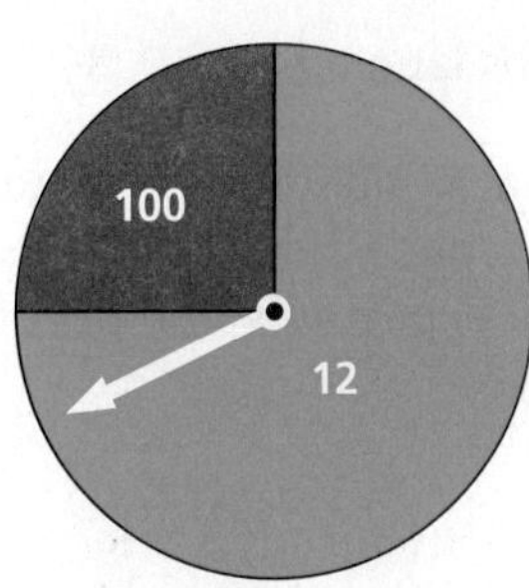

19.

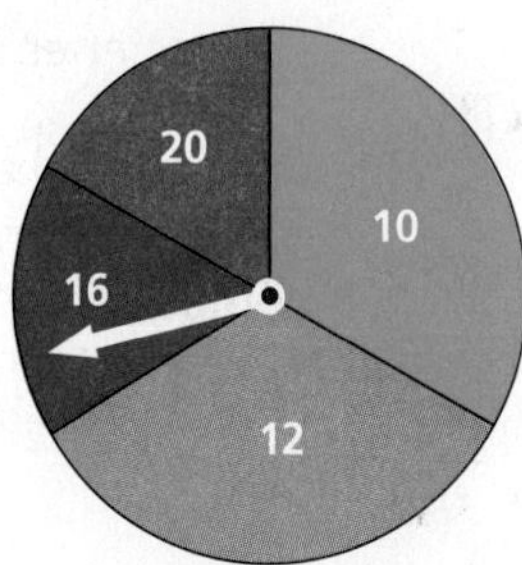

20.

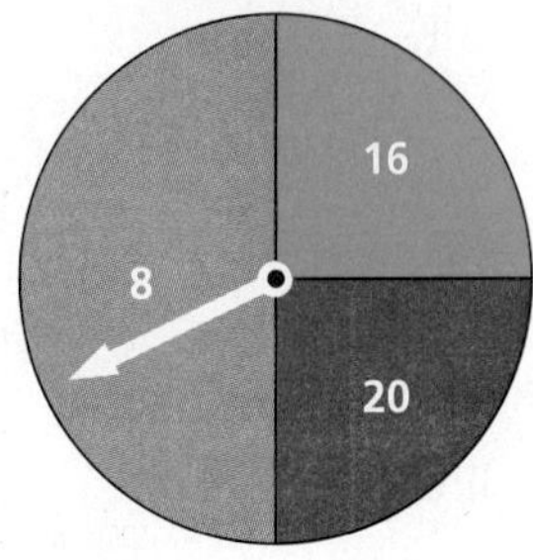

21.

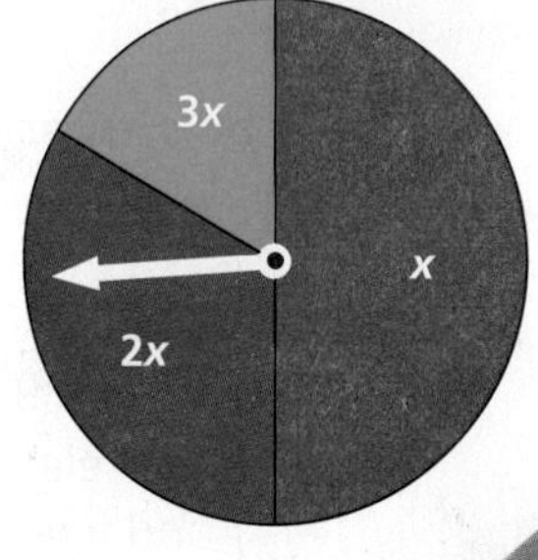

22. **Estimation** Jack has a bag of marbles for a game. There are 30 marbles in the bag, 8 are red, 12 are blue, and 10 are green. Each red marble is worth 5 points, each blue marble is worth 3 points and each green marble is worth 2 points. What is the approximate expected value of picking a marble from the bag?

23. **Write About It** Suppose that an item is insured for $10,000. The insurance company estimates that there is a 1% chance that they will have to pay out on the policy. If they need to make a profit of 50%, explain what they should charge for the policy.

Photodisc/Getty Images

24. **ERROR ANALYSIS** Camilla estimated the expected value of an 8-sided die with sides labeled 2, 3, 3, 6, 6, 6, 6, and 16 as follows:

$$2\left(\frac{1}{8}\right) + 3\left(\frac{1}{8}\right) + 6\left(\frac{1}{8}\right) + 16\left(\frac{1}{8}\right)$$

$$\frac{2 + 3 + 6 + 16}{8} = \frac{27}{8} \approx 3.4$$

Identify the error in the calculation of the expected value.

25. **Multi-Step** Most of the time, it takes Devon 32 minutes to get from work to his son's school. He has a 40% chance of hitting traffic on his way to pick his son up, which increases his travel time to 58 minutes.

a. What is Devon's average travel time?

b. Is the actual travel time for a given trip likely to be close to the average? Explain.

26. Which of the following has the highest expected value?

Ⓐ number cube with sides 1, 4, 4, 4, 10, 15

Ⓑ number cube with sides 2, 4, 6, 8, 10, 12

Ⓒ spinner divided into 5 equal sections labeled 3, 5, 7, 9, 11

Ⓓ spinner divided in 3 equal sections labeled 10, 10, 30

27. Gary and Ed are playing a game with a six-sided number cube labeled 1-6. If the cube lands on the numbers 1 or 2, they get 1 point. If the cube lands on any other number, they get 4 points. What is the expected value of rolling the number cube?

Ⓐ 1

Ⓑ 2

Ⓒ 3

Ⓓ 4

28. What is expected value?

Ⓐ the probability of an event.

Ⓑ the sum of all possible outcomes.

Ⓒ the weighted average of outcomes.

Ⓓ the relationship containing both direct and inverse variation.

CHALLENGE AND EXTEND

29. **Business** A shoe company has sales projections as shown below for three products. What is the expected value of the sales projections, in thousands?

Product	No. of Units Available	Expected Sales (as % of Units Available)	Price per Unit
A	450	25%	$59
B	320	60%	$79
C	275	15%	$119

30. **Write About It** Explain a situation in which you can use mathematics to make a decision. What type of mathematics is involved in making the decision?

Peter M. Fisher/Corbis

CHAPTER 8

SECTION 8B

MATHEMATICAL PRACTICES Look for regularity in repeated reasoning.

The Binomial and Normal Distributions

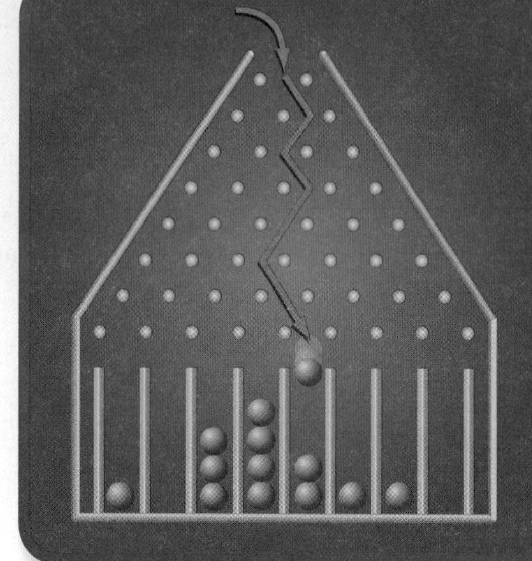

Bell of the Balls A bean machine, or Galton box, can be used to illustrate the normal distribution. Balls randomly bounce down a grid of pegs and collect in boxes. The piles of balls will resemble the bell curve of a normal distribution.

Use the figure to answer questions 1–3. The first 4 rows of pegs are shown.

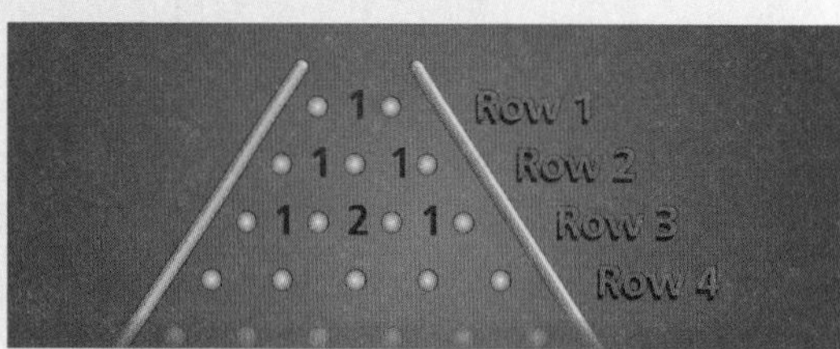

1. The blue numbers between the pegs indicate the number of possible paths for a ball to arrive at that location. Determine the numbers for Row 4.
2. What pattern do you recognize in the numbers?
3. Explain why for any row, there will be 1s in the first and last locations.
4. The numbers of paths to locations in the final row are shown. Directly below are box 1, box 2,..., box 8.

   1 7 21 35 35 21 7 1

   Find the probability that a ball will end up in box 4.
5. For a machine with $n + 1$ pegs in its final row, the probability of a ball ending up in box k is $P(\text{box } k) = \binom{n}{k} 0.5^k (1 - 0.5)^{n-k}$. Verify this formula for your answer to exercise 4.

Quiz for Lessons 8-5 Through 8-8

8-5 Sampling Distributions

1. The neighborhood association wants to know whether they should resurface the jogging trail at the local park. They survey the opinion of every other household on 3 of the 10 blocks in the neighborhood. What kind of sample is this?
2. According to a survey of a random sample of households, 62% of the neighborhood prefers not to add a bench to the park. The survey's margin of error is 8%. Determine whether the survey clearly projects the decision. Explain.

8-6 Binomial Distributions

3. Use the Binomial Theorem to expand $(m - 2n)^3$.

The spinner shown is spun 10 times.

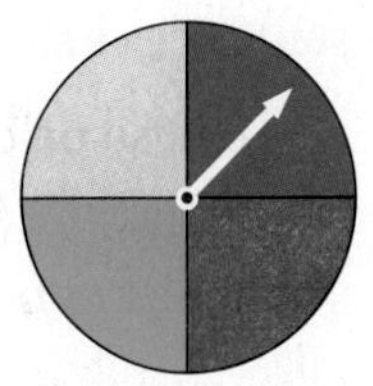

4. What is the probability that the spinner will land in the blue area exactly 5 times?
5. What is the probability that the spinner will land in the blue area at least 3 times?

A multiple-choice quiz has 5 questions. Each question has 3 possible answers. A student guesses the answer to each question. Find each probability.

6. The student answers all 5 questions correctly.
7. The student answers exactly 1 question correctly.
8. The student answers all 5 questions incorrectly.
9. The student answers at least 1 question correctly.

8-7 Fitting to a Normal Distribution

10. Scores on a test are normally distributed with a mean of 82 and a standard deviation of 6. Estimate the probability that a randomly selected student scored more than 85.
11. The weights in grams of a sample of 24 walnuts are shown. If the mean is 20 g and the standard deviation is 2.45 g, do the data appear to be normally distributed? Explain.

20	18	23	21	19	23
20	15	20	22	18	19
17	19	25	21	22	23
20	16	17	19	22	21

8-8 Analyzing Decisions

12. Suppose that an art dealer wants to insure a statue valued at $5000. The dealer estimates that there is a 2% chance that the insurance company will have to pay out on the policy. The company charges $110 for the policy. Should the dealer purchase the policy? Explain.

CHAPTER 8

Study Guide: Review

Vocabulary

biased sample
binomial experiment
binomial probability
Binomial Theorem
census
cluster sample
control group
controlled experiment
convenience sample
expected value
experiment
hypothesis testing
margin of error
null hypothesis
observational study
parameter
population
probability sample
random sample
randomized comparative experiment
sample
simple random sample
standard normal value
statistic
stratified sample
systematic sample
treatment group
variance

Complete the sentences below with vocabulary words from the list above.

1. A(n) ___?___ can also be called a weighted average.
2. A ___?___ is a sample where every member of the population being sampled has a nonzero probability of being selected.
3. ___?___ is used to determine whether the difference in two groups is likely to be caused by chance.

8-1 Measures of Central Tendency and Variation

EXAMPLES

■ **The probability distribution for the number of substitute teachers needed is given. Find the expected number of substitute teachers needed on any given day.**

Number of Substitutes *n*	0	1	2	3	4
Probability of *n* Substitutes	0.05	0.08	0.38	0.41	0.08

$0(0.05) + 1(0.08) + 2(0.38) + 3(0.41) + 4(0.08) = 2.39$

The expected number of substitutes is 2.39.

EXERCISES

Find the mean, median, and mode of each data set.

4. 5, 8, 0, 8, 6
5. 12, 15, 13, 13, 15, 12
6. The probability distribution for the number of arrests made in a small town on one day is given below. Find the expected number of arrests on any one day.

Number of Arrests *n*	0	1	2	3
Probability of *n* Arrests	0.65	0.22	0.1	0.03

8-2 Data Gathering

EXAMPLES

- **A mall wants to determine if staying open an additional hour on weekdays would interest shoppers. They survey random customers inside the mall one hour before closing each weekday. Are the results of the survey likely to be representative of the population? Explain.**

  No; although the survey is random, it does not consider shoppers that are in the mall earlier in the day. It also does not survey customers on the weekend, which may be interested in shopping later during the week.

EXERCISES

For exercises 7–9, determine whether the survey is likely to be representative of the population.

7. A coach asks every player on his basketball team in they think afterschool sports should be required for all students.
8. A city sends out surveys to random homeowners about the city's recycling plan.
9. A website asks customers if they prefer to shop online or go to one of their stores.
10. In a survey of 100 dentists, 63 said they would recommend a new type of floss. In a similar survey of 1,400 dentists, how many do you predict would recommend the floss?

8-3 Surveys, Experiments, and Observational Studies

EXAMPLES

- **Janet wants to determine if birds sing more on sunny days than on overcast days. Should Janet perform an experiment, or conduct an observational study? Explain.**

  Observational study; it is not practical for Janet to perform an experiment, because she has no control over the weather. It would also be very difficult to track particular birds. However, Janet can observe all birds in a particular area on sunny and overcast days.

EXERCISES

The studies described below are randomized comparative experiments. Describe the treatment, the treatment group, and the control group.

11. A psychologist wants to determine if working below fluorescent lights could cause lethargy. At a particular company new lights are installed, where half are fluorescent and half are incandescent. A month later, workers take a survey about their energy level while at work.
12. A dog food company wants to know if dogs prefer their brand of dog food to other brands. They send samples to 1,000 dog owners that use other brands. 500 of the samples were the company's brand, and 500 were not. They then send surveys to all the dog owners.

8-4 Significance of Experimental Results

EXAMPLES

A fertilizer company wants to test whether their fertilizer improves tomato plant yields better than other fertilizers. The results from several farms are shown in the table.

Total Tomato Yields

Their Fertilizer			Other Fertilizer		
141	202	190	154	193	180
187	165	171	196	169	165

- **State the null hypothesis.**

  The tomato yields from farms that use the company fertilizer will be the same as the farms that use other fertilizers.

- **Compare the results of the two groups. Does the company have enough evidence to reject the null hypothesis?**

  No; the tomato yields are too similar for the two groups. The medians differ by only 4.5 tomatoes.

EXERCISES

Jumpy-Jump inserts claim to increase a basketball player's vertical leap by about 2 inches. The data show the vertical leaps (in inches) for several players, with and without the inserts.

Vertical Leap (in.)

Without Insert				With Insert			
23	27	27	33	24	27	28	35
31	30	30	35	30	36	31	36

13. State the null hypothesis.
14. Compare the results of the two groups. Does the company have enough evidence to reject the null hypothesis?
15. A light bulb manufacturer claims that its bulbs last 400 hours. In a random sample of 3,000 bulbs, the mean was 390 hours with a standard deviation of 200 hours. Is there enough evidence to reject the claim?

8-5 Sampling Distributions

EXAMPLES

A travel website wants to survey about 1000 users about flight preferences. Classify each sample.

- **500 male members and 500 female members are emailed at random.**

  Stratified random sample; members are divided by gender then selected randomly.

- **The website posts the survey online, and uses the first 1000 respondents.**

  Self-selected sample; the users of the website voluntarily take the survey.

EXERCISES

In exercises 16 and 17, determine whether the survey clearly projects the winner. Explain your response.

16. A newspaper claims that 38% of voters will vote for Matthews in an election, and that 62% will vote for Harris. The margin of error is ±11%.
17. A website will have users vote for their all-time favorite flavor of ice cream, chocolate or vanilla. A survey shows that 53% will vote for vanilla, and 47% will vote for chocolate. The margin of error is ±5%.
18. A chef wants to open a restaurant. He wants to determine what type of food locals would most like to see offered. He surveys random locals walking around town on the weekend. What type of sample is this?

8-6 Binomial Distributions

EXAMPLES

Sheila bought 5 energy bars. Each has a 1 in 10 chance of winning a free energy bar.

- What is the probability that Sheila will win 3 energy bars?

$P(3) = {}_5C_3(0.1)^3(0.9)^{5-3}$ $\quad P(r) = {}_nC_r p^r q^{n-r}$

$= 10(0.001)(0.81) = 0.0081$

EXERCISES

Use the Binomial Theorem to expand each binomial.

19. $(5 + 2x)^3$ **20.** $(x - 2y)^4$

21. The probability of Ike making a free throw is 0.65. He shoots 75 free throws. Find the expected number of free throws made and the standard deviation.

22. A spinner is divided into 6 equal sections, numbered 1 through 6. It is spun 8 times. What is the probability that the spinner lands on 1 exactly 3 times? What is the probability that the spinner lands on 1 at least 2 times?

8-7 Fitting to a Normal Distribution

EXAMPLES

- **The scores of an algebra exam have a mean of 79 and a standard deviation of 7. Use the graph to estimate the probability that a score was less than 74.**

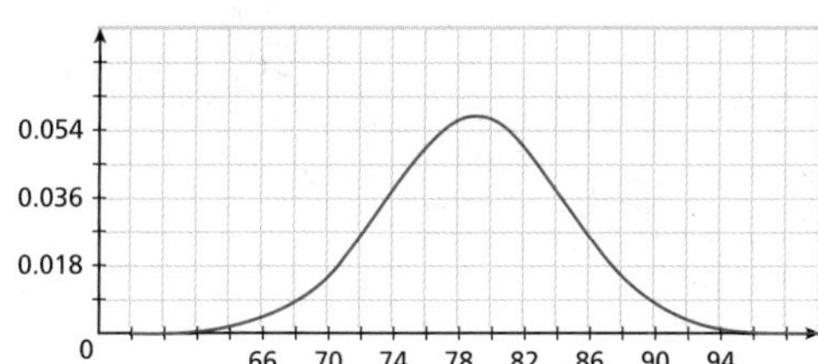

Each square on the grid has an area of $2(0.009) = 0.018$. There are about 8 squares below the curve for values of x less than 74. So, the probability is about $0.018(8) = 0.144$, or about 14%.

EXERCISES

The heights of players in a basketball league have a mean of 77 inches and a standard deviation of 4 inches. Estimate the given probability for the height of a randomly selected player.

23. at least 73 inches

24. at most 83 inches

25. between 69 inches and 75 inches

For a normally distributed random variable x with $\mu = 400$ and $\sigma = 25$, find each probability.

26. $x > 425$

27. $350 < x < 412.5$

28. $x < 375$ or $x > 450$

8-8 Analyzing Decisions

EXAMPLES

- **A carnival game involves tossing 3 coins for 2 ride tokens. If all 3 coins come up heads or tails, the player get 5 tokens. What is the expected value of the game?**

There are $2 \cdot 2 \cdot 2 = 8$ ways that three coins can be tossed. Two of these results are all heads and all tails, so $P(\text{player gets 5 tokens}) = 0.25$. So, there is a 25% chance of a net gain of 3 tokens, and a 75% chance of a net loss of 2 tokens.

$EV = 0.25(3) + 0.75(-2) = -0.75$

EXERCISES

What is the expected value of rolling the six-sided number cube as shown in the net below?

29.

30.

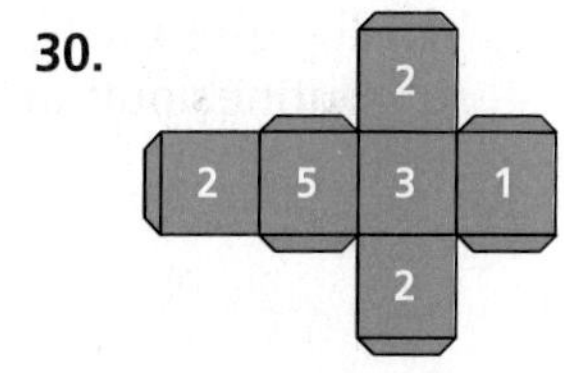

31. Beth has a quarter, a dime, and a nickel in her pocket. She pulls out two coins at random. What is the expected value of the coins?

CHAPTER 8

CHAPTER TEST

The number of natural satellites of major objects in the solar system (as of 2005) is given.

	Mercury	Venus	Earth	Mars	Jupiter	Saturn	Uranus	Neptune	Pluto
Satellites	0	0	1	2	63	33	27	13	1

Source: NASA Planetary Data System, 2005

1. Make a box-and-whisker plot of the data. Find the interquartile range.
2. Is 63 an outlier? Explain.
3. Identify the outlier in the following data set: 93, 107, 110, 103, 98, 95, 12, 111, 128, 99, 114, and 90. Describe how the outlier affects the mean and the standard deviation.
4. Use the Binomial Theorem to expand $(3x + y)^4$.

The probability of winning a carnival game is 15%. Elaine plays 10 times.

5. Find the probability that Elaine will win 2 times.
6. Find the probability that Elaine will win at least 2 times.
7. In a survey of 30 employees at a chain of bookstores, 5 employees said that they had reader fewer than 10 books in the last year. The chain has 372 employees. Predict the number of employees at the chain of bookstores who had read fewer than 10 books in the last year.

Explain whether the research topic is best addressed through an experiment or an observational study.

8. Does painting without a painter's mask put people at greater risk of respiratory problems?
9. Does using an exercise machine sold on television improve muscle growth?
10. An investment consultation firm claims that it will increase the value of its clients' investments by 17%. In a random sample of 50 clients of the firm, the average return on investments with minimal risk was 16.1% of the original investment, with a standard deviation of 3%. What is the z-value rounded to the nearest hundredth, and is there enough evidence to reject the firm's claim?
11. The owner of a plumbing company wants to know if his clients are satisfied with the company's service. He decides to ask 20 clients, randomly chosen from a list of his 43 clients, for their opinions of the company's service. What kind of sample is this?
12. If x is a normally distributed random variable with mean μ and standard deviation σ, then what is the probability that $x < \mu + \sigma$?
13. Dollie writes a computer subroutine to randomly output a number from an inputted list. She uses the list 1, 1, –1, 4, –2, –6, 13, –4.5. What is the expected value of the subroutine's output?

FOCUS ON SAT STUDENT-PRODUCED RESPONSES

Some questions on the SAT require you to enter your answer in a special grid. Your answers must be positive integers, fractions, or decimals. You cannot enter negative numbers or mixed numbers in the grid.

Some questions may have multiple answers; in these cases you may enter any one correct answer. If the solution is an inequality, be sure that you choose a number from the solution region.

You may want to time yourself as you take this practice test. It should take you about 9 minutes to complete.

1. The heights of people in a class are normally distributed with a mean of 68 inches and a standard deviation of 5 inches. Estimate the probability that the height of a randomly selected person from the class is more than 63 inches.

2. What is the expected value of an eight-sided die with sides 1, 1, 3, 4, 5, 6, 6, 10?

3. A theme park manager surveys every seventh person as they leave a rollercoaster ride, and finds that 31 out of the 35 people surveyed liked the ride. If 1155 unique riders ride the rollercoaster each day, predict the number of riders who liked the ride that day.

4. A claim is made that the mean of a data set will be 435. In a test of the claim, the mean among 41 trials is actually 468, with a standard deviation of 20. What is the z-value of the given data, rounded to the nearest hundredth?

5. A poll shows candidate A favored with 56% of the vote, and candidate B with 44% of the vote. What is the least percentage margin of error for which candidate B can claim that there is not a clearly-projected winner?

6. Nelson is bidding on an antique gumball machine. He plans to fix it, using parts that will cost him $25, and then resell it. He knows he can sell the fixed machine for $100. If there's a 5% chance that in the process he will accidentally break the machine further, making it unsalable, what is the maximum amount (in dollars) he should he bid?

CHAPTER 8

TEST TACKLER

Standardized Test Strategies

Short Response: Write Short Responses

Short-response test items are designed to measure understanding and reasoning skills. Typically, you must show how you solved the problem and explain your answer. Short-response questions are scored using a scoring rubric.

EXAMPLE 1

Short Response The data represent the number employees in each of a library's 6 branches.

{100, 44, 35, 20, 40, 75}

Are any of the data outliers?

Here are examples of how three different responses were scored using the scoring rubric shown.

2-point response:

I used a graphing calculator to find the 1-variable statistics for the data. The calculator showed that $\overline{x} = 52$, and $\sigma x = 26.365020557 \approx 26$. Then $3\sigma x \approx 78$. Because $52 - 78$ is negative, there are no outliers less than $52 - 78$. A library cannot have a negative number of employees. Values greater than $52 + 78 = 130$ would be outliers. There are no values greater than 130, so none of the data are outliers.

1-point response:

The mean of the data is 52 and the standard deviation is about 26. None of the data are outliers.

Notice that the correct answer is given, but no explanation is provided.

0-point response:

20 and 98 are outliers because 20 is much less than the other data values and 98 is much greater.

Notice that the student provided an incorrect response without showing any work.

Scoring Rubric

2 points: The student correctly solves the problem, showing all work. The student answers the question in a complete sentence, and provides an explanation.

1 point: The student correctly solves the problem but does not show all work, or does not provide an explanation.

1 point: The student gives an incorrect answer, but shows all work and provides an explanation for the answer.

0 points: The student gives no response or provides a solution without showing any work or explanation.

Never leave a short response test item blank. Showing your work and providing a reasonable explanation will result in at least partial credit.

Read each test item, and answer the questions that follow using this scoring rubric.

Scoring Rubric

- **2 points:** The student demonstrates a thorough understanding of the concept, correctly answers the question, and provides a complete explanation.
- **1 point:** The student shows all work and provides an explanation but answers the question incorrectly.
- **1 point:** The student correctly answers the question but does not show all work or does not provide an explanation.
- **0 points:** The student gives a response showing no work or explanation or gives no response.

Item A
Describe a real-world situation involving margin of error.

In a poll of voters, 38% of those surveyed said they would vote for Arujo, and 72% said they would vote for candidate Berne. The poll has a margin of error of 3%. So, the actual percent voting for Arujo is between 35% and 41%. The actual percent voting for Berne is between 69% and 75%. The survey clearly projects the outcome.

1. How would you score the student's response? Explain.
2. Rewrite the response so that it receives full credit.

Item B
Explain what expected value is. Give an example of a real-world situation involving expected value, and calculate the appropriate expected value.

The expected value is the sum of the outcomes and the probability. Suppose you roll a number cube. The expected value of the number cube is 32.

3. Score the response, and provide your reasoning for the score.
4. Give a response that would receive full credit.

Item C
In one family, the probability of having a brown-eyed child is 0.75. What is the probability that of their 3 children, at least two are brown-eyed?

The probability is the probability that exactly 2 of their children are brown-eyed or exactly 3 are brown-eyed, that is, $P(2) + P(3)$. The binomial probability of r successes is ${}_nC_2p^rq^{r-1}$.

$P(2) = {}_3C_2(0.75)^2(0.25)^1 = 3(0.5625)(0.25) = 0.421875.$

$P(3) = {}_3C_3(0.75)^3(0.25)^0 = 1(0.421875)(1) = 0.421875.$

$P(2) + P(3) = 2(0.421875) = 0.84375.$

The probability that at least two of their 3 children are brown-eyed is about 84%.

5. Should this response receive full credit? Explain your reasoning.

CHAPTER 8

STANDARDIZED TEST PREP

Learn It Online
State Test Practice

CUMULATIVE ASSESSMENT

Multiple Choice

1. Which is a factor of $-6x^3 - 2x + 6x + 2$?

Ⓐ $1 - x$

Ⓑ $x - 1$

Ⓒ $3x - 1$

Ⓓ $3x + 1$

2. What is the median of the test scores given?
$\{97, 78, 61, 90, 95, 96, 80, 67, 86, 88, 90, 92\}$

Ⓕ 85

Ⓖ 88

Ⓗ 89

Ⓙ 90

3. Which is the graph of the function $f(x) = 4\sqrt{x - 2} - 3$?

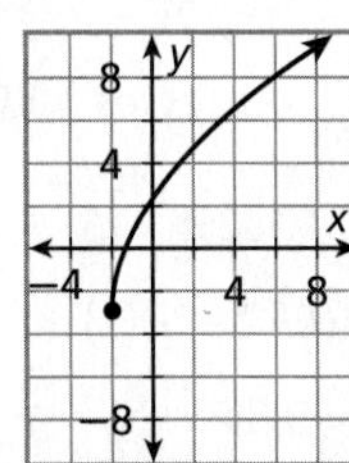

Ⓑ

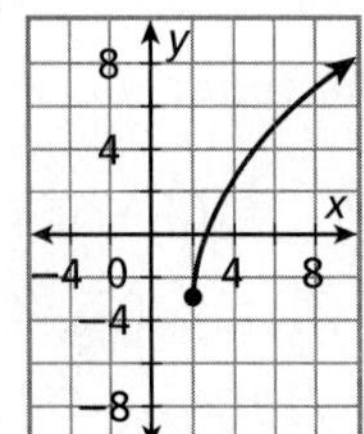

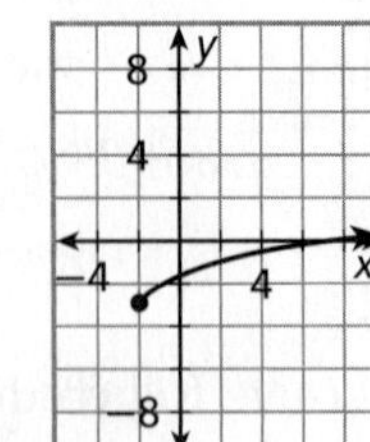

Ⓓ

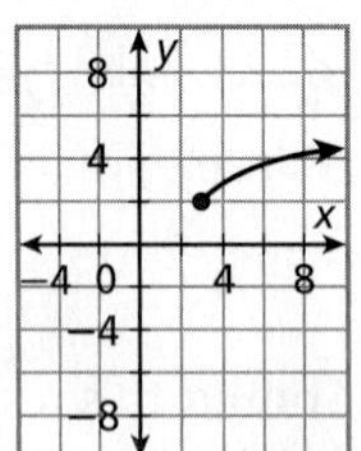

4. What is the remainder when $4x^2 + 2x + 5$ is divided by $x - 1$?

Ⓕ 0

Ⓖ 7

Ⓗ 11

Ⓙ $(x - 1)$

5. The population of a town was 35,478 in 2000 and has increased at a rate of 1.2% per year since then. Which expression represents the town's population *t* years after 2000?

Ⓐ $35{,}478(1.2)^t$

Ⓑ $35{,}478(1.012)^t$

Ⓒ $35{,}478(1.12)^t$

Ⓓ $35{,}478(0.012)^t$

6. If $\log_{16}[\log_3(\log_2 x)] = \frac{1}{4}$, then what is x?

Ⓕ 6

Ⓖ 24

Ⓗ 96

Ⓙ 512

7. What is $\log_{32} 2$?

Ⓐ 5

Ⓑ −5

Ⓒ 0.2

Ⓓ −0.2

8. Which equation is best represented by the following statement: *y* varies inversely as the square root of *x*?

Ⓕ $y = \frac{k}{\sqrt{x}}$

Ⓖ $y = \frac{k}{\sqrt{x^2}}$

Ⓗ $k = \sqrt{xy}$

Ⓙ $y = k\sqrt{x}$

9. Assume that all expressions are defined. Which expression is equivalent to $\frac{2x^2 - 5x - 3}{x^3 + x} + \frac{x - 3}{3x - x^2}$?

Ⓐ $\frac{2x + 1}{x^2 + 1}$

Ⓑ $\frac{(2x + 1)(3 - x)}{x^2 + 1}$

Ⓒ $\frac{(2x + 1)(2x)}{x^2 + 1}$

Ⓓ $\frac{6 - 2x}{x + 1}$

Gridded Response

10. For what x-values is the expression $\frac{(x+1)(x-1)}{(2-x)}$ undefined?

11. What is the value of z in the equation $\frac{z^2}{2z+1} = \frac{z^2}{3z+1}$?

12. The die below is rolled three times. What is the expected value of the sum?

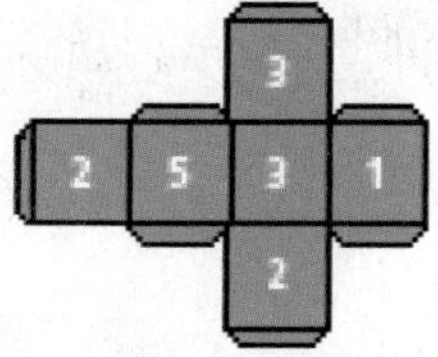

13. Two hundred people attended a test screening of a new television show. 32 said they would tune in to the show over alternatives if it were approved. If the expected television-viewing audience for the show's suggested timeslot is 5 million people, predict the number of people who would watch the show.

Short Response

14. Scores on a test are normally distributed with a mean of 82 and a standard deviation of 4.

    a. Estimate the probability that a randomly selected student scored less than 74.

    b. Estimate the probability that a randomly selected student scored more than 80.

15. A researcher is considering two methods of evaluating a new variety of anti-bacterial hand soap. In Method A, 50 people are told to use the new soap exclusively for a month, and report how many days they felt ill during the month.
    In Method B, 50 people are chosen at random, and asked whether they have tried the new soap and whether they got sick less often since using the new soap.
    Classify each method, and then explain which would be less reliable.

Extended Response

16. The editor of a cooking magazine wants to know the readers' favorite spices to use. The latest issue of the magazine included a survey, and 623 readers completed and returned the survey.

    a. Classify the sample.

    b. Identify the population and the sample.

    c. Is the sample likely to be representative of the population? Explain.

    d. Describe a method of conducting the survey that would be more representative of the population.

CHAPTER

9 Sequences and Series

COMMON CORE

Chapter Focus

- Represent sequences and series algebraically to solve problems.
- Prove statements by mathematical induction.

GOLDEN RECTANGLES

The Fibonacci sequence has connections to geometry, art, and architecture. Explore them by using golden rectangles.

Learn It Online
Chapter Project Online

SIME s.a.s/eStock Photo

ARE YOU READY?

Vocabulary

Match each term on the left with a definition on the right.

1. exponential function
2. function
3. linear equation
4. quadratic function

A. a pairing in which there is exactly one output value for each input value

B. an equation whose graph is a straight line

C. a function defined by a quotient of two polynomials

D. a function of the form $f(x) = ax^2 + bx + c$, where $a \neq 0$

E. a function of the form $f(x) = ab^x$, where $a \neq 0$ and $b \neq 1$

Simplify Radical Expressions

Simplify each expression.

5. $\sqrt{25} \cdot \sqrt{36}$
6. $\sqrt{121} - \sqrt{81}$
7. $\sqrt{\frac{1}{49}}$
8. $\frac{\sqrt{16}}{\sqrt{64}}$

Evaluate Powers

Evaluate.

9. $(-3)^3$
10. $(-5)^4$
11. $1 - (-2^3)^3$
12. $\frac{2^2 \cdot 2^7}{(2^2)^5}$

Solve for a Variable

Solve each equation for *x*.

13. $y = 12x - 5$
14. $y = -\frac{x}{3} + 1$
15. $y = -9 + x^2$
16. $y = -4(x^2 - 9)$

Evaluate Expressions

Evaluate each expression for $x = 2$, $y = 12$, and $z = 24$.

17. $\frac{y(y+1)}{3x}$
18. $z + (y - 1)x$
19. $y\left(\frac{x+z}{2}\right)$
20. $z\left(\frac{1-y}{1-x}\right)$

Counterexamples

Find a counterexample to show that each statement is false.

21. $n^2 = n$, where n is a real number
22. $n^3 \geq n^2 \geq n$, where n is a real number
23. $\frac{1}{n} > \frac{1}{n^2}$, where n is a real number
24. $\frac{2}{n} \neq \frac{n}{2}$, where n is a real number

CHAPTER 9

Study Guide: Preview

Where You've Been

Previously, you

- studied sets of numbers, including natural numbers and perfect squares.
- used patterns of differences or ratios to classify data.
- graphed and evaluated linear and exponential functions.

In This Chapter

You will study

- patterns of numbers, called *sequences,* and their sums, called *series.*
- patterns to determine whether sequences are arithmetic or geometric.
- how to write and evaluate sequences and series.

Where You're Going

You can use the skills learned in this chapter

- in future math classes, especially Precalculus and Calculus.
- in Physics classes to model patterns, such as the heights of bouncing objects.
- outside of school to calculate the growth of financial investments.

Key Vocabulary/Vocabulario

converge	convergir
diverge	divergir
explicit formula	fórmula explícita
finite sequence	sucesión finita
infinite sequence	sucesión infinita
iteration	iteración
limit	límite
recursive formula	fórmula recurrente
sequence	sucesión
series	serie
term of a sequence	término de una sucesión

Vocabulary Connections

To become familiar with some of the vocabulary terms in the chapter, consider the following. You may refer to the chapter, the glossary, or a dictionary if you like.

1. What does the word **sequence** mean in everyday usage? What might a number sequence refer to?
2. The word *finite* means "having definite or definable limits." Give examples of sentences that use the word *finite.* Explain what a **finite sequence** might refer to.
3. Using the previous definition of *finite,* give examples of sentences that use the word *infinite.* Explain what an **infinite sequence** might refer to.
4. What does a television series refer to? What might a mathematical **series** mean?
5. State what a term of a polynomial refers to. Then write a possible description for a **term of a sequence** .

CHAPTER 9

Writing Strategy: Write a Convincing Argument

Being able to write a convincing argument about a math concept shows that you understand the material well. You can use a four-step method to write an effective argument as shown in the response to the exercise below.

35. Write About It Describe the difference between theoretical probability and experimental probability. Give an example in which they may differ.

Step 1 **Identify the goal.**

The goal is to describe the difference between theoretical and experimental probability.

Step 2 **Provide a statement of response to the goal.**

Theoretical probability is based purely on mathematics, but experimental probability is based on the results of an experiment.

Step 3 **Provide the evidence to support your statement.**

In a coin toss, the theoretical probability of tossing heads is $\frac{\text{number of favorable outcomes}}{\text{number of outcomes in the sample space}} = \frac{1}{2}$.

The experimental probability of tossing heads is $\frac{\text{number of times the event occurs}}{\text{number of trials}}$.

In one trial, the result is either heads or tails, so the experimental probability will be 1 or 0. The theoretical probability is still $\frac{1}{2}$.

Step 4 **Summarize your argument.**

Because theoretical probability is based solely on the mathematical outcomes, it never changes. Experimental probability is based on actual results, so it may change with each trial of an experiment.

Try This

Use the four-step method described above to answer each question.

1. A number cube is rolled 20 times and lands on the number 3 twice. What is the fewest number of rolls needed for the experimental probability of rolling a 3 to equal the theoretical probability of rolling a 3? Explain how you got your answer.

2. Aidan has narrowed his college choices down to 9 schools. He plans to visit 3 or 4 schools before the end of his junior year. How many more ways can he visit a group of 4 schools than a group of 3 schools? Explain.

9-1 Introduction to Sequences

CC.9-12.F.IF.3 Recognize that sequences are functions…whose domain is a subset of the integers. *Also* CC.9-12.F.BF.2*

Objectives

Find the nth term of a sequence.

Write rules for sequences.

Vocabulary

sequence
term of a sequence
infinite sequence
finite sequence
recursive formula
explicit formula
iteration

Who uses this?

Sequences can be used to model many natural phenomena, such as the changes in a rabbit population over time.

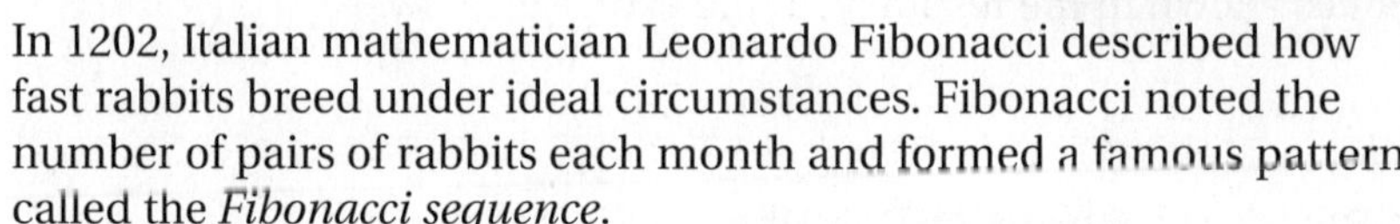

In 1202, Italian mathematician Leonardo Fibonacci described how fast rabbits breed under ideal circumstances. Fibonacci noted the number of pairs of rabbits each month and formed a famous pattern called the *Fibonacci sequence.*

A **sequence** is an ordered set of numbers. Each number in the sequence is a **term of the sequence**. A sequence may be an **infinite sequence** that continues without end, such as the natural numbers, or a **finite sequence** that has a limited number of terms, such as $\{1, 2, 3, 4\}$.

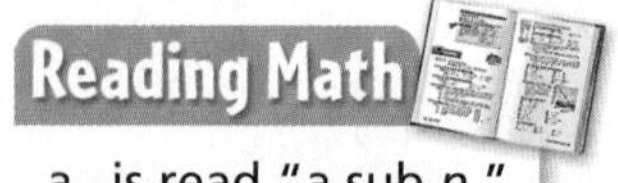

Reading Math

a_n is read "a sub n."

You can think of a sequence as a function with sequential natural numbers as the domain and the terms of the sequence as the range. Values in the domain are called *term numbers* and are represented by n. Instead of function notation, such as $a(n)$, sequence values are written by using subscripts. The first term is a_1, the second term is a_2, and the nth term is a_n. Because a sequence is a function, each number n has only one term value associated with it, a_n.

Term number	n	1	2	3	4	5	Domain
Term value	a_n	1	1	2	3	5	Range

In the Fibonacci sequence, the first two terms are 1 and each term after that is the sum of the two terms before it. This can be expressed by using the rule $a_1 = 1$, $a_2 = 1$, and $a_n = a_{n-2} + a_{n-1}$, where $n \geq 3$. This is a *recursive formula.* A **recursive formula** is a rule in which one or more previous terms are used to generate the next term.

EXAMPLE 1 Finding Terms of a Sequence by Using a Recursive Formula

Find the first 5 terms of the sequence with $a_1 = 5$ and $a_n = 2a_{n-1} + 1$ for $n \geq 2$.

The first term is given, $a_1 = 5$.

Substitute a_1 into the rule to find a_2. Continue using each term to find the next term.

n	$2a_{n-1} + 1$	a_n
1	*Given*	5
2	$2(5) + 1$	11
3	$2(11) + 1$	23
4	$2(23) + 1$	47
5	$2(47) + 1$	95

The first 5 terms are 5, 11, 23, 47, and 95.

CHECK IT OUT! **Find the first 5 terms of each sequence.**

1a. $a_1 = -5$, $a_n = a_{n-1} - 8$ **1b.** $a_1 = 2$, $a_n = -3a_{n-1}$

In some sequences, you can find the value of a term when you do not know its preceding term. An **explicit formula** defines the nth term of a sequence as a function of n.

EXAMPLE 2 Finding Terms of a Sequence by Using an Explicit Formula

Find the first 5 terms of the sequence $a_n = 2^n - 3$.

Make a table. Evaluate the sequence for $n = 1$ through $n = 5$.

n	$2^n - 3$	a_n
1	$2^1 - 3$	−1
2	$2^2 - 3$	1
3	$2^3 - 3$	5
4	$2^4 - 3$	13
5	$2^5 - 3$	29

The first 5 terms are −1, 1, 5, 13, and 29.

Check Use a graphing calculator.
Enter $y = 2^x - 3$ and make a table.

X	Y1	
1	-1	
2	1	
3	5	
4	13	
5	29	
6	61	
7	125	

X=1

Find the first 5 terms of each sequence.

2a. $a_n = n^2 - 2n$ **2b.** $a_n = 3n - 5$

You can use your knowledge of functions to write rules for sequences.

EXAMPLE 3 Writing Rules for Sequences

Write a possible explicit rule for the nth term of each sequence.

A **3, 6, 12, 24, 48, ...**

Examine the differences and ratios.

Ratios 2 2 2 2

Terms	3	6	12	24	48

1st differences 3 6 12 24

2nd differences 3 6 12

The ratio is constant. The sequence is exponential with a base of 2.

Look for a pattern with powers of 2.

$a_1 = 3 = 3(2)^0$, $a_2 = 6 = 3(2)^1$, $a_3 = 12 = 3(2)^2$, ...

A pattern is $3(2)^{n-1}$. One explicit rule is $a_n = 3(2)^{n-1}$.

Remember!

Linear patterns have constant first differences. Quadratic patterns have constant second differences. Exponential patterns have constant ratios.

B **2.5, 4, 5.5, 7, 8.5, ...**

Examine the differences.

Terms	2.5	4	5.5	7	8.5

1st differences 1.5 1.5 1.5 1.5

The first differences are constant, so the sequence is linear.

The first term is 2.5, and each term is 1.5 more than the previous.

A pattern is $2.5 + 1.5(n - 1)$, or $1.5n + 1$. One explicit rule is $a_n = 1.5n + 1$.

Write a possible explicit rule for the nth term of each sequence.

3a. 7, 5, 3, 1, −1, ... **3b.** $1, \frac{1}{2}, \frac{1}{3}, \frac{1}{4}, \frac{1}{5}, \ldots$

EXAMPLE 4 Physics Application

A ball is dropped and bounces to a height of 5 feet. The ball rebounds to 60% of its previous height after each bounce. Graph the sequence and describe its pattern. How high does the ball bounce on its 9th bounce?

Because the ball first bounces to a height of 5 feet and then bounces to 60% of its previous height on each bounce, the recursive rule is $a_1 = 5$ and $a_n = 0.6a_{n-1}$. Use this rule to find some other terms of the sequence and graph them.

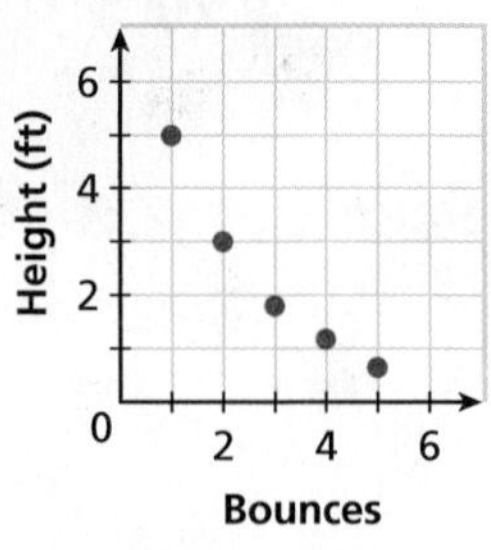

$a_2 = 0.6(5) = 3$

$a_3 = 0.6(3) = 1.8$

$a_4 = 0.6(1.8) = 1.08$

The graph appears to be exponential. Use the pattern to write an explicit rule.

$a_n = 5(0.6)^{n-1}$, where n is the bounce number

Use this rule to find the bounce height for the 9th bounce.

$a_9 = 5(0.6)^{9-1} \approx 0.084$ foot, or approximately 1 inch.

The ball is about 0.084 feet high on the 9th bounce.

Caution!

Do not connect the points on the graph because the number of bounces is limited to the set of natural numbers.

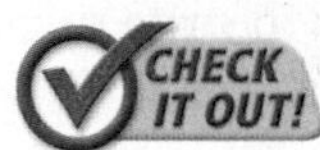

4. An ultra-low-flush toilet uses 1.6 gallons every time it is flushed. Graph the sequence of total water used after n flushes, and describe its pattern. How many gallons have been used after 10 flushes?

Recall that a fractal is an image made by repeating a pattern. Each step in this repeated process is an **iteration**, the repetitive application of the same rule.

EXAMPLE 5 Iteration of Fractals

The Sierpinski triangle is a fractal made by taking an equilateral triangle, removing an equilateral triangle from the center, and repeating for each new triangle. Find the number of triangles in the next 2 iterations.

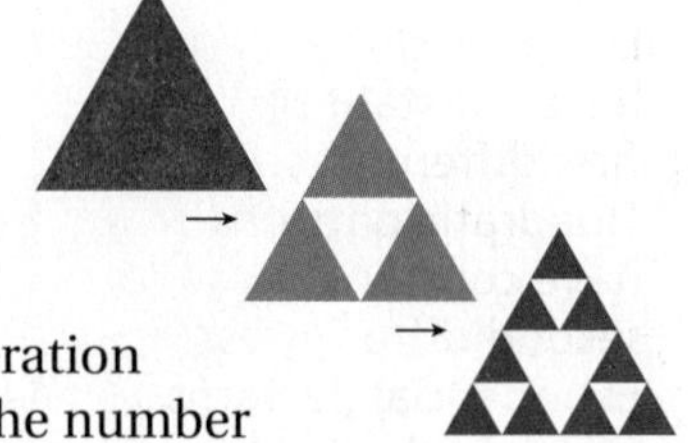

By removing the center of each triangle, each iteration turns every triangle into 3 smaller triangles. So the number of triangles triples with each iteration.

The number of triangles can be represented by the sequence $a_n = 3^{n-1}$.

The 4th and 5th terms are $a_4 = 3^{4-1} = 27$ and $a_5 = 3^{5-1} = 81$.

The next two iterations result in 27 and 81 triangles.

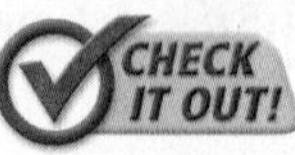

5. The Cantor set is a fractal formed by repeatedly removing the middle third of a line segment as shown. Find the number of segments in the next 2 iterations.

THINK AND DISCUSS

1. Explain the difference between a recursive rule and an explicit rule.
2. Identify three possible next terms for the sequence 1, 2, 4, ...
3. Describe how a sequence is a function. Do all sequences have the same domain? Explain.

4. **GET ORGANIZED** Copy and complete the graphic organizer. Summarize what you have learned about sequences.

Definition	Two types of sequences
Examples	Two possible formulas

Sequences

9-1 Exercises

GUIDED PRACTICE

1. **Vocabulary** A formula that uses one or more previous terms to find the next term is a(n) __?__ formula. (*explicit* or *recursive*)

SEE EXAMPLE 1

Find the first 5 terms of each sequence.

2. $a_1 = 1, a_n = 4a_{n-1} - 1$
3. $a_1 = 3, a_n = a_{n-1} + 11$
4. $a_1 = 500, a_n = \frac{a_{n-1}}{5}$

SEE EXAMPLE 2

5. $a_n = 12(n - 2)$
6. $a_n = \left(-\frac{1}{2}\right)^{n-1}$
7. $a_n = -3n^2$
8. $a_n = n(n - 1)$
9. $a_n = 4^{n-1}$
10. $a_n = (n + 1)^2$

SEE EXAMPLE 3

Write a possible explicit rule for the *n*th term of each sequence.

11. 6, 9, 12, 15, 18, ...
12. $\frac{1}{2}, \frac{2}{3}, \frac{3}{4}, \frac{4}{5}, \frac{5}{6}, \ldots$
13. 25, 15, 5, −5, −15, ...

SEE EXAMPLE 4

14. **Income** Billy earns $25,000 the first year and gets a 5% raise each year. Graph the sequence, and describe its pattern. How much will he earn per year after 5 years? 10 years?

SEE EXAMPLE 5

15. **Patterns** Find the number of segments in the next 2 terms of the pattern shown.

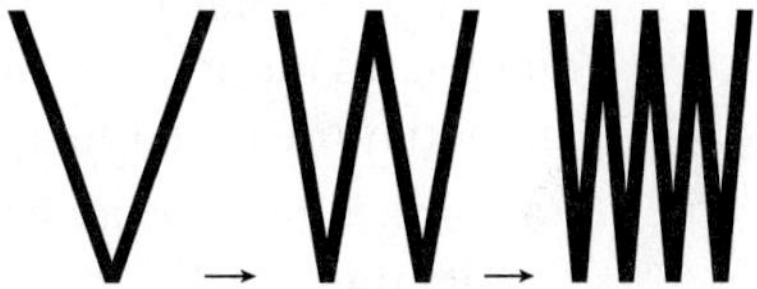

PRACTICE AND PROBLEM SOLVING

Find the first 5 terms of each sequence.

16. $a_1 = 7, a_n = a_{n-1} - 3$
17. $a_n = \frac{1}{n^2}$
18. $a_1 = 4, a_n = 1.5a_{n-1} - 2$
19. $a_n = (2)^{n-1} + 8$
20. $a_n = 2n^2 - 12$
21. $a_1 = -2, a_n = -3a_{n-1} - 1$

Independent Practice

For Exercises	See Example
16–18	1
19–21	2
22–24	3
25	4
26	5

Extra Practice

See Extra Practice for more Skills Practice and Applications Practice exercises.

Write a possible explicit rule for the *n*th term of each sequence.

22. 2, 8, 18, 32, 50, … **23.** 9, 5, 1, −3, −7, … **24.** 5, 0.5, 0.05, 0.005, …

25. Architecture Chairs for an orchestra are positioned in a curved form with the conductor at the center. The front row has 16 chairs, and each successive row has 4 more chairs. Graph the sequence and describe its pattern. How many chairs are in the 6th row?

26. Fractals Find the number of squares in the next 2 iterations of Cantor dust as shown.

Find the first 5 terms of each sequence.

27. $a_1 = 12,\ a_n = \frac{1}{2}a_{n-1} + 2$ **28.** $a_1 = 1,\ a_n = \frac{2}{a_{n-1}}$ **29.** $a_1 = -10,\ a_n = -a_{n-1} + 10$

30. $a_n = 2n^2 - 12$ **31.** $a_n = 8 - \frac{1}{10}n$ **32.** $a_n = 5(-1)^{n+1}(3)^{n\ 1}$

33. ///ERROR ANALYSIS/// Two attempts to find the first 5 terms of the sequence $a_1 = 3$ and $a_n = 2n + 1$ are shown. Which is incorrect? Explain the error.

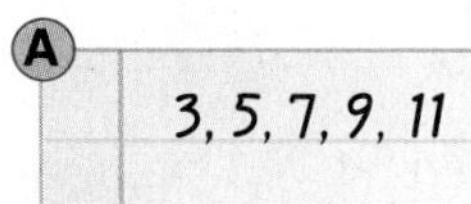

Write a possible explicit rule for each sequence, and find the 10th term.

34. $16, 4, 1, \frac{1}{4}, \frac{1}{16}, \ldots$ **35.** $\frac{15}{9}, \frac{14}{9}, \frac{13}{9}, \frac{12}{9}, \frac{11}{9}, \ldots$ **36.** −5.0, −2.5, 0, 2.5, 5.0, …

37. $1, -\frac{1}{2}, \frac{1}{3}, -\frac{1}{4}, \frac{1}{5}, \ldots$ **38.** 0.04, 0.4, 4, 40, 400, … **39.** 24, 21, 16, 9, 0, …

40. Fibonacci Recall from the lesson that the Fibonacci sequence models the number of pairs of rabbits after a certain number of months. The sequence begins 1, 1, …, and each term after that is the sum of the two terms before it.

a. Find the first 12 terms of the Fibonacci sequence.

b. How many pairs of rabbits are produced under ideal circumstances at the end of one year?

LINK

Math History

The Fibonacci sequence can also be used to discover the golden ratio. The ratios of successive terms become closer and closer to the golden ratio, $\frac{1+\sqrt{5}}{2}$.

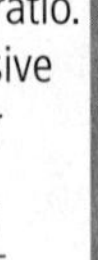

Find the number of dots in the next 2 figures for each dot pattern.

41.

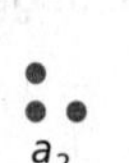

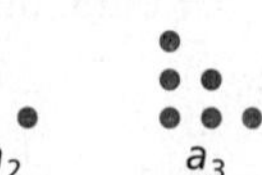

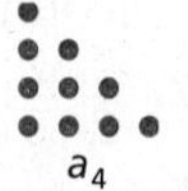

42.

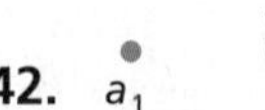

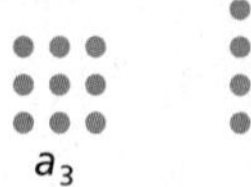

43. Chess Ronnie is scheduling a chess tournament in which each player plays every other player once. He created a table and found that each new player added more than one game.

a. Graph the sequence and describe its pattern. What are the next 2 terms in the sequence?

b. Use a regression to find an explicit rule for the sequence.

c. **What if…?** How would the schedule change if each player played every other player *twice*? Make a table, and describe how the sequence is transformed.

Single-Play Chess Tournament

Number of Players	Number of Games
1	0
2	1
3	3
4	6
5	10

MULTI-STEP TEST PREP

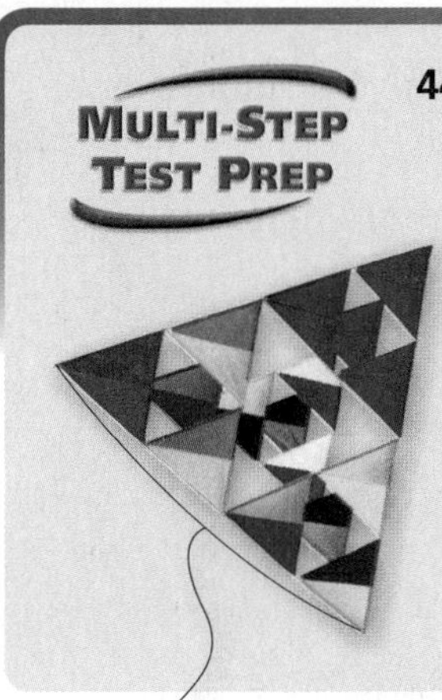

44. A kite is made with 1 tetrahedron in the first (top) layer, 3 tetrahedrons in the second layer, 6 tetrahedrons in the third layer, and so on. Each tetrahedron is made by joining six sticks of equal length.

a. The rule $a_n = a_{n-1} + 6n$ gives the number of sticks needed to make the nth layer of the kite, where $a_1 = 6$. Find the first five terms of the sequence.

b. Use regression to find an explicit rule for the sequence.

c. How many sticks are needed to build the 10th layer of the kite?

45. **Geometry** The sum of the interior angle measures for the first 5 regular polygons is shown.

Sum of Interior Angle Measures

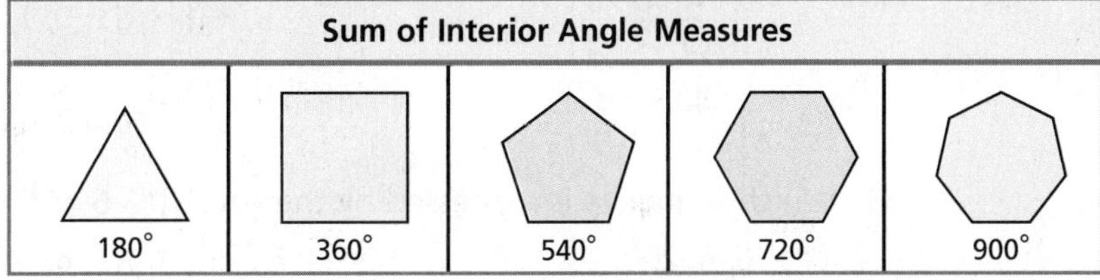

180°	360°	540°	720°	900°

a. Write an explicit rule for the nth term of the sequence of the sum of the angle measures. What is the sum of the measures of the interior angles of a 12-sided regular polygon?

b. Recall that all angles are congruent in a regular polygon. Make a table for the measure of an interior angle for each regular polygon. Graph the data, and describe the pattern.

c. Write an explicit rule for the nth term of the sequence described in part **b.**

d. Find the measure of an interior angle of a 10-sided regular polygon.

46. **Estimation** Estimate the 20th term of the sequence 7.94, 8.935, 9.93, 10.925, 11.92, ... Explain how you reached your estimate.

47. **Music** Music involves arranging different pitches through time. The musical notation below indicates the duration of various notes (and rests).

Symbols for Musical Notes and Rests

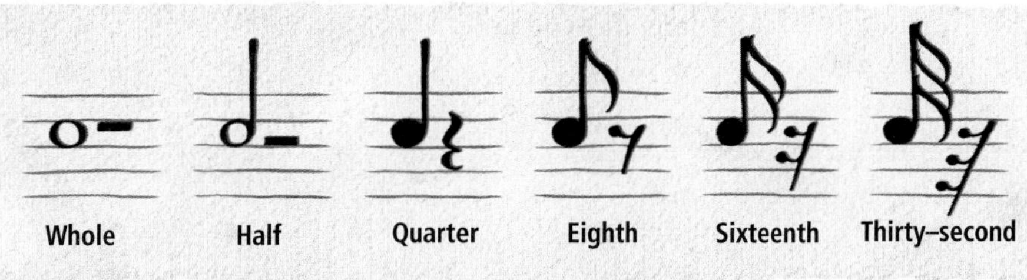

a. Write a numerical sequence that shows the progression of notes (and rests). Write a recursive formula and an explicit formula to generate this sequence.

b. In 4/4 time, a whole note represents 4 beats, a half note represents 2 beats, a quarter note represents 1 beat, and so on. Write a sequence for the number of beats that each note in the progression represents. Then write a recursive formula and an explicit formula to generate this sequence. How is this sequence related to the sequence in part **a**?

48. Critical Thinking Can the recursive rule and the explicit rule for a formula ever be the same?

49. Write About It Explain how an infinite sequence is different from a finite sequence.

50. Which is the next term in the sequence −9, −6, −3 , 0, ...?

Ⓐ −3 Ⓑ 0 Ⓒ 3 Ⓓ 6

51. Which rule describes the given sequence 4, 12, 36, 108, ...?

Ⓕ $a_n = 4 + 3n$

Ⓖ $a_n = 3 + 4n$

Ⓗ $a_1 = 4, a_n = 3a_{n-1}, n \geq 2$

Ⓙ $a_1 = 3, a_n = 4a_{n-1}, n \geq 2$

52. Which sequence is expressed by the rule $a_n = \frac{2n}{n+1}$?

Ⓐ $\frac{2}{3}, \frac{4}{5}, \frac{6}{7}, \frac{8}{9}, \frac{10}{11}, \ldots$

Ⓑ $1, \frac{4}{3}, \frac{3}{2}, \frac{8}{5}, \frac{5}{3}, \ldots$

Ⓒ $0, 1, 2, \frac{3}{2}, \frac{8}{5}, \ldots$

Ⓓ $2, \frac{3}{2}, \frac{8}{5}, \frac{5}{3}, \frac{12}{7}, \ldots$

53. Which sequence is expressed by the rule $a_1 = 6$ and $a_n = 12 - 2a_{n-1}, n \geq 2$?

Ⓕ 6, 4, 2, 0, −2, −4, ...

Ⓖ 0, 12, −12, 36, −60, ...

Ⓗ 6, 0, 12, −12, 36, ...

Ⓙ 6, 0, −6, −12, −18, ...

54. Gridded Response Find the next term in the sequence −32, 16, −8, 4, −2, ...

CHALLENGE AND EXTEND

Write an explicit rule for each sequence and find the 10th term.

55. $-\frac{2}{3}, \frac{5}{3}, 8, \frac{61}{3}, \frac{122}{3}, \ldots$

56. −2, 6, −12, 20, −30, ...

57. 0.9, 0.8, 0.6, 0.3, −0.1, ...

58. Geometry Draw 5 circles. Place 1 point on the first circle, 2 points on the second, 3 points on the third, and so forth. Then connect every point with every other point in each circle, and count the maximum number of nonoverlapping regions that are formed inside each circle.

a. Write the resulting sequence.

b. Although the sequence appears to double, the sixth circle has less than 32 possible regions. Try to find them all by carefully drawing this figure. How many did you get?

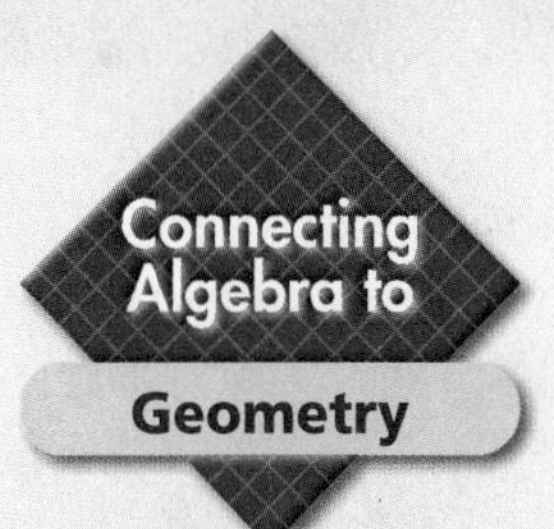

Geometric Patterns and Tessellations

Sequences of figures can often be described with number patterns.

Polygonal numbers can be represented by dots arranged in the form of polygons. The first four hexagonal numbers are illustrated. The sums show a pattern. The sequence for the total number of dots is 1, 6, 15, 28, ...

$n = 1$

1

$n = 2$

$1 + 5 = 6$

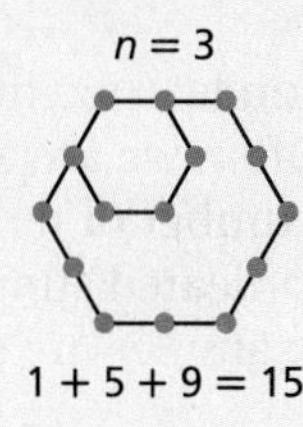

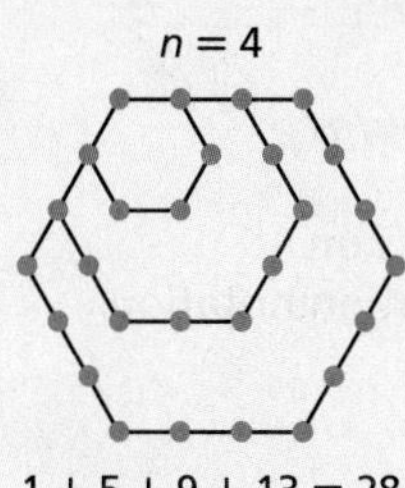

Example

The figure shows how regular hexagons can be used to tessellate, or cover, the plane. Write a sequence for the number of hexagons added at each stage. Describe the pattern in the sequence, and find the next term.

Show the number of hexagons added at each stage.

Level	1	2	3	4
Number of Hexagons	1	6	12	18

From the second term on, the number added appears to increase by 6 each time. The next level probably would have 24 hexagons. You can check your conjecture by constructing the next stage of the tessellation and counting the hexagons.

Try This

Write a sequence for the number of polygons added at each stage of the figure. Describe the pattern in the sequence, and find the next term.

1.

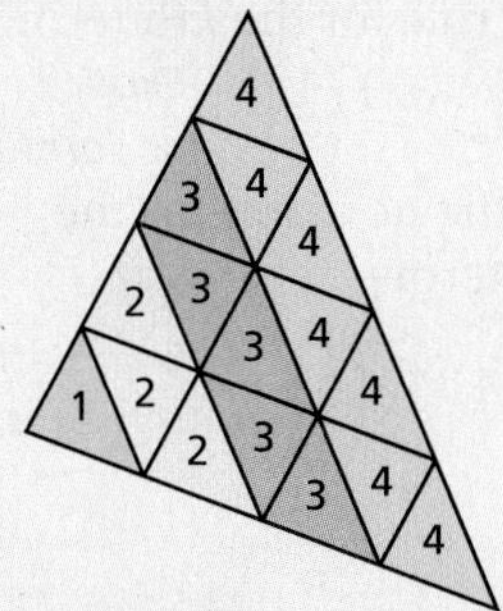

2.

4	4	4	4	4	4	4
4	3	3	3	3	3	4
4	3	2	2	2	3	4
4	3	2	1	2	3	4
4	3	2	2	2	3	4
4	3	3	3	3	3	4
4	4	4	4	4	4	4

3.

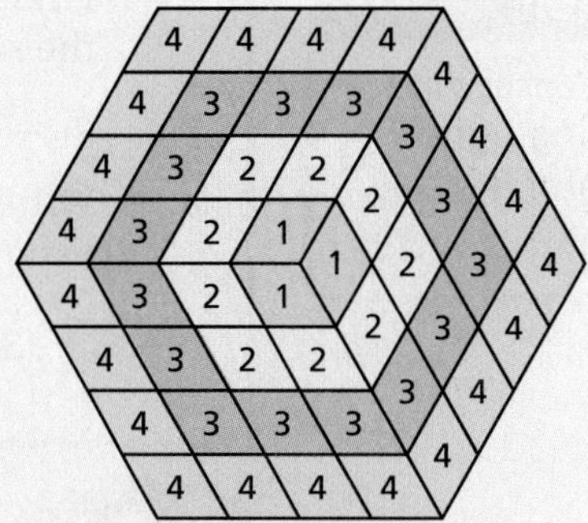

COMMON CORE

9-2 Series and Summation Notation

CC.9-12.F.IF.3 Recognize that sequences are functions ... whose domain is a subset of the integers.
Also **CC.9-12.F.BF.1a**

Objective
Evaluate the sum of a series expressed in sigma notation.

Vocabulary
series
partial sum
summation notation

Why learn this?
You can use sums of sequences to find the size of a house of cards. (See Example 4.)

You learned how to find the nth term of a sequence. Often we are also interested in the sum of a certain number of terms of a sequence. A **series** is the indicated sum of the terms of a sequence. Some examples are shown in the table.

Sequence	1, 2, 3, 4	2, 4, 6, 8, ...	$\frac{1}{2}, \frac{1}{3}, \frac{1}{4}, \frac{1}{5}, \frac{1}{6}$
Series	$1 + 2 + 3 + 4$	$2 + 4 + 6 + 8 + \cdots$	$\frac{1}{2} + \frac{1}{3} + \frac{1}{4} + \frac{1}{5} + \frac{1}{6}$

Because many sequences are infinite and do not have defined sums, we often find partial sums. A **partial sum**, indicated by S_n, is the sum of a specified number of terms of a sequence.

For the even numbers:

$S_1 = 2$ *Sum of first term*
$S_2 = 2 + 4 = 6$ *Sum of first 2 terms*
$S_3 = 2 + 4 + 6 = 12$ *Sum of first 3 terms*
$S_4 = 2 + 4 + 6 + 8 = 20$ *Sum of first 4 terms*

A series can also be represented by using **summation notation**, which uses the Greek letter $\sum$ (capital *sigma*) to denote the sum of a sequence defined by a rule, as shown.

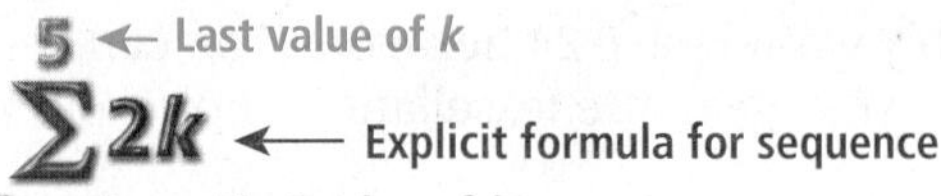

EXAMPLE  **Using Summation Notation**

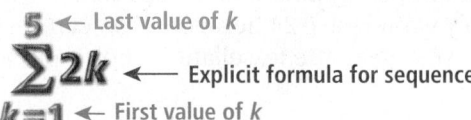

Write each series in summation notation.

A $3 + 6 + 9 + 12 + 15$

Find a rule for kth term of the sequence.

$a_k = 3k$ *Explicit formula*

Write the notation for the first 5 terms.

$\sum_{k=1}^{5} 3k$ *Summation notation*

B $\frac{1}{2} - \frac{1}{4} + \frac{1}{8} - \frac{1}{16} + \frac{1}{32} - \frac{1}{64}$

Find a rule for the kth term.

$a_k = (-1)^{k+1}\left(\frac{1}{2}\right)^k$ *Explicit formula*

Write the notation for the first 6 terms.

$\sum_{k=1}^{6} (-1)^{k+1}\left(\frac{1}{2}\right)^k$ *Summation notation*

Caution!
For sequences with alternating signs:
Use $(-1)^{k+1}$ if $a_1 = +$.
Use $(-1)^k$ if $a_1 = -$.

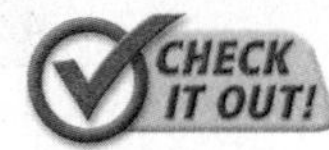

Write each series in summation notation.

1a. $\frac{2}{4} + \frac{2}{9} + \frac{2}{16} + \frac{2}{25} + \frac{2}{36}$ **1b.** $-2 + 4 - 6 + 8 - 10 + 12$

EXAMPLE 2 Evaluating a Series

Expand each series and evaluate.

A $\sum_{k=3}^{6} \frac{1}{2^k}$

$$\sum_{k=3}^{6} \frac{1}{2^k} = \frac{1}{2^3} + \frac{1}{2^4} + \frac{1}{2^5} + \frac{1}{2^6}$$ *Expand the series by replacing k.*

$$= \frac{1}{8} + \frac{1}{16} + \frac{1}{32} + \frac{1}{64}$$ *Evaluate powers.*

$$= \frac{8}{64} + \frac{4}{64} + \frac{2}{64} + \frac{1}{64} = \frac{15}{64}$$ *Simplify.*

Caution!

Watch out! A series can have a first value other than $k = 1$, such as in Example 2A, where k begins at 3.

B $\sum_{k=1}^{4} (10 - k^2)$

$$\sum_{k=1}^{4} (10 - k^2) = (10 - 1^2) + (10 - 2^2) + (10 - 3^2) + (10 - 4^2)$$ *Expand.*

$$= 9 + 6 + 1 + (-6)$$ *Simplify.*

$$= 10$$

Expand each series and evaluate.

2a. $\sum_{k=1}^{4} (2k - 1)$ **2b.** $\sum_{k=1}^{5} -5(2)^{k-1}$

Finding the sum of a series with many terms can be tedious. You can derive formulas for the sums of some common series.

In a *constant series,* such as $3 + 3 + 3 + 3 + 3$, each term has the same value.

$$\sum_{k=1}^{5} 3 = \underbrace{3 + 3 + 3 + 3 + 3}_{5 \text{ terms}} = 5 \cdot 3 = 15$$

The formula for the sum of a constant series is $\sum_{k=1}^{n} c = nc$, as shown.

$$\sum_{k=1}^{n} c = \underbrace{c + c + c + \cdots + c}_{n \text{ terms}} = nc$$

A *linear series* is a counting series, such as the sum of the first 10 natural numbers. Examine when the terms are rearranged.

$$\sum_{1}^{10} k = 1 + 2 + 3 + 4 + 5 + 6 + 7 + 8 + 9 + 10$$
$$= (1 + 10) + (2 + 9) + (3 + 8) + (4 + 7) + (5 + 6)$$
$$= \underbrace{11 + 11 + 11 + 11 + 11}_{5 \text{ terms}} = 5(11) = 55$$

Notice that 5 is half of the number of terms and 11 represents the sum of the first and the last term, $1 + 10$. This suggests that the sum of a linear series is $\sum_{k=1}^{n} k = \frac{n}{2}(1 + n)$, which can be written as $\sum_{k=1}^{n} k = \frac{n(n+1)}{2}$.

Similar methods will help you find the sum of a *quadratic series.*

Summation Formulas

CONSTANT SERIES	LINEAR SERIES	QUADRATIC SERIES
$\sum_{k=1}^{n} c = nc$	$\sum_{k=1}^{n} k = \frac{n(n+1)}{2}$	$\sum_{k=1}^{n} k^2 = \frac{n(n+1)(2n+1)}{6}$

EXAMPLE 3 Using Summation Formulas

Evaluate each series.

A $\sum_{k=5}^{10} 8$ *Constant series*

Method 1 Use the summation formula.

There are 6 terms.

$$\sum_{k=5}^{10} 8 = nc = 6(8) = 48$$

Method 2 Expand and evaluate.

$$\sum_{k=5}^{10} 8 = \underbrace{8 + 8 + 8 + 8 + 8 + 8}_{6 \text{ terms}} = 48$$

Caution!

When counting the number of terms, you must include both the first and the last. For example, $\sum_{k=5}^{10} 8$ has six terms, not five.
$k = 5, 6, 7, 8, 9, 10$

B $\sum_{k=1}^{5} k$ *Linear series*

Method 1 Use the summation formula.

$$\sum_{k=1}^{5} k = \frac{n(n+1)}{2} = \frac{5(6)}{2} = 15$$

Method 2 Expand and evaluate.

$$\sum_{k=1}^{5} k = 1 + 2 + 3 + 4 + 5 = 15$$

C $\sum_{k=1}^{7} k^2$ *Quadratic series*

Method 1 Use the summation formula.

$$\sum_{k=1}^{7} k^2 = \frac{n(n+1)(2n+1)}{6}$$
$$= \frac{7(7+1)(2 \cdot 7 + 1)}{6}$$
$$= \frac{56(15)}{6}$$
$$= 140$$

Method 2 Use a graphing calculator.

```
1²+2²+3²+4²+5²+6
²+7²
                140
```

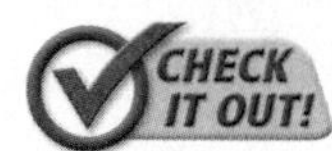

Evaluate each series.

3a. $\sum_{k=1}^{60} 4$ **3b.** $\sum_{k=1}^{15} k$ **3c.** $\sum_{k=1}^{10} k^2$

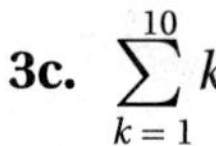

EXAMPLE 4 *Problem-Solving Application*

Ricky is building a card house similar to the one shown. He wants the house to have as many stories as possible with a deck of 52 playing cards. How many stories will Ricky's house have?

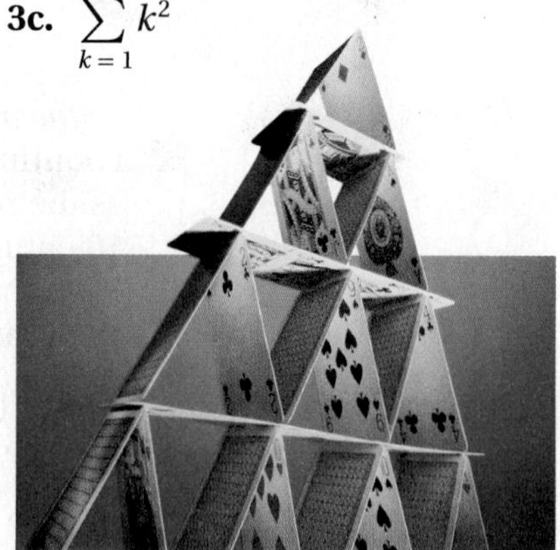

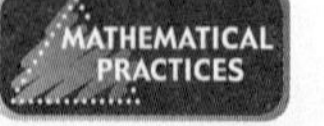

Make sense of problems and persevere in solving them.

1 Understand the Problem

The **answer** will be the number of stories, or rows, in the card house.

List the important information:

- He has 52 playing cards.
- The house should have as many stories as possible.

2 Make a Plan

Make a diagram of the house to better understand the problem. Find a pattern for the number of cards in each story. Write and evaluate the series.

Blow Up/Getty Images

3 Solve

Make a table and a diagram.

Row	1	2	3	4
Diagram				
Cards	2	5	8	11

The number of cards increases by 3 in each row. Write a series to represent the total number of cards in n rows.

$\sum_{k=1}^{n}(3k-1)$, where k is the row number and n is the total number of rows

Evaluate the series for several n-values.

$$\sum_{k=1}^{4}(3k-1) = [3(1)-1]+[3(2)-1]+[3(3)-1]+[3(4)-1] = 26$$

$$\sum_{k=1}^{5}(3k-1) = [3(1)-1]+[3(2)-1]+[3(3)-1]+[3(4)-1]+[3(5)-1] = 40$$

$$\sum_{k=1}^{6}(3k-1) = [3(1)-1]+[3(2)-1]+[3(3)-1]+[3(4)-1]+[3(5)-1]+[3(6)-1] = 57$$

Because Ricky has only 52 cards, the house can have at most 5 stories.

Look Back

Use the table to continue the pattern. The 5th row would have 14 cards. $S_5 = 2 + 5 + 8 + 11 + 14 = 40$. The next row would have more than 12 cards, so the total would be more than 52.

4. A flexible garden hose is coiled for storage. Each subsequent loop is 6 inches longer than the preceding loop, and the innermost loop is 34 inches long. If there are 6 loops, how long is the hose?

THINK AND DISCUSS

1. Explain the difference between a sequence and a series.
2. Explain what each of the variables represents in the notation $\sum_{k=m}^{n} k$.

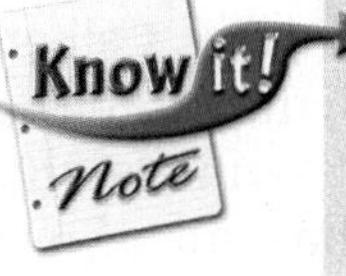

3. **GET ORGANIZED** Copy and complete the graphic organizer. Write the general notation and an example for each term.

	Sequence	Series
Notation		
Example		

9-2 Exercises

Learn It Online
Homework Help Online
Parent Resources Online

GUIDED PRACTICE

1. **Vocabulary** Give an example of *summation notation.*

SEE EXAMPLE 1

Write each series in summation notation.

2. $1 + \frac{1}{4} + \frac{1}{9} + \frac{1}{16} + \frac{1}{25}$
3. $-3 + 6 - 9 + 12 - 15$
4. $1 + 10 + 100 + 1000 + 10{,}000$
5. $100 + 95 + 90 + 85 + 80$

SEE EXAMPLE 2

Expand each series and evaluate.

6. $\sum_{k=1}^{5} k^3$
7. $\sum_{k=1}^{4} (-1)^{k+1} \frac{12}{k^2}$
8. $\sum_{k=5}^{10} -5k$

SEE EXAMPLE 3

Evaluate each series.

9. $\sum_{k=1}^{21} k$
10. $\sum_{k=1}^{20} k^2$
11. $\sum_{k=15}^{35} 6$

SEE EXAMPLE 4

12. **Finance** Melinda makes monthly car payments of $285 each month. How much will she have paid after 2 years? 5 years?

PRACTICE AND PROBLEM SOLVING

Independent Practice

For Exercises	See Example
13–16	1
17–19	2
20–22	3
23	4

Extra Practice

See Extra Practice for more Skills Practice and Applications Practice exercises.

Write each series in summation notation.

13. $1.1 + 2.2 + 3.3 + 4.4 + 5.5$
14. $\frac{1}{2} + \frac{2}{3} + \frac{3}{4} + \frac{4}{5} + \frac{5}{6}$
15. $11 - 12 + 13 - 14 + 15 - 16$
16. $1 + 2 + 4 + 8 + 16 + 32$

Expand each series and evaluate.

17. $\sum_{k=1}^{5} [8(k+1)]$
18. $\sum_{k=2}^{7} (-2)^k$
19. $\sum_{k=1}^{4} \frac{k-1}{k+1}$

Evaluate each series.

20. $\sum_{k=1}^{99} k$
21. $\sum_{k=11}^{88} 2.5$
22. $\sum_{k=1}^{25} k^2$
23. **Retail** A display of soup cans is arranged with 1 can on top and each row having an additional can. How many cans are in a display of 20 rows?

Write each series in summation notation.

24. $-1 + 4 - 9 + 16 - 25 + 36$
25. $25 + 24 + 23 + \cdots + 1$
26. $\frac{1}{3} + \frac{1}{9} + \frac{1}{27} + \frac{1}{81} + \frac{1}{243}$
27. $-800 - 80 - 8 - 0.8 - 0.08$
28. $10.8 + 10.5 + 10.2 + 9.9$
29. $9 - 16 + 25 - 36 + 49 - 64$
30. $-3.9 + 4.4 - 4.9 + 5.4 - 5.9$
31. $0 + 3.4 + 6.8 + 10.2 + 13.6$
32. $3 + \frac{3}{2} + 1 + \frac{3}{4} + \frac{3}{5}$
33. $1000 + 100 + 10 + 1 + \frac{1}{10}$
34. **Travel** The distance from St. Louis, Missouri, to Los Angeles, California, is 1596 miles. Michael plans to travel half the distance on the first day and half the remaining distance each day after that. Write a series in summation notation for the total distance he will travel in 5 days. How far will Michael travel in the 5 days?

35. **Safety** An employer uses a telephone tree to notify employees in the case of an emergency closing. When the office manager makes the decision to close, she calls 3 people. Each of these people calls 3 other people, and so on.

a. Make a tree diagram with 3 levels to represent the problem situation.

b. Write and evaluate a series to find the total number of people notified after 5 levels of calls.

c. **What if...?** Suppose that the phone tree involves calling 5 people at each level. How many more people would be notified after 5 levels of calls?

LINK

Math History

The Granger Collection, New York

At the age of 10, German mathematician Carl Friedrich Gauss discovered a quick method for adding the first 100 natural numbers. His method gave us the summation formula for a linear series.

Expand each series and evaluate.

36. $\sum_{k=1}^{6}(k^2+1)$

37. $\sum_{k=1}^{6}(-1)^k 5k$

38. $\sum_{k=3}^{6}\frac{1}{2k}$

39. $\sum_{k=1}^{6}(3k-2)$

40. $\sum_{k=6}^{11}12(k-2)$

41. $\sum_{k=1}^{5}\frac{k^2}{5k}$

42. **Architecture** A hotel is being built in the shape of a pyramid, as shown in the diagram. Each square floor is 10 feet longer and 10 feet wider than the floor above it.

a. Write a series that represents the total area of n floors of the hotel.

b. How many stories must the hotel be to have at least 50,000 square feet of floor area?

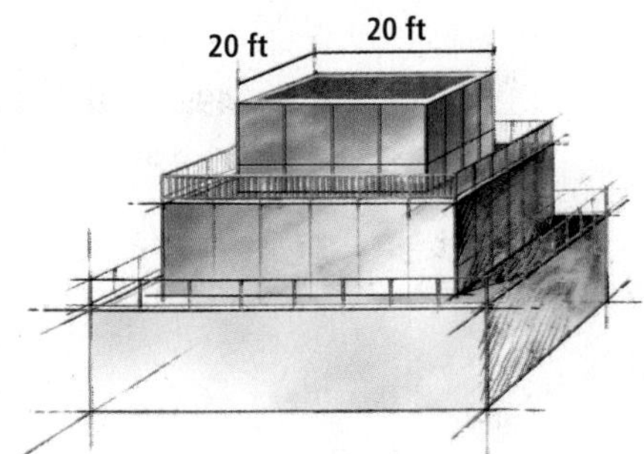

Estimation **Use mental math to estimate each sum. Then compare your answer to the sum obtained by using a calculator.**

43. $10 + 11 + 12 + \cdots + 29 + 30$

44. $1 + 3 + 5 + \cdots + 97 + 99$

45. $-2 + (-4) + (-6) + \cdots + (-98) + (-100)$

46. **Physics** The distance that an object falls in equal time intervals is represented in the table. Rules created by Leonardo da Vinci and Galileo are shown. (In this general case, specific units do not apply to time or distance.)

Distance Fallen in Each Time Interval

Time Interval	Leonardo's Rule	Galileo's Rule
1	1	1
2	2	3
3	3	5
4	4	7
5	5	9

a. Write the series for each rule for 5 intervals, and find the respective sums. What does the sum of the series for 5 intervals represent?

b. Write each series in summation notation. Then evaluate each series for $n = 10$.

c. By the current rule, the distance fallen in each interval is 1, 4, 9, 16, 25.... How do Leonardo's rule and Galileo's rule compare to the current rule?

47. **Critical Thinking** Some mathematical properties may be applied to series.

a. Evaluate $\sum_{k=1}^{10} 3n$ and $3\sum_{k=1}^{10} n$. Make a conjecture based on your answer.

b. Evaluate $\sum_{k=1}^{10} n + \sum_{k=1}^{10} 2$ and $\sum_{k=1}^{10}(n+2)$. Make a conjecture based on your answer.

MULTI-STEP TEST PREP

48. The series $\sum_{k=1}^{n}(3k^2 + 3k)$ gives the total number of sticks needed to make a tetrahedral kite with n layers.

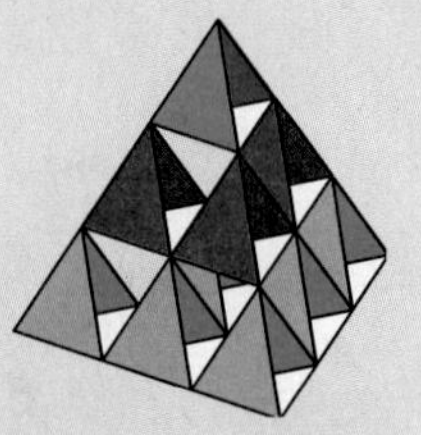

a. Expand and evaluate the series to find out how many sticks are needed to make a kite with 5 layers.

b. Use the properties

$$\sum_{k=1}^{n}(a_k + b_k) = \sum_{k=1}^{n}a_k + \sum_{k=1}^{n}b_k \text{ and } \sum_{k=1}^{n}ca_k = c\sum_{k=1}^{n}a_k$$

to rewrite the series as a multiple of a quadratic series plus a multiple of a linear series.

c. Use summation formulas to determine how many sticks are needed to make a kite with 17 layers.

49. **Multi-Step** Examine the pattern made by toothpick squares with increasing side lengths.

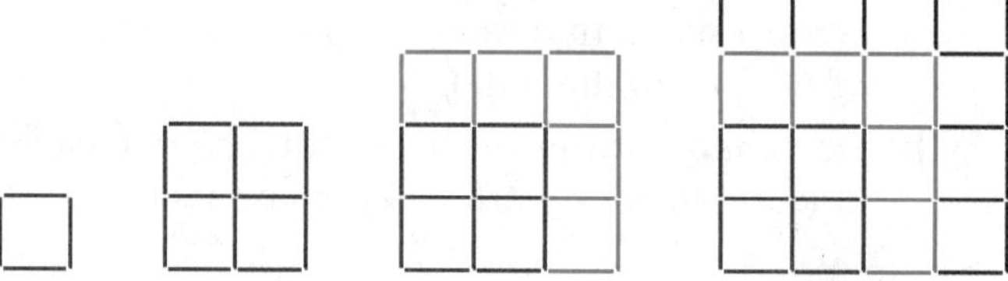

a. Write a sequence for the number of toothpicks added to form each new square.

b. Write and evaluate a series in summation notation to represent the total number of toothpicks in a square with a side length of 6 toothpicks.

50. **Critical Thinking** Are the sums of 1 + 3 + 5 + 7 + 9 and 9 + 7 + 5 + 3 + 1 the same? Do these series have the same summation notation? Explain.

51. **Write About It** Explain why S_n represents a partial sum and not a complete sum of the terms of a sequence.

TEST PREP

52. Which notation accurately reflects the series $\sum_{k=1}^{7}(-1)^k(3k)$?

Ⓐ 3 + 6 + 9 + 12 + 15 + 18 + 21

Ⓑ 3 − 6 + 9 − 12 + 15 − 18 + 21

Ⓒ −3 + 6 − 9 + 12 − 15 + 18 − 21

Ⓓ −3 − 6 − 9 − 12 − 15 − 18 − 21

53. Which notation accurately reflects the series $\frac{1}{2} + \frac{1}{4} + \frac{1}{6} + \frac{1}{8}$?

Ⓕ $\sum_{k=1}^{4}\frac{k}{2}$

Ⓖ $\sum_{k=1}^{4}\frac{1}{2^k}$

Ⓗ $\sum_{k=1}^{4}\frac{1}{2k}$

Ⓙ $\sum_{k=1}^{4}\frac{1}{k+2}$

54. What is the value of $\sum_{k=1}^{6}k^2$?

Ⓐ 36

Ⓑ 55

Ⓒ 91

Ⓓ 273

55. Find the sum of the series $\frac{1}{3} + \frac{1}{6} + \frac{1}{12} + \frac{1}{24}$.

Ⓕ $\frac{1}{45}$

Ⓖ $\frac{4}{45}$

Ⓗ $\frac{7}{12}$

Ⓙ $\frac{5}{8}$

Anthony Lysson

56. **Short Response** The number of cans in each row of a pyramidal stack is 1, 4, 9, 16, ... Would a sequence or series be used to find the number of cans in the 20th row? Explain.

CHALLENGE AND EXTEND

The product of a sequence of terms can be represented by using *pi notation,* which uses the Greek letter Π (capital *pi*). Expand each product and evaluate.

57. $\prod_{k=1}^{5} k$

58. $\prod_{k=1}^{4} (-1)^k$

Prove each summation property for the sequences a_k and b_k.

59. $\sum_{k=1}^{n} ca_k = c\sum_{k=1}^{n} a_k$

60. $\sum_{k=1}^{n} \left(a_k + b_k\right) = \sum_{k=1}^{n} a_k + \sum_{k=1}^{n} b_k$

61. **Critical Thinking** What might the sum of the sequence $1 - 1 + 1 - 1 + 1 - 1 + \cdots$ be if it continues forever? Explain.

Career Path

Steven Howe
Nursing student

Q: What high school math classes did you take?

A: Algebra 1, Geometry, Business Math, and Algebra 2

Q: Why did you decide to pursue a career in nursing?

A: I've always liked science, especially biology and anatomy. I also wanted a career where I can help people, so a job in medicine seemed perfect.

Q: How is math used in nursing?

A: Nurses have to make a lot of calculations to ensure that patients receive the correct dosages of medicine. They also use complicated instruments to measure and monitor different body functions.

Q: What are your future plans?

A: I'll finish my associate's degree in nursing at the end of the semester. I hope to get a job at one of the local hospitals.

Evaluate Sequences and Series

Graphing calculators have built-in features that help you generate the terms of a sequence and find the sums of series.

Use with Series and Summation Notation

Use appropriate tools strategically.

CC.9-12.F.BF.1a Determine an explicit expression, a recursive process, or steps for calculation from a context.

Activity

Use a graphing calculator to find the first 7 terms of the sequence $a_n = 1.5n + 4$. Then find the sum of those terms.

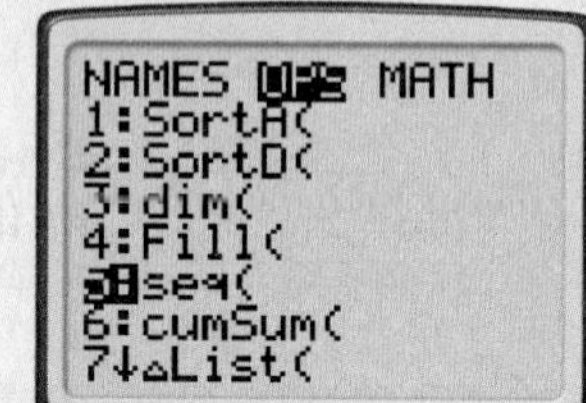

1 Find the first 7 terms of the sequence.

Enter the **LIST** operations menu by pressing 2nd STAT (LIST) and scrolling right to the **OPS** menu. Then select the sequence command **5:seq(**.

The sequence command takes the following four expressions separated by commas.

Enter the rule, using x as the variable. Enter 1 for the starting term and 7 for the ending term. Close the parentheses, and then press ENTER.

The terms of the sequence will be displayed in brackets. Use the arrow keys to scroll to see the rest of the terms.

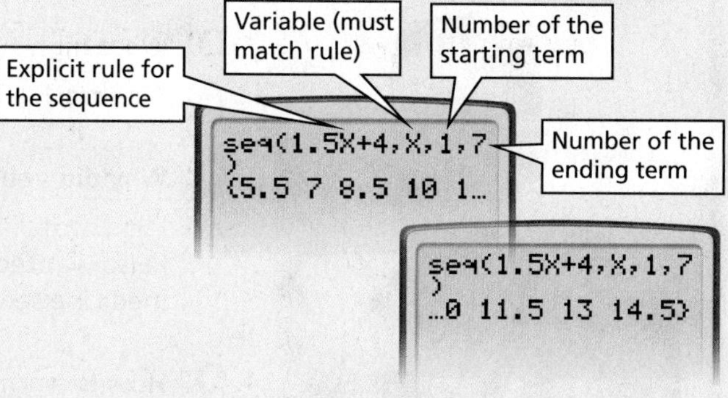

The first 7 terms are 5.5, 7, 8.5, 10, 11.5, 13, and 14.5.

2 Find the sum of the terms.

Enter the **LIST** math menu by pressing 2nd STAT (LIST), and scrolling right to the **MATH** menu. Then select the sum command **5:sum(**.

Follow the steps for entering a sequence as shown in Step 1.

The sum of the first 7 terms is 70.

sum(seq(1.5X+4,X,1,7))
70

Try This

Find the first 8 terms of each sequence. Then find the sum of those 8 terms.

1. $a_n = 2n^2 - 5$
2. $a_n = \frac{1}{4}(2)^{n-1}$
3. $a_n = 0.3n + 1.6$
4. $a_n = 20n$
5. $a_n = n^3 - 2n$
6. $a_n = 0.1(5)^n$
7. **Critical Thinking** Find the next 5 terms of the sequence 200, 182, 164, 146, 128, ... Then find the sum of those 5 terms.

9-3 Arithmetic Sequences and Series

CC.9-12.F.BF.2 Write...sequences both recursively and with an explicit formula, use them to model situations, and translate between the two forms.* *Also* **CC.9-12.F.LE.2**

Objectives
Find the indicated terms of an arithmetic sequence.

Find the sums of arithmetic series.

Vocabulary
arithmetic sequence
arithmetic series

Who uses this?

You can use arithmetic sequences to predict the cost of mailing letters.

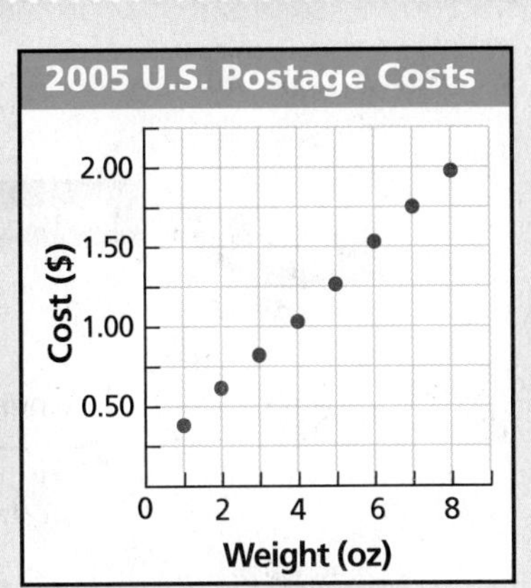

The cost of mailing a letter in 2005 based on its weight in ounces gives the sequence 0.37, 0.60, 0.83, 1.06, ... This sequence is called an **arithmetic sequence** because its successive terms differ by the same number d $(d \neq 0)$, called the *common difference.* For the mail costs, d is 0.23, as shown.

Term	a_1	a_2	a_3	a_4
Value	0.37	0.60	0.83	1.06

Differences 0.23 0.23 0.23

Recall that linear functions have a constant first difference. Notice also that when you graph the ordered pairs (n, a_n) of an arithmetic sequence, the points lie on a straight line. Thus, you can think of an arithmetic sequence as a linear function with sequential natural numbers as the domain.

EXAMPLE 1 Identifying Arithmetic Sequences

Determine whether each sequence could be arithmetic. If so, find the common first difference and the next term.

A $-3, 2, 7, 12, 17, \ldots$

$-3,\quad 2,\quad 7,\quad 12,\quad 17$

Differences 5 5 5 5

The sequence could be arithmetic with a common difference of 5. The next term is $17 + 5 = 22$.

B $-4, -12, -24, -40, -60, \ldots$

$-4,\quad -12,\quad -24,\quad -40,\quad -60$

Differences -8 -12 -16 -20

The sequence is not arithmetic because the first differences are not common.

Determine whether each sequence could be arithmetic. If so, find the common difference and the next term.

1a. $1.9, 1.2, 0.5, -0.2, -0.9, \ldots$ **1b.** $\frac{11}{2}, \frac{11}{3}, \frac{11}{4}, \frac{11}{5}, \frac{11}{6}, \ldots$

Each term in an arithmetic sequence is the sum of the previous term and the common difference. This gives the recursive rule $a_n = a_{n-1} + d$. You also can develop an explicit rule for an arithmetic sequence.

Notice the pattern in the table. Each term is the sum of the first term and a multiple of the common difference.

This pattern can be generalized into a rule for all arithmetic sequences.

Postage Costs per Ounce	
n	a_n
1	$a_1 = 0.37 + 0(0.23)$
2	$a_2 = 0.37 + 1(0.23)$
3	$a_3 = 0.37 + 2(0.23)$
4	$a_4 = 0.37 + 3(0.23)$
n	$a_n = 0.37 + (n - 1)(0.23)$

General Rule for Arithmetic Sequences

The nth term a_n of an arithmetic sequence is given by

$$a_n = a_1 + (n - 1)d$$

where a_1 is the first term and d is the common difference.

EXAMPLE 2 Finding the nth Term Given an Arithmetic Sequence

Find the 10th term of the arithmetic sequence 32, 25, 18, 11, 4, ...

Step 1 Find the common difference: $d = 25 - 32 = -7$.

Step 2 Evaluate by using the formula.

$a_n = a_1 + (n - 1)d$ — *General rule*

$a_{10} = 32 + (10 - 1)(-7)$ — *Substitute 32 for a_1, 10 for n, and −7 for d.*

$= -31$ — *Simplify.*

The 10th term is −31.

Check Continue the sequence.

n	1	2	3	4	5	6	7	8	9	10
a_n	32	25	18	11	4	−3	−10	−17	−24	−31 ✓

Find the 11th term of each arithmetic sequence.

2a. −3, −5, −7, −9, ...

2b. 9.2, 9.15, 9.1, 9.05, ...

Student to Student

Finding the nth Term

Diana Watson
Bowie High School

I like to check the value of a term by using a graphing calculator.

I enter the function for the nth, or general, term. For Example 2, enter y = 32 + (x − 1)(−7).

I then use the table feature. Start at 1 (for n = 1), and use a step of 1. Then find the desired term (y-value) as shown for n = 10.

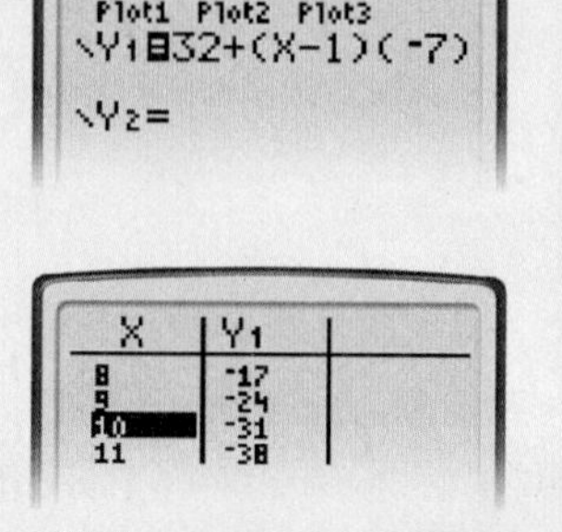

Lucca DiCecco/Alamy

EXAMPLE 3 Finding Missing Terms

Find the missing terms in the arithmetic sequence 11, ■, ■, ■, −17.

Step 1 Find the common difference.

$a_n = a_1 + (n-1)d$	*General rule*
$-17 = 11 + (5-1)d$	*Substitute −17 for a_n, 11 for a_1, and 5 for n.*
$-7 = d$	*Solve for d.*

Step 2 Find the missing terms using $d = -7$ and $a_1 = 11$.

$a_2 = 11 + (2-1)(-7)$	$a_3 = 11 + (3-1)(-7)$	$a_4 = 11 + (4-1)(-7)$
$= 4$	$= -3$	$= -10$

The missing terms are 4, −3, and −10.

3. Find the missing terms in the arithmetic sequence 2, ■, ■, ■, 0.

Because arithmetic sequences have a common difference, you can use any two terms to find the difference.

EXAMPLE 4 Finding the *n*th Term Given Two Terms

Find the 6th term of the arithmetic sequence with $a_9 = 120$ and $a_{14} = 195$.

Step 1 Find the common difference.

$a_n = a_1 + (n-1)d$	
$a_{14} = a_9 + (14-9)d$	*Let $a_n = a_{14}$ and $a_1 = a_9$. Replace 1 with 9.*
$a_{14} = a_9 + 5d$	*Simplify.*
$195 = 120 + 5d$	*Substitute 195 for a_{14} and 120 for a_9.*
$75 = 5d$	
$15 = d$	

Step 2 Find a_1.

$a_n = a_1 + (n-1)d$	*General rule*
$120 = a_1 + (9-1)(15)$	*Substitute 120 for a_9, 9 for n, and 15 for d.*
$120 = a_1 + 120$	*Simplify.*
$0 = a_1$	

Step 3 Write a rule for the sequence, and evaluate to find a_6.

$a_n = a_1 + (n-1)d$	*General rule*
$a_n = 0 + (n-1)(15)$	*Substitute 0 for a_1 and 15 for d.*
$a_6 = 0 + (6-1)15$	*Evaluate for n = 6.*
$= 75$	

The 6th term is 75.

CHECK IT OUT! **Find the 11th term of each arithmetic sequence.**

4a. $a_2 = -133$ and $a_3 = -121$ **4b.** $a_3 = 20.5$ and $a_8 = 13$

An **arithmetic series** is the indicated sum of the terms of an arithmetic sequence. You can derive a general formula for the sum of an arithmetic series by writing the series in forward and reverse order and adding the results.

$$S_n = a_1 \quad + (a_1 + d) + (a_1 + 2d) + \ldots + a_n$$
$$S_n = a_n \quad + (a_n - d) + (a_n - 2d) + \ldots + a_1$$
$$2S_n = \underbrace{(a_1 + a_n) + (a_1 + a_n) + (a_1 + a_n) \ldots + (a_1 + a_n)}_{(a_1 + a_n) \text{ is added } n \text{ times}}$$

$$2S_n = n(a_1 + a_n)$$

$$S_n = \frac{n(a_1 + a_n)}{2}, \text{ or } S_n = n\left(\frac{a_1 + a_n}{2}\right)$$

Sum of the First *n* Terms of an Arithmetic Series

WORDS	NUMBERS	ALGEBRA
The sum of the first *n* terms of an arithmetic series is the product of the number of terms and the average of the first and last terms.	The sum of $2 + 4 + 6 + 8 + 10$ is $5\left(\frac{2 + 10}{2}\right) = 5(6) = 30.$	$S_n = n\left(\frac{a_1 + a_n}{2}\right),$ where *n* is the number of terms, a_1 is the first term, and a_n is the *n*th term.

EXAMPLE 5 Finding the Sum of an Arithmetic Series

Find the indicated sum for each arithmetic series.

A S_{15} **for** $25 + 12 + (-1) + (-14) + \cdots$

Find the common difference.

$d = 12 - 25 = -13$

Find the 15th term.

$a_{15} = 25 + (15 - 1)(-13)$
$= -157$

Find S_{15}.

$S_n = n\left(\frac{a_1 + a_n}{2}\right)$ *Sum formula*

$S_{15} = 15\left(\frac{25 + (-157)}{2}\right)$ *Substitute.*

$= 15(-66) = -990$

Check Use a graphing calculator.

✓

B $\sum_{k=1}^{12} (3 + 4k)$

Find the 1st and 12th terms.

$a_1 = 3 + 4(1) = 7$

$a_{12} = 3 + 4(12) = 51$

Find S_{12}.

$S_n = n\left(\frac{a_1 + a_n}{2}\right)$

$S_{12} = 12\left(\frac{7 + 51}{2}\right)$

$= 348$

Check Use a graphing calculator.

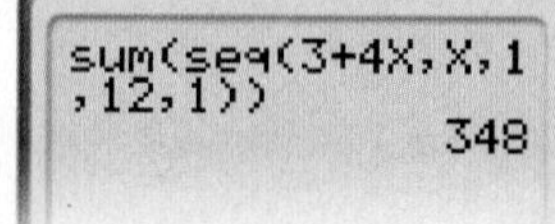

✓

Remember!

These sums are actually *partial sums.* You cannot find the complete sum of an infinite arithmetic series because the term values increase or decrease indefinitely.

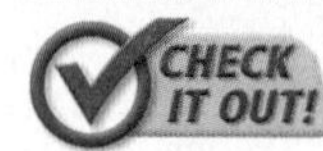

Find the indicated sum for each arithmetic series.

5a. S_{16} for $12 + 7 + 2 + (-3) + \cdots$ **5b.** $\sum_{k=1}^{15} (50 - 20k)$

EXAMPLE 6 Theater Application

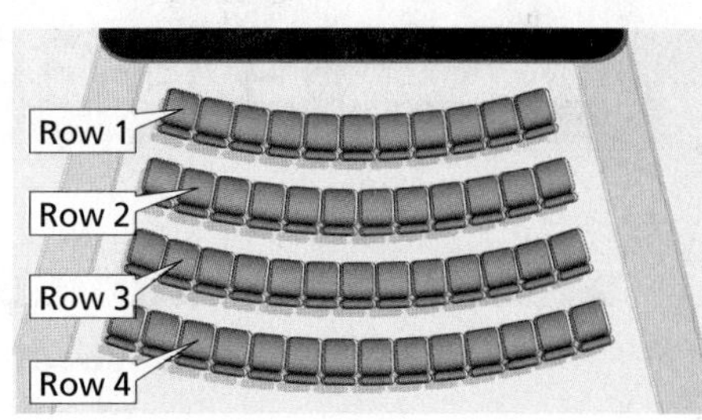

The number of seats in the first 14 rows of the center orchestra aisle of the Marquis Theater on Broadway in New York City form an arithmetic sequence as shown.

A How many seats are in the 14th row?

Write a general rule using $a_1 = 11$ and $d = 1$.

$a_n = a_1 + (n - 1)d$ *Explicit rule for nth term*

$a_{14} = 11 + (14 - 1)1$ *Substitute.*

$= 11 + 13$

$= 24$ *Simplify.*

There are 24 seats in the 14th row.

B How many seats in total are in the first 14 rows?

Find S_{14} using the formula for finding the sum of the first n terms.

$S_n = n\left(\frac{a_1 + a_n}{2}\right)$ *Formula for first n terms*

$S_{14} = 14\left(\frac{11 + 24}{2}\right)$ *Substitute.*

$= 14\left(\frac{35}{2}\right)$

$= 245$ *Simplify.*

There are 245 seats in rows 1 through 14.

6. What if...? Suppose that each row after the first had 2 additional seats.

a. How many seats would be in the 14th row?

b. How many total seats would there be in the first 14 rows?

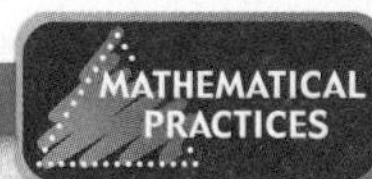

THINK AND DISCUSS

1. Compare an arithmetic sequence with a linear function.

2. Describe the effect that a negative common difference has on an arithmetic sequence.

3. Explain how to find the 6th term in a sequence when you know the 3rd and 4th terms.

4. Explain how to find the common difference when you know the 7th and 12th terms of an arithmetic sequence.

5. GET ORGANIZED Copy and complete the graphic organizer. Write in each rectangle to summarize your understanding of arithmetic sequences.

Definition	Characteristics
Arithmetic Sequences	
Examples	Formulas

9-3 Exercises

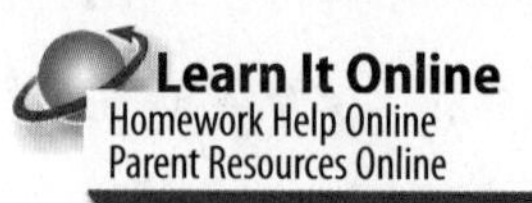

GUIDED PRACTICE

1. **Vocabulary** The expression 10 + 20 + 30 + 40 + 50 is an __?__. (*arithmetic sequence* or *arithmetic series*)

SEE EXAMPLE 1

Determine whether each sequence could be arithmetic. If so, find the common difference and the next term.

2. 46, 39, 32, 25, 18, ...
3. 28, 21, 15, 10, 6, ...
4. $\frac{12}{3}, \frac{10}{3}, \frac{8}{3}, \frac{6}{3}, \frac{4}{3}, \ldots$

SEE EXAMPLE 2

Find the 8th term of each arithmetic sequence.

5. 3, 8, 13, 18, ...
6. $10, 9\frac{3}{4}, 9\frac{1}{2}, 9\frac{1}{4}, \ldots$
7. −3.2, −3.4, −3.6, −3.8, ...

SEE EXAMPLE 3

Find the missing terms in each arithmetic sequence.

8. 13, ■, ■, 25
9. 9, ■, ■, ■, 37
10. 1.4, ■, ■, ■, −1

SEE EXAMPLE 4

Find the 9th term of each arithmetic sequence.

11. $a_4 = 27$ and $a_5 = 19$
12. $a_3 = 12.2$ and $a_4 = 12.6$
13. $a_3 = -5$ and $a_6 = -11$
14. $a_{10} = 100$ and $a_{20} = 50$
15. $a_7 = -42$ and $a_{11} = -28$
16. $a_4 = \frac{3}{4}$ and $a_8 = \frac{1}{2}$

SEE EXAMPLE 5

Find the indicated sum for each arithmetic series.

17. S_{15} for $5 + 9 + 13 + 17 + \cdots$
18. $\sum_{k=1}^{12} (-2 + 6k)$
19. S_{18} for $3.2 + 2.9 + 2.6 + 2.3 + \cdots$

SEE EXAMPLE 6

20. **Salary** Juan has taken a job with an initial salary of $26,000 and annual raises of $1250.
    a. What will his salary be in his 6th year?
    b. How much money in total will Juan have earned after six years?

PRACTICE AND PROBLEM SOLVING

Independent Practice

For Exercises	See Example
21–23	1
24–26	2
27–29	3
30–32	4
33–35	5
36	6

Extra Practice

See Extra Practice for more Skills Practice and Applications Practice exercises.

Determine whether each sequence could be arithmetic. If so, find the common difference and the next term.

21. 288, 144, 72, 36, 18, ...
22. −2, −12, −22, −32, −42, ...
23. 0.99, 0.9, 0.81, 0.72, ...

Find the 11th term of each arithmetic sequence.

24. 12, 11.9, 11.8, 11.7, ...
25. $\frac{2}{5}, \frac{3}{5}, \frac{4}{5}, 1, \ldots$
26. −3.0, −2.5, −2.0, −1.5, ...

Find the missing terms in each arithmetic sequence.

27. 77, ■, ■, ■, 33
28. −29, ■, ■, −2
29. 2.3, ■, ■, ■, 1.5

Find the 12th term of each arithmetic sequence.

30. $a_4 = 18.4$ and $a_5 = 16.2$
31. $a_4 = -2$ and $a_8 = 46$
32. $a_{22} = -49$ and $a_{25} = -58$

Find the indicated sum for each arithmetic series.

33. S_{15} for $-18 + (-16) + (-14) + \cdots$
34. $\sum_{k=1}^{20} (88 - 3k)$
35. $\sum_{k=1}^{14} \left(14 - \frac{1}{2}k\right)$

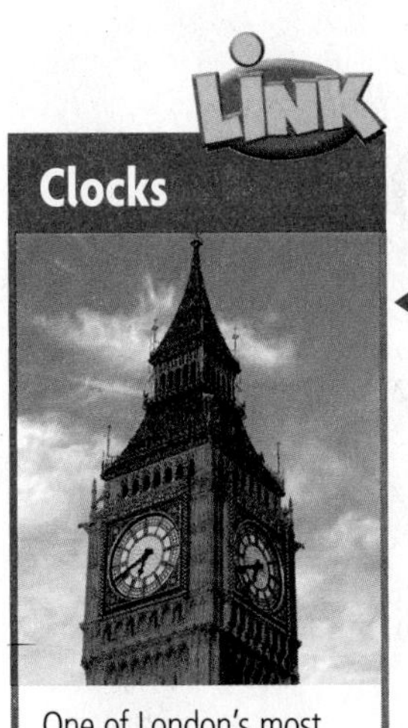

One of London's most recognizable landmarks, Big Ben sits atop the Palace of Westminister, where the British Parliament meets. The name Big Ben actually refers to the 13.8-ton bell that chimes the hours.

36. **Consumer Economics** Clarissa is buying a prom dress on layaway. She agrees to make a \$15 payment and increase the payment by \$5 each week.
   a. What will her payment be in the 9th week?
   b. How much money in total will Clarissa have paid after 9 weeks?

37. **Clocks** A clock chimes every hour. The clock chimes once at 1 o'clock, twice at 2 o'clock, and so on.
   a. How many times will the clock chime from 1 P.M. through midnight? in exactly one 24-hour period?
   b. **What if...?** Another clock also chimes once on every half hour. How does this affect the sequence and the total number of chimes per day?

Find the indicated sum for each arithmetic series.

38. $\sum_{k=1}^{16}(555 - 11k)$ 39. $\sum_{k=1}^{15}(4 - 0.5k)$ 40. $\sum_{k=1}^{18}\left(-33 + \frac{5}{2}k\right)$

41. S_{16} for $7.5 + 7 + 6.5 + 6.0 + \cdots$ 42. S_{18} for $2 + 9 + 16 + 23 + \cdots$

43. **Architecture** The Louvre pyramid in Paris, France, is built of glass panes. There are 4 panes in the top row, and each additional row has 4 more panes than the previous row.

   a. Write a series in summation notation to describe the total number of glass panes in n rows of the pyramid.
   b. If the pyramid were made of 18 complete rows, how many panes would it have?
   c. The actual pyramid has 11 panes less than a complete 18-row pyramid because of the space for the entrance. Find the total number of panes in the Louvre pyramid.

44. **Physics** Water towers are tall to provide enough water pressure to supply all of the houses and businesses in the area of the tower. Each foot of height provides 0.43 psi (pounds per square inch) of pressure.
   a. Write a sequence for the pressure in psi for each foot of height.
   b. What is the minimum height that supplies 50 psi, a typical minimum supply pressure?
   c. What is the minimum height that supplies 100 psi, which is a typical maximum pressure?
   d. Graph the sequence, and discuss the relationship between the height found for a pressure of 50 psi and the height found at 100 psi.

45. **Exercise** Sheila begins an exercise routine for 20 minutes each day. Each week she plans to add 5 minutes per day to the length of her routine.
   a. For how many minutes will she exercise each day of the 6th week?
   b. What happens to the length of Sheila's exercise routine if she continues this increasing pattern for 2 years?

46. **Geology** Every year the continent of North America moves farther away from Europe.

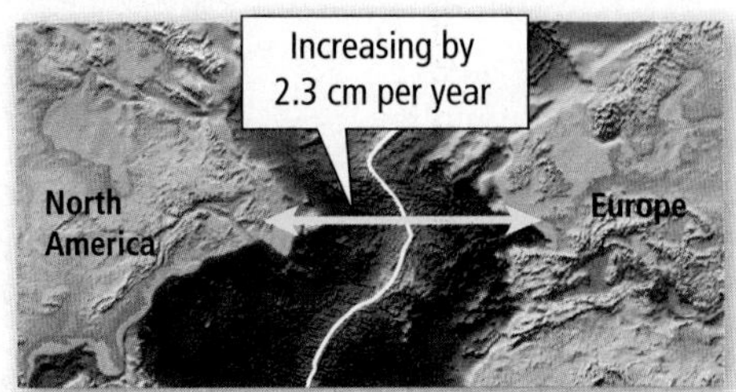

   a. How much farther from Europe will North America be in 50 years?
   b. How many years until an extra mile is added? (*Hint:* 1 mi ≈ 1609 m)

47. You can make a simple tetrahedral kite with one peak by using 4 tetrahedrons. You can also make long kites with multiple peaks by successively adding 3 tetrahedrons as shown.

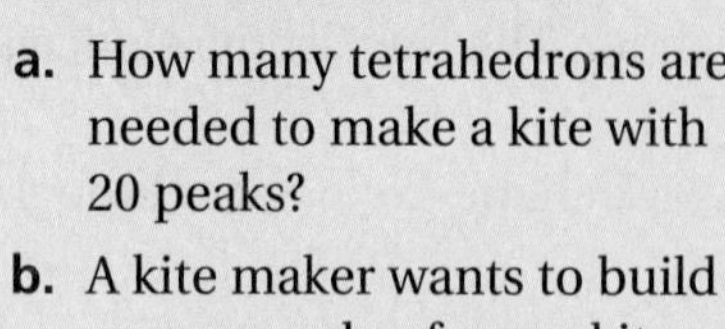

a. How many tetrahedrons are needed to make a kite with 20 peaks?

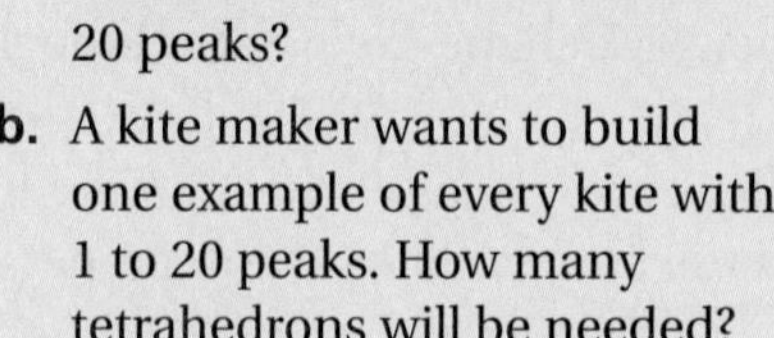

b. A kite maker wants to build one example of every kite with 1 to 20 peaks. How many tetrahedrons will be needed?

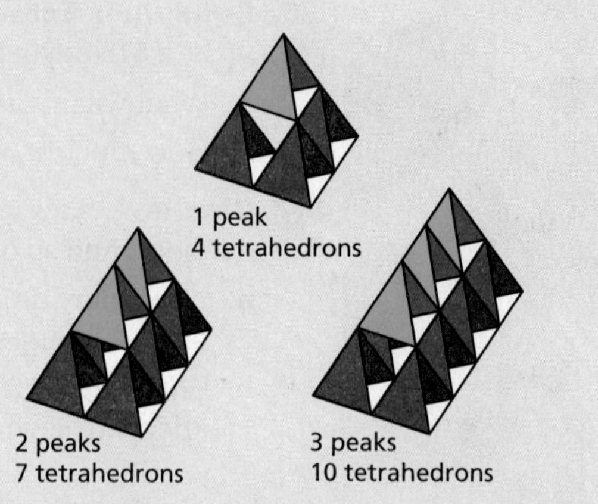

48. **Finance** The starting salary for a summer camp counselor is \$395 per week. In each of the subsequent weeks, the salary increases by \$45 to encourage experienced counselors to work for the entire summer. If the salary is \$710 in the last week of the camp, for how many weeks does the camp run?

49. **Sports** A town is planning a 5K race. The race route will begin at 1st street, travel 30 blocks down Main Street, and finish on 31st Street. The race planners want to have water stations at each turn. In addition, they want to place 5 more water stations evenly distributed between 1st Street and 31st Street on Main Street.

a. At what street intersections should the water stations be placed?

b. If each block is 0.1 mile, what is the maximum distance a runner will be from a water station while on Main Street?

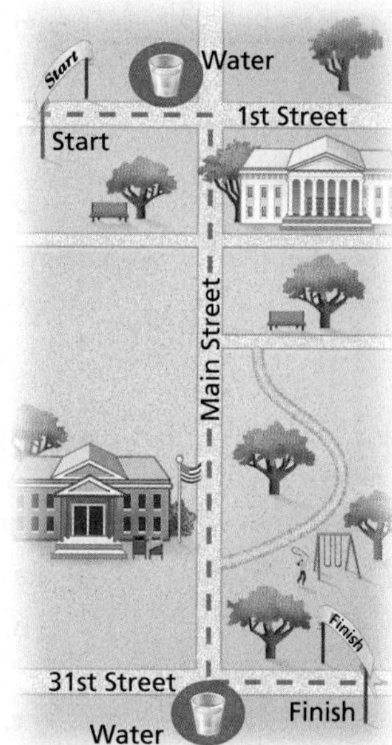

50. **Critical Thinking** What is the least number of terms you need to write the general rule for an arithmetic sequence? How many points do you need to write an equation of a line? Are these answers related? Explain.

51. **Write About It** An arithmetic sequence has a positive common difference. What happens to the nth term as n becomes greater and greater? What happens if the sequence has a negative common difference?

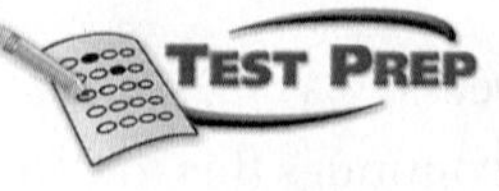

52. Which sequence could be an arithmetic sequence?

Ⓐ $\frac{1}{2}, \frac{1}{3}, \frac{1}{4}, \frac{1}{5}, \ldots$

Ⓑ 2.2, 4.4, 6.6, 8.8, ...

Ⓒ 2, 4, 8, 16, ...

Ⓓ 2, 4, 7, 11, ...

53. A catering company charges a setup fee of \$45 plus \$12 per person. Which of the following sequences accurately reflects this situation?

Ⓕ $a_n = 45 + 12(n - 1)$

Ⓖ 45, 57, 69, 81, 93, ...

Ⓗ $a_n = 57 + 12n$

Ⓙ 57, 69, 81, 93, 105, ...

Anthony Lysson

54. Which graph might represent the terms of an arithmetic sequence?

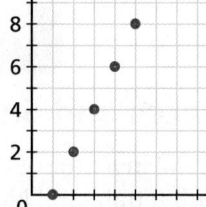

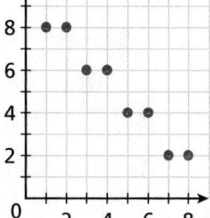

Ⓐ

Ⓑ

Ⓒ

Ⓓ

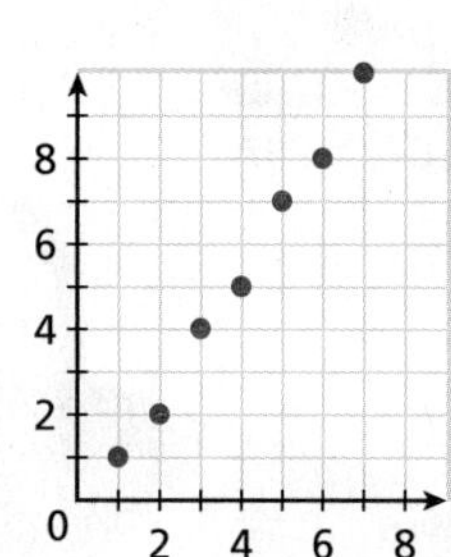

55. Given the arithmetic sequence 4, ■, ■, ■, 40, what are the three missing terms?

Ⓕ 11, 22, 33

Ⓖ 13, 22, 31

Ⓗ 14, 24, 34

Ⓙ 16, 24, 36

56. Which represents the sum of the arithmetic series 19 + 16 + 13 + 10 + 7 + 4?

Ⓐ $\sum_{k=1}^{6} 19 - 3k$

Ⓑ $\sum_{k=1}^{6} 19 - 4k$

Ⓒ $\sum_{k=1}^{6} (22 - 3k)$

Ⓓ $\sum_{k=1}^{6} [22 - 3(k - 1)]$

57. Gridded Response What is the 13th term of the arithmetic sequence 54, 50, 46, 42, ...?

CHALLENGE AND EXTEND

58. Consider the two terms of an arithmetic series a_n and a_m.

a. Show that the common difference is $d = \frac{a_n - a_m}{n - m}$.

b. Use the new formula to find the common difference for the arithmetic sequence with $a_{12} = 88$ and $a_{36} = 304$.

59. Find a formula for the sum of an arithmetic sequence that does NOT include the last term. When might this formula be useful?

60. The sum of three consecutive terms of an arithmetic sequence is 60. If the product of these terms is 7500, what are the terms?

61. Critical Thinking What does $a_{2n} = 2a_n$ mean and for what arithmetic sequences is it true?

CHAPTER 9

SECTION 9A

Look for regularity in repeated reasoning.

Exploring Arithmetic Sequences and Series

Go Fly a Kite! Alexander Graham Bell, the inventor of the telephone, is also known for his work with tetrahedral kites. In 1902, Bell used the kites to prove that it is possible to build an arbitrarily large structure that will fly. The kites are made up of tetrahedrons (four-sided triangular figures) with two sides covered with fabric. As shown in the figure, the size of a tetrahedral kite is determined by how many layers it has.

1 layer

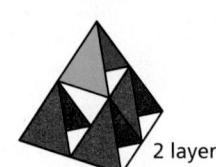

2 layers

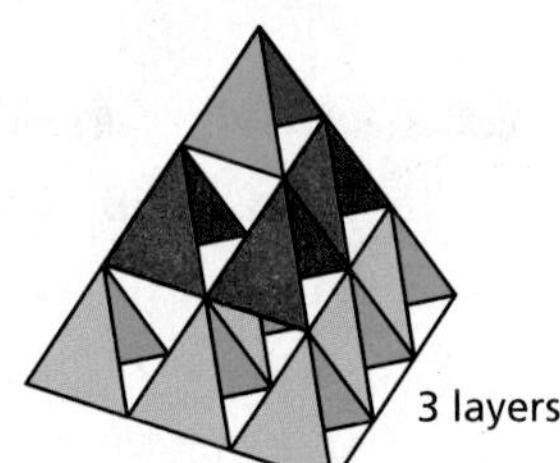

3 layers

1. The first layer of a tetrahedral kite has 1 tetrahedron, the second layer has 3 tetrahedrons, and the third layer has 6 tetrahedrons. Write a sequence that shows how many tetrahedrons are in each of the first 10 layers.
2. Write a recursive formula for the sequence.
3. Write an explicit rule for the nth term of the sequence.
4. How many tetrahedrons are there in the 25th layer?
5. Write a series in summation notation that gives the total number of tetrahedrons in a kite with 25 layers.
6. Evaluate the series in problem 5 to find the total number of tetrahedrons in a kite with 25 layers. (*Hint:* Use the properties

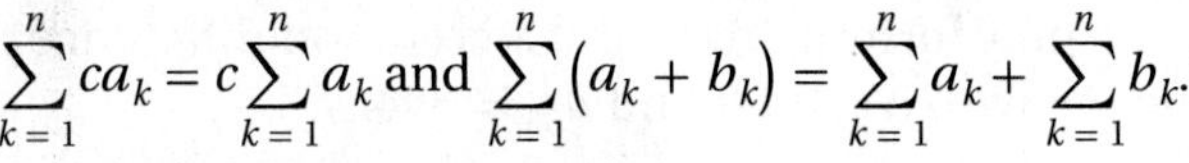

$\sum_{k=1}^{n} ca_k = c\sum_{k=1}^{n} a_k$ and $\sum_{k=1}^{n}\left(a_k + b_k\right) = \sum_{k=1}^{n} a_k + \sum_{k=1}^{n} b_k$.)

7. You see someone flying a large tetrahedral kite at a kite festival. You look up and estimate that the bottom layer of the kite contains between 100 and 110 tetrahedrons. How many layers does the kite have? How many tetrahedrons did it take to build the kite?

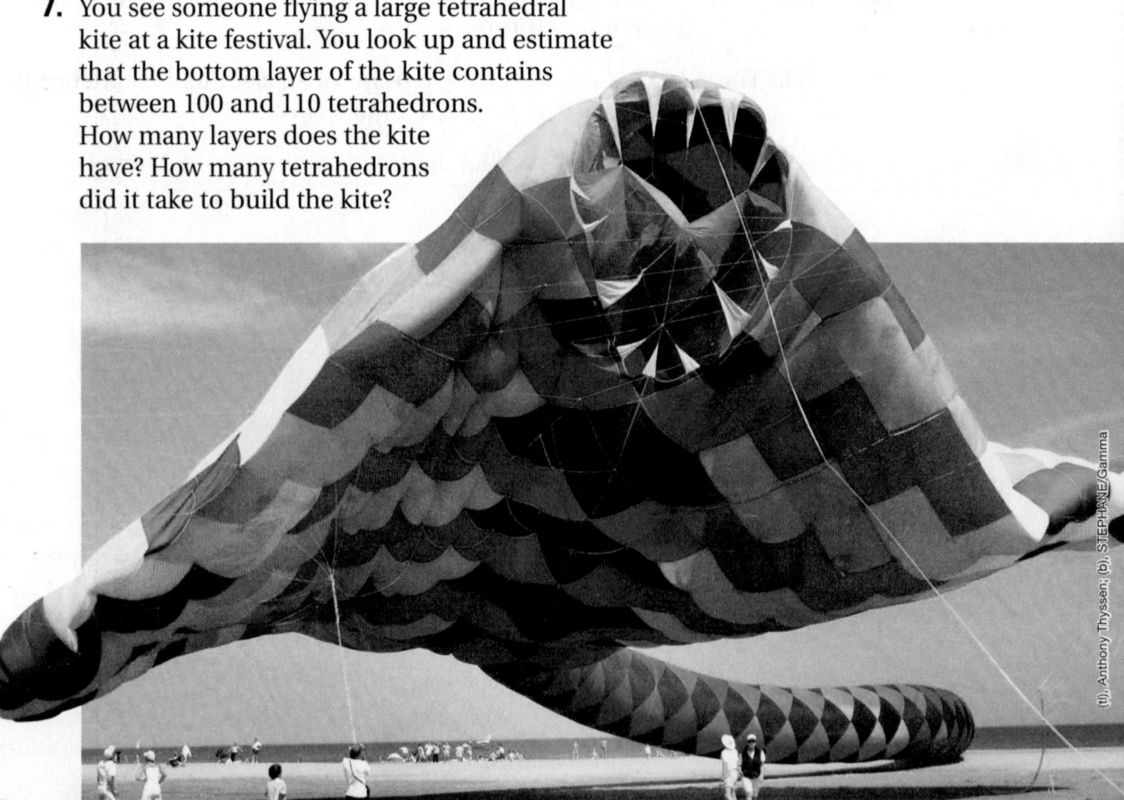

(tl), Anthony Thyssen; (b), STEPHANE/Gamma

READY TO GO ON?

CHAPTER 9

SECTION 9A

Quiz for Lessons 9-1 Through 9-3

9-1 Introduction to Sequences

Find the first 5 terms of each sequence.

1. $a_n = \frac{2}{3}n$
2. $a_n = 4^{n-1}$
3. $a_1 = -1$ and $a_n = 2a_{n-1} - 12$
4. $a_n = n^2 - 2n$

Write a possible explicit rule for the *n*th term of each sequence.

5. 8, 11, 14, 17, 20, ...
6. −2, −8, −18, −32, −50, ...
7. 1000, 200, 40, 8, $\frac{8}{5}$, ...
8. 437, 393, 349, 305, 261, ...
9. A car traveling at 55 mi/h passes a mile marker that reads mile 18. If the car maintains this speed for 4 hours, what mile marker should the car pass? Graph the sequence for *n* hours, and describe its pattern.

9-2 Series and Summation Notation

Expand each series and evaluate.

10. $\sum_{k=1}^{4}(-14 - 2k)$
11. $\sum_{k=1}^{4}\left(\frac{k}{k+2}\right)$
12. $\sum_{k=1}^{5}(-1)^k(k^2 - 2)$

Evaluate each series.

13. $\sum_{k=1}^{5}\frac{1}{2}$
14. $\sum_{k=1}^{40}k^2$
15. $\sum_{k=1}^{15}k$
16. The first row of a theater has 20 seats, and each of the following rows has 3 more seats than the preceding row. How many seats are in the first 12 rows?

9-3 Arithmetic Sequences and Series

Find the 8th term of each arithmetic sequence.

17. 10.00, 10.11, 10.22, 10.33, ...
18. −5, −13, −21, −29, ...
19. $a_2 = 57.5$ and $a_5 = 80$
20. $a_{10} = 141$ and $a_{13} = 186$

Find the missing terms in each arithmetic sequence.

21. −23, ■, ■, −89
22. 31, ■, ■, ■, 79

Find the indicated sum for each arithmetic series

23. S_{10} for 40 + 30 + 20 + 10 + ···
24. $\sum_{k=5}^{8}4k$
25. $\sum_{k=1}^{11}(0.5k + 5.5)$
26. S_{14} for −6 −1 + 4 + 9 + ···
27. Suppose that you make a bank deposit of $1 the first week, $1.50 the second week, $2 the third week, and so on. How much will you contribute to the account on the last week of the year (52nd week)? What is the total amount that you have deposited in the bank after one year?

COMMON CORE

9-4 Geometric Sequences and Series

CC.9-12.A.SSE.4 Derive the formula for the sum of a finite geometric series...and use the formula to solve problems.* *Also* **CC.9-12.F.BF.2*, CC.9-12.F.LE.2**

Objectives

Find terms of a geometric sequence, including geometric means.

Find the sums of geometric series.

Vocabulary

geometric sequence
geometric mean
geometric series

Who uses this?

Sporting-event planners can use geometric sequences and series to determine the number of matches that must be played in a tournament. (See Example 6.)

Serena Williams was the winner out of 128 players who began the 2003 Wimbledon Ladies' Singles Championship. After each match, the winner continues to the next round and the loser is eliminated from the tournament. This means that after each round only half of the players remain.

The number of players remaining after each round can be modeled by a *geometric sequence.* In a **geometric sequence**, the ratio of successive terms is a constant called the *common ratio* r $(r \neq 1)$. For the players remaining, r is $\frac{1}{2}$.

Term	a_1	a_2	a_3	a_4
Value	128	64	32	16

Ratios $\quad \frac{64}{128} = \frac{1}{2} \quad \frac{32}{64} = \frac{1}{2} \quad \frac{16}{32} = \frac{1}{2}$

Players in Each Round of Wimbledon

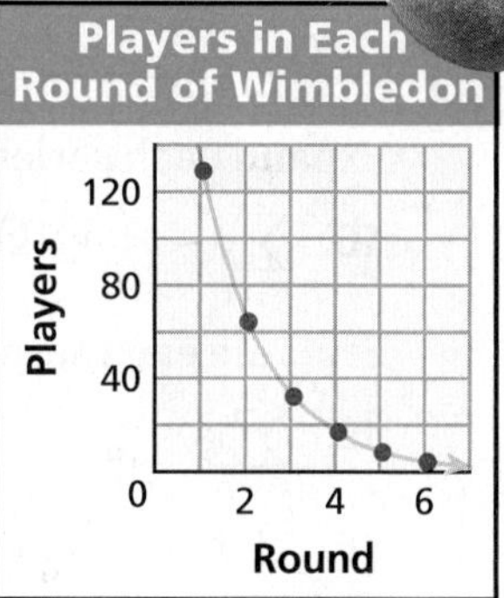

Recall that exponential functions have a common ratio. When you graph the ordered pairs (n, a_n) of a geometric sequence, the points lie on an exponential curve as shown. Thus, you can think of a geometric sequence as an exponential function with sequential natural numbers as the domain.

EXAMPLE 1 Identifying Geometric Sequences

Determine whether each sequence could be geometric or arithmetic. If possible, find the common ratio or difference.

A 8, 12, 18, 27, ...

8, 12, 18, 27

Diff. 4 6 9

Ratio $\frac{3}{2}$ $\frac{3}{2}$ $\frac{3}{2}$

It could be geometric, with $r = \frac{3}{2}$.

B 8, 16, 24, 32, ...

8, 16 24, 32

Diff. 8 8 8

Ratio 2 $\frac{3}{2}$ $\frac{4}{3}$

It could be arithmetic, with $d = 8$.

C 6, 10, 15, 21, ...

6, 10, 15, 21

Diff. 4 5 6

Ratio $\frac{5}{3}$ $\frac{3}{2}$ $\frac{7}{5}$

It is neither.

Determine whether each sequence could be geometric or arithmetic. If possible, find the common ratio or difference.

1a. $\frac{1}{4}, \frac{1}{12}, \frac{1}{36}, \frac{1}{108}, \ldots$

1b. 1.7, 1.3, 0.9, 0.5, ...

1c. −50, −32, −18, −8, ...

(tl), Reuters/CORBIS; (cl), PhotoDisc green/gettyimages

Each term in a geometric sequence is the product of the previous term and the common ratio, giving the recursive rule for a geometric sequence.

$$\underset{n\text{th term}}{a_n} = \underbrace{a_{n-1}}_{\text{Previous term}} \underset{\text{Common ratio}}{r}$$

You can also use an explicit rule to find the nth term of a geometric sequence. Each term is the product of the first term and a power of the common ratio as shown in the table.

Tennis Players in Each Round of Wimbledon

Round	1	2	3	4	n
Players	128	64	32	16	a_n
Formula	$a_1 = 128\left(\frac{1}{2}\right)^0$	$a_2 = 128\left(\frac{1}{2}\right)^1$	$a_3 = 128\left(\frac{1}{2}\right)^2$	$a_4 = 128\left(\frac{1}{2}\right)^3$	$a_n = 128\left(\frac{1}{2}\right)^{n-1}$

This pattern can be generalized into a rule for all geometric sequences.

General Rule for Geometric Sequences

The nth term a_n of a geometric sequence is

$$a_n = a_1 r^{n-1},$$

where a_1 is the first term and r is the common ratio.

EXAMPLE 2 Finding the nth Term Given a Geometric Sequence

Find the 9th term of the geometric sequence −5, 10, −20, 40, −80, ...

Step 1 Find the common ratio.

$$r = \frac{a_2}{a_1} = \frac{10}{-5} = -2$$

Step 2 Write a rule, and evaluate for $n = 9$.

$a_n = a_1 r^{n-1}$ *General rule*

$a_9 = -5(-2)^{9-1}$ *Substitute −5 for a_1, 9 for n, and −2 for r.*

$= -5(256) = -1280$

The 9th term is −1280.

Check Extend the sequence.

$a_5 = -80$ *Given*

$a_6 = -80(-2) = 160$

$a_7 = 160(-2) = -320$

$a_8 = -320(-2) = 640$

$a_9 = 640(-2) = -1280$ ✓

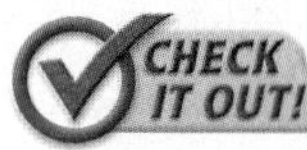

Find the 9th term of each geometric sequence.

2a. $\frac{3}{4}, -\frac{3}{8}, \frac{3}{16}, -\frac{3}{32}, \frac{3}{64}, \ldots$ **2b.** 0.001, 0.01, 0.1, 1, 10, ...

EXAMPLE 3 Finding the *n*th Term Given Two Terms

Find the 10th term of the geometric sequence with $a_5 = 96$ and $a_7 = 384$.

Step 1 Find the common ratio.

$a_7 = a_5 r^{(7-5)}$	*Use the given terms.*
$a_7 = a_5 r^2$	*Simplify.*
$384 = 96r^2$	*Substitute 384 for a_7 and 96 for a_5.*
$4 = r^2$	*Divide both sides by 96.*
$\pm 2 = r$	*Take the square root of both sides.*

Caution!

When given two terms of a sequence, be sure to consider positive and negative values for *r* when necessary.

Step 2 Find a_1.

Consider both the positive and negative values for *r*.

$a_n = a_1 r^{n-1}$		$a_n = a_1 r^{n-1}$	*General rule*
$96 = a_1(2)^{5-1}$	or	$96 = a_1(-2)^{5-1}$	*Use $a_5 = 96$ and $r = \pm 2$.*
$6 = a_1$		$6 = a_1$	

Step 3 Write the rule and evaluate for a_{10}.

Consider both the positive and negative values for *r*.

$a_n = a_1 r^{n-1}$		$a_n = a_1 r^{n-1}$	*General rule*
$a_n = 6(2)^{n-1}$	or	$a_n = 6(-2)^{n-1}$	*Substitute for a_1 and r.*
$a_{10} = 6(2)^{10-1}$		$a_{10} = 6(-2)^{10-1}$	*Evaluate for n = 6.*
$a_{10} = 3072$		$a_{10} = -3072$	

The 10th term is 3072 or −3072.

Find the 7th term of the geometric sequence with the given terms.

3a. $a_4 = -8$ and $a_5 = -40$ **3b.** $a_2 = 768$ and $a_4 = 48$

Geometric means are the terms between any two nonconsecutive terms of a geometric sequence.

Geometric Mean

If *a* and *b* are positive terms of a geometric sequence with exactly one term between them, the geometric mean is given by the following expression.

$$\sqrt{ab}$$

EXAMPLE 4 Finding Geometric Means

Find the geometric mean of $\frac{1}{2}$ and $\frac{1}{32}$.

$$\sqrt{ab} = \sqrt{\left(\frac{1}{2}\right)\left(\frac{1}{32}\right)}$$

$$= \sqrt{\frac{1}{64}} = \frac{1}{8} \quad \textit{Use the formula.}$$

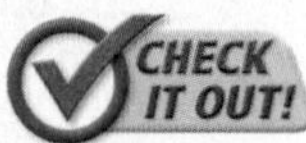

4. Find the geometric mean of 16 and 25.

The indicated sum of the terms of a geometric sequence is called a **geometric series**. You can derive a formula for the partial sum of a geometric series by subtracting the product of S_n and r from S_n as shown.

$$\begin{aligned} S_n &= a_1 + a_1 r + a_1 r^2 + \cdots + a_1 r^{n-1} \\ -rS_n &= \quad\; - a_1 r - a_1 r^2 - \cdots - a_1 r^{n-1} - a_1 r^n \\ \hline S_n - rS_n &= a_1 \qquad\qquad\qquad\qquad\qquad\quad - a_1 r^n \\ S_n(1-r) &= a_1(1-r^n) \\ S_n &= a_1\left(\frac{1-r^n}{1-r}\right) \end{aligned}$$

Sum of the First n Terms of a Geometric Series

The partial sum S_n of the first n terms of a geometric series $a_1 + a_2 + \cdots + a_n$ is given by

$$S_n = a_1\left(\frac{1-r^n}{1-r}\right),\ r \neq 1$$

where a_1 is the first term and r is the common ratio.

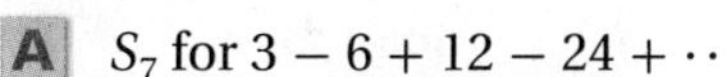

EXAMPLE 5 **Finding the Sum of a Geometric Series**

Find the indicated sum for each geometric series.

A S_7 for $3 - 6 + 12 - 24 + \cdots$

Step 1 Find the common ratio.

$$r = \frac{a_2}{a_1} = \frac{-6}{3} = -2$$

Step 2 Find S_7 with $a_1 = 3$, $r = -2$, and $n = 7$.

$$S_n = a_1\left(\frac{1-r^n}{1-r}\right) \quad \textit{Sum formula}$$

$$S_7 = 3\left(\frac{1-(-2)^7}{1-(-2)}\right) \quad \textit{Substitute.}$$

$$= 3\left(\frac{1-(-128)}{3}\right)$$

$$= 129$$

Check Use a graphing calculator.

```
sum(seq(3(-2)^(X
-1),X,1,7,1))
                129
```

✔

B $\sum_{k=1}^{5}\left(\frac{1}{3}\right)^{k-1}$

Step 1 Find the first term.

$$a_1 = \left(\frac{1}{3}\right)^{1-1} = \left(\frac{1}{3}\right)^0 = 1$$

Step 2 Find S_5.

$$S_n = a_1\left(\frac{1-r^n}{1-r}\right) \quad \textit{Sum formula}$$

$$S_5 = 1\left(\frac{1-\left(\frac{1}{3}\right)^5}{1-\left(\frac{1}{3}\right)}\right) \quad \textit{Substitute.}$$

$$= \left(\frac{1-\left(\frac{1}{243}\right)}{\frac{2}{3}}\right)$$

$$= \frac{242}{243}\cdot\frac{3}{2} = \frac{121}{81} \approx 1.49$$

Check Use a graphing calculator.

```
sum(seq((1/3)^(X
-1),X,1,5,1))
        1.49382716
```

✔

Remember!

These sums are partial sums because you are finding the sum of a finite number of terms.

Find the indicated sum for each geometric series.

5a. S_6 for $2 + 1 + \frac{1}{2} + \frac{1}{4} + \cdots$ **5b.** $\sum_{k=1}^{6} -3(2)^{k-1}$

EXAMPLE 6 Sports Application

The Wimbledon Ladies' Singles Championship begins with 128 players. The players compete until there is 1 winner. How many matches must be scheduled in order to complete the tournament?

Step 1 Write a sequence.

Let n = the number of rounds,

a_n = the number of matches played in the nth round, and

S_n = the total number of matches played through n rounds.

$a_n = 64\left(\frac{1}{2}\right)^{n-1}$ *The first round requires 64 matches, so $a_1 = 64$. Each successive match requires $\frac{1}{2}$ as many, so $r = \frac{1}{2}$.*

Remember!

Review solving exponential equations.

Step 2 Find the number of rounds required.

$1 = 64\left(\frac{1}{2}\right)^{n-1}$ *The final round will have 1 match, so substitute 1 for a_n.*

$\frac{1}{64} = \left(\frac{1}{2}\right)^{n-1}$ *Isolate the exponential expression by dividing by 64.*

$\left(\frac{1}{2}\right)^6 = \left(\frac{1}{2}\right)^{n-1}$ *Express $\frac{1}{64}$ as a power of $\frac{1}{2}$: $\frac{1}{64} = \left(\frac{1}{2}\right)^6$.*

$6 = n - 1$ *Equate the exponents.*

$7 = n$ *Solve for n.*

Step 3 Find the total number of matches after 7 rounds.

$$S_7 = 64\left(\frac{1-\left(\frac{1}{2}\right)^7}{1-\left(\frac{1}{2}\right)}\right) = 127$$ *Sum function for geometric series.*

127 matches must be scheduled to complete the tournament.

CHECK IT OUT!

6. **Real Estate** A 6-year lease states that the annual rent for an office space is \$84,000 the first year and will increase by 8% each additional year of the lease. What will the total rent expense be for the 6-year lease?

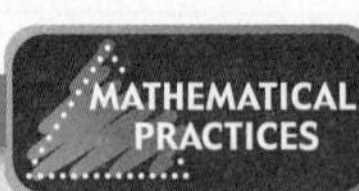

THINK AND DISCUSS

1. Find the next three terms of the geometric sequence that begins 3, 6, ... Then find the next three terms of the arithmetic sequence that begins 3, 6, ...
2. Compare the geometric mean of 4 and 16 with the mean, or average.

3. **GET ORGANIZED** Copy and complete the graphic organizer. In each box, summarize your understanding of geometric sequences.

Definition	Characteristics
Examples	Formulas

(Center: Geometric Sequences)

REUTERS/Ian Hodgson/CORBIS

9-4 Exercises

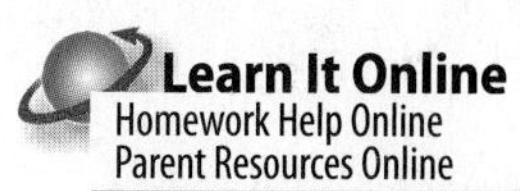

GUIDED PRACTICE

1. **Vocabulary** The term between two given terms in a geometric sequence is the ___?___. (*geometric mean* or *geometric series*)

SEE EXAMPLE 1

Determine whether each sequence could be geometric or arithmetic. If possible, find the common ratio or difference.

2. $-10, -12, -14, -16, \ldots$
3. $\frac{1}{2}, 1, 2, 3, \ldots$
4. $-320, -80, -20, -5, \ldots$

SEE EXAMPLE 2

Find the 10th term of each geometric sequence.

5. $2, 6, 18, 54, 162, \ldots$
6. $5000, 500, 50, 5, 0.5, \ldots$
7. $-0.125, 0.25, -0.5, 1, -2, \ldots$

SEE EXAMPLE 3

Find the 6th term of the geometric sequence with the given terms.

8. $a_4 = -12, a_5 = -4$
9. $a_2 = 4, a_5 = 108$
10. $a_3 = 3, a_5 = 12$

SEE EXAMPLE 4

Find the geometric mean of each pair of numbers.

11. 6 and $\frac{3}{8}$
12. 2 and 32
13. 12 and 192

SEE EXAMPLE 5

Find the indicated sum for each geometric series.

14. S_6 for $2 + 0.2 + 0.02 + \cdots$
15. $\sum_{k=1}^{5} (-3)^{k-1}$
16. S_5 for $12 - 24 + 48 - 96 + \cdots$
17. $\sum_{k=1}^{9} 256\left(\frac{1}{2}\right)^{k-1}$

SEE EXAMPLE 6

18. **Salary** In his first year, a math teacher earned $32,000. Each successive year, he earned a 5% raise. How much did he earn in his 20th year? What were his total earnings over the 20-year period?

PRACTICE AND PROBLEM SOLVING

Independent Practice

For Exercises	See Example
19–21	1
22–25	2
26–28	3
29–31	4
32–35	5
36	6

Extra Practice

See Extra Practice for more Skills Practice and Applications Practice exercises.

Determine whether each sequence could be geometric or arithmetic. If possible, find the common ratio or difference.

19. $-36, -49, -64, -81, \ldots$
20. $-2, -6, -18, -54, \ldots$
21. $2, 7, 12, 17, \ldots$

Find the 9th term of each geometric sequence.

22. $\frac{1}{2}, \frac{1}{10}, \frac{1}{50}, \frac{1}{250}, \frac{1}{1250}, \ldots$
23. $3, -6, 12, -24, 48, \ldots$
24. $3200, 1600, 800, 400, 200, \ldots$
25. $8, 24, 72, 216, 648, \ldots$

Find the 7th term of the geometric sequence with the given terms.

26. $a_4 = 54, a_5 = 162$
27. $a_5 = 13.5, a_6 = 20.25$
28. $a_4 = -4, a_6 = -100$

Find the geometric mean of each pair of numbers.

29. 9 and $\frac{1}{9}$
30. 18 and 2
31. $\frac{1}{5}$ and 45

Find the indicated sum for each geometric series.

32. S_6 for $1 + 5 + 25 + 125 + \cdots$
33. S_8 for $10 + 1 + \frac{1}{10} + \frac{1}{100} + \cdots$
34. $\sum_{k=1}^{6} -1\left(\frac{1}{3}\right)^{k-1}$
35. $\sum_{k=1}^{7} 8(10)^{k-1}$

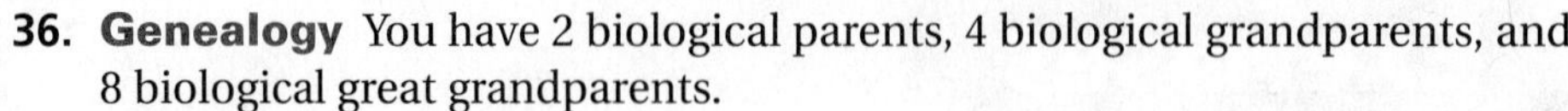

36. **Genealogy** You have 2 biological parents, 4 biological grandparents, and 8 biological great grandparents.

   a. How many direct ancestors do you have in the 6 generations before you? 12 generations?

   b. **What if...?** How does the explicit rule change if you are considered the first generation?

LINK

Collectibles

The most expensive rock'n'roll memorabilia ever purchased was John Lennon's Rolls Royce, with a price tag of $2.2 million.

Given each geometric sequence, (a) write an explicit rule for the sequence, (b) find the 10th term, and (c) find the sum of the first 10 terms.

37. $\frac{1}{16}, \frac{1}{8}, \frac{1}{4}, \frac{1}{2}, \ldots$

38. 4, 0.4, 0.04, 0.004, ...

39. 8, 16, 32, 64, ...

40. $-22, -11, -\frac{11}{2}, -\frac{11}{4}, \ldots$

41. 162, −54, 18, −6, ...

42. 12.5, 62.5, 312.5, 1562.5, ...

43. **Collectibles** Louis bought a vintage Rolling Stones concert shirt for $20. He estimates that the shirt will increase in value by 15% per year.

   a. How much is the shirt worth after 4 years? after 8 years?

   b. Does the shirt increase more in value during the first 4 years or the second 4 years? Explain.

44. **College Tuition** New grandparents decide to pay for their granddaughter's college education. They give the girl a penny on her first birthday and double the gift on each subsequent birthday. How much money will the girl receive when she is 18? 21? Will the money pay for her college education? Explain.

45. **Technology** You receive an e-mail asking you to forward it to 5 other people to ensure good luck. Assume that no one breaks the chain and that there are no duplications among the recipients. How many e-mails will have been sent after 10 generations, including yours, have received and sent the e-mail?

46. **Fractals** The Sierpinski carpet is a fractal based on a square. In each iteration, the center of each shaded square is removed.

   a. Given that the area of the original square is 1 square unit, write a sequence for the area of the nth iteration of the Sierpinski carpet.

   b. In which iteration will the area be less than $\frac{1}{2}$ of the original area?

47. **Paper** A piece of paper is 0.1 mm thick. When folded, the paper is twice as thick.

   a. Studies have shown that you can fold a piece of paper a maximum of 7 times. How thick will the paper be if it is folded on top of itself 7 times?

   b. Assume that you could fold the paper as many times as you want. How many folds would be required for the paper to be taller than Mount Everest (8850 m)?

48. **Measurement** Several common U.S. paper sizes are shown in the table.

   a. Examine the length and width measures for the different paper sizes. What interrelationships do you observe?

   b. How are the areas for each paper size (from A to E) mathematically related and what name is this relationship given?

Common U.S. Paper Sizes

U.S. Paper Size	Dimensions (in.)
A (letter)	$8\frac{1}{2} \times 11$
B (ledger)	11×17
C	17×22
D	22×34
E	34×44

Bettman/CORBIS

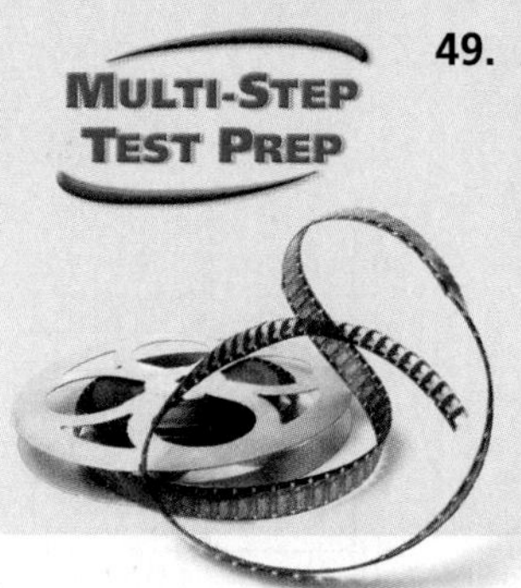

49. A movie earned $60 million in its first week of release and $9.6 million in the third week of release. The sales each week can be modeled by a geometric sequence.

a. Estimate the movie's sales in its second week of release.

b. By what percent did the sales decrease each week?

c. In what week would you expect sales to be less than $1 million?

d. Estimate the movie's total sales during its 8-week release period.

50. Biology The population growth of bacteria in a petri dish each hour creates a geometric sequence. After 1 hour there were 4 bacteria cells, and after 5 hours there were 324 cells. How many cells were found at hours 2, 3, and 4?

51. Critical Thinking Find an arithmetic sequence, a geometric sequence, and a sequence that is neither arithmetic nor geometric that begins 1, 4, ...

52. Finance Suppose that you pay $750 in rent each month. Suppose also that your rent is increased by 10% each year thereafter.

a. Write a series that describes the total rent paid each year over the first 5 years, and find its sum.

b. Use sigma notation to represent the series for the total rent paid each year over the first 10 years, and evaluate it.

53. Music The frequencies produced by playing C notes in ascending octaves make up a geometric sequence. C0 is the lowest C note audible to the human ear.

a. The note commonly called middle C is C4. Find the frequency of middle C.

b. Write a geometric sequence for the frequency of C notes in hertz where $n = 1$ represents C1.

c. Humans cannot hear sounds with frequencies greater than 20,000 Hz. What is the first C note that humans cannot hear?

Scale of C's

Note	Frequency (Hz)
C0	16.24
C1	32.7
C2	65.4
C3	130.8
C4	■

54. Medicine During a flu outbreak, a hospital recorded 16 cases the first week, 56 cases the second week, and 196 cases the third week.

a. Write a geometric sequence to model the flu outbreak.

b. If the hospital did nothing to stop the outbreak, in which week would the total number infected exceed 10,000?

55. Graphing Calculator Use the **SEQ** and **SUM** features to find each indicated sum of the geometric series $8 + 6 + 4.5 + \cdots$ to the nearest thousandth.

a. S_{10} **b.** S_{20} **c.** S_{30} **d.** S_{40}

e. Does the series appear to be approaching any particular value? Explain.

56. Critical Thinking If a geometric sequence has $r > 1$, what happens to the terms as n increases? What happens if $0 < r < 1$?

57. Write About It What happens to the terms of a geometric sequence when the first term is tripled? What happens to the sum of this geometric sequence?

58. Find the sum of the first 6 terms for the geometric series $4.5 + 9 + 18 + 36 + \cdots$.

Ⓐ 67.5 Ⓑ 144 Ⓒ 283.5 Ⓓ 445.5

59. Which graph might represent the terms of a geometric sequence?

Ⓕ

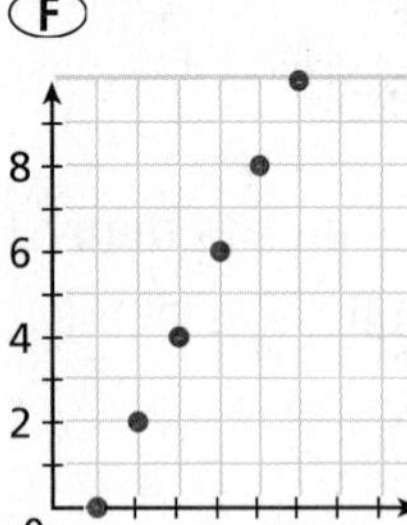

Ⓖ

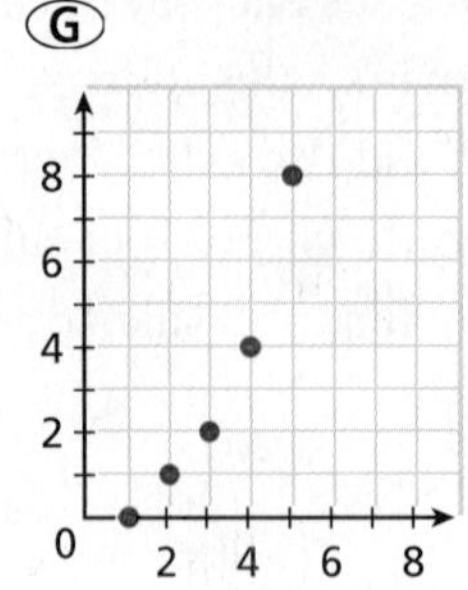

Ⓗ

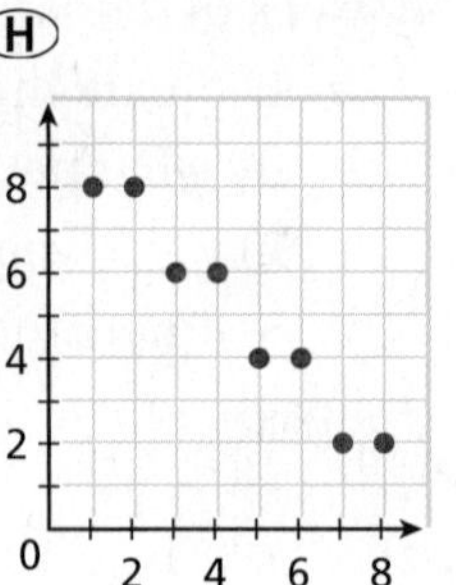

Ⓙ

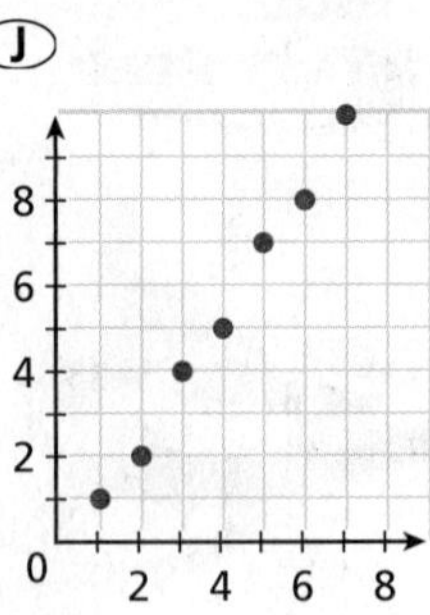

60. Find the first 3 terms of the geometric sequence with $a_7 = -192$ and $a_9 = -768$.

Ⓐ 3, −6, 12

Ⓑ −3, 12, −48

Ⓒ −3, 6, −12 or −3, −6, −12

Ⓓ 3, −12, 48 or −3, −12, −48

61. Which represents the sum of the series 10 − 15 + 22.5 − 33.75 + 50.625?

Ⓕ $\sum_{k=1}^{5} 10\left(\frac{3}{2}\right)^{k-1}$

Ⓖ $\sum_{k=1}^{5} 10\left(-\frac{3}{2}\right)^{k-1}$

Ⓗ $\sum_{k=1}^{5} -10\left(\frac{3}{2}\right)^{k-1}$

Ⓙ $\sum_{k=1}^{5} 10\left(-\frac{3}{2}\right)^{k}$

62. Short Response Why does the general rule for a geometric sequence use $n - 1$ instead of n? Explain.

CHALLENGE AND EXTEND

Graphing Calculator For each geometric sequence, find the first term with a value greater than 1,000,000.

63. $a_1 = 10$ and $r = 2$

64. $a_1 = \frac{1}{4}$ and $r = 4$

65. $a_1 = 0.01$ and $r = 3.2$

66. The sum of three consecutive terms of a geometric sequence is 73.5. If the product of these terms is 2744, what are the terms?

67. Consider the geometric sequence whose first term is 55 with the common ratio $\frac{1+\sqrt{5}}{2}$.

a. Find the next 5 terms rounded to the nearest integer.

b. Add each pair of successive terms together. What do you notice?

c. Make a conjecture about this sequence.

9-5 Algebra LAB

Explore Infinite Geometric Series

You can explore infinite geometric series by using a sequence of squares.

Use with Mathematical Induction and Infinite Geometric Series

MATHEMATICAL PRACTICES **Use appropriate tools strategically.**

CC.9-12.F.BF.2 Write...sequences both recursively and with an explicit formula, use them to model situations, and translate between the two forms.*

Activity

1. On a piece of graph paper, draw a 16×16 unit square. Note that its perimeter is 64 units.
2. Starting at one corner of the original square, draw a new square with side lengths half as long, or in this case, 8×8 units. Note that its perimeter is 32 units.
3. Create a table as shown at right. Fill in the perimeters and the cumulative sum of the perimeters that you have found so far.

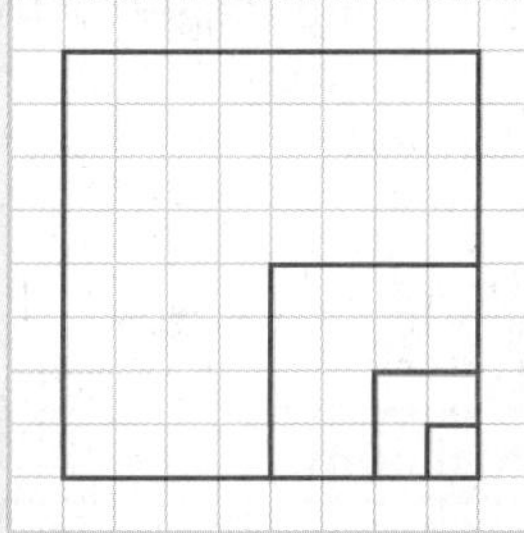

Square	Perimeter	Sum
16×16	64	64
8×8	32	96
4×4	■	■
2×2	■	■
1×1	■	■
$\frac{1}{2} \times \frac{1}{2}$	■	■

Try This

1. Copy the table, and complete the first 6 rows.
2. Use summation notation to write a geometric series for the perimeters.
3. Use a graphing calculator to find the sum of the first 20 terms of the series.
4. **Make a Conjecture** Make a conjecture about the sum of the perimeter series if it were to continue indefinitely.
5. Evaluate $\frac{64}{1 - \frac{1}{2}}$. How does this relate to your answer to Problem 4?
6. Copy and complete the table by finding the area of each square and the cumulative sums.
7. Use summation notation to write a geometric series for the areas.
8. Use a graphing calculator to find the sum of the first 10 terms of the series.
9. **Make a Conjecture** Make a conjecture about the sum of the area series if it were to continue indefinitely.
10. Evaluate $\frac{256}{1 - \frac{1}{4}}$. How does this relate to your answer to Problem 9?
11. **Draw a Conclusion** Write a formula for the sum of an infinite geometric sequence.

Square	Area	Sum
16×16	■	■
8×8	■	■
4×4	■	■
2×2	■	■
1×1	■	■
$\frac{1}{2} \times \frac{1}{2}$	■	■

COMMON CORE

9-5 Mathematical Induction and Infinite Geometric Series

CC.9-12.F.BF.2 Write…sequences both recursively and with an explicit formula, use them to model situations, and translate between the two forms.*

Objectives

Find sums of infinite geometric series.

Use mathematical induction to prove statements.

Vocabulary

infinite geometric series
converge
limit
diverge
mathematical induction

Why learn this?

You can use infinite geometric series to explore repeating patterns. (See Exercise 58.)

You learned how to find partial sums of geometric series. You can also find the sums of some infinite geometric series. An **infinite geometric series** has infinitely many terms. Consider the two infinite geometric series below.

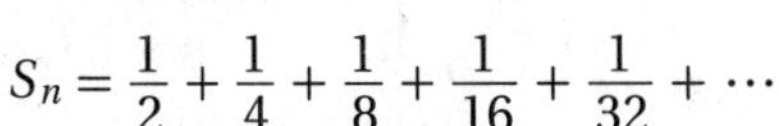

$$S_n = \frac{1}{2} + \frac{1}{4} + \frac{1}{8} + \frac{1}{16} + \frac{1}{32} + \cdots$$

Partial Sums						
n	1	2	3	4	5	6
S_n	$\frac{1}{2}$	$\frac{3}{4}$	$\frac{7}{8}$	$\frac{15}{16}$	$\frac{31}{32}$	$\frac{63}{64}$

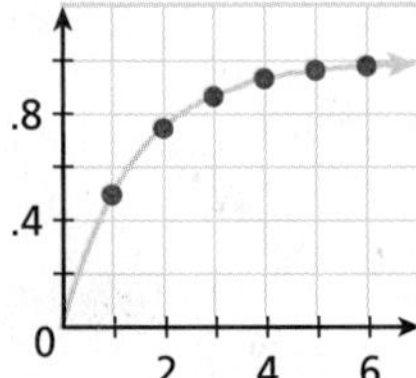

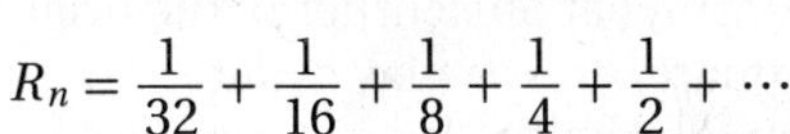

$$R_n = \frac{1}{32} + \frac{1}{16} + \frac{1}{8} + \frac{1}{4} + \frac{1}{2} + \cdots$$

Partial Sums						
n	1	2	3	4	5	6
R_n	$\frac{1}{32}$	$\frac{3}{32}$	$\frac{7}{32}$	$\frac{15}{32}$	$\frac{31}{32}$	$\frac{63}{32}$

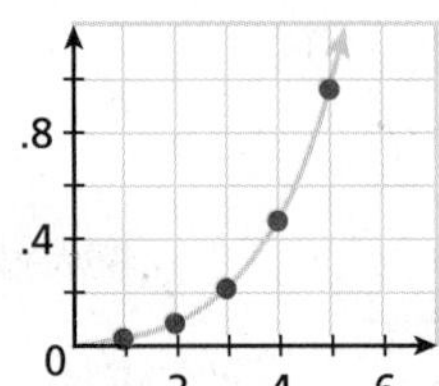

Notice that the series S_n has a common ratio of $\frac{1}{2}$ and the partial sums get closer and closer to 1 as n increases. When $|r| < 1$ and the partial sum approaches a fixed number, the series is said to **converge**. The number that the partial sums approach, as n increases, is called a **limit**.

For the series R_n, the opposite applies. Its common ratio is 2, and its partial sums increase toward infinity. When $|r| \geq 1$ and the partial sum does not approach a fixed number, the series is said to **diverge**.

EXAMPLE 1 Finding Convergent or Divergent Series

Determine whether each geometric series converges or diverges.

A $20 + 24 + 28.8 + 34.56 + \cdots$

$$r = \frac{24}{20} = 1.2, |r| \geq 1$$

The series diverges and does not have a sum.

B $1 + \frac{1}{3} + \frac{1}{9} + \frac{1}{27} + \frac{1}{81} + \cdots$

$$r = \frac{\frac{1}{3}}{1} = \frac{1}{3}, |r| < 1$$

The series converges and has a sum.

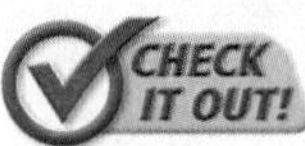

Determine whether each geometric series converges or diverges.

1a. $\frac{2}{3} + 1 + \frac{3}{2} + \frac{9}{4} + \frac{27}{8} + \cdots$ **1b.** $32 + 16 + 8 + 4 + 2 + \cdots$

If an infinite series converges, we can find the sum. Consider the series $S_n = \frac{1}{2} + \frac{1}{4} + \frac{1}{8} + \frac{1}{16} + \frac{1}{32} + \cdots$ from the previous page. Use the formula for the partial sum of a geometric series with $a_1 = \frac{1}{2}$ and $r = \frac{1}{2}$.

$$S_n = a_1\left(\frac{1 - r^n}{1 - r}\right) = \frac{1}{2}\left(\frac{1 - \left(\frac{1}{2}\right)^n}{1 - \frac{1}{2}}\right) = \frac{1\left(1 - \left(\frac{1}{2}\right)^n\right)}{2\left(\frac{1}{2}\right)} = \frac{1 - \left(\frac{1}{2}\right)^n}{1} = 1 - \left(\frac{1}{2}\right)^n$$

Graph the simplified equation on a graphing calculator. Notice that the sum levels out and converges to 1.

As n approaches infinity, the term $\left(\frac{1}{2}\right)^n$ approaches zero. Therefore, the sum of the series is 1. This concept can be generalized for all convergent geometric series and proved by using calculus.

Sum of an Infinite Geometric Series

The sum of an infinite geometric series S with common ratio r and $|r| < 1$ is

$$S = \frac{a_1}{1 - r},$$

where a_1 is the first term.

EXAMPLE 2 Finding the Sums of Infinite Geometric Series

Helpful Hint

You can graph a geometric series by using the sum formula: $S_n = a_1\left(\frac{1 - r^n}{1 - r}\right)$ with S_n as y and n as x and with values substituted for r and a_1.

Find the sum of each infinite geometric series, if it exists.

A $5 + 4 + 3.2 + 2.56 + \cdots$

$r = 0.8$ *Converges:* $|r| < 1$

$S = \frac{a_1}{1 - r}$ *Sum formula*

$= \frac{5}{1 - 0.8} = \frac{5}{0.2} = 25$

Check Graph $y = 5\left(\frac{1 - (0.8)^x}{1 - 0.8}\right)$ on a graphing calculator. The graph approaches $y = 25$. ✔

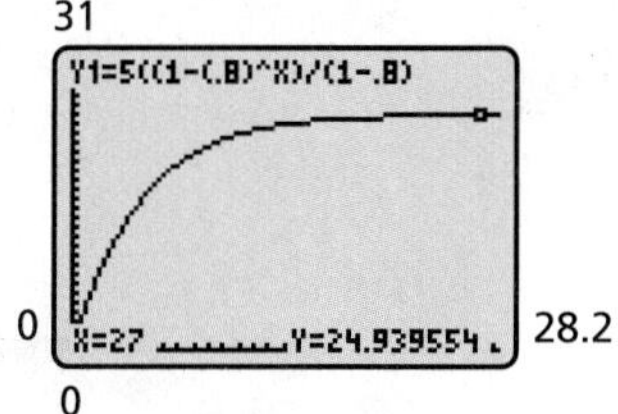

B $\sum_{k=1}^{\infty} \frac{2}{3^{k-1}}$

$\sum_{k=1}^{\infty} \frac{2}{3^{k-1}} = \frac{2}{1} + \frac{2}{3} + \frac{2}{9} + \cdots$ *Evaluate.*

$r = \frac{\frac{2}{3}}{2} = \frac{2}{6} = \frac{1}{3}$ *Converges:* $|r| < 1$

$S = \frac{a_1}{1 - r} = \frac{2}{1 - \frac{1}{3}} = \frac{2}{\frac{2}{3}} = \frac{6}{2} = 3$

Check Graph $y = 2\left(\frac{1 - \left(\frac{1}{3}\right)^x}{1 - \frac{1}{3}}\right)$ on a graphing calculator. The graph approaches $y = 3$. ✔

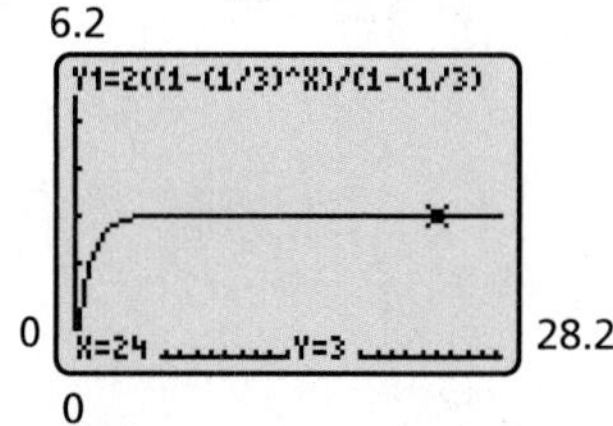

Find the sum of each infinite geometric series, if it exists.

2a. $25 - 5 + 1 - \frac{1}{5} + \frac{1}{25} - \cdots$ **2b.** $\sum_{k=1}^{\infty}\left(\frac{2}{5}\right)^k$

You can use infinite series to write a repeating decimal as a fraction.

EXAMPLE 3 Writing Repeating Decimals as Fractions

Write 0.232323... as a fraction in simplest form.

Step 1 Write the repeating decimal as an infinite geometric series.

$0.232323... = 0.23 + 0.0023 + 0.000023 + \cdots$ *Use the pattern for the series.*

Step 2 Find the common ratio.

$$r = \frac{0.0023}{0.23}$$

$$= \frac{1}{100}, \text{ or } 0.01$$ *$|r| < 1$; the series converges to a sum.*

Step 3 Find the sum.

$$S = \frac{a_1}{1 - r}$$ *Apply the sum formula.*

$$= \frac{0.23}{1 - 0.01} = \frac{0.23}{0.99} = \frac{23}{99}$$

Check Use a calculator to divide the fraction $\frac{23}{99}$. ✔

Remember!

Recall that every repeating decimal, such as 0.232323..., or $0.\overline{23}$, is a rational number and can be written as a fraction.

3. Write 0.111... as a fraction in simplest form.

You have used series to find the sums of many sets of numbers, such as the first 100 natural numbers. The formulas that you used for such sums can be proved by using a type of mathematical proof called **mathematical induction**.

Proof by Mathematical Induction

To prove that a statement is true for all natural numbers n,

Step 1 The base case: Show that the statement is true for $n = 1$.

Step 2 Assume that the statement is true for a natural number k.

Step 3 Prove that the statement is true for the natural number $k + 1$.

EXAMPLE 4 Proving with Mathematical Induction

Use mathematical induction to prove that the sum of the first n natural numbers is $1 + 2 + 3 + \cdots + n = \frac{n(n+1)}{2}$.

Step 1 Base case: Show that the statement is true for $n = 1$.

$$1 = \frac{n(n+1)}{2} = \frac{1(1+1)}{2} = \frac{2}{2} = 1$$ *The base case is true.*

Step 2 Assume that the statement is true for a natural number k.

$$1 + 2 + 3 + \cdots + k = \frac{k(k+1)}{2}$$ *Replace n with k.*

Step 3 Prove that it is true for the natural number $k + 1$.

$$1 + 2 + \cdots + k = \frac{k(k+1)}{2}$$

$$1 + 2 + \cdots + k + (k+1) = \frac{k(k+1)}{2} + (k+1) \quad \text{Add the next term } (k+1) \text{ to each side.}$$

$$= \frac{k(k+1)}{2} + \frac{2(k+1)}{2} \quad \text{Find the common denominator.}$$

$$= \frac{k(k+1) + 2(k+1)}{2} \quad \text{Add numerators.}$$

$$= \frac{(k+1)(k+2)}{2} \quad \text{Factor out } k+1.$$

$$= \frac{(k+1)[(k+1)+1]}{2} \quad \text{Write with } k+1.$$

Therefore, $1 + 2 + 3 + \cdots + n = \frac{n(n+1)}{2}$.

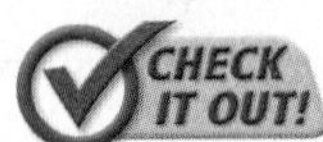

4. Use mathematical induction to prove that the sum of the first n odd numbers is $1 + 3 + 5 + \cdots + (2n - 1) = n^2$.

Mathematical statements that seem to be true may in fact be false. By finding a counterexample, you can disprove a statement.

EXAMPLE 5 Using Counterexamples

Helpful Hint

Often counterexamples can be found using special numbers like 1, 0, negative numbers, or fractions.

Identify a counterexample to disprove $2^n \geq n^2$, where n is a real number.

$2^0 \geq (0)^2$	$2^1 \geq (1)^2$	$2^4 \geq (4)^2$	$2^{-1} \geq (-1)^2$
$1 \geq 0$ ✔	$2 \geq 1$ ✔	$24 \geq 16$ ✔	$\frac{1}{2} \geq 1$ ✗

$2^n \geq n^2$ is not true for $n = -1$, so it is not true for all real numbers.

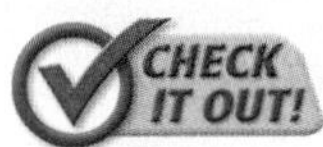

5. Identify a counterexample to disprove $\frac{a^2}{2} \leq 2a + 1$, where a is a real number.

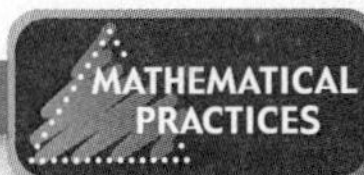

THINK AND DISCUSS

1. Explain how to determine whether a geometric series converges or diverges.

2. Explain how to represent the repeating decimal $0.8\overline{3}$ as an infinite geometric series.

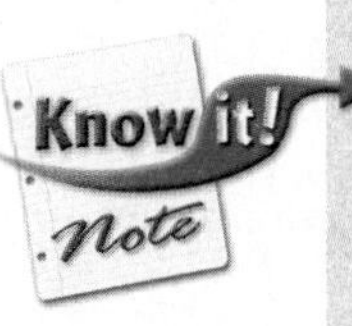

3. GET ORGANIZED Copy and complete the graphic organizer. Summarize the different infinite geometric series.

	Example	Common Ratio	Sum
Convergent Series			
Divergent Series			

9-5 Exercises

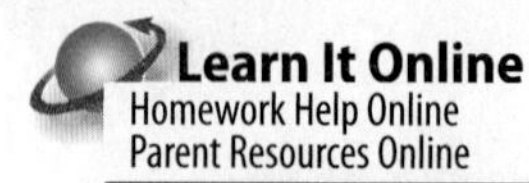

GUIDED PRACTICE

1. **Vocabulary** An infinite geometric series whose sum approaches a fixed number is said to __?__. (*converge* or *diverge*)

SEE EXAMPLE 1

Determine whether each geometric series converges or diverges.

2. $1 - \frac{1}{3} + \frac{1}{9} - \frac{1}{27} + \frac{1}{81} + \cdots$
3. $1 - 5 + 25 - 125 + 625 + \cdots$
4. $27 + 18 + 12 + 8 + \cdots$

SEE EXAMPLE 2

Find the sum of each infinite geometric series, if it exists.

5. $\frac{3}{4} + \frac{1}{2} + \frac{1}{3} + \frac{2}{9} + \cdots$
6. $\sum_{k=1}^{\infty} 4(0.25)^k$
7. $800 + 200 + 50 + \cdots$

SEE EXAMPLE 3

Write each repeating decimal as a fraction in simplest form.

8. $0.888\ldots$
9. $0.\overline{56}$
10. $0.131313\ldots$

SEE EXAMPLE 4

11. Use mathematical induction to prove that the sum of the first n even numbers is $2 + 4 + 6 + \cdots + 2n = n(n+1)$.

SEE EXAMPLE 5

Identify a counterexample to disprove each statement, where n is a real number.

12. $n^4 \geq 1$
13. $\log n > 0$
14. $n^3 \leq 3n^2$

PRACTICE AND PROBLEM SOLVING

Independent Practice

For Exercises	See Example
15–17	1
18–20	2
21–23	3
24	4
25–27	5

Extra Practice

See Extra Practice for more Skills Practice and Applications Practice exercises.

Determine whether each geometric series converges or diverges.

15. $3 + \frac{3}{5} + \frac{3}{25} + \frac{3}{125} + \frac{3}{625} + \cdots$
16. $5 + 10 + 20 + 40 + \cdots$
17. $2 - 4 + 8 - 16 + 32 + \cdots$

Find the sum of each infinite geometric series, if it exists.

18. $\sum_{k=1}^{\infty} 60\left(\frac{1}{10}\right)^k$
19. $\frac{8}{5} - \frac{4}{5} + \frac{2}{5} - \frac{1}{5} + \cdots$
20. $\sum_{k=1}^{\infty} 3.5^k$

Write each repeating decimal as a fraction in simplest form.

21. $0.\overline{6}$
22. $0.90909\ldots$
23. $0.541541541\ldots$
24. Use mathematical induction to prove $\frac{1}{1(2)} + \frac{1}{2(3)} + \frac{1}{3(4)} + \cdots + \frac{1}{n(n+1)} = \frac{n}{n+1}$.

Identify a counterexample to disprove each statement, where a is a real number.

25. $a^3 \neq -a^2$
26. $a^4 > 0$
27. $5a^2 > 2^a$
28. **/// ERROR ANALYSIS ///** Two possible sums for the series $\frac{1}{5} + \frac{2}{5} + \frac{4}{5} + \cdots$ are shown. Which is incorrect? Explain the error.

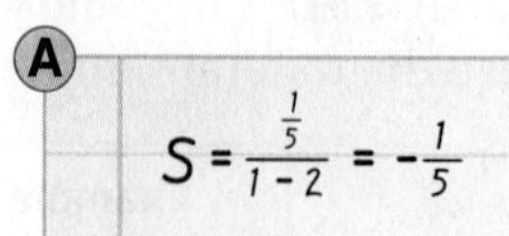

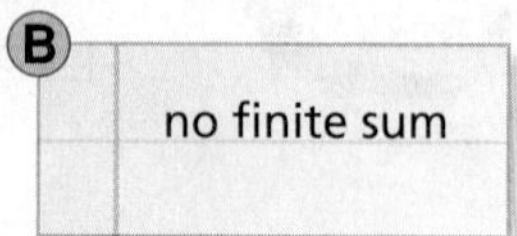

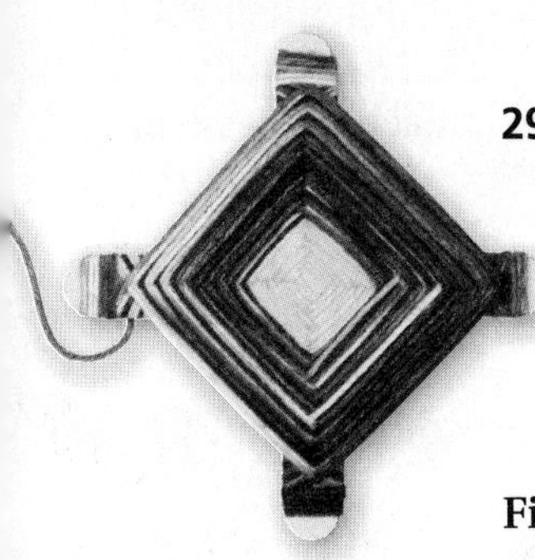

29. Art Ojos de Dios are Mexican holiday decorations. They are made of yarn, which is wrapped around sticks in a repeated square pattern. Suppose that the side length of the outer square is 8 inches. The side length of each inner square is 90% of the previous square's length. How much yarn will be required to complete the decoration? (Assume that the pattern is represented by an infinite geometric series.)

Find the sum of each infinite geometric series, if it exists.

30. $215 - 86 + 34.4 - 13.76 + \cdots$

31. $500 + 400 + 320 + \cdots$

32. $8 - 10 + 12.5 - 15.625 + \cdots$

33. $\sum_{k=1}^{\infty} -5\left(\frac{1}{8}\right)^{k-1}$

34. $\sum_{k=1}^{\infty} 2\left(\frac{1}{4}\right)^{k-1}$

35. $\sum_{k=1}^{\infty} \left(\frac{5}{3}\right)^{k-1}$

36. $-25 - 30 - 36 - 43.2 + \cdots$

37. $\sum_{k=1}^{n} 200(0.6)^{k-1}$

38. Geometry A circle of radius r has smaller circles drawn inside it as shown. Each smaller circle has half the radius of the previous circle.

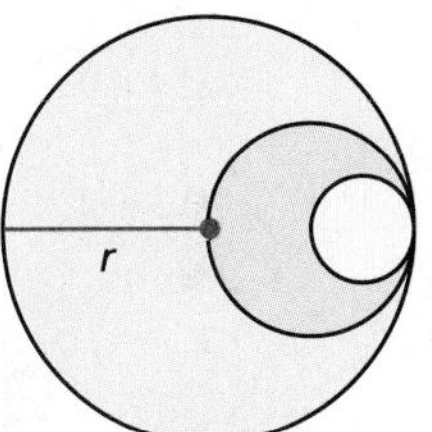

a. Write an infinite geometric series in terms of r that expresses the circumferences of the circles, and find its sum.

b. Find the sum of the circumferences for the infinite set of circles if the first circle has a radius of 3 cm.

Write each repeating decimal as a fraction in simplest form.

39. $0.\overline{4}$

40. $0.\overline{9}$

41. $0.\overline{123}$

42. $0.\overline{18}$

43. $0.\overline{5}$

44. $0.\overline{054}$

45. Music Due to increasing online downloads, CD sales have declined in recent years. Starting in 2001, the number of CDs shipped each year can be modeled by a geometric sequence.

a. Estimate the number of CDs that will be shipped in 2010.

b. Estimate the total number of CDs shipped from 2001 through 2010.

c. Suppose that the geometric series continued indefinitely. Find the total number of CDs shipped from 2001.

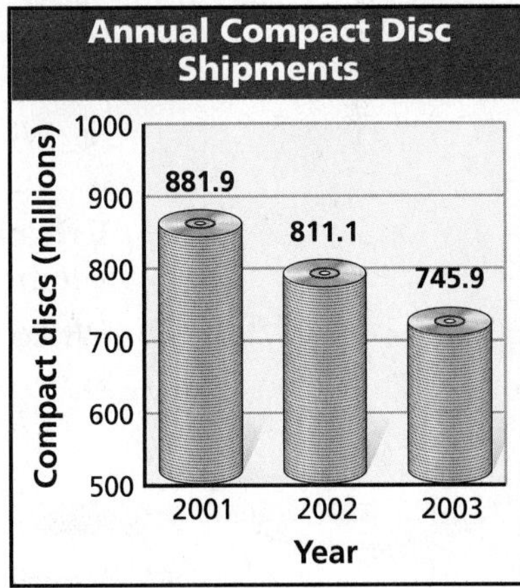

Use mathematical induction to prove each statement.

46. $1 + 2 + 4 + \cdots + 2^{n-1} = 2^n - 1$

47. $1 + 4 + \cdots + n^2 = \frac{n(n+1)(2n+1)}{6}$

48. $1(2) + 2(3) + 2(4) + \cdots + n(n+1) = \frac{n(n+1)(n+2)}{3}$

49. $\frac{1}{2} + \frac{1}{4} + \frac{1}{8} + \cdots + \left(\frac{1}{2}\right)^n = 1 - \left(\frac{1}{2}\right)^n$

Victoria Smith/HMH

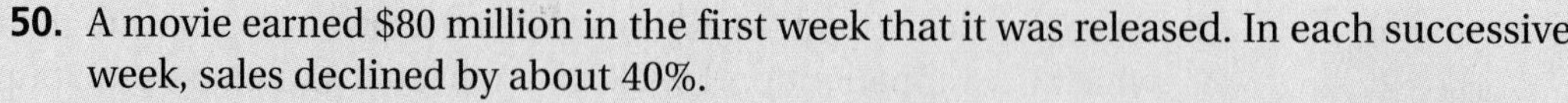

50. A movie earned $80 million in the first week that it was released. In each successive week, sales declined by about 40%.

a. Write a general rule for a geometric sequence that models the movie's sales each week.

b. Estimate the movie's total sales in the first 6 weeks.

c. If this pattern continued indefinitely, what would the movie's total sales be?

51. Game Shows Imagine that you have just won the grand prize on a game show. You can choose between two payment options as shown. Which would you choose, and why?

PRIZE PAYMENT OPTIONS

A.	B.
$1 million the first year and half of the previous year's amount for eternity	$100,000 a year for 20 years

Identify a counterexample to disprove each statement, where x is a real number.

52. $\frac{x^4}{x^3} \leq 2x$ **53.** $x^4 - 1 \geq 0$ **54.** $\ln x^5 > \ln x$

55. $2x^2 \leq 3x^3$ **56.** $2x^2 - x \geq 0$ **57.** $12x - x^2 > 25$

58. Geometry The midpoints of the sides of a 12-inch square are connected to form another concentric square as shown. Suppose that this process is continued without end to form a sequence of concentric squares.

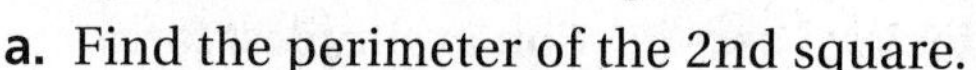

a. Find the perimeter of the 2nd square.

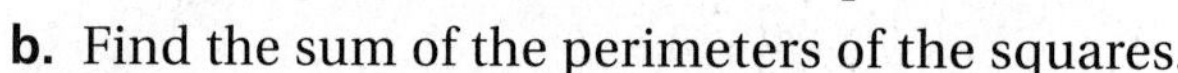

b. Find the sum of the perimeters of the squares.

c. Find the sum of the areas of the squares.

d. Write the sum of the perimeters in summation notation for the general case of a square with side length s. Then write the sum of the areas for the general case.

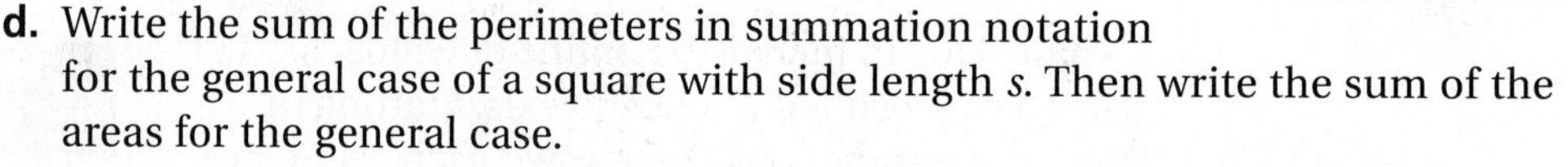

e. Which series decreases faster, the sum of the perimeters or the sum of the areas? How do you know?

59. Critical Thinking Compare the partial-sum S_n with the sum S for an infinite geometric series when $a_1 > 0$ and $r = \frac{4}{5}$. Which is greater? What if $a_1 < 0$?

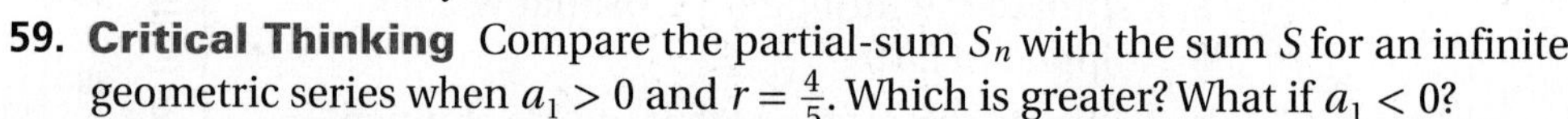

60. Write About It Why might the notation for a partial sum S_n change for the sum S for an infinite geometric series?

61. Which infinite geometric series converges?

Ⓐ $\sum_{k=1}^{\infty}\left(\frac{5}{4}\right)^k$ Ⓑ $\sum_{k=1}^{\infty}5\left(\frac{1}{4}\right)^k$ Ⓒ $\sum_{k=1}^{\infty}\frac{1}{4}(5)^k$ Ⓓ $\sum_{k=1}^{\infty}\left(\frac{1}{4}\right)^k 5^k$

62. What is the sum of the infinite geometric series $1 - \frac{1}{2} + \frac{1}{4} - \frac{1}{8} + \frac{1}{16} + \cdots$?

Ⓕ 2 Ⓖ $\frac{2}{3}$ Ⓗ $\frac{1}{2}$ Ⓙ $\frac{1}{3}$

63. An infinite geometric series has a sum of 180 and a common ratio of $\frac{2}{3}$. What is the first term of the series?

Ⓐ 60 Ⓑ 120 Ⓒ 270 Ⓓ 540

Ingram Publishing/Alamy

64. Which graph represents a converging infinite geometric series?

Ⓕ

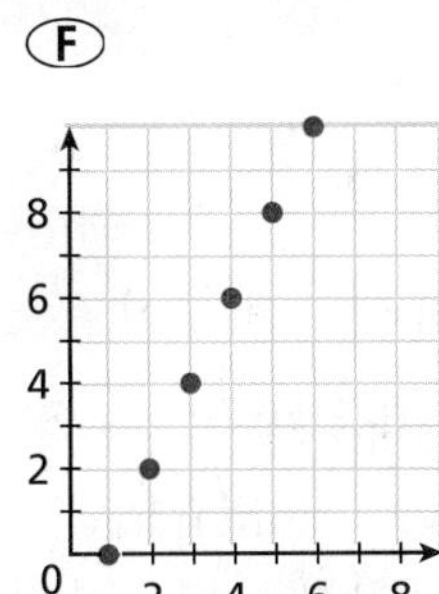

Ⓖ

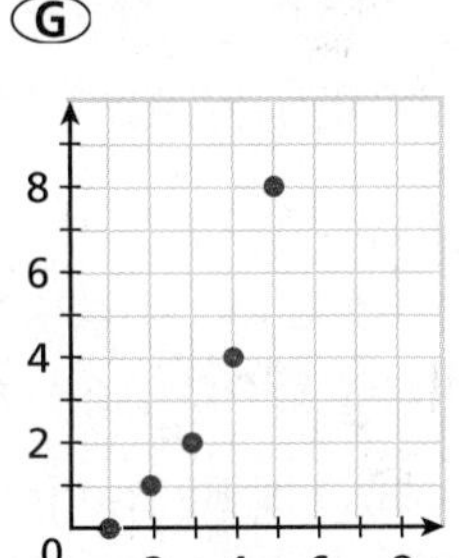

Ⓗ

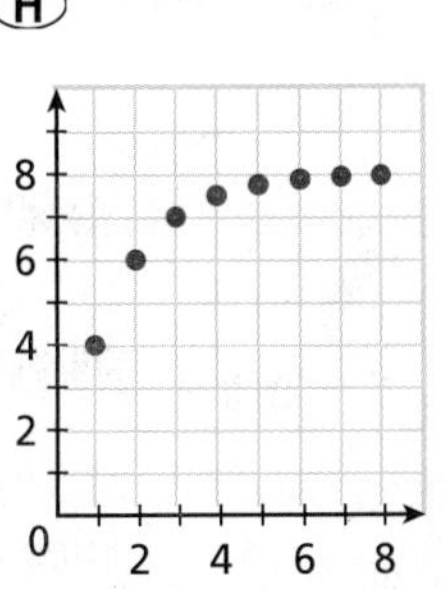

Ⓙ

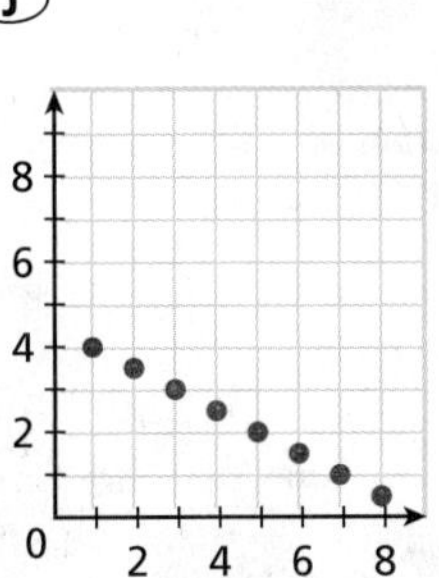

65. Extended Response Use mathematical induction to prove $3 + 5 + \cdots + (2n + 1) = n(n + 2)$. Show all of your work.

CHALLENGE AND EXTEND

Write each repeating decimal as a fraction in simplest form.

66. $0.1\overline{6}$ **67.** $0.41\overline{6}$ **68.** $0.5\overline{286}$

69. Critical Thinking Can an infinite arithmetic series approach a limit like an infinite geometric series? Explain why or why not.

70. Geometry Consider the construction that starts with a 12-inch square and contains concentric squares as indicated. Notice that a spiral is formed by the sequence of segments starting at a corner and moving inward as each midpoint is reached. A second similar spiral determines the area shown in blue.

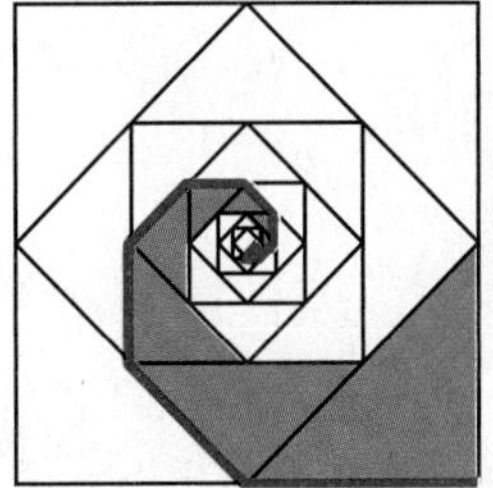

a. Use the sum of a series to find the length of the spiral indicated in red.

b. Use the sum of a series to find the polygonal area indicated in blue.

c. Is your answer to the sum of the polygonal area in part **b** reasonable? Explain.

CHAPTER 9

MULTI-STEP TEST PREP

SECTION 9B

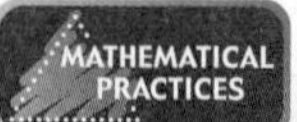

Reason abstractly and quantitatively.

Exploring Geometric Sequences and Series

Sticky Business Big-budget movies often have their greatest sales in the first weekend, and then weekend sales decrease with each passing week. After a movie has been released for a few weeks, movie studios may try to predict the total sales that the movie will generate.

1. Find the ratios of the sequences of weekend sales for *Spider-Man* and *Spider-Man 2*.
2. Write the rule for a geometric sequence that could be used to estimate the sales for *Spider-Man* in a given weekend.

Weekend Box Office Sales (million $)		
Weekend	***Spider-Man***	***Spider-Man 2***
1	114.9	115.8
2	71.4	45.2
3	45.0	24.8

3. Use the sequence from Problem 2 to predict *Spider-Man's* weekend sales for weeks 4 and 5.
4. Write and evaluate a series in summation notation to find *Spider-Man's* total weekend sales for the first 5 weekends of its release.
5. Suppose that the series from Problem 4 continued infinitely. Estimate the total weekend sales for *Spider-Man*. The actual total weekend sales for *Spider-Man* were about $311.1 million. How does this compare with your estimate?
6. Would a geometric sequence be a good model for the weekend sales of *Spider-Man 2*? Justify your answer.

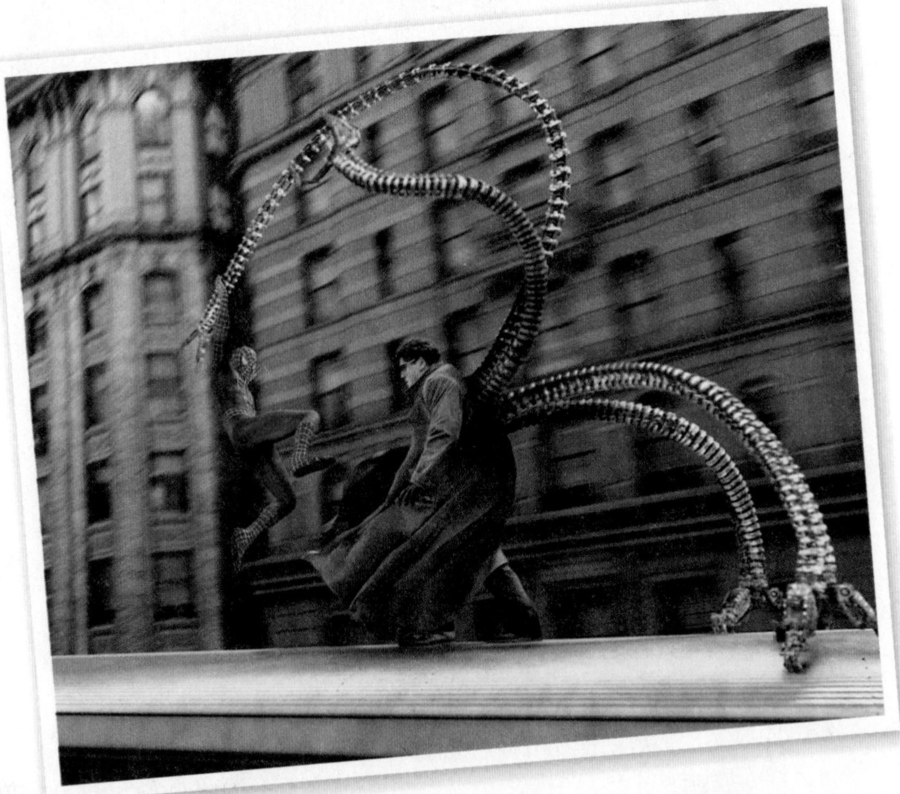

(t), Ingram Publishing/Alamy; (b), Sony Pictures/ZUMA

READY TO GO ON?

CHAPTER 9

SECTION 9B

Quiz for Lessons 9-4 Through 9-5

9-4 Geometric Sequences and Series

Find the 8th term of each geometric sequence.

1. $\frac{2}{5}, \frac{6}{5}, \frac{18}{5}, \frac{54}{5}, \ldots$
2. $-16, -40, -100, -250, \ldots$
3. $-1, 11, -121, 1331, \ldots$
4. $2, 20, 200, 2000, \ldots$

Find the 10th term of each geometric sequence with the given terms.

5. $a_1 = 3.3$ and $a_2 = 33$
6. $a_4 = -1$ and $a_6 = -4$
7. $a_6 = 20.25$ and $a_8 = 9$
8. $a_3 = 57$ and $a_5 = 513$

Find the geometric mean of each pair of numbers.

9. $\frac{1}{3}$ and $\frac{1}{27}$
10. 4.5 and 450
11. 32 and $\frac{1}{8}$

Find the indicated sum for each geometric series.

12. S_6 for $8 - 16 + 32 - 64 + \cdots$
13. S_5 for $1 + \frac{2}{3} + \frac{4}{9} + \frac{8}{27} + \cdots$
14. $\sum_{k=1}^{7} (8)^k$
15. $\sum_{k=1}^{5} 18\left(\frac{1}{6}\right)^{k-1}$
16. The cost for electricity is expected to rise at an annual rate of 8%. In its first year, a business spends \$3000 for electricity.
    a. How much will the business pay for electricity in the 6th year?
    b. How much in total will be paid for electricity over the first 6 years?

9-5 Mathematical Induction and Infinite Geometric Series

Find the sum of each infinite series, if it exists.

17. $25 + 20 + 16 + 12.8 + \cdots$
18. $15 - 18 + 21.6 - 25.92 + \cdots$
19. $\sum_{k=1}^{\infty} (-1)^k \left(\frac{2}{3}\right)^k$
20. $\sum_{k=1}^{\infty} 4(0.22)^k$

Use mathematical induction to prove $4 + 8 + 12 + \cdots + 4n = 2n(n + 1)$.

21. Step 1
22. Step 2
23. Step 3
24. A table-tennis ball is dropped from a height of 5 ft. The ball rebounds to 60% of its previous height after each bounce.
    a. Write an infinite geometric series to represent the distance that the ball travels after it initially hits the ground. (*Hint:* The ball travels up and down on each bounce.)
    b. What is the total distance that the ball travels after it initially hits the ground?

EXTENSION Area Under a Curve

CC.9-12.F.BF.2 Write…sequences both recursively and with an explicit formula, use them to model situations, and translate between the two forms.*

Objective
Approximate area under a curve by using rectangles.

Finding the area under a curve is an important topic in higher mathematics, such as calculus. You can approximate the area under a curve by using a series of rectangles as shown in Example 1.

EXAMPLE 1 Finding Area Under a Curve

Estimate the area under the curve $f(x) = -\frac{1}{2}x^2 + 2x + 3\frac{1}{8}$ over $0 \le x \le 5$.

Graph the function. Divide the area into 5 rectangles, each with a width of 1 unit.

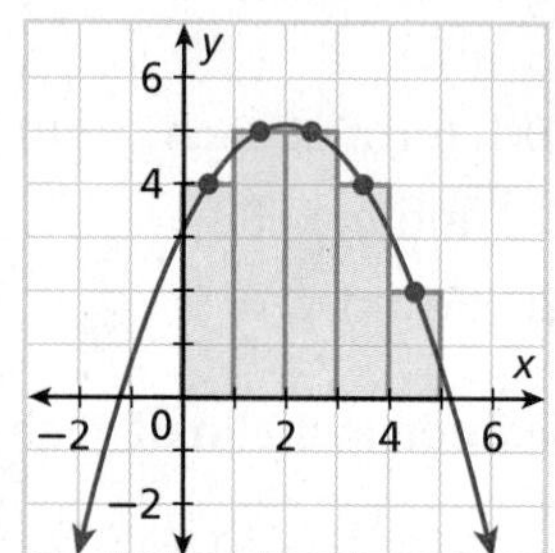

x	f(x)
0.5	4
1.5	5
2.5	5
3.5	4
4.5	2

Remember!
Area is measured in square units.

Find the height of each rectangle by evaluating the function at the center of each rectangle, as shown in the table.

Approximate the area by finding the sum of the areas of the rectangles.

$A \approx 1(4) + 1(5) + 1(5) + 1(4) + 1(2) = 20$

The estimate of 20 square units is very close to the actual area of $19\frac{19}{24}$ square units, which can be found by using calculus.

1. Estimate the area under the curve $f(x) = -x^2 + 5x + 5.75$ over $0 \le x \le 6$. Use 6 intervals.

You can formalize the procedure for finding the area under the curve of a function by using the sum of a series.

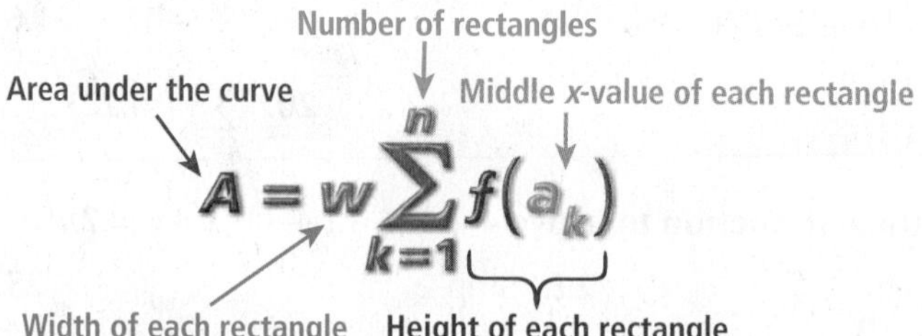

EXAMPLE 2 Finding Area Under a Curve by Using a Series

Use the sum of a series to estimate the area under the curve $f(x) = -x^2 + 50x$ over $0 \le x \le 50$.

Step 1 Graph the function.

Step 2 Divide the area into 5 rectangles, each with a width of 10 units.

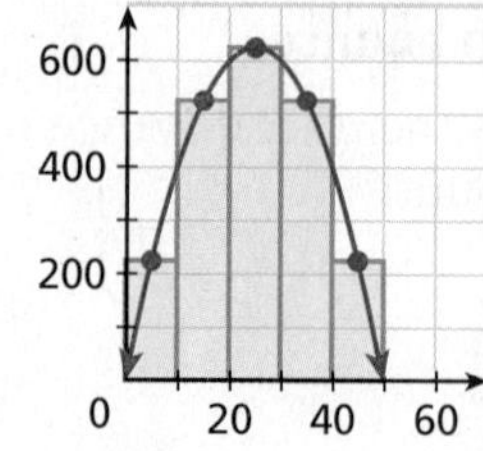

a_k	$f(a_k)$
$a_1 = 5$	225
$a_2 = 15$	525
$a_3 = 25$	625
$a_4 = 35$	525
$a_5 = 45$	225

Step 3 Find the value of the function at the center of each rectangle, as shown in the table.

Step 4 Write the sum that approximates the area.

$$A \approx 10\sum_{k=1}^{5} f(a_k) = 10\left[f(a_1) + f(a_2) + f(a_3) + f(a_4) + f(a_5)\right]$$
$$= 10\left[(225) + (525) + (625) + (525) + (225)\right]$$
$$= 10(2125) = 21{,}250$$

The estimated area is 21,250 square units.

2. Use the sum of a series to estimate the area under the curve $f(x) = -x^2 + 9x + 3$ over $0 \le x \le 9$. Use 3 intervals.

EXTENSION

Exercises

Estimate the area under each curve. Use 4 intervals.

1. $f(x) = -\frac{1}{2}x^2 + 12x + 2$ over $0 \le x \le 24$

2. $f(x) = -x^2 + 8x + 4$ over $0 \le x \le 8$

3. $f(x) = -\frac{1}{4}x^2 + 5x$ over $0 \le x \le 16$

4. $f(x) = -0.1x^2 + 20x$ over $0 \le x \le 200$

Use the sum of a series to estimate the area under each curve. Use 5 intervals.

5. $f(x) = -x^2 + 10x + 5$ over $0 \le x \le 10$

6. $f(x) = -x^2 + 30x$ over $0 \le x \le 20$

7. $f(x) = -\frac{1}{10}x^2 + 400$ over $0 \le x \le 50$

8. $f(x) = -0.2x^2 + 28x + 300$ over $0 \le x \le 150$

9. Physics The graph shows a car's speed versus time as the car accelerates. This realistic curve can be approximated by $v(t) = -0.1t^2 + 7.3t$, where v is the velocity in feet per second and t is the time in seconds.

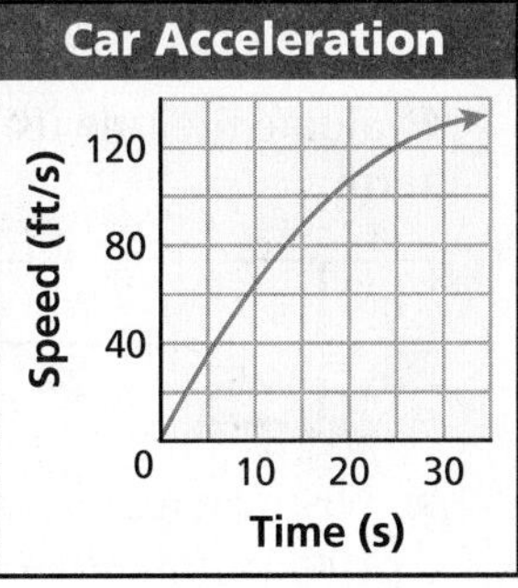

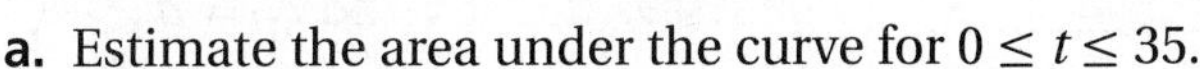

a. Estimate the area under the curve for $0 \le t \le 35$.

b. What does the area under the curve represent? Explain. (*Hint:* Consider the units of your answer to part **a.**)

10. Energy Conservation Daily electricity use peaks in the early afternoon and can be approximated by a parabola. Suppose that the rate of electricity use in kilowatts (kW) is modeled by the function $f(x) = -1.25x^2 + 30x + 700$, where x represents the time in hours.

a. Write a sum to represent the area under the curve for a domain of $0 \le x \le 24$.

b. Estimate the area under the curve.

11. Write About It Explain how the units of the values on the x-axis and the units of the values on the y-axis can be used to find the units that apply to the area under a curve.

12. Critical Thinking For a given function and domain, how would increasing the number of rectangles affect the approximation of the area under the curve?

CHAPTER 9

Study Guide: Review

Vocabulary

arithmetic sequence	geometric sequence	partial sum
arithmetic series	geometric series	recursive formula
converge	infinite geometric series	sequence
diverge	infinite sequence	series
explicit formula	iteration	summation notation
finite sequence	limit	term of a sequence
geometric mean	mathematical induction	

Complete the sentences below with vocabulary words from the list above.

1. A(n) __?__ has a common difference, and a(n) __?__ has a common ratio.
2. A series that has no limit __?__ , whereas a series that approaches a limit __?__ .
3. A(n) __?__ defines the *n*th term. A(n) __?__ defines the next term by using one or more of the previous terms.
4. A(n) __?__ continues without end, and a(n) __?__ has a last term.
5. Each step in a repeated process is called a(n) __?__ .

9-1 Introduction to Sequences

EXAMPLES

■ **Find the first 5 terms of the sequence with $a_1 = -52$; $a_n = 0.5a_{n-1} + 2$.**

Evaluate the rule using each term to find the next term.

n	1	2	3	4	5
a_n	−52	−24	−10	−3	0.5

■ **Write an explicit rule for the *n*th term of 100, 72, 44, 16, −12, ...**

Examine the differences or ratios.

Terms	100	72	44	16	−12
1st differences	28	28	28	28	

The first differences are constant, so the sequence is linear.

The first term is 100, and each term is 28 less than the previous term.

The explicit rule is $a_n = 100 - 28(n - 1)$.

EXERCISES

Find the first 5 terms of each sequence.

6. $a_n = n - 9$
7. $a_n = \frac{1}{2}n^2$
8. $a_n = \left(-\frac{3}{2}\right)^{n-1}$
9. $a_1 = 55$ and $a_n = a_{n-1} - 2$
10. $a_1 = 200$ and $a_n = \frac{1}{5}a_{n-1}$
11. $a_1 = -3$ and $a_n = -3a_{n-1} + 1$

Write a possible explicit rule for the *n*th term of each sequence.

12. −4, −8, −12, −16, −20, ...
13. 5, 20, 80, 320, 1280, ...
14. −24, −19, −14, −9, −4, ...
15. 27, 18, 12, 8, $\frac{16}{3}$, ...
16. **Sports** Suppose that a basketball is dropped from a height of 3 ft. If the ball rebounds to 70% of its height after each bounce, how high will the ball reach after the 4th bounce? the 9th bounce?

9-2 Series and Summation Notation

EXAMPLES

■ **Expand $\sum_{k=1}^{5}(-1)^{n+1}(11-2n)$, and evaluate.**

$$\sum_{k=1}^{5}(-1)^{n+1}(11-2n) = (-1)^2(11-2)$$
$$+ (-1)^3(11-4) + (-1)^4(11-6)$$
$$+ (-1)^5(11-8) + (-1)^6(11-10)$$
$$= 9 - 7 + 5 - 3 + 1$$
$$= 5 \quad \textit{Simplify.}$$

■ **Evaluate $\sum_{k=1}^{8} k^2$.**

Use summation formula for a quadratic series.

$$\sum_{k=1}^{8} k^2 = \frac{n(n+1)(2n+1)}{6}$$
$$= \frac{8(8+1)(2\cdot 8+1)}{6} = \frac{72(17)}{6} = 204$$

EXERCISES

Expand each series and evaluate.

17. $\sum_{k=1}^{4} k^2(-1)^k$

18. $\sum_{k=1}^{5}(0.5k+4)$

19. $\sum_{k=1}^{5}(-1)^{k+1}(2k-1)$

20. $\sum_{k=1}^{4}\frac{5k}{k^2}$

Evaluate each series.

21. $\sum_{k=1}^{8} -5$

22. $\sum_{k=1}^{10} k^2$

23. $\sum_{k=1}^{12} k$

24. **Finance** A household has a monthly mortgage payment of $1150. How much is paid by the household after 2 years? 15 years?

9-3 Arithmetic Sequences and Series

EXAMPLES

■ **Find the 12th term for the arithmetic sequence 85, 70, 55, 40, 25, ...**

Find the common difference:
$d = 70 - 85 = -15$.

$a_n = a_1 + (n-1)d$ *General rule*

$a_{12} = 85 + (12-1)(-15)$ *Substitute.*

$= -80$ *Simplify.*

■ **Find $\sum_{k=1}^{11}(-2-33k)$.**

Find the 1st and 11th terms.

$a_1 = -2 - 33(1) = -35$

$a_{11} = -2 - 33(11) = -365$

Find S_{11}.

$S_n = n\left(\frac{a_1 + a_n}{2}\right)$ *Sum formula*

$S_{11} = 11\left(\frac{-35-365}{2}\right)$ *Substitute.*

$= -2200$

EXERCISES

Find the 11th term of each arithmetic sequence.

25. 23, 19, 15, 11, ...

26. $\frac{1}{5}, \frac{3}{5}, 1, \frac{7}{5}, \frac{9}{5}, \ldots$

27. −9.2, −8.4, −7.6, −6.8, ...

28. $a_3 = 1.5$ and $a_4 = 5$

29. $a_6 = 47$ and $a_8 = 21$

30. $a_5 = -7$ and $a_9 = 13$

Find the indicated sum for each arithmetic series.

31. S_{18} for $-1 - 5 - 9 - 13 + \cdots$

32. S_{12} for $\frac{1}{3} + \frac{1}{6} + 0 - \frac{1}{6} + \cdots$

33. $\sum_{k=1}^{15}(-14+3k)$

34. $\sum_{k=1}^{15}\left(\frac{3}{2}k+10\right)$

35. **Savings** Kelly has $50 and receives $8 a week for allowance. He wants to save all of his money to buy a new mountain bicycle that costs $499. Write an arithmetic sequence to represent the situation. Then find whether Kelly will be able to buy the new bicycle after one year (52 weeks).

9-4 Geometric Sequences and Series

EXAMPLES

■ **Find the 8th term of the geometric sequence 6, 24, 96, 384, ….**

Find the common ratio. $r = \frac{24}{6} = 4$

Write a rule, and evaluate for $n = 8$.

$a_n = a_1 r^{n-1}$ *General rule*

$a_8 = 6(4)^{8-1} = 98{,}304$

■ **Find the 8th term of the geometric sequence with $a_4 = -1000$ and $a_6 = -40$.**

Step 1 Find the common ratio.

$a_6 = a_4 r^{(6-4)}$ *Use the given terms.*

$-40 = -1000r^2$ *Substitute.*

$\frac{1}{25} = r^2$ *Simplify.*

$\pm\frac{1}{5} = r$

Step 2 Find a_1 using both possible values for r.

$-1000 = a_1\left(\frac{1}{5}\right)^{4-1}$ or $-1000 = a_1\left(-\frac{1}{5}\right)^{4-1}$

$a_1 = -125{,}000$ or $a_1 = 125{,}000$

Step 3 Write the rule and evaluate for a_8 by using both possible values for r.

$a_n = a_1 r^{n-1}$ $a_n = a_1 r^{n-1}$

$a_n = -125{,}000\left(\frac{1}{5}\right)^{n-1}$ or $a_n = 125{,}000\left(-\frac{1}{5}\right)^{n-1}$

$a_8 = -125{,}000\left(\frac{1}{5}\right)^{8-1}$ $a_8 = 125{,}000\left(-\frac{1}{5}\right)^{8-1}$

$a_8 = -1.6$ $a_8 = -1.6$

■ **Find $\sum_{k=1}^{7} -2(5)^{k-1}$.**

Find the common ratio. $r = \frac{a_2}{a_1} = \frac{-6}{3} = -2$

Find S_7

$S_n = a_1\left(\frac{1-r^n}{1-r}\right)$ *Sum formula*

$S_7 = 3\left(\frac{1-(-2)^7}{1-(-2)}\right)$ *Substitute.*

$= 3\left(\frac{1-(-128)}{3}\right) = 129$

EXERCISES

Find the 8th term of each geometric sequence.

36. 40, 4, 0.4, 0.04, 0.004, …

37. $\frac{1}{18}, \frac{1}{6}, \frac{1}{2}, \frac{3}{2}, \ldots$

38. −16, −8, −4, −2, …

39. −6, 12, −24, 48, …

Find the 9th term of the geometric sequence with the given terms.

40. $a_3 = 24$ and $a_4 = 96$

41. $a_1 = \frac{2}{3}$ and $a_2 = -\frac{4}{3}$

42. $a_4 = -1$ and $a_6 = -4$

43. $a_3 = 4$ and $a_6 = 500$

Find the geometric mean of each pair of numbers.

44. 10 and 2.5

45. $\frac{1}{2}$ and 8

46. $\frac{\sqrt{3}}{96}$ and $\frac{\sqrt{3}}{6}$

47. $\frac{5}{12}$ and $\frac{125}{108}$

Find the indicated sum for each geometric series.

48. S_5 for $1 + \frac{1}{3} + \frac{1}{9} + \frac{1}{27} + \cdots$

49. S_6 for $-\frac{4}{5} + 8 - 80 + 800 + \cdots$

50. $\sum_{k=1}^{8} (4)^{k-1}$

51. $\sum_{k=1}^{7} -2(5)^{k-1}$

52. $\sum_{k=1}^{6} 60\left(-\frac{1}{2}\right)^{k-1}$

53. $\sum_{k=1}^{5} 18\left(\frac{1}{2}\right)^{k-1}$

54. Depreciation A new photocopier costs $9000 and depreciates each year such that it retains only 65% of its preceding year's value. What is the value of the photocopier after 5 years?

55. Rent A one-bedroom apartment rents for $650 a month. The rent is expected to increase by 6% per year.

a. What will be the annual rent expense on the apartment after 5 years?

b. What will be the total amount spent on rent if a person rents the apartment for the entire 5-year period?

9-5 Mathematical Induction and Infinite Geometric Series

EXAMPLES

Find the sum of each infinite series, if it exists.

■ $-9261 + 441 - 21 + 1 + \cdots$

$r = \frac{441}{-9261} = -\frac{1}{21}$ *Converges: $|r| < 1$*

$S = \frac{a_1}{1-r}$ *Sum formula*

$= \frac{-9261}{1-\left(-\frac{1}{21}\right)} = \frac{-9261}{\frac{22}{21}}$

$= -\frac{194{,}481}{22}$, or $-8840.0\overline{45}$

■ $\sum_{k=1}^{\infty} -5\left(\frac{7}{10}\right)^{k-1}$

$= -5 - \frac{35}{10} - \frac{245}{100} + \cdots$ *Evaluate.*

$r = \frac{-\frac{35}{10}}{-5} = \frac{7}{10}$ *Converges: $|r| < 1$*

$S = \frac{a_1}{1-r} = \frac{-5}{1-\frac{7}{10}} = \frac{-5}{\frac{3}{10}} = -\frac{50}{3}$, or $-16.\overline{6}$

■ **Use mathematical induction to prove $2 + 5 + \cdots + (3n-1) = \frac{n}{2}(3n+1)$.**

Step 1 Base case: Show that the statement is true for $n = 1$.

$2 = \frac{n}{2}(3n+1) = \frac{1}{2}(3 \cdot 1 + 1) = 2$ *True*

Step 2 Assume that the statement is true for a natural number k.

$2 + 5 + \cdots + (3k-1) = \frac{k}{2}(3k+1)$ *Replace n with k.*

Step 3 Prove that it is true for the natural number $k + 1$.

$2 + 5 + \ldots + (3k-1) + 3(k+1) - 1$ *Add to both sides.*

$= \frac{k}{2}(3k+1) + 3(k+1) - 1$

$= \frac{k(3k+1)}{2} + (3k + 3 - 1)$ *Multiply.*

$= \frac{3k^2 + k}{2} + \frac{2(3k+2)}{2}$ *Simplify and rewrite with like denominators.*

$= \frac{3k^2 + 7k + 4}{2}$ *Add.*

$= \frac{(k+1)(3k+4)}{2}$ *Factor.*

$= \frac{(k+1)}{2}(3(k+1)+1)$ *Write with k + 1.*

EXERCISES

Find the sum of each infinite series, if it exists.

56. $-2700 + 900 - 300 + 100 + \cdots$

57. $-1.2 - 0.12 - 0.012 - 0.0012 + \cdots$

58. $-49 - 42 - 36 - \frac{216}{7} + \cdots$

59. $4 + \frac{4}{5} + \frac{4}{25} + \frac{4}{125} + \cdots$

60. $\sum_{k=1}^{\infty} \frac{9}{3^k}$

61. $\sum_{k=1}^{\infty} -7\left(\frac{3}{5}\right)^k$

62. $\sum_{k=1}^{\infty} (-1)^{k+1}\left(\frac{1}{8^k}\right)$

63. $\sum_{k=1}^{\infty} \left(\frac{4}{3}\right)^k$

Use mathematical induction to prove each statement.

64. $2 + 4 + 8 + \cdots + 2^n = 2^{n+1} - 2$

65. $1 + 5 + 25 + \cdots + 5^{n-1} = \frac{5^n - 1}{4}$

66. $\frac{1}{3} + \frac{1}{15} + \cdots + \frac{1}{4n^2 - 1} = \frac{n}{2n+1}$

67. **Recreation** A child on a swing is let go from a vertical height so that the distance that he travels in the first back-and-forth swing is exactly 9 feet.

    a. If each swing decreases the distance by 85%, write an infinite geometric series that expresses the distance that the child travels in feet.

    b. What is the total distance that the child in the swing travels before the swing stops?

CHAPTER 9

CHAPTER TEST

Find the first 5 terms of each sequence.

1. $a_n = n^2 - 4$

2. $a_1 = 48$ and $a_n = \frac{1}{2}a_{n-1} - 8$

Write a possible explicit rule for the *n*th term of each sequence.

3. $-4, -2, 0, 2, 4, \ldots$

4. $54, 18, 6, 2, \frac{2}{3}, \ldots$

Expand each series and evaluate.

5. $\sum_{k=1}^{4} 5k^3$

6. $\sum_{k=1}^{7} (-1)^{k+1}(k)$

Find the 9th term of each arithmetic sequence.

7. $-19, -13, -7, -1, \ldots$

8. $a_2 = 11.6$ and $a_5 = 5$

9. Find 2 missing terms in the arithmetic sequence 125, ▇, ▇, 65.

Find the indicated sum for each arithmetic series.

10. S_{20} for $4 + 7 + 10 + 13 + \ldots$

11. $\sum_{k=1}^{12} (-9k + 8)$

12. The front row of a theater has 16 seats and each subsequent row has 2 more seats than the row that precedes it. How many seats are in the 12th row? How many seats in total are in the first 12 rows?

Find the 10th term of each geometric sequence.

13. $\frac{3}{256}, \frac{3}{64}, \frac{3}{16}, \frac{3}{4}, \ldots$

14. $a_4 = 2$ and $a_5 = 8$

15. Find the geometric mean of 4 and 25.

Find the indicated sum for each geometric series.

16. S_6 for $2 + 1 + \frac{1}{2} + \frac{1}{4} + \ldots$

17. $\sum_{k=1}^{6} 250\left(-\frac{1}{5}\right)^{k-1}$

18. You invest \$1000 each year in an account that pays 5% annual interest. How much is the first \$1000 you invested worth after 10 full years of interest payments? How much in total do you have in your account after 10 full years?

Find the sum of each infinite geometric series, if it exists.

19. $200 - 100 + 50 - 25 + \ldots$

20. $\sum_{k=1}^{\infty} 2\left(\frac{7}{8}\right)^k$

Use mathematical induction to prove $\frac{1}{2} + \frac{3}{2} + \frac{5}{2} + \cdots + \frac{2n-1}{2} = \frac{n^2}{2}$.

21. Step 1

22. Step 2

23. Step 3

FOCUS ON SAT

When you get your SAT scores, you are given the percentile in which your scores fall. This tells you the percentage of students that scored lower than you did on the same test. You'll see your percentile score at the national and state levels. They are usually not the same.

Read each problem carefully, and make sure that you understand what the question is asking. Before marking your final answer on the answer sheet, check that your answer makes sense in the context of the question.

You may want to time yourself as you take this practice test. It should take you about 8 minutes to complete.

1. The first term of a sequence is 6, and each successive term is 3 less than twice the preceding term. What is the sum of the first four terms of the sequence?

(A) 27

(B) 30

(C) 51

(D) 57

(E) 123

2. The first term of a sequence is 2, and the *n*th term is defined to be $3n - 1$. What is the average of the 7th, 10th, and 12th terms?

(A) 24.5

(B) 28

(C) 29

(D) 32

(E) 84

3. The first term of an arithmetic sequence is −5. If the common difference is 4, what is the 7th term of the sequence?

(A) −20,480

(B) −29

(C) 19

(D) 20

(E) 23

4. A population of 50 grows exponentially by doubling every 4 years. After how many years will the population have 1600 members?

(A) 20

(B) 16

(C) 10

(D) 6

(E) 5

5. Which of the following sequences can be expressed by the rule $a_n = \frac{n-1}{n+1}$?

(A) $3, 2, \frac{5}{3}, \frac{3}{2}, \frac{7}{5}, \ldots$

(B) $\frac{1}{2}, \frac{3}{4}, \frac{5}{6}, \frac{7}{8}, \frac{9}{10}, \ldots$

(C) $\frac{1}{3}, \frac{2}{4}, \frac{3}{5}, \frac{4}{6}, \frac{5}{7}, \ldots$

(D) $0, \frac{1}{3}, \frac{1}{2}, \frac{3}{5}, \frac{2}{3}, \ldots$

(E) $0, \frac{3}{2}, 3, \frac{5}{3}, 5, \ldots$

6. Which of the following sequences is a geometric sequence?

(A) −7, 14, −28, 56, −112, ...

(B) −4, −6, −8, −10, −12, ...

(C) −3, 1, −3, 1, −3, ...

(D) 4, 12, 48, 144, 576, ...

(E) 1, 4, 9, 16, 25, ...

CHAPTER 9

TEST TACKLER

Standardized Test Strategies

Short/Extended Response: Outline Your Response

Answering short and extended response items on tests is a lot like writing essays in English class. You can use an outline to plan your response to the question. Outlines help you organize the main points and the order in which they will appear in your answer. Outlining your response will help ensure that your explanation is clearly organized and includes all necessary information.

EXAMPLE 1

Short Response Ariana is saving money for a new car. She saves \$40 the first week, \$45 the second week, \$50 the third week, and so on. Explain whether an arithmetic or geometric sequence would best represent this situation. Use a sequence or series to determine the amount that she will save in the 8th week and the total amount that she will have saved after 8 weeks.

Create an outline for your response.

Outline

1. Explain whether arithmetic or geometric.
2. Write sequence and series.
3. Find amount saved in 8th week.
4. Find total saved after 8 weeks.

Follow the outline, and write out your response.

Include evidence to explain the answer for the first step.

An arithmetic sequence would best represent this situation because Ariana is adding \$5 each week to the amount that she saves. This would be an arithmetic sequence where the first term is 40 and the common difference is 5.

Clearly indicate which is the sequence and which is the series for the second step.

The sequence for the amount saved each week is $a_n = 40 + 5(n - 1)$. The series for the total amount saved is $\sum_{k=1}^{n}[40 + 5(k - 1)]$.

Show how you found the answers for the last two steps.

The amount saved in the 8th week is $a_8 = 40 + 5(8 - 1) = \$75$.

The total saved after 8 weeks is $\sum_{k=1}^{8}[40 + 5(k - 1)] = \$460$.

When you finish your response, check it against your outline to make sure that you did not leave out any details.

Read each test item and answer the questions that follow.

Item A

Short Response Explain how to determine whether an infinite geometric series has a sum.

1. What should be included in an outline of the response for this test item?
2. Read the two different outlines below. Which outline is the most useful? Why?

Student A

I. Definition of an infinite geometric series and the common ratio *r*.

II. Definition of the sum of an infinite geometric series.

III. Explain for which values of *r* that a sum exists.

Student B

A. Geometric series has a common ratio.

B. Common ratio has to be less than 1.

Item B

Extended Response A pattern for stacking cereal boxes is shown at right.

a. Explain how many boxes are in a 9-row display.

b. If 91 boxes are to be stacked in this display, explain how many rows the display will have.

3. Read the outline below. Identify any areas that need improvement. Rewrite the outline to make it more useful.

Outline

1. Find the number of boxes if there are 9 rows.
2. Find the number of rows needed for 91 boxes.

Item C

Extended Response A pattern of squares is created by doubling the dimensions of the previous square. Explain how to find the sum of the perimeters of the first 8 squares if the first square is 5 cm wide.

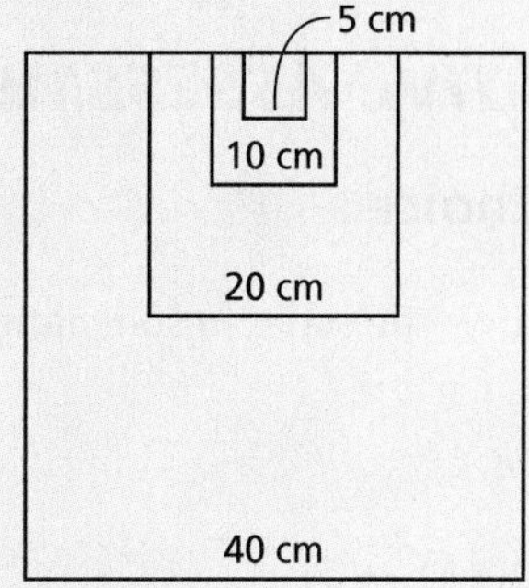

4. A student correctly gave the following response. Write an outline for a response to this question.

To find the perimeters of the first 8 squares, I need to determine the series.

$$4(5) + 4(10) + 4(20) + 4(40) + \cdots$$
$$4(5 + 10 + 20 + 40 + \cdots)$$
$$4 \cdot 5(1 + 2 + 4 + 8 + \cdots)$$
$$20(1 + 2 + 4 + 8 + \cdots)$$
$$20\sum_{n=1}^{8} 2^{(n-1)}$$

Now that I know that the first term is 20 and the common ratio is 2, I can use the formula $S_n = t_1\left(\frac{1 - r^n}{1 - r}\right)$, where t_1 is the first term and r is the common ratio.

$$S_n = 20\left(\frac{1 - 2^8}{1 - 2}\right)$$
$$= 20\left(\frac{1 - 256}{-1}\right)$$
$$= 20\left(\frac{-255}{-1}\right)$$
$$= 20(255) = 5100$$

So the sum of the perimeters of the first 8 squares is 5100 cm.

CHAPTER 9

STANDARDIZED TEST PREP

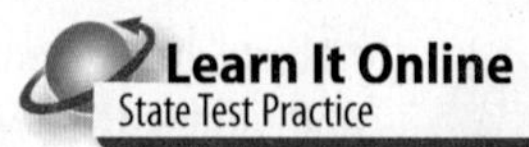

CUMULATIVE ASSESSMENT

Multiple Choice

1. Which shows the series in summation notation?

   $4 + 6 + 4 + 6 + 4$

   Ⓐ $\sum 24$

   Ⓑ $\sum_{n=0}^{5} [(-1)^n + 5]$

   Ⓒ $\sum_{n=1}^{4} [(-1)^n + 5]$

   Ⓓ $\sum_{n=1}^{5} [(-1)^n + 5]$

2. What is the expanded binomial?

   $(2x - y)^3$

   Ⓕ $x^3 - 3x^2y + 3xy^2 - y^3$

   Ⓖ $8x^3 - 12x^2y + 6xy^2 - y^3$

   Ⓗ $x^3 + 3x^2y + 3xy^2 + y^3$

   Ⓙ $8x^3 + 12x^2y + 6xy^2 + y^3$

3. Let $f(x) = x^3 + 2x^2 - 5x - 9$. Which function would show $f(x)$ reflected across the y-axis?

   Ⓐ $g(x) = -x^3 - 2x^2 + 5x + 9$

   Ⓑ $g(x) = -x^3 + 2x^2 + 5x - 9$

   Ⓒ $g(x) = 2x^3 + 4x^2 - 10x - 18$

   Ⓓ $g(x) = x^3 + 2x^2 - 5x - 5$

4. Which function shows exponential decay?

   Ⓕ $f(x) = -5x$

   Ⓖ $f(x) = 2.3(6.7)^x$

   Ⓗ $f(x) = 0.49(7.9)^x$

   Ⓙ $f(x) = 5.13(0.32)^x$

5. A ball is dropped from a height of 10 feet. On each bounce, the ball bounces 60% of the height of the previous bounce. Which expression represents the height in feet of the ball on the nth bounce?

   Ⓐ $10(0.6n)$

   Ⓑ $10(0.6)^{n-1}$

   Ⓒ $\frac{10 - n}{0.6}$

   Ⓓ $10(0.6)^n$

6. Which is the graph of the inequality $6x + 3y \geq 9x^2 - 3$?

   Ⓕ 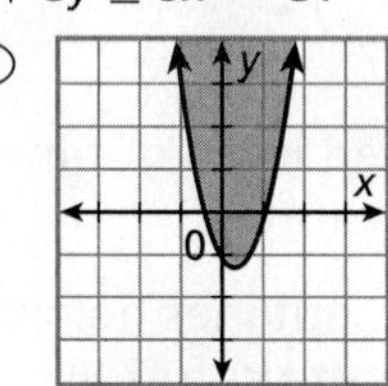

   Ⓗ 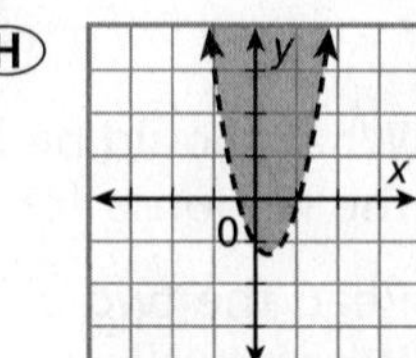

   Ⓖ 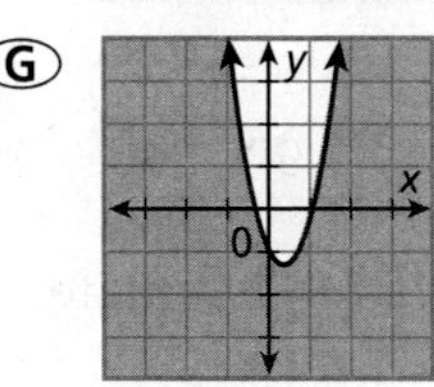

   Ⓙ 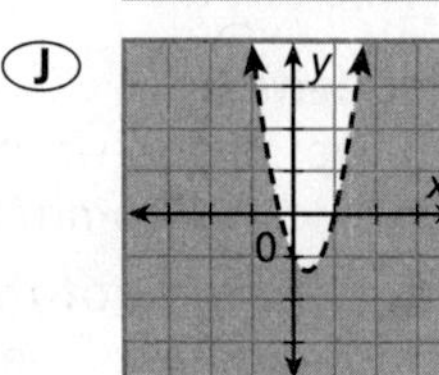

7. Gina opened a new deli. Her revenues for the first 4 weeks were \$2000, \$2400, \$2880, and \$3456. If the trend continues, which is the best estimate of Gina's revenues in the 6th week?

   Ⓐ \$3856

   Ⓑ \$4032

   Ⓒ \$4147

   Ⓓ \$4980

8. What is the 9th term in the sequence?

   $a_n = \frac{1}{2}(2^{n-1}) + 4$

   Ⓕ 36 Ⓗ 132

   Ⓖ 68 Ⓙ 260

9. Find the inverse of $f(x) = 4x - 5$.

   Ⓐ $f^{-1}(x) = -4x + 5$

   Ⓑ $f^{-1}(x) = \frac{1}{4}x + 5$

   Ⓒ $f^{-1}(x) = \frac{x + 5}{4}$

   Ⓓ $f^{-1}(x) = 5x - 4$

10. What transformation has been applied to f to get g?

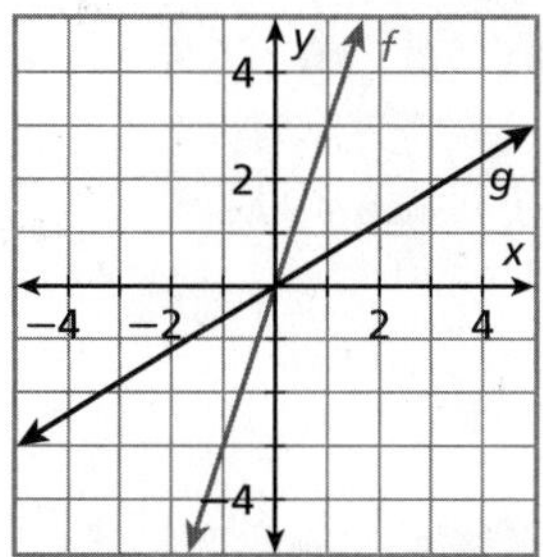

Ⓕ Horizontal compression by $\frac{1}{5}$

Ⓖ Horizontal stretch by 5

Ⓗ Vertical compression by $\frac{1}{3}$

Ⓙ Vertical stretch by 5

In Item 11, you may choose to graph, factor, complete the square, or use the Quadratic Formula to find the zeros.

11. Find the zeros of $f(x) = 2x^2 + 5x - 12$.

Ⓐ $-4, \frac{3}{2}$

Ⓑ $-2, 3$

Ⓒ $-\frac{3}{2}, 4$

Ⓓ $\frac{3}{2}, 2$

Gridded Response

12. Find the common ratio of the geometric sequence.

125, 50, 20, 8, ...

13. A card is drawn from a deck of 52. What is the probability of drawing a 10 or a diamond, to the nearest hundredth?

14. What is the sum of the arithmetic series?

$$\sum_{k=1}^{8} (7k - 3)$$

15. What is the y-value of the point that represents the solution to the given system of equations, to the nearest hundredth?

$$\begin{cases} 2y - 2 = 4x \\ 6 - x = 8y \end{cases}$$

Short Response

16. Use the function $f(x) = \sqrt[3]{5x}$ to answer the following questions.

   a. What is the domain and range?

   b. What is the inverse of $f(x)$?

   c. What is the domain and range of the inverse function?

   d. Graph $f(x)$ and $f^{-1}(x)$ on the same coordinate plane.

17. Use the infinite geometric series $\sum_{n=1}^{\infty} \frac{5}{4^{n-1}}$ to answer the following questions.

   a. Determine if the series converges or diverges.

   b. Find the sum of the infinite series, if it exists.

18. A grocery store display contains 3 cans on the top row and an additional can in each row forming a triangular shape.

   a. Would you use a sequence or a series to represent the number of cans in the nth row? Explain.

   b. How many cans are in the 12th row?

   c. What does the series $\sum_{k=1}^{n} (k + 2)$ represent? Explain.

Extended Response

19. A test to be on a trivia show has two parts. 60% of contestants pass the first part, and 20% pass the second part.

   a. Draw a tree diagram that gives the probabilities for a contestant's possible outcomes on the test.

   b. If a contestant must pass both parts of the test to be on the show, how many contestants out of a group of 50 would likely make the show? Show your work.

   c. Is it more likely that a contestant would pass both parts or fail both parts of the test? Explain.

Real-World CONNECTIONS

The Hoover Dam

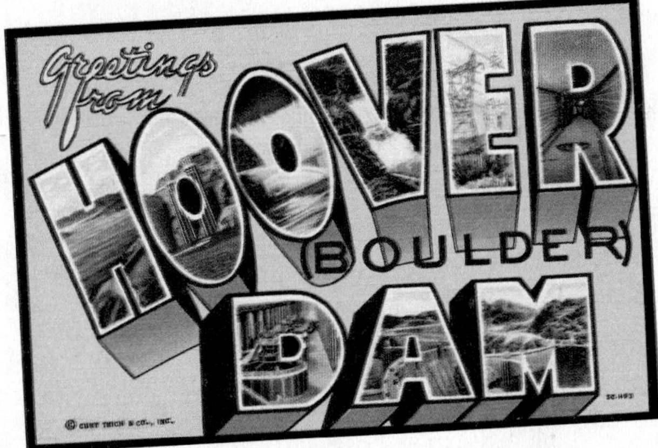

Since its completion in 1935, the Hoover Dam has often been cited as one of the seven engineering wonders of the world. Its 6.6 million tons of concrete tame the waters of the Colorado River and form Lake Mead, the largest man-made reservoir in the United States.

Choose one or more strategies to solve each problem. For 1 and 2, use the table.

Traffic Forecasts for the Hoover Dam			
Year	2007	2008	2009
Number of Cars per Day	16,300	16,780	17,260

1. The Hoover Dam serves as a bridge between the Nevada and Arizona sides of the Colorado River. Traffic analysts project that the traffic on the dam will increase according to an arithmetic sequence. How many cars, on average, would you predict to cross the dam each day in 2017?
2. Approximately how many vehicles will cross the dam in the years 2007 through 2017, inclusive? (*Hint:* Assume 365 days per year.)
3. Small trucks make up 18% of the traffic on the dam, and RVs account for another 4%. All trucks and RVs are inspected before they are allowed to cross.
   a. Assuming that other types of vehicles are not inspected, what is the probability that three consecutive vehicles arriving at a checkpoint will be inspected?
   b. What is the probability that 3 out of 5 vehicles arriving at a checkpoint will need to be inspected?

(b), Lester Lefkowitz/CORBIS; (cr), Lake County Museum/CORBIS

Silver and Gold Mining

Nevada's nickname is the Silver State, which is not surprising considering that more than 10 million ounces of the metal are mined in Nevada each year. Gold mining is also an essential part of Nevada's economy. In fact, if Nevada were a nation, it would rank third in the world in gold production behind South Africa and Australia.

Choose one or more strategies to solve each problem.

1. Nevada experienced a gold-mining boom from 1981 to 1990. During this period, the number of thousands of ounces of gold mined each year can be modeled by a geometric sequence in which $a_1 = 375$ (that is, 375,000 ounces were mined in 1981) and the common ratio is 1.35. Approximately how many ounces of gold were mined in 1990?
2. What was the total gold production in the years 1981 through 1990, inclusive?
3. In a particular mine, the probability of discovering a profitable quantity of gold in a sector is approximately 40%. What is the probability that the miners will discover a profitable quantity of gold in 3 of the next 4 sectors?

For 4, use the table.

4. Nevada experienced a silver boom during the 1990s. An industry analyst is collecting detailed data for all of the years from 1991 to 2000 in which silver production was outside of 1 standard deviation of the mean. For which years should she collect this data?

Nevada Silver Production

Year	Production (million oz)
1991	18.6
1992	19.7
1993	23.2
1994	22.8
1995	24.6
1996	20.7
1997	24.7
1998	21.5
1999	19.5
2000	23.2

CHAPTER

10 Trigonometric Functions

COMMON CORE

Chapter Focus

- Develop conceptual understanding of trigonometric functions.
- Solve problems with trigonometric functions and their inverses.

GEARING UP!

The shape and size of gear teeth determine whether gears fit together. You can use trigonometry to make a working model of a set of gears.

Learn It Online
Chapter Project Online

Vocabulary

Match each term on the left with a definition on the right.

1. acute angle
2. function
3. domain
4. reciprocal

A. the set of all possible input values of a relation or function
B. an angle whose measure is greater than 90°
C. a relation with at most one y-value for each x-value
D. an angle whose measure is greater than 0° and less than 90°
E. the multiplicative inverse of a number

Ratios

Use $\triangle ABC$ to write each ratio.

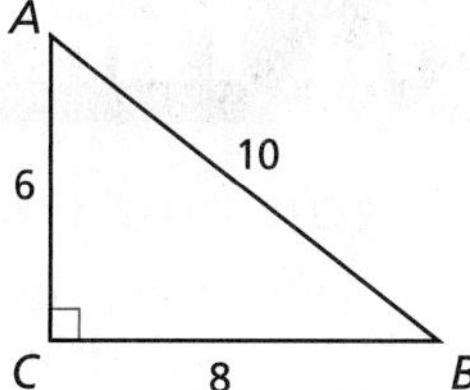

5. BC to AB
6. AC to BC
7. the length of the longest side to the length of the shortest side
8. the length of the shorter leg to the length of the hypotenuse

Classify Triangles

Classify each triangle as acute, right, or obtuse.

9. 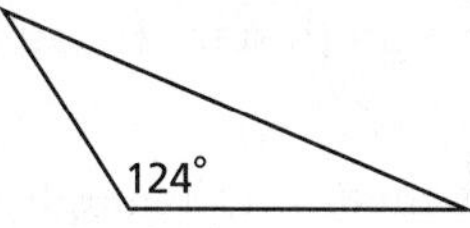

10. 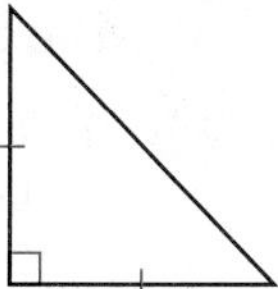

11. 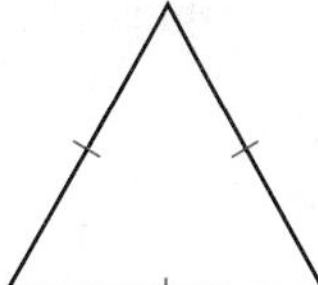

Triangle Sum Theorem

Find the value of x in each triangle.

12. 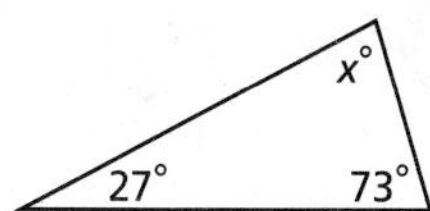

13. 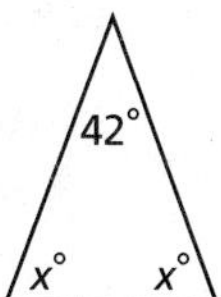

14. 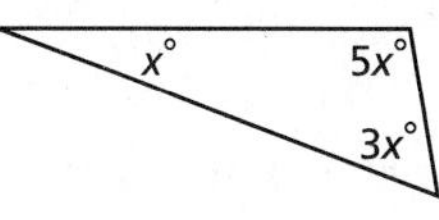

Pythagorean Theorem

Find the missing length for each right triangle with legs a and b and hypotenuse c. Round to the nearest tenth.

15. $a = 16$, $b = \blacksquare$, $c = 20$
16. $a = 3$, $b = 5$, $c = \blacksquare$
17. $a = 9$, $b = \blacksquare$, $c = 18$
18. $a = 7$, $b = 14$, $c = \blacksquare$

CHAPTER 10

Study Guide: Preview

Where You've Been

Previously, you

- used inverses of functions.
- measured indirectly using ratios and proportional reasoning.
- found equations of circles on the coordinate plane.

In This Chapter

You will study

- using trigonometric functions and their inverses.
- measuring indirectly using side lengths and angles of triangles.
- using angles of rotation and finding arc lengths of circles.

Where You're Going

You can use the skills in this chapter

- in other math classes, such as Precalculus.
- in scientific fields such as astronomy, forensics, geology, and engineering.
- outside of school in navigation, surveying, drafting, architecture, landscaping, and aviation.

Key Vocabulary/Vocabulario

angle of rotation	ángulo de rotación
coterminal angle	ángulo coterminal
initial side	lado inicial
radian	radián
reference angle	ángulo de referencia
standard position	posición estándar
terminal side	lado terminal
trigonometric function	función trigonométrica
unit circle	círculo unitario

Vocabulary Connections

To become familiar with some of the vocabulary terms in the chapter, consider the following. You may refer to the chapter, the glossary, or a dictionary if you like.

1. The word *trigonometry* comes from Greek words meaning "triangle measurement." What types of problems might you be able to solve by using **trigonometric functions** ?
2. What is a reference book? Based on this meaning of *reference*, what do you think a **reference angle** is?
3. What is a *rotation*? What do you think an **angle of rotation** is?
4. The origin of the word *unit* is a Latin word meaning "one." What do you think the radius of a **unit circle** is?

CHAPTER 10

Study Strategy: Learn Vocabulary

Understanding math terminology and vocabulary is important to learning and using new math concepts. You have already learned many new terms and as you progress in your studies of math, you will need to learn many more.

To learn new vocabulary:

- Look for the meaning of a new word through the context in which it is introduced.
- Use the prefix or suffix to determine the meaning of the root word.
- Relate the new term to familiar, everyday words.

Once you know what a word means, write its definition in your own words.

Vocabulary Word	Study Tips	Definition
Polynomial	Prefix *poly-*, meaning "many"	A monomial or a sum or difference of monomials
Conjunction	Prefix *con-*, meaning "connect" or "together"	A compound statement that uses the word *and*
Extraneous Solution	Relate to the word *extra*, meaning "not needed."	Extra roots that are not solutions to the original equation
Slope	Think of a *ski slope*.	The measure of the steepness of a line

polynomial = many
conjunction = connect or together
extraneous solution = not needed
slope = ski slope

Fill in the chart with information that can help you learn the vocabulary words.

	Vocabulary Word	Study Tips	Definition
1.	Trinomial	■	■
2.	Disjunction	■	■
3.	Variable	■	■
4.	Multiplicity	■	■

Use the given prefix's meaning to write the definition of the corresponding vocabulary words.

5. *dia-* through, across, between: diameter; diagonal

6. *trans-* across, beyond, through: transformation; translation

Special Right Triangles

Review the relationships of the side lengths of special right triangles below. You can use these relationships to find side lengths of special right triangles.

Special Right Triangles	
45°-45°-90° Triangle Theorem	In any 45°-45°-90° triangle, the length of the hypotenuse is $\sqrt{2}$ times the length of a leg.
30°-60°-90° Triangle Theorem	In any 30°-60°-90° triangle, the length of the hypotenuse is 2 times the length of the shorter leg, and the length of the longer leg is $\sqrt{3}$ times the length of the shorter leg.

Example

Find the unknown side lengths for the triangle shown.

The triangle is a 30°-60°-90° triangle, and the length of the hypotenuse is 8.

Step 1 Find the length of the shorter leg.

$8 = 2y$ *hypotenuse = 2 • shorter leg*

$4 = y$ *Solve for y, the length of the shorter leg.*

Step 2 Find the length of the longer leg.

$4\sqrt{3}$ *longer leg = $\sqrt{3}$ • shorter leg*

The length of the shorter leg is 4, and the length of the longer leg is $4\sqrt{3}$.

Check Use the Pythagorean Theorem.

$$4^2 + \left(4\sqrt{3}\right)^2 = 8^2$$

16 + 48	64
64	64 ✓

Find the unknown side lengths for each triangle.

1.

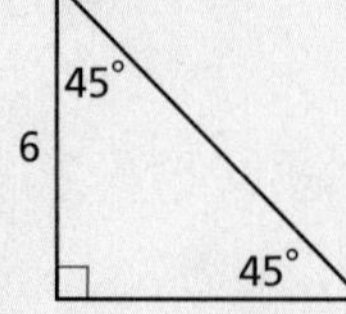

2.

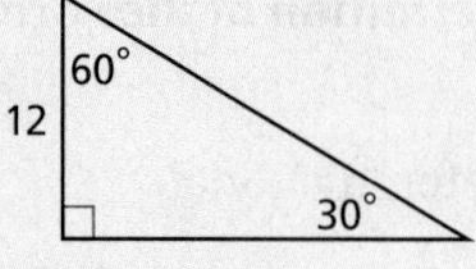

3.

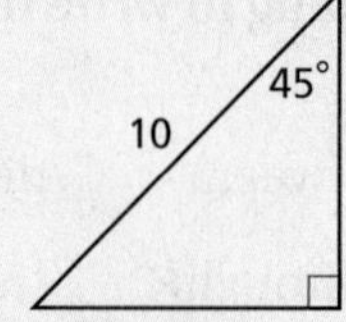

4.

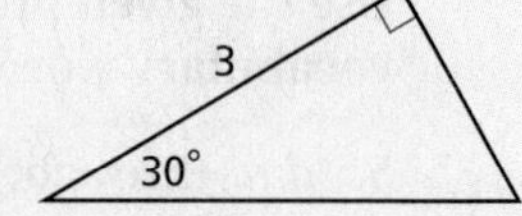

10-1 Right-Angle Trigonometry

CC.9-12.F.TF.3 ...Determine...the values of sine, cosine, tangent...express the values of sine, cosine, and tangent...in terms of their values for...any real number. *Also* **CC.9-12.F.TF.5***

Objectives

Understand and use trigonometric relationships of acute angles in triangles.

Determine side lengths of right triangles by using trigonometric functions.

Vocabulary

trigonometric function
sine
cosine
tangent
cosecant
secant
cotangent

Who uses this?

Trigonometry can be used to measure the heights of objects, such as an eruption of a geyser, that cannot be measured directly. (See Example 4.)

Trigonometry comes from Greek words meaning "triangle measurement." Trigonometry can be used to solve problems involving triangles.

A **trigonometric function** is a function whose rule is given by a trigonometric ratio. A *trigonometric ratio* compares the lengths of two sides of a right triangle. The Greek letter theta θ is traditionally used to represent the measure of an acute angle in a right triangle. The values of trigonometric ratios depend upon θ.

Trigonometric Functions

WORDS	NUMBERS	SYMBOLS
The **sine** (sin) of angle θ is the ratio of the length of the opposite leg to the length of the hypotenuse.	$\sin\theta = \frac{4}{5}$	$\sin\theta = \frac{\text{opp.}}{\text{hyp.}}$
The **cosine** (cos) of angle θ is the ratio of the length of the adjacent leg to the length of the hypotenuse.	$\cos\theta = \frac{3}{5}$	$\cos\theta = \frac{\text{adj.}}{\text{hyp.}}$
The **tangent** (tan) of angle θ is the ratio of the length of the opposite leg to the length of the adjacent leg.	$\tan\theta = \frac{4}{3}$	$\tan\theta = \frac{\text{opp.}}{\text{adj.}}$

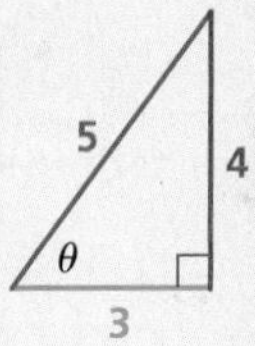

(Triangle with hypotenuse 5, legs 4 and 3, angle θ.)

The triangle shown at right is similar to the one in the table because their corresponding angles are congruent. No matter which triangle is used, the value of $\sin\theta$ is the same. The values of the sine and other trigonometric functions depend only on angle θ and not on the size of the triangle.

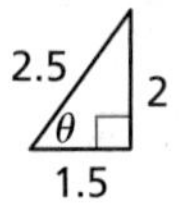

(Triangle with hypotenuse 2.5, legs 2 and 1.5, angle θ.)

$$\sin\theta = \frac{2}{2.5} = \frac{4}{5}$$

EXAMPLE 1 Finding Trigonometric Ratios

Find the value of the sine, cosine, and tangent functions for θ.

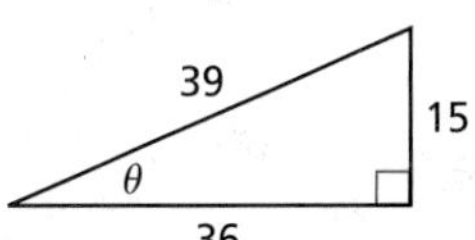

$$\sin\theta = \frac{\text{opp.}}{\text{hyp.}} = \frac{15}{39} = \frac{5}{13} \qquad \cos\theta = \frac{\text{adj.}}{\text{hyp.}} = \frac{36}{39} = \frac{12}{13} \qquad \tan\theta = \frac{\text{opp.}}{\text{adj.}} = \frac{15}{36} = \frac{5}{12}$$

1. Find the value of the sine, cosine, and tangent functions for θ.

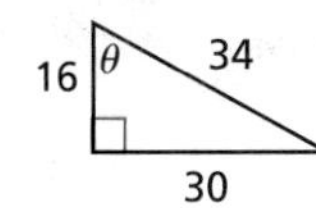

© John Elk III/Lonely Planet Images

You will frequently need to determine the value of trigonometric ratios for 30°, 60°, and 45° angles as you solve trigonometry problems. Recall from geometry that in a 30°-60°-90° triangle, the ratio of the side lengths is $1:\sqrt{3}:2$, and that in a 45°-45°-90° triangle, the ratio of the side lengths is $1:1:\sqrt{2}$.

Know it! Note

Trigonometric Ratios of Special Right Triangles

Diagram	Sine	Cosine	Tangent
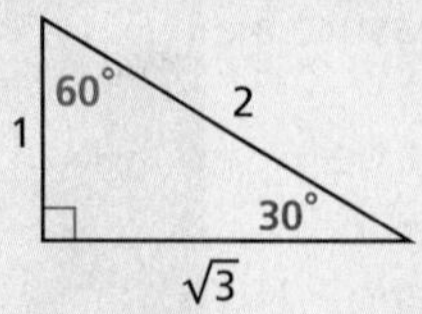	$\sin 30° = \frac{1}{2}$ $\sin 60° = \frac{\sqrt{3}}{2}$	$\cos 30° = \frac{\sqrt{3}}{2}$ $\cos 60° = \frac{1}{2}$	$\tan 30° = \frac{1}{\sqrt{3}} = \frac{\sqrt{3}}{3}$ $\tan 60° = \frac{\sqrt{3}}{1} = \sqrt{3}$
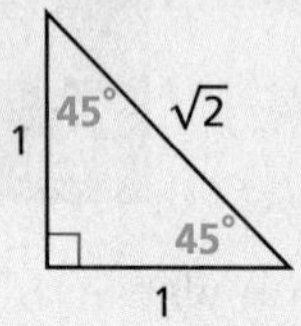	$\sin 45° = \frac{1}{\sqrt{2}} = \frac{\sqrt{2}}{2}$	$\cos 45° = \frac{1}{\sqrt{2}} = \frac{\sqrt{2}}{2}$	$\tan 45° = \frac{1}{1} = 1$

EXAMPLE 2 Finding Side Lengths of Special Right Triangles

Use a trigonometric function to find the value of *x*.

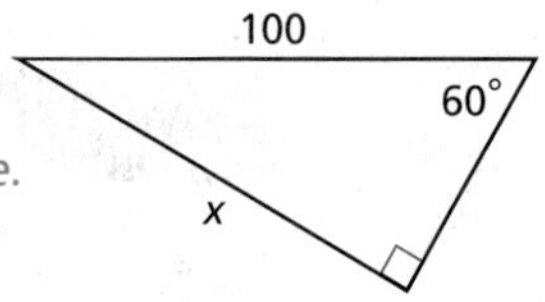

$\sin\theta = \frac{\text{opp.}}{\text{hyp.}}$ *The sine function relates the opposite leg and the hypotenuse.*

$\sin 60° = \frac{x}{100}$ *Substitute 60° for θ, x for opp., and 100 for hyp.*

$\frac{\sqrt{3}}{2} = \frac{x}{100}$ *Substitute $\frac{\sqrt{3}}{2}$ for sin 60°.*

$50\sqrt{3} = x$ *Multiply both sides by 100 to solve for x.*

CHECK IT OUT! 2. Use a trigonometric function to find the value of x.

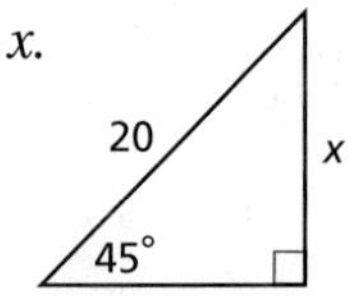

EXAMPLE 3 *Construction Application*

A builder is constructing a wheelchair ramp from the ground to a deck with a height of 18 in. The angle between the ground and the ramp must be 4.8°. To the nearest inch, what should be the distance *d* between the end of the ramp and the deck?

$\tan\theta = \frac{\text{opp.}}{\text{adj.}}$

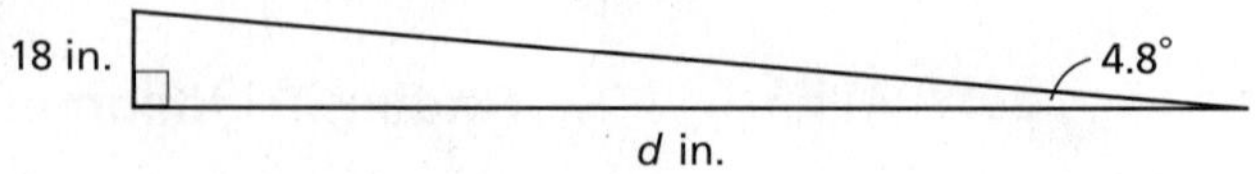

$\tan 4.8° = \frac{18}{d}$ *Substitute 4.8° for θ, 18 for opp., and d for adj.*

$d(\tan 4.8°) = 18$ *Multiply both sides by d.*

$d = \frac{18}{\tan 4.8°}$ *Divide both sides by tan 4.8°.*

$d \approx 214$ *Use a calculator to simplify.*

The distance should be about 214 in., or 17 ft 10 in.

Caution!

Make sure that your graphing calculator is set to interpret angle values as degrees. Press MODE. Check that **Degree** and not **Radian** is highlighted in the third row.

3. A skateboard ramp will have a height of 12 in., and the angle between the ramp and the ground will be 17°. To the nearest inch, what will be the length ℓ of the ramp?

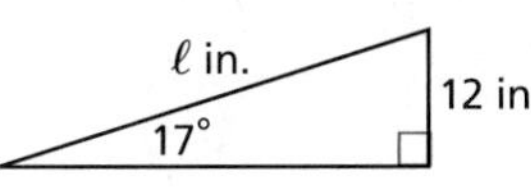

When an object is above or below another object, you can find distances indirectly by using the *angle of elevation* or the *angle of depression* between the objects.

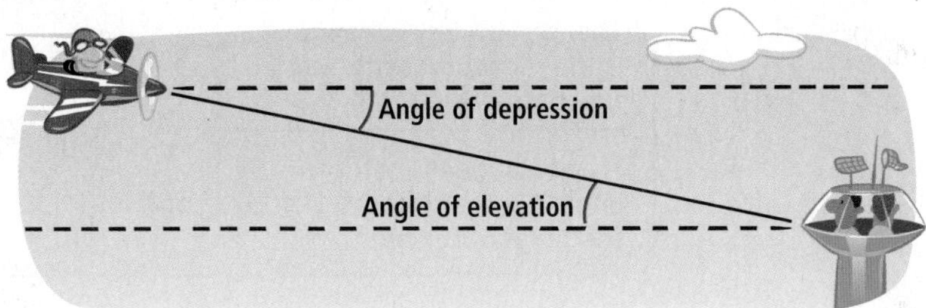

EXAMPLE 4 Geology Application

A park ranger whose eye level is 5 ft above the ground measures the angle of elevation to the top of an eruption of Old Faithful geyser to be 34.6°. If the ranger is standing 200 ft from the geyser's base, what is the height of the eruption to the nearest foot?

Step 1 Draw and label a diagram to represent the information given in the problem.

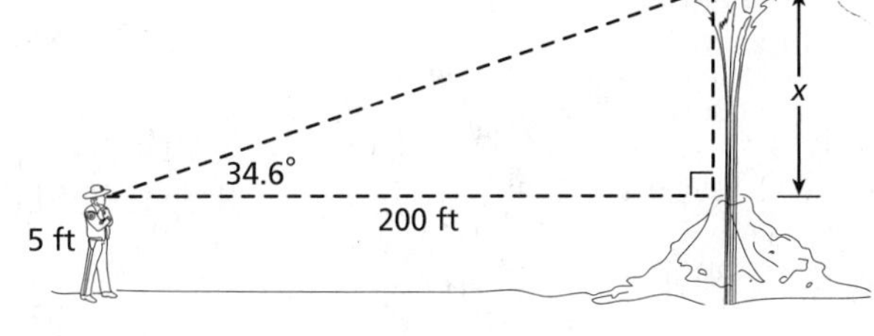

Step 2 Let x represent the height of the eruption compared with the ranger's eye level. Determine the value of x.

$\tan\theta = \frac{\text{opp.}}{\text{adj.}}$ *Use the tangent function.*

$\tan 34.6° = \frac{x}{200}$ *Substitute 34.6° for θ, x for opp., and 200 for adj.*

$200(\tan 34.6°) = x$ *Multiply both sides by 200.*

$138 \approx x$ *Use a calculator to solve for x.*

Step 3 Determine the overall height of the eruption.

$x + 5 = 138 + 5$
$= 143$

The ranger's eye level is 5 ft above the ground, so add 5 ft to x to find the overall height of the eruption.

The height of the eruption is about 143 ft.

4. A surveyor whose eye level is 6 ft above the ground measures the angle of elevation to the top of the highest hill on a roller coaster to be 60.7°. If the surveyor is standing 120 ft from the hill's base, what is the height of the hill to the nearest foot?

The reciprocals of the sine, cosine, and tangent ratios are also trigonometric ratios. They are the trigonometric functions *cosecant, secant,* and *cotangent.*

Reciprocal Trigonometric Functions

WORDS	NUMBERS	SYMBOLS
The **cosecant** (csc) of angle θ is the reciprocal of the sine function.	$\csc\theta = \frac{5}{4}$	$\csc\theta = \frac{1}{\sin\theta} = \frac{\text{hyp.}}{\text{opp.}}$
The **secant** (sec) of angle θ is the reciprocal of the cosine function.	$\sec\theta = \frac{5}{3}$	$\sec\theta = \frac{1}{\cos\theta} = \frac{\text{hyp.}}{\text{adj.}}$
The **cotangent** (cot) of angle θ is the reciprocal of the tangent function.	$\cot\theta = \frac{3}{4}$	$\cot\theta = \frac{1}{\tan\theta} = \frac{\text{adj.}}{\text{opp.}}$

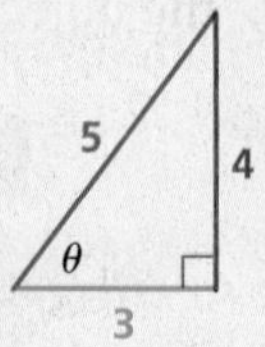

(Triangle with sides 3, 4, 5 and angle θ.)

EXAMPLE 5 Finding All Trigonometric Ratios

Find the values of the six trigonometric functions for θ.

(Right triangle with legs 14 and 48, angle θ.)

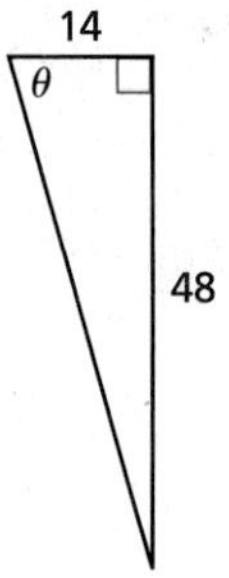

Step 1 Find the length of the hypotenuse.

$a^2 + b^2 = c^2$ *Pythagorean Theorem*

$c^2 = 14^2 + 48^2$ *Substitute 14 for a and 48 for b.*

$c^2 = 2500$ *Simplify.*

$c = 50$ *Solve for c. Eliminate the negative solution.*

Step 2 Find the function values.

$$\sin\theta = \frac{48}{50} = \frac{24}{25} \qquad \cos\theta = \frac{14}{50} = \frac{7}{25} \qquad \tan\theta = \frac{48}{14} = \frac{24}{7}$$

$$\csc\theta = \frac{1}{\sin\theta} = \frac{25}{24} \qquad \sec\theta = \frac{1}{\cos\theta} = \frac{25}{7} \qquad \cot\theta = \frac{1}{\tan\theta} = \frac{7}{24}$$

Helpful Hint

In each reciprocal pair of trigonometric functions, there is exactly one "**co**."

$\textbf{co}\text{secant}\,\theta = \frac{1}{\text{sine}\,\theta}$

$\text{secant}\,\theta = \frac{1}{\textbf{co}\text{sine}\,\theta}$

$\textbf{co}\text{tangent}\,\theta = \frac{1}{\text{tangent}\,\theta}$

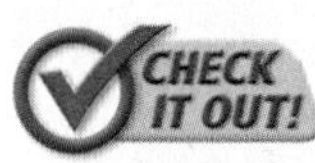

5. Find the values of the six trigonometric functions for θ.

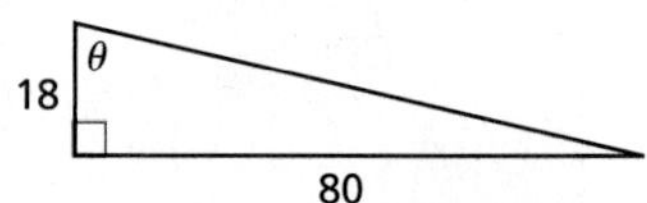

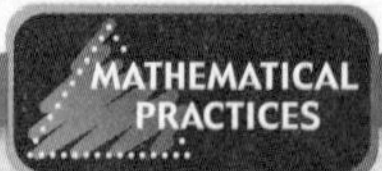

THINK AND DISCUSS

1. The sine of an acute angle in a right triangle is 0.6. Explain why the cosine of the other acute angle in the triangle must be 0.6.

2. If the secant of an acute angle in a right triangle is 2, which trigonometric ratio for that angle has a value of 0.5? Explain.

3. GET ORGANIZED Copy and complete the graphic organizer. For each trigonometric function, give the name, the side length ratio, and the reciprocal function.

	Sin	Cos	Tan
Function Name			
Side Length Ratio			
Reciprocal Function			

10-1 Exercises

GUIDED PRACTICE

1. **Vocabulary** The ratio of the length of the opposite leg to the length of the adjacent leg of an acute angle of a right triangle is the ___?___ of the angle. (*tangent* or *cotangent*)

SEE EXAMPLE 1

Find the value of the sine, cosine, and tangent functions for θ.

2. 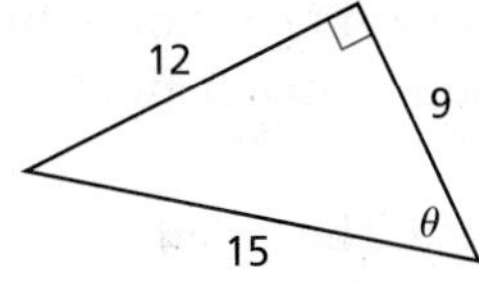

3. 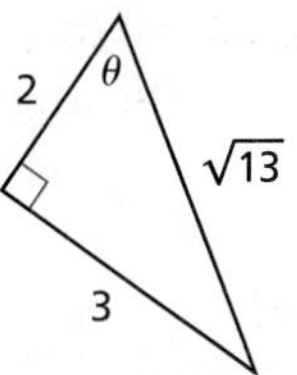

4. 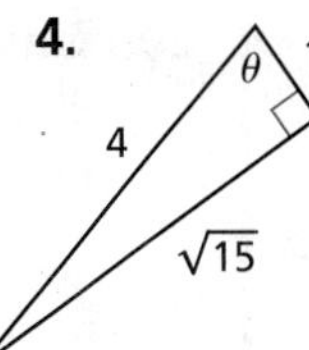

SEE EXAMPLE 2

Use a trigonometric function to find the value of x.

5. 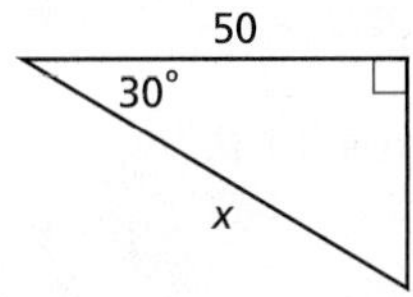

6. 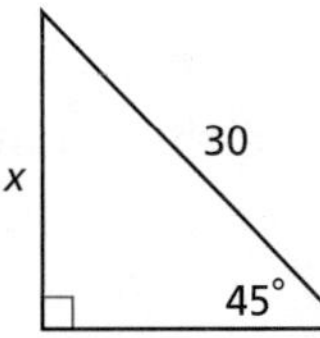

7. 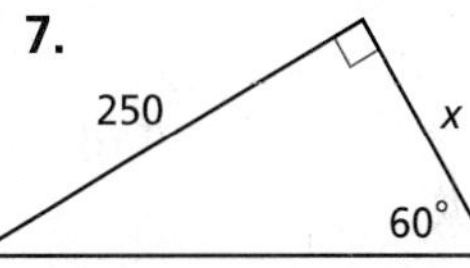

SEE EXAMPLE 3

8. **Engineering** An escalator in a mall must lift customers to a height of 22 ft. If the angle between the escalator stairs and the ground floor will be 30°, what will be the length ℓ of the escalator?

SEE EXAMPLE 4

9. **Recreation** The pilot of a hot-air balloon measures the angle of depression to a landing spot to be 20.5°. If the pilot's altitude is 90 m, what is the horizontal distance between the balloon and the landing spot? Round to the nearest meter.

SEE EXAMPLE 5

Find the values of the six trigonometric functions for θ.

10. 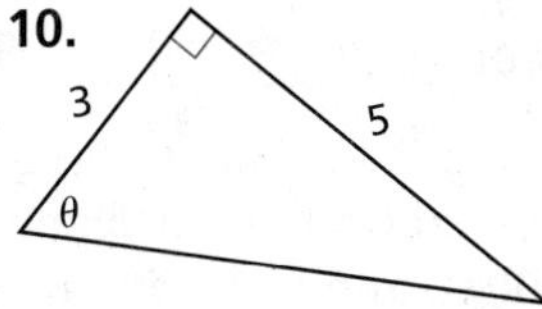

11. 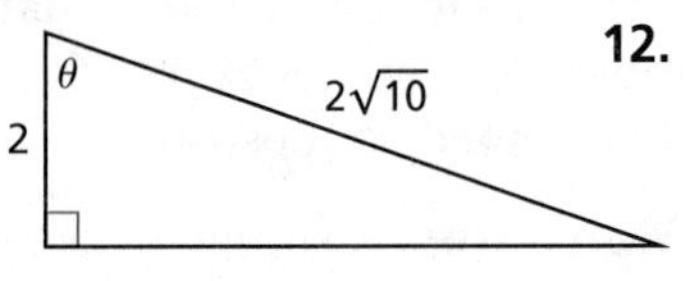

12. 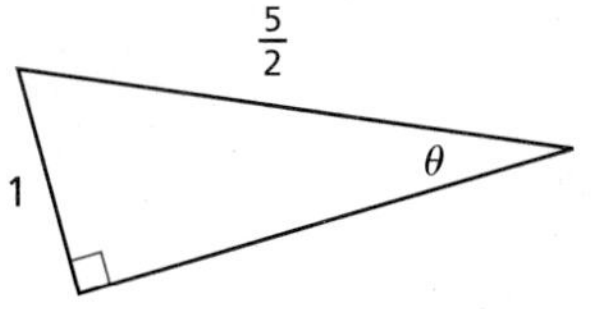

PRACTICE AND PROBLEM SOLVING

Independent Practice

For Exercises	See Example
13–15	1
16–18	2
19	3
20	4
21–23	5

Extra Practice

See Extra Practice for more Skills Practice and Applications Practice exercises.

Find the value of the sine, cosine, and tangent functions for θ.

13. 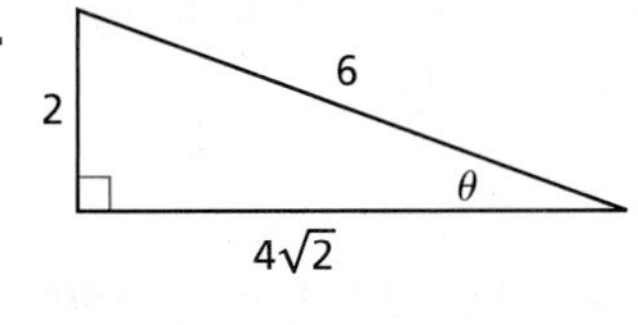

14. 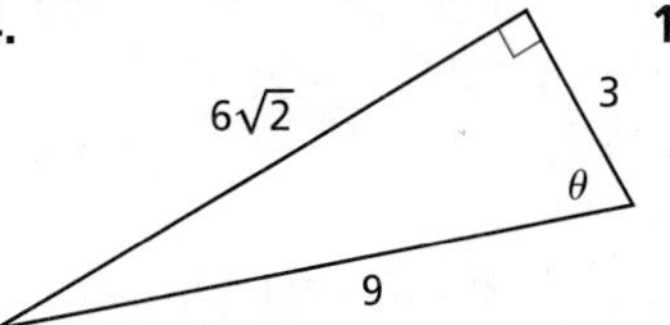

15. 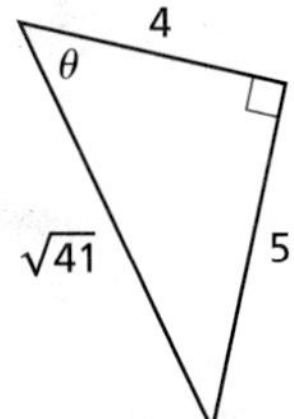

Use a trigonometric function to find the value of x.

16. 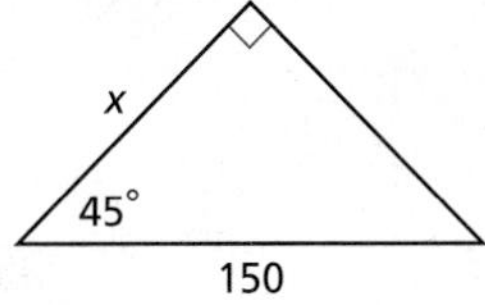

17. 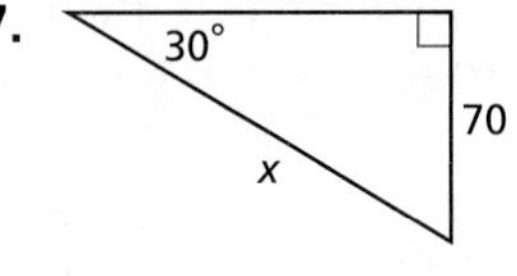

18. 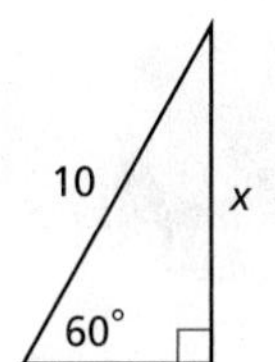

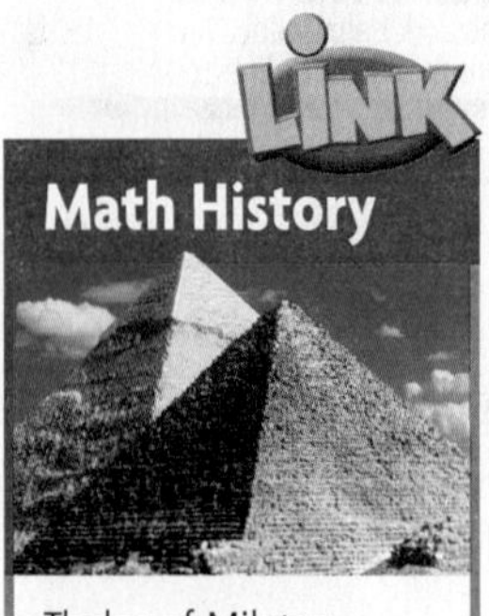

Thales of Miletus (624–547 B.C.E.) was a Greek mathematician reputed to have measured the height of the Egyptian pyramids by using the lengths of shadows and indirect measurement.

19. **History** Today, the Great Pyramid in Egypt is not as tall as when it was originally built. The square base of the pyramid has a side length of 230 m, and the sides of the pyramid meet the base at an angle of 52°.

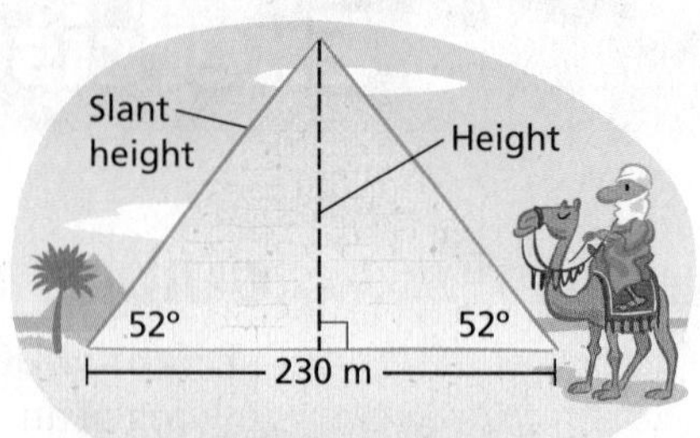

   a. What was the original height of the pyramid to the nearest meter?
   b. What was the original slant height of the pyramid to the nearest meter?

20. **Navigation** The top of the Matagorda Island Lighthouse in Texas is about 90 ft above sea level. The angle of elevation from a fishing boat to the top of the lighthouse is 10°.
   a. To the nearest foot, what is the distance d between the boat and the base of the lighthouse?
   b. **What if...?** After the boat drifts for half an hour, the angle of elevation has decreased to 4.5°. To the nearest foot, how much farther has the boat moved from the lighthouse?

Find the values of the six trigonometric functions for θ.

21. 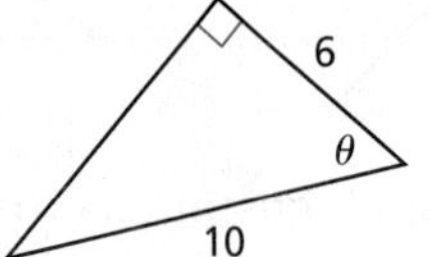

22. 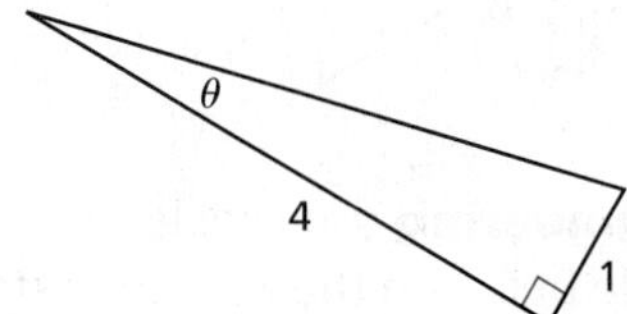

23. 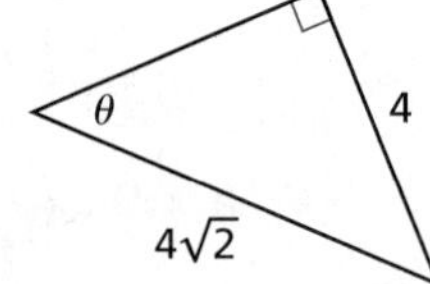

24. **Estimation** One factor that determines a ski slope's difficulty is the slope angle. The table shows the typical slope angles for the most common difficulty categories. For each category, estimate how many meters a skier descends for every 100 m that he or she moves forward horizontally. Explain how you determined your estimates.

Slope Ratings

Symbol	Difficulty	Slope Angle
●	Beginner	5° to 10°
■	Intermediate	10° to 20°
◆	Expert	20° to 35°

25. **Multi-Step** A supply package will be dropped from an airplane to an Arctic research station. The plane's altitude is 2000 ft, and its horizontal speed is 235 ft/s. The angle of depression to the target is 14°.
   a. To the nearest foot, what is the plane's horizontal distance from the target?
   b. The plane needs to drop the supplies when it is a horizontal distance of 500 ft from the target. To the nearest second, how long should the pilot wait before dropping the supplies?

MULTI-STEP TEST PREP

26. An observer on a sea cliff with a height of 12 m spots an otter through a pair of binoculars at an angle of depression of 5.7°.
   a. To the nearest meter, how far is the otter from the base of the cliff?
   b. Five minutes later, the observer sights the same otter at an angle of depression of 7.6°. To the nearest meter, how much closer has the otter moved to the base of the cliff?

27. **Surveying** Based on the measurements shown in the diagram, what is the width w of the river to the nearest foot?

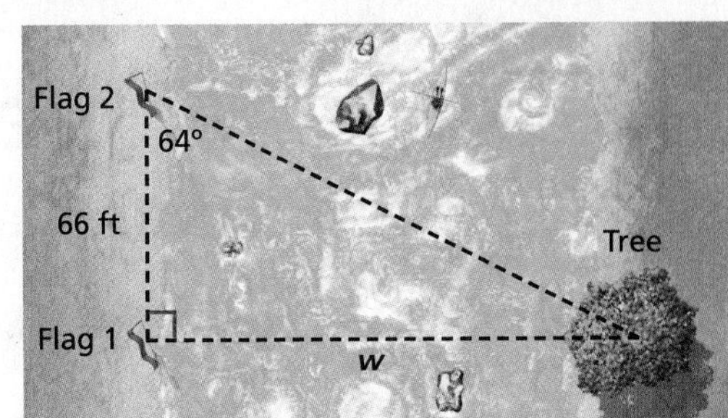

28. **Critical Thinking** Show that $\frac{\sin\theta}{\cos\theta} = \tan\theta$.

29. **Write About It** Suppose that you are given the measure of an acute angle in a right triangle and the length of the leg adjacent to this angle. Describe two different methods that you could use to find the length of the hypotenuse.

TEST PREP

Use the diagram for Exercises 30 and 31.

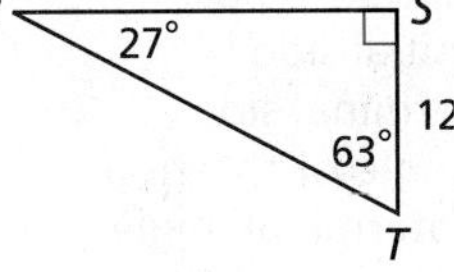

30. Which of the following is equal to $\cos 27°$?

(A) $\csc 63°$
(B) $\sec 63°$
(C) $\tan 63°$
(D) $\sin 63°$

31. Which expression represents the length of $\overline{RS}$?

(F) $12\cot 27°$
(G) $12\csc 27°$
(H) $12\sin 27°$
(J) $12\tan 27°$

32. If $\tan\theta = \frac{3}{4}$, what is $\cos\theta$?

(A) $\frac{3}{5}$
(B) $\frac{4}{5}$
(C) $\frac{5}{4}$
(D) $\frac{4}{3}$

CHALLENGE AND EXTEND

33. **Geometry** Two right triangles each have an acute angle with a sine ratio of 0.6. Prove that the triangles are similar.

34. For an acute angle of a right triangle, which trigonometric ratios are always greater than 1? Which are always less than 1? Explain.

35. **Geometry** A regular hexagon with sides of length 3 ft is inscribed in a circle.

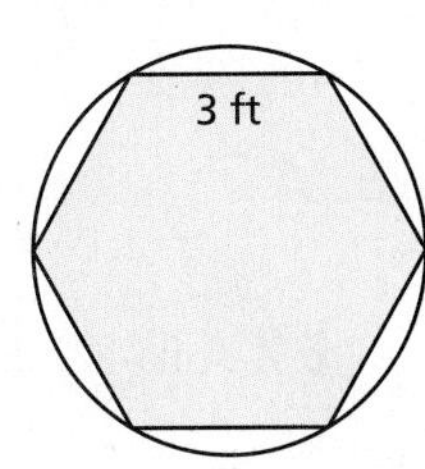

a. Use a trigonometric ratio to find the radius of the circle.

b. Determine the area of the hexagon.

36. Explain why the sine of an acute angle is equal to the cosine of its complement.

10-2 Angles of Rotation

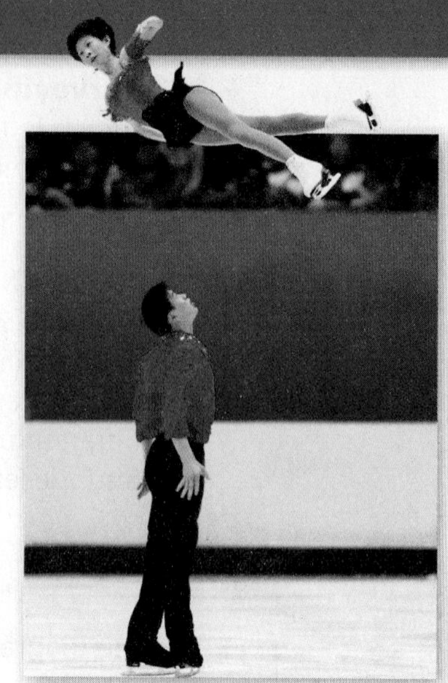

CC.9-12.F.TF.2 Explain how the unit circle in the coordinate plane enables the extension of trigonometric functions to all real numbers...

Objectives
Draw angles in standard position.

Determine the values of the trigonometric functions for an angle in standard position.

Vocabulary
standard position
initial side
terminal side
angle of rotation
coterminal angle
reference angle

Why learn this?
You can use angles of rotation to determine the rate at which a skater must spin to complete a jump. (See Exercise 51.)

Previously, you investigated trigonometric functions by using acute angles in right triangles. The trigonometric functions can also be evaluated for other types of angles.

An angle is in **standard position** when its vertex is at the origin and one ray is on the positive x-axis. The **initial side** of the angle is the ray on the x-axis. The other ray is called the **terminal side** of the angle.

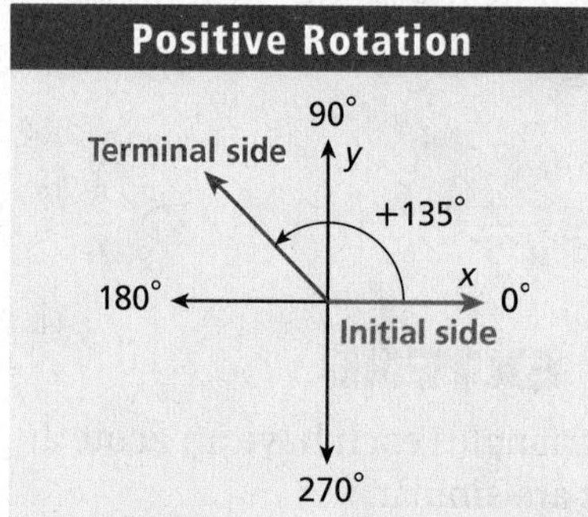

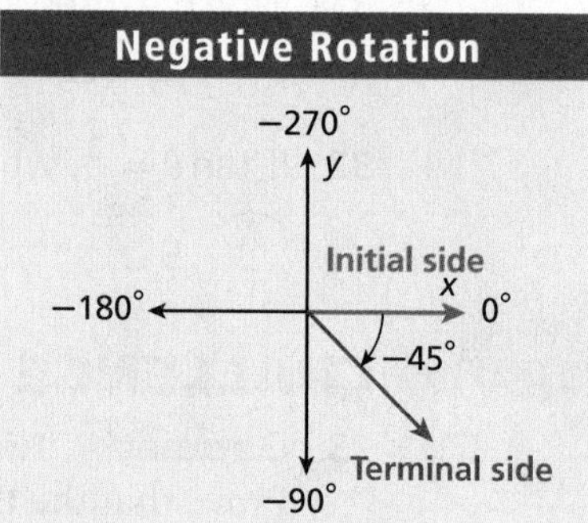

An **angle of rotation** is formed by rotating the terminal side and keeping the initial side in place. If the terminal side is rotated counterclockwise, the angle of rotation is positive. If the terminal side is rotated clockwise, the angle of rotation is negative. The terminal side can be rotated more than 360°.

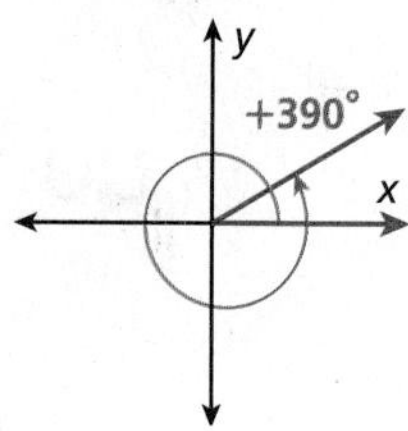

EXAMPLE 1 Drawing Angles in Standard Position

Remember!
A 360° rotation is a complete rotation. A 180° rotation is one-half of a complete rotation.

Draw an angle with the given measure in standard position.

A 300°

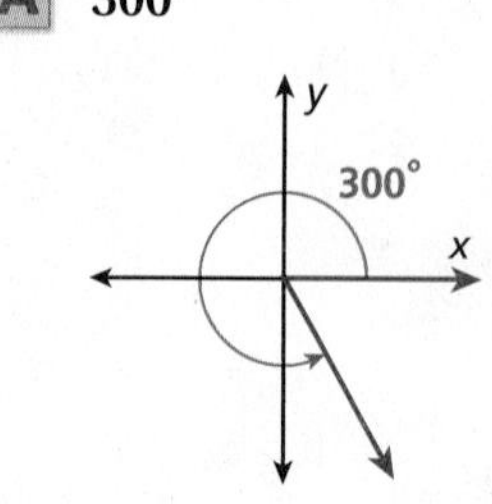

Rotate the terminal side 300° counterclockwise.

B −150°

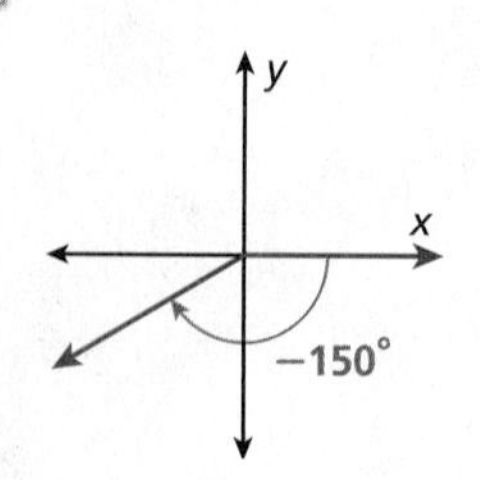

Rotate the terminal side 150° clockwise.

C 900°

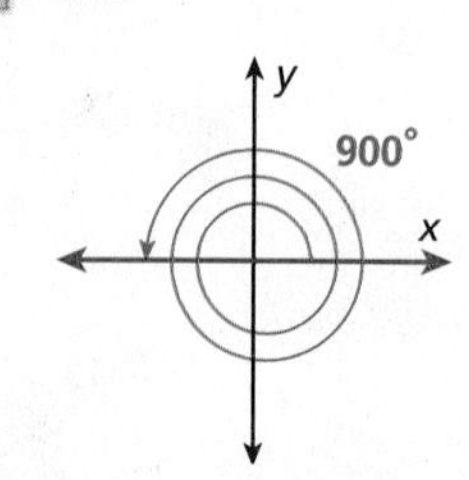

Rotate the terminal side 900° counterclockwise.
900° = 360° + 360° + 180°

Draw an angle with the given measure in standard position.

1a. 210° **1b.** 1020° **1c.** −300°

Photo by Rick Wilking/Reuters

Coterminal angles are angles in standard position with the same terminal side. For example, angles measuring 120° and −240° are coterminal.

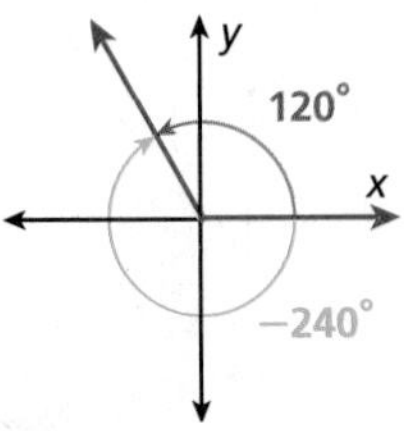

There are infinitely many coterminal angles. One way to find the measure of an angle that is coterminal with an angle θ is to add or subtract integer multiples of 360°.

EXAMPLE 2 Finding Coterminal Angles

Find the measures of a positive angle and a negative angle that are coterminal with each given angle.

A $\theta = 40°$

$40° + 360° = 400°$ *Add 360° to find a positive coterminal angle.*

$40° - 360° = -320°$ *Subtract 360° to find a negative coterminal angle.*

Angles that measure 400° and −320° are coterminal with a 40° angle.

B $\theta = 380°$

$380° - 360° = 20°$ *Subtract 360° to find a positive coterminal angle.*

$380° - 2(360°) = -340°$ *Subtract a multiple of 360° to find a negative coterminal angle.*

Angles that measure 20° and −340° are coterminal with a 380° angle.

Find the measures of a positive angle and a negative angle that are coterminal with each given angle.

2a. $\theta = 88°$ **2b.** $\theta = 500°$ **2c.** $\theta = -120°$

For an angle θ in standard position, the **reference angle** is the positive acute angle formed by the terminal side of θ and the x-axis. You will learn how to use reference angles to find trigonometric values of angles measuring greater than 90° or less than 0°.

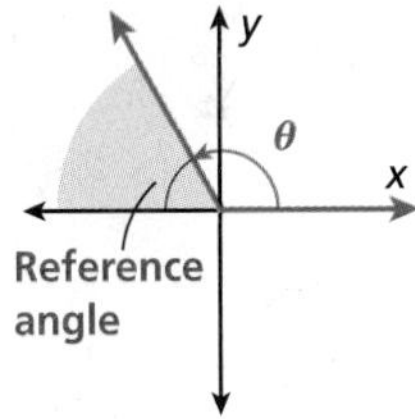

EXAMPLE 3 Finding Reference Angles

Find the measure of the reference angle for each given angle.

A $\theta = 150°$

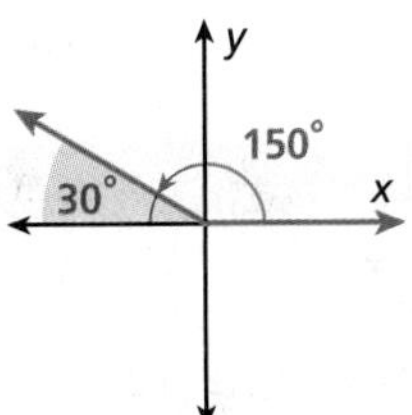

The measure of the reference angle is 30°.

B $\theta = -130°$

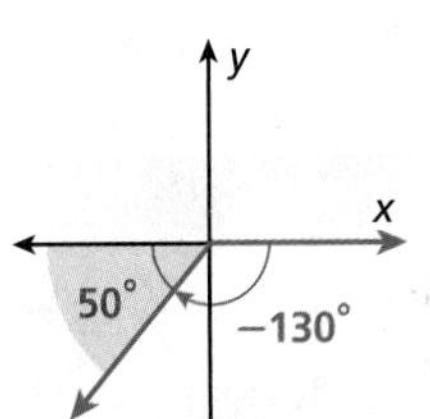

The measure of the reference angle is 50°.

C $\theta = 280°$

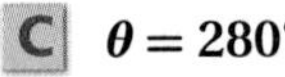

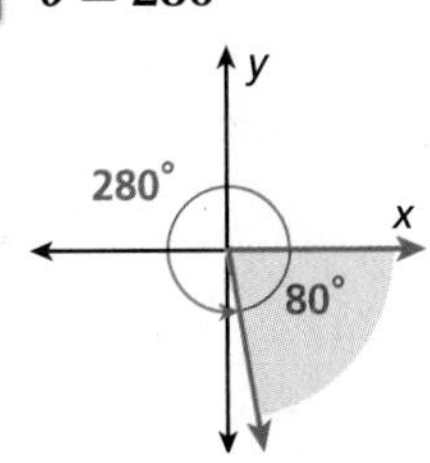

The measure of the reference angle is 80°.

Find the measure of the reference angle for each given angle.

3a. $\theta = 105°$ **3b.** $\theta = -115°$ **3c.** $\theta = 310°$

To determine the value of the trigonometric functions for an angle θ in standard position, begin by selecting a point P with coordinates (x, y) on the terminal side of the angle. The distance r from point P to the origin is given by $\sqrt{x^2 + y^2}$.

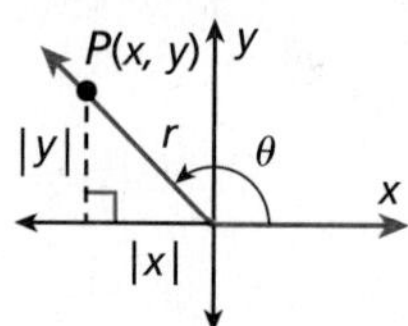

Trigonometric Functions

For a point $P(x, y)$ on the terminal side of θ in standard position and $r = \sqrt{x^2 + y^2}$,

SINE	COSINE	TANGENT
$\sin\theta = \frac{y}{r}$	$\cos\theta = \frac{x}{r}$	$\tan\theta = \frac{y}{x},\ x \neq 0$

EXAMPLE 4 Finding Values of Trigonometric Functions

$P(4, -5)$ is a point on the terminal side of θ in standard position. Find the exact value of the six trigonometric functions for θ.

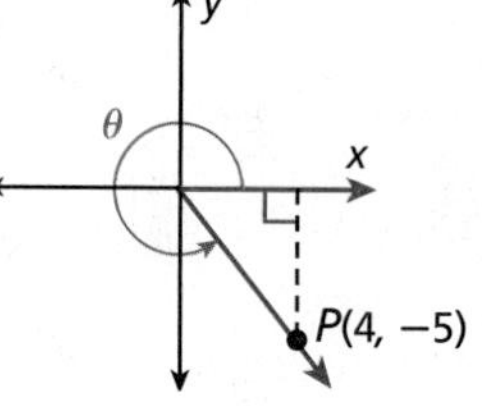

Step 1 Plot point P, and use it to sketch a right triangle and angle θ in standard position. Find r.

$$r = \sqrt{4^2 + (-5)^2} = \sqrt{16 + 25} = \sqrt{41}$$

Helpful Hint

Because r is a distance, its value is always positive, regardless of the sign of x and y.

Step 2 Find $\sin\theta$, $\cos\theta$, and $\tan\theta$.

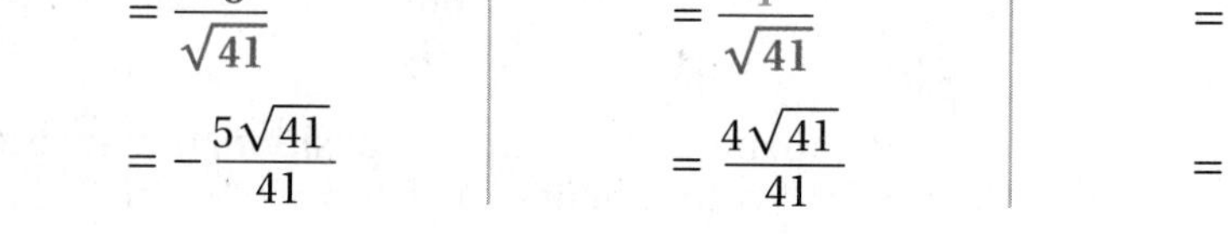

$$\sin\theta = \frac{y}{r} = \frac{-5}{\sqrt{41}} = -\frac{5\sqrt{41}}{41}$$

$$\cos\theta = \frac{x}{r} = \frac{4}{\sqrt{41}} = \frac{4\sqrt{41}}{41}$$

$$\tan\theta = \frac{y}{x} = \frac{-5}{4} = -\frac{5}{4}$$

Step 3 Use reciprocals to find $\csc\theta$, $\sec\theta$, and $\cot\theta$.

$$\csc\theta = \frac{1}{\sin\theta} = -\frac{\sqrt{41}}{5} \qquad \sec\theta = \frac{1}{\cos\theta} = \frac{\sqrt{41}}{4} \qquad \cot\theta = \frac{1}{\tan\theta} = -\frac{4}{5}$$

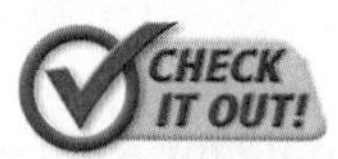

4. $P(-3, 6)$ is a point on the terminal side of θ in standard position. Find the exact value of the six trigonometric functions for θ.

THINK AND DISCUSS

1. Describe how to determine the reference angle of an angle whose terminal side is in Quadrant III.

2. **GET ORGANIZED** Copy and complete the graphic organizer. In each box, describe how to determine the given angle or position for an angle θ.

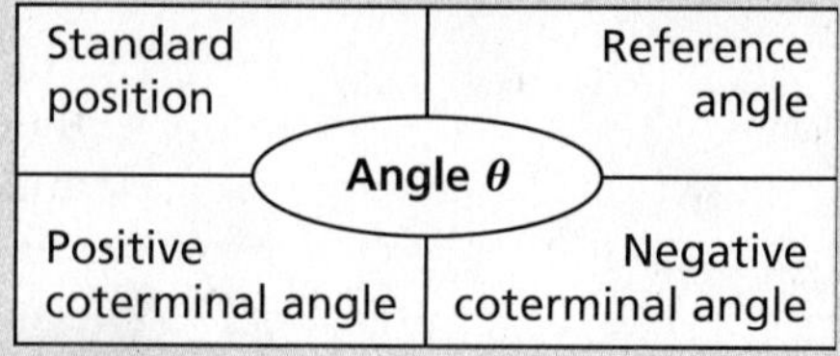

10-2 Exercises

Learn It Online
Homework Help Online
Parent Resources Online

GUIDED PRACTICE

1. **Vocabulary** If a 45° angle is in standard position, its __?__ side lies above the x-axis. (*initial* or *terminal*)

SEE EXAMPLE 1

Draw an angle with the given measure in standard position.

2. 60°
3. −135°
4. 450°
5. −1125°

SEE EXAMPLE 2

Find the measures of a positive angle and a negative angle that are coterminal with each given angle.

6. $\theta = 75°$
7. $\theta = 720°$
8. $\theta = -25°$
9. $\theta = -390°$

SEE EXAMPLE 3

Find the measure of the reference angle for each given angle.

10. $\theta = 95°$
11. $\theta = -250°$
12. $\theta = 230°$
13. $\theta = -160°$
14. $\theta = 345°$
15. $\theta = -130°$
16. $\theta = 15°$
17. $\theta = 220°$

SEE EXAMPLE 4

***P* is a point on the terminal side of θ in standard position. Find the exact value of the six trigonometric functions for θ.**

18. $P(-3, 2)$
19. $P(4, -2)$
20. $P(0, -6)$
21. $P(-3, -4)$
22. $P(5, -3)$
23. $P(1, 6)$
24. $P(-6, -5)$
25. $P(-3, 6)$

PRACTICE AND PROBLEM SOLVING

Independent Practice

For Exercises	See Example
26–29	1
30–33	2
34–41	3
42–49	4

Extra Practice

See Extra Practice for more Skills Practice and Applications Practice exercises.

Draw an angle with the given measure in standard position.

26. −120°
27. 225°
28. −570°
29. 750°

Find the measures of a positive angle and a negative angle that are coterminal with each given angle.

30. $\theta = 254°$
31. $\theta = 1020°$
32. $\theta = -165°$
33. $\theta = -610°$

Find the measure of the reference angle for each given angle.

34. $\theta = -25°$
35. $\theta = 50°$
36. $\theta = -185°$
37. $\theta = 200°$
38. $\theta = 390°$
39. $\theta = -95°$
40. $\theta = 160°$
41. $\theta = 325°$

***P* is a point on the terminal side of θ in standard position. Find the exact value of the six trigonometric functions for θ.**

42. $P(2, -5)$
43. $P(5, -2)$
44. $P(-4, 5)$
45. $P(4, 3)$
46. $P(-6, 2)$
47. $P(3, -6)$
48. $P(2, -4)$
49. $P(5, 4)$

50. **Recreation** A carousel has eight evenly spaced seats shaped like animals. During each ride, the carousel makes between 8 and 9 clockwise revolutions. At the end of one ride, the carousel stops so that the lion is in the position where the zebra was when the ride started. Through how many degrees did the carousel rotate on this ride?

51. **Multi-Step** A double axel is a figure-skating jump in which the skater makes 2.5 revolutions in the air. If a skater is in the air for 0.66 s during a double axel, what is her average angular speed to the nearest degree per second?

Determine the exact coordinates of point *P*.

52. 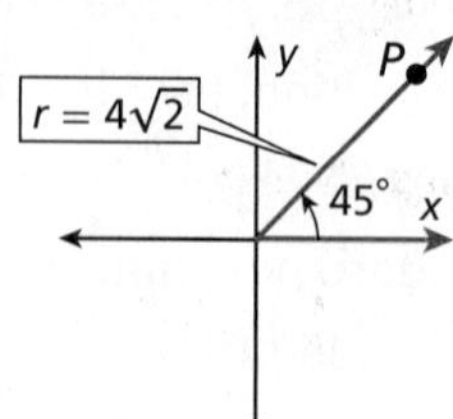

53. 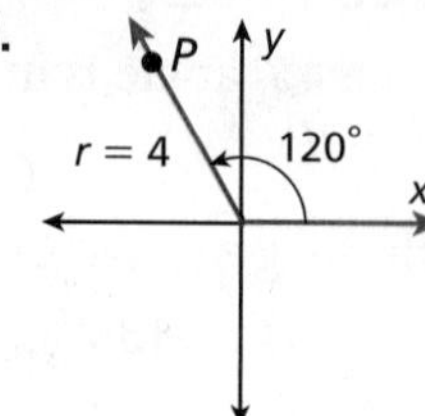

54. 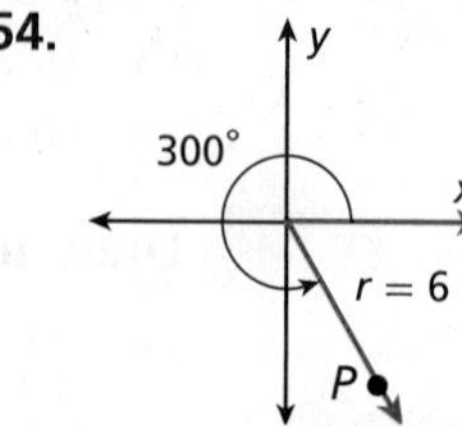

LINK

Fireworks

In professional fireworks displays, the chemicals that produce colored bursts of light are encased in spherical shells. In general, a firework rises about 100 ft for each inch of shell diameter.

55. **Fireworks** The horizontal distance x and vertical distance y in feet traveled by a firework can be modeled by the functions $x(t) = v(\cos\theta)t$ and $y(t) = -16t^2 + v(\sin\theta)t$. In these functions, v is the initial velocity of the firework, θ is the angle at which the firework is launched, and t is the time in seconds. A firework is launched with an initial velocity of 166 ft/s at an angle of 75°.

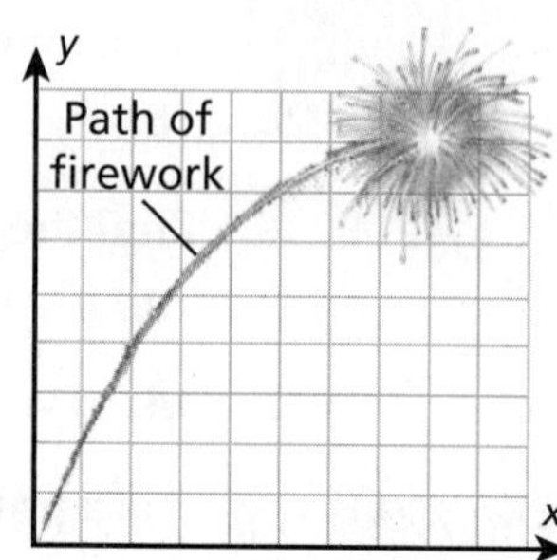

a. To the nearest foot, what is the maximum height that the firework will reach?

b. To achieve the greatest effect, the firework should explode when it reaches its maximum height. To the nearest second, how long after the launch should the firework explode?

c. To the nearest foot, what is the horizontal distance that the firework will have traveled when the maximum height is reached?

d. **What if...?** To the nearest foot, how much higher would the firework travel if it were fired at an angle of 90°?

56. **/// ERROR ANALYSIS ///** $P(2, -2)$ is a point on the terminal side of an angle θ in standard position. Two attempts at finding $\csc\theta$ are shown below. Which is incorrect? Explain the error.

A

$r = \sqrt{2^2 + (-2)^2} = \sqrt{8}$

$\csc\theta = \frac{\sqrt{8}}{2}$

$\csc\theta = \frac{2\sqrt{2}}{2} = \sqrt{2}$

B

$r = \sqrt{2^2 + (-2)^2} = \sqrt{8}$

$\csc\theta = \frac{\sqrt{8}}{-2}$

$\csc\theta = -\frac{2\sqrt{2}}{2} = -\sqrt{2}$

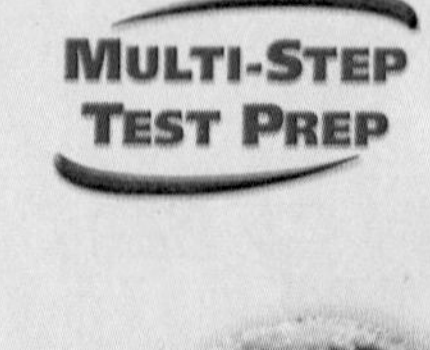

57. An aquarium has a cylindrical tank that rotates at a constant speed about an axis through the center of the cylinder's bases. In 1 minute, the tank rotates through an angle of 48°.

a. How long does it take the tank to make a complete rotation?

b. The tank rotates only during the aquarium's operating hours. If the aquarium is open from 9:30 A.M. to 6:00 P.M., how many rotations does the tank make in one day?

(cl), Steve Allen/Brand X Pictures/Alamy Photos; (bl), SuperStock

Use your calculator to find the value of each trigonometric function. Round to the nearest thousandth.

58. $\sin 260°$ **59.** $\cos(-130°)$ **60.** $\csc 200°$

Find all values of θ that have a reference angle with the given measure for $0° \leq \theta < 360°$.

61. $30°$ **62.** $55°$ **63.** $82°$

64. Critical Thinking Explain how the tangent of an angle in standard position is related to the slope of the terminal side of the angle.

65. Write About It Explain how to determine whether sin 225° is positive or negative without using a calculator.

TEST PREP

66. Which of the following angles have a reference angle with a measure of 30°?

I. $\theta = 120°$ II. $\theta = -150°$ III. $\theta = 330°$

Ⓐ III only Ⓑ I and II only Ⓒ II and III only Ⓓ I, II, and III

67. In standard position, the terminal side of $\angle P$ passes through point $(-3, 4)$, and the terminal side of $\angle Q$ passes through point $(3, 4)$. Which trigonometric function has the same value for both angles?

Ⓕ sine Ⓖ cosine Ⓗ tangent Ⓙ secant

68. Which angle in standard position is coterminal with an angle that measures $-120°$?

Ⓐ $\theta = 60°$ Ⓑ $\theta = 120°$ Ⓒ $\theta = 240°$ Ⓓ $\theta = 300°$

CHALLENGE AND EXTEND

***P* is a point on the terminal side of θ in standard position. Find the value of the sine, cosine, and tangent of θ in terms of *a* and *b*. Assume that *a* and *b* are positive.**

69. $P(a, b)$ **70.** $P\left(\frac{1}{a}, a\right)$ **71.** $P(a^2, ab)$

72. Write an expression that can be used to determine all of the coterminal angles of an angle that measures 50°.

73. For what values of θ, if any, are the six trigonometric functions undefined?

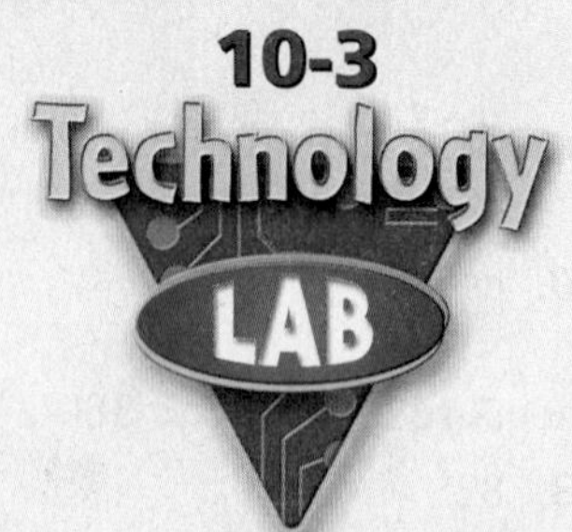

Explore the Unit Circle

A *unit circle* is a circle with a radius of 1 unit centered at the origin on the coordinate plane. You can use a graphing calculator to plot a unit circle based on the cosine and sine functions. You can then use the unit circle to explore the values of these functions for various angle measures.

Use with The Unit Circle

Use appropriate tools strategically.

CC.9-12.F.TF.2 Explain how the unit circle in the coordinate plane enables the extension of trigonometric functions to all real numbers... *Also* **CC.9-12.F.TF.3**

Use the sine and cosine functions to graph a unit circle, and use it to determine sin 30° and cos 30°.

1. Press MODE and make sure that the angle mode is set to **Degree**. Set the graphing mode to **Par** (Parametric).

2. Press Y=, and enter **cos(T)** for $\mathbf{X_{1T}}$ and **sin(T)** for $\mathbf{Y_{1T}}$.

```
Plot1 Plot2 Plot3
\X1T■cos(T)
 Y1T■sin(T)
\X2T=
```

3. Press WINDOW and set **Tmin** to 0, **Tmax** to 360, and **Tstep** to 2. Set **Xmin** and **Ymin** to −1, **Xmax** and **Ymax** to 1, and **Xscl** and **Yscl** to 0.1.

4. Press ZOOM and select **5:Zsquare**. A circle with a radius of 1 unit is displayed.

5. Press TRACE. Use the arrow keys to move the cursor to the point where **T=30**.

```
WINDOW
 Tmin=0
 Tmax=360
 Tstep=2
 Xmin=-1
 Xmax=1
 Xscl=.1
↓Ymin=-1
```

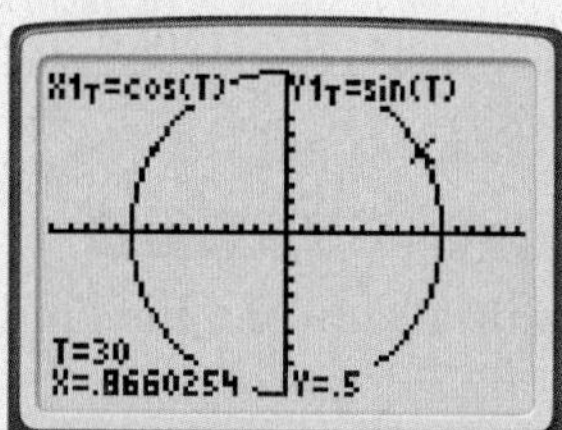

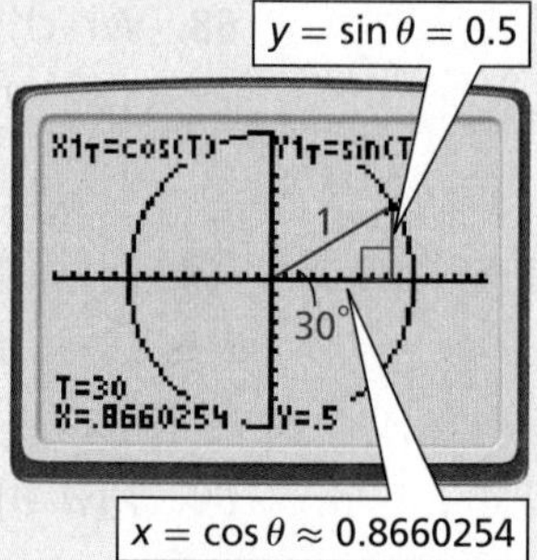

You know that $\sin 30° = \frac{1}{2} = 0.5$ and that $\cos 30° = \frac{\sqrt{3}}{2} \approx 0.8660254$. These values agree with those shown on the graph.

Notice that the unit circle can be used to define the cosine and sine functions. For an angle θ in standard position whose terminal side passes through point $P(x, y)$ on the unit circle, $\sin\theta = y$ and $\cos\theta = x$.

Try This

Use the unit circle on your graphing calculator to determine the values of the sine and cosine functions of each angle.

1. $\theta = 150°$
2. $\theta = 244°$
3. $\theta = 90°$
4. **Make a Conjecture** How can you verify that the unit circle displayed on your graphing calculator has a radius of 1 unit?
5. **Make a Conjecture** Use the graph of the unit circle to explain why the sine function is negative for an angle θ in standard position if the angle's terminal side lies in Quadrants III or IV.

COMMON CORE

10-3 The Unit Circle

CC.9-12.F.TF.2 Explain how the unit circle in the coordinate plane enables the extension of trigonometric functions to all real numbers... *Also* **CC.9-12.F.TF.1, CC.9-12.F.TF.4**

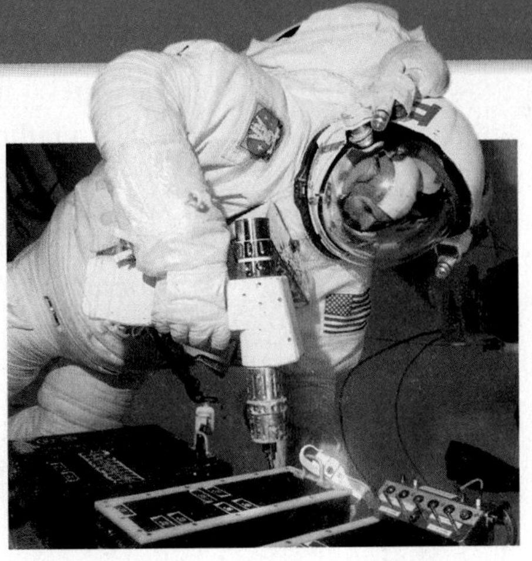

Objectives

Convert angle measures between degrees and radians.

Find the values of trigonometric functions on the unit circle.

Vocabulary

radian

unit circle

Who uses this?

Engineers can use angles measured in radians when designing machinery used to train astronauts. (See Example 4.)

So far, you have measured angles in degrees. You can also measure angles in *radians.*

A **radian** is a unit of angle measure based on arc length. Recall from geometry that an *arc* is an unbroken part of a circle. If a central angle θ in a circle of radius r intercepts an arc of length r, then the measure of θ is defined as 1 radian.

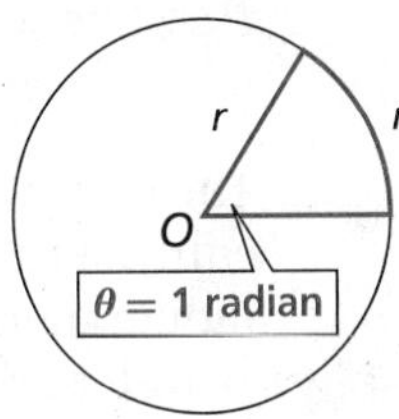

The circumference of a circle of radius r is $2\pi r$. Therefore, an angle representing one complete clockwise rotation measures 2π radians. You can use the fact that 2π radians is equivalent to 360° to convert between radians and degrees.

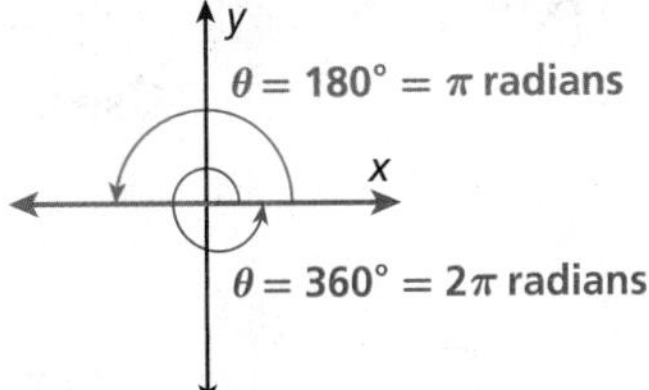

Converting Angle Measures

DEGREES TO RADIANS	RADIANS TO DEGREES
Multiply the number of degrees by $\left(\frac{\pi \text{ radians}}{180°}\right)$.	Multiply the number of radians by $\left(\frac{180°}{\pi \text{ radians}}\right)$.

EXAMPLE 1 Converting Between Degrees and Radians

Reading Math

Angles measured in radians are often not labeled with the unit. If an angle measure does not have a degree symbol, you can usually assume that the angle is measured in radians.

Convert each measure from degrees to radians or from radians to degrees.

A −45°

$$-45° \left(\frac{\pi \text{ radians}}{180°}\right) = -\frac{\pi}{4} \text{ radians} \qquad \textit{Multiply by } \left(\frac{\pi \text{ radians}}{180°}\right)$$

B $\frac{5\pi}{6}$ radians

$$\left(\frac{5\pi}{6} \text{ radians}\right)\left(\frac{180°}{\pi \text{ radians}}\right) = 150° \qquad \textit{Multiply by } \left(\frac{180°}{\pi \text{ radians}}\right)$$

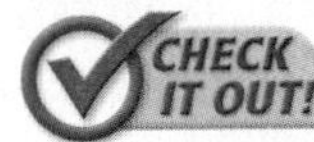

Convert each measure from degrees to radians or from radians to degrees.

1a. 80° **1b.** $\frac{2\pi}{9}$ radians **1c.** −36° **1d.** 4π radians

NASA Marshall Space Flight Center (NASA-MSFC)

A **unit circle** is a circle with a radius of 1 unit. For every point $P(x, y)$ on the unit circle, the value of r is 1. Therefore, for an angle θ in standard position:

$$\sin\theta = \frac{y}{r} = \frac{y}{1} = y$$

$$\cos\theta = \frac{x}{r} = \frac{x}{1} = x$$

$$\tan\theta = \frac{y}{x}$$

So the coordinates of P can be written as $(\cos\theta, \sin\theta)$.

The diagram shows the equivalent degree and radian measures of special angles, as well as the corresponding x- and y-coordinates of points on the unit circle.

The Unit Circle

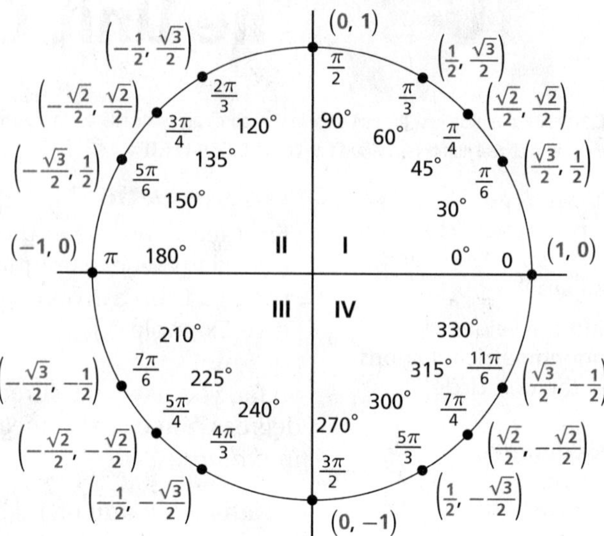

EXAMPLE  **Using the Unit Circle to Evaluate Trigonometric Functions**

Use the unit circle to find the exact value of each trigonometric function.

 $\cos 210°$

The angle passes through the point $\left(-\frac{\sqrt{3}}{2}, -\frac{1}{2}\right)$ on the unit circle.

$\cos 210° = x$ *Use* $\cos\theta = x$.

$= -\frac{\sqrt{3}}{2}$

 $\tan\frac{5\pi}{3}$

The angle passes through the point $\left(\frac{1}{2}, -\frac{\sqrt{3}}{2}\right)$ on the unit circle.

$\tan\frac{5\pi}{3} = \frac{y}{x}$ *Use* $\tan\theta = \frac{y}{x}$.

$= \frac{-\frac{\sqrt{3}}{2}}{\frac{1}{2}} = -\frac{\sqrt{3}}{2} \cdot \frac{2}{1} = -\sqrt{3}$

Use the unit circle to find the exact value of each trigonometric function.

2a. $\sin 315°$ **2b.** $\tan 180°$ **2c.** $\cos\frac{4\pi}{3}$

You can use reference angles and Quadrant I of the unit circle to determine the values of trigonometric functions.

Trigonometric Functions and Reference Angles
To find the sine, cosine, or tangent of θ:
Step 1 Determine the measure of the reference angle of θ.
Step 2 Use Quadrant I of the unit circle to find the sine, cosine, or tangent of the reference angle.
Step 3 Determine the quadrant of the terminal side of θ in standard position. Adjust the sign of the sine, cosine, or tangent based upon the quadrant of the terminal side.

The diagram shows how the signs of the trigonometric functions depend on the quadrant containing the terminal side of θ in standard position.

	QII	QI	
QII	$\sin\theta: +$ $\cos\theta: -$ $\tan\theta: -$	$\sin\theta: +$ $\cos\theta: +$ $\tan\theta: +$	QI
QIII	$\sin\theta: -$ $\cos\theta: -$ $\tan\theta: +$	$\sin\theta: -$ $\cos\theta: +$ $\tan\theta: -$	QIV

EXAMPLE 3 Using Reference Angles to Evaluate Trigonometric Functions

Use a reference angle to find the exact value of the sine, cosine, and tangent of 225°.

Step 1 Find the measure of the reference angle.

The reference angle measures 45°.

Step 2 Find the sine, cosine, and tangent of the reference angle.

$\sin 45° = \frac{\sqrt{2}}{2}$ *Use $\sin\theta = y$.*

$\cos 45° = \frac{\sqrt{2}}{2}$ *Use $\cos\theta = x$.*

$\tan 45° = 1$ *Use $\tan\theta = \frac{y}{x}$.*

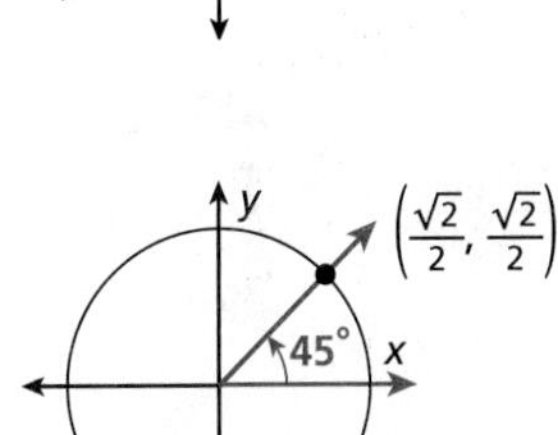

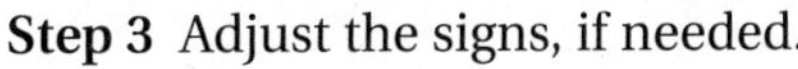

Step 3 Adjust the signs, if needed.

$\sin 225° = -\frac{\sqrt{2}}{2}$ *In Quadrant III, $\sin\theta$ is negative.*

$\cos 225° = -\frac{\sqrt{2}}{2}$ *In Quadrant III, $\cos\theta$ is negative.*

$\tan 225° = 1$ *In Quadrant III, $\tan\theta$ is positive.*

CHECK IT OUT! **Use a reference angle to find the exact value of the sine, cosine, and tangent of each angle.**

3a. 270° **3b.** $\frac{11\pi}{6}$ **3c.** −30°

If you know the measure of a central angle of a circle, you can determine the length s of the arc intercepted by the angle.

$$\frac{\text{radian measure of } \theta}{\text{radian measure of circle}} \rightarrow \frac{\theta}{2\pi} = \frac{s}{2\pi r} \leftarrow \frac{\text{arc length intercepted by } \theta}{\text{arc length intercepted by circle}}$$

$\theta = \frac{s}{r}$ *Multiply each side by 2π.*

$s = r\theta$ *Solve for s.*

Arc Length Formula

For a circle of radius r, the arc length s intercepted by a central angle θ (measured in radians) is given by the following formula.

$$s = r\theta$$

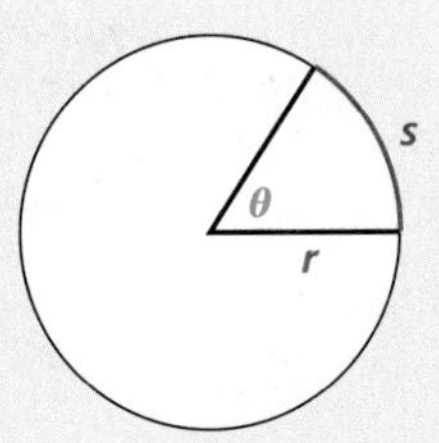

EXAMPLE 4 *Engineering Application*

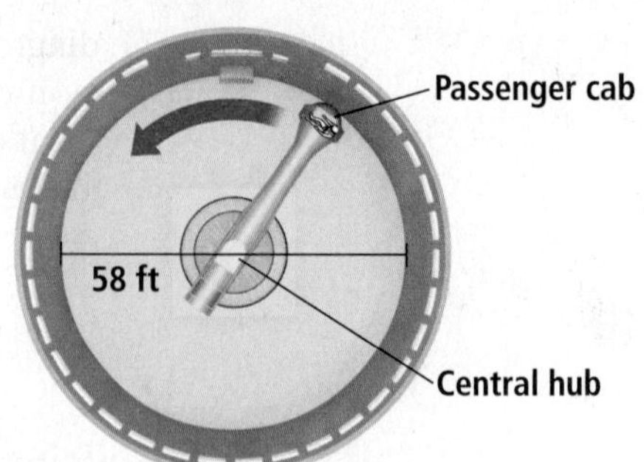

A human centrifuge is a device used in training astronauts. The passenger cab of the centrifuge shown makes 32 complete revolutions about the central hub in 1 minute. To the nearest foot, how far does an astronaut in the cab travel in 1 second?

Step 1 Find the radius of the centrifuge.

$$r = \frac{58}{2} = 29 \text{ ft}$$ *The radius is $\frac{1}{2}$ of the diameter.*

Step 2 Find the angle θ through which the cab rotates in 1 second.

$$\frac{\text{radians rotated in 1 s}}{1 \text{ s}} = \frac{\text{radians rotated in 60 s}}{60 \text{ s}}$$ *Write a proportion.*

$$\frac{\theta \text{ radians}}{1 \text{ s}} = \frac{32(2\pi) \text{ radians}}{60 \text{ s}}$$ *The cab rotates θ radians in 1 s and $32(2\pi)$ radians in 60 s.*

$$60 \cdot \theta = 32(2\pi)$$ *Cross multiply.*

$$\theta = \frac{32(2\pi)}{60}$$ *Divide both sides by 60.*

$$\theta = \frac{16\pi}{15}$$ *Simplify.*

Step 3 Find the length of the arc intercepted by $\frac{16\pi}{15}$ radians.

$$s = r\theta$$ *Use the arc length formula.*

$$s = 29\left(\frac{16\pi}{15}\right)$$ *Substitute 29 for r and $\frac{16\pi}{15}$ for θ.*

$$s \approx 97$$ *Simplify by using a calculator.*

The astronaut travels about 97 feet in 1 second.

4. An hour hand on Big Ben's Clock Tower in London is 14 ft long. To the nearest tenth of a foot, how far does the tip of the hour hand travel in 1 minute?

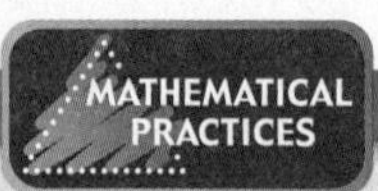

THINK AND DISCUSS

1. Explain why the tangent of a 90° angle is undefined.
2. Describe how to use a reference angle to determine the sine of an angle whose terminal side in standard position is in Quadrant IV.

3. **GET ORGANIZED** Copy and complete the graphic organizer. In each box, give an expression that can be used to determine the value of the trigonometric function.

	Acute Angle of Right Triangle	Angle of Rotation with $P(x, y)$	Angle with $P(x, y)$ on Unit Circle
$\sin\theta$			
$\cos\theta$			
$\tan\theta$			

10-3 Exercises

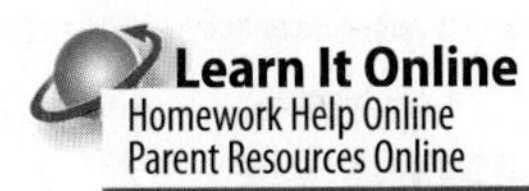

GUIDED PRACTICE

1. **Vocabulary** What is the radius of a *unit circle*? the circumference?

SEE EXAMPLE 1

Convert each measure from degrees to radians or from radians to degrees.

2. $30°$ 3. $-75°$ 4. $-150°$ 5. $135°$
6. $\frac{3\pi}{5}$ 7. $-\frac{5\pi}{8}$ 8. $-\frac{\pi}{3}$ 9. $\frac{4\pi}{9}$

SEE EXAMPLE 2

Use the unit circle to find the exact value of each trigonometric function.

10. $\sin 150°$ 11. $\tan 315°$ 12. $\cot \frac{11\pi}{6}$ 13. $\cos \frac{2\pi}{3}$

SEE EXAMPLE 3

Use a reference angle to find the exact value of the sine, cosine, and tangent of each angle.

14. $240°$ 15. $120°$ 16. $\frac{7\pi}{4}$ 17. $\frac{\pi}{3}$

SEE EXAMPLE 4

18. **Engineering** An engineer is designing a curve on a highway. The curve will be an arc of a circle with a radius of 1260 ft. The central angle that intercepts the curve will measure $\frac{\pi}{6}$ radians. To the nearest foot, what will be the length of the curve?

PRACTICE AND PROBLEM SOLVING

Independent Practice

For Exercises	See Example
19–26	1
27–30	2
31–34	3
35	4

Extra Practice

See Extra Practice for more Skills Practice and Applications Practice exercises.

Convert each measure from degrees to radians or from radians to degrees.

19. $240°$ 20. $115°$ 21. $-25°$ 22. $-315°$
23. $-\frac{\pi}{9}$ 24. $\frac{2\pi}{5}$ 25. $\frac{7\pi}{2}$ 26. $-\frac{4\pi}{3}$

Use the unit circle to find the exact value of each trigonometric function.

27. $\tan 300°$ 28. $\sin 120°$ 29. $\cos \frac{5\pi}{6}$ 30. $\sec \frac{\pi}{3}$

Use a reference angle to find the exact value of the sine, cosine, and tangent of each angle.

31. $225°$ 32. $135°$ 33. $\frac{11\pi}{6}$ 34. $-\frac{5\pi}{6}$

35. **Geography** New York City is located about 40° north of the equator. If Earth's radius is about 4000 miles, approximately how many miles south would a plane need to fly from New York City to reach the equator?

80°
60°
New York City
40°
20°
0°
Equator

Draw an angle with the given measure in standard position. Then determine the measure of its reference angle.

36. $\frac{\pi}{3}$ 37. $\frac{7\pi}{4}$ 38. $\frac{5\pi}{6}$

39. **Electronics** A DVD rotates through an angle of 20π radians in 1 second. At this speed, how many revolutions does the DVD make in 1 minute?

40. **Work** A cashier is unsure whether a group of customers ordered and ate a large or a medium pizza. All that remains is one crust, which has an arc length of about $4\frac{1}{4}$ in. All pizzas are divided into 12 equal pieces. If medium pizzas have a diameter of 12 in. and large pizzas have a diameter of 16 in., what size did the customers order? Explain how you determined your answer.

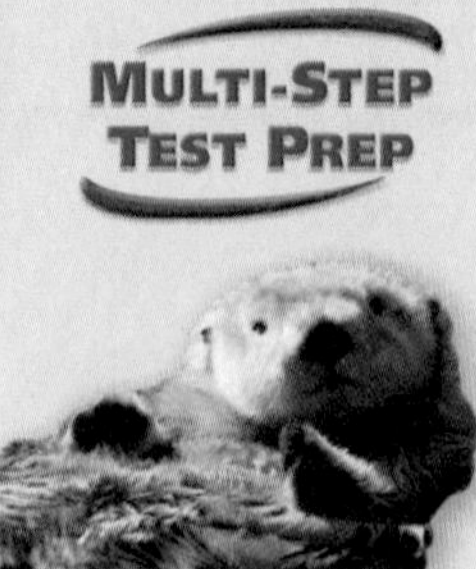

41. A railing along an observation deck at an aquarium has a length of 22 ft. The railing is shaped like an arc that represents $\frac{1}{8}$ of a circle.

a. What is the measure, to the nearest degree, of the central angle that intercepts the railing?

b. To the nearest foot, what is the radius of the circle on which the railing is based?

Find the measure of an angle that is coterminal with each given angle.

42. $\theta = \frac{\pi}{8}$ **43.** $\theta = \pi$ **44.** $\theta = \frac{3\pi}{4}$ **45.** $\theta = -\frac{4\pi}{3}$

46. Astronomy The table shows the radius of Earth and Pluto and the number of hours that each takes to rotate on its axis.

	Radius at Equator (km)	Rotational Period (h)
Earth	6378	24
Pluto	1195	153

a. How many days does it take Earth to rotate through an angle of 2π radians?

b. Through what angle, in radians, do Earth and Pluto rotate in 1 hour?

c. What if...? Suppose that a scientific expedition is sent to Pluto. In 1 hour, how much farther would a person at Earth's equator move than an astronaut at Pluto's equator, as a result of the bodies' rotations? Round to the nearest kilometer.

47. Quadrantal angles are angles whose terminal sides lie on the x- or y-axis in standard position. Explain how to use the unit circle to determine the sine of the quadrantal angles 0, $\frac{\pi}{2}$, π, and $\frac{3\pi}{2}$ radians.

48. Multi-Step A rear windshield wiper moves through an angle of 135° on each swipe. To the nearest inch, how much greater is the length of the arc traced by the top end of the wiper blade than the length of the arc traced by the bottom end of the wiper blade?

49. Critical Thinking If P is a point on the terminal side of θ in standard position, under what conditions are the coordinates of P equal to $(\cos\theta, \sin\theta)$?

50. Write About It Explain how to determine the value of $\sin(-\theta)$ if you know the value of $\sin\theta$.

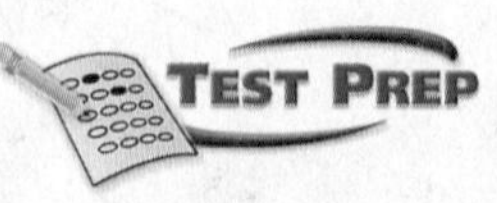

51. Which angle measure is closest to 2.5 radians?

(A) 90° (B) 120° (C) 150° (D) 225°

52. What is the value of $\cot\left(\frac{5\pi}{6}\right)$?

(F) $-\sqrt{3}$ (G) $-\frac{\sqrt{3}}{3}$ (H) $\frac{\sqrt{3}}{3}$ (J) $\sqrt{3}$

53. Short Response If the tangent of an angle θ is $-\sqrt{3}$ and the cosine of θ is $\frac{1}{2}$, what is the value of the other four trigonometric functions of θ? Explain how you determined your answer.

CHALLENGE AND EXTEND

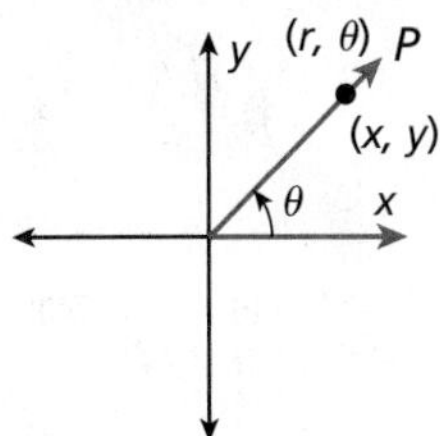

Polar Coordinates In the rectangular coordinate system, the coordinates of point P are (x, y). In the polar coordinate system, the coordinates of point P are (r, θ). Convert each point from polar coordinates to rectangular coordinates.

54. $\left(6\sqrt{2}, \frac{\pi}{4}\right)$ **55.** $\left(10, \frac{7\pi}{6}\right)$ **56.** $\left(5, \frac{5\pi}{3}\right)$

57. Photography A photographer taking nighttime photos of wildlife is using a searchlight attached to the roof of a truck. The light has a range of 250 m and can be rotated horizontally through an angle of 150°. Estimate the area of ground that can be lit by the searchlight without moving the truck. Explain how you determined your estimate.

58. What is the range of each of the six trigonometric functions for the domain $\{\theta \mid -90° < \theta < 90°\}$?

Career Path

Darryl Wright
Surveying Assistant

Q: What high school math classes did you take?

A: Algebra 1, Geometry, Algebra 2, and Trigonometry

Q: What do you like about surveying?

A: I like being outside and being in the construction industry. It's cool to see a bridge or building built where there wasn't anything before. I also like the high-tech instruments we get to use.

Q: How is math used in surveying?

A: Surveying is basically measuring a lot of distances and angles, so we use trigonometry and geometry all the time. I also do unit conversions to make sure the measurements are in the correct form.

Q: What are your future plans?

A: I'm taking classes at a community college and working toward an associate's degree in surveying. At the same time, I'm gaining work experience that will eventually help me become a licensed surveyor.

COMMON CORE

10-4 Inverses of Trigonometric Functions

CC.9-12.F.TF.6 (+) Understand that restricting a trigonometric function…allows its inverse to be constructed.
Also **CC.9-12.F.TF.7*** (+)

Objectives

Evaluate inverse trigonometric functions.

Use trigonometric equations and inverse trigonometric functions to solve problems.

Vocabulary

inverse sine function
inverse cosine function
inverse tangent function

Who uses this?

Hikers can use inverse trigonometric functions to navigate in the wilderness. (See Example 3.)

Jimmy Chin/National Geographic Image Collection

You have evaluated trigonometric functions for a given angle. You can also find the measure of angles given the value of a trigonometric function by using an *inverse trigonometric* relation.

Function	Inverse Relation
$\sin\theta = a$	$\sin^{-1} a = \theta$
$\cos\theta = a$	$\cos^{-1} a = \theta$
$\tan\theta = a$	$\tan^{-1} a = \theta$

Reading Math

The expression $\sin^{-1}$ is read as "the inverse sine." In this notation, $^{-1}$ indicates the *inverse* of the sine function, NOT the *reciprocal* of the sine function.

The inverses of the trigonometric functions are not functions themselves because there are many values of θ for a particular value of a. For example, suppose that you want to find $\cos^{-1}\frac{1}{2}$. Based on the unit circle, angles that measure $\frac{\pi}{3}$ and $\frac{5\pi}{3}$ radians have a cosine of $\frac{1}{2}$. So do all angles that are coterminal with these angles.

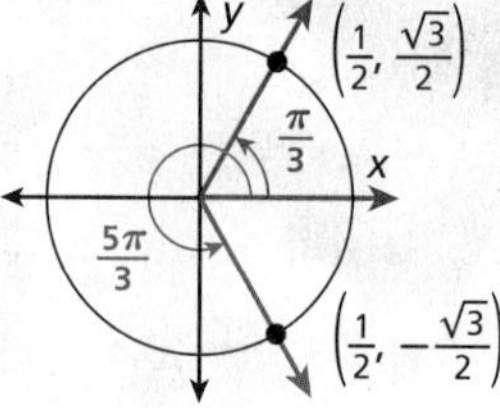

EXAMPLE 1 Finding Trigonometric Inverses

Find all possible values of $\sin^{-1}\frac{\sqrt{2}}{2}$.

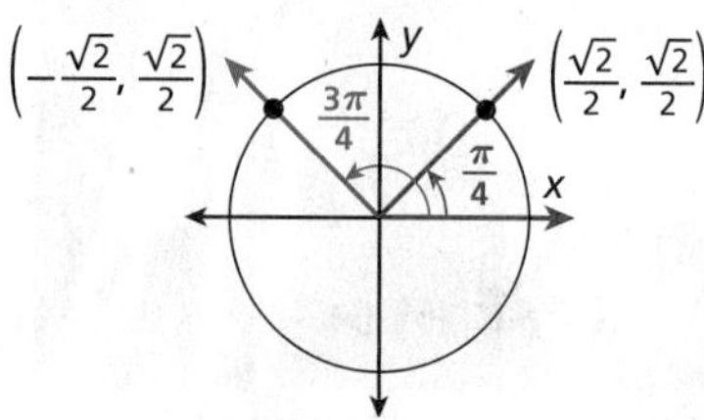

Step 1 Find the values between 0 and 2π radians for which $\sin\theta$ is equal to $\frac{\sqrt{2}}{2}$.

$$\frac{\sqrt{2}}{2} = \sin\frac{\pi}{4}, \quad \frac{\sqrt{2}}{2} = \sin\frac{3\pi}{4}$$

Use y-coordinates of points on the unit circle.

Step 2 Find the angles that are coterminal with angles measuring $\frac{\pi}{4}$ and $\frac{3\pi}{4}$ radians.

$$\frac{\pi}{4} + (2\pi)n, \quad \frac{3\pi}{4} + (2\pi)n$$

Add integer multiples of 2π radians, where n is an integer.

CHECK IT OUT!

1. Find all possible values of $\tan^{-1}1$.

Because more than one value of θ produces the same output value for a given trigonometric function, it is necessary to restrict the domain of each trigonometric function in order to define the inverse trigonometric functions.

Trigonometric functions with restricted domains are indicated with a capital letter. The domains of the Sine, Cosine, and Tangent functions are restricted as follows.

$\text{Sin}\,\theta = \sin\theta$ for $\left\{\theta \mid -\frac{\pi}{2} \le \theta \le \frac{\pi}{2}\right\}$ *θ is restricted to Quadrants I and IV.*

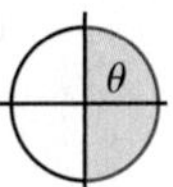

$\text{Cos}\,\theta = \cos\theta$ for $\{\theta \mid 0 \le \theta \le \pi\}$ *θ is restricted to Quadrants I and II.*

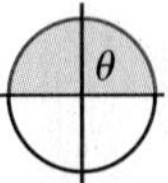

$\text{Tan}\,\theta = \tan\theta$ for $\left\{\theta \mid -\frac{\pi}{2} < \theta < \frac{\pi}{2}\right\}$ *θ is restricted to Quadrants I and IV.*

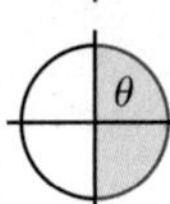

These functions can be used to define the inverse trigonometric functions. For each value of a in the domain of the inverse trigonometric functions, there is only one value of θ. Therefore, even though $\tan^{-1}1$ has many values, $\text{Tan}^{-1}1$ has only one value.

Inverse Trigonometric Functions

WORDS	SYMBOL	DOMAIN	RANGE
The **inverse sine function** is $\text{Sin}^{-1}a = \theta$, where $\text{Sin}\,\theta = a$.	$\text{Sin}^{-1}a$	$\{a \mid -1 \le a \le 1\}$	$\left\{\theta \mid -\frac{\pi}{2} \le \theta \le \frac{\pi}{2}\right\}$ $\{\theta \mid -90^\circ \le \theta \le 90^\circ\}$
The **inverse cosine function** is $\text{Cos}^{-1}a = \theta$, where $\text{Cos}\,\theta = a$.	$\text{Cos}^{-1}a$	$\{a \mid -1 \le a \le 1\}$	$\{\theta \mid 0 \le \theta \le \pi\}$ $\{\theta \mid 0^\circ \le \theta \le 180^\circ\}$
The **inverse tangent function** is $\text{Tan}^{-1}a = \theta$, where $\text{Tan}\,\theta = a$.	$\text{Tan}^{-1}a$	$\{a \mid -\infty < a < \infty\}$	$\left\{\theta \mid -\frac{\pi}{2} < \theta < \frac{\pi}{2}\right\}$ $\{\theta \mid -90^\circ < \theta < 90^\circ\}$

Reading Math

The inverse trigonometric functions are also called the arcsine, arccosine, and arctangent functions.

EXAMPLE 2 Evaluating Inverse Trigonometric Functions

Evaluate each inverse trigonometric function. Give your answer in both radians and degrees.

A $\text{Cos}^{-1}\frac{1}{2}$

$\frac{1}{2} = \text{Cos}\,\theta$ *Find the value of θ for $0 \le \theta \le \pi$ whose Cosine is $\frac{1}{2}$.*

$\frac{1}{2} = \text{Cos}\frac{\pi}{3}$ *Use x-coordinates of points on the unit circle.*

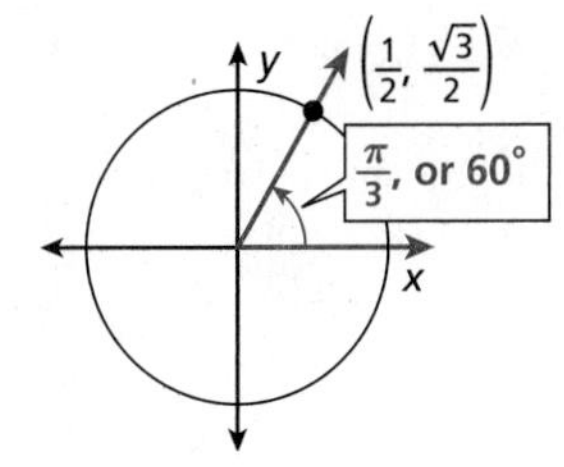

$\text{Cos}^{-1}\frac{1}{2} = \frac{\pi}{3}$, or $\text{Cos}^{-1}\frac{1}{2} = 60^\circ$

B $\text{Sin}^{-1}2$

The domain of the inverse sine function is $\{a \mid -1 \le a \le 1\}$. Because 2 is outside this domain, $\text{Sin}^{-1}2$ is undefined.

Evaluate each inverse trigonometric function. Give your answer in both radians and degrees.

2a. $\text{Sin}^{-1}\left(-\frac{\sqrt{2}}{2}\right)$ **2b.** $\text{Cos}^{-1}0$

You can solve trigonometric equations by using trigonometric inverses.

EXAMPLE 3 Navigation Application

A group of hikers plans to walk from a campground to a lake. The lake is 2 miles east and 0.5 mile north of the campground. To the nearest degree, in what direction should the hikers head?

Step 1 Draw a diagram.

The hikers' direction should be based on θ, the measure of an acute angle of a right triangle.

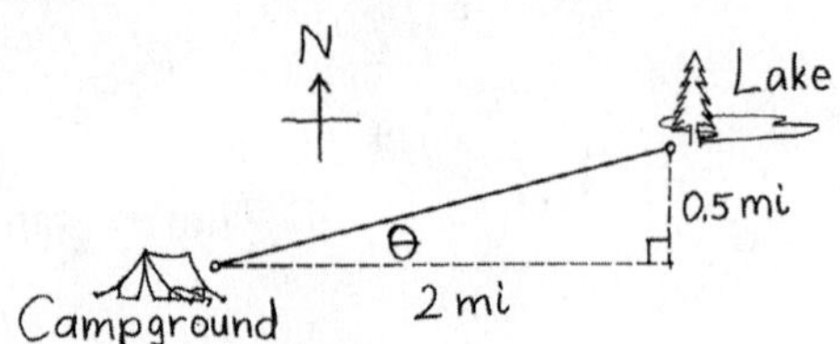

> **Caution!**
>
> If the answer on your calculator screen is 0.2449786631 when you enter $\tan^{-1}(0.25)$, your calculator is set to radian mode instead of degree mode.

Step 2 Find the value of θ.

$\tan\theta = \dfrac{\text{opp.}}{\text{adj.}}$ *Use the tangent ratio.*

$\tan\theta = \dfrac{0.5}{2} = 0.25$ *Substitute 0.5 for opp. and 2 for adj. Then simplify.*

$\theta = \text{Tan}^{-1}0.25$

$\theta \approx 14°$

The hikers should head 14° north of east.

CHECK IT OUT! **Use the information given above to answer the following.**

3. An unusual rock formation is 1 mile east and 0.75 mile north of the lake. To the nearest degree, in what direction should the hikers head from the lake to reach the rock formation?

EXAMPLE 4 Solving Trigonometric Equations

Solve each equation to the nearest tenth. Use the given restrictions.

A $\cos\theta = 0.6$, **for** $0° \le \theta \le 180°$

The restrictions on θ are the same as those for the inverse cosine function.

$\theta = \text{Cos}^{-1}(0.6) \approx 53.1°$ *Use the inverse cosine function on your calculator.*

B $\cos\theta = 0.6$, **for** $270° < \theta < 360°$

The terminal side of θ is restricted to Quadrant IV. Find the angle in Quadrant IV that has the same cosine value as 53.1°.

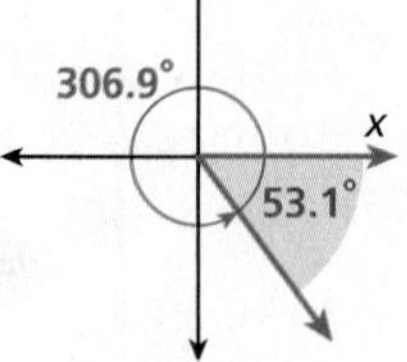

$\theta \approx 360° - 53.1° \approx 306.9°$ *θ has a reference angle of 53.1°, and $270° < \theta < 360°$.*

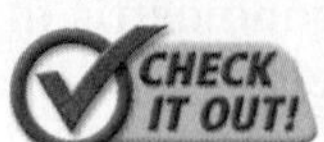

CHECK IT OUT! **Solve each equation to the nearest tenth. Use the given restrictions.**

4a. $\tan\theta = -2$, for $-90° < \theta < 90°$

4b. $\tan\theta = -2$, for $90° < \theta < 180°$

THINK AND DISCUSS

1. Given that θ is an acute angle in a right triangle, describe the measurements that you need to know to find the value of θ by using the inverse cosine function.
2. Explain the difference between $\tan^{-1}a$ and $\text{Tan}^{-1}a$.

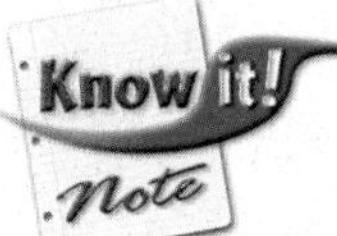

3. **GET ORGANIZED** Copy and complete the graphic organizer. In each box, give the indicated property of the inverse trigonometric functions.

Symbols	Domains
Associated quadrants	Ranges

Center: Inverse Trigonometric Functions

10-4 Exercises

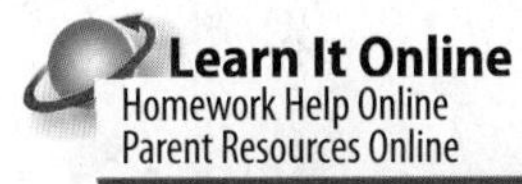

GUIDED PRACTICE

1. **Vocabulary** Explain how the inverse tangent function differs from the reciprocal of the tangent function.

SEE EXAMPLE 1

Find all possible values of each expression.

2. $\sin^{-1}\left(-\frac{1}{2}\right)$
3. $\tan^{-1}\frac{\sqrt{3}}{3}$
4. $\cos^{-1}\left(-\frac{\sqrt{2}}{2}\right)$

SEE EXAMPLE 2

Evaluate each inverse trigonometric function. Give your answer in both radians and degrees.

5. $\text{Cos}^{-1}\frac{\sqrt{3}}{2}$
6. $\text{Tan}^{-1}1$
7. $\text{Cos}^{-1}2$
8. $\text{Tan}^{-1}\left(-\sqrt{3}\right)$
9. $\text{Sin}^{-1}\frac{\sqrt{2}}{2}$
10. $\text{Sin}^{-1}0$

SEE EXAMPLE 3

11. **Architecture** A point on the top of the Leaning Tower of Pisa is shifted about 13.5 ft horizontally compared with the tower's base. To the nearest degree, how many degrees does the tower tilt from vertical?

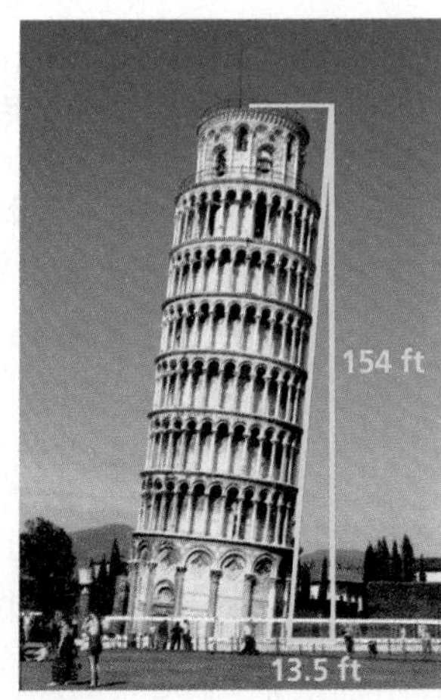

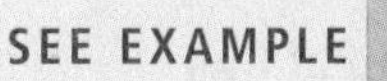

Solve each equation to the nearest tenth. Use the given restrictions.

12. $\tan\theta = 1.4$, for $-90° < \theta < 90°$
13. $\tan\theta = 1.4$, for $180° < \theta < 270°$
14. $\cos\theta = -0.25$, for $0 \le \theta \le 180°$
15. $\cos\theta = -0.25$, for $180° < \theta < 270°$

PRACTICE AND PROBLEM SOLVING

Independent Practice	
For Exercises	See Example
16–18	1
19–24	2
25	3
26–29	4

Extra Practice

See Extra Practice for more Skills Practice and Applications Practice exercises.

Find all possible values of each expression.

16. $\cos^{-1} 1$ **17.** $\sin^{-1} \frac{\sqrt{3}}{2}$ **18.** $\tan^{-1}(-1)$

Evaluate each inverse trigonometric function. Give your answer in both radians and degrees.

19. $\text{Sin}^{-1} \frac{\sqrt{3}}{2}$ **20.** $\text{Cos}^{-1}(-1)$ **21.** $\text{Tan}^{-1}\left(-\frac{\sqrt{3}}{3}\right)$

22. $\text{Cos}^{-1}\left(-\frac{\sqrt{3}}{2}\right)$ **23.** $\text{Tan}^{-1}\sqrt{3}$ **24.** $\text{Sin}^{-1}\sqrt{3}$

25. Volleyball A volleyball player spikes the ball from a height of 2.44 m. Assume that the path of the ball is a straight line. To the nearest degree, what is the maximum angle θ at which the ball can be hit and land within the court?

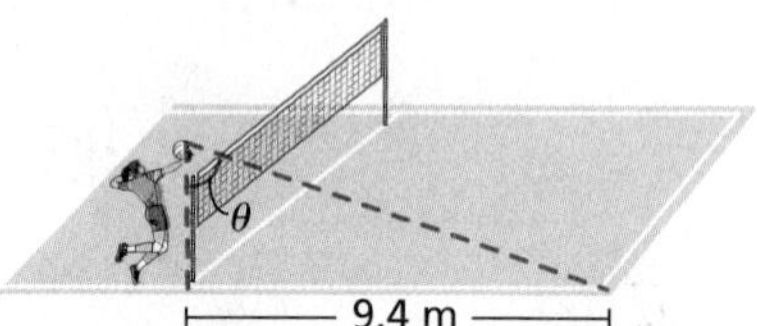

LINK

Aviation

A flight simulator is a device used in training pilots that mimics flight conditions as realistically as possible. Some flight simulators involve full-size cockpits equipped with sound, visual, and motion systems.

Solve each equation to the nearest tenth. Use the given restrictions.

26. $\sin\theta = -0.75$, for $-90° \le \theta \le 90°$ **27.** $\sin\theta = -0.75$, for $180° < \theta < 270°$

28. $\cos\theta = 0.1$, for $0° \le \theta \le 180°$ **29.** $\cos\theta = 0.1$, for $270° < \theta < 360°$

30. Aviation The pilot of a small plane is flying at an altitude of 2000 ft. The pilot plans to start the final descent toward a runway when the horizontal distance between the plane and the runway is 2 mi. To the nearest degree, what will be the angle of depression θ from the plane to the runway at this point?

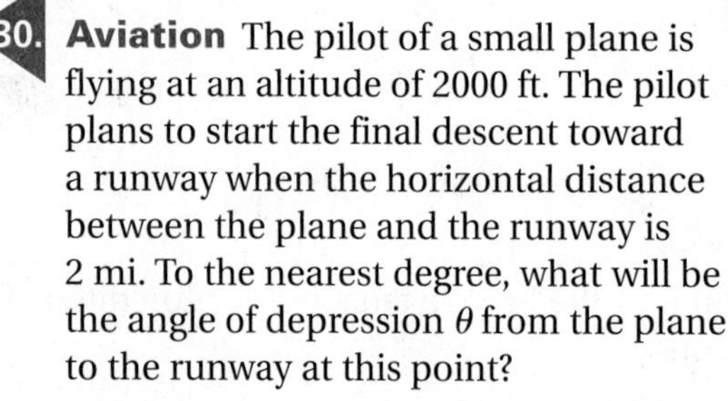

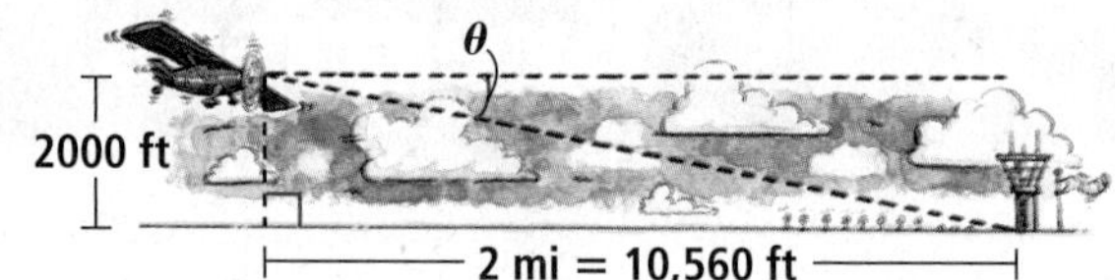

31. Multi-Step The table shows the dimensions of three pool styles offered by a construction company.

a. To the nearest tenth of a degree, what angle θ does the bottom of each pool make with the horizontal?

b. Which pool style's bottom has the steepest slope? Explain.

c. What if...? If the slope of the bottom of a pool can be no greater than $\frac{1}{6}$, what is the greatest angle θ that the bottom of the pool can make with the horizontal? Round to the nearest tenth of a degree.

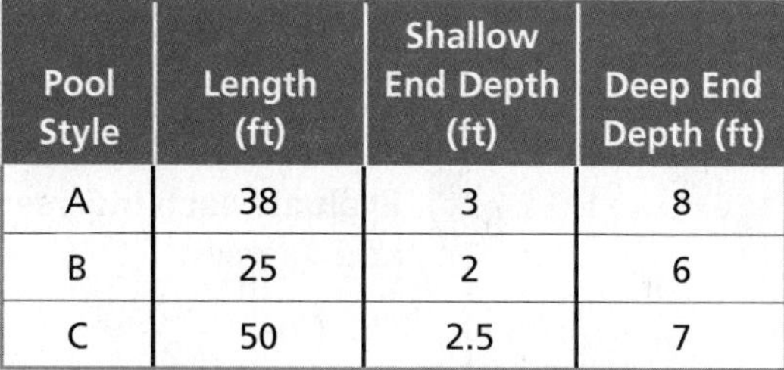

Pool Style	Length (ft)	Shallow End Depth (ft)	Deep End Depth (ft)
A	38	3	8
B	25	2	6
C	50	2.5	7

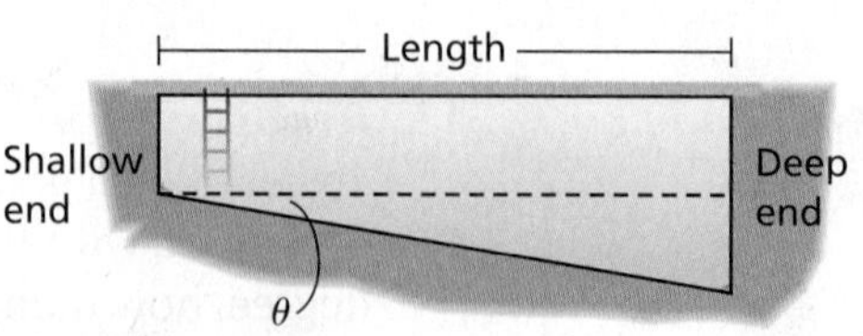

32. Navigation Lines of longitude are closer together near the poles than at the equator. The formula for the length ℓ of 1° of longitude in miles is $\ell = 69.0933\cos\theta$, where θ is the latitude in degrees.

a. At what latitude, to the nearest degree, is the length of a degree of longitude approximately 59.8 miles?

b. To the nearest mile, how much longer is the length of a degree of longitude at the equator, which has a latitude of 0°, than at the Arctic Circle, which has a latitude of about 66°N?

MULTI-STEP TEST PREP

33. Giant kelp is a seaweed that typically grows about 100 ft in height, but may reach as high as 175 ft.
    a. A diver positions herself 10 ft from the base of a giant kelp so that her eye level is 5 ft above the ocean floor. If the kelp is 100 ft in height, what would be the angle of elevation from the diver to the top of the kelp? Round to the nearest tenth of a degree.
    b. The angle of elevation from the diver's eye level to the top of a giant kelp whose base is 30 ft away is 75.5°. To the nearest foot, what is the height of the kelp?

Find each value.

34. $\text{Cos}^{-1}(\cos 0.4)$
35. $\tan(\text{Tan}^{-1} 0.7)$
36. $\sin(\text{Cos}^{-1} 0)$

37. **Critical Thinking** Explain why the domain of the Cosine function is different from the domain of the Sine function.

38. **Write About It** Is the statement $\text{Sin}^{-1}(\sin \theta) = \theta$ true for all values of θ? Explain.

TEST PREP

39. For which equation is the value of θ in radians a positive value?
    Ⓐ $\text{Cos}\,\theta = -\frac{1}{2}$　Ⓑ $\text{Tan}\,\theta = -\frac{\sqrt{3}}{3}$　Ⓒ $\text{Sin}\,\theta = -\frac{\sqrt{3}}{2}$　Ⓓ $\text{Sin}\,\theta = -1$

40. A caution sign next to a roadway states that an upcoming hill has an 8% slope. An 8% slope means that there is an 8 ft rise for 100 ft of horizontal distance. At approximately what angle does the roadway rise from the horizontal?
    Ⓕ 2.2°　Ⓖ 4.6°　Ⓗ 8.5°　Ⓙ 12.5°

41. What value of θ makes the equation $2\sqrt{2}(\text{Cos}\,\theta) = -2$ true?
    Ⓐ 45°　Ⓑ 60°　Ⓒ 135°　Ⓓ 150°

CHALLENGE AND EXTEND

42. If $\text{Sin}^{-1}\left(-\frac{\sqrt{2}}{2}\right) = -\frac{\pi}{4}$, what is the value of $\text{Csc}^{-1}(-\sqrt{2})$?

Solve each inequality for $\{\theta \mid 0 \le \theta \le 2\pi\}$.

43. $\cos\theta \le \frac{1}{2}$
44. $2\sin\theta - \sqrt{3} > 0$
45. $\tan 2\theta \ge 1$

CHAPTER 10

MULTI-STEP TEST PREP

SECTION 10A

MATHEMATICAL PRACTICES **Model with mathematics.**

Trigonometry and Angles

By the Sea The Monterey Bay Aquarium in California is visited by almost 2 million people each year. The aquarium is home to more than 550 species of plants and animals.

1. The window in front of the aquarium's Outer Bay exhibit is 54 ft long. Maria's camera has a viewing angle of 40°, as shown. To the nearest foot, how far would Maria need to stand from the window in order to include the entire window in a photo? This distance is labeled *d*.
2. Warty sea cucumbers may be found in Monterey Bay to a depth of about 64 m. A research vessel is anchored to the seafloor by a 70 m chain that makes an angle of 56° with the ocean's surface. Is the research vessel located over water that is too deep for warty sea cucumbers? Justify your answer.
3. A crystal jellyfish in a cylindrical aquarium tank is carried by a current in a circular path with a diameter of 2.5 m. In 1 min, the jellyfish is carried 26 cm by the current. At this rate, how long will it take the current to move the jellyfish in a complete circle? Round to the nearest minute.
4. A sea otter is released from the aquarium's rehabilitation program with a radio transmitter implanted in its abdomen. The transmitter indicates that the otter is 400 m west and 80 m south of an observation deck. How many degrees south of west should an aquarium worker standing on the deck aim his binoculars in order to see the otter? Round to the nearest degree.

READY TO GO ON?

Quiz for Lessons 10-1 Through 10-4

10-1 Right-Angle Trigonometry

Find the values of the six trigonometric functions for θ.

1.

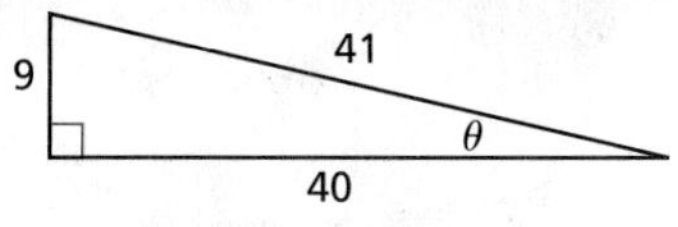

2.

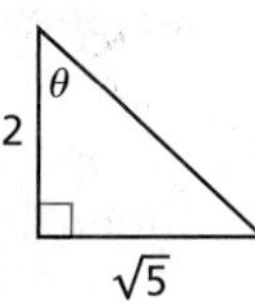

Use a trigonometric function to find the value of x.

3.

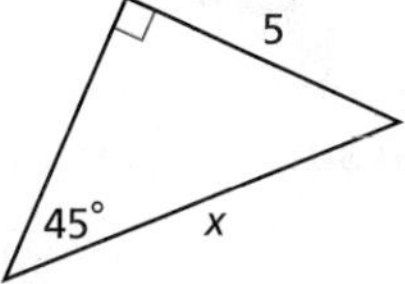

4.

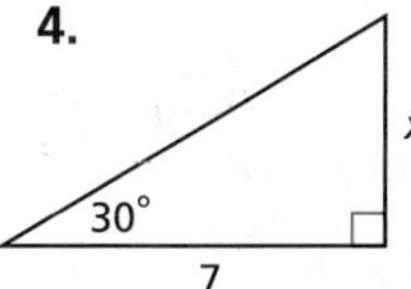

5. A biologist's eye level is 5.5 ft above the ground. She measures the angle of elevation to an eagle's nest on a cliff to be 66° when she stands 50 ft from the cliff's base. To the nearest foot, what is the height of the eagle's nest?

10-2 Angles of Rotation

Draw an angle with the given measure in standard position.

6. $-270°$

7. $405°$

Point P is a point on the terminal side of θ in standard position. Find the exact value of the six trigonometric functions for θ.

8. $P(12, -5)$

9. $P(-2, 7)$

10-3 The Unit Circle

Convert each measure from degrees to radians or from radians to degrees.

10. $-120°$

11. $63°$

12. $\frac{3\pi}{8}$

13. $-\frac{10\pi}{3}$

Use the unit circle to find the exact value of each trigonometric function.

14. $\cos 210°$

15. $\tan 120°$

16. $\cos\frac{\pi}{2}$

17. $\tan\frac{5\pi}{4}$

18. A bicycle tire rotates through an angle of 3.4π radians in 1 second. If the radius of the tire is 0.34 m, what is the bicycle's speed in meters per second? Round to the nearest tenth.

10-4 Inverses of Trigonometric Functions

Evaluate each inverse trigonometric function. Give your answer in both radians and degrees.

19. $\text{Sin}^{-1}\frac{\sqrt{3}}{2}$

20. $\text{Tan}^{-1}\left(-\frac{\sqrt{3}}{3}\right)$

21. A driver uses a ramp when unloading supplies from his delivery truck. The ramp is 10 feet long, and the bed of the truck is 4 feet off the ground. To the nearest degree, what angle does the ramp make with the ground?

10-5 The Law of Sines

CC.9-12.G.SRT.10 (+) Prove the Laws of Sines and Cosines and use them to solve problems. *Also* CC.9-12.G.SRT.11 (+)

Objectives

Determine the area of a triangle given side-angle-side information.

Use the Law of Sines to find the side lengths and angle measures of a triangle.

Who uses this?

Sailmakers can use sine ratios to determine the amount of fabric needed to make a sail. (See Example 1.)

A sailmaker is designing a sail that will have the dimensions shown in the diagram. Based on these dimensions, the sailmaker can determine the amount of fabric needed.

The area of the triangle representing the sail is $\frac{1}{2}bh$. Although you do not know the value of h, you can calculate it by using the fact that $\sin A = \frac{h}{c}$, or $h = c \sin A$.

$\text{Area} = \frac{1}{2}bh$ *Write the area formula.*

$\text{Area} = \frac{1}{2}bc \sin A$ *Substitute c sin A for h.*

This formula allows you to determine the area of a triangle if you know the lengths of two of its sides and the measure of the angle between them.

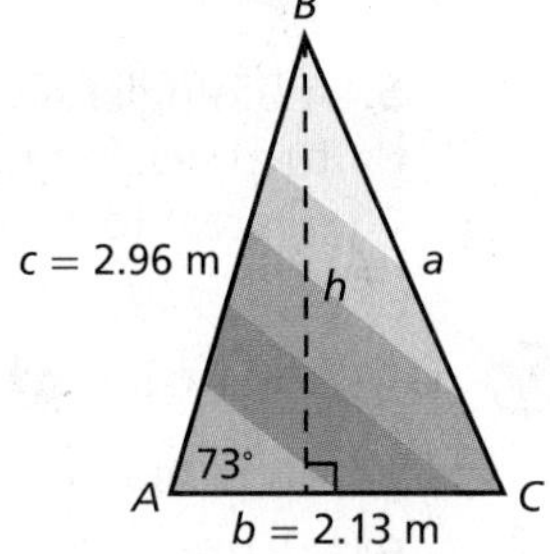

Helpful Hint

An angle and the side opposite that angle are labeled with the same letter. Capital letters are used for angles, and lowercase letters are used for sides.

Know it! Note — **Area of a Triangle**

For $\triangle ABC$,

$\text{Area} = \frac{1}{2}bc \sin A$

$\text{Area} = \frac{1}{2}ac \sin B$

$\text{Area} = \frac{1}{2}ab \sin C$

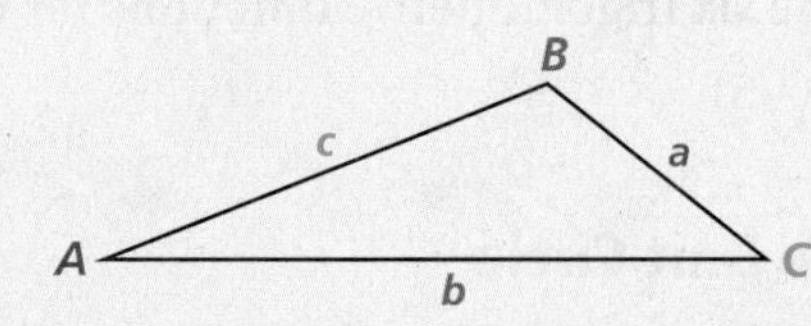

EXAMPLE 1 Determining the Area of a Triangle

Find the area of the sail shown at the top of the page. Round to the nearest tenth.

$\text{area} = \frac{1}{2}bc \sin A$ *Write the area formula.*

$= \frac{1}{2}(2.13)(2.96) \sin 73°$ *Substitute 2.13 for b, 2.96 for c, and 73° for A.*

≈ 3.014655113 *Use a calculator to evaluate the expression.*

The area of the sail is about 3.0 m^2.

1. Find the area of the triangle. Round to the nearest tenth.

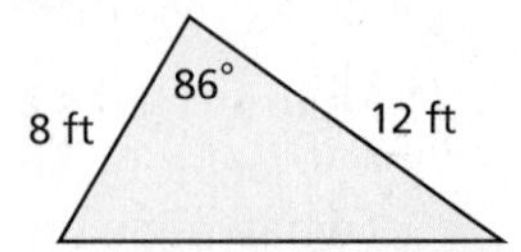

The area of $\triangle ABC$ is equal to $\frac{1}{2}bc\sin A$ or $\frac{1}{2}ac\sin B$ or $\frac{1}{2}ab\sin C$. By setting these expressions equal to each other, you can derive the Law of Sines.

$$\frac{1}{2}bc\sin A = \frac{1}{2}ac\sin B = \frac{1}{2}ab\sin C$$

$$bc\sin A = ac\sin B = ab\sin C$$ *Multiply each expression by 2.*

$$\frac{\cancel{b}\cancel{c}\sin A}{a\cancel{b}\cancel{c}} = \frac{\cancel{a}\cancel{c}\sin B}{\cancel{a}b\cancel{c}} = \frac{\cancel{a}\cancel{b}\sin C}{\cancel{a}\cancel{b}c}$$ *Divide each expression by abc.*

$$\frac{\sin A}{a} = \frac{\sin B}{b} = \frac{\sin C}{c}$$ *Divide out common factors.*

Law of Sines

For $\triangle ABC$, the Law of Sines states that

$$\frac{\sin A}{a} = \frac{\sin B}{b} = \frac{\sin C}{c}.$$

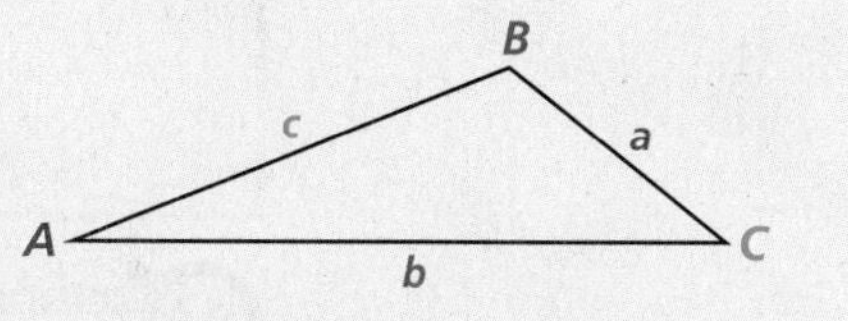

The Law of Sines allows you to solve a triangle as long as you know either of the following:

1. Two angle measures and any side length—angle-angle-side (AAS) or angle-side-angle (ASA) information
2. Two side lengths and the measure of an angle that is not between them—side-side-angle (SSA) information

EXAMPLE 2 **Using the Law of Sines for AAS and ASA**

Solve the triangle. Round to the nearest tenth.

A

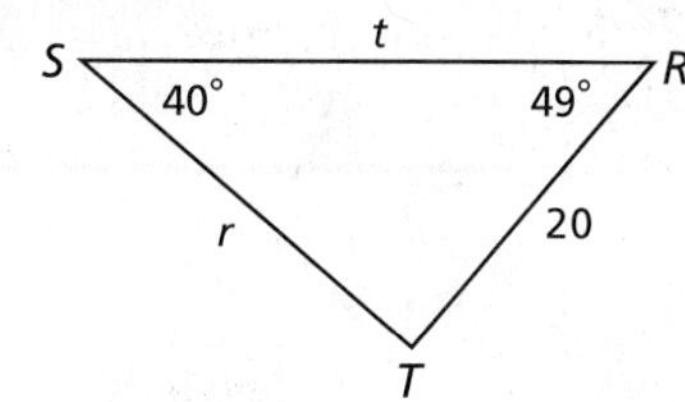

Step 1 Find the third angle measure.

$m\angle R + m\angle S + m\angle T = 180°$ *Triangle Sum Theorem*

$49° + 40° + m\angle T = 180°$ *Substitute 49° for m∠R and 40° for m∠S.*

$m\angle T = 91°$ *Solve for m∠T.*

Step 2 Find the unknown side lengths.

$\frac{\sin R}{r} = \frac{\sin S}{s}$	*Law of Sines*	$\frac{\sin S}{s} = \frac{\sin T}{t}$
$\frac{\sin 49°}{r} = \frac{\sin 40°}{20}$	*Substitute.*	$\frac{\sin 40°}{20} = \frac{\sin 91°}{t}$
$r\sin 40° = 20\sin 49°$	*Cross multiply.*	$t\sin 40° = 20\sin 91°$
$r = \frac{20\sin 49°}{\sin 40°}$	*Solve for the unknown side.*	$t = \frac{20\sin 91°}{\sin 40°}$
$r \approx 23.5$		$t \approx 31.1$

Reading Math

The expression "solve a triangle" means to find the measures of all unknown angles and sides.

Solve the triangle. Round to the nearest tenth.

B

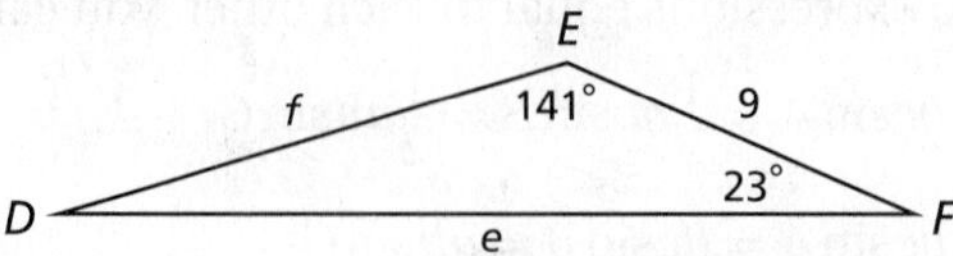

Step 1 Find the third angle measure.

$m\angle D = 180° - 141° - 23° = 16°$ *Triangle Sum Theorem*

Step 2 Find the unknown side lengths.

$\frac{\sin D}{d} = \frac{\sin E}{e}$ *Law of Sines* $\frac{\sin D}{d} = \frac{\sin F}{f}$

$\frac{\sin 16°}{9} = \frac{\sin 141°}{e}$ *Substitute.* $\frac{\sin 16°}{9} = \frac{\sin 23°}{f}$

$e = \frac{9 \sin 141°}{\sin 16°} \approx 20.5$ $f = \frac{9 \sin 23°}{\sin 16°} \approx 12.8$

Solve each triangle. Round to the nearest tenth.

2a.

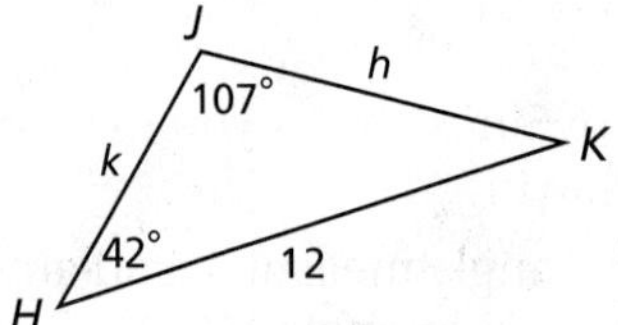

2b. M p N; 106°; 1.5; 56°; m; P

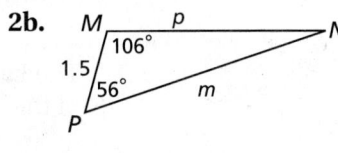

When you use the Law of Sines to solve a triangle for which you know side-side-angle (SSA) information, zero, one, or two triangles may be possible. For this reason, SSA is called the *ambiguous case.*

Ambiguous Case **Possible Triangles**

Given *a*, *b*, and m∠*A*,

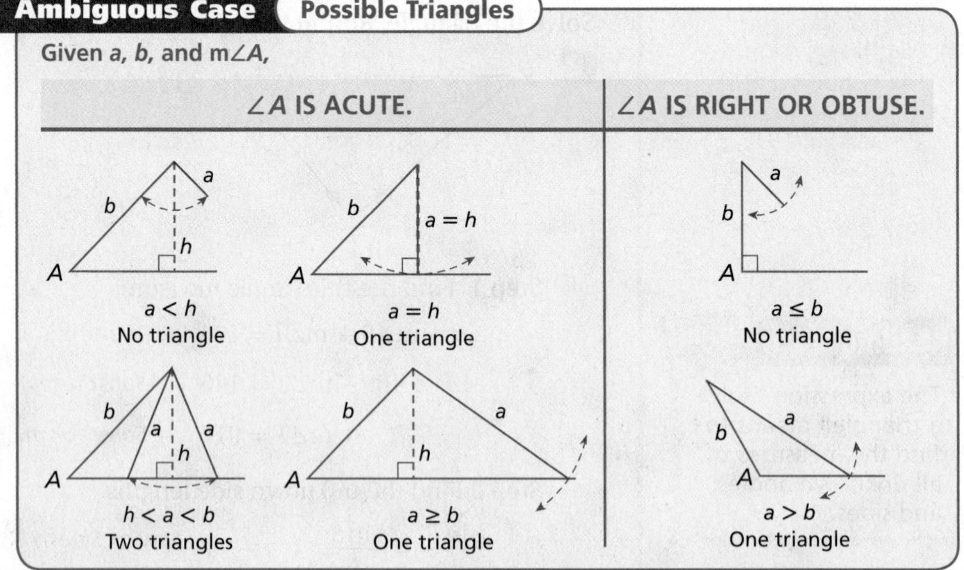

Remember!

When one angle in a triangle is obtuse, the measures of the other two angles must be acute.

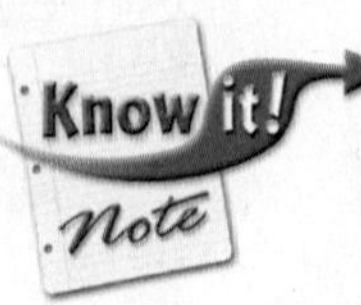

Solving a Triangle Given *a*, *b*, and m∠*A*
1. Use the values of *a*, *b*, and m∠*A* to determine the number of possible triangles.
2. If there is one triangle, use the Law of Sines to solve for the unknowns.
3. If there are two triangles, use the Law of Sines to find $m\angle B_1$ and $m\angle B_2$. Then use these values to find the other measurements of the two triangles.

EXAMPLE 3 Art Application

Maggie is designing a mosaic by using triangular tiles of different shapes. Determine the number of triangles that Maggie can form using the measurements $a = 11$ cm, $b = 17$ cm, and $m\angle A = 30°$. Then solve the triangles. Round to the nearest tenth.

Step 1 Determine the number of possible triangles. In this case, $\angle A$ is acute. Find h.

$\sin 30° = \frac{h}{17}$ — *$\sin\theta = \frac{\text{opp.}}{\text{hyp.}}$*

$h = 17\sin 30° \approx 8.5$ cm — *Solve for h.*

Because $h < a < b$, two triangles are possible.

Triangle 1

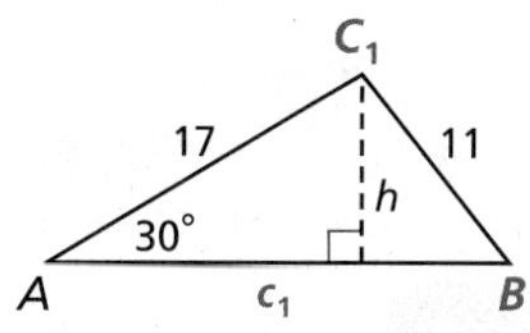

Triangle 2

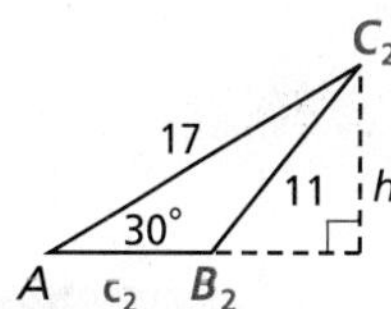

Step 2 Determine $m\angle B_1$ and $m\angle B_2$.

$\frac{\sin A}{a} = \frac{\sin B}{b}$ — *Law of Sines*

$\frac{\sin 30°}{11} = \frac{\sin B}{17}$ — *Substitute.*

$\sin B = \frac{17\sin 30°}{11}$ — *Solve for sin B.*

$\sin B \approx 0.773$

Let $\angle B_1$ represent the acute angle with a sine of 0.773. Use the inverse sine function on your calculator to determine $m\angle B_1$.

$m\angle B_1 = \text{Sin}^{-1}\left(\frac{17\sin 30°}{11}\right) \approx 50.6°$

Let $\angle B_2$ represent the obtuse angle with a sine of 0.773.

$m\angle B_2 = 180° - 50.6° = 129.4°$ — *The reference angle of $\angle B_2$ is 50.6°.*

Helpful Hint

Because $\angle B_1$ and $\angle B_2$ have the same sine value, they also have the same reference angle.

Step 3 Find the other unknown measures of the two triangles.

Solve for $m\angle C_1$.

$30° + 50.6° + m\angle C_1 = 180°$

$m\angle C_1 = 99.4°$

Solve for $m\angle C_2$.

$30° + 129.4° + m\angle C_2 = 180°$

$m\angle C_2 = 20.6°$

Solve for c_1.

$\frac{\sin A}{a} = \frac{\sin C_1}{c_1}$ — *Law of Sines*

$\frac{\sin 30°}{11} = \frac{\sin 99.4°}{c_1}$ — *Substitute.*

$c_1 = \frac{11\sin 99.4°}{\sin 30°}$ — *Solve for the unknown side.*

$c_1 \approx 21.7$ cm

Solve for c_2.

$\frac{\sin A}{a} = \frac{\sin C_2}{c_2}$

$\frac{\sin 30°}{11} = \frac{\sin 20.6°}{c_2}$

$c_2 = \frac{11\sin 20.6°}{\sin 30°}$

$c_2 \approx 7.7$ cm

3. Determine the number of triangles Maggie can form using the measurements $a = 10$ cm, $b = 6$ cm, and $m\angle A = 105°$. Then solve the triangles. Round to the nearest tenth.

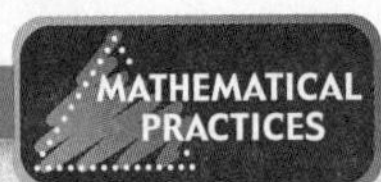

THINK AND DISCUSS

1. Explain how right triangle trigonometry can be used to determine the area of an obtuse triangle.
2. Explain why using the Law of Sines when given AAS or ASA is different than when given SSA.

3. **GET ORGANIZED** Copy and complete the graphic organizer. In each box, give the conditions for which the ambiguous case results in zero, one, or two triangles.

SSA: Given *a*, *b*, and m∠*A*			
Angle *A*	**0 triangles**	**1 triangle**	**2 triangles**
Obtuse			
Acute			

10-5 Exercises

GUIDED PRACTICE

SEE EXAMPLE 1

Find the area of each triangle. Round to the nearest tenth.

1. 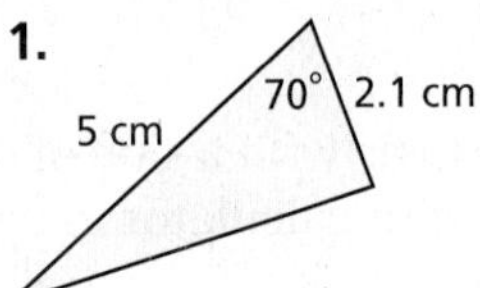

2. 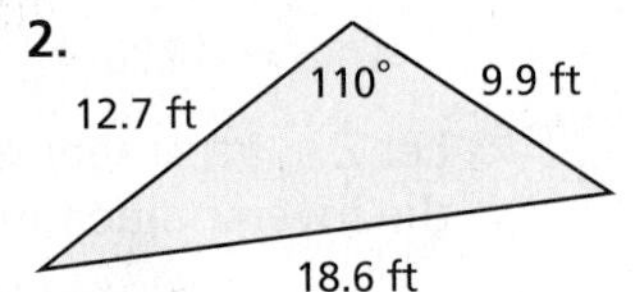

3. 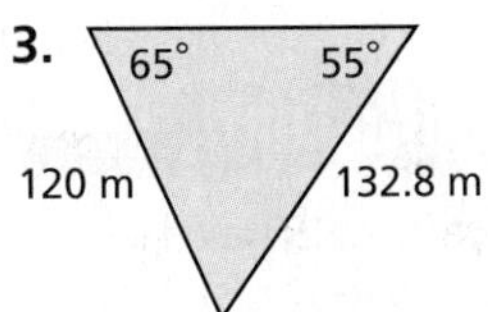

SEE EXAMPLE 2

Solve each triangle. Round to the nearest tenth.

4. 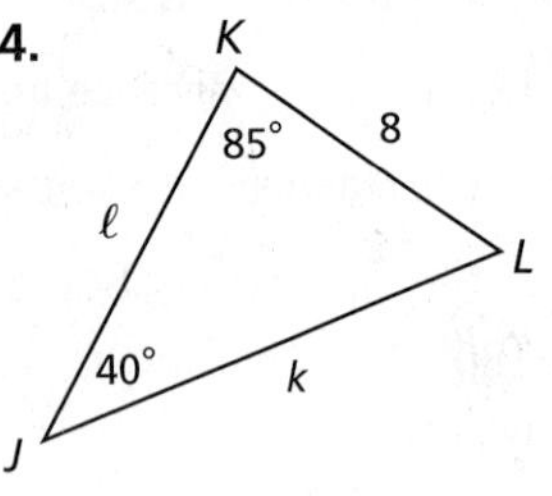

5. 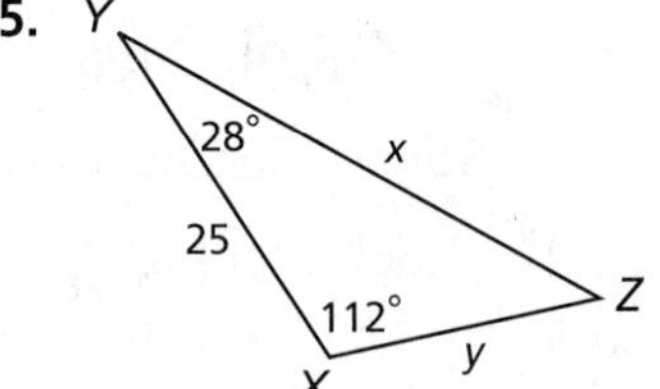

6. 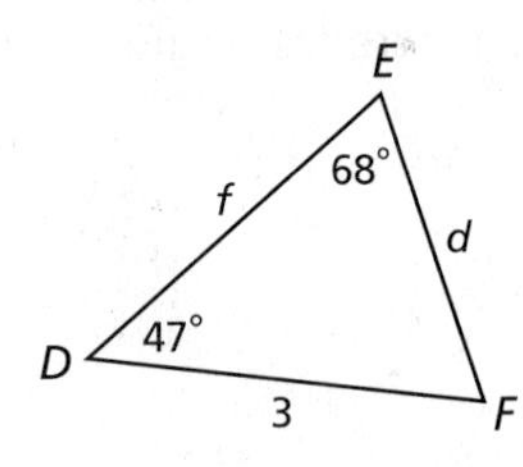

7. 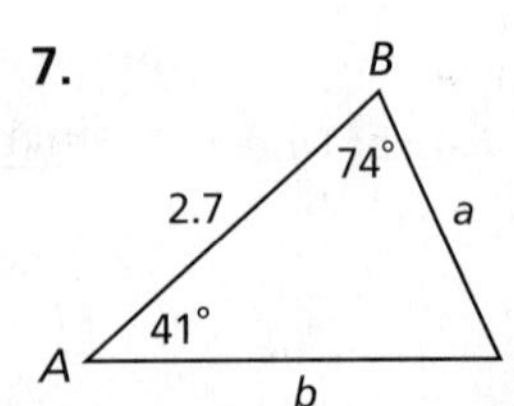

8. 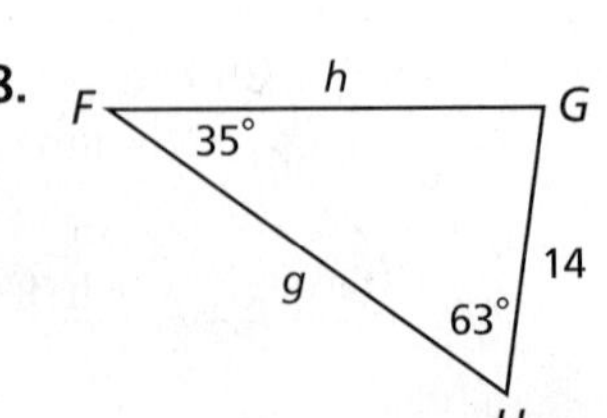

9. 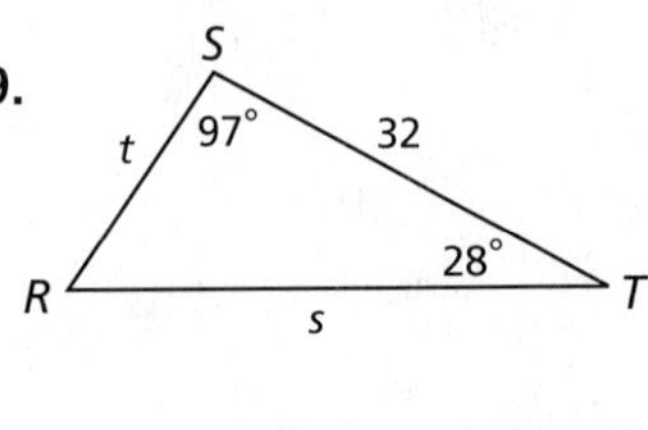

SEE EXAMPLE 3

Gardening **A landscape architect is designing triangular flower beds. Determine the number of different triangles that he can form using the given measurements. Then solve the triangles. Round to the nearest tenth.**

10. $a = 6$ m, $b = 9$ m, $m\angle A = 55°$
11. $a = 10$ m, $b = 4$ m, $m\angle A = 120°$
12. $a = 8$ m, $b = 9$ m, $m\angle A = 35°$
13. $a = 7$ m, $b = 6$ m, $m\angle A = 45°$

PRACTICE AND PROBLEM SOLVING

Independent Practice	
For Exercises	See Example
14–16	1
17–19	2
20–23	3

Extra Practice

See Extra Practice for more Skills Practice and Applications Practice exercises.

Find the area of each triangle. Round to the nearest tenth.

14.

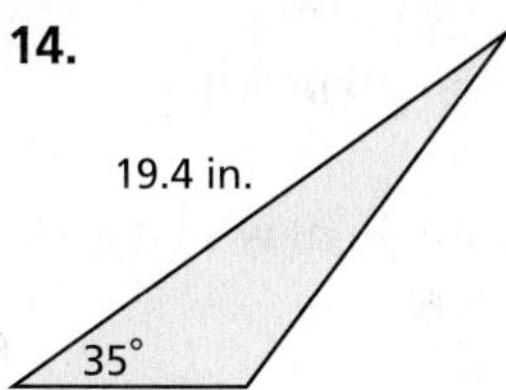

15.

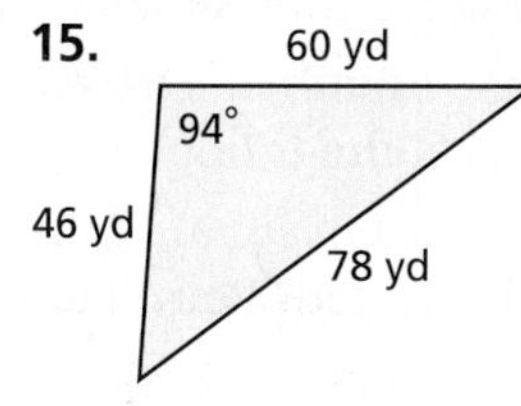

16.

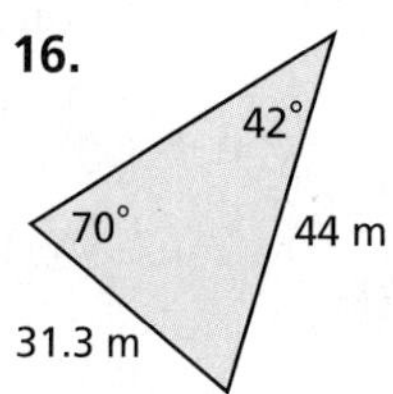

Solve each triangle. Round to the nearest tenth.

17.

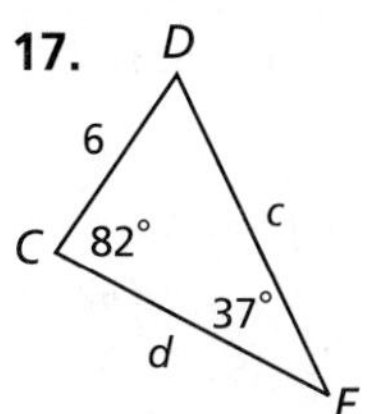

18.

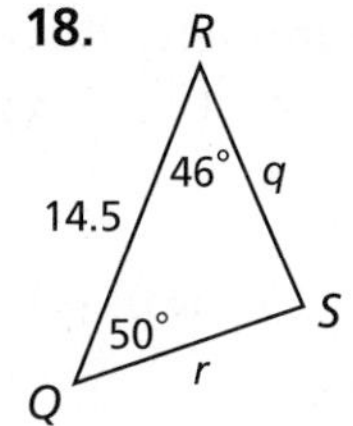

19.

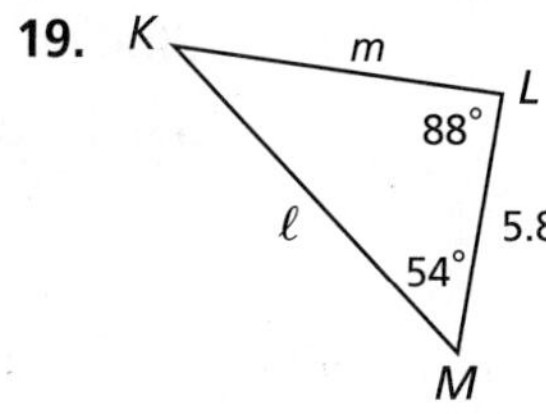

Art **An artist is designing triangular mirrors. Determine the number of different triangles that she can form using the given measurements. Then solve the triangles. Round to the nearest tenth.**

20. $a = 6$ cm, $b = 4$ cm, $m\angle A = 72°$

21. $a = 3.0$ in., $b = 3.5$ in., $m\angle A = 118°$

22. $a = 4.2$ cm, $b = 5.7$ cm, $m\angle A = 39°$

23. $a = 7$ in., $b = 3.5$ in., $m\angle A = 130°$

24. Astronomy The diagram shows the relative positions of Earth, Mars, and the Sun on a particular date. What is the distance between Mars and the Sun on this date? Round to the nearest million miles.

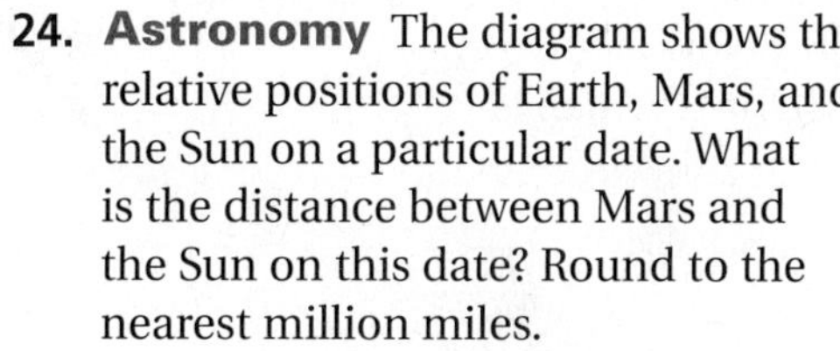

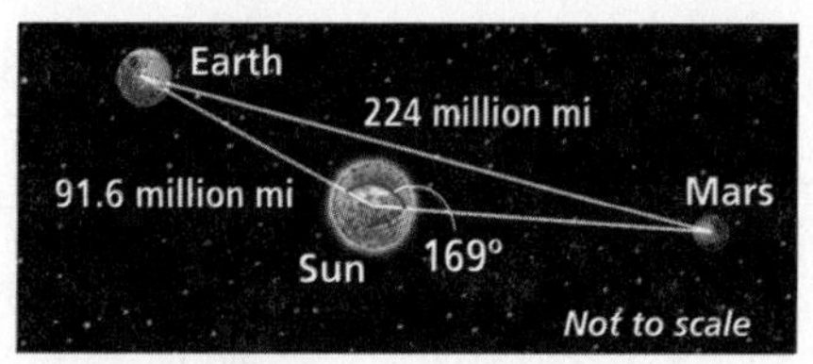

Use the given measurements to solve $\triangle ABC$. Round to the nearest tenth.

25. $m\angle A = 54°$, $m\angle B = 62°$, $a = 14$

26. $m\angle A = 126°$, $m\angle C = 18°$, $c = 3$

27. $m\angle B = 80°$, $m\angle C = 41°$, $b = 25$

28. $m\angle A = 24°$, $m\angle B = 104°$, $c = 10$

29. Rock Climbing A group of climbers needs to determine the distance from one side of a ravine to another. They make the measurements shown. To the nearest foot, what is the distance d across the ravine?

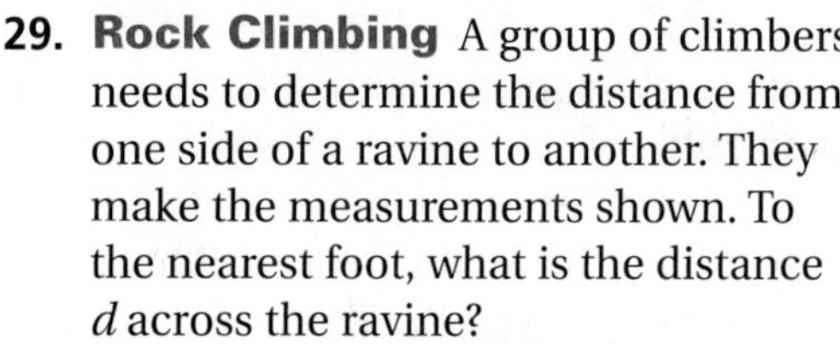

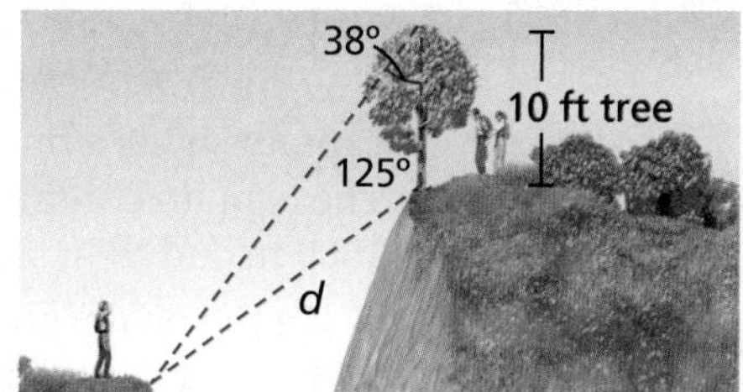

Determine the number of different triangles that can be formed using the given measurements. Then solve the triangles. Round to the nearest tenth.

30. $m\angle C = 45°$, $b = 10$, $c = 5$

31. $m\angle B = 135°$, $b = 12$, $c = 8$

32. $m\angle A = 60°$, $a = 9$, $b = 10$

33. $m\angle B = 30°$, $a = 6$, $b = 3$

34. Painting Trey needs to paint a side of a house that has the measurements shown. What is the area of this side of the house to the nearest square foot?

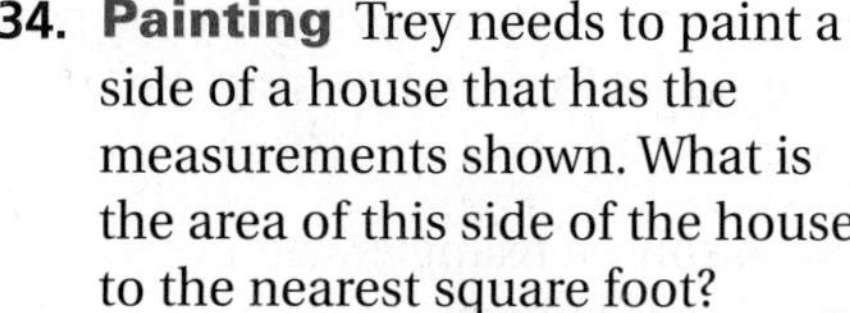

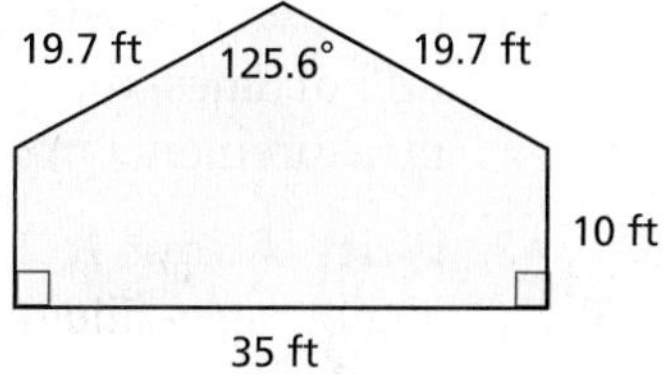

35. An emergency dispatcher must determine the position of a caller reporting a fire. Based on the caller's cell phone records, she is located in the area shown.

a. To the nearest tenth of a mile, what are the unknown side lengths of the triangle?

b. What is the area in square miles of the triangle in which the caller is located? Round to the nearest tenth.

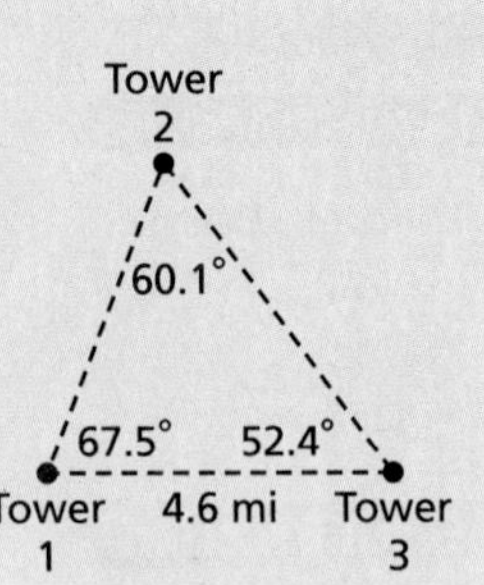

Find the indicated measurement. Round to the nearest tenth.

36. Find $m\angle B$.

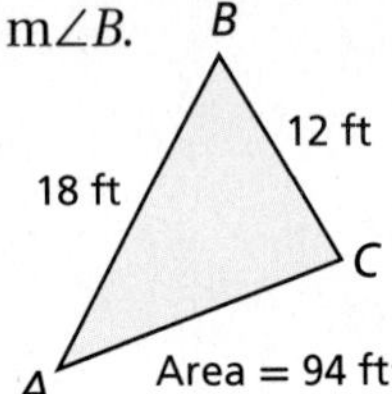

37. Find c.

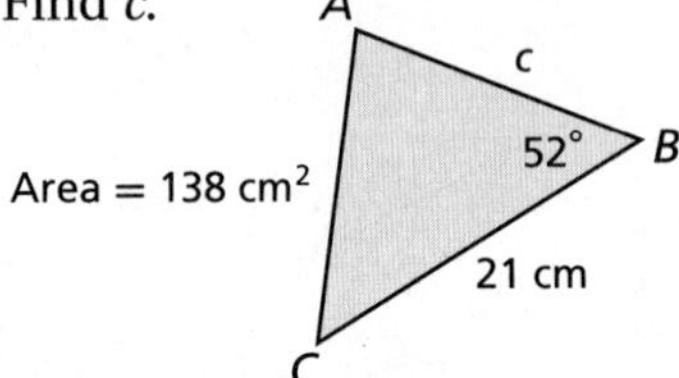

38. Multi-Step A new road will be built from a town to a nearby highway. So far, two routes have been proposed. To the nearest tenth of a mile, how much shorter is route 2 than route 1?

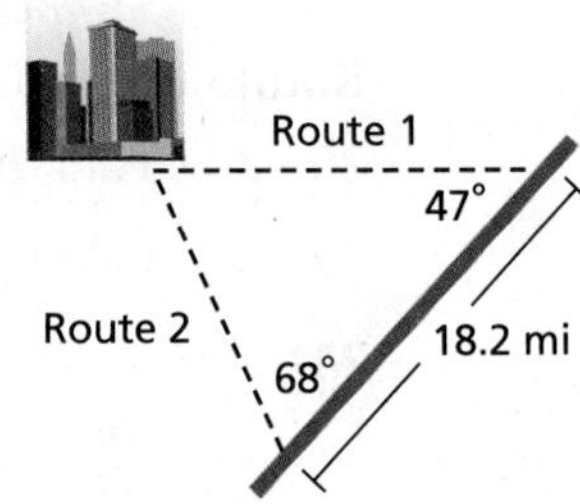

39. ///ERROR ANALYSIS/// Below are two attempts at solving $\triangle FGH$ for g. Which is incorrect? Explain the error.

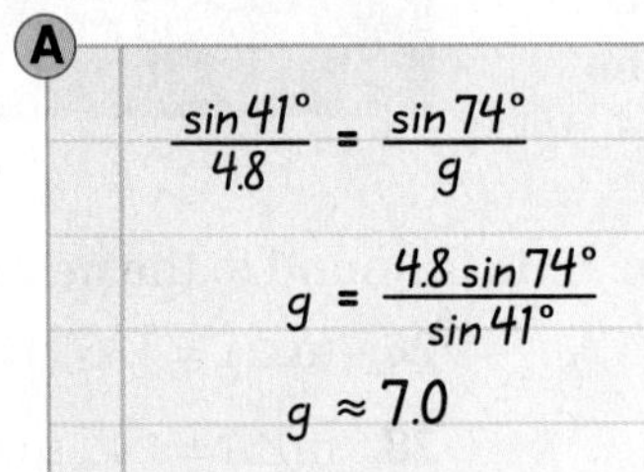

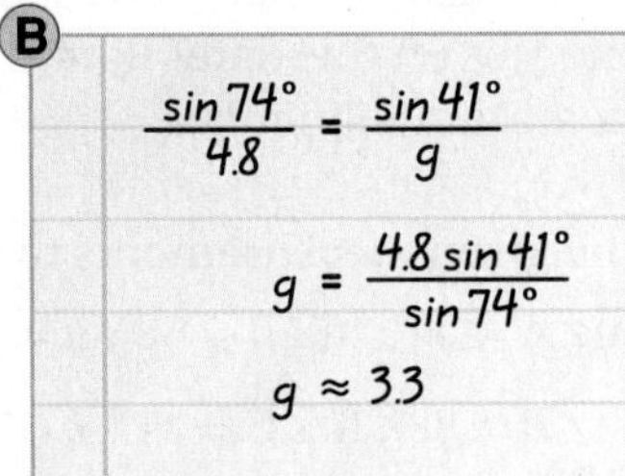

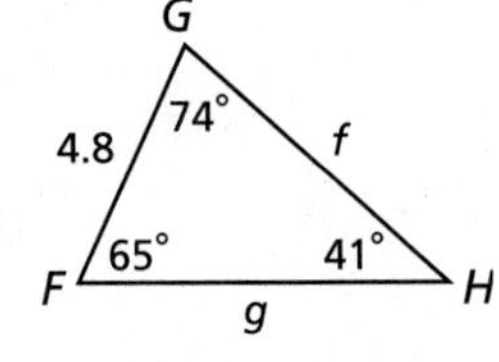

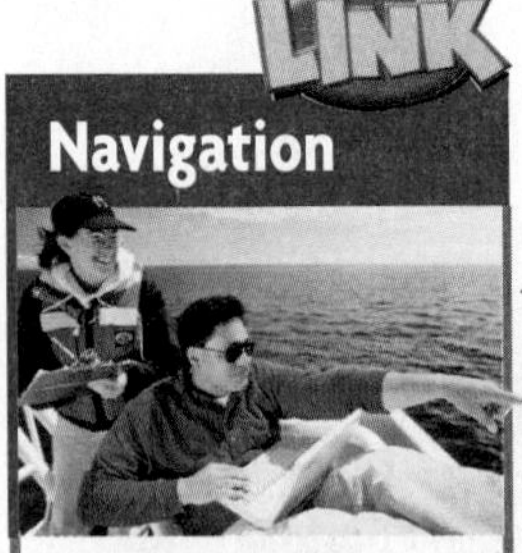

Navigation

Ship captains rely heavily on GPS technology. GPS stands for "Global Positioning System," a navigation system based on trigonometry and the use of satellites. The GPS can be used to determine information such as latitude and longitude.

40. Navigation As a tugboat travels along a channel, the captain sights a buoy at an angle of 28° to the boat's path. The captain continues on the same course for a distance of 1500 m and then sights the same buoy at an angle of 40°.

a. To the nearest meter, how far is the tugboat from the buoy at the second sighting?

b. To the nearest meter, how far was the tugboat from the buoy when the captain first sighted the bouy?

c. **What if...?** If the tugboat continues on the same course, what is the closest that it will come to the buoy? Round to the nearest meter.

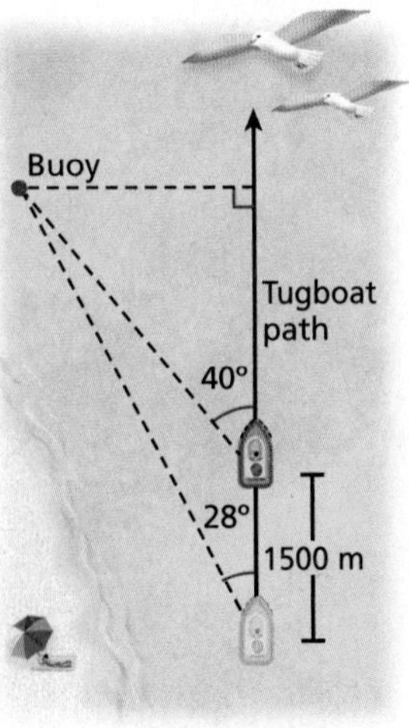

41. Critical Thinking How can you tell, without using the Law of Sines, that a triangle cannot be formed by using the measurements $m\angle A = 92°$, $m\angle B = 104°$, and $a = 18$?

42. Write About It Explain how to solve a triangle when angle-angle-side (AAS) information is known.

43. What is the area of $\triangle PQR$ to the nearest tenth of a square centimeter?

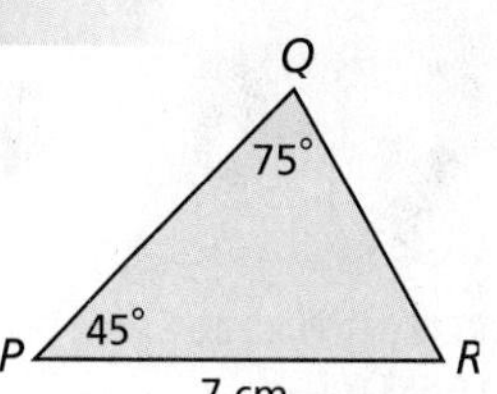

Ⓐ 2.4 cm^2　　Ⓒ 23.5 cm^2

Ⓑ 15.5 cm^2　　Ⓓ 40.1 cm^2

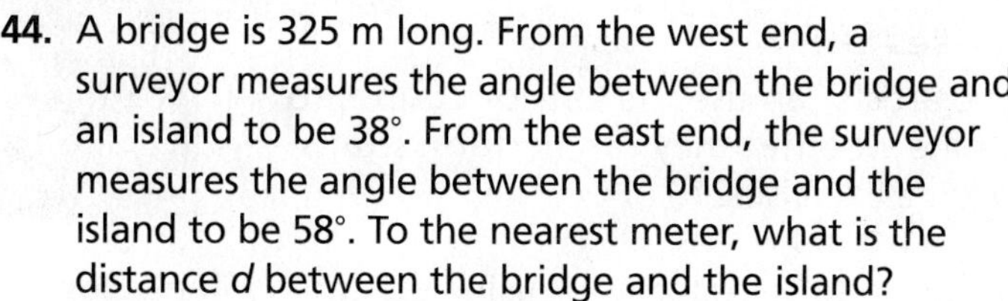
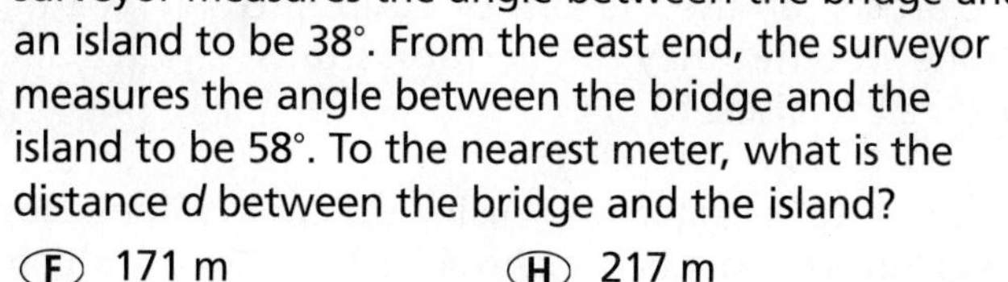

44. A bridge is 325 m long. From the west end, a surveyor measures the angle between the bridge and an island to be 38°. From the east end, the surveyor measures the angle between the bridge and the island to be 58°. To the nearest meter, what is the distance d between the bridge and the island?

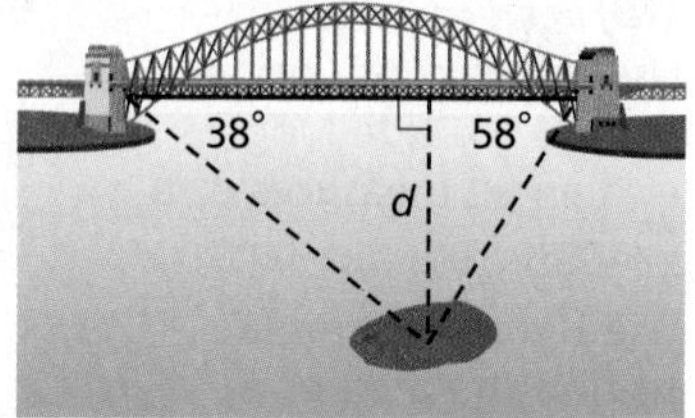

Ⓕ 171 m　　Ⓗ 217 m

Ⓖ 201 m　　Ⓙ 277 m

45. Short Response Examine $\triangle LMN$ at right.

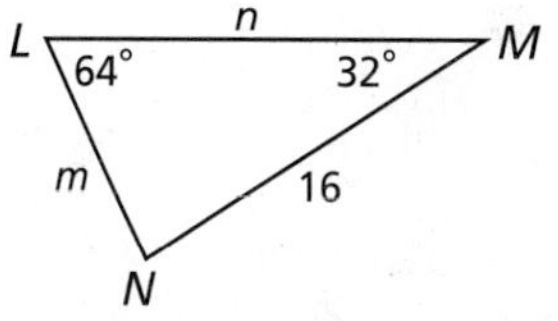

a. Write an expression that can be used to determine the value of m.

b. Is there more than one possible triangle that can be constructed from the given measurements? Explain your answer.

CHALLENGE AND EXTEND

46. What is the area of the quadrilateral at right to the nearest square unit?

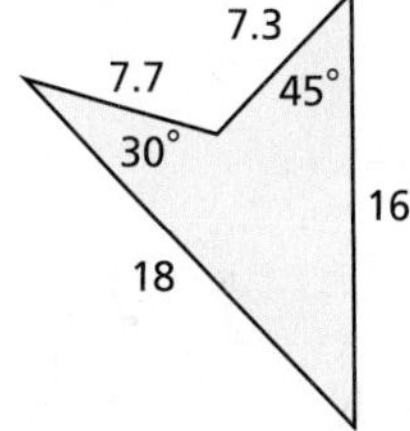

47. Critical Thinking The lengths of two sides of a triangle are $a = 3$ and $b = 2\sqrt{3}$. For what values of $m\angle A$ do two solutions exist when you solve the triangle by using the Law of Sines?

48. Multi-Step The map shows the location of two ranger stations. Each unit on the map represents 1 mile. A ranger at station 1 saw a meteor that appeared to land about 72° north of east. A ranger at station 2 saw the meteor appear to land about 45° north of west. Based on this information, about how many miles from station 1 did the meteor land? Explain how you determined your answer.

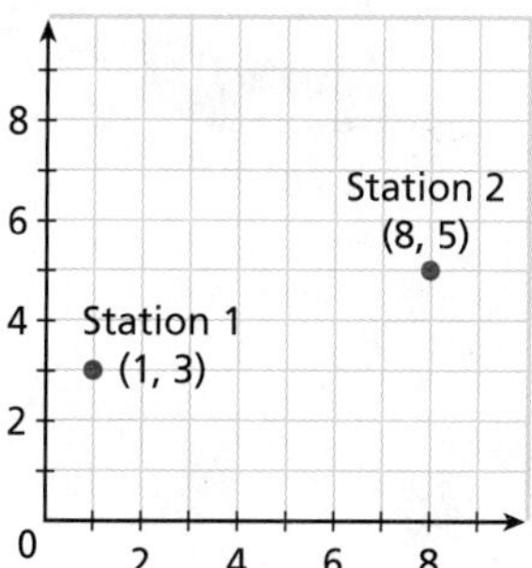

10-6 The Law of Cosines

CC.9-12.G.SRT.10 (+) Prove the Laws of Sines and Cosines and use them to solve problems.
Also **CC.9-12.G.SRT.11** (+)

Objectives

Use the Law of Cosines to find the side lengths and angle measures of a triangle.

Use Heron's Formula to find the area of a triangle.

Who uses this?

Trapeze artists can use the Law of Cosines to determine whether they can perform stunts safely. (See Exercise 27.)

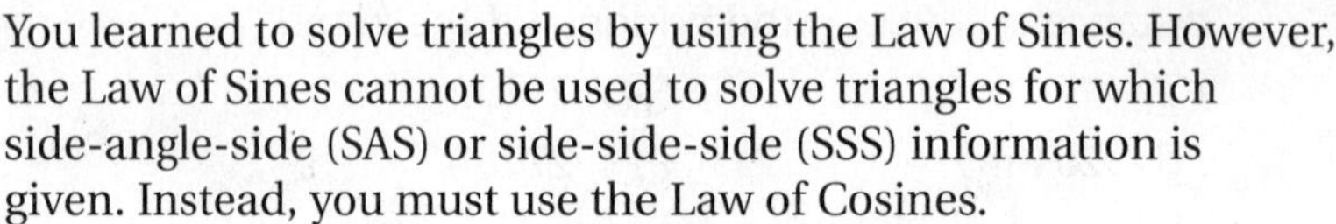

You learned to solve triangles by using the Law of Sines. However, the Law of Sines cannot be used to solve triangles for which side-angle-side (SAS) or side-side-side (SSS) information is given. Instead, you must use the Law of Cosines.

To derive the Law of Cosines, draw $\triangle ABC$ with altitude $\overline{BD}$. If x represents the length of $\overline{AD}$, the length of $\overline{DC}$ is $b - x$.

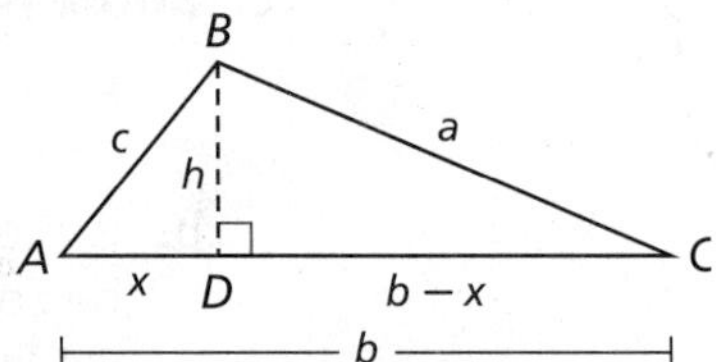

Write an equation that relates the side lengths of $\triangle DBC$.

$a^2 = (b - x)^2 + h^2$ *Pythagorean Theorem*

$a^2 = b^2 - 2bx + x^2 + h^2$ *Expand $(b - x)^2$.*

$a^2 = b^2 - 2bx + c^2$ *In $\triangle ABD$, $c^2 = x^2 + h^2$. Substitute c^2 for $x^2 + h^2$.*

$a^2 = b^2 - 2b(c\cos A) + c^2$ *In $\triangle ABD$, $\cos A = \frac{x}{c}$, or $x = c\cos A$. Substitute $c\cos A$ for x.*

$a^2 = b^2 + c^2 - 2bc\cos A$

The previous equation is one of the formulas for the Law of Cosines.

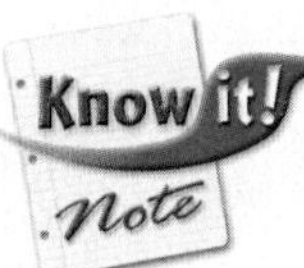

Law of Cosines

For $\triangle ABC$, the Law of Cosines states that

$a^2 = b^2 + c^2 - 2bc\cos A.$

$b^2 = a^2 + c^2 - 2ac\cos B.$

$c^2 = a^2 + b^2 - 2ab\cos C.$

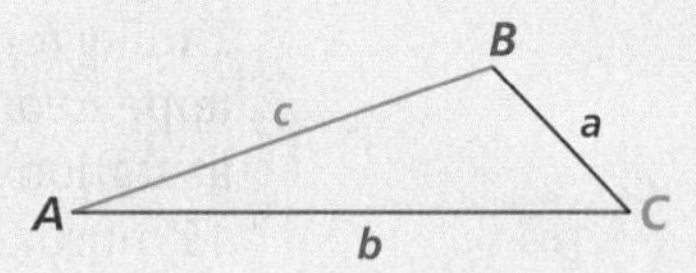

EXAMPLE 1 **Using the Law of Cosines**

Use the given measurements to solve $\triangle ABC$. Round to the nearest tenth.

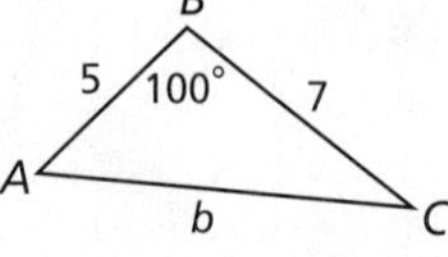

Step 1 Find the length of the third side.

$b^2 = a^2 + c^2 - 2ac\cos B$ *Law of Cosines*

$b^2 = 7^2 + 5^2 - 2(7)(5)\cos 100°$ *Substitute.*

$b^2 \approx 86.2$ *Use a calculator to simplify.*

$b \approx 9.3$ *Solve for the positive value of b.*

Step 2 Find an angle measure.

$\frac{\sin A}{a} = \frac{\sin B}{b}$ *Law of Sines*

$\frac{\sin A}{7} = \frac{\sin 100°}{9.3}$ *Substitute.*

$\sin A = \frac{7 \sin 100°}{9.3}$ *Solve for sin A.*

$m\angle A = \text{Sin}^{-1}\left(\frac{7 \sin 100°}{9.3}\right) \approx 47.8°$ *Solve for m∠A.*

Step 3 Find the third angle measure.

$47.8° + 100° + m\angle C \approx 180°$ *Triangle Sum Theorem*

$m\angle C \approx 32.2°$ *Solve for m∠C.*

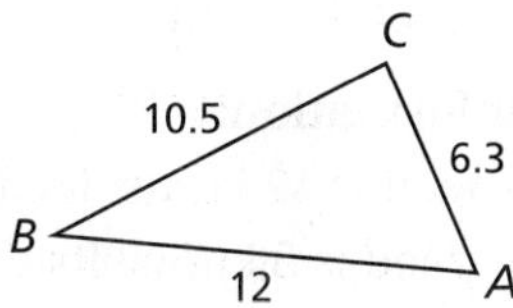

Remember!

The largest angle of a triangle is the angle opposite the longest side.

Step 1 Find the measure of the largest angle, ∠C.

$c^2 = a^2 + b^2 - 2ab\cos C$ *Law of Cosines*

$12^2 = 10.5^2 + 6.3^2 - 2(10.5)(6.3)\cos C$ *Substitute.*

$\cos C \approx 0.0449$ *Solve for cos C.*

$m\angle C \approx \text{Cos}^{-1}(0.0449) \approx 87.4°$ *Solve for m∠C.*

Step 2 Find another angle measure.

$b^2 = a^2 + c^2 - 2ac\cos B$ *Law of Cosines*

$6.3^2 = 10.5^2 + 12^2 - 2(10.5)(12)\cos B$ *Substitute.*

$\cos B \approx 0.8514$ *Solve for cos B.*

$m\angle B \approx \text{Cos}^{-1}(0.8514) \approx 31.6°$ *Solve for m∠B.*

Step 3 Find the third angle measure.

$m\angle A + 31.6° + 87.4° \approx 180°$ *Triangle Sum Theorem*

$m\angle A \approx 61.0°$ *Solve for m∠A.*

Use the given measurements to solve △ABC. Round to the nearest tenth.

1a. $b = 23$, $c = 18$, $m\angle A = 173°$ **1b.** $a = 35$, $b = 42$, $c = 50.3$

Student to Student

Solving Triangles

Stefan Maric
Wylie High School

If I solve a triangle using the Law of Sines, I like to use the Law of Cosines to check my work. I used the Law of Sines to solve the triangle below.

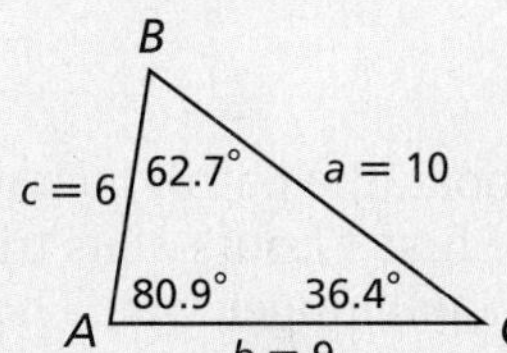

I can check that the length of side b really is 9 by using the Law of Cosines.

$b^2 = a^2 + c^2 - 2ac\cos B$	
9^2	$10^2 + 6^2 - 2(10)(6)\cos 62.7°$
81	81.0 ✔

The Law of Cosines shows that I was right.

EXAMPLE 2 Problem-Solving Application

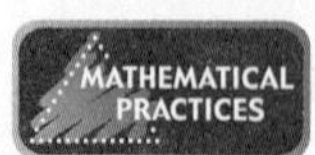

Make sense of problems and persevere in solving them.

A coast guard patrol boat and a fishing boat leave a dock at the same time on the courses shown. The patrol boat travels at a speed of 12 nautical miles per hour (12 knots), and the fishing boat travels at a speed of 5 knots. After 3 hours, the fishing boat sends a distress signal picked up by the patrol boat. If the fishing boat does not drift, how long will it take the patrol boat to reach it at a speed of 12 knots?

1 Understand the Problem

The **answer** will be the number of hours that the patrol boat needs to reach the fishing boat.

List the important information:

- The patrol boat's speed is 12 knots. Its direction is 15° east of north.
- The fishing boat's speed is 5 knots. Its direction is 130° east of north.
- The boats travel 3 hours before the distress call is given.

2 Make a Plan

Determine the angle between the boats' courses and the distance that each boat travels in 3 hours. Use this information to draw and label a diagram. Then use the Law of Cosines to find the distance d between the boats at the time of the distress call. Finally, determine how long it will take the patrol boat to travel this distance.

3 Solve

Step 1 Draw and label a diagram.

The angle between the boats' courses is $130° - 15° = 115°$. In 3 hours, the patrol boat travels $3(12) = 36$ nautical miles and the fishing boat travels $3(5) = 15$ nautical miles.

Step 2 Find the distance d between the boats.

$d^2 = p^2 + f^2 - 2pf\cos D$ *Law of Cosines*

$d^2 = 15^2 + 36^2 - 2(15)(36)\cos 115°$ *Substitute 15 for p, 36 for f, and 115° for D.*

$d^2 \approx 1977.4$ *Use a calculator to simplify.*

$d \approx 44.5$ *Solve for the positive value of d.*

Step 3 Determine the number of hours.

The patrol boat must travel about 44.5 nautical miles to reach the fishing boat. At a speed of 12 nautical miles per hour, it will take the patrol boat $\frac{44.5}{12} \approx 3.7$ hours to reach the fishing boat.

There are two solutions to $d^2 = 1977.4$. One is positive, and one is negative. Because d represents a distance, the negative solution can be disregarded.

4 Look Back

To reach the fishing boat, the patrol boat will have to travel a greater distance than it did during the first 3 hours of its trip. Therefore, it makes sense that it will take the patrol boat longer than 3 hours to reach the fishing boat. An answer of 3.7 hours seems reasonable.

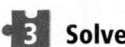

2. A pilot is flying from Houston to Oklahoma City. To avoid a thunderstorm, the pilot flies 28° off of the direct route for a distance of 175 miles. He then makes a turn and flies straight on to Oklahoma City. To the nearest mile, how much farther than the direct route was the route taken by the pilot?

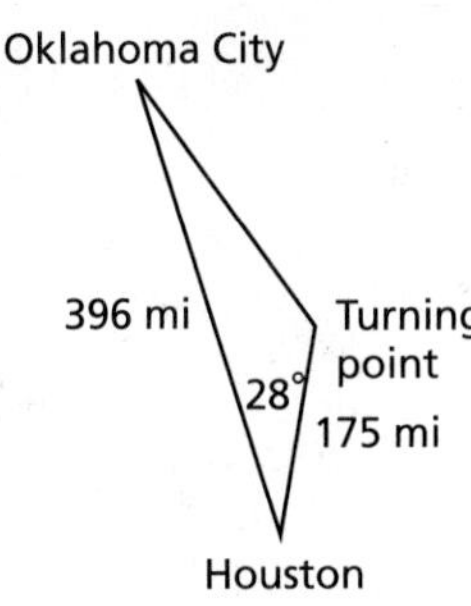

The Law of Cosines can be used to derive a formula for the area of a triangle based on its side lengths. This formula is called Heron's Formula.

Heron's Formula

For $\triangle ABC$, where s is half of the perimeter of the triangle, or $\frac{1}{2}(a + b + c)$,

Area $= \sqrt{s(s-a)(s-b)(s-c)}$

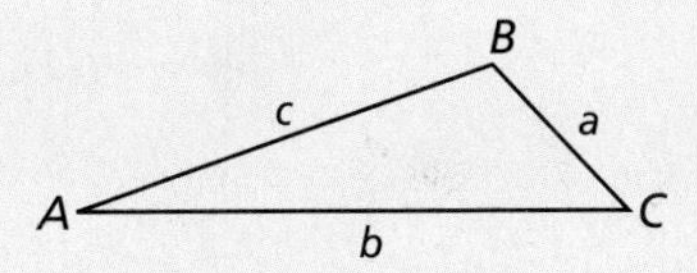

EXAMPLE 3 *Architecture Application*

A blueprint shows a reception area that has a triangular floor with sides measuring 22 ft, 30 ft, and 34 ft. What is the area of the floor to the nearest square foot?

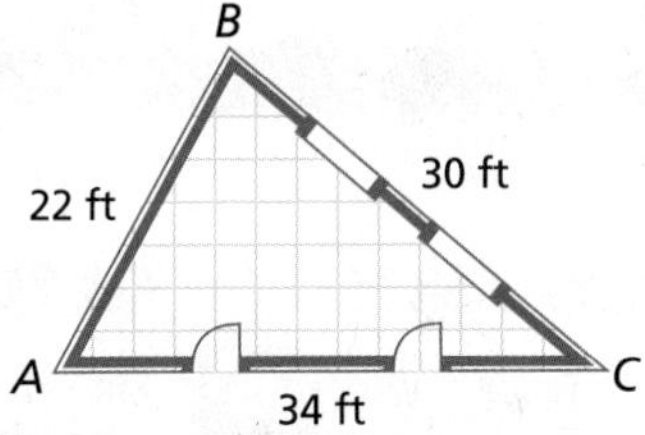

Step 1 Find the value of s.

$s = \frac{1}{2}(a + b + c)$ *Use the formula for half of the perimeter.*

$s = \frac{1}{2}(30 + 34 + 22) = 43$ *Substitute 30 for a, 34 for b, and 22 for c.*

Step 2 Find the area of the triangle.

$A = \sqrt{s(s-a)(s-b)(s-c)}$ *Heron's Formula*

$A = \sqrt{43(43-30)(43-34)(43-22)}$ *Substitute 43 for s.*

$A \approx 325$ *Use a calculator to simplify.*

The area of the floor is 325 ft^2.

Check Find the measure of the largest angle, $\angle B$.

$b^2 = a^2 + c^2 - 2ac\cos B$ *Law of Cosines*

$34^2 = 30^2 + 22^2 - 2(30)(22)\cos B$ *Substitute.*

$\cos B \approx 0.1727$ *Solve for cos B.*

$m\angle B \approx 80.1°$ *Solve for m∠B.*

Find the area of the triangle by using the formula area $= \frac{1}{2}ac\sin B$.

area $= \frac{1}{2}(30)(22)\sin 80.1° \approx 325 \text{ ft}^2$ ✔

3. The surface of a hotel swimming pool is shaped like a triangle with sides measuring 50 m, 28 m, and 30 m. What is the area of the pool's surface to the nearest square meter?

THINK AND DISCUSS

1. Explain why you cannot solve a triangle if you are given only angle-angle-angle (AAA) information.
2. Describe the steps that you could use to find the area of a triangle by using Heron's Formula when you are given side-angle-side (SAS) information.

3. **GET ORGANIZED** Copy and complete the graphic organizer. List the types of triangles that can be solved by using each law. Consider the following types of triangles: ASA, AAS, SAS, SSA, and SSS.

10-6 Exercises

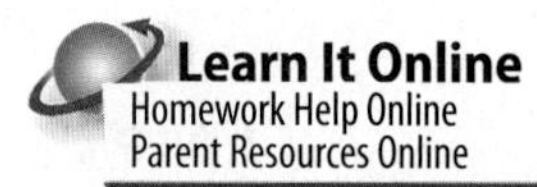

GUIDED PRACTICE

SEE EXAMPLE 1

Use the given measurements to solve each triangle. Round to the nearest tenth.

1. 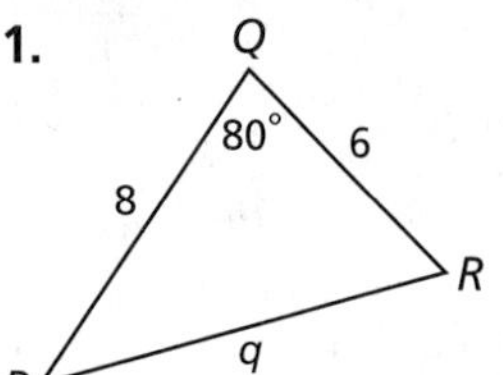

2. 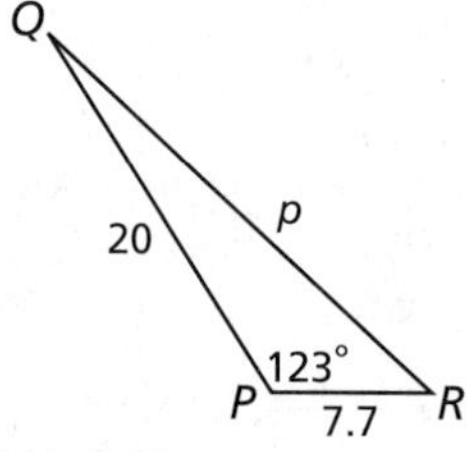

3. 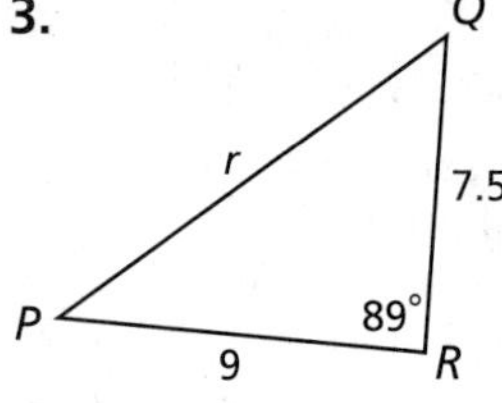

4. 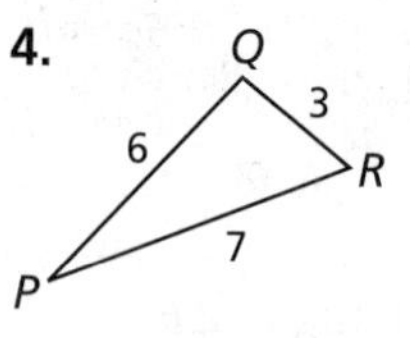

5. 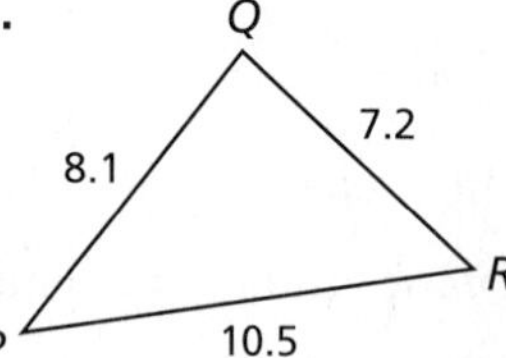

6. 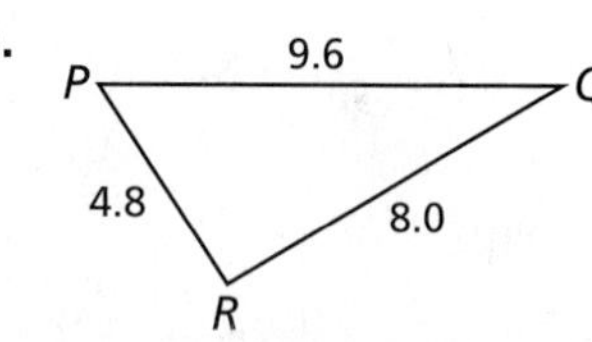

SEE EXAMPLE 2

7. **Recreation** A triangular hiking trail is being built in the area shown. At an average walking speed of 2 m/s, how many minutes will it take a hiker to make a complete circuit around the triangular trail? Round to the nearest minute.

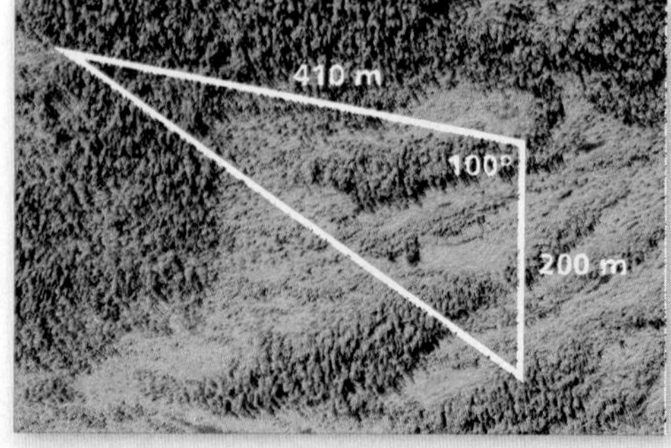

Jim Wark/Airphoto

SEE EXAMPLE 3

8. **Agriculture** A triangular wheat field has side lengths that measure 410 ft, 500 ft, and 420 ft. What is the area of the field to the nearest square foot?

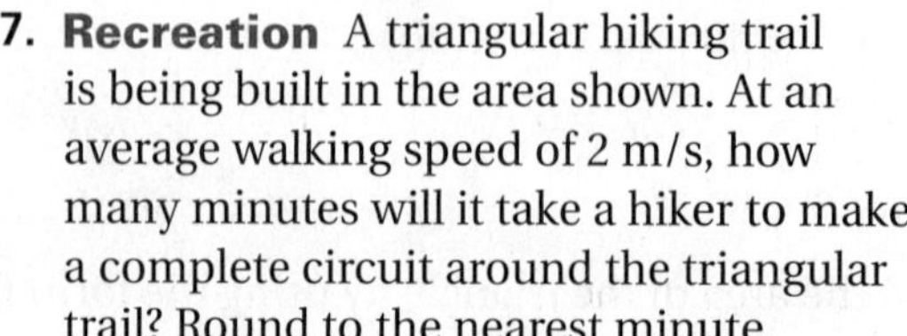

PRACTICE AND PROBLEM SOLVING

Independent Practice	
For Exercises	See Example
9–14	1
15	2
16	3

Extra Practice

See Extra Practice for more Skills Practice and Applications Practice exercises.

Use the given measurements to solve each triangle. Round to the nearest tenth.

9. 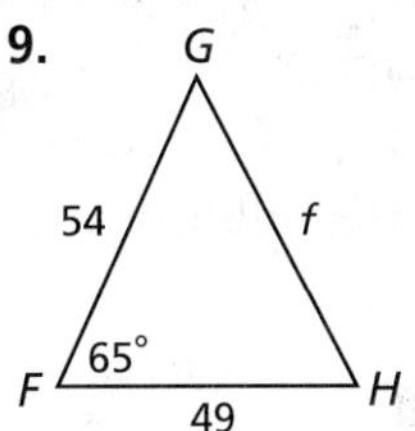

10. 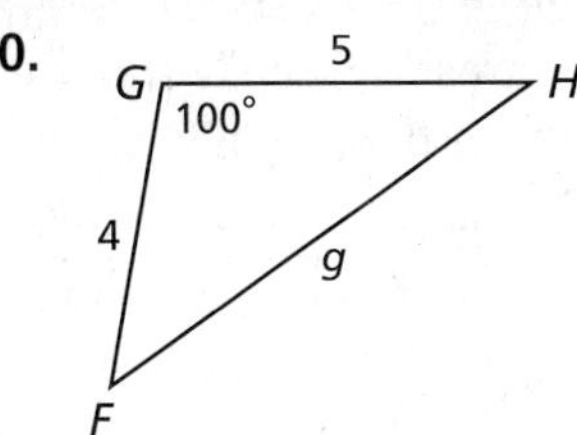

11. 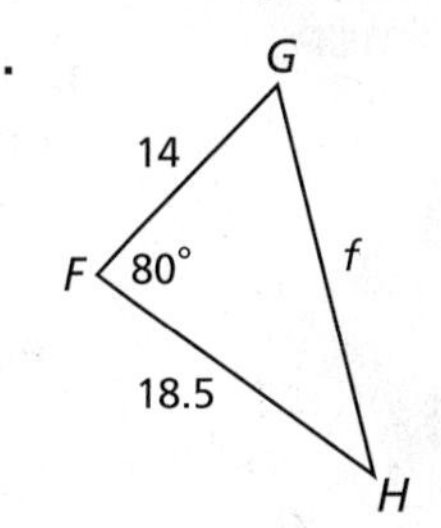

12. 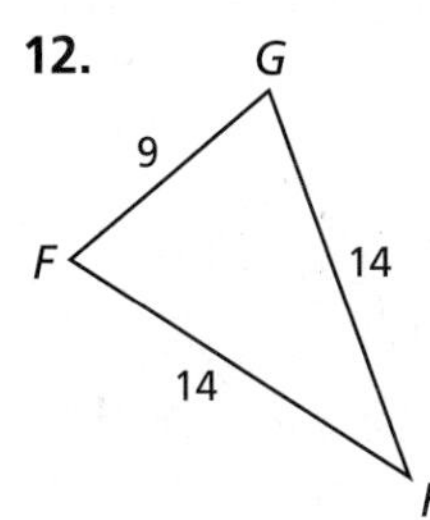

13. 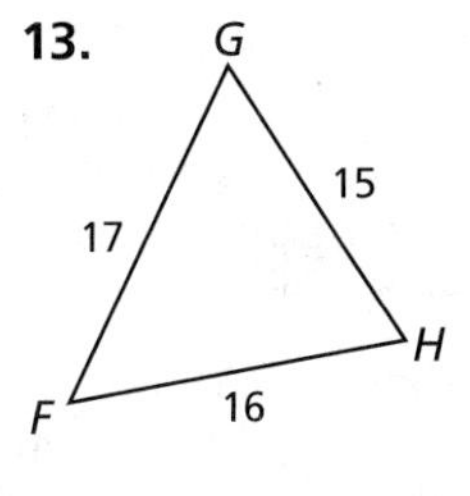

14. 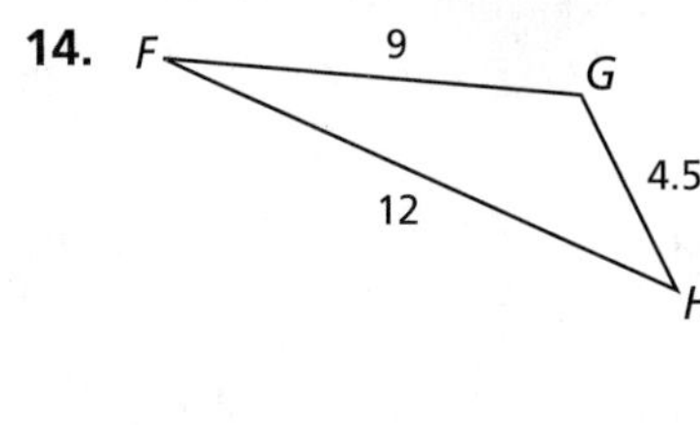

15. **Ecology** An ecologist is studying a pair of zebras fitted with radio-transmitter collars. One zebra is 1.4 mi from the ecologist, and the other is 3.5 mi from the ecologist. To the nearest tenth of a mile, how far apart are the two zebras?

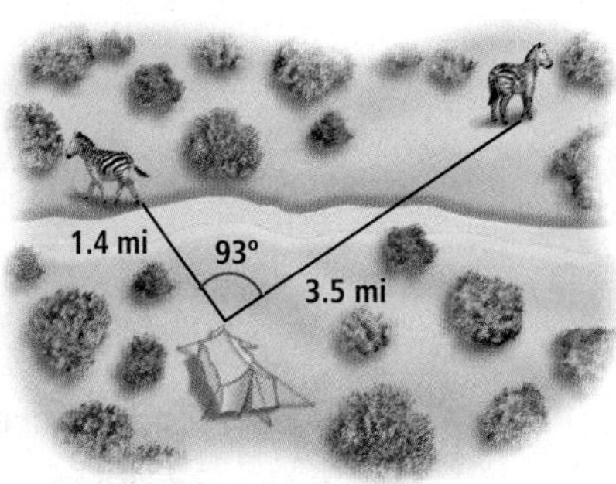

16. **Art** How many square meters of fabric are needed to make a triangular banner with side lengths of 2.1 m, 1.5 m, and 1.4 m? Round to the nearest tenth.

Use the given measurements to solve $\triangle ABC$. Round to the nearest tenth.

17. $m\angle A = 120°$, $b = 16$, $c = 20$

18. $m\angle B = 78°$, $a = 6$, $c = 4$

19. $m\angle C = 96°$, $a = 13$, $b = 9$

20. $a = 14$, $b = 9$, $c = 10$

21. $a = 5$, $b = 8$, $c = 6$

22. $a = 30$, $b = 26$, $c = 35$

23. **Commercial Art** A graphic artist is asked to draw a triangular logo with sides measuring 15 cm, 18 cm, and 20 cm. If she draws the triangle correctly, what will be the measures of its angles to the nearest degree?

24. **Aviation** The course of a hot-air balloon takes the balloon directly over points A and B, which are 500 m apart. Several minutes later, the angle of elevation from an observer at point A to the balloon is 43.3°, and the angle of elevation from an observer at point B to the balloon is 58.2°. To the nearest meter, what is the balloon's altitude?

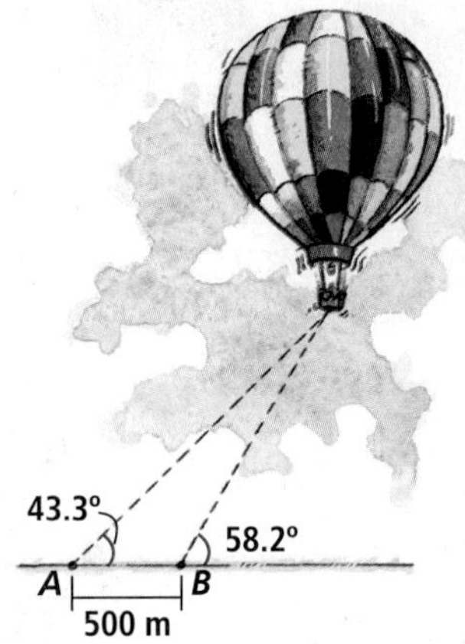

25. **Multi-Step** A student pilot takes off from a local airstrip and flies 70° south of east for 160 miles. The pilot then changes course and flies due north for another 80 miles before turning and flying directly back to the airstrip.
    a. How many miles is the third stage of the pilot's flight? Round to the nearest mile.
    b. To the nearest degree, what angle does the pilot turn the plane through in order to fly the third stage?

26. Phone records indicate that a fire is located 2.5 miles from one cell phone tower and 3.2 miles from a second cell phone tower.
    a. To the nearest degree, what are the measures of the angles of the triangle shown in the diagram?
    b. Tower 2 is directly east of tower 1. How many miles north of the towers is the fire? This distance is represented by n in the diagram.

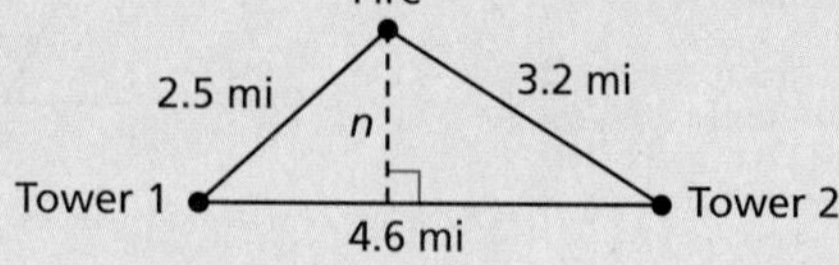

27. **Entertainment** Two performers hang by their knees from trapezes, as shown.
    a. To the nearest degree, what acute angles A and B must the cords of each trapeze make with the horizontal if the performer on the left is to grab the wrists of the performer on the right and pull her away from her trapeze?
    b. **What if...?** Later, the performer on the left grabs the trapeze of the performer on the right and lets go of his trapeze. To the nearest degree, what angles A and B must the cords of each trapeze make with the horizontal for this trick to work?

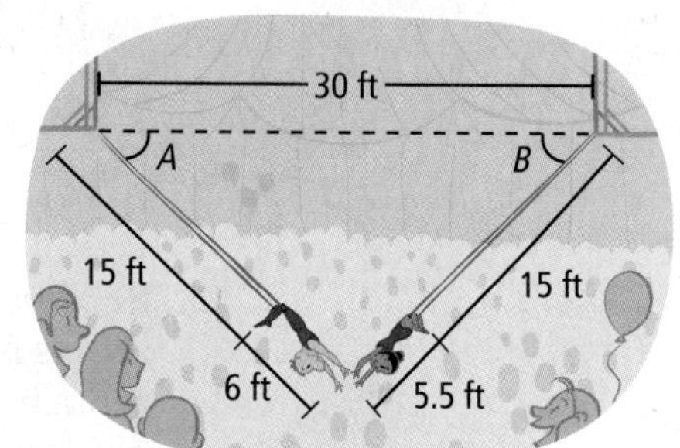

Find the area of the triangle with the given side lengths. Round to the nearest tenth.

28. 15 in., 18 in., 24 in.
29. 30 cm, 35 cm, 47 cm
30. 28 m, 37 m, 33 m
31. 3.5 ft, 5 ft, 7.5 ft
32. **Estimation** The adjacent sides of a parallelogram measure 3.1 cm and 3.9 cm. The measures of the acute interior angles of the parallelogram are 58°. Estimate the lengths of the diagonals of the parallelogram without using a calculator, and explain how you determined your estimates.

33. **Surveying** Barrington Crater in Arizona was produced by the impact of a meteorite. Based on the measurements shown, what is the diameter d of Barrington Crater to the nearest tenth of a kilometer?

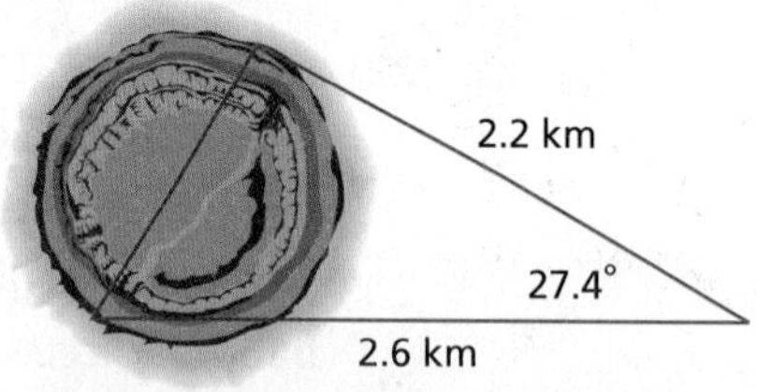

34. **Travel** The table shows the distances between three islands in Hawaii. To the nearest degree, what is the angle between each pair of islands in relation to the third island?

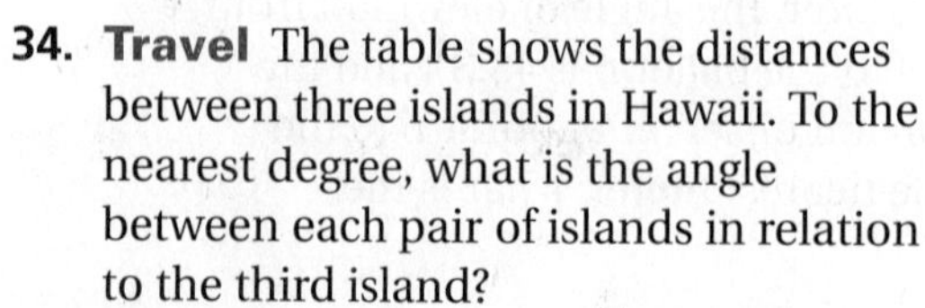

Distances Between Islands (mi)

	Kauai	Molokai	Lanai
Kauai	0	155.7	174.8
Molokai	155.7	0	26.1
Lanai	174.8	26.1	0

35. **Critical Thinking** Use the Law of Cosines to explain why $c^2 = a^2 + b^2$ for $\triangle ABC$, where $\angle C$ is a right angle.
36. **Critical Thinking** Can the value of s in Heron's Formula ever be less than the length of the longest side of a triangle? Explain.
37. **Write About It** Describe two different methods that could be used to solve a triangle when given side-side-side (SSS) information.

TEST PREP

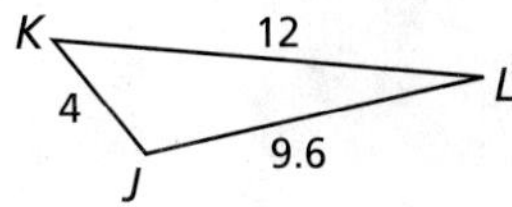

38. What is the approximate measure of $\angle K$ in the triangle shown?

Ⓐ 30°   Ⓒ 54°

Ⓑ 45°   Ⓓ 60°

39. For $\triangle RST$ with side lengths r, s, and t, which equation can be used to determine r?

Ⓕ $r = \sqrt{s^2 + t^2 - 2st \sin R}$ Ⓗ $r = \sqrt{s^2 + t^2 - 2st \cos R}$

Ⓖ $r = \sqrt{s^2 - t^2 - 2st \sin R}$ Ⓙ $r = \sqrt{s^2 - t^2 - 2st \cos R}$

40. A team of archaeologists wants to dig for fossils in a triangular area marked by three stakes. The distances between the stakes are shown in the diagram. Which expression represents the dig area in square feet?

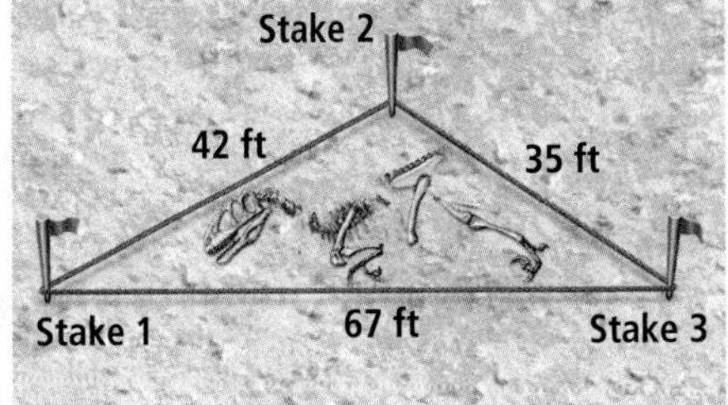

Ⓐ $\sqrt{72(30)(37)(5)}$

Ⓑ $\sqrt{48(6)(13)(19)}$

Ⓒ $\sqrt{144(42)(35)(67)}$

Ⓓ $\sqrt{144(102)(109)(77)}$

CHALLENGE AND EXTEND

41. Abby uses the Law of Cosines to find $m\angle A$ when $a = 2$, $b = 3$, and $c = 5$. The answer she gets is 0°. Did she make an error? Explain.

42. **Geometry** What are the angle measures of an isosceles triangle whose base is half as long as its congruent legs? Round to the nearest tenth.

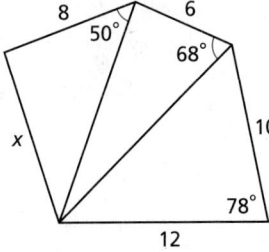

43. Use the figure shown to solve for x. Round to the nearest tenth.

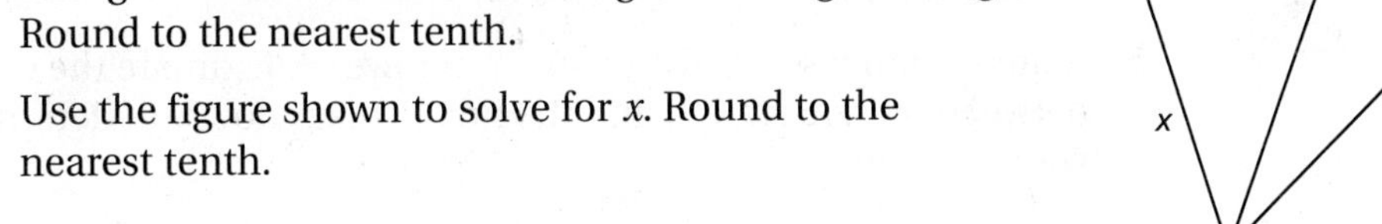

CHAPTER 10

MULTI-STEP TEST PREP

SECTION 10B

Model with mathematics.

Applying Trigonometric Functions

Where's the Fire? A driver dials 9-1-1 on a cell phone to report smoke coming from a building. Before the driver can give the building's address, the call is cut short. The 9-1-1 dispatcher is still able to determine the driver's location based on the driver's position in relation to nearby cell phone towers.

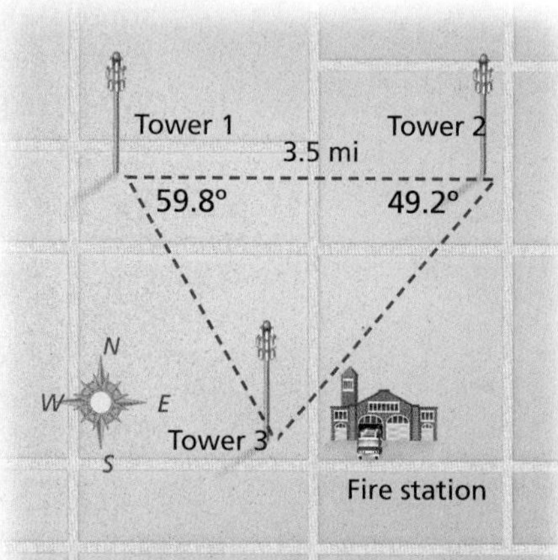

1. When the driver makes the call, he is located in the triangular area between the three cell phone towers shown. To the nearest tenth of a mile, what is the distance between tower 3 and each of the other towers?

2. What is the area in square miles of the triangle with the three cell phone towers at its vertices? Round to the nearest tenth.

3. The driver is 1.7 miles from tower 1 and 2.4 miles from tower 2 when the call is made. Make a sketch of the triangle with tower 1, tower 2, and the driver at its vertices. To the nearest tenth of a degree, what are the measures of the angles of this triangle?

4. Tower 2 is directly east of tower 1. How many miles east of tower 1 is the driver? How many miles south of tower 1 is the driver? Round to the nearest tenth.

5. A fire station is located 1 block from tower 3. Estimate the distance between the fire station and the fire. Explain how you determined your estimate.

READY TO GO ON?

Quiz for Lessons 10-5 and 10-6

10-5 The Law of Sines

Find the area of each triangle. Round to the nearest tenth.

1. 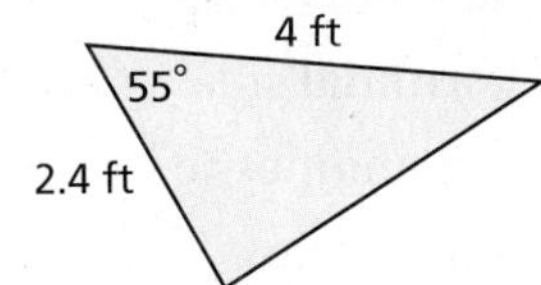

2. 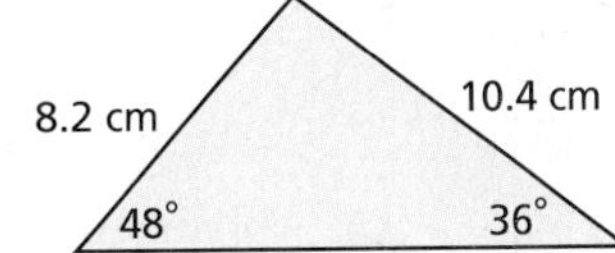

Solve each triangle. Round to the nearest tenth.

3. 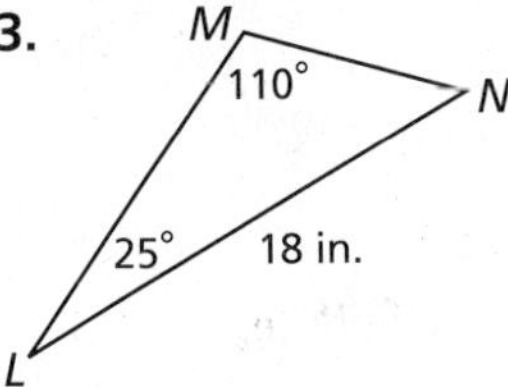

4. 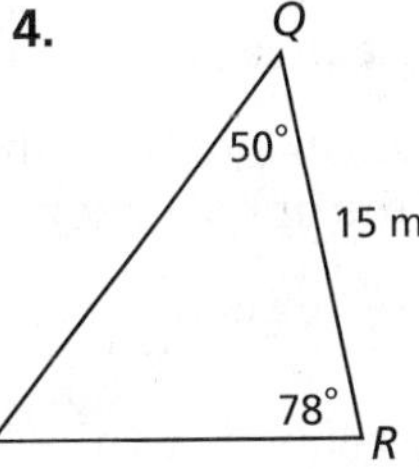

Derrick is designing triangular panes for a stained glass window. Determine the number of different triangles that he can form using the given measurements. Then solve the triangles. Round to the nearest tenth.

5. $a = 2.1$ cm, $b = 1.8$ cm, $m\angle A = 42°$
6. $a = 3$ cm, $b = 4.6$ cm, $m\angle A = 95°$
7. The rangers at two park stations spot a signal flare at the same time. Based on the measurements shown in the diagram, what is the distance between each park station and the point where the flare was set off? Round to the nearest tenth.

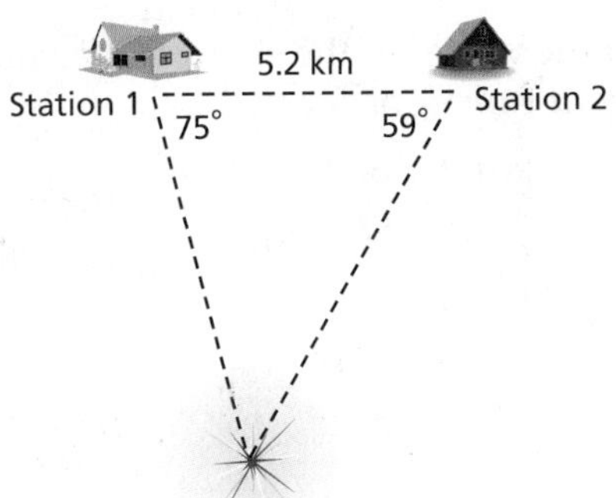

10-6 The Law of Cosines

Use the given measurements to solve each triangle. Round to the nearest tenth.

8. 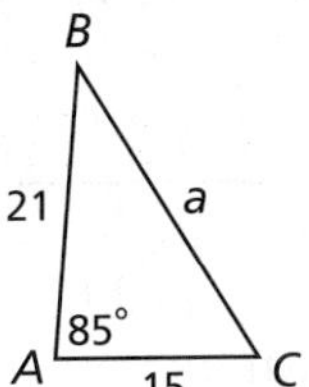

9. 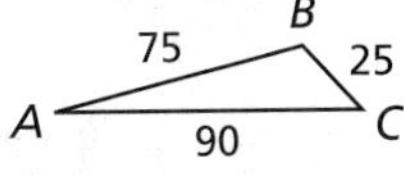

10. A civil engineer is working on plans for a new road called Pine Avenue. This road will intersect Market Boulevard and 3rd Street as shown. To the nearest degree, what is the measure of the angle that Pine Avenue will make with Market Boulevard?

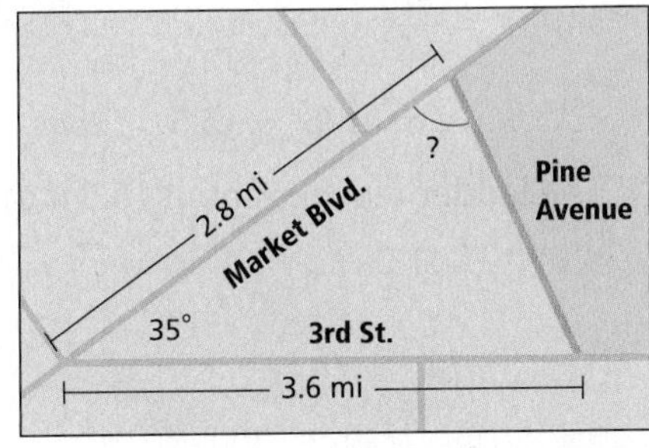

11. A school courtyard is shaped like a triangle. Its sides measure 25 yards, 27.5 yards, and 32 yards. What is the area of the courtyard to the nearest square yard?

CHAPTER 10

Study Guide: Review

Vocabulary

angle of rotation
cosecant
cosine
cotangent
coterminal angle
initial side
inverse cosine function
inverse sine function
inverse tangent function
radian
reference angle
secant
sine
standard position
tangent
terminal side
trigonometric function
unit circle

Complete the sentences below with vocabulary words from the list above.

1. A(n) ____?____ is a unit of angle measure based on arc length.

2. The ____?____ of an acute angle in a right triangle is the ratio of the length of the hypotenuse to the length of the opposite leg.

3. An angle in ____?____ has its vertex at the origin and one ray on the positive x-axis.

10-1 Right-Angle Trigonometry

EXAMPLES

■ **Find the values of the sine, cosine, and tangent functions for θ.**

$$\sin\theta = \frac{\text{opp.}}{\text{hyp.}} = \frac{8}{17}$$

$$\cos\theta = \frac{\text{adj.}}{\text{hyp.}} = \frac{15}{17}$$

$$\tan\theta = \frac{\text{opp.}}{\text{adj.}} = \frac{8}{15}$$

■ **A 16 ft ladder is leaned against a building as shown. How high up the building does the ladder reach?**

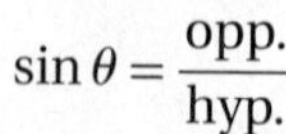

$$\sin\theta = \frac{\text{opp.}}{\text{hyp.}}$$

$$\sin 75^\circ = \frac{h}{16} \quad \textit{Substitute.}$$

$$h = 16\sin 75^\circ \approx 15.5 \quad \textit{Solve for h.}$$

The ladder reaches about 15.5 ft up the building.

EXERCISES

Find the values of the six trigonometric functions for θ.

4.

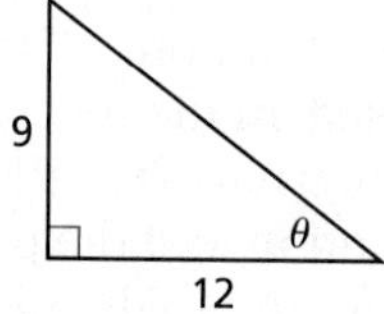

5.

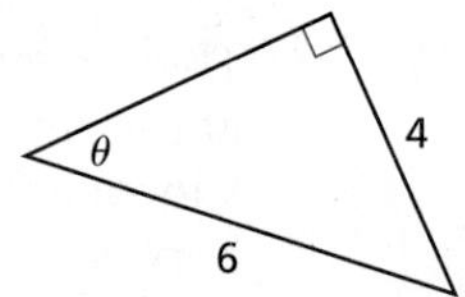

Use a trigonometric function to find the value of x.

6.

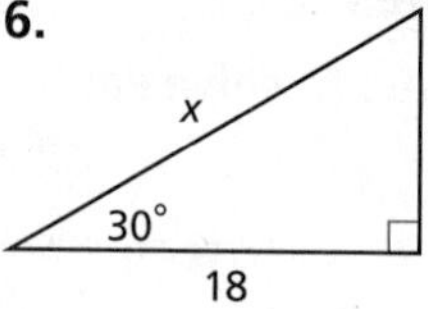

7.

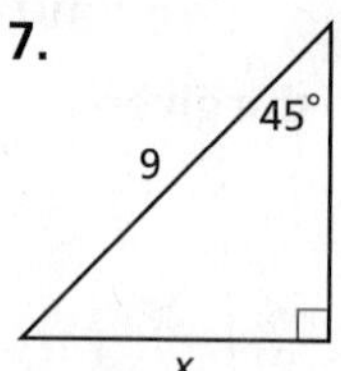

8. A support wire is being attached to a telephone pole as shown in the diagram. To the nearest foot, how long does the wire need to be?

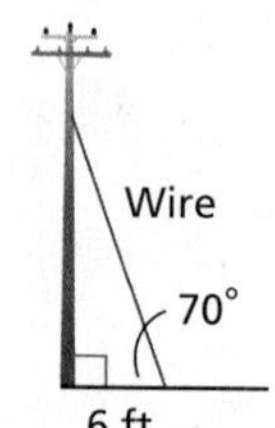

9. The angle of depression from a watchtower to a forest fire is 8°. If the watchtower is 25 m high, what is the distance between the base of the tower and the fire to the nearest meter?

10-2 Angles of Rotation

EXAMPLES

- **Draw a −290° angle in standard position.**

Rotate the terminal side 290° clockwise.

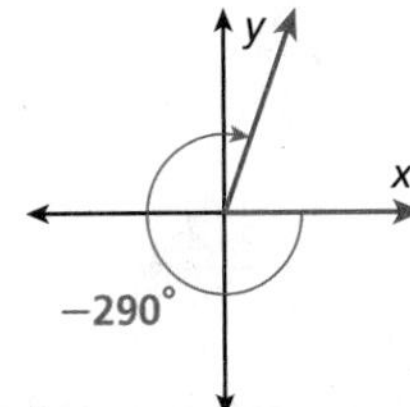

- **$P(-5, 12)$ is a point on the terminal side of θ in standard position. Find the exact value of the six trigonometric functions of θ.**

$r = \sqrt{(-5)^2 + (12)^2} = 13$ *Find r.*

$\sin\theta = \frac{y}{r} = \frac{12}{13}$ $\cos\theta = \frac{x}{r} = \frac{-5}{13} = -\frac{5}{13}$

$\tan\theta = \frac{y}{x} = \frac{12}{-5} = -\frac{12}{5}$ $\csc\theta = \frac{1}{\sin\theta} = \frac{13}{12}$

$\sec\theta = \frac{1}{\cos\theta} = -\frac{13}{5}$ $\cot\theta = \frac{1}{\tan\theta} = -\frac{5}{12}$

EXERCISES

Draw an angle with the given measure in standard position.

10. 195° **11.** −220° **12.** −450°

Find the measures of a positive angle and a negative angle that are coterminal with each given angle.

13. $\theta = 115°$ **14.** $\theta = 382°$ **15.** $\theta = -135°$

Find the measure of the reference angle for each given angle.

16. $\theta = 84°$ **17.** $\theta = 127°$ **18.** $\theta = -105°$

P is a point on the terminal side of θ in standard position. Find the exact value of the six trigonometric functions for θ.

19. $P(-4, 3)$ **20.** $P(5, 12)$ **21.** $P(-15, -8)$

22. $P(8, -3)$ **23.** $P(-9, -1)$ **24.** $P(-5, 10)$

10-3 The Unit Circle

EXAMPLES

Convert each measure from degrees to radians or from radians to degrees.

- −60°

$-60°\left(\frac{\pi \text{ radians}}{180°}\right) = -\frac{\pi}{3}$ radians

- $\frac{5\pi}{3}$ radians

$\left(\frac{5\pi}{3} \text{ radians}\right)\left(\frac{180°}{\pi \text{ radians}}\right) = 300°$

- **Use a reference angle to find the exact value of tan 150°.**

Step 1 The reference angle measures 30°.

Step 2 Find the tangent of the reference angle.

$\tan 30° = \frac{\sqrt{3}}{3}$

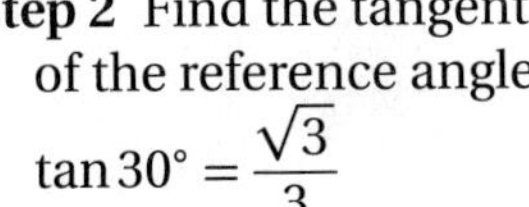

Step 3 Adjust the sign, if needed.

The tangent ratio is negative if the terminal side of the angle is in Quadrant II.

$\tan 150° = -\frac{\sqrt{3}}{3}$

EXERCISES

Convert each measure from degrees to radians or from radians to degrees.

25. 270° **26.** −120° **27.** 400°

28. $\frac{\pi}{6}$ **29.** $-\frac{\pi}{9}$ **30.** $\frac{9\pi}{4}$

Use the unit circle to find the exact value of each trigonometric function.

31. $\cos 240°$ **32.** $\tan\frac{3\pi}{4}$ **33.** $\sec 300°$

Use a reference angle to find the exact value of the sine, cosine, and tangent of each angle measure.

34. $\frac{7\pi}{6}$ **35.** 300° **36.** $-\frac{\pi}{3}$

37. A circle has a radius of 16 in. To the nearest inch, what is the length of an arc of the circle that is intercepted by a central angle of 80°?

38. The minute hand on a clock on a town hall tower is 1.5 meters in length.

a. Find the angle in radians through which the minute hand rotates in 10 minutes.

b. To the nearest tenth of a meter, how far does the tip of the minute hand travel in 10 minutes?

10-4 Inverses of Trigonometric Functions

EXAMPLES

■ **Evaluate $\text{Sin}^{-1}\left(-\frac{\sqrt{3}}{2}\right)$. Give your answer in both radians and degrees.**

$-\frac{\sqrt{3}}{2} = \text{Sin}\,\theta$ *Find the value of θ for $-\frac{\pi}{2} \le \theta \le \frac{\pi}{2}$.*

$-\frac{\sqrt{3}}{2} = \text{Sin}\left(-\frac{\pi}{3}\right)$ *Use y-coordinates of points on the unit circle.*

$\text{Sin}^{-1}\left(-\frac{\sqrt{3}}{2}\right) = -\frac{\pi}{3}$, or $\text{Sin}^{-1}\left(-\frac{\sqrt{3}}{2}\right) = -60°$

■ **A boat is 2.8 miles east and 1.3 miles north of a dock. To the nearest degree, in what direction should the boat head to reach the dock?**

Step 1 Draw a diagram.

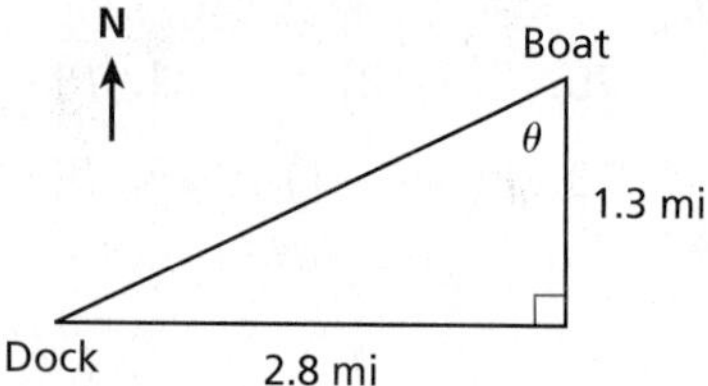

Step 2 Find the value of θ.

$\tan\theta = \frac{\text{opp.}}{\text{adj.}}$ *Use the tangent ratio.*

$\tan\theta = \frac{2.8}{1.3}$ *Substitute.*

$\theta = \text{Tan}^{-1}\left(\frac{2.8}{1.3}\right) \approx 65°$ *Solve for θ.*

The boat should head 65° west of south.

EXERCISES

Find all possible values of each expression.

39. $\tan^{-1}\sqrt{3}$

40. $\cos^{-1}\left(-\frac{\sqrt{3}}{2}\right)$

41. $\sin^{-1}\left(-\frac{\sqrt{2}}{2}\right)$

42. $\tan^{-1}\left(-\frac{\sqrt{3}}{3}\right)$

Evaluate each inverse trigonometric function. Give your answer in both radians and degrees.

43. $\text{Sin}^{-1}\left(-\frac{1}{2}\right)$

44. $\text{Tan}^{-1}\frac{\sqrt{3}}{3}$

45. $\text{Cos}^{-1}(-1)$

46. $\text{Sin}^{-1}\frac{\sqrt{2}}{2}$

47. A skateboard ramp is 39 inches long and rises to a height of 22 inches. To the nearest degree, what angle does the ramp make with the ground?

48. A parasail is a parachute that lifts a person into the air when he or she is towed by a boat. Shelley is parasailing at a height of 100 feet. If 152 feet of towline attaches her to the boat, what is the angle of depression from Shelley to the boat? Round to the nearest degree.

Solve each equation to the nearest tenth. Use the given restrictions.

49. $\sin\theta = 0.3$, for $-90° \le \theta \le 90°$

50. $\sin\theta = 0.3$, for $90° \le \theta \le 180°$

51. $\tan\theta = 2.2$, for $-90° < \theta < 90°$

52. $\tan\theta = 2.2$, for $180° \le \theta \le 270°$

10-5 The Law of Sines

EXAMPLES

■ **Find the area of the triangle. Round to the nearest tenth.**

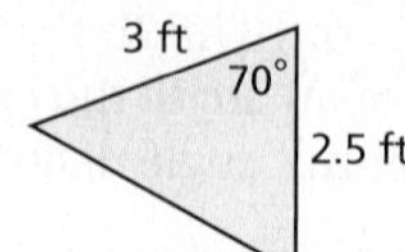

$\text{Area} = \frac{1}{2}ab\sin C$ *Use the area formula*

$= \frac{1}{2}(3)(2.5)\sin 70°$ *Substitute.*

$\approx 3.5\text{ ft}^2$ *Evaluate.*

EXERCISES

Find the area of each triangle. Round to the nearest tenth.

53.

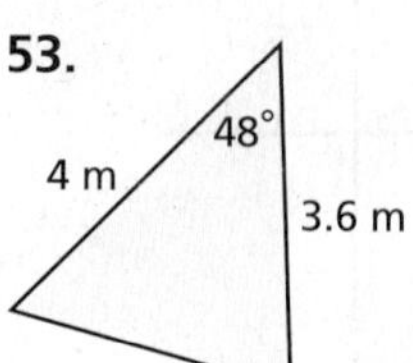

54.

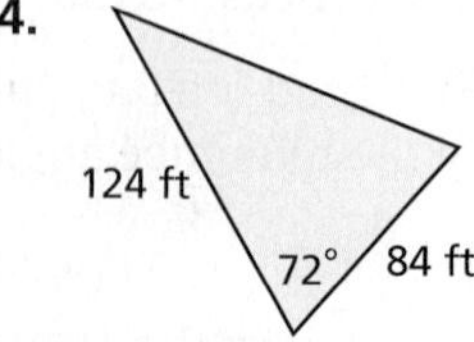

55.

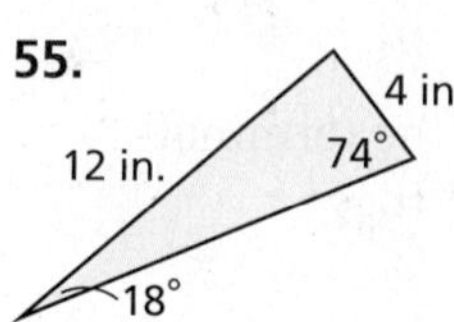

56.

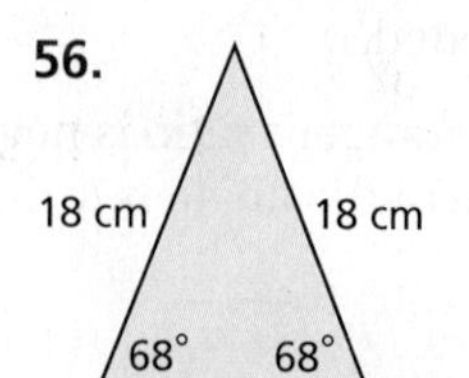

■ **Solve the triangle. Round to the nearest tenth.**

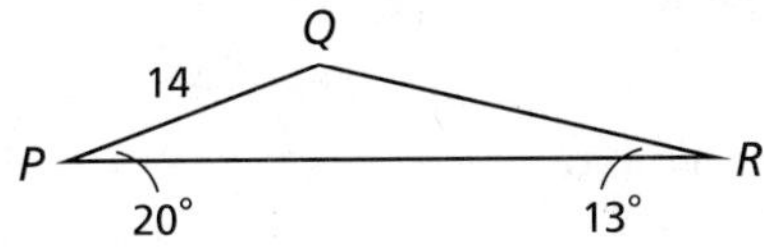

Step 1 Find the third angle measure.

$m\angle Q° = 180° - 20° - 13° = 147°$

Step 2 Use the Law of Sines to find the unknown side lengths.

$\frac{\sin P}{p} = \frac{\sin R}{r}$ $\quad$ $\frac{\sin Q}{q} = \frac{\sin R}{r}$

$\frac{\sin 20°}{p} = \frac{\sin 13°}{14}$ $\quad$ $\frac{\sin 147°}{q} = \frac{\sin 13°}{14}$

$p = \frac{14 \sin 20°}{\sin 13°}$ $\quad$ $q = \frac{14 \sin 147°}{\sin 13°}$

$p \approx 21.3$ $\quad$ $q \approx 33.9$

Solve each triangle. Round to the nearest tenth.

57. **58.**

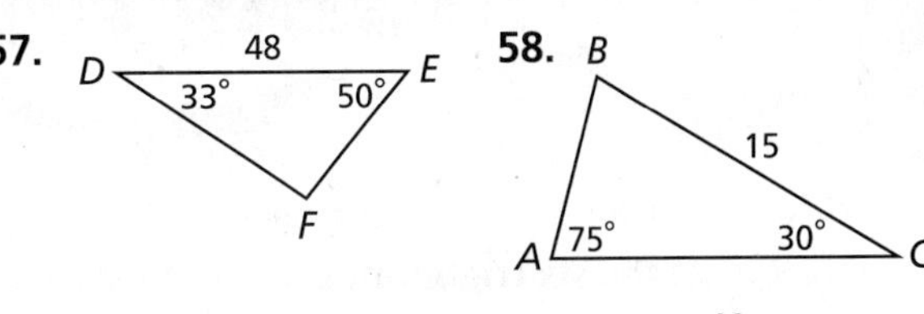

59. **60.**

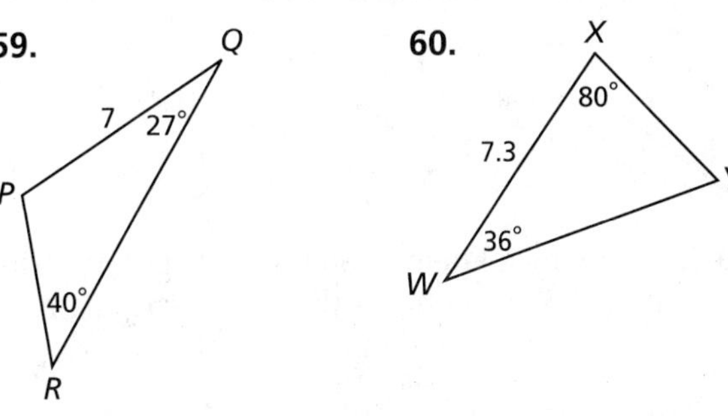

61. A graphic artist is designing a triangular logo. Determine the number of different triangles that he can form using the measurements $a = 14$ cm, $b = 16$ cm, and $m\angle A = 55°$. Then solve the triangles. Round to the nearest tenth.

10-6 The Law of Cosines

EXAMPLES

■ **Use the given measurements to solve $\triangle ABC$. Round to the nearest tenth.**

Step 1 Find the measure of the largest angle, $\angle B$.

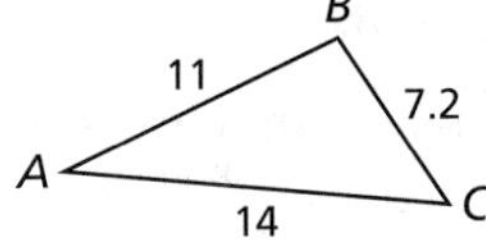

$b^2 = a^2 + c^2 - 2ac\cos B$

$14^2 = 7.2^2 + 11^2 - 2(7.2)(11)\cos B$

$m\angle B \approx 98.4°$

Step 2 Find another angle measure.

$a^2 = b^2 + c^2 - 2bc\cos A$

$7.2^2 = 14^2 + 11^2 - 2(14)(11)\cos A$

$m\angle A \approx 30.6°$

Step 3 Find the third angle measure.

$m\angle C \approx 180° - 30.6° - 98.4° \approx 51.0°$

■ **A triangular tile has sides measuring 4 in., 5 in., and 8 in. What is the area of the tile to the nearest square inch?**

$s = \frac{1}{2}(4 + 5 + 8) = 8.5$ *Find the value of s.*

$A = \sqrt{s(s-a)(s-b)(s-c)}$ *Heron's Formula*

$A = \sqrt{8.5(8.5-4)(8.5-5)(8.5-8)} \approx 8.2 \text{ in}^2$

EXERCISES

Use the given measurements to solve $\triangle ABC$. Round to the nearest tenth.

62. $m\angle C = 29°$, $a = 14$, $b = 30$

63. $m\angle A = 110°$, $b = 18$, $c = 12$

64. $a = 12$, $b = 3$, $c = 10$

65. $a = 7$, $b = 9$, $c = 11$

66. A bicycle race has a triangular course with the dimensions shown.

a. To the nearest tenth of a kilometer, how long is the race?

b. At an average speed of 28 km/h, how many hours will it take a rider to complete the race? Round to the nearest tenth.

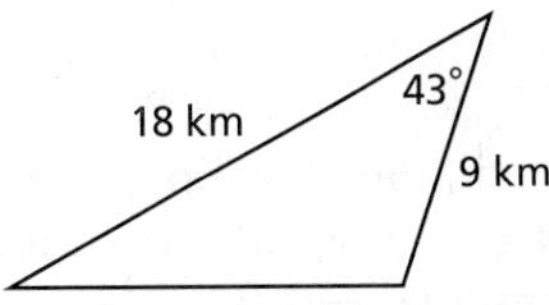

67. A triangular wading pool has side lengths that measure 10 ft, 12 ft, and 16 ft. What is the area of the pool's surface to the nearest square foot?

68. A triangular pennant has side lengths that measure 24 in., 24 in., and 8 in. What is the area of the pennant to the nearest square inch?

CHAPTER 10

CHAPTER TEST

Find the values of the six trigonometric functions for θ.

1. 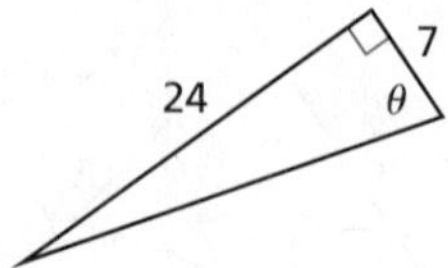

2. 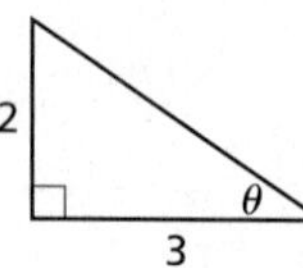

3. Katrina is flying a kite on 150 ft of string. The string makes an angle of 62° with the horizontal. If Katrina holds the end of the string 5 ft above the ground, how high is the kite? Round to the nearest foot.

Draw an angle with the given measure in standard position.

4. 100°

5. −210°

P is a point on the terminal side of θ in standard position. Find the exact value of the six trigonometric functions of θ.

6. $P(-32, 24)$

7. $P(-3, -7)$

Convert each measure from degrees to radians or from radians to degrees.

8. 310°

9. −36°

10. $\frac{2\pi}{9}$

11. $-\frac{5\pi}{6}$

Use the unit circle to find the exact value of each trigonometric function.

12. $\cos 210°$

13. $\tan \frac{11\pi}{6}$

Evaluate each inverse trigonometric function. Give your answer in both radians and degrees.

14. $\text{Cos}^{-1}\frac{\sqrt{2}}{2}$

15. $\text{Sin}^{-1}\left(-\frac{\sqrt{3}}{2}\right)$

16. A limestone cave is 6.2 mi south and 1.4 mi east of the entrance of a national park. To the nearest degree, in what direction should a group at the entrance head in order to reach the cave?

17. Find the area of $\triangle DEF$. Round to the nearest tenth.

18. Use the given measurements to solve $\triangle DEF$. Round to the nearest tenth.

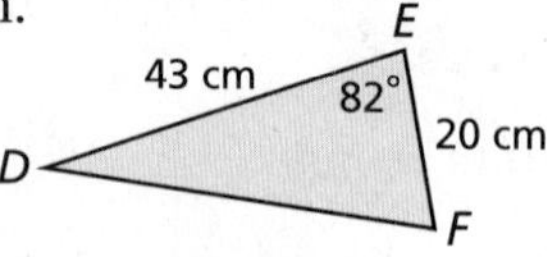

19. An artist is designing a wallpaper pattern based on triangles. Determine the number of different triangles she can form using the measurements $a = 28$, $b = 13$, and $m\angle A = 102°$. Then solve the triangles. Round to the nearest tenth.

20. Solve $\triangle LMN$. Round to the nearest tenth.

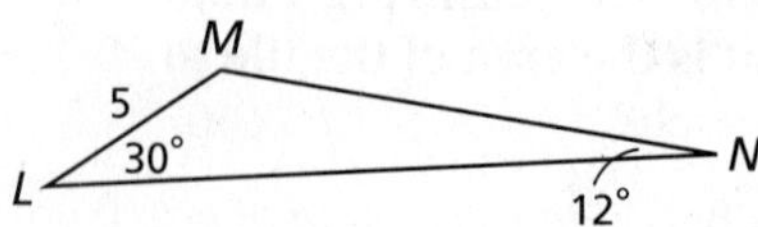

21. A lawn next to an office building is shaped like a triangle with sides measuring 16 ft, 24 ft, and 30 ft. What is the area of the lawn to the nearest square foot?

College Entrance Exam Practice

FOCUS ON SAT MATHEMATICS SUBJECT TESTS

Though both the SAT Mathematics Subject Tests Level 1 and Level 2 may include questions involving basic trigonometric functions, only the Level 2 test may include questions involving the Law of Sines, the Law of Cosines, and radian measure.

If you take the Level 1 test, make sure that your calculator is set to degree mode, because no questions will require you to use radians. If you take the Level 2 test, you will need to determine whether to use degree or radian mode as appropriate.

You may want to time yourself as you take this practice test. It should take you about 6 minutes to complete.

---

1. A right triangle has an angle measuring 22°. The shorter leg of the triangle has a length of 3 inches. What is the area of the triangle?

(A) 1.8 in^2

(B) 4.2 in^2

(C) 7.4 in^2

(D) 11.1 in^2

(E) 12.0 in^2

---

2. If $0 \le \theta \le \frac{\pi}{2}$ and $\cos^{-1}(\sin\theta) = \frac{\pi}{3}$, then what is the value of θ?

(A) $\frac{\pi}{6}$

(B) $\frac{\pi}{2}$

(C) $\frac{5\pi}{6}$

(D) $\frac{4\pi}{3}$

(E) $\frac{3\pi}{2}$

---

3. A triangle has side lengths of 7, 26, and 31. What is the measure of the smallest angle of the triangle?

(A) 8°

(B) 10°

(C) 26°

(D) 30°

(E) 40°

---

4. A manufacturer must produce a metal bar with a triangular cross section that meets the specifications shown. What is the length of side a?

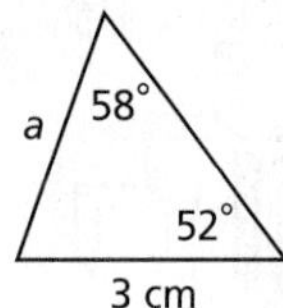

Note: Figure not drawn to scale

(A) 2.4 cm

(B) 2.6 cm

(C) 2.8 cm

(D) 3.2 cm

(E) 3.6 cm

---

5. If $\sin B = \frac{5}{9}$ in the figure below, what is $\tan A$?

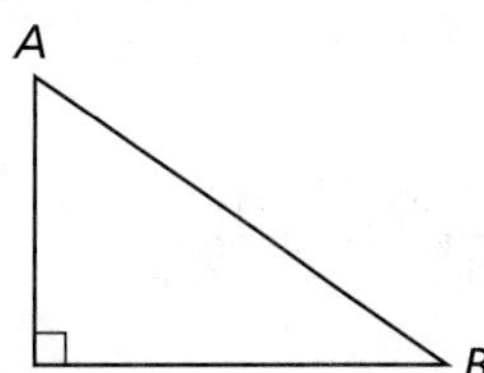

Note: Figure not drawn to scale

(A) 0.45

(B) 0.67

(C) 0.83

(D) 1.50

(E) 1.80

CHAPTER 10

TEST TACKLER

Standardized Test Strategies

Multiple Choice: Spatial-Reasoning Problems

Some problems test your ability to use spatial reasoning. To solve these problems, you must be able to recognize different views of geometric figures. Orthographic drawings and nets are two common ways of representing three-dimensional objects. An *orthographic drawing* usually presents three views of a three-dimensional object: top, front, and side. A *net* is a diagram that can be folded to form a three-dimensional figure.

EXAMPLE 1

The drawing shows the top view of a structure made from cubes as well as the number of cubes in each column of the structure. Which three-dimensional view represents the same structure?

3	2	1
2		
2		

Side

Front

(A)

(C)

(B)

(D)

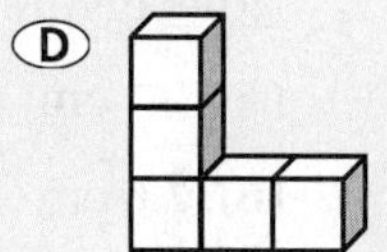

Start by sketching the top view of each answer choice.

Choice A

Choice B

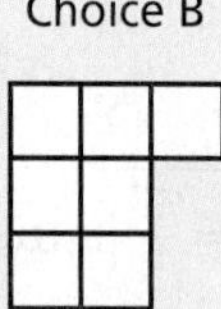

Choice C

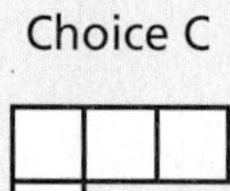

Choice D

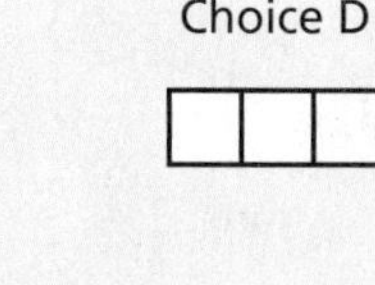

Choices B and D can be eliminated because their top views do not match the one given in the problem. Next, count the number of cubes in each column of choices A and C.

Choice A

3	2	1
2		
2		

Choice C

3	2	1
1		
1		

The two front columns of choice C have only 1 cube each instead of 2. Therefore, choice C can be eliminated. Each column of choice A, however, has the correct number of cubes.

The correct answer is choice A.

If you have trouble visualizing the geometric figures, make a quick sketch. Your sketch does not need to be exact, but it should show the sides or faces of the figures in the correct relationships to each other.

Read each test item and answer the questions that follow.

Item A

The front, top, and side views of a solid are shown below. What is the volume of the solid?

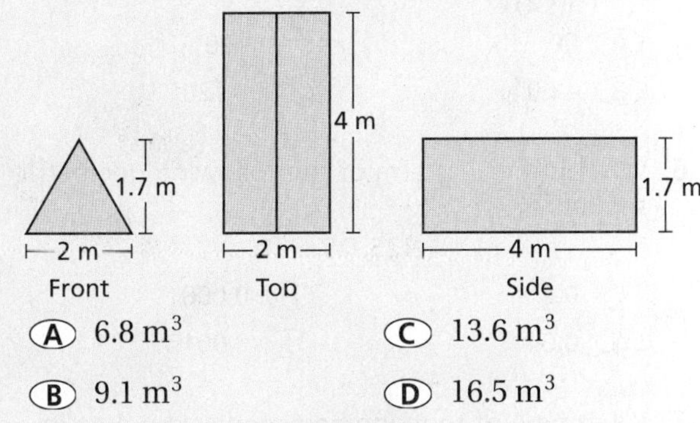

Ⓐ 6.8 m^3 Ⓒ 13.6 m^3

Ⓑ 9.1 m^3 Ⓓ 16.5 m^3

1. Make a sketch of the figure. What type of figure do the three views show?
2. How can you determine the volume of this figure?

Item B

What three-dimensional figure does this net represent?

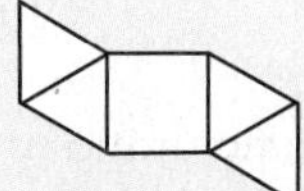

Ⓕ Square pyramid

Ⓖ Triangular pyramid

Ⓗ Rectangular prism

Ⓙ Triangular prism

3. What type and number of faces does the figure have?
4. What type and number of faces does each of the answer choices have?

Item C

Which of the following is the front view of the figure shown?

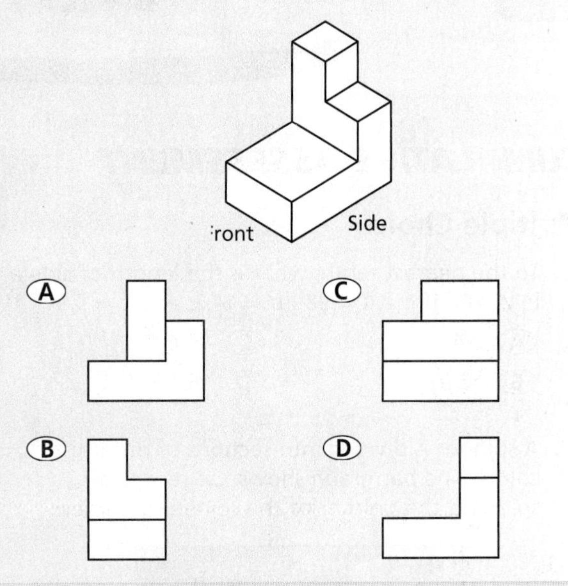

5. Make a sketch of the figure. Shade the faces on the front of the figure.
6. Describe the shapes of these faces.

Item D

Which is a true statement about the net of the cube shown?

Ⓕ The face with the star and the face with the circle are parallel.

Ⓖ The face with the heart and the face with the circle are perpendicular.

Ⓗ The faces with the triangles are parallel.

Ⓙ The face with the number 5 and the face with the star are perpendicular.

7. Which faces of the cube are opposite each other? Are opposite faces parallel or perpendicular to each other?
8. Can faces that share an edge be parallel to each other? Explain.

CHAPTER 10

STANDARDIZED TEST PREP

Learn It Online
State Test Practice

CUMULATIVE ASSESSMENT

Multiple Choice

1. To the nearest tenth, what is the length of side a in $\triangle ABC$ if $m\angle A = 98°$, $b = 14.2$, and $c = 5.9$?

Ⓐ 8.4
Ⓑ 12.9
Ⓒ 15.4
Ⓓ 16.1

2. A spinner is divided into sections of different colors. The bar graph shows the results of spinning the pointer of the spinner 50 times.

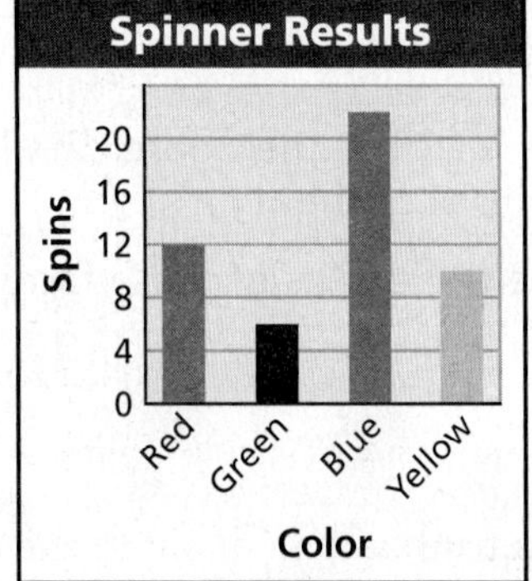

What is the experimental probability that the pointer of the spinner will land on a blue section?

Ⓕ 0.05
Ⓖ 0.22
Ⓗ 0.25
Ⓙ 0.44

3. If $-\frac{\pi}{2} \le \theta \le \frac{\pi}{2}$, what value of θ makes the equation $\sin^{-1}\left(\frac{1}{2}\right) = \theta$ true?

Ⓐ $\frac{\pi}{6}$
Ⓑ $\frac{\pi}{4}$
Ⓒ $\frac{\pi}{3}$
Ⓓ $\frac{5\pi}{6}$

4. The angle θ is in standard position. What is the measure of the reference angle for $\theta = 100°$?

Ⓕ $-260°$
Ⓖ $260°$
Ⓗ $80°$
Ⓙ $10°$

5. Evaluate the inverse trigonometric function $\text{Cos}^{-1}\left(-\frac{1}{2}\right)$.

Ⓐ $60°$
Ⓑ $-60°$
Ⓒ $120°$
Ⓓ $-120°$

6. What is the 7th term of the following geometric sequence?

125, 25, 5, 1, ...

Ⓕ 0.2
Ⓖ 0.04
Ⓗ 0.008
Ⓙ 0.0016

7. What type of function best models the data in the table?

x	−2	−1	0	1	2
y	6.35	11.6	29.35	59.6	102.35

Ⓐ linear
Ⓑ quadratic
Ⓒ cubic
Ⓓ square root

8. If $f(x) = \frac{3}{2}x - 4$ and $g(x) = \frac{1}{2}f(x)$, what is the y-intercept of $g(x)$?

Ⓕ -4
Ⓖ -2
Ⓗ $\frac{1}{2}$
Ⓙ $\frac{8}{3}$

9. What is the common ratio of the exponential function represented by the table?

x	−2	−1	0	1	2
y	2.56	3.2	4	5	6.25

Ⓐ 0.16
Ⓑ 0.25
Ⓒ 0.64
Ⓓ 1.25

10. What effect does a translation 3 units right have on the graph of $f(x) = 2x - 5$?

Ⓕ The slope increases.
Ⓖ The slope decreases.
Ⓗ The value of the y-intercept increases.
Ⓙ The value of the y-intercept decreases.

One way to check whether two expressions are equivalent is to substitute the same value for the variable in each expression. If the expressions simplify to different values, then they are *not* equivalent.

11. Which of the following is equivalent to $(x + 4)^3$?

(A) $x^3 + 64$

(B) $x^3 + 8x + 16$

(C) $4x^3 + 32x^2 + 64x$

(D) $x^3 + 12x^2 + 48x + 64$

12. What is $\cos\theta$?

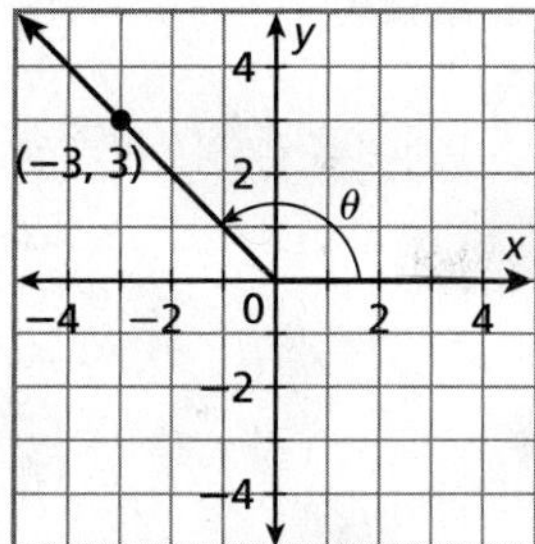

(F) −1

(G) $-\frac{\sqrt{2}}{2}$

(H) $\frac{\sqrt{2}}{2}$

(J) 1

13. What is the measure in degrees of an angle that measures $\frac{3\pi}{4}$ radians?

(A) 45°

(B) 90°

(C) 135°

(D) 180°

Gridded Response

14. To the nearest hundredth, what is the value of x in the triangle below?

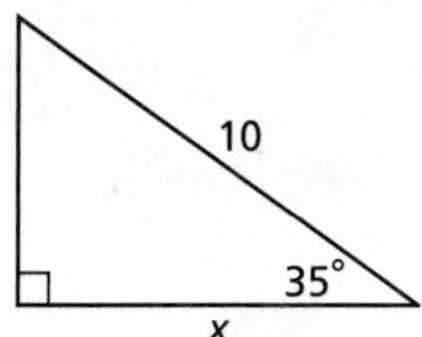

15. What is the 15th term of an arithmetic sequence with $a_{11} = 425$ and $a_{17} = 515$?

16. How many different triangles can be formed with the following measurements?

$a = 6.38$, $b = 4.72$, $m\angle A = 132°$

17. The function $h(t) = -4.9t^2 + 4.9t + 1.75$ models the height in meters of a lacrosse ball, where t is the time in seconds since the ball was thrown. Based on the model, what is the maximum height in meters that the ball will reach?

Short Response

18. Tickets for the water park cost \$12 for children under 13, \$20 for people ages 13 to 60, and \$15 for people over 60 years of age.

a. Write a function to represent the cost y in dollars of a ticket to the water park given a person's age x in years.

b. Graph the function.

19. What are the constraints on the region bounded by the quadrilateral below?

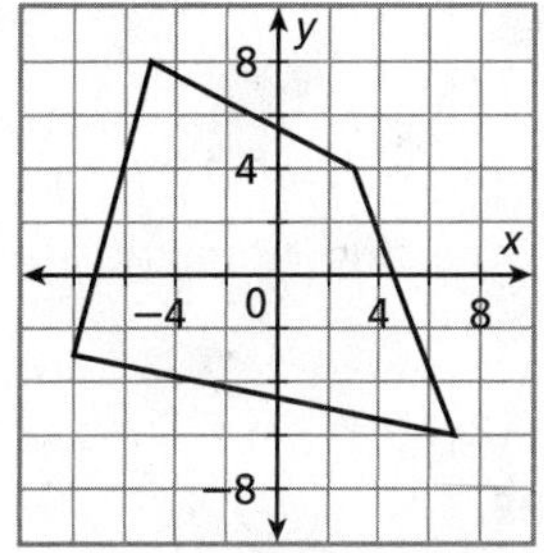

20. The table shows the number of Atlantic hurricanes for the years 1997–2004.

Atlantic Hurricanes			
Year	**Number**	**Year**	**Number**
1997	3	2001	9
1998	10	2002	4
1999	8	2003	7
2000	8	2004	9

a. Make a box-and-whisker plot of the hurricane data.

b. What is the mean number of hurricanes per year for the time period shown in the table?

Extended Response

21. The choir director at a high school wants to rent an auditorium for an upcoming performance. To pay for the auditorium, \$550 must be raised in ticket sales. The cost of the tickets will depend on the number of people who are expected to attend the performance.

a. Write a function to represent the number of dollars y a ticket should cost when x is the number of people who are expected to attend the performance.

b. What are the asymptotes of the function?

c. Graph the function.

d. What is a reasonable domain and range for the function? Explain.

e. How much should tickets cost if 250 people are expected to attend the performance?

CHAPTER

11 Trigonometric Graphs and Identities

COMMON CORE

Chapter

- Make connections among representations of trigonometric functions.
- Use reasoning to solve problems involving trigonometric ratios.

Spinning Wheels

You can use graphs of trigonometric functions and trigonometric identities to model the motion of a circle or a wheel in a variety of situations.

Learn It Online
Chapter Project Online

Martin Rogers/Getty Images

ARE YOU READY?

Vocabulary

Match each term on the left with a definition on the right.

1. cosecant
2. cosine
3. hypotenuse
4. tangent of an angle

A. the ratio of the length of the leg adjacent the angle to the length of the opposite leg

B. the ratio of the length of the leg adjacent the angle to the length of the hypotenuse

C. the ratio of the length of the leg opposite the angle to the length of the adjacent leg

D. the ratio of the length of the hypotenuse to the length of the leg opposite the angle

E. the side opposite the right angle

Divide Fractions

Divide.

5. $\dfrac{\frac{3}{5}}{\frac{5}{2}}$ 6. $\dfrac{\frac{3}{4}}{\frac{1}{2}}$ 7. $\dfrac{-\frac{3}{8}}{\frac{1}{8}}$ 8. $\dfrac{\frac{2}{3}}{-\frac{7}{4}}$

Simplify Radical Expressions

Simplify each expression.

9. $\sqrt{6} \cdot \sqrt{2}$ 10. $\sqrt{100 - 64}$ 11. $\dfrac{\sqrt{9}}{\sqrt{36}}$ 12. $\sqrt{\dfrac{4}{25}}$

Multiply Binomials

Multiply.

13. $(x + 11)(x + 7)$
14. $(y - 4)(y - 9)$
15. $(2x - 3)(x + 5)$
16. $(k + 3)(3k - 3)$
17. $(4z - 4)(z + 1)$
18. $(y + 0.5)(y - 1)$

Special Products of Binomials

Multiply.

19. $(2x + 5)^2$
20. $(3y - 2)^2$
21. $(4x - 6)(4x + 6)$
22. $(2m + 1)(2m - 1)$
23. $(s + 7)^2$
24. $(-p + 4)(-p - 4)$

CHAPTER 11

Study Guide: Preview

Where You've Been

In previous chapters, you

- solved problems involving triangles and trigonometric ratios.
- factored to solve quadratic equations.
- applied function models to solve real-world problems.
- solved equations by using algebra and graphs.

In This Chapter

You will study

- problems involving trigonometric functions.
- factoring to solve trigonometric equations.
- trigonometric function models of real-world problems.
- solving trigonometric equations by using algebra and graphs.

Where You're Going

You can use the skills in this chapter

- in your future math classes, particularly Calculus.
- in other classes, such as Physics, Biology, and Economics.
- outside of school to observe cyclical patterns and make conjectures.

Key Vocabulary/Vocabulario

amplitude	amplitud
cycle	ciclo
frequency	frecuencia
period	periodo
periodic function	función periódica
phase shift	cambio de fase
rotation matrix	matriz de rotación

Vocabulary Connections

To become familiar with some of the vocabulary terms in the chapter, consider the following. You may refer to the chapter, the glossary, or a dictionary if you like.

1. What does the word *amplify* mean? What might the **amplitude** of a pendulum swing refer to?
2. What does a **cycle** refer to in everyday language? Give examples of cyclical phenomena.
3. Give an example of something that occurs *frequently*. To describe how often something occurs, like brushing our teeth, we can say "we brush twice a day." Describe the **frequency** of your example.
4. What does **period** mean in everyday language? What might a **periodic function** refer to?
5. What result might you expect from using a **rotation matrix**?

CHAPTER 11

Study Strategy: Prepare for Your Final Exam

Math is a cumulative subject, so your final exam will probably cover all of the material that you have learned from the beginning of the course. Preparation is essential for you to be successful on your final exam. It may help you to make a study timeline like the one below.

2 weeks before the final:

- Look at previous exams and homework to determine areas I need to focus on; rework problems that were incorrect or incomplete.
- Make a list of all formulas and theorems that I need to know for the final.
- Create a practice exam using problems from the book that are similar to problems from each exam.

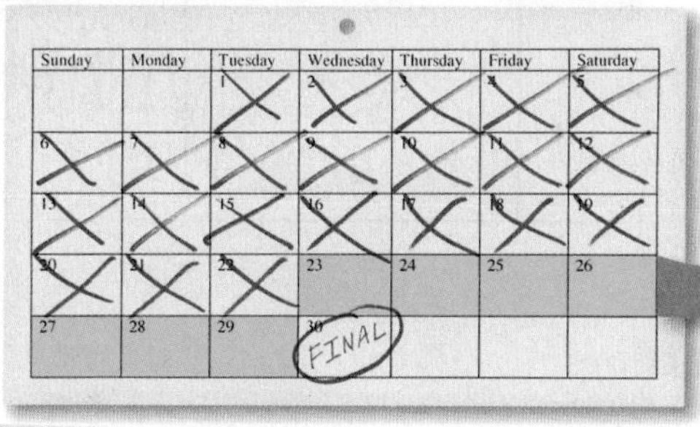

1 week before the final:

- Take the practice exam and check it. For each problem I miss, find two or three similar ones and work those.
- Work with a friend in the class to quiz each other on formulas, postulates, and theorems from my list.

1 day before the final:

- Make sure I have pencils and a calculator (check batteries!).

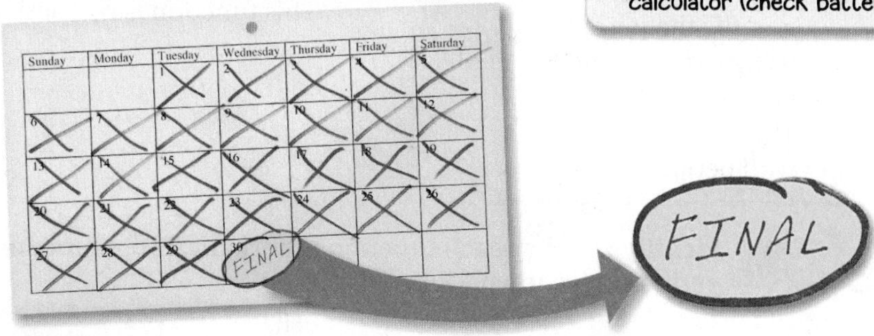

FINAL

1. Create a timeline that you will use to study for your final exam.

11-1 Graphs of Sine and Cosine

CC.9-12.F.IF.7 Graph functions expressed symbolically and show key features of the graph…* *Also* **CC.9-12.F.TF.5*, CC.9-12.F.BF.3, CC.9-12.F.IF.5*, CC.9-12.A.CED.2, CC.9-12.A.CED.3**

Objective
Recognize and graph periodic and trigonometric functions.

Vocabulary
periodic function
cycle
period
amplitude
frequency
phase shift

Why learn this?
Periodic phenomena such as sound waves can be modeled with trigonometric functions. (See Example 3.)

Periodic functions are functions that repeat exactly in regular intervals called **cycles**. The length of the cycle is called its **period**. Examine the graphs of the periodic function and nonperiodic function below. Notice that a cycle may begin at any point on the graph of a function.

EXAMPLE 

Identifying Periodic Functions

Identify whether each function is periodic. If the function is periodic, give the period.

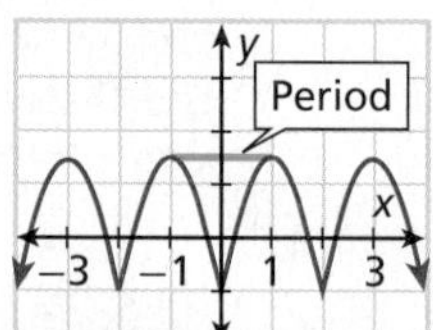

The pattern repeats exactly, so the function is periodic. Identify the period by using the start and finish of one cycle.

This function is periodic with period 2.

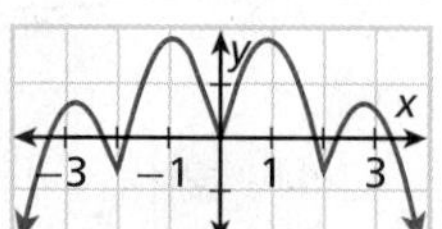

Although there is some symmetry, the pattern does not repeat exactly.

This function is not periodic.

Identify whether each function is periodic. If the function is periodic, give the period.

1a.

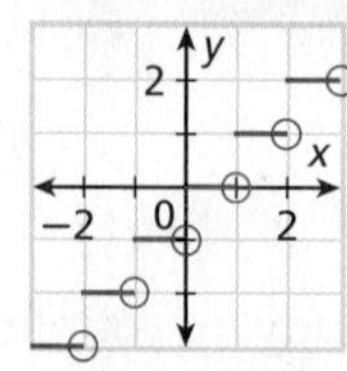

1b.

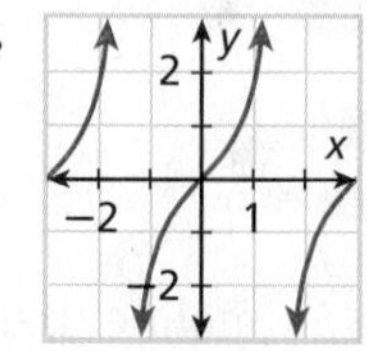

The trigonometric functions that you have studied are periodic. You can graph the function $f(x) = \sin x$ on the coordinate plane by using y-values from points on the unit circle where the independent variable x represents the angle θ in standard position.

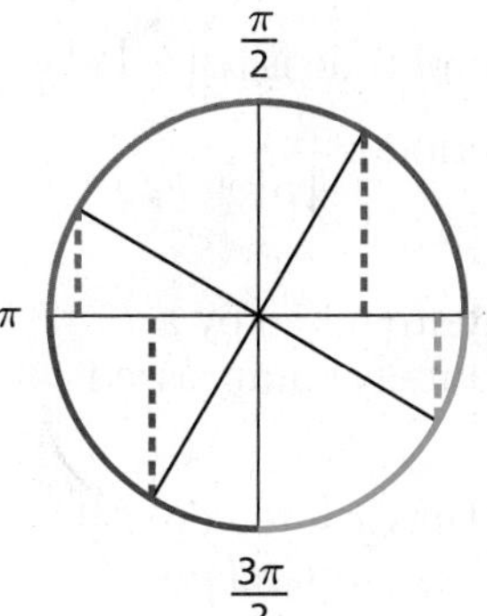

$x(=\theta)$	y
$\frac{\pi}{3}$	$\frac{\sqrt{3}}{2}$
$\frac{5\pi}{6}$	$\frac{1}{2}$
$\frac{4\pi}{3}$	$-\frac{\sqrt{3}}{2}$
$\frac{11\pi}{6}$	$-\frac{1}{2}$

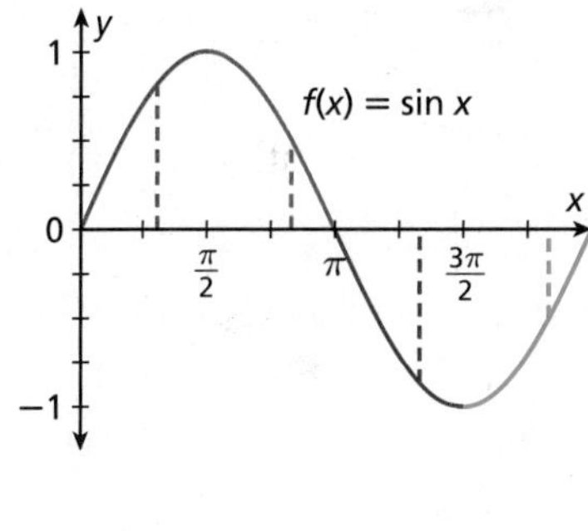

Similarly, the function $f(x) = \cos x$ can be graphed on the coordinate plane by using x-values from points on the unit circle.

The **amplitude** of sine and cosine functions is half of the difference between the maximum and minimum values of the function. The amplitude is always positive.

Characteristics of the Graphs of Sine and Cosine

FUNCTION	$y = \sin x$	$y = \cos x$
GRAPH		
DOMAIN	$\{x \mid x \in \mathbb{R}\}$	$\{x \mid x \in \mathbb{R}\}$
RANGE	$\{y \mid -1 \le y \le 1\}$	$\{y \mid -1 \le y \le 1\}$
PERIOD	2π	2π
AMPLITUDE	1	1

Helpful Hint

The graph of the sine function passes through the origin. The graph of the cosine function has y-intercept 1.

You can use the parent functions to graph transformations $y = a \sin bx$ and $y = a \cos bx$. Recall that a indicates a vertical stretch $(|a| > 1)$ or compression $(0 < |a| < 1)$, which changes the amplitude. If a is less than 0, the graph is reflected across the x-axis. The value of b indicates a horizontal stretch or compression, which changes the period.

Transformations of Sine and Cosine Graphs

For the graphs of $y = a \sin bx$ or $y = a \cos bx$ where $a \neq 0$ and x is in radians,

- the amplitude is $|a|$.
- the period is $\frac{2\pi}{|b|}$.

EXAMPLE 2 Stretching or Compressing Sine and Cosine Functions

Using $f(x) = \sin x$ as a guide, graph the function $g(x) = 3\sin 2x$. Identify the amplitude and period.

Step 1 Identify the amplitude and period.

Because $a = 3$, the amplitude is $|a| = |3| = 3$.

Because $b = 2$, the period is $\frac{2\pi}{|b|} = \frac{2\pi}{|2|} = \pi$.

Step 2 Graph.

The curve is vertically stretched by a factor of 3 and horizontally compressed by a factor of $\frac{1}{2}$.

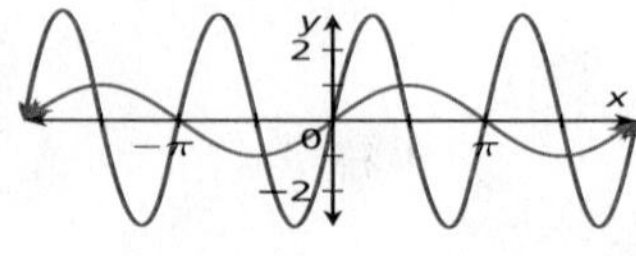

The parent function f has x-intercepts at multiples of π and g has x-intercepts at multiples of $\frac{\pi}{2}$.

The maximum value of g is 3, and the minimum value is −3.

2. Using $f(x) = \cos x$ as a guide, graph the function $h(x) = \frac{1}{3}\cos 2x$. Identify the amplitude and period.

Sine and cosine functions can be used to model real-world phenomena, such as sound waves. Different sounds create different waves. One way to distinguish sounds is to measure *frequency*. **Frequency** is the number of cycles in a given unit of time, so it is the reciprocal of the period of a function.

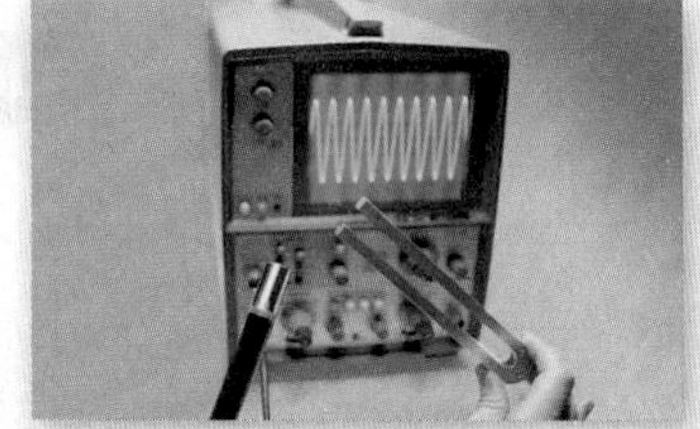

Hertz (Hz) is the standard measure of frequency and represents one cycle per second. For example, the sound wave made by a tuning fork for middle A has a frequency of 440 Hz. This means that the wave repeats 440 times in 1 second.

EXAMPLE 3 *Sound Application*

Use a sine function to graph a sound wave with a period of 0.005 second and an amplitude of 4 cm. Find the frequency in hertz for this sound wave.

Use a horizontal scale where one unit represents 0.001 second. The period tells you that it takes 0.005 seconds to complete one full cycle. The maximum and minimum values are given by the amplitude.

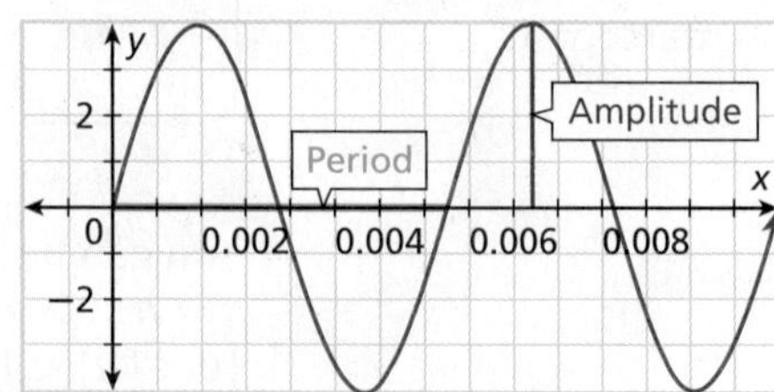

$$\text{frequency} = \frac{1}{\text{period}}$$

$$= \frac{1}{0.005} = 200 \text{ Hz}$$

The frequency of the sound wave is 200 Hz.

3. Use a sine function to graph a sound wave with a period of 0.004 second and an amplitude of 3 cm. Find the frequency in hertz for this sound wave.

Charles D. Winters

Sine and cosine can also be translated as $y = \sin(x - h) + k$ and $y = \cos(x - h) + k$. Recall that a vertical translation by k units moves the graph up $(k > 0)$ or down $(k < 0)$.

A **phase shift** is a horizontal translation of a periodic function. A phase shift of h units moves the graph left $(h < 0)$ or right $(h > 0)$.

EXAMPLE 4 Identifying Phase Shifts for Sine and Cosine Functions

Using $f(x) = \sin x$ as a guide, graph $g(x) = \sin\left(x + \frac{\pi}{2}\right)$. Identify the x-intercepts and phase shift.

Step 1 Identify the amplitude and period.

Amplitude is $|a| = |1| = 1$.

The period is $\frac{2\pi}{|b|} = \frac{2\pi}{|1|} = 2\pi$.

Step 2 Identify the phase shift.

$x + \frac{\pi}{2} = x - \left(-\frac{\pi}{2}\right)$ *Identify h.*

Because $h = -\frac{\pi}{2}$, the phase shift is $\frac{\pi}{2}$ radians to the left.

All x-intercepts, maxima, and minima of $f(x)$ are shifted $\frac{\pi}{2}$ units to the left.

Step 3 Identify the x-intercepts.

The first x-intercept occurs at $-\frac{\pi}{2}$. Because $\sin x$ has two x-intercepts in each period of 2π, the x-intercepts occur at $-\frac{\pi}{2} + n\pi$, where n is an integer.

Step 4 Identify the maximum and minimum values.

The maximum and minimum values occur between the x-intercepts. The maxima occur at $2\pi n$ and have a value of 1. The minima occur at $\pi + 2\pi n$ and have a value of -1.

Step 5 Graph using all of the information about the function.

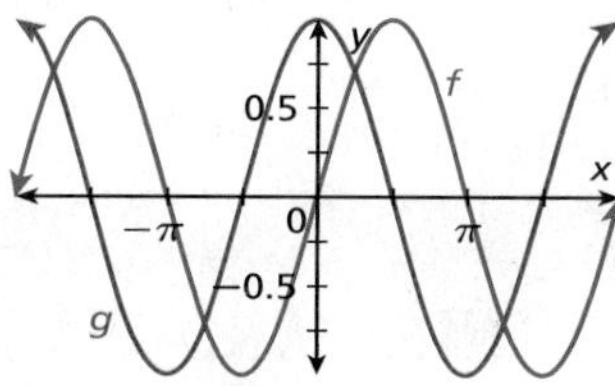

Helpful Hint

The repeating pattern is maximum, intercept, minimum, intercept,.... So intercepts occur twice as often as maximum or minimum values.

4. Using $f(x) = \cos x$ as a guide, graph $g(x) = \cos(x - \pi)$. Identify the x-intercepts and phase shift.

You can combine the transformations of trigonometric functions. Use the values of a, b, h, and k to identify the important features of a sine or cosine function.

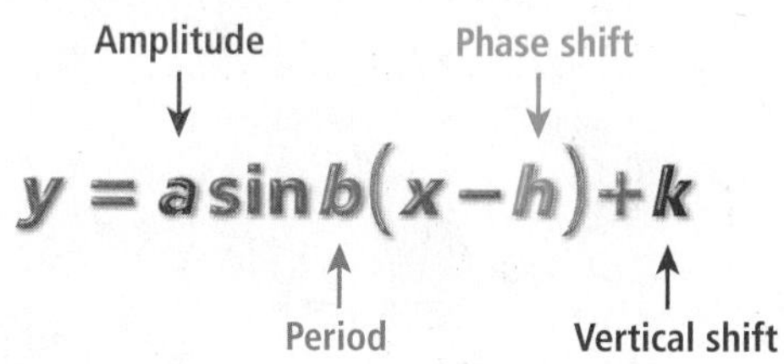

EXAMPLE 5 Entertainment Application

The Ferris wheel at the landmark Navy Pier in Chicago takes 7 minutes to make one full rotation. The height H in feet above the ground of one of the six-person gondolas can be modeled by $H(t) = 70 \sin \frac{2\pi}{7}(t - 1.75) + 80$, where t is time in minutes.

a. Graph the height of a cabin for two complete periods.

$$H(t) = 70 \sin \frac{2\pi}{7}(t - 1.75) + 80 \qquad a = 70,\ b = \frac{2\pi}{7},\ h = 1.75,\ k = 80$$

Step 1 Identify the important features of the graph.

Amplitude: 70

Period: $\frac{2\pi}{|b|} = \frac{2\pi}{\left|\frac{2\pi}{7}\right|} = 7$

The period is equal to the time required for one full rotation.

Phase shift: 1.75 minutes right

Vertical shift: 80

There are no x-intercepts.

Maxima: $80 + 70 = 150$ at 3.5 and 10.5

Minima: $80 - 70 = 10$ at 0, 7, and 14

Step 2 Graph using all of the information about the function.

b. What is the maximum height of a cabin?

The maximum height is $80 + 70 = 150$ feet above the ground.

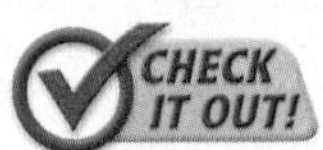

5. **What if...?** Suppose that the height H of a Ferris wheel can be modeled by $H(t) = -16 \cos \frac{\pi}{45}t + 24$, where t is the time in seconds.
   a. Graph the height of a cabin for two complete periods.
   b. What is the maximum height of a cabin?

THINK AND DISCUSS

1. **DESCRIBE** how the frequency and period of a periodic function are related. How does this apply to the graph of $f(x) = \cos x$?
2. **EXPLAIN** how the maxima and minima are related to the amplitude and period of sine and cosine functions.

3. **GET ORGANIZED** Copy and complete the graphic organizer. For each type of transformation, give an example and state the period.

Vertical compression	Horizontal stretch
Cosine Graphs	
Reflection	Phase shift

11-1 Exercises

GUIDED PRACTICE

1. **Vocabulary** Periodic functions repeat in regular intervals called __?__. (*cycles* or *periods*)

SEE EXAMPLE 1

Identify whether each function is periodic. If the function is periodic, give the period.

2. 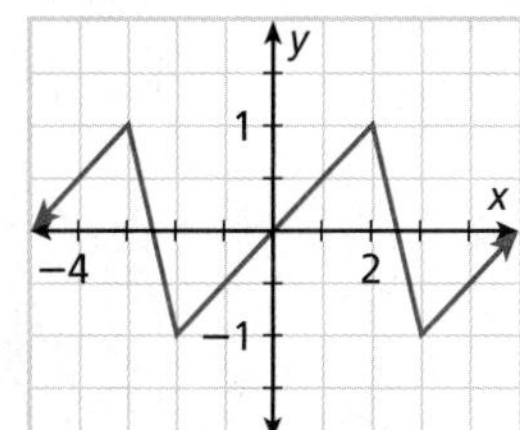

3. 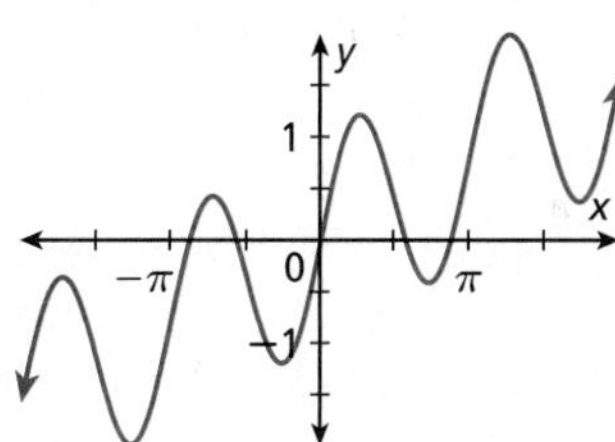

SEE EXAMPLE 2

Using $f(x) = \sin x$ or $f(x) = \cos x$ as a guide, graph each function. Identify the amplitude and the period.

4. $f(x) = 2\sin\frac{1}{2}x$
5. $h(x) = \frac{1}{4}\cos x$
6. $k(x) = \sin \pi x$

SEE EXAMPLE 3

7. **Sound** Use a sine function to graph a sound wave with a period of 0.01 second and an amplitude of 6 in. Find the frequency in hertz for this sound wave.

SEE EXAMPLE 4

Using $f(x) = \sin x$ or $f(x) = \cos x$ as a guide, graph each function. Identify the x-intercepts and the phase shift.

8. $f(x) = \sin\left(x + \frac{3\pi}{2}\right)$
9. $g(x) = \cos\left(x - \frac{\pi}{2}\right)$
10. $h(x) = \sin\left(x - \frac{\pi}{4}\right)$

SEE EXAMPLE 5

11. **Recreation** The height H in feet above the ground of the seat of a playground swing can be modeled by $H(\theta) = -4\cos\theta + 6$, where θ is the angle that the swing makes with a vertical extended to the ground. Graph the height of a swing's seat for $0° \le \theta \le 90°$. How high is the swing when $\theta = 60°$?

PRACTICE AND PROBLEM SOLVING

Independent Practice

For Exercises	See Example
12–13	1
14–17	2
18	3
19–22	4
23	5

Extra Practice

See Extra Practice for more Skills Practice and Applications Practice exercises.

Identify whether each function is periodic. If the function is periodic, give the period.

12. 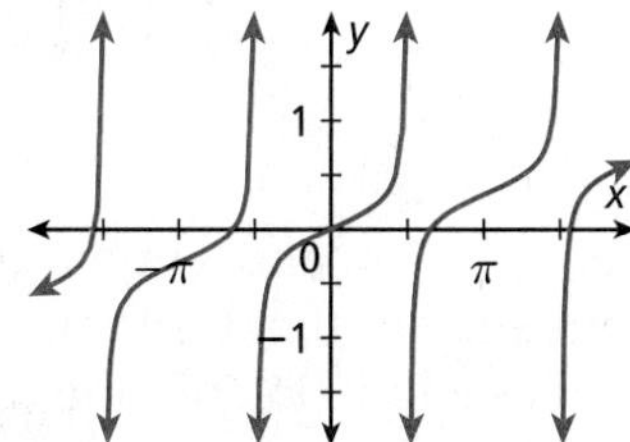

13. 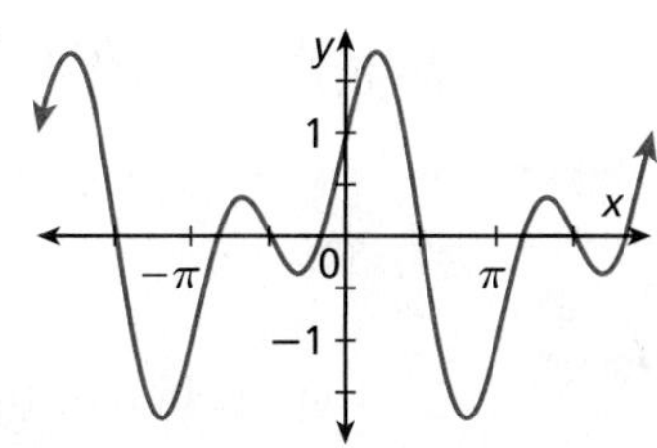

Using $f(x) = \sin x$ or $f(x) = \cos x$ as a guide, graph each function. Identify the amplitude and period.

14. $f(x) = 4\cos x$
15. $g(x) = \frac{3}{2}\sin x$
16. $g(x) = -\cos 4x$
17. $j(x) = 6\sin\frac{1}{3}x$

18. **Sound** Use a sine function to graph a sound wave with a period of 0.025 seconds and an amplitude of 5 in. Find the frequency in hertz for this sound wave.

Using $f(x) = \sin x$ or $f(x) = \cos x$ as a guide, graph each function. Identify the x-intercepts and phase shift.

19. $f(x) = \sin(x + \pi)$

20. $h(x) = \cos(x - 3\pi)$

21. $g(x) = \sin\left(x + \frac{3\pi}{4}\right)$

22. $j(x) = \cos\left(x + \frac{\pi}{4}\right)$

23. Oceanography The depth d in feet of the water in a bay at any time is given by $d(t) = \frac{3}{2}\sin\left(\frac{5\pi}{31}t\right) + 23$, where t is the time in hours. Graph the depth of the water. What are the maximum and minimum depths of the water?

LINK

Medicine

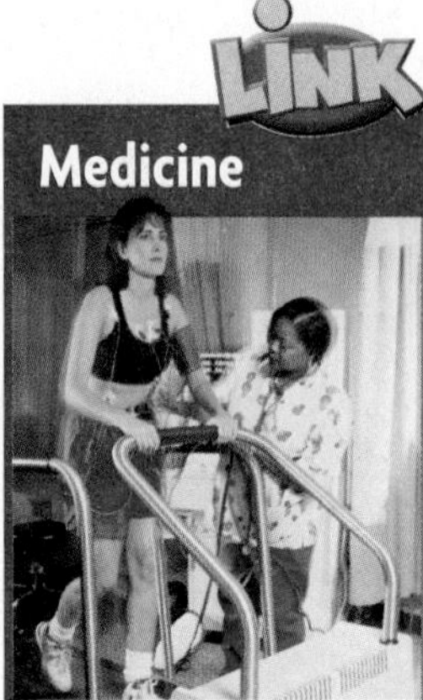

An EKG measures the electrical signals that control the rhythm of a beating heart. EKGs are used to diagnose and monitor heart disease.

24. Medicine The figure shows a normal adult electrocardiogram, known as an EKG. Each cycle in the EKG represents one heartbeat.

a. What is the period of one heartbeat?

b. The pulse rate is the number of beats in one minute. What is the pulse rate indicated by the EKG?

c. What is the frequency of the EKG?

d. How does the pulse rate relate to the frequency in hertz?

Adult EKG

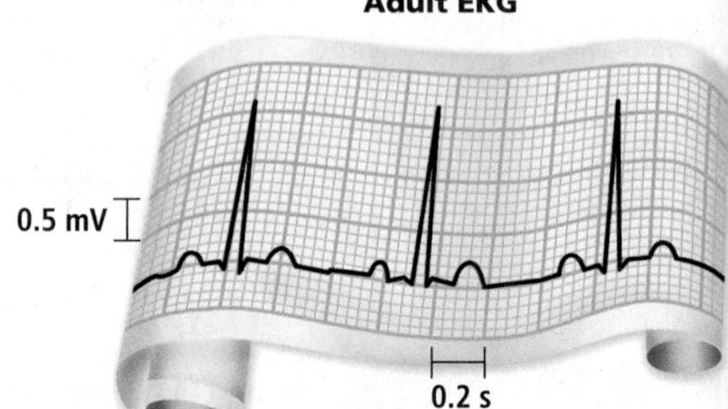

Determine the amplitude and period for each function. Then describe the transformation from its parent function.

25. $f(x) = \sin\left(x + \frac{\pi}{4}\right) - 1$

26. $h(x) = \frac{3}{4}\cos\frac{\pi}{4}x$

27. $h(x) = \cos(2\pi x) - 2$

28. $j(x) = -3\sin 3x$

Estimation Use a graph of sine or cosine to estimate each value.

29. $\sin 160°$

30. $\cos 50°$

31. $\sin 15°$

32. $\cos 95°$

Write both a sine and a cosine function for each set of conditions.

33. amplitude of 6, period of π

34. amplitude of $\frac{1}{4}$, phase shift of $\frac{2}{3}\pi$ left

Write both a sine and a cosine function that could be used to represent each graph.

35.

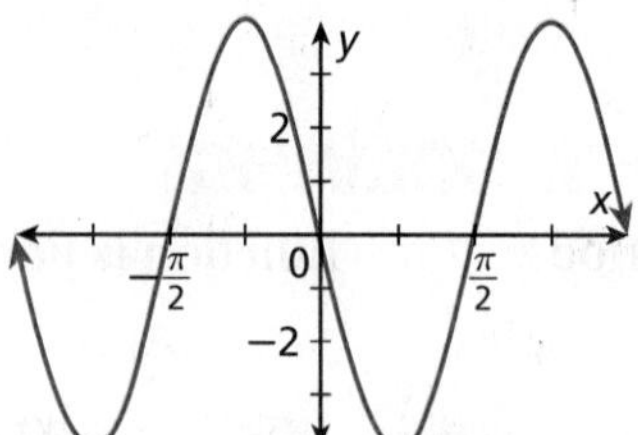

36.

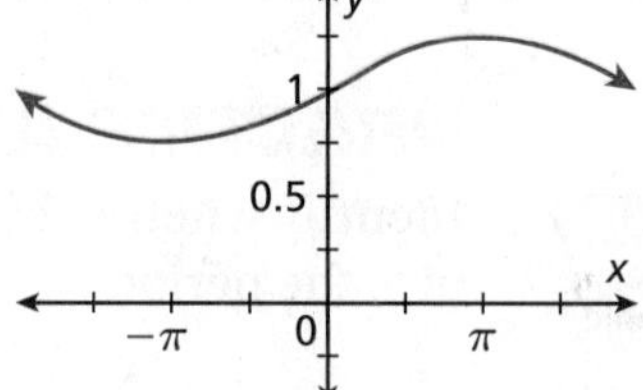

37. The tide in a bay has a maximum height of 3 m and a minimum height of 0 m. It takes 6.1 hours for the tide to go out and another 6.1 hours for it to come back in. The height of the tide h is modeled as a function of time t.

a. What are the period and amplitude of h? What are the maximum and minimum values?

b. Assume that high tide occurs at $t = 0$. What are $h(0)$ and $h(6.1)$?

c. Write h in the form $h(t) = a\cos bt + k$.

38. Critical Thinking Given the amplitude and period of a sine function, can you find its maximum and minimum values and their corresponding x-values? If not, what information do you need and how would you use it?

39. Write About It What happens to the period of $f(x) = \sin b\theta$ when $b > 1$? $b < 1$? Explain.

TEST PREP

40. Which trigonometric function best matches the graph?

Ⓐ $y = \frac{1}{2}\sin x$ Ⓒ $y = \frac{1}{2}\sin 2x$

Ⓑ $y = 2\sin x$ Ⓓ $y = 2\sin\frac{1}{2}x$

41. What is the amplitude for $y = -4\cos 3\pi x$?

Ⓕ -4 Ⓗ 4

Ⓖ 3 Ⓙ 3π

42. Based on the graphs, what is the relationship between f and g?

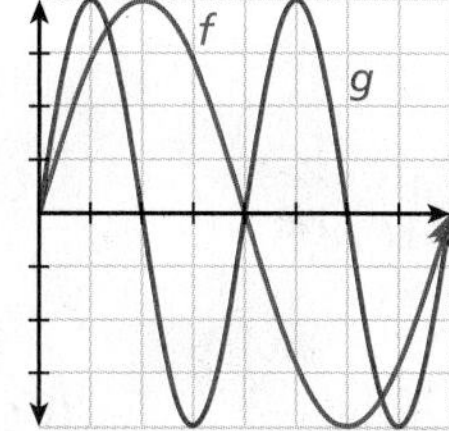

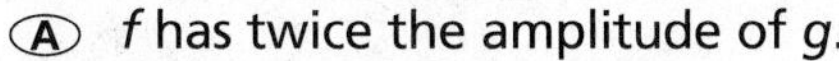
Ⓐ f has twice the amplitude of g.

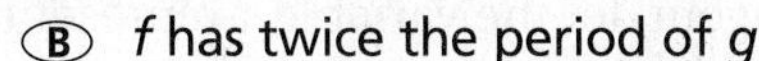
Ⓑ f has twice the period of g.

Ⓒ f has twice the frequency of g.

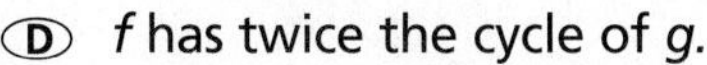
Ⓓ f has twice the cycle of g.

43. Short Response Using $y = \sin x$ as a guide, graph $y = -4\sin 2(x - \pi)$ on the interval $[0, 2\pi]$ and describe the transformations.

CHALLENGE AND EXTEND

44. Graph $f(x) = \text{Sin}^{-1} x$ and $g(x) = \text{Cos}^{-1} x$. (*Hint:* Use what you learned about graphs of inverse functions in a previous lesson and inverse trigonometric functions in a previous lesson.)

Consider the functions $f(\theta) = \frac{1}{2}\sin\theta$ and $g(\theta) = 2\cos\theta$ for $0° \le \theta \le 360°$.

45. On the same set of coordinate axes, graph $f(\theta)$ and $g(\theta)$.

46. What are the approximate coordinates of the points of intersection of $f(\theta)$ and $g(\theta)$?

47. When is $f(\theta) > g(\theta)$?

11-2 Graphs of Other Trigonometric Functions

CC.9-12.F.TF.5 Choose trigonometric functions to model periodic phenomena...* *Also* **CC.9-12.F.IF.5*, CC.9-12.F.IF.7*, CC.9-12.F.BF.3, CC.9-12.A.CED.2, CC.9-12.A.CED.3**

Objective
Recognize and graph trigonometric functions.

Why learn this?
You can use the graphs of reciprocal trigonometric functions to model rotating objects such as lights. (See Exercise 25.)

The tangent and cotangent functions can be graphed on the coordinate plane. The tangent function is undefined when $\theta = \frac{\pi}{2} + \pi n$, where n is an integer. The cotangent function is undefined when $\theta = \pi n$. These values are excluded from the domain and are represented by vertical asymptotes on the graph. Because tangent and cotangent have no maximum or minimum values, amplitude is undefined.

To graph tangent and cotangent, let the variable x represent the angle θ in standard position.

Characteristics of the Graphs of Tangent and Cotangent

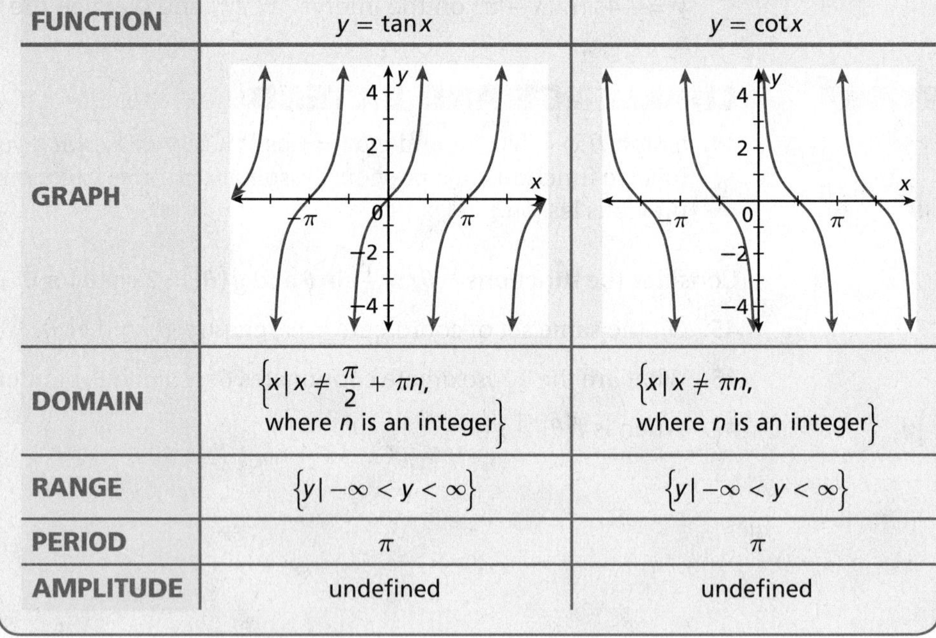

FUNCTION	$y = \tan x$	$y = \cot x$
GRAPH		
DOMAIN	$\left\{x \mid x \neq \frac{\pi}{2} + \pi n,\right.$ where n is an integer$\left.\right\}$	$\left\{x \mid x \neq \pi n,\right.$ where n is an integer$\left.\right\}$
RANGE	$\{y \mid -\infty < y < \infty\}$	$\{y \mid -\infty < y < \infty\}$
PERIOD	π	π
AMPLITUDE	undefined	undefined

Like sine and cosine, you can transform the tangent function.

Transformations of Tangent Graphs

For the graph of $y = a \tan bx$, where $a \neq 0$ and x is in radians,

- the period is $\frac{\pi}{|b|}$.
- the asymptotes are located at $x = \frac{\pi}{2|b|} + \frac{\pi n}{|b|}$, where n is an integer.

EXAMPLE 1 Transforming Tangent Functions

Using $f(x) = \tan x$ as a guide, graph $g(x) = \tan 2x$. Identify the period, x-intercepts, and asymptotes.

Step 1 Identify the period.

Because $b = 2$, the period is $\frac{\pi}{|b|} = \frac{\pi}{|2|} = \frac{\pi}{2}$.

Step 2 Identify the x-intercepts.

An x-intercept occurs at $x = 0$. Because the period is $\frac{\pi}{2}$, the x-intercepts occur at $\frac{\pi}{2}n$, where n is an integer.

Step 3 Identify the asymptotes.

Because $b = 2$, the asymptotes occur at $x = \frac{\pi}{2|2|} + \frac{\pi n}{|2|}$, or $x = \frac{\pi}{4} + \frac{\pi n}{2}$.

Step 4 Graph using all of the information about the function.

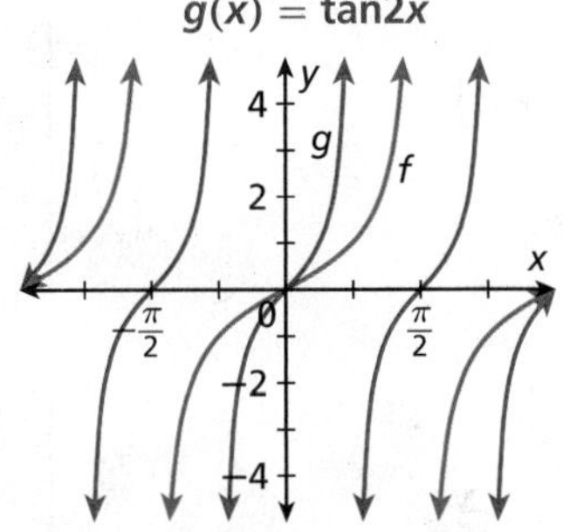

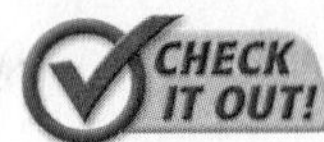

1. Using $f(x) = \tan x$ as a guide, graph $g(x) = 3\tan\frac{1}{2}x$. Identify the period, x-intercepts, and asymptotes.

Transformations of Cotangent Graphs

For the graph of $y = a\cot bx$, where $a \neq 0$ and x is in radians,

- the period is $\frac{\pi}{|b|}$.
- the asymptotes are located at $x = \frac{\pi n}{|b|}$, where n is an integer.

EXAMPLE 2 Graphing the Cotangent Function

Using $f(x) = \cot x$ as a guide, graph $g(x) = \cot 0.5x$. Identify the period, x-intercepts, and asymptotes.

Step 1 Identify the period.

Because $b = 0.5$, the period is $\frac{\pi}{|b|} = \frac{\pi}{|0.5|} = 2\pi$.

Step 2 Identify the x-intercepts.

An x-intercept occurs at $x = \pi$. Because the period is 2π, the x-intercepts occur at $x = \pi + 2\pi n$, where n is an integer.

Step 3 Identify the asymptotes.

Because $b = 0.5$, the asymptotes occur at

$$x = \frac{\pi n}{|0.5|} = 2\pi n.$$

Step 4 Graph using all of the information about the function.

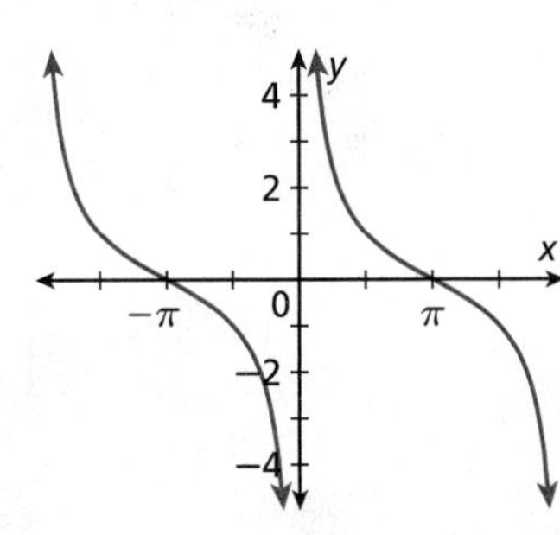

2. Using $f(x) = \cot x$ as a guide, graph $g(x) = -\cot 2x$. Identify the period, x-intercepts, and asymptotes.

Recall that $\sec \theta = \frac{1}{\cos \theta}$. So, secant is undefined where cosine equals zero and the graph will have vertical asymptotes at those locations. Secant will also have the same period as cosine. Sine and cosecant have a similar relationship. Because secant and cosecant have no absolute maxima or minima, amplitude is undefined.

Characteristics of the Graphs of Secant and Cosecant

FUNCTION	$y = \sec x$	$y = \csc x$
GRAPH		
DOMAIN	$\{x \mid x \neq \frac{\pi}{2} + \pi n$, where n is an integer$\}$	$\{x \mid x \neq \pi n$, where n is an integer$\}$
RANGE	$\{y \mid y \leq -1$, or $y \geq 1\}$	$\{y \mid y \leq -1$, or $y \geq 1\}$
PERIOD	2π	2π
AMPLITUDE	undefined	undefined

You can graph transformations of secant and cosecant by using what you learned in the previous lesson about transformations of graphs of cosine and sine.

EXAMPLE 3 Graphing Secant and Cosecant Functions

Using $f(x) = \cos x$ as a guide, graph $g(x) = \sec 2x$. Identify the period and asymptotes.

Step 1 Identify the period.

Because $\sec 2x$ is the reciprocal of $\cos 2x$, the graphs will have the same period.

Because $b = 2$ for $\cos 2x$, the period is $\frac{2\pi}{|b|} = \frac{2\pi}{|2|} = \pi$.

Step 2 Identify the asymptotes.

Because the period is π, the asymptotes occur at $x = \frac{\pi}{2|2|} + \frac{\pi}{|2|}n = \frac{\pi}{4} + \frac{\pi}{2}n$, where n is an integer.

Step 3 Graph using all of the information about the function.

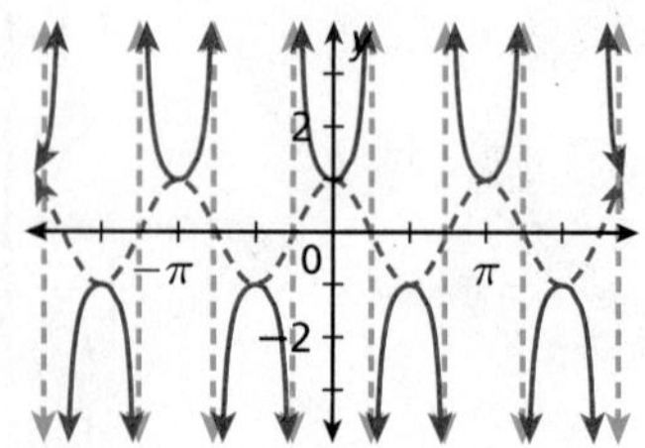

3. Using $f(x) = \sin x$ as a guide, graph $g(x) = 2 \csc x$. Identify the period and asymptotes.

THINK AND DISCUSS

1. **EXPLAIN** why $f(x) = \sin x$ can be used to graph $g(x) = \csc x$.
2. **EXPLAIN** how the zeros of the cosine function relate to the vertical asymptotes of the graph of the tangent function.

3. **GET ORGANIZED** Copy and complete the graphic organizer.

Function	Zeros	Asymptotes	Period
$y = \sec x$			
$y = \csc x$			
$y = \cot x$			
$y = \tan x$			

11-2 Exercises

GUIDED PRACTICE

SEE EXAMPLE 1

Using $f(x) = \tan x$ as a guide, graph each function. Identify the period, x-intercepts, and asymptotes.

1. $k(x) = 2\tan(3x)$
2. $g(x) = \tan\frac{1}{4}x$
3. $h(x) = \tan 2\pi x$

SEE EXAMPLE 2

Using $f(x) = \cot x$ as a guide, graph each function. Identify the period, x-intercepts, and asymptotes.

4. $j(x) = 0.25\cot x$
5. $p(x) = \cot 2x$
6. $g(x) = \frac{3}{2}\cot x$

SEE EXAMPLE 3

Using $f(x) = \cos x$ or $f(x) = \sin x$ as a guide, graph each function. Identify the period and asymptotes.

7. $g(x) = \frac{1}{2}\sec x$
8. $q(x) = \sec 4x$
9. $h(x) = 3\csc x$

PRACTICE AND PROBLEM SOLVING

Independent Practice

For Exercises	See Example
10–13	1
14–16	2
17–19	3

Extra Practice

See Extra Practice for more Skills Practice and Applications Practice exercises.

Using $f(x) = \tan x$ as a guide, graph each function. Identify the period, x-intercepts, and asymptotes.

10. $p(x) = \tan\frac{3}{2}x$
11. $g(x) = \tan\left(x + \frac{\pi}{4}\right)$
12. $h(x) = \frac{1}{2}\tan 4x$
13. $j(x) = -2\tan\frac{\pi}{2}x$

Using $f(x) = \cot x$ as a guide, graph each function. Identify the period, x-intercepts, and asymptotes.

14. $h(x) = 4\cot x$
15. $g(x) = \cot\frac{1}{4}x$
16. $j(x) = 0.1\cot x$

Using $f(x) = \cos x$ or $f(x) = \sin x$ as a guide, graph each function. Identify the period and asymptotes.

17. $g(x) = -\sec x$
18. $k(x) = \frac{1}{2}\csc x$
19. $h(x) = \csc(-x)$

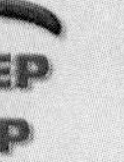

20. Between 1:00 P.M. ($t = 1$) and 6:00 P.M. ($t = 6$), the height (in meters) of the tide in a bay is modeled by $h(t) = 0.4 \csc \frac{5\pi}{31} t$.

a. Graph the function for the range $1 \leq t \leq 6$.

b. At what time does low tide occur?

c. What is the height of the tide at low tide?

d. What is the maximum height of the tide during this time span? When does this occur?

Find four values for which each function is undefined.

21. $f(\theta) = \tan \theta$ **22.** $g(\theta) = \cot \theta$ **23.** $h(\theta) = \sec \theta$ **24.** $j(\theta) = \csc \theta$

25. Law Enforcement A police car is parked on the side of the road next to a building. The flashing light on the car is 6 feet from the wall and completes one full rotation every 3 seconds. As the light rotates, it shines on the wall. The equation representing the distance a in feet is $a(t) = 6 \sec\left(\frac{2}{3}\pi t\right)$.

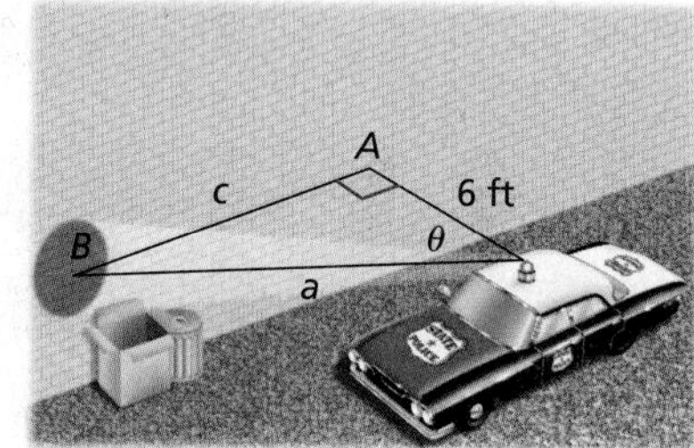

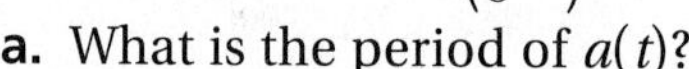

a. What is the period of $a(t)$?

b. Graph the function for $0 \leq t \leq 3$.

c. Critical Thinking Identify the location of any asymptotes. What do the asymptotes represent?

LINK
Math History

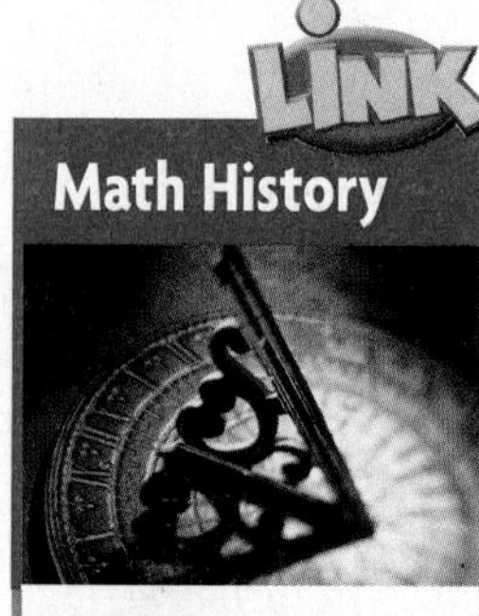

The Greek gnomon was a tall staff, but gnomon is also the part of a sundial that casts a shadow. Based on the variation of shadows at high noon, a gnomon can be used to determine the day of the year, in addition to the time of day.

26. Math History The ancient Greeks used a *gnomon,* a type of tall staff, to tell the time of day based on the lengths of shadows and the altitude θ of the sun above the horizon.

a. Use the figure to write a cotangent function that can be used to find the length of the shadow s in terms of the height of the gnomon h and the angle θ.

b. Graph your answer to part **a** for a gnomon of height 6 ft.

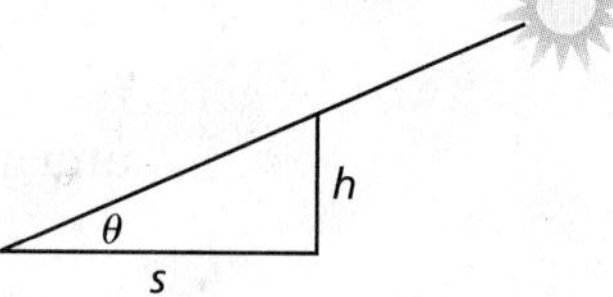

Complete the table by labeling each function as increasing or decreasing.

		$0 < x < \frac{\pi}{2}$	$\frac{\pi}{2} < x < \pi$	$\pi < x < \frac{3\pi}{2}$	$\frac{3\pi}{2} < x < 2\pi$
27.	$\sin x$	■	■	■	■
28.	$\csc x$	■	■	■	■
29.	$\cos x$	■	■	■	■
30.	$\sec x$	■	■	■	■
31.	$\tan x$	■	■	■	■
32.	$\cot x$	■	■	■	■

33. Critical Thinking Based on the table above, what do you observe about the increasing/decreasing relationship between reciprocal pairs of trigonometric functions?

34. **Critical Thinking** How do the signs (whether a function is positive or negative) of reciprocal pairs of trigonometric functions relate?

35. **Write About It** Describe how to graph $f(x) = 3\sec 4x$ by using the graph of $g(x) = 3\cos 4x$.

36. Which is NOT in the domain of $y = \cot x$?

Ⓐ $-\frac{\pi}{2}$ Ⓑ 0 Ⓒ $\frac{\pi}{2}$ Ⓓ $\frac{3\pi}{2}$

37. What is the range of $f(x) = 3\csc 2\theta$?

Ⓕ $\{y \mid y \le -1 \text{ or } y \ge 1\}$ Ⓗ $\{y \mid y \le -2 \text{ or } y \ge 2\}$

Ⓖ $\{y \mid y \le -3 \text{ or } y \ge 3\}$ Ⓙ $\{y \mid y \le -\frac{1}{2} \text{ or } y \ge \frac{1}{2}\}$

38. Which could be the equation of the graph?

Ⓐ $y = \tan 2x$ Ⓒ $y = 2\tan x$

Ⓑ $y = \cot 2x$ Ⓓ $y = 2\cot x$

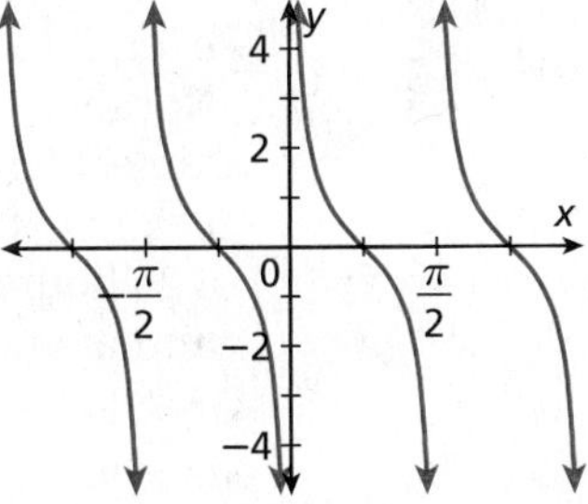

39. What is the period of $y = \tan\frac{1}{2}x$?

Ⓕ $\frac{\pi}{2}$ Ⓗ 2π

Ⓖ π Ⓙ 4π

40. The graph of which function has a period of $\frac{2\pi}{3}$ and an asymptote at $x = \frac{\pi}{2}$?

Ⓐ $y = \sec\frac{3}{2}x$ Ⓒ $y = \csc\frac{3}{2}x$

Ⓑ $y = \sec 3x$ Ⓓ $y = \csc 3x$

CHALLENGE AND EXTEND

Describe the period, local maximum and minimum values, and phase shift.

41. $f(x) = 4 - 3\csc \pi(x - 1)$ 42. $g(x) = 4\cot\frac{1}{2}\left(x - \frac{\pi}{2}\right)$ 43. $h(x) = 0.5\sec 2\left(x + \frac{\pi}{4}\right)$

44. $f(x) = 9 + 2\tan 3(x + \pi)$ 45. $g(x) = 0.62 + 0.76\sec x$ 46. $h(x) = \csc\frac{\pi}{2}\left(x + \frac{5}{7}\right)$

Graph each trigonometric function and its inverse. Identify the domain and range of the corresponding inverse function.

47. $f(x) = \text{Sec}\, x$ for $0 \le x \le \pi$ and $x \ne \frac{\pi}{2}$ 48. $f(x) = \text{Tan}\, x$ for $-\frac{\pi}{2} < x < \frac{\pi}{2}$

49. $g(x) = \text{Csc}\, x$ for $-\frac{\pi}{2} \le x \le \frac{\pi}{2}$ and $x \ne 0$ 50. $g(x) = \text{Cot}\, x$ for $0 < x < \pi$

CHAPTER 11

MULTI-STEP TEST PREP

SECTION 11A

MATHEMATICAL PRACTICES **Model with mathematics.**

Trigonometric Graphs

The Tide Is Turning Tides are caused by several factors, but the main factor is the gravitational pull of the Moon. As the Moon revolves around Earth, the Moon causes large bodies of water to swell toward it resulting in rising and falling tides. You can use trigonometric functions to develop a model of a simplified tide.

1. The highest tides in the world have been measured at the Bay of Fundy, in Nova Scotia, Canada. As shown in the table, high tides in the bay can reach heights of 16.3 m. Assume that it takes 6.25 hours for the tide to completely retreat and then another 6.25 hours for the tide to come back in. Write a periodic function based on the cosine function that models the height of the tide over time.

Tides at the Bay of Fundy

	Time (h)	Height (m)
High Tide	$t = 0$	16.3
Low Tide	$t = 6.25$	0

2. What are the amplitude, period, maximum and minimum values, and phase shift of the function?

3. Graph the function.

4. At time $t = 0$, the tide is at 16.3 m. What is the tide's height after 3 hours? after 9 hours?

5. Will a high tide occur at the same time each day at the Bay of Fundy? Why or why not?

6. It is possible to write a function that models the height of the tide based on the sine function. What is the function? What is the phase shift?

READY TO GO ON?

CHAPTER 11

SECTION 11A

Quiz for Lessons 11-1 Through 11-2

11-1 Graphs of Sine and Cosine

Identify whether each function is periodic. If the function is periodic, give the period.

1. 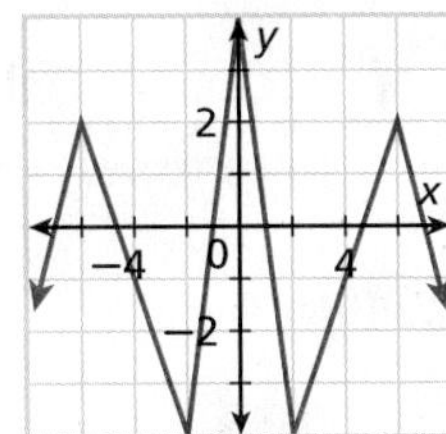

2. 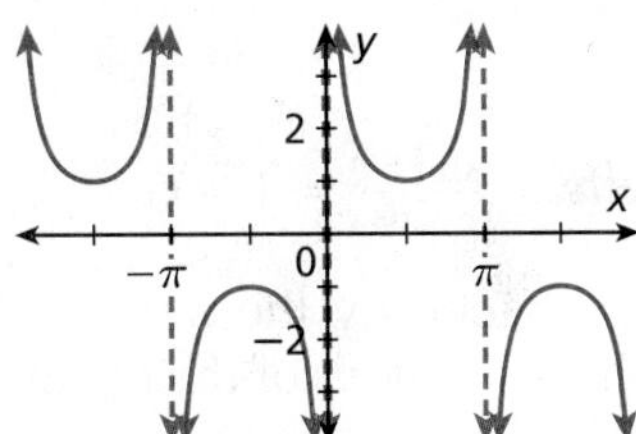

3. 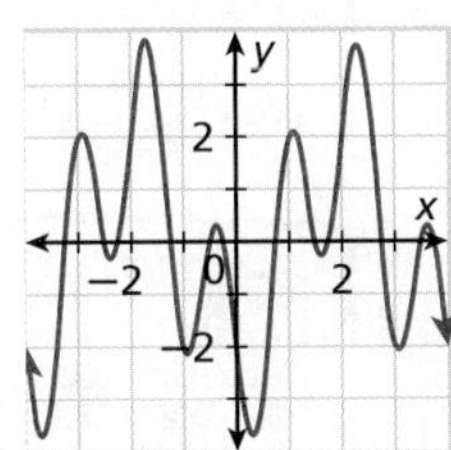

4. 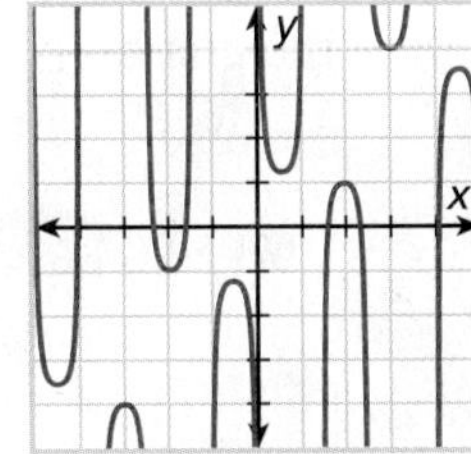

Using $f(x) = \sin x$ or $f(x) = \cos x$ as a guide, graph each function. Identify the amplitude and period.

5. $f(x) = \sin 4x$

6. $g(x) = -3 \sin x$

7. $h(x) = 0.25 \cos \pi x$

Using $f(x) = \sin x$ or $f(x) = \cos x$ as a guide, graph each function. Identify the x-intercepts and phase shift.

8. $f(x) = \cos\left(x - \frac{3\pi}{2}\right)$

9. $g(x) = \sin\left(x - \frac{3\pi}{4}\right)$

10. $h(x) = \cos\left(x + \frac{5\pi}{4}\right)$

11. The torque τ applied to a bolt is given by $\tau(x) = Fr \sin x$, where r is the length of the wrench in meters, F is the applied force in newtons, and x is the angle between F and r in radians. Graph the torque for a 0.5 meter wrench and a force of 500 newtons for $0 \le x \le \frac{\pi}{2}$. What is the torque for an angle of $\frac{\pi}{3}$?

11-2 Graphs of Other Trigonometric Functions

Using $f(x) = \tan x$ as a guide, graph each function. Identify the period, x-intercepts, and asymptotes.

12. $f(x) = \frac{1}{2} \tan 4x$

13. $g(x) = -2 \tan \frac{1}{2}x$

14. $h(x) = \tan \frac{1}{2}\pi x$

Using $f(x) = \cot x$ as a guide, graph each function. Identify the period, x-intercepts, and asymptotes.

15. $g(x) = -2 \cot x$

16. $h(x) = \cot 0.5x$

17. $j(x) = \cot 4x$

Using $f(x) = \cos x$ or $f(x) = \sin x$ as a guide, graph each function. Identify the period and asymptotes.

18. $f(x) = -2 \sec x$

19. $g(x) = \frac{1}{4} \csc x$

20. $h(x) = \sec \pi x$

Graph Trigonometric Identities

You can use a graphing calculator to compare graphs and make conjectures about trigonometric identities.

Use with Fundamental Trigonometric Identities

Use appropriate tools strategically.

CC.9-12.F.TF.8 Prove the Pythagorean identity $\sin^2(\theta) + \cos^2(\theta) = 1$ and use it to find $\sin(\theta)$, $\cos(\theta)$, or $\tan(\theta)$...

Determine whether $\frac{\sin^2 x}{1 - \cos x} = 1 + \cos x$ is a possible identity.

If the equation is an identity, there should be no visible difference in the graphs of the left- and right-hand sides of the equation.

1. Enter $\frac{\sin^2 x}{1 - \cos x}$ as **Y1** and $1 + \cos x$ as **Y2**. For **Y2**, select the mode represented by the 0 with a line through it. This will help you see the path of the graph.

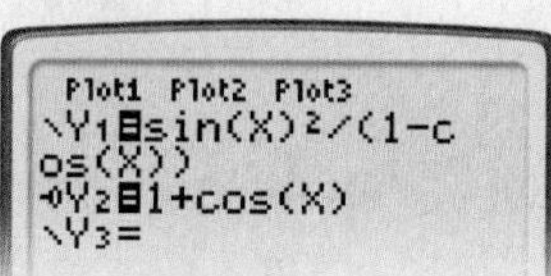

2. Set the graphing window by using ZOOM and **7:ZTrig.**

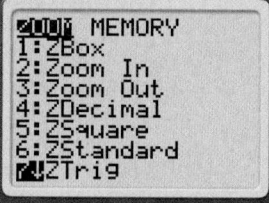

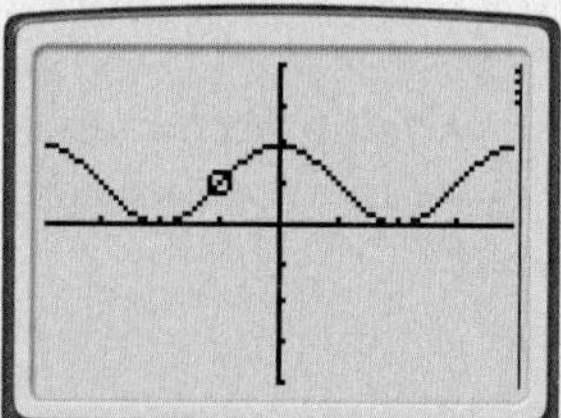

3. Watch the calculator as the graphs are generated. As **Y2** is being graphed, a circle will move along the path of the graph.

4. The path of the circle, **Y2**, traced the graph of **Y1**. The graphs appear to be the same.

   Because the graphs appear to be identical, $\frac{\sin^2 x}{1 - \cos x} = 1 + \cos x$ is most likely an identity. Use algebra to confirm.

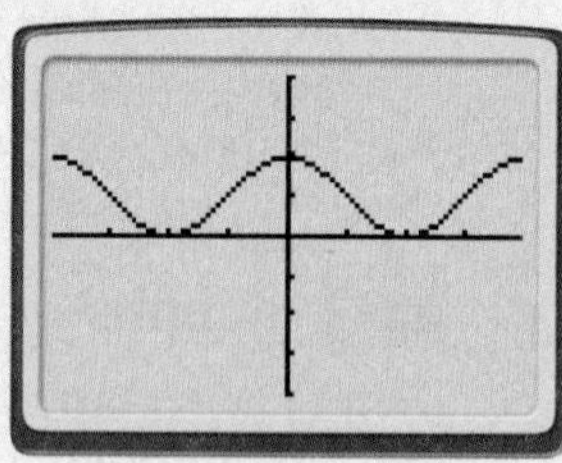

Try This

1. **Make a Conjecture** Determine whether $\sec x - \tan x \sin x = \cos x$ is a possible identity.
2. Prove or disprove your answer to Problem 1 by using algebra.
3. **Make a Conjecture** Determine whether $\frac{1 + \tan x}{1 + \cot x} = \tan x$ is a possible identity.
4. Prove or disprove your answer to Problem 3 by using algebra.

Angle Relationships

Angle relationships in circles and polygons can be used to solve problems.

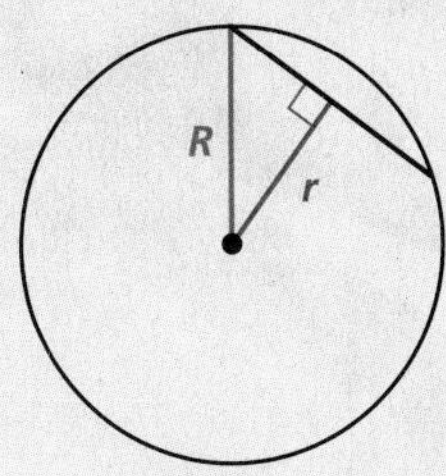

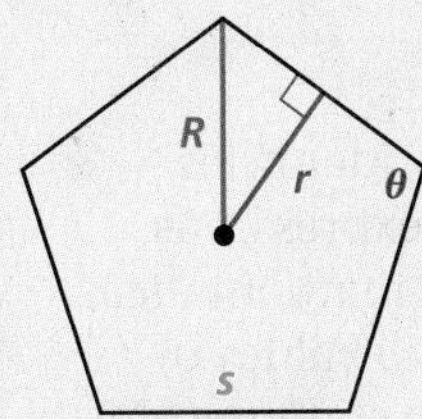

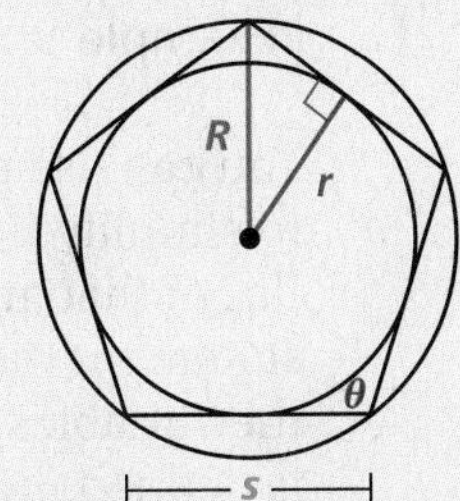

The figures show regular polygons. A **regular polygon** has sides of equal length and equal interior angles. Here are some useful relationships for regular polygons.

R bisects θ. $\qquad \theta = \left(\frac{n-2}{n}\right)180°$ $\qquad r = R\cos\left(\frac{180°}{n}\right)$ $\qquad s = 2r\tan\left(\frac{180°}{n}\right) = 2R\sin\left(\frac{180°}{n}\right)$

Example

A regular octagon is inscribed in a circle with a radius of 5 cm. What is the length of each side of the octagon?

Make a sketch of the problem.

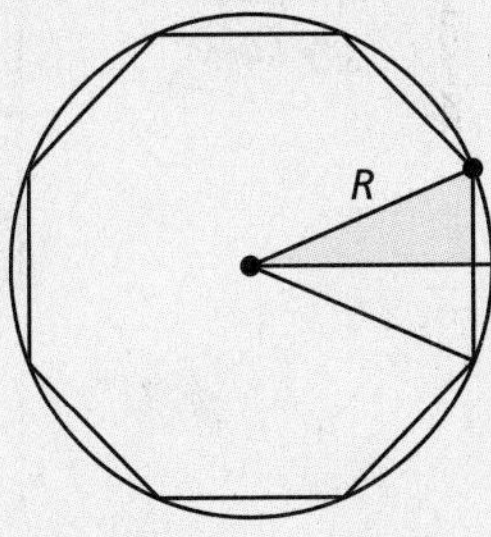

$s = 2R\sin\left(\frac{180°}{n}\right)$ *Choose a formula relating the radius of the circumscribed circle to the side length of the polygon.*

$s = 2(5)\sin\left(\frac{180°}{8}\right)$ *Substitute 5 for R and 8 for n.*

$s = 10\sin 22.5° \approx 3.83$ cm

Try This

Solve each problem. Round each answer to the nearest hundredth.

1. A circle is inscribed in an equilateral triangle with 8 in. sides. What is the diameter of the circle? What is the altitude of the triangle?
2. An isosceles right triangle is inscribed in a semicircle with a radius of 20 cm. What are the lengths of the three sides of the triangle?
3. The interior angles of a regular polygon each measure 150°. If this polygon is inscribed in a circle with a 10 in. diameter, how long is each side of the polygon?
4. Use the figure to find the side lengths of all three shaded triangles if the diameter of the circle is 10 cm. Round to the nearest hundredth if necessary.

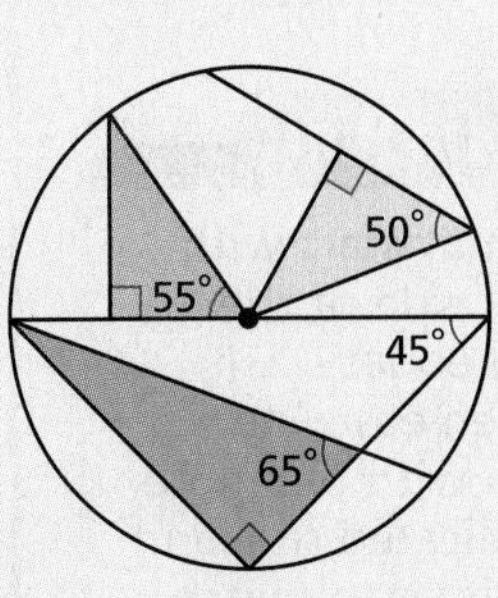

11-3 Fundamental Trigonometric Identities

CC.9-12.F.TF.8 Prove the Pythagorean identity $\sin^2(\theta) + \cos^2(\theta) = 1$ and use it to find $\sin(\theta)$, $\cos(\theta)$, or $\tan(\theta)$...

Objective
Use fundamental trigonometric identities to simplify and rewrite expressions and to verify other identities.

Who uses this?
Ski supply manufacturers can use trigonometric identities to determine the type of wax to use on skis. (See Example 3.)

You can use trigonometric identities to simplify trigonometric expressions. Recall that an identity is a mathematical statement that is true for all values of the variables for which the statement is defined.

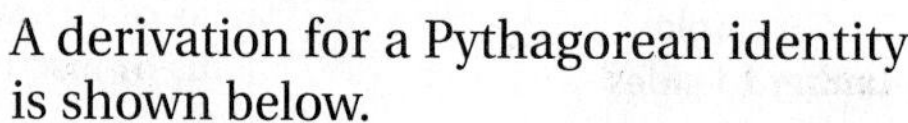

A derivation for a Pythagorean identity is shown below.

$x^2 + y^2 = r^2$	*Pythagorean Theorem*
$\frac{x^2}{r^2} + \frac{y^2}{r^2} = 1$	*Divide both sides by r^2.*
$\cos^2\theta + \sin^2\theta = 1$	*Substitute $\cos\theta$ for $\frac{x}{r}$ and $\sin\theta$ for $\frac{y}{r}$.*

Fundamental Trigonometric Identities

Reciprocal Identities	Tangent and Cotangent Ratio Identities	Pythagorean Identities	Negative-Angle Identities
$\csc\theta = \frac{1}{\sin\theta}$	$\tan\theta = \frac{\sin\theta}{\cos\theta}$	$\cos^2\theta + \sin^2\theta = 1$	$\sin(-\theta) = -\sin\theta$
$\sec\theta = \frac{1}{\cos\theta}$	$\cot\theta = \frac{\cos\theta}{\sin\theta}$	$1 + \tan^2\theta = \sec^2\theta$	$\cos(-\theta) = \cos\theta$
$\cot\theta = \frac{1}{\tan\theta}$		$\cot^2\theta + 1 = \csc^2\theta$	$\tan(-\theta) = -\tan\theta$

To prove that an equation is an identity, alter one side of the equation until it is the same as the other side. Justify your steps by using the fundamental identities.

EXAMPLE  **1**

Proving Trigonometric Identities

Helpful Hint
You may start with either side of the given equation. It is often easier to begin with the more complicated side and simplify it to match the simpler side.

Prove each trigonometric identity.

A $\sec\theta = \csc\theta\tan\theta$

$\sec\theta = \csc\theta\tan\theta$	*Choose the right-hand side to modify.*
$= \left(\frac{1}{\sin\theta}\right)\left(\frac{\sin\theta}{\cos\theta}\right)$	*Reciprocal and ratio identities*
$= \frac{1}{\cos\theta}$	*Simplify.*
$= \sec\theta$	*Reciprocal identity*

Duomo/CORBIS

Prove each trigonometric identity.

B $\csc(-\theta) = -\csc\theta$

$\csc(-\theta) = -\csc\theta$	*Choose the left-hand side to modify.*
$\dfrac{1}{\sin(-\theta)} =$	*Reciprocal identity*
$\dfrac{1}{-\sin\theta} =$	*Negative-angle identity*
$-\left(\dfrac{1}{\sin\theta}\right) = -\csc\theta$	
$-\csc\theta = -\csc\theta$	*Reciprocal identity*

Prove each trigonometric identity.

1a. $\sin\theta\cot\theta = \cos\theta$ **1b.** $1 - \sec(-\theta) = 1 - \sec\theta$

You can use the fundamental trigonometric identities to simplify expressions.

EXAMPLE 2 Using Trigonometric Identities to Rewrite Trigonometric Expressions

Rewrite each expression in terms of cos θ, and simplify.

A $\dfrac{\sin^2\theta}{1-\cos\theta}$

$\dfrac{1-\cos^2\theta}{1-\cos\theta}$	*Pythagorean identity*
$\dfrac{(1+\cos\theta)(1-\cos\theta)}{1-\cos\theta}$	*Factor the difference of two squares.*
$\dfrac{(1+\cos\theta)\cancel{(1-\cos\theta)}}{\cancel{1-\cos\theta}}$	*Simplify.*
$1+\cos\theta$	

B $\sec\theta - \tan\theta\sin\theta$

$\dfrac{1}{\cos\theta} - \left(\dfrac{\sin\theta}{\cos\theta}\right)\cdot\sin\theta$	*Substitute.*
$\dfrac{1}{\cos\theta} - \dfrac{\sin^2\theta}{\cos\theta}$	*Multiply.*
$\dfrac{1-\sin^2\theta}{\cos\theta}$	*Subtract fractions.*
$\dfrac{\cos^2\theta}{\cos\theta}$	*Pythagorean identity*
$\cos\theta$	*Simplify.*

Helpful Hint

If you get stuck, try converting all of the trigonometric functions into sine and cosine functions.

Rewrite each expression in terms of sin θ, and simplify.

2a. $\dfrac{\cos^2\theta}{1-\sin\theta}$ **2b.** $\cot^2\theta$

Student to Student — *Graphing to Check for Equivalent Expressions*

Julia Zaragoza
Oak Ridge
High School

I like to use a graphing calculator to check for equivalent expressions.

For Example 2A, enter $y = \dfrac{\sin^2\theta}{(1-\cos\theta)}$ *and* $y = 1 + \cos\theta$*. Graph both functions in the same viewing window.*

The graphs appear to coincide, so the expressions are most likely equivalent.

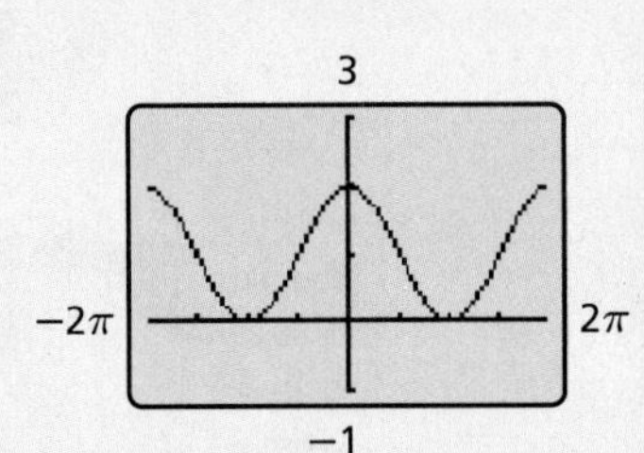

EXAMPLE 3 Sports Application

A ski supply company is testing the friction of a new ski wax by placing a waxed wood block on an inclined plane of wet snow. The incline plane is slowly raised until the wood block begins to slide.

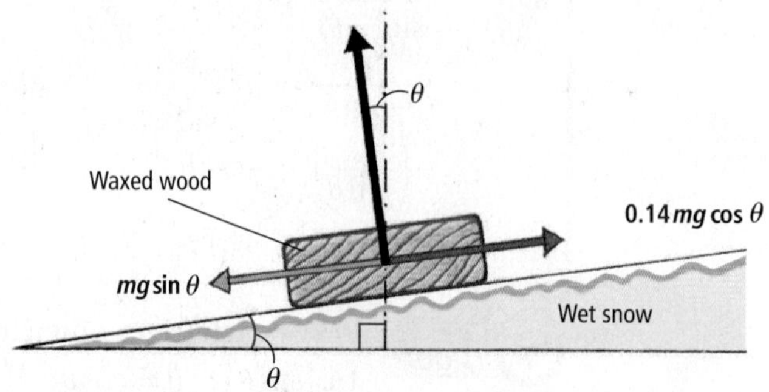

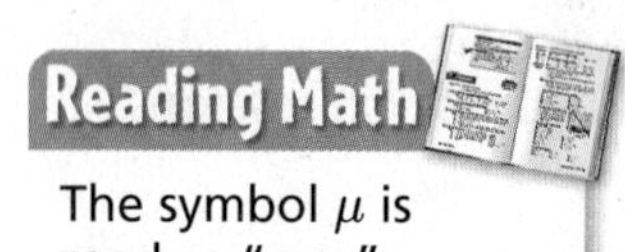

The symbol μ is read as "mu."

At the instant the block starts to slide, the component of the weight of the block parallel to the incline, $mg\sin\theta$, and the resistive force of friction, $\mu mg\cos\theta$, are equal. μ is the coefficient of friction. At what angle will the block start to move if $\mu = 0.14$?

Set the expression for the weight component equal to the expression for the force of friction.

$mg\sin\theta = \mu mg\cos\theta$

$\sin\theta = \mu\cos\theta$	*Divide both sides by mg.*
$\sin\theta = 0.14\cos\theta$	*Substitute 0.14 for μ.*
$\dfrac{\sin\theta}{\cos\theta} = 0.14$	*Divide both sides by $\cos\theta$.*
$\tan\theta = 0.14$	*Ratio identity*
$\theta \approx 8°$	*Evaluate inverse tangent.*

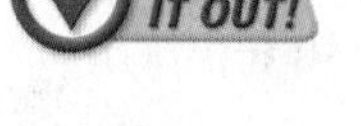

The wood block will start to move when the wet snow incline is raised to an angle of about 8°.

CHECK IT OUT!

3. Use the equation $mg\sin\theta = \mu mg\cos\theta$ to determine the angle at which a waxed wood block on a wood incline with $\mu = 0.4$ begins to slide.

THINK AND DISCUSS

1. **DESCRIBE** how you prove that an equation is an identity.
2. **EXPLAIN** which identity can be used to prove that $(1 - \cos\theta)(1 + \cos\theta) = \sin^2\theta$.

3. **GET ORGANIZED** Copy and complete the graphic organizer by writing the three Pythagorean identities.

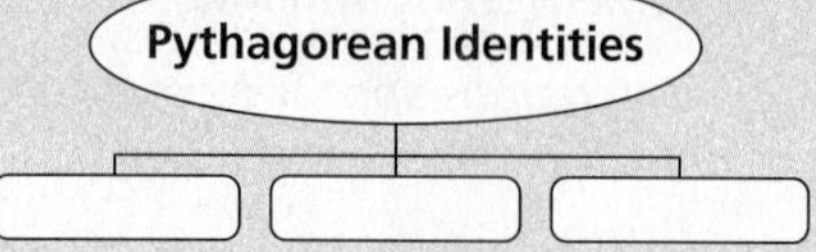

11-3 Exercises

Learn It Online
Homework Help Online
Parent Resources Online

GUIDED PRACTICE

SEE EXAMPLE 1

Prove each trigonometric identity.

1. $\sin\theta\sec\theta = \tan\theta$
2. $\cot(-\theta) = -\cot\theta$
3. $\cos^2\theta\left(\sec^2\theta - 1\right) = \sin^2\theta$

SEE EXAMPLE 2

Rewrite each expression in terms of $\cos\theta$, and simplify.

4. $\csc\theta\tan\theta$
5. $\left(1 + \sec^2\theta\right)\left(1 - \sin^2\theta\right)$
6. $\sin^2\theta + \cos^2\theta + \tan^2\theta$

SEE EXAMPLE 3

7. **Physics** Use the equation $mg\sin\theta = \mu mg\cos\theta$ to determine the angle at which a glass-top table can be tilted before a glass plate on the table begins to slide. Assume $\mu = 0.94$.

PRACTICE AND PROBLEM SOLVING

Independent Practice	
For Exercises	See Example
8–11	1
12–15	2
16	3

Extra Practice

See Extra Practice for more Skills Practice and Applications Practice exercises.

Prove each trigonometric identity.

8. $\sec\theta\cot\theta = \csc\theta$
9. $\dfrac{\sin\theta - \cos\theta}{\sin\theta} = 1 - \cot\theta$
10. $\tan\theta\sin\theta = \sec\theta - \cos\theta$
11. $\sec^2\theta\left(1 - \cos^2\theta\right) = \tan^2\theta$

Rewrite each expression in terms of $\sin\theta$, and simplify.

12. $\dfrac{\cos^2\theta}{1 + \sin\theta}$
13. $\dfrac{\tan\theta}{\cot\theta}$
14. $\cos\theta\cot\theta + \sin\theta$
15. $\dfrac{\sec^2\theta - 1}{1 + \tan^2\theta}$

16. **Physics** Use the equation $mg\sin\theta = \mu mg\cos\theta$ to determine the steepest slope of the street shown on which a car with rubber tires can park without sliding.

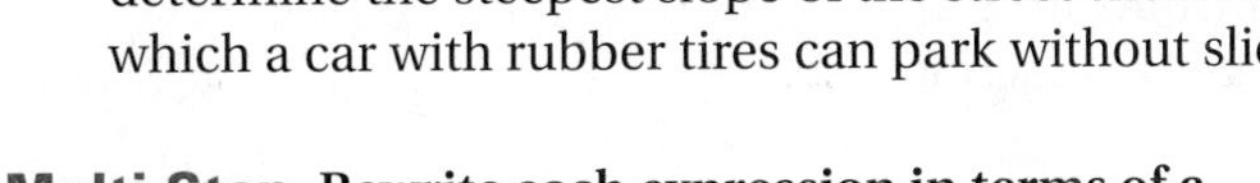

Multi-Step **Rewrite each expression in terms of a single trigonometric function.**

17. $\tan\theta\cot\theta$
18. $\sin\theta\cot\theta\tan\theta$
19. $\cos\theta + \sin\theta\tan\theta$
20. $\sin\theta\csc\theta - \cos^2\theta$
21. $\cos^2\theta\sec\theta\csc\theta$
22. $\cos\theta\left(\tan^2\theta + 1\right)$
23. $\csc\theta\left(1 - \cos^2\theta\right)$
24. $\csc\theta\cos\theta\tan\theta$
25. $\dfrac{\sin\theta}{1 - \cos^2\theta}$
26. $\dfrac{\sin^2\theta}{1 - \cos^2\theta}$
27. $\dfrac{\tan\theta}{\sin\theta\sec\theta}$
28. $\dfrac{\cos\theta}{\sin\theta\cot\theta}$
29. $\tan\theta\left(\tan\theta + \cot\theta\right)$
30. $\sin^2\theta + \cos^2\theta + \cot^2\theta$
31. $\sin^2\theta\sec\theta\csc\theta$

Verify each identity.

32. $\dfrac{\cos\theta - 1}{\cos^2\theta} = \sec\theta - \sec^2\theta$
33. $\sin^2\theta\left(\csc^2\theta - 1\right) = \cos^2\theta$
34. $\tan\theta + \cot\theta = \sec\theta\csc\theta$
35. $\dfrac{\cos\theta}{1 - \sin^2\theta} = \sec\theta$
36. $\dfrac{1 - \cos^2\theta}{\tan\theta} = \sin\theta\cos\theta$
37. $\dfrac{\csc^2\theta}{1 + \tan^2\theta} = \cot^2\theta$

Prove each fundamental identity without using any of the other fundamental identities. (*Hint:* Use the trigonometric ratios with *x*, *y*, and *r*.)

38. $\tan\theta = \dfrac{\sin\theta}{\cos\theta}$
39. $\cot\theta = \dfrac{\cos\theta}{\sin\theta}$
40. $1 + \cot^2\theta = \csc^2\theta$
41. $\csc\theta = \dfrac{1}{\sin\theta}$
42. $\sec\theta = \dfrac{1}{\cos\theta}$
43. $1 + \tan^2\theta = \sec^2\theta$

44. The displacement y of a mass attached to a spring is modeled by $y(t) = 5 \sin t$, where t is the time in seconds. The displacement z of another mass attached to a spring is modeled by $z(t) = 2.6 \cos t$.

a. The two masses are set in motion at $t = 0$. When do the masses have the same displacement for the first time?

b. What is the displacement at this time?

c. At what other times will the masses have the same displacement?

Graphing Calculator Use a graphing calculator to determine whether each of the following equations represents an identity. (*Hint:* You may need to rewrite the equations in terms of sine, cosine, and tangent.)

45. $(\csc\theta - 1)(\csc\theta + 1) = \tan^2\theta$

46. $\sec\theta - \cos\theta = \sin\theta$

47. $\cos\theta\left(\sec\theta + \cos\theta\csc^2\theta\right) = \csc^2\theta$

48. $\cot\theta(\cos\theta + \sin\theta\tan\theta) = \csc\theta$

49. $\cos\theta = 0.99\cos\theta$

50. $\sin\theta\cos\theta = \tan\theta - \tan\theta\sin^2\theta$

51. Physics A conical pendulum is created by a pendulum that travels in a circle rather than side to side and traces out the shape of a cone. The radius r of the base of the cone is given by the formula $r = \frac{g\tan\theta}{\omega^2}$, where g represents the force of gravity and ω represents the angular velocity of the pendulum.

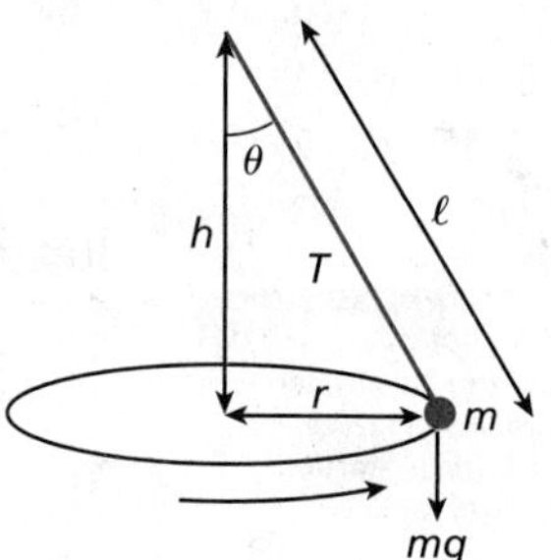

a. Use $\omega = \sqrt{\frac{g}{\ell\cos\theta}}$ and fundamental trigonometric identities to rewrite the formula for the radius.

b. Find a formula for ℓ in terms of g, ω, and a single trigonometric function.

Critical Thinking A function is called odd if $f(-x) = -f(x)$ and even if $f(-x) = f(x)$.

52. Which of the six trigonometric functions are odd? Which are even?

53. What distinguishes the graph of an odd function from an even function or a function that is neither odd nor even?

54. Determine whether the following functions are odd, even, or neither.

a.

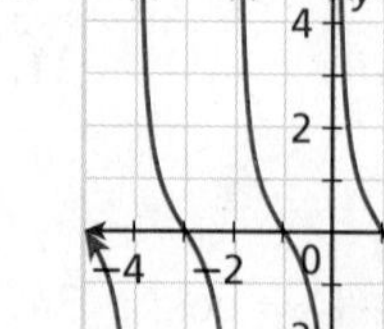

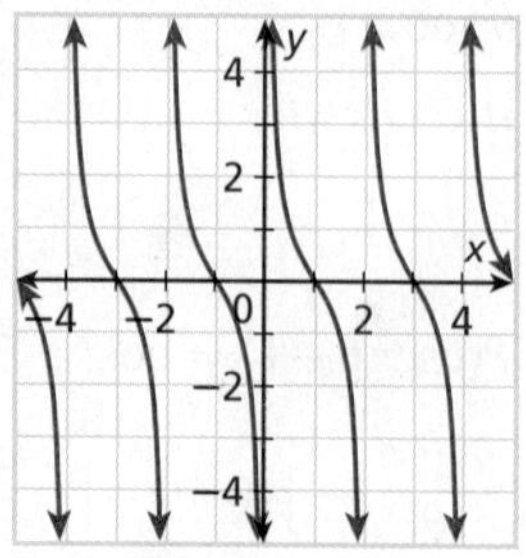

b.

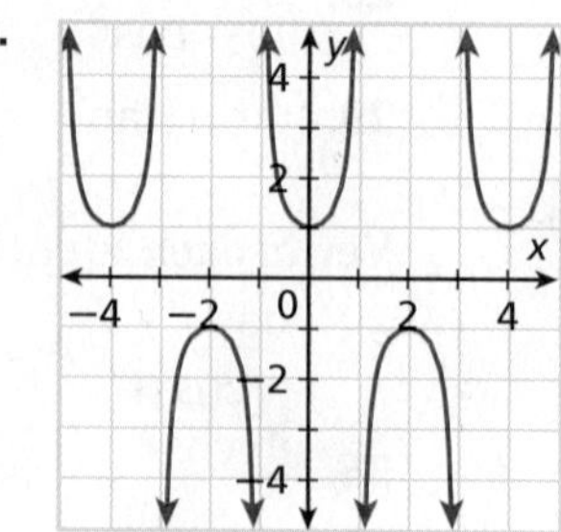

55. Critical Thinking In how many equivalent forms can $\tan\theta = \frac{\sin\theta}{\cos\theta}$ be expressed? Write at least three of its forms.

56. Write About It Use the fact that $\sin(-\theta) = -\sin\theta$ and $\cos(-\theta) = \cos\theta$ to explain why $\tan(-\theta) = -\tan\theta$.

57. Which expression is equivalent to $\sec\theta \sin\theta$?

Ⓐ $\sin\theta$ Ⓑ $\cos\theta$ Ⓒ $\csc\theta$ Ⓓ $\tan\theta$

58. Which expression is NOT equivalent to the other expressions?

Ⓕ $\sec\theta \csc\theta$ Ⓖ $\dfrac{1}{\sin\theta\cos\theta}$ Ⓗ $\dfrac{\tan\theta}{\sin^2\theta}$ Ⓙ $\dfrac{\cos^2\theta}{\cot\theta}$

59. Which trigonometric statement is NOT an identity?

Ⓐ $1 + \cos^2\theta = \sin^2\theta$ Ⓒ $1 + \tan^2\theta = \sec^2\theta$

Ⓑ $\csc^2\theta - 1 = \cot^2\theta$ Ⓓ $1 - \sin^2\theta = \cos^2\theta$

60. Which is equivalent to $1 - \sec^2\theta$?

Ⓕ $\tan^2\theta$ Ⓖ $-\tan^2\theta$ Ⓗ $\cot^2\theta$ Ⓙ $-\cot^2\theta$

61. **Short Response** Verify that $\sin\theta + \cot\theta\cos\theta = \csc\theta$ is an identity. Write the justification for each step.

CHALLENGE AND EXTEND

Write each expression as a single fraction.

62. $\dfrac{1}{\cos\theta} + \dfrac{1}{\cos^2\theta}$

63. $\dfrac{\cos\theta}{\sin\theta} + \dfrac{\sin\theta}{\cos\theta}$

64. $1 - \dfrac{\cos\theta}{\sin\theta}$

65. $\dfrac{1}{1 - \cos\theta} - \dfrac{\cos\theta}{1 - \cos^2\theta}$

Simplify.

66. $\dfrac{\frac{1}{\sin^2\theta} - 1}{\frac{\cos^2\theta}{\sin^2\theta}}$

67. $\dfrac{\frac{1}{\sin\theta} + \frac{1}{\cos\theta}}{\frac{1}{\sin\theta\cos\theta}}$

68. $\dfrac{\frac{1}{\sin\theta} - \frac{1}{\cos\theta}}{\frac{\sin\theta}{\cos\theta} - \frac{\cos\theta}{\sin\theta}}$

69. $\dfrac{1 - \frac{1}{\sin\theta}}{1 - \frac{1}{\sin^2\theta}}$

11-4 Sum and Difference Identities

CC.9-12.F.TF.9 (+) Prove the addition and subtraction formulas for sine, cosine, and tangent and use them to solve problems.

Objectives

Evaluate trigonometric expressions by using sum and difference identities.

Use a rotation transformation to perform rotations.

Vocabulary

rotation transformation

Why learn this?

You can use sum and difference identities to help form images made from rotations. (See Example 4.)

A transformation based on sum and difference identities can help find the coordinates of points rotated about the origin on a plane.

Sum and Difference Identities	
Sum Identities	**Difference Identities**
$\sin(A + B) = \sin A \cos B + \cos A \sin B$	$\sin(A - B) = \sin A \cos B - \cos A \sin B$
$\cos(A + B) = \cos A \cos B - \sin A \sin B$	$\cos(A - B) = \cos A \cos B + \sin A \sin B$
$\tan(A + B) = \dfrac{\tan A + \tan B}{1 - \tan A \tan B}$	$\tan(A - B) = \dfrac{\tan A - \tan B}{1 + \tan A \tan B}$

EXAMPLE  1

Evaluating Expressions with Sum and Difference Identities

Find the exact value of each expression.

A $\sin 75°$

$\sin 75° = \sin(30° + 45°)$ *Write 75° as the sum 30° + 45° because trigonometric values of 30° and 45° are known.*

$= \sin 30° \cos 45° + \cos 30° \sin 45°$ *Apply identity for sin(A + B).*

$= \frac{1}{2} \cdot \frac{\sqrt{2}}{2} + \frac{\sqrt{3}}{2} \cdot \frac{\sqrt{2}}{2}$ *Evaluate.*

$= \frac{\sqrt{2}}{4} + \frac{\sqrt{6}}{4} = \frac{\sqrt{2} + \sqrt{6}}{4}$ *Simplify.*

B $\cos\left(-\frac{\pi}{12}\right)$

$\cos\left(-\frac{\pi}{12}\right) = \cos\left(\frac{\pi}{6} - \frac{\pi}{4}\right)$ *Write $-\frac{\pi}{12}$ as the difference $\frac{\pi}{6} - \frac{\pi}{4}$.*

$= \cos\frac{\pi}{6}\cos\frac{\pi}{4} + \sin\frac{\pi}{6}\sin\frac{\pi}{4}$ *Apply the identity for cos(A − B).*

$= \frac{\sqrt{3}}{2} \cdot \frac{\sqrt{2}}{2} + \frac{1}{2} \cdot \frac{\sqrt{2}}{2}$ *Evaluate.*

$= \frac{\sqrt{6}}{4} + \frac{\sqrt{2}}{4} = \frac{\sqrt{2} + \sqrt{6}}{4}$ *Simplify.*

Helpful Hint

In Example 1B, there is more than one way to get $-\frac{\pi}{12}$. For example, $\left(\frac{\pi}{6} - \frac{\pi}{4}\right)$ or $\left(\frac{\pi}{4} - \frac{\pi}{3}\right)$.

Find the exact value of each expression.

1a. $\tan 105°$

1b. $\sin\left(-\frac{11\pi}{12}\right)$

Shifting the cosine function right π radians is equivalent to reflecting it across the x-axis. A proof of this is shown in Example 2 by using a difference identity.

Phase Shift Right π Radians

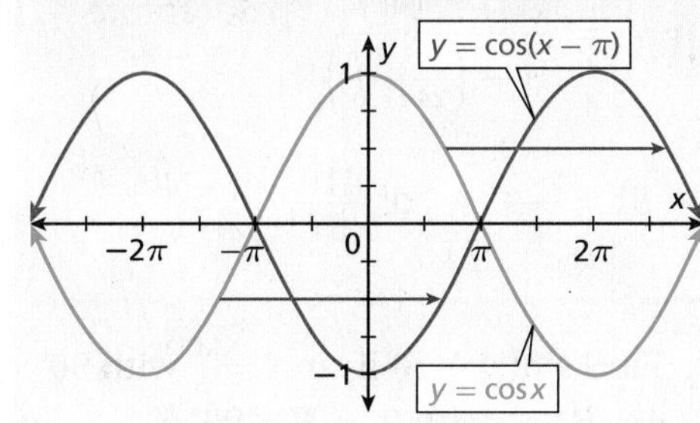

Reflection Across x-axis

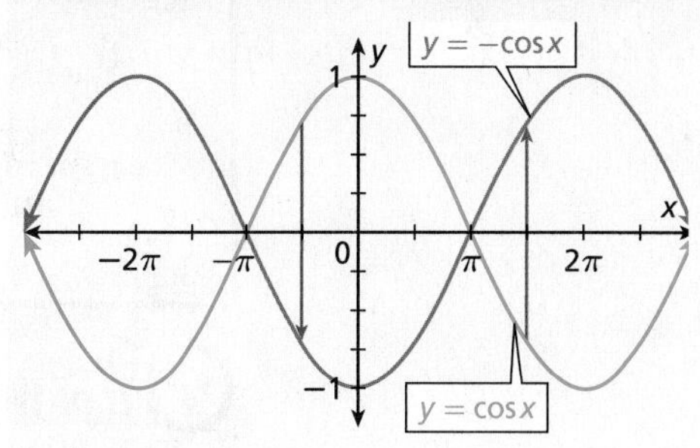

EXAMPLE 2 Proving Identities with Sum and Difference Identities

Prove the identity $\cos(x - \pi) = -\cos x$.

$\cos(x - \pi) = -\cos x$	*Choose the left-hand side to modify.*
$\cos x \cos \pi + \sin x \sin \pi =$	*Apply the identity for $\cos(A - B)$.*
$-1 \cdot \cos x + 0 \cdot \sin x =$	*Evaluate.*
$-\cos x = -\cos x$	*Simplify.*

2. Prove the identity $\cos\left(x + \frac{\pi}{2}\right) = -\sin x$.

EXAMPLE 3 Using the Pythagorean Theorem with Sum and Difference Identities

Find $\tan(A + B)$ if $\sin A = -\frac{7}{25}$ with $180° < A < 270°$ and if $\cos B = \frac{8}{17}$ with $0° < B < 180°$.

Step 1 Find $\tan A$ and $\tan B$.

Use reference angles and the ratio definitions $\sin A = \frac{y}{r}$ and $\cos B = \frac{x}{r}$. Draw a triangle in the appropriate quadrant and label x, y, and r for each angle.

In Quadrant III (QIII), $180° < A < 270°$ and $\sin A = -\frac{7}{25}$.

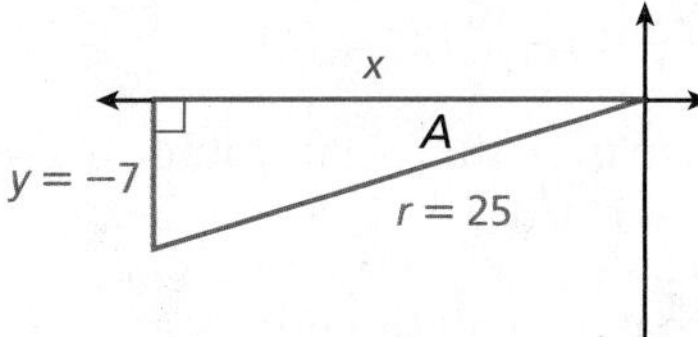

$x^2 + (-7)^2 = 25^2$

$x = -\sqrt{625 - 49} = -24$

Thus, $\tan A = \frac{y}{x} = \frac{7}{24}$.

In Quadrant I (QI), $0° < B < 180°$ and $\cos B = \frac{8}{17}$.

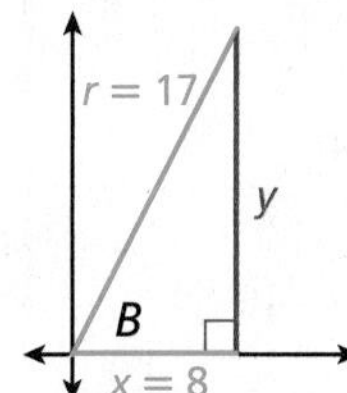

$8^2 + y^2 = 17^2$

$y = \sqrt{289 - 64} = 15$

Thus, $\tan B = \frac{y}{x} = \frac{15}{8}$.

Step 2 Use the angle-sum identity to find $\tan(A + B)$.

$$\tan(A+B) = \frac{\tan A + \tan B}{1 - \tan A \tan B}$$ *Apply identity for tan(A + B).*

$$= \frac{\left(\frac{7}{24}\right) + \left(\frac{15}{8}\right)}{1 - \left(\frac{7}{24}\right)\left(\frac{15}{8}\right)}$$ *Substitute $\frac{7}{24}$ for tan A and $\frac{15}{8}$ for tan B.*

$$\tan(A+B) = \frac{\frac{52}{24}}{1 - \frac{35}{64}}, \text{ or } \frac{416}{87}$$ *Simplify.*

3. Find $\sin(A - B)$ if $\sin A = \frac{4}{5}$ with $90° < A < 180°$ and if $\cos B = \frac{3}{5}$ with $0° < B < 90°$.

To rotate a point $P(x, y)$ through an angle θ, use a **rotation transformation**.

The sum identities for sine and cosine are used to derive the system of equations that yields the rotation transformation.

Using a Rotation Transformation

If $P(x, y)$ is any point in a plane, then the coordinates $P'(x', y')$ of the image after a rotation of θ degrees counterclockwise about the origin can be found by using the rotation transformation:

$$x' = x\cos\theta - y\sin\theta$$
$$y' = x\sin\theta + y\cos\theta$$

EXAMPLE 4 Using a Rotation Transformation

Find the coordinates of the points in the figure shown after a 30° rotation about the origin.

Use the rotation transformation with $\theta = 30°$. Since $\cos 30° = \frac{\sqrt{3}}{2}$ and $\sin 30° = \frac{1}{2}$, the transformation is

$$x' = \frac{\sqrt{3}}{2}x - \frac{1}{2}y$$
$$y' = \frac{1}{2}x + \frac{\sqrt{3}}{2}y$$

To find the coordinates of A', substitute the coordinates of $A(0, 2)$ into the system.

$$x' = \frac{\sqrt{3}}{2}(0) - \frac{1}{2}(2) = -1 \qquad y' = \frac{1}{2}(0) + \frac{\sqrt{3}}{2}(2) = \sqrt{3}$$

So, the image of A after a 30° rotation about the origin is $A'(-1, \sqrt{3})$.

The coordinates of all the points are $A'(-1, \sqrt{3})$, $B'(-2, 2\sqrt{3})$, $C'(1, \sqrt{3})$, and $D'(-2, 0)$. The points are graphed at right.

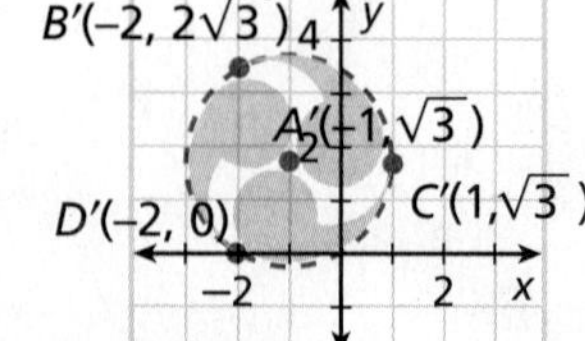

4. Find the coordinates of the points in the original figure after a 60° rotation about the origin.

THINK AND DISCUSS

1. **DESCRIBE** three different ways that you can use the difference identity to find the exact value of $\sin 15°$.
2. **EXPLAIN** the similarities and differences between the identity formulas for sine and cosine. How do the signs of the terms relate to whether the identity is a sum or a difference?

3. **GET ORGANIZED** Copy and complete the graphic organizer. For each type of function, give the sum and difference identity and an example.

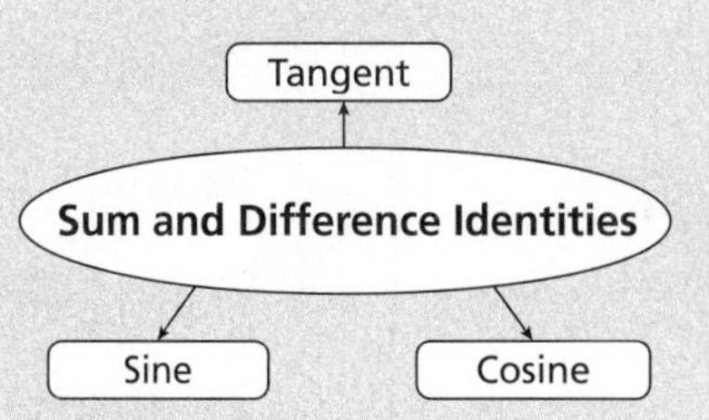

11-4 Exercises

GUIDED PRACTICE

1. **Vocabulary** A geometric rotation requires that a center point of rotation be defined. Which point and which direction does the rotation transformation assume?

SEE EXAMPLE 1

Find the exact value of each expression.

2. $\cos 105°$
3. $\sin \frac{11\pi}{12}$
4. $\tan \frac{\pi}{12}$
5. $\cos(-75°)$

SEE EXAMPLE 2

Prove each identity.

6. $\sin\left(\frac{\pi}{2} + x\right) = \cos x$
7. $\tan(\pi + x) = \tan x$
8. $\cos\left(\frac{3\pi}{2} - x\right) = -\sin x$

SEE EXAMPLE 3

Find each value if $\sin A = -\frac{12}{13}$ with $180° < A < 270°$ and if $\sin B = \frac{4}{5}$ with $90° < B < 180°$.

9. $\sin(A + B)$
10. $\cos(A - B)$
11. $\tan(A + B)$
12. $\tan(A - B)$

SEE EXAMPLE 4

13. Find the coordinates, to the nearest hundredth, of the vertices of triangle ABC with $A(0, 2)$, $B(0, -1)$, and $C(3, 0)$ after a 120° rotation about the origin.

PRACTICE AND PROBLEM SOLVING

Independent Practice

For Exercises	See Example
14–17	1
18–20	2
21–24	3
25	4

Extra Practice

See Extra Practice for more Skills Practice and Applications Practice exercises.

Find the exact value of each expression.

14. $\sin \frac{7\pi}{12}$
15. $\tan 165°$
16. $\sin 195°$
17. $\cos \frac{11\pi}{12}$

Prove each identity.

18. $\cos\left(\frac{3\pi}{2} + x\right) = \sin x$
19. $\sin\left(\frac{3\pi}{2} + x\right) = -\cos x$
20. $\tan(x - 2\pi) = \tan x$

Find each value if $\cos A = -\frac{12}{13}$ with $90° < A < 180°$ and if $\sin B = -\frac{4}{5}$ with $270° < B < 360°$.

21. $\sin(A + B)$
22. $\tan(A - B)$
23. $\cos(A + B)$
24. $\cos(A - B)$

25. Find the coordinates, to the nearest hundredth, of the vertices of figure ABC with $A(0, 2)$, $B(1, 2)$, and $C(0, 1)$ after a 45° rotation about the origin.

Find the exact value of each expression.

26. $\sin 165°$

27. $\tan(-105°)$

28. $\cos 195°$

29. $\sin(-15°)$

30. $\cos \frac{19\pi}{12}$

31. $\tan \frac{5\pi}{12}$

32. $\sin 255°$

33. $\tan 195°$

34. $\cos \frac{\pi}{12}$

Find the value for each unknown angle given that $0° \leq \theta \leq 180°$.

35. $\cos(\theta - 30°) = \frac{1}{2}$

36. $\cos(20° + \theta) = \frac{\sqrt{2}}{2}$

37. $\sin(180° - \theta) = \frac{1}{2}$

38. **Physics** Light enters glass of thickness t at an angle θ_i and leaves the glass at the same angle θ_i. However, the exiting ray of light is offset from the initial ray by a distance $\Delta = \left(\frac{\sin(\theta_i - \theta_r)}{\sin \theta_i \cos \theta_r}\right)t$, indicated in the figure shown.

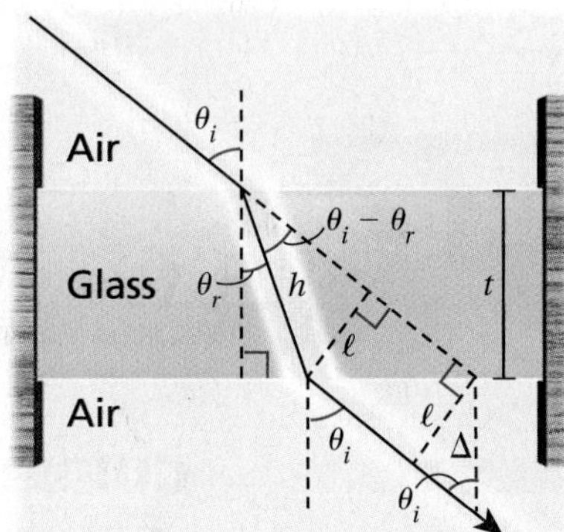

a. Write the formula for Δ in terms of tangent and cotangent by using the difference identities and other trigonometric identities.

b. Use the figure to write a ratio for $\sin(\theta_i - \theta_r)$.

Multi-Step **Find $\tan(A + B)$, $\cos(A + B)$, and $\sin(A - B)$ for each situation.**

39. $\sin A = -\frac{7}{25}$ with $180° < A < 270°$ and $\cos B = \frac{12}{13}$ with $0° < B < 90°$

40. $\sin A = -\frac{1}{3}$ with $270° < A < 360°$ and $\sin B = \frac{4}{5}$ with $0° < B < 90°$

41. The figure $PQRS$ will be rotated about the origin repeatedly to create the logo for a new product.

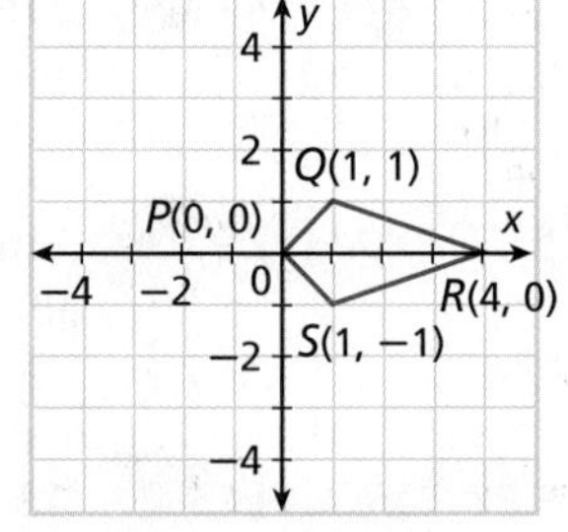

a. Write and simplify the rotation transformations for 90°, 180°, and 270° rotations.

b. Use your answers to part **a** to find the coordinates of the vertices of the figure after each of the three rotations.

c. Graph the three rotations on the same graph as $PQRS$ to create the logo.

42. **Critical Thinking** Is it possible to find the exact value of $\sin\left(\frac{11\pi}{24}\right)$ by using sum or difference identities? Explain.

MULTI-STEP TEST PREP

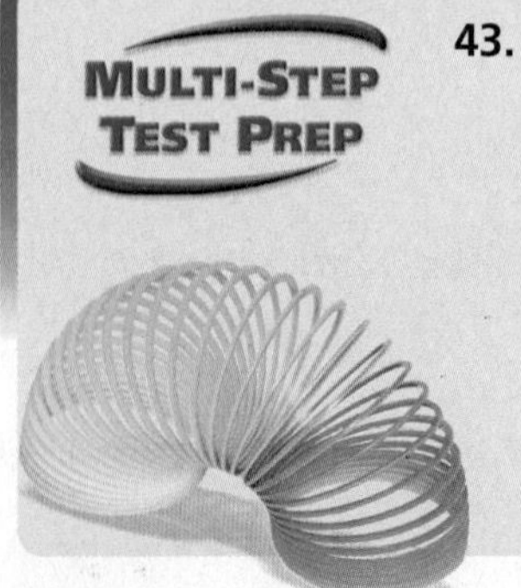

43. The displacement y of a mass attached to a spring is modeled by $y(t) = 4.2\sin\left(\frac{2\pi}{3}t - \frac{\pi}{2}\right)$, where t is the time in seconds.

a. What are the amplitude and period of the function?

b. Use a trigonometric identity to write the displacement, using only the cosine function.

c. What is the displacement of the mass when $t = 8$ s?

Sam Dudgeon/HMH

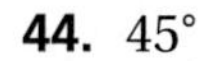

Geometry Find the coordinates, to the nearest hundredth, of the vertices of figure $ABCD$ with $A(0, 3)$, $B(1, 4)$, $C(2, 3)$, and $D(2, 0)$ after each rotation about the origin.

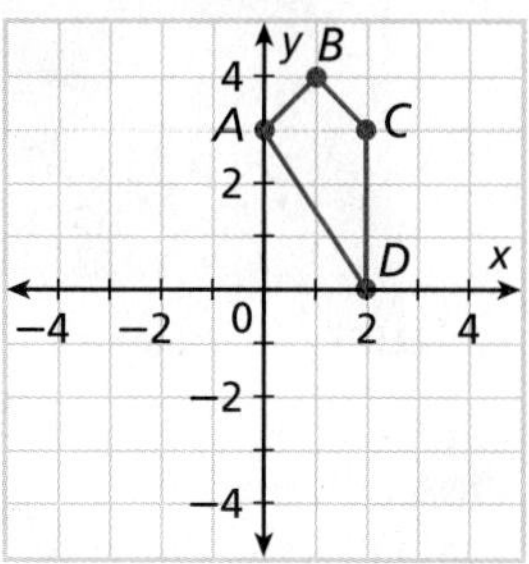

44. $45°$

45. $60°$

46. $120°$

47. $-30°$

48. **Write About It** In general, does $\sin(A + B) = \sin A + \sin B$? Give an example to support your response.

49. Which is the value of $\cos 15° \cos 45° - \sin 15° \sin 45°$?

Ⓐ $\frac{1}{2}$ Ⓑ $\frac{\sqrt{2}}{2}$ Ⓒ $-\frac{\sqrt{2}}{2}$ Ⓓ $\frac{2 + \sqrt{2}}{2}$

50. Which gives the value for x if $\sin\left(\frac{\pi}{2} + x\right) = \frac{1}{2}$?

Ⓕ $\frac{\pi}{6}$ Ⓖ $\frac{\pi}{4}$ Ⓗ $\frac{\pi}{3}$ Ⓙ $\frac{\pi}{2}$

51. Given $\sin A = \frac{1}{2}$ with $0° < A < 90°$ and $\cos B = \frac{3}{5}$ with $0° < B < 90°$, which expression gives the value of $\cos(A - B)$?

Ⓐ $\frac{3\sqrt{3} + 4}{10}$ Ⓑ $\frac{3\sqrt{3} - 4}{10}$ Ⓒ $\frac{3 + 4\sqrt{3}}{10}$ Ⓓ $\frac{3 - 4\sqrt{3}}{10}$

52. **Short Response** Find the exact value for $\sin(-15°)$. Show your work.

CHALLENGE AND EXTEND

53. Does the rotation transformation agree with the transformation for a reflection across the x-axis? Explain.

54. Derive the identity for $\tan(A + B)$.

55. Derive the rotation transformation by using the sum identities for sine and cosine and recalling from a previous lesson that any point $P(x, y)$ can be represented as $(r\cos\alpha, r\sin\alpha)$ by using a reference angle.

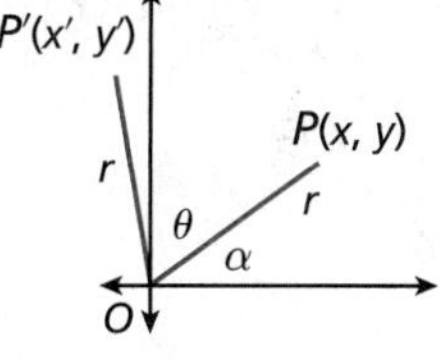

Find the angle by which a figure ABC with vertices $A(1, 0)$, $B(0, 2)$, and $C(-1, 0)$ was rotated to get $A'B'C'$.

56. $A'(0, 1)$, $B'(-2, 0)$, $C'(0, -1)$

57. $A'\left(\frac{\sqrt{2}}{2}, \frac{\sqrt{2}}{2}\right)$, $B'\left(-\sqrt{2}, \sqrt{2}\right)$, $C'\left(-\frac{\sqrt{2}}{2}, -\frac{\sqrt{2}}{2}\right)$

58. $A'(-1, 0)$, $B'(0, -2)$, $C'(1, 0)$

59. $A'\left(\frac{\sqrt{3}}{2}, \frac{1}{2}\right)$, $B'\left(-1, \sqrt{3}\right)$, $C'\left(-\frac{\sqrt{3}}{2}, -\frac{1}{2}\right)$

COMMON CORE

11-5 Double-Angle and Half-Angle Identities

CC.9-12.F.TF.9 (+) Prove the addition and subtraction formulas for sine, cosine, and tangent and use them to solve problems.

Objective
Evaluate and simplify expressions by using double-angle and half-angle identities.

Who uses this?
Double-angle formulas can be used to find the horizontal distance for a projectile such as a golf ball. (See Exercise 49.)

You can use sum identities to derive the *double-angle identities.*

$$\sin 2\theta = \sin(\theta + \theta)$$
$$= \sin\theta\cos\theta + \cos\theta\sin\theta$$
$$= 2\sin\theta\cos\theta$$

You can derive the double-angle identities for cosine and tangent in the same way. There are three forms of the identity for $\cos 2\theta$, which are derived by using $\sin^2\theta + \cos^2\theta = 1$. It is common to rewrite expressions as functions of θ only.

Know it! Note

Double-Angle Identities		
$\sin 2\theta = 2\sin\theta\cos\theta$	$\cos 2\theta = \cos^2\theta - \sin^2\theta$ $\cos 2\theta = 2\cos^2\theta - 1$ $\cos 2\theta = 1 - 2\sin^2\theta$	$\tan 2\theta = \dfrac{2\tan\theta}{1 - \tan^2\theta}$

EXAMPLE 1 **Evaluating Expressions with Double-Angle Identities**

Find $\sin 2\theta$ and $\cos 2\theta$ if $\cos\theta = -\frac{3}{4}$ and $90° < \theta < 180°$.

Step 1 Find $\sin\theta$ to evaluate $\sin 2\theta = 2\sin\theta\cos\theta$.

Method 1 Use the reference angle.

In QII, $90° < \theta < 180°$, and $\cos\theta = -\frac{3}{4}$.

$(-3)^2 + y^2 = 4^2$ — *Use the Pythagorean Theorem.*

$y = \sqrt{16 - 9} = \sqrt{7}$ — *Solve for y.*

$\sin\theta = \dfrac{\sqrt{7}}{4}$

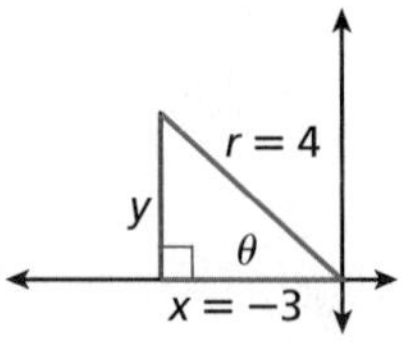

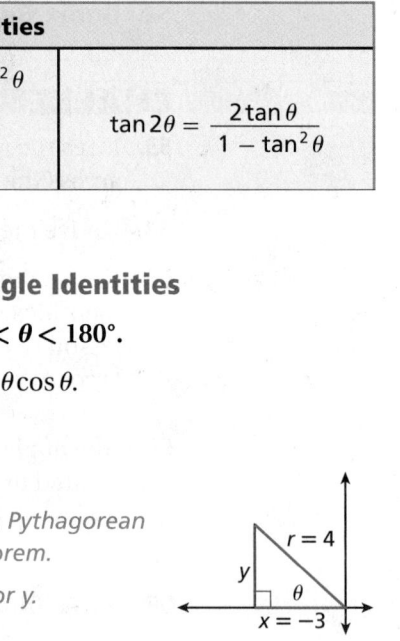

Caution!
The signs of x and y depend on the quadrant for angle θ.

	sin	cos
QI	+	+
QII	+	−
QIII	−	−
QIV	−	+

Method 2 Solve $\sin^2\theta = 1 - \cos^2\theta$.

$\sin^2\theta = 1 - \cos^2\theta$

$\sin\theta = \sqrt{1 - \left(-\frac{3}{4}\right)^2}$ — *Substitute $-\frac{3}{4}$ for $\cos\theta$.*

$= \sqrt{1 - \frac{9}{16}} = \frac{\sqrt{7}}{4}$ — *Simplify.*

$\sin\theta = \dfrac{\sqrt{7}}{4}$

Step 2 Find $\sin 2\theta$.

$\sin 2\theta = 2\sin\theta\cos\theta$	*Apply the identity for $\sin 2\theta$.*
$= 2\left(\frac{\sqrt{7}}{4}\right)\left(-\frac{3}{4}\right)$	*Substitute $\frac{\sqrt{7}}{2}$ for $\sin\theta$ and $-\frac{3}{4}$ for $\cos\theta$.*
$= -\frac{3\sqrt{7}}{8}$	*Simplify.*

Step 3 Find $\cos 2\theta$.

$\cos 2\theta = 2\cos^2\theta - 1$	*Select a double-angle identity.*
$= 2\left(-\frac{3}{4}\right)^2 - 1$	*Substitute $-\frac{3}{4}$ for $\cos\theta$.*
$= 2\left(\frac{9}{16}\right) - 1$	*Simplify.*
$= \frac{1}{8}$	

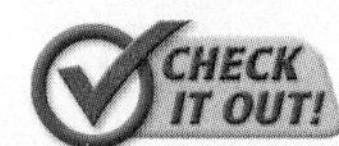

1. Find $\tan 2\theta$ and $\cos 2\theta$ if $\cos\theta = \frac{1}{3}$ and $270° < \theta < 360°$.

You can use double-angle identities to prove trigonometric identities.

EXAMPLE 2 Proving Identities with Double-Angle Identities

Prove each identity.

A $\sin^2\theta = \frac{1}{2}(1 - \cos 2\theta)$

$\sin^2\theta = \frac{1}{2}(1 - \cos 2\theta)$	*Choose the right-hand side to modify.*
$= \frac{1}{2}\left(1 - \left(1 - 2\sin^2\theta\right)\right)$	*Apply the identity for $\cos 2\theta$.*
$= \frac{1}{2}\left(2\sin^2\theta\right)$	*Simplify.*
$\sin^2\theta = \sin^2\theta$	

Helpful Hint

Choose to modify either the left side or the right side of an identity. Do not work on both sides at once.

B $(\cos\theta + \sin\theta)^2 = 1 + \sin 2\theta$

$(\cos\theta + \sin\theta)^2 = 1 + \sin 2\theta$	*Choose the left-hand side to modify.*
$\cos^2\theta + 2\cos\theta\sin\theta + \sin^2\theta =$	*Expand the square.*
$\left(\cos^2\theta + \sin^2\theta\right) + (2\cos\theta\sin\theta) =$	*Regroup.*
$1 + \sin 2\theta =$	*Rewrite using $1 = \cos^2\theta + \sin^2\theta$ and $\sin 2\theta = 2\sin\theta\cos\theta$.*
$1 + \sin 2\theta = 1 + \sin 2\theta$	

Prove each identity.

2a. $\cos^4\theta - \sin^4\theta = \cos 2\theta$

2b. $\sin 2\theta = \dfrac{2\tan\theta}{1 + \tan^2\theta}$

You can use double-angle identities for cosine to derive the *half-angle identities* by substituting $\frac{\theta}{2}$ for θ. For example, $\cos 2\theta = 2\cos^2\theta - 1$ can be rewritten as $\cos\theta = 2\cos^2\frac{\theta}{2} - 1$. Then solve for $\cos\frac{\theta}{2}$.

Half-Angle Identities

$$\sin\frac{\theta}{2} = \pm\sqrt{\frac{1-\cos\theta}{2}} \qquad \cos\frac{\theta}{2} = \pm\sqrt{\frac{1+\cos\theta}{2}} \qquad \tan\frac{\theta}{2} = \pm\sqrt{\frac{1-\cos\theta}{1+\cos\theta}}$$

Choose + or − depending on the location of $\frac{\theta}{2}$.

Half-angle identities are useful in calculating exact values for trigonometric expressions.

EXAMPLE 3 Evaluating Expressions with Half-Angle Identities

Use half-angle identities to find the exact value of each trigonometric expression.

A $\cos 165°$

$\cos\frac{330°}{2}$

$-\sqrt{\frac{1+\cos 330°}{2}}$ *Negative in QII*

$-\sqrt{\frac{1+\left(\frac{\sqrt{3}}{2}\right)}{2}}$ *$\cos 330° = \frac{\sqrt{3}}{2}$*

$-\sqrt{\left(\frac{2+\sqrt{3}}{2}\right)\left(\frac{1}{2}\right)}$ *Simplify.*

$-\frac{\sqrt{2+\sqrt{3}}}{2}$

Check Use your calculator.

```
cos(165)
         -.9659258263
-√(2+√(3))/2
         -.9659258263
```

B $\sin\frac{\pi}{8}$

$\sin\frac{1}{2}\left(\frac{\pi}{4}\right)$

$+\sqrt{\frac{1-\cos\left(\frac{\pi}{4}\right)}{2}}$ *Positive in QI*

$\sqrt{\frac{1-\frac{\sqrt{2}}{2}}{2}}$ *$\cos\frac{\pi}{4} = \frac{\sqrt{2}}{2}$*

$\sqrt{\left(\frac{2-\sqrt{2}}{2}\right)\left(\frac{1}{2}\right)}$ *Simplify.*

$\frac{\sqrt{2-\sqrt{2}}}{2}$

Check Use your calculator.

```
sin(π/8)
          .3826834324
√(2-√(2))/2
          .3826834324
```

Reading Math

In Example 3, the expressions $-\frac{\sqrt{2+\sqrt{3}}}{2}$ and $\frac{\sqrt{2-\sqrt{2}}}{2}$ are in reduced form and cannot be simplified further.

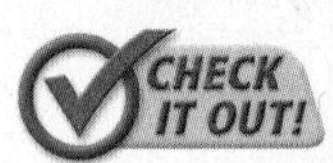

CHECK IT OUT! **Use half-angle identities to find the exact value of each trigonometric expression.**

3a. $\tan 75°$ **3b.** $\cos\frac{5\pi}{8}$

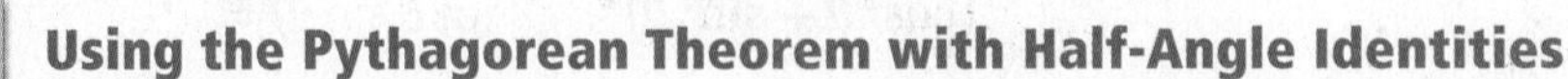

EXAMPLE 4 Using the Pythagorean Theorem with Half-Angle Identities

Find $\sin\frac{\theta}{2}$ and $\tan\frac{\theta}{2}$ if $\sin\theta = -\frac{5}{13}$ and $180° < \theta < 270°$.

Step 1 Find $\cos\theta$ to evaluate the half-angle identities.

Use the reference angle.

In QIII, $180° < \theta < 270°$, and $\sin\theta = -\frac{5}{13}$.

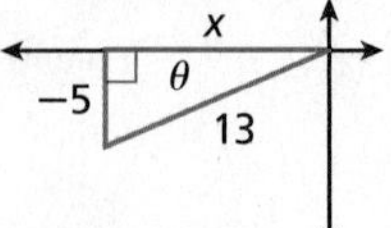

$x^2 + (-5)^2 = 13^2$ *Pythagorean Theorem*

$x = -\sqrt{169-25} = -12$ *Solve for the missing side x.*

Thus, $\cos\theta = -\frac{12}{13}$.

Step 2 Evaluate $\sin\frac{\theta}{2}$.

$\sin\frac{\theta}{2}$

$+\sqrt{\frac{1-\cos\theta}{2}}$ *Choose + for $\sin\frac{\theta}{2}$ where $90° < \frac{\theta}{2} < 135°$.*

$\sqrt{\frac{1-\left(-\frac{12}{13}\right)}{2}}$ *Evaluate.*

$\sqrt{\left(\frac{25}{13}\right)\left(\frac{1}{2}\right)}$ *Simplify.*

$\sqrt{\frac{25}{26}}$

$\frac{5\sqrt{26}}{26}$

Be careful to choose the correct sign for $\sin\frac{\theta}{2}$ and $\cos\frac{\theta}{2}$. If $180° < \theta < 270°$, then $90° < \frac{\theta}{2} < 135°$.

Step 3 Evaluate $\tan\frac{\theta}{2}$.

$\tan\frac{\theta}{2}$

$-\sqrt{\frac{1-\cos\theta}{1+\cos\theta}}$ *Choose − for $\tan\frac{\theta}{2}$ where $90° < \frac{\theta}{2} < 135°$.*

$-\sqrt{\frac{1-\left(-\frac{12}{13}\right)}{1+\left(-\frac{12}{13}\right)}}$ *Evaluate.*

$-\sqrt{\left(\frac{25}{13}\right)\left(\frac{13}{1}\right)}$ *Simplify.*

$-\sqrt{25}$

-5

CHECK IT OUT! **4.** Find $\sin\frac{\theta}{2}$ and $\cos\frac{\theta}{2}$ if $\tan\theta = \frac{4}{3}$ and $0° < \theta < 90°$.

THINK AND DISCUSS

1. **EXPLAIN** which double-angle identity you would use to simplify $\frac{\cos 2\theta}{\sin\theta + \cos\theta}$.
2. **DESCRIBE** how to determine the sign of the value for $\sin\frac{\theta}{2}$ and for $\cos\frac{\theta}{2}$.

3. **GET ORGANIZED** Copy and complete the graphic organizer. In each box, write one of the identities.

Double-Angle Identity for Cosine

11-5 Exercises

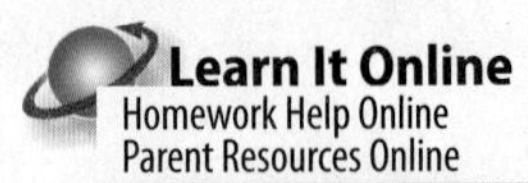

GUIDED PRACTICE

SEE EXAMPLE 1

Find $\sin 2\theta$, $\cos 2\theta$, and $\tan 2\theta$ for each set of conditions.

1. $\cos\theta = -\frac{5}{13}$ and $\frac{\pi}{2} < \theta < \pi$
2. $\sin\theta = \frac{4}{5}$ and $0° < \theta < 90°$

SEE EXAMPLE 2

Prove each identity.

3. $2\cos 2\theta = 4\cos^2\theta - 2$
4. $\sin^2\theta = 1 - \frac{\cos 2\theta + 1}{2}$
5. $\frac{1 + \cos 2\theta}{\sin 2\theta} = \cot\theta$
6. $\sin 2\theta = \frac{2\tan\theta}{1 + \tan^2\theta}$

SEE EXAMPLE 3

Use half-angle identities to find the exact value of each trigonometric expression.

7. $\cos 67.5°$
8. $\cos\frac{\pi}{12}$
9. $\tan\frac{3\pi}{8}$
10. $\sin 112.5°$

SEE EXAMPLE 4

Find $\sin\frac{\theta}{2}$, $\cos\frac{\theta}{2}$, and $\tan\frac{\theta}{2}$ for each set of conditions.

11. $\sin\theta = -\frac{24}{25}$ and $180° < \theta < 270°$
12. $\cos\theta = \frac{1}{4}$ and $270° < \theta < 360°$

PRACTICE AND PROBLEM SOLVING

Independent Practice

For Exercises	See Example
13–14	1
15–18	2
19–22	3
23–24	4

Extra Practice

See Extra Practice for more Skills Practice and Applications Practice exercises.

Find $\sin 2\theta$, $\cos 2\theta$, and $\tan 2\theta$ for each set of conditions.

13. $\cos\theta = -\frac{7}{25}$ and $90° < \theta < 180°$
14. $\tan\theta = \frac{20}{21}$ and $0 \le \theta \le \frac{\pi}{2}$

Prove each identity.

15. $\frac{\sin 2\theta}{\sin\theta} = 2\cos\theta$
16. $\cos^2\theta = \frac{1}{2}(1 + \cos 2\theta)$
17. $\tan\theta = \frac{1 - \cos 2\theta}{\sin 2\theta}$
18. $\tan\theta = \frac{\sin 2\theta}{1 + \cos 2\theta}$

Use half-angle identities to find the exact value of each trigonometric expression.

19. $\sin\frac{7\pi}{12}$
20. $\cos\frac{5\pi}{12}$
21. $\sin 22.5°$
22. $\tan 15°$

Find $\sin\frac{\theta}{2}$, $\cos\frac{\theta}{2}$, and $\tan\frac{\theta}{2}$ for each set of conditions.

23. $\tan\theta = -\frac{12}{35}$ and $\frac{3\pi}{2} < \theta < 2\pi$
24. $\sin\theta = -\frac{3}{5}$ and $180° < \theta < 270°$

Multi-Step **Rewrite each expression in terms of trigonometric functions of θ rather than multiples of θ. Then simplify.**

25. $\sin 3\theta$
26. $\sin 4\theta$
27. $\cos 3\theta$
28. $\cos 4\theta$
29. $\cos 2\theta + 2\sin^2\theta$
30. $\cos 2\theta + 1$
31. $\tan 2\theta(2 - \sec^2\theta)$
32. $\frac{\cos 2\theta}{\cos\theta + \sin\theta}$
33. $\frac{\cos\theta\sin 2\theta}{1 + \cos 2\theta}$
34. $\frac{\cos 2\theta - 1}{\sin^2\theta}$

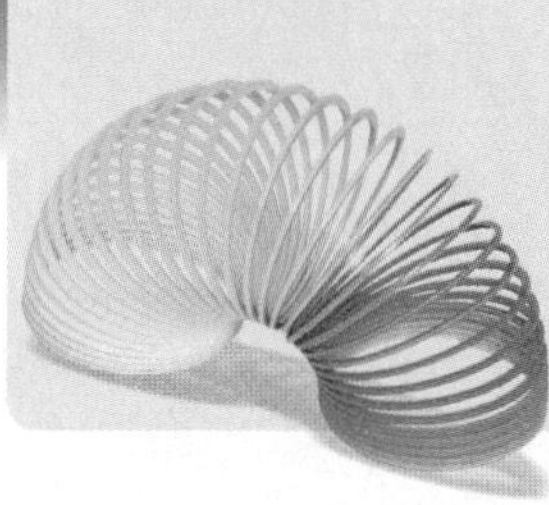

MULTI-STEP TEST PREP

35. The displacement y of a mass attached to a spring is modeled by $y(t) = 3.1 \sin 2t$, where t is the time in seconds.
    a. Rewrite the function by using a double-angle identity.
    b. The displacement w of another mass attached to a spring is given by $w(t) = 3.8 \cos t$. The two masses are set in motion at $t = 0$. When do the masses have the same displacement for the first time?
    c. What is the displacement at this time?

Multi-Step **Find $\sin 2\theta$, $\cos 2\theta$, $\tan 2\theta$, $\sin \frac{\theta}{2}$, $\cos \frac{\theta}{2}$, and $\tan \frac{\theta}{2}$ for each set of conditions.**

36. $\cos \theta = \frac{3}{8}$ and $\frac{\pi}{2} < \theta < \pi$

37. $\cos \theta = -\frac{\sqrt{5}}{3}$ and $180° < \theta < 270°$

38. $\sin \theta = \frac{2}{5}$ and $0° < \theta < 90°$

39. $\tan \theta = -\frac{1}{2}$ and $\frac{3\pi}{2} < \theta < 2\pi$

LINK

Physics

The Tevatron at Fermi National Accelerator Lab in Batavia, Illinois, uses superconducting magnets to study subatomic particles by colliding matter and antimatter inside of a ring with a diameter of 6.3 km.

Use half-angle identities to find the exact value of each trigonometric expression.

40. $\cos \frac{7\pi}{8}$

41. $\sin \frac{11\pi}{12}$

42. $\cos 105°$

43. $\sin(-15°)$

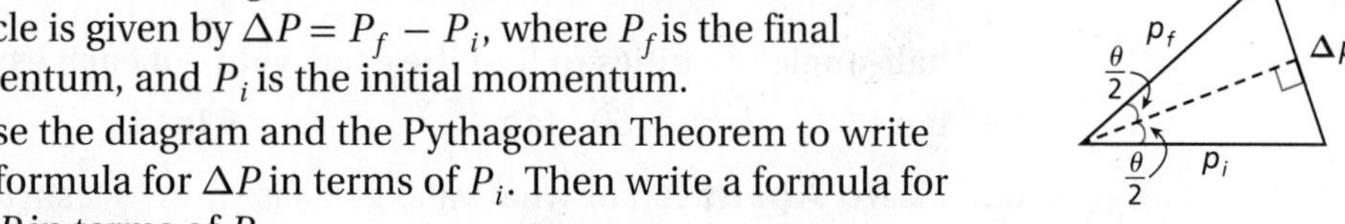

44. **Physics** The change in momentum of a scattered nuclear particle is given by $\Delta P = P_f - P_i$, where P_f is the final momentum, and P_i is the initial momentum.
    a. Use the diagram and the Pythagorean Theorem to write a formula for ΔP in terms of P_i. Then write a formula for ΔP in terms of P_f.
    b. Compare your two answers to part **a.** What does this tell you about the magnitude, or size, of the momentum before and after the "collision"?
    c. Write the formula for ΔP in terms of $\cos \theta$.

Prove each identity.

45. $\cos^2 \frac{\theta}{2} = \frac{\sin^2 \theta}{2(1 - \cos \theta)}$

46. $\cos 2\theta = \frac{1 - \tan^2 \theta}{1 + \tan^2 \theta}$

47. $\frac{\tan \theta + \sin \theta}{2 \tan \theta} = \cos^2 \frac{\theta}{2}$

48. **Graphing Calculator** Graph $y = \frac{(\cos x)(1 - \cos 2x)}{\sin 2x}$ to discover an identity. Then prove the identity.

49. **Multi-Step** A golf ball is hit with an initial velocity of v_0 in feet per second at an angle of elevation θ. The function $d(\theta) = \frac{{v_0}^2 \sin \theta \cos \theta}{16}$ gives the horizontal distance d in feet that the ball travels.
    a. Rewrite the function in terms of the double angle 2θ.
    b. Calculate the horizontal distance for an initial velocity of 80 ft/s for angles of 15°, 30°, 45°, 60°, and 75°.
    c. For a given velocity, what angle gives the maximum horizontal distance?
    d. **What if...?** If the initial velocity is 80 ft/s, through what approximate range of angles will the ball travel horizontally at least 175 ft?

50. **Critical Thinking** Explain how to find the exact value for $\sin 7.5°$.

51. **Write About It** How do you know when to use a double-angle or a half-angle identity?

Test Prep

52. What is the value of $\sin 2\theta$ if $\cos\theta = -\frac{\sqrt{2}}{2}$ and $90° < \theta < 180°$?

Ⓐ $\frac{1}{2}$ Ⓑ $\frac{\sqrt{2}}{2}$ Ⓒ 1 Ⓓ −1

53. What is the value for $\cos 2\theta$ if $\sin\theta = \cos\theta$?

Ⓕ 0 Ⓖ 1 Ⓗ $2\sin^2\theta$ Ⓙ $2\cos^2\theta$

54. What is the value for $\sin\frac{\theta}{2}$ if $\cos\theta = -\frac{12}{13}$ and $90° < \theta < 180°$?

Ⓐ $\frac{\sqrt{26}}{26}$ Ⓑ $-\frac{\sqrt{26}}{26}$ Ⓒ $\frac{5\sqrt{26}}{26}$ Ⓓ $-\frac{5\sqrt{26}}{26}$

55. What is the exact value for $\sin 157.5°$?

Ⓕ $-\frac{\sqrt{2-\sqrt{2}}}{2}$ Ⓖ $\frac{\sqrt{2-\sqrt{2}}}{2}$ Ⓗ $-\frac{\sqrt{2+\sqrt{2}}}{2}$ Ⓙ $\frac{\sqrt{2+\sqrt{2}}}{2}$

56. Short Response Verify that $\frac{\cos 2\theta}{\sin\theta + \cos\theta} = \cos\theta - \sin\theta$ for $0 \le \theta \le \frac{\pi}{2}$. Show each step in your justification process.

Challenge and Extend

57. Derive the double-angle formula for $\tan 2\theta$ by using the ratio identity for tangent and the double-angle identities for sine and cosine.

58. Derive the half-angle formula for $\tan\frac{\theta}{2}$ by using the ratio identity for tangent.

Use half-angle identities to find the exact value of each expression.

59. $\tan 7.5°$ **60.** $\tan\frac{\pi}{16}$ **61.** $\sin\frac{\pi}{24}$ **62.** $\cos 11.25°$

63. Write About It For what values of θ is $\sin 2\theta = 2\sin\theta$ true? Explain first by using graphs and then by solving the equation.

64. Derive the product-to-sum formulas $\sin A \sin B = \frac{1}{2}\left[\cos(A-B) - \cos(A+B)\right]$ and $\cos A \cos B = \frac{1}{2}\left[\cos(A+B) + \cos(A-B)\right]$ by using the angle sum and difference formulas.

11-6 Solving Trigonometric Equations

CC.9-12.F.TF.7 (+) Use inverse functions to solve trigonometric equations that arise in modeling contexts… and interpret them in terms of the context.* *Also* **CC.9-12.A.CED.1**

Objectives

Solve equations involving trigonometric functions.

Why learn this?

You can use trigonometric equations to determine the day of the year that the sun will rise at a given time. (See Example 4.)

Unlike trigonometric identities, most trigonometric equations are true only for certain values of the variable, called *solutions*. To solve trigonometric equations, apply the same methods used for solving algebraic equations.

EXAMPLE 1 Solving Trigonometric Equations with Infinitely Many Solutions

Find all of the solutions of $3\tan\theta = \tan\theta + 2$.

Method 1 Use algebra.

Solve for θ over one cycle of the tangent, $-90° < \theta < 90°$.

$3\tan\theta = \tan\theta + 2$

$3\tan\theta - \tan\theta = 2$ — *Subtract $\tan\theta$ from both sides.*

$2\tan\theta = 2$ — *Combine like terms.*

$\tan\theta = 1$ — *Divide by 2.*

$\theta = \tan^{-1}1$ — *Apply the inverse tangent.*

$\theta = 45°$ — *Find θ when $\tan\theta = 1$.*

Find all real number values of θ, where n is an integer.

$\theta = 45° + 180°n$ — *Use the period of the tangent function.*

Helpful Hint

Compare Example 1 with this solution:

$3x = x + 2$
$3x - x = 2$
$2x = 2$
$x = 1$

Method 2 Use a graph.

Graph $y = 3\tan\theta$ and $y = \tan\theta + 2$ in the same viewing window for $-90° \le \theta \le 90°$.

Use the intersect feature of your graphing calculator to find the points of intersection.

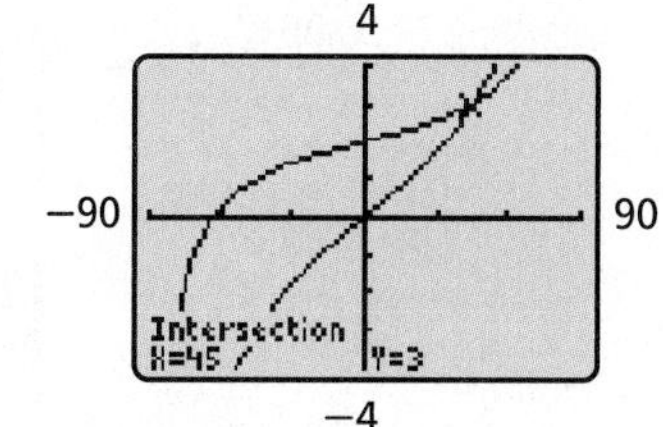

The graphs intersect at $\theta = 45°$. Thus, $\theta = 45° + 180°n$, where n is an integer.

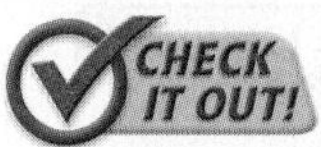

1. Find all of the solutions of $2\cos\theta + \sqrt{3} = 0$.

Some trigonometric equations can be solved by applying the same methods used for quadratic equations.

Cosmo Condina/TIPS Images

EXAMPLE 2 Solving Trigonometric Equations in Quadratic Form

Solve each equation for the given domain.

A $\sin^2\theta - 2\sin\theta = 3$ **for** $0 \le \theta < 2\pi$

$\sin^2\theta - 2\sin\theta - 3 = 0$	*Subtract 3 from both sides.*
$(\sin\theta + 1)(\sin\theta - 3) = 0$	*Factor the quadratic expression by comparing it with $x^2 - 2x - 3 = 0$.*
$\sin\theta = -1$ or $\sin\theta = 3$	*Apply the Zero Product Property.*

$\sin\theta = 3$ has no solution because $-1 \le \sin\theta \le 1$.

$\theta = \dfrac{3\pi}{2}$	*The only solution will come from $\sin\theta = -1$.*

Caution!

A trigonometric equation may have zero, one, two, or an infinite number of solutions, depending on the equation and domain of θ.

B $\cos^2\theta + 2\cos\theta - 1 = 0$ **for** $0° \le \theta < 360°$

The equation is in quadratic form but cannot easily be factored. Use the Quadratic Formula.

$\cos\theta = \dfrac{-(2) \pm \sqrt{(2)^2 - 4(1)(-1)}}{2(1)}$	*Substitute 1 for a, 2 for b, and −1 for c.*
$\cos\theta = -1 \pm \sqrt{2}$	*Simplify.*

$-1 - \sqrt{2} < -1$ so $\cos\theta = -1 - \sqrt{2}$ has no solution.

$\theta = \cos^{-1}(-1 + \sqrt{2})$	*Apply the inverse cosine.*
$\approx 65.5°$ or $294.5°$	*Use a calculator. Find both angles for $0° \le \theta < 360°$.*

Solve each equation for $0 \le \theta < 2\pi$.

2a. $\cos^2\theta + 2\cos\theta = 3$

2b. $\sin^2\theta + 5\sin\theta - 2 = 0$

You can often write trigonometric equations involving more than one function as equations of only one function by using trigonometric identities.

EXAMPLE 3 Solving Trigonometric Equations with Trigonometric Identities

Use trigonometric identities to solve each equation for $0 \le \theta < 2\pi$.

A $2\cos^2\theta = \sin\theta + 1$

$2(1 - \sin^2\theta) - \sin\theta - 1 = 0$	*Substitute $1 - \sin^2\theta$ for $\cos^2\theta$ by the Pythagorean identity.*
$-2\sin^2\theta - \sin\theta + 2 - 1 = 0$	*Simplify.*
$2\sin^2\theta + \sin\theta - 1 = 0$	*Multiply by −1.*
$(2\sin\theta - 1)(\sin\theta + 1) = 0$	*Factor.*
$\sin\theta = \dfrac{1}{2}$ or $\sin\theta = -1$	*Apply the Zero Product Property.*
$\theta = \dfrac{\pi}{6}$ or $\dfrac{5\pi}{6}$ or $\theta = \dfrac{3\pi}{2}$	

Check Use the intersect feature of your graphing calculator. A graph supports your answer.

2

0 2π

0 $\frac{\pi}{6}$ $\frac{5\pi}{6}$ $\frac{3\pi}{2}$

Use trigonometric identities to solve each equation for $0° \le \theta < 360°$.

B $\cos 2\theta + 3\cos\theta + 2 = 0$

$2\cos^2\theta - 1 + 3\cos\theta + 2 = 0$ — *Substitute $2\cos^2\theta - 1$ for $\cos 2\theta$ by the double-angle identity.*

$2\cos^2\theta + 3\cos\theta + 1 = 0$ — *Combine like terms.*

$(2\cos\theta + 1)(\cos\theta + 1) = 0$ — *Factor.*

$\cos\theta = -\frac{1}{2}$ — *Apply the Zero Product Property.*

or

$\cos\theta = -1$

$\theta = 120°$ or $240°$ or $\theta = 180°$

Check Use the intersect feature of your graphing calculator. A graph supports your answer.

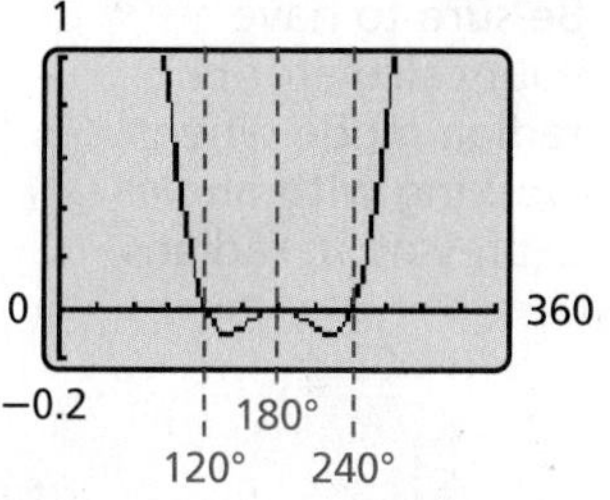

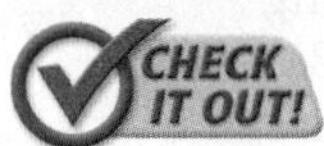

Use trigonometric identities to solve each equation for the given domain.

3a. $4\sin^2\theta + 4\cos\theta = 5$ for $0° \le \theta < 360°$

3b. $\sin 2\theta = -\cos\theta$ for $0 \le \theta < 2\pi$

EXAMPLE 4 *Problem-Solving Application*

Make sense of problems and persevere in solving them.

The first sunrise in the United States each day is observed from Cadillac Mountain on Mount Desert Island in Maine. The time of the sunrise can be modeled by $t(m) = 1.665\sin\frac{\pi}{6}(m + 3) + 5.485$, where t is hours after midnight and m is the number of months after January 1. When does the sun rise at 7 A.M.?

1 Understand the Problem

The **answer** will be months of the year.

List the important information:

- The function model is $t(m) = 1.665\sin\frac{\pi}{6}(m + 3) + 5.485$.
- Sunrise is at 7 A.M., which is represented by $t = 7$.
- m represents the number of months after January 1.

2 Make a Plan

Substitute 7 for t in the model. Then solve the equation for m by using algebra.

3 Solve

$$7 = 1.665 \sin \frac{\pi}{6}(m + 3) + 5.485 \qquad \textit{Substitute 7 for t.}$$

$$\frac{7 - 5.485}{1.665} = \sin \frac{\pi}{6}(m + 3) \qquad \textit{Isolate the sine term.}$$

$$\sin^{-1}(0.9\overline{099}) = \frac{\pi}{6}(m + 3) \qquad \textit{Apply the inverse sine.}$$

Sine is positive in Quadrants I and II. Compute both values.

QI: $\sin^{-1}(0.9\overline{099}) = \frac{\pi}{6}(m + 3)$

$$1.143 \approx \frac{\pi}{6}(m + 3)$$

$$\left(\frac{6}{\pi}\right)1.143 \approx m + 3$$

$$-0.817 \approx m$$

QII: $\pi - \sin^{-1}(0.9\overline{099}) = \frac{\pi}{6}(m + 3)$

$$\pi - 1.143 \approx \frac{\pi}{6}(m + 3)$$

$$\left(\frac{6}{\pi}\right)(\pi - 1.143) \approx m + 3$$

$$0.817 \approx m$$

The value $m = 0.817$ corresponds to late January and the value $m = -0.817$ corresponds to early December.

Caution!

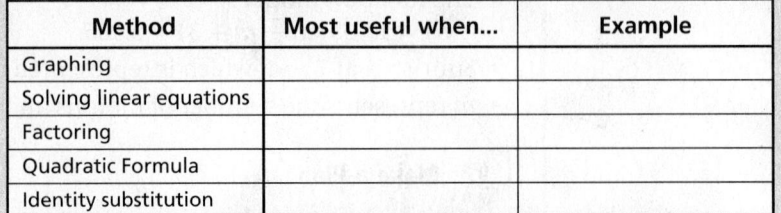

Be sure to have your calculator in radian mode when working with angles expressed in radians.

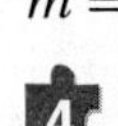

Look Back

Check your answer by using a graphing calculator. Enter $y = 1.665 \sin \frac{\pi}{6}(x + 3) + 5.485$ and $y = 7$. Graph the functions on the same viewing window, and find the points of intersection.

The graphs intersect at about 0.817 and −0.817.

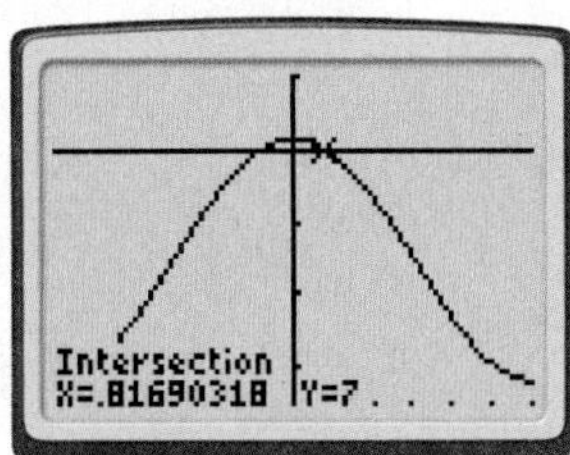

CHECK IT OUT!

4. The number of hours h of sunlight in a day at Cadillac Mountain can be modeled by $h(d) = 3.31 \sin \frac{\pi}{182.5}(d - 85.25) + 12.22$, where d is the number of days after January 1. When are there 12 hours of sunlight?

THINK AND DISCUSS

1. **DESCRIBE** the general procedure for finding all real-number solutions of a trigonometric equation.

2. **GET ORGANIZED** Copy and complete the graphic organizer. Write when each method is most useful, and give an example.

Method	Most useful when...	Example
Graphing		
Solving linear equations		
Factoring		
Quadratic Formula		
Identity substitution		

11-6 Exercises

Learn It Online
Homework Help Online
Parent Resources Online

GUIDED PRACTICE

SEE EXAMPLE 1

Find all of the solutions of each equation.

1. $6\cos\theta - 1 = 2$
2. $2\sin\theta - \sqrt{3} = 0$
3. $\cos\theta = \sqrt{3} - \cos\theta$

SEE EXAMPLE 2

Solve each equation for the given domain.

4. $2\sin^2\theta + 3\sin\theta = -1$ for $0 \le \theta < 2\pi$
5. $\cos^2\theta - 4\cos\theta + 1 = 0$ for $0° \le \theta < 360°$

SEE EXAMPLE 3

Multi-Step Use trigonometric identities to solve each equation for the given domain.

6. $2\sin^2\theta - \cos 2\theta = 0$ for $0° \le \theta < 360°$
7. $\sin^2\theta + \cos\theta = -1$ for $0 \le \theta < 2\pi$

SEE EXAMPLE 4

8. **Heating** The amount of energy from natural gas used for heating a manufacturing plant is modeled by $E(m) = 350\sin\frac{\pi}{6}(m + 1.5) + 650$, where E is the energy used in dekatherms, and m is the month where $m = 0$ represents January 1. When is the gas usage 825 dekatherms? Assume an average of 30 days per month.

PRACTICE AND PROBLEM SOLVING

Independent Practice	
For Exercises	See Example
9–12	1
13–14	2
15–16	3
17	4

Extra Practice

See Extra Practice for more Skills Practice and Applications Practice exercises.

Find all of the solutions of each equation.

9. $1 - 2\cos\theta = 0$
10. $\sqrt{3}\tan\theta - 3 = 0$
11. $2\cos\theta + \sqrt{3} = 0$
12. $2\sin\theta + 1 = 2 + \sin\theta$

Solve each equation for the given domain.

13. $2\cos^2\theta + \cos\theta - 1 = 0$ for $0 \le \theta < 2\pi$
14. $\sin^2\theta + 2\sin\theta - 2 = 0$ for $0° \le \theta < 360°$

Multi-Step Use trigonometric identities to solve each equation for the given domain.

15. $\cos 2\theta + \cos\theta + 1 = 0$ for $0° \le \theta < 360°$
16. $\cos 2\theta = \sin\theta$ for $0 \le \theta < 2\pi$
17. **Multi-Step** The amount of energy used by a large office building is modeled by $E(t) = 100\sin\frac{\pi}{12}(t - 8) + 800$, where E is the energy in kilowatt-hours, and t is the time in hours after midnight.
    a. During what time in the day is the electricity use 850 kilowatt-hours?
    b. When are the least and greatest amounts of electricity used? Are your answers reasonable? Explain.

Solve each equation algebraically for $0° \le \theta < 360°$.

18. $2\sin^2\theta = \sin\theta$
19. $2\cos^2\theta = \sin\theta + 1$
20. $\cos 2\theta - 2\sin\theta + 2 = 0$
21. $2\cos^2\theta + 3\sin\theta = 3$
22. $\cos^2\theta + \sin\theta - 1 = 0$
23. $2\sin^2\theta + \sin\theta = 0$

Solve each equation algebraically for $0 \le \theta < 2\pi$.

24. $\sin^2\theta - \sin\theta = 0$
25. $\cos^2\theta - 3\cos\theta = 4$
26. $\cos\theta(0.5 + \cos\theta) = 0$
27. $2\sin^2\theta - 3\sin\theta = 2$
28. $\cos^2\theta + \frac{1}{2}\cos\theta = 5$
29. $\sin^2\theta + 3\sin\theta + 3 = 0$
30. $\cos^2\theta + 4\cos\theta - 3 = 0$
31. $\tan^2\theta = \sqrt{3}\tan\theta$

32. **Sports** A baseball is thrown with an initial velocity of 96 feet per second at an angle θ degrees with a horizontal.

a. The horizontal range R in feet that the ball travels can be modeled by $R(\theta) = \frac{v^2 \sin 2\theta}{32}$. At what angle(s) with the horizontal will the ball travel 250 feet?

b. The maximum vertical height $H_{\max}$ in feet that the ball travels upward can be modeled by $H_{\max}(\theta) = \frac{v^2 \sin^2 \theta}{64}$. At what angle(s) with the horizontal will the ball travel 50 feet?

Performing Arts

Traditional Japanese kabuki theaters were round and were able to be rotated to change scenes. The stages were also equipped with trapdoors and bridges that led through the audience.

33. **Performing Arts** A theater has a rotating stage that can be turned for different scenes. The stage has a radius of 18 feet, and the area in square feet of the segment of the circle formed by connecting two radii as shown is $A = \frac{r^2}{2}(\theta - \sin \theta)$, with θ in radians.

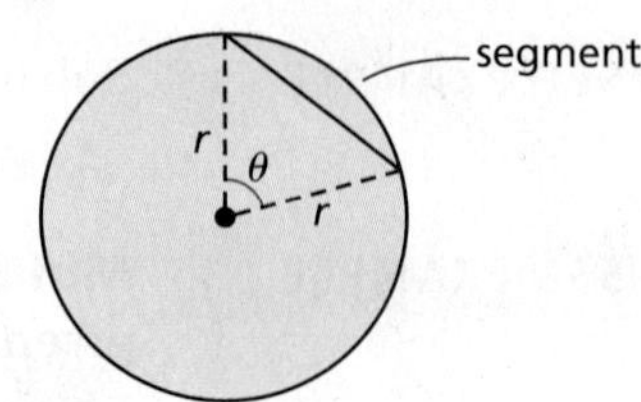

a. What angle gives a segment area of 92 square feet? How many such sets can simultaneously fit on the full rotating stage?

b. What angle gives a segment area of 50 square feet? About how many such sets can simultaneously fit on the full rotating stage?

34. **Oceanography** The height of the water on a certain day at a pier in Cape Cod, Massachusetts, can be modeled by $h(t) = 4.5 \sin \frac{\pi}{6.25}(t + 4) + 7.5$, where h is the height in feet and t is the time in hours after midnight.

a. On this particular day, when is the height of the water 5 feet?

b. How much time is there between high and low tides?

c. What is the period for the tide?

d. Does the cycle of tides fit evenly in a 24-hour day? Explain.

35. **/// ERROR ANALYSIS ///** Below are two solution procedures for solving $\sin^2 \theta - \frac{1}{2}\sin \theta = 0$ for $0° \le \theta < 360°$. Which is incorrect? Explain the error.

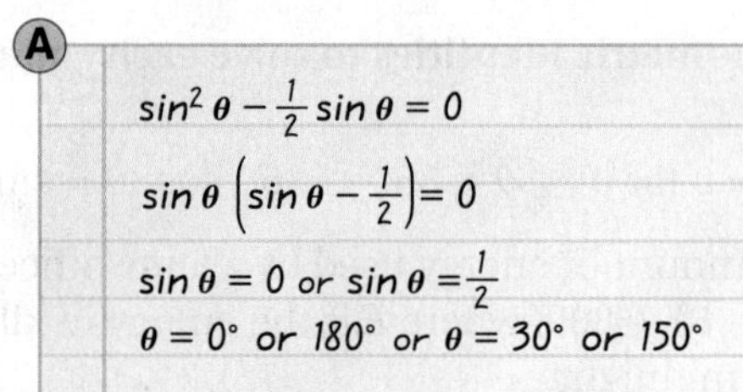

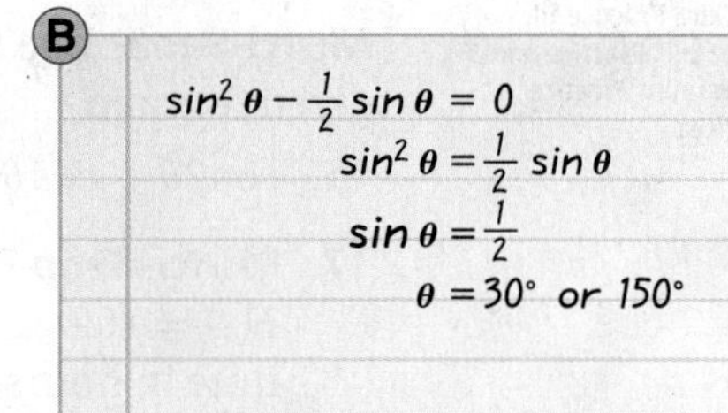

36. **Critical Thinking** What is the difference between a trigonometric equation and a trigonometric identity? Explain by using examples.

37. **Graphing Calculator** Use your graphing calculator to find all solutions of the equation $2 \cos x = 0.25x$.

MULTI-STEP TEST PREP

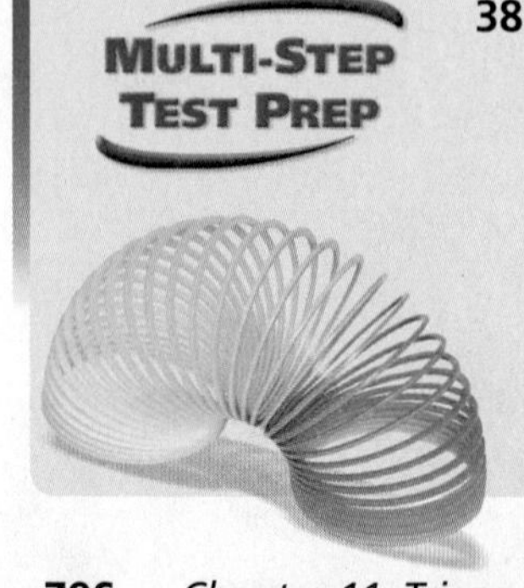

38. The displacement in centimeters of a mass attached to a spring is modeled by $y(t) = 2.9 \cos\left(\frac{2\pi}{3}t + \frac{\pi}{4}\right) + 3$, where t is the time in seconds.

a. What are the maximum and minimum displacements of the mass?

b. The mass is set in motion at $t = 0$. When is the displacement of the mass equal to 1 cm for the first time?

c. At what other times will the displacement be 1 cm?

(tl), Yuriko Nakao/Reuters/CORBIS; (b), Sam Dudgeon/HMH

Estimation Use a graphing calculator to approximate the solution to each equation to the nearest tenth of a degree for $0° \leq \theta < 360°$.

39. $\tan\theta - 12 = -1$

40. $\sin\theta + \cos\theta + 1.25 = 0$

41. $4\sin^2(2\theta - 30) = 4$

42. $\tan^2\theta + \tan\theta = 3$

43. $\sin^2\theta + 5\sin\theta = 3.5$

44. $\cos^2\theta - \cos 2\theta + 1 = 0$

45. **Write About It** How many solutions can a trigonometric equation have? Explain by using examples.

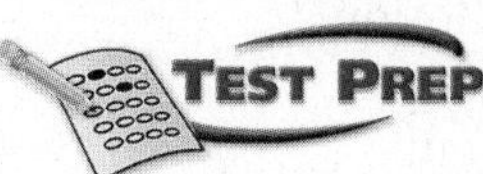

TEST PREP

46. Which values are solutions of $2\cos\theta + \sqrt{3} = 2\sqrt{3}$ for $0° \leq \theta < 360°$?

    (A) 30° or 150°
    (B) 30° or 330°
    (C) 60° or 120°
    (D) 60° or 320°

47. Which gives an approximate solution to $5\tan\theta - \sqrt{3} = \tan\theta$ for $-90° \leq \theta \leq 90°$?

    (F) −23.4°
    (G) −19.1°
    (H) 19.1°
    (J) 23.4°

48. Which value for θ is NOT a solution to $\sin^2\theta = \sin\theta$?

    (A) 0°
    (B) 90°
    (C) 180°
    (D) 270°

49. Which gives all of the solutions of $\cos\theta - 1 = -\frac{1}{2}$ for $0 \leq \theta < 2\pi$?

    (F) $\frac{2\pi}{3}$ or $\frac{5\pi}{3}$
    (G) $\frac{\pi}{3}$ or $\frac{2\pi}{3}$
    (H) $\frac{2\pi}{3}$ or $\frac{4\pi}{3}$
    (J) $\frac{\pi}{3}$ or $\frac{5\pi}{3}$

50. Which gives the solution to $\sin^2\theta - \sin\theta - 2 = 0$ for $0° \leq \theta < 360°$?

    (A) 90°
    (B) 270°
    (C) 90° or 270°
    (D) No solution

51. **Short Response** Solve $2\cos^2\theta + \cos\theta - 2 = 0$ algebraically. Show the steps in the solution process.

CHALLENGE AND EXTEND

Solve each equation algebraically for $0° \leq \theta < 360°$.

52. $9\cos^3\theta - \cos\theta = 0$

53. $4\cos^3\theta - \cos\theta = 0$

54. $16\sin^4\theta - 16\sin^2\theta + 3 = 0$

55. $\sin^2\theta - 4.5\sin\theta = 2.5$

56. $|\sin\theta| = \frac{1}{2}$

57. $|\cos\theta| = \frac{\sqrt{3}}{2}$

CHAPTER 11

MULTI-STEP TEST PREP

SECTION 11B

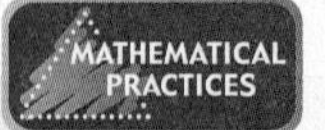

Model with mathematics.

Trigonometric Identities

Spring into Action Simple harmonic motion refers to motion that repeats in a regular pattern. The bouncing motion of a mass attached to a spring is a good example of simple harmonic motion. As shown in the figure, the displacement y of the mass as a function of time t in seconds is a sine or cosine function. The amplitude is the distance from the center of the motion to either extreme. The period is the time that it takes to complete one full cycle of the motion.

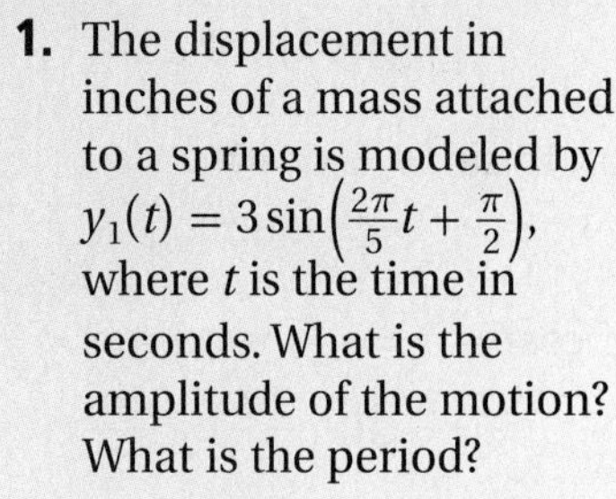

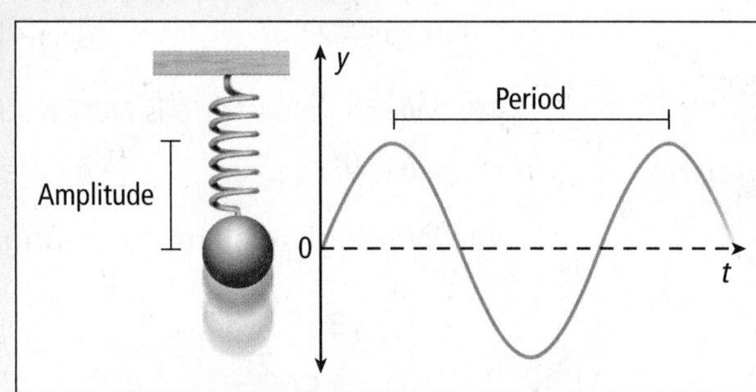

1. The displacement in inches of a mass attached to a spring is modeled by $y_1(t) = 3\sin\left(\frac{2\pi}{5}t + \frac{\pi}{2}\right)$, where t is the time in seconds. What is the amplitude of the motion? What is the period?
2. What is the initial displacement when $t = 0$ s? How long does it take until the displacement is 1.8 in.?
3. At what other times will the displacement be 1.8 in.?
4. Use trigonometric identities to write the displacement by using only the cosine function.
5. The displacement of a second mass attached to a spring is modeled by $y_2(t) = \sin\frac{2\pi}{5}t$. Both masses are set in motion at $t = 0$ s. How long does it take until both masses have the same displacement?
6. The displacement of a third mass attached to a spring is modeled by $y_3(t) = \cos\frac{\pi}{5}t$. The second and third masses are set in motion at $t = 0$ s. How long does it take until both masses have the same displacement?

CHAPTER 11

SECTION 11B

Quiz for Lessons 11-3 Through 11-6

11-3 Fundamental Trigonometric Identities

Prove each trigonometric identity.

1. $\sin^2\theta \sec\theta \csc\theta = \tan\theta$
2. $\sin(-\theta)\sec\theta \cot\theta = -1$
3. $\dfrac{\cot^2\theta - 1}{\cot^2\theta + 1} = 1 - 2\sin^2\theta$

Rewrite each expression in terms of a single trigonometric function.

4. $\cot\theta \sec\theta$
5. $\dfrac{1}{\cos(-\theta)}$
6. $\dfrac{\csc^2\theta}{\tan\theta + \cot\theta}$

11-4 Sum and Difference Identities

Find the exact value of each expression.

7. $\cos\dfrac{5\pi}{12}$
8. $\sin(-75°)$
9. $\tan 75°$

Find each value if $\sin A = \frac{1}{4}$ with $90° < A < 180°$ and if $\cos B = \frac{12}{13}$ with $270° < B < 360°$.

10. $\sin(A + B)$
11. $\cos(A + B)$
12. $\cos(A - B)$
13. Find the coordinates, to the nearest hundredth, of the vertices of figure $ABCD$ with $A(0, 0)$, $B(4, 1)$, $C(0, 2)$, and $D(-1, 1)$ after a $120°$ rotation about the origin.

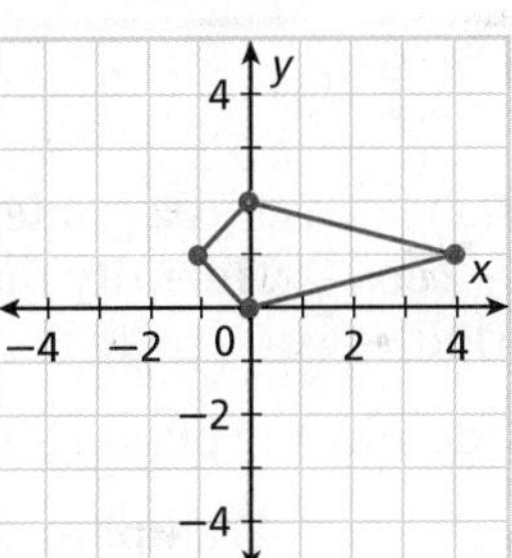

11-5 Double-Angle and Half-Angle Identities

Find each expression if $\cos\theta = -\frac{4}{5}$ and $180° < \theta < 270°$.

14. $\sin 2\theta$
15. $\cos 2\theta$
16. $\tan 2\theta$
17. $\sin\dfrac{\theta}{2}$
18. $\cos\dfrac{\theta}{2}$
19. $\tan\dfrac{\theta}{2}$
20. Use half-angle identities to find the exact value of $\cos 22.5°$.

11-6 Solving Trigonometric Equations

21. Find all solutions of $1 + 2\sin\theta = 0$ where θ is in radians.

Solve each equation for $0° \le \theta < 360°$.

22. $\cos 2\theta + 2\cos\theta = 3$
23. $8\sin^2\theta - 2\sin\theta = 1$

Use trigonometric identities to solve each equation for $0 \le \theta < 2\pi$.

24. $\cos 2\theta = 3\cos\theta + 1$
25. $\sin^2\theta + \cos\theta + 1 = 0$
26. The average daily *minimum* temperature for Houston, Texas, can be modeled by $T(x) = -15.85\cos\frac{\pi}{6}(x - 1) + 76.85$, where T is the temperature in degrees Fahrenheit, x is the time in months, and $x = 0$ is January 1. When is the temperature 65°F? 85°F?

CHAPTER

11 Study Guide: Review

Vocabulary

amplitude
cycle
frequency
period
periodic function
phase shift
rotation matrix

Complete the sentences below with vocabulary words from the list above.

1. The shortest repeating portion of a periodic function is known as a(n) ___?___.
2. The number of cycles in a given unit of time is called ___?___.
3. The ___?___ gives the length of a complete cycle for a periodic function.
4. A horizontal translation of a periodic function is known as a(n) ___?___.

11-1 Graphs of Sine and Cosine

EXAMPLES

■ **Using $f(x) = \cos x$ as a guide, graph $g(x) = -2\cos \frac{\pi}{2}x$. Identify the amplitude and period.**

Step 1 Identify the period and amplitude.

Because $a = -2$, amplitude is $|a| = |-2| = 2$.

Because $b = \frac{\pi}{2}$, the period is $\frac{2\pi}{|b|} = \frac{2\pi}{\left|\frac{\pi}{2}\right|} = 4$.

Step 2 Graph.

The curve is reflected over the x-axis.

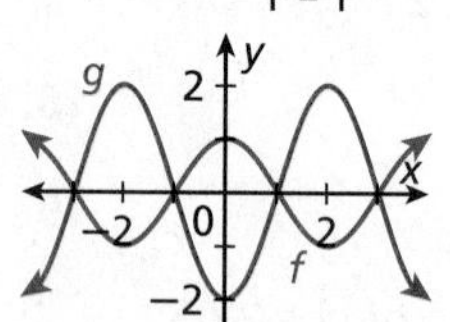

■ **Using $f(x) = \sin x$ as a guide, graph $g(x) = \sin\left(x - \frac{5\pi}{4}\right)$. Identify the x-intercepts and phase shift.**

The amplitude is 1. The period is 2π.

$-\frac{5\pi}{4}$ indicates a shift $\frac{5\pi}{4}$ units right.

The first x-intercept occurs at $\frac{\pi}{4}$. Thus, the intercepts occur at $\frac{\pi}{4} + n\pi$, where n is an integer.

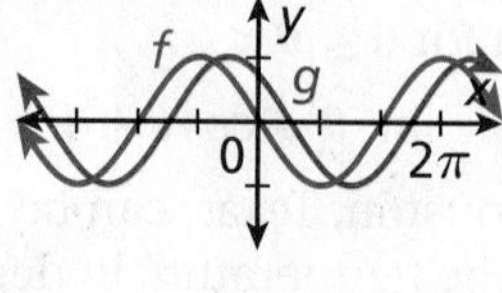

EXERCISES

Using $f(x) = \sin x$ or $f(x) = \cos x$ as a guide, graph each function. Identify the amplitude and period.

5. $f(x) = \cos 3x$
6. $g(x) = \cos \frac{1}{2}x$
7. $h(x) = -\frac{1}{3}\sin x$
8. $j(x) = 2\sin \pi x$
9. $f(x) = \frac{1}{2}\cos 2x$
10. $g(x) = \frac{\pi}{2}\sin \pi x$

Using $f(x) = \sin x$ or $f(x) = \cos x$ as a guide, graph each function. Identify the x-intercepts and phase shift.

11. $f(x) = \cos(x + \pi)$
12. $g(x) = \sin\left(x + \frac{\pi}{4}\right)$
13. $h(x) = \sin\left(x - \frac{3\pi}{2}\right)$
14. $j(x) = \cos\left(x + \frac{3\pi}{2}\right)$

Biology In photosynthesis, a plant converts carbon dioxide and water to sugar and oxygen. This process is studied by measuring a plant's carbon assimilation C (in micromoles of CO_2 per square meter per second). For a bean plant, $C(t) = 1.2\sin \frac{\pi}{12}(t - 6) + 7$, where t is time in hours starting at midnight.

15. Graph the function for two complete cycles.
16. What is the period of the function?
17. What is the maximum and at what time does it occur?

11-2 Graphs of Other Trigonometric Functions

EXAMPLE

- **Using $f(x) = \cot x$ as a guide, graph $g(x) = \cot \frac{\pi}{2}x$. Identify the period, x-intercepts, and asymptotes.**

  Step 1 Identify the period.

  Because $b = \frac{\pi}{2}$, the period is $\frac{\pi}{|b|} = \frac{\pi}{\left|\frac{\pi}{2}\right|} = 2$.

  Step 2 Identify the x-intercepts.

  The first x-intercept occurs at 1. Thus, the x-intercepts occur at $1 + 2n$, where n is an integer.

  Step 3 Identify the asymptotes.

  The asymptotes occur at $x = \frac{\pi n}{|b|} = \frac{\pi n}{\left|\frac{\pi}{2}\right|} = 2n$.

  Step 4 Graph.

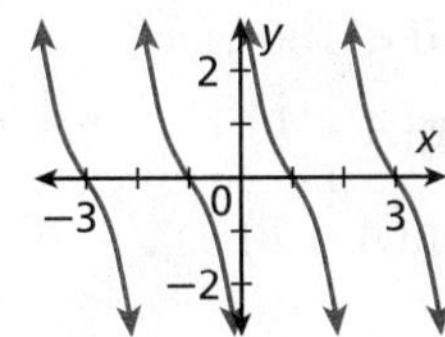

EXERCISES

Using $f(x) = \tan x$ or $f(x) = \cot x$ as a guide, graph each function. Identify the period, x-intercepts, and asymptotes.

18. $f(x) = \frac{1}{4}\tan x$

19. $g(x) = \tan \pi x$

20. $h(x) = \tan \frac{1}{2}\pi x$

21. $g(x) = 5\cot x$

22. $j(x) = -0.5\cot x$

23. $j(x) = \cot \pi x$

Using $f(x) = \cos x$ or $f(x) = \sin x$ as a guide, graph each function. Identify the period and asymptotes.

24. $f(x) = 2\sec x$

25. $g(x) = \csc 2x$

26. $h(x) = 4\csc x$

27. $j(x) = 0.2\sec x$

28. $h(x) = \sec(-x)$

29. $j(x) = -2\csc x$

11-3 Fundamental Trigonometric Identities

EXAMPLES

- **Prove $\frac{\tan\theta}{1-\cos^2\theta} = \sec\theta\csc\theta$.**

$\dfrac{\left(\frac{\sin\theta}{\cos\theta}\right)}{(\sin^2\theta)} =$	*Modify the left side. Apply the ratio and Pythagorean identities.*
$\left(\frac{\sin\theta}{\cos\theta}\right)\left(\frac{1}{\sin^2\theta}\right) =$	*Multiply by the reciprocal.*
$\left(\frac{1}{\cos\theta}\right)\left(\frac{1}{\sin\theta}\right) =$	*Simplify.*
$\sec\theta\csc\theta$	*Reciprocal identities*

- **Rewrite $\frac{\cot\theta + \tan\theta}{\csc\theta}$ in terms of a single trigonometric function, and simplify.**

$(\cot\theta + \tan\theta)\sin\theta$	*Given.*
$\left(\frac{\cos\theta}{\sin\theta} + \frac{\sin\theta}{\cos\theta}\right)\sin\theta$	*Ratio identities*
$\frac{\cos^2\theta + \sin^2\theta}{\cos\theta}$	*Add fractions and simplify.*
$\frac{1}{\cos\theta} = \sec\theta$	*Pythagorean and reciprocal identities*

EXERCISES

Prove each trigonometric identity.

30. $\sec\theta\sin\theta\cot\theta = 1$

31. $\frac{\sin^2(-\theta)}{\tan\theta} = \sin\theta\cos\theta$

32. $(\sec\theta + 1)(\sec\theta - 1) = \tan^2\theta$

33. $\cos\theta\sec\theta + \cos^2\theta\csc^2\theta = \csc^2\theta$

34. $(\tan\theta + \cot\theta)^2 = \sec^2\theta + \csc^2\theta$

35. $\tan\theta + \cot\theta = \sec\theta\csc\theta$

36. $\sin^2\theta\tan\theta = \tan\theta - \sin\theta\cos\theta$

37. $\frac{\tan\theta}{1-\cos^2\theta} = \sec\theta\csc\theta$

Rewrite each expression in terms of a single trigonometric function, and simplify.

38. $\cot\theta\sec\theta$

39. $\frac{\sec\theta\sin\theta}{\cot\theta}$

40. $\frac{\tan(-\theta)}{\cot\theta}$

41. $\frac{\cos\theta\cot\theta}{\csc^2\theta - 1}$

11-4 Sum and Difference Identities

EXAMPLES

■ **Find $\sin(A+B)$ if $\cos A = -\frac{1}{3}$ with $180° < A < 270°$ and if $\sin B = \frac{4}{5}$ with $90° < B < 180°$.**

Step 1 Find $\sin A$ and $\cos B$ by using the Pythagorean Theorem with reference triangles.

$180° < A < 270°$ $\quad$ $90° < B < 180°$

$\cos A = -\dfrac{1}{3}$ $\quad$ $\sin B = \dfrac{4}{5}$

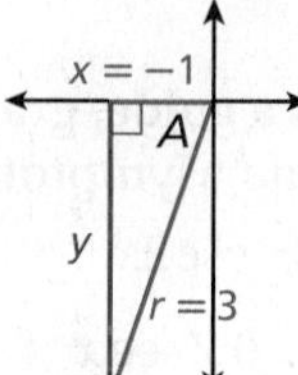

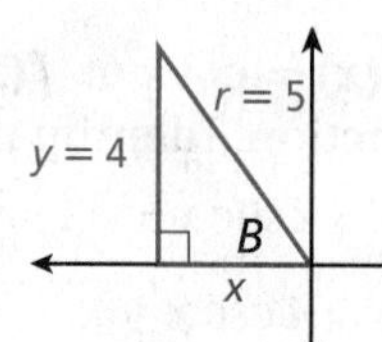

$y = -\sqrt{8}, \sin A = \dfrac{-\sqrt{8}}{3}$ $\quad$ $x = -3, \cos B = \dfrac{-3}{5}$

Step 2 Use the angle-sum identity.

$$\sin(A+B) = \sin A \cos B + \cos A \sin B$$

$$= \left(\frac{-\sqrt{8}}{3}\right)\left(\frac{-3}{5}\right) + \left(-\frac{1}{3}\right)\left(\frac{4}{5}\right)$$

$$= \frac{3\sqrt{8} - 4}{15}$$

■ **Find the coordinates to the nearest hundredth of the vertices of figure ABC with $A(0, 2)$, $B(1, 2)$, and $C(0, 1)$ after a 60° rotation about the origin.**

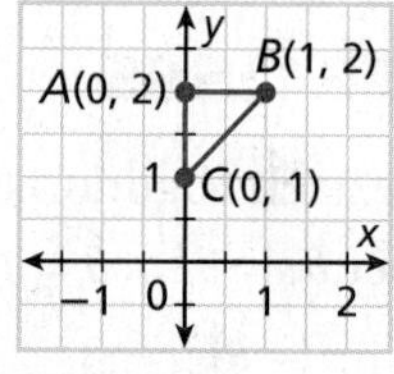

Step 1 Write matrices for a 60° rotation and for the points in the figure.

$$R_{60°} = \begin{bmatrix} \cos 60° & -\sin 60° \\ \sin 60° & \cos 60° \end{bmatrix} \quad \textit{Rotation matrix}$$

$$S = \begin{bmatrix} 0 & 1 & 0 \\ 2 & 2 & 1 \end{bmatrix} \quad \textit{Matrix of points}$$

Step 2 Find the matrix product.

$$R_{60°} \times S = \begin{bmatrix} \cos 60° & -\sin 60° \\ \sin 60° & \cos 60° \end{bmatrix} \begin{bmatrix} 0 & 1 & 0 \\ 2 & 2 & 1 \end{bmatrix}$$

$$\approx \begin{bmatrix} -1.73 & -1.23 & -0.87 \\ 1 & 1.87 & 0.5 \end{bmatrix}$$

Step 3 The approximate coordinates of the points after a 60° rotation are $A'(-1.73, 1)$, $B'(-1.23, 1.87)$, and $C'(-0.87, 0.5)$.

EXERCISES

Find the exact value of each expression.

42. $\sin \dfrac{19\pi}{12}$ $\quad$ **43.** $\cos 165°$

44. $\cos 15°$ $\quad$ **45.** $\tan \dfrac{\pi}{12}$

Find each value if $\tan A = \frac{3}{4}$ with $0° < A < 90°$ and if $\tan B = -\frac{5}{12}$ with $90° < B < 180°$.

46. $\sin(A+B)$ $\quad$ **47.** $\cos(A+B)$

48. $\tan(A-B)$ $\quad$ **49.** $\tan(A+B)$

50. $\sin(A-B)$ $\quad$ **51.** $\cos(A-B)$

Find each value if $\sin A = \frac{\sqrt{7}}{4}$ with $0° < A < 90°$ and if $\cos B = -\frac{5}{13}$ with $90° < B < 180°$.

52. $\sin(A+B)$ $\quad$ **53.** $\cos(A+B)$

54. $\tan(A-B)$ $\quad$ **55.** $\tan(A+B)$

56. $\sin(A-B)$ $\quad$ **57.** $\cos(A-B)$

Find the coordinates, to the nearest hundredth, of the vertices of figure $ABCD$ with $A(0, 0)$, $B(3, 0)$, $C(4, 2)$, and $D(1, 2)$ after each rotation about the origin.

58. 30° rotation $\quad$ **59.** 45° rotation

60. 60° rotation $\quad$ **61.** 90° rotation

Find the coordinates, to the nearest hundredth, of the vertices of figure $ABCD$ with $A(0, 0)$, $B(5, 2)$, $C(0, 4)$, and $D(-5, 2)$ after each rotation about the origin.

62. 120° rotation $\quad$ **63.** 180° rotation

64. 240° rotation $\quad$ **65.** 270° rotation

11-5 Double-Angle and Half-Angle Identities

EXAMPLES

Find each expression if $\sin\theta = \frac{1}{4}$ and $270° < \theta < 360°$.

■ $\sin 2\theta$

For $\sin\theta = \frac{1}{4}$ in QIV, $\cos\theta = -\frac{\sqrt{15}}{4}$.

$\sin 2\theta = 2\sin\theta\cos\theta$ *Identity for sin 2θ*

$= 2\left(\frac{1}{4}\right)\left(-\frac{\sqrt{15}}{4}\right) = -\frac{\sqrt{15}}{8}$ *Substitute.*

■ $\cos\frac{\theta}{2}$

$\cos\frac{\theta}{2} = \pm\sqrt{\frac{1+\cos\theta}{2}}$ *Identity for $\cos\frac{\theta}{2}$*

$= -\sqrt{\frac{1+\left(-\frac{\sqrt{15}}{4}\right)}{2}}$ *Negative for $\cos\frac{\theta}{2}$ in QII*

$= -\sqrt{\left(\frac{4-\sqrt{15}}{4}\right)\left(\frac{1}{2}\right)} = -\frac{\sqrt{4-\sqrt{15}}}{\sqrt{8}}$

EXERCISES

Find each expression if $\tan\theta = \frac{4}{3}$ and $0° < \theta < 90°$.

66. $\sin 2\theta$ **67.** $\cos 2\theta$

68. $\tan\frac{\theta}{2}$ **69.** $\sin\frac{\theta}{2}$

Find each expression if $\cos\theta = \frac{3}{4}$ and $\frac{3\pi}{2} < \theta < 2\pi$.

70. $\tan 2\theta$ **71.** $\cos 2\theta$

72. $\cos\frac{\theta}{2}$ **73.** $\sin\frac{\theta}{2}$

Use half-angle identities to find the exact value of each trigonometric expression.

74. $\sin\frac{\pi}{12}$ **75.** $\cos 75°$

11-6 Solving Trigonometric Equations

EXAMPLES

■ **Find all of the solutions of $3\cos\theta - \sqrt{3} = \cos\theta$.**

$3\cos\theta - \sqrt{3} = \cos\theta$

$3\cos\theta - \cos\theta = \sqrt{3}$ *Subtract tan θ.*

$2\cos\theta = \sqrt{3}$ *Combine like terms.*

$\cos\theta = \frac{\sqrt{3}}{2}$ *Divide by 2.*

$\theta = \cos^{-1}\left(\frac{\sqrt{3}}{2}\right)$ *Apply the inverse cosine.*

$\theta = 30°$ or $330°$ *Find θ for $0° \le \theta < 360°$.*

$\theta = 30° + 360°n$

or $330° + 360°n$

■ **Solve $6\sin^2\theta + 5\sin\theta = -1$ for $0° \le \theta < 360°$.**

$6\sin^2\theta + 5\sin\theta + 1 = 0$ *Set equal to 0.*

$(2\sin\theta + 1)(3\sin\theta + 1) = 0$ *Factor.*

$\sin\theta = -1$ or $\sin\theta = 3$ *Zero Product Property*

$\theta = 210°, 330°$ *$\sin\theta = 3$ has no solution since $-1 \le \sin\theta \le 1$.*

or $\approx 199.5°, 340.5°$

EXERCISES

Find all of the solutions of each equation.

76. $\sqrt{2}\cos\theta + 1 = 0$ **77.** $\cos\theta = 2 + 3\cos\theta$

78. $\tan^2\theta + \tan\theta = 0$ **79.** $\sin^2\theta - \cos^2\theta = \frac{1}{2}$

Solve each equation for $0 \le \theta < 2\pi$.

80. $2\cos^2\theta - 3\cos\theta = 2$ **81.** $\cos^2\theta + 5\cos\theta - 6 = 0$

82. $\sin^2\theta - 1 = 0$ **83.** $2\sin^2\theta - \sin\theta = 3$

Use trigonometric identities to solve each equation for $0 \le \theta < 2\pi$.

84. $\cos 2\theta = \cos\theta$ **85.** $\sin 2\theta + \cos\theta = 0$

86. Earth Science The number of minutes of daylight for each day of the year can be modeled with a trigonometric function. For Washington, D.C., S is the number of minutes of daylight in the model $S(d) = 180\sin(0.0172d - 1.376) + 720$, where d is the number of days since January 1.

a. What is the maximum number of daylight minutes, and when does it occur?

b. What is the minimum number of daylight minutes, and when does it occur?

CHAPTER

11

1. Using $f(x) = \cos x$ as a guide, graph $g(x) = \frac{1}{2}\cos 2x$. Identify the amplitude and period.
2. Using $f(x) = \sin x$ as a guide, graph $g(x) = \sin\left(x + \frac{\pi}{3}\right)$. Identify the x-intercepts and phase shift.
3. A torque τ in newton meters (N•m) applied to an object is given by $\tau(\theta) = Fr\sin\theta$, where r is the length of the lever arm in meters, F is the applied force in newtons, and θ is the angle between F and r in degrees. Find the amount and angle for the maximum torque and the minimum torque for a lever arm of 0.5 m and a force of 500 newtons, where $0° \le \theta \le 90°$.
4. Using $f(x) = \tan x$ as a guide, graph $g(x) = 2\tan \pi x$. Identify the period, x-intercepts, and asymptotes.
5. Using $f(x) = \cot x$ as a guide, graph $g(x) = \cot 4x$. Identify the period, x-intercepts, and asymptotes.
6. Using $f(x) = \sin x$ as a guide, graph $g(x) = \frac{1}{4}\csc x$. Identify the period and asymptotes.
7. Prove the trigonometric identity $\cot\theta = \cos^2\theta\sec\theta\csc\theta$.

Rewrite each expression in terms of a single trigonometric function.

8. $(\sec\theta + 1)(\sec\theta - 1)$
9. $\dfrac{\sin(-\theta)}{\cos(-\theta)}$

Find each value if $\tan A = \frac{3}{4}$ with $0° < A < 90°$ and if $\sin B = -\frac{12}{13}$ with $180° < B < 270°$.

10. $\sin(A + B)$
11. $\cos(A - B)$
12. Find the coordinates, to the nearest hundredth, of the vertices of figure $ABCD$ with $A(0, 1)$, $B(2, 1)$, $C(3, 3)$, and $D(-1, 3)$ after a 30° rotation about the origin.

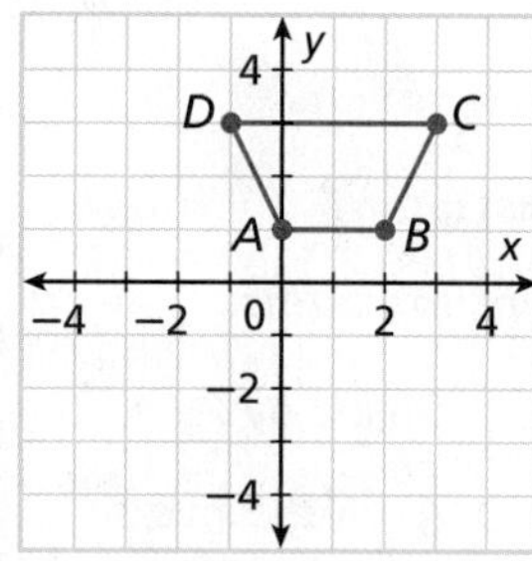

Find each expression if $\tan\theta = -\frac{12}{5}$ and $90° < \theta < 180°$.

13. $\sin 2\theta$
14. $\cos 2\theta$
15. $\cos\dfrac{\theta}{2}$
16. Use half-angle identities to find the exact value of $\sin\dfrac{3\pi}{8}$.
17. Find all of the solutions of $\tan\theta + \sqrt{3} = 0$.
18. Solve $2\sin^2\theta = \sin\theta$ for $0° \le \theta < 360°$.
19. Use trigonometric identities to solve $2\cos^2\theta + 3\sin\theta = 0$ for $0 \le \theta < 2\pi$.
20. The voltage at a wall plug in a home can be modeled by $V(t) = 156\sin 2\pi(60t)$, where V is the voltage in volts and t is time in seconds. At what times is the voltage equal to 110 volts?

College Entrance Exam Practice

FOCUS ON SAT MATHEMATICS SUBJECT TESTS

To help decide which standardized tests you should take, make a list of colleges that you might like to attend. Find out the admission requirements for each school. Make sure that you register for and take the appropriate tests early enough for colleges to receive your scores.

If your calculator malfunctions while you are taking an SAT Mathematics Subject Test, you may be able to have your score for that test canceled. To do so, you must inform a supervisor at the test center immediately when the malfunction occurs.

You may want to time yourself as you take this practice test. It should take you about 6 minutes to complete.

1. Identify the range of $f(x) = 3\sin x$.

(A) $-1 \leq f(x) \leq 1$

(B) $-3 < f(x) < 3$

(C) $0 \leq f(x) \leq 3$

(D) $-3 \leq f(x) \leq 3$

(E) $-\infty < f(x) < \infty$

2. If $2\sin^2\theta + 5\sin\theta = 3$, what could the value of θ be?

(A) $\frac{\pi}{6}$

(B) $\frac{\pi}{3}$

(C) $\frac{2\pi}{3}$

(D) $\frac{7\pi}{6}$

(E) $\frac{11\pi}{6}$

3. If $\sec\theta = 4$, what is $\tan^2\theta$?

(A) $\frac{1}{16}$

(B) 3

(C) 5

(D) 15

(E) 17

4. Given the figure, what is the value of $\cos(A - B)$?

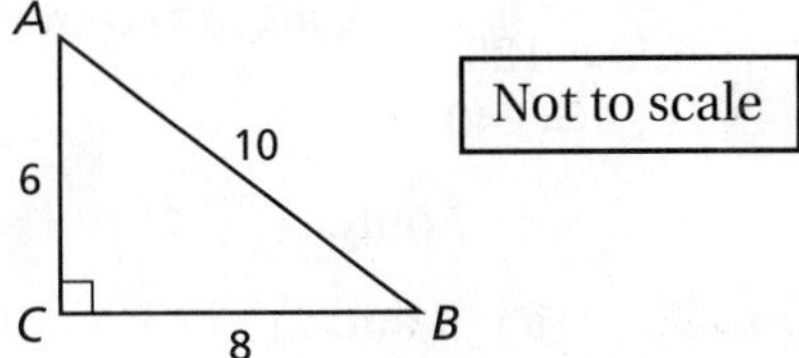

(A) 0

(B) $\frac{7}{25}$

(C) $\frac{24}{25}$

(D) 1

(E) $\frac{28}{25}$

5. If $\sin\theta = \frac{7}{9}$, what is $\cos 2\theta$?

(A) $-\frac{8\sqrt{2}}{9}$

(B) $-\frac{17}{81}$

(C) $\frac{17}{81}$

(D) $\frac{56\sqrt{2}}{81}$

(E) $\frac{8\sqrt{2}}{9}$

CHAPTER 11

TEST TACKLER

Standardized Test Strategies

Multiple Choice: Choose Answer Combinations

You may be given a test item in which you are asked to choose from a combination of statements. To answer these types of test items, try comparing each given statement with the question and determining whether the statement is true or false. If you determine that more than one of the statements is correct, choose the combination that contains each correct statement.

EXAMPLE 1

Which exact solution makes the equation $2\cos^2\theta - 3\cos\theta = 2$ true?

I. $\theta = 2°$
II. $\theta = 120°$
III. $\theta = 240°$

Look at each statement separately, and determine if it is true or false.

Ⓐ I only
Ⓑ II and III
Ⓒ II only
Ⓓ I, II, and III

As you consider each statement, mark it true or false.

Consider statement I: Substitute 2° for θ in the equation.

$$2\cos^2(2°) - 3\cos(2°) \approx -1.0006$$
$$\neq 2$$

Statement I is false.
So, the answer is ***not*** choice A or D.

Consider statement II: Substitute 120° for θ in the equation.

$$2\cos^2(120°) - 3\cos(120°) = 2$$

Statement II is true.
The answer *could be* choice B or C.

Consider statement III: Substitute 240° for θ in the equation.

$$2\cos^2(240°) - 3\cos(240°) = 2$$

Statement III is true.

Because both statements II and III are true, choice B is the correct response.

You can also use a table to keep track of whether the statements are true or false.

Statement	True/False
I	False
II	True
III	True

As you eliminate a statement, cross out the corresponding answer choice (s).

Read each test item and answer the questions that follow.

Item A

Which expression is equivalent to $\tan^2\theta$?

I. $\sec^2\theta - 1$

II. $\sec^2\theta + 1$

III. $\dfrac{1}{\csc^2\theta - 1}$

IV. $\dfrac{1-\cos^2\theta}{1-\sin^2\theta}$

Ⓐ I and II

Ⓑ II and III

Ⓒ I and III

Ⓓ I, III, and IV

1. What are some of the identities that involve the tangent function?
2. Determine whether statements I, II, III, and IV are true or false. Explain your reasoning.
3. Sally realized that statement III was true and selected choice B as her response. Do you agree? If not, what would you have done differently?

Item B

For the graph of $f(x) = 3\sin x + 2$, which of the statements are true?

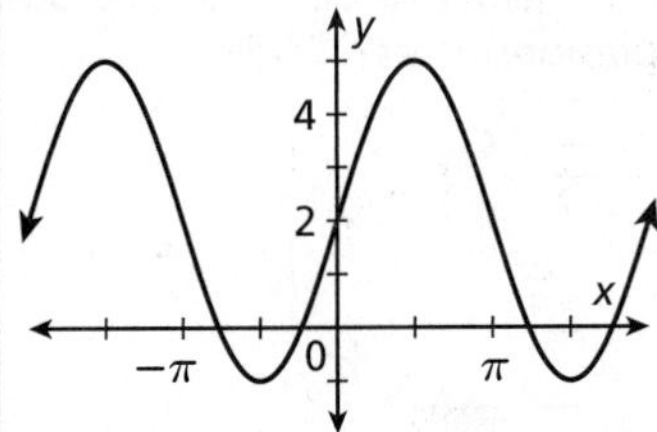

I. The function has a period of $\frac{2\pi}{3}$.

II. The function has an amplitude of 3.

III. The function has a period of 2π.

Ⓕ I only

Ⓖ III only

Ⓗ II only

Ⓙ II and III

4. How do you determine the period of a trigonometric function?
5. How do you determine the amplitude of a trigonometric function?
6. Using your response to Problems 4 and 5, which of the three statements are true? Explain.

Item C

Which identities do you need to use to prove that $\tan\theta\csc\theta = \sec\theta$?

I. $\tan\theta = \dfrac{\sin\theta}{\cos\theta}$

II. $\sec^2\theta = \tan^2\theta + 1$

III. $\csc\theta = \dfrac{1}{\sin\theta}$

Ⓐ I only

Ⓑ II only

Ⓒ I and II

Ⓓ I and III

7. Is statement I true or false? Can any answer choice be eliminated? Explain.
8. Is statement II true or false? Should you select the answer choice yet? Explain.
9. Is statement III true or false? Explain.
10. Which combination of statements is correct? How do you know?

Item D

For the graph of the function $f(x) = \sec 4x$, which are equations of some of the asymptotes?

I. $x = \dfrac{\pi}{8}$

II. $x = \dfrac{\pi}{2}$

III. $x = -\dfrac{3\pi}{4}$

Ⓕ I only

Ⓖ II and III

Ⓗ I, II, and III

Ⓙ I and III

11. Create a table, and determine whether each statement is true or false.
12. Using your table, which choice is the most accurate?

CHAPTER 11

STANDARDIZED TEST PREP

Learn It Online
State Test Practice

CUMULATIVE ASSESSMENT

Multiple Choice

1. What is the exact value of tan 15°?

Ⓐ $\frac{\sqrt{6}-\sqrt{2}}{4}$

Ⓑ $\frac{\sqrt{6}+\sqrt{2}}{4}$

Ⓒ $2+\sqrt{3}$

Ⓓ $2-\sqrt{3}$

2. Where do the asymptotes occur in the given equation?

$y = \frac{1}{3}\cot 2x$

Ⓕ $2\pi n$

Ⓖ $\frac{\pi n}{2}$

Ⓗ $3\pi n$

Ⓙ $\frac{\pi n}{3}$

3. What is the period of the given equation?

$y = 5\cos\frac{1}{3}x$

Ⓐ $\frac{2\pi}{5}$

Ⓑ $\frac{5}{3}$

Ⓒ $\frac{2\pi}{3}$

Ⓓ 6π

4. A movie has 14 dialogue scenes and 10 action scenes. If these are the only two types of scenes, what is the probability that a randomly selected scene will be an action scene?

Ⓕ $\frac{5}{12}$

Ⓖ $\frac{7}{12}$

Ⓗ $\frac{5}{7}$

Ⓙ $\frac{7}{5}$

5. What is the value of $f(x) = 3x^3 + 4x^2 + 7x + 10$ for $x = -2$?

Ⓐ −44

Ⓑ −12

Ⓒ 0

Ⓓ 36

6. Which graph shows an inverse variation function for which $y = 2$ when $x = -1$?

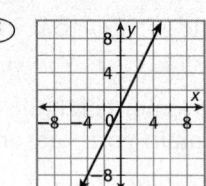

Ⓕ

Ⓗ 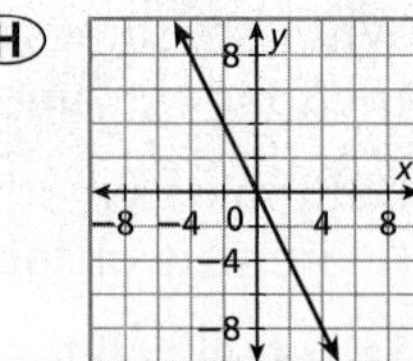

Ⓖ 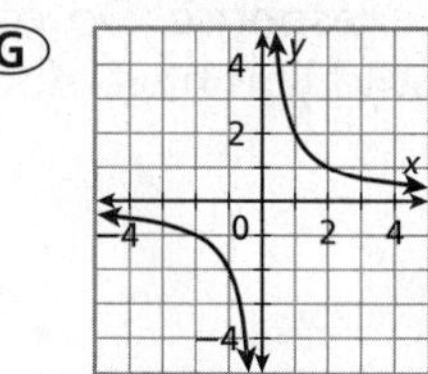

Ⓙ 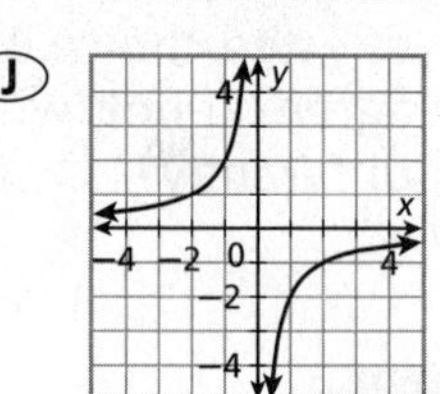

7. What is the exact value of cos157.5° using half-angle identities?

Ⓐ $-\frac{\sqrt{2-\sqrt{2}}}{2}$

Ⓑ $\frac{\sqrt{2-\sqrt{2}}}{2}$

Ⓒ $-\frac{\sqrt{2+\sqrt{2}}}{2}$

Ⓓ $\frac{\sqrt{2+\sqrt{2}}}{2}$

8. What type of function is $f(x) = -2x^3 - x + 10$?

Ⓕ cubic

Ⓖ exponential

Ⓗ quadratic

Ⓙ rational

9. Which is a solution of $2\cos\theta = 2\sin\theta$ for $\pi \le \theta \le 3\pi$?

(F) $\frac{\pi}{4}$

(G) π

(H) $\frac{5\pi}{4}$

(J) 3π

10. Identify the amplitude and the period of the function $f(x) = 4\cos 2x$.

(A) amplitude = 4; period = 2π

(B) amplitude = 2; period = 4

(C) amplitude = 4; period = π

(D) amplitude = $\frac{1}{4}$; period = 2

Gridded Response

11. What is the value of x?

$5\sqrt{2x - 7} + 4 = 9$

12. What is the value of $\cos\theta$? Round to the nearest thousandth.

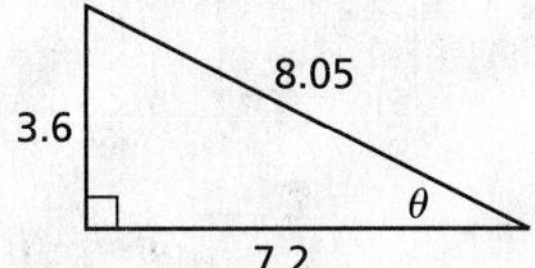

In Item 13, the answer will be a *y*-value only. It will be quickest and most efficient to isolate *x* in one equation and substitute for *x* in the second equation because then the first variable for which you obtain a value will be *y*.

13. What is the smallest y-value of a solution of the following system of equations?

$$\begin{cases} x - 4 = \frac{1}{4}y^2 \\ 2y = 8 - x \end{cases}$$

14. Find the sum of the arithmetic series $\sum_{k=1}^{14}(3k - 5)$.

Short Response

15. The chart below shows the names of the students on the academic bowl team.

Robin	Drew	Jim
Greg	Sarah	Mindy
Ashley	Tina	Justin
David	Amy	Kevin

a. Only 2 students can be chosen for the final academic bowl. How many different ways can the students be selected?

b. Explain why you solved the problem the way that you did.

16. Given the sequence:

4, 12, 36, 108, 324, ...

a. Write the explicit rule for the nth term.

b. Find the 10th term.

Extended Response

17. The chart below shows the grades in Mr. Bradshaw's class.

90	85	72	86	94	96
85	95	94	68	71	85
93	98	84	83	80	89

Round each answer to the nearest tenth.

a. Find the mean.

b. Find the median.

c. Find the mode.

d. Find the variance.

e. Find the standard deviation.

f. Find the range.

The Rock and Roll Hall of Fame

The Rock and Roll Hall of Fame in downtown Cleveland traces the history of rock music through live performances and interactive exhibits. Designed by renowned architect I. M. Pei, the 50,000-square-foot exhibition space houses everything from vintage posters to handwritten lyrics to John Lennon's report card.

Choose one or more strategies to solve each problem.
For 1 and 2, use the diagram.

1. Visitors enter the museum through an enormous glass entryway in the shape of a tetrahedron. The figure shows the dimensions of the tetrahedron. What is the pitch of the tetrahedron's slanted facade? (*Hint:* The pitch is shown in the figure by angle θ.)

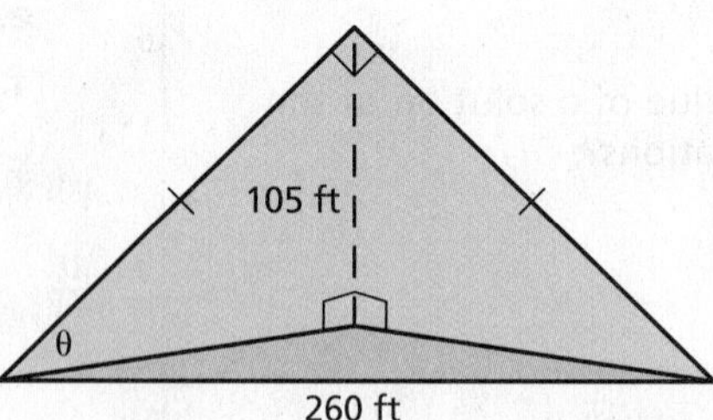

2. What is the area of the triangular floor space enclosed by the glass tetrahedron?
3. The Hall of Fame exhibits are displayed in an eight-story, 162-foot tower. Pei originally designed a 200-foot tower but had to reduce its height in order to meet the requirements of a nearby airport. From the top of the existing tower, an observer sights the entrance to the museum's plaza with an angle of depression of 18°. What would be the angle of depression to the entrance of the plaza from Pei's original tower?

Marblehead Lighthouse

Since its construction in 1821, Marblehead Lighthouse has stood at the entrance to Sandusky Bay, guiding sailors along Lake Erie's rocky shores. The 65-foot tower is one of Ohio's best-known landmarks and the oldest continuously operating lighthouse on the Great Lakes.

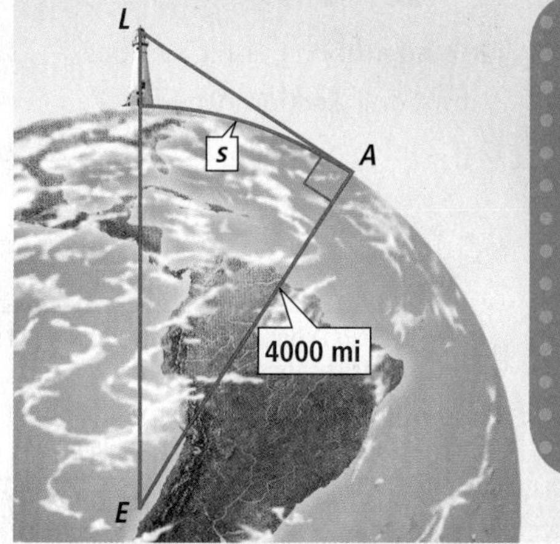

Choose one or more strategies to solve each problem.

1. The range of a lighthouse is the maximum distance at which its light is visible. In the figure, point A is the farthest point from which it is possible to see the light at the top of the lighthouse L. The distance along Earth s is the range. Assuming that the radius of Earth is 4000 miles, find the range of Marblehead Lighthouse.
2. In 1897, a new lighting system was installed in the lighthouse. A set of descending weights rotated the tower's lantern to produce a flashing light. The rotation could be modeled by the function $f(x) = \sin\frac{\pi}{5}x$, where x is the time in seconds since the weights were released. The light briefly flashed on whenever $f(x) = 1$. How many times per minute did the light flash?
3. Today the flashing light of Marblehead Lighthouse can be modeled by $g(x) = \sin\frac{\pi}{3}x$. How many seconds are there between each flash? Does the light flash more or less frequently than in 1897?

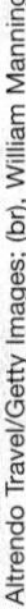

Real-World Connections

CHAPTER 12

Conic Sections

COMMON CORE

Chapter

- Develop conceptual understanding of conic sections.
- Applying algebraic representations of conic sections to solve problems.

CRACKING THE SUPER EGG

You can use conic sections to create your own super egg and discover the many different uses of super ellipses.

Learn It Online
Chapter Project Online

Vocabulary

Match each term on the left with a definition on the right.

1. vertex of a parabola
2. axis of symmetry
3. solution set of a system of equations
4. asymptote

A. a line that divides a plane figure or a graph into two congruent reflected halves
B. a line approached by the graph of a function
C. a line that is neither horizontal nor vertical
D. the turning point of a parabola
E. the set of points that make all equations in a system true

Circumference and Area of Circles

Find the circumference and area of each circle.

5. 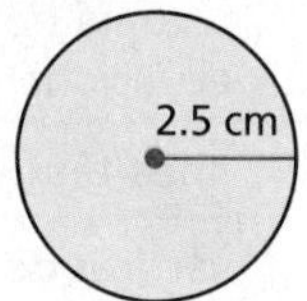

6. 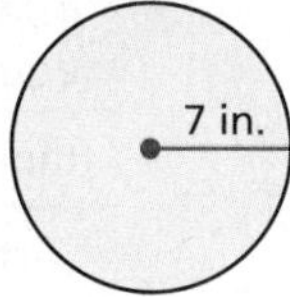

Area of Polygons

Find the area of each figure.

7. 15 in. / 7 in. / 6 in. / 7 in. / 15 in.

8. 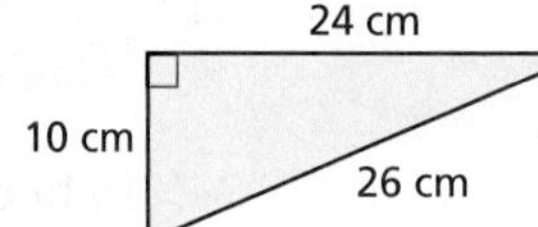

9. 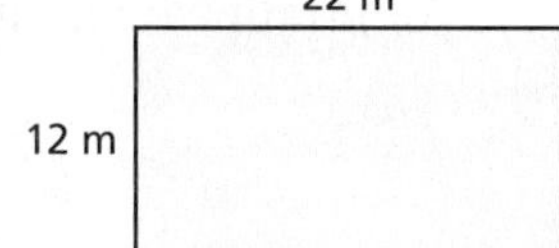

Find Areas in the Coordinate Plane

Find the area of each figure.

10. 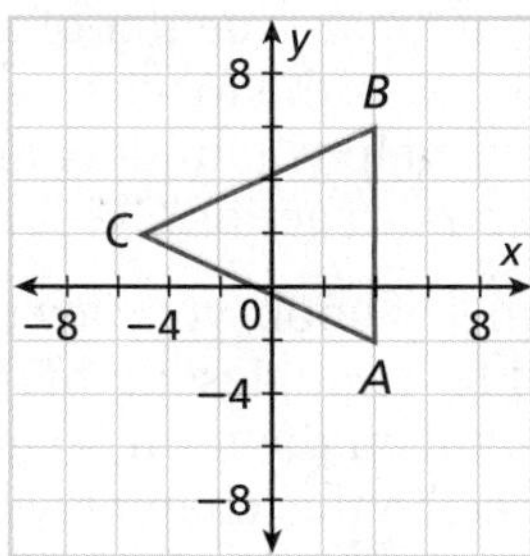

11. 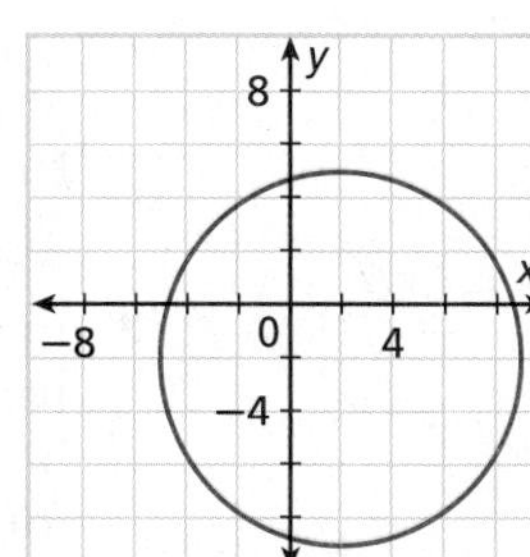

12. 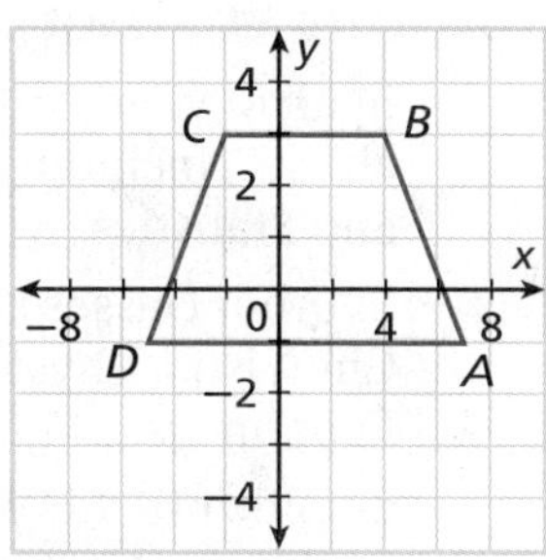

Complete the Square

Complete the square for each expression. Write the resulting expression as a binomial squared.

13. $x^2 - 4x + \blacksquare$

14. $x^2 - x + \blacksquare$

15. $x^2 + 6x + \blacksquare$

CHAPTER 12

Study Guide: Preview

Where You've Been

Previously, you

- graphed parabolas defined by quadratic functions.
- studied graphs of piecewise functions.
- solved systems of linear equations.

In This Chapter

You will study

- graphs of parabolas and other conic sections that are not functions.
- graphs of conic sections represented by two functions together.
- methods for solving systems of nonlinear equations.

Where You're Going

You can use the skills in this chapter

- in all of your future math classes, including Calculus and Statistics.
- in other classes such as Chemistry, Physics, and Economics.
- outside of school in engineering, architecture, astronomy, photography, and communications.

Key Vocabulary/Vocabulario

circle	círculo
conic section	sección cónica
directrix	directriz
ellipse	elipse
foci of an ellipse	focos de una elipse
foci of a hyperbola	focos de una hipérbola
focus of a parabola	foco de una parábola
hyperbola	hipérbola
nonlinear system of equations	sistema no lineal de ecuaciones
tangent line	línea tangente
vertices of an ellipse	vértices de una elipse
vertices of a hyperbola	vértices de una hipérbola

Vocabulary Connections

To become familiar with some of the vocabulary terms in the chapter, consider the following. You may refer to the chapter, the glossary, or a dictionary if you like.

1. When you use the word *focus* in most contexts, you mean a center of activity or attention. What is the focus of a painting? How can this help you understand a **focus** of a conic section?
2. In the geometry book, you saw the term *vertex* used for triangles. In this book you have already seen the term *vertex* used for parabolas. In this chapter, you will see the term **vertex** used for ellipses and hyperbolas. Why is the same term used in all of these different situations?
3. How often does a *tangent* touch a circle? Can curves other than circles also have **tangents**? What do you mean when you say that someone went "off on a tangent" during a discussion?

Reading Strategy: Interpret and Read Diagrams

Diagrams are informational tools. Be sure to read and understand the information provided in these visual aids before you attempt to work a problem.

Multi-Step Test Prep

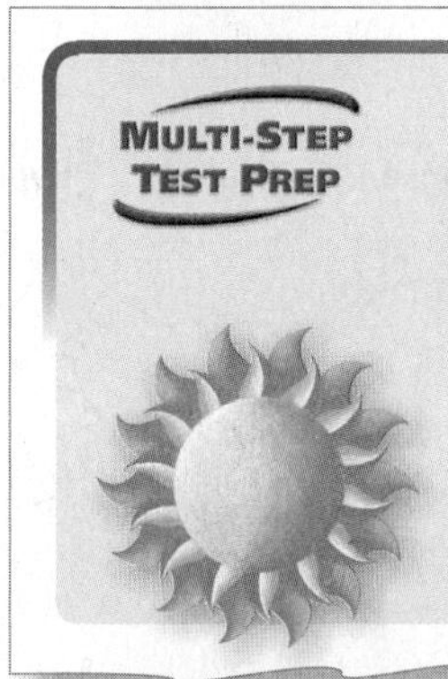

The figure shows the elliptical orbit of Mars, where each unit of the coordinate plane represents 1 million kilometers. As shown, the planet's maximum distance from the Sun is 249 million kilometers and its minimum distance from the Sun is 207 million kilometers.

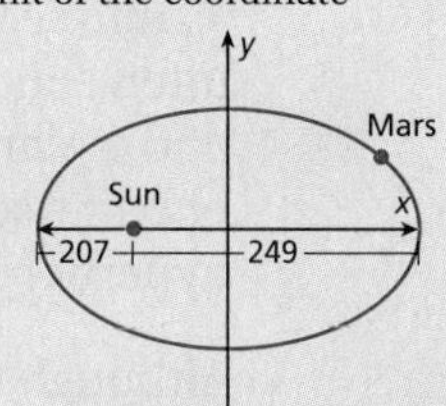

a. The Sun is at one focus of the ellipse. What are the coordinates of the Sun?

b. What is the length of the minor axis of the ellipse?

c. Write an equation that models the orbit of Mars.

1. **Examine the diagram.** A point labeled *Sun* lies on the major axis of what appears to be an ellipse. The distances from this point to the vertices are labeled 207 and 249.
2. **Reread the problem, and identify key information about the diagram.** Each unit represents 1 million kilometers. The Sun is at one focus of the ellipse.
3. **Interpret this information.** The labels 207 and 249 represent 207 million kilometers and 249 million kilometers. The length of the major axis can be found by adding these two measurements.
4. **Now you are ready to solve the problem.**

Try This

Read the problem below and examine the diagram. Then answer the questions below.

26. Engineering The main cables of a suspension bridge are ideally parabolic. The cables over a bridge that is 400 feet long are attached to towers that are 100 feet tall. The lowest point of the cable is 40 feet above the bridge.

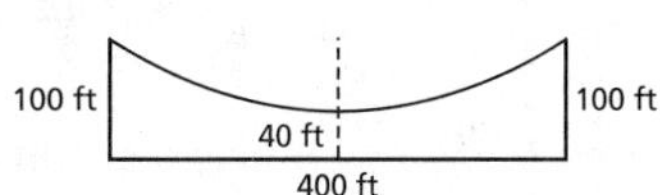

a. Find the coordinates of the vertex and the tops of the towers if the bridge represents the x-axis and the axis of symmetry is the y-axis.

1. What information is provided in the diagram?
2. What information regarding the diagram is provided in the problem?
3. What conclusions can you draw from the information related to the diagram?

12-1 Introduction to Conic Sections

CC.9-12.G.GPE.4 Use coordinates to prove simple geometric theorems algebraically.

Objectives
Recognize conic sections as intersections of planes and cones.

Use the distance and midpoint formulas to solve problems.

Vocabulary
conic section

Who uses this?
Archaeologists use distance and midpoint to organize excavation sites. (See Exercise 43.)

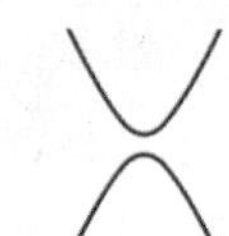

The parabola is one of a family of curves called *conic sections*. **Conic sections** are formed by the intersection of a double right cone and a plane. There are four types of conic sections: circles, ellipses, hyperbolas, and parabolas.

Although the parabolas you have studied are functions, most conic sections are not. This means that you often must use two functions to graph a conic section on a calculator.

A circle is defined by its center and its radius. An ellipse, an elongated shape similar to a circle, has two perpendicular axes of different lengths.

EXAMPLE 1 Graphing Circles and Ellipses on a Calculator

Graph each equation on a graphing calculator. Identify each conic section. Then describe the center and intercepts.

A $x^2 + y^2 = 25$

Step 1 Solve for y so that the expression can be used in a graphing calculator.

$y^2 = 25 - x^2$ *Subtract x^2 from both sides.*

$y = \pm\sqrt{25 - x^2}$ *Take the square root of both sides.*

Step 2 Use two equations to see the complete graph.

$y_1 = \sqrt{25 - x^2}$

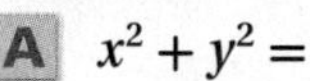

$y_2 = -\sqrt{25 - x^2}$

Use a square window on your graphing calculator for an accurate graph. The graphs meet and form a complete circle, even though it may not appear that way on your calculator.

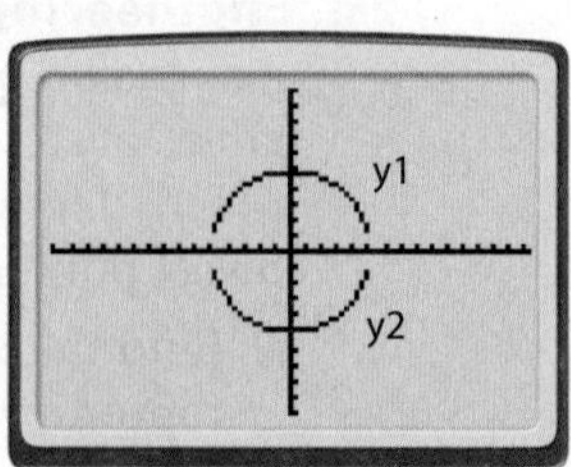

The graph is a circle with center (0, 0) and intercepts (5, 0), (−5, 0), (0, 5), and (0, −5).

Check Use a table to confirm the intercepts.

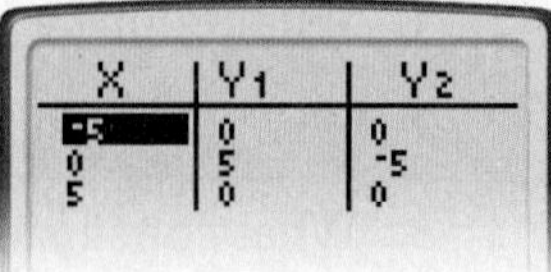

X	Y1	Y2
-5	0	0
0	5	-5
5	0	0

Remember!
When you take the square root of both sides of an equation, remember that you must include the positive and negative roots.

Graph each equation on a graphing calculator. Identify each conic section. Then describe the center and intercepts.

B $16x^2 + 9y^2 = 144$

Step 1 Solve for y so that the expression can be used in a graphing calculator.

$9y^2 = 144 - 16x^2$ *Subtract $16x^2$ from both sides.*

$y^2 = \frac{144 - 16x^2}{9}$ *Divide both sides by 9.*

$y = \pm\sqrt{\frac{144 - 16x^2}{9}}$ *Take the square root of both sides.*

Step 2 Use two equations to see the complete graph.

$y_1 = \sqrt{\frac{144 - 16x^2}{9}}$

$y_2 = -\sqrt{\frac{144 - 16x^2}{9}}$

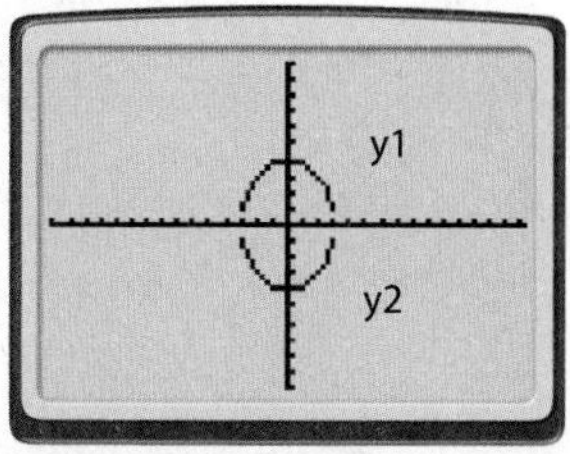

Use a square window on your graphing calculator. The graphs meet and form a complete ellipse, even though it may not appear that way on your calculator.

The graph is an ellipse with center $(0, 0)$ and intercepts $(3, 0)$, $(-3, 0)$, $(0, 4)$, and $(0, -4)$.

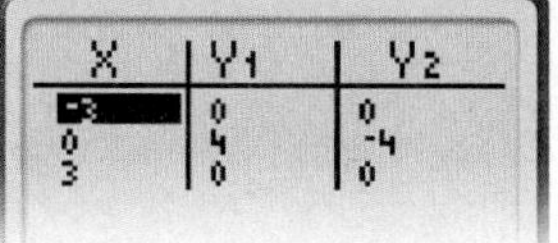

Check Use a table to confirm the intercepts.

Graph each equation on a graphing calculator. Identify each conic section. Then describe the center and intercepts.

1a. $x^2 + y^2 = 49$ **1b.** $9x^2 + 25y^2 = 225$

A parabola is a single curve, whereas a hyperbola has two congruent branches. The equation of a parabola usually contains either an x^2 term or a y^2 term, but not both. The equations of the other conics will usually contain both x^2 and y^2 terms.

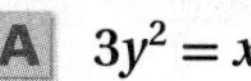

Graphing Parabolas and Hyperbolas on a Calculator

Graph each equation on a graphing calculator. Identify each conic section. Then describe the vertices and the direction that the graph opens.

A $3y^2 = x$

Step 1 Solve for y so that the expression can be used in a graphing calculator.

$y^2 = \frac{x}{3}$ *Divide both sides by 3.*

$y = \pm\sqrt{\frac{x}{3}}$ *Take the square root of both sides.*

Step 2 Use two equations to see the complete graph.

$y_1 = \sqrt{\frac{x}{3}}$ and $y_2 = -\sqrt{\frac{x}{3}}$

The graph is a parabola with vertex $(0, 0)$ that opens to the right.

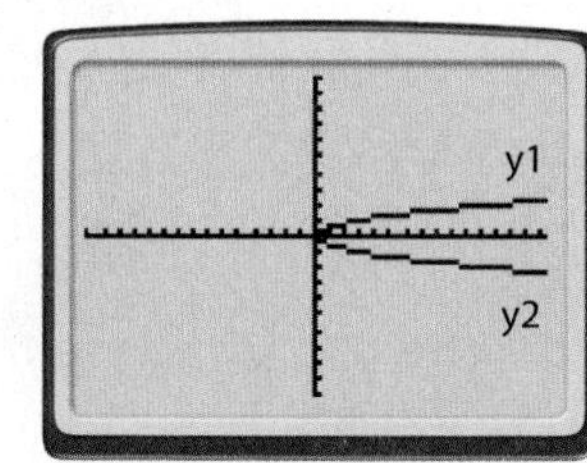

Graph each equation on a graphing calculator. Identify each conic section. Then describe the vertices and the direction that the graph opens.

B $x^2 - y^2 = 4$

Step 1 Solve for y so that the expression can be used in a graphing calculator.

$-y^2 = 4 - x^2$ *Subtract x^2 from both sides.*

$y^2 = -(4 - x^2)$ *Multiply both sides by −1.*

$y^2 = -4 + x^2$ *Distribute.*

$y^2 = x^2 - 4$ *Rearrange.*

$y = \pm\sqrt{x^2 - 4}$ *Take the square root of both sides.*

Helpful Hint

Because hyperbolas contain two curves that open in opposite directions, classify them as opening horizontally, vertically, or neither.

Step 2 Use two equations to see the complete graph.

$y_1 = \sqrt{x^2 - 4}$

$y_2 = -\sqrt{x^2 - 4}$

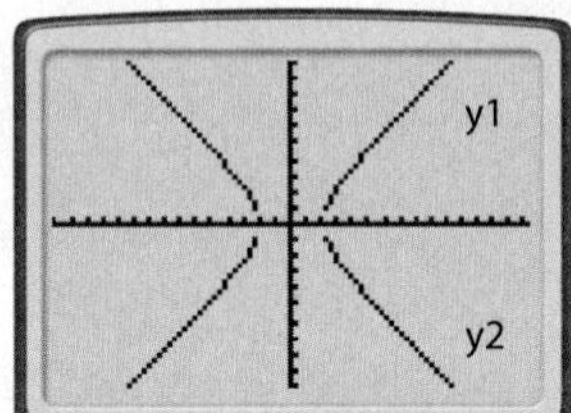

The graph is a hyperbola that opens horizontally with vertices at $(2, 0)$ and $(-2, 0)$.

Graph each equation on a graphing calculator. Identify each conic section. Then describe the vertices and the direction that the graph opens.

2a. $2y^2 = x$ **2b.** $x^2 - y^2 = 16$

Every conic section can be defined in terms of distances. You can use the Midpoint and Distance Formulas to find the center and radius of a circle.

Midpoint and Distance Formulas

FORMULA	EXAMPLE	GRAPH
The **midpoint** (x_M, y_M) of the segment with endpoints (x_1, y_1) and (x_2, y_2) is $(x_M, y_M) = \left(\frac{x_1 + x_2}{2}, \frac{y_1 + y_2}{2}\right)$.	The midpoint of the segment with endpoints (1, 2) and (5, 8) is $\left(\frac{1+5}{2}, \frac{2+8}{2}\right) = (3, 5)$.	(5, 8); (3, 5); (1, 2)
The **distance** d between the points with coordinates (x_1, y_1) and (x_2, y_2) is $d = \sqrt{(x_2 - x_1)^2 + (y_2 - y_1)^2}$.	The distance between the points (2, 1) and (6, 4) is $\sqrt{(6-2)^2 + (4-1)^2} = 5$.	(6, 4); (2, 1); 5; $4 - 1 = 3$; $6 - 2 = 4$

Because a diameter must pass through the center of a circle, the midpoint of a diameter is the center of the circle. The radius of a circle is the distance from the center to any point on the circle and equal to half the diameter.

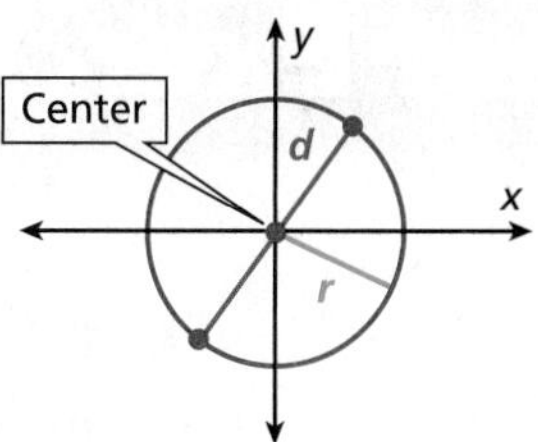

EXAMPLE 3 Finding the Center and Radius of a Circle

Find the center and radius of a circle that has a diameter with endpoints (3, 12) and (9, 4).

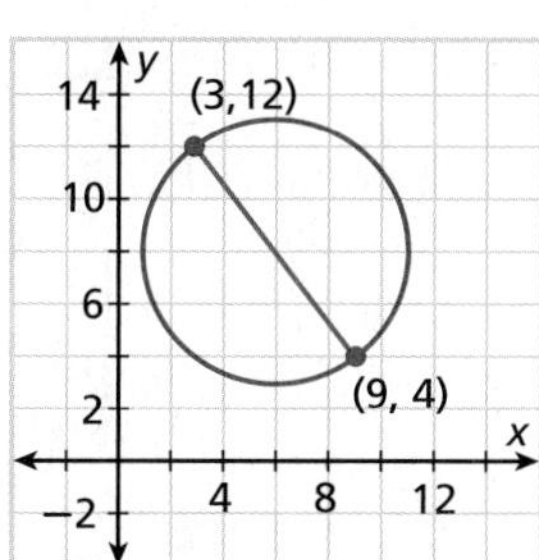

Step 1 Find the center of the circle.

Use the Midpoint Formula with the endpoints, (3, 12) and (9, 4).

$$\left(\frac{3+9}{2}, \frac{12+4}{2}\right) = (6, 8)$$

The center of the circle is (6, 8).

Step 2 Find the radius.

Use the Distance Formula with (6, 8) and (3, 12).

$$r = \sqrt{(6-3)^2 + (8-12)^2}$$
$$= \sqrt{3^2 + (-4)^2}$$
$$= \sqrt{9+16}$$
$$= 5$$

The radius of the circle is 5.

Check Use the other endpoint (9, 4) and the center (6, 8). The radius should equal 5 for any point on the circle.

$$r = \sqrt{(9-6)^2 + (4-8)^2} = 5 \checkmark$$

The radius is the same using (9, 4).

Helpful Hint

The midpoint formula uses averages. You can think of x_M as the average of the x-values and y_M as the average of the y-values.

3. Find the center and radius of a circle that has a diameter with endpoints (2, 6) and (14, 22).

THINK AND DISCUSS

1. If you know one endpoint and the midpoint of a line segment, how could you find the other endpoint of the segment?

2. Find the domain and range of each of the graphs in Examples 1 and 2.

3. GET ORGANIZED Copy and complete the graphic organizer. List the types of conic sections, and sketch an example of each.

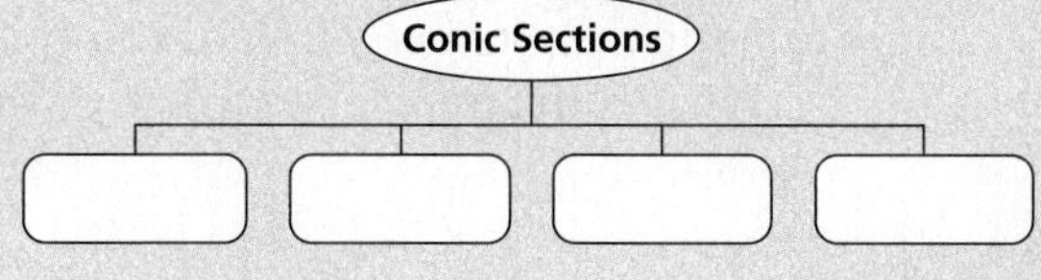

12-1 Exercises

Learn It Online
Homework Help Online
Parent Resources Online

GUIDED PRACTICE

1. **Vocabulary** What are the four different types of *conic sections*?

SEE EXAMPLE 1

Graph each equation on a graphing calculator. Identify each conic section. Then describe the center and intercepts.

2. $3x^2 + 3y^2 = 48$
3. $9x^2 + 16y^2 = 144$
4. $x^2 + y^2 = 36$

SEE EXAMPLE 2

Graph each equation on a graphing calculator. Identify each conic section. Then describe the vertices and the direction that the graph opens.

5. $5y^2 = x$
6. $x^2 = y^2 + 9$
7. $y^2 - x^2 = 25$
8. $12y = 6x^2$
9. $2x^2 - y^2 = 4$
10. $-y^2 = 4 + x$

SEE EXAMPLE 3

Find the center and radius of a circle that has a diameter with the given endpoints.

11. $(3, 6)$ and $(13, 30)$
12. $(-4, 1)$ and $(-16, -8)$
13. $(6, -9)$ and $(-8, 39)$

PRACTICE AND PROBLEM SOLVING

Independent Practice	
For Exercises	See Example
14–22	1
23–31	2
32–34	3

Extra Practice
See Extra Practice for more Skills Practice and Applications Practice exercises.

Graph each equation on a graphing calculator. Identify each conic section. Then describe the center and intercepts.

14. $49x^2 + 36y^2 = 1764$
15. $\frac{x^2}{9} + \frac{y^2}{9} = 1$
16. $243 - 3x^2 - 3y^2 = 0$
17. $\frac{x^2}{4} = 1 - \frac{y^2}{25}$
18. $4x^2 + 81y^2 = 324$
19. $\frac{4x^2}{25} + \frac{4y^2}{225} = 1$
20. $\frac{3}{4}x^2 + \frac{3}{4}y^2 = 75$
21. $4x^2 + 4y^2 = 81$
22. $x^2 + y^2 = \frac{4}{9}$

Graph each equation on a graphing calculator. Identify each conic section. Then describe the vertices and the direction that the graph opens.

23. $y = 2x^2$
24. $x^2 = y^2 + 64$
25. $x + 2y^2 = 0$
26. $x = \frac{2}{3}y^2$
27. $0 = 1 + \frac{x^2}{64} - \frac{y^2}{36}$
28. $5y^2 - 5x^2 = 180$
29. $x = 4y^2 - 3$
30. $y = 4 - \frac{x^2}{5}$
31. $9x^2 - 16y^2 = 144$

Find the center and radius of a circle that has a diameter with the given endpoints.

32. $(20, 21)$ and $(12, 6)$
33. $\left(\frac{9}{2}, \frac{5}{2}\right)$ and $\left(\frac{5}{2}, \frac{17}{2}\right)$
34. $(7, -5)$ and $(-1, 10)$

35. **Geometry** A circle has center $(-7, 10)$ and contains the point $(23, -6)$.
    a. Find the circumference and area of the circle.
    b. Find the other endpoint of the diameter with one endpoint $(23, -6)$.

36. The orbit of an asteroid can be modeled by the equation $16x^2 + 25y^2 = 400$.
    a. Graph the equation on a graphing calculator, and identify the conic section.
    b. Identify the x- and y-intercepts of the orbit.
    c. Suppose that each unit of the coordinate plane represents 50 million miles. What is the maximum width of the asteroid's orbit?

Use your graphing calculator to match each equation to one of the following graphs.

A. 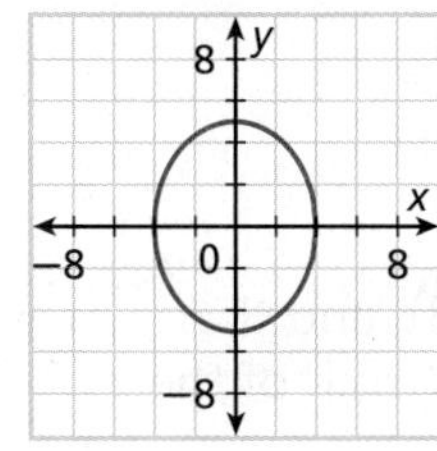

B. 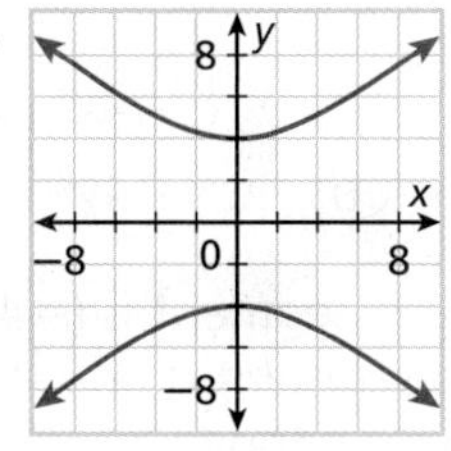

C. 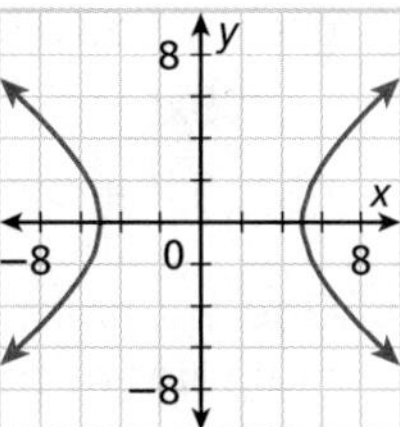

D. 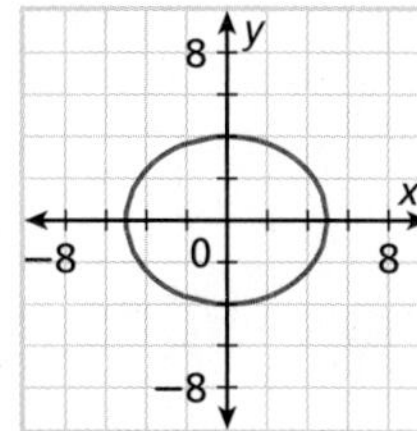

37. $16x^2 + 25y^2 = 400$

38. $16x^2 - 25y^2 = 400$

39. $25x^2 + 16y^2 = 400$

40. $25y^2 - 16x^2 = 400$

41. Geometry A quadrilateral has vertices $A(2, 3)$, $B(12, 3)$, $C(18, 11)$, and $D(8, 11)$.

a. Find the length of each side.

b. Classify the figure $ABCD$.

c. Find the area of $ABCD$.

42. Critical Thinking How can you tell if the graph of an equation in the form $ax^2 + by^2 = c$ is a circle or an ellipse?

43. Archaeology Archaeologists exploring an underwater site have set up a grid so that they can precisely label where any artifacts they discover were found. The archaeologists have found two treasure chests at points B and C and a ship's wheel at point A. Which treasure is the wheel closer to? Explain.

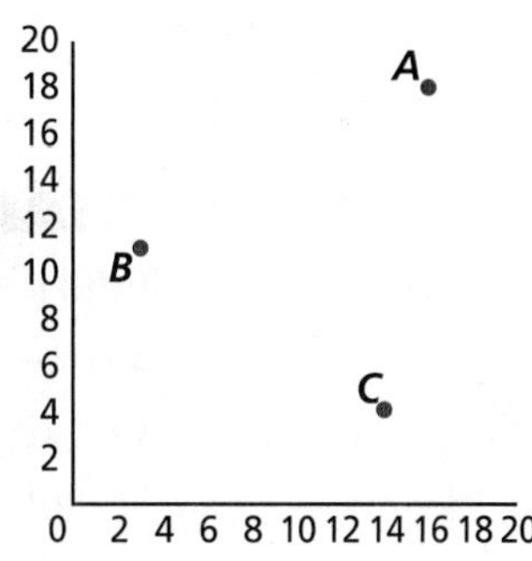

LINK

Archaeology

Chichén Itzá, in Yucatán, Mexico, was a major city of the Maya civilization. Its city center covers about 2 square miles and was used primarily for religious ceremonies. Today the ruins are the most visited archaeological site in Mexico.

44. ///ERROR ANALYSIS/// Which solution is incorrect? Explain the error. Find the distance between $(0, 0)$ and $(2, 3)$.

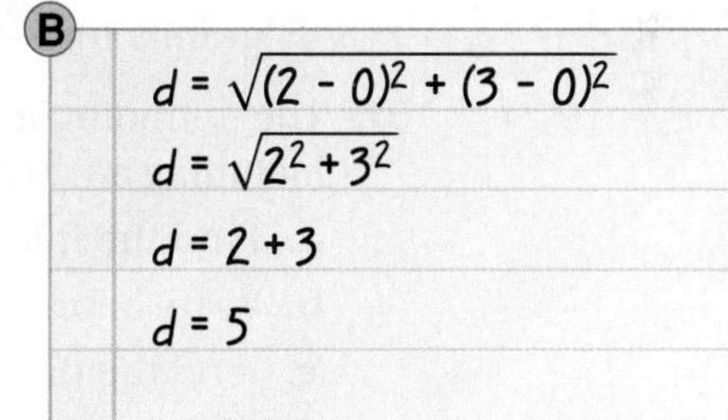

A

$d = \sqrt{(2-0)^2 + (3-0)^2}$

$d = \sqrt{2^2 + 3^2}$

$d = \sqrt{4 + 9}$

$d = \sqrt{13}$

B

$d = \sqrt{(2-0)^2 + (3-0)^2}$

$d = \sqrt{2^2 + 3^2}$

$d = 2 + 3$

$d = 5$

45. Geometry A triangle has vertices $A(8, 2)$, $B(13, 14)$, and $C(-4, 6)$.

a. Find the length of $\overline{AB}$.

b. Find the length of the segment joining the midpoints of $\overline{BC}$ and $\overline{AC}$.

c. Find the slopes of $\overline{AB}$ and the segment joining the midpoints of the other two sides. What do the slopes tell you about the two segments?

Tell whether each statement is sometimes, always, or never true. If it is sometimes true, give examples to support your answer.

46. A circle is a function.

47. The domain of a parabola is all real numbers.

48. The distance between two points is positive.

49. Write About It If a right triangle has a hypotenuse with length c and legs with lengths a and b, the Pythagorean Theorem states that $a^2 + b^2 = c^2$. Explain how the Distance Formula is related to the Pythagorean Theorem.

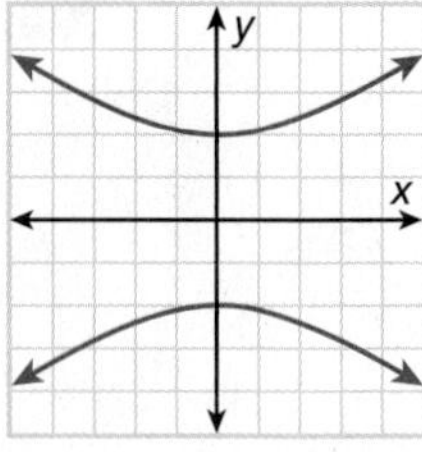

50. Which of the following could be the equation of the graph shown?

(A) $9x^2 - 4y^2 = 36$ (C) $9y^2 - 4x^2 = 36$

(B) $4x^2 + 9y^2 = 36$ (D) $9x^2 + 4y^2 = 36$

51. One endpoint of a line segment is $(-4, -8)$, and the midpoint of the line segment is $(2, -12)$. Which of the following is the other endpoint?

(F) $(-1, -10)$ (G) $(3, -2)$ (H) $(-8, 16)$ (J) $(8, -16)$

52. Which of the following are the *x*-intercepts of the graph of $4x^2 + 25y^2 = 100$?

(A) $(2, 0)$ and $(-2, 0)$ (C) $(5, 0)$ and $(-5, 0)$

(B) $(4, 0)$ and $(-4, 0)$ (D) $(10, 0)$ and $(-10, 0)$

53. What is the distance between the points $(-2, 6)$ and $(5, 30)$?

(F) $3\sqrt{145}$ (G) 31 (H) $3\sqrt{65}$ (J) 25

CHALLENGE AND EXTEND

Find *a* so that the two points are the given distance apart.

54. $(-5, 8)$ and $(3, a)$; 17

55. $(4, -10)$ and $(a, 5)$; 39

56. **Multi-Step** A degenerate conic is formed when a plane passes through the vertex of a hollow double cone. A point, a line, and a pair of intersecting lines are all degenerate conics.

a. The graph of $y^2 - x^2 = 0$ is a degenerate hyperbola. Graph $y^2 - x^2 = 0$.

b. What is the graph of $x^2 + y^2 = 0$?

c. Explain how a plane could intersect a hollow double cone to result in the graphs from parts **a** and **b**.

57. The midpoint and distance formulas can be extended to three dimensions by including an additional term in each formula for the variable *z*.

a. Find the midpoint of the segment with endpoints $(6, -3, -9)$ and $(12, 7, -13)$.

b. Write a formula to find the midpoint of a segment in three dimensions.

c. Find the distance between the points $(1, 2, 3)$ and $(5, 8, 10)$.

d. Write a formula to find the distance between two points in three dimensions.

12-2 Circles

CC.9-12.G.GPE.1 Derive the equation of a circle...using the Pythagorean Theorem...Find the center and radius of a circle given by an equation.

Objectives

Write an equation for a circle.

Graph a circle, and identify its center and radius.

Vocabulary

circle

tangent

Why learn this?

You can use circles to find locations within a given radius of an address. (See Example 3.)

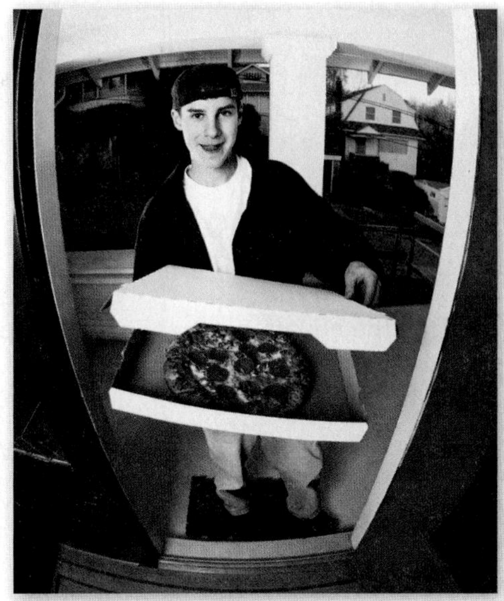

A **circle** is the set of points in a plane that are a fixed distance, called the radius, from a fixed point, called the center. Because all of the points on a circle are the same distance from the center of the circle, you can use the Distance Formula to find the equation of a circle.

EXAMPLE 1 Using the Distance Formula to Write the Equation of a Circle

Write the equation of a circle with center $(2, 1)$ and radius $r = 5$.

Use the Distance Formula with $(x_2, y_2) = (x, y)$, $(x_1, y_1) = (2, 1)$, and distance equal to the radius, 5.

$$d = \sqrt{(x_2 - x_1)^2 + (y_2 - y_1)^2}$$ *Use the Distance Formula.*

$$5 = \sqrt{(x - 2)^2 + (y - 1)^2}$$ *Substitute.*

$$5^2 = (x - 2)^2 + (y - 1)^2$$ *Square both sides.*

$$25 = (x - 2)^2 + (y - 1)^2$$

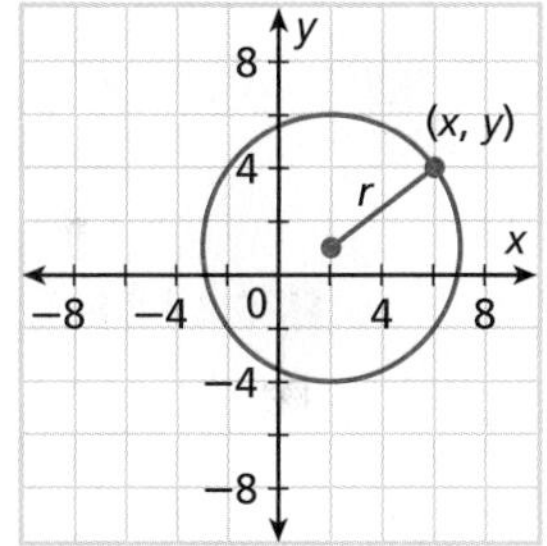

1. Write the equation of a circle with center $(4, 2)$ and radius $r = 7$.

Notice that r^2 and the center are visible in the equation of a circle. This leads to a general formula for a circle with center (h, k) and radius r.

Equation of a Circle

EQUATION	EXAMPLE	GRAPH
The equation of a circle with center (h, k) and radius r is $(x - h)^2 + (y - k)^2 = r^2$.	The equation of the circle with center $(5, -2)$ and radius $r = 8$ is $(x - 5)^2 + (y - (-2))^2 = 8^2$ or $(x - 5)^2 + (y + 2)^2 = 64$.	y; 4; r; x; −4; 0; 4; 8; 12; (h, k); −4; −8

EXAMPLE 2 Writing the Equation of a Circle

Write the equation of each circle.

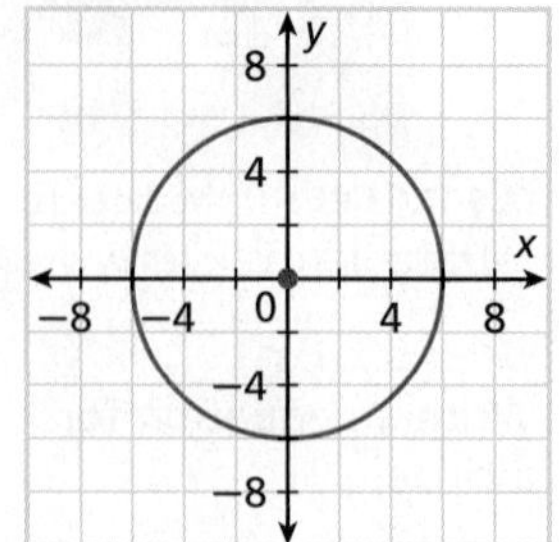

A **the graphed circle with center (0, 0) and radius $r = 6$**

$(x - h)^2 + (y - k)^2 = r^2$ *Equation of a circle*

$(x - 0)^2 + (y - 0)^2 = 6^2$ *Substitute.*

$x^2 + y^2 = 36$

Helpful Hint

If the center of the circle is at the origin, the equation simplifies to $x^2 + y^2 = r^2$.

B **the circle with center (2, 4) and containing the point (8, 12)**

$r = \sqrt{(8 - 2)^2 + (12 - 4)^2}$ *Use the Distance Formula to find the radius.*

$= \sqrt{6^2 + 8^2}$

$= \sqrt{100} = 10$

$(x - 2)^2 + (y - 4)^2 = 10^2$ *Substitute the values into the equation of a circle.*

$(x - 2)^2 + (y - 4)^2 = 100$

2. Find the equation of the circle with center (−3, 5) and containing the point (9, 10).

The location of points in relation to a circle can be described by inequalities. The points inside the circle satisfy the inequality $(x - h)^2 + (y - k)^2 < r^2$. The points outside the circle satisfy the inequality $(x - h)^2 + (y - k)^2 > r^2$.

EXAMPLE 3 *Consumer Application*

Raul and his friends are deciding where to have a pizza party based on the delivery area of the pizza restaurant. The restaurant is located at the point (−1, 2), and the letters represent the homes of Raul and his friends. Which houses are within a 3-mile radius of the restaurant and will get free delivery?

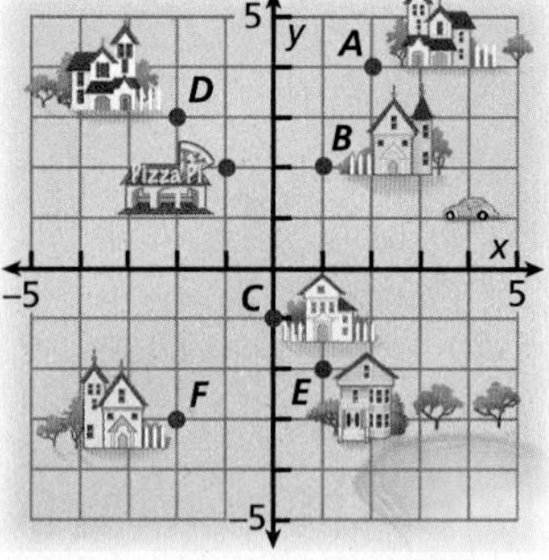

Graph the circle with center (−1, 2) and radius 3. The points inside the circle will satisfy the inequality $(x + 1)^2 + (y - 2)^2 < 3^2$.

Points D and B are within a 3-mile radius.

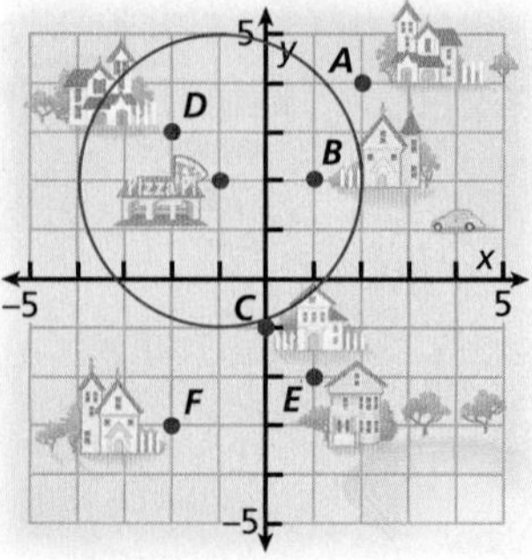

Check Point $C(0, -1)$ is near the boundary.

$(0 + 1)^2 + (-1 - 2)^2 < 3^2$

$(1)^2 + (-3)^2 < 3^2$

$1 + 9 < 9$ ✗ *Point C(0, −1) is not inside the circle.*

3. **What if...?** Which homes are within a 3-mile radius of a restaurant located at (2, −1)?

A **tangent** is a line in the same plane as the circle that intersects the circle at exactly one point. Recall from geometry that a tangent to a circle is perpendicular to the radius at the point of tangency.

EXAMPLE 4 Writing the Equation of a Tangent

Write the equation of the line that is tangent to the circle $25 = x^2 + y^2$ at the point $(3, 4)$.

Step 1 Identify the center and radius of the circle.

From the equation $25 = x^2 + y^2$, the circle has center $(0, 0)$ and radius $r = 5$.

Step 2 Find the slope of the radius at the point of tangency and the slope of the tangent.

$m = \frac{y_2 - y_1}{x_2 - x_1}$ *Use the slope formula.*

$m = \frac{4 - 0}{3 - 0}$ *Substitute $(3, 4)$ for (x_2, y_2) and $(0, 0)$ for (x_1, y_1).*

$m = \frac{4}{3}$ *The slope of the radius is $\frac{4}{3}$.*

Because the slopes of perpendicular lines are negative reciprocals, the slope of the tangent is $-\frac{3}{4}$.

Step 3 Find the slope-intercept equation of the tangent by using the point $(3, 4)$ and the slope $m = -\frac{3}{4}$.

$y - y_1 = m(x - x_1)$ *Use the point-slope formula.*

$y - 4 = -\frac{3}{4}(x - 3)$ *Substitute $(3, 4)$ for (x_1, y_1) and $-\frac{3}{4}$ for m.*

$y = -\frac{3}{4}x + \frac{25}{4}$ *Rewrite in slope-intercept form.*

The equation of the line that is tangent to $25 = x^2 + y^2$ at $(3, 4)$ is $y = -\frac{3}{4}x + \frac{25}{4}$.

Check Graph the circle and the line.

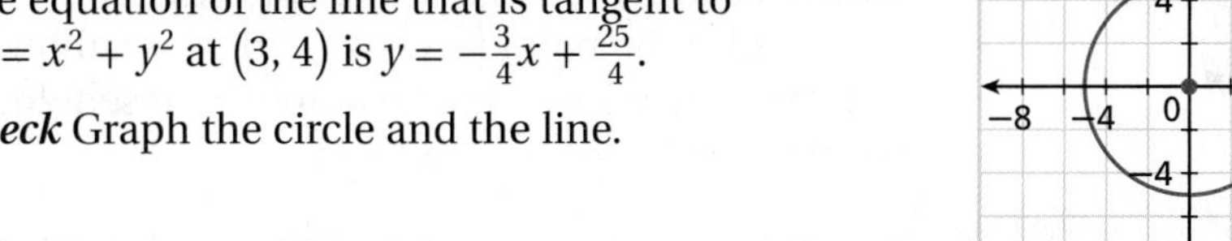

Remember!

You may want to review linear functions before writing equations for tangents.

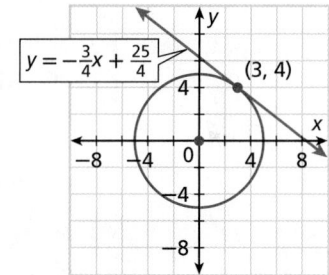

4. Write the equation of the line that is tangent to the circle $25 = (x - 1)^2 + (y + 2)^2$ at the point $(5, -5)$.

THINK AND DISCUSS

1. Explain the transformation of $x^2 + y^2 = 1$ that is necessary to get the equation $(x - h)^2 + (y - k)^2 = 1$.

2. Explain what happens to the radius if the equation of a circle changes from $x^2 + y^2 = 4$ to $x^2 + y^2 = 16$.

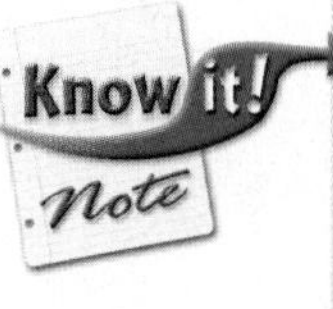

3. GET ORGANIZED Copy and complete the graphic organizer. Sketch each circle, and give its equation.

	$r = 1$	$r = 3$
Center (0, 0)		
Center (1, 2)		

12-2 Exercises

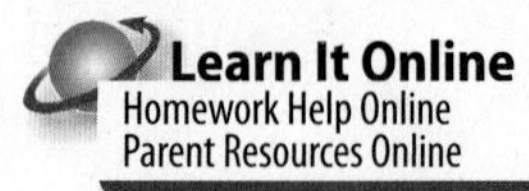

GUIDED PRACTICE

1. **Vocabulary** How can you recognize a *tangent* of a circle?

SEE EXAMPLE 1

Write the equation of each circle.

2. center $(6, -5)$ and radius $r = 4$
3. center $(-11, 3)$ and radius $r = 9$

SEE EXAMPLE 2

4. 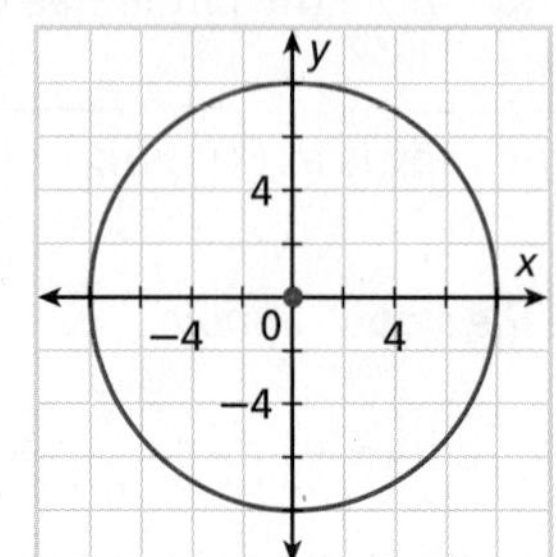

5. 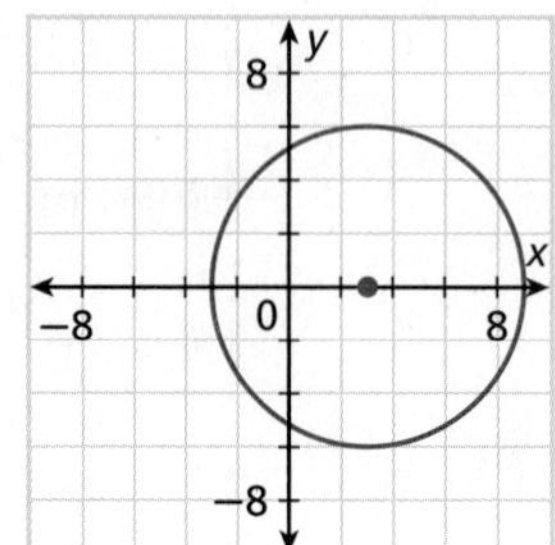

6. center $(-1, 9)$ and containing the point $(2, 5)$
7. center $(-2, -5)$ and containing the point $(-10, -20)$

SEE EXAMPLE 3

Depending on its strength, an earthquake can be felt in locations miles away from the epicenter.

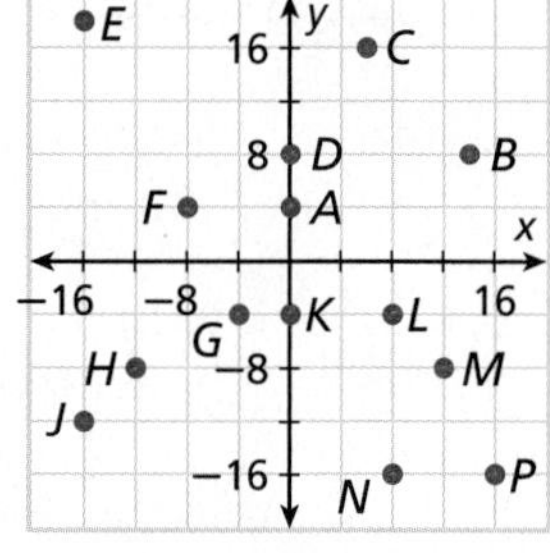

8. **Multi-Step** Suppose that the epicenter of the earthquake is located at the point $(5, -2)$ and the earthquake is felt up to 10 mi away. Which labeled points represent locations that are affected by the earthquake?
9. **Multi-Step** Suppose that the epicenter of the earthquake is located at the point $(-5, -7)$ and the earthquake is felt up to 8 mi away. Which labeled points represent locations that are affected by the earthquake?

SEE EXAMPLE 4

Multi-Step Write the equation of the line that is tangent to each circle at the given point.

10. $x^2 + y^2 = 100$; $(8, 6)$
11. $(x + 6)^2 + (y + 4)^2 = 25$; $(-9, -8)$

PRACTICE AND PROBLEM SOLVING

Independent Practice

For Exercises	See Example
12–13	1
14–17	2
18–19	3
20–21	4

Extra Practice

See Extra Practice for more Skills Practice and Applications Practice exercises.

Write the equation of each circle.

12. center $(3, 2)$ and radius $r = 7$
13. center $(5, 1)$ and radius $r = 10$

14. 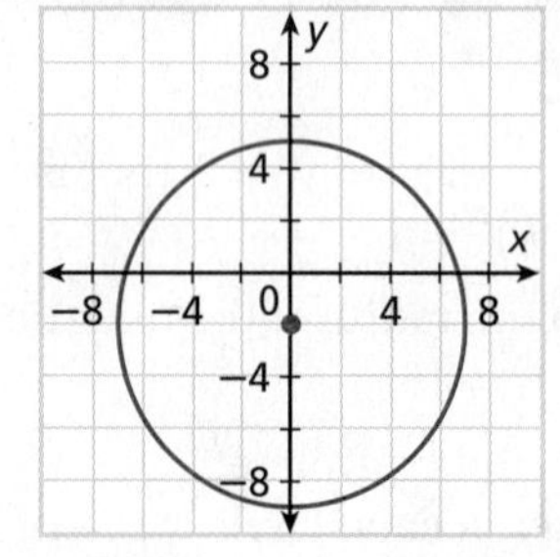

15. 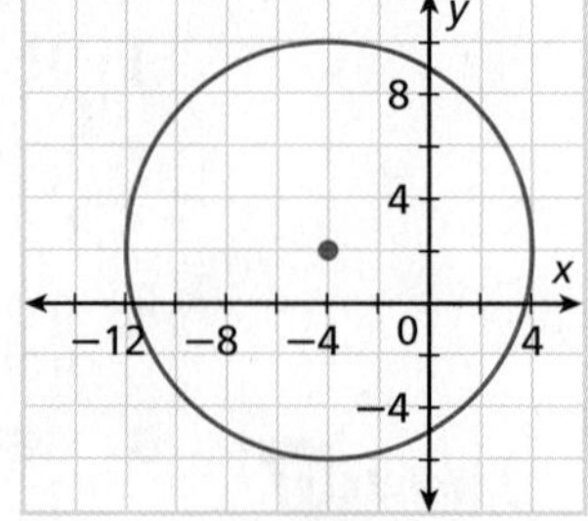

16. center $(12, -3)$ and containing the point $(-12, 7)$
17. center $(-6, -4)$ and containing the point $(-2, -1)$

Aida's puppy escaped from the backyard and is lost. Aida has created a map of places that the puppy may have gone.

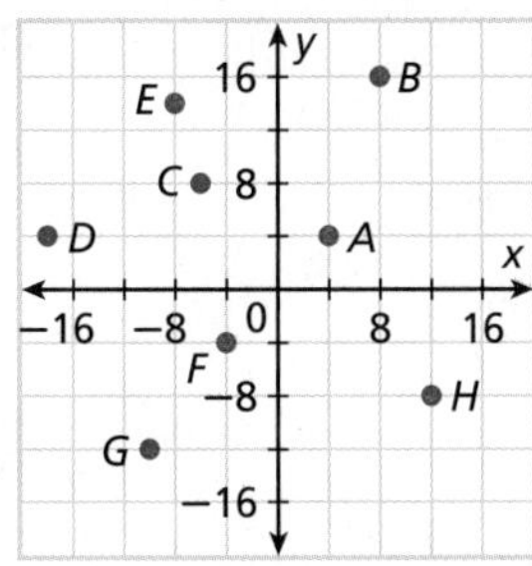

18. Multi-Step Suppose that Aida's house is located at the point $(3, 8)$. The puppy has been gone for 4 hours, and Aida estimates that the puppy cannot have traveled more than 12 miles. Which labeled points represent possible locations of the puppy?

19. Multi-Step Suppose that Aida's house is located at the point $(-6, 15)$. The puppy has been gone for 1 hour, and Aida estimates that the puppy cannot have traveled more than 3 miles. Which labeled points represent possible locations of the puppy?

Stonehenge, in southern England, is thought to have been built in three stages, from 2950-1600 B.C.E. It is not a single structure but consists of many stone, earth, and wood constructions.

Multi-Step Write the equation of the line that is tangent to each circle at the given point.

20. $x^2 + y^2 = 169, (-5, 12)$

21. $(x - 2)^2 + (y - 4)^2 = 289, (-15, 4)$

22. History The outermost ring of the ancient monument Stonehenge can be modeled by the equation $x^2 + y^2 = 27{,}225$. The Sarsen Circle, the center ring of stones usually associated with the monument, can be modeled by the equation $x^2 + y^2 = 2916$.

a. The Heel Stone is located outside of the circles, approximately at the point $(0, 300)$. Find the maximum and minimum distances, in feet, to the Heel Stone from both the outer and inner circles.

b. Graph the outer circle and the Sarsen Circle.

c. Two Station Stones surrounded by circular ditches are located within the outer circle. One stone is located at approximately $(-100, 100)$ and is surrounded by a ditch of radius 12 ft. Write an equation to model the ditch around this Station Stone.

Find the domain and range of each relation.

23. $x^2 + y^2 = 36$

24. $(x - 2)^2 + (y + 7)^2 = 81$

25. $(x + 2)^2 + (y)^2 = 9$

26. Geometry The circle with center $(2, 3)$ and the circle with center $(-1, -1)$ are tangent at the point $(5, 7)$.

a. Find an equation for the small circle.

b. Find an equation for the large circle.

c. Find the equation of the line that is tangent to both circles.

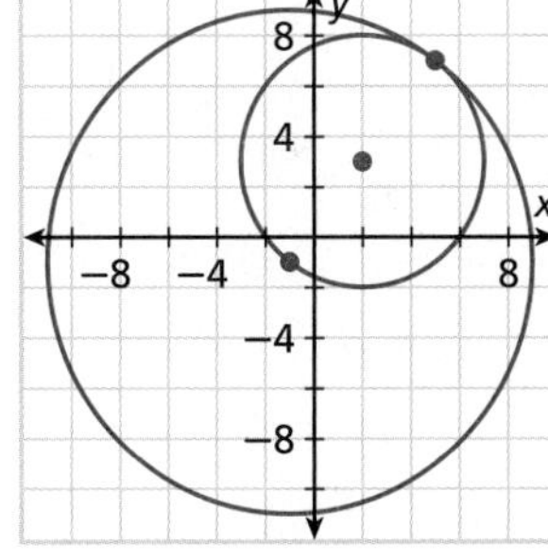

Geometry Find the center and radius of each circle.

27. $(x + 4)^2 + y^2 = 64$

28. $\left(x - \frac{2}{3}\right)^2 + \left(y - \frac{5}{8}\right)^2 = 49$

MULTI-STEP TEST PREP

29. The orbit of Venus is nearly circular. An astronomer develops a model for the orbit in which the Sun has coordinates $(-5, 20)$, the circular orbit of Venus passes through $(62, 20)$, and each unit of the coordinate plane represents 1 million miles.

a. Write an equation for the orbit of Venus.

b. How far is Venus from the Sun?

c. How far does Venus travel as it makes one complete orbit of the Sun?

30. **Entertainment** A radio station emits a signal that can be received by anyone within 120 miles of the station's transmitter. Write and graph an inequality for the region covered by the radio station with the transmitter located at $(0, 0)$.

31. **Critical Thinking** Is it possible to have two different lines that are tangent to the same circle at the same point? Explain.

32. **Write About It** How could you show that the line with equation $y = -\frac{5}{12}x + \frac{28}{3}$ is tangent to the circle with equation $169 = (x-3)^2 + (y+6)^2$ at the point $(8, 6)$?

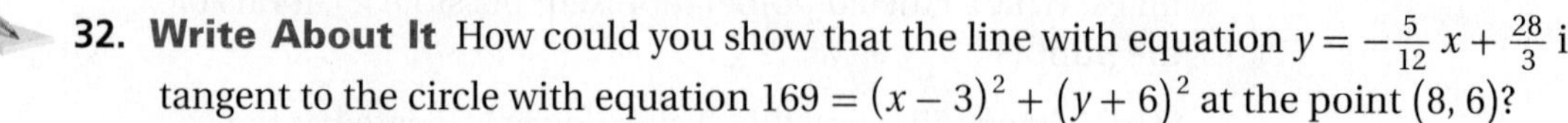

TEST PREP

33. Which of the following lines is tangent at $(13, 9)$ to the circle with center $(5, 3)$?

Ⓐ $y = \frac{3}{4}x - \frac{3}{4}$ Ⓑ $y = -\frac{3}{4}x + \frac{75}{4}$ Ⓒ $y = -\frac{4}{3}x + \frac{79}{3}$ Ⓓ $y = \frac{4}{3}x - \frac{25}{3}$

34. Which of the following points is inside the circle with the equation $121 = (x-5)^2 + (y+9)^2$?

Ⓕ $(12, 2)$ Ⓖ $(-8, 6)$ Ⓗ $(2, -6)$ Ⓙ $(-9, -3)$

35. **Short Response** Give the equation of a circle with center $(-4, 8)$ and radius $r = 9$.

CHALLENGE AND EXTEND

36. A *sphere* is the set of all points in three-dimensional space that are a fixed distance from a fixed point, called the center. The equation of a sphere with center (a, b, c) and radius r is $(x-a)^2 + (y-b)^2 + (z-c)^2 = r^2$. Write the equation of a sphere with center $(1, -3, 4)$ and radius 5.

37. The lines $y = -3x + 1$ and $y = 2x - 9$ each contain diameters of a particular circle. The point $(9, 19)$ is on the circle.

    a. Find the center of the circle.

    b. Write the equation of the circle.

Graph each system of inequalities.

38. $\begin{cases} x - 3y > -12 \\ (x-2)^2 + (y-1)^2 \le 49 \end{cases}$

39. $\begin{cases} (x-3)^2 + (y-2)^2 \le 36 \\ (x-4)^2 + (y+4)^2 \le 25 \end{cases}$

Surface Area and Volume

You can use formulas to find the surface area and volume of three-dimensional figures such as cylinders, cones, and spheres.

	Cylinder with radius r and height h	Cone with radius r and height h	Sphere with radius r
Solid			
Volume	$V = \pi r^2 h$	$V = \frac{1}{3}\pi r^2 h$	$V = \frac{4}{3}\pi r^3$
Surface Area	$S = 2\pi r(r + h)$	$S = \pi r\sqrt{r^2 + h^2} + \pi r^2$	$S = 4\pi r^2$

Example

Find the surface area and volume of the cone shown.

In order to use the formulas, identify the radius and height of the cone. $r = 5$ and $h = 12$. Find the surface area. Use the formula.

$S = \pi r\sqrt{r^2 + h^2} + \pi r^2$ *Formula for surface area of a cone.*

$S = \pi \cdot 5\sqrt{(5)^2 + (12)^2} + \pi(5)^2$ *Substitute 5 for r and 12 for h.*

$S = 90\pi$ *Simplify.*

Find the volume.

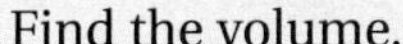

$V = \frac{1}{3}\pi r^2 h$ *Formula for the volume of a cone.*

$V = \frac{1}{3}\pi(5)^2(12)$ *Substitute 5 for r and 12 for h.*

$V = 100\pi$ *Simplify.*

Try This

Find the surface area and volume of each figure.

1.

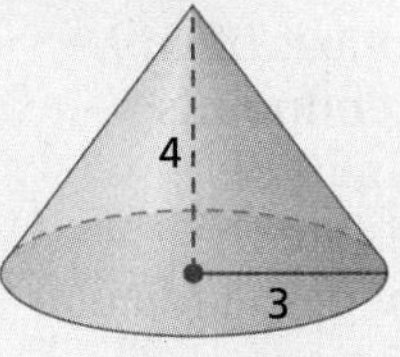

2.

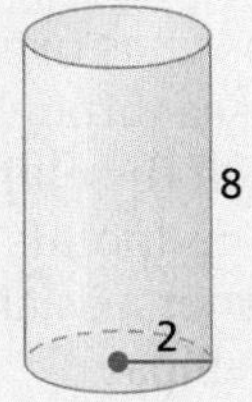

3.

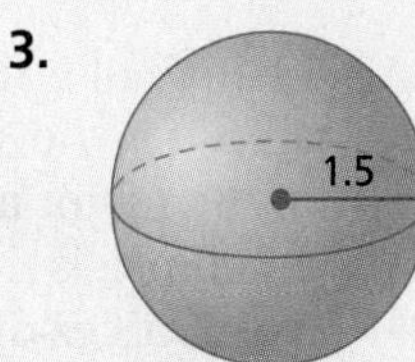

COMMON CORE

12-3 Ellipses

CC.9-12.G.GPE.3 (+) Derive the equations of ellipses and hyperbolas...

Objectives

Write the standard equation for an ellipse.

Graph an ellipse, and identify its center, vertices, co-vertices, and foci.

Vocabulary

ellipse
focus of an ellipse
major axis
vertices of an ellipse
minor axis
co-vertices of an ellipse

Who uses this?

The whispering gallery at the Chicago Museum of Science and Industry was designed by using an ellipse. (See Exercise 31.)

If you pulled the center of a circle apart into two points, it would stretch the circle into an ellipse.

An **ellipse** is the set of points $P(x, y)$ in a plane such that the sum of the distances from any point P on the ellipse to two fixed points F_1 and F_2, called the **foci** (singular: focus), is the constant sum $d = PF_1 + PF_2$. This distance d can be represented by the length of a piece of string connecting two pushpins located at the foci.

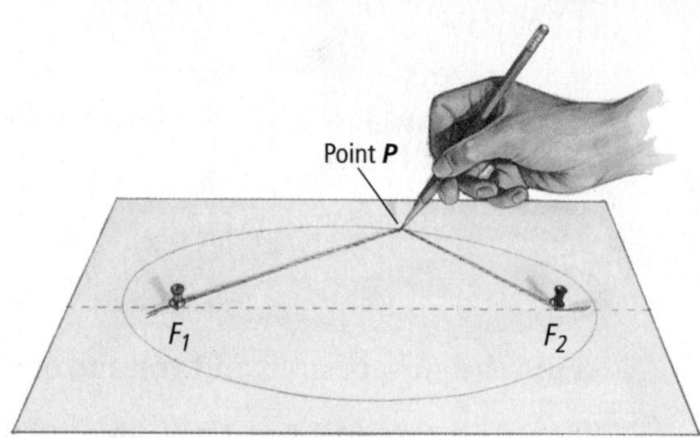

You can use the distance formula to find the constant sum of an ellipse.

EXAMPLE 1 Using the Distance Formula to Find the Constant Sum of an Ellipse

Find the constant sum for an ellipse with foci $F_1\left(-3, 0\right)$ and $F_2\left(3, 0\right)$ and the point on the ellipse $\left(0, 4\right)$.

$d = PF_1 + PF_2$ *Definition of the constant sum of an ellipse*

$d = \sqrt{(x_1 - x_3)^2 + (y_1 - y_3)^2} + \sqrt{(x_2 - x_3)^2 + (y_2 - y_3)^2}$ *Distance Formula*

$d = \sqrt{(-3 - 0)^2 + (0 - 4)^2} + \sqrt{(3 - 0)^2 + (0 - 4)^2}$ *Substitute.*

$d = \sqrt{25} + \sqrt{25}$ *Simplify.*

$d = 10$

The constant sum is 10.

1. Find the constant sum for an ellipse with foci $F_1\left(0, -8\right)$ and $F_2\left(0, 8\right)$ and the point on the ellipse $\left(0, 10\right)$.

Instead of a single radius, an ellipse has two axes. The longer axis of an ellipse is the **major axis** and passes through both foci. The endpoints of the major axis are the **vertices of the ellipse**. The shorter axis of an ellipse is the **minor axis**. The endpoints of the minor axis are the **co-vertices of the ellipse**. The major axis and minor axis are perpendicular and intersect at the center of the ellipse.

The standard form of an ellipse centered at (0, 0) depends on whether the major axis is horizontal or vertical.

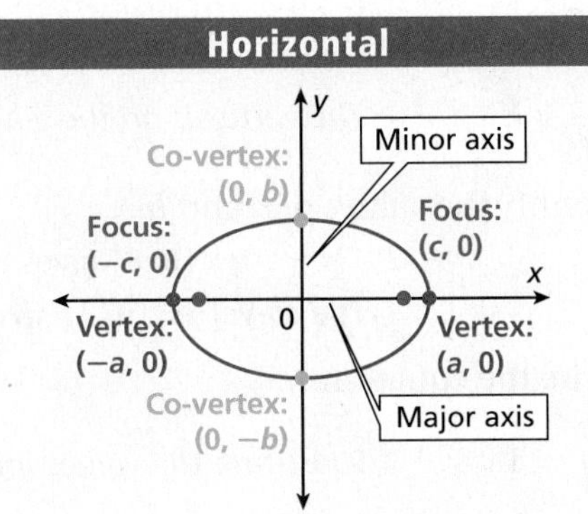

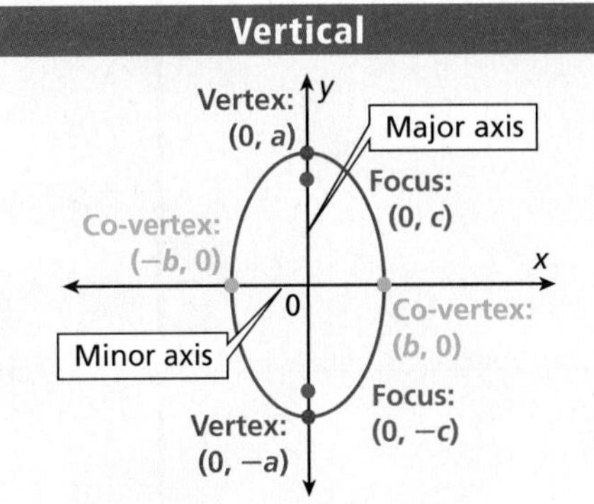

The values a, b, and c are related by the equation $c^2 = a^2 - b^2$. Also note that the length of the major axis is $2a$, the length of the minor axis is $2b$, and $a > b$.

Standard Form for the Equation of an Ellipse — Center at (0, 0)

MAJOR AXIS	HORIZONTAL	VERTICAL
Equation	$\frac{x^2}{a^2} + \frac{y^2}{b^2} = 1$	$\frac{y^2}{a^2} + \frac{x^2}{b^2} = 1$
Vertices	$(a, 0), (-a, 0)$	$(0, a), (0, -a)$
Foci	$(c, 0), (-c, 0)$	$(0, c), (0, -c)$
Co-vertices	$(0, b), (0, -b)$	$(b, 0), (-b, 0)$

EXAMPLE 2 Using Standard Form to Write an Equation for an Ellipse

Write an equation in standard form for each ellipse with center (0, 0).

A

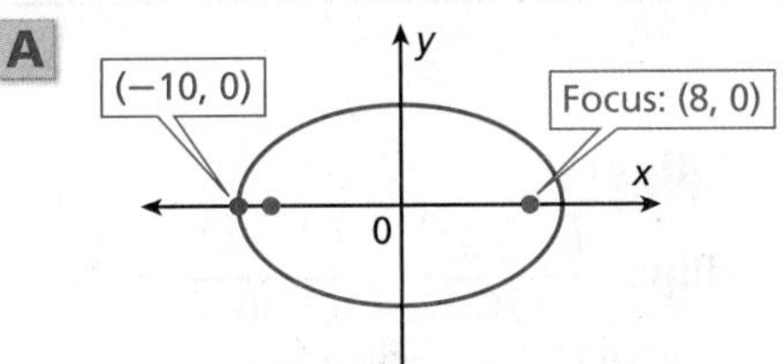

Step 1 Choose the appropriate form of equation.

$\frac{x^2}{a^2} + \frac{y^2}{b^2} = 1.$ *The horizontal axis is longer.*

Step 2 Identify the values of a and c.

$a = 10$ *The vertex $(-10, 0)$ gives the value of a.*

$c = 8$ *The focus $(8, 0)$ gives the value of c.*

Step 3 Use the relationship $c^2 = a^2 - b^2$ to find b^2.

$8^2 = 10^2 - b^2$ *Substitute 10 for a and 8 for c.*

$b^2 = 36$

Step 4 Write the equation.

$\frac{x^2}{100} + \frac{y^2}{36} = 1$ *Substitute the values into the equation of an ellipse.*

Write an equation in standard form for each ellipse with center $(0, 0)$.

B the ellipse with vertex $(0, 8)$ and co-vertex $(3, 0)$

Step 1 Choose the appropriate form of equation.

$$\frac{y^2}{a^2} + \frac{x^2}{b^2} = 1$$ *The vertex is on the y-axis.*

Step 2 Identify the values of a and b.

$a = 8$ *The vertex $(0, 8)$ gives the value of a.*

$b = 3$ *The co-vertex $(0, 3)$ gives the value of b.*

Step 3 Write the equation.

$$\frac{y^2}{64} + \frac{x^2}{9} = 1$$ *Substitute the values into the equation of an ellipse.*

CHECK IT OUT! Write an equation in standard form for each ellipse with center $(0, 0)$.

2a. Vertex $(9, 0)$ and co-vertex $(0, 5)$

2b. Co-vertex $(4, 0)$ focus $(0, 3)$

Ellipses may also be translated so that the center is not the origin.

Know it! Note

Standard Form for the Equation of an Ellipse Center at (h, k)

MAJOR AXIS	HORIZONTAL	VERTICAL
Equation	$\frac{(x-h)^2}{a^2} + \frac{(y-k)^2}{b^2} = 1$	$\frac{(y-k)^2}{a^2} + \frac{(x-h)^2}{b^2} = 1$
Vertices	$(h + a, k), (h - a, k)$	$(h, k + a), (h, k - a)$
Foci	$(h + c, k), (h - c, k)$	$(h, k + c), (h, k - c)$
Co-vertices	$(h, k + b), (h, k - b)$	$(h + b, k), (h - b, k)$

EXAMPLE 3 Graphing Ellipses

Graph the ellipse $\frac{(x-3)^2}{16} + \frac{(y-1)^2}{36} = 1$.

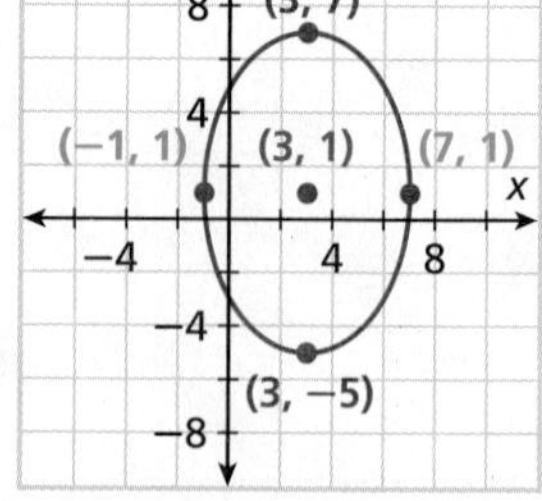

Step 1 Rewrite the equation as

$$\frac{(x-3)^2}{4^2} + \frac{(y-1)^2}{6^2} = 1.$$

Step 2 Identify the values of h, k, a, and b.

$h = 3$ and $k = 1$, so the center is $(3, 1)$.

$a = 6$ and $b = 4$; Because $6 > 4$, the major axis is vertical.

Step 3 The vertices are $(3, 1 \pm 6)$, or $(3, 7)$ and $(3, -5)$, and the co-vertices are $(3 \pm 4, 1)$, or $(7, 1)$ and $(-1, 1)$.

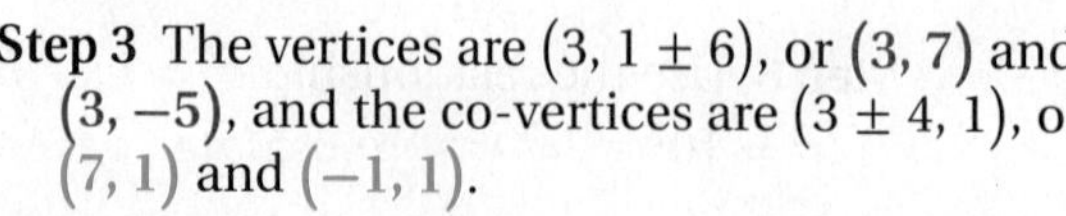

CHECK IT OUT! Graph each ellipse.

3a. $\frac{x^2}{64} + \frac{y^2}{25} = 1$

3b. $\frac{(x-2)^2}{25} + \frac{(y-4)^2}{9} = 1$

EXAMPLE 4 Engineering Application

A road passes through a tunnel in the form of a semi-ellipse. In order to widen the road to accommodate more traffic, engineers must design a larger tunnel that is twice as wide and 1.5 times as tall as the original tunnel. The design for the original tunnel can be modeled by the equation $\frac{x^2}{100} + \frac{y^2}{64} = 1$, measured in feet.

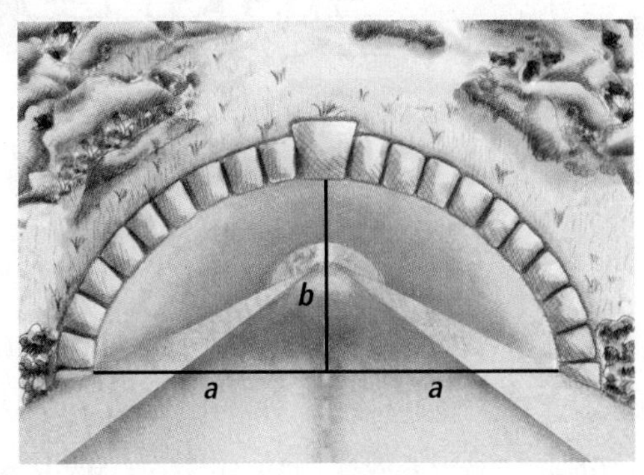

a. Find the dimensions of the larger tunnel.

Step 1 Find the dimensions of the original tunnel.

Because $100 > 64$, the major axis of the tunnel is horizontal.

$a^2 = 100$, so $a = 10$ and the width of the tunnel is $2a = 20$ ft.

$b^2 = 64$, so $b = 8$ and the height of the tunnel is 8 ft.

Step 2 Find the dimensions of the larger tunnel.

The width of the larger tunnel is $2(20) = 40$ ft.

The height is $1.5(8) = 12$ ft.

b. Write an equation for the design of the larger tunnel.

Step 1 Use the dimensions of the larger tunnel to find the values of a and b.

For the larger tunnel, $a = 20$ and $b = 12$.

Step 2 Write the equation.

The equation in standard form for the larger tunnel is $\frac{x^2}{20^2} + \frac{y^2}{12^2} = 1$, or $\frac{x^2}{400} + \frac{y^2}{144} = 1$.

Engineers have designed a tunnel with the equation $\frac{x^2}{64} + \frac{y^2}{36} = 1$, measured in feet. A design for a larger tunnel needs to be twice as wide and 3 times as tall.

4a. Find the dimensions for the larger tunnel.

4b. Write an equation for the design of the larger tunnel.

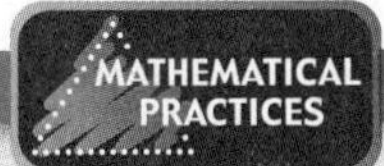

THINK AND DISCUSS

1. Explain where the foci are located in relation to the vertices.
2. Compare circles and ellipses by using lines of symmetry.

3. **GET ORGANIZED** Copy and complete the graphic organizer. Give an equation for each type of ellipse.

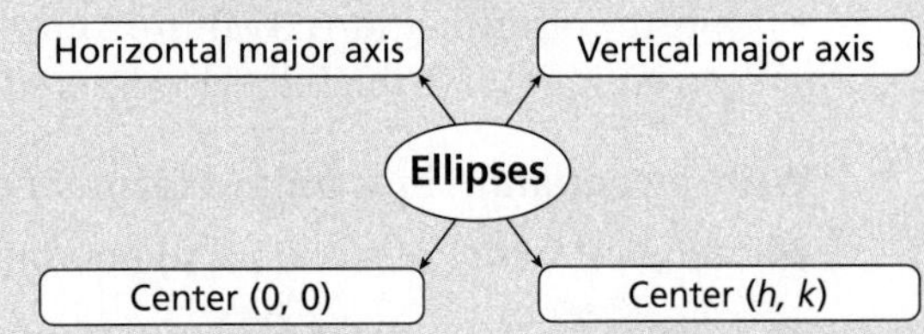

12-3 Exercises

Learn It Online
Homework Help Online
Parent Resources Online

GUIDED PRACTICE

1. **Vocabulary** How can you tell the difference between the *major axis* and the *minor axis* of an ellipse?

SEE EXAMPLE 1

Find the constant sum of an ellipse with the given foci and point on the ellipse.

2. $F_1(-5, 0)$, $F_2(5, 0)$, $P(0, -12)$
3. $F_1(0, -12)$, $F_2(0, 12)$, $P(9, 0)$

SEE EXAMPLE 2

Multi-Step Write an equation in standard form for each ellipse with center $(0, 0)$.

4. vertex $(-9, 0)$, co-vertex $(0, 7)$
5. vertex $(0, 25)$, focus $(0, -20)$
6. co-vertex $(10, 0)$, focus $(0, 24)$
7. vertex $(-7, 0)$, focus $(\sqrt{13}, 0)$

SEE EXAMPLE 3

Graph each ellipse.

8. $\frac{x^2}{36} + \frac{y^2}{81} = 1$
9. $\frac{x^2}{121} + \frac{y^2}{49} = 1$
10. $\frac{(x-5)^2}{16} + \frac{(y+2)^2}{36} = 1$
11. $\frac{(x+1)^2}{64} + \frac{(y-6)^2}{9} = 1$

SEE EXAMPLE 4

12. **Engineering** Engineers are building semi-elliptical bridges across two rivers. The larger river is 4 times as wide as the smaller river and must accommodate boats that are 3 times as tall. The equation for the bridge over the smaller river is $\frac{x^2}{225} + \frac{y^2}{144} = 1$, measured in feet.
    a. Find the dimensions of the larger bridge.
    b. Write an equation for the design of the larger bridge.

PRACTICE AND PROBLEM SOLVING

Independent Practice	
For Exercises	See Example
13–14	1
15–18	2
19–22	3
23	4

Extra Practice
See Extra Practice for more Skills Practice and Applications Practice exercises.

Find the constant sum of an ellipse with the given foci and point on the ellipse.

13. $F_1(-20, 0)$, $F_2(20, 0)$, $P(-21, 0)$
14. $F_1(0, -8)$, $F_2(0, 8)$, $P(9, 13.6)$

Multi-Step Write an equation in standard form for each ellipse with center $(0, 0)$.

15. vertex $(5, 0)$, co-vertex $(0, -2)$
16. co-vertex $(0, -8)$, focus $(6, 0)$
17. co-vertex $(4, 0)$, focus $(0, -3)$
18. vertex $(0, -9)$, focus $(0, 3\sqrt{5})$

Graph each ellipse.

19. $\frac{(x+2)^2}{169} + \frac{(y-7)^2}{25} = 1$
20. $\frac{(x-6)^2}{36} + \frac{(y-4)^2}{100} = 1$
21. $\frac{x^2}{256} + \frac{y^2}{196} = 1$
22. $\frac{x^2}{225} + \frac{y^2}{289} = 1$

23. **National Parks** South of the White House in Washington, D.C., is the President's Park South, or the Ellipse, which hosts events such as the White House Garden Tours. The Ellipse is 880 ft from north to south and 1057 ft from east to west. Write an equation for the Ellipse, centered at the origin.

Write an equation in standard form for each ellipse.

24. tangent to the x-axis at $(9, 0)$ and tangent to the y-axis at $(0, -6)$
25. center $(-4, 7)$, vertex $(-4, -3)$, focus $(-4, 0)$

26. **Estimation** An ellipse has a vertex at the point $(2.4, -6.1)$, focus $(0.35, -6.1)$, and center $(-4.5, -6.1)$. Estimate the coordinates of the co-vertices.

Write an equation for each graph, and give the domain and range. (*Hint:* The domain and range depend on the center and the lengths of the major and minor axes.)

27. 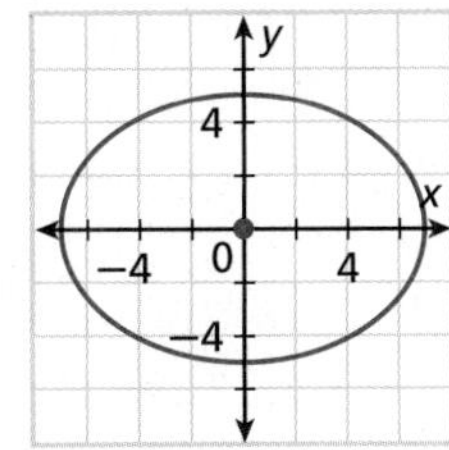

28. 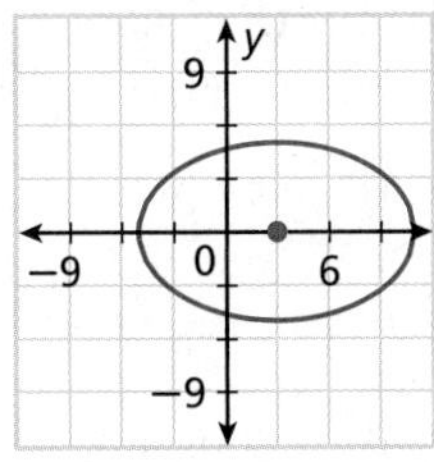

29. 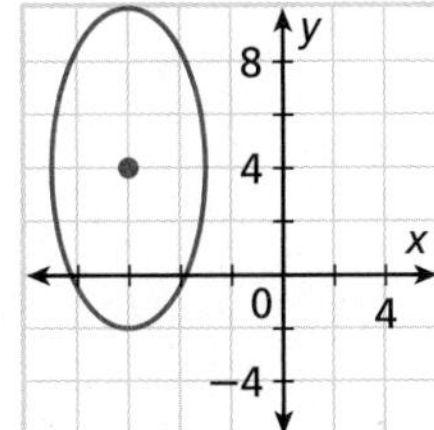

LINK

History

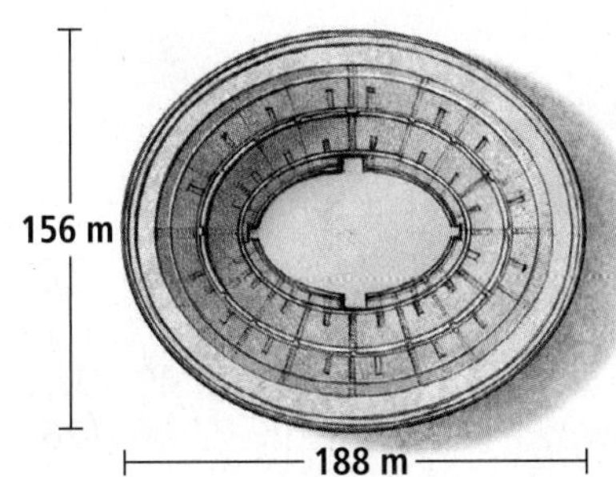

Located in Rome, Italy, the Colosseum was designed to hold as many as 50,000 spectators, who would arrive and leave through 80 entrances.

30. **History** The Roman Colosseum is shaped like a large ellipse, with an external width of 188 m and a length of 156 m. Write an equation that can be used to model the shape of the Colosseum.

31. **Architecture** As a result of their unique elliptical shapes, whispering galleries enable the smallest sound generated at one focus to be carried across the room to the other focus. The whispering gallery at the Chicago Museum of Science and Industry is 47 ft 4 in. long and 13 ft 6 in. wide.

   a. Supposing that the center of the floor of the whispering gallery is located at the origin, write an equation for the gallery floor.

   b. Find the coordinates of the foci. How far apart are they?

Find the center, vertices, co-vertices, foci, domain, and range of each ellipse.

32. $\frac{(x-1)^2}{225} + \frac{(y+5)^2}{324} = 1$

33. $9(x+9)^2 + 81(y+4)^2 = 729$

34. **Critical Thinking** An ellipse is defined by the distance $PF_1 + PF_2 = d$. Could the distance between the foci be less than $PF_1 + PF_2$? Explain.

35. **Geometry** The area of an ellipse in standard form is given by $A = \pi ab$.

   a. **Critical Thinking** How is the formula for the area of an ellipse related to the formula for the area of a circle?

   b. Find the area of $\frac{(x+2)^2}{169} + \frac{(y-7)^2}{25} = 1$.

MULTI-STEP TEST PREP

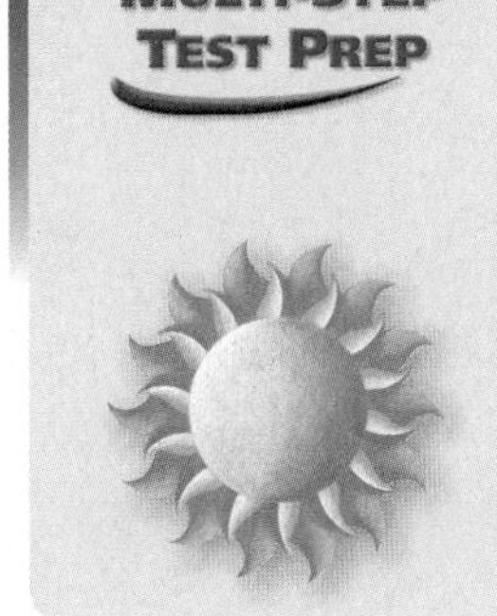

36. The figure shows the elliptical orbit of Mars, where each unit of the coordinate plane represents 1 million kilometers. As shown, the planet's maximum distance from the Sun is 249 million kilometers and its minimum distance from the Sun is 207 million kilometers.

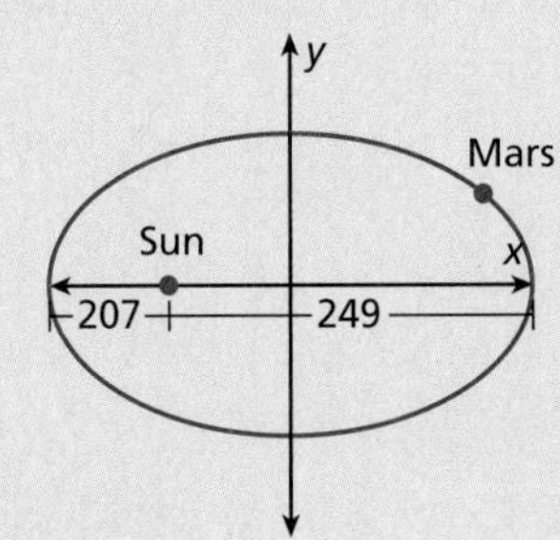

   a. The Sun is at one focus of the ellipse. What are the coordinates of the Sun?

   b. What is the length of the minor axis of the ellipse?

   c. Write an equation that models the orbit of Mars.

37. **Write About It** How is the distance $PF_1 + PF_2$ related to the length of the ellipse's major axis?

TEST PREP

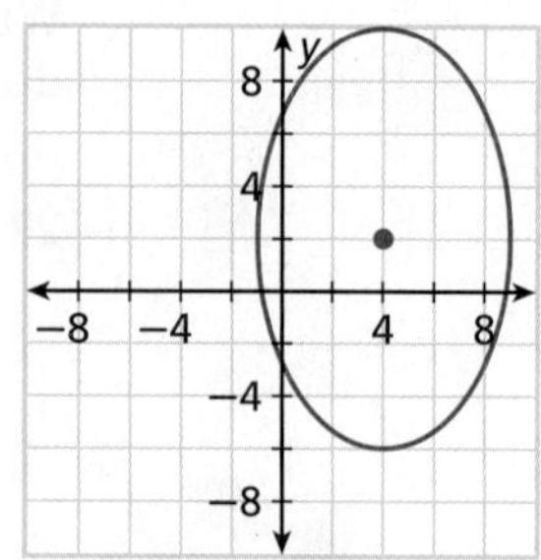

38. Which of the following is the equation for the graph?

Ⓐ $\dfrac{(x-4)^2}{25} - \dfrac{(y-2)^2}{64} = 1$

Ⓑ $25(x-4)^2 + 64(y-2)^2 = 1600$

Ⓒ $\dfrac{(x-4)^2}{64} + \dfrac{(y-2)^2}{25} = 1$

Ⓓ $64(x-4)^2 + 25(y-2)^2 = 1600$

39. The graph of which equation has the greatest distance between foci?

Ⓕ $\dfrac{(x-12)^2}{49} + \dfrac{(y+23)^2}{25} = 1$

Ⓗ $\dfrac{(x-1)^2}{20} + \dfrac{(y-1)^2}{150} = 1$

Ⓖ $\dfrac{x^2}{625} + \dfrac{y^2}{576} = 1$

Ⓙ $\dfrac{x^2}{175} + \dfrac{y^2}{225} = 1$

40. **Short Response** Give an equation for the ellipse with center $(2, -3)$, focus $(26, -3)$, and major axis length 50.

CHALLENGE AND EXTEND

41. The eccentricity of an ellipse is defined as $e = \frac{c}{a}$. Recall that $c^2 = a^2 - b^2$ for an ellipse in standard form.
    a. Find the eccentricity of the ellipse with equation $\frac{x^2}{841} + \frac{y^2}{400} = 1$.
    b. Find the equation of the ellipse with vertices $(13, 0)$ and $(-13, 0)$ and $e = \frac{5}{13}$.
    c. What are the possible values for the eccentricity of an ellipse?
    d. Describe the relationship between eccentricity and the shape of an ellipse.

42. **Astronomy** The path that the Moon travels around Earth is an ellipse with Earth at one focus. The length of the major axis is about 477,700 mi, and the length of the minor axis is about 476,980 mi.
    a. Write an equation for the Moon's orbit.
    b. Find the minimum and maximum distances from Earth to the Moon.

43. Write an equation for an ellipse with foci $F_1\,(-3, 0)$ and $F_2\,(3, 0)$ and a constant sum of 10. (*Hint:* Use $d = PF_1 + PF_2$ and the point (x, y).)

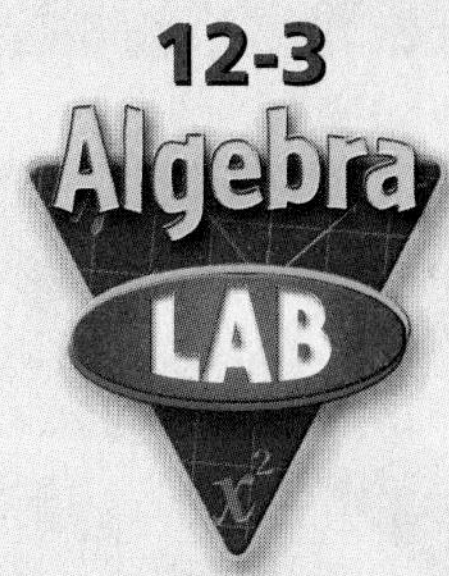

Locate the Foci of an Ellipse

You have seen how an ellipse is defined by its foci and how to draw an ellipse given the foci. You can find the foci of a given ellipse by using a compass.

Use appropriate tools strategically.

Use with Ellipses

CC.9-12.G.GPE.3 (+) Derive the equations of ellipses and hyperbolas…

Activity

Find the foci of the ellipse with major axis length 20 and minor axis length 12.

1. Graph the ellipse so that the center is at $(0, 0)$. Mark the endpoints of the major axis: $(-10, 0)$ and $(10, 0)$. Mark the endpoints of the minor axis at $(0, -6)$ and $(0, 6)$. Draw the ellipse.

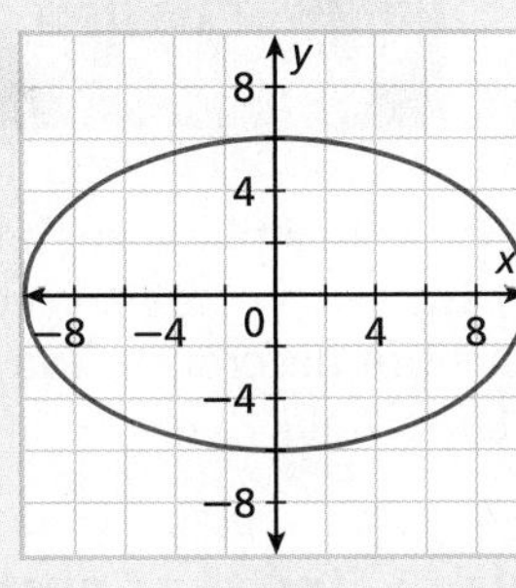

2. Use a compass to draw a circle with radius 10 units centered at $(0, 0)$.

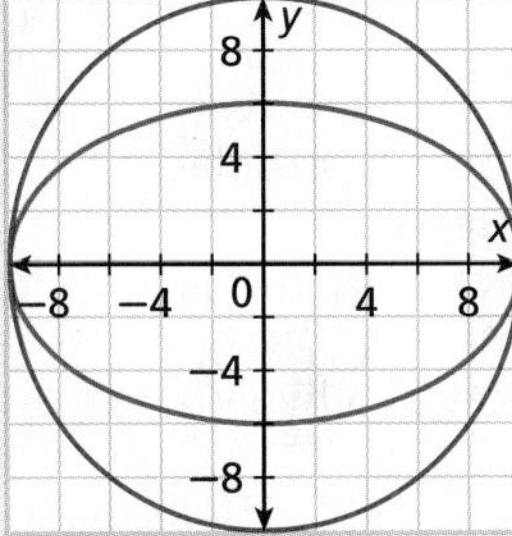

3. Draw the line with equation $y = 6$ on the graph. Mark the points where the line intersects the circle.

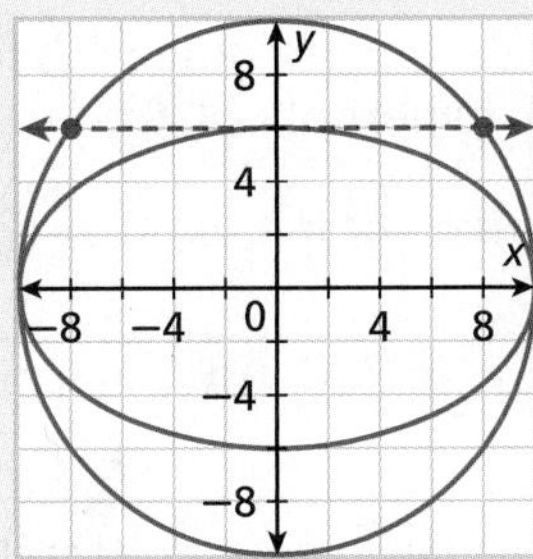

4. Draw lines from the points where $y = 6$ intersects the circle perpendicular to the x-axis. The foci of the ellipse are the points where the perpendicular lines intersect the x-axis. Where are the foci of your ellipse? Check by using the formula $c^2 = a^2 - b^2$.

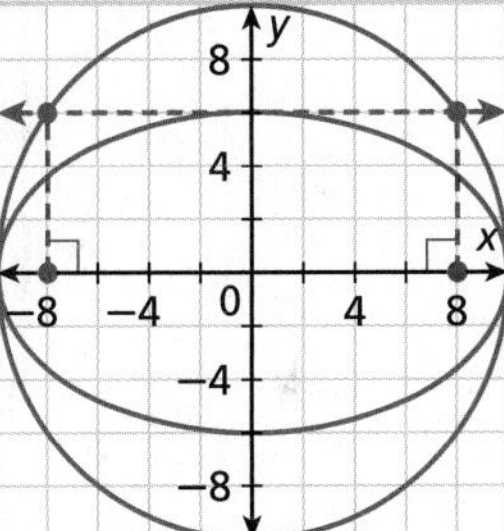

Try This

Use a compass to find the foci of each ellipse with a horizontal major axis.

1. major axis length 26, minor axis length 10
2. major axis length 34, minor axis length 16

Use a compass to find the foci of each ellipse with a vertical major axis.

3. major axis length 25, minor axis length 24
4. major axis length 20, minor axis length 12
5. **Critical Thinking** In Step 3 above, what other line could you have drawn to get the same foci?
6. **Critical Thinking** Why does this method of locating the foci of an ellipse work?

12-4 Hyperbolas

CC.9-12.G.GPE.3 (+) Derive the equations of ellipses and hyperbolas…

Objectives

Write the standard equation for a hyperbola.

Graph a hyperbola, and identify its vertices, co-vertices, center, foci, and asymptotes.

Vocabulary

hyperbola
focus of a hyperbola
branch of a hyperbola
transverse axis
vertices of a hyperbola
conjugate axis
co-vertices of a hyperbola

Who uses this?

Biologists use hyperbolas to locate and track whales based on the sounds that the whales make. (See Exercise 33.)

What would happen if you pulled the two foci of an ellipse so far apart that they moved outside the ellipse? The result would be a *hyperbola*, another conic section.

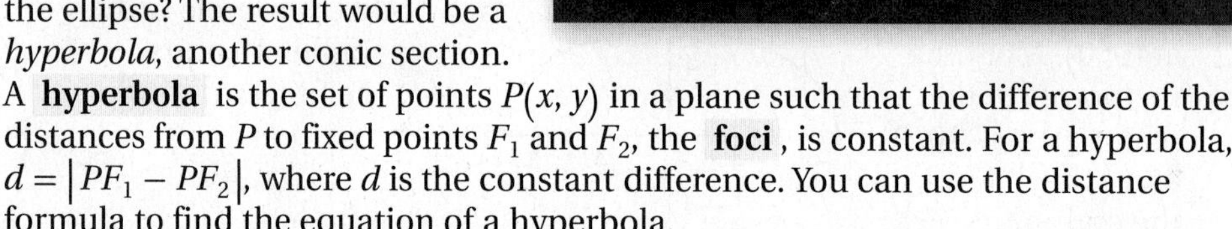

A **hyperbola** is the set of points $P(x, y)$ in a plane such that the difference of the distances from P to fixed points F_1 and F_2, the **foci**, is constant. For a hyperbola, $d = |PF_1 - PF_2|$, where d is the constant difference. You can use the distance formula to find the equation of a hyperbola.

EXAMPLE 1 Using the Distance Formula to Find the Constant Difference of a Hyperbola

Find the constant difference for a hyperbola with foci $F_1\ (-5, 0)$ and $F_2\ (5, 0)$ and the point on the hyperbola $(4, 0)$.

$d = |PF_1 - PF_2|$ *Definition of the constant difference of a hyperbola*

$= \left|\sqrt{(x_1 - x_3)^2 + (y_1 - y_3)^2} - \sqrt{(x_2 - x_3)^2 + (y_2 - y_3)^2}\right|$ *Distance Formula*

$= \left|\sqrt{(-5 - 4)^2 + (0 - 0)^2} - \sqrt{(5 - 4)^2 + (0 - 0)^2}\right|$ *Substitute.*

$= |\sqrt{81} - \sqrt{1}|$ *Simplify.*

$= 8$

The constant difference is 8.

1. Find the constant difference for a hyperbola with foci at $F_1\ (0, -10)$ and $F_2\ (0, 10)$ and the point on the hyperbola $(6, 7.5)$.

As the graphs in the following table show, a hyperbola contains two symmetrical parts called **branches**.

A hyperbola also has two axes of symmetry. The **transverse axis** of symmetry contains the vertices and, if it were extended, the foci of the hyperbola. The **vertices of a hyperbola** are the endpoints of the transverse axis.

The **conjugate axis** of symmetry separates the two branches of the hyperbola. The **co-vertices of a hyperbola** are the endpoints of the conjugate axis. The transverse axis is not always longer than the conjugate axis.

The standard form of the equation of a hyperbola depends on whether the hyperbola's transverse axis is horizontal or vertical.

Horizontal	Vertical
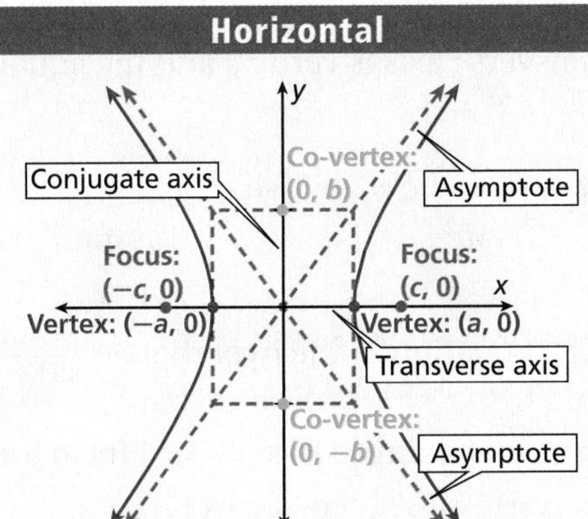	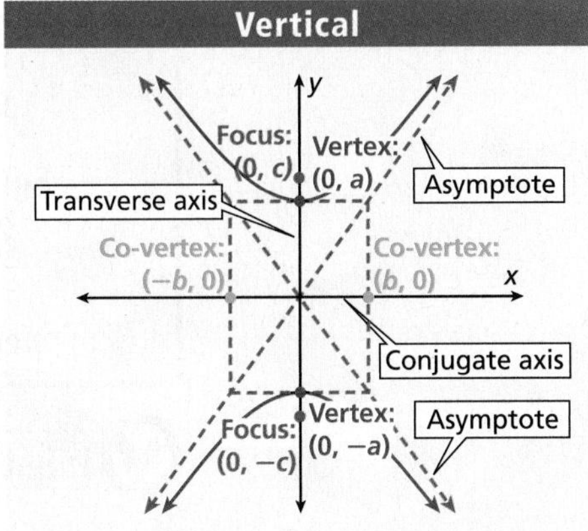

The values a, b, and c are related by the equation $c^2 = a^2 + b^2$. Also note that the length of the transverse axis is $2a$ and the length of the conjugate axis is $2b$.

Standard Form for the Equation of a Hyperbola Center at (0, 0)

TRANSVERSE AXIS	HORIZONTAL	VERTICAL
Equation	$\frac{x^2}{a^2} - \frac{y^2}{b^2} = 1$	$\frac{y^2}{a^2} - \frac{x^2}{b^2} = 1$
Vertices	$(a, 0), (-a, 0)$	$(0, a), (0, -a)$
Foci	$(c, 0), (-c, 0)$	$(0, c), (0, -c)$
Co-vertices	$(0, b), (0, -b)$	$(b, 0), (-b, 0)$
Asymptotes	$y = \pm\frac{b}{a}x$	$y = \pm\frac{a}{b}x$

EXAMPLE 2 Writing Equations of Hyperbolas

Write an equation in standard form for each hyperbola.

A

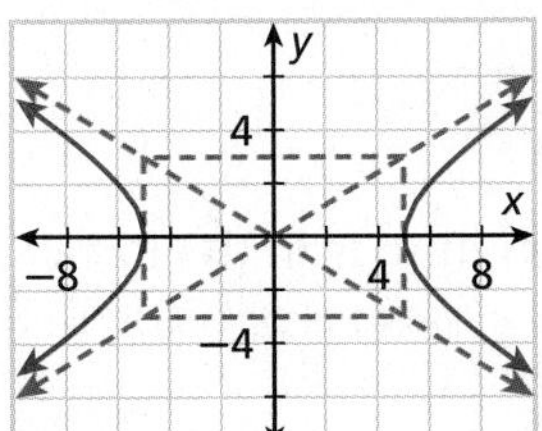

Step 1 Identify the form of the equation.

The graph opens horizontally, so the equation will be in the form $\frac{x^2}{a^2} - \frac{y^2}{b^2} = 1$.

Step 2 Identify the center and vertices.

The center of the graph is $(0, 0)$, the vertices are $(-5, 0)$ and $(5, 0)$, and the co-vertices are $(0, -3)$ and $(0, 3)$. So $a = 5$ and $b = 3$.

Step 3 Write the equation.

Because $a = 5$ and $b = 3$, the equation of the graph is $\frac{x^2}{5^2} - \frac{y^2}{3^2} = 1$, or $\frac{x^2}{25} - \frac{y^2}{9} = 1$.

Write an equation in standard form for each hyperbola.

B **the hyperbola with center $(0, 0)$, vertex $(0, 12)$, and focus $(0, 20)$**

Step 1 Because the vertex and the focus are on the vertical axis, the transverse axis is vertical and the equation is in the form $\frac{y^2}{a^2} - \frac{x^2}{b^2} = 1$.

Step 2 $a = 12$ and $c = 20$; Use $c^2 = a^2 + b^2$ to solve for b^2.

$20^2 = 12^2 + b^2$ *Substitute 12 for a and 20 for c.*

$256 = b^2$

Step 3 The equation of the hyperbola is $\frac{y^2}{144} - \frac{x^2}{256} = 1$

Write an equation in standard form for each hyperbola.

2a. Vertex $(0, 9)$, co-vertex $(7, 0)$

2b. Vertex $(8, 0)$, focus $(10, 0)$

As with circles and ellipses, hyperbolas do not have to be centered at the origin.

Standard Form for the Equation of a Hyperbola Center at (h, k)

TRANSVERSE AXIS	HORIZONTAL	VERTICAL
Equation	$\frac{(x-h)^2}{a^2} - \frac{(y-k)^2}{b^2} = 1$	$\frac{(y-k)^2}{a^2} - \frac{(x-h)^2}{b^2} = 1$
Vertices	$(h + a, k), (h - a, k)$	$(h, k + a), (h, k - a)$
Foci	$(h + c, k), (h - c, k)$	$(h, k + c), (h, k - c)$
Co-vertices	$(h, k + b), (h, k - b)$	$(h + b, k), (h - b, k)$
Asymptotes	$y - k = \pm\frac{b}{a}(x - h)$	$y - k = \pm\frac{a}{b}(x - h)$

EXAMPLE 3 Graphing a Hyperbola

Find the vertices, co-vertices, and asymptotes of each hyperbola, and then graph.

A $\frac{y^2}{25} - \frac{x^2}{36} = 1$

Step 1 The equation is in the form $\frac{y^2}{a^2} - \frac{x^2}{b^2} = 1$, so the transverse axis is vertical with center $(0, 0)$.

Step 2 Because $a = 5$ and $b = 6$, the vertices are $(0, 5)$ and $(0, -5)$ and the co-vertices are $(6, 0)$ and $(-6, 0)$.

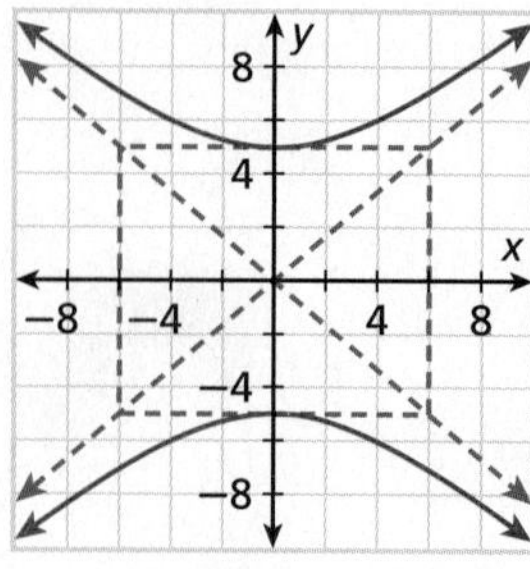

Step 3 The equations of the asymptotes are $y = \frac{5}{6}x$ and $y = -\frac{5}{6}x$.

Step 4 Draw a box by using the vertices and co-vertices. Draw the asymptotes through the corners of the box.

Step 5 Draw the hyperbola by using the vertices and the asymptotes.

Find the vertices, co-vertices, and asymptotes of each hyperbola, and then graph.

B $\dfrac{(x-2)^2}{16} - \dfrac{(y+3)^2}{49} = 1$

Step 1 The equation is in the form $\frac{(x-h)^2}{a^2} - \frac{(y-k)^2}{b^2} = 1$ so the transverse axis is horizontal with center $(2, -3)$.

Step 2 Because $a = 4$ and $b = 7$, the vertices are $(6, -3)$ and $(-2, -3)$ and the co-vertices are $(2, 4)$ and $(2, -10)$.

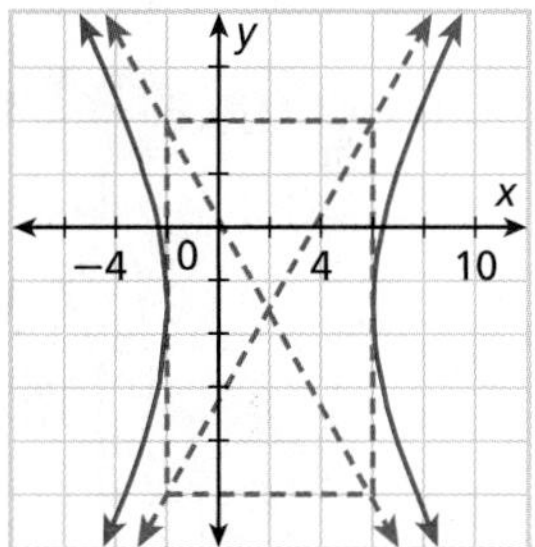

Step 3 The equations of the asymptotes are $y + 3 = \frac{7}{4}(x-2)$ and $y + 3 = -\frac{7}{4}(x-2)$.

Step 4 Draw a box by using the vertices and co-vertices. Draw the asymptotes through the corners of the box.

Step 5 Draw the hyperbola by using the vertices and the asymptotes.

Caution!

The graph of the hyperbola must pass through the vertices and approach both of the asymptotes.

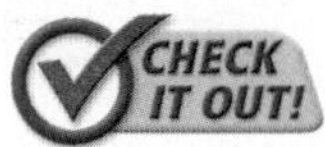

Find the vertices, co-vertices, and asymptotes of each hyperbola, and then graph.

3a. $\dfrac{x^2}{16} - \dfrac{y^2}{36} = 1$

3b. $\dfrac{(y+5)^2}{9} - \dfrac{(x-1)^2}{1} = 1$

Notice that as the parameters change, the graph of the hyperbola is transformed.

Parameter	Transformation
h	Translates the graph left for $h > 0$ and right for $h < 0$
k	Translates the graph up for $k > 0$ and down for $k < 0$
a	Stretches the graph in the direction of the transverse axis; as a increases, the vertices move farther apart.
b	Stretches the graph in the direction of the conjugate axis; as b increases, the co-vertices move farther apart.

MATHEMATICAL PRACTICES

THINK AND DISCUSS

1. When is the transverse axis of a hyperbola shorter than its conjugate axis?

2. How do you tell when a hyperbola has a horizontal transverse axis?

3. GET ORGANIZED Copy and complete the graphic organizer. Label all of the parts of the hyperbola.

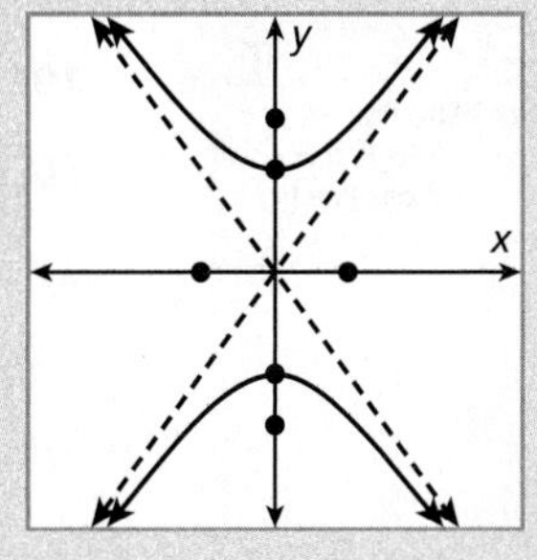

12-4 Exercises

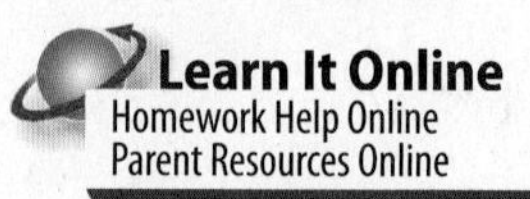

GUIDED PRACTICE

1. **Vocabulary** The vertices of a hyperbola lie on the __?__ (*transverse axis* or *conjugate axis*).

SEE EXAMPLE 1

Find the constant difference for a hyperbola with the given foci and point on the hyperbola.

2. $F_1(-13, 0)$, $F_2(13, 0)$, $P(5, 0)$
3. $F_1(0, -17)$, $F_2(0, 17)$, $P(0, -15)$

SEE EXAMPLE 2

Write an equation in standard form for each hyperbola.

4. center $(0, 0)$, vertex $(0, 5)$, and focus $(0, 13)$
5. center $(0, 0)$, vertex $(9, 0)$, and co-vertex $(0, 7)$
6. 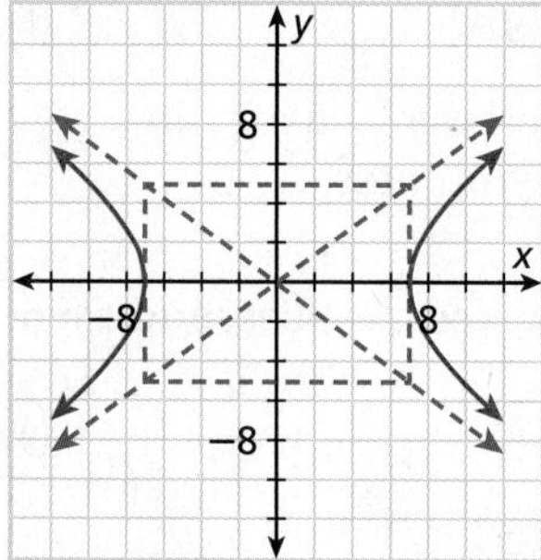

7. 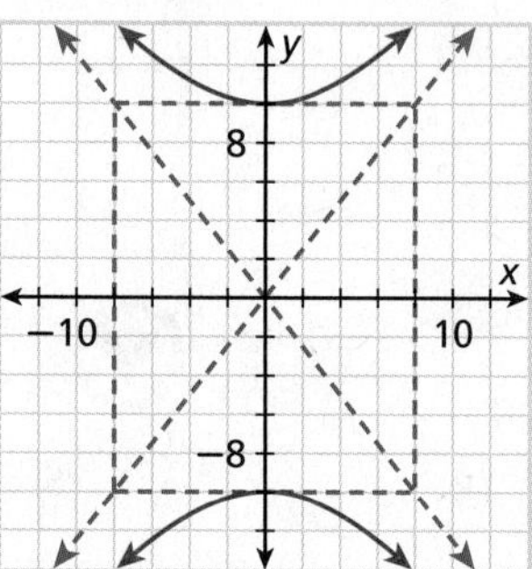

SEE EXAMPLE 3

Find the vertices, co-vertices, and asymptotes of each hyperbola, and then graph.

8. $\frac{x^2}{49} - \frac{y^2}{36} = 1$
9. $\frac{x^2}{25} - \frac{y^2}{64} = 1$
10. $\frac{y^2}{25} - \frac{x^2}{36} = 1$
11. $\frac{y^2}{100} - \frac{x^2}{81} = 1$
12. $\frac{(x-4)^2}{9} - \frac{(y-3)^2}{64} = 1$
13. $\frac{(x-4)^2}{16} - \frac{(y+6)^2}{49} = 1$
14. $\frac{(y+8)^2}{36} - \frac{(x+3)^2}{25} = 1$
15. $\frac{(y+7)^2}{4} - \frac{x^2}{25} = 1$

PRACTICE AND PROBLEM SOLVING

Independent Practice

For Exercises	See Example
16–17	1
18–21	2
22–29	3

Extra Practice

See Extra Practice for more Skills Practice and Applications Practice exercises.

Find the constant difference for a hyperbola with the given foci and point on the hyperbola.

16. $F_1(0, -10)$, $F_2(0, 10)$, $P(0, 6)$
17. $F_1(-29, 0)$, $F_2(29, 0)$, $P(21, 0)$

Write an equation in standard form for each hyperbola.

18. center $(0, 0)$, vertex $(15, 0)$, co-vertex $(0, -13)$
19. center $(0, 0)$, vertex $(-8, 0)$, focus $(17, 0)$
20. 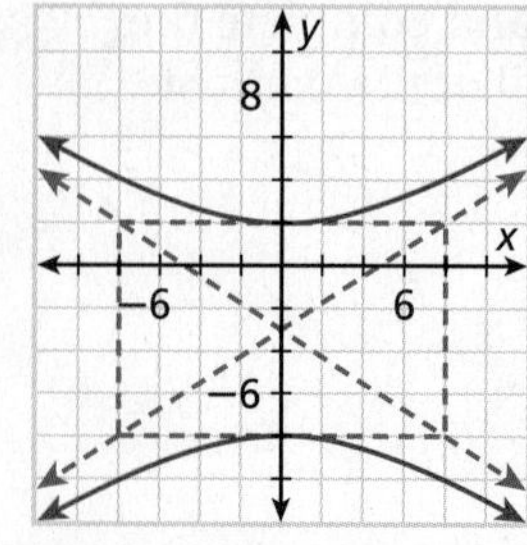

21. 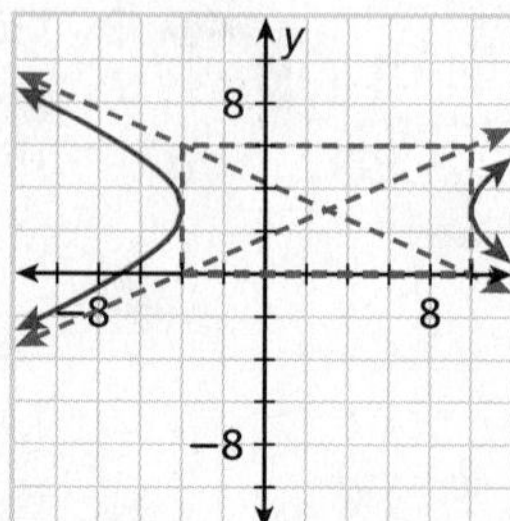

Find the vertices, co-vertices, and asymptotes of each hyperbola, and then graph.

22. $\frac{x^2}{64} - \frac{y^2}{36} = 1$ 23. $\frac{y^2}{25} - \frac{x^2}{81} = 1$ 24. $\frac{y^2}{81} - \frac{x^2}{16} = 1$ 25. $\frac{x^2}{4} - \frac{y^2}{121} = 1$

26. $\frac{(y-1)^2}{64} - \frac{(x+2)^2}{36} = 1$ 27. $\frac{(x+5)^2}{25} - \frac{(y-3)^2}{16} = 1$

28. $\frac{(y-8)^2}{25} - \frac{(x+6)^2}{36} = 1$ 29. $\frac{(x-6)^2}{9} - \frac{(y-2)^2}{16} = 1$

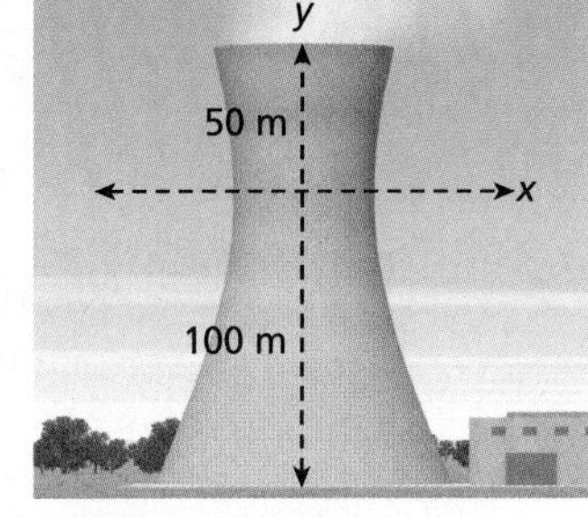

30. **Architecture** If the x-axis is placed at a height of 100 meters, the outer edge of a cooling tower can be modeled by the hyperbola $\frac{x^2}{900} - \frac{y^2}{1600} = 1$, measured in meters. If the tower is 150 meters tall, find the width of the cooling tower at the top.

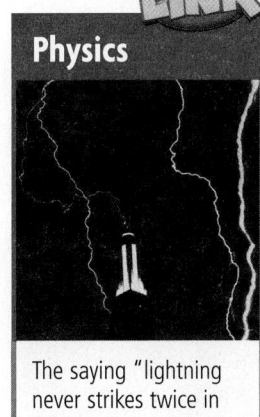

Physics

The saying "lightning never strikes twice in the same place" is often disproven. The Empire State Building is struck by lightning about 100 times each year and serves as a lightning rod for the surrounding area.

31. **Critical Thinking** What happens to the graph of $\frac{x^2}{a^2} - \frac{y^2}{16} = 1$ as the values of a increase? What happens to the graph of $\frac{x^2}{16} - \frac{y^2}{b^2} = 1$ as the values of b increase?

32. **Physics** Two people standing 10,000 feet apart see lightning strike. One person hears the thunder 5 seconds after the other person. Because sound travels at 1100 feet per second, one person is 5500 feet farther from the lightning strike than the other. The possible locations of the strike then form a hyperbola with the two people at the foci. Place the origin midway between the two people, and write an equation that could be used to represent the possible locations of the lightning strike.

33. **Biology** Two underwater listening devices 12,000 feet apart detect a whale call. One device detects the call 2 seconds before the other. The possible locations of the whale form a hyperbola with the two devices at the foci.
   a. If the speed of sound in water is 5000 feet per second, write an equation for the possible locations of the whale. (*Hint:* Place the origin midway between the devices.)
   b. **What if...?** Could the location of the whale be more precisely located if there were a third listening device? Explain.

34. **Critical Thinking** How could you identify the domain and range of a hyperbola? Explain.

35. **Critical Thinking** Consider a hyperbola with equation $\frac{(y-k)^2}{a^2} - \frac{(x-h)^2}{b^2} = 1$. Which parameter—$a$, b, or c—has the greatest value? Which has the least value? Explain.

36. **Write About It** Suppose you have two hyperbolas that are the same except that the transverse axis and conjugate axis are switched. How does switching the axes affect the equations of the asymptotes for the two hyperbolas? Why?

37. A comet's path as it approaches the Sun is modeled by one branch of the hyperbola $\frac{y^2}{900} - \frac{x^2}{44{,}896} = 1$, where the Sun is at the corresponding focus. Each unit of the coordinate plane represents 1 million miles.
   a. Find the coordinates of the Sun, assuming that it is at the focus with nonnegative coordinates.
   b. How close does the comet come to the Sun?
   c. When the comet is far from the Sun, the comet's path can be modeled by the hyperbola's asymptotes. Write the equations of the asymptotes.

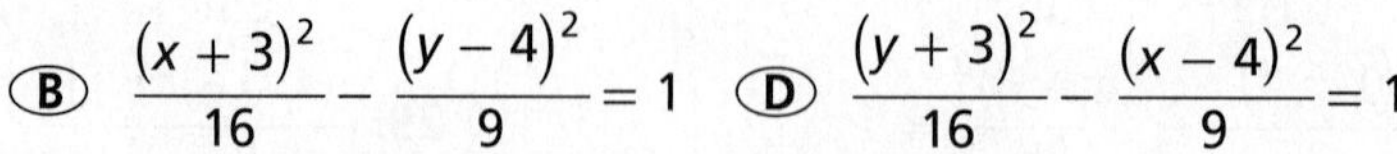

TEST PREP

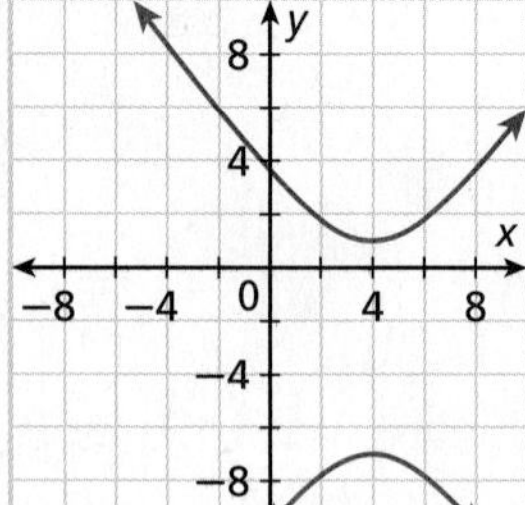

38. Which of the following is the equation of the graph shown?

Ⓐ $\dfrac{(x-3)^2}{16} - \dfrac{(y+4)^2}{9} = 1$ Ⓒ $\dfrac{(y-3)^2}{16} - \dfrac{(x+4)^2}{9} = 1$

Ⓑ $\dfrac{(x+3)^2}{16} - \dfrac{(y-4)^2}{9} = 1$ Ⓓ $\dfrac{(y+3)^2}{16} - \dfrac{(x-4)^2}{9} = 1$

39. Which of the following is an asymptote of the graph of $1 = \dfrac{x^2}{4} - \dfrac{y^2}{9}$?

Ⓕ $y = -\dfrac{2}{3}x$ Ⓖ $y = \dfrac{3}{2}x$ Ⓗ $y = -\dfrac{9}{4}x$ Ⓙ $y = \dfrac{4}{9}x$

40. The graph of which of the following equations will have the greatest distance between foci?

Ⓐ $\dfrac{(x-6)^2}{36} - \dfrac{(y+2)^2}{81} = 1$ Ⓒ $\dfrac{(y+115)^2}{49} - \dfrac{(x-225)^2}{100} = 1$

Ⓑ $\dfrac{(x+22)^2}{45} - \dfrac{(y-36)^2}{125} = 1$ Ⓓ $\dfrac{(y-59)^2}{90} - \dfrac{(x+76)^2}{95} = 1$

41. What is the length of the conjugate axis of the hyperbola with equation $\dfrac{x^2}{49} - \dfrac{y^2}{121} = 1$?

Ⓕ 7 Ⓖ 11 Ⓗ 14 Ⓙ 22

CHALLENGE AND EXTEND

Write an equation in standard form for each hyperbola.

42. co-vertex $(-12, 0)$, asymptote $y = -\dfrac{4}{3}x$

43. vertex $(27, -9)$, asymptote $y + 9 = -\dfrac{3}{5}(x - 7)$

44. The eccentricity of a hyperbola is defined as $e = \frac{c}{a}$. Recall that $c^2 = a^2 + b^2$ for a hyperbola in standard form.

   a. Find the eccentricity of $\frac{(x-4)^2}{144} - \frac{(y+2)^2}{1225} = 1$.

   b. Find the equation of a hyperbola with vertices $(0, 6)$ and $(0, -6)$, and eccentricity $e = \frac{4}{3}$.

   c. What are the possible values for the eccentricity of a hyperbola?

   d. Describe the relationship between eccentricity and the shape of a hyperbola.

45. Use the distance formula to write the equation of a hyperbola with foci at $F_1(-5, 0)$ and $F_2(5, 0)$ and $d = 8$. (*Hint:* Use $d = PF_1 - PF_2$ and the point (x, y).)

COMMON CORE

12-5 Parabolas

CC.9-12.G.GPE.2 (+) Derive the equation of a parabola given a focus and directrix.

Objectives

Write the standard equation of a parabola and its axis of symmetry.

Graph a parabola, and identify its focus, directrix, and axis of symmetry.

Vocabulary

focus of a parabola
directrix

Why learn this?

Parabolas are used with microphones to pick up sounds from sports events. (See Example 4.)

The graph of a quadratic function is a parabola. Because a parabola is a conic section, it can also be defined in terms of distance.

A parabola is the set of all points $P(x, y)$ in a plane that are an equal distance from both a fixed point, the **focus**, and a fixed line, the **directrix**. A parabola has an axis of symmetry perpendicular to its directrix and that passes through its vertex. The vertex of a parabola is the midpoint of the segment connecting the focus and the directrix.

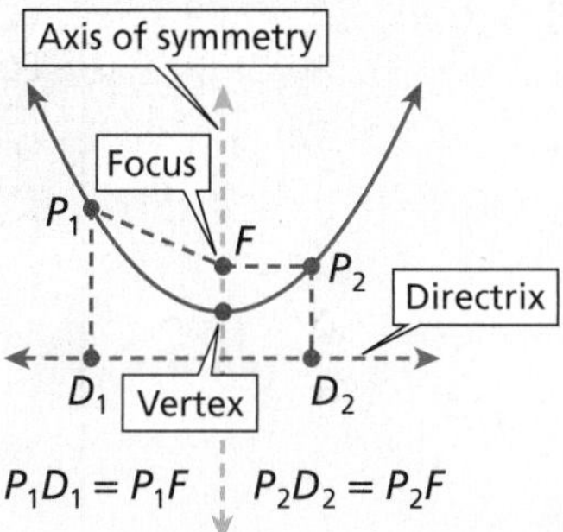

EXAMPLE 1 Using the Distance Formula to Write the Equation of a Parabola

Use the Distance Formula to find the equation of a parabola with focus $F(0, 3)$ and directrix $y = -3$.

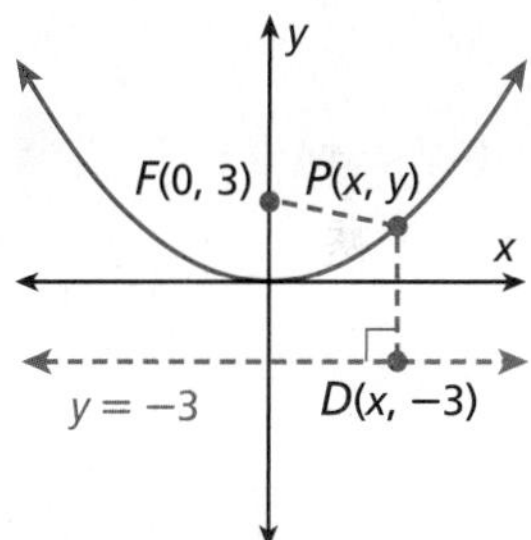

$PF = PD$	*Definition of a parabola*
$\sqrt{(x - x_1)^2 + (y - y_1)^2} = \sqrt{(x - x_2)^2 + (y - y_2)^2}$	*Distance Formula*
$\sqrt{(x - 0)^2 + (y - 3)^2} = \sqrt{(x - x)^2 + (y + 3)^2}$	*Substitute (0, 3) for (x_1, y_1) and (x, −3) for (x_2, y_2).*
$\sqrt{x^2 + (y - 3)^2} = \sqrt{(y + 3)^2}$	*Simplify.*
$x^2 + (y - 3)^2 = (y + 3)^2$	*Square both sides.*
$x^2 + y^2 - 6y + 9 = y^2 + 6y + 9$	*Expand.*
$x^2 - 6y = 6y$	*Subtract y^2 and 9 from both sides.*
$x^2 = 12y$	*Add 6y to both sides.*
$y = \frac{1}{12}x^2$	*Solve for y.*

Remember!

The distance from a point to a line is defined as the length of the line segment from the point perpendicular to the line.

1. Use the Distance Formula to find the equation of a parabola with focus $F(0, 4)$ and directrix $y = -4$.

Previously, you have graphed parabolas with vertical axes of symmetry that open upward or downward. Parabolas may also have horizontal axes of symmetry and may open to the left or right.

The equations of parabolas use the parameter p. The $|p|$ gives the distance from the vertex to both the focus and the directrix.

Standard Form for the Equation of a Parabola Vertex at (0, 0)

AXIS OF SYMMETRY	HORIZONTAL $y = 0$	VERTICAL $x = 0$
Equation	$x = \frac{1}{4p}y^2$	$y = \frac{1}{4p}x^2$
Direction	Opens right if $p > 0$ Opens left if $p < 0$	Opens upward if $p > 0$ Opens downward if $p < 0$
Focus	$(p, 0)$	$(0, p)$
Directrix	$x = -p$	$y = -p$
Graph	$D(-p, y)$, $P(x, y)$, $F(p, 0)$, $x = -p$	$F(0, p)$, $P(x, y)$, $y = -p$, $D(x, -p)$

EXAMPLE 2 **Writing Equations of Parabolas**

Write the equation in standard form for each parabola.

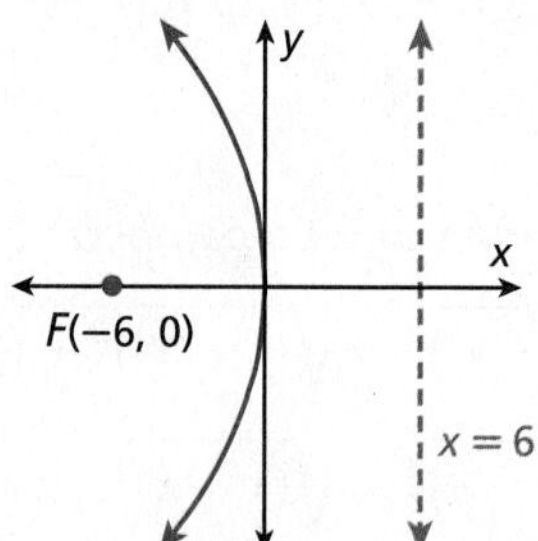

Step 1 Because the axis of symmetry is horizontal and the parabola opens to the left, the equation is in the form $x = \frac{1}{4p}y^2$ with $p < 0$.

Step 2 The distance from the focus $(-6, 0)$ to the vertex $(0, 0)$ is 6, so $p = -6$ and $4p = -24$.

Step 3 The equation of the parabola is $x = -\frac{1}{24}y^2$.

Check Use your graphing calculator. The graph of the equation appears to match.

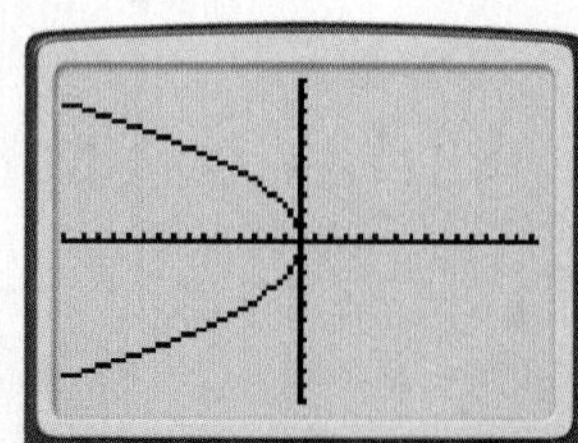

Write the equation in standard form for each parabola.

B the parabola with vertex $(0, 0)$ and directix $y = -2.5$.

Step 1 Because the directrix is a horizontal line, the equation is in the form $y = \frac{1}{4p}x^2$. The vertex is above the directrix, so the graph will open upward.

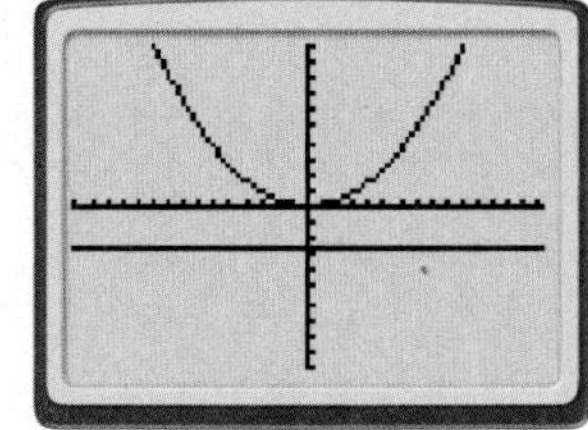

Step 2 Because the directrix is $y = -2.5$, $p = 2.5$ and $4p = 10$.

Step 3 The equation of the parabola is $y = \frac{1}{10}x^2$.

Check Use your graphing calculator.

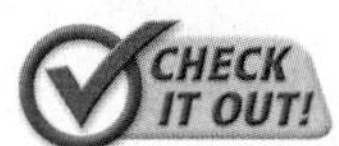

Write the equation in standard form for each parabola.

2a. vertex $(0, 0)$, directrix $x = 1.25$

2b. vertex $(0, 0)$, focus $(0, -7)$

The vertex of a parabola may not always be the origin. Adding or subtracting a value from x or y translates the graph of a parabola. Also notice that the values of p stretch or compress the graph.

Standard Form for the Equation of a Parabola Vertex at (h, k)

AXIS OF SYMMETRY	HORIZONTAL $y = k$	VERTICAL $x = h$
Equation	$x - h = \frac{1}{4p}(y - k)^2$	$y - k = \frac{1}{4p}(x - h)^2$
Direction	Opens right if $p > 0$ Opens left if $p < 0$	Opens upward if $p > 0$ Opens downward if $p < 0$
Focus	$(h + p, k)$	$(h, k + p)$
Directrix	$x = h - p$	$y = k - p$
Graph	y; $y = k$; $F(h + p, k)$; (h, k); x; $x = h - p$	$x = h$; y; $F(h, k + p)$; (h, k); $y = k - p$; x

EXAMPLE 3 Graphing Parabolas

Find the vertex, value of p, axis of symmetry, focus, and directrix of the parabola $x - 2 = -\frac{1}{16}(y + 5)^2$. Then graph.

Step 1 The vertex is $(2, -5)$.

Step 2 $\frac{1}{4p} = -\frac{1}{16}$, so $4p = -16$ and $p = -4$.

Step 3 The graph has a horizontal axis of symmetry, with equation $y = -5$, and opens left.

Step 4 The focus is $\left(2 + (-4), -5\right)$, or $(-2, -5)$.

Step 5 The directrix is a vertical line $x = 2 - (-4)$, or $x = 6$.

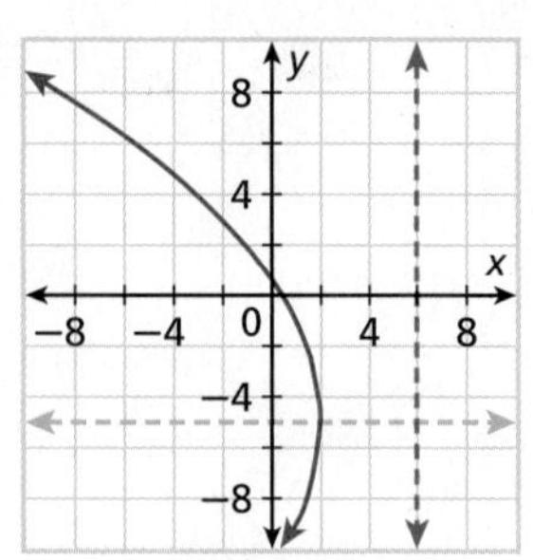

Find the vertex, value of p, axis of symmetry, focus, and directrix of each parabola. Then graph.

3a. $x - 1 = \frac{1}{12}(y - 3)^2$ **3b.** $y - 4 = -\frac{1}{2}(x - 8)^2$

Light or sound waves collected by a parabola will be reflected by the curve through the focus of the parabola, as shown in the figure. Waves emitted from the focus will be reflected out parallel to the axis of symmetry of a parabola. This property is used in communications technology.

EXAMPLE  Using the Equation of a Parabola

Engineers are constructing a parabolic microphone for use at sporting events. The surface of the parabolic microphone will reflect sounds to the focus of the microphone at the end of a part called a feedhorn. The equation for the cross section of the parabolic microphone dish is $x = \frac{1}{32}y^2$, measured in inches. How long should the engineers make the feedhorn?

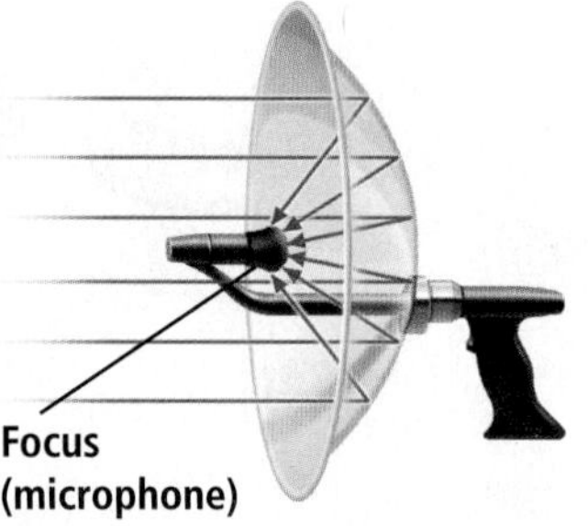

The equation for the cross section is in the form $x = \frac{1}{4p}y^2$, so $4p = 32$ and $p = 8$. The focus should be 8 inches from the vertex of the cross section. Therefore, the feedhorn should be 8 inches long.

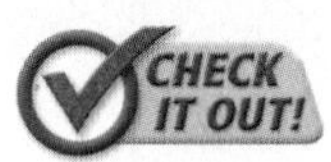

4. Find the length of the feedhorn for a microphone with a cross section equation $x = \frac{1}{44}y^2$.

THINK AND DISCUSS

1. By using the standard form of a parabola's equation, how can you tell which direction a parabola opens?

2. How does knowing the value of p help you in finding the focus and the directrix of a parabola?

3. GET ORGANIZED Copy and complete the graphic organizer. Sketch an example and give an equation for each type of parabola.

Opens upward	Opens right
Parabola	
Opens downward	Opens left

12-5 Exercises

Learn It Online
Homework Help Online
Parent Resources Online

GUIDED PRACTICE

1. **Vocabulary** Describe the relationship between a parabola and its *directrix*.

SEE EXAMPLE 1

Use the distance formula to find the equation of a parabola with the given focus and directrix.

2. $F(0, -5)$, $y = 5$
3. $F(7, 0)$, $x = -7$
4. $F(-3, 0)$, $x = 6$

SEE EXAMPLE 2

Write the equation in standard form for each parabola.

5.

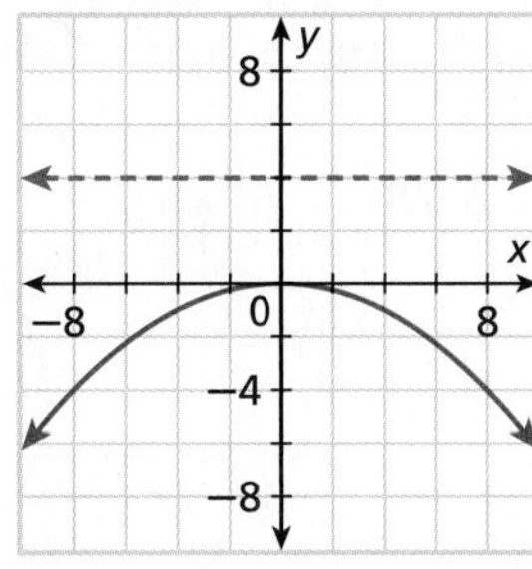

6.

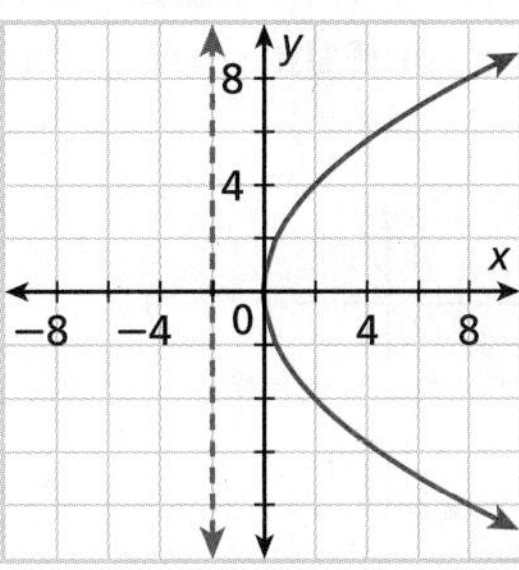

7.

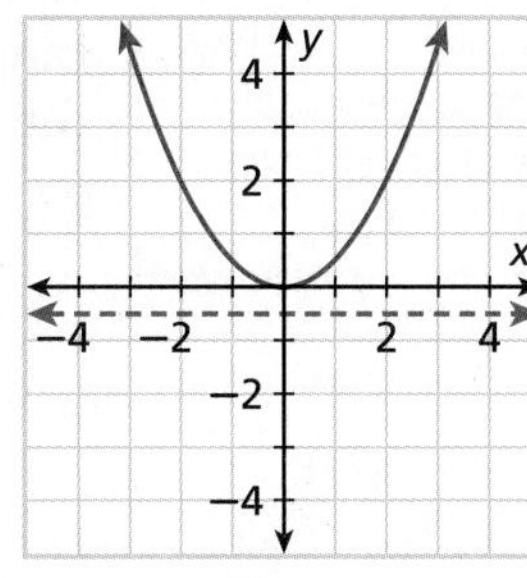

8. vertex $(0, 0)$, focus $(0, 1)$
9. vertex $(0, 0)$, focus $(-8, 0)$

SEE EXAMPLE 3

Find the vertex, value of *p*, axis of symmetry, focus, and directrix of each parabola, and then graph.

10. $y = \frac{1}{32}(x + 2)^2$
11. $x = \frac{1}{24}(y - 4)^2$
12. $y + 1 = \frac{1}{16}(x - 2)^2$

SEE EXAMPLE 4

13. **Communications** The equation for the cross section of a parabolic satellite TV dish is $y = \frac{1}{38}x^2$, measured in inches. How far is the focus from the vertex of the cross section?

PRACTICE AND PROBLEM SOLVING

Independent Practice

For Exercises	See Example
14–16	1
17–21	2
22–24	3
25	4

Extra Practice

See Extra Practice for more Skills Practice and Applications Practice exercises.

Use the distance formula to find the equation of a parabola with the given focus and directrix.

14. $F(0, 3)$, $y = -5$
15. $F(-2, 0)$, $x = 8$
16. $F(7, 0)$, $x = -1$

Write the equation in standard form for each parabola.

17.

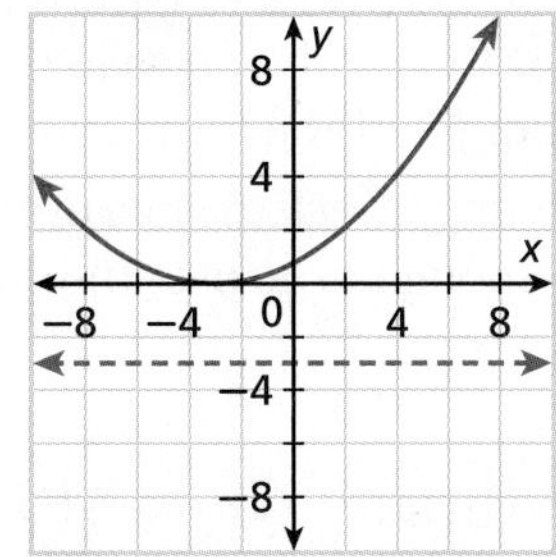

18.

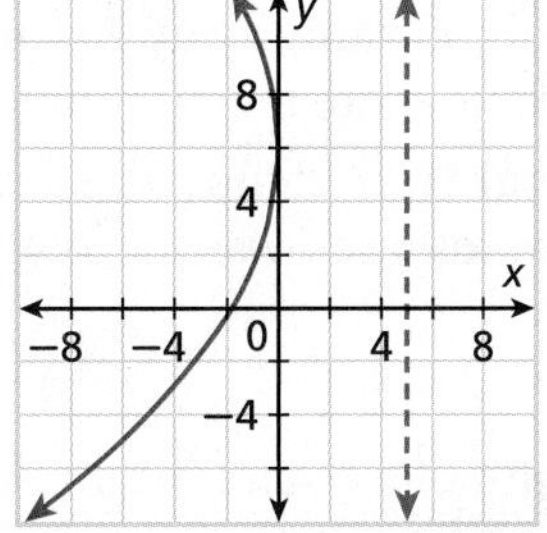

19.

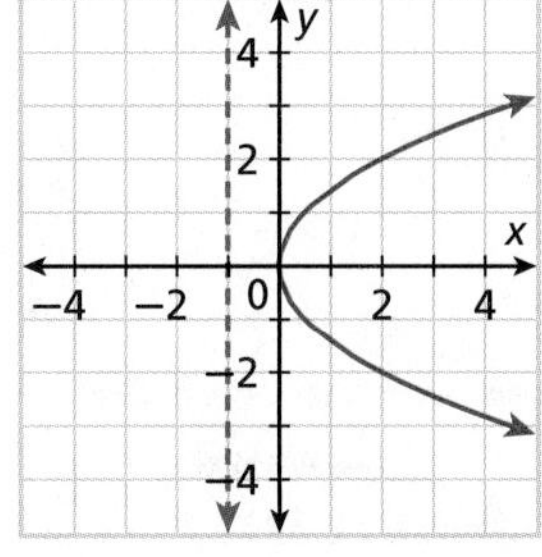

20. vertex $(0, 0)$, focus $\left(\frac{1}{2}, 0\right)$
21. vertex $(0, 0)$, focus $(0, -6)$

Find the vertex, value of *p*, axis of symmetry, focus, and directrix of each parabola, and then graph.

22. $y = \frac{1}{8}(x - 1)^2$
23. $x = 2y^2 + 1$
24. $x - 2 = \frac{1}{2}(y + 1)^2$

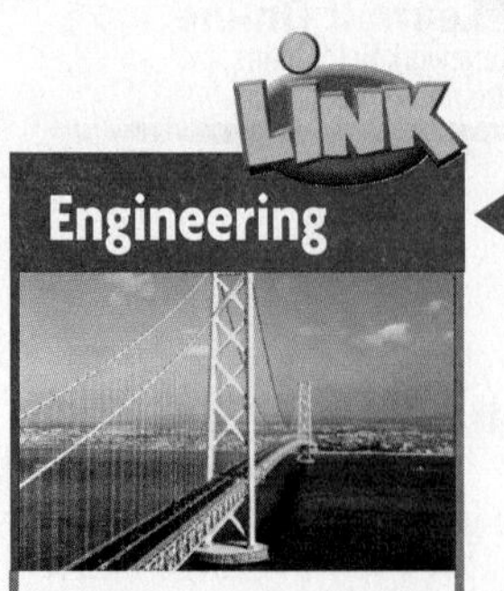

The Akashi-Kaikyo Bridge is the longest suspension bridge in the world with a main span of 1991 m. Also known as the Pearl Bridge, it connects the Kobe region of Japan to Awaji Island.

25. **Communications** Find an equation for a cross section of a parabolic microphone whose feedhorn is 9 inches long if the end of the feedhorn is placed at the origin.

26. **Engineering** The main cables of a suspension bridge are ideally parabolic. The cables over a bridge that is 400 feet long are attached to towers that are 100 feet tall. The lowest point of the cable is 40 feet above the bridge.

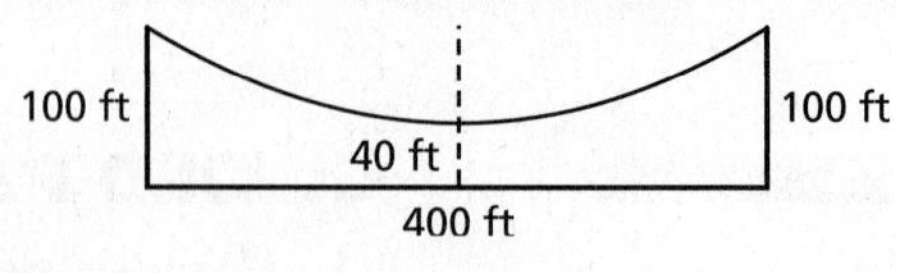

 a. Find the coordinates of the vertex and the tops of the towers if the bridge represents the x-axis and the axis of symmetry is the y-axis.
 b. Find an equation that can be used to model the cables.

Write the equation in standard form for each parabola, and give the domain and range. (*Hint:* Find the domain and range by using the vertex and the direction that the parabola opens.)

27.

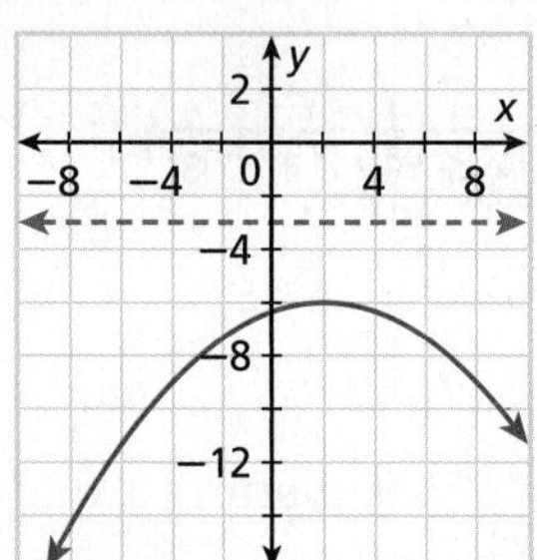

28.

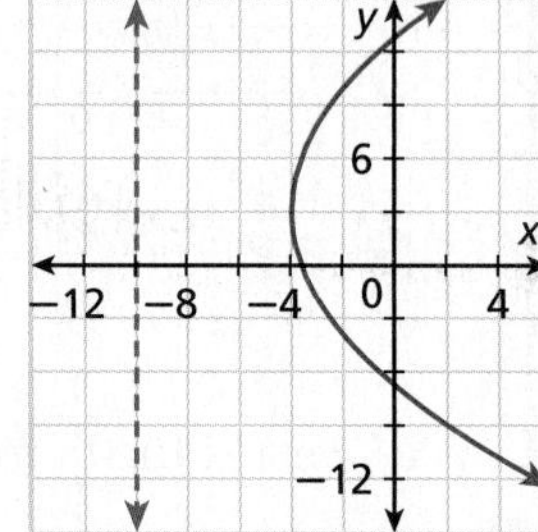

29. vertex $(-7, -3)$, focus $(2, -3)$

30. vertex $(5, -2)$, focus $(5, -8)$

31. focus $(0, 0)$, directrix $y = 10$

32. focus $(2, 6)$, directrix $y = -8$

33. focus $(4, -5)$, directrix $x = 12$

34. focus $(-3, 1)$, directrix $x = -15$

35. **Engineering** A spotlight has parabolic cross sections.
 a. Write an equation for a cross section of the spotlight if the bulb is 5 inches from the vertex and the vertex is placed at the origin.
 b. Write an equation for a cross section of the spotlight if the bulb is 4 inches from the vertex and the bulb is placed at the origin.
 c. If the spotlight has a diameter of 24 inches at its opening, find the depth of the spotlight if the bulb is 5 inches from the vertex.

36. **Sports** When a football is kicked, the path that the ball travels can be modeled by a parabola.
 a. A placekicker kicks a football, which reaches a maximum height of 8 yards and lands 50 yards away. Assuming that the football was at the origin when it was kicked, write an equation for the height of the football.
 b. **What if...?** If the placekicker was trying to kick the ball over a 10-foot-high goalpost 40 yards away, was the football high enough to go over the goalpost? Explain.

MULTI-STEP TEST PREP

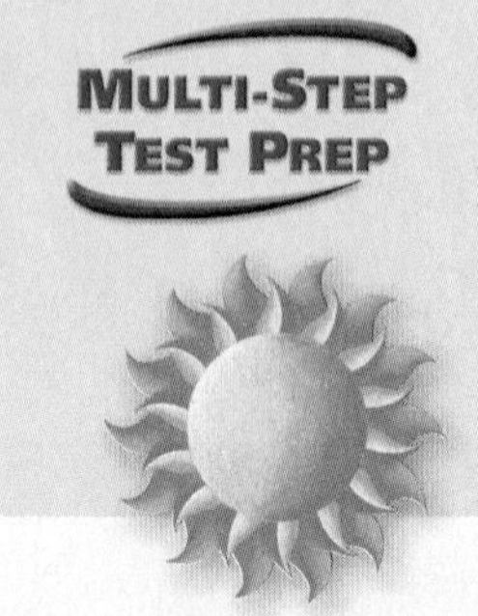

37. The path of a comet is modeled by the parabola $y = -\frac{1}{532}(x + 96)^2 + 174$, where each unit of the coordinate plane represents 1 million kilometers.
 a. The Sun is at the focus of the parabolic path. Find the coordinates of the Sun.
 b. How close does the comet come to the Sun?
 c. What are the coordinates of the comet when it is at its closest point to the Sun?

Graph each equation. Identify the vertex, value of p, axis of symmetry, focus, and directrix for each equation.

38. $20(y-2) = (x+6)^2$

39. $y = -2(x+4)^2 + 5$

40. $(y+7)^2 = \frac{x}{16}$

41. $x + 3 = \frac{1}{8}(y-2)^2$

42. **Critical Thinking** Find the distance d from the focus to the points on the parabola that are on the line perpendicular to the axis of symmetry and through the focus. Explain your answer.

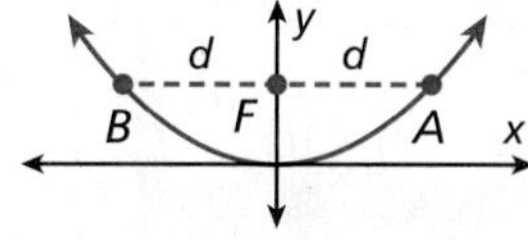

43. **Write About It** Explain how changing the value of p will affect the vertex, focus, and directrix of the parabola $y - k = \frac{1}{4p}(x-h)^2$.

TEST PREP

44. The graph of which of the following parabolas opens to the left?

Ⓐ $16y - 4x^2 = 12$ Ⓑ $16y + 4x^2 = 12$ Ⓒ $16x - 4y^2 = 12$ Ⓓ $16x + 4y^2 = 12$

45. Which of the following is the axis of symmetry for the graph of $x - 4 = \frac{1}{8}(y+2)^2$?

Ⓕ $x = 0$ Ⓖ $y = -2$ Ⓗ $x = 4$ Ⓙ $y = 8$

46. Which of the following graphs has the directrix $y = 4$?

Ⓐ $y + 3 = \frac{1}{4}(x-1)^2$

Ⓒ $x - 5 = \frac{1}{4}(y+4)^2$

Ⓑ $y - 5 = \frac{1}{4}(x+2)^2$

Ⓓ $x + 3 = \frac{1}{4}(y-2)^2$

47. **Short Response** What are the coordinates of the focus for the graph of $x - 3 = \frac{1}{16}y^2$?

CHALLENGE AND EXTEND

Write the equation in standard form for each parabola.

48. vertex $(6, 8)$, contains the point $(4, -2)$, axis of symmetry $x = 6$

49. focus $(6, 5)$, axis of symmetry $x = 6$, contains the point $(10, 5)$

Multi-Step The latus rectum of a parabola is the line segment perpendicular to the axis of symmetry through the focus, with endpoints on the parabola. Find the length of the latus rectum of each parabola.

50. $y = \frac{1}{8}x^2$

51. $y - k = \frac{1}{4p}(x-h)^2$

CHAPTER 12

MULTI-STEP TEST PREP

SECTION 12A

MATHEMATICAL PRACTICES **Model with mathematics.**

Understanding Conic Sections

The Solar System Johannes Kepler (1571–1630) is generally credited as the first astronomer to recognize the role of the conic sections in describing our solar system. Kepler's first law of planetary motion states that the path of every planet is an ellipse with the Sun at one focus.

1. Although the orbit of Earth around the Sun is elliptical, it very closely resembles a circle. The orbit can be modeled by $x^2 + y^2 = 8649$, where the Sun is at the origin and each unit of the coordinate plane represents 1 million miles. How far does Earth travel in 1 year as it makes one complete orbit?

2. The figure shows the elliptical orbit of Mercury, whose minimum distance to the Sun is 29 million miles and whose maximum distance to the Sun is 43 million miles. According to Kepler's laws, the average distance of a planet to the Sun is equal to half the length of the orbit's major axis. What is the average distance of Mercury to the Sun?

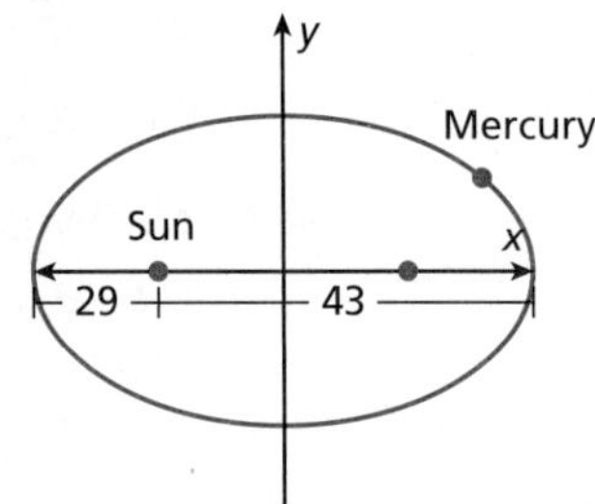

3. Write an equation that models the orbit of Mercury.

4. A comet that passes through the solar system just once has a path that is modeled by a hyperbola or a parabola. Astronomers discover a comet whose path is modeled by $\frac{x^2}{2500} - \frac{y^2}{37{,}500} = 1$, with the Sun at one focus. How close will the comet come to the Sun?

5. The path of another comet is modeled by $336(x - 89) = (y - 62)^2$, with the Sun at the focus. In this model, what are the coordinates of the Sun? How close will this comet come to the Sun?

READY TO GO ON?

CHAPTER 12

SECTION 12A

Quiz for Lessons 12-1 Through 12-5

12-1 Introduction to Conic Sections

1. The delivery area of a furniture store extends to the locations $(-7, 12)$ and $(5, -4)$. Write an equation for the delivery area of the store if a line between the locations represents a diameter of the delivery area.

Identify and describe each conic section.

2. $\frac{(x+2)^2}{64} + \frac{(y-8)^2}{64} = 1$
3. $25x^2 + 36y^2 = 900$
4. $x = \frac{y^2}{3} + 2$
5. $\frac{y^2}{25} - \frac{x^2}{25} = 1$

12-2 Circles

Write the equation of each circle.

6. center $(-3, 7)$ and radius $r = 12$
7. center $(4, -2)$ and containing the point $(-4, 13)$
8. Write the equation of the line that is tangent to $x^2 + y^2 = 225$ at $(9, -12)$.

12-3 Ellipses

Find the center, vertices, co-vertices, and foci of each ellipse. Then graph.

9. $\frac{x^2}{81} + \frac{y^2}{100} = 1$
10. $4(x-2)^2 + 16(y+3)^2 = 64$
11. Write the equation of the ellipse with center $(3, 5)$, vertex $(-10, 5)$, and focus $(8, 5)$.
12. A semi-elliptical bridge over a stream that is 30 feet wide must be 12 feet high at its highest point to accommodate boat traffic. Write an equation for a cross section of the bridge.

12-4 Hyperbolas

Find the center, vertices, co-vertices, foci, and asymptotes for each hyperbola. Then graph.

13. $\frac{y^2}{49} - \frac{x^2}{25} = 1$
14. $\frac{(x-5)^2}{36} - \frac{(y+3)^2}{9} = 1$
15. Write the equation of the hyperbola with vertices $(2, 3)$ and $(2, 9)$ and co-vertex $(7, 6)$.

12-5 Parabolas

Find the vertex, value of *p*, axis of symmetry, focus, and directrix for each parabola. Then graph.

16. $x = -\frac{1}{12}y^2$
17. $y = 2(x+3)^2 + 4$
18. Write the equation of the parabola with focus $(5, 2)$ and directrix $x = 1$.
19. A cross section of a parabolic microphone has the equation $35x = y^2$, where x and y are measured in inches. How far from the vertex of the microphone should the feedhorn be placed?

12-6 Identifying Conic Sections

CC.9-12.G.GPE.1 Derive the equation of a circle…using the Pythagorean Theorem…Find the center and radius of a circle given by an equation.

Objectives

Identify and transform conic sections.

Use the method of completing the square to identify and graph conic sections.

Why learn this?

The path of an airplane in a dive can be modeled by a branch of a hyperbola or a parabola. (See Example 4.)

© Chuck Eckert/Alamy

Previously, you have learned about the four conic sections. Recall the equations of conic sections in standard form. In these forms, the characteristics of the conic sections can be identified.

Know it! Note

Standard Forms for the Conic Sections with Center (h, k)

	HORIZONTAL AXIS	VERTICAL AXIS
Circle	$(x-h)^2+(y-k)^2=r^2$	
Ellipse	$\frac{(x-h)^2}{a^2}+\frac{(y-k)^2}{b^2}=1$	$\frac{(x-h)^2}{b^2}+\frac{(y-k)^2}{a^2}=1$
Hyperbola	$\frac{(x-h)^2}{a^2}-\frac{(y-k)^2}{b^2}=1$	$\frac{(y-k)^2}{a^2}-\frac{(x-h)^2}{b^2}=1$
Parabola	$x-h=\frac{1}{4p}(y-k)^2$	$y-k=\frac{1}{4p}(x-h)^2$

EXAMPLE 1 Identifying Conic Sections in Standard Form

Identify the conic section that each equation represents.

A $\frac{(x-7)^2}{5^2}-\frac{(y+2)^2}{2^2}=1$

This equation is of the same form as a hyperbola with a horizontal transverse axis.

B $y-3=\frac{1}{12}(x-4)^2$

This equation is of the same form as a parabola with a vertical axis of symmetry.

C $\frac{(x-1)^2}{8^2}+\frac{(y-1)^2}{10^2}=1$

This equation is of the same form as an ellipse with a vertical major axis.

Identify the conic section that each equation represents.

1a. $x^2+(y+14)^2=11^2$ **1b.** $\frac{(y-6)^2}{2^2}-\frac{(x-1)^2}{21^2}=1$

Student to Student — *Classifying Conic Sections*

Mercedes Raya
Central High School

I can classify an equation in standard form just by looking. This is a good way for me to check my work.

Only one squared term	→	*it's a parabola.*
A squared term minus a squared term	→	*it's a hyperbola.*
A squared term plus a squared term	→	*it's a circle or an ellipse.*

All conic sections can be written in the general form $Ax^2 + Bxy + Cy^2 + Dx + Ey + F = 0$. The conic section represented by an equation in general form can be determined by the coefficients.

Classifying Conic Sections

For an equation of the form $Ax^2 + Bxy + Cy^2 + Dx + Ey + F = 0$
(A, B, and C do not all equal 0.)

CONIC SECTION	COEFFICIENTS
Circle	$B^2 - 4AC < 0$, $B = 0$, and $A = C$
Ellipse	$B^2 - 4AC < 0$ and either $B \neq 0$ or $A \neq C$
Hyperbola	$B^2 - 4AC > 0$
Parabola	$B^2 - 4AC = 0$

EXAMPLE 2 Identifying Conic Sections in General Form

Identify the conic section that each equation represents.

A $6x^2 + 9y^2 + 12x - 15y - 25 = 0$

$A = 6, B = 0, C = 9$ — *Identify the values for A, B, and C.*

$B^2 - 4AC$

$0^2 - 4(6)(9)$ — *Substitute into $B^2 - 4AC$.*

-216 — *Simplify. The conic is either a circle or an ellipse.*

$A \neq C$ — *The conic is not a circle.*

Because $B^2 - 4AC < 0$ and $A \neq C$, the equation represents an ellipse.

B $4x^2 + 4xy + y^2 - 12x + 8y + 36 = 0$

$A = 4, B = 4, C = 1$ — *Identify the values for A, B, and C.*

$B^2 - 4AC$

$4^2 - 4(4)(1)$ — *Substitute into $B^2 - 4AC$.*

0 — *Simplify.*

Because $B^2 - 4AC = 0$, the equation represents a parabola.

Identify the conic section that each equation represents.

2a. $9x^2 + 9y^2 - 18x - 12y - 50 = 0$

2b. $12x^2 + 24xy + 12y^2 + 25y = 0$

If you are given the equation of a conic in standard form, you can write the equation in general form by expanding the binomials.

If you are given the general form of a conic section, you can use the method of completing the square to write the equation in standard form.

EXAMPLE 3 Finding the Standard Form of the Equation for a Conic Section

Find the standard form of each equation by completing the square. Then identify and graph each conic.

A $x^2 - 12x - 16y + 36 = 0$

$x^2 - 12x + \blacksquare = 16y - 36 + \blacksquare$ — *Prepare to complete the square in x.*

$x^2 - 12x + \left(\frac{-12}{2}\right)^2 = 16y - 36 + \left(\frac{-12}{2}\right)^2$ — *Add $\left(-\frac{12}{2}\right)^2$, or 36, to both sides to complete the square.*

$(x-6)^2 = 16y$ — *Factor and simplify.*

$\frac{1}{16}(x-6)^2 = y$ — *Divide both sides by 16.*

$y = \frac{1}{16}(x-6)^2$ — *Rewrite in standard form.*

Because the conic is of the form $y - k = \frac{1}{4p}(x-h)^2$, it is a parabola with vertex $(6, 0)$ and $p = 4$, and it opens upward. The focus is $(6, 4)$ and the directrix is $y = -4$.

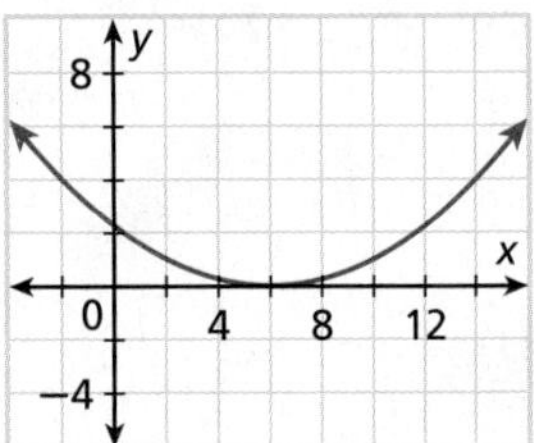

B $x^2 + 4y^2 + 4x - 24y + 36 = 0$

$x^2 + 4x + \blacksquare + 4y^2 - 24y + \blacksquare = -36 + \blacksquare + \blacksquare$ — *Rearrange to prepare for completing the square in x and y.*

$x^2 + 4x + \blacksquare + 4(y^2 - 6y + \blacksquare) = -36 + \blacksquare + \blacksquare$ — *Factor 4 from the y terms.*

$x^2 + 4x + \left(\frac{4}{2}\right)^2 + 4\left[y^2 - 6y + \left(-\frac{6}{2}\right)^2\right] = -36 + \left(\frac{4}{2}\right)^2 + 4\left(-\frac{6}{2}\right)^2$ — *Complete both squares.*

$(x+2)^2 + 4(y-3)^2 = 4$ — *Factor and simplify.*

$\frac{(x+2)^2}{4} + \frac{(y-3)^2}{1} = 1$ — *Divide both sides by 4.*

Because the conic is of the form $\frac{(x-h)^2}{a^2} + \frac{(y-k)^2}{b^2} = 1$, it is an ellipse with center $(-2, 3)$, horizontal major axis length 4, and minor axis length 2. The co-vertices are $(-2, 4)$ and $(-2, 2)$, and the vertices are $(-4, 3)$ and $(0, 3)$.

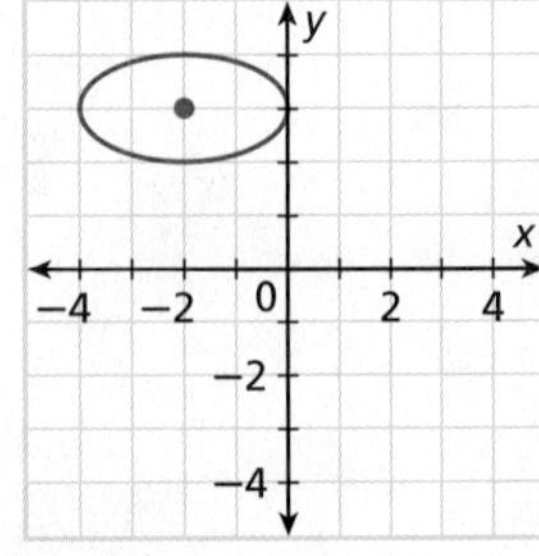

Remember!

You must factor out the leading coefficient of x^2 and y^2 before completing the square.

Find the standard form of each equation by completing the square. Then identify and graph each conic.

3a. $y^2 - 9x + 16y + 64 = 0$

3b. $16x^2 + 9y^2 - 128x + 108y + 436 = 0$

EXAMPLE 4 Aviation Application

At an air show, an airplane makes a dive that can be modeled by the equation $-4x^2 + 16y^2 - 16x + 32y - 64 = 0$, measured in hundreds of feet, with the ground represented by the x-axis. How close to the ground does the airplane pass?

The graph of $-4x^2 + 16y^2 - 16x + 32y - 64 = 0$ is a conic section. Write the equation in standard form.

$$-4x^2 - 16x + \blacksquare + 16y^2 + 32y + \blacksquare = 64 + \blacksquare + \blacksquare$$

Rearrange to prepare for completing the square in x and y.

$$-4\left(x^2 + 4x + \blacksquare\right) + 16\left(y^2 + 2y + \blacksquare\right) = 64 + \blacksquare + \blacksquare$$

Factor −4 from the x terms and 16 from the y terms.

$$-4\left[x^2 + 4x + \left(\frac{4}{2}\right)^2\right] + 16\left[y^2 + 2y + \left(\frac{2}{2}\right)^2\right] = 64 - 4\left(\frac{4}{2}\right)^2 + 16\left(\frac{2}{2}\right)^2$$

Complete both squares.

$$16(y+1)^2 - 4(x+2)^2 = 64$$ *Simplify.*

$$\frac{(y+1)^2}{4} - \frac{(x+2)^2}{16} = 1$$ *Divide both sides by 64.*

Because the conic is of the form $\frac{(y-k)^2}{a^2} - \frac{(x-h)^2}{b^2} = 1$, it is a hyperbola with vertical transverse axis length 4 and center $(-2, -1)$. The vertices are then $(-2, 1)$ and $(-2, -3)$. Because distance above ground is always positive, the airplane will be on the upper branch of the hyperbola. The relevant vertex is $(-2, 1)$ with y-coordinate 1.

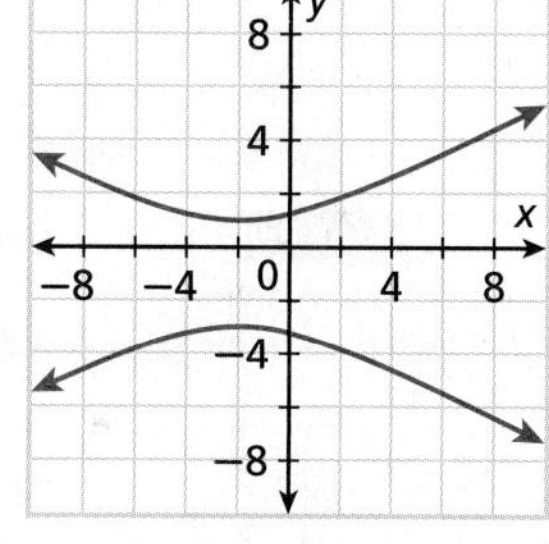

The minimum height of the plane is 100 feet.

4. An airplane makes a dive that can be modeled by the equation $-16x^2 + 9y^2 + 96x + 36y - 252 = 0$, measured in hundreds of feet. How close to the ground does the airplane pass?

THINK AND DISCUSS

1. In the equation $Ax^2 + Bxy + Cy^2 + Dx + Ey + F = 0$, if $B = 0$, what must be true about either A or C for the equation to represent a parabola?

2. When solving by completing the square, what must be added to both sides of the equation if one side has $5x^2 - 30x$? Explain.

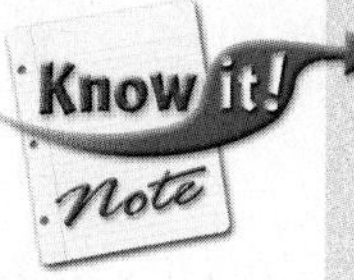

3. GET ORGANIZED Copy and complete the graphic organizer. Give an example of coefficients for each conic section in general form.

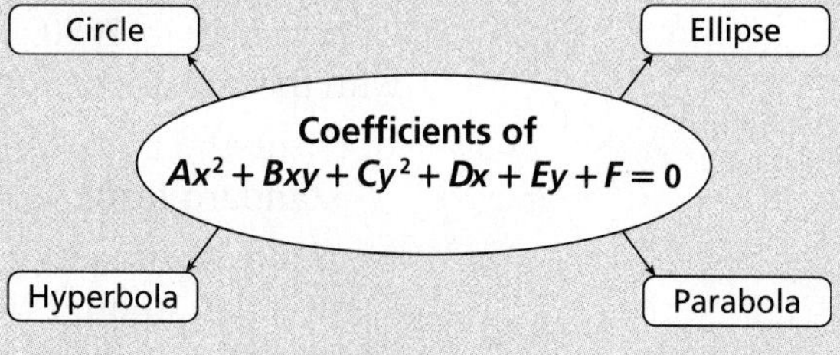

12-6 Exercises

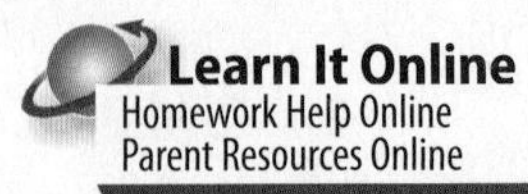

GUIDED PRACTICE

Identify the conic section that each equation represents.

SEE EXAMPLE 1

1. $\frac{(x+4)^2}{2^2} + \frac{(y-3)^2}{3^2} = 1$
2. $\frac{(x-8)^2}{5^2} - \frac{y^2}{5^2} = 1$
3. $y + 9 = 4(x-1)^2$
4. $(x-2)^2 + (y-6)^2 = 13^2$

SEE EXAMPLE 2

5. $12x^2 + 18y^2 - 8x + 9y - 10 = 0$
6. $-4y^2 + 15x + 12y - 8 = 0$
7. $10x^2 + 15xy + 10y^2 + 15x + 25y + 9 = 0$
8. $6x^2 = 14x + 12y^2 - 16y + 20$

SEE EXAMPLE 3

Find the standard form of each equation by completing the square. Then identify and graph each conic.

9. $x^2 + y^2 - 16x + 10y + 53 = 0$
10. $x^2 + 14x - 12y + 97 = 0$
11. $25x^2 + 9y^2 + 72y - 81 = 0$
12. $16x^2 + 36y^2 + 160x - 432y + 1120 = 0$

SEE EXAMPLE 4

13. **Multi-Step** A moth is circling an outdoor light in a path that can be modeled by the equation $4x^2 + 9y^2 - 108y = -288$, measured in inches. How close does the moth pass to a lizard located at the origin?

PRACTICE AND PROBLEM SOLVING

Independent Practice

For Exercises	See Example
14–17	1
18–21	2
22–31	3
32	4

Extra Practice

See Extra Practice for more Skills Practice and Applications Practice exercises.

Identify the conic section that each equation represents.

14. $\frac{(y-11)^2}{2^2} - \frac{(x+15)^2}{9^2} = 1$
15. $x - 4 = \frac{1}{16}(y-3)^2$
16. $(x+2)^2 + (y-4)^2 = 3^2$
17. $\frac{(x+2)^2}{6^2} + \frac{(y-7)^2}{8^2} = 1$
18. $12x^2 - 18y^2 - 18x - 12y + 12 = 0$
19. $7x^2 + 28x - 29y - 16 = 0$
20. $-12x^2 - 3y^2 + 7x + 9y - 5 = 0$
21. $12x^2 + 9y^2 - 2xy + 9 = 8y - 3y^2$

Find the standard form of each equation by completing the square. Then identify and graph each conic.

22. $x^2 + 20x - 4y + 100 = 0$
23. $x^2 + y^2 - 8y - 33 = 0$
24. $9x^2 + 36y^2 - 72x - 180 = 0$
25. $25x^2 - 4y^2 - 72y - 424 = 0$
26. $x^2 - 2x - 20y - 79 = 0$
27. $x^2 + y^2 + 10x + 4y + 9 = 0$
28. $64x^2 + 49y^2 + 256x - 196y - 2684 = 0$
29. $9x^2 - 4y^2 + 18x + 56y - 223 = 0$
30. $y^2 + 6x + 12y - 6 = 0$
31. $x^2 + y^2 - 5x + 9y + 10.5 = 0$
32. **Astronomy** Scientists find that the path of a comet as it travels around the Sun can be modeled by the function $225x^2 + 64y^2 + 7650x + 50{,}625 = 0$, with the Sun as one focus.
    a. Write the equation in standard form.
    b. If measurements are in millions of miles, about how close will the comet come to the sun?

Comet C/2001 Q4

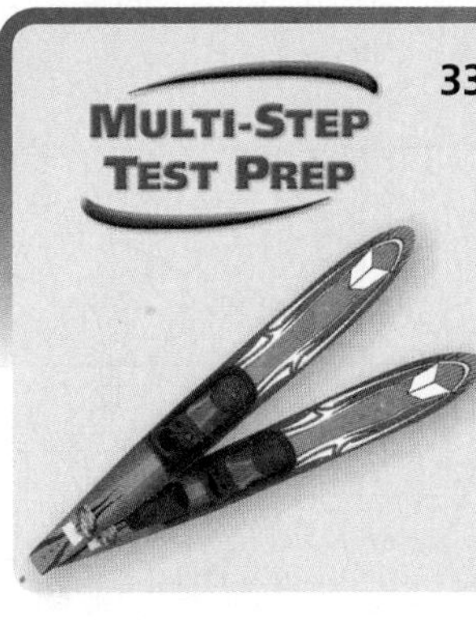

33. A water-skier is towed along a path that can be modeled by $25x^2 + 4y^2 + 300x - 24y + 836 = 0$. Each unit of the coordinate plane represents 10 m.
   a. What is the shape of the water-skier's path?
   b. The edge of a dock is represented by the y-axis. How close does the water-skier come to the dock?
   c. A second water-skier is towed along the same path. What is the maximum possible distance between the two water-skiers?

Write each equation in the form $Ax^2 + Bxy + Cy^2 + Dx + Ey + F = 0$.

34. $(x-7)^2 + (y+12)^2 = 81$
35. $\dfrac{(x-5)^2}{25} + \dfrac{(y+8)^2}{36} = 1$
36. $\dfrac{(x+10)^2}{49} - \dfrac{(y-6)^2}{81} = 1$

Determine whether the origin lies inside, outside, or on the graph of each equation.

37. $36x^2 + 4y^2 - 432x + 1152 = 0$
38. $4x^2 + 36y^2 - 48x = 0$
39. $16x^2 + 64y^2 - 192x + 16y - 447 = 0$
40. $3x^2 + 3y^2 = 147$

LINK
Math History

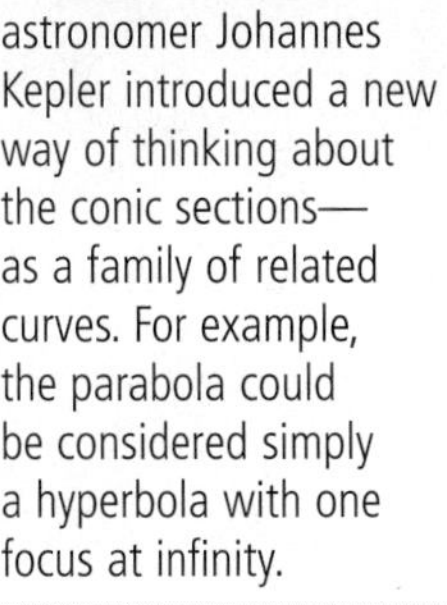

In 1604, German astronomer Johannes Kepler introduced a new way of thinking about the conic sections—as a family of related curves. For example, the parabola could be considered simply a hyperbola with one focus at infinity.

41. **Multi-Step** A model of the solar system includes a satellite orbiting the Moon on a path that can be modeled by the equation $6x^2 + 6y^2 = 24$, measured in centimeters (1 cm:10,000 km). If the Moon is located at the point $(0, 38.4)$, how close will the satellite pass to the Moon in the model?

42. **Critical Thinking** What does the graph of $x^2 - xy = 0$ look like? Explain.

43. **Agriculture** A farmer is planning to fence in part of the farm. Placing the farmhouse at the origin, the farmer finds that the path for the fence can be modeled by the equation $x^2 + y^2 - 80x - 60y - 37{,}500 = 0$, measured in feet.
   a. Write the equation in standard form.
   b. Find the area enclosed by the fence.
   c. Is the farmhouse inside or outside of the fence?

44. **/// ERROR ANALYSIS ///** In which case below was the conic section $4y^2 + 3x - 12y = 2x^2 + 18$ identified incorrectly? Explain the error.

A

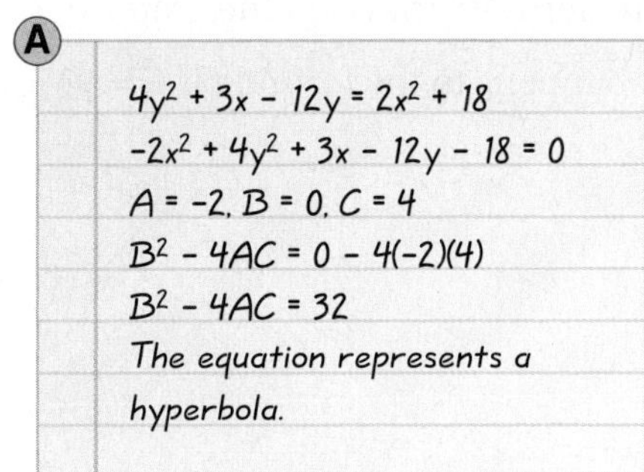

$4y^2 + 3x - 12y = 2x^2 + 18$
$-2x^2 + 4y^2 + 3x - 12y - 18 = 0$
$A = -2,\ B = 0,\ C = 4$
$B^2 - 4AC = 0 - 4(-2)(4)$
$B^2 - 4AC = 32$
The equation represents a hyperbola.

B

$4y^2 + 3x - 12y = 2x^2 + 18$
$A = 2,\ B = 0,\ C = 4$
$B^2 - 4AC = 0 - 4(2)(4)$
$B^2 - 4AC = 32$
$A \neq C$
The equation represents an ellipse.

45. **Sports** The path followed by a baseball after it is hit can be modeled by the equation $2x^2 - 800x + 1000y - 4000 = 0$, measured in feet.
   a. Write the equation in standard form.
   b. What is the maximum height of the ball?
   c. What was the height of the ball when it was hit?
   d. **What if...?** How would changing the 4000 in the equation to 5000 change your answers to parts **b** and **c**?

46. **Write About It** Compare the equations and graphs of parabolas and hyperbolas.

47. Which of the following is the equation for the graph shown?

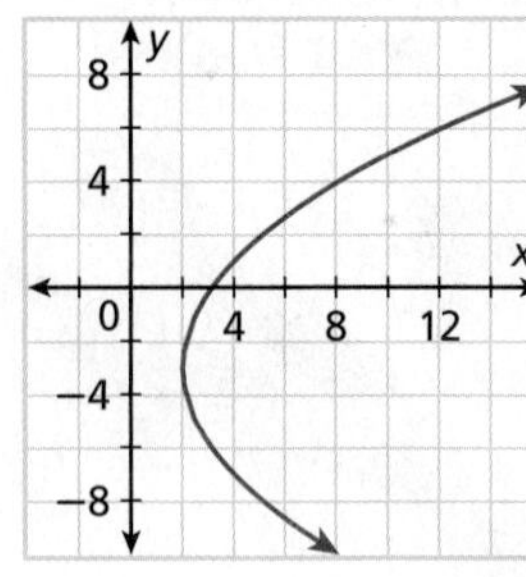

Ⓐ $3y^2 - 24x + 18y + 75 = 0$
Ⓑ $5x^2 + 30x - 40y + 125 = 0$
Ⓒ $2x^2 - 3y^2 + 18x - 24y + 75 = 0$
Ⓓ $3x^2 + 2y^2 - 24x + 18y + 125 = 0$

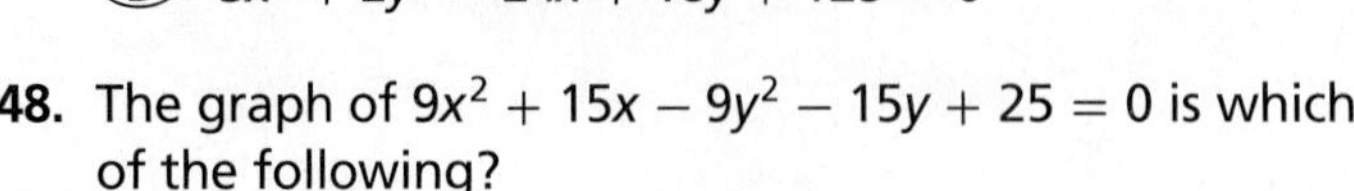

48. The graph of $9x^2 + 15x - 9y^2 - 15y + 25 = 0$ is which of the following?

Ⓕ Circle　　Ⓖ Ellipse
Ⓗ Hyperbola　　Ⓙ Parabola

49. Which of the following is the equation for the graph shown?

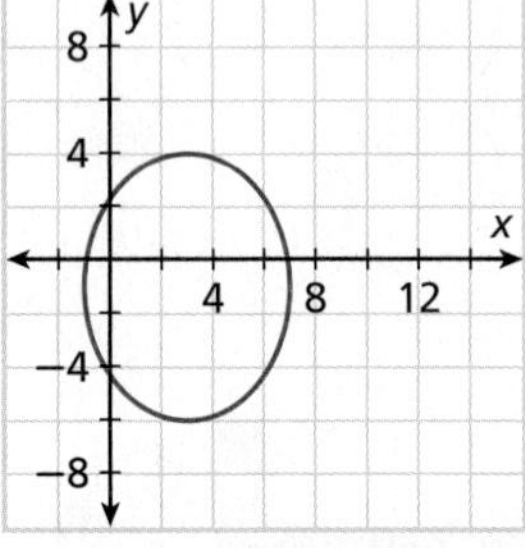

Ⓐ $25x^2 + 25y^2 - 150x + 32y - 159 = 0$
Ⓑ $25x^2 - 150x + 32y = 159$
Ⓒ $25x^2 - 150x = 16y^2 - 32y + 159$
Ⓓ $16y^2 + 32y - 159 = 150x - 25x^2$

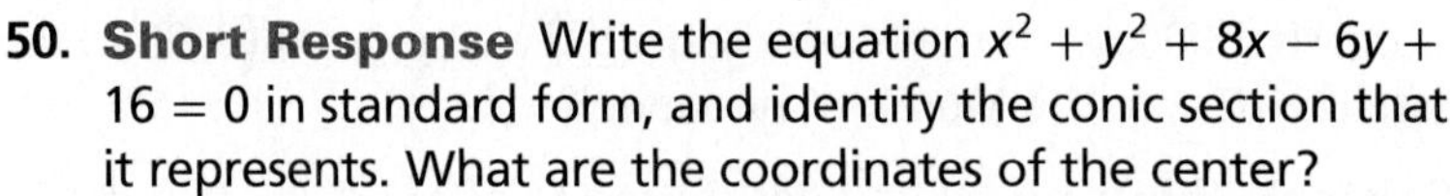

50. **Short Response** Write the equation $x^2 + y^2 + 8x - 6y + 16 = 0$ in standard form, and identify the conic section that it represents. What are the coordinates of the center?

CHALLENGE AND EXTEND

In order to graph the general form of conic sections, $Ax^2 + Bxy + Cy^2 + Dx + Ey + F = 0$, use the quadratic formula,

$$y = \frac{-(Bx + E) \pm \sqrt{(Bx + E)^2 - 4C(Ax^2 + Dx + F)}}{2C}$$, **and a graphing calculator.**

51. Graph $4x^2 + 8xy - 9y^2 - 36 = 0$.

52. Graph $9x^2 - 12xy + 16y^2 - 144 = 0$.

53. What effect does the term Bxy have on the graph?

54. **What if...?** What happens to the formula if $C = 0$?

Conic-Section Art

You can use graphs of conic sections to design and create pictures on the coordinate grid.

Use appropriate tools strategically.

CC.9-12.G.GPE.1 Derive the equation of a circle…using the Pythagorean Theorem… Find the center and radius of a circle given by an equation.

Learn It Online
Lab Resources Online

Use with Identifying Conic Sections

Create a picture of a dragonfly by using one circle and six ellipses.

1 Graph the head by using $x^2 + (y - 5)^2 = 1$.

Solve for y, $y = \pm\sqrt{1 - x^2} + 5$, and graph. There are two ways to enter the two halves of the circle into the calculator.

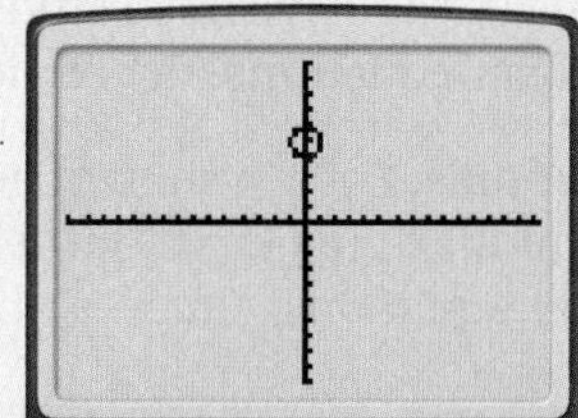

```
Plot1 Plot2 Plot3
\Y1=√(1-X^2)+5
\Y2=-√(1-X^2)+5
```

2 The part of the equation $\{-1, 1\}$ represents $\pm$ and can be used to graph both halves of a conic section at one time.

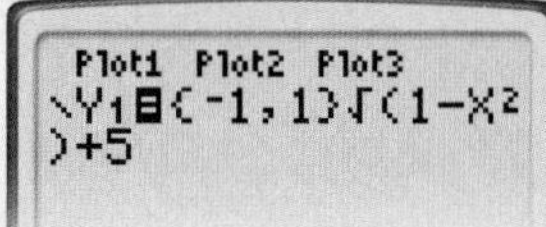

3 Graph the body parts and one right wing by using $x^2 + \frac{(y-2)^2}{4} = 1$, $x^2 + \frac{(y+4)^2}{16} = 1$, *and* $\frac{(x-6)^2}{25} + (y-1)^2 = 1$.

4 Graph the other right wing and left wings by using $\frac{(x-5)^2}{16} + (y-3)^2 = 1$, $\frac{(x+6)^2}{25} + (y-1)^2 = 1$, *and* $\frac{(x+5)^2}{16} + (y-3)^2 = 1$.

5 The dragonfly is now complete.

Turn off the axes by using the **Format** function and setting **AxesOff**.

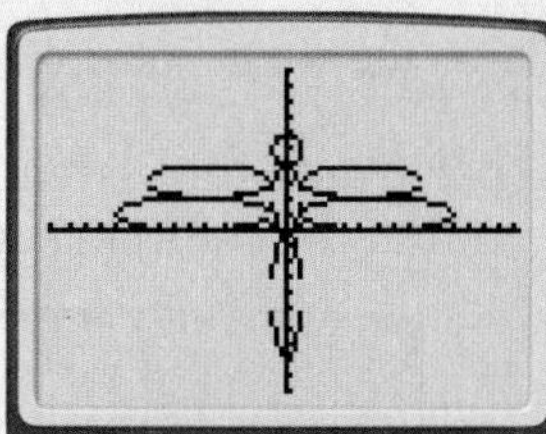

Try This

1. Create your own picture by using the graphs of conic sections. Use at least four conic sections. You may also use lines if necessary.
2. Trade equations with a classmate, and attempt to re-create his or her picture by using only the equations.

12-7 Solving Nonlinear Systems

CC.9-12.A.REI.7 Solve a…system consisting of a linear equation and a quadratic equation…

Objective
Solve systems of equations in two variables that contain at least one second-degree equation.

Vocabulary
nonlinear system of equations

Who uses this?
Harbormasters can solve nonlinear systems to ensure that ships traveling in a variety of patterns do not collide. (See Example 4.)

A **nonlinear system of equations** is a system in which at least one of the equations is not linear. You have been studying one class of nonlinear equations, the conic sections.

The solution set of a system of equations is the set of points that make all of the equations in the system true, or where the graphs intersect. For systems of nonlinear equations, you must be aware of the number of possible solutions.

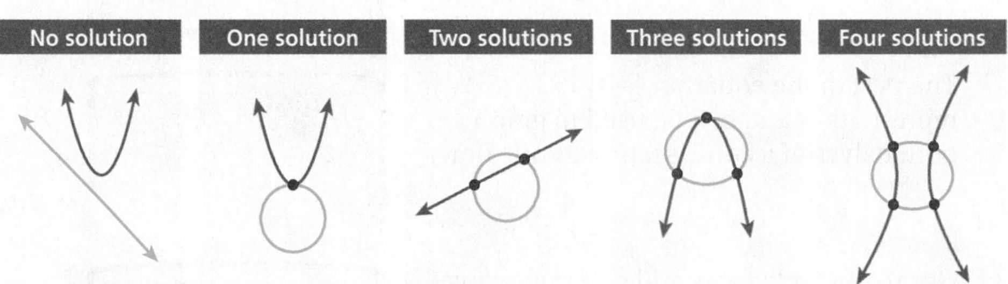

You can use your graphing calculator to find solutions to systems of nonlinear equations and to check algebraic solutions.

EXAMPLE 1 Solving a Nonlinear System by Graphing

Solve $\begin{cases} 2x - y = 1 \\ y + 7 = 2(x+1)^2 \end{cases}$ **by graphing.**

The graph of the first equation is a line, and the graph of the second equation is a parabola, so there may be as many as two points of intersection.

Step 1 Solve each equation for *y*.

$y = 2x - 1$ *Solve the first equation for y.*

$y = 2(x+1)^2 - 7$ *Solve the second equation for y.*

Step 2 Graph the system on your calculator, and use the intersect feature to find the solution set.

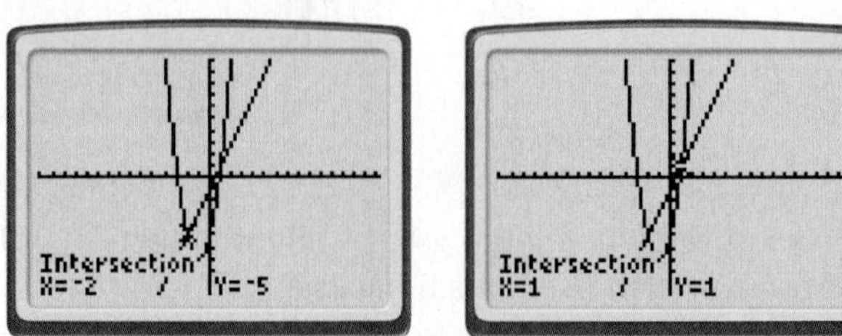

The points of intersection are $(-2, -5)$ and $(1, 1)$.

Check Substitute the points into each equation.

Check $(-2, -5)$.

y	$2x - 1$
-5	$2(-2) - 1$
-5	-5 ✔

y	$2(x+1)^2 - 7$
-5	$2(-2+1)^2 - 7$
-5	-5 ✔

Check $(1, 1)$.

y	$2x - 1$
1	$2(1) - 1$
1	1 ✔

y	$2(x+1)^2 - 7$
1	$2(1+1)^2 - 7$
1	1 ✔

The solution set of the system is $\{(-2, -5), (1, 1)\}$.

1. Solve $\begin{cases} 3x + y = 4.5 \\ y = \frac{1}{2}(x-3)^2 \end{cases}$ by graphing.

The substitution method for solving linear systems can also be used to solve nonlinear systems algebraically.

EXAMPLE 2 Solving a Nonlinear System by Substitution

Solve $\begin{cases} x^2 + y^2 = 25 \\ y + 5 = \frac{1}{2}x^2 \end{cases}$ **by using the substitution method.**

The graph of the first equation is a circle, and the graph of the second equation is a parabola. There may be as many as four points of intersection.

Step 1 It is simplest to solve for x^2 because both equations have x^2 terms.

$x^2 = 2y + 10$ *Solve for x^2 in the second equation.*

Step 2 Use substitution.

$(2y + 10) + y^2 = 25$ *Substitute this value into the first equation.*

$y^2 + 2y - 15 = 0$ *Simplify, and set equal to 0.*

$(y - 3)(y + 5) = 0$ *Factor.*

$y = 3$ or $y = -5$

Step 3 Substitute 3 and -5 into $x^2 = 2y + 10$ to find values for x.

$x^2 = 2(3) + 10$
$x^2 = 16$
$x = \pm 4$
$(4, 3)$ and $(-4, 3)$ are solutions.

$x^2 = 2(-5) + 10$
$x^2 = 0$
$x = 0$
$(0, -5)$ is a solution.

The solution set of the system is $\{(4, 3), (-4, 3), (0, -5)\}$.

Check Use a graphing calculator. The graph supports that there are three points of intersection.

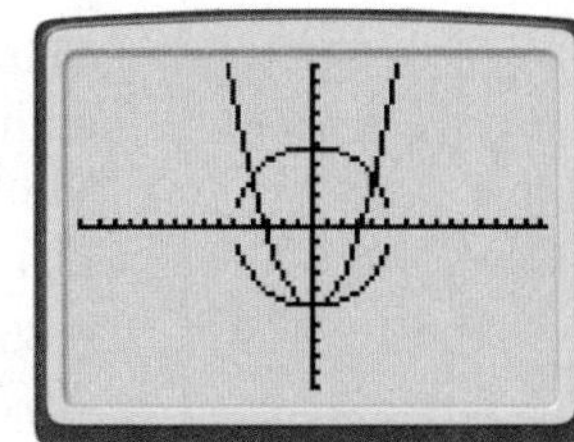

Solve each system of equations by using the substitution method.

2a. $\begin{cases} x + y = -1 \\ x^2 + y^2 = 25 \end{cases}$

2b. $\begin{cases} x^2 + y^2 = 25 \\ y - 5 = -x^2 \end{cases}$

The elimination method can also be used to solve systems of nonlinear equations.

EXAMPLE 3 Solving a Nonlinear System by Elimination

Solve $\begin{cases} 25x^2 + 9y^2 = 225 \\ 16x^2 - 9y^2 = 144 \end{cases}$ by using the elimination method.

The graph of the first equation is an ellipse, and the graph of the second equation is a hyperbola. There may be as many as four points of intersection.

Remember!

In Example 3, you can check your work on a graphing calculator.

Step 1 Eliminate y.

$$\begin{array}{rl} 25x^2 + 9y^2 = 225 & \\ + \ 16x^2 - 9y^2 = 144 & \textit{Add the equations.} \\ \hline 41x^2 \qquad = 369 & \\ x^2 = 9, \text{ so } x = \pm 3 & \textit{Solve for x.} \end{array}$$

Step 2 Find the values for y.

$$\begin{array}{rl} 25(9) + 9y^2 = 225 & \textit{Substitute 9 for } x^2. \\ 225 + 9y^2 = 225 & \textit{Simplify.} \\ y = 0 & \end{array}$$

The solution set of the system is $\{(3, 0), (-3, 0)\}$.

3. Solve $\begin{cases} 25x^2 + 9y^2 = 225 \\ 25x^2 - 16y^2 = 400 \end{cases}$ by using the elimination method.

EXAMPLE 4 *Problem-Solving Application*

Make sense of problems and persevere in solving them.

A tour boat travels around a small island in a pattern that can be modeled by the equation $36x^2 + 25y^2 = 900$, with the island at the origin. Suppose that a fishing boat approaches the island on a path that can be modeled by the equation $y - 3 = \frac{1}{5}x^2$. Is there any danger of collision?

1 Understand the Problem

There is a potential danger of a collision if the two paths cross.
The paths will cross if the graphs of the equations intersect.
List the important information:

- $36x^2 + 25y^2 = 900$ represents the path of the tour boat.
- $y - 3 = \frac{1}{5}x^2$ represents the path of the fishing boat.

2 Make a Plan

To see if the graphs intersect, solve the system $\begin{cases} 36x^2 + 25y^2 = 900 \\ y - 3 = \frac{1}{5}x^2 \end{cases}$.

3 Solve

The graph of the first equation is an ellipse, and the graph of the second equation is a parabola. There may be as many as four points of intersection.

$x^2 = 5y - 15$ *Solve the second equation for x^2.*

$36(5y - 15) + 25y^2 = 900$ *Substitute this value into the first equation.*

$25y^2 + 180y - 1440 = 0$ *Simplify, and set equal to 0.*

$$y = \frac{-180 \pm \sqrt{180^2 - 4(25)(-1440)}}{2(25)}$$ *Use the quadratic formula.*

$y = \dfrac{-180 \pm 420}{50}$, or $y = 4.8$ and $y = -12$

Substitute $y = 4.8$ and $y = -12$ into $x^2 = 5y - 15$ to find the values for x.

$x^2 = 5(4.8) - 15$ $\quad$ $x^2 = 5(-12) - 15$

$x^2 = 9$, or $x = \pm 3$ $\quad$ $x^2 = -75$ *There are no real values of $\sqrt{-75}$.*

The real solutions to the system are $(3, 4.8)$ and $(-3, 4.8)$.

4 Look Back

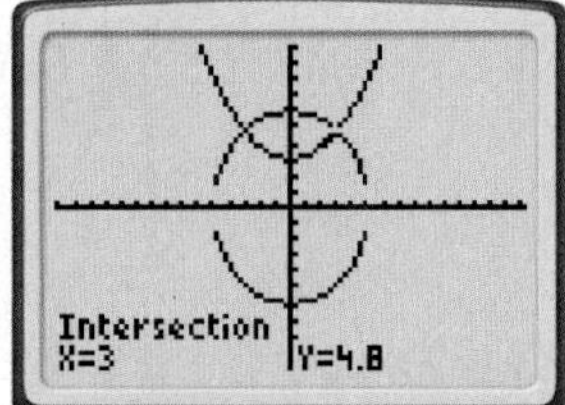

The graph supports that there are two points of intersection. Because the paths intersect, the boats are in danger of colliding if they arrive at the intersections $(3, 4.8)$ or $(-3, 4.8)$ at the same time.

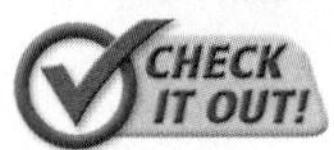

4. What if...? Suppose the paths of the boats can be modeled by the system $\begin{cases} 36x^2 + 25y^2 = 900 \\ y + 2 = -\frac{1}{10}x^2 \end{cases}$.
Is there any danger of collision?

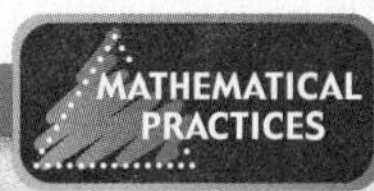

THINK AND DISCUSS

1. What can you tell about the graphs if the system has no solution?
2. Describe the steps for solving a nonlinear system of equations by graphing.

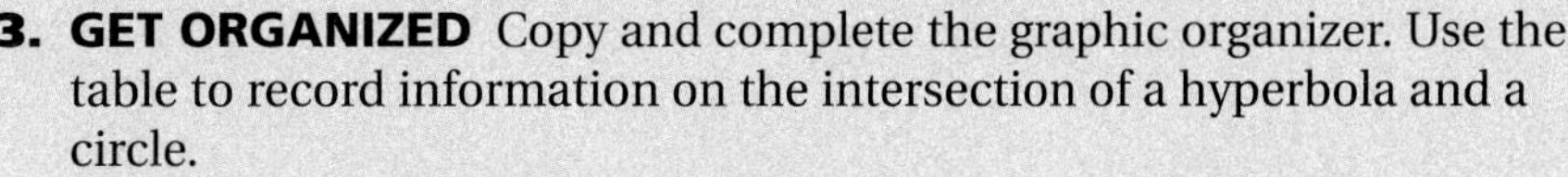

3. **GET ORGANIZED** Copy and complete the graphic organizer. Use the table to record information on the intersection of a hyperbola and a circle.

	Graph	Example
No Solution		
One Solution		
Two Solutions		
Three Solutions		
Four Solutions		

12-7 Exercises

Learn It Online
Homework Help Online
Parent Resources Online

GUIDED PRACTICE

1. **Vocabulary** How is a *nonlinear system of equations* different from a linear system of equations?

SEE EXAMPLE 1

Solve each system of equations by graphing.

2. $\begin{cases} y + 3x = 0 \\ y - 6 = -3x^2 \end{cases}$

3. $\begin{cases} y + 2 = \frac{1}{4}(x - 4)^2 \\ x - y = 6 \end{cases}$

4. $\begin{cases} y + 2x = 10 \\ x = \frac{1}{8}(y - 2)^2 \end{cases}$

SEE EXAMPLE 2

Solve each system of equations by using the substitution method.

5. $\begin{cases} y + x = 17 \\ x^2 + y^2 = 169 \end{cases}$

6. $\begin{cases} x^2 + y^2 = 25 \\ y - x = 7 \end{cases}$

7. $\begin{cases} x^2 + y^2 = 36 \\ x + 2y = 16 \end{cases}$

8. $\begin{cases} x^2 + y^2 = 100 \\ x + 2 = \frac{1}{8}y^2 \end{cases}$

9. $\begin{cases} x^2 + y^2 = 36 \\ y + 6 = \frac{1}{3}x^2 \end{cases}$

10. $\begin{cases} x^2 + y^2 = 25 \\ y - 6.25 = -\frac{1}{4}x^2 \end{cases}$

SEE EXAMPLE 3

Solve each system of equations by using the elimination method.

11. $\begin{cases} x^2 + y^2 = 20 \\ 4x^2 + y^2 = 68 \end{cases}$

12. $\begin{cases} 9x^2 + 5y^2 = 45 \\ 6y^2 - 27x^2 = 54 \end{cases}$

13. $\begin{cases} 4x^2 + 3y^2 = 12 \\ 5x^2 + 6y^2 = 30 \end{cases}$

SEE EXAMPLE 4

14. **Radio** The range of a radio station is bounded by the circle with equation $x^2 + y^2 = 2025$. A stretch of highway near the station is modeled by the equation $y - 15 = \frac{1}{20}x^2$. At what points does a car on the highway enter or exit the broadcast range of the station?

PRACTICE AND PROBLEM SOLVING

Independent Practice

For Exercises	See Example
15–17	1
18–23	2
24–29	3
30	4

Extra Practice

See Extra Practice for more Skills Practice and Applications Practice exercises.

Solve each system of equations by graphing.

15. $\begin{cases} 2y - x = 10 \\ y - 3 = \frac{1}{8}(x + 4)^2 \end{cases}$

16. $\begin{cases} x - 6 = -\frac{1}{6}y^2 \\ 2x + y = 6 \end{cases}$

17. $\begin{cases} y^2 - x^2 = 36 \\ 2x + y = -\frac{3}{2} \end{cases}$

Solve each system of equations by using the substitution method.

18. $\begin{cases} x^2 + y^2 = 13 \\ x - y = 1 \end{cases}$

19. $\begin{cases} y^2 - 4x^2 = 16 \\ y - x = 4 \end{cases}$

20. $\begin{cases} x^2 - y^2 = 16 \\ x + y^2 = 4 \end{cases}$

21. $\begin{cases} y = \frac{1}{4}(x - 3)^2 \\ 3x - 2y = 13 \end{cases}$

22. $\begin{cases} -3 = 2x^2 - y \\ x^2 - 36 = 9y^2 \end{cases}$

23. $\begin{cases} x^2 + y^2 = 8 \\ x^2 - y = 6 \end{cases}$

Solve each system of equations by using the elimination method.

24. $\begin{cases} 2x^2 + 3y^2 = 83 \\ 4x^2 - 2y^2 = -34 \end{cases}$

25. $\begin{cases} \frac{x^2}{5} + \frac{y^2}{3} = 15 \\ x^2 + y^2 = 20 \end{cases}$

26. $\begin{cases} x^2 + y^2 = 16 \\ y^2 - 2x^2 = 16 \end{cases}$

27. $\begin{cases} x - y = 7 \\ x^2 - y = 7 \end{cases}$

28. $\begin{cases} 4x^2 + y^2 = 1 \\ -x^2 + y^2 = 1 \end{cases}$

29. $\begin{cases} x^2 + y^2 = 9 \\ x^2 - 4y^2 = 4 \end{cases}$

30. **Multi-Step** While waiting to land, an airplane is traveling above the airport in a holding pattern that can be modeled by the equation $49x^2 + 64y^2 = 3136$, with the air traffic control tower at the origin. Suppose that another plane approaches the airport at the same altitude as the first plane on a path that can be modeled by the equation $y - 6 = \frac{1}{4}x^2$. Should the air traffic controller at the airport be concerned? If so, what are the possible points of collision?

Solve each system of equations by using any method.

31. $\begin{cases} y = x^2 \\ x = y^2 \end{cases}$
32. $\begin{cases} 5x^2 + 4y^2 = 216 \\ 3x^2 + 6y^2 = 162 \end{cases}$
33. $\begin{cases} 8y - x = 2 \\ x - 10 = -4y^2 \end{cases}$
34. $\begin{cases} y - x^2 = 2 \\ 4y - x^2 = 20 \end{cases}$

35. $\begin{cases} x^2 + 4y^2 = 36 \\ x^2 + y^2 = 9 \end{cases}$
36. $\begin{cases} \dfrac{x^2}{16} - \dfrac{y^2}{9} = 1 \\ \dfrac{y^2}{25} - \dfrac{x^2}{4} = 1 \end{cases}$
37. $\begin{cases} x + 6 = \dfrac{1}{2}y^2 \\ x - 4 = -\dfrac{1}{8}y^2 \end{cases}$
38. $\begin{cases} \dfrac{x^2}{16} + \dfrac{y^2}{25} = 1 \\ \dfrac{x^2}{16} + \dfrac{y^2}{4} = 1 \end{cases}$

39. $\begin{cases} x - 3 = 2y^2 \\ y^2 - 9x^2 = 36 \end{cases}$
40. $\begin{cases} x^2 + y^2 = 100 \\ x + 5y = 10 \end{cases}$
41. $\begin{cases} 3x^2 - 6y^2 = 204 \\ 4x^2 - 2y^2 = 368 \end{cases}$
42. $\begin{cases} 4x^2 + 9y^2 = 36 \\ 2x + 3y = 6 \end{cases}$

43. **Physics** A speeding driver sees a parked police car at time $t = 0$ and starts to decelerate while the police car accelerates as the officer chases the driver. The distance that the driver has traveled in feet after t seconds can be modeled by the function $d(t) = 250 + 125t - 1.2t^2$. The distance that the police car has traveled in feet after t seconds can be modeled by the function $d(t) = 4.2t^2$. How long does it take the police car to catch the driver?

LINK

Geology

One of the largest earthquakes ever recorded occurred in December 2004 off the coast of Indonesia. The quake caused a giant tsunami that wreaked havoc in Sri Lanka, Thailand, and other countries.

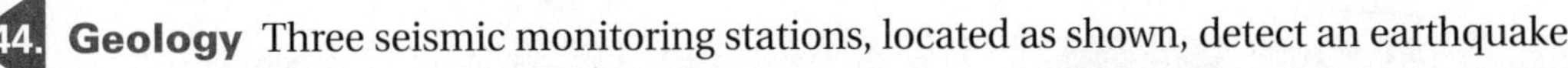

44. **Geology** Three seismic monitoring stations, located as shown, detect an earthquake.
   a. Suppose that the epicenter of the earthquake is 30 miles closer to station 2 than to station 1. Use 30 as the constant difference and Stations 1 and 2 as the foci to write an equation for the possible locations of the earthquake.
   b. Suppose that the epicenter of the earthquake is 40 miles closer to station 2 than to station 3. Use 40 as the constant difference and stations 2 and 3 as the foci to write an equation for the possible locations of the earthquake.
   c. Find the coordinates of the epicenter of the earthquake to the nearest mile.

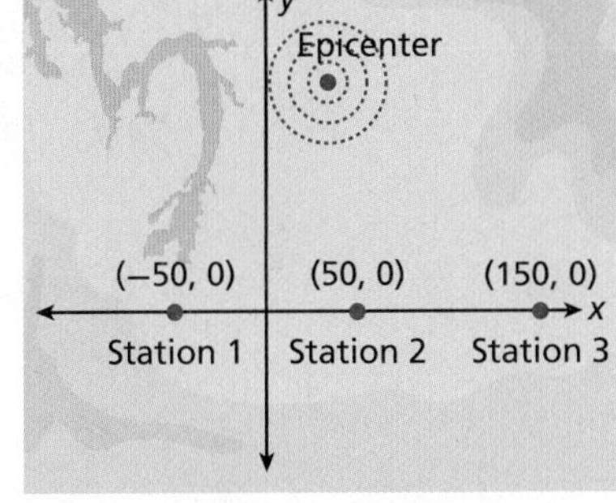

45. **Estimation** Use your graphing calculator to estimate the points of intersection of $x^2 - 4y^2 + 7x = 0$ and $x^2 - y + 5x - 24 = 0$.

46. **Critical Thinking** What must be true in order for two parabolas to have exactly four points of intersection? Explain.

MULTI-STEP TEST PREP

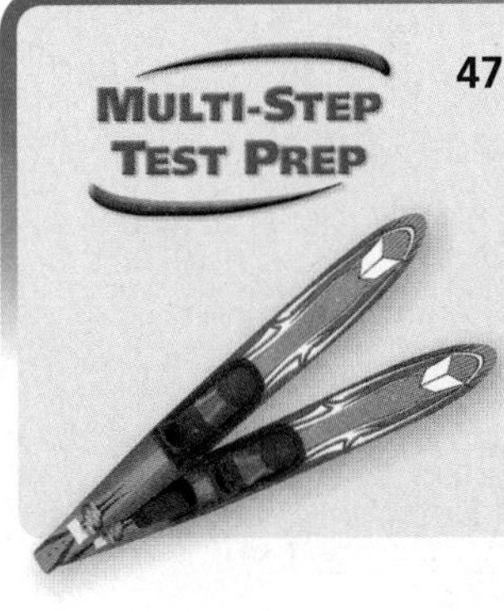

47. A water-skiing exhibition takes place in a body of water modeled by the first and second quadrants of the coordinate plane. A water-skier is towed along a path that can be modeled by $-x^2 + 4y^2 + 8x - 8y - 16 = 0$.
   a. What is the shape of the water-skier's path?
   b. A second water-skier's path is modeled by $x^2 + y^2 - 8x - 8y + 23 = 0$. Is there a chance that the two water-skiers will collide? If so, where?

48. **Astronomy** An asteroid is traveling toward Earth on a path that can be modeled by the equation $y = \frac{1}{28}x^2 - 7$. It approaches a satellite in orbit on a path that can be modeled by the equation $\frac{x^2}{49} + \frac{y^2}{51} = 1$. What are the coordinates of the points where the satellite and asteroid might collide?

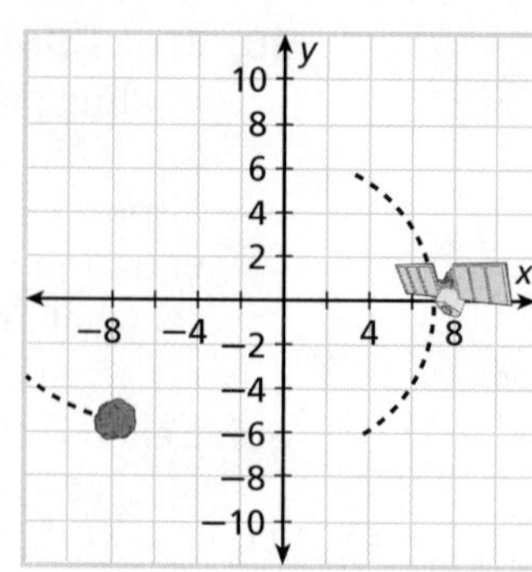

49. **Recreation** Ice skaters Bianca and Mark are performing a routine in which Bianca skates in a path that can be modeled by the equation $x + 2 = \frac{y^2}{4}$ and Mark skates in a path that can be modeled by the equation $\frac{(x+4)^2}{4} + \frac{y^2}{9} = 1$. When the pair meets, they will perform a lift. What are the coordinates of the point where the pair will perform a lift?

50. **Multi-Step** The lake at a resort has an island near the center. A tour boat's path on the lake can be modeled by the equation $16x^2 + 9y^2 = 36$, with the island at the origin. If a canoe's path on the lake can be modeled by the equation $8x + 5y^2 = 20$, find the coordinates of the points on the lake where the boats might meet.

51. **Write About It** How would the value of a in the system $\begin{cases} x^2 - y^2 = 25 \\ \frac{x^2}{a^2} + \frac{y^2}{9} = 1 \end{cases}$ affect the number of solutions for the system?

TEST PREP

52. Which of the following points is a solution to the system $\begin{cases} 4x^2 + 5y^2 = 189 \\ 8y^2 - 2x = 60 \end{cases}$?

Ⓐ (3, −6) Ⓑ (−3, −6) Ⓒ (6, −3) Ⓓ (−6, −3)

53. How many solutions does the system $\begin{cases} \frac{x^2}{16} + \frac{y^2}{9} = 144 \\ x = 3(y-2)^2 \end{cases}$ have?

Ⓕ 1 Ⓖ 2 Ⓗ 3 Ⓙ 4

54. For which value of k will the system $\begin{cases} x^2 + y^2 = 25 \\ 5(y+k) = x^2 \end{cases}$ have exactly one solution?

Ⓐ $k = -5$ Ⓑ $k = 0$ Ⓒ $k = 5$ Ⓓ $k = 25$

CHALLENGE AND EXTEND

Solve each system of equations by any method.

55. $\begin{cases} x^2 + y^2 = 25 \\ 3x^2 + 2y^2 = 66 \\ x + y^2 = 13 \end{cases}$

56. $\begin{cases} 6x^2 - 3y^2 = 204 \\ y + 10 = \frac{1}{3}x^2 \\ 25x^2 - 36(y-2)^2 = 900 \end{cases}$

57. $\begin{cases} x^2 + y^2 = 25 \\ xy = 12 \\ y^2 - x - 8y + 19 = 0 \end{cases}$

Graph each system of inequalities.

58. $\begin{cases} y - 5 < -\frac{1}{8}x^2 \\ y + 5 \geq \frac{1}{6}x^2 \end{cases}$

59. $\begin{cases} x^2 + y^2 \leq 36 \\ y + 6 > x^2 \end{cases}$

60. $\begin{cases} \frac{x^2}{9} + \frac{y^2}{36} \leq 1 \\ \frac{x^2}{25} + \frac{y^2}{9} \geq 1 \end{cases}$

61. **Economics** Industry analysts predict that the demand curve for a new software product can be modeled by the function $D(p) = 5000 - 0.2p^2$, where p is the price of the product and $D(p)$ is the number of products that can be sold at p. The analysts also predict that the supply curve for the new product can be modeled by the function $S(p) = 0.3p^2$, where p is the price of the product and $S(p)$ is the number of products that companies will supply at p. Predict the price for the new product.

Career Path

Shawn Innes
Actuarial Science major

Q: What math classes did you take in high school?

A: In high school, I took algebra, geometry, and precalculus.

Q: What do actuaries do?

A: Basically, actuaries evaluate the likelihood of certain events and try to find creative ways to reduce the chances of undesirable outcomes. Actuaries are involved in many different industries such as business and finance, health, retirement planning, and insurance.

Q: How do you become an actuary?

A: To become a full actuary, a series of exams must be completed. These exams cover topics like calculus, economics, and finance.

Q: What are your future plans?

A: I'd like to work at the consulting firm where I interned. They specialize in retirement planning and benefits. There, I tested formulas used to calculate pensions for client companies.

CHAPTER 12

MULTI-STEP TEST PREP

SECTION 12B

Model with mathematics.

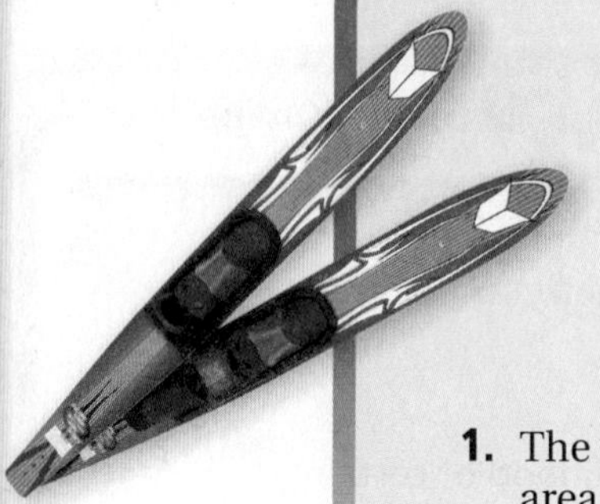

Applying Conic Sections

Water-skiing A water-skiing team is planning an exhibition on a lake. The figure shows the performance area that has been roped off on the lake and the location of the viewing stand. Each unit of the coordinate plane represents 10 ft.

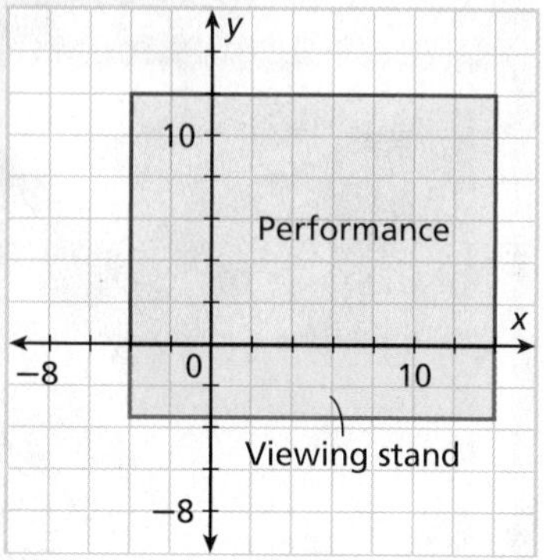

y
10
Performance
x
−8
0
10
Viewing stand
−8

1. The first water-skier enters the performance area, and the boat tows her along a path modeled by $16x^2 + 25y^2 - 96x - 300y + 644 = 0$. What is the shape of the path? Explain.

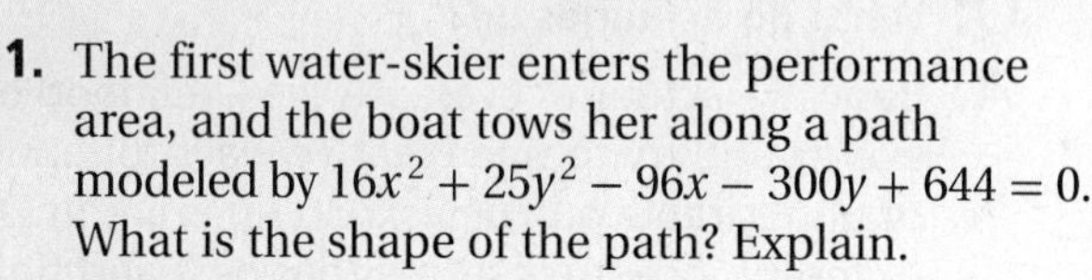

2. How close to the viewing stand does the water-skier pass?

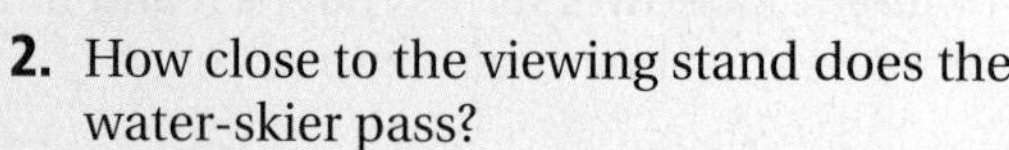

3. During this routine, the water-skier will pass directly in front of what percentage of the viewers?

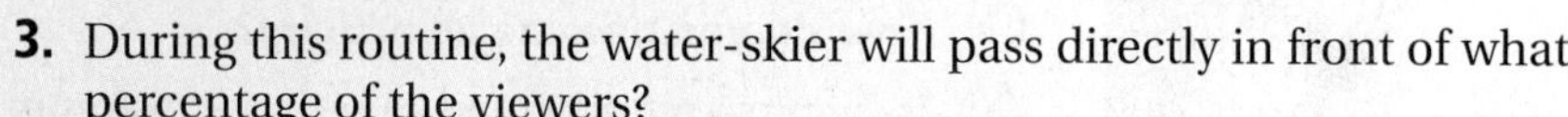

4. A second water-skier enters the performance area. The boat tows him along a path modeled by $x^2 + y^2 - 20x - 12y + 132 = 0$. What is the shape of the path? Explain.
5. Is there a chance that the second water-skier will collide with the first? If so, where?
6. A third water-skier is towed along a path modeled by $x^2 - 14x - 8y + 129 = 0$. At what points does the water-skier enter and exit the performance area?
7. Is there a chance that this water-skier will collide with the others? If so, where?

READY TO GO ON?

Quiz for Lessons 12-6 and 12-7

12-6 Identifying Conic Sections

Identify the conic section that each equation represents.

1. $\frac{6x^2}{9} + \frac{8y^2}{12} = 1$
2. $8(y-4) - 3(x+4)^2 = 1$
3. $\frac{(y-2)^2}{9} = \frac{(x+5)^2}{16} + 1$
4. $(y-2)^2 - 3(x+7) = 0$
5. $2x^2 + 4y^2 - 12y = 18$
6. $7x^2 - 5xy - 3y^2 + 7x - 6 = 0$
7. $9x^2 + 12xy + 16y^2 - 5x + 2y = 0$
8. $x^2 + y^2 - 4x + 6y - 11 = 0$

Write each equation in the form $Ax^2 + Bxy + Cy^2 + Dx + Ey + F = 0$.

9. $y - 5 = \frac{1}{4}(x+8)^2$
10. $\frac{(y-3)^2}{9} - \frac{(x+5)^2}{5} = 1$

Find the standard form of each equation by completing the square. Then identify the conic.

11. $x^2 + y^2 - 6x - 8y + 15 = 0$
12. $3x^2 + 4y^2 - 18x + 8y + 19 = 0$
13. $5y^2 - x - 60y + 176 = 0$
14. $2x^2 - 6y^2 - 16x - 24y = 4$

12-7 Solving Nonlinear Systems

Solve each system of equations by graphing.

15. $\begin{cases} 8y + 3x^2 = 56 \\ y = \frac{1}{4}x^2 - 3 \end{cases}$
16. $\begin{cases} 2x - 8 = y^2 \\ 3x - 3y = -12 \end{cases}$
17. $\begin{cases} x^2 + y^2 = 169 \\ 5y - 12x = 0 \end{cases}$

Solve each system by using the substitution or elimination method.

18. $\begin{cases} x^2 - 2y^2 = 28 \\ 3y - x = 0 \end{cases}$
19. $\begin{cases} 2x^2 + 3y^2 = 21 \\ x^2 - 9y = 0 \end{cases}$
20. $\begin{cases} 8x^2 + 4y^2 = 32 \\ 10x^2 + 6y^2 = 60 \end{cases}$

21. A team of stunt racing boats is performing a series of stunts along paths shown in the graph. During the performance, the lead boat moves in a path that can be modeled by the equation $\frac{x^2}{9} + \frac{y^2}{4} = 1$. Two other boats race in formation along each of the branches of the equation $\frac{x^2}{9} - \frac{y^2}{4} = 1$. At what points are the boats in danger of colliding?

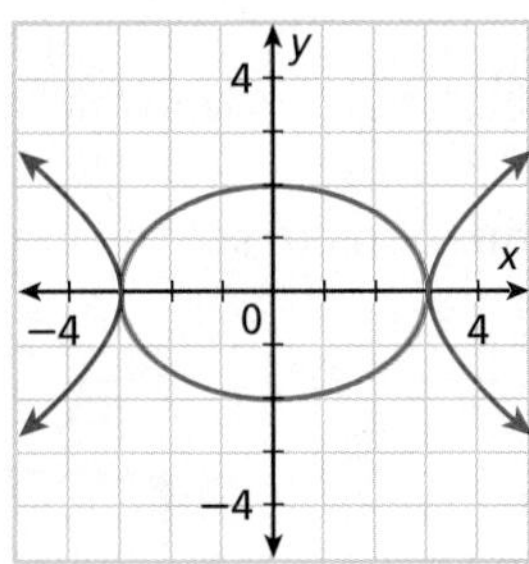

22. Find n so that the system $\begin{cases} \frac{x^2}{9} + \frac{y^2}{16} = 1 \\ y - n = x^2 \end{cases}$ has exactly three solutions.

CHAPTER 12

Study Guide: Review

Vocabulary

branch of a hyperbola	ellipse	nonlinear system of equations
circle	foci of an ellipse	tangent
conic section	foci of a hyperbola	transverse axis
conjugate axis	focus of a parabola	vertices of an ellipse
co-vertices of an ellipse	hyperbola	vertices of a hyperbola
co-vertices of a hyperbola	major axis	
directrix	minor axis	

Complete the sentences below with vocabulary words from the list above.

1. The line containing the vertices and the foci of a hyperbola is the ___?___ of symmetry of the hyperbola.

2. A line in the same plane as a circle that intersects the circle in exactly one point is a(n) ___?___.

3. A parabola is the set of all points P(*x*, *y*) that are equidistant from both a fixed point, called the ___?___, and a fixed line, called the ___?___.

4. A(n) ___?___ is formed by the intersection of a double right cone and a plane.

12-1 Introduction to Conic Sections

EXAMPLE

■ **Graph $4x^2 + 25y^2 = 100$ on a graphing calculator. Identify and describe the conic section.**

Solve for *y* so that the expression can be used in a graphing calculator.

$25y^2 = 100 - 4x^2$ *Subtract $4x^2$ from both sides.*

$y^2 = \frac{100 - 4x^2}{25}$ *Divide both sides by 25.*

$y = \pm\sqrt{\frac{100 - 4x^2}{25}}$ *Take the square root of both sides.*

Use two equations to see the complete graph.

$y_1 = \sqrt{\frac{100 - 4x^2}{25}}$ and $y_2 = -\sqrt{\frac{100 - 4x^2}{25}}$

The graph is an ellipse with center (0, 0), *y*-intercepts 2 and −2, and *x*-intercepts 5 and −5.

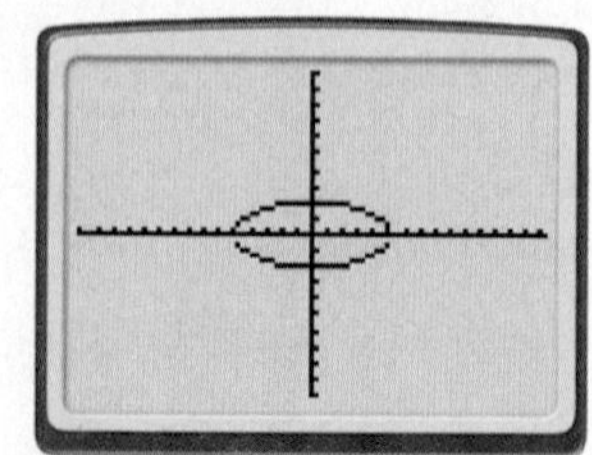

EXERCISES

Graph each equation on a graphing calculator. Identify and describe the conic section.

5. $x^2 + y^2 = 81$

6. $\frac{x^2}{25} - \frac{y^2}{4} = 1$

7. $x = \frac{1}{4}(y + 1)^2$

8. $8x^2 + 25y^2 = 98$

9. Which equation is represented by the graph?

A. $16x^2 - 16y^2 = 256$

B. $16y^2 = 9x^2 + 144$

C. $9x^2 + 16y^2 = 256$

D. $9y^2 - 16x^2 = 144$

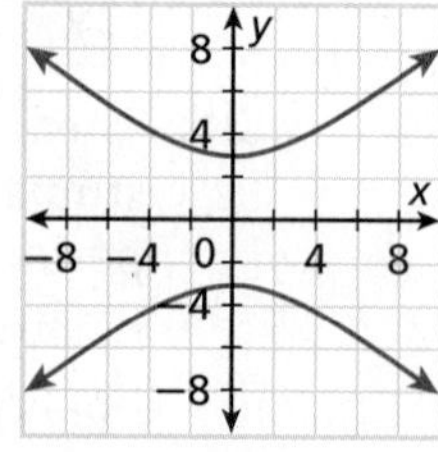

Find the center and the radius of a circle that has a diameter with the given endpoints.

10. (−9, −3) and (15, −3)

11. (−4, 1) and (20, −6)

12-2 Circles

EXAMPLES

- **Write the equation of the circle with center $(-5, 9)$ and radius $r = 16$.**

Substitute into the general equation of a circle, $(x - h)^2 + (y - k)^2 = r^2$.

$$(x - (-5))^2 + (y - 9)^2 = 16^2$$

$$(x + 5)^2 + (y - 9)^2 = 256 \qquad \textit{Simplify.}$$

- **Write an equation of the line that is tangent at (12, 9) to the circle with equation $x^2 + y^2 = 225$.**

The circle has center $(0, 0)$. The tangent is perpendicular to the radius at the point of tangency.

Find the slope of the radius and the slope of the tangent.

$$m_r = \frac{9 - 0}{12 - 0} = \frac{9}{12} = \frac{3}{4} \qquad \textit{The slope of the radius is } \tfrac{3}{4}.$$

$$m_t = -\frac{4}{3} \qquad \textit{Use the negative reciprocal.}$$

$$y - 9 = -\frac{4}{3}(x - 12) \qquad \textit{Use point-slope form.}$$

EXERCISES

Find the center and the radius of each circle.

12. $(x - 6)^2 + y^2 = 361$
13. $(x + 12)^2 + (y - 4)^2 = 15$

Write the equation of each circle.

14. center $(8, -7)$ and radius $r = 14$
15. center $(3, 6)$ and containing the point $(7, -2)$
16. diameter with endpoints $(2, 5)$ and $(-8, 11)$

Write an equation of the line that is tangent to the given circle at the given point.

17. $x^2 + y^2 = 34$ at $(3, 5)$
18. $(x + 3)^2 + y^2 = 16$ at $(-3, 4)$
19. $(x - 2)^2 + (y + 7)^2 = 44$ at $(6, -2)$
20. $(x + 4)^2 + (y - 1)^2 = 89$ at $(1, -7)$

12-3 Ellipses

EXAMPLE

- **Graph $\frac{(x + 1)^2}{25} + \frac{(y - 4)^2}{9} = 1$. Then find the foci of the ellipse.**

Rewrite the equation as $\frac{(x + 1)^2}{5^2} + \frac{(y - 4)^2}{3^2} = 1$.

The center is $(-1, 4)$. Because $5 > 3$, the major axis is horizontal, $a = 5$ and $b = 3$. The vertices are $(-1 \pm 5, 4)$, or $(-6, 4)$ and $(4, 4)$. The co-vertices are $(-1, 4 \pm 3)$ or $(-1, 7)$ and $(-1, 1)$.

In an ellipse, $c^2 = a^2 - b^2$. In this ellipse, $c^2 = 5^2 - 3^2 = 16$, so $c = 4$.

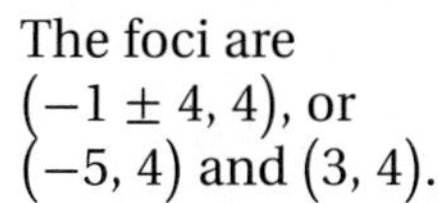

The foci are $(-1 \pm 4, 4)$, or $(-5, 4)$ and $(3, 4)$.

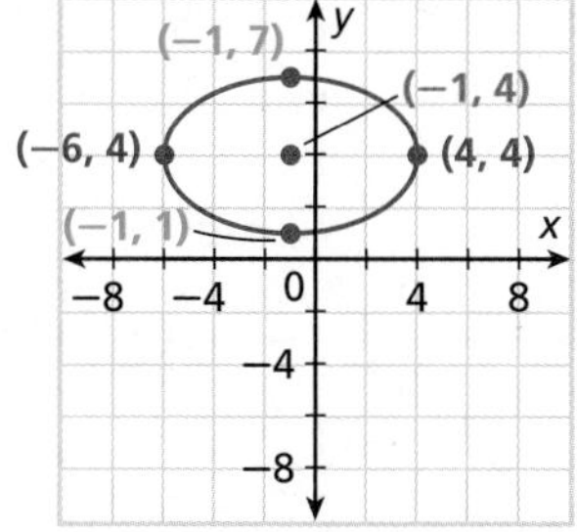

EXERCISES

Find the center, vertices, co-vertices, and foci of each ellipse. Then graph.

21. $\frac{x^2}{9} + \frac{y^2}{36} = 1$
22. $25x^2 + 64y^2 = 1600$
23. $\frac{(x - 3)^2}{49} + \frac{(y + 2)^2}{64} = 1$

Find the equation of each ellipse.

24.

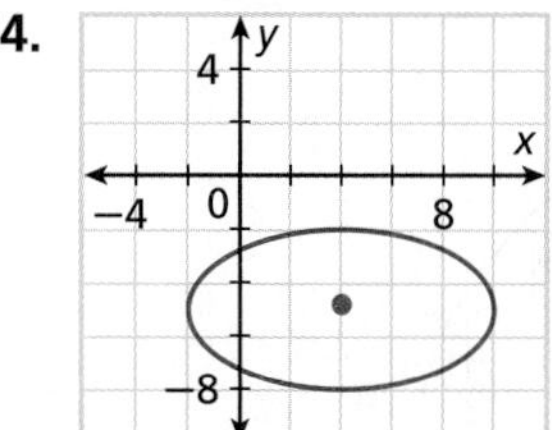

25. co-vertices at $(12, 0)$ and $(-12, 0)$ and major axis length 30
26. vertices at $(-8, 3)$ and $(4, 3)$ and foci at $(-5, 3)$ and $(1, 3)$

12-4 Hyperbolas

EXAMPLE

- **Find the center, vertices, co-vertices, foci, and asymptotes of $\frac{y^2}{16} - \frac{x^2}{9} = 1$. Then graph.**

The equation is in the form $\frac{y^2}{a^2} - \frac{x^2}{b^2}$, so the transverse axis is vertical. The center is $(0, 0)$.

Because $a = 4$ and $b = 3$, the vertices are $(0, 4)$ and $(0, -4)$ and the co-vertices are $(3, 0)$ and $(-3, 0)$. The equations of the asymptotes are $y = \frac{4}{3}x$ and $y = -\frac{4}{3}x$.

In a hyperbola, $c^2 = a^2 + b^2$. In this hyperbola, $c^2 = 4^2 + 3^2 = 25$, so $c = 5$ and the foci are $(0, 5)$ and $(0, -5)$.

Draw a box by using the vertices and co-vertices. Draw the asymptotes through the corners of the box. Draw the hyperbola by using the vertices and the asymptotes.

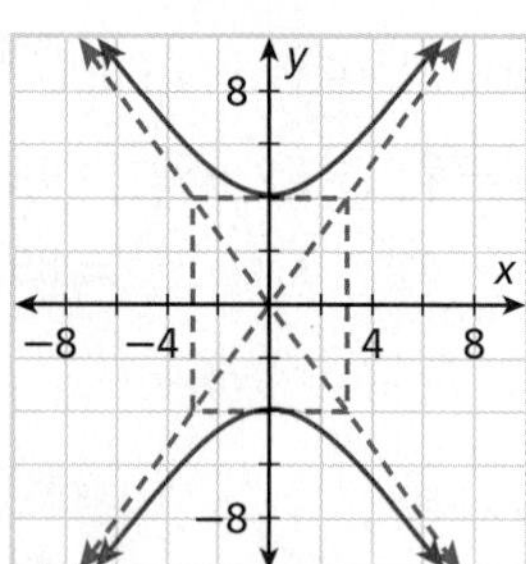

EXERCISES

Find the center, vertices, co-vertices, foci, and asymptotes of each hyperbola, and then graph.

27. $\frac{x^2}{25} - \frac{y^2}{49} = 1$

28. $64y^2 - 36x^2 = 2304$

29. $\frac{(x-3)^2}{4} - \frac{(y+6)^2}{49} = 1$

Write an equation in standard form for each hyperbola.

30.

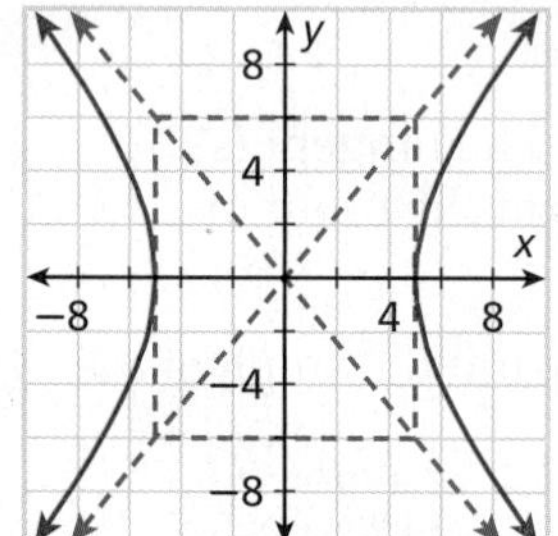

31. vertices $(11, 0)$ and $(-11, 0)$ and conjugate axis length 8

32. co-vertices $(6, 0)$ and $(-6, 0)$ and asymptotes $y = \frac{5}{6}x$ and $y = -\frac{5}{6}x$

33. length of transverse axis 10 and foci at $(-7, 18)$ and $(-7, -8)$

12-5 Parabolas

EXAMPLE

- **Find the vertex, value of p, axis of symmetry, focus, and directrix of $x - 2 = -\frac{1}{16}(y+3)^2$. Then graph.**

The equation is in the form $x - h = \frac{1}{4p}(y - k)^2$ with $p < 0$, so the graph opens to the left.

The vertex is $(2, -3)$, and the axis of symmetry is $y = -3$.

Because $\frac{1}{4p} = -\frac{1}{16}$, $p = -4$. The focus is $(2 - 4, -3)$, or $(-2, -3)$.

The directrix is $x = 2 + 4$, or $x = 6$.

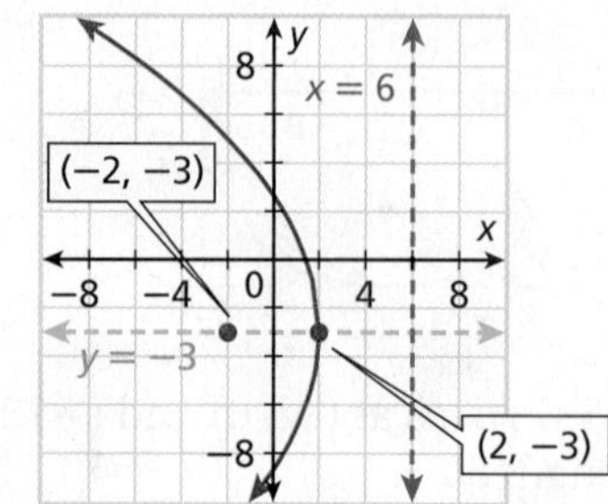

EXERCISES

Find the vertex, value of p, axis of symmetry, focus, and directrix for each parabola. Then graph.

34. $y = -\frac{1}{12}x^2$

35. $x = 2y^2$

36. $y - 5 = (x + 4)^2$

37. $x - 4 = -\frac{1}{6}(y + 2)^2$

Write the equation in standard form for each parabola.

38.

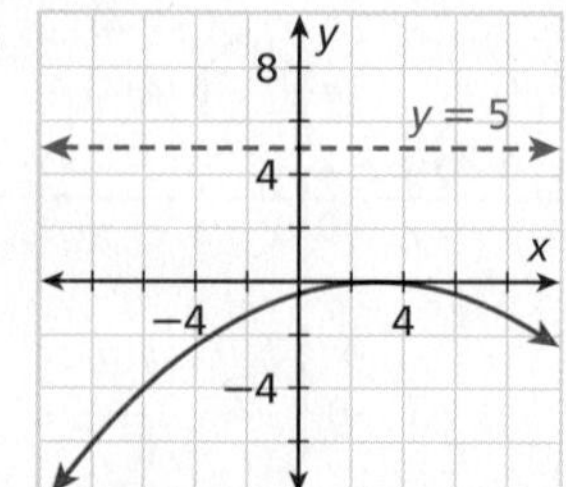

39. vertex $(4, 6)$, axis of symmetry $y = 6$, $p = -2.5$

40. focus $(12, -4)$ and directrix $x = 6$

12-6 Identifying Conic Sections

EXAMPLES

- **Identify the conic section represented by $3x^2 + 5xy - 8y^2 + 3x - 5y = 2$.**

$A = 3, B = 5, C = -8$ *Identify values of A, B, and C.*

$B^2 - 4AC = 5^2 - 4(3)(-8) = 121$ *Substitute.*

Because $B^2 - 4AC > 0$, the equation represents a hyperbola.

- **Find the standard form of the equation by completing the square. Then identify the conic.**

$y^2 - 4x - 10y = -13$

$y^2 - 10y + \blacksquare = 4x - 13 + \blacksquare$ *Rearrange.*

$y^2 - 10y + \left(\frac{10}{2}\right)^2 = 4x - 13 + \left(\frac{10}{2}\right)^2$ *Add $\left(\frac{10}{2}\right)^2$ to both sides.*

$(y - 5)^2 = 4x + 12$ *Factor, and simplify.*

$x + 3 = \frac{1}{4}(y - 5)^2$ *Rewrite in standard form.*

The equation represents a parabola.

EXERCISES

Identify the conic section that each equation represents.

41. $\frac{x^2}{12} = 1 - \frac{y^2}{9}$

42. $(x - 5)^2 = \frac{2}{3}(y + 4)^2 + 1$

43. $(x - 8)^2 = \frac{1}{12}(y + 5)$

44. $7x^2 + 7y^2 - 15x = 25$

45. $15x^2 - 6xy + 9y^2 - 12x - 12y + 15 = 0$

Find the standard form of each equation by completing the square. Then identify and graph each conic.

46. $y^2 - 4x + 12y = -24$

47. $2x^2 + 6y^2 + 16x = -20$

48. $x^2 + y^2 + 10x - 8y + 5 = 0$

49. $4x^2 - 8y^2 + 8x - 48y - 100 = 0$

12-7 Solving Nonlinear Systems

EXAMPLE

- **Solve $\begin{cases} x^2 - y^2 = 16 \\ y^2 - x = 4 \end{cases}$ by using the substitution method.**

The graph of the first equation is a hyperbola. The graph of the second equation is a parabola. There may be as many as four points of intersection.

It is simplest to solve for y^2 because both equations have y^2 terms.

$y^2 = x + 4$ *Solve the second equation for y^2.*

$x^2 - (x + 4) = 16$ *Substitute this value into the first equation.*

$(x - 5)(x + 4) = 0$ *Simplify, and factor.*

$x = 5$ or $x = -4$

$y^2 = 5 + 4 = 9$ or $y^2 = -4 + 4 = 0$ *Substitute.*

$y = \pm 3$ when $x = 5$ and $y = 0$ when $x = -4$. The solution set is $\{(5, 3), (5, -3), (-4, 0)\}$.

EXERCISES

Solve each system of equations by graphing.

50. $\begin{cases} y + 6 = \frac{1}{2}(x - 2)^2 \\ y + 2x = -2 \end{cases}$

51. $\begin{cases} 25x^2 + 16y^2 = 400 \\ 16y = -5(x - 4)^2 \end{cases}$

Solve each system by using the substitution method.

52. $\begin{cases} 2x^2 - 2y^2 = 56 \\ x^2 + y^2 = 100 \end{cases}$

53. $\begin{cases} 2x^2 - y^2 = 14 \\ y - 2x = -4 \end{cases}$

Solve each system by using the elimination method.

54. $\begin{cases} 4y^2 - 8x^2 = 16 \\ 4x^2 + 5y^2 = 20 \end{cases}$

55. $\begin{cases} 3x^2 - 2y^2 = 76 \\ 5x^2 + 3y^2 = 228 \end{cases}$

Solve each system by using any method.

56. $\begin{cases} 3x^2 + 5y^2 = 192 \\ 3y - x = 16 \end{cases}$

57. $\begin{cases} \frac{x^2}{25} - \frac{y^2}{16} = 1 \\ 30x^2 + 20y^2 = 600 \end{cases}$

CHAPTER 12

1. The transmission of a radio signal can be received at the locations $(1, -10)$ and $(-11, 6)$. Write an equation for the range of the signal if a line between the locations represents a diameter of the range.
2. Write the equation of the line that is tangent to $(x + 2)^2 + (y - 8)^2 = 40$ at $(3, -1)$.
3. Find the center, vertices, co-vertices, and foci of the ellipse with equation $49(x + 4)^2 + 16(y-2)^2 = 784$. Then graph.
4. A shelter for a patch of young strawberry plants is constructed in the form of an ellipse. If the shelter is 4.5 feet high at its highest point and the patch is 19 feet wide, write an equation for the ellipse.
5. Find the center, vertices, co-vertices, foci, and asymptotes of the hyperbola with equation $\frac{x^2}{25} - \frac{y^2}{144} = 1$. Then graph.
6. Write the equation of the hyperbola with vertices $(0, 7)$ and $(0, -7)$ and conjugate axis length 28.
7. Find the vertex, value of p, axis of symmetry, focus, and directrix of the parabola with equation $y + 4 = \frac{1}{24}(x - 2)^2$. Then graph.
8. The filament of a flashlight bulb is located at the focus, which is 0.75 centimeters from the vertex of the flashlight's parabolic reflector. Write an equation for the cross section of the parabolic reflector if the vertex is at the origin and the reflector is pointed to the left.

Identify the conic section that each equation represents.

9. $\frac{x - 2}{4} = \frac{(y + 5)^2}{12}$
10. $1 - \frac{(x + 5)^2}{8} = \frac{(y - 4)^2}{8}$
11. $7x^2 + 5xy - 2y^2 + 8x - 26 = 0$

Find the standard form of each equation by completing the square. Then identify the conic.

12. $x^2 + y^2 - 16x + 20y + 124 = 0$
13. $6x^2 + 4y^2 + 84x - 24y + 306 = 0$

Find the solutions to the system by using the substitution or elimination method.

14. $\begin{cases} 2y - 3x = 1 \\ x + 4 = \frac{1}{4}(y - 2)^2 \end{cases}$
15. $\begin{cases} y + x = 2 \\ x^2 + y^2 = 52 \end{cases}$
16. $\begin{cases} 3x^2 - 4y^2 = 143 \\ 5x^2 - 5y^2 = 280 \end{cases}$

17. Two trapeze artists are swinging through the air along the paths shown in the graph. One performer releases the swing and travels in a path that can be modeled by the equation $y = -\frac{1}{4}x^2 + 16$. The performer's partner moves along a path that can be modeled by the equation $y = \frac{1}{2}x^2 + 16$. At what point will the performer be caught by his partner?

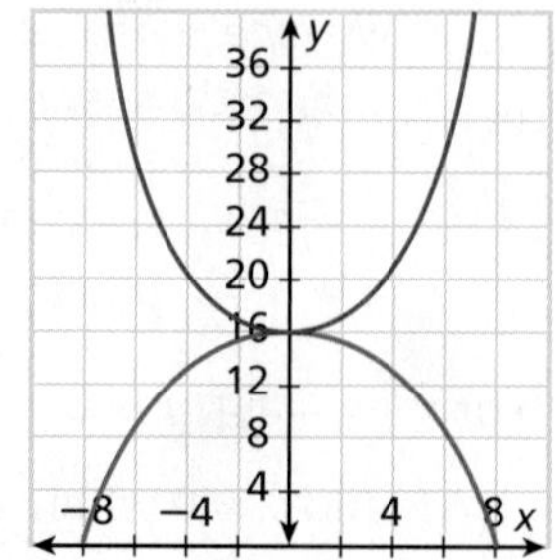

CHAPTER 12

FOCUS ON SAT MATHEMATICS SUBJECT TESTS

The topics covered on each SAT Mathematics Subject Tests vary only slightly each time the test is administered. You can find out the general distribution of questions across topics and then determine which areas need more of your attention when you are studying for the test.

To prepare for the SAT Mathematics Subject Tests, start reviewing course material a couple of months before your test date. Take sample tests to find the areas you might need to focus on more. Remember that you are not expected to have studied all of the topics on the test.

You may want to time yourself as you take this practice test. It should take you about 6 minutes to complete.

1. The graph of the equation $x^2 + y^2 - 2x + 3y + 8 = 0$ is which of the following?

(A) Parabola

(B) Circle

(C) Hyperbola

(D) Ellipse

(E) Point

2. What is the length of the major axis of the ellipse with equation $\frac{(x-1)^2}{4} + (y+3)^2 = 9$?

(A) 2

(B) 3

(C) 4

(D) 6

(E) 12

3. What is the distance from the focus to the vertex of a parabola with equation $x = \frac{1}{12}(y-1)^2$?

(A) 3

(B) 6

(C) 12

(D) 48

(E) 144

4. Which of the following is the equation of an asymptote of the graph of $\frac{(y+2)^2}{9} - \frac{(x-5)^2}{4} = 1$?

(A) $y+2 = \frac{3}{2}(x-5)$

(B) $y+2 = \frac{2}{3}(x-5)$

(C) $y+2 = \frac{9}{4}(x-5)$

(D) $y = \frac{3}{2}x$

(E) $y = \frac{2}{3}x$

5. The circle with equation $x^2 + y^2 + sx + ty + 33 = 0$ has center $(4, 5)$. What is $\frac{s}{t}$?

(A) $-\frac{5}{4}$

(B) $-\frac{4}{5}$

(C) $\frac{4}{5}$

(D) $\frac{5}{4}$

(E) There is not enough information to determine the answer.

CHAPTER 12

TEST TACKLER

Standardized Test Strategies

Multiple Choice: Context-Based Test Items

You will encounter some multiple-choice test items where the problem statement does not give you an actual problem to solve but requires you to use the answer choices provided to determine which choice fits the context of the problem statement. Depending on the problem, you can use a variety of methods, such as substitution, graphing, or elimination, to obtain the correct answer.

EXAMPLE 1

Which of the following equations, when graphed, has x-intercepts at $(5, 0)$ and $(-5, 0)$?

Ⓐ $2x^2 + 25y^2 = 150$

Ⓑ $8x^2 + 50y^2 = 200$

Ⓒ $5x^2 + 5y^2 = 100$

Ⓓ $4x^2 + 5y^2 = 50$

Although there are many equations that have x-intercepts at $(5, 0)$ and $(-5, 0)$, you need to select the equation from the four choices given. For this problem, you can use either of these two methods:

Substitution Method Substitute $x = 5$ and $y = 0$ into the equation, and simplify. Then substitute $x = -5$ and $y = 0$ into the equation, and simplify. Find which equation makes a true statement with the given x-intercepts.

Try choice A: $2x^2 + 25y^2 = 150$; $2(5)^2 + 25(0)^2 = 50$
Because the first equation does not make a true statement, $150 \neq 50$, choice A is incorrect.

Try choice B: $8x^2 + 50y^2 = 200$; $8(5)^2 + 50(0)^2 = 200$; $8(-5)^2 + 50(0)^2 = 200$
Because both equations make a true statement, choice B is correct.

Try choice C and choice D to confirm that you found the correct answer.

Graphing Method Solve each equation in the answer choices for y. Then graph each equation on a graphing calculator. Look for the graph that intersects the x-axis at $(5, 0)$ and $(-5, 0)$.

Try choice A: $2x^2 + 25y^2 = 150$

$$y = \pm\sqrt{\frac{(150 - 2x^2)}{25}}$$

When graphed on a calculator, the graph crosses the x-axis at about (8.5, 0) and (–8.5, 0). Choice A is incorrect.

Try choice B: $8x^2 + 50y^2 = 200$

$$y = \pm\sqrt{\frac{(200 - 8x^2)}{50}}$$

When graphed on a calculator, the graph crosses the x-axis at (5, 0) and (–5, 0). Choice B is the correct answer.

Try choice C and choice D to confirm that you found the correct answer.

Underline the context of the problem statement to make sure that you are clear about what is being asked.

Read each test item and answer the questions that follow.

Item A

Which equation, when graphed, is a parabola that opens to the right?

Ⓐ $4y - 2x^2 = 6$

Ⓑ $4y + 2x^2 = 6$

Ⓒ $4x - 2y^2 = 6$

Ⓓ $4x + 2y^2 = 6$

1. On a coordinate grid, sketch two or three parabolas that open to the right. Can they all be represented by the same equation? If not, what do these equations have in common?
2. From what you know about parabolas, can any of the answer choices be eliminated? Explain.
3. Describe how to determine which answer choice is correct.

Item B

The graph of which of the following ellipses has the smallest distance between foci?

Ⓕ $\frac{(x+16)^2}{64} + \frac{(y-9)^2}{25} = 1$

Ⓖ $\frac{x^2}{4} + \frac{y^2}{81} = 1$

Ⓗ $\frac{(x-1)^2}{1} + \frac{(y-1)^2}{100} = 1$

Ⓙ $\frac{x^2}{289} + \frac{y^2}{169} = 1$

4. If you read only the problem statement and not the answer choices, can you solve the problem? Explain.
5. How can you find the distance between foci if you know *a* and *b*?

Item C

Which of the following points is inside the circle described by the following equation?

$$(x-2)^2 + (y-6)^2 = 9$$

Ⓐ $(0, 0)$

Ⓑ $(-2, 4)$

Ⓒ $(5, 6)$

Ⓓ $(3, 5)$

6. Describe how you can use your graphing calculator to determine the correct answer.
7. Can you use algebra to determine the correct answer? If so, describe your method.

Item D

A power outage affects areas *L*, *M*, and *N*. Which of the following best describes the power outage?

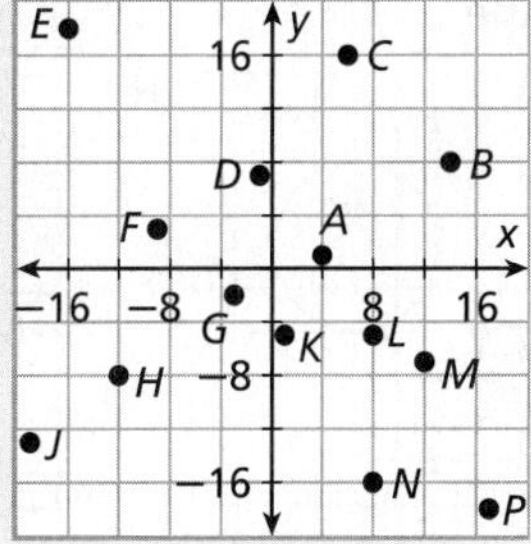

Ⓕ The main generator is located at $(12, -9)$ and shuts down power up to 9 miles away.

Ⓖ The main generator is located at $(4, -6)$ and shuts down power up to 8 miles away.

Ⓗ The main generator is located at $(10, -3)$ and shuts down power up to 5 miles away.

Ⓙ The main generator is located at $(-8, -15)$ and shuts down power up to 15 miles away.

8. What does the problem state about areas *L*, *M*, and *N*? What can you interpret about the areas not mentioned?
9. A student found that areas *L* and *M* are within the circle described by choice H. Can the student stop working and select choice H as the correct response? Explain.
10. Describe a method that you can use to determine the correct answer.

CHAPTER 12

STANDARDIZED TEST PREP

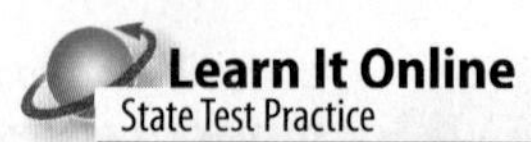

CUMULATIVE ASSESSMENT

Multiple Choice

1. Which conic section does the equation $\frac{x^2}{20} + \frac{y^2}{52} = 1$ represent?

   (A) Circle

   (B) Parabola

   (C) Hyperbola

   (D) Ellipse

2. Which is the graph of $(x + 2)^2 + (y - 2)^2 = 16$?

   (F) 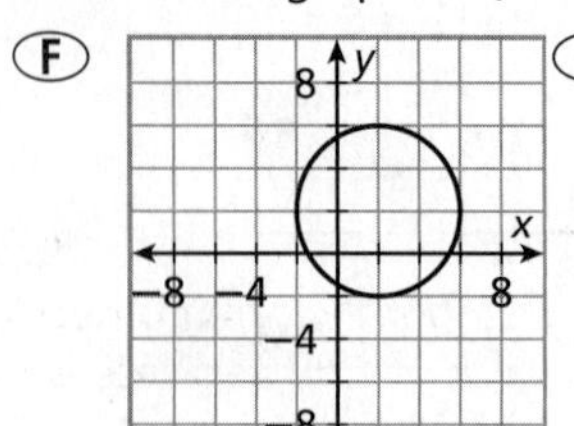

   (H) 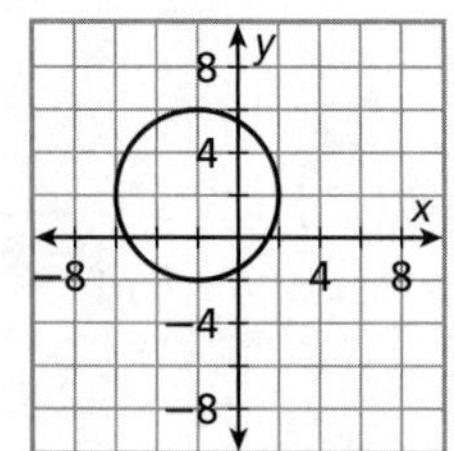

   (G) 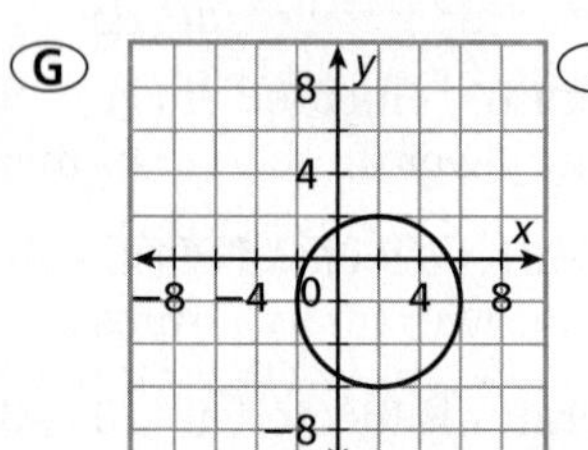

   (J) 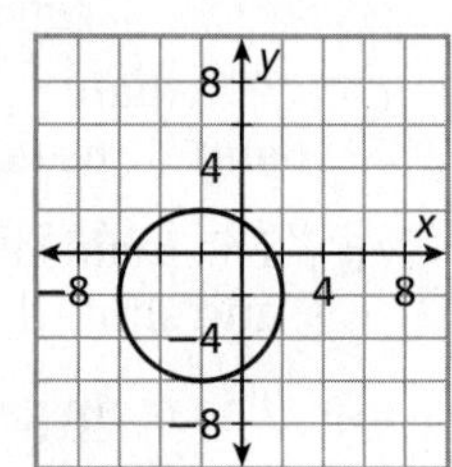

3. What system of linear inequalities can be used to represent the graph?

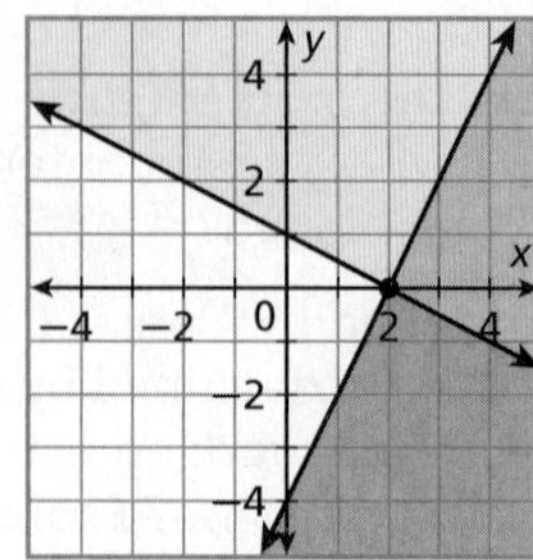

   (A) $\begin{cases} y \leq 2x - 4 \\ 2y \geq -x + 2 \end{cases}$

   (C) $\begin{cases} y \leq 2x - 4 \\ 2y \leq -x + 2 \end{cases}$

   (B) $\begin{cases} y < 2x - 4 \\ 2y > -x + 2 \end{cases}$

   (D) $\begin{cases} y < 2x - 4 \\ 2y < -x + 2 \end{cases}$

4. What equation can be used to represent the graph?

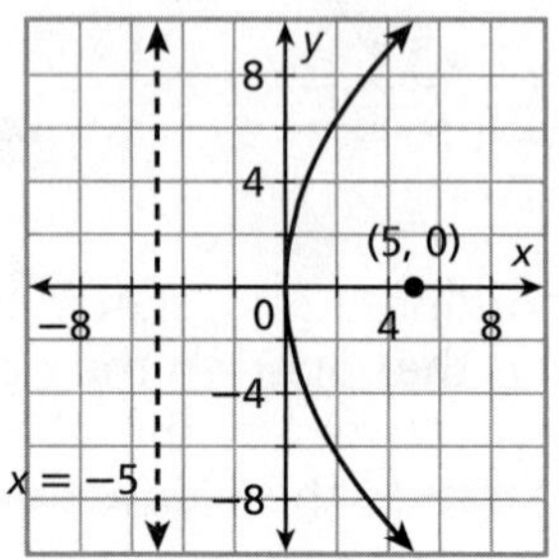

   (F) $x = -\frac{1}{20}y^2$

   (G) $x = \frac{1}{20}y^2$

   (H) $y = \frac{1}{20}x^2$

   (J) $y = -\frac{1}{20}x^2$

5. Solve $\begin{cases} x^2 + 4y^2 = 64 \\ x + 8 = \frac{1}{2}y^2 \end{cases}$ by using the substitution method.

   (A) $\{(-8, 0), (0, 4), (0, -4)\}$

   (B) $\{(0, -8), (4, 0), (-4, 0)\}$

   (C) $\{(-8, 0), (0, 4)\}$

   (D) $\{(0, 4), (0, -4)\}$

6. Find all of the roots of the polynomial equation $x^5 + x^4 - x^3 - x^2 - 20x - 20 = 0$.

   (F) $\sqrt{5}, -\sqrt{5}, -1$

   (G) $i, -i, \sqrt{5}, -\sqrt{5}, -1$

   (H) $2i, -2i, \sqrt{5}, -\sqrt{5}, -1$

   (J) $4i, -4i, \sqrt{5}, -\sqrt{5}, -1$`

7. At age 20, Jon invested $50 at 6.75% compounded continuously. Jon is now 50. What is the present value of Jon's investment?

   (A) $4,545.67

   (B) $378.81

   (C) $17,534.57

   (D) $2,314.46

In Item 15, recall that the notation $(f \circ g)(x)$ is equivalent to $f(g(x))$. Begin by substituting the value for x into the function $g(x)$.

8. Simplify.

$\frac{x+1}{3x+4} + \frac{x-1}{4x-7}$

Ⓕ $\frac{2x}{7x-3}$

Ⓖ $\frac{7x^2-17x-11}{(3x+4)(4x-7)}$

Ⓗ $\frac{7x^2+17x-11}{(3x+4)(4x-7)}$

Ⓙ $\frac{7x^2-2x-11}{(3x+4)(4x-7)}$

9. What is the inverse of the function $f(x) = \frac{7x-4}{3}$?

Ⓐ $f^{-1}(x) = \frac{3}{7x-4}$

Ⓑ $f^{-1}(x) = \frac{3x+4}{7}$

Ⓒ $f^{-1}(x) = \frac{3}{7}x - \frac{3}{4}$

Ⓓ $f^{-1}(x) = \frac{3}{7}x - \frac{4}{7}$

10. Solve for x: $3^{2x-1} = 27^{x+4}$.

Ⓕ 5

Ⓖ $\frac{7}{5}$

Ⓗ −2

Ⓙ −13

Gridded Response

11. What is the x-intercept of the axis of symmetry of the function $f(x) = 5x^2 - \frac{1}{2}x - 4$?

12. Evaluate.

$\log_{256} 16$

13. Solve for x.

$\frac{8}{x+4} - \frac{2}{x} = \frac{5}{x+4}$

14. Simplify.

$\left(\sqrt[3]{2^9}\right)^2$

15. Given $f(x) = 3x^2 - 1$ and $g(x) = \frac{1}{x+5}$, what is the value of $(f \circ g)(-6)$?

Short Response

16. A hyperbola has center $(3, -5)$, focus $(-10, -5)$, and vertex $(15, -5)$.

a. Write the equation for the hyperbola.

b. What are the equations of the asymptotes of the hyperbola?

17. The approximate heart rate of an adult can be modeled by $f(x) = -(x-5)^2 + 75$, where x is the age (in tens) of the person.

a. Find the inverse for the function, and explain what it represents.

b. Approximate the age of a person whose heart rate is 65.

18. Solve the system of equations by using any method.

$$\begin{cases} x^2 - 2y = 1 \\ 2x + \sqrt{y} = 2 \end{cases}$$

a. What is the solution of the system?

b. Explain your choice of method.

Extended Response

19. Joan's grandmother gave her a diamond necklace valued at \$4500. The value of the necklace is predicted to appreciate 7.5% per year.

a. Write a function to model the predicted growth in the value of the necklace.

b. Graph the function.

c. What is the predicted value of the necklace in 10 years?

d. Based on the model, what was the value of the necklace 30 years ago?

Real-World CONNECTIONS

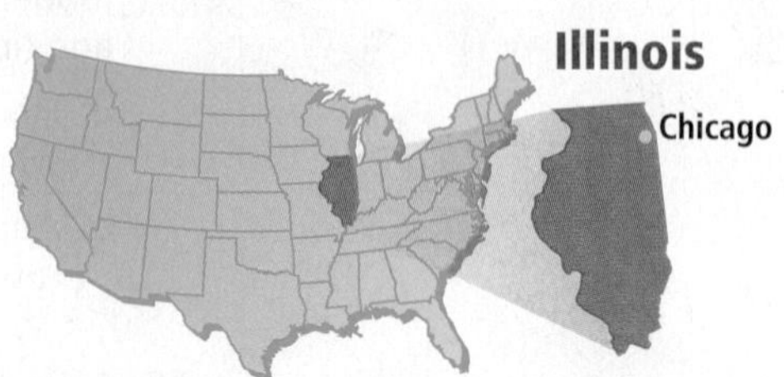

The First Ferris Wheel

The organizers of the 1893 World's Fair in Chicago wanted an attraction that would outdo the Eiffel Tower, which had been built four years earlier for the Paris World's Fair. A bridge builder named George Ferris met the challenge by designing a colossal wheel that could carry more than 2100 passengers at a time. During the fair, 1.5 million visitors paid the 50-cent fee for a 20-minute ride on Ferris's wheel.

Choose one or more strategies to solve each problem. For 1, use the table.

Building Ferris's Wheel

Date	Total Number of Cars Attached
June 10, 1893	1
June 11, 1893	6
June 13, 1893	21

1. Each car of the wheel could carry up to 60 passengers. Because of the cars' enormous size, it took several days to hang all of the cars on the wheel. Develop a model to predict the number of cars that had been attached to the wheel by June 14, 1893.
2. As the wheel revolved, the paths of the cars could be modeled by $x^2 + y^2 - 250y = 0$. Find the diameter of the wheel.
3. Approximately how many feet has a car traveled after one complete revolution of the wheel?
4. A car starts at the bottom of the wheel. After 2 min 15 s, the car's horizontal distance to the central axle is 125 ft. How long does it take the car to make one complete revolution?

Soldier Field

Chicago's Soldier Field was built in 1924 as a multipurpose sports stadium. Since 1970, it has been the home of the National Football League's Chicago Bears. In 2003, a new 61,500-seat stadium was built within the shell of the original structure so that the historic colonnades and exterior walls of the old Soldier Field could be preserved.

Choose one or more strategies to solve each problem.

1. The renovated stadium can be modeled by an ellipse centered at the origin, a vertex at $(425, 0)$, and a focus at $(301, 0)$, measured in feet. Find the length and width of the stadium to the nearest foot.

For 2, use the diagram.

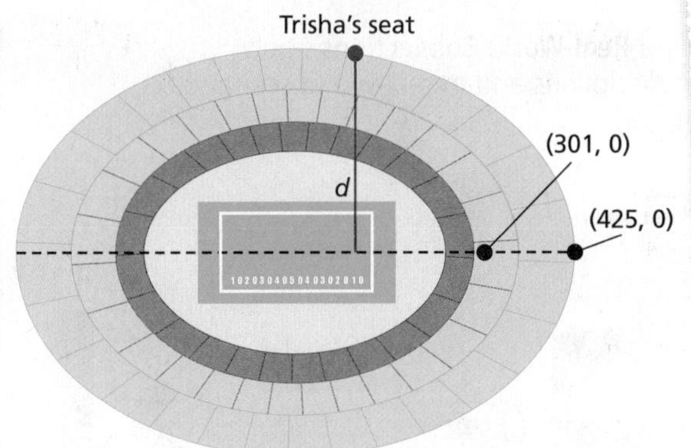

2. Trisha bought tickets to a Bears game. As shown, her seat is on the 20-yard line, in the last row of the stadium. What is the horizontal distance d to the nearest foot from her seat to the middle of the playing field?

3. During the game, a player makes a kick from the 40-yard line. The ball reaches a maximum height of 9 yards and lands 60 yards away. If the path of the ball is modeled by a parabola, does the ball clear the 10-foot-tall goalpost located 50 yards away? If so, by how many feet?

(t), Jim Wark/Airphoto; (b), John Gress/Reuters/CORBIS

COMMON CORE

Mastering the *Standards*

for Mathematical Practice

The topics described in the Standards for Mathematical Content will vary from year to year. However, the *way* in which you learn, study, and think about mathematics will not. The Standards for Mathematical Practice describe skills that you will use in all of your math courses.

Mathematical Practices

1. *Make sense of problems and persevere in solving them.*
2. *Reason abstractly and quantitatively.*
3. *Construct viable arguments and critique the reasoning of others.*
4. *Model with mathematics.*
5. *Use appropriate tools strategically.*
6. *Attend to precision.*
7. *Look for and make use of structure.*
8. *Look for and express regularity in repeated reasoning.*

4 Model with mathematics.

Mathematically proficient students can apply... mathematics... to... problems... in everyday life, society, and the workplace...

In your book

Multi-Step Test Prep and **Real-World Connections** apply mathematics to other disciplines and in real-world scenarios.

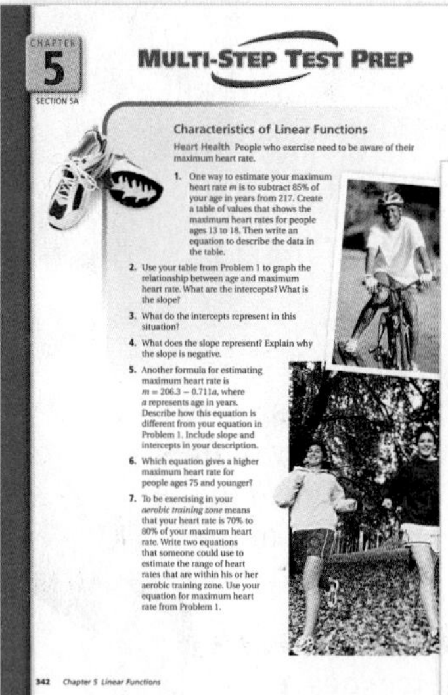

CHAPTER 5

SECTION 5A

MULTI-STEP TEST PREP

Characteristics of Linear Functions

Heart Health People who exercise need to be aware of their maximum heart rate.

1. One way to estimate your maximum heart rate m is to subtract 85% of your age in years from 217. Create a table of values that shows the maximum heart rates for people ages 13 to 18. Then write an equation to describe the data in the table.
2. Use your table from Problem 1 to graph the relationship between age and maximum heart rate. What are the intercepts? What is the slope?
3. What do the intercepts represent in this situation?
4. What does the slope represent? Explain why the slope is negative.
5. Another formula for estimating maximum heart rate is $m = 206.3 - 0.711a$, where a represents age in years. Describe how this equation is different from your equation in Problem 1. Include slope and intercepts in your description.
6. Which equation gives a higher maximum heart rate for people ages 75 and younger?
7. To be exercising in your *aerobic training zone* means that your heart rate is 70% to 80% of your maximum heart rate. Write two equations that someone could use to estimate the range of heart rates that are within his or her aerobic training zone. Use your equation for maximum heart rate from Problem 1.

342 *Chapter 5 Linear Functions*

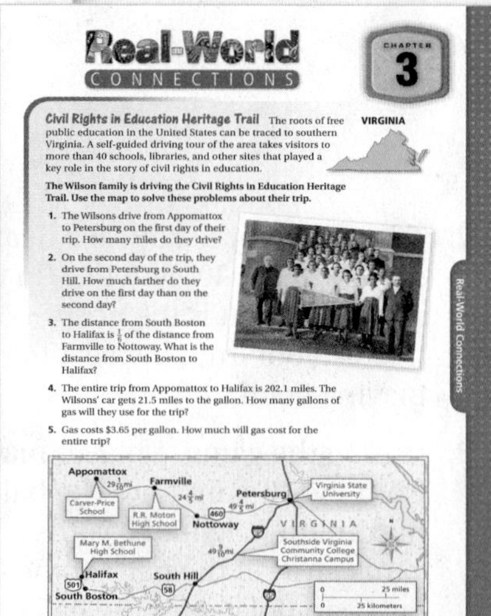

Real-World CONNECTIONS

CHAPTER 3

Civil Rights in Education Heritage Trail The roots of free public education in the United States can be traced to southern Virginia. A self-guided driving tour of the area takes visitors to more than 40 schools, libraries, and other sites that played a key role in the story of civil rights in education.

VIRGINIA

The Wilson family is driving the Civil Rights in Education Heritage Trail. Use the map to solve these problems about their trip.

1. The Wilsons drive from Appomattox to Petersburg on the first day of their trip. How many miles do they drive?
2. On the second day of the trip, they drive from Petersburg to South Hill. How much farther do they drive on the first day than on the second day?
3. The distance from South Boston to Halifax is $\frac{1}{6}$ of the distance from Farmville to Nottoway. What is the distance from South Boston to Halifax?
4. The entire trip from Appomattox to Halifax is 202.1 miles. The Wilsons' car gets 21.5 miles to the gallon. How many gallons of gas will they use for the trip?
5. Gas costs $3.65 per gallon. How much will gas cost for the entire trip?

Real-World Connections 199

PhotoDisc/Getty Images

Student Handbook

Student Handbook

Lesson 1-1 **Perform the given translation on the point $(-3, 4)$. Give the coordinates of the translated point.**

1. 3 units right **2.** 5 units up **3.** 2 units left, 2 units down

Use a table to perform each transformation of $y = f(x)$. Use the same coordinate plane as the original function.

4. reflection across the y-axis

5. translation 2 units up

6. vertical compression by a factor of $\frac{1}{2}$

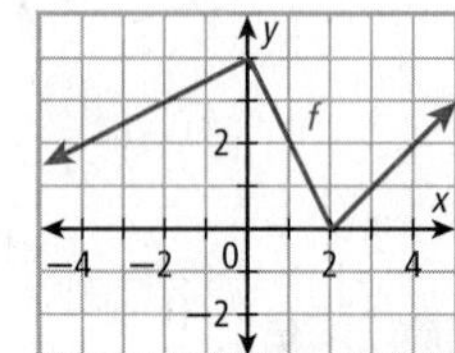

Lesson 1-2 **Identify the parent function for g from its function rule. Then graph g on your calculator and describe what transformation of the parent function it represents.**

7. $g(x) = (x + 3)^3$ **8.** $g(x) = \sqrt{x - 4}$ **9.** $g(x) = x^2 + 3$

Graph the data from the table. Describe the parent function and the transformation that best approximates the data set.

10.

x	−2	−1	0	1	2
y	−4	−0.5	0	0.5	4

11.

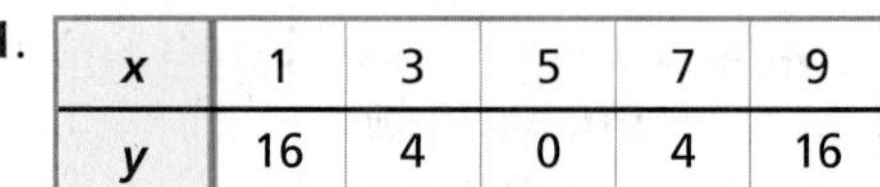

x	1	3	5	7	9
y	16	4	0	4	16

Lesson 1-3 **Let $g(x)$ be the indicated transformation of $f(x)$. Write the rule for $g(x)$.**

12. $f(x) = \frac{4}{7}x + 1$; vertical translation 3 units down

13. $f(x) = -4x + 9$; horizontal stretch by a factor of 4

14. linear function defined in the table; reflection across the y-axis

x	−1	0	2	5
y	−17	−11	1	19

Lesson 1-4 **Let $g(x)$ be the indicated transformation of $f(x) = x$. Write the rule for $g(x)$.**

15. vertical stretch by a factor of 2 followed by a horizontal shift 2 units right

16. horizontal shift 5 units left followed by a reflection across the x-axis

17. vertical stretch by a factor of $\frac{3}{2}$ followed by a vertical shift 8 units down

18. If the points in a scatter plot have a positive correlation, then the r-value is ____?____ . If the points have no correlation, then the r-value is ____?____.

19. Make a scatter plot of the data shown in the table.

x	0	2	3	4	6	9
y	18	15	14	10	5	1

20. Find the correlation coefficient and the equation of the line of best fit. Draw the line of best fit on your scatter plot.

Mastering the Standards

for Mathematical Practice

The topics described in the Standards for Mathematical Content will vary from year to year. However, the *way* in which you learn, study, and think about mathematics will not. The Standards for Mathematical Practice describe skills that you will use in all of your math courses.

Mathematical Practices

1. *Make sense of problems and persevere in solving them.*
2. *Reason abstractly and quantitatively.*
3. *Construct viable arguments and critique the reasoning of others.*
4. *Model with mathematics.*
5. *Use appropriate tools strategically.*
6. *Attend to precision.*
7. *Look for and make use of structure.*
8. *Look for and express regularity in repeated reasoning.*

5 Use appropriate tools strategically.

Mathematically proficient students consider the available tools when solving a... problem... [and] are... able to use technological tools to explore and deepen their understanding...

In your book

Algebra Labs and **Technology Labs** use concrete and technological tools to explore mathematical concepts.

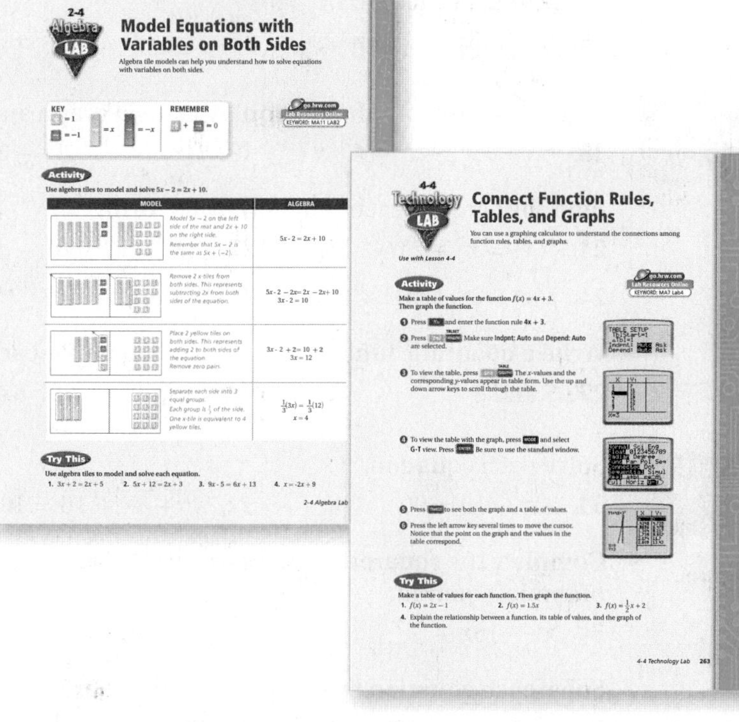

2-4 Algebra LAB

Model Equations with Variables on Both Sides

Algebra tile models can help you understand how to solve equations with variables on both sides.

KEY: = 1; = −1; = x; = $-x$. REMEMBER: + = 0

go.hrw.com Lab Resources Online KEYWORD: MA11 LAB2

Activity

Use algebra tiles to model and solve $5x - 2 = 2x + 10$.

MODEL		ALGEBRA
	Model $5x - 2$ on the left side of the mat and $2x + 10$ on the right side. Remember that $5x - 2$ is the same as $5x + (-2)$.	$5x - 2 = 2x + 10$
	Remove 2 x-tiles from both sides. This represents subtracting 2x from both sides of the equation.	$5x - 2 - 2x = 2x - 2x + 10$ $3x - 2 = 10$
	Place 2 yellow tiles on both sides. This represents adding 2 to both sides of the equation. Remove zero pairs.	$3x - 2 + 2 = 10 + 2$ $3x = 12$
	Separate each side into 3 equal groups. Each group is $\frac{1}{3}$ of the side. One x-tile is equivalent to 4 yellow tiles.	$\frac{1}{3}(3x) = \frac{1}{3}(12)$ $x = 4$

Try This

Use algebra tiles to model and solve each equation.

1. $3x + 2 = 2x + 5$ 2. $5x + 12 = 2x + 3$ 3. $9x - 5 = 6x + 13$ 4. $x = -2x + 9$

2-4 Algebra Lab

4-4 Technology LAB

Connect Function Rules, Tables, and Graphs

You can use a graphing calculator to understand the connections among function rules, tables, and graphs.

Use with Lesson 4-4

go.hrw.com Lab Resources Online KEYWORD: MA7 Lab4

Activity

Make a table of values for the function $f(x) = 4x + 3$. Then graph the function.

1. Press and enter the function rule **4x + 3**.
2. Press TBLSET. Make sure **Indpnt: Auto** and **Depend: Auto** are selected.
3. To view the table, press TABLE. The x-values and the corresponding y-values appear in table form. Use the up and down arrow keys to scroll through the table.
4. To view the table with the graph, press MODE and select **G-T** view. Press ENTER. Be sure to use the standard window.
5. Press to see both the graph and a table of values.
6. Press the left arrow key several times to move the cursor. Notice that the point on the graph and the values in the table correspond.

Try This

Make a table of values for each function. Then graph the function.

1. $f(x) = 2x - 1$ 2. $f(x) = 1.5x$ 3. $f(x) = \frac{1}{2}x + 2$
4. Explain the relationship between a function, its table of values, and the graph of the function.

4-4 Technology Lab 263

Extra Practice Chapter 2 ■ Skills Practice

Lesson 2-1

Graph each function by using a table.

1. $f(x) = \frac{1}{2}x^2 - 4$
2. $f(x) = 2x^2 - x + 3$
3. $f(x) = -x^2 - 3x$

Using the graph of $f(x) = x^2$ as a guide, describe the transformations, and then graph each function.

4. $g(x) = (x + 2)^2 + 1$
5. $g(x) = -2x^2$
6. $g(x) = \frac{1}{4}x^2$

Use the description to write each quadratic function in vertex form.

7. The parent function $f(x) = x^2$ is vertically stretched by a factor of 3 and translated 6 units right to create g.
8. The parent function $f(x) = x^2$ is reflected across the x-axis and translated 12 units down to create g.

Lesson 2-2

Identify the axis of symmetry for the graph of each function.

9. $f(x) = 2x^2 + 1$
10. $f(x) = (x + 3)^2 - 5$
11. $f(x) = 3(x - 2)^2$

For each function, (a) determine whether the graph opens upward or downward, (b) find the axis of symmetry, (c) find the vertex, (d) find the y-intercept, and (e) graph the function.

12. $f(x) = 2x^2 - 4x + 5$
13. $f(x) = -\frac{1}{2}x^2 - 2x + 3$
14. $f(x) = -x^2 - 8x - 6$

Find the minimum or maximum value of each function. Then state the domain and range of the function.

15. $f(x) = 3x^2 + 60x + 294$
16. $f(x) = -2x^2 + 28x - 95$
17. $f(x) = 2x^2 + 14x + 30$

Lesson 2-3

Find the zeros of each function by using a graph and a table.

18. $f(x) = x^2 + 5x + 6$
19. $f(x) = x^2 - 3x - 28$
20. $f(x) = -x^2 + 12x - 20$

Find the zeros of each function by factoring.

21. $f(x) = x^2 + 2x - 35$
22. $f(x) = x^2 - 8x - 9$
23. $f(x) = 2x^2 - 9x$
24. $f(x) = x^2 + 10x + 25$
25. $f(x) = x^2 - 49$
26. $f(x) = x^2 - 12x + 36$

Write a quadratic function in standard form for each given set of zeros.

27. 5 and 8
28. −3 and 1
29. 6 and 6
30. 12 and 0

Lesson 2-4

Solve each equation.

31. $4x^2 - 10 = 90$
32. $x^2 + 8x + 16 = 10$
33. $x^2 + 4x + 4 = 8$

Complete the square for each expression. Write the resulting expression as a binomial squared.

34. $x^2 - 16x + ■$
35. $x^2 + 22x + ■$
36. $x^2 + 7x + ■$

Solve each equation by completing the square.

37. $x^2 + 8x = -10$
38. $x^2 - 12x = 13$
39. $x^2 + 20 = 10x$
40. $2x^2 + 12x = 14$
41. $3x^2 - 18 = 48x$
42. $x^2 - 5 = 2x$

Write each function in vertex form, and identify its vertex.

43. $f(x) = x^2 - 2x + 17$
44. $f(x) = x^2 + 4x - 8$
45. $f(x) = 4x^2 - 24x + 31$

Lesson 2-5

Express each number in terms of *i*.

46. $2\sqrt{-81}$ **47.** $-\sqrt{-144}$ **48.** $\sqrt{-128}$ **49.** $5\sqrt{-48}$

Solve each equation.

50. $169 + x^2 = 0$ **51.** $2x^2 = -200$ **52.** $x^2 = -90$

Find the zeros of each function.

53. $f(x) = x^2 + 8x + 20$ **54.** $f(x) = x^2 - 14x + 65$ **55.** $f(x) = x^2 - 2x + 46$

Find each complex conjugate.

56. $12i$ **57.** $3 - 6i$ **58.** $10i - 3$ **59.** $2\sqrt{7} - 10i$

Lesson 2-6

Find the zeros of each function by using the Quadratic Formula.

60. $f(x) = x^2 - 10x + 3$ **61.** $f(x) = 2x^2 + 5x + 1$ **62.** $f(x) = -x^2 + 8x - 3$

63. $f(x) = x^2 - 6x + 40$ **64.** $f(x) = x^2 + 7x + 13$ **65.** $f(x) = 2x^2 - 9x + 25$

Find the type and number of solutions for each equation.

66. $x^2 + 8x = -16$ **67.** $x^2 + 3 = 10x$ **68.** $5 + 2x^2 = 12x$ **69.** $4x^2 + 2x = -9$

Lesson 2-7

Graph each inequality.

70. $y \geq (x + 3)^2 + 2$ **71.** $y < 2x^2 - 4x - 1$ **72.** $y < -x^2 + 11x - 24$

Solve each inequality.

73. $x^2 + 13x + 20 < -2$ **74.** $x^2 - 11x \geq -10$ **75.** $x^2 + 6x + 3 > 10$

76. $x^2 - 2x - 20 > 28$ **77.** $2x^2 - 9x \leq 5$ **78.** $3x^2 + 1 \geq 4x$

Lesson 2-8

Determine whether each data set could represent a quadratic function. Explain.

79.

x	3	4	5	6	7
y	−2	−5	−6	−5	−2

80.

x	−2	−1	0	1	2
y	−5	2	3	4	11

81.

x	−6	−5	−4	−3	−2
y	19	10	7	10	19

Write a quadratic function that fits each set of points.

82. $(-2, 0)$, $(1, 6)$, and $(3, -10)$ **83.** $(-4, -25)$, $(0, -9)$, and $(2, 5)$

Lesson 2-9

Graph each complex number.

84. -3 **85.** $2i$ **86.** $2 + 4i$ **87.** $-3 - 3i$

Find each absolute value.

88. $|6 + 9i|$ **89.** $|-3 + 4i|$ **90.** $|-7i|$

Simplify. Write the result in the form $a + bi$.

91. $(3 + 7i) + (-2 + 3i)$ **92.** $(-9 - 4i) + (5 + i)$ **93.** $(10 + 6i) - (3i - 12)$

94. $-3i(9 - 2i)$ **95.** $(2 - i)(4 + 3i)$ **96.** $(6 + 4i)(4 - 5i)$

97. $\dfrac{11 + 3i}{2 + i}$ **98.** $\dfrac{-44 - 40i}{-8 + 2i}$ **99.** $\dfrac{5 + 12i}{3 + 2i}$

Extra Practice Chapter 3 ■ Skills Practice

Lesson 3-1

Identify the degree of each monomial.

1. $7x^2$
2. $-12x$
3. $2x^3y^3$
4. 8

Rewrite each polynomial in standard form. Then identify the leading coefficient, degree, and number of terms. Name the polynomial.

5. $5x^2 + 6 + 9x - 10x^3$
6. $3 - 12x^4 - 6x^2$
7. $14x + 15x^5$

Add or subtract. Write your answer in standard form.

8. $(12x^2 + 4x - 9) + (3x^3 - 7x^2 - 1)$
9. $(34 + 8x^3 - 9x^2) - (3x^3 + 10x^2 - 4x - 4)$

Graph each polynomial function on a calculator. Describe the graph, and identify the number of real zeros.

10. $f(x) = 5x^3 + 4x - 6$
11. $g(x) = 2x^4 - 12x + 3$
12. $h(x) = 3x^3 - 4x + 1$

Lesson 3-2

Find each product.

13. $3ab(2a^2 - 5ab + 9b)$
14. $-5cd^3(8d + 3c - c^2d)$
15. $(x + 3)(2x^2 - x + 6)$
16. $(2x - 1)(-x^2 + 5x + 5)$
17. $(2x + 6)^3$
18. $(y - 2)^4$

Expand each expression.

19. $(x - y)^5$
20. $(y + 4)^4$
21. $(2x + y)^5$
22. $(x - 2y)^4$

Lesson 3-3

Divide by using long division.

23. $(6x^2 + 7x - 2) \div (x + 4)$
24. $(2x^2 - 9x + 10) \div (2x - 1)$

Divide by using synthetic division.

25. $(3x^3 + 4x^2 - 8) \div (x - 2)$
26. $(2x^3 + 3x^2 - 6x - 4) \div (x - 1)$

Use synthetic division to evaluate the polynomial for the given value.

27. $P(x) = -2x^3 + 7x^2 - 3x - 9$ for $x = -2$
28. $P(x) = 6x^3 - 7x^2 + 10$ for $x = 0.5$

Lesson 3-4

Determine whether the given binomial is a factor of the polynomial $P(x)$.

29. $(x + 2)$; $P(x) = 3x^3 + 11x^2 + 2x - 16$
30. $(x - 4)$; $P(x) = 12x^3 + 9x^2 - 2x + 8$
31. $(x + 1)$; $P(x) = x^4 - 3x^3 + 10x + 4$
32. $(x - 3)$; $P(x) = x^3 - 3x^2 - 4x + 12$

Factor each expression.

33. $2x^3 + 12x^2 - 4x - 24$
34. $2x^3 + 5x^2 - 18x - 45$
35. $4x^3 + 12x^2 + 12x + 36$
36. $a^3 + 27$
37. $128b - 2b^4$
38. $4c^5 + 32c^2$

Lesson 3-5

Solve each polynomial equation by factoring.

39. $2x^3 + 3x^2 - 8x - 12 = 0$
40. $-3x^3 + 30x^2 + 5x - 50 = 0$

Identify the roots of each equation. State the multiplicity of each root.

41. $x^3 + 15x^2 + 75x + 125 = 0$
42. $x^3 - 2x^2 - 32x + 96 = 0$
43. $8x^3 - 12x^2 + 6x - 1 = 0$
44. $4x^3 + 16x^2 - 25x - 100 = 0$

Identify all of the real roots of each equation.

45. $2x^4 - x^3 - 14x^2 - 5x + 6 = 0$
46. $6x^3 - 11x^2 - 19x - 6 = 0$

Lesson 3-6

Write the simplest polynomial function with the given zeros.

47. $-1, 1, 4$ **48.** $-3, \frac{1}{2}, \frac{1}{3}$ **49.** $-3, 1, \frac{2}{3}$ **50.** $-5, 1, 2$

Solve each equation by finding all roots.

51. $x^4 - 5x^3 + 15x^2 - 45x + 54 = 0$ **52.** $2x^4 + 5x^3 - 10x^2 + 10x + 8 = 0$

Write the simplest polynomial function with the given zeros.

53. $3, \sqrt{5}$ **54.** $1 + i, 2$ **55.** $-2, 2i$ **56.** $1, \sqrt{2}, i$

Lesson 3-7

Identify the leading coefficient, degree, and end behavior.

57. $P(x) = 7x^3 - 12x^2 + 9x - 10$ **58.** $Q(x) = -3x^5 + 8x^4 - 16x + 1$

Identify whether the function graphed has an odd or even degree and a positive or negative leading coefficient.

59.

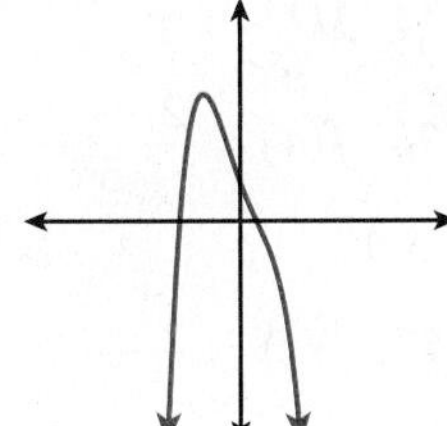

60.

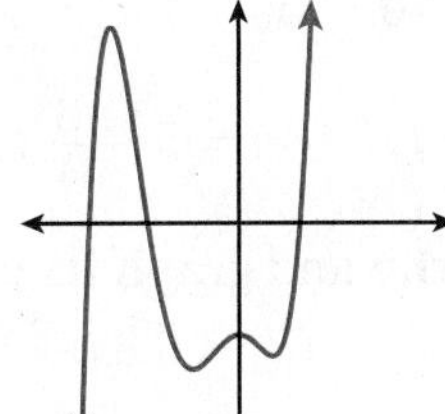

61.

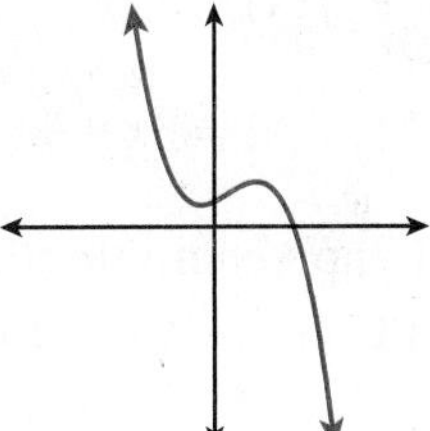

Graph each function.

62. $Q(x) = -4x^3 - 12x^2 + x + 3$ **63.** $R(x) = 2x^4 + x^3 - 19x^2 - 9x + 9$

Graph each function on a calculator, and estimate the local maxima and minima.

64. $S(x) = -2x^4 + x^3 + 5x^2 + 6$ **65.** $T(x) = x^3 + 5x^2 + 3x + 1$

Lesson 3-8

For $f(x) = 2x^3 - 3$, write the rule for each function and sketch the graph.

66. $g(x) = f(x) + 6$ **67.** $h(x) = f(x - 2)$ **68.** $j(x) = f(-x)$ **69.** $k(x) = \frac{1}{2}f(x)$

Let $f(x) = -3x^4 + 2x^2 - 7x + 10$. Write a function g that performs each transformation.

70. Reflect $f(x)$ across the y-axis. **71.** Reflect $f(x)$ across the x-axis.

Let $f(x) = x^3 - 7x^2 + 5$. Graph f and g on the same coordinate plane. Describe g as a transformation of f.

72. $g(x) = f(x + 4)$ **73.** $g(x) = -2f(x)$ **74.** $g(x) = f(-x) - 3$

Write a function that transforms $f(x) = 3x^3 - 5x^2 + x + 1$ in each of the following ways. Support your solution by using a graphing calculator.

75. Stretch vertically by a factor of 3 and move 1 unit to the right.

76. Reflect across the y-axis and move 1 unit down.

Lesson 3-9

Use finite differences to determine the degree of the polynomial that best describes the data.

77.

x	−2	−1	0	1	2	3
y	−24	−4	6	12	20	36

78.

x	−2	−1	0	1	2	3
y	−27	0	9	12	69	288

Extra Practice Chapter 4 ▪ Skills Practice

Lesson 4-1

Tell whether the function shows growth or decay. Then graph.

1. $f(x) = 12(2.4)^x$
2. $f(x) = 20\left(\frac{4}{5}\right)^x$
3. $f(x) = 0.25(5)^x$

Explain whether each function is exponential.

4. $f(x) = 4x^9$
5. $f(x) = 0.6^x$
6. $f(x) = 10(0)^x$

Lesson 4-2

Graph the relation and connect the points. Then graph the inverse. Identify the domain and range of each relation.

7.

x	1	2	3	4
y	−1	0	2	4

8.

x	−3	−1	2	4
y	−3	−1	−1	−3

Use inverse operations to write the inverse of each function.

9. $f(x) = 15x$
10. $f(x) = x + 9$
11. $f(x) = \frac{x}{7}$
12. $f(x) = 3x + 2$
13. $f(x) = 5 - \frac{3}{4}x$
14. $f(x) = \frac{2x+1}{5}$

Graph each function. Then write and graph its inverse.

15. $f(x) = 2x + 4$
16. $f(x) = 0.8x + 1$
17. $f(x) = \frac{4x-5}{3}$

Lesson 4-3

Write each exponential equation in logarithmic form.

18. $3^5 = 243$
19. $51^0 = 1$
20. $16^{1.5} = 64$
21. $7^x = 343$

Write each logarithmic equation in exponential form.

22. $\log_{64}512 = 1.5$
23. $\log_2 0.125 = -3$
24. $\log_4 x = 70$
25. $\log_x 12 = 3$

Evaluate by using mental math.

26. $\log_{10}1000$
27. $\log_5 0.2$
28. $\log_{0.5}0.125$
29. $\log_{1.1}1.21$

Use the given *x*-values to graph each function. Then graph its inverse. Describe the domain and range of the inverse function.

30. $f(x) = 4^x$; $x = -2, -1, 0, 1, 2$
31. $f(x) = 0.2^x$; $x = -2, -1, 0, 1, 2$

Lesson 4-4

Express as a single logarithm. Simplify, if possible.

32. $\log_2 10 + \log_2 12.8$
33. $\log_4 8 + \log_4 2$
34. $\log_5 1.25 + \log_5 4$
35. $\log_6 144 - \log_6 4$
36. $\log 10{,}000 - \log 100$
37. $\log_8 8 - \log_8 1$

Simplify, if possible.

38. $\log_8 64^4$
39. $\log_7 49^5$
40. $\log_9 1^4$
41. $\log_3 3^{5x+8}$
42. $4^{\log_4 12}$
43. $\log_{1.4}1.4^5$

Evaluate.

44. $\log_4 256$
45. $\log_4\left(\frac{1}{64}\right)$
46. $\log_3 7$
47. $\log_4 13$

Lesson 4-5

Solve and check.

48. $3^{x+1} = 9^4$ **49.** $32^{x-2} = 8^x$ **50.** $9^x = 12$ **51.** $3.5^{2x-1} = 15$

Solve.

52. $\log_6(4x - 9) = \log_6(x)$ **53.** $\log_7(10x + 13) = 3$ **54.** $\log(20x) - \log 4 = 2$

55. $\log_9 x^3 = 8$ **56.** $\log x + \log(2x - 1) = 1$ **57.** $\log_3\left(\frac{2}{x}\right) + 2 = 0$

Use a table and a graph to solve.

58. $3^{4x-3} = 243$ **59.** $3^x 4^x \geq 1728$ **60.** $\log x^3 = x - 94$ **61.** $3\log x^2 < 6$

Lesson 4-6

Graph.

62. $f(x) = e^x - 1$ **63.** $f(x) = -2e^x + 3$ **64.** $f(x) = 2 - e^{-x}$ **65.** $f(x) = 1.5e^{x+1}$

Simplify.

66. $\ln e^{20}$ **67.** $\ln e^{2x+10}$ **68.** $e^{\ln 5x^2}$ **69.** $e^{2\ln 2x}$

Lesson 4-7

Make a table of values and graph each function. Describe the asymptote, the domain, and the range. Tell how the graph is transformed from the graph of $f(x) = 4^x$.

70. $g(x) = 4^x - 2$ **71.** $h(x) = 4^{x+2}$ **72.** $j(x) = 4^{x-1} - 4$

Graph each exponential function. Find the y-intercept, the asymptote, the domain, and the range. Describe how the graph is transformed from the graph of its parent function.

73. $g(x) = -\frac{1}{2}(3^x)$ **74.** $h(x) = 3(2^{-x})$ **75.** $j(x) = 5e^{x+1}$

Graph each logarithmic function. Find the asymptote. Then describe how the graph is transformed from the graph of its parent function.

76. $g(x) = -4\log x$ **77.** $h(x) = 3\ln(3 - x)$ **78.** $j(x) = \ln(0.5x) - 3$

Write each transformed function by using the given parent function and the indicated transformations.

79. The parent function $f(x) = 6^x$ is horizontally stretched by a factor of 3 and translated 4 units to the left.

80. The parent function $f(x) = \log x$ is vertically compressed by a factor of $\frac{1}{5}$, reflected across the y-axis, and translated 10 units down.

Lesson 4-8

Determine whether f is an exponential function of x. If so, find the constant ratio.

81.

x	−2	−1	1	2	3
y	0.4	2	10	50	250

82.

x	−2	−1	0	1	2
y	−17	−2	13	28	43

83.

x	−2	−1	0	1	2
y	4	2	1	0.5	0.25

84.

x	−2	−1	0	1	2
y	−6	1	12	37	54

Extra Practice Chapter 5 ■ Skills Practice

Lesson 5-1

Given: y varies directly as x. Write and graph each direct variation function.

1. $y = 8$ when $x = 2$
2. $y = 21$ when $x = 3$
3. $y = 4$ when $x = 2.5$

Given: y varies inversely as x. Write and graph each inverse variation function.

4. $y = 4$ when $x = 2$
5. $y = 4$ when $x = \frac{1}{2}$
6. $y = \frac{3}{5}$ when $x = 10$

Determine whether each data set represents a direct variation, an inverse variation, or neither.

7.

x	1	3	6
y	2.5	7.5	15

8.

x	2	4	8
y	6	10	18

9.

x	2	8	20
y	5	1.25	0.5

Lesson 5-2

Simplify. Identify any x-values for which the expression is undefined.

10. $\dfrac{6x^3}{27x^2 + 12x}$
11. $\dfrac{x^2 - x - 2}{3x - 6}$
12. $\dfrac{-x^2 + 16}{-x^2 - 9x - 20}$

Multiply or divide. Assume that all expressions are defined.

13. $\dfrac{4xy^3}{5x^2} \cdot \dfrac{20x^3y^2}{-16xy^7}$
14. $\dfrac{x^2 - 9}{2x + 10} \cdot \dfrac{x + 5}{x - 3}$
15. $\dfrac{x - 4}{2x^2} \cdot \dfrac{x}{x^2 - x - 12}$
16. $\dfrac{3x^3}{4x + 4} \div \dfrac{9x}{x + 1}$
17. $\dfrac{12x^3y^6}{9xy} \div \dfrac{6y^2}{3x}$
18. $\dfrac{x^2 - 16}{x^2 + 4x + 3} \div \dfrac{x - 4}{x + 1}$

Lesson 5-3

Find the least common multiple for each pair.

19. $6x^3y$ and $2xy^2$
20. $x^2 + 5x$ and $x^2 - 25$
21. $x^2 - 3x - 18$ and $x^2 - 5x - 6$

Add or subtract. Identify any x-values for which the expression is undefined.

22. $\dfrac{x + 9}{2x + 1} + \dfrac{3x + 6}{2x + 1}$
23. $\dfrac{2}{x + 3} + \dfrac{4x}{x^2 - 9}$
24. $\dfrac{1}{x^2 + 6x + 8} + \dfrac{1}{x^2 - 6x - 16}$
25. $\dfrac{x - 6}{x + 5} - \dfrac{8x + 7}{x + 5}$
26. $\dfrac{x}{x + 1} - \dfrac{3}{x + 4}$
27. $\dfrac{7}{x - 9} - \dfrac{2x - 6}{x^2 - 13x + 36}$

Simplify. Assume that all expressions are defined.

28. $\dfrac{\frac{3x}{3x + 21}}{\frac{9x^2}{x + 7}}$
29. $\dfrac{\frac{x}{x - 1}}{\frac{10x^2}{-4x + 4}}$
30. $\dfrac{\frac{1}{x - 2}}{\frac{x + 3}{x^2 - 4}}$

Lesson 5-4

Using the graph of $f(x) = \frac{1}{x}$ as a guide, describe the transformation and graph each function.

31. $g(x) = \dfrac{1}{x - 4}$
32. $g(x) = \dfrac{1}{x} + 6$
33. $g(x) = \dfrac{1}{x + 2} - 5$

Identify the zeros and asymptotes of each function. Then graph.

34. $f(x) = \dfrac{x^2 - 5x - 24}{2x + 1}$
35. $f(x) = \dfrac{2x^2 - 3x - 2}{x - 4}$
36. $f(x) = \dfrac{-3x^2 + 8x - 4}{x^2 - 25}$

Identify holes in the graph of each function. Then graph.

37. $f(x) = \dfrac{x^2 - 4x - 21}{x + 3}$
38. $f(x) = \dfrac{x^2 - 4x - 5}{x^2 - 25}$
39. $f(x) = \dfrac{x^2 - 3x}{4x - 12}$

Lesson 5-5

Solve each equation.

40. $12 + \frac{2}{3x} = 6$

41. $x - \frac{1}{x} = \frac{35}{x}$

42. $\frac{x}{x+1} + \frac{x}{4} = \frac{3x}{4x+4}$

43. $\frac{x-1}{x-4} = \frac{x+6}{x}$

44. $\frac{6x}{x+5} = \frac{2x-20}{x+5}$

45. $\frac{4}{x-4} = \frac{-x}{x-4} + \frac{x}{2}$

Solve each inequality by using a graph and a table.

46. $\frac{2x+1}{x} \geq 3$

47. $\frac{4}{x+3} < 2$

48. $\frac{x-4}{2x} \geq 2$

Solve each inequality algebraically.

49. $\frac{3}{x+2} \leq 1$

50. $\frac{10}{x-2} < 2$

51. $\frac{15}{x+3} \leq 1$

Lesson 5-6

Simplify each expression. Assume all variables are positive.

52. $\sqrt[3]{343x^9}$

53. $\sqrt[5]{\frac{x^5}{32}}$

54. $\sqrt[4]{\frac{x^8y^4}{10}}$

Write each expression in radical form, and simplify.

55. $81^{\frac{3}{2}}$

56. $243^{\frac{2}{5}}$

57. $(-8)^{\frac{4}{3}}$

Write each expression using rational exponents.

58. $\sqrt[5]{10^2}$

59. $\sqrt[4]{17^3}$

60. $\left(\sqrt[5]{8}\right)^3$

Simplify each expression.

61. $8^{\frac{1}{2}} \cdot 8^{\frac{5}{2}}$

62. $\frac{4^{\frac{7}{2}}}{4^{\frac{1}{2}}}$

63. $\left(100^{\frac{1}{2}}\right)^3$

Lesson 5-7

Graph each function, and identify its domain and range.

64. $f(x) = \sqrt{x-4} + 1$

65. $f(x) = -\frac{1}{2}\sqrt{x}$

66. $f(x) = 2\sqrt[3]{x+2}$

Using the graph of $f(x) = \sqrt{x}$ as a guide, describe the transformation and graph each function.

67. $g(x) = \sqrt{x-8}$

68. $g(x) = -6\sqrt{x}$

69. $g(x) = \frac{1}{3}\sqrt{x} + 2$

Graph each inequality.

70. $y \geq \sqrt{x+2} - 3$

71. $y < 2\sqrt{-x}$

72. $y > -4\sqrt[3]{x} + 4$

Lesson 5-8

Solve each equation.

73. $\sqrt{2x+10} = 10$

74. $\sqrt{4x+4} = 2\sqrt{4x-9}$

75. $3\sqrt[3]{x} = \sqrt[3]{7x+40}$

76. $\sqrt{2x+48} = x$

77. $2x + 5 = \sqrt{4x+10}$

78. $x + 6 = \sqrt{4x+21}$

79. $(3x-5)^{\frac{1}{2}} = 4$

80. $(x-4)^{\frac{1}{3}} = -2$

81. $(8x-7)^{\frac{1}{2}} = x$

Solve each inequality.

82. $\sqrt{x-7} < 3$

83. $\sqrt{3x+1} + 2 \leq 6$

84. $\sqrt{2x-3} > 5$

Extra Practice Chapter 6 ■ Skills Practice

Lesson 6-1

Match each situation to its corresponding graph. Sketch a possible graph of the situation if the situation does not match any of the given graphs.

Graph A

Graph B

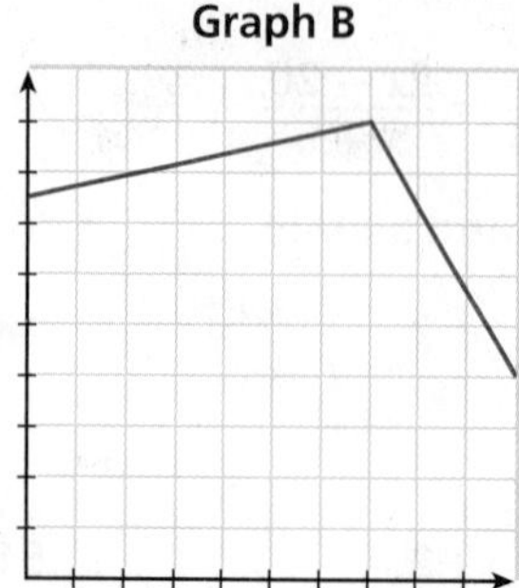

Graph C

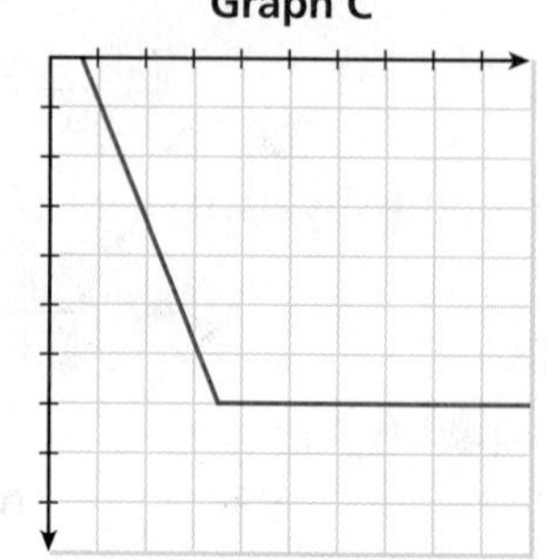

Graph D

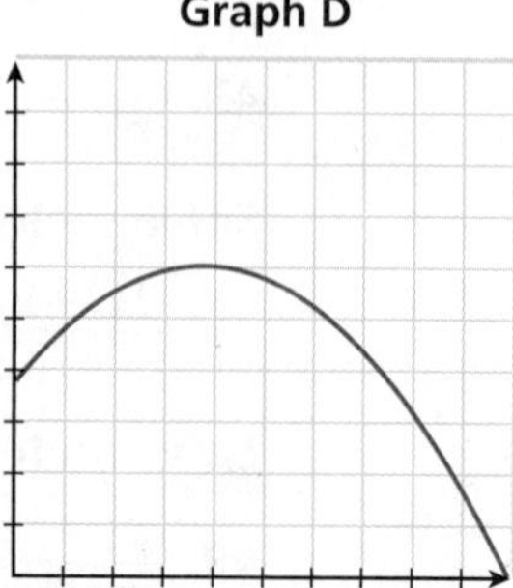

1. A state senator's high approval rating is rising steadily but then drops sharply after a scandal.
2. The value of an antique chair increases steadily.
3. Sales of a valuable stock dip and then recover.
4. A scuba diver descends to 60 ft below sea level and swims around at that depth.

Lesson 6-2

Compare the end behavior for each pair of functions.

5. $y = -3x^2 + 10x$ and $y = -3(2)^x$

6. $f(x) = e^{-x}$ and $g(x) = x^5 + 1$

7. Larry charges $40 per hour for tutoring. Tutor-Express charges as shown in the table. For how many hours will the costs be the same?

Tutor-Express				
Tutoring (h)	1	2	3	4
Cost ($)	80	110	140	170

Lesson 6-3

Evaluate each piecewise function for $x = -2$ and $x = 5$.

8. $f(x) = \begin{cases} 10 & \text{if } x \le -4 \\ 7 & \text{if } -4 < x \le 2 \\ 3 & \text{if } x > 2 \end{cases}$

9. $g(x) = \begin{cases} x + 2 & \text{if } x < 0 \\ 4 - x & \text{if } x \ge 0 \end{cases}$

10. $h(x) = \begin{cases} x^2 - 3 & \text{if } x \le 2 \\ x + 1 & \text{if } x > 2 \end{cases}$

Lesson 6-4

Graph each function.

11. $f(x) = \begin{cases} 4 & \text{if } x < -1 \\ -1 & \text{if } x \ge -1 \end{cases}$

12. $g(x) = \begin{cases} 2x - 4 & \text{if } x \le 2 \\ -2x + 2 & \text{if } x > 2 \end{cases}$

13. $h(x) = \begin{cases} 2 & \text{if } x < 3 \\ x^2 - 7 & \text{if } x \ge 3 \end{cases}$

Given $f(x) = \begin{cases} 2x - 2 & \text{if } x < 1 \\ -3x & \text{if } x \ge 1 \end{cases}$, write the rule for each function.

14. $g(x)$, a vertical stretch by a factor of 3

15. $h(x)$, a reflection across the y-axis

Identify the x- and y-intercepts of $f(x)$. Without graphing $g(x)$, identify its x- and y-intercepts.

16. $f(x) = -3x + 6$ and $g(x) = f(-2x)$

17. $f(x) = (x - 3)^2$ and $g(x) = -2f(x)$

Lesson 6-5

Given $f(x)$, graph $g(x)$.

18. $f(x) = \frac{1}{2}x - 4$ and $g(x) = f(-x) + 2$
19. $f(x) = |x + 2|$ and $g(x) = \frac{1}{2}f(x - 1) - 4$

Given $f(x) = -2x + 5$ and $g(x) = 4x^2 - 11$, find each function.

20. $(f + g)(x)$
21. $(f - g)(x)$
22. $(g - f)(x)$

Given $f(x) = x - 3$ and $g(x) = x^2 + 3x - 18$, find each function.

23. $(fg)(x)$
24. $\left(\frac{f}{g}\right)(x)$
25. $\left(\frac{g}{f}\right)(x)$

Given $f(x) = \frac{1}{2}x + 5$ and $g(x) = -2x^2$, find each value.

26. $f(g(2))$
27. $g(f(2))$
28. $g(f(-6))$

Given $f(x) = \sqrt{x}$, $g(x) = 2x + 3$, and $h(x) = x^2 + 20$, write each composite function. State the domain of each.

29. $f(g(x))$
30. $g(f(x))$
31. $g(h(x))$

Lesson 6-6

Use the horizontal-line test to determine whether the inverse of each relation is a function.

32.

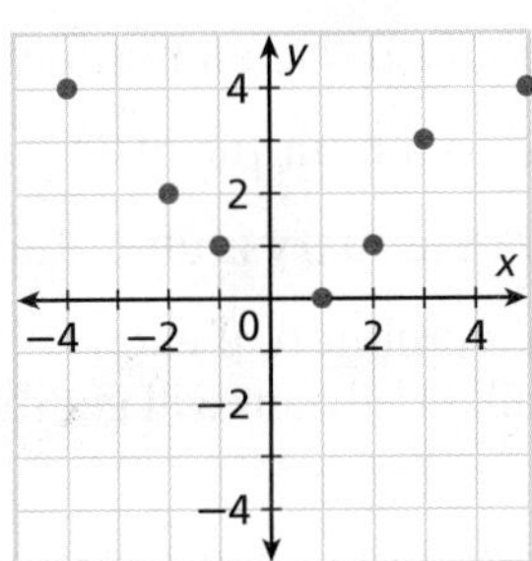

33.

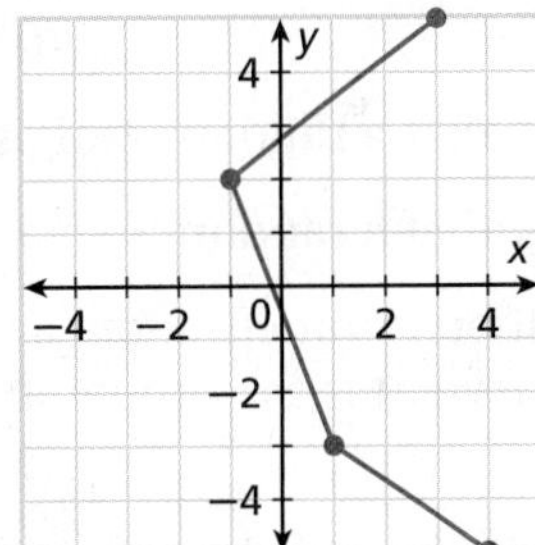

34.

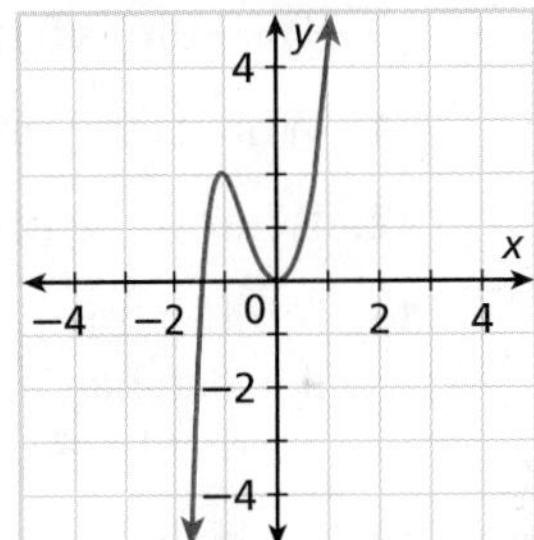

Find the inverse of each function. Determine whether the inverse is a function, and state its domain and range.

35. $f(x) = \frac{1}{2}x - 7$
36. $g(x) = 10 - x^2$
37. $h(x) = \frac{3}{4 + x}$

Determine by composition whether each pair of functions are inverses.

38. $f(x) = \frac{3}{4}x^2$ and $g(x) = \sqrt{\frac{4}{3}x}$ for $x \geq 0$
39. $f(x) = \frac{12x + 1}{5}$ and $g(x) = \frac{5}{12x - 1}$

Lesson 6-7

Use constant differences or ratios to determine which parent function would best model the given data set.

40.

x	y
1	6
3	−12
5	−30
7	−48
9	−66

41.

x	y
2	−3
4	6
6	21
8	42
10	69

42.

x	y
0	0.5
1	2
2	8
3	32
4	128

Extra Practice Chapter 7 ■ Skills Practice

Lesson 7-1

1. When text messaging on a telephone, pressing a 3 types D, E, F, or 3. Pressing a 7 types P, Q, R, S, or 7. How many messages are possible by pressing a 3, a 7, and then a 3?

2. At a company, each employee has an ID that consists of 2 digits followed by a letter. The letters Q and X are not used. How many employee IDs are possible?

3. If there are 8 finalists in a talent show, how many ways can a winner and a runner-up be chosen?

4. Jim's soccer team has 18 members. How many ways can the coach choose a right forward, a center forward, and a left forward?

5. Erin's health club offers 7 types of aerobics classes. She plans to attend 4 classes this week. How many ways can she choose 4 classes that are all different?

6. Francesca can take 4 of her 14 books on a trip. How many ways can she choose them?

Lesson 7-2

Two number cubes are rolled. Find each probability.

7. Both cubes roll the same number.

8. The sum is greater than 8.

9. The sum is 8 or less.

10. Both cubes roll even numbers.

11. What is the probability that a random 2-digit number is a multiple of 7?

12. What is the probability that a randomly selected day in January is after the 20th?

13. A mother is making different lunches for each of her 3 children. If each child grabs a lunch bag at random, what is the probability that all 3 children will get the correct bag?

14. A teacher writes MATHEMATICS on a piece of paper and then cuts out each letter and puts them all in a bag. She will draw two letters at random. What is the probability that she will select an M and an A?

The shaded region is vertically centered in the flag. Find each probability.

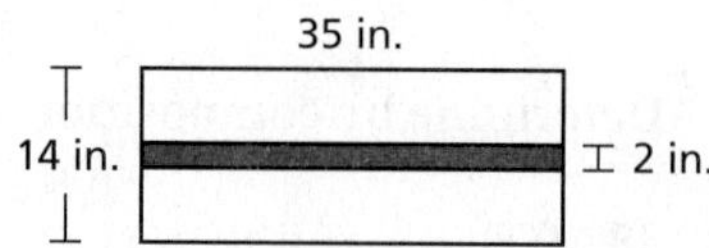

15. a random point inside the flag is in the shaded region

16. a random point inside the flag is above the shaded region

A marble is drawn from a bag and then its color is recorded in the table.

17. Find the experimental probability of drawing a blue marble.

18. Find the experimental probability of drawing a pink or a yellow marble.

Marble Drawing Experiment

Color	Times Drawn
Pink	12
Green	10
Blue	16
Yellow	12

Lesson 7-3

Find each probability.

19. rolling a number greater than or equal to 4 on a number cube twice in a row
20. drawing a face card from a deck, replacing it, and drawing a number card
21. Two number cubes are rolled—one blue and one yellow. Find the probability that the yellow cube is even, and the sum is 7. Explain why the events are dependent.

The table shows the results of a schoolwide survey on the homecoming dance. Find each probability.

Homecoming Dance Location Survey		
	Girls	Boys
Gymnasium	67	58
Cafeteria	53	37

22. A student who prefers the cafeteria is a girl.
23. A surveyed student is male and prefers the gymnasium.

A bag contains 18 beads—5 blue, 6 yellow, and 7 red. Determine whether the events are independent or dependent. Find the indicated probability.

24. selecting a yellow and then a blue bead when they are chosen with replacement
25. selecting a yellow and then a blue bead when they are chosen without replacement

Lesson 7-4

The table shows the side dish chosen with the lunch plate and the supper plate at a diner on one day.

	Salad	Fries	Broccoli	Total
Lunch	26	47	9	82
Supper	42	29	34	105
Total	68	76	43	187

26. Make a table of the joint and marginal relative frequencies. Round to the nearest hundredth where appropriate.
27. If you are given that a customer ordered a lunch plate, what is the probability that fries were chosen as the side dish?
28. If you are given that a customer ordered broccoli with the meal plate, what is the probability that it was the supper plate?

Lesson 7-5

29. A table was chosen at random in the cafeteria, and there were 2 freshmen, 5 sophomores, 7 juniors, and 2 seniors eating there. A student is chosen at random from the table. What is the probability of choosing a freshman or a senior?

The numbers 1–20 are written on cards and placed in a bag. Find each probability.

30. choosing a number less than 10 or choosing a multiple of 5
31. choosing 20 or choosing an odd number
32. In an apartment building with 50 residents, 16 residents have cats, 28 residents are students, and 9 of the students have cats. What is the probability that a resident is a student or has a cat?
33. There are 8 couples in a dance competition, and each of the 3 judges must pick the couple they believe should win. Suppose the judges picked randomly. What is the probability that at least 2 judges picked the same couple?

Lesson **8-1**

Find the mean, median, and mode of each data set.

1. $\{3, 7, 8, 2, 8, 4\}$
2. $\{12, 9, 8, 15, 16, 12, 13\}$
3. $\{7, 31, 20, 12, 18\}$
4. Find the expected value of the raffle prize.

Raffle Prizes				
Value	$0	$5	$20	$200
Probability	0.76	0.16	0.06	0.02

Make a box-and-whisker plot of the data. Find the interquartile range.

5. $\{3, 5, 7, 6, 5, 2, 3\}$
6. $\{12, 15, 18, 10, 9, 15, 16\}$

Find the variance and standard deviation.

7. $\{8, 12, 10, 6, 9\}$
8. $\{14, 15, 10, 8, 12, 13\}$
9. $\{6, 33, 37, 28, 1\}$

Lesson **8-2**

Determine whether the survey is likely to be representative of the population.

10. A student asks the members of the math team whether math classes should be required for all four years of high school.
11. A state sends out surveys to random city governments about the city's parking plans.
12. A website asks customers if they prefer to read news online or in a print magazine.
13. In a survey of 100 town residents, 63 said they prefer the library's new hours. If you were able to survey all 23,000 residents of the town, how many would you expect to prefer the library's new hours?

Lesson **8-3**

Determine whether each situation is an experiment or an observational study.

14. A farmer wants to know if a new fertilizer affects the weight of the fruit produced by strawberry plants. She applies the fertilizer to 10 rows of plants and does not apply the fertilizer to 10 other rows of plants.
15. A researcher compares incomes of people who live in rural areas with incomes of people who live in large cities.

Explain whether each research topic is best addressed through an experiment or an observational study. Then explain how you would set up the experiment or the observational study.

16. Does living on a farm reduce allergies?
17. Does reducing the fat in a particular recipe make it less appealing?

Lesson **8-4**

To test the redesign of its Web site, an online bookseller assembled users and randomly divided them into two groups. One group used the new Web site to make an online purchase and the other group used the old website to do the same transaction. The times for the transactions are shown below.

Time to Complete (minutes)

New Web Site	Old Web Site
3, 5, 6.5, 4, 7, 3, 4, 5, 5.5, 3.5	6, 8, 9, 4.5, 10, 6, 5, 8, 6.5, 6

18. State the null hypothesis.
19. Compare the results of the two groups. Does the company have enough evidence to reject the null hypothesis?
20. A tire manufacturer claims that one brand of tires will last 50,000 miles. In a random sample of 100 tires, the mean was 45,000 miles with a standard deviation of 7000 miles. Is there enough evidence to reject this claim?

Lesson 8-5

Classify each sample.

21. A store owner in a mall wants to determine whether a new brand of shoes will sell in her store. She surveys random people in the mall on the weekend.

22. A city councilor wants to know how residents in the city will react to a new policy. He surveys residents by mailing a random sample of voters.

23. The director of the student theater group wants to know which of three plays will have the largest student audience. He randomly chooses 20 freshman, 20 sophomores, 20 juniors, and 20 seniors in the hall between classes.

Determine whether the survey clearly projects the winner. Explain your response.

24. A polling company claims that 38% of voters will vote for Tucci in an election, and that 64% will vote for Gonzales. The margin of error is ±9%.

25. A website will have users vote for the cutest of three dog photos. A survey shows that 53% will vote for Photo 1, and 47% will vote for Photo 3. The margin of error is ±5%.

Lesson 8-6

Use the Binomial Theorem to expand each binomial.

26. $(x + 4)^5$ **27.** $(2x - 3)^4$ **28.** $(2a + 7b)^3$

29. Patrick takes a multiple-choice quiz that has 4 questions. There are 5 answer choices for each question. What is the probability that he will get at least 2 answers correct by guessing?

Lesson 8-7

Scores on a test are normally distributed with a mean of 82 and a standard deviation of 6. Use the table below to find the probability of a randomly selected student having the given score.

z	−2.5	−2	−1.5	−1	−0.5	0	0.5	1	1.5	2	2.5
Probability	0.01	0.02	0.07	0.16	0.31	0.5	0.69	0.84	0.93	0.98	0.99

30. below 82 **31.** above 94 **32.** between 70 and 79

For a normally distributed random variable x with $\mu = 240$ and $\sigma = 12$, find each probability.

33. $x < 216$ **34.** $228 < x < 252$ **35.** $x < 222$ or $x > 270$

Lesson 8-8

What is the expected value of rolling the six-sided number cube as shown in the net below?

36.

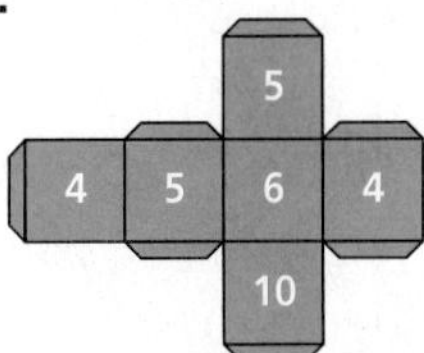

37.

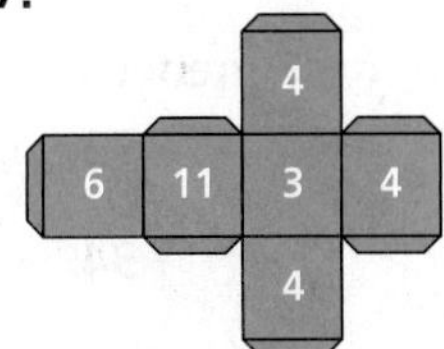

38.

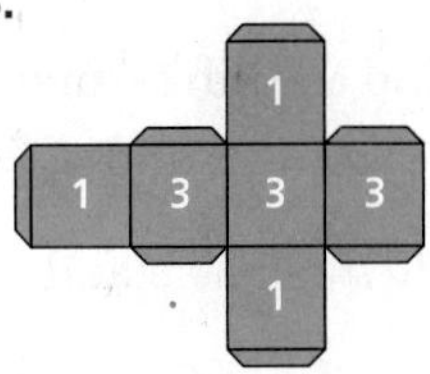

39. You roll the number cubes from Exercises 37 and 38. Find the expected value for the sum.

Extra Practice Chapter 9 ■ Skills Practice

Lesson 9-1

Find the first 5 terms of each sequence.

1. $a_1 = 16, a_n = 0.25a_{n-1}$
2. $a_1 = -1, a_n = 3a_{n-1} + 1$
3. $a_1 = 2, a_2 = 5, a_n = 2a_{n-1} + a_{n-2}$
4. $a_n = 5(n - 1)$
5. $a_n = 3^n - 4$
6. $a_n = (n + 2)^2$

Write a possible explicit rule for the *n*th term of each sequence.

7. 5, 1, −3, −7, −11, ...
8. 7, 9, 13, 21, 37, ...
9. $\frac{3}{4}, \frac{3}{2}, \frac{9}{4}, 3, \frac{15}{4}, \ldots$
10. $60, 30, 15, \frac{15}{2}, \ldots$

Lesson 9-2

Write each series in summation notation.

11. $\frac{1}{2} + \frac{1}{4} + \frac{1}{6} + \frac{1}{8} + \frac{1}{10}$
12. $0 + 3 + 8 + 15 + 24 + 35$
13. $50 + 41 + 32 + 23 + 14 + 5$
14. $-4 - 2 + 0 + 2 + 4$

Expand each series and evaluate.

15. $\sum_{k=1}^{5}(12k - 7)$
16. $\sum_{k=1}^{4}\frac{(2k)^2}{2}$
17. $\sum_{k=1}^{5}\frac{k - 2}{k + 1}$

Evaluate each series.

18. $\sum_{k=1}^{55}k$
19. $\sum_{k=15}^{25}12$
20. $\sum_{k=1}^{18}k^2$

Lesson 9-3

Determine whether each sequence could be arithmetic. If so, find the common difference and the next term.

21. 15.5, 28, 40.5, 53, 65.5, ...
22. 9.67, 9.34, 9.01, 8.68, ...
23. $\frac{1}{2}, 2, \frac{9}{2}, 8, \frac{25}{2}, \ldots$
24. 2, 4, 6, 4, 2, ...

Find the 8th term of each arithmetic sequence.

25. 4.5, 6, 7.5, 9, 10.5, ...
26. 74, 68, 62, 56, 50, ...
27. $5, 5\frac{2}{5}, 5\frac{4}{5}, 6\frac{1}{5}, 6\frac{3}{5}, \ldots$

Find the missing terms in each arithmetic sequence.

28. 13, ■, ■, 37, ...
29. 9.5, ■, ■, ■, −0.5, ...
30. 10, ■, ■, ■, 26, ...

Find the 9th term of each arithmetic sequence.

31. $a_3 = 29$ and $a_6 = 56$
32. $a_4 = 16$ and $a_7 = -2$
33. $a_{10} = 30.5$ and $a_{14} = 38.5$
34. $a_5 = 3\frac{1}{3}$ and $a_7 = 2\frac{2}{3}$

Find the indicated sum for each arithmetic series.

35. S_{12} for 18, 21, 24, 27, 30, ...
36. S_{15} for 20, 18.5, 17, 15.5, 14, ...
37. $\sum_{k=1}^{9}(5k + 8)$
38. $\sum_{k=1}^{20}(-2.75k + 15)$

Lesson 9-4

Determine whether each sequence could be geometric or arithmetic. If possible, find the common ratio or difference.

39. 7, 14, 28, 56, 112, ...

40. 7, 14, 21, 28, 35, ...

41. $\frac{2}{3}, 1\frac{1}{3}, 2\frac{2}{3}, 5\frac{1}{3}, 10\frac{2}{3}, \ldots$

42. 25.5, 31, 36.5, 42, 47.5, ...

43. −3, 6, 21, 42, 69, ...

44. $4, 1, \frac{1}{4}, \frac{1}{16}, \frac{1}{64}, \ldots$

Find the 7th term of each geometric sequence.

45. 5, 10, 20, 40, 80, ...

46. 200, 100, 50, 25, 12.5, ...

47. −1, 3, −9, 27, −81, ...

48. 7, 70, 700, 7000, ...

Find the 8th term of the geometric sequence with the given terms.

49. $a_4 = 4$, $a_5 = 8$

50. $a_4 = 16$, $a_6 = 256$

51. $a_3 = 125$, $a_5 = 5$

52. $a_4 = 4$, $a_7 = 864$

Find the geometric mean of each pair of numbers.

53. 4 and 36

54. $\frac{1}{4}$ and $\frac{1}{9}$

55. 72 and 288

56. 10 and 20

Find the indicated sum for each geometric series.

57. S_8 for 5, −15, 45, −135, ...

58. S_6 for $\frac{3}{4}$, 3, 12, 48, ...

59. $\sum_{k=1}^{5} 12(2)^{k-1}$

60. $\sum_{k=1}^{7} (-4)^{k-1}$

Lesson 9-5

Determine whether each geometric series converges or diverges.

61. $\frac{5}{2}, \frac{5}{8}, \frac{5}{32}, \frac{5}{128}, \ldots$

62. 0.1, 0.5, 2.5, 12.5, 62.5, ...

63. 1, 1.3, 1.69, 2.197, 2.8561, ...

64. 1, 0.7, 0.49, 0.343, 0.2401, ...

Find the sum of each infinite geometric series, if it exists.

65. 1.1, 1.21, 1.331, 1.4641, ...

66. 1.8, 1.62, 1.458, 1.3122, ...

67. 7, 0.7, 0.07, 0.007, ...

68. $\sum_{k=1}^{\infty} \frac{1}{2}\left(\frac{3}{2}\right)^k$

69. $\sum_{k=1}^{\infty} 8\left(\frac{4}{10}\right)^k$

70. $\sum_{k=1}^{\infty} 100(0.95)^k$

Write each repeating decimal as a fraction in simplest form.

71. $0.\overline{4}$

72. $0.\overline{26}$

73. $0.\overline{892}$

Identify a counterexample to disprove each statement, where the variable is a real number.

74. $4a^3 \geq 8a^2$

75. $5^{2n} \geq 5^n$

76. $x^2 > (x-1)^2$

77. $|x+1| \geq |x|$

Lesson 10-1

Find the value of the sine, cosine, and tangent functions for θ.

1.

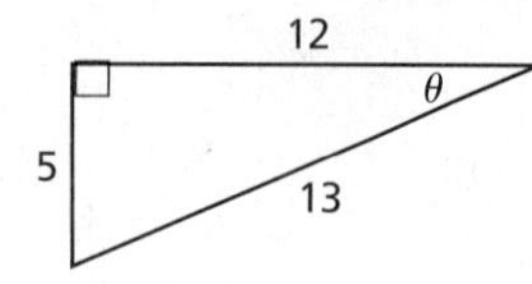

2.

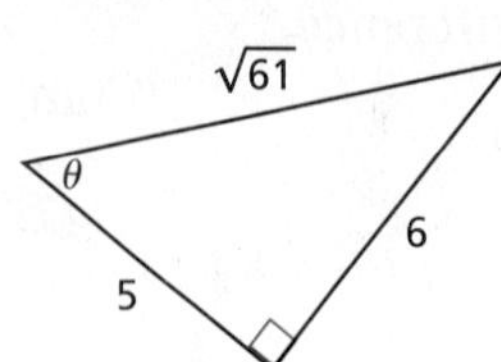

3.

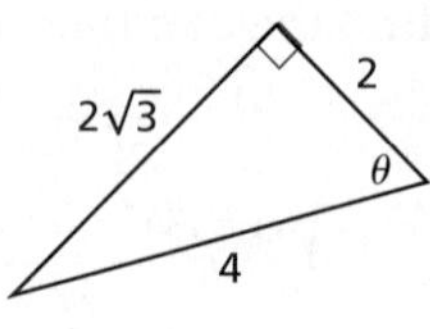

Use a trigonometric function to find the value of x.

4.

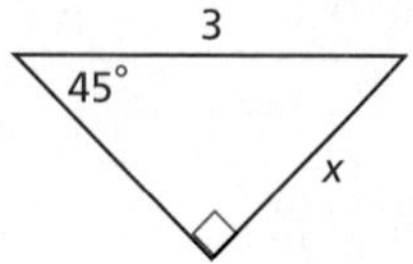

5.

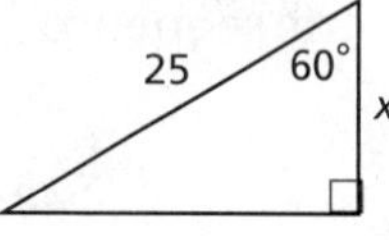

6.

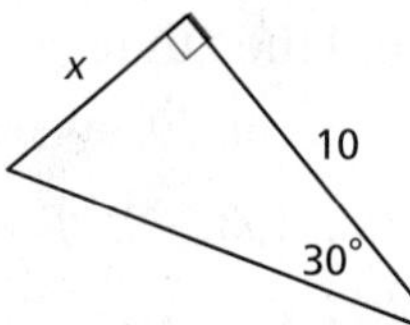

Find the values of the six trigonometric functions for θ.

7.

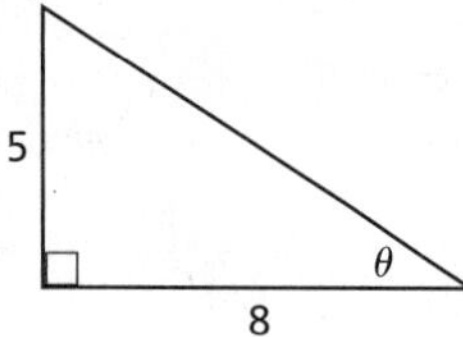

8.

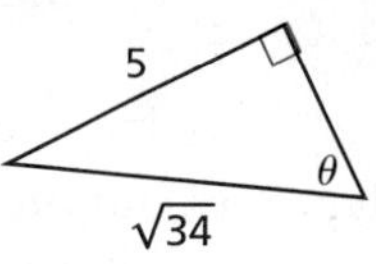

9.

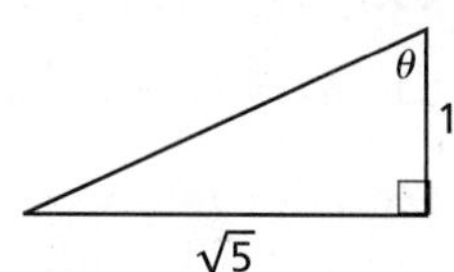

Lesson 10-2

Draw an angle with the given measure in standard position.

10. $-30°$ **11.** $240°$ **12.** $410°$ **13.** $-350°$

Find the measures of a positive angle and a negative angle that are coterminal with each given angle.

14. $\theta = 20°$ **15.** $\theta = 400°$ **16.** $\theta = -125°$ **17.** $\theta = -385°$

Find the measure of the reference angle for each given angle.

18. $\theta = -120°$ **19.** $\theta = 175°$ **20.** $\theta = 110°$ **21.** $\theta = 385°$

P is a point on the terminal side of θ in standard position. Find the exact value of the six trigonometric functions for θ.

22. $P(2, 3)$ **23.** $P(-1, 4)$ **24.** $P(-1, -1)$ **25.** $P(2, -8)$

Lesson 10-3

Convert each measure from degrees to radians or from radians to degrees.

26. $60°$ **27.** $-135°$ **28.** $90°$ **29.** $-10°$

30. $-\frac{3\pi}{2}$ **31.** $\frac{\pi}{10}$ **32.** $\frac{\pi}{18}$ **33.** $-\frac{3\pi}{8}$

Use the unit circle to find the exact value of each trigonometric function.

34. $\cos 150°$ **35.** $\tan \frac{7\pi}{4}$ **36.** $\sin \frac{7\pi}{6}$ **37.** $\cos 315°$

38. $\sin \frac{2\pi}{3}$ **39.** $\cos 270°$ **40.** $\csc \frac{4\pi}{3}$ **41.** $\cot 225°$

Use a reference angle to find the exact value of the sine, cosine, and tangent of each angle.

42. $-150°$ **43.** $210°$ **44.** $315°$ **45.** $330°$

46. $\frac{\pi}{4}$ **47.** $-\frac{7\pi}{6}$ **48.** $\frac{5\pi}{4}$ **49.** $\frac{5\pi}{3}$

Lesson 10-4

Find all possible values of each expression.

50. $\tan^{-1}(-\sqrt{3})$ **51.** $\cos^{-1}\frac{1}{2}$ **52.** $\sin^{-1}\left(-\frac{\sqrt{3}}{2}\right)$

Evaluate each inverse trigonometric function. Give your answer in both radians and degrees.

53. $\text{Tan}^{-1}(-1)$ **54.** $\text{Sin}^{-1}\frac{1}{2}$ **55.** $\text{Cos}^{-1}\left(-\frac{\sqrt{2}}{2}\right)$

Solve each equation to the nearest tenth. Use the given restrictions.

56. $\sin\theta = 0.8$, for $-90^\circ \le \theta \le 90^\circ$

57. $\sin\theta = 0.8$, for $90^\circ < \theta < 180^\circ$

58. $\tan\theta = 2.1$, for $-90^\circ < \theta < 90^\circ$

59. $\tan\theta = 2.1$, for $180^\circ < \theta < 270^\circ$

Lesson 10-5

Find the area of each triangle. Round to the nearest tenth.

60.

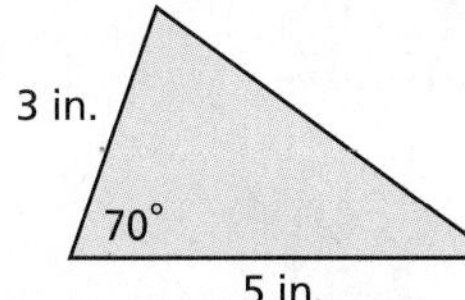

61.

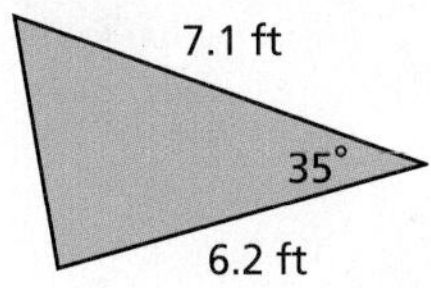

62.

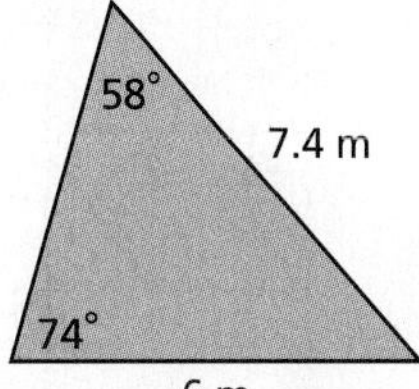

Solve each triangle. Round to the nearest tenth.

63.

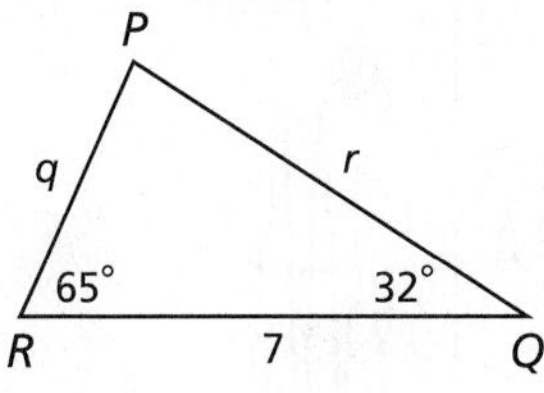

64.

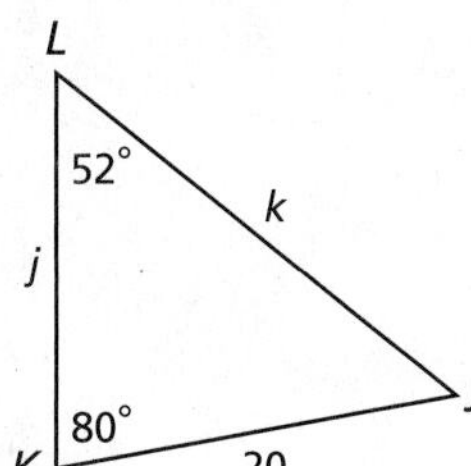

65.

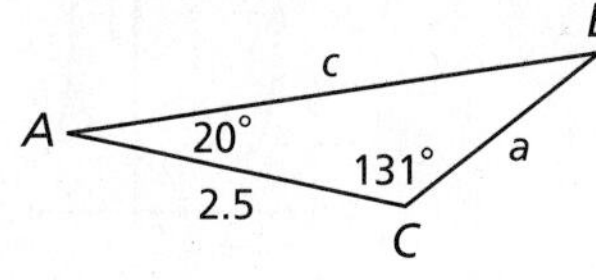

66.

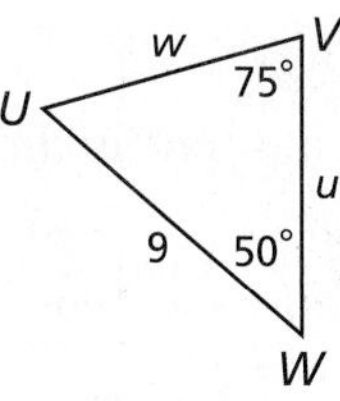

67.

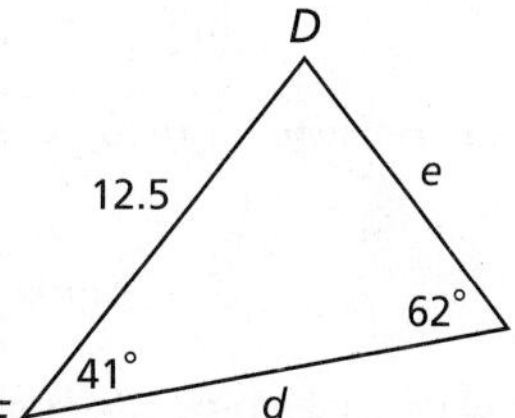

68.

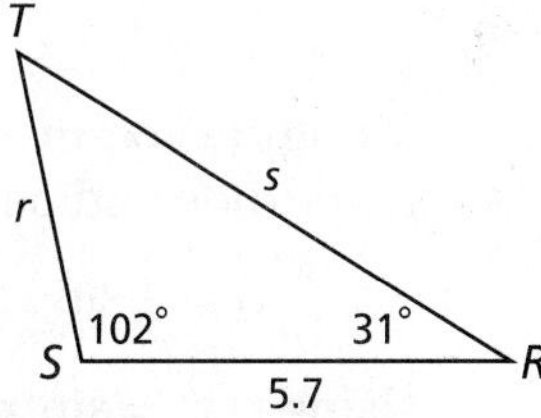

Lesson 10-6

Use the given measurements to solve each triangle. Round to the nearest tenth.

69.

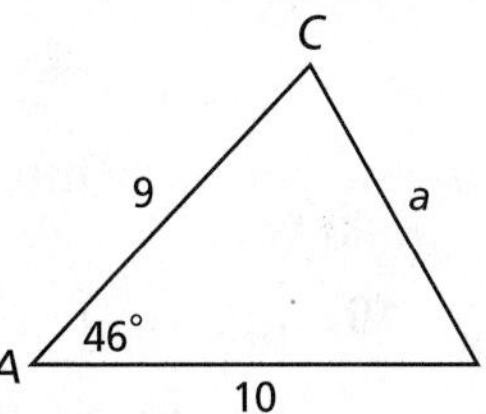

70.

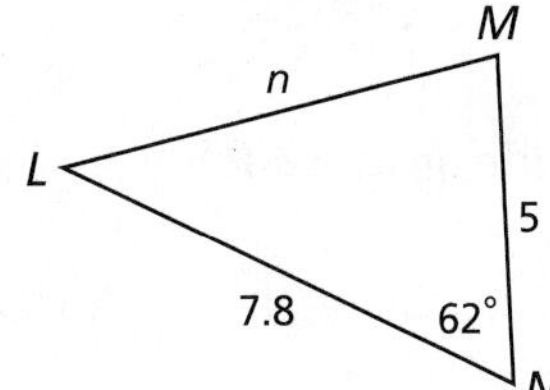

71.

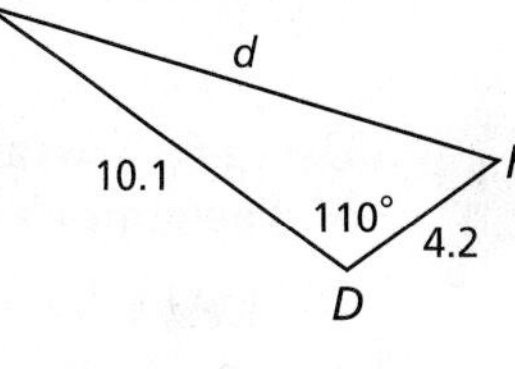

72.

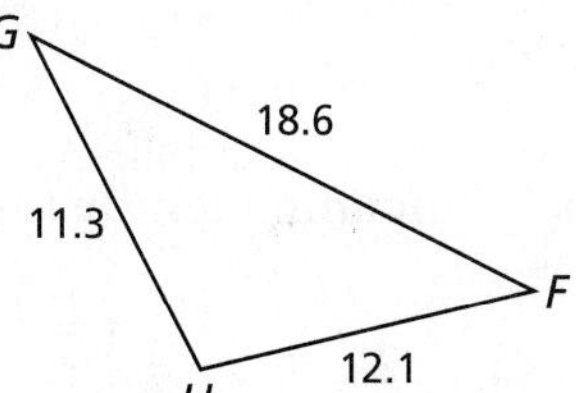

73.

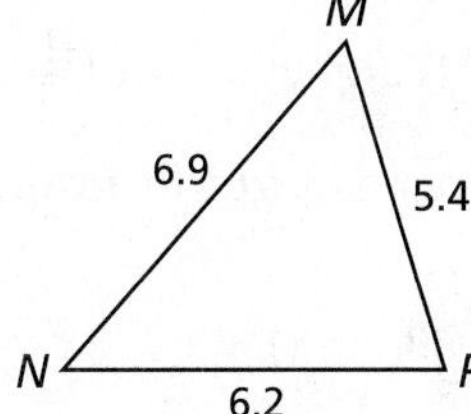

74.

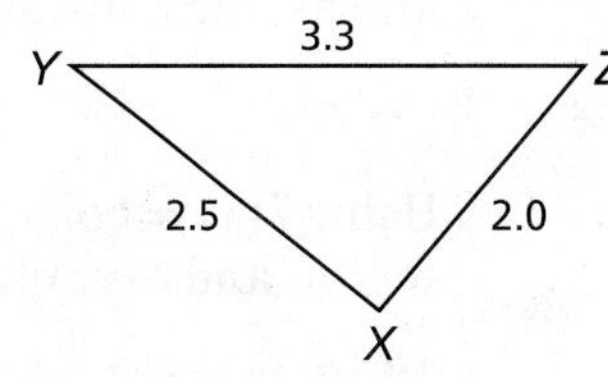

Lesson 11-1

Identify whether each function is periodic. If the function is periodic, give the period.

1. 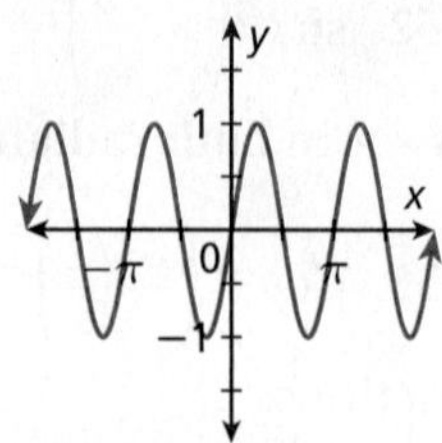

2. 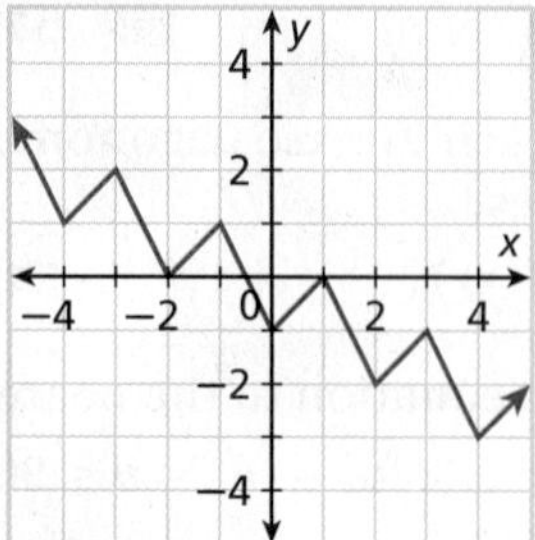

3. 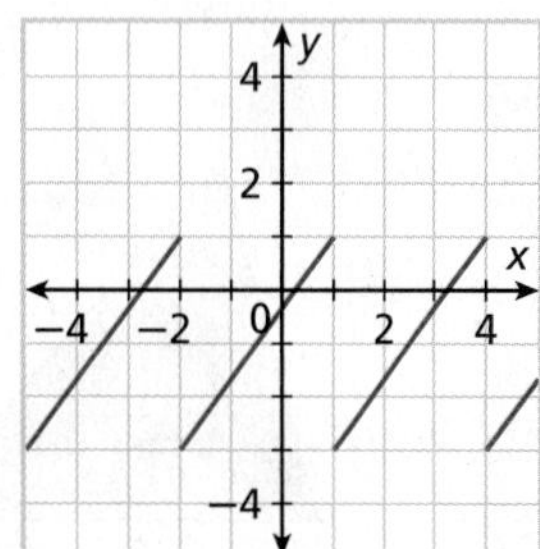

4. 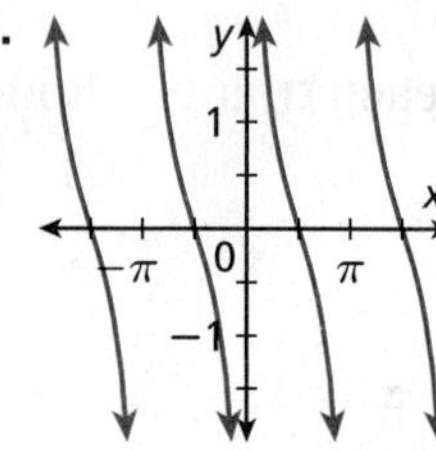

5. 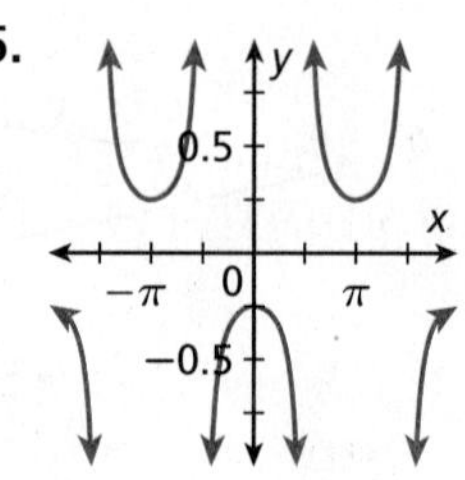

6. 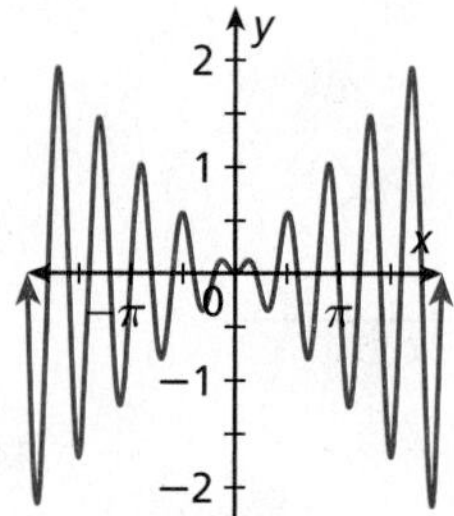

Using $f(x) = \sin x$ or $f(x) = \cos x$ as a guide, graph each function. Identify the amplitude and period.

7. $f(x) = \frac{1}{2}\sin 2x$
8. $g(x) = 3\cos\frac{1}{2}x$
9. $h(x) = 2\cos \pi x$

Using $f(x) = \sin x$ or $f(x) = \cos x$ as a guide, graph each function. Identify the x-intercepts and phase shift.

10. $f(x) = \cos\left(x + \frac{\pi}{2}\right)$
11. $g(x) = \sin(x - \pi)$
12. $h(x) = \sin\left(x + \frac{\pi}{4}\right)$

Lesson 11-2

Using $f(x) = \tan x$ as a guide, graph each function. Identify the period, x-intercepts, and asymptotes.

13. $g(x) = 2\tan 2x$
14. $g(x) = \frac{1}{2}\tan 3x$
15. $h(x) = -\tan \pi x$

Using $f(x) = \cot x$ as a guide, graph each function. Identify the period, x-intercepts, and asymptotes.

16. $g(x) = \frac{1}{2}\cot 2x$
17. $g(x) = -\cot\frac{1}{2}x$
18. $h(x) = \cot 3x$

Using $f(x) = \cos x$ or $f(x) = \sin x$ as a guide, graph each function. Identify the period and asymptotes.

19. $g(x) = \sec\frac{1}{2}x$
20. $g(x) = \csc 2x$
21. $h(x) = \frac{1}{4}\sec x$

Lesson 11-3

Prove each trigonometric identity.

22. $\sec(-\theta) = \sec\theta$
23. $\dfrac{1-\cos\theta}{\sin\theta} = \dfrac{\sin\theta}{1+\cos\theta}$
24. $\tan^2\theta\,(1-\sin^2\theta) = \sin^2\theta$

Rewrite each expression in terms of cos θ and simplify.

25. $\sec\theta\,(1-\sin^2\theta)$
26. $\dfrac{\sin^2\theta}{1+\cos\theta}$
27. $\dfrac{\csc\theta-\sin\theta}{\cot\theta}$

Rewrite each expression in terms of sin θ and simplify.

28. $\dfrac{\tan\theta+1}{\sec\theta+\csc\theta}$
29. $\dfrac{\cot\theta}{\csc\theta}$
30. $1-\cot\theta\cos\theta\sin\theta$

Lesson 11-4

Find each value if $\sin A = \frac{12}{13}$ with $0° < A < 90°$ and if $\cos B = -\frac{3}{5}$ with $90° < B < 180°$.

31. $\sin(A+B)$
32. $\cos(A-B)$
33. $\tan(A+B)$

Find the coordinates, to the nearest hundredth, of the vertices of figure $ABCD$ with $A(-2,-2)$, $B(-2,3)$, $C(1,3)$, and $D(1,-2)$ after each rotation about the origin.

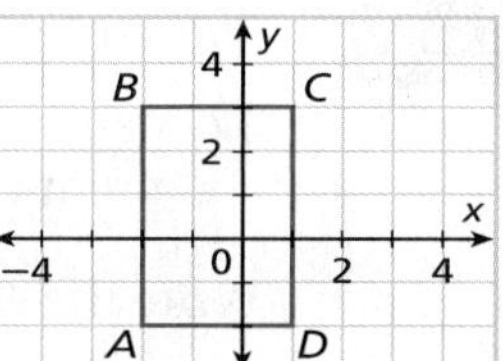

34. 135°
35. 270°

Lesson 11-5

Find sin 2θ, cos 2θ, and tan 2θ for each set of conditions.

36. $\sin\theta = \frac{12}{13}$ and $0° < \theta < 90°$
37. $\cos\theta = -\frac{3}{5}$ and $180° < \theta < 270°$
38. $\tan\theta = -\frac{3}{2}$ and $\frac{3\pi}{2} < \theta < 2\pi$
39. $\sin\theta = \frac{1}{3}$ and $\frac{\pi}{2} < \theta < \pi$

Prove each identity.

40. $\dfrac{\cos 2\theta}{\cos\theta+\sin\theta} = \cos\theta - \sin\theta$
41. $\dfrac{\cos\theta\sin 2\theta}{1+\cos 2\theta} = \sin\theta$
42. $\cos 2\theta + 2\sin^2\theta = 1$
43. $(\sin\theta - \cos\theta)^2 = 1 - \sin 2\theta$

Find $\sin\frac{\theta}{2}$, $\cos\frac{\theta}{2}$, and $\tan\frac{\theta}{2}$ for each set of conditions.

44. $\sin\theta = \frac{3}{5}$ and $90° < \theta < 180°$
45. $\tan\theta = -\frac{7}{24}$ and $270° < \theta < 360°$
46. $\tan\theta = -\frac{\sqrt{5}}{2}$ and $\frac{\pi}{2} < \theta < \pi$
47. $\cos\theta = \frac{1}{5}$ and $0 < \theta < \frac{\pi}{2}$

Lesson 11-6

Find all of the solutions of each equation.

48. $2\cos\theta = \sqrt{2}$
49. $2\sin\theta + 5 = 6$
50. $3\tan\theta = 2\tan\theta - 1$
51. $\tan\theta = 2\tan\theta - \sqrt{3}$

Solve each equation for the given domain.

52. $\cos^2\theta - 3\cos\theta - 4 = 0$ for $0 \le \theta < 2\pi$
53. $2\sin^2\theta - 5\sin\theta + 2 = 0$ for $0 \le \theta < 2\pi$
54. $\sin^2\theta + 3\sin\theta + 1 = 0$ for $0° \le \theta < 360°$
55. $\cos^2\theta + 4\cos\theta - 2 = 0$ for $0° \le \theta < 360°$

Use trigonometric identities to solve each equation for the given domain.

56. $\cos 2\theta + 3\cos\theta = 1$ for $0 \le \theta < 2\pi$
57. $\cos 2\theta + 5\sin\theta = -2$ for $0 \le \theta < 2\pi$
58. $2\sin^2\theta = 3 - 3\cos\theta$ for $0° \le \theta < 360°$
59. $\sin 2\theta = \cos\theta$ for $0° \le \theta < 360°$

Lesson 12-1

Graph each equation on a graphing calculator. Identify each conic section. Then describe the center and intercepts.

1. $4x^2 + 16y^2 = 64$
2. $x^2 + y^2 = 4$
3. $4x^2 + 4y^2 = 100$

Graph each equation on a graphing calculator. Identify each conic section. Then describe the vertices and the direction that the graph opens.

4. $x^2 = y^2 + 16$
5. $-10y^2 = x$
6. $2y^2 - x^2 = 5$

Find the center and radius of a circle that has a diameter with the given endpoints.

7. $(-2, -1)$ and $(6, 3)$
8. $(-4, 0)$ and $(2, 8)$
9. $(2, 1)$ and $(8, -1)$

Lesson 12-2

Write the equation of each circle.

10. center $(-4, 3)$ and radius $r = 3$
11. center $(4, 6)$ and radius $r = 9$
12. center $(-3, 3)$ and containing the point $(-3, 0)$
13. center $(2, -5)$ and containing the point $(4, -3)$

Write the equation of the line that is tangent to each circle at the given point.

14. $(x + 2)^2 + (y + 4)^2 = 25; (-5, 0)$
15. $(x - 4)^2 + y^2 = 100; (10, 8)$

Lesson 12-3

Find the constant sum of an ellipse with the given foci and point on the ellipse.

16. $F_1(0, 4), F_2(0, -4), P(3, 0)$
17. $F_1(6, 0), F_2(-6, 0), P(0, 8)$

Write an equation in standard form for each ellipse with center (0, 0).

18. vertex $(0, 6)$, co-vertex $(5, 0)$
19. co-vertex $(0, 5)$, focus $(12, 0)$

Graph each ellipse.

20. $\frac{x^2}{16} + \frac{y^2}{49} = 1$
21. $\frac{x^2}{100} + \frac{y^2}{36} = 1$
22. $\frac{(x-3)^2}{25} + \frac{(y+2)^2}{64} = 1$

Lesson 12-4

Find the constant difference for a hyperbola with the given foci and point on the hyperbola.

23. $F_1(-15, 0), F_2(15, 0), P(12, 0)$
24. $F_1(0, 16), F_2(0, -16), P(0, 10)$

Write an equation in standard form for each hyperbola.

25.

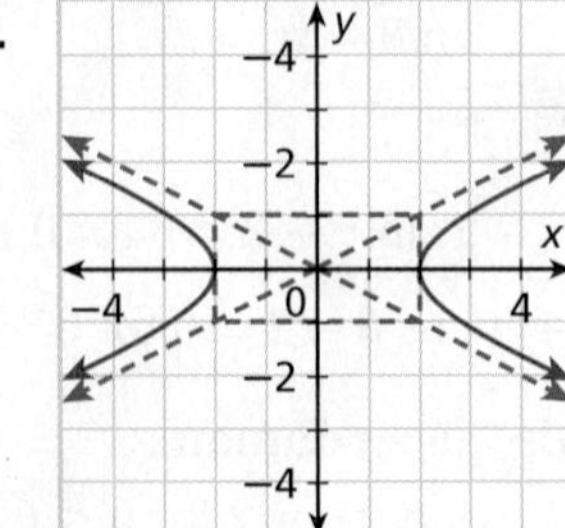

26.

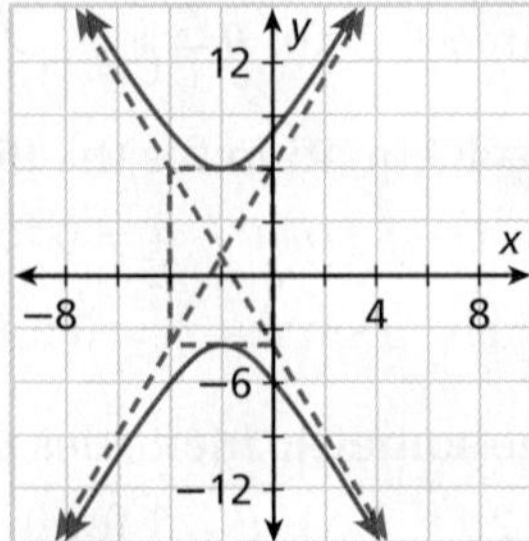

Find the vertices, co-vertices, and asymptotes of each hyperbola, and then graph.

27. $\frac{x^2}{25} - \frac{y^2}{9} = 1$
28. $\frac{(x-4)^2}{16} - \frac{(y+2)^2}{4} = 1$
29. $\frac{(y-2)^2}{9} - (x-2)^2 = 1$

Lesson 12-5

Use the distance formula to find the equation of a parabola with the given focus and directrix.

30. $F(8, 0), x = -8$ **31.** $F(0, 9), y = -9$ **32.** $F(-2, 0), x = 4$

Write the equation in standard form for each parabola.

33.

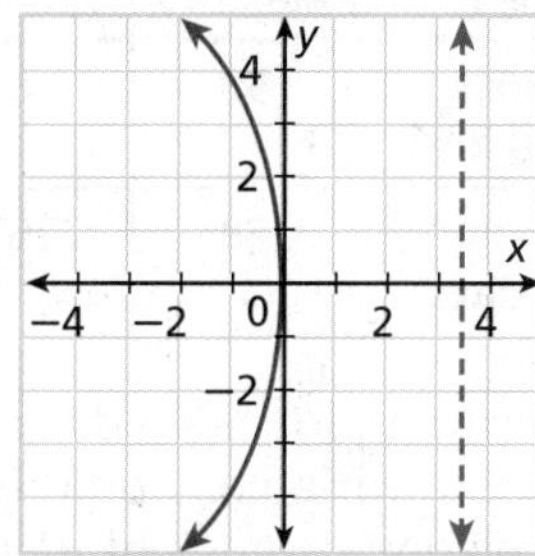

34.

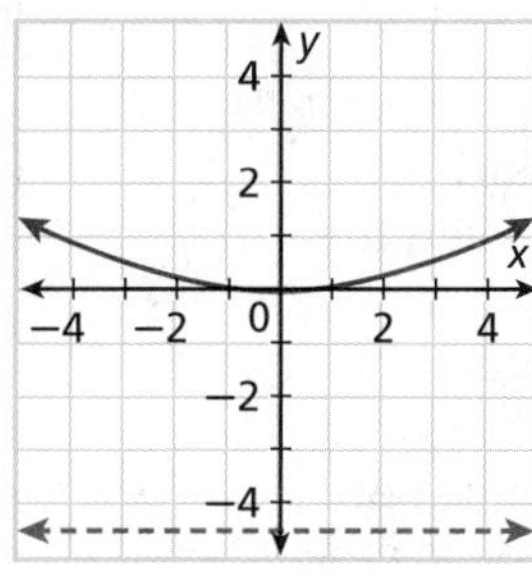

35.

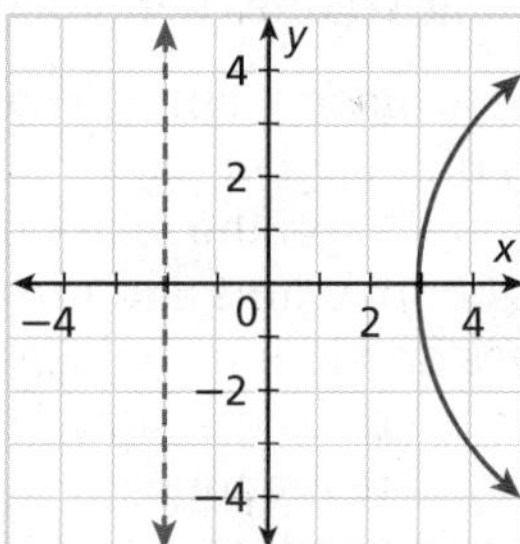

Find the vertex, value of *p*, axis of symmetry, focus, and directrix of each parabola.

36. $y = \frac{1}{20}(x - 1)^2$ **37.** $x = -\frac{1}{12}(y + 4)^2$ **38.** $y - 5 = \frac{1}{26}(x + 3)^2$

Lesson 12-6

Identify the conic section that each equation represents.

39. $\frac{(x + 9)^2}{144} + \frac{(y - 2)}{81} = 1$ **40.** $x^2 + (y - 7)^2 = 81$ **41.** $x + 3 = \frac{1}{6}(y - 6)^2$

42. $4x^2 + 8xy + 5y^2 + 3x + 7 = 0$ **43.** $-2x^2 + 8xy - 8y^2 + 20x = 0$

Find the standard form of each equation by completing the square. Then identify and graph each conic.

44. $4x^2 + 9y^2 - 8x + 72y + 112 = 0$ **45.** $-4x^2 + y^2 + 16x - 4y - 28 = 0$

Lesson 12-7

Solve each system of equations by graphing.

46. $\begin{cases} \frac{(x - 3)^2}{25} + \frac{(y + 2)^2}{64} = 1 \\ 5y + 8x = -26 \end{cases}$ **47.** $\begin{cases} y = -\frac{1}{2}x^2 + 3 \\ y = \frac{1}{2}x - 7 \end{cases}$

48. $\begin{cases} (x + 1)^2 + (y + 4)^2 = 16 \\ x - y = 7 \end{cases}$ **49.** $\begin{cases} 16x^2 + 25y^2 = 400 \\ 20y = 3x^2 \end{cases}$

Solve each system of equations by using the substitution method.

50. $\begin{cases} x^2 + y^2 = 100 \\ y = 3x - 10 \end{cases}$ **51.** $\begin{cases} 4x^2 - 16y^2 = 64 \\ 2y + 12 = 3x \end{cases}$ **52.** $\begin{cases} x^2 + y^2 = 36 \\ 36x^2 + 49y^2 = 1764 \end{cases}$

Solve each system of equations by using the elimination method.

53. $\begin{cases} x^2 + y^2 = 18 \\ x^2 - 5y^2 = -36 \end{cases}$ **54.** $\begin{cases} 3x^2 + 2y^2 = 98 \\ 9x^2 + 4y^2 = 244 \end{cases}$ **55.** $\begin{cases} 4x^2 + 6y^2 = 118 \\ 2y^2 - 2x^2 = -14 \end{cases}$

Extra Practice Chapter 1 ▪ Applications Practice

1. **Recreation** A bowling alley charges $4.00 to rent shoes and $2.75 per game. As part of a promotion, the alley lowers the price of shoes to $3.00. What kind of transformation describes the change in the total cost of bowling x games per person? *(Lesson 1-1)*

2. **Sports** Each team in a soccer league plays each of the other teams one time during a season. Graph the relationship between the number of teams and the total number of games and identify which parent function best describes the data. Then use the graph to estimate the total number of games per season when there are 8 teams in the league. *(Lesson 1-2)*

Total Number of Games per Season					
Teams	4	6	10	12	14
Games	6	15	45	66	91

3. The table below shows properties of the element aluminum. Graph the volume as a function of mass. Then use your graph to estimate the volume of 10 grams of aluminum. *(Lesson 1-3)*

Aluminum Properties				
Mass (g)	54	121.5	220	297
Volume (cm^3)	20	45	80	110

Careers Use the following information for Exercises 4 and 5.

At a spa each masseur earns $80 per day plus $15 per massage. Starting next month, the per-massage fee will be raised to $30. *(Lesson 1-3)*

4. Write $f(x)$ to represent the original earnings and $g(x)$ to represent the new earnings.

5. Graph $f(x)$ and $g(x)$ on the same coordinate plane. Describe the transformation.

6. **Astronomy** The table below shows the distances from four planets to the Sun and the time it takes in Earth days for each planet to complete its revolution around the Sun.

Planet	Mercury	Venus	Earth	Mars
Distance (million km)	58	108	150	228
Revolution (Earth days)	88	225	365	687

Make a scatter plot using distance as the independent variable. Find the line of best fit and correlation coefficient. *(Lesson 1-4)*

7. The cost for several large-screen televisions are shown below. *(Lesson 1-4)*

Large-Screen Televisions			
Size (in.)	Cost ($)	Size (in.)	Cost ($)
52	1150	47	1200
46	880	50	1050
54	1200	55	1600
50	990	52	1480

a. Make a scatter plot of the data with size as the independent variable.

b. Find the correlation coefficient and the equation of best fit. Draw the line of best fit on your scatter plot.

c. Predict the cost of a 60 inch television.

Construction **Use the following information for Exercises 1 and 2.**

A landscape designer is using square stepping stones in a backyard. The function $f(x) = 8x^2$ represents the area in square inches that will be covered by 8 stepping stones with side length x inches. *(Lesson 2-1)*

1. Write a function g for the area that will be covered by 16 stepping stones with side length x inches. Describe g as a transformation of f.
2. The landscape designer decides to use smaller stones with a side length of $(x - 2)$ inches. Write a function h for the area that will be covered by 8 of the smaller stones. Describe h as a transformation of f.

Entertainment **Use the following information for Exercises 3 and 4.**

Part of a roller coaster's path can be modeled by the function $f(x) = -\frac{4}{49}x^2 + \frac{40}{7}x$, where x is the horizontal distance in feet the roller coaster has traveled and f is its height in feet above the ground. *(Lesson 2-2)*

3. What is the roller coaster's maximum height above the ground on this part of the path?
4. How far has the roller coaster traveled horizontally when it reaches its maximum height?

Sports **Use the following information for Exercises 5–7.**

A kickball player kicks a ball from ground level with an initial vertical velocity of 24 ft/s.

5. Write a function in standard form for the ball's height h in feet, where t is the time in seconds after the ball is thrown. *(Lesson 2-3)*
6. How long is the ball in the air? *(Lesson 2-3)*
7. Complete the square to rewrite h in vertex form. What is the ball's maximum height? *(Lesson 2-4)*
8. **School** In a student's science fair project, he claims that the height h in feet above the ground of an object shot from a catapult can be modeled by $h(t) = 16t^2 - 32t + 32$, where t is the time in seconds after the object is shot. What are the zeros of this function? Explain why the values of the zeros indicate that the student's model is incorrect. *(Lesson 2-5)*
9. **Forestry** A wind gust blows a cone from a branch on a redwood tree. The cone's height h in meters above the ground can be modeled by $h(t) = -4.9t^2 - t + 75$, where t is the time in seconds since the cone broke from the branch. To the nearest tenth of a second, how long does the cone fall before hitting the ground? *(Lesson 2-6)*
10. **Business** The weekly profit p in dollars generated by a smoothie stand can be modeled by the function $p(c) = -302c^2 + 1635c - 1712$, where c is the cost in dollars per smoothie. For what range of smoothie costs will the stand generate at least \$450 per week? *(Lesson 2-7)*
11. **Law Enforcement** The table shows the cost of speeding tickets in a certain town, based on how many miles per hour over the speed limit the driver was traveling. Find a quadratic model for the fine given the number of miles per hour over the speed limit. Estimate the fine for a driver traveling 8 mi/h over the speed limit. *(Lesson 2-8)*

Miles per Hour over the Speed Limit	Fine ($)
5	55
10	70
15	95
20	130

12. **Fractals** A fractal can be generated from the formula $Z_{n+1} = (Z_n)^2 + 0.4$. Find the value of Z_2 for this fractal given that $Z_1 = 0.5 - 0.5i$ and $Z_2 = (Z_1)^2 + 0.4$.

Extra Practice Chapter 3 ■ Applications Practice

Manufacturing **Use the following information for Exercises 1 and 2.**

A company produces globes in two different sizes. The large globes have a radius of x inches, and the small globes have a radius of $x - 2$ inches. *(Lesson 3-1)*

1. Write functions to find the volume of each globe size.
2. Evaluate each function for $x = 8$.

Business **Use the following information for Exercises 3 and 4.**

Mr. Schwartz models the number of items his business sold during its first 10 years as $N(x) = 0.07x^3 + 9x^2 - 16x + 80$. His average profit per item (in dollars) can be modeled as $P(x) = 0.5x + 10$. *(Lesson 3-2)*

3. Write a polynomial $T(x)$ that can be used to model the total profit for his company during these years.
4. Evaluate $T(4)$ and explain its significance.
5. **Entertainment** The concert attendance for a music group can be described by the function $F(x) = \frac{1}{4}x^3 + 2x^2 + 50$, where x is the number of concerts since its debut. Use synthetic division to find the number of people who attended the fourth concert. *(Lesson 3-3)*

Sports **Use the following information for Exercises 6 and 7.**

The manager of a basketball team charted the team's progress for the season. For each game, she took the team's points and subtracted the points that the other team scored. The team's performance can be modeled by the function $P(x) = x^3 - 9x^2 + 18x$, where x represents the number of games since the start of the season. *(Lesson 3-4)*

6. Find the zeros of the function. What do they represent?
7. Write the function in factored form.
8. **Packaging** A company packages its ink pens in a box whose length is 3 inches longer than its width and whose height is 2 inches shorter than its width. The volume of the box is 18 in^3. What are the dimensions of the box? *(Lesson 3-5)*
9. **Medicine** A medicine capsule is shaped like a cylinder with a hemisphere at each end. The cylindrical portion of the capsule is 3 cm long, and the volume is $\frac{9}{4}\pi$ cm^3. Find the radius of the capsule. *(Lesson 3-6)*

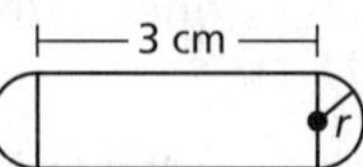

Investing **Use the following information for Exercises 10–12.**

Sharon tracked the closing value of a stock that she owns each day over a 25-day period. On average, the stock followed the curve $F(x) = -0.005x^3 + 0.05x^2 + x + 31.25$. *(Lesson 3-7)*

10. Graph the function on a graphing calculator.
11. What is the maximum value that the stock hit, and on approximately what day did it occur?
12. What is the y-intercept of the graph, and what does it signify?

School **Use the following information for Exercises 13 and 14.**

The enrollment of students at a school each year since 2000 can be modeled by the function $S(x) = -0.005x^5 + 0.07x^4 - 0.5x^2 + 278$. *(Lesson 3-8)*

13. Write the function $T(x) = S(x) - 50$.
14. Graph S and T on the same coordinate plane. Describe T as a transformation of S.
15. **Government** The table below shows the number of city employees during a 6-year period. Use a polynomial model to estimate the number of city employees in 2007. *(Lesson 3-9)*

Year	City Employees
2000	165
2001	168
2002	181
2003	210
2004	261
2005	340

School Use the following information for Exercises 1–3.

A school's honor society was founded in 1970 with 120 members. Since then, the society membership has increased by about 10% each year. *(Lesson 4-1)*

1. Write a function representing the number of members each year since the club's founding (1970 = year 0).
2. Graph the function through the year 2005.
3. In which year did the number of members exceed 1000?

Chemistry Use the following information for Exercises 4–6.

A glass was filled with 6 inches of water and left out on the counter. The amount of water in inches left in the glass after d days is $f(d) = 6 - 0.2d$. *(Lesson 4-2)*

4. Write the inverse function $f^{-1}(d)$.
5. After how many days was there 3.4 inches of water left in the glass?
6. After how many days was the glass empty?

Biology Use the following information for Exercises 7 and 8.

The number of bacteria in a culture after t hours is $f(t) = 3^{\frac{t}{2}}$. *(Lesson 4-3)*

7. How many bacteria are in the culture after 10 hours?
8. Replace $f(t)$ with y and write the function in logarithmic form.

Sound Use the following information for Exercises 9 and 10.

The loudness L of sound in decibels is given by $L = 10\log\left(\frac{I}{I_0}\right)$, where I is the intensity of sound and I_0 is the intensity of the softest audible sound. *(Lesson 4-4)*

9. Rewrite this equation as the difference of two logarithms.
10. When is the equation undefined?

11. **Investing** A stock is losing value at a rate of 5% per month. An investor made an initial purchase of $1500 worth of stock. The value of her shares of stock after m months is $A = 1500(0.95)^m$. Solve for m to find how many months it will take for the stockholder's shares to be worth less than $1000. *(Lesson 4-5)*
12. **Economics** Ivy's parents invested $2700 for college in an account that receives 3.5% interest compounded continuously. What will the total amount of their investment be when Ivy starts college in 8 years? *(Lesson 4-6)*
13. **Physics** Americium-241, a radioactive element used in smoke detectors, has a half-life of 7370 years. Find the decay constant, then use the decay function $N(t) = N_0 e^{-kt}$ to determine the amount of atoms that remain from a sample of 1000 atoms after 20,000 years. *(Lesson 4-6)*

Art Use the following information for Exercises 14–16.

A small painting by Mondrian was valued at $10,500 in the year 2000. Since then its value has been increasing by 3% each year. The value of the painting x years after the year 2000 is $V = 10{,}500(1.03)^x$. Write a function for each transformation described below and explain the effect on the graph of the parent function. *(Lesson 4-7)*

14. The initial value in 2000 is adjusted to $9500.
15. The value is $1500 more each year.
16. The value of the painting increases by 3% every 2 years.
17. **Business** The table gives the number of employees at a company in the years since it was founded. Find a logarithmic model for the data. Predict when the company will have 60 employees. *(Lesson 4-8)*

Company Employees

Years since Founding	1	2	3	4	5	6
Employees	12	26	34	40	44	48

Extra Practice Chapter 5 ■ Applications Practice

1. **Physics** The amount of force F exerted by an object varies directly as the object's acceleration a. An object accelerating at 5 m/s^2 exerts a force of 10 Newtons. How much force would the same object exert at an acceleration of 7 m/s^2? *(Lesson 5-1)*

2. **Transportation** The time t required for a bus to travel a certain distance varies inversely as its average speed r. It takes the bus 2.2 h to travel between two cities at 50 mi/h. How long would the same drive take at 40 mi/h? *(Lesson 5-1)*

Recreation Use the following information for Exercises 3 and 4.

At a carnival booth, contestants can win a prize by throwing a dart at a square board. The total area of the board in square feet can be represented by the expression $4x^2 + 24x + 36$. *(Lesson 5-2)*

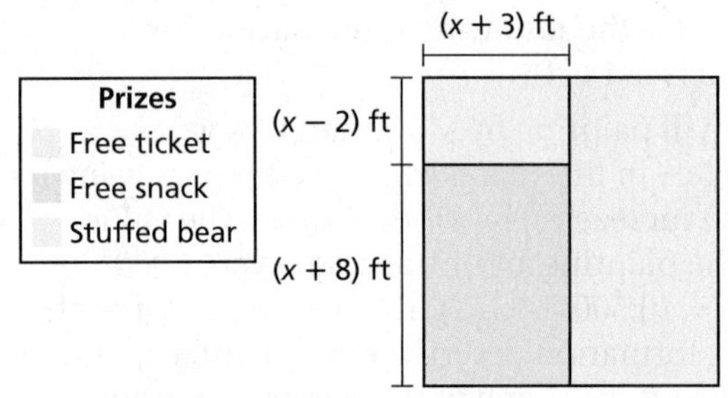

3. If a dart hits the board at random, what is the probability in terms of x of winning a bear?

4. If a dart hits the board at random, what is the probability in terms of x of winning a snack?

5. **Fitness** Geoff ran a 6 mi race for charity. During the first 4 mi of the race, he averaged 6 mi/h. During the last 2 mi, he averaged 5.5 mi/h. What was Geoff's average speed in miles per hour for the entire race? Round to the nearest hundredth. *(Lesson 5-3)*

School Use the following information for Exercises 6 and 7.

A science class is taking a field trip to a planetarium. Admission costs \$8 per student, plus there is a tour charge of \$80 per class. *(Lesson 5-4)*

6. Write and graph a function to represent the total average cost of the field trip per student.

7. Find the total average cost per student if 25 students go on the field trip.

8. **Travel** A tour boat travels 12 mi up a river and 12 mi down the river in a total of 5.5 h. In still water, the boat travels at an average speed of 5.5 mi/h. Based on this information, what is the speed of the river's current? *(Lesson 5-5)*

9. **Carpentry** A carpenter can build a cabinet in 4 h. When his son assists him, they can build the same type of cabinet in 2.5 h. About how long would it take the carpenter's son to build a cabinet by himself? *(Lesson 5-6)*

10. **Measurement** A large cubic storage box has a volume of $166\frac{3}{8}$ ft^3. The box is labeled with a strip of tape that wraps once around the entire box. What is the length of the tape that labels the box? *(Lesson 5-6)*

Physics Use the following information for Exercises 11 and 12.

The period of a pendulum is the time it takes for the pendulum to complete one back-and-forth swing. The function $f(x) = 2\pi\sqrt{\frac{x}{32}}$ gives the period f of a pendulum in seconds where x is the length of the pendulum in feet. *(Lesson 5-7)*

11. Write a function g for the period of a pendulum of length $(x + 2)$ ft.

12. Describe the function g as a transformation of f.

13. **Geometry** The length of a diagonal d of a rectangular prism is given by $d = \sqrt{\ell^2 + w^2 + h^2}$, where ℓ is the length, w is the width, and h is the height. What is the minimum height in inches of a box with a length of 15 in. and a width of 12 in. that will hold a 20 in. baton? Round your answer to the nearest tenth. *(Lesson 5-8)*

1. **Ecology** The table shows the population of a colony of penguins over a 6-year period. Use a graph and an equation to predict the number of penguins in the colony in 2010. *(Lesson 6-1)*

Penguin Colony Population	
Year	Population
2000	112
2001	123
2002	135
2003	149
2004	164
2005	180

2. **Depreciation** The value V of Tom's car t years after buying it is given by the function $V\ 21{,}000(0.81)^{t/2}$. His friend thinks that a better function to describe this situation is $V\ 21{,}000\ \ 1200t$. Graph both functions for $0 < t < 16$. How do the functions compare? *(Lesson 6-2)*

3. **Shipping** A shipping company charges different rates depending on the weight of the package to be shipped. *(Lesson 6-3)*

Shipping Costs	
Weight (lb)	Cost ($)
Under 2	$3.50
2 to 7	$6.00
More than 7	$9.00

Write and graph a piecewise function to represent shipping costs for packages up to 10 lb.

Recreation **Use the following information for Exercises 4 and 5.**

The zoo charges $7.00 per person for admittance. For groups of 20 people or more, the zoo charges $6.00 per person plus a one-time administrative fee of $10. *(Lesson 6-4)*

4. Write a function to represent the cost of admittance to the zoo for x people.

5. The zoo decides to raise the group administrative fee by $5. Write the resulting function. How does this affect the graph?

Politics **Use the following information for Exercises 6 and 7.**

Approximately 2 in 3 people surveyed support a bill to raise the salaries of local police officers. Of those who support the bill, 60% also support a raise in taxes to pay for the bill. *(Lesson 6-5)*

6. Write a composite function for the number of people who support the bill and think that taxes should be raised.

7. The total number of people who support both the bill and the tax is 90. How many people were surveyed?

Scouting **Use the following information for Exercises 8–10.**

The graph shows the number of merit badges that scouts from the same troop have earned, based on the number of years they have been in the troop. *(Lesson 6-6)*

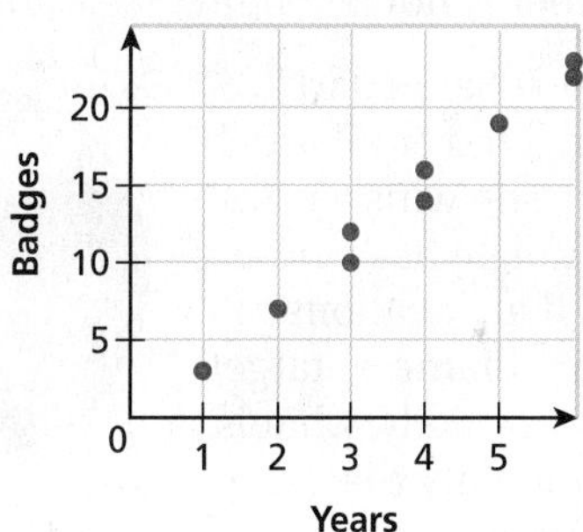

8. Graph the inverse of $f(x)$.

9. Is $f(x)$ a function? Is its inverse a function?

10. Use your graph to predict how long a scout has been in the troop if he has earned 36 badges.

Nutrition **Use the following information for Exercises 11 and 12.**

The table shows the number of Calories and grams of fat in selected sandwiches. *(Lesson 6-7)*

Sandwich Nutrition Information					
Fat (g)	6	8	12	15	20
Calories	372	396	442	477	535

11. Write a function that models the data.

12. Use your model to predict the number of Calories in a sandwich containing 25 grams of fat.

Extra Practice Chapter 7 ■ Applications Practice

Music Use the following information for Exercises 1 and 2.

Serialism is a form of music in which the composer arranges each of the 12 tones in an octave to form a musical phrase. *(Lesson 7-1)*

1. How many ways can the 12 tones of an octave be arranged?
2. How many different musical phrases could a composer create by arranging only 5 of the 12 tones of an octave?
3. **Drama** A drama class is performing the Greek tragedy *Antigone,* by Sophocles. Of the 15 students in the class, 6 will make up the chorus. How many different ways can the chorus be selected? *(Lesson 7-1)*
4. **Holidays** Of December's 31 days, the 25th and the 31st are holidays. What is the probability that a randomly chosen day in December is not a holiday? *(Lesson 7-2)*
5. **Games** If Sara's dart lands in a red equilateral triangle, she wins a prize. Each triangle has a base of 2 in. If all locations on the 12 in. diameter target are equally likely, what is the probability that Sara wins a prize? *(Lesson 7-2)*

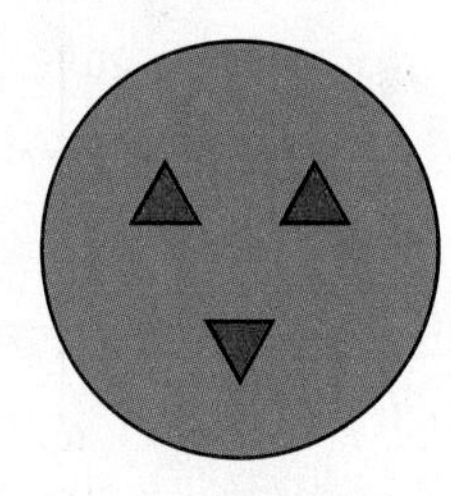

Literature Use the following information for Exercises 6 and 7.

The works of Chilean poet Pablo Neruda have been published in many languages. The school library has copies of two of his books in both English and Spanish. The table shows how many times each book has been checked out. *(Lesson 7-3)*

Books Checked Out		
	Canto General	*Extravagario*
English	23	27
Spanish	17	14

6. What is the probability that *Canto General* was checked out in Spanish?
7. What is the probability that a student who checked out a Pablo Neruda book selected *Extravagario* in English?

Basketball Use the following information for Exercises 8–11.

The table shows the numbers of points scored by the top three scorers in last week's basketball tournament that were made as 1-point shots (free throws), 2-point shots, and 3-point shots. *(Lesson 7-4)*

	1-point	2-point	3-point
Tina	11	38	21
Stella	7	24	42
Misha	17	46	6

8. What is the total number of points scored by the three girls?
9. What is the joint relative frequency that represents points scored by Misha as 2-point shots?
10. What is the marginal relative frequency of the points that were made as 3-point shots?
11. Given that a point was scored by a free throw, what it the probability that Misha scored that point?

Immigration Use the following information for Exercises 12 and 13.

A group of 100 immigrants was studied over a one-year period. During the study, 63 of the immigrants found jobs, and 14 returned to their country of origin. Of the immigrants who found jobs, 6 of them returned to their countries before the end of the study. *(Lesson 7-5)*

12. What is the probability that an immigrant found a job or returned to his or her country of origin?
13. What is the probability that an immigrant did not find a job or returned to his country of origin?

Basketball **Use the following information for Exercises 1–3.**

The table below shows the number of points scored by Tracy McGrady and Yao Ming of the Houston Rockets during the same 5 games of the 2005 season. *(Lesson 8-1)*

Points Scored					
Game	1	2	3	4	5
Tracy McGrady	28	36	25	37	27
Yao Ming	15	20	30	8	33

1. Find the mean of both sets of data.
2. Find the standard deviation of both sets of data.
3. Determine whether there is an outlier. If so, describe how it affects the mean and standard deviation.

Exercise **Use the following information for Exercises 4 and 5. You plan to report on the level of physical activity of students in your school.** *(Lesson 8-2)*

4. Describe how you could choose a representative sample of students.
5. Write an unbiased question you could use to collect information on how many hours per week a student exercises.
6. **Pets** Describe how you would set up a randomized, controlled experiment to investigate the hypothesis below. Include any precautions you would take to ensure that your conclusions are valid. *(Lesson 8-3)*

   Dog food with added Omega-3 fatty acids will give dogs a shiny coat.
7. **Marketing** A marketing firm claims that its ad campaign will increase sales for a sneaker brand by 12%. In a random sample of 16 stores, the average increase in sales was 10.5% with a standard deviation of 4%. Find the z-value, rounded to the nearest hundredth. Is there enough evidence to reject the marketing firm's claim? *(Lesson 8-4)*
8. **Quality Control** The manager of a book publisher has received a shipment of books from the printer. He want to examine the books to determine the quality of the printing. Classify each sampling method. Which is most accurate? Which is least accurate? *(Lesson 8-5)*

Method A Open the first box and examine the books on top.

Method B Open each box and examine a randomly selected book from each.

Method C Open several randomly selected boxes and examine every book in each.

Nutrition **Use the following information for Exercises 9 and 10.**

At a frozen yogurt store, 75% of customers ask for a cup, while the others ask for a cone. At closing time, the store has 7 people waiting and only 2 cones left. *(Lesson 8-6)*

9. What is the probability that exactly 2 people will want cones?
10. What is the probability that no more than 2 people will want cones?

Manufacturing **A machine is used to fill boxes of cereal. An analysis of samples shows that the amount of cereal in each box varies. The weights are normally distributed with a mean of 20 ounces and a standard deviation of 0.25 ounce.** *(Lesson 8-7)*

11. Find the z-scores for weights of 19.4 ounces and 10.4 ounces.
12. What is the probability that a randomly selected cereal box weighs at most 19.4 ounces?
13. What is the probability that a randomly selected cereal box weighs between 19.4 and 20.4 ounces?
14. Beth has 3 quarters, a dime, and 6 pennies in her pocket. She pulls out two coins at random. What is the expected value of the coins?
15. **Insurance** Suppose that an item is insured for $12,000. The insurance company estimates that there is a 1% chance that they will have to pay out on the policy. What is the expected loss on the policy?

Extra Practice Chapter 9 ■ Applications Practice

Housing Use the following information for Exercises 1 and 2.

Lily moved into her apartment in 2001, when the rent was $650. Every year since then, the landlord has raised the rent by 5%. *(Lesson 9-1)*

1. Graph the sequence and describe its pattern.
2. How much will Lily's rent be in 2010?
3. **Fractals** Find the number of red circles in the next 2 terms of the fractal. *(Lesson 9-1)*

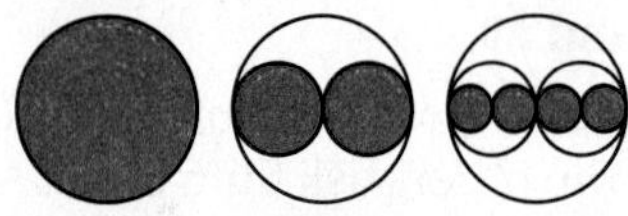

4. **Awards** A local charity started its Volunteer Hall of Fame by inducting the first honoree in 1997. The next year it inducted 2 new members, and in 1999 it inducted 3 new members. Each year since then, it has added one more member than it did the previous year. How many members will the Volunteer Hall of Fame have in 2009? *(Lesson 9-2)*

Fractals Use the following information for Exercises 5 and 6.

The number of circles in the first iteration of the fractal is $3^0 = 1$. The number of circles in the second iteration of the fractal is $3^0 + 3^1 = 4$. The number of circles in the third iteration of the fractal is $3^0 + 3^1 + 3^2 = 13$. *(Lesson 9-2)*

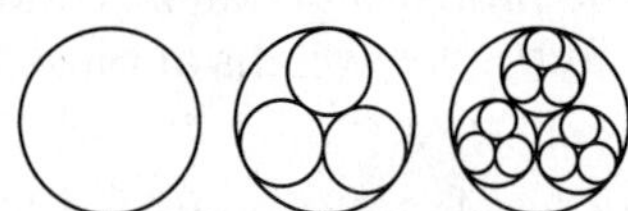

5. Use summation notation to write an expression for the number of circles in the nth iteration of the fractal.
6. Find the number of circles in the 5th iteration of the fractal.

Fitness Use the following information for Exercises 7–9.

When a member first joins a health club, he or she pays $240 for the first year. Each year after that, the yearly fee is reduced by $10. *(Lesson 9-3)*

7. What is the yearly fee for the 7th year?
8. How much will a member have paid after belonging to the health club for 10 years?
9. If a member has paid a total of $2450 in fees, how long has she been a member of the health club?

Communication Use the following information for Exercises 10–12.

The Parent Teacher Association spreads news using a phone tree. The president and vice president start the phone tree by calling 3 people each. Each of the 6 people called then have 3 new people to call, and so on, until every member of the PTA has been called. *(Lesson 9-4)*

10. Write a sequence to describe the phone tree.
11. How many people are on the 5th row of the phone tree?
12. It takes a total of 6 rows to finish the phone tree. Write an expression in summation notation to express the number of people called in the entire phone tree. How many members does the Parent Teacher Association have?

Business Use the following information for Exercises 13 and 14.

The table shows the annual revenue generated by a new product in its first 4 years. *(Lesson 9-5)*

Annual Revenue				
Year	2001	2002	2003	2004
Sales (thousand $)	375	225	135	81

13. Assume that the trend continues. Estimate the revenue generated in 2008.
14. Assume that the sales trend continues indefinitely. Estimate the total revenue the product will generate.

1. **Aviation** A plane is flying at an altitude of 6500 ft. The pilot sights the runway of an airport at an angle of depression of 6°. To the nearest tenth of a mile, what is the horizontal distance from the plane to the runway? *(Lesson 10-1)*

2. **Architecture** Thomas stands 250 m from the base of the Sears Tower in Chicago. His eye level is 1.75 m above the ground, and he measures the angle of elevation to the top of the tower to be 60.4°. Based on this information, what is the height of the Sears Tower to the nearest meter? *(Lesson 10-1)*

Recreation Use the following information for Exercises 3 and 4.

A Ferris wheel makes one complete revolution in 40 s. *(Lesson 10-2)*

3. Through what angle, in degrees, does a car of the Ferris wheel rotate in 70 s?

4. How long does it take a car of the Ferris wheel to rotate through an angle of 792° ?

5. **Landscape Design** A path through a park is shaped like an arc of a circle with a radius of 25 ft. The central angle that intercepts the path measures $\frac{\pi}{2}$ radians. To the nearest foot, how long is the path? *(Lesson 10-3)*

6. **Entertainment** A standard circus ring is 42 ft in diameter. A clown on a bicycle rides once around the circumference of the ring in 10 s. To the nearest tenth of a foot, how far does the clown travel in 1 second? *(Lesson 10-3)*

7. **Astronomy** Venus is approximately 108 million km from the Sun and takes 225 days to complete an orbit. Based on this information, how far does Venus travel in its nearly circular orbit around the Sun in 1 day? Round to the nearest million kilometers. *(Lesson 10-3)*

8. **Construction** The entrance to a store is 6 in. above the level of the sidewalk. A contractor is building an access ramp to the entrance that will cover a horizontal distance of 6 ft. To the nearest degree, what angle will the ramp make with the sidewalk? *(Lesson 10-4)*

9. **Safety** The "1-to-4" rule states that when a ladder is leaning against a wall, the bottom of the ladder should be 1 ft away from the wall for every 4 ft that the top of the ladder rises on the wall. To the nearest degree, what angle should the ladder make with the ground? *(Lesson 10-4)*

10. **Surveying** A surveyor is measuring a triangular plot of land, as shown. To the nearest foot, what is the distance between stakes 1 and 2? *(Lesson 10-5)*

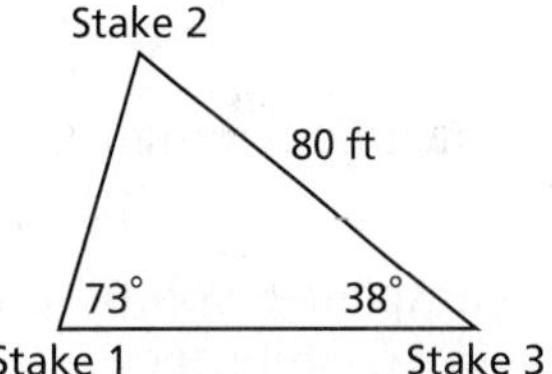

Hobbies Use the following information for Exercises 11 and 12.

Andrew uses pieces of wood to build triangular picture frames. Determine the number of triangles he can form using the given side and angle measurements. Then solve the triangles. Round to the nearest tenth. *(Lesson 10-5)*

11. $a = 10.5$ cm, $b = 12$ cm, $m\angle A = 60°$

12. $a = 8$ cm, $b = 15$ cm, $m\angle A = 44°$

13. **Hiking** Anne and Keisha leave their campsite at the same time. Anne hikes due east at 2 mi/h. Keisha heads 65° east of north at 3 mi/h. To the nearest tenth of a mile, what is the distance d between the hikers after 3 hours? *(Lesson 10-6)*

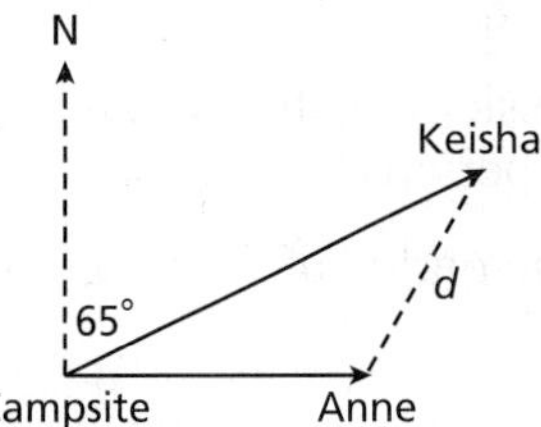

14. A museum has a triangular window with sides measuring 9 ft, 11 ft, and 14 ft. What is the area of the window to the nearest square foot? *(Lesson 10-6)*

Extra Practice Chapter 11 ■ Applications Practice

1. **Sound** Use a sine function to graph a sound wave with a period of 0.006 second and an amplitude of 5 cm. Find the frequency in hertz for this sound wave. *(Lesson 11-1)*

Recreation Use the following information for Exercises 2–4.

As a cyclist rides her bike, the height in inches above the ground of one of the pedals is modeled by $H(t) = 6\cos 2\pi t + 12$, where t is the time in seconds. *(Lesson 11-1)*

2. Graph the height of the pedal for two complete periods.
3. What is the maximum and minimum height of the pedal?
4. How many complete revolutions does the pedal make in one minute?

Use the following information for Exercises 5 and 6.

As a swimming pool is drained, the depth of the water in feet is modeled by $D(t) = 1.05 \cot \frac{\pi}{8}\left(t + \frac{1}{2}\right)$, where t is the time in hours. *(Lesson 11-2)*

5. Graph the depth of the water in the swimming pool for $0 \le t \le 3$.
6. What is the starting depth of the water? Round to the nearest inch.

Use the following information for Exercises 7 and 8.

The minute hand of a clock begins on the 12 and moves around the dial. The slope of the line represented by the minute hand is given by the function $S(t) = -\tan 2\pi(t - 0.25)$, where t is the time in hours. *(Lesson 11-2)*

7. Graph the slope of the minute hand for six complete periods.
8. What is the period of the function?
9. **Physics** Use the equation $mg\sin\theta = \mu mg\cos\theta$ to determine the angle at which a steel table can be tilted before a copper pan on the table begins to slide. Assume $\mu = 0.53$ and round your answer to the nearest degree. *(Lesson 11-3)*

Geometry Use the following information for Exercises 10 and 11.

Find the coordinates, to the nearest hundredth, of the vertices of $\triangle ABC$ after the given rotation. *(Lesson 11-4)*

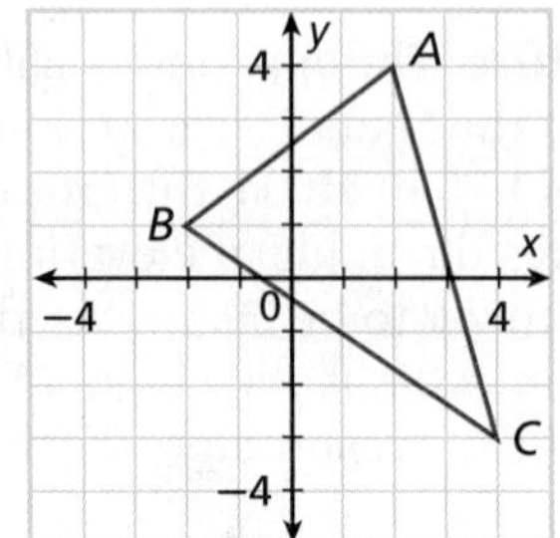

10. A 60° rotation about the origin
11. A 135° rotation about the origin

Physics Use the following information for Exercises 12 and 13.

The horizontal component of the acceleration of an object sliding down a frictionless inclined plane is $a(\theta) = 9.8\sin\theta\cos\theta$, where θ is the angle of the inclined plane and where acceleration is measured in meters per second per second $\left(\frac{m}{s^2}\right)$. *(Lesson 11-5)*

12. Rewrite the function in terms of the double angle 2θ.
13. Graph the function for $0 \le \theta \le \frac{\pi}{2}$. For what angle does the object have the greatest acceleration in the horizontal direction?
14. The population in thousands of a seaside town is modeled by $P(t) = 10\sin\frac{\pi}{180}(t - 160) + 15$, where t is the day of the year and $t = 0$ represents January 1. How many days after January 1 is the population equal to 22,000? *(Lesson 11-6)*
15. The temperature in New York City during one day in the summer is modeled by $F(t) = 16\sin\frac{\pi}{12}(t - 8) + 68$, where F is the temperature in degrees Fahrenheit and t is the time in hours after midnight. At what times during the day is the temperature 80°F? *(Lesson 11-6)*

Geometry **Use the following information for Exercises 1–3.**

A circle has center $(7, 8)$ and contains the point $(11, 11)$. *(Lesson 12-1)*

1. Find the circumference of the circle.
2. Find the area of the circle.
3. Find the other endpoint of the diameter with one endpoint $(11, 5)$.

Design **Use the following information for Exercises 4–6.**

Grace is designing a courtyard for a client. The courtyard will include a small circular fountain inside a large circular patio, which will be surrounded by a square fence. The plans have been overlaid on a coordinate plane, as shown below. *(Lesson 12-2)*

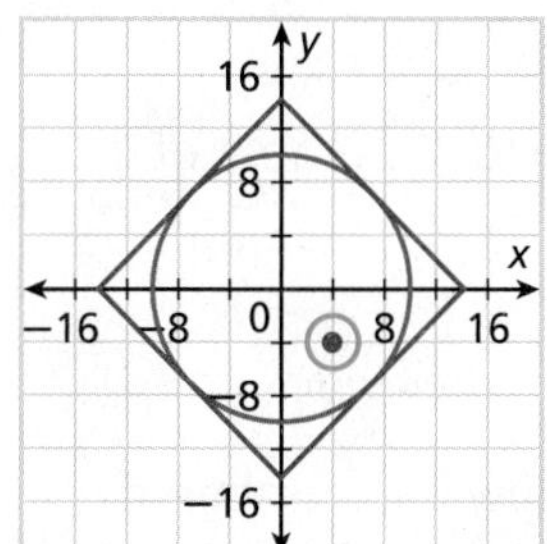

4. Find an equation for the fountain.
5. Find an equation for the circular patio.
6. Each side of the fence is tangent to the patio. Find the equation for the part of the fence that passes through the point $\left(-5\sqrt{2}, 5\sqrt{2}\right)$.

Architecture **Use the following information for Exercises 7 and 8.**

The Oval Office in the White House has a major axis 35 ft 10 in. long and a minor axis 29 ft long. *(Lesson 12-3)*

7. Suppose that the center of the floor of the Oval Office is located at the origin. Write an equation that can be used to model the office floor.
8. Find the coordinates of the foci.

9. **Sports** Two people watching a baseball game are seated 2000 feet apart. One person hears the crack of the bat 1 second before the other person. Because sound travels at 1100 feet per second, one person must be 1100 feet closer to the bat than the other. The possible locations of the batter form a hyperbola with the two people as foci. Write an equation that could be used to represent the possible locations of the batter. (*Hint:* Place the origin midway between the two people.) *(Lesson 12-4)*

10. **Recreation** A half-pipe, similar to those used by skateboarders, is parabolic in shape. Use the intersection of the ground and the center of the half-pipe as the origin and write an equation to model the shape of the curved interior of the structure. *(Lesson 12-5)*

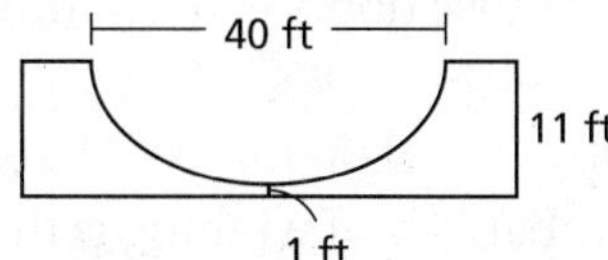

Fitness **Use the following information for Exercises 11 and 12.**

A runner is running on a track. His path in yards can be modeled by the equation $x^2 - 160x + 4y^2 - 160y + 7840 = 0$. *(Lesson 12-6)*

11. Write the equation in standard form by completing the square.
12. There is a drinking fountain in the center of the track. What are the coordinates of the fountain? What is the farthest distance that a runner would have to travel from the track to the fountain?

13. **Ecology** A water tank has spilled, and the flooded area in square feet can be modeled by the equation $x^2 + y^2 = 225$. Near the spilled tank, there is a garden whose shape can be modeled by the equation $\frac{(x-9)^2}{25} + \frac{(y-6)^2}{36} = 1$. At what points do the boundaries of the spill and the garden intersect? *(Lesson 12-7)*

Problem Solving Handbook

Draw a Diagram

You can draw a diagram that represents the information in a problem to help you understand and solve the problem.

Problem Solving Strategies

Draw a Diagram	Make a Table
Make a Model	Solve a Simpler Problem
Guess and Test	Use Logical Reasoning
Work Backward	Use a Venn Diagram
Find a Pattern	Make an Organized List

EXAMPLE

Carmen is participating in an online contest to win a car. She is given a choice of three doors. Each door leads to another level with three doors, and each of those leads to another level with three doors. Behind one of those final doors is the grand prize of a new car. What is the probability of winning the car if she chooses doors at random?

1 Understand the Problem

List the important information.

- She begins with three doors.
- Each of those doors leads to three other doors, and each of those doors leads to another three doors.
- One of the final doors leads to the car.
- The probability of winning is the number of cars divided by the total number of final door choices.

The answer will be the probability of finding the car.

2 Make a Plan

Use a tree diagram to show the possible door choices. This will show the number of possible paths Carmen could choose.

3 Solve

Draw the tree diagram. Draw three doors to represent the original three doors. Draw three more doors for each door and connect them with lines. Repeat to have three rows of doors.

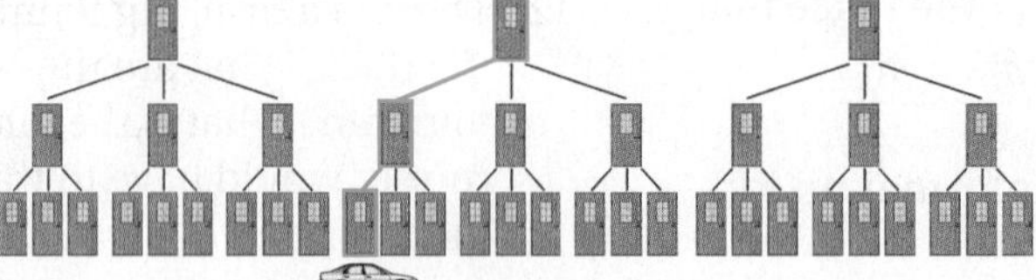

The highlighted path shows that there is exactly one way to win the car.

The total number of paths is 27.

The probability of winning the car is $\frac{1}{27} \approx 3.7\%$.

4 Look Back

Check that you drew your diagram correctly. Does the diagram accurately represent the information given in the question?

PRACTICE

1. Bob has a green, a blue, a red, and a yellow marble in a bag. He randomly selects one marble at a time from the bag until the bag is empty. What is the probability that the blue marble is chosen immediately before the red one?

Problem-Solving Handbook

Make a Model

For problems that involve objects, it is sometimes useful to make a model to help you solve the problem.

Problem Solving Strategies

Draw a Diagram	Make a Table
Make a Model	Solve a Simpler Problem
Guess and Test	Use Logical Reasoning
Work Backward	Use a Venn Diagram
Find a Pattern	Make an Organized List

EXAMPLE

Ryan created a pyramid with a square base out of cans of soup for a store display. When he had finished, he needed to know the number of cans that he had used. The pyramid has four levels. The top level has one can, and each row beneath it has one additional can added to each side length. How many cans are in the pyramid?

Understand the Problem

List the important information.

- There are four levels.
- The top level has one can.
- The side length increases by one as you go down each level.

The answer will be the number of cans in the pyramid.

Make a Plan

You can use blocks to make a model of the problem. Use the blocks to create the pyramid in the problem. Remember to count the number of blocks as you go.

3 Solve

Since each level has one can added to the side length, the side length of the bottom level is 4. Make a 4-by-4 square of blocks for the base. Count the number of blocks used. The level above has side lengths of 3, so make a 3-by-3 square on top of the base. Count the number of blocks used in this level. Continue to the top of the pyramid. The total number of blocks is the sum of the blocks at each level: $16 + 9 + 4 + 1 = 30$.

Look Back

Make sure the pyramid matches the given information. There should be four levels increasing by one in side length as you go down the pyramid.

PRACTICE

1. Paul wants to make a pyramid with an equilateral triangle base out of cans. Paul has 25 cans. He wants the pyramid to have one can on the top, and he wants the number of cans on each side of the following triangle layers to increase by one. How tall can Paul make the pyramid? How many cans will he have left over?
2. A display of cereal boxes is arranged with 1 box on top and each row having an additional box. How many boxes are in a display of 9 rows?

Guess and Test

One way to solve a problem is to guess the answer and test to see whether it is correct. You can continue to guess and test until you find the correct answer.

Problem Solving Strategies

Draw a Diagram	Make a Table
Make a Model	Solve a Simpler Problem
Guess and Test	Use Logical Reasoning
Work Backward	Use a Venn Diagram
Find a Pattern	Make an Organized List

EXAMPLE

Tom is playing a game where he draws marbles out of a bag. Red marbles are worth 3 points, and blue ones are worth 2 points. Tom drew 8 marbles and won 20 points. How many marbles of each color does Tom have?

1 Understand the Problem

List the important information.

- Red marbles are worth 3 points.
- Blue marbles are worth 2 points.
- The total number of points is 20.
- The total number of marbles is 8.

2 Make a Plan

Start with a guess in which the total number of marbles is 8. Test to see whether the total number of points is 20.

3 Solve

Make a first guess of 3 red and 5 blue, and find the total number of points.

Guess: 3 red and 5 blue

Test: $(3 \times 3) + (5 \times 2) = 19$

The number of points is too small. Increase the number of red marbles and decrease the number of blue marbles.

Guess: 5 red and 3 blue

Test: $(5 \times 3) + (3 \times 2) = 21$

The number of points is too high. Decrease the number of red marbles and increase the number of blue marbles.

Guess: 4 red and 4 blue

Test: $(4 \times 3) + (4 \times 2) = 20$

Tom should have drawn 4 red marbles and 4 blue marbles.

4 Look Back

Test the answer to see whether the number of marbles satisfies the question.

4 red marbles and 4 blue marbles are 8 marbles and are worth 20 points.

PRACTICE

1. Fred has 7 coins. All the coins are nickels or dimes. The total value of the coins is \$0.55. How many of each type of coin does he have?

2. The sum of Beth's age and Brian's age is 20. Three times Beth's age plus 2 times Brian's age is 55. How old are Beth and Brian?

Work Backward

Sometimes in a problem you are given an end result and asked to find a fact that leads to the result. In these cases, you can work backward to solve the problem.

Problem Solving Strategies

Draw a Diagram	Make a Table
Make a Model	Solve a Simpler Problem
Guess and Test	Use Logical Reasoning
Work Backward	Use a Venn Diagram
Find a Pattern	Make an Organized List

EXAMPLE

Laura is delivering meals to retirement communities. She dropped off 2 less than $\frac{1}{2}$ of the meals at the first community. Then she dropped off $\frac{1}{3}$ of the remaining meals plus 2 at the second community. She has 8 meals left. How many meals did she have to start?

1 Understand the Problem

List the important information.

- Laura delivered $\frac{1}{2}$ of the meals minus 2 at the first community.
- Laura delivered $\frac{1}{3}$ of the meals plus 2 at the second community.
- She has 8 meals left.

The answer will be the number of meals that she had at the start.

2 Make a Plan

Start with the 8 meals and work backward through the given information to determine the beginning number of meals.

3 Solve

She has 8 meals at the end, so start with 8 meals.

She delivered $\frac{1}{3}$ of the meals plus 2 at the second community, so add 2 to the number of meals and multiply by $\frac{3}{2}$ to undo giving $\frac{1}{3}$ away. $\quad \frac{3}{2}(8 + 2) = 15$

She had 15 meals before she visited the second community.

She delivered $\frac{1}{2}$ of the meals minus 2 at the first community, so subtract 2 and multiply by 2 to undo giving $\frac{1}{2}$ away. $\quad 2(15 - 2) = 26$

Laura started with 26 meals.

4 Look Back

Use the starting amount of 26 meals and work from the beginning of the problem following the steps.

Start: 26

Subtract $\frac{1}{2}$ of the meals plus 2 more: 15

Subtract $\frac{2}{3}$ of the meals minus 2 more: 8

PRACTICE

1. A tree is growing in Danny's yard. When Danny first observed the tree, he noticed that the number of branches on the tree had doubled that year. The year after, the number of branches tripled minus 3. The year after that, the tree doubled its number of branches, plus 6. How many branches did the tree originally have if it currently has 120 branches?

Find a Pattern

When the pieces of information in a problem have a relationship, you can find a pattern to help solve the problem.

Problem Solving Strategies

Draw a Diagram	Make a Table
Make a Model	Solve a Simpler Problem
Guess and Test	Use Logical Reasoning
Work Backward	Use a Venn Diagram
Find a Pattern	Make an Organized List

EXAMPLE

Fred has 3 homework problems the first day of school. The second day he has 5. The third day he has 7. The fourth day he has 9. If this pattern continues, how many homework problems will Fred have on the tenth day of school?

Understand the Problem

List the important information.

- On day 1 he has 3 homework problems, on day 2 he has 5 homework problems, on day 3 he has 7 homework problems, and on day 4 he has 9 homework problems.

The answer will be the number of homework problems Fred will have on day 10.

Make a Plan

Find a pattern by comparing the number of homework problems Fred has each day. Then use this pattern to determine the number of homework problems he will have on day 10.

Solve

Organize the data and find the pattern.

Day	Number of Homework Problems	Pattern
1	3	$3 + 2(1 - 1)$
2	5	$3 + 2(2 - 1)$
3	7	$3 + 2(3 - 1)$
4	9	$3 + 2(4 - 1)$

The pattern is that he gains 2 homework problems each day. Since he has 3 problems the first day and the number of days that have passed is the day number minus 1, the number of homework problems Fred has on the day n is $3 + 2(n - 1)$. The number of homework problems Fred will have on day 10 is $3 + 2(10 - 1) = 21$.

Look Back

Since the pattern is that he gains 2 homework problems each day, continue the data in a table to make sure that he will have 21 homework problems on the tenth day. Check that the formula you developed satisfies the information given in the question.

PRACTICE

1. Joseph is making signs for his student council election campaign. He made 1 sign the first day, 4 signs the second day, 7 signs the third day, and 10 signs the fourth day. How many signs will he make on the tenth day?
2. A flower is growing in a field. In year 1 there are two flowers in the field, in year 2 there are 3, in year 3 there are 5, in year 4 there are 9, in year 5 there are 17, and in year 6 there are 33. How many flowers will there be in year 11?

Make a Table

When you are solving problems that involve a large amount of data, it is often useful to make a table to organize and analyze the data.

Problem Solving Strategies

Draw a Diagram	**Make a Table**
Make a Model	Solve a Simpler Problem
Guess and Test	Use Logical Reasoning
Work Backward	Use a Venn Diagram
Find a Pattern	Make an Organized List

EXAMPLE

Peter, Michael, and Lisa work at the same shop. Peter works every 2 days, Michael works every 4 days, and Lisa works every 5 days. They all worked today. In how many days will they all work together again? How many days will each person work between now and when they all work together next?

1 Understand the Problem

List the important information.

- Peter works every 2 days, Michael every 4 and Lisa every 5.
- They all worked together today.

The answers will be:

- the number of days until they work together again and
- the number of days each person will work between now and then.

2 Make a Plan

Make a table, using ✔'s to show the days each person works.

3 Solve

Start with a ✔ in each person's row on day 0. For Peter, place a ✔ every 2 days. For Michael, place a ✔ every 4 days. For Lisa, place a ✔ every 5 days.

Day	0	1	2	3	4	5	6	7	8	9	10	11	12	13	14	15	16	17	18	19	20
Peter	✔		✔		✔		✔		✔		✔		✔		✔		✔		✔		✔
Michael	✔				✔				✔				✔				✔				✔
Lisa	✔					✔					✔					✔					✔

They will all work together again in 20 days. Peter will work nine, Michael will work 4, and Lisa will work 3 days between now and then.

Look Back

Check the information in the table. Make sure that no mistakes have been made in counting and that the data matches the information given in the question.

PRACTICE

1. If Peter works every 3 days, Michael works every 5 days, and Lisa works every 6 days, when will the next day be that they all work together if they all worked together today? How many days will each person work between now and when they all work together next?

2. A restaurant receives a shipment of produce every 2 days, a shipment of meat every 9 days, and a shipment of frozen food every 12 days. When will be the next day that all three shipments arrive if all three shipments arrived today? How many of each type of shipment will the restaurant receive between now and then?

Solve a Simpler Problem

When solving a complex problem, it is sometimes helpful to write a simpler problem, solve it, and then use a similar method to solve the complex problem.

Problem Solving Strategies

Draw a Diagram	Make a Table
Make a Model	**Solve a Simpler Problem**
Guess and Test	Use Logical Reasoning
Work Backward	Use a Venn Diagram
Find a Pattern	Make an Organized List

EXAMPLE

In a garden, there are 2 flowers, 1 red and 1 blue. Each year, the number of red flowers increases by 1 and the number of blue flowers increases by 2. What percent of the flowers will be red 10 years from now?

 **Understand the Problem**

List the important information.

- The field begins with 1 red and 1 blue flower.
- Each year, the number of red flowers increases by 1.
- Each year, the number of blue flowers increases by 2.

The answer will be the percent of red flowers after 10 years have passed.

 **Make a Plan**

Solve a simpler problem: Find the pattern in the number of red flowers and the total number of flowers in ten years.

 **Solve**

Make a table. Separate the two patterns. Identify each pattern and develop a formula.

Year	Red Flowers	Pattern	Blue Flowers	Total Flowers	Pattern
0	1	$1 + (0)$	1	2	$2 + 3(0)$
1	2	$1 + (1)$	3	5	$2 + 3(1)$
2	3	$1 + (2)$	5	8	$2 + 3(2)$
3	4	$1 + (3)$	7	11	$2 + 3(3)$

If n is the nth year, then the number of red flowers is $1 + n$ and the total number of flowers is $2 + 3n$. The percent of flowers that are red is the ratio of the number of red flowers to the total number of flowers.

So the percent of red flowers in the nth year is $\frac{1+n}{2+3n}$, and in 10 years the percent of flowers that are red is $\frac{1+10}{2+3(10)} = \frac{11}{32} = 34.375\%$.

 **Look Back**

Check that the answer is reasonable. Since the blue flowers grow faster than the red flowers and the garden starts with an equal number of each, there should be more blue flowers than red flowers. Therefore, the percent of red flowers should be less than 50%.

PRACTICE

1. In a field of flowers, there are 2 flowers; 1 yellow and 1 orange. Each year, the number of yellow flowers increases by 3, and the number of orange flowers increases by 4. What percent of the flowers will be yellow in 20 years?

Use Logical Reasoning

Use logical reasoning to help you solve problems by identifying the facts and using them to draw conclusions.

Problem Solving Strategies

Draw a Diagram	Make a Table
Make a Model	Solve a Simpler Problem
Guess and Test	**Use Logical Reasoning**
Work Backward	Use a Venn Diagram
Find a Pattern	Make an Organized List

EXAMPLE

Friends Jeff, Luca, Linda, and Blair are each a different age between 11 and 14. Each person has a different favorite color and sport. The sports are baseball, football, tennis and hockey. The colors are red, blue, green, and yellow. Jeff is 11 and likes to play baseball. The football player is the oldest and dislikes red. The hockey player's favorite color is blue. Linda does not play football. Blair likes the color green, plays tennis, and is a year younger than Linda. Find each person's age, favorite color, and sport.

1 Understand the Problem

List the important information.

- Jeff is 11 and likes to play baseball.
- The football player is the oldest and dislikes red.
- The hockey player's favorite color is blue.
- Linda does not play football.
- Blair likes the color green, plays tennis, and is a year younger than Linda.

The answer will be each person's age, favorite color, and sport.

2 Make a Plan

Start with the given clues. Use logical reasoning to make a table of the facts.

3 Solve

Make a table. Work with the clues one at a time. Place a ✔ in a box if the clue matches the person and an *X* if it does not.

	R	Bl	G	Y	Ba	F	T	H	11	12	13	14
Jeff	✔	X	X	X	✔	X	X	X	✔	X	X	X
Luca	X	X	X	✔	X	✔	X	X	X	X	X	✔
Linda	X	✔	X	X	X	X	X	✔	X	X	✔	X
Blair	X	X	✔	X	X	X	✔	X	X	✔	X	X

Jeff is 11, plays baseball, and likes red. Luca is 14, plays football, and likes yellow. Linda is 13, plays hockey, and likes blue. Blair is 12, plays tennis, and likes green.

4 Look Back

Compare your answer to the clues in the problem. Make sure none of the conclusions conflict with the clues.

PRACTICE

1. Friends Bob, Gary, Roxanne, and Robin have last names that begin with the letters *B, S, T,* and *H*. Their ages are 10, 12, 14, and 16, and their hair colors are blond, black, brown, and red. Bob's last initial is *B*. Robin is a teenager. Roxanne does not have red hair. Bob is 2 years older than Roxanne. The oldest has the last initial *S* and brown hair. Gary's last initial comes before Roxanne's in the alphabet. Gary is 10 and has black hair. Find each person's last initial, age, and hair color.

Use a Venn Diagram

Venn diagrams can be useful in solving problems with sets that overlap each other.

Problem Solving Strategies

Draw a Diagram	Make a Table
Make a Model	Solve a Simpler Problem
Guess and Test	Use Logical Reasoning
Work Backward	**Use a Venn Diagram**
Find a Pattern	Make an Organized List

EXAMPLE

There were three science lectures that students could attend, one on physics, one on chemistry, and one on biology. Four students attended all lectures, 6 students went to both the biology and physics lectures, 10 students went to both the chemistry and physics lectures, and 16 students went to both the chemistry and biology lectures. If a total of 30 students attended the physics lecture, 50 students attended the chemistry lecture, and 60 students attended the biology lecture, how many students went to at least one lecture?

1 Understand the Problem

List the important information.

- all lectures: 4
- biology and physics: 6
- chemistry and physics: 10
- chemistry and biology: 16
- physics: total of 30
- chemistry: total of 50
- biology: total of 50

The answer will be the number of students that went to at least one lecture.

2 Make a Plan

Use a Venn diagram to show the number of students that attended each lecture.

3 Solve

Draw and label three overlapping circles. In the section where all the circles overlap, place a 4 because 4 students attended all the lectures. In each section where only two circles overlap, place the number of students that went to both those two lectures. Calculate the number of students that went to only one lecture by taking the number of students that attended each lecture and subtracting the number that also attended other lectures. The sum of the numbers in each circle should be the total number of students that attended that lecture.

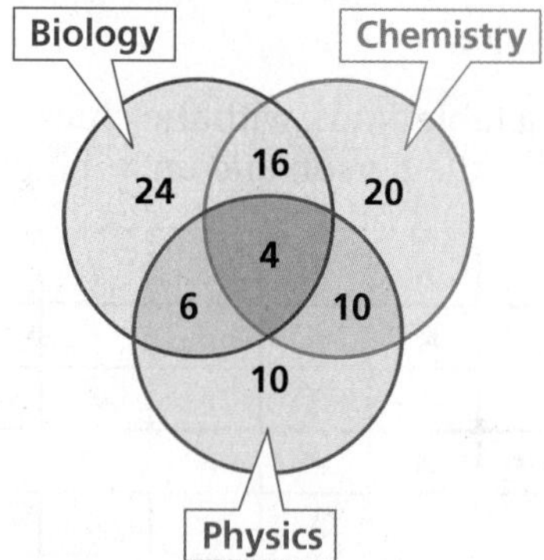

The total number of students is the sum of the numbers in all the circles.

Therefore, the number of students is $24 + 6 + 10 + 16 + 4 + 10 + 20 = 90$.

4 Look Back

Check your Venn diagram against the initial data to make certain that the diagram agrees with the question asked.

PRACTICE

1. In summer school the math courses offered were Algebra, Geometry, and Calculus. Three students took all three courses, 5 students took only Algebra and Geometry, 1 student took only Calculus and Geometry, and 10 students took only Algebra and Calculus. If there were 28 students in Algebra, 24 students in Geometry, and 30 students in Calculus, how many students took at least one math course?

Make an Organized List

When you are solving a problem that contains a lot of information, it may be helpful to make an organized list to record the possible outcomes.

Problem Solving Strategies

Draw a Diagram	Make a Table
Make a Model	Solve a Simpler Problem
Guess and Test	Use Logical Reasoning
Work Backward	Use a Venn Diagram
Find a Pattern	**Make an Organized List**

EXAMPLE

Pete's Pizza has four toppings to choose from: pepperoni, ham, extra cheese, and mushrooms. How many possible pizzas are there if you can have 0, 1, 2, 3, or 4 toppings and cannot get the same topping twice?

1 Understand the Problem

List the important information.

- There are 4 possible toppings.
- A pizza can have 0 to 4 toppings.
- You cannot have the same topping twice.

The answer will be the number of pizzas that are possible.

Make a Plan

Make an organized list of the possible combinations of toppings. List all the possible combinations.

3 Solve

Make a column for each number of toppings on the pizza. Let P = pepperoni, H = ham, C = extra cheese, and M = mushrooms.

0 Toppings	1 Topping	2 Toppings	3 Toppings	4 Toppings
Plain Cheese	P	PH	PHC	PHCM
	H	PC	PHM	
	C	PM	PCM	
	M	HC	HCM	
		HM		
		CM		

Adding the number of choices yields 16 possible pizzas.

Look Back

Make sure all the possible choices are shown in the table and that none repeat.

PRACTICE

1. Pete's Pizza has decided that customers may repeat toppings but choose no more than a total of two toppings per pizza. How many pizzas are now possible?
2. Calvin has a bag with 5 balls inside. The balls are all distinct and labeled A through E. How many three-letter "words" can he create by randomly removing a ball and not replacing it? (Consider a word to be any permutation of three letters.)
3. Matty is going to run some errands. She may stop by the cleaners, the video store, and the grocery store. If she plans to make at least 1 stop, how many possible routes can she take?

1-1

Check It Out!

1a. $(3, 3)$ **b.** $(-2, 1)$

2a.

$x + 3$	x	y
1	−2	4
2	−1	0
3	x	2
5	x	2

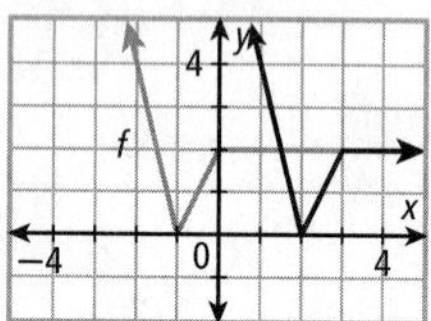

b.

x	y	$-y$
−2	4	−4
−1	0	x
x	2	−2
x	2	−2

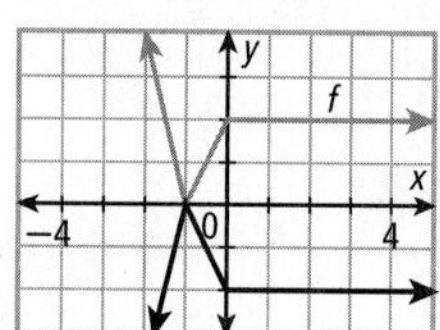

3.

x	y	$2y$
−1	3	6
0	0	0
2	2	4
4	2	4

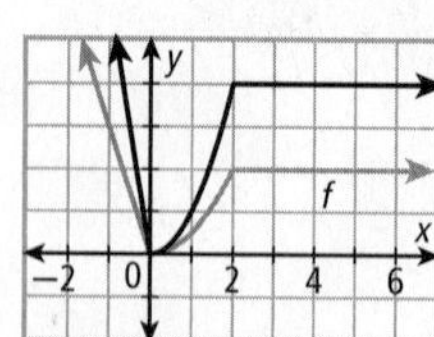

4. vertical compression by a factor of $\frac{3}{4}$

Recording Studio Fees

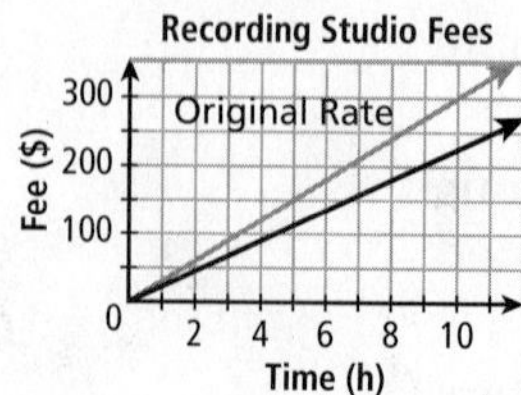

Exercises

1. compression **3.** $(4, -1)$

5.

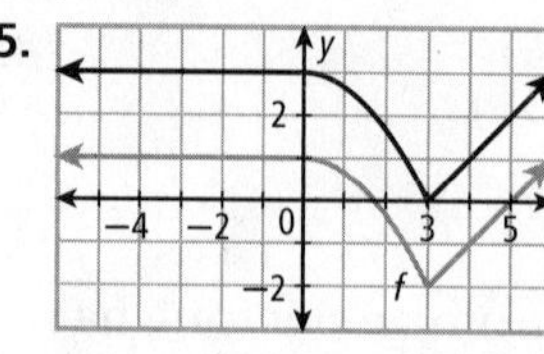

7.

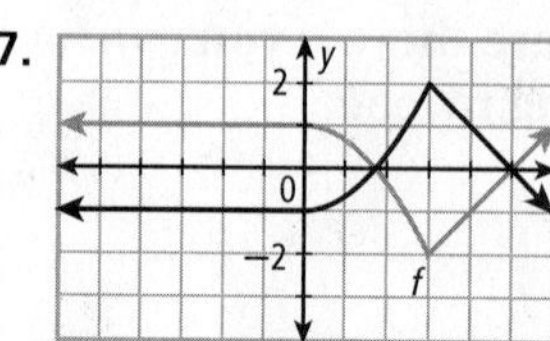

9.

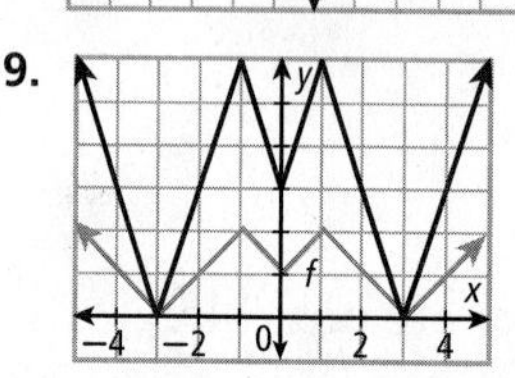

11. vertical compression by a factor of $\frac{1}{2}$ **13.** horizontal shift right 5 units **15.** $(3, 5)$

17.

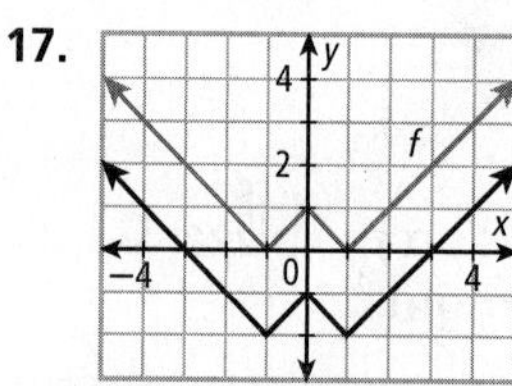

21.

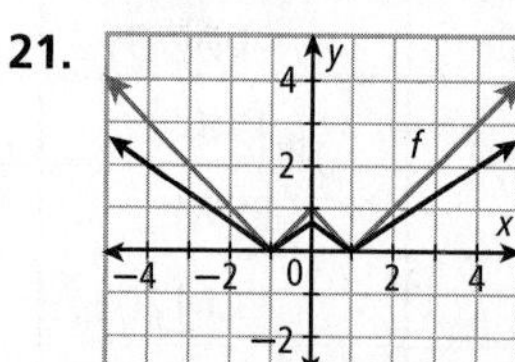

25. vertical shift down 5 units **27.** horizontal stretch by a factor of 2 **29.** 10 square units; the same as the original **31.** 7 square units; smaller than the original **33.** 10 square units; the same as the original **35.** 30 square units; larger than the original **37a.** vertical translation **b.** horizontal compression **c.** the increase in the per-hour labor rate

39.

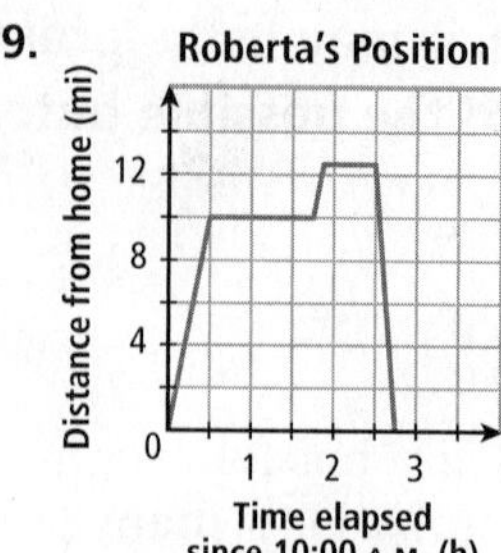

41.

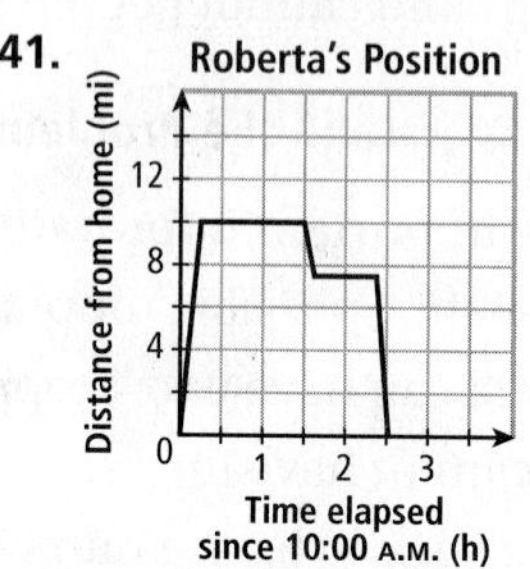

43. The library is half as far from Roberta's house. **47.** H **49.** H **53a.** $c(n) = 0.37n$ **b.** vertical stretch **c.** 15 in 1999 and 13 in 2002 **d.** The number of letters that can be mailed for $5.00 must be rounded down to the nearest whole number.

1-2

Check It Out!

1a. cubic; translation 2 units up **b.** quadratic; reflection across the y-axis

2. linear; vertical stretch by a factor of 3

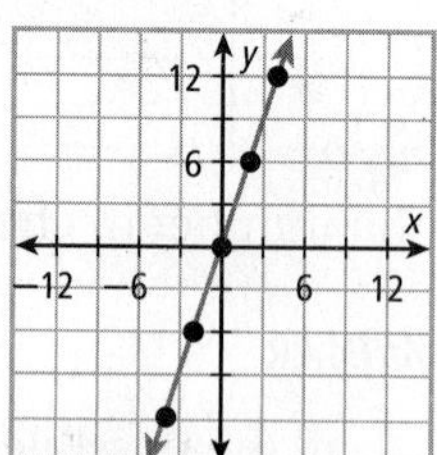

3. linear; about $72

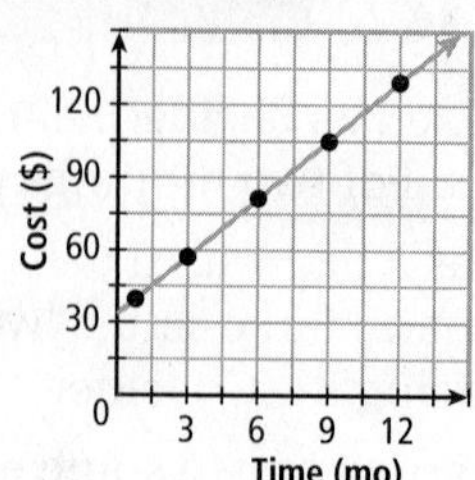

Exercises **3.** quadratic; translation 1 unit left **5.** square root; translation 3 units left **7.** linear; translation $\sqrt{2}$ units down
9. cubic; vertical compression or horizontal stretch **11.** quadratic; translation 1 unit down
13. cubic; translation 3 units up
15. square root; vertical stretch or horizontal compression
17. D: $\{x \mid x \geq 0\}$; R: $\{y \mid y \geq 0\}$; vertical stretch by a factor of 3
19. D: $\{x \mid x \geq 0\}$; R: $\{y \mid y \leq 0\}$; reflection across the x-axis
21. D: $\{x \mid x \in \mathbb{R}\}$; R: $\{y \mid y \leq 1\}$; reflection across the x-axis and then a vertical shift up 1 unit
23. \$195 **25.** quadratic; horizontal shift right 7 units **27.** linear; reflection across the y-axis and a vertical shift down 1 unit
29. linear; $\approx$ 1500 pixels
31. quadratic; $\approx$ 1417 pixels
33. Cubic; D: $\{\ell \mid \ell \geq 0\}$; R: $\{y \mid y \geq 0\}$; the domain and range are restricted.
35. Linear; D: $\{n \mid n \in \mathbb{N}\}$; R: $\{y \mid y \in \mathbb{N}\}$; the domain and range are restricted.
37. Square root; D: $\{a \mid a \geq 0\}$; R: $\{y \mid y \geq 0\}$; the domain and range are the same.
39a. linear **b.** cubic
c. quadratic **d.** square root
e. linear; horizontal stretch by a factor of 2 and a vertical shift up 3 units **43.** H **45.** G
47. quadratic **49.** linear

1-3

Check It Out!

1a. $g(x) = 3(x - 2) + 1$
b. $g(x) = -(x + 2)$
2. $g(x) = \frac{1}{4}(3x + 2)$
3. $g(x) = \frac{1}{2}(x + 8)$
4a. $S(n) = 25n - 75$
b.

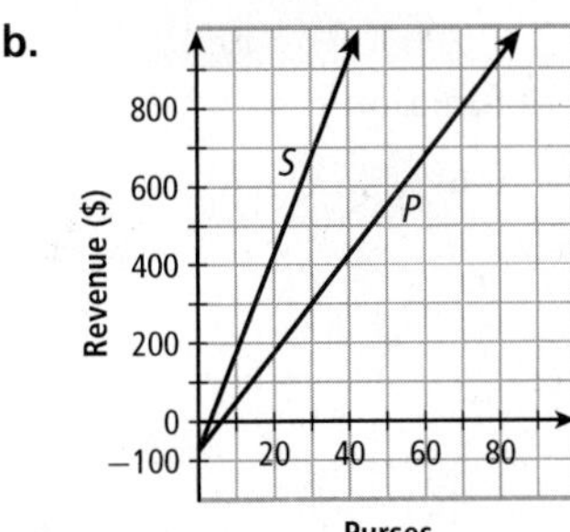

4c. horizontal compression by a factor of $\frac{1}{2}$

Exercises **1.** $g(x) = -\frac{3}{2}x + 2$
3. $g(x) = x - 6$
5. $g(x) = \frac{2}{3}x - 6$
7a. $D(n) = .0.60n + 5.00$
b.

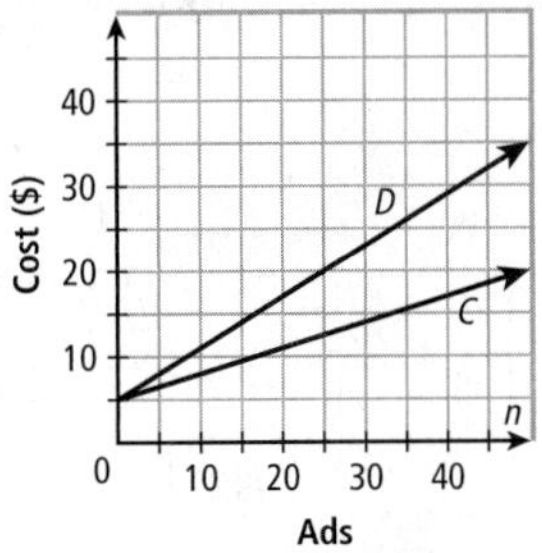

c. horizontal compression by a factor of $\frac{1}{2}$
9. $g(x) = \frac{1}{2}x - 4$
11. $g(x) = 1.2(-0.5x + 0.5)$
13. $g(x) = \frac{1}{2.75}(x + 1)$
15a. $g(x) = 0.15x + 0.35$
b.

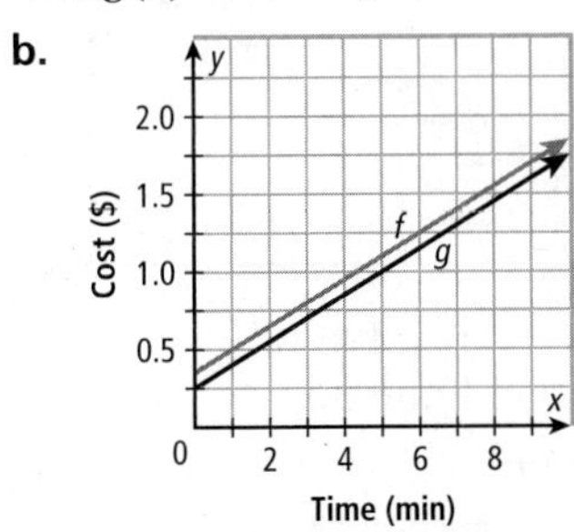

c. vertical shift up 0.1 unit
17. $g(x) = 2x$
19. $T(n) = 0.10\left(\frac{n}{15}\right) = \frac{n}{150}$; vertical stretch by a factor of 1.6
21a. $g(x) = -x - 2$
b. $h(x) = -x + 2$

23a. 22.125; 20; 23; 59 **b.** Mean, median, and mode are increased by 7. Range stays the same.
c. All are multiplied by 4.
d. Mean, median, and mode are multiplied by 2, and 5 is added. Range is multiplied by 2. **25.** H
27. F

1-4

Check It Out!

1.

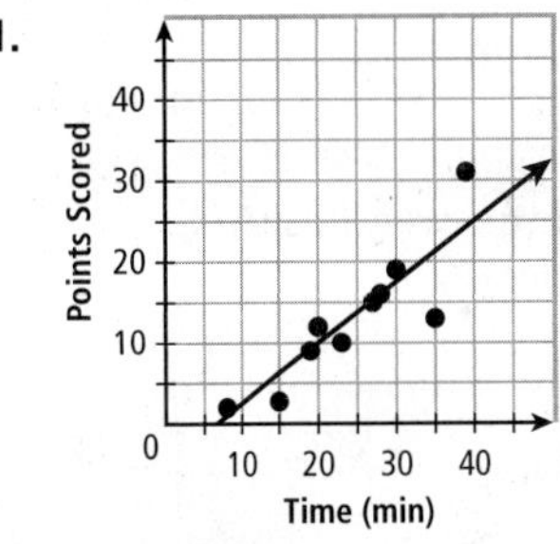

Possible answer: $p = 0.75m - 5$
2a.

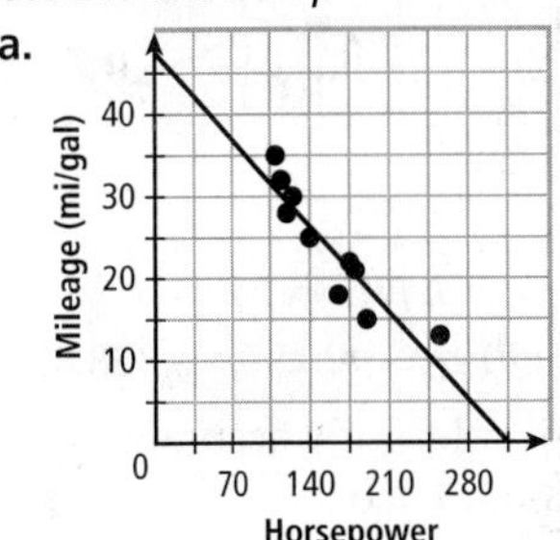

b. $r \approx -0.916$; $y \approx -0.15x + 47.5$; for a 1-unit increase in hp, gas mileage drops $\approx$ 0.15 mi/gal
c. $\approx$ 16.0 mi/gal **3.** $\approx$ 10 g; not close to the 15 g in the table.

Exercises **1a.** a weak positive linear correlation between data sets
b. a strong negative linear correlation between data sets
c. virtually no correlation between the data sets
3a–b.

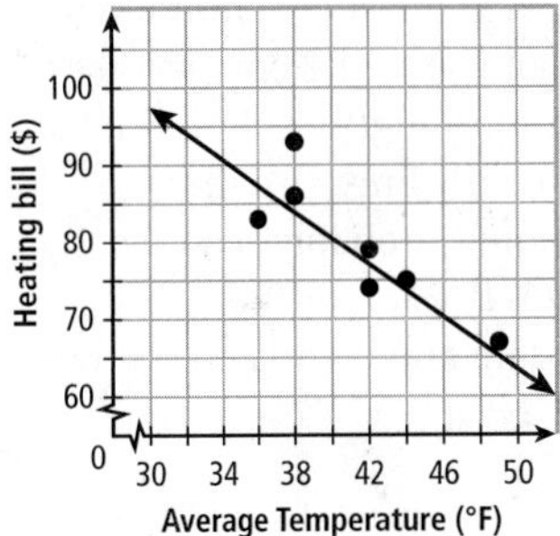

$r \approx -0.864$; $h \approx -1.68t + 148.88$
c. \$81.68; the correlation coefficient is fairly close to -1, so the prediction is somewhat close to the actual value.

5.

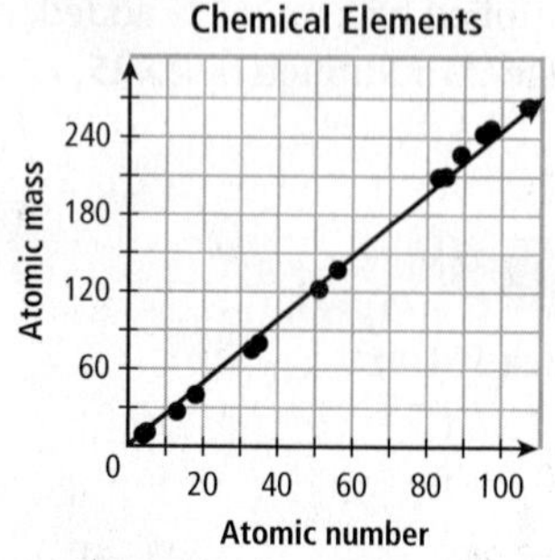

Possible answer: positive; $w = 2.5n - 5.5$

7a–b.

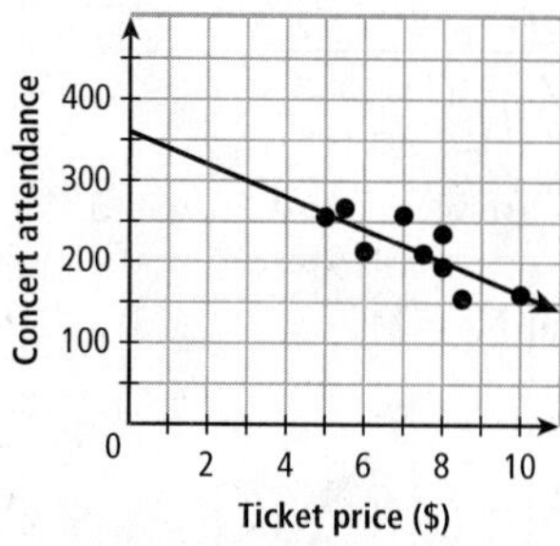

$r \approx -0.801$ $a \approx -20.95p + 368.89$
c. 180 people; fairly accurate.
9. $r \approx 0$ **11.** $r \approx 0.9$
13. Possible answers:
13a. $s = 95.5 - p$
b. $s = 100.5 - p$;

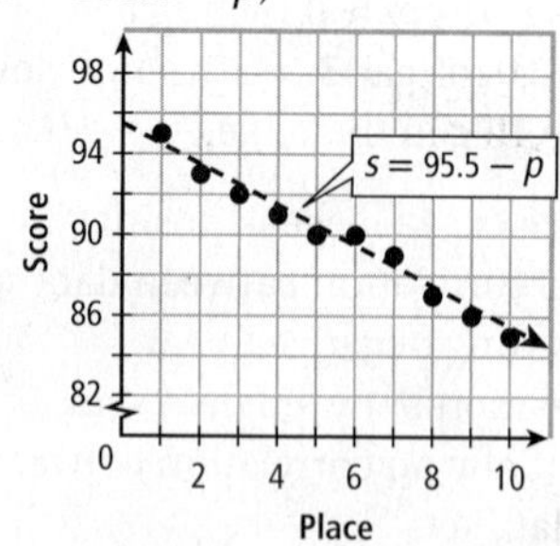

15a. $r = 0.994$; $y \approx 1.20x - 3.66$
b. A 1 cm increase in femur length corresponds to a 1.2 cm increase in humerus length. **c.** 44.7 cm; the data is nearly linear, so the prediction is probably accurate.
19. C **21.** B **23a.** $r = 0$
b. The data appear related but not linear.

Study Guide: Review

1. parent function
2. translation
3. correlation
4. (0, –5)
5. (5, 1)
6.

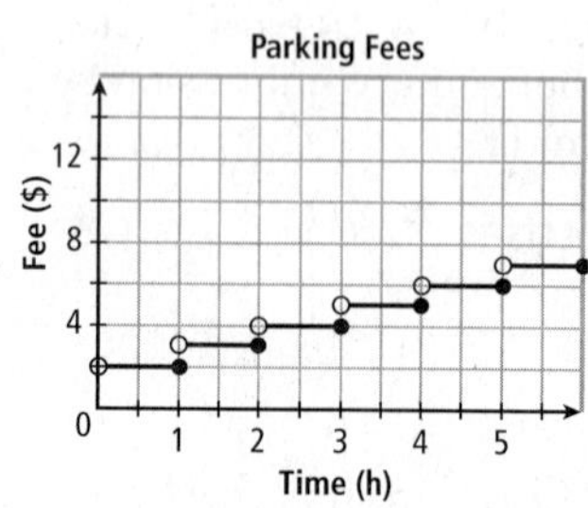

vertical compression by a factor of $\frac{1}{2}$

7.

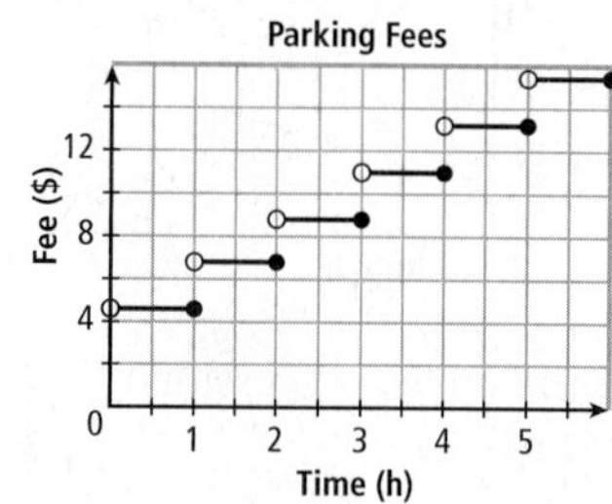

vertical stretch by a factor of 1.1

8.

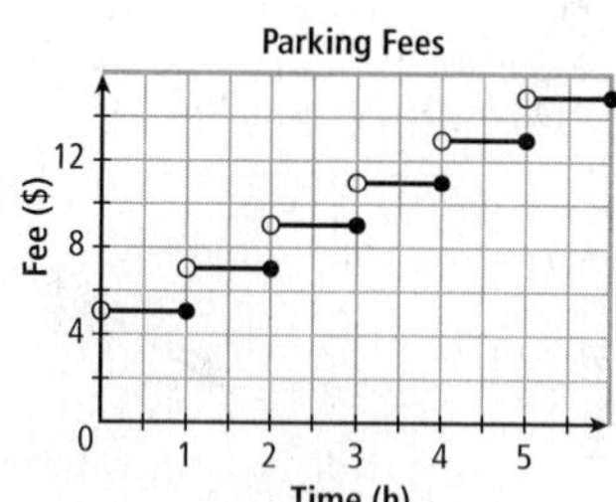

translation 1 unit up

9. quadratic function

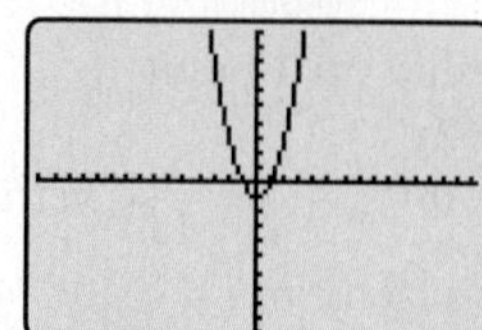

translation 1 unit down

10. square-root function

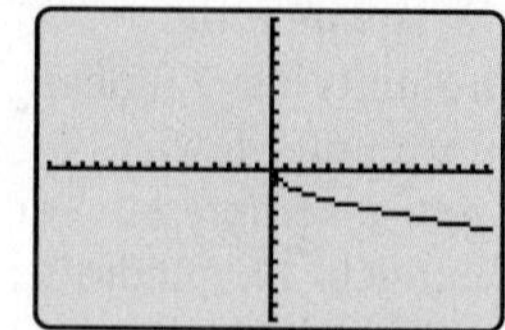

reflection across the x-axis

11.

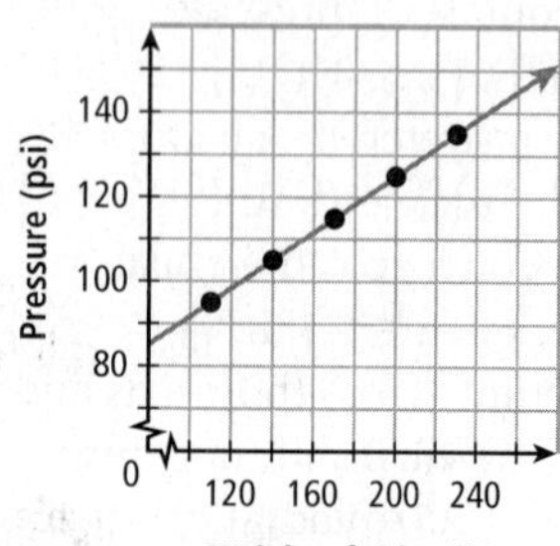

linear function; about 90 psi
12. $g(x) = x - 8$
13. $g(x) = 3x + 15$
14. $g(x) = x - 4$
15. $g(x) = -x - 5$
16. $g(x) = -x - 12$
17a.

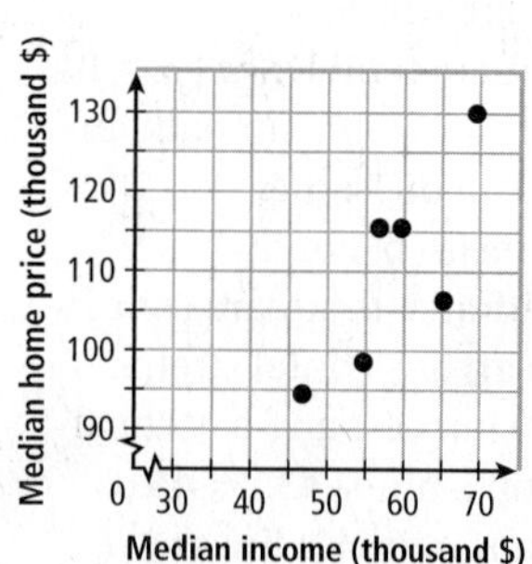

b. $r = 0.800$; $P = 1.279I + 35.074$

Mastering the Standards

for Mathematical Practice

The topics described in the Standards for Mathematical Content will vary from year to year. However, the *way* in which you learn, study, and think about mathematics will not. The Standards for Mathematical Practice describe skills that you will use in all of your math courses.

Mathematical Practices

1. *Make sense of problems and persevere in solving them.*
2. *Reason abstractly and quantitatively.*
3. *Construct viable arguments and critique the reasoning of others.*
4. *Model with mathematics.*
5. *Use appropriate tools strategically.*
6. *Attend to precision.*
7. *Look for and make use of structure.*
8. *Look for and express regularity in repeated reasoning.*

1 Make sense of problems and persevere in solving them.

Mathematically proficient students start by explaining to themselves the meaning of a problem... They analyze givens, constraints, relationships, and goals. They make conjectures about the form... of the solution and plan a solution pathway...

In your book

Focus on Problem Solving describes a four-step plan for problem solving. The plan is introduced at the beginning of your book, and practice with the plan appears throughout the book.

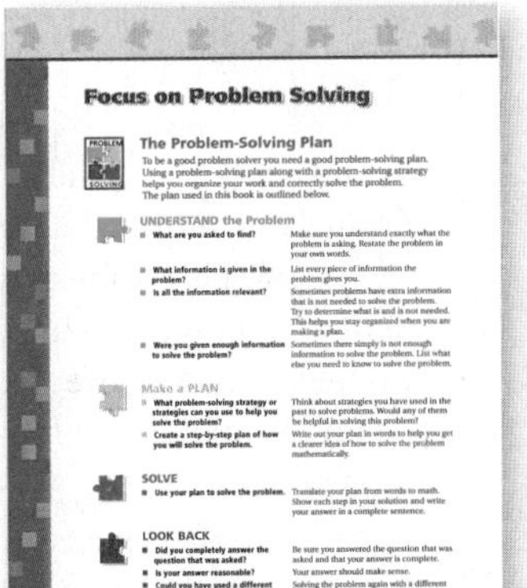

Focus on Problem Solving

The Problem-Solving Plan

To be a good problem solver you need a good problem-solving plan. Using a problem-solving plan along with a problem-solving strategy helps you organize your work and correctly solve the problem. The plan used in this book is outlined below.

UNDERSTAND the Problem

What are you asked to find?	Make sure you understand exactly what the problem is asking. Restate the problem in your own words.
What information is given in the problem?	List every piece of information the problem gives you.
Is all the information relevant?	Sometimes problems have extra information that is not needed to solve the problem. Try to determine what is and is not needed. This helps you stay organized when you are making a plan.
Were you given enough information to solve the problem?	Sometimes there simply is not enough information to solve the problem. List what else you need to know to solve the problem.

Make a PLAN

What problem-solving strategy or strategies can you use to help you solve the problem?	Think about strategies you have used in the past to solve problems. Would any of them be helpful in solving this problem?
Create a step-by-step plan of how you will solve the problem.	Write out your plan in words to help you get a clearer idea of how to solve the problem mathematically.

SOLVE

Use your plan to solve the problem.	Translate your plan from words to math. Show each step in your solution and write your answer in a complete sentence.

LOOK BACK

Did you completely answer the question that was asked?	Be sure you answered the question that was asked and that your answer is complete.
Is your answer reasonable?	Your answer should make sense.
Could you have used a different strategy to solve the problem?	Solving the problem again with a different strategy is a good way to check your answer.
Did you learn anything that could help you solve similar problems in the future?	You may want to take notes about this kind of problem and the strategy you used to solve it.

xx *Focus On Problem Solving*

EXAMPLE 5 *Problem-Solving Application*

PROBLEM SOLVING

The cost to place an ad in a newspaper for one week is a linear function of the number of lines in the ad. The costs for 3, 5, and 10 lines are shown. Write an equation in slope-intercept form that represents the function. Then find the cost of an ad that is 18 lines long.

City Gazette

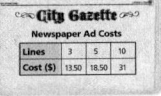

Newspaper Ad Costs

Lines	3	5	10
Cost ($)	13.50	18.50	31

1 Understand the Problem

- The **answer** will have two parts—an equation in slope-intercept form and the cost of an ad that is 18 lines long.
- The ordered pairs given in the table satisfy the equation.

2 Make a Plan

First, find the slope. Then use point-slope form to write the equation. Finally, write the equation in slope-intercept form.

3 Solve

Step 1 Choose any two ordered pairs from the table to find the slope.

$$m = \frac{y_2 - y_1}{x_2 - x_1} = \frac{18.50 - 13.50}{5 - 3} = \frac{5}{2} = 2.5 \quad \textit{Use (3, 13.50) and (5, 18.50).}$$

Step 2 Substitute the slope and any ordered pair from the table into the point-slope form.

$$y - y_1 = m(x - x_1)$$
$$y - 31 = 2.5(x - 10) \quad \textit{Use (10, 31).}$$

Step 3 Write the equation in slope-intercept form by solving for y.

$$y - 31 = 2.5(x - 10)$$
$$y - 31 = 2.5x - 25 \quad \textit{Distribute 2.5.}$$
$$y = 2.5x + 6 \quad \textit{Add 31 to both sides.}$$

Step 4 Find the cost of an ad containing 18 lines by substituting 18 for x.

$$y = 2.5x + 6$$
$$y = 2.5(18) + 6 = 51$$

The cost of an ad containing 18 lines is $51.

4 Look Back

Check the equation by substituting the ordered pairs (3, 13.50) and (5, 18.50).

y	$= 2.5x + 6$
13.50	2.5(3) + 6
13.5	7.5 + 6
13.5	13.5✓

y	$= 2.5x + 6$
18.50	2.5(5) + 6
18.5	12.5 + 6
18.5	18.5✓

Comstock/Getty Images

2-1

Check It Out!

1.

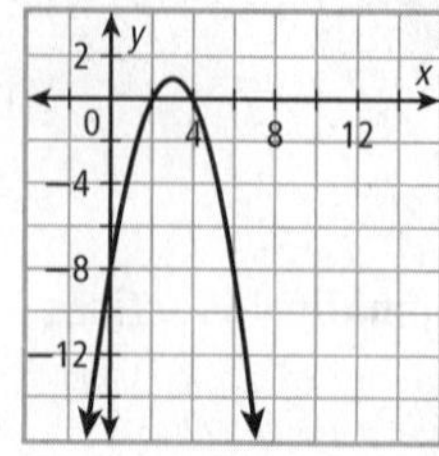

x	−1	1	3	5	7
$g(x)$	−15	−3	1	−3	−15

2a.

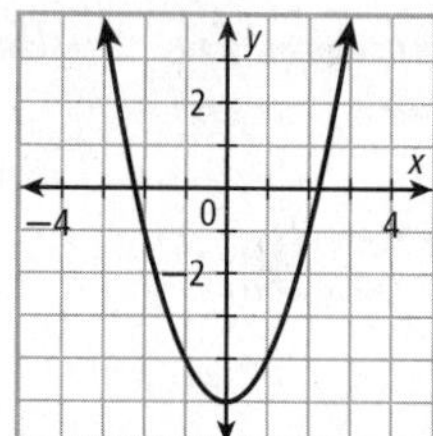

g is f translated 5 units down.

b.

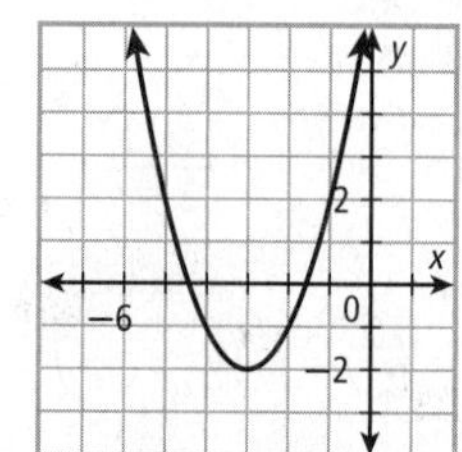

h is f translated 3 units left and 2 units down.

3a.

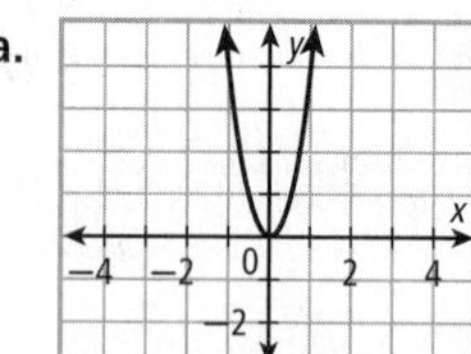

g is a horizontal compression of f by a factor of $\frac{1}{2}$.

b.

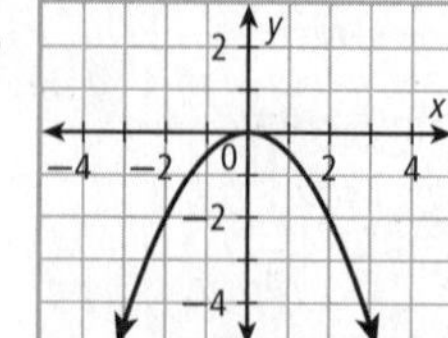

h is f reflected across the x-axis and vertically compressed by a factor of $\frac{1}{2}$. **4a.** $g(x) = \frac{1}{3}(x - 2)^2 - 4$ **b.** $g(x) = -(x + 5)^2 + 1$ **5.** Vertical compression by a factor of $\frac{13}{15}$; the braking distance will be less with optimally inflated new tires than with tires having more wear.

Exercises 1. vertex

3.

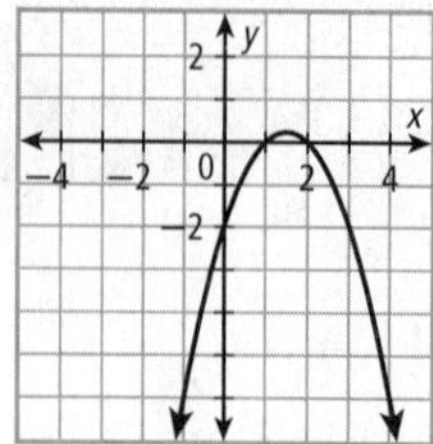

5. d is f translated 4 units right. **7.** h is f translated 1 unit left and 3 units down. **9.** h is a horizontal stretch of f by a factor of 8. **11.** h is f reflected across the x-axis and horizontally compressed by a factor of $\frac{1}{5}$. **13.** d is f reflected across the x-axis and vertically compressed by a factor of $\frac{2}{3}$. **15.** $h(x) = -x^2 - 6$

17.

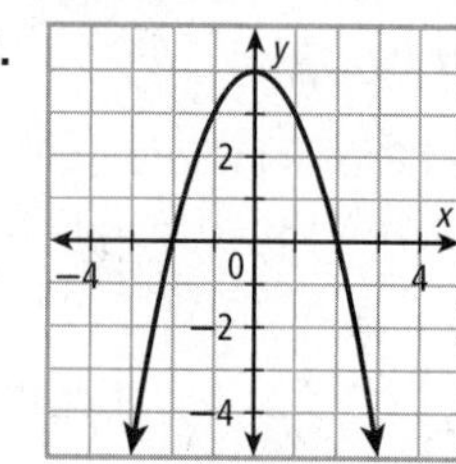

19.

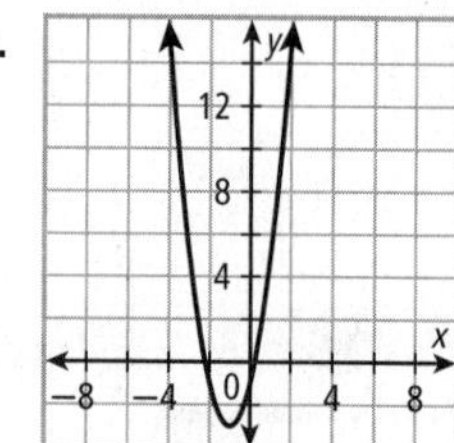

21. h is f translated 5 units left. **23.** g is f translated 4 units left and 3 units down. **25.** j is f translated 4 units right and 9 units down. **27.** h is f reflected across the x-axis and vertically stretched by a factor of 20. **29.** $g(x) = -\frac{1}{2}(x - 1)^2$ **31.** Vertical translation; at any given speed, the gas mileage for an SUV is 18 mi/gal less than for a compact car. **33.** p is f reflected across the x-axis and translated 4 units right. **35.** h is f vertically stretched by a factor of 4 and translated 2 units down. **37.** g is f horizontally compressed by a factor of $\frac{1}{3}$ and translated 1 unit up. **39.** C **41.** A **43.** horizontal line; linear or constant function

45a. vertical compression by a factor of 0.38 and translation 3.5 units right and 59 units up **b.** $y = -6.08(t - 4)^2 + 95$ **47.** J **49.** G **51.** translation 6 units right and 6 units up: $y = -3(x - 3)^2 + 3$

2-2

Check It Out! 1. $x = 3$

2a.

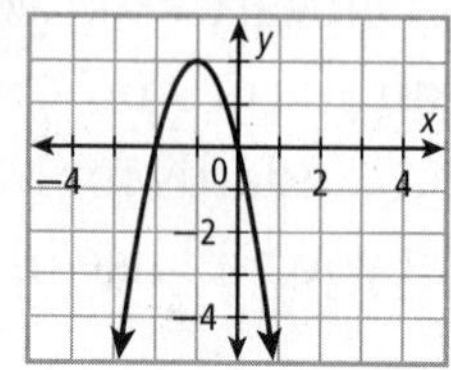

downward; $x = -1$; $(-1, 2)$; 0

b.

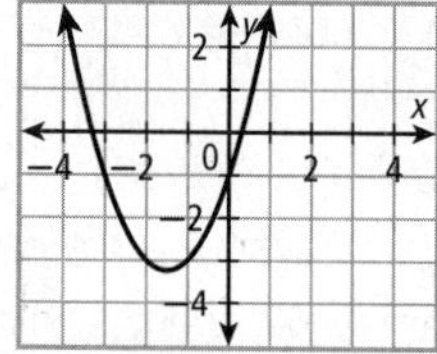

upward; $x = -\frac{3}{2}$; $\left(-\frac{3}{2}, -\frac{13}{4}\right)$; −1

3a. minimum: −6; D: $\mathbb{R}$; R: $\{y \mid y \geq -6\}$ **b.** maximum: −4; D: $\mathbb{R}$; R: $\{y \mid y \leq -4\}$ **4.** 30.0 mi/gal at 49 mi/h

Exercises 1. minimum **3.** $x = 0$ **5.** downward; $x = -1$; $(-1, -7)$; −8 **7.** downward; $x = 2$; $(2, 3)$; −1 **9.** maximum: $\frac{1}{4}$; D: $\mathbb{R}$; R: $\left\{y \mid y \leq \frac{1}{4}\right\}$ **11.** 3.125 m **13.** $x = 1$ **15.** upward; $x = -\frac{1}{2}$; $\left(-\frac{1}{2}, -\frac{9}{4}\right)$; −2 **17.** upward; $x = 2$; $(2, -6)$; −4 **19.** upward; $x = -\frac{1}{3}$; $\left(-\frac{1}{3}, -\frac{25}{3}\right)$; −8 **21.** downward; $x = 0$; $(0, -2)$; −2 **23.** upward; $x = -2$; $(-2, 1)$; 2 **25.** maximum: 9; D: $\mathbb{R}$; R: $\{y \mid y \leq 9\}$ **27.** maximum: −4; D: $\mathbb{R}$; R: $\{y \mid y \leq -4\}$ **29.** minimum: 0; D: $\mathbb{R}$; R: $\{y \mid y \geq 0\}$ **31.** 64 ft **33a.** 562.5 mm **b.** 93.75 to 1 **c.** 168.75 m **35.** minimum: ≈ −3.029771 **37.** minimum: ≈ −1.253333 **41a.** about 1.6 s **b.** about 45 ft **43.** G **45.** G

2-3

Check It Out! 1. −3,1 **2a.** −1, 6 **b.** 0, 8 **3.** 3 s **4a.** $x = 2$ **b.** $x = -\frac{3}{5}$, $x = \frac{3}{5}$ **5.** Possible answer: $f(x) = x^2 - 25$

Exercises 1. roots **3.** 2, 4 **5.** 1, 6 **7.** −4, 0 **9.** −2, 8 **11.** 4 s **13.** $x = 2$ **19.** −3, 2 **21.** −8, −3 **23.** 0, 9 **25.** −8, 1 **27.** 4 s **29.** $x = -\frac{9}{2}$, $x = \frac{9}{2}$ **31.** $x = -\frac{1}{2}, x = \frac{1}{2}$ **33.** $x = \frac{2}{7}$ **37.** 0, 6 **39.** 6 **41.** 11 **43.** 5, 6 **45.** −7, −2 **47a.** $h(t) = -16t^2 + 16t + 5$ **b.** 1.25 s **49.** $x = -5, x = -1$ **51.** $x = -\frac{1}{3}$ **53.** $x = -2, x = 3$ **55a.** $(0, -16)$ **b.** −16 **c.** −4, 4 **57a.** $(1, 2)$ **b.** 0 **c.** 0, 2 **59a.** $\left(-\frac{1}{6}, -4\frac{1}{12}\right)$ **b.** −4 **c.** $-1\frac{1}{3}$, 1 **61.** 20 ft by 4 ft **63.** 10 m by 5 m **67.** B **69.** C **71.** $x = 0, x = \frac{3}{2}$ **73.** $x = \frac{1}{4}, x = \frac{1}{2}$ **75a.** $(a + b)(a^2 - ab + b^2) = a^3 - a^2b + ab^2 + a^2b - ab^2 + b^3 = a^3 + b^3$ **b.** $(2x + 3)(4x^2 - 6x + 9)$ **c.** $a^3 - b^3 = (a - b)(a^2 + ab + b^2)$ **d.** $(x - 1)(x^2 + x + 1)$

2-4

Check It Out! 1a. $x = \pm\frac{5}{2}$ **b.** $x = -11, x = 3$ **2a.** $x^2 + 4x + 4 = (x + 2)^2$ **b.** $x^2 - 4x + 4 = (x - 2)^2$ **c.** $x^2 + 3x + \frac{9}{4} = \left(x + \frac{3}{2}\right)^2$ **3a.** $x = \frac{9 \pm \sqrt{89}}{2}$ **b.** $x = -1, x = 9$ **4a.** $f(x) = (x + 12)^2 + 1; (-12, 1)$ **b.** $g(x) = 5(x - 5)^2 + 3; (5, 3)$

Exercises 1. $\left(\frac{b}{2}\right)^2$ **3.** $x = 1, x = 9$ **5.** $x^2 + 14x + 49 = (x + 7)^2$ **7.** $x^2 - 9x + \frac{81}{4} = \left(x - \frac{9}{2}\right)^2$ **9.** $x = 2, x = 4$ **11.** $x = -2 \pm 2\sqrt{7}$ **13.** $x = -2 \pm \frac{\sqrt{46}}{2}$ **15.** $g(x) = (x - 5)^2 - 14; (5, -14)$ **17.** $f(x) = (x + 4)^2 - 26; (-4, -26)$ **19.** $h(x) = 3(x - 2)^2 - 16; (2, -16)$ **21.** $x = -7, x = 13$ **23.** $x^2 - 18x + 81 = (x - 9)^2$ **25.** $x^2 - \frac{1}{2}x + \frac{1}{16} = \left(x - \frac{1}{4}\right)^2$ **27.** $x = 2 \pm \sqrt{3}$ **29.** $x = 2, x = 6$ **31.** $x = -1 \pm \frac{2\sqrt{3}}{3}$ **33.** $g(x) = (x + 7)^2 + 22; (-7, 22)$ **35.** $f(x) = (x + 2)^2 - 11; (-2, -11)$ **37.** $h(x) = 2(x + 1.5)^2 + 20.5; (-1.5, 20.5)$ **39a.** about 12.3 s **b.** about 2.3 s **41.** $x = \pm\sqrt{3}$ **43.** $x = \pm 5$ **45.** $x = -13 \pm \sqrt{7}$ **47.** $x = \frac{-3 \pm 5\sqrt{2}}{2}$ **49.** $x = \frac{-3 \pm \sqrt{5}}{3}$ **51.** $x = -5, x = -3$ **53.** $x = \frac{-2 \pm \sqrt{7}}{3}$ **55.** $x = \frac{7 \pm \sqrt{57}}{2}$ **57.** $x = -3 \pm \sqrt{5}$ **59.** $x = 4 \pm 2\sqrt{10}$ **61a.** 1.7 s **b.** 71 ft/s **65.** $x = \pm 7.416$ **67.** $x = \pm 4.192$ **69.** $x = \pm 1.528$ **73.** B **75.** A **77.** 2.5 **79.** $b = \pm 24$ **81.** $b = \pm 18$ **83.** $2\sqrt{5} \pm 1$ **85a.** 135,000 ft^2 **b.** 450 ft by 300 ft **c.** 129,600 ft^2

2-5

Check It Out! 1a. $2i\sqrt{3}$ **b.** $12i$ **c.** $-i\sqrt{7}$ **2a.** $x = \pm 6i$ **b.** $x = \pm 4i\sqrt{3}$ **c.** $x = \pm\frac{5}{3}i$ **3a.** $x = -4; y = -\frac{3}{10}$ **b.** $x = -\frac{8}{5}; y = -\frac{\sqrt{6}}{6}$ **4a.** $-2 \pm 3i$ **b.** $4 \pm i\sqrt{2}$ **5a.** $9 + i$ **b.** $\sqrt{3} - i$ **c.** $8i$

Exercises 1. imaginary **3.** $2i$ **5.** $12i$ **7.** $x = \pm 6i$ **9.** $x = \pm 11i$ **11.** $x = 1; y = -1$ **13.** $-3 \pm 5i$ **15.** $\sqrt{5} - 5i$ **17.** $6 - i\sqrt{2}$ **19.** $-i\sqrt{10}$ **21.** $5i\sqrt{2}$ **23.** $x = \pm 4i$ **25.** $x = \pm 8i$ **27.** $x = -3; y = -5$ **29.** $\frac{3 \pm i\sqrt{7}}{8}$ **31.** $\frac{3 \pm i\sqrt{21}}{3}$ **33.** $-\frac{\sqrt{3}}{2} + 2i$ **35.** $-1 - \frac{i}{10}$ **37.** $1 - 14i$ **39.** $-2\sqrt{5} - 4i$ **41.** $9 + i\sqrt{2}$ **43.** $c = 0, d = 5$ **45.** $c = \pm 2, d = 4$ **47.** $x = \pm 9i$ **49.** $x = \pm 12i$ **51.** $x = \pm 2i\sqrt{2}$ **53.** $x = -5 \pm 2i$ **55.** $x = -1 \pm 2i$ **57.** $x = 12 \pm i\sqrt{5}$ **59.** always true **61.** sometimes true **63.** sometimes true **65.** sometimes true **67.** $-1 \pm 4i$ **69.** $-8 \pm 3i$ **71.** $8 \pm 2i$ **73.** The complex conjugate of a real number a is the number a. **75a.** $t = \frac{7}{2} \pm \frac{\sqrt{3}}{2}i$ **b.** no **c.** 196 ft **77.** F **79.** G **81.** When $a < 0$, the 2 solutions are imaginary and complex. When $a > 0$, the 2 solutions are real and complex.

2-6

Check It Out! 1a. $\frac{-3 \pm \sqrt{37}}{2}$ **b.** $4 \pm \sqrt{6}$ **2.** $\frac{1}{6} \pm \frac{\sqrt{95}}{6}i$ **3a.** 1 distinct real solution **b.** 2 distinct nonreal complex solutions **c.** 2 distinct real solutions **4.** 449 ft

Exercises 3. $\frac{2 \pm \sqrt{7}}{3}$ **5.** −6, 1 **7.** $\pm\frac{\sqrt{38}}{2}$ **9.** $-3 \pm i\sqrt{3}$ **11.** $-2 \pm i\sqrt{6}$ **13.** $\frac{-7 \pm i\sqrt{111}}{20}$ **15.** 2 distinct real solutions **17.** 14 in. and 20 in. **19.** −6, 0 **21.** $-1 \pm \sqrt{10}$ **23.** $\pm\frac{\sqrt{21}}{7}$ **25.** $\frac{-1 \pm i\sqrt{3}}{2}$ **27.** $\frac{-7 \pm 3\sqrt{17}}{4}$ **29.** $\frac{2 \pm 2i\sqrt{2}}{3}$ **31.** 2 distinct real solutions **33.** 1 distinct real solution **35.** 2 distinct real solutions **37a.** 9 s **b.** 6 s **39.** $\frac{1 \pm \sqrt{3}}{2}$ **41.** $\frac{-3 \pm \sqrt{17}}{4}$ **43.** $\frac{1 \pm i\sqrt{87}}{2}$ **45.** $x = -2, x = 5$ **47.** $x = -2.5, x = 1.5$ **49.** $x = -3, x = 7$ **51.** $x = \pm 5$ **53.** $x = 8$ **55.** 3 in. **57.** $c = -36$ **61.** B **63.** C **65.** 15 cm and 8 cm

2-7

Check It Out!

1a.

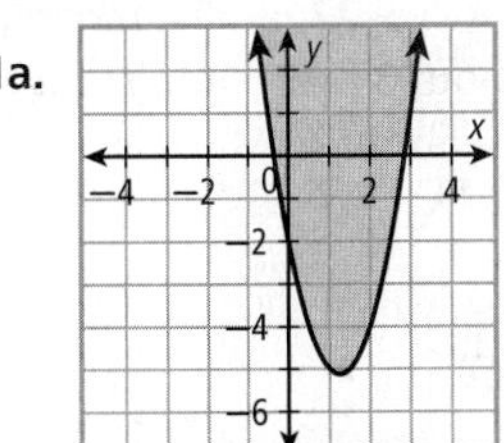

b.

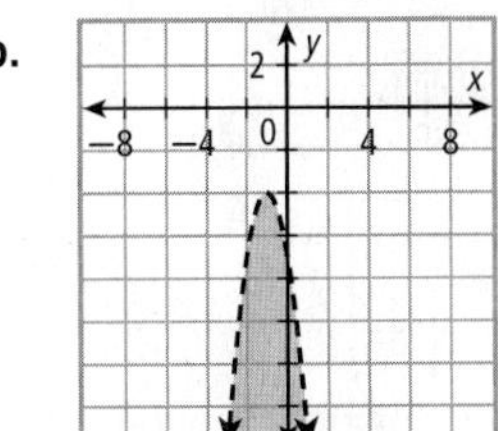

2a. $-1 < x < 2$ **b.** $x \leq 0$ or $x \geq 2.5$ **3a.** $x \leq 2$ *or* $x \geq 4$ **b.** $x < -1$ or $x > 2.5$ **4.** fewer than 14 or more than 36 people

Exercises

3.

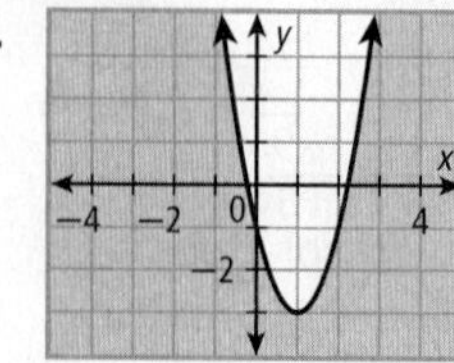

5. $0 \le x \le 5$ **7.** $1.5 \le x \le 3$ **9.** $-8 < x < -5$ **11.** a range of costs between about \$21.78 and \$48.22

13.

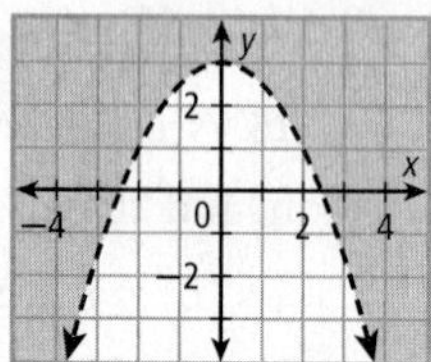

15.

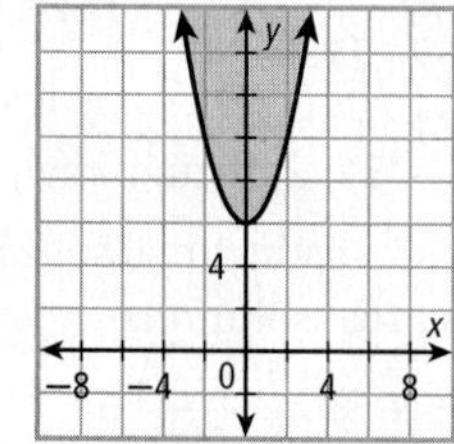

17.

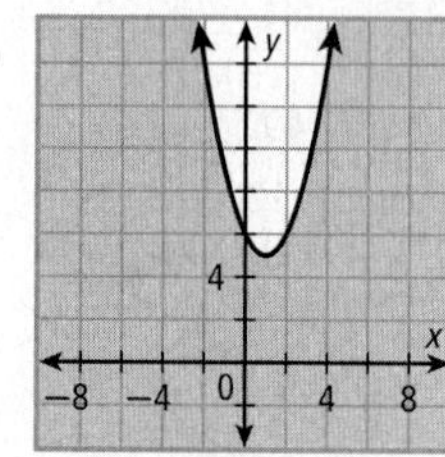

19. $x \le -1$ or $x \ge -0.5$ **21.** $x < -2$ or $x > 4$ **23.** $2 < x < 10$ **25.** $-1 \le x \le 2.5$ **27.** at distances less than about 3 ft and at distances greater than about 102 ft

29.

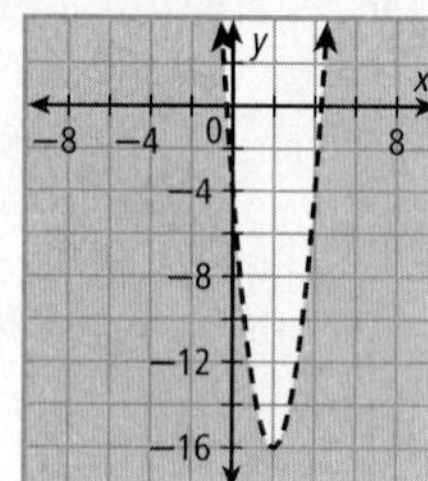

33.

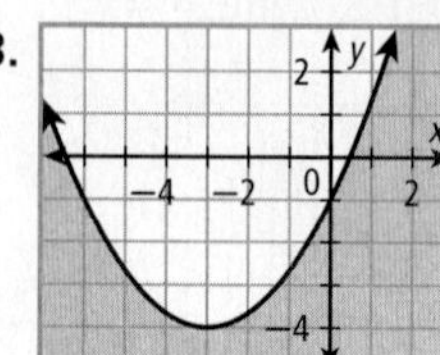

35. $-3 \le x \le 8$ **37.** $\frac{-1-\sqrt{17}}{4} < x < \frac{-1+\sqrt{17}}{4}$ **39.** $-1 - \frac{\sqrt{6}}{3} < x < -1 + \frac{\sqrt{6}}{3}$ **41.** $\frac{-5-\sqrt{61}}{6} \le x \le \frac{-5+\sqrt{61}}{6}$ **43.** $x \le \frac{1-\sqrt{6}}{5}$ or $x \ge \frac{1+\sqrt{6}}{5}$ **45.** $x < 3$ or $x > 9$ **47.** a distance between 0 ft and about 31 ft **49.** A **51a.** $A(x) = -\frac{1}{2}x^2 + 10x$ **b.** $3.7 \le x \le 16.3$ **c.** $0 < x \le 5.5$ or $14.5 \le x \le 20$ **53b.** a width between 5 ft and 15 ft **c.** a width of 10 ft **55.** $0.9 \le x \le 14.1$ **57.** $x \le -2.2$ or $x \ge 0.7$ **59.** It is not **63.** J **65.** $x < -3$ or $x > -1$ **69.** 121.5 square units

2-8

Check It Out! 1a. Quadratic; second differences are constant for equally spaced x-values. **b.** Not quadratic; first differences are constant so the function is linear. **2.** $f(x) = -x^2 + 4x - 3$ **3.** $L(d) \approx 14.3d^2 - 112.4d + 430.1$; about 446 ft

Exercises 3. Not quadratic; second differences are not constant for equally spaced x-values. **5.** $y = x^2 - 2x - 3$ **7.** $y = x^2 - 3x + 4$ **9.** $y = -\frac{1}{2}x^2 + 4x - 3$ **11.** $C(x) \approx 0.0098x^2 + 0.62x + 3.8$; about \$31.20 **13.** Quadratic; second differences are constant for equally spaced x-values. **15.** $y = \frac{4}{3}x^2 - x - \frac{7}{3}$ **17.** $y = 0.5x^2 - 3x - 8$ **19.** $y \approx -3.7x^2 + 216x + 781$; about \$3290 million, or \$3.29 billion **21.** The function is $A(b) = \left(\frac{1}{2}h\right)b$, which is linear. **23.** The function is $A(s) = s^2$, which is quadratic. **25.** -3 **27.** -1 **29a.** $p(s) = -0.125s^2 + 5.25s - 35.05$ **b.** \$18.95 **c.** a maximum point; the price and size of the most expensive pizza **d.** \$9.95; $-$\$1.05 **31.** not quadratic **33.** quadratic; $y = 5x^2 + 2x$ **35.** not quadratic **39a.** $y \approx -10.7x + 208.1$ **b.** no **c.** linear; $y = 4x + 8$ **41.** $t(n) = \frac{1}{2}n^2 + \frac{1}{2}n$ **43b.** $y \approx 0.5x + 3$ **c.** $y \approx -0.13x^2 + 2.8x - 6$ **45.** B **47.** D **49.** $y = 2x^2 - 5$

2-9

Check It Out!

1.

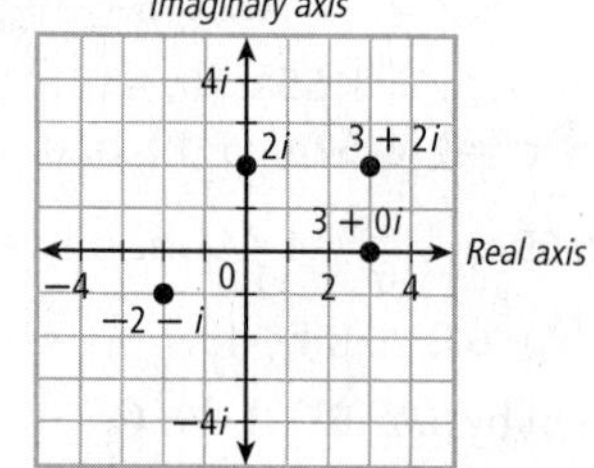

2a. $\sqrt{5}$ **b.** $\frac{1}{2}$ **c.** 23 **3a.** $-3 - i$ **b.** $-3 - 3i$ **c.** 8

4a.

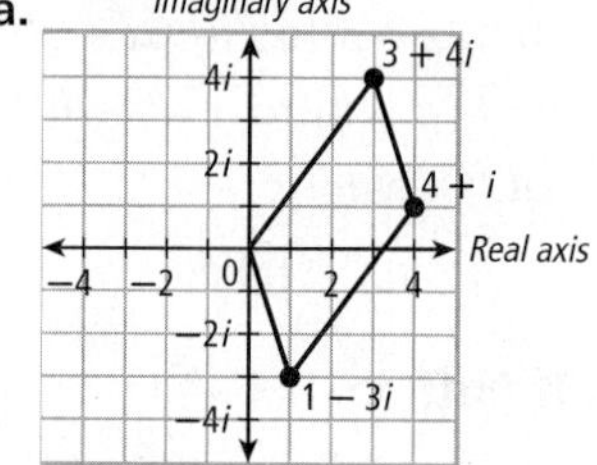

$4 + i$

b.

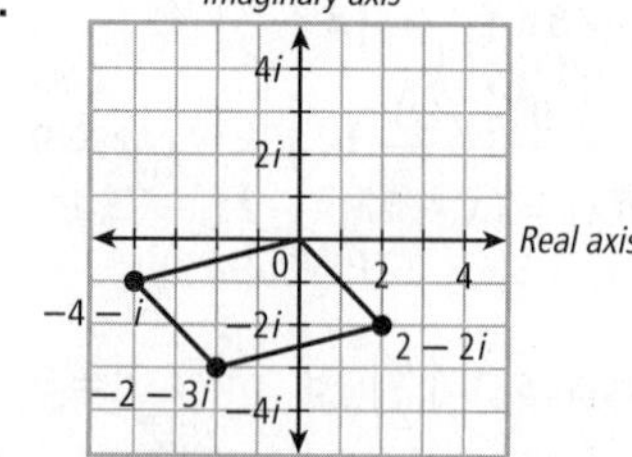

$-2 - 3i$

5a. $10 + 6i$ **b.** $20 - 28i$ **c.** 13 **6a.** $-\frac{1}{2}i$ **b.** -1 **7a.** $-8 + 3i$ **b.** $\frac{7}{5} + \frac{1}{5}i$

Exercises **1.** real; imaginary
3, 5.

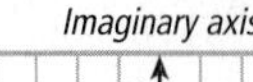

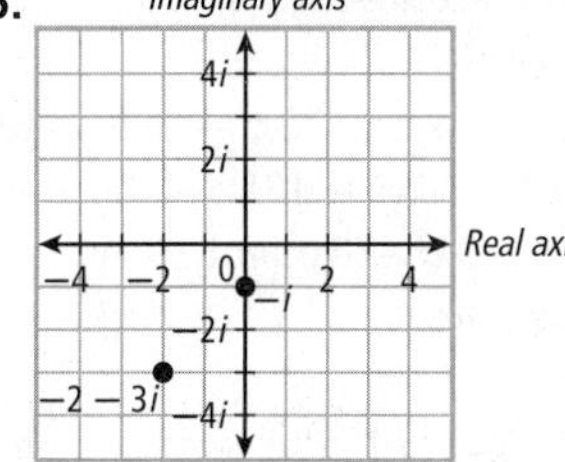

7. 33.3 **9.** 13 **11.** 15 **13.** $3 - 5i$ **15.** $-9 + 15i$ **17.** $-28 - 19i$ **19.** $-3 - i$ **21.** 5 **23.** $37 - 5i$ **25.** $8 + 6i$ **27.** $-i$ **29.** -1 **31.** $\frac{21}{10} + \frac{17}{10}i$ **33.** $4 - i$ **35.** $-2 + \frac{1}{2}i$
37, 39.

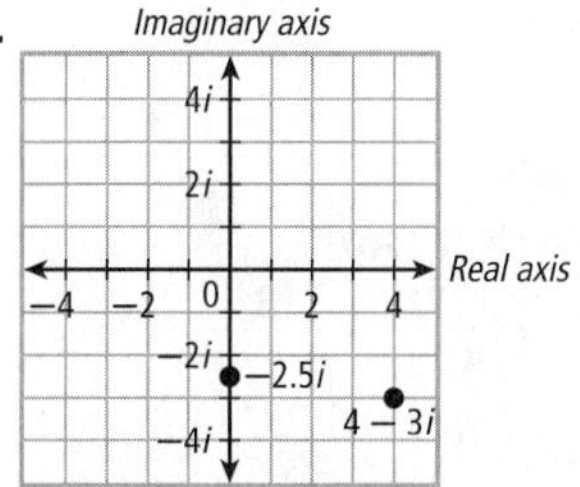

41. 18 **43.** 10 **45.** $2\sqrt{29}$ **47.** $-11 + 7i$ **49.** $28 + 41i$ **51.** $-4 + 9i$ **53.** $4 + 6i$ **55.** $48 + 12i$ **57.** 53 **59.** $24 + 78i$ **61.** $-i$ **63.** -5 **65.** $\frac{13}{10} - \frac{11}{10}i$ **67.** $4 + i$ **69.** $\frac{3}{4} + \frac{9}{4}i$ **71.** $3i$ **73.** $-2 - i$ **75.** $\sqrt{10}$ **77.** $2\sqrt{10}$ **79.** 0 **81.** $\frac{\sqrt{10}}{2}$ **83.** $\sqrt{11}$ **85.** $9.5 + 2.9i$ **87.** $-9.7 + 1.3i$ **89.** $-1 + 4i$ **91.** $-5 + 12i$ **93.** $10 - 5i$ **95.** 0 **97.** $1 - 12i$ **99.** $\frac{26}{37} + \frac{8}{37}i$ **101.** $\frac{8}{13} + \frac{12}{13}i$ **103.** $Z_{eq} = \frac{7}{4} - i$ **105.** always true **107.** always true **109.** A is incorrect. **113.** D **115.** C **119.** $\frac{ac + bd}{c^2 + d^2} + \frac{(bc - ad)}{c^2 + d^2}i$

Study Guide: Review

1. imaginary number; complex number **2.** zero of a function **3.** vertex of a parabola **4.** discriminant **5.** minimum value

6.
7.

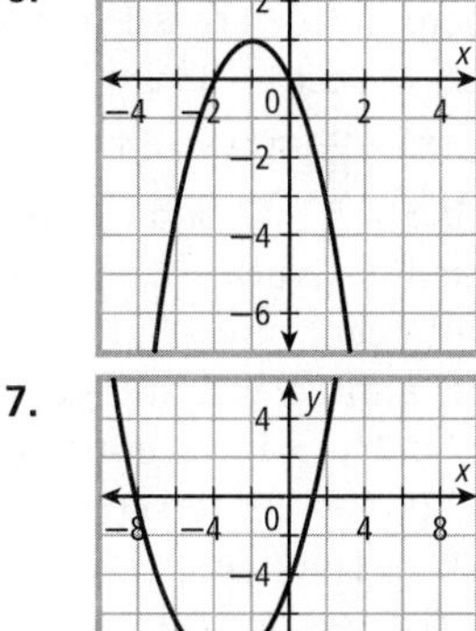

8. g is f vertically stretched by a factor of 4 and translated 2 units right. **9.** g is f reflected across the x-axis, vertically stretched by a factor of 2, and translated 1 unit left. **10.** g is f vertically compressed by a factor of $\frac{1}{3}$ and translated 3 units down. **11.** g is f reflected across the x-axis and translated 2 units left and 6 units up. **12.** Possible answer: $g(x) = -x^2 - 3$ **13.** Possible answer: $g(x) = 2(x - 4)^2$ **14.** Possible answer: $g(x) = \frac{1}{4}(x + 1)^2$ **15.** opens upward; $x = 2$; $(2, -1)$; 3 **16.** opens upward; $x = -1$; $(-1, 2)$; 3 **17.** opens upward; $x = 1.5$; $(1.5, -2.25)$; 0 **18.** opens upward; $x = 2$; $(2, 2)$; 4 **19.** minimum: 5 **20.** maximum: 4.5 **21.** minimum: -5.25 **22.** maximum: 18 **23.** maximum: 12 **24.** minimum: 7 **25.** $x = -1$ or $x = 8$ **26.** $x = 2$ or $x = 3$ **27.** $x = -12$ or $x = 12$ **28.** $x = 0$ or $x = 21$ **29.** $x = 2$ **30.** $x = -1$ or $x = -3$ **31.** $x = 2$ or $x = -16$ **32.** $x = -\frac{1}{3}$ **33.** Possible answer: $f(x) = x^2 + x - 6$ **34.** Possible answer: $f(x) = x^2 - 1$ **35.** Possible answer: $f(x) = x^2 - 9x + 20$ **36.** Possible answer: $f(x) = x^2 + 5x + 6$ **37.** Possible answer: $f(x) = x^2 + 10x + 25$ **38.** Possible answer: $f(x) = x^2 - 9x$ **39.** $x = 4$ or $x = 12$ **40.** $x = -14$ or $x = -6$ **41.** $x = -2$ or $x = 8$

42. $x = 7 \pm \sqrt{62}$ **43.** $f(x) = (x - 2)^2 + 5$; $(2, 5)$ **44.** $g(x) = (x + 1)^2 - 8$; $(-1, -8)$ **45.** $x = \pm 9i$ **46.** $x = \pm 5i$ **47.** $x = -3 \pm i$ **48.** $x = -6 \pm 3i$ **49.** $x = 7 \pm i\sqrt{26}$ **50.** $x = 11 \pm 2i\sqrt{3}$ **51.** $-5i - 4$ **52.** $3 - i\sqrt{5}$ **53.** $\frac{3 \pm \sqrt{41}}{2}$ **54.** $5 \pm 2i\sqrt{3}$ **55.** $\frac{5}{2} \pm \frac{i\sqrt{11}}{2}$ **56.** $-\frac{3}{2} \pm i\frac{\sqrt{3}}{2}$ **57.** $\frac{5}{2} \pm i\frac{\sqrt{15}}{2}$ **58.** 1 distinct real solution **59.** 2 real solutions **60.** 2 nonreal complex solutions **61.** 2 real solutions **62.** 2 nonreal complex solutions **63.** 2 nonreal complex solutions

64.

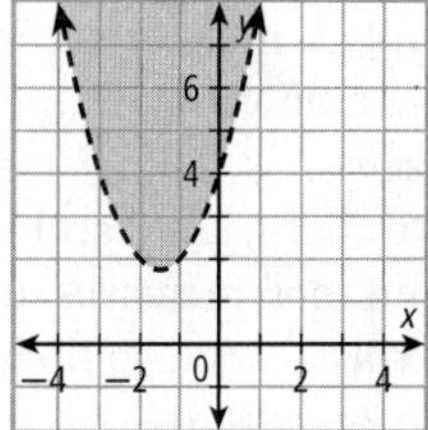

65.

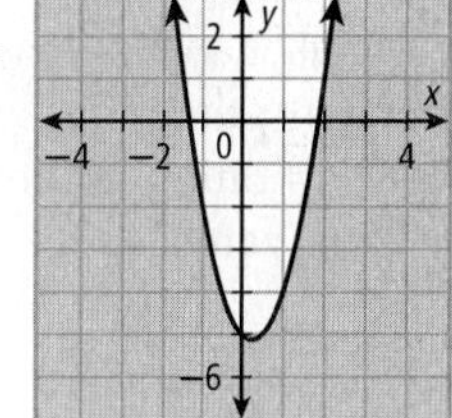

66. $x \le -3$ or $x \ge 1$ **67.** $-4 < x < -1$ **68.** $x < 1$ or $x > 5$ **69.** $-3 \le x \le 3$ **70.** $-\sqrt{3} < x < \sqrt{3}$ **71.** $-2 \le x \le \frac{2}{3}$ **72.** $y = -x^2 - 3x + 6$ **73.** $y = -2x^2 + x$ **74.** $y \approx 0.000188x^2 - 0.0112x + 0.182$ **75.** ≈ 0.074 in. **76.** $y \approx 0.360x^2 - 11.9x + 105$ **77.** ≈ 37.8 ohms **78.** 3 **79.** $2\sqrt{5}$ **80.** 20 **81.** 7 **82.** $7 + 4i$ **83.** $6 + 2i$ **84.** -6 **85.** $-20 - 15i$ **86.** $46 + 28i$ **87.** 13 **88.** $9 - 19i$ **89.** $-57 - 51i$ **90.** 1 **91.** $-5i$ **92.** $-\frac{9}{2} + i$ **93.** $\frac{7}{25} + \frac{26}{25}i$ **94.** $2 - 6i$ **95.** $4 + 5i$

3-1

Check It Out! **1a.** 3 **b.** 0 **c.** 5 **d.** 9 **2a.** $-2x^2 + 4x + 2$; -2; 2; 3; quadratic trinomial **b.** $x^3 - 18x^2 + 2x - 5$; 1; 3; 4; cubic polynomial with 4 terms **3a.** $16x^3 - 30x^2 + 6x - 16$ **b.** $5x^3 - 9x^2 - 3x + 14$ **4.** $f(4) = 3.8398$; $f(17) = 1.6368$; the concentration of dye after 4 s; the concentration of dye after 17 s **5a.** From left to right, the graph increases, decreases slightly, and then increases again. It crosses the x-axis 3 times, so there appear to be 3 real zeros. **b.** From right to left, the graph decreases and then increases. It does not cross the x-axis, so there are no real zeros. **c.** From left to right, the graph decreases and then increases. It crosses the x-axis twice, so there appear to be 2 real zeros. **d.** From left to right, the graph alternately decreases and increases, changing direction 3 times. It crosses the x-axis 4 times, so there appear to be 4 real zeros.

Exercises **1.** The leading coefficient of a polynomial is the number being multiplied by the variable with the greatest degree. **3.** 5 **5.** 6 **7.** $3x^2 + 5x - 4$; 3; 2; 3; quadratic trinomial **9.** $4x^4 + 8x^2 - 3x + 1$; 4; 4; 4; quartic with 4 terms **11.** $3x^2 + 12x + 3$ **13.** $-5x^2 - 7x - 5$ **15.** From left to right, the graph increases. It crosses the x-axis once, so there appears to be 1 real zero. **17.** From left to right, the graph decreases. It crosses the x-axis once, so there appears to be 1 real zero. **19.** 8 **21.** 0 **23.** $2x^4 + 3x^3 + x^2 - 7x$; 2; 4; 4; quartic with 4 terms **25.** $2x^3 + 10x - 9$; 2; 3; 3; cubic trinomial **27.** $x^3 + x^2$ **29.** $5y^3 - 3y^2 + 2y + 2$ **31a.** $d(1) = -3$; $d(2) = -28$ **33.** From left to right, the graph increases. There is 1 real zero. **35.** The graph decreases, increases, and then decreases. There is 1 real zero. **41.** $S(x) = 4\pi x^2 + 8\pi x$ **43.** $S(x) = 5\pi x^2 + \frac{31}{2}\pi x + 12\pi$ **45a.** \$12.04 **b.** \$27.52 **47.** sometimes true **49.** sometimes true **51a.** The x-intercepts are -3, 1, and 4. **b.** The x-intercepts are -1, -2, 3, and 1. **c.** The x-intercepts are 0, -1, and 2. **d.** The x-intercepts are -2 and 3. **e.** The x-intercepts are $-\frac{1}{2}$, 0, and $\frac{1}{2}$. **53.** Yes **55.** J **57.** J

3-2

Check It Out!
1a. $12c^3d^3 - 18c^2d^3 + 42c^2d^4$
b. $6x^2y^4 + x^2y^3 - 28x^2y^2 + 30x^2y$
2a. $9b^3 - 9b^2c - 4bc^2 + 4c^3$
b. $x^4 + x^3 - 21x^2 + 13x - 2$
3. $T(x) = -0.00008x^4 - 0.0028x^3 + 0.028x^2 + 0.3x + 9$
4a. $x^4 + 16x^3 + 96x^2 + 256x + 256$
b. $8x^3 - 12x^2 + 6x - 1$
5a. $x^3 + 6x^2 + 12x + 8$
b. $x^5 - 20x^4 + 160x^3 - 640x^2 + 1280x - 1024$
c. $81x^4 + 108x^3 + 54x^2 + 12x + 1$

Exercises
1. $-20c^3d^5 - 12c^4d^4$
3. $5x^3y + 8x^2y - 7xy$
5. $x^3 + x^2y - 3xy^2 + y^3$
7. $3x^5 + 15x^4 + 16x^3 - 3x^2 + 6x - 2$
9. $-0.02x^4 - 0.3x^3 + 4.4x^2 - 14.2x + 20$
11. $x^4 + 4x^3y + 6x^2y^2 + 4xy^3 + y^4$
13. $x^3 - 9x^2y + 27xy^2 - 27y^3$
15. $16x^4 + 32x^3y + 24x^2y^2 + 8xy^3 + y^4$
17. $32x^5 - 80x^4y + 80x^3y^2 - 40x^2y^3 + 10xy^4 - y^5$
19. $6x^4 + 27x^3 - 18x^2$
21. $12r^5 + 28r^4 - 60r^3 + 28r^2$
23. $6x^3 + 7x^2y - 16xy^2 + 10y^3$
25. $12x^4 + 17x^3 + 8x^2 + x - 2$
27. $8x^3 - 24x^2 + 24x - 8$
29. $x^4 - 4x^3y + 6x^2y^2 - 4xy^3 + y^4$
31. $x^4 - 12x^3y + 54x^2y^2 - 108xy^3 + 81y^4$ **33.** $x^5 + 5x^4y + 10x^3y^2 + 10x^2y^3 + 5xy^4 + y^5$
35. equivalent **37.** not equivalent
39. $T(x) =-0.0003x^4 - 0.0164x^3 + 2.572x^2 - 14.12x + 116.2$
41. $p^3 - 6p^2q + 12pq^2 - 8q^3$
43. $x^6 + x^4y^3 + x^3y^3 + xy^6$
45. $5x^3y + x^2y - 9xy + 10x^3 + 2x^2 - 18x$
47. $3x^4 - 24x^3 + 72x^2 - 96x + 48$
49. $-x^5 - 14x^3 - 45x^2 + 30x - 450$
51. $2x^6 - 3x^5 - 8x^4 + 12x^3 + 14x - 21$
53. No
55a. $f(n) = \frac{1}{4}n^4 + n^3 + \frac{5}{4}n^2 + \frac{1}{2}n$
b. 7098 **59.** J **61.** H
63. $x^{10} - 10x^9 + 45x^8 - 120x^7 + 210x^6 - 252x^5 + 210x^4 - 120x^3 + 45x^2 - 10x + 1$
65. $m^6 - 3m^4n^2 + 3m^2n^4 - n^6$
67. $B(x) = x - 3$
69. $B(x) = x^3 + 1$

3-3

Check It Out!
1a. $5x + 1 - \frac{13}{3x + 1}$
b. $x + 8 - \frac{4}{x - 3}$
2a. $6x - 23 + \frac{63}{x + 3}$ **b.** $x + 3$
3a. $P(-3) = 4$
b. $P\left(\frac{1}{5}\right) = 5$ **4.** $y - 5$

Exercises **3.** $x + 2 + \frac{1}{x - 1}$
5. $7x - 2$ **7.** $x - 6$
9. $P(-8) = 42$ **11.** $P(-1) = 6$
13. $x + 4$ **15.** $x^2 - 1$
17. $\frac{1}{2}x^3 - 2x^2 - \frac{7}{2}$
19. $x + 4 + \frac{2}{x + 1}$
21. $x + 1 - \frac{2}{x + 8}$
23. $2x + 14 - \frac{1}{x - \frac{1}{2}}$
25. $P(4) = 9$
27. $P\left(-\frac{1}{3}\right) = \frac{5}{3}$
29. $I(t) = 0.5t^2 + 4t$
31. $a = 2$; $b = 8$; $c = 29$
33. $a = 3$; $b = 9$; $c = -4$
35. $x - 2$
37. $D(h) = \frac{1}{\pi} - \frac{4}{\pi h} + \frac{20}{\pi h^2}$
39. $y^2 + 5$ **41.** $x^2 - 5x - 12$
43. $t - 4$ **45.** $x^3 + 3x^2 - 10x - 1$
47. $x^3 - x^2 + 3x - 4 + \frac{1}{x - 6}$
49. Solution B is correct. **53.** B
55. D **57.** $P(-4) = -1{,}189{,}150$
59. $P(1) = 0$ **61.** $k = 18$

3-4

Check It Out!

1a. no **b.** yes
2a. $(x+3)(x-3)(x-2)$
b. $(x^2+4)(2x+1)$
3a. $(2+z^2)(4-2z^2+z^4)$
b. $2x^2(x-2)(x^2+2x+4)$
4. $x = 1, 3, 4$; $V(x) = (x-1)(x-3)(x-4)$

Exercises

1. yes **3.** yes
5. $(x+2)(x-2)(x+5)$
7. $2(x+2)(x-2)(x-1)$
9. $3(x-2)(4x+1)$
11. $2t^4(t+3)(t^2-3t+9)$
13. $(3+x)(9-3x+x^2)$
15. $(y-5)(y^2+5y+25)$
17. no **19.** yes
21. $(b+2)(b-2)(4b+3)$
23. $(x+3)(x-3)(3x+1)$
25. $(x+2)(x-2)(5x-1)$
27. $(s-1)(s+1)(s^2+s+1)(s^2-s+1)$
29. $6x(x-3)(x^2+3x+9)$
31. $y^2(y+3)(y^2-3y+9)$
33. $x^2(x^2-7)(x^2-7)$
35. $(x-2)(x+2)(4x+1)$
37. $x(2x^2-1)(2x^2-3)(2x^2+3)$
39. $a = 3$; $d = 72$
41. $P(x) = (x-2)(x^3+5x+1)$
43. $P(x) = (x+2)(2x^4-6x+3)$
45a. $f(t) = -t(t-8)(t-18)(t-18)$ **b.** \$2,535,000
c. $f(15) = -945$
47. $B(x) = x^3-2x^2+4x-8$ **51.** J
53. $[(x-3)+2][(x-3)^2 - 2(x-3)+4]$; $(x-1)(x^2-8x+19)$
57. $(3x-5)(3x-5)$
59. $\left(x-\frac{22}{3}\right)\left(x+\frac{35}{6}\right)$

3-5

Check It Out!

1a. $x = 0, -1, 6$ **b.** $x = -5, 2, 5$
2a. $x = 2$ with multiplicity 4
b. $x = 0$ with multiplicity 3; $x = -1$ with multiplicity 1; $x = 6$ with multiplicity 2 **3.** 2 ft
4. $x = -\frac{1}{2}, 1 \pm \sqrt{5}$

Exercises

3. $x = 6, -6, 1, -1$
5. $x = 0, \frac{1}{3}, -4$
7. $x = -5, -2, 2, 5$
9. $x = -2$, 2 with multiplicity 3
11. $x = -6, \pm\sqrt{5}$ **13.** $x = -5, 1, 4$
15. $x = -3, 3$ **17.** $x = -8, 0, 8$
19. $x = \frac{5}{2}, \pm\sqrt{2}$ **21.** $x = 0$ with multiplicity 2; $x = 8$ with multiplicity 3 **23.** 3 in. by 3 in.
25. $x = -\frac{4}{3}, \pm\sqrt{2}$ **27a.** $\pm1, \pm2, \pm4$
b. $x = -2, 2$ **c.** 2 **d.** $x = -2.62, -0.38$ **29.** $x = 3, 2 \pm\sqrt{2}$
31. $x = -5, -2, 3, 5$
33. $x = -1, 0, 1, 2 \pm \sqrt{5}$ **35a.** 126 ft
b. The coaster passes through 2 tunnels within the first 100 s.
c. Possible answer: $h(t) = 3(t-3)(t-5)$ **41.** F **43.** H
45. $k = -18$ **47.** $k = 6$

3-6

Check It Out!

1a. $P(x) = x^3-4x^2-4x+16$
1b. $x^3 - \frac{11}{3}x^2 + 2x$
2. $x = -5, 1, 2i, -2i$
3. $P(x) = x^5-5x^4+9x^3-17x^2+20x+12$ **4.** $r = 9$ ft

Exercises

1. $P(x) = x^3 - \frac{10}{3}x^2 + 3x - \frac{2}{3}$
3. $P(x) = x^3 - \frac{1}{2}x^2 - 4x + 2$
5. $x = 2, \frac{2 \pm \sqrt{2i}}{3}$
7. $P(x) = x^3-4x^2+6x-4$
9. $P(x) = x^5-2x^4+2x^3-4x^2-8x+16$
11. $P(x) = x^3-3x-2$
13. $P(x) = x^3+3x^2-6x-8$
15. $x = 1, 3$ **17.** $x = \frac{3}{2}, 2i, -2i$
19. $x = 1, -1, \pm\sqrt{3}$
21. $P(x) = x^5+3x^4-13x^3-39x^2+40x+120$ **23.** $r = 9$ ft
25. $x = 2, -4, -1$
27. $x = -1$ **29.** $x = 3, \frac{-1 \pm i\sqrt{3}}{2}$
31. $x = 0, 7, 3 \pm 2i$
33. $x = \pm3i, \pm i\sqrt{5}$ **35.** $x = -1, 2, 3$
37a. $x^3-6x^2-243 = 0$ **b.** 9 m
c. They are complex.
39. $P(x) = x^4+12x^2-64$
41. $P(x) = x^3-4x^2+5x-2$
43. $P(x) = x^4-6x^3+18x^2-54x+81$
45. never true **47.** Sometimes true
49. $x = 0$ or $x \approx \pm0.537$
51. $x \approx -0.782, 0.975, 3.965$
53. $r = 6$ **57.** B **59.** D **61.** D
63. $f(3i) = 0$; $f(-\sqrt{3}) = -36 - 12\sqrt{3}$ **65.** $x = \pm3i$
67. $(a+bi)(a-bi)$
69. $(a+bi)(a-bi)(a^4-2a^2b^2+b^4)$
71. $x^4+2x^2+1 = 0$; $\pm i$

3-7

Check It Out!

1a. 2; 5; as $x \to -\infty$, $P(x) \to -\infty$, as $x \to +\infty$, $P(x) \to \infty$ **b.** -3; 2; as $x \to -\infty$, $P(x) \to -\infty$ as $x \to +\infty$, $P(x) \to -\infty$
2a. odd; negative **b.** even; positive
3a.

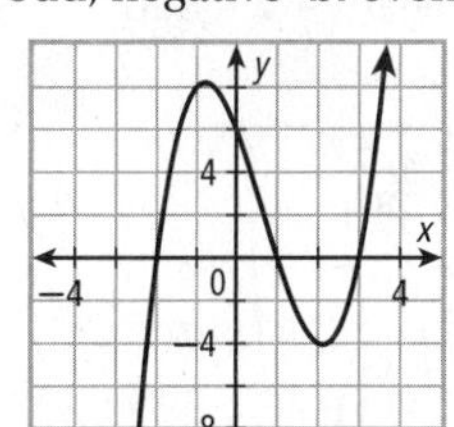

b.

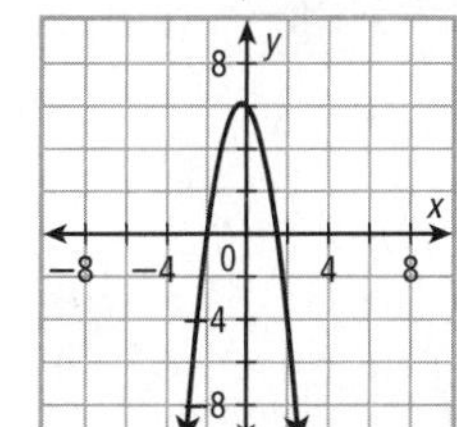

4a.

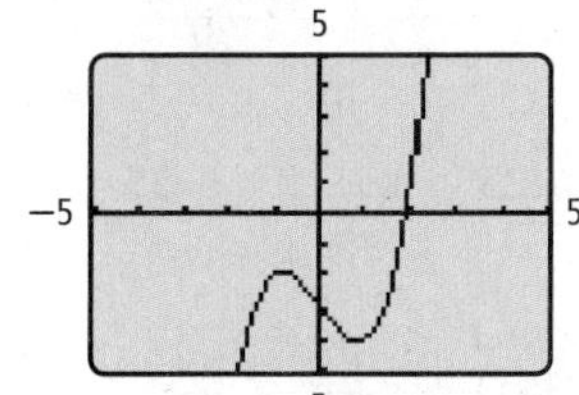

min = -4.0887; max = -1.9113
b.

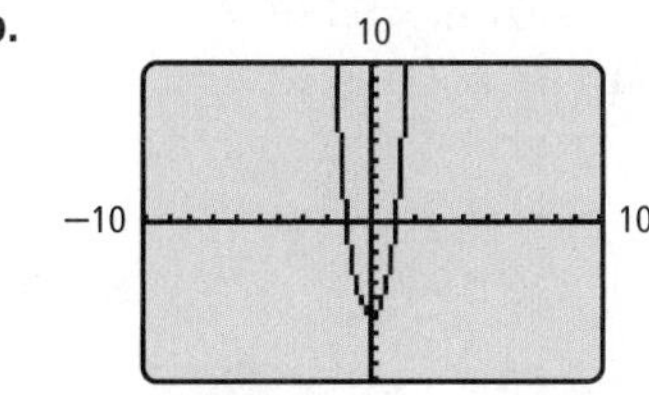

min = 6
5. 420.1 ft³

Exercises

1. A graph "turns around" at a turning point.
3. -2; 7; $x \to -\infty$ $Q \to +\infty$, $x \to +\infty$ $Q \to -\infty$ **5.** 3; 2; $x \to \infty$ $S \to +\infty$, $x \to +\infty$ $S \to +\infty$ **7.** even; positive
9. even; negative
11. 

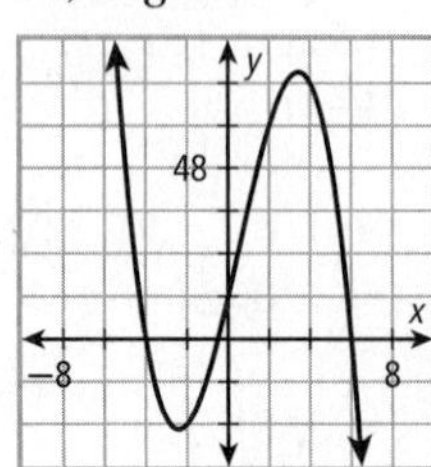

13. max = -2.9098; min = -14.0902
15. 2; 3; $x \to -\infty$ $P \to -\infty$, $x \to +\infty$ $P \to +\infty$
17. -1; 5; $x \to -\infty$ $R \to \infty$ $x \to +\infty$ $R \to +\infty$
19. even; negative **21.** odd; negative
23.

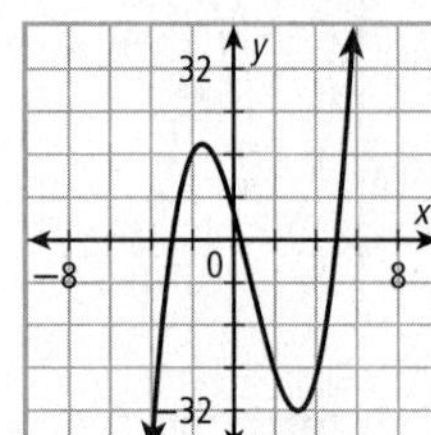

25.

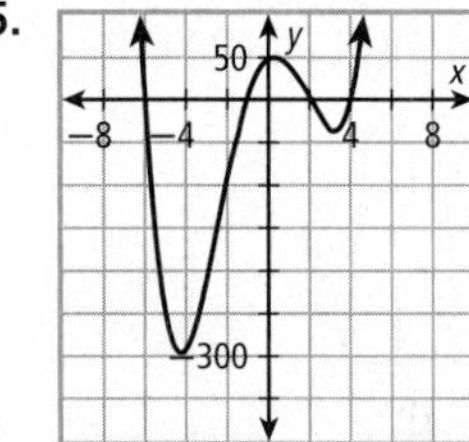

27. min = 20 **29.** max = -1
31. 3.425 L; 0.5 s **33.** B **35.** A
37. $+\infty$; $+\infty$ **39.** $+\infty$; $+\infty$
41. $-\infty$; $-\infty$
45a. $V(x) = -\frac{1}{3}x^3 + \frac{10}{3}x^2$
b. ≈ 49.4 in^3 **c.** approximately 6.7 in. × 3.3 in. × 6.7 in.
49. H

3-8

Check It Out!

1a. $g(x) = x^3 - 1$

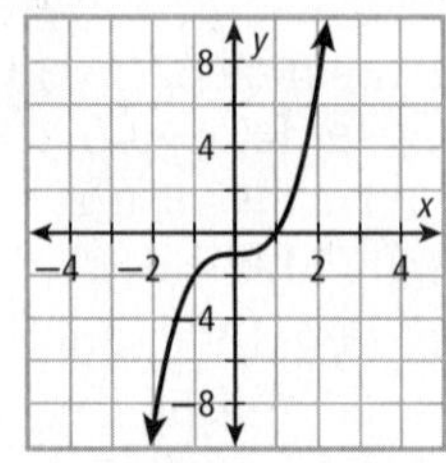

b. $g(x) = x^3 + 6x^2 + 12x + 12$

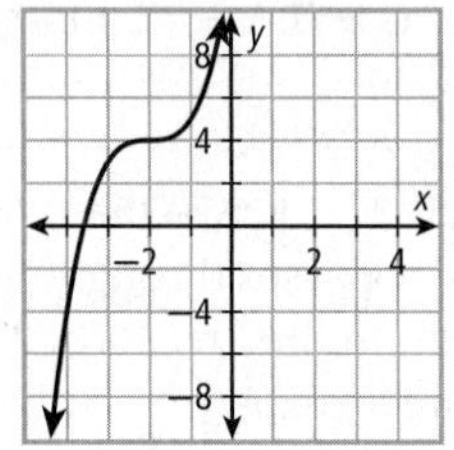

2a. $g(x) = -x^3 + 2x^2 + x - 2$
b. $g(x) = -x^3 - 2x^2 + x + 2$
3a. vertical compression

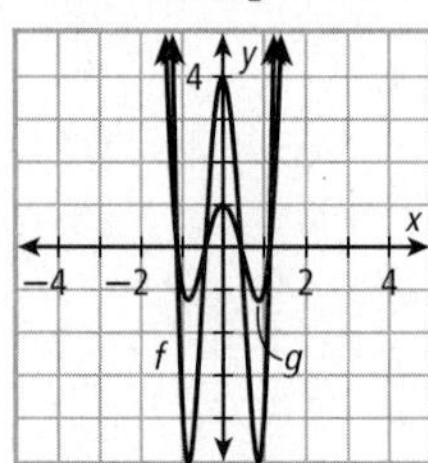

b. horizontal stretch

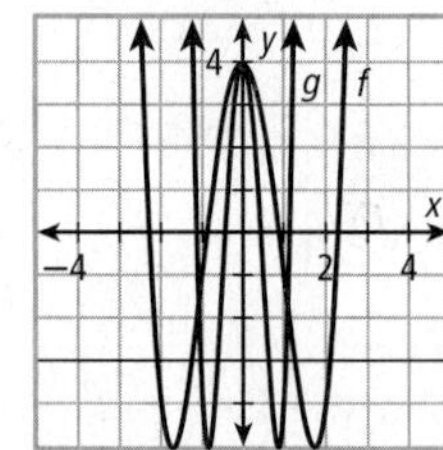

4a. $g(x) = 4(x - 3)^3 - 1$
$= 4x^3 - 3x^2 + 108x - 109$

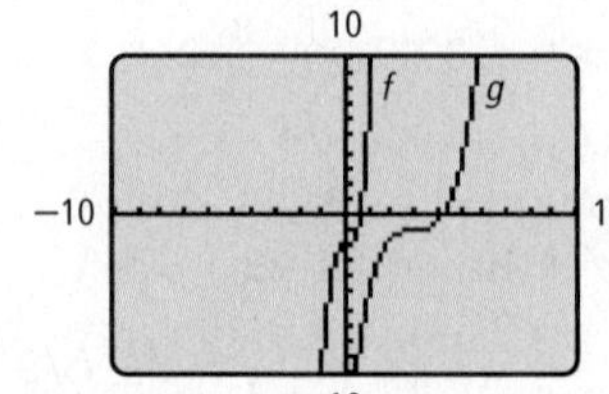

b. $g(x) = -8(x + 3)^3 + 2$
$= -8x^3 - 96x^2 - 384x - 510$

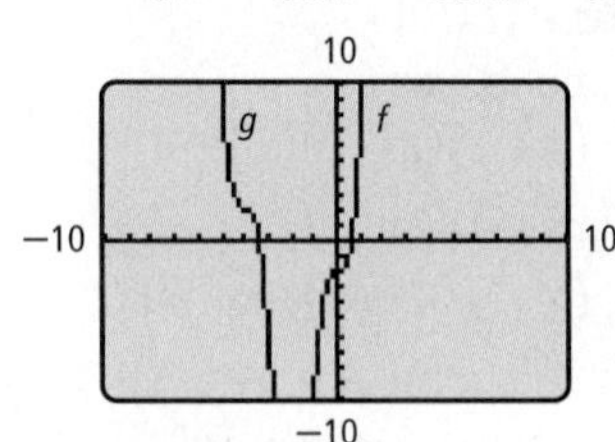

5. $g(x) = 0.01x^3 + 0.55x^2 - 5.85x + 134.25$
Possible answer: The model represents the number of sales since March.

Exercises

1. $g(x) = x^4 - 4$ **3.** $j(x) = 81x^4 - 8$
5. $g(x) = x^3 + 3x^2 + 2x + 1$
7. horizontal stretch **9.** horizontal compression and vertical shift
11. $g(x) = -32x^3 + 2$
13. $c(x) = 4x^3 - 6x + 60$; the cost has doubled.
15. $h(x) = x^3 - 9x^2 + 27x - 31$
17. $g(x) = -x^3 + 2x^2 - 5x + 3$
19. vertical stretch
21. horizontal stretch
23. $g(x) = \frac{1}{3}x^4 - 1$
25. $V\left(\frac{2}{3}x\right) = \frac{8}{27}x^3 + \frac{4}{3}x^2 + \frac{2}{3}x + 8$
27a. $v > 2.04$ **b.** $G(v) = 0.24v^2 + 2.4v + 6$; a shift 5 units left
c. $v \geq 0$ **d.** a vertical stretch
31. B **33.** B **35.** shift right 2 units
37. shift right 3 units and up 8 units

3-9

Check It Out!

1. cubic **2.** $f(x) = 0.001x^3 - 0.113x^2 + 4.134x - 24.867$
3. $\approx \$11{,}482.84$

Exercises **1.** linear **3.** quartic
5. 831 patients **7.** quartic
9. $f(x) = 0.821x^2 - 1.821x + 23.357$
13a. $f(x) = 0.019x^3 - 0.185x^2 + 0.95x + 12.056$; $R^2 = 0.9944$

b. $f(x) = 0.0075x^4 - 0.071x^3 + 0.143x^2 + 0.604x + 12.083$; $R^2 = 0.9967$ **c.** no **15.** yes **17.** C **19.** $f(x) = x^3 - 5x + 4$

Study Guide: Review

1. monomial **2.** synthetic division **3.** multiplicity **4.** end behavior **5.** $-3x^3 + 4x^2 + 6x + 7$; -3; 3; 4: cubic polynomial with 4 terms **6.** $-x^5 + 2x^4 + 5x^3 + 8x$; -1; 5; 4: quintic polynomial with 4 terms **7.** $9x^2 - 11x + 1$; 9; 2; 3: quadratic trinomial **8.** $x^4 - 6x^2$; 1; 4; 2: quartic binomial **9.** $8x^3 + x^2 - 4x$ **10.** $-5x^3 + 6x^2 + 10x - 1$ **11.** $-6x^2 - x + 9$ **12.** $-4x^4 - x^3 - 3$ **13.** From left to right, it alternately increases and decreases, changing direction 3 times and crossing the x-axis 2 times. There appear to be 2 real zeros. **14.** From left to right, it increases, decreases slightly, and then increases again. It crosses the x-axis 1 time. There appears to be 1 real zero. **15.** From left to right, it alternately decreases and increases, changing direction 3 times. It crosses the x-axis 4 times. There appear to be 4 real zeros. **16.** From left to right, it increases, decreases, and then increases again. It crosses the x-axis 3 times. There appear to be 3 real zeros. **17.** $15x^3 - 10x^2$

18. $-6t^3 + 18t^2 - 3t$ **19.** $a^3b^2 - a^2b^2 + a^2b^3$ **20.** $x^3 - 4x^2 + x + 6$ **21.** $2x^4 + 3x^3 - 5x^2 + 2x + 5$ **22.** $x^3 - 9x^2 + 27x - 27$ **23.** $x^5 + 4x^4 - 3x^3 - 11x^2 + 4x$ **24.** $16x^4 + 32x^3 + 24x^2 + 8x + 1$ **25.** $4\pi x^4 - 4\pi x^3 - 12\pi x^2$ **26.** $x^2 - 7x + 16 - \frac{39}{x+2}$ **27.** $4x^3 + 2x^2 + 4x + 1 + \frac{5}{2x-1}$ **28.** $x^2 - x + \frac{2}{x-3}$ **29.** $x^2 + 2x + 6 + \frac{11}{x-2}$ **30.** $x^2 + 2x + 2$ in.; remainder 2 in. **31.** no **32.** yes **33.** yes **34.** $(x-1)(x-4)(x+4)$ **35.** $(x-2)(2x-1)(2x+1)$ **36.** $3(x+3)(x^2-3x+9)$ **37.** $2(2x-1)(x^2+2x+1)$ **38.** 1, 2 **39.** -2, $-2 \pm \sqrt{3}$ **40.** -1 **41.** $-3, 3, \pm\sqrt{3}$ **42.** $-1, \pm\sqrt{2}$ **43.** $1, 2 \pm 2\sqrt{2}$ **44.** 2 m **45.** $P(x) = x^3 - 3x^2 - 10x + 24$ **46.** $P(x) = x^3 - \frac{1}{2}x^2 - \frac{13}{2}x - 3$ **47.** $P(x) = x^3 + x^2 - 2x - 2$ **48.** $P(x) = x^3 + 3x^2 + x + 3$ **49.** $P(x) = x^4 - 5x^2 + 6$ **50.** $P(x) = x^4 - 2x^3 + 2x^2 - 8x - 8$ **51.** $1, -2i, 2i$ **52.** $-i, i, -\sqrt{2}, \sqrt{2}$ **53.** $\pm 4, \pm\frac{1}{2}i$ **54.** $\pm\sqrt{5}, -3$ **55.** -2; 3; as $x \to -\infty, f(x) \to +\infty$; as $x \to +\infty, f(x) \to -\infty$ **56.** 1; 4; as $x \to \pm\infty, f(x) \to +\infty$

57. -3; 6; as $x \to \pm\infty, f(x) \to -\infty$ **58.** 7; 5; as $x \to -\infty, f(x) \to -\infty$, as $x \to +\infty, f(x) \to +\infty$

59.

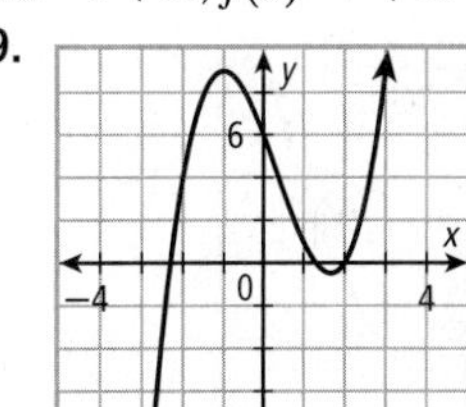

60.

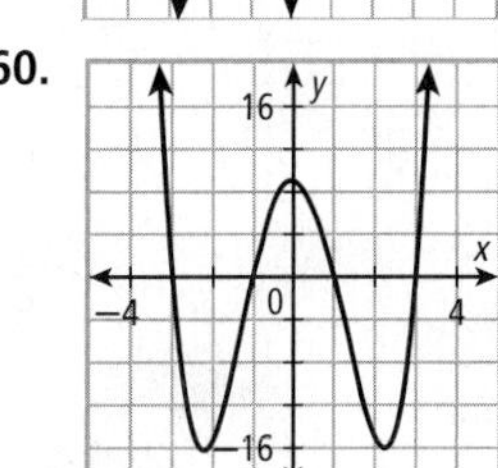

61.

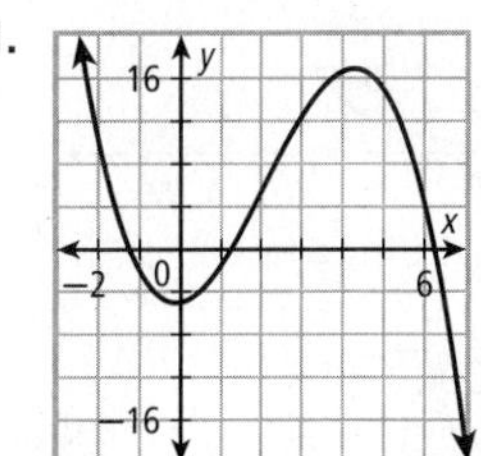

62. $g(x) = 2x^4 - 12x^2 + 1$ **63.** $g(x) = -x^4 + 6x^2 + 6$ **64.** $g(x) = (-x-3)^4 + 6(-x-3)^2 - 4$ **65.** $f(x) \approx -6\frac{2}{3}x^4 + 80x^3 - 328\frac{1}{3}x^2 + 575x - 72$ **66.** $f(x) \approx 80.5x^3 - 523.5x^2 + 1790x + 544$

4-1

Check It Out!

1. growth

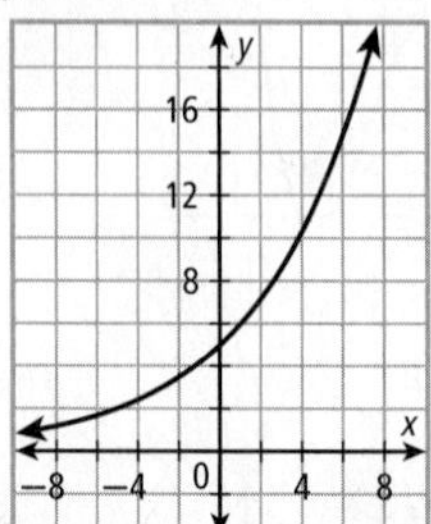

2. $P(t) = 350(1.14)^t$

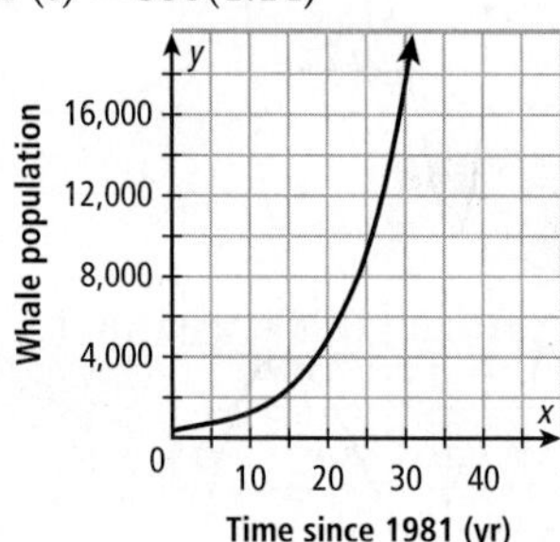

30.9 yr

3. $v(t) = 1000(0.85)^t$

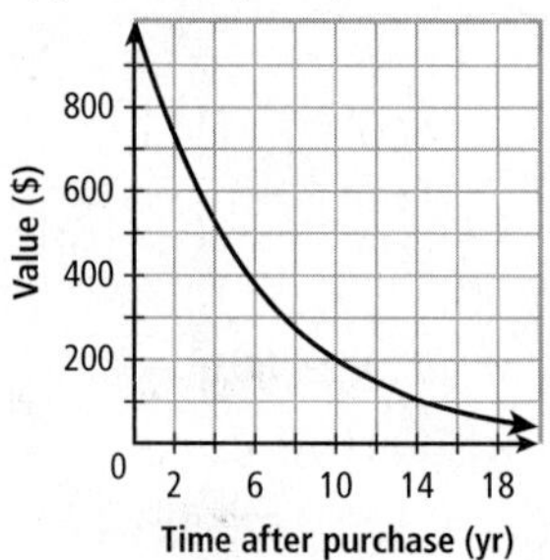

14.2 yr

Exercises **1.** exponential decay.

3. growth

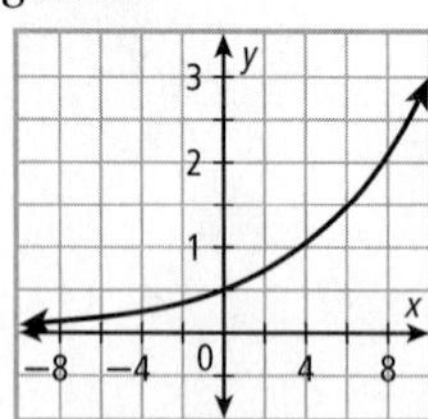

5a. $f(x) = 150(2^x)$

b.

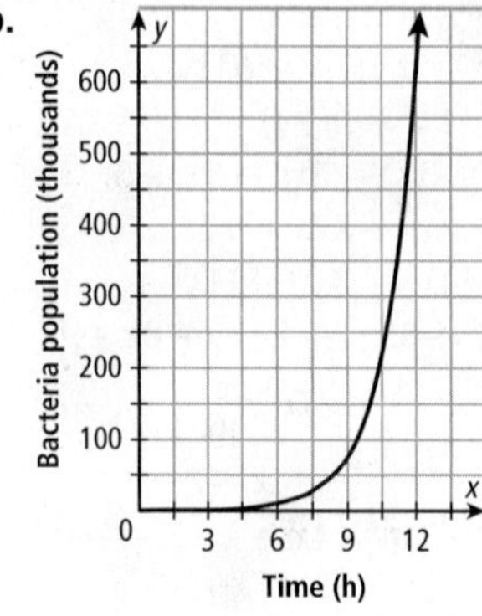

c. $\approx 600{,}000$

7. decay **9.** growth

11a. $f(x) = 10(0.95)^x$ **c.** ≈ 6 units

d. 13.6 min. **13.** no

15. $\approx \$12{,}000{,}000$ **17.** ≈ 5.8 yr

19. 15.63; 6.25; ...; 0.03; 0.01

21a. ≈ 3146 **b.** 12th month

25. $(34.868, 100]$ **27a.** 17%

b. $A(t) = 500(0.83)^t$ **c.** ≈ 36.8 mg

29. 3^x **31.** B **37.** $x > 22.76$

39. 2; $(2, 4)$, $(\approx -0.767, \approx 0.588)$

4-2

Check It Out!

1.

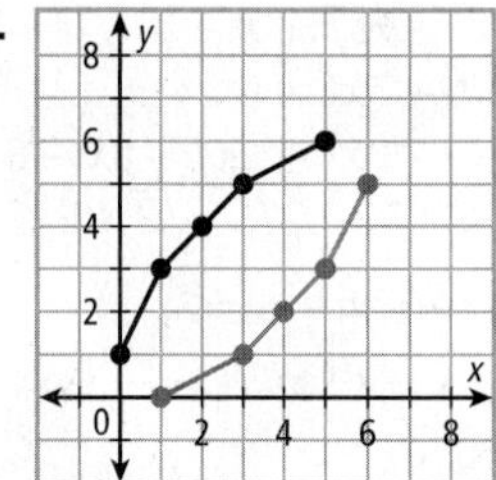

relation: D: $\{1 \le x \le 6\}$;

R: $\{0 \le y \le 5\}$

inverse: D: $\{0 \le y \le 5\}$;

R: $\{1 \le x \le 6\}$

2a. $f^{-1}(x) = 3x$ **b.** $f^{-1}(x) = x - \frac{2}{3}$

3. $f^{-1}(x) = \frac{x+7}{5}$

4. $f^{-1}(x) = \frac{3}{2}x - 3$

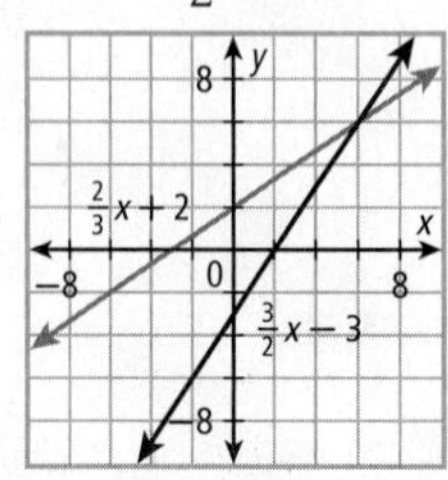

5. inverse: $z = 6t - 6$; 36 oz of water

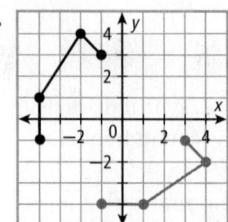

Exercises

1. relation

3.

relation: D: $\{-1 \le x \le 4\}$;

R: $\{-4 \le y \le -1\}$

inverse: D: $\{-4 \le y \le -1\}$;

R: $\{-1 \le x \le 4\}$

5. $f^{-1}(x) = \frac{1}{4}x$ **7.** $f^{-1}(x) = x + 2\frac{1}{2}$

9. $f^{-1}(x) = 2(x - 3)$

11. $f^{-1}(x) = -\frac{2}{3}x + 1$

13. $f^{-1}(x) = \frac{2}{3}x + \frac{5}{3}$

15.

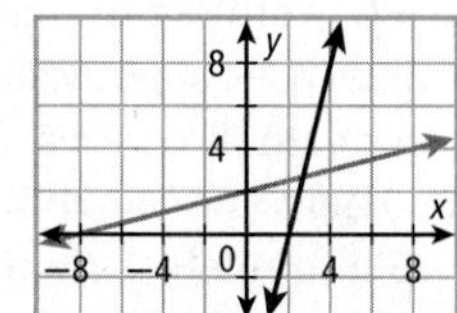

$f^{-1}(x) = 4(x - 2)$

17. $F = \frac{9}{5}C + 32$; 61° F

19.

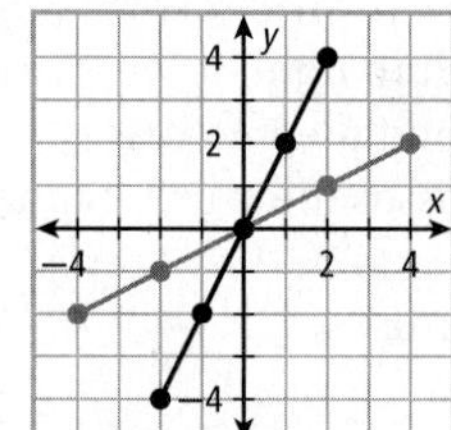

relation: D: $\{-4 \le x \le 4\}$;

R: $\{-2 \le y \le 2\}$

inverse: D: $\{-2 \le y \le 2\}$;

R: $\{-4 \le x \le 4\}$

21. $f^{-1}(x) = x + 1\frac{3}{4}$

23. $f^{-1}(x) = -\frac{1}{32}x + \frac{21}{32}$

25. $f^{-1}(x) = 5x - 60$

27. $f^{-1}(x) = -3x + 6$

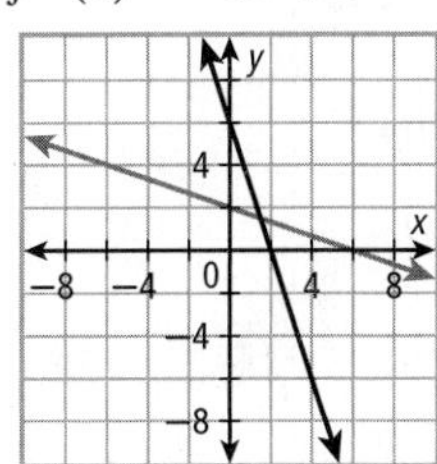

29. 22 **31a.** $f^{-1}(x) = \frac{212 - x}{1.85}$
b. 6500 ft **c.** 27,946 ft

33. (4, 2), (2, 4), (−3, −1), (−1, −3)

35. $f(x) = \frac{10}{12.59}x$; $f^{-1}(x) = 1.259x$; 31.48 s **37.** B **39.** yes **41.** always

43. never **45.** always

47a. $P = \frac{147}{340}d + 14.7$

b. D: $\{d \mid d \geq 0\}$; R: $\{P \mid P \geq 14.7\}$

c. $d = \frac{340}{147}P - 34$; depth as a function of pressure **49.** F

51.

x	1	2	3	4	5
y	0	1	2	3	4

53. $y = -\frac{b}{a}x + \frac{c}{a}$

4-3

Check It Out! 1a. $\log_9 81 = 2$
b. $\log_3 27 = 3$ **c.** $\log_x 1 = 0$
2a. $10^1 = 10$ **b.** $12^2 = 144$
c. $\left(\frac{1}{2}\right)^{-3} = 8$ **3a.** −5 **b.** −1

4.

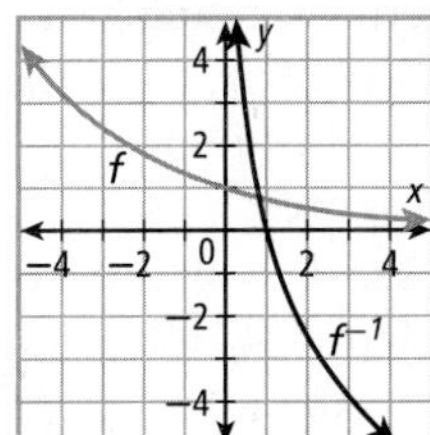

$f(x)$: D: ℝ; R: $\{y \mid y > 0\}$; $f^{-1}(x)$: D: $\{x \mid x > 0\}$; R: ℝ **5.** about 3.8

Exercises

1. x **3.** $\log_4 8 = 1.5$ **5.** $\log_3 243 = x$
7. $x^3 = -16$ **9.** $6^3 = x$ **11.** −2 **13.** 2
15. $f(x)$: D: ℝ, R: $\{y \mid y > 0\}$; $f^{-1}(x)$: D: $\{x \mid x > 0\}$; R: ℝ
17. $\log_x 32 = 2.5$ **19.** $\log_{1.2} 1 = 0$

21. $5^4 = 625$ **23.** $4.5^0 = 1$ **25.** 0 **27.** 3
29. $f(x)$: D: ℝ, R: $\{y \mid y > 0\}$; $f^{-1}(x)$: D: $\{x \mid x > 0\}$; R: ℝ **31.** no **33.** 1
35. yes **37a.** orange **b.** lemon
c. grapefruit **39.** C **41.** A **43.** 6
47a. $2^{11} = 2048$ Hz, $\log_2 2048 = 11$
b. 3 octaves lower

4-4

Check It Out!
1a. $\log_5 (625 \bullet 25) = 6$
b. $\log_{\frac{1}{3}} 3 = -1$ **2.** $\log_7 7 = 1$
3a. $4 \log 10 = 4$ **b.** $4 \log_5 5 = 4$
c. $-5 \log_2 2 = -5$ **4a.** 0.9 **b.** $8x$
5a. 1.5 **b.** $1.\overline{3}$ **6.** ≈ 63

Exercises

1. $\log_5 3125 = 5$ **3.** $\log_3 81 = 4$
5. $\log 100 = 2$ **7.** 2 **9.** 6 **11.** $\frac{x}{2} + 5$
13. 5 **15.** −1.5 **17.** ≈ 1.43
19. 2 times as large **21.** $\log 10 = 1$
23. $\log 10 = 1$ **25.** $\log_{1.5} 3.375 = 3$
27. 0.2 **29.** $7 + x$ **31.** 4 **33.** 1.5
35. ≈ 3.16 times as intense
37. $\log_b m + \log_b n = \log_b mn$
39. $n\log_b b^m = mn$
41. 0 **43.** $-\frac{3}{2}$ **45.** 1
47. $10^{-7} - 10^{-7.6}$
49. $t = \log_{1.08}\left(\frac{50}{40}\right)$; 2.9
55a. ≈ 0.2 **b.** ≈ 2.6 **c.** ≈ 2.4
57. sometimes **59.** always
61. always **63.** sometimes **65.** B
67. H **71.** $\{x \mid x > 1\}$ **73.** $\{x \mid x > 0\}$
75. $\{x \mid -1 \leq x < 0\}$ **77.** x **79.** ∅

4-5

Check It Out!
1a. 1.5 **b.** ≈ −1.565 **c.** ≈ 1.302
2. day 18 **3a.** 5 **b.** 2 **4a.** $x = 2$
b. $x < 2$ **c.** $x = 1000$

Exercises

1. exponential equation **3.** $x = -2$
5. $x \approx 1.661$ **7.** $x \approx 0.503$ **9.** $x = \frac{1}{8}$
11. $x = 108$ **13.** $x = \frac{9}{13}$ **15.** $x = 2$
17. $x = 3.5$ **19.** $x = 100$ **21.** $x = -5$
23. $x = 0.8$ **25.** ≈ 7.595
27. ≈ 41 min **29.** $x = 30$ **31.** ≈ 2.73
33. $x = 20$ **35.** $x < 1$ **37.** $x = 4$

39. $x = 4$ **41.** 24 keys below concert A **43.** 0 **47a.** 11 km; 25 km **b.** greater **49.** J **51.** no
53. $\{x \mid 0 < x < 12\}$

4-6

Check It Out!
1.

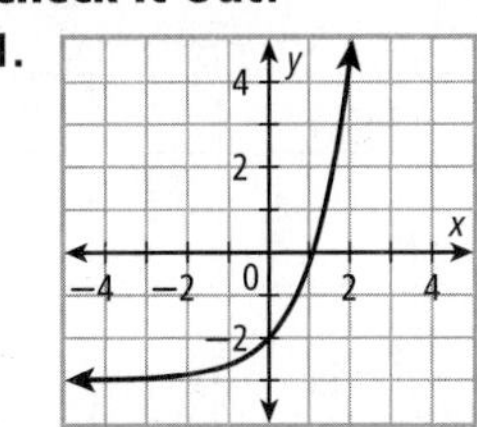

2a. 3.2 **b.** x^2 **c.** $x + 4y$
3. \$132.31 **4.** ≈ 47.6 days

Exercises

1. $f(x) = \ln x$; natural logarithm

3.

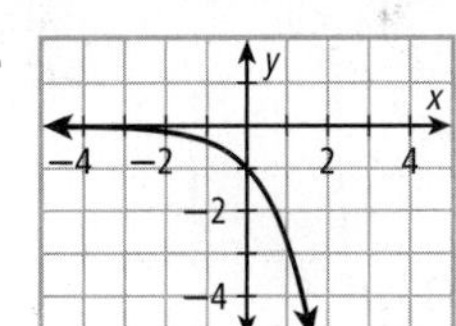

5.

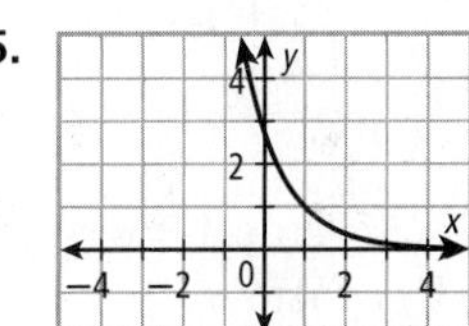

7. $x - y$ **9.** $2x$ **11.** \$9465.87

13.

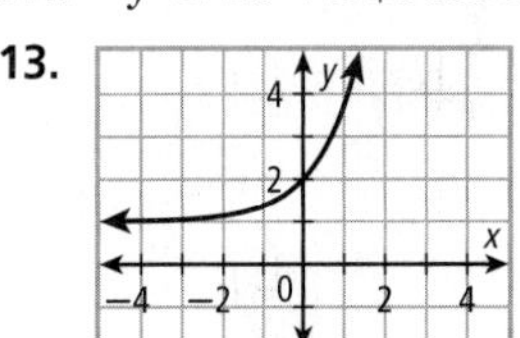

15.

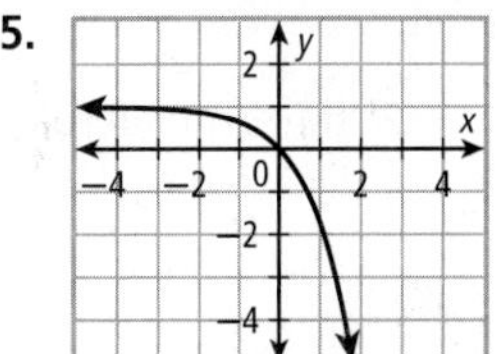

17. 0 **19.** $c + 2$ **21.** \$5553.55
23a. They are reciprocals.
25a. ≈ 2.4 min **b.** ≈ 2.8 min
c. room: ≈ 17.4 min
27. B **29.** C **31.** $x = \frac{e}{5} \approx 0.54$
33. $x = \frac{e^5}{\sqrt{10}} \approx 47$
35. $\{x \mid x > 0\}$ **37b.** 2

41. C **43.** A **45.** 4; yes
47a. $f(x) = \ln(-x)$ **b.** $f(x) = -\ln x$
c. $f(x) = -\ln(-x)$
d. one asymptote: $x = 0$

Check It Out!

1.

x	-2	-1	0	1	2
$j(x)$	$\frac{1}{16}$	$\frac{1}{8}$	$\frac{1}{4}$	$\frac{1}{2}$	1

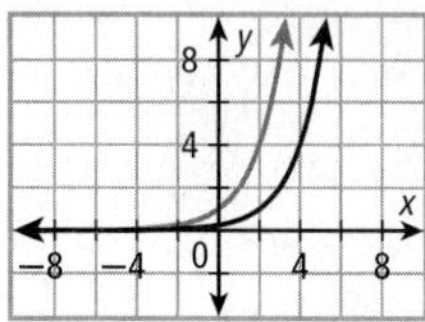

$y = 0$; $j(x) = 2^x$ translation 2 units right

2a.

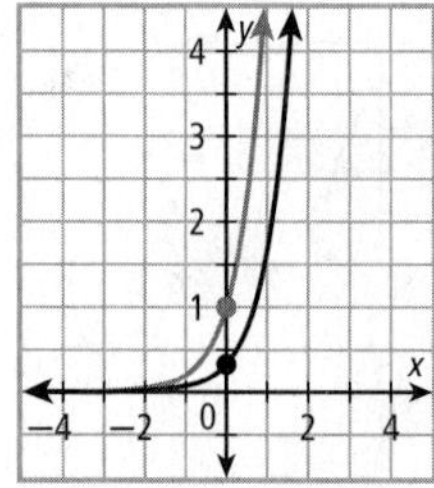

$\frac{1}{3}$; $y = 0$; $f(x) = 5^x$ vertical compression by a factor of 3

b.

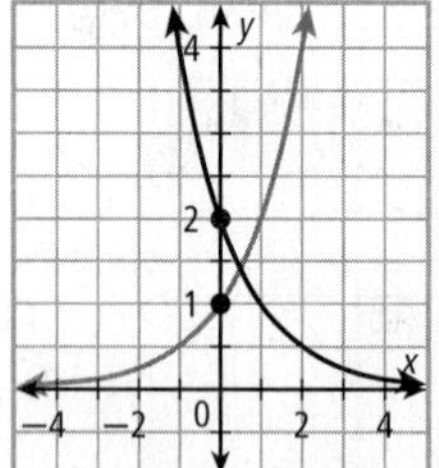

2; $y = 0$; $j(x) = 2^x$ reflection across y-axis and vertical stretch by a factor of 2

3.

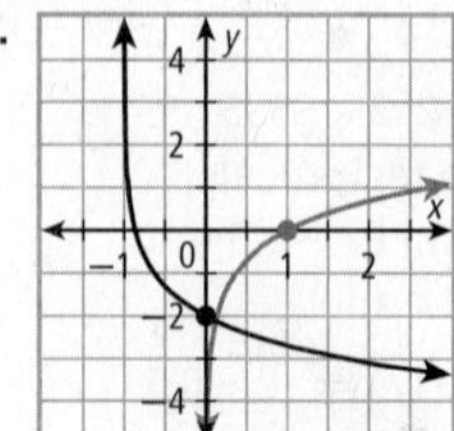

$x = -1$; translation of $f(x) = \ln x$ 1 unit left, reflection across the x-axis, and translation 2 units down; D: $\{x \mid x > -1\}$

4. $g(x) = 2\log(x + 3)$
5. $t = 38{,}679$ yr; no

Exercises

1.

x	-2	-1	0	1	2
$g(x)$	2.1	2.3	3	5	11

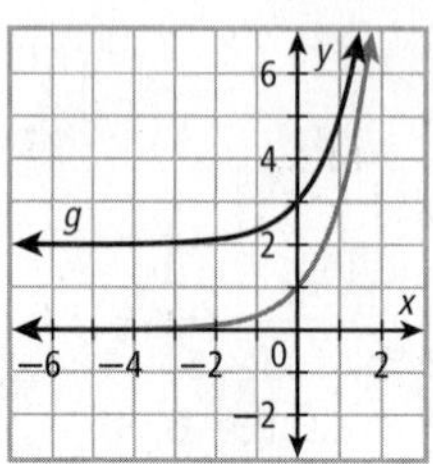

$y = 2$; translation 2 units up; R: $\{y \mid y > 2\}$

3.

x	-3	-2	-1	0	1
$j(x)$	0.11	0.33	1	3	9

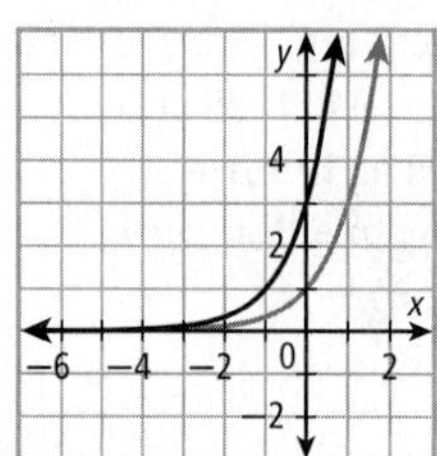

$y = 0$; translation 1 unit left

5. $\frac{1}{3}$; $y = 0$; vertical compression by a factor of $\frac{1}{3}$

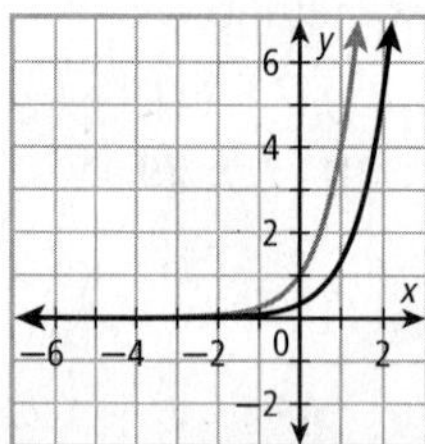

7. -2; $y = 0$; vertical stretch by a factor of 2 and reflection across the x-axis; R: $\{y \mid y < 0\}$

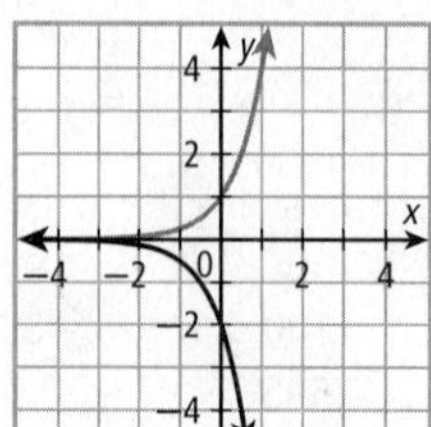

9. 1; $y = 0$; horizontal compression by a factor of $\frac{1}{2}$

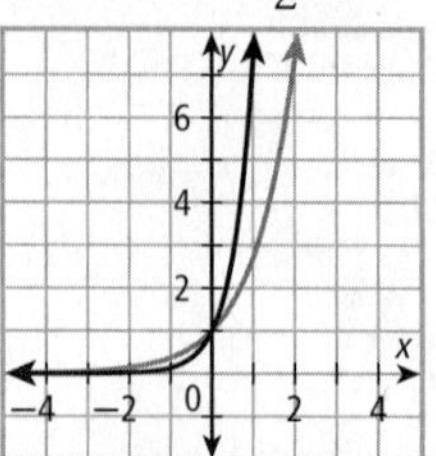

11. $x = -3$; translation 3 units left and vertical stretch by a factor of 2.5; D: $\{x \mid x > -3\}$

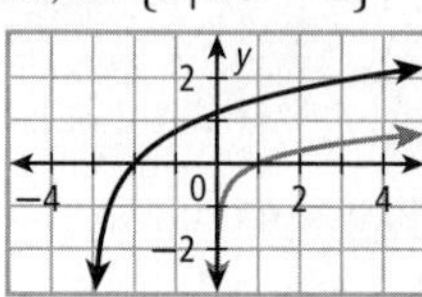

13. $g(x) = -0.7^{\left(\frac{x}{3} + 2\right)}$

15. translated 1 unit left, stretched vertically by a factor of 3, and translated 6 units up; D: $\{t \mid t \geq 0\}$; after about 39 years

17.

x	-2	-1	0	1	2
$h(x)$	1	5	25	125	625

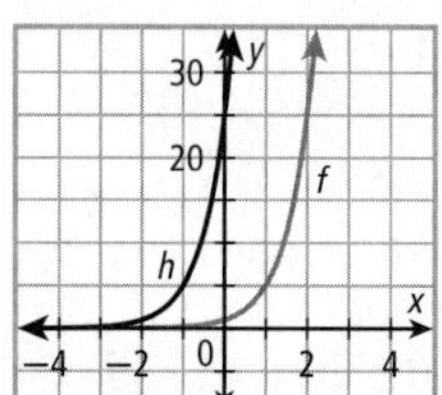

$y = 0$; translation 2 units left

19. 4; $y = 0$; vertical stretch by a factor of 4 **21.** -0.25; $y = 0$; vertical compression by a factor of 0.25 and reflection across the x-axis; R: $\{y \mid y < 0\}$ **23.** 4; $y = 0$; vertical stretch by a factor of 4 and reflection across the y-axis
25. $x = 5$; translation 5 units right; D: $\{x \mid x > 5\}$ **27.** $x = 0$; vertical stretch by a factor of 4 and reflection across the x-axis
29. $f(x) = \ln(4x + 3) - 0.5$
31. ≈ 47 yr **33.** A **35.** D **37.** F
39. D: $\{x \mid x \geq -3\}$; R: $\mathbb{R}$; x-intercept: -2; y-intercept: 2.39 **41.** always

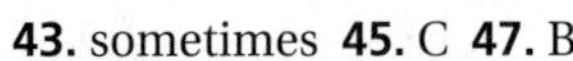

43. sometimes **45.** C **47.** B
51a. $N(t) = 419(0.99)^t$
b. $N(t) = 419(0.99)^{\frac{m}{12}}$
c. 413 **53.** H

4-8

Check It Out!

1a. yes; 1.5 **b.** no
2. $B(t) \approx 199(1.25)^t$; ≈ 10.3 min
3. $S(t) \approx 0.59 + 2.64 \ln t$; ≈ 16.6 min

Exercises

1. exponential regression **3.** yes; $\frac{2}{3}$
5. yes; $\frac{4}{3}$ **7.** $P(t) \approx 621.6 + 1221 \ln t$; ≈ 421 mo **9.** no **11.** yes; $\frac{1}{2}$
13. $T(t) \approx 4.45(1.165)^t$; ≈ 2011
15. yes; $f(x) = 1.55(7.54)^x$
19. $s(t) = 68.24(3.69)^t$; ≈ 46.5 million **23a.** 20.5 mi/h; 36.8 mi/h; 84.0 mi/h **b.** $s = 100(0.8^t)$
25a. exponential **b.** linear **27.** F
29. $f(x) = 7.68(2.5)^x$

Study Guide: Review

1. natural logarithmic function
2. asymptote
3. inverse relation
4. growth **5.** growth
6. decay **7.** growth
8. growth
9. $P(t) = 765(1.02)^t$
10.

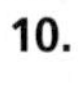

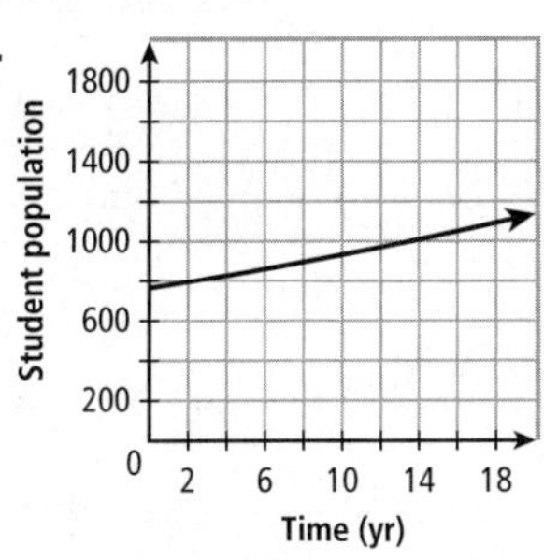

11. ≈ 845 **12.** ≈ 13.5 yr
13.

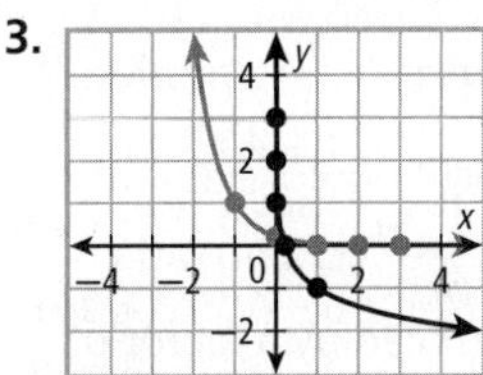

14. $P_T = P_L(1 - 0.03)$
15. $P_L = \frac{P_T}{0.97}$ **16.** $K = \frac{8}{5}M$; 40 km
17. $\log_3 243 = 5$ **18.** $\log_9 1 = 0$
19. $\log_{\frac{1}{3}} 27 = -3$ **20.** $2^4 = 16$
21. $10^1 = 10$ **22.** $0.6^2 = 0.36$
23. 2 **24.** 2 **25.** −1 **26.** −2 **27.** 0
28.

x	−2	−1	0	1	2
y	4	2	1	0.5	0.25

D: $\{x \mid x > 0\}$; R: $\mathbb{R}$
29. $\log_2 128 = 7$
30. $\log 1{,}000{,}000 = 6$
31. $\log_2 64 = 6$ **32.** $\log 100 = 2$
33. $\log_5 5^4 = 4$ **34.** $9 \log 10 = 9$
35. 10 times **36.** −1 **37.** $x \geq -6$
38. $x > 10$ **39.** 17.67 quarters, or 4.4 yr **40.** $k = 0.0346$
41. $g(x) = -3e^x - 2$ **42.** 0.6; $y = 0$; vertically compressed by a factor of $\frac{3}{5}$ and horizontally compressed by a factor of $\frac{1}{6}$ **43.** 0.5; $x = -0.5$; translated $\frac{1}{2}$ unit left and vertically stretched by a factor of 2
44. $V(t) = 5300(1 - 0.35)^t$
45. vertically stretched by a factor of 3500 **46.** $f(x) \approx 11.26(1.05)^x$
47. $f(x) \approx -97.8 + 56.4 \ln x$
48. The exponential function; $r^2 \approx 0.94$ versus $r^2 \approx 0.60$ for the logarithmic function

Selected Answers ■ Chapter 5

5-1

Check It Out!

1. $y = 0.5x$

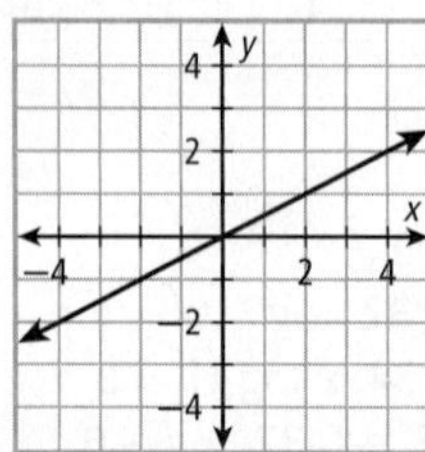

2. 6.25 in. **3.** 1.6 m

4. $y = \frac{40}{x}$

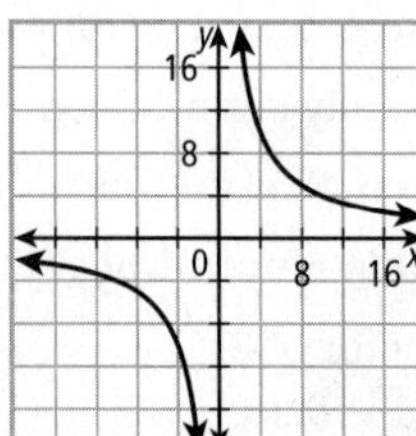

5. $83\frac{1}{3}$ working hours

6a. inverse **b.** direct **7.** 20 L

Exercises **1.** indirect variation **3.** $y = -9x$ **5.** 12 ft **7.** 6 ft **9.** $y = \frac{14}{x}$ **11.** $y = -\frac{5}{x}$ **13.** neither **15.** direct **17.** $y = \frac{1}{2}x$ **19.** $y = -3x$ **21.** 88 Cal **23.** 0.2 kg **25.** $y = \frac{10.5}{x}$ **27.** 5 days **29.** neither **31.** 1.375 atm **33.** sometimes **35.** always **37a.** $s = \frac{6300}{t}$ **b.** 30 s **39a.** $I = 0.02Pt$ **b.** True Federal Bank **c.** \$30 **41.** $x = 5$; $y = 4.4$; $z = 2$ **45.** D **47.** D **49.** 24 **51.** $y \approx 7$

5-2

Check It Out!

1a. $2x^9; x \neq 0$ **b.** $\frac{1}{x-1}; x \neq -\frac{4}{3}$ and $x \neq 1$ **c.** $\frac{(2x+1)}{(2x-3)}; x \neq -\frac{2}{3}$ and $x \neq \frac{3}{2}$ **2a.** $-2; x \neq 5$ **b.** $\frac{-x}{2x-1}$; $x \neq 3$ and $x \neq \frac{1}{2}$ **3a.** $\frac{2x^3}{3}$ **b.** $\frac{2}{x-2}$ **4a.** $\frac{3y}{x^2}$ **b.** $\frac{4(x-4)}{x+3}$ **5a.** no solution **b.** $x = 4$

Exercises

3. $\frac{(2x+5)}{(2x-7)}; x \neq \frac{1}{3}$ and $x \neq \frac{7}{2}$ **5.** $\frac{-1}{x-5}; x \neq -4$ and $x \neq 5$ **7.** $6x$; defined for all real values of x **9.** $\frac{2(x-2)}{(x+5)}$ **11.** $\frac{x^7y^4}{3}$ **13.** $\frac{(x+5)^2}{(2x-3)(x+2)}$ **15.** no solution **17.** $x = -1$ **19.** $\frac{4}{x+5}; x \neq \frac{1}{2}$ and $x \neq -5$ **21.** $\frac{-3}{x-4}; x \neq -6$ and $x \neq 4$ **23.** $-4; x \neq -5$ **25.** $\frac{(x-4)(2x-1)}{(x-3)(x+4)}$ **27.** $\frac{3(2x-5)}{x}$ **29.** $\frac{x+1}{x-1}$ **31.** $\frac{x+3}{x+5}$ **33.** $x = 2$ **35.** $\frac{\pi r^2}{\pi (5r)^2}; \frac{1}{25}$ **37.** $\frac{4x-3}{2x-1}$ **39.** $2x^2y^2$ **41.** $\frac{3}{x+1}$ **43a.** square prism: $\frac{h}{1}$; cylinder: $\frac{h}{1}$ **b.** square prism: $\frac{2s+4h}{sh}$; cylinder: $\frac{2r+2h}{rh}$ **c.** The ratio would be reduced by a factor of $\frac{1}{2}$. **45.** Student A **47.** D **49.** A **51.** $\frac{2(x^2+5x+25)}{x^2-5x+25}$ **53.** $\frac{2(x+1)(x+2)}{x^2+1}$

5-3

Check It Out!

1a. $\frac{9x+4}{x^2-3}; x \neq \pm\sqrt{3}$ **b.** $\frac{x^2+3x-3}{3x-1}; x \neq \frac{1}{3}$ **2a.** $12x^5y^7$ **b.** $(x+2)(x-2)(x+3)$ **3a.** $\frac{15x-4}{6(x-1)}; x \neq 1$ **b.** $\frac{x+2}{x+3}$; $x \neq -3$ **4a.** $\frac{15x^2-20x-6}{(2x+5)(5x-2)}$; $x \neq -\frac{5}{2}$ and $x \neq \frac{2}{5}$ **b.** $\frac{x+4}{x-8}$; $x \neq \pm 8$ **5a.** $\frac{1}{x}$ **b.** 10 **c.** $\frac{3(x-2)}{2x(x+4)}$ **6.** 42.4 mi/h

Exercises

3. $\frac{-2x-7}{4x+5}; x \neq -\frac{5}{4}$ **5.** $16x^4y^3$ **7.** $\frac{2(4x^2+x-8)}{(x+6)(2x-1)}$; $x \neq -6$ and $x \neq \frac{1}{2}$ **9.** $\frac{2x^2-4x-1}{(x+3)(x-3)}; x \neq \pm 3$ **11.** $\frac{-1}{x-4}; x \neq \pm 4$ **13.** $\frac{(2x-3)(x+2)}{4x-3}$ **15.** $\frac{3(x+2)}{2x^2}$ **17.** $\frac{2(2x-3)}{4x-7}; x \neq \frac{7}{4}$ **19.** $\frac{x^2-2x+2}{2x+7}; x \neq -\frac{7}{2}$ **21.** $(4x-5)(4x+5)(x+1)$ **23.** $\frac{7(2x-3)}{3(x-2)}; x \neq 2$ **25.** $\frac{-(2x+3)(x-2)}{(x-3)(x+3)}; x \neq \pm 3$ **27.** $\frac{1}{x-2}; x \neq 2$ and $x \neq 4$ **29.** $\frac{(3x-2)(x+3)}{(5x+1)(x+2)}$ **31.** 0.6 °C/min **33.** $\frac{x^2+6x-6}{(x+4)(x-3)}; x \neq -4$ and $x \neq 3$ **35.** $\frac{5x-9}{(x-5)(x+4)(x+3)}; x \neq -4$, $x \neq -3$, and $x \neq 5$ **37.** $\frac{2x^2-13x+9}{(x-1)(x-2)}; x \neq 1$ and $x \neq 2$ **39.** $\frac{2(4x^3-6x^2-3x-4)}{(3x+4)(2x-3)}$; $x \neq -\frac{4}{3}$ and $x \neq \frac{3}{2}$ **41.** $\frac{-9x^2-52x+7}{(x+7)(x+6)(x+1)}; x \neq -7$, $x \neq -6$, and $x \neq -1$ **43.** $\frac{24}{(x+2)^2}$ **45.** $\frac{7(x-3)}{6x(x-1)}$ **49.** D **51.** A **53.** $\frac{-5x^2-15x+6}{(x+2)(x-2)}$ **55.** $\frac{-4}{(x+2)^2(x-2)}$ **57.** $6x^2+4x+20$ **59.** $\frac{8}{5}$

Extension

Check It Out!

1. The set of positive integers is only closed under addition and multiplication. When adding positive integers a and b, movement is to the right from point a to point b by b units, which represents a positive integer and each unit is an integer. Since positive integers are closed under addition, multiplication is also closed, as multiplication of positive integers can be rewritten as repeated addition. Positive integers are not closed under subtraction. Counterexample: for $a = 5$ and $b = 7$, $a - b = 5 - 7 = -2$, which is a negative integer. Positive integers are not closed under division. Counterexample: for $a = 3$ and $b = 8$, $\frac{a}{b} = \frac{3}{8}$, which is not a positive integer.

2. The set of negative rational numbers is closed under addition. Since the addition of negative integers is always negative, the addition of negative rational numbers will result in a negative rational number as well. The set of negative rational numbers is not closed under subtraction. Counterexample: $\frac{a}{b} - \frac{c}{d} = -\frac{1}{2} - \left(-\frac{3}{4}\right) = -\frac{1}{2} + \frac{3}{4} = -\frac{2}{4} + \frac{3}{4} = \frac{1}{4}$. Since the result is a positive rational number, negative rational numbers are not closed under subtraction. The set of negative rational numbers is not closed under multiplication. Since the product of two negative numbers is always a positive, then the product of two rational numbers will never result in a negative rational number. The same is true of division of negative rational numbers. A division of two negative numbers will result in a positive number, so the set of negative rational numbers is not closed under division.

3. The set of polynomials is closed under subtraction. Since subtraction can be rewritten as addition for the coefficients of like terms and polynomials are closed under addition, they are closed under subtraction for real-number coefficients.

4. The set of rational expressions is closed under multiplication. Let $f(x)$, $g(x)$, $p(x)$ and $q(x)$ be polynomial expressions and $g(x) \neq 0$ and $q(x) \neq 0$: $\frac{f(x)}{g(x)} \cdot \frac{p(x)}{q(x)} = \frac{f(x) \cdot p(x)}{g(x) \cdot q(x)}$. Since the product of polynomials is closed under multiplication, the rational expressions are closed under multiplication.

Exercises

1. Not closed; counterexample: $a = 4$ and $b = 9$, $\frac{a}{b} = \frac{4}{9}$, which is not a whole number. **3.** Not closed; counterexample: $a = 10$, $b = 14$; $a - b = 10 - 14 = -4$, which is a negative even number. **5.** Closed. Let $2a$ represent an even integer and $2b$ represent an even integer. Then $2a + 2b = 2(a + b)$, which is an even integer. **9.** Showing one counterexample is enough to prove that a set is not closed, but one example isn't sufficient to show that a set is closed.

11. $-1 \times -1 = 1$
$-1 \times 1 = -1$
$1 \times -1 = -1$
$1 \times 1 = 1$

13. the set of integers itself

15a. 12 **b.** Yes; any time has an 'hour number' in the set 1 through 12, and that digit plus any number of hours is another number in the set.

5-4

Check It Out!

1a. g is f translated 4 units left.

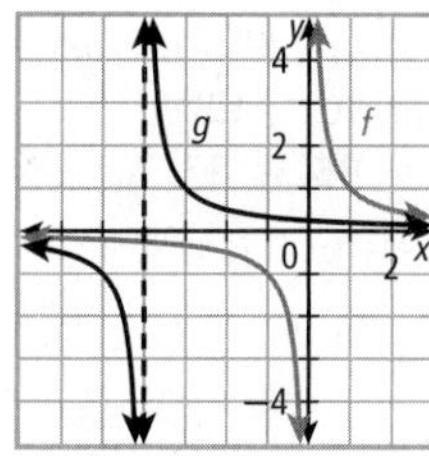

b. g is f translated 1 unit up.

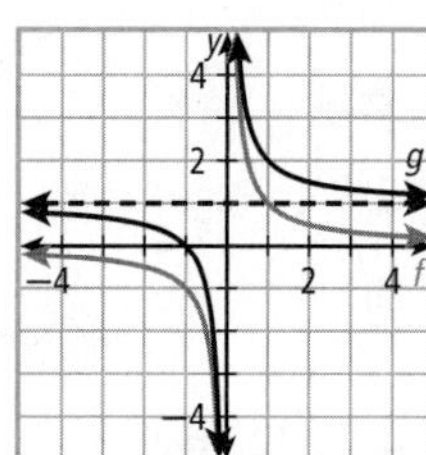

2. asymptotes: $x = 3$, $y = -5$; D: $\{x \mid x \neq 3\}$; R: $\{y \mid y \neq -5\}$

3. zeros: $-6, -1$; asymptote: $x = -3$

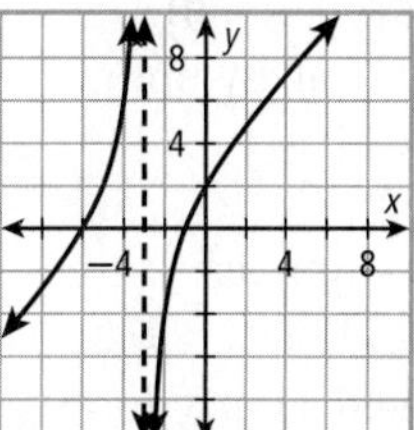

4a. zeros: $-5, 3$; asymptote: $x = 1$

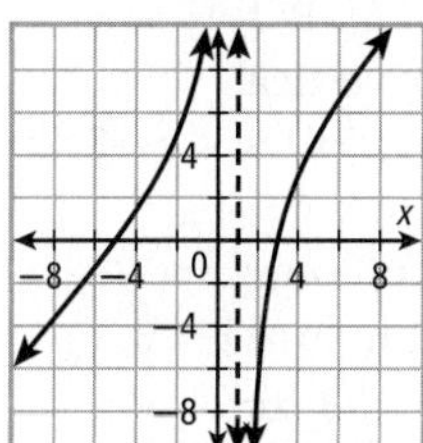

b. zero: 2; asymptotes: $x = -1$, $x = 0$, $y = 0$

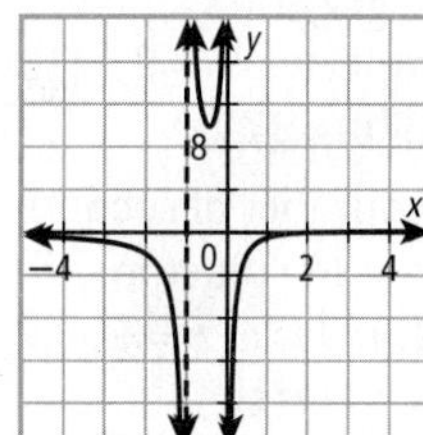

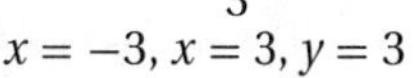
c. zeros: $-\frac{1}{3}$, 0; asymptotes: $x = -3$, $x = 3$, $y = 3$

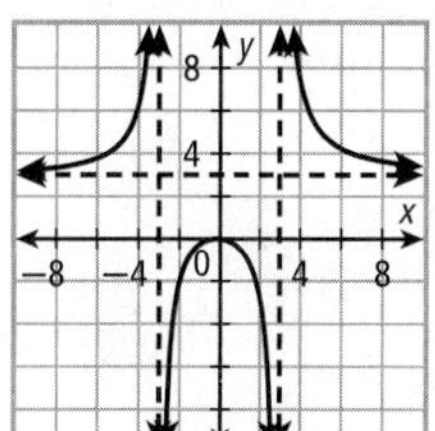

5. hole at $x = 2$

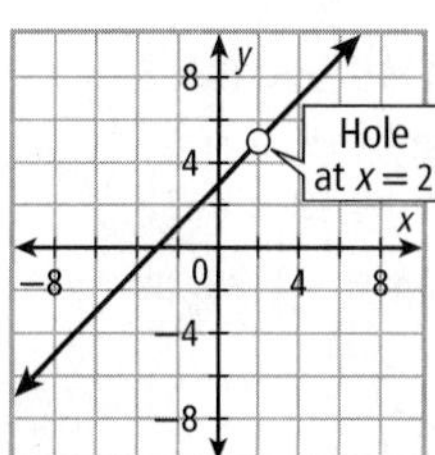

Exercises **1.** discontinuous
3. g is f translated 5 units left.
5. asymptotes: $x = 0$, $y = -1$; D: $\{x \mid x \neq 0\}$; R: $\{y \mid y \neq -1\}$

7. asymptotes: $x = 2$, $y = -8$; D: $\{x | x \neq 2\}$; R: $\{y | y \neq -8\}$
9. zeros: 0, 5; vertical asymptote: $x = 2$ **11.** zeros: -2, -1; asymptote: $x = 3$
13. zero: $-\frac{2}{5}$; asymptotes: $x = -1$, $y = 5$ **15.** hole at $x = 2$
17. g is f translated 5 units down.
19. g is f vertically stretched by a factor of 2. **21.** asymptotes: $x = 0$, $y = 5$; D: $\{x | x \neq 0\}$; R: $\{y | y \neq 5\}$
23. zeros: -2, 5; vertical asymptote: $x = 2$ **25.** zeros: -2, 2; vertical asymptote: $x = -3$
27. zero: 3; asymptotes: $x = -2$, $x = 2$, $y = 0$ **29.** hole at $x = 0$
31. hole at $x = 7$ **33.** zero: -1; asymptotes: $x = 0$, $y = 1$; hole at $x = 3$ **35.** zero: $\frac{5}{6}$; asymptotes: $x = \frac{2}{3}$, $y = -2$
37. zero: 0; asymptotes: $x = 3$, $x = -3$, $y = 0$ **43b.** ≈ 17 g
47b. $t = 12$; the number of seconds the driver spent at the pit stop **c.** 57 s **51.** F **53.** holes at $x = 1$, $x = 2$, $x = 3$

5-5

Check It Out! 1a. $x = 3$ **b.** $x = -2$ **c.** $x = -3$, $x = 2$ **2a.** no solution **b.** $x = -6$ **3.** 1.5 mi/h
4. about 24 min **5a.** $3 < x \leq 4$ **b.** $x = -5$
6a. $x \leq \frac{1}{2}$ or $x > 2$
b. $x < -3$ or $x > -\frac{3}{2}$
Exercises 3. $w = \frac{1}{11}$
5. $x = -1$, $x = 6$ **7.** $k = 1$
9. $x = 0$, $x = 7$ **11.** 2.4 mi/h
13. $-5 < x < 0$ **15.** $x < 0$ or $x > 1$
17. $x < 4$ or $x \geq 8$ **19.** $x = 1$
21. $a = \frac{22}{3}$ **23.** $z = 2$, $z = 7$
25. $x = -8$ **27.** $x = -2$ **29.** about 6 h
31. $x = -3$
33. $x < 0$ or $x > \frac{1}{6}$
35. $-10 < x < -7$ **37a.** 2003 **b.** 18 hits **c.** 170 hits **39.** $z = 0$
41. $x = -5$ **43.** $a = 2$ **45.** $-1 < x < 1$
47. $x = \pm 0.45$ **49.** $x = 0$, $x = 2$
51a. 2001 winner: $\frac{500}{s}$; 2002 winner: $\frac{500}{s + 25}$ **b.** 141 mi/h

55. G **57b.** about 13 h **59.** all real numbers except -3, 0, and 3
61. $x < -21$ or $3 < x < 4$

5-6

Check It Out! 1a. no real roots **b.** ± 1 **c.** 5 **2a.** $2x$ **b.** $\frac{\sqrt[4]{27}}{3}x^2$ **c.** x^3
3a. 4 **b.** 32 **c.** 125
4a. $81^{\frac{3}{4}}$ **b.** 1000 **c.** $5^{\frac{1}{2}}$ **5a.** 6 **b.** $-\frac{1}{2}$ **c.** 25 **6.** 32 cm from the bridge
Exercises 1. 3 **3.** ± 5 **5.** $2x$
7. $\frac{5x^2\sqrt[3]{36}}{6}$ **9.** $x^3\sqrt[3]{x}$ **11.** $-2x\sqrt{10}$
13. 216 **15.** -3 **17.** $9^{\frac{10}{5}} = 9^2 = 81$
19. $5^{\frac{1}{2}}$ **21.** 169 **23.** 2 **25.** $\frac{1}{5}$ **27.** $-\frac{1}{5}$
29. 44 in. **31.** 2 **33.** $3x$
35. $\frac{x^2\sqrt[3]{4}}{10}$ **37.** $2x^3\sqrt[3]{7}$
39. $x^2\sqrt[5]{x^3}$ **41.** 8 **43.** 10,000
45. $14^{\frac{3}{3}} = 14^1 = 14$ **47.** $144^{\frac{1}{2}} = 12$
49. 64 **51.** $\frac{2}{3}$ **53.** $\frac{9}{7}$ **55.** $5^{\frac{1}{9}}$, or $\sqrt[9]{5}$
57. \$1189 **59a.** about 18% **b.** about 12.6 g **61a.** $\frac{2\pi\sqrt{Lg}}{g}$
b. 1.2 s **63.** $(5x)^{\frac{7}{2}}$ **65.** $11^{\frac{3}{2}}x^{12}$
67. $5\sqrt[4]{125x^3}$ **69.** $b\sqrt[3]{a^2b}$
71. $b\sqrt[4]{4a^3b^2}$ **73.** always
75. never **77.** 2 and 3; about 2.62
79. -5 and -4; about -4.31
81. A is incorrect. **85.** A **87.** A
89. $20^{\frac{1}{8}}$ **91.** $a < -1$ or $0 < a < 1$

5-7

Check It Out! 1a. D: $\{x | x \in \mathbb{R}\}$; R: $\{y | y \in \mathbb{R}\}$

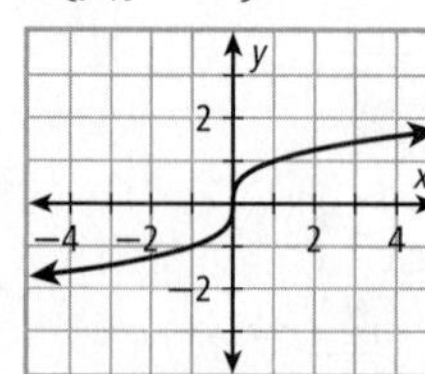

b. D: $\{x | x \geq -1\}$; R: $\{y | y \geq 0\}$

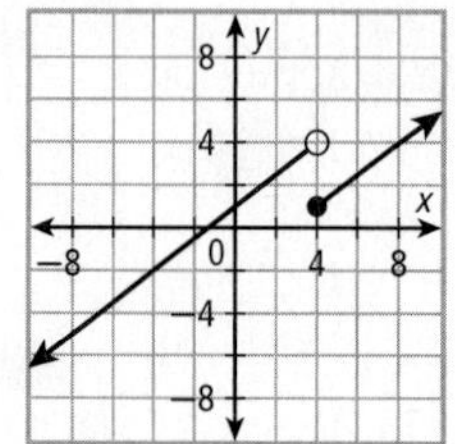

2a. g is f translated 1 unit up.

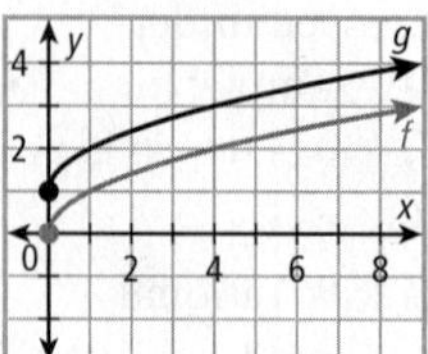

b. g is f vertically compressed by a factor of $\frac{1}{2}$.

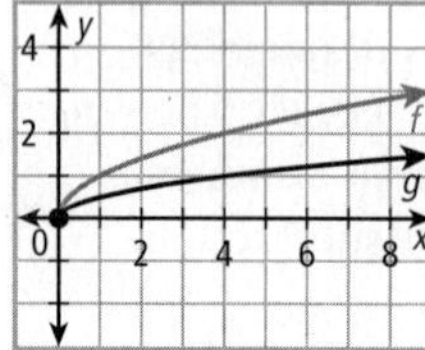

3a. g is f reflected across the y-axis and translated 3 units up.

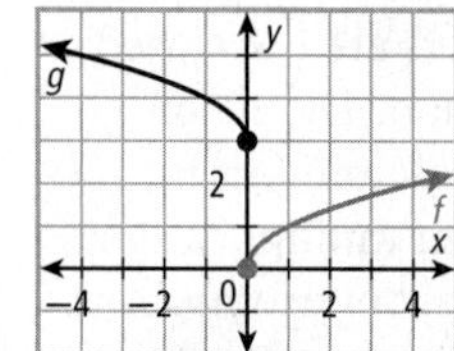

b. g is f vertically stretched by a factor of 3, reflected across the x-axis, and translated 1 unit down.

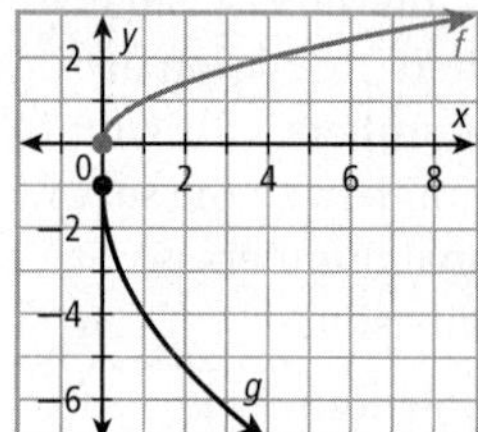

4. $g(x) = -2\sqrt{x} + 1$
5. $h(x) = \sqrt{\frac{256}{25}x}$; about 23 ft/s
6a.

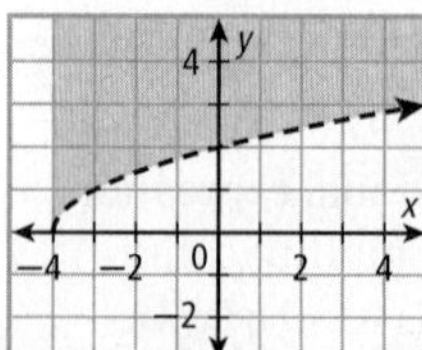

b.

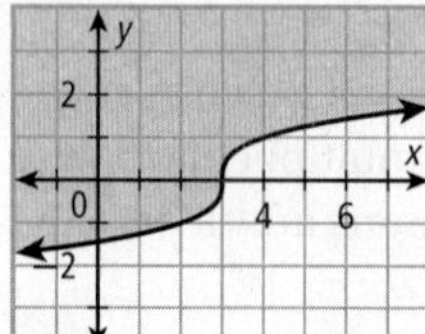

Exercises 3. D: $\{x|x \geq 0\}$; R: $\{y|y \geq -1\}$ **5.** D: $\{x|x \in \mathbb{R}\}$; R: $\{y|y \in \mathbb{R}\}$ **7.** D: $\{x|x \in \mathbb{R}\}$; R: $\{y|y \in \mathbb{R}\}$ **9.** h is f vertically stretched by a factor of 3. **11.** g is f compressed vertically by a factor of $\frac{1}{2}$ and translated 1 unit down. **13.** j is f reflected across the y-axis and then translated 3 units right. **15.** h is f reflected across the y-axis, horizontally compressed by a factor of $\frac{1}{2}$, and then translated 2 units left. **17.** $g(x) = 4\sqrt{(x+5)} - 2$

19. $g(x) = \frac{6}{5}\sqrt{\frac{5}{9}x}$; about 2.2 mi

21.

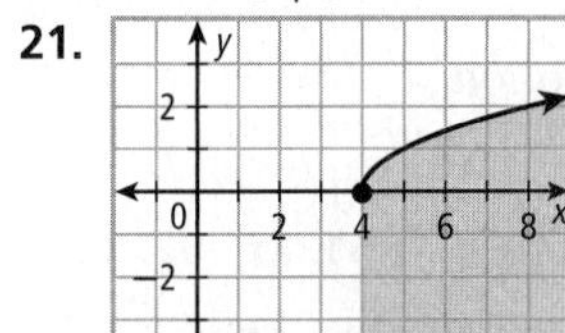

23.

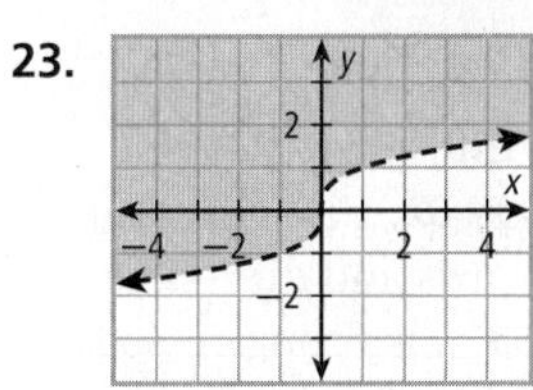

25. D: $\{x|x \geq 0\}$; R: $\{y|y \leq 0\}$ **27.** D: $\{x|x \in \mathbb{R}\}$; R: $\{y|y \in \mathbb{R}\}$ **29.** D: $\{x|x \in \mathbb{R}\}$; R: $\{y|y \in \mathbb{R}\}$ **31.** h is f translated 4 units right. **33.** g is f horizontally compressed by a factor of $\frac{1}{3}$ and then translated 5 units left. **35.** j is f translated 4 units left and 1 unit down. **37.** h is f reflected across the y-axis, vertically stretched by a factor of 3, and then translated 2 units up.

39. $g(x) = \frac{1}{3}\sqrt{x+3}$

41. $g(x) = -\sqrt{x+1} - 4$

43.

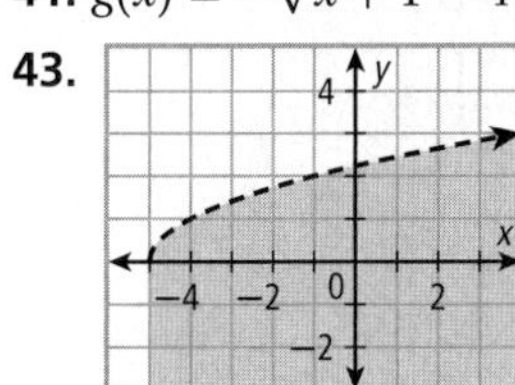

45.

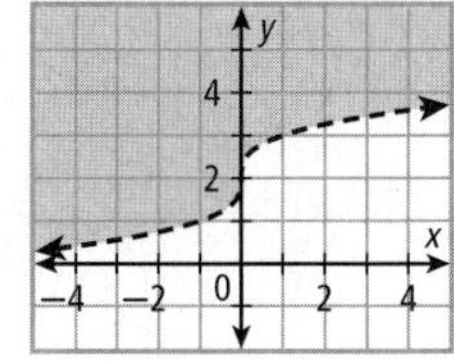

47a. $\approx$ 762 beats/min **b.** $\approx$ 58 beats/min **49.** a vertical stretch by a factor of 3 followed by a translation 1 unit right and 9 units down **51.** D **53.** A **55a.** about 373 km **b.** It will appear to decrease by about 76 km. **57.** yes **59c.** by a factor of 4 **61.** sometimes **63.** never **65.** yes **67b.** about 346 m/s **c.** −273.15°C **69.** 1.4 s **73.** D **75.** A **79.** $f(x) = -2\sqrt{\frac{1}{5}(x+3)} + 4$

5-8

Check It Out! 1a. $x = 2$ **b.** $x = 4$ **c.** $x = 39$ **2a.** $x = 6$ **b.** $x = 2$ **3a.** $x = 1$ **b.** $x = -4, x = 3$ **4a.** $x = 22$ **b.** $x = 5$ **c.** $x = 3$ **5a.** $3 \leq x \leq 12$ **b.** $x \geq -1$ **6.** If the car were traveling 30 mi/h, its skid marks would have measured about 43 ft. Because the actual skid marks measure less than 43 ft, the car was not speeding.

Exercises 1. No; the expression under the radical does not contain a variable. **3.** $x = 12$ **5.** $x = 5$ **7.** $x = 3$ **9.** $x = 10$ **11.** $x = 8$ **13.** $x = 4, x = 5$ **15.** $x = -1$ **17.** $x = 14$ **19.** $x = 5$ **21.** $x = -\frac{3}{4}$ **23.** $-5 \leq x \leq 20$ **25.** $\frac{-5}{2} \leq x < 10$ **27.** $x = 93$ **29.** $x = 18$ **31.** $x = 38$ **33.** $x = 6$ **35.** $x = \frac{7}{3}$ **37.** $x = 4$ **39.** $x = 25$ **41.** $x = 7$ **43.** $3 \leq x \leq 19$ **45.** about 1.5 tons **47.** $A = \pi r^2$ **49.** $E = \frac{1}{2}mv^2$ **51a.** 5 m **b.** 25.6 m/s^2 **53a.** $r \leq \sqrt{\frac{A}{\pi}}$ **b.** no **55.** $x \approx 5.84$ **57.** $x \approx 2.35$ **59.** 995 g **63.** H **65.** F **67.** always true **69.** always true **71.** $x = 9$ **73.** $x = 10$

Extension

Check It Out!

1.

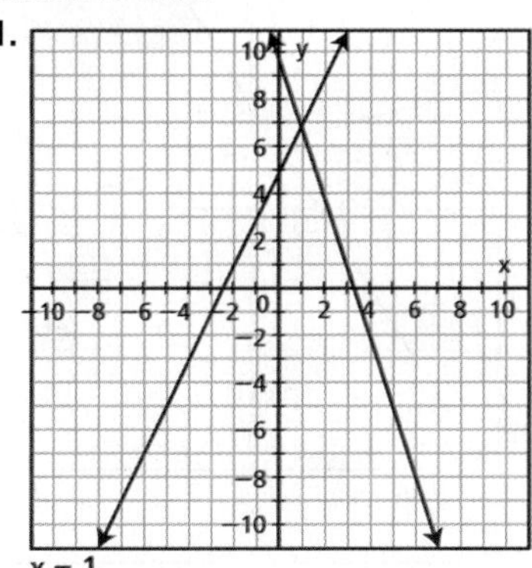

x = 1

2.

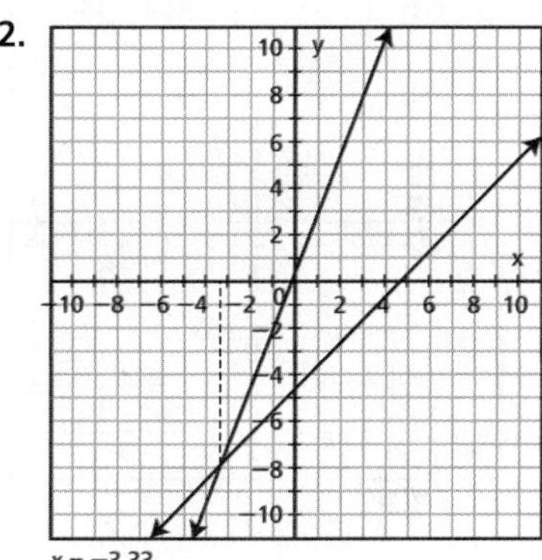

x = −3.33

3.

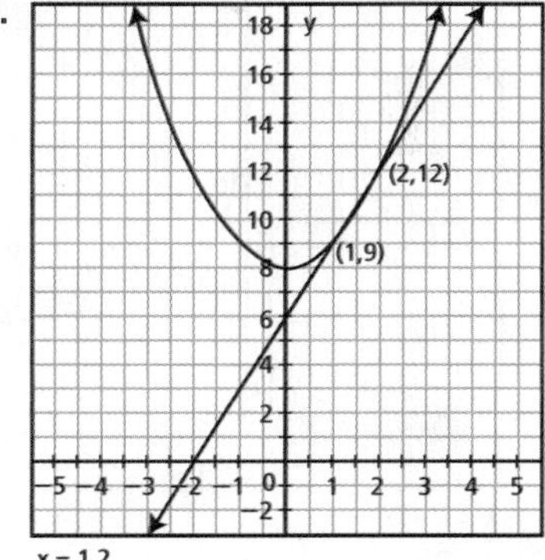

x = 1,2

4.

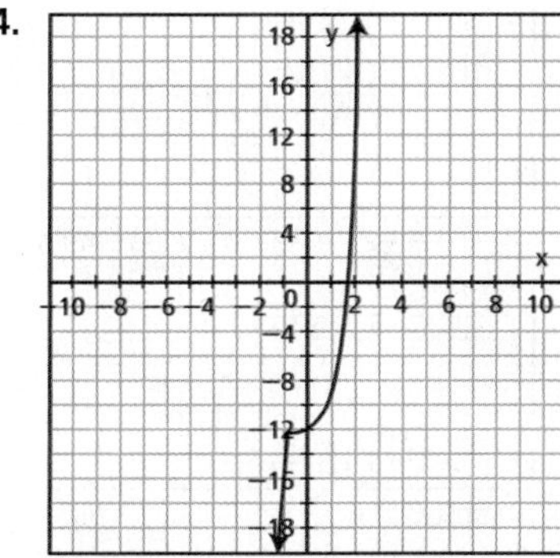

Since the graphs share all points, there are an infinite number of solutions.

Exercises

1.

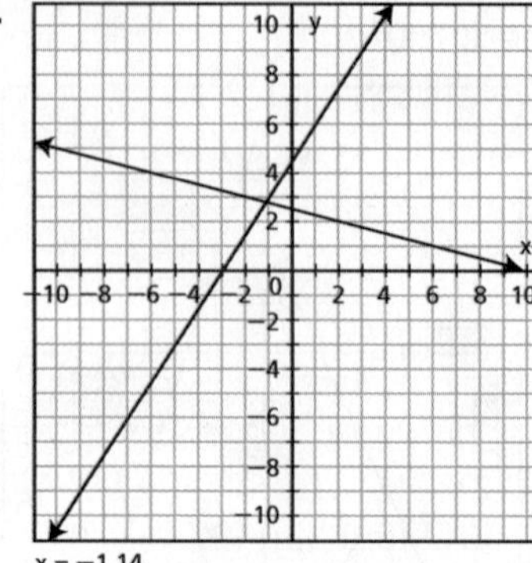

$x = -1.14$

3.

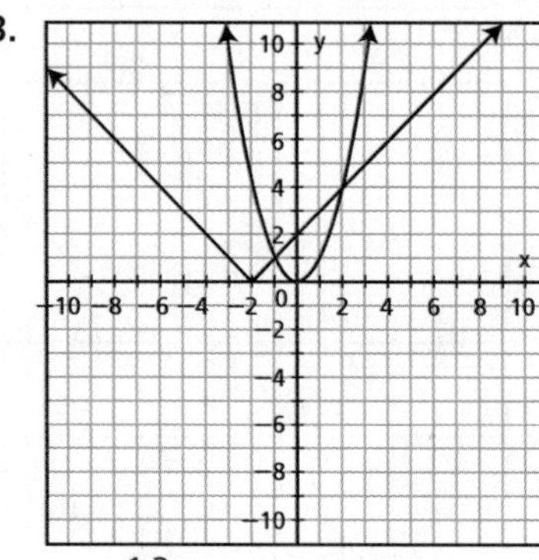

$x = -1, 2$

5.

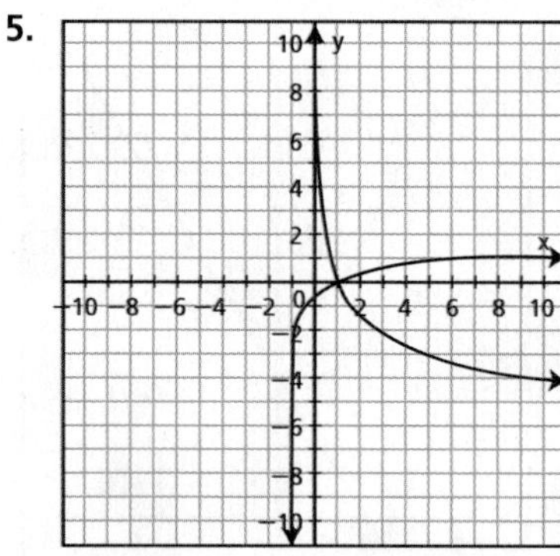

$x = 0.86$

7.

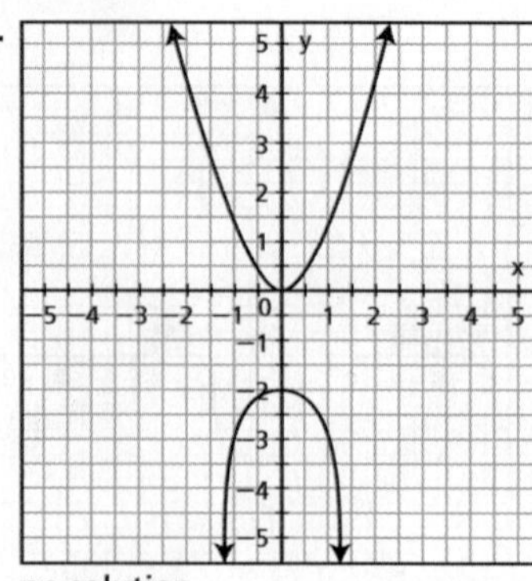

no solution

9.

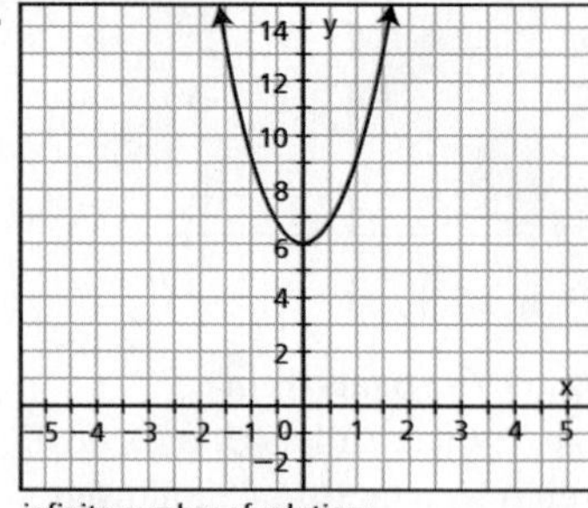

infinite number of solutions

11. Equations will have undefined values for any terms that contain variables in the denominator. Any value of x that makes the denominator 0 will make the equation undefined and any intersections given by a calculator at those points need to be discarded.

Study Guide: Review

1. rational function **2.** direct variation; constant of variation **3.** $y = \frac{1}{3}x$ **4.** $y = 4x$ **5.** 306 tiles **6.** \$2000 **7.** $y = \frac{6}{x}$ **8.** $y = \frac{4}{x}$ **9.** 24 ohms **10.** inverse variation **11.** $\frac{8}{3x^2}; x \neq 0$ **12.** $\frac{2x^3}{x+4}; x \neq -4$ **13.** $\frac{x-3}{x+1}; x \neq -4, x \neq -1$ **14.** $\frac{3}{x-5}$ **15.** $\frac{-x}{(x-4)(x+3)}$ **16.** $\frac{x-1}{x+1}$ **17.** $\frac{3x-1}{x-3}$ **18.** $\frac{2x}{y}$ **19.** $\frac{2(x+5)}{x+3}$ **20.** 1 **21.** $\frac{x+3}{3(x+4)}$ **22.** $\frac{x^2+12}{x^2+4}$ **23.** $\frac{2x}{(x+3)(x-3)}; x \neq \pm 3$ **24.** $\frac{2(x+1)}{(x+2)(x-2)}; x \neq \pm 2$ **25.** $\frac{8x^2+4x+45}{(3x+7)(4x-1)}; x \neq -\frac{7}{3}, x \neq \frac{1}{4}$ **26.** $(x-3)^2(x+3)$ **27.** $(x-5)(x+2)(x+7)$ **28.** $\frac{2x-3}{x+4}; x \neq -4$ **29.** $\frac{x^2-10x-25}{(x+5)(x-5)}; x \neq \pm 5$ **30.** $\frac{-(x^2-3x-1)}{(x-3)(x+2)}; x \neq -2, x \neq 3$ **31.** $\frac{6x^2-16x-7}{(2x+1)(3x-1)}; x \neq -\frac{1}{2}, x \neq \frac{1}{3}$ **32.** $\frac{8(x-6)}{5(x+2)}$ **33.** $\frac{2x-3}{x(x-3)}$ **34.** $\frac{(x-2)^2}{4x}$ **35.** ≈ 548 mi/h **36.** g is f translated 4 units right. **37.** g is f translated 2 units right and 3 units up. **38.** asymptotes: $x = 1, y = -3$; D: $\{x \mid x \neq 1\}$; R: $\{y \mid y \neq -3\}$ **39.** asymptotes: $x = -2, y = 1$; D: $\{x \mid x \neq -2\}$; R: $\{y \mid y \neq 1\}$ **40.** zeros: 0, 3; asymptote: $x = -4$ **41.** zero: 3; asymptotes: $x = -5, x = -1, y = 0$ **42.** zero: 2; asymptotes: $x = -3$, $y = 2$ **43.** zeros: −3, 3; asymptote: $x = 2$ **44.** hole at $x = -3$ **45.** $x = -2$ or $x = 3$ **46.** no solution **47.** $x = 2$ **48.** $x = 0$ **49.** $x < -\frac{4}{3}$ or $x > 0$ **50.** $x < 3$ or $x > \frac{7}{2}$ **51.** $3x^2$ **52.** $3x^3$ **53.** $2x\frac{\sqrt[3]{9}}{3}$ **54.** $(-27)^{\frac{2}{3}}$ **55.** $16^{\frac{3}{4}}$ **56.** $9^{\frac{3}{2}}$ **57.** 17 **58.** 81 **59.** $\frac{1}{2}$ **60.** D: $\{x \mid x \geq 0\}$; R: $\{y \mid y \geq 5\}$ **61.** D: $\mathbb{R}$; R: $\mathbb{R}$ **62.** g is f reflected across the x-axis and translated 1 unit up. **63.** h is f compressed horizontally by a factor of $\frac{1}{4}$. **64.** j is f reflected across the y-axis and translated 8 units right. **65.** k is f reflected across the x-axis, compressed vertically by a factor of $\frac{1}{2}$, and translated 1 unit up. **66.** $g(x) = 3\sqrt{x+4}$

67.

68.

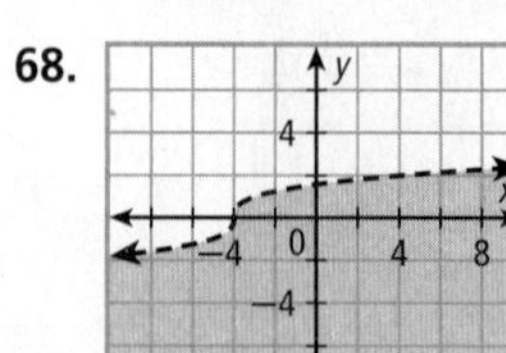

69. $x = 19$ **70.** $x = 109$ **71.** $x = 9$ **72.** $x = 2$ **73.** $x = 2$ or $x = 8$ **74.** $x = 8$ **75.** $x = 0.5$ **76.** $x = 85$ **77.** $x = 7$ **78.** $x = -219$ **79.** $4 \leq x \leq 13$ **80.** $x > 9$ **81.** $0 \leq x < 12$ **82.** $x > -7$ **83.** ≈ 1.6 m **84.** 60.3 m^3

Mastering the Standards

for Mathematical Practice

The topics described in the Standards for Mathematical Content will vary from year to year. However, the *way* in which you learn, study, and think about mathematics will not. The Standards for Mathematical Practice describe skills that you will use in all of your math courses.

Mathematical Practices

1. *Make sense of problems and persevere in solving them.*
2. *Reason abstractly and quantitatively.*
3. *Construct viable arguments and critique the reasoning of others.*
4. *Model with mathematics.*
5. *Use appropriate tools strategically.*
6. *Attend to precision.*
7. *Look for and make use of structure.*
8. *Look for and express regularity in repeated reasoning.*

④ Model with mathematics.

Mathematically proficient students can apply... mathematics... to... problems... in everyday life, society, and the workplace...

In your book

Multi-Step Test Prep and **Real-World Connections** apply mathematics to other disciplines and in real-world scenarios.

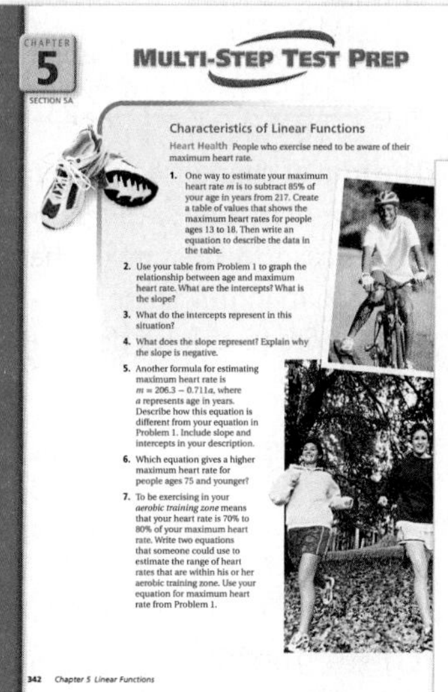

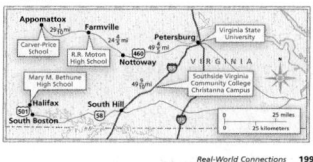

CHAPTER 5 SECTION 5A

MULTI-STEP TEST PREP

Characteristics of Linear Functions

Heart Health People who exercise need to be aware of their maximum heart rate.

1. One way to estimate your maximum heart rate m is to subtract 85% of your age in years from 217. Create a table of values that shows the maximum heart rates for people ages 13 to 18. Then write an equation to describe the data in the table.
2. Use your table from Problem 1 to graph the relationship between age and maximum heart rate. What are the intercepts? What is the slope?
3. What do the intercepts represent in this situation?
4. What does the slope represent? Explain why the slope is negative.
5. Another formula for estimating maximum heart rate is $m = 206.3 - 0.711a$, where a represents age in years. Describe how this equation is different from your equation in Problem 1. Include slope and intercepts in your description.
6. Which equation gives a higher maximum heart rate for people ages 75 and younger?
7. To be exercising in your *aerobic training zone* means that your heart rate is 70% to 80% of your maximum heart rate. Write two equations that someone could use to estimate the range of heart rates that are within his or her aerobic training zone. Use your equation for maximum heart rate from Problem 1.

342 *Chapter 5 Linear Functions*

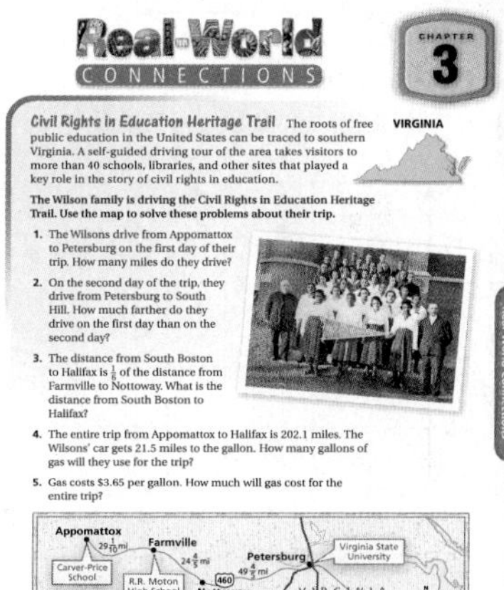

Real-World CONNECTIONS

CHAPTER 3

Civil Rights in Education Heritage Trail The roots of free public education in the United States can be traced to southern Virginia. A self-guided driving tour of the area takes visitors to more than 40 schools, libraries, and other sites that played a key role in the story of civil rights in education.

VIRGINIA

The Wilson family is driving the Civil Rights in Education Heritage Trail. Use the map to solve these problems about their trip.

1. The Wilsons drive from Appomattox to Petersburg on the first day of their trip. How many miles do they drive?
2. On the second day of the trip, they drive from Petersburg to South Hill. How much farther do they drive on the first day than on the second day?
3. The distance from South Boston to Halifax is $\frac{1}{6}$ of the distance from Farmville to Nottoway. What is the distance from South Boston to Halifax?
4. The entire trip from Appomattox to Halifax is 202.1 miles. The Wilsons' car gets 21.5 miles to the gallon. How many gallons of gas will they use for the trip?
5. Gas costs \$3.65 per gallon. How much will gas cost for the entire trip?

Real-World Connections 199

PhotoDisc/Getty Images

6-1

Check It Out!

1.

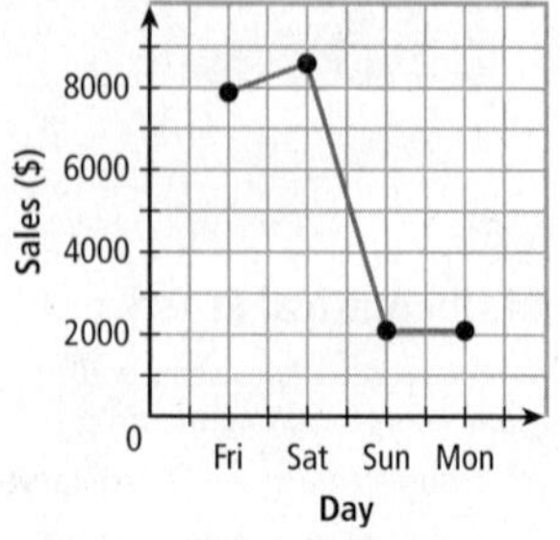

b.

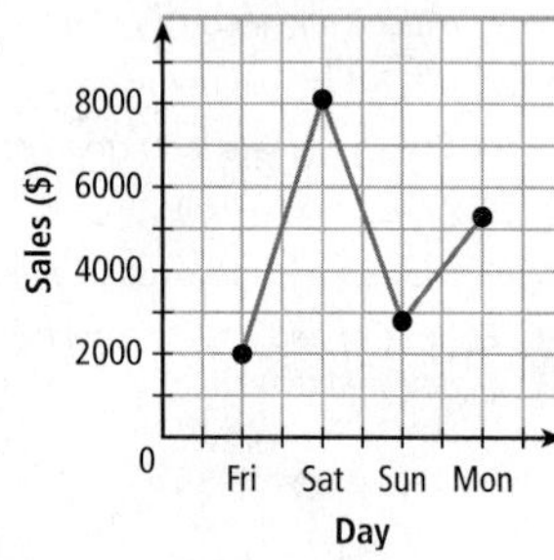

2.

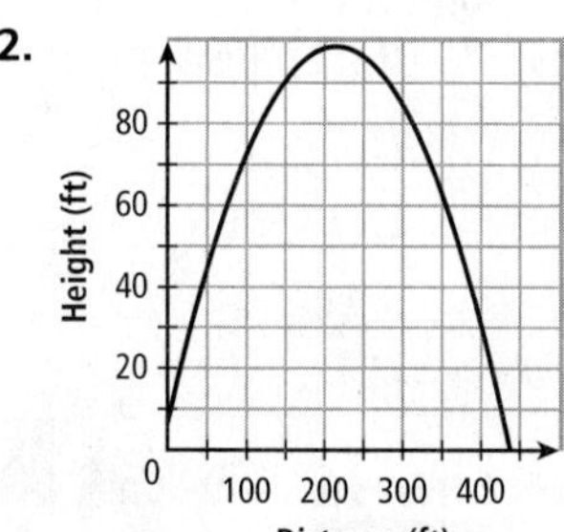

$h(x) = -0.002x^2 + 0.86x + 6.55$

3.

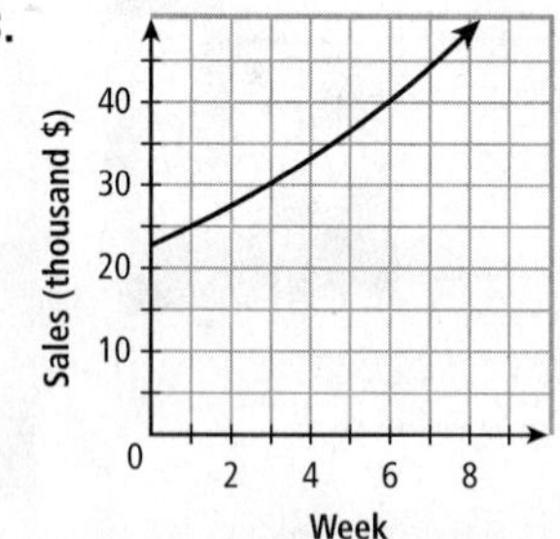

$f(x) \approx 22{,}727.15(1.1)^x$; 8 weeks

Exercises **1.** graph D **3.** graph B

5.

Enrollment Costs	
Credit Hours	**Cost ($)**
1	397.75
2	616.15
3	834.55
4	1053.00
5	1271.40

$C = 179.35 + 218.4x$

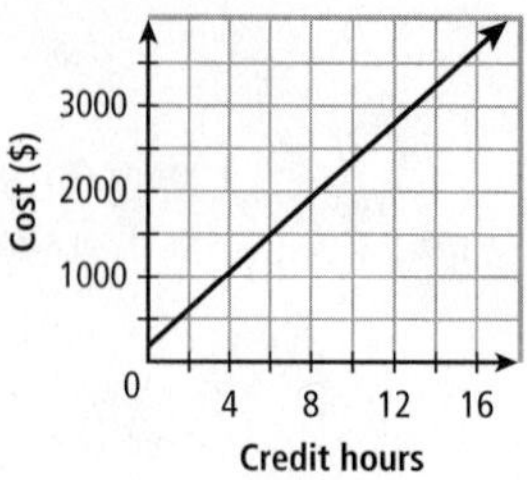

7. graph C **9.** graph D **11.** $T(t) = -0.02375t^2 + 0.525t + 101.1$
13a. $W(t) = 3t + 4$; The whale weighs 4 tons at birth and gains 3 tons per month. **15.** $14
17. exponential function
19a. $C(t) = -3t^2 + 21t + 24$
b. ≈ 61 **c.** 8 h after opening
21b. $h(t) \approx 0.0071t^3 - 0.1714t^2 + 2.1t + 2.071$ **c.** during year 15
25. C **29.** $C(p) = 1.065(0.8p - 10)$

6-2

Check It Out!

1. Mike's average rate of change is
$$m = \frac{(124-20)}{(5-1)} = \frac{104}{4} = 26$$
John's average rate of change is
$$m = \frac{(204-25)}{(8-1)} = \frac{179}{7} \approx 25.57$$
The rate of change is the average amount of money saved per week. In this case, Mike's rate of change is larger than John's, so he saves about $0.43 more than John per week.

2.

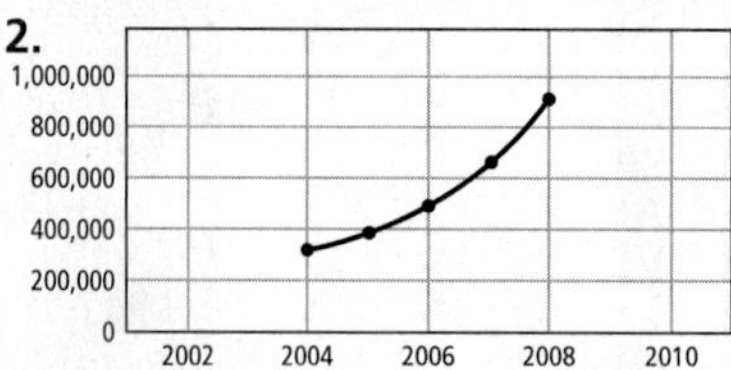

3. $f(x) = 916.67x^3 - 5{,}485{,}750x^2 + 10{,}942{,}873{,}333.33x - 7{,}276{,}079{,}455{,}500$

Exercises **1.** The slope is always a rate of change. By definition, the slope shows the ratio of change in the behavior of the function $f(x)$ by comparing its vertical movement against its horizontal movement.

3.

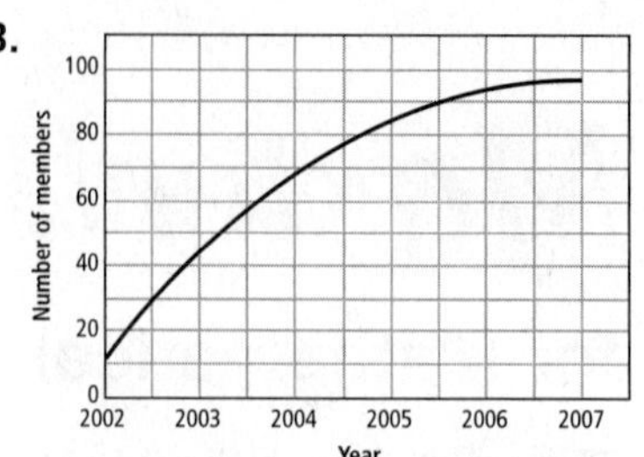

5. Company A charges $0.75 per rental with a monthly fee of $10.00. Company B charges $1.50 per rental with a monthly fee of $5.00. The rate of change is larger for Company B. While the monthly charge is less, Company A will be cheaper when a customer rents at least 7 videos per month.
7. As $x \to +\infty$, $f(x) \to -\infty$ and $g(x) \to +\infty$ and as $x \to -\infty$, $f(x) \to +\infty$ and $g(x) \to -\infty$.
9. As $x \to +\infty$, $f(x) \to -\infty$ and $g(x) \to +\infty$ and as $x \to -\infty$, $f(x) \to 0$; as $x \to 0$, $g(x) \to -\infty$.
11. $f(x) = 3x^2$
13. $f(x)$ has an absolute maximum at $f(x) = 3$. $g(x)$ has a local maximum at $g(x) = 0$.
15. As $x \to +\infty$, $f(x) \to -\infty$ and as $x \to -\infty$, $f(x) \to 0$
17. As $x \to +\infty$, $f(x) \to +\infty$ and as $x \to -\infty$, $f(x) \to +\infty$
19. Both graphs are linear, but the graph that shows Ann's hourly progress is steeper. The slope of 62 represents Ann's average speed of 62 miles per hour. The slope of 58 represents Jo's average speed of 58 miles per hour.

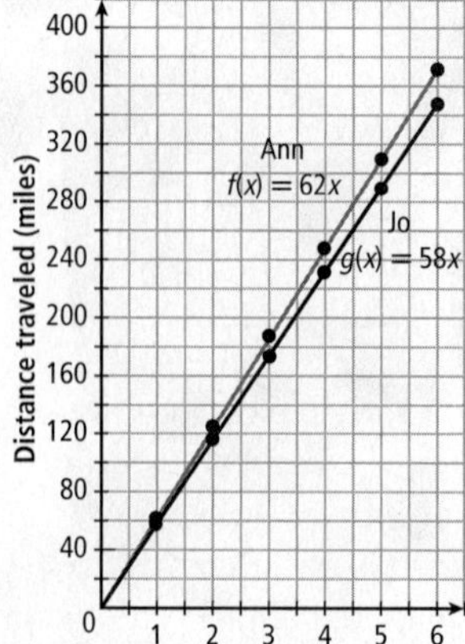

21. The end behavior of all three functions remains the same. The rate at which the function increases as $x \to +\infty$ is the only variation in the end behavior of the functions.
23. B
25. C

6-3

Check It Out!

1.

Time Range (h)	Green Fee ($)
[8 A.M. – noon)	28
[noon – 4 P.M.)	24
[4 P.M. – 9 P.M.)	12

The green fee is $28 from 8 A.M. up to noon, $24 from noon up to 4 P.M., and $12 from 4 P.M. up to 9 P.M.
2a. 15; 15 **b.** 4; 13

3a.

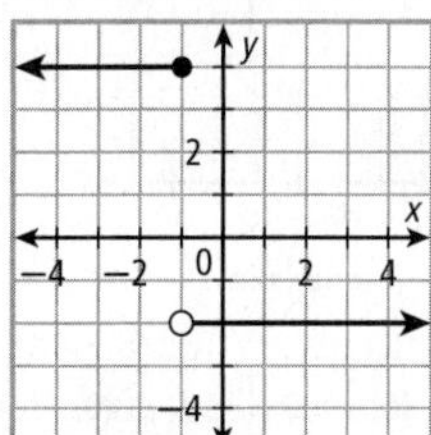

b.

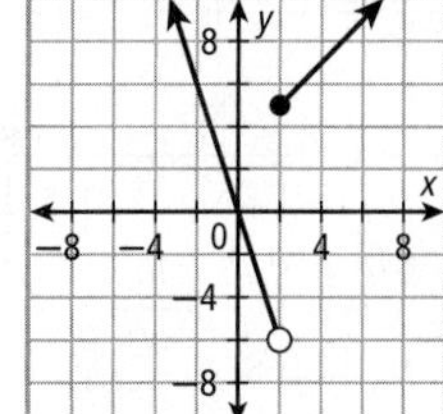

4.

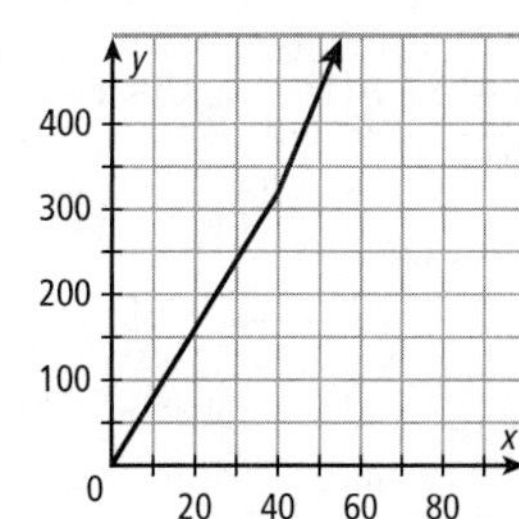

$f(h) = \begin{cases} 8h & \text{if } 0 \le h \le 40 \\ 12(h-40) + 320 & \text{if } h > 40 \end{cases}$

Exercises **1.** Step functions are a subset of piecewise functions. A step function is a piecewise function that is constant over each interval in its domain. **3.** The price per yard is $10 for less than 5 yd^3, $7 for 5 yd^3 up to 25 yd^3, and $4 for 25 yd^3 or more.

Topsoil Prices	
Price per Cubic Yard ($)	Volume (yd^3)
10	$0 \le x < 5$
7	$5 \le x < 25$
4	$x \ge 25$

5. −39; −5

7.

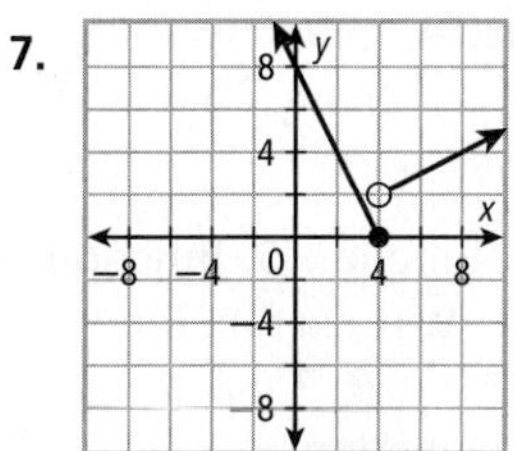

9.

Buffet Prices	
Price ($)	Age (yr)
0	$0 < x < 3$
2	$3 \le x < 8$
5	$8 \le x < 18$
8	$18 \le x$

The buffet is free for children under 3, $2 for children from 3 up to 8, $5 for children from 8 up to 18, and $8 for adults. **11.** 1; 5; 5

13.

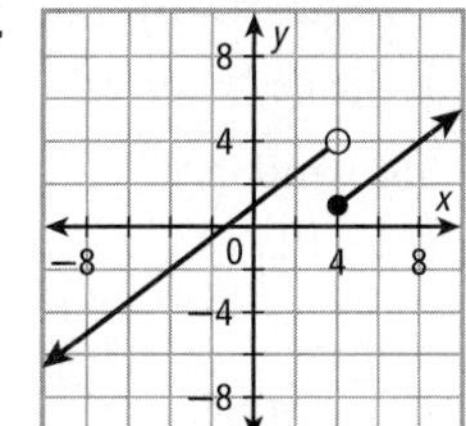

15. $f(x) = \begin{cases} 30 & \text{if } 0 < x \le 15 \\ 50 & \text{if } 15 < x \le 50 \\ 75 & \text{if } x > 50 \end{cases}$

17. $f(x) = \begin{cases} \frac{6}{5}x - 3 & \text{if } x < 5 \\ \frac{2}{5}x + 2 & \text{if } x \ge 5 \end{cases}$

19. $f(x) = \begin{cases} 6 & \text{if } x \le 4 \\ 6 + 3(x-4) & \text{if } x > +4 \end{cases}$

21. $f(x) = \begin{cases} +x & \text{if } x \ge 0 \\ -x & \text{if } x < 0 \end{cases}$

23. $h(x) = \begin{cases} 2x - 4 & \text{if } x \ge 0 \\ -2x - 4 & \text{if } x < 0 \end{cases}$

27a. $d(t) = \begin{cases} 18t & \text{if } 0 \le t \le 10 \\ 16.5(t-10) + 180 & \text{if } 10 < t \le 20 \end{cases}$

b. First half; the slope is steeper.
29. D: $\mathbb{R}$; R: $\{y \mid y \ge -4\}$ **33.** C **35.** B
37. $f(x) = 4 + 1.5(\lceil x \rceil - 1)$; $11.50

6-4

Check It Out!

1. $g(x) = \begin{cases} \left(\frac{x}{2}\right)^2 & \text{if } x \le 0 \\ \frac{x}{2} - 3 & \text{if } x > 0 \end{cases}$

2a. $f(x)$: x-int. = −6, y-int. = 4; $g(x)$: x-int. = −6, y-int. = −4
b. $f(x)$: x-int. = ±3, y-int. = −9; $g(x)$: x-int. = ±3, y-int. = −3

3.

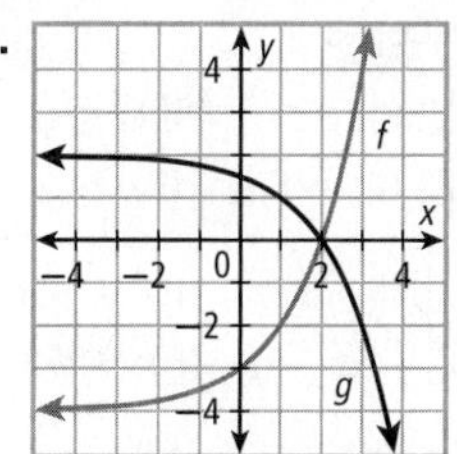

4. $f(x) = \begin{cases} 6.50 & \text{if } x < 12 \\ 9.50 & \text{if } x \ge 12 \end{cases}$

Exercises

1. $g(x) = \begin{cases} x + 3 & \text{if } x \le -6 \\ 4(x+6) & \text{if } x > -6 \end{cases}$

3. $f(x)$: x-int. = −3, y-int. = 12; $g(x)$: x-int. = −3, y-int. = 2

5.

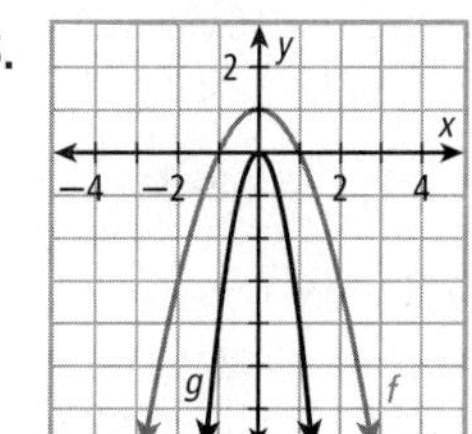

7. $T(x) = \begin{cases} 0.024x + 100 & \text{if } 0 < x \le 10{,}000 \\ 0.060x + 100 & \text{if } x > 10{,}000 \end{cases}$

9. $h(x) = \begin{cases} \left(\frac{x}{2}\right)^2 & \text{if } x < 2 \\ 2x & \text{if } x \ge 2 \end{cases}$

11. $f(x)$: x-int. = 6, y-int. = 9; $g(x)$: x-int. = 6, y-int. = 6

13. $f(x)$: x-int. = 5, y-int. = 2; $g(x)$: x-int. = 2.5, y-int. = 2
15. $f(x)$: x-int. = 0, y-int. = 0; $g(x)$: x-int. = 1, y-int. = −4
17.

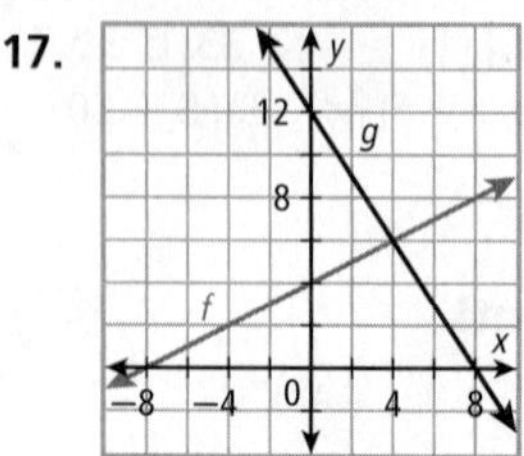

19a. $f(n) = \begin{cases} 16.2n & \text{if } n \le 50 \\ 360 + 9n & \text{if } n > 50 \end{cases}$

b. $f(n) = \begin{cases} 14.2n & \text{if } n \le 50 \\ 360 + 7n & \text{if } n > 50 \end{cases}$

21a. n x-intercepts

23a. $T(n) = \begin{cases} 2.8n & \text{if } n \le 8 \\ 3.6n - 6.4 & \text{if } n > 8 \end{cases}$

25. $f(x) - 7 = \begin{cases} 2^x - 8 & \text{if } x \le -3 \\ -5x - 4 & \text{if } x > -3 \end{cases}$

27b. $C(x) = \begin{cases} 1.29x & \text{if } 0 < x < 4 \\ 0.85(1.29x) & \text{if } 4 \le x < 7 \\ 0.7(1.29x) & \text{if } x \ge 7 \end{cases}$

c. horizontal stretch by a factor of 2 **29.** x-int: 2; y-int: 3 **33.** J **35a.** 28 **b.** 56

6-5

Check It Out! **1a.** $(f + g)(x) = x^2$ **b.** $(f - g)(x) = -x^2 + 10x - 12$ **2a.** $(fg)(x) = x^3 + 2x^2 - 4x - 8$ **b.** $\left(\frac{g}{f}\right)(x) = x - 2, x \ne -2$ **3a.** 15 **b.** 9 **4a.** $f(g(x)) = 3\sqrt{x} + 2, x \ge 0$ **b.** $g(f(x)) = \sqrt{3x - 4} + 2, x \ge \frac{4}{3}$ **5a.** $f(c) = 0.68c$ **b.** \$168.64

Exercises **3.** $-x^2 + 13x + 13$ **5.** $2x^3 + 4x^2 + 2x$ **7.** $\frac{1}{2x}, x \ne 0$ or -1 **9.** −68 **11.** $4x^2 - 12x + 9$; $\mathbb{R}$ **13.** $x + 1$; $x \ge -1$ **15.** $3x^2 + 5x - 2$ **17.** $2x^2 + 2x - 4$ **19.** $2x^4 + 10x^3 + 4x^2 - 40x - 48$ **21.** $\frac{1}{x - 2}, x \ne -2$ or 2 **23.** $\frac{x + 3}{2}, x \ne -2$ **25.** −11 **27.** −17 **29.** −59 **31.** $\frac{4x + 3}{4x + 6}; x \ne -\frac{3}{2}$ **33a.** $C(x) = 4\left(\frac{x}{9}\right) + 100$ **b.** 630 ft^2

35a. $f(p) = p - 10$ **b.** $g(p) = 0.85p$ **c.** $f(g(p)) = 0.85p - 10$; $g(f(p)) = 0.85p - 8.5$ **d.** 15% **e.** \$31.65 **37a.** $D(t) = 704 \cdot 1.05^t$ **b.** about 3043 **c.** about 2020 **39.** 4 **41.** 2 **43.** no **45.** B **47.** B **49.** $g(x) = \frac{3}{2}x^2 + 5$ **51a.** 12 ft **b.** 8 ft

6-6

Check It Out! **1.** function **2.** $f^{-1}(x) = \sqrt[3]{x + 2}$; function; D: $\mathbb{R}$; R: $\mathbb{R}$ **3a.** yes **b.** no

Exercises **1.** function **3.** function **5.** $y = \pm\sqrt{x + 9}$; not a function; D: $\{x \mid x \ge -9\}$; R: $\mathbb{R}$ **7.** no **9.** not a function **11.** function **13.** $f^{-1}(x) = \frac{\sqrt[3]{x}}{2}$; function; D: $\mathbb{R}$; R: $\mathbb{R}$ **15.** $f^{-1}(x) = \frac{6}{5}x - \frac{9}{5}$; function; D: $\mathbb{R}$; R: $\mathbb{R}$ **17.** $f^{-1}(x) = (x - 5)^2 - 8$; function; D: $\{x \mid x \ge 5\}$; R: $\{y \mid y \ge -8\}$ **19.** no **21.** yes **23a.** $d(t) = \frac{t - 20}{2.5}$ **b.** within 4 mi **25.** $y = \frac{5}{x} - 4$; D: $\{x \mid x \ne 0\}$; R: $\{y \mid y \ne -4\}$ **27.** $y = x^3 + 12$; D: $\mathbb{R}$; R: $\mathbb{R}$ **29.** $y = \log_7 x$; D: $\{x \mid x > 0\}$; R: $\mathbb{R}$ **31.** $y = \ln\left(\frac{x}{3}\right) - 5$; D: $\{x \mid x > 0\}$; R: $\mathbb{R}$ **33.** g and h **35.** f and h **37a.** $a(h) = \left(\frac{h - 19}{3}\right)^2$ **b.** about 20.25 mo **39a.** $t(d) = \frac{\sqrt{d^2 - 1600}}{3}$ **b.** ≈ 1833.28 s (about 31 min) **41a.** $h(s) = \frac{s - 18\pi}{6\pi}$ **b.** 23.53 cm **43a.** $s = \sqrt{A}$ **c.** ≈ 894 ft **47.** J **49.** G **53.** $y = e^{\frac{3x-3}{x+1}}$ **55.** $f^{-1}(g^{-1}(x)) \ne (f(g(x)))^{-1}$

6-7

Check It Out! **1a.** square root **b.** exponential **2.** $f(x) = \frac{1}{2}x^2 + \frac{5}{2}x + 8$ **3.** $f(x) \approx -0.2x^2 + 23.99x + 5.28$

Exercises **1.** linear **3.** exponential **5a.** $V(t) \approx 0.08t^2 - 2.04t + 60.86$ **b.** about \$51.68 **7.** quadratic **9.** $f(x) \approx -0.009x^2 + 2.28x - 55.31$

11a. $y \approx 34.37x + 85{,}851.76$ **b.** about 2594 ft^2 **15a.** $V(t) \approx 6126.9(1.016)^t$ **b.** about 34,611 ft^3 **17a.** $f(x) \approx 75.95(1.055^x)$ **b.** about 5.5%/yr **c.** The model predicts \$160.65, which is about \$5 more than the actual FCI. **d.** about 2008 **21.** B **23.** D **25.** $f(x) \approx x^{0.5}$; $f(x) = \sqrt{x}$

Study Guide: Review

1. one-to-one function **2.** step function **3.** composition of functions
4.

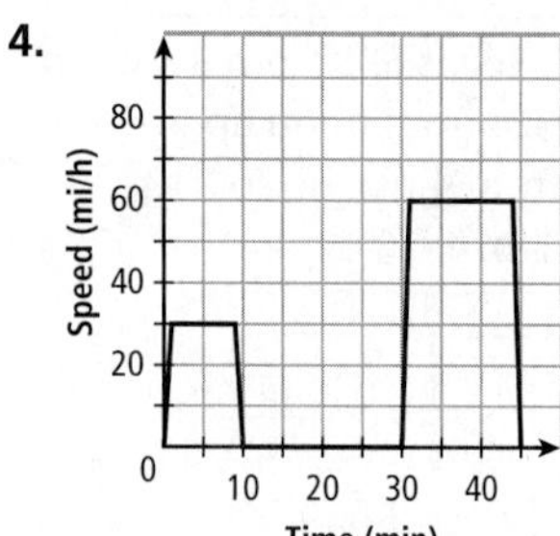

5.

Guests	10	20	30	40	50
Appetizers	160	200	240	280	320

$y = 4x + 120$

6a.

Radius (in.)	1.5	2	2.5	3	4
Time (s)	3	5	7.5	10.5	18

$y = x^2 + \frac{1}{2}x$ **b.** 52.5 s
7. As $x \to +\infty$, $g(x) \to -\infty$. As $x \to -\infty$, $g(x) \to +\infty$.
8. As $x \to +\infty$, $h(x) \to 0$. As $x \to -\infty$, $h(x) \to 0$.
9.

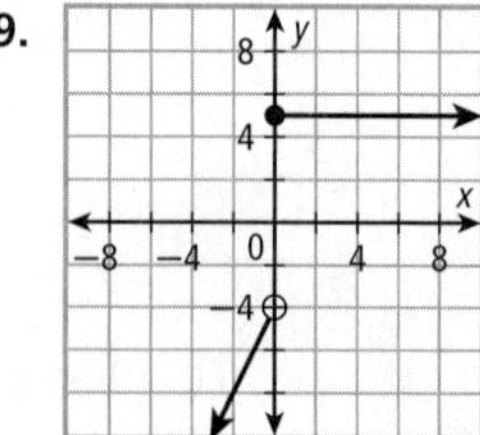

10.

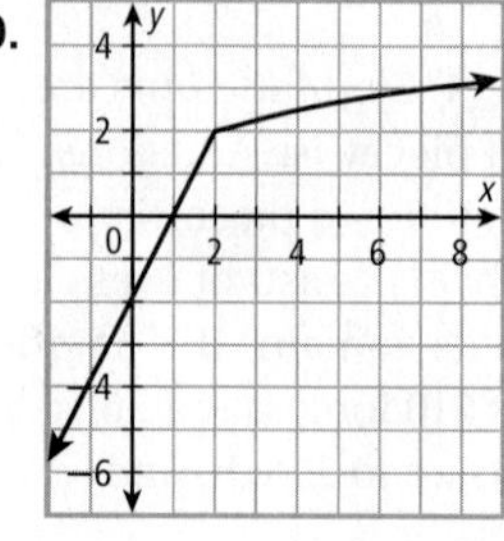

11. $f(x) = \begin{cases} \frac{5}{2}x - 4 & \text{if } x < 4 \\ -\frac{3}{2}x + 8 & \text{if } x \geq 4 \end{cases}$

12. $f(x) =$
$\begin{cases} 6 & 0 < x \leq 8 \\ 6 + 1.5(x - 8) & 8 < x \leq 48 \end{cases}$

13. $h(x) = \begin{cases} 2x & \text{if } x \leq 3 \\ -4x + 18 & \text{if } x > 3 \end{cases}$

14. $g(x) = \begin{cases} 3(x - 7) + 2 & \text{if } x \leq 7 \\ (x - 7)^2 & \text{if } x > 7 \end{cases}$

15.

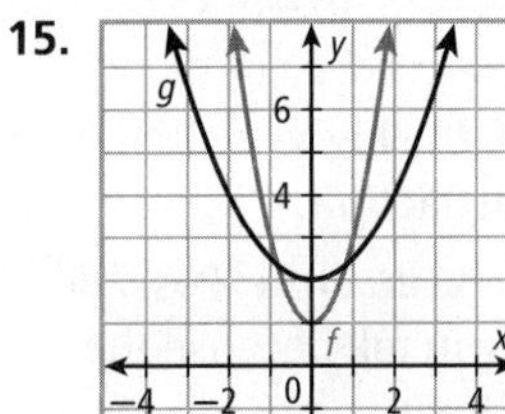

16. $x^2 - 4x - 21$ **17.** $x^2 - 6x - 7$
18. $-x^2 + 6x + 7$
19. $x^3 - 12x^2 + 21x + 98$

20. $x + 2, x \neq 7$ **21.** $\frac{1}{x+2}, x \neq 7$ or -2 **22.** $-10; -\frac{8}{3}$ **23.** 2; undefined
24. $g(f(x)) = \frac{8}{x-1}$; D: $\{x \mid x \neq 1\}$
25. $f(g(x)) = \frac{8}{x+1} - 2$;
D: $\{x \mid x \neq -1\}$
26. $P(x) = 1.09(x + 30)$ **27.** function
28. $f^{-1}(x) = \frac{-x+5}{8}$; function;
D: $\mathbb{R}$; R: $\mathbb{R}$ **29.** $y = \pm 3\sqrt{x} - 6$;
not a function; D: $\{x \mid x \geq 0\}$; R: $\mathbb{R}$
30. $f^{-1}(x) = \frac{5}{2x} - 4$; function;
D: $\{x \mid x \neq 0\}$; R: $\{y \mid y \neq -4\}$
31. $f^{-1}(x) = (x-3)^2 + 5$; function;
D: $\{x \mid x \geq 3\}$; R: $\{y \mid y \geq 5\}$ **32.** no
33. yes **34.** $r = \sqrt{\frac{A}{4\pi}}$; r is the radius for a sphere with a given surface area.
35a. $f(x) = 23.96(1.02)^x$
b. $\approx$ 129.0 million gal **c.** $\approx$ 37°F

7-1

Check It Out! **1a.** 120 **b.** 73,116,160 **2a.** 336 **b.** 20 **3.** 28

Exercises **1.** important; permutation **3.** 225 **5.** 1320 **7.** 5985 **9.** 12 **11.** 72 **13.** 20 **15.** 71,916,768 **17.** 1 **19.** 6 **21.** 72 **23.** 6700 **25.** 35 **27.** > **29.** <

33a.

President	A	A	A	A	A	A	A	A	A	A	A	A
Vice President	B	B	B	C	C	C	D	D	D	E	E	E
Secretary	C	D	E	B	D	E	B	C	E	B	C	D

b.

President	B	B	B	B	B	B	B	B	B	B	B	B
Vice President	A	A	A	C	C	C	D	D	D	E	E	E
Secretary	C	D	E	A	D	E	A	C	E	A	C	D

60 ways

c. 60 **d.** 10; 60; 10 **37.** A **39.** D **41.** 1365 **43.** $({}_{30}C_{12})({}_{18}C_2)$

7-2

Check It Out! **1a.** $\frac{5}{36}$ **b.** 0 **c.** $\frac{5}{12}$ **2.** $\frac{16}{25}$ **3.** $\frac{1}{28}$ **4.** $\frac{16}{225}$ **5a.** $\frac{9}{26}$ **b.** $\frac{19}{26}$

Exercises **1.** theoretical probability **3.** $\frac{1}{4}$ **5.** $\frac{1}{4}$ **7.** $\frac{303}{365}$ **9.** $\frac{1}{220}$ **11.** $\frac{1}{9}$ **13.** $\frac{3}{5}$ **15.** $\frac{4}{5}$ **17.** $\frac{1}{56}$ **19.** $\approx\frac{1}{42}$ **21.** never **23a.** $\frac{\pi}{4}$ **25a.** 0.68; 0.84; 0.76; 0.64 **b.** 0.73 **27.** $\frac{2}{5}$ **29.** June; ≈ 0.13 **31.** no; yes **33.** $\frac{1}{2}$ **37.** G **39.** H

7-3

Check It Out! **1a.** $\frac{1}{36}$ **b.** $\frac{1}{8}$ **2.** $\frac{5}{36}$ **3a.** ≈ 0.014 **b.** ≈ 0.186 **4a.** independent; $\frac{3}{20}$ **b.** dependent; $\frac{1}{6}$ **c.** dependent; $\frac{1}{12}$

Exercises **1.** independent **3.** $\frac{1}{8}$ **5.** The probability that the yellow cube shows a multiple of 3 increases from $\frac{1}{3}$ if the product is 6; $\frac{1}{2}$ **7.** $\frac{1}{100}$ **9.** dependent; $\frac{9}{38}$ **11.** $\frac{1}{12}$ **13.** The probability that the product is 8 increases from $\frac{1}{18}$ if the blue cube is less than 3; $\frac{1}{36}$ **15.** ≈ 0.72 **17.** dependent; $\frac{1}{6}$ **19.** independent **21.** independent **23a.** ≈ 0.61 **b.** ≈ 0.05 **25a.** $\frac{625}{1296}$ **b.** $\frac{1}{36}$ **c.** $\frac{1}{6}$ **27.** ≈ 0.6 **29.** 40 **33.** F **35.** 7

7-4

Check It Out!

1.

	Fiction	Nonfiction	Total
Hardcover	0.133	0.248	0.381
Paperback	0.448	0.171	0.619
Total	0.581	0.419	1

2a.

		Ballet		
		Yes	No	Total
Tap	Yes	0.19	0.26	0.45
	No	0.43	0.12	0.55
	Total	0.62	0.38	1

b. 0.69 or 69%

3. Al's Driving has the best pass rate, about 64%, versus 61% for Drive Time and 50% for Crash Course.

Exercises **1.** marginal

3.

	Under-classmates	Upper-classmates	Total
Morning	0.16	0.28	0.44
Afternoon	0.36	0.2	0.56
Total	0.52	0.48	1

5a.

		Play Sport		
		Yes	No	Total
Play instrument	Yes	0.23	0.19	0.42
	No	0.25	0.33	0.58
	Total	0.48	0.52	1

b. 0.55

c. 0.48

7.

	Students	Adults	Total
T-Shirts	0.267	0.383	0.65
Sweatshirts	0.117	0.233	0.35
Total	0.384	0.616	1

9a.

	Satisfied	Dissatisfied	Total
Team 1	0.17	0.07	0.24
Team 2	0.29	0.1	0.39
Team 3	0.29	0.08	0.37
Total	0.75	0.25	1

b. Team 1: 0.71; Team 2: 0.74; Team 3: 0.78

c. Team 3 has the highest rate of customer satisfaction.

11. Maria made an error; Possible answer: You can tell because the four relative frequencies have a sum of 1.1, rather than 1.

13a.

		Work less than 5 miles from home?		
		Yes	No	Total
Use new system?	Yes	0.2	0.27	0.47
	No	0.37	0.17	0.54
	Total	0.57	0.44	1

b. 0.35

c. 0.57

15. C

17.

	Yes	No	Total
Children	0.125	0.1	0.225
Teenagers	0.725	0.05	0.775
Total	0.85	0.15	1

19. 10 children

21. 0

7-5

Check It Out! **1a.** Each student can vote only once. **b.** 75% **2a.** $\frac{4}{13}$ **b.** $\frac{8}{13}$ **3.** $\frac{31}{40}$ **4.** ≈ 0.1524

Exercises **1.** inclusive events **3.** $\frac{3}{5}$ **5.** $\frac{4}{5}$ **7.** $\frac{7}{9}$ **9.** $\frac{54}{65}$ **11.** ≈ 0.92 **13.** $\frac{1}{2}$ **15.** $\frac{1}{4}$ **17.** $\frac{32}{49}$ **19.** $1 - 0.75^{13} \approx 0.976$ **21.** 0.37;

experimental **23.** 87%; 100% **25b.** 4.16%; 52.24% **27.** 0.49 **29a.** 0.42 **b.** 0.02 **c.** 0.44; it is the sum of the probabilities. **31.** D **33.** D **35.** ≈ 0.12 **37.** $\frac{13}{18}$ **39.** 0.9 **41.** 0.2

Study Guide: Review

1. dependent events
2. permutation
3. conditional relative frequency
4. 7,000,000 **5.** 792 **6.** 2,162,160 **7.** 604,800 **8.** 20 **9.** $\frac{5}{36}$ **10.** $\frac{5}{18}$ **11.** $\frac{1}{2}$ **12.** $\frac{11}{12}$ **13.** $\frac{1}{210}$ **14.** $\frac{1}{10{,}000}$ **15.** $\frac{5}{24}$ **16.** ≈ 0.21 **17.** $\frac{1}{5}$ **18.** $\frac{4}{5}$ **19.** $\frac{7}{25}$ **20.** $\frac{13}{25}$ **21.** $\frac{1}{4}$ **22.** $\frac{3}{4}$ **23.** $\frac{1}{4}$ **24.** $\frac{1}{2}$ **25.** $\frac{1}{216}$ **26.** $\frac{6}{25}$ **27.** $\frac{11}{21}$ **28.** $\frac{1}{13}$ **29.** $\frac{13}{31}$ **30.** $\frac{14}{99}$

31.

		Went to beach		
		Yes	No	
Joined a sports team	Yes	0.278	0.25	0.528
	No	0.306	0.167	0.472
		0.583	0.417	1

32. $\frac{10}{21} \approx 0.476$ **33.** $\frac{6}{15} = 0.4$ **34.** Each coupon offers only 1 discount. **35.** $\frac{5}{6}$ **36.** $\frac{7}{13}$ **37.** $\frac{1}{2}$ **38.** $\frac{7}{10}$

8-1

Check It Out! 1a. 6.5; 7; no mode **b.** 4.2; 5; 2 and 6 **2.** 0.37

3.

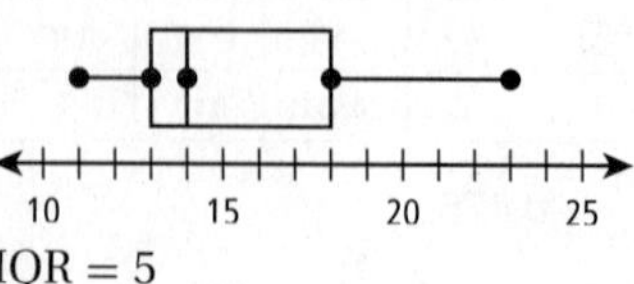

IQR = 5

4. 1.4; ≈ 1.6 **5.** 19; the mean increases from ≈ 4.3 to ≈ 5.4, and the standard deviation increases from ≈ 2.2 to ≈ 4.3.

Exercises 1. variance **3.** 5.375; 6; 6 **5.** $0.36

7.

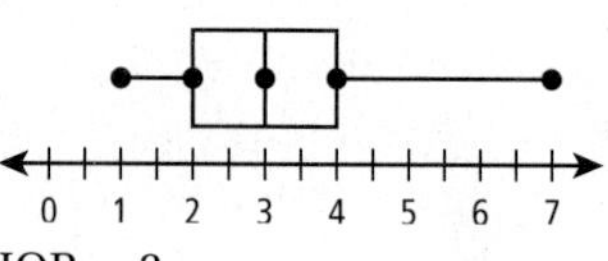

IQR = 2

9. 0.8; 0.89 **11.** 142.92; 11.95 **13.** $23.1\overline{6}$; 20.5; no mode **15.** 15; 15; no mode

17.

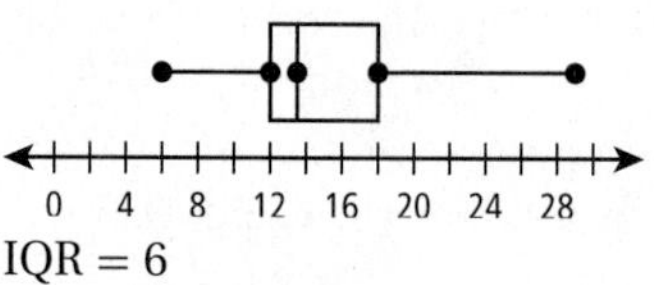

IQR = 6

19.

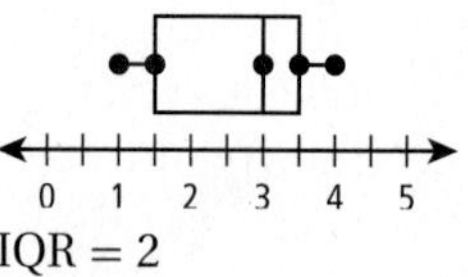

IQR = 2

21. 343.71; 18.54 **23.** 58; the mean increases from ≈ 19.8 to ≈ 22.8, and the standard deviation increases from ≈ 5.6 to ≈ 11.5. **25.** the mean; 37° is an outlier and affects the mean greatly. **27.** 15; $Q_1 - 1.5(IQR) = 79 - 1.5(90 - 79) = 62.5$; $15 < 62.5$ **29.** < 0.3 min or > 6.9 min; none **31.** Ruth **35.** – $0.499 **37.** B **39a.** 12.25 **b.** $\frac{13}{36}$ **c.** $\frac{23}{36}$ **d.** no **41.** D **43.** C **45.** 1

8-2

Check It Out! 1. There is a 1:1 ratio of perch to walleye; no **2.** Yes; people visiting a news site online are more likely to be interested in news and subscribe to a daily newspaper. **3.** No; people in a restaurant on a Tuesday night are much more likely to eat out often. **4.** 77 phone calls **5.** No, he is not justified in his evaluation because the sample size was too small. He has about a 24% chance of not opening a prize in five boxes.

Exercises 1. biased **3.** Yes; a student that has not gone home from school by 5PM is probably at the school for some kind of extracurricular activity, which is likely to be a sport. **5.** No; the sample chosen is a convenience sample, which is not likely to be representative of the population. The sample overrepresents students who get to school early in the morning, and who are more likely to have time to eat breakfast at school and make the issue a priority. **7.** No; the sample is not likely to be representative of the population because it underrepresents students who don't purchase food frequently in the cafeteria, perhaps because of the lack of variety. **9.** 175 employees **11.** The chef did not make a good decision. If there are about 1200 customers a week, then there is an average of one-seventh of that, about 171, a night. There were only 110 customers that night, so it was a slow night and therefore a relatively small sample that was not representative of the total customers. Also, more customers may have ordered the dish because it was offered at a discounted price, and not necessarily because it sounded good to them. **13.** 281 employees; 70 randomly chosen employees **15.** all of the junk mail that the family receives; the junk mail received during one week **17.** No; a random sample is likely to be representative of the population. **19.** Yes; the sample is not likely to be representative of the population because only people with a strong feeling one way or the other will choose to respond to the survey. **23.** Yes; this method is not likely to under or overrepresent any group because a wide range of spectators will be surveyed. **25.** No; this method overrepresents people who are likely to enjoy bake sales. **27.** 200 students **29.** 565 students **31.** 520 students **33.** Possible answer: No, this was not a good decision because the sample is biased. The sample contains only dog owners, who are more likely to favor an off-leash area. The town could make a better decision by surveying every twenty-fifth person who enters the park each evening for a week. **35.** F **37.** 100 students chosen from 504 students; in this sample, about 1 in every 5 students is surveyed, where the other method results in about 1 in every 7 students surveyed. The greater fraction of students surveyed, the more accurate the results are likely to be. **39.** No; about 4% of the discs are defective.

8-3

Check It Out! 1. It is an observational study because an observation is being conducted without controlling the environment in any way. **2.** treatment: using the old and new websites to make purchases; treatment group: users of the website using the new website to make purchases; control group: users of the website using the old website to make purchases. **3.** 1000 mg of vitamin is not known to have any negative effects, so conduct an experiment. Randomly choose one group of people to take the supplements, randomly choose another group of people to not take the supplements, and monitor the cholesterol levels in both groups. **4.** Method A: experiment. Method B: survey. Method C: observational study; Method B is least reliable, because there is no basis for comparison. Method C has a comparison group, but the members are self-selected, which could lead to bias. In method A, the members of each group are randomly selected, so method A is the most reliable.

Exercises **1.** experimental **3.** The caretaker applies a treatment (giving half the elephants the new food) to some of the individuals (elephants). The situation is an example of an experiment. **5.** The treatment in this study is *drinking no more soft drinks*. The treatment group consists of the fifty students who stopped drinking soft drinks, and the control group consists of the fifty students who continued to consume soft drinks. **7.** The treatment (exposing pets to second-hand smoke) may affect the pets' health, so it is not ethical to assign individuals to a treatment group. Instead, perform an observational study; Possible answer: Randomly choose one group of pets who are already exposed to second-hand smoke. Randomly choose another group of pets that are not exposed to second-hand smoke. Monitor the health of the pets in both groups at regular intervals. **9.** The treatment (installing more stoplights on a road) is impractical. Perform an observational study; Possible answer: Randomly choose a number of different roads already with stoplights to gather data about the number of accidents vs. the number of stoplights presently installed per mile.

11. The treatment is eating chicken before a baseball game. Since the treatment is not harmful to the subjects, use an experiment. Possible answer: Have a player eat chicken before some games of baseball, and not others. Record the player's number of home runs. Repeat for many games, across several players. **13.** In method A, the researcher gives one group a treatment by asking them to drink coffee, so the method is an experiment. In method B, the researcher asks questions about people's self-reported regular habits. This method is a survey. In method C, the researcher observes people who are already either coffee-drinkers or noncoffee-drinkers, but does not impose a treatment. This is an observational study. Method B is least reliable, because there is no basis for comparison. Method C has a comparison group, but the groupings are based on self-reports, which could lead to bias. In method A, the members of each group are randomly selected, which makes the two groups theoretically similar except for the variable — whether or not they are coffee-drinkers. This method is most reliable. **15.** experiment **17.** experiment **19.** The treatment in this study is *switching the volunteers to the new drug*. The treatment group consists of the volunteers taking the new drug, and the control group consists of the volunteers continuing with the old drug. **21.** The treatment in this study is *feeding the people the new recipe*. The treatment group consists of the people served the new recipe, and the control group consists of the people served the old recipe. **23.** Riley is correct. Mr. Johnson is investigating the effect of the exposure to the weather, so that is the treatment. The part of the deck with the sealant is the control group because it is not exposed to the weather. **25.** experiment

27. experiment **29.** observational study **31.** In method A, the researcher gives each group a treatment, so the method is an experiment. In method B, the researcher asks questions about ointments that people have used before. This method is a survey. In method C, the researcher observes people who have chosen different ointments, but does not impose a treatment. This is an observational study. Method B is least reliable, because there is no basis for comparison. Method C has a comparison group, but the groupings are based on self-reports, which could lead to bias. In method A, the members of each group are randomly selected, which makes the two groups theoretically similar except for the variable, the different ointments. This method is most reliable. **33.** J

8-4

Check It Out! **1a.** The students in the morning class will have the same test scores as the students in the afternoon class. **b.** Yes; there is a large difference in the test scores of the two classes. The teacher does have enough evidence to reject the null hypothesis, so she can conclude that students in her afternoon class perform better on tests.
2. Calculate the z-value: $\dfrac{2600 - 3000}{\frac{300}{\sqrt{40}}}$

$\approx \dfrac{-400}{47.43} \approx -8.43$

Because $|z| = 8.43 > 1.96$, you can rejnect the claim of the tax preparer. **3a.** The test scores will be the same for both groups of new employees at Company A. **b.** There is a large difference in the two groups that is unlikely to be caused by chance. The labor union should reject the null hypothesis, which means that the professional development program is working to increase test scores at Company A.

Exercises **1.** chance **3a.** The test scores will be the same for both groups of new employees at Company A. **b.** There is a large difference in the two groups that is unlikely to be caused by chance. The labor union should reject the null hypothesis, which means that the professional development program is working to increase test scores at Company A. **5.** −2.65; yes **7a.** The levels of the substance will be the same for residents of both cities. **b.** The data is spread about evenly in the two groups, so any difference is likely to caused by chance. The null hypothesis cannot be rejected based on these results. **9a.** The potassium levels will be the same in treated and untreated plants. **b.** The data are spread about evenly in the two groups, so any difference is likely to caused by chance. The null hypothesis cannot be rejected based on these results. **11a.** −3.57 **b.** yes **13a.** −1.00 **b.** no **15.** Claim I is a candidate for hypothesis testing, but not claim II. Claim I can be tested and a degree of certainty about its truth can be established. Claim II can't be tested at all; there's no way to test today whether it will rain tomorrow. It can only be shown to be true or false by waiting. **17.** Mandy is incorrect because she miscalculated the z-value. In the third-to-last step, she did not flip the fraction in the denominator before multiplying it by −2. **19.** H **21.** Billy is correct. The fact that their results fall well outside the expected range only makes it unlikely that they performed the experiment wrong; their results are not in and of themselves conclusive proof of incorrectly conducting the experiment.

8-5

Check It Out! **1.** self-selected **2a.** Method A is a self-selected sample. Method B is a convenience sample. Method C is a cluster sample. Method A is the least accurate because only people who are willing to volunteer their opinions are chosen. Method B is also inaccurate because only students and only those in the cafeteria are surveyed. Method C is the most accurate because different groups are randomly chosen and then all members of the chosen group are surveyed. **3.** Yes; while there is overlap between the intervals for Chang and Harris, their intervals, which are from 28% to 34%, do not overlap the interval for Gonzalez, which is 35% to 41%.

Exercises **1.** margin of error **3.** simple random **5.** Method A is a simple random sample. Method B is a stratified sample. Method C is a cluster sample. Method A is the most accurate, because every member of the population is equally likely to be in the sample. Because there is not an equal number of students in each class, in Method B some classes will be overrepresented and others underrepresented. Method C is the least accurate, because freshman and juniors have no chance of being included. **7.** Yes; 36% ± 9% = 27% to 45% and 64% ± 9% = 55% to 73%. The intervals do not overlap, so the survey clearly projects the winner.

9. stratified **11.** convenience **13.** systematic **15.** systematic **17.** Method A is a stratified sample. Method B is a self-selected sample. Method C is a simple random sample. Method C is the most accurate and Method B is the least accurate.

21. No; 55% ± 6% = 49% to 61% and 45% ± 6% = 39% to 51%. The intervals overlap, so the survey does not clearly indicate the majority's preference.

23. B **25.** D **29.** b, c, and d; b: Do you prefer the taste of sample A or sample B?; c: Would you rather read a book or watch a movie?; d: Do you enjoy watching music videos?

8-6

Check It Out! **1a.** $x^5 - 5x^4y + 10x^3y^2 - 10x^2y^3 + 5xy^4 - y^5$ **b.** $a^3 + 6a^2b + 12ab^2 + 8b^3$ **2a.** $\frac{2}{9} \approx 0.22$ **b.** $\frac{47}{128} \approx 0.37$ **3a.** ≈ 0.98 **b.** ≈ 0.09

Exercises **1.** 2 **3.** $27x^3 + 135x^2 + 225x + 125$ **5.** $x^6 + 6x^5y + 15x^4y^2 + 20x^3y^3 + 15x^2y^4 + 6xy^5 + y^6$ **7.** ≈ 0.026 ≈ 0.181 **9.** $y^4 + 20y^3 + 150y^2 + 500y + 625$ **11.** $1024 + 3840x + 5760x^2 + 4320x^3 + 1620x^4 + 243x^5$ **13.** ≈ 0.86 **15.** $\frac{3}{8}; \frac{1}{8}$ **17.** $x^5 - 5x^4y + 10x^3y^2 - 10x^2y^3 + 5xy^4 - y^5$ **19.** $256k^4 - 256k^3 + 96k^2 - 16k + 1$ **21.** 0.384 **23.** $\frac{8}{27}$ **25.** $\frac{1}{16}; \frac{5}{16}$ **27.** ≈ 0.989 **29.** ≈ 0.94 **33a.** $\frac{82}{365}$ **b.** ≈ 0.14 **c.** ≈ 0.19 **35.** ≈ 0.03 **37.** ≈ 0.59 **39.** ≈ 0.3 **41.** B **43.** B **45.** ≈ 0.29 **47a.** ≈ 0.67 **b.** ≈ 0.62

Extension

Check it Out! **1.** ≈ 97.7%

Exercises **1.** ≈ 95.4% **3.** ≈ 68.2% **5.** ≈ 47.7% **7.** ≈ 15.9%

8-7

Check it Out! **1.** 0.19 **2.** 0.98 **3.** No, 14 out of 18 values fall below the mean.

Exercises

1. The standard normal value of a statistic is found by subtracting the mean from the statistic and dividing the result by the standard deviation. **3.** 0.31 **5.** 0.14 **7.** Yes; see the table below. The projected number of data values below each z-value is close to the actual number. The data appears to be normally distributed.

z	Area Below z	x	Values Below x	
			Projected	Actual
-2	0.02	0.3	1	0
-1	0.16	0.4	5	3
0	0.5	0.5	15	17
1	0.84	0.6	25	24
2	0.98	0.7	29	29

9. 0.02 **11.** 0.06 **13.** No; see the table below. There should be more values under 45 inches. **15.** 0.99 **17.** 0.16 **19.** 0.04 **21.** B **23.** 10 **25.** $\mu = 20$ and $\sigma = 4$

8-8

Check it Out!

1. 2.67 **2.** Route A: $0.60(16) + 0.40(25) = 9.6 + 10 = 19.6$ minutes; Route B: $0.20(40) + 0.80(10) = 8 + 8 = 16$ minutes; Route C: $0.90(20) + 0.1(32) = 21.2$ minutes. He should take Route B. **3.** College A: $0.75 \cdot 0.30 = 0.225$; College B: $0.70 \cdot 0.40 = 0.280$; College C: $0.70 \cdot 0.45 = 0.315$. She has a higher probability of being accepted in College C with a financial aid.

Exercises

1. expected value

3. $2\left(\frac{1}{6}\right) + 3\left(\frac{1}{6}\right) + 4\left(\frac{2}{6}\right) + 8\left(\frac{1}{6}\right) + 12\left(\frac{1}{6}\right) =$

$\frac{2 + 3 + 8 + 8 + 12}{6} = \frac{33}{6} = 5.5$

5. $7 + 5.5 = 12.56$

7. Category A: $500(0.1) + (-100)(0.9) = -\$40$ Category B: $100(0.3) + (-20)(0.7) = \$16$ Category C: $50(0.6) + 0(0.4) = \$30$ Category C has the highest expected value.

9. $5\left(\frac{1}{2}\right) + 1\left(\frac{1}{2}\right) = \frac{6}{2} = 3$

11. $3 + 4.5 = 7.5$

13. $2000(0.001) + 150(0.02) = 5$; a fair price would be \$5 per ticket.

15. $5\left(\frac{4}{8}\right) + 9\left(\frac{2}{8}\right) + 12\left(\frac{2}{8}\right) =$

$\frac{20 + 18 + 24}{8} = \frac{62}{8} = 7.75$

17. 17.15

19. $16\left(\frac{1}{6}\right) + 20\left(\frac{1}{6}\right) + 10\left(\frac{2}{6}\right) + 12\left(\frac{2}{6}\right) =$

$\frac{16 + 20 + 20 + 24}{6} \approx 13.33$

21. $\frac{5x}{3}$

23. Sample answer: The expected loss on the policy is $\$10{,}000(0.01) = \$100$. In order to break even, they would need to charge \$100 for the policy. In order to make a profit of 50%, they would need to charge \$200. **25a.** $0.6(32) + 0.4(58) = 19.2 + 23.2 = 42.4$ **b.** The average travel time is 42.4 minutes. The actual trip will be closer to one of the values 32 or 58, since Devon either will or won't encounter traffic. The expected value helps make decisions between two or more routes, but the result is not necessarily close to the actual time on any given trip.

Study Guide: Review

1. expected value **2.** population sample **3.** hypothesis testing **4.** mean: 5.4; median: 6; mode: 8 **5.** mean: $13.\overline{3}$; median: 13; modes: 12, 13, and 15 **6.** 0.51

7.

28 36 44 52 60 68 76 84

IQR = 35

8. [5.4, 9.6] **9.** yes **10.** The mean decreases from 75.5 to 69.3, and the standard deviation increases from ≈ 21.5 to ≈ 25.1. **11.** not representative; basketball players are likely to prefer sports **12.** representative **13.** not representative; customers who prefer stores aren't likely to be at the website **14.** $\frac{63}{100} \times 1400 = 882$ **15.** treatment: working below fluorescent light, treatment group: group working below fluorescent lights, control group: group working under incandescent light **16.** treatment: receiving the company's brand of dog food, treatment group: those receiving the company's brand, control group: those receiving the other brands **17.** The vertical leap for both groups will be the same. **18.** The quartiles for the first group is 27, 30.5, and 34, versus 27.5, 30.5, and 35.5 for the second group. There is not a large difference, so we cannot reject the nul hypothesis. **19.** $|z| \approx 2.74 > 1.96$. There is enough evidence to reject the claim with 95% certainty. **20.** $62\% - 11\% = 51\%$. $38\% + 11\% = 49\%$. $51\% > 49\%$, so the survey clearly projects a winner. **21.** $53\% - 5\% = 48\%$. $47\% + 5\% = 52\%$. $48\% < 52\%$, so the survey does not clearly project a winner. **22.** convenience sample. **23.** $125 + 150x + 60x^2 + 8x^3$ **24.** $x^4 - 8x^3y + 24x^2y^2 - 32xy^3 + 16x^4$ **25.** 48.75; ≈ 4.13 **26.** ≈ 0.10; ≈ 0.40 **27.** 0.66 **28.** 0.93 **29.** 0.48 **30.** 0.16 **31.** 0.67 **32.** 0.18 **33.** 3.33 **34.** 2.5 **35.** 26.67

9-1

Check It Out! **1a.** −5, −13, −21, −29, −37 **b.** 2, −6, 18, −54, 162 **2a.** −1, 0, 3, 8, 15 **b.** −2, 1, 4, 7, 10 **3a.** $a_n = 9 - 2n$ **b.** $a_n = \frac{1}{n}$

4.

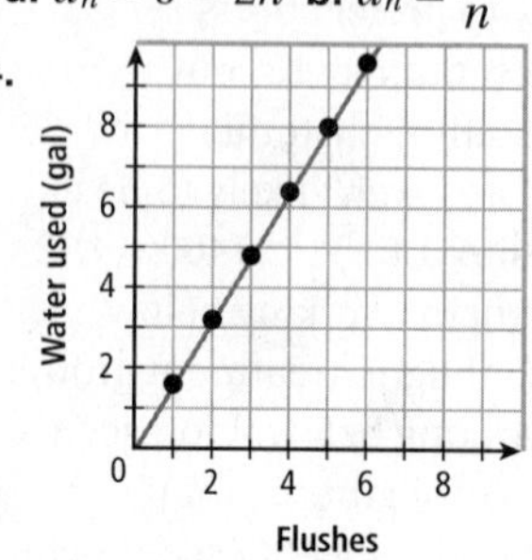

The graph shows the points lie on a line with positive slope; 16 gal. **5.** 8, 16

Exercises **1.** recursive **3.** 3, 14, 25, 36, 47 **5.** −12, 0, 12, 24, 36 **7.** −3, −12, −27, −48, −75 **9.** 1, 4, 16, 64, 256 **11.** $a_n = 3 + 3n$ **13.** $a_n = 35 - 10n$ **15.** 16, 32 **17.** −2, 5, −16, 47, −142 **19.** 9, 10, 12, 16, 24 **21.** $1, \frac{1}{4}, \frac{1}{9}, \frac{1}{16}, \frac{1}{25}$ **23.** $a_n = 13 - 4n$ **25.** linear with a slope of 4; 36 **27.** 12, 8, 6, 5, $4\frac{1}{2}$ **29.** 10, 20, −10, 20, −10 **31.** 7.9, 7.8, 7.7, 7.6, 7.5 **33.** B is incorrect. The formula is explicit, not recursive. **35.** $a_n = \frac{16}{9} - \frac{1}{9}n$; $\frac{2}{3}$ **37.** $a_n = \frac{(-1)^{n+1}}{n}$; $-\frac{1}{10}$ **39.** $a_n = 25 - n^2$; −75 **41.** 15, 21 **43a.** 15, 21 **b.** $a_n = \frac{1}{2}n^2 - \frac{1}{2}n$ **c.**

Players	1	2	3	4	5
Games	0	2	6	12	20

The sequence is twice the previous sequence. The function is a vertical stretch by a factor of 2.

45a. $a_n = 180(n - 2)$ for $n \geq 3$; 1800° **c.** $a_n = \frac{180(n-2)}{n}$ for $n \geq 3$ **47a.** $1, \frac{1}{2}, \frac{1}{4}, \frac{1}{8}, \frac{1}{16}, \frac{1}{32}$; $a_1 = 1, a_n = \frac{1}{2}a_{n-1}$; $a_n = \left(\frac{1}{2}\right)^{n-1}$ **b.** $4, 2, 1, \frac{1}{2}, \frac{1}{4}, \frac{1}{8}$; $a_1 = 4, a_n = \frac{1}{2}a_{n-1}$; $a_n = 4\left(\frac{1}{2}\right)^{n-1}$

51. H **53.** H **55.** $a_n = \frac{n^3}{3} - 1$; $\frac{997}{3}$ **57.** $a_n = -0.05n^2 + 0.05n + 0.9$; −3.6 **59.** $\frac{(x-3)}{(x+2)}$ **61.** $\frac{1}{x+5}$

9-2

Check It Out! **1a.** $\sum_{k=1}^{5} \frac{2}{(k+1)^2}$ **b.** $\sum_{k=1}^{6} (-1)^k (2k)$ **2a.** $1 + 3 + 5 + 7 = 16$ **b.** $-5 - 10 - 20 - 40 - 80 = -155$ **3a.** 240 **b.** 120 **c.** 385 **4.** 294 in., or $24\frac{1}{2}$ ft

Exercises **1.** $\sum_{k=1}^{n} k$ **3.** $\sum_{k=1}^{5} (-1)^k (3k)$ **5.** $\sum_{k=1}^{5} [100 - 5(k-1)]$ **7.** $12 - 3 + \frac{4}{3} - \frac{3}{4} = 9\frac{7}{12}$ **9.** 231 **11.** 126 **13.** $\sum_{k=1}^{5} 1.1k$ **15.** $\sum_{k=1}^{6} (-1)^{k+1} (k + 10)$ **17.** $16 + 24 + 32 + 40 + 48 = 160$ **19.** $0 + \frac{1}{3} + \frac{2}{4} + \frac{3}{5} = \frac{43}{30}$ **21.** 195 **23.** 210 cans **25.** $\sum_{k=1}^{25} (26 - k)$ **27.** $\sum_{k=1}^{5} -800\left(\frac{1}{10}\right)^{k-1}$ **29.** $\sum_{k=1}^{6} (-1)^{k+1} (k + 2)^2$ **31.** $\sum_{k=1}^{5} 3.4k - 3.4$, or $\sum_{k=1}^{5} 3.4(k - 1)$ **33.** $\sum_{k=1}^{5} \frac{1000}{10^{k-1}}$ **35b.** $\sum_{k=1}^{5} 3^k = 3 + 9 + 27 + 81 + 243 = 363$ **c.** 3542 **37.** $-5 + 10 - 15 + 20 - 25 + 30 = 15$ **39.** $1 + 4 + 7 + 10 + 13 + 16 = 51$ **41.** $\frac{1}{5} + \frac{2}{5} + \frac{3}{5} + \frac{4}{5} + 1 = 3$ **43.** 420 **45.** −2550 **47a.** Both equal 165; $\sum_{k=1}^{n} ca_k = c\sum_{k=1}^{n} a_k$. **b.** Both equal 75; $\sum_{k=1}^{n} (a_k + b_k) = \sum_{k=1}^{n} a_k + \sum_{k=1}^{n} b_k$. **49. a.** $a_n = 4n$ **b.** $\sum_{k=1}^{6} 4k$; 84 toothpicks **53.** H **55.** J **57.** $1 \cdot 2 \cdot 3 \cdot 4 \cdot 5 = 120$ **59.** $\sum_{k=1}^{n} ca_k = ca_1 + ca_2 + \cdots + ca_n = c(a_1 + a_2 + \cdots + a_n) = c\sum_{k=1}^{n} a_k$

9-3

Check It Out! **1a.** arithmetic; $d = -0.7$; −1.6 **b.** not arithmetic **2a.** −23 **b.** 8.7 **3.** $\frac{3}{2}, 1, \frac{1}{2}$ **4a.** −25 **b.** 8.5 **5a.** −408 **b.** −1650 **6a.** 37 seats **b.** 336 total seats

Exercises **1.** arithmetic series **3.** not arithmetic **5.** 38 **7.** −4.6 **9.** 16, 23, 30 **11.** −13 **13.** −17 **15.** −35 **17.** 495 **19.** 11.7 **21.** not arithmetic **23.** arithmetic; −0.09; 0.63 **25.** $\frac{12}{5}$ **27.** 66, 55, 44 **29.** 2.1, 1.9, 1.7 **31.** 94 **33.** −60 **35.** 143.5 **37a.** 78; 156 **b.** adds 1 to each term of the sequence; adds 24 to the total number per day **39.** 0 **41.** 60 **43a.** $\sum_{k=1}^{n} 4k$ **b.** 684 **c.** 673 **45.** 45 minutes; after 2 years, her exercise routine would be over 8 h long, which is not realistic. **47a.** 61 **b.** 650 **49a.** 6th, 11th, 16th, 21st, and 26th Streets **b.** 0.25 mi **53.** J **55.** G **57.** 6

9-4

Check It Out! **1a.** geometric; $r = \frac{1}{3}$ **b.** arithmetic; $d = -0.4$ **c.** neither **2a.** $\frac{3}{1024}$ **b.** 100,000 **3a.** −1000 **b.** $\frac{3}{4}$ or $-\frac{3}{4}$ **4.** 20 **5a.** $\frac{63}{16}$ **b.** −189 **6.** $616,218.04

Exercises **1.** geometric mean **3.** neither **5.** 39,366 **7.** 64 **9.** 324 **11.** $\frac{3}{2}$ **13.** 48 **15.** 61 **17.** 511 **19.** neither **21.** arithmetic; $d = 5$ **23.** 768 **25.** 52,488 **27.** 30.375 **29.** 1 **31.** 3 **33.** 11.111111 **35.** 8,888,888 **37.** $a_n = \frac{1}{16}(2)^{n-1}$; $a_{10} = 32$; $S_{10} = \frac{1023}{16} \approx 63.94$ **39.** $a_n = 8(2)^{n-1}$; $a_{10} = 4096$;

$S_{10} = 8184$ **41.** $a_n = 162\left(-\frac{1}{3}\right)^{n-1}$; $a_{10} = -\frac{2}{243}$; $S_{10} = 121\frac{121}{243}$ ≈ 121.5 **43a.** \$34.98; \$61.18 **45.** 2,441,406 **47a.** 12.8 mm **b.** 27 folds **49a.** \$24 million **b.** 60% **c.** week 6 **d.** about \$99.93 million **53a.** about 261.6 Hz **b.** $a_n \approx 16.3(2)^n$ **c.** C11 **55a.** 30.198 **b.** 31.899 **c.** 31.994 **d.** 32.000 **e.** Yes, the series appears to be approaching 32. **59.** G **61.** G **63.** $a_{18} = 1,310,720$ **65.** $a_{17} \approx 1,208,925.82$ **67a.** 89, 144, 233, 377, 610 **b.** Their sum is the next term.

9-5

Check It Out! 1a. diverges **b.** converges **2a.** $\frac{125}{6}$ **b.** $\frac{2}{3}$ **3.** $\frac{1}{9}$

4. Step 1: $\sum_{k=1}^{1}(2k-1) = 1;\ 1^2 = 1$

Step 2: $1 + 3 + \cdots + (2k-1) = k^2$

Step 3: $1 + 3 + \cdots + (2k-1) + [2(k+1)-1]$
$= k^2 + [2(k+1)-1]$
$= k^2 + 2k + 1$
$= (k+1)^2$

5. $a = 5$: $\frac{5^2}{2} \stackrel{?}{\le} 2(5) + 1$
$12.5 \not\le 11$

Exercises 1. converge **3.** diverges **5.** $\frac{9}{4}$ **7.** $1066\frac{2}{3}$ **9.** $\frac{56}{99}$

11. Step 1: $2 \cdot 1 = n(n+1)$
$= 1(1+1) = 2$

Step 2: $2 + 4 + \cdots + 2(k)$
$= (k)(k+1)$

Step 3: $2 + 4 + \cdots + 2k + 2(k+1) = k(k+1) + 2(k+1)$
$= k^2 + k + 2k + 2$
$= k^2 + 3k + 2$
$= (k+1)(k+2)$

13. Possible answer: $n = 1$ **15.** converges **17.** diverges **19.** $\frac{16}{15}$ **21.** $\frac{2}{3}$ **23.** $\frac{541}{999}$ **25.** $a = 0$ **27.** $a = 0$ **29.** 320 in., or $26\frac{2}{3}$ ft **31.** 2500 **33.** $-\frac{40}{7}$ **35.** No sum exists. **37.** 500 **39.** $\frac{4}{9}$ **41.** $\frac{41}{333}$ **43.** $\frac{5}{9}$ **45a.** about 415.0 million **b.** about 6.2 billion **c.** about 11 billion **53.** $x = \frac{1}{2}$ **55.** $x = -2$ **57.** $x = 0$ **59.** For $a_1 > 0$, $S > S_n$, and both sums are positive. For $a_1 < 0$, $S_n > S$, and both sums are negative. **61.** B **63.** A **67.** $\frac{5}{12}$ **69.** No; the partial sums will approach infinity if $d > 0$ and negative infinity if $d < 0$.

Study Guide: Review

1. arithmetic; geometric **2.** diverges; converges **3.** explicit formula; recursive formula **4.** infinite sequence; finite sequence **5.** iteration **6.** −8, −7, −6, −5, −4 **7.** $\frac{1}{2}, 2, \frac{9}{2}, 8, \frac{25}{2}$ **8.** $1, -\frac{3}{2}, \frac{9}{4}, -\frac{27}{8}, \frac{81}{16}$ **9.** 55, 53, 51, 49, 47 **10.** 200, 40, 8, $\frac{8}{5}, \frac{8}{25}$ **11.** −3, 10, −29, 88, −263 **12.** $a_n = -4n$ **13.** $a_n = 5(4)^{n-1}$ **14.** $a_n = 5n - 29$ **15.** $a_n = 27\left(\frac{2}{3}\right)^{n-1}$ **16.** 0.72 ft, or 8.6 in.; 0.12 ft, or 1.5 in. **17.** $-1 + 4 - 9 + 16 = 10$ **18.** $4.5 + 5.0 + 5.5 + 6.0 + 6.5 = 27.5$ **19.** $1 - 3 + 5 - 7 + 9 = 5$ **20.** $5 + \frac{5}{2} + \frac{5}{3} + \frac{5}{4} = \frac{125}{12}$ **21.** −40 **22.** 385 **23.** 78 **24.** \$27,600; \$207,000 **25.** 17 **26.** $\frac{21}{5}$ **27.** −1.2 **28.** 29.5 **29.** −18 **30.** 23 **31.** −630 **32.** −7 **33.** 150 **34.** 330 **35.** 50, 58, 66, 74,...; no, because he will have a total savings of only \$458 **36.** 0.000004 **37.** $\frac{243}{2}$ **38.** $-\frac{1}{8}$ **39.** 768 **40.** 98,304 **41.** $\frac{512}{3}$ **42.** ±32 **43.** 62,500 **44.** 5 **45.** 2 **46.** $\frac{\sqrt{3}}{24}$ **47.** $\frac{25}{36}$ **48.** $\frac{121}{81}$ **49.** 72,727.2 **50.** 21,845 **51.** −39,062 **52.** $\frac{315}{8} = 39.375$ **53.** $\frac{279}{8} = 34.875$ **54.** \$1044.26 **55.** \$9847.32; \$43,969.32 **56.** −2025 **57.** $-\frac{4}{3}$ or $-1.\overline{3}$ **58.** −343 **59.** 5 **60.** 4.5 **61.** $-\frac{21}{2}$ **62.** $\frac{1}{9}$ **63.** No sum exists.

64. Step 1: $2^1 = 2^{1+1} - 2 = 2$

Step 2: $2 + \cdots + 2^k = 2^{k+1} - 2$

Step 3: $2 + \cdots + 2^k + 2^{k+1}$
$= 2^{k+1} - 2 + 2^{k+1}$
$= 2(2^{k+1}) - 2$
$= 2^{k+2} - 2 = 2^{k+1+1} - 2$

65. Step 1: $5^{1-1} = \frac{5^1 - 1}{4} = 1$

Step 2: $1 + \cdots + 5^{k-1} = \frac{5^k - 1}{4}$

Step 3: $1 + \cdots + 5^{k-1} + 5^k$
$= \frac{5^k - 1}{4} + 5^k$
$= \frac{5^k - 1}{4} + \frac{4(5^k)}{4}$
$= \frac{5^k + 4(5^k) - 1}{4}$
$= \frac{5(5^k) - 1}{4} = \frac{5^{k+1} - 1}{4}$

66. Step 1: $\frac{1}{4(1^2) - 1}$
$= \frac{1}{2(1) + 1}$
$= \frac{1}{3}$

Step 2: $\frac{1}{3} + \cdots + \frac{1}{4k^2 - 1}$
$= \frac{k}{2k + 1}$

Step 3: $\frac{1}{3} + \cdots + \frac{1}{4k^2 - 1} + \frac{1}{4(k+1)^2 - 1}$
$= \frac{k}{2k+1} + \frac{1}{4(k+1)^2 - 1}$
$= \frac{k}{2k+1} + \frac{1}{4k^2 + 8k + 3}$
$= \frac{k}{2k+1} + \frac{1}{(2k+1)(2k+3)}$
$= \frac{k(2k+3)}{(2k+1)(2k+3)} + \frac{1}{(2k+1)(2k+3)}$
$= \frac{k(2k+3) + 1}{(2k+1)(2k+3)}$
$= \frac{2k^2 + 3k + 1}{(2k+1)(2k+3)}$
$= \frac{(2k+1)(k+1)}{(2k+1)(2k+3)}$
$= \frac{k+1}{2k+2+1}$
$= \frac{k+1}{2(k+1)+1}$

67a. $\sum_{k=1}^{\infty} 9(0.85)^{k-1}$ **b.** 60 ft

10-1

Check It Out! 1. $\sin\theta = \frac{15}{17}$; $\cos\theta = \frac{8}{17}$; $\tan\theta = \frac{15}{8}$ **2.** $x = 10\sqrt{2}$ **3.** 41 in. **4.** 220 ft **5.** $\sin\theta = \frac{40}{41}$; $\cos\theta = \frac{9}{41}$; $\tan\theta = \frac{40}{9}$; $\csc\theta = \frac{41}{40}$; $\sec\theta = \frac{41}{9}$; $\cot\theta = \frac{9}{40}$

Exercises 1. tangent **3.** $\sin\theta = \frac{3\sqrt{13}}{13}$; $\cos\theta = \frac{2\sqrt{13}}{13}$; $\tan\theta = \frac{3}{2}$ **5.** $x = \frac{100\sqrt{3}}{3}$ **7.** $x = \frac{250\sqrt{3}}{3}$ **9.** 241 m **11.** $\sin\theta = \frac{3\sqrt{10}}{10}$; $\cos\theta = \frac{\sqrt{10}}{10}$; $\tan\theta = 3$; $\csc\theta = \frac{\sqrt{10}}{3}$; $\sec\theta = \sqrt{10}$; $\cot\theta = \frac{1}{3}$ **13.** $\sin\theta = \frac{1}{3}$; $\cos\theta = \frac{2\sqrt{2}}{3}$; $\tan\theta = \frac{\sqrt{2}}{4}$ **15.** $\sin\theta = \frac{5\sqrt{41}}{41}$; $\cos\theta = \frac{4\sqrt{41}}{41}$; $\tan\theta = \frac{5}{4}$ **17.** $x = 140$ **19a.** 147 m **b.** 187 m **21.** $\sin\theta = \frac{4}{5}$; $\cos\theta = \frac{3}{5}$; $\tan\theta = \frac{4}{3}$; $\csc\theta = \frac{5}{4}$; $\sec\theta = \frac{5}{3}$; $\cot\theta = \frac{3}{4}$ **23.** $\sin\theta = \frac{\sqrt{2}}{2}$; $\cos\theta = \frac{\sqrt{2}}{2}$; $\tan\theta = 1$; $\csc\theta = \sqrt{2}$; $\sec\theta = \sqrt{2}$; $\cot\theta = 1$ **25a.** 8022 ft **b.** 32 s **27.** 135 ft **31.** F **35a.** 3 ft **b.** $13.5\sqrt{3}$ ft^2

10-2

Check It Out!

1a.

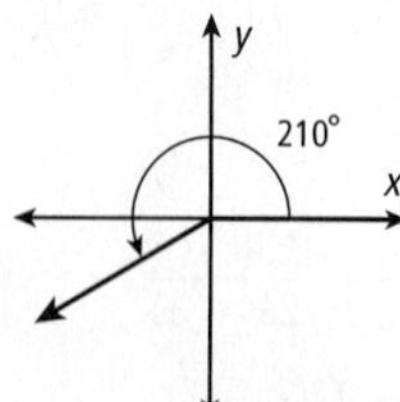

b.

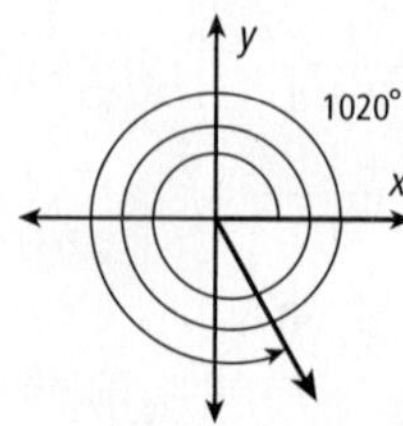

c.

2a. Possible answer: 448°; −272° **b.** Possible answer: 860°; −220° **c.** Possible answer: 240°; −480° **3a.** 75° **b.** 65° **c.** 50° **4.** $\sin\theta = \frac{2\sqrt{5}}{5}$; $\cos\theta = -\frac{\sqrt{5}}{5}$; $\tan\theta = -2$; $\csc\theta = \frac{\sqrt{5}}{2}$; $\sec\theta = -\sqrt{5}$; $\cot\theta = -\frac{1}{2}$

Exercises 1. terminal

3.

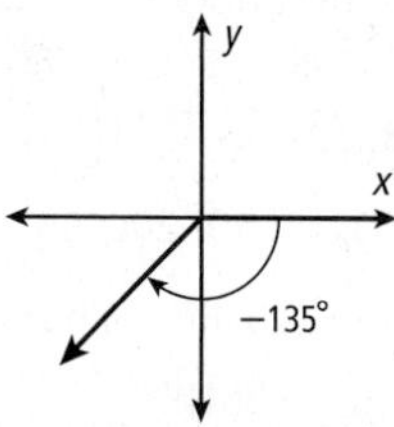

5.

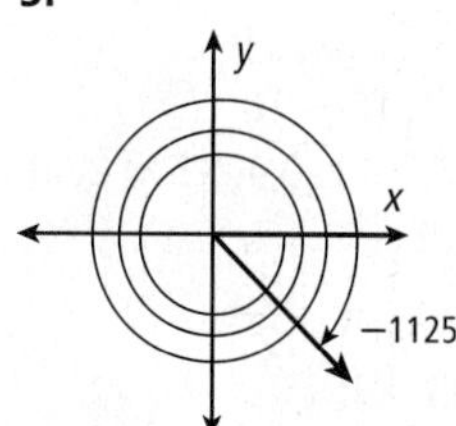

11. 70° **13.** 20° **15.** 50° **17.** 40° **19.** $\sin\theta = -\frac{\sqrt{5}}{5}$; $\cos\theta = \frac{2\sqrt{5}}{5}$; $\tan\theta = -\frac{1}{2}$; $\csc\theta = -\sqrt{5}$; $\sec\theta = \frac{\sqrt{5}}{2}$; $\cot\theta = -2$ **21.** $\sin\theta = -\frac{4}{5}$; $\cos\theta = -\frac{3}{5}$; $\tan\theta = \frac{4}{3}$; $\csc\theta = -\frac{5}{4}$; $\sec\theta = -\frac{5}{3}$; $\cot\theta = \frac{3}{4}$ **23.** $\sin\theta = \frac{6\sqrt{37}}{37}$; $\cos\theta = \frac{\sqrt{37}}{37}$; $\tan\theta = 6$; $\csc\theta = \frac{\sqrt{37}}{6}$; $\sec\theta = \sqrt{37}$; $\cot\theta = \frac{1}{6}$ **25.** $\sin\theta = \frac{2\sqrt{5}}{5}$; $\cos\theta = -\frac{\sqrt{5}}{5}$; $\tan\theta = -2$; $\csc\theta = \frac{\sqrt{5}}{2}$; $\sec\theta = -\sqrt{5}$; $\cot\theta = -\frac{1}{2}$

27.

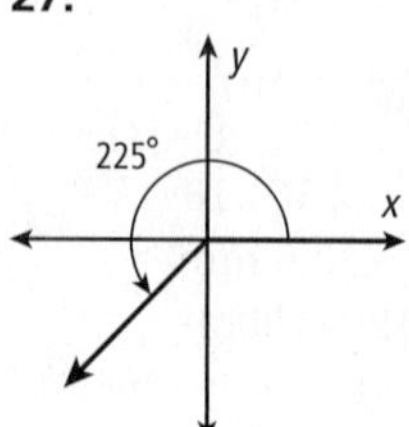

29.

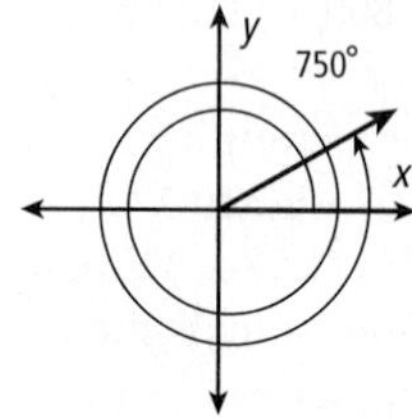

35. 50° **37.** 20° **39.** 85° **41.** 35° **43.** $\sin\theta = -\frac{2\sqrt{29}}{29}$; $\cos\theta = \frac{5\sqrt{29}}{29}$; $\tan\theta = -\frac{2}{5}$; $\csc\theta = -\frac{\sqrt{29}}{2}$; $\sec\theta = \frac{\sqrt{29}}{5}$; $\cot\theta = -\frac{5}{2}$ **45.** $\sin\theta = \frac{3}{5}$; $\cos\theta = \frac{4}{5}$; $\tan\theta = \frac{3}{4}$; $\csc\theta = \frac{5}{3}$; $\sec\theta = \frac{5}{4}$; $\cot\theta = \frac{4}{3}$ **47.** $\sin\theta = -\frac{2\sqrt{5}}{5}$; $\cos\theta = \frac{\sqrt{5}}{5}$; $\tan\theta = -2$; $\csc\theta = -\frac{\sqrt{5}}{2}$; $\sec\theta = \sqrt{5}$; $\cot\theta = -\frac{1}{2}$ **49.** $\sin\theta = \frac{4\sqrt{41}}{41}$; $\cos\theta = \frac{5\sqrt{41}}{41}$; $\tan\theta = \frac{4}{5}$; $\csc\theta = \frac{\sqrt{41}}{4}$; $\sec\theta = \frac{\sqrt{41}}{5}$; $\cot\theta = \frac{5}{4}$ **51.** 1364°/s **53.** $(-2, 2\sqrt{3})$ **55a.** 402 ft **b.** 5 s **c.** 215 ft **d.** 29 ft **57a.** 7.5 min **b.** 68 rotations **59.** −0.643 **61.** 30°, 150°, 210°, 330° **63.** 82°, 98°, 262°, 278° **67.** F **69.** $\sin\theta = \frac{b\sqrt{a^2+b^2}}{a^2+b^2}$; $\cos\theta = \frac{a\sqrt{a^2+b^2}}{a^2+b^2}$; $\tan\theta = \frac{b}{a}$ **71.** $\sin\theta = \frac{b\sqrt{a^2+b^2}}{a^2+b^2}$; $\cos\theta = \frac{a\sqrt{a^2+b^2}}{a^2+b^2}$; $\tan\theta = \frac{b}{a}$ **73.** sine and cosine: none; tangent and secant: for $\theta = 90°$ for $\theta = 270°$ and all angles coterminal with these angles; cosecant and cotangent: for $\theta = 0°$ for $\theta = 180°$ and all angles coterminal with these angles.

10-3

Check It Out! 1a. $\frac{4\pi}{9}$ radians **b.** 40° **c.** $-\frac{\pi}{5}$ radians **d.** 720°
2a. $-\frac{\sqrt{2}}{2}$ **b.** 0 **c.** $-\frac{1}{2}$
3a. sin 270° = −1; cos 270° = 0; tan 270°: undefined
b. $\sin\frac{11\pi}{6} = -\frac{1}{2}$; $\cos\frac{11\pi}{6} = \frac{\sqrt{3}}{2}$; $\tan\frac{11\pi}{6} = -\frac{\sqrt{3}}{3}$
c. $\sin(-30°) = -\frac{1}{2}$; $\cos(-30°) = \frac{\sqrt{3}}{2}$; $\tan(-30°) = -\frac{\sqrt{3}}{3}$ **4.** 1.5 ft

Exercises 1. 1 unit; 2π units
3. $-\frac{5\pi}{12}$ radians **5.** $\frac{3\pi}{4}$ radians
7. −112.5° **9.** 80° **11.** −1 **13.** $-\frac{1}{2}$
15. $\sin 120° = \frac{\sqrt{3}}{2}$; $\cos 120° = -\frac{1}{2}$; $\tan 120° = -\sqrt{3}$
17. $\sin\frac{\pi}{3} = \frac{\sqrt{3}}{2}$; $\cos\frac{\pi}{3} = \frac{1}{2}$; $\tan\frac{\pi}{3} = \sqrt{3}$ **19.** $\frac{4\pi}{3}$ radians
21. $-\frac{5\pi}{36}$ radians **23.** −20°
25. 630° **27.** $-\sqrt{3}$ **29.** $-\frac{\sqrt{3}}{2}$
31. $\sin 225° = -\frac{\sqrt{2}}{2}$; $\cos 225° = -\frac{\sqrt{2}}{2}$; $\tan 225° = 1$
33. $\sin\frac{11\pi}{6} = -\frac{1}{2}$; $\cos\frac{11\pi}{6} = \frac{\sqrt{3}}{2}$; $\tan\frac{11\pi}{6} = -\frac{\sqrt{3}}{3}$ **35.** about 2793 mi
37. reference angle: $\frac{\pi}{4}$
39. 600 revolutions/min
41a. 45° **b.** 28 ft **51.** C
53. $\sin\theta = -\frac{\sqrt{3}}{2}$; $\csc\theta = -\frac{2\sqrt{3}}{3}$; $\sec\theta = 2$; $\cot\theta = -\frac{\sqrt{3}}{3}$
55. $\left(-5\sqrt{3}, -5\right)$

10-4

Check It Out! 1. $\frac{\pi}{4} + (2\pi)n$ or $\frac{5\pi}{4} + (2\pi)n$, where n is an integer
2a. $-\frac{\pi}{4}$ or −45° **b.** $\frac{\pi}{2}$ or 90°
3. 37° north of east **4a.** $\theta = -63.4°$ **b.** $\theta = 116.6°$

Exercises 3. $\frac{\pi}{6} + (2\pi)n$ and $\frac{7\pi}{6} + (2\pi)n$, where n is an integer
5. $\frac{\pi}{6}$; 30° **7.** undefined **9.** $\frac{\pi}{4}$; 45°
11. 5° **13.** $\theta = 234.5°$ **15.** $\theta = 255.5°$
17. $\frac{\pi}{3} + (2\pi)n$ and $\frac{2\pi}{3} + (2\pi)n$, where n is an integer **19.** $\frac{\pi}{3}$; 60°
21. $-\frac{\pi}{6}$; −30° **23.** $\frac{\pi}{3}$; 60° **25.** 75°
27. $\theta = 228.6°$ **29.** $\theta = 275.7°$
31a. style A: 7.5°; style B: 9.1°; style C: 5.1° **b.** style B **c.** 9.5°
33a. 84.0° **b.** 121 ft **35.** 0.7
39. A **41.** C **43.** $\frac{\pi}{3} \le \theta \le \frac{5\pi}{3}$
45. $\frac{\pi}{8} \le \theta < \frac{\pi}{4}$ or $\frac{5\pi}{8} \le \theta < \frac{3\pi}{4}$ or $\frac{9\pi}{8} \le \theta < \frac{5\pi}{4}$ or $\frac{13\pi}{8} \le \theta < \frac{7\pi}{4}$

10-5

Check It Out! 1. 47.9 ft²
2a. m∠K = 31°; $k \approx 6.5$; $h \approx 8.4$
b. m∠N = 18°; $m \approx 4.7$; $p \approx 4.0$
3. 1 triangle; m∠B ≈ 35.4°; m∠C ≈ 39.6°; $c \approx 6.6$ cm

Exercises 1. 4.9 cm² **3.** 6900.5 m²
5. m∠Z = 40°; $x \approx 36.1$; $y \approx 18.3$
7. m∠C = 65°; $a \approx 2.0$; $b \approx 2.9$
9. m∠R = 55°; $s \approx 38.8$; $t \approx 18.3$
11. 1 triangle; m∠B ≈ 20.3°; m∠C ≈ 39.7°; $c \approx 7.4$ m
13. 1 triangle; m∠B ≈ 37.3°; m∠C ≈ 97.7°; $c \approx 9.8$ m
15. 1376.6 yd² **17.** m∠D = 61°; $c \approx 9.9$; $d \approx 8.7$ **19.** m∠K = 38°; $\ell \approx 9.4$; $m \approx 7.6$ **21.** 0 triangles
23. 1 triangle; m∠B ≈ 22.5°; m∠C ≈ 27.5°; $c \approx 4.2$ in.
25. m∠C = 64°; $b \approx 15.3$; $c \approx 15.6$
27. m∠A = 59°; $a \approx 21.8$; $c \approx 16.7$
29. 21 ft **31.** 1 triangle; m∠A ≈ 16.9°; m∠C ≈ 28.1°; $a \approx 4.9$ **33.** 1 triangle; m∠A = 90°; m∠C = 60°; $c \approx 5.2$
35a. distance from tower 1 to tower 2: 4.2 mi; distance from tower 2 to tower 3: 4.9 mi **b.** 8.9 mi²
37. 16.7 cm **39.** B is incorrect.
43. B **45b.** no **47.** 0° < m∠A < 60°

10-6

Check It Out! 1a. $a \approx 40.9$; m∠B ≈ 3.9°; m∠C ≈ 3.1°
b. m∠A ≈ 43.4°; m∠B ≈ 55.6°; m∠C ≈ 81.0° **2.** 34 mi **3.** 367 m²

Exercises 1. $q \approx 9.1$; m∠P ≈ 40.5°; m∠R ≈ 59.5° **3.** $r \approx 11.6$; m∠P ≈ 40.3°; m∠R ≈ 50.7°
5. m∠P ≈ 43.2°; m∠Q ≈ 86.5°; m∠R ≈ 50.3° **7.** 9 min **9.** $f \approx 55.5$; m∠G ≈ 53.1°; m∠H ≈ 61.9°
11. $f \approx 21.2$; m∠G ≈ 59.2°; m∠H ≈ 40.8° **13.** m∠F ≈ 54°; m∠G ≈ 59.6°; m∠H ≈ 66.4°
15. 3.8 mi **17.** m∠B ≈ 26.3°; m∠C ≈ 33.7°; $a \approx 31.2$
19. m∠A ≈ 51.3°; m∠B ≈ 32.7°; $c \approx 16.6$ **21.** m∠A ≈ 38.6°; m∠B ≈ 92.9°; m∠C ≈ 48.5°
23. 74°, 46°, and 60° **25a.** 89 mi **b.** 38° **27a.** m∠A = 43°; m∠B = 44° **b.** m∠A = 28°; m∠B = 41°
29. 524.6 cm² **31.** 7.3 ft² **33.** 1.2 km
39. H **41.** No, Abby did not make an error. A triangle cannot be formed from sides that measure 2 units, 3 units, and 5 units.
43. $x = 9.9$

Study Guide: Review

1. radian **2.** cosecant
3. standard position
4. $\sin\theta = \frac{3}{5}$; $\cos\theta = \frac{4}{5}$; $\tan\theta = \frac{3}{4}$; $\csc\theta = \frac{5}{3}$; $\sec\theta = \frac{5}{4}$; $\cot\theta = \frac{4}{3}$
5. $\sin\theta = \frac{2}{3}$; $\cos\theta = \frac{\sqrt{5}}{3}$; $\tan\theta = \frac{2\sqrt{5}}{5}$; $\csc\theta = \frac{3}{2}$; $\sec\theta = \frac{3\sqrt{5}}{5}$; $\cot\theta = \frac{\sqrt{5}}{2}$
6. $x = 12\sqrt{3}$ **7.** $x = \frac{9\sqrt{2}}{2}$
8. 18 ft **9.** 178 m
10.

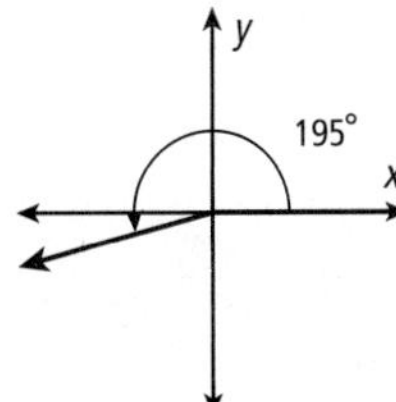

11.

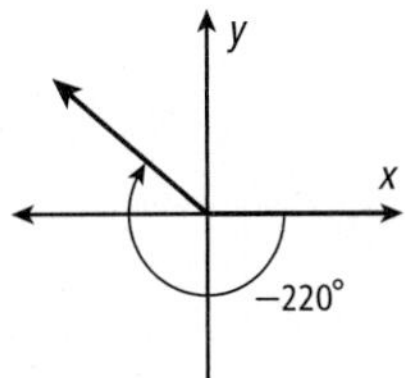

12.

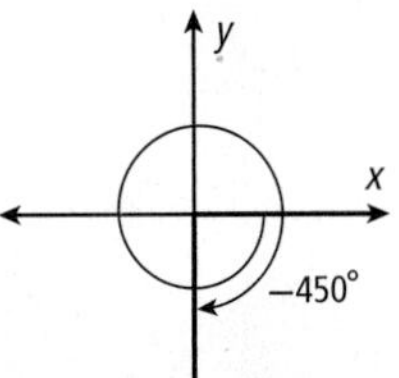

13. Possible answer: 475°; −245°
14. Possible answer: 22°; −338°
15. Possible answer: 225°; −495°
16. 84° **17.** 53° **18.** 75°
19. $\sin\theta = \frac{3}{5}$; $\cos\theta = -\frac{4}{5}$; $\tan\theta = -\frac{3}{4}$; $\csc\theta = \frac{5}{3}$; $\sec\theta = -\frac{5}{4}$; $\cot\theta = -\frac{4}{3}$
20. $\sin\theta = \frac{12}{13}$; $\cos\theta = \frac{5}{13}$; $\tan\theta = \frac{12}{5}$; $\csc\theta = \frac{13}{12}$; $\sec\theta = \frac{13}{5}$; $\cot\theta = \frac{5}{12}$
21. $\sin\theta = -\frac{8}{17}$; $\cos\theta = -\frac{15}{17}$; $\tan\theta = \frac{8}{15}$; $\csc\theta = -\frac{17}{8}$; $\sec\theta = -\frac{17}{15}$; $\cot\theta = \frac{15}{8}$
22. $\sin\theta = -\frac{3\sqrt{73}}{73}$; $\cos\theta = \frac{8\sqrt{73}}{73}$; $\tan\theta = -\frac{3}{8}$; $\csc\theta = -\frac{\sqrt{73}}{3}$; $\sec\theta = \frac{\sqrt{73}}{8}$; $\cot\theta = -\frac{8}{3}$
23. $\sin\theta = -\frac{\sqrt{82}}{82}$; $\cos\theta = -\frac{9\sqrt{82}}{82}$; $\tan\theta = \frac{1}{9}$; $\csc\theta = -\sqrt{82}$; $\sec\theta = -\frac{\sqrt{82}}{9}$; $\cot\theta = 9$
24. $\sin\theta = \frac{2\sqrt{5}}{5}$; $\cos\theta = -\frac{\sqrt{5}}{5}$; $\tan\theta = -2$; $\csc\theta = \frac{\sqrt{5}}{2}$; $\sec\theta = -\sqrt{5}$; $\cot\theta = -\frac{1}{2}$

25. $\frac{3\pi}{2}$ radians **26.** $-\frac{2\pi}{3}$ radians
27. $\frac{20\pi}{9}$ radians **28.** 30° **29.** −20°
30. 405° **31.** $-\frac{1}{2}$ **32.** −1 **33.** 2
34. $\sin\frac{7\pi}{6} = -\frac{1}{2}$; $\cos\frac{7\pi}{6} = -\frac{\sqrt{3}}{2}$; $\tan\frac{7\pi}{6} = \frac{\sqrt{3}}{3}$ **35.** $\sin 300° = -\frac{\sqrt{3}}{2}$; $\cos 300° = \frac{1}{2}$; $\tan 300° = -\sqrt{3}$
36. $\sin\left(-\frac{\pi}{3}\right) = -\frac{\sqrt{3}}{2}$; $\cos\left(-\frac{\pi}{3}\right) = \frac{1}{2}$; $\tan\left(-\frac{\pi}{3}\right) = -\sqrt{3}$
37. 22 in. **38a.** $\frac{\pi}{3}$ radians **b.** 1.6 m
39. $\frac{\pi}{3} + (2\pi)n$ and $\frac{4\pi}{3} + (2\pi)n$, where n is an integer
40. $\frac{5\pi}{6} + (2\pi)n$ and $\frac{7\pi}{6} + (2\pi)n$, where n is an integer
41. $\frac{5\pi}{4} + (2\pi)n$ and $\frac{7\pi}{4} + (2\pi)n$, where n is an integer
42. $\frac{5\pi}{6} + (2\pi)n$ and $\frac{11\pi}{6} + (2\pi)n$, where n is an integer
43. −30°; $-\frac{\pi}{6}$ radians **44.** 30°; $\frac{\pi}{6}$ radians **45.** 180°; π radians
46. 45°; $\frac{\pi}{4}$ radians **47.** 34°
48. 41° **49.** 17.5° **50.** 162.5°
51. 65.6° **52.** 245.6° **53.** 5.4 m^2
54. 4953.1 ft^2 **55.** 24.0 $in.^2$
56. 112.5 cm^2 **57.** $m\angle F = 97°$; $d \approx 26.3$; $e \approx 37.0$ **58.** $m\angle B = 75°$; $b = 15$; $c \approx 7.8$ **59.** $m\angle P = 113°$; $p \approx 10.0$; $q \approx 4.9$ **60.** $m\angle Y = 64°$; $w = 4.8$; $x = 8.0$ **61.** 2 triangles; $m\angle B_1 \approx 69.4°$; $m\angle C_1 \approx 55.6°$; $c_1 \approx 14.1$ cm; $m\angle B_2 \approx 110.6°$; $m\angle C_2 \approx 14.4°$; $c_2 \approx 4.3$ cm
62. $m\angle A \approx 20.9°$; $m\angle B \approx 130.1°$; $c \approx 19.0°$ **63.** $m\angle B \approx 43.0°$; $m\angle C \approx 27.0°$; $a \approx 24.8$
64. $m\angle A \approx 125.7°$; $m\angle B \approx 11.7°$; $m\angle C \approx 42.6°$ **65.** $m\angle A \approx 39.4°$; $m\angle B \approx 54.7°$; $m\angle C \approx 85.9°$
66a. 40.0 km **b.** 1.4 h **67.** 60 ft^2
68. 95 $in.^2$

Mastering the Standards

for Mathematical Practice

The topics described in the Standards for Mathematical Content will vary from year to year. However, the *way* in which you learn, study, and think about mathematics will not. The Standards for Mathematical Practice describe skills that you will use in all of your math courses.

Mathematical Practices

1. *Make sense of problems and persevere in solving them.*
2. *Reason abstractly and quantitatively.*
3. *Construct viable arguments and critique the reasoning of others.*
4. *Model with mathematics.*
5. *Use appropriate tools strategically.*
6. *Attend to precision.*
7. *Look for and make use of structure.*
8. *Look for and express regularity in repeated reasoning.*

5 Use appropriate tools strategically.

Mathematically proficient students consider the available tools when solving a... problem... [and] are... able to use technological tools to explore and deepen their understanding...

In your book

Algebra Labs and **Technology Labs** use concrete and technological tools to explore mathematical concepts.

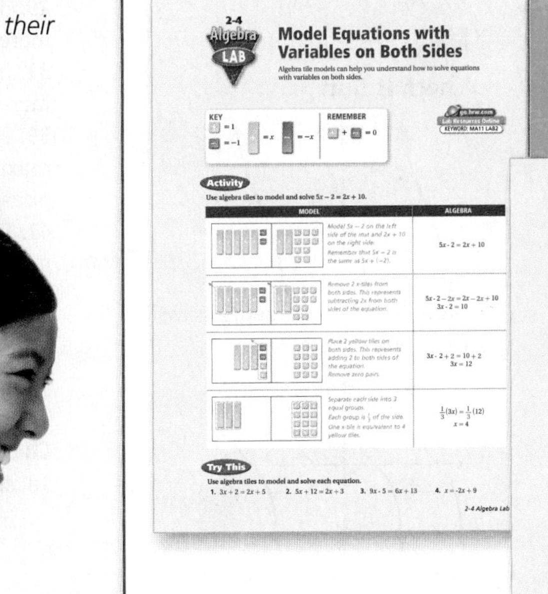
2-4 Algebra LAB

Model Equations with Variables on Both Sides

Algebra tile models can help you understand how to solve equations with variables on both sides.

KEY: = 1; = −1; = x; = $-x$
REMEMBER: + = 0

go.hrw.com Lab Resources Online KEYWORD: MA11 LAB2

Activity

Use algebra tiles to model and solve $5x - 2 = 2x + 10$.

MODEL	ALGEBRA
Model $5x - 2$ on the left side of the mat and $2x + 10$ on the right side. Remember that $5x - 2$ is the same as $5x + (-2)$.	$5x - 2 = 2x + 10$
Remove 2 x-tiles from both sides. This represents subtracting $2x$ from both sides of the equation.	$5x - 2 - 2x = 2x - 2x + 10$ $3x - 2 = 10$
Place 2 yellow tiles on both sides. This represents adding 2 to both sides of the equation. Remove zero pairs.	$3x - 2 + 2 = 10 + 2$ $3x = 12$
Separate each side into 3 equal groups. Each group is $\frac{1}{3}$ of the side. One x-tile is equivalent to 4 yellow tiles.	$\frac{1}{3}(3x) = \frac{1}{3}(12)$ $x = 4$

Try This

Use algebra tiles to model and solve each equation.

1. $3x + 2 = 2x + 5$ 2. $5x + 12 = 2x + 3$ 3. $9x - 5 = 6x + 13$ 4. $x = -2x + 9$

2-4 Algebra Lab

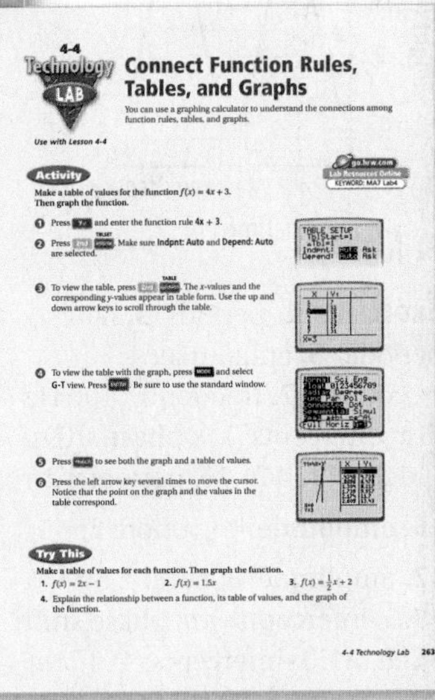
4-4 Technology LAB

Connect Function Rules, Tables, and Graphs

You can use a graphing calculator to understand the connections among function rules, tables, and graphs.

Use with Lesson 4-4

go.hrw.com Lab Resources Online KEYWORD: MA7 Lab4

Activity

Make a table of values for the function $f(x) = 4x + 3$. Then graph the function.

1. Press and enter the function rule **4x + 3**.
2. Press TBLSET. Make sure **Indpnt: Auto** and **Depend: Auto** are selected.
3. To view the table, press TABLE. The x-values and the corresponding y-values appear in table form. Use the up and down arrow keys to scroll through the table.
4. To view the table with the graph, press MODE and select **G-T** view. Press . Be sure to use the standard window.
5. Press to see both the graph and a table of values.
6. Press the left arrow key several times to move the cursor. Notice that the point on the graph and the values in the table correspond.

Try This

Make a table of values for each function. Then graph the function.

1. $f(x) = 2x - 1$ 2. $f(x) = 1.5x$ 3. $f(x) = \frac{1}{2}x + 2$
4. Explain the relationship between a function, its table of values, and the graph of the function.

4-4 Technology Lab 263

Getty Images/Image Source

11-1

Check It Out! 1a. not periodic **b.** periodic; 3

2.

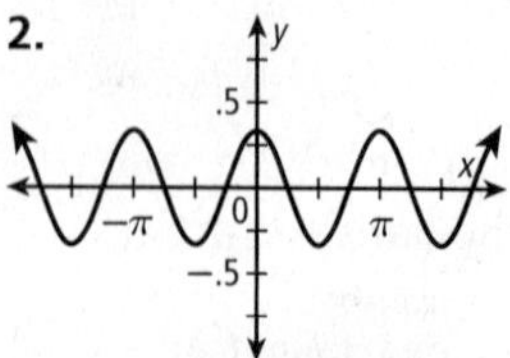

amplitude: $\frac{1}{3}$; period: π

3.

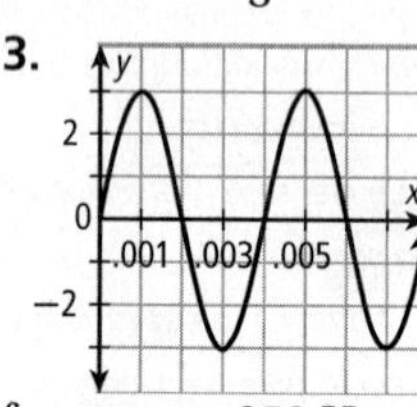

frequency: 250 Hz

4.

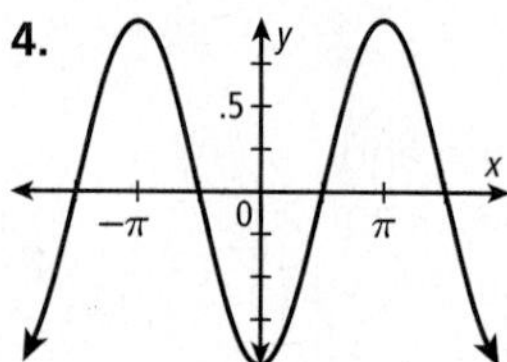

x-intercepts: $\frac{\pi}{2} + n\pi$; phase shift: π right

5a.

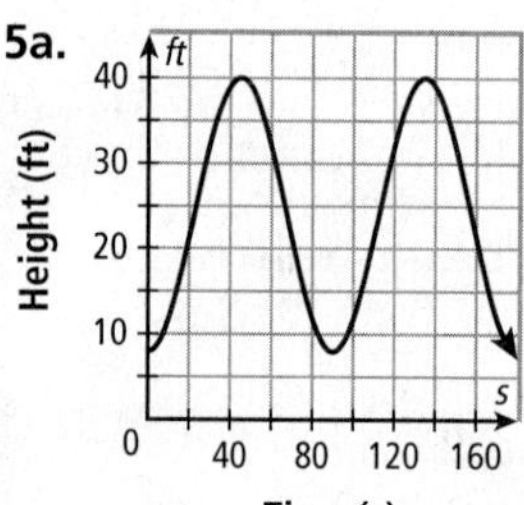

b. 40 ft

Exercises 1. periods **3.** not periodic **5.** amplitude: $\frac{1}{4}$; period: 2π **7.** frequency: 100 Hz **9.** x-intercepts: πn; phase shift: $\frac{\pi}{2}$right **11.** 4 ft **13.** periodic; 2π **15.** amplitude: $\frac{3}{2}$; period: 2π **17.** amplitude: 6; period: 6π **19.** x-intercepts: πn; phase shift: π left **21.** x-intercepts: $\frac{\pi}{4} + \pi n$; phase shift: $\frac{3\pi}{4}$ left **23.** max.: 24.5 ft; min.: 21.5 ft **25.** amplitude: 1; period: 2π; phase shift $\frac{\pi}{4}$ left and vertical shift 1 down **27.** amplitude: 1; period: 1; horizontal compression and vertical shift 2 down **29.** ≈ 0.3 **31.** ≈ 0.25 **33.** $f(x) = 6 \sin 2x$; $f(x) = 6 \cos 2x$ **35.** $f(x) = -4 \sin 2x$; $g(x) = 4 \cos 2\left(x + \frac{\pi}{4}\right)$ **37a.** period: 12.2; amplitude: 1.5; max.: 3; min.: 0 **b.** $h(0) = 3$; $h(6.1) = 0$ **c.** $h(t) = 1.5 \cos \frac{2\pi}{12.2}t + 1.5$ **39.** The period decreases for $b > 1$ and increases for $b < 1$ because the period is given by $\frac{2\pi}{b}$. **41.** H **43.** phase shift π right, horizontal compression, vertical stretch, and reflection across the x-axis amplitude: 4; period: π; x-intercepts $0, \frac{\pi}{2}, \pi, \frac{3\pi}{2}$, and 2π; max.: 4, min.: -4

45.

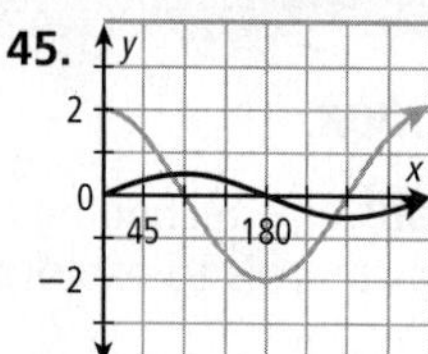

47. $76° < \theta < 256°$

11-2

Check It Out!

1.

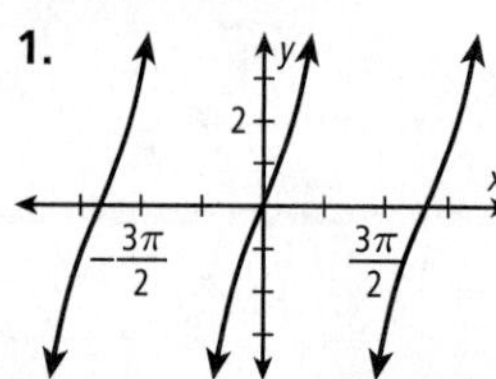

period: 2π; x-intercepts: $2\pi n$; asymptotes: $\pi + 2\pi n$

2.

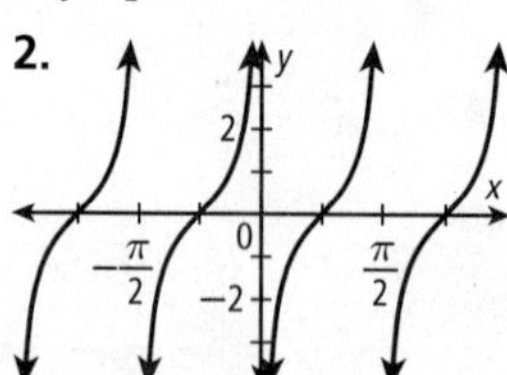

period: $\frac{\pi}{2}$; x-intercepts: $\frac{\pi}{4} + \frac{\pi}{2}n$; asymptotes: $\frac{\pi}{2}n$

3.

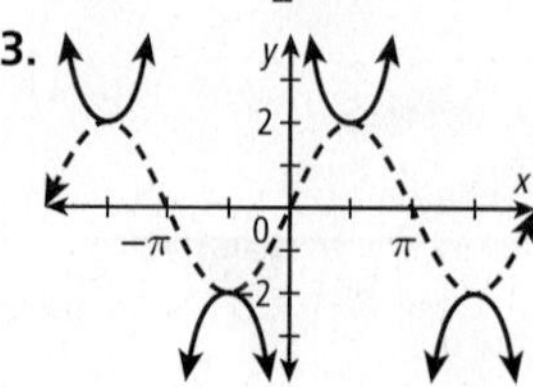

period: 2π; asymptotes: πn

Exercises 1. period: $\frac{\pi}{3}$; x-intercepts: $\frac{\pi}{3}n$; asymptotes: $\frac{\pi}{6} + \frac{\pi}{3}n$ **3.** period: $\frac{1}{2}$; x-intercepts: $\frac{1}{2}n$; asymptotes: $\frac{1}{4} + \frac{1}{2}n$ **5.** period: $\frac{\pi}{2}$; x-intercepts: $\frac{\pi}{4} + \frac{\pi}{2}n$; asymptotes: $\frac{\pi}{2}n$ **7.** period: 2π; asymptotes: $\frac{\pi}{2} + \pi n$ **9.** period: 2π; asymptotes: πn **11.** period: π; x-intercepts: $\frac{3\pi}{4} + \pi n$; asymptotes: $\frac{\pi}{4} + \pi n$ **13.** period: 2; x-intercepts: $2n$; asymptotes: $1 + 2n$ **15.** period: 4π; x-intercepts: $2\pi + 4\pi n$; asymptotes: $4\pi n$ **17.** period: 2π; asymptotes: $\frac{\pi}{2} + \pi n$ **19.** period: 2π; asymptotes: πn **21.** $\frac{\pi}{2}, \frac{3\pi}{2}$; $-\frac{\pi}{2}, \frac{5\pi}{2}$ **23.** $\frac{\pi}{2}, \frac{3\pi}{2}$; $-\frac{\pi}{2}, \frac{5\pi}{2}$ **25a.** 3 s **c.** $t = \frac{3}{4}$ and $t = \frac{9}{4}$ **27.** increasing; decreasing; decreasing; increasing **29.** decreasing; decreasing; increasing; increasing **31.** increasing; increasing; increasing; increasing **37.** G **39.** H **41.** period: 2; local maximum: 1; local minimum: 7; phase shift: 1 right **47.** D: $\{x \mid x \leq -1 \text{ or } x \geq 1\}$; R: $\left\{y \mid 0 \leq y \leq \pi \text{ and } y \neq \frac{\pi}{2}\right\}$ **49.** D: $\{x \mid x \leq -1 \text{ or } x \geq 1\}$; R: $\{y \mid -\frac{\pi}{2} \leq y \leq \frac{\pi}{2} \text{ and } y \neq 0\}$

11-3

Check It Out!

1a. $\sin\theta \cot\theta = \sin\theta\left(\frac{\cos\theta}{\sin\theta}\right) = \cos\theta$

b. $1 - \sec(-\theta) = 1 - \frac{1}{\cos(-\theta)} = 1 - \frac{1}{\cos\theta} = 1 - \sec\theta$

2a. $1 + \sin\theta$ **b.** $\frac{1}{\sin^2\theta} - 1$ **3.** $\theta \approx 22°$

Exercises

1. $\sin\theta \sec\theta = \sin\theta\left(\frac{1}{\cos\theta}\right) = \frac{\sin\theta}{\cos\theta} = \tan\theta$

3. $\cos^2\theta(\sec^2\theta - 1) = \cos^2\theta(\tan^2\theta)$
$= \cos^2\theta\left(\frac{\sin\theta}{\cos\theta}\right)^2$
$= \cos^2\theta\left(\frac{\sin^2\theta}{\cos^2\theta}\right)$
$= \sin^2\theta$
5. $1 + \cos^2\theta$ **7.** $\theta \approx 43°$
9. $\frac{\sin\theta - \cos\theta}{\sin\theta} = \frac{\sin\theta}{\sin\theta} - \frac{\cos\theta}{\sin\theta}$
$= 1 - \cot\theta$
11. $\sec^2\theta(1 - \cos^2\theta) = \left(\frac{1}{\cos^2\theta}\right)(\sin^2\theta)$
$= \frac{\sin^2\theta}{\cos^2\theta}$
$= \tan^2\theta$
13. $\frac{\sin^2\theta}{1 - \sin^2\theta}$ **15.** $\sin^2\theta$ **17.** 1
19. $\sec\theta$ **21.** $\cot\theta$ **23.** $\sin\theta$
25. $\csc\theta$ **27.** 1 **29.** $\sec^2\theta$ **31.** $\tan\theta$
33. $\sin^2\theta(\csc^2\theta - 1) = \sin^2\theta\cot^2\theta$
$= \sin^2\theta\left(\frac{\cos^2\theta}{\sin^2\theta}\right)$
$= \cos^2\theta$
35. $\frac{\cos\theta}{1 - \sin^2\theta} = \frac{\cos\theta}{\cos^2\theta} =$
$\frac{1}{\cos\theta} = \sec\theta$
39. $\cot\theta = \frac{x}{y} = \frac{r\cos\theta}{r\sin\theta}$
$= \frac{\cos\theta}{\sin\theta}$
43. $x^2 + y^2 = r^2$
$\frac{x^2}{x^2} + \frac{y^2}{x^2} = \frac{r^2}{x^2}$
$1 + \left(\frac{y}{x}\right)^2 = \left(\frac{r}{x}\right)^2$
$1 + \tan^2\theta = \sec^2\theta$
45. no **47.** yes **49.** no
51a. $r = \ell\sin\theta$ **b.** $\ell = \frac{g}{\omega^2}\sec\theta$
55. an infinite number of equivalent forms **57.** D **59.** A
63. $\frac{1}{\sin\theta\cos\theta}$ **65.** $\frac{1}{1 - \cos^2\theta}$
67. $\sin\theta + \cos\theta$ **69.** $\frac{\sin\theta}{\sin\theta + 1}$

11-4

Check It Out! **1a.** $-2 - \sqrt{3}$
b. $\frac{\sqrt{2} - \sqrt{6}}{4}$
2. $\cos\left(\frac{\pi}{2} + x\right) = \cos\left(\frac{\pi}{2}\right)\cos x - \sin\left(\frac{\pi}{2}\right)\sin x$
$= (0)\cos x - (1)\sin x$
$= -\sin x$
3. $\frac{24}{25}$ **4.** $A'(-\sqrt{3}, 1)$, $B'(-2\sqrt{3}, 2)$, $C'(0, 2)$, $D'(-\sqrt{3}, -1)$

Exercises **1.** A rotation matrix assumes a counterclockwise rotation about the origin.
3. $\frac{\sqrt{6} - \sqrt{2}}{4}$ **5.** $\frac{\sqrt{6} - \sqrt{2}}{4}$
7. $\tan(\pi + x) = \frac{\tan\pi + \tan x}{1 - \tan\pi\tan x}$
$= \frac{0 + \tan x}{1 - 0}$
$= \tan x$
9. $\frac{16}{65}$ **11.** $\frac{16}{63}$ **13.** $A'(-1.73, -1)$, $B'(-0.87, 0.5)$, $C'(-1.5, 2.60)$
15. $\sqrt{3} - 2$ **17.** $\frac{-\sqrt{2} - \sqrt{6}}{4}$
19. $\sin\left(\frac{3\pi}{2} + x\right) = \sin\frac{3\pi}{2}\cos x + \cos\frac{3\pi}{2}\sin x$
$= (-1)\cos x + (0)\sin x$
$= -\cos x$
21. $\frac{63}{65}$ **23.** $-\frac{16}{65}$ **25.** $A'(-1.41, 1.41)$, $B'(-0.71, 2.12)$, $C'(-0.71, 0.71)$
27. $2 + \sqrt{3}$ **29.** $\frac{\sqrt{2} - \sqrt{6}}{4}$
31. $2 + \sqrt{3}$ **33.** $2 - \sqrt{3}$ **35.** $\theta = 90°$
37. $\theta = 30°$ or $150°$
39. $\frac{204}{253}; -\frac{253}{325}; \frac{36}{325}$
41a. $\begin{bmatrix} 0 & -1 \\ 1 & 0 \end{bmatrix} \begin{bmatrix} -1 & 0 \\ 0 & -1 \end{bmatrix}; \begin{bmatrix} 0 & 1 \\ -1 & 0 \end{bmatrix};$
b. $P'(0, 0)$, $Q'(-1, 1)$, $R'(0, 4)$, $S'(1, 1)$; $P''(0, 0)$, $Q''(-1, -1)$, $R''(-4, 0)$, $S''(-1, 1)$; $P'''(0, 0)$, $Q'''(1, -1)$, $R'''(0, -4)$, $S'''(-1, -1)$
43a. 4.2; 3 **b.** $y(t) = -4.2\cos\frac{2\pi}{3}t$
c. 2.1 **45.** $A'(-2.60, 1.5)$, $B'(-2.96, 2.87)$, $C'(-1.60, 3.23)$, $D'(1, 1.73)$ **47.** $A'(1.50, 2.60)$, $B'(2.87, 2.96)$, $C'(3.23, 1.60)$, $D'(1.73, -1)$ **49.** A **51.** A
57. 45° **59.** 30°

11-5

Check It Out! **1.** $\frac{4\sqrt{2}}{7}; -\frac{7}{9}$
2a. Possible answer:
$\cos^4\theta - \sin^4\theta$
$= (\cos^2\theta + \sin^2\theta)(\cos^2\theta - \sin^2\theta)$
$= (1)(\cos 2\theta) = \cos 2\theta$
b. Possible answer:
$\frac{2\tan\theta}{1 + \tan^2\theta} = \frac{2\left(\frac{\sin\theta}{\cos\theta}\right)}{\sec^2\theta}$
$= \frac{2\left(\frac{\sin\theta}{\cos\theta}\right)}{\frac{1}{\cos^2\theta}} \cdot \frac{\left(\frac{\cos^2\theta}{1}\right)}{\left(\frac{\cos^2\theta}{1}\right)}$
$= 2\left(\frac{\sin\theta}{\cos\theta}\right)\left(\frac{\cos^2\theta}{1}\right)$
$= 2\sin\theta\cos\theta = \sin 2\theta$
3a. $\sqrt{7 + 4\sqrt{3}}$ **b.** $-\frac{\sqrt{2 - \sqrt{2}}}{2}$
4. $\frac{\sqrt{5}}{5}; \frac{2\sqrt{5}}{5}$

Exercises **1.** $-\frac{120}{169}; -\frac{119}{169}; \frac{120}{119}$
3. $2\cos 2\theta = 2(2\cos^2\theta - 1)$
$= 4\cos^2\theta - 2$
5. $\frac{1 + \cos 2\theta}{\sin 2\theta} = \frac{1 + (2\cos^2\theta - 1)}{(2\sin\theta\cos\theta)}$
$= \frac{2\cos^2\theta}{2\sin\theta\cos\theta}$
$= \frac{\cos\theta}{\sin\theta} = \cot\theta$
7. $\frac{\sqrt{2 - \sqrt{2}}}{2}$ **9.** $\sqrt{\frac{2 + \sqrt{2}}{2 - \sqrt{2}}}$
11. $\frac{4}{5}; -\frac{3}{5}; -\frac{4}{3}$
13. $-\frac{336}{625}; -\frac{527}{625}; \frac{336}{527}$
15. $\frac{\sin 2\theta}{\sin\theta} = \frac{(2\sin\theta\cos\theta)}{\sin\theta}$
$= 2\cos\theta$
17. $\frac{1 - \cos 2\theta}{\sin 2\theta} = \frac{1 - (1 - 2\sin^2\theta)}{2\sin\theta\cos\theta}$
$= \frac{2\sin^2\theta}{2\sin\theta\cos\theta}$
$= \frac{\sin\theta}{\cos\theta} = \tan\theta$
19. $\frac{\sqrt{2 + \sqrt{3}}}{2}$ **21.** $\frac{\sqrt{2 - \sqrt{2}}}{2}$

23. $\frac{\sqrt{37}}{37}$; $-\frac{6\sqrt{37}}{37}$; $-\frac{1}{6}$
25. $3\sin\theta\cos^2\theta - \sin^3\theta$
27. $\cos\theta(1 - 4\sin^2\theta)$ **29.** 1
31. $2\tan\theta$ **33.** $\sin\theta$
35a. $y(t) = 6.2 \sin t \cos t$
b. about 0.66 s **c.** about 3.00 m
37. $\frac{4\sqrt{5}}{9}$; $\frac{1}{9}$; $4\sqrt{5}$; $\frac{\sqrt{18+6\sqrt{5}}}{6}$; $-\frac{\sqrt{18-6\sqrt{5}}}{6}$; $-\frac{\sqrt{3+\sqrt{5}}}{\sqrt{3-\sqrt{5}}}$
39. $-\frac{4}{5}$; $\frac{3}{5}$; $-\frac{4}{3}$; $\sqrt{\frac{5-2\sqrt{5}}{10}}$; $-\sqrt{\frac{5+2\sqrt{5}}{10}}$; $-\sqrt{\frac{5-2\sqrt{5}}{5+2\sqrt{5}}}$
41. $\frac{\sqrt{2-\sqrt{3}}}{2}$ **43.** $-\frac{\sqrt{2-\sqrt{3}}}{2}$
49a. $d(\theta) = \frac{v_0^2 \sin 2\theta}{32}$
b. 100 ft; ≈ 173 ft; 200 ft; ≈ 173 ft; 100 ft **c.** 45° **d.** $30.52° < \theta < 59.48°$
53. F **55.** G
59. $\sqrt{\frac{2-\sqrt{2+\sqrt{3}}}{2+\sqrt{2+\sqrt{3}}}}$
61. $\frac{1}{2}\sqrt{2-\sqrt{2+\sqrt{3}}}$

11-6

Check It Out! 1. 150° + 360n°, 210° + 360n° **2a.** 0 **b.** ≈ 21.9°, ≈ 158.1° **3a.** 60°, 300° **b.** 90°, 210°, 270°, 330° **4.** late March and late September

Exercises 1. 60° + 360n°, 300° + 360n° **3.** 30° + 360n°, 330° + 360n° **5.** ≈ 74.5° or 285.5° **7.** π **9.** 60° + 360n°, 300° + 360n° **11.** 150° + 360n°, 210° + 360n° **13.** $\frac{\pi}{3}$, π, or $\frac{5\pi}{3}$ **15.** 90°, 120°, 240°, 270° **17a.** 10:00 A.M. and 6:00 P.M. **19.** 30°, 150°, 270° **21.** 30°, 90°, 150° **23.** 0°, 180°, 210°, 330° **25.** π **27.** $\frac{7\pi}{6}$, $\frac{11\pi}{6}$ **29.** no solution **31.** 0, $\frac{\pi}{3}$, π, $\frac{4\pi}{3}$ **33a.** $\approx\frac{\pi}{2}$; 4 sets **b.** $\approx\frac{2\pi}{5}$; 5 sets **35.** B is incorrect **37.** $x \approx -4.165, -1.797, 1.395, 5.464, 6.831$ **39.** ≈ 84.8°, ≈ 264.8° **41.** 60°, 150°, 240°, 330° **43.** 38.5°, 141.5° **47.** J **49.** J **51.** $\theta \approx 38.7°$ or 321.3°. **53.** 90°, 270°, 120°, 240°, 60°, 300° **55.** 210°, 330° **57.** 30°, 150°, 210°, 330°

Study Guide: Review

1. cycle **2.** frequency **3.** period **4.** phase shift **5.** amplitude: 1; period: $\frac{2\pi}{3}$ **6.** amplitude: 1; period: 4π **7.** amplitude: $\frac{1}{3}$; period: 2π **8.** amplitude: 2; period: 2 **9.** amplitude: $\frac{1}{2}$; period: π **10.** amplitude: $\frac{\pi}{2}$; period: 2 **11.** x-intercepts: $\frac{\pi}{2} + \pi n$; phase shift: π left **12.** x-intercepts: $\frac{3\pi}{4} + \pi n$; phase shift: $\frac{\pi}{4}$ left **13.** x-intercepts: $\frac{\pi}{2} + \pi n$; phase shift: $\frac{3\pi}{2}$ right **14.** x-intercepts: πn; phase shift: $\frac{3\pi}{2}$ left
15.

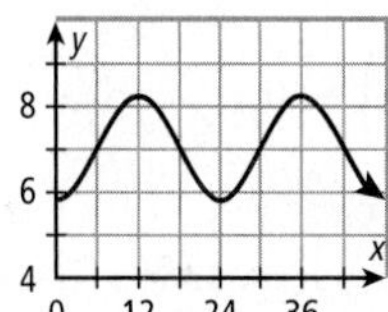

16. 24 h **17.** 8.2; noon **18.** period: π; x-intercepts: πn; asymptotes: $\frac{\pi}{2} + \pi n$ **19.** period: 1; x-intercepts: n; asymptotes: $\frac{1}{2} + n$ **20.** period: 2; x-intercepts: $2n$; asymptotes: $1 + 2n$ **21.** period: π; x-intercepts: $\frac{\pi}{2} + \pi n$; asymptotes: πn
22. period: π; x-intercepts: $\frac{\pi}{2} + \pi n$; asymptotes: πn **23.** period: 1; x-intercepts: $\frac{1}{2} + n$; asymptotes: n
24. period: 2π; asymptotes: $\frac{\pi}{2} + \pi n$
25. period: π; asymptotes: $\frac{\pi}{2}n$
26. period: 2π; asymptotes: πn
27. period: 2π; asymptotes: $\frac{\pi}{2} + \pi n$
28. period: 2π; asymptotes: $\frac{\pi}{2} + \pi n$
29. period: 2π; asymptotes: $\pi + \pi n$
30. $\sec\theta\sin\theta\cot\theta = \left(\frac{1}{\cos\theta}\right)\sin\theta\left(\frac{\cos\theta}{\sin\theta}\right) = \left(\frac{\cos\theta}{\cos\theta}\right)\left(\frac{\sin\theta}{\sin\theta}\right) = 1$

31. $\frac{\sin^2(-\theta)}{\tan\theta} = \frac{(-\sin\theta)(-\sin\theta)}{\frac{\sin\theta}{\cos\theta}} = (\sin\theta)(\sin\theta)\left(\frac{\cos\theta}{\sin\theta}\right) = \sin\theta\cos\theta$

32. $(\sec\theta + 1)(\sec\theta - 1) = \sec^2\theta - 1 = \tan^2\theta$

33. $\cos\theta\sec\theta + \cos^2\theta\csc^2\theta = 1 + \cos^2\theta\frac{1}{\sin^2\theta} = 1 + \cot^2\theta = \csc^2\theta$

34. $(\tan\theta + \cot\theta)^2 = \tan^2\theta + 2\tan\theta\cot\theta + \cot^2\theta = \tan^2\theta + 2 + \cot^2\theta = (\tan^2\theta + 1) + (1 + \cot^2\theta) = \sec^2\theta + \csc^2\theta$

35. $\tan\theta + \cot\theta = \frac{\sin\theta}{\cos\theta} + \frac{\cos\theta}{\sin\theta} = \frac{\sin^2\theta + \cos^2\theta}{\sin\theta\cos\theta} = \frac{1}{\sin\theta\cos\theta} = \sec\theta\csc\theta$

36. $\sin^2\theta\tan\theta = (1 - \cos^2\theta)\tan\theta = \tan\theta - \cos^2\tan\theta = \tan\theta - \cos^2\theta\left(\frac{\sin\theta}{\cos\theta}\right) = \tan\theta - \sin\theta\cos\theta$

37. $\frac{\tan\theta}{1 - \cos^2\theta} = \frac{\left(\frac{\sin\theta}{\cos\theta}\right)}{(\sin^2\theta)} = \left(\frac{\sin\theta}{\cos\theta}\right)\left(\frac{1}{\sin^2\theta}\right) = \left(\frac{1}{\cos\theta}\right)\left(\frac{1}{\sin\theta}\right) = \sec\theta\csc\theta$

38. $\csc\theta$ **39.** $\tan^2\theta$ **40.** $-\tan^2\theta$
41. $\sin\theta$ **42.** $\frac{-\sqrt{2}-\sqrt{6}}{4}$
43. $\frac{-\sqrt{2}-\sqrt{6}}{4}$ **44.** $\frac{\sqrt{6}+\sqrt{2}}{4}$
45. $2 - \sqrt{3}$ **46.** $-\frac{16}{65}$ **47.** $-\frac{63}{65}$
48. $\frac{56}{33}$ **49.** $\frac{16}{63}$ **50.** $-\frac{56}{65}$ **51.** $-\frac{33}{65}$
52. $\frac{36 - 5\sqrt{7}}{52}$ **53.** $\frac{-15 - 12\sqrt{7}}{52}$
54. $\frac{5\sqrt{7} + 36}{15 - 12\sqrt{7}}$ **55.** $\frac{5\sqrt{7} - 36}{15 + 12\sqrt{7}}$
56. $\frac{-36 - 5\sqrt{7}}{52}$ **57.** $\frac{-15 + 12\sqrt{7}}{52}$

58. $\approx \begin{bmatrix} 0 & 2.60 & 2.46 & -0.13 \\ 0 & 1.50 & 3.73 & 2.23 \end{bmatrix}$

59. $\approx \begin{bmatrix} 0 & 2.12 & 1.41 & -0.71 \\ 0 & 2.12 & 4.24 & 2.12 \end{bmatrix}$

60. $\approx \begin{bmatrix} 0 & 1.5 & 0.27 & -1.23 \\ 0 & 2.60 & 4.46 & 1.87 \end{bmatrix}$

61. $\begin{bmatrix} 0 & 0 & -2 & -2 \\ 0 & 3 & 4 & 1 \end{bmatrix}$

62. $\approx \begin{bmatrix} 0 & -4.23 & -3.46 & 0.77 \\ 0 & 3.33 & -2 & -5.33 \end{bmatrix}$

63. $\begin{bmatrix} 0 & -5 & 0 & 5 \\ 0 & -2 & -4 & -2 \end{bmatrix}$

64. $\approx \begin{bmatrix} 0 & -0.77 & 3.46 & 4.23 \\ 0 & -5.33 & -2 & 3.33 \end{bmatrix}$

65. $\begin{bmatrix} 0 & 2 & 4 & 2 \\ 0 & -5 & 0 & 5 \end{bmatrix}$ **66.** $\frac{24}{25}$

67. $-\frac{7}{25}$ **68.** $\frac{1}{2}$ **69.** $\frac{\sqrt{5}}{5}$ **70.** $-3\sqrt{7}$
71. $\frac{1}{8}$ **72.** $-\frac{\sqrt{14}}{4}$ **73.** $\frac{\sqrt{2}}{4}$
74. $\frac{\sqrt{2-\sqrt{3}}}{2}$ **75.** $\frac{\sqrt{2-\sqrt{3}}}{2}$
76. $135° + 360n°$, $225° + 360n°$
77. $180° + 360n°$ **78.** $0° + 180n°$, $135° + 180n°$ **79.** $60° + 180n°$, $120° + 180n°$ **80.** $\frac{2\pi}{3}, \frac{4\pi}{3}$
81. 0 **82.** $\frac{\pi}{2}, \frac{3\pi}{2}$ **83.** $\frac{3\pi}{2}$
84. $0, \frac{2\pi}{3}, \frac{4\pi}{3}$ **85.** $\frac{\pi}{2}, \frac{7\pi}{6}, \frac{3\pi}{2}, \frac{11\pi}{6}$
86a. 900 min; late June **b.** 540 min; late December

12-1

Check It Out!

1a.

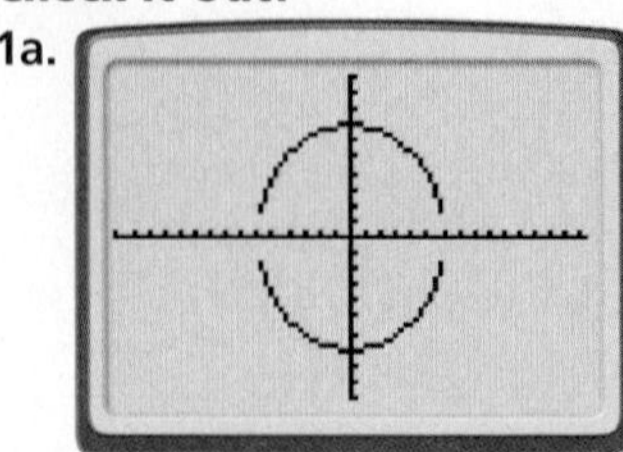

circle; center: (0, 0); intercepts: (0, ±7), (±7, 0)

b.

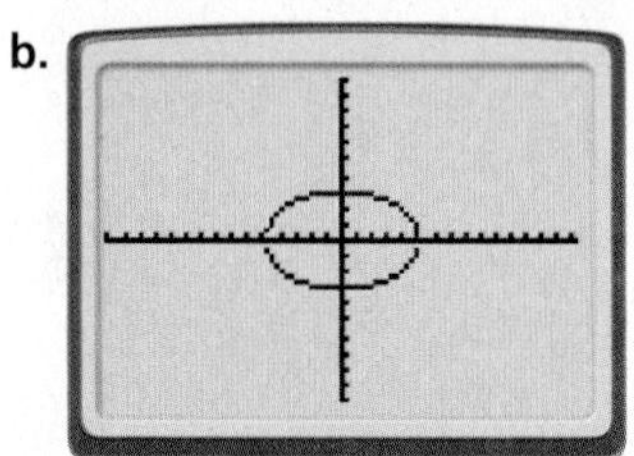

ellipse; center: (0, 0); intercepts: (±5, 0), (0, ±3)

2a.

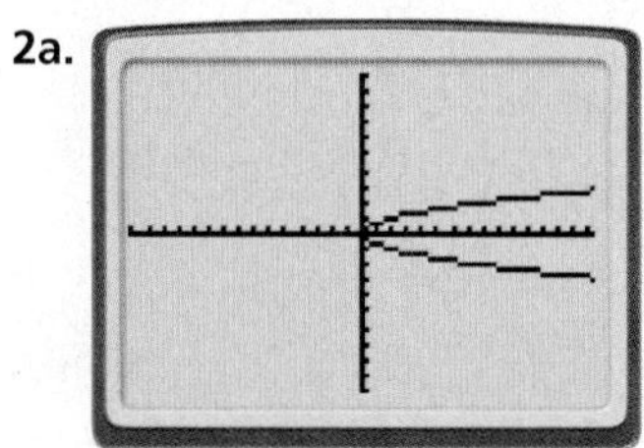

parabola; vertex: (0, 0); opens right

b.

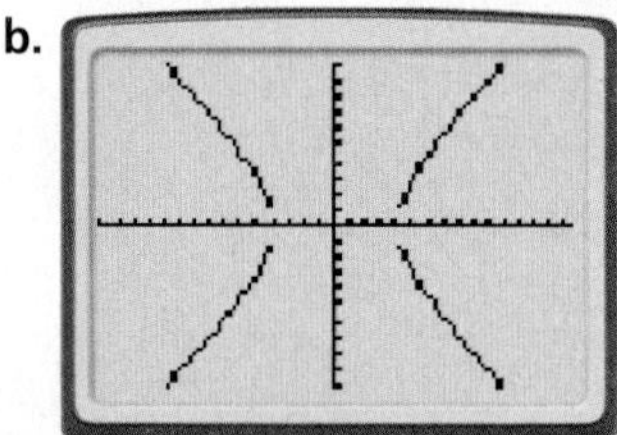

hyperbola; vertices: (±4, 0); opens horizontally **3.** Center: (8, 14); $r = 10$

Exercises **1.** circles, ellipses, hyperbolas, and parabolas **3.** ellipse; center: (0, 0); intercepts: (0, ±3), (±4, 0) **5.** parabola; vertex: (0, 0); opens right **7.** hyperbola; vertices: (0, ±5); opens vertically **9.** hyperbola; vertices: $(\pm\sqrt{2}, 0)$; opens horizontally **11.** center: (8, 18); $r = 13$ **13.** center: (−1, 15); $r = 25$ **15.** circle; center: (0, 0); intercepts: (0, ±3), (±3, 0) **17.** ellipse; center: (0, 0); intercepts: (0, ±5), (±2, 0) **19.** ellipse; center: (0, 0); intercepts: $\left(0, \pm\frac{15}{2}\right), \left(\pm\frac{5}{2}, 0\right)$ **21.** circle; center: (0, 0); intercepts: $\left(0, \pm\frac{9}{2}\right), \left(\pm\frac{9}{2}, 0\right)$ **23.** parabola; vertex: (0, 0); opens upward **25.** parabola; vertex: (0, 0); opens left **27.** hyperbola; vertices: (0, ±6); opens vertically **29.** parabola; vertex: (−3, 0); opens right **31.** hyperbola; vertices: (±4, 0); opens horizontally **33.** center: $\left(\frac{7}{2}, \frac{11}{2}\right)$; $r = \sqrt{10}$ **35a.** $C = 68\pi$; $A = 1156\pi$ **b.** (−37, 26) **37.** D **39.** A **41a.** $AB = 10$; $AD = 10$; $BC = 10$; $CD = 10$ **b.** rhombus **c.** 80 square units **43.** C **45a.** 13 units **b.** 6.5 units **c.** $\frac{12}{5}$; $\frac{12}{5}$ **47.** Sometimes true **51.** J **53.** J **55.** $a = -32$ or 40 **57. a.** (9, 2, −11) **b.** $\left(\frac{x_1 + x_2}{2}, \frac{y_1 + y_2}{2}, \frac{z_1 + z_2}{2}\right)$ **c.** $d = \sqrt{101}$ **d.** $d = \sqrt{(x_2 - x_1)^2 + (y_2 - y_1)^2 + (z_2 - z_1)^2}$

12-2

Check It Out!
1. $(x - 4)^2 + (y - 2)^2 = 49$
2. $(x + 3)^2 + (y - 5)^2 = 169$
3. C, E **4.** $y = \frac{4}{3}x - \frac{35}{3}$

Exercises
3. $(x + 11)^2 + (y - 3)^2 = 81$
5. $(x - 3)^2 + y^2 = 36$
7. $(x + 2)^2 + (y + 5)^2 = 289$
9. K, H, G **11.** $y = -\frac{3}{4}x - \frac{59}{4}$
13. $(x - 5)^2 + (y - 1)^2 = 100$
15. $(x + 4)^2 + (y - 2)^2 = 64$
17. $(x + 6)^2 + (y + 4)^2 = 25$
19. E **21.** $x = -15$
23. $\{x \mid -6 \le x \le 6\}$; $\{y \mid -6 \le y \le 6\}$
25. $\{x \mid -5 \le x \le 1\}$; $\{y \mid -3 \le y \le 3\}$
27. (−4, 0); 8
29a. $(x + 5)^2 + (y - 20)^2 = 4489$
b. 67 million mi **c.** 134π million mi
31. No **33.** C **35.** $(x + 4)^2 + (y - 8)^2 = 81$ **37a.** (2, −5)
b. $(x - 2)^2 + (y + 5)^2 = 625$

12-3

Check It Out! **1.** 20
2a. $\frac{x^2}{81} + \frac{y^2}{25} = 1$ **b.** $\frac{y^2}{25} + \frac{x^2}{16} = 1$

3a.

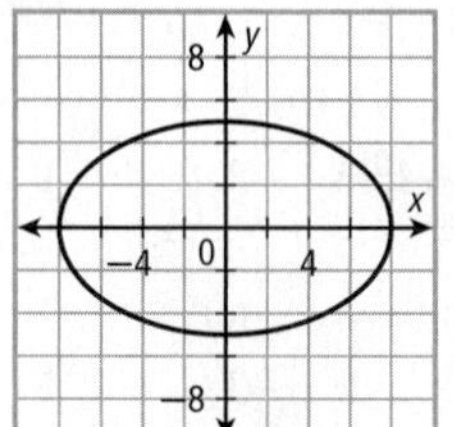

b.

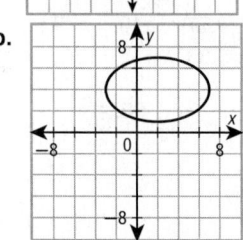

4a. width: 32 ft; height: 18 ft
b. $\frac{x^2}{256} + \frac{y^2}{324} = 1$

Exercises **1.** The major axis of an ellipse is always longer than the minor axis of an ellipse. **3.** 30
5. $\frac{y^2}{625} + \frac{x^2}{225} = 1$ **7.** $\frac{x^2}{49} + \frac{y^2}{36} = 1$

9.

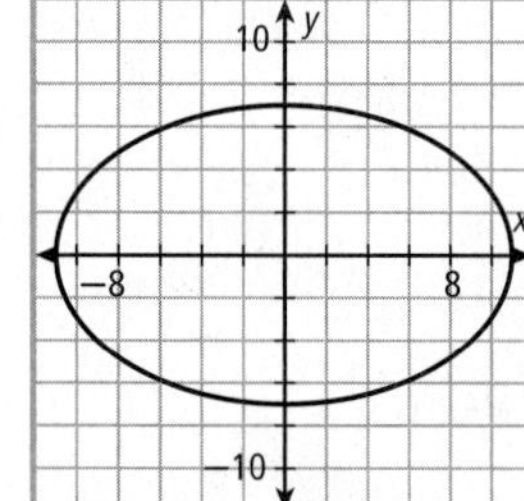

11.

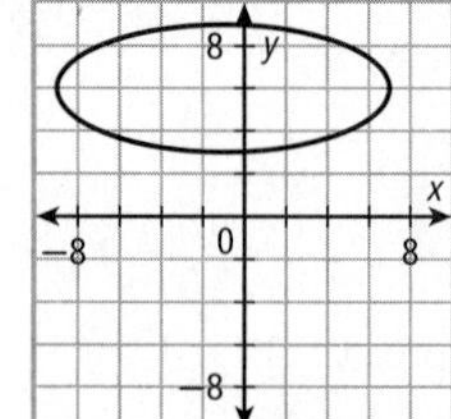

13. 42 **15.** $\frac{x^2}{25} + \frac{y^2}{4} = 1$
17. $\frac{y^2}{25} + \frac{x^2}{16} = 1$

19.

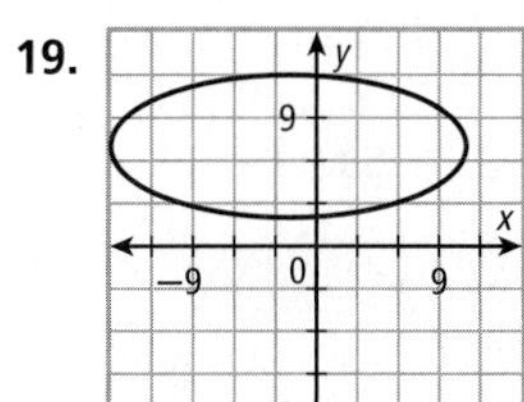

21.

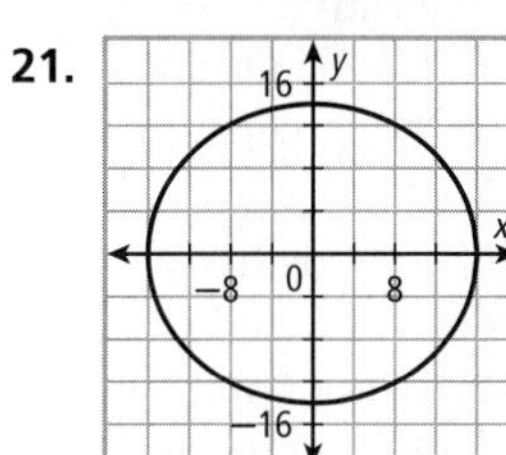

23. $\frac{x^2}{279{,}312.25} + \frac{y^2}{193{,}600} = 1$

25. $\frac{(y-7)^2}{100} + \frac{(x+4)^2}{51} = 1$

27. $\frac{x^2}{49} + \frac{y^2}{25} = 1$; D: $\{x \mid -7 \le x \le 7\}$; R: $\{y \mid -5 \le y \le 5\}$

29. $\frac{(y-4)^2}{36} + \frac{(x+6)^2}{9} = 1$; $\{x \mid -9 \le x \le -3\}, \{y \mid -2 \le y \le 10\}$

31a. $\frac{9x^2}{5041} + \frac{16y^2}{729} = 1$ **b.** $(\pm 22.68, 0)$; ~45.36 ft **33.** center: $(-9, -4)$; vertices: $(0, -4)$, $(-18, -4)$; co-vertices: $(-9, -7)$, $(-9, -1)$; foci: $(-9 \pm 6\sqrt{2}, -4)$; D: $\{x \mid -18 \le x \le 0\}$; R: $\{y \mid -7 \le y \le -1\}$ **35a.** Instead of r^2, the formula for the area of an ellipse uses the values of a and b because an ellipse can be defined by a and b rather than a radius. **b.** 65π **37.** The length of an ellipse's major axis is equal to the distance $PF_1 + PF_2$. **39.** H

41a. $\frac{21}{29}$ **b.** $\frac{x^2}{169} + \frac{y^2}{144} = 1$ **c.** $0 < e < 1$ **43.** $\frac{x^2}{25} + \frac{y^2}{16} = 1$

12-4

Check It Out! 1. 12

2a. $\frac{y^2}{81} - \frac{x^2}{49} = 1$ **b.** $\frac{x^2}{64} - \frac{y^2}{36} = 1$

3a. vertices: $(\pm 4, 0)$; co-vertices: $(0, \pm 6)$; asymptotes: $y = \pm\frac{3}{2}x$

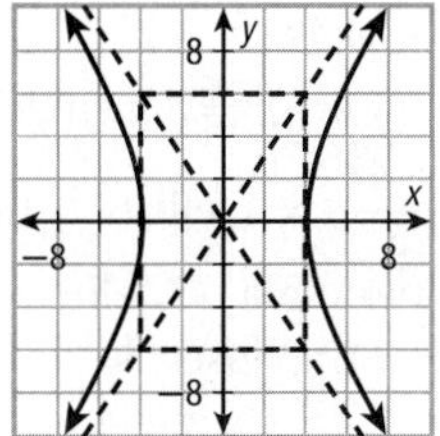

b. vertices: $(1, -4)$, $(1, -6)$; co-vertices: $(4, -5)$, $(-2, -5)$; asymptotes: $y = \pm\frac{1}{3}(x-1) - 5$

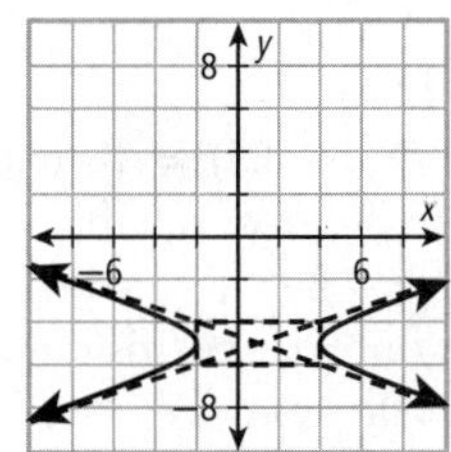

Exercises 1. transverse axis **3.** 30 **5.** $\frac{x^2}{81} - \frac{y^2}{49} = 1$

7. $\frac{y^2}{100} - \frac{x^2}{64} = 1$

9. vertices: $(\pm 5, 0)$; co-vertices: $(0, \pm 8)$; asymptotes: $y = \pm\frac{8}{5}x$

11. vertices: $(0, \pm 10)$; co-vertices: $(\pm 9, 0)$; asymptotes: $y = \pm\frac{10}{9}x$

13. vertices: $(8, -6)$, $(0, -6)$; co-vertices: $(4, 1)$, $(4, -13)$; asymptotes: $y = \pm\frac{7}{4}(x-4) - 6$

15. vertices: $(0, -5)$, $(0, -9)$; co-vertices: $(\pm 5, -7)$; asymptotes: $y = \pm\frac{2}{5}x - 7$ **17.** 42

19. $\frac{x^2}{64} - \frac{y^2}{225} = 1$

21. $\frac{(x-3)^2}{49} - \frac{(y-3)^2}{9} = 1$

23. vertices: $(0, \pm 5)$; co-vertices: $(\pm 9, 0)$; asymptotes: $y = \pm\frac{5}{9}x$

25. vertices: $(\pm 2, 0)$; co-vertices: $(0, \pm 11)$; asymptotes: $y = \pm\frac{11}{2}x$

27. vertices: $(0, 3)$, $(-10, 3)$; co-vertices: $(-5, 7)$, $(-5, -1)$; asymptotes: $y = \pm\frac{4}{5}(x+5) + 3$

29. vertices: $(9, 2)$, $(3, 2)$; co-vertices: $(6, 6)$, $(6, -2)$; asymptotes: $y = \pm\frac{4}{3}(x-6) + 2$

33b. Yes **35.** $c^2 = a^2 + b^2$, so c always has the greatest value. There is not enough information given to determine whether a or b has the least value. **37a.** $(0, 214)$ **b.** 184 million mi **c.** $y \approx \pm 0.142x$

39. G **41.** J

43. $\frac{(x-7)^2}{400} - \frac{(y+9)^2}{144} = 1$

45. $\frac{x^2}{16} - \frac{y^2}{9} = 1$

12-5

Check It Out! 1. $y = \frac{1}{16}x^2$

2. a. $x = -\frac{1}{5}y^2$ **b.** $y = -\frac{1}{28}x^2$

3a. vertex: $(1, 3)$; $p = 3$; axis of symmetry: $y = 3$; focus: $(4, 3)$; directrix: $x = -2$

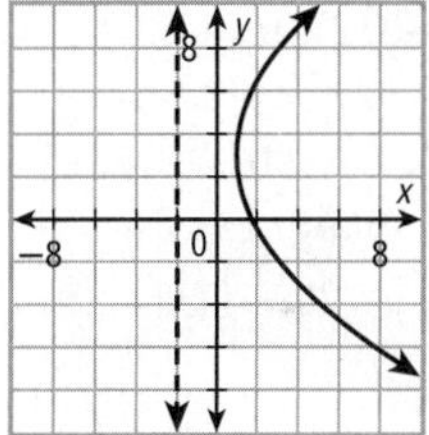

b. vertex: $(8, 4)$; $p = -\frac{1}{2}$; axis of symmetry: $x = 8$; focus: $(8, 3.5)$; directrix: $y = 4.5$

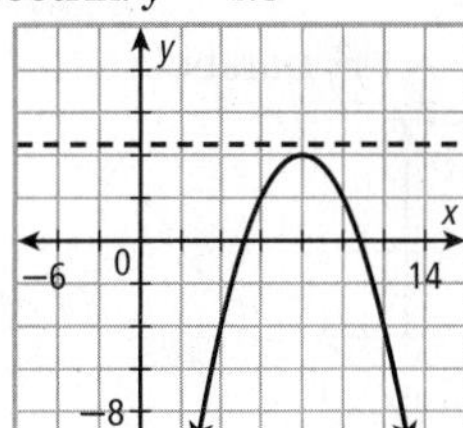

4. 11 in.

Exercises 3. $x = \frac{1}{28}y^2$

5. $y = -\frac{1}{16}x^2$ **7.** $y = \frac{1}{2}x^2$

9. $x = -\frac{1}{32}y^2$ **11.** vertex: $(0, 4)$; $p = 6$; axis of symmetry: $y = 4$; focus: $(6, 4)$; directrix: $x = -6$

13. 9.5 in **15.** $x - 3 = -\frac{1}{20}y^2$
17. $y = \frac{1}{12}(x + 3)^2$ **19.** $x = \frac{1}{4}y^2$
21. $y = -\frac{1}{24}x^2$ **23.** vertex: (1, 0); $p = \frac{1}{8}$; axis of symmetry: $y = 0$; focus: $\left(\frac{9}{8}, 0\right)$; directrix: $x = \frac{7}{8}$
27. $y + 6 = -\frac{1}{12}(x - 2)^2$; D: $\{x \mid x \in \mathbb{R}\}$; R: $\{y \mid y \leq -6\}$
29. $x + 7 = \frac{1}{36}(y + 3)^2$; D: $\{x \mid x \geq -7\}$; R: $\{y \mid y \in \mathbb{R}\}$
31. $y - 5 = -\frac{1}{20}x^2$; D: $\{x \mid x \in \mathbb{R}\}$; R: $\{y \mid y \leq 5\}$ **33.** $x - 8 = -\frac{1}{16}(y + 5)^2$; D: $\{x \mid x \leq 8\}$; R: $\{y \mid y \in \mathbb{R}\}$ **35a.** $y = \frac{1}{20}x^2$ **b.** $y + 4 = \frac{1}{16}x^2$ **c.** 7.2 in
37a. (−96, 41) **b.** 133 million km **c.** (−96, 174) **39.** vertex: (−4, 5); $p = -\frac{1}{8}$; axis of symmetry: $x = -4$; focus: $\left(-4, 4\frac{7}{8}\right)$; directrix: $y = 5\frac{1}{8}$
41. vertex: (−3, 2); $p = 2$; axis of symmetry: $y = 2$; focus: (−1, 2); directrix: $x = -5$
45. G **47.** (7, 0) **49.** $y - 7 = -\frac{1}{8}(x-6)^2$ or $y - 3 = \frac{1}{8}(x - 6)^2$
51. $4p$

12-6

Check It Out! 1a. circle **b.** hyperbola **2a.** circle **b.** parabola **3a.** $x = \frac{1}{9}(y + 8)^2$; parabola

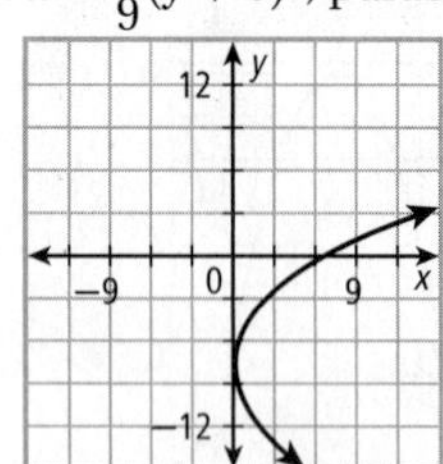

b. $\frac{(x - 4)^2}{9} + \frac{(y + 6)^2}{16} = 1$; ellipse

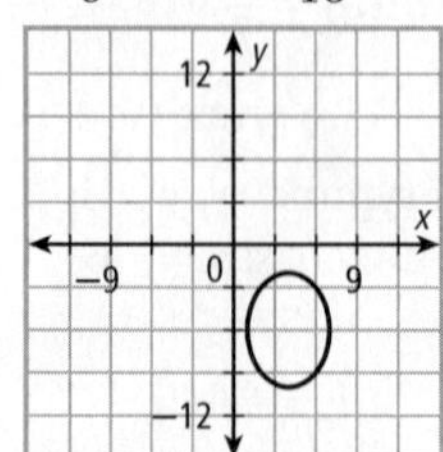

4. 200 ft

Exercises 1. ellipse **3.** parabola **5.** ellipse **7.** ellipse
9. $(x - 8)^2 + (y + 5)^2 = 36$; circle
11. $\frac{x^2}{9} + \frac{(y + 4)^2}{25} = 1$; ellipse
13. 4 in **15.** parabola **17.** ellipse
19. parabola **21.** ellipse
23. $x^2 + (y - 4)^2 = 49$; circle
25. $\frac{x^2}{4} - \frac{(y + 9)^2}{25} = 1$; hyperbola
27. $(x + 5)^2 + (y + 2)^2 = 20$; circle
29. $\frac{(x + 1)^2}{4} - \frac{(y - 7)^2}{9} = 1$; hyperbola
31. $(x - 2.5)^2 + (y + 4.5)^2 = 16$; circle
33a. ellipse **b.** 40 m **c.** 100 m
35. $36x^2 + 25y^2 - 360x + 400y + 1600 = 0$ **37.** outside **39.** inside
41. 36.4 cm **43a.** $(x - 40)^2 + (y - 30)^2 = 40{,}000$ **b.** $40{,}000\pi$
c. inside **45a.** $y - 84 = -\frac{1}{500}(x-200)^2$ **b.** 84 ft **c.** 4 ft
47. A **49.** D
53. It rotates the graph.

12-7

Check It Out! 1. (0, 4.5)
2a. (−4, 3), (3, −4)
b. (0, 5), (±3, −4) **3.** no solution
4. yes, at (±4, −3.6)

Exercises 3. (4, −2), (8, 2)
5. (12, 5), (5, 12) **7.** no solution
9. (0, −6), $\left(\pm 3\sqrt{3}, 3\right)$
11. (±4, 2), (±4, −2)
13. no solution
15. (0, 5), (−4, 3)
17. (2.5, −6.5), (−4.5, 7.5)
19. (0, 4), $\left(\frac{8}{3}, \frac{20}{3}\right)$ **21.** (5, 1), (7, 4)
23. (±2, −2), $\left(\pm\sqrt{7}, 1\right)$ **25.** no solution **27.** (0, −7), (1, −6)
29. $\left(2\sqrt{2}, \pm 1\right), \left(-2\sqrt{2}, \pm 1\right)$
31. (0, 0), (1, 1) **33.** (6, 1), (−26, −3)
35. (0, ±3) **37.** (2, ±4)
39. no solution **41.** (10, ±4), (−10, ±4) **43.** 25 s **45.** (2.8, −2.6), (3.3, 2.9), (−7.9, −1.3), (−8.1, 1.5)

47a. hyperbola **b.** yes; approximately (6.69, 2.68), (1.31, 2.68) **49.** (−2, 0) **53.** G

Study Guide: Review

1. transverse axis **2.** tangent line
3. focus; directrix **4.** conic section **5.** circle with center (0, 0) and radius $r = 9$ **6.** hyperbola with center (0, 0) and intercepts (5, 0) and (−5, 0) **7.** parabola with vertex (0, −1), opening in the positive x-direction **8.** ellipse with center (0, 0), and intercepts (±3.5, 0), and (0, ≈ ±1.98) **9.** B
10. center: (3, −3); $r = 12$
11. center: (8, −2.5); $r = 12.5$
12. center: (6, 0); $r = 19$
13. center: (−12, 4); $r = \sqrt{15}$
14. $(x - 8)^2 + (y + 7)^2 = 196$
15. $(x - 3)^2 + (y - 6)^2 = 80$
16. $(x + 3)^2 + (y - 8)^2 = 34$
17. $y - 5 = -\frac{3}{5}(x - 3)$
18. $y = 4$ **19.** $y + 2 = -\frac{4}{5}(x - 6)$
20. $y + 7 = \frac{5}{8}(x - 1)$
21. center: (0, 0); vertices: (0, ±6); co-vertices: (±3, 0); foci: $\left(0, \pm 3\sqrt{3}\right)$
22. center: (0, 0); vertices: (±8, 0); co-vertices: (0, ±5); foci: $\left(\pm\sqrt{39}, 0\right)$
23. center: (3, −2); vertices: (3, 6), (3, −10); co-vertices: (10, −2), (−4, −2); foci: $\left(3, -2 \pm \sqrt{15}\right)$
24. $\frac{(x - 4)^2}{36} + \frac{(y + 5)^2}{9} = 1$
25. $\frac{x^2}{144} + \frac{y^2}{225} = 1$
26. $\frac{(x + 2)^2}{36} + \frac{(y - 3)^2}{27} = 1$
27. center: (0, 0); vertices: (±5, 0); co-vertices: (0, ±7); foci: $\left(\pm\sqrt{74}, 0\right)$; asymptotes: $y = \pm\frac{7}{5}x$
28. center: (0, 0); vertices: (0, ±6); co-vertices: (±8, 0); foci: (0, ±10); asymptotes: $y = \pm\frac{3}{4}x$ **29.** center: (3, −6); vertices: (5, −6), (1, −6); co-vertices: (3, 1), (3, −13); foci: $\left(3 \pm \sqrt{53}, -6\right)$; asymptotes:

$y + 6 = \pm\frac{7}{2}(x - 3)$ **30.** $\frac{x^2}{25} - \frac{y^2}{36} = 1$
31. $\frac{x^2}{121} - \frac{y^2}{16} = 1$ **32.** $\frac{y^2}{25} - \frac{x^2}{36} = 1$
33. $\frac{(y-5)^2}{25} - \frac{(x+7)^2}{144} = 1$
34. vertex: (0, 0); $p = -3$; axis of symmetry: $x = 0$; focus: (0, −3); directrix: $y = 3$ **35.** vertex: (0, 0); $p = \frac{1}{8}$; axis of symmetry: $y = 0$; focus: $\left(\frac{1}{8}, 0\right)$; directrix: $x = -\frac{1}{8}$
36. vertex: (−4, 5); $p = \frac{1}{4}$; axis of symmetry: $x = -4$; focus: $\left(-4, 5\frac{1}{4}\right)$; directrix: $y = 4\frac{3}{4}$ **37.** vertex: (4, −2); $p = -1.5$; axis of symmetry: $y = -2$; focus: (2.5, −2); directrix: $x = 5.5$
38. $y = -\frac{1}{20}(x - 3)^2$
39. $x - 4 = -\frac{1}{10}(y - 6)^2$
40. $x - 9 = \frac{1}{12}(y + 4)^2$ **41.** ellipse
42. hyperbola **43.** parabola
44. circle **45.** ellipse
46. $x + 3 = \frac{1}{4}(y + 6)^2$; parabola
47. $\frac{(x+4)^2}{6} + \frac{y^2}{2} = 1$; ellipse
48. $(x + 5)^2 + (y - 4)^2 = 36$; circle
49. $\frac{(x+1)^2}{8} - \frac{(y+3)^2}{4} = 1$; hyperbola **50.** (2, −6), (−2, 2)
51. (4, 0), (0, −5)
52. (8, ±6), (−8, ±6)
53. (3, 2), (5, 6) **54.** (0, 2), (0, −2)
55. (6, 4), (6, −4), (−6, 4), (−6, −4)
56. (2, 6), (−7, 3) **57.** no solution

Glossary/Glosario

ENGLISH / **SPANISH** / **EXAMPLES**

---

absolute value of a complex number The absolute value of $a + bi$ is the distance from the origin to the point (a, b) in the complex plane and is denoted $|a + bi| = \sqrt{a^2 + b^2}$.

valor absoluto de un número complejo El valor absoluto de $a + bi$ es la distancia desde el origen hasta el punto (a, b) en el plano complejo y se expresa $|a + bi| = \sqrt{a^2 + b^2}$.

$|2 + 3i| = \sqrt{2^2 + 3^2} = \sqrt{13}$

---

absolute value of a real number The absolute value of x is the distance from zero to x on a number line, denoted $|x|$.

$$|x| = \begin{cases} x & \text{if } x \geq 0 \\ -x & \text{if } x < 0 \end{cases}$$

valor absoluto de un número real El valor absoluto de x es la distancia desde cero hasta x en una recta numérica y se expresa $|x|$.

$$|x| = \begin{cases} x & \text{si } x \geq 0 \\ -x & \text{si } x < 0 \end{cases}$$

$|3| = 3$
$|-3| = 3$

---

absolute-value function A function whose rule contains absolute-value expressions.

función de valor absoluto Función cuya regla contiene expresiones de valor absoluto.

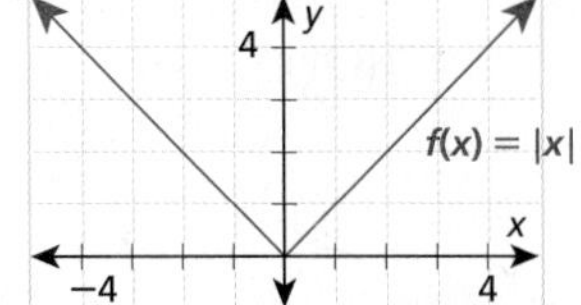

---

accuracy The closeness of a given measurement or value to the actual measurement or value.

exactitud Cercanía de una medida o un valor a la medida o el valor real.

---

acute angle An angle that measures greater than 0° and less than 90°.

ángulo agudo Ángulo que mide más de 0° y menos de 90°.

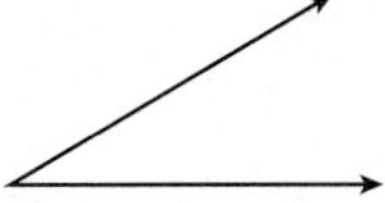

---

additive inverse of a matrix A matrix where each entry is the opposite of each entry in another matrix. Two matrices are additive inverses if their sum is the zero matrix.

inverso aditivo de una matriz Matriz en la cual cada entrada es el opuesto de cada entrada en otra matriz. Dos matrices son inversos aditivos si su suma es la matriz cero.

$\begin{bmatrix} 1 & -2 \\ 0 & 4 \end{bmatrix}$ and $\begin{bmatrix} -1 & 2 \\ 0 & -4 \end{bmatrix}$ are additive inverses.

---

address The location of an entry in a matrix, given by the row and column in which the entry appears. In matrix A, the address of the entry in row i and column j is a_{ij}.

dirección Ubicación de una entrada en una matriz, indicada por la fila y la columna en las que aparece la entrada. En la matriz A, la dirección de la entrada de la fila i y la columna j es a_{ij}.

In the matrix $A = \begin{bmatrix} 2 & 3 \\ 4 & 1 \end{bmatrix}$,
the address of the entry 2 is a_{11},
the address of the entry 3 is a_{12}.

---

amplitude The amplitude of a periodic function is half the difference of the maximum and minimum values (always positive).

amplitud La amplitud de una función periódica es la mitad de la diferencia entre los valores máximo y mínimo (siempre positivos).

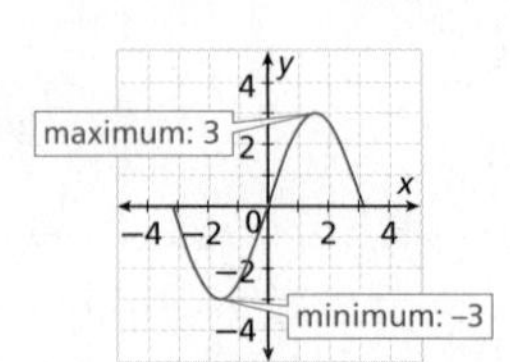

amplitude $= \frac{1}{2}\left[3 - (-3)\right] = 3$

ENGLISH	SPANISH	EXAMPLES
angle of depression The angle formed by a horizontal line and a line of sight to a point below.	**ángulo de depresión** Ángulo formado por una recta horizontal y una línea visual a un punto inferior.	
angle of elevation The angle formed by a horizontal line and a line of sight to a point above.	**ángulo de elevación** Ángulo formado por una recta horizontal y una línea visual a un punto superior.	
angle of rotation An angle formed by a rotating ray, called the terminal side, and a stationary reference ray, called the initial side.	**ángulo de rotación** Ángulo formado por un rayo en rotación, denominado lado terminal, y un rayo de referencia estático, denominado lado inicial.	Terminal side, 135°, 45°, Initial side
arc An unbroken part of a circle consisting of two points on the circle, called the endpoints, and all the points on the circle between them.	**arco** Parte continua de un círculo formada por dos puntos del círculo denominados extremos y todos los puntos del círculo comprendidos entre éstos.	R, S
arc length The distance along an arc measured in linear units.	**longitud de arco** Distancia a lo largo de un arco medida en unidades lineales.	10 ft, D, 90°, C $m\widehat{CD} = 5\pi$ ft
arithmetic sequence A sequence whose successive terms differ by the same nonzero number d, called the *common difference.*	**sucesión aritmética** Sucesión cuyos términos sucesivos difieren en el mismo número distinto de cero d, denominado *diferencia común.*	4, 7, 10, 13, 16, ... +3 +3 +3 +3 $d = 3$
arithmetic series The indicated sum of the terms of an arithmetic sequence.	**serie aritmética** Suma indicada de los términos de una sucesión aritmética.	$4 + 7 + 10 + 13 + 16 + \ldots$
asymptote A line that a graph approaches as the value of a variable becomes extremely large or small.	**asíntota** Línea recta a la cual se aproxima una gráfica a medida que el valor de una variable se hace sumamente grande o pequeño.	Asymptote
augmented matrix A matrix that consists of the coefficients and the constant terms in a system of linear equations.	**matriz aumentada** Matriz formada por los coeficientes y los términos constantes de un sistema de ecuaciones lineales.	System of equations: $3x + 2y = 5$, $2x - 3y = 1$ Augmented matrix: $\left[\begin{array}{cc\|c} 3 & 2 & 5 \\ 2 & -3 & 1 \end{array}\right]$
axis of symmetry A line that divides a plane figure or a graph into two congruent reflected halves.	**eje de simetría** Línea que divide una figura plana o una gráfica en dos mitades reflejadas congruentes.	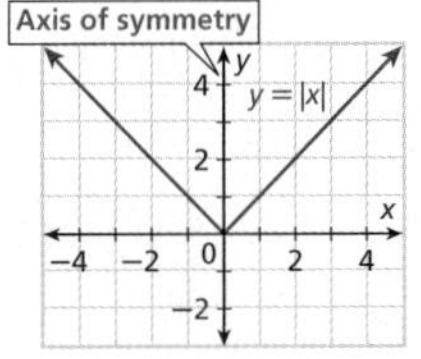

ENGLISH	SPANISH	EXAMPLES

B

base of an exponential function The value of b in a function of the form $f(x) = ab^x$, where a and b are real numbers with $a \neq 0$, $b > 0$, and $b \neq 1$.	**base de una función exponencial** Valor de b en una función del tipo $f(x) = ab^x$, donde a y b son números reales con $a \neq 0$, $b > 0$, y $b \neq 1$.	$f(x) = 5(2)^x$ ↑ base
biased sample A sample that does not fairly represent the population.	**muestra no representativa** Muestra que no representa adecuadamente una población.	
binomial A polynomial with two terms.	**binomio** Polinomio con dos términos.	$x + y$ $2a^2 + 3$ $4m^3n^2 + 6mn^4$
binomial experiment A probability experiment consists of n identical and independent trials whose outcomes are either successes or failures, with a constant probability of success p and a constant probability of failure q, where $q = 1 - p$ or $p + q = 1$.	**experimento binomial** Experimento de probabilidades que comprende n pruebas idénticas e independientes cuyos resultados son éxitos o fracasos, con una probabilidad constante de éxito p y una probabilidad constante de fracaso q, donde $q = 1 - p$ o $p + q = 1$.	A multiple-choice quiz has 10 questions with 4 answer choices. The number of trials is 10. If each question is answered randomly, the probability of success for each trial is $\frac{1}{4} = 0.25$ and the probability of failure is $\frac{3}{4} = 0.75$.
binomial probability In a binomial experiment, the probability of r successes $(0 \leq r \leq n)$ is $P(r) = {}_nC_r \cdot p^r q^{n-r}$.	**probabilidad binomial** En un experimento binomial, la probabilidad de r éxitos $(0 \leq r \leq n)$ es $P(r) = {}_nC_r \cdot p^r q^{n-r}$.	In the binomial experiment above, the probability of randomly guessing 6 problems correctly is $P = {}_{10}C_6\,(0.25)^6\,(0.75)^4 \approx 0.016$.
Binomial Theorem For any positive integer n, $(x + y)^n = {}_nC_0\, x^n y^0 + {}_nC_1\, x^{n-1} y^1 + {}_nC_2\, x^{n-2} y^2 + \cdots + {}_nC_{n-1}\, x^1 y^{n-1} + {}_nC_n\, x^0 y^n$	**Teorema de los binomios** Dado un entero positivo n, $(x + y)^n = {}_nC_0\, x^n y^0 + {}_nC_1\, x^{n-1} y^1 + {}_nC_2\, x^{n-2} y^2 + \cdots + {}_nC_{n-1}\, x^1 y^{n-1} + {}_nC_n\, x^0 y^n$	$(x + 2)^4 = {}_4C_0\, x^4 2^0 + {}_4C_1\, x^3 2^1 + {}_4C_2\, x^2 2^2 + {}_4C_1\, x^1 2^3 + {}_4C_4\, x^0 2^4 = x^4 + 8x^3 + 24x^2 + 32x + 16$
box-and-whisker plot A method of showing how data is distributed by using the median, quartiles, and minimum and maximum values; also called a *box plot.*	**gráfica de mediana y rango** Método para demostrar la distribución de datos utilizando la mediana, los cuartiles y los valores mínimos y máximos; también llamado *gráfica de caja.*	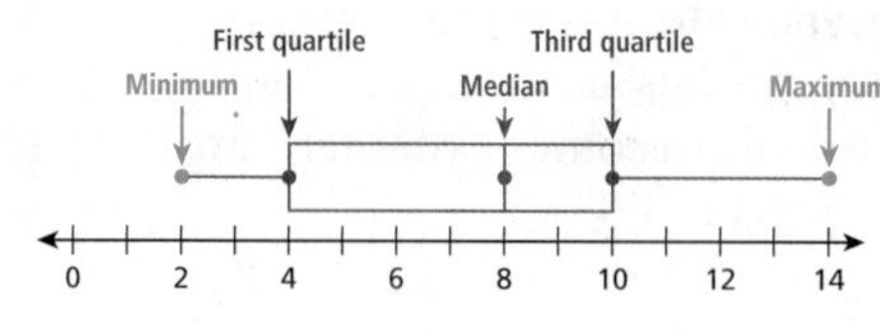
branch of a hyperbola One of the two symmetrical parts of the hyperbola.	**rama de una hipérbola** Una de las dos partes simétricas de la hipérbola.	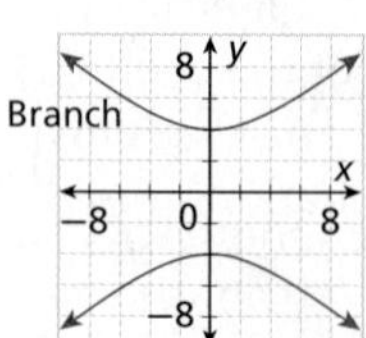

ENGLISH	SPANISH	EXAMPLES

census A survey of an entire population.	**censo** Estudio de una población entera.	
circle The set of points in a plane that are a fixed distance from a given point called the center of the circle.	**círculo** Conjunto de puntos en un plano que se encuentran a una distancia fija de un punto determinado denominado centro del círculo.	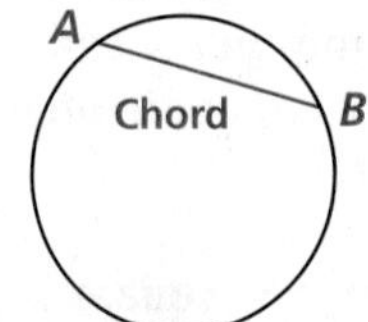
circumference The distance around a circle.	**circunferencia** Distancia alrededor del círculo.	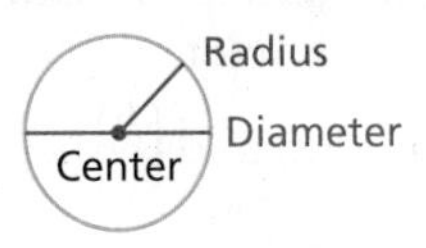
cluster sample A sample in which the population is first divided into groups, a sample of the groups is randomly chosen, and all members of the chosen groups are surveyed.	**muestra por grupos** Muestra en la que la población se divide primeramente en grupos, se elige al azar una muestra de los grupos y se estudia a todos los miembros de los grupos elegidos.	
coefficient matrix The matrix of the coefficients of the variables in a linear system of equations.	**matriz de coeficientes** Matriz de los coeficientes de las variables en un sistema lineal de ecuaciones.	System of equations: $2x + 3y = 11$, $5x - 4y = 16$; Coefficient matrix: $\begin{bmatrix} 2 & 3 \\ 5 & -4 \end{bmatrix}$
coefficient of determination The number R^2, with $0 \le R^2 \le 1$, that shows the fraction of the data that are close to the curve of best fit and, thus, how well the curve fits the data.	**coeficiente de determinación** El número R^2, con $0 \le R^2 \le 1$, que muestra la fracción de los datos cercanos a la línea de mejor ajuste y, por lo tanto, cuánto se ajusta la línea de mejor ajuste a los datos.	
combination A selection of a group of objects in which order is *not* important. The number of combinations of r objects chosen from a group of n objects is denoted ${}_nC_r$.	**combinación** Selección de un grupo de objetos en la cual el orden *no* es importante. El número de combinaciones de r objetos elegidos de un grupo de n objetos se expresa así: ${}_nC_r$.	For 4 objects *A, B, C,* and *D,* there are ${}_4C_2 = 6$ different combinations of 2 objects: *AB, AC, AD, BC, BD, CD.*
combined variation A relationship containing both direct and inverse variation.	**variación combinada** Relación que contiene variaciones directas e inversas.	$y = \frac{kx}{z}$, where k is the constant of variation
common difference In an arithmetic sequence, the nonzero constant difference of any term and the previous term.	**diferencia común** En una sucesión aritmética, diferencia constante distinta de cero entre cualquier término y el término anterior.	In the arithmetic sequence 3, 5, 7, 9, 11, ..., the common difference is 2.
common logarithm A logarithm whose base is 10, denoted $\log_{10}$ or just log.	**logaritmo común** Logaritmo de base 10, que se expresa $\log_{10}$ o simplemente log.	$\log 100 = \log_{10}100 = 2$, since $10^2 = 100$.

ENGLISH	SPANISH	EXAMPLES
common ratio In a geometric sequence, the constant ratio of any term and the previous term.	**razón común** En una sucesión geométrica, la razón constante r entre cualquier término y el término anterior.	In the geometric sequence 32, 16, 18, 4, 2 ..., the common ratio is $\frac{1}{2}$.
complement of an event All outcomes in the sample space that are not in an event E, denoted $\overline{E}$.	**complemento de un suceso** Todos los resultados en el espacio muestral que no están en el suceso E y se expresan $\overline{E}$.	In the experiment of rolling a number cube, the complement of rolling a 3 is rolling a 1, 2, 4, 5, or 6.
completing the square A process used to form a perfect-square trinomial. To complete the square of $x^2 + bx$, add $\left(\frac{b}{2}\right)^2$.	**completar el cuadrado** Proceso utilizado para formar un trinomio cuadrado perfecto. Para completar el cuadrado de $x^2 + bx$, hay que sumar $\left(\frac{b}{2}\right)^2$.	$x^2 + 6x + \blacksquare$ Add $\left(\frac{6}{2}\right)^2 = 9$. $x^2 + 6x + 9$ $(x + 3)^2$ *is a perfect square.*
complex conjugate The complex conjugate of any complex number $a + bi$, denoted $\overline{a + bi}$, is $a - bi$.	**conjugado complejo** El conjugado complejo de cualquier número complejo $a + bi$, expresado como $\overline{a + bi}$, es $a - bi$.	$\overline{4 + 3i} = 4 - 3i$ $\overline{4 - 3i} = 4 + 3i$
complex fraction A fraction that contains one or more fractions in the numerator, the denominator, or both.	**fracción compleja** Fracción que contiene una o más fracciones en el numerador, en el denominador, o en ambos.	$\dfrac{\frac{1}{2}}{1 + \frac{2}{3}}$
complex number Any number that can be written as $a + bi$, where a and b are real numbers and $i = \sqrt{-1}$.	**número complejo** Todo número que se puede expresar como $a + bi$, donde a y b son números reales e $i = \sqrt{-1}$.	$4 + 2i$ $5 + 0i = 5$ $0 - 7i = -7i$
complex plane A set of coordinate axes in which the horizontal axis is the real axis and the vertical axis is the imaginary axis; used to graph complex numbers.	**plano complejo** Conjunto de ejes cartesianos en el cual el eje horizontal es el eje real y el eje vertical es el eje imaginario; se utiliza para representar gráficamente números complejos.	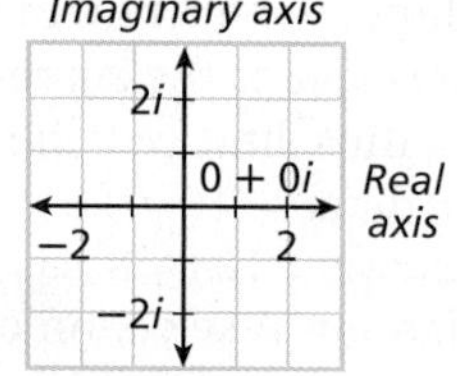
composite figure A plane figure made up of triangles, rectangles, trapezoids, circles, and other simple shapes, or a three-dimensional figure made up of prisms, cones, pyramids, cylinders, and other simple three-dimensional figures.	**figura compuesta** Figura plana compuesta por triángulos, rectángulos, trapecios, círculos y otras formas simples, o figura tridimensional compuesta por prismas, conos, pirámides, cilindros y otras figuras tridimensionales simples.	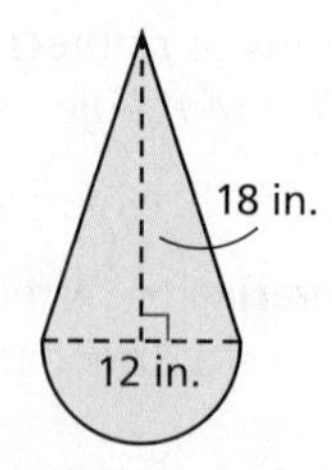
composition of functions The composition of functions f and g, written as $(f \circ g)(x)$ and defined as $f(g(x))$ uses the output of $g(x)$ as the input for $f(x)$.	**composición de funciones** La composición de las funciones f y g, expresada como $(f \circ g)(x)$ y definida como $f(g(x))$ utiliza la salida de $g(x)$ como la entrada para $f(x)$.	If $f(x) = x^2$ and $g(x) = x + 1$, the composite function $(f \circ g)(x) = (x + 1)^2$.
compound event An event made up of two or more simple events.	**suceso compuesto** Suceso formado por dos o más sucesos simples.	In the experiment of tossing a coin and rolling a number cube, the event of the coin landing heads and the number cube landing on 3.

ENGLISH	SPANISH	EXAMPLES
compression A transformation that pushes the points of a graph horizontally toward the y-axis or vertically toward the x-axis.	**compresión** Transformación que desplaza los puntos de una gráfica horizontalmente hacia el eje y o verticalmente hacia el eje x.	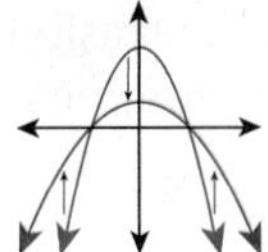
conditional probability The probability of event B, given that event A has already occurred or is certain to occur, denoted $P(B \mid A)$; used to find probability of dependent events.	**probabilidad condicional** Probabilidad del suceso B, dado que el suceso A ya ha ocurrido o es seguro que ocurrirá, expresada como $P(B \mid A)$; se utiliza para calcular la probabilidad de sucesos dependientes.	
conditional relative frequency The ratio of a joint relative frequency to a related marginal relative frequency in a two-way table.	**frecuencia relativa condicional** Razón de una frecuencia relativa conjunta a una frecuencia relativa marginal en una tabla de doble entrada.	
congruent Having the same size and shape, denoted by ≅.	**congruente** Que tiene el mismo tamaño y forma, expresado por ≅.	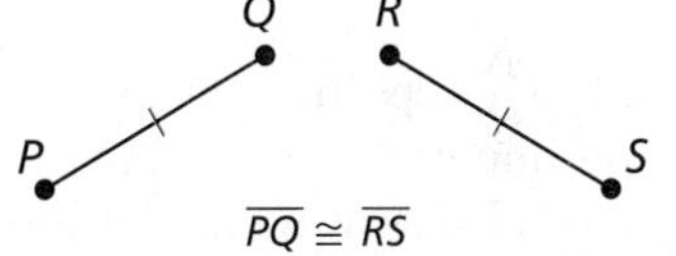 $\overline{PQ} \cong \overline{RS}$
conic section A plane figure formed by the intersection of a double right cone and a plane. Examples include circles, ellipses, hyperbolas, and parabolas.	**sección cónica** Figura plana formada por la intersección de un cono regular doble y un plano. Algunos ejemplos son círculos, elipses, hipérbolas y parábolas.	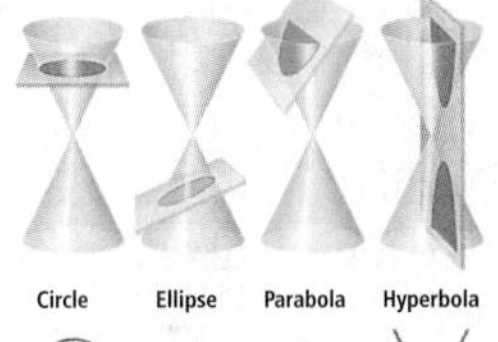
conjugate axis The axis of symmetry of a hyperbola that separates the two branches of the hyperbola.	**eje conjugado** Eje de simetría de una hipérbola que separa las dos ramas de la hipérbola.	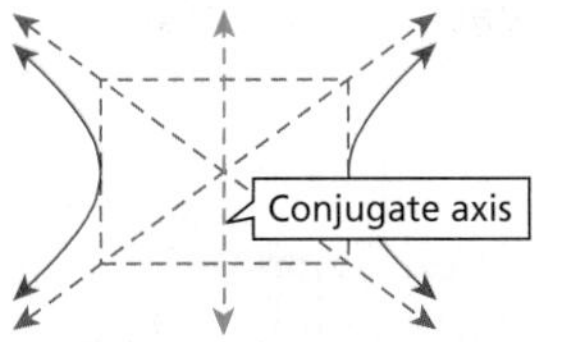
constant function A function of the form $f(x) = c$, where c is a constant.	**función constante** Función del tipo $f(x) = c$, donde c es una constante.	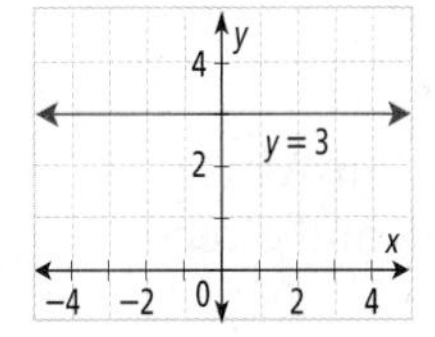
constant matrix The matrix of the constants in a linear system of equations.	**matriz de constantes** Matriz de las constantes de un sistema lineal de ecuaciones.	System of equations: $\begin{cases} 2x + 3y = 11 \\ 5x - 4y = 16 \end{cases}$ Constant matrix: $\begin{bmatrix} 11 \\ 16 \end{bmatrix}$
constant of variation The constant k in direct, inverse, joint, and combined variation equations.	**constante de variación** La constante k en ecuaciones de variación directa, inversa, conjunta y combinada.	$y = 5x$ ↑ constant of variation

ENGLISH	SPANISH	EXAMPLES
constraint One of the inequalities that define the feasible region in a linear-programming problem.	**restricción** Una de las desigualdades que definen la región factible en un problema de programación lineal.	Constraints: $x > 0$ $y > 0$ $x + y \leq 8$ $3x + 5y \leq 30$ 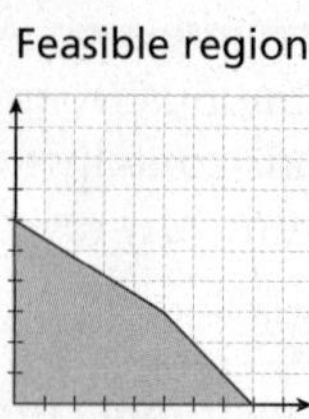
continuous data Data that can take on any real-value measurement within an interval.	**datos continuos** Datos obtenidos por medición que pueden asumir cualquier valor real dentro de un intervalo.	The quantity of water in a glass as the water evaporates is continuous data.
continuous function A function whose graph is an unbroken line or curve with no gaps or breaks.	**función continua** Función cuya gráfica es una línea recta o curva continua, sin espacios ni interrupciones.	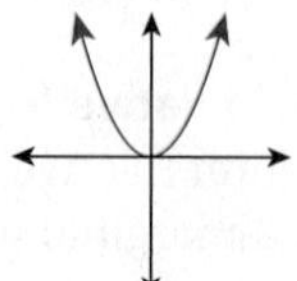
contradiction An equation that has no solutions.	**contradicción** Ecuación que no tiene soluciones.	$x + 1 = x$ $1 = 0$ ✗
control group In a controlled experiment, the group that does not receive treatment. This group is used for comparison.	**grupo de control** En un experimento controlado, el grupo que no está expuesto a la manipulación; es el grupo que sirve como comparación.	
controlled experiment An experiment in which two groups are studied under conditions that are identical except for one variable.	**experimento controlado** Experimento en el que se estudia a dos grupos bajo condiciones que son idénticas, excepto por una variable.	
converge An infinite series converges when the partial sums approach a fixed number.	**convergir** Una sucesión o serie infinita converge cuando las sumas parciales se aproximan a un número fijo.	$\frac{1}{2} + \frac{1}{4} + \frac{1}{8} + \frac{1}{16} + \ldots$ converges to 1.
convenience sample A sample based on members of the population that are readily available.	**muestra de conveniencia** Una muestra basada en miembros de la población que están fácilmente disponibles.	A reporter surveys people he personally knows.
correlation A measure of the strength and direction of the relationship between two variables or data sets.	**correlación** Medida de la fuerza y dirección de la relación entre dos variables o conjuntos de datos.	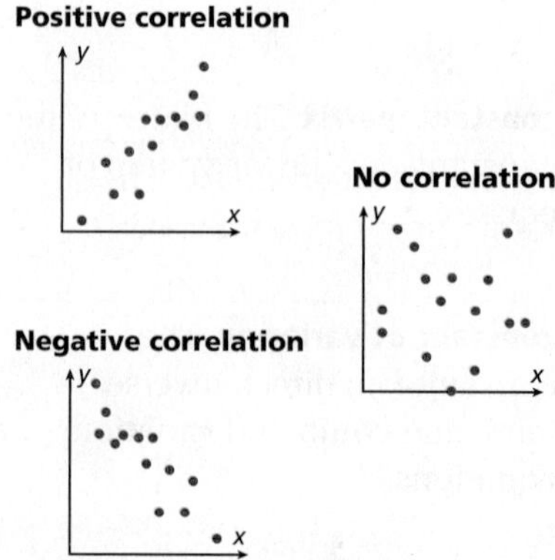

ENGLISH	SPANISH	EXAMPLES
correlation coefficient A number r, where $-1 \le r \le 1$, that describes how closely the points in a scatter plot cluster around the least-squares line.	**coeficiente de correlación** Número r, donde $-1 \le r \le 1$, que describe a qué distancia de la recta de mínimos cuadrados se agrupan los puntos de un diagrama de dispersión.	An r-value close to 1 describes a strong positive correlation. An r-value close to 0 describes a weak correlation or no correlation. An r-value close to -1 describes a strong negative correlation.
cosecant In a right triangle, the cosecant of angle A is the ratio of the length of the hypotenuse to the length of the side opposite A. It is the reciprocal of the sine function.	**cosecante** En un triángulo rectángulo, la cosecante del ángulo A es la razón entre la longitud de la hipotenusa y la longitud del cateto opuesto a A. Es la inversa de la función seno.	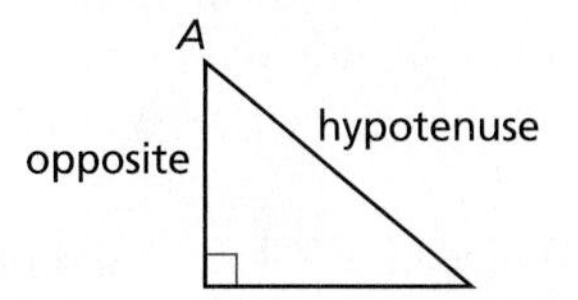 $\csc A = \frac{\text{hypotenuse}}{\text{opposite}} = \frac{1}{\sin A}$
cosine In a right triangle, the cosine of angle A is the ratio of the length of the side adjacent to angle A to the length of the hypotenuse. It is the reciprocal of the secant function.	**coseno** En un triángulo rectángulo, el coseno del ángulo A es la razón entre la longitud del cateto adyacente al ángulo A y la longitud de la hipotenusa. Es la inversa de la función secante.	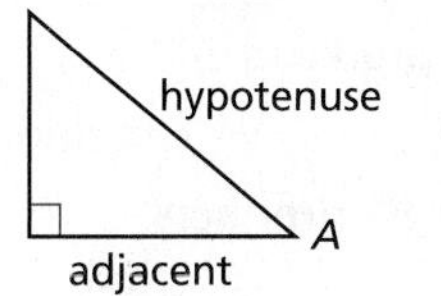 $\cos A = \frac{\text{adjacent}}{\text{hypotenuse}} = \frac{1}{\sec A}$
cotangent In a right triangle, the cotangent of angle A is the ratio of the length of the side adjacent to A to the length of the side opposite A. It is the reciprocal of the tangent function.	**cotangente** En un triángulo rectángulo, la cotangente del ángulo A es la razón entre la longitud del cateto adyacente a A y la longitud del cateto opuesto a A. Es la inversa de la función tangente.	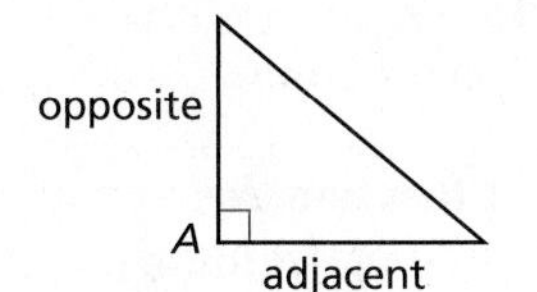 $\cot A = \frac{\text{adjacent}}{\text{opposite}} = \frac{1}{\tan A}$
coterminal angles Two angles in standard position with the same terminal side.	**ángulos coterminales** Dos ángulos en posición estándar con el mismo lado terminal.	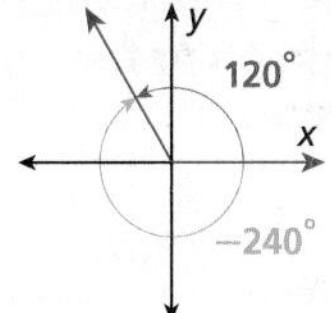
counterexample An example that proves that a conjecture or statement is false.	**contraejemplo** Ejemplo que demuestra que una conjetura o enunciado es falso.	
co-vertices of a hyperbola The endpoints of the conjugate axis.	**co-vértices de una hipérbola** Extremos de un eje conjugado.	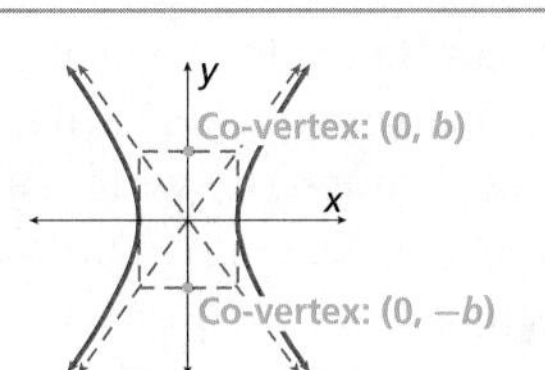
co-vertices of an ellipse The endpoints of the minor axis.	**co-vértices de una elipse** Extremos del eje menor.	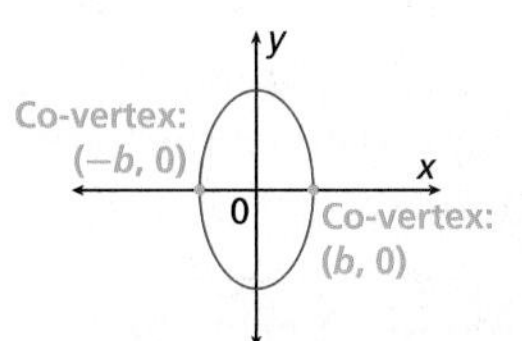

ENGLISH	SPANISH	EXAMPLES
Cramer's rule A method of solving systems of linear equations by using determinants.	**regla de Cramer** Método para resolver sistemas de ecuaciones lineales utilizando determinantes.	For the system $\begin{cases} x - y = 3 \\ 2x - y = -1 \end{cases}$, $D = \begin{vmatrix} 1 & -1 \\ 2 & -1 \end{vmatrix} = 1(-1) - 2(-1) = 1$; $x = \dfrac{\begin{vmatrix} c_1 & b_1 \\ c_2 & b_2 \end{vmatrix}}{D} = \dfrac{\begin{vmatrix} 3 & -1 \\ -1 & -1 \end{vmatrix}}{1} = \dfrac{-3 - 1}{1} = -4$; $y = \dfrac{\begin{vmatrix} a_1 & c_1 \\ a_2 & c_2 \end{vmatrix}}{D} = \dfrac{\begin{vmatrix} 1 & 3 \\ 2 & -1 \end{vmatrix}}{1} = \dfrac{-1 - 6}{1} = -7$
critical values Values that separate the number line into intervals that either contain solutions or do not contain solutions.	**valores críticos** Valores que separan la recta numérica en intervalos que contienen o no contienen soluciones.	
cross products In the statement $\frac{a}{b} = \frac{c}{d}$, *bc* and *ad* are the cross products.	**productos cruzados** En el enunciado $\frac{a}{b} = \frac{c}{d}$, *bc* y *ad* son los productos cruzados.	$\frac{1}{2} = \frac{3}{6}$ Cross products: $2 \cdot 3 = 6$ and $1 \cdot 6 = 6$
cube-root function The function $f(x) = \sqrt[3]{x}$.	**función de raíz cúbica** La función $f(x) = \sqrt[3]{x}$.	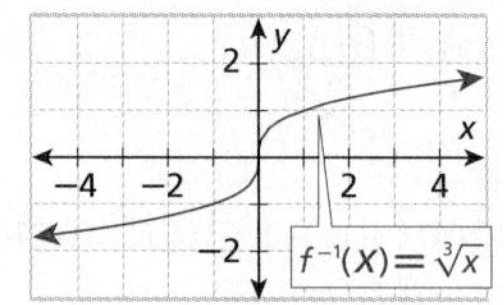
cubic function A polynomial function of degree 3.	**función cúbica** Función polinomial de grado 3.	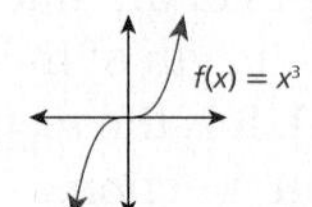
cycle of a periodic function The shortest repeating part of a periodic graph or function.	**ciclo de una función periódica** La parte repetida más corta de una gráfica o función periódica.	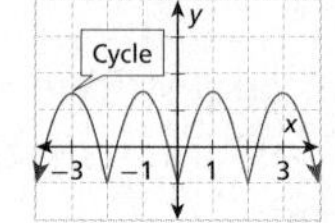

D

ENGLISH	SPANISH	EXAMPLES
decay factor The base $1 - r$ in an exponential expression.	**factor decremental** Base $1 - r$ en una expresión exponencial.	$2(0.93)^t$ ↑ decay factor (representing $1 - 0.07$)
degenerate conic A degenerate conic is formed when a plane passes through the vertex of a hollow double cone. A point, a line, and a pair of intersecting lines are all degenerate conics.	**cónica degenerada** Una cónica degenerada se forma cuando un plano atraviesa el vértice de un cono doble hueco. Un punto, una línea y un par de líneas secantes son cónicas degeneradas.	A point is a circle with no radius.
degree of a monomial The sum of the exponents of the variables in the monomial.	**grado de un monomio** Suma de los exponentes de las variables del monomio.	$4x^2y^5z^3$ Degree: $2 + 5 + 3 = 10$; 5 Degree: 0 $(5 = 5x^0)$
degree of a polynomial The degree of the term of the polynomial with the greatest degree.	**grado de un polinomio** Grado del término del polinomio con el grado máximo.	$3x^2y^2 + 4xy^5 - 12x^3y^2$ Degree 6 (Degree 4, Degree 6, Degree 5)

ENGLISH	SPANISH	EXAMPLES
dependent events Events for which the occurrence or nonoccurrence of one event affects the probability of the other event.	**sucesos dependientes** Dos sucesos son dependientes si el hecho de que uno de ellos se cumpla o no afecta la probabilidad del otro.	From a bag containing 3 red marbles and 2 blue marbles, drawing a red marble, and then drawing a blue marble without replacing the first marble.
dependent system A system of equations that has infinitely many solutions.	**sistema dependiente** Sistema de ecuaciones que tiene infinitamente muchas soluciones.	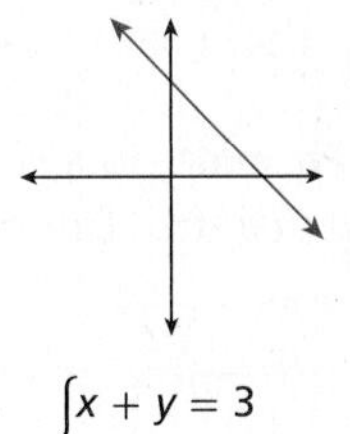 $\begin{cases} x + y = 3 \\ 2x + 2y = 6 \end{cases}$
dependent variable The output of a function; a variable whose value depends on the value of the input, or independent variable.	**variable dependiente** Salida de una función; variable cuyo valor depende del valor de la entrada, o variable independiente.	$y = 2x + 1$ ↑ dependent variable
determinant A real number associated with a square matrix. The determinant of $A = \begin{bmatrix} a & b \\ c & d \end{bmatrix}$ is $\lvert A \rvert = ad - bc$.	**determinante** Número real asociado con una matriz cuadrada. El determinante de $A = \begin{bmatrix} a & b \\ c & d \end{bmatrix}$ es $\lvert A \rvert = ad - bc$.	$\begin{vmatrix} 2 & -1 \\ 3 & 4 \end{vmatrix} = 2(4) - (-1)(3) = 11$
difference of two squares A polynomial of the form $a^2 - b^2$, which may be written as the product $(a + b)(a - b)$.	**diferencia de dos cuadrados** Polinomio del tipo $a^2 - b^2$, que se puede expresar como el producto $(a + b)(a - b)$.	$x^2 - 4 = (x + 2)(x - 2)$
dimensions of a matrix A matrix with m rows and n columns has dimensions $m \times n$, read "m by n."	**dimensiones de una matriz** Una matriz con m filas y n columnas tiene dimensiones $m \times n$, expresadas "m por n".	$\begin{bmatrix} -3 & 2 & 1 & -1 \\ 4 & 0 & -5 & 2 \end{bmatrix}$ Dimensions 2×4
direct variation A linear relationship between two variables, x and y, that can be written in the form $y = kx$, where k is a nonzero constant.	**variación directa** Relación lineal entre dos variables, x e y, que puede expresarse en la forma $y = kx$, donde k es una constante distinta de cero.	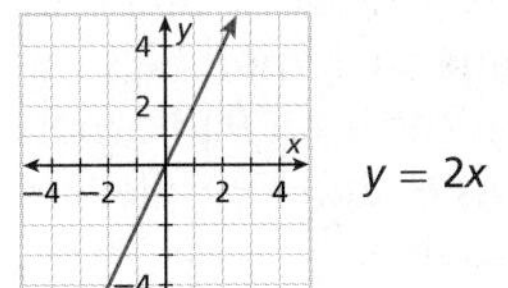 $y = 2x$
directrix A fixed line used to define a *parabola.* Every point on the parabola is equidistant from the directrix and a fixed point called the *focus.*	**directriz** Línea fija utilizada para definir una *parábola.* Cada punto de la parábola es equidistante de la directriz y de un punto fijo denominado *foco.*	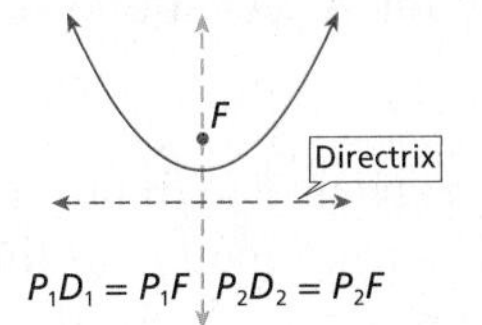
discontinuous function A function whose graph has one or more jumps, breaks, or holes.	**función discontinua** Función cuya gráfica tiene uno o más saltos, interrupciones u hoyos.	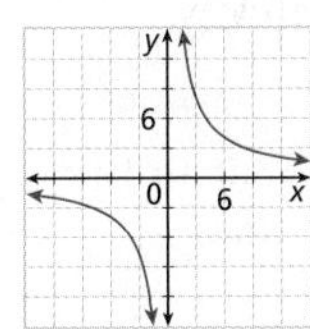
discrete data Data that cannot take on any real-value measurement within an interval.	**datos discretos** Datos que no admiten cualquier medida de valores reales dentro de un intervalo.	the number of pennies in a jar over time

ENGLISH	SPANISH	EXAMPLES
discriminant The discriminant of the quadratic equation $ax^2 + bx + c = 0$ is $b^2 - 4ac$.	**discriminante** El discriminante de la ecuación cuadrática $ax^2 + bx + c = 0$ es $b^2 - 4ac$.	The discriminant of $2x^2 - 5x - 3$ is $(-5)^2 - 4(2)(-3) = 25 + 24 = 49$.
disjunction A compound statement that uses the word *or*.	**disyunción** Enunciado compuesto que contiene la palabra *o*.	John will walk to work OR he will stay home.
Distance Formula In a coordinate plane, the distance from (x_1, y_1) to (x_2, y_2) is $d = \sqrt{(x_2 - x_1)^2 + (y_2 - y_1)^2}$.	**Fórmula de distancia** En un plano cartesiano, la distancia desde (x_1, y_1) hasta (x_2, y_2) es $d = \sqrt{(x_2 - x_1)^2 + (y_2 - y_1)^2}$.	The distance from (2, 1) to (6, 4) is $d = \sqrt{(6-2)^2 + (4-1)^2} = \sqrt{4^2 + 3^2} = \sqrt{9 + 16} = 5$.
diverge An infinite series diverges when the partial sums do not approach a fixed number.	**divergir** Una serie infinita diverge cuando las sumas parciales no se aproximan a un número fijo.	$1 + 2 + 4 + 8 + 16 + \ldots$ diverges.
domain The set of all possible input values of a relation or function.	**dominio** Conjunto de todos los posibles valores de entrada de una función o relación.	The domain of the function $f(x) = \sqrt{x}$ is $\{x \mid x \geq 0\}$.

ENGLISH	SPANISH	EXAMPLES
element of a set An item in a set.	**elemento de un conjunto** Componente de un conjunto.	4 is an element of the set of even numbers. $4 \in \{\text{even numbers}\}$
elimination A method used to solve systems of equations in which one variable is eliminated by adding or subtracting two equations of the system.	**eliminación** Método utilizado para resolver sistemas de ecuaciones por el cual se elimina una variable sumando o restando dos ecuaciones del sistema.	
ellipse The set of all points *P* in a plane such that the sum of the distances from *P* to two fixed points F_1 and F_2, called the foci, is constant.	**elipse** Conjunto de todos los puntos *P* de un plano tal que la suma de las distancias desde *P* hasta los dos puntos fijos F_1 y F_2, denominados focos, es constante.	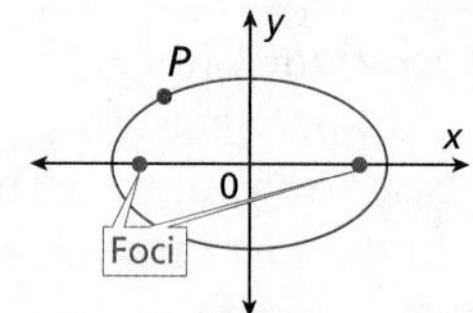
empty set A set with no elements.	**conjunto vacío** Conjunto sin elementos.	The solution set of $\|x\| < 0$ is the empty set, $\{\ \}$, or $\varnothing$.
end behavior The trends in the *y*-values of a function as the *x*-values approach positive and negative infinity.	**comportamiento extremo** Tendencia de los valores de *y* de una función a medida que los valores de *x* se aproximan al infinito positivo y negativo.	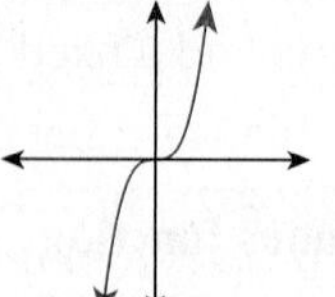 End behavior: $f(x) \to \infty$ as $x \to \infty$; $f(x) \to -\infty$ as $x \to -\infty$
entry Each value in a matrix; also called an element.	**entrada** Cada valor de una matriz; también denominado elemento.	3 is the entry in the first row and second column of $A = \begin{bmatrix} 2 & 3 \\ 0 & 1 \end{bmatrix}$, denoted a_{12}.

ENGLISH	SPANISH	EXAMPLES
equally likely outcomes Outcomes are equally likely if they have the same probability of occurring. If an experiment has n equally likely outcomes, then the probability of each outcome is $\frac{1}{n}$.	**resultados igualmente probables** Los resultados son igualmente probables si tienen la misma probabilidad de ocurrir. Si un experimento tiene n resultados igualmente probables, entonces la probabilidad de cada resultado es $\frac{1}{n}$.	If a coin is tossed, and heads and tails are equally likely, then $P(\text{heads}) = P(\text{tails}) = \frac{1}{2}$.
equation A mathematical statement that two expressions are equivalent.	**ecuación** Enunciado matemático que indica que dos expresiones son equivalentes.	$x + 4 = 7$ $2 + 3 = 6 - 1$ $(x - 1)^2 + (y + 2)^2 = 4$
evaluate To find the value of an algebraic expression by substituting a number for each variable and simplifying by using the order of operations.	**evaluar** Calcular el valor de una expresión algebraica sustituyendo cada variable por un número y simplificando mediante el orden de las operaciones.	Evaluate $2x + 7$ for $x = 3$. $2x + 7$ $2(3) + 7$ $6 + 7$ 13
event An outcome or set of outcomes in a probability experiment.	**suceso** Resultado o conjunto de resultados en un experimento de probabilidad.	In the experiment of rolling a number cube, the event "an odd number" consists of the outcomes 1, 3, and 5.
expected value The weighted average of the numerical outcomes of a probability experiment.	**valor esperado** Promedio ponderado de los resultados numéricos de un experimento de probabilidad.	The table shows the probability of getting a given score by guessing on a three-question quiz. **Score**: 0, 1, 2, 3 **Probability**: 0.42, 0.42, 0.14, 0.02 The expected value is a score of $0(0.42) + 1(0.42) + 2(0.14) + 3(0.02) = 0.76$.
experiment An operation, process, or activity in which outcomes can be used to estimate probability.	**experimento** Una operación, proceso o actividad cuyo resultado se puede usar para estimar la probabilidad.	Tossing a coin 10 times and noting the number of heads.
experimental probability The ratio of the number of times an event occurs to the number of trials, or times, that an activity is performed.	**probabilidad experimental** Razón entre la cantidad de veces que ocurre un suceso y la cantidad de pruebas, o veces, que se realiza una actividad.	Kendra made 6 of 10 free throws. The experimental probability that she will make her next free throw is $P(\text{free throw}) = \frac{\text{number made}}{\text{number attempted}} = \frac{6}{10}$.
explicit formula A formula that defines the nth term a_n, or general term, of a sequence as a function of n.	**fórmula explícita** Fórmula que define el enésimo término a_n, o término general, de una sucesión como una función de n.	Sequence: 4, 7, 10, 13, 16, 19, ... Explicit formula: $a_n = 1 + 3n$
exponent The number that indicates how many times the base in a power is used as a factor.	**exponente** Número que indica la cantidad de veces que la base de una potencia se utiliza como factor.	$3^4 = 3 \cdot 3 \cdot 3 \cdot 3 = 81$ ↑ exponent
exponential decay An exponential function of the form $f(x) = ab^x$ in which $0 < b < 1$. If r is the rate of decay, then the function can be written $y = a(1 - r)^t$, where a is the initial amount and t is the time.	**decremento exponencial** Función exponencial del tipo $f(x) = ab^x$ en la cual $0 < b < 1$. Si r es la tasa decremental, entonces la función se puede expresar como $y = a(1 - r)^t$, donde a es la cantidad inicial y t es el tiempo.	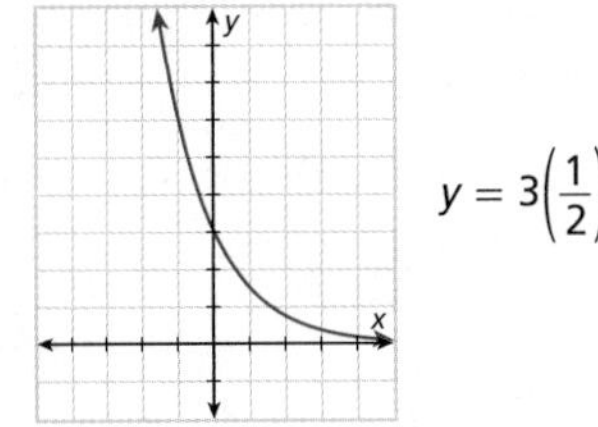 $y = 3\left(\frac{1}{2}\right)^x$

ENGLISH	SPANISH	EXAMPLES
exponential equation An equation that contains one or more exponential expressions.	**ecuación exponencial** Ecuación que contiene una o más expresiones exponenciales.	$2^{x+1} = 8$
exponential function A function of the form $f(x) = ab^x$, where a and b are real numbers with $a \neq 0$, $b > 0$, and $b \neq 1$.	**función exponencial** Función del tipo $f(x) = ab^x$, donde a y b son números reales con $a \neq 0$, $b > 0$ y $b \neq 1$.	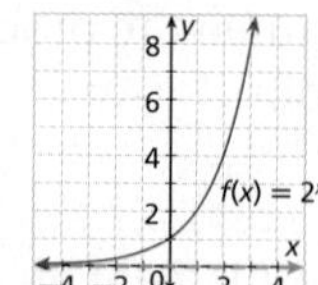
exponential growth An exponential function of the form $f(x) = ab^x$ in which $b > 1$. If r is the rate of growth, then the function can be written $y = a(1 + r)^t$, where a is the initial amount and t is the time.	**crecimiento exponencial** Función exponencial del tipo $f(x) = a$ b^x en la que $b > 1$. Si r es la tasa de crecimiento, entonces la función se puede expresar como $y = a(1 + r)^t$, donde a es la cantidad inicial y t es el tiempo.	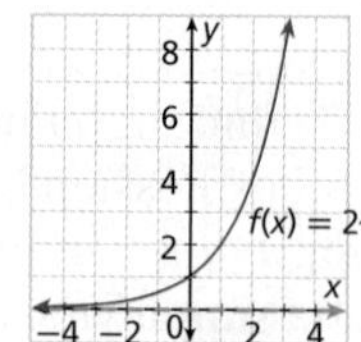
exponential regression A statistical method used to fit an exponential model to a given data set.	**regresión exponencial** Método estadístico utilizado para ajustar un modelo exponencial a un conjunto de datos determinado.	
extraneous solution A solution of a derived equation that is not a solution of the original equation.	**solución extraña** Solución de una ecuación derivada que no es una solución de la ecuación original.	To solve $\sqrt{x} = -2$, square both sides; $x = 4$. ***Check*** $\sqrt{4} = -2$ is false; so 4 is an extraneous solution.

ENGLISH	SPANISH	EXAMPLES
Factor Theorem For any polynomial $P(x)$, $(x - a)$ is a factor of $P(x)$ if and only if $P(a) = 0$.	**Teorema del factor** Dado el polinomio $P(x)$, $(x - a)$ es un factor de $P(x)$ si y sólo si $P(a) = 0$.	$(x - 1)$ is a factor of $P(x) = x^2 - 1$ because $P(1) = 1^2 - 1 = 0$.
factorial If n is a positive integer, then n factorial, written $n!$, is $n \cdot (n-1) \cdot (n-2) \cdot \ldots \cdot 2 \cdot 1$. The factorial of 0 is defined to be 1.	**factorial** Si n es un entero positivo, entonces el factorial de n, expresado como $n!$, es $n \cdot (n-1) \cdot (n-2) \cdot \ldots \cdot 2 \cdot 1$. Por definición, el factorial de 0 será 1.	$7! = 7 \cdot 6 \cdot 5 \cdot 4 \cdot 3 \cdot 2 \cdot 1 = 5040$ $0! = 1$
factoring The process of writing a number or algebraic expression as a product.	**factorización** Proceso por el que se expresa un número o expresión algebraica como un producto.	$x^2 - 4x - 21 = (x - 7)(x + 3)$
family of functions A set of functions whose graphs have basic characteristics in common. Functions in the same family are transformations of their parent function.	**familia de funciones** Conjunto de funciones cuyas gráficas tienen características básicas en común. Las funciones de la misma familia son transformaciones de su función madre.	Some members of the family of quadratic functions with the parent function $f(x) = x^2$ are: $f(x) = 3x^2$ $f(x) = x^2 + 1$ $f(x) = (x - 2)^2$ 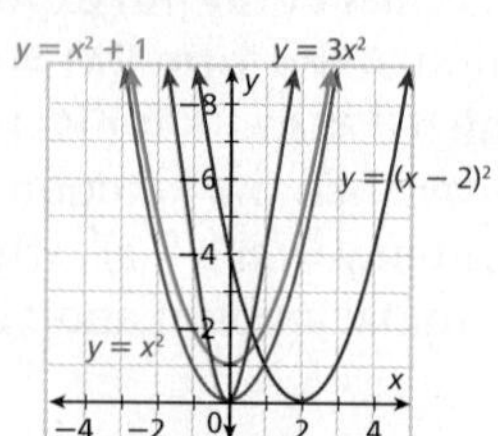

ENGLISH	SPANISH	EXAMPLES
favorable outcome The occurrence of one of several possible outcomes of a specified event or probability experiment.	**resultado favorable** Cuando se produce uno de varios resultados posibles de un suceso específico o experimento de probabilidad.	In the experiment of rolling an odd number on a number cube, the favorable outcomes are 1, 3, and 5.
feasible region The set of points that satisfy the constraints in a linear-programming problem.	**región factible** Conjunto de puntos que cumplen con las restricciones de un problema de programación lineal.	Constraints: $x > 0$ $y > 0$ $x + y \leq 8$ $3x + 5y \leq 30$ Feasible region 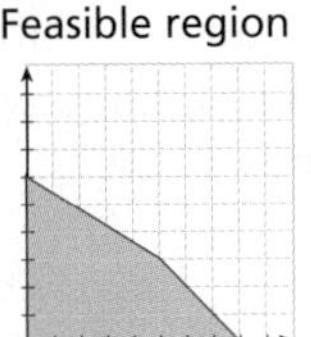
Fibonacci sequence The infinite sequence of numbers beginning with 1, 1 such that each term is the sum of the two previous terms.	**sucesión de Fibonacci** Sucesión infinita de números que comienza con 1, 1 de forma tal que cada término es la suma de los dos términos anteriores.	1, 1, 2, 3, 5, 8, 13, 21, ...
finite sequence A sequence with a finite number of terms.	**sucesión finita** Sucesión con un número finito de términos.	1, 2, 3, 4, 5
finite set A set with a definite, or finite, number of elements.	**conjunto finito** Conjunto con un número de elementos definido o finito.	$\{2, 4, 6, 8, 10\}$
first differences The differences between y-values of a function for evenly spaced x-values.	**primeras diferencias** Diferencias entre los valores de y de una función para valores de x espaciados uniformemente.	x: 0, 1, 2, 3 y: 3, 7, 11, 15 first differences +4 +4 +4
first quartile The median of the lower half of a data set, denoted Q_1. Also called *lower quartile.*	**primer cuartil** Mediana de la mitad inferior de un conjunto de datos, expresada como Q_1. También se llama *cuartil inferior.*	Lower half: 18, (23), 28, | Upper half: 36, 42, 49 First quartile
focus (pl. foci) of a hyperbola One of two fixed points F_1 and F_2 that are used to define a hyperbola. For every point P on the hyperbola, $PF_1 - PF_2$ is constant.	**foco de una hipérbola** Uno de los dos puntos fijos F_1 y F_2 utilizados para definir una hipérbola, Para cada punto P de la hipérbola, $PF_1 - PF_2$ es constante.	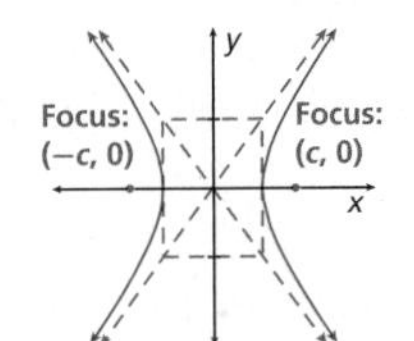
focus (pl. foci) of an ellipse One of two fixed points F_1 and F_2 that are used to define an ellipse. For every point P on the ellipse, $PF_1 + PF_2$ is constant.	**foco de una elipse** Uno de los dos puntos fijos F_1 y F_2 utilizados para definir una elipse. Para cada punto P de la elipse, $PF_1 + PF_2$ es constante.	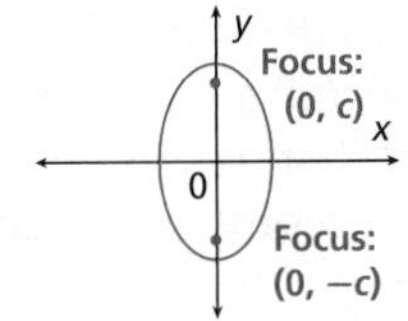
focus (pl. foci) of a parabola A fixed point F used with a *directrix* to define a *parabola.*	**foco de una parábola** Punto fijo F utilizado con una *directriz* para definir una *parábola.*	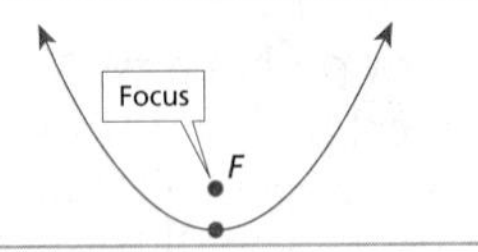
frequency of a data value The number of times the value appears in the data set.	**frecuencia de un valor de datos** Cantidad de veces que aparece el valor en un conjunto de datos.	In the data set 5, 6, 6, 6, 8, 9, the data value 6 has a frequency of 3.

ENGLISH	SPANISH	EXAMPLES
frequency of a periodic function The number of cycles per unit of time. Also the reciprocal of the period.	**frecuencia de una función periódica** Cantidad de ciclos por unidad de tiempo. También es la inversa del periodo.	The function $y = \sin(2x)$ has a period of π and a frequency of $\frac{1}{\pi}$.
function A relation in which every input is paired with exactly one output.	**función** Una relación en la que cada entrada corresponde exactamente a una salida.	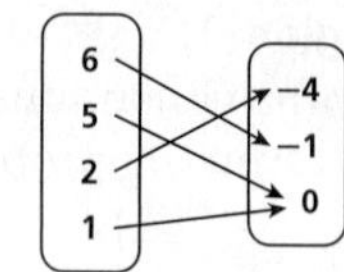
function notation If x is the independent variable and y is the dependent variable, then the function notation for y is $f(x)$, read "f of x," where f names the function.	**notación de función** Si x es la variable independiente e y es la variable dependiente, entonces la notación de función para y es $f(x)$, que se lee "f de x", donde f nombra la función.	equation: $y = 2x$ function notation: $f(x) = 2x$
function rule An algebraic expression that defines a function.	**regla de función** Expresión algebraica que define una función.	$f(x) = 2x^2 + 3x - 7$ ↑ function rule
Fundamental Counting Principle For n items, if there are m_1 ways to choose a first item, m_2 ways to choose a second item after the first item has been chosen, and so on, then there are $m_1 \cdot m_2 \cdot \ldots \cdot m_n$ ways to choose n items.	**Principio fundamental de conteo** Dados n elementos, si existen m_1 formas de elegir un primer elemento, m_2 formas de elegir un segundo elemento después de haber elegido el primero, y así sucesivamente, entonces existen $m_1 \cdot m_2 \cdot \ldots \cdot m_n$ formas de elegir n elementos.	If there are 4 colors of shirts, 3 colors of pants, and 2 colors of shoes, then there are $4 \cdot 3 \cdot 2 = 24$ possible outfits.

ENGLISH	SPANISH	EXAMPLES
general form of a conic section $Ax^2 + Bxy + Cy^2 + Dx + Ey + F = 0$, where A and B are not both 0.	**forma general de una sección cónica** $Ax^2 + Bxy + Cy^2 + Dx + Ey + F = 0$, donde A y B no son los dos 0.	A circle with a vertex at (1, 2) and radius 3 has the general form $x^2 + y^2 - 2x - 4y - 4 = 0$.
geometric mean In a geometric sequence, a term that comes between two given nonconsecutive terms of the sequence. For positive numbers a and b, the geometric mean is $\sqrt{ab}$.	**media geométrica** En una sucesión geométrica, un término que se encuentra entre dos términos no consecutivos dados de la sucesión. Dados los números positivos a y b, la media geométrica es $\sqrt{ab}$.	The geometric mean of 4 and 9 is $\sqrt{4(9)} = \sqrt{36} = 6$.
geometric probability A form of theoretical probability determined by a ratio of geometric measures such as lengths, areas, or volumes.	**probabilidad geométrica** Una forma de la probabilidad teórica determinada por una razón de medidas geométricas, como longitud, área o volumen.	 The probability of the pointer landing on red is $\frac{2}{9}$.

ENGLISH	SPANISH	EXAMPLES
geometric sequence A sequence in which the ratio of successive terms is a constant r, called the common ratio, where $r \neq 0$ and $r \neq 1$.	**sucesión geométrica** Sucesión en la que la razón de los términos sucesivos es una constante r, denominada razón común, donde $r \neq 0$ y $r \neq 1$.	1, 2, 4, 8, 16, ... (• 2 • 2 • 2 • 2) $r = 2$
geometric series The indicated sum of the terms of a geometric sequence.	**serie geométrica** Suma indicada de los términos de una sucesión geométrica.	$1 + 2 + 4 + 8 + 16 + \ldots$
glide reflection A composition of a translation and a reflection across a line parallel to the translation vector.	**deslizamiento con inversión** Composición de una traslación y una reflexión sobre una línea paralela al vector de traslación.	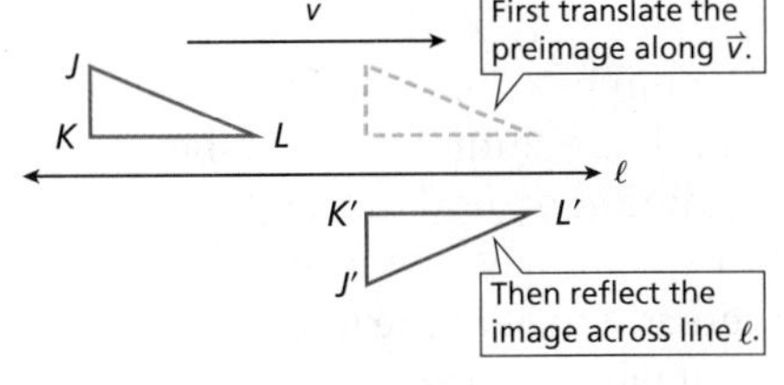
grade A measure of the steepness of surfaces, expressed as a percent.	**grado** Medida de la inclinación de las superficies, expresada como un porcentaje.	A ramp that rises 1 foot for every 5 feet of the horizontal distance has a grade of 20%.
greatest common factor (GCF) The product of the greatest integer and the greatest power of each variable that divides evenly into each term.	**máximo común divisor (MCD)** Producto del entero mayor y la potencia mayor de cada variable que divide exactamente cada término.	The GCF of $4x^3y$ and $6x^2y$ is $2x^2y$. The GCF of 27 and 45 is 9.
greatest-integer function A function denoted by $f(x) = [x]$ or $f(x) = \lfloor x \rfloor$ in which the number x is rounded down to the greatest integer that is less than or equal to x.	**función de entero mayor** Función expresada como $f(x) = [x]$ o $f(x) = \lfloor x \rfloor$ en la cual el número x se redondea hacia abajo hasta el entero mayor que sea menor que o igual a x.	$\lfloor 4.98 \rfloor = 4$ $\lfloor -2.1 \rfloor = -3$
growth factor The base $1 + r$ in an exponential expression.	**factor de crecimiento** La base $1 + r$ en una expresión exponencial.	$12{,}000(1 + 0.14)^t$ — growth factor ($1 + 0.14$)

H

ENGLISH	SPANISH	EXAMPLES
half-life The half-life of a substance is the time it takes for one-half of the substance to decay into another substance.	**vida media** La vida media de una sustancia es el tiempo que tarda la mitad de la sustancia en desintegrarse y transformarse en otra sustancia.	Carbon-14 has a half-life of 5730 years, so 5 g of an initial amount of 10 g will remain after 5730 years.
half-plane The part of the coordinate plane on one side of a line, which may include the line.	**semiplano** Parte del plano cartesiano de un lado de una línea, que puede incluir la línea.	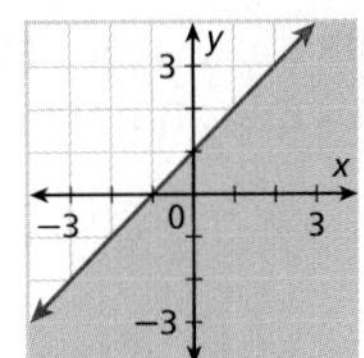

ENGLISH	SPANISH	EXAMPLES
Heron's Formula A triangle with side lengths a, b, and c has area $A = \sqrt{s(s-a)(s-b)(s-c)}$, where s is one-half the perimeter, or $s = \frac{1}{2}(a+b+c)$.	**fórmula de Herón** Un triángulo con longitudes de lado a, b y c tiene un área $A = \sqrt{s(s-a)(s-b)(s-c)}$, donde s es la mitad del perímetro ó $s = \frac{1}{2}(a+b+c)$.	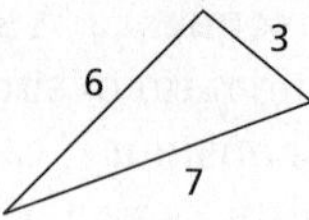 $s = \frac{1}{2}(3+6+7) = 8$ $A = \sqrt{8(8-3)(8-6)(8-7)}$ $= \sqrt{80} = 4\sqrt{5}$ square units
hole (in a graph) An omitted point on a graph. If a rational function has the same factor $x - b$ in both the numerator and the denominator, and the line $x = b$ is not a vertical asymptote, then there is a hole in the graph at the point where $x = b$.	**hoyo (en una gráfica)** Punto omitido en una gráfica. Si una función racional tiene el mismo factor $x - b$ tanto en el numerador como en el denominador, y la línea $x = b$ no es una asíntota vertical, entonces hay un hoyo en la gráfica en el punto donde $x = b$.	$f(x) = \frac{(x-2)(x+2)}{(x+2)}$ has a hole at $x = -2$. 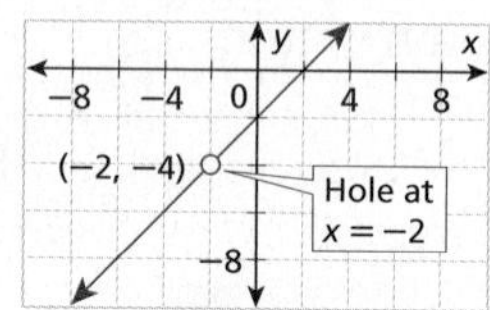
horizontal line A line described by the equation $y = b$, where b is the y-intercept.	**línea horizontal** Línea descrita por la ecuación $y = b$, donde b es la intersección con el eje y.	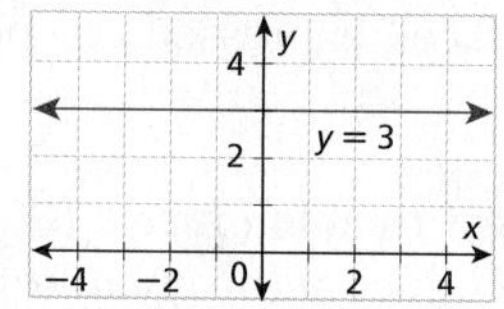
horizontal line test If a horizontal line crosses the graph of a function f at more than one point, then the inverse is not a function.	**prueba de la línea horizontal** Si una línea horizontal cruza la gráfica de una función f en más de un punto, entonces la inversa no es una función.	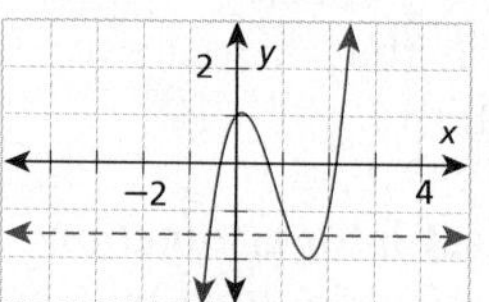 The inverse is not a function.
hyperbola The set of all points P in a plane such that the difference of the distances from P to two fixed points F_1 and F_2, called the foci, is a constant $d = \lvert PF_1 - PF_2 \rvert$.	**hipérbola** Conjunto de todos los puntos P en un plano tal que la diferencia de las distancias de P a dos puntos fijos F_1 y F_2, llamados focos, es una constante $d = \lvert PF_1 - PF_2 \rvert$.	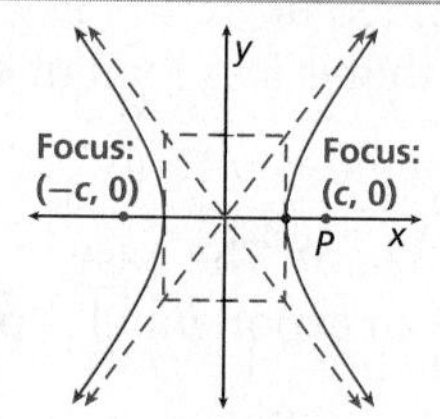
hypothesis testing A type of testing used to determine whether the difference in two groups is likely to be caused by chance.	**comprobación de hipótesis** Tipo de comprobación que sirve para determinar si el azar es la causa probable de la diferencia entre dos grupos.	

I

imaginary axis The vertical axis in the complex plane, it graphically represents the purely imaginary part of complex numbers.	**eje imaginario** Eje vertical de un plano complejo. Representa gráficamente la parte puramente imaginaria de los números complejos.	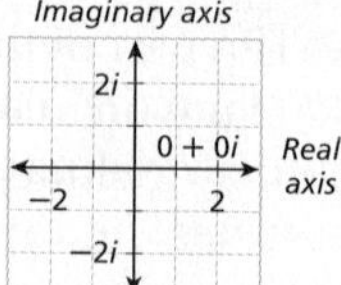

ENGLISH	SPANISH	EXAMPLES
imaginary number The square root of a negative number, written in the form *bi*, where *b* is a real number and *i* is the imaginary unit, $\sqrt{-1}$. Also called a *pure imaginary number.*	**número imaginario** Raíz cuadrada de un número negativo, expresado como *bi*, donde *b* es un número real e *i* es la unidad imaginaria, $\sqrt{-1}$. También se denomina *número imaginario puro.*	$\sqrt{-16} = \sqrt{16} \cdot \sqrt{-1} = 4i$
imaginary part of a complex number For a complex number of the form $a + bi$, the real number *b* is called the imaginary part, represented graphically as *b* units on the imaginary axis of a complex plane.	**parte imaginaria de un número complejo** Dado un número complejo del tipo $a + bi$, el número real *b* se denomina parte imaginaria y se representa gráficamente como *b* unidades en el eje imaginario de un plano complejo.	$5 + 6i$ (real part: 5; imaginary part: 6i)
imaginary unit The unit in the imaginary number system, $\sqrt{-1}$.	**unidad imaginaria** Unidad del sistema de números imaginarios, $\sqrt{-1}$.	$\sqrt{-1} = i$
inclusive events Events that have one or more outcomes in common.	**sucesos inclusivos** Sucesos que tienen uno o más resultados en común.	In the experiment of rolling a number cube, rolling an even number and rolling a number less than 3 are inclusive events because the outcome 2 is both even and less than 3.
inconsistent system A system of equations or inequalities that has no solution.	**sistema inconsistente** Sistema de ecuaciones o desigualdades que no tiene solución.	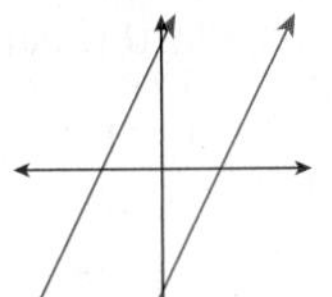 $\begin{cases} y = 2.5x + 5 \\ y = 2.5x - 5 \end{cases}$ is inconsistent.
independent events Events for which the occurrence or non-occurrence of one event does not affect the probability of the other event.	**sucesos independientes** Dos sucesos son independientes si el hecho de que se produzca o no uno de ellos no afecta la probabilidad del otro suceso.	From a bag containing 3 red marbles and 2 blue marbles, drawing a red marble, replacing it, and then drawing a blue marble.
independent system A system of equations that has exactly one solution.	**sistema independiente** Sistema de ecuaciones que tiene exactamente una solución.	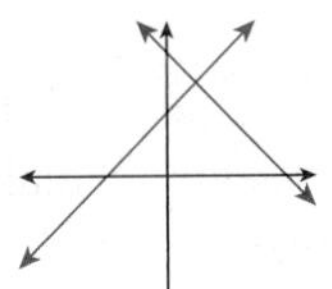 $\begin{cases} y = -x + 4 \\ y = x + 2 \end{cases}$ Solution: (1, 3)
independent variable The input of a function; a variable whose value determines the value of the output, or dependent variable.	**variable independiente** Entrada de una función; variable cuyo valor determina el valor de la salida, o variable dependiente.	$y = 2x + 1$ (independent variable: x)
index In the radical $\sqrt[n]{x}$, which represents the *n*th root of *x*, *n* is the index. In the radical $\sqrt{x}$, the index is understood to be 2.	**índice** En el radical $\sqrt[n]{x}$, que representa la enésima raíz de *x*, *n* es el índice. En el radical $\sqrt{x}$, se da por sentado que el índice es 2.	The radical $\sqrt[3]{8}$ has an index of 3.

ENGLISH	SPANISH	EXAMPLES
indirect measurement A method of measurement that uses formulas, similar figures, and/or proportions.	**medición indirecta** Método para medir objetos mediante fórmulas, figuras semejantes y/o proporciones.	
inequality A statement that compares two expressions by using one of the following signs: <, >, ≤, ≥, or ≠.	**desigualdad** Enunciado que compara dos expresiones utilizando uno de los siguientes signos: <, >, ≤, ≥, ó ≠.	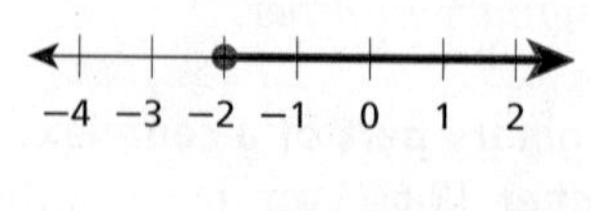 $x \geq -2$
infinite geometric series A geometric series with infinitely many terms.	**serie geométrica infinita** Serie geométrica con una cantidad infinita de términos.	$\frac{1}{10} + \frac{1}{100} + \frac{1}{1000} + \frac{1}{10,000} + \dots$
infinite sequence A sequence with infinitely many terms.	**sucesión infinita** Sucesión con infinitos términos.	1, 3, 5, 7, 9, 11, ...
infinite set A set with an unlimited, or infinite, number of elements.	**conjunto infinito** Conjunto con un número de elementos ilimitado o infinito.	The set of all integers is an infinite set.
initial side The ray that lies on the positive x-axis when an angle is drawn in standard position.	**lado inicial** El rayo que se encuentra en el eje positivo x cuando se traza un ángulo en la posición estándar.	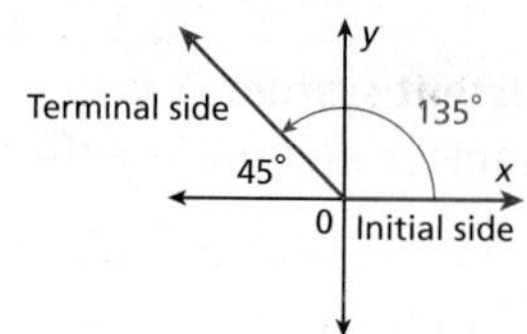
integer A member of the set of whole numbers and their opposites.	**entero** Miembro del conjunto de números cabales y sus opuestos.	... −3, −2, −1, 0, 1, 2, 3 ...
interquartile range (IQR) The difference of the third (upper) and first (lower) quartiles in a data set, representing the middle half of the data.	**rango entre cuartiles** Diferencia entre el tercer cuartil (superior) y el primer cuartil (inferior) de un conjunto de datos, que representa la mitad central de los datos.	Lower half Upper half 18, (23), 28, | 29, (36), 42 First quartile Third quartile Interquartile range: 36 − 23 = 13.
interval notation A way of writing the set of all real numbers between two endpoints. The symbols [and] are used to include an endpoint in an interval, and the symbols (and) are used to exclude an endpoint from an interval.	**notación de intervalo** Forma de expresar el conjunto de todos los números reales entre dos extremos. Los símbolos [y] se utilizan para incluir un extremo en un intervalo y los símbolos (y) se utilizan para excluir un extremo de un intervalo.	Interval notation — Set-builder notation (a, b) — $\{x \mid a < x < b\}$ $(a, b]$ — $\{x \mid a < x \leq b\}$ $[a, b)$ — $\{x \mid a \leq x < b\}$ $[a, b]$ — $\{x \mid a \leq x \leq b\}$
inverse cosine function If the domain of the cosine function is restricted to $[0, \pi]$, then the function $\text{Cos}\,\theta = a$ has an inverse function $\text{Cos}^{-1} a = \theta$, also called *arccosine.*	**función coseno inverso** Si el dominio de la función coseno se restringe a $[0, \pi]$, entonces la función $\text{Cos}\,\theta = a$ tiene una función inversa $\text{Cos}^{-1} a = \theta$, también llamada *arco coseno.*	$\text{Cos}^{-1} \frac{1}{2} = \frac{\pi}{3}$

ENGLISH	SPANISH	EXAMPLES

inverse function The function that results from exchanging the input and output values of a one-to-one function. The inverse of $f(x)$ is denoted $f^{-1}(x)$.

función inversa Función que resulta de intercambiar los valores de entrada y salida de una función uno a uno. La función inversa de $f(x)$ se expresa $f^{-1}(x)$.

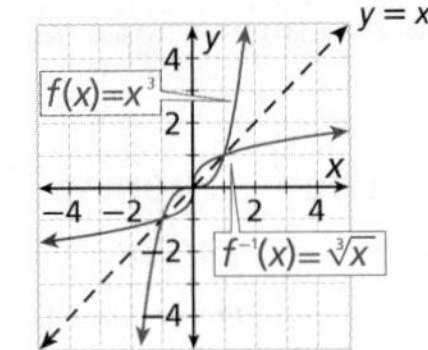

inverse relation The inverse of the relation consisting of all ordered pairs (x, y) is the set of all ordered pairs (y, x). The graph of an inverse relation is the reflection of the graph of the relation across the line $y = x$.

relación inversa La inversa de la relación que consta de todos los pares ordenados (x, y) es el conjunto de todos los pares ordenados (y, x). La gráfica de una relación inversa es el reflejo de la gráfica de la relación sobre la línea $y = x$.

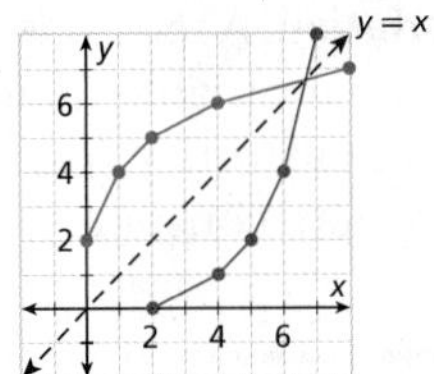

inverse sine function If the domain of the sine function is restricted to $\left[-\frac{\pi}{2}, \frac{\pi}{2}\right]$, then the function $\text{Sin}\,\theta = a$ has an inverse function, $\text{Sin}^{-1} a = \theta$, also called *arcsine.*

función seno inverso Si el dominio de la función seno se restringe a $\left[-\frac{\pi}{2}, \frac{\pi}{2}\right]$, entonces la función $\text{Sen}\,\theta = a$ tiene una función inversa, $\text{Sen}^{-1} a = \theta$, también llamada *arco seno.*

$\text{Sin}^{-1} \frac{\sqrt{3}}{2} = \frac{\pi}{3}$

inverse tangent function If the domain of the tangent function is restricted to $\left(-\frac{\pi}{2}, \frac{\pi}{2}\right)$, then the function $\text{Tan}\theta = a$ has an inverse function, $\text{Tan}^{-1} a = \theta$, also called *arctangent.*

función tangente inversa Si el dominio de la función tangente se restringe a $\left(-\frac{\pi}{2}, \frac{\pi}{2}\right)$, entonces la función $\text{Tan}\theta = a$ tiene una función inversa, $\text{Tan}^{-1} a = \theta$, también llamada *arco tangente.*

$\text{Tan}^{-1}\sqrt{3} = \frac{\pi}{3}$

inverse variation A relationship between two variables, x and y, that can be written in the form $y = \frac{k}{x}$, where k is a nonzero constant and $x \neq 0$.

variación inversa Relación entre dos variables, x e y, que puede expresarse en la forma $y = \frac{k}{x}$, donde k es una constante distinta de cero y $x \neq 0$.

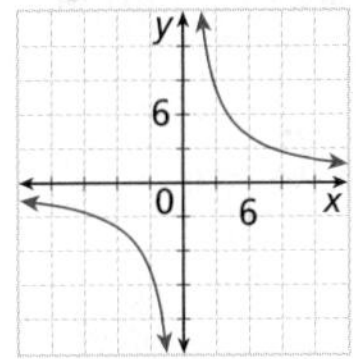

$y = \frac{24}{x}$

irrational number A real number that cannot be expressed as the ratio of two integers.

número irracional Número real que no se puede expresar como una razón de enteros.

$\sqrt{2}, \pi, e$

iteration The repetitive application of the same rule.

iteración Aplicación repetitiva de la misma regla.

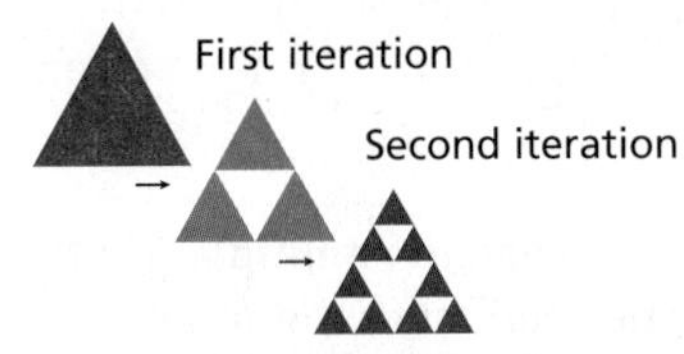

Glossary/Glosario

ENGLISH | SPANISH | EXAMPLES

joint relative frequency The ratio of the frequency in a particular category divided by the total number of data values.

frecuencia relativa conjunta La razón de la frecuencia en una determinada categoría dividida entre el número total de valores.

joint variation A relationship among three variables that can be written in the form $y = kxz$, where k is a nonzero constant.

variación conjunta Relación entre tres variables que se puede expresar de la forma $y = kxz$, donde k es una constante distinta de cero.

$y = 3xz$

Law of Cosines For $\triangle ABC$ with side lengths a, b, and c,
$a^2 = b^2 + c^2 - 2bc \cos A$
$b^2 = a^2 + c^2 - 2ac \cos B$
$c^2 = a^2 + b^2 - 2ab \cos C$.

Ley de cosenos Dado $\triangle ABC$ con longitudes de lado a, b y c,
$a^2 = b^2 + c^2 - 2bc \cos A$
$b^2 = a^2 + c^2 - 2ac \cos B$
$c^2 = a^2 + b^2 - 2ab \cos C$.

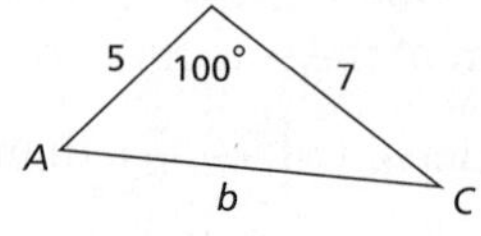

$b^2 = 7^2 + 5^2 - 2(7)(5) \cos 100°$
$b^2 \approx 86.2$
$b \approx 9.3$

law of large numbers The tendency of experimental probability to approach theoretical probability as the number of trials gets very large.

Ley de los números grandes Tendencia de la probabilidad experimental a acercarse a la probabilidad teórica cuando el número de pruebas es muy grande.

The more times you toss a coin, the closer the experimental probability will be to $\frac{1}{2}$.

Law of Sines For $\triangle ABC$ with side lengths a, b, and c,
$\frac{\sin A}{a} = \frac{\sin B}{b} = \frac{\sin C}{c}$.

Ley de senos Dado $\triangle ABC$ con longitudes de lado a, b y c,
$\frac{\text{sen } A}{a} = \frac{\text{sen } B}{b} = \frac{\text{sen } C}{c}$.

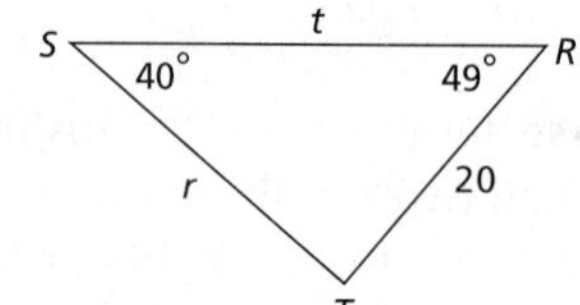

$\frac{\sin 49°}{r} = \frac{\sin 40°}{20}$
$r = \frac{20 \sin 49°}{\sin 40°} \approx 23.5$

leading coefficient The coefficient of the first term of a polynomial in standard form.

coeficiente principal Coeficiente del primer término de un polinomio en forma estándar.

$3x^2 + 7x - 2$
Leading coefficient

least common denominator (LCD) The least common multiple of two or more given denominators.

mínimo común denominador (mcd) Mínimo común múltiplo de dos o más denominadores dados.

The LCD of $\frac{3}{4}$ and $\frac{5}{6}$ is 12.

least common multiple (LCM) The product of the smallest positive number and the lowest power of each variable that divides evenly into each term.

mínimo común múltiplo (mcm) El producto del número positivo más pequeño y la potencia más baja de cada variable que divide exactamente cada término.

The LCM of 10 and 18 is 90.
The LCM of $2x^2$ *and* $5x^3$ *is* $10x^3$.

ENGLISH	SPANISH	EXAMPLES
least-squares line The line of fit for which the sum of the squares of the residuals is as small as possible.	**recta de mínimos cuadrados** Recta de ajuste para la cual la suma de los cuadrados de los residuos es la menor posible.	
limit For an infinite arithmetic series that converges, the number that the partial sums approach.	**límite** Para un serie que coverge, el número que se aproximan las sumas.	The series $\frac{1}{2} + \frac{1}{4} + \frac{1}{8} + \frac{1}{16} + \ldots$ has a limit of 1.
line of best fit The line that comes closest to all of the points in a data set.	**línea de mejor ajuste** Línea que más se acerca a todos los puntos de un conjunto de datos.	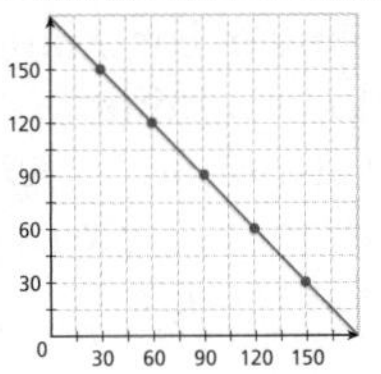
linear equation in one variable An equation that can be written in the form $ax = b$, where a and b are constants and $a \neq 0$.	**ecuación lineal en una variable** Ecuación que puede expresarse en la forma $ax = b$, donde a y b son constantes y $a \neq 0$.	$x + 1 = 7$
linear function A function that can be written in the form $f(x) = mx + b$, where x is the independent variable and m and b are real numbers. Its graph is a line.	**función lineal** Función que puede expresarse en la forma $f(x) = mx + b$, donde x es la variable independiente y m y b son números reales. Su gráfica es una línea.	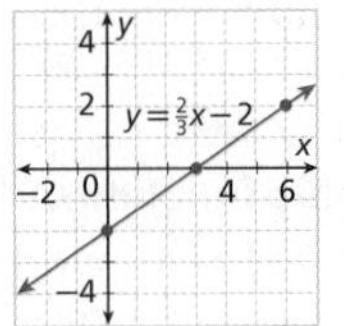
linear inequality in two variables An inequality that can be written in one of the following forms: $y < mx + b$, $y > mx + b$, $y \leq mx + b$, $y \geq mx + b$, or $y \neq mx + b$, where m and b are real numbers.	**desigualdad lineal en dos variables** Desiqualdad que puede expresarse de una de las siguientes formas: $y < mx + b$, $y > mx + b$, $y \leq mx + b$, $y \geq mx + b$, o $y \neq mx + b$, donde m y b son números reales.	$2x + 3y \leq 6$ $y > \frac{1}{2}x - 7$
linear programming A method of finding a maximum or minimum value of a linear function, called the *objective function*, that satisfies a given set of conditions, called *constraints*.	**programación lineal** Método para calcular un valor máximo o mínimo de una función lineal, denominada *función objetiva*, que cumple con una serie dada de condiciones, denominadas *restricciones*.	Constraints: $x \geq 0$, $40x + 60y \leq 1440$, $y \geq \frac{1}{3}x$, $y \leq 16$ Feasible Region 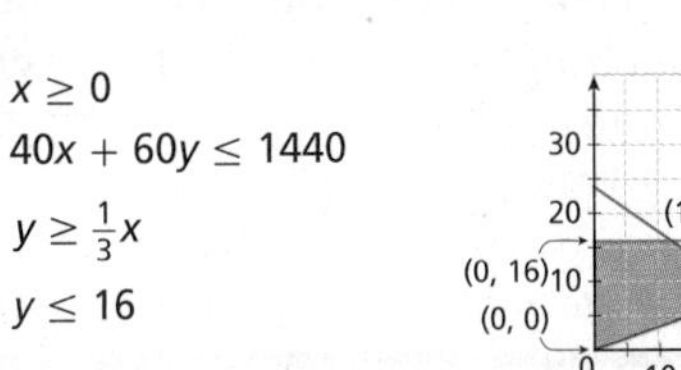 For the given constraints, the objective function $P = 18x + 25y$ is maximized at $(24, 8)$.
linear regression A statistical method used to fit a linear model to a given data set.	**regresión lineal** Método estadístico utilizado para ajustar un modelo lineal a un conjunto de datos determinado.	

ENGLISH	SPANISH	EXAMPLES
linear system A system of equations containing only linear equations.	**sistema lineal** Sistema de ecuaciones que contiene sólo ecuaciones lineales.	$\begin{cases} y = 2x + 1 \\ x + y = 8 \end{cases}$
local maximum For a function f, $f(a)$ is a local maximum if there is an interval around a such that $f(x) < f(a)$ for every x-value in the interval except a.	**máximo local** Dada una función f, $f(a)$ es el máximo local si hay un intervalo en a tal que $f(x) < f(a)$ para cada valor de x en el intervalo excepto a.	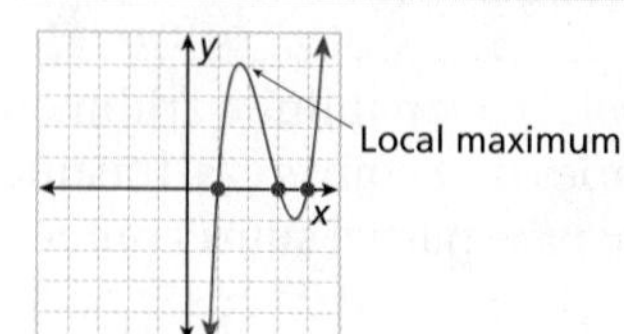
local minimum For a function f, $f(a)$ is a local minimum if there is an interval around a such that $f(x) > f(a)$ for every x-value in the interval except a.	**mínimo local** Dada una función f, $f(a)$ es el mínimo local si hay un intervalo en a tal que $f(x) > f(a)$ para cada valor de x en el intervalo excepto a.	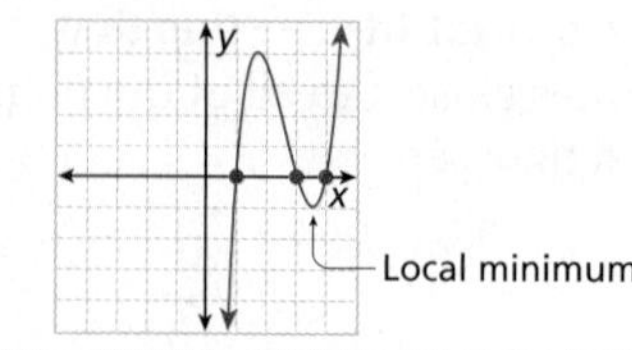
logarithm The exponent that a specified base must be raised to in order to get a certain value.	**logaritmo** Exponente al cual debe elevarse una base determinada a fin de obtener cierto valor.	$\log_2 8 = 3$, because 3 is the power that 2 is raised to in order to get 8; or $2^3 = 8$.
logarithmic equation An equation that contains a logarithm of a variable.	**ecuación logarítmica** Ecuación que contiene un logaritmo de una variable.	$\log x + 3 = 7$
logarithmic function A function of the form $f(x) = \log_b x$, where $b \neq 1$ and $b > 0$, which is the inverse of the exponential function $f(x) = b^x$.	**función logarítmica** Función del tipo $f(x) = \log_b x$, donde $b \neq 1$ y $b > 0$, que es la inversa de la función exponencial $f(x) = b^x$.	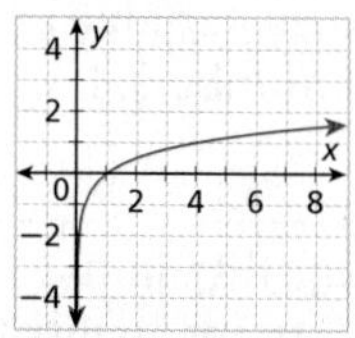 $f(x) = \log_4 x$
logarithmic regression A statistical method used to fit a logarithmic model to a given data set.	**regresión logarítmica** Método estadístico utilizado para ajustar un modelo logarítmico a un conjunto de datos determinado.	
logistic function An exponential growth function that tapers off at an asymptote.	**función logística** Función de crecimiento exponencial que disminuye en una asíntota.	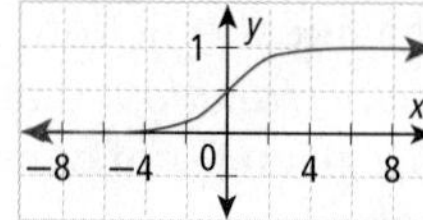

M

ENGLISH	SPANISH	EXAMPLES
major axis The longer axis of an ellipse. The foci of the ellipse are located on the major axis, and its endpoints are the *vertices of the ellipse.*	**eje mayor** El eje más largo de una elipse. Los focos de la elipse se encuentran sobre el eje mayor y sus extremos son los *vértices de la elipse.*	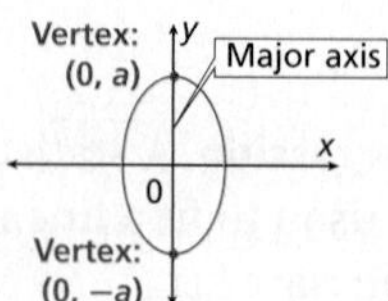
margin of error In a random sample, it defines an interval, centered on the sample percent, in which the population percent is most likely to lie.	**margen de error** En una muestra aleatoria, define un intervalo, centrado en el porcentaje de muestra, en el que es más probable que se encuentre el porcentaje de población.	

Glossary/Glosario

ENGLISH	SPANISH	EXAMPLES
marginal relative frequency The sum of the joint relative frequencies in a row or column of a two-way table.	**frecuencia relativa marginal** La suma de las frecuencias relativas conjuntas en una fila o columna de una tabla de doble entrada.	
mathematical induction A type of mathematical proof. To prove that a statement is true for all natural numbers n, first show that the statement is true for $n = 1$; then assume it is true for some number k and prove that it is true for $k + 1$. It follows that the statement is true for all values of n.	**inducción matemática** Tipo de demostración matemática. Para demostrar que un enunciado se cumple para todos los números naturales n, primero se demuestra que el enunciado se cumple para $n = 1$; luego se supone que se cumple para un número k y se demuestra que se cumple para $k + 1$. Por lo tanto, el enunciado se cumplirá para todos los valores de n.	
matrix A rectangular array of numbers.	**matriz** Arreglo rectangular de números.	$\begin{bmatrix} 1 & 0 & 3 \\ -2 & 2 & -5 \\ 7 & -6 & 3 \end{bmatrix}$
matrix equation An equation of the form $AX = B$, where A is the coefficient matrix, X is the variable matrix, and B is the constant matrix of a system of equations.	**ecuación matricial** Ecuación del tipo $AX = B$, donde A es la matriz de coeficientes, X es la matriz de variables y B es la matriz de constantes de un sistema de ecuaciones.	System of equations: $\begin{matrix} 2x + 3y = 7 \\ 4x - 6y = 5 \end{matrix}$ Matrix equation: $\begin{bmatrix} 2 & 3 \\ 4 & -6 \end{bmatrix}\begin{bmatrix} x \\ y \end{bmatrix} = \begin{bmatrix} 7 \\ 5 \end{bmatrix}$
matrix product The product of two matrices, where each entry in P_{ij} is the sum of the products of consecutive entries in row i in matrix A and column j in matrix B.	**producto matricial** Producto de dos matrices, donde cada entrada de P_{ij} es la suma de los productos de las entradas consecutivas de la fila i de la matriz A y de la columna j de la matriz B.	$\begin{bmatrix} 1 & 2 \\ 3 & 4 \end{bmatrix}\begin{bmatrix} 5 & 6 \\ 7 & 8 \end{bmatrix} = \begin{bmatrix} 1(5) + 2(7) & 1(6) + 2(8) \\ 3(5) + 4(7) & 3(6) + 4(8) \end{bmatrix}$ $= \begin{bmatrix} 19 & 22 \\ 43 & 50 \end{bmatrix}$
maximum value of a function The y-value of the highest point on the graph of the function.	**máximo de una función** Valor de y del punto más alto en la gráfica de la función.	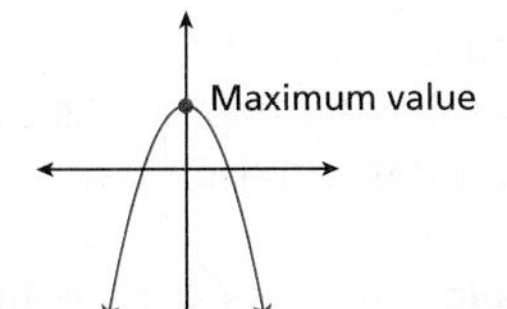
mean The sum of all the values in a data set divided by the number of data values. Also called the *average*.	**media** Suma de todos los valores de un conjunto de datos dividida entre el número de valores de datos. También llamada *promedio*.	Data set: 4, 6, 7, 8, 10 Mean: $\frac{4 + 6 + 7 + 8 + 10}{5} = \frac{35}{5} = 7$
measure of central tendency A measure that describes the center of a data set.	**medida de tendencia dominante** Medida que describe el centro de un conjunto de datos.	the mean, median, or mode
measure of variation A measure that describes the spread of a data set.	**medida de variación** Medida que describe la amplitud de un conjunto de datos.	the range, variance, standard deviation, or interquartile range

ENGLISH	SPANISH	EXAMPLES
median of a data set For an ordered data set with an odd number of values, the median is the middle value. For an ordered data set with an even number of values, the median is the average of the two middle values.	**mediana de un conjunto de datos** Dado un conjunto de datos ordenados con un número impar de valores, la mediana es el valor del medio. Dado un conjunto de datos ordenados con un número par de valores, la mediana es el promedio de los dos valores del medio.	8, 9, (9), 12, 15 Median: 9 4, 6, (7, 10), 10, 12 Median: $\frac{7+10}{2} = 8.5$
midpoint The point that divides a segment into two congruent segments.	**punto medio** Punto que divide un segmento en dos segmentos congruentes.	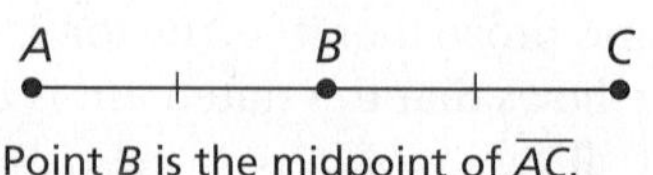 Point B is the midpoint of $\overline{AC}$.
minimum value of a function The y-value of the lowest point on the graph of the function.	**mínimo de una función** Valor de y del punto más bajo en la gráfica de la función.	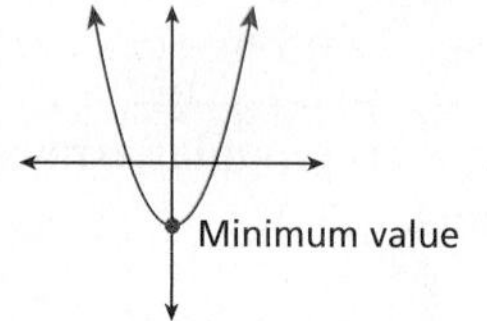
minor axis The shorter axis of an ellipse. Its endpoints are the *co-vertices of the ellipse.*	**eje menor** El eje más corto de una elipse. Sus extremos son los *co-vértices de la elipse.*	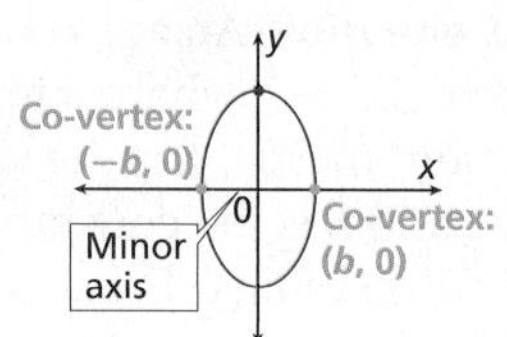
mode The value or values that occur most frequently in a data set; if all values occur only once, the data set is said to have no mode.	**moda** El valor o los valores que se presentan con mayor frecuencia en un conjunto de datos. Si todos los valores se presentan con la misma frecuencia, se dice que el conjunto de datos no tiene moda.	Data set: 3, 6, (8, 8), 10 Mode: 8 Data set: 2, (5, 5), (7, 7) Modes: 5 and 7 Data set: 2, 3, 6, 9, 11 No mode
monomial A number or a product of numbers and variables with whole-number exponents, or a polynomial with one term.	**monomio** Número o producto de números y variables con exponentes de números cabales, o polinomio con un término.	$8x, 9, 3x^2y^4$
multiple root A root r is a multiple root when the factor $(x - r)$ appears in the equation more than once.	**raíz múltiple** Una raíz r es una raíz múltiple cuando el factor $(x - r)$ aparece en la ecuación más de una vez.	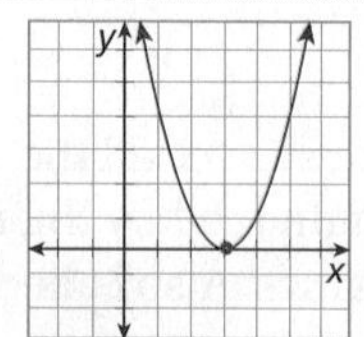 3 is a multiple root of $P(x) = (x - 3)^2$.
multiplicative identity matrix A square matrix with 1 in every entry of the main diagonal and 0 in every other entry.	**matriz de identidad multiplicativa** Una matriz cuadrada que contiene 1 en cada entrada de la diagonal principal y 0 en las demás entradas.	$\begin{bmatrix} 1 & 0 \\ 0 & 1 \end{bmatrix}, \begin{bmatrix} 1 & 0 & 0 \\ 0 & 1 & 0 \\ 0 & 0 & 1 \end{bmatrix}$

ENGLISH	SPANISH	EXAMPLES
multiplicative inverse of a square matrix The multiplicative inverse of square matrix A, if it exists, is notated A^{-1}, where the product of A and A^{-1} is the identity matrix.	**inverso multiplicativo de una matriz cuadrada** El inverso multiplicativo de una matriz cuadrada A, si existe, se escribe A^{-1}, donde el producto de A y A^{-1} es la matriz de identidad.	The multiplicative inverse of $A = \begin{bmatrix} -2 & 5 \\ 1 & -3 \end{bmatrix}$ is $A^{-1} = \begin{bmatrix} -3 & -5 \\ -1 & -2 \end{bmatrix}$, because $AA^{-1} = A^{-1}A = \begin{bmatrix} 1 & 0 \\ 0 & 1 \end{bmatrix}$.
multiplicity If a polynomial $P(x)$ has a multiple root at r, the multiplicity of r is the number of times $(x - r)$ appears as a factor in $P(x)$.	**multiplicidad** Si un polinomio $P(x)$ tiene una raíz múltiple en r, la multiplicidad de r es la cantidad de veces que $(x - r)$ aparece como factor en $P(x)$.	For $P(x) = (x - 3)^2$, the root 3 has a multiplicity of 2.
mutually exclusive events Two events are mutually exclusive if they cannot both occur in the same trial of an experiment.	**sucesos mutuamente excluyentes** Dos sucesos son mutuamente excluyentes si ambos no pueden ocurrir en la misma prueba de un experimento.	In the experiment of rolling a number cube, rolling a 3 and rolling an even number are mutually exclusive events.

N

ENGLISH	SPANISH	EXAMPLES
natural logarithm A logarithm with base e, written as ln.	**logaritmo natural** Logaritmo con base e, que se escribe ln.	$\ln 5 = \log_e 5 \approx 1.6$
natural logarithmic function The function $f(x) = \ln x$, which is the inverse of the natural exponential function $f(x) = e^x$. Domain is $\{x \mid x > 0\}$; range is all real numbers.	**función logarítmica natural** Función $f(x) = \ln x$, que es la inversa de la función exponencial natural $f(x) = e^x$. El dominio es $\{x \mid x > 0\}$; el rango es todos los números reales.	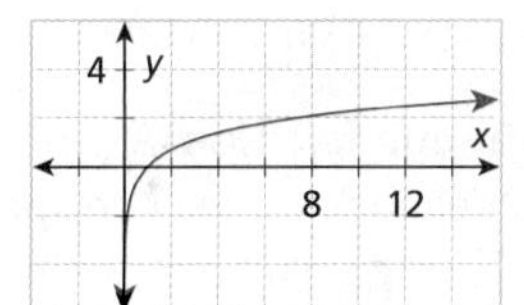
natural number A counting number.	**número natural** Número que sirve para contar.	1, 2, 3, 4, 5, 6, ...
negative exponent A base raised to a negative exponent is equal to the reciprocal of that base raised to the opposite exponent: $b^{-n} = \frac{1}{b^n}$.	**exponente negativo** Una base elevada a un exponente negativo es igual al recíproco de dicha base elevado al exponente opuesto: $b^{-n} = \frac{1}{b^n}$.	$5^{-3} = \frac{1}{5^3} = \frac{1}{125}$
net A diagram of the faces of a three-dimensional figure arranged in such a way that the diagram can be folded to form the three-dimensional figure.	**plantilla** Diagrama de las caras de una figura tridimensional que se puede plegar para formar la figura tridimensional.	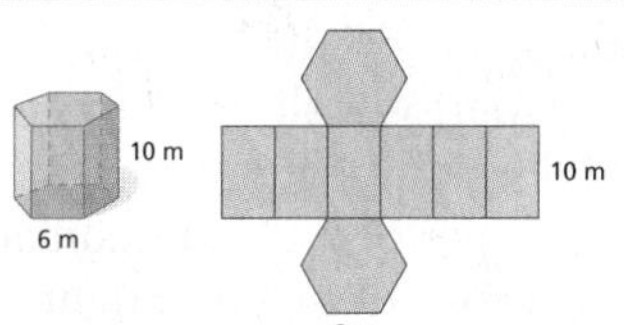
nonlinear system of equations A system in which at least one of the equations is not linear.	**sistema no lineal de ecuaciones** Sistema en el cual por lo menos una de las ecuaciones no es lineal.	$\begin{cases} y = 2x^2 \\ y = -3x^2 + 5 \end{cases}$

ENGLISH	SPANISH	EXAMPLES
nth root The nth root of a number a, written as $\sqrt[n]{a}$ or $a^{\frac{1}{n}}$, is a number that is equal to a when it is raised to the nth power.	**enésima raíz** La enésima raíz de un número a, que se escribe como $\sqrt[n]{a}$ o $a^{\frac{1}{n}}$, es un número igual a a cuando se eleva a la enésima potencia.	$\sqrt[5]{32} = 2$, because $2^5 = 32$.
null hypothesis An assumption in statistics that there is no difference between the two groups being tested.	**hipótesis nula** En estadística, una suposición que indica que no hay diferencias entre los dos grupos puestos a prueba.	

O

ENGLISH	SPANISH	EXAMPLES
objective function The function to be maximized or minimized in a linear programming problem.	**función objetiva** Función que se debe maximizar o minimizar en un problema de programación lineal.	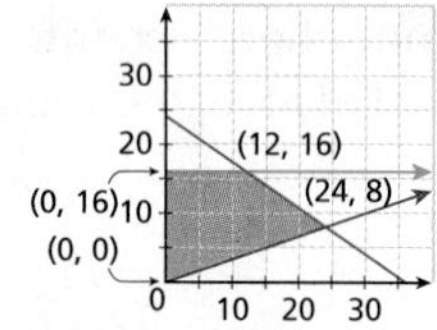 The objective function $P = 18x + 25y$ is maximized at $(24, 8)$.
observational study A study that observes individuals and measures variables without controlling the individuals or their environment in any way.	**estudio de observación** Estudio que permite observar a individuos y medir variables sin controlar a los individuos ni su ambiente.	
one-to-one function A function in which each y-value corresponds to only one x-value. The inverse of a one-to-one function is also a function.	**función uno a uno** Función en la que cada valor de y corresponde a sólo un valor de x. La inversa de una función uno a uno es también una función.	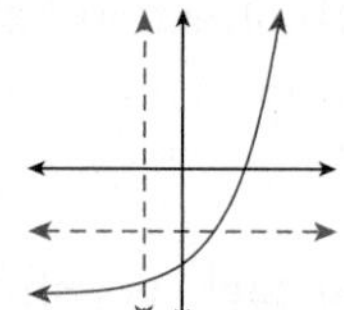
order of operations A process for evaluating expressions: First, perform operations in parentheses or other grouping symbols. Second, evaluate powers and roots. Third, perform all multiplication and division from left to right. Fourth, perform all addition and subtraction from left to right.	**orden de las operaciones** Proceso para evaluar las expresiones: Primero, realizar las operaciones entre paréntesis u otros símbolos de agrupación. Segundo, evaluar las potencias y las raíces. Tercero, realizar todas las multiplicaciones y divisiones de izquierda a derecha. Cuarto, realizar todas las sumas y restas de izquierda a derecha.	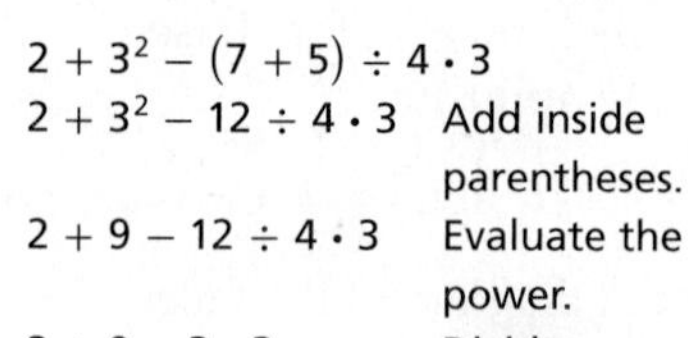 $2 + 3^2 - (7 + 5) \div 4 \cdot 3$ $2 + 3^2 - 12 \div 4 \cdot 3$ Add inside parentheses. $2 + 9 - 12 \div 4 \cdot 3$ Evaluate the power. $2 + 9 - 3 \cdot 3$ Divide. $2 + 9 - 9$ Multiply. $11 - 9$ Add. 2 Subtract.
ordered triple A set of three numbers that can be used to locate a point (x, y, z) in a three-dimensional coordinate system.	**tripleta ordenada** Conjunto de tres números que se pueden utilizar para ubicar un punto (x, y, z) en un sistema de coordenadas tridimensional.	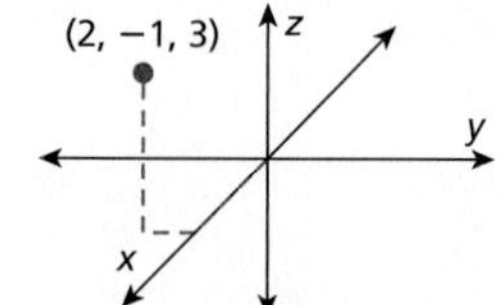

ENGLISH	SPANISH	EXAMPLES

origin The intersection of the x- and y-axes in a coordinate plane. The coordinates of the origin are $(0, 0)$.

origen Intersección de los ejes x e y en un plano cartesiano. Las coordenadas de origen son $(0, 0)$.

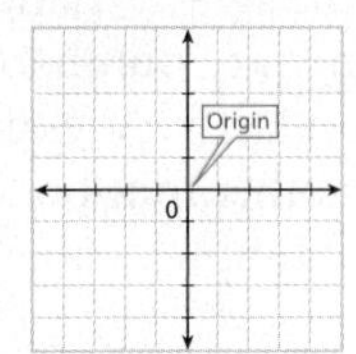

outcome A possible result of a probability experiment.

resultado Resultado posible en un experimento de probabilidad.

In the experiment of rolling a number cube, the possible outcomes are 1, 2, 3, 4, 5, and 6.

outlier A data value that is far removed from the rest of the data. A value less than $Q_1 - 1.5(\text{IQR})$ or greater than $Q_3 + 1.5(\text{IQR})$ is considered to be an outlier.

valor extremo Valor de datos que está muy alejado del resto de los datos. Un valor menor que $Q_1 - 1.5(\text{IQR})$ o mayor que $Q_3 + 1.5(\text{IQR})$ se considera un valor extremo.

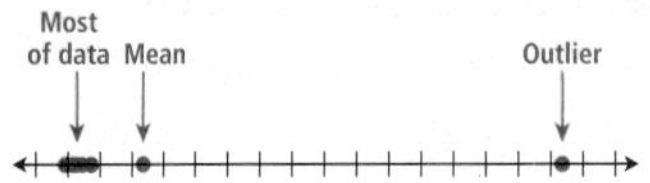

P

parabola The shape of the graph of a quadratic function. Also, the set of points equidistant from a point F, called the *focus*, and a line d, called the *directrix*.

parábola Forma de la gráfica de una función cuadrática. También, conjunto de puntos equidistantes de un punto F, denominado *foco*, y una línea d, denominada *directriz*.

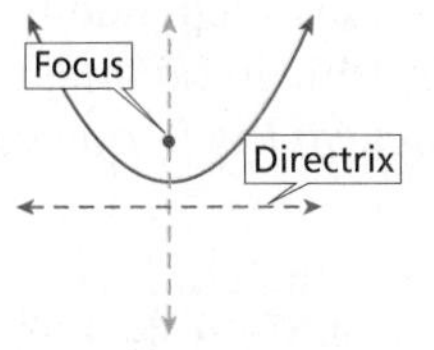

parameter One of the constants in a function or equation that may be changed. Also the third variable in a set of parametric equations.

parámetro Una de las constantes en una función o ecuación que se puede cambiar. También es la tercera variable en un conjunto de ecuaciones paramétricas.

$y = (x - h)^2 + k$

h and k are parameters

parametric equations A pair of equations that define the x- and y-coordinates of a point in terms of a third variable called a parameter.

ecuaciones paramétricas Par de ecuaciones que definen las coordenadas x e y de un punto en función de una tercera variable denominada parámetro.

$x(t) = t + 1$

$y(t) = -2t$

parent function The simplest function with the defining characteristics of the family. Functions in the same family are transformations of their parent function.

función madre La función más básica con las características de la familia. Las funciones de la misma familia son transformaciones de su función madre.

$f(x) = x^2$ is the parent function for $g(x) = x^2 + 4$ and $h(x) = 5(x + 2)^2 - 3$.

partial sum Indicated by $S_n = \sum_{i=1}^{n} a_i$, the sum of a specified number of terms n of a sequence whose total number of terms is greater than n.

suma parcial Expresada por $S_n = \sum_{i=1}^{n} a_i$, la suma de un número específico n de términos de una sucesión cuyo número total de términos es mayor que n.

For the sequence $a_n = n^2$, the fourth partial sum of the infinite series $\sum_{k=1}^{\infty} k^2$ is

$\sum_{k=1}^{4} k^2 = 1^2 + 2^2 + 3^2 + 4^2 = 30.$

ENGLISH	SPANISH	EXAMPLES
Pascal's triangle A triangular arrangement of numbers in which every row starts and ends with 1 and each other number is the sum of the two numbers above it.	**triángulo de Pascal** Arreglo triangular de números en el cual cada fila comienza y termina con 1 y cada uno de los demás números es la suma de los dos números que están encima de él.	1 1 1 1 2 1 1 3 3 1 1 4 6 4 1
perfect square A number whose positive square root is a whole number.	**cuadrado perfecto** Número cuya raíz cuadrada positiva es un número cabal.	36 is a perfect square because $\sqrt{36} = 6$.
perfect-square trinomial A trinomial whose factored form is the square of a binomial. A perfect-square trinomial has the form $a^2 - 2ab + b^2 = (a - b)^2$ or $a^2 + 2ab + b^2 = (a + b)^2$.	**trinomio cuadrado perfecto** Trinomio cuya forma factorizada es el cuadrado de un binomio. Un trinomio cuadrado perfecto tiene la forma $a^2 - 2ab + b^2 = (a - b)^2$ o $a^2 + 2ab + b^2 = (a + b)^2$.	$x^2 + 6x + 9$ is a perfect-square trinomial, because $x^2 + 6x + 9 = (x + 3)^2$.
period of a periodic function The length of a cycle measured in units of the independent variable (usually time in seconds). Also the reciprocal of the frequency.	**periodo de una función periódica** Longitud de un ciclo medido en unidades de la variable independiente (generalmente el tiempo en segundos). También es la inversa de la frecuencia.	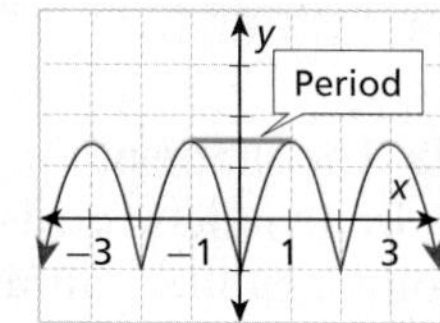
periodic function A function that repeats exactly in regular intervals, called *periods*.	**función periódica** Función que se repite exactamente a intervalos regulares denominados *periodos*.	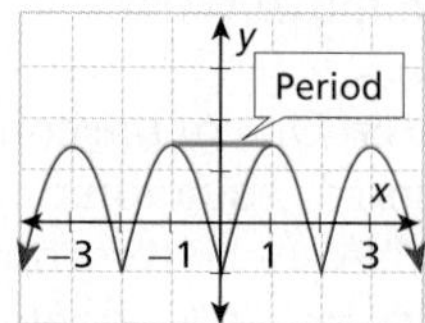
permutation An arrangement of a group of objects in which order is important. The number of permutations of r objects from a group of n objects is denoted ${}_nP_r$.	**permutación** Arreglo de un grupo de objetos en el cual el orden es importante. El número de permutaciones de r objetos de un grupo de n objetos se expresa ${}_nP_r$.	For 4 objects *A, B, C,* and *D*, there are ${}_4P_2 = 12$ different permutations of 2 objects: *AB, AC, AD, BC, BD, CD, BA, CA, DA, CB, DB,* and *DC*.
phase shift A horizontal translation of a periodic function.	**cambio de fase** Traslación horizontal de una función periódica.	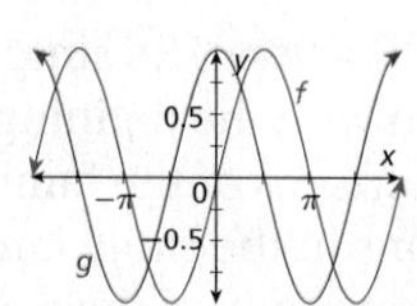g is a phase shift of f $\frac{\pi}{2}$ units left.
piecewise function A function that is a combination of one or more functions.	**función a trozos** Función que es una combinación de una o más funciones.	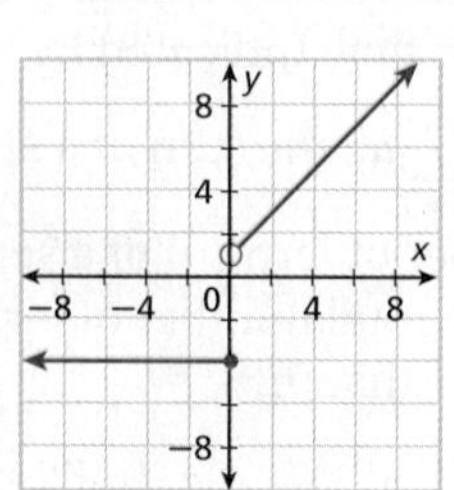$f(x) = \begin{cases} -4 & \text{if } x \le 0 \\ x + 1 & \text{if } x > 0 \end{cases}$

ENGLISH	SPANISH	EXAMPLES

point-slope form The point-slope form of a linear equation is $y - y_1 = m(x - x_1)$, where m is the slope and (x_1, y_1) is a point on the line.

forma de punto y pendiente La forma de punto y pendiente de una ecuación lineal es $y - y_1 = m(x - x_1)$, donde m es la pendiente y (x_1, y_1) es un punto en la línea.

The equation of the line through (2, 1) with slope 3 is $y - 1 = 3(x - 2)$.

---

polynomial A monomial or a sum or difference of monomials.

polinomio Monomio o suma o diferencia de monomios.

$2x^2 + 3x - 7$

---

polynomial function A function whose rule is a polynomial.

función polinomial Función cuya regla es un polinomio.

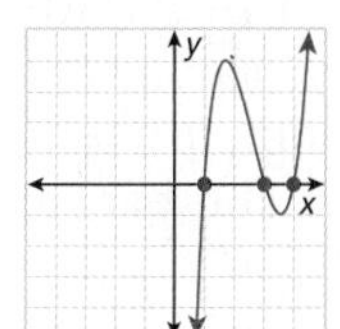

$f(x) = x^3 - 8x^2 + 19x - 12$

---

population The entire group of objects or individuals considered for a survey.

población Grupo completo de objetos o individuos que se desea estudiar.

In a survey about the study habits of high school students, the population is all high school students.

---

probability A number from 0 to 1 (or 0% to 100%) that is the measure of how likely an event is to occur.

probabilidad Número entre 0 y 1 (o entre 0% y 100%) que describe cuán probable es que ocurra un suceso.

A bag contains 3 red marbles and 4 blue marbles. The probability of choosing a red marble is $\frac{3}{7}$.

---

probability distribution for an experiment The function that pairs each outcome with its probability.

distribución de probabilidad para un experimento Función que asigna a cada resultado su probabilidad.

A number cube is rolled 10 times. The results are shown in the table.

Outcome	1	2	3	4	5	6
Probability	$\frac{1}{10}$	$\frac{1}{5}$	$\frac{1}{5}$	0	$\frac{3}{10}$	$\frac{1}{5}$

---

probability sample A sample in which every member of the population being sampled has a nonzero probability of being selected.

muestra de probabilidad Muestra en la que cada miembro de la población que se estudia tiene una probabilidad distinta de cero de ser elegido.

---

proportion A statement that two ratios are equal; $\frac{a}{b} = \frac{c}{d}$.

proporción Enunciado que establece que dos razones son iguales; $\frac{a}{b} = \frac{c}{d}$.

$\frac{2}{3} = \frac{4}{6}$

---

pure imaginary number *See* imaginary number.

número imaginario puro *Ver* número imaginario.

$3i$

Q

quadratic equation An equation that can be written in the form $ax^2 + bx + c = 0$, where a, b, and c are real numbers and $a \neq 0$.

ecuación cuadrática Ecuación que se puede expresar como $ax^2 + bx + c = 0$, donde a, b y c son números reales y $a \neq 0$.

$x^2 + 3x - 4 = 0$
$x^2 - 9 = 0$

ENGLISH | **SPANISH** | **EXAMPLES**

Quadratic Formula The formula $x = \frac{-b \pm \sqrt{b^2 - 4ac}}{2a}$, which gives solutions, or roots, of equations in the form $ax^2 + bx + c = 0$, where $a \neq 0$.

fórmula cuadrática La fórmula $x = \frac{-b \pm \sqrt{b^2 - 4ac}}{2a}$, que da soluciones, o raíces, para las ecuaciones del tipo $ax^2 + bx + c = 0$, donde $a \neq 0$.

The solutions of $2x^2 - 5x - 3 = 0$ are given by

$$x = \frac{-(-5) \pm \sqrt{(-5)^2 - 4(2)(-3)}}{2(2)}$$

$$= \frac{5 \pm \sqrt{25 + 24}}{4} = \frac{5 \pm 7}{4};$$

$x = 3$ or $x = -\frac{1}{2}$.

---

quadratic function A function that can be written in the form $f(x) = ax^2 + bx + c$, where a, b, and c are real numbers and $a \neq 0$, or in the form $f(x) = a(x - h)^2 + k$, where a, h, and k are real numbers and $a \neq 0$.

función cuadrática Función que se puede expresar como $f(x) = ax^2 + bx + c$, donde a, b y c son números reales y $a \neq 0$, o como $f(x) = a(x - h)^2 + k$, donde a, h y k son números reales y $a \neq 0$.

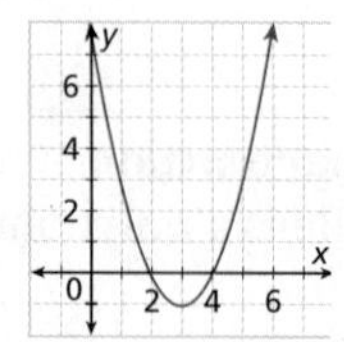

$f(x) = x^2 - 6x + 8$

---

quadratic inequality in two variables An inequality that can be written in one of the following forms:
$y < ax^2 + bx + c$,
$y > ax^2 + bx + c$,
$y \leq ax^2 + bx + c$,
$y \geq ax^2 + bx + c$,
or $y \neq ax^2 + bx + c$,
where a, b, and c are real numbers and $a \neq 0$.

desigualdad cuadrática en dos variables Desigualdad que puede expresarse de una de las siguientes formas:
$y < ax^2 + bx + c$,
$y > ax^2 + bx + c$,
$y \leq ax^2 + bx + c$,
$y \geq ax^2 + bx + c$,
o $y \neq ax^2 + bx + c$,
donde a, b y c son números reales y $a \neq 0$.

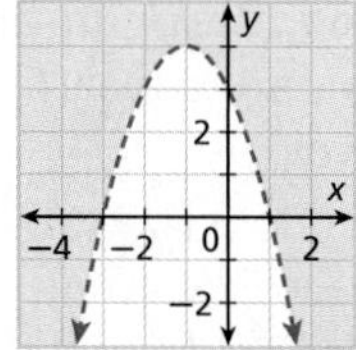

$y > -x^2 - 2x + 3$

---

quadratic model A quadratic function used to represent a set of data.

modelo cuadrático Función cuadrática que se utiliza para representar un conjunto de datos.

x	4	6	8	10
$f(x)$	27	52	89	130

A quadratic model for the data is $f(x) = x^2 + 3.3x - 2.6$.

---

quadratic regression A statistical method used to fit a quadratic model to a given data set.

regresión cuadrática Método estadístico utilizado para ajustar un modelo cuadrático a un conjunto de datos determinado.

R

radian A unit of angle measure based on arc length. In a circle of radius r, if a central angle has a measure of 1 radian, then the length of the intercepted arc is r units.

2π radians $= 360°$
1 radian $\approx 57°$

radián Unidad de medida de un ángulo basada en la longitud del arco. En un círculo de radio r, si un ángulo central mide 1 radián, entonces la longitud del arco abarcado es r unidades.

2π radianes $= 360°$
1 radián $\approx 57°$

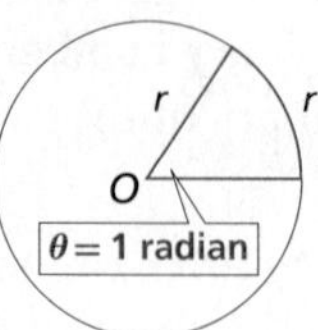

---

radical An indicated root of a quantity.

radical Raíz indicada de una cantidad.

$\sqrt{36} = 6$, $\sqrt[3]{27} = 3$

ENGLISH	SPANISH	EXAMPLES
radical equation An equation that contains a variable within a radical.	**ecuación radical** Ecuación que contiene una variable dentro de un radical.	$\sqrt{x+3}+4=7$
radical function A function whose rule contains a variable within a radical.	**función radical** Función cuya regla contiene una variable dentro de un radical.	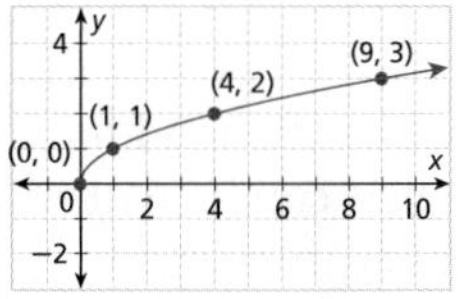 (graph: points (0, 0), (1, 1), (4, 2), (9, 3)) $f(x)=\sqrt{x}$
radical inequality An inequality that contains a variable within a radical.	**desigualdad radical** Desigualdad que contiene una variable dentro de un radical.	$\sqrt{x+3}\le 7$
radical symbol The symbol $\sqrt{}$ used to denote a root. The symbol is used alone to indicate a square root or with an index, $\sqrt[n]{}$, to indicate the *n*th root.	**símbolo de radical** Símbolo $\sqrt{}$ que se utiliza para expresar una raíz. Puede utilizarse solo para indicar una raíz cuadrada, o con un índice, $\sqrt[n]{}$, para indicar la enésima raíz.	$\sqrt{36}=6,\ \sqrt[3]{27}=3$
radicand The expression under a radical sign.	**radicando** Número o expresión debajo del signo de radical.	$\sqrt{x+3}-2$ (arrow to $x+3$: Radicand)
randomized comparative experiment An experiment in which the individuals are assigned to the control group or the treatment group at random, in order to minimize bias.	**experimento comparativo aleatorizado** Experimento en el que se elige al azar a los individuos para el grupo de control o para el grupo experimental, a fin de minimizar el sesgo.	
range of a data set The difference of the greatest and least values in the data set.	**rango de un conjunto de datos** La diferencia del mayor y menor valor en un conjunto de datos.	The data set $\{3, 3, 5, 7, 8, 10, 11, 11, 12\}$ has a range of $12-3=9$.
range of a function or relation The set of output values of a function or relation.	**rango de una función o relación** Conjunto de los valores de salida de una función o relación.	The range of $y=x^2$ is $\{y \mid y\ge 0\}$.
rate A ratio that compares two quantities measured in different units.	**tasa** Razón que compara dos cantidades medidas en diferentes unidades.	$\frac{55\text{ miles}}{1\text{ hour}}=55\text{ mi/h}$
ratio A comparison of two quantities by division.	**razón** Comparación de dos cantidades mediante una división.	$\frac{1}{2}$ or 1:2
rational equation An equation that contains one or more rational expressions.	**ecuación racional** Ecuación que contiene una o más expresiones racionales.	$\frac{x+2}{x^2+3x-1}=6$
rational exponent An exponent that can be expressed as $\frac{m}{n}$ such that if *m* and *n* are integers, then $b^{\frac{m}{n}}=\sqrt[n]{b^m}=\left(\sqrt[n]{b}\right)^m$.	**exponente racional** Exponente que se puede expresar como $\frac{m}{n}$ tal que, si *m* y *n* son números enteros, entonces $b^{\frac{m}{n}}=\sqrt[n]{b^m}=\left(\sqrt[n]{b}\right)^m$.	$4^{\frac{3}{2}}=\sqrt{4^3}=\sqrt{64}=8$ $4^{\frac{3}{2}}=\left(\sqrt{4}\right)^3=2^3=8$

ENGLISH	SPANISH	EXAMPLES
rational expression An algebraic expression whose numerator and denominator are polynomials and whose denominator has a degree ≥ 1.	**expresión racional** Expresión algebraica cuyo numerador y denominador son polinomios y cuyo denominador tiene un grado ≥ 1.	$\frac{x+2}{x^2+3x-1}$
rational function A function whose rule can be written as a rational expression.	**función racional** Función cuya regla se puede expresar como una expresión racional.	$f(x) = \frac{x+2}{x^2+3x-1}$
rational inequality An inequality that contains one or more rational expressions.	**desigualdad racional** Desigualdad que contiene una o más expresiones racionales.	$\frac{x+2}{x^2+3x-1} \geq 6$
rational number A number that can be written in the form $\frac{a}{b}$, where a and b are integers and $b \neq 0$.	**número racional** Número que se puede expresar como $\frac{a}{b}$, donde a y b son números enteros y $b \neq 0$.	$3, 1.75, 0.\overline{3}, -\frac{2}{3}, 0$
rationalizing the denominator A method of rewriting a fraction by multiplying by another fraction that is equivalent to 1 in order to remove radical terms from the denominator.	**racionalizar el denominador** Método que consiste en escribir nuevamente una fracción multiplicándola por otra fracción equivalente a 1 a fin de eliminar los términos radicales del denominador.	$\frac{1}{\sqrt{2}}\left(\frac{\sqrt{2}}{\sqrt{2}}\right) = \frac{\sqrt{2}}{2}$
real axis The horizontal axis in the complex plane; it graphically represents the real part of complex numbers.	**eje real** Eje horizontal de un plano complejo. Representa gráficamente la parte real de los números complejos.	Imaginary axis; $2i$; $0 + 0i$; Real axis; -2; 2; $-2i$
real number A rational or irrational number. Every point on the number line represents a real number.	**número real** Número racional o irracional. Cada punto de la recta numérica representa un número real.	$-5, 0, \frac{2}{3}, \sqrt{2}, 3.1, \pi$
real part of a complex number For a complex number of the form $a + bi$, a is the real part.	**parte real de un número complejo** Dado un número complejo del tipo $a + bi$, a es la parte real.	$5 + 6i$ — Real part (5), Imaginary part (6i)
reciprocal For a real number $a \neq 0$, the reciprocal of a is $\frac{1}{a}$. The product of reciprocals is 1.	**recíproco** Dado el número real $a \neq 0$, el recíproco de a es $\frac{1}{a}$. El producto de los recíprocos es 1.	$\frac{1}{2}$ is the reciprocal of 2. $\frac{5}{3}$ is the reciprocal of $\frac{3}{5}$.
recursive formula A formula for a sequence in which one or more previous terms are used to generate the next term.	**fórmula recurrente** Fórmula para una sucesión en la cual uno o más términos anteriores se utilizan para generar el término siguiente.	For the sequence 5, 7, 9, 11, ..., a recursive formula is $a_1 = 5$ and $a_n = a_{n-1} + 2$.
reduced row-echelon form A form of an augmented matrix in which the coefficient columns form an identity matrix.	**forma escalonada reducida por filas** Forma de matriz aumentada en la que las columnas de coeficientes forman una matriz de identidad.	$\left[\begin{array}{cc\|c} 1 & 0 & -1 \\ 0 & 1 & 3 \end{array}\right]$

ENGLISH	SPANISH	EXAMPLES

reference angle For an angle in standard position, the reference angle is the positive acute angle formed by the terminal side of the angle and the x-axis.

ángulo de referencia Dado un ángulo en posición estándar, el ángulo de referencia es el ángulo agudo positivo formado por el lado terminal del ángulo y el eje x.

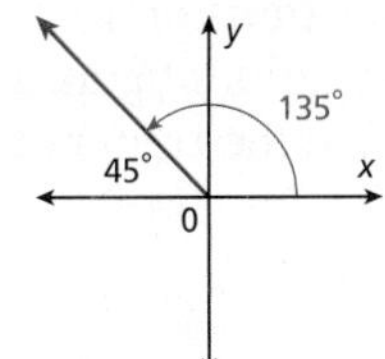

reflection A transformation that reflects, or "flips," a graph or figure across a line, called the line of reflection, such that each reflected point is the same distance from the line of reflection but is on the opposite side of the line.

reflexión Transformación que refleja, o invierte, una gráfica o figura sobre una línea, llamada la línea de reflexión, de manera tal que cada punto reflejado esté a la misma distancia de la línea de reflexión pero que se encuentre en el lado opuesto de la línea.

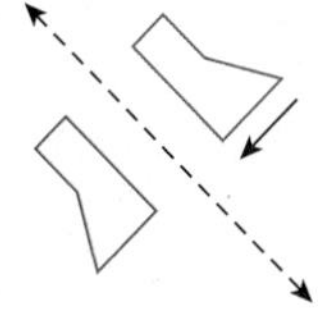

reflection matrix A matrix used to reflect a figure across a specified *line of symmetry*.

matriz de reflexión Matriz utilizada para reflejar una figura sobre un *eje de simetría* específico.

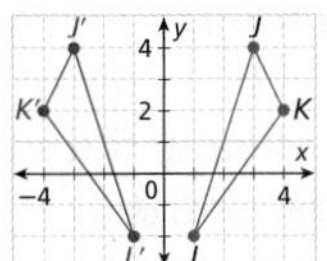

Matrix $\begin{bmatrix} -1 & 0 \\ 0 & 1 \end{bmatrix}$ was used to reflect the figure across the y-axis.

regression The statistical study of the relationship between variables.

regresión Estudio estadístico de la relación entre variables.

relation A set of ordered pairs.

relación Conjunto de pares ordenados.

$\{(0, 5), (0, 4), (2, 3), (4, 0)\}$

replacement set A set of numbers that can be substituted for a variable.

conjunto de reemplazo Conjunto de números que pueden sustituir una variable.

The solution set of $y = x + 3$ for the replacement set $\{1, 2, 3\}$ is $\{4, 5, 6\}$.

right angle An angle that measures 90°.

ángulo recto Ángulo que mide 90°.

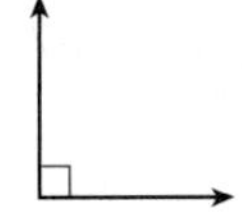

right triangle A triangle with one right angle.

triángulo rectángulo Triángulo con un ángulo recto.

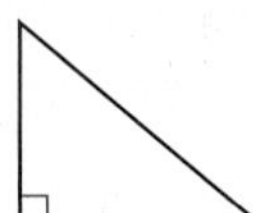

rigid transformation A transformation that does not change the size or shape of a figure.

transformación rígida Transformación que no cambia el tamaño o la forma de una figura.

Reflections, rotations, and translations are rigid transformations.

root of an equation Any value of the variable that makes the equation true.

raíz de una ecuación Cualquier valor de la variable que transforme la ecuación en verdadera.

The roots of $(x - 2)(x + 1) = 0$ are 2 and -1.

roster notation A way of representing a set by listing the elements between braces, { }.

notación de lista Forma de representar un conjunto enumerando los elementos entre llaves, { }.

The first 5 positive odd numbers are $\{1, 3, 5, 7, 9\}$.

ENGLISH | **SPANISH** | **EXAMPLES**

rotation A transformation that rotates or turns a figure about a point called the center of rotation.

rotación Transformación que hace rotar o girar una figura sobre un punto llamado centro de rotación.

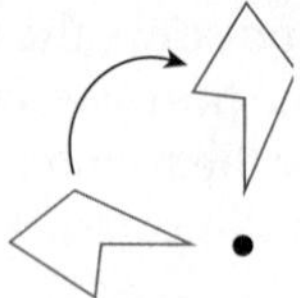

---

rotation transformation
A transformation used to rotate a figure about the origin.

Transformatión de rotación
transformatión utilizada para rotar una figura sobre el origen.

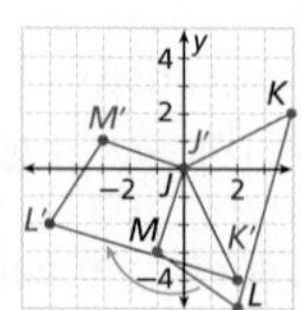

The system $\begin{cases} x' = x\cos 90 - y\sin 90 \\ y' = x\sin 90 + y\cos 90 \end{cases}$ was used to rotate the figure 90° clockwise.

---

row operation An operation performed on a row of an augmented matrix that creates an equivalent matrix.

operación por filas
Operación realizada en una fila de una matriz aumentada que crea una matriz equivalente.

$$\left[\begin{array}{cc|c} 2 & 0 & -2 \\ 0 & 1 & 3 \end{array}\right] = \left[\begin{array}{cc|c} \frac{1}{2}(2) & \frac{1}{2}(0) & \frac{1}{2}(-1) \\ 0 & 1 & 3 \end{array}\right]$$

$$= \left[\begin{array}{cc|c} 1 & 0 & -1 \\ 0 & 1 & 3 \end{array}\right]$$

---

row-reduction method The process of performing elementary row operations on an augmented matrix to transform the matrix to reduced row echelon form.

método de reducción por filas Proceso por el cual se realizan operaciones elementales de filas en una matriz aumentada para transformar la matriz en una forma reducida de filas escalonadas.

$$\left[\begin{array}{cc|c} 2 & 0 & -2 \\ 0 & 1 & 3 \end{array}\right] = \left[\begin{array}{cc|c} \frac{1}{2}(2) & \frac{1}{2}(0) & \frac{1}{2}(-1) \\ 0 & 1 & 3 \end{array}\right]$$

$$= \left[\begin{array}{cc|c} 1 & 0 & -1 \\ 0 & 1 & 3 \end{array}\right]$$

S

sample A part of the population.

muestra Una parte de la población.

In a survey about the stud habits of high school students, a sample is a survey of 100 students.

---

sample space The set of all possible outcomes of a probability experiment.

espacio muestral Conjunto de todos los resultados posibles en un experimento de probabilidades.

In the experiment of rolling a number cube, the sample space is 1, 2, 3, 4, 5, 6 .

---

scalar A number that is multiplied by a matrix.

escalar Número que se multiplica por una matriz.

$$3\begin{bmatrix} 1 & -2 \\ 2 & 3 \end{bmatrix} = \begin{bmatrix} 3 & -6 \\ 6 & 9 \end{bmatrix}$$

↑ scalar

---

scatter plot A graph with points plotted to show a possible relationship between two sets of data.

diagrama de dispersión Gráfica con puntos que se usa para demostrar una relación posible entre dos conjuntos de datos.

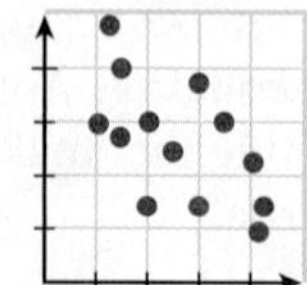

ENGLISH	SPANISH	EXAMPLES
secant of an angle In a right triangle, the ratio of the length of the hypotenuse to the length of the side adjacent to angle A. It is the reciprocal of the cosine function.	**secante de un ángulo** En un triángulo rectángulo, la razón entre la longitud de la hipotenusa y la longitud del cateto adyacente al ángulo A. Es la inversa de la función coseno.	hypotenuse; A; adjacent leg; $\sec A = \frac{\text{hypotenuse}}{\text{adjacent}} = \frac{1}{\cos A}$
second differences Differences between first differences of a function.	**segundas diferencias** Diferencias entre las primeras diferencias de una función.	x: 0, 1, 2, 3; y: 1, 4, 9, 16; first differences +3 +5 +7; second differences +2 +2
self-selected sample A sample in which members volunteer to participate.	**muestra de voluntarios** Muestra en la que los miembros se ofrecen voluntariamente para participar.	
sequence A list of numbers that often form a pattern.	**sucesión** Lista de números que generalmente forman un patrón.	1, 2, 4, 8, 16, ...
series The indicated sum of the terms of a sequence.	**serie** Suma indicada de los términos de una sucesión.	1 + 2 + 4 + 8 + 16 + ...
set A collection of items called elements.	**conjunto** Grupo de componentes denominados elementos.	$\{1, 2, 3\}$
set-builder notation A notation for a set that uses a rule to describe the properties of the elements of the set.	**notación de conjuntos** Notación para un conjunto que se vale de una regla para describir las propiedades de los elementos del conjunto.	$\{x \mid x > 3\}$ is read, "The set of all x such that x is greater than 3."
Sierpinski triangle A fractal formed from a triangle by removing triangles with vertices at the midpoints of the sides of each remaining triangle.	**triángulo de Sierpinski** Fractal formado a partir de un triángulo al cual se le recortan triángulos cuyos vértices se encuentran en los puntos medios de los lados de cada triángulo restante.	
simple event An event consisting of only one outcome.	**suceso simple** Suceso que contiene sólo un resultado.	In the experiment of rolling a number cube, the event consisting of the outcome 3 is a simple event.
simple random sample A sample selected from a population so that each member of the population has an equal chance of being selected.	**muestra aleatoria simple** Muestra seleccionada de una población tal que cada miembro de ésta tenga igual probabilidad de ser seleccionada.	Mr. Hansen chose a random sample of the class by writing each student's name on a slip of paper, mixing up the slips, and drawing five slips without looking.

ENGLISH	SPANISH	EXAMPLES

simulation A model of an experiment, often one that would be too difficult or time-consuming to actually perform.

simulación Modelo de un experimento; generalmente se recurre a la simulación cuando realizar dicho experimento sería demasiado difícil o llevaría mucho tiempo.

A random number generator is used to simulate the roll of a number cube.

---

sine In a right triangle, the ratio of the length of the side opposite $\angle A$ to the length of the hypotenuse.

seno En un triángulo rectángulo, razón entre la longitud del cateto opuesto a $\angle A$ y la longitud de la hipotenusa.

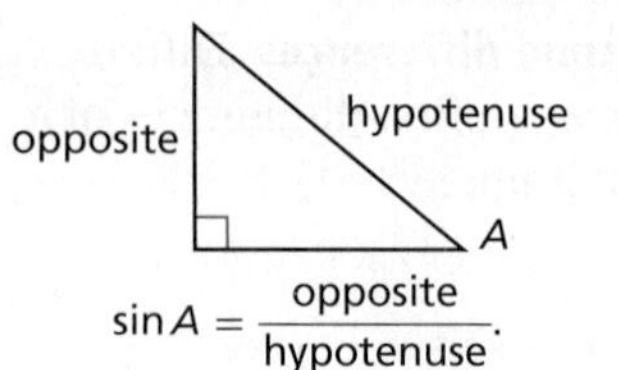

$\sin A = \dfrac{\text{opposite}}{\text{hypotenuse}}$.

---

slope A measure of the steepness of a line. If (x_1, y_1) and (x_2, y_2) are any two points on the line, the slope of the line, known as m, is represented by the equation $m = \dfrac{y_2 - y_1}{x_2 - x_1}$.

pendiente Medida de la inclinación de una línea. Dados dos puntos (x_1, y_1) y (x_2, y_2) en una línea, la pendiente de la línea, denominada m, se representa con la ecuación $m = \dfrac{y_2 - y_1}{x_2 - x_1}$.

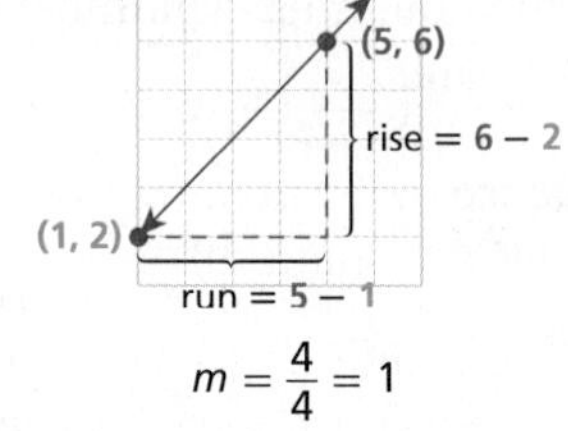

---

slope-intercept form The slope-intercept form of a linear equation is $y = mx + b$, where m is the slope and b is the y-intercept.

forma de pendiente-intersección La forma de pendiente-intersección de una ecuación lineal es $y = mx + b$, donde m es la pendiente y b es la intersección y.

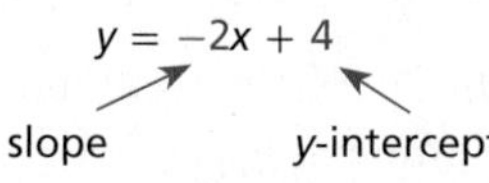

---

solution set of an equation The set of values that make an equation true.

conjunto solución de una ecuación Conjunto de valores que hacen verdadero un enunciado.

The solution set of $x^2 = 9$ is $\{-3, 3\}$.

---

solving a triangle Using given measures to find unknown angle measures or side lengths of a triangle.

resolución de un triángulo Utilizar medidas dadas para hallar las medidas desconocidas de los ángulos o las longitudes de los lados de un triángulo.

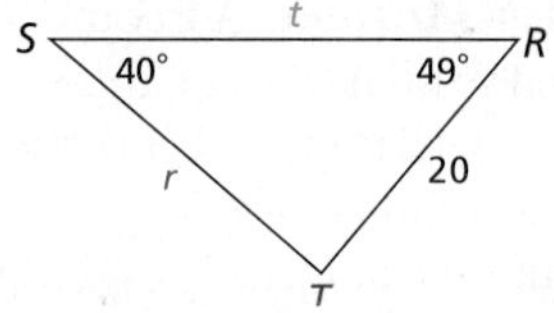

$49° + 40° + m\angle T = 180°$

$m\angle T = 91°$

$\dfrac{\sin 49°}{r} = \dfrac{\sin 40°}{20}$ $\qquad$ $\dfrac{\sin 91°}{t} = \dfrac{\sin 40°}{20}$

$r \approx 23.5$ $\qquad$ $t \approx 31.1$

---

special right triangle A 45°-45°-90° triangle or a 30°-60°-90° triangle.

triángulo rectángulo especial Triángulo de 45°-45°-90° o triángulo de 30°-60°-90°.

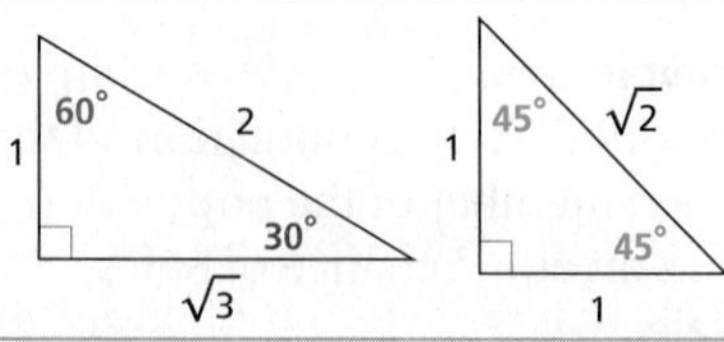

---

square matrix A matrix with the same number of rows as columns.

matriz cuadrada Matriz con el mismo número de filas y columnas.

$\begin{bmatrix} 1 & 2 \\ 0 & -3 \end{bmatrix}, \begin{bmatrix} 1 & -3 & 1 \\ 2 & 0 & -2 \\ 0 & 1 & 3 \end{bmatrix}$

---

square-root function A function whose rule contains a variable under a square-root sign.

función de raíz cuadrada Función cuya regla contiene una variable bajo un signo de raíz cuadrada.

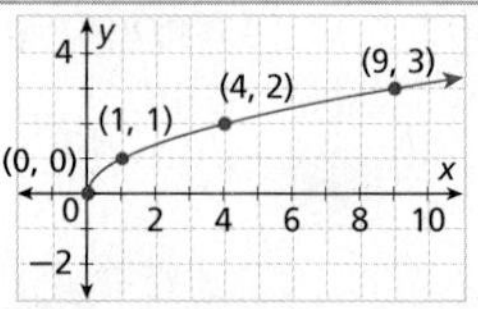

$f(x) = \sqrt{x}$

ENGLISH	SPANISH	EXAMPLES
standard deviation A measure of dispersion of a data set. The standard deviation σ is the square root of the variance.	**desviación estándar** Medida de dispersión de un conjunto de datos. La desviación estándar σ es la raíz cuadrada de la varianza.	Data set: $\{6, 7, 7, 9, 11\}$ Mean: $\frac{6+7+7+9+11}{5} = 8$ Variance: $\frac{1}{5}(4+1+1+1+9) = 3.2$ Standard deviation: $\sigma = \sqrt{3.2} \approx 1.8$
standard form of a polynomial A polynomial in one variable is written in standard form when the terms are in order from greatest degree to least degree.	**forma estándar de un polinomio** Un polinomio de una variable se expresa en forma estándar cuando los términos se ordenan de mayor a menor grado.	$3x^3 - 5x^2 + 6x - 7$
standard form of a quadratic equation $ax^2 + bx + c = 0$, where a, b, and c are real numbers and $a \neq 0$.	**forma estándar de una ecuación cuadrática** $ax^2 + bx + c = 0$, donde a, b y c son números reales y $a \neq 0$.	$2x^2 + 3x - 1 = 0$
standard normal value A value that indicates how many standard deviations above or below the mean a particular value falls, given by the formula $z = \frac{x-\mu}{\sigma}$, where z is the standard normal value, x is the given value, μ is the mean, and σ is the standard deviation of a standard normal distribution.	**valor normal estándar** Valor que indica a cuántas desviaciones estándar por encima o por debajo de la media se encuentra un determinado valor, dado por la fórmula $z = \frac{x-\mu}{\sigma}$, donde z es el valor normal estándar, x es el valor dado, μ es la media y σ es la desviación estándar de una distribución normal estándar.	
standard position An angle in standard position has its vertex at the origin and its initial side on the positive x-axis.	**osición estándar** Ángulo cuyo vértice se encuentra en el origen y cuyo lado inicial se encuentra sobre el eje x.	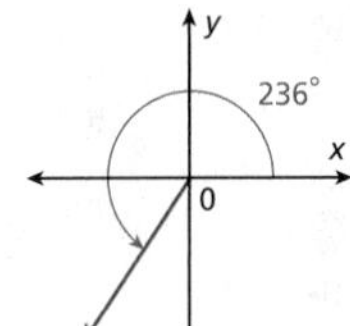
statistic A number that describes a sample.	**estadística** Número que describe una muestra.	
step function A piecewise function that is constant over each interval in its domain.	**función escalón** Función a trozos que es constante en cada intervalo en su dominio.	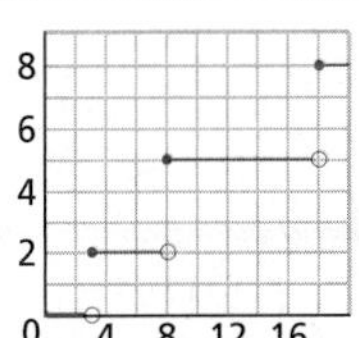
stratified sample A sample in which a population is divided into distinct groups and members are selected at random from each group.	**muestra estratificada** Muestra en la que población está dividida en grupos diferenciados y los miembros de cada grupo se seleccionan al azar.	Ms. Carter chose a stratified sample of her school's student population by randomly selecting 30 students from each grade level.
stretch A transformation that pulls the points of a graph horizontally away from the y-axis or vertically away from the x-axis.	**estiramiento** Transformación que desplaza los puntos de una gráfica en forma horizontal alejándolos del eje y o en forma vertical alejándolos del eje x.	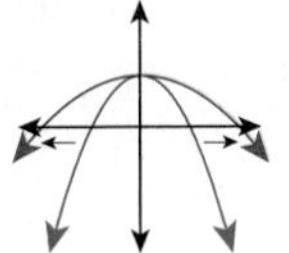

ENGLISH	SPANISH	EXAMPLES
substitution A method used to solve systems of equations by solving an equation for one variable and substituting the resulting expression into the other equation(s).	**sustitución** Método utilizado para resolver sistemas de ecuaciones resolviendo una ecuación para una variable y sustituyendo la expresión resultante en las demás ecuaciones.	$\begin{cases} 2x + 3y = -1 \\ x - 3y = 4 \end{cases}$ Solve for x. $x = 4 + 3y$ Substitute into the first equation and solve. $2(4 + 3y) + 3y = -1$ $y = -1$ Then solve for x. $x = 4 + 3(-1) = 1$
summation notation A method of notating the sum of a series using the Greek letter $\sum$ (capital *sigma*).	**notación de sumatoria** Método de notación de la suma de una serie que utiliza la letra griega $\sum$ (SIGMA mayúscula).	$\sum_{k=1}^{5} 3k = 3 + 6 + 9 + 12 + 15 = 45$
synthetic division A shorthand method of dividing by a linear binomial of the form $(x - a)$ by writing only the coefficients of the polynomials.	**división sintética** Método abreviado de división que consiste en dividir por un binomio lineal del tipo $(x - a)$ escribiendo sólo los coeficientes de los polinomios.	$(x^3 - 7x + 6) \div (x - 2)$ $\begin{array}{r\|rrrr} 2 & 1 & 0 & -7 & 6 \\ & & 2 & 4 & 6 \\ \hline & 1 & 2 & -3 & \boxed{0} \end{array}$ $(x^3 - 7x + 6) \div (x - 2) = x^2 + 2x - 3$
system of equations A set of two or more equations that have two or more variables.	**sistema de ecuaciones** Conjunto de dos o más ecuaciones que contienen dos o más variables.	$\begin{cases} 2x + 3y = -1 \\ x^2 = 4 \end{cases}$
system of linear inequalities A system of inequalities in two or more variables in which all of the inequalities are linear.	**sistema de desigualdades lineales** Sistema de desigualdades en dos o más variables en el que todas las desigualdades son lineales.	$\begin{cases} 2x + 3y \geq -1 \\ x - 3y < 4 \end{cases}$
systematic sample A sample based on selecting one member of the population at random and then selecting other members by using a pattern.	**muestra sistemática** Muestra en la que se elige a un miembro de la población al azar y luego se elige a otros miembros mediante un patrón.	Mr. Martin chose a systematic sample of customers visiting a store by selecting one customer at random and then selecting every tenth customer after that.

ENGLISH	SPANISH	EXAMPLES
tangent of an angle In a right triangle, the ratio of the length of the leg opposite $\angle A$ to the length of the leg adjacent to $\angle A$.	**tangente de un ángulo** En un triángulo rectángulo, razón entre la longitud del cateto opuesto a $\angle A$ y la longitud del cateto adyacente a $\angle A$.	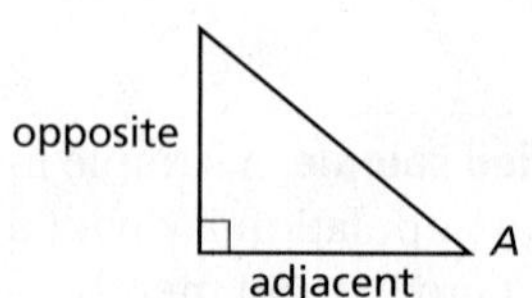 $\tan A = \frac{\text{opposite}}{\text{adjacent}}$
tangent line A line that is in the same plane as a circle and intersects the circle at exactly one point.	**línea tangente** Línea que está en el mismo plano que un círculo y corta al círculo en exactamente un punto.	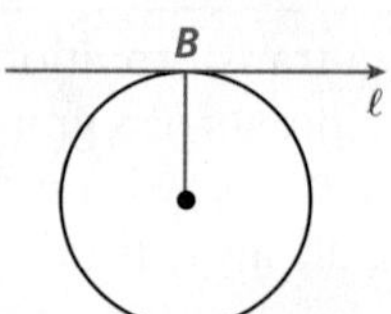

ENGLISH	SPANISH	EXAMPLES

term of a sequence An element or number in the sequence.

término de una sucesión Elemento o número de una sucesión.

5 is the third term in the sequence 1, 3, 5, 7, ...

---

terminal side For an angle in standard position, the ray that is rotated relative to the positive x-axis.

lado terminal Dado un ángulo en una posición estándar, el rayo que rota en relación con el eje positivo x.

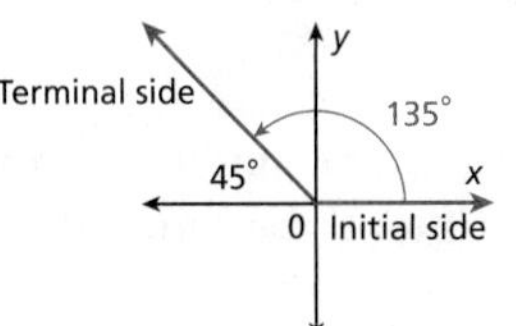

---

theoretical probability The ratio of the number of equally likely outcomes in an event to the total number of possible outcomes.

probabilidad teórica Razón entre el número de resultados igualmente probables de un suceso y el número total de resultados posibles.

The theoretical probability of rolling an odd number on a number cube is $\frac{3}{6} = \frac{1}{2}$.

---

third quartile The median of the upper half of a data set. Also called *upper quartile.*

tercer cuartil La mediana de la mitad superior de un conjunto de datos. También se llama *cuartil superior.*

Lower half Upper half

Third quartile

---

three-dimensional coordinate system A space that is divided into eight regions by an x-axis, a y-axis, and a z-axis. The locations, or coordinates, of points are given by ordered triples.

sistema de coordenadas tridimensional Espacio dividido en ocho regiones por un eje x, un eje y y un eje z. Las ubicaciones, o coordenadas, de los puntos son dadas por tripletas ordenadas.

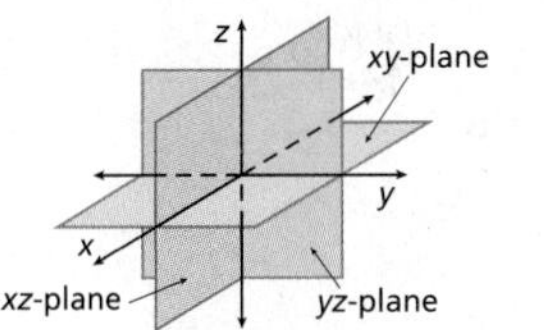

---

transformation A change in the position, size, or shape of a figure or graph.

transformación Cambio en la posición, tamaño o forma de una figura o gráfica.

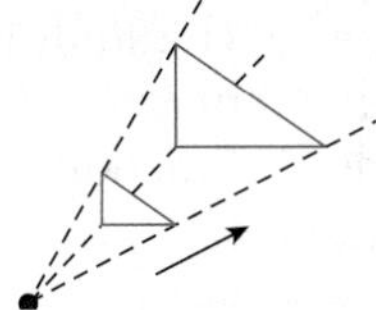

---

translation A transformation that shifts or slides every point of a figure or graph the same distance in the same direction.

traslación Transformación en la que todos los puntos de una figura se mueven la misma distancia en la misma dirección.

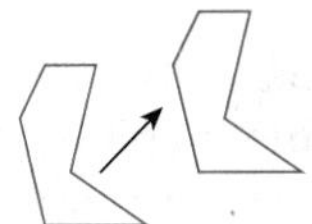

---

translation matrix A matrix used to translate points on the coordinate plane.

matriz de traslación Matriz utilizada para trasladar puntos en el plano cartesiano.

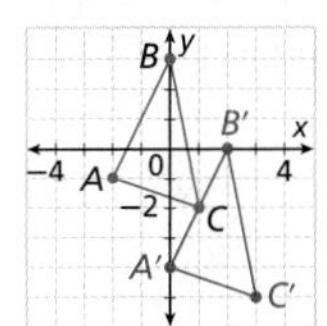

Matrix $\begin{bmatrix} -2 & -2 & -2 \\ 3 & 3 & 3 \end{bmatrix}$ is used to translate the figure 2 units left and 3 units up.

---

transpose A matrix that reverses the rows and columns of a matrix.

transposición Matriz que invierte las filas y columnas de una matriz.

$\begin{bmatrix} 1 & 2 \\ 3 & 4 \\ 5 & 6 \end{bmatrix}$ is the transpose of $\begin{bmatrix} 1 & 3 & 5 \\ 2 & 4 & 6 \end{bmatrix}$.

ENGLISH	SPANISH	EXAMPLES
transverse axis The axis of symmetry of a hyperbola that contains the vertices and foci.	**eje transversal** Eje de simetría de una hipérbola que contiene los vértices y focos.	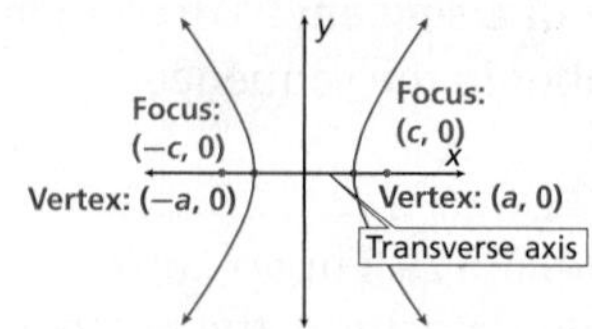
treatment group In a controlled experiment, the group that receives treatment.	**grupo experimental** En un experimento controlado, el grupo que está expuesto a la manipulación.	
trial In probability, a single repetition or observation of an experiment.	**prueba** En probabilidad, una sola repetición u observación de un experimento.	In the experiment of rolling a number cube, each roll is one trial.
trigonometric function A function whose rule is given by a trigonometric ratio.	**función trigonométrica** Función cuya regla es dada por una razón trigonométrica.	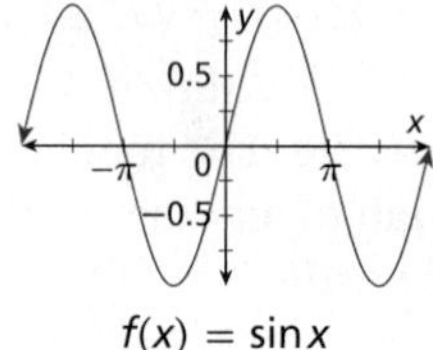 $f(x) = \sin x$
trigonometric ratio Ratio of the lengths of two sides of a right triangle.	**razón trigonométrica** Razón entre dos lados de un triángulo rectángulo.	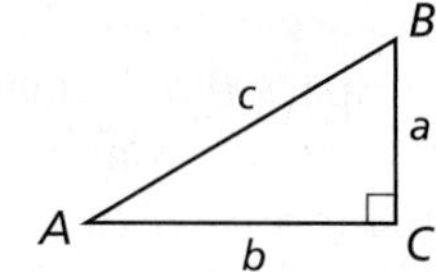 $\sin A = \frac{a}{c}$, $\cos A = \frac{b}{c}$, $\tan A = \frac{a}{b}$
trigonometry The study of the measurement of triangles and of trigonometric functions and their applications.	**trigonometría** Estudio de la medición de los triángulos y de las funciones trigonométricas y sus aplicaciones.	
trinomial A polynomial with three terms.	**trinomio** Polinomio con tres términos.	$4x^2 + 3xy - 5y^2$
turning point A point on the graph of a function that corresponds to a local maximum (or minimum) where the graph changes from increasing to decreasing (or vice versa).	**punto de inflexión** Punto de la gráfica de una función que corresponde a un máximo (o mínimo) local donde la gráfica pasa de ser creciente a decreciente (o viceversa).	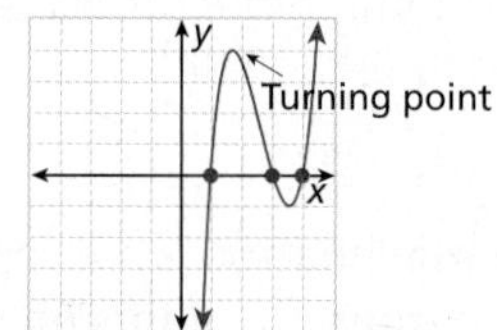

ENGLISH	SPANISH	EXAMPLES
unit circle A circle with a radius of 1, centered at the origin.	**círculo unitario** Círculo con un radio de 1, centrado en el origen.	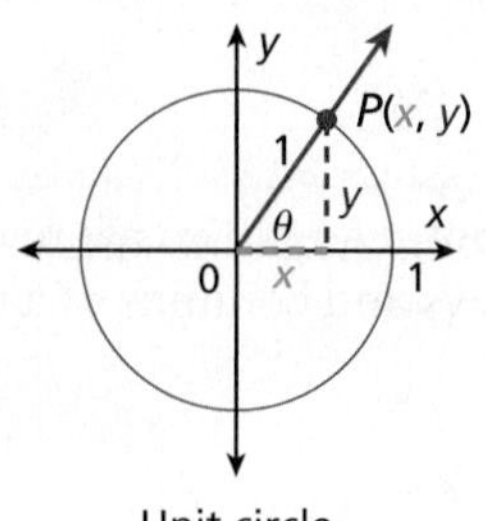 Unit circle

ENGLISH	SPANISH	EXAMPLES

variable A symbol used to represent a quantity that can change.

variable Símbolo utilizado para representar una cantidad que puede cambiar.

$2x + 3$
↑
variable

---

variable matrix The matrix of the variables in a linear system of equations.

matriz de variables Matriz de las variables de un sistema lineal de ecuaciones.

System of equations: $\begin{cases} 2x + 3y = -1 \\ x - 3y = 4 \end{cases}$

Variable matrix: $\begin{bmatrix} x \\ y \end{bmatrix}$

---

variance The average of squared differences from the mean. The square root of the variance is called the *standard deviation.*

varianza Promedio de las diferencias cuadráticas en relación con la media. La raíz cuadrada de la varianza se denomina *desviación estándar.*

Data set: is $\{6, 7, 7, 9, 11\}$

Mean: $\frac{6 + 7 + 7 + 9 + 11}{5} = 8$

Variance: $\frac{1}{5}(4 + 1 + 1 + 1 + 9) = 3.2$

Venn diagram A diagram used to show relationships between sets.

diagrama de Venn Diagrama utilizado para mostrar la relación entre conjuntos.

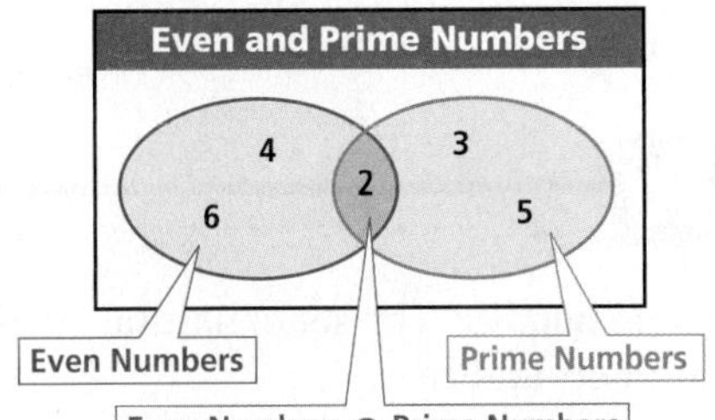

---

vertex form of a quadratic function A quadratic function written in the form $f(x) = a(x - h)^2 + k$, where a, h, and k are constants and (h, k) is the vertex.

forma en vértice de una función cuadrática Una función cuadrática expresada en la forma $f(x) = a(x - h)^2 + k$, donde a, h y k son constantes y (h, k) es el vértice.

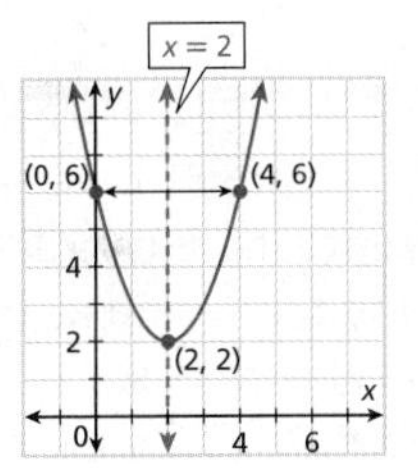

$f(x) = (x - 2)^2 + 2$

---

vertex of a hyperbola (vertices) The endpoints of the transverse axis of the hyperbola.

vértice de una hipérbola Extremos del eje transversal de la hipérbola.

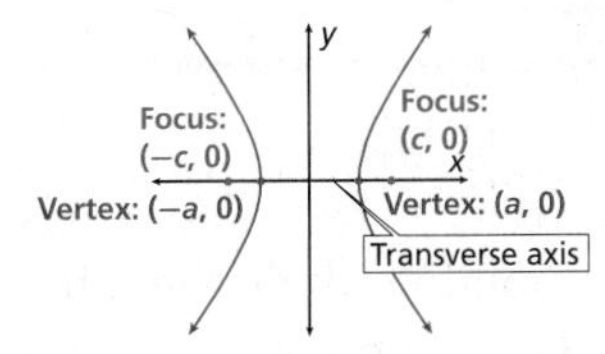

---

vertex of an absolute-value graph The point where the axis of symmetry intersects the graph.

vértice de una gráfica de valor absoluto Punto donde en el eje de simetría interseca la gráfica.

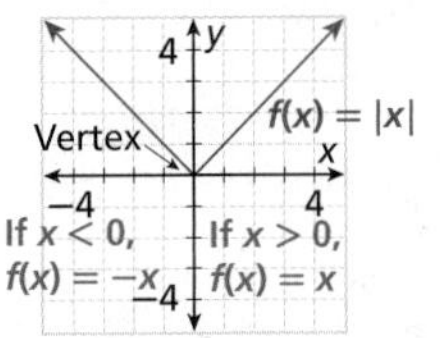

---

vertex of an ellipse (vertices) The endpoints of the major axis of the ellipse.

vértice de una elipse Extremos del eje mayor de la elipse.

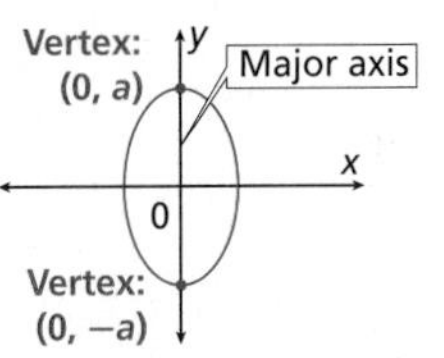

ENGLISH | **SPANISH** | 

vertex of a parabola The highest or lowest point on the parabola.

vértice de una parábola Punto más alto o más bajo de una parábola.

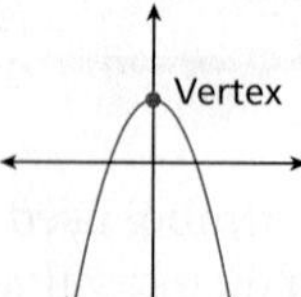

vertical line A line whose equation is $x = a$, where a is the x-intercept. The slope of a vertical line is undefined.

línea vertical Línea cuya ecuación es $x = a$, donde a es la intersección con el eje x. La pendiente de una línea vertical es indefinida.

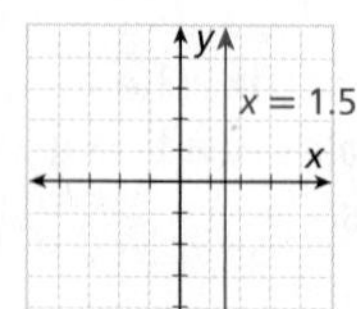

vertical-line test A test used to determine whether a relation is a function. If any vertical line crosses the graph of a relation more than once, the relation is not a function.

prueba de la línea vertical Prueba utilizada para determinar si una relación es una función. Si una línea vertical corta la gráfica de una relación más de una vez, la relación no es una función.

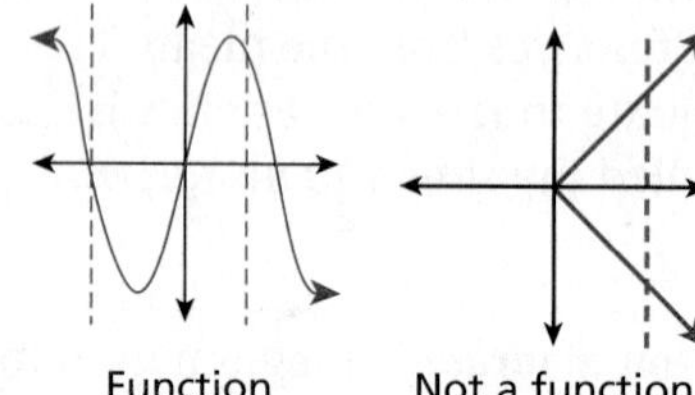
Function | Not a function

whole number The set of natural numbers and zero.

número cabal Conjunto de los números naturales y cero.

0, 1, 2, 3, 4, 5, ...

x-intercept The x-coordinate(s) of the point(s) where a graph intersects the x-axis.

intersección con el eje *x* Coordenada(s) x de uno o más puntos donde una gráfica corta el eje x.

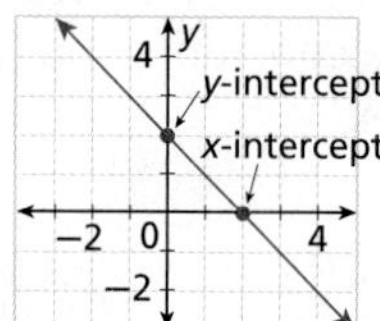

y-intercept The y-coordinate(s) of the point(s) where a graph intersects the y-axis.

intersección con el eje *y* Coordenada(s) y de uno o más puntos donde una gráfica corta el eje y.

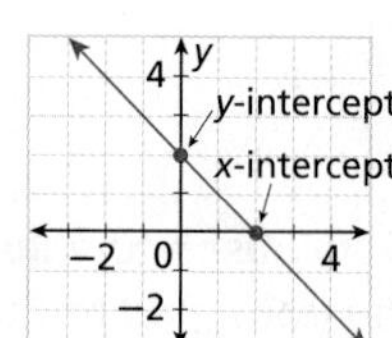

ENGLISH	SPANISH	EXAMPLES

Z

z-axis The third axis in a three-dimensional coordinate system.

eje z Tercer eje en un sistema de coordenadas tridimensional.

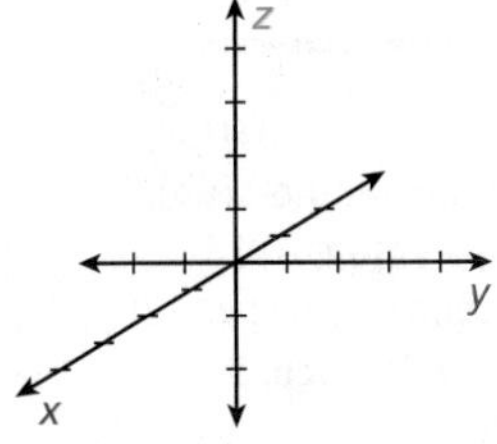

zero exponent For any nonzero real number x, $x^0 = 1$.

exponente cero Dado un número real distinto de cero x, $x^0 = 1$.

$5^0 = 1$

zero of a function For the function f, any number x such that $f(x) = 0$.

cero de una función Dada la función f, todo número x tal que $f(x) = 0$.

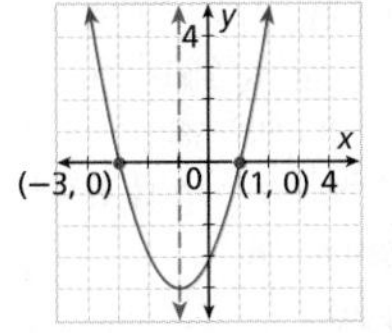

The zeros of $f(x) = x^2 + 2x - 3$ are -3 and 1.

Index 

A

Index

B

C

E

Index

Index

T

U

V

Index